A DICTIONARY OF SCOTTISH EMIGRANTS TO CANADA BEFORE CONFEDERATION

DONALD WHYTE
F.H.G., F.S.G.

ONTARIO GENEALOGICAL SOCIETY
TORONTO 1986

ISBN 0-920036-09-0

Canadian Cataloguing in Publication Data

Whyte, Donald.
  Dictionary of Scottish emigrants to Canada before Confederation

Bibliography: p.
Includes index.
ISBN 0-920036-09-0

1. Scots — Canada — Directories. 2. Canada — Emigration and immigration —
Directories. 3. Scotland — Emigration and immigration — Directories. I. Ontario
Genealogical Society. II. Title.

FC106.S3W49 1985   971′.004963′025   C85-099188-9
F1035.S4W49 1985

This book was published with the assistance of a grant from the Ontario Ministry
of Culture and Recreation.

Word Processing: Barb and Joe Goski — Ottawa, Ontario
Typesetting: Graph Comp Design — Ottawa, Ontario
Design and Layout: Graphic Centre Caspari — Ottawa, Ontario
Printing: The Hearn/Kelly Printing Co. Ltd. — London, Ontario

TO
THE MEMORY OF
THE IMMIGRANT SCOTS PIONEERS
WHOSE VISION OF
A TRANSCONTINENTAL NATION
BROUGHT PURPOSE TO CANADIAN UNITY

CONTENTS

ACKNOWLEDGEMENTS

Grateful acknowledgements are made to the following persons and institutions for permission to quote from copyright material:

The Public Archives of Canada, Ottawa, Ont.
The Public Archives of Nova Scotia, Halifax, N.S.
The New Brunswick Museum, Fredericton, N.B.
Genealogical Association of Nova Scotia.
The MacMillan Company of Canada (division of Gage Publishing, Ltd.), Toronto, Ont.
Wilfred Laurier University Press, Waterloo, Ont.
News Publishing Co., Truro, N.S.
The Advocate Printing & Publishing Co., Ltd., Pictou, N.S.
West Elgin Historical & Genealogical Association, Ont.
The late Miss Cora Mimnaugh, Inverness, Que.
George H. Cook, Saint John, N.B.
Rae Fleming, Woodville, Ont.
Mrs Margery E. Pewtress, Cobourg, Ont.

Mrs Jean S. McGill, Toronto, Ont.
J. Douglas Ross, Willowdale, Ont.
The Clan MacLeod Society of Glengarry, Ont.
Norman A. McDonald, Big Bras d'Or, Cape Breton, N.S.
Mrs Norma Frew, Brantford, Ont.
James O. St. Clair, and the Mabou Gaelic & Historical Society, Mabou, Cape Breton, N.S.
The Hector Publishing Co., Ltd., New Glasgow, N.S.
The Scottish Genealogy Society, Edinburgh, Scotland.
The Scottish Record Office, Edinburgh, Scotland.
The Scottish Record Society, Edinburgh, Scotland.

ACKNOWLEDGEMENTS

INTRODUCTION

The idea of compiling information about Scottish emigration was discussed over thirty years ago, soon after the formation of the Scottish Genealogy Society, and it was intended that such a project would be a corporate effort. Little was done, however, until 1961, when the writer commenced work on emigrants. After commencing files on various countries, he came to the conclusion that he should personally confine his researches to North America. As a result a volume titled *A Dictionary of Scottish Emigrants to the U.S.A.* was published at Baltimore by the Magna Carta Book Company in 1972. It covered a cross-section of emigrants up to 1855. The volume was soon out of print and was re-issued in 1981.

During the compilation of the U.S.A. volume, which was planned as an ongoing project, it became evident that the pressures of earning a living would – for a time at least – restrict the work. By the time the volume was published the compiler was undertaking genealogical enquiries and author's research, and the labour left no leisure for compiling information about Scottish emigrants. He had already filed some 2,500 cards relating to Scots who had emigrated to Canada. The fact that little or no progress was made during the years he had to abandon the work, confirmed his view that it required deep personal commitment, and was too intricate to be carried out as a corporate effort on a voluntary basis.

In 1977, convinced that a work on Scottish emigrants to Canada would be a tremendous value, the writer discussed the matter with the Council of the Scottish Genealogy Society, of which he was then Chairman, and obtained their blessing to resume research on his own account. Coverage to 1855 had seemed a reasonable terminus, as statutory registration of births, deaths and marriages, commenced in Scotland that year, and thereafter information is more easily found, but as the work progressed he came to the conclusion that 1867 was a more intelligible break for Canadians. As now published the work contains 12,501 entries, which with dependents not separately listed, records over 30,000 names, most of these being of actual emigrants.

It was desirable that the following facts be established: NAME, PARENTAGE, PLACE OF ORIGIN, DATES OF BIRTH AND DEATH, DESTINATION, DATE and SHIP, OCCUPATION, WIFE/HUSBAND, PARENTAGE, DATE OF MARRIAGE, CHILDREN, and sources of information. In practise it has not always been possible to obtain full details, but what has been recorded should be of value to genealogists, biographers and historians. At no stage has the compiler imagined he could give precise statistics about Scottish emigration to Canada.

Except in the case of widows, or of female emigrants who married in Canada, children are listed under the fathers. When more information about children than name and age was available, separate cross-referenced entries were made in the case of those born in Scotland, while children born in Canada are simply named. Where no dates are available it cannot be guaranteed that children are in order of birth, and no claim is made for completeness of issue. Wives born in Scotland also have separate entries, cross-referenced to their maiden surnames. Widows are shown under their maiden surnames, with guide entries thus:

ADAM, Mrs Robert. See DOW, Helen.

In some cases it has not been possible to determine relationships, and it is possible that some emigrants have more than one entry. Alexander Bannerman, b 1805, Kildonan, Sutherland, who settled in Grey County, Ontario, before 1844, might be the same man who appears in 1854 at Lot 30, Con 25, Brant Township, Bruce County, but the compiler has made no assumptions. Likewise one is tempted to think that Donald McDonald, b North Uist, 1803, is the same as Donald McDonald, who had a son James, M.L.A., but the entries cannot be joined without further information. To take another example, Marion Ross, ca. 1815-34, may have been the wife of William

McDonald, 1782–1867, as their names appear on adjacent tombstones at Baillie Cemetery, Lovat, Pictou County, N.S., but evidence is lacking.

Surnames with the prefix Mc and Mac are lumped together, separation being a doubtful exercise. Variations in spelling are common in old records, and many people who insist their surname has always been spelled in a particular way, are often surprised to find their ancestors appearing in parochial registers, shipping lists and other documents under numerous variants. With so many entries with the same surname and forename, each one has been numbered to facilitate easy reference.

Some critics may fault certain entries and split hairs over what constitutes an emigrant. The writer has taken the view that a Scot who moved to Canada and returned home at a later date should be included, as he may have contributed when there to history or culture. Moreover the link with Canada may not have been severed, as children may have remained. A good example is the Rev. Andrew Walker Herdman, who ministered in Nova Scotia, and returned to Scotland to become minister of Rattray. He left issue in Canada including two sons who became clergymen. Similarly, public officials and discharged soldiers are included, especially if listed in Canadian biographical works.

The principle that an emigrant should be shown under the country to which he first moved has been followed as far as possible. In the U.S.A. volume already mentioned, Scots who went to the Mohawk Valley in New York State in 1773, appear, and are shown as having settled in Upper Canada after the Revolutionary War. The present work contains many who settled first in Canada, then moved to the U.S.A. However, in many cases the port of entry has not been established and residence in Canada has been the deciding factor. Consideration of these points will confirm that the volume on that country and this work are in some measure complementary. At one period it was suggested that the emigrants should simply be listed in a work on North America. This would doubtless be attractive from a publisher's standpoint, but

the special place of the Scots in Canada – the country's third largest ethnic group – seemed to warrant a separate publication. It is doubted if any other ethnic group in Canada can refer to a work of this kind.

In respect of information, this work will be found superior to the volume published on the U.S.A. This is due mainly to two factors. The experience gained in compiling and editing the U.S.A. book has been invaluable. But the main reason is that the bulk of emigration of Scots to Canada was during the period following the Revolutionary War and our closing date of 1867, and the documentation is better. The compiler could have gone on indefinitely, but costs of publication had to be borne in mind. This work covers only a good cross-section of emigrants, but if it meets with success, supplementary volumes can be considered, including some additional indices to the present work. A balance had to be struck between what was desirable from an academic point of view, and what was feasible from an economic standpoint. Genealogists – and this work is primarily genealogical – will recognise that the work is an aid to research, not a substitute, and will in general find few problems in consulting this *Dictionary*.

An area of difficulty may occasionally be place-names. In making entries it seemed best to give locations which are understandable today. There seems no good reason why before certain years Ontario should be called Upper Canada, or Prince Edward Island called the Isle of St John. The same considerations have applied in respect of boundaries of townships and counties which have been changed. In too many cases the writer has not even been in the fortunate position of giving township and county, and has been obliged to state simply the province: even on occasion merely 'Canada.' Where an entry gives the place of arrival as Quebec, that is his only known destination; where QUE, the emigrant settled in the province. In the case of large towns like Hamilton and Kingston, it did not seem requisite to state the county or township. Similarly, where a Scottish county town is given as the place of origin – not always the place of birth – the shire is not entered. Counties without a town or burgh of the same name, for example Argyll, have not usually been given the suffix *shire*.

One special feature of this work is that many entries have been made through direct correspondence with descendants of Scottish emigrants, in order to record as much unpublished material as possible. Appeals for information were made in various provinces. For assistance with this thanks are due to Miss Marjorie Goodfellow, columnist of the *Sherbrooke Gazette*; to Terrence Punch, former editor of the genealogical *Newsletter* of the Nova Scotia Historical Society; and to J. Brian Gilchrist, for a notice in the *Toronto Sunday Star*, which brought numerous letters.

It would not be possible to acknowledge every letter received, but the following must be thanked for assistance: Archie A. MacNeil, Vancouver, B.C.; Mrs Nina G. Ross, New Westminster, B.C.; Eric Leighton, Truro, N.S.; William B. McEwen, Stockton Springs, Maine, and Miss Patricia L. Belier, Fredericton, N.B., for information about emigrants to the Maritimes. The following sent detailed information about individual families: Mrs R.E. Bowley, Peterborough, Ont.; Donald W. McLean, Fredericton, N.B.; Mrs Jean Lye, Sudbury, Ont.; Mrs Louise Hope, Claremont, Ont.; Mrs Catherine St. John, Mississauga, Ont.; Mrs Jean Edward, Parkham, Ont.; Stephen E. Wood, Whitby, Ont.; Mrs. E.A. Walker, Barrie, Ont.; Mrs. Florence Denning, Turner Valley, Alberta; Mrs A. Connally, Montreal, Que.; Alexander Martin, Winnipeg, Man.; Rev. Donald McKenzie, Ottawa, Ont.; Robert K. Stevens, Embassy-Rome, A.P.O., New York; Mrs Brenda Merriman, Puslinch, Ont.; and Dr George A. Neville, Ottawa, Ont.

Among colleagues and friends in the genealogical world who have helped in various ways must be mentioned Miss Sheila Ford, Dumfries, who supplied extracts from old newspapers she was indexing; Miss Donna L. Baker, Kitchener (now Mrs Edison C. Breckenridge, Springville, Utah), for taking trouble to locate maps and books of interest; Peter Bower, formerly of the Public Archives of Canada, now Provincial Archivist of Manitoba, for several acts of kindness;

Francis L. Leeson, of the Surname Archive, Ferring, East Sussex, England, for information about government assisted emigrants of 1815; the Rev. Ronald Mattson, of Minneapolis, Minnesota, for the gift of a valuable book; Scottish professional genealogists Ms Sheila Pitcairn and James A. Thompson, for many useful pieces of information; and to William M. Lawson, formerly of Paisley College of Technology, for valuable notes on the Benbecula people who sailed on the *Lulan* in 1848, access to his manuscript collections, and advice about Gaelic place-names.

Apart from voluminous correspondence, the compiler has researched widely, and the sources are given in keyed references, with the bibliography shown at the end of this work. Acknowledgements to holders of copyright material are made at the beginning. Particular thanks are due to the Public Archives of Canada; the Provincial Archives of Nova Scotia; the Scottish Record Office, Edinburgh; the National Library of Scotland, Edinburgh; the Public Library, Rosemount Viaduct, Aberdeen; the Mitchell Library, Glasgow; and the Library of the Scottish Genealogy Society, Edinburgh.

Finally, I have pleasure in extending thanks to the Executive Council and Publications Committee of Ontario Genealogical Society, for the interest shown in this work. The publication of a work of national importance by a provincial genealogical society – albeit Canada's largest – is worthy of the highest commendation. Several members have been actively involved in the production of the work, and particular thanks are due to Mrs Marie Charbonneau, former chairperson, and Mrs Ruth Holt, co-chairperson of the Publications Committee; Bill Zuefelt, project manager; Jim Kennedy, editor of *Families*, and Mrs Claudia McArthur, office administrator.

DONALD WHYTE

4 Carmel Road,
Kirkliston,
West Lothian,
Scotland,
EH29 9DD

ABBREVIATIONS AND EXPLANATIONS

adm	admitted
app	appointed
appr	apprentice, or apprenticed
asgn	assigned
b	born
bap	baptized
bro/o	brother of
Bt	Baronet
bur	buried
ca	*circa* or about
CE	Civil Engineer
ch	children
Ch	Church
Co	County, company
Con	Concession
coun	council, or councillor
cous	cousin
d	died or dead
d/o	daughter of
dec	deceased
dep	deported
dept	department
desc	descended, or descendant
dist	district
dsp	died *sine prole*, or without issue
dy	died young
educ	educated
emig	emigrated, or emigrant
emp	employed
estab	established
ex	out of – applied to port from which a ship sailed
FC	Free Church
FRGS	Fellow of the Royal Geographical Society
FRS	Fellow of the Royal Society
FRSC	Fellow of the Royal College of Surgeons
G	Great
GD	Gifts and Deposits (series of manuscripts in the Scottish Record Office, Edinburgh)
Gen	General
Gfa	Grandfather
Gmo	Grandmother
Gov	Governor
gr	granted
grad	graduated
gr-s	grandson
gr-s/o	grandson of
HEICS	Honourable East India Company's Service
hus/o	husband of
ind	inducted
indt	indentured
inf	infant
Is	Island
JP	Justice of the Peace
k	killed
KC	Kings Councillor
KCB	Knight Commander of the Bath
KCMG	Knight Commander of St. Michael and St. George
LLD	Doctor of Laws
LRSC	Licentiate of the Royal College of Surgeons
Lt	Lieutenant
m	married
Maj	Major
matric	matriculated
MD	Doctor of Medicine
min	minister
MLA	Member of the Legislative Assembly
MLC	Member of the Legislative Council
MP	Member of Parliament
MPP	Member of the Provincial Parliament
nat	native
natr	naturalised
NE	New England
neph	nephew
n i	not identified
nr	near

OPR	Old Parochial Register (in the care of the Registrar General for Scotland, Edinburgh)	s/o	son of
		SGSL	Scottish Genealogy Society Library
ord	ordained	Sgt	Sergeant
par	parish	sis/o	sister of
poss	possibly	sist	sister
Pres	President	sld	sailed
Presb	Presbytery or Presbyterian	SRO	Scottish Record Office
prob	probably	stld	settled
Prof	Professor	succ	succeeded
prom	promoted	supp	supposed
QC	Queen's Councillor	trans	translated (term used when a clergyman is called and admitted to another benefice)
qv	see entry for that person elsewhere in dictionary		
		Ts	Tombstone
RA	Royal Artillery	Twp	Township
rel	related	UEL	United Empire Loyalist
rep	represented, or representative	Univ	University
res	resided, or residing	unm	unmarried
ret	retired	UP	United Presbyterian
retr	returned	wid/o	widow of
RN	Royal Navy	WS	Writer to the Signet
s	son (not abbreviated when used initially or finally)	<	Before (year)
		>	After (year)

NOTE: Punctuation has been curtailed in the text, and marks indicating possessive case have been omitted in the interests of economy.

Countries
AUS	Australia
CAN	Canada
ENG	England
FRA	France
GER	Germany
IOM	Isle of Man
IRL	Ireland
NZ	New Zealand
SCT	Scotland
USA	United States
WLS	Wales

Canada
ALB	Alberta
BC	British Columbia
MAN	Manitoba
NB	New Brunswick
NFD	Newfoundland
NS	Nova Scotia
NWT	N.W. Territories
ONT	Ontario
PEI	Prince Edward Island
QUE	Quebec
SAS	Saskatchewan
YUK	Yukon

United States
AK	Alaska
AL	Alabama
AR	Arkansas
AZ	Arizona
CA	California
CO	Colorado
CT	Connecticut
DC	District of Columbia
DE	Delaware
FL	Florida
GA	Georgia
HI	Hawaii
IA	Iowa
ID	Idaho
IL	Illinois
IN	Indiana
KS	Kansas
KY	Kentucky
LA	Louisiana
MA	Massachusetts

MD	Maryland	ESS	Essex
ME	Maine	GLS	Gloucestershire
MI	Michigan	HAM	Hampshire
MN	Minnesota	HEF	Herefordshire
MO	Missouri	HRT	Hertfordshire
MS	Mississippi	HUN	Huntingdonshire
MT	Montana	KEN	Kent
NC	North Carolina	LAN	Lancashire
ND	North Dakota	LEI	Leicestershire
NE	Nebraska	LIN	Lincolnshire
NH	New Hampshire	LND	London
NJ	New Jersey	MDX	Middlesex
NM	New Mexico	NBL	Northumberland
NV	Nevada	NFK	Norfolk
NY	New York	NRY	Yks North Riding
OH	Ohio	NTH	Northamptonshire
OK	Oklahoma	NTT	Nottinghamshire
OR	Oregon	OXF	Oxfordshire
PA	Pennsylvania	RUT	Rutland
RI	Rhode Island	SAL	Shropshire
SC	South Carolina	SFK	Suffolk
SD	South Dakota	SOM	Somerset
TN	Tennessee	SRY	Surrey
TX	Texas	SSX	Sussex
UT	Utah	STS	Staffordshire
VA	Virginia	WAR	Warwickshire
VT	Vermont	WES	Westmorland
WA	Washington	WIL	Wiltshire
WI	Wisconsin	WOR	Worcestershire
WV	West Virginia	WRY	Yks West Riding
WY	Wyoming	YKS	Yorkshire

Wales

AGY	Anglesey
BRE	Brecknockshire
CAE	Caernarvon
CGN	Cardiganshire
CMN	Carmarthen
DEN	Denbighshire
FLN	Flintshire
GLA	Glamorgan
MER	Merioneth
MGY	Montgomeryshire
MON	Monmouthshire
PEM	Pembroke
RAD	Radnorshire

England

BDF	Bedfordshire
BKM	Buckinghamshire
BRK	Berkshire
CAM	Cambridgeshire
CHS	Cheshire
CON	Cornwall
CUL	Cumberland
DBY	Derbyshire
DEV	Devon
DOR	Dorset
DUR	Durham
ERY	Yks East Riding

Ireland

ANT	Antrim
ARM	Armagh
CAR	Carlow
CAV	Cavan
CLA	Clare
COR	Cork
DON	Donegal
DOW	Down
DRY	Derry
DUB	Dublin
FER	Fermanagh
GAL	Galway
KER	Kerry
KID	Kildare
KIK	Kilkenny
LDY	Londonderry
LET	Leitrim
LEX	Leix (Queens)
LIM	Limerick
LOG	Longford
LOU	Louth
MAY	Mayo
MEA	Meath
MOG	Monaghan
OFF	Offaly (Kings)
ROS	Roscommon
SLI	Sligo

TIP	Tipperary		LKS	Lanark
TYR	Tyrone		MLN	Midlothian
WAT	Waterford		MOR	Moray
WEM	West Meath		NAI	Nairn
WEX	Wexford		OKI	Orkney Isles
WIC	Wicklow		PEE	Peebles
			PER	Perth
Scotland			RFW	Renfrew
ABD	Aberdeen		ROC	Ross and Cromarty
ANS	Angus		ROX	Roxburgh
ARL	Argyll		SEL	Selkirk
AYR	Ayr		SHI	Shetland
BAN	Banff		STI	Stirling
BEW	Berwick		SUT	Sutherland
BUT	Bute		WIG	Wigtown
CAI	Caithness		WLN	West Lothian
CLK	Clackmannan			
DFS	Dumfries		**Islands**	
DNB	Dunbarton		ALD	Alderney
ELN	East Lothian		CHI	Channel Island
FIF	Fife		GSY	Guernsey
INV	Inverness		IOM	Isle of Man
KCD	Kincardine		IOW	Isle of Wight
KKD	Kirkcudbright		JSY	Jersey
KRS	Kinross		SRK	Sark

A

1 ABERCROMBY, Robert. From Greenyards, Bannockburn, STI. s/o William A. and Agnes Spence. To QUE, 1754; stld Montreal. **SA x 69**.

2 ADAM, Archibald, b ca 1790. From ANS. To NS, 1842; stld Bedford, Halifax Co, NS. m Martha Smith, 1851, ch. **DC 2 Jan 1981**.

3 ADAM, David, ca 1832-86. From Lintrathen, ANS. s/o Thomas A, farmer in Clintlaw, and wife Ellen. To ONT, and d Morris City, MAN. **Ts Lintrathen**.

4 ADAM, Hugh, 3 Apr 1804–10 Jul 1894. From Paisley, RFW. s/o James A. and Isabel McDougal. To Dalhousie Twp, Lanark Co, ONT, prob <1840. Weaver, farmer and engraver. m Marion Black, qv, ch: 1. Hugh, jr, b 14 Mar 1834; 2. James, b 31 May 1836; 3. Mary, b 5 May 1845. **DC 26 Sep 1979**.

5 ADAM, Margaret. From Leslie, ABD. d/o Robert A. and Helen Dow, qv. To ONT, 1848; stld Middlesex Co. Wife of James Milne, qv. **DC 21 Mar 1981**.

ADAM, Mrs Robert. See DOW, Helen.

6 ADAMS, Alexander, ca 1785–12 Jul 1845. Poss from ABD, and rel to Harvey A, qv. To QUE <1817; stld Matapedia, Bonaventure Co. Moved in 1825 to Caraquet, Gloucester Co, NB, and in 1827 to Restigouche, Bonaventure Co. Farmer and shipowner. m Catherine Henderson, 1796–1864, from Miramichi, Northumberland Co, NB, ch: 1. Harvey, b 11 Jan 1822; 2. Elizabeth, b 29 May 1823; 3. Barbara, b 7 Jan 1826; 4. Isabella, b 29 May 1827; 5. Christina, b 10 Dec 1829; 6. James, b 25 Dec 1832; 7. Mary, b 10 Oct 1835; 8. Alexander John, b 5 Dec 1841. **DC 17 Oct 1981**.

7 ADAMS, Alexander, b 23 Dec 1810, Nether Mains, Echt, ABD. s/o John A, qv, and Elizabeth Gillespie, qv. To Campbellton, Restigouche Co, NB, 1817. m Barbara, d/o Alexander Adams, qv, and Catherine Henderson. **DC 17 Oct 1981**.

8 ADAMS, Ann, 1822–9 Nov 1873. From Thornhill, DFS. d/o Alexander A. To QUE on the *David of London*, ex Greenock, 19 May 1821; stld Ramsay Twp, Lanark Co, ONT. wife of John Gemmill, qv. **OSG 26**.

9 ADAMS, George. To Hudson Bay and Red River <1815. Pioneer settler. **LSS 192**.

10 ADAMS, Harvey. Poss from ABD, and rel to Alexander A, qv. To QUE, <1817; stld Matapedia, Bonaventure Co. Pioneer British settler. **DC 17 Oct 1981**.

11 ADAM(S), John, b ca 1785. From Echt par, ABD. To Campbellton, Restigouche Co, NB, 1817. wife Elizabeth Gillespie, qv with him, and ch: 1. John, jr, qv; 2. William, b 18 Dec 1808, who went to Australia; 3. Alexander, qv; 4. Peter, qv. **DC 17 Oct 1981**.

12 ADAMS, John, jr, b 29 Mar 1807, Nether Mains, Echt, ABD. s/o John A, qv, and Elizabeth Gillespie, qv. To Campbellton, Restigouche Co, NB, 1817. m Margaret McDonald. Son James. **DC 17 Oct 1981**.

13 ADAMS, John. From Aberdeen. bro/o Robert A, qv. To Mission Point, Restigouche Co, NB, prob 1773. m Mary, d/o Col Thomas Busteed, from Cork, IRL. **SR 15**.

14 ADAMS, Peter, b 13 June 1813, Tillioch, Echt par, ABD. s/o John A, qv, and Elizabeth Gillespie, qv. To Campbellton, Restigouche Co, NB, 1817. m Elizabeth, d/o Alexander Adams, qv, and Catherine Henderson. **DC 17 Oct 1981**.

15 ADAMS, Robert. From Aberdeen. bro/o John A, qv. To Mission Point, Restigouche Co, NB, ca 1774, and acquired land on the south side of the Restigouche River. m Elizabeth, d/o Col Thomas Busteed, Battery Point. Dau Mary, b 14 Apr 1790, first white child b on the Restigouche. **SR 15**.

16 ADAMS, Thomas. From ROX. To QUE on the *Sarah Mary Ann*, 1831; stld Dumfries Twp, Waterloo Co, ONT. **HGD 60**.

17 ADAMS, William. To QUE on the *Alexander*, 1816; stld Lot 22, Con 1, Bathurst Twp, Lanark Co, ONT. **HCL 233**.

18 ADAMSON, Alexander. From Glenelg, Moidart, INV. To PEI on the *Lucy*, ex Loch nan Uamh, Arisaig, 12 Jul 1790. Tenant. Family with him. **PLL**.

19 ADAMSON, Donald. From Moidart, INV. To PEI on the *Jane*, ex Loch nan Uamh, Arisaig, 12 Jul 1790. Pedlar. Wife and inf with him. **PLJ**.

20 ADAMSON, Edmund. From Arienskill, poss in Moidart, INV. To PEI on the *Jane*, ex Loch nan Uamh, Arisaig, 12 Jul 1790. Wife with him. **PLJ**.

21 ADAMSON, James William, 10 Sep 1796–9 Aug 1880. To Pictou Co, NS, 1817. Applied for gr of land, 1820. m Sep 1824, Mary Thain. **NSN 7/2**.

22 ADAMSON, Lachlan. From Glenuig, Moidart, INV. To PEI on the *Lucy*, ex Loch nan Uamh, Arisaig, 12 Jul 1790. Tenant. Wife with him, and 2 ch. **PLL**.

23 AFFLECK, Eliza, d 17 Jul 1857. From Balmaghie, KKD. d/o — A, farmer in Dinnans. To Colchester, Essex Co, ONT. m John Murray. **DGH 21 Aug 1857**.

24 AFFLECK, Robert. To Galbraith, Lanark Twp, Lanark Co, ONT, 1820. Weaver. Wife with him, and 9 ch, incl Robert, jr, qv. **HCL 65**.

25 AFFLECK, Robert, jr. s/o Robert A, qv. To Galbraith, Lanark Twp, Lanark Co, ONT, 1820. m Mary Borrowman, qv. **HCL 65**.

AIKIN. See also AITKEN, AITKIN.

26 AIKIN, William. To Pictou Co, NS, <1775. **HPC App B**.

27 AINSLIE, Agnes, ca 1778–4 Nov 1856. From Kirk Yetholm, ROX. wid/o William Hood. To York Co, ONT, 1831; stld Scarborough. Owned west half of Lot 1, Con 4, Markham Twp. Son William, qv. **DC 27 Aug 1975**.

28 AINSLIE, James, d 31 Dec 1873. From Begbie, Haddington, ELN. To Galt, Waterloo Co, ONT, ca 1841. Printer, and became proprietor of the *Dumfries Reformer* newspaper. **HGD 219**.

29 AINSLIE, Robert Forrest, ca 1811–8 June 1862. Poss from BEW. s/o Capt John A, HEICS, and Sarah Geddes. To Hamilton, ONT, <1840, but d Glasgow, Scotland. Gentleman. m Eliza Borren, ch: 1. Allan, b 1839, d inf; 2. George, 1841-58; 3. Robert John Gordon, 1843-48. **DC 20 Jul 1982**.

30   AINSLIE, Thomas. From Jedburgh, ROX. To QUE, <1766; stld Woodfield. Collector of Customs. m Mary Potts. Son Thomas Philip, b 21 Aug 1766. **Jedburgh OPR 792/4**.

31   AIRD, Isabella, b 1 Apr 1820. From Kirkmichael, AYR. d/o William A, qv, and Mary Hunter, qv. To QUE on the *George Cannon*, 1829; stld Montreal. m (i) Robert —; (ii) Joseph Tanner, ch.   **DC 15 Jul 1979**.

32   AIRD, John, b 20 Nov 1817. From Kirkmichael, AYR. s/o William A, qv, and Mary Hunter, qv. To QUE on the *George Cannon*, 1829. m (ii) Mary McIntyre Thom.   **DC 15 Jul 1979**.

33   AIRD, Mary, b 7 Aug 1809. From Kirkmichael, AYR. d/o William A, qv, and Mary Hunter, qv. To QUE on the *George Cannon*, 1829; stld Montreal. m Robert Dalgleish, qv.   **DC 15 Jul 1979**.

34   AIRD, Robert, b. 1753. From Kilmarnock, AYR. s/o John A, merchant, and Ann Campbell. To Montreal, QUE, 1782. Merchant. m 18 Feb 1782, Janet Findley, qv, ch: 1. John, 1784–1823; 2. Martha, b 25 Aug 1786; 3. Anna, b 9 Mar 1788; 4. Rosina, b 23 Mar 1791; 5. Janet, b 18 Jul 1793; 6. William, b 9 Jun 1795; 7. Robert, b 5 Nov 1799; 8. James, b 5 Oct 1803; 9. Findley, b 8 Oct 1806.   **Kilmarnock OPR 597/3; SGC 143**.

35   AIRD, William, 1785–1860. From Kirkmichael, AYR. To QUE on the *George Cannon*, 1829; stld Montreal. Wife Mary Hunter, qv, with him, and ch: 1. David, b 28 Aug 1807; 2. Mary, qv; 3. William, b 1 Jul 1811; 4. Margaret, b 2 Sep 1814; 5. James, b 8 Oct 1815; 6. John, qv; 7. Isabella, qv.   **DC 15 Jul 1979**.

36   AITCHISON, Andrew, 14 Feb 1831–Feb 1895. From Lauder, BEW. bro/o Ebenezer A, qv. To Niagara, Lincoln Co, ONT, 1852; later to Guelph, Wellington Co. m Elizabeth Ann Bathgate, qv, ch: 1. Andrew; 2. William; 3. Ebenezer; 4. Peter; 5. Ann; 6. Simon; 7. Margaret; 8. John Alexander.   **EHE 43**.

37   AITCHISON, Ebenezer. From Lauder, BEW. bro/o Andrew A, qv. To Niagara, Lincoln Co, ONT, ca 1852; later to Dumfries Twp, Wellington Co, **EHE 43**.

38   AITCHISON, Elizabeth, b ca 1796. From Annan, DFS. To Chatham, Northumberland Co, NB, ca 1816. Wife of John McLean, qv.   **DC 2 Jun 1978**.

39   AITCHISON, Isobel. To Dumfries Twp, Waterloo Co, ONT, 1832. Wife of Rev William Proudfoot, qv. **HGD 214**.

40   AITCHISON, Janet. From Lauder, BEW. sis/o Andrew A, qv, and of Ebenezer A, qv. To Niagara, Lincoln Co, ONT, ca 1852; later to Dumfries Twp, Wellington Co.   **EHE 43**.

41   AITCHISON, William, d 1875. From Annan, DFS. To New Annan, Colchester Co, NS, 1832. m Margaret Miller, qv, ch: 1. James, 1825–1911; 2. Agnes; 3. Rachel; 4. Christine; 5. Ann; 6. Jane; 7. Euphemia; 8. Elizabeth; 9. Mary Laidlaw; 10. Ellen; 11 Jennie. **SG xxvii/2 76**.

AITKEN. See also AIKEN, AIKIN.

42   AITKEN, Isabella, 14 Dec 1820–15 Jun 1899. Prob from Glasgow. d/o John A, qv, and wife Margaret. To

QUE, 1832, and stld Lanark Co, ONT. m David Turnbull, qv.   **DC 21 Jan 1960**.

43   AITKEN, Jeanie. Prob from Glasgow. d/o John A, qv, and wife Margaret. To QUE, 1832; stld Lanark Co, ONT.   **DC 21 Jan 1961**.

44   AITKEN, John, b ca 1725. From Caerlaverock, DFS. To Georgetown, Kings Co, PEI, on the *Lovely Nellie*, ex Carsethorn Bay, May 1775. Wife Margaret Lowden, qv, with him, and ch: 1. James, aged 17; 2. Gideon, aged 7; 3. Margaret, aged 4; 4. Agnes, aged 2.   **ELN**.

45   AITKEN, John. Prob from Glasgow. To QUE, 1832; stld Lanark Co, ONT. Wife Margaret with him, and ch: 1. William, qv; 2. Margaret, qv; 3. Jeanie, qv; 4. Mary, qv; 5. Isabella, qv.   **DC 21 Jan 1960**.

46   AITKEN, Margaret. Prob from Glasgow. d/o John A, qv, and wife Margaret, qv. To QUE, 1832; stld Lanark Co, ONT.   **DC 21 Jan 1961**.

47   AITKEN, Mary. Prob from Glasgow. d/o John A, qv, and wife Margaret, qv. To QUE, 1832; stld Lanark Co, ONT.   **DC 21 Jan 1960**.

48   AITKEN, Rev Roger. Poss from ABD. Episcopal min at St Johns, Aberdeen, 1781–1813. To NS, as missionary for the Society for the Propagation of the Gospel. Served at Lunenburg, 1817-19; Liverpool, 1820; again at Lunenburg, 1821-24. Hon MA, Marischall Coll, Aberdeen, 1809.   **FAM ii 398; SNQ ii/2 138**.

49   AITKEN, Thomas, 1781–18 Oct 1848. From AYR. To Hamilton, ONT. m Esther Bryan, qv.   **Ts Mt Albion**.

50   AITKEN, Thomas, b 1799. From Bo'ness, WLN. s/o James A, merchant. Grad MA Univ of Glasgow, 1818. To Halifax, NS, 1828. Missionary, and became rector of Halifax Academy.   **RGG 9; FES vii 613**.

51   AITKEN, William. Prob from Glasgow. s/o John A, qv, and wife Margaret. To QUE, 1832. stld Lanark Co, ONT.   **DC 21 Jan 1961**.

52   AITKEN, Rev William Cuthbert, 28 Feb 1834–13 Dec 1913. From Torphichen, WLN. s/o Robert A, farmer, Silver Mine, and Anne Anderson. Educ Bathgate Academy and Univ of Edinburgh. App by Colonial Committee to Cobourg, Northumberland Co, ONT, 1864. Min at Vaughan, York Co, from 1865, and trans to St James's, Newcastle, Northumberland Co, NB, 1880. m 8 May 1867, Jane, d 1927, d/o Joseph Vaughan Noble and Sarah McQuarrie, ch: 1. Sarah Noble, b 1 Mar 1868; 2. Annie Anderson, b 19 Apr 1870; 3. Robert Traven Donaldson, b 23 Apr 1873; 4. Joseph Mauns, b 26 Feb 1878; 5. William Maxwell, 1879–1964, newspaper magnate, cr Bart, 1916, and raised to peerage, 1917; 6. Arthur Noble, b 26 Jul 1883; 7. Jean Noble, b 11 Sep 1885; 8. Allan Anderson, b 15 Sep 1887; 9. Laura Katherine, b 24 Feb 1892.   **FES vii 624**.

53   AITKENHEAD, James. To QUE on the *George Canning*, ex Greenock, 14 Apr 1821; stld prob Lanark Co, ONT.   **HCL 239**.

AITKIN. See also AITKEN, AIKIN.

54   AITKIN, Ann, b ca 1765. From Edinburgh. To QUE, 1822; stld Beckwith Twp, Lanark Co, ONT. Wife of Rev George Buchanan, qv.   **HCL 192**.

55   AITKIN, Daniel. To NS, prob <1814; stld Guysborough Co. m 19 Dec 1814, Charity, d/o John Jamieson and Charlotte Morrison.   **NSN 25/122**.

56 AITKIN, Robert. From ROX. To QUE on the *Sarah Mary Jane*, 1831; stld Blue Lake, Dumfries Twp, Waterloo Co, ONT. **HGD 60**.

57 ALDCORN, William, b ca 1806. To St Gabriel de Valcartier, QUE, prob <1855. **Census 1861**.

58 ALEXANDER, George. From Balmedie, ABD. s/o James A, farmer, and Ann Simpson. To Drummond Co, QUE, ca 1820, and was sometime in Durham, Grey Co, ONT. Formerly Capt, RN. m 1830, Ann Richards. Son James, res Ulverton, QUE. **MGC 2 Aug 1979**.

59 ALEXANDER, George, b 21 May 1814. From Banff. s/o George A, merchant. Matric Marischall Coll, Aberdeen, 1827. To Gore, Perth Co, ONT; later to Barrie, Simcoe Co. Pres of the Provincial Agricultural Association, 1857; MLA 1858-67; senator, 1873-90. **FAM ii 463; SNQ vi/1 89**.

60 ALEXANDER, George, d ca 1858. To Toronto, ONT. Farmer. Son Andrew. **SH**.

61 ALEXANDER, Sir James Edward, 1803-85. From Westerton, STI. s/o Alexander A. of Powis, CLK. Matric Univ of Glasgow, 1817, and attended Royal Military Academy. Held several staff appointments in the army. App Commander-in-Chief of the Forces in Canada, 1847, and lived in the country until 1855, when he held the rank of Lt Col. Travel-writer and biographer; CB, 1873; General, 1881. **MOT 21; IBD 6; CBD 22; GMA 9823; MDB 6**.

62 ALEXANDER, John. Prob from STI and poss rel to Peter A, qv. To McNab Twp, Renfrew Co, ONT, 1825. **EMT 18**.

63 ALEXANDER, John, 12 May 1817–10 Apr 1882. Poss from Paisley, RFW. To Toronto, ONT, ca 1844, later to Peoria, IL. m ca 1842, Mary Montgomery, qv, ch: 1. Gilbert, b ca 1844; 2. Mary, b ca 1846; 3. Jane, b ca 1847; 4. John, b 30 Mar 1849; 5. Robert Henry, b 31 Mar 1856; 6. Sarah, b 1859; 7. William, b 1861; 8. Thomas Montgomery, b 18 June 1862; 9. Charles, b 1864; 10. Agnes, b 1866. **DC 10 Sep 1974**.

64 ALEXANDER, Michael, b 1813. To ONT <1840, but stld Bristol Twp, Pontiac Co, QUE, 1849. m Margaret Hammond, ch: 1. William; 2. Elizabeth Ann; 3. James; 4. Edward; 5. Jennie. **DC 21 Mar 1981**.

65 ALEXANDER, Peter. Prob from STI and poss rel to John A, qv. To McNab Twp, Renfrew Co, ONT, 1825. **EMT 18**.

66 ALEXANDER, Robert, b 16 Jul 1776, Nerston, East Kilbride, LKS. s/o Robert A. and Jean Aiken. To QUE, ex Greenock, May 1823. Went to Albany, NY, and stld eventually at Jackson, Washington Co. Farmer. m Mary Strang, qv, ch: 1. Cathrine, b 30 May 1806; 2. Robert, b 7 Jan 1808; 3. Maxwell, b 17 Jan 1810; 4. Jean, b 17 Apr 1812; 5. William, b 12 Sep 1814; 6. James, twin; 7. Mary, b 30 Apr 1817; 8. Barbara, b 6 Apr 1819; 9. John b 9 May 1821; 10. Orlando Strang, b 17 May 1813. **East Kilbride OPR 643/2-3; LDW 27 Sep 1975**.

67 ALEXANDER, Rev Thomas, From Aberdeen. s/o James A, tailor. Grad MA Marischall Coll, 1824. To ONT 1835 to become Presb min at Cobourg, Northumberland Co. Later at Grey, Mount Pleasant and Burford. **FAM ii 441; SNQ ii/2 171**.

68 ALEXANDER, Sir William, 1604-38. From Menstrie, STI. s/o Sir William A, 1567–1640, who had a charter of NS, NB, etc, 1821, and of Janet Erskine. To Port Royal, NS, 1629, with a group of settlers, but retr to SCT, 1631. Lord of Session, 1635, and Viscount Canada. m Lady Margaret, d/o William, Marquess of Douglas, ch: 1. William, Earl of Stirling, dsp; 2. Catherine; 3. Jean; 4. Margaret; 5. Lucy. **SP viii 178; MDB 718**.

69 ALLAN, Adam, 1757–1823. From Dumfries. To NB and d there. Militiaman. **MDB 7**.

70 ALLAN, Alexander, 1775–16 Jul 1855. From Aberdeen. s/o Alexander A, brick and tile manufacturer, Old Machar par. To Preston Twp, Waterloo Co, ONT, 1843. Advocate in Aberdeen; Town Clerk of Preston and superintendent of Wellington Dist Schools. m 7 Oct 1824, Ann Davidson, qv, and had, prob with other ch: 1. Alexander, alumnus Marischall Coll, Aberdeen, 1839-43; 2. Ann, qv; 3. William, res Salem; 4. Absolom Shade, Sheriff of Wellington Co. **SAA 81; FAM ii 508; EHE 11**.

71 ALLAN, Andrew, 1822–1901. From Saltcoats, AYR. s/o Capt Alexander A, shipmaster, and Jean Crawford. Joined business of bro Hugh, qv, at Montreal, QUE, 1846, and succ him in presidency of Montreal Ocean Steamship Co. m 1846, Isabelle Ann, d/o John Smith. Son Andrew Alexander, 1860–1919, Shipowner and financier. **MDB 7**.

72 ALLAN, Ann. From Aberdeen. d/o Alexander A, qv, and Ann Davidson, qv. To Preston Twp, Waterloo Co, ONT, 1843. m at Salem, 26 Aug 1863, Thomas McQueen, farmer, Pilkington Twp. **SAA 81**.

73 ALLAN, Ann, 27 Feb 1780–14 Dec 1855. From Bargour, Mauchline, AYR. d/o Andrew A. and Elizabeth Muir. To Amherstburg, Essex Co, ONT, 1852. wid/o John Paton, 1776–1844, whom she m 1 Jul 1803, ch: 1. Elizabeth, qv; 2. Alexander, 1805-80, res Crosby, ENG; 3. Andrew, 1807-70, d AYR; 4. John, qv; 5. James, 1811-53; 6. David, qv; 7. Rev William, d Nottingham, ENG; 8. Janet, 1817-21; 9. Robert, 1819-70; 10. Allan, 1821-30; 11. Thomas, 1823-31; 12. Janet, 1825-26; 13. Annie, twin, d 1849. **DC 30 Sep 1960**.

74 ALLAN, Charles, d 13 Jan 1859. From Bendochy, PER. To Pilkington Twp, Wellington Co, ONT, 1833. Carpenter, builder and first reeve of Pilkington. Later warden of Wellington Co. m Grace Irons, qv, ch: 1. Charles, b 1828; 2. Adam Ferguson; 3. Henrietta; 4. James; 5. Jemina; 6. Grace; 7. David, dy. **EHE 120; DC 7 Jun 1980**.

75 ALLAN, Rev Daniel, 1812-84. From ROC. Educ Aberdeen. App by Glasgow Colonial Society, 1836, to ONT, and ord min at Stratford, Perth Co, and Woodstock, Oxford Co, 21 Oct 1838. Joined FC, 1844, and was later min at North Easthope. d at Goderich. **FES vii 624; PCM 14**.

76 ALLAN, Francis, b ca 1793. From Corstorphine, MLN. To QUE ex Greenock, 1815; stld Scotch Line, Lanark Co. Clerk, teacher and farmer. Wife Janet Cowie, qv, with him, and 1 child. **SEC 1; HCL 231**.

77 ALLAN, George. From Lethendy, PER. bro/o Charles A, qv. To Elora, Nichol Twp, Wellington Co, prob <1840. **EHE 121**.

78   ALLAN, George, ca 1831–27 Nov 1854. From Monzie, PER. s/o Campbell A. and Jane Cloudsly. To CAN, prob ONT, and d there.   **Ts Monzie**.

79   ALLAN, Henrietta. From Lethendy, PER. sis/o Charles A, qv. To Elora, Nichol Twp, Wellington Co, ONT, prob <1840.   **EHE 121**.

80   ALLAN, Sir Hugh, 29 Sep 1810–9 Dec 1882. From Saltcoats, AYR. s/o Capt Alexander A, shipmaster, and Jean Crawford. To Montreal, QUE, 1826. Shipowner, and founded the 'Allan Line.' Pres of Merchants' Bank and of the Montreal Telegraph Co. Knighted 1871. Involved in attempt to finance and gain control of the building of the Canadian Pacific Railway, which caused 'The Pacific Scandal' of 1873. m 13 Sep 1844, Matilda, d/o John Smith, Montreal, and d Edinburgh, SCT. Son Sir Hugh Montague, 1860–1951, financier.   **BNA 1157; SNQ v/1 70; SGC 385; CBD 24; MDB 8**.

81   ALLAN, James. From Logiealmond, PER. s/o James A, farmer, Braconesk, and Janet Gorrie. To Montreal, QUE, <1835.   **Ts Moneydie**.

82   ALLAN, James. From Lethendy, PER. bro/o Charles A, qv. To Elora, Nichol Twp, Wellington Co, ONT, prob <1840. Blacksmith.   **EHE 121**.

83   ALLAN, James Glen, ca 1816–12 Jan 1886. From Edinburgh. s/o Francis A, upholsterer, and Isabella Sheach. To NS.   **Ts Old Calton**.

84   ALLAN, Janet, 24 Jul 1836–15 Nov 1922. From Thurso, CAI. To South Ely, Shefford Co, QUE, 1842, poss with parents. m Hugh Munroe, qv, and d Melbourne, Richmond Co.   **MGC 2 Aug 1979**.

85   ALLAN, John, 3 Jan 1746–7 Feb 1805. From Edinburgh. s/o William A, qv, and Isabella Maxwell, qv. To Halifax, NS, 1749. Farmer, merchant and MLA, rep Cumberland Co, 1775-76. Fled to Maine to escape treason charge and became an Indian agent. m Mary, d/o Mark Patton, Halifax. Son William, 1770–1814.   **MLA 10**.

86   ALLAN, John, b ca 1791. From Cockburnspath, BEW. To QUE, ex Greenock, 1815, and stld 1816 in Burgess Twp, Lanark Co, ONT. Labourer, later farmer.   **SEC 1; HCL 15**.

87   ALLAN, John. From Bannockburn, STI. To QUE, 1822; stld Leeds Twp, Megantic Co, QUE, 1825. Farmer. ch with him: 1. Margaret, d 1838; 2.John; 3. William; 4. Charles, b ca 1824.   **AMC 130**.

88   ALLAN, John. From Logiealmond, PER. s/o James A, farmer, Braconesk, and Janet Gorrie. To Montreal, QUE, <1835.   **Ts Moneydie**.

89   ALLAN, John, d 28 Jun 1850. From Westbarns, Dunbar, ELN. s/o James A. To Ingersoll Twp, Oxford Co, ONT.   **DGH 25 Jul 1850**.

90   ALLAN, Margaret. Prob from Tayport, FIF. To Heron Is, Restigouche Co, NB, 1826. Wife of Alexander Dutch, qv.   **DC 13 Oct 1980**.

91   ALLAN, Margaret. To Leeds Twp, Megantic Co, QUE, 1831. m William Oliver, qv.   **AMC 147**.

92   ALLAN, Robert, 1797–4 Mar 1852. From Alves par, MOR. To Baltimore, Hamilton Twp, Northumberland Co, ONT, ca 1835. Farmer. m Helen Henry, qv, ch: 1. Janet, b 16 Jul 1823; 2. Jane, b 11 Aug 1825; 3. George,

b 6 Aug 1827; 4. Helen, b 2 Oct 1830; 5. Christian, b 23 May 1833; 6. Alexander, b ca 1835; 7. Isabella, b ca 1836; 8. Robert, b ca 1837.   **DC 7 Sep 1979**.

93   ALLAN, William, 1720-90. From Edinburgh. To Halifax, NS, 1749; moved to Fort Lawrence, 1752. Soldier and farmer. Wife Isabella Maxwell, qv, with him and s John.   **MLA 10**.

94   ALLAN, William, 1770–11 Jul 1853. From Huntly Moss, ABD. s/o Alexander A. and Margaret Mowat. To Niagara, Lincoln Co, ONT, <1798; later to Toronto. Postmaster, Collector of Customs and Major, 3rd York Militia. An incorporator of the ill-fated Bank of Upper Canada, and first pres of the St Andrew's Society of Toronto. m Leah Tyrer. Son George William, 1822–1901, lawyer.   **BNA 410, 730**.

95   ALLAN, William, b 1790. From LKS. To ONT 1830. m Elizabeth Fleming, qv, ch: William, jr, qv.   **DC 15 Jun 1977**.

96   ALLAN, William, jr, b ca 1805. From LKS. s/o William A, qv, and Elizabeth Fleming, qv. To ONT, 1830. m Elizabeth Hood, qv. Dau Hannah Watt, b 23 Oct 1827.   **DC 15 Jun 1977**.

97   ALLAN, William. From Logiealmond, PER. s/o James A, farmer, Braconesk, and Janet Gorrie. To Montreal, QUE, <1835.   **Ts Moneydie**.

98   ALLAN, William, 7 Sep 1817–24 May 1901. From King Edward par, ABD. Enlisted in 93rd Foot, 17 Aug 1837, and served in IRL and CAN. Discharged at QUE, 31 Jan 1848, and stld Ancaster Twp, Wentworth Co, ONT. Went later to Forest Twp, Sanilac Co, MI. Farmer. m Mary, 1825–1909, d/o Robert Fowler and Mary Fletcher, ch: 1. Janet, 1853–1935; 2. George Alexander, 1854–1925; 3. Elizabeth, 1856–1909; 4. Harmon, 1858–1944; 5. Emma, 1862–1929; 6. Sarah; 7. David, 1867–1901.   **DC 18 Jul 1979**.

99   ALLEN, Charles Edward, 16 Nov 1810–4 Jul 1885. Prob from PER. s/o John Lee A. of Errol Park. To Montreal, QUE. WS, and unm.   **HWS 60**.

100   ALLEN, Rev James, 20 Jul 1817–14 Jan 1881. From Dunbar, ELN. s/o Richard A, schoolmaster. Educ Univ of Edinburgh, 1833-40, and studied divinity. To Halifax, NS, as probationer, 1845. Ord to Covehead Presb Ch, Queens Co, PEI, 1846. m Grace Jane McDonald, ch: 1. John R; 2. Dr Archibald; 3. Maggie, d inf; 4. Maggie, d 1873; 5. Emma.   **DC 11 Apr 1981**.

101   ALLEN, James. To Pictou, NS, on the *Lady Gray*, ex Cromarty, ROC, arr 16 Jul 1841.   **DC 15 Jul 1979**.

102   ALLEN, John, b 1781. To Charlottetown, PEI, on the *Humphreys*, ex Tobermory, 14 Jul 1806. Wife Francis, aged 25, with him, and ch: 1. Thomas, aged 4; 2. Maria, aged 2.   **PLH**.

103   ALLEN, Margaret. From Aberdeen. To Shelburne Co, NS, <1776. m John McLean, qv.   **DC 5 Mar 1979**.

104   ALSTON, Christina, b 21 Jun 1821. From Glasgow. d/o John A, qv, and Janetty Dickson, qv. To QUE, 1834; stld Lanark Co, ONT. m James Drysdale, qv.   **Barony OPR 622/8; DC 20 May 1962**.

105   ALSTON, John, 10 Sep 1795–14 Nov 1846. From Linlithgow, WLN. s/o James A. and Christian Edgar. To Lanark Twp, Lanark Co, ONT, 1834. Shoemaker, sometime in Calton, Glasgow. m Janetty Dickson, qv, ch: 1. Christian, b 1821; 2. James; 3. Janet, b 1824; 4. Elizabeth, b 1828. **DC 26 Oct 1970**.

106 ALVES, Alexander. From Forres, MOR. To Chatham, Deux-Montagnes, QUE, 1833. m Janet McHattie, qv, ch: 1. Helen, qv; 2. James, qv; 3. John, b 1812, carpenter, stld York Co, ONT, and later Cincinnati, OH; 4. Alexander, stld Wells, Somerset, ENG; 5. William, b 1816, stld York Co, ONT, later Rochester, NY; 6. Janet, qv. **DC 17 Dec 1981**.

107 ALVES, Helen, b ca 1810. From Forres, MOR. d/o Alexander A, qv, and Janet McHattie, qv. To Chatham, Deux-Montagnes Co, QUE, 1833. m Alexander Kerr, qv. **DC 17 Dec 1981**.

108 ALVES, James, b 1811. From Forres, MOR. s/o Alexander A, qv, and Janet McHattie, qv. To York Co, ONT, 1832; stld later Parry Sound. m twice, ch incl: 1. Frank; 2. Gordon; 3. Agnes; 4. Lloyd. **DC 17 Dec 1981**.

109 ALVES, Janet, b 1818. From Forres, MOR. d/o Alexander A, qv, and Janet McHattie, qv. To Chatham, Deux-Montagnes Co, QUE, 1833. m Thomas Marks, from IRL. **DC 17 Dec 1981**.

110 AMOS, Adam, 1791–1886. From ROX. s/o James A, qv, and Janet Armstrong, qv. To Botsford, Westmorland Co, NB, Apr 1820. m Ellen Craig, qv, ch: 1. James, 1815-89; 2. John, 1819-78; 3. Robert, 1822–1907; 4. Janet, 1825–1907; 5. William, 1827–1907; 6. Elizabeth, 1827–1919; 7. Isabella, 1829–1909; 8 Adam, b 1832; 9. Thomas Oulton, 1834–1921; 10. Margaret, 1839–1914, unm; 11. David, 1841–1919. **DC 11 Dec 1979**.

111 AMOS, Elizabeth. From ROX. d/o James A, qv, and Janet Armstrong, qv. To Botsford, Westmorland Co, NB, 1820. m David Murray, ch. **DC 11 Dec 1979**.

112 AMOS, Flora, 1818-97. From Is Colonsay, ARL. d/o Malcolm A, qv, and Ellen Gillis, qv. To PEI, 1819; stld Nine Mile Creek, Queens Co. m Archibald Shaw, Brudenell, ch. **DC 25 Oct 1980**.

113 AMOS, James, ca 1770–12 Aug 1855. From ROX. To Botsford, Westmorland Co, NB, Apr 1820. Farmer. m Janet Armstrong, qv, ch: 1. Adam, qv; 2. Janet, qv; 3. James Robert, qv; 4. Elizabeth, qv. **DC 11 Dec 1979**.

114 AMOS, James Robert, 1799–22 Apr 1880. From ROX. s/o James A, qv, and Janet Armstrong, qv. To Botsford, Westmorland Co, NB, Apr 1820. m there, Mary, 1792–1870, ch: 1. James, b 1828; 2. George, b 1830; 3. Alexander, 1831-69; 4. Thomas, b 1836. **DC 11 Dec 1979**.

115 AMOS, Janet Armstrong, 1794–28 May 1884. From ROX. d/o James A, qv, and Janet Armstrong, qv. To Botsford, Westmorland Co, NB, ca 1834. m Adam Scott, qv. **DC 11 Dec 1979**.

116 AMOS, Joseph, b 31 Oct 1811. From Is Colonsay, ARL. s/o Malcolm A, qv, and Ellen Gillis, qv. To PEI, 1819; stld Nine Mile Creek, Queens Co; moved ca 1863, to Lower Derby, Northumberland Co, NB. m Catherine, d/o Alexander McNeil, qv, and Margaret McFee, qv, ch: 1. Margaret, 1839–1916, unm; 2. Flora, 1841–1920; 3. Ellen, 1843–1914; 4. Sarah, 1846–1931; 5. Malcolm,

1848–1920; 6. Annie, 1850–1940; 7. John Alexander, 1855–1941. **DC 25 Oct 1980**.

117 AMOS, Malcolm, b ca 1789. From Is Colonsay, ARL. To PEI, 1819; stld Lot 65, Nine Mile Creek, Queens Co. Farmer. m 9 Feb 1806, Ellen Gillis, qv, ch: 1. Joseph, qv; 2. Robert, qv; 3. Margaret, qv; 4. Flora, qv; 5. Janet, 1819-95; 6. John, b 1820, dy; 7. Ewen, b 1825; 8. John, 1828–1914. **SG xx/1 23; DC 25 Oct 1980**.

118 AMOS, Margaret, ca 1816–21 Feb 1846. From Is Colonsay, ARL. d/o Malcolm A, qv, and Ellen Gillis, qv. To PEI, 1819; stld Nine Mile Creek, Queens Co. m 1841, Malcolm James Ferguson, ch s John. After she d her husband m her yr sist Janet. **DC 25 Oct 1980**.

119 AMOS, Robert, ca 1815–14 Jan 1900. From Is Colonsay, ARL. s/o Malcolm A, qv, and Ellen Gillis, qv. To PEI, 1819; stld Nine Mile Creek, Queens Co. m Margaret, d/o Alexander McNeil, qv, and Margaret McFee, qv, ch: 1. Malcolm, 1849-60; 2. John, b ca 1853; 3. Jessie, b ca 1856; 4. Flora, 1858–1915; 5. Ellen, 1860–1925. **DC 25 Oct 1980**.

120 ANDERSON, Agnes, 2 Nov 1844–12 Jan 1904. From Hawick, ROX. d/o William A, qv, and Helen Scott, qv. To King Twp, York Co, ONT, ca 1846. m Walter Reid, Reidsville, Ayr, Waterloo Co. **DC 2 Aug 1979**.

121 ANDERSON, Alexander, b 22 Jun 1768. Prob from MOR. To Flat River, PEI, on the *John & Elizabeth*, arr 30 Jul 1775; stld poss Kings Co. m at Rustico, 1789, ch. **DC 27 Jul 1980**.

122 ANDERSON, Alexander, ca 1794–28 Jan 1824. From Strathspey. To NS and d there leaving a widow and child. **VSN No 456**.

123 ANDERSON, Alexander, b ca 1772. From Fortingall, PER. bro/o Christian Ann A, qv. To Charlottetown, PEI, on the *Clarendon*, ex Oban, 6 Aug 1808; stld Hillsborough River. Farmer. Wife Isobel, aged 32, with him, and ch: 1. James, aged 10; 2. Ann, aged 8; 3. Christian, aged 6; 4. Isobel, aged 4. **CPL; DC 11 Apr 1981**.

124 ANDERSON, Alexander, b ca 1790. From Crieff, PER. To Beckwith Twp, Lanark Co, ONT, 1820; moved to Monaghan Twp, Northumberland Co, 1834. m Catherine Kennedy. **DC 21 Mar 1981**.

125 ANDERSON, Alexander. From Petty, INV. To East Williams Twp, Middlesex Co, ONT, 1832. Son William, mill-owner, Mexico. **PCM 43**.

126 ANDERSON, Alexander. From Ellen par or Cruden par, ABD. To ONT <1850. m Elizabeth Freure. **DC 23 Jun 1980**.

127 ANDERSON, Alexander. From ABD. Neph of John A of Candacraig. To ONT <1855. **SH**.

128 ANDERSON, Andrew, 10 Mar 1810–20 May 1885. From LKS. s/o Andrew A. and Martha Mahon. To Sydney Mines, Cape Breton Co, NS, ca 1834. Mine manager. m Elizabeth Crawford Logan, ch: 1. Andrew, b 1830; 2. Janet, b 1832; 3. Elizabeth, b 1835; 4. Martha, b 1837; 5. Jane, b 1840; 6. John, b 1842; 7. George, b 1844; 8. James, b 1847; 9. Rebecca, b 1849; 10. William, b 1852; 11. Margaret, b 1854; 12. Mary, b 1857; 13. Robert, b 1858. **DC 20 May 1980**.

129   ANDERSON, Ann. From SUT. To Pictou Co, NS, 1822; stld nr Lansdowne. Wife of Donald Bethune, qv. **DC 10 Feb 1980.**

130   ANDERSON, Ann, ca 1801–23 Jan 1869. From ABD. To Hamilton, ONT. m William Grassie, qv.   **Ts Mt Albion.**

131   ANDERSON, Ann Cruden. From Ellon, ABD. s/o James A. in Kirktown of Logie. To Hamilton, ONT, ca 1854. m Rev William Masson, qv.   **FES vi 387.**

132   ANDERSON, Beatrice. From LKS. To Lanark Co, ONT, 1820. Wife of Archibald Nairn, qv.   **DC 21 Mar 1980.**

133   ANDERSON, Catherine, 1803–25 May 1871. From Kenmore, PER. To Esquesing Twp, Halton Co, ONT, 1821. Wife of Malcolm McPherson, qv.   **EPE 74.**

134   ANDERSON, Christian. From Ellon par or Cruden par, ABD. To Lincoln Co, ONT, <1850. m William Cavers, farmer, Wellandport.   **DC 23 Jun 1980.**

135   ANDERSON, Christian Ann, ca 1784–12 May 1876. From Fortingall, PER. sis/o Alexander A, qv. To Charlottetown, PEI, on the *Clarendon*, ex Oban, 6 Aug 1808; stld Hillsborough River. Wife of Archibald McGregor, qv.   **CPL; DC 11 Apr 1981.**

136   ANDERSON, Christina. From Dalkeith, MLN. To Leeds Twp, Megantic Co, QUE, 1831. Wife of David McIntosh, qv.   **AMC 144.**

137   ANDERSON, David. From Petty, INV. To East Williams Twp, Middlesex Co, ONT, 1832.   **PCM 43.**

138   ANDERSON, Duncan. From Comrie, PER. To Montreal, QUE, on the *Curlew*, ex Greenock, 21 Jul 1818; stld prob Lanark Co, ONT. Ch with him: 1. Eliza, aged 9; 2. Peter, aged 3.   **BCL.**

139   ANDERSON, Rev Duncan, 1828–1903. From Monymusk, ABD. Educ Kings Coll, Aberdeen, and grad MA 1818. To QUE, 1854, and became min of St Andrews Ch, Lévis. Author and ornithologist.   **KCG 300; MDB 13.**

140   ANDERSON, Edward, d 28 Dec 1840. From Stenrishill, Wamphray, DFS. To Oakville, Halton Co, ONT, and d there.   **DGH 25 Feb 1841.**

141   ANDERSON, Elspeth. From Ellon par or Cruden par, ABD. To Lincoln Co, ONT, <1850. m Andrew Dalrymple.   **DC 23 Jun 1980.**

142   ANDERSON, Mrs Grace Thorburn, ca 1788–15 Dec 1857. From Elizatown, DFS. To Rae Is, NFD. wid/o John Anderson.   **DGH 15 Jan 1858.**

143   ANDERSON, Hugh. From Aberdeen. To St Anns, Victoria Co, NS, 1850. Sea-Capt. Went later to Melbourne, AUS, but stld Auckland, North Is, NZ. m Margaret, d/o Rev Norman MacLeod, qv, and Mary MacLeod, qv, ch.   **DC 15 Feb 1980.**

144   ANDERSON, James. Prob rel to William A, qv, and to Robert A, qv. To QUE on the *Commerce*, ex Greenock, Jun 1820.   **HCL 238.**

145   ANDERSON, Rev James, 5 Jul 1834–14 Jul 1913. From Kenmore, PER. s/o Duncan A, farmer, and Janet McEwen. Educ Univ of St Andrews, 1851-52. To NS, 1866, and was min of Wallace and Pugwash, Cumberland Co. Adm to St James's, Newcastle,

Northumberland Co, NB, 1873. Retr to SCT and was min at Alvie, INV, 1880–1913. m (i) 1865, Barbara Grant, 1832-83; (ii) 1888, Jessie, d/o Rev Daniel Munro, min at Insh.   **SAM 114; FES vi 357, vii 608, 613.**

146   ANDERSON, James. From Scroggiehill, Elgin. s/o James A. and Elspet Gow. To ONT <1855. Farmer. **SH.**

147   ANDERSON, James. From Logie Buchan, ABD. To Toronto, ONT, 1835; stld Scott Twp. Retr to SCT 1837. m Margaret Davidson, qv, and had, poss with other ch: 1. Jean, b Scott Twp, 7 Mar 1836; 2. Alexander, b 10 Feb 1838; 3. William Alexander, b 9 Jan 1843, Newhills, baker, who emig later to Toronto.   **Newhills OPR 226/2; DC 16 Apr 1978.**

148   ANDERSON, Janet. To Williams Twp, Middlesex Co, ONT, <20 Mar 1834, when m James McDonald, qv.   **PCM 18.**

149   ANDERSON, Janet. To ONT <1845, and m — McFarlane, ch: 1. Helen; 2. James; 3. Janet; 4. Matthew; 5. Thomas; 6. Robert.   **SH.**

150   ANDERSON, Jean. From Huntley, ABD. To ONT, 1854; stld poss Wentworth Co. m Robert Wilson, qv.   **DC 23 Nov 1981.**

151   ANDERSON, John. To Halifax, NS, <1775. Dau Elizabeth, b <1780.   **DC 5 Jan 1966.**

152   ANDERSON, John, ca 1790–17 Jul 1810. From Cellardyke, Kilrenny, FIF. s/o James A, shipmaster, and Margaret Millar. To Halifax, NS, and d there.   **Ts Kilrenny.**

153   ANDERSON, John. From Glasgow. To ONT, ca 1810. m Elizabeth —. Dau Elizabeth Gilmore, b Barrhead, 9 Mar 1809.   **DC 16 Jul 1969.**

154   ANDERSON, John. To QUE, 1818; stld Con 7, Beckwith Twp, Lanark Co, ONT.   **HCL 34.**

155   ANDERSON, John. From Kenmore, PER. To Montreal, QUE, on the *Sophia*, ex Greenock, 26 Jul 1818; stld prob Beckwith Twp, Lanark Co, ONT. Wife Isabelle with him, and ch: 1. Donald, aged 13; 2. Hugh, aged 11; 3. Margaret, aged 9; 4. Peter, aged 6; 5. James, aged 4; 6. Robert, aged 2.   **SPL.**

156   ANDERSON, John, b 1767. From Rothes, ABD. To Halifax, NS, 1819; stld Musquodoboit Harbour. m Annie Reach, qv, ch: 1. Alexander; 2. Peter; 3. John; 4. William, qv; 5. James; 6. Charles; 7. George; 8. Annie; 9. Jobina.   **HNS iii 521.**

157   ANDERSON, John. From Eskdalemuir, DFS. To Montreal, QUE, prob <1830. m Miss Le Beau, and had, poss with other ch: 1. William, merchant in Montreal, later in Port Hope, Durham Co, ONT; 2. Jane.   **GSO 18.**

158   ANDERSON, John. From Petty, INV. To East Williams Twp, Middlesex Co, ONT, 1832. Son James R, physician.   **PCM 43.**

159   ANDERSON, John, b ca 1805. To Frontenac Co, ONT, <1838. m Sarah Douglas, ch: 1. Mary Ann, b 1838; 2. Isabella, b 1841; 3. James, b 1844; 4. John, b 1846; 5. Almetia, b 1849; 6. Sarah, b 1851; 7. William, b 1853; 8. Emily, b 1857.   **DC 25 Jan 1981.**

160   ANDERSON, Rev John, b 1832. From Abernathy, INV. To Ottawa, ONT, 1839. m Margaret Kennedy, ch. **DC 4 Mar 1965.**

161 ANDERSON, John, ca 1830–6 Nov 1854. From Cockhall, Fowlis par, ANS. s/o John A, farmer, and Marjory Piggot. To ONT and d Gloucester, Carleton Co. **Ts Fowlis**.

162 ANDERSON, John, ca 1809–1 Feb 1859. From Swinton, BEW. s/o John A, feuar, and Isabella Aitchison. To Kingston, ONT, and d there. **Ts Swinton**.

163 ANDERSON, John Paterson. From Colmonell, AYR. s/o John A. of Dalgarroch House, to whom he was served heir. To QUE <1851.

164 ANDERSON, Kate. Prob from PER. To McNab Twp, Renfrew Co, ONT, 1825. **DC 3 Jan 1980**.

165 ANDERSON, Margaret, ca 1780–30 Aug 1872. From LKS. To Lanark Co, ONT, 1820. Wife of George Waddell, qv. **DC 27 Jan 1977**.

166 ANDERSON, Martha. To Truro, Colchester Co, NS, <1760. m John Morrison, farmer and MLA. **MLA 254**.

167 ANDERSON, Mary, 1803-72. From Kettins, ANS. To Ancaster Twp, Wentworth Co, ONT, <1845, later to Pilkington Twp, Wellington Co. Wife of Alexander Watson, qv. **EHE 41**.

168 ANDERSON, Peter. From Kenmore, PER. To Montreal, QUE, on the *Sophia*, ex Greenock, 26 Jul 1818; stld prob Beckwith Twp, Lanark Co, ONT. Wife Christian with him and ch: 1. Donald, aged 9; 2. Grace, aged 7; 3. John, aged 5; 4. Ann, aged 3; 5. Peter, aged 2; 6. James, aged 9 mo. **SPL**.

169 ANDERSON, Peter, ca 1806–1 May 1887. From Tomnagrew, Dunkeld, PER. To Reach Twp, Ontario Co, ONT, ca 1840. Farmer. m Catherine Ferguson, qv, ch: 1. Catherine McAlpine, b ca 1848; 2. Jane, b ca 1850; 3. Jessie M, b ca 1852; 4. Elizabeth, b ca 1854; 5. Isabella, b ca 1858; 6. Patience, b ca 1862. **DC 31 Jan 1982**.

170 ANDERSON, Robert, b ca 1760. To Baddeck dist, Victoria Co, NS, 1786. Joiner, Left ch. **CBC 1818**.

171 ANDERSON, Robert. Prob rel to James A, qv, and William A, qv. To QUE on the *Commerce*, ex Greenock, Jun 1820. **HCL 238**.

172 ANDERSON, Robert, d 15 May 1840. From DFS. s/o Dr James A. of Mounie. To Georgina Twp, York Co, ONT. **DGH 17 Sep 1840**.

173 ANDERSON, Robert, b ca 1807. From LKS. To Montreal, QUE, 1840. **SGC 565**.

174 ANDERSON, Robert, 8 Feb 1846–29 Apr 1904. From Hawick, ROX. s/o William A, qv, and Helen Scott, qv. To King Twp, York Co, ONT, ca 1846. Worked as a cooper, and farmed at Donegal Village, Perth Co. m (i) Ellen Johnston; (ii) Annie Reid. **DC 2 Aug 1979**.

175 ANDERSON, Robert, b 23 Mar 1807. From Ellon par or Cruden par, ABD. To Niagara, Lincoln Co, ONT, <1850. m Sarah Oxborrow, and had, poss with other ch: 1. Robert; 2. Thomas; 3. William; 4. Walter; 5. Sarah. **DC 23 Jun 1980**.

176 ANDERSON, Thomas, 1748–1841. To Halifax, NS, on the *Duke of York*, ex Liverpool, 16 Mar 1772. m Mary Redburn, 1748–1828. **DC 12 May 1980**.

177 ANDERSON, Thomas Brown, 1796–28 May 1873. From Edinburgh. s/o Peter and Magdalene A. To Montreal, QUE, 1827. m Ann, d/o John Richardson and wid/o David Ogden, ch. **Ts Buccleuch**.

178 ANDERSON, William, b 1785. From Aberdalgie, PER. To Hudson Bay, ca 1812, and prob to Red River. **RRS 13**.

179 ANDERSON, William, b ca 1778. From Edinburgh. To QUE, poss on the *Atlas*, ex Greenock, 11 Jul 1815; stld ONT. Farmer and gardener. Wife Ann McKenzie, qv, with him, and 3 ch. **SEC 1**.

180 ANDERSON, William, 27 Apr 1804–17 Mar 1883. From Rothes, ABD. s/o John A, qv, and Annie Reach, qv. To Halifax, NS, 1819; stld Musquodoboit Harbour. Surveyor. m 1827, Eliza, d/o John Bayer and Margaret Bolong, ch: 1. John, dy; 2. Ann, b 1829; 3. Eliza M, b 1831; 4. Catherine; 5. Sarah Jane, b 1835; 6. Alexander, b 1837; 7. Mary, b 1839; 8. Isabelle, b 1841; 9. Charles, b 1843; 10. William, b 1843; 11. John, b 1845; 12. James Farquhar, b 1854. **HNS iii 521**.

181 ANDERSON, William. Prob rel to James A, qv, and Robert A, qv. To QUE on the *Commerce*, ex Greenock, Jun 1820. **HCL 238**.

182 ANDERSON, William. From Petty, INV. To East Williams Twp, Middlesex Co, ONT, 1832. **PCM 43**.

183 ANDERSON, Rev William, 1813-47. From Airdrie, LKS. To Inverness, Megantic Co, QUE, arr Oct 1844. Congregational min. **AMC 53**.

184 ANDERSON, William, d 19 Jun 1868. From Greenock, RFW. To Toronto, ONT, ca 1840. m Eliza Bowden Dalling, qv, and had, with other ch, s Robert, b 1843. **SCN**.

185 ANDERSON, William, 30 Dec 1818–27 Dec 1901. From Hawick, ROX. To King Twp, York Co, ONT, ca 1846. Farmer. m Helen Scott, qv, ch: 1. Agnes, qv; 2. Robert, qv; 3. Walter, b King Twp, 2 Jun 1847, d inf; 4. Margery, 1848-94; 5. Walter, 1850-67; 6. Margaret, 1852–1927; 7. Thomas, 1854–1914; 8. John, b 1856, res Brantford; 9. Hugh, 1858–1942; 10. Janet, 1860–1938, b Elma Twp, Perth Co. **DC 2 Aug 1979**.

186 ANDERSON, William, 1804-72. From AYR. To Caledon Twp, Peel Co, ONT, <1840. **DC 21 Apr 1980**.

187 ANDERSON, William James, 2 May 1812–15 May 1873. Grad MD Univ Edinburgh, and was LRCS. To NS, 1833, later to QUE. Physician, journalist and historian. **MDB 14**.

188 ANDREW, David, b ca 1751. From AYR. To QUE on the *Friendship*, ex Port Glasgow, 30 Mar 1775. Ship carpenter, 'going out to build vessels.' **LSF**.

189 ANDREW, Thomas. From Glasgow. bro/o John A, maltman. To NS <1830; stld Horton, Kings Co. Son Thomas. **HNS iii 678**.

190 ANGUS, Robert B. From Bathgate, WLN. To Montreal, QUE, 1852. Banker, and shareholder, St Paul and Manitoba railroad syndicate. **BNA 1076**.

191 ANGUS, Thomas, b ca 1780. From Stromness, OKI. To Hudson Bay, ca 1813, and prob to Red River. **RRS 13**

192 ANNAN, Ebenezer, ca 1820–24 Jun 1847. From KRS. s/o Dr A. To Liverpool, Queens Co, NS. *The Scotsman*, 17 Jul 1847.

193 ANNAND, William. From BAN. To Halifax, NS, <1808, with wife Jane Russell, qv. Merchant. Son William, 1808-87, farmer, newpaperman and MLA **MLA 14; MDB 16**.

194 ANNEL, Magnus, d 1795. Prob from OKI. To CAN <1780, and emp by HBCo. **ERT iii 10**.

195 ARBUCKLE, Neil. To Belfast, Queens Co, PEI, <1833. Schoolmaster. **HP 28**.

196 ARBUCKLES, Charles. From Falkirk, STI. Served as an NCO in 82nd Regt, and was gr 200 acres in Pictou Co, NS. m a d/o Barnabus McGee, pioneer settler, ch. **HPC App F**.

197 ARCHIBALD, David. To Truro, Colchester Co, NS, <1800. Son Col David. **HT 62**.

198 ARCHIBALD, Hugh, 1815–1904. From Saltcoats, AYR. s/o William A, qv, and Isabel Wood, qv. To River Louison, Restigouche Co, NB, 1831. Farmer. m Isabella Sutherland, 1828–1905, ch: 1. Alexander S, b 16 May 1868; 2. Janet Ferguson, b 1870; 3. Robina Wood, b 1872. **DC 1 Oct 1979**.

199 ARCHIBALD, Isabella, ca 1818–8 Jun 1874. From Saltcoats, AYR. d/o William A, qv, and Isabel Wood, qv. To Restigouche Co, NB, 1831. m 2 Apr 1846, Alexander Winton, 1810–1904, an Ulster-Scot, ch: 1. William, b 1847; 2. Nancy, b 1849; 3. John, b 1852; 4. Hugh, b 1854; 5. Isabella, b 1856; 6. Alexander, b 1858; 7. Janet, b 1859. **DC 1 Oct 1979**.

200 ARCHIBALD, Jane, ca 1829–ca 1857. From Saltcoats, AYR. d/o William A, qv, and Isabel Wood, qv. To Restigouche Co, NB, 1831. m Archibald Black, qv. **DC 1 Oct 1979**.

201 ARCHIBALD, John Wood, ca 1821–18 May 1890. From Saltcoats, AYR. s/o William A, qv, and Isabel Wood, qv. To River Louison, Restigouche Co, NB, 1831. Farmer. m Agnes, d/o James Calderwood, qv, and Margaret Crookshanks, qv, ch: 1. Margaret, b 1851; 2. Isabella Jane, b 1852; 3. James, b 1854; 4. Agnes, b 1855; 5. Martha, b 1857; 6. Elizabeth, b 1859; 7. John, b 1860. **DC 1 Oct 1979**.

202 ARCHIBALD, Margaret, b 27 Jul 1818. Prob from Tullibody, CLK. To Trafalgar Twp, Halton Co, ONT, after her m 13 Aug 1841, to John Marshall, qv. **DC 31 Mar 1980**.

203 ARCHIBALD, Martha. From Ardrossan par, AYR. d/o Hugh A, sailor, and Jeanet Cowan. To River Louison, Restigouche Co, NB, <1829. m John Campbell, qv. **DC 1 Oct 1979**.

204 ARCHIBALD, Martha, ca 1824–23 Apr 1900. From Saltcoats, AYR. d/o William A, qv, and Isabel Wood, qv. To Restigouche Co, NB, 1831. m Nathaniel McNair, jr, qv. **DC 1 Oct 1979**.

205 ARCHIBALD, Robert, 1816–5 May 1879. From Saltcoats, AYR. s/o William A, qv, and Isabel Wood, qv. To River Louison, Restigouche Co, NB, 1831. Farmer and Postmaster for the Archibald Settlement. m Catherine Black, qv, ch: 1. Elizabeth, b 1844; 2. William, b 1846; 3. James, b 1848; 4. Robert, b 1851; 5. Jane, b 1853; 6. Isabella, b 1855; 7. Catherine, b 1859; 8. Martha, b 1861; 9. Hugh, b 1866, bur New Mills. **CUC 21; DC 1 Oct 1979**.

206 ARCHIBALD, Rev Robert, 1804–13 Jun 1884. From Tullibody, Alloa. s/o Robert A, farmer, and Janet Henderson. Educ Univ of Glasgow, and ord min of Chatham, Northumberland Co, NB, 1834. Retr to SCT 1846, and was afterwards min at Kilbarchan, RFW, and at New Monkland, LKS. m 1833, Anne, d 1870, d/o William Hutton and Catherine Fotheringham, ch. **FES iii 272, vii, 608**.

207 ARCHIBALD, Thomas, ca 1830–ca 1860. From Saltcoats, AYR. s/o William A, qv, and Isabel Wood, qv. To River Louison, Restigouche Co, NB, 1831. Farmer. m his cousin Mary, d/o John Campbell, qv, and Martha Archibald, qv. Son William, b 1859. **DC 1 Oct 1979**.

208 ARCHIBALD, William, b 1 Oct 1781, Ardrossan par, AYR. s/o Hugh A, sailor, and Jeanet Cowan. To River Louison, Restigouche Co, NB, June 1831. Farmer. m Isabel Wood, qv, ch: 1. Hugh, qv; 2. Robert, qv; 3. Isabella, qv; 4. William, qv; 5. Martha, qv; 6. John Wood, qv; 7. Jane, qv; 8. Thomas, qv; 9. James, ca 1832–ca 1864, killed in American Civil War; 10. Margaret; 11. Elizabeth. **DC 1 Oct 1979**.

209 ARCHIBALD, William, jr, 1820-97. From Saltcoats, AYR. s/o William A, qv, and Isabel Wood, qv. To Restigouche Co, NB, 1831. Farmer. m 13 Jun 1846, Helen McNichol, qv, ch: 1. Isabella, b 1848; 2. Ellen, b 1850; 3. Hugh, b 1851; 4. Elizabeth, b 1853; 5. Martha, b 1861; 6. Mary, b 1855; 7. Donald, b 1857; 8. William, b 1863; 9. Robert, b 1864; 10. James, b 1867; 11. Mary; 12. Barbara. **DC 1 Oct 1979**.

210 ARGO, Adam L. Prob from New Deer, ABD. bro/o James A, qv, and Barbara A, qv. To York Co, ONT, 1835; stld Winternourne. **EHE 88**.

211 ARGO, Barbara. From New Deer, ABD. sis/o Adam A, qv, and James A, qv. To ONT, 1836; stld Bon Accord, Nichol Twp, Wellington Co. Wife of Alexander Watt, qv. **EHE 88**.

212 ARGO, James. Prob from New Deer, ABD. bro/o Adam A, qv, and Barbara A, qv. To York Co, ONT, 1835; later to Eramosa Twp, Wellington Co. **EHE 88**.

213 ARKLEY, John. From Kingsfield, Linlithgow. To QUE, prob 1822; moved to Leeds Twp, Megantic Co, QUE, 1825. Farmer. m (i) Margaret, d/o John Allan, qv, ch: 1. John, res Barton, VT; 2. James; 3. William, res Santa Barbara, CA. m (ii) Margaret Mann, with further ch: 4. Robert; 5. Annie; 6. George; 7. Margaret; 8. Isabella, b 1856; 9. Alexander, physician, Essex Junction, VT; 10. Elsie; 11. Harriet. **AMC 130**.

214 ARMOUR, Hugh, 1796–1822. From Kilmarnock, AYR. bro/o Robert A, qv, and Shaw A, qv. To Montreal, QUE, prob 1803, and d St Thérèsa de Blainville. Merchant. **SGC 267**.

215 ARMOUR, Robert, ca 1781–1857. From Kilmarnock, AYR. bro/o Hugh A, qv, and Shaw A, qv. To Montreal, QUE, 1798. Publisher and bookseller; Treasurer, St Gabriel St Ch, 1815-17, and sometime Cashier, Bank of Canada. m 1806, Elizabeth Harvie, qv, ch: 1. Robert; 2. Mary, b 1808; 3. Andrew Harvie, b 1809; 4. John, b 1815; 5. Agnes Hunter. **SGC 265; MDB 19**.

216 ARMOUR, Shaw. From Kilmarnock, AYR. bro/o Robert A, qv, and Hugh A, qv. To Montreal, QUE, prob 1803; later to Cobourg, Northumberland Co, ONT. Discount clerk, Bank of Canada. **SGC 267**.

217 ARMSTRONG, Alexander Scott, d 3 Feb 1855. From Dumfries. s/o Christopher A. To London, Westminster Twp, Middlesex Co, ONT. **DGC 3 Apr 1855**.

218 ARMSTRONG, Christopher, b ca 1764. From Nethermiln, Glencairn, DFS. bro/o Thomas A, qv, and William A, qv. To Georgetown, Kings Co, PEI, on the *Lovely Nellie*, ex Annan, 1774. **ELN**.

219 ARMSTRONG, Christopher. From DFS. To Falmouth, Hants Co, NS, <1840. Sometime of RE, and became farmer and fruit grower. Son John. **HNS iii 649**.

220 ARMSTRONG, James, b 12 Oct 1791. From Westerkirk par, DFS. bro/o John A, qv. To ONT prob <1810. **DC 26 Oct 1981**.

221 ARMSTRONG, James. From Edinburgh. To Perth, Lanark Co, ONT, 1854. Farmer. m Helen Mitchell. Son William. **DC 4 Mar 1965**.

222 ARMSTRONG, Janet, ca 1775–29 Nov 1865. From ROX. To Botsford, Westmorland Co, NB, 1820. Wife of James Amos, qv. **DC 11 Dec 1979**.

223 ARMSTRONG, Janet, 22 Aug 1798–27 Nov 1829. From Castleton, ROX. d/o John A and Isabell Marshall. To Scotch Lake, York Co, NB, 1819. Wife of John Oliver, qv. **DC 16 Jul 1979**.

224 ARMSTRONG, Jasper, 1796–1 Dec 1869. From Irongray, KKD. To Miramichi, Northumberland Co, NB, 1830. **DC 14 Jan 1980**.

225 ARMSTRONG, John. From Westerkirk, DFS. bro/o James A, qv, ONT. To NB <1810. **DC 26 Oct 1981**.

226 ARMSTRONG, John, d 3 June 1818, 'in prime of life.' From Langholm, DFS. To ONT. **DGH 18 Aug 1818**.

227 ARMSTRONG, John, 1802-67. From Todhillwood, Canonbie par, DFS. Said desc from Johnie A. of Gilnockie, a celebrated border chief of the 16th century. To Toronto, ONT, 1823. Axe manufacturer. ch. **CAE 17**.

228 ARMSTRONG, John, ca 1805–21 May 1861. From Glenzier Hall, Canonbie par, DFS. To Hamilton, ONT, prob <1850. Wife Margaret, 1808-63. **CAE 6, 10**.

229 ARMSTRONG, Mary, b ca 1812. To QUE <1833; later to NY and to Liberty Co, TX. m (i) David Middleton, ch: 1. Mary Jane, b QUE, 1834; 2. David, b 1836; 3. Sarah Ann, b 1840. m (ii) 1841, at Galveston, TX, Malcolm Chisholm, with further ch: 4. Anne, b 1842. **DC 7 Sep 1963**.

230 ARMSTRONG, Peter. To ONT, 1812; stld Drummond Twp, Lanark Co. Farmer, ch by wife Tibby, whom he m 1818. **HCL 45**.

231 ARMSTRONG, Simon, ca 1785–28 Mar 1857. From Harlawrigg, Canonbie par, DFS. To ONT prob <1835; stld St Mary's, Blanshard Twp, Perth Co. **DGH 19 Jun 1857**.

232 ARMSTRONG, Thomas, b ca 1757. From Nethermiln, Glencairn, DFS. bro/o Christopher A, qv, and of William A, qv. To Georgetown, Kings Co, PEI, on the *Lovely Nellie*, ex Annan. **ELN**.

233 ARMSTRONG, Thomas. From Castleton, ROX. To Queensbury par, York Co, NB, prob 1819. m Agnes Murray, qv, ch: 1. Adam; 2. James, alive 1877; 3. Charles; 4. Catherine; 5. Elizabeth. **DC 16 Jul 1979**.

234 ARMSTRONG, Walter, ca 1779–8 Apr 1842. From Westerkirk, DFS. s/o James A, tenant in Rigg, and Janet Borthwick. To Galt Twp, Waterloo Co, ONT. **Ts Westerkirk**.

235 ARMSTRONG, William, b ca 1759. From Nethermiln, Glencairn, DFS. bro/o Christopher A, qv, and of Thomas A, qv. To Georgetown, PEI, on the *Lovely Nellie*, ex Annan, 1774. **ELN**.

236 ARMSTRONG, William, b 10 Jul 1811. From Castleton, ROX. s/o Adam A. and Jane Nichol. To ONT 1827. Schoolteacher. **DC 16 Nov 1981**.

237 ARNOT, Lamont. Gr-s of John A, Prestonpans, ELN. To Bathurst, Lanark Co, ONT, <1853. **SH**.

238 ARNOTT, James, 1794–1864. From Glasgow. To ONT, ca 1839; stld Lanark Co, and d Rosetta. Weaver and farmer. m Margaret Horn, qv, ch: 1. Margaret, qv; 2. James Horn, qv; 3. George, b 1831; 4. John. **DC 2 Nov 1979**.

239 ARNOTT, James Horn, 1819–16 Feb 1896. From Glasgow. s/o James A, qv, and Margaret Horn, qv. To Lanark Co, ONT, ca 1839. m Janet Baird, 1 Aug 1848. **DC 2 Nov 1979**.

240 ARNOTT, Margaret, 21 Apr 1828–13 Apr 1885. From Glasgow. d/o James A, qv, and Margaret Horn, qv. To Lanark Co, ONT, ca 1839, and d Bagot, MAN. m John Machan, qv. **DC 2 Nov 1979**.

241 ARTHUR, Jean, b 6 Sep 1795. From Boghall, Houston and Kilellan par, RFW. d/o James A, weaver, and Elizabeth Shaw. To PEI, 1820. Wife of William Fyfe, qv. **DC 6 Apr 1979**.

242 ARTHUR, Margaret, b ca 1820. From OKI. To Pictou, NS, <1855. m George Johnston, s/o John James Hamilton, qv. Son Howard Hamilton, b 1855. **HNS iii 240**.

243 ATHOLE, Francis. Prob from Stranraer, WIG. To Halifax, NS, <1838. **SH**.

244 AULD, James, b 1831. To Hamilton, Northumberland Co, ONT. **Ts Mt Albion**.

245 AULD, Jane, 1768–1840. From AYR. d/o Robert A, qv, and Jean Fisset, qv. To Richmond Bay, PEI, on the *Falmouth*, ex Greenock, 8 Apr 1770; stld Stanhope, Queens Co. m Murdoch McLeod, qv, 2 Jan 1788. **DC 28 May 1980**.

246 AULD, Janet, 1775–10 Jul 1851. From Whitburn, WLN. To PEI, later to Pictou Co, NS. m (i) Rev Peter Gordon, qv; (ii) Rev James Drummond MacGregor, qv. **PAC 235; HNS iii 191, 393**.

247 AULD, John, ca 1766–7 Sep 1842. From AYR. s/o Robert A, qv, and Jean Fisset, qv. To Richmond Bay, PEI, on the *Falmouth*, ex Greenock, 8 Apr 1770; stld Stanhope, Queens Co, and d Covehead. m 7 Jul 1796, Margaret, d/o John Miller, qv, ch: 1. William, b 1797; 2. John; 3. David; 4. Robert; 5. Francis; 6. Edward; 7. George; 8. Jean; 9. Margaret; 10. Catherine; 11. Isabella. **DC 28 May 1980**.

248 AULD, John. From Irvine, AYR. s/o John A, shipmaster, and Margaret Begg. To Montreal, QUE, <21 Mar 1846. Merchant. *Ayr Sasines*, **328, 137**.

249 AULD, Robert, ca 1735–ca 1810. From AYR. To Richmond Bay, PEI, on the *Falmouth*, ex Greenock, 8 Apr 1770; stld Lot 34, Stanhope, Queens Co. Blacksmith and farmer. m Jean Fisset, qv, ch: 1. John, qv; 2. Jane, qv; 3. William; 4. Mary, b ca 1772; 5. Ann or Agnes, b ca 1775; 6. Robert, jr; 7. Isabella, 1779–1869; 8. David, d 1814; 9. Elizabeth or Betsy, res Vernon River. **DC 27 Jul 1980**.

250 AUSTIN, Mary. From Milton Mills, Moffat, DFS. d/o John A. To Galt, Dumfries Twp, Waterloo Co, ONT. m there 1856, Thomas Whittiker. *Carlisle Patriot*, **19 Apr 1856**.

B

251 BABINGTON, Benjamen, d 17 Feb 1848. From Dumfries. s/o Rev Charles B, Episcopal clergyman there, 1871-40. To Wentworth Co, ONT, and d Dundas. Partner, firm of James Bell Ewart & Co. **DGH 30 Mar 1848**.

252 BABINGTON, Lilias, d 23 Mar 1843. From Dumfries. Prob rel to Rev Charles B, Episcopalian clergyman there. To Dundas, Wentworth Co, ONT. m William J. Syme. **DGH 23 Mar 1843**.

253 BADENOCH, Alexander. Poss from Edinburgh. Gr-s of Alexander Forsyth, tailor in Calton. To QUE <1825. Merchant. **SH**.

254 BAILEY, Charles. From LKS. To QUE on the *Prompt*, ex Greenock, 4 Jul 1820; stld Dalhousie Twp, Lanark Co, ONT. **HCL 68**.

255 BAILLIE, Christy, ca 1798–25 Mar 1843. From Clyne par, SUT. To Earltown, Colchester Co, NS, <1830. Wife of Alexander McDonald, qv. **DC 19 Mar 1981**.

256 BAILLIE, Donald, ca 1796–13 Sep 1875. From SUT. To Pictou Co, NS, 1814. Wife Elspie, ca 1816–ca 1910. Both bur at Lovat. **DC 27 Oct 1979**.

257 BAILLIE, Hugh. To Restigouche Co, NB, ca 1768. Indian trader, sometime partnership with George Walker, qv. Sold his property to John Schoolbred, 1773. **SR 13**.

258 BAILLIE, John. From Sutherland. Served in 82nd Regt and was gr 150 acres in Pictou Co, NS, 1784. **HPC App F**.

259 BAILLIE, John, ca 1805–7 Dec 1881. From Clyne, SUT. To Pictou, NS, and stld Gairloch. Wife Margaret, ca 1796–3 Sep 1869. Both bur at Lovat. **DC 27 Oct 1979**.

260 BAILLIE, Margaret. From Barrowfield, Glasgow. To QUE, ex Greenock, summer 1815. Wife of Farquhar Smith, qv. **SEC 4**.

261 BAILLIE, Robert, ca 1757–19 Aug 1832. From Clyne, SUT. To Pictou, NS, 1814. Bur at Lovat. **DC 27 Oct 1979**.

262 BAILLIE, William, ca 1760–20 Mar 1847. From SUT, poss Clyne par. To Colchester Co, NS <1830; stld nr Earltown. m Christian Sutherland, qv. Son George, 1805-30. **DC 19 Mar 1981**.

263 BAILLIE, William, ca 1800–14 Sep 1874. From Clyne, SUT. To Pictou Co, NS; stld West River. Wife Janet, ca 1809–5 Oct 1881. Both bur Lovat. **DC 27 Oct 1979**.

264 BAIN, Donald, b ca 1751. To Charlottetown, PEI, on the *Elizabeth & Ann*, ex Thurso, arr 8 Nov 1806. Family with him: 1. James, aged 18; 2. Donald, aged 16; 3. Robert, aged 14; 4. William, aged 10; 5. Janet, aged 7; 6. John, aged 5; 7. Christian, aged 4. **PLEA**.

265 BAIN, Elizabeth, 1813–1 Sep 1882. From Glasgow. d/o William B, qv, and Janet Ross, qv. To Lanark Co, ONT, poss 1821. m Dr Alexander Munro, qv. **DC 2 Nov 1979**.

266 BAIN, Helen, 1805–4 Sep 1882. Prob from Cromarty par, ROC. To ONT, poss 1830. Wife of Thomas Hood, qv. **DC 27 Dec 1979**.

267 BAIN, Hugh, b ca 1790. From Strathglass, INV. To Pictou, NS, on the *Sarah*, ex Fort William, June 1801. **PLS**.

268 BAIN, James, 1 May 1817–18 May 1908. From Edinburgh. s/o James B. and Frances Brodie. To Toronto, ONT, 1846. Bookseller and stationer. m Joanna Watson, qv, ch: 1. James, 1842–1908, Librarian, Toronto Public Library; 2. Robert, b 1844; 3. Margaret, b 1845; 4. Mary, 1847-79; 5. John, 1849-79; 6. William, 1851-52; 7. Donald, 1853–1931. m (ii) 6 Dec 1854, Jessie Laurie, 1833-88, with further ch: 8. Jessie, 1855–1909; 9. Francis, 1857–1940; 10. Alexander, 1859–1903; 11. William, d inf; 12. Thomas, 1863–1950; 13. Amelia, 1865–1924; 14. Helen, 1867–1945; 15. Duncan, d inf; 16. Kenneth, d inf; 17. Jane, 1875–1962; 18. May, d 1876. **DC 27 Mar 1979**.

269 BAIN, Rev James, ca 1801–9 Dec 1885. From Kinkell, PER. Secession min at Kirkcaldy, FIF, 1826-53, when he went to Scarborough, York Co, ONT. Min of St Andrews Ch there until 1874. d at Markham. **UPC ii 360**.

270 BAIN, John. From BAN. Gr-s of Thomas B, wright in Keith. To Canada <1854. Cabinetmaker. **SH**.

271 BAIN, Mary Cullen, 8 Nov 1818–28 May 1900. From PER. d/o William B, qv, and Janet Ross, qv. To Lanark Co, ONT. m 4 Jan 1839, John Gillies, qv. **DC 2 Nov 1979**.

272 BAIN, Thomas, b 14 Dec 1834. From Denny, STI. To West Flamborough, Wentworth Co, ONT, 1837. m 25 Jun 1874, Helen, d/o John Weir. **DC 29 Sep 1964**.

273 BAIN, Thomas Middleton. From ROC. To Pictou, NS, ca 1853; stld New Glasgow, Pictou Co. Foreman with Acadia Coal Company. m Ann Campbell, qv. Son James, b 1860. **HNS iii 95**.

274 BAIN, Walter. To QUE on the *George Canning*, ex Greenock, 14 Apr 1821; stld prob Lanark Co, ONT. **HCL 239**.

275 BAIN, William, 1781–9 Feb 1832. From PER. To Lanark Co, ONT, poss 1821. m Janet Ross, qv, ch: 1. Elizabeth, qv; 2. Mary Cullen, qv; 3. William, b 16 Oct 1821. **DC 2 Nov 1979**.

276 BAIN, William, b ca 1783. From Forres, MOR. To CAN, 1834. Bookbinder. m Mary Mackenzie, qv, ch. **SG x/1 26**.

277 BAIN, William, b ca 1816. To Plympton Twp, Lambton Co, ONT, <1848. Storekeeper. m Agnes Spiers,

qv, ch: 1. James, b ca 1840; 2. Mary, b ca 1841;
3. William, b ca 1845; 4. George, b ca 1848; 5. Robert,
b ca 1855; 6. John, b ca 1857.   **DC 7 Nov 1979**.

278   BAIRD, Agnes, 27 Sep 1813–10 Sep 1875. From
Rutherglen, LKS. d/o William B, qv, and Margaret
Lochhead. To Montreal, QUE, on the *Royal George*, ex
Greenock, Jan 1827; stld Sarnia, Lambton Co, ONT.
m — Leach.   **DC 19 Nov 1978**.

279   BAIRD, Archibald, b ca 1772. From Rutherglen,
LKS. s/o John B. and Janet Jackson. To Montreal, QUE,
on the *Royal George*, ex Greenock, Jan 1827; stld
Sarnia, Lambton Co, ONT. Prob widower. ch with him:
1. John, 1803-81; 2. Janet, qv; 3. James; 4. William;
5. Elizabeth; 6. Agnes.   **DC 19 Nov 1978**.

280   BAIRD, Alexander, b 17 Mar 1823. From
Kirkintilloch, DNB. s/o James B, qv, and Janet Fergus,
qv. To Waterloo Co, ONT, 1841. m Janet Gordon, qv.
DC 2 Dec 1979.

281   BAIRD, Daniel, d 1852. From Dunning, PER.
s/o John B and Janet Roy. To ONT <1824, and
d Torbolton Twp, Carleton Co. Sometime Lt, RN.
m Helen McAra.   **DC 10 Nov 1978**.

282   BAIRD, Elizabeth, 27 Mar 1804–2 Jun 1843. From
Rutherglen, LKS. d/o William B, qv, and Margaret
Lochhead. To Montreal, QUE, on the *Royal George*, ex
Greenock, Jan 1827; stld Sarnia, Lambton Co, ONT, later
St Clair Co, MI. m Richard Allington.   **DC 19 Nov 1978**.

283   BAIRD, Elizabeth. To Pictou, NS, on the *London*,
arr 14 Jul 1848.   **DC 15 Jul 1979**.

284   BAIRD, George, 1825-73. From Kirkintilloch, DNB.
s/o James B, qv, and Janet Fergus, qv. To Waterloo Co,
ONT, 1841, and d at Plattsville. m Jessie Scott,
1824-93.   **DC 2 Dec 1979**.

285   BAIRD, Henry, 25 Jul 1808–27 Jan 1877. From
Rutherglen, LKS. s/o William B, qv, and Margaret
Lochhead. To Montreal, QUE, on the *Royal George*, ex
Greenock, Jan 1827; stld Sarnia, Lambton Co, ONT, later
St Clair Co, MI. Blacksmith. m 8 Feb 1833, Elizabeth
Schriener. Son William.   **DC 19 Nov 1978**.

286   BAIRD, James. Prob from LKS. To QUE on the
Brock, ex Greenock, Jul 1820; stld prob Lanark Co,
ONT.   **HCL 238**.

287   BAIRD, James, b ca 1786. From Kirkintilloch,
DNB. To Waterloo Co, ONT, 1841. Farmer. m Janet
Fergus, qv, ch: 1. Jean, 1814-22; 2. Mary, qv; 3. James,
1818-49, d in TX; 4. John, qv; 5. Alexander, qv;
6. George, qv; 7. Janet, 1827-67; 8. Thomas, qv;
9. Matthew, 1832-35; 10. Hugh, 1835–1904.
DC 2 Dec 1979.

288   BAIRD, Janet, 2 Oct 1808–29 May 1843. From
Rutherglen, LKS. d/o Archibald B, qv. To Montreal, QUE,
on the *Royal George*, ex Greenock, Jan 1827; stld
Sarnia, Lambton Co, ONT. m James Low, qv.
DC 19 Nov 1978.

289   BAIRD, Rev John, ca 1818–27 Sep 1874. From
STI. s/o Robert B, carpenter. Matric Univ of Glasgow
and grad MA 1834. Min of Secession Ch and UP Ch at
Jedburgh, 1843-53. Presb min at Pickering, ONT, 1854;
later at Port Stanley.   **RGG 28; GMA 13293; UPC ii 257**.

290   BAIRD, John, 8 Mar 1820–17 Oct 1891. From
Kirkintilloch, DNB. s/o James B, qv, and Janet Fergus,

qv. To Waterloo Co, ONT, 1841, and d New York City.
m Agnes Russell.   **DC 2 Dec 1979**.

291   BAIRD, John, 3 Nov 1833–5 Jan 1909. From
Glasgow. To Sherbrooke, QUE. m Ellen Paisley, qv.
MGC 2 Aug 1979.

292   BAIRD, Margaret, 7 Mar 1800–24 Jan 1879. From
Rutherglen, LKS. d/o William B, qv, and Margaret
Lochhead. To Montreal, QUE, on the *Royal George*, ex
Greenock, Jan 1827; stld Sarnia, Lambton Co, ONT, later
St Clair Co, MI. m James Young.   **DC 19 Nov 1978**.

293   BAIRD, Matthew, Prob from LKS. To Lanark Co,
ONT, <1850. m Ann Robertson. Dau Mary.   **DC 5 Feb
1981**.

294   BAIRD, Robert. Poss from LKS. Rel to William B,
qv. To Ramsay Twp, Lanark Co, ONT, 1821.   **HCL 85**.

295   BAIRD, Susan, 1815-91. From Rutherglen, LKS.
d/o William B, qv, and Margaret Lochhead. To Montreal,
QUE, on the *Royal George*, ex Greenock, Jan 1827; stld
Sarnia, Lambton Co, ONT, later St Clair Co, MI.
m William Westbrook.   **DC 19 Nov 1978**.

296   BAIRD, Thomas, 1829–1905. From Kirkintilloch,
DNB. s/o James B, qv, and Janet Fergus, qv. To
Waterloo Co, ONT, 1841, and d there. m Margaret Millar,
qv, ch.   **DC 2 Dec 1979**.

297   BAIRD, William, 9 Nov 1776–9 Mar 1855. From
Rutherglen, LKS. s/o John B. and Janet Jackson. To
Montreal, QUE, on the *Royal George*, ex Greenock, Jan
1827; stld Sarnia, Lambton Co, ONT, later St Clair Co,
MI. Weaver. m 22 Apr 1797, Margaret, d before 1827;
d/o Henry Lochhead and Margaret Bark, ch: 1. John,
d inf; 2. Margaret, qv; 3. Janet, remained in SCT;
4. Elizabeth, qv; 5. Henry, qv; 6. Agnes, qv; 7. William,
qv; 8. Susan, qv.   **DC 19 Nov 1978**.

298   BAIRD, William. Poss from LKS. Rel to Robert B,
qv. To Ramsay Twp, Lanark Co, ONT, 1821.   **HCL 85**.

299   BAIRD, William, jr, 20 Jul 1813–10 Sep 1875.
From Rutherglen, LKS. s/o William B, qv, and Margaret
Lochhead. To Montreal, QUE, on the *Royal George*, ex
Greenock, Jan 1827; stld Sarnia, Lambton Co, ONT, later
St Clair Co, MI. m 26 Oct 1846, Charlotte Earle.
DC 19 Nov 1978.

300   BAIRD, William. To Pictou, NS, on the *Hope*, ex
Glasgow, 5 Apr 1848. Wife Margaret with him, and ch:
1. Margaret; 2. Mary; 3. Gavin; 4. Jane, 5. Robertson;
6. Janet. They went later to USA.   **DC 12 Jul 1979**.

301   BALFOUR, William, ca 1759–2 Dec 1811. From
Edinburgh. To John B. To Fredericton, NB. Lt Gen
British Army at Fort Howe, 1784, and in 1811 became
President and Commander-in-Chief of the Province.
DGC 11 Feb 1812; MDB 32.

302   BALLANTINE, David, 10 Oct 1803–23 Aug 1853.
From Port Dundas, Glasgow. s/o David B. and Mary
Hodge. To Stratford, Perth Co, ONT, 1841; later to
Dundas. Engineer and millwright. m Mary Murray, qv.
Dau Mary Hodge, qv.   **NDF 12**.

303   BALLANTINE, Mary Hodge, b ca 1830. From
Glasgow. d/o David B, qv, and Mary Murray, qv. To Perth
Co, ONT, 1841. m Nelson, a merchant, son of Robert
Keefer and Lavinia Lawrason, and res Burlington, Halton
Co. ch: 1. Robert; 2. Alexander; 3. Mary; 4. dau.
NDF 177.

304   BALLANTYNE, Daniel. To Ballantyne's Cove, Antigonish Co, NS, <1800. m Ellen, d/o George Morrison and Jane Forbes, ch: 1. George; 2. John; 3. James; 4. William; 5. David; 6. Thomas; 7. Alexander; 8. Jane; 9. Nellie; 10. Margaret; 11. Ann; 12. Janet.   **HCA 78**.

305   BALLANTYNE, David. Served in 82nd Regt as NCO, and was gr 200 acres in Pictou Co, NS, 1784. Moved later to Cape George, Antigonish Co, where he left ch.   **HPC App F**.

306   BALLANTYNE, David. To QUE on the *Commerce*, ex Greenock, Jun 1820; stld poss Lanark Co, ONT. **HCL 238**.

307   BALLANTYNE, Robert Michael, 24 Apr 1825–8 Feb 1894. Born Edinburgh. s/o Alexander B, master printer, and Randall Scott Grant. Educ Edinburgh Academy, 1835-37. To York Factory, Hudson Bay, on the *Prince Rupert*, ex Gravesend, Jun 1841. Appr as a clerk with the HBCo and served at York Factory, Norway House and Seven Islands. Retr to SCT 1847 and subsequently wrote *Hudson Bay* and other books of travel and adventure, suited for young people. m at Edinburgh, 31 Jul 1866, Jane Dickson, b 1846, d/o Rev William Grant, min at Cavers, and Jane Dickson. ch. **IBD 20; CBD 64; EAR 81; MDB 32**.

308   BALLENDEN, John, d 1856. From Stennes, OKI. To Montreal, QUE. Emp with HBCo. ch by a half-breed woman who d 1853.   **LDW 7 Apr 1979**.

309   BALMAIN, Hannah. From Inverkeithing, FIF. To QUE, ex Greenock, summer 1815; stld ONT. Wife of John McNab, qv.   **SEC 2**.

310   BALMER, Robert. From Cessford, ROX. s/o Richard B, mason. To Montreal, QUE, <1855. Merchant.   **SH**.

311   BANNATYNE, Andrew Graham Bellenden, 31 Oct 1829–18 May 1889. From South Ronaldshay, OKI. s/o James B. To MAN, 1846. Emp with HBCo at Norway House and was a mem of the Council of Assiniboia, 1868. m Annie, d/o Andrew McDermott.   **BNA 1091; MDB 32**.

312   BANNERMAN, Adam. To Grey Co, ONT, ca 1855. m Catherine Furlong, and had, poss with other ch: 1. Alexander; 2. John; 3. George.   **DC 3 Sep 1979**.

313   BANNERMAN, Alexander, b 22 Jun 1791. From Loist, Kildonan, SUT. s/o John B, tenant, and Janet Sutherland. To Fort Churchill, Hudson Bay, on the *Prince of Wales*, ex Stromness, 28 Jun 1813. Went to York Factory and thence to Red River.   **Kildonan OPR 52/1; LSS 186; RRS 27; LSC 323**.

314   BANNERMAN, Alexander, b ca 1798. From Duible, Kildonan, SUT. s/o William B, qv, and Barbara Gunn, qv. To York Factory, Hudson Bay, arr 26 Aug 1815, thence to Red River. m Janet, d/o William McKay, qv, ch: 1. John, b ca 1832; 2. David; 3. Alexander; 4. Selkirk; 5. James; 6. Donald.   **DC 3 Sep 1979**.

315   BANNERMAN, Alexander, b ca 1805. To West Gwillimbury, Simcoe Co, ONT, poss via Red River. m Catherine —, b ca 1809, ch: 1. Alexina, b ca 1838; 2. Jane, b ca 1842; 3. Adam, b ca 1844; 4. Mary, b ca 1846; 5. Betsy, b ca 1849; 6. Joanna, b ca 1850; 7. Donald, b 1851.   **DC 3 Sep 1979**.

316   BANNERMAN, Alexander, b ca 1805. From Kildonan par, SUT. To Grey Co, ONT, <1844; stld Blanchard. m Sarah Burgess, ch: 1. William; 2. Andrew; 3. Alexander; 4. Esther; 5. James; 6. Sarah; 7. John. **DC 3 Sep 1979**.

317   BANNERMAN, Alexander. Poss from SUT. Stld Lot 33, Con 25, Brant Twp, Brant Co, ONT, 1854. **DC 3 Sep 1979**.

318   BANNERMAN, Sir Alexander, 1783–1864. From Aberdeen. s/o Thomas B, merchant. Educ Marischall Coll, Aberdeen, 1801-05. Banker and MP, 1833. To Charlottetown, PEI, 1851. Lt Gov of PEI, and cr KB. Ret 1854, but was Gov of NFD, 1857-63.   **BNA 705; FAM ii 388; MDB 32**.

319   BANNERMAN, Andrew, b 1816. To West Gwillimbury, Simcoe Co, <1851. m 7 Jan 1851, Ann McLelland, and stld Sullivan Twp, Grey Co.   **DC 3 Sep 1979**.

320   BANNERMAN, Christian, 1794–1813. From Loist, Kildonan, SUT. d/o John B, tenant, and Janet Sutherland. To Fort Churchill, Hudson Bay, on the *Prince of Wales*, ex Stromness, 28 Jun 1813, and d there. **Kildonan OPR 52/1; LSS 186; RRS 27; LSC 323**.

321   BANNERMAN, Christian, b ca 1793. From Kildonan, SUT. To York Factory, Hudson Bay, arr 26 Aug 1815; stld Red River.   **LSC 327**.

322   BANNERMAN, Christian, b 28 Jan 1797, Badflaich, Kildonan par, SUT. d/o Donald B, qv, and Christian Gordon, qv. To Fort Churchill, Hudson Bay, on the *Prince of Wales*, ex Stromness, 28 Jun 1813. Went to York Factory, 1814, thence to Red River.   **Kildonan OPR 52/1; LSS 185; RRS 26; LSC 321**.

323   BANNERMAN, Donald, ca 1764–24 Sep 1813. From Badflaich, Kildonan par, SUT. hus/o Christian Gordon, qv. To Fort Churchill, Hudson Bay, on the *Prince of Wales*, ex Stromness, 28 Jun 1813, and d there. ch with him: 1. William, qv; 2. Christian, qv; 3. Donald.   **LSS 185; RRS 26; LSC 321**.

324   BANNERMAN, Donald. Prob from SUT. To Pictou, NS, on the *Lady Gray*, ex Cromarty, ROC, arr 16 Jul 1841.   **DC 15 Jul 1979**.

325   BANNERMAN, Elizabeth, b ca 1791, Dalhalmy, Kildonan par SUT. d/o John B, tenant, and Bessie Bannerman. To Fort Churchill, Hudson Bay, on the *Prince of Wales*, ex Stromness, 28 Jun 1813. Went to York Factory, 1814, thence to Red River. Left settlement and arr Holland River, 6 Sep 1815.   **LSS 186; RRS 27; LSC 323**.

326   BANNERMAN, Ellen, ca 1804–2 Feb 1871. From Helmsdale, SUT. To Simcoe Co, ONT, ca 1830. m at Loth, SUT, 10 Apr 1828, Alexander Murray, qv. **DC 28 Nov 1980**.

327   BANNERMAN, George, b ca 1792. From Kildonan, SUT. To Fort Churchill, Hudson Bay, on the *Prince of Wales*, ex Stromness, 28 Jun 1813. Went to York Factory, 1814, thence to Red River. Pioneer settler.   **LSS 186; RRS 27; LSC 322**.

328   BANNERMAN, Gordon. From Kintradwell or Loth, SUT. To Barneys River, Pictou Co, NS, 1822. Farmer. m Wilhelmina Sutherland, qv, ch: 1. Roderick, b 18 Dec

1818; 2. Margaret, b 17 Jun 1821; 3. John, b 10 Jun 1823; 4. Ann, b 18 Jun 1824. **DC 3 Sep 1979**.

329 BANNERMAN, Hugh, b 1 May, 1793, Dalhalmie, Kildonan par, SUT. s/o John B. and Bessie Bannerman. To Fort Churchill, Hudson Bay, on the *Prince of Wales*, ex Stromness, 28 Jun 1813. Went to York Factory, 1814, thence to Red River. Left settlement and arr Holland River, 6 Sep 1815. **Kildonan OPR 52/1; LSS 186; RRS 27; LSC 323**.

330 BANNERMAN, Isabel, 1793–1858. From Duible, Kildonan, SUT. d/o William B, qv, and Barbara Gunn, qv. To Fort Churchill, Hudson Bay, on the *Prince of Wales*, ex Stromness, 28 Jun 1813. Went to York Factory, 1814, thence to Red River. m 5 Jan 1815, Robert Sutherland, qv. **Kildonan OPR 52/1; LSS 186; RRS 27; LSC 323**.

331 BANNERMAN, James, 1822-57. From East Helmsdale, SUT. s/o John B. To Barneys River, Pictou Co, NS, <1855. m 1856, Jane McLeod. **LDW 6 Jun 1972**.

332 BANNERMAN, John, b 1760. From Kildonan, SUT. To York Factory, Hudson Bay, arr 26 Aug 1815, thence to Red River. Wife Catherine McKay, qv, with him, and s Alexander, aged 1. **LSC 326**.

333 BANNERMAN, John, ca 1790–1814. From Duible, Kildonan, SUT. s/o William B, tenant, and Barbara Gunn. To Fort Churchill, Hudson Bay, on the *Prince of Wales*, ex Stromness, 28 Jun 1813, and d there. **LSS 186; RRS 27; LSC 323**.

334 BANNERMAN, John, b ca 1808. To Innisfil Twp, Simcoe Co, <30 Nov 1843, when he m Christiana McKay, West Gwillimbury. ch: 1. James; 2. Angus; 3. George; 4. William; 5. Andrew; 6. John; 7. Christiana; 8. Jennette; 9. Isabella; 10. Robert; 11. Elizabeth; 12. Alice. **DC 3 Sep 1979**.

335 BANNERMAN, John. Prob from SUT. To Pictou, NS, on the *Lady Gray*, ex Cromarty, ROC, arr 16 Jul 1841. Weaver. **DC 15 Jul 1979**.

336 BANNERMAN, Mary. From Kildonan par, SUT. To Fort Churchill, Hudson Bay, on the *Prince of Wales*, ex Stromness, 28 Jun 1813. Went to York Factory, 1814, and thence to Red River. **LSS 185; RRS; LSC 323**.

337 BANNERMAN, Robertina, b ca 1800. To ONT <1850. **DC 3 Sep 1979**.

338 BANNERMAN, Simon. From Kildonan par, SUT. s/o Donald B. and Elizabeth Mackay. To NS, 1822. m 13 Dec 1816, Margaret Sutherland. **LDW 6 Jun 1972**.

339 BANNERMAN, William, b 1760. From Duible, Kildonan par, SUT. To York Factory, Hudson Bay, arr 26 Aug 1815, thence to Red River. m Barbara Gunn, qv, ch: 1. John, qv; 2. Isobel, b 1793, prob dy; 3. Ann, b ca 1796; 4. William, b 12 Jun 1796; 5. Alexander, qv; 6. Donald, b ca 1800; 7. George, b ca 1806. **LSC 326, Kildonan OPR 52/1**.

340 BANNERMAN, William, b 4 Dec 1791. From Badflaich, Kildonan par, SUT. s/o Donald B, qv, and Christy Gordon, qv. To Fort Churchill, Hudson Bay, on the *Prince of Wales*, ex Stromness, 28 Jun 1813. Went to York Factory, 1814, thence to Red River. Moved to Gwillimbury, Simcoe Co, ONT, 1815. Wife Ann with him. **LSC 185; RRS 26; LSC 321**.

341 BANNERMAN, William. Prob from SUT. To Pictou, NS, on the *Lady Gray*, ex Cromarty, ROC, arr 16 Jul 1841. **DC 15 Jul 1979**.

342 BANSLEY, James, d 7 Jul 1854. From Alloa, CLK. s/o James B. and Jean Carmichael, 1810-91. To Toronto, ONT, and d there. **Ts Alloa**.

343 BARBER, Jane, d 16 Aug 1847. From Corsock Mill, Parton, KKD. To 'Neilson Hall,' Harwich, Kent Co, ONT. Wife of Alexander Fergusson, qv. **DGH 14 Oct 1847**.

344 BARBER, Thomas, b 1784. From Torthorwald, DFS. To QUE on the *Atlas*, ex Greenock, 11 Jul 1815; stld Lot 8, Con 10, Burgess Twp, Lanark Co, ONT. Tailor, later farmer. Wife Janet Hannah, qv, with him and 4 ch. **SEC 1; HCL 15, 232**.

345 BARCLAY, Elizabeth, 1805-71. From Cupar, FIF. d/o Rev George B, qv, and Janet Tullis, qv. To Pickering Twp, York Co, ONT, 1816. m (i) 1851, John Millar, 1785–1851, without ch; (ii) 1861, James Hamilton, 1808-85, without ch. **BOP 43**.

346 BARCLAY, Francis, d 13 Mar 1860. From Canonbie par, DFS. To ONT, and d Innisfil, Simcoe Co, leaving ch. **CAE 4**.

347 BARCLAY, Rev George, 3 Jul 1780–10 Aug 1857. From Cupar, FIF. s/o George B. and Elizabeth Gibson. To Pickering Twp, York Co, ONT, 1816. Baptist min, Markham and Whitby, and schoolmaster. m Janet Tullis, qv, ch: 1. George, qv; 2. Jane, qv; 3. James, 1807-08; 4. Margaret, qv; 5. Nancy, qv; 6. James, qv; 7. David Lyons, 1819–1904; 8. William Sleigh, 1821-92; 9. Eli Gorham, 1825-93. **BOP 2, 5, 6**.

348 BARCLAY, George jr, 1801-82. From Cupar, FIF. s/o Rev George B, qv, and Janet Tullis, qv. To Pickering Twp, York Co, ONT, 1816. Farmer. Jailed for sedition, 1837, but later pardoned. m (i) Jane Willson, 1809-70, ch: 1. Jane, b 1832; 2. Nancy, 1834–1929; 3. Joshua, 1836-95; 4. Dr George, 1837-88; 5. William, 1840–1910; 6. Catherine, b 1841; 7. John Willson, 1843-94; 8. David, 1845–1937; 9. Eli Robert, 1846–1936; 10. Arthur, 1850–1931. m (ii) Mary Jane Sicily. **BOP 11, 15**.

349 BARCLAY, James, 1815-69. From Cupar, FIF. s/o Rev George B, qv, and Janet Tullis, qv. To Pickering Twp, York Co, ONT, 1816. Farmer. m Hannah Caroline Parnham, 1818–1904, ch: 1. Almira Evalina, 1838-79; 2. George James, 1840–1903, res Oshawa; 3. Ann Jane, 1842–1909; 4. Eli David, 1844-89; 5. William Henry, 1846–1900; 6. Albert Ernest, 1850–1928; 7. Walter Franklin, 1853-72; 8. Lyman Theophilus, 1855–1925; 9. Carolina Matilda, 1858-79; 10. Helena Louise Josephine, 1861–1945. **BOP 53**.

350 BARCLAY, Jane or Janet, 1803-38. From Cupar, FIF. d/o Rev George B, qv, and Janet Tullis, qv. To Pickering Twp, York Co, ONT, 1816. m Randall Spencer Bently, 1800-93, farmer, Claremont, ch: 1. Lavina, 1823–1906; 2. William, 1825–1902; 3. Maria, 1827–1901; 4. Nancy, 1830-84; 5. George, 1832–1920; 6. Jane, 1835-36; 7. Randall Spencer, b 1838. **BOP 38, 41**.

351 BARCLAY, John, ca 1758–3 Apr 1838. Prob from Moy par, INV. To London Twp, Middlesex Co, ONT, 1828. m Margaret McBean, qv. Dau Margaret, 1795–1879. **PCM 50**.

352 BARCLAY, Rev John, 9 Jul 1795–29 Sep 1826.
From Kettle, FIF. s/o Rev Peter B, par min, and Margaret
Duddingston. To Kingston, ONT, 1821. First min of St
Andrew's Ch there. **FES v 160, vii 625.**

353 BARCLAY, Rev John, ca 1812–22 Sep 1887. From
AYR. s/o John B, merchant. Matric Univ of Glasgow,
1827, and grad MA 1832. Min of St Andrew's Presb Ch,
Toronto, 1842-70. DD, Glasgow, 1855. Ret 1870. **GMA
12083; RGG 33; FES vii 625; SNQ vi/1 49.**

354 BARCLAY, Margaret, 1810-92. From Cupar, FIF.
d/o Rev George B, qv, and Janet Tullis, qv. To Pickering
Twp, York Co, ONT, 1816. Dressmaker. m Robert Barrie,
1811-58, ch: 1. Jane, b 1834; 2. George, 1836-39;
3. John, b 1838; 4. Ann, b 1840; 5. Charles, 1842-43;
6. Robert Hugh, b 1844; 7. Betsy Maria, b 1847;
8. Margaret Ellen, b 1849; 9. Alexander Campbell,
b 1851; 10. Ida, b 1855. **BOP 44.**

355 BARCLAY, Nancy, 1812-96. From Cupar, FIF.
d/o Rev George B, qv, and Janet Tullis, qv. To Pickering
Twp, York Co, ONT, 1816. m Abraham Knowles, 1803-78,
ch: 1. Mary, 1832-68; 2. George, 1834–1918, res
Pasadena, CA; 3. William, b 1836, went to IA; 4. Daniel,
1838-39; 5. Richard, b 1840; 6. Jane Barclay, 1842-98;
7. Charles, 1844-77; 8. Anna, b 1847; 9. Henry,
b 1849. **BOP 49.**

356 BAKER, Archibald, b 18 Aug 1808. From
Sanquhar, DFS. s/o Thomas B, burgess, and Sarah
Johnston. To ONT <1840. Merchant and magistrate.
MSK 90.

357 BARNET, Elizabeth, b ca 1790. From Auchterarder,
PER. d/o John Barnet and Amelia Motherwell. To
Torbolton, Carleton Co, ONT, 1821. Wife of David
McLaren, qv. **DC 10 Mar 1981.**

358 BARNSTON, George, 1800–14 Mar 1883. From
Edinburgh. To Montreal, QUE, 1820. Fur trader and
naturalist. Crossed the Rockies in the service of the
HBCo, and ret as chief factor, 1867. s/o Dr James,
d 1858, Professor of Botany at McGill Coll, Montreal.
DGH 18 Jul 1858; MDB 35.

359 BARR, Alexander. From Knapdale, ARL. To Lobo
Twp, Middlesex Co, ONT, 1836. **PCM 39.**

360 BARR, Angus. To Belfast, Queens Co, PEI,
<1811. **HP 74.**

361 BARR, Ann. Prob from AYR. To Brant Co, ONT,
<1850. Wife of David Campbell, qv. **DC 5 Mar 1980.**

362 BARR, Elizabeth, 1819–1922. Born Glasgow.
d/o James B, qv, and Janet Love, qv. To Pictou, NS,
ca 1830, and d Rush City, MN. m prob in NB in 1838,
Capt Donald Bannerman, shipowner in Liverpool.
FNQ iv 12.

363 BARR, Henry. From RFW. To ONT <1830. Wife
Margaret, ca 1802–27 Jul 1869, with him. She
m (ii) Rev James Smith, a Baptist preacher.
DC 27 Oct 1979.

364 BARR, James, 1770–1860. From Torbolton, AYR.
s/o Matthew B, merchant in Kilbarchan, RFW, and Janet
McCuaig. To Pictou, NS, ca 1830. Retr later to SCT and
stld Govan, LKS. m Janet Love, qv, ch: 1. Janet, d unm
1873; 2. Margaret, qv; 3. Elizabeth, qv. **FNQ iv 12-22.**

365 BARR, Rev John, ca 1839–11 Aug 1870. From
LKS. s/o William B, husbandman. Matric Univ of

Glasgow, 1852, and studied further at Queens Coll,
Kingston, ONT, 1857-62. Adm min of Laprairie, QUE,
1867. **GMA 16222; FES vii 625.**

366 BARR, Margaret, 1802-88. From Tarbolton, AYR.
d/o James B, qv, and Janet Love, qv. To Pictou, NS, ca
1830, and d St Paul, MN. Wife of James Malcolm, qv.
FNQ iv 12-22.

367 BARR, Margaret, b 28 Aug 1827. From Partick,
Glasgow. To ONT ca 1846. m John S. Robertson, qv.
DC 23 Feb 1981.

368 BARR, Peter, b ca 1788. From Houston, RFW. To
Hudson Bay, ca 1813, and prob to Red River. **RRS 13.**

369 BARR, Peter. To QUE on the *Commerce*, ex
Greenock, Jun 1820; stld Lot 6, Con 6, Darling Twp,
Lanark Co, ONT. Pioneer settler. **HCL 76, 239.**

370 BARRIE, Christina, b 18 Nov 1804, poss in
Manchester, ENG. d/o William B. and Margaret Wilson.
Ex Greenock, 30 Apr 1841, and arr Montreal, QUE,
18 Jun 1841. Stld Kingsey Twp, QUE. m at Linlithgow,
15 Dec 1826, William Dickson, qv. **DC 13 Jan 1980.**

371 BARRIE, Thomas, b ca 1777. From Dundee, ANS.
To QUE, ex Greenock, summer 1815; stld Lot 11, Con 1,
Bathurst Twp, Lanark Co, ONT. Shoemaker, later farmer.
Wife Agnes Whale, qv, with him, and 9 ch. **SEC 2;
HCL 16.**

372 BARRIE, Rev William, ca 1800–28 Jul 1879.
From Strathmiglo, FIF. Called to Johnshaven, KCD,
United Secession Ch, but went to Wellington Co, ONT.
Min at Eramosa and Nichol from 1843. DD, Monmouth
Coll, IL. **UPC i 80.**

373 BARRON, George, ca 1803–6 Apr 1891. From
Savoch, ABD. To Whitby, Ontario Co, ONT, <1835, later
to Peel Twp and Nichol Twp. Farmer and Ch elder.
m Elspet Watt, qv. **EHE 92, 104.**

374 BARRON, Jessie, b 1813. From Aberdeen. To QUE
<1851, and stld later in Toronto. m John Bonallie, qv.
DC 7 Feb 1980.

375 BARROWMAN, Alexander, ca 1822–17 Dec 1884.
From Edinburgh. s/o Robert B. and Elizabeth Stevenson.
To Montreal, QUE. **Ts Greyfriars.**

376 BARTLEMAN, Peter, 1795–1881. From
Haddington, ELN. To Bruce Co, ONT, 1822; stld Brant
Twp. Wheelwright and cabinet-maker. **LDW 16 Jun
1968.**

377 BARTON, John, d 12 Mar 1857. From Hoddam
par, DFS. To Stratford, Perth Co, ONT. Killed at swing
bridge over Desjardines Canal. **DGH 1 May 1857.**

378 BATCHELOR, George. To NS <28 Jan 1818, when
he m Mary Ann, d/o George Hay. **NSS No 1296.**

379 BATHGATE, Elizabeth Ann. To Dumfries Twp,
Wellington Co, ONT, <1855. m Andrew Aitchison, qv.
EHE 43.

380 BAXTER, Alexander. Poss from ARL. To
Aldborough Twp, Elgin Co, ONT, prob 1818. Farmer.
PDA 93.

381 BAXTER, David, ca 1799–10 Feb 1848. From
Dornock Mill, DFS. s/o Robert B. and Elizabeth Irving,
qv. To Halifax, NS, and d there. **Ts Dornock.**

BAXTER, Mrs Robert. See IRVING, Elizabeth.

382   BAXTER, John. To Aldborough Twp, Elgin Co, ONT, 1819; moved to Mosa Twp, 1832.   **PCM 14**.

383   BAXTER, John, 1807-71. From ARL. To Caledon Twp, Peel Co, ONT, <1840. Wife Mary, 1811-79, from Kilfinan, ARL.   **DC 21 Apr 1980**.

384   BAXTER, Sarah, 1804-70. From ARL. To Caledon Twp, Peel Co, ONT, <1840. Wife of Archibald Ferguson, qv.   **DC 21 Apr 1980**.

385   BAYNE, George Thomas, ca 1790–1 Aug 1876. From PER. To Ottawa, ONT, 1826. Timekeeper, Rideau Canal Locks; later dairy farmer. m Elizabeth Robertson, ch: 1. David, dy; 2. Mary, dy; 3. Margery Smith, qv; 4. Robert, qv; 5. John, qv; 6. Jean; 7. Mary Ann; 8. David; 9. Elizabeth.   **DC 3 May 1967**.

386   BAYNE, Rev James, ca 1816–9 Dec 1876. From Dunbar, ELN. s/o Rev Andrew B, Antiburgher min. To Londonderry, Colchester Co, NS, ca 1842; later to Pictou. Missionary, teacher, and became min of Prince Street Presb Ch, Pictou. ch incl: 1. Rev Ernest, of Mabou; 2. Herbert Andrew; 3. George Arthur, engineer; 4. James A, res Moncton, NB.   **UPC i 528; HNS iii 447**.

387   BAYNE, John, 1825–1908. From PER. s/o George Thomas B, qv, and Elizabeth Robertson. To Ottawa, ONT, 1826. m 1853, Margaret Richardson, 1834–1913, d/o James Dunlop, qv, and Cochrane Ray Richardson, qv.   **DC 3 May 1967**.

388   BAYNE, Rev John, 16 Nov 1806–3 Nov 1859. Born Greenock, RFW. s/o Rev Kenneth B, min of the Gaelic Ch, and Margaret Hay. Matric Univ of Glasgow, 1819, and was an asst min in the OKI before being ind Presb min of Galt, Waterloo Co, ONT, 1835. Joined FC and became its leader.   **GMA 10319; FES iii 200, vii 625; HGD 116; MDB 37**.

389   BAYNE, Margery Smith, ca 1823–11 Nov 1857. From PER. d/o George Thomas B, qv, and Elizabeth Robertson, qv. To Ottawa, ONT, 1826. m 1846, William Pollock, qv.   **DC 3 May 1967**.

390   BAYNE, Robert, 1825-99. From PER. s/o George Thomas B, qv, and Elizabeth Robertson, qv. To Ottawa, ONT, 1826. m 1854, Margaret Moffat, 1832–1909, from Belfast, IRL, ch.   **DC 3 May 1967**.

391   BAYNE, Thomas, 1819-90. From Dunbar, ELN. To Pictou, NS, 1840. Merchant. m Elizabeth, d/o George Hunter, Hants Co, ch: 1. Charles, estate agent, Halifax; 2. Andrew, estate agent; 3. George H, 1859–1903; 4. Alexander McLeod, dy.   **HNS iii 447**.

392   BEAN, Alexander. To Restigouche Co, NB, ca 1784; stld prob Mission Point. Discharged soldier, 42nd Regt.   **SR 15**.

393   BEATON, Alexander, b ca 1771. From Badenoch, INV. s/o Angus B, qv, and Isabel McDonald, qv. To Pictou, NS, on the *Dove*, ex Fort William, Jun 1801. Farmer at Little Judique, Inverness Co. m Ann McDonald, ch: 1. Isabel; 2. Angus; 3. John; 4. Alexander; 5. Ronald; 6. Allan, dy; 7. Janet; 8. Catherine; 9. Catriona; 10. Sara.   **PLD; MP 112**.

394   BEATON, Alexander. From Lochaber, INV. s/o Alexander B, qv, and first wife Mary MacDonald. To Pictou, NS, 1804; stld Mabou, Inverness Co. m Christy MacDonald, from Antigonish Co, ch: 1. Sara;

2. Mary; 3. Catherine; 4. Alexander; 5. Angus; 6. Anne; 7. Margaret; 8. Donald; 9. Mary; 10. Isabel.   **MP 162**.

395   BEATON, Alexander. From Lochaber, INV. s/o John B. To Pictou, NS, 1804, stld Mabou, Inverness Co. m (i) Mary MacDonald, ch: 1. Alexander, qv; 2. Archibald; 3. James. m (ii) Anne MacInnes, further ch: 4. John, qv; 5. Margaret, qv; 6. Sara, qv; 7. Catherine, qv; 8. Mrs Mackenzie.   **MP 162**.

396   BEATON, Alexander, ca 1797–1830. From Lochaber, INV. s/o Finlay 'Mor' B, qv, and Margaret McLaren, qv. To PEI, ca 1805. Moved to Mabou, Inverness Co, NS, 1809. m Anne, d/o Murdock MacPherson, South West Mabou.   **MP 213**.

397   BEATON, Alexander, b 1753. To Port Hood dist, Inverness Co, NS, 1806. Farmer, m, ch.   **CBC 1818**.

398   BEATON, Alexander, b ca 1779. To Port Hood, Inverness Co, NS, 1810. Mason, m, ch.   **CBC 1818**.

399   BEATON, Alexander, b ca 1782. To Port Hood dist, Inverness Co, NS, 1816. Farmer, m, ch.   **CBC 1818**.

400   BEATON, Alexander. From INV. s/o Donald B, qv, and Mary Campbell. To Mabou, Inverness Co, NS, prob <1820. m Catherine Campbell, ch: 1. Donald; 2. Alexander; 3. John; 4. Angus; 5. Dougald; 6. Mary; 7. Catherine; 8. Sara; 9. Anne.   **MP 153**.

401   BEATON, Alexander. To Antigonish Co, NS, 1802, and poss went to Inverness Co.   **DC 17 May 1982**.

402   BEATON, Angus. From Is Skye, INV. s/o Malcolm B. To Orwell Bay, PEI, on the *Polly*, ex Portree, arr 7 Aug 1803; stld Flat River. m Margaret McPhee, qv, ch: 1. Malcolm; 2. Peter; 3. Donald; 4. Angus; 5. John; 6. Samuel; 7. Neil.   **DC 9 Oct 1980**.

403   BEATON, Angus. From Badenoch, INV. s/o Donald B, qv, abd Miss MacDonald. To Pictou, NS, on the *Dove*, ex Fort William, Jun 1801; stld Inverness Co, NS. m Isabel MacDonald, qv, ch: 1. Alexander, qv; 2. Angus, qv; 3. Donald, qv; 4. Marian; 5. Ann; 6. Archibald, qv; 7. John, qv; 8. Finlay, qv; 9. Margaret, qv; 10. Catherine, qv; 11. Sara.   **PLD; MP 95**.

404   BEATON, Angus, jr. From Badenoch, INV. s/o Angus B, qv, and Isabel MacDonald, qv. To Pictou, NS, on the *Dove*, ex Fort William, Jun 1801; stld Little Judique, Inverness Co. Farmer. m Mary, d/o Donald MacDonald, ch: 1. Angus, postmaster; 2. Donald; 3. Alexander.   **PLD; MP 137**.

405   BEATON, Angus. Prob from Is Skye, INV. To PEI, poss 1803. Son Angus, alive 1811.   **HP 74**.

406   BEATON, Angus, b 1790. To Inverness Co, NS, 1806; stld nr Port Hood. Farmer, m <1818.   **CBC 1818**.

407   BEATON, Angus, b 1777. To Inverness Co, NS, 1806; stld nr Port Hood. Farmer, m, ch.   **CBC 1818**.

408   BEATON, Angus. From INV. s/o Finlay 'Mor' B, qv, and Margaret MacLaren, qv. To NS, 1809. m (i) Isabel, d/o Angus Cameron, ch: 1. Margaret; 2. Isabel. m (ii) Margaret Stuart, qv, further ch: 3. Alexander; 4. Donald; 5. Finlay; 6. Archibald; 7. Mary; 8. Flora; 9. Catherine; 10. Sarah.   **MP 218**.

409   BEATON, Angus, b ca 1771. To Port Hood dist, Inverness Co, NS, 1816. Farmer, m, ch.   **CBC 1818**.

410   BEATON, Angus, b ca 1772. To Port Hood dist, Inverness Co, NS, 1816. Farmer, m, ch.   **CBC 1818**.

411   BEATON, Angus 'Cleireach'. From INV. s/o Donald B, qv, and Mary Campbell. To Inverness Co, NS, 1817; stld Port Hastings. m Charlotte MacPherson, qv, ch: 1. Mary; 2. Catherine; 3. Sara; 4. Anne; 5. Jessie; 6. John; 7. Murdock; 8. Donald; 9. Angus.   **MP 158**.

412   BEATON, Ann. From Badenoch, INV. d/o Angus B, qv, and Isabel MacDonald, qv. To Pictou, NS, on the *Dove*, ex Fort William, Jun 1801; stld Inverness Co. m John Gillis, qv.   **MP 147, 343**.

413   BEATON, Anne. From INV. d/o Donald B, qv, and Mary Campbell. To Mabou, Inverness Co, NS, prob <1820. m Alexander Beaton, qv.   **MP 162, 176**.

414   BEATON, Archibald, b 1787. From Badenoch, INV. s/o Angus B, qv, and Isabel MacDonald, qv. To Pictou, NS, on the *Dove*, ex Fort William, Jun 1801; stld Little Judique, Inverness Co. m (i) Miss MacDonald, ch: 1. Angus; 2. Margaret; 3. Catherine; 4. Anne or Nancy; 5. Mary; 6. Isabel; 7. Sara. By a second wife: 8. Donald; 9. Christina.   **PLD; MP 143**.

415   BEATON, Archibald, b ca 1798. From Lochaber, INV. s/o Finlay Mor B, qv, and Margaret MacLaren, qv. To PEI, ca 1805, but stld Mabou, Inverness Co, NS, 1809. m Catherine MacPhee, qv, ch: 1. Angus; 2. Alexander; 3. Finlay; 4. Donald, b 1844; 5. Archibald; 6. Margaret; 7. Mairearad.   **MP 213**.

416   BEATON, Archibald. From Achluachrach, Glenspean, INV. s/o Finlay Mor B, qv, and Margaret MacLaren, qv. To PEI, ca 1805, but moved to Mabou Coal Mines, Inverness Co, NS. m Catherine, d/o Archibald MacPhee, qv, and Margaret Cameron, qv, ch: 1. Angus; 2. Alexander; 3. Finlay; 4. Donald; 5. Archibald; 6. Margaret; 7. Margaret.   **MP 213, 782**.

417   BEATON, Catherine, b 1796. From Badenoch, INV. d/o Angus B, qv, and Isabel MacDonald, qv. To Pictou, NS, on the *Dove*, ex Fort William, Jun 1801; stld Little Judique, Inverness Co. m Finlay MacDonald, qv.   **PLD; MP 147, 580**.

418   BEATON, Catherine. From Lochaber, INV. d/o Alexander B, qv, and second wife Ann MacInnes. To Pictou, NS, 1804; stld Mabou, Inverness Co. m Donald MacDonald.   **MP 175**.

419   BEATON, Catherine, 1801–29 Oct 1886. From Is Coll, ARL. To NS, ca 1822. m Angus Campbell, qv. **DC 31 Jul 1961**.

420   BEATON, Catherine. From INV. d/o Donald B, qv, and Mary Campbell. To Mabou, Inverness Co, NS, prob <1820. m John Rankin, qv.   **MP 162, 814**.

421   BEATON, Colin. From Is Mull, ARL. To Pickering, York Co, ONT, 1832. m Christian Mackinnon, qv. Son Alexander, 1838–1932, physician.   **DC 30 Aug 1977**.

422   BEATON, Donald. From Is Skye, INV. To Belfast, Queens Co, PEI, prob 1803.   **HP 74**.

423   BEATON, Donald, b 1746. From Lochaber, INV. s/o Alexander B. and Flora Cameron. To East Point, Kings Co, PEI, 1772. ch.   **MP 176**.

424   BEATON, Donald, 1769–26 Mar 1867. From Badenoch, INV. s/o Angus B, qv, and Isabel MacDonald, qv. To Pictou, NS, on the *Dove*, ex Fort William, Jun

1801; stld Little Judique, Inverness Co. Farmer. m Sara, d/o Angus Cameron, ch: 1. Donald; 2. Angus; 3. Alexander; 4. Finlay; 5. Margaret; 6. Mary; 7. Isabel; 8. Anne.   **PLD; MP 95**.

425   BEATON, Donald or Daniel, b ca 1778. To Port Hood dist, Inverness Co, NS, 1806. Farmer, m, ch. **CBC 1818**.

426   BEATON, Donald or Daniel, b ca 1786. To Port Hood dist, Inverness Co, NS, 1816. Farmer, m, ch. **CBC 1818**.

427   BEATON, Donald. From INV. s/o Alexander B. and Anne MacBain. To Mabou, Inverness Co, NS, prob <1805. m Miss MacDonald, ch: 1. Alexander; prob remained in SCT; 2. Donald, prob remained in SCT; 3. Angus, qv; 4. Margaret.   **MP 88**.

428   BEATON, Donald, b ca 1793. To Port Hood dist, Inverness Co, NS, ca 1806. Farmer, unm.   **CBC 1818**.

429   BEATON, Donald. From INV. s/o John B. To South West Mabou, Inverness Co, NS, ca 1817. m Mary, d/o Angus Campbell, ch: 1. John, soldier; 2. Donald, qv; 3. Alexander, qv; 4. Angus, qv; 5. Anne, qv; 6. Catherine, qv.   **MP 147**.

430   BEATON, Donald, b 1823. From Is Mull, ARL. s/o Duncan B, qv, and Jessie McDonald. To York Co, ONT, and stld Kleinburg <1844. m Marjery Grant, qv. **DC 15 Nov 1972**.

431   BEATON, Donald 'Ban'. From INV. s/o Donald B, qv, and Mary Campbell. To South West Mabou, Inverness Co, NS, prob <1820. m Catherine, d/o Alasdair MacDonald, ch: 1. Angus; 2. Alexander; 3. John; 4. Donald; 5. Catherine; 6. Mary.   **MP 147**.

432   BEATON, Donald 'Morair'. From Is Skye, INV. s/o Alexander B. To Becket Brook, North East Mabou, Inverness Co, NS, <1810. Farmer. m Margaret Beaton, ch: 1. Donald; 2. Alexander; 3. Angus; 4. Catherine, dy; 5. Mary.   **MP 89**.

433   BEATON, Dougald. From Is Skye, INV. s/o Alexander B. To Mabou, Inverness Co, NS, prob <1810. Farmer. m Miss MacDonald, ch: 1. Donald; 2. Alexander; 3. Angus, dy; 4. John; 5. Mary; 6. Catherine; 7. Margaret; 8. Anne.   **MP 90**.

434   BEATON, Duncan, ca 1791–22 Aug 1850. From Is Mull, ARL. To York Co, ONT, <1844; stld Kleinburg. m Jessie McDonald. Son Donald, qv.   **DC 15 Nov 1972**.

435   BEATON, Farquhar. Prob from INV. To Montreal, QUE, prob arr Sep 1802. Petitioned for land on the Ottawa River, ONT, 6 Aug 1804.   **DC 15 Mar 1980**.

436   BEATON, Finlay 'Mor', b 1765. From Achluachrach, Glenspean, INV. s/o Alexander B. and Flora Cameron. To PEI ca 1805. Moved 1809 to Mabou, Inverness Co, NS. m Margaret MacLaren, qv, ch: 1. John, qv; 2. Sara, qv; 3. Alexander, qv; 4. Archibald, qv; 5. Angus, qv; 6. Mary.   **CBC 1818; MP 190**.

437   BEATON, Finlay, b ca 1792. From Badenoch, INV. s/o Angus B, qv, and Isabel MacDonald, qv. To Pictou, NS, on the *Dove*, ex Fort William, Jun 1801; stld Little Judique, Inverness Co; later Monk's Head, Pomquet, Antigonish Co. m Ann MacDonald, qv, ch: 1. Angus; 2. Mary; 3. Margaret; 4. Donald; 5. Alexander;

6. Patrick; 7. Catherine, 1834-1916; 8. Allan; 9. Anne; 10. Alexander Og; 11. Isabel; 12. Angus Og. **PLD; MP 127**.

438 BEATON, Hugh. To Pictou, NS, on the *Lady Gray*, ex Cromarty, ROC, arr 16 Jul 1841. **DC 15 Jul 1979**.

439 BEATON, Isabel. From Lochaber, INV. d/o Finlay B. To South West River, Mabou, Inverness Co, NS, 1805. Wife of Donald 'Ban Onorach' MacDonald, qv. **MP 176, 562**.

440 BEATON, James, b 10 Nov 1830. From Liaba, Kilninian and Kilmore par, Is Mull, ARL. s/o Neil B, qv, and Mary McNiven, qv. To ONT, poss <1848; stld Vaughan Twp, York Co. m 1857, Christina, d/o Archibald McDougall, qv, and his wife Catherine, ch. **DC 25 Feb 1976**.

441 BEATON, Jessie. From Lochaber, INV. d/o Finlay B. To Mabou, Inverness Co, NS, prob <1810. m John Rankin. **MP 176, 810**.

442 BEATON, John, b ca 1789. From Badenoch, INV. s/o Angus B, qv, and Isabel MacDonald, qv. To Pictou, NS, on the *Dove*, ex Fort William, Jun 1801; stld Little Judique, Inverness Co. Farmer. m Margaret Beaton, qv, ch: 1. Donald; 2. Finlay; 3. John; 4. Archibald; 5. Alexander; 6. Angus; 7. Angus Og; 8. Mary; 9. Mary, jr; 10. Isabel; 11. Anne. **PLD; MP 106**.

443 BEATON, John. From Is Skye, INV. To Belfast, Queens Co, PEI, prob 1803. **HP 74**.

444 BEATON, John, b 1 Nov 1800. From Lochaber, INV. s/o Alexander B, qv, and second wife Anne MacInnes. To Pictou, NS, 1804; stld South West Mabou River, later Mull River. Farmer and mill-owner. m Ellen Whitehead, ch: 1. Alexander; 2. James; 3. James; 4. John; 5. William; 6. Alexander, jr; 7. Elizabeth; 8. Abigail; 9. Catherine; 10. Jane; 11. Agnes; 12. Anne; 13. Thomas. **MP 168**.

445 BEATON, John, b ca 1785. To Port Hood dist, Inverness Co, NS, 1806. Farmer, m, ch. **CBC 1818**.

446 BEATON, John, b ca 1801. To Inverness Co, NS, 1809; stld prob Mabou. Farmer. **CBC 1818**.

447 BEATON, John, 1794–1865. From Lochaber, INV. s/o Finlay Mor B, qv, and Margaret MacLean, qv. To PEI ca 1805; and to Mabou, Inverness Co, NS, 1809. m 8 Sep 1819, Mary MacDonald, qv, ch: 1. Donald, b 1821; 2. Angus, b 1823; 3. Finlay, b 1825, dy; 4. Margaret, b 1827; 5. Ronald, b 1829; 6. John, b 1831; 7. Alexander, b 1836, dy; 8. Alexander J, b 1837. **CBC 1818; HP 191**.

448 BEATON, Margaret, b 1794. From Badenoch, INV. d/o Angus B, qv, and Isabel MacDonald, qv. To Pictou, NS, on the *Dove*, ex Fort William, Jun 1801; stld Little Judique, Inverness Co. m Angus Cameron, qv. **PLD; MP 95, 257**.

449 BEATON, Margaret. From Locaber, INV. d/o Alexander B, qv, and his second wife Anne MacInnes. To Pictou, NS, prob 1804; stld Little Judique, Inverness Co. m John Beaton, qv. **MP 171**.

450 BEATON, Mary. From Lochaber, INV. d/o Finlay B. To Mabou, Inverness Co, NS, prob 1805. m Angus Dubh Cameron, qv. **MP 176, 238**.

451 BEATON, Neil, b ca 1797. From Liaba, Kilninian

and Kilmore par, Is Mull, ARL. Prob s/o Lawrence B. and Ann Mackinnon. To ONT <1848. m Mary McNiven, qv, ch: 1. Ann; 2. James, qv; 3. John, b 1832; 4. William, b 1834; 5. Lachlan, b 1838; 6. Jane, b 1846. **DC 25 Feb 1976**.

452 BEATON, Samuel. From Is Skye, INV. To Queens Co, PEI, prob 1803. **HP 74**.

453 BEATON, Sara, b ca 1795. From Lochaber, INV. d/o Finlay Mor B, qv, and Margaret MacLaren, qv. To PEI ca 1805; and moved to Mabou, Inverness Co, NS, 1809. m Ronald MacDonald. **MP 213, 508**.

454 BEATON, Sara. From Lochaber, INV. d/o Alexander B, qv, and second wife Anne MacInnes. To Pictou, NS, 1804; stld Mabou, Inverness Co. m William MacGillivray. **MP 175**.

455 BEATTIE, Agnes, 1830–1914. Poss from DFS. To Melbourne, Richmond Co, QUE, prob <1854. m Robert McMorine, qv. **MGC 15 Jul 1980**.

456 BEATTIE, Andrew, b ca 1792. From Corrie Mill, n i, but poss in DFS. To QUE, ex Greenock, summer 1815; stld ONT. Teacher. **SEC 2**.

457 BEATTIE, Charles, ca 1802–17 Jun 1884. From Canonbie, DFS. To Melbourne, Richmond Co, QUE, prob <1850. m Elizabeth Murray, qv. **MGC 15 Jul 1980**.

458 BEATTIE, Francis, ca 1796–29 Sep 1828. From DFS. s/o Francis B, hatter, and Elizabeth Brown. To Port Hope, Durham Co, ONT, and d there. **DGC 23 Dec 1828; MSM 299**.

459 BEATTIE, George. From Aberdeen. To Elora, Nichol Twp, Wellington Co, ONT, 1835. ch: 1. Mrs William Hastings; 2. Mrs Robert Pritchard; 3. Mrs John Simpson; 4. James; 5. Elizabeth; 6. Mrs Andrew Hudson; 7. Georgina, d inf; 8. Mrs John Mutrie; 9. Mrs Thomas Pritchard; 10. William T, went to SAS; 11. George, farmer, Elora; 12. Mrs W.J. Patterson; 13. Rev John A, Miama, MAN. **EHE 91**.

460 BEATTIE, Grace. To QUE, <1849; stld Melbourne, Richmond Co. m Pipe Major Dougald Campbell, qv. **MGC 2 Aug 1979**.

461 BEATTIE, Isabella, ca 1794–1883. From Castleton, ROX. d/o John B. To York Co, NB, ca 1820; moved to Middlesex Co, ONT, 1836. m John Oliver, qv, 8 Dec 1837. **DC 16 Jul 1979**.

462 BEATTIE, James, ca 1799–18 Jul 1821. From DFS. To NB, 1820, but joined relatives at Truro, Colchester Co, NS. d of a fall from his horse the day he was to marry. **NSS No 2729**.

463 BEATTIE, James, ca 1819–24 Oct 1843. From Sarkshields, Kirkpatrick-Fleming, DFS. s/o James B. and Jane Broach. To Whitby, Ontario Co, ONT, and d there. **Ts Kirkpatrick-Fleming**.

464 BEATTIE, Janet, 12 Oct 1825–11 Nov 1915. From DFS. To QUE and stld Sherbrooke. m Malcolm Ross, qv. **MGC 2 Aug 1979**.

465 BEATTIE, John, ca 1792–8 May 1842. From Langholm, DFS. To Streetsville, Peel Co, ONT. Miller. **DGH 7 Jul 1842**.

466 BEATTIE, Jane, 1820–29 May 1900. From Annan, DFS. To Melbourne, Richmond Co, QUE, <1845. m Donald Stalker, qv. **MGC 15 Jul 1980**.

467   BEATTIE, Robina, ca 1805–18 Feb 1859. From Lochmaben, DFS. To Montreal, QUE. m Thomas Knubley.   **DGH 18 Mar 1859**.

468   BEATTIE, Simon, 1822-88. From DFS. To Melbourne, Richmond Co, QUE, <1850. m Catherine McMorine, qv, ch: 1. Nicoles, 1850-87; 2. Elizabeth, 1852-54; 3. William G, 1865–1905; 4. Mary, 1869-85.   **MGC 15 Jul 1980**.

469   BEATTIE, Simon. From DFS. Neph of James B, Newbie, Annan. To Markham Twp, York Co, ONT, poss <1854. Farmer. m (i) 1862, Mary, d/o George Miller, qv; (ii) Janet, d 1869, d/o Robert Sommerville, farmer, Stonehouse.   **CAE 5, 7, 18**.

470   BEATTIE, William. From Liddesdale, ROX. To York Co, NB, ca 1820; moved 1836 to Westminster Twp, Middlesex Co, ONT. Farmer. m Janet Hogg, qv, ch: 1. John; 2. William; 3. Catherine; 4. Margaret; 5. Jane; 6. James; 7. Isabella; 8. Andrew; 9. Edward; 10. Janet; 11. Nancy; 12. David; 13. Mary; 14. Peter; 15. George.   **DC 16 Jul 1979**.

471   BEATTIE, William. To QUE on the *David of London*, ex Greenock, 19 May 1821; stld poss Lanark Co, ONT.   **HCL 239**.

472   BEATTIE, William, b ca 1800. From ABD. To Guelph Twp, Wellington Co, ONT, 1839. m Elizabeth McDonald, qv, ch: 1. John, b 1821; 2. Jean, b 1827.   **SG xxiv/2 53**.

473   BEATTON, William. From Kinghorn, FIF. s/o Alexander B, schoolmaster. To QUE <1853; stld Haldimand Twp, Northumberland Co, ONT.   **SH**.

474   BECK, William, d Jun 1832. From DFS. To QUE, and d there of cholera. Mariner.   **DGC 14 Aug 1832**.

475   BECKET, Jane: To Peterborough Co, ONT, <1850. m David Fife, qv.   **DC 5 Feb 1968**.

476   BECKET, Janet. To Peterborough Co, ONT, <1850. m Thomas Fife, qv.   **DC 5 Feb 1968**.

477   BECKET, Mary A. To Peterborough Co, ONT, <1850. m William Fife, qv.   **DC 5 Feb 1968**.

478   BECKWITH, John, d ca 1822. Prob from Edinburgh. s/o Maj Gen John B, of Viscount Bury's Regt, and Janet Wishart. To Halifax, NS, <1829. Son Lt Col John Charles.   **SH**.

479   BEGG, Alexander, 7 May 1825–Mar 1905. From Watten, CAI. s/o Andrew B. and Jane Taylor. To Belleville, Hastings Co, ONT, 1846. Farmer, teacher, and journalist who became associated with the North-West.   **MDB 43; DC 15 Mar 1980**.

480   BEITH, Alexander, sr. From Campbeltown, ARL. To ONT, 1835. Farmer. Son Alexander, jr, qv.   **DC 29 Sep 1974**.

481   BEITH, Alexander, jr. From Campbeltown, ARL. s/o Alexander B, qv. To ONT, 1835. Farmer. m Catherine, d/o Alexander McTaggart, qv, ch: 1. Robert; 2. James.   **DC 29 Sep 1974**.

482   BELL, Alice. From Melrose, ROX. sis/o Janet B, qv. To Waterloo Co, ONT, <1836; stld North Dumfries Twp. m Suibhne McDonald, qv.   **DC 26 Sep 1981**.

483   BELL, Angus. To Belfast, Queens Co, PEI, <1825. Farmer and elder of St John's Ch, Belfast.   **HP 41**.

484   BELL, Angus, From Is Islay, ARL. To Megantic Co, QUE, <1850. ch: 1. Angus; 2. Christiana; 3. Malcolm; 4. Donald; 5. Ronald; 6. Kate; 7. John.   **AMC 49**.

485   BELL, Basil H. From ELN. To Pictou, NS, <1847. Teacher of Classics, Pictou Academy. m Mary, d/o Adam Carr, Albion Mines. Son Adam Carr, b 1847.   **HNS iii 173**.

486   BELL, Dugald, b ca 1781. Prob from Is Colonsay, ARL. To Charlottetown, PEI, on the *Spencer*, 22 Sep 1806. Relatives with him incl: 1. Mary, aged 15; 2. Nelly, aged 12; 3. Catherine, aged 10; 4. Duncan, aged 7; 5. Janet, aged 5; 6. Margaret, b 1806.   **PLSN; HP 74**.

487   BELL, Duncan, b ca 1728. Prob from Is Colonsay, ARL. To Charlottetown, PEI, on the *Spencer*, ex Oban, 22 Sep 1806. Prob father of Dougald B, qv.   **PLSN**.

488   BELL, Flora, b ca 1797. Prob from Is Colonsay, ARL. To Charlottetown, PEI, on the *Spencer*, ex Oban, 22 Sep 1806. Poss rel to Dougald B, qv.   **PLSN**.

489   BELL, Flora, 1813-52. From Is Islay, ARL. To Oro Twp, Simcoe Co, ONT, ca 1833. m Malcolm Galbraith, qv.   **GSO 26**.

490   BELL, Herbert, 30 Nov 1818–15 Feb 1876. From Middlebie par, DFS. To Alberton, Prince Co, PEI, 1840. Shipbuilder, merchant, farmer and politician. m 1849, Jane Bowness.   **BNA 718; DC 21 Mar 1981**.

491   BELL, Janet, ca 1796–Nov 1830. From DFS. To Miramichi, Northumberland Co, NB. m Christopher Wishart, qv.   **DC 4 Dec 1978**.

492   BELL, Janet. From Melrose, ROX. m there in 1834, John Young, qv, and went with him to ONT.   **DC 26 Sep 1981**.

493   BELL, John. To PEI, prob 1803; stld Belfast, Queens Co. Petitioner for Dr MacAulay, 1811.   **HP 74**.

494   BELL, John. From Annandale, DFS. To Tatamagouche, Colchester Co, NS, 1806. Farmer at Willow Ch, later New Annan, which he named. ch: 1. Irvine; 2. William; 3. Gavin; 4. James; 5. Robert.   **HT 36, 42**.

495   BELL, John. From Paisley, RFW. s/o David B, weaver. To CAN <1832. Weaver.   **SH**.

496   BELL, John, b 29 Aug 1810. From Is Colonsay, ARL. s/o Angus B. and Peggy McFaden. To East Gwillimbury Twp, York Co, ONT, 1836; thence to Mariposa Twp, Victoria Co, and in 1855 to Elderslie Twp, Bruce Co. m Margaret McAlder, qv, ch: 1. Catherine, b 1837; 2. Archibald, b 20 Sep 1838; 3. Angus, b 1840; 4. Margaret, b 1844; 5. Sarah, b 1846; 6. Flora, b 1848; 7. Hector, b 1850; 8. Mary, b 1852; 9. John, b 1852; 10. Christina, b 1855.   **DC 30 Jul 1979**.

497   BELL, John, ca 1804–26 Aug 1849. From Tinwald, DFS. s/o David B, wheelwright, Amisfield Town. To St John, NB. Millwright.   **DGH 8 Nov 1849**.

498   BELL, Joseph, ca 1807–9 May 1838. From DFS. To St. John, NB, and d there. Mason.   **DGC 25 Jul 1838**.

499   BELL, Lachlan, d 30 Sep 1854. From Carluke, LKS. s/o John B, 1774–1862, and Jane Shaw. To CAN, prob ONT, and d there.   **Ts Carluke**.

500 BELL, Malcolm, b ca 1741. Prob from Is Colonsay, ARL. To Charlottetown, PEI, on the *Spencer*, ex Oban, 22 Sep 1806. ch with him: 1. Archibald, aged 25; 2. Angus, aged 24; 3. Janet, aged 18. **PLSN; HP 74**.

501 BELL, Marion, b ca 1772. Prob from Is Colonsay, ARL. To Charlottetown, PEI, on the *Spencer*, ex Oban, 22 Sep 1806. **PLSN**.

502 BELL, Mary, b 1779. Prob from Ecclefechan, DFS. To NB, 1817. Wife of James Johnston, qv. **DC 5 Apr 1979**.

503 BELL, Mary, ca 1792–3 Sep 1867. From Hoddam, DFS. To Ayr, Waterloo Co, ONT, and d there. wid/o Andrew Rome, joiner, who d 1832. **Ts Middlebie**.

504 BELL, Minto, b 20 June 1790. From Bedrule, ROX. d/o William B, Menlaws. To QUE, ca 1832; stld ONT. Wife of George G, qv. **DC 11 Aug 1976**.

505 BELL, Rev Patrick, 1801–22 Apr 1869. From Mid Leoch, Auchterhouse, ANS. s/o George B, farmer. Educ Univ of St Andrews, 1819-20, and became a family tutor. To Fergus, Wellington Co, ONT, 1833, but retr to SCT, 1837. Inventor of a reaping machine and became min of Carmylie, ANS, 1843. m 1859, Jane, d/o Alexander Lawson, Dundee; ch: 1. Jessie, b 1860; 2. John, b 1862; 3. Jane, b 1865. **IBD 27; CBD 86; SAM 63; FES v 434**.

506 BELL, Peter, 1824-53. From Dalton, DFS. s/o Robert B. in Almagill, and Mary Blackstock. To ONT ca 1850, and d nr Darlington, Durham Co. **Ts Dalton**.

507 BELL, Thomas. From DFS. To Richibucto, Kent Co, NB. m Janet Jardine, qv. **DGC 24 Feb 1836**.

608 BELL, Rev William, 20 May 1780–16 Aug 1857. From Airdrie, LKS. To QUE on the *Rothiemurchus*, 1817; stld Perth, Drummond Twp, Lanark Co, ONT. Pioneer Secession min in the Rideau settlements, teacher, and author of *Hints to Emigrants* (1824). Wife with him. ch: 1. William, storekeeper; 2. John, bank teller and militiaman; 3. Robert, appr printer, 1823, later merchant; 4. Andrew, matric Univ of Glasgow, 1824; 5. James, bank agent; 6. Mrs John C. Malloch; 7. Rev George, b 1819, min at Walkerton. **GMA 11402; HCL 41, *et passim*; MDB 47; FES vii 626**.

509 BELL, William, 20 Apr 1811–27 Mar 1889. From Cambusnethan, LKS. To Chesley, Elderslie Twp, Bruce Co, ONT. m Cecilia Smith, qv. **Ts Carbarns**.

510 BELL, William, ca 1812–ca 1841. From DFS. s/o James B. and Sophia Bell. To QUE. **Ts Dumfries**.

511 BELL, William. s/o — B. and — Renwick (d/o Robert R, wright in Jedburgh, ROX). To Niagara, Lincoln Co, ONT, <1842. **SH**.

512 BENNETT, Agnes, 1808–13 Jun 1899. From Dunfermline, FIF. Prob d/o Thomas B. To Wentworth Co, ONT, ca 1833. Wife of Peter Somerville, qv. **DC 4 Oct 1980**.

513 BENNETT, Christian. From Dunfermline, FIF. d/o Thomas B. To Wentworth Co, ONT, 1841. Wife of Robert Somerville, qv. **DC 4 Oct 1980**.

514 BENNETT, Henry. From ROX. To Dundas Co, ONT, 1852. Dau Elizabeth. **DC 1 Jan 1968**.

515 BENNETT, William. To QUE on the *Commerce*, ex Greenock, Jun 1820; stld prob Lanark Co, ONT. **HCL 238**.

516 BENNETT, William. Heir in 1858 to William Schoolbred, Kinnesswood, KRS. To ONT. **SH**.

517 BENNIE, James. Prob from Glasgow. Rel to William B, qv, and to John B, qv. To Ramsay Twp, Lanark Co, ONT, ca 1821; stld Lot 26, Con 8. **RPE 105; HCL 83, 217**.

518 BENNIE, John. Prob from Glasgow. Rel to William B, qv, and to James B, qv. To Ramsay Twp, Lanark Co, ONT, ca 1821. **RPE 105**.

519 BENNIE, William. Prob from Glasgow. Rel to James B, qv, and to John B, qv. To Ramsay Twp, Lanark Co, ONT, ca 1821. **RPE 105**.

520 BENVIE, James. Prob rel to Samuel B, qv. To Halifax, NS, <1810; stld Musquodoboit Valley. Discharged soldier, farmer, militiaman and magistrate. Son Andrew, farmer, Salt Springs. **HNS iii 177**.

521 BENVIE, Samuel. Prob rel to James B, qv. To Halifax, NS, and stld Musquodoboit Valley <1810. m Martha, b 1792, sis/o Hon William McKeen, ch: 1. Adam, b 1830; 2. Peter Hutchinson, b 1832, stld with bro Adam at Mabou, Inverness Co; 3. Margaret, b 1834. **MP ii 79**.

522 BERRY, Patrick. To Pictou Co, NS, <8 Nov 1775. **HPC App B**.

523 BERTRAM, Alexander, 1811–31 Aug 1875. From BEW. To Montreal, QUE, 1831. Chief of fire brigade. **SGC 618**.

524 BERTRAM, George. From BEW. bro/o Alexander B, qv. To Montreal, QUE, 1831. Veterinary surgeon, sometime in partnership with James Turner, qv. **SGC 619**.

525 BERTRAM, Henry. Prob rel to William B, qv. To QUE on the *Commerce*, ex Greenock, Jun 1820; stld prob Lanark Co, ONT. **HCL 239**.

526 BERTRAM, John, 1829–1906. From Eddleston, PEE. s/o Alexander B. To Dundas Co, ONT, 1852. Millwright and toolmaker. m Elizabeth, d/o Henry Bennett, qv, and had, poss with other ch: 1. Alexander, 1853–1926, army officer, KB 1916; 2. Henry; 3. James. **DC 29 Sep 1964**.

527 BERTRAM, William. Prob rel to Henry B, qv. To QUE on the *Commerce*, ex Greenock, Jun 1820; stld prob Lanark Co, ONT. **HCL 239**.

528 BEST, Isabella. Poss from Edinburgh. Niece of Barbara Playfair. To Wolfville, Kings Co, NS, <1844. **SH**.

529 BEST, Jacob. To St Armand, Missisquoi Co, QUE, ca 1820. **DC 11 Feb 1980**.

530 BETHUNE, Beth, b ca 1791. From Uig, Is Skye, INV. to York Factory, Hudson Bay, on the *Edward & Anne*, ex Stornoway, Lewis, arr 24 Sep 1811. Pioneer settler, Red River. **LSS 184; RRS 13, 26; LSC 321**.

531 BETHUNE, Catherine. From Glenelg, INV. To QUE on the *Liscard*, 1849; stld Glengarry Co, ONT. Wife of Donald MacLeod, qv. **MG 30, 317**.

532   BETHUNE, Donald. From SUT. To Pictou Co, NS, 1822; stld nr Lansdowne. m Anne Anderson, qv. **DC 10 Feb 1980**.

533   BETHUNE, Ewen, b ca 1793. From Glenelg, INV. To QUE, ex Greenock, summer 1815; stld prob Lanark Co, ONT. Labourer, unm.   **SEC 6**.

534   BETHUNE, James. From Kilmorack, INV. To Pictou Co, NS, on the *Dove*, ex Fort William, Jun 1801. Labourer.   **PLD**.

535   BETHUNE, John. From Kilmorack, INV. To Pictou, NS, on the *Dove*, ex Fort William, Jun 1801. Labourer. **PLD**.

536   BETHUNE, John. To Pictou, NS, on the *Ellen*, ex Loch Laxford, SUT, 22 May 1848. Wife Ann with him, and ch: 1. Marion; 2. Barbara; 3. John; 4. Ann; 5. Johann.   **DC 15 Jul 1979**.

537   BETHUNE, Mary. To Richmond Co, NS, <1850. Wife of Roderick Bethune, qv.   **MLA 30**.

538   BETHUNE, Roderick. To Loch Lomond, Richmond Co, NS, <1850. m Mary Bethune, qv. Son John Lemuel, 1850–1913, MLA.   **MLA 30**.

539   BEVERIDGE, David, d 29 May 1861. From Maxwelltown, KKD. To Hawkesbury Twp, Prescott Co, ONT. Dau Maggie.   **CAE 6, 11**.

540   BEVERIDGE, John Adamson, b 1836. From Dumfermline, FIF. s/o Andrew B. and — Spratt. To ONT, ca 1852. m Eliza Sherwin.   **LDW 28 Feb 1965**.

541   BEVERIDGE, Margaret. From Dumfries. d/o David B, merchant, and Margaret McKinnell. To ONT <1864. m Rev James Mair, qv.   **FES vii 645**.

542   BIGGAR, Agnes, 1823–1901. d/o John B, qv, and Mary Rodgerson, qv. To PEI, prob <1836. m Richard Elliott.   **DC 25 Nov 1981**.

543   BIGGAR, James, d 29 Jul 1856. From Barbui, Irongray par, DFS. To Brant Co, ONT; stld Mount Pleasant.   **DGC 25 Nov 1856**.

544   BIGGAR, James, 1829–1907. From DFS. s/o John B, qv, and Mary Rodgerson, qv. To PEI, prob <1836. m Elizabeth d/o Joseph Davison, qv, and Ann Whitehead, ch: 1. John Frederick, dy; 2. Joseph, 1859–1937; 3. Thomas, 1861-94; 4. Agnes, 1866–1951; 5. Mary, 1864–1922; 6. Eliza, 1870–1952; 7. Margaret, 1873–1936.   **DC 25 Nov 1981**.

545   BIGGAR, James, d 18 Dec 1875. Prob from DFS. bro/o Thomas B, qv. To PEI, prob <1836. m Eliza Hutton.   **DC 25 Nov 1981**.

546   BIGGAR, John, 1799–1865. From Langholm, DFS. To PEI <1836; stld poss Breadalbane, Queens Co. m Mary Rodgerson, qv, ch: 1. Agnes, qv; 2. John, jr, qv; 3. James, qv; 4. Jane; 5. Mary; 6. Robert; 7. Johanna; 8. Thomas.   **DC 25 Nov 1981**.

547   BIGGAR, John, jr, 1827–1906. s/o John B, qv, and Mary Rodgerson, qv. To PEI, prob <1836. m (i) Miss Holmes; (ii) Jane Anderson.   **DC 25 Nov 1981**.

548   BIGGAR, Thomas, b 14 Feb 1815. Prob from DFS. bro/o James B, qv. To PEI, prob <1836. m Margaret McKay, ch: 1. Janet, b Stanley Bridge, 1840; 2. Catherine, b 1841; 3. Robert, 1842-59; 4. Mary

Ann, 1844-96; 5. John M, 1847-76; 6. William, 1848-80; 7. Christy Isobel, 1850–1947; 8. Elizabeth, 1852-80.   **DC 25 Nov 1981**.

549   BILSLAND, Jane Margaret, ca 1808–22 Dec 1894. From Glasgow. To QUE on the *Prompt*, ex Greenock, 4 Jul 1820; stld Dalhousie Twp, Lanark Co, ONT. Wife of James Hood, qv.   **DC 10 Mar 1980**.

550   BIRKMYRE, Rev John, ca 1796–6 Jun 1864. From Kilbarchan, RFW. s/o Capt William B. Matric Univ of Glasgow, 1812, and grad MA, 1816. Min of St Pauls Ch, Fredericton, NB, 1832-41. Retr to SCT and was min of Dean par, Edinburgh, 1844-64. DD, Glasgow 1840. Son William Frederick, actuary, Glasgow.   **RGG 45; GMA 8549; FES i 30, vii 608**.

551   BIRRELL, Ebenezer, ca 1801–27 Feb 1887. From Portmoak, KRS. s/o John B, portioner in Kinnesswood, and Christopher Arnott. To ONT and d at 'Maple Hall.' **Ts Portmoak**.

552   BIRRELL, John, 6 Apr 1815–12 Feb 1875. From Lerwick, SHI. s/o Ralph B, collector of Excise, and Eliza Thomson. To Montreal, QUE, ca 1835; later to London, Middlesex Co, ONT. Merchant. m Maria Louisa Sunley, ch: 1. George; 2. Elizabeth.   **Lerwick OPR 5/1**.

553   BIRRELL, Ralph, b 17 Dec 1816. From Lerwick, SHI. s/o Ralph B. and Eliza Thomson. To Montreal, QUE, ca 1835; later to London, Middlesex Co, ONT. m Hermoine, d/o Samuel Peters, surveyor, ch.   **Lerwick OPR 5/1**.

554   BISHOP, Archibald. From Edinburgh. To Huron Twp, Bruce Co, ONT. MPP, South Huron, 1873. **BNA 802**.

555   BISSET, Rev John, 1761–1810. From Breechin, ANS. s/o Rev John B. and Elizabeth Angus. Grad MA Marischall Coll, Aberdeen, 1779, and became Episcopal clergyman. To St. John, NB, 1786; later rector of Shrewsbury, MD, and asst rector of Trinity par, New York. Became Professor of Belles Lettres, Columbia Coll, and d at London.   **FAM iii 349; FES v 376**.

556   BLACK, Alexander, 1775–4 Oct 1854. From Glasgow. To QUE >1815, and stld English River. m Agnes Donald, qv, ch: 1. John, 1802-41; 2. Josiah, qv.   **Ts Russeltown Flats**.

557   BLACK, Allan, b 1806. From Dunganichy, Is Benbecula, INV. s/o John B. and Mary Wilson. To Pictou, NS, on the *Lulan*, ex Glasgow, 17 Aug 1848. m (i) Kirsty MacLellan, ch: 1. John, b 1838; 2. Mary, remained in Benbecula. m (ii) Margaret MacDonald, qv, with further ch: 3. Duncan, b 1846.   **DC 12 Jul 1979**.

558   BLACK, Archibald, ca 1822–ca 1859. From Kings Corse, Kilbride par, Is Arran, BUT. s/o James B, qv, and Elizabeth McMillan, qv. To Nash Creek, Restigouche Co, NB, 1829. m Jane Archibald, qv, and had dau Mary, b 1852.   **DC 1 Oct 1979**.

559   BLACK, Archibald. From ARL. To North Dorchester Twp, Middlesex Co, ONT, 1844.   **PCM 67**.

560   BLACK, Archibald. From ARL. Prob bro/o John B, qv. To Middlesex Co, ONT, 1846; stld Adelaide Twp. **PCM 28**.

561   BLACK, Archie. From Is Jura, ARL. Prob rel to Hugh B, qv. To Ekfrid Twp, Middlesex Co, ONT, 1832. **PCM 31**.

562 BLACK, Catherine, 1820–1901. From Kilbride par, Is Arran, BUT. d/o James B, qv, and Elizabeth McMillan, qv. To Nash Creek, Restigouche Co, NB, 1829. m Robert Archibald, qv. **DC 1 Oct 1979**.

563 BLACK, Catherine, 1810-50. From Is Mull, ARL. To Caledon Twp, Peel Co, ONT, <1840. Wife of Neil Lamont, qv. **DC 21 Apr 1980**.

564 BLACK, David. bro/o Mary B. To ONT <1855. **SH**.

565 BLACK, Donald. From Is Jura, ARL. To Ekfrid Twp, Middlesex Co, ONT, 1852. **PCM 31**.

566 BLACK, Rev Edward, 10 Dec 1793–9 May 1845. From Penninghame, WIG. s/o Rev James B, par min, and Isabella Paterson. Educ Univ of Edinburgh. To Montreal, QUE, as asst to Rev Henry Esson, qv, St Gabriel St Ch. Seceded 1831, and estab St Pauls Ch. DD, Edinburgh 1837. m (i) Eliza Craw, qv; (ii) Williamina McMillan, qv. ch incl: 1. Rev William McMillan, min at Anwoth, KKD; 2. Mrs John Greensheilds. **DGH 31 Jan 1840; SGC 340; FES ii 375, vii 627**.

567 BLACK, Euphemia, b ca 1778. From Dalavich or Kilmichael-Glassary par, ARL. To York Co, ONT, 1818, but stld Mosa Twp, Middlesex Co. Wife of John McKellar, qv. **DC 29 Oct 1979**.

568 BLACK, George, d 21 May 1839. From Penninghame, WIG. s/o Rev James B, par min, and Isabella Paterson. To Montreal, QUE, and d there. **DGH 5 Jun 1839; FES ii 375**.

569 BLACK, Hugh. From Is Jura, ARL. Prob rel to Archie B, qv. To Ekfrid Twp, Middlesex Co, ONT, 1832. **PCM 31**.

570 BLACK, Isabella, 1786–1877. From Lismore, ARL. d/o Duncan B. and Isabella Mackenzie. To Pictou, NS, on the *Economy*, ex Tobermory, 1 Oct 1819. m at Glasgow, 19 Jul 1808, John McLean, poet, qv. **DC 13 Apr 1966**.

571 BLACK, Isabelle, b 18 Feb 1815. From Kaimflat, Ednam, ROX. d/o John b, qv, and Helen Hunter, qv. To Sophiasburgh, Prince Edward Co, ONT, 1817. m William Vader. **DC 9 Jun 1980**.

572 BLACK, James, b 1780. From King's Corse, Kilbride, Is Arran, BUT. To Dalhousie, NB, 1829; stld Nash Creek, Restigouche Co. m Elizabeth McMillan, qv, ch: 1. Catherine, qv; 2. Archibald, qv; 3. Donald or Daniel, b 1825. **MAC 9**.

573 BLACK, James. To Simcoe Co, ONT, 1847; stld Stroud. m Mary Latimer, qv, ch: 1. Robert; 2. Sarah; 3. William; 4. Margaret; 5. James, jr, qv; 6. Johnston. **DC 21 Mar 1981**.

574 BLACK, James, jr. s/o James B, qv, and Mary Latimer, qv. To Simcoe Co, ONT, 1847; stld Stroud. m Mary Ann Ostler, ch: 1. Robert John, 1862–1912; 2. William James; 3. Annie Maria; 4. Andrew, 1868-93; 5. Anson; 6. Minnie, d inf. **DC 21 Mar 1981**.

575 BLACK, Janet. From ARL. To Aldborough Twp, Middlesex Co, ONT, 1818. Wife of Archibald McKellar, qv, and acted as midwife in the Scottish settlements. **PCM 23**.

576 BLACK, John. To QUE, ca 1784. Shipbuilder and MLA. **MDB 59**.

577 BLACK, John, 1760–1833. From Aberdeen. To St John, NB, 1786. Purchasing agent. Retr to SCT, 1806, and bought estate of Forresthill, Aberdeen, from father-in-law. m Jane, d London, 1866, d/o Alexander and Jean Stephen of Pitmeddan, ch: 1. Alexander; 2. William; 3. Thomas, 1801-25; 4. George, 1804-58. **SNQ viii/1 99**.

578 BLACK, John. From ARL. Prob bro/o Archibald B. To Adelaide Twp, Middlesex Co, ONT, 1846. **PCM 28**.

579 BLACK, John, ca 1794–4 May 1820. From Glasgow. To NS and d there. **NSS No 1950**.

580 BLACK, John. From Kilmartin par, ARL. To ONT 1816. Wife Janet Campbell, qv, with him, and dau Janet. **DC 29 Oct 1979**.

581 BLACK, John, d 10 Aug 1841. From Glasgow. To Montreal, QUE. Emp with Watson, Black & Co. **DGH 31 Jan 1840**.

582 BLACK, John, 12 Apr 1788–19 Jan 1857. From Kaimflat, Ednam, ROX. s/o John B. and Mary Wilson. To Sophiasburgh, Prince Edward Co, ONT, 1817. Farmer. m Helen Sinclair, qv, ch: 1. John, jr, qv; 2. Isabelle, qv; 3. Mary, qv; 4. William, b 22 Apr 1819; 5. Agnes, b 22 Jul 1821; 6. Charles, b 25 Jul 1824; 7. Jane, b 25 Mar 1827; 8. Margaret Ann, b 15 Sep 1830; 9. Helen, b 23 Mar 1833. **DC 9 Jun 1980**.

583 BLACK, John, jr, b 7 Aug 1813. From Kaimflat, Ednam, ROX. s/o John B, qv, and Helen Hunter, qv. To Sophiasburgh, Prince Edward Co, ONT, 1817. m Sarah Ann Vancleaf. **DC 9 Jun 1980**.

584 BLACK, John. bro/o Marion Scotland B, qv. To Toronto, ONT, <1850. **SH**.

585 BLACK, John, d 11 Jul 1857. From Dunkeld, PER. s/o Rev John B, Congregational min there, 1813-57. To Lanark Co, ONT, and was drowned in the River Clyde. **DGH 7 Aug 1857**.

586 BLACK, Rev John, 8 Jan 1818–11 Feb 1882. From Garwaldshiels, Eskdalemuir, DFS. s/o William B, farmer, and Margaret Halliday. To Toronto, ONT, <1851, and studied at Knox Coll. Ord in Presb Ch and became pioneer min of that faith in MAN. DD, Queen's Univ. **BNA 1047; FES vii 655; MDB 59**.

587 BLACK, John, 11 Mar 1817–3 Feb 1879. From St Andrew's, FIF. s/o John B, shipowner, and Janet Smith. To Assiniboia, MAN, 1839. Emp with HBCo and became Recorder of Rupert's Land. Sometime in Australia, but d St Andrews, MAN. m 1854, Margaret, d/o Alexander Christie, poss Alexander C, 1793–1872, qv. **Ts St Andrew's, FIF**.

588 BLACK, Josiah, 1815-95. From Glasgow. To QUE >1815. s/o Alexander B, qv, and Agnes Donald, qv. m Ann Wylie, qv. **Ts Russelltown Flats**.

589 BLACK, Margaret. From Old Cumnock, AYR. To ONT, 1833. Wife of Allan Hunter, qv. **Old Cumnock OPR 610/4; LDW 30 Aug 1976**.

590 BLACK, Marion, 9 Dec 1804–23 Feb 1879. From Paisley, RFW. To Dalhousie Twp, Lanark Co, ONT, prob <1840. Wife of Hugh Adam, qv. **DC 26 Sep 1979**.

591 BLACK, Marion Scotland. sis/o John B, qv. To Toronto, ONT, <1850. m — Stow. **SH**.

592   BLACK, Mary, b 22 Oct 1816. From Kaimflat, Ednam, ROX. d/o John B, qv, and Helen Hunter, qv. To Sophiasburgh, Prince Edward Co, ONT, 1817. m Robert Ferguson Pegan.   **DC 9 Jun 1980**.

593   BLACK, Samuel, ca 1785–8 Jan 1841. From ABD. s/o John B. and Mary Leith. To Montreal, QUE, 1802. Clerk with XYCo and later with NWCo. Opposed to NWCo/HBCo merger, 1821, and was not emp by the united company until 1823. Explored Finlay River, 1824, and app a chief factor, 1837. Shot by an Indian nr the mouth of the Columbia River.   **SH; MDB 59**.

594   BLACK, Walter. From DFS. To QUE on the *George Canning*, ex Greenock, 14 Apr 1821; stld Lot 21, Con 7, Ramsay Twp, Lanark Co, ONT. Wheelwright and farmer. Wife Mary with him, and several ch, incl: 1. John; 2. Mary.   **HCL 73, 82, 239**.

595   BLACK, William, b 1727. From Paisley, RFW. To Cumberland Co, NS, 1774. m Elizabeth Stocks, from Huddersfield, YKS, ENG, ch: 1. John; 2. William; 3. Thomas; 4. Richard; 5. Sarah.   **DC 21 Mar 1981**.

596   BLACK, William, 1770–1866. From Aberdeen. To NB <1819. Pres and administrator of NB, 1829-31, and three times Mayor of St John. m a d/o Lt Col Christopher Billop.   **MDB 60**.

597   BLACK, William. From Is Arran, BUT. To Dalhousie, NB, prob 1829.

598   BLACK, William. From ARL. To Ekfrid Twp, Middlesex Co, ONT, 1832. ch: 1. Malcolm; 2. Donald; 3. Dugal; 4. Alexander; 5. Nicol; 6. Nancy; 7. Christy.   **PCM 30**.

599   BLACKADDER, Francis. Prob from STI. To QUE <1841, when described as 'a promising young man.'   **DJL 6**.

600   BLACKBURN, Christopher. Poss from Killearn, PER. bro/o Hugh B, qv. To Malbaie, QUE, <1770.   **LDW 8 Jun 1978**.

601   BLACKBURN, Hugh. bro/o Christopher B, qv. Poss from Killearn, PER. To Malbaie, QUE, <1770.   **LDW 8 Jun 1978**.

602   BLACKBURN, John, b ca 1820. Prob from RFW. s/o Robert B, qv. To Lanark Co, ONT, poss <1841; stld Lot 13, Con 5, Darling Twp. Farmer. m Mrs Mather, ch: 1. Robina, b ca 1845; 2. John, b ca 1846; 3. Jane, b ca 1848; 4. Allan, b 1850.   **DC 5 Feb 1981**.

603   BLACKBURN, Margaret, ca 1813-61. From Elderslie, RFW. d/o William B. and Margaret Spier. To Lanark Co, ONT, ca 1841. Wife of Matthew Reid, qv, m 21 Jun 1835.   **DC 8 Sep 1980**.

604   BLACKBURN, Robert, b ca 1783. Prob from RFW. To Lanark Co, ONT, ca 1841. Joiner. Son John.   **DC 5 Feb 1981**.

605   BLACKBURN, Robert, b ca 1815. From RFW. To QUE on the *Carleton*, ex Glasgow, arr 5 Jun 1842; stld Lanark Co, ONT. Carpenter. m Bethia Craig, qv, and had, poss with other ch: 1. Robert, b ca 1837; 2. Matilda, b ca 1845; 3. Elizabeth, b ca 1848.   **DC 5 Feb 1981**.

606   BLACKBURN, Stevenson, b 1815. From Elderslie, RFW. s/o Robert B, millwright, and Agnes Stevenson. To Lanark Co, ONT, <1842. Stationer, tailor and later farmer. m Mary McCreadie, qv, ch: 1. Jean,

b Johnstone, 1840; 2. Mary, b 1842, Lanark Co, ONT; 3. Agnes, b 1844; 4. Stevenson, jr, b ca 1846; 5. Jessie, b ca 1848.   **Abbey OPR 559/8; DC 5 Feb 1981**.

607   BLACKBURN, William, d 12 Jun 1841. From Glasgow. s/o William B, weaver. Matric Univ of Glasgow, 1807. To Kemptville, Leeds and Grenville Co, ONT.   **GMA 7355**.

608   BLACKHALL, Elspet, 1777–6 Aug 1853. To QUE <1840, and went to Wellington Co, ONT. Wife of James Davidson, qv.   **EHE 11**.

609   BLACKIE, Charles, b ca 1738. From Milnbank, Southwick, Kirkbean, KKD. To Georgetown, Kings Co, PEI, on the *Lovely Nellie*, ex Annan, 1774; poss later to NS. m Janet Herries, qv, and had, poss with other ch: 1. John, b ca 1768; 2. William, b ca 1770; 3. James, b ca 1772; 4. Ann, b ca 1774; 5. Charles, 1783–1869, res Upper Stewiacke, Colchester Co, NS.   **ELN; NSN 24/87**.

610   BLACKLAY, William, ca 1813–21 Aug 1834. From Drumcriel, Durrisdeer, DFS. To Toronto, ONT.   **DGC 15 Oct 1834**.

611   BLACKLOCK, Ambrose, 17 May 1784–5 Oct 1866. From DFS. To St Andrew's, Stormont Co, ONT. Surgeon, RN, War of 1812; MLA, 1828-30. m 15 May 1816, Catherine, 1798–1878, d/o Capt Ranald Macdonell and Marjery Robertson, ch: 1. John James, physician; 2. Thomas Robertson.   **SDG 153, 347, 451**.

612   BLACKLOCK, Thomas, b 1778. From Ecclefechan, DFS. To PEI, 1821; moved to Westmorland Co, NB. Schoolteacher. m Jennie Hall, qv, ch.   **DC 17 Apr 1981**.

613   BLACKWOOD, James. Prob from LKS. To QUE on the *Commerce*, ex Greenock, Jun 1820; stld Lanark Co, ONT.   **HCL 238**.

614   BLACKWOOD, John. Prob from Glasgow. To Montreal, QUE, ca 1800. Ship's carpenter. m Mary Munroe, ch: 1. Robert, d ca 1890; 2. Alexander, 1811-84; 3. Barbara.   **DC 2 Jul 1979**.

615   BLACKWOOD, John. Prob from LKS. Neph of Thomas B, qv. To Montreal, QUE, prob <1842; later to ONT. Merchant.   **SGC 497**.

616   BLACKWOOD, Martha. Poss from RFW. To QUE on the *Atlas*, ex Greenock, 11 Jul 1815; stld Burgess Twp, Lanark Co, ONT. Wife of William Wallace.   **SEC 3**.

617   BLACKWOOD, Thomas, 10 Feb 1773–22 Nov 1842. From AYR. To QUE, 1791; moved to Montreal, 1797. Merchant, treas. of Montreal Savings Bank and a director of the General Hospital. Son James.   **SGC 244**.

618   BLACKWOOD, Rev Robert, ca 1785–12 Dec 1857. From KRS. To Shubenacadie, Hants Co, NS, 1816, later to Tatamagouche, Colchester Co, NS. Clergyman. m Ann McAra, qv, ch: 1. Jessie; 2. David, res Halifax; 3. William.   **HT 81, 110, 111**.

619   BLAIKIE, Charles. From KKD or DFS. To NS <26 Aug 1783, when gr 300 acres on West River, Pictou Co.   **HPC App A and D**.

620   BLAIKIE, John. From KKD or DFS. To Pictou, NS; stld east side of West River <12 Feb 1783, when listed as capable of bearing arms. Son Harris, res Stewiacke, Colchester Co.   **HPC App D and E; HNS iii 558**.

BLAIN. See also BLAIND, BLAND.

621 BLAIN, David, 1832-91. From Ayr. To Kingston, ONT, <1856; later to Toronto. Lawyer and Liberal politician, West York. **BNA 741**.

622 BLAIN, James. To QUE on the *Brock*, ex Greenock, 1820; stld prob Dalhousie Twp, Lanark Co, ONT. **HCL 238**.

BLAIND. See also BLAIN, BLAND.

623 BLAIND, Eliza. From Glasgow. To Bath Village, Lennox Co, ONT. m Rev John Smith, qv. **DGC 30 Sep 1835**.

624 BLAIND, William Kelly, Mar 1799-24 Oct 1855. From DFS. s/o Samuel B, draper and furrier, and Mary Kelly. To Hastings Co, ONT, and stld Belleville, 1832. Schoolteacher. ch incl: 1. William, b 10 Dec 1820; 2. Jane. **MSM 288; DGC 29 Jan 1856**.

BLAIR, Hon A J. See FERGUSSON, Adam Johnston.

625 BLAIR, Andrew. From AYR. To NS <1840. Son Andrew, land surveyor. **DC 15 Mar 1980**.

626 BLAIR, Archibald. Cousin of Archibald B, Merchiston, Edinburgh. To Cayuga, Haldimand Co, ONT, <1837. **SH**.

627 BLAIR, Dugald, ca 1815-23 Dec 1855. From RFW. Matric Univ of Glasgow, 1830, and grad MD 1839. Sometime physician in Greenock, and d St Stephen, Charlotte Co, NB. **GMA 12676**.

628 BLAIR, Elizabeth. From PER. To McNab Twp, Renfrew Co, ONT, 1825. **DC 3 Jun 1980**.

629 BLAIR, James, b 13 Oct 1814. From Castleton, ROX. s/o Thomas B, qv, and Violet Oliver, qv. To Scotch Lake, York Co, NB, ca 1819; later to Westminster Twp, Middlesex Co, ONT. Farmer. m Jean Oliver, qv. **DC 16 Jul 1979**.

630 BLAIR, John, b 1815. Poss from DNB. s/o — B. and Christian McGregor, 1774-1873. To QUE, ca 1829; stld Cushing. **DC 28 Jan 1961**.

631 BLAIR, John. To QUE on the *David of London*, ex Greenock, 19 May 1821; stld prob Lanark Co, ONT. **HCL 239**.

632 BLAIR, Robert, b ca 1725. From New Abbey, KKD. To Georgetown, Kings Co, PEI, on the *Lovely Nellie*, ex Annan, 1774. Sailor. **ELN**.

633 BLAIR, Sarah. From Hawick, ROX. To QUE, ex Greenock, Jul 1815, and stld ONT. Wife of Robert Newall, qv. **SEC 1**.

634 BLAIR, Thomas. From Castleton, ROX. To York Co, NB, ca 1819; moved in 1836 to Westminster Twp, Middlesex Co, ONT. Farmer. m Violet Oliver, qv. Son James, qv. **DC 16 Jul 1979**.

635 BLAIR, William, b ca 1744. From Colvend, KKD. To Georgetown, Kings Co, PEI, on the *Lovely Nellie*, ex Carsethorn, May 1775. Mariner. **ELN**.

636 BLAIR, William, d 1821. To ONT, poss 1812; stld Lot 23, Con 3, Bathurst Twp, Lanark Co, ONT. Farmer and brickmaker. **HCL 54**.

BLAND. See also BLAIN, BLAIND.

637 BLAND, Mary, ca 1809-23 Feb 1834. From DFS. Poss d/o Robert B, linen merchant. To Kingston, ONT. m Rev John Smith, qv. **DGC 30 Sep 1835**.

638 BLUE, Archibald. To PEI, ca 1803; stld Belfast. Petitioner for Dr MacAulay, 1811. **HP 74**.

639 BLUE, Archibald, ca 1845-1910. From Killean and Kilchenzie par, Kintyre, ARL. s/o Donald B, qv, and Mary McConachy, qv. To Elderslie Twp, Bruce Co, ONT, <1855. Farmer. m Ann Bell, qv, 1851-1927, and d at Chesley, ch: 1. Alexander, 1881-1941; 2. Lachlan, 1885-1944; 3. Janet 1888-1948. **DC 6 Jan 1982**.

640 BLUE, Donald, 1794-1874. From Is Arran, BUT. To Megantic Co, QUE, <1840; moved later to ONT. m 1824, Ann McKillop, qv, ch: 1. Donald; 2. Dugald; 3. Jane; 4. Catherine. **AMC 132**.

641 BLUE, Donald, 1814-19 Nov 1900. From Killean and Kilchenzie par, Kintyre, ARL. To Elderslie Twp, Bruce Co, ONT, <1855. Farmer. m Mary McConechy, qv, ch: 1. Archibald, qv; 2. Janet, 1849-1937, d Winnipeg. **DC 6 Jan 1982**.

642 BLUE, James, b ca 1814. From Killean and Kilchenzie par, Kintyre, ARL. To Elderslie Twp, Bruce Co, ONT, <1855, with relatives. Bur St Andrews Cemetery, Chesley. **DC 6 Jan 1982**.

643 BLUE, John. To Pictou, NS, on the *Hope*, ex Glasgow, 5 Apr 1848; but went to USA. **DC 12 Jul 1979**.

644 BLUE, John. Poss from North Knapdale, ARL. To Aldborough Twp, Elgin Co, ONT, prob <1830. m Mary McTavish, qv. Son Archibald, 1840-1914, b Oxford, Kent Co, journalist. **PDA 42**.

645 BLUE, Katie. Prob from Knapdale, ARL. To Aldborough Twp, Elgin Co, ONT, poss 1819. m John MacIntyre, qv. **DC 23 Nov 1981**.

646 BLUE, Marion, d 1857. From Campbeltown, ARL. To QUE, 1830; stld Richmond Co. Wife of Gilbert Stalker, qv. **DC 7 Mar 1980**.

647 BLUE, Neil. From ARL. To QUE, ex Greenock, arr Oct 1830; stld Leggat's Point. Wife Mary with him, ch: 1. Dougald; 2. Malcolm; 3. Alexander; 4. John. **DC 2 Mar 1980**.

648 BLUE, Neil. From ARL. To Ekfrid Twp, Middlesex Co, ONT, ca 1839. Tailor. **PCM 31**.

649 BOAG, Rev William, ca 1770-26 May 1856. From Dovehill, Glasgow. Relief Ch min respectively at Castle Douglas, Strathkinnes and Dunning. Ch of Scotland min at Airdrie, LKS, 1845-52; trans to Pulteneytown, Wick. To Norvaltown, Montreal, QUE, 1853. **UPC i 206, ii 594**.

650 BOAK, Sir Robert, 1822-1904. From Leith, MLN. To Halifax, NS, 1831. Merchant, Robert Boak & Sons, and Pres of the Legislative Council of NS. **MDB 65**.

651 BOGIE, Andrew, 15 Aug 1834-25 Dec 1907. From Dysart, FIF. s/o James B, qv, and Agnes Reid, qv. To Ashfield Twp, Huron Co, ONT, ca 1848. Sailor, m 14 Sep 1859, Martha Sallows, 1837-1924, ch: 1. William, b 1861; 2. Sarah, 1862-1917; 3. Mary, b 1864; 4. Thomas, b 1866; 5. Robert, 1869-1953; 6. Agnes, 1872-1957; 7. Alexander, 1882-1971. **DC 4 Aug 1979**.

652   BOGIE, Annie, b 11 Feb 1837. From Dysart, FIF. d/o James B, qv, and Agnes Reid, qv. To Ashfield Twp, Huron Co, ONT, ca 1848. m — Middleton, and went to WI <1861.   **Dysart OPR 426/5; DC 15 Jul 1979**.

653   BOGIE, Christian, b 23 Nov 1838. From Dysart, FIF. d/o James B, qv, and Agnes Reid, qv. To Ashfield Twp, Huron Co, ONT, ca 1848. m — Stoddart, and went to WI <1861.   **Dysart OPR 426/5; DC 15 Jul 1979**.

654   BOGIE, James, ca 1810–ca 1858. From Pathhead, Dysart, FIF. s/o James B, Kirkcaldy. To Ashfield Twp, Huron Co, ONT, ca 1848. Sailor, later farmer. m Agnes Reid, qv, ch: 1. James, qv; 2. Andrew, qv; 3. Annie, qv; 4. Christian, qv; 5. Johanna, qv; 6. William, 1844-60; 7. Robert, qv; 8. Alexander, 1848–1901; 9. David, 1850–1918.   **DC 15 Aug 1979**.

655   BOGIE, James, jr, b 9 Sep 1832. From Dysart par, FIF. s/o James B, qv, and Agnes Reid, qv. To Ashfield Twp, Huron Co, ONT, ca 1848. m Mary Ann Clark, ca 1859.   **Dysart OPR 426/5; DC 15 Jul 1979**.

656   BOGIE, Johanna, b 4 Sep 1841. From Dysart par, FIF. d/o James B, qv, and Agnes Reid, qv. To Ashfield Twp, Huron Co, ONT, ca 1848. m William Green, d 1860, at Goderich, and after his d went to WI and m — Stoddart.   **Dysart OPR 426/5; DC 15 Jul 1979**.

657   BOGIE, Robert, b 15 Aug 1846. From Dysart par, FIF. s/o James B, qv, and Agnes Reid, qv. To Ashfield Twp, Huron Co, ONT, ca 1848. m and went to WI >1861.   **Dysart OPR 426/5; DC 15 Jul 1979**.

658   BONALLIE, Archibald. From Dysart, FIF. s/o William B. and Margaret Miller. To QUE prob <1851; stld Sherbrooke Co. Farmer.   **DC 7 Feb 1980**.

659   BONALLIE, Benjamen. From Dysart, FIF. s/o William B. and Margaret Miller. To QUE prob <1851. m Sarah Gilpin, who d 1922, ch.   **DC 7 Feb 1980**.

660   BONALLIE, Isabella. From Dysart, FIF. d/o William B. and Margaret Miller. To QUE prob <1851; stld Valcartier Twp. m — Currigan.   **DC 7 Feb 1980**.

661   BONALLIE, John, 1814-84. From Dysart, FIF. s/o William B. and Margaret Miller. To QUE ca 1845; later to Toronto, ONT. Ship chandler. m Jessie Barron, qv, ch.   **DC 7 Feb 1980**.

662   BONALLIE, William. From Dysart, FIF. s/o William B. and Margaret Miller. To QUE prob <1851.   **DC 7 Feb 1980**.

BONAR. See also BONNAR.

663   BONAR, Margaret. From Glasgow. To Grey Co, ONT, ca 1845. Wife of Abraham Creighton, qv. **DC 30 Aug 1977**.

664   BONE, Adam, 12 Jul 1821–4 Jan 1904. From Dalry, AYR. s/o David B. and Agnes Kerr. To Brantford Twp, Brant Co, ONT, prob 1852. Shoemaker. m Jean Heron, qv, ch: 1. David, qv; 2. Jean, 1843–1931; 3. Agnes, b 1845; 4. Adam, jr, qv; 5. Margaret, qv; 6. Mary, qv; 7. Ann, 1853–1935; 8. James, b 1855, dy; 9. Lizzie, b 1858, went to AZ.   **DC 27 Jun 1979**.

665   BONE, Adam, jr, 1 Dec 1846–20 Oct 1922. From Dalry, AYR. s/o Adam B, qv, and Jean Heron, qv. To Brantford Twp, Brant Co, ONT, 1852. Shoemaker.

m 16 Nov 1869, Isabelle Davidson, 1842-91, ch: 1. Helen Jane, 1870–1919; 2. George Adam, 1878–1958.   **DC 27 Jun 1979**.

666   BONE, David, 14 Jun 1842–24 Dec 1916. From Dalry, AYR. s/o Adam B, qv, and Jean Heron, qv. To Brantford Twp, Brantford Co, ONT, ca 1852. m at Chesley, Elderslie Twp, Bruce Co, 26 Sep 1870, Elizabeth Shea, 1853–1928, ch: 1. Catherine, called Kate, 1871–1943; 2. David, 1872–1948; 3. James E, 1874–1959; 4. Mary, 1877–1955; 5. Clara, 1881–1920; 6. Annie, b 1883; 7. Helen Isabel, or Nellie, b 1885; 8. Florence, 1889–1958; 9. Adam, 1890–1952; 10. John Heron, 1892–1972.   **DC 27 Jun 1979**.

667   BONE, James, 9 Oct 1829–28 Jan 1903. From Dalry, AYR. s/o David B. and Agnes Kerr. To Paris, Brant Co, ONT, 1852. Master tanner. m in 1854, Christina Scott, 1829–1903, ch: 1. Agnes, 1857–1953; 2. Margaret, 1861-82; 3. David Robert, 1865–1931; 4. Elizabeth, 1867–1945; 5. Isabel, b 1870; 6. James, 1875–1946.   **DC 17 Jun 1979**.

668   BONE, Margaret, 9 Feb 1849–5 Dec 1909. From Dalry, AYR. d/o Adam B, qv, and Jean Heron, qv. To Brantford Twp, Brant Co, ONT, prob 1852. m John S. McTavish.   **DC 27 Jun 1979**.

669   BONE, Mary, 7 Apr 1851–28 Aug 1876. From Dalry, AYR. d/o Adam B, qv, and Jean Heron, qv. To Brantford Twp, Brant Co, ONT, prob 1852. m Joseph Hall.   **DC 27 Jun 1979**.

BONNAR. See also BONAR.

670   BONNAR, James Turnbull, b 5 Aug 1810. From Dunfermline, FIF. s/o David B, and rel to Thomas B, wright. To King Twp, York Co, ONT, prob <1850. m Mary Kennedy, qv. Son Robert Andrew, 1860–1932, criminal lawyer.   **SH; Ts Dunfermline**.

671   BONNAR, Thomas. From Dunfermline, FIF. s/o Thomas B, wright, d 1832, and Catherine McIlwraith, 1799–1875. To QUE <1832. Sometime Sgt, 71st Regt.   **SH; Ts Dunfermline**.

672   BONNER, William, b ca 1815. To QUE, 1846; stld Pittsburgh Twp, Frontenac Co, ONT. Wife Jane, b IRL, ca 1815, with him. ch: 1. Maria, b ca 1842; 2. William, b ca 1846; 3. Isabella, b ca 1848; 4. Matthew, b ca 1850.   **DC 13 Mar 1980**.

673   BONYMAN, Edward. From BAN. bro/o John B, qv, and James B, qv. To Tatamagouche, Colchester Co, NS, <1835. Farmer. ch, incl: 1. John; 2. Alexander.   **HT 68**.

674   BONYMAN, James. From BAN. bro/o Edward B, qv, and John B, qv. To Tatamagouche, Colchester Co, NS, 1836. Farmer.   **HT 68**.

675   BONYMAN, John. From Rothiemay, ABD. bro/o Edward B, qv, and James B, qv. To NS 1828; stld French River, Tatamagouche, Colchester Co. Farmer and magistrate. ch incl: 1. James; 2. John.   **HT 68**.

676   BONYMAN, Susan. From BAN. Prob sis/o Edward B, qv, John B, qv, and James B, qv. To Tatamagouche, Colchester Co, NS, <1840. m Robert Cooper, qv. **HT 68**.

677   BORLAND, John. To Pictou, NS, on the *Hope*, ex Glasgow, 5 Apr 1848. Wife Jane with him, and ch: 1. Janet; 2. John; 3. Isabella.   **DC 12 Jul 1979**.

678 BORLAND, Robert. To Pictou, NS, on the *Hope*, ex Glasgow, 5 Apr 1848. Wife Elizabeth with him, and ch: 1. Robert; 2. John; 3. Elizabeth; 4. Joseph; 5. John; 6. Jane; 7. Janet; 8. John, yr; 9. Isabella. They went later to USA. **DC 12 Jul 1979**.

679 BORROWMAN, Alexander, ca 1822–17 Dec 1884. From Edinburgh. s/o Robert B. and Elizabeth Stevenson. To Montreal, QUE, and d there. **Ts Greyfriars**.

680 BORROWMAN, James. To QUE on the *George Canning*, ex Greenock, 14 Apr 1821; stld Lanark Twp, Lanark Co, ONT. Farmer. **HCL 239**.

681 BORROWMAN, James, 24 Feb 1800–24 May 1876. From LKS. To Oshawa Village, Ontario Co, ONT, <1854. m Margaret Murray, qv. **DC 6 Sep 1979**.

682 BORROWMAN, Mary, 1813–1916. Prob d/o James B, qv. To Lanark Co, ONT, 1821. m Robert Affleck, jr, qv. **HCL 65**.

683 BORROWMAN, William. To QUE on the *George Canning*, ex Greenock, 14 Apr 1821; stld Lanark Twp, Lanark Co, ONT. **HCL 225**.

684 BORTHWICK, George, 26 Feb 1822–14 Nov 1906. From Edinburgh. s/o Dr George B. Educ Edinburgh Academy, 1830-37, and awarded Mathematics Medal. To CAN, 1840. Subsequently a merchant in Liverpool and New York. m 1859, Mary Elizabeth, d/o Matthew Norman MacDonald Hume of Bernisdale, WS. **EAR 59; HWS 198**.

685 BORTHWICK, Rev Hugh John, b ca 1825. s/o John B, schoolteacher. Educ Univ of Edinburgh and Queen's College, Kingston, ONT. Ord 1853 and became min of Chelsea, QUE, 1862. Went to Calf Mountain, MAN, as missionary, 1864, and was adm min of Mountain City, 1881. m 1848, Maria Taylor, qv. **FES vii 656**.

686 BORTHWICK, Rev John Douglas, 1832–14 Jan 1912. From Glencorse, MLN. To ONT 1850; stld later Montreal, QUE. Schoolteacher and ord to Ch of Eng, 1866. Incumbent of St Mary's, Hochelaga, and author of educational books. **MDB 69**.

687 BORTHWICK, Thomas, b 13 Dec 1808. From Edinburgh. Wife Annie deceased. To ONT 1834, with ch: 1. John, b 24 Jun 1826; 2. David, b ca 1828; 3. Jessie, b ca 1830; 4. Mary, b ca 1832. **DC 31 Aug 1979**.

688 BOSS, Andrew. To QUE on the *Brock*, ex Greenock, 1820; stld poss Lanark Co, ONT. **HCL 238**.

689 BOW, William, b 18 May 1825. From Aberdeen. To Dundas Co, ONT, ca 1840. **DC 4 Mar 1965**.

690 BOWER, David. To QUE on the *Commerce*, ex Greenock, Jun 1820; and stld Lanark Co, ONT. **HCL 63, 239**.

691 BOWES, James. From Glamis, ANS. To QUE on the *David of London*, ex Greenock, 19 May 1821; stld Lot 21, Con 6, Lanark Twp, Lanark Co, ONT. Engraver and blockmaker, later farmer. m Margaret Monteith, qv, ch: 1. Lillias, b 1794; 2. Thomas, b 1796; 3. Margaret, b 1797; 4. James, jr, b 1799, stld Lot 20; 5. John, b 1802, stld Lot 23, Con 7, Ramsay Twp; 6. Jessie, b 1805; 7. Robert, stld Lot 21, Con 7, Lanark Co; 8. William; 9. Catherine. **HCL 72, 86, 239; DC 6 Dec 1979**.

692 BOWES, James, 1798–1873. From LKS, poss Lesmahagow. To Scarborough, York Co, ONT, ca 1833. **DC 29 Mar 1981**.

693 BOWES, Thomas. Prob from ANS. To QUE on the *David of London*, ex Greenock, 19 May 1821; stld prob Lanark Co, ONT. **HCL 239**.

694 BOWIE, Margaret, d 6 Sep 1847. From AYR. d/o William B. To ONT, and d Kemptville, Leeds and Grenville Co. m Maj Robert Hamilton, qv. **DGH 28 Oct 1847**.

695 BOWMAN, David, 1808-87. From Montrose, ANS. s/o Alexander B. and Euphemia Birnie. To Esquesing Twp, Halton Co, ONT, ca 1850. Farmer. m Alison Moore, ch: 1. Alexander; 2. David; 3. Euphemia; 4. Janet; 5. Elizabeth; 6. Catherine; 7. David; 8. Martha; 9. William; 10. Allan; 11. Agnes; 12. Alison. **DC 24 Nov 1979**.

696 BOWMAN, John. To Pictou, NS, on the *Hope*, ex Glasgow, 5 Apr 1848. Wife Mary with him, and ch: 1. John; 2. Mary. They may have gone to USA. **DC 12 Jul 1979**.

697 BOYD, Alexander. From Arisaig, INV. To Pictou, NS, on the *Dove*, ex Fort William, Jun 1801. Labourer. **PLD**.

698 BOYD, Ann, 1798–1888. From Jedburgh, ROX. d/o Alexander B. To Leeds Twp, Megantic Co, QUE, 1831. Wife of Ayton Kinnaird, qv, whom she m at Edinburgh, 17 Dec 1817. **DC 2 Mar 1982**.

699 BOYD, Catherine. From Bornish, Is South Uist, INV. To West Williams Twp, Middlesex Co, ONT, 1849. Wife of James McIntyre, qv. **WLC**.

700 BOYD, Donald. From Is North Uist, INV. To West Williams Twp, Middlesex Co, ONT, ca 1848. Sailor. **PCM 48**.

701 BOYD, Hugh. From Arisaig, INV. To Pictou, NS, on the *Dove*, ex Fort William, Jun 1801. Labourer. **PLD**.

702 BOYD, James Tower, b ca 1830. From Aberdeen. s/o George B, merchant in Ceylon. Appr advocate, 1829; alumnus, Marischall Coll, 1847-51. To Brantford Twp, Brant Co, ONT. **FAM iii 539; SAA 390**.

703 BOYD, John. Poss from ABD. To South River, Antigonish Co, NS, <1800. m Margaret McPherson, qv, ch: 1. Christina; 2. Hugh; 3. Angus; 4. Catherine; 5. John; 6. Alexander; 7. Sarah; 8. Angus Og; 9. Mary. **HCA 79**.

704 BOYD, John. From Arisaig, INV. To Pictou, NS, on the *Dove*, ex Fort William, Jun 1801; went later to Antigonish Co, and d Morristown. Wife Catherine with him, and ch: 1. Anne; 2. Angus; 3. Angus Og; 4. John, b 1794. **PLD; VSN No 1204**.

705 BOYD, John. Prob rel to Samuel B, qv. To QUE on the *Commerce*, ex Greenock, Jun 1820; stld prob Lanark Co, ONT. **HCL 239**.

706 BOYD, John. To Oshawa Village, ONT, <1854. Saddler. Wife Euphemia, 1819-54, native of Perth. **DC 6 Sep 1979**.

707 BOYD, Margaret, ca 1735–Jan 1792. From Birnie par, MOR. To Flat River, PEI, on the *John and Elizabeth*, arr 30 Jul 1775; stld St Peter's Bay. Wife of John Dingwell, qv. **DC 27 Jul 1980**.

708   BOYD, Mary. From Arisaig, INV. Prob wife of Alexander B, qv. To Pictou, NS, on the *Dove*, ex Fort William, Jun 1801. **PLD**.

709   BOYD, Mary. From Arisaig, INV. Prob wife of Hugh B, qv. To Pictou, NS, on the *Dove*, ex Fort William, Jun 1801. **PLD**.

710   BOYD, Mary, b ca 1797. From Arisaig, INV. Poss d/o Hugh B, qv. To Pictou, NS, on the *Dove*, ex Fort William, Jun 1801. **PLD**.

711   BOYD, Mary, 1795–7 Oct 1869. From Jedburgh, ROX. d/o Alexander B, shoemaker, and his wife, the wid/o Alexander Fraser. To Leeds Twp, Megantic Co, QUE, 1822. m John Lambie, qv. **AMC 143; DC 11 Feb 1980**.

712   BOYD, Robert, b ca 1750. From AYR. To QUE on the *Friendship*, ex Port Glasgow, 30 Mar 1775. Ship carpenter, 'going to build vessels.' **LSF**.

713   BOYD, Samuel. Prob rel to John B, qv. To QUE on the *Commerce*, ex Greenock, Jun 1820; stld Lanark Co, ONT. **HCL 239**.

714   BOYD, Susannah, 1798–1868. From Is Pabbay, off Lewis, ROC, but b IRL. To Melbourne, Richmond Co, QUE, poss 1841. Wife of Evander McIver, qv. **MGC 15 Jul 1980**.

715   BOYES, Thomas. From Hamilton, LKS. To PEI <1794. Sometime Capt, 26th Regt, later of Royal Lanarkshire Militia. m Elizabeth Campbell, ch: 1. Elizabeth Mary; 2. Thomas William, b 3 May 1795; 3. Adam Duncan, b 19 Jun 1798; 4. John, b Hamilton, 16 Mar 1800; 5. Jane, b 30 Oct 1801; 6. Grace, twin with Jane; 7. Charles Robert, b 12 Sep 1803; 8. Catherine Augusta Smith, b 20 Oct 1812.   **Hamilton OPR 647/3**.

716   BOYLE, Angus. From Lochaber, INV. s/o Duncan B. To Beauly, Antigonish Co, NS, <1810. Prob discharged soldier. m Miss Dougall, ch: 1. Alexander; 2. Angus; 3. Duncan; 4. Donald; 5. Andrew; 6. Patrick; 7. John; 8. Kate; 9. Lucy. **HCA 82; MP 224**.

717   BOYLE, Angus. From Lochaber, INV. s/o Duncan B. To CAN on the *Earl of Dalhousie*, 1821; stld Mabou, Inverness Co, NS. Tailor, later farmer. m Isabel MacDonell, qv, ch: 1. Duncan; 2. Archibald; 3. Alexander, went to MN; 4. Donald; 5. John; 6. Angus; 7. Dougald Robert, b 1847; 8. Margaret; 9. Catherine; 10. Mary; 11. Anne.   **MP 224**.

718   BOYLE, David, b ca 1790. From Johnstone, RFW. To CAN <1829; stld prob ONT. Son Archibald, b ca 1826.   **SG xxiii/2 53**.

719   BOYLE, David, 1 May 1842–14 Feb 1911. From Greenock, RFW. s/o John Borland B. and Ann Anderson. To Salem, Nichol Twp, Wellington Co, ONT. Schoolteacher, Middlebrook, Pilkington Twp, 1865-71; Headmaster, Elora Public School, 1871-81; museum curator and archaeologist; LLD, Toronto 1909. m 24 May 1867, Martha S. Frankland, from Bingley, YKS, ENG, ch: 1. Susanna Peel; 2. John B; 3. James Frankland, d 1917; 4. Anne Anderson; 5. Robert. **EHE 164; MDB 78**.

720   BRACKENRIDGE, Agnes, b ca 1780. From Edinburgh. To QUE on the *Atlas*, ex Greenock, 11 Jul 1815; stld Bathurst Twp, Lanark Co, ONT. Wife of William Old, qv. **SEC 1**.

721   BRAIDEN, James. Poss from Glasgow. To QUE on the *Commerce*, ex Greenock, Jun 1820; stld Dalhousie Twp, Lanark Co, ONT. Son James with him.   **HCL 66, 239**.

722   BRAIDEN, Robert, b 1737. From Dumfries. To Georgetown, PEI, on the *Lovely Nellie*, ex Carsethorn, May 1775. Labourer. Wife Jean Kirkpatrick, qv, with him, and ch: 1. James, aged 7; 2-3. William and David, aged 4; 4. Edward, b 1774.   **ELN**.

723   BRAIDWOOD, James. To QUE on the *George Canning*, ex Greenock, 14 Apr, 1821; stld prob Lanark Co, ONT. **HCL 239**.

724   BRAKE, Isabella. From Premnay, ABD. To Elora, Nichol Twp, Wellington Co, ONT, 1836. Wife of William Gerrie, qv. **EHE 93**.

725   BRAND, Christina, 27 Jul 1801–28 May 1887. From Drumlithie, KCD. To Bayside, Whitby Twp, ONT. m William Gordon, qv. **DC 6 Sep 1979**.

726   BRAND, Jane, 10 Jul 1823–23 Jul 1902. From New Cumnock, AYR. To Richmond Co, QUE, 1847; stld Windsor Mills. Wife of Hugh Farquhar, qv.   **DC 11 Nov 1981**.

727   BRANDER, John, ca 1799–24 May 1869. From Speymouth, MOR. To Newcastle, Northumberland Co, NB, ca 1830. **DC 14 Jan 1980**.

728   BRANDER, William, ca 1793–3 Aug 1817. To NS and d there. **NSS No 1142**.

729   BRASH, John, b ca 1781. From Port Dundas, Glasgow. To QUE, ex Greenock, on the *Atlas*, 11 Jul 1815; stld Lot 3, Con 10, Burgess Twp, Lanark Co, ONT. Ploughman, later farmer. Wife Catherine McLean, qv, with him, and 3 ch. **SEC 1; HCL 15, 232**.

730   BREARCLIFFE, Matthew, d 30 Jan 1856. From Bagbie, KKD. s/o Matthew B. To St Andrews, Charlotte Co, NB, and d there. **DGC 4 Mar 1856**.

731   BRECHIN, James, d 1796. From Aberdeen. To Halifax, NS. Son James. **NER liv 147**.

732   BRECHIN, Robert, 1818–20 Oct 1897. From Glasgow. To Hants Co, NS, prob <1850. Wife Mary, 1821-75. **DC 20 Jan 1981**.

733   BREMNER, George. To QUE on the *David of London*, ex Greenock, 19 May 1821; stld poss Lanark Co, ONT. **HCL 65**.

734   BREMNER, James. From ROC. Prob rel to John B, qv. To East Williams Twp, Middlesex Co, ONT, 1831. **PCM 43**.

735   BREMNER, James John, b 23 May 1828. From Keith, BAN. s/o Dr Alexander B, surgeon, 3rd Buffs. To Halifax, NS, <1854, when Lt, 1st Halifax Regt. Became Lt Col, 1865. Organised 66th Fusiliers, which he commanded until 1886. m d/o Judge Des Barres. **HNS iii 528**.

736   BREMNER, John. From ROC. Prob rel to James B, qv. To East Williams Twp, Middlesex Co, ONT, 1831. **PCM 43**.

737   BREWSTER, John, 25 Jul 1783–15 Jul 1861. From Perth. To ONT, 1834, and d Westport, Leeds Co. Before emig was a farm grieve nr Dingwall, ROC. m Ann Roy, ch. **DC 15 Jun 1982**.

738 BRIGG, Andrew, b ca 1740. From Kirkbean, KKD. To Georgetown, Kings Co, PEI, on the *Lovely Nellie*, ex Carsethorn, May 1775. Blacksmith. Wife Margaret Griver, qv, with him. **ELN**.

739 BRIMS, Helen. From Thurso, CAI. d/o Donald B, fisherman. To CAN <1855. m William Calder. **SH**.

740 BROACH, Andrew. From Lochmaben, DFS. Prob s/o John B, d 1855, and Janet Tweedie. To Winnipeg, MAN, <1855. **Ts Lochmaben**.

741 BROAD, John, b ca 1769. From Redford, MLN. To QUE, ex Greenock, summer 1815, and stld ONT. Farmer. Wife Isobel Stevenson, qv, with him, and 6 ch. **SEC 2**.

742 BROADFOOT, Agnes, 1790–1864. From Penpont, DFS. d/o William B. To Guelph Twp, Wellington Co, ONT, 1836. Wife of Thomas Martin, qv. **DC 31 Dec 1979**.

743 BROADFOOT, Alexander, ca 1800–10 Mar 1887. Prob from KKD. To ONT, 1833; stld Tuckersmith Twp, Huron Co. Farmer. m (i) Margaret Carnochan, qv, at least two ch: 1. Margaret, qv; 2. Susan or Sarah. m (ii) Marion McMillan, qv, further ch: 3. Marion, 1846–1929; 4. Agnes, 1852-90; 5. Alexander, b 1854, physician, WI; 6. William, 1856–1922; 7. Robert, 1863–1927. **DC 26 May 1979**.

744 BROADFOOT, Alexander, d 22 Apr 1851. From Airdrie, Kirkbean, KKD. To Toronto, ONT, and stld Port Hope. Ch: 1. Robert, d Toronto, 23 Aug 1835; 2. Alexander; 3. David, d 6 Apr 1836, Port Hope; 4. Eliza, ca 1816–2 Aug 1835, d Little Falls, NY, on way to CAN. **DGC 16 Sep and 28 Oct 1835, and 25 May 1836**.

745 BROADFOOT, Anna. From Kingarth, BUT. d/o Walter B. m 24 Jul 1866, Rev John Ferries, qv, and stld Brandon, MAN. **FES vi 420**.

746 BROADFOOT, Jean, 1818–1914. From DFS. To ONT, 1834. Wife of Daniel Galbraith, qv. **DC 9 Mar 1980**.

747 BROADFOOT, John, 1828–1901. From KKD. s/o Samuel B, qv, and Jean Hastings, qv. To Nichol Twp, Wellington Co, ONT, 1833. Councillor and reeve. m Ellen Munroe, 1831–1900, ch: 1. Mrs Alexander Martin; 2. Bella; 3. David M; 4. Samuel; 5. Janet; 6. Mrs James Kilpatrick; 7. John; 8. Mrs R. B. Blyth. **DC 11 Nov 1981**.

748 BROADFOOT, Margaret. Prob from KKD. d/o Alexander B, qv. To ONT, 1833; stld Tuckersmith Twp, Huron Co, 1833. m Robert, s/o James Ferguson, d 1838, and Helen Esther Laidlaw, qv. **DC 26 May 1979**.

749 BROADFOOT, Margaret. From Airdrie, Kirkbean, KKD. Prob rel to Alexander B, qv. To Port Hope, Durham Co, ONT, <1838. m Donald Mackay, Cromartie Farm, Pickering Twp, York Co. **DGC 28 Mar 1838**.

750 BROADFOOT, Samuel, 7 Apr 1821–1 Feb 1888. From Urr par, KKD. s/o Alexander B. and Susan Gibson. To ONT, 1841. Millwright. m 2 Jun 1843, Sarah Moore, ch. **DC 3 Jan 1972**.

751 BROADFOOT, Samuel, 1780–1872. From Penpont, KKD. s/o William B. To Nichol Twp, Wellington Co, ONT, 1833. Shepherd, later farmer and merchant, Lot 10, Con 10. m (i) Jean Hastings, qv, ch: 1. William, 1823–1901, farmer; 2. Mrs Thomas Black; 3. John, qv; 4. Thomas, dy; 5. Mrs Matthew Anderson; 6. James. m (ii) 1836, Mary Haxton, further ch: 7. Mrs Alexander Anderson; 8. Mrs James Cowan; 9. Mrs Alexander McCready; 10. Mrs Alexander Miller; 11. George; 12. Mary; 13. Samuel, b 1853. **DC 31 Dec 1979**.

752 BROCKETT, Christian. From Lesmahagow, LKS. To Oro Twp, Simcoe Co, ONT, 1831. Wife of James Tudhope, qv. **DC 5 Aug 1979**.

753 BROCKIE, Ann. From ABD. To Bon Accord, Nichol Twp, Wellington Co, ONT, 1836. Wife of Archibald Cummings, qv. **EHE 94**.

754 BROCKIE, John. From Belhelvie, ABD. To Bon Accord, Nichol Twp, Wellington Co, ONT, ca 1837. Farmer. Wife with him, and ch: 1. John, went to Paisley, Bruce Co; 2. George, went also to Paisley; 3. William, went also to Paisley, 1854; 4. James; 5. Alexander; 6. David; 7. Archibald; 8. Margaret; 9. Catherine. **EHE 95, 102**.

755 BRODIE, Angus, 1774–1870. Born Kintyre, ARL, but emig from Laggan, Is Arran, BUT. Sld on the *Caledonia*, ex Greenock, 25 Apr 1829, arr QUE. m Isabella Walker, qv, ch: 1. Neil, qv; 2. Catherine, qv; 3. Janet, qv; 4. Marion, qv; 5. Mary, qv; 6. Isabella; 7. Margaret; 8. Ann; 9. Elizabeth. **AMC 132; MAC 32**.

756 BRODIE, Ann, 1779–1863. From Kilbirnie, AYR. d/o Robert B. in Bankside, and Margaret Burns. To QUE, summer 1803; stld Côte St Pierre, Montreal. m Apr 1803, Hugh Brodie, qv. **DC 1 Apr 1979**.

757 BRODIE, Ann, b 15 Jul 1817. From Kilbirnie, AYR. d/o Robert B, qv, and Janet Crawford, qv. To QUE on the *True Briton*, 1822; stld Montreal. m William Gardener, qv. **DC 1 Apr 1979**.

758 BRODIE, Barbara, ca 1787–22 Feb 1877. From Kilbirnie, AYR. d/o Robert B. in Bankside, and Margaret Burns. To Montreal, QUE, 1819; stld later Chateauguay Co. m James Holmes, qv. **DC 1 Apr 1979**.

759 BRODIE, Catherine, b ca 1825. From Laggan, Is Arran, BUT. d/o Angus B, qv, and Isabella Walker, qv. To QUE on the *Caledonia*, ex Greenock, 25 Apr 1829; stld Inverness, Megantic Co, QUE. m Alexander McGillvray, qv. **AMC 12; MAC 32**.

760 BRODIE, Elizabeth. From Peterhead, ABD. d/o William B. To Ottawa, ONT, 1834. m Thomas Thomson, qv, ch. **DC 16 Aug 1973**.

761 BRODIE, George. From Peterhead, ABD. Uncle of Elizabeth B, qv. To Ottawa, ONT, 1834. **DC 16 Aug 1973**.

762 BRODIE, Hugh, ca 1780–1852. From Kilbirnie, AYR. To Montreal, QUE, 1803; stld Côte St Pierre, Montreal. Farmer and fruit grower. m Ann Brodie, qv, ch: 1. Mary, b 10 Nov 1804; 2. Robert, b 1 May 1809; 3. Hugh, b 14 Mar 1811. **SGC 269; DC 1 Apr 1974**.

763 BRODIE, Hugh. Prob from ARL. To Ekfrid Twp, Middlesex Co, ONT, 1832. ch: 1. Sarah; 2. Nancy; 3. Mary; 4. Betsy; 5. Euphemia; 6. Jessie. **PCM 30**.

764 BRODIE, James, b 15 Jul 1817. From Kilbirnie, AYR. s/o Robert B, qv, and Janet Crawford, qv. To QUE, 1822, on the *True Briton*, and stld Montreal. m Mary Symons. **DC 1 Apr 1979**.

765 BRODIE, Janet, b 1774. From Bankhead, Kilbirnie, AYR. d/o Robert B. and Margaret Burns. To QUE, 1815; stld Point aux Trembles, Montreal Is. Wife of John McConnochie, qv. **DC 1 Apr 1979**.

766 BRODIE, Janet, b ca 1778. From Glasgow. To Charlottetown, PEI, on the *Clarendon*, ex Oban, 6 Aug 1808. Spinster. Son George, aged 4, with her. **CPL**.

767 BRODIE, Janet, b 21 Nov 1811. From Kilbirnie, AYR. d/o Robert B, qv, and Elizabeth Peebles. To QUE on the *True Briton*, 1822; stld Montreal. m William Greig. **DC 1 Apr 1979**.

768 BRODIE, Janet, 1827–1905. From Lagganton, Is Arran, BUT. d/o Angus B, qv, and Isabella Walker, qv. To QUE on the *Caledonia*, ex Greenock, 25 Apr 1829; stld Inverness, Megantic Co. m Thomas McCammon. **AMC 11; MAC 32**.

769 BRODIE, Jean, 1819–1906. From Kilbirnie, AYR. d/o Robert B, qv, and Janet Crawford, qv. To QUE on the *True Briton*, 1822; stld Montreal. Missionary to Labrador <1867, when she became superintendent of a female school at the House of Industry and Refuge at Montreal. **DC 1 Apr 1979**.

770 BRODIE, Margaret, b 24 Aug 1813. From Kilbirnie, AYR. d/o Robert B, qv, and Elizabeth Peebles. To QUE on the *True Briton*, 1822; stld Montreal. m John McIntosh. **DC 1 Apr 1979**.

771 BRODIE, Marion, 1829–1908. From Mid Sannox, Is Arran, BUT. d/o Angus B, qv, and Isabella Walker, qv. To QUE on the *Caledonia*, ex Greenock, 25 Apr 1829; stld Inverness, Megantic Co, QUE. m John Dugald McKenzie, qv. **AMC 12; MAC 32**.

772 BRODIE, Mary, 8 Jan 1786–3 Apr 1876. From Kilbirnie, AYR. d/o Robert B. and Margaret Burns. To Montreal, QUE, 1820; stld Dundee, Huntingdon Co, QUE. Wife of Alexander Gardiner, qv, whom she m 27 Feb 1805. **DC 1 Apr 1979**.

773 BRODIE, Mary, 1821-99. From Kilbirnie, AYR. d/o Robert B, qv, and Janet Crawford, qv. To QUE, 1822, on the *True Briton*; stld Montreal. m Robert, d 1886, s/o Hugh Brodie, qv, and Ann Brodie, qv. **DC 1 Apr 1979**.

774 BRODIE, Neil, 1824-74. From Laggan, Is Arran, BUT. s/o Angus B, qv, and Isabella Walker, qv. To QUE on the *Caledonia*, ex Greenock, 25 Apr 1829; stld Inverness, Megantic Co, QUE. Mayor of Inverness, 1858-64. m Barbara, d/o Sinclair Goudie, qv, ch: 1. Catherine; 2. Angus; 3. Sinclair; 4. Neil; 5. John Sinclair; 6. Isabella Barbara; 7. George; 8. William. **AMC 12, 138; MAC 32**.

775 BRODIE, Rev Neil, ca 1834–21 Mar 1907. From Lochgilphead, ARL. s/o Peter B, merchant. Matric Univ of Glasgow, 1848, and studied theology, 1853-57. To Cape Breton as missionary, 1863, and adm min of Gairloch, Pictou Co, NS, 1868. Trans to Lochiel, Glengarry Co, ONT. Retr to SCT and was min at Stenscholl, Is Skye, 1886-90. **GMA 15572; FES vii 181, 613, 627**.

776 BRODIE, Robert, b 1782. From Bankside, Kilbirnie, AYR. s/o Robert B. and Margaret Burns. To CAN, 1822 on the *True Briton*, and stld Montreal.

Farmer. m (i) 1809, Elizabeth, d/o James Peebles, ch: 1. Robert, jr, qv; 2. Janet, qv; 3. Margaret, qv. m (ii) 1817, Janet Crawford, qv, further ch: 4. James, qv; 5. Ann, qv; 6. Jean, qv; 7. Mary, qv; 8. Barbara, b 1824; 9. William, b 1825; 10. Agnes, b 1827; 11. Elizabeth, b 1829; 12. William, yr, b 1831. **DC 1 Apr 1979**.

777 BRODIE, Robert, jr, 8 Oct 1810–12 Jan 1862. From Kilbirnie, AYR. s/o Robert B, qv, and Elizabeth Peebles. To QUE on the *True Briton*, 1822; stld Montreal. m Jean Boyd. **DC 1 Apr 1979**.

778 BRODIE, Robert. Prob from ARL. To Ekfrid Twp, Middlesex Co, ONT, 1832. ch: 1. Donald; 2. Murdock; 3. Sara; 4. Christy; 5. Mrs McEwan. **PCM 30**.

779 BROOKE, James, ca 1776–5 Apr 1833. From Glasgow. To Lanark Co, ONT, 1820. m Barbara Newbigging, qv. ch with them: 1. James b 1807; 2. Robert. **DC 27 Jan 1977**.

780 BROOKE, Rev John, 1801-82. From Slamannan, STI. Educ Univ of Edinburgh, and ord min of New Richmond, NB, 1839; trans to St Paul's, Fredericton, 1843. DD, Univ of NB, 1856. **FES vii 608**.

781 BROTHERSTON, Robert. Poss from PEE. To QUE <1849; stld prob Gaspé East. **SH**.

782 BROW, Elizabeth. From DFS. To ONT <1848. Wife of William Irving, qv. **LDW 15 Mar 1971**.

783 BROW, Mary, ca 1775–8 May 1862. From Middlebie par, DFS. To Richibucto, Kent Co, NB. m William Johnstone, qv. **CAE 8**.

784 BROWN, Adam, 3 Apr 1826–16 Jan 1926. From Edinburgh. To Montreal, QUE, 1833; later to Hamilton, ONT. Merchant and politician. **MDB 84**.

785 BROWN, Agnes. Prob from AYR. To Pictou, NS, prob 1830. m William Stewart, miller, qv. **HNS iii 391**.

786 BROWN, Agnes, b ca 1778. From Balgray, Applegarth par, DFS, but b Tundergarth par. To QUE, 1832; stld St Augustin, Deux-Montagnes Co. Wife of James Dobie, qv. **DC 3 Feb 1981**.

787 BROWN, Alexander, d 18 Sep 1826. From Greenock, RFW. To NS and d there. **VSN No 1854**.

788 BROWN, Alexander, d 22 Sep 1844. From Applegarth par, DFS. To Charlottetown, PEI, ca 1822. Master of the Central Academy, Charlottetown. **DGH 7 Nov 1844**.

789 BROWN, Alexander, 1787–1858. From ARL. To Caledon Twp, Peel Co, ONT, <1840. Wife Rachael, 1782–1876, with him. **DC 21 Apr 1980**.

790 BROWN, Rev Andrew. 22 Aug 1763–19 Feb 1834. From Sillerknowes, Biggar, LKS. s/o Richard B, weaver, and Isabella Forrest. Matric Univ of Glasgow, 1776. Became min of Presb Ch, Halifax, NS, 1787. Retr to SCT and was min at Lochmaben, 1795-99; New Greyfriars, Edinburgh, 1799–1800; St Giles, Edinburgh, 1800-34. Prof of Belles Lettres, Univ of Edinburgh, 1801-34, and Moderator of the General Assembly of Ch of SCT, 1813. m (i) 1792, Daniela, d/o George Cranstoun, ch: (ii) 1805, Mary, d/o Dr Gregory Grant; (iii) 1830, Mary Ogilvie, wid/o Dr Andrew Pearson. **GMA 3628; FES i 34, 72, ii 214, vii 613**.

791   BROWN, Andrew. Prob from LKS. To QUE on the *George Canning*, ex Greenock, 14 Apr 1821; stld prob Lanark Co, ONT. **HCL 239**.

792   BROWN, Archibald, 14 Mar 1801–13 Aug 1885. From Jedburgh, ROX. s/o Thomas B. To South Elmsley Twp, Leeds Co, ONT, 1831; and d Kitley Twp. Farmer. m Mary Rutherford, qv, ch: 1. Isabel, 1824-72; 2. Margaret, b 1828; 3. Thomas, b 1831; 4. Elizabeth, b 1833; 5. Mary, b 1836; 6. James, b 1838; 7. Ellen, b 1841; 8. George, 1843–1915; 9. Ann Josephine, 1850–1943. **DC 9 Nov 1981**.

793   BROWN, Betty. From Anstruther, FIF. To Glen Morris, South Dumfries Twp, Brant Co, ONT, 1818. Wife of James Sharp, qv. **DC 31 Jan 1982**.

794   BROWN, Cecilia. To QUE on the *David of London*. ex Greenock, 19 May 1821; stld Ramsay Twp, Lanark Co, ONT. Wife of Walter Gardner jr, qv. **HCL 83**.

795   BROWN, Charles. From Is Arran, BUT. To Dalhousie, NB, prob <1840; stld Escuminac, Bonaventure Co, QUE. **MAC 9**.

796   BROWN, Clementine. Poss from OKI. To Megantic Co, QUE, 1842. m Thomas Johnstone, qv. **AMC 48**.

797   BROWN, Christian. From Killin, PER. To QUE, ex Greenock, summer 1815; stld ONT. Wife of Archibald McLaren, qv. **SEC 3**.

798   BROWN, David. To QUE <1818; stld St Henri, Levis. **DC 11 Feb 1980**.

799   BROWN, David. From ROX. To CAN on the *Sarah Mary Jane*, 1831; stld Dumfries Twp, Waterloo Co, ONT. **HGD 60**.

800   BROWN, Donald, b 1766. To QUE on the *Oughton*, arr Jul 1804; stld Baldoon, Dover Twp, Kent Co, ONT. Drover. Wife Marion with him, aged 35, and ch: 1. Hector, b 1797; 2. Flora; 3. Alexander. m (ii) Catherine, wid/o John Buchanan, qv. **UCM 268, 302; DC 4 Oct 1979**.

801   BROWN, Donald, 1798–1886. From Is Islay, ARL. To Cape Breton Is, NS, ca 1832; moved to ONT, 1851, and stld Fenelon Twp, Victoria Co. m Catherine Sinclair, ch: 1. Dougald, 1831–1915; 2. Neil, 1835–1911; 3. Christena, 1839–1918; 4. Flora, 1842-74; 5. Janet; 6. Kate. **EC 31**.

802   BROWN, Duncan, 1781–1821. Prob from ARL. To Aldborough Twp, Elgin Co, ONT, poss 1818. Son John, 1811-21. **PDA 41**.

803   BROWN, Duncan, 1813-78. From Is Islay, ARL. bro/o John B, qv. To Cape Breton Is, NS, ca 1832, later to Georgina Twp, York Co, ONT. **EC 31**.

804   BROWN, Ellen, b ca 1810. To St Gabriel de Valcartier, QUE, prob <1855. **Census 1861**.

805   BROWN, Elizabeth. From Knapdale, ARL. To ONT 1846. Wife of Duncan Graham, qv. **SG xxvi/3 92**.

806   BROWN, Elizabeth, 1831–1924. From Paisley, RFW. To York Co, ONT, <1855. Wife of James Watt Galbraith, qv. **GSO 14**.

807   BROWN, Flora, b ca 1748. To Charlottetown, PEI, on the *Spencer*, ex Oban, 22 Sep 1806. Wife of Duncan Munn, qv. **PLSN**.

808   BROWN, George. Served in 82nd Regt as NCO and was gr 200 acres at Fraser's Mountain, Pictou Co, NS, 1784. **HPC App F**.

809   BROWN, George. From LKS. To QUE on the *Prompt*, ex Greenock, 4 Jul 1820; stld Dalhousie Twp, Lanark Co, ONT. **HCL 68**.

810   BROWN, George, b 1829. From Edinburgh. To Perth Co, ONT, ca 1850; stld Molesworth. Moved in 1888 to Heppner, OR. m Mary, d/o John Mitchell, ch. **DC 3 Aug 1982**.

811   BROWN, Isabella. From Is Colonsay, ARL. To PEI, 1840. Wife of Peter McCalder, qv. **DC 23 Jul 1964**.

812   BROWN, James, ca 1776–23 May 1845. From Glasgow. To QUE <1795; later to Montreal. Bookseller and proprietor of the *Montreal Gazette*. Son John O, auctioneer. **SGC 270**.

813   BROWN, James, 1790–1870. From ANS. To NB 1808; stld St Andrews, Charlotte Co. Farmer, poet and politician. **MDB 86**.

814   BROWN, James, b ca 1753. To Pictou, NS, 1815. Mason, unm, 1816. **INS 39**.

815   BROWN, James, b 8 Apr 1822. From Duns, BEW. bro/o William B, qv. To Montreal, QUE, 1848. Partner with Archibald Swan, qv, in wholesale dry goods business; later on his own account. ch. **SGC 568**.

816   BROWN, James, b 1825. From DFS. To Martintown, Glengarry Co, ONT, 1831. **DC 4 Mar 1965**.

817   BROWN, James, 1813-71. From Aberdeen. To Dalhousie, Restigouche Co, NB, and d St John. **DC 14 Jan 1980**.

818   BROWN, James, 1802-40. Prob from ARL. To Caledon Twp, Peel Co, ONT, poss <1835. m Mary McBride, qv. **DC 21 Apr 1980**.

819   BROWN, James. From Motherwell or Crossford, LKS. To Dalhousie Twp, Lanark Co, ONT, <1840; later to Perth Co. Postmaster. Motherwell, Fullerton Twp, named in his honour. Son James. **DC 13 Jan 1978**.

820   BROWN, James, b ca 1832. From AYR prob Ochiltree. Stepson of Alexander McCosh, qv. Stld Huron Twp, Bruce Co, ONT, 1853. **DC 3 Apr 1967**.

821   BROWN, James. From Kintail, ROC. To Stormont Co, ONT, <1850. m Catherine McGillis, Williamstown. Son John, Reeve, Roxborough Twp, 1874. **SDG 254**.

BROWN, Mrs James. See NICOL, Helen.

822   BROWN, Jane or Jean, 15 Aug 1819–27 Aug 1898. From Kilmaurs, AYR. d/o David B. and Jane Stinson. To ONT 1854; stld Binbrook Twp, Wentworth Co, later Chatham Twp, Kent Co. Wife of James McDonald Dunlop, qv, whom she m 16 Dec 1842. **DC 22 Mar 1982**.

823   BROWN, Jane, b ca 1836. From AYR, prob Ochiltree. Step-dau of Alexander McCosh, qv. Stld Huron Twp, Bruce Co, ONT, 1853. **DC 3 Apr 1967**.

824   BROWN, Janet, 1776–1821. From Bathgate, WLN. To QUE on the *David of London*, ex Greenock, 19 May 1821; stld Lanark Co, ONT. Wife of James Dick, qv. **Ts Kirkton; HCL 71, 228**.

825   BROWN, Janet, b 23 Jan 1816. From DFS. d/o Samuel B, qv, and Elizabeth Murray, qv. To Pictou Co,

NS, 1823. m 20 Mar 1841, Richard, s/o Thomas Tanner and Rachel Clarke, ch: 1. Rachel; 2. Elizabeth; 3. Thomas; 4. William F, b 1854; 5. Charles E. **HNS iii 695**.

826   BROWN, Janet. From Dalbeattie, KKD. d/o Robert and Margaret B. To CAN, ca 1842. Wife of Alexander Murray, qv.   **DC 22 Nov 1981**.

827   BROWN, Janet, b ca 1812. To St Gabriel de Valcartier, QUE, prob <1855.   **Census 1861**.

828   BROWN, John, d 12 Sep 1825. From Glasgow. To NS and d there.   **VSN No 1315**.

829   BROWN, John, 1795–1877. From Is Islay, ARL. bro/o Duncan B, qv. To Cape Breton Is, NS, ca 1832; later to Georgina, York Co, ONT.   **EC 31**.

830   BROWN, John, 26 Mar 1799–21 Jan 1875. From South Knapdale, ARL. To Dalhousie Lake, Lanark Co, ONT, ca 1835. m Isobella Whyte, qv, ch: 1. Duncan, b 16 May 1823; 2. Ann, b 25 Mar 1827; 3. John, b 16 Jul 1829; 4. Catherine; 5. Mary.   **DC 13 Feb 1978**.

831   BROWN, John. To Dundas Co, ONT, ca 1840. m Mary Gray.   **DC 4 Apr 1965**.

832   BROWN, John, d 24 Dec 1863. From Kirkmahoe, DFS. To Perth, Lanark Co, ONT, prob <1854. Mason. m a d/o David Jardine, Kirkton of Tinwald, DFS, ch. **CAE 9**.

833   BROWN, John, d 27 Feb 1869. From Sanquhar, DFS. To ONT, and stld Sarnia, Lambton Co. **DGC 26 Mar 1869**.

834   BROWN, Rev John, b ca 1775. From Orwell, KRS. s/o John B, farmer. Matric Univ of Glasgow, 1789. Missionary of the Secession Ch, and became min at Londonderry, Colchester Co, NS.   **GMA 4913**.

835   BROWN, John James. Prob from FIF. Gr-s of William B, sawyer in Pennylide, St Andrews. To NB <1855. Sea captain.   **SH**.

836   BROWN, John Moore, d 19 Aug 1849. From Aberdeen. s/o Principal William Laurence B. and Ann Elizabeth Brown, his cousin. Grad MA Marischall Coll, Aberdeen, 1814. To ONT and d Hamilton. Physician. **DGH 4 Oct 1848; FAM ii 30, 416, 419**.

837   BROWN, Katherine, b ca 1812. Poss from ARL. To QUE, ca 1828; stld Three Rivers, later NY, and finally WI. m Gavin Argyle Campbell, qv.   **DC 16 Apr 1960**.

838   BROWN, Lawrence, ca 1745–ca 1805. Prob from PER. To Richmond Bay, PEI, on the *Falmouth*, ex Greenock, 8 Apr 1770; stld prob Queens Co. Weaver. m Jean Jamieson, qv, ch: 1. Helen; 2. Jane; 3. John; 4. Elizabeth; 5. William; 6. Margaret; 7. Catherine; 8. Janet; 9. Isabella; 10. Mary; 11. Ann; 12. Rebecca; 13. James.   **DC 28 May 1980**.

839   BROWN, Margaret, b ca 1811. To St Gabriel de Valcartier, QUE, prob <1855.   **Census 1861**.

840   BROWN, Margaret, b 6 Jan 1822. From SEL. d/o James B. and Helen Nicol, qv. To North Dumfries Twp, Waterloo Co, ONT, ca 1857. Wife of John Fairbairn, qv, whom she m 5 Aug 1848.   **DC 7 Dec 1981**.

841   BROWN, Mary. From ABD. To Elora, Nichol Twp, Wellington Co, ONT, 1836. m James Philp, qv.   **EHE 92**.

842   BROWN, Nancy, b ca 1783. Prob from Is Colonsay, ARL. To Charlottetown, PEI, on the *Spencer*, ex Oban, 22 Sep 1806.   **PLSN**.

843   BROWN, Neil. Prob from ARL. To Ekfrid Twp, Middlesex Co, ONT, poss <1850.   **PCM 31**.

844   BROWN, Nicolas, d 8 Jun 1841. To Cornwall, Stormont Co, ONT. m John Aitken, farmer.   **DGH 9 Dec 1841**.

845   BROWN, Peter. From Knapdale, ARL. To Lobo Twp, Middlesex Co, ONT, 1829. ch: 1. Archibald; 2. James; 3. John; 4. Duncan; 5. Margaret; 6. Flora. **PCM 39**.

846   BROWN, Peter. From Aberdeen. To Fergus Twp, Wellington Co, ONT, 1835, but retr later to Aberdeen. Auctioneer.   **EHE 89**.

847   BROWN, Robert, ca 1803–4 Jul 1861. From CAI. To Pictou, NS. Bur with wife Isabella and inf s John Thomas, at Salt Springs.   **DC 27 Oct 1979**.

848   BROWN, Samuel, b 23 May 1789. From Dumfries. To Pictou Co, NS, 1823. m Elizabeth Murray, qv, and had with other ch a dau Janet, qv. **HNS iii 695**.

849   BROWN, Sarah, 1796–1874. From ARL. To Caledon Twp, Peel Co, ONT, <1840. Wife of Alexander McLeish, qv.   **DC 21 Apr 1980**.

850   BROWN, Thomas. To Antigonish Co, NS, prob <1810. m Miss McLeod, ch: 1. Mary; 2. John; 3. Kenneth; 4. Thomas; 5. Donald; 6. Betsy; 7. Ann; 8. Nancy; 9. Sarah.   **HCA 84**.

851   BROWN, Thomas, ca 1752–19 Feb 1839. From FIF. To Pictou Co, NS, and bur with wife Ann, ca 1771–1841, at Salt Springs.   **DC 27 Oct 1979**.

852   BROWN, Thomas, b ca 1819. To St Gabriel de Valcartier, QUE, prob <1855.   **Census 1861**.

853   BROWN, William. Prob from Balmaghie, KKD. To QUE <1764. Co-proprietor of the *Quebec Gazette*. **MDB 564; ENA 21**.

854   BROWN, William, b ca 1793. From Kilmaurs, AYR. To Hudson Bay, ca 1813, and prob to Red River. **RRS 13**.

855   BROWN, William. To QUE on the *Commerce*, ex Greenock, 11 May 1821; stld prob Lanark Co, ONT. **HCL 238**.

856   BROWN, William. From Rannoch, PER. To Antigonish Co, NS, 1824; stld McMillan. Pioneer settler.   **HCA 16**.

857   BROWN, William, 1811-77. From Carluke, LKS. To PEI 1844. m Jane Wilson, qv, and emig with ch: 1. William; 2. James; 3. Samuel; 4. Elizabeth. **DC 2 Dec 1981**.

858   BROWN, William, 1 Mar 1824–4 Jul 1883. From Duns, BEW. bro/o James B, qv. To Montreal, QUE, 1845. Nurseryman at Côte des Neiges, and author. **SGC 571**.

859   BROWN, William, b ca 1814. To St Gabriel de Valcartier, QUE, prob <1855.   **Census 1861**.

860   BROWN, William, b ca 1834. Prob from Ochiltree, AYR. Stepson of Alexander McCosh, qv. To QUE on the

Glasgow, ex Glasgow, 23 Apr 1853; stld Huron Twp, Bruce Co. **LDW 20 May 1967**.

861 BROWNING, Archibald. From LKS. Rel to John B, qv. To Lanark Co, ONT, 1821; stld Lavant Twp, Lot 5, Con 7, and Lot 6, Con 11. Farmer. **HCL 76**.

862 BROWNING, John. From LKS. Rel to Archibald B, qv. To Lanark Co, ONT, 1821; stld Lavant Twp, Lot 5, Con 7, and Lot 6, Con 8. **HCL 76**.

863 BROWNLEE, James, d ca 1840. From Cambusnethan, LKS. To Kingston, ONT, 1826. Blacksmith. m Margaret or Peggy Thomson, qv, ch s Robert, qv. **DC 13 Feb 1978**.

864 BROWNLEE, Robert, 1806–1900. From Cambusnethan par, LKS. s/o James B, qv, and Margaret or Peggy Thomson, qv. To Kingston, ONT, 1826. m Mary Dunlop, qv. **DC 13 Feb 1978**.

BROWNLEY. See also BROWNLEE, BROWNLIE.

865 BROWNLEY, Robert, b ca 1753. To Inverness Co, NS, 1781; stld at Mabou. Cooper, unm. **CBC 1818**.

866 BROWNLIE, John, ca 1791–6 Jul 1846. From Hamilton, LKS. To Scarborough, York Co, ONT, ca 1833. **DGH 29 Mar 1846**.

867 BRUCE, Catherine, b ca 1782. From Kildonan, SUT. To York Factory, Hudson's Bay, with Donald McKay, qv, poss her husband. Arr 26 Aug 1815, and went to Red River. **LSC 326**.

868 BRUCE, Donald. From SUT. To Pictou, NS, on the *Harmony*, 1822; stld Barney's River, Pictou Co. Son George, qv. **HNS iii 256**.

869 BRUCE, Donald, b ca 1790. From Is Skye, INV. To CAN; stld prob PEI. m Ann Matheson, qv, ch: 1. John; 2. Malcolm, qv; 3. Angus; 4. John; 5. Margaret; 6. Flora. **DC 1 Aug 1979**.

870 BRUCE, Fanny. From Kilmarnock, AYR. sis/o Dr James B, physician in Liverpool. To Montreal, QUE, <1850. m John Smith, merchant. **Ayr Sasines, 350, 263**.

871 BRUCE, George, 1810–1901. From SUT. s/o Donald B, qv. To Pictou, NS, on the *Harmony*, 1822; stld Barney's River, Pictou Co. Son Hector. **HNS iii 256**.

872 BRUCE, George. From Wick, CAI. To Guelph, Wellington Co, ONT, 1836. Farmer. m Elizabeth Taylor, qv. Son John, qv. **DC 11 Nov 1981**.

873 BRUCE, Helen, d 1870. From Edinburgh, but res in Peebles before going to ONT, 1832. m ca 1805, David McEwan, qv, and d at Chatham, Kent Co. **DC 23 Mar 1979**.

874 BRUCE, James, 20 Jul 1811–20 Nov 1863. From Broomhall, Dunfermline, FIF. s/o Thomas B, 7th Earl of Elgin and 10th Earl of Kincardine. To Halifax, NS, ex Liverpool, arr 20 Jan 1847. Gov Gen of CAN, 1847-54. m (i) 1841, Elizabeth Mary, d/o Charles Lennox Cumming-Bruce of Dunphail, ch. Succ his father same year. m (ii) 1846, Lady Mary Louisa, d/o John George Lambton, 1st Earl of Durham, further ch. **BNA 608; SP iii 494; SDG 191; MDB 215**.

875 BRUCE, John, b ca 1754. From Aultsmoral, Clyne, SUT. To Fort Churchill, Hudson Bay, on the *Prince of*

Wales, ex Stromness, 28 Jun 1813. Went to York Factory, 1814, thence to Red River. Pioneer settler. **LSS 186; RSS 27; LSC 323**.

876 BRUCE, John, b 1826. From Wick, CAI. s/o George B, qv, and Elizabeth Taylor, qv. To Guelph Twp, Wellington Co, ONT, 1836. Farmer. m Mary Scroggie, ch: 1. Mrs. Thomas Randall; 2. George; 3. John; 4. Mrs George Broadfoot; 5. James; 6. Mrs. Samuel Broadfoot; 7. Alexander; 8. Isabella; 9. William; 10. Margaret; 11. Donald; 12. Baxter; 13. Stewart; 14. Robert; 15. George. **DC 11 Nov 1981**.

877 BRUCE, Malcolm, b 1811. From Is Skye, INV. s/o Donald B, qv, and Ann Matheson, qv. To CAN, 1841; stld prob PEI. m Barbara Fraser, qv. **DC 1 Aug 1979**.

878 BRUCE, Robert, 1802-85. From Aberdeen. To QUE, 1835. Market gardener, and left fortune for educational purposes. **MDB 87**.

879 BRUCE, William, 7 Nov 1833–7 Mar 1927. From Unst par, SHI. To ONT with parents, 1838. Educ Hamilton, ONT, and Oberlin Coll, OH. Became famous astronomer and founded Elmwood Observatory. m Janette Blair. Son William Blair, 1859–1906, landscape and portrait painter. **MDB 89; ENA 22**.

880 BRUNTON, Mary, 1805–19 Mar 1890. From ROX. To North Monaghan Twp, Peterborough Co, ONT, <1851. Wife of George Young, qv. **DC 25 Mar 1981**.

881 BRUNTON, Rev William, ca 1767–12 Aug 1839. Born Newbattle, MLN. Burgher min at Aberdeen, and went to Montreal, QUE, 1820. Presb min at Lachine. **UPC i 3**.

882 BRYAN, Esther, ca 1765–20 Nov 1848. From AYR. To Hamilton, ONT. Wife of Thomas Aitken, qv. **Ts Mt Albion**.

883 BRYCE, George. From Kilmadock, PER. To Brant Co, ONT, <1844; stld Mount Pleasant. m Katherine Margaret Henderson, qv. Son Rev George, 1844–1931, Pres of Royal Society of Canada, 1909. **BNA 848; FES vii 656; MDB 89**.

884 BRYCE, James, b ca 1773. From West Calder, MLN. To QUE on the *Atlas*, ex Greenock, 11 Jul 1815; stld Lot 13, Con 1, Bathurst Twp, Lanark Co, ONT. Farmer. Wife Jane Purdie, qv, with him, and ch: 1. James, b ca 1800; 2-3. Harriet, dy, and Sophia, twins, b ca 1802; 4. John, b ca 1804; 5-6. Mary and Margaret, b 1807. **SEC 1; HCL 16, 232**.

885 BRYCE, John. From Symington, LKS. s/o Thomas B, 1758–1837, and wife Agnes. To Toronto, ONT. ch. **Ts Symington**.

886 BRYCE, William. To Lanark Co, ONT, 1821; stld Lots 7 & 8, Con 3, North Sherbrooke Twp. Farmer. Son William. **HCL 74**.

887 BRYDEN, David. Poss from DFS. To NS <1800, poss later to USA. m (i) Sarah Fisher, ch: 1. David; 2. James; 3. Rhoda; 4. Sarah; 5. Andrew. m (ii) Elizabeth Gemmel Skeed. **NSN 28/230; DC 7 Mar 1978**.

888 BRYDEN, John. From AYR. Gr-s of John B. To NB <1844. **SH**.

889 BRYDEN, Robert. From KKD or DFS. To NS, and stld Middle River, Pictou Co, <12 Feb 1783, when listed as capable of bearing arms. Some descendants stld Tatamagouche, Colchester Co, 1835.   **HPC App D and E; HT 72**.

890   BRYDEN, Robert. From Ruthwell par, DFS. To Waterloo Co, ONT, poss <1853. Schoolteacher.   **CAE 7**.

891   BRYDON, David. From Aberlosk, Yarrow, SEL. s/o Adam B, and Margaret Armstrong. To ONT with his family, 1847.   **Ts Yarrow**.

892   BRYDON, Robert, 1805-80. From ROX. To Guelph, Wellington Co, 1831; stld 'Paisley Block.' Farmer. m Helen Elliott, qv, ch: 1. Janet; 2. Mrs John Richardson; 3. Robert, jr, farmer, Eramosa Twp; 4. William; 5. James; 6. George; 7. Mrs John Johnston; 8. John; 9. Mrs William McCandless; 10. Walter; 11. Donald.   **DC 11 Nov 1981**.

893   BRYDON, Robert. From Yarrow par, SEL. To ONT, prob 1847. Teacher.   **Ts Yarrow**.

894   BRYMER, Arthur, ca 1777–10 Jul 1847. From Fochabers, MOR. To Richmond Co, NS, <1840. MLA, 1846-47.   **MLA 44**.

895   BRYMER, Douglas, 3 Jul 1823–18 Jun 1902. From Greenock, RFW. s/o Alexander B, of Stirling, and Elizabeth Fairlie. To QUE, 1857. Farmer there, but moved to ONT and became journalist. App first Dominion archivist, 1872. LLD and FRS, CAN. m Jean, d 1884, d/o William Thomson. Son William, 1855–1925, art teacher.   **SGC 633; MDB 89**.

896   BRYMER, John Fairlie, 1815–7 Jun 1829. From Greenock, RFW. s/o Alexander B. and Elizabeth Fairlie. To QUE, and killed there.   **Ts Greenock**.

897   BRYSON, James. From Paisley, RFW. To QUE on the *David of London*, ex Greenock, 19 May 1821; stld Lot 11, Con 10, Ramsay Twp, Lanark Co, ONT. Farmer. ch incl: 1. George, lumberman and MLA, after whom the village of Bryson is named; 2. Robert, lumberman, Fort Coulonge, QUE.   **HCL 70, 85**.

898   BUCHAN, Rev Alexander, 1795–18 Jul 1875. From Foulis, PER. Educ Univ of Edinburgh. Ord min of Leeds and St Syvestre, Megantic Co, QUE, 17 Oct 1842. Retr to SCT and was min at Stanley, 1851-54, when trans to Bannockburn. Retr to CAN, 1856, and was min at Stirling, Hastings Co.   **FES iv 298, vii 628; AMC 109**.

899   BUCHAN, David. From Perth. s/o James B, merchant. Matric Univ of Glasgow, 1819. To Toronto, ONT.   **GMA 10283**.

900   BUCHAN, Janet, 1805-92. From Deerness, OKI. To St Catharines, Lincoln Co, ONT, via New York, 1849. Wife of Thomas Irvine, qv, whom she m 11 Feb 1834.   **DC 11 Nov 1981**.

901   BUCHAN, John. From Crimongorth, Crimond, ABD. s/o John B, farmer, and Elizabeth Milne. To ONT ca 1837.   **DC 20 Oct 1976**.

902   BUCHANAN, Ann. From Edinburgh. d/o Rev George B, qv, and Ann Aitkin, qv. To Beckwith Twp, Lanark Co, ONT, 1823. m Peter McLaurin, qv.   **HCL 192**.

903   BUCHANAN, Annie, b 1806. From Carnish, Uig par, Is Lewis, ROC. d/o Norman B. and Kirsty McDonald. To QUE, 1851; stld Weedon, Wolfe Co. Wife of Malcolm MacAulay, qv.   **DC 25 May 1979; WLC**.

904   BUCHANAN, Catherine, d 1912. From Is Lewis, ROC. d/o Kenneth B. and Peggy Nicholson. To QUE, ca 1852; stld prob Wolfe Co. m Charles Smith, qv.   **WLC**.

905   BUCHANAN, Catherine. From STI. To Halifax, NS, 1795. Wife of Alexander McDougall, qv.   **MLA 210**.

906   BUCHANAN, Andrew. Prob from STI. bro/o George B, qv. To Montreal, QUE, <1831, when he went to McNab Twp, Renfrew Co, ONT. Sawyer and miller, Madawaska River.   **HCL 106**.

907   BUCHANAN, Donald. To PEI ca 1803; stld nr Belfast. Petitioner for Dr MacAulay, 1811.   **HP 74**.

908   BUCHANAN, Duncan, b 1758. From Scarsdale, Flodigarry, Is Skye, INV. To Orwell Bay, PEI, on the *Polly*, ex Portree, arr 7 Aug 1803; stld Belfast. m Flora McLeod.   **DC 22 Jun 1965**.

909   BUCHANAN, Duncan. Prob from STI. A minor, poss s/o Peter B, qv. To McNab Twp, Renfrew Co, ONT, 1825.   **DC 3 Jan 1980**.

910   BUCHANAN, Elizabeth. From Edinburgh. d/o Rev George B. qv, and Ann Aitkin, qv. To Beckwith Twp, Lanark Co, ONT, 1823. Schoolteacher at Perth, Drummond Twp. m Archibald Campbell, Rideau Ferry.   **HCL 192**.

911   BUCHANAN, Rev George, ca 1763–12 Sep 1835. Prob from PER. Missionary in ARL before being ord min of Strathkinnes Relief Ch, FIF, 1808. Min of Cameronian Ch, Linktown, 1816-18. Became military chaplain and went to QUE. Adm min of Beckwith Twp, Lanark Co, ONT, 1822, and preached in a barn before the building of St Andrews Presb Ch, 7th Line, 1832. m Ann Aitkin, qv, ch: 1. George; 2. David, catechist in Jamaica, d 1842; 3. Margaret, qv; 4. Ann, qv; 5. Jessie; 6. Elizabeth, qv; 7. Helen, qv; 8. Mary; 9. Isabella, qv; 10. Julia.   **UPC i 205; HCL 40, 192-4; MGC 2 Aug 1979**.

912   BUCHANAN, George. Prob from STI. bro/o Andrew B, qv. To Montreal, QUE, <1831, when he moved to McNab Twp, Renfrew Co, ONT. Sawyer and miller, Madawaska River. m a sis/o George Powell.   **HCL 106**.

913   BUCHANAN, Helen, 1805-30. From Edinburgh. d/o Rev George B, qv, and Ann Aitkin, qv. To Beckwith Twp, Lanark Co, ONT, 1823. Schoolteacher at Perth, Drummond Co. m John Ferguson, Perth.   **HCL 192**.

914   BUCHANAN, Isabella. From Edinburgh. d/o Rev George B, qv, and Ann Aitkin, qv. To Beckwith Twp, Lanark Co, ONT, 1823. m 1832, Anthony Philips.   **HCL 192**.

915   BUCHANAN, Isaac, 21 Jul 1810–1 Oct 1883. From Glasgow. s/o Peter B, manufacturer, who succeeded to the estate of Auchmar, and — Buchanan. To Toronto, ONT, 1830, as rep of firm of William Guild & Co, merchants, and estab branch there, also in Hamilton and London. Economist and MLA. m Agnes Jarvis, qv, ch: 1. Peter, b Toronto, 1844; 2. Jane Milligan, b Gorbals, 25 Feb 1846; 3. Robert Andrew Washington, b New York, 29 Feb 1848; 4. Margaret Douglas, b Gourock, 12 Jan 1850; 5. Harris, res Pittsburgh, USA, 1870; 6. James Isaac, res Pittsburgh, 1870; 7. Douglas, res Vandergrift Buildings, 323 Fourth Ave, Pittsburgh, 1893, when adm mem of the Buchanan Society, Glasgow.   **Glasgow OPR 644-1/38; BNA 540**.

916 BUCHANAN, James, b 1801. From Torlum, Is Benbecula, INV. s/o Donald B, (s of Alexander B.) and Catherine McDonald. To East Williams Twp, Middlesex Co, ONT, ca 1852. Wife Flora with him, and ch: 1. Ann, b 1829; 2. Donald, b 1836; 3. James, b 1838; 4. John, b 1840; 5. Norman, b 1846. **PCM 44; WLC**.

917 BUCHANAN, James, b 1807. From Torlum, Is Benbecula, INV. s/o Duncan B, (s of Alexander B.) and Mary McPherson. To East Williams Twp, Middlesex Co, ONT, ca 1852. m Ann McDonald, qv, ch: 1. Penny, b 1834; 2. Mary, b 1836; 3. Ann, b 1839; 4. Alexander, b 1841; 5. Marion, b 1844; 6. Catherine, b 1846; 7. Donald, b 1848; 8. Duncan, b 1851; 9. Ranald, b 1854; 10. Penny, yr. **PCM 44; WLC**.

918 BUCHANAN, Janet. From Kenmore, PER. To NB 1816. Wife of Andrew Somerville, qv. **LDW 16 Dec 1980**.

919 BUCHANAN, Jessie. From Edinburgh. d/o Rev George B, qv, and Ann Aitkin, qv. To Beckwith Twp, Lanark Co, ONT, 1823. m Duncan Campbell, Rideau Ferry. **HCL 192**.

920 BUCHANAN, John. To PEI ca 1803; stld nr Belfast. Petitioner for Dr MacAulay, 1811. **HP 74**.

921 BUCHANAN, John, 1762–1805. Poss from PER. To QUE on the *Oughton*, arr Jul 1804; stld Baldoon, Dover Twp, Kent Co, ONT. Farmer. Wife–prob second–Catherine, with him, and ch: 1. Marion, b 1785; 2. Alexander, b 1787; 3. Robert, 1794–1804; 4. Catherine, b 1796; 5. Donald, b 1798. 6. Nellie, b 1800; 7. John, b 1802. Widow m (ii) Donald Brown, qv. **UCM 267, 302; DC 4 Oct 1979**.

922 BUCHANAN, John. Poss from STI. A minor, poss s/o Peter B, qv. To McNab Twp, Renfrew Co, ONT, 1825. **DC 3 Jan 1980**.

923 BUCHANAN, John. From Is Skye, INV. To NS <1850; stld Baddeck River, Victoria Co. Farmer. Dau Elizabeth. **HNS iii 336**.

924 BUCHANAN, Malcolm. To PEI ca 1803; stld nr Belfast. Petitioner for Dr MacAulay, 1811. **HP 74**.

925 BUCHANAN, Margaret. From Edinburgh. d/o Rev George B, qv, and Ann Aitkin, qv. To Beckwith Twp, Lanark Co, ONT, 1823. m John Dewar. **HCL 192**.

926 BUCHANAN, Neil, b 1802. From Crulivig, Uig par, Is Lewis, ROC. s/o Donald B. and Ann McKay. To QUE, 1851; stld Scotstown, Compton Co, QUE. m (i) Effie Smith, ch: 1. John, b 1830. Neil m (ii) Isabella McLeod, ch: 2. Ann, b 1838. m (iii) Mary McArthur, see ADDENDA, ch: 3. Effie, b 1843; 4. Annabella, b 1848; 5. Margaret, b 1851; 6. Neil, b 1857. **WLC**.

927 BUCHANAN, Patrick, b ca 1803. From Leny, PER. To ONT, 1818. Merchant. m Lucy Baker, ch: 1. Margaret; 2. Janet; 3. Lucy Ann; 4. Elizabeth. **DC 4 Mar 1965**.

928 BUCHANAN, Peter. From Cragan, Ballinluig, PER. To McNab Twp, Renfrew Co, ONT, 1825. **EMT 18**.

929 BUCHANAN, Peter, 1802–11 Dec 1868. From PER. To Esquesing Twp, Halton Co, ONT, prob <1830. Bur Acton. **EPE 74**.

930 BUCHANAN, Robert. From Glasgow. To QUE <1836; stld Aubigny. Merchant. **DC 11 Feb 1980**.

931 BUCHANAN, Robert, 1819–1902. From Paisley, RFW. s/o Walter B. To Puslinch Twp, Wellington Co, ONT, 1849. Wright and farmer, Lots 11-13, Con 5. m Mary Jane Budgeon, 1836-92, ch: 1. Agnes; 2. Mary; 3. Walter, farmer; 4. James; 5. Lydia. **DC 11 Nov 1982**.

932 BUCHANAN, Sarah, 1783–1877. From Oban, ARL. To Port Hawkesbury, NS, 1819; stld Upper Southeast Mabou, Inverness Co, 1820. d at West Bay. Wife of Peter MacFarlane, qv. **MP ii 412**.

933 BUCHANAN, William. From Lochgilphead, ARL. To Westminster Twp, Middlesex Co, ONT, 1832. Son Malcolm. **PCM 51**.

934 BUCKLEY, Marion, b ca 1740. From New Abbey, KKD. To Georgetown, Kings Co, PEI, on the *Lovely Nellie*, ex Carsethorn, May 1775. Wife of Joseph Grieve, qv. **ELN**.

935 BUDGE, John, 1816-74. From CAI. To St John, NB. *The Highlander*, 21 Feb 1874.

936 BUIST, Henry, ca 1804–19 Dec 1876. From Strathmiglo, FIF. s/o Henry B. of Pittuncarty, and Rachel Robertson. To CAN, prob ONT. **Ts Strathmiglo**.

937 BULLIANS, James, b ca 1779. From PER. To Pictou, NS, on the *Commerce*, ex Port Glasgow, 10 Aug 1803. Farmer. **PLC**.

938 BULLOCH, James. To QUE on the *Commerce*, ex Greenock, Jun 1820; stld prob Lanark Co, ONT. **HCL 238**.

939 BULLOCK, Thomas. To QUE on the *Commerce*, ex Greenock, Jun 1820; stld prob Lanark Co, ONT. **HCL 238**.

940 BURDEN, Ann, d 1838. From PER. To Megantic Co, QUE. m — Gould, ch: 1. Jean; 2. Margaret; 3. William. **AMC 148**.

941 BURGESS, John. s/o James B. and Helen Graham. To CAN on the *Ellen McCarthy*, 1830; prob stld NB. Wife Janet Masterton, qv, with him. **DC 4 Oct 1979**.

942 BURGESS, William. To Pictou, NS, on the *London*, arr 14 Jul 1848. **DC 15 Jul 1979**.

943 BURN, David, d 2 Mar 1840. To Northumberland Co, ONT. Merchant. **DGH 1 May 1840**.

944 BURN, Hannah King, d 9 Jun 1828. From Edinburgh. d/o James B, merchant, and — Wilson. To St John, NB. m Daniel McIntosh, merchant. **Ts St Cuthbert's, Edinburgh**.

945 BURNET, Alexander, b ca 1802. To CAN, ex Greenock, 8 May 1833; stld Oshawa, East Whitby Twp, Ontario Co, ONT. Millwright. m Janet Thornton, qv, ch: 1. Andrew, b 1829; 2. Joseph, qv; 3. Alexander, b 1834; 4. Robert, b 1837; 5. Margaret, b 1846. **DC 18 Jan 1980**.

946 BURNET, Arthur, b ca 1833. Rel to Alexander B, qv. To East Whitby Twp, Ontario Co, ONT. Planer. By wife Margaret, ch: 1. Jane, b ca 1859; 2. Jessie; 3. John; 4. Margaret; 5. Christian; 6. Andrew. **DC 18 Jan 1980**.

947 BURNET, Catherine, 1799–13 Feb 1891. From Glasgow. To Melbourne, Richmond Co, QUE. m Robert McMorine, qv. **MGC 15 Jul 1980**.

948 BURNET, Janet, b ca 1800. From Traquair, PEE, but prob b Ettrick par, SEL. To Dumfries Twp, Waterloo Co, ONT, 1824. Wife of William Scott, qv. **DC 17 Mar 1980**.

949 BURNET, Joseph, 27 Mar 1832–13 Feb 1906. s/o Alexander B, qv, and Janet Thornton, qv. To Oshawa, East Whitby Twp, Ontario Co, ONT, 1833. Miller. m (i) Margaret Strickland, d 1859; (ii) Phoebe Park. **DC 18 Jan 1980**.

950 BURNETT, Alexander. From ABD. To Niagara, Lincoln Co, ONT, via NY, 1832; later to Galt, Waterloo Co. Shop asst. **HGD 97**.

951 BURNETT, Alexander, 1805-92. From ABD. To Winterbourne, Waterloo Co, ONT, 1835; moved to Pilkington Twp, 1850, and stld Lot 5, Con 3. Farmer. m Jean Sangster, qv, ch: 1. Jane; 2. John; 3. James; 4. George; 5. Samuel; 6. Mary Ann; 7. Elsie; 8. Sarah; 9. Alexander; 10. William; 11. Robert. **DC 11 Nov 1981**.

952 BURNIE, William, d 11 Dec 1824. From Moffat, DFS. To Chatham, Northumberland Co, NB. Merchant. **DGC 22 Feb 1825**.

953 BURNS, Alexander, 1807-90. From AYR. s/o Thomas B, qv, and Janet Wallace, qv. To Esquesing Twp, Halton Co, ONT, prob 1820; stld Lot 3, Con 6, Eramosa Twp, Wellington Co, 1826. Farmer. m Margaret Aitken, 1830, ch: 1. Elizabeth, b 1832; 2. Thomas, b 1834; 3. Alexander, b 1836; 4. Andrew, b 1838; 5. Alexander, b 1843; 6. John, b 1846; 7. Robert, b 1848; 8. William, b 1851. **DC 11 Dec 1981**.

954 BURNS, Gavin, d 5 Jul 1837. Capt of the brig *Glasgow*, of Greenock. To Montreal, QUE, and d there 'in the prime of life.' **DGC 16 Aug 1837**.

955 BURNS, Rev George, 1790–1876. From Bo'ness, WLN. s/o John B, Surveyor of Customs, and Grizel Ferrier. To St John, NB, 1816, and ord as min of St Andrews Ch there. Retr to SCT 1831, and was min at Tweedsmuir, later of Corstorphine FC. m 1827 Esther, d/o Rev J. Struthers, Edinburgh, ch: 1. Jane Briggs, b 1828; 2. Esther Struthers, b 1830; 3. George Ferrier, 1833–1911, d Toronto; 4. Robert Briggs, d inf, 1839. **AFC i 109; FES i 296, vii 609**.

956 BURNS, George F, b ca 1831. Educ Edinburgh Academy, 1844-46, and went to ONT, prob Bruce Co. **EAR 122**.

957 BURNS, Grace. From PER or ANS. To Montreal, QUE, arr Jun 1842; stld North Easthope, Perth Co, ONT. Wife of Andrew Easson, qv. **DC 15 Jul 1978, 24 May 1979**.

958 BURNS, Rev John, d 1822. From Fenwick, AYR. Itinerant min and went to ONT 1803. Became pastor of United Secession Ch at Stamford, Welland Co. **UPC ii 142n**.

959 BURNS, John. To Halifax, NS, <6 Nov 1825, when he m Charlotte, d/o Nathaniel Hatfield. **VSN No 1410**.

960 BURNS, John, b 1805. From AYR. s/o Thomas B, qv, and Janet Wallace, qv. To Esquesing Twp, ONT, <1835. Was educ Univ of Edinburgh and became editor of the *Record*, in Toronto. **DC 11 Dec 1981**.

961 BURNS, John, b ca 1817. To New Germany, Lunenburg Co, NS, ca 1852. m Charlotte, b 1830, d/o John Ellis Crandall and Deborah Dimock. **NSN 27/190**.

962 BURNS, Rev Robert, 13 Feb 1789–19 Sep 1869. From Bo'ness, WLN. s/o John B, Surveyor of Customs, and Grizel Ferrier. Educ Univ of Edinburgh. Min of St George's, Paisley, 1811-43; of St George's FC, 1843-45; and of Knox Ch, Toronto, ONT, 1845-56, when app Prof of Ch History in Knox Coll. m (i) 1814, Janet Orr, ch: 1. Agnes, 1816-20; 2. John, dy; 3. James Orr, matric Univ of Glasgow, 1840; 4. William; 5. Robert Ferrier, qv. m (ii) 1844, Elizabeth Bell, d/o Thomas Bonar. **AFC i 109; FES iii 176; GMA 14269; MDB 94**.

963 BURNS, Rev Robert Ferrier, 23 Dec 1826–5 Apr 1896. From Paisley, RFW. s/o Robert B, qv, and Janet Orr. Matric Univ of Glasgow, 1840. Min of Chalmers Presb Ch, Kingston, ONT, 1847-55; Knox Presb Ch, St Catherine's, 1855-67; Scottish Ch, Chicago, 1867-70; Côte Street Ch, Montreal, 1870-75; Fort Massey Presb Ch, Halifax, NS, 1875. **BNA 862; GMA 14288; FES iii 176, vii 628; MDB 94**.

964 BURNS, Thomas, 1775–1861. From AYR. To Esquesing Twp, Halton Co, ONT, 1820. Farmer there and in Eramosa Twp, Wellington Co. m Janet Wallace, qv, ch: 1. John, qv; 2. Alexander, qv; 3. Thomas, b 1811, res Acton. **DC 11 Dec 1981**.

965 BURNSIDE, Henry. From Glasgow. To NS <1795, stld East River, Pictou Co. Discharged soldier, 42nd Regt, and gr land. Son James moved to Antigonish Co, 1826. **HNS iii 569**.

966 BURR, Robert, d 1895. To Fergus Twp, Wellington Co, ONT, 1846. Farmer and was Assessor and Collector for West Garafraxa Twp. m Margaret Wilson, ch: 1. John; 2. Margaret; 3. William; 4. Mrs De Guerre. **DC 11 Dec 1981**.

967 BURRY, Mary. From Dunkeld, PER. To QUE on the *Albion*, ex Greenock, 5 Jun 1829; stld Hamilton Range, Megantic Co, QUE. Wife of Thomas McKenzie, qv. **AMC 22**.

968 BURT, George, ca 1795–1863. From Glasgow, but b FIF. bro/o John B, qv. To Guelph Twp, Wellington Co, ONT, 1828; stld Con 6, Erin Twp. Farmer. m Bethia Wilson, qv, ch: 1. George, d 1839; 2. Rebecca, b 1846; 3. James Wilson, stock-breeder; 4. William; 5. James; 6. David; 7. Ellen; 8. Mrs. Henry Hills. **DC 11 Dec 1981**.

969 BURT, John. From Glasgow, but prob b FIF. bro/o George B, qv. To Erin Twp, Wellington Co, ONT, <1840. Schoolteacher. **DC 11 Dec 1981**.

970 BURT, William. To Pictou, NS, on the *Lulan*, ex Glasgow, 17 Aug 1848, and may have gone to PEI. **DC 12 Jul 1979**.

971 BUTLER, John. To Pictou, NS, on the *London*, arr 11 Apr 1848. Wife Mary with him, and ch: 1. Sally; 2. John; 3. Hugh; 4. James; 5. Jane; 6. Henry. **DC 15 Jul 1979**.

972 BYDE, Janet. From Glasgow. To Paris Village, Brant Co, ONT, 1840. wid/o John Edmiston, ch: 1. Archibald, qv; 2. James, qv; 3. John, qv; 4. Walter, qv. **GNL 6/16; DC 1 Feb 1980**.

C

973 CADDELL, William James, b 1810. To Halifax, NS; later to Hants Co and stld nr Admiral Rock. m Mary Bartlett, ch: 1. Capt John; 2. Alexander; 3. James; 4. William; 5. Frank; 6. Margaret; 7. Jessie. **NSN 16/7**.

974 CADENHEAD, Alexander Shirrefs, 3 Jul 1823– 22 May 1883. From Aberdeen. s/o Alexander C, advocate, and Jane Shirrefs. To Nichol Twp, Wellington Co, ONT, 1841; res later in Fergus. Clerk of Court and later Crown Land Agent. m Mary Arbuthnott Fordyce, qv, ch: 1. Alexander, res Burlington; 2. Arthur Dingwall, went to MAN; 3. James Shirrefs; 4. James Brebner, 1862-64; 5. John Arbuthnott, went to MAN; 6. George Morison; 7. Elizabeth; 8. Magdalene Dingwall, 1866-67. **NDF 35; SAA 110**.

975 CAIE, Robert. From ABD. To Meil Creek, Richibucto, Kent Co, NB, 1820. Wife Isabella, 1778–1861, bur Chatham. **DC 21 Mar 1981**.

976 CAIRNS, Elizabeth. Poss from BEW or SEL. To PEI poss ca 1840. Wife of William Mabon, qv. **DC 17 Jan 1980**.

977 CAIRNS, Janet, b 24 Apr 1785. From Wilton par, ROX. To ONT ca 1834. Wife of Andrew Dryden, qv, m ca 1802. **SG xv/3 49; DC 28 Jan 1968**.

978 CAIRNS, Robert. From Broombush, Lockerbie, DFS. To Kings Co, PEI, ca 1840. Wife Mary Carruthers d 'Broombush,' St Peter's Road, 1868. **DGH 13 Nov 1868**.

979 CAIRNS, Thomas. From Dumfries. To Bedeque, Prince Co, PEI, <1841. m Agnes Wilson, qv. **DGH 25 Nov 1841**.

980 CALDER, Ann, ca 1774–28 Aug 1816. From Tongue par, SUT. d/o William C, catechist. To Pictou, NS, on the *Prince William*, of Newcastle, arr Sep 1815. m (i) John McKay, Reay Fencibles, d 1811, ch: 1. John, b 1794, may have d in SCT; 2. Donald; 3. William, 1800-88; 4. Barbara, d 1835; 5. Sophia; 6. Amelia Harriet, 1808-98; 7. Johanna. m (ii) — McIntosh. **DC 6 Aug 1979**.

981 CALDER, Elizabeth, b ca 1800. From Breachlich, Dalcross, INV. To ONT, 1832. m John Fraser, qv. **DC 14 Sep 1966**.

982 CALDER, Janet. From Islay, ARL. To ONT <1855; stld Oro Twp, Simcoe Co. Wife of Henry McCuaig, qv. **DC 9 Oct 1979**.

983 CALDER, John. From ABD. To Nichol Twp, Wellington Co, ONT, 1835. ch: 1. Eliza; 2. Barbara; 3. Kirstie; 4. Alexander; 5. John; 6. Mary; 7. Margaret; 8. Isabella; 9. William; 10. Jemima; 11. Georgina. **EHE 91**.

984 CALDER, Margaret, ca 1830-72. From Lagavulin, Is Islay, ARL. To Eldon Twp, Victoria Co, ONT, 1852. Wife of Archibald MacMillan, qv. **EC 160**.

985 CALDER, Nellie. From INV. To Halifax, NS, on the brig *John*, arr 4 Jun 1784. Wife of Alexander McKay, qv. **CP 35**.

986 CALDERWOOD, James. To Restigouche Co, NB, ca 1831. Wife Margaret Crookshank, qv, with him, and dau Agnes, b 7 Nov 1827. **DC 1 Oct 1979**.

987 CALDWELL, David, ca 1781–ca 1850. From Barony par, Glasgow. To QUE, 1820; stld Lanark Co, ONT. Farmer. m Mary Ann Vaughan, qv, ch: 1. Ann, b 1813; 2. Mary, b 1815; 3. John, b 1817; 4. Jane, b 1819; 5. Jean, b 1822; 6. Maria, b 1824; 7. Caroline, b 1826; 8. David Henry, b 1828; 9. Abraham V, b 1832; 10. Isaac James, b 1834. **DC 17 Nov 1973**.

988 CALDWELL, Isabella. sis/o Jane C, qv. To CAN <1840; stld prob ONT. **GNL 6/16**.

989 CALDWELL, Joseph, d 1826. Poss from RFW. To Restigouche Co, NB, ca 1820; stld opp Heron Is. ch: **CUC 5**.

990 CALDWELL, James. Poss from RFW. s/o William C. and Jean Brodie. To Montreal, QUE, <1840. **DC 23 Mar 1979**.

991 CALDWELL, Jane, b 27 Sep 1808. sis/o Isabella C, qv. To CAN <1840; stld prob ONT. **GNL 6/16**.

992 CALDWELL, William. Prob from RFW. To QUE on the *Earl of Buckinghamshire*, ex Greenock, 29 Apr 1821; stld Lot 24, Con 2, Lanark Co, ONT. Sons Alexander and Boyd, lumbermen. **HCL 73, 166**.

993 CALDWELL, William, b ca 1765. To Kingston, ONT. Soldier. ch: 1. Jane, b 27 Dec 1808; 2. Isabella. **DC 1 Feb 1980**.

994 CALDWELL, William, b ca 1793. Prob from RFW. To QUE on the *Earl of Buckinghamshire*, ex Greenock, 29 Apr 1821; stld Darling Twp, Lanark Co, ONT. Woollen weaver. **DC 10 Nov 1978**.

CALHOUN. See also COLQUHOUN.

995 CALHOUN, Angus. To Aldborough Twp, Elgin Co, ONT, 1859. **PDA 68**.

996 CALL, Richard. To Magog, Stanstead Co, QUE, <1837. m Venia Turner, ch: **DC 11 Feb 1980**.

997 CALLACHAN, Elizabeth. From Peterhead, ABD. To QUE on the *Champlain of Quebec*, Sep 1831. Went to Leeds Co, ONT; later to Bromley and Wilberforce Twps, Renfrew Co. Wife of Robert Robertson Smith, qv. **DC 15 Sep 1979**.

998 CALLIE, Christina, ca 1796–30 Jun 1869. From Dornoch, SUT. To Pictou Co, NS, and bur Salt Springs. Wife of John Rettie, qv. **DC 27 Oct 1979**.

999 CALVERT, Elizabeth, ca 1769–28 Apr 1854. From Dalton, DFS. To ONT and d New Dublin Mills. Wife of James Pearson, qv. **Ts Dalton**.

1000 CALVERT, John, 1795–1843. From DFS. To York Co, ONT, <1843; stld Markham. m Elizabeth Wilson, qv, ch: 1. Kirsty, 1820-94; 2. George, b ca 1828; 3. John, 1832–1913; 4. Jonathan, 1835-99; 5. William, 1836–1913; 6. Margaret, b ca 1839; 7. Janet, b ca 1841. **DC 17 Apr 1978**.

1001 CAMERON, Alexander, ca 1729–15 Aug 1831. From Lochbroom, ROC. To Pictou, NS, on the *Hector*, ex Loch Broom, arr 17 Sep 1773. Witnessed Battle of Culloden, 1746. Gr land at Lochbroom, Pictou Co. Farmer. By wife Janet ch: 1. Alexander, qv; 2. Christiana, qv; 3. John; 4. Lilias; 5. Roderick; 6. Duncan; 7. Annabel; 8. Margaret. **HPC App C; NSN 11/1**.

1002 CAMERON, Alexander. From Lochbroom, ROC. s/o Alexander C, qv. To Pictou, NS, on the *Hector*, ex

Loch Broom, arr 17 Sep 1773; stld Lochbroom, Pictou Co. Farmer and Ch elder. **HPC App C**.

1003 CAMERON, Alexander. Served in the 84th Regt and following discharge in 1784, was gr 100 acres on the east side of East River, Pictou Co, NS. **HPC App C**.

1004 CAMERON, Alexander. To Pictou Co, NS, <1 Apr 1793, when gr 300 acres on west branch of East River. **HPC App H**.

1005 CAMERON, Alexander. From Lochaber, INV. To Antigonish Co, NS, ca 1797, and stld Salt Springs. m Miss Cameron, ch: 1. Catherine; 2. Sarah; 3. Mary; 4. Isabel. **HCA 89**.

1006 CAMERON, Alexander. From Kilmorack, INV. To Pictou, NS, on the *Dove*, ex Fort William, Jun 1801. Tenant. **PLD**.

1007 CAMERON, Alexander. From Kilmorack, INV. To Pictou, NS, on the *Dove*, ex Fort William, Jun 1801. Labourer. **PLD**.

1008 CAMERON, Alexander. From Urquhart, INV. To Pictou, NS, on the *Sarah*, ex Fort William, Jun 1801. Farmer. Wife Helen with him, and ch: 1. Alexander, labourer; 2. Ann, aged 13; 3. Flory, aged 7; 4. Mary, aged 3. **PLS**.

1009 CAMERON, Alexander. From Lochielhead, INV. To Montreal, QUE, ex Fort William, 3 Jul 1802; stld E ONT. **MCM 1/4 26**.

1010 CAMERON, Alexander. From Salachen, Ardgour, ARL. To Montreal, QUE, ex Fort William, 3 Jul 1802; stld E ONT. **MCM 1/4 26**.

1011 CAMERON, Alexander. From Thornhill, PER. To Montreal, QUE, ex Fort William, 3 Jul 1802; stld E ONT. Wife and 2 ch with him. **MCM 1/4, 26**.

1012 CAMERON, Alexander. From Gortnecorn, Ardnamurchan, ARL. To Montreal, QUE, ex Fort William, 3 Jul 1802; stld E ONT. **MCM 1/4 26**.

1013 CAMERON, Alexander. From Ardnabie, ni, INV. To Montreal, QUE, ex Fort William, 3 Jul 1802; stld E ONT. **MCM 1/4 24**.

1014 CAMERON, Alexander, b ca 1752. To Charlottetown, PEI, on the *Rambler*, ex Torbermory, 20 Jun 1806. Wife Catherine with him, aged 38, and ch: 1. Jean, aged 20; 2. Hugh, aged 17; 3. John, aged 15; 4. Janet, aged 14; 5. Sarah, aged 12; 6. James, aged 5; 7. Catherine, aged 2 mo. **PLR**.

1015 CAMERON, Alexander, b ca 1778. To Charlottetown, PEI, on the *Rambler*, ex Tobermory, 20 Jun 1806. Wife Mary, aged 23, with him, and dau Catherine, b 1805. **PLR**.

1016 CAMERON, Alexander, 1768–1835. To Pictou Co, NS, <1810; stld Loch Broom. m Janet Archibald, 1769–1835, and had with other ch: 1. Daniel; 2. Janet. **NSN 9/1**.

1017 CAMERON, Alexander, b 1801. From Greenock, RFW. s/o Allan C, qv, and Agnes Morrison. To NS, 1810; stld Low Point, and later River Denys, Inverness Co. m Janet, d/o Robert Bull. **DC 23 Feb 1980**.

1018 CAMERON, Alexander. Prob from INV. To Pictou Co, NS, <1815; stld West Branch Lake, East River. ch: 1. Donald, res Elgin; 2. Kenneth, tailor. **PAC 12**.

1019 CAMERON, Alexander. To Lanark Co, ONT, 1815; stld Burgess Twp. **HCL 15**.

1020 CAMERON, Alexander, ca 1788–2 Oct 1859. From Abernethy, INV. Poss s/o Angus C. and Janet Ross. Discharged from 103rd Regt as a Colour Sgt, 1818, and gr land in Lot 12, Con 5, Bathurst Twp, Lanark Co, ONT. Farmer. m Margaret Grant, ch: 1. Ewan, b ca 1820; 2. John, b ca 1822; 3. James, b ca 1824; 4. Alexander, b ca 1829; 5. Catherine, b ca 1830; 6. Robert, b ca 1831; 7. William, b ca 1833; 8. John, b ca 1837. **DC 18 Jul 1979**.

1021 CAMERON, Alexander. Poss from Lochaber, INV. To Aldborough Twp, Elgin Co, ONT, <1820. Farmer. **PDA 92**.

1022 CAMERON, Alexander. From Lochaber, INV. To London Twp, Middlesex Co, ONT, <1830. Son John, barrister, Strathroy. **PCM 50**.

1023 CAMERON, Alexander. Poss from Lochaber, INV. To Lobo Twp, Middlesex Co, ONT, 1838. ch: 1. John; 2. Archie; 3. Mrs. A. Barclay; 4. Mrs B.B. Harris. **PCM 40**.

1024 CAMERON, Alexander. Poss from ARL. To Aldborough Twp, Elgin Co, ONT, 1840. ch. **PDA 67**.

1025 CAMERON, Rev Alexander, ca 1817–1 Apr 1886. From Strontian, ARL. s/o Donald C, joiner. Educ Univs of Edinburgh and Glasgow. To MAN, 1850, and was FC min there. Retr to SCT and was FC min at Ardersier, INV, 1854-86. m Jessie Cameron. **GMA 14707; AFC i 111**.

1026 CAMERON, Alexander, d 1 Jul 1866. From Chirnside, BEW. s/o Alexander C. and Janet Paxton. To NS prob <1854, and d L'Ardoise, Richmond Co. **Ts Chirnside**.

1027 CAMERON, Allan. Prob from Achosnich, Ardnamurchan, ARL. To Cape Breton Is, NS, 1810. Dau Margaret. **DC 23 Feb 1980**.

1028 CAMERON, Allan. From Lochaber, INV. s/o Dougald and Jane C. To Antigonish Co, NS, prob <1810. ch: 1. Hugh, qv; 2. John. **HCA 85**.

1029 CAMERON, Allan. From Greenock, RFW. s/o Ewen C. To NS 1810; stld Low Point, later River Denys, Inverness Co. m Agnes Morrison, ch: 1. Charles; 2. Alexander, qv; 3. Donald; 4. Archibald. **DC 23 Feb 1980**.

1030 CAMERON, Allan, d ca 1870. From Lochaber, INV. s/o Donald C. To Mabou, Inverness Co, NS, ca 1826. Miller. m (i) Christina, d/o James and Sarah Hawley, ch: 1. Ann; 2. Margaret, b 1852; 3. Donald, went to AUS; 4. James, shipbuilder; 5. George. m (ii) Christina MacPherson, wid/o Archibald MacDonald, no ch. **MP ii 90**.

1031 CAMERON, Angus. From Glenturret, INV. bro/o John C, qv. To Montreal, QUE, ex Fort William, 3 Jul 1802; stld E ONT. **MCM 1/4 24**.

1032 CAMERON, Angus, b ca 1746. To NS on the *Rambler*, ex Tobermory, Is Mull, 20 Jun 1806. Wife Ann, aged 50, with him, and ch: 1. Donald, aged 30; 2. Alexander, aged 20; 3. Sarah, aged 19; 4. Ann, aged 17; 5. Flora, aged 15; 6. Allan, aged 12; 7. Angus, aged 10. **PLR**.

1033 CAMERON, Angus, b ca 1768. To Inverness Co, NS, 1806; stld Port Hood dist. Farmer, m and ch. **CBC 1818**.

1034 CAMERON, Angus, b ca 1782. To Inverness Co, NS, 1806; stld Port Hood dist. Farmer, m and ch. **CBC 1818**.

1035 CAMERON, Angus, b ca 1768. From Auchleeks, ARL. To Charlottetown, PEI, on the *Clarendon*, ex Oban, 6 Aug 1808. Wife Ann, aged 27, with him, and ch: 1. Mary, aged 5; 2. Euphemia, aged 3. Labourer. **CPL**.

1036 CAMERON, Angus, 1782–11 Aug 1876. From BAN. s/o James C, farmer, and Janet Farquharson. To Montreal, QUE, <1810. Emp with NWCo, and was app a chief factor at the merger with HBCo, 1821. Later a chief factor, and retr SCT. m Elizabeth Morrison, and d Firhall, Nairn. **MDB 103**.

1037 CAMERON, Angus, ca 1762–23 Aug 1847. From Kinlochleven, ARL. To ONT, and d Seymour, Northumberland Co. Poss sometime army officer. **DGH 23 Sep 1847**.

1038 CAMERON, Angus, b 1785. To Pictou Co, NS, 1815. Labourer. **INS 37**.

1039 CAMERON, Angus, b 1786. To Pictou Co, NS, 1815. Labourer. Poor person, 1816. **INS 37**.

1040 CAMERON, Angus. To QUE <1808; stld Drummond Twp, Lanark Co, ONT, 1816. Discharged soldier; inn-keeper. Son Malcolm, b 1808, storekeeper and politician, Perth. **HCL 157**.

1041 CAMERON, Angus, b ca 1796. From Lochaber, INV. s/o Ewen C. and Margaret Gillies. To Inverness Co, NS, <1820; gr land east side of Upper South West River. m Margaret Beaton, qv, ch: 1. Hugh; 2. Archibald; 3. Alexander; 4. Angus; 5. Donald; 6. Isabel; 7. Sara; 8. Anne; 9. Catherine; 10. Margaret; 11. Mary. **MP 257**.

1042 CAMERON, Angus 'Donn'. From Lochaber, INV. s/o Angus 'Dubh' C, qv, and Mary Beaton, qv. To Mabou, Inverness Co, NS, prob 1805. m (i) Mary, d/o Alexander Beaton, qv, and Ann Beaton, ch: 1. Angus Og. m (ii) Catherine, d/o Archibald Kennedy, further ch: 2. Donald; 3. John; 4. Alexander; 5. Finlay; 6. Sara; 7. Mary; 8. Catherine. **MP 239**.

1043 CAMERON, Angus 'Dubh'. From Lochaber, INV. To Mabou, Inverness Co, NS, prob 1805. m Mary Beaton, qv, ch: 1. Angus 'Donn,' qv; 2. John 'Donn,' qv; 3. Margaret, qv; 4. Anne, qv; 5. Margaret, jr, qv; 6. Sara, qv; 7. Ann, jr, qv; 8. Jessie. **MP 238**.

1044 CAMERON, Ann, 1764–1854. From Loch Sunart, ARL. To Cape Breton Is, NS, 1784, with husband Donald McIntyre, qv, and widowed shortly afterwards. She obtained land at Princeville, Inverness Co, and farmed successfully there. **WLC**.

1045 CAMERON, Ann, b ca 1797. From Kilmorack, INV. Poss d/o Alexander C, tenant, qv. To Pictou, NS, on the *Dove*, ex Fort William, Jun 1801. m John Fraser, qv. **PLD; PAC 67**.

1046 CAMERON, Ann, b ca 1820. Prob from Snizort, Is Skye, INV. To Kinloss Twp, Bruce Co, ONT, 1852. Wife of Norman Nicolson, qv. **DC 12 Apr 1979**.

1047 CAMERON, Mrs Ann, b 1756. To Pictou Co, NS, 1815. Widow, maintained by friends, 1816. **INS 37**.

1048 CAMERON, Anne. Poss from Is Muck, INV. To Montreal, QUE, ex Fort William, 3 Jul 1802; stld E ONT. **MCM 1/4 25**.

1049 CAMERON, Anne. From Lochaber, INV. d/o Angus 'Dubh' C, qv, and Mary Beaton, qv. To Mabou, Inverness Co, NS, ca 1805. m Alexander MacDonald, who was drowned at Broad Cove. **MP 256**.

1050 CAMERON, Anne, jr. From Lochaber, INV. d/o Angus 'Dubh' C, qv, and Mary Beaton, qv. To Mabou, Inverness Co, NS, ca 1805. m — MacDonald, South River, Antigonish Co. **MP256**.

1051 CAMERON, Archibald. Served in 82nd Regt and was gr 150 acres in Pictou Co, NS, 1784. **HPC App F**.

1052 CAMERON, Archibald, 1769–1861. From ARL. bro/o Charles C, qv. To Miramichi, Northumberland Co, NB, 1802. Wife Mary, 1769–1854, with him, ch: 1. Archibald; 2. John; 3. Donald; 4. Hugh; 5. Alexander; 6. James; 7. Murdock; 8. Dougald, dy. **DC 4 Dec 1978**.

1053 CAMERON, Archibald. From Lochaber, INV. To Kouchibouguac, Kent Co, NB, <1830. Farmer. m Mary Cameron, qv. Son Hugh. **DC 15 Nov 1980**.

1054 CAMERON, Archibald. From Lochgilphead, ARL. Rel to Hector C, qv. To Westminster Twp, Middlesex Co, ONT, 1836. **PCM 52**.

1055 CAMERON, Betsy, 1772–1826. Prob from INV. d/o James and Margaret C. To Pictou Co, NS. Bur Old Elgin. **DC 20 Nov 1976**.

1056 CAMERON, Catherine. From Glengarry, INV. To Montreal, QUE, ex Fort William, 3 Jul 1802; stld E ONT. **MCM 1/4 24**.

1057 CAMERON, Catherine. From Lochaber, INV. d/o Donald C, soldier, and Christina Cameron. To South East Mabou, Inverness Co, NS, 1831; prob later to Antigonish Co. Wife of Angus MacDonald, qv. **HCA 194; MP 554**.

1058 CAMERON, Catherine. From INV. To QUE ca 1830, and stld Madoc Twp, Hastings Co, ONT. m James Ellis, stonemason. **DC 18 Nov 1981**.

1059 CAMERON, Catherine, ca 1816–9 Jun 1894. From ARL. To QUE, <1850, and bur Flodden Station. m Donald McLean, qv. **MGC 15 Jul 1980**.

1060 CAMERON, Charles. From ARL. bro/o Archibald C, qv. To Miramichi, Northumberland Co, NB, 1802. m 26 Jul 1808, Sarah Russell. **DC 4 Dec 1978**.

1061 CAMERON, Christiana. From Lochbroom, ROC. d/o Alexander C, qv. To Pictou, NS, on the *Hector*, ex Loch Broom, arr 17 Sep 1773. m Alexander McKay, qv. **HPC App C**.

1062 CAMERON, David, 1804-72. From PER. To CAN, 1838, and became an emp of HBCo. Superintendent of coal mines at Nanaimo, Vancouver Is, BC; Judge of Supreme Court, 1853. **MDB 104**.

1063 CAMERON, Donald. From INV. To Pictou, NS, on the *Hector*, ex Loch Broom, arr 17 Sep 1773. Discharged soldier, 78th Regt, and pioneer settler, East

River, where he was drowned. m Mary McDonald, qv, ch: 1. John; 2. Hugh; 3. Mary. The family being RCs moved to Antigonish Co. **HPC App A and C**.

1064   CAMERON, Donald. To Pictou Co, NS, <26 Aug 1783; gr 100 acres on west side of East River. **HPC App A**.

1065   CAMERON, Donald. From Urquhart par, INV. bro/o Finlay C, qv, and Samuel C, qv. Served in 84th Regt and gr 150 acres on East River of Pictou, NS, 1784. ch: 1. Donald; 2. Duncan, drummer-boy in 84th; 3. Alexander; 4. Mary. **SG iii/4 98; CP 51; HPC App G**.

1066   CAMERON, Donald. From INV. To Pictou Co, NS, 1801; stld Fraser's Mountain. Farmer. Son Alexander. **HNS iii 231**.

1067   CAMERON, Donald, b ca 1778. To Western Shore, Inverness Co, NS, 1808. Farmer, m, ch. **CBC 1818**.

1068   CAMERON, Donald, b ca 1750. From Kilmorack, INV. To Pictou Co, NS, 1801. Gr 300 acres, 1816. **NSN 17/3**.

1069   CAMERON, Donald. From Kilmorack, INV. To Pictou, NS, on the *Dove*, ex Fort William, Jun 1801. Tenant. Wife Katherine with him, ch: 1. Margaret; 2. Catherine; 3. James, aged 13; 4. Hugh, aged 11, 5. Isobel, aged 7. **PLD**.

1070   CAMERON, Donald. From Drimnasallie, Fort William, INV. To Montreal, QUE, ex Fort William, 3 Jul 1802; stld E ONT. **MCM 1/4 23**.

1071   CAMERON, Donald. From Kenlocharkaig, INV. To Montreal, QUE, ex Fort William, 3 Jul 1802; stld E ONT. Wife with him and 2 ch. **MCM 1/4 24**.

1072   CAMERON, Donald. From Kirktown, INV. To Montreal, QUE, ex Fort William, 3 Jul 1802; stld E ONT. **MCM 1/4 26**.

1073   CAMERON, Donald. To Pictou, NS, poss 1802. Dau Jane, d 1868. **NSN 19/1**.

1074   CAMERON, Donald, b ca 1762. From Kilmorack, INV. Poss s/o Hugh C. Soldier, 1776-84, 1809, 1814-15, sometime of 84th and 79th Regts, and was wounded at Waterloo. To Pictou, NS, 1816, and stld West River, where gr 300 acres. m Margaret, d/o David McKenzie, ch: 1. William; 2. Hugh. **SG xxvi/1 23; DC 31 Mar 1979**.

1075   CAMERON, Donald, ca 1803–15 Aug 1837. From Rynatine, Abernethy, INV. s/o Nathaniel C, farmer, and Marjory Grant. To ONT. **Ts Abernethy**.

1076   CAMERON, Donald. From Lochaber, INV. s/o John C. To Inverness Co, NS, 1825; stld River Denys. Farmer. m Betsy, d/o Ewen Cameron, ch: 1. John Donald, 1830–1916; 2. Ann; 3. Alexander; 4. Isable. **MP ii 117**.

1077   CAMERON, Donald. Prob from INV. bro/o Peter C, qv. Led about 670 highlanders to QUE and to Glengarry Co, ONT, 1821-24. Gr land in Thorah and Eldon Twps, 1826, but was impeded in his desire to bring in emigrants because of a settlement within one year clause imposed by the Executive Council, which resulted in disputes. **EC 9; DC 21 Mar 1980**.

1078   CAMERON, Donald, 1793–1823. From Kilmichael-Glassary, ARL. To Caledon Twp, Peel Co, ONT,

<1840. Wife Christina McLeven, qv, with him. **DC 21 Apr 1980**.

1079   CAMERON, Donald, b 1800. From Balemore, North Uist, INV. To East Williams Twp, Middlesex Co, ONT, <1850. m Catherine McLellan who d in Scotland, ch: 1. Kate, b 1826; 2. John, b 1828; 3. Ann, b 1829; 4. Rachel; 5. Ewen, b 1834. **PCM 43**.

1080   CAMERON, Donald Roy. To Pictou Co, NS, prob <1790; stld on east branch of East River. Farmer. **PAC 201**.

1081   CAMERON, Dougald, 1810–23 Jul 1870. From Lochaber, INV. s/o Alexander C. To Lochaber, Antigonish Co, NS, <8 Jan 1840, m Mary McEachern, 1822-94. Son Archibald, 1845–1915. **DC 9 Feb 1981**.

1082   CAMERON, Duncan, d 1838. Prob from Glenmoriston, INV. bro/o John Dougald C, qv, and Janet C, qv. To York Co, ONT, 1801. Merchant, and commanded the York Volunteers, 1812. Provincial Secretary, 1817-38. **MDB 104**.

1083   CAMERON, Duncan. From Achnacarry, INV. Prob rel to John C, qv. To Montreal, QUE, ex Fort William, 3 Jul 1802; stld E ONT. **MCM 1/4 26**.

1084   CAMERON, Duncan. From Drimnasallie, Fort William, INV. To Montreal, QUE, ex Fort William, 3 Jul 1802; stld E ONT. **MCM 1/4 26**.

1085   CAMERON, Duncan. Prob from Morven, ARL. To Chambly, QUE, <1804. By wife Mary had son John, b 1804. **DC 15 Jul 1974**.

1086   CAMERON, Duncan. From Dull, PER. To Montreal, QUE, on the *Curlew*, ex Greenock, 21 Jul 1818; stld prob Beckwith Twp, Lanark Co, ONT. Wife Margaret with him, ch: 1. Isabella, b 1804; 2. Donald, b 1813. **BCL**.

1087   CAMERON, Duncan, d 1842. To ONT ca 1836; stld York Mills, Toronto. Ret as Lt Col of 79th Regt in 1820, and in 1838 commanded 1st Regt North York Militia. ch. **MDB 104**.

1088   CAMERON, Duncan. From Is South Uist, INV. To East Williams Twp, Middlesex Co, ONT, ca 1849. Res latterly in MI. **PCM 44**.

1089   CAMERON, Elizabeth. From Killin, PER. To QUE, ex Greenock, summer 1815; stld ONT. Wife of Hugh Fraser, qv. **SEC 4**.

1090   CAMERON, Emily, d 2 Mar 1858. From ARL. To NB 1802. m Farquhar McRae, qv, and d Bay du Vin, Northumberland Co. **DC 14 Jan 1980**.

1091   CAMERON, Ewen. From Kinlochmoiar, INV. To Pictou, NS, on the *Dove*, ex Fort William, Jun 1801. Farmer. ch: 1. Roderick; 2. Eliza, aged 14; 3. Mary, aged 4; 4. Margaret; 5. Christian, aged 1 ½. **PLD**.

1092   CAMERON, Ewen, ca 1800–28 Apr 1897. From Is Skye, INV. To PEI 1829; stld Point Prim, Queens Co. m Ann MacDonald, and had, prob with other ch: 1. Roderick, master mariner; 2. Alexander, master mariner; 3. Jessie. **HP 35**.

1093   CAMERON, Ewen. From Is Skye, INV. To Cape Mabou, Inverness Co, NS, <1840; later to PEI. ch: 1. Murdock; 2. Michael; 3. Mary; 4. Sara; 5. Effie. **MP 225**.

1094 CAMERON, Ewen Morley, 4 Apr 1787–15 Jan 1888. From Fort William, INV. To Port Stanley, Elgin Co, ONT, 1819. ch: 1. Ewen Morley; 2. Charles; 3. Alexander. **DC 13 Aug 1974**.

1095 CAMERON, Finlay. From Urquhart and Glenmoriston par, INV. bro/o Donald C, qv, and Samuel C, qv. To CAN <1776. Joined 84th Regt and on discharge, 1784, was gr 400 acres on east side of East River. Drowned soon afterwards. ch. **SG iii/4 98; HPC App G**.

1096 CAMERON, Finlay. From Lochbroom, ROC. To Pictou, NS, on the *Dove*, ex Fort William, Jun 1801. Labourer. **PLD**.

1097 CAMERON, Finlay. From Dull par, PER. To Montreal, QUE, on the *Curlew*, ex Greenock, 21 Jul 1818; stld prob Beckwith Twp, Lanark Co, ONT. Wife Janet with him. **BCL**.

1098 CAMERON, Hector. From Lochgilphead, ARL. Rel to Archibald C, qv. To Westminster Twp, Middlesex Co, ONT, 1836. **PCM 52**.

1099 CAMERON, Hugh. From Lochaber, INV. To Antigonish Co, NS, prob <1800. Uncle of Bishop John Cameron. **MP 265**.

1100 CAMERON, Hugh. From Kilmorack, INV. To Pictou, NS, on the *Dove*, ex Fort William, Jun 1801. Farmer. **PLD**.

1101 CAMERON, Hugh. From Kiltarlity, INV. To Pictou, NS, on the *Dove*, ex Fort William, Jun 1801. Wife Ann with him, ch: 1. Mary, aged 8; 2. James, aged 3. **PLD**.

1102 CAMERON, Hugh, 1801–10 Jan 1882. From INV. To Centerdale, Pictou Co, NS, 1803. m 31 Jul 1832, Elizabeth McIntosh, 1809-89, ch: 1. John A, b 15 Jun 1833; 2. Samuel, b 1 Nov 1834; 3. John, b 4 Jul 1836; 4. Donald, b 14 Apr 1838; 5. Helen, b 30 Apr 1840; 6. William Alexander, b 15 Apr 1842; 7. David McIntosh, b 4 May 1844; 8. Hugh, b 18 Jun 1847. **PAC 33**.

1103 CAMERON, Hugh. From Lochaber, INV. To Montreal, QUE, but stld Finch Twp, Stormont Co, ONT, 1808. Son Duncan. **SDG 84**.

1104 CAMERON, Hugh. From Lochaber, INV. s/o Dougald and Jane C. To Antigonish Co, NS, prob <1810. m Margaret Gillis, ch: 1. Christy; 2. Dougald, b 1802; 3. Catherine; 4. John; 5. Hugh Og. **HCA 85**.

1105 CAMERON, Hugh. From Lochaber, INV. s/o Allan C, qv. To NS <1810; stld South River, Antigonish Co. m Jane McMillan, ch: 1. Allan; 2. John; 3. Margaret; 4. Jessie; 5. Katie Bell. **HCA 85**.

1106 CAMERON, Isobel, b ca 1789. From Kilmorack, INV. To Pictou, NS, on the *Dove*, ex Fort William, Jun 1801. **PLD**.

1107 CAMERON, Isobel. From Kilmorack, INV. To Pictou, NS, on the *Dove*, ex Fort William, Jun 1801. Spinster. **PLD**.

1108 CAMERON, Isabel. From Lochaber, INV. To Inverness Co, NS, prob 1816. Wife of Hugh McMaster, qv. **CBC 1818; WLC**.

1109 CAMERON, James. Prob from INV. To East River, Pictou Co, NS, <18 Dec 1797. Discharged soldier, 84th Regt, and gr 300 acres. **HPC App H**.

1110 CAMERON, James. From Kiltarlity, INV. To Pictou, NS, on the *Dove*, ex Fort William, Jun 1801. Wife Janet with him, ch: 1. James, aged 6; 2. Donald, aged 2. **PLD**.

1111 CAMERON, James, b 1793. To Pictou, NS, 1815; res Mount Thom, 1816. Sawyer, m with 2 ch, and poor. **INS 39**.

1112 CAMERON, James. To Springville, Pictou Co, NS, prob <1815. Son James. **PAC 34**.

1113 CAMERON, James, ca 1817–28 Jan 1851. Neph of Angus C, qv, from BAN. To Montreal, QUE, 1817. Clerk with HBCo at Timiskaming and became a chief trader in 1849. He d at Kirkmichael, BAN, SCT. **MDB 105**.

1114 CAMERON, James. Poss from ARL. To Metcalfe Twp, Middlesex Co, ONT, 1854. Farmer and magistrate. ch: 1. Alexander; 2. Mary J, res Strathroy; 3. James W. **PCM 26**.

1115 CAMERON, Jane, ca 1760–2 Mar 1828. From Strathglass, INV. To Pictou, NS. m William Fraser. Bur Old Elgin. **DC 20 Mar 1976**.

1116 CAMERON, Janet. Prob from Glenmoriston, INV. sis/o Duncan C, qv, and John Dougald C, qv. To ONT prob 1801 and res at Gore Vale, nr Toronto, 1838. **MDB 104**.

1117 CAMERON, Janet. From Glenelg, INV. To QUE, summer 1815; stld prob E ONT. Wife of John McRae, qv. **SEC 5**.

1118 CAMERON, Janet, ca 1791–6 May 1869. From Aberfeldy, PER. To ONT 1817, and d Breadalbane, Lochiel Twp, Glengarry Co. m James Lothian, qv. **DC 27 Oct 1979**.

1119 CAMERON, Janet, b ca 1823. Poss from INV. Niece of Lachlan C, qv. To Eldon Twp, Victoria Co, ONT, 1826. m Ronald Gilchrist, ch: 1. Mary; 2. Betsy; 3. James; 4. Margaret; 5. John; 6. Hugh; 7. Donald; 8. Ann; 9. Catherine; 10. Jessie. **EC 36**.

1120 CAMERON, Janet. From Fort Augustus, INV. To Greenfield, Kenyon Twp, Glengarry Co, ONT, 1837. m Ranald McIsaac McDonald, qv. **DC 14 Jun 1968**.

1121 CAMERON, Jean, b 1780. From Is Rum, ARL. To Gut of Canso, Cape Breton Is, NS, on the *Saint Lawrence*, ex Tobermory, 11 Jul 1828. **SLL**.

1122 CAMERON, Jenet. From Kilmorack, INV. To Pictou Co, NS, on the *Dove*, ex Fort William, Jun 1801. Spinster. **PLD**.

1123 CAMERON, John, b ca 1748. To Western Shore, Inverness Co, NS, 1800. Widower and farmer. **CBC 1818**.

1124 CAMERON, John, b ca 1787. From Kilmorack, INV. To Pictou, NS, on the *Dove*, ex Fort William, Jun 1801. Labourer. **PLD**.

1125 CAMERON, John. From Kenmore, PER. To Montreal, QUE, ex Fort William, 3 Jul 1802; stld E ONT. Wife with him, ch: 1. John; 2. Donald; 3. Ewen. **MCM 1/4 24**.

1126 CAMERON, John. From Glentureet, INV. bro/o Angus C, qv. To Montreal, QUE, ex Fort William, 3 Jul 1802; stld E ONT. **MCM 1/4 24**.

1127   CAMERON, John. From Glenelg, INV. To Montreal, QUE, ex Fort William, 3 Jul 1802; stld E ONT. **MCM 1/4 26**.

1128   CAMERON, John. From Achnacarry, INV. Prob rel to Duncan C, qv. To Montreal, QUE, ex Fort William, 3 Jul 1802; stld E ONT. Wife with him. **MCM 1/4 26**.

1129   CAMERON, John. Poss from Is Muck, INV. To Montreal, QUE, ex Fort William, 3 Jul 1802; stld E ONT. **MCM 1/4 26**.

1130   CAMERON, John. From Kinlochiel, INV. To Montreal, QUE, ex Fort William, INV; stld E ONT, 1802. **MCM 1/4 26**.

1131   CAMERON, John 'Donn'. From Lochaber, INV. s/o Angus 'Dubh' C, qv, and Mary Beaton. To South West Mabou, Inverness Co, NS, 1805. m Anne McKillop, qv, ch: 1. Angus; 2. Donald; 3. Archibald; 4. Alexander; 5. Duncan; 6. John; 7. Mary; 8. Catherine; 9. Margaret. **MP 249**.

1132   CAMERON, John, b ca 1746. From ARL. To Charlottetown, PEI, on the *Rambler*, ex Tobermory, 20 Jun 1806. Wife Ann, aged 60, with him, ch: 1. Donald, aged 30; 2. Alexander, aged 20; 3. Sara, aged 19; 4. Ann, aged 17; 5. Allan, aged 12; 6. Flora, aged 15; 7. Angus, aged 10; 8. Donald, b 1806.   **PLR**.

1133   CAMERON, John, b ca 1785. To Charlottetown, PEI, on the *Rambler*, ex Tobermory, 20 Jun 1806. **PLR**.

1134   CAMERON, John, b 1778. To Inverness Co, NS, 1806; stld nr Port Hood. Farmer, ch. **CBC 1818**.

1135   CAMERON, John 'Ruadh'. From Achintee, Fort William, INV. To Antigonish Co, NS, 1801. m Christy MacDonald, qv, and had, poss with other ch: 1. Dugald; 2. Rev John, 1826–1910, Bishop of Antigonish; 3. Jane; 4. Allan. **HCA 58, 87**.

1136   CAMERON, John. To Pictou Co, NS, 1815; res Lower Settlement. Labourer, 1816. **INS 37**.

1137   CAMERON, John, b 1806. From Lochaber, INV. To Lochaber, Antigonish Co, NS, 1816. Wife Jane with him. **DC 9 Feb 1981**.

1138   CAMERON, John. From Breadalbane, PER. To Côte St Charles, QUE, 1815; thence to East Hawkesbury, Prescott Co, ONT. Wife with him, ch: 1. Johanna; 2. Marjorie; 3. Annie; 4. Eliza; 5. Marjorie, yr; 6. Annie; 7. Katherine; 8. Margaret; 9. Colin; 10. John; 11. Dougal. **SMB**.

1139   CAMERON, John, 1796–1828. To Black River, Northumberland Co, NB, prob <1820. Farmer, lumberman and commissioner for highways. m ca 1827, Mary McNaughton, ch. **DC 21 Mar 1981**.

1140   CAMERON, John. From Lochaber, INV. s/o Donald C. To Mabou, Inverness Co, NS, ca 1826. Farmer, and teacher of Hillsborough-Mabou Combined School. m Ann, d/o John MacLean, Strathlorne, ch: 1. Ann, b 1845; 2. Murdoch, b 1847; 3. Angus, b 1850, d in AUS; 4. Catherine, b 1853; 5. Donald, 1856–1920, said to have inherited property in SCT. **MP ii 92**.

1141   CAMERON, John. From Johnstone, RFW. s/o Duncan C. To Cape Breton Co, NS, <1830. **SH**.

1142   CAMERON, John 'Ruadh'. Prob from Lochaber,

INV. To Antigonish Co, NS, prob 1830. m Miss McMillan, ch: 1. Donald; 2. Mrs Angus McDougall; 3. Mrs Duncan 'Ruadh' Stewart; 4. Mrs James Stewart; 5. Mrs Donald Murray; 6. Mrs MacInnes. **HCA 85**.

1143   CAMERON, John 'Squire'. To Antigonish Co, NS, ca 1830. m Margaret McMillan, qv, ch: 1. Donald; 2. John. **HCA 85**.

1144   CAMERON, John. From Is Tyree, ARL. To Cape Breton Is, NS, 1831. Wife Janet McCallum, qv, with him, ch. **DC 4 Mar 1981**.

1145   CAMERON, John. Prob from Lochaber, INV. To Lobo Twp, Middlesex Co, ONT, 1838. ch: 1. Malcolm; 2. John. **PCM 40**.

1146   CAMERON, John 'Roy'. From Is Benbecula, INV. To East Williams Twp, Middlesex Co, ONT, 1848. **PCM 44**.

1147   CAMERON, John. From Is South Uist, INV. To West Williams Twp, Middlesex Co, ONT, 1849; stld Centre Road. **PCM 48**.

1148   CAMERON, John. From Glenelg, INV. To ONT ca 1850; stld prob Glengarry Co, ONT. m Mary McPhee, ch: 1. Jessie; 2. Margaret; 3. Donald. **DC 27 Jul 1982**.

1149   CAMERON, John Dugald, ca 1777–21 Mar 1857. From Glenmoriston, INV. To Nipigon, Algoma Dist, ONT, 1795. Emp with NWCo and was in charge of Lake Winnipeg dist, 1811. Partner, 1813. He was a chief factor with HBCo >1821. Ret to Grafton, Northumberland Co, ONT, 1844, ch by an Indian woman. **MDB 105**.

1150   CAMERON, John McAlpine. To Dundas, Wentworth Co, ONT, <1822. Emp with the Canada Company. m Nancy Foy. Son Sir Matthew Crooks, 1822-87, lawyer and Conservative politician. **BNA 604; MDB 107**.

1151   CAMERON, Julia, 15 Oct 1829–15 Jun 1909. From Is Mull, ARL. To QUE, prob <1850. m Peter MacNaughton, qv. **MGC 15 Jul 1980**.

1152   CAMERON, Lachlan. From Lochaber, INV. s/o Dougald and Jane C. To Antigonish Co, NS, prob <1810. m Ann McGillivray, ch: 1. Dougald; 2. John; 3. Lachlan; 4. Margaret; 5. Ann. **HCA 87**.

1153   CAMERON, Lachlan, b ca 1796. Poss from INV. To Eldon Twp, Victoria Co, ONT, 1826. Discharged soldier, 26th Regt, later farmer and landowner. m Ann Gilchrist, ch: 1. Jane, b 1833; 2. Betsy, b 1835; 3. Euphemia, b 1837; 4. John, b 1839; 5. Margaret, b 1840; 6. Hugh, b 1843; 7. Nancy, b 1847; 8. Ann. **EC 35**.

1154   CAMERON, Lachlan, ca 1819–ca 1870. Prob from INV. Neph of Lachlan C, qv. To Eldon Twp, Victoria Co, ONT, 1826. Farmer. m Flora Gillespie, ch: 1. Mary, b 1847; 2. Sarah; 3. Lachlan; 4. Hugh; 5. Dougald; 6. Archie; 7. Sandy; 8. John; 9. Jessie; 10. Jane; 11. Flora. **EC 36**.

1155   CAMERON, Malcolm. From Is North Uist, INV. To West Williams Twp, Middlesex Co, ONT, ca 1848; stld Con 10. **PCM 48**.

1156   CAMERON, Malcolm. From Is Benbecula, INV. To East Williams Twp, Middlesex Co, ONT, 1848. **PCM 44**.

1157   CAMERON, Margaret. From Kilmorack, INV. Poss

rel to Hugh C, qv. To Pictou, NS, on the *Dove*, ex Fort William, Jun 1801. **PLD**.

1158 CAMERON, Margaret. From Glengarry, INV. To Montreal, QUE, ex Fort William, 3 Jul 1802; stld E ONT. **MCM 1/4 26**.

1159 CAMERON, Margaret, b ca 1755. From Kilmallie par, INV. To Montreal, QUE, ex Fort William, arr Sep 1802; stld Lachine, and later in Stormont Co, ONT. Wife of Allan McMillan of Glenpeanmore, qv, whom she m 1774. **MCM 1/4 12**.

1160 CAMERON, Margaret. From Fincastle, PER, but b INV. To NS, 1803; stld Antigonish Co. m (i) Charles Gordon, who d SCT, leaving ch s Donald, qv, stld PEI. m (ii) — Robertson. **BP 10**.

1161 CAMERON, Margaret. From Lochaber, INV. d/o Angus 'Dubh' C, qv, and Mary Beaton, qv. To Mabou, Inverness Co, NS, ca 1805. m — MacGillivray. **MP 256**.

1162 CAMERON, Margaret, b ca 1797. From Kilmorack, INV. Poss rel to Hugh C, qv. To Pictou, NS, on the *Dove*, ex Fort William, Jun 1801. **PLD**.

1163 CAMERON, Marion. From Glenelg, INV. To QUE, ex Greenock, summer 1815; stld prob Lanark Co, ONT. Wife of Kenneth McRae, qv. **SEC 8**.

1164 CAMERON, Marjery. Prob from Glengarry, INV. To Montreal, QUE, 1802; stld E ONT. **MCM 1/4 24**.

1165 CAMERON, Mary. From Letterfinlay, Loch Lochy, INV. To Montreal, QUE, 1802; stld E ONT. **MCM 1/4 23**.

1166 CAMERON, Mary. Prob from Glengarry, INV. To Montreal, QUE, 1802; stld E ONT. **MCM 1/4 24**.

1167 CAMERON, Mrs Mary, b ca 1756. To Charlottetown, PEI, on the *Rambler*, ex Tobermory, 20 Jun 1806. Poss mother of John C, qv. **PLR**.

1168 CAMERON, Mary. From Lochaber, INV. To Kouchibouguac, Kent Co, NB, <1830. m Archibald Cameron, qv, her cous. **DC 15 Nov 1980**.

1169 CAMERON, Mary, 1813-91. Poss from INV. To Williamstown, Glengarry Co, ONT, <19 Nov 1841, when m Donald McMaster. m (ii) Angus MacDonald. **DC 14 Aug 1979**.

1170 CAMERON, Mary, ca 1793–ca 1855. From Killearnan, ROC. To Ashfield Twp, Huron Co, ONT, 1845. Wife of Murdoch MacDonald, qv. **DC 15 Jul 1979**.

1171 CAMERON, Nancy, b ca 1815. To Huron Twp, Bruce Co, ONT, <1853. m Hugh Cameron, farmer. **DC 18 May 1982**.

1172 CAMERON, Peter. Prob from INV. bro/o Donald C, land agent, qv. To Eldon Twp, Victoria Co, ONT, prob <1830. **DC 21 Mar 1980**.

1173 CAMERON, Samuel. From Urquhart and Glenmoriston, INV. bro/o Donald C, qv, and Finlay C, qv. Served in 84th Regt, and on discharge was gr 300 acres on west side of East River, Pictou Co, NS, ca 1784. Son Samuel, also of 84th, gr 100 acres on east side of river. **HPC App G; SG iii/4 98**.

1174 CAMERON, Samuel. From Lochaber, INV. s/o John C. To Inverness Co, NS, prob <1825; stld River Denys. **MP ii 117**.

1175 CAMERON, Samuel. From Lochaber, INV. To Lobo Twp, Middlesex Co, ONT, ca 1832. ch: 1. John; 2. Duncan; 3. Donald; 4. Alexander; 5. Mrs. McNeil. **PCM 40**.

1176 CAMERON, Sara. From Lochaber, INV. d/o Angus 'Dubh' C, qv, and Mary Beaton, qv. To Little Judique, Inverness Co, NS, poss 1805. Wife of Donald Beaton, qv. **MP 256**.

1177 CAMERON, Thomas, 10 Jan 1766–24 Jun 1842. From Govan, Glasgow. s/o Lachland C. and Janet Hill. To QUE, 1821; stld Elmsley Twp, Lanark Co, ONT. m Agnes Hill, qv, ch: 1. Robert, b 27 May 1798; 2. Agnes, 1799–1823; 3. Janet, b 15 May 1801; 4. Mary, b 2 Apr 1803; 5. Margaret, b 21 Apr 1805; 6. Isabella, b 1 Jun 1808; 7. Hugh, 1810-12; 8. James, b 1 Apr 1813; 9. Hugh, b 4 May 1814; 10. James, yr, b 4 Dec 1816; 11. Christina, b 2 Feb 1821. **DC 17 May 1974**.

1178 CAMERON, William, 1756–24 Oct 1835. From INV. To NS, and stld East Forks, Middle River. m Christian Fraser, qv, ch: 1. John, 1799–1863; 2. William, alive 1826. **PAC 35**.

1179 CAMERON, William, b ca 1791. To Pictou, NS, 1815. Labourer, 1816. **INS 37**.

1180 CAMERON, William. Prob from INV. To Westminster Twp, Middlesex Co, ONT, <1840; res later Strathroy. **PCM 55**.

1181 CAMERON, William. Prob from Lochaber, INV. To Durham Co, ONT, poss <1850; stld Orono. Went later to Port Elgin, Bruce Co. m Johanna Stark. Son Donald Alexander, 1864–1925, banker. **DC 30 Aug 1977**.

1182 CAMPBELL, Adam Lothian. Poss from Breadalbane, PER. To ONT 1815. Wife Janet, ca 1782–3 Oct 1868, with him. Son Robert res Breadalbane, Lochiel Twp, Glengarry Co. **DC 27 Oct 1979**.

1183 CAMPBELL, Agnes, 1792–1885. From Lochgoilhead, ARL. d/o Archibald C. To QUE, ex Greenock, 28 Jun 1828; stld North Sherbrooke, Lanark Co, ONT. m John McDougall, qv. **DC 21 Jan 1960**.

1184 CAMPBELL, Agnes. Prob from Paisley, RFW. d/o — C. and — Hart. To St John, NB, <1825. **SH**.

1185 CAMPBELL, Alan, b 1795. Prob from Mull, ARL. To Mull River, Inverness Co, NS. m Mary McCallum, and had, prob with other ch: 1. Neil; 2. Norman. **NSN 27/190**.

1186 CAMPBELL, Alexander, b ca 1786. From Mull, ARL. To Charlottetown, PEI, on the *Clarendon*, ex Oban, 6 Aug 1808. Labourer. bro/o Sarah C, qv, and Mary C, qv. **CPL**.

1187 CAMPBELL, Alexander. Prob from ARL. s/o Mrs Isabella C, qv. To Aldborough Twp, Elgin Co, ONT, poss 1818. Farmer. Moved later to Huron Co. ch: 1. Dugald; 2. Mrs Angus McLarty. **PDA 64**.

1188 CAMPBELL, Alexander. From Glengarry, INV. To Antigonish Co, NS, prob <1820. ch: 1. John; 2. Angus; 3. Donald; 4. Alexander; 5. Mrs McGee. **HCA 91**.

1189 CAMPBELL, Alexander. Prob from LKS. To QUE 1821; stld Lanark Co, ONT. **HCL 74**.

1190 CAMPBELL, Alexander, 1795–1884. From NAI. To Talbot Twp, Elgin Co, ONT, <1820. m Nancy McArthur, qv. **DC 24 Aug 1963**.

1191   CAMPBELL, Alexander. From Lochaber, INV. s/o Malcolm C. To Inverness Co, NS, 1821; stld Black River. Farmer. m Lucy Kennedy, qv, ch: 1. Malcolm; 2. Finlay; 3. Alexander; 4. Angus; 5. Donald; 6. Anne; 7. Mary; 8. Margaret; 9. Flora; 10. Catherine.   **MP 273**.

1192   CAMPBELL, Alexander, b 1808. From INV. bro/o John C, qv. To Pictou Co, NS, and stld Mount Thom.   **NSN 11/2**.

1193   CAMPBELL, Alexander. From Is Eigg, INV. To Glengarry Co, ONT, <1828; later to Victoria Co, and stld Eldon Twp.   **DC 21 Mar 1980**.

1194   CAMPBELL, Alexander. From Lochgilphead, ARL. To Lobo Twp, Middlesex Co, ONT, 1829. ch: 1. Duncan A; 2. Archibald; 3. Mrs Alexander Campbell.   **PCM 39**.

1195   CAMPBELL, Alexander, ca 1809–15 Oct 1879. From INV. To Pictou Co, NS, prob <1830; bur Hill Cemetery, West River Station. Wife Catherine, 1812–1901.   **DC 10 Feb 1980**.

1196   CAMPBELL, Alexander. Prob from ARL. To Eldon Twp, Victoria Co, ONT, <1830. Stonemason. ch: 1. James; 2. Peter; 3. John; 4. Alexander; 5. Duncan; 6. Donald; 7. Charles.   **DC 21 Mar 1980**.

1197   CAMPBELL, Alexander. From ARL. To East Williams Twp, Middlesex Co, ONT, 1831.   **PCM 1197**.

1198   CAMPBELL, Alexander, b 1814. From Roseneath, DNB. s/o Robert C, qv, and Jean McFarlane, qv. To Ekfrid Twp, Middlesex Co, ONT, 1833.   **PCM 32**.

1199   CAMPBELL, Alexander. From ARL. To QUE 1818; stld Metcalfe Twp, Middlesex Co, ONT, 1835. Mechanic.   **PCM 24**.

1200   CAMPBELL, Alexander, 1810–27 Feb 1899. From Aberdeen. To Truro, Colchester Co, NS, prob <1840. Land surveyor, MLA. m Miss McNab, niece of Joseph Howe, and d Galt, Waterloo Co, ONT.   **MLA 53**.

1201   CAMPBELL, Alexander. From ARL. To Aldborough Twp, Elgin Co, ONT, 1840.   **PDA 67**.

1202   CAMPBELL, Alexander, 16 Jan 1806–26 Feb 1892. From Glasgow. s/o Peter C. To QUE, 1842; stld North Sherbrooke, Lanark Co, ONT. m Agnes, 1800-77. d/o Neil McVean, ch: 1. Mary; 2. Harriet; 3. Peter; 4. Agnes, dy.   **DC 21 Jan 1960**.

1203   CAMPBELL, Alexander, ca 1826–2 Dec 1909. From Is Skye, INV. s/o Archibald C. and Margaret McLean. To Broad Cove, Inverness Co, NS. Lawyer, farmer, merchant, and MLA. m (i) Mary, d/o John MacLean, Strathlorne; (ii) Ella, sis/o Principal Grant.   **MLA 53**.

1204   CAMPBELL, Alexander. To Pictou, NS, on the *Lady Gray*, ex Cromarty, arr 16 Jul 1841.   **DC 15 Jul 1979**.

1205   CAMPBELL, Alexander, b 17 Apr 1820. From SUT. s/o Donald C. To London, Middlesex Co, ONT, <1847. Builder, firm of Craig & Campbell. m 1 Jan 1847, Helen McPherson, qv, ch: 1. Lilias, b 13 Oct 1847; 2. Donald, b 23 Apr 1849; 3. James, b 27 Sep 1851; 4. Alexander, b 28 Dec 1852; 5. Lachlan, b 29 Jan 1855; 6. Elsie, b 7 Dec 1856; 7. Helen, b 7 Dec 1858; 8. John, b 14 Jul 1860; 9. Margaret, b 12 Apr 1862.   **DC 7 Apr 1980**.

1206   CAMPBELL, Alexander, d 1893. From PER. s/o Capt James C. of Glenfalloch. To Simcoe Co, ONT, prob <1850; moved to Mosa Twp, Middlesex Co.   **PCM 24**.

1207   CAMPBELL, Allan, b 1795. From Tenga, Kilninian and Kilmore par, Is Mull, ARL. s/o Hugh C. and Grace McColl. To Mull River, Inverness Co, NS, 1820. Farmer, storekeeper and lay preacher. m Mary McCallum, qv, ch: 1. Norman, qv; 2. Hugh, qv; 3. Neil, b 1830.   **MP ii 119, 413**.

1208   CAMPBELL, Angus, b 1809. From Is Rum, ARL. To Gut of Canso, Cape Breton Is, NS, on the *Saint Lawrence*, ex Tobermory, 11 Jul 1811.   **SLL**.

1209   CAMPBELL, Angus. To QUE on the *Elvira*, 1816; stld Lot 25, Con 9, Bathurst Twp, Lanark Co, ONT.   **HCL 234**.

1210   CAMPBELL, Angus, b ca 1770. To St Andrew's dist, Cape Breton Is, 1816. Farmer, m and ch.   **CBC 1818**.

1211   CAMPBELL, Angus, 1795–19 Apr 1901. From Applecross, ROC. To PEI 1818; later to Cape Breton Is, NS. Farmer. m Catherine Beaton, qv.   **DC 31 Jul 1961**.

1212   CAMPBELL, Angus. From Badenoch, INV. To QUE via New York, 1819; stld Ekfrid Twp, Middlesex Co, ONT, 1821. ch: 1. John, qv; 2. Malcolm; 3. Mrs John McIntosh.   **PCM 29**.

1213   CAMPBELL, Angus. From Lochaber, INV. To Glencoe, Inverness Co, NS, prob <1820. m Catherine Nicholson, qv, ch: 1. Duncan; 2. Elizabeth; 3. Isabel; 4. Anne; 5. Janet; 6. Catherine; 7. Margaret.   **MP 176**.

1214   CAMPBELL, Angus. From Lochaber, INV. To Mabou, Inverness Co, NS, prob <1820. ch: 1. John; 2. Donald; 3. Duncan; 4. Janet; 5. Marcella; 6. Mrs Duncan MacDonald; 7. Mrs Alexander Mackinnon.   **HCA 92**.

1215   CAMPBELL, Angus. From Lochaber, INV. s/o Malcolm C. To Inverness Co, NS, 1821; stld Black River. m Catherine MacDonald, qv, ch: 1. Malcolm; 2. Donald; 3. Angus; 4. Flora; 5. Catherine; 6. Mary; 7. Alexander.   **MP 281**.

1216   CAMPBELL, Angus. To Antigonish Co, NS, prob <1830; stld Brierly Brook. m Miss MacDonald, ch: 1. Alexander; 2. John; 3. Donald; 4. Margaret; 5. Mary; 6. Catherine; 7. Sarah.   **HCA 93**.

1217   CAMPBELL, Angus, 'An Gobha Ban.' Prob from Lochaber, INV. Rel to Archibald 'Brewer' C, qv. To Mabou, Inverness Co, NS, 1831. m Catherine MacDonald, qv, ch: 1. Alexander; 2. Janet; 3. Anne; 4. Sara.   **MP 291**.

1218   CAMPBELL, Angus. From Lochaber, INV. s/o Dougald C. and Mary Beaton. To South West Mabou Ridge, Inverness Co, NS, 1838. m Anne MacDonald, qv, ch: 1. Angus; 2. John; 3. Hugh; 4. Dougald; 5. Mary; 6. Catherine; 7. Anne; 8. Janet; 9. Alexander.   **MP 295**.

1219   CAMPBELL, Angus. From Lochaber, INV. To Antigonish Co, NS, <1840; later to Dunakin, Inverness Co. Piper. m Catherine, d/o John Campbell, ch: 1. John; 2. Donald; 3. Sara; 4. Patrick; 5. Dougald; 6. Charles; 7. John Og.   **MP 309**.

1220   CAMPBELL, Angus, b 1820. From Lochaber, INV. s/o Duncan C. and Anne MacKillop, qv. To Mabou, Inverness Co, NS. m 11 Sep 1854, Flora, d/o John MacDonald, ch: 1. Duncan; 2. Cassie; 3. Janet; 4. Mary. **MP 327**.

1221   CAMPBELL, Angus, ca 1794–12 Sep 1854. From Glenelg, INV. To Glengarry Co, ONT, <1844. m Mary Margaret McGinnis, qv. Dau Catherine. **MG 291**.

1222   CAMPBELL, Angus. From Is Eigg, INV. To Brantford, Brant Co, ONT, prob <1845. m Catherine MacEachern, qv. **MP 638**.

1223   CAMPBELL, Angus, 1834–14 Aug 1920. From South Dell, Ness par, Is Lewis, ROC. s/o Kenneth C, qv, and Gormelia McLeod. To QUE ca 1854. Served with HBCo in NWT for 7 years, and d Lingwick, Compton Co, QUE. m Catherine, d/o John McFarlane and Mary Morrison, ch: **DC 22 Jun 1979**.

1224   CAMPBELL, Ann. From Glenelg, INV. To QUE, ex Greenock, summer 1815; stld prob Lanark Co, ONT. Wife of Malcolm McLeod, qv. **SEC 7**.

1225   CAMPBELL, Ann. From Glenelg, INV. To QUE, ex Greenock, summer 1815; stld prob Lanark Co, ONT. Wife of Duncan McLellan, qv. **SEC 8**.

1226   CAMPBELL, Ann. From Killin, PER. To QUE, ex Greenock, on the *Atlas*, 12 Jul 1815; stld North Elmsley Twp, Lanark Co, ONT. Wife of Donald McDonald, qv. **SEC 4**.

1227   CAMPBELL, Ann, 12 May 1785–26 Mar 1874. From Tenga, Kilninian and Kilmore par, Is Mull, ARL. d/o Hugh C. and Grace McColl. To Inverness Co, NS, 1819. Wife of Parlan MacFarlane, qv. **MP 413**.

1228   CAMPBELL, Ann. From Is Tyree, ARL. d/o Dougald C, Saltcoats, AYR. To Lake Ainslie, Inverness Co, NS, 1820. Wife of Hugh McDonald, qv. **DC 23 Feb 1980**.

1229   CAMPBELL, Ann. Prob from ROC. To Pictou, NS, ca 1853. m Thomas Middleton Bain, qv. **HNS iii 95**.

1230   CAMPBELL, Annie, b 1800. From ARL. To ONT, 1818; stld Eldon Twp, Victoria Co, ONT. Wife of Archibald McMillan, qv. **EC 58**.

1231   CAMPBELL, Archibald, 1808–13 Mar 1898. From Lochaber, INV. To Pictou, NS, on the *Nymph*, ex Aberdeen, 1816. m 28 Jan 1839, Mary, d/o Donald Chisholm, ch. **NSN 25/123**.

1232   CAMPBELL, Archibald. From ARL. To Aldborough Twp, Elgin Co, ONT, prob 1818. Farmer. Son Archibald. **PDA 93**.

1233   CAMPBELL, Archibald. From Inveraray, ARL. To NFD <1820. m Barbara MacCorquodale, qv. Son Archibald, 1798–1845, West India merchant. **SG xi/1 14**.

1234   CAMPBELL, Archibald, 27 May 1784–3 Apr 1857. From Cosanrochaid, North Knapdale, ARL. d/o Donald C, dec, and Isabella McLellan, qv. To Lobo Twp, Middlesex Co, ONT, 1819; later to Caradoc Twp. Farmer. m Christian Graham, ch: 1-3. Duncan, Neil and Alexander, who did not come to CAN; 4. Isabel, b 1815; 5. Margaret; 6. James. m (ii) Isabella, d/o Dugal Morrison, ch: 7. Archibald M, b 1829; 8. Janette; 9. Donald; 10. Malcolm, stld Lot 23, Con 10, Caradoc

Twp; 11. John; 12. Mary, 1830-48. **PCM 36; DC 20 Jul 1982**.

1235   CAMPBELL, Archibald. To Lanark Co, ONT, 1821; stld Lot 6, Con 6, North Sherbrooke Twp. **HCL 74**.

1236   CAMPBELL, Archibald. From ARL. s/o John and Catherine C. To Eldon Twp, Victoria Co, ONT, 1830. **EC 38**.

1237   CAMPBELL, Archibald. To Antigonish Co, NS, <1830; stld Brierly Brook. m Mary Chisholm, ch: 1. Catherine; 2. Jessie; 3. Sarah; 4. Theresa; 5. John; 6. John; 7. Angus; 8. William. **HCA 93**.

1238   CAMPBELL, Archibald, ca 1804–22 Aug 1841. From Tayvallich, North Knapdale, ARL. bro/o Peter C. To ONT 1830. Wife Mary with him and inf dau Sarah. **DC 21 Mar 1974**.

1239   CAMPBELL, Archibald. Poss from Glenlyon, PER. bro/o John C. To ONT prob 1832. Son Joseph, miller, Vernon Twp, Muskoka Co. **DC 1 Aug 1975**.

1240   CAMPBELL, Archibald. From Killin, PER. s/o Hugh C. and Christian McEwen. To ONT 1833. **DC 21 Jul 1970**.

1241   CAMPBELL, Sir Archibald, 12 Mar 1769–6 Oct 1843. From PER. s/o Lt Archibald C, military officer, and Margaret Small. Served in British Army and distinguished himself in the Burmese War. Lt Gov of NB 1831-37. Knighted 1814, and cr Bart 1831. m Helen, d/o Capt John McDonald, 84th Regt, and had with other ch: 1. Rev Archibald, d 1831. 2. Sir John, 1807-55, 2nd Bart. **SN iii 694**.

1242   CAMPBELL, Archibald, 1814-94. Prob from ARL. bro/o Colin C, qv. To Caledon Twp, Peel Co, ONT, <1840. Wife Catherine Mackinnon, qv. **DC 21 Apr 1980**.

1243   CAMPBELL, Archibald, 1819-37. From Craignish, ARL. To Caledon Twp, Peel Co, ONT, <1840. **DC 21 Apr 1980**.

1244   CAMPBELL, Archibald. From Duirnish, Is Skye, INV. To Cape Breton Co, NS, <1840. Schoolmaster. m Matilda McLeod, qv, ch: 1. Rev Ewen, held ministries in Lewis; 2. Donald, drowned at sea; 3. Alexander, politician, Inverness Co, NS; 4. John Charles; 5. Christian; 6. Ann; 7. Margaret. *McLeod Muniments*; **FES vii 203**.

1245   CAMPBELL, Archibald 'Brewer.' Prob from Lochaber, INV. Rel to Angus 'An Gobha Ban' C, qv. To Mabou Coal Mines, Inverness Co, NS, <1835. m Margaret, d/o Donald MacDonald, ch: 1. Angus; 2. Donald; 3. Alexander; 4. Archibald; 5. Sara; 6. Mary; 7. Anne; 8. Ellen; 9. John. **MP 289**.

1246   CAMPBELL, Archibald. From ARL. Prob bro/o John C, qv. To Adelaide Twp, Middlesex Co, ONT, 1845; went later to Port Huron. Army officer during American Civil War. **PCM 28**.

1247   CAMPBELL, Catherine, ca 1766–26 May 1846. From Lochbroom, ROC. To Pictou Co, NS, <1810; bur Salt Springs. Wife of William McDonald, qv. **DC 22 Jun 1980**.

1248   CAMPBELL, Catherine. Poss from ARL. To QUE, ex Greenock, summer 1815; stld ONT. Wife of Peter McDougall, qv. **SEC 3**.

1249 CAMPBELL, Catherine. From Strathglass or Glen Urquhart, INV. d/o Flora C. To Pictou, NS, on the *Sarah*, ex Fort William, Jun 1801; stld Irish Mountain. Wife of John McMillan, qv. **PLS; CP 86**.

1250 CAMPBELL, Catherine. From Is Mull, ARL. d/o Hugh C, Tenga, Kilninian and Kilmore par, and Grace McColl. To Port Hood, Inverness Co, NS. 1803; stld later Mull River. Wife of John Livingstone, qv. **MP ii 240**.

1251 CAMPBELL, Catherine. From Kilmonivaig par, INV. d/o Dugald C. To South West River, Inverness Co, NS, 1805. Wife of Alexander MacDonald, qv. **MP 562**.

1252 CAMPBELL, Catherine, b ca 1765. From Kilfinichen, Is Mull, ARL. To Hudson Bay and Red River <1815. **RRS 25**.

1253 CAMPBELL, Catherine. From Is Muck, INV. To Cape Breton Is, NS, prob <1820. Wife of Lauchlin MacMillan, qv. **NSN 32/379**.

1254 CAMPBELL, Catherine, 1819–1901. From ARL. To Caledon Twp, Peel Co, ONT, <1840. Wife of James McBride, qv. **DC 21 Apr 1980**.

1255 CAMPBELL, Mrs Catherine. To ONT <1831. Widow. ch with her: 1. Peter; 2. Archie; 3. Neil; 4. John; 5. James; 6. Alister; 7. Sandy. **DC 16 Sep 1975**.

1256 CAMPBELL, Charles, b ca 1788. From Caliach, Kilmore, Is Mull, ARL. To Hudson Bay and Red River <1815. Pioneer settler. Wife Catherine Livingstone, qv, with him, and ch: 1. Mary, aged 2; 2. Alexander, inf. **RRS 24**.

1257 CAMPBELL, Charles. To Antigonish Co, NS, prob <1830; stld Brierly Brook. m Miss MacDonald, ch: 1. Daniel; 2. Kate; 3. Mary; 4. Alexander. **HCA 92**.

1258 CAMPBELL, Charles James, 6 Nov 1819–17 Apr 1906. From Is Skye, INV. s/o Capt John C. and Isabella McRae. To NS 1830; stld Victoria Co. Shipowner, officer of militia and MLA. m 1843, Jane Ingram, ch. **BNA 678; MLA 54**.

1259 CAMPBELL, Christian. From Killin, PER. To QUE, ex Greenock, summer 1815; stld ONT. Wife of Duncan McArthur, qv. **SEC 4**.

1260 CAMPBELL, Christian. From Killin, PER. To QUE, ex Greenock, summer 1815; stld ONT. Wife of John McDonald, qv. **SEC 4**.

1261 CAMPBELL, Christian, b ca 1778. To Pictou Co, NS, 1815; res Middle River, 1816. Servant. **INS 38**.

1262 CAMPBELL, Christian. From Comrie par, PER. To Montreal, QUE, on the *Curlew*, ex Greenock, 19 May 1818; stld Beckwith Twp, Lanark Co, ONT. Wife of Robert Ferguson, qv. **BCL; DC 29 Dec 1981**.

1263 CAMPBELL, Christian. Prob from PER. Poss wife of Peter C, qv. To McNab Twp, Renfrew Co, ONT, 1825. **DC 3 Jan 1980**.

1264 CAMPBELL, Christian. Prob from PER. Rel to Peter C, qv. To McNab Twp, Renfrew Co, ONT, 1825. **DC 3 Jan 1825**.

1265 CAMPBELL, Christina. From Is Harris, INV. To Cape Breton Is, NS, 1831. Wife of Norman McAskill, qv. **DC 19 Mar 1964**.

1266 CAMPBELL, Christina, ca 1784–23 Dec 1844. d/o Donald C, dec, and Isabella McLellan, qv. To Caradoc Twp, Middlesex Co, ONT, ca 1821. m Dugald Smith, qv. **PCM 35**.

1267 CAMPBELL, Christine. From ARL. d/o Alexander C. and Jean Wilson. To QUE on the *Earl of Buckinghamshire*, ex Greenock, 29th Apr 1821; stld Almonte Village, Ramsay Twp, Lanark Co, ONT. Wife of Lachlan McLean, qv, m 1804. **DC 8 Aug 1978**.

1268 CAMPBELL, Christy McArthur, d 1882. From Eneclate, Uig par, Is Lewis, ROC. d/o Malcolm C. alias McArthur, and Ann McLeod. To Winslow Twp, Compton Co, QUE, 1851; stld Stornoway. m Donald MacDonald, qv. **TFT 15; WLC**.

1269 CAMPBELL, Colin, 1752–1834. Born Inveraray, ARL. s/o David C. of Belmont, Corstorphine, WS, of the Balcardine family, and his first wife. To Shelburne Twp, NS, 1783; later to St Andrew's, Charlotte Co, NB. Loyalist from NY. Collector of Customs, Probate Judge and MLA, 1793–1818. m (i) 1794, Alice, d/o Robert Hogg, Shelburne, and wid/o Col Samuel Campbell, Wilmington, SC; m (ii) 1796, Elizabeth, d/o Richard Hardy, Shelburne. ch: 1. John, 1797–1870, MP Queen's Co, 1845-60; 2. Colin, 1798–1878, of Weymouth, NS, Notary Public. **MLA 54**.

1270 CAMPBELL, Colin, b 1758. From Rannoch, PER. To Charlottetown, PEI, on the *Clarendon*, ex Oban, 6 Aug 1808. Wife Catherine aged 45, with him, and ch: 1. Catherine, aged 20; 2. Margaret, aged 18; 3. Isobell, aged 16; 4. Mary, aged 14; 5. Janet, aged 11; 6. Elizabeth, aged 9; 7. Archibald, aged 4; 8. Christian, aged 1. **CPL**.

1271 CAMPBELL, Colin, b ca 1790. From ARL. To York Factory, Hudson Bay, on the *Edward & Anne* ex Stornoway, Lewis, ROC, arr 24 Sep 1811. Labourer and pioneer settler at Red River, 1812. **LSS 184; RRS 26; LSC 321**.

1272 CAMPBELL, Colin. From ARL, poss Is Islay. To ONT 1813; stld Nottawasaga, Simcoe Co, m and ch: 1. Colin, b 1820; 2. Alexander, b 1826; 3. Allan, b 1833. **DC 6 Apr 1982**.

1273 CAMPBELL, Colin, b 1790. To St Andrew's dist, Cape Breton Co, NS, 1817. Farmer, m, ch. **CBC 1818**.

1274 CAMPBELL, Colin. From PER, poss Killin. Prob s/o Duncan C, qv, and wife Kitty. To McNab Twp, Renfrew Co, ONT, 1825. **DC 3 Jan 1980**.

1275 CAMPBELL, Colin, d 1831. From PER, poss Dull par. To Osgoode Twp, Carleton Co, ONT, <1831. Farmer. Killed while felling a tree. m Margaret Dow, qv. Dau Margaret, 1832–1914. **DC 1 Aug 1975**.

1276 CAMPBELL, Sir Colin, ca 1776–13 Jun 1847. From ARL. s/o John C. of Melfort and Colina Campbell. Held several staff appointments in the British Army, and with the rank of Maj-Gen was in 1833 app Governor of NS. Forced to resign and was recalled 1840. KCB, 1814. **BNA 507; MDB 108**.

1277 CAMPBELL, Colin. Prob from ARL. bro/o Archibald C, 1814-94, qv. To Caledon Twp, Peel Co, ONT, <1840. **DC 21 Apr 1980**.

1278 CAMPBELL, Colin. From Bornish, Is South Uist, INV. To West Williams Twp, Middlesex Co, ONT, 1849; stld Con 14. m Effie McIntyre. **PCM 48**.

1279 CAMPBELL, Daniel, b ca 1783. To Charlottetown, PEI, on the *Elizabeth & Ann*, ex Thurso, arr 8 Nov 1806. **PLEA**.

1280 CAMPBELL, Daniel, b ca 1788. From Rhu, DNB. To Hudson Bay, ca 1813, and prob to Red River. **RRS 13**.

1281 CAMPBELL, Daniel, d 1869. From ARL. To Caledon Twp, Peel Co, ONT, <1840. Wife Nancy, 1811-51. **DC 21 Apr 1980**.

1282 CAMPBELL, David, 1825–1907. From AYR. bro/o Thomas C, qv. To Brantford Twp, Brant Co, ONT, <1850; later in Oakland Twp. Farmer. m 25 Jun 1847, Ann Barr, qv, ch: 1. Janet Barr, 1848–1908; 2. Isabella, 1850-85; 3. James, 1852-83; 4. Annie, 1854–1944; 5. George, 1856–1934; 6. Jennie, 1861–1932; 7. David, 1864–1945; 8. John, 1868–1950; 9. Maggie, 1871–1951. **DC 5 Mar and 23 Sep 1980**.

1283 CAMPBELL, Donald. From Glenelg, INV. To QUE, 1796; stld Lot 36, Con 6, Lochiel Twp, Glengarry Co, ONT. **MG 211**.

1284 CAMPBELL, Donald, b ca 1782. From Is Mull, ARL. To Charlottetown, PEI, on the *Clarendon*, ex Oban, 8 Aug 1808. Labourer. m Ann McLean, qv, ch: 1. Alexander, b 8 Feb 1811; 2. Mary, b 7 Feb 1819. **CPL; DC 11 Apr 1981**.

1285 CAMPBELL, Donald. Prob from ARL. To Charlottetown, PEI, <1810. Wife Grace Stewart, qv, with him. Son Peter b 20 Sep 1810. **DC 11 Apr 1981**.

1286 CAMPBELL, Donald, b 1783. To Port Hood dist, Inverness Co, NS, 1812. Farmer, and widower by 1818. ch. **CBC 1818**.

1287 CAMPBELL, Donald, b ca 1765. From Glenelg, INV. To QUE, ex Greenock, summer 1815; stld prob Lanark Co, ONT. Farmer. Wife Catherine Morrison, qv, with him, and 6 ch. **SEC 7**.

1288 CAMPBELL, Donald. From PER. bro/o Duncan C, qv. To QUE on the *Lady of the Lake*, Sep 1816; stld Lot 3, Con 3, Drummond Twp, Lanark Co, ONT. Farmer. m Janet Robertson, qv. **HCL 20, 237**.

1289 CAMPBELL, Donald, b ca 1774. To Western Shore, Inverness Co, NS, 1817. Trader, m, ch. **CBC 1818**.

1290 CAMPBELL, Donald. From ARL. To Aldborough Twp, Elgin Co, ONT, prob 1818. Farmer. **PDA 93**.

1291 CAMPBELL, Donald, ca 1793–1 Feb 1870. From ROC. To Miramichi, Northumberland Co, NB, 1819, and d Tabusintac. **DC 4 Oct 1978**.

1292 CAMPBELL, Donald, 1823–18 Mar 1887. To St Anne's, Victoria Co, NS, poss <1850; moved ca 1860 to Waipu, NZ. m (i) Sarah, d/o Donald MacLeod, qv, and Ann Morrison, qv; m (ii) Catherine Campbell. **DC 20 Mar 1981**.

1293 CAMPBELL, Donald. From ARL. To QUE 1828; stld Lochabar, Ottawa Co. Farmer. **ELB 1**.

1294 CAMPBELL, Donald. From Lochgilphead, ARL. To Lobo Twp, Middlesex Co, ONT, 1829. ch: 1. John 'Ban'; 2. Janet; 3. Mary. **PCM 39**.

1295 CAMPBELL, Donald, b ca 1795. To Antigonish Co, NS, <1830. m Sarah MacDonald, ch: 1. John; 2. Donald. **HCA 90**.

1296 CAMPBELL, Donald. From North Uist, INV. To Inverness Co, NS, ca 1831. ch with him: 1. Murdoch, b 1806; 2. Edward, b 1808, stld Campbell's Mountain; 3. Ronald; 4. John; 5. Donald; 6. Annie. **DC 20 Jul 1960**.

1297 CAMPBELL, Donald. From North Knapdale, ARL. To Caradoc Twp, Middlesex Co, ONT, 1830. m Mary 'Ban' McNeil, ch: 1. John; 2. Duncan; 3. Donald; 4. Malcolm; 5. Mrs Malcolm Campbell; 6. Mary; 7. Isabella. **PCM 34**.

1298 CAMPBELL, Donald. From ARL. To East Williams Twp, Middlesex Co, ONT, 1833. **PCM 43**.

1299 CAMPBELL, Donald, b 1815. From Is Islay, ARL. To Eldon Twp, Victoria Co, ONT, ca 1835. Farmer and lumberman. m Catherine Smith, qv, ch: 1. John; 2. Kate; 3. Donald; 4. Mary; 5. Margaret; 6. Bessie; 7. Archie; 8. Malcolm. **EC 46**.

1300 CAMPBELL, Donald, ca 1804–19 Aug 1881. From Is Skye, INV. To Glengarry Co, ONT, <1838. m Meriom MacLeod, qv, ch: 1. Catherine, 1838–1924; 2. Kenneth; 3. Anne, 1844–1906; 4. Malcolm, 1852-82; 5. Sarah, d 1885; 6. John D; 7. Mary; 8. Flora; 9. Isabella, 1860-87. **MG 292**.

1301 CAMPBELL, Donald. From ARL. To Caradoc Twp, Middlesex Co, ONT, <1840; moved to Adelaide Twp. **PCM 28**.

1302 CAMPBELL, Donald. From Lochaber, INV. s/o Dugald C. and Mary Beaton. To Glencoe, Inverness Co, NS, ca 1840. m Catherine Hutchinson, ch: 1. Donald; 2. James; 3. Samuel; 4. Dougald; 5. Angus; 6. Thomas; 7. Jane; 8. Mary; 9. John. **MP 304**.

1303 CAMPBELL, Donald, b ca 1806. Prob from ARL. To Caledon Twp, Peel Co, ONT, ca 1841; moved to Bentinck Twp, Grey Co, and stld Lot 10, Con 1. Farmer. Wife Isabella with him and ch: 1. Robert; 2. John; 3. Colin; 4. Thomas; 5. Christina. Others b ONT: 6. Catherine; 7. Isabella; 8. Daniel; 9. George. **DC 18 May 1982**.

1304 CAMPBELL, Donald, b 1816. From Eneclate, Uig par, Is Lewis, ROC. s/o Malcolm C. alias McArthur, and Ann McLeod. To Winslow Twp, Compton Co, QUE, 1851. Township clerk. m Isabella McLeod, see ADDENDA, ch: 1. Effie, b 1840; 2. Margaret, b 1844; 3. Marion, b 1848; 4. Ann, b 1849; 5. Isabella, b 1854; 6. Kirsty, b 1856; 7. Donald John, b 1858; 8. Ewen McLean, b 1856. **WLC**.

1305 CAMPBELL, Donald. From Lochaber, INV. s/o Duncan C. and Anne MacKillop, qv. To Mabou, Inverness Co, NS, <1854. m Catherine, d/o Malcolm Campbell, ch: 1. Duncan; 2. Malcolm; 3. Donald; 4. Allan; 5. Alexander; 6. Catherine. **MP 328**.

CAMPBELL, Mrs Donald. See McLELLAN, Isabella.

1306 CAMPBELL, Sir Donald, 1800-50. From Polmont Bank, STI. s/o Angus C. and Lillias Buchanan. Succeeded his uncle, Niall C. as 16th Capt of Dunstaffnage, 1829, and was cr Bart, 1836. Lt Gov of PEI, 1847-50. m 1825, Caroline Eliza, d/o Sir William Plomer, Snaresbrook, ESS, ch, for which see *Burke's Landed Gentry*, 1972, iii 141.

1307 CAMPBELL, Donald D. From Lochranza, Is Arran, BUT. s/o Dugald C, qv, and Mary McKillop, qv. To

Inverness, Megantic Co, QUE, 1831; later to Listowel, Perth Co, ONT. Farmer, storekeeper and first mayor of Listowel. m Catherine Ferguson. **AMC 38**.

1308   CAMPBELL, Dougald, 1819-97. From Is Islay, ARL. Served in 79th Regt and discharged at QUE; stld Melbourne, Richmond Co. Tailor and piper. m Grace Beattie, qv, ch: 1. Alexander; 2. John; 3. Charles; 4. William; 5. Janet; 6. Annie; 7. Mary; 8. Emma. **MGC 2 Aug 1979**.

1309   CAMPBELL, Dougald B. From ARL. To Aldborough Twp, Elgin Co, ONT, 1846. **PDA 67**.

1310   CAMPBELL, Dugald, d 1857. From Knapdale, ARL. To QUE on the *Mars*, ex Tobermory, 28 Jul 1818; stld Aldborough Twp, Elgin Co, ONT. Farmer, and pioneered the Baptist Ch there. Son Archibald. **PCM 15; PDA 17, 24**.

1311   CAMPBELL, Dugald. From Lochranza, Is Arran, BUT. To Inverness, Megantic Co, QUE, 1831. Schoolteacher. m Mary McKillop, qv, ch: 1. Catherine, 1822-95; 2. Jane, qv; 3. Peter, qv; 4. Donald D, qv; 5. Dugald, jr, qv. **AMC 38; MAC 35**.

1312   CAMPBELL, Dugald, jr. From Lochranza, Is Arran, BUT. s/o Dugald C, qv, and Mary McKillop, qv. To Inverness, Megantic Co, QUE, 1831. m Eliza Layfield. **AMC 38**.

1313   CAMPBELL, Duncan, b ca 1781. To St Andrew's dist, Cape Breton Is, NS, ca 1805, and became a farmer. **CBC 1818**.

1314   CAMPBELL, Duncan, ca 1771-1854. Prob from Breadalbane, PER. bro/o Isabella C, qv. To Queens Co, PEI, poss 1808, when he m Margaret Dewar, qv. Son Peter, b 25 Dec 1809, and others. **DC 11 Apr 1981**.

1315   CAMPBELL, Duncan. From Breadalbane, PER. To Breadalbane, Lochiel Twp, Glengarry Co, ONT, 1815. **SDG 131**.

1316   CAMPBELL, Duncan, b ca 1781. From Carey, Abernethy, PER. To QUE ex Greenock, summer 1815; stld ONT. Farmer. Wife Katherine Dewar, qv, with him, and 2 ch. **SEC 3**.

1317   CAMPBELL, Duncan. From PER. bro/o Donald C, qv. To QUE on the *Lady of the Lake*, Sep 1816; stld Lot 3, Con 3, Drummond Twp, Lanark Co, ONT. **HCL 20, 237**.

1318   CAMPBELL, Duncan. From Killin, PER. To Montreal, QUE, on the *Curlew*, ex Greenock, 21 Jul 1821; stld prob Beckwith Twp, Lanark Co, ONT. Wife Catherine with him, and ch: 1. John, aged 10; 2. Elizabeth, aged 8; 3. Janet, aged 6. **BCL**.

1319   CAMPBELL, Duncan, ca 1802-92. From Greenock. s/o Archibald C, cooper. To Montreal, QUE, 1820. Clerk to a firm of wholesalers, who sent him to Simcoe Co, ONT, where he stld and became a banker and Commissioner of Crown Lands. m Clara, d/o Capt James Marshall Perkins, RN, ch. **LDW 15 Sep 1980**.

1320   CAMPBELL, Duncan. To Lanark Co, ONT, 1821; stld Lot 7, Con 2, North Sherbrooke Twp. **HCL 74**.

1321   CAMPBELL, Duncan. From Lochearnhead, PER. To Montreal, QUE, on the *Niagara*, ex Greenock, arr 28 May 1825; stld McNab Twp, Renfrew Co, ONT. Wife Helen Watt, qv, with him, and ch: 1. Isobel; 2. Cathrine; 3. Alexander; 4. Margaret. **EMT 18**.

1322   CAMPBELL, Duncan. From PER. A minor, poss rel to Duncan C, qv, and Helen Watt, qv. To McNab Twp, Renfrew Co, ONT. **DC 3 Jan 1980**.

1323   CAMPBELL, Duncan. From PER, poss Killin. To McNab Twp, Renfrew Co, ONT, 1825. Wife Kitty with him. **DC 3 Jan 1980**.

1324   CAMPBELL, Duncan, jr. From PER, poss Killin. To McNab Twp, Renfrew Co, ONT, 1825. **DC 3 Jan 1980**.

1325   CAMPBELL, Duncan. From ARL. To Ekfrid Twp, Middlesex Co, ONT, 1830. Weaver. **PCM 30**.

1326   CAMPBELL, Duncan, ca 1788-7 Nov 1846. From Lochgilphead, ARL. To QUE on the *River of London*, ex Greenock, 1830; stld Headles Creek, Lobo Twp, Middlesex Co, ONT. m Margaret Mitchell Campbell, ch: 1. John; 2. Peter; 3. Archibald; 4. Donald; 5. Duncan; 6. Robert; 7. Alexander; 8. Sarah; 9. Christy. **PCM 39; DC 1 Aug 1979**.

1327   CAMPBELL, Duncan. From ARL. To East Williams Twp, Middlesex Co, ONT, 1831. Assessor, 1842. **PCM 43**.

1328   CAMPBELL, Duncan 'Laird'. From ARL. To Mosa Twp, Middlesex Co, ONT, 1831. Farmer. Wife with him. ch incl: 1. Duncan, reeve; 2. Euphemia; 3. Peter, moved to Metcalfe Twp; 4. Donald, moved to Metcalfe Twp, 1850. **PCM 24, 26**.

1329   CAMPBELL, Duncan, 1781-1864. From PER, poss Dull par. To Osgoode Twp, Carleton Co., ONT, 1832. Farmer. m Janet Dow, qv, ch: 1. Thomas, 1838-1911; 2. John; 3. Janet; 4. Catherine; 5. Margaret. **DC 1 Aug 1975**.

1330   CAMPBELL, Duncan, ca 1768-13 May 1837. From Breadalbane, PER. To Halton Co, ONT, 1833; stld Esquesing Twp, and bur Boston Cemetery. **EPE 75**.

1331   CAMPBELL, Duncan. From ARL. To Mosa Twp, Middlesex Co, ONT, 1843. **PCM 24**.

1332   CAMPBELL, Duncan, ca 1766-25 Jun 1858. From Carwhin, Breadalbane, PER. To Esquesing Twp, Halton Co, ONT, prob <1845; d Puslinch Twp, Wellington Co, ONT. **EPE 74**.

1333   CAMPBELL, Duncan. From ARL. To Adelaide Twp, Middlesex Co, ONT, 1849. ch: 1. Duncan A, reeve of Adelaide Twp; 2. Archibald; 3. Donald S.; 4. Isabella; 5. Sarah; 6. Emma. **PCM 28**.

1334   CAMPBELL, Duncan. From Edinburgh. To Lincoln Co, ONT; stld Niagara. Physician. Dau Jane, d Edinburgh, 17 May 1850. **DGH 23 May 1850**.

1335   CAMPBELL, Duncan. To Halifax Co, NS, <1850. Wife Catherine with him. Son Alexander, b 1852, MD, Professor of Medicine at Dalhousie Coll. **HNS iii 119**.

1336   CAMPBELL, Duncan. Prob from ARL. To Cape Breton Is, NS, <1850. m Julia McMillan, qv. Dau Margaret, res Whycocomagh, 1867. **NSN 22/10**.

1337   CAMPBELL, Duncan. From Oban, ARL. s/o John C, Lochnell. Educ Edinburgh High School and Edinburgh Institution. To Brantford, Brant Co, ONT, ca 1850. Railroadman, m and ch. **HSC 54**.

1338   CAMPBELL, Duncan B. From ARL. To Aldborough Twp, Middlesex Co, ONT, 1819; moved to Metcalfe Twp, 1832. **PCM 26**.

1339 CAMPBELL, Duncan D. From ARL. To Caradoc Twp, Middlesex Co, ONT, <1840, when stld Adelaide Twp. **PCM 28**.

1340 CAMPBELL, Duncan M. From ARL. To Metcalfe Twp, Middlesex Co, ONT, 1831. **PCM 26**.

1341 CAMPBELL, Duncan Neil, ca 1793–24 May 1879. From Kintyre, ARL. To McKillop Twp, Huron Co, ONT, <1855. m Mary Campbell, qv. Son John Colin, qv. **DC 8 Feb 1970 and 16 Jun 1980**.

CAMPBELL, Mrs Duncan. See MACKILLOP,

1342 CAMPBELL, Effie, b 1821. From South Dell, Ness, Is Lewis, ROC. d/o Kenneth C, and Gormelia McLeod. To QUE, 1855. Wife of John Morrison, qv. **DC 22 Jun 1979**.

1343 CAMPBELL, Elizabeth. Prob from Glasgow. To Pictou Co, NS, 1821. m at Glasgow, 1819, Lachlan McLean, qv. **PAC 53**.

1344 CAMPBELL, Elizabeth. From PER, poss Killin. Prob d/o Duncan C, qv, and wife Kitty. To McNab Twp, Renfrew Co, ONT, 1825. **DC 3 Jan 1980**.

1345 CAMPBELL, Elizabeth. From Edinburgh. sis/o Rev A.J.C. C, Geelong, AUS. To Montreal, QUE, where m Rev Henry Esson, qv. **SGC 283**.

1346 CAMPBELL, Euphemia. From Is Skye, INV. To PEI, 1842; stld Queens Co. Wife of Alexander 'Mor' Munro, qv. **SPI 118**.

1347 CAMPBELL, Flora. From INV. Said rel to family of Lochnell. To Inverness Co, NS, ca 1822; stld Whycocomagh. Wife of Colin McNiven, qv. **DC 23 Feb 1980**.

1348 CAMPBELL, Flora, 1808–14 Mar 1891. From Harris, INV. To Victoria Co, NS, 1841. Wife of Malcolm McDonald, qv. **DC 22 Jun 1979**.

1349 CAMPBELL, Gavin Argyle, b ca 1809. From ARL. To QUE ca 1828; stld Three Rivers. Shipowner. m ca 1827, Katherine Brown, qv, ch: 1. Peter Shepard, 1829–1919; 2. Mary, 1832–1922; 3. William, 1834–1918; 4. Catherine, b 1836; 5. Robert, b 1838; 6. James M, b 1840; 7. John, 1844–1913. **DC 16 Apr 1960**.

1350 CAMPBELL, George, b ca 1778. From Creich par, SUT. To Fort Churchill, Hudson Bay, on the *Prince of Wales*, ex Stromness, 28 Jun 1813; thence to Red River. Wife Helen, aged 20, with him, and dau Bell, aged 1. **LSS 184; RRS 27; LSC 323**.

1351 CAMPBELL, George William, 19 Oct 1810–30 May 1882. From DNB. s/o Robert C, Chamberlain of Roseneath. Matric Univ of Glasgow, 1823. To Montreal, QUE, ca 1830. Physician and Professor of Surgery. Dau Margaret. **GMA 11317; Ts Roseneath**.

1352 CAMPBELL, Gormelia, b 1806. From Aird, Is Benbecula, INV. wid/o Alexander MacIntyre. To Pictou, NS, on the *Lulan*, ex Glasgow, 17 Aug 1848, with her ch: 1. Peter, b 1829; 2. Donald, b 1831; 3. Ann, b 1833; 4. Angus, b 1835; 5-6. John and Peggy, twins, b 1842. **DC 12 Jul 1979**.

1353 CAMPBELL, Grace. From Lochgilphead, ARL. sis/o John C, from Strathaven, qv. To QUE on the *Ada*, 1831; stld Ayr Village, Waterloo Co, ONT, later Ekfrid Twp, Middlesex Co. m David Graham, qv. **DC 3 Aug 1979**.

1354 CAMPBELL, Harriet, 1793–10 Nov 1863. From Killundine, Morven, ARL. d/o Hugh C. To Flat River, Queens Co, PEI. m Allan MacDougall, qv. **SPI 42**.

1355 CAMPBELL, Hector, b ca 1776. Prob from Is Colonsay, ARL. To Charlottetown, PEI, on the *Spencer*, ex Oban, 22 Sep 1806. ch with him: 1. Neil, aged 3; 2. John, aged 1. **PLSN**.

1356 CAMPBELL, Hector, b 1778. To St Andrews dist, Cape Breton Is, NS, ca 1810. Farmer, m and ch. **CBC 1818**.

1357 CAMPBELL, Hugh. From Is Mull, ARL. s/o Allan C, qv, and Mary MacCallum, qv. To Mull River, Inverness Co, NS, 1820. Storekeeper. m Jane MacMillan. **MP ii 120**.

1358 CAMPBELL, Hugh. From Dalbraick, Dunblane, PER. To McNab Twp, Renfrew Co, ONT, 1825. **EMT 18**.

1359 CAMPBELL, Hugh. From Killin, PER. s/o Hugh C. and Christian McEwen. To ONT 1833, and was drowned soon after arrival. **DC 21 Jul 1970**.

1360 CAMPBELL, Humphrey, b 1808. From Roseneath, DNB. s/o Robert C, qv, and Jean McFarlane, qv. To Ekfrid Twp, Middlesex Co, ONT, 1833. Twp warden. **PCM 32**.

1361 CAMPBELL, Isabel. From Moidart, INV. To NS <1820. Wife of Angus MacDonald, qv. **MP 502**.

1362 CAMPBELL, Isobella, d 26 Jun 1869. Prob from Breadalbane, PER. sis/o Duncan C, qv. To Queens Co, PEI, <21 Dec 1810, when m Donald McGregor, jr, qv. **DC 11 Apr 1981**.

1363 CAMPBELL, Mrs Isobella, ca 1764–26 Apr 1846. Prob from ARL. To Aldborough Twp, Elgin Co, ONT, prob 1818. ch: 1. Duncan, qv; 2. Alexander, qv; 3. Dugald; 4. Mrs Dugald MacDougall; 5. Mrs Alexander McPherson. **PDA 63**.

1364 CAMPBELL, James. To Pictou Co, NS, <8 Nov 1775. **HPC App B**.

1365 CAMPBELL, James, b ca 1743. From PER. s/o Alexander C. and Mary Cameron. To PEI <1770. Private secretary. m a sis/o James Townsend, from BRK, ENG, ch: 1. Archibald; 2. James; 3. John; 4. George; 5. Eliza, 1781–1830; 6. Caroline; 7. Sarah. **DC 1 Oct and 3 Nov 1966**.

1366 CAMPBELL, James. From Garabeg, Urquhart, INV. To Pictou Co, NS; stld East Branch of East River, 1819. m Elizabeth Fraser, ch: 1. Elizabeth; 2. Catherine; 3. Grace; 4. Mary Ann. **PAC 52**.

1367 CAMPBELL, James, ca 1797–6 Mar 1864. From Breadalbane, PER. To Halton Co, ONT, 1817; stld Esquesing Twp, and bur Boston cemetery. **EPE 75**.

1368 CAMPBELL, James. To Lanark Twp, Lanark Co, ONT, ca 1820. Manufacturer, later farmer. m Jean Whyte, qv, ch. **HCL 65**.

1369 CAMPBELL, James, d 1828. From Shian, Kenmore, PER. s/o Alexander C, tenant, and Marion M. Campbell. To ONT. **Ts Kenmore**.

1370 CAMPBELL, James. From PER, poss Killin. Prob s/o Archibald C, qv, and wife Kitty. To McNab Twp, Renfrew Co, ONT. **DC 3 Jan 1980**.

1371   CAMPBELL, James. From ARL. To Ottawa Co, QUE, 1828; stld Lochaber. Farmer, Lot 21, Range 2. **ELB 1**.

1372   CAMPBELL, James, 1804-44. From ARL. To Caledon Twp, Peel Co, ONT, <1840. Wife Margaret, 1782–1862, prob also from ARL. **DC 21 Apr 1820**.

1373   CAMPBELL, James, b ca 1800. From Edinburgh. s/o William C. and Elizabeth Grant. To Toronto, ONT, ca 1840. Publisher. Son William J. **MGC 2 Aug 1979**.

1374   CAMPBELL, Rev James, 1782–7 Jun 1859. Born Creich, SUT. Min of Kildonan, 1824-45. To Pictou, NS. m 22 Mar 1821, Johanna Polson, d/o Rev Alexander Urquhart, min of Rogart par, and Wilhelmina Polson, ch: 1. Alexandrina, b 21 Mar 1822; 2. Isabella, b 27 Sep 1825; 3. George, b 5 May 1827; 4. Mrs Sutherland. **FES vii 91**.

1375   CAMPBELL, James Ellice. To Montreal, QUE, <1800. Fur-trader, NWCo, and claimed descent from the Campbells of Breadalbane. Lumber merchant and ship owner. m d/o John McDonald of Gart, qv. Son James Reid, res Inverardine, Cornwall, ONT. **SGC 268**.

1376   CAMPBELL, Jane. From Glasgow. To QUE ex Greenock, summer 1815; stld Bathurst Twp, Lanark Co, ONT. Wife of John McLeod, qv. **SEC 3**.

1377   CAMPBELL, Jane, 1825–2 Feb 1895. From Lochranza, Is Arran, BUT. d/o Dugald C, qv, and Mary McKillop, qv. To Inverness, Megantic Co, QUE, 1831. m John McKinnon, jr, qv. **AMC 40; MAC 35**.

1378   CAMPBELL, Jane, 13 Apr 1827–20 Apr 1897. From Strathaven, LKS. d/o John C, qv, and Jane McPherson, qv. To Southwold Twp, Elgin Co, ONT, 1835. m Mathew Gilbert, Yarmouth Twp, Elgin Co, 26 Feb 1846, ch: 1. Martha Jane, 1847–1922; 2. John Arthur, 1853–1900; 3. Mary Elizabeth, 1860–1928. **DC 3 Aug 1979**.

1379   CAMPBELL, Janet, 1783–1837. From Is Islay, ARL. To Eldon Twp, Victoria Co, ONT, <1830. Wife of Duncan McCuaig, qv. **EC 90**.

1380   CAMPBELL, Janet. From Kilmartin, ARL. To ONT 1816. Wife of John Black, qv. **DC 29 Oct 1979**.

1381   CAMPBELL, Jessie. From ARL. Prob sis/o Mary C, qv. To Adelaide Twp, Middlesex Co, ONT, 1845. m John Black, and stld at Port Huron. **PCM 28**.

1382   CAMPBELL, John. From Is Shona, Loch Moidart, INV. To PEI on the *Jane*, ex Loch nan Uamh, Arisaig, 12 Jul 1790. Family with him. **PLJ**.

1383   CAMPBELL, John, 1788–6 Jun 1833. From ROC. s/o John C. To Black River, Northumberland Co, NS, prob 1804. Farmer and magistrate. ch: **DC 30 Jul 1980**.

1384   CAMPBELL, John, b ca 1752. From Is Mull, ARL. To Charlottetown, PEI, on the *Clarendon*, ex Oban, 6 Aug 1808. Labourer. Wife Isobel, aged 56, with him, and family: 1. Roderick, aged 31; 2. Donald, aged 25; 3. Alexander, aged 9. **CPL**.

1385   CAMPBELL, John. From Is Islay, ARL. To Belfast, PEI, <1811, when a petitioner for Dr Macaulay. Son John, b 1789. **DC 5 Mar 1979; HP 74**.

1386   CAMPBELL, John, b ca 1786. To Port Hood dist,

Inverness Co, NS, ca 1816. Farmer, m and ch. **CBC 1818**.

1387   CAMPBELL, John, b 1807. From INV. bro/o Alexander C, qv. To Pictou Co, NS; stld Mount Thom. m Christy MacQuarrie. **NSN 11/2**.

1388   CAMPBELL, John, b 1797. From Kilfinichen, Is Mull, ARL. To Hudson Bay and Red River <1815. **RRS 24**.

1389   CAMPBELL, John, b 1800. From Kilfinichen, Is Mull, ARL. To Hudson Bay and Red River <1815. **RRS 24**.

1390   CAMPBELL, John. Prob from Lochaber, INV. s/o Donald 'Ban' C. To Inverness Co, NS, Jun 1816; stld Glenora Falls. m Mary Campbell, qv, ch: 1. Angus; 2. Dougald; 3. Catherine; 4. Anne; 5. Mary; 6. Kate. **MP 292**.

1391   CAMPBELL, John, b 1767. To Western Shore, Inverness Co, NS, 1817. Farmer, m and ch. **CBC 1818**.

1392   CAMPBELL, John. From Killin, PER. To Montreal, QUE, on the *Sophia*, ex Greenock, 26 Jul 1818; stld prob Beckwith Twp, Lanark Co, ONT. Wife Mary with him, and ch: 1. Janet, aged 16; 2. Peter; 3. Donald, aged 12; 4. John, aged 10; 5. Catherine, aged 7; 6. Susan, aged 12. **SPL**.

1393   CAMPBELL, John. To Aldborough Twp, Elgin Co, ONT, prob 1818. Farmer. **PDA 93**.

1394   CAMPBELL, John. From Paisley, RFW. To Lanark Twp, Lanark Co, ONT, 1820. **HCL 225**.

1395   CAMPBELL, John. From Badenoch, INV. s/o Angus C, qv. To QUE, via New York, 1819; moved to Ekfrid Twp, Middlesex Co, ONT, 1821. ch: 1. Angus, JP, d 1904; 2-3. John and George, twins; 4. Jane; 5. Letitia; 6. Elizabeth; 7. Bella. **PCM 29**.

1396   CAMPBELL, John. From Loch Awe, ARL. To Lobo Twp, Middlesex Co, ONT, 1824. ch: 1. Sylvester, qv; 2. John. **PCM 39**.

1397   CAMPBELL, John. Prob from Ardrossan par, AYR. To River Louison, Restigouche Co, NB, ca 1826. Farmer. m Martha Archibald, qv. Dau Mary, b ca 1836. **DC 1 Oct 1979**.

1398   CAMPBELL, John, 1791–1851. From North Knapdale, ARL. s/o Donald C, dec, and Isabella McLellan, qv. To Caradoc Twp, Middlesex Co, ONT, <1827; stld Lot 12, Con 5. Farmer. m Nancy Galbraith, ch: 1. Donald, stld East Williams Twp; 2. Archibald; 3. Malcolm; 4. Alexander; 5. Isabella; 6. Christina; 7. Mary; 8. Nancy; 9. John. **PCM 36**.

1399   CAMPBELL, John 'Brock'. From ARL. To QUE on the *Huntly*, 1828; stld Eldon Twp, Victoria Co, ONT. **DC 21 Mar 1980**.

1400   CAMPBELL, John, b 1823. Prob from ARL. To Sydney, Cape Breton Co, NS, poss <1840. By wife Christina had ch: 1. Murdoch; 2. Alexander. **NSN 6/2**.

1401   CAMPBELL, John. To Antigonish Co, NS, poss <1830. m Miss Campbell, ch: 1. Kate; 2. Hannah; 3. John, res Brierly Brook. **HCA 93**.

1402   CAMPBELL, John. From Pluscardine, MOR. s/o John C. and Margaret Asher. To Montreal, QUE, prob 1831; stld ONT. Wife Margaret Faulkiner, qv, with him. **DC 22 Sep 1979**.

1403   CAMPBELL, John, called 'Iain Dubh Beag'. From ARL. To Ekfrid Twp, Middlesex Co, ONT, 1832. **PCM 31**.

1404   CAMPBELL, John. From ARL. To Mosa Twp, Middlesex Co, ONT, 1832.   **PCM 24**.

1405   CAMPBELL, John. To Inverness, Megantic Co, QUE, ca 1830.   **AMC 42**.

1406   CAMPBELL, John. From INV. To QUE on the *Zephyr*, ex Cromarty, 16 Jun 1833.   **DC 25 Aug 1980**.

1407   CAMPBELL, John, 10 Jun 1795–24 Feb 1876. From Killin, PER. s/o Joseph C. and Ann McDiarmid. stld Osgoode Twp, Carleton Co, ONT, 1833. Hostler and mail-driver. m Elizabeth McAlpin, qv, ch: 1. Joseph McAlpin; 2. Hugh; 3. Daniel; 4. John Robert; 5. Jeannie; 6. Anne; 7. Alpin.   **DC 22 Nov 1978**.

1408   CAMPBELL, John, ca 1792–27 Sep 1868. Poss b nr Oban, ARL, but emig from Strathaven, LKS. To Southwold Twp, Elgin Co, ONT, 1835. Shoemaker. m Jane McPherson, qv, ch: 1. Nancy, qv; 2. John, qv; 3. Mary, qv; 4. Jane, qv; 5. Lachlin, qv; 6. Neil, qv; 7. Dugald, b ONT 1836; 8. Grace, b 1839.   **DC 3 Aug 1979**.

1409   CAMPBELL, John, jr, 6 Dec 1821–6 Mar 1892. From Strathaven, LKS. s/o John C, qv, and Jane McPherson, qv. To Southwold Twp, Elgin Co, ONT, 1835, and d Yarmouth Twp. Farmer and owner of a travelling thrashing mill. m 20 Feb 1849, Lydia Robins, from ENG, ch: 1. Lydia Ann, 1850–1919; 2. John, 1852-55; 3. Daniel, 1855-71; 4. Mary, d inf 1858; 5. Jennie, 1859–1938; 6. Grace, 1862–1945; 7. Neil, 1866–1943; 8. George, 1869–1921.   **DC 3 Aug 1979**.

1410   CAMPBELL, John. From Is Skye, INV. To Fairview, Mariposa Twp, Victoria Co, ONT, <1840. Farmer. m Miss McLean, and had, poss with other ch: 1. John; 2. Donald; 3. Mary; 4. Euphemia; 5. Katie; 6. Norman L, b 1841.   **EC 48**.

1411   CAMPBELL, John. To Toronto, ONT, <1841. Retr to SCT and res Stranraer, WIG.   **SH**.

1412   CAMPBELL, John (1). To Pictou, NS, on the *Lady Gray*, ex Cromarty, ROC, arr 16 Jul 1841.   **DC 15 Jul 1979**.

1413   CAMPBELL, John (2). To Pictou, NS, on the *Lady Gray*, ex Cromarty, ROC, arr 16 Jul 1841.   **DC 15 Jul 1979**.

1414   CAMPBELL, John, ca 1813–22 Apr 1888. From Is Skye, INV. To Victoria Co, NS, 1841. ch: **DC 22 Jun 1979**.

1415   CAMPBELL, John. From North Knapdale, ARL. To Caradoc Twp, Middlesex Co, ONT, 1841. ch: 1. John, res Sarnia; 2. Donald, farmer; 3. Archibald; 4. Christie; 5. Mary; 6. Margaret.   **PCM 35**.

1416   CAMPBELL, John. From ARL. Prob bro/o Archibald C, qv. To Adelaide Twp, Middlesex Co, ONT, 1845.   **PCM 28**.

1417   CAMPBELL, John. From Is Skye, INV. To Eldon Twp, Victoria Co, ONT, <1850; stld Glenarm. Hotelier. m Mary Ferguson, ch: 1. Jack; 2. Kenneth; 3. Angus; 4. Daniel; 5. Colin; 6. Mary; 7. Annie.   **EC 41**.

1418   CAMPBELL, John. From ARL. To Aldborough Twp, Elgin Co, ONT, 1850.   **PDA 68**.

1419   CAMPBELL, John. From Lochaber, INV. s/o Duncan C. and Ann McKillop, qv. To Mabou, Inverness Co, NS, <1854. m Catherine, d/o John MacPherson, MacAra's Brook, Antigonish Co, and Flora Grant, ch: 1. Duncan; 2. John; 3. Daniel; 4. Donald; 5. John Duncan; 6. Anne; 7. Flora; 8. Mary; 9. Catherine Anne; 10. Elizabeth; 11. Colin.   **MP 327**.

1420   CAMPBELL, John, 6 Jun 1827–22 Apr 1874. From Greenock, RFW. s/o Rollo C. and Elizabeth Steel. To Montreal, QUE. Barrister. m Catherine Theresa Desiree McGowan, qv, ch: 1. Rolinda St Helena, b 1851; 2. Alexia, d NY, 1854.   **LDW 21 Aug 1978**.

CAMPBELL, Mrs John. See MACRAE, Isabella.

1421   CAMPBELL, John Ann, ca 1789–24 Apr 1857. From Galston, AYR. d/o John C. and Helen Carnduff. To ONT, ca 1846, and d Eversley, York Co. Wife of Thomas Gillies, qv, m at Galston, 24 Jun 1806.   **DC 17 Nov 1979**.

1422   CAMPBELL, John C, d 11 May 1879. From LKS. s/o Daniel C. and Elizabeth Taylor. To ONT, 1843; later to Saratoga Twp, MN. Weaver. m Mary Robertson, ch: 1. John Robert, qv; 2. Elizabeth; 3. Joseph; 4. Mary Ann; 5. Marion.   **DC 3 Mar 1968**.

1423   CAMPBELL, John Colin, 20 Oct 1820–24 Oct 1864. From Kintyre, ARL. s/o Duncan Neil C, qv, and Mary Campbell, qv. To McKillop Twp, Huron Co, ONT. m Elizabeth, d/o Peter McMillan, qv, and Mary Keith, qv. Dau Flora, 1856–1922.   **DC 8 Feb 1970 and 16 Jun 1980**.

1424   CAMPBELL, John Robert, 3 May 1839–21 Oct 1921. From Edinburgh. s/o John R. C, qv, and Mary Robertson. To ONT, 1843; later to Saratoga Twp, MN. Farmer and landowner. m 1873, Anna, d/o Olie Ulvestad and Anna Westad, ch: 1. Edward Alexander, 1887–1926; 2. Mary Buffam, 1833–1951.   **DC 3 Mar 1968**.

1425   CAMPBELL, Julia. From ARL. d/o Edward C. and Peggy McLean. To NS, ca 1820. m Daniel MacMillan, qv.   **DC 1 Jul 1968**.

1426   CAMPBELL, Kenneth. From Is Eigg, INV. To Glengarry Co, ONT, <1828; stld later Eldon Twp, Victoria Co.   **DC 21 Mar 1980**.

1427   CAMPBELL, Kenneth, b 1801. From South Dell, Is Lewis, ROC. s/o Angus C. and Margaret Murray. To Lingwick Twp, Compton Co, QUE, 1863. m (i) Gormelia McLeod; (ii) Mary Smith. ch: 1. Roderick, who remained in Lewis; 2. Effie, qv; 3. Norman, qv; 4. Ann, b 1826; 5. Mary, qv; 6. Murdo, b 1829; 7. John, b 1831; 8. Angus, b 1834.   **WLC**.

1428   CAMPBELL, Lachlan. From Cleadale, Is Eigg, INV. To QUE on the *British Queen*, ex Arisaig, 16 Aug 1790; stld nr Montreal. Tenant. Wife and ch with him. **QCC 103**.

1429   CAMPBELL, Lachlin, 25 Jun 1829–10 Aug 1906. From Strathaven, LKS. s/o John C, qv, and Jane McPherson, qv. To Southwold Twp, Elgin Co, ONT, 1835, and d St Thomas. Sheriff of Elgin Co. m Nancy Black, ch: 1. John L; 2. Duncan; 3. Mrs Cochran; 4. Agnes; 5. Neil, d 1906; 6. Dougald, d 1908.   **DC 3 Aug 1979**.

1430   CAMPBELL, Malcolm, b ca 1798. From

Kilfinichen, Is Mull, ARL. To Hudson Bay and Red River, <1815. **RRS 24**.

1431   CAMPBELL, Malcolm, 10 Jul 1786–30 Dec 1865. From Killisport, Knapdale, ARL. s/o Donald C, dec, and Isabella McLellan, qv. To Middlesex Co, ONT, 1819; stld Lobo Twp, but moved to Caradoc Twp. Farmer. m Mary Smith, qv, ch: 1. Christian, b 1812; 2. Donald, b 1814; 3. John, b 1816; 4. Malcolm, b 1818; 5. Duncan, b 1820; 6. Isabella, b 1821; 7. Mary Ann; 8. Archie, b 1823; 9. Margaret, b 1828; 10. Joseph, b 1830; 11. Benjamin, b 1831; 12. Catherine, b 1834. **PCM 36; DC 20 Jul 1982**.

1432   CAMPBELL, Malcolm, called 'Callum Mor'. From ARL. To Ekfrid Twp, Middlesex Co, ONT, ca 1832. ch: 1. Archibald; 2. Mrs Angus McEachern; 3. Mrs Thomas Campbell. **PCM 30**.

1433   CAMPBELL, Malcolm, b 1812. From Roseneath, DNB. s/o Robert C, qv, and Jean McFarlane, qv. To Ekfrid Twp, Middlesex Co, ONT, via NY, 1834; stld Thames River, Lot 6. Farmer and schoolteacher, Aldborough Twp, later in Ekfrid Twp. Reeve, and lay preacher of the Baptist faith. **PCM 33**.

1434   CAMPBELL, Malcolm. From Is Lewis, INV. To QUE, ex Stornoway, arr 4 Aug 1851; stld Huron Twp, Bruce Co, ONT, 1852. Head of family.   **DC 5 Apr 1967**.

1435   CAMPBELL, Margaret. From ARL, prob Knapdale. d/o Donald C, dec, and Isabella McLennan, qv. To Caradoc Twp, Middlesex Co, ONT, ca 1821. m Duncan McDonald.   **PCM 35**.

1436   CAMPBELL, Margaret. From Glenelg, INV. To QUE, ex Greenock, summer 1815; stld prob Lanark Co, ONT. Wife of John McGillivray, qv.   **SEC 8**.

1437   CAMPBELL, Margaret. Prob from PER. Rel to Peter C, qv. To McNab Twp, Renfrew Co, ONT, 1825. **DC 3 Jan 1980**.

1438   CAMPBELL, Margaret, 1823–86. From ARL. To Nassagaweya Twp, Halton Co, ONT, <1849. Wife of Archibald McPhail, qv.   **DC 9 Nov 1981**.

1439   CAMPBELL, Marion. From INV. d/o 'the Laird of Skriegh.' To Pictou, NS, on the *Hector*, ex Loch Broom, arr 17 Sep 1773. Wife of Alexander Fraser, qv, Middle River.   **HPC App A and C**.

1440   CAMPBELL, Marion. From Glenelg, INV. To QUE, summer 1815, ex Greenock; stld prob ONT. Wife of John McRae, qv.   **SEC 5**.

1441   CAMPBELL, Marjery. From Killin, PER. To QUE on the *Dorothy*, ex Greenock, 12 Jul 1815; stld Elmsley Twp. Lanark Co, ONT. Wife of Alexander McDonald, qv.   **SEC 4**.

1442   CAMPBELL, Mary, 1808–45. Prob from North Knapdale, ARL. To Aldborough Twp, Elgin Co, ONT, prob 1819. m Malcolm McIntyre, qv.   **PDA 41**.

1443   CAMPBELL, Mary. From PER, poss Killin, and perhaps inf d/o Duncan C, qv, and Helen Watt, qv. To McNab Twp, Renfrew Co, ONT, 1825.   **DC 3 Jan 1980**.

1444   CAMPBELL, Mary, ca 1794–8 Jun 1891. From Kintyre, ARL. To McKillop Twp, Huron Co, ONT. Wife of Duncan Campbell, qv.   **DC 8 Feb 1970**.

1445   CAMPBELL, Mary. From Finlarig, PER. To QUE

ex Greenock, summer 1815; stld prob Lanark Co, ONT. Wife of Peter Morison, qv.   **SEC 8**.

1446   CAMPBELL, Mary. Prob from Lochaber, INV. d/o Dougald C. To Inverness Co, NS, Jun 1816; stld Glenora Falls. Wife of John Campbell, qv.   **MP 292**.

1447   CAMPBELL, Mary. From ARL, prob Knapdale. d/o Donald C, dec, and Isabella McLellan, qv. To Caradoc Twp, Middlesex Co, ONT, ca 1821. m Dugald Graham.   **PCM 35**.

1448   CAMPBELL, Mary, d 10 Feb 1878. From Is Skye, INV. To Wycocomaugh, Inverness Co, NS. Wife of Murdoch McLeod, qv.   **DC 19 Nov 1977**.

1449   CAMPBELL, Mary. From Glen Roy, INV. d/o Donald C. To Mabou Ridge, Inverness Co, NS, 1816. Wife of Alexander 'Ruadh' MacDonald, qv. **MP 512**.

1450   CAMPBELL, Mary, 27 Dec 1823–27 Jan 1862. From Strathaven, LKS. d/o John C, qv, and Jane McPherson, qv. To Southwold Twp, Elgin Co, ONT, 1835, and d Port Burwell. m Capt Alexander McBride, ch: 1. Mary; 2. John; 3. Ann; 4. Amelia; 5. Grace. **DC 3 Aug 1979**.

1451   CAMPBELL, Mary. From ARL. Prob sis/o Jessie C, qv. To Adelaide Twp, Middlesex Co, ONT, 1845. m Archibald Campbell.   **PCM 28**.

1452   CAMPBELL, Mary, b 1819. From ARL. To Halton Co, ONT, <1849; stld Erin Twp, Wellington Co. Wife of John McPhail, qv.   **DC 9 Nov 1981**.

1453   CAMPBELL, Mary. From Lochaber, INV. d/o Duncan C. and Anne MacKillop, qv. To Mabou, Inverness Co, NS, <1854. m John Welsh, carpenter, without ch.   **MP 330**.

1454   CAMPBELL, Mary, b 1826. From South Dell, Ness, Is Lewis, ROC. d/o Kenneth C, qv, and Gormelia McLeod. To QUE, 1855. Wife of Donald Murray, qv. **DC 22 Jun 1975**.

1455   CAMPBELL, Moses, b 1723. From PER. s/o Maj Allan C. To Glengarry Co, ONT, <1800.   **MG 403**.

CAMPBELL, Mrs. See COLVIN, Catherine.

1456   CAMPBELL, Murdoch. To Antigonish Co, NS, prob <1830. m Miss MacDonald, ch: 1. Daniel; 2. John; 3. Catherine; 4. Jessie; 5. Margaret.   **HCA 92**.

1457   CAMPBELL, Murdoch, 1806–16 Sep 1879. From Is North Uist, INV. s/o Donald C, qv. To Inverness Co, NS, 1831. m 1831, Mary Mackinnon, qv, ch: 1. John, b 1832; 2. Donald, b 1834; 3. Belle, b 1836; 4. Alexander, b 1839; 5. Anne, b 1842.   **DC 16 Apr 1960**.

1458   CAMPBELL, Murdock, ca 1782–1819. From ROC. To Pictou Co, NS, 1803. Bur Salt Springs. m Catherine Cameron who d 21 Jan 1871.   **DC 27 Oct 1979**.

1459   CAMPBELL, Nancy. Poss from Glenlyon, PER. To QUE, prob 1818; stld Chatham Twp, Argenteuil Co. Wife of Alexander McGibbon, qv.   **DC 30 Jun 1971**.

1460   CAMPBELL, Nancy. From ARL, prob Knapdale. d/o Donald C, dec, and Isabella McLellan, qv. To Caradoc Twp, Middlesex Co, ONT, ca 1821. m Donald McGugan.   **PCM 35**.

1461 CAMPBELL, Nancy, 8 Feb 1819–14 Sep 1891. From Strathaven, LKS. d/o John C, qv, and Jane McPherson, qv. To Southwold Twp, Elgin Co, ONT, 1835. m (i) Donald Leitch, Yarmouth Twp, Elgin Co, ch: 1. Jane, 1839–1910; 2. John, 1845-71; 3. Dr Archibald, 1846–1927; 4. Lachlin; 5. Mary. m (ii) Duncan Munro, no ch. **DC 3 Aug 1979**.

1462 CAMPBELL, Neil, b 1777. To Charlottetown, PEI, on the *Rambler*, ex Tobermory, 20 Jun 1806; stld Queens Co. m Janet McGilveray, qv, ch: 1. Margaret, b 7 Nov 1806; 2. James, b 7 Aug 1808; 3. Mary, b 5 Dec 1814; 4. Isabella, b 5 Jul 1812; 5. Thomas, b 3 Mar 1819. **PLR; DC 11 Apr 1981**.

1463 CAMPBELL, Neil, b ca 1791. From Torin Uichdrich, Kilfinichen, Is Mull, ARL. To Hudson Bay and Red River, <1815. **RRS 24**.

1464 CAMPBELL, Neil. To QUE on the *Brock*, ex Greenock, Jul 1820; stld Dalhousie Twp, Lanark Co, ONT. Pioneer settler. **HCL 66, 238**.

1465 CAMPBELL, Neil, 1809-80. Poss from PER. To Montreal, QUE. m Elizabeth, d/o James Fisher, qv, and Elizabeth Haggart, qv, ch: 1. Elizabeth, b 1839; 2. Christina, b 1840; 3. Catherine; 4. Euphemia. **DC 26 Mar 1979**.

1466 CAMPBELL, Neil. From ARL. To QUE, 1828; stld Lochaber, Ottawa Co. Farmer, Lot 22, Range 2. m Catherine McCallum, qv. Son Archie, b ca 1820, came out in 1832. **ELB 1**.

1467 CAMPBELL, Neil. From ARL. s/o John and Catherine C. To Eldon Twp, Victoria Co, ONT, 1830; stld Lot 9, Con 2. **EC 38**.

1468 CAMPBELL, Neil, 12 Aug 1832–24 May 1872. From Strathaven, LKS. s/o John C, qv, and Jane McPherson, qv. To Southwold Twp, Elgin Co, ONT, 1835; later to Yarmouth Twp. Farmer. m Margaret Farrel. Dau Jane d 1928, ID. **DC 3 Aug 1979**.

1469 CAMPBELL, Neil. From ARL. To Mosa Twp, Middlesex Co, ONT, prob <1840; stld Newbury. **PCM 24**.

1470 CAMPBELL, Neil. From ARL. To Adelaide Twp, Middlesex Co, ONT, 1845; went later to AUS. **PCM 28**.

1471 CAMPBELL, Nelly, 1770–1851. From ARL. Said desc from the family of Duntroon. To ONT and bur Fingal, Southwold Twp, Elgin Co. **SG xxiii/3 50**.

1472 CAMPBELL, Norman. From Is Mull, ARL. s/o Allan C, qv, and Mary MacCallum, qv. To Mull River, Inverness Co, NS, 1820. m Ann, d/o Donald Cameron, River Denys. Dau Catherine. **MP ii 120**.

1473 CAMPBELL, Norman, b 1823. From South Dell, Ness, Is Lewis, ROC. s/o Kenneth C, qv, and Gormelia McLeod. To QUE, 1855. **DC 22 Jun 1975**.

1474 CAMPBELL, Patrick, b 1752. To Baddeck dist, Victoria Co, NS, 1812; stld prob Middle River. Farmer, m and ch: 1. John, b ca 1793; 2. Angus, b ca 1795; 3. Roderick, b ca 1799. **CBC 1818**.

1475 CAMPBELL, Peter, 1786–1847. From ARL. To Lanark Co, ONT, 1817; stld nr Perth, Drummond Twp. ch incl: 1. Rev Robert, b 1835, min and historian of St Gabriel St Ch, Montreal; 2. Rev Alexander, b 1837, min at Beachburg; 3. John. **SGC 612, 638**.

1476 CAMPBELL, Peter. From Killin, PER. To McNab Twp, Renfrew Co, ONT, 1825. **EMT 18**.

1477 CAMPBELL, Peter, b 1826. From Lochranza, Is Arran, BUT. s/o Dugald C, qv, and Mary McKillop, qv. To Inverness, Megantic Co, QUE; later to Listowel, Perth Co, ONT. m Aimee McKenzie. **AMC 38; MAC 35**.

1478 CAMPBELL, Peter. From ARL. s/o John and Catherine C. To Eldon Twp, Victoria Co, ONT, 1830; stld Lot 9, Con 2. **EC 38**.

1479 CAMPBELL, Peter, 1767–1840. From ARL. To Caledon Twp, Peel Co, ONT, prob <1830. Wife Mary, 1782–1862, prob also from ARL. **DC 21 Apr 1980**.

1480 CAMPBELL, Rachel. From ARL. To NS on the *Highland Lad*, 1826; stld nr Port Hastings, Inverness Co. Wife of John MacQuarrie, qv. **DC 28 Jul 1981**.

1481 CAMPBELL, Rachel. From Port Glasgow, RFW. d/o Colin C. m Adam Ferrie, qv, 3 Jun 1805, and stld Montreal, QUE, 1829. **SGC 474**.

1482 CAMPBELL, Robert, 1808-94. From Glenlyon, PER. To Red River, MAN, ca 1832, in the service of the HBCo. Became a chief factor. Explored in the Mackenzie River Basin and discovered Upper Yukon River. Latterly a rancher in MAN. m ca 1860, Eleanora Stirling, ch. **MDB 110; DC 10 Jan 1980**.

1483 CAMPBELL, Robert, b 1763. From Roseneath, DNB. To NY on the *Czar*, 1834; stld Ekfrid Twp, Middlesex Co, ONT. m Jean McFarlane, qv, ch: 1. Duncan, b 1794; 2. John, b 1797; 3. Robert, qv; 4. Christina, b 1801; 5. Donald, b 1804; 6. Mary, b 1806; 7. Humphrey, qv; 8. Dugald, b 1810; 9. Malcolm, qv; 10. Alexander, qv. **PCM 32**.

1484 CAMPBELL, Robert, jr, b 1799. From Roseneath, DNB. s/o Robert C, qv, and Jean McFarlane, qv. To Ekfrid Twp, Middlesex Co, ONT, 1840. Superintendent of schools. ch: 1. Robert, teacher; 2. Mrs John P. Corneil; 3. Jessie; 4. Jennie; 5. Humphrey, poet; 6. Mary; 7. Angus, res nr London; 8. Malcolm, bank agent, Glencoe; 9. George, Reeve of Ekfrid. **PCM 32**.

1485 CAMPBELL, Robert. s/o James C. and Jean Torrie. To Montreal, QUE, <1855. Millwright. **SH**.

1486 CAMPBELL, Roderick. From Is Mull, ARL. To Queens Co, PEI, 1808. m Mary McPhaill, qv. Son Donald, b 1814. **DC 11 Apr 1981**.

1487 CAMPBELL, Rollo, 17 Dec 1803–2 Jan 1871. From Dunning, PER. To Montreal, QUE, 1822. Printer and publisher. **MDB 110**.

1488 CAMPBELL, Samuel. From Tulloch, Loch Laggan, INV. To Pictou Co, NS, <1803, when he moved to South West Mabou, Inverness Co. m Jane MacGregor, qv, ch: 1. Donald; 2. Malcolm, went to MN; 3. John; 4. Samuel; 5. Mary. **MP 311**.

1489 CAMPBELL, Sarah. From Is Skye, INV. To Victoria Co, NS, 1829; later to Inverness Co. Wife of Donald MacPherson, qv. **DC 23 Feb 1980**.

1490 CAMPBELL, Sylvester. From Loch Awe, ARL. s/o John C, qv. To Lobo Twp, Middlesex Co, ONT, 1824. m Isabella, d/o Donald Lamont, qv. **PCM 39**.

1491 CAMPBELL, Tamerlane. To Carleton Co, NB, <1790. Formerly officer in 42nd Regt. **DC 3 Feb 1981**.

1492 CAMPBELL, Thomas. Prob from INV. To Cape Breton Is, NS, <1837, but moved to Ekfrid Twp, Middlesex Co, ONT. Later in Lobo Twp, and d Strathroy, Adelaide Twp. m Miss Campbell. **PCM 30**.

1493 CAMPBELL, Thomas, 4 Jul 1829–24 May 1904. From AYR. bro/o David C, qv. To Brantford Twp, Brant Co, ONT, <1850. m 14 Mar 1852, Lydia Robertson, ch: 1. James, b 1853; 2. Sarah, b 1855; 3. John, b 1857; 4. Isobell, b 1858; 5. William, b 1860; 6. Alfred, b 1861; 7. Robert, b 1862; 8. Thomas, b 1864; 9. Ann, b 1866; 10. Alexander, b 1867; 11. George, b 1872; 12. Mary, b 1874. **DC 5 Mar and 23 Sep 1980**.

1494 CAMPBELL, Thomas Dugald. Prob from PER. Cous and heir of Donald McGregor of Balhaldie. To CAN <1855. **SH**.

1495 CAMPBELL, Lord William, ca 1730-78. From ARL. s/o John, 4th Duke of Argyll, and Hon Mary Bellenden. Governor of NS 1766-73, and afterwards of SC. **SP i 385; MDB 110**.

1496 CAMPBELL, William, b 1751. From Brownmoor, Annan, DFS. s/o — C, dec, and Catherine Colvin, qv. To Georgetown, PEI, on the *Lovely Nellie*, ex Annan, 1774; moved to Pictou Co, NS, and farmed at East River. m Martha Henderson, qv, ch: 1. Alexander, stld Tatamagouche, Colchester Co; 2. William; 3. James; 4. George; 5. Thomas; 6. Margaret; 7. Hannah. **ELN; HPC App D and E; HT 35**.

1497 CAMPBELL, Sir William, 1758–18 Jan 1834. From Caithness. s/o Capt Alexander C, RN. To Guysborough, NS, 1784, later to Sydney, Cape Breton Is. Moved to Toronto, ONT, where he built a mansion in 1822. Soldier, lawyer and contractor; MLA, 1799–1806, and became Chief Justice of Upper Canada. m 5 Jun 1785, Hannah, d/o Joseph and Ruth Hadley, Chedabucto. Dau Elizabeth Amelia. **BNA 459-83; MLA 57; MDB 110**.

1498 CAMPBELL, William, b ca 1788. From Glenelg, INV. To QUE, ex Greenock, summer 1815; stld prob Lanark Co, ONT. Farmer. Wife Christian McLellan, qv, with him, and 4 ch. **SEC 8**.

1499 CAMPBELL, William 'Squire', 1801–7 Jun 1872. From Pluscardine, MOR. s/o John C. and Margaret Asher. To Montreal, QUE, arr 26 May 1831; stld Thurlow Twp, Hastings Co, ONT, 1834. Stonemason, later farmer. m Isabella Masson, qv, ch: 1. Flora McDonnell, b 9 Aug 1828; 2. Elizabeth, b 19 Feb 1830; 3. William, b 16 Oct 1831; 4. John, b 30 May 1833; 5. Isabella, b 4 May 1835; 6. Margaret, b 10 Jan 1837; 7. Alexander, b 14 Jul 1839; 8. Helen, b 22 Dec 1841. **DC 22 Sept 1979**.

1500 CAMPBELL, William, ca 1812–24 Jun 1873. From ARL. To Pictou Co, NS, 1841; stld East Forks, Middle River. m Margaret Thompson, qv, ch: 1. Jessie; 2. Mary; 3. Janet; 4. Effie; 5. Jane Ruth; 6. Margaret. **PAC 36**.

1501 CAMPBELL, William, 1832-74. From Newton-Stewart, WIG. To Hamilton, ONT. m Mary Clark, qv. **Ts Mt Albion**.

1502 CAMPBELL, William, b ca 1796. From Port Ellen, Is Islay, ARL. To Eldon Twp, Victoria Co, ONT, <1850. Stonemason. m Miss Hunter, ch: 1. Archibald; 2. Duncan; 3. Anne; 4. Betsy. **EC 50**.

1503 CAMPBELL, William. Prob from Glasgow. Gr-s of William C, moulder there. To Toronto, ONT, <1853. Upholsterer. **SH**.

1504 CAMPBELL, William Edward, b 7 Sep 1807. From DFS. To ONT 1829; stld Toronto. Blacksmith. m Jane Murray, qv. **DC 7 Jul 1981**.

1505 CANDLISH, Charles. Poss from ARL. To Sherbrooke Co, QUE, ca 1840; stld afterwards Drummond Co, and latterly at Longueil, Huntingdon Co. Son Charles William, b Lisgar. **MGC 2 Aug 1979**.

1506 CANNON, Robert. To QUE on the *Commerce*, ex Greenock, 11 May 1821; stld Lot 17, Con 2, Lanark Twp, Lanark Co, ONT. Cooper, innkeeper and later Postmaster at Hopetown. **HCL 65, 239**.

1507 CANNON, William, 1791–1841. From Glasgow. To Ramsay Twp, Lanark Co, ONT, 1835. Naval surgeon, then practised medicine in CAN. m Margaret King, qv. Son Rev Dr Andrew, Professor of Theology. **OSG 27**.

1508 CARDESHAM, Ellen, b ca 1810. To St Gabriel de Valcartier, QUE, <1860. **Census 1861**.

1509 CARGILL, Arthur. From Milton, Kinettles, ANS. To NY on the *Lady Kinnaird*, 1837; stld CAN, prob ONT. Farmer. **DC 18 Apr 1862**.

1510 CARLAW, Isabella, 8 Jan 1820–9 Jul 1897. Prob from Sanquhar par, DFS. d/o Alexander C. and Jane Tweedie. To Cornwall Twp, Stormont Co, ONT, 1854. Wife of George Law, qv, m 4 Sep 1835. **DC 20 Jan 1980**.

1511 CARLOW, John A, b 13 Feb 1840. From STI. To QUE 1853. Cashier, Grand Trunk Railway, ch. **DC 29 Sep 1964**.

1512 CARLYLE, Alexander. From DFS. Rel to Thomas C, 1795–1881, the famous author. To Brant Co, ONT, via NY, ca 1843. m Janet Clowe, qv, ch: 1. Jane; 2. Thomas; 3. Jessie; 4. John; 5. Alexander; 6. William; 7. Robert. **DC 23 Sep 1980**.

1513 CARLYLE, George. Poss from DFS. bro/o Walter C, qv. To ONT, 1840; stld prob Dundas Co. **DC 4 Mar 1965**.

1514 CARLYLE, Janet, d 20 Jul 1883. From Ecclefechan, DFS. d/o James C, stonemason, and Margaret Aitken. To Hamilton, ONT, ca 1844. m — Hanning, from Manchester, ENG. **CAE 48**.

1515 CARLYLE, Walter. Poss from DFS. bro/o George C, qv. To ONT, 1840; stld prob Dundas Co. **DC 4 Mar 1965**.

1516 CARLYLE, William, ca 1820–17 Jul 1903. From Eaglesfield, Ecclefechan, DFS. To Toronto, ONT, 1849. Master builder, alderman and JP. **CAE 74**.

1517 CARMICHAEL, Archibald, b ca 1791. Poss from ARL. To Eldon Twp, Victoria Co, ONT, <1830. Wife Margaret with him. ch: 1. Duncan, b 1820; 2-3. Hugh and Isabella, b 1826; 4. Margaret, b 1829; 5. Mary, b 1830; 6. Archibald, b 1836. **EC 52**.

1518 CARMICHAEL, Charles, d 1790. From Creag an Fhitich, Kilmonivaig par, INV. Rel to Hugh C, qv, prob his brother. To QUE on the *Gentian*, ex Oban, 1820; stld Lobo Twp, Middlesex Co, ONT. ch: 1. John; 2. Hugh; 3. Donald; 4. Catherine; 5. Mary. **PCM 38**.

1519 CARMICHAEL, Daniel or Donald, b 1787. From Oban, ARL. s/o Duncan and Flora C. To Victoria Co, NS, 1811; stld Inverness Co. m Sarah, d/o David Ross, Margaree, 1820, ch: 1. Mary; 2. David; 3. Elizabeth; 4. Duncan; 5. Margaret; 6. Jacob; 7. Ann, unm; 8. Melinda; 9. Catherine; 10. Flora; 11. John; 12. Sarah. **DC 23 Feb 1980**.

1520 CARMICHAEL, Donald. From PER. Prob s/o James C, qv, and Mary Sinclair, qv. To McNab Twp, Renfrew Co, ONT, 1825. **DC 3 Jan 1980**.

1521 CARMICHAEL, Dugald. From Caolasraide, South Knapdale, ARL. To Lobo Twp, Middlesex Co, ONT, 1842; later to Petrolia, Lambton Co. ch: 1. John; 2. Mrs Anderson; 3. Mrs Barry; 4. Mrs Butterworth. **PCM 39**.

1522 CARMICHAEL, Hector, 1822–22 Jun 1879. To Victoria Co, NS, 1828. m Mary Smith, 1831–1905. **DC 22 Jun 1979**.

1523 CARMICHAEL, Hugh, b 1796. From Creag an Fhitich, Kilmonivaig par, INV. Rel to Charles C, prob his bro. To QUE on the *Gentian*, ex Oban, 1820; stld Lobo Twp, Middlesex Co, ONT. ch: 1. Allan; 2. Duncan; 3. Donald; 4. Hugh; 5. Charles; 6. Alexander; 7. John, went to KS; 8. Peter; 9. James; 10. Betsy; 11. Catherine; 12. Susan. **PCM 38**.

1524 CARMICHAEL, Hugh. From Lismore and Appin par, ARL. s/o Allan C. and Catherine McIntyre. To Lobo Twp, Middlesex Co, ONT, 1825. m d/o Malcolm Campbell, qv, and Mary Smith, qv. **DC 16 Jan 1976**.

1525 CARMICHAEL, James. From PER. Served in 82nd Regt as NCO, and was gr 200 acres in Pictou Co, NS, 1784. ch. **HPC App F**.

1526 CARMICHAEL, James. From Edinburgh. To Montreal on the *Niagara*, ex Greenock, arr 28 May 1825; stld Flat River, McNab Twp, Renfrew Co, ONT. Farmer. Wife Mary Sinclair, qv, with him, and ch: 1. Duncan; 2. James. **EMT 18, 22**.

1527 CARMICHAEL, James. To Pictou, NS, on the *Lulan*, ex Glasgow, 17 Aug 1848. Wife Jessie with him. Part-owner of the ship, with Capt George McKenzie, New Glasgow, Pictou Co. **DC 12 Jul 1979**.

1528 CARMICHAEL, Janet. Poss from PER. To ONT <1818. m Alexander Thompson, qv. **DC 2 Sep 1981**.

1529 CARMICHAEL, John. From Comrie par, PER. To Montreal, QUE, on the *Curlew*, ex Greenock, 21 Jul 1818; stld prob Beckwith Twp, Lanark Co, ONT. Wife Ann with him. **BCL**.

1530 CARMICHAEL, John, 1784–1867. From PER. To Middlesex Co, ONT, 1818; stld London Twp. Farmer and surveyor. m Mary McLaren, qv, ch: 1. Peter; 2. Mary; 3. Alexander; 4. John; 5. Duncan, b 1817; 6. Andrew; 7. James; 8. Elgin; 9. Jennie; 10. Archibald. **PCM 50**.

1531 CARMICHAEL, Lt John, d 1828. To Charlottetown, PEI. Sometime Colonial Secretary. **DGC 16 Dec 1828**.

1532 CARMICHAEL, John. From PER. A minor, prob s/o James C, qv, and Mary Sinclair, qv. To McNab Twp, Renfrew Co, ONT, 1825. **DC 3 Jan 1980**.

1533 CARMICHAEL, Mary. To Charlottetown, PEI, on the *Humphreys*, ex Tobermory, 14 Jul 1806. Wife of or wid/o — McDonald. ch with her: 1. Lachlin, aged 11; 2. Flora, aged 9; 3. Penny, aged 7; 5. Mary, aged 4. **PLH**.

1534 CARMICHAEL, Mary. From Is Mull, ARL. To ONT ca 1854. Wife of Donald Lamont, qv. **DC 7 Jan 1982**.

1535 CARNIE, James, ca 1816–27 Jul 1849. From Kirkmaiden, WIG. To Hamilton, ONT. **DGH 6 Sep 1849**.

1536 CARNOCHAN, Grace, b 12 Jan 1829. From Girthon par, KKD. d/o Samuel C, qv, and Agnes Hawthorn, qv. To Huron Co, ONT, 1833. m William McGeogh. **DC 27 Jun 1981**.

1537 CARNOCHAN, James, ca 1797–ca 1884. From KKD. bro/o Joseph C. To Miramichi, Northumberland Co, NB, ca 1816. Farmer. m Jane, d/o John Cowden, qv, and Martha Gibson, qv, and wid/o Adam Gillis, ch: 1. John, b 1825; 2. William, b 1827; 3-4. Mary and Martha, twins, b 1829; 5. James, b 1831; 6. Alexander, 1834–1900; 7. Joseph, b 1835; 8. Robert, 1837–1907. **DC 25 Feb 1982**.

1538 CARNOCHAN, James, 1 Mar 1814–16 Mar 1891. From Girthon par, KKD. s/o Samuel C, qv, and Mary Halliday. To Huron Co, ONT, 1832. m Jane Landsborough, qv. **DC 27 Jun 1981**.

1539 CARNOCHAN, Jane, 8 Jan 1816–6 Dec 1899. From Girthon par, KKD. d/o Samuel C, qv, and Mary Halliday. To Huron Co, ONT, 1833. Wife of James Dickson, qv. **DC 27 Jun 1981**.

1540 CARNOCHAN, Margaret, 1 Feb 1810–1 Aug 1844. Born Little Barley, Girthon par, KKD. d/o Samuel C, qv, and Mary Halliday. To Huron Co, ONT, 1833. m Alexander Broadfoot, qv. **DC 27 Jun 1981**.

1541 CARNOCHAN, Robert, 20 Dec 1811–26 Oct 1886. From Girthon par, KKD. s/o Samuel C, qv, and Mary Halliday. To Tuckersmith Twp, Huron Co, ONT, 1832. m Agnes Landsborough, qv. **DC 27 Jun 1981**.

1542 CARNOCHAN, Samuel, 23 May 1785–5 Mar 1859. From Anwoth par, but b Girthon par, KKD. s/o James C. in Largies, and Sarah Houston. To Tuckersmith Twp, Huron Co, ONT, 1832. m (i) Mary, 1780–1820, d/o John Halliday, ch: 1. Sarah, qv; 2. Margaret, qv; 3. Robert, qv; 4. James, qv; 5. Jane, qv; 6. Isabella, 1818-84, d Culcaigrie, unm; 7. Mary, b 1820, remained in SCT. Samuel m (ii) Agnes Hawthorn, qv, with further ch: 9. Samuel, jr, qv; 10. Grace, qv; 11. John, 1834-94; 12. William, 1840–1911; 13. Eliza, b ca 1842. **Ts Anwoth; DC 26 May and 27 Jun 1981**.

1543 CARNOCHAN, Samuel, jr, 15 Dec 1826–21 Aug 1893. From Girthon par, KKD. s/o Samuel C, qv, and Agnes Hawthorn, qv. To Huron Co, ONT, 1833. m Margaret Little, 1838-99. **DC 27 Jun 1981**.

1544 CARNOCHAN, Sarah, 10 Nov 1807–17 Feb 1869. From Girthon par, KKD. d/o Samuel C, qv, and Mary Halliday. To Huron Co, ONT, 1833. m Adam Black, 1802-53. **DC 27 Jun 1981**.

1545 CARNS, David, b ca 1753. To QUE on the *Amity's Desire*, ex London, 26 Apr 1774. Attorney-at-law. **NER lxiii 342**.

1546 CARNS, Jane, b ca 1756. sis/o David C, qv. To QUE on the *Amity's Desire*, ex London, Apr 1774. Spinster. **DC 21 Mar 1981**.

1547 CARR, Andrew. To Mosa Twp, Middlesex Co, ONT, prob <1840; stld Wardsville. **PCM 24**.

1548   CARR, George, 1792–1834. From LKS. To Nelson Twp, Halton Co, ONT, ca 1826; stld Lot 3, Con 1. Farmer. m Ann Hogg, qv, ch: 1. Janet, qv; 2. George, dy; 3. Elizabeth, dy.   **DC 21 Mar 1981.**

1549   CARR, J. From DFS. To Pictou Co, NS, <1823. Dau Agnes.   **VSN No 286.**

1550   CARR, Janet. From LKS. d/o George C, qv, and Ann Hogg, qv. To Nelson Twp, Halton Co, ONT, ca 1826. m Robert Bartley Taylor.   **DC 21 Mar 1981.**

1551   CARR, Janet, 1800-42. From LKS. d/o William C. and Agnes Hogg. To Nelson Twp, Halton Co, ONT, ca 1826. m William Wilson, qv.   **DC 21 Mar 1981.**

1552   CARRUTHERS, Agnes, 1825–13 Mar 1860. From Kilmarnock, AYR. d/o John C. and Agnes Hamilton. To ONT. m — Robb.   **Ts Kilmarnock.**

1553   CARRUTHERS, Andrew. From Dalton par, DFS. s/o James C. in Nutholm. To QUE on the *Triton*, Jun 1847. ch James and Mary d on voyage.   **Ts Dalton.**

1554   CARRUTHERS, Andrew, ca 1814–4 Oct 1877. From St Mungo par, DFS. Prob rel to William C, qv. To ONT and d 36 Maitland St, Toronto. Postal worker.   **CAE 39.**

1555   CARRUTHERS, John, 1813–8 Mar 1889. From Ecclefechan, DFS. To Kingston, ONT, <1837. Wholesale grocer and somtime Pres of Board of Trade. Contested Kingston against Sir John A. Macdonald, qv. ch.   **CAE 53.**

1556   CARRUTHERS, Mary. Poss from DFS. To Tatamagouche, Colchester Co, NS, ca 1840. Wife of David Williamson, qv.   **HT 71.**

1557   CARRUTHERS or CRUTHERS, Mary, b ca 1817. From Kelso, ROX. d/o Peter and Mary C. To Normanby Twp, Grey Co, ONT, 1854. Wife of Robert Jeffrey, qv.   **DC 31 Dec 1979.**

1558   CARRUTHERS, William, ca 1801–11 Sep 1872. From St Mungo par, DFS. Prob rel to Andrew C, qv. To Medonte Twp, Simcoe Co, ONT.   **CAE 27.**

1559   CARRWELL, Robert. From Glasgow. bro/o Thomas C. To Ramsay Twp, Lanark Co, ONT, <1855.   **SH.**

1560   CARSON, Charles, b ca 1753. From Colvend, KKD. Prob bro/o John C, qv. To Georgetown, Kings Co, PEI, on the *Lovely Nellie*, ex Carsethorn, May 1775. Labourer.   **ELN.**

1561   CARSON, Elizabeth. From Edinburgh. d/o William C, writer there, formerly in DFS. To Invermay, Guelph Twp, Wellington Co, ONT. m 8 Jul 1836, Thomas W. Valentine, Irvineside.   **DGC 31 Aug 1836.**

1562   CARSON, Jane, ca 1830–28 Jan 1857. Prob from DFS. To Port Hope, Durham Co, ONT. m James McHolm.   **DGH 27 Feb 1857.**

1563   CARSON, Jane Maxwell. From DFS. d/o William C, writer there, later in Edinburgh. m 14 Apr 1834, John Kennedy, qv, and stld Invermay, Guelph Twp, Wellington Co, ONT.   **DGC 16 Apr 1834.**

1564   CARSON, John, b ca 1753. From Colvend, KKD. Prob bro/o Charles C, qv. To Georgetown, Kings Co, PEI, on the *Lovely Nellie*, ex Carsethorn, May 1775. Labourer.   **ELN.**

1565   CARSON, Robert. From DFS. s/o James C, master mariner, and Elspeth Cowan. To NS <1855, and d there.   **Ts Dumfries.**

1566   CARSON, Samuel. To Aldborough Twp, Elgin Co, ONT.   **PDA 67.**

1567   CARSON, William, ca 1770–26 Feb 1843. Prob from Deebank, now Argrennan, Tongland par, KKD. Educ Edinburgh, and went to St John's, NFD. Physician and politician.   **DGH 27 Apr 1843; MDB 117.**

1568   CARSEWELL, Hugh, d 1840. To Montreal, QUE, 1833. Teacher. m Margaret Home. Son Robert.   **DC 29 Sep 1974.**

1569   CARSEWELL, John. Prob from ARL. To Mosa Twp, Middlesex Co, ONT, 1830.   **PCM 23.**

1570   CARSEWELL, Robert. To QUE on the *David of London*, ex Greenock, 19 May 1821; stld Lanark Co, ONT.   **HCL 70.**

1571   CARTER, John. From ABD. To Guelph, Wellington Co, ONT, <1855. m Margaret Wilson, qv. Dau Margaret.   **DC 18 Apr 1962.**

1572   CASSIE, Rev John. From ABD. Grad MA, King's Coll, ABD, 1827, and became UP min at Port Hope, Durham Co, ONT.   **KCG 283.**

1573   CATANACH, John, d 8 Jul 1816. To Montreal, QUE, <1791. Emp as baker by William Logan, qv.   **SGC 249.**

1574   CATHRO, Peter, b 14 Nov 1775. From Dundee, ANS. To CAN, ca 1800.   **DC 3 May 1977.**

1575   CAVEN, John. From Kirkcolm, WIG. To Galt Twp, Waterloo Co, ONT, 1847; stld Ayr. Schoolteacher. Son William, qv.   **MGC 2 Aug 1979.**

1576   CAVEN, Rev William, 1830–1904. From Kirkholm, WIG. s/o John C, qv. To Galt, Waterloo Co, ONT, 1847; stld Ayr. Became min of St Marys Presb Ch, Downie, Perth Co. Principal of Knox Coll, Toronto, 1873, and played an important part in forming the UP Ch in CAN, 1875. m 1856, Margaret, d/o John Goldie, qv, ch.   **BNA 826; MDB 138.**

1577   CAW, Rev David, 1797–4 Oct 1864. From Methven, PER. s/o William C. Matric Univ of Glasgow, 1821. Min of Savoch of Deer United Secession Ch, 1830-32. To Broadalbin, ONT, and min there 1832-46; trans to Paris, Brant Co.   **GMA 10721; UPC i 145.**

1578   CHALMERS, Alexander, 1804–1902. From Hamilton, LKS. s/o Robert C. C, qv, and Isabella Forrest, qv. To ONT ca 1842; stld Lambton Co. m Rebecca Shaw, qv.   **DC 12 Jul 1979.**

1579   CHALMERS, Gabriel, 12 Jan 1778–17 Sep 1858. From Cummertrees, DFS. s/o John C. and Mary Dickson. To Smiths Falls, North Elmsley Twp, Lanark Co, ONT, 1837. Blacksmith, farmer, and JP. Wife Margaret Mundle, qv, with him, and ch: 1. Mary, qv; 2. Jean Beattie, b 18 Jul 1808; 3. John, b 18 Nov 1811; 4. Edward, b 13 Feb 1814; 5. Agnes, b 3 Jun 1816; 6. Jemima, b 5 Apr 1818; 7. Margaret, b 17 Jun 1820; 8. Henry, b 10 Sep 1822; 9. Janet, b 7 Oct 1824; 10. Hugh Gabriel, b 11 Nov 1826; 11. Thomas Andrew, b 12 May 1833.   **DGH 19 Nov 1858; DC 14 Jan 1980.**

1580   CHALMERS, Isabella, 1816–7 Dec 1893. From

Hamilton, LKS. d/o Robert C. C, qv, and Isabella Forrest, qv. To QUE on the *Commerce*, ex Greenock, 11 May 1821; stld Dalhousie Twp, Lanark Co, ONT. m William Purdom, b 1812. **DC 12 Jul 1979**.

1581 CHALMERS, James, 1801–8 Mar 1886. From Hamilton, LKS. s/o Robert C. C, qv, and Isabella Forrest, qv. To QUE on the *Commerce*, ex Greenock, 11 May 1821; stld Dalhousie Twp, Lanark Co, ONT. m Isabella Cameron, 1808-86. **DC 12 Jul 1979**.

1582 CHALMERS, Jamesie, d 18 Aug 1837. From Newfieldburn, Ruthwell, DFS. d/o Gabriel C. and Mary Dickson. To Smiths Falls, Lanark Co, ONT. **Ts Ruthwell**.

1583 CHALMERS, Marion, 1817–19 Oct 1876. From Hamilton, LKS. d/o Robert C. C, qv, and Isabella Forrest, qv. To QUE on the *Commerce*, ex Greenock, 11 May 1821. m James Barrie, 1815-83. **DC 12 Jul 1979**.

1584 CHALMERS, Mary, b 7 Sep 1806. From Cummertrees, DFS. d/o Gabriel C, qv, and Margaret Mundle, qv. To Smiths Falls, Lanark Co, ONT, Apr 1837. Wife of Edward Clint, qv. **DC 14 Jan 1980**.

CHALMERS, Mrs. See MASSON, Elizabeth.

1585 CHALMERS, Robert C, 1776–1868. From Hamilton, LKS. To QUE on the *Commerce*, ex Greenock, 11 May 1821; stld Dalhousie Twp, Lanark Co, ONT. Farmer. m Isabella Forrest, qv, ch: 1. Annie; 2. James, qv; 3. Christine; 4. Alexander, qv; 5. Robert, jr, qv; 6. Isabella, qv; 7. Marion, qv; 8. William, b ONT. **SG xxvii/2 83; DC 12 Jul 1979**.

1586 CHALMERS, Robert, jr, 1810-97. From Hamilton, LKS. s/o Robert C. C, qv, and Isabella Forrest, qv. To QUE on the *Commerce*, ex Greenock, 11 May 1821; stld Dalhousie Twp, Lanark Co, ONT. Moved to Lambton Co, 1836. m Elizabeth Thom. **DC 12 Jul 1979**.

1587 CHAMBERS, Edward, b ca 1798. From OKI. To CAN <1828, poss Hudson Bay, but retr to SCT. Again to CAN, ca 1840, prob to Port Hope, Durham Co. Moved to Monaghan Twp, Northumberland Co. m Jane, d/o Thomas Vincent, Albany, ch: 1. Sophia, qv; 2. Jane, qv; 3. Edward, jr, qv; 4. Margaret, qv; 5. Jessie, b ca 1839; 6. Thomas, alive 1883; 7. George, b ca 1843; 8. John, b ca 1845; 9. Harriet, b ca 1847; 10. Joseph, b ca 1849. **DC 12 Jul 1979 and 31 Jan 1982**.

1588 CHAMBERS, Edward, jr, ca 1833–14 Dec 1908. From OKI. To Port Hope, Durham Co, ONT, ca 1840; stld South Monaghan Twp, Northumberland Co, later Verulam Twp, Victoria Co. Farmer. m Mary Jane, 1838–1919, d/o George Wood and Isabella Rebecca Colton, ch: 1. Amelia, b ca 1857; 2. Joseph, b ca 1859; 3. George, b ca 1860; 4. James Henry, b 1860; 5. David, b ca 1860; 6. Lillian, b ca 1865; 7. Alfred Edward, b ca 1867; 8. Frederick Charles, b 1869; 9. Thomas Vincent. **DC 31 Jan 1982**.

1589 CHAMBERS, Jane, b ca 1831, OKI. d/o Edward C, qv, and Jane Vincent. To Port Hope, Durham Co, ca 1840; stld later South Monaghan Twp, Northumberland Co. m Andrew Finnie, qv. **DC 31 Jan 1982**.

1590 CHAMBERS, John, b ca 1793. From Walls, OKI. To Hudson Bay, ca 1813, and prob to Red River. **RRS 13**.

1591 CHAMBERS, Margaret, ca 1836–9 Mar 1916. From OKI. d/o Edward C, qv, and Jane Vincent. To Port Hope, Durham Co, ONT, ca 1840; stld later South Monaghan Twp, Northumberland Co. m Robert, s/o George Wood and Isabella Rebecca Colton, ch. **DC 31 Jan 1982**.

1592 CHAMBERS, Robert. Stld Tatamagouche, Colchester Co, NS, 1806. Discharged soldier, and farmer. ch: 1. Samuel; 2. James, shipbuilder. **HT 41, 59**.

1593 CHAMBERS, Sophia, b ca 1828. From OKI. d/o Edward C, qv, and Jane Vincent. To ONT ca 1840; stld Port Hope, Durham Co, later South Monaghan Twp, Northumberland Co. m George Whittington, farmer, Harwich Twp, Kent Co, ch. **DC 31 Jan 1982**.

1594 CHARLES, Lewis. Poss from INV. Said rel to Simon McTavish, Albany fur-trader. To Montreal, QUE, <1800. Landscape gardener. ch. **SGC 269**.

1595 CHARTERS, Mary Jane. From ROX. d/o Thomas C. To St John, NB, <19 Aug 1845, when m Alexander Jardine, merchant. **DGH 25 Sep 1845**.

1596 CHASE, Elizabeth. Cabin passenger on the *London*, arr Pictou, NS, 11 Apr 1848. Unm. **DC 15 Jul 1979**.

1597 CHEP, James, b ca 1806. To ONT <2 May 1833, when m Charlotte, d/o Caleb Reynolds. ch: 1. Charlotte, 1839-75; 2. Henrietta, b 1841; 3. Catherine, b ca 1844; 4. Elizabeth, b ca 1849, prob Ancaster. **DC 5 Apr 1982**.

1598 CHESSER, Margaret. Poss from Edinburgh. To Brockville, Elizabethtown Twp, Leeds Co, ONT, 1854. Wife of Thomas Hislop, qv. **DC 28 Jun 1980**.

1599 CHEYNE, Rev George, ca 1800–1 Apr 1878. From Auchterless, ABD. s/o William C, farmer. Grad MA Marischall Coll, Aberdeen, 1822. To Hamilton, ONT, 1831. Presb min at Amherstburg, Essex Co, later at Saltfleet and Binbrook, Wentworth Co. Joined FC 1844. **FAM ii 434; SNQ ii/2 171**.

1600 CHEYNE, Jane. To CAN, 1826. Wife of Ralph Mabon, qv. **SG xxvii/4 170**.

1601 CHEYNE, Miss, ca 1750–8 Jan 1821. From Edinburgh. d/o Charles C, merchant, and Ann Gordon, of the family of Park. To NS and d Lunenburg, Lunenburg Co. **NSS No 2176**.

1602 CHISHOLM, Alexander. From INV. To Glengarry Co, ONT, 1790; stld Loch Garry. m Mary McDonell. Son Kenneth. **DC 4 Mar 1965**.

1603 CHISHOLM, Alexander. From Urquhart and Glenmoriston par, INV. bro/o John C, qv. To Salt Springs, Antigonish Co, NS, >1781. **SG iii/4 97**.

1604 CHISHOLM, Alexander. From Kenleoid, Ardchattan and Muckairn par, ARL. To PEI on the *Lucy*, ex Loch nan Uamh, Arisaig, 12 Jul 1790. Wife with him, and 2 ch. **PLL**.

1605 CHISHOLM, Alexander 'Gow'. From Strathglass, INV. bro/o Rev William C, qv. To Antigonish Co, NS, <1800. m Margaret, d/o Alexander Chisholm, ch: 1. Alexander; 2. Donald; 3. Archibald; 4. William; 5. John, res Cape Breton Is; 6. Peggy; 7. Kate. **HCA 100**.

1606 CHISHOLM, Alexander. Prob from Strathglass, INV. To Antigonish Co, NS, poss <1800. m Christine MacDonald, ch: 1. John; 2. Alexander; 3. John Og; 4. Hugh; 5. Ann; 6. Catherine; 7. Isobella. **HCA 105**.

1607 CHISHOLM, Alexander. From Strathglass, INV. To Antigonish Co, NS, ca 1800; stld Malignant Cove. m Ann McInnes, ch: 1. Alexander; 2. John; 3. Kenneth; 4. Donald; 5. Ann. **HCA 111**.

1608 CHISHOLM, Alexander, b ca 1776. To Western Shore, Inverness Co, NS, 1801. Farmer, m and ch. **CBC 1818**.

1609 CHISHOLM, Alexander. From Strathglass, INV. To Pictou, NS, on the *Sarah*, ex Fort William, Jun 1801. Labourer. Wife Margaret with him, and dau Margaret. **PLS**.

1610 CHISHOLM, Alexander. From Strathglass, INV. To Pictou, NS, on the *Sarah*, ex Fort William, Jun 1801. Farmer. **PLS**.

1611 CHISHOLM, Alexander, b ca 1791. Poss s/o Colin C, qv. To Western Shore, Inverness Co, NS, 1801. Farmer, unm. **CBC 1818**.

1612 CHISHOLM, Alexander. From Erchless, Kintail, ROC and INV. To Pictou, NS, on the *Dove*, ex Fort William, Jun 1801. Labourer. **PLD**.

1613 CHISHOLM, Alexander. From Strathglass, INV. To Pictou, NS, on the *Sarah*, ex Fort William, Jun 1801. Farmer. Wife Mary with him, and ch: 1. Duncan; 2. Catherine; 3. Patrick. **PLS**.

1614 CHISHOLM, Alexander. From Kilmorack, INV. To Pictou, NS, on the *Sarah*, ex Fort William, Jun 1801. Farmer. Wife Helen with him, and ch: 1. Catherine; 2. Margaret, aged 14; 3. Ann, aged 12; 4. Alexander, aged 10; 5. Helen, aged 8; 6. Isobel, aged 6; 7. Colin, aged 2; 8. inf. **PLS**.

1615 CHISHOLM, Alexander, ca 1770–6 Jul 1834. Prob from Strathglass, INV. To Pictou Co, NS. Bur Old Elgin. **DC 20 Nov 1976**.

1616 CHISHOLM, Alexander. From INV. To Antigonish Co, NS, prob <1810; stld Salt Springs. m Mary Chisholm, ch: 1. Kenneth. m (ii) Mary MacPhee, further ch: 2. Donald; 3. Samuel; 4. Kenneth; 5. Roderick; 6. Annie; 7. Christina; 8. Alexander G; 9. Duncan; 10. Archibald; 11. John; 12. Amelia; 13. Janet. **HCA 108**.

1617 CHISHOLM, Alexander, d 19 Oct 1854. Rel to James Sutherland, qv. Capt in Royal African Corps <1817, and stld Glengarry Co, ONT, 1818. MLA. m Janet, d/o Alexander McDonall of Leek, and Jean Chisholm. **SDG 167**.

1618 CHISHOLM, Alexander 'Ban'. From Strathglass, INV. bro/o John 'Ban' C, qv. To NS 1821; stld Long Point, Inverness Co. m Catherine McQuarrie, ch: 1. Neil, res Port Hastings; 2. John 'Ruadh', merchant and schoolteacher, Port Hastings. **WLC**.

1619 CHISHOLM, Alexander. From Is Skye, INV. s/o Donald C, dec, and Mary McPherson, qv. To Margaree Forks, Inverness Co, NS, 1832; later to Kewstoke, Whycocomagh. m Christy MacAskill, Cape North, ch: 1. Norman, dy; 2. Hugh; 3. Daniel; 4. Ann. Prob others. **MP ii 186**.

1620 CHISHOLM, Alexander 'Og'. From Is Skye, INV. s/o Donald C, dec, and Mary McPherson, qv. To Margaree Forks, Inverness Co, NS, 1832. Son Donald, res Glendyer. **MP ii 186**.

1621 CHISHOLM, Angus. From Is Skye, INV. s/o Donald C, dec, and Mary McPherson, qv. To Margaree Forks, Inverness Co, NS, 1832. Son Daniel. **MP ii 186**.

1622 CHISHOLM, Angus Kenneth. From Strathglass, INV. To Antigonish Co, NS, ca 1833; stld Brierly Brook. Wife Isobel Chisholm, qv, with him, and ch: 1. Nancy; 2. Kenneth; 3. William; 4. John, qv. Others b NS were: 5. Margaret; 6. Donald; 7. Catherine; 8. Isobel; 9. Valentine; 10. Duncan; 11. Finlay. **NSN 28/230**.

1623 CHISHOLM, Ann, b ca 1827. From Strathglass, INV. d/o Donald C, qv, and Isabella Chisholm, qv. To Monks Head, Antigonish Co, NS, 1832. m Angus, s/o William MacDonald, Marshy Hope. **HCA 117**.

1624 CHISHOLM, Anne. From Strathglass, INV. To Montreal, QUE, ex Fort William, 3 Jul 1802; stld E ONT. **MCM 1/4 26**.

1625 CHISHOLM, Archibald. From Lochbroom, ROC. To Pictou, NS, on the *Hector*, ex Loch Broom, arr 17 Sep 1773; stld East River. Joined 2nd Batt, Royal Highland Emigrant Regt. m a d/o Alexander Ross, qv. **HPC App C**.

1626 CHISHOLM, Archibald. Prob from Strathglass, INV. To NS, prob <1800; stld Antigonish Co. m Margaret Chisholm, ch: 1. Alexander; 2. Colin; 3. William; 4. Angus. **HCA 103**.

1627 CHISHOLM, Archibald. From Kilmorack, INV. To Pictou, NS, on the *Sarah*, ex Fort William, Jun 1801. Farmer. Wife Catherine with him, and ch: 1. Isobel; 2. Ann; 3. Catherine, aged 12. **PLS**.

1628 CHISHOLM, Archibald. From Kilmorack, INV. To Pictou, NS, on the *Sarah*, ex Fort William, Jun 1801. Tenant. Wife Ann with him, and an inf. **PLS**.

1629 CHISHOLM, Archibald. From Kiltarlity, INV. Prob rel to Colin C, qv. To Pictou, NS, on the *Sarah*, ex Fort William, Jun 1801. Labourer. **PLS**.

1630 CHISHOLM, Archibald. From Strathglass, INV. To NS prob 1803; stld Lismore, Antigonish Co. Farmer. m Ann, sis/o Rev Archibald McDonell, Judique, ch: 1. John; 2. Archibald; 3. Catherine. **HCA 99**.

1631 CHISHOLM, Catherine, ca 1730–2 Jan 1828. From INV. To NS, and d Douglas, Hants Co. **VSN No. 1664**.

1632 CHISHOLM, Catherine, ca 1790–20 Apr 1874. Prob from INV. To Pictou Co, NS. Bur Old Elgin. m Donald Shaw, qv. **DC 20 Nov 1976**.

1633 CHISHOLM, Catherine, d 17 Mar 1882. From INV. To NS <1832; stld Pictou Co. m John Shortt, qv. Bur at Salt Springs. **DC 27 Oct 1979**.

1634 CHISHOLM, Christine. From Strathglass, INV. To NS <1850; stld Guysborough Co. m Colin Chisholm, qv. **HNS iii 330**.

1635 CHISHOLM, Colin. From Kiltarlity, INV. Prob rel to Archibald C, qv. To Pictou, NS, on the *Sarah*, ex Fort William, Jun 1801. Labourer. **PLS**.

1636 CHISHOLM, Colin, b ca 1763. To Western Shore, Inverness Co, NS, 1801. Farmer, m and ch.   **CBC 1818**.

1637 CHISHOLM, Colin, b ca 1798. Poss s/o Colin C, qv. To Western Shore, Inverness Co, NS, 1801. Farmer, unm.   **CBC 1818**.

1638 CHISHOLM, Colin, b 1827. From Kilmuir, Is Skye, INV. s/o Donald C, dec, and Mary McPherson, qv. To Margaree Forks, Inverness Co, NS, 1832; later to Brook Village Rear. Farmer. m Anne Mackinnon, qv, ch: 1. Malcolm, 1855–1940; 2. Alexander, 1857–1953; 3. Dan Hugh, b 1862; 4. Flora, 1864–1952; 5. Donald Hugh, 1866–1958; 6. Malcolm 'Young', 1868–1924, went to MT; 7. Mary, 1869–1923; 8. Kitty Ann, b 1871, dy.   **MP ii 186**.

1639 CHISHOLM, Colin. Prob from Strathglass, INV. To Antigonish Co, NS, <1840. m Catherine Chisholm. **HCA 105**.

1640 CHISHOLM, Colin. From Strathglass, INV. To Guysborough Co, NS, <1850. m Christine Chisholm, qv.   **HNS iii 330**.

1641 CHISHOLM, Colin. Prob from Strathglass, INV. To Antigonish Co, NS, <1840. m Kate McIntosh, ch: 1. Mary, b 1837; 2. Rt Rev Colin, b 1840; 3. Donald, b 1842; 4. Isabella, b 1844; 5. Alexander, b 1850; 6. Catherine, b 1848; 7. Alexander Og, b 1850; 8. Duncan, b 1852, physician; 9. William; 10. John, b 1855; 11. Annie, b 1857; 12. Catherine, b 1859; 13. Archibald Francis, b 1862.   **HCA 105**.

1642 CHISHOLM(E), David, ca 1796–24 Sep 1842. From ROC. To Montreal, QUE, 1822. Journalist and historian.   **MDB 136**.

1643 CHISHOLM, Donald. From Strathglass, INV. To Pictou, NS <1788; stld Mallgnant Cove, Antigonish Co. m Catherine d/o Col Gillis, ch: 1. Sarah; 2. Mrs Alexander Gillis, Arisaig; 3. Mrs John Gillis.   **HCA 110**.

1644 CHISHOLM, Donald. From Strathglass, INV. To Pictou Co, NS, <18 Dec 1797; stld East River, where was gr 350 acres. Son Donald, jr, gr 400 acres. **HPC App H**.

1645 CHISHOLM, Donald, 1742–26 Feb 1842. From INV. To NS, and stld West Branch, East River, Pictou Co. Farmer. Bur Old Elgin. By wife Elizabeth, 1770–1859, ch: 1. James, dy; 2. Peter, dy; 3. Hugh, 1798–1820; 4. Catherine.   **PAC 39; DC 20 Nov 1976**.

1646 CHISHOLM, Donald. From Strathglass, INV. bro/o Rev William C, qv. To Antigonish Co, NS, <1800. Discharged soldier. By wife Rose ch: 1. Colin; 2. John; 3. Archie; 4. Alexander.   **HCA 100**.

1647 CHISHOLM, Donald 'Mor'. From INV. To Antigonish Co, NS, poss <1800; stld South Side Harbour. m a sis/o Rev Colin Grant, Arisaig, ch: 1. Alexander; 2. Rev John, b 1800; 3. Mrs John MacRae; 4. Colin.   **HCA 103**.

1648 CHISHOLM, Donald. From Strathglass, INV. To South River, Antigonish Co, NS, ca 1800. m Miss Chisholm, ch: 1. Donald; 2. John; 3. Alexander; 4. William; 5. Jane; 6. Mrs William Chisholm; 7. Mrs Donald Mackenzie.   **HCA 112**.

1649 CHISHOLM, Donald, 1754–1840. From Strathglass, INV. To NS on the *Aurora*, ex Fort William,

3 Jun 1803. Wife Flora, 1755–1841, with him, ch: 1. Donald Og, 1776–1869, genealogist; 2. Margaret; 3. Roderick; 4. Catherine; 5. Alexander.   **HCA 97**.

1650 CHISHOLM, Donald. From Strathglass, INV. s/o Kenneth C. To Monks Head, Antigonish Co, NS, 1832. m Isabella Chisholm, qv, ch: 1. Kenneth, qv; 2. Ann, qv; 3. John, qv; 4. William, qv; 5. Margaret, b Antigonish Co; 6. Donald; 7. Catherine; 8. Isabella; 9. Valentine; 10. Finlay; 11. Duncan.   **HCA 117**.

CHISHOLM, Mrs Donald. See McPHERSON, Mary.

1651 CHISHOLM, Duncan. From Strathglass, INV. To Little Harbour, Pictou Co, NS, <1800. ch: 1. William, qv; 2. Robert, qv; 3. Alexander; 4. Mrs Donald MacIntosh.   **HCA 98**.

1652 CHISHOLM, Duncan. From Kilmorack, INV. To Pictou, NS, on the *Sarah*, ex Fort William, Jun 1801. Labourer. Wife Ann with him.   **PLS**.

1653 CHISHOLM, Duncan. From Kilmorack, INV. To Pictou, NS, on the *Sarah*, ex Fort William, Jun 1801. Farmer. Wife Ann with him, and an inf.   **PLS**.

1654 CHISHOLM, Duncan. From Strathglass, INV. To NS 1801; stld Malignant Harbour, Antigonish Co. ch: 1. Barbara; 2. Duncan; 3. Christy; 4. Colin; 5. Rory; 6. John; 7. Ellen; 8. Donald; 9. Bella; 10. Angus. **HCA 114**.

1655 CHISHOLM, Finlay. From Strathglass, INV. bro/o Rev William C, qv. To Antigonish Co, NS, <1800. m Miss Chisholm, ch: 1. Donald; 2. Finlay; 3. Colin; 4. Kate; 5. Isabella; 6. Mary; 7. Eliza; 8. John.   **HCA 100**.

1656 CHISHOLM, Isabella. From Strathglass, INV. To Monks Head, Antigonish Co, NS, 1832. Wife of Donald Chisholm, qv.   **HCA 117**.

1657 CHISHOLM, Isobel. From Strathglass, INV. To Antigonish Co, NS, ca 1833; stld Brierly Brook. Wife of Angus Kenneth Chisholm, qv.   **NSN 28/230**.

1658 CHISHOLM, James. From Urquhart and Glenmoriston par, INV. To Pictou, NS, on the *Sarah*, ex Fort William, Jun 1801. Farmer. Wife Martha with him, ch: 1. Isobel, aged 14; 2. Mary, aged 12; 3. James, aged 10; 4. Catherine, aged 7; 5. John, aged 5; 6. Ewen, aged 2.   **PLS**.

1659 CHISHOLM, James. From Kilmorack, INV. To Pictou, NS, on the *Dove*, ex Fort William, Jun 1801. Labourer.   **PLD**.

1660 CHISHOLM, James Sutherland. To Montreal, QUE. Served heir to Donald Macdonell Chisholm of Chisholm, d 1858, in lands in ROC and in INV. **SH; SDG 167**.

1661 CHISHOLM, Jean. From Crasky, Strathglass, INV. To Antigonish Co, NS, ca 1813. Wife of John Fraser, qv.   **HCA 133**.

1662 CHISHOLM, Jenette. From Kilmorack, INV. To Pictou, NS, on the *Sarah*, ex Fort William, Jun 1801. **PLS**.

1663 CHISHOLM, John. From Strathglass, INV. To Pictou Co, NS, 1784; stld East Branch, East River. Discharged soldier, 84th Regt; gr 300 acres. Drowned with Finlay Cameron, qv, 1785. ch: 1. John, jr; 2. Belle; 3. Nancy; 4. Margaret; 5. John; 6. Archibald. **HPC App G; PAC 41**.

1664   CHISHOLM, John. From Strathglass, INV. To Pictou Co, NS, <1788. ch: 1. Mary; 2. Malcolm; 3. William. **HCA 10**.

1665   CHISHOLM, John. From INV. To Pictou Co, NS, <18 Dec 1797; stld East River. Prob discharged soldier, and gr 300 acres. **HPC App H**.

1666   CHISHOLM, John. From Urquhart and Glenmoriston par, INV. bro/o Alexander C, qv. To Salt Springs, Antigonish Co, NS, >1781. Son John, jr, qv. **SG iii/4 97**.

1667   CHISHOLM, John, jr. From Urquhart and Glenmoriston par, INV. s/o John C, qv. To Salt Springs, Antigonish Co, NS, >1781. m Mary Livingston, qv, ch. **SG iii/4 97**.

1668   CHISHOLM, John 'Donn'. Prob from Strathglass, Inverness Co, NS, <1801; stld South Side Harbour. m Miss Chisholm, and had, with other ch: 1. Alexander; 2. John; 3. Colin; 4. Kenneth. **HCA 104**.

1669   CHISHOLM, John. From Kilmorack, INV. Poss rel to William C, qv. To Pictou, NS, on the *Dove*, ex Fort William, Jun 1801. Labourer. **PLD**.

1670   CHISHOLM, John. From Kilmorack, INV. To Pictou, NS, on the *Sarah*, ex Fort William, Jun 1801. Farmer. Wife Catherine with him, ch: 1. Donald; 2. Colin; 3. William; 4. Margaret. **PLS**.

1671   CHISHOLM, John, b ca 1786. From Strathglass, INV. To Pictou, NS, on the *Sarah*, ex Fort William, Jun 1801. **PLS**.

1672   CHISHOLM, John. From Kiltarlity, INV. To Pictou, NS, on the *Sarah*, ex Fort William, Jun 1801. Wife Flora with him, ch: 1. John; 2. Roderick; 3. Archibald. **PLS**.

1673   CHISHOLM, John, b 1766. From Strathglass, INV. To Pictou, NS, on the *Sarah*, ex Fort William, Jun 1801; stld Western Shore, Inverness Co. Farmer. Wife Ann with him, ch: 1. John, b ca 1793; 2. Alexander, b ca 1795, carpenter; 3. Colin; 4. Donald, b ca 1799. **PLS; CBC 1818**.

1674   CHISHOLM, John. From Strathglass, INV. s/o Austin C. To Gaspereaux Lake, Kings Co, NS, prob <1810. m Miss MacPherson, ch: 1. Austin; 2. Donald; 3. Duncan; 4. Rory; 5. Ann; 6. Peggy; 7. Mrs Colin Fraser. **HCA 113**.

1675   CHISHOLM, John. From Strathglass, INV. To Antigonish Co, NS, prob <1820; stld Brierly Brook. m Margaret MacPherson, ch: 1. Hugh; 2. Donald; 3. Duncan; 4. Margaret. **HCA 109**.

1676   CHISHOLM, John 'Ban'. From Strathglass, INV. bro/o Alexander 'Ban' C, qv. Stld Inverness Co, NS, poss 1821. Son Christopher. **WLC**.

1677   CHISHOLM, John, b ca 1828. From Strathglass, INV. s/o Donald C, qv, and Isabella Chisholm, qv. To Monks Head, Antigonish Co, NS, 1832. m (i) Janet Chisholm, ch; (ii) Janet MacDonald, with further ch. **HCA 117**.

1678   CHISHOLM, John, b ca 1832. From Strathglass, INV. s/o Angus Kenneth C, qv, and Isobel C, qv. To

Antigonish Co, NS, ca 1833; stld Brierly Brook. m (ii) Elizabeth McLean, ch: 1. Margaret; 2. Angus; 3. John; 4. Bella; 5. Colin; 6. Valentine; 7. Kenneth; 8. Anne; 9. Daniel; 10. Florence.   **NSN 28/234**.

1679   CHISHOLM, John 'Donn'. Prob from Strathglass, INV. To Antigonish Co, NS, <1840. m Catherine, d/o Rory 'Ban' McNeil.   **HCA 105**.

1680   CHISHOLM, Katherine. From Kilmorack, INV. To Pictou, NS, on the *Dove*, ex Fort William, Jun 1801. Spinster. **PLD**.

1681   CHISHOLM, Kenneth. From Strathglass, INV. To Pictou, NS, on the *Dove*, ex Fort William, Jun 1801. Labourer. Wife and ch with him. **PLD**.

1682   CHISHOLM, Kenneth, b ca 1825. From Strathglass, INV. s/o Donald C, qv, and Isabella Chisholm, qv. To Monks Head, Antigonish Co, NS, 1832. m Catherine MacIntosh, ch: 1. John C; 2. Angus; 3. Janet; 4. Ann; 5. Isabel; 6. Christine; 7. Alexander; 8. John; 9. John H. **HCA 117**.

1683   CHISHOLM, Margaret. From Kilmorack, INV. Poss rel to Archibald C, qv. To Pictou, NS, on the *Sarah*, ex Fort William, Jun 1801. Spinster. **PLS**.

1684   CHISHOLM, Mary. From Strathglass, INV. Prob wife of Alexander C, farmer, qv. To Pictou, NS, on the *Sarah*, ex Fort William, Jun 1801. Spinster. **PLS**.

1685   CHISHOLM, Mary. From INV. To Pictou Co, NS, <1816; stld Hopewell. m Roderick McLean, qv. **PAC 150**.

1686   CHISHOLM, Michael. Prob from INV. To Antigonish Co, NS, <1832, when he moved to PEI. m Miss MacPherson, and had ch. **HP 38**.

1687   CHISHOLM, Neil, d 1849. Poss from ARL. To Ekfrid Twp, Middlesex Co, ONT, 1832. **PCM 31**.

1688   CHISHOLM, Robert. From Strathglass, INV. s/o Duncan C, qv. To Little Harbour, Pictou Co, NS, <1800. m Sarah Mackinnon, ch: 1. Duncan; 2. Robert; 3. Daniel; 4. Mrs Floyd; 5. Kate. **HCA 98**.

1689   CHISHOLM, Roderick. From Strathglass, INV. To Pictou, NS, on the *Nora*, ex Fort William, 1801; stld Marydale, Antigonish Co. Pioneer settler. **HCA 14**.

1690   CHISHOLM, Roderick. From Kilmorack, INV. To Pictou, NS, on the *Dove*, ex Fort William, Jun 1801. Labourer. **PLD**.

1691   CHISHOLM, Roderick. From INV. To Long Point, Inverness Co, NS, <1820. m Isabella Chisholm, ch: 1. Alexander, 1847–1915; 2. Dr Donald, went to St Louis, MO; 3. Colin, b 1850, barrister and MLA. **HNS iii 641; MLA 62**.

1692   CHISHOLM, Rory 'Mor'. From INV. To South Side Harbour, Antigonish Co, NS, poss <1800. m Catherine, d/o Donald Chisholm, ch: 1. Colin; 2. Daniel Rory; 3. William; 4. Kate; 5. Isabella; 6. Mary; 7. Isabella; 8. Donald; 9. John, merchant. **HCA 104**.

1693   CHISHOLM, Rory. From Strathglass, INV. To Pictou, NS, on the *Sarah*, ex Fort William, Jun 1801. Tenant. Wife Mary with him, and ch: 1. Mary; 2. Christian, aged 12. **PLS**.

1694   CHISHOLM, Thomas, b ca 1738. From Kirkbean,

KKD. To Georgetown, Kings Co, PEI, on the *Lovely Nellie*, ex Carsethorn, May 1775. Farmer.   **ELN**.

1695   CHISHOLM, William. From Strathglass, INV. s/o Duncan C, qv. To Little Harbour, Antigonish Co, NS, <1802. m Miss MacDonald.   **HCA 98**.

1696   CHISHOLM, Rev William, ca 1775–3 Aug 1819. From Strathglass, INV. bro/o Finlay C, qv, Donald C, qv, and Alexander 'Gow' C, qv. To Antigonish Co, NS, <1800. Became RC priest, and d at Georgeville. **HCA 99**.

1697   CHISHOLM, William. From Kiltarlity, INV. To Pictou, NS, on the *Dove*, ex Fort William, Jun 1801. Labourer.   **PLD**.

1698   CHISHOLM, William. From Kilmorack, INV. Prob rel to John C, qv. To Pictou, NS, on the *Dove*, ex Fort William, Jun 1801. Labourer.   **PLD**.

1699   CHISHOLM, William. From Strathglass, INV. To Pictou, NS, on the *Sarah*, ex Fort William, Jun 1801. Wife Catherine with him, ch: 1. Catherine, aged 9; 2. Ann, aged 4; 3. Alexander, aged 3.   **PLS**.

1700   CHISHOLM, William. From Kilmorack, INV. To Pictou, NS, on the *Sarah*, ex Fort William, Jun 1801. Farmer. Wife Mary with him, ch: 1. Alexander; 2. Donald; 3. Margaret; 4. Catherine; 5. Kenneth, aged 8; 6. William, aged 4; 7. Colin, aged 3; 8. inf. **PLS**.

1701   CHISHOLM, William, b ca 1797. Poss rel to Colin C, qv. To Western Shore, Inverness Co, NS, 1816. Farmer, unm.   **CBC 1818**.

1702   CHISHOLM, William, b ca 1758. To Western Shore, Inverness Co, NS, 1817. Farmer, m and had ch.   **CBC 1818**.

1703   CHISHOLM, William, b ca 1831. From Strathglass, INV. s/o Donald C, qv, and Isabella C, qv. To Monks Head, Antigonish Co, NS, 1832. m (i) Margaret MacDonald, ch; (ii) Elizabeth MacLean, with further ch.   **HCA 117**.

1704   CHISHOLM, William. To Pictou, NS, on the *Lady Gray*, ex Cromarty, ROC, arr 16 Jul 1841.   **DC 15 Jul 1979**.

1705   CHRISTIE, Alexander, 1793–1872. From Aberdeen. s/o Alexander C, merchant. Matric Marishcall Coll, Aberdeen, 1812. To CAN prob <1820, and became an emp of HBCo. App Gov of Assiniboia, 1833. m a Cree woman and retr to SCT, 1849. Sons James T. and William Joseph, educ Marischall Coll.   **FAM ii 415, 491, 506; MDB 138**.

1706   CHRISTIE, Alexander James, d 1843. From ABD. Prob s/o Alexander C. To CAN, 1817. Physician, farmer and journalist.   **MDB 138**.

1707   CHRISTIE, David, 1818-80. Educ Edinburgh High School and emig to Brant Co, ONT. Farmer and politician. Became Secretary of State for CAN. m (i) 1850, Isabel, d/o Robert Turnbull; (ii) 1860, Margaret, d/o William Turnbull.   **BNA 602; MDB 138**.

1708   CHRISTIE, Donald, 1796–14 Sep 1844. From Killin par, PER. s/o Donald C. and Jean McIntyre. To ONT <1835; stld prob Ontario Co. m (i) Christian Campbell, ch: 1. Donald, b ca 1830; 2. Malcolm, b ca 1832; 3. Helen, b ca 1835. m (ii) Mary Munro. **DC 31 Jan 1982**.

1709   CHRISTIE, Duncan. To Oxford Co, ONT, <1853. m Eliza Pearson.   **DC 4 Mar 1965**.

1710   CHRISTIE, Hugh, 1756–1838. From Lochaber, INV. To Martintown, Glengarry Co, ONT, <1816. Son John, qv.   **SMB**.

1711   CHRISTIE, Jean, b ca 1800. From Killin, PER. d/o Donald C. and Jean McIntyre. To Reach Twp, Ontario Co, ONT, ca 1835. Wife of Archibald McDiarmid, qv. **DC 31 Jan 1982**.

1712   CHRISTIE, Rev James, 4 Oct 1828–12 Feb 1902. From Kildrummy, ABD. s/o William C, par schoolmaster. Grad MA Kings Coll, Aberdeen, 1846. Min of Wallace and Pugwash, Cumberland Co, NS, 1859-64. Went as missionary to Comax, BC, 1887, and Denman Is. Later at Wellington. He d in Victoria.   **KCG 298; FES vii 614, 657**.

1713   CHRISTIE, John, b ca 1791. To QUE on the *Eliza*, ex Greenock, 3 Aug 1815; stld Bathurst Twp, Lanark Co, ONT. Farmer, Lot 2, Con 2. Wife Isobel Wright, qv, with him.   **SEC 1; HCL 233**.

1714   CHRISTIE, John, ca 1796–1872. From Lochaber, INV. s/o Hugh C, qv. To Martintown, Glengarry Co, ONT, <1816. m Janet McArthur.   **SMB**.

1715   CHRISTIE, John, 22 Nov 1795–19 Jun 1864. From MacDuff, BAN. s/o Alexander C. and Janet Christie. To Halifax, NS, on the *Brilliant*, Mar 1830. Went to Stanstead Twp, Richelieu Co, QUE, via Derby, VT. Stonemason. Wife Magdalene Lumsden, qv, with him. ch: 1. Alexander, 1821-65; 2. Catherine, 1823-88; 3. John, 1824-85; 4. Jessie, dy; 5. Robina, 1828-75; 6. Anna Gibb, 1830–1912; 7. Penelope, 1832–1906; 8. Margaret, 1834-59; 9. George, 1836-39.   **DC 12 Jan 1980**.

1716   CHRISTIE, John, b ca 1812. From Glasgow. To NS <1834; stld Bras d'Or Lake, Cape Breton Is. Merchant, with William Gammell, qv. m Ann Smith, qv. Son John H, b 1834, merchant, postmaster and shipbuilder.   **HNS iii 418**.

1717   CHRISTIE, John, d 21 Oct 1857. From Killin, PER. s/o Donald C. and Jean McIntyre. To Reach Twp, Ontario Co, ONT, 1845. Farmer. m Jean McLaren, qv, ch: 1. John, b 1829; 2. Duncan, b 1831; 3. Jane, b 1834; 4. Donald; 5. James; 6. Elizabeth, b 1843.   **DC 12 Jul 1979**.

1718   CHRISTIE, John, 1798–24 Feb 1881. From Killin, PER. To Reach Twp, Ontario Co, ONT, ca 1840. Farmer. m 24 Jan 1824, Janet McAlpin, who d in SCT, ch: 1. Duncan, b ca 1824; 2. Donald, b 1829; 3. Hugh, b 1830; 4. Jane, b 1832; 5. John, b 1835.   **DC 12 Jul 1979**.

1719   CHRISTIE, Kate. From Is Arran, BUT. To QUE on the *Margaret*, 1832; stld Inverness, Megantic Co, QUE.   **MAC 42**.

1720   CHRISTIE, Lewis, 19 Nov 1832–4 Dec 1910. Prob from ABD. To South Gower, Grenville Co, ONT. Farmer. m 29 Apr 1856, at South Gower, Jane Bennet, from Co Mayo, IRL, b 1833.   **DC 29 Dec 1974**.

1721   CHRISTIE, Margaret. From Breadalbane, PER. To Martintown, Glengarry Co, ONT. Wife of Donald McDonald, qv.   **SMB**.

1722   CHRISTIE, Mary A. From Is Arran, BUT. To QUE

on the *Margaret*, 1832; stld Inverness, Megantic Co, QUE. **MAC 42**.

1723   CHRISTIE, Peter. From Killin, PER. s/o Donald C. and Jean McIntyre. To ONT <1836. m Miss Christie, ch: 1. Donald; 2. John; 3. Duncan; 4. Peter; 5. James; 6. Jane; 7. Hugh; 8. Lucy; 9. Christina; 10. Catherine; 11. Margaret; 12. Mary. **DC 12 Jul 1979**.

1724   CHRISTIE, Robert, 1780–1877. bro/o Rev Thomas C, qv. To Dumfries Twp, Waterloo Co, ONT, 1834. Son Hon David, Speaker in the Canadian Senate. **HGD 213**.

1725   CHRISTIE, Rev Thomas. bro/o Robert C, qv. To Dumfries Twp, Waterloo Co, ONT, 1832. Missionary of the United Secession Ch, and res West Flamborough. **HGD 214**.

1726   CHRISTIE, William M, ca 1819–14 Jun 1900. From Huntly, ABD. To ONT, 1848. Baker. m Mary Jane, d/o James McMullen, ch. **DC 29 Sep 1964**.

1727   CHRISTIELAW, William. Prob from LKS. To Lanark Co, ONT, 1821; stld Lot 1, Con 1, North Sherbrooke Twp. **HCL 74**.

1728   CLAPPERTON, Elizabeth. To Montreal, QUE, 1812. m Andrew Leishman, qv. **DC 1 Apr 1974**.

1729   CLARK, Mrs Agnes, ca 1747–12 Jun 1826. From KKD. wid/o James C. To NS and d there. **VSN No 1721**.

1730   CLARK, Alexander. From Comrie, PER. To Montreal, QUE, on the *Curlew*, ex Greenock, 21 Jul 1818. Wife Janet with him, and dau Mary, aged 9. **BCL**.

1731   CLARK, Alexander. From INV. To East Williams Twp, Middlesex Co, ONT, 1832. **PCM 43**.

1732   CLARK, Alexander. From Grantown-on-Spey, MOR. To Port Dover, Norfolk Co, ONT, 1841. Farmer. Son Dr Daniel, b 29 Aug 1835, surgeon, became Superintendent of the Lunatic Asylum at Toronto in 1875. **BNA 1189**.

1733   CLARK, Catherine, ca 1828–21 Dec 1856. From Tain, ROC. d/o John C. To Woodstock, Oxford Co, ONT, and d at the res of her bro John C, qv. **DGH 23 Jan 1857**.

1734   CLARK, Charles. From Aberdeen. To Mill Brook, Tatamagouche, Colchester Co, NS, <1849. Farmer. **HT 82**.

1735   CLARK, Donald. From Comrie par, PER. To Montreal, QUE, on the *Curlew*, ex Greenock, 21 Jul 1818; stld prob Beckwith Twp, Lanark Co, ONT. Wife Margaret with him. **BCL**.

1736   CLARK, George, 1827–29 May 1905. From Insch par, ABD. To Tatamagouche, Colchester Co, NS, 1847. Hardware merchant and MLA. m (i) 1856, Agnes Aitcheson; (ii) 1873, Elizabeth Bell. **HT 82; SNQ viii/1 189; MLA 65**.

1737   CLARK, Isabella, ca 1810–28 Dec 1857. From Kingussie, INV. d/o Capt William C. of Dalnavert, and Margaret Shaw. To Kingston, ONT, <1850. m her cousin, John Alexander McDonald, qv. **DC 5 Mar 1982**.

1738   CLARK, James, d 1901. From Aberdeen. bro/o John C, qv. To Halifax, NS, arr 1843; stld

Tatamagouche, Colchester Co. Farmer and magistrate. Son Sydney. **HT 81**.

1739   CLARK, Jane P. From Ayr. To QUE. m William C. Hunter, b Montreal. Son Archibald M. b Brome, 1863. **MGC 2 Aug 1979**.

1740   CLARK, John, ca 1799–7 Nov 1847. From Dunscore, DFS. To QUE, and d Chateau Richer, Montmorency Co. Physician. **DGH 9 Dec 1847**.

1741   CLARK, John. From Aberdeen. bro/o James C, qv. To Halifax, NS, arr 1843; stld Mill Brook, Tatamagouche, Colchester Co. Farmer and storekeeper. **HT 81**.

1742   CLARK, John. To Pictou, NS, on the *Hope*, ex Glasgow, 5 Apr 1848. **DC 12 Jul 1979**.

1743   CLARK, John. From Tain, ROC. s/o John C. To Woodstock, Oxford Co, ONT, <1855. **DGH 23 Jan 1857**.

1744   CLARK, Joseph, b ca 1730. From Sanquhar, DFS. To Georgetown, Kings Co, PEI, on the *Lovely Nellie*, ex Carsethorn, May 1775. Joiner. Wife Ann Wilkie, qv, with him, and ch: 1. Ann, aged 4; 2. Joseph, b ca 1772. **ELN**.

1745   CLARK, Margaret, ca 1792–18 Aug 1881. From Inveraray, ARL. d/o Daniel C. and Janet McGregor. To QUE, and d Kirks Ferry. m — Allan. **LDW 30 May 1972**.

1746   CLARK, Margaret, b ca 1830. From Is Tyree, ARL. d/o Hugh C. and Christina McLean. To Tiverton, Kincardine Twp, Bruce Co, ONT. m John McLean. **LDW 8 Mar 1970**.

1747   CLARK, Margaret. From Kingussie, INV. d/o Capt William C. of Dalnavert, and Margaret Shaw. To Kingston, ONT, prob <1850. m — Greene. **DC 2 Mar 1982**.

1748   CLARK, Maria, d 1893. From Kingussie, INV. d/o Capt William C. of Dalnavert, and Margaret Shaw. To Kingston, ONT, <1850. m — Macpherson, her cousin, ch. **CSL 184**.

1749   CLARK, Mary, 1834–31 Dec 1877. From Fyvie, ABD. To Hamilton Twp, Northumberland Co, ONT. m William Campbell, qv. **Ts Mt Albion**.

1750   CLARK, Robert. From INV. To Pictou Co, NS, 1784, and had grants of land on East River. Discharged soldier, 84th Regt. **HPC App G and H**.

1751   CLARK, Robert. From Aberdeen. To NS <1849; stld Mill Brook, Tatamagouche, Colchester Co. Farmer. **HT 82**.

1752   CLARK, Thomas, ca 1770–1837. From Dumfries. To ONT <1807, when 'for military services' he was gr land by the Crown the entire twp of Nichol, Wellington Co. MLC for 29 years. m Mary Margaret, 1792–1837, d/o Robert Kerr, army surgeon. **EHE 50**.

1753   CLARK, Thomas W, ca 1829–19 Jun 1869. From Ruthwell, DFS. s/o George C. and Mary Wilson. To Victoria, BC, and d there. **Ts Ruthwell**.

1754   CLARK, Walter, d 1853. To ONT <1838; stld Brant Co. Farmer. Son John, b 1840. **DC 23 Sep 1980**.

1755   CLARK, William, b ca 1743. From Caerlaverock, DFS. To Georgetown, Kings Co, PEI, on the *Lovely*

Nellie, ex Carsethorn, May 1775. Gardener. Went to Pictou, NS, and stld west side of West River. Listed as capable of bearing arms, 1783. Wife Grizel Kissock, qv, with him, and inf s John. **ELN; HPC App D and E.**

1756 CLARK, William, b ca 1796. To Inverness Co, NS, 1816; stld Port Hood dist. Unm. **CBC 1818.**

1757 CLARK, William. From Aberdeen. To NS <1849; stld Mill Brook, Tatamagouche, Colchester Co. Farmer. **HT 82.**

1758 CLARK, Rev William Brown, 1805-93. Born Biggar, LKS, and educated Univ of Edinburgh. Schoolmaster in Yarrow, SEL, but studied theology and became missionary in Edinburgh. Ord min of Half-Morton, DFS, 1839. Joined FC 1843, and was min at Maxwelltown until 1853, when adm to Chalmers Church, Quebec. Res. 1874, and app Professor of Church History, Quebec. s/o William C, merchant, m (i) 1836, Jane Brown; (ii) Amelia Torrance or Gibb, d 1893. ch: 1. Elizabeth Glover; 2. Bethia Barbara, both by first wife. **AFC i 121; FES ii 235.**

1759 CLARK, Sir William Mortimer, 24 May 1836–11 Aug 1917. Born Aberdeen. s/o John C, manager of the Aberdeen Insurance Co, and Jane Mortimer. Matric Marischall Coll, Aberdeen, 1850, and grad BA, Univ of Edinburgh. Adm WS 1859. To Toronto, ONT, <1866. Lawyer and Lt Gov of ONT. m Helen, d/o Gilbert Gordon, Peterborough, ch. **FAM ii 556; HWS 110.**

1760 CLARKE, John. From Petty, INV. To East Williams Twp, Middlesex Co, ONT, prob 1833. **PCM 43.**

1761 CLARKE, R. Douglas. From Edinburgh. To Halifax, NS, 1809. Merchant. m Wilhelmina Delmolitor Davis, ch. **HNS iii 446.**

1762 CLARKE, Thomas, ca 1774–6 Oct 1835. To CAN <1820, and d at Falls of Niagara, leaving relatives in DFS. Hon Col. **DGC 25 Nov 1835.**

1763 CLARKSON, John. To Pictou, NS, on the *Lulan*, ex Glasgow, 17 Aug 1848. Wife with him. **DC 12 Jul 1979.**

1764 CLEGHORN, Archibald, d 25 Sep 1840. From Leith, MLN. To New Glasgow, Pictou Co, NS. *The Witness*, **7 Nov 1840.**

1765 CLEGHORN, George, b ca 1819. Poss from MLN. To NB <1854. m Agnes Hogg, qv, ch: 1. Elizabeth, b 1845; 2. Jane, b 1846; 3. Jessie, b 1848; 4. George, b 1851; 5. John, b 1854. **DC 10 Jun 1981.**

1766 CLEGHORN, William. Prob from Edinburgh. bro/o Isobel C. To Montreal, QUE, <1841. **SH.**

1767 CLELAND, Robert. From Perth. s/o John C, surgeon. To Montreal, QUE, <1855. Banker. **SH.**

1768 CLEPHANE, George, d 17 Feb 1851. From Carslogie, Cupar, FIF. s/o Andrew C, Advocate, and Anna Maria Douglas. Educ Edinburgh Academy, 1826-33, and went to CAN. **EAR 37.**

1769 CLERK, Agnes, b ca 1819. To St Gabriel de Valcartier, QUE, prob <1855. **Census 1861.**

1770 CLERK, Elizabeth, b ca 1823. To St Gabriel de Valcartier, QUE, prob <1855. **Census 1861.**

1771 CLERK, George Edward, 18 Mar 1815–20 Sep 1875. From Penicuik, MLN. Second s/o Sir George C. of Penicuik, 6th Bart, and Maria Law. To Montreal, QUE, 1847. Journalist. m 27 Nov 1849, Marie Louise Elizabeth, d/o Casimer Dupuis, Montreal, and had, with other ch: 1. George Edward, 1850–1906; 2. Charles François, 1851–1927; 3. Henry Joseph, 1856–1929; 4. Edmund Antoine, 1858–1921; 5. Alexander Marie Joseph, 1870–1932. **DC 20 Feb 1978.**

1772 CLERK, Samuel, b ca 1802. To St Gabriel de Valcartier, QUE, prob <1855. **Census 1861.**

1773 CLEZIE, George. Prob from BEW. To Toronto, ONT, <1840. **DC 24 Sep 1979.**

1774 CLINT, Edward. From DFS, poss Cummertrees par. To Lanark Co, ONT, 1837; stld Smiths Falls, North Elmsley Twp. Wife Mary Chalmers, qv, with him. **DC 14 Jan 1980.**

1775 CLOUSTON, Edward, 1759–1810. From OKI. s/o Capt Robert C. of Nisthouse, and Margaret Isbister. Served with the HBCo and retr to Stromness, 1798. d without lawful issue. **TFC 120.**

1776 CLOUSTON, James Stewart, 1826-74. From Smoogro, OKI. s/o Edward C. and Ann Rose Stewart. To CAN, ca 1842, and emp as a clerk with the HBCo. Served at Moose Factory and became a chief trader. m Margaret, d/o Robert Miles, chief factor, ch: 1. Sir Edward Seaborne, 1849–1912, banker, Montreal; 2. Robert; 3. William, 1861–1934. **TFC 116; DC 21 Mar 1971.**

1777 CLOUSTON, Robert. From Orphir, OKI. To Red River, MAN, <1831. m Nancy, d/o James Sutherland, qv. **DC 21 Mar 1971.**

1778 CLOUSTON, Robert, 1820–13 Aug 1858. From Smoogro, OKI. s/o Edward C. and Ann Rose Stewart. To CAN, 1842. Clerk, later chief trader, HBCo. m Jessy, d/o Donald Ross, qv, chief trader. **TFC 116; DC 21 Mar 1971.**

1779 CLOUSTON, Thomas. From OKI. To Hudson Bay, 1813. Labourer. m Isabella Kerr. Son Thomas, b Stromness, OKI, 15 Nov 1813. **Stromness OPR 30/2.**

1780 CLOWE, Janet. To Brant Co, ONT, <1850. m Alexander Carlyle, qv. **DC 23 Sep 1980.**

1781 CLUBB, Alexander, b 1818. From ABD. Rel to John C, qv. To ONT prob <1854. Stone-cutter, cabinet-maker and farmer. Wife Jane Reed, qv, with him, and ch: 1. Alexander, b 25 Nov 1845; 2. George, b 6 Feb 1848. **DC 20 Sep 1979.**

1782 CLUBB, John, b 1822. From ABD. Rel to Alexander C, qv. To ONT <1854. Shoemaker. Wife Helen, b 1824, with him. **DC 20 Sep 1979.**

1783 CLUGSTON, Rev John, 1796–21 Jan 1877. From Glasgow. s/o James C, craftsman. Matric Univ of Glasgow, 1816. To QUE and was min there. Son Rev James, b QUE, 1831, became FC min at Stewarton, AYR. **GMA 9621; AFC i 122.**

1784 CLUNESS, David. From Petty, INV. To East Williams Twp, Middlesex Co, ONT, 1832. ch. **PCM 43.**

1785 CLYMIE, Duncan. From LKS. Prob rel to John C, qv. To QUE on the *Prompt*, ex Greenock, summer 1820; stld Lanark Co, ONT. **HCL 238.**

1786 CLYMIE, John. From LKS. Prob rel to John C, qv. To QUE on the *Prompt*, ex Greenock, summer 1820; stld Lanark Co, ONT. **HCL 238**.

1787 COATES, James, d 8 Oct 1823. Prob from DFS. Mate of the *John & Mary*, of Newcastle, and d at Quebec. **DGC 23 Dec 1823**.

1788 COBB, William. To Ramsay Twp, Lanark Co, ONT, 1821. **HCL 86**.

1789 COBBAN, James, ca 1800–26 Feb 1857. From Aberdeen. s/o James C, merchant. Grad MA Marischall Coll, Aberdeen, 1818, and became a surgeon in the RN. Stld Trafalgar Twp, Halton Co, ONT, 1832, and practiced medicine. m 9 Jan 1836, at Dundas, Catharine Ann, d/o Capt Thomas Jarmy and Sarah Pierce, ch: 1. Elizabeth Martha, b ca 1837; 2. Mary, b 1839; 3. Matthew Whyte, b ca 1840; 4. Sarah Isabella, b 1843; 5. Agnes Anne, b 1845; 6. Maria Louisa, 1847-48; 7. Charles, b ca 1850. **FAM ii 422; DC 15 May 1982**.

1790 COCHRAN, John. From KKD. To Lanark Co, ONT, <1820. Dau Elizabeth. **MDB 530**.

1791 COCHRANE, James. From Paisley, RFW. To Megantic Co, QUE, 1828. Discharged soldier. **DC 11 Feb 1980**.

1792 COCHRANE, Rupert John, d 1831. Prob from Edinburgh. To Halifax, NS. m Isabella MacComb Clarke, d 1851, ch: 1. Bayard Clarke, RE, d Bermuda, 1864; 2. Rupert Inglis, 34th Regt, d 1864, Lucknow, India. **Ts St Johns, Edinburgh**.

1793 COCHRANE, Rev William, ca 1829–29 May 1879. From Rothesay, BUT. s/o John C, craftsman. Matric Univ of Glasgow, 1847. Adm min of Elgin, ONT, 1866; trans to Port Hope, 1868. Demitted his charge 1871, and was afterwards at Middleville. **FES vii 630**.

1794 COCK, Rev Daniel, b ca 1730. From Roberton, LKS. s/o James C. Matric Univ of Glasgow, 1744, and was Secession min at Cartsdyke, Greenock, 1752-69. Min at Truro, Colchester Co, NS, 1771–1805. **GMA 1060; UPC ii 169**.

1795 COCKBURN, George Ralph Richardson, b 15 Feb 1834. From Edinburgh. Educ Edinburgh High School and Edinburgh Univ, where he grad MA in 1858. To Toronto as teacher, and in 1861 was app Principal of Upper Canada Coll. **CEG 231; BNA 1177**.

1796 COCKBURN, Henry G. Day, b 1820. From Edinburgh. s/o Henry C. and Elizabeth McDowall, of the Castle Semple family. Educ Edinburgh Academy, 1828-35, and went to Hamilton, ONT. **EAR 50**.

1797 COCKBURN, John, b ca 1782. From Mellerstain, BEW. To QUE, ex Greenock, summer 1815; stld ONT. Shepherd. Wife Jane Whitehead, qv, with him, and 7 ch. **SEC 2**.

1798 COCKBURN, Joseph. From Cupar, FIF. To Georgina Twp, York Co, ONT, ca 1825. m Elizabeth Leslie, qv. Son James. **DC 8 Nov 1981**.

1799 COLLANS, Robert, ca 1816–18 Apr 1842. From Maxwelltown, DFS. To Bonavista, NFD, and d there. **DGH 26 May 1842**.

1800 COLLEDGE, William Wilson, b ca 1825. From Glasgow. s/o William C, lawyer. Matric Univ of Glasgow,

1841. To ONT; stld Westminster Twp, Middlesex Co. Farmer and mining engineer at Byron. **GMA 14360**.

1801 COLLIE, Janet. Prob from DFS. To Pictou Co, NS, 1816; stld East Forks and m Thomas Halliday, qv. **PAC 123**.

1802 COLLINS, Robert, b 22 Aug 1801. From Paisley, RFW. To ONT <1855. m Margaret McColl, qv. **DC 7 Apr 1972**.

COLQUHOUN. See also CALHOUN.

1803 COLQUHOUN, Alexander. To QUE, 1804. Soldier, War of 1812. **DC 4 Mar 1965**.

1804 COLQUHOUN, Archibald. From Dundee, ANS. s/o Rev Malcolm C, min of the Gaelic Chapel there. To Georgetown, Chateauguay Co, QUE, 1833. Moved later to Otonabee and Mulmar, Peterborough Co, ONT. **FES v 333, vii 630**.

1805 COLQUHOUN, James. To QUE on the *Commerce*, ex Greenock, Jun 1820; stld prob Lanark Co, ONT. **HCL 238**.

1806 COLQUHOUN, Malcolm. From ARL. To Ekfrid Twp, Middlesex Co, ONT, 1849. **PCM 31**.

1807 COLQUHOUN, Mary, b ca 1809. Poss from LKS. To Darling Twp, Lanark Co, ONT, ca 1843. Wife of Colin Wilson, qv. **DC 5 Feb 1981**.

1808 COLQUHOUN, Sarah. From Appin par, ARL. To ONT 1831. m Samuel McColl, qv. **DC 20 Nov 1960**.

1809 COLQUHOUN, Walter, b ca 1788. From Rhu, DNB. To Hudson Bay, ca 1813, and prob to Red River. **RRS 13**.

1810 COLTON, Barbara, b ca 1780. From Glasgow. To QUE on the *George Canning*, ex Greenock, 14 April 1821; stld Ramsay Twp, Lanark Co, ONT. Wife of James Yuill, qv. **DC 7 Dec 1981**.

1811 COLVILLE, John, 12 Mar 1812–14 Dec 1878. Poss from PER. To Hamilton, ONT. m Elizabeth Menzies, qv. **Ts Mt Albion**.

1812 COLVIN, Catherine, 1710–1809. From Lockerbie, DFS. To Georgetown, Kings Co, PEI, on the *Lovely Nellie*, ex Annan, 1774; moved to Pictou Co, NS, later to Colchester Co. wid/o Alexander Waugh, by whom she had, poss with other ch: 1. Wellwood, qv; and also wid/o — Campbell, by whom she had further ch: 2. William, qv; 3. Margaret, b 1749. **ELN; HT 35**.

1813 COLVIN, William. From INV. To Lobo Twp, Middlesex Co, ONT, ca 1832. ch: 1. William; 2. Alexander; 3. Mrs Caverhill; 4. Mrs McIvor; 5. Mrs McQueen; 6. Mrs Ross; 7. Mrs McBane. **PCM 40**.

1814 COMMON, Mary, b 8 Oct 1797. From Southdean, ROX. d/o James C. and Isabella Wood. To Guelph, Wellington Co, ONT, <1830. **LDW 15 Oct 1975**.

1815 COMRIE, Duncan. From Comrie, PER. To Otonabee Twp, Peterborough Co, ONT, 1829. m 15 Nov 1819, Christian McCowan, ch: 1. William, b 26 Aug 1820. m (ii) 9 Sep 1826, Janet Millar, qv, with further ch: 2. Margaret, b 6 Aug 1827; 3. Christian, b ONT 29 Aug 1829. **DC 13 Sep 1982**.

1816 COMRIE, Peter. From Comrie, PER. To Montreal, QUE, on the *Curlew*, ex Greenock, 21 Jul 1818; stld prob

Beckwith Twp, Lanark Co, ONT. Wife Jane with him, and ch: 1. Peter; 2. John, inf. **BCL**.

1817   CONN, William, 1789–1863. From AYR. To NS prob <1830; stld Cumberland Co. Wife Mary, 1798–1876.   **DC 29 Oct 1980**.

1818   CONNELL, Colin, b ca 1786. To Charlottetown, PEI, on the *Humphreys*, ex Tobermory, 14 Jul 1806. **PLH**.

1819   CONNELL, John, b 9 Sep 1824. From Clyde Street, Glasgow. To ONT <1847.   **DC 15 Jun 1977**.

1820   CONNON, Thomas, 14 Feb 1832–10 Jan 1899. Born Tillyeve, Udny, ABD, but family had moved to Elfhill, Stonehaven, KCD. To ONT and stld Elora, Nichol Twp, Wellington Co, 1853. Wholesale grocer and pioneer photographer. m Jean Keith, qv, ch: 1. Elizabeth; 2. John Robert, b 1862, photographer and historian; 3. Thomas G, res Goderich. **EHE 190**.

1821   COOK, Archibald. From Mid Kiscadale, Is Arran, BUT. To Inverness, Megantic Co, QUE, 1831. m Mary McKelvie, qv, ch: 1. Robert, qv; 2. James, d Isle of Man, 1870; 3. Mary, qv; 4. Alexander, prob emig later; 5. John, qv; 6. Catherine, qv; 7. Archibald, jr, qv; 8. Peter, qv; 9. Elizabeth, unm. **AMC 39; MAC 37**.

1822   COOK, Archibald, jr, b 1820. From Kiscadale, Is Arran, BUT. s/o Archibald C, qv, and Mary McKelvie, qv. To Inverness, Megantic Co, QUE, 1831. m 1852, Susan Ellis. **AMC 39; MAC 37**.

1823   COOK, Archibald, b 1799. From Drimaginear, Is Arran, BUT. To Dalhousie, NB, <1840. m Margaret Murphy or Murchie, qv, ch: 1. John, b 1826; 2. Archibald, b 1827; 3. Margaret, b 1831.   **MAC 9**.

1824   COOK, Catherine. From Kilmory, Is Arran, BUT. d/o Archibald C, qv, and Mary McKelvie, qv. To Inverness, Megantic Co, QUE, 1831. m Malcolm McKillop, qv. **AMC 39; MAC 37**.

1825   COOK, Catherine. From Is Arran, BUT. d/o Malcolm and Catherine C. To QUE, 1832; stld Hull, Ottawa Co. Wife of Archibald McMaster, qv.   **DC 23 Apr 1967**.

1826   COOK, Catherine, b 1787. From Stragail, Is Arran, BUT. To Nash Creek, Restigouche Co, NB, 1831. **MAC 9**.

1827   COOK, Catherine, 1793–1890. From Clayned, Kilmory, Is Arran, BUT. To Dalhousie, NB, 1832; stld Point la Nim. Wife of John McCurdy, qv, whom she m 1819. **MAC 20**.

1828   COOK, Christina. From Is Arran, BUT. To Megantic Co, QUE, 1851. Wife of James Stuart, qv. **AMC 49**.

1829   COOK, Daniel, b 1783. From Kilmory par, Is Arran, BUT. To Dalhousie, NB; stld Nash Creek, Restigouche Co, 1829. **MAC 9**.

1830   COOK, Daniel or Donald, 1796–1863. From Is Arran, BUT. To Benjamen River, Restigouche Co, NB, 1824. **MAC 11**.

1831   COOK, Daniel or Donald, 1828-89. From Corriecrevie, Kilmory par, Is Arran, BUT. s/o John C, qv, and Catherine Crawford, qv. To Restigouche Co, NB, 1829; stld Addington par, later Black Point. Blacksmith.

m Margaret, 1834-92, d/o William Archibald, qv, and Isabel Wood, qv, ch: 1. Catherine, 1857–1913; 2. William Archibald, 1859-86; 3. John, 1860-70; 4. James Finlay, ca 1863–1937, d Vancouver, BC; 5. Isabella, b ca 1867; 6. Mary, 1869–1949, d CA; 7. David, 1870–1925; 8. Martha, 1872–1958; 9. Margaret Jane, 1872–1958; 10. Agnes, 1878-92; 11. Elizabeth, 1880–1969. **DMC 1 Oct 1979**.

1832   COOK, Elizabeth, 1819–5 Apr 1894. From Corriecrevie, Kilmory par, Is Arran, BUT. d/o Duncan C. and Elizabeth Stewart. To NB, ca 1852; stld Dundee, Restigouche Co. Wife of William Mackinnon, qv, whom she m 1 Jul 1838. **DC 1 Oct 1980**.

1833   COOK, Finlay, 1821–1907. From Corriecrevie, Kilmory par, Is Arran, BUT. s/o John C, qv, and Catherine Crawford, qv. To Benjamen River, Restigouche Co, NB, 1829; moved to Maria, Bonaventure Co, QUE, later to Belledune, Gloucester Co, NB. Commission merchant. m (?) Agnes Turner, ch: 1. Catherine, d inf; 2. John, d inf; 3. James, d inf; 4. Agatha, 1861–1921, went to San Francisco; 5. William, 1866–1933. **DMC 1 Oct 1979**.

1834   COOK, James, 1822-55. From Corriecrevie, Kilmory par, Is Arran, BUT. s/o John C, qv, and Catherine Crawford, qv. To Benjamen River, Restigouche Co, NB, 1829. Farmer there. m 5 Sep 1855, Elizabeth Currie, qv, ch: 1. John, 1857-90; 2. Catherine, 1859-96; 3. Donald, b 1861; 4. Robert, 1862–1938; 5. Elizabeth, 1864–1948; 6. Mary Jane, 1867–1946; 7. James, 1870–1920. **DMC 1 Oct 1979**.

1835   COOK, Janet, 17 Jan 1834–30 Dec 1905. Poss from Glasgow. To ONT ca 1852, and d Oak River, MAN. Wife of John Henry, qv. **DC 20 Nov 1980**.

1836   COOK, John, 1775–1864. From North Kiscadale, Kilbride, Is Arran, BUT. To Blackland, Restigouche Co, NB, 1829, and d New Mills. m Helen Kennedy, qv, ch: 1. John, jr, qv; 2. James, b 1812; 3. Peter, b 1813; 4. Mary, b 1816; 5. Neil, 1817-96; 6. Alexander; 7. Helen, 1819–1912; 8. Catherine, b 1830. **MAC 10; DC 6 May 1967**.

1837   COOK, John, jr, 10 Oct 1810–8 Feb 1879. From North Kiscadale, Kilbride, Is Arran, BUT. s/o John C, qv, and Helen Kennedy, qv. To Blackland, Restigouche Co, NB, 1829; later to River Charlo. Magistrate and officer of militia. m 1839, Margaret McPherson, qv. **CUC 15; DC 28 Apr 1981**.

1838   COOK, John, 1784–1873. From Clauchog, Kilmory par, Is Arran, BUT. To Dickie, Restigouche Co, NB, 1829. m Margaret Mackinnon, qv, ch: 1. Mary, b Sliddery, 1815; 2. William, b Torrilin, 1817; 3. Margaret, 1819-73; 4. John, b 1822; 5. Ann, 1825-96; 6. Elizabeth, 1827-93. **MAC 11**.

1839   COOK, John, 1788–2 May 1869. From Kilmory par, Is Arran, BUT. s/o Malcolm C. and Margaret Stuart. To Benjamen River, Restigouche Co, NB, 1829. Farmer. m Catherine Crawford, qv, ch: 1. John, qv; 2. Mary, b 1819, dy; 3. Finlay, qv; 4. James, qv; 5. Mary, qv; 6. Daniel or Donald, qv. **MAC 11; DC 1 Oct 1979**.

1840   COOK, John, 1797–1881. From Is Arran, BUT. To NB prob <1840; stld Restigouche Co. Wife Margaret, 1826-90, with him. **MAC 12**.

1841 COOK, John, 1818-76. From Corriecrevie, Kilmory par, Is Arran, BUT. s/o John C, qv, and Catherine Crawford, qv. To Benjamen River, Restigouche Co, NB, Jun 1829; stld Durham par. Had ch by wife Catherine. **DC 1 Oct 1979**.

1842 COOK, John, 1805-73. From Is Arran, BUT. To Restigouche Co, NB, prob <1840. ch with him: 1. Archibald, 1824-93; 2. Isabel, 1829–1911. **MAC 12**.

1843 COOK, John, b ca 1819. From Kiscadale, Is Arran, BUT. s/o Archibald C, qv, and Mary McKelvie, qv. To Inverness, Megantic Co, QUE, 1831. m 1859, Abigail Chesley. **AMC 39; MAC 37**.

1844 COOK, John, called 'Johnny Red'. From Is Arran, BUT. To Restigouche Co, NB, prob <1840. m Mary Ferguson, qv. **MAC 12**.

1845 COOK, Rev John, ca 1804–31 Mar 1892. From Sanquhar, DFS. s/o John C, craftsman. Matric Univ of Glasgow, 1820. To QUE, and was min of St Andrews Ch, 1838-88. Moderator of the first General Assembly of the Presb Ch of Canada, and one of the founders of Queens Univ, Kingston. Principal of Morin Coll, QUE. LLD, 1880, Queens Univ, and subject of a commemorative stamp, 1975. m Eliza Airth, ch: 1. John, lawyer, d unm; 2. Robert, dy; 3. William; 4. Archibald. **GMA 10521; MDB 153; MGC 2 Aug 1979**.

1846 COOK, Mary, b 1801. From Kilmory, Is Arran, BUT. d/o John C. and Margaret Robison. To Restigouche Co, NB, 1831. Wife of Peter Murchie or Murphy, qv. **MAC 25; DC 6 May 1967**.

1847 COOK, Mary, b 1815. From Kiscadale, Is Arran, BUT. d/o Archibald C, qv, and Mary McKelvie, qv. To Inverness, Megantic Co, QUE, 1831. m John Dingwall. **AMC 39; MAC 37**.

1848 COOK, Mary, 1825–4 Oct 1879. From Corriecrevie, Kilmory par, Is Arran, BUT. d/o John C, qv, and Catherine Crawford, qv. To Benjamen River, Restigouche Co, NB, 1829. m 12 Sep 1848, James McMillan, qv. **DMC 1 Oct 1979**.

1849 COOK, Mary, d 1842. From Kiscadale, Is Arran, BUT. sis/o John C, qv. To Inverness, Megantic Co, QUE, 1831. Wife of James Stewart, qv. **AMC 39; MAC 38**.

1850 COOK, Peter, 1814–1859. From Arran, BUT. To NB ca 1831; later to Galt, Waterloo Co, ONT. Partner in foundry, and Secretary of School Board, 1855. **HGD 247**.

1851 COOK, Peter, b 1824. From Kiscadale, Is Arran, BUT. s/o Archibald C, qv, and Mary McKelvie, qv. To Inverness, Megantic Co, QUE, 1831. m Catherine Currie, qv. **AMC 39; MAC 37**.

1852 COOK, Robert, 1809-81. From Auchenchairn, Kilbride, Is Arran, BUT. To Restigouche Co, NB, 1832; stld Archibald Settlement. Wife Catherine McMillan, qv, with him, and s Neil, b 1831. **MAC 12**.

1853 COOK, Robert, b 1809. From Kiscadale, Is Arran, BUT. s/o Archibald C, qv, and Mary McKelvie, qv. To Inverness, Megantic Co, QUE, 1831. m Esther McCammon. **AMC 39; MAC 37**.

1854 COOK, William, 1809-53. From Cloined, Kilmory par, Is Arran, BUT. s/o John C. and Margaret Robison. Farmer. To Blackland, Restigouche Co, NB, 1829.

m Elizabeth Hamilton, qv, ch: 1. John, 1833-58; 2. Janet, 1836–1919; 3. Archibald, 1839–1909; 4. William, 1841–1917; 5. Catherine, 1842–1930; 6. Donald, b 1847; 7. Annie; 8. Elizabeth, b 1850; 9. Margaret, d 1923. **DC 6 Nov 1983**.

COOPER. See also COWPER.

1855 COOPER, George. From ABD. bro/o Robert C, qv. To French River, Tatamagouche, Colchester Co, NS, 1834. Farmer. **HT 70**.

1856 COOPER, James, b 16 Jul 1770. To ONT 1774. Farmer and soldier during War of 1812. Son Daniel. **DC 29 Sep 1964**.

1857 COOPER, John, b ca 1786. From Sanda, OKI. To York Factory, Hudson Bay, on the *Edward & Anne*, ex Stornoway, Lewis, arr 24 Sep 1811. Pioneer settler, Red River, 1812. **LSS 184; RRS 26; LSC 321**.

1858 COOPER, Magdalene, 1796–1853. From Dundee, ANS. To Collingwood Twp, Grey Co, ONT, ca 1848. Wife of George Reekie, qv. **DC 24 May 1979**.

1859 COOPER, Robert. From ABD. bro/o George C, qv. To French River, Tatamagouche, Colchester Co, NS, 1834. Farmer. m Susan Bonyman, qv, ch: 1. James; 2. William; 3. Mary. **HT 68**.

1860 COOPER, Ross Henry, 1814-91. From Aberdeen. To Cumberland Co, NS. Bur Methodist Cemetery, Pugwash. **DC 29 Oct 1980**.

COPELAND. See also COUPLAND.

1861 COPELAND, Joseph. From Kirkbean, KKD. To Cornwall, Stormont Co, ONT. Farmer. Son Robert, engineer, d 1860. **DGC 3 Apr 1860**.

1862 COPELAND, Margaret, d 7 Sep 1849. From Kirkbean, KKD. d/o Joseph C. in Prestonmill. To Cornwall, Stormont Co, ONT. m John Bell. **DGH 15 Nov 1849**.

1863 CORBET, Alexander. From Port Ban, Arisaig, INV. To PEI on the *Lucy*, ex Loch nan Uamh, 12 Jul 1790. Carpenter. **PLL**.

1864 CORBET, Ann. From Mingarry, Ardnamurchan, ARL. To Antigonish Co, NS, 1829. Wife of Allan 'Mor' MacDonald, qv. **HCA 200**.

1865 CORBET, Christy. From Ardachie, nr Fort William, INV. Poss d/o John C, qv. To Montreal, QUE, ex Fort William, 3 Jul 1802; stld E ONT. **MCM 1/4 23**.

1866 CORBET, John. From Ardachie, nr Fort William, INV. To Montreal, QUE, ex Fort William, 3 Jul 1802; stld E ONT. Wife with him and s William. **MCM 1/4 23**.

1867 CORMACK, Alexander. From Wick, CAI. To Chatham, Northumberland Co, NB, prob <1840. **DC 14 Jan 1980**.

1868 CORMACK, James. From SUT. bro/o William C, qv. To QUE <1851; prob stld Montreal. **SH**.

1869 CORMACK, William. From SUT. bro/o James C, qv. To Montreal, QUE, prob <1851. Merchant. Retr to SCT and was in business at Tongue, later Thurso. **SH**.

1870 CORRIGAL, Jacob, d 8 Mar 1844. From Kirkwall, OKI. To CAN 1790, and joined HBCo, serving first at Albany Factory. Journeyed to Sturgeon Lake from Osnaburgh House in 1794. Master at Lake St Ann and at

Martins Fall between 1794 and 1812, and later again at Martins Fall. App Sheriff HBCo Territories, 1823. Ret to Cobourg, ONT. By wife Mary had ch: 1. William; 2. Charlotte; 3. Elizabeth; 4. Catherine; 5. Ann, alive 1855. **LDW 19 Jan 1979**.

1871 CORSON, Elizabeth, d 1 Dec 1857. From Durrisdeer, DFS. d/o Adam C. in Coshogle. To Pembroke Twp, Renfrew Co, ONT. Wife of W. Kennedy. **DGH 8 Jan 1858**.

1872 CORSON, James, d Mar 1833. From Durrisdeer, DFS. s/o Adam C. in Coshogal. To Port Hope, Durham Co, ONT. **DGC 7 Aug 1833**.

1873 CORSAN, James, ca 1798–30 Sep 1885. From Glasgow. To Washington, nr Ayr, Waterloo Co, ONT. Merchant. m Elizabeth Nisbet, ch: 1. Elizabeth; 2. Thomas, 1821-26; 3. Agnes, dy; 4. John, dy; 5. James, d AUS, 1855. **Ts Anderston**.

1874 CORT, John, d ca 1785. From Aberdeen. To Miramichi, Northumberland Co, NB, 1765, and gr land. Pioneer lumberman and fisherman in association with William Davidson, qv, and assisted in attracting settlers. **BNA 266; DC 25 Feb 1982**.

1875 COULTART, Robert, b ca 1754. From Kirkgunzeon, KKD. To Georgetown, Kings Co, PEI, on the *Lovely Nellie*, ex Annan, 1774. Labourer. **ELN**.

COUPLAND. See also COPELAND.

1876 COUPLAND, Alexander, b ca 1753. From Kelton par, KKD. To Georgetown, Kings Co, PEI, on the *Lovely Nellie*, ex Annan, 1774. Labourer. **ELN**.

1877 COUPLAND, George, ca 1832–11 Oct 1854. From Mouswald par, DFS. s/o George C, farmer, and Isabella Dickson. To Scarborough, York Co, ONT, and d there. **Ts Mouswald**.

1878 COURT, James, ca 1812–14 Feb 1883. From Glasgow. s/o John C, law clerk, and Grace Blackwood. To Montreal, QUE, <1842. Emp as an accountant for a time with his uncle Thomas Blackwood, qv. m Mrs McIntosh or Bent, and d at Glasgow. **SGC 449**.

1879 COUTTS, Rev David, ca 1802–6 Apr 1884. From Monzie, PER. s/o Henry C, farmer. Matric Univ of Glasgow, 1822. Probationer of Secession Ch, then studied medicine. To ONT, and became Presb min, latterly at Brampton, Peel Co. **GMA 10903**.

1880 COUTTS, Henrietta, ca 1775–22 Mar 1864. From ABD. To Halifax, NS, <27 Jan 1824, when m Alexander Garden, qv. Stld later Hants Co. **VSN No 442; DC 20 Jan 1981**.

1881 COUTTS, Margaret. From Clashindrich, Glengairn, ABD. To Tilbury East, Kent Co, ONT, <1841. Wife of Alexander McGregor, qv. **SG ix/3 14**.

1882 COWAN, Alexander. From Tarbert, ARL. To Caradoc Twp, Middlesex Co, ONT, 1847. **PCM 35**.

1883 COWAN, David, ca 1830–13 Jan 1882. From Rattray, PER. s/o William C, joiner, and Julia Sim. To Toronto, ONT. Merchant. **Ts Rattray**.

1884 COWAN, Dugald. From Tarbert, ARL. To Caradoc Twp, Middlesex Co, ONT, 1847. **PCM 35**.

1885 COWAN, James, b 1785. From Sundhope, Yarrow, SEL. s/o William C. and Isabella Scott. To Galt

Twp, Waterloo Co, ONT, 1829. m Margaret Nichol, qv, ch. **DC 9 May 1979**.

1886 COWAN, John. From Tarbert, ARL. To Caradoc Twp, Middlesex Co, ONT, 1847. **PCM 35**.

1887 COWAN, Mary, 1837–23 Feb 1896. From Rattray, PER. Poss d/o William C, joiner, and Julia Sim. To Toronto, ONT. m John Hillock. **Ts Rattray**.

1888 COWAN, Ronald. From Tarbert, ARL. To Caradoc Twp, Middlesex Co, ONT, 1847; later to Strathroy, Adelaide Twp. **PCM 35**.

1889 COWAN, William. From STI. s/o John C. To ONT 1817. m Janet Wallace, qv. **DC 4 Dec 1970**.

1890 COWDEN, John, d 1819. Poss from RFW. To St John, NB, on the *Alexander*, ex Greenock, spring 1816; stld Miramichi, Northumberland Co. m Martha Gibson, qv, and had, poss with other ch: 1. Jane, 1800-80; 2. John, whose family went to USA 1844; 3. Mrs John Clark; 4. Alexander Allan, b ca 1817. **DC 25 Feb 1982**.

1891 COWIE, Andrew, 1798–21 Oct 1890. From BAN. To NS <1830; stld Liverpool, Queens Co. Tanner and shipowner; MLA. m 8 Jan 1820, Janet More. **MLA 74**.

1892 COWIE, Ann, 13 Feb 1820–21 Mar 1884. From Lonmay, ABD. To Uxbridge Twp, York Co, ONT, ca 1820. Wife of John Milne, qv. **DC 12 Sep 1979**.

1893 COWIE, Christine, 1823-86. From Glasgow. d/o John C, qv, and Bethia Cowie. To QUE on the *Bowling*, 1842; stld East Williams Twp, Middlesex Co, ONT. m 1846, Donald McDonald, qv. **DC 10 Nov 1981**.

1894 COWIE, Elizabeth, 1819–1905. From Glasgow. d/o William C. and Christina Jackson. To QUE on the *Bowling*, 1842; stld East Williams Twp, Middlesex Co, ONT. m William Turnbull, qv. **DC 10 Nov 1981**.

1895 COWIE, George. To Pictou, NS, on the *Lulan*, ex Glasgow, 17 Aug 1848. **DC 12 Jul 1979**.

1896 COWIE, Janet, 1817-88. From Springbank, Glasgow. d/o William C. and Christina Jackson. To QUE on the *Bowling*, 1842; stld East Williams Twp, Middlesex Co, ONT. m Robert Turnbull. **DC 10 Nov 1981**.

1897 COWIE, John, 1794–1877. From Springbank, Glasgow. s/o William C. and Christina Jackson. To QUE on the *Bowling*, 1842; stld East Williams Twp, Middlesex Co, ONT. Weaver. m Bethia Cowie, 1796–1842, a relative, who d on the voyage, ch: 1. William, remained in SCT; 2. Christine, qv; 3. Marian, 1832-99, unm; 4-5. John Bryce, qv, and Robert, qv, identical twins. **DC 10 Nov 1981**.

1898 COWIE, John Bryce, 1835–1901. From Glasgow. s/o John C, qv, and Bethia Cowie. To QUE on the *Bowling*, 1842; stld East Williams Twp, Middlesex Co, ONT. m Christine Turnbull, qv, ch. **DC 10 Nov 1981**.

1899 COWIE, Margaret. From Carnwath, LKS. To QUE on the *Atlas*, ex Greenock, 11 Jul 1815; stld North Elmsley Twp, Lanark Co, ONT. Wife of James Taylor, qv. **SEC 2**.

1900 COWIE, Robert, 1835–1920. From Glasgow. s/o John C, qv, and Bethia C. To QUE on the *Bowling*, 1842; stld East Williams Twp, Middlesex Co, ONT. m Isabella McArthur, 1842–1918, ch. **DC 10 Nov 1981**.

1901 COWIE, Janet. From Corstorphine, MLN. To QUE,

ex Greenock, 1815; stld Scotch Line, Lanark Co, ONT. Wife of Francis Allan, qv. **SEC 1; HCL 231**.

COWPER. See also COOPER.

1902   COWPER, George C. To Owen Sound, Grey Co, ONT. Newspaper editor. m Jessie, d/o John Dalzier. Son James Alexander. **DC 29 Sep 1964**.

1903   COWPER, Janet, d 19 Nov 1871. From MOR. To NB prob <1850. m Alexander Laing. **DC 14 Jan 1980**.

1904   COWPER, Margaret, b 1802. From Edinburgh. d/o James C. and Elizabeth Gray. To Ottawa, ONT, <1830. m Findlay Sinclair. **DC 2 Aug 1982**.

1905   COX, Helen, ca 1827–21 May 1868. From Annan, DFS. d/o James C, blacksmith, and Helen Jackson. To Hamilton, ONT, 1855. Wife of William Edgar, qv. **CAE 19**.

1906   CRABB, Ann Grace. From KKD. To QUE, 1845; stld Pilkington Twp, Wellington Co, ONT. Wife of Robert Haig, qv. **EHE 39**.

1907   CRAIG, Agnes. From DFS. To Moncton, Westmorland Co, NB, <1840. m Thomas Mitchell Brown, ch: 1. William; 2. Eunice; 3. Sarah Elizabeth, went to Norfolk, ONT; 4. Robert, dy. **DC 2 Mar 1980**.

1908   CRAIG, Bethia. From Paisley, RFW. To QUE on the *Carleton*, ex Glasgow, arr 5 Jun 1842; stld Lanark Co, ONT. Wife of Robert Blackburn, qv. **DC 5 Feb 1981**.

1909   CRAIG, Ellen, 1795–1875. From ROX. To Botsford, Westmorland Co, NB, 1820. Wife of Adam Amos, qv. **DC 11 Dec 1979**.

1910   CRAIG, Samuel. To QUE on the *Alexander*, 1816; stld Lot 12, Con 3, Drummond Twp, Lanark Co, ONT. **HCL 233**.

1911   CRAIG, William. To Lanark Co, ONT, 1821; stld Lot 3, Con 2, Darling Twp. Cooper and farmer. **HCL 76**.

1912   CRAIG, William, b 20 Jul 1793. s/o John C. and Janet Gibson. To ONT ca 1820. m Christina Swan. **DC 13 Feb 1978**.

1913   CRAIK, Agnes, b 1813. Prob from Edinburgh. d/o William C, qv, and Agnes Denham, qv. To Franklin Twp, Huntingdon Co, QUE, <1815. m Alexander, s/o John Blackwood, qv, and Mary Munroe. **DC 2 Jul 1979**.

1914   CRAIK, Jane, 5 May 1830–9 Apr 1913. From West Barns, Dunbar, ELN. To ONT 1843, and d at Strange, York Co. m Archibald Gillies, qv. **DC 17 Nov 1979**.

1915   CRAIK, William. Prob from Edinburgh. To Franklin Twp, Huntingdon Co, QUE, <1815. m Agnes Denham, qv, ch: 1. Bell; 2. Agnes, qv; 3. David; 4. Andrew; 5. William; 6. James; 7. Robert; 8. John; 9. Mary. **DC 2 Jul 1979**.

1916   CRAIL, Agnes. From Edinburgh. To QUE on the *Earl of Buckinghamshire*, ex Greenock, 28 Apr 1821; stld prob Dalhousie Twp, Lanark Co, ONT. Wife of John Dunlop, qv. **DC 13 Feb 1978**.

1917   CRAM, John. From Comrie par, PER. To Montreal, QUE, on the *Curlew*, ex Greenock, 21 Jul

1818; stld prob Beckwith Twp, Lanark Co, ONT. Wife Isabella with him, and dau Mary, aged 3. **BCL**.

1918   CRANSTON, Robert. From ROX. To CAN on the *Sarah Mary Jane*, 1831; stld Dumfries Twp, Waterloo Co, ONT. Farmer. **HGD 60**.

1919   CRAW, Eliza M, d 1 May 1828. To Montreal, QUE. m Rev Edward Black, qv. **DGC 17 Jun 1828**.

1920   CRAWFORD, Alexander. From Is Arran, BUT. s/o William C. and Katherine Shaw. To PEI <1850. m Ellen McLaren, qv. **AMC 82**.

1921   CRAWFORD, Andrew, d 15 Aug 1846. From Port Glasgow, RFW. s/o Dr William C. To Montreal, QUE. Physician. **Ts Port Glasgow**.

1922   CRAWFORD, Andrew. From Paisley, RFW. s/o Ninian C, 1791–1853, shawl-maker. To Montreal, QUE, <1853. **Ts Renfrew**.

1923   CRAWFORD, Catherine, 1788–2 Oct 1876. From Sliddery, Kilmory par, Is Arran, BUT. d/o Donald C. and Catherine Currie. To Benjamen River, Restigouche Co, NB, 1829, and d New Mills. Wife of John Cook, qv, m 19 May 1817. **MAC 11; DMC 1 Oct 1979**.

1924   CRAWFORD, Donald. From Is Arran, BUT. To PEI <1850. m Mary Kelso. **AMC 82**.

1925   CRAWFORD, Donald. From Lochgilphead, ARL. Rel to Duncan C, qv. To Westminster Twp, Middlesex Co, ONT, 1832. **PCM 51**.

1926   CRAWFORD, Donald or Daniel. From Balimenoch, Kilmory par, Is Arran, BUT. To Inverness, Megantic Co, QUE, 1831. m Margaret McKinnon, ch: 1. Mary, b 1796; 2. James, b 1797; 3. William, b 1800; 4. Ann, b 1803; 5. Donald, b 1804; 6. Dugald, b 1806; 7. Janet, b 1808; 8. Catherine, b 1811; 9. Alexander. **AMC 42; MAC 41**.

1927   CRAWFORD, Duncan. From Lochgilphead, ARL. Rel to Donald C, qv. To Westminster Twp, Middlesex Co, ONT, 1832. **PCM 51**.

1928   CRAWFORD, George. From Airth, STI. s/o Hugh C, 1801-95, and Jane Learmonth. To Montreal, QUE. Policeman. **Ts Airth**.

1929   CRAWFORD, Henry. From Airth, STI. s/o Hugh C, 1801-95, and Jane Learmonth. To Montreal, QUE, and later to NFD. **Ts Airth**.

1930   CRAWFORD, Hugh. To East Williams Twp, Middlesex Co, ONT, 1831. Son Hector, b 1832. **PCM 44**.

1931   CRAWFORD, Isabella. From Corrie Burn, Is Arran, BUT. d/o William C. and Katherine Shaw, and wid/o Peter Gordon. To QUE on the *Albion*, ex Greenock, 5 Jun 1829; stld Inverness, Megantic Co, QUE. ch: 1. Peter; 2. Isabella, 1775–1847; 3. William. **AMC 21; MAC 34**.

1932   CRAWFORD, James. From Lochgilphead, ARL. To Lobo Twp, Middlesex Co, ONT. ch: 1. Duncan; 2. James; 3. John; 4. Janet; 5. Mrs William Anderson. **PCM 39**.

1933   CRAWFORD, James, 1799–1879. From Is Arran, BUT. To Dalhousie, NB, prob 1833; stld Escuminac, Bonaventure Co, QUE. m Mary Stewart, qv. Son James, b 1832. **MAC 13**.

1934 CRAWFORD, James. From RFW. s/o Hugh C, servant at Castle Semple. To Hamilton, ONT, <1850. **SH**.

1935 CRAWFORD, Janet. From LKS. To North Sherbrooke Twp, Lanark Co, ONT, 1821. Poss wife of James Gilmour, qv. **DC 1 Apr 1968**.

1936 CRAWFORD, Janet. From Kilbirnie, AYR. To QUE on the *True Briton*, 1822; stld Montreal. Wife of Robert Brodie, qv. **DC 1 Apr 1979**.

1937 CRAWFORD, Janet. Prob from Dalry, AYR. d/o David C. and Ann Hunter. To Pictou, NS, on the *Hope*, ex Glasgow, 5 Apr 1848. Wife of Robert Cullen, qv. **PAC 12; DC 12 Jul 1979**.

1938 CRAWFORD, Jean, 1789–1884. From Tarbert, ARL. To Aldborough Twp, Elgin Co, ONT, 1843. Wife of Robert Morrison, qv. **DC 14 Feb 1980**.

1939 CRAWFORD, Jean, 1784–1828. From Glasgow. To Oakville, Halton Co, ONT, 1844. Wife of Thomas Nisbet, qv. **Nisbet Chart**.

1940 CRAWFORD, Jean. From Ayr. To ONT 1852, and d Amherstburg Twp, Essex Co. Wife of John Gibb, qv. **DC 5 Jun 1981**.

1941 CRAWFORD, John. From Caolasraide, South Knapdale, ARL. To Caradoc Twp, Middlesex Co, ONT, 1835. ch: 1. Archie; 2. Duncan. **PCM 35**.

1942 CRAWFORD, John. To Mosa Twp, Middlesex Co, ONT, 1837. ch incl: 1. Dr James, res Detroit; 2. Rev John, res Niagara Falls. **PCM 21**.

1943 CRAWFORD, Katherine. From Is Arran, BUT. d/o William and Katherine C. To Megantic Co, QUE, <1840. Prob m Duncan McMillan, qv. **AMC 82; MAC 32**.

1944 CRAWFORD, Malcolm. From Caolasraide, South Knapdale, ARL. To Caradoc Twp, Middlesex Co, ONT, 1842. ch: 1. Archie; 2. Dugald; 3. Dr Allan; 4. Malcolm; 5. Mrs Archibald Fletcher. **PCM 35**.

1945 CRAWFORD, Mary, d 1830. From Corrie Burn, Is Arran, BUT. d/o William C. and Katherine Shaw, and wid/o John McKillop, qv. To QUE on the *Albion*, ex Greenock, 5 Jun 1829; stld Inverness, Megantic Co. ch: 1. Peter, qv; 2. Donald, qv; 3. Catherine, qv; 4. John 'Banker', b 1804, unm; 5. Mary, qv; 6. Malcolm, qv; 7. Alexander, qv; 8. William; 9. Isabella, dy. **AMC 21; MAC 33**.

1946 CRAWFORD, Robert. From Paisley, RFW. s/o Ninian C, 1791–1853, shawl-maker. To Montreal, QUE, <1853. **Ts Renfrew**.

1947 CREAM, Thomas Neill, 27 May 1850–15 Nov 1892. From Glasgow. s/o William C, qv, and Mary Elder, qv. To QUE, 1854. Emp with father until 1872, when commenced study of medicine at McGill Univ. Grad MD 1876. MRCPS Edin, 1878. Abortionist and mass murderer, suspected as 'Jack the Ripper.' Hanged at Newgate, London, ENG. **MGC 2 Aug 1979**.

1948 CREAM, William, d 12 May 1887. From Glasgow. To QUE 1854. Manager of shipbuilding firm; later timber merchant. m Mary Elder, qv, and had, with other ch, s Thomas Neill, qv. **MGC 2 Aug 1979**.

1949 CREECH, Mary, b 1827, prob in FIF. To ONT ca 1855. Wife of James Kelly. qv. **DC 1 Dec 1980**.

CREIGHTON. See also CRICHTON.

1950 CREIGHTON, Abraham. From Glasgow. To Grey Co, ONT, ca 1845. Wife Margaret Bonar, qv. Son David, qv. **DC 30 Aug 1977**.

1951 CREIGHTON, David, 1843–1917. From Glasgow. s/o Abraham C, qv, and Margaret Bonar, qv. To Grey Co, ONT, ca 1845. Journalist and Conservative politician. m 1873, Jane Elizabeth Kramer, ch: 1. Charles D; 2. Jennie A; 3. P. May; 4. Stella. **DC 30 Aug 1977**.

1952 CREIGHTON, Elizabeth, 1801–2 Nov 1880. From Dryfesdale, DFS. To West Farnham, Brome Co, QUE, <1846. Wife of Joseph Kirkpatrick, qv. **DC 17 Nov 1981**.

1953 CRERAR, Peter, ca 1786–5 Jan 1857. From Breadalbane, PER. To Pictou, NS, prob <1830. Deputy Surveyor and Registrar of Deeds. **DGH 23 Jan 1857**.

CRICHTON. See also CREIGHTON.

1954 CRICHTON, Ann. From Perth. To CAN, 1817; stld Ottawa, 1826. Wife of Thomas McKay, qv. **MDB 462**.

1955 CRICHTON, John, ca 1801–16 Apr 1854. From Chirnside, BEW. s/o John C, slater, and Margaret Purves. To Brockville, Leeds Co, ONT, and d there. **Ts Chirnside**.

1956 CRINGEN, Isabella, b ca 1798. From Sanquhar, DFS. To Eldon Twp, Victoria Co, ONT, 1831. Wife of Robert Williamson, qv. **EC 223**.

1957 CRINKLAW, James, 1777–1864. From ROX. To Westminster Twp, Middlesex Co, ONT, 1833. By a first wife, ch: 1. Margaret, b 1804, Lochmaben, DFS; 2. William, soldier; 3. Elizabeth, b 1807; 4. John, b 1809, Minto, ROX; 5. Mary, b 1811. m (ii) Janet Smith, qv, with further ch: 6. Martha, b 1815; 7. Agnes, b 1818; 8. George, b 1820; 9. Georgina, b 1821, went to McHenry Co, IL; 10. James, b 1823; 11. Walter, b 1825; 12. David, b 1826; 13. Janet, b 1829; 14. Christina, b 1831; 15. Joseph, b 1835; 16. Robert, b 1837. **DC 11 Nov 1981**.

CRISTIE. See also CHRISTIE.

1958 CRISTIE, Mary A, b 1828. From Is Arran, BUT. To QUE on the *Margaret*, 1832; stld Megantic Co, QUE. m Joseph McNey. **AMC 42**.

1959 CROCKETT, John, ca 1743–21 Feb 1790. From Thorneyhill, Colvend par, DFS. To Georgetown, Kings Co, PEI, on the *Lovely Nellie*, which he is supposed to have built, ex Annan, 1774. Moved to Middle River, Pictou Co, NS. Carpenter, later farmer, and gr 500 acres on east side of river. Listed 1783 as capable of bearing arms. m Margaret Young, qv, ch: 1. James, 1768–1830; 2. William, qv; 3. Joseph, b 1773; 4. John. **ELN; HPC App A, D, and E; PAC 44**.

1960 CROCKETT, John. To PEI poss <1840. m Ellen Stewart. **SG xix/3 95**.

1961 CROCKETT, William, b ca 1769. From Colvend, KKD. s/o John C, qv, and Margaret Young, qv. To Georgetown, Kings Co, PEI, on the *Lovely Nellie*, ex Annan, 1774; stld later Middle River, Pictou Co, NS. Farmer. m Mary, d/o Alexander McLean, Marshdale, ch, incl s James. **ELN; PAC 44**.

1962 CROIL, James, 4 Sep 1821–28 Nov 1916. From Glasgow. s/o James C, merchant. Matric Univ of

Glasgow, 1838. To Williamsburg, Dundas Co, ONT, 1845; moved to Montreal, QUE, 1870. Farmer, carpenter, and editor of the *Presbyterian*, afterwards *Presbyterian Record*. m Christian Elizabeth, d/o Matthew Richardson. **GMA 13894; SDG 382; MDB 163**.

1963 CROLL, Andrew, ca 1820–18 Jun 1848. From St Andrews, FIF. s/o Charles C. and Janet Mitchell. To QUE and was drowned there. **Ts St Andrews**.

1964 CROMAR, Alexander. From ABD. To Bon Accord, Nichol Twp, Wellington Co, ONT, 1836. ch: 1. Robert; 2. Anne. **EHE 94**.

1965 CROMAR, Robert. From ABD. To Bon Accord, Nichol Twp, Wellington Co, ONT, arr 17 Sep 1836, but stld Upper Pilkington Twp. Farmer. m Elizabeth, d/o Edward Thomas Day, and Mary Ross, ch: 1. Alexander; 2. George; 3. Henry, res Beaverton; 4. Mrs Robert Fisher; 5. Mrs George Cumming; 6. Mrs E.B. Armstrong; 7. Mrs George Renton. **EHE 97**.

1966 CROMBIE, James, 1818–1 Jul 1876. To Galt, Waterloo Co, ONT, prob <1840; stld Preston. Woolen manufacturer. **HGD 239**.

1967 CROMBIE, John, 1794–1870. From Stoneykirk, WIG. To ONT 1819; stld Lot 21, Con 3, Chinguacousy Twp, Peel Co. Teacher and physician. m Miss Waite, from Fairfield, NY. **DC 21 Mar 1981**.

1968 CROMBIE, Rev John, b 13 Nov 1820. From Fyvie, ABD, but prob b Aberdeen. s/o John C. Grad MA Marischall Coll, Aberdeen, 1842, and completed his studies at Edinburgh. To Inverness, Inverness Co, QUE, as missionary, 1854. Ord at Laguerre, 1855, and ind to Inverness, 1856. Trans to Smiths Falls, Lanark Co, ONT, 1869, and was there until he resigned in 1887. Moderator of the Synod of Montreal and Ottawa, 1881, and DD, Presb Coll, Montreal, 1895. **FAM ii 505; SGC 551; AMC 120**.

1969 CRON, John, ca 1809–24 Apr 1851. From Kirkpatrick-Fleming, DFS. s/o John C, blacksmith, and Agnes Wise. To Markham, York Co, ONT. **Ts Kirkpatrick-Fleming**.

1970 CRON, Matthew, ca 1780–19 Jan 1844. From Hyberries, Cummertrees, DFS. s/o James C. and Janet Paterson, of Mouswald par. To Edwardsburgh, Grenville Co, ONT. Miller. **DGH 21 Mar 1844; Ts Mouswald**.

1971 CRON, William. From DFS. To Dover Twp, Kent Co, ONT, <1855. Farmer. m Mary Johnstone, qv. **CAE 4**.

1972 CROOK, Sarah, ca 1833–20 Feb 1913. From Glasgow. To Melbourne, Richmond Co, QUE. m William Martyn, 1835–1911, a native of Cornwall, ENG. **MGC 15 Jul 1980**.

1973 CROOKS, Francis. From Kilmarnock, AYR. To Niagara, Lincoln Co, ONT, <1800. ch: 1. Ramsay, fur-trader; 2. William, qv; 3. James, qv; 4. Matthew, stld Ancaster; 5. Francis, jr, qv; 6. John, res Ancaster; 7. Janet. **DC 23 Sep 1980**.

1974 CROOKS, Francis, jr, d 1845. From Kilmarnock, AYR. s/o Francis C, qv. To Grimsby, Lincoln Co, ONT, <1800. m Mary Stagg, who d 1845, ch: 1. Mary; 2. Eliza; 3. William; 4. Charles. **DC 23 Sep 1980**.

1975 CROOKS, James, 1778–1860. From Kilmarnock,

AYR. s/o Francis C, qv. To Lincoln Co, ONT, prob 1794; stld Niagara, later Flamborough. Merchant and MLA; served in War of 1812. Son Adam, 1827-82, QC, MLA. **SNQ vi/1 49; DC 23 Sep 1980**.

1976 CROOKS, William, b 1776. From Kilmarnock, AYR. s/o Francis C, qv. To Grimsby, Lincoln Co, ONT, <1800. Merchant, shipowner, and served in War of 1812. m Mary Butler. **DC 23 Sep 1980**.

CROOKSHANK. See also CRUICKSHANK.

1977 CROOKSHANK, Margaret. Poss from Is Arran, BUT. To Restigouche Co, NB, ca 1831. Wife of James Calderwood, qv. **DC 1 Oct 1979**.

1978 CROSBIE, Euphemia, d 23 Mar 1847. From Balmaghie par, KKD. To Waterloo Co, ONT, d Dumfries. Wife of John McNaught, qv. **DGH 20 May 1847**.

1979 CROSS, Rev Archibald, 1821–11 Apr 1900. From East Calder, MLN. s/o Alexander C, farmer, and Jane Peacock. Burgher min at West Linton, PEE, 1848-52. To Oxford Co, ONT, and became UP Ch min at Ingersoll and Woodstock. Trans to Newton and Newcastle, Durham Co. Resigned 1875, and retr to SCT. m Christian Rattray, and d Newington, Edinburgh. **UPC i 561**.

1980 CROZIER, Isabel. From Yarrow par, SEL. To ONT, summer 1831. Wife of William Waldie, qv. **DC 12 Oct 1979**.

1981 CRUDEN, Euphemia Buchan, 25 Jan 1821–19 Feb 1876. From Logie-Buchan, ABD. d/o Rev George C, par min, and Sophia Fraser. To ONT. m Charles S. Ross, Receiver-General. **FES vi 197**.

CRUICKSHANK. See also CROOKSHANK.

1982 CRUICKSHANK, George. From Rothes, MOR. To Montreal, QUE, 1842. Was in Demerara for a short period, but retr to Montreal. Later in Streetsville, Peel Co, ONT, and Three Rivers, QUE. m a d/o James Turner, qv. **SGC 570**.

1983 CRUICKSHANK, James, d 29 Jun 1853. From Insch or Culsamond, ABD. To ONT 1836; stld Nichol Twp, Wellington Co. Moved to Pilkington Twp. Farmer. m Margaret Mennie, qv, ch: 1. Barbara; 2. Andrew; 3. Elizabeth; 4. George. **EHE 39**.

1984 CRUICKSHANK, Jean, b 1794. From Grantown-on-Spey, MOR. wid/o Donald McPherson, Chelsea pensioner. To Puslinch Twp, Wellington Co, ONT, 1848. ch: 1. James, qv; 2. Thomas, b 1821; 3. William, b 1823; 4. Elspet, b 1826; 5. John, b 1828; 6. Mary, b 1831; 7. Ann, b 1833. **DC 7 Apr 1975**.

1985 CRUICKSHANK, Rev John, 1803–13 Jun 1892. From Fordyce, BAN. Grad MA Kings Coll, Aberdeen, 1821, and was Murray lecturer there in 1827. Ord 1828 and called to St Andrews Presb Ch, Ottawa, ONT. Trans to Brockville, 1843, and to Niagara, 1846. Retr to SCT and was min at Turriff, ABD. m at Beckwith Twp, Lanark Co, ONT, 1 Aug 1838, Katherine Fellows, from Rockcliffe, who d 1909, ch: 1. Katherine Margaret, 1839-40; 2. Charlotte, b 1841; 3. William John, b 1842; 4. May Amelia, b 1844; 5. Margaret, b 1846; 6. Alexander Imlach, b 1848; 7. James Clark, b 1851; 8. Thomas Fellows, b 1853; 9. Katherine Laura, b 1861. **KCG 278; SNQ iii/2 154; FES vi 273, vii 631**.

1986 CRUICKSHANK, Robert, b 21 Apr 1743. From

Arbroath, ANS. s/o George C. and Isobel Wallace. To Montreal, QUE. **FES v 442**.

1987 CRUICKSHANK, Robert. From INV. To West Williams Twp, Middlesex Co, ONT, ca 1850. **PCM 47**.

1988 CRUICKSHANK, Robert Cromarty, 9 Sep 1801–1 Mar 1850. Born Dunnet, CAI, but emig from South Ronaldsay, OKI. To Hudson Bay, 1818, and emp with HBCo. Went to Megantic Co, QUE, 1825. Carpenter. m 1 Jan 1832, Caroline Glanville, b London, ENG, 1813, d/o John Yeoman Cooke and Mary Ann Glanville, ch: 1. Mary Ann, b 1832; 2. Helen, b 1835; 3. William, b 1837; 4. Caroline, b 1839; 5. Robert Cromarty, b 1841; 6. John Yeoman, b 1842; 7. James Cromarty, b 1845; 8. Andrew Dunn, b 1847, went to MI; 9. Henry Frederick, b 1849; 10. Frederick, b 1851; 11. Charles Glanville, b 1853, physician, went to NM. **AMC 135; DC 11 Feb 1980**.

1989 CUBITT, Lt Col Thomas, d 15 Mar 1840. To Kingston, ONT, and d there. **DGH 1 May 1840**.

1990 CUDDIE, Thomas, b ca 1793. From Corstorphine, MLN. To QUE, ex Greenock, summer 1815; stld Scotch Line, Lanark Co, ONT. Gardener, later farmer. m Marion Fyffe, qv. **SEC 1; HCL 12, 231**.

1991 CULLEN, Robert. Prob from AYR. s/o Thomas C. To Pictou, NS, on the *Hope*, ex Glasgow, 5 Apr 1848; stld Big Brook, later Stellarton. m Janet Crawford, qv, ch: 1. Thomas; 2. David; 3. Anne; 4. Jane; 5. Margaret; 6. Elizabeth; 7. Martha; 8. John; 9. William. **PAC 12; DC 12 Jul 1979**.

1992 CULLEN, Robert. Prob from AYR. To Ottawa, ONT, later to Wellington Co. m Margaret Linton, qv. Dau Elizabeth, b 1841. **LDW 20 May 1967**.

1993 CULLEN, William, ca 1792–15 Oct 1847. From Anderston, Glasgow. To Charlottetown, PEI, <1829. Clerk to the House of Assembly. **DGH 4 Nov 1847**.

1994 CULLEN, Rev William, b 1839. From LKS. s/o John C, merchant. Matric Univ of Glasgow, 1854, and studied theology, 1858-62. To PEI 1863, and adm min of St Peters Road Ch, Georgetown. Went to AUS for health reasons and was min at Bright and Buckland, Victoria. **GMA 16474; FES vii 587, 619**.

1995 CULTON, Anthony, b ca 1745. From Troqueer par, KKD. To Georgetown, Kings Co, PEI, on the *Lovely Nellie*, ex Carsethorn, May 1775; stld later East River, Pictou Co, NS. Farmer, and gr 500 acres on west side of river. Listed as capable of bearing arms, 1783. m Janet McCaughter, qv, ch: 1. Marion, b ca 1763; 2. Robert, b ca 1765; 3. Janet, b ca 1769; 4. John, b ca 1771; 5. Ann, b ca 1773. **ELN; HPC App A, C and D; HNS iii 670**.

1996 CUMMIN, Ann, ca 1793–9 Jan 1832. From Kiltarlity, INV. To Pictou, NS, on the *Diligence*, 1820; moved to London Twp, Middlesex Co, ONT, 1830. Wife of James Fraser, missionary, qv. **DC 11 Mar 1979**.

1997 CUMMING, Archibald. Prob rel to Paul C, qv. To QUE on the *Commerce*, ex Greenock, Jul 1820; stld prob Lanark Co, ONT. **HCL 239**.

1998 CUMMING, Cuthbert, 1787–1870. From BAN. To CAN, 1804, and became a clerk with the NWCo at Fort Dauphin. After merger with HBCo became a chief trader at Swan River and Montreal. Retr to Colborne, AUS,

1844. m 1842, at Pic, Lake Superior, Jane, d/o Thomas McMurray, fur-trader, ch. **MDB 166**.

1999 CUMMING, Daniel. To QUE on the *Commerce*, ex Greenock, Jul 1820; stld prob Lanark Co, ONT. **HCL 239**.

2000 CUMMING, John. To QUE on the *Commerce*, ex Greenock, Jul 1820; stld prob Lanark Co, ONT. Son John with him. **HCL 239**.

2001 CUMMING, Margaret, b 1774. From Is Arran, BUT. To Dalhousie, NB, 1830; stld Restigouche Co. m James Hamilton, qv. **MAC 14**.

2002 CUMMING, Margaret, 1797–1880. From Kingscorse, Is Arran, BUT. To Charlo, Restigouche Co, NB, 1828. Wife of John Hamilton, qv. **MAC 15**.

2003 CUMMING, Paul. Prob rel to Archibald C, qv. To QUE on the *Commerce*, ex Greenock, Jul 1820; stld prob Lanark Co, ONT. **HCL 239**.

2004 CUMMING, Robert, b 1821. From Kintyre, ARL. s/o Robert C. and Barbara Milloy. To Chatham, Kent Co, ONT. m Rose McNaughton. Son Neil Thomas. **LDW 5 Nov 1970**.

2005 CUMMINGS, Archibald. From ABD. To Bon Accord, Nichol Twp, Wellington Co, ONT, 1836. Wife Ann Brockie, qv, with him, and ch: 1. Alexander; 2. George; 3. Archibald; 4. James; 5. Christina; 6. Annie. **EHE 94**.

2006 CUMMINGS, Maggie, d 8 Dec 1879. From Is Skye, INV. To Inverness Co, NS. m William David McLeod. **DC 19 Nov 1977**.

2007 CUMMINGS, William, b 18 Mar 1791. Poss from Blair Drummond, PER. s/o James C. and Rebecca Gordon. To ONT <1830; stld prob Esquesing Twp, Halton Co. m Margaret, b Armagh, IRL, d/o William Bell. Dau Rebecca. **DC 15 Feb 1971**.

2008 CUNNINGHAM, Alexander, 20 Dec 1813–12 Jul 1871. From Greenfoot, Kilwinning, AYR. s/o John and Barbara C. To Lambton Co, ONT, <1840, and stld Dresden. **DC 12 May 1980**.

2009 CUNNINGHAM, David. To Tatamagouche, Colchester Co, NS, <1820. Farmer. **HT 47,n**.

2010 CUNNINGHAM, George, b 14 Nov 1804. From Duns, BEW. s/o Rev George C, par min, and Hyndmer Barclay. To CAN, prob ONT. **FES ii 10**.

2011 CUNNINGHAM, George, 1816–20 Jun 1887. From SEL. To ONT <1839, poss first to Dumfries Twp, Waterloo Co, but stld <1850 in Hullett Twp, Huron Co. m Agnes Wright, qv, ch: 1. Walter, 1839–1910; 2. Margaret, 1840–1908; 3. Isabella, b 1844; 4. Thomas, b 1846; 5. James, b 1849; 6. George, b 1852, went to St Paul, MN; 7. Andrew, 1854–1909; 8. Agnes, 1856–1944. **DC 20 Jul 1979**.

2012 CUNNINGHAM, John. From AYR. s/o — C. and — Millar. To CAN <1843. **SH**.

2013 CUNNINGHAM, Robert Glasgow, 9 Feb 1812–12 Jan 1854. From Greenfoot, Kilwinning, AYR. s/o John and Barbara C. To Huron Co, ONT, ca 1835; stld Goderich. m Hannah Reid, ch: 1. John; 2. Charles. **DC 12 May 1980**.

2014 CURRAN, John. From KKD, poss Castle Douglas. To Toronto, ONT, <1857. Drover, later inn-keeper.

m Nicolas, d/o Teady Gormaly, and had, prob with other ch: 1. Jane, b 1852; 2. John, b 1854. **DC 3 Dec 1981**.

2015 CURRIE, Andrew, ca 1821–1905. From Eaglesham, RFW. Prob s/o Robert C. and Elizabeth Fulton. To Bruce Co, ONT, 1851. Farmer. m Margaret McGillivray, qv, ch: 1. Robert; 2. Mary; 3. Susan; 4. Duncan. **DC 15 Jan 1977**.

2016 CURRIE, Annie. From Is Arran, BUT. Prob rel to Ronald C, qv. To Inverness, Megantic Co, QUE, <1840; later to Lillooet, BC. **MAC 44**.

2017 CURRIE, Archibald, b 1782. To St Andrews dist, Cape Breton Is, NS, 1814. Farmer, m and ch. **CBC 1818**.

2018 CURRIE, Archibald, b ca 1798. From Is Arran, BUT. Prob rel to John C, qv. To NB ca 1818; petitioned 9 Feb 1821 for 150 acres–Lot 68–on the south side of Restigouche River, Restigouche Co. **DC 31 May 1980**.

2019 CURRIE, Archibald. From Is Arran, BUT. To QUE on the *Favourite*, 1846; stld Megantic Co, QUE, but d in LA. m 7 Sep 1830, Margaret Taylor, ch: 1. Catherine, qv; 2. John, b 1833; 3. William, ca 1835–ca 1862; 4. Neil, 1841-58; 5. Janet, qv; 6. Archibald, d 1897. m (ii) Janet Hamilton, rel to Peter H, qv, with further ch: 7. Ronald, b ca 1849; 8. Margaret; 9. Annie. **AMC 44, 49; MAC 43**.

2020 CURRIE, Archibald. From Kintyre, ARL. To Ekfrid Twp, Middlesex Co, ONT, 1849; went later to MI. **PCM 31**.

2021 CURRIE, Archibald, ca 1798–ca 1882. From Is South Uist, INV. s/o John C. To East Williams Twp, Middlesex Co, ONT, ca 1849. m Eliza McEachan, qv, ch: 1. John, b 1817; 2. Donald, remained in Scotland and res Benbecula; 3. Catherine, qv; 4. Marion, b 1824; 5. Mary, qv; 6. Allan, b 1828; 7. Flora, b 1830; 8. Simon; 9. Marion, b 1835; 10. Alexander, b 1839. **PCM; WLC**.

2022 CURRIE, Barbara, 1831–1903. From Is Islay, ARL. To Oro Twp, Simcoe Co, ONT, prob <1853. m William Smith, qv. **DC 21 Mar 1980**.

2023 CURRIE, Catherine, b 1831. From Kilmory par, Is Arran, BUT. d/o Archibald C, qv, and Margaret Taylor. To QUE on the *Favourite*, 1846; stld Inverness, Megantic Co, QUE. m 1853, Peter Cook, qv; (ii) James Butler. **AMC 49; MAC 43**.

2024 CURRIE, Catherine, b 1821. From Is South Uist, INV. d/o Archibald C, qv, and Eliza McEachan, qv. To East Williams Twp, Middlesex Co, ONT, ca 1849. m Malcolm Wilson. **WLC**.

2025 CURRIE, Cathrine, b 1780. Prob from Is Colonsay, ARL. To Charlottetown, PEI, on the *Spencer*, ex Oban, 22 Sep 1806. **PLSN**.

2026 CURRIE, Donald, b 1790. From Lochgilphead, ARL. To ONT, 1831. Wife Catherine with him, ch: 1. Archibald, b 1819; 2-3. Mary and Alexander, b 1822; 4. Donald, b 1823; 5. Robert, b 1826; 6. Christina. **DC 18 Sep 1981**.

2027 CURRIE, Donald. From ARL. To Aldborough Twp, Elgin Co, ONT, 1850. **PDA 75**.

2028 CURRIE, Donald 'Ruadh'. From INV. Gr-s of Lachlan MacMhuirich, b 1741, Bard of Clanranald. To

Cape Breton Co, NS, 1840; stld East Bay. ch: 1. Nial; 2. Lachlan; 3. Michael, 1855–1936; 4. Joseph; 5. John; 6. Catherine. **DC 28 Oct 1962**.

2029 CURRIE, Duncan, b 1773. To St Andrews dist, Cape Breton Is, NS, 1814. Farmer, m and had ch. **CBC 1818**.

2030 CURRIE, Elizabeth, b 29 Oct 1775. From Greenock, RFW. To CAN, 1820; stld prob ONT. Wife of Alexander Hill, qv. **SCN; DC 13 Jan 1962**.

2031 CURRIE, Elizabeth, d 1911. Prob from Is Arran, BUT. To Benjamen River, Restigouche Co, NB, poss <1840. m James Cook, qv. **DMC 1 Oct 1979**.

2032 CURRIE, Flora. From Kilmory, Is Arran, BUT. To QUE, and stld Hull, Ottawa Co. m 10 Jun 1828, Neil Currie, qv. **DC 24 Nov 1981**.

2033 CURRIE, Gavin, 1800-69. From Annandale, DFS. s/o — C. and — Irving. To Tatamagouche, Colchester Co, NS, <1820. Farmer and mariner. m Hannah, 1810–1902, d/o Francis Wilson, qv, and had, poss with other ch: 1. James; 2. Thomas; 3. John. **HT 43**.

2034 CURRIE, Henrietta. From Annandale, DFS. d/o — C. and — Irving. To Tatamagouche, Colchester Co, NS, <1825. m Wellwood, gr-s of Wellwood Waugh, qv. **HT 46**.

2035 CURRIE, Hugh. Rel to John C, qv. To Lanark Co, ONT, 1821; stld Lot 6, Con 4, North Sherbrooke Twp. **HCL 74**.

2036 CURRIE, James, b ca 1776. Prob from Is Colonsay, ARL. To Charlottetown, PEI, on the *Spencer*, ex Oban, 22 Sep 1806. Dau Mary, aged 7 mo with him. **PLSN**.

2037 CURRIE, James, b ca 1781. Prob from Is Colonsay, ARL. To Charlottetown, PEI, on the *Spencer*, ex Oban, 22 Sep 1806. Son James, aged 2 with him. **PLSN**.

2038 CURRIE, James. From Annandale, DFS. s/o — C. and — Irving. To Tatamagouche, Colchester Co, NS, <1820. Gardener. **HT 43**.

2039 CURRIE, Jane, b ca 1785. Prob from Is Colonsay, ARL. To Charlottetown, PEI, on the *Spencer*, ex Oban, 22 Sep 1806. **PLSN**.

2040 CURRIE, Janet, b ca 1751. Prob from Is Colonsay, ARL. To Charlottetown, PEI, on the *Spencer*, ex Oban, 22 Sep 1806. **PLSN**.

2041 CURRIE, Janet, b 1838. From Kilmory, Is Arran, BUT. d/o Archibald C, qv, and Margaret Taylor. To QUE on the *Favourite*, 1846; stld Inverness, Megantic Co, QUE. m Lachlan McCurdie, qv. **AMC 42; MAC 43**.

2042 CURRIE, Jean. From Shisken, Is Arran, BUT. To QUE on the *Margaret*, 1832; stld Inverness, Megantic Co, QUE. Wife of Donald Henry, qv. ch with her: 1. Janet; 2. Margaret; 3. Donald. **MAC 42**.

2043 CURRIE, Jean Walls. From Inverkeithing, FIF. d/o Robert C. and Elizabeth Stewart. To ONT 1846. m Robert Cook. **DC 21 Mar 1981**.

2044 CURRIE, John. To QUE on the *Alexander*, 1816; stld Lot 16, Con 4, Bathurst Twp, Lanark Co, ONT. **HCL 233**.

2045 CURRIE, John, 1796–1816. From Is Arran, BUT. Prob rel to Archibald C, qv. To NB, ca 1816. Petitioned 9 Feb 1821 for 150 acres–Lot 67–on the south side of the Restigouche River, Restigouche Co. By wife Dorothy, b 1805, ch: 1. Margaret; 2. Ann; 3. Dorothy Ann; 4. David; 5. Neil; 6. John; 7. Catherine; 8. Alexander; 9. Mary; 10. Eliza. **DC 31 May 1980**.

2046 CURRIE, John. Rel to Hugh C, qv. To Lanark Co, ONT, 1821; stld Lot 6, Con 4, North Sherbrooke Twp. **HCL 74**.

2047 CURRIE, John, 1796–1869. From Annandale, DFS. s/o — C. and — Irving. To Tatamagouche, Colchester Co, NS, <1820; stld Waughs River. Farmer and schoolteacher. Son Wellwood. **HT 46**.

2048 CURRIE, John, 1803-84. From Corriecrevie, Kilmory par, Is Arran, BUT. To Nash Creek, Restigouche Co, NB, 1834. m Elspeth Fergusson, qv. Dau Elspa d Rio Vista, CA, 1918. **MAC 13**.

2049 CURRIE, John. From Is Islay, ARL. To Simcoe Co, ONT, prob <1853. Wife Catherine McAllister, qv, with him. Son John, 1862–1931, soldier and politician. **DC 30 Aug 1977**.

2050 CURRIE, Margaret. From Annandale, DFS. d/o — C. and — Irving. To Tatamagouche, Colchester Co, NS, <1825. m Samuel, s/o William Wauch, qv, and Elizabeth Rood. **HT 46**.

2051 CURRIE, Margaret, 1785–1857. From Knapdale, ARL. To Ekfrid Twp, Middlesex Co, ONT, 1823. Wife of Neil Galbraith. **GSO 33**.

2052 CURRIE, Margaret, ca 1807–27 Feb 1902. From Is Mull, ARL. To Queens Co, PEI, <1836. m Rev Samuel MacLeod, qv. **SPI 159**.

2053 CURRIE, Margaret. From Is Arran, BUT. To Inverness, Megantic Co, QUE, <1840. m Peter McKillop, qv. **AMC 21**.

2054 CURRIE, Mary. From Annandale, DFS. d/o — C. and — Irving. To Tatamagouche, Colchester Co, NS, <1825. m John Shannon. **HT 46**.

2055 CURRIE, Mary, b 1826. From Is South Uist, INV. d/o Archibald C, qv, and Eliza McEachan, qv. To East Williams Twp, Middlesex Co, ONT, ca 1849. m Hector McLennan, qv. **WLC**.

2056 CURRIE, Neil, b ca 1794. From Is Arran, BUT. To Restigouche Co, NB, ca 1819. Petitioned 9 Feb 1821 for 150 acres–Lot 74–on the south side of Restigouche River. **DC 31 May 1980**.

2057 CURRIE, Neil. Prob from Kilmory, Is Arran, BUT. To QUE, 1828; stld Hull, Ottawa Co. m Flora Grant, qv, ch: 1. Mary; 2. John; 3. Peter; 4. David; 5. Daniel; 6. Alexander; 7. Flora; 8. Elizabeth. **DC 24 Nov 1981**.

2058 CURRIE, Peter. From ARL. To East Williams Twp, Middlesex Co, ONT, 1831. Son Rev Peter. **PCM 43**.

2059 CURRIE, Ronald. From Is Arran, BUT. Prob rel to Margaret C, qv. To Inverness, Megantic Co, QUE, <1840; later to Lillooet, BC. **MAC 44**.

2060 CURRIE, William, 1785–1869. From Annandale, DFS. s/o — C. and — Irving. To Tatamagouche, Colchester Co, NS, 1809. Farmer and innkeeper. m Hannah Wilson, wid/o Alexander Waugh, qv. **HT 43**.

2061 CURRY, Isabella. From Hamilton, LKS. To Clyde River, Shelburne Co, NS, <1770. Wife of Gavin Lyle, qv. **DC 18 Jul 1981**.

2062 CUTHBERT, James, d 1798. From Castle Hill, INV. s/o Alexander and Beatrix C. To QUE ca 1765. Formerly Capt, 15th Regt, and acquired the Seigniory of Berthier. Built St Andrews Chapel at Montreal, the first Protestant edifice in the province. m Catherine Cairns, ch: 1. James, 1769–1849; 2. Ross, 1776–1861; 3. Caroline. **SGC 63; MDB 168**.

2063 CUTHBERT, William, ca 1796–3 Aug 1854. From AYR. To New Richmond, Bonaventure Co, QUE. Merchant. **Ts Greenock**.

2064 CUTHBERTSON, Grizel or Grace. To QUE on the *Prompt*, ex Greenock, 4 Jul 1820; stld Lanark Twp, Lanark Co, ONT. Wife of Robert Penman, qv. **DC 22 Oct 1980**.

2065 CUTHBERTSON, Marion. From Kilmaurs, AYR. To Galt, Waterloo Co, ONT, and stld Dumfries Twp. Wife of John Dickie, qv. **DD 5**.

2066 CUTT, James, 23 Apr 1833–22 Apr 1880. From North Ronaldsay, OKI. s/o James C. and Isabella Swanney. To ONT ca 1855, and stld Blanshard Twp, Perth Co. m Christina Muir, qv, ch: 1. Isabella, b 1855; 2. James, b 1857; 3. John, 1860–1945; 4. Robert Hall, 1862–1928; 5. Thomas, 1864–1904; 6. Mary Christina, b 1866. **DC 20 Jul 1979**.

D

2067 DALGARNO, Andrew. From ABD. To Elora, Nichol Twp, Wellington Co, ONT, 1836. m Kirstie Calder, ch: 1. Andrew, res Arthur Twp; 2. John, res Sullivan Twp, Grey Co; 3. Margaret; 4. Barbara; 5. Beatrice. **EHE 92**.

2068 DALGLEISH, Janet, 8 Feb 1766–19 Aug 1850. From Stow, MLN. d/o George D. and Helen Tait. To Sandwich, Windsor, Essex Co, ONT, <1848, and d Cuyahoga Falls, OH. wid/o Thomas Gray, 1766–1833. **DC 14 Jan 1975**.

2069 DALGLEISH, Penny, b ca 1805. From Is Rum, ARL. Prob d/o Simon D, qv. To Gut of Canso, Cape Breton Is, NS, on the *Saint Lawrence*, ex Tobermory, 11 Jul 1828. **SLL**.

2070 DALGLEISH, Robert, d 4 Jul 1877. From MLN. To Montreal, QUE, 1828. Served in the military secretariat for 45 years. m Mary, d/o William Aird. **SGC 487**.

2071 DALGLEISH, Simon, b ca 1766. From Is Rum, ARL. To Gut of Canso, Cape Breton Is, NS, on the *Saint Lawrence*, ex Tobermory, 11 Jul 1828. **SLL**.

DALHOUSIE, Earl of. See RAMSAY, George.

2072 DALLAS, Alexander Grant, ca 1818–2 Jan 1882. To CAN and entered service of the HBCo, 1850. App chief factor at Fort Victoria, Vancouver Is, BC. Gov of Ruperts Land, 1862, in succ to George Simpson, qv. Retr to SCT. m Amelia, d/o Sir James Douglas, qv. **MDB 170**.

2073 DALLING, Eliza Bowden, 10 Feb 1818–23 Jan 1905. From Greenock, RFW. d/o Robert D, customs officer. To Toronto, ONT, ca 1840. m William Anderson, qv. **SCN**.

2074   DALRYMPLE, Barbara. sis/o Eliza D, qv. To QUE on the *Bruce*, ex Aberdeen, arr 13 Aug 1817. Teacher of a school for young ladies. **DC 6 Jan 1977**.

2075   DALRYMPLE, Christian. sis/o Eliza D, qv. To QUE on the *Bruce*, ex Aberdeen, arr 13 Aug 1817. m Dr Alexander Skakel, qv. **DC 6 Jan 1977**.

2076   DALRYMPLE, Eliza, 1799–1889. sis/o Barbara D, qv, and Christian D, qv. To QUE on the *Bruce*, ex Aberdeen, arr 13 Aug 1817. **DC 6 Jan 1977**.

2077   DALRYMPLE, James, 1827–1910. From FIF. To Hamilton, ONT, 1853. Farmer. m Mary Coleville Saunders, qv, ch: 1. James S, 1856-92; 2. Margaret Jane, 1858-92; 3. Christine E, 1862–1943; 4. George T, 1864–1918; 5. Mary Ann, 1867–1936; 6. Arthur Edward, 1875–1947. **DC 31 Dec 1979**.

2078   DALRYMPLE, Mary. sis/o Barbara D, qv, Christian D, qv, and Eliza D, qv. To QUE on the *Bruce*, ex Aberdeen, arr 13 Aug 1817. **DC 6 Aug 1977**.

2079   DALRYMPLE, Robert, 1794–1875. From Leslie, FIF. s/o John D, and Jean Will. To Montreal, QUE, ca 1814. Cabin boy. m 1822, Ann Elizabeth Farrar, ch: 1. Ann; 2. Christian; 3. John; 4. Elizabeth; 5. Robert; 6. Caroline; 7. Jane; 8. Mary; 9. George; 10. James; 11. Christian. **DC 26 Sep 1977**.

2080   DALZEILL, Catherine, 1808-93. From Kirkconnel, DFS. To Huron Co, ONT, ca 1855. Wife of William Laidlaw, qv. **DC 26 May 1979**.

2081   DALZEILL, John, ca 1798–13 Mar 1859. From Courstein, Annandale, DFS. To South Dumfries Twp, Brant Co, ONT, and d there. **DGH 8 Apr 1859**.

2082   DARLING, Agnes. From Edington, Chirnside par, BEW. To Leeds Twp, Megantic Co, QUE, 1834. Wife of William Kinghorn, qv, m 12 Jun 1815. **Chirnside OPR 730/1-2**.

2083   DARLING, David, ca 1797–7 Jul 1881. From ROX. s/o Robert D. and Ann Scott. To Esquesing Twp, Halton Co, ONT. m 16 Aug 1866, Margaret, d/o John Dewar, qv, and Emily Knight, qv, and had, prob with other ch: 1. Annie B; 2. Emily H. **DC 24 Nov 1979**.

2084   DARLING, James. From Edinburgh. To ONT, 1854; stld Huron Twp, Bruce Co. Stone-cutter. m Helen Eliza Gillon Hill, qv, ch: 1. Helen; 2. John, druggist. **DC 5 Jan 1962**.

2085   DARLING, H.W. From Edinburgh. bro/o Robert D, qv, and William D, qv. To Montreal, QUE, 1839. Pres of the Bank of Commerce. **SGC 673**.

2086   DARLING, Robert. From Edinburgh. bro/o H.W. and William D, qv. To Montreal, QUE, prob 1839. Dry goods merchant. **SGC 673**.

2087   DARLING, William, 1819–1 Nov 1885. From Edinburgh. bro/o H.W. and Robert D, qv. To Montreal, QUE, 1839. Hardware merchant. m Mary Davidson, qv, and res Bloomfield House, Hochelaga. They had, prob with other ch: 1. William; 2. Andrew, res Toronto; 3. Mrs G.T. Ross. **SGC 673**.

2088   DARLING, Rev William Stewart, ca 1818–19 Jan 1886. To Orillia Twp, Simcoe Co, ONT, <1846. Ch of Eng clergyman and author. **MDB 170**.

2089   DARROCH, Angus, b 1746. From Is Colonsay, ARL. To Charlottetown, PEI, on the *Spencer*, ex Oban, 22 Sep 1806. Wife Effy McAlister, qv, with him, and ch: 1. Duncan, qv; 2. Malcolm, b ca 1786. **PLSN; DC 18 Nov 1981**.

2090   DARROCH, Archibald, b 1786. From Is Colonsay, ARL. Prob bro/o James D, qv. To Charlottetown, PEI, on the *Spencer*, ex Oban, 22 Sep 1806. **PLSN**.

2091   DARROCH, Cathrine, b 1776. From Is Colonsay, ARL. To Charlottetown, PEI, on the *Spencer*, ex Oban, 22 Sep 1806. **PLSN**.

2092   DARROCH, Duncan, ca 1777–19 Feb 1853. From Is Colonsay, ARL. s/o Angus D, qv. To Charlottetown, PEI, on the *Spencer*, ex Oban, 22 Sep 1806. m Margaret McMillan, qv. Son John, b 1803. **PLSN; DC 18 Nov 1981**.

2093   DARROCH, James, b ca 1774. From Is Colonsay, ARL. Prob bro/o Archibald D, qv. To Charlottetown, PEI, on the *Spencer*, ex Oban, 22 Sep 1806. **PLSN**.

2094   DARROCH, Nancy, b ca 1783. From Is Colonsay, ARL. Prob rel to Angus D, qv. To Charlottetown, PEI, on the *Spencer*, ex Oban, 22 Sep 1806. **PLSN**.

2095   DARROCH, Rachel, b 1769. From Is Colonsay, ARL. To Charlottetown, PEI, on the *Spencer*, ex Oban, 22 Sep 1806. **PLSN**.

2096   DARROCH, Rev William, d 16 Jun 1865. To Kingston, ONT, <1858. Educ Queens Coll, 1858-61, and was adm first min of St Matthews Ch, Montreal, QUE, 1861. **FES vii 631**.

2097   DAVIDSON, Ann, ca 1804–17 Sep 1878. From Aberdeen. d/o James D, qv, and Elspet Blackhall, qv. To Preston Twp, Waterloo Co, ONT, 1843. m Alexander Allan, qv. **SAA 80; EHE 10**.

2098   DAVIDSON, Arthur. From ABD, poss Clatt. To Montreal, QUE, <1800. Judge of the Court of Kings Bench. m Jane, d/o Maj Malcolm Fraser, 78th Regt, and had, prob with other ch: 1. Jane; 2. Eliza or Elizabeth. **SGC 148**.

2099   DAVIDSON, David, ca 1821–1851. From Brechin, ANS. To St Johns, NFD. Ships carpenter. **Ts Brechin**.

2100   DAVIDSON, Elsie. From Aberdeen. d/o James D, qv, and Elspet Blackhall, qv. To Wellington Co, ONT, prob <1840. m William McKenzie, and retr later to SCT. **EHE 10**.

2101   DAVIDSON, Grizel or Grace, b ca 1770. From Kilbride par, Is Arran, BUT. To Dalhousie, NB, 1826. Wife of John Hamilton, qv. d at Irving, SCT. **MAC 17**.

2102   DAVIDSON, Harriet. To Montreal, QUE, prob <1854. m Alexander McGibbon, who became Inspector of Indian Agencies in the NWT. **SGC 567**.

2103   DAVIDSON, Hugh. To Chatham, Northumberland Co, NB, 1842. m Margaret Ruelle, ch: 1. Thomas; 2. William; 3. Barbara; 4. James. **DC 15 Apr 1975**.

2104   DAVIDSON, Isabella, ca 1775–14 Feb 1846. From Urr, KKD. To Cobourg, Northumberland Co, ONT. Wife of John Roddick, qv. **DGH 26 Mar 1846**.

2105   DAVIDSON, Isabella. From Aberdeen. d/o James D, qv, and Elspet Blackhall, qv. To Wellington Co, ONT, but stld Galt, Waterloo Co. m Absolom Shade,

b Wyoming Co, PA, 1793, pioneer settler at Galt.
HGD 19; EHE 10.

2106 DAVIDSON, James. From Edinburgh. To Pictou
Co, NS, <1775. Teacher, and commenced the first
sabbath school in Canada at Lyons Brook. **HNS iii 219;
HPC App B**.

2107 DAVIDSON, James. From ROX. To CAN on the
Sarah Mary Jane, 1831; stld nr Paris, Dumfries Twp,
Waterloo Co, ONT. **HGD 60**.

2108 DAVIDSON, James, 31 Mar 1776–15 Aug 1852.
From Aberdeen, but native of Walthamstow, ESS. To
Wellington Co, ONT, prob <1840. Cotton thread
manufacturer. m Elspet Blackhall, qv, ch: 1. John, qv;
2. James; 3. William, merchant in Liverpool;
4. Alexander, merchant in Malta; 5. Ann, qv;
6. Elizabeth; 7. Isabella, qv; 8. Mary, qv; 9. Elsie,
qv. **EHE 10**.

2109 DAVIDSON, James Ironside, b 8 Jun 1818. From
Monquhitter, ABD. To ONT. Farmer and Liberal
politician. **SNQ ix/1 26**.

2110 DAVIDSON, John, ca 1805–30 Nov 1877. From
Aberdeen. s/o James D, qv, and Elspet Blackhall, qv. To
Woolwich Twp, Waterloo Co, ONT, 1834, but moved to
Galt and became storekeeper, post-master, bank agent
and capt of militia. m Miss Tassie. **HGD 245,n;
EHE 10**.

2111 DAVIDSON, Rev John, 1813–2 Feb 1890. From
Paisley, RFW. s/o James D, craftsman. Matric Univ of
Glasgow, 1828, and studied theology. Min at La Prairie,
1844-49; New Richmond, NB, 1851; North Williamsburg,
1858. Declined to join Union, 1875. **GMA 12300;
FES vii 631**.

2112 DAVIDSON, John, 1831–1902. Poss from ABD.
s/o John D. and Elizabeth Gordon. To Dundee, QUE,
1835. Journalist. m 1861, Matilda Davidson, his
sist-in-law, d/o John Stott. **DC 4 Mar 1965**.

2113 DAVIDSON, John Alexander, 1810-88. From
Aberdeen, but b Putney, SRY. s/o Alexander D. and
Sarah Alexander. To Nichol Twp, Wellington Co, ONT,
1835. m Catherine Robeson Middleton, qv, ch: 1. Sarah;
2. Robert; 3. James, d NY; 4. Catherine; 5. Christina;
6. Annie; 7. William; 8. Hadassah. **EHE 89; DC 7 Jun
1980**.

2114 DAVIDSON, Kenneth, 1774–24 Nov 1874. From
ROC. To Pictou Co, NS, prob <1830; bur Hill Cemetery,
West River Station. m Isabella Fraser, qv. **DC 10 Feb
1980**.

2115 DAVIDSON, Lachlan. From Dunachton, Alvie,
INV. s/o Samuel D. and Isabella Grant. To Cannington,
nr Lindsay, Victoria Co, ONT. **Ts Alvie**.

2116 DAVIDSON, Margaret, 1795–1875. From Is
Arran, BUT. To Inverness, Megantic Co, QUE, 1843. Wife
of Peter McKenzie, qv. **AMC 40; MAC 40**.

2117 DAVIDSON, Margaret. From Kintore, ABD. To
Toronto, ONT, 1835, but retr to SCT, 1837. m at Udny,
6 Jun 1835, James Anderson, qv. **Udny OPR 249/2;
DC 16 Apr 1978**.

2118 DAVIDSON, Margaret Tweeddale, 10 Jul 1815–
12 Apr 1861. From Paisley, RFW. d/o Rev Elliot William
D. and Mary McTaggart. To Halifax, NS, 1848. Wife of
Rev Alexander F, qv. **FES ii 377; MDB 239**.

2119 DAVIDSON, Mary. From Aberdeen. d/o James D,
qv, and Elspet Blackhall, qv. To Wellington Co, ONT,
prob <1840. m John, s/o Andrew Geddes, Crown Land
Agent. **EHE 10**.

2120 DAVIDSON, Mary. From Edinburgh. To Montreal,
QUE, prob <1850. m William Darling, qv. **SGC 673**.

2121 DAVIDSON, Mary, d 7 Oct 1868. From
Dryfesdale, DFS. d/o — D, schoolmaster. To Huron Twp,
Bruce Co, ONT. m R. Jardine. **DGH 13 Nov 1868**.

2122 DAVIDSON, Samuel, d 21 Jul 1842. From Alloa,
CLK. To Belleville Twp, Hastings Co, ONT. Physician.
DGH 15 Sep 1842.

2123 DAVIDSON, Thomas, b ca 1778. To Little Bras
D'Or dist, Cape Breton Is, NS, <1810. Servant.
CBC 1818.

2124 DAVIDSON, Thomas. To QUE on the *Commerce*,
ex Greenock, Jun 1820; stld prob Lanark Co, ONT.
HCL 238.

2125 DAVIDSON, Thomas. Prob from Shotts par, LKS.
To Peterborough Co, ONT, ca 1828; stld Con 8,
Otonabee Twp. Farmer. m Helen Shearer, qv. **DC 7 Jan
1981**.

2126 DAVIDSON, William, ca 1740–17 Jun 1790. From
Bellie par, MOR. s/o John Godsman and — Davidson.
Changed surname to Davidson on emig to Halifax, NS,
1764. Stld Miramichi, Northumberland Co, NB, and gr
land along with John Cort, qv. Pioneer fisherman and
lumberman, shipbuilder and MLA. m Sarah, d/o Dr
Phineas Nevers, ch. **BNA i 265; MLA 83**.

2127 DAVIDSON, William, b 1780. From Ednam, ROX.
s/o Matthew D. and Agnes Hogg. To ONT <1830. Son
Ninian, merchant in QUE. **LDW 19 Apr 1970**.

2128 DAVIS, John, d 9 Dec 1826. From Paisley, RFW.
To Halifax, NS. **VSN No 1970**.

2129 DAVISON, Joseph, 1792–1878. Prob from STI.
s/o — D. and Ann Richardson. To PEI <1850. m Ann,
d/o William Whitehead, qv, and Mary Hosea, qv, ch:
1. Joseph, b 1819; 2. William, b 1821; 3. Mary Ann,
b 1824; 4. John, b 1826; 5. Margaret, b 1829;
6. Andrew, b 1832; 7. Elizabeth, b 1834; 8. Fred,
b 1836. **DC 25 Nov 1981**.

2130 DAWSON, Alexander, b ca 1765. From
Overtown, Ordiquhil, BAN. s/o John D. To Pictou Co,
NS, <1820. Son John William, 1820-99, geologist and
naturalist, knighted 1884. **BNA 818; CBD 285;
MDB 176**.

2131 DAWSON, Rev Aneas McDonell, 30 Jul 1810–
29 Dec 1894. From Portsoy, BAN. s/o John D. in
Redhaven, and Anne McDonell. Educ Paris and Blairs
Coll, KCD. Ord to RC priesthood and went to QUE,
1854. Hon Vicar-General of Ottawa, 1890; LLD Queens
Univ; author and historian. **MDB 172**.

2132 DAWSON, George, 1813-83. From Falkirk, STI.
To Lincoln Co, ONT, <1826. Appr typesetter at Niagara,
and went later to Rochester and Albany, NY. Editor of
Rochester *Democrat*, 1836. **SAS 40**.

2133 DAWSON, J.A. Cabin passenger on the *Lulan*, ex
Glasgow, 17 Aug 1848, bound for Pictou, NS.
DC 12 Jul 1979.

2134 DAWSON, Richard. To QUE prob <1850. Son Richard, res Lachute. **MGC 2 Aug 1979**.

2135 DAWSON, Simon James, 1820–20 Nov 1902. From BAN. To QUE, 1851. Engineer on projects on the St Maurice River; later Government surveyor, Red River, and engaged in road-making. MLA, Algoma, ONT, 1875-78. **BNA 1083**.

2136 DAWSON, William, d 14 Jul 1863. From PER. s/o John D, 1800-83, farmer, and Elizabeth McNab. To ONT and d Ojibwa, Middlesex Co. **Ts Tullibody**.

2137 DEAN, James, d 1872. To QUE; later to ONT. Shipbuilder. m Anne Coffin. Son John. **DC 29 Sep 1964**.

2138 DEANS, James. From ROX. To CAN on the *Sarah Mary Jane*, 1831; stld Dumfries Twp, Waterloo Co, ONT. **HGD 60**.

2139 DEANS, Walter. From ROX. Poss rel to James D, qv. To CAN on the *Sarah Mary Jane*, 1831; stld Dumfries Twp, Waterloo Co, ONT. **HGD 60**.

2140 DEAS, Rev William, ca 1807–1862. Prob from Perth. To Adelaide Twp, Middlesex Co, ONT. **Ts Perth**.

2141 DEIVER, Donald, b ca 1788. From Foss, PER. To Charlottetown, PEI, on the *Clarendon*, ex Oban, 6 Aug 1808. Wife Margaret, aged 20, with him. Labourer. **CPL**.

2142 DEMPSTER, George. From Alloa, CLK. s/o — D. and Helen Duncan or Traquair. To Montreal, QUE, <1848. Merchant. **DGH 7 Dec 1848**.

2144 DEMPSTER, Robert, 10 Jul 1815–23 Jun 1889. From Balerno, MLN. s/o Robert D. and Margaret Purdie. To ONT <1844; stld 1865 at Oshawa, East Whitby Twp. Carpenter. m Lillias Tennant, qv, ch: 1. Robert, b ca 1843; 2. Marion; 3. Margaret; 4. Sarah; 5. George; 6. Jessie; 7. Lillias. **DC 18 Jan 1980**.

2145 DENHAM, Agnes. Prob from Edinburgh. To Franklin Twp, Huntingdon Co, QUE, <1813. Wife of William Craik, qv. **DC 2 Jul 1979**.

2146 DENHAM, Helen, 30 Oct 1793–10 May 1887. From DFS. d/o Humphrey D. and Mary Laidlaw. To QUE ca 1832; stld Buckingham. Went to Barton Twp, Wentworth Co, ONT. Wife of James Paisley, qv. **DC 11 Jul 1979**.

2147 DENHAM, Wilhelmina, d 31 Jan 1826. From Edinburgh. d/o Thomas D, H.M. General Register House. To Queenston, Lincoln Co, ONT. m Francis Hall, CE. ***Dumfries Monthly Magazine,* Mar 1826**.

2148 DENNISON, John, ca 1781–7 Dec 1824. To NS and d there. **VSN No 848**.

2149 DENNISTOUN, Alexander, 6 Sep 1821–2 Nov 1895. From Edinburgh. s/o James D. of Dennistoun and Colgrain, and Mary Ramsay Oswald. Educ Edinburgh Academy and Loretto School, Musselburgh. To ONT, ca 1840, and engaged in the lumber trade, but was sometime in Montreal, QUE, where he founded the first golf club in North America, 1873. m 1866, Margaret, d/o John Redpath, of Terrace Bank, Montreal, and retr to SCT. **EAR 2149**.

2150 DENNISTOUN, Robert, b 13 Jan 1815. From DNB. s/o James D. of Dennistoun and Colgrain, and Mary Ramsay Oswald. Educ Edinburgh Academy and came to ONT 1834. Stld Victoria Co. Farmer and became lawyer in Peterborough. Judge, 1868. m 24 Dec 1839, Maxwell Hamilton. Son James Frederick, 1841-86, QC. **BNA 914; EAR 55**.

2151 DEVINE, Rev James. From Aberdeen. Grad MA Kings Coll, Aberdeen, 1840. Became Episcopal min and went to CAN. **KCG 293**.

DEWAR, —. See McKERCHAR, Mrs Alexander.

2152 DEWAR, Alexander, b ca 1783. From Glenartney, PER. s/o Archibald D, qv, and wife Margaret. To Beckwith Twp, Lanark Co, ONT, 1819; later to Plympton Twp, Lambton Co. Transferred the 'quigrich' or head of St Fillans crozier, to the National Museum of Antiquities of SCT, 1876. **IFB 73; HCL 34**.

2153 DEWAR, Alexander. Prob from PER. To Mosa Twp, Middlesex Co, ONT, 1830. **PCM 24**.

2154 DEWAR, Andrew, ca 1835-59. From Kilmany, FIF. s/o James D. in Gauldry, and Ann Ness. To Toronto, ONT. **Ts Kilmany**.

2155 DEWAR, Archibald. From Glenartney, Comrie par, PER. s/o Alexander D, Breadalbane. To Montreal, QUE, on the *Curlew*, ex Greenock, 21 Jul 1818; stld Beckwith Twp, Lanark Co, ONT, later Plympton Twp, Lambton Co. Farmer. Wife Margaret with him, and sons Duncan and Archibald. Son Alexander, qv, followed. **BCL; IFB 72; HCL 33**.

2156 DEWAR, Catherine. Poss from Lochearnhead, PER. To Montreal, QUE, on the *Niagara*, ex Greenock, arr 28 May 1825; stld McNab Twp, Renfrew Co, ONT. Wife of Alexander McNab, qv. **EMT 22**.

2157 DEWAR, Donald. From Dull par, PER. To Kings Co, PEI, <1820. m Jun 1782, Elizabeth Irving, ch: 1. Duncan, b 1784; 2. Margaret, b 1787; 3. John, b 1789; 4. Donald, b 1792; 5. Robert, b 1802; 6. Betty, b 1804; 7. Jessie. **DC 14 Jul 1982**.

2158 DEWAR, Donald. Prob from Glenelg, INV. To Glengarry Co, ONT, 1832; stld nr Dunvegan. Wife Jessie McLeod, qv. **MG 30**.

2159 DEWAR, Donald. From Knapdale, ARL. To Lobo Twp, Middlesex Co, ONT, 1838. **PCM 39**.

2160 DEWAR, John. From Comrie par, PER. To Montreal, QUE, on the *Curlew*, ex Greenock, 21 Jul 1818; stld Derry, Beckwith Twp, Lanark Co, ONT. Farmer. Prob the man who m Margaret Buchanan, qv. **HCL 194; BCL**.

2161 DEWAR, John. Poss from ARL. To Lobo Twp, Middlesex Co, ONT, 1828. **PCM 39**.

2162 DEWAR, John, 25 Sep 1803–24 Apr 1871. From Shenavail, Dull par, PER. s/o John D. and May McDonald. To ONT 1830, stld Esquesing Twp, Halton Co, Lot W7, Con 1. m Emily Knight, qv, ch: 1. John, jr, qv; 2. Margaret; 3. James; 4. Robert; 5. David; 6. May; 7. Duncan; 8. Amelia Ann; 9. Jane. **DC 24 Nov 1979**.

2163 DEWAR, John, jr, 22 Aug 1829–1 Nov 1888. From Shenavail, Dull par, PER. s/o John D, qv, and Emily Knight, qv. To Esquesing Twp, Halton Co, ONT, 1830. Teacher and lawyer, QC 1868. m 1874, Jane, d/o Robert Somerville, politician, Huntingdon, QUE. **DC 24 Nov 1979**.

2164 DEWAR, John. From Glenelg, INV. To QUE on the *Liscard*, 1849; stld Glengarry Co, ONT. Farmer. m Mary Ann MacLeod, qv, ch: 1. Malcolm; 2. Norman; 3. Katie; 4. Sarah; 5. Mary Ann; 6. Harriet; 7. Margaret; 8. Christie. **MG 355.**

2165 DEWAR, John 'Ban'. From Glenelg, INV. To QUE, 1796; stld Lot 29, Con 7, Lochiel Twp, Glengarry Co, ONT. **MG 211.**

2166 DEWAR, Katherine. From Carey, PER. To QUE, ex Greenock, summer 1815; stld ONT. Wife of Duncan Campbell, qv. **SEC 3.**

2167 DEWAR, Malcolm. From Comrie par, PER. To Montreal, QUE, on the *Curlew*, ex Greenock, 21 Jul 1818; stld Derry, Beckwith Twp, Lanark Co, ONT. Farmer. Lot 23, Con 7. Wife Ann with him, and ch: 1. Ann, aged 5; 2. Alexander, aged 2. **BCL; HCL 33.**

2168 DEWAR, Margaret, b ca 1770. Prob from Breadalbane, PER. To Queens Co, PEI, poss 1808. Wife of Duncan Campbell, qv. **DC 11 Apr 1981.**

2169 DEWAR, Margaret, b ca 1790. From Killin, PER. To QUE, ex Greenock, summer 1815; stld ONT. Wife of Alexander McLaurin, qv. **SEC 4.**

2170 DEWAR, Peter. From Comrie, PER. To Montreal, QUE, on the *Curlew*, ex Greenock, 21 Jul 1818; stld Beckwith Twp, Lanark Co, ONT. **BCL; HCL 33.**

2171 DEWAR, Thomas. Prob from PER. To Aldborough Twp, Elgin Co, ONT, <1820. Farmer. Son Thomas. **PDA 92.**

2172 DICHMAN, Thomas, b 1795. From LKS. s/o John and Margaret D. To QUE on the *David of London*, ex Greenock, 19 May 1821; stld Lanark Twp, Lanark Co, ONT. Wife Catherine Donaldson, qv, with him. **LDW 4 Mar 1970.**

2173 DICK, Alexander, 1792–1868. From FIF. To Northumberland Co, NB, prob <1840. **DC 14 Jan 1980.**

2174 DICK, James, 1779–1821. From Bathgate, WLN. s/o John and Janet D. To QUE on the *David of London*, ex Greenock, 19 May 1821. He was drowned at Prescott, and his wife Janet Brown, qv, continued on to Lanark Co, ONT, and stld Lot 13, Con 9, Lanark Twp. ch: 1. Margaret, qv; 2. Janet, b 1801; 3. John, qv; 4. James; 5. Jane, b 1807; 6-7. Agnes and Elizabeth, twins, b 1809; 8. William, b 1812; 9. Robert, qv; 10. Catherine, b 1816; 11. Alexander, b 1818. **Ts Kirkton; HCL 71.**

2175 DICK, John, b ca 1751. From AYR. To QUE on the *Friendship*, ex Port Glasgow, 30 Mar 1775. Ship carpenter, 'going out to build vessels.' **LSF.**

2176 DICK, John, b 1803. From Bathgate, WLN. s/o James D, qv, and Janet Brown, qv. To QUE on the *David of London*, ex Greenock, 19 May 1821; stld Lanark Twp, Lanark Co, ONT. m Mary Gemmill. **Ts Kirkton; HCL 71; DC 6 Dec 1978.**

2177 DICK, Margaret, b 1800. From Bathgate, WLN. d/o James D, qv, and Janet Brown, qv. To QUE on the *David of London*, ex Greenock, 19 May 1821; stld Lanark Twp, Lanark Co, ONT. m Robert Stead, ch. **HCL 71; DC 6 Dec 1978.**

2178 DICK, Robert, b 1814. From Bathgate, WLN. s/o James D, qv, and Janet Brown, qv. To QUE on the *David of London*, ex Greenock, 19 May 1821; stld Lanark Twp, Lanark Co, ONT. Went later to USA and stld subsequently at Chicago, IL. Inventor of a method of using gummed labels to address newspapers. **HCL 71; DC 6 Dec 1978.**

2179 DICK, Robert. To Pictou, NS, on the *London*, arr 14 Jul 1848. **DC 15 Jul 1979.**

2180 DICKEY, Abraham. To QUE on the *Alexander*, 1816; stld Lot 2, Con 4, Drummond Twp, Lanark Co, ONT. **HCL 233.**

2181 DICKIE, James, b 3 Oct 1809, Langmuir, Kilmaurs, AYR. s/o John D, qv, and Marion Cuthbertson, qv. To Galt, Waterloo Co, ONT, 1833; stld Dumfries Twp. m Jane McDonald, from Blenheim, ch: 1. John, b 1838; 2. James; 3. Marion; 4. Donald; 5. Elizabeth; 6. Jane; 7. Alexander. **DD 14.**

2182 DICKIE, John. From AYR. To Miramichi, Northumberland Co, NB, <1822, when he moved to Restigouche Co. Farmer. ch incl: 1. David; 2. John; 3. Mrs William Fleming. **CUC 6.**

2183 DICKIE, John. To ONT, 1820; stld Oshawa, Durham Co. m Rebecca, d/o Thomas Fowke. Son Henry. **DC 29 Sep 1964.**

2184 DICKIE, John, ca 1777–30 Nov 1848. From Langmuir, Kilmaurs, AYR. s/o John D, farmer, and Janet Caldwell. To Galt, Waterloo Co, ONT, 1833; stld Dumfries Twp. Farmer. m 1805, Marion Cuthbertson, qv, ch: 1. John, qv; 2. James, qv; 3. David, b 14 Sep 1811; 4. William, qv; 5. Alexander, b 8 Oct 1815; 6. Margaret, qv; 7. Janet, b 2 Mar 1820; 8. Robert, b 1 Jun 1822; 9. Marion. **DD 5.**

2185 DICKIE, John, jr, b 26 Feb 1807. From Langmuir, Kilmaurs, AYR. s/o John D, qv, and Marion Cuthbertson, qv. To Galt, Waterloo Co, ONT, 1833; stld Dumfries Twp. Farmer. m Janet Miller, qv, ch: 1. John, b 1830; 2. James, b 1834; 3. David, b 1841; 4. William, b 1842; 5. Marion, b 1843; 6. Jean, b 1845; 7. Janet, b 1845; 8. Jane, d inf; 9. William; 10. Alexander. **DD 14.**

2186 DICKIE, Margaret, b 20 Jan 1818, Laigh Langmuir, Kilmaurs, AYR. d/o John D, qv, and Marion Cuthbertson, qv. To Galt, ONT, 1833; stld Dumfries Twp, Waterloo Co. m Robert Dickie, qv. **DD 14.**

2187 DICKIE, Robert. From Sorn, AYR. To Puslinch Twp, Wellington Co, ONT, 1839; stld later Dumfries Twp, Waterloo Co. m Margaret Dickie, qv, ch: 1. William, 1839-54; 2. John, b 1841; 3. Marion, b 1843; 4. George, b 1845; 5. Jane, b 1847; 6. Margaret, 1850-71; 7. James, d inf; 8. Jean; 9. Jessie; 10. Annie. **DD 14.**

2188 DICKIE, William, ca 1785–ca 1845. From Langmuir, Kilmaurs, AYR. s/o John D. and Janet Caldwell. To Galt, ONT, 1833; stld Dumfries Twp, Waterloo Co. Farmer, Con 12. m Janet Howie, qv, ch: 1. Janet, b 1818; 2. Agnes, b 1825; 3. Elizabeth, b 1827; 4. Margaret Cunningham, b 1830; 5. William, b 1835; 6. Marian, b 1837. **DD 14.**

2189 DICKIE, William, b 9 Sep 1813, Langmuir, Kilmaurs, AYR. s/o John D, qv, and Marion Cuthbertson, qv. To Galt, ONT, and stld Dumfries Twp,

Waterloo Co. Farmer. m 1840, Margaret Heastie, ch:
1. John, b 1841; 2. Jane, b 1844; 3. Marion, b 1846;
4. James, b 1848; 5. Margaret, b 1850.   **DD 14**.

2190   DICKSON, Elizabeth, 1809-78. Poss from DFS.
d/o James D, qv, and Jean Ross. To Chatham,
Northumberland Co, NB, 1822; stld Napan. m John
Jardine, qv.   **DC 2 Jun 1978**.

2191   DICKSON, Elizabeth, ca 1821–12 Apr 1874. From
Canonbie, DFS. To Melbourne, Richmond Co, QUE,
<1843; bur Danville. Wife of John Goodfellow, qv.
MGC 15 Jul 1980.

2192   DICKSON, George, ca 1809–14 May 1845. From
Shaw, Tundergarth, DFS. s/o Andrew D. and Janet
Bryden. To Dumfries Twp, Waterloo Co, ONT.
Ts Tundergarth.

2193   DICKSON, Herbert, b ca 1812. Poss from DFS.
s/o James D, qv, and Jean Ross. To Chatham,
Northumberland Co, NB, 1822; stld Napan. Farmer. By
wife who d <1871, ch: 1. David, b ca 1845; 2. Mathew,
b ca 1850; 3. James, b ca 1854; 4. Janet, b ca 1858;
5. Robert, b ca 1860; 6. Jane, b ca 1862.   **DC 2 Jun
1978**.

2194   DICKSON, James, ca 1770–1868. Poss from
DFS. To Chatham, Northumberland Co, NB, 1822; stld
Napan. Farmer. m Jean Ross, 1780–1857, from ENG,
ch: 1. James, jr, qv; 2. Elizabeth, qv; 3. Herbert, qv;
4. John, qv; 5. Robert, qv; 6. Joseph, qv; 7. William,
qv; 8. Jonathan, qv; 9. Thomas.   **DC 2 Jun 1978**.

2195   DICKSON, James, d 1783. To Halifax, NS.
Hospital surgeon.   **ERT iii 74**.

2196   DICKSON, James, b ca 1790. From Harray, OKI.
To Hudson Bay, ca 1813, and prob to Red River.
RRS 13.

2197   DICKSON, James, ca 1807–ca 1887. Poss from
DFS. s/o James D, qv, and Jean Ross. To Chatham,
Northumberland Co, NB, 1822; stld Napan. m Janet Orr,
qv, ch: 1. Mary, b 1836; 2. James, b 1839; 3. Alexander,
b 1843; 4. Agnes, b 1839; 5. David, b 1847;
6. Margaret, b 1855; 7. Janet, b 1857.   **DC 2 Jun
1978**.

2198   DICKSON, James, ca 1826–23 Aug 1857. From
Urr par, KKD. To Hamilton, ONT, and d there at Duke
Street.   **DGH 18 Sep 1857**.

2199   DICKSON, James, d 1895. From KKD or DFS. To
Huron Co, ONT, 1833. MP Huron and Bruce, 1861-67.
m Jane Carnochan, qv.   **DC 27 Jun 1981**.

2200   DICKSON, Janetty, 4 Sep 1795–20 Feb 1877.
From Linlithgow, WLN. d/o Joseph D, woolcomber, and
Janet Henderson. To Lanark Co, ONT, 1834. Wife of
John Alston, qv, m at Calton, Glasgow, 31 Dec 1819.
Barony OPR 622/16.

2201   DICKSON, Jean, d 1844. From Antons Hill,
Eccles, BEW. d/o James D. To Halifax, NS, 1804.
m 1797, Lt Col Martin Hunter, app Brig Gen of the
forces in the Maritimes, 1803.   **LDW 16 Feb 1960**.

2202   DICKSON, John, b ca 1812. Poss from DFS.
s/o James D, qv, and Jean Ross. To Chatham,
Northumberland Co, NB, 1822; stld Napan. By wife Mary
had ch: 1. William, b ca 1841; 2. James, b ca 1843;
3. Jane, b ca 1844; 4. Elizabeth, b 1846; 5. John,
b ca 1849; 6. Sarah, b ca 1850.   **DC 2 Jun 1978**.

2203   DICKSON, John, ca 1815–16 Sep 1847. From
DFS. To Hamilton, ONT.   **Ts Mt Albion**.

2204   DICKSON, Jonathan, b ca 1822. Poss from DFS.
s/o James D, qv, and Jean Ross. To Chatham,
Northumberland Co, NB, ca 1822; stld Napan. Farmer.
m (i) Mary; (ii) Susan. ch: 1. James, b 1850; 2. George,
b ca 1852; 3. David, b ca 1854; 4. John, b ca 1856;
5. Jane, b ca 1859; 6. Mary, b ca 1861; 7. Elizabeth,
b ca 1863; 8. Clement, b ca 1865; 9. Thomas,
b ca 1868; 10. James, yr.   **DC 2 Jun 1978**.

2205   DICKSON, Joseph, b ca 1815. Poss from DFS.
s/o James D, qv, and Jean Ross. To Chatham,
Northumberland Co, NB, 1822; stld Napan. Farmer. By
wife Mary had ch: 1. Jonathan, b ca 1851; 2. William,
b ca 1852; 3. James, b ca 1855; 4. Mary, b ca 1859.
DC 2 Jun 1978.

2206   DICKSON, Robert, ca 1767–20 Jun 1823. To
Montreal, QUE, 1781. Furtrader, Michilimackinac, and
later associated with Lord Selkirk's Red River colony.
m To-to-uin, a Sioux woman, ch.   **MDB 189**.

2207   DICKSON, Robert, b ca 1814. Poss from DFS.
s/o James D, qv, and Jean Ross. To Chatham,
Northumberland Co, NB, 1822; stld Napan. Farmer. By
wife Mary had ch: 1. David, b ca 1843; 2. Elizabeth,
b ca 1845.   **DC 2 Jun 1978**.

2208   DICKSON, Robert, ca 1804–5 Jan 1865. From
DFS. To Morrison, Puslinch Twp, Wellington Co, ONT.
DGH 3 Feb 1865.

2209   DICKSON, Thomas, ca 1775–21 Jan 1825. From
DFS. To Queenston, Lincoln Co, ONT. m Archange,
1780–1829, d/o Hon Alexander Grant, qv. ch: 1. John
Alexander, d 1821; 2. Mary Theresa, alive 1836.
**DGC 18 Sep 1821, 15 Mar 1825, 28 Apr 1829, 16 Nov
1836**.

2210   DICKSON, William, 1769–19 Feb 1846. From
DFS. To Niagara, Lincoln Co, ONT, 1792. Lawyer, soldier,
and MLC. Purchased former Indian lands formed into
Dumfries Twp, 1816, and promoted settlements at Galt,
where he lived 1827-36. ch incl: 1. Robert, 1796–1846,
MLA, d Leghorn, Italy; 2. William, b 1799; 3. Walter H,
b 1805, Canadian senator, 1867.   **HGD 15, 51;
MDB 189, 199**.

2211   DICKSON, William, b ca 1819. Poss from DFS.
s/o James D, qv, and Jean Ross. To Chatham,
Northumberland Co, NB, 1822; stld Napan. Farmer.
m Elizabeth Gillis, 1844, ch: 1. William, b ca 1846;
2. Mary Ann, b ca 1850; 3. James, b ca 1854;
4. Elizabeth, b ca 1859; 5. Agnes, b ca 1860;
6. Alexander, b ca 1862.   **DC 2 Jun 1978**.

2212   DICKSON, William, 15 Jul 1804–30 Jun 1891.
From Linlithgow, WLN. s/o James D. and Ann Smith. To
Kingsey Twp, Drummond Co, QUE, 1841; later to
Richmond. Farmer. m Christina Barrie, qv, and had with
other ch: 1. John, b 12 Jan 1831; 2. Ann, b 21 Apr 1833;
3. William, b 23 Oct 1838, d Goldendale, WA; 4. John
Mitchell, b 13 Mar 1841; 5. Christina; 6. George.
MGC 2 Aug 1979; DC 13 Jan 1980.

2213   DICKSON, William. From Galashiels, SEL. To
Renfrew Co, ONT, 1835. Lumberman. m Marian Forrest.
Son Robert.   **DC 29 Sep 1964**.

2214   DINGWALL, Magdalene, 15 Feb 1786–24 Feb

1846. From Aberdeen. d/o Alexander D, stocking-manufacturer, and Elizabeth Douglass. To Wellington Co, ONT, 1836, and d 'Belsyde,' Fergus. m 9 Sep 1813, her cous, Alexander Dingwall Fordyce, qv. **NDF 62, 418; SAA 186; SNQ viii/1 121.**

2215   DINGWALL, Alexander, 20 Feb 1766–20 Jan 1841. From Birnie par, MOR. s/o John D, qv, and Margaret Boyd, qv. To Flat River, PEI, on the *John & Elizabeth*, arr 30 Jul 1775; stld St Peters Bay, Kings Co, later Bay Fortune. m Margaret Morrow, East Point, and had, poss with other ch: 1. Isabella, b 1787; 2. Margaret. **DC 27 Jul 1980.**

2216   DINGWELL, James, 18 Feb 1759–24 Jan 1841. From Birnie par, MOR. s/o John D, qv, and Margaret Boyd, qv. To Flat River, PEI, on the *John & Elizabeth*, arr 30 Jul 1775; stld St Peters Bay. m 1792, Margaret Saunderson, and had, poss with other ch: 1. Margaret; 2. Charles. **DC 27 Jul 1980.**

2217   DINGWELL, John, ca 1730–ca 1824. From Rashbrook, Birnie par, MOR, but poss b INV. To Flat River, PEI, on the *John & Elizabeth*, arr 30 Jul 1775; stld St Peters Bay, Kings Co. Farmer. m Margaret Boyd, qv, ch: 1. John, 1756-77, Ensign, Royal Highland Emigrants; 2. James, qv; 3. Robert, b 6 Mar 1763; 4. Alexander, qv; 5. Anna, b 3 May 1768; 6. Joseph, qv; 7. William, b 16 May 1773. **DC 27 Jul 1980.**

2218   DINGWELL, Joseph, 18 Mar 1771–9 Feb 1815. From Birnie par, MOR. s/o John D, qv, and Margaret Boyd, qv. To Flat River, PEI, on the *John & Elizabeth*, arr 30 Jul 1775; stld St Peters Bay, Kings Co, later Bay Fortune. m Margaret, 1775–1857, d/o William McKie, qv, ch. **DC 27 Jul 1980.**

2219   DINWIDDIE, Margaret, ca 1774–15 May 1860. From DFS. To Pictou, NS, on *Thomsons Packet*; stld Colchester Co. m William Johnston, qv. **CAE 5.**

2220   DIXON, James. From Ettrick par, SEL. To Galt, Waterloo Co, ONT, <1830. Schoolteacher. Son Rev John, min at Yonkers, NY. **HGD 89.**

2221   DIXON, Margaret, b 9 Mar 1817. To NB on the *St Andrew*, Jul 1843. Wife of William Craig, from Northumberland. **DC 15 May 1977.**

2222   DIXON, William. From Lockerbie, DFS. To Hamilton, ONT. Gardener. m Margaret Auld. Son James. **DC 29 Sep 1964.**

2223   DOBIE, Agnes, 1 Mar 1802–23 Apr 1894. To Leeds Twp, Megantic Co, QUE, <1840. m William P. Learmonth, qv. **DC 11 Feb 1980.**

2224   DOBIE, James, b ca 1775. From Balgray, Applegarth par, DFS, but b Dryfesdale par. To QUE, 1832; stld St Augustin, Deux-Montagnes Co. m Agnes Brown, qv, ch: 1. Thomas, b 7 Apr 1800; 2. James, b 3 Aug 1804; 3. Robert, b 26 Mar 1808; 4. Mary, b 13 Jun 1810; 5. David, b 25 Jun 1812; 6-7. Joseph and Agnes, b 23 Jan 1816. **DC 3 Feb 1981.**

2225   DOBIE, Rev Robert, 1826–28 Apr 1888. From STI. s/o John D. Matric Univ of Glasgow, 1841, and also attended Univ of St Andrews, 1847-48. To Montreal, QUE, 1852. Ord min of Osnabruck, Stormont Co, ONT, 1853; trans to Milton, 1872. Declined to join the Union of 1875. m Annie Eve, d/o William Cline. Son William. **GMA 14392; SAM 108; FES vii 631; DC 29 Sep 1964.**

DOBIE, Mrs William. See WALKER, Margaret.

2226   DOBSON, Francis. From SEL. To NS <17 Jun 1818, when m Euphemia Turnbull, qv. **NSS No 1376.**

2227   DODDS, William, ca 1812–24 Aug 1890. From Kirkinner, WIG. To Nine Mile River, Hants Co, NS, 1847. Wife Agnes, 1811–1909, with him, and s George, 1838-57. **DC 20 Jan 1981.**

2228   DODS, Mary, b 14 Oct 1824. From ROX. d/o Peter D, qv, and Margaret Miller, qv. To McKillop Twp, Huron Co, ONT, <22 Jun 1849, when m Robert McMillan, qv. **DC 26 May 1979.**

2229   DODS, Peter, 1793–1869. From ROX. To ONT <1840; stld prob Huron Co. m Margaret Miller, qv. Dau Mary, qv. **DC 26 May 1979.**

2230   DODS, Thomas, d ca 1830. From STI. To QUE on the *David of London*, ex Greenock, 19 May 1821; stld Lanark Co, ONT. Farmer. m Helen Maxwell, qv, ch: 1. Thomas, b 6 Dec 1803; 2. John, b 3 Jun 1805; 3. Crawford, b 20 Oct 1809; 4. James, b 21 Apr 1811; 5. William, b 2 Aug 1815; 6. David Chrystal, b 16 Apr 1818; 7. Charles Murray, b 27 Jul 1819. **SG xxvi/3 80; DC 1 Nov 1979.**

2231   DOIG, Margaret Wingate, b ca 1820. From STI. d/o Henry D. and Jean McInnes. To Montreal, QUE, on the *Cluthe*, ex Glasgow, 1851. Wife of James Stewart, qv. **DC 10 Nov 1966.**

2232   DON, William, ca 1791–1850. From Strathcathro, ABD. s/o Alexander D. in Ballownie, and Jean Hood. To Montreal, QUE. **Ts Strathcathro.**

2233   DONALD, Agnes, 1776–1 Jan 1854. Prob from Glasgow. To QUE >1815, and stld English River. Wife of Alexander Black, qv. **Ts Russeltown Flats.**

2234   DONALD, Alexander, 28 Apr 1845–3 Jan 1927. From ABD. To ONT, and moved ca 1867 to MO. Emp with Central Branch Shops, Pacific Railroads. **LDW 15 Dec 1970.**

2235   DONALD, James, b ca 1771. From Athol, PER. To Charlottetown, PEI, on the *Clarendon*, ex Oban, 6 Aug 1808. Wife Isobel McDonald, qv, with him, and ch, surnamed McDonald: 1. Donald, aged 10; 2. Margaret, aged 8; 3. Elizabeth, aged 4; 4. John, aged 2. **CPL.**

2236   DONALD, James. Prob from LKS. To QUE on the *Prompt*, ex Greenock, summer 1820; stld Dalhousie Twp, Lanark Co, ONT. **HCL 68.**

2237   DONALD, Jane, ca 1783–23 Jul 1855. Prob from ABD. To Hamilton, ONT. Wife of William Innes, qv. **Ts Mt Albion.**

2238   DONALD, Jean, 19 Mar 1769–13 Dec 1829. From Glasgow. To QUE on the *Earl of Buckinghamshire*, ex Greenock, 9 Apr 1821; stld Lot 1, Con 8, Lanark Twp, Lanark Co, ONT. Wife of Alexander McVicar, qv. **DC 18 May 1982.**

2239   DONALD, John, 1799–1882. From Hamilton, LKS. s/o John D. and Agnes Wilson, qv. To QUE on the *Prompt*, ex Greenock, 4 Jul 1820; stld Dalhousie Twp, Lanark Co, ONT. Farmer. m Marion Duncan, qv, ch: 1. Agnes, b 1822; 2. Jeanette, b 1824; 3. John, 1826-82; 4. Thomas, d 1893; 5. Andrew, drowned in Lake Huron, 1870; 6. Jean; 7. Matthew; 8. James;

9. Frank; 10. Barbara; 11. Elizabeth; 12. Marion.
DC 11 Nov 1981.

2240 DONALD, Rev William, 6 Jun 1807–20 Feb 1871. From Edinginght Grange, BAN. s/o John D, farmer, and Janet McHattie. Grad MA Kings Coll, Aberdeen, 1832. Schoolmaster at Huntly. To St John, NB, arr 18 Jun 1849, and adm min of St Andrews Ch. m (i) —, d 1850, leaving ch; (ii) 1852, Louisa Agnes, 1826-92, d/o Hugh Wilson, Edinburgh, with further ch. **KCG 287; FES vii 609**.

2241 DONALDSON, Agnes. From PER. d/o David D, qv, and Mary Hutchinson, qv. To Pictou Co, NS, 1849; later to Tatamagouche, Colchester Co. Wife of William Menzie, qv. **HT 83**.

2242 DONALDSON, Andrew, b ca 1785. From Kinglassie, FIF. bro/o Thomas D, qv. To QUE on the *Elvira*, summer 1815; stld Lot 23, Con 4, South Elmsley Twp, Leeds Co, ONT. **SEC 6; HCL 234**.

2243 DONALDSON, Andrew, jr, b ca 1789. From Kinglassie, FIF. bro/o Andrew D, qv. To QUE on the *Elvira*, summer 1815; stld prob Lanark Co, ONT. **SEC 6**.

2244 DONALDSON, Catherine. From LKS. d/o William D. and Agnes Thomson. To QUE on the *David of London*, ex Greenock, 19 May 1821; stld Lanark Co, ONT. m 26 Jan 1817, Thomas Dichman, qv, ch. **LDW 4 Mar 1970**.

2245 DONALDSON, Cecilia. From PER. d/o David D, qv, and Mary Hutchinson, qv. To Pictou Co, NS, 1849; later to Tatamagouche, Colchester Co. m James Semple. **HT 83**.

2246 DONALDSON, David, 1807-91. From PER. To Pictou Co, NS, 1849; later to Tatamagouche, Colchester Co. m Mary Hutchinson, qv, ch: 1. Robert, went to NZ; 2. John, went to NZ; 3. George, went to NZ; 4. William, farmer, French River; 5. David, farmer, French River; 6. Agnes, qv; 7. Elizabeth, qv; 8. Cecilia, qv; 9. Jane; 10. Mary. **HT 83**.

2247 DONALDSON, Duncan, d 5 Feb 1877. From PER. To Harvey Hill, Inverness Twp, Megantic Co, QUE, <1850. m Mary A. Hancock, d 1893, ch: 1. John; 2. Peter; 3. Harriet; 4. Elizabeth; 5. Mary A; 6. Jane; 7. Janet; 8. Joseph. **AMC 135**.

2248 DONALDSON, Eliza. To London, Westminster Twp, Middlesex Co, ONT, <17 Mar 1834, when m John Sinclair, qv. **PCM 14**.

2249 DONALDSON, Elizabeth. From PER. d/o David D, qv, and Mary Hutchinson, qv. To Pictou Co, NS, 1854; later to Tatamagouche, Colchester Co. Wife of Thomas Malcolm, qv. **HT 83**.

2250 DONALDSON, Isobella, b ca 1798. From Kinglassie, FIF. sis/o Andrew D, qv. To QUE on the *Elvira*, summer 1815; stld prob Lanark Co, ONT. **SEC 6**.

2251 DONALDSON, James, b ca 1792. From Kinglassie, FIF. bro/o Andrew D, qv. To QUE on the *Elvira*, summer 1815; stld Lot 22, Con 3, South Elmsley Twp, Leeds Co, ONT. Farmer. **SEC 6; HCL 233**.

2252 DONALDSON, Margaret, b ca 1794. From Kinglassie, FIF. sis/o Andrew D, qv. To QUE on the *Elvira*, summer 1815; stld prob Lanark Co, ONT. **SEC 6**.

2253 DONALDSON, Sarah. From Edinburgh. d/o Alexander D. To CAN <1841. **SH**.

2254 DONALDSON, Thomas, b ca 1798. From Kinglassie, FIF. bro/o Andrew D, qv. To QUE on the *Elvira*, summer 1815; stld Lot 22, Con 5, South Elmsley Twp, Leeds Co, ONT. **SEC 6; HCL 234**.

2255 DONNAHUE, Deborah. From Kilwinning, AYR, but prob of Irish extraction. To QUE on the *Commerce*, ex Greenock, 20 Jun 1821; stld Lanark Co, ONT. Wife of Robert Love, qv. **DC 26 Sep 1979**.

2256 DOUGALL, James. From Paisley, REW. s/o John D. To Windsor, Essex Co, ONT. Nurseryman, but later joined his bro John D, qv, in business in Toronto and Montreal. **SGC 444**.

2257 DOUGALL, Janet. d/o Henry D. and Margaret Harvie, qv. To Montreal, QUE, on the *Ann Henzell*, 1844; stld Hamilton, ONT, later Exeter. m John Strang, qv. **DC 19 Sep 1960**.

2258 DOUGALL, John, 8 Jul 1808–19 Aug 1886. From Paisley, RFW. s/o John D. To Montreal, QUE, 1826. Muslin manufacturer and agent for Paisley shawls. Had business interests in Toronto, ONT. Editor of the *Canada Temperence Advocate* from 1835, and founder of the *Weekly Witness*, 1846. m Elizabeth, d 1883, d/o John Redpath, qv, and had with other ch: 1. John, editor; 2. James Duncan, journalist, Flushing, Long Is. NY; 3. Mrs A.M. Cochrane, NY; 4. Susan; 5. Lily. **SGC 443; MDB 193; MGC 15 Jul 1980**.

   DOUGALL, Mrs Margaret. See HARVEY, Janet.

2259 DOUGLAS, Alexander. From Dull par, PER. To Montreal, QUE, on the *Curlew*, ex Greenock, 21 Jul 1818; stld prob Beckwith Twp, Lanark Co, ONT. Wife Elizabeth with him. **BCL**.

2260 DOUGLAS, Ann, b ca 1766. To Pictou, NS, 1815; res Rogers Hill, 1816. Widow, with 1 child. **INS 39**.

2261 DOUGLAS, Colin. From Beauly, INV. To Pictou, NS, on the *Hector*, ex Loch Broom, arr 17 Sep 1773, with wife Catherine and ch: 1. Margaret; 2. Alexander. Two others d on voyage. Stld Middle River. Farmer and deacon. **HPC App A and C**.

2262 DOUGLAS, David, 30 Jun 1799–12 Jul 1834. From Scone, PER. s/o John D, mason, and Jean Drummond. To US and CAN, 1823, as rep of the London Horticultural Society, and made an expedition to the Columbia dist. Journey from Fort Vancouver to Hudson Bay, 1827. Species of pine named after him. He d in Is Hawaii, the result of an accident. **Scone OPR 394A/1; IBD 107; CBD 309; MDB 194**.

2263 DOUGLAS, Donald, b ca 1773. From SUT. To Pictou Co, NS, 1803; stld Concord. m Margaret Grant, qv, ch: 1. Alexander; 2. Donald; 3. James; 4. Catherine; 5. Elizabeth; 6. Margaret; 7. Christy. **PAC 130**.

2264 DOUGLAS, Donald, b 1792. To Pictou, NS; res Rogers Hill, 1816. Blacksmith. **INS 39**.

2265 DOUGLAS, George. To QUE on the *Commerce*, ex Greenock, Jun 1820; stld prob Lanark Co, ONT. **HCL 238**.

2266 DOUGLAS, Rev George, 14 Oct 1825–11 Feb 1894. From Ashkirk, SEL. s/o John D, qv, and Mary Hood, qv. To Montreal, QUE, 1831. Studied medicine but became Methodist clergyman and Principal of the Wesleyan Theological Coll. LLD, McGill Univ, 1870, and DD, Victoria Univ, 1884. **BNA 839; SGC 329; MDB 194**.

2267 DOUGLAS, James, b ca 1718. From New Abbey, KKD. To Georgetown, Kings Co, PEI, on the *Lovely Nellie*, ex Carsethorn, May 1775. Labourer. Wife Janet Neish, qv, with him, and s James, aged 8. **ELN**.

2268 DOUGLAS, James. From BEW. s/o John D. of Burnhouses, and —, d/o John Wilson of Middenhill. To Charlottetown, PEI, <1794. Comptroller of Customs. Son Samuel James. **SH**.

2269 DOUGLAS, Sir James, 14 Aug 1803–2 Aug 1877. From Lanark, but prob b West Indies. s/o John D, merchant, and — Ritchie. To QUE on the brig *Matthews*, ex Liverpool, 1819. Joined NWCo as a clerk, and continued with HBCo after 1821. Became the leading man on the Pacific coast. Gov of Vancouver Is from 1851, and Gov of BC, 1858-63, when knighted. m Amelia, d/o William Connolly, and had with other ch: 1. Hon James, MLA, rep Victoria; 2. Jane; 3. Agnes; 4. Alice; 5. Martha. **BNA 1107, 1121; MDB 195; ENA 21**.

2270 DOUGLAS, James, 20 May 1800–14 Apr 1886. From Brechin, ANS. To QUE, 1826; stld Beauport. MD, Edinburgh, and MRCS. Superintendent of Beauport Asylum. m Elizabeth Ferguson. Son James, 1837–1918, metalurgist and historian. **MDB 195; DC 30 Aug 1977**.

2271 DOUGLAS, James. From DFS. bro/o John D, qv. To Percy Twp, Northumberland Co, ONT, prob 1834. Wife d ca 1845. Dau Harriet James, b ca 1844. **DC 18 Jan 1972**.

2272 DOUGLAS, James, ca 1815–12 Dec 1883. From Mouswald, DFS. s/o James D. and Mary Kerr. To QUE, ex Liverpool, 1850; stld West Farnham, Brome Co, QUE. Farmer. m Janet Kirkpatrick, qv, ch: 1. Robert, qv; 2. Mary, d inf; 3. Margaret, qv; 4. Mary, qv; 5. Elizabeth Creighton, 1852-54; 6. William James, 1854–1930; 7. George Carlton, b 1859, went to CA; 8. Janet Elizabeth, b 1863, went to CO. **DC 17 Nov 1981**.

2273 DOUGLAS, Rev James Struthers, 1818–18 Jun 1884. s/o John D, blacksmith, and Mary Turner. Trained as a physician, but entered ministry as pastor of St Andrews Ch, Peterborough, ONT, 1858. Missionary to Presb of Toronto, 1864-67. Retr to SCT and was min successively at Birsay and North Yell. m 1856, Anna McCrate, ch: 1. Anna Maria, b 1856; 2. Thomas F, b 1859; 3. George Alexander, b 1860; 4. Arthur Pringle, b 1862; 5. Clara Newcombe, b 1865; 6. Edith Emma, b 1867; 7. Mary A, b 1870; 8. Catherine Elizabeth, b 1872; 9. James R, b 1874; 10. John F, b 1875; 11. David H, b 1878; 12. Christian, b 1880. **FES vii 304, 632**.

2274 DOUGLAS, John, b ca 1750. From Kirkbean, KKD. Prob bro/o William D, qv. To Georgetown, Kings Co, PEI, on the *Lovely Nellie*, ex Carsethorn, May 1775. Labourer. **ELN**.

2275 DOUGLAS, John. bro/o Robert D, qv. To Caledonia, Queens Co, NS, 1815. **NSN 5/2**.

2276 DOUGLAS, John. To QUE on the *Commerce*, ex Greenock, Jun 1820; stld prob Lanark Co, ONT. **HCL 238**.

2277 DOUGLAS, John, b ca 1800. From Ashkirk, SEL. bro/o William D, schoolteacher, VT, d 1829. To Montreal, QUE, 1831. Miller. m Mary Hood, qv, ch: 1. James, b 13 Mar 1821; 2. John, b 11 Sep 1823; 3. George, qv. **Ashkirk OPR 781/4; SGC 329**.

2278 DOUGLAS, John. From DFS. bro/o James D, qv. To Percy Twp, Northumberland Co, ONT, 1834. Farmer and clerk of the Divisional Court of Percy. m Mary Haining, qv, ch: 1. Elisabeth, b 1836; 2. Mary, b 1839; 3. Margaret, b 1842. **DC 18 Jan 1972**.

2279 DOUGLAS, John Moffat, b 26 May 1839. Prob from BEW. Poss s/o John D, and sis/o Janet D. To ONT. Senator. **DC 3 Jan 1979**.

2280 DOUGLAS, Margaret. From PER. To QUE ca 1834; later to Puslinch Twp, Wellington Co, ONT. wid/o — McRobbie. **DC 31 Jul 1979**.

2281 DOUGLAS, Margaret. From DFS. sis/o John D, qv, and of James D, qv, of Percy Twp, Northumberland Co, ONT. To Richibucto, Kent Co, NB, prob <1840. m — McClelland. Son Robert alive 1861. **DC 18 Jan 1972**.

2282 DOUGLAS, Margaret, 23 Jul 1846–21 Aug 1878. From DFS. d/o James D, qv, and Janet Kirkpatrick, qv. To QUE, ex Liverpool, 1850; stld West Farnham, Brome Co, QUE. **DC 17 Nov 1981**.

2283 DOUGLAS, Mary, 1799–1859. From KKD. Foster d/o Thomas Halliday, qv, and said rel to Thomas Douglas, Earl of Selkirk, qv. To Queens Co, PEI, 1806. m — Halliday, ch. **SPI 42**.

2284 DOUGLAS, Mary, 1 Dec 1848–8 Mar 1932. From DFS. d/o James D, qv, and Janet Kirkpatrick, qv. To QUE, ex Liverpool, 1850; stld West Farnham, Brome Co, QUE. m James Pendlebury, who d 1883. **DC 17 Nov 1981**.

2285 DOUGLAS, Mary Stuart, 1811-89. Prob from Aberdeen. d/o Rev George D, Methodist preacher. To QUE. m Alexander Macdonald, 1808-71, qv. **DC 6 Jan 1977**.

2286 DOUGLAS, Robert. From Forneth, Blairgowrie par, PER. To St John, NB, 1813. Son John b 1806. **DC 1 May 1806**.

2287 DOUGLAS, Robert, ca 1799–22 Feb 1871. From DFS. To St John, NB, ca 1821. **CAE 27**.

2288 DOUGLAS, Robert. bro/o John D, qv. To Port George, Annapolis Co, NS, ca 1825. **NSN 5/2**.

2289 DOUGLAS, Robert, 13 Nov 1841–20 May 1912. From DFS. s/o James D, qv, and Janet Kirkpatrick, qv. To QUE, ex Liverpool, 1850; stld West Farnham, Brome Co, QUE. m Sarah Louise Loud, d 1816. **DC 17 Nov 1981**.

2290 DOUGLAS, Thomas, 20 Jun 1771–8 Apr 1820. From St Marys Is, KKD. Eldest surviving s/o Dunbar Hamilton D, 4th Earl of Selkirk. 5th Earl of Selkirk, 1779. Author, politician, and coloniser. Organised schemes for Scottish settlements at Dover and Chatham, ONT; PEI, and Red River Assiniboia. Visited Maritimes and Montreal, 1803-4, and in 1815 came to Montreal and

Red River, via NY. Retr to SCT, 1818. m 1807, Jean, d/o James Wedderburn of Colville, ch.   **SN iii 431; SP vii 523**.

2291 DOUGLAS, William, 1753–13 Feb 1835. From Kirkbean, KKD. Prob bro/o John D, qv. To Georgetown, Kings Co, PEI, on the *Lovely Nellie*, ex Carsethorn, May 1775. Labourer. m Catherine Miller, qv, ch: 1. Thomas, b ca 1780; 2. William, b ca 1782; 3. James, b ca 1783; 4. Robert b ca 1784; 5. David, b ca 1786; 6. John, b ca 1787; 7. Kitty, b ca 1790; 8. Nellie, b ca 1793; 9. Betsy, b ca 1796; 10. George, b ca 1800.   **ELN; DC 13 Jan 1982**.

2292 DOUGLAS, William, b 1790. To Pictou Co, NS, 1815; res Rogers Hill, 1816. Labourer, m, with two ch. **INS 38**.

2293 DOUGLAS, William. From Wishaw, LKS. s/o James D. To CAN, 1857; stld prob ONT. **DC 27 Dec 1981**.

12294 DOULL, John. From CAI. To PEI <1840; later to New Glasgow, Pictou Co, NS, but seems to have retr to PEI. Son James, b 1840. **HNS iii 669**.

2295 DOULL, Robert, b 1828. From Wick, CAI. To Pictou, NS, prob <1850. Merchant, banker, magistrate and officer of militia. **BNA 681**.

2296 DOUSE, William. To Queens Co, PEI, <1830. Agent for Thomas Douglas, Earl of Selkirk, qv, and erected mills at Pinette. **HP 50**.

2297 DOW, Alexander, 1803-97. From Glen Quaich, Dull par, PER. s/o Thomas D, qv, and Janet McEwan, qv. To Osgoode Twp, Carleton Co, ONT, 1832, but moved to Metcalfe Twp. Farmer. m (i) Christine McTavish; (ii) Isabelle Brodie, 1817-61, ch.   **DC 1 Aug 1975**.

2298 DOW, Catherine, b 28 Jun 1811. From Auchinderran, Marnoch, BAN. d/o William D, qv, and Margaret Lumsden, qv. To QUE on the *Brilliant*, ex Aberdeen, 8 Aug 1832; stld Whitby Twp, Ontario Co, ONT. m George Milne, farmer, ch.   **DC 4 Feb 1982**.

2299 DOW, Elspet, 25 Nov 1814–13 Dec 1913. From Auchinderran, Marnoch, BAN. d/o William D, qv, and Margaret Lumsden, qv. To QUE on the *Brilliant*, ex Aberdeen, 8 Aug 1832; stld Whitby Twp, Ontario Co, ONT. m 9 Jul 1840, James Wallace, qv.   **DC 4 Feb 1982**.

2300 DOW, Helen. From Premnay, ABD. To Middlesex Co, ONT, 1848; stld Nissouri Twp. wid/o Robert Adam. **DC 21 Mar 1981**.

2301 DOW, James, 1812–1900. From Glen Quaich, Dull par, PER. s/o Thomas D, qv, and Janet McEwan, qv. To Osgoode Twp, Carleton Co, ONT, 1832; later to Vernon Twp, Muskoka Dist. Farmer. m Janet Robertson, qv, ch: 1. Jessie R, 1852–1921; 2. Thomas, 1855-61; 3. Charles Alexander, 1856–1947; 4. John Russell, 1859–1955.   **DC 1 Aug 1975**.

2302 DOW, James, b ca 1820. From Mortlach, BAN. s/o Thomas D, qv, and Jane D, qv. To Nichol Twp, Wellington Co, ONT, 1833. m Elspeth Grant, ch. **DC 4 Oct 1979**.

2303 DOW, Jane, 1800-81. From Mortlach, BAN. Prob rel to William D, 1777–1855, qv. To ONT, 1833; stld Nichol Twp, Wellington Co. Wife of Thomas Dow, qv. **DC 4 Oct 1979**.

2304 DOW, Janet. From Alloway, AYR. To QUE, prob 1821; stld Lanark Co, ONT. m John Robertson, qv. **SG xx/1 11**.

2305 DOW, Janet, 1805-94. From Glen Quaich, Dull par, PER. d/o Thomas D, qv, and Janet McEwan, qv. To Osgoode Twp, Carleton Co, ONT, 1832. Wife of Donald Campbell, qv.   **DC 1 Aug 1975**.

2306 DOW, John, 1799–1879. From Glen Quaich, Dull par, PER. s/o Thomas D, qv, and Janet McEwan, qv. To Osgoode Twp, Carleton Co, ONT, 1832. Farmer, and Reeve of Osgoode, 1855-71. m Katherine Campbell, ch.   **DC 1 Aug 1975**.

2307 DOW, John, 9 Aug 1816–7 Oct 1858. From Auchinderran, Marnoch, BAN. s/o William D, qv, and Margaret Lumsden, qv. To QUE on the *Brilliant*, ex Aberdeen, 8 Aug 1832; stld Whitby Twp, Ontario Co, ONT. m 7 Nov 1848, Catherine Isabella Ball, 1824–1900, ch: 1. William Gerrard, 1849–1937; 2. John Ball, 1851–1910; 3. Margaret Lumsden, 1853–1937; 4. Jean Gertrude, 1855-91; 5. Katherine Isabella, 1858–1953. **DC 4 Feb 1982**.

2308 DOW, Margaret, 1802-85. From Glen Quaich, Dull par, PER. d/o Thomas D, qv, and Janet Lumsden, qv. To Osgoode Twp, Carleton Co, ONT, <1831. Wife of Colin Campbell, qv.   **DC 1 Aug 1975**.

2309 DOW, Margaret, 18 May 1809–8 Jul 1848. From Auchinderran, Marnoch par, BAN. d/o William D, qv, and Margaret Lumsden, qv. To QUE on the *Brilliant*, ex Aberdeen, 8 Aug 1832; stld Whitby Twp, Ontario Co, ONT. Wife of James Murray, by whom she had two sons who emig with her: 1. James, b 1830; 2. William, b 1832.   **DC 4 Feb 1982**.

2310 DOW, Margaret, b ca 1823. From Marnoch par, BAN. d/o Thomas D, qv, and Jane D, qv. To Nichol Twp, Wellington Co, ONT, 1833. m John McDonald, ch. **DC 4 Oct 1979**.

2311 DOW, Mary. From Alloway, AYR. To QUE, prob 1821; stld Lanark Co, ONT. m William Robertson, qv. **SG xx/1 11**.

2312 DOW, Peter, 1832–1913. From Marnoch par, BAN. s/o Thomas D, qv, and Jane D, qv. To Nichol Twp, Wellington Co, ONT. m Agnes Wilson, 1832–1903, ch: 1. Thomas, 1859-62; 2. William George, 1866–1927, physician, Owen Sound; 3. Janet Wilson, 1866–1945; 4. Rev James Andrew, 1868–1934; 5. Jane Isabella, 1870–1927; 6. Agnes, 1872–1941; 7. Mary Ann, 1874–1951; 8. Peter Frederick, 1878–1903. **DC 4 Oct 1979**.

2313 DOW, Robina, 15 Mar 1813–2 Sep 1884. From Auchinderran, Marnoch, BAN. d/o William D, qv, and Margaret Lumsden, qv. To QUE on the *Brilliant*, ex Aberdeen, 8 Aug 1832; stld Whitby Twp, Ontario Co, ONT. m 5 Feb 1835, Dr Jonathan Foote, 1804-85, from VT, ch.   **DC 4 Feb 1982**.

2314 DOW, Thomas, 1770–1854. From Glen Quaich, Dull par, PER. To Osgoode Twp, Carleton Co, ONT, 1832. Farmer, Lot 36, Con 9. m Janet McEwan, qv, ch: 1. Thomas, b ca 1798; 2. John, qv; 3. Margaret, qv; 4. Alexander, qv; 5. Janet, qv; 6. James, qv.   **DC 1 Aug 1975**.

2315 DOW, Thomas, 1787–1870. b Aberdeen, but emig from BAN to Nichol Twp, Wellington Co, ONT,

1833. Stonemason, later farmer. m Jane Dow, qv, ch: 1. James, qv; 2. William, qv; 3. Margaret, qv; 4. Isabel, b ca 1824; 5. Thomas, jr, qv; 6. Peter, qv; 7. Janet, qv. **DC 4 Oct 1979**.

2316 DOW, Thomas, 7 Jun 1818–13 Apr 1894. From Auchinderran, Marnoch, BAN. s/o William D, qv, and Margaret Lumsden, qv. To QUE on the *Brilliant*, ex Aberdeen, 8 Aug 1832; stld Whitby Twp, Ontario Co, ONT. m Eliza Harriet Chesebro, 1821-94, ch: 1. Leonara Levanche, 1847-73; 2. Eliza, d inf; 3. Clara Ronina, 1848–1945; 4. Alexander, d inf; 5. Susan Eliza, 1870-87. **DC 4 Oct 1979**.

2317 DOW, Thomas, jr, d 1877. From Marnoch, BAN. s/o Thomas D, qv, and Jane D, qv. To Nichol Twp, Wellington Co, ONT, 1833. Farmer. m Margaret McDonald, ch: 1. Jane, 1851-77; 2. Thomas; 3. Sarah, b 1855; 4. Janet, 1856-74; 5. Mary, b 1858; 6. Margaret, d 1880; 7. James, res MI; 8. Peter, res MAN. **DC 4 Oct 1979**.

2318 DOW, William, 1777–1855. From Auchinderran, Marnoch, BAN. s/o William D. and Margaret Gerrard. To QUE on the *Brilliant*, ex Aberdeen, 8 Aug 1832; stld Whitby Twp, Ontario Co, ONT. Farmer. m Margaret Lumsden, qv, ch: 1. William, jr, qv; 2. Margaret, qv; 3. Catharine, qv; 4. Robina, qv; 5. Elspet, qv; 6. John, qv; 7. Thomas, qv; 8. James, b 1820; 9. Alexander, b 1821; 10. Magdalene, b 1823; 11. Helen, b 1826. **Marnoch OPR 161/1; DC 4 Oct 1979**.

2319 DOW, William, jr, 28 Oct 1807–19 Sep 1843. From Auchinderran, Marnoch, BAN. s/o William D, qv, and Margaret Lumsden, qv. To QUE on the *Brilliant*, ex Aberdeen, 8 Aug 1832; stld Whitby Twp, Ontario Co, ONT. Farmer. m Elizabeth Strathearn, qv, ch: 1. David, 1837-85; 2. Margaret Lumsden, b 1838; 3. William, 1840-61; 4. Agnes, b 1841; 5. John Strathearn, d 1855. **Marnoch OPR 161/1; DC 4 Feb 1982**.

2320 DOW, William, 1822–1914. From Marnoch par, BAN. s/o Thomas D, qv, and Jane D, qv. To Nichol Twp, Wellington Co, ONT, 1833. m Mary Wilson, qv, ch: 1. Thomas, 1850–1933; 2. Margaret, 1851-94; 3. Robert, 1853–1946; 4. Jane, 1855–1947, unm; 5. William, 1859–1933; 6. James, b 1862. **DC 4 Oct 1979**.

2321 DOW, William. From Muckhart par, PER. s/o William D, 1765–1844, and Ann Mason, 1780–1852. To Montreal, QUE, and d there. **Ts Muckhart**.

2322 DOWIE, Alexander. From St Monance, FIF. s/o William D, sailor. To Montreal, QUE, <1846. **SH**.

2323 DOWNIE, George Hart, ca 1828–16 May 1867. From Edinburgh. s/o John Macleay D. and Marion Hart. To Algoma Dist, ONT, and d Lefroy. m Agnes Rankin Wilson, qv, and had, poss with other ch: 1. Jean Woodburn, 1856–1932; 2. George Hart, d NY, 1924; 3. Maria Hope, 1860–1946. **Ts Grange, Edinburgh**.

2324 DOWNIE, Malcolm. To Aldborough Twp, Elgin Co, ONT, 1818; moved to Mosa Twp, 1832. ch: 1. Neil A, teacher; 2. Dr Colin, res Chicago. **PCM 23; PDA 93**.

2325 DOWNS, Thomas William, b ca 1802. From Glasgow. To CAN, 1824. Wife Marion Thomson, qv, with him. **SG xxvii/4 170**.

2326 DRIPPS, Rev Matthew, 1767–12 May 1828. From Kilmarnock, AYR. To Shelburne, Shelburne Co, NS, 1804. Dau Maria. **DGC 11 Nov 1828; NSN 39/49**.

2327 DROVER, John, d 1852. From PER. To CAN, 1852, but drowned when landing. Widow Marion Traquair, qv, went with family to ONT and stld Tuckersmith Twp, Huron Co. ch: 1. John, b ca 1840; 2. Hannah, b 19 Mar 1842; 3. Marion, b ca 1843; 4. Margaret, b ca 1845; 5. Wilhelmina, b ca 1847. **DC 6 Dec 1967**.

2328 DRUMMOND, Duncan. From Comrie, PER. To Otonabee Twp, Peterborough Co, ONT, 1829. Wife and ch with him. **DC 13 Sep 1982**.

2329 DRUMMOND, Sir George Alexander, 11 Feb 1829–2 Feb 1910. From Edinburgh. s/o George D, builder, and Margaret Pringle. Educ Edinburgh High School and went to Montreal, QUE. Partner, John Redpath & Sons, sugar refiners; farmer; senator; philanthropist, KCMG 1904, KCVO 1908. m (i) 1857, Helen, d/o John Redpath, qv, ch: 1. Maurice; 2. Huntly; 3. Edgar; 4. Arthur; 5. George. m (ii) 1884, Grace Julia, d/o A. Davidson Parker, Montreal, ch: 6. Julian, d 1886; 7. Guy, killed 1914-18 war. **HSC 61; MDB 199**.

2330 DRUMMOND, Malcolm. From Comrie par, PER. To Montreal, QUE, on the *Curlew*, ex Greenock, 21 Jul 1818; stld prob Beckwith Twp, Lanark Co, ONT. Wife Christian with him, and ch: 1. Malcolm, aged 6; 2. Margaret, aged 2. **BCL**.

2331 DRUMMOND, Peter. Prob from PER. To Montreal, QUE, on the *Niagara*, ex Greenock, arr 28 May 1825; stld McNab Twp, Renfrew Co, ONT. **EMT 18**.

2332 DRUMMOND, Thomas, 1810-82. Poss from PER. To PEI <1836; stld Brookfield. m Margaret Gourley, qv, ch: 1. Isabel, d unm; 2. Thomas; 3. James, 1836–1913; 4. John, 1842–1910; 5. Mary Ann, 1845–1928; 6. Margaret, 1848–1908; 7. Jane. **DC 25 Nov 1981**.

2333 DRUMMOND, Rev William, ca 1740–1777. From Madderty, PER. To Richmond Bay, PEI, on the *Falmouth*, ex Greenock, 8 Apr 1770, and went later to Canaan, CT. Missionary, and went out with a party of emigrants sponsored by Sir James Montgomery of Stanhope. He left a *Diary* of the trip. **DC 28 May 1980**.

2334 DRYBURGH, John, ca 1810–ca 1878. From Murraygate, Dundee, ANS. To Toronto, ONT, <1856. Wood plane-maker. Sons William and John, plane-makers in Toronto. **DC 1 Jan 1982**.

2335 DRYDEN, Andrew, b ca 1777. Prob from Hawick par, ROX. To ONT ca 1834. m Janet Cairns, qv, ch: 1. Anne; 2. Thomas; 3. John; 4. Robert; 5. Jane; 6. Andrew; 7. William; 8. James; 9. Walter. **SG xv/3 49; DC 17 Jan 1967**.

2336 DRYNON, William. Poss from AYR. To QUE on the *David of London*, ex Greenock, 19 May 1819; stld Lanark Co, ONT. **HCL 239**.

2337 DRYSDALE, Alexander, d 1 Oct 1873. From Lasswade, MLN. s/o John D. of Viewfield, and Jessie Sceales. To 'Jessiefield,' Garafraxa Twp, Wellington Co, ONT, 1835. Farmer, magistrate and officer of militia. Retr to SCT, 1864, and stld Castelau House, Dunbar. m Janet Dingwall Fordyce, qv, ch: 1. John; 2. Alexander

Adolphus, 1852-79; 3. Magdalene Dingwall, d 1881;
4. Jessie Gordon; 5. Elizabeth Agnes, d inf; 6. Janet
Castelau, d 1868; 7. Elizabeth Sceales; 8. Mary
Arbuthnott.   **NFD 73, 133; EAR 23**.

2338   DRYSDALE, Alicia Murray. From Edinburgh.
d/o William D, watch and clock maker, Lothian Street,
and Rebecca Murray. To New Glasgow, Pictou Co, NS,
1836, when m Rev John Stewart, qv.   **FES vii 608,
618**.

2339   DRYSDALE, Christina, ca 1789–26 Nov 1872.
From Carnock, FIF. d/o James D, qv, and Christian
Fergus, qv. To North Burgess Twp, Lanark Co, ONT,
ca 1822. m Thomas Moodie, qv.   **DC 18 Mar 1968**.

2340   DRYSDALE, George. To New Annan, Colchester
Co, NS. m Margaret Shearer, qv. Son Arthur,
1857–1922, QC, MLA.   **MLA 109**.

2341   DRYSDALE, James, ca 1758–25 Mar 1852. From
Glendevon, PER. To QUE on the *Dorothy*, ex Greenock,
12 Jul 1815; stld Lot 6, Con 10, Burgess Twp, Lanark
Co, ONT, Apr 1816. Farmer. m Christian Fergus, qv, ch:
1. Christina, qv; 2. Robert, qv; 3. James; 4. Elizabeth;
5. Jane; 6. Isabel; 7. Margaret; 8. Helen.   **SEC 4;
HCL 15, 232; DC 24 Sep 1969**.

2342   DRYSDALE, James, ca 1817–16 Nov 1899. From
Glasgow. s/o Robert D, qv, and Margaret Thomson, qv.
To QUE on the *Commerce*, 1820. Carpenter. m Christina
Alston, qv, ch: 1. Margaret Dunlop; 2. John Alston;
3. Robert; 4. Janet Robertson; 5. James; 6. Christina
Gerry; 7. Elizabeth Pullar; 8. William (adopted);
9. Isabella (adopted).   **HCL 238; DC 7 Apr 1962**.

2343   DRYSDALE, Robert, 15 Jul 1792–15 Jul 1882.
From Dollar, CLK. s/o James D, qv, and Christian
Fergus, qv. To QUE on the *Commerce*, Jun 1820; stld
Perth Twp, Lanark Co, ONT. m Margaret Thomson, qv,
ch: 1. James, qv; 2. Robert, jr, qv; 3. Alexander;
4. Christina; 5. Ann; 6. Andrew; 7. John; 8. Janet;
9. William; 10. Francis.   **DC 5 May 1962**.

2344   DRYSDALE, Robert, jr, b ca 1819. From Dollar,
CLK. s/o Robert D, qv, and Margaret Thomson, qv. To
QUE on the *Commerce*, Jun 1820; stld Lanark Co, ONT.
m Christina Moodie.   **DC 5 May 1962**.

2345   DRYSDALE, Thomas. From Edinburgh.
s/o William D, watch and clock maker, Lothian Street,
and Rebecca Murray. To QUE <1834. Watchmaker.
Ts Old Calton; SH.

2346   DUFF, Alexander, 16 Jul 1771–10 Jun 1809.
From Foveran, ABD. s/o Rev William D, par min, and
Ann Mitchell. To Amherstburg, Essex Co, ONT.
Merchant.   **FES vi 194**.

2347   DUFF, Alexander, b ca 1830. Prob from
Dunscore, DFS. s/o James D. and Agnes Kerr. To
Markham, York Co, ONT, <28 Feb 1858, when m Maria,
aged 26, d/o James Osborne and Cynthia Nole.
DC 24 Mar 1982.

2348   DUFF, Rev Archibald, 23 Apr 1810–19 Nov 1883.
From Aberdeen. s/o Archibald D, dancing master. Matric
Marischall Coll, 1825. To Montreal, QUE, <1836.
Grocer, but studied at Glasgow and became a
Congregational min at Fraserburgh, Liverpool and Wick.
Came again to CAN as a min of the Evangelical Union,
and stld Cowansville, Missiquoi Co, QUE, later in

Sherbrooke. DD, VT, 1879. ch: 1. Rev Archibald,
Bradford, YKS; 2. John, accountant in Montreal.
FAM ii 456; SNQ i/2 154.

2349   DUFF, James. To Pictou Co, NS, <1831; stld nr
MacIntyre. m Sarah Johnson.   **NSN 32/359**.

2350   DUFF, James, 2 Mar 1818–25 Apr 1900. From
Logiealmond, PER. To Halton Co, ONT, prob <1850; stld
Esquesing Twp. m (as his second wife), Margaret
McKenzie, qv.   **EPE 76**.

2351   DUFF, Jeanette, b ca 1800. To ONT <1853; stld
Lambton Co. Wife of Archibald Jamieson, qv.   **DC 1 Oct
1981**.

2352   DUFF, John. From Kilmorack, INV. To Pictou, NS,
on the *Sarah*, ex Fort William, Jun 1801. Labourer. Wife
Cathrine with him and an inf.   **PLS**.

2353   DUFF, John, ca 1840–1905. To Wellington Co,
ONT, 1850. Farmer and importer of Clydesdale horses.
m Elizabeth Stewart, ch.   **DC 9 Nov 1981**.

2354   DUFF, William. From Falkirk, STI. s/o Robert D.
To Carbonear, NFD. Fish merchant. m Mary Thomson,
qv, and had with other ch a son William, b 1872,
merchant, Bridgewater, Lunenburg Co, NS.
HNS iii 644.

2355   DUNBAR, Alexander, 3 Feb 1758–4 Jan 1832.
From Croy, INV. bro/o Robert D, qv, and William D, qv.
To Pictou Co, NS, 1784, and was gr 200 acres on west
branch of East River. Discharged soldier, 84th Regt.
m Elizabeth Grant, qv, ch: 1. John, 1784–1848, bur
Old Elgin; 2. James, 1791–1868.   **HPC App H; PAC 53,
55; NSN 30/296**.

2356   DUNBAR, Elizabeth, 1784–1870. From Dufftown,
BAN. To ONT 1833; stld Nichol Twp, Wellington Co. Wife
of John Munro, qv.   **DC 31 Dec 1979**.

2357   DUNBAR, George Home, d Oct 1839. From
Edinburgh. s/o Prof George D. To Niagara Twp, Lincoln
Co, ONT, and d there. Lt, 93rd Highlanders.
DGH 15 Nov 1839.

2358   DUNBAR, John, ca 1782–15 Nov 1829. Prob
from INV. To Pictou, NS. Bur Old Elgin. m Janet
Monroe.   **DC 20 Nov 1976**.

2359   DUNBAR, Robert. From INV. bro/o Alexander D,
qv, and William D, qv. To East River, Pictou Co, NS,
<18 Dec 1797, and gr 450 acres. Prob discharged
soldier.   **HPC App H**.

2360   DUNBAR, William, 1755–3 Sep 1831. From INV.
bro/o Alexander D, qv, and Robert D, qv. To Pictou Co,
NS, and stld Big Brook, west branch of East River, 1785.
m Amelia Rose, qv. ch: 1. James; 2. Donald; 3. Rev
Hugh, PEI; 4. Alexander; 5. Christy; 6. Isabella; 7. Kitty;
8. Elizabeth; 9. Jessie.   **PAC 48; DC 20 Nov 1976**.

2361   DUNCAN, Alexander, ca 1771–10 Apr 1823. To
Halifax, NS, and d there.   **VSN No 134**.

2362   DUNCAN, David. From Aberdeen. To Mission
Point, Restigouche River, NB, 1773. Emp with John
Schoolbred, merchant. Son John, qv.   **SR 13**.

2363   DUNCAN, David, b ca 1790. From Kinglassie,
FIF. To QUE, ex Greenock, summer 1815; prob stld
Lanark Co, ONT. Farmer. Wife Jean, bro/o Andrew
Donaldson, qv, did not embark.   **SEC 6**.

2364 DUNCAN, David. From Kincardine O'Neil, ABD. s/o George D, forester. To QUE, 1853, on the *James Boyd*. m Christina Mortimer, qv, ch: 1. David; 2. Peter; 3. Christina; 4. Margaret. **DC 29 Nov 1977**.

2365 DUNCAN, James, 18 Jun 1815–19 Dec 1876. From Rutherglen, LKS, but poss b ENG. s/o Sgt William D, qv, and Philadelphia Stubberfield. To QUE on the *Prompt*, ex Greenock, 4 Jul 1820; stld Dalhousie Twp, Lanark Co, ONT, later Innisfil, Simcoe Co. m Margaret Hood, qv, ch: 1. William, b 1847; 2. Jane, b 1848; 3. Philadelphia, b 1851; 4. John, b 1854; 5. Margaret, b 1856; 6. Janet, b 1859; 7. Elizabeth, b 1862; 8. Hannah, b 1864; 9. Hannah, b 1865; 10. Robert, b 1869; 11. Joseph, b 1872. **DC 11 Aug 1980**.

2366 DUNCAN, James. Prob from Banchory, ABD. To CAN <1837. Labourer, but owned some property in Aberdeen. Son John, blacksmith. **SH**.

2367 DUNCAN, Rev James. To Bayfield, ONT, ca 1840. Clergyman and poet. Dau Anna, authoress. **DC 1 Jan 1968**.

2368 DUNCAN, John. From Aberdeen. s/o David D, qv. To Mission Point, Restigouche River, NB, 1773. m 30 Mar 1790, Elizabeth Morton, from Nepisiquit. **SR 16**.

2369 DUNCAN, John. From LKS. To QUE on the *Prompt*, ex Greenock, 4 Jul 1820; stld Dalhousie Twp, Lanark Co, ONT. **HCL 68**.

2370 DUNCAN, John Morrison, ca 1795–3 Oct 1825. From Glasgow. s/o Andrew D, printer to the Univ, 1811-27. Matric Univ of Glasgow, 1806, and grad BA, 1816. To CAN and USA 1818, and d at Glasgow. Author. Son John Morrison, 1826-94, advocate. **GMA 7144; MDB 205**.

2371 DUNCAN, Jean, 1788–1871. From Auchterhouse, ANS. d/o Charles D. and Janet Whyte. To QUE, 1841; stld Argenteuil Co, nr Lachute. Wife of David Low, qv, whom she m 12 Dec 1819. **DC 15 Jan 1982**.

2372 DUNCAN, Margaret, 1774–1837. From Kilmory par, Is Arran, BUT. To Restigouche Co, NB, <1834. Wife of Thomas McMillan, qv. **MAC 23**.

2373 DUNCAN, Marion. From Hamilton, LKS. To QUE on the *Prompt*, ex Greenock, 4 Jul 1820; stld Dalhousie Twp, Lanark Co, ONT. Wife of John Donald, qv. **DC 11 Nov 1981**.

2374 DUNCAN, Mary, b ca 1804. From SHI. sis/o Robert D, qv. To ONT <1853. m (i) James Hughson, ch; (ii) George Martin, with further ch. **SCN**.

2375 DUNCAN, Robert, b 1802. From SHI. bro/o Mary D, qv. To ONT <1853. **SCN**.

2376 DUNCAN, Robert, ca 1810–ca 1867. From Meigle, PER. s/o Robert D, farmer. Matric Univ of Glasgow, 1820, and became licentiate of the Ch of Scotland. Missionary to ONT, 1832, but may have retr to SCT. **GMA 10555; FES vii 632**.

2377 DUNCAN, Thomas, ca 1775–ca 1825. From Bedlay, Cadder par, LKS. To QUE, ex Greenock, summer 1815; stld Lochiel Twp, Glengarry Co, ONT. Wife Isabella McDonald, qv, with him and ch: 1. Isabella, b ca 1806; 2. Annie, b 3 Dec 1807; 3. Thomas, jr, qv; 4. Donald McDonald, b 21 Jan 1812. **SEC 1; DC 26 Jun 1981**.

2378 DUNCAN, Thomas, jr, b 23 Feb 1810. From Cadder par, LKS, but poss b RFW. s/o Thomas D, qv, and Isabella McDonald, qv. To QUE, ex Greenock, summer 1815; stld Lochiel Twp, Glengarry Co, ONT. m Harriete Fraser. Dau Sophia Sterling, b 1853. **SEC 1; DC 26 Jun 1981**.

2379 DUNCAN, Thomas, ca 1808–13 Dec 1892. From Perth. To Hamilton, ONT. Wife Jessie d 5 May 1888. **Ts Mt Albion**.

2380 DUNCAN, William, 1771–1843. From Rutherglen, LKS. To QUE on the *Prompt*, ex Greenock, 4 Jul 1820; stld Dalhousie Twp, Lanark Co, ONT. Went later to Innisfil, Simcoe Co. Discharged soldier, later farmer. m Philadelphia Stubberfield, ch: 1. James, qv; 2. Thomas, b 1817; 3. Janet. **DC 11 Aug 1980**.

2381 DUNCANSON, James, 1750–1802. Poss from Aberdeen. To Horton Twp, Kings Co, NS, ca 1773. Blacksmith. By wife Isabel ch: 1. James; 2. Mary, b 1773; 3. George, b 1774; 5. William, b ca 1782. **DC 9 Oct 1980**.

2382 DUNDAS, George, 12 Nov 1819–18 Mar 1880. From Dundas, South Queensferry, WLN. s/o James D. of that Ilk and Hon Mary Tufton Duncan. Served in the army and was MP for WLN. Lt Gov of PEI, 1859-70; later of St Vincent and of the Windward Is. CMG. m 1859, Mary, d/o Rev W.A. Clark, Belford Hall, Northumberland, no ch. **MDB 206**.

2383 DUNDAS, William, d 20 Aug 1842. From Ochtertyre, PER. s/o James D, WS, and Elizabeth Graham. To Lincoln Co, ONT, and d Niagara Falls. Sometime of HEIC Civil Service, Bengal. **DGH 22 Sep 1842**.

2384 DUNLOP, James, ca 1813–27 Jul 1869. From Paisley, RFW. To Sherbrooke Twp, Lanark Co, ONT, 1821; stld Lot 12, Con 3. Moved in 1834 to Plympton Twp, Lambton Co. **HCL 74; DC 27 Oct 1979**.

2385 DUNLOP, James, b 10 Mar 1810. From Brookside, Gifford, ELN. s/o Peter D. and Jean Wood. To QUE, ex Greenock, 22 Jun 1833; stld Perth, ONT, afterwards White Lake, and in 1843 at Nepean Twp, Carleton Co. m 3 Jun 1833, Cochrane Ray Richardson, qv. Dau Margaret Richardson, b 1834. **DC 15 Aug 1967**.

2386 DUNLOP, James, 1 Nov 1852–6 Sep 1941. From Dreghorn, AYR. s/o James McDonald D, qv, and Jane Brown, qv. To Binbrook Twp, Wentworth Co, ONT, 1854; later Hamilton. Merchant. m 13 Nov 1877, Mary Ann, 1858–1936, d/o Robert Wilson, qv, and Jean Anderson, qv, ch: 1. Annie Webster, 1879–1944; 2. Hugh McDonald, 1880–1965; 3. Ethel Beatrice, 1885–1978; 4. Frank Anderson, 1889–1978. **DC 23 Nov 1981**.

2387 DUNLOP, James McDonald, 16 Aug 1820–10 Oct 1904. From Dreghorn, AYR. s/o Hugh D, farmer, and Jean Dickie. To ONT, 1854; stld Binbrook Twp, Wentworth Co, later Dresden, Chatham Twp, Kent Co. m Jane Brown, qv, ch: 1. Jane, b 27 Apr 1843; 2. Hugh, b 12 Jan 1845; 3. Agnes, b 4 Apr 1848; 4. David, b 15 Feb 1850; 5. James, qv; 6. Mary B, b 9 Mar 1855; 7. Dr John W, b 16 Apr 1857; 8. Mathieson R, b 1 Jul 1863. **DC 23 Nov 1981 and 22 Mar 1982**.

2388 DUNLOP, John. From Edinburgh. To QUE on the *Earl of Buckinghamshire*, ex Greenock, 28 Apr 1821; stld prob Dalhousie Lake, Lanark Co, ONT. Tailor. Wife Margaret Crail, qv, with him. Dau Mary, qv. **DC 13 Feb 1978**.

2389 DUNLOP, Mary. From Edinburgh. d/o John D, qv, and Agnes Crail, qv. To QUE on the *Earl of Buckinghamshire*, ex Greenock, 28 Apr 1821; stld prob Dalhousie Twp, Lanark Co, ONT. m Robert Brownlee, qv. **DC 13 Feb 1978**.

2390 DUNLOP, Robert Graham, ca 1789–28 Feb 1841. From Garbraid, Greenock, RFW. s/o Alexander D. of Keppoch, and Janet Graham. Half-pay officer, and emig to Huron Tract, ONT, 1833. Registrar of Huron, and MP 1835-41. m June 1835, Louisa McColl, qv. **DC 19 Mar 1981**.

2391 DUNLOP, William 'Tiger', 1792–29 Jun 1848. From Garbraid, Greenock, RFW. s/o Alexander D. of Keppoch, and Janet Graham. Matric Univ of Glasgow, 1806, and studied medicine. Asst Surgeon in 89th Regt in CAN, War of 1812. Author and newspaper editor in India and in ENG, 1817-26, when he came again to CAN to become principal asst to John Galt, qv, of the Canada Company. Stld 'Garbraid', nr Goderich. MP, and is regarded historically as the father of Huron Co, ONT. **BNA 445; GMA 7018; MDB 207**.

2392 DUNN, Agnes. From Dundee, ANS, but lived in Duntocher, DNB before emig to QUE, ca 1832. Wife of William Shaw, qv. **DC 8 May 1979**.

2393 DUNN, Andrew. From STI. To Leeds Twp, Megantic Co, QUE, 1830. m Elizabeth, d/o William Oliver, qv, ch: 1. Janet; 2. Mary; 3. James; 4. William; 5. Agnes; 6. Margaret; 7. Elizabeth. **AMC 135**.

2394 DUNN, James. Poss from Edinburgh. To St Johns, NFD, <1835. **SH**.

2395 DUNN, Robert. From Glasgow. Served as NCO in 82nd Regt and was gr 200 acres in Pictou Co, NS, 1784. ch. **HPC App F**.

2396 DUNN, Simon. Prob from RFW. To Ramsay Twp, Lanark Co, ONT, 1821. Lumberman. **HCL 86, 165**.

2397 DUNN, William. To Ingersoll, Oxford Co, ONT, 1842. m Annie Reid. Son Thomas Weir, b 1856, stld QUE. **MGC 2 Aug 1979**.

2398 DUNOON or DENOON, Hugh, b 18 Sep 1762. From Killearnan, ROC. s/o Rev David D, par min, and Mary Inglis. To Pictou Co, NS, <1 Apr 1793, and gr land on East River. Discharged soldier, farmer, merchant and immigration agent. **HPC App H; FES vii 12**.

2399 DUNSMUIR, Robert, 31 Aug 1825–12 Apr 1889. From Hurlford, Riccartoun par, AYR. s/o James D. To Fort Vancouver, BC, as a coal consultant, 1851. Became coalmaster and industrialist; MLA, 1882. m Joanna Olive White, qv, ch: 1. Elizabeth; 2. Agnes; 3. James, 1851–1920, Premier of BC; 4. Alexander; 5. Marion; 6. Mary; 7. Jessie; 8. Effie; 9. Joan; 10. Maud. **BNA 1121; MDB 208**.

2400 DURIE, Rev William, 1804–12 Sep 1847. b Glasgow. s/o William D, merchant, and Janet Gillespie. Matric Univ of Glasgow, 1817. Relief Ch min at Earlston, 1834-43, when adm to Ch of Scotland. Asst min at Cardross until 1847, when emig to Ottawa to become min of St Andrews Ch there. Unm. **GMA 9908; FES vii 632**.

2401 DUTCH, Alexander. Prob from Tayport, FIF. bro/o George D, qv. To Heron Is, Restigouche Co, NB, 1826. m Margaret Allan, qv, and had with other ch: 1. George, qv; 2. John, first white child b on Heron Is. **DC 13 Oct 1980**.

2402 DUTCH, George. Prob from Tayport, FIF. bro/o Alexander D, qv. To Heron Is, Restigouche Co, NB, 1826 and 1842. Sawyer and shipbuilder. Moved to Seaside, on mainland, opp Heron Is. **DC 13 Oct 1980**.

2403 DUTCH, George, b ca 1824. Prob from Tayport, FIF. s/o Alexander D, qv, and Margaret Allan, qv. To Heron Is, Restigouche Co, NB, 1826. m 1848, Margaret Connacher. Son Robert C, 1861–1937. **CUC 5, 43**.

2404 DUTHIE, John. From Aberdeen. To Mission Point, Restigouche River, NB, ca 1773. Fisherman and emp sometime with John Schoolbred, merchant. **SR 14**.

E

EADIE. See also EDIE.

2405 EADIE, Andrew, 1794–1866. From Buttergask, Ardoch par, PER. s/o Robert E. and Isabel Sharpe. To Brant Co, ONT, prob <1820; stld Mount Pleasant. **SG xxviii/1 41; DC 8 Sep 1979**.

2406 EADIE, Isabel, b 13 Nov 1807. From Buttergask, Ardoch par, PER. d/o Robert E. and Isabel Sharpe. To Brant Co, ONT, prob <1855. **DC 8 Sep 1979**.

2407 EADIE, John, 1796–1857. From Buttergask, Ardoch par, PER. s/o Robert E. and Isabel Sharpe. To Brant Co, ONT, prob <1855; stld Mount Pleasant. **DC 8 Sep 1979**.

2408 EADIE, Robert, 13 Apr 1798–5 May 1882. From Buttergask, Ardoch par, PER. s/o Robert E. and Isabel Sharpe. To ONT, 1842; stld Oakland Twp, Brant Co. Farmer. m (i) Eliza McLaws, qv, and had with other ch: Robert, jr, qv. m (ii) Margaret France, poss from Glasgow. **SG xxvi/4 142; DC 23 Sep 1980**.

2409 EADIE, Robert, jr. From Glasgow. s/o Robert E, qv, and Eliza McLaws, qv. To ONT, 1842; stld Oakland Twp, Brant Co. m 1851, Martha Swift, ch: 1. Emily, unm; 2. Ebenezer, farmer; 3. Dr Andrew; 4. James. **DC 23 Sep 1980**.

2410 EADIE, Thomas, b 15 Apr 1813. From Buttergask, Ardoch par, PER. s/o Robert E. and Isabel Sharpe. To Brant Co, ONT, prob <1855; stld poss Turnberry, Huron Co. ch: 1. David; 2. Isabel; 3. Colin; 4. Beatrix; 5. Janet; 6. Margaret; 7. Agnes. **DC 8 Sep 1979**.

2411 EADIE, William, 1792–1872. From Buttergask, Ardoch par, PER. s/o Robert E. and Isabel Sharpe. To Brant Co, ONT, prob <1820; stld Mount Pleasant. **SG xxviii/1 41**.

2412 EADY, Ann, 24 Jan 1813–1 Oct 1877. From Dunnottar par, KCD. To NS prob <1854, and d Rockford, IL. m George Keith, qv, ch. **DC 29 Jan 1981**.

EASSON. See also ESSON.

2413 EASSON, Andrew. Prob from Burnside, Alyth, PER. To Montreal, QUE, Jun 1842; stld Con 3, North Easthope, Perth Co, ONT. Farmer. Wife Grace Burns, qv, with him, and ch: 1. William; 2. Andrew; 3. Jean; 4. Isabel; 5. Kathren; 6. Elspeth, qv.   **DC 15 Jul 1978 and 24 May 1979**.

2414   EASSON, Elspeth, 3 Aug 1834–24 Apr 1920. Prob from Burnside, Alyth, PER. d/o Andrew E, qv, and Grace Burns, qv. To Montreal, QUE, Jun 1842; stld North Easthope, Perth Co, ONT. m John Thomson, qv.   **DC 15 Jul 1978 and 24 May 1979**.

2415   EASSON, James. To Lanark Co, ONT, 1821; stld Lot 13, Con 2, North Sherbrooke Twp, where estab 1836.   **HCL 74**.

2416   EASTON, Alexander, ca 1784–20 Dec 1867. From Broadhopelee, Liddesdale, DFS. To Dumfries Twp, Waterloo Co, ONT.   **CAE 18**.

2417   EASTON, George. From LKS. Prob rel to Thomas E, qv. To QUE on the *Prompt*, ex Greenock, 4 Jul 1820; stld Dalhousie Twp, Lanark Co, ONT.   **HCL 68**.

2418   EASTON, Margaret, ca 1765–23 Jan 1826. From Forfar, ANS. d/o John E. and Elizabeth Wallace. To NB <1826. Wife of David Mathie.   **Ts Forfar**.

2419   EASTON, Rev Robert, 1773–1831. From Overhall, Hawick, ROX. s/o Andrew E. and Mary Kedzie. Educ Univ of Edinburgh, and the Associate (Burgher) Hall. Secession min at Morpeth, 1798–1802. To Montreal, QUE, and became min of a Secession congregation at St Peter Street. Ret 1824.   **SGC 176; FES vii 632; THS 1828, 38**.

2420   EASTON, Thomas. From LKS. Prob rel to George E, qv. To QUE on the *Prompt*, ex Greenock, 4 Jul 1820; stld Dalhousie Twp, Lanark Co, ONT.   **HCL 68**.

2421   EASTOR, James, ca 1793–1 Aug 1817. From Falkirk, STI. To Liverpool, Queens Co, NS. **NSS No 1147**.

2422   EATON, George. Prob from LKS. To Lanark Co, ONT, 1821; stld Lot 6, Con 1, North Sherbrooke Twp. **HCL 74**.

2423   ECKFORD, Henry, b 1775. From Irvine, AYR. To QUE, ca 1791, and learned shipbuilding under his uncle, John Black, qv. Went to New York, where he built ships of quality.   **SAS 31**.

2424   EDDIE, Alexander. From Nairn. To Ekfrid Twp, Middlesex Co, ONT, ca 1840.   **PCM 30**.

2425   EDDIE, John. From Nairn. To Ekfrid Twp, Middlesex Co, ONT, ca 1840.   **PCM 30**.

2426   EDGAR, James. From Keithock, Brechin, ANS. To QUE 1840, and stld Sherbrooke. Wife Grace Matilda Fleming, qv, with him. Son James David, 1841-99, res Toronto, lawyer and Liberal politician.   **BNA 744**.

2427   EDGAR, Jean, b 17 Apr 1798, Burnfoot, Middlebie par, DFS. d/o William E. and Janet Bell. To Scarborough Twp, York Co, ONT, ca 1832. m 13 Jan 1826, David Thomson, qv.   **Middlebie OPR 841/1; LDW 22 Jan 1976**.

2428   EDGAR, William, ca 1782–6 Oct 1855. From Annan, DFS. Prob s/o David E. To Hamilton, ONT, and d there. Carpenter.   **DGC 13 Nov 1855**.

2429   EDGAR, William, 8 Jan 1821–5 Jan 1877. From Landheads, Annan, DFS. s/o James E, joiner, and Margaret Minto. To Hamilton, ONT, prob 1854. Joiner,

later contractor (Edgar & Melville), alderman and railway projector. m 1849, Helen Cox, qv, ch: 1. James, 1850-69; 2. John; 3. Andrew, res Montreal, QUE; 4. David; 5. George Minto, d inf, 1866; 7. Mrs William Edgar, Winston; 8. Mrs Ernest Alexander, Montreal. **CAE 4, 19, 38, 71**.

EDIE. See also EADIE.

2430   EDIE, Charles, b 1836. From The Mount, Monimail, FIF. s/o Robert E. and Margaret Aitken. To CAN <1855.   **DC 6 Apr 1979**.

2431   EDMISTON, Archibald, From Glasgow. s/o John E. and Janet Byde, qv. To Paris Village, Brant Co, ONT, 1840; later to Blenheim Twp, Oxford Co. Baker and farmer, Con 5.   **DC 1 Feb 1980**.

2432   EDMISTON, James. From Glasgow. s/o John E. and Janet Byde, qv. To Paris Village, Brant Co, ONT, 1840. Baker.   **DC 1 Feb 1980**.

EDMISTON, Mrs John. See BYDE, Janet.

2433   EDMISTON, John. From Glasgow. s/o John E. and Janet Byde, qv. To Paris Village, Brant Co, ONT, 1840. Baker.   **DC 1 Feb 1980**.

2434   EDMISTON, Walter, b 21 Apr 1819. From Glasgow. s/o John E. and Janet Byde, qv. To Paris Village, Brant Co, ONT, 1840. Baker, and farmer Con 5. m 11 Jan 1846, Eliza Graham, ch: 1. James, b 1846; 2. John, b 1847; 3. Frances, b 1850; 4. Janet, b 1852; 5. Mary Ann, b 1854; 6. Walter, b 1865; 7. William, b 1859; 8. Eliza Jane, b 1861; 9. Alexander, b 1863; 10. Andrew, b 1866; 11. George, b 1868.   **DC 1 Feb 1980**.

2435   EDMOND, Jane, ca 1791–17 Jun 1855. From Glasgow. Prob sis/o Margaret E, qv. To Hamilton, ONT.   **Ts Mt Albion**.

2436   EDMOND, Janet E, ca 1768–15 Jan 1835. Prob from STI. To Montreal, QUE, 1796, to m her maternal cous, William Logan, qv. Retr to SCT 1815, and d at Clarkston, Polmont, STI.   **SGC 130; Ts Polmont**.

2437   EDMOND, Margaret, ca 1807–3 Nov 1871. From Glasgow. Prob sis/o Jane E, qv. To Hamilton, ONT. **Ts Mt Albion**.

2438   EDMONSTONE, William. From STI. bro/o Archibald E. To Montreal, QUE, <1855. Merchant.   **SH**.

2439   EDWARDS, Andrew. To Lanark Co, ONT, 1821; stld Lot 12, Con 3, North Sherbrooke Twp.   **HCL 74**.

2440   EDWARDS, John S, ca 1800–28 Dec 1868. From Stotfield, Kinnedar par, MOR. s/o James E. and Elspet Bannerman. To Clarence Twp, Russell Co, ONT, <1840.   **Ts Kinnedar; DC 27 Oct 1979**.

2441   ELDER, Donald, b ca 1785. To Charlottetown, PEI, on the *Elizabeth & Ann*, arr 8 Nov 1806.   **PLEA**.

2442   ELDER, H.W. From Edinburgh. To Ottawa, ONT. Educ Edinburgh and went later to QUE. Teacher at Marlow and at Stanstead Academy. Son John Wallace, b 1862, customs officer, Beebe.   **MGC 2 Aug 1979**.

2443   ELDER, Mary. From Dunfermline, FIF. To Brantford, Brant Co, ONT, <1851. m Ebenezer Roy, merchant.   **SH**.

2444   ELDER, Mary. From Glasgow. To QUE 1854. Wife of William Cream, qv.   **MGC 2 Aug 1979**.

ELGIN, 8th Earl of. See BRUCE, James.

2445   ELLICE, Edward, 1781–17 Sep 1863.
s/o Alexander E, merchant at Schenectady, NY, and —
Phyn. Grad BA and MA at Marischal Coll, Aberdeen, and
went to Montreal, QUE, 1803. Fur-trader with XYCo and
NWCo. Played a part in uniting the NWCo with the HBCo
in 1821. Became MP for Coventry, ENG, and purchased
the estate of Ardochy, Glengarry, SCT. Deputy Gov
HBCo, 1858-63. DCL St Andrews. m 1809, Lady
Hannah, d/o Charles, 1st Earl Grey, ch, s Edward,
1810-80, politician. m (ii) 1843, Lady Ann, widow of
Thomas, 1st Earl of Leicester.   **FAM ii 381;**
DC 13 Feb 1978.

2446   ELLIOT, Francis. To Winchester Twp, Dundas Co,
ONT, <1855.   **DC 4 Mar 1965**.

2447   ELLIOT, John. Prob from ROX. To NS <1810.
Son Samuel.   **HNS iii 217**.

2448   ELLIOT, Rev Joseph, 1810-85. From ROX. Ord to
Congregational Ch, 1836, and min at Bury St Edmunds,
ENG. To CAN ca 1855. Author.   **MDB 217**.

2449   ELLIOT, Margaret, ca 1797–4 Aug 1836. From
Thickside, Eskdalemuir, DFS. d/o James E, shepherd,
and Margaret Brydon. To QUE. Wife of Thomas Nicol.
Ts Eskdalemuir.

2450   ELLIOT, George, 1821-88. From PEE. s/o William
E, qv, and Janet Tait, qv. To Guelph Twp, Wellington Co,
ONT, 1831. Farmer, Con 6. m Margaret Cleghorn, ch:
1. William C; 2. John; 3. Mrs Eli Ridolls; 4. Mrs George
Whitelaw; 5. Mrs John McIntosh; 6. Christina;
7. Mrs Thomas Whitelaw; 8. Robert G; 9. Elizabeth.
DC 11 Nov 1981.

2451   ELLIOT, Helen, 1819–1901. From PEE.
d/o William E, qv, and Janet Tait, qv. To Guelph Twp,
Wellington Co, ONT, 1831. m Robert Brydon, qv.
DC 11 Nov 1981.

2452   ELLIOT, Isabelle, 1829–1913. From PEE.
d/o William E, qv, and Janet Tait, qv. To Guelph Twp,
Wellington Co, ONT, 1831. m John Renton, qv.
DC 11 Nov 1981.

2453   ELLIOT, James, 1825-93. From PEE. s/o William
E, qv, and Janet Tait, qv. To Guelph Twp, Wellington Co,
ONT, 1831; later to MAN. Farmer. m Margaret Murdock,
b 1832, ch: 1. William; 2. James; 3. Mrs Fraser; 4. Mrs
England; 5. Jessie; 6. Margaret.   **DC 11 Nov 1981**.

2454   ELLIOT, John, b 23 Apr 1819. To Digby Co, NS,
1819; stld Long Is. m Lucy Ann Buckman, 28 Oct 1838,
ch.   **DC 20 Jan 1982**.

2455   ELLIOT, Margaret, 1823–1906. From PEE.
d/o William E, qv, and Janet Tait, qv. To Guelph Twp,
Wellington Co, ONT, 1831. m Thomas Anderson.
DC 11 Nov 1981.

2456   ELLIOT, Robert, 1817–1905. From PEE.
s/o William E, qv, and Janet Tait, qv. To Guelph Twp,
Wellington Co, ONT, 1831. Farmer. m Jane Richardson,
1815-90, ch: 1. William, dy; 2. Janet; 3. Jane;
4. William R, cattle-breeder; 5. Agnes; 6. Mrs James
McIntosh; 7. John.   **DC 11 Nov 1981**.

2457   ELLIOT, William, 1779–1866. From PEE. To
QUE, 1831; stld Lot 16, Con 3B, Guelph Twp, Wellington
Co, ONT. Farmer. m Janet Tait, qv, ch: 1. Janet, dy;

2. William, 1815-67; 3. Robert, qv; 4. Helen, qv;
5. George, qv; 6. Margaret, qv; 7. James, qv; 8.
Isabella, qv.   **DC 11 Nov 1981**.

2458   ELLIS, David, ca 1820-51. From Arbroath, ANS.
s/o Fletcher E, farmer, and Madeline Davidson. To St
Johns, NFD. Ship carpenter.   **Ts Arbroath Abbey**.

2459   ELLIS, John, 1811-95. From Kintore, ABD. To
Chatham, Northumberland Co, NB. m Jane Robertson,
1838–1923.   **DC 14 Jan 1980**.

2460   ELLIS, Richard. To QUE on the *Fame*, 1815; stld
Lot 4, Con 8, Drummond Twp, Lanark Co, ONT. Sons
Richard, jr, and Edward.   **HCL 233**.

2461   EMSLIE, George, ca 1803–19 Oct 1869. From
Aberdeen. To QUE on the *Fania*, ex Glasgow, 3ᵒ Jun
1834; thence to Montreal and stld Bon Accord, Nichol
Twp, Wellington Co, ONT. Schoolteacher and dry goods
merchant. m Agnes Gibbon, qv, ch: 1. Mrs Robert
Philip; 2. Margaret, qv; 3. William; 4. George;
5. Alexander; 6. Gordon; 7. Mrs David Spragge.
EHE 64.

2462   EMSLIE, Jean, b ca 1800. From Aberdeen.
sis/o George E, qv, and Agnes Gibbon, qv. To Bon
Accord, Nichol Twp, Wellington Co, ONT, 1835. Wife of John Gibbon, qv.
EHE 90.

2463   EMSLIE, Margaret. From ABD. To Nichol Twp,
Wellington Co, ONT, 1835. m William Gibbon, qv.
EHE 90.

2464   EMSLIE, Margaret, 30 Jan 1831–2 May 1916.
From Aberdeen. d/o George E, qv, and Agnes Gibbon,
qv. To QUE on the *Fania*, ex Glasgow, 30 Jun 1834; stld
Bon Accord, Nichol Twp, Wellington Co, ONT. m James
Middleton, qv.   **EHE 64; DC 7 Jun 1980**.

2465   EMSLIE, Thomas. To QUE <1790. m at
Edinburgh, 9 Dec 1790, Marion, d/o the dec James
Williamson of Cardrona, PEE.   **Edinburgh**
OPR 685-1/52.

2466   ENGLAND, William, ca 1738–29 Dec 1822.
To Montreal, QUE, <1789. Cooper. Son James,
fur-trader.   **SGC 76**.

2467   ERSKINE, Alexander, 1783–31 Dec 1863. To
Ramsay Twp, Lanark Co, ONT, summer 1832. Farmer.
Dau Jean, qv.   **DC 17 Oct 1979**.

2468   ERSKINE, James M, ca 1783–1 Mar 1824. To NS
and d at sea between Granville and Annapolis.
VSN No 566.

2469   ERSKINE, Jean, 1810–20 Apr 1891.
d/o Alexander E, qv. To Ramsay Twp, Lanark Co,
ONT, summer 1832. m 14 Nov 1828, Peter Young, qv.
DC 17 Oct 1979.

2470   ESDAILE, John, b 9 Dec 1813. From Perth.
s/o Rev Dr James E, min of the East Ch, and Margaret
Blair. To Montreal, QUE, prob 1833. Wholesale merchant
with bro Robert, qv.   **SGC 495; FES iv 232**.

2471   ESDAILE, Robert, 21 Nov 1816–5 Jul 1882. From
Perth. s/o Rev Dr James E. and Margaret Blair. To
Montreal, QUE, arr Jun 1833. Wholesale merchant with
bro John, qv, later broker. m Nancy, d/o John McKenzie,
qv, and had, prob with other ch, s Robert.   **SGC 495;**
FES iv 232.

2472 ESDALE, Charles. To QUE on the *Commerce*, ex Greenock, Jun 1820; stld prob Lanark Co, ONT. **HCL 239**.

2473 ESKDALE, Edward, ca 1815–28 Aug 1834. From Kirkmichael, DFS. s/o Robert E, farmer in Parkgate, and Agnes Nicolson. To Grosse Is, QUE, and d there. **Ts Kirkmichael**.

2474 ESPLIN, Charles, b ca 1800, Cortachy, ANS. To Montreal, QUE, ca 1834. Millwright. **SGC 623**.

ESSON. See also EASSON.

2475 ESSON, Adam. From ABD. Uncle of John E, qv. To Halifax, NS, <1823. Grocer. **MLA 112**.

2476 ESSON, Rev Henry, ca 1793–11 May 1853. b Balnacraig, Aboyne, ABD. s/o Robert E. Grad MA Marischall Coll, Aberdeen, 1811. Ord by Presb of Aberdeen and became min of St Gabriel St Ch, Montreal, QUE, 1817. Founded and taught at Montreal Academic Institution. Chaplain, St Andrews Society of Montreal, 1835, and in 1844 app Professor of Philosophy at Knox Coll, Toronto. m 1823, Mary, d/o Campbell Sweeney; (ii) 1842, Elizabeth Campbell, qv. **FAM ii 401; SGC 276; SNQ ii/2 171; FES vii 632**.

2477 ESSON, John, 1804–4 Mar 1863. From Aberdeen. s/o Charles E. and Elizabeth Whyte, and neph of Adam E, qv. To Halifax, NS, 1823. Wholesale and retail grocer, and MLA. m 10 Jan 1836, Harriet Ann, d/o Thomas and Harriet Leonard. **MLA 112**.

2478 EWART, George Graham. From Edinburgh. s/o Robert E, saddler, and Charlotte Ritchie. To Stratford, Perth Co, ONT, <1854. Teacher. **SH**.

2479 EWART, Robert Brunton, ca 1809–13 Apr 1852. From Edinburgh. s/o Robert E, saddler, and Charlotte Ritchie. To Stratford, Perth Co, ONT, ca 1835. **Ts St Cuthberts**.

2480 EWING, Helen, 1833–10 May 1887. From Galston, AYR. d/o James E, dec, and Jean Wilson, qv. To ONT, ca 1856, and d at Hastings. m James Christie. **DC 12 Aug 1980**.

2481 EWING, Isabella, b 1845. From Galston, AYR. d/o James E, dec, and Jean Wilson, qv. To Peterborough, ONT, ca 1856. m William Cameron. **DC 12 Aug 1980**.

2482 EWING, James. From Leadhills, LKS. To QUE, ca 1823; stld Pike River. Wife with him and dau Margaret, qv. **MGC 2 Aug 1979**.

2483 EWING, Jane Hood, 1847–5 Oct 1917. From Galston, AYR. d/o James E, dec, and Jean Wilson, qv. To Peterborough Co, ONT, ca 1856. m William Houston. **DC 12 Aug 1980**.

2484 EWING, John, 9 Feb 1817–6 Sep 1904. To QUE, and stld Melbourne, Sherbrooke Co. m Jessie Smith, qv. Both bur Maple Grove. **MGC 2 Aug 1979**.

2485 EWING, Capt John, d 18 Jan 1835. From Dumfries. To QUE, ca 1830. Sometime of 24th Regt. **DGH 28 Jan 1835**.

2486 EWING, John Leckie, ca 1832–19 Mar 1893. From Kippen, STI. s/o William E. Matric Univ of Glasgow, 1847. To ONT, later MAN. **GMA 15235**.

2487 EWING, Margaret, b 9 Mar 1817. From Leadhills, LKS. d/o James E, qv. To QUE, ca 1823; stld Pike River. m William Graham, ch: 1. Francis, res New York City; 2. Jennie; 3. James, d ca 1887. **MGC 2 Aug 1979**.

2488 EWING, Margaret Ann, 1837–24 Nov 1892. From Galston, AYR. d/o James E, dec, and Jean Wilson, qv. To ONT, ca 1856. m Capt Manson, master mariner, Toronto. **DC 12 Aug 1980**.

EWING, Mrs James. See WILSON, Jean.

2489 EWING, William. From Glasgow. To Montreal, QUE, <1852. Clerk. m Elizabeth McAulay, qv. **SH**.

F

2490 FAICKNY, Mr. Cabin passenger on the *Lulan*, ex Glasgow, 17 Aug 1848, bound for Pictou, NS. **DC 12 Jul 1979**.

2491 FAIR, Christine. From Haddington, ELN. To Leeds Twp, Megantic Co, QUE, 1841. Wife of Robert Learmonth, qv. **DC 15 Feb 1980**.

2492 FAIR, John. To QUE on the *Brock*, ex Greenock, summer 1820; stld prob Lanark Co, ONT. **HCL 238**.

2493 FAIRBAIRN, Elizabeth, b 13 May 1817. From ROX. d/o Robert F. and Kate Scott. To QUE <1850. m William Bell Grieve, qv. **DC 11 Aug 1976**.

2494 FAIRBAIRN, Rev John, 11 Feb 1808–3 Apr 1895. From Halyburton, Greenlaw par, BEW. s/o John F, farmer, and Jessie Johnston. To Ramsay Twp, Lanark Co, ONT, and was min there 1833-42, when he retr to SCT to become min at Greenlaw Chapel, BEW. m (i) Maria Wilson, qv, with a s John, merchant in Rockhampton, Queensland. m (ii) Agnes Copland, 1811-87. **FES ii 20, vii 633; HCL 203**.

2495 FAIRBAIRN, John, ca 1823–7 Oct 1880. From Selkirk, SEL. To North Dumfries Twp, Waterloo Co, ONT, ca 1857. m Margaret Brown, qv, ch: 1. John, b 1848; 2. James, b 1850; 3. Andrew, b 1853; 4. Thomas, 1856–1929; 5. George Nicol, b 1858; 6. Robert, 1859–1929; 7. George, 1861-98; 8. David, b 1862; 9. William, b 1863; 10. Archibald; 11. Charles. **DC 7 Dec 1981**.

2496 FAIRBAIRN, Robert. From Edinburgh. To CAN, prob ONT, <1851. Joiner. m Helen Milne, qv. **SH**.

2497 FAIRIE, Janet, 10 Oct 1812–26 May 1892. From Ecclesmachan par, WLN. To Montreal, QUE, 1832; stld Durham. Moved later to Orrock Twp, Shelburne Co, MN. m 27 Jan 1828, Robert Orrock, qv. **Kirkliston OPR 667/2; LDW 23 Dec 1978**.

2498 FAIRLIE, John. To Pictou, NS, on the *Lulan*, ex Glasgow, 17 Aug 1848. **12 Jul 1979**.

2499 FAIRN, Benjamen. To NS 1783; stld Granville, Annapolis Co. Farmer. ch: 1. Nancy Ann, b 8 Dec 1778; 2. Elizabeth; 3. Sarah; 4. William, 1788–1871; 5. Zeruriah, b ca 1790; 6. Henry, 1792–1825; 7. Benjamin. **HNS iii 427**.

FALCONER. See also FALKNER and FAULKINER.

2500 FALCONER, Alexander. From Lochbroom, ROC. To Pictou, NS, on the *Hector*, ex Loch Broom, arr 17 Sep 1773; stld nr Hopewell, Pictou Co. **HPC App C**.

2501   FALCONER, Hector. To Pictou, NS, on the *Ellen*, ex Loch Laxford, SUT, 22 May 1979. Wife Mary with him and ch: 1. Flora; 2. Catherine; 3. Alexander; 4. Hughina; 5. Mary; 6. Mary; 7. James; 8. Johan; 9. Peter.   **DC 15 Jul 1979**.

2502   FALCONER, Rev James, 1806-56. From Paisley, RFW. Min of Associate Congregation, Paisley, 1837-39; of Martyrs Ch there, 1840-43, when he became min of Martyrs FC. Trans to Wigtown, 1844, and in 1851 came to CAN.   **FES iii 178**.

2503   FALCONER, John Redpath, ca 1825–13 Feb 1903. Poss from Kirkmichael, PER. To ONT <1864; stld Lot 17, Con 10, Kinloss Twp, Bruce Co. Farmer. m Ann McLean, 1836–1911, from Co Tyrone, IRL, ch: 1. Edward McLean, b 16 Apr 1865; 2. George Alexander, b 14 Apr 1867; 3. John Thomas, b 1869; 4. Janet; 5. Mary Murray, b 1872; 6. Catherine Jane, b 6 Jan 1877; 7. William James, b 9 Jan 1880.   **DC 28 Oct 1981**.

2504   FALCONER, Margaret, ca 1785–23 Jun 1864. Prob from INV. To Pictou Co, NS; bur Old Elgin. **DC 20 Nov 1976**.

2505   FALCONER, William, ca 1739–16 Sep 1804. From Essil, Speymouth, MOR. To CAN and emp with HBCo at Fort Severn. m Ann Morrison, 1754–1840, and retr to Garmouth, SCT.   **Ts Essil**.

2506   FALKIN, William. To Pictou, NS, on the *Hope*, ex Glasgow, 5 Apr 1848. Wife Elizabeth with him, and ch: 1. Margaret; 2. John; 3. Jane; 4. Tabitha. **DC 12 Jul 1979**.

FALKNER. See also FALCONER and FAULKINER.

2507   FALKNER, Alexander, ca 1752–24 Jul 1812. Poss from INV. To Pictou Co, NS; bur Old Elgin. **DC 20 Nov 1976**.

FARISH. See also FARRISH.

2508   FARISH, Francis, ca 1772–17 Jul 1842. From Annan, DFS. To Montreal, QUE, ca 1830. Son James res Hamilton, ONT.   **SH; DGH 28 Aug 1842**.

2509   FARISH, Jane, ca 1799–1832. From Gretna, DFS. d/o Archibald F. and Mary Moffat. To Montreal, QUE.   **Ts Gretna**.

FARISH, Mrs. See SWAN, Mary.

2510   FARISH, William, d 17 Aug 1847. From Annan, DFS. Prob s/o Francis R, qv. To Hamilton, ONT. Merchant.   **DGH 16 Sep 1847**.

2511   FARLINGER, Nicholas. s/o John F. To Dundas Co, ONT, 1819. m (i) Miss Perry, and had with other ch: 1. James; 2. Thomas; 3. Sarah Ann. m (ii) Martha Jane, d/o Edward Aubrey, with further ch: 4. Edward; 5. Nelson; 6. Catherine.   **DC 4 Mar 1965**.

2512   FARQUHAR, Adam, b 29 Sep 1825. From New Cumnock, AYR. s/o John F. and Catherine Stitt, qv. To Richmond Co, QUE, 1847; stld Windsor Mills. m Agnes Findlay, qv.   **DC 11 Nov 1981**.

2513   FARQUHAR, Gilbert, 9 Mar 1824–16 Dec 1897. From New Cumnock, AYR. s/o John F. and Catherine Stitt, qv. To Richmond Co, QUE, 1847; stld Windsor Mills. m Agnes Wilson, qv.   **DC 11 Nov 1981**.

2514   FARQUHAR, Hugh, 21 Mar 1821–24 Dec 1904. From New Cumnock, AYR. s/o John F. and Catherine

Stitt, qv. To Richmond Co, QUE, 1847; stld Windsor Mills. m Jane Brand, qv, ch.   **DC 11 Nov 1981**.

2515   FARQUHARSON, Rev Alexander, 29 May 1793–25 Jan 1858. From Strathardale, PER. s/o John F, farmer. App with the sanction of the Glasgow Colonial Committee as a Gaelic-speaking licentiate of the Ch of Scotland to min in Cape Breton Is, NS, 1833. Ord at Plaster Cove, 11 Sep 1833, and ind to pastorate of Middle River and Lake Ainslie, Nov 1834. m Ann Mackenzie. Son Rev Alexander, min at Sydney, Cape Breton Co.   **FES vii 607; MGC 2 Aug 1979**.

2516   FARQUHARSON, John. To Hudson Bay and Red River <1815. Pioneer settler.   **LSS 192; LSC 327**.

FARRISH. See also FARISH.

2517   FARRISH, Robert, ca 1827–17 Jan 1875. From DFS. To Bruce Co, ONT, prob <1857. m Mary Hunter, b 1840, who m afterwards Henry Richardson. ch: 1. Henry, b 1860; 2. Ellen, b ca 1861; 3. Janet, b 1864; 4-5. Elizabeth and Mary, b 1867; 6. Robert D, b 1872; 7. Sydney Belle, b 1874.   **DC 30 Apr 1980**.

2518   FASKEN, Christina. From Forgue, ABD. d/o William F, qv, and Margaret Mitchell, qv. To Nichol Twp, Wellington Co, ONT, 1829; later to Pilkington Twp. m William Atkinson.   **EHE 42**.

2519   FASKEN, George, ca 1820–18 Apr 1883. From Forgue, ABD. s/o William F, qv, and Margaret Mitchell, qv. To ONT and stld Pilkington Twp, Wellington Co, 1844. m Sarah, 1824-96, d/o Joseph Carder, ch: 1. William; 2. Joseph; 3. John; 4. James; 5. Samuel; 6. Margaret; 7. Rev George, d 1894; 8. Alexander. **EHE 42**.

2520   FASKEN, Isabella. From Forgue, ABD. d/o William F, qv, and Margaret Mitchell, qv. To Pilkington Twp, Wellington Co, ONT, prob <1845. m Alexander McCrae.   **EHE 42**.

2521   FASKEN, John. From Forgue, ABD. s/o William F, qv, and Margaret Mitchell, qv. To Nichol Twp, Wellington Co, ONT, 1839; stld later Pilkington Twp. m Christina Wilson.   **EHE 42**.

2522   FASKEN, Jean. From Forgue, ABD. d/o William F, qv, and Margaret Mitchell, qv. To Pilkington Twp, Wellington Co, ONT, prob <1845. m John Gordon, Minto Twp.   **EHE 42**.

2523   FASKEN, Margaret. From Forgue, ABD. d/o William F, qv, and Margaret Mitchell, qv. To Nichol Twp, Wellington Co, ONT, 1839; later to Pilkington Twp. m Samuel Card, Guelph.   **EHE 42**.

2524   FASKEN, Marion. From Forgue, ABD. d/o William F, qv, and Margaret Mitchell, qv. To ONT, and stld Pilkington Twp, Wellington Co, 1844. m Alexander McDonald, Guelph.   **EHE 42**.

2525   FASKEN, Robert, 1820–5 Nov 1896. From Forgue, ABD. s/o William F, qv, and Margaret Mitchell. To ONT 1844; stld Pilkington Twp, Wellington Co. m Isabella Milne, qv, ch: 1. John; 2. Mary; 3. Ann; 4. Robert; 5. Margaret; 6. David; 7. William; 8. Isabella; 9. Alexander.   **EHE 42**.

2526   FASKEN, William. From Forgue, ABD. To Nichol Twp, Wellington Co, ONT, 1839. Mason, architect and contractor, Pilkington Twp. m Margaret Mitchell, qv, ch:

1. Christian, qv; 2. John, qv; 3. Margaret, qv;
4. William, dy; 5. Alexander, went to MO; 6. Robert, qv;
7. George, qv; 8. Marion, qv; 9. Isabella, qv; 10. Jean,
qv; 11. James, went to MN. **EHE 42**.

FAULKINER. See also FALCONER and FALKNER.

2527 FAULKINER, Margaret. From MOR. To Montreal,
QUE, prob 1831; stld ONT. Wife of John Campbell, qv.
DC 22 Sep 1979.

2528 FEE, Catherine. From Is Arran, BUT. To
Inverness, Megantic Co, QUE, <1840. m John
Hamilton, qv. **AMC 42; MAC 42**.

2529 FELFERD, John. From Kincardine par, PER. To
Montreal, QUE, on the *Sophia*, ex Greenock, 26 Jul
1818; stld prob Beckwith Twp, Lanark Co, ONT. Wife
Janet with him, and ch: 1. John, aged 2; 2. Elizabeth,
aged 2 mo. **SPL**.

2530 FENTON, Alexander, b 1775. From ANS. To
Wolfes Cove, QUE, on the *Blonde*, 1842; thence to
Miramichi, NB, and stld nr Chatham. Farmer.
m (ii) Annie Gruar, qv, ch: 1. David, qv; 2. John, qv;
3. Margaret, b ca 1825; 4. Ellen, qv; 5. Marjorie,
b ca 1829, unm; 6. Mary, qv. **DC 18 June 1978**.

2531 FENTON, Alexander, jr, 1789–1869. From ANS.
s/o Alexander F, qv, by first wife. To QUE, ca 1833; but
stld nr Chatham, NB. m (i) 1834, Margaret Newland, ch:
1. Jane, b 1835. m (ii) 9 Mar 1840, Christina McLeod,
further ch: 2. David; 3. William McLeod; 4. Mary K;
5. Ann. **DC 18 Jun 1978**.

2532 FENTON, David, b 1819. From ANS.
s/o Alexander F, qv, and Margaret Gruar, qv. To Wolfes
Cove, QUE, on the *Blonde*, 1842; but stld nr Chatham,
NB. Carpenter. By wife Jane ch: 1. Mary, b ca 1858, dy;
2. Ann b ca 1859; 3. David, b ca 1861; 4. Alexander,
b ca 1863. **DC 18 Jun 1978**.

2533 FENTON, Ellen, 1827–1906. From ANS.
d/o Alexander F, qv, and Annie Gruar, qv. To Wolfes
Cove, QUE, on the *Blonde*, 1842; but stld nr Chatham,
NB. m 25 Oct 1850, John Bremner, 1818-86, ch:
1. David Fenton, dy 1853; 2. Mary Ann, b 1852;
3. Catherine, b ca 1854; 4. Ellen, b ca 1857; 5. James,
b ca 1859; 6. Alexander, b 1861; 7. David, b ca 1863;
8. John, b ca 1865; 9. Edwin, b ca 1875. **DC 18 Jun
1978**.

2534 FENTON, John, b ca 1822. From ANS.
s/o Alexander F, qv, and Annie Gruar, qv. To Wolfes
Cove, QUE, on the *Blonde*, 1842; but stld Chatham, NB.
By wife Agnes, d 1901, ch: 1. Peter, b 31 Dec 1857;
2. Margaret Ann, b 3 Feb 1860; 3. David, b ca 1863;
4. Mary, b ca 1868; 5. Catherine, b ca 1870; 6. James,
b ca 1873. **DC 18 Jun 1978**.

2535 FENTON, Margaret, b ca 1825. From ANS.
d/o Alexander F, qv, and Annie Gruar, qv. To Wolfes
Cove, QUE, on the *Blonde*, 1842; stld nr Chatham, NB.
m 29 Mar 1850, William Rennie. **DC 18 Jun 1978**.

2536 FENTON, Mary, b 23 Jul 1831. From Dundee,
ANS. d/o Alexander F, qv, and Annie Gruar, qv. To Wolfes
Cove, QUE, on the *Blonde*, 1842, but stld nr Chatham,
NB. m 16 Dec 1853, Dudley, farmer and militiaman,
s/o Dudley Perley and Ann Gillis, ch: 1. Dudley;
2. Helen; 3. Alexander; 4. Margaret; 5. Hannah Pickard;
6. Thomas Horsfield; 7. Alexander Fenton, b 1869;

8. James Walls; 9. Catherine Mary Ellen; 10. Annie.
DC 18 Jun 1978.

2537 FENWICK, Rev Kenneth Mackenzie, 1826–1903.
To ONT <1843. Congregational min. ch: 1. Helen;
2. Jessie; 3. George S; 4. Arthur; 5. Isabella Hune,
b 1843. **DC 6 Jan 1977**.

2538 FERGUS, Christian, ca 1767–25 Jun 1849. From
Dollar par, CLK. Prob d/o James F. To QUE on the
Commerce, ex Greenock, Jun 1820; stld Perth Twp,
Lanark Co, ONT. Wife of James Drysdale, qv,
m at Dollar, 13 Jan 1787. **DC 18 Mar 1968**.

2539 FERGUS, Janet, 1790–23 Oct 1854. From
Campsie, STI. To Waterloo Co, ONT, 1841. Wife of
James Baird, qv. **DC 2 Dec 1979**.

2540 FERGUSON, Alexander, d 1803. From PER, prob
Atholl. bro/o Robert F, qv. To Eel River, Restigouche Co,
NB, 1794. Pioneer fish trader. **SR 15**.

2541 FERGUSON, Alexander, ca 1765–29 Dec 1817.
From Glenmoriston, INV. To Hants Co, NS, prob <1810.
m Eleanor Grant, qv. **DC 20 Jan 1981**.

2542 FERGUSON, Alexander, b 20 Jun 1779. From
Balquhidder, PER. s/o Duncan Donald F. and Helen
Stewart, his second wife. To ONT, ca 1818; stld poss
Bathurst Twp, Lanark Co. Farmer. Bur Prestonville,
Perth. **DC 11 Jan 1980**.

2543 FERGUSON, Alexander. Prob rel to William F, qv.
To QUE on the *Commerce*, ex Greenock, Jun 1820; stld
prob Lanark Co, ONT. **HCL 238**.

2544 FERGUSON, Alexander, 1810–1 May 1846. From
Edinburgh. To Montreal, QUE, ca 1829. Contributor to
the Montreal *Herald*. m Miss Orkney. **SGC 504**.

2545 FERGUSON, Alexander, 1791–1870. From ARL.
To Caledon Twp, Peel Co, ONT, <1840. Wife Janet,
1805-77, prob also from ARL. **DC 21 Apr 1980**.

2546 FERGUSON, Alexander. From ARL. To Victoria
Co, ONT, <1853; stld Manilla. m Annie McFadyen, qv.
Son Alexander Hugh, 1853–1911, surgeon, became
professor at Univ of Illinois. **DC 5 Jun 1979**.

2547 FERGUSON, Angus. Prob from Greenock, RFW.
Rel to Alexander F, merchant, who emig to USA. To NFD
<1843, but retr later to SCT. Clerk. **SH**.

2548 FERGUSON, Angus R. To NS <1850; stld Cape
Breton Is. m Margaret J McAskill, Antigonish Co. Son
John A, engineer. **HNS iii 235**.

2549 FERGUSON, Ann. From Glasgow. To QUE, 1828;
stld later Halifax Twp, Megantic Co, QUE. m 1832,
Gabriel Kerr, ch. **AMC 141**.

2550 FERGUSON, Archibald, ca 1753–5 Mar 1838.
From RFW. To QUE <1775. Merchant-tailor and officer
of militia. m Rebecca Hamby. **DC 18 Apr 1982**.

2551 FERGUSON, Archibald, 1791–1882. From ARL.
To Caledon Twp, Peel Co, ONT, <1840. Wife Sarah
Baxter, qv, with him. **DC 21 Apr 1980**.

2552 FERGUSON, Catherine, 1795–1870. From Ross,
Is Mull, ARL. To Caledon Twp, Peel Co, ONT, <1840.
Wife of Alexander Stewart, qv. **DC 21 Apr 1980**.

2553 FERGUSON, Catherine, 1820–11 May 1899. From
Ardeonaig, Killin par, PER. d/o Donald F. and Jean

Christie. To Reach Twp, Ontario Co, ONT, prob <1840.
m Peter Anderson, qv.   **DC 31 Jan 1982**.

2554   FERGUSON, Catherine, b 1815. From Kirkibost,
Is North Uist, INV. d/o Neil F, qv, and Margaret McLean,
qv. To Cape Breton Co, NS, on the Tay, ex Loch Maddy,
22 Aug 1841. m Ewan MacKenzie, qv.   **DC 19 Apr 1968**.

2555   FERGUSON, Christian, 1817-67. From Is Arran,
BUT. To Black Point, Restigouche Co, 1841. Wife of Peter
Stewart, qv.   **MAC 26**.

2556   FERGUSON, Christina. To Victoria Co, ONT,
<1851; stld Woodville. m Hector MacCrimmon, qv.
DC 5 Sep 1981.

2557   FERGUSON, Colin. From Melfort, ARL. Rel to
Duncan F, qv. To Westminster Twp, Middlesex Co, ONT,
1832. **PCM 51**.

2558   FERGUSON, Colin. Prob from ARL. To
Aldborough Twp, Elgin Co, ONT, <1820. Farmer. m Miss
Buchanan. Son John.   **PDA 51, 93**.

2559   FERGUSON, David, 28 Feb 1820–5 Apr 1859.
From Bathgate, WLN. s/o James F. and Mary Alexander.
To Montreal, QUE, and d Point St Charles.
Ts Bathgate.

2560   FERGUSON, Donald or Daniel. From Kincardine
par, PER. To Montreal, QUE, on the *Sophia*, ex
Greenock, 26 Jul 1818; stld Lot 9W, Con 4, Beckwith
Twp, Lanark Co, ONT. Farmer. Wife Catherine with him,
and ch: 1. Alexander, aged 15, stld later Lot 3, Con 4W;
2. John, aged 4; 3. Elizabeth, aged 7; 4. Catherine,
aged 5.   **SPL**.

2561   FERGUSON, Donald or Daniel. From Kincardine
par, PER. bro/o Peter F, qv. To QUE on the *Sophia*, ex
Greenock, 26 Jul 1818; stld Lot 8W, Con 1, Beckwith
Twp, Lanark Co, ONT. Farmer. Wife Mary with him.
SPL.

2562   FERGUSON, Donald, b ca 1730. From Comrie
par, PER. To Montreal, QUE, on the *Curlew*, ex
Greenock, 21 Jul 1818; stld Lot 22W, Con 5, Beckwith
Twp, Lanark Co, ONT. Farmer. m Christian Stewart, qv,
ch: 1. Duncan, qv; 2. John, qv; 3. James, qv;
4. Robert, qv; 5. Hugh.   **BCL; DC 29 Dec 1981**.

2563   FERGUSON, Donald. Prob from ARL. To Mosa
Twp, Middlesex Co, ONT, 1828.   **PCM 23**.

2564   FERGUSON, Donald, ca 1810–9 Jun 1854. From
Clyne, SUT. To NS poss <1840; stld near Earltown,
Colchester Co. Dau Nancy, 1828-40.   **DC 19 Mar 1981**.

2565   FERGUSON, Donald, b ca 1775. From Baleshare,
Is North Uist, INV. To Cape Breton Co, NS, <1848. Wife
Christina with him, and ch: 1. John, qv; 2. Margaret,
b ca 1820; 3. Flora, b ca 1825; 4. Alexander, b ca 1830;
5. Ann, b ca 1834.   **WLC**.

2566   FERGUSON, Donald, ca 1772–5 Nov 1872. Prob
from Balquhidder, PER. To ONT <1850. ch: 1. John,
b 2 Oct 1808; 2. Duncan, b 3 Jun 1813; 3. Peter,
b 27 May 1816; 4. Margaret, b 12 Oct 1819.
DC 21 Mar 1981.

2567   FERGUSON, Donald, b 1827. From Portnahaven,
Is Islay, ARL. s/o Malcolm F, qv, and wife Nancy. To
Minto Twp, Wellington Co, ONT, ca 1854; stld Lot 97,
Con D. Wife Mary with him. ch incl: 1. Malcolm;
2. John.   **RFS 147**.

2568   FERGUSON, Duncan. To Glengarry Co, ONT,
1794; stld Lot 8, Con 15, Lancaster Twp.   **MG 56**.

2569   FERGUSON, Duncan, b 1797. From Comrie par,
PER. s/o Donald F, qv, and Christian Stewart, qv. To
Montreal, QUE, on the *Curlew*, ex Greenock, 21 Jul
1818; stld Lot 23E, Con 5, Beckwith Twp, Lanark Co,
ONT. Farmer. m Ann McLaren, qv.   **BCL; HCL 33;
DC 29 Dec 1981**.

2570   FERGUSON, Duncan. From Strathyre,
Balquhidder par, PER. To Montreal, QUE, on the *Sophia*,
ex Greenock, 26 Jul 1818; stld Lot 8W, Con 1, Beckwith
Twp, Lanark Co, ONT. Farmer. Wife Isabella with him,
and ch: 1. Robert, aged 10; 2. John, aged 8.   **SPL**.

2571   FERGUSON, Duncan. Prob from ARL. To
Aldborough Twp, Elgin Co, ONT, <1820. Farmer.
PDA 93.

2572   FERGUSON, Duncan. Prob from PER. To QUE on
the *Duchess of Richmond*, 1821; stld Lot 7W, Con 6,
Beckwith Twp, Lanark Co, ONT. Farmer. Wife and ch with
him.   **DC 29 Dec 1981**.

2573   FERGUSON, Duncan. From ARL. Prob bro/o
John F, qv. To Mosa Twp, Middlesex Co, ONT,
1828.   **PMC 23**.

2574   FERGUSON, Duncan, 1749–1835. From
Kilmichael-Glassary, ARL. To Caledon Twp, Peel Co, ONT,
prob <1830.   **DC 21 Apr 1980**.

2575   FERGUSON, Duncan. From Melfort, ARL. Rel to
Colin C, qv. To Westminster Twp, Middlesex Co, ONT,
1832. **PCM 51**.

2576   FERGUSON, Duncan. From ARL. To Aldborough
Twp, Elgin Co, ONT, 1850. Farmer. ch.   **PDA 68**.

2577   FERGUSON, Duncan, ca 1785–20 Oct 1853.
From Logiealmond, PER. s/o John F, tacksman of
Coynichan, and Margaret McDougal. To ONT and
d Lanark Co.   **Ts Tullichettle, Comrie**.

2578   FERGUSON, George. To Glengarry Co, ONT,
1794; stld Lot 12, Con 15, Lancaster Twp.   **MG 56**.

2579   FERGUSON, Hugh, d 1871. b PER but emig from
DFS. stld Derby, Miramichi River, Northumberland Co,
NB.   **DC 14 Jan 1980**.

2580   FERGUSON, Hugh. From ARL. To Mosa Twp,
Middlesex Co, ONT.   **PMC 23**.

2581   FERGUSON, James. To Glengarry Co, ONT, 1794;
stld Lot 7, Con 16, Lancaster Twp.   **MG 56**.

2582   FERGUSON, James. To Pictou Co, NS, 1815, res
Harbourmouth, Pictou, 1816. Mason, in poor
circumstances.   **INS 39**.

2583   FERGUSON, James. From Comrie par, PER.
s/o Donald F, qv, and Christian Stewart, qv. To Montreal,
QUE, on the *Curlew*, ex Greenock, 21 Jul 1818; stld
Lot 23, Con 4, Beckwith Twp, Lanark Co, ONT. Farmer.
Wife Christian McLaren, qv, with him, and ch:
1. Catherine, aged 4; 2. Robert, aged 2.   **BCL; HCL 33;
DC 29 Dec 1981**.

2584   FERGUSON, James. Prob from ARL. To
Aldborough Twp, Elgin Co, ONT, <1820. Farmer.
PDA 94.

2585   FERGUSON, James, 1806-96. From

Levenhorroch, Kilmory par, Is Arran, BUT. To Dalhousie, NB, 1826; stld Benjamen River, Restigouche Co. **MAC 13**.

2586 FERGUSON, James, d 19 Oct 1856. From Girthon par, KKD. s/o William F, farmer in Grobdale. To Huron Co, ONT, ca 1853, and d Tuckersmith Twp. **DGC 18 Nov 1856**.

2587 FERGUSON, Janet, 1815–1901. From Killiecrankie, PER. To Toronto, 1851. Wife of Charles Rogers, qv. **DC 29 Dec 1981**.

2588 FERGUSON, John. To Glengarry Co, ONT, 1794; stld Lot 6, Con 15, Lochiel Twp. **MG 56**.

2589 FERGUSON, John, ca 1730–6 Feb 1824. To Hants Co, NS, prob <1800; bur Presb Cemetery, Nine Mile River. **DC 20 Jan 1981**.

2590 FERGUSON, John. From Blair Atholl, PER. To PEI <1807; stld prob Queens Co. m Isabella Stewart. Son Donald, 1839–1909, farmer and politician. **DC 30 Aug 1977**.

2591 FERGUSON, John, b ca 1765. From Callender, PER. To QUE, ex Greenock, summer 1815; stld Lot 23, Con 1, Bathurst Twp, Lanark Co, ONT. Farmer. Wife Catherine McIntyre, qv, embarked with him, and 7 ch. **SEC 2; HCL 16, 230**.

2592 FERGUSON, John, b 22 Jul 1781. From Balquhidder, PER. s/o Duncan Donald F. and Helen Stewart, his second wife. To QUE on the *Caledonia*, 1816; stld Lot 23, Con 4, Bathurst Twp, Lanark Co, ONT. Farmer. **HCL 44, 234; DC 11 Jan 1980**.

2593 FERGUSON, John. From Comrie par, PER. s/o Donald F, qv, and Christian Stewart. To QUE on the *Curlew*, ex Greenock, 21 Jul 1818; stld Lot 23W, Con 4, Beckwith Twp, Lanark Co, ONT. Farmer. m Mary McGregor, qv. **BCL; DC 29 Dec 1981**.

2594 FERGUSON, John, b ca 1743. From Leckuary, Kilmichael-Glassary, ARL. To QUE on the *Mars*, ex Tobermory, 28 May 1818; stld Aldborough Twp, Elgin Co, ONT. m Catherine Campbell, ch: 1. Iver, remained at Leckuary; 2. John; 3. Margaret, b 1769; 4. Duncan; 5. James; 6. Donald. **DC 15 Mar 1982**.

2595 FERGUSON, John, b 1802. From Levenhorroch, Kilmory par, Is Arran, BUT. To Dalhousie, NB, 1826; stld Benjamen River, Restigouche Co. **MAC 13**.

2596 FERGUSON, John. From ARL. Prob bro/o Duncan F, qv. To Mosa Twp, Middlesex Co, ONT, 1828. **PCM 23**.

2597 FERGUSON, John, 1813-87. From AYR. To Bathurst, Gloucester Co, NB, 1836. Rep of firm of Pollock, Gilmore & Co, Glasgow, also militiaman and Conservative politician. **BNA 697; SNQ vi/1 49**.

2598 FERGUSON, John, b 1775. From Kilbride Bennan, Is Arran, BUT. To Dalhousie, NB, <1834; stld Restigouche Co. m 20 Mar 1800, Catherine McMillan, qv, ch: 1. Catherine, b 1801; 2. Elspa, b 1807; 3. William, 1810-63; 4. Janet, 1812-87; 5. Ebenezer, 1816-83; 6. Mary, 1823-89. **MAC 13**.

2599 FERGUSON, John, ca 1799–21 May 1868. From Clyne, SUT. To NS, poss <1840; stld nr Earltown, Colchester Co. m Maria Sutherland, qv, and had, with

other ch: 1. Catherine, ca 1842-58; 2. Donald, ca 1847-58. **DC 19 Mar 1981**.

2600 FERGUSON, John. To Pictou, NS, on the *Lulan*, ex Glasgow, 17 Aug 1848. **DC 12 Jul 1979**.

2601 FERGUSON, John, b 6 May 1815. From Baleshare, North Uist, INV. s/o Donald and Christina F. To Cape Breton Co, NS, <1848. Capt, Cape Breton Militia, and MLA. m 1848, Eliza, d/o John Thompson, Sydney. **MLA 116**.

2602 FERGUSON, John Dugald, b 1825. From Greenock, RFW. To Campbelltown, Restigouche Co, NB, <1855. Ship architect. **DC 18 Jan 1972**.

2603 FERGUSON, Malcolm, b ca 1793. From Portnahaven, Is Islay, BUT. To Minto Twp, Wellington Co, ONT, ca 1854. Farmer. Wife Nancy with him, and ch: 1. Donald, qv; 2. Malcolm, jr, qv; 3. Archibald. **RFS 147**.

2604 FERGUSON, Malcolm, jr, 1834–1914. From Portnahaven, Is Islay, ARL. s/o Malcolm F, qv, and wife Nancy. To Minto Twp, Wellington Co, ONT, ca 1854. m Catharine Ross, qv, ch: 1. Malcolm; 2. Alexander; 3. Ann, went to ND; 4. Donald; 5. Margaret; 6. Florence, d inf; 7. John; 8. Catherine. **RFS 147, 185**.

2605 FERGUSON, Malcolm, d 1901. Prob from ARL. To Cape Breton Co, NS, <1855. m Mary McLean, qv, ch: 1. John; 2. Daniel; 3. Kate; 4. Archibald, b Port Morien, 1863; 5. Christie; 6. Donald Hugh; 7. Angus; 8. John; 9. Alexander. **HNS iii 330**.

2606 FERGUSON, Margaret. From Aberdeen. d/o John F, merchant. To ONT, Jun 1822. m 1818, Lt James Grierson, qv. **DC 10 Nov 1978**.

2607 FERGUSON, Mary, 1800-78. From Feorline, Kilmory par, Is Arran, BUT. To Benjamen River, Restigouche Co, NB, 1829. Wife of Charles McAllister, qv. **MAC 19**.

2608 FERGUSON, Mary, b 1784. From West Bennan, Is Arran, BUT. To Dayfield, Restigouche Co, NB, 1832. m (i) 7 Jul 1824, John Murphy, ch: 1. Donald, 1811-32; 2. Catherine, 1818-94; 3. Mary, 1819–1902. m (ii) John Cook, qv. **MAC 12**.

2609 FERGUSON, Neil, 1789–1867. From Kirkibost, Is North Uist, INV. s/o Donald F. To Cape Breton Co, NS, on the *Tay*, ex Loch Maddy, 22 Aug 1841; stld Sydney. Tacksman and shore officer. m 1812, Margaret McLean, qv, ch: 1. Catherine, qv; 2. John, b 1822; 3. Christina; 4. Angus; 5. Margaret, b 1822; 6. Donald, b 1826. **DC 18 May 1968; WLC**.

2610 FERGUSON, Neil, b ca 1781. From Dunganichy, Is Benbecula, INV. To Pictou, NS, on the *Lulan*, ex Glasgow, 17 Aug 1848. m Janet Ferguson, who d <1848, ch: 1. Catherine, b 1820; 2. Donald, b 1823; 3. Somerled, b 1825; 4. Margaret, b 1827; 5. Angus, b 1828; 6. Fergus, b 1832. **DC 12 Jul 1979**.

2611 FERGUSON, Patrick, b 1768. From Is Mull, ARL. To Charlottetown, PEI, on the *Clarendon*, ex Oban, 6 Aug 1808. Labourer. **CPL**.

2612 FERGUSON, Patrick or Peter, 1768–5 Aug 1849. From Balquhidder, PER. s/o Duncan Donald F. and Margaret McGregor. To QUE on the *Jane*, Aug 1818; stld

Drummond Twp, Lanark Co, ONT. Farmer. m Margaret McGregor, ch: 1. Mary, 1804-93; 2. Duncan, 1805-65; 3. Peter, 1811-64; 4. Margaret, 1813-79; 5. Agnes, 1817-90. **DC 11 Jan 1980**.

2613 FERGUSON, Peter. From Glenmoriston, INV. To Glengarry Co, ONT, prob <1800. **LDW 10 Nov 1975**.

2614 FERGUSON, Peter. To Glengarry Co, ONT, 1794; stld Lot 9, Con 15, Lancaster Twp. **MG 56**.

2615 FERGUSON, Peter. From Kincardine par, PER. bro/o Donald or Duncan F, qv. To QUE on the *Sophia*, ex Greenock, 26 Jul 1818; stld Beckwith Twp, Lanark Co. Wife Janet with him. **SPL**.

2616 FERGUSON, Rev Peter, 1807-63. From Bridge of Teith, PER. s/o Peter F. Matric Univ of Glasgow, 1822. To West Williamsburg, Dundas Co, ONT. Min there, 1831; trans to Esquesing, Halton Co, 1832. Joined Ch of Scotland, 1834. **GMA 11035**.

2617 FERGUSON, Robert, 1768-1851. From PER. bro/o Alexander F, qv. To Eel River, Restigouche Co, NB, 1796. Chief clerk with his bro and helped expand the fish trade. Purchased 1,000 acres in 1810, and built 'Athol House.' Dau Elizabeth. **SR 15, 17**.

2618 FERGUSON, Robert, 1777-1856. From Balquhidder, PER. s/o Peter F. and Helen Stewart. To QUE on the *Caledonia*, Jul 1816; stld Bathurst Twp, Lanark Co, ONT. Farmer. m Margaret Buchanan, ch: 1. Duncan; 2. Margaret; 3. Helena; 4. James; 5. Agnes or Nancy; 6. Elizabeth. **HCL 234; DC 18 May 1982**.

2619 FERGUSON, Robert. From Comrie, PER. s/o Donald F, qv, and Christian Stewart, qv. To Montreal, QUE, on the *Curlew*, ex Greenock, 21 Jul 1818; stld Beckwith Twp, Lanark Co, ONT. Wife Christian Campbell, qv, with him. **BCL; HCL 33**.

2620 FERGUSON, Robert. From Kincardine par, PER. To QUE on the *Sophia*, ex Greenock, 26 Jul 1818; stld Lot 9E, Con 4, Beckwith Twp, Lanark Co, ONT. Farmer. Wife Jane with him. **SPL**.

2621 FERGUSON, Robert. To QUE on the *Commerce*, ex Greenock, Jun 1820; stld prob Lanark Co, ONT. **HCL 239**.

2622 FERGUSON, Robert. To Pictou, NS, on the *Lady Gray*, ex Cromarty, arr 16 Jul 1841. **DC 15 Jul 1979**.

2623 FERGUSON, Roderick. From Is North Uist, INV. To East Williams Twp, Middlesex Co, ONT, 1848. Schoolteacher. ch: 1. Angus, principal teacher of a school at St Thomas; 2. Roderick, teacher; 3. Neil, teacher; 4. Mrs Cruickshank. **PCM 48**.

2624 FERGUSON, Susan, 10 May 1812-3 Mar 1885. From Cummertrees, DFS. To Ottawa, ONT, <1846. Wife of John Hannah, qv. **DC 27 May 1981**.

2625 FERGUSON, Thomas, 1809-57. From Caerlaverock, DFS. To Moncton, Westmorland Co, NB, and d there, ch. **CAE 1**.

2626 FERGUSON, William. Prob rel to Alexander F, qv. To QUE on the *Commerce*, ex Greenock, Jun 1820; stld prob Lanark Co, ONT. **HCL 238**.

2627 FERGUSON, William, ca 1779-2 Sep 1857. From Cummertrees, DFS. To Quaker Hill, Uxbridge Twp, Ontario Co, ONT, ca 1830. m Mary Graham, 1782-1858. **DC 9 Jun 1980**.

2628 FERGUSON, William, ca 1824-6 Jun 1848. From Dumfries. s/o James F, writer. To Hamilton, ONT, and d there. **DGH 29 Jun 1848**.

2629 FERGUSON, William Erskine, b ca 1800. s/o John F, Aberdeen. Matric Marischall Coll, Aberdeen, 1817, and completed his studies at St Andrews. To ONT ca 1822 as catechist app by the Colonial Committee. Later Inspector of Schools in Dundas Co. **FAM ii 430; SAM 62; FES vii 633**.

2630 FERGUSSON, Adam, 1783-26 Sep 1862. From Cupar, FIF. s/o Neil F. of Pitcullo, Advocate, and Agnes Colquhoun. To Woodhill, Fergus Twp, Wellington Co, ONT, 1831 and 1833. Advocate at the Scottish Bar, farmer and author. m (i) 1811, Jemima Johnston Blair, d 1824, d/o and heiress of Maj James Johnston, HEICS, ch: 1. Neil James, 1814-62, of Balthayock, PER; 2. Adam Johnston, qv; 3. David, qv; 4. John, qv; 5. James Scott, qv; 6. George Douglas, qv; 7. Robert, qv. m (ii) 1833, Jessy Tower. **BNA 537; EAR 16; FAS 69; MDB 60, 227**.

2631 FERGUSSON, Adam Johnston, 4 Nov 1816-29 Dec 1867. From Edinburgh. s/o Adam F, qv, and Jemima Blair Johnston. To Guelph Twp, Wellington Co, ONT, 1833. Lawyer and Liberal politician. Assumed surname of Blair in 1862 on d of bro Neil James of Balthayock. **EAR 16; MDB 60**.

2632 FERGUSSON, Alexander. From Corsock Mill, Parton, KKD. To Harwich, Kent Co, ONT, <1847. m Jane Barber, qv, ch. **DGH 14 Oct 1847**.

2633 FERGUSSON, David, 1817-60. s/o Adam F, qv, and Jemima Blair Johnston. Educ Edinburgh Academy, 1825-30. To Fergus Twp, Wellington Co, ONT, 1833. **EAR 30**.

2634 FERGUSSON, Elspeth or Elizabeth, 1807-93. From Kilmory par, Is Arran, BUT. To Nash Creek, Restigouche Co, NB, 1834. m 20 Jan 1828, John Currie, qv. **MAC 13**.

2635 FERGUSSON, George Douglas, 1822-15 Sep 1895. From Edinburgh. s/o Adam F, qv, and Jemima Blair Johnston. Educ Edinburgh Academy, 1831-33. To Fergus Twp, Wellington Co, ONT, 1833. Banker and landowner. m Charlotte Legge, from Gananoque, Leeds Co. **EAR 65**.

2636 FERGUSSON, James, d 1 Jul 1836. From DFS. s/o John F. To Toronto, ONT. Merchant. **DGC 24 Aug 1836**.

2637 FERGUSSON, James Scott, 1820-7 Jul 1850. From Edinburgh. s/o Adam F, qv, and Jemima Blair Johnston. Educ Edinburgh Academy, 1827-32. To Port Dover, Norfolk Co, ONT, and in business there. m Miss McDonald, from Gananoque, Leeds Co. **EAR 44**.

2638 FERGUSSON, Janet, 1780-1854. From Kilbride Bennan, Is Arran, BUT. To Restigouche Co, NB, prob <1840. m 11 Jul 1819, Alexander McKenzie, qv. **MAC 20**.

2639 FERGUSSON, John, 1772-1840. From PER. To PEI, 1808; stld Marshfield. Farmer. m Margaret Robertson, qv, ch: 1. Margaret, b 1809; 2. Donald, cattle-breeder. **HP 103**.

2640 FERGUSSON, John, 1819-1 Jul 1849. From Edinburgh. s/o Adam F, qv, and Jemima Blair Johnston.

Educ Edinburgh Academy, 1825-29. Went to Niagara, Lincoln Co, ONT. d on a business trip to China. **EAR 30**.

2641 FERGUSSON, Capt Thomas, ca 1809–14 Oct 1857. From Caerlaverock, DFS. To Moncton, Westmorland Co, NB, and d there, leaving a widow and 5 ch. **DGH 13 Nov 1857**.

2642 FERGUSSON, Robert, 1824–11 Oct 1883. From Edinburgh. s/o Adam F, qv, and Jemima Blair Johnston, qv. Educ Edinburgh Academy, 1832-33, and came to CAN. Emp with Bank of British North America, and subsequently their agent in New York. Later on board of Union Bank of London and became Governor. m Georgina Hobson, Baltimore. **EAR 70**.

2643 FERRIE, Adam, 15 Mar 1777–24 Dec 1863. From Irvine, AYR. s/o James F. and Jane Robertson. To Montreal, QUE, ex Greenock, 5 Jun 1829. Merchant and MLA. Went to ONT, 1833, and stld Hamilton, 1835. m Rachel Campbell, qv, and had, prob with other ch: 1. Colin Campbell; 2. Janet; 3. Mrs Alexander Ewing. **SGC 474; MDB 228; DC 5 Apr 1982**.

2644 FERRIE, John. From Glasgow. Poss rel to Adam F, qv. To Hamilton, ONT, <1855. Dry goods merchant. m Emily Brown. Son Campbell. **DC 19 Sep 1960**.

2645 FERRIE, Rev William, 8 Mar 1815–29 Dec 1903. From Kilconquhar, FIF. s/o Rev Prof William F, and Elizabeth McCormack. Attended Univ of St Andrew, 1828-29, and matric Univ of Glasgow, 1831. Min at Anstruther Easter, 1839-43, when joined FC. To St John, NB, and min there 1851-61. Went to NY, but came again to CAN as min at Prescott and Spencerville, ONT, 1863. Later min at Mongaup Valley, NY, and d Monticello. m Jessie F.S. Taylor. **SAM 78; GMA 12754; FES v 181; AFC i 153; MDB 228**.

2646 FERRIER, Abraham, b ca 1782. From Waterside, Fenwick par, AYR. To QUE, prob on the *Atlas*, ex Greenock, 11 Jul 1815; stld Burgess Twp, Lanark Co, ONT. Weaver, labourer, and became farmer. Wife Christian Rowal, qv, with him, and 4 ch. **SEC 3; HCL 15**.

2647 FERRIER, Alexander David, 13 Nov 1813–4 Aug 1890. From Belsyde, Linlithgow, WLN. s/o Louis Henry F, qv, and Charlotte Munro, d 1822. To QUE <1835, when he moved to Nichol Twp, Wellington Co, ONT. County Clerk of Wellington, later MPP. m Magdalene Dingwall Fordyce, qv, without ch. **BNA 756; NDF 85; EAR 7**.

2648 FERRIER, James, 22 Oct 1800–30 May 1888. From Auchtermuchty, FIF. s/o George F. and Elizabeth Bayne. To Montreal, QUE, 1821. Engaged in banking and commerce and became a Canadian senator, 1867. Dau Mrs W.S. McFarlane. **BNA 602; SGC 327; Ts Auchtermuchty**.

2649 FERRIER, John, b ca 1784. From Waterside, Fenwick par, AYR. To QUE on the *Atlas*, ex Greenock, 11 Jul 1815; stld Lot 7, Con 10, Burgess Twp, Lanark Co, ONT. Weaver and labourer, later farmer. Wife Charlotte McGlashan, qv, with him, and 4 ch. **SEC 3; HCL 15, 232**.

2650 FERRIER, Louis Henry, 5 Aug 1776–28 Jan 1833. From Belsyde, Linlithgow, WLN. s/o Maj Gen Ilay F, Scots Brigade, and Jane McQueen. To QUE, <1830.

Advocate at the Scottish Bar, 1798, and became Collector of Customs at QUE. m Charlotte Munro, ch: 1. Ilay, Brevet Maj, 48th Madras NI; 2. Katherine; 3. Jane; 4. Charlotte; 5. Alexander David, qv; 6. George Abercrombie, d unm. **NDF 86; FAS 71**.

2651 FERRIES, Rev John, 23 Oct 1836–13 Jun 1903. From Edinkillie, MOR. s/o Rev Peter F, par min, and Mary Ann Grace Smith. Matric Univ of Glasgow, 1852, and grad BA 1855. Succ father as min of Edinkillie, 1865, and later became min of Presb Ch at Brandon, MAN. m Anna Broadfoot, qv, ch. **GMA 16088; RGG 190; FES vi 420, vii 656**.

2652 FERRIS, James Moir, ca 1813–21 Apr 1870. From Aberdeen. s/o James M, tradesman. Matric Marischall Coll, Aberdeen, 1827. To Montreal, QUE, <1834. Teacher and newspaper editor. m Sarah Robertson, qv. **FAM ii 465; MDB 465**.

2653 FETTES, Rev James, 1819-96. From Edinburgh. Studied there at New Coll, and was ord at Montreal, QUE, 1848. Retr to SCT, 1850, and adm FC min at Ladhope, SEL. m 1846, Mary Gordon Huie. **AFC i 153**.

2654 FETTES, William, b ca 1840. From ANS. To Grey Co, ONT, <1865. m Mary McPhail, ch. **DC 11 Nov 1981**.

FIFE. See also FYFE.

2655 FIFE, Alexander, b 24 Nov 1815. From Tulliallan, FIF. s/o John F, qv, and Agnes Graham Hutchison, qv. To Peterborough Co, ONT, 1820. m Margaret Eason. **DC 11 Dec 1967**.

2656 FIFE, David, 22 Aug 1805–9 Jan 1877. From Tulliallan, FIF. s/o John F, qv, and Agnes Graham Hutchison, qv. To Peterborough Co, ONT, 1820. Farmer, and originator of 'Fife Red Wheat,' 1842. m Jane Becket, qv, ch. **DC 11 Dec 1967**.

2657 FIFE, Hutchison, b 12 Jun 1812. From Tulliallan, FIF. s/o John F, qv, and Agnes Graham Hutchison, qv. To Peterborough Co, ONT, 1820. **DC 11 Dec 1967**.

2658 FIFE, James, b 8 Oct 1803. From Tulliallan, FIF. s/o John F, qv, and Agnes Graham Hutchison, qv. To Peterborough Co, ONT, 1820. m Elizabeth Malcolm, qv. **DC 11 Dec 1967**.

2659 FIFE, John, b Sep 1763. From Tulliallan, FIF. s/o William F, qv, and Martha Adam. To Peterborough Co, ONT, 1820. Farmer. m (i) 1790, Katherine Robertson; (ii) 25 Nov 1796, Agnes Graham Hutchison, qv, ch: 1. John, jr, qv; 2. James, b 1799, d inf; 3. Thomas, b 1801, dy; 4. James, qv; 5. David, qv; 6. William, qv; 7. Thomas, qv; 8. Hutchison, qv; 9. Alexander, qv; 10. Robert, b 1815, dy. **DC 11 Dec 1967 and 10 Jun 1977**.

2660 FIFE, John, jr, b 31 Aug 1797. From Tulliallan, FIF. s/o John F, qv, and Agnes Graham Hutchison, qv. To Peterborough Co, ONT, 1820. m Eliza Carter, from IRL. **DC 11 Dec 1967 and 5 Feb 1968**.

2661 FIFE, Thomas, b 11 Dec 1809. From Tulliallan, FIF. s/o John F, qv, and Agnes Graham Hutchison, qv. To Peterborough Co, ONT, 1820. m Janet Becket, qv. **DC 11 Dec 1967**.

2662 FIFE, William, b 10 Aug 1807. From Tulliallan, FIF. s/o John F, qv, and Agnes Graham Hutchison, qv. To

Peterborough Co, ONT, 1820. m Mary A. Becket, qv.
DC 11 Dec 1967.

2663 FINDELSON, Mary, d 1844. From Is Skye, INV.
To Baddeck, Victoria Co, NS, 1841. Wife of Donald
McPherson, qv. **HNS iii 517**.

2664 FINDLAY, Agnes, d 1907. From New Cumnock,
AYR. To Richmond Co, QUE, 1847; stld Windsor Mills.
Wife of Adam Farquhar, qv, whom she m 5 Dec 1845.
DC 11 Nov 1981.

2665 FINDLAY, Ann, d 1843. From Cullen, BAN.
d/o George and Ann F. To Kingston, ONT. **Ts Cullen**.

2666 FINDLAY, James, ca 1799–1883. From LKS,
poss Strathaven. To Scarborough, York Co, ONT,
ca 1833. **DC 29 Mar 1981**.

2667 FINDLAY, James. From New Machar par, ABD.
To Nichol Twp, Wellington Co, ONT, 1836. m Margaret
Ruxton, qv, ch: 1. Agnes; 2. William, auctioneer;
3. John, went to BC; 4. David; 5. James; 6. Alexander,
d Toronto; 7. Robert, res Sudbury, ONT; 8. Charles, res
Shoal Lake, MAN. **EHE 92**.

2668 FINDLAY, Jane, ca 1829–24 Jan 1908. From
ABD. To Ashburn Village, East Whitby Twp, Ontario Co,
ONT, ca 1854. m James Lawrence, qv. **DC 23 Jul
1979**.

2669 FINDLAY, John. To QUE on the *David of London*,
ex Greenock, 19 May 1821; stld Lanark Co, ONT.
HCL 70.

2670 FINDLAY, John, b 27 Oct 1818. From Crofthead,
Galston, AYR. s/o Francis F. and Janet Craig. To Oxford
Co, ONT, ca 1852; stld Morpeth. **SCN**.

2671 FINDLAY, Thomas, b ca 1823. From Crofthead,
Galston, AYR. s/o Francis F. and Janet Craig. To Oxford
Co, ONT, ca 1854. **SCN**.

2672 FINDLEY, Janet. From Kilmarnock, AYR. To
Montreal, QUE, 1782. Wife of Robert Aird, qv.
LDW 14 Jan 1976.

2673 FINLAY, Hugh, ca 1732–26 Dec 1801. To QUE,
1760. Postmaster there, and in 1774 app Deputy
Postmaster General of British North America. Left a
Journal. **BNA 406; MDB 230**.

2674 FINLAY, James, d 1797. To Montreal, QUE,
<1766. Pioneer fur-trader on the Saskatchewan River
and partner in firm of Finlay & Gregory, later Gregory
McLeod & Co. Associated with NWCo. Finlay River, a
tributary of the Peace, named after him. m ca 1765,
Christina Youel, ch: 1. James, 1766–1830; 2. Ann;
3. Christy; 4. John, 1774–1833. By a Chippewa woman
he had: 5. Jacques, 1768–1828, pioneer fur-trader at
Spokane. **SGC 111; BNA 956; ENA 16; MDB 230;
DC 27 Feb 1972**.

2675 FINLAY, James. From Rothes, MOR. To Halifax,
NS <26 Apr 1825, when he m Elspet Sherar. qv. **VSN
No 1126**.

2676 FINLAY, William, b Stromness, OKI. To Hudson
Bay, ca 1812, and prob to Red River. **RRS 13**.

2677 FINLAYSON, Donald. To NS prob 1853.
m Annabella Murchison. Son Duncan, b 1867, lawyer.
HNS iii 56.

2678 FINLAYSON, Duncan, ca 1796–25 Jul 1862.
From Dingwall, ROC. s/o John F, qv. To CAN <1815.
Emp by HBCo and served in Labrador, Red River and on
the Columbia. Chief factor 1831, and Gov of Assiniboia,
1838-44. Ret 1859. m a d/o Geddes Simpson, London,
ENG. **MDB 231**.

2679 FINLAYSON, John. From Glenelg, INV. To QUE
on the *Nephton*, 1802; stld Chambly Mountain. Moved in
1812 to Williamstown. **SAS 18**.

2680 FINLAYSON, John. From Dingwall, ROC. To
Montreal, QUE, <1800. Became emp of HBCo, and a
chief factor in 1846. ch: 1. Nicol, qv; 2. Duncan, qv.
MDB 231.

2681 FINLAYSON, Nicol, 1795–17 May 1877. From
Dingwall, ROC. s/o John F, qv. To CAN <1821, and
joined HBCo as a clerk. Took part in explorations in
northern Labrador and estab Fort Chimo, Ungava Bay.
m 10 Aug 1829, Elizabeth Kennedy, ch. **DC 21 Mar
1981**.

2682 FINLAYSON, Rachel, 1816-91. From Branahuie,
Is Lewis, ROC. d/o Donald F. To Lingwick Twp, Compton
Co, QUE, ca 1842. Wife of William McLeod, qv. **WLC**.

2683 FINLAYSON, Roderick, ca 1818–30 Jan 1892.
From Lochalsh, ROC. To NY, 1828, but went to Montreal
and Lachine, QUE. Joined HBCo prob 1837, and took
part in the founding of Fort Victoria on the Pacific coast.
Chief trader, 1850; chief factor, 1859; MLC 1851-63.
m 1849, Sarah, d/o John Work, chief factor, Fort
Simpson. **MDB 231**.

2684 FINNIE, Andrew, 1820–19 Jun 1908. To ONT
<1848; stld prob South Monaghan Twp, Northumberland
Co. m Jane Chambers, qv, ch: 1. Edward, b ca 1849;
2. George, b ca 1851; 3. John, b ca 1853; 4. Juliet,
b ca 1854; 5. Andrew, b ca 1857; 6. Walter, b ca 1859;
7. Jane, b ca 1862; 8. James, b ca 1864; 9. Janet,
b ca 1866; 10. Mary Ann, b ca 1868; 11. Sophia,
b ca 1870; 12. Sophia, b 1872. **DC 31 Jan 1982**.

2685 FINNIE, Robert, b 1830. To Montreal, QUE,
<1844; later to New Orleans, LA. m Ellen, d/o Robert
and Alison Dryden, ch: 1. Alison E; 2. Walter Forsyth;
3. Isabella Jean; 4. Mary R; 5. Robert Dryden; 6. Earl
S. **SG xxiii/1 12; DC 14 Oct 1979**.

2686 FINNIS, Andrew, ca 1795–6 Nov 1871. From
DFS. To Gloucester Co, NB, prob <1840; stld Madisco.
Wife Mary, 1793–1871. **DC 14 Jan 1980**.

2687 FINNIS, Henry, ca 1764–5 Nov 1834. From
Dalton, DFS. To Miramichi, Northumberland Co, NB.
m Jean Graham. 1760–1832. Son Matthew, 1800-32,
d Edinburgh. **Ts Dalton**.

2688 FISHER, Alexander, d <1800. From Dunkeld,
PER. bro/o Duncan F, qv, James F, qv, and John F, qv.
To Montreal, QUE, prob <1780. Inn-keeper, St Mary
Street. m a sis/o Hon Alexander Grant, L'Orignal, ch,
(confused at source). **SGC 72, 77, 142**.

2689 FISHER, Ann. From PER, poss Killin par. Prob
rel to Cathrine F, qv. To McNab Twp, Renfrew Co, ONT,
1825. **DC 3 Jan 1980**.

2690 FISHER, Cathrine. From PER, poss Killin par.
Prob rel to Ann F, qv. To McNab Twp, Renfrew Co, ONT,
1825. **DC 3 Jan 1980**.

2691   FISHER, Christian, 1793–1862. From Kenmore par, PER. d/o James F, qv, and Elizabeth Haggart, qv. To Montreal, QUE, <1808; stld later at Ormstown. m Alexander Mills, ch: 1. James, b 1822; 2. Robert, b 1826; 3. Alexander, b 1828; 4. Christina, b 1830; 5. Andrew, b 1833; 6. Elizabeth, b 1835.   **DC 26 Mar 1979**.

2692   FISHER, Christian. From PER, prob Lochearnhead. A minor, and poss d/o Donald F, qv, and Margaret McEwen, qv. To McNab Twp, Renfrew Co, ONT, 1825.   **EMT 23**.

2693   FISHER, Christine, 1 May 1782–16 Apr 1877. From Killin, PER. d/o John F. and Margaret Brown. To Oro Twp, Simcoe Co, ONT, 1832. Wife of John McPherson, qv.   **DC 8 Nov 1981**.

2694   FISHER, Donald, 1791–1866. From Kenmore, PER. s/o James F, qv, and Elizabeth Haggart, qv. To Montreal, QUE, <1808; later to Norfolk Co, ONT.   **DC 26 Mar 1979**.

2695   FISHER, Donald. From Lochearnhead, PER. To Montreal, QUE, on the *Niagara*, ex Greenock, arr 28 May 1825; stld McNab Twp, Renfrew Co, ONT. Wife Margaret McEwan, qv, with him, and ch: 1. Cathrine; 2. Margaret.   **EMT 18, 22**.

2696   FISHER, Duncan, ca 1753–5 Jul 1820. From Dunkeld, PER. bro/o Alexander F, qv, James F, qv, and John F, qv. To Montreal, QUE, ca 1776. Cordiner. m Catherine, d/o Rev Philip Embury, pioneer of Methodism in North America, ch, (confused at source).   **SGC 72**.

2697   FISHER, Finlay, ca 1756–28 Jul 1815. From PER. cous of Alexander F, qv, Duncan F, qv, James F, qv, and John F, qv. To Montreal, QUE, ca 1776. Schoolmaster.   **SGC 72**.

2698   FISHER, Rev George, ca 1823–17 Jan 1909. From Kells, KKD. s/o William F, farmer. Matric Univ of Glasgow, 1838, and ord for Secession Church. Became min of Esquesing, Halton Co, ONT, but later renounced connection.   **GMA 13876**.

2699   FISHER, James. From Dunkeld, PER. bro/o Alexander F, qv, Duncan F, qv, and John F, qv. To Montreal, QUE, prob <1780.   **SGC 72**.

2700   FISHER, James, b 1759. From Kenmore par, PER. s/o Donald F. and Janet Hay. To Montreal, QUE, <1808; stld Pointe-Longue. Farmer. m Elizabeth Haggart, qv, ch: 1. Donald, qv; 2. John, qv; 3. Christian, qv; 4. Janet, qv; 5. Alexander, 1798–1864, res Lawers, PER; 6. Peter, 1800-50; 7. Elizabeth, 1808-80; 8. James, bur Montreal, 1856; 9. Catherine, who went to SCT and res Acharn, PER.   **DC 26 Mar 1979**.

2701   FISHER, James. Poss from PER. To Aldborough Twp, Elgin Co, ONT, 1852. Son John.   **PDA 68**.

2702   FISHER, James, 6 Nov 1840–10 May 1927. From Dull par, PER. To Toronto, ONT, <1855, and educ Univ there, grad BA, 1862, and MA, 1872. Lawyer.   **MDB 232**.

2703   FISHER, Janet, b 1796. From Kenmore par, PER. d/o James F, qv, and Elizabeth Haggart, qv. To Montreal, QUE, <1808. m Edmund Haney, ch.   **DC 26 Mar 1979**.

2704   FISHER, Janet. From Lochearnhead, PER. To Montreal, QUE, on the *Niagara*, ex Greenock, arr 28 May 1825; stld McNab Twp, Renfrew Co, ONT. Wife of Malcolm McLaren, qv.   **EMT 18**.

2705   FISHER, Janet, ca 1785–18 Jan 1854. From PER. To McNab Twp, Renfrew Co, ONT, poss <1825. Wife of John McCallum, qv.   **DC 22 Aug 1978**.

2706   FISHER, Janet. From PER, poss Lochearnhead. A minor, poss d/o Donald F, qv, and Margaret McEwan, qv. To Montreal, QUE, on the *Niagara*, ex Greenock, arr 28 May 1825; stld McNab Twp, Renfrew Co, ONT.   **EMT 23**.

2707   FISHER, Janet, 1812-50. From PER. To Osgoode Twp, Carleton Co, ONT, ca 1831. Wife of Duncan McNab, qv.   **DC 1 Aug 1979**.

2708   FISHER, John. From Dunkeld, PER. bro/o Alexander F, qv, Duncan F, qv, and James F, qv. To Montreal, QUE, ca 1780.   **SGC 72**.

2709   FISHER, John, 1794–1858. From Kenmore par, PER. s/o James F, qv, and Elizabeth Haggart, qv. To Montreal, QUE, <1808; stld later QUE. m Rose, d/o Satchwell Leney, engraver, New York City and Longue-Pointe, QUE, ch.   **DC 26 Mar 1979**.

2710   FISHER, John. From Perth. s/o — F. and — Hepburn. To Plympton Twp, Lambton Co, ONT, <1846.   **SH**.

2711   FISHER, Malcolm. From Balquhidder par, PER. To Montreal, QUE, on the *Curlew*, ex Greenock, 21 Jul 1818; stld prob Beckwith Twp, Lanark Co, ONT. Wife Christian with him, ch: 1. Janet, aged 14; 2. John, aged 13; 3. Donald, aged 11; 4. Ann, aged 9; 5. Malcolm, aged 4; 6. Mary, aged 1.   **BCL**.

2712   FISHER, Mary. From PER, prob Lochearnhead. A minor, poss d/o Donald F, qv, and Margaret McEwan, qv. To McNab Twp, Renfrew Co, ONT, 1825.   **DC 3 Jan 1980**.

2713   FISHER, William. From Glasgow. To Halifax, NS, <12 Jun 1824, when he m Mary, third d/o of Alexander Phillips.   **VSN No 601**.

2714   FISHER, William, ca 1813–11 Jun 1850. From Rerrick, KKD. To Essex Co, ONT, and d Colchester, leaving ch.   **DGH 25 Jul 1850**.

2715   FISSET, Jean, b ca 1745. From AYR. To Richmond Bay, PEI, on the *Falmouth*, ex Greenock, 8 Apr 1770; stld Stanhope, Queens Co. Wife of Robert Auld, qv.   **DC 28 May 1980**.

2716   FLECK, Alexander. From Ayr. To ONT, prob <1850. Machinist. m Lilias Walker. Son Alexander.   **DC 29 Sep 1964**.

2717   FLEMING, Charles. To QUE on the *Commerce*, ex Greenock, Jun 1820; stld prob Lanark Co, ONT.   **HCL 239**.

2718   FLEMING, David, b ca 1825. From Kirkcaldy, FIF. s/o Andrew Greig F. and Elizabeth Arnot. To Montreal, QUE, on the *Brilliant*, ex Broomielaw, Glasgow, 24 Apr 1845; stld Kingston, ONT.   **DC 1 Jan 1968**.

2719   FLEMING, Elizabeth, b ca 1768. From LKS. To ONT, 12 May 1830. Wife of William Allan, qv.   **DC 1 Jun 1977**.

2720   FLEMING, Gavin, b 1826. From Falkirk, STI. To Dumfries Twp, Waterloo Co, ONT, <1851. Merchant,

Treasurer of South Dumfries and Liberal politician, rep North Brant. **BNA 752; HGD 213**.

2721 FLEMING, Grace Matilda, b 14 Jun 1819. From Carriden, WLN. d/o Rev David F, par min, and Grace Ross. To Sherbrooke, QUE, 1840, after m to James Edgar, qv. **BNA 744; FES i 199**.

2722 FLEMING, James. From ABD. bro/o John F, qv. To Montreal, QUE, prob <1810. m Ann Cuthbert, d 1860, author and teacher. **MDB 235**.

2723 FLEMING, James, d 26 Jan 1852. From Aberdeen. To Toronto, ONT. Seedsman. **Aberdeen OPR 168A/37**.

2724 FLEMING, John, ca 1786–30 Jul 1832. From ABD. To Montreal, QUE, 1803. Merchant and bibliophile. Pres of Bank of Montreal, 1830-32. **SGC 267; MDB 235**.

2725 FLEMING, John. From PER. To Woodbridge, York Co, ONT, arr May 1843. Farmer. m Margaret Robertson. Son Christopher Alexander. **DC 29 Sep 1964**.

2726 FLEMING, John, 1820–21 Jan 1877. From Dunfermline, FIF. To Galt, Waterloo Co, ONT, ca 1835. Merchant and MLC. **HGD 232**.

2727 FLEMING, Margaret, ca 1797–ca 1857. From Blair Atholl, PER. To Grey Twp, Huron Co, ONT, 1852. Wife of Alexander Stewart, qv. **DC 15 May 1969**.

2728 FLEMING, Sir Sandford, 7 Jul 1827–22 Jul 1915. From Kirkcaldy, FIF. s/o Andrew Greig F. and Elizabeth Arnot. To QUE on the *Brilliant*, ex Broomielaw, Glasgow, 24 Apr 1845; stld Montreal and Ottawa. Civil Engineer, Northern Railway, 1852; Inter-Colonial Railway, 1867; Canadian Pacific Railway, 1871. Inventor of Standard Time and promoter of Pacific Cable. Designed Canada's first postage stamp. Pres of Royal Society of CAN, 1888; LLD, St Andrews, 1884, and other honours. CMG 1877; KCMG 1897. m Ann Jean, d/o Sheriff Hall, Peterborough, ch: 1. Frank A; 2. Hugh; 3. Lily; 4. Minnie; 5. Sandford Hall; 6. Walter. **BNA 1067; SG xv/3 52; MDB 236; DC 26 Sep 1964 and 1 Jan 1968**.

2729 FLEMING, William, b ca 1790. Poss from LKS. To PEI, 1817; moved to Miramichi, Northumberland Co, NB. Petitioned for 150 acres (Lot 66) on south side of the Restigouche River, 9 Feb 1821. Became miller and magistrate. m a d/o John Dickie, qv. **CUC 6; DC 31 May 1980**.

2730 FLEMING, William. To Pictou Co, NS, on the *Lulan*, ex Glasgow, 17 Aug 1848. Wife Elizabeth with him, ch: 1. Alexander; 2. Janet; 3. Hugh; 4. Elizabeth. **DC 12 Jul 1979**.

2731 FLETCHER, Rev Alexander, 1791–1836. From Is Skye, INV. To Pictou, NS, 1816; later to Martintown, Glengarry Co, ONT. Teacher, but ord min of Martintown, 1819. Min of Williamstown, 1822-24, and d at Plantagenet. **SDG 121; FES vii 633**.

2732 FLETCHER, Andrew, Poss from PER. To Aldborough Twp, Elgin Co, ONT, prob 1818. Farmer. **PDA 93**.

2733 FLETCHER, Archibald, ca 1788–1831. From Glenorchy, ARL. To Montreal, QUE, 1823. ch incl: 1. John, qv; 2. Mrs George Winks. **SGC 439**.

2734 FLETCHER, Archibald. From Caolasraide, South Knapdale, ARL. To Caradoc Twp, Middlesex Co, ONT, 1842. ch: 1. Archie; 2. Neil; 3. Dugald; 4. Duncan; 5. Nancy; 6. Mary; 7. Margaret; 8. Jennie. **PCM 35**.

2735 FLETCHER, Elizabeth. From Callander, PER. To QUE, Jul 1815, ex Greenock; stld ONT. Wife of Malcolm McVean, qv. **SEC 1**.

2736 FLETCHER, Hugh. From Appin, ARL. To Ekfrid Twp, Middlesex Co, ONT, 1849. ch. **PCM 31**.

2737 FLETCHER, John, b 23 May 1815, Greenock, RFW. s/o Archibald F, qv. To Montreal, QUE, 1823. Served in Montreal Light Infantry, 1837-39, as a sergeant, and later became chief of Fire Brigade. Officer of Militia, 1847; afterwards of 100th Regt. Awarded CMG. **SGC 440**.

2738 FLETT, John. From OKI. To Hudson Bay and Red River <1815. Pioneer settler. **LSS 193; LSC 193**.

2739 FLINN, John. Prob from Glasgow. To QUE on the *Brock*, ex Greenock, Jul 1820; stld Lanark Co, ONT. **HCL 238**.

2740 FLOOD, John, b ca 1781. From Anderston, Glasgow. To QUE on the *Atlas*, ex Greenock, 11 Jul 1815; stld Lot 23, Con 7, Bathurst Twp, Lanark Co, ONT. Weaver, later farmer. Wife Janet McKechnie, qv, with him, and ch: 1. James, b ca 1800; 2. John, b ca 1812. **SEC 1; HCL 16, 231-2**.

2741 FOLEY, John. To Pictou, NS, on the *London*, arr 11 Apr 1848. Wife Elizabeth with him. **DC 15 Jul 1979**.

2742 FOOTE, David, 27 Jun 1823–10 Oct 1891. From Millhaugh, Kettins par, ANS. To QUE, 1842, and after working on the Rideau Canal stld Fergus, Garafraxa Twp, Wellington Co, ONT. Builder and farmer. m Barbara Smart, d 1880, ch: 1. Mrs. Sharpe; 2. Annie, teacher; 3. Mrs Henry Wissler; 4. Mrs J.D. Maitland; 5. Bella; 6. Mary, teacher; 7. James, drowned on the Columbia River, 1885; 8. David. **EHE 130**.

2743 FOOTE, George. From Millhaugh, Kettins, ANS. s/o David F. To NS, 1818; stld prob Pictou Co. **DC 1 Aug 1982**.

2744 FOOTE, John. Poss from Kettins par, ANS. Served as a corporal in 82nd Regt and was gr land in Pictou Co, NS, 1784. **HPC App F; DC 1 Aug 1982**.

2745 FOOTE, Robert, b 12 Mar 1761. From Aberdeen. To Halifax, NS, 1780. Soldier, later farmer at Lower Horton, Kings Co. m Elizabeth Kinnie, b 1761, ch: 1. Margaret, b 3 Dec 1786; 2. Elizabeth, b 10 Sep 1788; 3. Robert, b 15 Sep 1790; 4. Ruth, b 25 Oct 1792; 5. John, b 25 Feb 1795; 6. Caleb, b 13 Nov 1796; 7. Nancy, b 10 Nov 1798; 8. Lucy, b 3 Dec 1799; 9. Mary Ann, b 21 May 1802; 10. William, b Mar 1804; 11. Jeremiah, b 16 Mar 1806. **NSN 12/2; DC 1 Aug 1982**.

2746 FORBES, Alexander, ca 1755–1848. From ROC. Served in 38th Regt and was discharged at New York, 1783; stld Shelburne Co, NS, and gr land. m 1790, Phoebe Dennis, ch. **DC 16 Nov 1981**.

2747 FORBES, Alexander. Poss from PER. To Aldborough Twp, Elgin Co, ONT, poss 1818. Farmer, and in 1820, assessor. **PDA 92**.

2748 FORBES, Alexander, ca 1793–30 Mar 1851.

From STI. s/o Maj Arthur F, North Carolina Highlanders, and Jessie Campbell. To Kingston, ONT. Sometimes Maj, 79th Highlanders. **Ts Stirling**.

2749 FORBES, Rev Alexander, ca 1807–30 Oct 1881. From Monymusk, ABD. s/o Rev Robert F, par min, and Rachel Copland. To Inverness Twp, QUE. Teacher and clergyman. d at Waterton, ONT. **FES vi 177**.

2750 FORBES, Rev Alexander, b ca 1820. From Old Machar, ABD. s/o Alexander F. Grad MA Kings Coll, Aberdeen, 1840. Missionary to NB, 1854, and became min of St Johns, Dalhousie, 1855. Trans to Inverness, ONT, 1859, and ret <1875. **FES vii 634**.

2751 FORBES, Annie, ca 1790–24 Feb 1885. Prob from Moy, INV. d/o — F. and — Mackenzie. To London Twp, Middlesex Co, ONT. **PCM 50**.

2752 FORBES, Cecilia, 1770–1867. From PER, poss Logierait. sis/o Donald F, qv. To Halifax, NS, 1817; stld NB, later Ancaster Twp, Wentworth Co, ONT. Spinster. **DC 11 Dec 1981**.

2753 FORBES, Charles. From Kilmorack, INV. To Pictou, NS, on the *Dove*, ex Fort William, Jun 1801. Labourer. **PLD**.

2754 FORBES, Daniel, ca 1789–11 Jun 1877. From Dull par, PER. bro/o Margaret F, qv, PEI. To QUE ca 1811; later to Waddington, Lawrence Co, NY. Farmer. m (i) Janet Kennedy, qv, ch: 1. Christiana, b 7 Feb 1812; 2. Elizabeth, d inf 1814; 3. Elizabeth, b 6 Dec 1815; 4. Jane, b 7 Jun 1818; 5. Margaret Maria, b 28 Jul 1820; 6. Daniel, b 12 Dec 1822; 7. Alexander Duncan, b 21 Dec 1824; 8. William Wallace, b 9 Feb 1827; 9. Lucretia Myers, b 11 Jul 1829. m (ii) Margaret Davidson. **LDW 7 Dec 1974**.

2755 FORBES, Daniel, ca 1787–29 Apr 1855. From Perth. To Esquesing Twp, Halton Co, ONT, prob <1845. Wife Christy, ca 1792–1850. **EPE 74**.

2756 FORBES, Daniel, 1820-82. From PER, poss Logierait. To ONT prob <1856; d Caledonia, Haldimand Co. m Catherine, 1826-97, and had, poss with other ch: 1. James, 1856–1918; 2. Charles, 1860–1924; 3. Frederick, 1865–1898. **DC 11 Dec 1981**.

2757 FORBES, Donald, b ca 1790. From Foss, PER. To Charlottetown, PEI, on the *Clarendon*, ex Oban, 6 Aug 1808. Labourer. **CPL**.

2758 FORBES, Donald, 1794–1861. From PER, poss Logierait. bro/o Cecilia F, qv. To Halifax, NS, 1817; stld NB, but went later to Ancaster Twp, Wentworth Co, ONT. Son Robert, 1818-91, teacher. **DC 11 Dec 1981**.

2759 FORBES, Duncan, ca 1807–2 Sep 1882. Prob from Moy, INV. s/o — F. and — Mackenzie. To London Twp, Middlesex Co, ONT, 1830. Wife Elizabeth, 1815-91. **PCM 50**.

2760 FORBES, George, b 26 Dec 1825. From Logie Coldstone, ABD. s/o Charles F. and Jane Farquharson. To Toronto, 1845; stld later Plympton Twp, Lambton Co. m Mary O, d/o John Thain, d 1844, and Mary Ann Oxenham. **DC 4 Oct 1979**.

2761 FORBES, Harry, b 8 Oct 1836. From Logie Coldstone, ABD. Poss rel to George F, qv. To Tilbury Twp, Essex Co, ONT. Agriculturalist. **DC 4 Oct 1979**.

2762 FORBES, James. From Kilmorack, INV. To Pictou, NS, on the *Dove*, ex Fort William, Jun 1801. Labourer. **PLD**.

2763 FORBES, Isobel, b 23 Mar 1813. From Monymusk, ABD. d/o Rev Robert F, par min, and Rachel Copland. To QUE. Unm. **FES vi 177**.

2764 FORBES, Jane Inglis, 1807-85. From ABD. To Bon Accord, Nichol Twp, Wellington Co, ONT, 1835. Wife of William Tytler, qv. **EHE 93**.

2765 FORBES, John. From Urquhart and Glenmoriston par, INV. To Pictou, NS, <1 Apr 1797, when he was at east branch of East River. ch. **HPC App H**.

2766 FORBES, John. From Kilmorack, INV. To Pictou, NS, on the *Dove*, ex Fort William, Jun 1801. Labourer. **PLD**.

2767 FORBES, John. From ROC. To East Williams Twp, Middlesex Co, ONT, 1831. **PCM 43**.

2768 FORBES, John, 1802-86. From Aberdeen. To QUE, but stld Sydney, Cape Breton Co, NS, <1853. Schoolmaster, postmaster and magistrate. m Jennet Yeoman, qv. Son John, b 1854. **HNS iii 243**.

2769 FORBES, Margaret, b ca 1786. From Dull par, PER. To Charlottetown, PEI, on the *Clarendon*, ex Oban, 6 Aug 1808. Wife of Duncan Kennedy, qv. **DC 11 Apr 1981**.

2770 FORBES, Margaret, 6 Feb 1793–29 Jan 1890. From Eastwood par, RFW. d/o John and Janet F. To Dalhousie Twp, Lanark Co, ONT, 1821. m 2 Jun 1815, James Machan, qv. **DC 2 Nov 1979**.

2771 FORBES, Margaret, b ca 1796. From Foss, PER. To Charlottetown, PEI, on the *Clarendon*, ex Oban, 6 Aug 1808. Wife of Duncan Kennedy, qv. **CPL; NSN 27/193**.

2772 FORBES, Margaret, b 23 Mar 1806. From Monymusk, ABD. d/o Rev Robert F, par min, and Rachel Copland. To QUE. **FES vi 177**.

2773 FORBES, Mary. From INV. Niece of Donald McDonald, qv, Middle River. To Pictou on the *Hector*, ex Loch Broom, arr 17 Sep 1773. m William McLeod, McLellans Brook. **HPC App C**.

2774 FORBES, Mary, 1803–17 Aug 1880. From Logie, Fetteresso, KCD. To Osprey Twp, Grey Co, ONT, 1854. Wife of John Hendry, qv. **DC 8 Nov 1981**.

2775 FORBES, Sophia Horn, d 20 Nov 1858. From Edinburgh. d/o Alexander F. and Catherine Marshall Munro. To Montreal, QUE. m James Grant. **Ts St Cuthberts**.

2776 FORBES, William, d 4 Mar 1838. From Kilmorack, INV. To Pictou Co, NS, 1801. Bur Salt Springs. **DC 27 Oct 1979**.

2777 FORBES, Rev William G, ca 1801–20 Sep 1886. From North Ronaldsay, OKI. To Halifax, NS, 1847. Schoolteacher, but studied theology and became FC min at Port Hastings, River Inhabitants and River Denys, in Cape Breton Is, 1851. Resigned 1881. Son Henry. **DC 11 Apr 1981**.

2778 FORBES, Williamina. From ROX. To Inverness Twp, Megantic Co, QUE, ca 1835. Wife of Alexander Melrose. **DC 11 Feb 1980**.

2779 FORD, John. Prob from PER and rel to Thomas F, qv. To Aldborough Twp, Elgin Co, ONT, poss 1814. Pioneer settler. **PDA 92**.

2780 FORD, Thomas. Prob from PER and rel to John F, qv. To Aldborough Twp, Elgin Co, ONT, poss 1814; stld Lot B, Con 12. Pioneer settler. **PDA 24, 92**.

2781 FORDYCE, Alexander Dingwall, 7 Feb 1786– 23 Feb 1852. From Aberdeen. s/o Arthur Dingwall F, advocate, and Janet Morison. To 'Lescraigie,' Nichol Twp, Wellington Co, ONT, 1836. Alumnus, Marischall Coll, Aberdeen, 1800. Merchant, farmer and Warden of Wellington. m Magdalene Dingwall, qv, ch: 1. Arthur, 1814-45, merchant in Calcutta, India; 2. Elizabeth; 3. Janet Dingwall, qv; 4. Alexander Dingwall, b London, ENG, but also emig to Wellington Co and was the family historian; 5. William, 1820-21; 6. Charlotte, 1822-23; 7. Agnes, 1824-30; 8. Magdalene Dingwall, qv; 9. James Morison, 1828-47; 10. Mary Arbuthnott, qv. **NDF 117; FAM ii 383; SAA 186; SNQ viii/1 120**.

2782 FORDYCE, Janet Dingwall, 18 Jan 1819–1 Oct 1840. Born Pulmore, Aberdeen. d/o Alexander Dingwall F, qv, and Magdalene Dingwall, qv. To Nichol Twp, Wellington Co, ONT, 1836. m Alexander Drysdale, qv. **NDF 74, 133**.

2783 FORDYCE, Magdalene Dingwall, 17 Jun 1826–13 Sep 1872. From Aberdeen. d/o Alexander Dingwall F, qv, and Magdalene Dingwall, qv. To Wellington Co, ONT, 1836. m 22 Mar 1850, Alexander David Ferrier, qv. **NDF 136**.

2784 FORDYCE, Mary Arbuthnott, 1 Apr 1831–31 Jan 1884. Born Millburn Cottage, Aberdeen. d/o Alexander Dingwall F, qv, and Magdalene Dingwall, qv. To Nichol Twp, Wellington Co, ONT, 1836. m 31 May 1850, Alexander Shirrefs Cadenhead, qv, and d at Fergus. **NDF 136**.

2785 FOREST, Robert. From LKS. To QUE on the *Prompt*, ex Greenock, 4 Jul 1820; stld Dalhousie Twp, Lanark Co, ONT. **HCL 68**.

2786 FORESTER, James, ca 1792–23 Mar 1859. From DFS. To Halifax, NS, where he was emp with HM Ordnance Office. Ret to SCT and d Kingholm Cottage, DFS. **DGH 1 Apr 1853**.

2787 FORESTER, Robert. From Glasgow. To Montreal, QUE, prob <1854. Wholesale grocer, sometime in partnership with Archibald Moir, qv. **SGC 573**.

2788 FORGIE, Gilbert, To QUE on the *Commerce*, ex Greenock, Jun 1820; stld prob Lanark Co, ONT. **HCL 239**.

2789 FORGUE, Jane. From Govan, Glasgow. To Kingston, ONT, <1829. Wife of William Lyall, qv. **DC 7 Jun 1980**.

2790 FORREST, Alexander. To New Glasgow, Pictou Co, NS, <1842. Physician. Son Rev John, b 1842, pastor of St Johns Ch, Halifax, 1866-81. **HNS iii 36**.

2791 FORREST, George, ca 1818–1 Sep 1866. To PEI and d at Southport. **DGH 28 Sep 1866**.

2792 FORREST, Isobella. From Hamilton, LKS. To QUE on the *Commerce*, ex Greenock, Apr 1821; stld Dalhousie Twp, Lanark Co, ONT. Wife of Robert C. Chalmers, qv. **DC 12 Jul 1979**.

2793 FORREST, James S. From Annan, DFS. To Hamilton, ONT, <1854. Grocer, in partnership with son-in-law Robert Pool. **CAE 3**.

2794 FORREST, Rev Robert, ca 1768–17 Mar 1846. From Dunbar, ELN. Educ Univ of Edinburgh and Associated Burgher Theological Hall. Burgher min at Saltcoats, AYR, 1798–1802. To Montreal, via NY, and min there 1804. Trans to Pearl Street Ch, NY, and was later in Stamford, DE. **SGC 169; UPC ii 309; FES vii 634**.

2795 FORREST, William John, ca 1828–9 Sep 1873. From Annan, DFS. s/o John F. in Longmeadow. To ONT; stld Kamouraska and d Ottawa. Civil Engineer. **Ts Annan**.

FORRESTER. See also FORESTER.

2796 FORRESTER, Rev Alexander, 1805–20 Apr 1869. From Kirkliston par, WLN. s/o John F. Educ Univ of Edinburgh and ord 1835. Joined FC 1843. Min of Paisley Middle par, RFW, and called to Chalmers Ch, Halifax, NS, 1848. Noted teacher; DD, Princeton, 1859. d at NY. m 1841, Margaret Tweeddale Davidson, qv, ch: 1. Isabella Margaret Monteith, b 20 Sep 1842; 2. Mary, b 27 Feb 1847; 3. Jessie Louisa, d 1908; 4. Alexander, dy; 5. John Charles Dalrymple Hay, dy. **FES ii 377; AFC i 159; MDB 239**.

2797 FORRESTER, Charles, 1775–21 Jan 1871. From Lockerbie, DFS. To Fergus, Wellington Co, ONT, 1851. Son Andrew. **CAE 24**.

2798 FORSYTH, Alexander. Prob from ABD. Matric Marischall Coll, Aberdeen, 1811. To Halifax, NS, <1817, when awarded Hon MA by Kings Coll, Aberdeen. **FAM ii 412; KCG 276**.

2799 FORSYTH, Alexander, b 8 Nov 1825. To CAN <1850. m Anna Shackleton, qv, ch: 1. Janet, b 12 Oct 1844; 2. Isabella, b 12 Apr 1846; 3. Thomas, b 9 Jul 1847. **SG xxvii/2 84**.

2800 FORSYTH, George, 1755–1806. From Huntly, ABD. s/o William F. and Jean Phyn. To Niagara, Lincoln Co, ONT, prob <1800. Merchant. m Miss Tenbroeck. Dau Mary Ann, res Brechin, Angus, SCT, and d unm. **MDB 240**.

2801 FORSYTH, George, b ca 1793. To ONT prob <1830; stld Peterborough Co. **DC 8 Nov 1981**.

2802 FORSYTH, James, 1759–1843. From Huntly, ABD. s/o William F. and Jean Phyn. To Niagara, Lincoln Co, ONT, <1800, but afterwards went to London, ENG, and was in the service of Lloyds. **MDB 240**.

2803 FORSYTH, James. To QUE on the *Commerce*, ex Greenock, Jun 1820; stld prob Lanark Co, ONT. **HCL 239**.

2804 FORSYTH, John, 1762–29 Dec 1837. From Huntly, ABD. s/o William F. and Jean Phyn. To Montreal, QUE, 1779. Head of the firm of Forsyth, Richardson & Co. MLC 1827. m Margaret, d/o Charles Grant, fur-trader, qv, ch: 1. William; 2. John Blackwood; 3. Jane Prescott. **SGC 85; MDB 240**.

2805 FORSYTH, John, ca 1789–17 Sep 1814. To Halifax, NS, 1813. **DC 14 May 1982**.

2806 FORSYTH, Joseph, 1764–1813. From Huntly, ABD. s/o William F. and Jean Phyn. To QUE <1784, and

stld Kingston, ONT. Merchant. m (i) Miss Bell, ch;
(ii) Alicia, d/o James Robins, with further ch. Son William
matric Marischall Coll, Aberdeen, 1811. **MDB 240;
FAM ii 412**.

2807 FORSYTH, Margaret, 6 Sep 1827–4 Jun 1886.
Prob from LKS. d/o Menan F, qv, and Alison Meikle, qv.
To Dummer Twp, Peterborough Co, ONT, <1833.
m William Moore, ch. **DC 8 Nov 1981**.

2808 FORSYTH, Mary, ca 1790–13 Jul 1876. From
BEW. To ONT poss <1830; stld Peterborough Co. Wife
of James McFee, qv. **DC 8 Nov 1981**.

2809 FORSYTH, Menan, 15 Jul 1795–4 Sep 1876.
Prob from LKS. To Dummer Twp, Peterborough Co, ONT,
<1830. Farmer. m Alison Meikle, qv, ch: 1. John,
1819-99, unm; 2. Elizabeth, b 1824, dy; 3. Margaret, qv;
4. David, 1833–1913; 5. Alison, 1840–1927; 6. Janet,
1842–1911; 7. George Alexander, b 1842. **DC 8 Nov
1981**.

2810 FORSYTH, Thomas, 1761–19 Mar 1832. From
Huntly, ABD. s/o William F. and Jean Phyn. To Montreal,
QUE, prob <1784. Partner, Forsyth, Richardson & Co.
d unm. **SGC 85; MDB 240; Ts Huntly**.

2811 FORSYTH, William, b 1737. To Sherbrooke,
QUE. Parks superintendent and horticulturalist.
MGC 2 Aug 1979.

2812 FOSTER, John, 6 Nov 1811–22 Apr 1893. To
Charlottetown, PEI, ca 1839. Ret army officer. m Sarah
McEachern, qv, ch: 1. Elizabeth, b Leith, 3 Mar 1832,
dy; 2. Louisa, b 10 May 1834; 3. Maria Elizabeth,
b 13 Jul 1835; 4. Jane, b 6 Mar 1837; 5. Sarah,
b 29 Jun 1838, dy; 6. John A, b 5 Mar 1840;
7. Sarah, b NB, 16 Dec 1841; 8. Allan, b 10 Apr 1844;
9. Anne, b 24 Dec 1845; 10. Janet, b 26 Aug 1847;
11. Elizabeth, b 28 Jun 1849. **SCN**.

2813 FOSTER, Robert, b 1821. To ONT ca 1847;
moved to WI, ca 1858. By wife Lilly ch: 1. William,
b 1844; 2. James, b 1849, CAN; 3. John R, b 1851;
4. Martha, b 1854; 5. Robert, b 1857; 6. Lilly, b WI;
7. Sarah, b 1861; 8. Catherine, b 1864. **DC 21 Mar
1981**.

2814 FOULIS, George, 14 Oct 1828–31 Jan 1905.
From Papa Westray, OKI. s/o George F. and Jane Leslie.
To Yarmouth Co, NS, spring 1852. Wife Barbara McKay,
qv, with him. ch. **DC 4 May 1979**.

2815 FOULIS, Thomas. From Papa Westray, OKI.
Uncle of George F, qv. To Yarmouth Co, NS, <1839. Sea
captain. m (i) Sara Main, d 1854, d/o Thomas Goudey
and Elizabeth Harris, ch: 1. Elizabeth J; 2. Sarah K;
3. Jessie, b 7 Oct 1846. m (ii) Martha Alice, d/o David
Rose. **DC 4 May 1979**.

2816 FOWLER, John. Served in 82nd Regt and was gr
land in Pictou Co, NS, 1784. **HPC App F**.

2817 FOWLIE, Colin M, ca 1839–29 May 1893. From
Old Deer, ABD. To QUE and stld Melbourne, Sherbrooke
Co. m Helen McKenzie. Both bur Maple Grove.
MGC 2 Aug 1979.

2818 FOWLIE, George, 15 Sep 1793–2 Dec 1843.
From ABD. To Northumberland Co, NB, 1816; stld Little
Miramichi River. Farmer, carpenter and millwright.
m 13 Aug 1828, Jane, 1809-98, d/o Samuel McKnight,
ch: 1. James, 1828–1923; 2. George, 1831-99;

3. Robert, b 1832; 4. Elizabeth Halliday, 1834–1911;
5. Samuel, 1836-75; 6. Alexander, b 1838; 7. Isabella,
b 1840; 8. Mary, 1841–1937; 9. Francis, 1843–1912.
DC 2 May 1981.

2819 FOYER, Janet, 1787–1874. To Fergus, ONT,
<1849. Wife of David Galbraith, qv. **DC 9 Mar 1980**.

2820 FRANCE, Margaret, 1833–1914. From
Cockburnspath, BEW. d/o Richard F. in Ninewells Mill,
and Isabella Wilson. To ONT prob <1855; stld Brant Co.
m Robert Eadie, qv. **DC 8 Sep 1979**.

2821 FRANCE, Robert, ca 1826–25 Feb 1862. From
Cockburnspath, BEW. s/o Richard F. in Ninewells Mill,
and Isabella Wilson. To Fenelon Falls, Victoria Co, ONT,
prob <1858. **Ts Cockburnspath**.

2822 FRANCIS, William. To QUE on the *Commerce*,
ex Greenock, Jun 1820; stld prob Lanark Co, ONT.
HCL 239.

2823 FRASER, Alexander, b ca 1732. From Beauly,
INV. Said to have been rel to the Lovat Frasers. To
Pictou, NS, on the *Hector*, ex Loch Broom, arr 17 Sep
1773; stld Middle River, Pictou Co. m Marion Campbell,
qv, ch: 1. Alexander, jr, qv; 2. Simon, qv; 3. Katherine,
qv; 4. Isabella, qv; 5. Hugh, qv; 6. David; 7. William.
HPC App A and C.

2824 FRASER, Alexander, jr. From Beauly, INV.
s/o Alexander F, qv, and Marion Campbell, qv. To Pictou,
NS, on the *Hector*, ex Lochbroom, arr 17 Sep 1773; stld
Middle River, Pictou Co. Farmer. **HPC A and C**.

2825 FRASER, Alexander, ca 1730–1790. From
Kirkhill, Kilmorack, INV. s/o Andrew F. To Halifax, NS, on
the brig *John*, arr 4 Jun 1784; stld McLellans Brook,
Pictou Co. Farmer. Wife prob d Kirkhill. ch: 1. Alexander,
jr; 2. Peter, qv; 3. Ann, qv; 4. Catherine, qv; 5. Isabella,
qv; 6. Mary, qv. **CP 33; HPC App 1; SG iii/4 98**.

2826 FRASER, Alexander. Poss from INV. To
Montreal, QUE, <1791. Prob served in 78th Regt.
SGC 111.

2827 FRASER, Alexander. From INV. To Antigonish
Co, NS, prob <1800. m Miss Kell, ch: 1. James;
2. Malcolm; 3. Hugh; 4. John; 5. Donald; 6. Kate;
7. Sarah. **HCA 134**.

2828 FRASER, Alexander, ca 1800–11 Jan 1846. From
Kiltarlity, INV. Poss s/o John F, qv. To Pictou Co, NS,
1801. Bur Hill Cemetery, West River Station. m Mary
Gordon, qv. **DC 10 Feb 1976**.

2829 FRASER, Alexander. To Pictou, NS, on the
Sarah, ex Fort William, Jun 1801. Tacksman. Wife
Medley with him, and ch: 1. Mary, aged 12; 2. Elizabeth,
aged 6; 3. Margaret, aged 3. **PLS**.

2830 FRASER, Alexander. From Kiltarlity, INV. To
Pictou, NS, on the *Dove*, ex Fort William, Jun 1801.
Labourer. Wife with him, and s Robert, aged 12. **PLD**.

2831 FRASER, Alexander. From Kilmorack, INV. To
Pictou, NS, on the *Dove*, ex Fort William, Jun 1801.
Farmer. Wife Margaret with him, and ch: 1. Mary, aged
14; 2. Margaret, aged 9; 3. Janet, aged 7; 4. Alexander,
aged 5; 5. Robert, aged 3. **PLD**.

2832 FRASER, Alexander. From Kirkhill, INV. To
Pictou, NS, on the *Dove*, ex Fort William, Jun 1801.
Labourer. **PLD**.

2833　FRASER, Alexander. From INV. To Pictou Co, NS, ca 1801; stld McLellans Brook. Son Hector, qv. **HNS iii 417**.

2834　FRASER, Alexander. From Fort Augustus, INV. To Montreal, QUE, ex Fort William, 3 Jul 1802; stld E. ONT. Wife and 2 ch with him. **MCM 1/4 25**.

2835　FRASER, Alexander. Prob from INV. To Pictou Co, NS, <1810; stld Big Brook. Farmer. ch: 1. Hugh A; 2. James. **PAC 11**.

2836　FRASER, Alexander, 1776–1853. From Fort Augustus, INV. To Charlottenburg, Glengarry Co, ONT, <1812. Farmer; Quartermaster of Canadian Fencible Regt, 1812; MLA, 1828-34; Warden of Stormont, Dundas and Glengarry, and Registrar. m Ann, 1797–1861, d/o Archibald Macdonell of Leek, ch: 1. Archibald; 2. Ann; 3. Catherine; 4. Isabella; 5. Mary. **SGD 154; MDB 245**.

2837　FRASER, Alexander, b 1815. From Glen Convinth, Kiltarlity, INV. s/o James F, qv, and Ann Cummin, qv. To Pictou, NS, on the *Diligence*, 1820; went later to London Twp, Middlesex Co, ONT, and stld Lot 34, Con 20, East Williams Twp. Farmer. Sold out to James McFarlane, 1844, and went then to Vancouver, BC. **DC 11 Mar 1979**.

2838　FRASER, Alexander, 1792–1864. From Strathdores, INV. s/o James F. To Dundee, Glengarry Co, ONT. m Nancy Fraser, ch: 1. James Grant, b 1816; 2. John; 3. Alexander; 4. Peter; 5. William; 6. Nancy, b 1833; 7. Margaret, b 1835; 8. Robert, b 1837. **DC 4 Mar 1965**.

2839　FRASER, Alexander. From INV. To Pictou, NS, prob <1830; stld later Antigonish Co. m Miss MacInnes, who m (ii) — Dunbar. ch: 1. Malcolm; 2. Alexander 'Og'; 3. John 'Ruadh'; 4. Elizabeth; 5. Ann. **HCA 137**.

2840　FRASER, Alexander. From Dornoch, SUT. To Lobo Twp, Middlesex Co, ONT, ca 1832. ch: 1. Hugh; 2. Archibald; 3. Donald; 4. Annie; 5. Mary; 6. Kate; 7. Bella; 8. Margaret. **PCM 40**.

2841　FRASER, Alexander. Prob from ABD. To Bon Accord, Nichol Twp, Wellington Co, ONT, 1837. Wife with him. ch: 1. George, qv; 2. William; 3. Jane; 4. Mary. **EHE 95**.

2842　FRASER, Alexander. Prob from INV. To Antigonish Co, NS, prob <1840. m Sarah Clarke, ch: 1. Sarah; 2. Rachel; 3. Helen; 4. David; 5. James; 6. Simon; 7. Hugh; 8. George; 9. John. **HCA 139**.

2843　FRASER, Alexander, ca 1801–31 Jan 1874. From Boleskine, INV. bro/o Sheriff F, Ottawa. To Ingersoll, Oxford Co, ONT. *The Highlander*, 14 Mar 1874.

2844　FRASER, Rev Alexander, 28 Aug 1804–21 Jun 1883. From Kirkhill, INV. s/o Rev Donald F, par min, and Jean Gordon. Educ Univ of Edinburgh and succ father as min of Kirkhill in 1837. Joined the FC in 1843, and in 1846 visited 'CAN and USA' to aid Highland settlers in organising congregations. d at Kirkhill, unm. **FES vi 474**.

2845　FRASER, Alexander, 24 Aug 1824–23 Oct 1883. From INV. s/o John F, qv, and Lillias Fraser. To Montreal, QUE, 1843. Mission secretary there. Moved to Cobourg Twp, Northumberland Co, ONT, <1850. m 25 Jun 1850, at Toronto, Mary Mead, d/o Benjamen Torrance, qv, ch:

1. Mary Lillias, b 1851; 2. Selina Elizabeth, 1853-74; 3. John Edward, b 1855; 4. William Torrance, b 1857; 5. Theresa Gordon; 6. Frederick Laing; 7. Amy Millicent; 8. Annabella Jane; 9. Alice Mead; 10. Edith Constance; 11. Madeline Follett; 12. Stuart Alexander. **SGC 480; DC 18 Jul 1979**.

2846　FRASER, Alexander Roderick, 1804-84. From Glenelg, INV. s/o John F, qv, and Margaret McRae, qv. To QUE on the *Eliza*, ex Greenock, 3 Aug 1815; stld Hawkesbury Twp, Prescott Co, ONT, 1816. m Janet Robertson, qv, ch. **DC 19 Feb 1980**.

2847　FRASER, Alexander R, 1747–1832. From INV. To Pictou Co, NS, 1818; stld West River. m Annabella Munro, qv. Both bur Salt Springs. **DC 27 Oct 1979**.

2848　FRASER, Andrew, 1814–6 Mar 1894. From Glenelg, INV. s/o John F, qv, and Margaret McRae, qv. To QUE on the *Eliza*, ex Greenock, 3 Aug 1815; stld West Hawkesbury Twp, Prescott Co, ONT, 1816. Farmer. m a d/o John Fraser, Lachine, QUE, ch. **DC 19 Feb 1980**.

2849　FRASER, Ann. From Kirkhill, Kilmorack, INV. d/o Alexander F, qv. To Halifax, NS, on the brig *John*, arr 4 Jun 1784; stld McLellans Brook, Pictou Co. m Donald 'Ban' Fraser, McLellans Mountain, ch. **SG iii/4 98**.

2850　FRASER, Ann. From Erchless, INV. Prob rel to Margaret F, qv. To Pictou, NS, on the *Sarah*, ex Fort William, Jun 1801. Spinster. **PLS**.

2851　FRASER, Ann. From Kilmorack, INV. Prob wife or rel of Simon F, labourer, qv. To Pictou, NS, on the *Sarah*, ex Fort William, Jun 1801. Spinster. **PLS**.

2852　FRASER, Annie. From Beauly, INV. d/o Malcolm F. To Pictou Co, NS, 1832. m Alexander MacLeod, qv. **PAC 156**.

2853　FRASER, Archibald, 1806–19 Jan 1846. Poss from INV. s/o James F. and Ann Campbell. To Lanark Co, ONT, <9 Feb 1828, when m Mary, d/o John Halliday, qv, and Margaret Johnston, qv. ch: 1. James, 1828–1910; 2. Margaret, b 1830; 3. Ann, b 1832; 4. John, b 1834; 5. Mary Ann, b 1836; 6. William, b 1839; 7. Janet, b 1842; 8. Archibald, 1845-99. **DC 3 Nov 1982**.

2854　FRASER, Archibald, ca 1815–7 Jul 1893. From Paisley, RFW. To Nine Mile River, Hants Co, NS, prob <1840. **DC 20 Jan 1981**.

2855　FRASER, Barbara, b 1816. From ROC. To CAN, 1841; stld prob PEI. Wife of Malcolm Bruce, qv. **DC 1 Aug 1979**.

2856　FRASER, Catherine. From Kirkhill, Kilmorack, INV. d/o Alexander F, qv. To Halifax, NS, on the brig *John*, arr 4 Jun 1784; stld McLellans Brook, Pictou Co. m John McBain. **CP 33**.

2857　FRASER, Catherine, ca 1792–10 Feb 1870. From Beauly, INV. d/o William F, qv, and Marion McKinnon, qv. To Pictou Co, NS; stld Big Brook, west branch, East River. m James MacIntosh, 1794–1860, McLellans Brook. Son James, 1833–1905. **PAC 61**.

2858　FRASER, Catherine. From Strathglass, INV. To Pictou, NS, on the *Sarah*, ex Fort William, Jun 1801. Spinster. **PLS**.

2859　FRASER, Catherine, ca 1805–18 Oct 1880. From

Dornoch, SUT. To Pictou, NS, 1810. m Hugh McDonald, qv. **DC 10 Feb 1980**.

2860 FRASER, Catherine, b 1806. From Glenelg, INV. d/o John F, qv, and Margaret McRae, qv. To QUE on the *Eliza*, ex Greenock, 3 Aug 1815; stld West Hawkesbury Twp, Prescott Co, ONT, 1816. m Kenneth MacKenzie, Glen Sandfield. **DC 19 Feb 1980**.

2861 FRASER, Catherine. From INV. sis/o Simon F, qv, and of Donald F, qv. To South River, Antigonish Co, NS, <1820. m Donald, s/o John Chisholm. **HCA 136**.

2862 FRASER, Catherine, ca 1823–25 Jun 1865. From Gorbals, Glasgow. d/o John F. and Mary Johnston. To St Catharines, Lincoln Co, ONT, <1854, when she m Hope McNiven, qv. **DC 22 Jun 1968 and 5 Sep 1979**.

2863 FRASER, Charles. Prob from INV. To Pictou, NS, on the *Hector*, ex Glasgow, arr 17 Sep 1773; stld Cornwallis, later Fishers Grant, Pictou Co. Farmer. **HPC App C**.

2864 FRASER, Christian. From INV. To Pictou Co, NS, and stld East Forks, Middle River. Wife of William Cameron, qv. **PAC 36**.

2865 FRASER, Christie, ca 1804–7 Jul 1897. Prob from INV. To Pictou Co, NS, prob <1830. m Donald McIntosh, qv. **DC 10 Feb 1980**.

2866 FRASER, Christina or Christy, ca 1750–23 May 1826. From INV. sis/o James 'Mor' F, qv. To Pictou, NS, on the *Hector*, ex Loch Broom, arr 17 Sep 1773. Wife of Donald McKay, qv, pioneer settler, East River. **HPC App A; SG iii/4 96**.

2867 FRASER, Colin, *alias* Duncan. From OKI. To CAN <1828. Personal piper to Sir George Simpson, qv. **LDW 15 Feb 1968**.

2868 FRASER, Daniel. To Restigouche Co, NB, <1830; stld Matapedia. Landowner, farmer, fish and timber merchant, with over 100 employees. Warden, Bonaventure Co. **SR 21**.

2869 FRASER, Daniel. To QUE <1826. Merchant tailor. m Elizabeth Mitchell, qv. **SH**.

2870 FRASER, Donald, 1768–1821. From Kiltarlity, INV. Prob s/o Hugh F, qv. To Pictou, NS, on the *Hector*, ex Loch Broom, arr 17 Sep 1773. m Margaret Table, 1776–1854. **SG iii/4 9**.

2871 FRASER, Donald. From Ardnafouran, Arisaig, INV. To QUE on the *British Queen*, ex Arisaig, 16 Jun 1790; stld nr Montreal. Blacksmith. Wife and family with him. **QCC 103**.

2872 FRASER, Donald. From Kilmarnock, INV. To Pictou, NS, on the *Dove*, ex Fort William, Jun 1801. Labourer. **PLD**.

2873 FRASER, Donald. From Kilmorack, INV. To Pictou, NS, on the *Dove*, ex Fort William, Jun 1801. Labourer. **PLD**.

2874 FRASER, Donald. Prob from Glengarry, INV. To Montreal, QUE, ex Fort William, 3 Jul 1802; stld E ONT. Wife and child with him. **MCM 1/4 23**.

2875 FRASER, Donald, 1782–1859. Prob from INV. To Pictou, NS, 1803. By wife Elizabeth ch: 1. Hugh; 2. Jane. **PAC 58**.

2876 FRASER, Donald. To Orwell Bay, PEI, on the *Polly*, ex Portree, Is Skye, INV, 7 Aug 1803; stld nr Belfast. m Christene McTavish, qv. Dau Isobell. **HP 36**.

2877 FRASER, Donald, ca 1781–26 Feb 1868. From INV. To Pictou Co, NS, and bur Hill Cemetery, West River Station. **DC 10 Feb 1980**.

2878 FRASER, Donald, ca 1769–26 Aug 1857. From Gairloch, ROC. To Pictou Co, NS, prob <1810. Bur Churchville. Wife Janet, ca 1774–10 Mar 1851, also from Gairloch. **DC 22 Jun 1980**.

2879 FRASER, Donald. From INV. bro/o Simon F, qv. To South River, Antigonish Co, NS, <1820. m Margaret MacGillivray, qv, ch: 1. Alexander, miller; 2. Donald; 3. John. **HCA 136**.

2880 FRASER, Donald, 28 Jan 1812–1888. From Glen Convinth, Kiltarlity, INV. s/o James F, qv, and Ann Cummin, qv. To Pictou, NS, on the *Diligence*, 1820; stld later London Twp, Middlesex Co, ONT. m Isabella Ross, and stld afterwards at Bosanquet Twp, Lambton Co. Farmer and surveyor. **PCM 17; DC 11 Mar 1979**.

2881 FRASER, Donald. Prob from INV. To Westminster Twp, Middlesex Co, ONT, 1833. ch: 1. Malcolm, barrister; 2. James H, barrister. **PCM 55**.

2882 FRASER, Donald, 1804–97. From INV. s/o James F. To ONT. m 20 Feb 1833, Margaret McBain, ch: 1. Duncan, b 1834; 2. James, b 1835; 3. John, b 1839; 4. Anna, b 1841; 5. Mary; 6. Isabella, b 1846; 7. Margaret; 8. William, b 1848; 9. Nancy, b 1853. **DC 4 Mar 1965**.

2883 FRASER, Rev Donald, 15 Jan 1826–13 Feb 1892. From INV. s/o John F, qv, and Lillias Fraser. Grad MA Kings Coll, Aberdeen, 1842, and completed his studies at Knox Coll, Toronto, ONT. Ord Côté Street Ch, Montreal, QUE, 1851. Trans to Inverness High FC, 1859, and adm to Marylebone Presb Ch, London, ENG, 1870. DD, Aberdeen, 1872. m 1853, Theresa Isabella Gordon. **SGC 479; KCG 295; SNQ i/2 169; AFC ii 160; MDB 245**.

2884 FRASER, Donald, 1821–1912. From Knockbain, ROC. To ONT, 1854; stld Scott Twp, York Co, and later Minto Twp, Wellington Co. Farmer. m Elizabeth Ross, qv, ch: 1. James, 1848-51; 2. Margaret C, 1850–1949; 3. Elizabeth, 1856–1958. **RFS 134**.

2885 FRASER, Rev Donald Allan, 24 Nov 1793–7 Feb 1845. From Torosay, Is Mull, ARL. s/o Rev Alexander F, par min, and Isabella McLean. Educ High School and Univ of Edinburgh. To Halifax, NS, 1817, and was min successively at McLellans Mountain and Lunenburg. Adm to St Andrews Ch, NFD, 1842. m Catherine Isabella McLean, qv, ch: 1. Alexander, 1819-59; 2. Hector McLean, 1821–1904; 3. Allan, 1823-59; 4. Isabella McLean, 1824-62; 5. James Oliphant, 1826–1904; 6. James Nutting, 1824-62; 7. Charles Leonard, 1830-72; 8. John McLean, 1831–1908; 9. William, 1833-89; 10. Archibald, 1835-69; 11. Henry McLean. **FES iv 124, vii 659; RAM 6**.

2886 FRASER, Duncan, b 1780. To QUE <1824, when he stld Megantic Co. Discharged soldier. **AMC 135**.

2887 FRASER, Elizabeth, b ca 1784. Prob from Borrobol, Kildonan, SUT. Aunt of Margaret, wife of William S, qv. To Fort Churchill, Hudson Bay, on the

Prince of Wales, ex Stromness, 28 Jun 1813. Went to York Factory, 1814, and thence to Red River.   **LSS 184; RRS 26; LSC 321.**

2888   FRASER, Elizabeth. From Fort Augustus, INV. To QUE, ex Greenock, summer 1815; stld prob Lanark Co, ONT. Wife of John McDonald, qv.   **SEC 8.**

2889   FRASER, Elizabeth. To Pictou Co, NS, <1855; stld Caribou. m Caleb, s/o Noah Priest. Son John, b 1866.   **HNS iii 245.**

2890   FRASER, Ellen, b 1799. From Beauly, INV. d/o William F, qv, and Marion Mackinnon, qv. To Pictou Co, NS, 1801; stld Big Brook, west branch of East River.   **PAC 61.**

2891   FRASER, Ellen, 1806-98. From Glenelg, INV. d/o John F, qv, and Margaret McRae, qv. To QUE on the *Eliza*, ex Greenock, 3 Aug 1815; stld West Hawkesbury Twp, Prescott Co, ONT, 1816. m Donald McPhee.   **DC 19 Feb 1980.**

2892   FRASER, George. Prob from ABD. s/o Alexander F, qv. To Elora, Nichol Twp, Wellington Co, ONT, 1836. m Isabella Mair.   **EHE 92.**

2893   FRASER, Hector. From INV. s/o Alexander F, qv. To Pictou Co, NS, ca 1801; stld McLellans Brook. Moved in 1838 to Sutherlands River. Son James Hector, b ca 1828.   **HNS iii 417.**

2894   FRASER, Helen. From Beauly, INV. To Pictou, NS, on the *Hector*, ex Loch Broom, arr 17 Sep 1773. Wife of Colin McKay, qv.   **HPC App A and C.**

2895   FRASER, H. From Kirkhill, INV. To Pictou, NS, on the *Dove*, ex Fort William, Jun 1801. Dau aged 8 with her.   **PLD.**

2896   FRASER, Hugh. From INV. s/o Alexander F, qv, and Marion Campbell, qv. To Pictou, NS, on the *Hector*, ex Loch Broom, arr 17 Sep 1773; stld Middle River. Farmer.   **HPC App C.**

2897   FRASER, Hugh. From Kiltarlity, INV. To Pictou, NS, on the *Hector*, ex Loch Broom, arr 17 Sep 1773; stld east side of East River, and gr 400 acres, 1783. m Sophia Macpherson, qv. Son Alexander, 1784–1829.   **HPC App A and C; SG iii/4 96.**

2898   FRASER, Hugh, b ca 1741. From Kiltarlity, INV. To Pictou, NS, on the *Hector*, ex Loch Broom, arr 17 Sep 1773; stld McLellans Brook, Pictou Co. Weaver and farmer. Wife Rebecca Patterson, qv, with him, ch: 1. Donald, miller; 2. Mary, qv; 3. Jane, qv. Son 'Squire' John, qv, emig later.   **HPC App C.**

2899   FRASER, Hugh, 1761–1841. From Aird, INV. To Pictou Co, NS, ca 1801; stld West Branch Lake, East River. Farmer and carpenter. ch: 1. Mary; 2. Alexander; 3. Hugh; 4. James, dy; 5. Isabella.   **PAC 11, 80; DC 20 Nov 1976.**

2900   FRASER, Hugh 'Mor', 1780–5 Aug 1872. From Strathglass, INV. Rel to James 'Mor' F, qv, East River. To Pictou Co, NS, <1810; stld McLellans Brook. Moved later to East River St Marys. Farmer. m 1818, Mary, d/o Donald 'Ban' Fraser, and Ann Fraser. Dau Nancy, d 1911.   **CP 35; SG iii/4 96.**

2901   FRASER, Hugh, 1785–1879. From INV. To Pictou Co, NS, <1810; stld nr Big Brook, west branch of East River. m Elspeth McDonald, 1806-79, ch: 1. William,

b 1828; 2. John, b 1829; 3. Jane, b 1831; 4. Alexander, b 1834; 5. Finlay, b 1835, killed in American Civil War; 6. Hugh, 1837–1919; 7. Margaret, 1839-68; 8. Donald, b 1842; 9. David Ross, 1844-73.   **PAC 82.**

2902   FRASER, Hugh. To CAN, 1810, as soldier, Royal Engineers, and served during War of 1812. Gr land nr Ottawa, but moved later to Pembroke Twp, Renfrew Co, ONT. Land surveyor. m Elizabeth Celves. Son Alexander, 1830–1903, b Goulbourn Twp, Carleton Co, financier.   **DC 30 Aug 1977.**

2903   FRASER, Hugh. To Middlesex Co, ONT, <6 Aug 1833, when he m Margaret McGregor, qv.   **PCM 17.**

2904   FRASER, Hugh. From INV. To East Williams Twp, Middlesex Co, ONT, 1832.   **PCM 43.**

2905   FRASER, Hugh 'Mor'. From Petty, INV. To East Williams Twp, Middlesex Co, ONT, 1832.   **PCM 43.**

2906   FRASER, Hugh. To Pictou, NS, on the *Lady Grey*, ex Cromarty, ROC, arr 16 Jul 1841.   **DC 16 Jul 1841.**

2907   FRASER, Hugh, ca 1788–7 Dec 1860. From INV. To Pictou Co, NS, and stld Mount Thom. m Nancy Stuart, qv. Both bur at Salt Springs.   **DC 27 Oct 1979.**

2908   FRASER, Hugh, called Evan, b 1794. From Beauly, INV. s/o William F, qv, and Marion Mackinnon, qv. To Pictou Co, NS, 1801.   **PAC 61.**

2909   FRASER, Hugh, b ca 1771. From Killin, PER. To QUE, ex Greenock, summer 1815; stld ONT. Carpenter. Wife Elizabeth Cameron, qv, with him, and 5 ch.   **SEC 4.**

2910   FRASER, Hugh Graham, 15 Mar 1814–31 Jul 1901. From Edinburgh. s/o John F. and Isabella Munro. To Margaree, Inverness Co, <1846, when he m Ann Mavina, 1821-98, d/o John Crowdis and Sarah Hart. ch: 1. John Andrew, 1848–1912; 2. Annie I, 1850–1934; 3. David Thomas, 1852–1926; 4. Hugh, 1854–1901; 5. James W, 1858–1937; 6. Alfie M, 1860–1937; 7. Lydia Margaret, 1864–1943.   **DC 16 Feb 1962.**

FRASER, Mrs Hugh. See GRANT, Ann.

2911   FRASER, Isabella. From INV. s/o Alexander F, qv, and Marion Campbell, qv. To Pictou, NS, on the *Hector*, ex Loch Broom, arr 17 Sep 1773; stld Middle River. m David McLean, qv, East River.   **HPC App C.**

2912   FRASER, Isabel, 1818-37. From Glen Convinth, Kiltarlity, INV. d/o James F, qv, and Ann Cummin, qv. To Pictou, NS, on the *Diligence*, 1820; moved 1830 to London Twp, Middlesex Co, ONT. Said to have m Andrew Allen.   **DC 11 Mar 1979.**

2913   FRASER, Isabel, 6 May 1827–27 Jan 1900. From Kennowaird, Petty, INV. d/o John F, qv, and Elizabeth Calder, qv. To North Dumfries Twp, Waterloo Co, ONT, 1832. m 1843, Robert Mackenzie, qv.   **DC 5 Dec 1966.**

2914   FRASER, Isabella. From Kirkhill, Kilmorack, INV. d/o Alexander F, qv. To Halifax, NS, on the *John*, arr 4 Jun 1784; stld McLellans Brook, Pictou Co. m Donald MacGregor, qv.   **CP 33.**

2915   FRASER, Isabella, ca 1806–5 Nov 1881. From INV. To Pictou Co, NS, prob <1830. m Kenneth Davidson, qv.   **DC 10 Feb 1980.**

2916   FRASER, James. From INV. Said rel to the Lovat

Frasers. To Halifax, NS, 1780. Merchant and mem of the Executive Council of NS. Son Benjamen, b 1812, physician. **HNS iii 469**.

2917 FRASER, James 'Culloden'. Served in the 84th Regt and after discharge, 1784, was gr 100 acres on west side of the east branch of East River, Pictou Co, NS. m Nancy, d/o John Robertson, qv, ch. **HPC App G**.

2918 FRASER, James 'Mor'. From Aird or Strathglass, INV. To Pictou Co, NS, 1784, and stld east branch of the East River. Discharged soldier, 84th Regt, and gr 350 acres. m Mary, d/o Donald Cameron, qv, East River, ch: 1. Hugh; 2. Margaret; 3. James 'Og'; 4. John; 5. Janet; 6. Donald; 7. Christie; 8. Alexander; 9. Simon. **HPC App C and G; CP 51**.

2919 FRASER, Rev James. Chaplain, 71st Highlanders. Became min of a pioneer Scottish congregation at Shelburne, NS, and did mission work in NB. **FES vii 612**.

2920 FRASER, James. From Kilmorack, INV. To Pictou, NS, on the *Dove*, ex Fort William, Jun 1801. Labourer. **PLD**.

2921 FRASER, James, 7 Mar 1802–8 May 1884. From Boleskine, INV. To Pictou Co, NS, 1804; stld New Glasgow. Merchant, postmaster, militiaman and politician. He was elected chieftain of the Frasers in British North America at a rally in Ottawa, 1867. m 1826, Elizabeth, d/o Rev Peter Gordon, qv, Pictou. **MLA 128; MDB 246**.

2922 FRASER, James, 1785–1868. From INV. To Esquesing Twp, Halton Co, ONT. Pioneer settler, and town clerk of Esquesing. m Jennet Stirrat, ch: 1. John Stirrat; 2. James Oliver; 3. Mary Bowman; 4. David; 5. William; 6. Alexander; 7. Jane; 8. George; 9. Jennet. **DC 21 Apr 1967**.

2923 FRASER, James, d ca 1850. From Speyside, INV. s/o Donald F. and Abigail McPherson. To Cornwallis, Kings Co, NS. Discharged soldier. Son John McPherson, alive 1879. **NSN 40/64**.

2924 FRASER, James. Prob from Glasgow. To Lanark Co, ONT, 1816; stld Lot 18, Con 1, Bathurst Twp. **HCL 16**.

2925 FRASER, James, 18 Jan 1792–30 Apr 1869. From Glen Convinth, INV. s/o Donald F. To Pictou, NS, on the *Diligence*, 1820; stld Pictou Co. Moved 1830 to London Twp, Middlesex Co, ONT. Farmer, teacher and missionary. m (i) Ann Cummin, qv, ch: 1. Donald, qv; 2. Alexander, qv; 3. Isabel, qv; 4. William, b 1822, hotel-keeper, Stratford; 5. Margaret, b 1824; 6. Ann, b 1826; 7. Janet, b 1828; 8. James, jr, b 1830. m (ii) 1832, Margery McBain, qv, further ch: 9. John, b 1833; 10. Christiana, b 1834; 11. Mary, b 1835; 12. Abigail, b 1839; 13. Margery, b 1840. **DC 11 Mar 1979**.

2926 FRASER, James, 1830–ca 1866. From Flemington, Fort George, INV. s/o John F, qv, and Elizabeth Calder, qv. To North Dumfries Twp, Waterloo Co, ONT. Cooper. m Mary Ann McAvoy, ch: 1. Elizabeth, 1857–1942; 2. John; 3. Jean, a nun, d 1919; 4. James. **DC 5 Dec 1966 and 17 Jan 1967**.

2927 FRASER, James, 1816–78. Prob from INV. To

Dundee, Glengarry Co, ONT, 1836. m Harriet Grant, ch: 1. Duncan; 2. Alexander; 3. Annie; 4. Ellen; 5. Jane. **DC 4 Mar 1965**.

2928 FRASER, James, 1789–11 Mar 1857. From Dores par, INV. s/o James F. To Dundee, Glengarry Co, ONT, poss 1836. m Isabella Grant, ch: 1. Nancy; 2. James; 3. Margaret; 4. William, b 1822; 5. Alexander, b 1823; 6. Hugh, b 1827; 7. Isabella, b 1831; 8. John. **DC 4 Mar 1965**.

2929 FRASER, James. From ABD. To Elora, Nichol Twp, Wellington Co, ONT, 1836. Moved later to Milton Twp, Halton Co. **EHE 92**.

2930 FRASER, Rev James, 1800–8 Apr 1874. From Fodderty, ROC. Educ Aberdeen and Edinburgh, and became schoolmaster at Lochinver, SUT. To NS, 1837, as missionary, and was adm min of Boulardarie, Victoria Co. m Jessie Morrison, qv. Son John A, 1840–1909, MLA. **FES vii 607; MLA 129**.

2931 FRASER, James. Prob from INV. To Winchester Twp, Dundas Co, ONT, <1840. **DC 4 Mar 1965**.

2932 FRASER, James. To Eldon Twp, Victoria Co, <1853; stld Lot 22, Con 8. Farmer. Son John. **EC 58**.

2933 FRASER, James, b 26 Nov 1813. From Easter Whitehill, Gamrie, BAN. s/o James F. and Barbara Ross. To Arthur Twp, Wellington Co, ONT, 1854. Wright, contractor and builder. m ca 1836, Barbara Joss, qv, ch: 1. Alexander, b 1837; 2. Barbara, b 1838; 3. Margaret, b 1841; 4. James Wernham, b 1844; 5. Mary Stuart, b 1846; 6. John, b 1848; 7. Bathia, b 1850; 8. Isabella, b 1853, d inf; 9. Isabella; 10. Jean; 11. Janet. **DC 12 Nov 1968**.

2934 FRASER, James, 1826–1908. From Fordyce, BAN. To Hamilton, ONT, 1853; stld Sullivan Twp, later Holland Twp, Grey Co, ONT. Yeoman. m Jean Mitchell, qv, ch: 1. Alexander, b 1851; 2. Janet, b 1853; 3. James, b 1855; 4. John, b 1857; 5. William, b 1859; 6. Mary A, 1870-72. **DC 17 Aug 1982**.

2935 FRASER, Jane. From Kiltarlity, INV. d/o Hugh F, qv. To Pictou, NS, on the *Hector*, ex Loch Broom, arr 17 Sep 1773. m John Fraser, Merigomish. **HPC App C**.

2936 FRASER, Jane. From ROC. To QUE on the *Cleopatra*, 14 Jun 1831; stld ONT. Wife of David Urquhart, qv. **DC 27 Dec 1979**.

2937 FRASER, Jane, 1829-70. From Inverness. d/o John F, qv, and Lillias Fraser. To Montreal, QUE, <1846. m James Torrance. **DC 18 Jul 1979**.

2938 FRASER, Janet. From Strathglass, INV. sis/o John F, qv. To James River, Antigonish Co, NS, prob <1830. m John Chisholm, ch. **HCA 101, 136**.

2939 FRASER, Janet, 31 Jul 1819–21 Oct 1893. From Dingwall, ROC. d/o Donald F, road contractor. To QUE, prob on the *Brilliant*, ex Cromarty, arr 23 May 1842. Wife of Alexander Ross, jr, qv. **RFS, 77, 82, 122**.

2940 FRASER, Jean, 1773–1839. Born Lochbroom par, ROC. d/o Hugh F. and Ann Grant, qv. To Pictou, NS, on the *Hector*, arr 17 Sep 1773. She was the youngest passenger, and lived at Truro, Colchester Co, with her mother. m David Page, silversmith, ch. **DC 19 Nov 1979**.

2941   FRASER, John 'Squire', 1766–30 Jul 1850. Poss s/o Hugh F, INV. To Pictou, NS, on the *Hector*, ex Loch Broom, arr 17 Sep 1773; stld McLellans Brook, Pictou Co. Farmer. m Katherine Fraser, qv, Middle River, ch. **HPC App C; SG iii/4 95**.

2942   FRASER, John, b ca 1750. From AYR. To QUE on the *Friendship*, ex Port Glasgow, 30 Mar 1775. Ship carpenter, 'going out to build vessels.' **LSF**.

2943   FRASER, John, called 'Iain Ruadh.' Prob from Kirkhill, INV. To Halifax, NS, on the *John*, arr 4 Jun 1784; stld Springville, Pictou Co, and gr 300 acres in 1793. Discharged soldier, later farmer. m Catherine, d/o John Robertson, qv, and Margaret McKay, qv, ch: 1. James; 2. Donald; 3. William; 4. Mary; 5. Margaret; 6. Nancy; 7. Jessie; 8. Catherine; 9. Christie. **HPC App H; HNS iii 486; CP 59**.

2944   FRASER, John. Prob from INV. Capt, 82nd Regt, and gr land in Pictou Co, NS. App magistrate, 15 Oct 1784. ch incl: 1. Major Simon; 2. John, collector. **HPC App F**.

2945   FRASER, John. From INV. Served as NCO in 82nd Regt and was gr 200 acres at Fishers Grant, Pictou Co, NS, 1784. Moved to French River, ch. **HPC App F**.

2946   FRASER, John, ca 1765–23 Feb 1842. From Kiltarlity, INV. To Pictou Co, NS, 1801; bur Hill Cemetery, West River Station. **DC 10 Feb 1980**.

2947   FRASER, John, 1796–13 Oct 1887. From Beauly, INV. s/o William F, qv, and Marion Mackinnon, qv. To Pictou, NS, 1801; stld Big Brook, west branch of East River. Farmer. m Ann Cameron, qv, ch: 1. Hugh, 1823–1905; 2. John, b 1824; 3. William, blacksmith; 4. Catherine; 5. Margaret. **PAC 61**.

2948   FRASER, John, ca 1789–30 Apr 1861. From SUT. To Pictou Co, NS, and bur Lansdowne. Wife Christie Sutherland, qv. **DC 10 Feb 1980**.

2949   FRASER, John. From Kiltarlity, INV. To Pictou, NS, on the *Sarah*, ex Fort William, Jun 1801. Farmer. Wife Christian with him, and ch: 1. William; 2. Bell; 3. Ann, aged 3. **PLS**.

2950   FRASER, John. From Kirkhill, INV. To Pictou, NS, on the *Sarah*, ex Fort William, Jun 1801. Labourer. Wife Christian with him, and dau Isobel, aged 2. **PLS**.

2951   FRASER, John, ca 1773–11 Feb 1870. Prob from INV. To Pictou Co, NS, 1802, and bur Salt Springs. Wife Janet d 17 Feb 1870. **DC 27 Oct 1979**.

2952   FRASER, John. From Crasky, Strathglass, INV. To Antigonish Co, NS, ca 1813. m Jean Chisholm, qv, and had with other ch: 1. Rev William, qv; 2. Jean; 3. David; 4. Angus; 5. Simon; 6. John; 7. Colin; 8. Thomas; 9. Austin. **HCA 56, 133**.

2953   FRASER, John. From Strathglass, INV. To South Side Harbour, Antigonish Co, NS, poss <1815. m Miss MacDonald, ch: 1. William, d at sea, ch; 2. Catherine. **HCA 138**.

2954   FRASER, John, b 1772. To Pictou Co, NS, 1815; stld West River, 1816. Weaver, m with 5 ch, and 'very poor.' **INS 38**.

2955   FRASER, John, b 1776. To Pictou Co, NS, 1815. Res Rogers Hill, 1816. Weaver, m with 6 ch. **INS 39**.

2956   FRASER, John, 1783–1862. From Glenelg, INV. To QUE on the *Eliza*, ex Greenock, 3 Aug 1815; stld West Hawkesbury Twp, Prescott Co, ONT, 1816. Tailor and farmer. m Margaret McRae, qv, ch: 1. Alexander Roderick, qv; 2. Catherine, qv; 3. Ellen, qv; 4. Ann, b 1811, unm; 5. Andrew, qv; 6. John; 7. Donald, b Sorel, QUE, 1815; 8. Alexander William, 1818–1900, farmer; 9. William, 1820-52. **SEC 5; DC 21 Jan and 19 Feb 1980**.

2957   FRASER, John, 1796–1875. From Dores par, INV. s/o James F. To Dundee, Glengarry Co, ONT, 1818. m 1824, Isabella, d/o John Seaton, ch: 1. Nancy; 2. Isabella; 3. Mary; 4. James, b 1833; 5. John, b 1835; 6. Donald J, b 1837; 7. William; 8. Alexander, b 1841; 9. Jane, b 1844; 10. Margaret, b 1846; 11. Thomas, b 1852; 12. Elizabeth, b 1855. **DC 4 Mar 1965**.

2958   FRASER, John, 21 Dec 1799–12 Sep 1893. From Fort Augustus, INV. To NS, 1820. Studied law at Fredericton, NB, and went to Miramichi, Northumberland Co. Moved ca 1827 to Bathurst, Gloucester Co. Postmaster at Cross Point, 1846; Collector of Customs, magistrate and officer of militia. m 1837, Elizabeth, d/o Robert Ferguson, qv, ch. **SR 22**.

2959   FRASER, John. From Inverness. To Halifax, NS, ca 1820; stld later at Miramichi, Northumberland Co, NB. Shipbuilder. Son John James, 1829-96, Premier of NB, 1878-82. **BNA 696**.

2960   FRASER, John. bro/o William F, qv. To Leeds Twp, Megantic Co, QUE, <1824. Farmer. **AMC 135**.

2961   FRASER, John, 22 Aug 1795–21 Dec 1852. From Bucht, Kilbhean, Inverness. s/o Alexander F, merchant, and Annabella Munro. To Montreal, QUE, 1837. Emp by the Canada Company and d at London, Middlesex Co, ONT. m (i) Lillias Fraser, Kirkhill, who d 1835, ch: 1. Alexander, qv; 2. Rev Donald, qv; 3. Rev William, qv; 4. Jane, qv; 5. Isabella, 1827-87, d Brighton, ENG; 6. John, 1832-71, d Baghdad; 7. Annabella, d inf. m (ii) 1839, Selina, d/o John Torrance, qv, further ch: 8. David Torrance, 1840–1902; 9. Edward, d 1852; 10. Lillias, 1845-91. **DC 18 Jul 1979 and 29 May 1982**.

2962   FRASER, John, b 17 Nov 1799. From Braes of Dunvormie, Logie Easter, ROC. To North Dumfries Twp, Waterloo Co, ONT. Farmer. m 16 Jun 1826, Elizabeth Calder, qv, ch: 1. Isabel, qv; 2. Margaret, dy; 3. James, qv; 4. John, b 1833; 5. Simon, 1835-60; 6. Alexander, 1837-98; 7. Jane, 1841-64; 8. Malcolm, 1843-64. **DC 14 Sep and 5 Dec 1966**.

2963   FRASER, John, ca 1788–25 Jan 1850. From ROC. To Pictou Co, NS, prob <1830; stld Mount Thom. m Margaret Monroe, qv. **DC 19 Mar 1981**.

2964   FRASER, John. From Strathglass, INV. bro/o Janet F, qv. To James River, Antigonish Co, NS, prob <1830. m Miss Chisholm, ch: 1. Alexander; 2. Rory; 3. Rev James, Georgeville; 4. Dr John, res New York; 5. Donald; 6. William; 7. Ellen; 8. Isabel; 9. Mary; 10. Mrs MacIsaac, Cape George. **HCA 137**.

2965   FRASER, John. From INV. To South River, Antigonish Co, NS, poss <1830. m Miss MacDonald, and had, prob with other ch: 1. William; 2. Archibald. **HCA 134**.

2966   FRASER, John. Prob from INV. To Montreal, QUE, <1844, when he moved to Westminster Twp, Middlesex Co, ONT. Lay preacher. **PCM 55**.

2967   FRASER, John. From INV. To Middlesex Co, ONT, 1849; stld McGillivray Twp.   **PCM 56**.

2968   FRASER, Rev John, ca 1824–5 May 1894. From Grantown-on-Spey, MOR. To Chatham, Kent Co, ONT, <1850, and ord there. Trans to Goderich, Huron Co, 1856. Retr to SCT <1862, and stld Glasgow. **UPC ii 89**.

2969   FRASER, John L. From INV. To Hamilton, ONT, ca 1835; stld St Georges. m Mary Clerk, ch: 1. Col John, farmer in Brantford Twp, Brant Co, and officer of militia; 2. Kate.   **DC 23 Sep 1980**.

2970   FRASER, Katherine, 1766–1823. From Kirkhill, INV. d/o Alexander F, qv, and Margaret Campbell, qv. To Pictou, NS, on the *Hector*, ex Loch Broom, arr 17 Sep 1773. m (i) Alexander Ross; (ii) 'Squire' John Fraser, qv.   **HPC App C; SG iii/4 95**.

2971   FRASER, Kenneth, ca 1737-92. From SUT. To Pictou, NS, on the *Hector*, ex Loch Broom, arr 17 Sep 1773; stld Londonderry, Colchester Co, later Horton, Kings Co. Went back to Pictou and gr land on east side of Middle River, 1783. ch.   **HPC App A and C**.

2972   FRASER, Lydia, 1739–1805. From Bunchrew, Inverness. d/o Donald F, farmer, and Isobel Fraser. To Halifax, NS, prob on the *John*, arr 4 Jun 1784; stld Pictou Co. Wife of Simon Fraser, qv.   **NDF App p lii**.

2973   FRASER, Malcolm, 26 May 1733–14 Jun 1815. Prob from INV. s/o Donald F. and Janet McIntosh. Served with 78th Regt at Louisbourg and Quebec and acquired seigniory of Mount Murray at Malbaie, QUE. Later Capt, Royal Highland Emigrants. m Marie Allaire, ch: 1. Angélique, b ca 1760; 2. Alexander, 1761–1837, fur-trader; 3. Joseph, b ca 1765; 4. Jane.   **MDB 247; DC 17 Apr 1979**.

2974   FRASER, Malcolm. From Beauly, INV. To Pictou Co, NS, 1833; stld Telford, New Glasgow. m (i) Annie Chisholm, ch: 1. Alexander; 2. Elizabeth. m (ii) Catherine Munro, with further ch: 3. Malcolm; 4. Thomas; 5. Mary; 6. Margaret; 7. Annie; 8. James; 9. Sarah; 10. Emily.   **PAC 157**.

2975   FRASER, Malcolm, d ca 1858. Poss from PER. To QUE ca 1853; stld Rimouski East. Farmer. Wife Alice with him. Son Peter, 1846–1940, lumberman, West Effingham, Addington Co, ONT, acted as a guide in the Weslemkoon Lake area.   **DC 12 May 1980**.

2976   FRASER, Margaret. From Kilmorack, INV. To Pictou, NS, on the *Dove*, ex Fort William, Jun 1801. Spinster. **PLD**.

2977   FRASER, Margaret. From Ercless, INV. Prob rel to Ann F, qv. To Pictou, NS, on the *Sarah*, ex Fort William, Jun 1801. Spinster. **PLS**.

2978   FRASER, Margaret, 30 Nov 1787–28 Nov 1864. Prob from INV. To PEI, 1803; stld Vernon River. m 1804, Jeremiah, 1780–1857, s/o Jeremiah Enman and Margaret Benoit, ch.   **HP 87**.

2979   FRASER, Margaret. From SUT. To Ramsay Twp, Lanark Co, ONT, ca 1831. Wife of Angus Sutherland, qv.   **DC 11 Mar 1980**.

2980   FRASER, Mary. From Kiltarlity, INV. d/o Hugh F, qv. To Pictou, NS, on the *Hector*, ex Loch Broom, arr 17 Sep 1773. m — Cameron, Merigomish. **HPC App C**.

2981   FRASER, Mary. From Kilmorack, INV. To Pictou, NS, on the *Dove*, ex Fort William, Jun 1801. A dau with her. **PLD**.

2982   FRASER, Mary. From Glasgow. d/o John F. and Mary Johnston, m at Gorbals, 1818. To Ingersoll, Oxford Co, ONT, <1850.   **DC 22 Jun 1968**.

2983   FRASER, Mary, b ca 1805. From Nairn. d/o John F. and Christie Kennedy. To Glengarry Co, ONT, 1832. Wife of Alexander Grant, qv.   **DC 18 Jul 1963**.

2984   FRASER, Mrs Mary. From Kirkhill, INV. To Pictou, NS, on the *Dove*, ex Fort William, Jun 1801. **PLD**.

2985   FRASER, Nancy or Ann, ca 1777–5 Aug 1859. From Kilmorack, INV. d/o Kenneth F, sometime in Glasgow. To Pictou, NS, <1812. Wife of Hector McLean, qv.   **SG xii/1 26**.

2986   FRASER, Paul, d 1855. From INV. bro/o Alexander F, qv, Glengarry Co, ONT. To CAN, 1819, and entered service of NWCo. After merger of 1821 was a clerk with HBCo. In charge of Athabaska dept, 1825-32, and later of New Caledonia dist. Chief trader, 1843. **MDB 247**.

2987   FRASER, Peter. From Kirkhill, INV. s/o Alexander F, qv, McLellans Brook, Pictou Co, NS. To Halifax, NS, on the brig *John*, arr 4 Jun 1784; stld McLellans Brook. Farmer. m Margaret, d/o Colin Douglas, qv. **SG iii/4 95**.

2988   FRASER, Roderick. From INV. To Antigonish Co, NS, poss <1840. m Janet McArthur, ch: 1. John; 2. Christina; 3. Margaret; 4. Archibald; 5. Alexander; 6. Daniel; 7. Charles; 8. Sarah; 9. Mary; 10. Malcolm; 11. Marie; 12. Isabel; 13. Mary, jr; 14. Mary Margaret. **HCA 134**.

2989   FRASER, Ronald. From Is Eigg, INV. To Arisaig Mountain, Antigonish Co, NS, 1823. m Miss MacIsaac, ch: 1. Malcolm; 2. Donald; 3. Alexander, called Sandy; 4. George; 5. Angus; 6. Mary.   **HCA 135**.

2990   FRASER, Simon. From INV. s/o Alexander F, qv, and Marion Campbell, qv. To Pictou, NS, on the *Hector*, ex Loch Broom, arr 17 Sep 1773; stld Middle River, Pictou Co. Farmer, and gr 500 acres on east side of river, 26 Aug 1783. By wife Jane, who m (ii) William Wright, ch: 1. Alexander; 2. Hugh; 3. Catherine; 4. Robert Marshall; 5. Isabella, res Port Hood; 6. Frances, unm; 7. John, drowned off NFD. **HPC App A and C; DC 23 Feb 1980**.

2991   FRASER, Simon, 1740-87. From Kirkhill, INV. To Halifax, NS, prob on the *John*, arr 4 Jun 1784; stld East River, Pictou Co. Farmer. m Lydia Fraser, qv, and had, poss with other ch: 1. Thomas, d 1802; 2. John, d 1812; 3. Donald, d 1813, unm; 4. William, qv; 5. Mrs Thomas McKenzie.   **HPC App I; NDF App p lii**.

2992   FRASER, Simon, ca 1760–6 May 1839. Prob from Boleskine and Abertarff par, INV. s/o Capt Alexander F. To Montreal, QUE, ca 1789. Fur-trader, and became partner of NWCo, 1795. Ret in 1800 after serving at Grand Portage, and purchased Bellevue, Lake of Two Mountains. d at St Annes, Montreal. Simon m Catherine, d 1846, d/o Donald Mackay, qv.   **MDB 248**.

2993   FRASER, Simon. From Kilmorack, INV. To Pictou, NS, on the *Sarah*, ex Fort William, Jun 1801. Labourer. **PLS**.

2994 FRASER, Simon, b 1792. To Pictou Co, NS, 1815; res Lower Settlement, 1816. Blacksmith. **INS 38**.

2995 FRASER, Simon. From INV. bro/o Donald F, qv. To South River, Antigonish Co, NS, <1820. m Catherine MacDonald, ch: 1. Donald; 2. John; 3. Alexander; 4. Jessie; 5. Kate; 6. Margaret; 7. Mary. **HCA 136**.

2996 FRASER, Simon, ca 1791–9 Sep 1857. From Inverness. To Pictou Co, NS, prob <1825. Bur Churchville. **DC 22 Jun 1980**.

2997 FRASER, Simon, d 30 Aug 1811. To QUE, and d Perth, Lanark Co, ONT. **DGC 17 Sep 1811**.

2998 FRASER, Rev Simon, 1806–6 Sep 1887. From Boleskine and Abertarff par, INV. s/o Simon F, shepherd, and Bessie Fraser. Grad MA Kings Coll, Aberdeen, 1830, and was librarian there until 1834. Ord min of Alnwick and Glenelg, Northumberland Co, NB, 1835. Retr to SCT and was min of Fortrose FC, Black Isle, 1840-67. m Eliza Ross, ch. **KCG 285; AFC i 161; FES vii 9**.

2999 FRASER, Rev Simon Cumming, b ca 1814. Grad MA Kings Coll, Aberdeen, 1835. Ord 1844 and went to QUE. Min at St Charles, Bell Alliance, but joined FC 1845. Min at Port Neuf, QUE, 1846-47; McNab and Horton, ONT, 1849-57; McNab, 1859-68; and at Thorold, 1871-76. Ret 1877. Dau Mrs Alexander Hill. **KCG 290; FES vii 634; AMC 109**.

3000 FRASER, Thomas. From INV. To QUE, ca 1763. Prob discharged soldier. m Elizabeth Cole. Son Augustin. **DC 1 Apr 1981**.

3001 FRASER, Thomas. From Lochbroom, ROC. To Pictou, NS, on the *Hector*, ex Loch Broom, arr 17 Sep 1773. **HPC App C**.

3002 FRASER, Thomas. To Halifax, NS, on the *John*, arr 4 Jun 1784; stld Pictou Co, NS, prob nr New Glasgow. **HPC App I**.

3003 FRASER, Thomas. From Urquhart and Glenmoriston par, INV. Prob served in 82nd Regt. Gr 200 acres at head of west branch of East River, Pictou Co, NS, 1793. **HPC App H**.

3004 FRASER, Rev Thomas, ca 1792–15 Jul 1884. From Kilbarchan, RFW. s/o Thomas F, merchant. Matric Univ of Glasgow, 1809. Relief Ch min at Kings Park, Dalkeith, 1819-26. To Niagara, Lincoln Co, ONT, 1827. Went to USA ca 1829, where he was with the Dutch Reformed Ch. Min in Lanark Co, ONT, 1844-61, when he withdrew from active duty. **GMA 7796; UPC i 561; FES vii 634**.

3005 FRASER, Thomas, 1803-76. To Pictou Co, NS, and stld Elgin. m (i) Miss Blackie, Rogers Hill, ch: 1. John Thomas; 2. William; 3. Mary; 4. Christy; 5. Jane; 6. Christy; 7. James Duncan. m (ii) Mary McPhee, wid/o Daniel McDonald, and had further ch: 8. Angus; 9. Robert; 10. Howard; 11. Jennie; 12. Peter, res CA. **PAC 145**.

3006 FRASER, William. From SUT. To Pictou, NS, on the *Hector*, ex Loch Broom, arr 17 Sep 1773. **HPC App C**.

3007 FRASER, William 'Og'. To Halifax, NS, prob on the *John*, arr 4 Jun 1784; stld nr New Glasgow, Pictou Co. **HPC App I**.

3008 FRASER, William, 1773–1859. From Kirkhill, INV. s/o Simon F, qv, and Lydia F, qv. To Halifax, NS, prob on the *John*, arr 4 Jun 1784; stld East River, Pictou Co. Farmer, and a ch elder for over 50 years. m Mary McGregor, ch: 1. Simon; 2. Donald; 3. James; 4. Lydia; 5. Isobel; 6. Rebecca; 7. Jane; 8. Mary. **NDF App p lii**.

3009 FRASER, William. From Inverness. To Pictou Co, NS, <1 Apr 1797, when gr 350 acres at Big Brook, west branch of East River. ch. **HPC App H**.

3010 FRASER, William. From INV. To Pictou Co, NS, <1800. Surveyor. m Sarah Fraser, qv, ch: 1. William, res McLellans Brook; 2. John 'Collier'; 3. Mrs John Mackay. **HPC App C**.

3011 FRASER, William, jr, b 1797. From Beauly, INV. To Pictou Co, NS, 1801; stld Big Brook, west branch of East River. Gr 320 acres, 1811. Farmer and sawyer. m Jane, d/o Donald Fraser, qv, and wife Elizabeth, ch: 1. Donald, b 1827, shoemaker; 2. Marion, b 1829; 3. Simon, b 1832, went to AUS and was knighted; 4. William, b 1835; 5. Betsy. **PAC 58; DC 20 Nov 1976**.

3012 FRASER, William. From Beauly, INV. Said desc from the Lovat Frasers. To Pictou Co, NS, 1801; stld Big Brook, west branch of East River, and gr 100 acres 1811. m Marion McKinnon, qv, ch: 1. Catherine, qv; 2. Hugh, called Evan, qv; 3. John, qv; 4. William, jr, qv; 5. Ellen, qv; 6. Allan; 7. Alexander; 8. Simon; 9. James. **PAC 61**.

3013 FRASER, William. From Fort Augustus, INV. To Montreal, QUE, ex Fort William, 3 Jul 1802; stld E ONT. Wife and 2 ch with him. **MCM 1/4 25**.

3014 FRASER, William 'Deacon'. To Pictou Co, NS, ca 1810; stld nr Big Brook, west branch of East River. Farmer. Dau Annie alive 1869. **PAC 11**.

3015 FRASER, William, b ca 1785. To Pictou Co, NS, 1815; res Pictou Town, 1816. Schoolmaster, 'able to support himself.' **INS 39**.

3016 FRASER, Rev William, ca 1778–4 Oct 1851. From Crasky, Strathglass, INV. s/o John F, qv, and Jean Chisholm, qv. Educ Scots Coll, Valladolid, Spain, and ord to RC priesthood, 1804. He served at Fort William and at Lismore, and in 1822 went to Halifax, NS. Missionary, Grand Narrows and Antigonish Co; Vicar Apostolic of NS, 1825; Bishop of Halifax, 1843, and of Arichat, 1844. **CP 62; HCA 56, 133; MP 493; SG iii/4 98; MDB 248**.

3017 FRASER, William. bro/o John F, qv. To Leeds Twp, Megantic Co, QUE, <1824. Farmer, Lot 3, 8th Range. **AMC 135**.

3018 FRASER, Rev William. Prob from INV. To Breadalbane, Lochiel Twp, Glengarry Co, ONT. Baptist min there, 1831-50; farmer and schoolteacher. **SDG 131; MG 443**.

3019 FRASER, William, d 8 Feb 1874. From INV. s/o James F. To ONT. m 20 Feb 1833, Isabella McLean, ch: 1. James; 2. John W, b 1836; 3. Jane; 4. James; 5. Alexander; 6. Lachlan; 7. Nancy; 8. William, b 1852. **DC 4 Mar 1965**.

3020 FRASER, William, ca 1794–9 Oct 1867. From

Glenmoriston, INV. To Nine Mile River, Hants Co, NS, prob <1840. Wife Janet, 1800-90, native of Paisley, RFW. **DC 20 Jan 1981**.

3021 FRENCH, Thomas, 10 Apr 1830–20 Jun 1858. From Carnwath, LKS. s/o John F. in Lampits, and Jane Herbert. To CAN, prob ONT. **Ts Carnwath**.

3022 FRIEND, Mary. From West Kilbride, AYR. To QUE, ex Greenock, summer 1815; stld North Burgess Twp, Lanark Co, ONT. Wife of James Miller, qv. **SEC 3**.

3023 FULLARTON, Alexander, b 20 Apr 1817. From Saltcoats, AYR. s/o Fergus F, qv, and Mary Fullerton, qv. To Pictou, NS, 1818; stld West River Road. Farmer. By wife Mary ch: 1. Margaret, b 1845; 2. Jane, b 1846; 3. Mary, b 1848; 4. Catherine, b 1849; 5. Flora, b 1851; 6. James William, b 1852; 7. Alexander, b 1854; 8. Annie, b 1855; 9. Harriet, b 1858; 10. Jessie. **DC 24 Mar 1979**.

3024 FULLARTON, Daniel, 17 Dec 1808–Mar 1857. From Saltcoats, AYR. s/o Fergus F, qv, and Mary Fullerton, qv. To Pictou Co, NS, 1818; stld West River. Farmer and tanner. m Harriet Olding. Son George, d 1 May 1908. **DC 24 Mar 1979**.

3025 FULLARTON, Fergus, 7 Jan 1778–23 Feb 1835. From Is Arran, BUT. s/o Donald F, farmer in Whitefarland. Res for some time in Ardrossan par, AYR. To Pictou Co, NS, 1818; stld Lyons Brook, West River. Farmer; purchased 174 acres. m Mary Fullarton, qv, ch: 1. Jane, qv; 2. Margret, dy; 3. Daniel, qv; 4. John, qv; 5. Margret, dy; 6. Mary, dy; 7. Alexander, qv; 8. James; 9. William, b 1821; 10. David, b 1825, lumberman. **DC 24 Mar 1979; HNS iii 246**.

3026 FULLARTON, Jane, 29 Jan 1804–1 Jun 1873. From Ardrossan, AYR. d/o Fergus F, qv, and Mary Fullerton, qv. To Pictou Co, NS, 1818. m Thomas Renton, qv. **HNS iii 247; DC 24 Mar 1979**.

3027 FULLARTON, John, 20 Mar 1811–17 Sep 1882. From Saltcoats, AYR. s/o Fergus F, qv, and Mary Fullerton, qv. To Pictou Co, NS, 1818; stld West River Road. Farmer and landowner. m Barbara Harris, 1815-84, in 1835, ch: 1. Jessie, 1841–1900; 2. John, 1839-64; 3. James, 1841–1900; 4. Dr Thomas; 5. Daniel, 1845-69; 6. George, 1847-74; 7. Mary Jane, 1848–1929; 8. Robert, 1850–1929; 9. Caroline, 1853–1916; 10. Margaret, 1854-98; 11. Adah, 1856–1929; 12. Louis Wentworth, d inf 1859; 13. Abram, 1860-99. **DC 24 Mar 1979**.

3028 FULLEN, Thomas. To QUE on the *Alexander*, 1816; stld Lot 16, Con 9, Bathurst Twp, Lanark Co, ONT. **HCL 233**.

FULLERTON. See also FULLARTON.

3029 FULLERTON, James, b 1793. From Kilmichael, Is Arran, BUT. s/o James F. To QUE on the *Albion*, ex Greenock, 5 Jun 1829; stld Inverness, Megantic Co, QUE. Blacksmith. m Janet Murphy, qv, ch: 1. James, jr, qv; 2. Mary; 3. Janet; 4. Archibald; 5. Jane, qv; 6. Peter; 7. Neil; 8. Alexander; 9. John; 10. Charles. **AMC 12, 21; MAC 34**.

3030 FULLERTON, James, jr, b 6 Apr 1822. From Corrie, Is Arran, BUT. s/o James F, qv, and Janet Murphy, qv. To QUE on the *Albion*, ex Greenock, 5 Jun 1829; stld Inverness, Megantic Co, QUE. Farmworker,

later farmer. m 18 Mar 1851, Mary McMillan, qv, ch: 1. James; 2. Hadley; 3. Mary Janet; 4. Neil Eugene. **AMC 21, 137; MAC 34**.

3031 FULLERTON, James. Prob from AYR. To St John, NB, <1820. Heir portioner to Rev Daniel McNaught, d 1819. Relief Ch min at Biggar, LKS. **SH; UPC ii 410**.

3032 FULLERTON, Jane. From Corrie, Is Arran, BUT. d/o James F, qv, and Mary Murphy, qv. To QUE on the *Albion*, ex Greenock, 5 Jun 1829; stld Inverness, Megantic Co, QUE. m John McKelvie. **AMC 21; MAC 35**.

3033 FULLERTON, Mary, 14 May 1782–10 May 1847. From Is Arran, BUT. d/o Donald F. and Margaret Stuart. To Pictou Co, NS, 1818; stld Lyons Brook, West River. Wife of Fergus Fullarton, qv, whom she m 4 Jun 1803. **DC 24 Mar 1979**.

3034 FULLERTON, Robert, 30 May 1785–23 Apr 1807. From Dalry, AYR. s/o Rev John F, par min, and Helen Donald. Sometime HEICS, d PEI. **FES iii 85**.

3035 FULTON, James. Prob rel to John F, qv. To Pictou Co, NS, <1776. **HPC App C**.

3036 FULTON, James, d 21 Sep 1816. From Paisley, RFW. To NS, and d aboard the ship *Protector*. **NSS No 898**.

3037 FULTON, John. Prob rel to James F, qv. To Pictou Co, NS, <1776. **HPC App B**.

FYFE. See also FIFE.

3038 FYFE, Elizabeth. From Turriff, ABD. To Huntingdon Village, QUE, 1836. Wife of William Rose, qv. **DC 11 Nov 1979**.

3039 FYFE, Margaret, 25 Dec 1845–21 Apr 1860. From Kintore, ABD. To ONT 1854. Wife of Robert Pirie, whom she m at Skene, 14 Dec 1845. **DC 22 Aug 1974**.

3040 FYFE, William, b 23 Mar 1794, South Kirktoun, par of Houston and Kilellan, RFW. s/o Robert F. and Isobell Millar. To PEI, 1820. m Jean Arthur, qv. **DC 6 Apr 1979**.

3041 FYFFE, Marion. From Corstorphine, MLN. To Lanark Co, ONT, < Jul 1817. Wife of Thomas Cuddie, qv. **SEC 1; HCL 12, 231**.

G

3042 GAIR, Christian, b 1755. To Charlottetown, PEI, on the *Elizabeth & Ann*, ex Thurso, arr 8 Nov 1806. Wife of George Logan, qv. **PLEA**.

GAIRDNER. See also GARDINER and GARDNER.

3043 GAIRDNER, Robert Hunter. From Edinburgh. s/o Robert G, solicitor. To QUE <1836. Lawyer. **SH**.

3044 GALBRAITH, Alexander, 1811-55. From Killean par, ARL. s/o John G. and Margaret McGill, qv, 1834. m Isobel Mitchell, qv. **DC 9 Mar 1980**.

3045 GALBRAITH, Alexander, d 1843. From Glasgow. To Carleton Place, Lanark Co, ONT, 1821. By a first wife ch: 1. Daniel, qv; 2. Margaret, qv. m (ii) Mrs Stephenson. **GSO 11**.

3046 GALBRAITH, Angus, b 1781. From ARL. To Dunwich Twp, Elgin Co, ONT, prob <1854. **GSO 33**.

3047   GALBRAITH, Angus, 1796–1888. From Is Islay, ARL. To ONT, ca 1833, stld Oro Twp, Simcoe Co. m Annabella McPhail, qv, ch: 1. Flora, 1832–1916; 2. John; 3. Malcolm, b 1839; 4. Elizabeth, b 1841; 5. Mary, b 1843; 6. Neil, b 1848.   **GSO 26; DC 9 Mar 1980**.

3048   GALBRAITH, Angus, b 1828. From Is Colonsay, ARL. To Bruce Co, ONT, ca 1852. Farmer. By wife Mary, b 1834, ch: 1. Angus, b 1858; 2. Catharine, 1860-83; 3. Lindsay, b 1862; 4. Malcolm, 1864-95.   **GSO 28; DC 9 Mar 1980**.

3049   GALBRAITH, Archibald, d 1874. From Knapdale, ARL. Prob s/o Alexander G. and Mary Leitch. To NY on the *Perseverance*, arr 17 Aug 1833; stld Southwold Twp, Elgin Co, ONT. By his second wife Mary Campbell, 1783–1862, he had, prob with other ch: 1. Neil, qv; 2. Malcolm, qv; 3. John, qv.   **GSO 33**.

3050   GALBRAITH, Archibald, 1834-89. From Is Colonsay, ARL. To Bruce Co, ONT, ca 1852. By his first wife ch: 1. Duncan, 1842–1909; 2. John, 1858-87; 3. Kate, b 1845. m (ii) Margaret McNeil, from PEI, further ch: 4. Hugh, 1857–1918; 5. John, 1858-87; 6. Donald, 1859–1916; 7. Archie, b 1860; 8. Roderick; 9. Mary; 10. Esther; 11. Maggie; 12. Flora, 1862–1947.   **DC 9 Mar 1980**.

3051   GALBRAITH, Christina, b 1831. From Is Colonsay, ARL. To Bruce Co, ONT, ca 1852. m A. McCalder. Son Neil, b 1855.   **DC 9 Mar 1980**.

3052   GALBRAITH, David. To Fergus, Wellington Co, ONT, <1849. Storekeeper. m Janet Foyer, qv, ch: 1. William, 1821-57; 2. Robert John, 1832-62.   **DC 9 Mar 1980**.

3053   GALBRAITH, David. From Paisley, RFW. s/o David G. and Jean Whitehill. To QUE, poss 1853; stld Ormstown, Chateauguay Co.   **GSO 14**.

3054   GALBRAITH, David, 1830–1902. From Glasgow. To ONT, ca 1854. Dancing master. m Carthina Stewart, ch: 1. John; 2. Agnes; 3. Isobel; 4. Janet; 5. Hannah; 6. Annie, 1862–1933; 7. Mary, 1863–1933; 8. Christina.   **DC 9 Mar 1980**.

3055   GALBRAITH, Daniel, 1805-51. From Killean par, ARL. s/o John G. and Margaret McGill, qv. To ONT, 1834. m Jean Broadfoot, qv.   **DC 9 Mar 1980**.

3056   GALBRAITH, Daniel, 1815-80. From Glasgow. s/o Alexander G, qv. To Carleton Place, Lanark Co, ONT, 1821. Farmer, railroad director and Liberal politician. m 1850, Janet McFarlane, 1822-95, ch: 1. Hannah, 1853–1903; 2. Margaret, 1855–1910; 3. Ellen, b 1858; 4. Robert, b 1860; 5. Phoebe; 6. Nellie, unm.   **BNA 752; DC 9 Mar 1980**.

3057   GALBRAITH, Donald, 1763–1847. From Is Islay, ARL. To Oro Twp, Simcoe Co, ONT.   **GSO 26; DC 9 Mar 1980**.

3058   GALBRAITH, Donald, 1808-80. To Darlington Twp, Durham Co, ONT, <1852; bur Bowmanville. Wife Catherine, 1809-83, with him.   **GSO 13**.

3059   GALBRAITH, Donald, 1812-96. From Is Colonsay, ARL. To Bruce Co, ONT, ca 1852. m Margaret McDougall, qv, ch: 1. Mary, 1860–1911; 2. Malcolm, 1862–1934; 3. John, 1864–1924; 4. Flora, 1870-94; 5. Effie.   **DC 9 Mar 1980**.

3060   GALBRAITH, Donald, b ca 1820. Prob from ARL. To ONT prob <1854; stld Dunwich Twp, Elgin Co. m Isobel Thomson, ch: 1. Margaret, b ca 1854; 2. Angus, b ca 1858; 3. Mary, 1861–1956; 4. Isobel, b 1866.   **GSO 33**.

3061   GALBRAITH, Donald, 1824-76. From Is Colonsay, ARL. To Bruce Co, ONT, ca 1852. By wife Christina, 1832-87, ch: 1. Angus, 1853-77; 2. Annie, b 1858; 3. John, 1858-87.   **GSO 28; DC 9 Mar 1980**.

3062   GALBRAITH, Hester. Prob from Is Mull, ARL. To Mariposa Twp, Victoria Co, ONT, 1847. Wife of John McFee, qv.   **LDW 30 Jan 1974**.

3063   GALBRAITH, James Watt, 1823-73. From Abbey par, Paisley, RFW. s/o David G. and Jean Whitehill. To York Co, ONT, prob <1855. m Elizabeth Brown, qv, ch: 1. Margaret, b 1858; 2. Jane, b 1859; 3. David, b 1860; 4. Mary, b 1862; 5. John, b 1863; 6. James, b 1865; 7. Alexander, b 1867; 8. Elizabeth, b 1869; 9. Catharine, b 1870; 10. Isabella.   **GSO 14**.

3064   GALBRAITH, Janet, 1811-85. From Is Islay, ARL. To Bruce Co, ONT, ca 1840. m Angus McPhail, 1811-63. Dau Mary, b 1842.   **GSO 29; DC 9 Mar 1980**.

3065   GALBRAITH, John. To QUE on the *Commerce*, ex Greenock, Jun 1820; stld Lot 10, Con 4, Ramsay Twp, ONT. Farmer. m Martha Cochrane, ch: 1. Daniel, b ca 1822; 2. Agnes, b ca 1824.   **HCL 239; GSO 11**.

3066   GALBRAITH, John, 1803-86. From Is Islay, ARL. Prob bro/o Angus G, qv. To Oro Twp, Simcoe Co, ONT, ca 1833. Innkeeper.   **GSO 26; DC 9 Mar 1980**.

3067   GALBRAITH, John, 1805-49. From Knapdale, ARL. s/o Archibald G, qv. To ONT poss <1830; stld Dunwich Twp, Elgin Co, 1835. m Christina McCallum, qv, ch: 1. Archibald, 1828–1902; 2. Mary, 1832–1904; 3. John, 1835-98; 4. Daniel, 1840–1916; 5. Neil, 1835-98; 6. James, 1844–1918; 7. Sarah, 1846–1922; 8. Duncan, 1848–1920.   **GSO 33**.

3068   GALBRAITH, John. From ARL. To West Williams Twp, Middlesex Co, ONT, 1847; stld Con 9.   **PCM 46**.

3069   GALBRAITH, John, 1809-92. From Kilberry, ARL. s/o Lachlan G. and Mary McPhail. To ONT, 1847; stld poss Bruce Co. m Margaret McMillan, qv, ch: 1. Mary, 1841-50; 2. Duncan, 1843-59; 3. Donald, 1845–1907; 4. Margaret, 1846–1912; 5. Lachlan, 1849–1927; 6. Elizabeth, 1853–1932; 7. Mary, 1855–1935.   **DC 9 Mar 1980**.

3070   GALBRAITH, John, b 1821. From Is Colonsay, ARL. To Bruce Co, ONT, ca 1852. m Margaret Cameron, ch: 1. Euphemia, b 1853; 2. Pearl, b 1855; 3. Duncan, b 1857; 4. James, b 1858; 5. Sarah, b 1860; 6. Janet, b 1862; 7. Margaret, b 1864; 8. Angus, b 1868; 9. Elizabeth, b 1870.   **GSO 28; DC 9 Mar 1980**.

3071   GALBRAITH, John, b 1824. From Coldstream, BEW. s/o John and Margaret G. To ONT prob <1850; stld later Toronto. m (i) Christina Taylor, ch: 1. Christina, d inf; 2. Margaret, b 1856; 3. Agnes, b 1858; 4. Christina, b 1860; 5. Jane, b 1862; 6. Beatrix, b 1864; 7. John, b 1867; 8. Janet, b 1870. m (ii) M. Veitch, with further ch: 9. Anna, b 1875; 10. Alexandra, b 1876; 11. Alison, b 1877; 12. Malcolm, b 1880.   **GSO 18**.

3072   GALBRAITH, John, 1826–1921. To Beverley Twp,

Wentworth Co, ONT, ca 1851. m Janet Gibb, qv, ch:
1. Isabella, b ca 1847; 2. John, 1851-91; 3. Janet,
1853–1923; 4. William, b ca 1855; 5. James, b ca 1857;
6. Margaret, b ca 1859; 7. David, b 1861; 8. Agnes,
b 1866; 9. George, b 1868; 10. Minnie, b 1871.
GSO 24; DC 9 Mar 1980.

3073 GALBRAITH, John, b 1829. To Guelph Twp,
Wellington Co, ONT, 1848. By wife Mary, 1831-80, ch:
1. William, 1849-86; 2. Janet, b 1850; 3. James,
1852-94; 4. John, b 1854; 5. Stephen, b 1859;
6. Alfred, b 1862. **DC 9 Mar 1980**.

3074 GALBRAITH, John. From ARL. To Carleton Place,
Lanark Co, ONT, <1831. m Ellen Stewart, qv. Son David,
1831–1912. **DC 9 Mar 1980**.

3075 GALBRAITH, John, 1815-79. From ARL. s/o John
G. and Margaret McGill, qv. To ONT, 1834. Importer of
Clydesdale horses. m Flora MacConnachie, qv.
DC 9 Mar 1980.

3076 GALBRAITH, Lachlan, 1796–1868. From Is Islay,
ARL. To Oro Twp, Simcoe Co, ONT, poss 1833. By wife
Catherine, b 1820, ch: 1. John, b 1846; 2. Mary, b 1849;
3. Archibald, b 1851; 4. Lachlan, 1852-74; 5. Margaret,
b 1855; 6. Sarah, b 1858; 7. Ann, b 1860; 8. Flora,
b 1862; 9. Sarah, jr, b 1864; 10. Catharine, b 1866;
11. Donald, b 1868. **GSO 26; DC 9 Mar 1980**.

3077 GALBRAITH, Malcolm, 1799–1883. From Is
Gigha, ARL. s/o Colin G. To ONT, 1845; stld
Bowmanville, Durham Co. Lawyer. m Isobella
MacDonald Keith, qv, ch: 1. Mary Ann, b 1837;
2. Malcolm, b 1838; 3. John Keith, 1839-90, lawyer;
4. Isobella, b 1841; 5. Flora, b 1851; 6. Catherine Jane,
b 1853; 7. Donald E, b 1855; 8. Joseph N, b 1860.
GSO 13; DC 9 Mar 1980.

3078 GALBRAITH, Malcolm, b ca 1800. From
Knapdale, ARL. s/o Archibald G, qv. To Port Talbot, ONT,
1823; stld Ekfrid Twp, Middlesex Co. Farmer and
roadmaster. m Catherine McCallum, 1802-78, ch:
1. Mary, 1836–1922; 2. Margaret, 1838–1921.
GSO 33; PCM 30.

3079 GALBRAITH, Malcolm, b ca 1815. From Is Islay,
ARL. To Oro Twp, Simcoe Co, ONT, prob 1833. m Flora
Bell, qv, ch: 1. Donald, b 1838; 2. Flora, b 1839; 3. Neil,
1844-65; 4. Sarah, 1846–1916; 5. John, b 1847;
6. Lachlan, b 1852. **GSO 26; DC 9 Mar 1980**.

3080 GALBRAITH, Margaret, b 1 Nov 1771. From
Kintyre, ARL. d/o Henry G. and Agnes Armour. To
Miramichi, Northumberland Co, NB, 1821; later to
Restigouche Co. Wife of Nathaniel McNair, qv, whom
she m 24 Apr 1802. **DC 7 Feb 1981**.

3081 GALBRAITH, Margaret, 1818–1907. From
Glasgow. d/o Alexander G, qv. To Carleton Place, Lanark
Co, ONT, 1821. m (i) Duncan McIntosh; (ii) Donald
McLean, Ramsay Twp, later in Renfrew Co. **DC 9 Mar
1980**.

3082 GALBRAITH, Mary, 1819-85. From Kilberry, ARL.
d/o Lachlan G. and Mary McPhail. To Bruce Co, ONT,
1847. m Alexander McLeish, qv. **GSO 31**.

GALBRAITH, Mrs John. See McGILL, Margaret.

3083 GALBRAITH, Neil, 1812-66. Prob from Is Islay,
ARL. To Oro Twp, Simcoe Co, ONT, poss 1833. By wife
Mary ch: 1. Rhona, b 1849; 2. Donald, b 1851; 3. John,

b 1853; 4. Margaret, b 1855; 5. Catharine, b 1858;
6. Angus, b 1860; 7. Mary, b 1862; 8. Sarah, b 1864;
9. Neil, 1867–1956; 10. Archibald. **GSO 26;
DC 9 Mar 1980**.

3084 GALBRAITH, Neil. To Egremont Twp, Grey Co,
ONT. By wife Janet, b 1829, ch: 1. John, b 1856;
2. Ann, b 1858; 3. Duncan, b 1860. **GSO 25;
DC 9 Mar 1980**.

3085 GALBRAITH, Neil, d 1860. From Crinan, ARL. To
Dunwich Twp, Middlesex Co, ONT, ca 1819; moved to
Ekfrid Twp, 1831. m Margaret Currie, qv, ch: 1. Daniel or
Donald, 1819-94; 2. Mary, 1820-97; 3. John, 1822-64;
4. Neil, 1826-75; 5. Jane, 1827-99; 6. Margaret,
1830–1922; 7. George, b 1832; 8. Malcolm,
1839–1914. **PCM 29, 46; GSO 33**.

3086 GALBRAITH, Robert, 1820-99. From Kilbarchan,
RFW. s/o John G. and Janet Caldwell. To Wellington Co,
ONT, 1852, and stld Guelph. Tailor. m Frances,
d/o William Heather, ch: 1. John, 1855-60; 2. Janet,
1856–1941; 3. Marianne, 1858-59; 4. William,
1860–1931; 5. Robert, grad Queens Univ, 1896; 6. Fanny
Sophia, 1867–1949. **GSO 21**.

3087 GALBRAITH, Thomas, 1822-99. From
Coldstream, BEW. s/o John and Margaret G. To
Montreal, QUE, <1845; later to Port Hope, Durham Co,
ONT. Merchant and journalist. m Jane, d/o John
Anderson, qv, Montreal, ch: 1. John Anderson,
1846–1914, engineer and scientist, LLD, 1903;
2. William, 1848–1925; 3. Thomas, 1849–1922;
4. Jane Anderson, 1851-88; 5. James, 1853-56;
6. Robert Alfred, 1858-76; 7. James, b 1858, twin,
d inf. **GSO 18**.

3088 GALBRAITH, Walter, b 1782. To Howard Twp,
Kent Co, ONT, <1851. By wife Elizabeth, b 1803, ch:
1. Walter, b ca 1829; 2. Agnes, b ca 1832; 3. William,
b ca 1837; 4. Jane, b ca 1844. **DC 9 Mar 1980**.

3089 GALBRAITH, William, 1832–1905. From
Sighthill, Glasgow. s/o John G, miller, and Christian
Craig. To Front Street, Toronto, ONT, ca 1855. Merchant.
m Janet Grey Wright, qv, ch: 1. John, 1857–1939;
2. Jeannie Muir, 1858-97; 3. Christian Craig, 1860–1947;
4. William, 1862–1920; 5. Robert S, 1864–1944;
6. Janet W, 1866–1947; 7. Catherine, b 1868; 8. James
Richardson, 1870–1927; 9. Margaret Wardrop,
1871–1960; 10. Ronald Wright, 1876-77. **GSO 20**.

3090 GALE, Rev Alexander, 1802–6 Apr 1854. From
Logie-Coldstone, ABD. s/o John G, farmer. Grad MA,
Marischall Coll, Aberdeen, 1819. To QUE, 1827. Min at
Amherstburg, ONT, 1828-31; at Lachine, Montreal,
1832-33; trans to Hamilton, ONT, 1833. App Principal of
Toronto Academy and Professor of Classics at Knox Coll,
1846. Joined FC, 1844, and was Moderator of Synod,
1853. **FAM ii 423; FES vii 634**.

GALLIE. See also GALLY.

3091 GALLIE, James Begg. Prob from Invergordon,
ROC. To NS <1847. **SH**.

3092 GALLOWAY, Rev George, 1814–11 Nov 1844.
Born Peterhead, ABD. s/o James G, shoemaker. Grad
Marischall Coll, Aberdeen, 1833. App by Glasgow
Colonial Committee as 'Missionary at large to Upper
Canada.' Min at Markham, York Co, 1840-44.
FAM ii 470; SNQ ii/2 171; FES vii 634.

3093   GALLOWAY, Jessie. From Sanquhar, DFS. To Eldon Twp, Victoria Co, ONT, 1831. Wife of James Williamson, qv. **EC 223**.

GALLY. See also GALLIE.

3094   GALLY, Flora, b 1799. To Pictou Co, NS, 1815; res Pictou Town, 1816. unm servant, 'able to support herself.' **INS 39**.

3095   GALT, Sir Alexander Tilloch, 6 Sep 1817–19 Sep 1893. From Irvine, AYR. s/o John G, qv, and Elizabeth Tilloch, qv. To Kingston, ONT, 1826. Served with the British and American Land Co, 1833-56. MLA, rep Sherbrooke Co, 1849-50. Retr for Sherbrooke Town, 1853, and was Finance Minister, 1858-62, 1864-66. Delegate to Confederation conferences and Pres of Grand Trunk Railway. m (i) Elizabeth, d/o John Torrance, qv, and Elizabeth Fisher, ch: 1. Elliott, 1850–1928. m (ii) Amy Torrance, her sist, with further ch: 2. John, 1856–1932; 3. Amy; 4. Catherine; 5. Selina; 6. Evelyn, authoress; 7. Mabel; 8. Oneida; 9. Muriel, a nurse in World War I; 10. Annie. **BNA 590; IBD 156; MDB 255; DC 1 Jan 1968**.

3096   GALT, John, 2 May 1799–11 Apr 1839. From Irvine, AYR. s/o Capt John G. and Jean Thomson. To ONT, 1826. Commissioner for the Canada Company, 1826-29, and promoted settlements around Guelph, Wellington Co. Negotiated with William Dickson, qv, the road from Galt (named in his honour) to Guelph. Author. m 1813, Elizabeth Tilloch, qv, ch: 1. John, jr, qv; 2. Thomas, qv; 3. Alexander Tilloch, qv. **HGD 48; IBD 156; CBD 394; MBD 255; DC 1 Jan 1968**.

3097   GALT, John, jr, b 1814. From Irvine, AYR. s/o John G, qv, and Elizabeth Tilloch, qv. To ONT, 1826. Registrar at Goderich, Huron Co. m Helen, d/o Daniel Lizars, qv, ch: 1. Agnes, b 1844; 2. Blanch, b 1847; 3. Jane Helen, b 1857; 4. Magdalena, b 1859; 5. John, 1861–1938, Postmaster at Goderich. **DC 1 Jan 1968**.

3098   GALT, Sir Thomas, 17 Aug 1815–19 Jun 1901. From Irvine, AYR, but b London, ENG. s/o John G, qv, and Elizabeth Tilloch, qv. To Goderich Twp, Huron Co, ONT, 1826, but stld later at Toronto. Lawyer, and became Chief Justice of CAN, 1887. Knighted, 1888. m Louisa, d/o James Marshall Perkins, RN, ch: 1. Elizabeth Alice; 2. Ada; 3. Alexander Casimer; 4. George Frederick, 1855–1928; 5. Thomas Percival; 6. Frederick William; 7. Clarence Campbell; 8. Louisa Ethel; 9. Edith; 10. Hubert. **BNA 910; MDB 256; DC 1 Jan 1968**.

3099   GALT, William, ca 1787–4 Nov 1830. From Kilmarnock, AYR. To Montreal, QUE, <1825. Merchant. **Ts Glasgow Necropolis**.

GAMMEL. See also GAMMELL, GEMMEL, GEMMELL, GEMMIL, GEMMILL.

3100   GAMMEL, Thomas. To QUE on the *Commerce*, ex Greenock, Jun 1820; stld Lanark Co, ONT, poss Ramsay Twp. **HCL 239**.

3101   GAMMELL, Robert, b ca 1770. From AYR. Prob bro/o William G, qv. To Little Bras D'Or dist, Cape Breton Co, NS, <1815. Farmer. Widower with ch in 1818. **CBC 1818**.

3102   GAMMELL, William, b ca 1772. From AYR. Prob bro/o Robert G, qv. To Little Bras D'Or dist Cape Breton

Co, NS, <1815. Farmer and merchant, widowed by 1818. **CBC 1818; HNS iii 418**.

3103   GARDEN, Alexander, ca 1775–17 Nov 1857. From ABD. To Halifax, NS, <1824; stld later Nine Mile River, Hants Co. m Henrietta Coutts, qv. **VSN No 442; DC 20 Jan 1981**.

GARDINER. See also GAIRDNER and GARDNER.

3104   GARDINER, Alexander, 25 Feb 1782–19 Oct 1862. From Burnbrae, Kilmacolm, AYR. s/o John B, farmer, and Janet Hatridge. To Montreal, QUE, ex Port Glasgow, 1820; stld Dundee, Huntingdon Co. m Mary Brodie, qv, ch: 1. Barbara, 1805-36; 2. John, 1807-30; 3. Mary, 1808-30; 4. Robert, 1809-33; 5. Alexander, 1812-75; 6. James, 1815-49; 7. William, qv; 8. Margaret; 9. Robert David, 1818-49; 10. Rev Hugh; 11. Charles, 1822-42; 12. Joseph, 1825-91; 13. Peter, 1828-94; 14. John, 1830-34. **DC 1 Apr 1979**.

3105   GARDINER, Janet. From Tundergarth par, DFS. To QUE, ex Greenock, summer 1815; stld prob Lanark Co, ONT. Wife of Thomas Scott, qv. **SEC 6**.

3106   GARDINER, William, b 20 Feb 1814. From Kilbirnie, AYR. s/o Alexander G, qv, and Mary Brodie, qv. To Montreal, QUE, 1820. m Ann Brodie, qv. **DC 1 Apr 1979**.

3107   GARDNER, Rev Alexander. From Leslie par, ABD. Grad MA, Kings Coll, Aberdeen, 1827. To Hamilton, ONT, 1836, and became min of St Andrews Presb Ch, Fergus, Wellington Co. **KCG 283; FES vii 634; EHE 93**.

3108   GARDNER, Archibald, 11 Mar 1836–25 Jul 1875. From Paisley, RFW. s/o Archibald G. of Nethercommon, and Elizabeth Wylde. To Montreal, QUE. **Ts Paisley**.

3109   GARDNER, Mary. From Shotts par, LKS. To Clarke Twp, Durham Co, ONT, 1835. Wife of Thomas Waddell, qv. **Shotts OPR 655/4**.

3110   GARDNER, Robert, b ca 1783. From Paisley, RFW. To QUE on the *Atlas*, ex Greenock, 11 Jul 1815; stld Lot 4, Con 10, North Burgess Twp, Lanark Co, ONT. Farmer. May have left settlement <1820. **SEC 2; HCL 15, 230, 232**.

3111   GARDNER, Walter. To QUE on the *David of London*, ex Greenock, 19 May 1821; stld Lot 26, Con 7, Ramsay Twp, Lanark Co, ONT. Wife Mary Lindsay, qv, with him, and s Walter, jr, qv. **HCL 83**.

3112   GARDNER, Walter, jr. From Greenock on the *David of London*, 19 May 1821; arr QUE; stld Ramsay Twp, Lanark Co, ONT. Wife Cecilia Brown, qv, with him. **HCL 83, 239**.

3113   GARDNER, William. From Glasgow. To Lanark Co, ONT, 1824. Farmer. m Mary McKerrow. Son Frank. **DC 29 Sep 1964**.

3114   GARROW, David, b 1 Oct 1796. From Aberlour, BAN. s/o Patrick G. and Beatrix McDonald. To Ingersoll Twp, Oxford Co, ONT, 1855; stld Lot 15, Con 1. Farmer. m Margaret Grant, d 1855, ch: 1. Peter, dy; 2. James, dy; 3. John, dy; 4. David, 1841-62; 5. Alexander, 1843–1912; 6. Isabella, 1844–1918, went to NE; 7. Elizabeth, 1846–1915; 8. Ernest Donald, 1851–1909, stld NE. **DC 15 Jul 1967 and 23 Mar 1968**.

3115   GARROW, Margaret, 1811-64. From Raploch, STI.

To ONT, ca 1850. m William Graham, qv.   **DC 18 Dec 1982**.

3116   GATHERER, Adam. To Montreal, QUE, <1841, when he moved to Elora, Nichol Twp, Wellington Co, ONT. Dau Mrs Joseph Laird.   **EHE 118**.

3117   GASS, John. From DFS. bro/o Robert G, qv, and Joseph G, qv. To Pictou Co, NS, 1816. ch: 1. Henderson, saddler in Tatamagouche, Colchester Co; 2. Robert, shoemaker, Tatamagouche, d 1894.   **HT 79**.

3118   GASS, Joseph. From DFS. bro/o John G, qv, and Robert G, qv. To Pictou Co, NS, 1816; moved to Cape John, 1842. Son Robert.   **HT 79**.

3119   GASS, Robert. From DFS. bro/o John G, qv, and Joseph G, qv. To Pictou Co, NS, 1816.   **HT 79**.

3120   GEDDES, Andrew, 2 Jun 1782–7 Mar 1865. From BAN. To QUE 1834; moved later to Hamilton, ONT. Went to Elora, Nichol Twp, 1844, when he became Crown Land Agent for Wellington Co. ch: 1. James; 2. Capt John; 3. Andrew; 4. Margaret; 5. May, d 1833; 6. Anne, d 1891.   **EHE 123**.

3121   GEDDES, Charles, 1749–27 Sep 1810. From Edinburgh. s/o James G, clock and watchmaker, and Lilias Gray. To Halifax, NS, and d there. Watchmaker. Heir of line and provision general to his father, 18 Nov 1784.   **SH**.

3122   GEDDES, James, 1 Sep 1809–28 May 1883. From Aberdeen. s/o Andrew G, merchant. Matric Marischall Coll, Aberdeen, 1823, and adm advocate, 1831. To CAN, prob ONT. m Cecilia Byng Clarke, d 1896.   **FAM ii 451; SAA 199**.

3123   GEDDES, James. To London, Westminster Twp, Middlesex Co, ONT, 1844. Left ch.   **PCM 55**.

3124   GEDDIE, John. From BAN. To Pictou, NS, 1817. Clockmaker. m Mary Menzies, qv. Son John, 1815-72, Presb missionary in South Seas, d Geelong, AUS.   **MDB 260; DC 21 Mar 1981**.

3125   GEGGIE, Rev James, 1793–3 Jan 1863. Born Chirnside, BEW. s/o James G. Educ Univ of Edinburgh, and studied theology. Joined Ch of Scotland and ord for mission work in CAN, 1837. Adm min of Valcartier, QUE, 1841. Joined FC, 1844, and held charges at Edwardsburgh, Dalhousie, and Spencerville.   **FES vii 634**.

3126   GEIKIE, Rev Archibald. From Edinburgh. Poss rel of Rev Archibald Constable G, qv. To Lambton Co, ONT, and was min at Moore Twp and Sarnia Twp. Son Walter Bayne, qv.   **DC 15 Mar 1980**.

3127   GEIKIE, Rev Archibald Constable, 22 Jul 1821–29 Jul 1898. From Edinburgh. s/o Archibald G, perfumer. Matric Univ of Glasgow, 1840. To Waterloo Co, ONT, and was min at Kitchener, later at Galt. Went to Bathurst, NSW, AUS, 1861.   **GMA 14237**.

3128   GEIKIE, David, b ca 1815, prob Edinburgh. To Newcastle, Northumberland Co, NB, <1844. m Jessie Harvey, qv. Dau Agnes, b 27 Oct 1844.   **LDW 1 Apr 1972**.

3129   GEIKIE, Walter Bayne, 8 May 1830–12 Jan 1917. Born Edinburgh. s/o Rev Archibald G, qv. To Lambton Co, ONT. Physician and teacher on staff of Victoria Univ, Cobourg, 1856-70, and from 1878–1903, Dean of Faculty of Medicine at Trinity Coll, Toronto. m 1854, Frances Miriam, d/o James Woodhouse, and had, poss with other ch: 1. Walter Woodhouse; 2. Archibald James; 3. Annie Laurie; 4. Ethel Frances.   **MDB 260; DC 15 Mar 1980**.

GEMMEL. See also GAMMELL, GEMMELL, GEMMIL and GEMMILL.

3130   GEMMEL, James, 26 Oct 1814–5 Apr 1881. From Kilmarnock, AYR. To Toronto, ONT, <1834, and d in MT, leaving ch.   **SCN**.

3131   GEMMEL, John, ca 1818–12 Jul 1864. From Balmaghie, KKD. s/o John G. in Finninness, and Helen Symington. To ONT and stld poss Simcoe Co.   **Ts Anwoth**.

3132   GEMMEL, John James, ca 1834–28 Nov 1890. From Paisley, RFW. s/o John G, writer. Matric Univ of Glasgow, 1850. To Ottawa, ONT. Lawyer.   **GMA 15868**.

3133   GEMMEL, Robert, ca 1827–1 Apr 1863. From Balmaghie, KKD. s/o John G. in Finninness, and Helen Symington. To ONT; stld Orillia Twp, Simcoe Co.   **Ts Anwoth**.

3134   GEMMEL, Thomas, b ca 1828. From Paisley, RFW. s/o Andrew and Mary G. To East Whitby Twp, Ontario Co, ONT. m 24 Sep 1860, Elizabeth, d/o Hugh and Elizabeth McInally, from Tyrone, IRL.   **DC 18 Jan 1980**.

3135   GEMMELL, Ivie, 1796–1885. From Ochiltree par, AYR. s/o William G. in Muirston, and Margaret Smith. To ONT poss 1853, and d Compton Co, QUE. Son James, 1835-97, farmer, Compton Co.   **DC 12 Jan 1980**.

3136   GEMMELL, Rev John, 1760–1844. From Dunlop, AYR. s/o Andrew G, farmer. Matric Univ of Glasgow, 1773, and became min of a 'Lifter' congregation at Dalry, 1789. Later printer in Beith, and poss MD, Glasgow, 1818. To QUE on the *David of London*, ex Greenock, 19 May 1821; stld Dalhousie Twp, Lanark Co, ONT. ch incl: 1. John R, printer, who became clerk of Lambton County Court; 2. Grizel or Grace.   **OSG 27; GMA 3293; FES vii 634; HCL 196, 222, 239**.

3137   GEMMILL, James. From Paisley, RFW. To Ramsay Twp, Lanark Co, ONT; stld Lot 5, Con 11.   **HCL 86**.

3138   GEMMILL, John. From Catrine, AYR. To QUE on the *David of London*, ex Greenock, 19 May 1821; stld Clayton, Ramsay Twp, Lanark Co, ONT.   **OSG 27**.

3139   GEMMILL, John, ca 1790–1852. From RFW. s/o John G. of Holehouse, and Mary Dunlop. Clerk with uncle Alexander Steven in Port Glasgow, then tread manufacturer in Beith, AYR. To QUE on the *David of London*, ex Greenock, 19 May 1821; stld Lot 15, Con 9, Ramsay Twp, Lanark Co, ONT. Farmer and merchant. m (i) Ann Adams, qv, ch: 1. John Alexander, qv; 2. James, dy; 3. Mary Ann, dy. m (ii) Margaret Muirhead, Longue Point, Montreal, with further ch: 4. Mary, dy; 5. James Dunlop, b 1833, who succeeded to his father's property at Almonte; 6. William Muirhead, d inf.   **OSG 26; HCL 239**.

3140   GEMMILL, John Alexander, 26 Oct 1816–15 Feb 1876. From Glasgow. s/o John G, qv, and Ann Adams, qv. To QUE on the *David of London*, ex Greenock,

19 May 1821; stld Ramsay Twp, Lanark Co, ONT, and d at Birchendale, Pakenham. Merchant and author. m 1845, Janet, d/o Dr William Cannon, qv, and Margaret King, qv. Son John Alexander, b 1846, lawyer in Ottawa. **OSG 27**.

3141 GENTLE, Andrew, ca 1747–14 Feb 1835. From Dunblane, PER. To QUE and d there. m Mary Yale, 1760–1847. Dau Mary. **DC 4 Jan 1982**.

3142 GERRIE, Mary. From Premnay, ABD. d/o William G, qv, and Isabella Brake, qv. To Nichol Twp, Wellington Co, ONT, 1836. m David Keith, Chesley. **EHE 93**.

3143 GERRIE, William, ca 1777–4 Mar 1861. From Leslie, ABD. To Bon Accord, Nichol Twp, Wellington Co, ONT, 1836. m Clementina Stewart, qv, ch: 1. Alexander; 2. William; 3. John; 4. Adam, res Eramosa; 5. James, d Elora, 1894; 6. Janet; 7. Dorothy; 8. Isabella; 9. Margaret. **EHE 93**.

3144 GERRIE, William. From Premnay, ABD. To Elora, Nichol Twp, Wellington Co, ONT, 1836; moved later to Brant. m Isabella Brake, qv, ch: 1. William, res Fergus; 2. James, res Elora; 3. John, res Fergus; 4. Mary, qv; 5. Andrew; 6. Peter, farmer nr Fergus; 7. Alexander; 8. Thomas, went to Oakland, CA; 9. George; 10. Isabella; 11. Margaret. **EHE 93**.

3145 GIBB, Hugh, b 1844. From Ayr. s/o William G, qv, and Mary Thomson, qv. To ONT 1854; stld poss Malden Twp, Essex Co. m Mary McGuire, ch: 1. Andrew William, 1871–1936; 2. Hugh; 3. James A, 1873–1937; 4. Mary Elizabeth; 5. Anna, b 1875; 6. Carrie, 1881–1975; 7. Stella. **DC 5 Jun 1981**.

3146 GIBB, James. From Carluke, LKS. s/o John G, farmer in Hillhead, and Jean Lawson, 1756–1839. To QUE <1826. Wife d 1856, aged 61. Son James Lawson, 1831-33. **Ts Carluke**.

3147 GIBB, James, 29 Jul 1812–29 Sep 1894. From Ayr. bro/o William G, qv, and John G, qv. To ONT 1849, and d Amherstburg Twp, Essex Co. m Mary Manson, qv, ch. **DC 5 Jun 1981**.

3148 GIBB, James D, 1832–1917. From Ayr. s/o William G, qv, and Mary Thomson, qv. To ONT 1854; stld poss Malden Twp, Essex Co. m (i) Mary Dube; (ii) Mrs James Gibb, wid/o a cous. **DC 5 Jun 1981**.

3149 GIBB, Janet, 2 Oct 1820–16 Dec 1854. From Wishaw, LKS. To Waterloo Co, ONT, ca 1842. m 3 Jul 1837, Archibald Watson, qv. **DC 31 Jul 1979**.

3150 GIBB, Janet, 1827-81. To Beverley Twp, Wentworth Co, ONT, ca 1851. m John Galbraith, qv. **GSO 24**.

3151 GIBB, John. From Carluke, LKS. s/o John G, farmer in Hillhead, and Jean Lawson, 1756–1839. To Montreal, QUE, <1826. **Ts Carluke**.

3152 GIBB, John, 9 Jul 1804–5 Apr 1864. From Ayr. bro/o William G, qv, and James G, qv. To ONT, 1852, and d Amherstburg Twp, Essex Co. m Jean Crawford, qv, ch. **DC 5 Jun 1981**.

3153 GIBB, Marion, ca 1757–20 May 1823. From LKS, prob Larkhall. To QUE, prob <1817. wid/o Andrew Torrance. **DC 13 Jul 1980**.

3154 GIBB, Thomas. From Carluke, LKS. s/o John G,

farmer in Hillhead, and Jean Lawson, 1756–1839. To Montreal, QUE, <1826. **Ts Carluke**.

3155 GIBB, William, 2 Jun 1810–12 Sep 1891. From Ayr. bro/o John G, qv, and James G, qv. To ONT, 1854, and d Amherstburg, Essex Co. m Mary Thomson, qv, ch: 1. James D, qv; 2. Jane; 3. William, d 1908; 4. Hugh, qv; 5. Agnes; 6. Catherine, 1846–1909; 7. Mary; 8. John. **DC 5 Jun 1981**.

3156 GIBBON, Agnes, ca 1806–2 Jul 1889. From Cullerlie, Echt par, ABD. To QUE on the *Fania*, ex Glasgow, 30 Jun 1834; stld Bon Accord, Nichol Twp, Wellington Co, ONT. Wife of George Emslie, qv. **EHE 64**.

3157 GIBBON, George, b ca 1762. From Sandwick, OKI. To York Factory, Hudson Bay, on the *Edward & Anne*, ex Stornoway, arr 24 Sep 1811. Went to Red River. Labourer. **LSS 184; RRS 26; LSC 321**.

3158 GIBBON, John. From Aberdeen. To Bon Accord, Nichol Twp, Wellington Co, ONT, 1835. Son William, qv. **EHE 101**.

3159 GIBBON, John, 1798–1860. From ABD. To Elora, Nichol Twp, Wellington Co, ONT, 1835. Dry goods merchant and farmer. m Jean Emslie, qv, ch: 1. William, qv; 2. John, d 1849; 3. George. **EHE 90**.

3160 GIBBON, William. From ABD, poss Garioch. s/o John G, qv, and Jean Emslie, qv. To QUE on the *Fania*, ex Glasgow, 30 Jun 1834; stld Bon Accord, Nichol Twp, Wellington Co, ONT. m Margaret Emslie, qv, ch: 1. William; 2. Helen; 3. Jean; 4. Agnes. **EHE 65, 90**.

3161 GIBBON, William, b 26 Mar 1826. From Aberdeen. s/o John G, qv. To Bon Accord, Nichol Twp, Wellington Co, ONT, 1835, stld Lot 5, Con 11. Farmer. m Susanna, d/o William Reynolds, ch: 1. Jane Elmslie, d 1895; 2. William Reynolds, d 1882; 3. John Brown; 4. Francis Henry, res MAN; 5. George, d inf; 6. Mary Eliza; 7. Susanna Margaret, res Stratford; 8. Owen Henry, d 1888; 9. Agnes Emily; 10. Arthur Playford; 11. Herbert Addison, res Seattle. **EHE 101**.

3162 GIBBONS, William. To QUE on the *Commerce*, ex Greenock, Jun 1820; stld Lanark Co, ONT. **HCL 238**.

3163 GIBSON, Adam, b ca 1743. From Kirkbean, KKD. Prob bro/o James G, qv. To Georgetown, Kings Co, PEI, on the *Lovely Nellie*, ex Carsethorn, May 1775. Chapman. **ELN**.

3164 GIBSON, Rev Hamilton, ca 1807–19 Oct 1885. From Carluke, LKS. Educ at Glasgow and became asst min of the Tron Ch there. To Waterloo Co, ONT, 1850. Min at Galt. Trans to Bayfield, Huron Co, 1860. Wife d 1875. **FES vii 635**.

3165 GIBSON, James, b ca 1730. From Kirkbean, KKD. Prob bro/o Adam G, qv. To Georgetown, Kings Co, PEI, on the *Lovely Nellie*, ex Carsethorn, May 1775. Chapman. **ELN**.

3166 GIBSON, James, b ca 1794. From Muirkirk, AYR. Prob bro/o Peter G, qv. To QUE, ex Greenock, summer 1815; stld ONT. Labourer. **SEC 4**.

3167 GIBSON, James, b ca 1775. From Broadbedyke, ni, but poss in DFS. To QUE, ex Greenock, summer 1815; stld prob Lanark Co, ONT. Farmer. Wife Helen Little, qv, with him, and 5 ch. **SEC 2**.

3168   GIBSON, James, b ca 1798. From LKS, poss Lesmahagow. To Scarborough, York Co, ONT, 1833. **DC 29 Mar 1981.**

3169   GIBSON, Martha, 1819-61. From Greenock, RFW. To St John, NB, on the *Alexander*, ex Greenock, spring 1816; stld Miramichi, Northumberland Co. Wife of John Cowden, qv. **DC 25 Feb 1982.**

3170   GIBSON, Mary, b 1819. To Lanark Co, ONT, prob <1840. m John McDougall, qv. **DC 2 Nov 1979.**

3171   GIBSON, Peter, b ca 1792. From Muirkirk, AYR. Prob bro/o James G, qv. To QUE, ex Greenock, summer 1815; stld prob Lanark Co, ONT. Labourer. **SEC 4.**

3172   GIBSON, Robert, b ca 1761. From Edinburgh. To QUE on the *Baltic Merchant*, ex Greenock, 12 Jul 1815; stld Lot 15, Con 1, Bathurst Twp, Lanark Co, ONT. Stockingmaker, later farmer. Wife Janet with him, and 5 ch. **SEC 8; HCL 12, 16, 232.**

3173   GIBSON, Thomas, b 8 Jan 1825. From Greenlaw, BEW. To Huron Co, ONT, 1854; stld Howick. Millwright, and MPP for East Huron. **BNA 796; SNQ ii/2 53.**

3174   GIBSON, William. From Glamis, ANS. To Toronto Twp, Peel Co, ONT, 1827. m Mary Sinclair, qv. Son Sir John Morison, 1842–1929, soldier and Lt Gov of ONT, 1908-14. **BNA 794.**

3175   GIBSON, William, 1815–1900. From DFS. To ONT <1840; stld Burritt's Rapids, later Morrisburg, Dundas Co. Grist miller; MLA. ch incl: 1. Ralph; 2. Matthew. **SDG 247.**

3176   GIBSON, William, 1827–25 Dec 1858. From Arbroath, ANS. s/o Alexander G. and Jean Mill. To Toronto, ONT. **Ts Arbroath.**

3177   GIFFEN, William, ca 1822–15 May 1890. From Kilmarnock, AYR. To Sherbrooke Co, QUE, ca 1843, but went later to ONT and d Adelaide Twp, Middlesex Co. Farmer. m Mary Ann Pitt, qv, ch: 1. Annabella, 1844–1927, d Bosanquet Twp; 2. James, 1846–1916, d Strathroy; 3. William Pitt; 4. Mary, 1854-73; 5. Susan, b 1858. **DC 31 Dec 1981.**

3178   GIFFORD, Arthur. From SHI. s/o Andrew G, Busta, Delting par. To Toronto, ONT, <1841. **SH; DC 21 Nov 1975.**

3179   GILCHRIST, Alexander, ca 1818–21 Nov 1867. From Carluke, LKS. s/o James G, Gilfoot, and Margaret Smith. To St John, NB, prob <1848. Merchant. **Ts Carluke.**

3180   GILCHRIST, Allan. To East Williams Twp, Middlesex Co, ONT, 1831. **PCM 44.**

3181   GILCHRIST, Archibald. From Is Islay, ARL. To ONT, 1854; stld prob Oro Twp, Simcoe Co. m Ellen McCuaig, qv, ch. **DC 9 Oct 1979.**

3182   GILCHRIST, Elizabeth, called Betty, 1814-72. From Glenegedale, Kildalton par, Is Islay, ARL. d/o Dugald G. and Grace Johnston. To Grey Co, ONT, poss 1854. Wife of Donald McCuaig or McLeod, qv, whom she m 21 Dec 1839. **LDW 4 Jun 1976.**

3183   GILCHRIST, Jean, b 11 Jan 1805. From Kilmarnock, AYR. To QUE on the *Renfrewshire*, ex Glasgow, 1842; stld Elgin Co, ONT. Wife of John McLean, qv. **DC 1 Dec 1980.**

3184   GILCHRIST, John. From ARL. To West Williams Twp, Middlesex Co, ONT, <1850. **PCM 47.**

3185   GILCHRIST, Margaret, d 3 Apr 1847. Poss from DFS. To Kingston, ONT, and d there. m Rev James Williamson. **DGH 20 May 1847.**

3186   GILCHRIST, Margaret Forrest, ca 1815–28 Aug 1848. From Carluke, LKS. d/o James G, Gilfoot, and Margaret Smith. **Ts Carluke.**

3187   GILCHRIST, Thomas, ca 1813–17 Dec 1856. From Carluke, LKS. s/o James G, Gilfoot, and Margaret Smith. To St John, NB. Merchant. **Ts Carluke.**

3188   GILCHRIST, Thomas, b 1812. From Leith, MLN. s/o — G. and Rebecca Wilson, who later m Charles Frederick Schlaberg. To QUE, 1828; stld Argenteuil Co, nr Lachute. **DC 15 Jan 1982.**

3189   GILKISON, William, 4 Mar 1777–23 Apr 1833. From Irvine, AYR. s/o David G, shipmaster, and Mary Walker. To ONT, 1796, and commanded a NWCo schooner on Lake Erie. Fought in War of 1812, and retr to SCT for a period. Again to ONT, 1832, and founded town of Elora, named after a family ship. m Isabella, d/o Comm Alexander Grant, qv, and had, poss with other ch: 1. David, d 1851; 2. Alexander Grant, d 1849; 3. William Galt, matric Univ of Glasgow, 1821, and d in India; 4. Robert, shipbuilder; 5. Archibald, matric Univ of Glasgow, 1826, d 1876; 6. Jasper Tough, 1814–1906; 7. Daniel Mercer, d 1861. **GMA 10830 and 11837; EHE 57.**

3190   GILL, Mary. From Earlston, BEW. To Hamilton, ONT, 1852. Wife of William Wadell Wood, qv. **DC 23 Sep 1980.**

3191   GILL, William. From Galashiels, SEL. To Dundas Co, ONT, <1851. m Alison Saunderson. Son Robert, b Dundas, 30 Sep 1851. **Galashiels OPR 775/2.**

3192   GILLAN, John. To QUE on the *David of London*, ex Greenock, 19 May 1821; stld Ramsay Twp, Lanark Co, ONT. Teacher. **HCL 86, 180, 239.**

3193   GILLANDERS, Alexander. From Kishorn, Applecross, ROC. s/o Lachlan G, farmer, and Margaret Mackenzie, 1783–1832. To ONT prob <1844. **Ts Kishorn.**

3194   GILLESPIE, Alexander, 1819–30 Jul 1865. From LKS. s/o Alexander Gillespie of Sunnyside. Educ Edinburgh Academy, 1829-36, and awarded medal for mathematics. Became merchant in CAN. **EAR 56.**

3195   GILLESPIE, Charles, b ca 1803. From Bodinglea, Roberton par, LKS. s/o John G. and Catherine Hope. To Milton, Shefford Co, QUE. Schoolmaster and postmaster. m Widow Watson, ch. **MGC 2 Aug 1979.**

3196   GILLESPIE, Dugald. From Is Islay, ARL. bro/o John G, qv. To NC, but stld Eldon Twp, Victoria Co, ONT, 1828. **EC 60.**

3197   GILLESPIE, Elizabeth, b ca 1785. From Echt par, ABD. To Campbellton, Restigouche Co, NB, 1817. Wife of John Adam(s), qv. **DC 17 Oct 1981.**

3198   GILLESPIE, George, 1772–1842. From Milnholm, Douglas, LKS. s/o Alexander G. and Grizel Paterson. To Montreal, QUE, ca 1790. Served with NWCo, and became partner in firm of Parker, Gerrard, Ogilvie & Co, later Gillespie, Moffat & Co, and rep them at

Michilimackinac. Ret >1812 to his estate of Biggar Park, LKS. m 1818, Helen Hamilton, 1790–1869, ch: 1. Alexander of Biggar Park; 2. Jane, dy; 3. Sir John, 1822–1901, WS; 4. Grizel Paterson, d 1860; 5. George Hamilton, 1827–1900; 6. Helen Jane, d 1899; 7. Walter, 1830-98; 8. Thomas James, dy.   **SGC 264; HWS 164; Gillespie Chart; MDB 265; Ts Wiston**.

3199   GILLESPIE, Helen. From PER. To Egremont Twp, Grey Co, ONT, <1835. m William Reid, qv.   **DC 20 Feb 1978**.

3200   GILLESPIE, John. From Wiston, LKS. To QUE, 1826; stld Abbotsford, Rouville Co. m 1799, Catherine Hope, qv.   **MGC 15 Jul 1980**.

3201   GILLESPIE, John. From Is Islay, ARL. bro/o Dugald G, qv. To NC, but stld Eldon Twp, Victoria Co, ONT, 1828. ch: 1. John; 2. Flora; 3. Sarah, 1835–1927.   **EC 60**.

3202   GILLESPIE, Robert, 1785–1863. From LKS. s/o Alexander G. of Milnholm, Douglas, and Grizel Paterson. To Montreal, QUE, ca 1800. Partner of firm of Gillespie & Moffat, merchants, and office bearer of St Gabriel Street Ch. Ret to ENG, 1822. m (i) 1815, Anne Agnes, d/o Robert Kerr, Niagara, ch: 1. Robert, 1818–1901, of Bitteswell House, LEI; 2. Alexander, 1823-52; 3. Thomas Clark, d 1891; 4. Elizabeth, dy; 5. Mary Anne, dy; 6. Ellen; 7. Catherine, dy; 8. Anne Agnes. m (ii) Caroline Matilda, d 1879, d/o Dr Daniel Arnoldi, Montreal.   **SGC 264; Gillespie Chart; MDB 265; Ts Wiston**.

3203   GILLESPIE, Robert, b ca 1805. From Bodinglea, Roberton par, LKS. s/o John G. and Catherine Hope. To QUE and stld Abbotsford, St-Hyacinthe. Store-keeper and farmer. m Lydia Paterson, qv.   **MGC 2 Aug 1979**.

3204   GILLESPIE, William David, 24 Jun 1819–19 Apr 1848. From Edinburgh. s/o Dr Alexander G, 30 York Place. Educ Edinburgh Academy, 1828-35, and went to Hudson Bay territory. d in Italy.   **EAR 50**.

3205   GILLIES, Alexander, b ca 1772. To Western Shore, Inverness Co, NS, 1802. Farmer. ch.   **CBC 1818**.

3206   GILLIES, Alexander, b ca 1786. To Inverness, Inverness Co, NS, 1806. Farmer, ch.   **CBC 1818**.

3207   GILLIES, Alexander, b 1791. From Balivanich, Is Benbecula, INV. To Pictou, NS, on the *Lulan*, ex Glasgow, 17 Aug 1848. Wife Flora, b 1801, with him, and dau Isabella, qv.   **DC 12 Jul 1979**.

3208   GILLIES, Angus, b 1800. To St Andrews dist, Cape Breton Co, NS, ca 1817. Farmer.   **CBC 1818**.

3209   GILLIES, Annabel, 1826-93. From Plockton, ROC. sis/o Kenneth G, qv. To Aldborough Twp, Elgin Co, ONT, 1851; stld Huron Twp, Bruce Co, 1852. Wife of Peter McKenzie, qv.   **DC 25 Dec 1981**.

3210   GILLIES, Archibald. From ARL. Prob bro/o Duncan G, qv. To Mosa Twp, Middlesex Co, ONT, 1832.   **PCM 24**.

3211   GILLIES, Archibald, 15 Jan 1821–22 Apr 1913. From Galston, AYR. s/o Thomas G, qv, and John Ann Campbell, qv. To ONT, 1843; stld York Co, and d Toronto. m Jane Craik, qv, ch: 1. Thomas, 1853–1922; 2. Robert, 1855–1933; 3. Margaret, 1858-62; 4. Archibald, d inf 1862; 5. Johanna, 1862–1929;

6. Margaret, 1864–1937; 7. Jean, 1867–1941; 8. Laurie, 1869–1957; 9. John, 1871–1942; 10. Agnes, d 1944.   **DC 11 Dec 1979**.

3212   GILLIES, Colin. Poss from ARL, and prob rel to John G, qv. To Aldborough Twp, Elgin Co, ONT, <1820. Farmer.   **PDA 92**.

3213   GILLIES, Donald, b 1753. To Western Shore, Inverness Co, NS, 1796. Farmer. ch incl Donald, jr, b 1783.   **CBC 1818**.

3214   GILLIES, Donald. From Knoydart, INV. To Pictou, NS, on the *Dove*, ex Fort William, Jun 1801. Farmer. Wife Ann with him, and ch: 1. Alexander, aged 3; 2. Hugh, aged 2.   **PLD**.

3215   GILLIES, Donald, b ca 1794. To St Andrews dist, Cape Breton Co, NS, 1802. Farmer.   **CBC 1818**.

3216   GILLIES, Donald. From Is Tyree, ARL. To NS, 1825; stld Whycocomagh, Inverness Co. m Mary Gillies. Son Neil, b 1835.   **HNS iii 210**.

3217   GILLIES, Duncan. From Arisaig, INV. To PEI on the *Jane*, ex Loch nan Uamh, 12 Jul 1790. Family with him.   **PLJ**.

3218   GILLIES, Duncan. From North Morar, INV. To QUE on the *British Queen*, ex Arisaig, 16 Aug 1790; stld nr Montreal. Tenant. Wife and ch with him.   **QCC 103**.

3219   GILLIES, Duncan, b 1768. To Western Shore, Inverness Co, NS, 1798. Farmer, m and had ch.   **CBC 1818**.

3220   GILLIES, Duncan, b 1773. To St Andrews dist, Cape Breton Co, NS, 1817. Farmer, m and had ch.   **CBC 1818**.

3221   GILLIES, Duncan. From ARL. To Aldborough Twp, Elgin Co, ONT, prob 1818.   **PDA 59**.

3222   GILLIES, Duncan. From ARL. To Mosa Twp, Middlesex Co, ONT, 1823. Widowed mother with him.   **PMC 24**.

3223   GILLIES, Duncan. From ARL. Prob bro/o Archibald G, qv. To Mosa Twp, Middlesex Co, ONT, 1832.   **PCM 24**.

3224   GILLIES, Elizabeth, 1838–1928. From Galston, AYR. d/o John G, qv, and Jean Struthers, qv. To King Twp, York Co, ONT, ca 1842. m Daniel Peterman, farmer, Collingwood.   **DC 11 Dec 1979**.

3225   GILLIES, Florence. From Knoydart, INV. To QUE, ex Greenock, summer 1815; stld prob Lanark Co, ONT. Wife of Ronald McDonell, qv.   **SEC 7**.

3226   GILLIES, George, b ca 1800. From Stornoway, Is Lewis, ROC. To Guelph, Wellington Co, ONT, ca 1852; stld Huron Twp, Bruce Co. Sailor, railwayman and farmer. By wife Sarah, ch: 1. George, b 1836; 2. Jessie, b 1842; 3. Christina, b 1846; 4. Margaret, b 1849; 5. John; 6. Donald.   **WLC**.

3227   GILLIES, Grizel or Grace, 13 Apr 1814–6 Sep 1880. From Galston, AYR. d/o Thomas G, qv, and John Ann Campbell, qv. To ONT, poss 1854, and d North Keppel Twp, Grey Co. m Robert Young, qv.   **DC 17 Nov 1979**.

3228   GILLIES, Hugh, b 1770. To Western Shore, Inverness Co, NS, 1797. Farmer, m and had ch.   **CBC 1818**.

3229 GILLIES, Isabella, b 1826. From Balivanich, Is Benbecula, INV. d/o Alexander G, qv, and wife Flora. To Pictou, NS, on the *Lulan*, ex Glasgow, 17 Aug 1848. Wife of John Morrison, qv. **DC 12 Jul 1979**.

3230 GILLIES, James 'Deffy'. Served as NCO in 82nd Regt, and was gr 200 acres in Pictou Co, NS, 1784. Moved to Merigomish Is. ch. **HPC App F**.

3231 GILLIES, James, 1786–1851. s/o George and Janet G. To QUE on the *David of London*, ex Greenock, 19 May 1821; stld Lot 10, Con 5, Lanark Twp, Lanark Co, ONT. Weaver and farmer. m Helen Stark, qv, ch: 1. John, qv; 2. George, b 1813; 3. James, lumber merchant; 4. Isabella, b 1820. **HCL 70, 168; DC 2 Nov 1979**.

3232 GILLIES, John. From Burard, North Morar, INV. To QUE on the *British Queen*, ex Arisaig, 16 Aug 1790; stld nr Montreal. Tenant. Wife and ch with him. **QCC 103**.

3233 GILLIES, John, b 1776. To Western Shore, Inverness Co, NS, 1802. Farmer. ch. **CBC 1818**.

3234 GILLIES, John. From Is Skye, INV. To Orwell Cove, PEI, 1803; stld nr Belfast. Petitioner for Dr MacAulay, 1811. **HP 74**.

3235 GILLIES, John, b 1784. To Western Shore, Inverness Co, NS, 1805. Farmer, m and had ch. **CBC 1818**.

3236 GILLIES, John, b 1778. To Western Shore, Inverness Co, NS, 1811. Farmer. ch. **CBC 1818**.

3237 GILLIES, John, b 1791. To St Andrews dist, Cape Breton Co, NS, 1817. Farmer. **CBC 1818**.

3239 GILLIES, John, b 1778. To St Andrews dist, Cape Breton Co, NS, 1818. Farmer; m and had ch. **CBC 1818**.

3240 GILLIES, John. Poss from ARL, and prob rel to Colin G, qv. To Aldborough Twp, Elgin Co, ONT, <1820. Farmer. **PDA 92**.

3241 GILLIES, John, 1811-88. s/o James G, qv, and Helen Stark, qv. To QUE on the *David of London*, ex Greenock, 19 May 1821; stld Lanark Twp, Lanark Co, ONT. Lumberman. m Mary Cullen Bain, qv. **HCL 70; DC 2 Nov 1979**.

3242 GILLIES, John. From Is Islay, ARL. To QUE, prob <1841; stld Megantic Co. m Christiana McEachern, ch: 1. Peter; 2. Mary; 3. John; 4. Malcolm; 5. Flora; 6. Annabella; 7. Rev Archibald, Presb min in NZ. **AMC 49**.

3243 GILLIES, John, 5 Oct 1810–31 Mar 1888. From Galston, AYR, but said b ARL. s/o Thomas G, qv, and John Ann Campbell, qv. To ONT ca 1842; stld King Twp, york Co. Farmer. m Jean Struthers, qv, ch; 1. Elizabeth, qv; 2. Thomas, d inf 1842; 3. Johanna, 1844-96; 4. Jane, b 1845; 5. John, 1847-64; 6. Thomas, JP, 1849–1939; 7. Ellen, 1851–1940; 8. James, 1852–1932; 9. Grace; 10. John, 1850–1932; 11. Mary, 1854–1920; 12. Bella, 1860–1950; 13. Hugh, d inf 1861; 14. Robert, d inf 1863. **DC 11 Dec 1979**.

3244 GILLIES, John, b 1805. From INV. To NS <1845; stld Irish Cove, Cape Breton Co. m Mary Isabella McLean, qv. Son Joseph Alexander, b 1849, KC. **HNS iii 280**.

3245 GILLIES, John, b 1811. From Tomluachrach, Is Benbecula, INV. s/o John 'Ban' G. and wife Isabella. To Pictou, NS, on the *Lulan*, ex Glasgow, 17 Aug 1848. Wife Ann MacEachan, qv, with him, and ch: 1. Flora; 2. Margaret, b 1840; 3. John, b 1842; 4. Christina, b 1844; 5. Catherine. **DC 12 Jul 1979**.

3246 GILLIES, Kenneth. From Plockton, ROC. bro/o Annabel G, qv. To QUE, 1851; stld 1852, Lots 33-34, Con 1, Huron Twp, Bruce Co, ONT. Farmer. **DC 25 Dec 1981**.

3247 GILLIES, Malcolm, ca 1817–ca 1897. From Dunganichy, Is Benbecula, INV. s/o Alexander G. and Christy McLellan. To West Williams Twp, Middlesex Co, ONT, ca 1852. m Marion McIntyre, qv, ch: 1. Catherine, b 1837; 2. Matthew, b 1839; 3. Christy, b 1841; 4. John, b 1844; 5. Flora, b 1847; 6. Mary, b 1850; 7. Kirsty, b 1851. **PCM 48; WLC**.

3248 GILLIES, Mary. From Morar, INV. To Pictou, NS, on the *Dove*, ex Fort William, Jun 1801. Poss wife of Angus G, qv. **PLD**.

3249 GILLIES, Neil. From Knapdale, ARL. To Lobo Twp, Middlesex Co, ONT, 1836. ch: 1. John; 2. Flora; 3. Joanna. **PCM 39**.

3250 GILLIES, Peter. From Keppoch, Arisaig, INV. To PEI on the *Jane*, ex Loch nan Uamh, 12 Jul 1790. Wife with him, and 3 ch. **PLJ**.

3251 GILLIES, Peter, 1815-99. From Timsgarry, Uig par, Is Lewis, ROC. s/o Angus G. and Christy Matheson. To QUE <1855; stld Lingwick Twp, Compton Co. m (i) Margaret McLean, qv, ch: 1. Marion, b 1843; 2. Sarah, b 1846; 3. John, b 1850; 4. Mary, b 1852; 5. Catherine, b 1854; 6. Peter, b Gould, QUE, 1859; 7. Margaret. m (ii) Margaret Thomson, who went with him to Lewis <1899. **MGC 2 Aug 1979; WLC**.

3252 GILLIES, Rev Robert, ca 1800–15 Nov 1848. From Brechin, ANS. s/o Provost Colin G. Grad MA Kings Coll, Aberdeen 1825. Min of Caerlaverock par, DFS, 1833-46, when deposed. Went to ONT and d there. m 1833, Margaret Ann Irvine, ch. **KCG 281; FES ii 260; DGH 4 Jan 1849**.

3253 GILLIES, Thomas, ca 1783–16 May 1867. From Galston, AYR. s/o Daniel G. and Grace Crawford. To ONT ca 1846, and stld York Co. Agricultural labourer and mason. m John Ann Campbell, qv, ch: 1. Helen, 1807-25; 2. Daniel, b 6 Nov 1808, who poss remained in SCT; 3. John, qv; 4. Thomas, b Sornbeg, 10 Nov 1812, dy; 5. Grizel or Grace, qv; 6. Ann, 1816-65, remained in SCT; 7. Isobel, 1818-43; 8. Archibald, qv; 9. Helen, qv. **DC 17 Nov 1979**.

3254 GILLIES, William. From Tray, South Morar, INV. To PEI on the *Jane*, ex Loch nan Uamh, Arisaig, 12 Jul 1790. Tenant. Wife with him. **PLJ**.

3255 GILLIS, Alexander. From Arisaig, INV. To Pictou, NS, on the *Dove*, ex Fort William, Jun 1801. Labourer. **PLD**.

3256 GILLIS, Angus. From Morar, INV. To Pictou, NS, on the *Dove*, ex Fort William, Jun 1801. Labourer. **PLD**.

3257 GILLIS, Angus, b 1758. To Mabou, Inverness Co, NS, 1806. Farmer, m and had ch. **CBC 1818**.

3258   GILLIS, Angus. From Morar, INV. To Antigonish Co, NS, poss <1820. ch by a first wife: 1. John; 2. Catherine; 3. Ann. m (ii) Mary MacDonald, ch: 4. Hugh; 5. Andrew. **HCA 139**.

3259   GILLIS, Angus. From Morar, INV. s/o Malcolm G. To NS, 1821; stld Margaree, Inverness Co, 1823. Son Hugh, qv. **DC 30 Apr 1978**.

3260   GILLIS, Rev Angus, 1807–5 Oct 1851. From Moidart, INV. s/o Alastair 'Ban' G. and Mary Cameron. Educ Lismore and at Valladolid, Spain. Ord to RC priesthood, 1840. Served at Braemar, Chapeltown and Glenmoriston. To NS, ca 1846, and was in Antigonish Co and Inverness Co. **MP 372**.

GILLIS, Angus. See MACDONALD, Angus.

3261   GILLIS, Catherine. From Knoydart, INV. To Antigonish Co, NS, 1810. Wife of Alexander 'Mor' MacPherson, qv. **HCA 343**.

3262   GILLIS, Donald. From Morar, INV. s/o — G. and — MacGillivray. To Pictou Co, NS, ca 1793, but stld Antigonish Co. Pioneer settler. m Christy MacDonald, wid/o John Smith. Son Alexander. **HCA 144**.

3263   GILLIS, Donald. From Is Skye, INV. To PEI, poss 1803; stld nr Belfast. Petitioner for Dr MacAulay, 1811. **HP 74**.

3264   GILLIS, Donald, b ca 1788. Prob s/o Angus G, qv. To Mabou, Inverness Co, NS, 1806. Farmer, m and had ch. **CBC 1818**.

3265   GILLIS, Donald 'Ban'. From INV. To Williams Point, Antigonish Co, NS, poss <1820. m Miss MacGillivray, ch: 1. John; 2. Angus; 3. Ann; 4. Mrs John 'Ban' MacGillivray; 5. Mrs William MacGillivray; 6. Margaret. **HCA 147**.

3266   GILLIS, Duncan. From Aberchalder, INV. To Montreal, QUE, ex Fort William, 3 Jul 1802; stld E ONT. **MCM 1/4 25**.

3267   GILLIS, Duncan, b ca 1801. To Port Hood dist, Inverness Co, NS, 1805, and became farmer. **CBC 1818**.

3268   GILLIS, Duncan. From Morar, INV. To Antigonish Co, NS, poss <1820; stld South River. ch: 1. Donald; 2. Hugh; 3. John; 4. Angus; 5. William; 6. Allan; 7. Mrs Donald McGillivray. **HCA 141**.

3269   GILLIS, Ellen, b ca 1786. From Is Colonsay, ARL. To PEI, 1819. Wife of Malcolm Amos, qv. **DC 19 Sep 1977**.

3270   GILLIS, Hugh. From Morar, INV. To Pictou, NS, 1801; stld South West Mabou, Inverness Co, 1805. Gr 400 acres. m (i) Mary Gillis, qv, ch: 1. Angus; 2. Donald; 3. Duncan; 4. John; 5. Mary; 6. Catherine. m (ii) Mary MacLellan, no ch. **MP 358**.

3271   GILLIS, Hugh. Prob from ARL. To Antigonish Co, NS, poss <1815. Son Donald. **HCA 147**.

3272   GILLIS, Hugh, b 1818. From Morar, INV. s/o Angus G, qv. To NS, 1821; stld Margaree, Inverness Co, 1823. Farmer. Son Malcolm Hugh, 1856–1929, farmer and Gaelic poet. **DC 30 Apr 1978**.

3273   GILLIS, Hugh 'Mor'. Prob from INV. To Arisaig, Antigonish Co, NS, poss <1840. m Margaret, d/o Alexander McDonald, ch: 1. Peter; 2. Duncan;

3. Archibald, dy; 4. Ronald, dy; 5. Hugh, went to Los Angeles; 6. William; 7. Catherine; 8. Duncan; 9. Ronald; 10. Elizabeth; 11. Mary; 12. Katherine; 13. Christy; 14. Margaret. **HCA 141**.

3274   GILLIS, John 'Ban'. From Morar, INV. bro/o Angus G, qv. To Miramichi, Northumberland Co, NB, <1789, later to NS, and stld Pictou Co, afterwards Antigonish Co. m Flora MacGillivray, qv, ch: 1. John 'Ruadh', qv; 2. Donald; 3. Angus; 4. Lachlan; 5. Alexander; 6. Allan. **HCA 143**.

3275   GILLIS, John 'Ruadh'. From Morar, INV. s/o John 'Ban' G, qv, and Flora MacGillivray, qv. To NS, 1791; stld Antigonish Co. m Christy MacDonald, ch: 1. John 'Og'; 2. Colin; 3. Lachlan; 4. Angus; 5. Alexander; 6. Ann. **HCA 144**.

3276   GILLIS, John. Poss from Is Skye, INV. To PEI, ca 1803; stld nr Belfast. Petitioner for Dr Macaulay, 1811. **HP 74**.

3277   GILLIS, John, b ca 1791. Prob s/o Angus G, qv. To Mabou, Inverness Co, NS, 1806. Trader, m and ch. **CBC 1818**.

3278   GILLIS, John. From Moidart, INV. To Mabou, Inverness Co, NS, poss 1810. m Anne Beaton, qv, ch: 1. Angus; 2. Donald; 3. Peter; 4. Margaret; 5. John; 6. Mary. **CBC 1818; MP 343**.

3279   GILLIS, John, 1832–1931. Prob from Is Skye, INV. To PEI <1840, and d Charlottetown. Master mariner. **HP 59**.

3280   GILLIS, Katherine. From Arisaig, INV. To Pictou, NS, on the *Dove*, ex Fort William, Jun 1801. Spinster. **PLD**.

3281   GILLIS, Malcolm, 1805–30 Oct 1884. From Is Skye, or Is Raasay, INV. bro/o John G. To Charlottetown, PEI, <1840; stld Hartsville, Queens Co. Farmer. m (i) Catherine McEwen, who d in SCT, ch: 1. Jessie, 1829–99; 2. Margaret, 1832–88, unm; m (ii) Harriet Matheson, qv, with further ch: 3. John, 1840–1925; 4. John 'Og', 1847–85; 5. Mary Ann, d 1906; 6. Alexander, b 1852; 7. Dr Angus, b 1855, res Salem, OR; 8. Ronald, res Moncton, NB; 9. Christian, b 1858; 10. Roderick, res Hammondvale, NB. **DC 16 Aug 1982**.

3282   GILLIS, Margaret. From INV. To Antigonish Co, NS, poss <1805. m John Smith, qv. **HCA 362**.

3283   GILLIS, Mary. From Mallaig, INV. d/o Martin G. To Pictou Co, NS, 1801; later to South West Mabou, Inverness Co. Wife of Hugh Gillis, qv. **MP 358**.

3284   GILLIS, Mary. Prob from Glengarry, INV. To Montreal, QUE, ex Fort William, 3 Jul 1802; stld E ONT. **MCM 1/4 24**.

3285   GILLIS, Murdoch. From Is Skye, INV. To PEI, poss 1803; stld Orwell Cove. **HP 73**.

3286   GILLIS, Peter. From INV, prob Morar or Arisaig. To Antigonish Co, NS, <1815. m Miss MacDonald, ch: 1. Angus; 2. Lachlan; 3. Duncan; 4. John; 5. Catherine; 6. Sarah; 7. Ann. **HCA 147**.

3287   GILMORE, Jane. To Wallace, Cumberland Co, NS, <28 Mar 1827, when m Elijah Tuttle. **VSN No 2171**.

3288 GILMOUR, Andrew. To Pictou, NS, on the *Hope*, ex Glasgow, 5 Apr 1848. Wife Ann with him, and ch: 1. Jane; 2. Robert; 3. Ann; 4. Helen. **DC 12 Jul 1979**.

3289 GILMOUR, Boyd. Prob from AYR. To Vancouver, BC, <1850. Mineralogist, HBCo. **DC 27 Feb 1968**.

3290 GILMOUR, Catherine, b ca 1783. From St Andrews par, Glasgow. To QUE, ex Greenock, summer 1821; stld prob Lanark Co, ONT. Wife of George Watt, qv. **RPE 62**.

3291 GILMOUR, David, b 1816. From Glasgow. s/o William G, merchant. Matric Univ of Glasgow, 1831. To QUE. **GMA 12816**.

3292 GILMOUR, James. Rel to William G, qv. To QUE on the *Earl of Buckinghamshire*, ex Greenock, 29 Apr 1821; stld Lot 4, Con 2, North Sherbrooke Twp, Lanark Co, ONT. Son James. **RPE 97; HCL 74**.

3293 GILMOUR, John. From Paisley, RFW. bro/o William G, merchant. To Ramsay Twp, Lanark Co, ONT, <1833. **SH**.

3294 GILMOUR, John, d 1851. To QUE, prob <1813, later to Eldon Twp, Victoria Co, ONT. Son James. **EC 61**.

3295 GILMOUR, William. Rel to James G, qv. To Lanark Co, ONT, 1821; stld Lot 4, Con 2, North Sherbrooke Twp. **HCL 74**.

3296 GILRAY, Catherine T, b 1834. From PER. d/o John G. and wife Mary. See Mrs Mary G. To Vaughan Twp, York Co, ONT, ca 1846. m Anthony Bowes, b 1814. Son Thomas. **DC 11 Jan 1980**.

3297 GILRAY, Christina, b 1831. From PER. d/o Mrs Mary G, qv. To Vaughan Twp, York Co, ONT, ca 1846. m Alexander Armour, b 1818. **DC 11 Jan 1980**.

3298 GILRAY, James, b 1827. From PER. s/o Mrs Mary G, qv. To Vaughan Twp, York Co, ONT, ca 1846. m Ann Jared, b 1831. **DC 11 Jan 1980**.

3299 GILRAY, Jane, 1822–25 Oct 1890. From PER. d/o Mrs Mary G. To Vaughan Twp, York Co, ONT, ca 1846. m (i) 29 Nov 1841, Charles Webster, qv; (ii) 1867, James Young. Jane was bur at Mount Pleasant, Toronto. **DC 24 Nov 1979 and 11 Jan 1980**.

3300 GILRAY, Mrs Mary, b ca 1790. From PER. Wife of or wid/o John G. To Vaughan Twp, York Co, ONT, ca 1846. ch with her: 1. Jane, qv; 2. James, qv; 3. Christina, qv; 4. Catherine T, qv. **DC 11 Jan 1980**.

3301 GILRAY, Robert, b 1816, Montreal, QUE, but went to SCT with his father John G, soldier. To ONT 1845; stld Epping, Euphrasia Twp, Grey Co. Son Rev Alexander, 1843–1915, b PER. **DC 11 Jan 1980**.

3302 GILROY, George. To Lanark Co, ONT, 1821; stld Lot 4, Con 2, North Sherbrooke Twp. **HCL 74**.

3303 GLADSTONE, Isabella. From Merton, BEW. To Guelph Twp, Wellington Co, ONT, 1833. Wife of Andrew Whitelaw, qv. **SG xxiv/2 53**.

3304 GLASHAN, John Cadenhead, ca 1844–14 Mar 1932. From ABD. To ONT, prob with parents, 1853. Schoolteacher and mathematician, later Inspector of Schools, Middlesex Co. LLD, Toronto, and FRS Canada. **MDB 267**.

3305 GLASS, Henry. To QUE on the *Commerce*, ex Greenock, Jun 1820; stld Lanark Village, Lanark Co, ONT. Storekeeper. m Christina, d/o Angus Cameron, storekeeper at Perth, Drummond Twp. **HCL 59, 64, 191, 238**.

3306 GLASSFURD, Rev Peter, ca 1800–29 Aug 1873. From Glasgow. s/o Robert G, merchant, and Jean MacDougall. Matric Univ of Glasgow, 1816. To Vaughan Twp, York Co, ONT, 1854. Relief and UP min at Alnwick, 1838-42; min at Leitholm, 1842-49; min at Albion and Vaughan. m 1856, Anna, d/o James Harris, qv, ch: 1. Robert; 2. Dr William; 3. Charles; 4. Emma; 5. Jean. **UPC ii 276; GMA 9731**.

3307 GLEN, Rev Andrew, 1796–1863. From Lochwinnoch, RFW. s/o William G, farmer. Educ Univ of Glasgow and Associate Burgher, Theological Hall. To Montreal, and ord min of St Peter Street Ch, 1818; trans to Terrebonne, River Du Chene and Richmond, but retr to SCT and became FC min at Glenbervie, KCD. **AFC i 169; GMA 9453; FES vii 635**.

3308 GLEN, Joseph. To Pictou Co, NS, <1776. **HPC App B**.

3309 GLEN, Margaret. From Templeton, Kilmarnock, AYR. To Penobscot, ME, ca 1767, but stld St Andrews, Charlotte Co, NB. Wife of Matthew Lymburner, qv. **DC 11 Nov 1981**.

3310 GLEN, William. From Paisley, RFW. To Sydenham Twp, Grey Co, ONT, <1854; stld Lot 8, Con B. m Janet Wilson, ch: 1. William, b 8 May 1854; 2. David, b 2 Nov 1846. **Abbey, Paisley, OPR 559/7**.

3311 GLENDINNING, James. From DFS. To Kent Co, NB, prob <1840. m Elizabeth Hannay, qv, ch. Absconded with his sist-in-law, Margaret Hannay, <1861. **DC 5 Aug 1980**.

3312 GLENDINNING, John. To Galloway, NB, on the *Dykes*, May 1817. **DC 7 Feb 1972**.

3313 GLENDINNING, Mary, 1767–1847. From Westerkirk, DFS. To Scarborough, ONT, 1795. Wife of David Thomson, qv, m 30 Nov 1787. **LDW 22 Jan 1976**.

3314 GLENNIE, James, 1750–23 Nov 1817. From St Andrews, FIF. Educ Univ of St Andrews, 1766-67, and at Royal Military Academy. Served in British Army, and after discharge stld Fredericton, NB. Mathematician and politician, rep Sunbury. **SAM 17; MDB 267**.

3315 GLOSSOP, Daniel. From Saltcoats, AYR. To Lanark Co, ONT, poss 1821; stld Lanark Twp. Shoemaker. **HCL 225**.

3316 GODSMAN, Alexander, ca 1753–13 Jan 1819. From BAN. To NS. **NSS No 1523**.

GODSMAN, William. See DAVIDSON, William.

3317 GOLDIE, James, b ca 1750. From AYR. To QUE on the *Friendship*, ex Port Glasgow, 30 Mar 1775. Ship carpenter, 'going out to build vessels.' **LSF**.

3318 GOLDIE, John, 21 Mar 1793–23 Jul 1886. From Kirkoswald, AYR. To ONT, 1844, stld Ayr Village, Waterloo Co. Naturalist. m Margaret Dunlop Smith, qv, ch. **MDB 269; MGC 2 Aug 1979**.

3319 GOLLAN, Fanny, 1801–21 Dec 1877. Poss from

Applecross, ROC. To Belfast, PEI, ca 1830. Wife of Donald Mackenzie, qv. **DC 9 Oct 1980**.

3320 GOODFELLOW, Adam, d 1827. From Midlem, Bowden par, ROX. Prob s/o William G. and Agnes Simson, qv. To West Gwillimbury Twp, Simcoe Co, ONT, <1827. Farmer, Lot 8, Con 6. m Janet McKenzie. Son John, b 1821. **MGC 2 Aug 1979**.

3321 GOODFELLOW, Archibald. Poss from ROX. To Cavan Twp, Durham Co, ONT, 1824. Farmer and merchant. **MGC 2 Aug 1979**.

3322 GOODFELLOW, James, b ca 1778. From Bowden par, ROX. Prob s/o William G. and Agnes Simson, qv. To ONT prob <1827, and stld Bolton, nr Toronto. **MGC 2 Aug 1979**.

3323 GOODFELLOW, John, ca 1792–16 Nov 1876. From Midlem, Bowden par, ROX. Prob s/o William G. and Agnes Simson, qv. To West Gwillimbury, Simcoe Co, ONT, prob <1827. Farmer, Lot 14, Con 7. m 1824, Catherine, d/o Col Tivy, ch: 1. William; 2. Thomas; 3. James; 4. Adam; 5. Peter; 6. Susannah; 7. Joseph; 8. Robert; 9. Samuel; 10. John; 11. Anne. Prob also dau Agnes by a previous wife. **MGC 2 Aug 1979**.

3324 GOODFELLOW, James. From Eckford par, ROX. To Albion Twp, Peel Co, ONT, <25 Feb 1819, when gr 100 acres. Farmer. m Margaret Hay, qv, ch: 1. Adam, b 16 Nov 1810; 2. Christian, b 15 Aug 1812; 3. Mary, b 17 Oct 1814; 4. William; 5. Margaret; 6. Agnes; 7. James, b 1824. **MGC 2 Aug 1979**.

3325 GOODFELLOW, John, b ca 1793. From ROX. To Markham, York Co, ONT, 1819. Farmworker. **MGC 2 Aug 1979**.

3326 GOODFELLOW, John, 1818–1902. From ROX. To Melbourne, Richmond Co, QUE, <1843. Farmer. m Elizabeth Dickson, qv, ch: 1. Elizabeth, b 28 Aug 1843; 2. William, b 19 Apr 1845; 3. Janet, 1854–75; 4. Mary, b 20 May 1855; 5. Margaret, b 6 Sep 1860. **MGC 15 Jul 1980**.

3327 GOODFELLOW, Robert, 1787–31 May 1865. From Lilliesleaf, ROX. s/o Adam G. and Jean Hall. To St Gabriel de Valcartier, QUE, ca 1821. Farmer and miller. m Janet Thomson, ch: 1. Janet, b 26 Mar 1821; 2. Helen, b 14 Dec 1822; 3. Marion, b 20 Sep 1825; 4. Robert, b 16 Sep 1827; 5. Margaret, bap 18 Oct 1829; 6. William, bap 18 Oct 1829; 7. John, bap 15 Jan 1832; 8. Thomas Thomson, b 27 Jan 1836. **Lilliesleaf OPR 795/1; MGC 2 Aug 1979**.

3328 GOODFELLOW, John, 21 Apr 1825–29 Apr 1900. From ROX. s/o Robert and Rachel G. To ONT, Aug 1843, and stld Innisfil, Simcoe Co. Farmer. m (i) 31 Oct 1850, Margaret Cross, ch: 1. Mary, b 1852; 2. Elizabeth, b 1854; 3. Susannah, b 1855; 4. Isabelle, b 1857; 5. Agnes, b 1859; 6. Margaret, b 1861. m (ii) 16 Apr 1862, Esther, d/o William and Jane McCullough, further ch: 7–8. Jane and Rachel, b 1862; 9. Fanny, b 1864; 10. Robert, b 1865; 11. Annie, b 1868; 12. Jemina, b 1870; 13. Willie, b 1872; 14. William, b 1875; 15. Flora, b 1877; 16. Alexander, b 1879; 17. Christena May, b 1886. **DC 11 Aug 1980**.

3329 GOODFELLOW, William. Poss from ROX. To Albion Twp, Peel Co, ONT, 1832. Farmer, Lot 10, Con 4. **MGC 2 Aug 1979**.

GOODFELLOW, Mrs William. See SIMSON, Agnes.

3330 GORDON, Adam. From Aberdeen. To Pictou, NS, <1823, when m Agnes, d/o J. Carr, qv. **VSN No 286**.

3331 GORDON, Alexander 'Picture', 1765–12 Oct 1849. From Glasgow. s/o Alexander G, merchant, and Isabel Fleming. Matric Univ of Glasgow, 1776. Merchant and patron of the arts. To Gilston, ONT, and d there. m Elizabeth, 1772–1849, d/o Thomas Buchanan of Ardoch. **GMA 3634; OEC No 343**.

3332 GORDON, Alexander, 6 Nov 1781–*post* 1841. From Cairnfield, BAN. Eldest s/o Alexander G. and Jean Gordon. Ret from army and went to QUE on the *Earl of Dalhousie*, ex Greenock, 26 Aug 1827. Stld Mount Dorchester, Queenston, Lincoln Co, ONT. m 1805, Elizabeth Robinson, ch: 1. William, b 8 May 1806; 2. George Robinson, 1807–25; 3. Alexander, jr, qv; 4. Elizabeth Mary, 1808–25; 5. Jessie Mercer, 1810–60; 6. Penelope Garden Campbell, 1813–70. *Gordoniana*, **Kings Coll, Aberdeen**.

3333 GORDON, Alexander, jr, 1812–61. From Cairnfield, BAN. s/o Alexander G, qv, and Elizabeth Robinson. To Whirlpool Farm, Stamford, Lincoln Co, ONT, prob <1827. m Jessie, d/o James Laing, Jamaica, ch: 1. Malcolm Alexander, d 1901; 2. Alexander, d inf; 3. Jessie, d unm 1921; 4. Elizabeth; 5. Louisa; 6. Francis Hawtrey, b 1853, alive 1936. *Gordoniana*, **Kings Coll, Aberdeen**.

3334 GORDON, Andrew, 10 Oct 1822–10 Apr 1883. From Elgin, MOR. To QUE on the *Berbice*, spring 1848; stld Dundas, ONT. Moved to Elora, Nichol Twp, Wellington Co, 1849. m Mary Skieff, qv, ch: 1. John, res Brooklyn, NY; 2. Mrs Robert Tribe; 3. Isabella; 4 George; 5. William; 6. Joseph Gibson, res Preston. **EHE 134**.

3335 GORDON, Charles, ca 1783–Jul 1844. From Avoch, Black Isle, ROC. To Grey Co, ONT, ca 1842. Formerly Capt, 93rd Regt. m in ENG, 26 Apr 1814, Mary Russell, ch: 1. Elizabeth, b 30 Jun 1816; 2. Thomas, b 15 Nov 1819; 3. Charles, jr, qv; 4. Mary Sophia, b 19 Aug 1823; 5. Robert, b 3 Feb 1827; 6. John Adam, b 4 May 1828; 7. Hugh, b 11 Dec 1831. **DC 11 Mar 1980**.

3336 GORDON, Charles, jr, 22 Apr 1821–29 Mar 1888. Born Kildonan, SUT. s/o Charles G, qv, and Mary Russell. To Sydenham Twp, Grey Co, ONT, ca 1844. m Georgina McKay. **DC 11 Mar 1980**.

3337 GORDON, Charles, b Edinburgh, ca 1786. To Charlottetown, PEI, on the *Clarendon*, ex Oban, ARL, 6 Aug 1808. Surgeon. **CPL**.

3338 GORDON, Christian or Christy, b ca 1770. From Badflaich, Kildonan, SUT. Wife of Donald Bannerman, qv. To Fort Churchill, Hudson Bay, on the *Prince of Wales*, ex Stromness, 28 Jun 1813. Went to York Factory, 1814, thence to Red River. Left the settlement and arr Holland River, ONT, 6 Sep 1815. **LSS 185; RRS 26; LSC 321; Kildonan OPR 52/1**.

3339 GORDON, Donald, 1762–1819. From Blair Atholl, PER. s/o Charles G. and Margaret Cameron. To Pictou, NS, on the *Commerce*, ex Port Glasgow, 10 Aug 1803; stld Brudenell, Kings Co, PEI. Farmer, and patriarch of

the Brudenell Gordons. m (i) Christina McLaren, qv, ch:
1. Isobel, qv; 2. Henry, qv; 3. James, qv; 4. Donald,
b 1802; 5. Betsy. m (ii) Jessie McLaren, Hermitage,
further ch: 6. John; 7. Peter; 8. Jessie; 9. Charles,
dy. **PLC; BP 3, 8, 30**.

3340 GORDON, Donald 'Ruadh', d 1871. From Dull
par, PER. s/o Henry G. To Kings Co, PEI, <1820.
BP 10.

3341 GORDON, Donald, 1771–1827. To Pictou Co, NS,
<1827; stld Elgin. m Janet McLean, 1775–1825. Son
Donald, 1827-66; res Big Brook, west branch, East
River. **PAC 93**.

3342 GORDON, Donald. From Is Skye, INV. s/o Patrick
G. To Charlottetown, PEI, on the *Mary Kennedy*, ex
Portree, arr Jun 1829. m Mary McDonald, qv.
DC 21 Oct 1978.

3343 GORDON, Donald. To Pictou, NS, on the *Lady
Grey*, ex Cromarty, ROC, arr 16 Jul 1841. **DC 15 Jul
1979**.

3344 GORDON, Donald Brown. From ABD. To PEI
<1850. **SH**.

3345 GORDON, George, b ca 1786. To Charlottetown,
PEI, on the *Elizabeth & Ann*, ex Thurso, arr 8 Nov
1806. **PLEA**.

3346 GORDON, George, ca 1779–15 Sep 1849. From
SUT. To Pictou Co, NS; stld Six Mile Brook. m Catherine
Grant, qv. **DC 10 Feb 1980**.

3347 GORDON, George. From Glasgow. s/o William G,
plasterer. To ONT <1855. **SH**.

3348 GORDON, Helen. From ABD. d/o Lt Francis G,
Mill of Lumphart, Old Meldrum. To Pictou, NS, <1820.
m James Monro, qv. **NDF 202**.

3349 GORDON, Henry, 1788–1864. From Fincastle,
PER. s/o Donald G, qv, and Christian McLaren, qv. To
Pictou, NS, on the *Commerce*, ex Port Glasgow, 10 Aug
1803; stld Brudenell, Kings Co, PEI. m (i) Margaret
McDonald, East River, ch: 1. Daniel; 2. Capt James, d in
OR; 3. Belle; 4. Elizabeth; 5. John. m (ii) ca 1852, Betsy
Stewart, wid/o Neil McQuarrie, further ch: 6. Henry;
7. Oswald; 8. Frederick. **PLC; BP 30**.

3350 GORDON, Rev Henry, 1790–13 Dec 1880. From
Edinburgh. s/o Thomas G, WS, and Letitia McVeigh.
Studied law and was adm WS, 1 Jul 1825. App
missionary by Glasgow Colonial Society and adm min of
Newmarket and King, York Co, ONT, 1834. Trans to
Gananoque, 1837, and joined FC there, 1844. Moderator
of Free Presb Ch in CAN, 1854. Min without charge,
1869-80. **HWS 167; FES vii 635**.

3351 GORDON, Isabella, ca 1787–19 Nov 1853. From
Clyne, SUT. To Pictou Co, NS, poss 1802; stld New
Lairg. m Donald Sutherland, qv. **DC 10 Feb 1980**.

3352 GORDON, Isobel, 1796–1817. From Fincastle,
PER. d/o Donald G, qv, and Christina McLaren, qv. To
Pictou, NS, on the *Commerce*, ex Port Glasgow, 10 Aug
1803; stld Brudenell, Kings Co, PEI. m her cous, James
McLaren, qv. **PLC; BP 30, 53**.

3353 GORDON, James, 1800-86. From Fincastle, PER.
s/o Donald G, qv, and Christina McLaren, qv. To Pictou,
NS, on the *Commerce*, ex Port Glasgow, 10 Aug 1803;
stld Brudenell, Kings Co, PEI. m Betsy Stewart,

1804-80, Brackley Point, ch: 1. Margaret; 2. Daniel;
3. Isabel; 4. Christina; 5. Elizabeth; 6. Jessie; 7. Grace;
8. James; 9. Dr John A; 10. William; 11. Matilda L.
PLC; BP 30, 32.

3354 GORDON, James, b 8 May 1806. From
Cairnfield, BAN. s/o Alexander G, qv, and Elizabeth
Robinson, qv. To ONT <1830. m Margaret, d/o William
Mylne, Grand River. *Gordoniana*, **Kings Coll,
Aberdeen**.

3355 GORDON, Rev James. Poss from ABD. To
Kingston, ONT, <1848, prob with parents. Educ Queens
Coll, Kingston, 1848-53, and grad MA. Became min at
Markham, York Co, ONT, 1854; later at North
Doncaster. **FES vii 635**.

3356 GORDON, James Ross, ca 1827–1910. Prob
from ANS. s/o James G. and Sarah Ross. To ONT ca
1855. **LDW 5 Jun 1974**.

3357 GORDON, Jane, b 1780. From Carsphairn, KKD.
To Burlington, Nelson Twp, Halton Co, ONT, 1817. Wife
of William Sinclair, qv. **DC 18 Feb 1980**.

3358 GORDON, Janet. From KKD. To Waterloo Co,
ONT, <1855. m Alexander Baird, qv. **DC 2 Dec 1979**.

3359 GORDON, John, b 5 May 1797. From Gifford,
ELN. s/o Benjamen G, carrier in Saltoun, and Katherine
Finlayson. To Montreal, QUE, 1832; stld Howick, English
River. Shoemaker, farmer. m Sarah Henderson, qv, ch:
1. Isabella, b 15 Aug 1818; 2. Elizabeth, b 4 Oct 1820;
3. William, b 17 Aug 1822; 4. Benjamen, b 28 Jun 1824;
5. John, b 9 Sep 1825; 6. George, b 25 Oct 1827;
7. Sarah Ann, b 5 Jan 1830; 8. James, b at sea, Jun
1832; 9. Janet, b Howick, ca 1834; 10. Jessie, b ca
1836. **DC 3 Jun 1981**.

3360 GORDON, John G. From Kildonan, SUT. To
Pictou, NS, 1816. Son William, qv. **DC 30 Aug 1977**.

3361 GORDON, Joseph. Prob rel to William G, qv. To
London, Westminster Twp, Middlesex Co, ONT,
<1840. **PCM 55**.

3362 GORDON, Margaret. From Uig, Is Skye, INV.
d/o Donald G. To PEI on the *Mary Kennedy*, arr Jun
1829; stld Vernon River. m Donald MacDonald, qv.
HP 37.

3363 GORDON, Mary, ca 1801–6 Jan 1872. From INV.
To Pictou Co, NS, prob <1820. m Alexander Fraser.
DC 10 Feb 1976.

3364 GORDON, Rev Peter, d 2 Apr 1809. From
Brechin, ANS. To Pictou, NS, 1805, as probationer, and
was ord min of St Peters, Kings Co, PEI, 1807. m Janet
Auld, qv, who m (ii) Rev Dr James Drummond
McGregor, qv. Dau Elizabeth. **UPC i 572,n**.

3365 GORDON, Peter. From Is Skye, INV. To PEI,
poss on the *Mary Kennedy*, 1829; stld Uigg, Vernon
River. Son Rev John A, 1847–1933, MA, DD, Baptist
clergyman. **HP 37**.

GORDON, Mrs Peter. See CRAWFORD, Isabella.

3366 GORDON, Robert D, d 9 Jan 1857. From Castle
Douglas, KKD. s/o Hugh G. To Hamilton, ONT.
DGH 2 Feb 1857.

3367 GORDON, Thomas, d 1895. From Dornoch, SUT.
To NS, 1826. Moved to London, Westminster Twp,

Middlesex Co, ONT, 1852, where he held many public positions. **PCM 55**.

3368　GORDON, Thomas. From Cragon, Inverallan, MOR. Tacksman. To Hants Co, NS, 1804. m Anna Grant, qv, ch: 1. Margaret, b 25 Nov 1777; 2. James, b 26 Oct 1779. **Cromdale OPR 128B/2**.

3369　GORDON, Thomas. From Buittle, KKD. s/o John G, farmer, and Agnes Templeton. To QUE <1853; stld Three Rivers, St Maurice Co. **Ts Calton, Edinburgh**.

3370　GORDON, William, 1790–1868. To Pictou Co, NS, and stld Glengarry. m Margaret Sutherland, ch: 1. Janet; 2. Robert, 1822–1905; 3. Charles; 4. Donald; 5. Daniel; 6. Josiah. **PAC 90**.

3371　GORDON, William. From Kildonan, SUT. s/o John G. G, qv. To Pictou Co, NS, 1816. Merchant. Son Rev Daniel Miner, 1845–1925, Vice-Chancellor and Principal of Queens Univ, Kingston, ONT. **DC 30 Aug 1977**.

3372　GORDON, William. Poss from FIF. To Lanark Co, ONT, 1820. Leader of a group of emigrants sponsored by the Abercrombie Friendly Society. **HCL 63**.

3373　GORDON, William, b 10 May 1818. From Corrie Burn, Is Arran, BUT. s/o Peter G. and Isabella Crawford, qv. To QUE on the *Albion*, ex Greenock, 5 Jun 1829; stld Inverness, Megantic Co. Moved later to Lowell, MA, and to CA. m 1 Sep 1852, Mary, d/o Sinclair Goudie, qv. Son Robert. **AMC 21, 138; MAC 35**.

3374　GORDON, William, 4 Feb 1797–18 Dec 1876. From Brechin, ANS. To Bayside, Whitby Twp, ONT. m Christina Brand, qv. Dau Jean, 1837–1915. **DC 6 Sep 1979**.

3375　GORDON, William. Prob rel to Joseph G, qv. To London, Westminster Twp, Middlesex Co, ONT, <1840. **PCM 55**.

3376　GOUDIE, Sinclair. From Shetland Is. To Lower Ireland, Megantic Co, QUE, 1826; later to Inverness Twp. Carpenter. m Catherine McKillop, qv, ch: 1. John; 2. Catherine; 3. Mary; 4. Barbara; 5. Isabella, schoolteacher; 6. Margery. **AMC 35, 60, 138**.

3377　GOURLAY, Elizabeth. From KKD. d/o Peter G. and Helen Sproat. To CAN, prob ONT, <1855. m William Henry. **SH**.

3378　GOURLAY, Robert Fleming, 24 Mar 1778–1 Aug 1863. From Ceres, FIF. s/o Oliver G. and Janet Fleming. Educ Univ of St Andrews, 1794-95. To Kingston, ONT, <1817. Pioneer journalist, land agent and pamphleteer. Visited Scotch Line settlers in Lanark Co, ONT, 1817. Banished for agitation. Author of a valuable *Statistical Account of Canada*, published London, 1822. Sometime in native land and in USA, but retr to CAN, 1856. **BNA 417; SAM 43; SDG 140; MDB 274; HCL 25, 44**.

3379　GOURLAY, William. To QUE on the *David of London*, ex Greenock, 19 May 1821; stld Lanark Co, ONT. **HCL 70**.

3380　GOURLEY, George, b 1821. s/o William G. To Perth Twp, Lanark Co, ONT, <1840. m Mary Robson. **DC 10 Oct 1967**.

3381　GOURLEY, Margaret, 1807-75. Poss from PER. To PEI <1836. Wife of Thomas Drummond, qv. **DC 25 Nov 1981**.

3382　GOW, John, b ca 1770. From Strathbran, PER. To Charlottetown, PEI, on the *Clarendon*, ex Oban, 6 Aug 1808. Labourer. **CPL**.

3383　GOW, John. From Comrie, PER. To Montreal, QUE, on the *Curlew*, ex Greenock, 21 Jul 1818; stld prob Beckwith Twp, Lanark Co, ONT. Wife Janet with him. **BCL**.

3384　GOW, Peter, b 20 Nov 1818. From Johnstone, RFW. s/o John G, shoemaker, and Agnes Ferguson. To Brockville, ONT, 1842; moved to Guelph, Wellington Co, 1844. Tanner and miller, mayor of Guelph and MPP. m 1857, Mary Maxwell Smith, ch. **BNA 1171**.

3385　GOWANLOCK, Andrew, b 1835, Yethouse, Southdean, ROX. s/o William G, qv, and Christian Laidlaw, qv. To ONT 1842; stld prob Bruce Co. m Betsy Laidlaw, ch. **DC 15 Oct 1975**.

3386　GOWANLOCK, Elizabeth Oliver, 1829–1907. From Southdean, ROX. d/o William G, qv, and Christian Laidlaw, qv. To ONT, 1842; stld prob Bruce Co, and d Port Elgin. m James Rowand, MP for West Bruce, ch. **DC 15 Oct 1975**.

3387　GOWANLOCK, George, ca 1789–26 Jul 1856. From Redhall, Lochmaben par, DFS. To Caradoc Twp, Middlesex Co, ONT. Farmer. m Janet Robertson, qv. **DGC 5 Aug 1856**.

3388　GOWANLOCK, Robert, 1825–1906. From Southdean, ROX. s/o William G, qv, and Christian Laidlaw, qv. To ONT, 1842; stld prob Bruce Co. m Jane Armstrong, and d at Brant, ch. **DC 15 Oct 1975**.

3389　GOWANLOCK, Walter, b 1839. From Southdean, ROX. s/o William G, qv, and Christian Laidlaw, qv. To ONT 1842 and stld prob Bruce Co. m Mary Rogan, ch. **DC 15 Oct 1975**.

3390　GOWANLOCK, William, 1798–1888. From Chesters, Southdean, ROX. To ONT 1842; stld prob Bruce Co, and d Port Elgin. m Christian Laidlaw, qv, ch: 1. Robert, qv; 2. Helen, d 1906; 3. Elizabeth Oliver, qv; 4. Christian, b 1831; 5. William, qv; 6. Andrew, qv; 7. James; 8. Walter, qv; 9. John, b CAN. **DC 15 Oct 1975**.

3391　GOWANLOCK, William, jr, b 1833. From Southdean, ROX. s/o William G, qv, and Christian Laidlaw, qv. To ONT 1842; stld prob Bruce Co. d at Brant, having m Jane Armstrong, ch. **DC 15 Oct 1975**.

3392　GRAHAM, Alexander, ca 1787–23 Sep 1862. From SUT. To Pictou Co, NS; stld Six Mile Brook. m Christy Munro, qv. **DC 27 Oct 1979**.

3393　GRAHAM, Alexander, 1 Sep 1814–8 Nov 1901. From Knapdale, ARL. s/o John G, qv, and Nancy Ann Livingston, qv. To QUE, 1837; moved to Lobo Twp, Middlesex Co, ONT, and in 1871 to Washington Co, KS. m Janet, d/o John McLellan, qv, and Katherine McVicar, qv, ch. **DC 25 Jan 1964**.

3394　GRAHAM, Alexander, b 1819. From South Knapdale, ARL. s/o Duncan G, dec, and Catherine Livingstone, qv. To ONT 1846; stld prob Huron Co. m Anne Tolmie, qv. **SG xxvi/3 92**.

3395　GRAHAM, Alexander. Poss from PER, and prob rel to William G, qv. To Aldborough Twp, Elgin Co, ONT, 1860. **PDA 68**.

3396   GRAHAM, Angus. From Is Lewis, INV. To QUE, ex Stornoway, arr 4 Aug 1851; stld Huron Twp, Bruce Co, ONT, 1852. Head of family.   **DC 5 Apr 1967**.

3397   GRAHAM, Archibald. From ARL. To Brampton Co, ONT, 1831; stld Boston Mills. Wife Martha with him, and ch: 1. Flora; 2. Mary; 3. Nancy; 4. John; 5. David.   **DC 29 Apr 1981**.

3398   GRAHAM, Charles, 1772–1841. From Rerrick, KKD. s/o William G, mason in Dundrennan, and Janet Kirkpatrick. To Pictou, NS, 1815. m Marion Hyslop, qv, ch: 1. Andrew, b 1796; 2. William, b 1797; 3. Robert, b 1799; 4. John, b 1801; 5. Charles, b 1803; 6. Nathaniel, b 1805; 7. James, b 1807; 8. Janet, b 1809; 9. Maxwell, b 1811; 10. George; 11. David, b 1815.   **DC 28 Dec 1975**.

3399   GRAHAM, Christie, b 1829. From South Knapdale, ARL. d/o Duncan G, dec, and Catherine Livingstone, qv. To ONT, 1846; stld prob Huron Co. m James McVicar.   **SG xxvi/3 92**.

3400   GRAHAM, David. From Lochgilphead, ARL. To QUE on the *Ada*, 1831; stld Ayr Village, Waterloo Co, later Ekfrid Twp, Middlesex Co. m Grace Campbell, qv, ch: 1. John; 2. Donald; 3. Duncan; 4. Anne; 5. Catherine; 6. Grace; 7. Mary; 8. Margaret. **DC 3 Aug 1979**.

3401   GRAHAM, David, ca 1808–2 Aug 1847. From DFS. s/o John G, Newbigging. To York Co, ONT, and d Scarborough. Surgeon.   **DGH 1 Jun 1848**.

3402   GRAHAM, Donald. From SUT. To Pictou, NS, on the *Hector*, ex Loch Broom, arr 17 Sep 1773. **HPC App C**.

3403   GRAHAM, Donald. To PEI, prob <1830; stld Orwell River. Schoolmaster in the Belfast area.   **HP 28**.

3404   GRAHAM, Donald. Prob from ARL. To Ekfrid Twp, Middlesex Co, ONT, 1834.   **PCM 30**.

3405   GRAHAM, Donald. From Knapdale, ARL. To Caradoc Twp, Middlesex Co, ONT, 1835.   **PCM 35**.

3406   GRAHAM, Donald, 1807-91. From Ballachulish, ARL. bro/o John G, qv. To Dutton, Dunwich Twp, Elgin Co, ONT, 1841. Farmer.   **DC 15 Jul 1979**.

3407   GRAHAM, Donald, 4 Feb 1821–26 Aug 1902. From Lochhead, South Knapdale, ARL. s/o Duncan G. and Catherine Livingstone, qv. To Lobo Twp, Middlesex Co, ONT, <1851. Brickmaker, weaver and farmer. m 1861, Ann, d/o Norman Smith and Christena McDonald, ch: 1. Christena, b 11 Jun 1862; 2. Duncan, b 11 Apr 1863; 3. Donald, b 24 Aug 1865; 4. Angus, b 17 Jul 1866; 5. Kate, b 11 Jun 1870; 6. Margaret, b 28 May 1872; 7. James, b 5 Mar 1874; 8. Norman, b 4 May 1876; 9. Normina, b 2 May 1878.   **SG xxvi/3 92; DC 13 Nov 1979**.

3408   GRAHAM, Dugald. From Knapdale, ARL. To Lobo Twp, Middlesex Co, ONT, 1829. ch: 1. Donald; 2. Duncan; 3. Alexander; 4. Sarah; 5. Ishbel; 6. Margaret.   **PCM 38**.

3409   GRAHAM, Dugald. Poss from PER. bro/o Robert G, qv. To Mosa Twp, Middlesex Co, ONT, 1832. **PCM 24**.

3410   GRAHAM, Duncan 'Mor'. From Knapdale, ARL. To Lobo Twp, Middlesex Co, ONT, 1828. ch: 1. Neil;

2. Duncan; 3. Alexander; 4. Dugald; 5. Mary; 6. Flora; 7. Margaret.   **PCM 39**.

3411   GRAHAM, Duncan, b ca 1812. From Knapdale, ARL. s/o John G, qv, and Nancy Ann Livingston, qv. To QUE, 1837; later to Lobo Twp, Middlesex Co, ONT. m Mary Campbell Ferguson.   **DC 1 Mar 1964**.

3412   GRAHAM, Duncan. Poss from PER. To Mosa Twp, Middlesex Co, ONT, 1832. ch: 1. Archibald, farmer, Glencoe; 2. Angus, res Thamesville; 3. Duncan, drowned in Lake Huron; 4. Donald, stld Metcalfe Twp, qv, 1832.   **PCM 24, 26**.

3413   GRAHAM, Duncan, b 1823. From South Knapdale, ARL. s/o Duncan G, dec, and Catherine Livingstone, qv. To ONT 1846; stld prob Huron Co. m Elizabeth Brown, qv.   **SG xxvi/3 92**.

GRAHAM, Mrs Duncan. See LIVINGSTONE, Catherine.

3414   GRAHAM, Elizabeth. From Paisley, RFW. To Ashdale, Antigonish Co, NS, <1830. m Thomas Goodwill, naval officer. Son Rev John, 1831–1905, missionary, New Hebrides.   **FES vii 619**.

3415   GRAHAM, Elizabeth, b 1823. From LKS. d/o — G. and Elizabeth Hood, qv, who m (ii) William Allan, jr, qv. To ONT, May 1830.   **DC 15 Jun 1977**.

3416   GRAHAM, Flora, b ca 1810. From Knapdale, ARL. d/o John G, qv, and Nancy Ann Livingston, qv. To QUE, 1837; later to Lobo Twp, Middlesex Co, ONT. m John Clark.   **DC 1 Mar 1964**.

3417   GRAHAM, Rev Hugh, 1758–1829. From West Calder par, MLN. Educ Edinburgh. To NS <1810, and d at Stewiacke, Colchester Co. Presb min and author. **MDB 275**.

3418   GRAHAM, Hugh. Prob from Edinburgh. s/o Hugh G. sometime in British West Indies. To ONT <1846. **SH**.

3419   GRAHAM, Janet, 1820–27 Jan 1895. Poss from SUT. To Pictou Co, NS. m James McKay, qv. **DC 10 Feb 1980**.

3420   GRAHAM, Jean, 1800-48. From Rerrick, KKD. d/o Andrew G, mason, and Janet Maxwell. To Pictou, NS, prob <1830.   **DC 28 Dec 1975**.

3421   GRAHAM, John, 11 Mar 1748–28 Sep 1803. Poss from PER. To Antigonish Co, NS, prob 1784. By wife Isobel, 1755–1824, ch: 1. John, b 1778; 2. William, b 1780; 3. Peter, b 1782; 4. James, b 1785; 5. Janet, b 1788; 6. Eunice, b 1791; 7. David, b 1793; 8. Mary, b 1796; 9. Sarah, b 1799; 10. Isabella, b 1802. **NSN 32/373**.

3422   GRAHAM, John. From INV. To Inverness Co, NS, <1795; stld Grand Judique. Farmer. m Margaret MacDonald, ch: 1. Ronald; 2. Stephen; 3. David; 4. Alexander; 5. John; 6. Angus; 7. Isabel; 8. Margaret; 9. Effie; 10. Annie.   **CBC 1818; WLC**.

3423   GRAHAM, John, 1791–1864. To Pictou Co, NS, prob <1830; bur Hill Cemetery, West River Station. m Ellen Sutherland, qv.   **DC 10 Feb 1980**.

3424   GRAHAM, John. From Knapdale, ARL. To Caradoc Twp, Middlesex Co, ONT, 1833. ch: 1. Alexander; 2. Hugh; 3. John; 4. Donald; 5. Archie; 6. Mary; 7. Nancy; 8. Christie.   **PCM 35**.

3425   GRAHAM, John, 1805-90. Prob from ARL. To Caledon Twp, Peel Co, ONT, <1835. Wife Ann McCallum, qv, with him.   **DC 21 Apr 1980**.

3426   GRAHAM, John, ca 1785–14 Aug 1844. From Knapdale, ARL, s/o Alexander G. and Flora McEwen. To Beauharnois Twp, Huntingdon Co, QUE, 1837; later to Middlesex Co, ONT, and stld Lobo Twp. Weaver. m Nancy Ann Livingston, qv, ch: 1. Katie, qv; 2. Flora, qv; 3. Duncan, qv; 4. Alexander, qv.   **DC 25 Jan and 1 Mar 1964**.

3427   GRAHAM, John, 1808-92. From Ballachulish, ARL. bro/o Donald G, qv. To Dutton, Dunwich Twp, Elgin Co, ONT, 1841. Farmer.   **DC 15 Jul 1979**.

3428   GRAHAM, John. Poss from ARL. To Ekfrid Twp, Middlesex Co, ONT, prob <1850.   **PCM 31**.

3429   GRAHAM, John, 1815-76. From Barvas par, Is Lewis, ROC. s/o Michael G. and Effie McLeod. To Whitton Twp, Compton Co, QUE, 1863. m Mary Paterson, qv, ch: 1. Angus, b 1859; 2. Effie, b 1859; 3. Donald, b 1861; 4. Alexander, b 1863; 5. John, b 1866; 6. Norman, b 1869; 7. Murdo, b 1870.   **WLC**.

3430   GRAHAM, Kate, b 1815. From South Knapdale, ARL. d/o Duncan G, dec, and Catherine Livingstone, qv. To ONT, 1846; stld prob Huron Co. m John McLeod, qv.   **SG xxvi/3 92**.

3431   GRAHAM, Katie, b ca 1808. From Knapdale, ARL. d/o John G. and Nancy Ann Livingston, qv. To QUE, 1837; later to Lobo Twp, Middlesex Co, ONT. m Michael Bolyn.   **DC 1 Mar 1964**.

3432   GRAHAM, Margaret, b ca 1738. From St Mungo par, DFS. To Georgetown, Kings Co, PEI, on the *Lovely Nellie*, ex Carsethorn, May 1775. Wife of David Irvine, qv.   **ELN**.

3433   GRAHAM, Margaret. From ARL. To QUE on the *Gestian*, ex Oban, 1820; stld Lobo Twp, Middlesex Co, ONT. Wife of Alexander Stewart, qv.   **PCM 41**.

3434   GRAHAM, Mary, 1774–1858. From Is Arran, BUT. To Restigouche Co, NB, prob 1829. Wife of Angus Sillars, qv.   **MAC 27**.

3435   GRAHAM, Mary, b 1815. From South Knapdale, ARL. d/o Duncan G, dec, and Catherine Livingstone, qv. To ONT, 1846; stld prob Huron Co. Wife of Allan McConnell, qv.   **SG xxvi/3 92**.

3436   GRAHAM, Peter. To Lobo Twp, Middlesex Co, ONT, <1840. m Jane Thomson, ch: 1. Mary; 2. Margaret; 3. Annie; 4. Archibald, d 1883; 5. Duncan, d 1903; 6. Janet; 7. Peter, d 1891.   **PCM 40**.

3437   GRAHAM, Robert. Poss from PER. bro/o Dugald G, qv. To Mosa Twp, Middlesex Co, ONT, 1832.   **PCM 24**.

3438   GRAHAM, Robert, 1820-47. From Pollockshaws, RFW. To QUE on the *Anchor*, summer 1847, and d soon after arrival. m Isabella Wilson, qv, ch: 1. David; 2. John; 3. James; 4. Robert; 5. William; 6. Elizabeth; 7. Jane; 8. Margaret.   **DC 22 Nov 1981**.

3439   GRAHAM, Roderick, 1800-69. From ARL. To Caledon Twp, Peel Co, ONT, <1840.   **DC 21 Apr 1840**.

3440   GRAHAM, Roger. Poss from ARL. To Ekfrid Twp, Middlesex Co, ONT, 1831.   **PCM 31**.

3441   GRAHAM, Samuel, 11 Jul 1819–15 Jan 1902. From Paisley, RFW. s/o Samuel G. and Jane Thomson. To ONT 1837; stld poss Elgin Co, and d at Rodney.   **SG xxvii/2 78**.

3442   GRAHAM, Walter, 1796–14 Dec 1854. From Lochmaben, DFS. To NS, and stld prob Colchester Co.   **DGC 30 Jan 1855**.

3443   GRAHAM, William, b 1750. From Dryfesdale, DFS. To Georgetown, Kings Co, PEI, on the *Lovely Nellie*, ex Carsethorn, May 1775. Labourer.   **ELN**.

3444   GRAHAM, William, 12 Dec 1752–11 Aug 1814. From Forteviot, PER. s/o John G, tenant farmer, and Jean Barclay. Served in Loyal American Rangers, ca 1780; afterwards as Capt in the Duke of Cumberlands Regt of Foot. Gr land in NS and disbanded at Guysborough. Also gr land in York Co, ONT. Res Guysborough, 1784-94, then moved to York Co, ONT. Capt, later Lt Col of York Militia. m Unis Elizabeth Taylor, 3 Aug 1789, ch: 1. Jane Elizabeth, b 1790; 2. John Elias, b 1792; 3. William, b 1796; 4-5. Adam and Peter, b 10 Jul 1799; 6. Margaret, b 1800, Whitchurch, York Co.   **Ts Forteviot; LDW 9 Aug 1970**.

3445   GRAHAM, William. Prob from PER. To McNab Twp, Renfrew Co, ONT, 1825.   **DC 3 Jan 1980**.

3446   GRAHAM, William, ca 1803–16 May 1871. From SUT. To Pictou Co, NS. Wife Ann, 1805–9 Dec 1877, with him. Both bur Salt Springs.   **DC 27 Oct 1979**.

3447   GRAHAM, William, 1806–16 May 1874. From Raploch, STI. To Hamilton, ONT, ca 1844; stld Lot 22N, Con 12, Blenheim Twp, Oxford Co. Weaver and farmer. m Margaret Garrow, qv, ch: 1. Rev John, Wesleyan preacher in MI; 2. Mary, 1839–1920; 3. William, 1841-52; 4. James, b 1843; 5. Edward, 1844-82; 6. Margaret, 1847-92; 7. Annie, 1852–1924; 8. Elizabeth, d 1871.   **DC 18 Dec 1982 and 16 Feb 1983**.

3448   GRAHAM, William. Poss from PER, and prob rel to Alexander G, qv. To Aldborough Twp, Elgin Co, ONT, 1860.   **PDA 68**.

3449   GRAHAME, David, b 1831. From Edinburgh. s/o James G, lawyer, 29 Ann Street. Educ Edinburgh Academy, 1840-44, and came to CAN. Drowned at the Falls of Niagara.   **EAR 108**.

3450   GRAHAME, Jeffrey, b 1829. From Edinburgh. s/o James G, lawyer, 29 Ann Street. Edinburgh Academy, 1840-46, and came to CAN.   **EAR 108**.

3451   GRAHAME, John. To QUE on the *Commerce*, ex Greenock, Jun 1820; stld Lot 17, Con 10, Ramsay Twp, Lanark Co, ONT. Leader of a group of emigrants sponsored by the Glasgow Emigration Society.   **HCL 61, 80, 238**.

3452   GRAHAME, William Richard, 1807–15 Oct 1867. From Moat, Annan, DFS. s/o Rev James G, WS, and Janet Graham. Matric Univ of Glasgow, 1819. To Muirdrum, Vaughan Twp, York Co, ONT, <1840. Farmer. Son Thomas, b Vaughan, 20 Mar 1840.   **SH; GMA 10376; HWS 172**.

3453   GRANGER, William. To QUE on the *Prompt*, ex Greenock, 4 Jul 1820; stld Lanark Co, ONT. Leader of a group of emigrants.   **HCL 62, 238**.

3454 GRANT, —. From INV. To Pictou Co, NS. Carpenter. m Sophia McDonald. Son Donald, builder and manufacturer. **BNA 680.**

3455 GRANT, Mrs A. Cabin passenger on the *Lulan*, ex Glasgow, 17 Aug 1848, bound for Pictou, NS. **DC 15 Jul 1979.**

3456 GRANT, Alexander, 1733–8 May 1813. From Glenmoriston, INV. s/o Patrick G. and Isobel Grant. To ONT <1773, and became Commodore of the Western Lakes. MLC, Upper Canada, 1792, and app Administrator, 1805. m 1774, Theresa, d/o Charles Barthe, and d Grosse Pointe, MI. They had, prob with other ch: 1. Isabelle; 2. Archange. **MDB 276; DGC 2 Nov 1813.**

3457 GRANT, Alexander, ca 1734–18 Apr 1810. From Glenmoriston, INV. To Nine Mile River, Hants Co, NS, poss <1800. m Margaret Mitchell, qv. **DC 20 Jan 1981.**

3458 GRANT, Alexander. From Urquhart and Glenmoriston par, INV. Prob rel to John M, farmer, qv. To Pictou, NS, on the *Sarah*, ex Fort William, Jun 1801. **PLS.**

3459 GRANT, Alexander. From Urquhart and Glenmoriston par, INV. To Pictou, NS, on the *Sarah*, ex Fort William, Jun 1801. Farmer. Wife Hannah with him, and ch: 1. Alexander, aged 4; 2. Isobel, aged 1 ½. **PLS.**

3460 GRANT, Alexander. Poss from Kilchrenan, ARL. To Montreal, QUE, ex Fort William, 3 Jul 1802; stld E ONT. Wife and family with him. **MCM 1/4 23.**

3461 GRANT, Alexander. From Urquhart and Glenmoriston par, INV. To QUE <1820; stld 'Duldraeggan', L'Orignal, Ottawa River. Fur-trader and farmer. **LDW 15 Jul 1962.**

3462 GRANT, Alexander, b 1805. From Nairn. s/o James G. and Marjorie McPhail. To Glengarry Co, ONT, 1832. Farmer. m Mary Fraser, qv, ch: 1. John, b 1827; 2. Marjorie, b 1829; 3. James; 4. Christina; 5. Mary; 6. Isabella; 7. Alexander; 8. Donald, b 1855. **DC 18 Jul 1963.**

3463 GRANT, Angus, b 1777. To Richmond Co, NS, 1801. **CBC 1818.**

3464 GRANT, Angus. From Urquhart and Glenmoriston par, INV. To Pictou, NS, on the *Sarah*, ex Fort William, Jun 1801. Farmer. Son Duncan, aged 11, with him. **PLS.**

3465 GRANT, Ann. From INV. To Pictou, NS, on the *Hector*, ex Loch Broom, arr 17 Sep 1773; stld Truro, Colchester Co. wid/o Hugh Fraser, who d 1773, and by whom she had a posthumous dau, Jean, qv. m (ii) Nathaniel Polly, further ch. **HPC App C.**

3466 GRANT, Anna. From Cragon, Inverallan, MOR. To Hants Co, NS, 1804. Wife of Thomas Gordon, qv. **Cromdale OPR 128B/2.**

3467 GRANT, Anne. From Levishie, nr Invermoriston, INV. Prob rel to John G, qv. To Montreal, QUE, ex Fort William, 3 Jul 1802; stld E ONT. **MCM 1/4 23.**

3468 GRANT, Barbara. From Golspie, SUT. d/o Alexander G, weaver. To Montreal, QUE, ca 1831; later to ONT. Wife of Alexander Mackenzie, qv, whom she m Feb 1826. **DC 11 Mar 1982.**

3469 GRANT, Catherine, d 28 May 1873. To Pictou Co, NS; stld Six Mile Brook. Wife of George Gordon, qv. **DC 10 Feb 1980.**

3470 GRANT, Charles, ca 1730–84. From MOR. s/o James G. of Kincorth. To QUE <1770. Merchant. m Jane Holmes, and had with other ch: 1. Frederick, of Ecclesgreig, KCD; 2. Charles, 1784–1843, fur-trader; 3. Margaret. **MDB 275.**

3471 GRANT, Christina, 1753–1818. From Beauly, INV. Prob d/o James G. To Pictou, NS, on the *Hector*, ex Loch Broom, arr 17 Sep 1773. m Roderick McKay, blacksmith, qv, East River pioneer. **HPC App A; SG iii/4 96.**

3472 GRANT, Cuthbert, d 1799. From Lethendry, Cromdale, INV. s/o David G. and Margaret Grant. To Montreal, QUE, prob <1785. Fur-trader and became partner of NWCo. Half-breed s Cuthbert James, 1796–1854, 'Warden of the Plains.' **BNA 985; MDB 276; DC 17 May 1978.**

3473 GRANT, David Alexander. Prob from INV. s/o David G. To QUE <1782; stld Longueuil, Huntingdon Co. Discharged soldier, 84th Regt; Sieur de Longueuil. m Marie Charlotte Josephte Le Moyne, Baroness de Longueuil. Son Charles William, b Quebec, 1782. **DC 1 Aug 1979.**

3474 GRANT, Donald. From SUT. To Pictou, NS, on the *Hector*, ex Loch Broom, arr 17 Sep 1773. Went to PEI, later to Knoydart, Antigonish Co, NS. m Catherine MacDonald, qv, and had, poss with other ch: 1. John, qv; 2. Dougald, deaf-mute, remained in SCT; 3. Mary; 4. Mrs Mackenzie, PEI; 5. Mrs MacDougall, PEI. **HPC App C; HCA 154.**

3475 GRANT, Donald. From Kenleoid, nr Taychreggan, ARL. To PEI on the *Jane*, ex Loch nan Uamh, 12 Jul 1790. Family with him. **PLJ.**

3476 GRANT, Donald. From Urquhart and Glenmoriston par, INV. To Pictou, NS, on the *Sarah*, ex Fort William, Jun 1801. Farmer. Wife Sarah with him, and ch: 1. Alexander, aged 9; 2. Christian, aged 6; 3. Isobel, aged 3. **PLS.**

3477 GRANT, Donald. From Urquhart and Glenmoriston par, INV. To Pictou, NS, on the *Sarah*, ex Fort William, Jun 1801. Labourer. Wife Margaret with him, and ch: 1. Elizabeth; 2. Patrick, aged 8; 3. Catherine, aged 6; 4. William, aged 4; 5. Robert, aged 2. **PLS.**

3478 GRANT, Donald. From Dalcataig, Loch Ness, INV. To Montreal, QUE, ex Fort William, 3 Jul 1802. Petitioned for land on Ottawa River, ONT, 6 Aug 1804. Wife with him. **MCM 1/4 23; DC 15 Mar 1980.**

3479 GRANT, Donald, 1777–1865. Prob from INV. To ONT, ca 1831; stld Eldon Twp, Victoria Co, 1837. Farmer, Con 4. By wife Catherine had ch: 1. John, 1811-73; 2. Hector, unm; 3. Andrew, farmer nr Lorneville; 4. Christine; 5. Donald; 6. Catherine. **EC 36.**

3480 GRANT, Mrs Donald. From Glenelg, INV. sis/o John Dewar, qv. To QUE on the *Liscard*, 1849; stld Glengarry Co, ONT. **MG 355.**

3481   GRANT, Eleanor, ca 1772–14 Oct 1818. From Urquhart and Glenmoriston par, INV. To Hants Co, NS, prob <1810. Wife of Alexander Ferguson, qv. **DC 20 Jan 1981**.

3482   GRANT, Eliza. From Drumnadrochit, INV. To Montreal, QUE, ex Fort William, 3 Jul 1802; stld E ONT. **MCM 1/4 23**.

3483   GRANT, Elizabeth, b 4 May 1762. From Croy, INV. To Pictou Co, NS, ca 1784; stld East River. m Alexander Dunbar, qv. **NSN 30/296; DC 20 Nov 1976**.

3484   GRANT, Elizabeth Jane, 1788–21 Jan 1867. From Advie, MOR. d/o James G. and Ann Stewart. To Sombra Twp, Lambton Co, ONT, via New York and Erie Canal, 1837. Wife of Peter Grant, qv. **Cromdale OPR 128b/2; Ts Advie; DC 4 Oct 1979**.

3485   GRANT, Ellen, ca 1774–23 Feb 1876. From SUT. To Pictou Co, NS. Wife of Joseph McLeod, qv. **DC 27 Oct 1979**.

3486   GRANT, Finlay. Prob from INV. To Pictou Co, NS, ca 1801. m Ann Fraser. Son John, b 1831. **HNS iii 382**.

3487   GRANT, Flory. From Dundreggan, Glenmoriston, INV. Poss rel to Mary G, qv, and Isabella G, qv. To Montreal, QUE, ex Fort William, 3 Jul 1802; stld E ONT. **MCM 1/4 23**.

3488   GRANT, Hugh. From INV. To ONT, 1828. m Mary Robinson, ch: 1. Isabella; 2. Margaret; 3. Charles; 4. Mary; 5. William; 6. Jessie. **DC 4 Mar 1965**.

3489   GRANT, Isabella. From Dundreggan, Glenmoriston, INV. Poss rel to Flory G, qv, and Mary G, qv. To Montreal, QUE, ex Fort William, 3 Jul 1802; stld E ONT. **MCM 1/4 23**.

3490   GRANT, Isabella. Prob from INV. d/o Alexander G. To Pictou Co, NS, ca 1820; stld East River. m 2 Nov 1822, Hugh McLennan, of Antigonish Co. **NSS No 2858**.

3491   GRANT, Isabella, 1798–1911. From Urquhart and Glenmoriston par, INV. To QUE, 1822; stld Lancaster Twp, Glengarry Co, ONT. Wife of Peter Grant, qv. **DC 2 Jan 1980**.

3492   GRANT, Isabella. From Glasgow. To Toronto, ONT, <1853. Wife of Alexander Sellar, qv. **LDW 16 Apr 1970**.

3493   GRANT, James, b ca 1726. From Glenurquhart, INV. To Pictou, NS, on the *Hector*, ex Loch Broom, arr 17 Sep 1773; stld Kings Co, later Grahams Pond, Caribou, Pictou Co. Farmer also at Upper Settlement, East River. Wife with him and ch: 1. Alexander; 2. Margaret; 3. Mary; 4. Jane, b 1771; 4. Robert. **HPC App C**.

3494   GRANT, James. Prob from INV. To Antigonish Co, NS, <1820. m Miss Chisholm, ch: 1. John; 2. William; 3. Alexander; 4. Duncan. **HCA 153**.

3495   GRANT, James. From BAN. To Pictou, NS, 1826; stld Stellarton. Schoolmaster. m Mary Munro, qv, and had, poss with other ch: 1. Rev. George Martin, d 1916; 2. Rev George Monro, CMG, min at Georgetown, PEI, later Principal of Queens Coll, Kingston, ONT. **FES vii 636; DC 1 Jan 1968**.

3496   GRANT, James. From Strathspey. To Westminster Twp, Middlesex Co, ONT, 1830. Son James, farmer, London Twp. **PCM 55**.

3497   GRANT, James, 1 Aug 1822–5 May 1887. From Edinburgh. s/o Capt G, Gordon Highlanders. To NFD, 1832, with his father. Retr to SCT, 1839. Draughtsman and military novelist. **CBD 429**.

3498   GRANT, James. From Inverness. To Martintown, Glengarry Co, ONT, ca 1832. Physician. m Jane Ord, qv. Son Sir James Alexander, qv. **MDB 277**.

3499   GRANT, James, 1826–17 Jun 1864. From Duthil, INV. s/o Rev William G. and Mary Garioch. To Sombra Twp, Lambton Co, ONT, ca 1851; stld Duthill. Physician, formerly army surgeon. m Jane McPherson, qv. **FES vi 361; DC 4 Oct 1979**.

3500   GRANT, Sir James Alexander, 1831–5 Feb 1820. From Inverness. s/o Dr James G, qv, and Jane Ord, qv. To Martintown, Glengarry Co, ONT, ca 1832. Physician and politician. KCMG 1887. m 1856, Maria, d/o Edward Malloch. **BNA 746; MDB 277**.

3501   GRANT, Jane, ca 1804–23 Nov 1869. From Advie, MOR. d/o William G. To Sombra Twp, Lambton Co, ONT, 1836, via New York and Erie Canal. m 28 Nov 1828, James Reid, qv. **DC 4 Oct 1979**.

3502   GRANT, Janet. From Redcastle, ROC. To Pictou, NS, on the *Sarah*, ex Fort William, Jun 1801. Spinster. **PLS**.

3503   GRANT, Jean, ca 1750–29 Jan 1789. From Knockando, MOR. To Merigomish, Pictou Co, NS, poss 1788. Wife of John McNeil, qv. **DC 18 Jul 1981**.

3504   GRANT, John, ca 1754–23 Aug 1817. From Glenmoriston, INV. To Montreal, QUE, 1771; stld Lachine. Fur-trader, carrier, and forwarding agent for the NWCo. m 30 Jul 1777, Margaret Beattie, and had, poss with other ch: 1. James Charles; 2. Margaret; 3. Mrs Donald Duff. **SGC 230; MDB 278**.

3505   GRANT, John. From SUT. s/o Donald G, qv, and Catherine MacDonald, qv. To Pictou, NS, on the *Hector*, ex Lochbroom, arr 17 Sep 1773. Sometime in PEI, but stld Knoydart, Antigonish Co, NS. m Catherine MacDonald, ch: 1. Angus; 2. Dougald; 3. Colin, dy; 4. Rev Donald; 5. Donald; 6. Duncan; 7. Sarah; 8. Catherine. **HCA 154**.

3506   GRANT, John. From Urquhart and Glenmoriston par, INV. To Pictou, NS, on the *Sarah*, ex Fort William, Jun 1802. Farmer. **PLS**.

3507   GRANT, John. From Strathglass, INV. To Pictou, NS, on the *Sarah*, ex Fort William, Jun 1801. Farmer. Wife Catherine with him, and ch: 1. James, aged 10; 2. John, aged 8; 3. Alexander, aged 6; 4. Donald, aged 4. **PLS**.

3508   GRANT, John. To Pictou, NS, 1801; stld Sunny Brae, East River. Son William, clergyman. **PAC 70**.

3509   GRANT, John. From Levishie, Glenmoriston, INV. Poss rel to Anne G, qv. To Montreal, QUE, ex Fort William, 3 Jul 1802; stld E ONT. **MCM 1/4 23**.

3510   GRANT, John. Poss from Appin, ARL. To Montreal, QUE, ex Fort William, 3 Jul 1802; stld E ONT. **MCM 1/4 23**.

3511 GRANT, John. Prob from INV. To Antigonish Co, NS, <1820. m Miss Fraser, ch: 1. Alexander; 2. John; 3. Isabella; 4. Janet; 5. Mary. **HCA 153**.

3512 GRANT, John, b ca 1783. To Pictou, NS, 1815; res Pictou Town, 1816. House carpenter, unm. **INS 39**.

3513 GRANT, John, 6 May 1791–20 May 1890. From Grantown-on-Spey, MOR. To Pictou, NS, <1830; d Telford. m Sophia 'Tailor' MacDonald, 1802-93. **DC 10 May 1962**.

3514 GRANT, Katherine, b 1767. From Kildonan, SUT. To Fort Churchill, Hudson Bay, on the *Prince of Wales*, ex Stromness, 28 Jun 1813. Went to York Factory, thence to Red River. Wife of John Sutherland, qv. stld later Bradford, Simcoe Co, ONT. **LSS 184; RRS 26; LSC 321; DC 11 Sep 1977**.

3515 GRANT, Kenneth, d 1857. Prob from Fodderty, ROC. s/o William G, d 1857, Polla, Strathpeffer, and Isabella Ross. To Galt Twp, Waterloo Co, ONT, and d there. **Ts Fodderty**.

3516 GRANT, John, b 16 Jun 1824. From Advie, MOR. s/o Peter G, qv, and Elizabeth Jane Grant, qv. To Sombra Twp, Lambton Co, ONT, 1837. m Margaret, d/o John McDonald, qv, Dover Twp, Kent Co, and Catherine McLean, qv. **DC 4 Oct 1979**.

3517 GRANT, Malcolm, 20 Oct 1828–25 Jun 1856. From OKI. s/o Malcolm G. and Margaret Norquoy. To Orford Twp, Kent Co, ONT, 1849. Farmer. m at Hamilton, ONT, 25 Jun 1856, Martha, d/o James Lather and Betsy Newport, Haldimand Co, emigrants from LAN, ENG, ch: 1. Janet, 1857-59; 2. Jane, 1859-61; 3. Elizabeth, 1860–1922; 4. John, 1862–1946, rancher, Touchet, WA; 5. James, 1865–1950, rancher, Walla Walla, WA; 6. Jessie, d 1855; 7. Malcolm, 1870–1905; 8. George, 1873–1939, physician, ND; 9. William, b ca 1875; 10. Isaac, 1876-83; 11. Edward, 1882–1920, physician, Roblin, MAN; 12. Alfred, b 1882, barrister, Edmonton, ALB. **DC 23 Feb 1980**.

3518 GRANT, Marcus. Poss from ARL. To Ekfrid Twp, Middlesex Co, ONT, prob <1850. **PCM 31**.

3519 GRANT, Margaret. Prob from SUT. To Pictou Co, NS, 1803; stld Concord. Wife of Donald Douglas, qv. **PAC 130**.

3520 GRANT, Margaret. From Glenmoriston, INV. To ONT, 1816. Wife of Allan MacDonald, qv. **DC 4 Mar 1965**.

3521 GRANT, Mary. From Dundreggan, Glenmoriston, INV. Poss rel to Flory G, qv, and Isabella G, qv. To Montreal, QUE, ex Fort William, 3 Jul 1802; stld E ONT. **MCM 1/4 23**.

3522 GRANT, Patrick. From Urquhart and Glenmoriston par, INV. Prob rel to Angus G, qv. To Pictou, NS, on the *Sarah*, ex Fort William, Jun 1801. Farmer. **PLS**.

3523 GRANT, Peter, 1764–20 Jul 1848. From INV. To Montreal, QUE, 1784. Clerk with NWCo, later partner. Ret <1807, and res Ste Anne, Bout de l'Isle. **MDB 278**.

3524 GRANT, Peter. Prob from INV. Served in 84th Regt and after discharge, 1784, was gr land on east side of east branch of East River, Pictou Co, NS. Son Alexander. **HPC App G; PAC 94**.

3525 GRANT, Peter. To Pictou Co, NS, ca 1784; stld Little Harbour. Discharged soldier, gr land. ch incl: 1. John; 2. Joseph. **HNS iii 172**.

3526 GRANT, Peter, 1791–1881. From Glenmoriston, INV. s/o Finlay G. To QUE, 1822, and stld Lancaster Twp, Glengarry Co, ONT. Farmer. m Isabella Grant, qv, ch: 1. Ellen, b 1827; 2. Hannah; 3. Bella; 4. Margaret, 1832–1922; 5. Anna, 1839-64; 6. Elizabeth, d unm 1916; 7. Allan, d unm 1926; 8. Donald. **DC 2 Jan 1980**.

3527 GRANT, Peter. Prob from INV. To Halifax, NS, <1830; stld later at Pictou. Schoolteacher and book-keeper, afterwards farmer. Son John, farmer. **HNS iii 248**.

3528 GRANT, Peter, 1747–1 Apr 1816. From Aberdeen. To Halifax, NS. **NSS No 1032**.

3529 GRANT, Peter, 1786–26 Mar 1852. From Advie, MOR. s/o William G. To Sombra Twp, Lambton Co, ONT, via New York and Erie Canal, 1837; stld Lot 10, Con 9. Farmer. Wife Elizabeth Jane Grant, qv, with him, and surviving ch: 1. Jane Ann Mary, b 30 Jun 1820; 2. Elspet, b 4 Apr 1822; 3. John, b 16 Apr 1824; 4. William, b 20 Sep 1828; 5. Ann, b 7 Aug 1830; 6. Elizabeth, b 25 Mar 1832. **Cromdale OPR 128b/2; Ts Advie; DC 4 Oct 1979**.

3530 GRANT, Robert, ca 1752–16 Aug 1801. From Lethendry, Cromdale, MOR. s/o David G. and Margaret Grant. To Montreal, QUE, <1784. Fur-trader in Red River area and became partner, NWCo. Retr to SCT, 1793, and later purchased estate of Kincorth, in Dyke and Moy par. m 5 Dec 1795, Anne, d/o Rev Lewis Grant, Cromdale. ch. **FES vi 358; MDB 279; Ts Cromdale**.

3531 GRANT, Robert Patterson, 12 Apr 1814–13 Nov 1892. From Inverness. s/o Lewis G, bookseller. To NS, 1835; stld Pictou Co. Banker, merchant and shipowner; MLA, 1859-63. m 1840, Annie, d/o James Carmichael, New Glasgow. **MLA 144**.

3532 GRANT, Roderick, b ca 1795. To Eldon Twp, Victoria Co, ONT, ca 1833. Farmer. **EC 65**.

3533 GRANT, Rory. Prob from INV. To Antigonish Co, NS, poss <1815. m (i) Christy Fraser; (ii) Christy Chisholm, ch: 1. John; 2. Angus; 3. Duncan. **HCA 153**.

3534 GRANT, Mrs R. To Pictou, NS, on the *Lulan*, ex Glasgow, 17 Aug 1848. **DC 12 Jul 1979**.

3535 GRANT, William, 1741–5 Oct 1805. Poss from INV. To QUE, 1763. Forwarding agent; Deputy Receiver-General for QUE, 1777, and MLA, 1791. Purchased several seignories. m 1770, Mrs Charles Jacques Le Moyn, Baroness de Longueuil. **MDB 279**.

3536 GRANT, Sir William, 3 Oct 1752–23 May 1832. From Elchies, MOR. s/o James G, farmer. To QUE, 1775. Lawyer, and became Attorney-General of the province. Went to ENG, where he was knighted, 1799. Lord Rector of Aberdeen Univ, 1809; DCL, Oxford 1820. **SAS 22; FAM ii 19; MDB 279**.

3537 GRANT, William, 1743–20 Nov 1810. From Blairfindie, Kirkmichael, BAN. To QUE <1777. Fur-trader, with Campion & Co, and res Three Rivers, where he owned property. **MDB 279**.

3538 GRANT, William. From Kilmorack, INV. To

Pictou, NS, on the *Sarah*, ex Fort William, Jun 1801. Labourer. **PLS**.

3539   GRANT, William. Prob from INV. To Antigonish Co, NS, prob <1815. Son Alexander. **HCA 152**.

3540   GRANT, William, b ca 1766. To Pictou, NS, 1815; stld West River, 1816. Labourer, m, with 7 ch. 'Very poor, but industrious.' **INS 38**.

3541   GRANT, William. To Pictou, NS, on the *Lulan*, ex Glasgow, 17 Aug 1848. **DC 12 Jul 1979**.

3542   GRASSIE, George, ca 1763–27 Apr 1823. From Aberdeen. To Halifax, NS, <1790. Wine merchant, magistrate and MLA. m 21 Mar 1793, Mary Eliza Shatford Lawson. **MLA 144**.

3543   GRASSIE, William, ca 1795–15 Nov 1877. Poss from ABD. To Hamilton, ONT. m Ann Anderson, qv, ch. **Ts Mount Albion**.

3544   GRAY, Alexander, 1796–12 Apr 1879. From ARL. To QUE on the *Mars*, ex Tobermory, 28 Jul 1818; stld Aldborough Twp, Elgin Co, ONT. Farmer. m Catherine McLarty, qv, ch: 1. Neil; 2. Dougald; 3. Angus; 4. Mary; 5. Catherine; 6. Belle; 7. Donald.   **PDA 24, 43**.

3545   GRAY, Rev Archibald, 1764–1826. From Forres, MOR. Missionary and min in Shetland Is, before going to Halifax, NS, 1796. Min of St Matthews Ch there. m 14 Dec 1802, Ann, d/o Dr Michael Head. Son Rev Archibald, Episcopal clergyman. **FES vii 300; DGC 24 Oct 1826**.

3546   GRAY, Archibald. From Knapdale, ARL. To Lobo Twp, Middlesex Co, ONT, 1836. **PCM 39**.

3547   GRAY, Archibald, ca 1833–15 Oct 1904. Prob from Glasgow. s/o Lachlan and Euphemia G. To Sarnia Twp, Lambton Co, ONT, ca 1854. m Isabella McKenzie, qv, ch: 1. Mary Livingstone, b 1854; 2. John, b 1855; 3. Euphemia, b 1857; 4. Lachlan, b 1859; 5. James, went to Detroit; 6. Archibald; 7. Annie.   **DC 30 Jul 1980**.

3548   GRAY, Catharine. From New Machar, ABD. To Bon Accord, Nichol Twp, Wellington Co, ONT, ca 1837. Wife of Thomas Gray, qv. **EHE 95**.

3549   GRAY, Catherine. From Dornoch, SUT. To Halifax, NS, <1840. Wife of Robert MacDonald, qv. **MLA 201**.

3550   GRAY, Donald or Daniel, 1777–8 Nov 1857. From INV. To Colchester Co, NS, 1801; later Hopewell, Pictou Co. Farmer and millwright. m Nancy McDonald, qv, ch: 1. John, qv; 2. William; 3. Alexander; 4. Donald, 1823-77; 5. Margaret; 6. Janet; 7. Isabel; 8. Mary; 9. Catherine; 10. Nancy.   **PAC 97; HNS iii 181**.

3551   GRAY, George, b ca 1755. From Banff. To QUE on the *Eliza*, ex Greenock, 3 Aug 1815; stld Lot 4, Con 2, Bathurst Twp, Lanark Co, ONT. Wife Isobel Lesley, qv, with him, and 8 ch, incl John, b ca 1795. **SEC 8; HCL 233**.

3552   GRAY, George, 10 Jun 1793–13 Sep 1850. From Galashiels, SEL. s/o Thomas G. and Janet Dalgleish, qv. To Windsor, Sandwich Twp, Essex Co, ONT, <1848; d Cuyahoga Falls, OH. m 13 Nov 1828, in Lancaster, ENG, Mary Vickers, 1799–1875, ch: 1. Thomas, b 1829; 2. Elizabeth, b 1831; 3. William, b 1833; 4. James,

b 1835; 5. George, b 1838; 6. Mary Helen, b 1841; 7. John, b 1844.   **DC 14 Jan 1975**.

3553   GRAY, Isabella, 1768–1853. From Fort William, INV. d/o Archibald G, merchant. To Montreal, QUE, on the *Friends*, ex Fort William, 3 Jun 1802. Wife of Archibald McMillan of Murlaggan, qv, m 1794. **MCM 1/4 18**.

3554   GRAY, James, 1829–13 Jul 1879. From Huntly, ABD. To Northumberland Co, NB. Bur at Chatham. **DC 14 Nov 1980**.

3555   GRAY, James. From ROC. To East Williams Twp, Middlesex Co, ONT, <1850. **PCM 43**.

3556   GRAY, Jean, b ca 1808. From Evelix, Dornoch, SUT. d/o Robert G. and Sarah Munro. To Toronto, ONT, prob <1840. m William Mackay. **DC 21 Mar 1981**.

3557   GRAY, John. From INV. s/o Donald G, qv, and Nancy McDonald, qv. To Pictou, NS, 1801; stld Colchester Co, and later at Hopewell, Pictou Co. m 1831, Isabella Fraser. Son John Andrew, b 1853. **HNS iii 181, 390; PAC 97**.

3558   GRAY, John. From ARL. To Lobo Twp, Middlesex Co, ONT, 1819. ch: 1. Malcolm; 2. John; 3. Angus; 4. Duncan; 5. Dugald; 6. Janet; 7. Betsy; 8. Margaret. **PCM 39**.

3559   GRAY, Rev John. From Elgin, MOR. To ONT, ca 1844. Studied at Knox Coll, Toronto, and became min at Orillia, Simcoe Co, 1851. DD, Knox Coll, 1885. **SGC 525**.

3560   GRAY, John, ca 1819–22 Jan 1863. From Lennel, Coldstream, BEW. s/o John G, feuar, and Janet Dodds. To ONT, and d there. **Ts Old Lennel**.

3561   GRAY, Margaret, 15 Mar 1835–1 Feb 1917. Poss from PER. To Dundas, Wentworth Co, ONT, <1855. m Thomas J McLaren, qv. **DC 20 Feb 1981**.

3562   GRAY, Margaret McKenzie, d 20 Mar 1788. From Edinburgh. d/o Alexander G, WS, and Margaret Alves. To Montreal, QUE, and d there. *Dumfries Journal*, **9 Jul 1788; HWS 174**.

3563   GRAY, Neil. From Knapdale, ARL. To Lobo Twp, Middlesex Co, ONT, 1836. **PCM 39**.

3564   GRAY, Robert, d 1828. From Glasgow. To Charlottetown, PEI, 1787. Had fought in American Revolutionary War with the rank of Capt. Became Treasurer of the Council of PEI. m Mary Burns, and had, prob with other ch: 1. John Hamilton, 1812-87, Premier of PEI, 1863-65; 2. Elizabeth. **NSN 39/46; DC 21 Mar 1981**.

3565   GRAY, Robert. Prob from AYR. To St John, NB, on the *Magog*, ex Ayr, arr 30 Apr 1849. Wife Margaret with him, and ch: 1. James, aged 9; 2. Thomas, aged 6; 3. Jane, aged 5; 4. Robert, aged 3. **DC 29 Jan 1980**.

3566   GRAY, Thomas. From New Machar, ABD. To Bon Accord, Nichol Twp, Wellington Co, ONT, ca 1837. Farmer. m Catherine Gray, qv, ch: 1. William; 2. Jane, went to IA; 3. Christina; 4. David, res Grand Rapids, MI; 5. Barbara; 6. James; 7. George, d IA; 8. Catherine. **EHE 95**.

GRAY, Mrs Thomas. See DALGLEISH, Janet.

3567   GRAY, Thomasina, b ca 1770. From Fort William, INV. d/o Archibald G, merchant. To Montreal, QUE, ex Fort William, on the *Friends*, 3 Jun 1802; stld prob Argenteuil Co.   **MCM 1/4 26.**

3568   GRAY, William, 1810-91. From Brodick, Is Arran, BUT. To Dalhousie, NB, 1832; stld Escuminac, Bonaventure Co, QUE.   **MAC 14.**

3569   GREENHILL, David, ca 1812–3 Nov 1873. From Cupar, FIF. s/o David G, millwright, and Agnes Hill. To Hamilton, ONT.   **Ts Cupar.**

3570   GREENHILL, John, ca 1810–15 Feb 1868. From Cupar, FIF. s/o David G, millwright, and Agnes Hill. To ONT, and d Binbrook, Wentworth Co.   **Ts Cupar.**

3571   GREENHORN, Elizabeth. To Pictou, NS, on the *Hope*, ex Glasgow, 5 Apr 1848.   **DC 12 Jul 1979.**

3572   GREENHORN, John. To Pictou, NS, on the *Hope*, ex Glasgow, 5 Apr 1848. Wife Margaret with him, and ch: 1. Anne; 2. John.   **DC 12 Jul 1979.**

3573   GREENSHIELDS, James Blackwood. From LKS. s/o James G. and Jean Gillespie. To Montreal, QUE, <1820.   **DC 23 Jul 1979.**

3574   GREENSHIELDS, Janet, ca 1815–28 Jan 1894. Poss from Kilmarnock, AYR. To QUE <1845. m Andrew Houston Young, qv.   **Ts Irvine.**

3575   GREGOR, Mary, b ca 1822. To St Gabriel de Valcartier, QUE, prob <1855.   **Census 1861.**

3576   GREIG, James. Prob from Dollar, CLK. s/o Peter G, Forrester Mill. To CAN, prob ONT, <1854.   **SH.**

GREY. See also GRAY.

3577   GREY, Betty, b ca 1795. Prob from Kildonan, SUT. To Fort Churchill, Hudson Bay, on the *Prince of Wales*, ex Stromness, 28 Jun 1813. Went to York Factory, spring 1814; thence to Red River. Left settlement and arr Holland River, 6 Sep 1815.   **LSS 185; RRS 26; LSC 322.**

3578   GREY, Jane or Jean, b ca 1790. Prob from Kildonan, SUT. To Fort Churchill, Hudson Bay, on the *Prince of Wales*, ex Stromness, 28 Jun 1813. Went to York Factory, spring 1814; thence to Red River. Left settlement and arr Holland River, 6 Sep 1815.   **LSS 185; RRS 26; LSC 322.**

3579   GRIERSON, James, d 1856. From Edinburgh. s/o Comm James G, RN, and wife Elizabeth. Sometime Lt, RN. d Torbolton Twp, Carleton Co, ONT, having emig 1822. m Margaret Ferguson, qv.   **DC 10 Nov 1978.**

3580   GRIERSON, Janet, b ca 1817. From Kirkton par, DFS. To ONT, ca 1843; stld prob Grey Co. Wife of George Reid, qv.   **DC 8 Mar 1977.**

3581   GRIERSON, John, 1783–14 Feb 1851. From Edinburgh. s/o Comm James G, RN, and wife Elizabeth. Sometime Lt, RN. To ONT, Jun 1822, and d Torbolton Twp, Carleton Co. m Ann Gronton.   **DC 10 Nov 1978.**

3582   GRIEVE, David, d 1 Mar 1843. From Edinburgh. s/o Thomas G, merchant. To Liverpool, Queens Co, NS. Physician.   **DGH 20 Apr 1843.**

3583   GRIEVE, George, 1779–1849. From Roberton par, ROX. s/o John G. in Hoscoat. To QUE, ca 1832; stld prob Beauharnois. Wife Minto Bell, qv, with him, and s William Bell, qv.   **DC 11 Aug 1976.**

3584   GRIEVE, Margaret, d 1 Jul 1864. From Branxholm Braes, ROX. d/o James G. To 'Braes', Newmarket, York Co, ONT.   **DGH 5 Aug 1864.**

3585   GRIEVE, Joseph, b ca 1738. From New Abbey, KKD. To Georgetown, Kings Co, PEI, on the *Lovely Nellie*, ex Carsethorn, May 1775. Weaver. Wife Marion Buckley, qv, with him, and ch: 1. John, aged 10; 2. Robert, aged 8; 3. Mary, aged 3.   **ELN.**

3586   GRIEVE, William, ca 1825–4 Aug 1878. From Borthwick Wa's, Roberton par, ROX. s/o Walter G, tenant in Southfield, and Christian Elliot. To ONT, and d Keppel Twp, Grey Co.   **THS 1938/81; Ts Borthwick Wa's.**

3587   GRIEVE, William Bell, 1818-85. From Roberton par, ROX. s/o George G, qv, and Minto Bell, qv. To QUE, ca 1832; stld prob Lennox, ONT. m Elizabeth Fairbairn, qv.   **DC 11 Aug 1976.**

3588   GRIGOR, Rev Colin, d 1864. From ROC. Educ Aberdeen and app missionary by the Colonial Committee. To QUE, and ord min of L'Orignal, Prescott Co, ONT, 1844. Trans to Guelph, Wellington Co, and in 1857 to Plantagenet, Prescott Co.   **FES vii 636.**

3589   GRIVER, Margaret, b ca 1742. From Kirkbean, KKD. To Georgetown, Prince Co, PEI, on the *Lovely Nellie*, ex Carsethorn, May 1775. Wife of Andrew Brigg, qv.   **ELN.**

3590   GRUAR, Annie, b 1790. From Dundee, ANS. To Wolfes Cove, QUE, on the barque *Blonde*, 1842; later to Miramichi, Northumberland Co, NB, and stld Chatham. Second wife of Alexander Fenton, qv.   **DC 18 Jun 1978.**

3591   GUILD, William. Poss from ABD. To Musquodoboit Valley, Halifax Co, NS, ca 1780. m Jessie Kirk. Dau Christina.   **NSN 6/6.**

3592   GUNN, Alexander. From Thurso, CAI. To ONT, 1851. Dau Diana.   **DC 29 Sep 1964.**

3593   GUNN, Alexander, b ca 1756. From Ascaig, Kildonan, SUT. To Fort Churchill, Hudson Bay, on the *Prince of Wales*, ex Stromness, 28 Jun 1813. Went to York Factory, 1814; thence to Red River.   **LSS 184; RRS 27; LSC 322.**

3594   GUNN, Alexander, b ca 1764. From Kildonan, SUT. To Fort Churchill, Hudson Bay, on the *Prince of Wales*, ex Stromness, 28 Jun 1813. Went to York Factory, 1814; thence to Red River. Left settlement and arr Holland River, 6 Sep 1815. Wife Christina d Fort Churchill, 20 Sep 1814. Son William, qv.   **LSS 184; RRS 26; LSC 321.**

3595   GUNN, Angus, b ca 1793. From SUT. s/o Donald G, qv. To Fort Churchill, Hudson Bay, on the *Prince of Wales*, ex Stromness, 28 Jun 1813. Wife Janet with him. Trekked to Red River, spring 1814. Left settlement and arr Holland River, 6 Sep 1815. LSS 185; RRS 26; LSC 322.

3596   GUNN, Archibald, b ca 1795. To Pictou, NS, 1815; res Mount Thom, 1816. Unm labourer, 'very poor.' **INS 39.**

3597   GUNN, Barbara, b ca 1766. From Kildonan, SUT. Wife of William Bannerman, qv. To York Factory, Hudson Bay, arr 26 Aug 1815, and went to Red River. **LSC 326.**

3598   GUNN, Benjamen. To Pictou, NS, on the *Ellen*, ex Lochlaxford, SUT, 22 May 1979. Wife Flora with him, and s Donald. **DC 15 Jul 1979.**

3599 GUNN, Betsy, 1809–15 Apr 1892. From CAI. sis/o John G, qv. To Pictou Co, NS. m 6 Jun 1844, as his second wife, Alexander Ross, qv, Big Brook. **PAC 98**.

3600 GUNN, Christian, b ca 1765. From Kildonan, SUT. Wife of Alexander McBeth, qv. To York Factory, Hudson Bay, arr 26 Aug 1815, and went to Red River. **LSC 326**.

3601 GUNN, Mrs Christian, b ca 1775. From Kildonan, SUT. To York Factory, Hudson Bay, arr 26 Aug 1815, and stld Red River. Widow. **LSC 323**.

3602 GUNN, Christina, 1801-75. From CAI or SUT. To Wentworth Co, ONT, ca 1841; stld later Sydenham Twp, Grey Co. Wife of Alexander Sutherland, qv. **DC 11 Mar 1980**.

3603 GUNN, David. From CAI. bro/o John G, qv. To Pictou Co, NS, <1820. **PAC 98**.

3604 GUNN, Donald, b ca 1750. From Borrobol, Kildonan par, SUT. To Fort Churchill, Hudson Bay, on the *Prince of Wales*, ex Stromness, 28 Jun 1813. Went to Red River, but left settlement with wife and one dau, and arr Holland River, 6 Sep 1815. By wife Janet, b 1763, ch: 1. Angus, qv; 2. Catherine, d 29 Aug 1813; 3. Esther, qv; 4. George, qv; 5. Christian. **LSS 185; RSS 26; LSC 322**.

3605 GUNN, Donald, 1797–30 Nov 1878. From Halkirk, CAI. To Hudson Bay, and emp by HBCo at York Factory, Severn and Oxford House. Later at Red River. Magistrate and MLC, MAN; historian and naturalist. m 1819, Margaret, d/o James Swain, York Factory. Son John. **BNA 1199; MDB 286**.

3606 GUNN, Donald, b 1791. From ARL. To Eldon Twp, Victoria Co, ONT, 1830; stld Lot 11, Con 2. Farmer. By wife Flora had ch: 1. Robert; 2. John; 3. Elizabeth, b 1834. **EC 66**.

3607 GUNN, Elizabeth, b ca 1792. To Pictou Co, NS, 1815; res Mount Thom, 1816. Widow, poor, with one child. **INS 39**.

3608 GUNN, Esther, b ca 1790. From Kildonan par, SUT. d/o Donald G, qv. To Fort Churchill, Hudson Bay, on the *Prince of Wales*, ex Stromness, 28 Jun 1813. Went to York Factory, 1814; thence to Red River. Left settlement and arr Holland River, 6 Sep 1815. **LSS 185; RRS 26; LSC 322**.

3609 GUNN, George, b ca 1799. From Borrobol, Kildonan, SUT. s/o Donald G, qv. To Fort Churchill, Hudson Bay, on the *Prince of Wales*, ex Stromness, 28 Jun 1813. Went to York Factory, 1814; and on to Red River. Left settlement and arr Holland River, 6 Sep 1815. **LSS 185; RRS 26; LSC 322**.

3610 GUNN, George M, d 1883. From Dornoch, SUT. bro/o William G, qv. To Oxford Co, ONT, 1832; moved to Westminster Twp, Middlesex Co, ONT, 1842, and res London. **PCM 55**.

3611 GUNN, Hugh, ca 1807–7 May 1885. From CAI. To Colchester Co, NS, prob <1840; bur East Earltown. m Jennie McKay, qv, and had, prob with other ch: 1. Margaret, 1847-60; 2. Isabella, 1850-64. **DC 22 Jun 1980**.

3612 GUNN, Isabel. From CAI. sis/o John G, qv. To Pictou Co, NS, prob <1820. m Donald Grant, Marshdale, ch: 1. Jessie Bell; 2. Daniel; 3. David; 4. Alexander; 5. John; 6. Catherine Gray; 7. Peter William; 8. Margaret Elizabeth. **PAC 98**.

3613 GUNN, John, ca 1794–29 Jan 1841. From CAI. To Pictou, NS, and bur Salt Springs. **DC 27 Oct 1979**.

3614 GUNN, John. From CAI. bro/o David G, qv, and of Isabel G, qv. To Pictou Co, NS, prob <1820. m Nancy McKay, Foxbrook, ch: 1. Daniel; 2. Colin; 3. Catherine. **PAC 98**.

3615 GUNN, John. To QUE on the *Brock*, ex Greenock, Jul 1820; stld prob Lanark Co, ONT. **HCL 238**.

3616 GUNN, John. To QUE, ex Glasgow, Jul 1830, and stld ONT. **DC 4 Nov 1979**.

3617 GUNN, Rev John, 1806–2 Nov 1870. From Farr, SUT. Matric Kings Coll, Aberdeen, 1825. To Cape Breton Co, NS, as missionary, 1838. Adm Presb min of Broad Cove. **FES vii 607**.

3618 GUNN, McKenzie. To Pictou, NS, on the *Ellen*, ex Lochlaxford, SUT, 22 May 1848. Wife Marion with him, and ch: 1. John; 2. Mary; 3. Jane; 4. Donald; 5. Robert; 6. Angus; 7. William. **DC 15 Jul 1979**.

3619 GUNN, Margaret, 28 Dec 1802–20 Jun 1887. sis/o John G, David G, and Isabel G, qv. To Pictou Co, NS, prob <1820. m Sylvanus Keith, qv. **PAC 98**.

3620 GUNN, Margaret. Poss from ROC. To ONT, 1811; and stld Eldon Twp, Victoria Co. Wife of Alexander Munro, qv. **EC 200**.

3621 GUNN, Mary. From Kildonan, SUT. sis/o Robert G, piper, qv. To Fort Churchill, Hudson Bay, on the *Prince of Wales*, ex Stromness, 28 Jun 1813. Went to York Factory, 1814; thence to Red River. **LSS 186; RSS 27; LSC 323**.

3622 GUNN, Robert, b ca 1784. To Charlottetown, PEI, on the *Elizabeth & Ann*, ex Thurso, arr 8 Nov 1806. **PLEA**.

3623 GUNN, Robert. From Kildonan par, SUT. To Fort Churchill, Hudson Bay, on the *Prince of Wales*, ex Stromness, 28 Jun 1813. Piper. Went to York Factory, 1814; thence to Red River. Left settlement and arr Holland River, 6 Sep 1815. **LSS 186; RRS 27; LSC 323**.

3624 GUNN, Robert John, b 17 Feb 1814. From Watten, CAI. s/o Rev Alexander G. and Elizabeth Arthur. To ONT. Physician. **FES vii 139**.

3625 GUNN, William, b ca 1798, Kildonan, SUT. s/o Alexander G, qv. To Fort Churchill, Hudson Bay, on the *Prince of Wales*, ex Stromness, 28 Jun 1813. Went to York Factory, 1814, and to Red River. **LSS 184; RRS 26; LSC 321**.

3626 GUNN, William, 23 Jul 1802–16 Dec 1856. From Lanark. To Montreal, QUE, prob with parents, 1804. Became bank agent in Quebec. m Elizabeth, d/o William Irwin, Argyle, NY, and by her who d 1886, ch: 1. Sarah; 2. Isabella Ann; 3. Henry Esson, dy; 4. Jessie; 5. Jane. **SGC 482**.

3627 GUNN, William, ca 1818-44. From Perth. Neph of Lt George Mackenzie, Royal Perth Militia, who d 1856. To ONT. Merchant. **Ts Perth**.

3628   GUNN, William. From Dornoch, SUT. bro/o George G, qv. To Oxford Co, ONT, 1832; moved to London, Westminster Twp, Middlesex Co, ONT, 1842, and d soon afterwards. **PCM 55**.

3629   GUNN, William. To Pictou, NS, on the *Lady Gray*, ex Cromarty, ROC, arr 16 Jul 1841. **DC 15 Jul 1979**.

3630   GUNN, William. To Pictou, NS, on the *Ellen*, ex Lochlaxford, SUT, 22 May 1848. Wife Christy with him and s Donald. **DC 15 Jul 1979**.

3631   GUTHRIE, Donald, b 8 May 1840. From Edinburgh. s/o Hugh G. To Toronto, ONT, 1855. Became lawyer, and in 1876, MPP for South Wellington. **BNA 1170**.

3632   GUTHRIE, George Edward, 29 Aug 1812–14 Dec 1901. From Huntleywood, Gordon, BEW. s/o William G. and Janet Mercer. To New Glasgow, Terrebonne Co, QUE, 1833. Farmer. m (i) Mary Smythe, qv, ch: 1. Janet; 2. Andrew, went to CA; 3. Mary. m (ii) Mary Beattie, from IRL, with further ch: 4. George, 1844–1900; 5. Alexander, 1848–91; 6. James, dy; 7. Ann. **DC 22 Jul 1979**.

3633   GUTHRIE, Mary, 1819–1912. From Tannadice, ANS. To Ormestown, Dorchester Co, QUE, 1847. Wife of John Reid, qv. **DC 21 Jul 1969**.

H

HACKET. See also HALKETT.

3634   HACKET, Janet. From Old Deer, ABD. To ONT, 1854. Wife of John Pirie, qv. **DC 22 Aug 1974**.

3635   HAGGART, Archibald, b ca 1802. From Callelochan, Acharn, Kenmore par, PER. To North Monaghan Twp, Peterborough Co, ONT, prob <1846. Farmer. Wife Isabella, b ca 1791, with him, and ch: 1. Isabella, b ca 1831; 2. Janet, b ca 1833. **DC 25 Mar 1981**.

3636   HAGGART, Elizabeth, 1770–1846. From Kenmore par, PER. To Montreal, QUE, <1808; stld Longue-Pointe. Wife of James Fisher, qv, whom she m 1790. **DC 26 Mar 1979**.

3637   HAGGART, James, 1777–1833. From Kenmore, PER. s/o Donald H. and Janet McKerchar. To Pictou Co, NS, ca 1812; stld Piedmont Valley. m Janet Robertson, qv, ch. **DC 27 May 1981**.

3638   HAGGART, John. From Breadalbane, PER. To Bathurst Twp, Lanark Co, ONT, <1830; stld nr Perth. Stonemason and miller. Son John Graham, 1836–1913, MPP and Postmaster General, 1888-92. **BNA 752; HCL 145**.

3639   HAIG, James, b ca 1822. From BEW. bro/o Thomas H, qv. To ONT, 1836. **SG xxvi/3 91**.

3640   HAIG, John, b ca 1780. Prob from Preston, BEW. To Colborne, Northumberland Co, ONT, 1833. ch: 1. David; 2. Joseph; 3. Thomas; 4. James; 5. Samuel; 6. Alexander; 7. John. **SG xxvi/3 91**.

3641   HAIG, Robert. From Auchenblae, Laurencekirk, KCD. To QUE, arr 10 Aug 1845; stld Pilkington Twp, Wellington Co, ONT. m Ann Grace Crabb, qv, ch; 1. James, b 1818; 2. Alexander, res Grand Rapids, MI;

3. William, b 1829; 4. Ann; 5. Robert, Postmaster of Elora, Nichol Twp. **EHE 39**.

3642   HAIG, Thomas, b ca 1807. From BEW. bro/o James H, qv. To ONT, 1836. Discharged soldier. ch: 1. Samuel; 2. John; 3. Thomas Allan; 4. William; 5. Peter; 6. James; 7. David; 8. Isabella; 9. Margaret. **SG xxvi/3 91**.

3643   HAIG, Rev Thomas, 1817-66. b Glasgow. s/o Thomas H. Matric Univ of Glasgow, 1838. App by Glasgow Colonial Committee as missionary. Min at Brockville, Leeds Co, ONT, 1848-51; trans to Beauharnois, QUE, 1851. Ret to Lachine, 1858. **GMA 14030; FES vii 636**.

3644   HAIGHLE, Robert, ca 1801–ca 1841. From KKD. To ONT, ca 1835; stld Cobourg Twp, Northumberland Co, later Dummer Twp, Peterborough Co. Farmer. m Janet Lelland, qv, ch: 1. Margaret, b 1827; 2. Mary; 3. Elizabeth, b 1837. **DC 29 Oct 1979**.

3645   HAINING, Mary. From Crossmichael, KKD. To Percy Twp, Northumberland Co, ONT, 1834. Wife of John Douglas, qv. **DC 18 Jan 1972**.

3646   HAIR, William. From Kintyre, ARL. To Westminster Twp, Middlesex Co, ONT, 1838. ch: 1. Archibald; 2. James. **PCM 52**.

3647   HALDANE, John, d 11 Oct 1857. To Montreal, QUE, 1798. Fur-trader with XYCo, later with NWCo and HBCo, with whom he became chief factor of Columbia dist, and later of Lake Superior dist. Ret 1827 and d Edinburgh, SCT. **MDB 291**.

3648   HALDANE, John. From Edinburgh. To Goderich, Huron Co, ONT, <1835. Lawyer and farmer. Son John, militiaman, 1837. **DC 1 Jan 1968**.

3649   HALEY, Richard, 1820-96. Prob from Glasgow. To Windsor, Hants Co, NS, <1855. Farmer. By wife Eliza, ch incl George, b 1863, farmer. **HNS iii 610**.

HALKETT. See also HACKET.

3650   HALKETT, Rev Andrew, 2 Nov 1810–1 Sep 1874. From Edinburgh. s/o Samuel H, merchant, and Euphemia Wallace. Educ High School and Univ of Edinburgh. To St John, NB, 1843, and ord min of St Andrews Ch. Trans to Brechin, ANS, SCT, 1847. m Frances Ann, d 1896, d/o William Taylor, Fredericton, in 1844, ch: 1. James Brooke, b 1845; 2. Sarah Taylor, 1847-86; 3. William, 1849-54; 4. Andrew, 1851-52; 5. Frances Ann, b 1853; 5. Andrew, b 1854, naturalist; 6. Ellen Eliza, b 1856; 7. William, 1858–1908; 8. Robert Moir, b 1862; 9. Charles Samuel, b 1866. **FES v 378, vii 609**.

3651   HALKETT, John, 1768–12 Nov 1852. From Pitfirrane, FIF. s/o Sir John H, 4th Bart, and Lady Mary Hamilton. Adm advocate, 1789. Stockholder of HBCo, 1810, later committee mem. Associated with Lord Selkirks Red River scheme, and was one of his executors. Author, and d Brighton, ENG. m (i) 1794, Ann, d 1805, d/o William Todd of Millhill, without ch. m (ii) Lady Katherine Douglas, 1778–1848, sis/o Thomas Douglas, qv, Earl of Selkirk, ch. **LSS 24; SP vii 523; FAS 93; SG vii/3 15; MDB 291**.

3652   HALL, Helen. From Largs, AYR. To Montreal, QUE, where she m 1835, William Hutchison, qv. **SGC 489**.

3653   HALL, James. From Dollar, CLK. To QUE on the *Commerce*, ex Greenock, Jun 1820; stld Lanark Co, ONT. Son James, jr, b 1806, civil engineer, merchant and Sheriff of Peterborough. **BNA 1168; HCL 238**.

3654   HALL, James, ca 1790–ca 1868. From Kelso par, ROX. To Thurlow Twp, Hastings Co, ONT, 1823. Wife Isabella with him. Farmer. ch: 1. Andrew, b ca 1816; 2. Adam, b ca 1818; 3. Isabella Easton, b 1821; 4. Harriet, b ca 1825; 5. James, b ca 1826; 6. John, b 1828; 7. Margaret, b ca 1830; 8. George, b 1833; 9. Elizabeth, b ca 1835. **DC 20 Jan 1980**.

3655   HALL, Jennie. From Ecclefechan, DFS. To NB, 1833. Wife of Thomas Blacklock, qv. **DC 17 Apr 1981**.

3656   HALL, John. From Inchinnan, RFW. s/o Robert H. and Margaret Barr. To NFD <1821. Shipmaster. **Ts Inchinnan**.

3657   HALL, John Sharp, 7 Feb 1798–30 Sep 1885. s/o Rev James H, min at Lesmahagow, LKS, and Margaret Hay. Matric Univ of Glasgow, 1811, and adm WS, 1821. To Halifax, NS, and d Bedford, QUE. m Margaret Fleming, who d 30 Sep 1885. **GMA 8419; FES iii 315; HWS 181**.

3658   HALIBURTON, John. Poss from ABD. To Restigouche River, NB, ca 1774, and acquired land on the south bank. **SR 15**.

3659   HALIBURTON, John B, 1814-80. From Dunkeld, PER. To ONT, ca 1845, and d Waterdown, Wentworth Co. Farmer. m Elizabeth McIntyre, qv, ch: 1. David, 1842-96; 2. Margaret, 1844–1935; 3. Barbara, 1848–1935; 4. Elizabeth, 1851–1911. **DC 2 Jun 1980**.

3660   HALLIDAY, Andrew, ca 1798–23 Mar 1865. From Brydekirk, DFS. To Haldimand Twp, Northumberland Co, ONT. Tea-dealer. m Janet Halliday, qv. Dau Barbara. **CAE 12, 13**.

3661   HALLIDAY, James, d 12 Apr 1846. From Annan, DFS. s/o William H. To Haldimand Twp, Northumberland Co, ONT. Physician. **DGH 18 Jun 1846**.

3662   HALLIDAY, Janet, ca 1798–12 Jan 1865. From New Park, Annan. d/o William H, farmer. To Haldimand Twp, Northumberland Co, ONT. Wife of Andrew Halliday, qv. **CAE 12, 13**.

3663   HALLIDAY, John, ca 1778–21 Mar 1870. From Hutton and Corrie par, DFS. To QUE, ex Greenock, summer 1815; stld Bathurst Twp, Lanark Co, ONT. Schoolmaster. Wife Margaret Johnston, qv, with him, and 7 ch. **SEC 2; HCL 41, 43, 230; CAE 23**.

3664   HALLIDAY, John, d 18 May 1858. From Brydekirk, DFS. s/o Andrew H. To Haldimand Twp, Northumberland Co, ONT. **DGH 25 Jun 1858**.

3665   HALLIDAY, John, ca 1808–28 Dec 1855. From DFS. To NFD, prob <1830. **DGC 19 Feb 1856**.

3666   HALLIDAY, Margaret, 1778–16 Sep 1868. From DFS. To Lanark Co, ONT, 1821; moved in 1858 to Sarnia Twp, Lambton Co. m Walter Lyle. **CAE 19**.

3667   HALLIDAY, Thomas. Poss from KKD. To Queens Co, PEI, 1806; stld Belfast dist. Stonemason. Left ch and was foster-father of Mary Douglas, qv. **SPI 42**.

3668   HALLIDAY, Thomas, 1791–1867. From DFS. To Pictou Co, NS, and stld Glengarry. m Janet Collie, qv. Son John, 1822–1902. **PAC 123**.

3669   HALLIDAY, William, ca 1793–11 Dec 1855. From Duncow, Kirkmahoe, DFS. To Sullivan Twp, Grey Co, ONT; stld Bloomfield. **DGC 22 Jan 1856**.

3670   HAMBLETON, Charles, 1766–1828. To QUE <1795, when he m Froisine Rollet. Navigator, and lightman of Green Is, 1809-27. **SG xxv/2 57**.

3671   HAMILTON, Alexander. From Galston, AYR. bro/o James H. To ONT <1850. **SH**.

3672   HAMILTON, Alexander. To Montreal, QUE, on the *Royal George*, ex Greenock, Jan 1827; stld Sarnia, Lambton Co, ONT. Wife and ch with him. **DC 19 Nov 1978**.

3673   HAMILTON, Andrew, b ca 1802. Prob from Rutherglen, LKS. s/o Thomas H. m 28 May 1827, Isabella McBain, qv. To McNab Twp, Renfrew Co, ONT, 1827. **LDW 2 Jul 1973**.

3674   HAMILTON, Archibald, b 1802. From Kingscorse, Kilbride par, BUT. To Restigouche Co, NB, 1829; stld Black Point. m Elizabeth McMillan, qv, ch: 1. Mary, b Mid Kiscade, 1826; 2. James, 1828-51. **MAC 16**.

3675   HAMILTON, Catherine Ann, 1808-80. From Knockankelly, Kilbride par, Is Arran, BUT. d/o John H, qv, and Catherine Kennedy, qv. To Blackland, Restigouche Co, NB, 1829. m Hugh, s/o John McKenzie, qv. **DC 23 May 1980**.

3676   HAMILTON, David. To QUE on the *Commerce*, ex Greenock, Jun 1820; stld prob Lanark Co, ONT. **HCL 239**.

3677   HAMILTON, Elizabeth, 1811-74. From Corrie, Kilbride par, Is Arran, BUT. To Restigouche Co, NB, 1826; stld Black Point. Wife of William McMillan, qv. **MAC 23**.

3678   HAMILTON, Elizabeth. From Is Arran, BUT. To Blackland, Restigouche Co, NB, 1829. Wife of William Cook, qv. **DC 6 Nov 1967**.

3679   HAMILTON, Elizabeth. From Is Arran, BUT. sis/o James H, baker. To Restigouche Co, NB, 1834. m Peter Hamilton, jr, qv. **CUC 24**.

3680   HAMILTON, Elizabeth. From Is Islay, ARL. To Kincardine, Bruce Co, ONT, <1865; stld later Huron Twp, Bruce Co. Wife of Peter MacDonald, qv. **DC 25 Dec 1981**.

3681   HAMILTON, George, b ca 1815. From Edinburgh. s/o Thomas H. and Maria Helen Colquhoun. To ONT <1858. **SH**.

3682   HAMILTON, James, b 1774. From Is Arran, BUT. To Dalhousie, NB, 1830; stld Charlo, Restigouche Co. m Margaret Cumming, qv, ch: 1. James F, 1811-88; 2. Margaret, b 1819. **MAC 14**.

3683   HAMILTON, James, b 1776. From Is Arran, BUT. To Charlo, Restigouche Co, NB, <1836. Weaver. m Mary McBride, qv, ch: 1. Mary, b 1799; 2. James, 1803-84; 3. Elizabeth, b 1806; 4. Robert, b 1808; 5. Margaret, 1810-87; 6. Anna, 1812-94; 7. Christina, b 1817. **MAC 14**.

3684   HAMILTON, James. From Cummertrees, DFS. To Watford, Lambton Co, ONT, ca 1845. Wife Mary McLean, qv, with him. **DC 18 Jul 1979**.

3685   HAMILTON, James, 1800-73. From Mid

Kiscadale, Kilbride par, Is Arran, BUT. s/o James H. To Blackland, Restigouche Co, NB, <1841. Farmer. m Catherine Kennedy, qv, ch: 1. Margaret, 1837–1911; 2. Catherine, 1839–1913; 3. Helen, 1842–1916; 4. Janet, d inf, 1844; 5. David, 1846–1917. **MAC 15; DC 6 Nov 1967**.

3686 HAMILTON, James, b 1819, Rutherglen par, LKS. s/o William H. Served as private in 29th Regt for over 14 years, and discharged at Dinapore, India. Held Punjab Medal and two clasps. To Crosshill, McNab Twp, Renfrew Co, ONT. **LDW 2 Jul 1973**.

3687 HAMILTON, John, b ca 1765. From Is Arran, BUT. To Dalhousie, NB, 1831. m 2 Apr 1785, Catherine Jamieson, qv, ch: 1. Janet, b 1787; 2. Mary, b 1790; 3. John, b 1792; 4. James, b 1795; 5. Margaret, b 1798; 6. Catherine, b 1802. **MAC 14**.

3688 HAMILTON, John, 1769–1848. From Kingscorse, Kilbride par, Is Arran, BUT. To Dalhousie, NB, 1826. Shoemaker. m Grizel or Grace Davidson, qv, 1798, ch: William, 1811–87. **MAC 17**.

3689 HAMILTON, John, b 1773. From Largiemore, Kilbride, Is Arran, BUT. To Blackland, Restigouche Co, NB, 1829. m Catherine Kennedy, qv, and had, poss with other ch: 1. Elizabeth, b 1797; 2. Catherine Ann, qv; 3. William, 1812–87; 4. Margaret, qv. **MAC 15**.

3690 HAMILTON, John, 1788–1868. From Kingscorse, Is Arran, BUT. s/o James H. To Blackland, Restigouche Co, NB, 1828. m Margaret Cumming, qv, ch: 1. James, 1821–96; 2. Catherine, b 1823; 3. Anne, b 1827; 4. John, 1828–1911; 5. Elizabeth, 1835–1902. **MAC 15; DC 6 Nov 1967**.

3691 HAMILTON, John. From Mannyguil, Is Arran, BUT. bro/o Peter H, qv. To Inverness, Megantic Co, QUE, 1831. Shoemaker. m Catherine Fee, qv. **AMC 42; MAC 42**.

3692 HAMILTON, John F, 24 Aug 1805–23 Jan 1892. From Strathhaven, LKS. To ONT, 1852; stld Amherstburg, Essex Co, but moved to Almont, Lapeer Co, MI. m 25 Aug 1825, Elizabeth Paton, qv. **DC 30 Sep 1960**.

3693 HAMILTON, John James. From Glasgow. To Pictou, NS, <1819. Son George Johnston, b 1819. **HNS iii 240**.

3694 HAMILTON, Malcolm, b ca 1830. To QUE, ex Glasgow, on the *Sophia*, 1847. **LC 10 Sep 1966**.

3695 HAMILTON, Margaret, 1802–83. From Kingscorse, Kilbride, Is Arran, BUT. To Pointe-à-la-Garde, Bonaventure Co, QUE, 1831. m Daniel McNeish, qv. **MAC 24**.

3696 HAMILTON, Margaret, 1815–59. From Largiemore, Kilbride par, Is Arran, BUT. d/o John H, qv, and Catherine Kennedy, qv. To Blackland, Restigouche Co, NB, 1829. m Angus, s/o Angus McLean, qv, and Mary Sinclair, qv, ch: 1. Margaret, 1835–56; 2. Mary, 1837–1919; 3. Angus, 1838–1908; 4. William, b ca 1841; 5. John, 1842–1912; 6. Daniel, 1845–1911; 7. Neil, ca 1848–71; 8. Elizabeth, 1850–1939; 9. James, 1853–95; 10. David, 1854–1929; 11. Hugh, ca 1855–ca 1860. **RCP 7**.

3697 HAMILTON, Mary, b 1787. From Torrilin, Kilmory par, Is Arran, BUT. To Dalhousie, NB, 1829. Wife of William Jamieson, qv. **MAC 17**.

3698 HAMILTON, Mary. From Paisley, RFW. d/o Edward H, baker. To Inverness Co, NS, <1840; stld Lake Ainslie. m John McInnes, qv. **DC 30 Aug 1977**.

3699 HAMILTON, Peter, 1755–1836. From Kingscorse, Kilbride par, Is Arran, BUT. Poss s/o Thomas H. To Dalhousie, NB, Apr 1829, on the *Cassaro*; stld Charlo River, Restigouche Co. Farmer. m Isabella McKelvie, qv, ch: 1. Margaret; 2. James, 1793–1865, sailor; 3. William, b 1799; 4. Archibald, b 1802; 5. Peter, jr, qv; 6. Alexander, 1808–94. **MAC 16; DC 6 Nov 1967**.

3700 HAMILTON, Peter, jr, 1805–99. From Kingscorse, Kilbride par, Is Arran, BUT. s/o Peter H, qv, and Isabella McKelvie, qv. To Dalhousie, NB, on the *Cassaro*, Apr 1829; stld Charlo River. Fisherman and magistrate. m Elizabeth Hamilton, qv. Son Peter. **CUC 24**.

3701 HAMILTON, Peter, b 1800. From Kilbride, Is Arran, BUT. To Dalhousie, NB, 1828. **MAC 16**.

3702 HAMILTON, Peter, b 1810. From Mannyguil, Is Arran, BUT. bro/o John H, qv. To Inverness, Megantic Co, QUE, 1831. m Ann McCurdie, qv. Son Donald stld Lillooet, BC. **AMC 42, 80; MAC 42**.

3703 HAMILTON, Robert, 25 Feb 1750–8 Mar 1809. From Bolton, ELN. s/o Rev John H, par min, and Jane Wright. To Carleton Is, Frontenac Co, ONT, 1780. Merchant in Kingston, and MLC, 1792. m (i) Catherine Askin, d 1796, wid/o John Robertson, ch: 1. Robert, 1786–1865; 2. George, 1790–1858, founder of the city of Hamilton, Ont; 3. James, 1790–1858; 4. Alexander, 1792–1839; 5. Samuel. m (ii) 1797, Mary Herkimer, wid/o Neil McNeil, with further ch: 6. Joseph, 1798–1847; 7. Peter Hunter, 1800–57; 8. Hon John, 1802–82, pioneer of steam navigation on Lake Ontario and the Upper St Lawrence; 9. Mary. **BNA 539; FES i 357; MDB 297**.

3704 HAMILTON, Robert, d <1847. To ONT. Formerly Major, 78th Regt. m Margaret Bowie, qv. **DGH 28 Oct 1847**.

3705 HAMILTON, Robert, ca 1789–1875. From Lesmahagow, LKS, but poss b Glasgow. To Scarborough, York Co, ONT, 1830. Weaver, later farmer. m Elisabeth Stobo, qv, ch: 1. Elisabeth, b 1 Jul 1817; 2. Janet, b Dec 1818; 3. Agnes, b 15 Oct 1821; 4. Robert, b 11 Apr 1826; 5. Margaret, b 3 Mar 1827; 6. James, b Glasgow, 5 Jul 1829. **DC 29 Mar 1981**.

3706 HAMILTON, Rev Robert, b ca 1830. From STI. s/o Alexander H, farmer. Matric Univ of Glasgow, 1846. Licentiate of UP Ch and became min at Motherwell, Perth Co, ONT. **GMA 15200**.

3707 HAMILTON, Robert Douglas, 1783–1857. Prob from LKS. To Scarborough, York Co, Ont, 1827. Physician and author. **DC 29 Mar 1981**.

3708 HAMILTON, Thomas. From LKS. Gr-s of Lt James H. of Dowan, nr Glasgow. To Halifax, NS, <1789. **SH**.

3709 HAMILTON, William, 1799–1888. From Mid Kiscadale, Kilbride par, Is Arran, BUT. To Charlo, Restigouche Co, NB, <1832. m Mary Margaret McKelvie, qv. **MAC 16**.

3710 HAMILTON, William. From Greenock, RFW. s/o Capt John H, d Irvine, 1848, and Grace Davidson. To Dalhousie, NB. m Jane McEwan, ch: 1. William, 1845–1905; 2. Grace Davidson, 1853–1923, d Greenock. **Ts Greenock**.

3711 HAMMOND, Henry. To QUE on the *Commerce*, ex Greenock, Jun 1820; stld prob Lanark Co, ONT. **HCL 238**.

3712 HANDYSIDE, David, 11 Aug 1794–15 Mar 1855. From Edinburgh. To Montreal, QUE, <1830. Merchant and distiller. m Melinda Adams, d 1848, from Burlington, VT, and had with other ch: 1. Charles, res Lachine; 2. Mrs Joseph Jones. **SGC 499**.

3713 HANNAH, James. To QUE on the *Brook*, ex Greenock, Jul 1820; stld prob Lanark Co, ONT. **HCL 238**.

3714 HANNAH, Janet. From Torthorwald, DFS. To QUE on the *Atlas*, ex Greenock, 11 Jul 1815; stld Burgess Twp, Lanark Co, ONT. Wife of Thomas Barber, qv. **SEC 1**.

3715 HANNAH, John. From Cummertrees, DFS. To Ottawa, ONT, <1846. m Susan Ferguson, qv, and had, prob with other ch: 1. William H, qv; 2. James F, 1847–1913, farmer Woodlake, MN; 3. Thomas F, farmer. **DC 27 May 1981**.

3716 HANNAH, William H, b 20 Mar 1839. From Cummertrees, DFS. s/o John H, qv, and Susan Ferguson, qv. To Ottawa, ONT, <1846. m Sarah Sampson. **DC 27 May 1981**.

3717 HANNAY, Elizabeth, 14 Feb 1817–1 Mar 1902. From Creetown, KKD. s/o William H, qv, and Mary Murray, qv. To Kent Co, NB, <1830. m James Glendinning, qv. **DC 5 Aug 1980**.

3718 HANNAY, James, 20 Jan 1815–16 Sep 1883. From Creetown, KKD. s/o William H, qv, and Mary Murray, qv. To Kent Co, NB, <1830. Merchant and hotelier. m Christabel Brunskull, d/o Jonathan and Christabel Gail, ch. **DC 5 Aug 1980**.

3719 HANNAY, Rev James, 18 Feb 1799–8 Jun 1855. From Stoneykirk, WIG. s/o Thomas H. Matric Univ of Glasgow, 1814. Ch of Scotland missionary at Richibucto, Kent Co, NB, 1833-45. Retr to SCT and was min at Milngavie, DNB, 1847-55. m (i) Susan McDowall, qv. (ii) Jane Salter. Son James, 1842–1910, historian. **GMA 9384; FES iii 361, vii 609**.

3720 HANNAY, Margaret, b 17 Jan 1828. From Glasgow. d/o William H, qv, and Mary Murray, qv. To Kent Co, NB, <1830. Absconded with her brother-in-law, James Glendinning, qv. **DC 5 Aug 1980**.

3721 HANNAY, Mary, 21 Apr 1827–24 May 1902. From Creetown, KKD. d/o William H, qv, and Mary Murray, qv. To Kent Co, NB, <1830. m John Mundle, qv. **DC 5 Aug 1980**.

3722 HANNAY, Robert, 22 May 1819–7 Mar 1864. From Creetown, KKD. s/o William H, qv, and Mary Murray, qv. To Kent Co, NB, <1830. Hotelier. m (i) Sarah Agnes, d/o James Hudson and Elizabeth Graham, St Nicolas River; (ii) her sist Mary, by whom he had ch. He d at Richibucto. **DC 5 Aug 1980**.

3723 HANNAY, William, ca 1793–5 Dec 1869. From Creetown, KKD. To NB, ex Glasgow, <1830, and d Kingston, Kent Co. Farmer and merchant. m Mary Murray, qv, ch: 1. James, qv; 2. Elizabeth, qv; 3. Robert, qv; 4. William Carson, qv; 5. John, b 5 Jul 1823; 6. Mary, qv; 7. Margaret, qv; 8. Euphemia Sophia, b Galway, Kent Co, 5 Jun 1830; 9. Jessie, b 28 Aug 1832. **DC 5 Aug 1980**.

3724 HANNAY, William Carson, 24 Aug 1821–18 Jul 1887. From Creetown, KKD. s/o William H, qv, and Mary Murray, qv. To Kent Co, NB, <1830. m Mary Room, d/o David Mundle, qv, and Mary Room, qv, ch. **DC 5 Aug 1980**.

3725 HARDIE, Henry. From Corstorphine, MLN. s/o James H, 1720–1802, farmer, West Craigs, and Susan Young. To QUE. Drowned in the St Lawrence River. **Ts Gogar**.

3726 HARDY, Elizabeth. Prob from ROX. d/o James H. and Elizabeth Hunter. To Pictou Co, NS, ex Greenock, arr 28 Oct 1814. Wife of Robert Oliver, qv. **OM 4/3**.

3727 HARDY, Isobel, d 14 Sep 1849. From Newlands of Brodie, Dyke and Moy par, MOR. wid/o Alexander Masson. To Montreal, QUE, ca 1831; later to Hastings Co, ONT, and d Roslin. Son Alexander. **DC 20 Jun 1980**.

3728 HARDY, Jane, b ca 1795, prob Deeside, ABD. To Halifax, NS, <1820. m — Murray, merchant, and had ch. **HNS iii 638**.

3729 HARGRAVE, James, 1798–1856. From ROX. To CAN <1820. Served with NWCo, and >1821 with HBCo. Chief trader, 1833, and chief factor, 1844, York Factory. He was at Sault Ste Marie in 1854, and retr to Brockville Twp, Leeds Co, ONT. m at Glasgow, SCT, 8 Jan 1840, Letitia MacTavish, qv, ch, son Joseph James, d 1894, author of *Red River*. m (ii) Margaret Alcock. **MDB 299; DC 28 Oct 1978**.

3730 HARKNESS, Elizabeth, ca 1828–11 Mar 1882. From Hawick, ROX. d/o Thomas H, qv, and Helen Scott, qv. To ONT; stld prob Galt, Waterloo Co. wid/o James Anderson. m (ii) Dr Montgomery, Kingston, ONT. **THS 1936/27**.

3731 HARKNESS, Gideon. From Hawick, ROX. s/o Thomas H, qv, and Helen Scott, qv. To Galt, Waterloo Co, ONT; later to Owen Sound, Grey Co. m at Roxburgh, 11 Feb 1842, Margaret Scott, qv, ch. **THS 1937/74**.

3732 HARKNESS, Rev James, 1789–25 Feb 1835. From Sanquhar, DFS. s/o James H, qv. Matric Univ of Glasgow, 1801. Asst min at St Quivox, AYR, and emig to QUE, 1820. Min of St Andrews Ch there. **GMA 6233**.

3733 HARKNESS, James, d 23 Aug 1841. From Holestane, Durrisdeer, DFS. s/o William H. To Montreal, QUE, and d Dewillville, Chateauguay River. **DGH 23 Sep 1841**.

3734 HARKNESS, Jane, d 1840. From Woodhall, Dornock, DFS. To Martintown, Glengarry Co, ONT. m Thomas Gray, innkeeper. **DGH 30 Jul 1840**.

3735 HARKNESS, John, ca 1802–11 Aug 1833. From Lochmaben, DFS. s/o George H. and Martha Tweedie. To CAN, and d there. **Ts Lochmaben**.

3736   HARKNESS, Mary, 1824-78. From Hawick, ROX. d/o Thomas H, qv, and Helen Scott, qv. To ONT, poss Galt, Waterloo Co. m James Young.   **THS 1936/27**.

3737   HARKNESS, Thomas, ca 1786–18 Dec 1858. Prob s/o James H, mason, and Elizabeth Oliver, Hawick, ROX. To ONT; stld poss Galt, Waterloo Co. m Helen Scott, qv, ch: 1. Mary, qv; 2. Elizabeth, qv; 3. Gideon, qv; 4. Daniel, d inf.   **THS 1936/27, 1937/74**.

3738   HARKNESS, Walter, ca 1801–3 Jan 1834. From Dumfries. s/o William H. in Holestane, Durrisdeer par. To Montreal, QUE. Surgeon.   **Ts Dumfries; DGC 19 Feb 1834**.

3739   HARPER, Nicol, b ca 1778. From Birsay, OKI. To York Factory, Hudson Bay, on the *Edward & Anne*, ex Stornoway, arr 24 Sep 1811. Labourer. Pioneer settler, Red River.   **LSS 184; RRS 26; LSC 321**.

3740   HARPER, William, b 13 Jan 1813. To Campbellton, Restigouche Co, NB, <4 Apr 1844, when he m Catherine Young.   **DC 18 Jan 1972**.

3741   HARRIS, Alexander. From ABD. To Nichol Twp, Wellington Co, ONT, 1835.   **EHE 90**.

3742   HARRIS, Matthew. Prob rel to Robert H, qv. To Pictou Co, NS, <1776.   **HPC App B**.

3743   HARRIS, Robert. Prob rel to Matthew H, qv. To Pictou Co, NS, <1776.   **HPC App B**.

3744   HARRIS, William Cron, 2 Jun 1825–28 Mar 1893. From Fern, ANS. s/o Rev David H, par min, and Grace Dow. To Oshawa, Ontario Co, ONT. m Jean, d/o William Gordon, qv, and Christina Brand, qv. **FES v 396; DC 6 Sep 1979**.

3745   HARRISON, David, b ca 1735. From Ecclefechan, Hoddam par, DFS. To Georgetown, Kings Co, PEI, on the *Lovely Nellie*, ex Annan, 1774. Wheelwright. Wife Janet Henderson, qv, with him, and ch: 1. Grizel, aged 19; 2. Agnes, aged 17; 3. Helen, aged 13; 4. Janet aged 9; 5. Margaret, aged 7.   **ELN**.

3746   HARROWER, John. From Blair Drummond, PER. To Esquesing Twp, Halton Co, ONT, prob <1852. Farmer.   **DC 15 Feb 1971**.

3747   HARROWER, Peter. From Blair Drummond, PER. To Goderich, Huron Co, ONT, prob <1852.   **DC 15 Feb 1971**.

3748   HART, James, b ca 1793. To QUE on the *Earl of Buckinghamshire*, ex Greenock, 28 Apr 1821; stld Ramsay Twp, Lanark Co, ONT. Wife Mary, b ca 1793, with him. ch: 1. Marion, b SCT; 2. Margaret; 3. Mary, b 1827; 4. Thomas, b 1834.   **DC 18 Dec 1978 and 5 Mar 1979**.

3749   HART, James. From Paisley, RFW. s/o James H, weaver. To St John, NB, <1825.

3750   HART, James Robert. To Lanark Co, ONT, <1839. Wife Julia with him, and dau Janet, b 1820. **DC 18 Dec 1978**.

3751   HART, John, 6 Nov 1808–23 Oct 1881. From Paisley, RFW. To QUE on the *Carleton*, ex Glasgow, arr 5 Jun 1842; stld Perth, Drummond Twp, Lanark Co, ONT. Merchant and leader of a group of emigrants. m Jean Mason Semple, 1808-81, b London, ENG, ch: 1. John Semple, 1833–1917; 2. Rev Thomas, qv;

3. Margaret Richmond, 1837–1914; 4. William, 1841–1914; 5. Richmond James, 1844-92; 6. Jane Ann, b 1846; 7. Caroline, 1847-80; 8. Samuel Richmond, b 1849; 9. Annie, 1851–1920.   **DC 19 Apr 1982**.

3752   HART, Rev Thomas, 6 Sep 1835–17 Aug 1912. b Paisley, RFW. s/o John H, qv, and Jean Mason Semple. To Perth, Drummond Twp, Lanark Co, ONT, with parents. 1842. Educ Perth and Queens Univ, Kingston, where he grad BA and MA, 1860 and 1868. Professor of Classics at Manitoba Coll, Winnipeg. m 1872, Isabella, d/o Judge G. Malloch and Isabella Margaret Bell, ch.   **FES vii 657; DC 19 Apr 1982**.

3753   HARVEY, Alexander, b ca 1815. From ANS. s/o John H. of Kinnettles, and Angelica Dingwall Fordyce. To Fergus, Wellington Co, ONT, ca 1835; later to Qu'Appelle, in the north-west. Farmer, merchant and magistrate. m 15 Aug 1839, Matilda, d/o Sebastian Shade and Hannah Hunt, ch: 1. Sebastian Alexander, res Chicago; 2. Absolom Inglis Edward; 3. Omar Frederick Hildebrand; 4. Angelica Elizabeth, 1843-45; 5. Isabella Matilda; 6. Angelica Caroline; 7. Hannah Jane. **NDF 160-168**.

3754   HARVEY, Janet. From Largie, Insch par, ABD. To Galt, Wellington Co, ONT, 1838. wid/o John Robertson, by whom she had a dau Jane, qv, and wife of James Sims, qv.   **EHE 124**.

3755   HARVEY, Jessie, b ca 1817. Prob from DFS. To Newcastle, Northumberland Co, NB, ca 1825. m David Geikie, qv.   **LDW 1 Apr 1972**.

3756   HARVEY, John. From Midlem, Bowden, ROX. s/o John M, mason. To Kingston, ONT, <1827.   **SH**.

3757   HARVEY, John, ca 1802–6 Apr 1868. From DFS. To Newcastle, Northumberland Co, NB, and stld Douglastown.   **DC 4 Oct 1978**.

3758   HARVIE, Archibald, b 1743. From Dalry, AYR. s/o James H. in Dogartmill. To NS, <1800.   **Dalry OPR 587/1**.

3759   HARVIE, Charles, 2 Mar 1821–25 Sep 1891. From STI. s/o John H, qv, and Agnes Miller, qv. To South Orillia Twp, Simcoe Co, ONT, 1832. Farmer. m Marian McLeod, qv, ch: 1. Margaret, 1846–1915; 2. John C, 1849–1928; 3. Donald, 1852–1940; 4. Charles Sanderson, 1854–1918; 5. William McLeod, 1856–1919; 6. Agnes Jane, 1858–1939; 7. Alexander Raymond, 1860–1925; 8. James Norman, 1865–1946. **DC 8 Nov 1981**.

3760   HARVIE, Elizabeth, d 1823. From Kilmarnock, AYR. Prob sis/o Andrew H. To Montreal, QUE, <1806. m Robert Armour, qv.   **SGC 265**.

3761   HARVIE, James, b 1746. From Dalry, AYR. s/o James H. in Dogartmill. To NS <1800.   **Dalry OPR 587/1**.

3762   HARVIE, John, 30 Jun 1788–14 Mar 1873. From STI. To South Orillia Twp, Simcoe Co, ONT, 1832; stld Lot 9W, Con 1. Miller. m Agnes Miller, qv, ch: 1. James, remained in SCT; 2. John, jr, qv; 3. Andrew, 1816-96; 4. Robert, qv; 5. Charles, qv; 6. William, qv; 7. Margaret, qv; 8. Thomas Lockerby, qv.   **DC 8 Nov 1981**.

3763   HARVIE, John, jr, 1814-97. From STI. s/o John H, qv, and Agnes Miller, qv. To South Orillia Twp,

Simcoe Co, ONT, 1832. m 1838, Ellen Thompson.
DC 8 Nov 1981.

3764   HARVIE, Margaret, 1828–20 Mar 1866. From STI. d/o John H, qv, and Agnes Miller, qv. To South Orillia Twp, Simcoe Co, ONT, 1832. m John Rutherford.   **DC 8 Nov 1981**.

3765   HARVIE, Margaret. d/o Andrew H. and Margaret Shirra. To Montreal, QUE, on the *Ann Henzell*, 1844; stld Hamilton, ONT, later London, Middlesex Co. wid/o Henry Dougall, farmer. ch with her: 1. William; 2. Margaret; 3. Henry; 4. Janet, qv; 5. James; 6. Ellen; 7. David. Eld s John remained in SCT.   **DC 19 Sep 1960**.

3766   HARVIE, Robert, 1798–1889. From Is Arran, BUT. To Doaktown, Northumberland Co, NB, <1831, when he stld Nash Creek, Restigouche Co. Wife Mary Strahan, qv, with him. m (ii) Mary Murchie. ch incl: 1. Margaret, b 1830; 2. Andrew, 1837-91, carpenter and magistrate.   **CUC 15; MAC 17**.

3767   HARVIE, Robert, 1819–14 Apr 1890. From STI. s/o John H, qv, and Agnes Miller, qv. To South Orillia Twp, Simcoe Co, ONT, 1832. m 1845, Alison Rutherford.   **DC 8 Nov 1981**.

3768   HARVIE, Thomas Lockerby, 1830-86. From STI. s/o John H, qv, and Agnes Miller, qv. To South Orillia Twp, Simcoe Co, ONT, 1832. m Sarah Suter.   **DC 8 Nov 1981**.

3769   HARVIE, William, 1826–1909. From STI. s/o John H, qv, and Agnes Miller, qv. To South Orillia Twp, Simcoe Co, ONT, 1832. m Elizabeth McMillan. **DC 8 Nov 1981**.

3770   HASTIE, Agnes. From KKD. To ONT, ca 1842; stld prob Tuckersmith Twp, Huron Co. Wife of George Sproat, qv.   **DC 29 Oct 1979**.

3771   HASTIE, Alexander, 24 Apr 1805–13 Aug 1864. From Carnock, FIF. s/o Robert H. To CAN, 1822, but returned to SCT, 1827. Rep of mercantile house of Robert Hastie & Co. Provost of Glasgow, 1846; MP 1847 and 1852. m Anne, d/o Robert Napier of Shandon, engineer, ch.   **IBD 206; OEC 446B**.

3772   HASTINGS, James, 1815–1902. From Thornhill, DFS. To Westmorland Co, NB, 1841. m 1842, Isobel Murray, who d 1887.   **DC 17 Apr 1981**.

3773   HASTINGS, Jean, d 1834. From Penpont, DFS. To Nichol Twp, Wellington Co, ONT, 1833. Wife of Samuel Broadfoot, qv.   **DC 11 Nov 1981**.

3774   HATTIE, Alexander, 1757–1842. bro/o George H, qv, and William H, qv. To Halifax, NS; stld Barneys River, Pictou Co. Farmer, lumberman, mason and miller. m 1790, Catherine, d/o Joseph McDonald, ch: 1. William; 2. Jane; 3. John; 4. Elizabeth; 5. Alexander; 6. John, jr; 7. Rebecca; 8. James; 9. Daniel; 10. George; 11. Hugh; 12. Janet.   **HFM 7, 12**.

3775   HATTIE, George. bro/o Alexander H, qv, and William H, qv. To Halifax, NS, 1786; stld Barneys River, Pictou Co, afterwards Newport, Hants Co. Estate factor. m Mary Ann Maxwell Jadis, ch: 1. Margaret or Peggy; 2. Jane; 3. Fanny; 4. Mary; 5. Ann; 6. Eunice.   **HFM 2**.

3776   HATTIE, William. bro/o Alexander H, qv, and George H, qv. To Halifax, NS, 1786; stld Barneys River, Pictou Co. Farmer, unm.   **HFM 2**.

3777   HAWTHORN, Agnes, 1800–26 Aug 1847. From Girthon par, KKD. To Tuckersmith Twp, Huron Co, ONT, 1832. Wife of Samuel Carnochan, qv.   **DC 27 Jun 1981**.

3778   HAY, David D, b 1828. From Dundee, ANS. To Montreal, QUE, 1844; stld Bowmanville, Durham Co, ONT. Moved to Lefroy, Simcoe Co, then to Elma, Perth Co. Farmer, merchant at Listowel, and immigration agent.   **BNA 796**.

3779   HAY, James, ca 1826–22 Dec 1906. From BAN. To Campbellford, Hastings Co, ONT, <1850. **DC 17 Dec 1970**.

3780   HAY, Jean, 1792–1864. Poss from Edinburgh. d/o Alexander H. and Jean Tuck. To CAN. **Ts Canongate**.

3781   HAY, John, b ca 1783. From St Vigeans, ANS. To QUE on the *Atlas*, ex Greenock, 11 Jul 1815; stld Lot 25, Con 1, Bathurst Twp, Lanark Co, ONT. Farm labourer. **SEC 3; HCL 16, 230**.

3782   HAY, John. To QUE on the *Commerce*, ex Greenock, Jun 1820; stld prob Lanark Co, ONT. **HCL 238**.

3783   HAY, John. From PER. To McNab Twp, Renfrew Co, ONT, 1825.   **DC 3 Jan 1981**.

3784   HAY, John, 15 Mar 1822–7 Aug 1878. From BAN. To Campbellford, Hastings Co, ONT, 1842. m Mary Strachan, qv.   **DC 17 Dec 1970**.

3785   HAY, John, b 1793. s/o John H. To Rawdon Twp, Hastings Co, ONT, ca 1844; moved later to E. Seymour Twp, Northumberland Co. m Ann Watson, 1819. **DC 23 Mar 1979**.

3786   HAY, Rev John, 1827–31 Jul 1866. From Perth. Prob s/o John H, 1785–1860. Educ Univs of Edinburgh and St Andrews. Min of Stanley Chapel, PER, 1854-58. Missionary in ONT, 1858, and adm min of Mount Forest Ch, Wellington Co, 1861. Resigned 1866, and d at Kincardine.   **SAM 105; FES iv 252, vii 637**.

3787   HAY, Margaret. Prob from ROX. To Albion Twp, Peel Co, ONT, <1819. Wife of James Goodfellow, qv. **Eckford OPR 787/1; MGC 2 Aug 1979**.

3788   HAY, Marjory. From Bawds, Urquhart par, MOR. To PEI, but stld Blackes Rock, Northumberland Co, NB. Wife of Robert Logie, qv.   **LDW 24 Jun 1973**.

3789   HAY, Peter, ca 1789–16 Jul 1854. From Slains par, ABD. To QUE on the *Amity*, ex Aberdeen, spring 1835; stld Seymour, Northumberland Co, ONT, later Upper Pilkington, Wellington Co. Farmer and millwright. m Janet Shand, qv, ch: 1. William; 2. Ann; 3. James; 4. John, d MT; 5. George, d 1900; 6. Alexander; 7. Charles, res Elora; 8. Robert.   **EHE 97**.

3790   HAY, Robert, b 1808. From Tippermuir, PER. To Toronto, ONT, 1831. Cabinet-maker, and became master furniture maker, sawyer and landowner.   **BNA 810**.

3791   HAY, Thomas. From Glasgow. To Lobo Twp, Middlesex Co, ONT, 1842. ch: 1. Donald; 2. Samuel; 3. John; 4. Ann; 5. Jessie.   **PCM 40**.

3792   HAY, William, b 1765. From Lanmay, ABD. To QUE, ex Greenock, summer 1815; stld Con 14, Lochiel Twp, Glengarry Co, ONT. Farmer. Wife Ann Jameson, qv, with him, and 9 ch: 1. John; 2. James; 3. Alexander; 4. William.   **SEC 4; DC 27 Jul 1982**.

3793 HAY, William, 27 May 1818–30 May 1888. From Peterhead, ABD. To St Johns, NFD, 1847; later to Toronto, ONT. Architect of public buildings, incl St Michaels Coll, Toronto. Retr to SCT, 1860, and d Portobello, MLN. **MDB 307**.

3794 HAY, William, b ca 1842. To St Gabriel de Valcartier, QUE, prob <1855. **Census 1861**.

3795 HAYMAN, William, d 1829. From INV. To Halifax, NS, 1783; stld Country Harbour, later Tatamagouche, Colchester Co. Discharged soldier, and became farmer. ch: 1. David; 2. Mrs Murphy; 3. Mrs Smith; 4. Mrs Cameron; 5. Mrs Donald Cameron; 6. Mrs Matatall; 7. Donald; 8. William; 9. John; 10. Mrs Langille; 11. Frederick; 12. Margaret. **HNS iii 38; NSN 5/2**.

3796 HEDDLE, Robert, 4 Oct 1826–28 Aug 1860. From OKI. s/o Robert H. of Melsetter and Cletts. Educ Edinburgh Academy, 1834-42. To CAN ca 1845, but retr because of ill-health. Farmer and naturalist. m Jane, d/o Dr Duguid, Kirkwall. **EAR 79**.

3797 HEDDLE, Sinclair. From SHI. To QUE, 1812, later to Inverness Twp, Megantic Co. Tailor. m 1813, Ann Mann, ch: 1. Ann; 2. William; 3. Thomas; 4. Jessie; 5. Christina; 6. Margaret; 7. John. **AMC 139**.

3798 HEADRICK, Isabella, 1817–1 Aug 1907. From Rutherglen, LKS. d/o James H, qv, and Sarah Somerville, qv. To QUE on the *George Canning*, ex Greenock, 14 Apr 1821; stld Lanark Twp, Lanark Co, ONT. m Eustas Barber, 1811–1900, ch. **DC 8 Nov 1981**.

3799 HEADRICK, James, ca 1789–8 Dec 1868. From Rutherglen, LKS. To QUE on the *George Canning*, ex Greenock, 14 Apr 1821; stld Lanark Twp, Lanark Co, ONT. Moved to Pakenham Twp, 1833. Weaver and farmer. m Sarah Somerville, qv, ch: 1. James, jr, qv; 2. David, 1811-89, unm; 3. Elizabeth, b 1813, dy; 4. William, qv; 5. Isabella, qv; 6. John, qv; 7. Archibald, b 1821, res McNab Twp, Renfrew Co; 8. Elizabeth, 1823–1905; 9. Janet, 1825–1908; 10. Robert, 1830-63; 11. Peter, b 1831, went to USA; 12. Sarah, 1833-97. **DC 25 Jun 1975 and 8 Nov 1981**.

3800 HEADRICK, James, jr, ca 1809–19 Aug 1882. From Rutherglen, LKS. s/o James H, qv, and Sarah Somerville, qv. To QUE on the *George Canning*, ex Greenock, 14 Apr 1821; stld Lanark Twp, Lanark Co, ONT. m Frances Switzer, 1825-90, ch. **DC 8 Nov 1981**.

3801 HEADRICK, John, 1820–12 Apr 1898. From Rutherglen, LKS. s/o James H, qv, and Sarah Somerville, qv. To QUE on the *George Canning*, ex Greenock, 14 Apr 1821; stld Lanark Twp, Lanark Co, ONT. m Ellen Gleeson, 1829–1906, ch. **DC 8 Nov 1981**.

3802 HEADRICK, John, ca 1811–1901. From Glasgow. To Drummond Twp, Lanark Co, ONT, 1831. m Margaret McKenzie, qv, ch: 1. David, prob remained in SCT; 2. William; 3. Janet; 4. Isabel; 5. John, prob dy. **SG xxiii/1 11; DC 8 Aug 1979**.

3803 HEADRICK, William, ca 1815–11 Sep 1880. From Rutherglen, LKS. s/o James H, qv, and Sarah Somerville, qv. To QUE on the *George Canning*, ex Greenock, 14 Apr 1821; stld Lanark Twp, Lanark Co, ONT. m Agnes McNab, ch. **DC 8 Nov 1981**.

3804 HENDERSON, Alexander, b 18 Oct 1805. From ABD. To Toronto, ONT, 1834; later to USA. **DC 22 Jan 1981**.

3805 HENDERSON, Alexander. To QUE <1837; stld prob Montreal. m Mary Chipchase, ch: 1. George, 1840–1932, moved to NC; 2. Mary, 1858-96, also went to NC; 3. Margaret. **DC 10 Mar 1981**.

3806 HENDERSON, Alexander. From Jedburgh, ROX. To Chinguacousy Twp, Peel Co, ONT, <1841. **LDW 28 Nov 1970**.

3807 HENDERSON, David, b ca 1798. From Is Arran, BUT. To Restigouche Co, NB, ca 1813. Petitioned for 150 acres of Lot 72 on the south side of the Restigouche River, 9 Feb 1821. **DC 31 May 1980**.

3808 HENDERSON, David, ca 1824–16 Sep 1861. From Galashiels, SEL. s/o Alexander H. and Jane Fairlie. To Markham, York Co, ONT, and d there. **Ts Galashiels**.

3809 HENDERSON, David. Prob from Jedburgh, ROX. To Chinguacousy Twp, Peel Co, ONT, <1841. **LDW 28 Nov 1970**.

3810 HENDERSON, Donald. Prob from Knoydart, INV. To QUE on the *British Queen*, ex Arisaig, 16 Aug 1790; stld nr Montreal. Servant. **QCC 103**.

3811 HENDERSON, Donald. From INV. To East Williams Twp, Middlesex Co, ONT, 1832. **PCM 43**.

3812 HENDERSON, Duncan, b ca 1752. To Charlottetown, PEI, on the *Rambler*, ex Tobermory, 20 Jun 1806. Wife Isabella, aged 30, with him, ch: 1. Donald, aged 10; 2. Janet, aged 8; 3. John, aged 5; 4. Mary, aged 3; 5. Isabel, aged 1. **PLR**.

3813 HENDERSON, Duncan, b ca 1759. To Charlottetown, PEI, on the *Humphreys*, ex Tobermory, 14 Jul 1806. Wife Sarah, aged 47, with him, and ch: 1. Mary, aged 20; 2. Donald, aged 18; 3. Janet, aged 12; 4. John, aged 2. **PLH**.

3814 HENDERSON, George, b 1781. From Merton, BEW. To Guelph Twp, Wellington Co, ONT, 1833. m Elizabeth Hewitt, qv, ch: 1. Richard; 2. Isabella; 3. Thomas, b 1832. **SG xxiv/2 53**.

3815 HENDERSON, George Alexander, 20 Oct 1813– 6 Apr 1888. Poss from CAI. To NS, ca 1839, and d Kingsley, MAN. m 1839, Christena McKay, qv, ch. **DC 7 Nov 1980**.

3816 HENDERSON, Helen called Nellie, 1734-95. From Lockerbie, DFS. To Georgetown, PEI, on the *Lovely Nellie*, ex Annan, 1774; moved to Pictou Co, NS, later to Colchester Co. Wife of Wellwood Waugh, qv, whom she m 1760. **ELN; HT 32**.

3817 HENDERSON, Isabelle. From ABD. To Miramichi, Northumberland Co, NB, 1832. m William Yorston, qv. **MGC 2 Aug 1979**.

3818 HENDERSON, James. Prob from ARL. To Delaware Twp, Middlesex Co, ONT, ca 1852. **PCM 57**.

3819 HENDERSON, Jane, b 21 Jun 1783. From Peterhead, ABD. To Lanark Co, ONT, 1841; stld Merrickville. Wife of Charles McRitchie, qv, whom she m 25 Dec 1814. **DC 10 Oct 1982**.

3820 HENDERSON, Janet, b ca 1731. From Ecclefechan, Hoddam par, DFS. To Georgetown, Kings Co, PEI, on the *Lovely Nellie*, ex Annan, 1774. Wife of David Harrison, qv. **ELN**.

3821 HENDERSON, John. To QUE on the *Commerce*, ex Greenock, Jun 1820; stld prob Lanark Co, ONT. **HCL 239**.

3822 HENDERSON, Jean. From Westerkirk, DFS. To Scarborough Twp, York Co, ONT, ca 1802. Wife of Andrew Thomson, qv. **LDW 22 Jan 1976**.

3823 HENDERSON, John, b 1804. From Sliddery, Kilmory par, Is Arran, BUT. To Dalhousie, NB, <1844; stld Charlo, Restigouche Co. m Mary Ritchie, qv, ch: 1. Mary, 1829–1919; 2. Archibald; 3. Nancy, 1836-89. **MAC 17**.

3824 HENDERSON, John. From ROX. Prob rel to Thomas H, qv, and William H, qv. To QUE on the *Sarah Mary Jane*, 1831; stld Dumfries Twp, Waterloo Co, ONT. **HGD 60**.

3825 HENDERSON, Katherine Margaret. From PER. To Mount Pleasant, Brant Co, ONT, <1844. Wife of George Bryce, qv. **FES vii 656**.

3826 HENDERSON, Martha, b ca 1766. From Hoddam, DFS. d/o Thomas H, qv, and Margery Hogg, qv. To Georgetown, Kings Co, PEI, on the *Lovely Nellie*, ex Carsethorn, May 1775; stld later in Pictou Co, NS. m William Campbell, qv. **ELN; HT 35**.

3827 HENDERSON, Peter, 28 Jan 1795–18 Apr 1829. From Falkirk, STI. s/o James H, Rosebank, and Catherine Wyse. To St Johns, NFD, <1820. Merchant. **Ts Falkirk**.

3828 HENDERSON, Sarah, b 13 Jul 1792. From Gifford, ELN, but b poss Glencarse, PER. To Montreal, QUE, 1832; stld English River. Wife of John Gordon, qv, whom she m at Saltoun, ELN, 25 May 1817. **DC 3 Jun 1981**.

3829 HENDERSON, Thomas, b ca 1742. From Hoddam par, DFS. To Georgetown, Kings Co, PEI, on the *Lovely Nellie*, ex Carsethorn, May 1775. Joiner. Wife Margery Hogg, qv, with him, and ch: 1. Martha, qv; 2. Hannah, aged 3; 3. Thomas. **ELN**.

3830 HENDERSON, Thomas. From ROX. Prob rel to John H, qv, and William H, qv. To QUE on the *Sarah Mary Jane*, 1831; stld Dumfries Twp, Waterloo Co, ONT. **HGD 60**.

3831 HENDERSON, William, 1783–1883. From SHI. To QUE, 1799; stld Frampton, Bruce Co. m at QUE Anglican Cathedral, Maria Dickson. Son Gilbert. **DC 11 Feb 1980**.

3832 HENDERSON, William. From ROX. Prob rel to John H, qv, and Thomas H, qv. To QUE on the *Sarah Mary Jane*, 1831; stld Dumfries Twp, Waterloo Co, ONT. **HGD 60**.

3833 HENDERSON, William. From Craigie, Dalmeny par, WLN. s/o James H, contractor, d 1835. To QUE. **Ts Dalmeny**.

3834 HENDERSON, Rev William, 18 Aug 1800–6 Jun 1868. Prob from ABD. Grad MA, Kings Coll, Aberdeen, 1822, and became a teacher at Coldstream Academy, BEW. Ord min of Union Ch, Aberdeen. App by Colonial Committee as missionary to Salisbury, Moncton and Shediac, NB, 1841. Adm min of St James' Ch, Newcastle, 1844. DD, Queens, 1868. m 1857, d/o Rev Joseph Purdie, Clydevale, LKS. **KCG 279; FES vii 610**.

HENDRY. See also HENRY.

3835 HENDRY, Alexander, ca 1804–21 Apr 1839. From Aberdeen. s/o William H, house-painter. To CAN, ca 1830. Alumnus, Marischall Coll, 1821, and adm to Society of Advocates of Aberdeen, 1826. m Jane, d/o Capt Alexander Burnett, HEICS. **FAM ii 429; SAA 221**.

3836 HENDRY, Alexander, 1797–1874. From Portlethen, KCD. To Osprey Twp, Grey Co, ONT, 1854, and d Collingwood Twp. **DC 8 Nov 1981**.

3837 HENDRY, Alexander, 10 Jul 1839–4 Oct 1922. From Logie, Fetteresso, KCD. s/o John H, qv, and Mary Forbes, qv. To Osprey Twp, Grey Co, ONT, 1854. m 1871, Sarah Mullin. **DC 8 Nov 1981**.

3838 HENDRY, Rev Donald, 1774–1847. From Corrygills, Is Arran, BUT. To Inverness Twp, Megantic Co, QUE, 1831. Clergyman and farmer. m Elizabeth Kelso, qv, no ch. **AMC 12; MAC 39**.

3839 HENDRY, Francis, b ca 1786. To Pictou Co, NS, 1815; res West River, 1816. Shoemaker. m with 2 ch. **INS 38**.

3840 HENDRY, George, 17 Dec 1845–14 Nov 1914. From Logie, Fetteresso, KCD. s/o John H, qv, and Mary Forbes, qv. To Osprey Twp, Grey Co, ONT, 1854. m Mary White. **DC 8 Nov 1981**.

3841 HENDRY, James, 6 Oct 1830–31 Aug 1917. From Logie, Fetteresso, KCD. s/o John H, qv, and Mary Forbes, qv. To Osprey Twp, Grey Co, ONT, 1854. m 1855, Margaret Dick. **DC 8 Nov 1981**.

3842 HENDRY, John, 1800–7 Jan 1877. From Fetteresso, KCD. To ONT, 1854; stld Lot 11, Con 2, Osprey Twp, Grey Co. Farmer of 113 acres. m Mary Forbes, qv, ch: 1. James, qv; 2. Ann, qv; 3. John, 1835–1906; 4. William, 1837-39; 5. Alexander, qv; 6. Mary, qv; 7. George, qv; 8. William, qv. **DC 8 Nov 1981**.

3843 HENDRY, Mary, 14 Jul 1841–22 Nov 1916. From Logie, Fetteresso, KCD. d/o John H, qv, and Mary Forbes, qv. To Osprey Twp, Grey Co, ONT, 1854. m William Lloyd, 1835–1908. **DC 8 Nov 1981**.

3844 HENDRY, William, 2 Mar 1849–8 Jul 1941. From Logie, Fetteresso, KCD. s/o John H, qv, and Mary Forbes, qv. To Osprey Twp, Grey Co, ONT, 1854. m Johanna Galloway, 1854–1911. **DC 8 Nov 1981**.

3845 HENLY, Rory, b ca 1758. Poss from INV. To Western Shore, Inverness Co, NS, 1799. Farmer, m and ch. **CBC 1818**.

3846 HENNING, Barbara. From Colvend, KKD. To Georgetown, Kings Co, PEI, on the *Lovely Nellie*, ex Annan, 1774. **ELN**.

HENRY. See also HENDRY.

3847 HENRY, Alexander. To Halifax Co, NS, <1840; stld Upper Musquodoboit. Ship's carpenter, later surveyor. m Sarah Fisher. **NSN 8/2**.

3848 HENRY, Donald. From Shisken, Is Arran, BUT. To Inverness, Megantic Co, QUE, 1831. m 12 Feb 1832, Jean Currie, qv. **MAC 12**.

3849 HENRY, Donald. From Is Arran, BUT. To Megantic Co, QUE, ca 1831. Dau Kate. **AMC 42**.

3850   HENRY, Flora. From Corrigills, Kilbride, Is Arran, BUT. To Inverness, Megantic Co, QUE, 1839. Wife of Donald Shaw, qv.   **AMC 48; MAC 42**.

3851   HENRY, Francis, b ca 1786. To Pictou, NS, 1815; stld West River, Pictou Co, NS, 1816. ch.   **INS 38**.

3852   HENRY, Rev George, ca 1709-95. Chaplain of a Scottish regt, and present at the fall of Quebec. He organised the first Presb church in CAN in a room at the Jesuit's Barracks, Quebec, 1765.   **SGC 22; FES vii 637**.

3853   HENRY, George, d 26 Sep 1820. Poss from Aberdeen. To NS, and drowned nr Sydney, Cape Breton Co.   **NSS No 2100**.

3854   HENRY, Helen. From Alves par, MOR. To Baltimore, Hamilton Twp, Northumberland Co, ONT, ca 1835. Wife of Robert Allan, qv, m 19 Jun 1822. **DC 27 Sep 1979**.

3855   HENRY, Janet. To QUE on the *Margaret*, 1832; stld Megantic Co, QUE. m 1836, James Kerr, qv. **AMC 42**.

3856   HENRY, John, ca 1779–1 Mar 1813. From Aberdeen. s/o William H, weaver, and Margaret Petrie. To Halifax, NS, and d there.   **Ts St Nicolas, Aberdeen**.

3857   HENRY, John, 22 Jun 1828–13 Sep 1888. From DFS. To ONT, ca 1852; stld prob nr Hamilton. Moved to MAN, 1879. m Janet Cook, qv, ch: 1. Elizabeth, b 1853, d inf; 2. Edward, 1853-54; 3. John, 1855–1907; 4. Joseph, 1857-96; 5. Edward, b 1858; 6. William, 1860-81; 7. Charles, 1862-97; 8. Elizabeth, b 1863, d inf; 9. Alexander, b 1865; 10. Samuel, 1872–1947; 11. Thomas, b 1874; 12. Jessie Ellen, 1878–1962; 13. Mary, 1878–1932, an adopted child.   **DC 20 Nov 1980**.

3858   HENRY, Margaret. From Is Arran, BUT. sis/o Janet H, qv. To QUE on the *Margaret*, 1832; stld Megantic Co.   **AMC 42**.

3859   HENRY, Mary. From Is Arran, BUT. To Inverness, Megantic Co, QUE, 1848. Wife of John Kelso, qv. **AMC 49; MAC 44**.

3860   HENRY, Rev Thomas. Educ Univ of Edinburgh and emig to QUE. Was min at Lachute in 1841, and joined the FC in 1845.   **FES vii 637**.

3861   HENRY, William. To Lower Ireland, Megantic Co, QUE, <1829. Pioneer settler. m Margaret McKenzie. **AMC 34**.

3862   HENRY, William. From Is Arran, BUT. To QUE on the *Caledonia*, ex Greenock, 25 Apr 1829; stld Inverness Twp, Megantic Co. Carpenter.   **AMC 12**.

3863   HEPBURN, William. To Winchester Twp, Dundas Co, ONT, <1855.   **DC 4 Mar 1965**.

3864   HERALD, Rev James, ca 1830–5 Mar 1896. b Kirriemuir, ANS. s/o John H. Educ Marischall Coll, Aberdeen, 1845-49. To ONT and adm min of Dundas, 1858.   **FAM ii 530; FES vii 637**.

3865   HERD, Mary, b ca 1830. From ANS. To CAN, ca 1854; stld prob ONT. Wife of James Lawson. **DC 29 Dec 1980**.

3866   HERDMAN, Rev Andrew Walker, 5 Sep 1822–7 Aug 1894. From Rattray, PER. s/o Rev William H, par

min, and Sophia Walker. Educ Madras Coll and Univ of St Andrews. To Pictou, NS, and became min of St Andrews Ch, 1853. Retr to SCT and adm min of Rattray, 1879. m 4 Oct 1849, Elizabeth Close, Pictou, ch: 1. William Close, b 1851; 2. Andrew Walker, b 1853; 3. Rev James Chalmers, 1855–1910, min of Presb Ch, Calgary; 4. Elizabeth Rate, b 1857; 5. Mary Sophia, b 1859, Canadian missionary to India; 6. John Robert, b 1861; 7. Edward Gordon, b 1863; 8. Rev Arthur Wentworth Knox, b 1865, min at Winnipeg.   **SAM 91; FES iv 172, vii 615, 658**.

3867   HERMISTON, Isabella, b 30 Nov 1818. To ONT <8 Nov 1837, when m George Ramsey, qv.   **DC 15 Apr 1980**.

3868   HERON, Jean, 1821–2 Feb 1894. From Dalry, AYR. To Brantford Twp, Brant Co, ONT, prob 1852. Hatmaker. m Adam Bone, qv.   **DC 27 Jun 1979**.

3869   HERON, Robert, d 1834. Poss from DFS. To Toronto, ONT. Printer.   **DGC 5 Nov 1834**.

3870   HERRIES, Janet, b ca 1738. From Milnbank, Southwick, Kirkbean, KKD. To Georgetown, Kings Co, PEI, on the *Lovely Nellie*, ex Annan, 1774. Wife of Charles Blackie, qv.   **ELN**.

3871   HERVEY, James. From Greenock, RFW. To Montreal, QUE, <1846.   **Ts Greenock**.

3872   HERVEY, Michael. To CAN <1535, and explored the St Lawrence River with Jacques Cartier.   **SAS 16**.

3873   HETHERINGTON, James, d 5 Mar 1863. From Annan, DFS. To Hamilton, ONT, prob <1840. Sawyer. **CAE 9**.

3974   HEWITT, Elizabeth. From Merton, BEW. To Guelph Twp, Wellington Co, ONT, 1833. Wife of George Henderson, qv.   **SG xxiv/2 53**.

3875   HEYMER, James, b 20 Jan 1807. From Stitchel, ROX. s/o James H. and Mary Hastings. To QUE, ex Leith, 1830. Moved to NY, ca 1836. Nail-maker. m Ellen Peirson, from ENG, ch: 1. Robert Bruce; 2. Mary Eliza; 3. Eliza Sarah; 4. William John; 8. Mary Elizabeth; 9. William S.   **DC 17 May 1977**.

3876   HILL, Agnes, 19 Sep 1775–Jan 1847. From Govan, Glasgow. d/o Ninian H. and Mary Walker. To QUE, 1821; stld North Elmsley Twp, Lanark Co, ONT. Wife of Thomas Cameron, qv.   **DC 17 May 1974**.

3877   HILL, Alexander, b 1779. From Skipness, ARL. s/o Daniel H. and Mary Campbell. To Lanark Co, ONT, ca 1820. Wife Elizabeth Currie, qv, or Curry, with him, and ch: 1. Daniel, b 2 Apr 1807; 2. Agnes, b 6 Jun 1808; 3. Alexander, qv; 4. Mary, b 16 Aug 1812; 5. John, b 26 Jan 1814; 6. Archibald Newall, qv; 7. Elizabeth, b 17 Nov 1818.   **DC 13 Jan 1962**.

3878   HILL, Alexander, jr, b 1811. From Skipness, ARL. s/o Alexander H, qv, and Elizabeth Currie, qv. To ONT, ca 1820, and stld Lanark Co. m Agnes Hood, qv, ch.   **DC 10 Mar 1820**.

3879   HILL, Andrew. To Lanark Co, ONT, 1821; stld Lot 13, Con 2, Darling Twp. Farmer and innkeeper. **HCL 76**.

3880   HILL, Archibald Newall, b 20 Aug 1816. From Glasgow. s/o Alexander H, qv, and Elizabeth Currie, qv.

To Lanark Co, ONT, ca 1820. m 21 Feb 1840, Isabella, d/o James Hood, qv, and Jane Margaret Bilsland, qv, ch. **DC 10 Mar 1980**.

3881 HILL, Daniel. From Wallacetown, Ayr. s/o James H, weaver, and Mary Eadie. To St Johns, NFD, <1850. **Ayr Sasines, 351, 248**.

3882 HILL, Ellen. Prob from Blaigowrie, PER. To Hastings Co, ONT, <1850. Wife of Daniel or Donald McInroy, qv. **DC 10 Nov 1981**.

3883 HILL, Helen Eliza Gillon. Poss from Linlithgow, WLN. To Seaforth Village, Huron Co, ONT, 1854. Wife of James Darling, qv. **DC 5 Jan 1962**.

3884 HILL, Margaret Sinclair. From Linlithgow, WLN. To Seaforth Twp, Huron Co, ONT, 1854. Wife of Alexander Young, qv. **DC 2 Jan 1962**.

3885 HILL, Robert, 1803-88. To QUE, 1828; stld later Inverness, Megantic Co, QUE. m (i) Jane Andrews; (ii) Miss Wallace. ch: 1. Alexander; 2. Mary Ann; 3. Jane; 4. Eliza; 5. David; 6. Charlotte; 7. Matilda; 8. Sarah; 9. Samuel; 10. William; 11. Caroline; 12. Robert; 13. Isabella; 14. Allan. **AMC 140**.

3886 HILL, Rev Thomas, ca 1789-17 Mar 1824. From Hawick, ROX. s/o David H, carrier, and Agnes Waugh. Min of the Burgher Ch. To Montreal, QUE, ca 1824. **SGC 326**.

3887 HILLHOUSE, William P, b 29 Jan 1833. From Ayr. To QUE, ca 1850; stld later Brome Co. m Elizabeth Pibus, and had, poss with other ch: 1. William Mills, b Bondville, 1859; 2. Eva E; 3. Alvin Percival. **MGC 2 Aug 1979**.

HISLOP. See also HYSLOP.

3888 HISLOP, Thomas, 29 Dec 1823-26 Jun 1895. From Edinburgh. s/o Walter H. and Isabella Aitchison. To Brockville, Elizabethtown Twp, Leeds Co, ONT, ca 1854. Railway agent. m Margaret Chesser, qv, ch: 1. Elizabeth, b 1 Mar 1851; 2. Isabella, b 30 Apr 1853; 3. James, dy; 4. Fanny, b 3 Nov 1857; 5. William B, b 30 Nov 1859; 6. John B, b 4 Jan 1861; 7. Margaret, b 17 Apr 1866. **DC 28 Jun 1980**.

3889 HOGG, Alexander, ca 1808-5 May 1853. Poss from SEL. To Montreal, QUE, 1833; stld later Parma, NY. By wife Sarah, ch: 1. John, b 1830; 2. James A, 1833-1912; 3. Sarah, b 1836; 4. Jane, b 1838; 5. Isabella. **LDW 22 Oct 1980**.

3890 HOGG, Agnes, b 1826. Poss from MLN. To NB, 1854. Wife of George Cleghorn, qv. **DC 10 Jun 1981**.

3891 HOGG, Ann, 1796-1862. Prob from LKS. To Nelson Twp, Halton Co, ONT, ca 1826. Wife of George Carr, qv. **DC 21 Mar 1981**.

3892 HOGG, David. From Edinburgh. To ONT. m Isabella Inglis, qv. Son William Drummond. **DC 29 Sep 1964**.

3893 HOGG, David, ca 1804-19 Apr 1849. From Broughty Ferry, ANS. To St John, NB, <1828. Moved in 1838 to Hobart, Tasmania. Master blacksmith. m Elizabeth E, d/o Andrew Barnes, shipowner, and Katherine Eustace, ch: 1. Catherine, b 1829, St John; 2. Andrew; 3. David; 4. John Stuart; 5. Mary; 6. James Eustace, b 1838; 7. George Barnes; 8. Annie; 9. Louisa; 10. Thomas; 11. William; 12. Charles. **DC 11 Nov 1981**.

3894 HOGG, Janet, ca 1789-12 Jun 1874. From DFS. To QUE and stld Melbourne, Sherbrooke Co. Wife of Andrew Wilson, qv. **MGC 2 Aug 1979**.

3895 HOGG, Janet. From Liddesdale, ROX. To York Co, NB, ca 1820; later to Middlesex Co, ONT. Wife of William Beattie, qv. **DC 16 Jul 1979**.

3896 HOGG, Rev John, 1823-3 Mar 1877. b Yarrow, SEL. s/o Thomas H, farmer. Educ Univ of Glasgow, 1839, and ord to Relief Ch, Dumfries, 1846. To Hamilton, ONT, 1851. Min at Detroit, MI, 1859, but joined Ch of Scotland and retr to CAN. Adm min of Guelph, ONT, 1861. **GMA 14041; UPC i 219; FES vii 637**.

3897 HOGG, Margery, b ca 1742. From Hoddam par, DFS. To Georgetown, Kings Co, PEI, on the *Lovely Nellie*, ex Carsethorn, May 1775. Wife of Thomas Henderson, qv. **ELH**.

3898 HOGGAN, James, d 27 Feb 1834. From Waterside, Thornhill, DFS. To ONT. **DGC 23 Apr 1834**.

3899 HOGGAN, John McMurdo, ca 1812-5 Sep 1848. From Middlebie par, DFS. s/o James H. of Waterside. To ONT. **DGH 19 Oct 1848**.

HOLLIDAY. See HALLIDAY.

3900 HOLM, Hector. To Pictou, NS, on the *Lady Gray*, ex Cromarty, ROC, arr 16 Jul 1841. Son Hector with him. **DC 15 Jul 1979**.

3901 HOLMES, James, 1874-10 Aug 1848. From Lochwinnoch, RFW. s/o John H. and Margaret Orr. To Montreal, QUE, ca 1820; stld later Chateauguay Co. Farmer. m Barbara Brodie, qv, ch: 1. Margaret, qv; 2. John, d 1822; 3. Robert, d 1845; 4. Barbara, d 1894; 5. Mary Ann, 1826-1909. **DC 1 Apr 1979 and 18 May 1982**.

3902 HOLMES, John. From ROC. To Pictou Co, NS, 1803, with wife Christy. Son John, qv. **MLA 162**.

3903 HOLMES, John, jr, qv, 1789-3 Jun 1876. From ROC. s/o John H, qv, and wife Christy. To Pictou Co, NS, 1803. Deputy Commissioner of Crown Lands, JP, and MLA. m 1814, Christina Fraser. Son Simon Hugh, 1831-1919, MLA. **BNA 683; MLA 162**.

3904 HOLMES, Margaret, b 17 Jun 1810. From Port Glasgow, RFW. d/o James H, qv, and Barbara Brodie, qv. To Montreal, QUE, 1819. m 22 Jun 1833, William Parkyn, engineer, ch. **DC 1 Apr 1979**.

3905 HOLMES, Margaret, d 1 Jan 1841. From Edinburgh. To Goderich, Huron Co, ONT, 1833. wid/o Daniel Lizars, engraver. **DGH 25 Feb 1841**.

3906 HONEYMAN, Mr. Cabin passenger on the *Lulan*, ex Glasgow, 17 Aug 1848, bound for Pictou, NS. **DC 12 Jul 1979**.

3907 HOOD, Agnes, 5 Mar 1811-16 Feb 1872. From Bridgeton, Glasgow. d/o James H, qv, and Jane Margaret Bilsland, qv. To QUE on the *Prompt*, ex Greenock, 4 Jul 1820; stld Dalhousie Twp, Lanark Co, ONT. m 6 Apr 1832, Alexander Hill, qv. **DC 10 Mar 1980**.

3908 HOOD, David. bro/o William Hood, qv. To QUE <1845, with parents who farmed nr St Philippe de Laprairie. Operated saw and planing mills. Son David. **SGC 634**.

3909 HOOD, Elizabeth, 17 Dec 1773–9 Aug 1856. From Kelso, ROX. s/o William H. and Hannah Clarke. To QUE on the *Prompt*, ex Greenock, 4 Jul 1820; stld Dalhousie Twp, Lanark Co, ONT. m John Todd, qv. **DC 10 Mar 1980.**

3910 HOOD, Elizabeth, ca 1801-75. From Glasgow. Poss d/o James H, qv. To QUE on the *Prompt*, ex Greenock, 4 Jul 1820; stld Dalhousie Twp, Lanark Co, ONT. m (i) — Graham; (ii) William Allan, jr, qv. **DC 15 Jun 1977 and 10 Mar 1980.**

3911 HOOD, Isabella, 1786–27 Sep 1842. Prob from Cromarty par, ROC. Perhaps sis/o Thomas H, qv. To Scott Twp, Ontario Co, ONT, poss 1830. Wife of Hugh Mustard, qv. **DC 27 Dec 1979.**

3912 HOOD, James, 6 Apr 1776–30 Jul 1859. From Kelso, ROX. s/o William H. and Hannah Clarke. To QUE on the *Prompt*, ex Greenock, 4 Jul 1820; stld Dalhousie Twp, Lanark Co, ONT. Discharged soldier, 89th Regt, and lay preacher. m (i) 28 May 1798, Elizabeth Jones, ch: 1. William, qv; 2. Elizabeth, b 1801; 3. Hannah, d 1830; 4. Jane, d ca 1862. m (ii) 14 Nov 1808, Jane Margaret Bilsland, qv, further ch: 5. Jean, qv; 6. Agnes, qv; 7. James, 1812-27; 8. Isabel, 1814-16; 9. Robert, 1816-20; 10. Margaret, qv; 11. Isobella, 1821-47; 12. Annie, 1823–1912; 13. Mary, 1827–1910; 14. Janet, 1829-30. **HCL 238; DC 10 Mar 1980.**

3913 HOOD, Jean, 31 Aug 1809–24 Feb 1899. From Bridgeton, Glasgow. d/o James H, qv, and Jane Margaret Bilsland, qv. To QUE on the *Prompt*, ex Greenock, 4 Jul 1820; stld Dalhousie Twp, Lanark Co, ONT. m 1830, James Jack, qv. **DC 10 Mar 1980.**

3914 HOOD, Margaret, 8 Dec 1814–8 Aug 1871. From Bridgeton, Glasgow. d/o James H, qv, and Jane Margaret Bilsland, qv. To QUE on the *Prompt*, ex Greenock, 4 Jul 1820; stld Dalhousie Twp, Lanark Co, ONT. m (i) Davidson, s/o John Todd, qv, and Elizabeth Hood, qv, ch. m (ii) James, s/o William Hood and Jane Graham, further ch. **DC 10 Mar 1980.**

3915 HOOD, Margaret, 13 Jul 1827–5 Apr 1914. From Glasgow. d/o Dr William H. and Jean Graham. To ONT, 1844; stld Innisfil, Simcoe Co. m 22 Feb 1847, James Duncan, qv. **DC 11 Aug 1980.**

3916 HOOD, Mary, ca 1789–1869. From Glasgow. d/o William H. To QUE on the *Prompt*, ex Greenock, 4 Jul 1820; stld Dalhousie Twp, Lanark Co, ONT. Wife of William Jack, qv. **DC 10 Mar 1980.**

3917 HOOD, Mary, b ca 1800. From Ashkirk, SEL. Prob sis/o Andrew H, miller, Ashkirk Mill. To Montreal, QUE, 1831. Wife of John Douglas, qv. **Ashkirk OPR 781/4.**

3918 HOOD, Robert, b ca 1782. Prob from Innerleithen, PEE. To QUE, ex Greenock, summer 1815; stld prob Lanark Co, ONT. Ploughman. Wife Helen Scott, qv, with him, and 3 ch. **SEC 2.**

3919 HOOD, Thomas, 1793–20 Sep 1868. From Cromarty par, ROC. Perhaps bro/o Isabella H, qv. To ONT, poss 1830. m Helen Bain, qv. **DC 27 Dec 1979.**

HOOD, Mrs William. See AINSLIE, Agnes.

3920 HOOD, William, 1799–28 Feb 1874. From Glasgow. s/o James H, qv, and first wife Elizabeth Jones. To QUE on the *Prompt*, ex Greenock, 4 Jul 1820; stld Dalhousie Twp, Lanark Co, ONT. Farmer and schoolteacher. m Martha Park, qv, ch: 1. Marion, 1826–1906; 2. James, 1828–1910; 3. Elizabeth, 1830-94; 4. Martha Park, 1832–1917; 5. William, 1834–1922; 6. Margaret, 1836–1917; 7. Andrew, 1838–1924; 8. John, 1841-86; 9. David, 1846–1912; 10. Gemmill, 1843-63. **HCL 238; DC 10 and 21 Mar 1980.**

3921 HOOD, William, Jun 1805–13 May 1887. From Kirk Yetholm, ROX. s/o William H, dec, and Agnes Ainslie, qv. To York Co, ONT, 1831; stld Lots 31 and 32, Scarborough Twp. Farmer. m Elizabeth Rutherford, qv, and had, with other ch: 1. William, b 9 Sep 1827; 2. Walter, b 15 Aug 1829; 3. Elizabeth, b 9 Sep 1831, in CAN; 4. Adam; 5. Andrew. **DC 27 Aug 1975.**

3922 HOOD, William. To QUE <1845, with parents who farmed nr St Philippe de Laprairie. Engineer, and manager of sawmills after d of bro David H, qv. Went to Muskoka, 1878. **SGC 634.**

3923 HOPE, Catherine. From Wiston, LKS. To QUE, 1826, and stld Abbotsford, Bouville Co. Wife of John Gillespie, qv. **MGC 15 Jul 1980.**

3924 HOPE, Jane, ca 1793–21 Mar 1878. From Hutton and Corrie par, DFS. To PEI, ca 1818. Wife of James Corrie Jardine, qv. **DC 6 Apr 1979.**

3925 HOPKINS, William, b ca 1845. To St Gabriel de Valcartier, QUE, poss <1853. **Census 1861.**

3926 HOPKIRK, Henry Glassford, ca 1819–12 Nov 1842. From Edinburgh. s/o John Glassford H, WS, and Jessie Hamilton, and neph of James H, qv. To Kingston, ONT, and d there. **DGH 22 Dec 1842; HWS 195.**

3927 HOPKIRK, James, ca 1800–15 Oct 1859. From Glasgow. s/o John H. of Dalbeth and Easterhill, merchant, and Christian Glassford. Matric Univ of Glasgow, 1816, and grad LL.B, 1826. Adm advocate, 1825. To Kingston, ONT, and d there. **GMA 9609; RGG 273; OEC 166; FAS 105.**

3928 HORN, Margaret, 1800–28 Jan 1854. Prob from Glasgow. To ONT ca 1839; stld Lanark Co, and d Rosetta. Wife of James Arnott, qv. **DC 2 Nov 1979.**

3929 HORNE, Adam Grant, ca 1831–ca 1903. From Edinburgh. To CAN, 1851. Served with HBCo at Fort Rupert, and was assigned to the Pacific coast. Conducted several explorations and has been described as 'Canada's Davy Crockett.' Later opened his own store at Nanaimo. **DC 21 Mar 1981.**

3930 HORNE, Alexander, ca 1772–8 Feb 1867. From Kirkintilloch, DNB. To Pictou Co, NS, ca 1801; stld Middle River. ch: 1. Ellen, b ca 1802; 2. Barbara; 3. Bennet; 4. Thomas, 1808-95; 5. Nancy. **DC 18 Nov 1979.**

3931 HOSSACK, Donald. From Dundee, ANS. To Miramichi, Northumberland Co, NB, 1835. Wife Margaret McLay, qv, with him, and ch: 1. Alexander; 2. Donald; 3. Ann; 4. Jane, 1829–1904. **DC 4 Dec 1978.**

3932 HOSEA, Mary, 1772–1860. From Bannockburn, STI. To NB, 1820; stld later PEI. Wife of William Whitehead, qv. **DC 25 Nov 1981.**

3933 HOUSTON, James. To Pictou, NS, on the *Hope*,

ex Glasgow, 5 Apr 1848. Wife Jane with him, and s James. **DC 12 Jul 1979**.

3934 HOUSTON, Mary. From Greddock Mill, Creetown, KKD. To ONT, 1845; stld prob York Co. m 27 Mar 1845, James Kellock, qv. **DGH 10 Apr 1845**.

3935 HOWAT, Agnes, d 1846. Prob rel to Elizabeth H, qv. To Pictou, NS. Drowned in wreck of *Sutlej*, of Pictou, bound for Fall River. **DGH 30 Jul 1846**.

3936 HOWAT, Charles Douglas, ca 1815–12 May 1843. From DFS. s/o Alexander H, Dean of Guild, and Elizabeth McGuffog. To Kingston, ONT. **DGH 13 Jul 1843; MSM 122**.

3937 HOWAT, Elizabeth, d 1846. Prob rel to Agnes H. To Pictou, NS. Drowned in wreck of *Sutlej*, of Pictou, bound for Fall River. **DGH 30 Jul 1846**.

3938 HOWAT, Helen. From DFS. d/o Alexander H, Dean of Guild, and Elizabeth McGuffog. To Kingston, ONT, <1843, when m David Martin. **DGH 13 Jul 1843**.

3939 HOWAT, Isabella, 1768–29 Feb 1844. From BAN. d/o James H, qv. To Flat River, PEI, on the *John & Elizabeth*, arr 30 Jul 1775; stld Queens Co. m James McGregor, qv. **DC 27 Jul 1980**.

3940 HOWAT, James. From BAN. To PEI on the *John & Elizabeth*, arr 30 Jul 1775; stld Flat River, Queens Co. ch with him: 1. Isabella, qv; 2. James, b 1772. m (ii) Mrs Muttart, with further ch. **SG xix/3 95; DC 27 Jul 1980**.

3941 HOWIE, James. From AYR. To Colchester Twp, Essex Co, ONT, ca 1852. Son David, b Muirkirk, ca 1845. **DC 9 Jan 1971**.

3942 HOWITT, John, ca 1799–26 Aug 1852. From AYR. To Pictou Co, NS, prob <1830; bur Churchville. **DC 22 Jun 1980**.

3943 HUGHES, John. To QUE on the *David of London*, ex Greenock, 19 May 1821; stld poss Lanark Co, ONT. **HCL 239**.

3944 HUGHSTON, Joshua. Poss from OKI. To St John, NB, <1800. Wife Sarah with him. Dau Jemima. **NER viii 98**.

3945 HUME, Archibald. To Montreal, QUE, <1830. Chandler and soap manufacturer. Retr to SCT. **SGC 378**.

3946 HUMPHREY, Thomas, ca 1811–28 Jun 1877. From Stromness, OKI. To Halifax, NS, <1832. Retr to SCT and res Edinburgh. **Ts Warriston**.

3947 HUNTER, Alexander. s/o John H. and Catherine Fotheringham. To NB <1830. **SH**.

3948 HUNTER, Allan. From Old Cumnock, AYR. bro/o John H, qv. To ONT, 1833. Shoemaker. m (i) 19 Jul 1822, Elizabeth Chessy, ch: 1. Katherine, b 1822; 2. Andrew, b 1824; 3. James, b 1826; 4. Thomas, b 1828; 5. James, b 1830. m (ii) Margaret Black, qv. **Old Cumnock OPR 610/4; LDW 30 Aug 1976**.

3949 HUNTER, Andrew, b 1797. From Paisley, RFW. s/o John H, weaver, and Christian McFarlane. To QUE <1830. **DC 15 Oct 1972**.

3950 HUNTER, Duncan, 1814–24 Jul 1890. From Port Ellen, Is Islay, ARL. s/o Lachlan H. and Mary McLeod or McCuaig. To QUE, ex Port Glasgow, 17 Jul 1842; stld Brampton dist, Peel Co, ONT, later Chinguacousy Twp. Farmer. m Catherine McLeod, qv, or McCuaig, ch: 1. Flora; 2. Hugh, dy; 3. Mary; 4. Alexander, dy; 5. Catherine; 6. Duncan; 7. Anne; 8. William, 1861–1935. **DC 29 Dec 1981**.

3951 HUNTER, Edward, ca 1819–20 Sep 1847. From Dunnichen, ANS. s/o Andrew H, par schoolmaster, and Margaret Irons. To Montreal, QUE, and d there. **Ts Dunnichen**.

3952 HUNTER, Elizabeth, b 1844. From Lamlash, Is Arran, BUT. d/o James H, qv, and Ann McKelvie, qv. To QUE on the *Bowly*, 1846; stld Inverness, Megantic Co. m William Dempsey. **AMC 49; MAC 43**.

3953 HUNTER, Francis, 1762–1853. From Alloa, CLK. To Halifax, NS, ex London, 1792, but stld QUE, 1794, and Montreal, 1831. Merchant. m, ch: 1. Francis, merchant, in partnership with bro-in-law John Fisher; 2. Mrs George Rhynas; 3. Mrs Alexander Miller; 4. Mrs Fisher. **SGC 429**.

3954 HUNTER, George, d 6 Jul 1854. From Polwarth, BEW. s/o John H, tenant of Godscroft. To NFD, and d La Poile. Surgeon. **Ts Polwarth**.

3955 HUNTER, Helen, 20 Jul 1789–19 Dec 1856. Poss from MLN. To Sophiasburgh Twp, Prince Edward Co, ONT, 1817. Wife of John Black, qv. **DC 30 Jun 1979**.

3956 HUNTER, Helen. Prob from Lilliesleaf, ROX. To Camden, Addington Co, ONT, <1845. m Mack Hermiston. **SH**.

3957 HUNTER, James. From Is Arran, BUT. To QUE on the *Bowly*, 1846; stld Inverness, Megantic Co. m Ann McKelvie, qv, wid/o James McKinnon, ch: 1. James; 2. Elizabeth, qv. **AMC 49; MAC 43**.

3958 HUNTER, Jane. From LKS. To QUE on the *George Canning*, ex Greenock, 14 Apr 1821. m at Govan, Robert Purdon, qv. **DC 26 Nov 1980**.

3959 HUNTER, Jane, 1797–1880. From ARL. To Caledon Twp, Peel Co, ONT, <1840. Wife of Alexander McFarlane, qv. **DC 21 Apr 1980**.

3960 HUNTER, Mrs Jane Douglas, d 5 Aug 1858. From Southerness, Kirkbean, KKD. wid/o Robert H. To Winchester Twp, Dundas Co, ONT. **DGH 1 Oct 1858**.

3961 HUNTER, Janet. To ONT, 1831. Wife of John Johnston, qv. **DC 30 Nov 1979**.

3962 HUNTER, John, b ca 1797. From Is Arran, BUT. To Restigouche Co, NB, ca 1817. Petitioned for 150 acres of Lot 71 on the south side of the Restigouche River, 9 Feb 1821. **DC 31 May 1980**.

3963 HUNTER, John. To Compton Co, QUE, ca 1825. Son Thomas W, res Hereford, Compton Co. **MGC 2 Aug 1979**.

3964 HUNTER, John. From Old Cumnock, AYR. To ONT 1833. Woollen weaver. m Margaret Linton, qv, ch: 1. Andrew, b DFS, 1821; 2. Robert, b AYR, 1823; 3. Jane, b 1826; 4. Janet, b 1832. **Old Cumnock OPR 610/4; LDW 30 Aug 1976**.

3965 HUNTER, Rev John. App by Colonial Committee, 1848, and adm min at Woodstock and Richmond, NB, 1849. **FES vii 610**.

3966 HUNTER, John. From Newton-upon-Ayr. s/o Hugh H. To CAN <1855. Moulder. **SH**.

3967 HUNTER, Margaret. From Hawick, ROX. d/o Robert H, grocer, and Jane Fleming. To ONT, 1849. m Alexander Purdom, qv. **THS 1848/23**.

3968 HUNTER, Mary, 1781–1862. From Kirkmichael, AYR. d/o David H. To QUE on the *George Canning*, 1829, stld Montreal. Wife of William Aird, qv. **DC 15 Jul 1979**.

3969 HUNTER, Peter, 1746–1805. Poss from Auchterarder, PER. Served in 60th Rifles and reached rank of Colonel. App Commander-in-Chief of the Forces in CAN, 1799, and Lt Gov of Upper Canada. d unm. **BNA 311; SAS 17**.

3970 HUNTER, Robert. From Kilmarnock, AYR. bro/o William H, qv. To Montreal, QUE, <1789. **SGC 78**.

3971 HUNTER, Thomas. Prob rel to William H, qv. To Lanark Co, ONT, 1816; stld Lot 7, Con 10, Drummond Twp. Farmer. **HCL 20**.

3972 HUNTER, William. From Kilmarnock, AYR. bro/o Robert H, qv. To Montreal, QUE, <1789. Treas of St Gabriel Street Ch <1803. m Isabella Cowan, wid/o William Stewart, qv. Son William, notary. **SGC 77**.

3973 HUNTER, William. Prob rel to Thomas H, qv. To Lanark Co, ONT, 1816; stld Lot 7, Con 10, Drummond Twp. Farmer. **HCL 20**.

3974 HUTCHISON, Agnes Graham, b ca 1775. From Kincardine-on-Forth, PER. Poss d/o Thomas H. To Peterborough Co, ONT, 1820. m John Fife, qv. **DC 11 Dec 1967 and 10 Jun 1977**.

3975 HUTCHISON, Alexander, 1806–10 Apr 1884. Poss from MOR. To Oakville Twp, Halton Co, ONT, 1825; stld Fergus, Wellington Co. Cooper, later farmer. d West Garafraxa Twp. m Ann, 1820-77, from YKS, ENG, d/o Francis Vickers and Mary Brook, ch: 1. David, b 23 Oct 1847; 2. Mary, b 1 Feb 1850; 3. Alexander, b 20 Nov 1851; 4. Ann, b 20 Jul 1853; 5. Eliza, b 9 Apr 1855. **DC 19 Nov 1981**.

3976 HUTCHISON, Matthew, 1766–1846. From Greenock, RFW. To Guysborough Co, NS, ca 1789. m 1806, Ann Cook, from New England, ch. **DC 10 Nov 1981**.

3977 HUTCHISON, Matthew, b 17 May 1827. From Largs, AYR. To Montreal, QUE, prob <1853; later to Goderich, Huron Co, ONT. Baker, later manager of flour mills. m Helen Ogilvie. **SGC 569**.

3978 HUTCHISON, Robina. From Edinburgh. To New York on the *Science*, 1833; stld Colborne Twp, Huron Co, ONT. Wife of Daniel Lizars, qv. **St Cuthberts OPR 685-2/35**.

3979 HUTCHISON, Thomas, d 13 Oct 1845. From Tinwald, DFS. To ONT, and prob stld Norfolk Co. **DGH 27 Nov 1845**.

3980 HUTCHISON, William, 12 Sep 1809–6 Aug 1875. From Kilwinning, AYR. To Montreal, QUE, 1833; moved to Cobourg, Northumberland Co, ONT, 1857. Master builder and contractor. m 1835, Helen Hall, qv, ch. **SGC 489**.

3981 HUTCHINSON, Mary, 1802-95. From PER. To Pictou Co, NS, 1849; stld later French River, Tatamagouche, Colchester Co. Wife of David Donaldson, qv. **HT 83**.

3982 HUTSON, James. From Castlelaw, Ashkirk, SEL. To ONT, 1830. Labourer. m Margaret Stoddart, qv, ch: 1. Walter, b 9 May 1823; 2. Isabel, b 24 Oct 1825; 3. James, b 24 Apr 1828; 4. Robert, b 15 Apr 1834; 5. John, b 8 Nov 1839; 6. George Stoddart, d 7 May 1845. **Ashkirk OPR 781/4**.

3983 HYNDMAN, Donald. From ARL, poss Campbelltown. To Ekfrid Twp, Middlesex Co, ONT, 1831. ch: 1. Peter; 2. Gilbert; 3. Neil. **PCM 30**.

3984 HYNDMAN, Peter. From Skipness, ARL. To ONT, 1846; stld poss Erin Twp, Wellington Co. m Jean McVannel, qv, ch: 1. Christina; 2. Duncan; 3. James, b ca 1844. **DC 16 Mar 1978**.

3985 HYNDMARSH, Jane, 1795–20 Sep 1856. From Roxburgh or Morebattle, ROX. To Glenelg Twp, Grey Co, ONT, ca 1850. Wife of Adam Weir, qv. **DC 28 Dec 1981**.

HYSLOP. See also HISLOP.

3986 HYSLOP, Edward, d 1847. From DFS. To Onslow, Colchester Co, NS. Journalist. m Janet Weir, 1794–1869. **CAE 20**.

3987 HYSLOP, Marion, 1771–1851. From Rerrick, KKD. To Pictou Co, NS, 1815. Wife of Charles Graham, qv. **DC 28 Dec 1975**.

3988 HYSLOP, Richard, ca 1786–28 Dec 1868. Poss from DFS. To Earltown, Colchester Co, NS, <1845. Wife predeceased him. ch incl: 1. John, 1824-60; 2. Edward, alive 1868. **NSN 11/2, 30/311**.

3989 HYSLOP, William, ca 1835–6 Dec 1855. From Middlebie par, DFS. s/o John H, Blackwoodridge Limeworks. To Durham Co, ONT, and d Port Hope. **DGC 22 Jan 1856**.

I

3990 IMMERSON, Richard. Poss from PER. To QUE on the *Lady of the Lake*, Sep 1816; stld prob Lanark Co, ONT. **HCL 237**.

3991 INCHES, Andrew Small, 29 Apr 1817–31 Oct 1897. From Dunkeld, PER. s/o James I, qv, and Janet Small, qv. To St John, NB, 1833. m 1863, Margaret Dougall. **DC 2 Mar 1980**.

3992 INCHES, James, Jul 1784–23 Aug 1847. From Dunkeld, PER. s/o James I, merchant, and Helen Blair. To St John, NB, 1832, but retr to SCT, 1841. m Janet Small, qv, ch: 1. Charles Hood, 1815-92; 2. Andrew Small, qv; 3. Keir, 1818-38; 4. Robert Peddie, 1821-22; 5. Jane Stewart, qv; 6. Julius Legendre, qv; 7. Helen Blair, 1826-33; 8. Elder Baird, 1827-35; 9. Alexander Mackenzie, 1829-64; 10. Jessie, 1831-35; 11. James Archibald, qv; 12. Patrick Robertson, b NB, 1835. **DC 2 Mar 1980; Ts Dunkeld**.

3993 INCHES, James Archibald, 12 Aug 1832–25 May 1878. From Newtyle, ANS. s/o James I, qv, and Janet Small, qv. To St John, NB, 1833. m 9 Sep 1854, Charlotte L. Wooffendale. **DC 2 Mar 1980**.

3994 INCHES, Jane Stewart, 7 Nov 1822–17 Jun

1891. From Dunkeld, PER, but b Stenton, ELN.
d/o James I, qv, and Janet Small, qv. To St John, NB,
1833, and d Omaha, NE. m at Dublin, 5 Jan 1842,
W. Prest.   **DC 2 Mar 1980**.

3995   INCHES, Julius Legendre, 8 Jun 1824–19 Aug
1900. From Dunkeld, PER. s/o James I, qv, and Janet
Small, qv. To St John, NB, 1833. m 20 Dec 1849,
Frances Jane Everett, at Fredericton.   **DC 2 Mar 1980**.

3996   INGLIS, George, b 26 May 1804. Prob from
Stow par, MLN. To Dummer Twp, Peterborough Co, ONT,
via ME, summer 1832. m Isabel Matheson, qv, ch:
1. Margaret, b 23 Aug 1832; 2. Robert, b 9 Jul 1836;
3. James, b 15 May 1838; 4. Helen, b 2 Jun 1841;
5. Agnes, b 19 Oct 1842; 6. George, b 28 Nov 1846;
7. Daniel, b 28 May 1849.   **DC 14 Jul 1980**.

3997   INGLIS, Isabella. From CLK. d/o Robert I. To
ONT. Wife of David Hogg, qv.   **DC 29 Sep 1964**.

3998   INGLIS, John. From Hamilton, LKS. To ONT,
prob <1855; stld Dundas. ch incl: 1. John; 2. James;
3. Robert; 4. Annie.   **DC 23 Nov 1981**.

3999   INGLIS, John, b 1803. To Huron Twp, Bruce Co,
ca 1851. Farmer. Wife Elizabeth with him, and ch.
DC 25 Dec 1981.

4000   INGRAM, George, 1778–1849. From Gordon,
BEW. s/o George I, feuar, and Susan Fairbairn. To
Medonte Twp, Simcoe Co, ONT, 1833. Farmer, Con 3.
m Alison White, qv, ch: 1. George, jr, qv; 2. Robert,
1811-36; 3. James, qv.   **DC 5 Aug 1979**.

4001   INGRAM, George, jr, 1808-67. From Gordon,
BEW. s/o George I, qv, and Alison White, qv. To
Medonte Twp, Simcoe Co, ONT, 1833. Farmer, Con 3.
m Catherine Tudhope, qv, ch: 1. Christian, 1843–1927;
2. Alison, 1845-65; 3. George, 1846–1917; 4. James,
1848–1916; 5. Robert, 1850–1925; 6. Alexander,
1852–1910; 7. Susanna, 1855-59; 8. Jane, 1858–1930;
9. Margaret, 1862–1963, d Toronto, unm.   **DC 5 Aug
1979**.

4002   INGRAM, James, 1812-36. From Gordon, BEW.
s/o George I, qv, and Alison White, qv. To Medonte Twp,
Simcoe Co, ONT, 1833. Farmer, Lot 49, Con 3.
m Elizabeth Tudhope, qv, ch.   **DC 5 Aug 1979**.

4003   INKSTER, James. From OKI. To Red River, MAN,
prob <1830. Blacksmith. m Elizabeth, d/o James
Sutherland, HBCo.   **DC 21 Mar 1981**.

4004   INKSTER, John, 1799–30 Jun 1874. From OKI.
To Ruperts Land, 1819. Stonemason with HBCo, later
farmer and merchant. m 20 Jan 1826, Mary, d/o William
Sinclair, chief factor. Son Colin, b 1843, Red River, MLC,
MAN.   **BNA 1097; DC 21 Mar 1981**.

4005   INNES, Ann, 1813–9 Dec 1894. From ABD. To
Hamilton, ONT.   **Ts Mt Albion**.

4006   INNES, Isobella, d ca 1884. From ABD. To
Hamilton, ONT. Second wife of Robert Watt, qv.
Ts Mt Albion.

4007   INNES, James, b 1 Feb 1833, Huntly, ABD.
s/o James I, mason, and Elspet Fordyce. To Wellington
Co, ONT, 1853. Teacher, reporter and journalist. Became
editor and publisher of the Guelph *Mercury*, 1862. MPP,
rep South Wellington, later Eramosa.   **Huntly
OPR 202/3; BNA 1135; SNG x/1 137**.

4008   INNES, Kenneth, ca 1797–13 Apr 1864. From
Lochbroom par, ROC. To Pictou Co, NS, 1803. Bur at
Salt Springs.   **DC 27 Oct 1979**.

4009   INNES, Robert. From Inverness, but rel to the
family Innes of Stow, MLN. To Pictou, NS, on the
Hector, ex Loch Broom, arr 17 Sep 1773; stld Windsor,
Hants Co, later Minudie, Cumberland Co. Wife Janet
with him, and s Duncan.   **HPC App C; NSN 18/4**.

4010   INNES, Robert. From ABD. To Restigouche River,
NB, ca 1774, and got land on south side of the river.
SR 15.

4011   INNES, William, b ca 1783. Prob from ABD. To
Hamilton, ONT. m Jane Donald, qv.   **Ts Mt Albion**.

4012   INNES, William, ca 1830–30 Sep 1865. Prob
from ABD. To Hamilton, ONT.   **Ts Mt Albion**.

4013   INNESS, Robert. From Thurso, CAI. Served in
76th Regt and in 1785 was gr 100 acres in Shelburne
Co, NS. Sometime of Catherines River, and moved
<1787 to Hunts Point, Queens Co. m 1775, in SCT,
Margaret Sutherland, qv, ch: 1. Robert; 2. Nancy;
3. Margaret; 4. William, b 1788.   **LC 22 Dec 1962**.

4014   IRELAND, William, ca 1773–1822. From
Dunfermline, FIF. To Montreal, QUE, 1791. m Anastasia
Genery. Son William, b 1807, sec-treas, Queens Univ,
Kingston, ONT.   **SGC 139**.

4015   IRETON, John. To QUE on the *Commerce*, ex
Greenock, Jun 1820; stld prob Lanark Co, ONT.
HCL 238.

4016   IRONS, Grace. From Lethendy, PER. To
Pilkington Twp, Wellington Co, ONT, 1833. Wife of
Charles Allan, qv.   **DC 7 Jun 1980**.

4017   IRVINE, Alexander. To CAN, 1826. Wife Jane
Cheyne, qv, with him.   **SG xxvii/4 170**.

4018   IRVINE, Christopher, b ca 1750. From
Ecclefechan, DFS. To Pictou Co, NS, 1820; stld Mount
Thom. Innkeeper. m Margaret McQueen, wid/o Jonathan
Radcliffe.   **SG viii/1 26**.

4019   IRVINE, David, b ca 1738. From St Mungo par,
DFS. To Georgetown, Kings Co, PEI, on the *Lovely
Nellie*, ex Carsethorn, May 1775. Labourer. Wife
Margaret Graham, qv, with him, and ch: 1. William,
aged 11; 2. Jean, aged 7; 3. James, aged 3.   **ELN**.

4020   IRVINE, James, ca 1792–29 Sep 1856. From
DFS. To Richibucto, Kent Co, NB, and d there, ch.
DGC 28 Oct 1856.

4021   IRVINE, Janet. To Pictou, NS, on the *London*, arr
14 Jul 1848.   **DC 15 Jul 1979**.

4022   IRVINE, Thomas, 1809-90. From Deerness, OKI.
To NY, 1849; thence to St Catharines, Lincoln Co, ONT.
m Janet Buchan, qv, ch: 1. Thomas, b 1835; 2. Edward,
b 1838; 3. George, b 1841; 4. Janet, b 1846.
DC 11 Nov 1981.

4023   IRVING, Elizabeth, ca 1770–6 Sep 1853. From
Dornock, DFS. To New Annan, Colchester Co, NS.
wid/o Robert Baxter, d 1806. Son David, qv.
Ts Dornock.

4024   IRVING, James. From Hoddam par, DFS. To
ONT, prob <1853. Joiner. m at Lockerbie, 7 Jun 1860,
Margaret, d/o James Davidson, parochial schoolmaster
at Dryfesdale.   **CAE 5**.

4025 IRVING, John. From DFS. To ONT <1855. m Margaret Wylie, qv. Dau Margaret res Cornwall, Stormont Co. **SDG 243**.

4026 IRVING, Mary Crone. From Ecclefechan, DFS. Rel to Edward I, schoolmaster in Annan. To Cornwall Twp, Stormont Co, ONT, 1818. Wife of Dr William Johnstone, qv. **SDG 445**.

4027 IRVING, Paulus Aeamilius, 23 Sep 1714–22 Apr 1796. From DFS. s/o William I. of Bonshaw. Commanded 15th Regt at Quebec, and in 1764 was app a member of the first council of the province. President and Administrator, 1766, but dismissed by Sir Guy Carleton, and returned to Britain. m Judith, d/o Capt William Westfield. Son Paulus Aeamilius, 1751–1828, Major, 47th Regt. **BNA 314; MDB 340**.

4028 IRVING, William, ca 1810–17 Jan 1874. From Raeburn, Kirkpatrick-Fleming, DFS. s/o David I, farmer. To ONT <1848, and d Kingston. m Elizabeth Brow, qv, ch: 1. William, b 1833; 2. Mary; 3. Catherine; 4. Bella; 5. Elizabeth. **CAE 32**.

4029 ISBISTER, Joseph, d ca 1771. From Harray, OKI. s/o Adam I, portioner of Isbister, and Helen McKenley. Joined HBCo marine service, ca 1725. Later served as chief trader at Fort Albany and established Henlay House, 120 miles up the Albany River. Served also at Prince of Wales Fort, on the Churchill River, ca 1748. He ret 1756. ch all lost at sea except dau Mrs Madden, who res at Chelsea, ENG. **TFC 107**.

4030 ISBISTER, Magnus, b ca 1790. From OKI. To York Factory, Hudson Bay, on the *Edward & Ann*, ex Stornoway, arr 24 Sep 1811. Labourer. Original settler, Red River, 1812. **LSS 184; RRS 26; LSC 321**.

4031 ISBISTER, Samuel. From OKI. To Hudson Bay <1854. Emp with HBCo. Son Samuel, seaman. **SH**.

4032 ISLES, James, ca 1751–2 May 1827. From PER. To NS and d there. **VSN No 2228**.

4033 IVALL, Mrs Anne. Prob from MOR. To QUE, ca 1836. Son Alexander, b ca 1830, with her. **DC 23 Aug 1982**.

J

4034 JACK, Hannah Clark, ca 1819–20 Mar 1911. From Barony par, Glasgow. d/o William J, qv, and Mary Hood, qv. To QUE on the *Prompt*, ex Greenock, 4 Jul 1820; stld Dalhousie Twp, Lanark Co, ONT. m Thomas Park, b 1817, s/o William Duncan and Phyllis Stubberfield. **DC 10 Mar 1980**.

4035 JACK, Isabella, ca 1820–20 Sep 1862. From Barony par, Glasgow. d/o William J, qv, and Mary Hood, qv. To QUE on the *Prompt*, ex Greenock, 4 Jul 1820; stld Dalhousie Twp, Lanark Co, ONT. m 1 May 1843, Joseph Gemmill, 1823–1906, s/o William Hood and Jane Graham. **DC 10 Mar 1980**.

4036 JACK, James, b ca 1792. From Kelso, ROX. Prob s/o John J. and Helen Pace. To St Gabriel de Valcartier, QUE, <1830. Farmworker. m Isabella Kerr, qv, and had, prob with other ch: 1. John, b 22 May 1820; 2. James, b 28 Aug 1822; 3. Margaret; 4. Ellen. **Eckford OPR 787a/2; Census 1861; MGC 2 Aug 1979**.

4037 JACK, James, 1 Jan 1808–22 Dec 1894. From Barony par, Glasgow. s/o William J, qv, and Mary Hood, qv. To QUE on the *Prompt*, ex Greenock, 4 Jul 1820; stld Dalhousie Twp, Lanark Co, ONT. Farmer. m Jean Hood, qv, ch: 1. William, 1832–1914; 2. James Hood, b 1833; 3. Margaret, 1835–1917; 4. John, 1839–1918; 5. Thomas, 1845–80; 6. Agnes, 1844–1928; 7. Mary; 8. Ignacius, b 1850; 9. Elizabeth, b 1852. **DC 10 and 21 Mar 1980**.

4038 JACK, John. From Knockbain, INV. To Pictou, NS, on the *Dove*, ex Fort William, Jun 1801. Labourer. **PLD**.

4039 JACK, John Whyte, b 31 Dec 1810. From Barony par, Glasgow. s/o William J, qv, and Mary Hood, qv. To QUE on the *Prompt*, ex Greenock, 4 Jul 1820; stld Dalhousie Twp, Lanark Co, ONT. m (i) Jane Hood, ch: 1. Jane, b 1835; 2. William, b 1836; 3. Gemmill, 1839–1918; 4. Thomas, b 1842; 5. Jane, b 1846; 6. Mary, b 1848; 7. William, b 1850; 8. Kerr, b 1852; 9. David, b 1854; 10. Elmira, b 1858; 11. Graham, b ca 1859. By second wife Susan, no ch. **DC 10 and 21 Mar 1980**.

4040 JACK, Martha, b 1820. From Avoch, ROC. d/o Hugh and Mary J. To Mornington Twp, Perth Co, ONT. Wife of Thomas Urquhart, qv. **DC 15 Jul 1974**.

4041 JACK, William, ca 1789–1 Jul 1860. From Glasgow. To QUE on the *Prompt*, ex Greenock, 4 Jul 1820; stld Dalhousie Twp, Lanark Co, ONT. Discharged soldier, farmer. m 1811, Mary Hood, qv, ch: 1. James, qv; 2. John Whyte, qv; 3. William, jr, qv; 4. Hannah Clark, qv; 5. Isabella, qv; 6. Thomas. **HCL 68, 238; DC 10 Mar 1980**.

4042 JACK, William, jr, 1816-92. From Barony par, Glasgow. To QUE on the *Prompt*, ex Greenock, 4 Jul 1820; stld Dalhousie Twp, Lanark Co, ONT. Farmer. m 1844, Hannah, b 1825, d/o William Hood and Jane Graham, ch: 1. Jane, b 1845; 2. William, b 1847; 3. Mary, b 1850; 4. Hannah, b 1852; 5. Elizabeth, b 1858; 6. Margaret, b 1858; 7. Jane or Jessie, b 1859; 8. Isabella, 1861–1946; 9. Thomas, 1864–1960; 10. James, b 1868, res Edmonton, ALB. **DC 10 and 21 Mar 1980**.

4043 JACK, William Brydone, 1819-86. From Tinwald, DFS. Matric Univ of St Andrews, 1835, and grad MA. To Fredericton, NB, 1840. Prof of Mathematics in Kings Coll, afterwards Univ of NB, of which he became pres. m 19 Dec 1844, Marion Ellen, d/o Hon Charles Jeffrey Peters, Attorney-General. **BNA 839; SAM 89; DGH 20 Feb 1845**.

4044 JACKSON, Alexander, ca 1758–7 Apr 1828. To NS and d there. **VSN 2839**.

4045 JACKSON, Archibald, ca 1802-73. From Lochgilphead, ARL. bro/o John J, qv. To Eldon Twp, Victoria Co, ONT, 1831; stld Lot 4, Con 2. m Catherine McCorquodale, qv, ch: 1. Janet, b 1833; 2. Donald, b 1835; 3. Catherine, b 1837; 4. Duncan, b 1838; 5. Christina, b 1840; 6. John, b 1842; 7. Hugh, b 1843. **EC 256; DC 21 Feb 1980**.

4046 JACKSON, George. From Aberdeen. To Pictou Co, NS, <1850. Merchant. Son James William. **HNS iii 252**.

4047 JACKSON, James. From ARL. To Metcalfe Twp,

Middlesex Co, ONT, prob <1844. Schoolteacher. m d/o Archibald 'Dalbuidhe' McCallum, qv. **PCM 27**.

4048 JACKSON, James. From Blairgowrie, PER. To ONT, 1843, with wife Jane Rutherford, qv. Dau Catherine, d 1913. **DC 23 Mar 1979**.

4049 JACKSON, John. From Lochgilphead, ARL. bro/o Archibald J, qv. To Mariposa Twp, Victoria Co, ONT, 1857, later to Eldon Twp. m Elizabeth Niven, qv, ch: 1. Donald, 1836–1924; 2. Christine; 3. Lawrence; 4. Alexander, lawyer; 5. Elizabeth. **EC 256**.

4050 JACKSON, Joseph. From Kilspindie, PER. s/o Thomas J, 1756–1827, and Margaret Grimman, 1762–1838. To CAN, prob ONT, <1855. **Ts Kilspindie**.

4051 JACKSON, Matthew. To QUE on the *Fame*, 1815; stld Lot 8, Con 9, Drummond Twp, Lanark Co, ONT. **HCL**.

JAFFRAY. See also JEFFERY and JEFFREY.

4052 JAFFRAY, Peter, 1800–15 Nov 1864. From STI. To ONT, 1844, and stld Galt, Waterloo Co. Printer, and part-owner of a newspaper. **HGD 219**.

4053 JAFFRAY, Robert, 23 Jan 1832–16 Dec 1914. From Bannockburn, STI. s/o William J. and Margaret Heugh. To Toronto, 1852. Master grocer and a director of the Toronto *Globe*. m 1860, Sarah, d/o John Bugg, ch. **MDB 344**.

4054 JAMES, Robert. To QUE on the *Commerce*, ex Greenock, Jun 1820; stld prob Lanark Co, ONT. **HCL 239**.

4055 JAMESON, Ann. From Lonmay, ABD. To QUE, ex Greenock, summer 1815; stld ONT. Wife of William Hay, qv. **SEC 4**.

4056 JAMESON, Hugh, d 1811. To Montreal, QUE. Asst Commissary and Storekeeper. **DGC 24 Sep 1811**.

4057 JAMIESON, Rev Andrew, 14 Apr 1814–24 Jun 1885. From Edinburgh where he was educ. s/o Robert J, baker, and Marion Ewart. To Gatineau, QUE, 1832. Ord as a deacon of the Anglican Ch by Rev John Strachan, qv, and was missionary in York Co, ONT. Ord to the priesthood, 1843, and served at Walpole Is. Went to Algonac, St Clair Co, MI. m (i) 1837, Lois Andrus, ch: 1. Mary M, b 1838; 2. Martha S, b 1840; 3. Robert A, 1843–1910; 4. Richard E, 1845–1918; 5. George A, 1848-85; 6. William A, dy; 7. Walter Noble, dy. m (ii) 1871, Margery Courtenay, with further ch: 8. Jessie Louisa, 1874–1932. **DC 15 Sep 1978 and 5 Jul 1979**.

4058 JAMIESON, Archibald, ca 1833–22 May 1849. From ROX. s/o Archibald J, Roadhead, Hawick. To Grey Co, ONT. Killed by lightning nr Owen Sound, along with Walter McFarlane, qv. **DGH 5 Jul 1849**.

4059 JAMIESON, Archibald, ca 1801–ca 1874. From Glasgow. To Lambton Co, ONT, <1853. Farmer. m Jeanette Duff, qv, ch: 1. Jeanette, b ca 1831; 2. Archibald, b ca 1834; 3. James Duff, 1838–1910; 4. Isabella, b ca 1840. **SG xxix/4 139**.

4060 JAMIESON, Catherine, b ca 1765. From Is Arran, BUT. To Dalhousie, NB, 1831. Wife of John Hamilton, qv. **MAC 14**.

4061 JAMIESON, David, 1800–21 Oct 1886. From Dunfermline, FIF. To Simcoe Co, ONT, <1832; bur Craighurst. m Margaret Muir, qv. Son David, 1832-80. **DC 10 Dec 1981**.

4062 JAMIESON, Euphemia. From Callander, PER. To QUE on the *Eliza*, ex Greenock, 3 Aug 1815; stld North Elmsley Twp, Lanark Co, ONT. Wife of James McLaren, qv. **SEC 1**.

4063 JAMIESON, James. Poss from ARL. To Aldborough Twp, Elgin Co, ONT, 1849; stld Con 6. m Jeanette McKellar, qv, ch: 1. Peter; 2. James; 3. Archibald; 4. Samuel, dy. **PDA 64**.

4064 JAMIESON, James Duff, 8 Mar 1838–4 Mar 1910. From Glasgow. s/o Archibald J. and Jeanette Duff. To QUE, 1850; stld later Bosanquet Twp, Lambton Co, ONT, ca 1900. Farmer. m Annabella, 1844–1927, d/o William Giffen, Sherbrooke Twp, and Mary Ann Pitt. ch: 1. Mary, 1866–1941; 2. William, 1869–1931; 3. Archibald, 1873–1952; 4. George, b 1877; 5. James, b 1871; 6. Albert, b 1876; 7. Walter, b 1881. **DC 26 Oct 1980**.

4065 JAMIESON, Janet, b ca 1797. From Muirkirk, AYR. sis/o William J, qv. To QUE, summer 1815; stld ONT. **SEC 6**.

4066 JAMIESON, Jean, alive 1807. Poss from AYR. d/o John J, qv. To Richmond Bay, PEI, on the *Falmouth*, ex Greenock, 8 Apr 1770; stld Queens Co. m 21 Dec 1770, Lawrence Brown, qv. **DC 28 May 1980**.

4067 JAMIESON, John. Poss from AYR. To Richmond Bay, PEI, on the *Falmouth*, ex Greenock, 8 Apr 1770; stld Queens Co. Wife with him, and ch: 1. Alexander, drowned in Tracadie harbour, 1771; 2. Jean, qv; 3. Catherine. **DC 28 May 1980**.

4068 JAMIESON, John, b ca 1781. From Muirkirk, AYR. To QUE, ex Greenock, summer 1815; stld prob Lanark Co, ONT. Shoemaker. **SEC 8**.

4069 JAMIESON, John, 22 Jun 1794–1 Jan 1848. From Abington, LKS. s/o James J. and Mary Gillespie. To Montreal, QUE, 1815. Partner, Gillespie & Moffat, merchants. m a d/o Samuel Hatt, of Chambly, and d Edinburgh, SCT, leaving £600 to establish a bursary at the Univ of Edinburgh to benefit boys of his native district. **SGC 429; Ts Biggar**.

4070 JAMIESON, John. From Kilmarnock, AYR. To St John, NB, <15 Nov 1825, when m Eleanor Agnes, d/o the dec John Cook, res of Halifax, NS. **VSN No 1424**.

4071 JAMIESON, John. From AYR. To ONT, 1854; stld prob Huron Co. m Ann Lang, qv, ch. **DC 26 May 1979**.

4072 JAMIESON, Mary Ann Kerr, 16 Mar 1841–1 Jan 1900. From Dreghorn, AYR. d/o Rev John Campbell J. and Mary Young. To Victoria, BC. m Thomas Reid. **FES iii 89**.

4073 JAMIESON, William, b ca 1787. From Muirkirk, AYR. bro/o Janet J, qv. To QUE, summer 1815; stld ONT. **SEC 6**.

4074 JAMIESON, William, b 1783. From Torrilin, Kilmory par, Is Arran, BUT. To Dalhousie, NB, 1829. m 21 Feb 1817, Mary Hamilton, qv, ch: 1. Donald, b 1818; 2. William, b 1821; 3. James, 1823-96; 4. Peter, 1826–1902. **MAC 17**.

4075 JARDINE, James Corrie, b 19 Feb 1794, Corrie Halls, par of Hutton and Corrie, DFS. s/o Andrew J. and Isabella Corrie. To PEI, ca 1818. m Jane Hope, qv. Dau Isabella with them. **DC 6 Apr 1979**.

4076 JARDINE, Janet. From DFS. To Richibucto, Kent Co, NB. m there, 22 Dec 1835, Thomas Bell, qv. **DGC 24 Feb 1836**.

4077 JARDINE, John. From Newmains, Lochmaben, DFS. To Galt, Waterloo Co, ONT. Farmer. m Catherine Johnstone, qv, who d there 1845. **DGH 20 Nov 1845**.

4078 JARDINE, John, 1802-78. Prob from DFS. To Chatham, Northumberland Co, NB, <15 Aug 1828, when m Elizabeth Dickson, qv. Farmer. **DC 2 Jun 1978**.

4079 JARDINE, Joseph, b ca 1815. From DFS. To Hamilton, ONT. Wife Agnes, 1815-72. **Ts Mt Albion**.

4080 JARDINE, Margaret, 1 Apr 1810–17 Nov 1830. From DFS. Rel to Joseph J, qv. To Hamilton, ONT. **Ts Mt Albion**.

4081 JARDINE, Rev Thomas, 10 May 1823–2 Aug 1894. From Glasgow. s/o William J, craftsman, and Agnes Hunter. To Halifax, NS, 1856, and became min of St Matthews Ch. Retr to SCT, 1862, and adm min of Ardsheen *quod sacra* par, AYR. m 1857, Jessie, d/o Rev Hugh Dewar, Stonehouse, ch. **GMA 1419; FES ii 330, vii 615**.

4082 JARVIS, Agnes. From Glasgow. d/o Robert J, merchant. To Toronto, ONT, 1844. Wife of Isaac Buchanan, qv. **Glasgow OPR 644-1/38**.

JEFFREY. See also JAFFREY.

4083 JEFFREY, John, b 11 Apr 1759. From Edinburgh. To Yarmouth Co, NS, ca 1784. Discharged soldier, 4th Batt, Royal Artillery. **DC 31 Dec 1981**.

4084 JEFFREY, Isabella, 1844-1919. From Kelso, ROX. d/o Robert J, qv, and Mary Cruthers, qv. To ONT, 1854; stld Normanby Twp, Grey Co. m Robert Stephenson, qv. **DC 3 Jul 1981**.

4085 JEFFREY, Peter, 1853-1928. From Kelso, ROX. s/o Robert J, qv, and Mary Cruthers, qv. To Normanby Twp, Grey Co, ONT, 1854. Rancher and farmer. m 1877, Barbara Jane Chambers, 1858-1935. **DC 31 Dec 1979**.

4086 JEFFREY, Robert, ca 1817–ca 1888. From Kelso, ROX. s/o William and Isabel J. To Normanby Twp, Grey Co, ONT, 1854; stld Lot 24, Con 6. Farmer. m Mary Cruthers, qv, ch: 1. Isabelle, b 1846; 2. Jessie, b 1847; 3. William, 1849-57; 4. Peter, jr, qv; 5. Robert, jr, qv; 6. James, 1857–1929; 7. Christopher, b ca 1860; 8. Margaret, 1863-1911. **DC 31 Dec 1979**.

4087 JEFFREY, Robert, jr, 1854-1922. From Kelso, ROX. s/o Robert J, qv, and Mary Cruthers, qv. To Normanby Twp, Grey Co, ONT, 1854. Stonemason and farmer. m Margaret Deans, 1854-1925, ch: 1. Mary Jean, 1894–1969; 2. Robert Leslie, 1901-62; 3. Ethel Margaret, 1904-79. **DC 3 Jul 1981**.

4088 JEFFREYS, Joseph, b ca 1795. From Edinburgh. Poss bro/o Thomas J, qv. To QUE, ex Greenock, summer 1815; stld prob Lanark Co, ONT. Farmer. **SEC 6**.

4089 JEFFREYS, Thomas, b ca 1793. From Edinburgh. Poss bro/o Joseph J, qv. To QUE, ex Greenock, summer

1815; stld prob Lanark Co, ONT. Wife Isobella Wilson, qv, with him, and 1 child. **SEC 6**.

4090 JENNINGS, Rev John, 8 Oct 1814–Feb 1876. From Glasgow. Matric Univ of St Andrews, 1828, and studied at the Theological Hall of the United Associate Synod. To Toronto, ONT, and was pastor of a church there for thirty-six years. Editor of the *Canadian Presbyterian Magazine*. ch. **BNA 858; SAM 78; MDB 348**.

4091 JESSIMAN, Alexander, 1807–19 Feb 1889. From Huntly, ABD. To NB, ca 1834; stld Douglastown, Northumberland Co. Carpenter and farmer. m 1835, Elizabeth Anderson, ch: 1. Son, d 1836, inf; 2. Catherine, 1838-44; 3. William, b 1840; 4. Ann, b 1842; 5. Elizabeth, 1845-81; 6. Mary, 1846–1942; 7. Alexander, 1854–1929. **DC 2 May 1981**.

4092 JOHNSON, Adam Gordon, ca 1781–ca 1843. Prob from DFS. bro/o John J. To Montreal, QUE, and d there. **DGH 22 Jun 1843**.

4093 JOHNSON, Alexander, b ca 1778. To St Andrews dist, Cape Breton Co, NS, ca 1807. Farmer, m and ch. **CBC 1818**.

4094 JOHNSON, Alexander, d 1874. From Tarbet, ARL. s/o Archibald J, qv. To Aldborough Twp, Middlesex Co, ONT, 1820; stld Lobo Twp. ch: 1. Hugh, d 1896; 2. Mary, res Beaverton, MI; 3. Stephen; 4. Thomas; 5. Dr Alexander; 6. Dr Archibald; 7. Eliza, res Port Huron; 8. John, res Beaverton, MI. **PCM 40**.

4095 JOHNSON, Alexander. From ARL. To North Dorchester Twp, Middlesex Co, ONT, 1844. **PCM 57**.

4096 JOHNSON, Angus, b ca 1770. To St Andrews dist, Cape Breton Co, NS, 1810. Farmer, m and ch. **CBC 1818**.

4097 JOHNSON, Archibald, d 1821. From Caolasraide, South Knapdale, ARL. To Aldborough Twp, Middlesex Co, ONT, 1820; stld Lobo Twp. Drowned in Thames River, ch: 1. Alexander, qv; 2. Effie, qv; 3. Donald, qv; 4. Hugh, qv; 5. Nancy, qv; 6. Isabella, qv; 7. Margaret, qv; 8. John, qv; 9. Dugald, qv; 10. Archibald, jr, qv; 11. Mary, b ONT. **PCM 41**.

4098 JOHNSON, Archibald, jr, b ca 1819. From Tarbet, ARL. s/o Archibald J, qv. To Aldborough, Middlesex Co, ONT, 1820; stld Lobo Twp. m Isabella, d/o Neil McKeith, qv, Komoka, ch: 1. Donald; 2. Archibald; 3. John; 4. Maggie. **PCM 41**.

4099 JOHNSON, Donald, b 1768. To St Andrews dist, Cape Breton Co, NS, 1810. Farmer, m and ch incl Donald, b 1801. **CBC 1818**.

4100 JOHNSON, Donald, d 1877. From Tarbet, ARL. s/o Archibald J, qv. To Aldborough Twp, Middlesex Co, ONT, 1820; stld Lobo Twp. m Mary Lamont, ch: 1. Catherine; 2. Effie; 3. Maggie; 4. Mary; 5. Bella, d 1903; 6, Donald, went to IA; 7. Nancy; 8. Alexander, d 1879; 9. Archie, d IA. **PCM 41**.

4101 JOHNSON, Donald, b 1780. From Forsinan, Is South Uist, INV. To West Williams Twp, Middlesex Co, ONT, 1849; stld Centre Road. Wife Margaret d SCT, ch: 1. Murdo, b 1811; 2. Neil, b 1815; 3. Ann, b 1816; 4. John, b 1820; 5. Kirsty, b 1826. **PCM 48; WLC**.

4102 JOHNSON, Donald. Prob from ARL. To Ekfrid

Twp, Middlesex Co, ONT, 1849. ch: 1. Archie; 2. Mrs D. McGugan. **PCM 30**.

4103 JOHNSON, Dugald. From Tarbet, ARL. s/o Archibald J, qv. To Aldborough Twp, Middlesex Co, ONT, 1820; stld later Lobo Twp. Went to St Louis, MO, 1844. **PCM 41**.

4104 JOHNSON, Effie, d 1893. From Tarbet, ARL. d/o Archibald J, qv. To Aldborough Twp, Middlesex Co, ONT, 1820; stld later Lobo Twp. m John Sinclair, ch. **PCM 41**.

4105 JOHNSON, Elizabeth, 1800–25 Oct 1874. From Glasgow. To QUE, 1832; stld Medonte Twp, Simcoe Co, ONT. Wife of Gavin Turner, qv. **DC 8 Nov 1981**.

4106 JOHNSON, Gavin, b ca 1752. From Bothwell par, LKS. To Georgetown, Kings Co, PEI, on the *Lovely Nellie*, ex Carsethorn, May 1775. Schoolmaster. **ELN**.

4107 JOHNSON, Hugh, d 1883. From Tarbet, ARL. s/o Archibald J, qv. To Aldborough Twp, Middlesex Co, ONT, 1820; stld Lobo Twp. m Julia Leitch, ch: 1. Margaret; 2. Archibald; 3. Malcolm, res St Thomas; 4. Julia, d 1871; 5. Donald; 6. Colin; 7. John, res Harvey, IL; 8. Hugh D, res Strathroy, Adelaide Twp; 9. Sarah, d 1897; 10. Bella, d 1897. **PCM 41**.

4108 JOHNSON, Isabella, d 1847. From Tarbet, ARL. d/o Archibald J, qv. To Aldborough Twp, Middlesex Co, ONT, 1820; stld Lobo Twp. m Duncan Lamont, ch. **PCM 41**.

4109 JOHNSON, J, d 11 Feb 1846. Prob from DFS. To Norfolk Co, ONT. Sometime Lt Col, Bombay Engineers. **DGH 26 Mar 1846**.

4110 JOHNSON, James, b ca 1815. From Balivanich, Is Benbecula, INV. s/o John and Ann J, sometime in Uachdar. To Cape Breton Is, NS, ca 1842. Wife Ann McLeod, qv, with him, and dau Catherine, inf. **LDW 9 Sep 1973**.

4111 JOHNSON, John, ca 1804-97. From Tarbet, ARL. s/o Archibald J, qv. To Aldborough Twp, Middlesex Co, ONT, 1820; stld Lobo Twp. m Isabella Leitch, ch: 1. Archibald, civil engineer, d 1900; 2. Sarah; 3. Margaret; 4. Hugh, d 1873; 5. Donald, d 1860; 6. Mary, d 1881; 7. Dugald; 8. Helena. **PCM 41**.

4112 JOHNSON, Nancy, d 1901. From Tarbet, ARL. d/o Archibald J, qv. To Aldborough Twp, Middlesex Co, ONT, 1820; stld Lobo Twp. m Donald McArthur. **PCM 41**.

4113 JOHNSON, Neil, b 1800. From Kallin, Is Grimsay, off Benbecula, INV. s/o John and Ann J. To Cape Breton Is, NS, 1842. m Catherine McDonald, qv, ch: 1. Alexander, b 1825; 2. John, b 1827; 3. Samuel, b 1829; 4. Ann, b 1831; 5. Donald, b 1835; 6. Ranald, b 1836; 7. Effie, b 1838; 8. Catherine, b 1840. **LDW 9 Sep 1973; WLC**.

4114 JOHNSON, Margaret. From Tarbet, ARL. d/o Archibald J, qv. To Aldborough Twp, Middlesex Co, ONT, 1820; stld Lobo Twp. m Archibald, s/o Dugald Campbell, qv, ch. **PCM 41**.

4115 JOHNSON, Roderick, b ca 1770. To St Andrews dist, Cape Breton Co, NS, 1817. Farmer, m and ch. **CBC 1818**.

4116 JOHNSTON, Alexander. Poss from DFS. s/o George J. To Brant Co, ONT, <1847. Dau Margaret. **DC 23 Sep 1980**.

4117 JOHNSTON, Alexander, 1781–30 Jan 1861. To Windsor, Hants Co, NS. **DC 4 Dec 1978**.

4118 JOHNSTON, Angus. From Is South Uist, INV. To QUE on the *Admiral*, ex Lochboisdale, Aug 1851; stld ONT. Crofter who resisted the clearances on the Gordon estates. **DC 21 Mar 1981**.

4119 JOHNSTON, Catherine, 1789–13 Apr 1860. Poss from Rothesay, BUT. To Nassagaweya Twp, Halton Co, ONT, <1849. Wife of Archibald McPhail, qv. **DC 9 Nov 1981**.

4120 JOHNSTON, George, ca 1791–20 Sep 1875. From Aberdeen. To Montreal, QUE, ca 1813. Baker. Dau Mrs William Muir. **SGC 435**.

4121 JOHNSTON, James. Prob from DFS. To Tatamagouche, Colchester Co, NS, <1810. **HT 43**.

4122 JOHNSTON, James, b ca 1781. Prob from Ecclefechan par, DFS. To Northumberland Co, NB, 1817. Wife Mary Bell, qv, with him, and ch: 1. William, b 1805; 2. Thomas, b 1807; 3. Alexander, b 1813; 4. Robert, b 1815. **SG xxv/2 58; DC 27 Feb 1978**.

4123 JOHNSTON, James. From Bridge of Weir, RFW, but poss b in IRL, ca 1820. To QUE on the *Albion*, 5 Jun 1829; stld Megantic Co. Son William. **AMC 22**.

4124 JOHNSTON, James. Prob from Edinburgh. Rel to James J, spirit dealer there, who d 1850. To NFD. Surgeon. **SH**.

4125 JOHNSTON, Janet, b ca 1715. From DFS. To Georgetown, Kings Co, PEI, on the *Lovely Nellie*, ex Carsethorn, May 1775. **ELN**.

4126 JOHNSTON, Janet, 3 May 1793–7 Mar 1860. From Park, Closeburn, DFS. To Brockville, Leeds Co, ONT. m Matthew McDougall. **DGC 8 May 1860**.

4127 JOHNSTON, John, b ca 1789. Poss from Craighouse, Is Jura, ARL. To QUE on the *Atlas*, ex Greenock, 11 Jul 1815; stld prob Lanark Co, ONT. **SEC 8; HCL 232**.

4128 JOHNSTON, John, ca 1801–19 Mar 1865. From Moffat, DFS. Prob rel to William J, qv. To Pictou, NS, on the brig *Thomsons Packet*, 1821; stld New Annan, Colchester Co. **CAE 2**.

4129 JOHNSTON, John. To Dundas Co, ONT, <1853. m Mary McLean, qv. Son Adam, 1853–1915, lawyer, Morrisburg. **SDG 442**.

4130 JOHNSTON, John. To Campbellford, Seymour Twp, Northumberland Co, ONT, prob 1831. Land patented in Lot 12, Con 9, 15 May 1858. m Janet Hunter, qv, ch: 1. Elizabeth, b 1843; 2. Agnes, b 1843; 3. John, b 20 Nov 1845; 4. David, b 1847; 5. Daniel, b 1849. **DC 28 Dec 1979**.

4131 JOHNSTON, John. From Is North Uist, INV. To East Williams Twp, Middlesex Co, ONT, 1848. **PCM 44**.

4132 JOHNSTON, Margaret. From Hutton and Corrie par, DFS. To QUE, summer 1815; stld Scotch Line, Lanark Co, ONT. Wife of John Halliday, qv. **SEC 2; HCL 230**.

4133 JOHNSTON, Murdoch. From Is Coll, ARL. bro/o Capt William J, 2nd Madras Infantry. To QUE, ex Liverpool, 7 Jul 1847; stld Mara Twp, Simcoe Co, ONT. Wife emig with him and d Montreal. ch: 1. Alexander, d on the voyage; 2. Donald, d at Montreal; 3. Isabella, d at Montreal; 4. William; 5. James, b 1835; 6. Lachlan, d 1919; 7. John M, 1832-94, res Barrie; 8. Sarah; 9. Neil, dy, Toronto. **DC 16 May 1982**.

4134 JOHNSTON, Neil. Prob from ARL. To Aldborough Twp, Elgin Co, ONT, <1820. Farmer. **PDA 94**.

4135 JOHNSTON, Peter. Poss from ARL. To Aldborough Twp, Elgin Co, ONT, 1849. **PDA 75**.

4136 JOHNSTON, Robert. To QUE on the *Brock*, ex Greenock, 9 Jul 1820; stld prob Lanark Co, ONT. **HCL 238**.

4137 JOHNSTON, Robert, ca 1793–31 Jan 1869. From Hoddam, DFS. To Richibucto, Kent Co, NB. **DC 4 Oct 1978**.

4138 JOHNSTON, Robert. Prob from Troqueer, KKS. To Fergus, Wellington Co, ONT, <1851. Leather merchant. **SH**.

4139 JOHNSTON, Robert, ca 1801–21 Jun 1877. From Watchhill, Annan, DFS. To PEI <1855, and d Dover East, ONT. **CAE 39**.

4140 JOHNSTON, Robert L, 1770–1868. From DFS. Said desc from Annandale family. To Metcalfe Twp, Middlesex Co, ONT, 1832, and gr 750 acres. ch: 1. Robina; 2. Eleanor; 3. Col William, res Strathroy. **PCM 27**.

4141 JOHNSTON, Stewart Soutar, 1800-46. From DFS. To Windsor, Essex Co, ONT. Teacher, and claimed descent from Annandale family. **DGH 12 Mar 1846**.

4142 JOHNSTON, William, d 20 May 1828. From DFS. To PEI. Attorney-General. Son George, d 1835, res Kinharvie House, New Abbey, KKD. **DGC 1 Jul 1828**.

4143 JOHNSTON, William, ca 1795–22 Dec 1867. From Broats, Kirkpatrick-Fleming, DFS. To Richibucto, Kent Co, NB. m Mary Brow, qv. **CAE 18**.

4144 JOHNSTON, William, ca 1782–18 Oct 1852. From Beech Hill, Annan, DFS. To ONT and d there. m <1808, Janet Howet, ch: 1. John, d 1834; 2. Thomas, d 1876. **Ts Annan**.

4145 JOHNSTON, William, b ca 1778. Prob from Stobo, PEE. To QUE, ex Greenock, summer 1815; stld Lot 16, Con 1, Bathurst Twp, Lanark Co, ONT. Farmer. Wife Janet Nicol, qv, with him, and 1 ch. **SEC 6; HCL 16**.

4146 JOHNSTON, William, d 12 Feb 1859. From Hermitage of Spottes, Urr par, KKD. s/o John J. To Cobourg Twp, Northumberland Co, ONT. **DGH 18 Mar 1859**.

4147 JOHNSTON, William, d <1860. From Moffat, DFS. Prob rel to John J, qv. To Pictou, NS, on *Thomsons Packet*, 1821; stld New Annan, Colchester Co. m Margaret Dinwiddie, qv. **CAE 5**.

4148 JOHNSTON, William, 6 Mar 1840–13 Jan 1917. From Airdsgreen, Glenbuck, Muirkirk, AYR. To Blanshard Twp, Perth Co, ONT, ca 1859. Township clerk and historian. **MDB 352**.

4149 JOHNSTONE, Agnes, ca 1808–20 Feb 1878. From Lamberton Toll, BEW. To Wellington Co, ONT, 1851, and d at Guelph. Wife of John Paterson, qv. **DC 29 Dec 1970**.

4150 JOHNSTONE, Alexis. From Is Skye, INV. To Sydney Mines, Cape Breton Co, NS, <1855, when m Neal McNab, coal-cutter. ch: 1. Jane; 2. Daniel; 3. Mary; 4. Margaret; 5. William. **NSN 10/2**.

4151 JOHNSTONE, Catherine, d 16 Aug 1845. From Lochmaben, DFS. To Galt, Dumfries Twp, Waterloo Co, ONT. Wife of John Jardine, qv. **DGH 20 Nov 1845**.

4152 JOHNSTONE, Ebenezer Wilson, 22 Sep 1813–26 Aug 1839. From Dalry, AYR. s/o Rev Thomas J, par min, and Jane Wilson. To ONT and d at Skeldon. **FES iii 86**.

4153 JOHNSTONE, Elizabeth. From Annan, DFS. sis/o John J, mariner. To PEI <1854. m W. Anderson. **SH**.

4154 JOHNSTONE, Isaac. From OKI. bro/o Thomas J, qv, and Margaret J, qv. To Megantic Co, QUE, 1842. **AMC 48**.

4155 JOHNSTONE, James Chevalier de, ca 1720–ca 1800. From Edinburgh. s/o James J, merchant-burgess. Aide-de-Camp to Prince Charles Edward Stuart during the '45 Rebellion. Went to France, and thence to CAN in the French service. Fought at Louisbourg and was present at the capitulation of QUE. Retr to France, where he wrote his *Memoirs* of the Rebellion. **SN ii 580; IBD 245; CBD 539; MDB 352**.

4156 JOHNSTONE, Mrs Janet, 1771–1841. From Ruthwell, DFS. wid/o Francis Johnstone, d 1827. To Whitchurch, York Co, ONT, with ch: 1. Jean, qv; 2. Nicolas, qv. **Ts Ruthwell**.

4157 JOHNSTONE, Jean, ca 1781–17 Jul 1859. From DFS. To St John's, NFD, and d there. Wife of William Porteous. **DGH 12 Aug 1859**.

4158 JOHNSTONE, Jean, ca 1809–1864. From Ruthwell, DFS. d/o Mrs Janet J, qv. To Whitchurch, York Co, ONT, <1841. m James Rae. **Ts Ruthwell**.

4159 JOHNSTONE, John, 1828-75. Prob from AYR. To Port Morien, Cape Breton Co, NS, 1855. m Margaret Taylor, qv. **NSN 7/3**.

4160 JOHNSTONE, John, 1794–21 Oct 1871. From DFS. To Flatlands, Restigouche Co, NB, ca 1821. **DC 14 Jan 1980**.

4161 JOHNSTONE, John, ca 1801–15 Mar 1864. From Dryfesdale par, DFS. s/o William J, Millhill. To CAN, prob ONT. **DGH 6 May 1864**.

4162 JOHNSTONE, Margaret, d ca 1830. From Pefferlaw, Chirnside, BEW. d/o William J. and Jean Fife. To ONT, ca 1820. Wife of John Lyall, qv. **DC 5 Aug 1970**.

4163 JOHNSTONE, Margaret. From OKI. sis/o Thomas J, qv, and Isaac J, qv. To Megantic Co, QUE, 1842. m William Macdonald, qv. **AMC 48**.

4164 JOHNSTONE, Mary, d 29 Sep 1859. From Barrasgate, Cummertrees par, DFS. To Dover Twp, Kent Co, ONT. Wife of William Cron, qv. **CAE 4**.

4165 JOHNSTONE, Nicolas, ca 1811–22 Jul 1868. From Ruthwell, DFS. d/o Mrs Janet J, qv. To Stouffville, Whitchurch, York Co, ONT, <1841. **Ts Ruthwell**.

4166 JOHNSTONE, Robert, b 1790. From Pefferlaw, Chirnside, BEW. s/o William J. and Jean Fife. To ONT, ca 1820; stld Georgina Twp, York Co, ONT. **DC 5 Aug 1970**.

4167 JOHNSTONE, Robert. From Annan, DFS. bro/o John J, mariner. To CAN <1854; poss PEI. **SH**.

4168 JOHNSTONE, Thomas. From OKI. bro/o Isaac J, qv, and Margaret J, qv. To Megantic Co, QUE, 1842. m Clementine Brown, qv, ch: 1. Thomas; 2. Jane; 3. Mary; 4. William. **AMC 48**.

4169 JOHNSTONE, Walter. From Tundergarth, DFS. To PEI, <1850. Teacher. Son John, of Birmingham, ENG, inventor. **CAE 46**.

4170 JOHNSTONE, William, 1788–1875. From Ecclefechan, Hoddam par, DFS. To Cornwall Twp, Stormont Co, ONT, 1818. Physician, educ Edinburgh. m Mary Crone Irving, qv. **SDG 445**.

4171 JOHNSTONE, William, b 19 Sep 1784. From Pefferlaw, Chirnside, BEW. s/o William J. and Jean Fife. To Georgina Twp, York Co, ONT, ca 1819; stld Con 7. Commander, RB, ret. Miller and storekeeper. **DC 5 Aug 1970**.

4172 JONES, Anthony Hart. Prob from Edinburgh. bro/o William J, shipmaster in Leith. To Argyle, Yarmouth Co, NS, <1898. ch: 1. Constance; 2. Margaret; 3. Ann. **SH**.

4173 JONES, Henry. Poss from RFW. To Montreal, QUE, on the *Royal George*, ex Greenock, Jan 1827; stld Sarnia, Lambton Co, ONT. Leader of a small group of emigrants. By first wife had ch: 1. Henry; 2. John; 3. Thomas; 4. Robert; 5. Bessie; 6. Julia. m (ii) Susan Phinney, qv. **DC 19 Nov 1978**.

4174 JONES, Robert. From Paisley, RFW. s/o William J, Hawkhead Mills, and Margaret Locke. To PEI, 1809; stld Pinette River, Queens Co. Draughtsman, cabinet-maker, farmer and militiaman. m Hannah Simpson, qv, ch. **HP 78**.

4175 JORDAN, Martin. To Hudson Bay and Red River <1815. Pioneer settler. **LSS 192; LSC 327**.

4176 JOSS, Barbara, b 5 Jul 1816. From Gamrie, BAN. d/o John J. and Margaret Mansen. To Arthur, Wellington Co, ONT. m ca 1836, James Fraser, qv. **DC 12 Nov 1968**.

4177 JUDGE, Peter Jack, ca 1824–11 Feb 1906. From Irvine, AYR. s/o James and Drusilla J. To Halifax, NS, ca 1844. Mariner. m (i) 25 May 1847, Maria Ann Williams, 1825-75, ch: 1. Charlotte, b 1848; 2. James Williams, b 1850; 3. William, 1852–1933; 4. Sophia Jane, 1854–1936; 5. George Philip, 1857–1933; 6. Charles Edward, 1859–1947; 7. Thomas Peter, 1862-65; 8. John Albert, 1864–1936; 9. Henry Foster, b 1866; 10. Thomas Samuel, 1868–1945; 11. Richard Holt, 1869–1913. m (ii) Susan Lang, 1836–1907, further ch: 12. Frank Hire, 1878–1918. **SG xxvii/4; DC 28 Jun and 19 Aug 1981**.

4178 JUNOR, Christian, ca 1823–20 Apr 1905. From Rosemarkie, ROC. d/o James and Mary J. To QUE on the *John McKenzie*, ex Glasgow, arr 25 Jun 1857; stld Scott Twp, York Co, ONT, later Minto Twp, Wellington Co. Wife of Roderick Ross, qv. **RFS 158**.

K

4179 KAY, John. From Kilmarnock, AYR. bro/o Robert K, solicitor there. To Montreal, QUE, <26 Jul 1853. *Ayr Sasines*, 373, 74.

4180 KAY, Mungo, 1775–1818. To Montreal, QUE. Editor of the *Herald* newspaper. **DGC 24 Nov 1818**.

4181 KAY, William. To Montreal, QUE, <1793. Neph of Alexander Hutchison, wine merchant in Edinburgh. Son William. **SH**.

4182 KEAN, John. To Megantic Co, QUE; stld Halifax Twp. m Elizabeth Russell, qv, ch: 1. Robert; 2. Rev John. **AMC 49**.

4183 KEAY, Rev Peter, 1823-73. From Glasgow. s/o Peter K. To Woodstock and Northampton, Carleton Co, NB, 1854, as missionary. Adm min of Nashwaak Ch, 1854, and trans to Greenock Ch, St Andrews, Charlotte Co, 1868. **FES vii 610**.

4184 KEILL, George, 1799–1820. From Montrose, ANS. s/o James K. in Mains of Dun. To Wallace, Cumberland Co, NS, <1820. Wife Agnes Mathew drowned in Wallace Harbour. Both bur Methodist cemetery, Wallace. **DC 29 Oct 1980**.

4185 KEIR, Rev John, ca 1779–12 Oct 1858. From STI. s/o John K, farmer. Matric Univ of Glasgow, 1799, and became min of Secession Ch. To NS 1810, and was min at Princetown and Royalty. Professor of Theology and DD. **GMA 6059**.

4186 KEITH, Alexander, 5 Oct 1795–14 Dec 1873. From Halkirk, CAI. s/o Donald K. and Christian Brims. To Halifax, NS, 1812. Brewer, Mayor of Halifax, 1843, 1853-54, and MLC, 1843-73. ch. **BNA 676; DC 21 Mar 1981**.

4187 KEITH, Ann. From Kinknockie, Old Deer, ABD. sis/o John K, qv. To Nichol Twp, Wellington Co, ONT, ca 1838. m Hugh Fraser, shoemaker in Salem. **EHE 96**.

4188 KEITH, Catharine. From Kinknockie, Old Deer, ABD. sis/o John K, qv. To Nichol Twp, Wellington Co, ONT, ca 1838. m James Walker, Garafraxa Twp. **EHE 96**.

4189 KEITH, Daniel, 1791–1868. From RFW. To Chatham, Northumberland Co, NB, ca 1822. **DC 14 Jan 1980**.

4190 KEITH, David. From Kinknockie, Old Deer, ABD. bro/o John K, qv. To Nichol Twp, Wellington Co, ONT, ca 1838, later to Chesley, Bruce Co. Blacksmith. ch. **EHE 96**.

4191 KEITH, Elizabeth, b 1828. From ABD. sis/o Mary K, qv. To Ontario Co, ONT, prob ca 1854. m James Stocks, qv. **DC 23 Jul 1979**.

4192 KEITH, George, 1780–22 Jan 1859. From Auchterless, ABD. s/o James K, farmer, Nether Third, and Isabella Bruce. To Montreal, QUE, ca 1800. Clerk with NWCo in Athabaska dept, and became a partner. After merger with HBCo, 1821, became a chief factor. He retr to SCT and d Aberdeen. **MDB 360**.

4193 KEITH, George. From Kinknockie, Old Deer, ABD. bro/o John K, qv. To Nichol Twp, Wellington Co, ONT, ca 1838; stld later Belleville. Manufacturer. **EHE 96**.

4194 KEITH, George, b 7 May 1819. From Crimond par, ABD. To NS, prob <1854, but moved to Rockford, IL, <1860. Wife Ann Eady, qv, with him. **DC 29 Jan 1981**.

4195 KEITH, Helen. From Kinknockie, Old Deer, ABD. sis/o John K, qv. To Nichol Twp, Wellington Co, ONT, ca 1838. m Alexander Hamilton. **EHE 96**.

4196 KEITH, Isobella MacDonald. Prob from Is Ghiga, ARL. To ONT, 1834. Wife of Malcolm Galbraith, qv. **DC 9 Mar 1980**.

4197 KEITH, James, 1784–27 Jan 1851. From Auchterless, ABD. s/o James K, farmer in Nether Third, and Isabella Bruce. To Montreal, QUE, ca 1800. Clerk with NWCo, and became a partner, 1814. After the union with HBCo, 1821, was a chief factor at English River, Fort Chipewyan, and Montreal. Retr 1845 and d Aberdeen, SCT. m a d/o Geddes Mackenzie Simpson, Stamford Hill, MDX, ENG. **SH; MDB 360**.

4198 KEITH, Jean, d 1909. From Old Deer, ABD. d/o John K, qv, and Christian Watt, qv. To Elora, Nichol Twp, Wellington Co, ONT, 1834. m 4 Nov 1854, Thomas Connon, qv. **EHE 85, 190**.

4199 KEITH, John. Poss from CAI. To Inverness Co, NS, <1819; stld Mull River. Farmer. m <1823, Margaret Ness, qv, ch: 1. James, went to AUS; 2. Sarah; 3. Isobel; 4. Eliza; 5. Matilda; 6. George; 7. David, 1848–1918, d UT. **MP ii 247**.

4200 KEITH, John, 12 Jan 1809–11 Jul 1878. From Kinknockie, Old Deer, ABD. To QUE on the *Fania*, ex Glasgow, 30 Jun 1834; stld Bon Accord, Nichol Twp, Wellington Co, ONT. Cabinet-maker and farmer. m Christina Watt, qv, ch: 1. Jean, qv; 2. Mrs James Henderson; 3. John, jr, qv; 4. Alexander, res Grand Rapids, MI; 5. Mrs David Steven; 6. George; 7. Elsie. **EHE 85**.

4201 KEITH, John, jr. From Old Deer, ABD. s/o John K, qv, and Christian Watt, qv. To QUE on the *Fania*, ex Glasgow, 30 Jun 1834; stld Bon Accord, Nichol Twp, Wellington Co, ONT. m Ann Argo. **EHE 85**.

4202 KEITH, Mary. Poss from ARL. To Woodstock, Oxford Co, ONT, <1830. Wife of Peter McMillan, qv. **DC 16 Jun 1980**.

4203 KEITH, Mary, 1831–1907. From ABD. sis/o Elizabeth K, qv. To Ashburn Village, East Whitby Twp, Ontario Co, ONT, <1854. m Andrew Lawrence, jr, qv. **DC 23 Jul 1979**.

4204 KEITH, Sylvanus, 31 May 1796–11 Feb 1882. From Dornoch, SUT. To Pictou, NS, <1825; stld Big Brook, west branch of East River, later Albion Mines. m Margaret Gunn, qv, ch: 1. Catherine; 2. James, 1829–1907; 3. Margaret; 4. Donald, b 1832; 5. Barbara, 1834–76; 6. Betsy, 1835–64; 7. Isabel, 1840–1911; 8. David, b 1843; 9. Sylvanus. **PAC 98**.

4205 KEITH, William. From Kinknockie, Old Deer, ABD. bro/o John K, qv. To Nichol Twp, Wellington Co, ONT, ca 1838; later to Garafraxa Twp. Dau Mrs John Simpson, res Shoal Lake, MAN. **EHE 96**.

4206 KELLEY, Donald. From Stornoway, Is Lewis, ROC. To PEI <1840. Teacher in Uigg school, Queens Co. Dau Catherine, 1840–1915. **HP 85**.

4207 KELLOCK, James. From Thornhill, Morton par, DFS. To ONT, Apr 1845; stld prob York Co. Ironmonger. m Mary Houston, qv. **DGH 10 Apr 1845**.

4208 KELLY, James, b 1822. From Glasgow. To ONT, ca 1855. Wife Mary Creech, qv, with him, and ch: 1. James, b 1848; 2. Jane or Janet, b 1850. **DC 1 Dec 1850**.

4209 KELLY, Robert, ca 1812–6 May 1876. From Glasgow. To ONT <1840, when m at Welland, Charlotte Bacon, from Niagara. Sailor, later farmer. **DC 29 Jun 1979**.

4210 KELSO, Alexander. From North Sannox, Is Arran, BUT. To QUE on the *Caledonia*, ex Greenock, 25 Apr 1829; stld Inverness Village, Megantic Co, QUE. Wife Janet Kerr, qv, with him, and ch: 1. John; 2. Margaret, b 1820; 3. Elizabeth, qv; 4. Catherine, b 1825; 5. Janet, b 1825. **AMC 11; MAC 31**.

4211 KELSO, Ann, b 20 Sep 1823. From Is Arran, BUT. d/o Robert K, qv, and Catherine Kelso, qv. To QUE on the *Caledonia*, ex Greenock, 25 Apr 1829; stld Megantic Co. m 10 Jan 1848, Malcolm McKillop, qv. **AMC 11; MAC 30**.

4212 KELSO, Archibald, b 1779. From Is Arran, BUT. To Nash Creek, Restigouche Co, NB, 1829. Wife Mary McMillan, qv, with him, and ch: 1. Catherine, b 1818; 2. Ann, b 1820; 3. John, 1822–80; 4. Margaret, b Kilbride par, 1825. **MAC 18**.

4213 KELSO, Archibald, b 1825. From Is Arran, BUT. s/o John K, qv, and Mary Henry, qv. To Inverness, Megantic Co, QUE, 1848. m 28 Apr 1858, Isabella McGillvray, qv, ch: 1. Mary; 2. Angus, d aged 20; 3. John; 4. Robert; 5. Helen; 6. Isobel. **AMC 49; MAC 44**.

4214 KELSO, Catherine, 1778–1847. From Glen Sannox, Is Arran, BUT. To QUE on the *Caledonia*, ex Greenock, 25 Apr 1829; stld Inverness, Megantic Co. Wife of Donald McKillop, qv. **AMC 10; MAC 29**.

4215 KELSO, Catherine, b 1819. From Laggan, Is Arran, BUT. d/o Robert K, qv, and Catherine Kelso, qv. To QUE on the *Caledonia*, ex Greenock, 25 Apr 1829; stld Inverness, Megantic Co. m 4 Sep 1838, James McKillop, qv. **AMC 11; MAC 30**.

4216 KELSO, Catherine, 1787–1868. From Laggan, Is Arran, BUT. To QUE on the *Caledonia*, ex Greenock, 25 Apr 1829; stld Inverness, Megantic Co. Wife of Robert Kelso, qv. **AMC 11; MAC 30**.

4217 KELSO, Elizabeth, 1773–1849. From Corrygills, Is Arran, BUT. To Inverness Twp, Megantic Co, QUE, 1831. Wife of Rev Donald Hendry, qv. **AMC 12; MAC 39**.

4218 KELSO, Elizabeth, b 1819. From Laggan, Is Arran, BUT. d/o Robert K, qv, and Catherine K, qv. To QUE on the *Caledonia*, ex Greenock, 25 Apr 1829; stld Inverness Twp, Megantic Co. m A. Robertson. **AMC 339; MAC 30**.

4219 KELSO, Elizabeth, b 1829. From Is Arran, BUT. d/o John K, qv, and Mary Henry, qv. To Inverness,

Megantic Co, QUE, 1848. m James McGillvray, qv.
AMC 49; MAC 44.

4220 KELSO, Elizabeth, b 1823. From North Sannox, Is Arran, BUT. d/o Alexander K, qv, and Janet Kerr, qv. To QUE on the *Caledonia*, ex Greenock, 25 Apr 1829; stld Inverness Village, Megantic Co, QUE. m — Baldwin. **AMC 11; MAC 31**.

4221 KELSO, James, b 1810. From Laggan, Is Arran, BUT. s/o Robert K, qv, and Catherine K, qv. To QUE on the *Caledonia*, ex Greenock, 25 Apr 1829; stld Inverness, Megantic Co. Farmer. m Isabella McKelvie, qv. **AMC 11; MAC 30**.

4222 KELSO, Janet, d 1858. From Is Arran, BUT. To QUE on the *Newfoundland*, ex Greenock, 12 Jun 1829; stld Inverness, Megantic Co. Wife of Peter Sillers, sr, qv. **AMC 22; MAC 35**.

4223 KELSO, Janet. From Is Arran, BUT. To QUE, 1831; stld Inverness, Megantic Co. wid/o Kerr and wife of James McKinnon, qv, whom she m in 1838. **AMC 39, 146; MAC 32**.

4224 KELSO, John. From North Sannox, Is Arran, BUT. To Inverness Twp, Megantic Co, QUE, 1831. m Ann McMillan, qv, ch: 1. John, b 1824; 2. Mary, qv; 3. William, qv. **AMC 39; MAC 38**.

4225 KELSO, John. From Is Arran, BUT. To Inverness, Megantic Co, QUE, 1848. m Mary Henry, qv, ch: 1. Archibald, qv; 2. Margaret, qv; 3. Elizabeth, qv; 4. John, jr, qv. **AMC 49; MAC 44**.

4226 KELSO, John, jr, b 1834. From Catacull, Is Arran, BUT. s/o John K, qv, and Mary Henry, qv. To Inverness, Megantic Co, QUE, 1848. m Eliza J. Cochrane. **AMC 49; MAC 44**.

4227 KELSO, Margaret, b 1827. From Is Arran, BUT. d/o John K, qv, and Mary Henry, qv. To Inverness, Megantic Co, QUE, 1848. m Duncan McGillvray, qv. **AMC 49; MAC 44**.

4228 KELSO, Mary. From North Sannox, Is Arran, BUT. d/o John K, qv, and Ann McMillan, qv. To Inverness Twp, Megantic Co, QUE, 1831. m — Douglas, ONT. **MAC 39; MAC 38**.

4229 KELSO, Mary, b 1816. From Laggan, Is Arran, BUT. d/o Robert K, qv, and Catherine K, qv. To QUE on the *Caledonia*, ex Greenock, 25 Apr 1829; stld Inverness, Megantic Co. m Angus McGillvray, jr, qv. **AMC 11; MAC 30**.

4230 KELSO, Robert, 1782–1858. From Laggan, Is Arran, BUT. To QUE on the *Caledonia*, ex Greenock, 25 Apr 1829; stld Inverness, Megantic Co. Farmer. m Catherine Kelso, qv, ch: 1. James, qv; 2. Margaret, b 1813, d unm; 3. Mary, qv; 4. Catherine, qv; 5. Elizabeth, qv; 6. Ann, qv; 7. Mrs Joseph Wallis. **AMC 11; MAC 30**.

4231 KELSO, William, 1787–1856. From Mid Sannox, Is Arran, BUT. To QUE on the *Caledonia*, ex Greenock, 25 Apr 1829; stld Inverness Twp, Megantic Co. Wife Mary McKillop, with him, and ch: 1. Mary, 1810-80; 2. Alexander, 1815-48; 3. Catherine, 1817-98; 4. James, 1821-98; 5. Margaret, 1826-92; 6. William, 1829-92. **AMC 11; MAC 31**.

4232 KELSO, William. From North Sannox, Is Arran, BUT. s/o John K, qv, and Ann McMillan, qv. To

Inverness, Megantic Co, QUE, 1831. m Miss Harvey, Leeds Twp. **AMC 39; MAC 38**.

4233 KEMP, Alexander, 1793–1876. From Gairloch, ROC. s/o William K, qv. To Boulardarie, Victoria Co, NS, 1821; later to Waipu, NZ. Wife Annabella, 1803-76, with him. ch: 1. Donald, drowned 1860; 2. Duncan, drowned 1860; 3. Jessie, 1831-89; 4. Alexander, 1831–1907, twin. **DC 25 Sep 1981**.

4234 KEMP, Rev Alexander Ferrie, 1822–4 May 1884. From Greenock, RFW. s/o Simon K, teacher in Kirkton, and Grace Ferrie, his first wife. Educ Univ of Edinburgh, and Presb Coll, London. Ord at Bolton, LAN, 1851, and was sometime chaplain to the 26th Regt, Cameronians. To Montreal, QUE, 1854. Min of St Gabriel Street Ch. Trans to Hamilton, ONT, 1865. Later app Prof of Philosophy at Olivet Coll, MI. Author. ch. **SGC 552; MDB 361; FES vii 486; DC 24 Oct 1978**.

4235 KEMP, Duncan. From Gairloch, ROC. Poss s/o William K, qv. To Boulardie, Victoria Co, NS, 1821; later to Waipu, NZ. Wife Mary Morrison, qv, with him. ch: 1. Catherine; 2. Isabella; 3. Margaret; 4. Mary; 5. John. **DC 25 Sep 1981**.

4236 KEMP, Gregor, d 1861. From Gairloch, ROC. s/o William K, qv. To Boulardarie, Victoria Co, NS, 1821. Went to NZ on the *Ellen Lewis*, ex St Anns, 1 Dec 1859, and stld Waipu. Drowned when the *William Pope* was lost between Waipu and Auckland. m Mary McGregor, qv, ch: 1. Ann; 2. Mary; 3. Alexander; 4. Catherine; 5. Johanna; 6. Jessie, 1840-94; 7. Jane. **DC 25 Sep 1981**.

4237 KEMP, William. From Gairloch, ROC. To Boulardarie, Victoria Co, NS, 1821. Wife Mary with him, and ch: 1. Alexander, qv; 2. Gregor, qv; 3. Margaret. **NSN 20/2**.

4238 KEMPT, Sir James, 25 Jan 1775–20 Dec 1854. b Canongate, Edinburgh. s/o Gavin K, merchant there and at Botley Hill, Southampton, and Sarah Walker. Army career incl aide-de-camp to Sir Ralph Abercromby. GCB, 1815, and was Gov Gen of NS, 1820-28. Gov Gen of CAN, 1828-30; PC, 1830; prom to General, 1841. d at South Audley, London, ENG. **BNA 495; Canongate OPR 585-3/9**.

4239 KENNEDY, Agnes, 1823–1906. From Dundee, ANS. To Collingwood Twp, Grey Co, ca 1848. Wife of John Reekie, qv. **DC 24 May 1979**.

4240 KENNEDY, Alexander, ca 1781–6 Jun 1832. From OKI. To CAN 1798, and entered the service of HBCo. Emp at Cumberland House, 1813-19, and became a chief factor >1821. Served on the Columbia River, and d London, ENG. **MDB 362; DC 21 Mar 1981**.

4241 KENNEDY, Alexander. From Laddie, nr Loch Garry, INV. To Montreal, QUE, ex Fort William, 3 Jul 1802; stld E ONT. Wife and 2 ch with him. **MCM 1/4 26**.

4242 KENNEDY, Alexander. From PER. To Glengarry Co, ONT, 1816. Son John. **DC 4 Mar 1965**.

4243 KENNEDY, Alexander. From Lochaber, INV. To Antigonish Co, NS, prob <1830. m Margaret Chisholm, ch: 1. Thomas; 2. Rory; 3. Alexander; 4. John; 5. Mary; 6. Ann; 7. Mrs Donald 'Ban' MacDonald, Glenroy. **HCA 158**.

4244 KENNEDY, Alexander, 27 Jun 1790–20 May 1879. From Baladuill, Is Tyree, ARL. s/o Neil K. and Catharine McLean. To QUE on the *Conrad*, ex Greenock, 18 Jun 1850; stld West Gwillimbury Twp, Simcoe Co, ONT. m Isabel McKinnon, qv, ch: 1. Neil, qv; 2. Mary, b 15 Mar 1819; 3. Alexander, b 13 May 1821; 4. Angus, qv; 5. Flora, b 16 Mar 1826; 6. Hugh, qv; 7. Hector, b 2 Apr 1828; 8. Catherine, b 1824; 9. Isabella, qv. **SG xxx/1 31**.

4245 KENNEDY, Andrew, ca 1802–30 Aug 1859. From Maxwelltown, KKD. To Murray Harbour, Kings Co, PEI. **DGH 21 Oct 1859**.

4246 KENNEDY, Angus. From Lochaber, INV. To Antigonish Co, NS, prob <1830. Teacher. m Janet MacDonald, ch: 1. Alexander; 2. John; 3. Samuel; 4. John, jr. **HCA 158**.

4247 KENNEDY, Angus, 14 Dec 1823–5 Apr 1911. From Baladuill, Is Tyree, ARL. s/o Alexander K, qv, and Isabel McKinnon, qv. To QUE on the *Conrad*, ex Greenock, 18 Jun 1850; stld Proton Twp, Grey Co, ONT. m Flora McDougall, qv, ch: 1. Alexander, b 28 Feb 1859; 2. Archie; 3. John Alexander; 4. Lachlan, d 1903; 5. Bella; 6. Neil; 7. Angus, b 1868; 8. Hugh; 9. Malcolm; 10. Margaret, b 1876; 11. John; 12. Duncan, d 1957. **DC 30 Sep 1980**.

4248 KENNEDY, Anne. From Aberchalder, INV. Poss rel to Donald McPhee, qv. To Montreal, QUE, ex Fort William, arr Sep 1802; stld E ONT. **MCM 1/4 23**.

4249 KENNEDY, Anne. From Fort Augustus, INV. To QUE, ex Greenock, summer 1815; stld ONT. Wife of Allan McDonell, qv. **SEC 4**.

4250 KENNEDY, Archibald. To QUE on the *Alexander*, 1816; stld Lot 12, Con 3, Drummond Twp, Lanark Co, ONT. **HCL 233**.

4251 KENNEDY, Catherine, b 1771. From Auchenchairn, Kilbride, Is Arran, BUT. To Blackland, Restigouche Co, NB, <1829. Wife of John Hamilton, qv. **MAC 15**.

4252 KENNEDY, Catherine, 1803–95. From Mid Kiscadale, Kilbride par, Is Arran, BUT. To Blackland, Restigouche Co, NB, <1841. Wife of James Hamilton, qv. **MAC 15**.

4253 KENNEDY, Catherine, 1815–84. From PER, poss Blairgowrie par. To Hamilton, ONT, 1852. Wife of James Saunders, qv. **DC 31 Dec 1979**.

4254 KENNEDY, David, 1828–31 Jul 1903. From AYR. To Derby Twp, Bruce Co, ONT, and d at Tara. Pioneer settler and author. **MDB 362**.

4255 KENNEDY, Donald. From Is Canna, INV. bro/o John 'Ruadh' K, qv. To Cape Breton Is, NS, 1791. Farmer. m Mary, d/o Donald McLeod, qv, from Is Eigg, ch: 1. Mary; 2. Donald; 3. Ann; 4. Sarah; 5. Catherine; 6. Bridget; 7. Angus; 9. Elizabeth. **WLC**.

4256 KENNEDY, Donald. From Achluachrach, Glen Spean, INV. To Montreal, QUE, ex Fort William, 3 Jul 1802; stld E ONT. Wife with him. **MCM 1/4 23**.

4257 KENNEDY, Donald. From Lewiston, Urquhart and Glenmoriston par, INV. To Montreal, QUE, ex Fort William, 3 Jul 1802; stld E ONT. Wife and 3 ch with him. **MCM 1/4 24**.

4258 KENNEDY, Donald. From Laddy, nr Loch Garry, INV. To Montreal, QUE, ex Fort William, 3 Jul 1802; stld E ONT. Wife and 2 ch with him. **MCM 1/4 23**.

4259 KENNEDY, Donald. From Kinlochlochy, INV. To Montreal, QUE, ex Fort William, 3 Jul 1802; stld E ONT. Wife and 4 ch with him. **MCM 1/4 23**.

4260 KENNEDY, Donald. From Inchlaggan, Glengarry, INV. To Montreal, QUE, ex Fort William, 3 Jul 1802; stld E ONT. Wife with him, and family: 1. Angus; 2. Alexander; 3. Allan. **MCM 1/4 24**.

4261 KENNEDY, Donald, b ca 1758. From PER. To Pictou, NS, on the *Commerce*, ex Port Glasgow, 10 Aug 1803. Farmer. Wife Margaret, aged 35, with him, and ch: 1. Janet, aged 10; 2. John, aged 8; 3. Robert, aged 6; 4. David, aged 3. **PLC**.

4262 KENNEDY, Donald, 1804-88. From Blair Atholl, PER. To Beckwith Twp, Lanark Co, ONT, 1818. Surveyor and architect. m Janet, d/o George Buckam. Son George. **DC 29 Sep 1964**.

4263 KENNEDY, Donald. From Lochaber, INV. To Antigonish Co, NS, prob <1830. m Sarah Campbell, ch: 1. Angus; 2. Christina; 3. Mary. **HCA 158**.

4264 KENNEDY, Donald. To Pictou, NS, on the *London*, arr 11 Apr 1848. Wife Jane with him, and ch: 1. Thomas W; 2. Elizabeth. **DC 15 Jul 1979**.

4265 KENNEDY, Duncan. From Aberchalder, INV. To Montreal, QUE, ex Fort William, 3 Jul 1802; stld E ONT. Wife and 3 ch with him. **MCM 1/4 23**.

4266 KENNEDY, Duncan, b ca 1783. From Dull par, PER. To Charlottetown, PEI, on the *Clarendon*, ex Oban, 6 Aug 1808. Labourer. Wife Margaret Forbes, qv, with him. ch: 1. Jane, qv; 2. Christine, b PEI; 3. Mrs McGregor; 4. Daniel. **CPL; DC 11 Apr 1981**.

4267 KENNEDY, Effie. From INV. To Montreal, QUE, ex Fort William, 3 Jul 1802; stld E ONT. **MCM 1/4 24**.

4268 KENNEDY, Elizabeth Whigham, 1816-92. From KKD. s/o Robert K. and Robina Henderson. To Guelph Twp, Wellington Co, ONT, <1842. m Robert Martin, qv. **DC 31 Dec 1979**.

4269 KENNEDY, Ewen. From Aberchalder, INV. To Montreal, QUE, ex Fort William, 3 Jul 1802; stld E ONT. Wife with him. **MCM 1/4 23**.

4270 KENNEDY, Ewen. From Invergarry, INV. Prob rel to Peggy K, qv. To Montreal, QUE, ex Fort William, 3 Jul 1802; stld E ONT. Wife with him. **MCM 1/4 26**.

4271 KENNEDY, Helen, 1786–1865. From North Kiscadale, Kilbride par, Is Arran, BUT. To Blackland, Restigouche Co, NB, 1829. Wife of John Cook, qv. **MAC 9**.

4272 KENNEDY, Helen, b 1796. From Kilbride par, Is Arran, BUT. To Blackland, Restigouche Co, NB, 1829. Wife of Donald McNicol, qv. **MAC 26**.

4273 KENNEDY, Hugh, b 2 Apr 1828. From Baladhuill, Is Tyree, ARL. s/o Alexander K, qv, and Isabel McKinnon, qv. To QUE on the *Conrad*, ex Greenock, 18 Jun 1850; stld Carrick Twp, later Bruce Twp, Bruce Co, ONT. m Mary Brown, d 1895, ch: 1. Alexander, b 1855; 2. Catherine, b 1857; 3. Donald, b 1858; 4. Hugh, b 1860; 5. Isabella, b 1864; 6. John, b 1866;

7. Flora, b 1867; 8. Mary, b 1870; 9. Neil, b 1876;
10. Albert, b 1877. **DC 30 Sep 1980**.

4274 KENNEDY, Isabella, b 1843. From Baladhuill, Is
Tyree, ARL. d/o Alexander K, qv, and Isabel McKinnon,
qv. To QUE on the *Conrad*, ex Greenock, 18 Jun 1850;
stld West Gwillimbury Twp, Simcoe Co, ONT, later
Carrick Twp, Bruce Co. m 30 Dec 1858, John, b 1830,
s/o Peter and Elspeth Butchart. **DC 30 Sep 1980**.

4275 KENNEDY, James. From Portree, Is Skye, INV.
s/o Donald K. To PEI, arr Jul 1841. m Ann Nicolson,
qv. **DC 13 Jul 1968**.

4276 KENNEDY, James, ca 1825–18 Aug 1858. From
Dumfries. To Toronto, ONT, 1845. Nurseryman.
DGH 1 Oct 1858.

4277 KENNEDY, John 'Ruadh'. From Is Canne, INV.
bro/o Donald K, qv. To Cape Breton Is, NS, <1810; stld
River Inhabitants, Inverness Co. Farmer. **WLC**.

4278 KENNEDY, Jane, b 1807. From Foss, Dull par,
PER. d/o Duncan K, qv, and Margaret Forbes, qv. To
Charlottetown, PEI, on the *Clarendon*, ex Oban, 6 Aug
1808. m Alexander Scott. **CPL; DC 11 Apr 1981**.

4279 KENNEDY, John. From Inchlaggan, Glengarry,
INV. To Montreal, QUE, ex Fort William, 3 Jul 1802; stld
E ONT. Wife with him, and family: 1. Ewen; 2. Mary;
3. Alexander; 4. Janet; 5. Angus. **MCM 1/4 24**.

4280 KENNEDY, John. From Invervigar, Boleskine and
Abertarff par, INV. To Montreal, QUE, ex Fort William,
3 Jul 1802; stld E ONT. Wife with him, and family:
1. Duncan; 2. Alexander. **MCM 1/4 24**.

4281 KENNEDY, John, b ca 1770. From Foss, PER. To
Charlottetown, PEI, on the *Clarendon*, ex Oban, 6 Aug
1808. Wife Janet, aged 30, with him, and ch: 1. Janet,
aged 8; 2. Donald, aged 6; 3. Elizabeth, aged 4;
4. Duncan, aged 1. **CPL**.

4282 KENNEDY, John. From Dull par, PER. To
Montreal, QUE, on the *Curlew*, ex Greenock, 21 Jul
1818; stld Beckwith Twp, Lanark Co, ONT. Farmer. Wife
Mary with him, and ch: 1. James, aged 10; 2. Mary,
aged 8.

4283 KENNEDY, John. From Lochaber, INV. To
Antigonish Co, NS, <1830. m Miss MacDonald, ch:
1. Alexander; 2. Annie; 3. Margaret; 4. Mary;
5. Elizabeth. **HCA 158**.

4284 KENNEDY, John 'Ruadh'. From Lochaber, INV. To
Antigonish Co, NS, <1820; moved later to Broad Cove,
Inverness Co. Farmer. m Elizabeth Fraser, and had, prob
with other ch: 1. Jessie; 2. Mary. **HCA 158; MP 191,
221**.

4285 KENNEDY, John. From New Abbey, KKD.
s/o David K. of Knocknalling. To ONT <1834. m at
Pleasance, Dumfries, 14 Aug 1834, Jane Maxwell
Carson, qv. **DGC 16 Apr 1834**.

4286 KENNEDY, John. Poss from PER. To Galt,
Waterloo Co, ONT, <1840. Lime-burner. m Helen
Rintoul. **HGD 116**.

4287 KENNEDY, John. To Aldborough Twp, Elgin Co,
ONT, 1854. **PDA 68**.

4288 KENNEDY, Joseph, b ca 1794. From Foss, PER.
To Charlottetown, PEI, on the *Clarendon*, ex Oban,
6 Aug 1808. Labourer. **CPL**.

4289 KENNEDY, Katherine, ca 1787–ca 1872. From
Fort William, INV. Prob d/o Donald K. To Pictou, NS, on
the *Good Intent*, 1816; stld Antigonish Co. Wife of
Alexander 'Breac' MacDonald, qv. **HCA 190**.

4290 KENNEDY, Lachlan. From Lochaber, INV.
bro/o Lucy K, qv. To ONT, ca 1821, poss via NS.
MP 273.

4291 KENNEDY, Lucy. From Lochaber, INV.
sis/o Lachlan K, qv. To Inverness Co, NS, 1821; stld
Black River. Wife of Alexander Campbell, qv. **MP 272**.

4292 KENNEDY, Margaret, ca 1796–14 Sep 1842.
From Dull par, PER. To QUE, ca 1812; later to
Waddington, St Lawrence Co, NY. Wife of Daniel Forbes,
qv, m 12 Mar 1811. **LDW 7 Dec 1974**.

4293 KENNEDY, Mary. From Laddie, nr Loch Garry,
INV. To Montreal, QUE, ex Fort William, 3 Jul 1802; stld
E ONT. **MCM 1/4 24**.

4294 KENNEDY, Mary. From Bowmore, Is Islay, ARL.
To King Twp, York Co, ONT, prob <1850. m James
Turnbull Bonnar, qv, 29 Dec 1835. **DC 22 May 1982**.

4295 KENNEDY, Neil, b 16 Dec 1816. From Baladhuill,
Is Tyree, ARL. s/o Alexander K, qv, and Isabel
McKinnon, qv. To QUE on the *Conrad*, ex Greenock,
18 Jun 1850; stld Carrick Twp, later Bruce Twp, Bruce
Co, ONT. m 28 Jan 1846, Christina McLean, qv, ch:
1. Flora, b 1847; 2. Ann, b 1850; 3. Isabella, b 1852.
DC 30 Sep 1980.

4296 KENNEDY, Peggy. From Invergarry, INV. Prob rel
to Ewen K, qv. To Montreal, QUE, ex Fort William, 3 Jul
1802; stld E ONT. **MCM 1/4 26**.

4297 KENNEDY, Rachel. To Guelph, ONT, ca 1842.
Wife of Alexander Stewart, qv. **LDW 4 Jun 1973**.

4298 KENNEDY, Robert. To QUE, spring 1818; stld
Beckwith Twp, Lanark Co, ONT. **HCL 33**.

4299 KENNEDY, Sophia, d 3 Dec 1841. From
Durrisdeer, DFS. d/o William K. in Murryhill. To New
Edinburgh Village, Russell Co, ONT. **DGH 28 Apr 1842**.

4300 KENNEDY, Susannah, ca 1786–10 Aug 1873.
From PER. To PEI prob <1808; stld Queens Co.
m Donald McGregor, qv. **DC 11 Apr 1981**.

4301 KENNEDY, Thomas, ca 1820–8 Feb 1842. From
Durrisdeer, DFS. s/o William K. in Murryhill. To New
Edinburgh Village, Russell Co, ONT. **DGH 28 Apr 1842**.

4302 KENNEDY, William. To Pictou Co, NS, <1776.
HPC App B.

4303 KENNEDY, William. From DFS. To QUE, 1832;
later to Spencerville, Grenville Co, ONT. Millwright.
m Agnes Stark. Son Sir John, 1838–1921, engineer,
Montreal. **DC 30 Aug 1977**.

4304 KENNEDY, William, 1799–1849. From Paisley,
RFW. To CAN, 1838, as private secretary to John George
Lambton, 1st Earl of Durham, British High
Commissioner. Went later to TX, and was British Consul
at Galveston. Author. d at Paris. **IBD 253**.

KENNEDY, Mrs W. See CORSON, Elizabeth.

4305 KENT, James, ca 1749–1825. From Alloa, CLK.
To Colchester Co, NS, <1770. Farmer and MLA.
m 1774, Margaret Williams. **MLA 178**.

4306 KENT, John. From Alloa, CLK. Prob rel to James K, qv. To NS <1820; stld Lower Stewiacke, Colchester Co. Son Edward, b 1823, res Tatamagouche. **HT 77**.

4307 KER, Rev Andrew, b ca 1775. From Falkirk, STI. s/o Robert K, farmer. Matric Univ of Glasgow, 1789. Licentiate of Secession Ch, missioned to USA, 1799, but declined and later became min at Economy, Colchester Co, NS. **GMA 4892**.

4308 KER, Isabella, 31 Jan 1789–7 Feb 1821. From Stobo, PEE. d/o Rev Alexander K, par min, and Katherine Williamson. To QUE <1818, when m James Kerr, qv. **FES i 291**.

4309 KER, Margaret. Poss from Madderty par, PER. To Montreal, QUE, on the *Niagara*, ex Greenock, arr 28 May 1825; stld McNab Twp, Renfrew Co, ONT. Wife of James McFarlane, qv. **EMT 18**.

4310 KERR, Alexander. From Urinbeg, Is Arran, BUT. s/o Hugh K, qv, and Euphemia Kerr, qv. To Inverness, Megantic Co, QUE, 1831. m Margery McKillop, qv. **AMC 39; MAC 37**.

4311 KERR, Alexander. Prob from Forres, MOR. To Chatham, Deux-Montagnes, QUE, 1833. Farmer. m Helen Alves, qv. **DC 17 Dec 1981**.

4312 KERR, Alexander. From Assynt, SUT. To Oxford Co, ONT, <20 Sep 1847; stld nr Woodstock. *MacLeod Muniments*, Box 36.

4313 KERR, Alexander, b 17 Jun 1835. From Dunipace, STI. s/o Alexander K, and Janet Reid. To Huron Co, ONT, 1854. m 1860, Helen Lapslie, ch: 1. Elizabeth; 2. Alexander; 3. Janet; 4. John; 5. Archie; 7. Jean; 8. William. **DC 4 Mar 1965**.

4314 KERR, Andrew, b ca 1793. To St Gabriel de Valcartier, QUE, prob <1855. Prob hus/o Ellen Whalens, qv. **Census 1861**.

4315 KERR, Cathel. To Pictou, NS, on the *Ellen*, ex Lochlaxford, SUT, 22 May 1848. Wife Ann with him, and ch: 1. John; 2. George; 3. Bell; 4. William; 5. Barbara. **DC 15 Jul 1979**.

4316 KERR, Catherine, 1795–1874. From South Sannox, Is Arran, BUT. To QUE on the *Caledonia*, ex Greenock, 25 Apr 1829; stld Inverness, Megantic Co. Wife of Neil McMillan, qv. **AMC 11; MAC 32**.

4317 KERR, Catherine, 1802-75. From Corrie, Is Arran, BUT. To Blackland, Restigouche Co, NB, 1832. Wife of John McCormack, qv. **MAC 19**.

4318 KERR, Catherine, b ca 1815. To St Gabriel de Valcartier, QUE, poss <1855. **Census 1861**.

4319 KERR, Colin, 1788–11 May 1834. Poss from ARL. To Aldborough Twp, Elgin Co, ONT, 1818. **PDA 41**.

4320 KERR, Daniel, b 1791. From Kilbride Bennan, Is Arran, BUT. To Dalhousie, NB, 1827. m 9 Apr 1816, Ann Sinclare, qv, and had, poss with other ch: 1. Mary; 2. Alexander, 1818-90; 3. Ann, b 1820; 4. John, b 1822; 5. Donald, b 1824. **MAC 18**.

4321 KERR, Donald. From Is Arran, BUT. To Megantic Co, QUE, 1831. m Catherine, prob d/o Mrs Isabel Stewart, qv. **AMC 42**.

4322 KERR, Donald. From Urinbeg, Is Arran, BUT. s/o Hugh K, qv, and Euphemia Kerr, qv. To Inverness Twp, Megantic Co, QUE, 1831. m Catherine Cameron, Upper Ireland Twp. **AMC 39; MAC 36**.

4323 KERR, Donald. From Monachar, Is Arran, BUT. To Inverness, Megantic Co, QUE, prob <1840. **MAC 41**.

4324 KERR, Donald, 1831-1907. From Dugary, Is Arran, BUT. s/o Finlay K, qv, and Annie McFee, qv. To Inverness Twp, Megantic Co, QUE, 1842. m Margery Kerr. **AMC 40; MAC 40**.

4325 KERR, Donald. To Pictou, NS, on the *Ellen*, ex Lochlaxford, SUT, 22 May 1848. Wife Sarah with him, and ch: 1. William; 2. John; 3. Flora; 4. Cathy. **DC 15 Jul 1979**.

4326 KERR, Elizabeth, b ca 1835. From Dugary, Is Arran, BUT. d/o Finlay K, qv, and Annie McFee, qv. To Inverness Twp, Megantic Co, QUE, 1842. m William Greenlay. **AMC 40; MAC 40**.

4327 KERR, Euphemia. From Urinbeg, Is Arran, BUT. To Inverness Twp, Megantic Co, QUE, 1831. Wife of Hugh Kerr, qv. **AMC 39; MAC 36**.

4328 KERR, Euphemia. From Is Arran, BUT. d/o John K. and Janet Kelso, qv. To Megantic Co, QUE, 1831. m John McGillivray. **AMC 39**.

4329 KERR, Finlay, 1791–1871. From Dugary, Is Arran, BUT. To Inverness Twp, Megantic Co, QUE, 1842. m Annie McFee, qv, ch: 1. John, qv; 2. Donald, qv; 3. Flora, qv; 4. Elizabeth, qv; 5. Malcolm, qv; 6. James, d at sea, 1842. **AMC 40; MAC 40**.

4330 KERR, Flora, b 1834. From Dugary, Is Arran, BUT. d/o Finlay K, qv, and Annie McFee, qv. To Inverness, Megantic Co, QUE, 1842. m Donald Kerr. **AMC 40; MAC 40**.

4331 KERR, Hugh. From Urinbeg, Is Arran, BUT. To Inverness Twp, Megantic Co, QUE, 1831. m Euphemia Kerr, qv, ch: 1. John; 2. Alexander, qv; 3. Isabella, qv; 4. James, qv; 5. Malcolm, drowned at Quebec Wharf; 6. Catherine; 7. Donald, qv; 8. Hugh. **AMC 39; MAC 36**.

4332 KERR, Isabella, b ca 1798. From Maxton, ROX. To St Gabriel de Valcartier, QUE, <1830. m 21 Nov 1819, James Jack, qv. **Maxton OPR 798/1; Census 1861**.

4333 KERR, Isabella. From Urinbeg, Is Arran, BUT. d/o Hugh K, qv, and Euphemia Kerr, qv. To Megantic Co, QUE, 1831. m Donald McEachern, qv. **AMC 39; MAC 36**.

4334 KERR, James, ca 1765–5 May 1846. From Leith, MLN. s/o Robert K. Matric Univ of Glasgow, 1787, and was adm to the English Bar. To QUE, 1787. Judge of Kings Bench, 1807, and pres of the Legislative Council, 1831. m Isabella Ker, qv. **GMA 4771; MDB 365**.

4335 KERR, James, d 1830. From DFS. Stld Kings Co, NS. Sometime Col, Queens Rangers. **NSN 27/193**.

4336 KERR, James, ca 1810–25 Jan 1879. From DFS. To Northumberland Co, NB, 1816; stld nr Chatham. **DC 14 Jan 1980**.

4337 KERR, James. From Urinbeg, Is Arran, BUT. s/o Hugh K, qv, and Euphemia Kerr, qv. To Inverness,

Megantic Co, QUE, 1831. m Janet Henry, qv.   **AMC 39; MAC 36**.

4338   KERR, James, b ca 1821. To St Gabriel de Valcartier, QUE, prob <1855. Prob s/o Andrew K, qv, and Ellen Whalens, qv.   **Census 1861**.

4339   KERR, James, 15 Feb 1827–27 Feb 1883. From Dunipace, STI. s/o Alexander K. and Janet Reid. To QUE on the *Ann Rankine*, 1851; stld Huron Co, ONT. Farmer. m 29 Apr 1851, Isabel, d/o Peter Campbell and Janet Mitchell, ch: 1. Janet, b 1853; 2. Alexander, b 1854; 3. Mary Jane, b 1859; 4. John, b 1861; 5. James, b 1865; 6. Isabella, b 1868; 7. William Archibald, b 1872.   **DC 4 Mar 1965**.

4340   KERR, Janet. From North Sannox, Is Arran, BUT. d/o John K. To QUE on the *Caledonia*, ex Greenock, 25 Apr 1829; stld Inverness Village, Megantic Co. Wife of Alexander Kelso, qv.   **AMC 11; MAC 31**.

4341   KERR, John, ca 1809–21 Jul 1874. From DFS. To NB, 1818, and d Kirkhill, New Bandon, Northumberland Co. Collector of Customs.   **DGC 1 Sep 1874**.

4342   KERR, John. Poss from ARL. To Aldborough Twp, Elgin Co, ONT, 1818. Farmer.   **PDA 59**.

4343   KERR, John. From ROX. To QUE on the *Sarah Mary Jane*, 1831; stld Dumfries Twp, Waterloo Co, ONT.   **HGD 460**.

4344   KERR, John. From Swinton par, BEW. To Fredericton, NB, 1834; stld Stanley, York Co. m Jane Turnbull, qv, ch: 1. Jane, b 27 Dec 1827; 2. Janet Caroline, b 20 Mar 1830; 3. Harriet, 4. Thomas, b 18 Oct 1834; 5. James, b 9 Aug 1837; 6. John, b 15 Apr 1840; 7. William, b 24 Jun 1842; 8. Mary Ann, b 21 Sep 1845; 9. George, b 25 Apr 1848. **Swinton OPR, 755/3; DC 19 Jun 1980**.

4345   KERR, John, 1826–1903. From Dugary, Is Arran, BUT. s/o Finlay K, qv, and Annie McFee, qv. To Inverness Twp, Megantic Co, QUE, 1842. m Mary Groves.   **AMC 40; MAC 40**.

4346   KERR, John, 1820–1906. From Dunipace, STI. s/o Alexander K. and Janet Reid. To CAN on the *Susan*, 1852; stld Huron Co, ONT. m Janet Lapslie, no ch. **DC 4 Mar 1965**.

4347   KERR, John. Neph of Mary Lamont, Edinburgh. To Three Rivers, QUE, <1854.   **SH**.

4348   KERR, John, b ca 1823. To St Gabriel de Valcartier, QUE, prob <1855.   **Census 1861**.

4349   KERR, John Campbell, b ca 1793. From Edinburgh. Rel to John K, solicitor there. To QUE on the *Atlas*, ex Greenock, 11 Jul 1815; stld Lot 21, Con 1, Bathurst Twp, Lanark Co, ONT. Saddler, farmer. **SEC 2; SH; HCL 232**.

4350   KERR, Katherine, b ca 1778. From Auchiuellan, Kilmartin par, ARL. To Otonabee Twp, Peterborough Co, ONT, ca 1819. Wife of Malcolm McFarlane, qv. **DC 13 Sep 1982**.

4351   KERR, Malcolm, b 1836. From Dugary, Is Arran, BUT. s/o Finlay K, qv, and Annie McFee, qv. To Inverness Twp, Megantic Co, QUE, 1842. m Janet McKinnon.   **AMC 40; MAC 40**.

4352   KERR, Margaret, b ca 1819. To St Gabriel de Valcartier, QUE, <1855.   **Census 1861**.

4353   KERR, Mary, 1804-88. From Kilmory, Is Arran, BUT. To Restigouche Co, NB, 1829; stld Point la Nim. Wife of John McNeish, qv, m 2 Mar 1826.   **MAC 24**.

4354   KERR, Mary, 1810-95. From West Bennan, Is Arran, BUT. To Charlo, Restigouche Co, NB, 1845. **MAC 18**.

4355   KERR, Mary. From Is Arran, BUT. d/o John K, qv, and Janet Kelso, qv. To Megantic Co, QUE, 1831. m Neil Fullerton, and went later to IA.   **AMC 39**.

4356   KERR, Mary, 1808-48. From Lingerton, Kilmichael-Glassary, ARL. To Southwold Twp, Elgin Co, ONT, 1833. m 24 Mar 1832, Duncan McCormaig, qv. **DC 18 Jul 1979**.

4357   KERR, Mary. From Monacher, Is Arran, BUT. Poss a widow. To Inverness Twp, Megantic Co, QUE, prob <1840.   **MAC 41**.

4358   KERR, Norman. From Achmelvich, Assynt, SUT. s/o Cathel K. To QUE on the *Panama*, ex Loch Laxford, 19 Jun 1847. Went to Zorra, Oxford Co, ONT.   *McLeod Muniments*, **Box 36**.

4359   KERR, Peter, b 1805. From West Bennan, Kilmory, Is Arran, BUT. To Dalhousie, NB, 1828. **MAC 18**.

4360   KERR, Robert. Poss from ARL. To Aldborough Twp, Elgin Co, ONT, prob 1818. Farmer.   **PDA 93**.

4361   KERR, Robert, b ca 1824. To St Gabriel de Valcartier, QUE, prob <1855.   **Census 1861**.

4362   KERR, Samuel, ca 1779–16 Feb 1872. From DFS. To St John, NB, prob <1840.   **CAE 27**.

4363   KERR, Thomas. Prob from BEW. To Pictou, NS, <1820; stld Middle River. Millwright. ch: 1. Francis; 2. George; 3. Frank; 4. Hardy; 5. William. **HNS iii 142**.

4364   KERR, Thomas, d 12 Aug 1847. From Sanquhar, DFS, where he was an accountant with the British Linen Bank. To Montreal, QUE.   **DGH 23 Sep 1847**.

4365   KERR, William, ca 1775–4 Apr 1845. From Stranraer, WIG. s/o Bailie John K. To Hinchinbrooke Twp, Frontenac Co, ONT. Farmer at Arvie.   **DGH 20 Feb 1845**.

4366   KETCHEN, Rev James, 1797–1871. From DFS. s/o John K, landowner, and Grace Mitchell. Educ Univ of Edinburgh, and was app missionary by the Glasgow Colonial Society, 1831. To Belleville, Hastings Co, ONT, and Presb min there until 1844, when he retr to SCT. FC min at Mordington, BEW, 1844-71, and d unm. **AFC i 201; FES vii 638**.

4367   KETTLES, Charles. Prob from PER. To ONT, <1844.   **DC 21 Mar 1981**.

4368   KIDD, Alexander, b ca 1781. From Blackburn, WLN. To QUE on the *Baltic Merchant*, ex Greenock, 12 Jul 1815; stld Lot 18, Con 1, Bathurst Twp, Lanark Co, ONT. Cartwright and farmer. Wife Christian White, qv, with him, and 7 ch.   **SEC 8; HCL 16, 232**.

4369   KIDD, Rev James, 8 Feb 1826–17 May 1894. From New Deer, ABD. s/o James K, beadle, and Joan Henderson. Grad MA, Kings Coll, Aberdeen 1851. Min at Richmond, Carleton Co, NB, 1861-68. Trans to a charge in ONT, but retr to SCT and became min of Bressay,

Shetland Is. m Elizabeth Lillian Neal, of Richmond, ch:
1. James William, b 1873; 2. Samuel Neal Theodore,
b 1878. **KCG 303; FES vii 281, 610**.

4370   KILGOUR, Alexander. From FIF. To QUE <1850;
stld Clarendon Twp, Pontiac Co. Stonemason. m Janet
Norval, qv. Son Alexander, b ca 1838. **DC 21 Mar 1981**.

4371   KILGOUR, William. Poss from FIF. To QUE
<1840; stld Beauharnois. m Ann Wilson. Son Robert,
1847–1918, manufacturer, Toronto. **DC 30 Aug 1977**.

4372   KILPATRICK, John. To QUE on the *George
Canning*, ex Greenock, 14 Apr 1821; stld Lanark Co,
ONT. **HCL 239**.

4373   KING, Rev Andrew, 1793–24 Feb 1874. From
Glasgow. s/o John K, craftsman, and Janet Lennox.
Grad MA Univ of Glasgow, 1831, and became a teacher.
Ord 1830 and was min of Torphichen, WLN, 1836-43.
Joined FC and adm to St Stephens, Glasgow. To Halifax,
NS, 1848, and was Prof of Theology at the Presb Coll
there until 1871. m 27 Apr 1848, Matilda Ferguson, and
d Helensburgh, SCT. **RGG 311; GMA 6867; FES i 232,
iii 466, vii 615**.

4374   KING, Mrs Catherine. From Kincardine par, PER.
To Montreal, QUE, on the *Sophia*, ex Greenock, 26 Jul
1818; stld prob Beckwith Twp, Lanark Co, ONT. **SPL**.

4375   KING, Mrs Christian. From Kincardine par, PER.
To Montreal, QUE, on the *Sophia*, ex Greenock, 26 Jul
1818; stld prob Beckwith Twp, Lanark Co, ONT. **SPL**.

4376   KING, Duncan. From Kincardine par, PER. To
Montreal, QUE, on the *Sophia*, ex Greenock, 26 Jul
1818; prob stld Beckwith Twp, Lanark Co, ONT. Wife
Christian with him. **SPL**.

4377   KING, Isabella, b ca 1834. From Yetholm, ROX.
d/o Ralph K. and Mary Scott. To Hamilton Twp,
Northumberland Co, ONT. m 31 Oct 1860, James Watt,
qv. **DC 18 Jan 1980**.

4378   KING, James. To Ramsay Twp, Lanark Co, ONT,
ca 1821; stld Lot 11, Con 10. Farmer. **HCL 85**.

4379   KING, James. From Motherwell, LKS. s/o John
K. in Windmillhill. To Montreal, QUE, <1850, when
served heir to his father. **SH**.

4380   KING, John. From Tyrie, ABD. To QUE and
d there. Sometime of RHA. Son John, QC, father of
William Lyon Mackenzie King, 1874–1950, Prime
Minister of CAN. **DC 18 Sep 1975**.

4381   KING, John. To QUE on the *Fame*, 1815; stld
Lot 3, Con 7, Drummond Twp, Lanark Co, ONT.
HCL 233.

4382   KING, John. From Kincardine par, PER. To
Montreal, QUE, on the *Sophia*, ex Greenock, 26 Jul
1818; stld prob Beckwith Twp, Lanark Co, ONT. **SPL**.

4383   KING, John. From Kincardine par, PER. To
Montreal, QUE, on the *Sophia*, ex Greenock, 26 Jul
1818. Wife Janet with him, and ch: 1. Robert, aged 15;
2. Mary, aged 13; 3. Janet, aged 11; 4. John,
aged 2 ½. **SPL**.

4384   KING, John. From DFS. To Colchester Co, NS,
<1841. Magistrate. By wife Sarah Ann had with other ch
s Edwin David, b 1841, barrister. **HNS iii 141**.

4385   KING, Rev John Mark, 25 May 1829–5 Mar
1899. From Yetholm, ROX. s/o Ralph K. and Mary Scott.
Grad MA, Univ of Edinburgh, 1854, and was ord as a
Presb min in CAN, poss at Toronto. Principal of
Manitoba Coll, Winnipeg, 1883-99; DD, Knox Coll, 1882.
m 1873, Janet, d/o Hugh Skinner. **CEG 229; MDB 368**.

4386   KING, Joseph. To QUE on the *Alexander*, 1816;
stld Lot 12, Con 9, Bathurst Twp, Lanark Co, ONT.
HCL 233.

4387   KING, Margaret, 1784–1866. From Glasgow.
d/o John K, merchant. To Ramsay Twp, Lanark Co,
ONT, 1835. Wife of Dr William Cannon, RN, qv.
OSG 27.

4388   KING, William Scott, b ca 1836. From Yetholm,
ROX. s/o Ralph K. and Mary Scott. To Hamilton Twp,
Northumberland Co, ONT. m Ellen Jane Morrison, qv.
DC 18 Jan 1980.

4389   KING, Warden, d 1823. From Gourock, RFW.
s/o John K. and Margaret Warden. To Montreal, QUE,
1832, and became an ironfounder in partnership with
George Rogers. **SGC 524; Ts Gourock**.

4390   KINGHORN, John, 17 Aug 1823–16 Dec 1916.
From Edington, Chirnside par, BEW. s/o William K, qv,
and Agnes Darling, qv. To Leeds Twp, Megantic Co,
QUE, 1834. Farmer, 5th range. m 2 Feb 1847, Elizabeth,
d/o James Hutchison and Mary McMillan, ch.
Chirnside OPR 730/1; AMC 142.

4391   KINGHORN, William. From Edington, Chirnside
par, BEW. s/o William, 1756–1823, and wife Dorothy. To
Leeds Twp, Megantic Co, QUE, 1834. Hedger, later
farmer. m Agnes Darling, qv, ch: 1. William, b 16 Mar
1816, stld Rockford, IL; 2. Barbara, 1817-19; 3. Peterina
Macindoe, b 25 Jul 1819, named after Rev Peter
Macindoe, Cameronian preacher; 4. Dorothy, b 13 May
1821, res Rockford, IL; 5. John, qv; 6. Barbara, jr;
7. George. **Chirnside OPR 730/1-2; AMC 142;
Ts Chirnside**.

4392   KINLEYSIDE, Robert, ca 1813–14 Jan 1850.
From Whitsome par, BEW. s/o John K. and Helen
Thompson. Drowned off the coast of Labrador.
Ts Whitsome.

4393   KINMOND, Margaret, b 14 Jun 1793. From Errol
par, PER. To ONT, 1832. Wife of John Sharp, qv.
DC 31 Aug 1979.

4394   KINNEAR, Ayton, 1800-85. From Edinburgh.
s/o Robert K. To Megantic Co, QUE, 1831. Baker,
confectioner and miller. m Ann Boyd, qv, and had with
other ch: 1. James, qv; 2. Mary Fraser, 1820–1916;
3. Ayton, b 1825; 4. Alexander, 1829-70. **DC 2 Mar
1980**.

4395   KINNEAR, David, ca 1807–20 Nov 1862. From
Edinburgh. s/o George K, banker. Adm advocate, 1829,
but came to QUE and stld Drummondville. Editor of the
Montreal Gazette, and later of the *Montreal Herald*.
FAS 118; MDB 371.

4396   KINNEAR, James, 9 Oct 1818–28 Nov 1901.
From Edinburgh. s/o Ayton K, qv, and Mary Boyd, qv.
To QUE, 1831; stld Osgood Valley, Megantic Co. Miller,
shopkeeper and JP. m 1842, Harriet Wilson, and had
with other ch: 1. John L; 2. William; 3. George F;
4. James; 5. Maria. **AMC 142; MGC 2 Aug 1977**.

4397 KIRBY, Mrs. To Pictou Co, NS, 1815; res Little Harbour, 1816. Widow, with ch, and re-married. **INS 38.**

4398 KIRK, James. From Dumfries. To NS <1822; stld Lismore, Pictou Co. Son Adam, b 1822, merchant. **HNS iii 512.**

4399 KIRK, James. From St Andrews, FIF. s/o James K, 1749–1829, and Elspeth Russell, 1751–1832. To St John, NB. Merchant. **Ts St Andrews.**

4400 KIRK, John, d 21 Jun 1824. To NB, and d Letang. Capt of the ship *Nancy*, of Dumfries. **DGC 10 Aug 1824.**

4401 KIRKCUDBRIGHT, Mary, b ca 1843. To St Gabriel de Valcartier, QUE, prob <1856. **Census 1861.**

4402 KIRKHOPE, Jane, b ca 1793. To St Gabriel de Valcartier, QUE, prob <1856. **Census 1861.**

4403 KIRKLAND, Peggy, b 3 May 1794. From Is Islay, ARL. d/o William K, Bowmore par, and Marion McVoran. To Victoria Co, ONT, poss 1830. Wife of Archibald Sinclair, qv. **DC 21 Feb 1980.**

4404 KIRKNESS, Peter, 12 Dec 1825–19 May 1904. From OKI. To ONT, and d Mount Forest, Wellington Co. **SG xxii/1 24.**

4405 KIRKPATRICK, Andrew, 1829-68. From Torthorwald, DFS. s/o Joseph K, qv, and Elizabeth Creighton, qv. To West Farnham, Brome Co, QUE, <1846. m Ellen Berry. **DC 17 Nov 1981.**

4406 KIRKPATRICK, Isabella, 1833–1917. From Torthorwald, DFS. d/o Joseph K, qv, and Elizabeth Creighton, qv. To West Farnham, Brome Co, QUE, <1846. m William Quackenbush, who d 1904. **DC 17 Nov 1981.**

4407 KIRKPATRICK, Janet, 25 Feb 1815–24 May 1881. From Torthorwald, DFS. d/o Robert K, farmer, Beacon Hill, and Margaret Young. To QUE, ex Liverpool, 1850; stld West Farnham, Brome Co, QUE. Wife of James Douglas. **DC 17 Nov 1981.**

4408 KIRKPATRICK, Janet, b 1837. From Torthorwald, DFS. d/o Joseph K, qv, and Elizabeth Creighton, qv. To West Farnham, Brome Co, QUE, <1846. m Robert Burnet. **DC 17 Nov 1981.**

4409 KIRKPATRICK, Jean, b ca 1748. From Dumfries. To Georgetown, Kings Co, PEI, on the *Lovely Nellie*, ex Carsethorn, May 1775. Wife of Robert Braiden, qv. **ELN.**

4410 KIRKPATRICK, Joseph, 1 Mar 1805–31 Dec 1885. From Torthorwald, DFS. s/o Robert K, farmer, Beacon Hill, and Margaret Young. To West Farnham, Brome Co, QUE, <1846. m Elizabeth Creighton, qv, ch: 1. Andrew, 1825-28; 2. Robert, 1827–1909; 3. Andrew, qv; 4. John, 1831-62; 5. Isabella, qv; 6. Margaret, qv; 7. Janet, qv; 8. Mary, qv; 9. David, 1841–1918. **DC 17 Nov 1981.**

4411 KIRKPATRICK, Margaret, 1835–1910. From Torthorwald, DFS. d/o Joseph K, qv, and Elizabeth Creighton, qv. To West Farnham, Brome Co, QUE, <1846. m George Steinhour, who d 1914. **DC 17 Nov 1981.**

4412 KIRKPATRICK, Mary, 1839–1916. From Torthorwald, DFS. d/o Joseph K, qv, and Elizabeth Creighton, qv. To West Farnham, Brome Co, QUE,

<1846. m Alexander Grant, who d 1900. **DC 17 Nov 1981.**

4413 KIRKPATRICK, Samuel. To Aldborough Twp, Elgin Co, ONT, <1850. Postmaster at New Glasgow. m Effie, d/o Donald McGugan, qv, and Mary McIntyre, ch: 1. Thomas W, reeve; 2. Dr John; 3. Daniel, res West Lorne; 4 Henrietta, schoolteacher; 5. Mary. **PDA 28-29.**

4414 KIRKPATRICK, Sarah, 1806-51. Prob from Penpont, DFS. To ONT, ca 1842. Wife of John McNaught, qv. **DC 23 Oct 1981.**

4415 KIRKWOOD, David, ca 1833-70. From Glasgow. To Ekfrid Twp, Middlesex Co, ONT. m Elizabeth Phillips. **DC 15 Jul 1979.**

4416 KIRKWOOD, Matthew. To QUE on the *Commerce*, ex Greenock, Jun 1820; stld prob Lanark Co, ONT. **HCL 239.**

4417 KIRKWOOD, Mary, b ca 1793. Prob from ROX. To NS, 1817. Wife of Henry Leck, qv, m at Morebattle, ROX, 22 Nov 1812. **DC 1 Aug 1981.**

4418 KISSOCK, Elizabeth. To Kingston, ONT, ca 1805. m ca 1804, James Torrance, qv. **DC 18 Jul 1979.**

4419 KNIGHT, David, ca 1790–1874. From PER, poss Caputh. bro/o Emily K, qv. To Halton Co, ONT, prob 1830; stld Esquesing Twp. Farmer. m Catherine Moore, ch: 1. James; 2. John; 3. Robert; 4. Ephraim; 5. Amy. **EPE 75; DC 24 Nov 1979.**

4420 KNIGHT, Emily, ca 1805–2 Apr 1897. From PER, poss Caputh. sis/o David K, qv. To Esquesing Twp, Halton Co, ONT, 1830. Wife of John Dewar, qv. **DC 24 Nov 1979.**

4421 KNOX, Annie, 1824-96. From Hawick, ROX. To Winnipeg, MAN, 1854. Wife of Charles Scott, qv. **THS 1936/96.**

4422 KNOX, Catherine, b ca 1824. To St Gabriel de Valcartier, QUE, prob <1855. **Census 1861.**

4423 KNOX, Alison, b ca 1807. To St Gabriel de Valcartier, QUE, prob <1855. **Census 1861.**

4424 KNOX, John, b ca 1815. To St Gabriel de Valcartier, QUE, prob <1855. **Census 1861.**

4425 KNOX, Rev Robert, 1794–3 May 1825. Educ Univ of Edinburgh, where he grad MA, 1820. To Halifax, NS, and was asst min at St Matthews Ch until 1823. Retr to SCT and was ind to Ordiquill, BAN, 26 Sep 1823. **FES vi 292, vii 615; CEG 219.**

4426 KNOX, Rollo Campbell, ca 1827–24 Jul 1843. From Kilwinning, AYR. s/o James K. To Montreal, QUE, and was drowned there. **DGH 24 Aug 1843.**

4427 KNOX, Walter, b ca 1812. To St Gabriel de Valcartier, QUE, prob <1855. **Census 1861.**

4428 KNOX, William, b ca 1809. To St Gabriel de Valcartier, QUE, prob <1855. **Census 1861.**

4429 KYDD, Cecilia, 1803-89. From Brechin, ANS. To QUE, 1850; stld Bristol. Wife of David Smith, qv. **DC 15 Mar 1971.**

4430 KYLE, Jane. From Glasgow. To QUE, 1821; stld Lanark Co, ONT. Wife of John Robertson, qv. **SG xx/1 11.**

L

4431 LAIDLAW, Andrew, 28 May 1794–16 Aug 1874. From Ettrick par, SEL. s/o James L, qv, and Helen Scott. To Halton Co, ONT, ca 1818; stld Esquesing. m Agnes Quarrie, qv, ch: 1. James, 1816-18; 2. Isabella, 1818-91; 3. Helen, 1820-45; 4. James, 1822–1906; 5. George, 1823–1908; 6. Mary, 1826-44; 7. Robert B, 1828–1901; 8. Jane, 1830–1906; 9. Elizabeth, 1832–1901; 10. Margaret, 1834–1915; 11. William, 1836-40. **LDW 15 Mar 1968**.

4432 LAIDLAW, Christian, b ca 1800. From Southdean, ROX. To ONT, 1842; stld prob Bruce Co. Wife of William Gowanlock, qv. **DC 15 Oct 1975**.

4433 LAIDLAW, Douglas, b ca 1790. From Rulewater, ROX. s/o William L. and Helen Douglas. To CAN, where m Elizabeth Ross. Dau Mary Douglas. **DC 15 Oct 1975**.

4434 LAIDLAW, Elizabeth, ca 1781–20 Jul 1875. From Kirklandhill, Kirkconnel, DFS. Prob d/o Robert L. and Marion McCririck. To ONT, 1842; stld McKillop Twp, Huron Co. Wife of Robert McMillan, qv. **DC 26 May 1979**.

4435 LAIDLAW, George, ca 1828–6 Aug 1889. From ROC. s/o George L. To CAN <1850. Railway builder and farmer. **MDB 381**.

4436 LAIDLAW, Helen Esther, 1814-95. From Kirkconnel, DFS. Rel to Mary L, qv. To ONT, 1844; stld McKillop Twp, Huron Co. m (i) James Ferguson, from Loughborough, LEI, ch; (ii) James McDowell, qv. **DC 26 May 1979**.

4437 LAIDLAW, James, b 5 Apr 1763. From Hopehouse, Selkirk par, SEL. s/o Robert L. and Betty Biggar. To Halton Co, ONT, ca 1818; stld Esquesing Twp. Farmer. m Helen Scott, ch: 1. Mary, b 6 Sep 1791; 2. Robert, b 28 Sep 1792; 3. Andrew, qv; 4. James, jr, qv; 5. William, qv; 6. Walter, qv. **LDW 15 Mar 1968**.

4438 LAIDLAW, James, jr, 28 May 1796–23 Jul 1886. From Ettrick par, Selkirk par, SEL. s/o James L, qv, and Helen Scott. To Halton Co, ONT, ca 1818; stld Esquesing Twp. m Annie Henderson, ch: 1. James; 2. John; 3. Alexander; 4. Rev Robert J; 5. Margaret. **LDW 15 Mar 1968**.

4439 LAIDLAW, James. From Duns, BEW. To ONT, ca 1850; stld Gananoque Village, Leeds Co, ONT; later to Jacksonville, FL, and Hamilton, ONT. m Elizabeth Nuttal. **DC 23 Nov 1981**.

4440 LAIDLAW, Janet, ca 1793–26 Apr 1861. From Eskdalemuir, DFS. wid/o William Park in Halmains. To Durham, Grey Co, ONT, and d there. **Ts Eskdalemuir**.

4441 LAIDLAW, Rev John, d 1824. From Kelso, ROX. Min of Relief Ch successively at Banff, and at Dunning, PER. To Musquodoboit, Halifax Co, NS. Min there, but went to PA, ca 1820, and d Pittsburgh. **UPC ii 593**.

4442 LAIDLAW, John, ca 1790–31 Jan 1862. From Kirklandhill, Kirkconnel, DFS. s/o Robert L. and Marion McCririck. To ONT, 1834; stld Huron Co. Unm. **DC 26 May 1979**.

4443 LAIDLAW, John Douglas, b 1835. From Rulewater, ROX. s/o James L, tenant, and Isabella Turnbull. To Toronto, ONT. Grain merchant and storekeeper. m Ann McKeggie, ch. **LDW 15 Oct 1975**.

4444 LAIDLAW, Margaret. From Kirkconnel, DFS. To McKillop Twp, Huron Co, ONT, <1850. m James McMichael, qv, 1856. **DC 26 May 1979**.

4445 LAIDLAW, Mary, ca 1790–15 Sep 1880. From Kirklandhill, Kirkconnel, DFS. Prob d/o Robert L. and Marion McCririck. To McKillop Twp, Huron Co, ONT. Wife of Walter McMillan, qv. **DC 26 May 1979**.

4446 LAIDLAW, Robert. From ROX. To QUE on the *Sarah Mary Jane*, 1831; stld Paisley Block, Dumfries Twp, Waterloo Co, ONT. Son James with him. **HGD 60**.

4447 LAIDLAW, Thomas, 1825–1902. From ROX. s/o Robert L. and Elizabeth Irvine. To Guelph Twp, Wellington Co, ONT, 1831. Farmer. m Janet Martin, qv, ch: 1. Elizabeth Irvine, 1862–1933; 2. Thomas Robert, 1869-71. **DC 31 Dec 1979**.

4448 LAIDLAW, Walter, 23 Oct 1799–3 May 1873. From Ettrick par, SEL. s/o James L, qv, and Helen Scott. To Esquesing Twp, Halton Co, ONT, 1818. m Margaret Robertson, b 1810, ch: 1. Ellen, b 1828; 2. James, b 1830; 3. Catherine, b 1833; 4. Dr Alexander, 1835-65; 5. Robert, b 1837; 6. William, b 1839; 7. Duncan, 1841–1906; 8. Margaret, 1842–1919; 9. Walter, d inf, 1844. **LDW 15 Mar 1968**.

4449 LAIDLAW, William, 31 Jan 1798–5 Jan 1839. From Ettrick par, SEL. s/o James L, qv, and Helen Scott. To Halton Co, ONT, ca 1818; stld Esquesing Twp. m Mary Scott, d 1868; ch: 1. James; 2. Ellen; 3. John S; 4. Robert; 5. Thomas; 6. Jane, d 1866. **LDW 15 Mar 1968**.

4450 LAIDLAW, William, ca 1804–13 Sep 1870. From Kirklandhill, Kirkconnel, DFS. Prob s/o Robert L. and Marion McCririck. To ONT, ca 1855; stld Turnberry, Huron Co. Farmer. m Catherine Dalzeill, qv, ch: 1. Jane, b 1829; 2. Robert; 3. James, b 1833; 4. Alexander, 1836-58; 5. Marion, b 1838; 6. John, b 1841; 7. Margaret, b 1844; 8. Catherine, b 1849. **DC 26 May 1979**.

4451 LAING, Alexander, b ca 1778. From Old Deer, ABD. s/o George L. To QUE, ex Greenock, summer 1815; stld Beech Ridge, Chateauguay Co. Accountant in Montreal, later farmer. m 9 May 1809, Ann Watt, qv, ch: 1. John, qv; 2. Elizabeth, qv; 3. Alexander, 1814-20; 4. Jean, qv; 5. Margaret, b 17 Feb 1817; 6. James, b 26 Dec 1818; 7. George, b 24 Feb 1822; 8. Ann, b 1 May 1824. **SEC 4; DC 29 Oct 1978 and 27 May 1980**.

4452 LAING, Elizabeth, b 21 May 1812. From Old Deer, ABD. d/o Alexander L, qv, and Ann Watt, qv. To QUE, ex Greenock, summer 1815; stld Valetta, East Tilbury Twp, Kent Co, ONT. m 1827, James Ainslie, farmer, Beech Ridge, Chateauguay Co, QUE, ch. **SEC 4; DC 29 Oct 1978 and 27 May 1980**.

4453 LAING, Elizabeth, 1817–25 Jun 1902. From MOR. To Oshawa Village, Ontario Co, ONT. Wife of William Smith, qv. **DC 6 Sep 1979**.

4454 LAING, Jean, b 28 Jun 1815, Greenock, RFW. d/o Alexander L, qv, and Ann Watt, qv, both from ABD. To QUE, ex Greenock, summer 1815; stld Comber, Essex Co, ONT. m William, b 1815, s/o Richard Stacey, from Wexford, IRL, ch: 1. Elizabeth, b 1844; 2. Ann, b 1846; 3. Mary Jane, b 1848; 4. James, b 1851; 5. Alexander, b 1855; 6. William Richard, b 1860. **SEC 4; DC 29 Oct and 27 May 1980**.

4455   LAING, John, b 3 Nov 1810. From Old Deer, ABD. s/o Alexander L, qv, and Ann Watt, qv. To QUE, summer 1815, ex Greenock; stld Valetta, East Tilbury Twp, Kent Co, ONT. Farmer. m 16 Jul 1840, Mary Ann, d/o William Hope and Isabella Ainslie, ch: 1. Ann, b 20 May 1841; 2. Isabella, b 8 Apr 1843; 3. Alexander, b 13 Jan 1845; 4. Elizabeth, b 3 Feb 1847; 5. William, b 1 May 1849; 6. James, b 5 Feb 1851; 7. John, b 14 Jan 1853; 8. Mary Jane, b 1 Jan 1855; 9. George, b 3 Apr 1857; 10. Ellen Eliza, b 24 Apr 1859; 11. Albert Thomas, b 27 Jan 1863; 12. Walter Charles, b 6 Jun 1865. **SEC 4; DC 29 Oct 1978 and 27 May 1980**.

4456   LAING, Rev John, b 1828. From ROC. To ONT, poss with parents, 1843. Studied at Knox Coll and Kings Coll, Toronto. Ord min of Scarborough, 1854. Trans to Cobourg, 1860; to Ladies Coll, Ottawa, 1872, and to Dundas, 1873. ch. **BNA 870**.

4457   LAING, Miss, d 5 Oct 1838. From OKI. d/o Robert L. To Gore Twp, Perth Co, ONT. m Alexander Mackenzie Shaw, Glenshaw. **DGC 21 Nov 1838**.

4458   LAIRD, Alexander. From RFW. To Queens Co, PEI, 1819. Farmer and Liberal politician. ch incl: 1. Alexander, b 1830, politician; 2. David, 1833–1914, journalist, and became Lt Gov of NWT. **BNA 715-717**.

4459   LAIRD, Francis O. From Ballater, ABD. To Sarnia Twp, Lambton Co, ONT. m Eliza Patterson, qv. Son Alexander, 1853–1915, banker. **DC 30 Aug 1977**.

4460   LAMB, Ann, b 1817. From Kincardine par, PER. d/o James L, qv, and Elizabeth McFarlane, qv. To QUE, 1831; stld Ottawa Co. m Alexander Gordon, St Andrews. **DJL 2**.

4461   LAMB, Elizabeth. From Glasgow. sis/o James L. To Halifax, NS, 1828; moved to Westmorland Co, NB. **DC 17 Apr 1981**.

4462   LAMB, Eloise. Poss from BEW. gr-d/o Robert L. in Templehall. To Fredericton, NB, <1829. **SH**.

4463   LAMB, Helen, b Aug 1813. From Kincardine par, PER. d/o James L, qv, and Elizabeth McFarlane, qv. To QUE, 1831; stld Lochaber, Ottawa Co. m John Edwards, Rockland, Russell Co, ONT, ch: 1. Alexander; 2. John; 3. James; 4. William; 5. Margaret. **DJL 2**.

4464   LAMB, James. From Glasgow. bro/o Elizabeth L, qv. To Halifax, NS, 1828; moved to Westmorland Co, NB. Stonecutter. m Janet, d/o John Murray, qv. **DC 17 Apr 1981**.

4465   LAMB, James, 21 Jul 1776–8 Jun 1855. From Thornhill, PER. s/o John L. and Mary McArthur. To QUE, 1831; stld Lochaber, Ottawa Co. Farmer. Wife Elizabeth McFarlane, qv, with him, and ch: 1. John, qv; 2. Elizabeth, dy; 3. Helen, qv; 4. William, qv; 5. Ann, qv; 6. Margaret, qv; 7. Janet, qv; 8. James, qv. **DJL 1**.

4466   LAMB, James, jr, 26 Aug 1829–16 Apr 1914. From Kincardine par, PER. s/o James L, qv, and Elizabeth McFarlane, qv. To QUE, 1831; stld Lochaber, Ottawa Co. Farmer. m Sarah Ann Baker, ch: 1. Margaret Baker, 1856-88; 2. James Edgar, 1858-92; 3. John Dewar, 1860-90; 4. Peter Osborne, 1862–1940; 5. Elizabeth Ann, 1864-83; 6. Helen Edwards, 1867–1952; 7. Lucy Janet, 1872–1955; 8. Francis Dorothy, 1878–1948. **DJL 3**.

4467   LAMB, Janet, b Apr 1824. From Kincardine par, PER. d/o James L, and Elizabeth McFarlane, qv. To QUE, 1831; stld Lochaber, Ottawa Co. m Alexander McLean, ch: 1. Janet; 2. Mary; 3. Elizabeth; 4. Margaret; 5. Alexander. **DJL 2**.

4468   LAMB, John. From LKS. To QUE on the *Prompt*, ex Greenock, 4 Jul 1820; stld Lanark Co, ONT. **HCL 238**.

4469   LAMB, John, 8 Oct 1809–10 May 1895. From Kincardine par, PER. s/o James L, qv, and Elizabeth McFarlane, qv. To QUE, 1831; stld Lochaber, Ottawa Co. Millwright. m Mary Dewar, 1811-85, ch: 1. Elizabeth Jane, 1836-68; 2. Catherine, b 1838; 3. James Byrne, 1841–1923; 4. William Alexander, 1843–1935; 5. Mary, 1846-47; 6. Mary Ann, b 1848; 7. John Harcus, 1850–1936. **DJL 2**.

4470   LAMB, Margaret, b Oct 1820. From Kincardine par, PER. d/o James L, qv, and Elizabeth McFarlane, qv. To QUE, 1831; stld Lochaber, Ottawa Co. m John McLean, ch: 1. Florence; 2. Jennie; 3. Jennie; 4. James; 5. William; 6. John; 7. Donald. **DJL 2**.

4471   LAMB, William, 6 Aug 1815–1894. From Kincardine par, PER. s/o James L, qv, and Elizabeth McFarlane, qv. To QUE, 1831; stld Lochaber, Ottawa Co, later Clarence Creek, Russell Co, ONT. Farmer. m Margaret Gordon, d 1902, ch: 1. William; 2. James; 3. John; 4. Helen; 5. Gordon, 1865–1950, res Goderich, Huron Co, ONT. **DJL**.

4472   LAMBIE, Rev James, 1805–16 Sep 1847. Born Tarbolton, AYR. s/o James L, farmer. Matric Univ of Glasgow, 1818, and grad MA, 1822. To Pickering and Whitby, ONT, 1841. **GMA 10055; FES vii 638**.

4473   LAMBIE, John, 1797–1865. From AYR. To Leeds Twp, Megantic Co, QUE, ca 1815. m Mary Boyd, qv. **DC 2 Mar 1982**.

4474   LAMOND, Alexander. To PEI, poss 1803; stld nr Belfast. Petitioner for Dr MacAulay, 1811. **HP 74**.

4475   LAMOND, Jane. Rel to Marion L, qv. To Pictou, NS, on the *Ellen*, ex Lochlaxford, SUT, 22 May 1848. **DC 15 Jul 1979**.

4476   LAMOND, John. Poss from North Uist, INV. To Mira River, Cape Breton Co, NS, 1828. Dau Maria, qv. **DC 7 Oct 1964**.

4477   LAMOND, Margaret, ca 1770–5 Jun 1840. From PER. To Halton Co, ONT, prob 1817; stld Esquesing Twp. Bur Boston cemetery. m John Stewart, qv. **EPE 75**.

4478   LAMOND, Maria. Poss from North Uist, INV. d/o John L, qv. To Mira River, Cape Breton Co, NS, 1828. m Hector McNeil, qv. **DC 7 Oct 1964**.

4479   LAMOND, Marion. Rel to Jane L, qv. To Pictou, NS, on the *Ellen*, ex Lochlaxford, SUT, 22 May 1848. **DC 15 Jul 1979**.

4480   LAMONT, Archibald, 1810–1900. From Is Mull, ARL. s/o Duncan L, qv, and Mary MacArthur, qv. To Markham Twp, York Co, ONT, 1821; moved to Caledon Twp, and later to Saugeen Twp, Bruce Co. Farmer. m Margaret McKechnie, qv, and had, with other ch: 1. Sarah; 2. William; 3. Robert; 4. Donald; 5. Alexander; 6. John, sometime in Santa Fé, NM. **DC 7 Jan 1982**.

4481 LAMONT, Archibald. From Is Islay, ARL. To Caradoc Twp, Middlesex Co, ONT, 1841. ch: 1. Donald; 2. John, res Strathroy; 3. Archie, farmer; 4. Mrs D.A. Campbell. **PCM 35**.

4482 LAMONT, Catherine, b ca 1794. From Is Mull, ARL. Step-d/o John McEachern, qv, and d/o his wife Margaret. To Charlottetown, PEI, on the *Clarendon*, ex Oban, 6 Aug 1808. **CPL**.

4483 LAMONT, Donald. From Caolasraide, South Knapdale, ARL. To Lobo Twp, Middlesex Co, ONT, 1820. ch: 1. Duncan; 2. Peter; 3. John; 4. Mary; 5. Isabella; 6. Rachel; 7. Christie. **PCM 38**.

4484 LAMONT, Donald. From Is Mull, ARL. To ONT, ca 1854; stld poss York Co. Wife Mary Carmichael, qv, with him, and s Duncan Carmichael, qv. **DC 7 Jan 1982**.

4485 LAMONT, Duncan, 1802-67. From Caolasraide, South Knapdale, ARL. To Lobo Twp, Middlesex Co, ONT, 1820. Deacon of the Baptist Ch. **PCM 15**.

4486 LAMONT, Duncan, 20 Jun 1778–14 Aug 1821. From Is Ulva, Kilninian and Kilmore par, Is Mull, ARL. To QUE, 1821, and d on the passage from Lachine to Kingston, ONT. m Mary McArthur, qv, ch: 1. Flora, b 1803; 2. John, b 1804; 3. Duncan, b 1805; 4. Donald; 5. Archibald, qv; 6. Marion, b 1811; 7. Sarah, qv; 8. Catherine, b 1813, poss d inf; 9. Catherine, b 1814; 10. Kirsty, b 1816; 11. Hector, b 1821. **DC 26 Feb 1981 and 7 Jan 1982**.

4487 LAMONT, Duncan Carmichael, 1837–4 Oct 1917. From Is Mull, ARL. s/o Donald L, qv, and Mary Carmichael, qv. To Cheltenham, Peel Co, ONT, ca 1854, and d Orangeville, Dufferin Co. m Margaret Robson Henderson, and had with other ch: 1. John Henderson, 1865–1936, Judge of the Supreme Court; 2. Catherine. **DC 7 Jan 1982**.

4488 LAMONT, Hector. From Is South Uist, INV. To QUE on the *Admiral*, ex Lochboisdale, 17 Aug 1851; stld ONT. Crofter. **DC 21 Mar 1981**.

4489 LAMONT, Rev Hugh, 1835–26 May 1897. From Is Iona, ARL. Educ Univ of Edinburgh, and Queens Coll, Kingston, ONT. Ord min of Finch Twp, Stormont Co, ONT, 1865. Retr to SCT and was min at Kilmeny, Is Islay, ARL, 1870-72. Re-adm to Finch and was later at Dalhousie Mills, NB, Lake Megantic, QUE, and Little Metis. **FES iv 77; vii 638**.

4490 LAMONT, Joseph. To QUE on the *Brock*, ex Greenock, 9 Jul 1820; stld prob Lanark Co, ONT. **HCL 238**.

4491 LAMONT, Neil, 1788–1853. From Is Mull, ARL. To Caledon Twp, Peel Co, ONT, <1840. Wife Catherine Black, qv, with him. **DC 21 Apr 1980**.

4492 LAMONT, Neil, b 1792. From Is Tyree, ARL. s/o John L. To Bruce Co, ONT, 1850. Farmer. **DC 21 Mar 1981**.

4493 LAMONT, Neil. From ARL. To Lobo Twp, Middlesex Co, ONT, 1850. ch: 1. Archibald; 2. Mary; 3. Euphemia; 4. Lily; 5. Nettie; 6. Annie; 7. Hannah; 8. Ella. **PCM 39**.

4494 LAMONT, Norman. From Cowal dist, ARL. To Lobo Twp, Middlesex Co, ONT, via NY, 1831, and d Strathroy, Adelaide Twp, ch. **PCM 39**.

4495 LAMONT, Peter, b 1800. From Is Tyree, ARL. s/o John L. To Bruce Co, ONT, 1850. Farmer of 500 acres. m Ann McLean, ch. **DC 21 Mar 1981**.

4496 LAMONT, Samuel. From Bowmore, Is Islay, ARL. To Fort Churchill, Hudson Bay, on the *Prince of Wales*, 1813. Went to York Factory, Apr 1814, thence to Red River. **LSS 186; RRS 27; LSC 323**.

4497 LAMONT, Sarah, 1812-95. From Torosay, Is Mull, ARL. d/o Duncan L, qv, and Mary McArthur, qv. To QUE, 1821; stld Markham Twp, York Co, ONT, later Saugeen Twp, Bruce Co. m 1839, Joseph Schell, who d 1879, ch. **DC 7 Jan 1982**.

4498 LANDELL, George Richardson, 2 May 1785– 6 Aug 1834. s/o Rev James L, par min, and Janet Heriot. Sometime Lt of Marines, and lost arm at Trafalgar. To Montreal, QUE, and d there. **FES ii 39; Ts Coldingham**.

4499 LANDSBOROUGH, Agnes, 1812-99. From KKD, poss Girthon par. To Huron Co, ONT, 1833. m Robert Carnochan, qv. **DC 27 Jun 1981**.

4500 LANDSBOROUGH, Jane, 1815-99. From KKD, poss Girthon par. To Huron Co, ONT, 1833. m James Carnochan, qv. **DC 27 Jun 1981**.

4501 LANDSBURGH, Eliza. From Lochenbreck, KKD. To Hamilton, ONT, <29 Jul 1844, when m John Landsburgh. **DGH 17 Oct 1844**.

4502 LANG, Andrew. To QUE on the *Earl of Buckinghamshire*, ex Greenock, 29 Apr 1821; stld Lanark Co, ONT. **HCL 73**.

4503 LANG, Ann. From Kilbirnie, AYR. To ONT, 1854; stld prob Huron Co. m (i) John Jamieson, qv; (ii) John McMillan, qv. **DC 26 May 1979**.

4504 LANG, Arthur. Prob from LKS. To QUE on the *Earl of Buckinghamshire*, ex Greenock, 29 Apr 1821; stld Lanark Co, ONT, at Lot 14, Con 10, Ramsay Twp. Farmer and schoolteacher. Wife and ch with him. **HCL 80, 85, 180**.

4505 LANG, Daniel. From ARL. s/o Hector L, qv, and wife Isabella. To Aldborough Twp, Elgin Co, ONT, 1853. Farmer, fisherman and local politician. m 1868, Ann Jane Graham, ch: 1. Hector, MLA; 2. Col Malcolm, MP; 3. A. Wilson; 4. Daniel, barrister; 5. Mrs J.B. Ferguson; 6. Mrs Elmer E. Hench; 7. Belle, res St Thomas. **PDA 31**.

4506 LANG, Rev Gavin, 1791–25 Aug 1869. Born Paisley, RFW. s/o Robert L. and Euphemia Morrison. Matric Univ of Glasgow, 1814. Ord 1829 and made min of Shelburne, NS, 1829. Retr to SCT and was min at Glasford, LKS, 1832-69. m 1829, Anna Robertson, ch: 1. David Marshall, 1830–1912; 2. Anna Hamilton, 1831–1908; 3. Robert, d inf; 4. Rev John Marshall, 1834–1909; 5. Rev Gavin, 1835–1919, min of St Andrews Ch, Montreal; 6. Sir Robert, 1836–1913; 7. Euphemia Morrison, b 1838; 8. Elizabeth Stobie, b 1840; 9. Jane, b 1841; 10. Margaret Wiseman, b 1843; 11. Rev James Paisley, b 1846; 12. Alexander, b 1848, London manager of the Bank of Montreal. **BNA 872; GMA 9093; FES iii 255, vii 615**.

4507 LANG, Hector. From ARL. To ONT, 1853; stld Aldborough Twp, Elgin Co, ONT. Wife Isabella with him, and ch: 1. Malcolm, sailor, drowned 1858; 2. Daniel, qv; 3. Christina; 4. Mary; 5. Flora; 6. Isabella.   **PDA 30**.

4508   LANG, Isabel, b ca 1804. To St Gabriel de Valcartier, QUE, prob <1855.   **Census 1861**.

4509   LANG, John. Prob from LKS, and s/o Arthur L, qv. To QUE on the *Earl of Buckinghamshire*, ex Greenock, 29 Apr 1821; stld Ramsay Twp, Lanark Co, ONT. Sawyer at Almonte.   **HCL 81**.

4510   LANG, John, b ca 1803. To St Gabriel de Valcartier, QUE, prob <1855.   **Census 1861**.

4511   LANG, Robert, b 1834. From Lesmahagow, LKS. To ONT, 1833. m Marion Watson, qv, ch: 1. Janet; 2. James; 3. William; 4. Robert, b ONT, 1834. **DC 6 May 1978**.

4512   LANGMUIR, John Woodburn, b 6 Nov 1835, Warwick Mains, Irvine, AYR. To ONT, 1849. Founder of the Toronto General Trust Company.   **SNQ vi/1 50**.

4513   LATIMER, Mary. To Simcoe Co, ONT, 1847; stld Stroud. Wife of Colin Black, qv.   **DC 21 Mar 1981**.

4514   LAUCHLAND, William, b ca 1835. From Beith, AYR. To Oshawa Twp, Durham Co, ONT. m Ann Jane, d/o James Barclay, qv, and Hannah Carolyn Parnham, ch: 1. Carolyn Isabel, 1868-94; 2. James Parnham, 1869-93; 3. Anne Louise, 1872-74; 4. William George, b 1873; 5. Ada Florence, b 1875, d inf; 6. Dr Lyman Craig, 1878–1935, res Dundas; 7. Norman Lee, 1881–1950; 8. Harold Stanley, 1884-86.   **BOP 57**.

LAURENCE. See also LAWRENCE.

4515   LAURENCE, George C. From Melrose, ROX. To Port Hood, Inverness Co, NS, <1840. Sheriff of Inverness Co. m Helen Turnbull, qv, with at least two ch: 1. Henry T, 1841–1916, MLA; 2. Frederick Andrew, 1843–1912, MLA.   **MLA 184**.

LAURIE. See also LAWRIE.

4516   LAURIE, Alexander. To Pictou, NS, on the *London*, arr 14 Jul 1848.   **DC 15 Jul 1979**.

4517   LAURIE, Andrew, 1823-43. From Caerlaverock, DFS. s/o William L. and Janet Hunter. To St Johns, NFD, and d there.   **Ts Caerlaverock**.

4518   LAURIE, Jean. Poss from Kilmarnock, AYR. d/o Robert L. To CAN <1853.   **SH**.

4519   LAURIE, Robert, ca 1790–20 Jan 1838. From Cummertrees, DFS. s/o David L, Kelhead Quarry, and Elspeth Watson. To Tatamagouche, Colchester Co, NS. **Ts Cummertrees**.

4520   LAVEROCK, James, ca 1824–21 Jul 1864. From Kennoway, FIF. To Montreal, QUE; later to Howick, Chateauguay Co. Baker.   **DC 19 Nov 1982**.

4521   LAW, George, 11 Mar 1812–16 Dec 1871. From Blackieburn, Crawfordjohn, LKS, but sometime of Wanlockhead, DFS. To Cornwall Twp, Stormont Co, ONT, 1854; later to Sciota Twp, Dakota Co, MN, USA. Lead-miner, later farmer. m Isabella Carlaw, qv, ch: 1. James, b 1836; 2. Jane, b 1838; 3. Margaret, b 1840; 4. John, b 1842; 5. Margaret, b 1844; 6. Ebenezer, b 1847; 7. Archibald, b 1851; 8. Walter Tweedie, b 1855; 9. Agnes Dalziel, b 1859; 10. George, b 1862. **DC 20 Jan 1980**.

4522   LAW, Rev George. From Fetteresso, KCD. Matric Kings Coll, Aberdeen, 1850. To NS, 1863, as missionary. Adm min at Chinguacousy, York Co, ONT, 1866. **FES vii 639**.

4523   LAW, James, 1812-68. From Kirkoswald, AYR. To Montreal, QUE, 1831. Merchant with firm of Isaac Buchanan & Co. Unm.   **SGC 502**.

LAWRENCE. See also LAURENCE.

4524   LAWRENCE, Andrew, ca 1796–30 Apr 1884. From Newton of Kinmundy, Old Deer, ABD. To QUE on the *Beatrice*, Apr 1854; stld Ashburn, East Whitby Twp, Durham Co, ONT. m (i) 19 Aug 1826, Mary Murray, 1805-26, ch: 1. Andrew, jr, qv. m (ii) 18 Dec 1828, Mary Ann Sim, qv, further ch: 2. James, qv; 3. John, qv; 4. Isabella, 1840–1921, unm; 5. William, b 24 Sep 1843; 6. Charles, b 3 Apr 1849, dy.   **DC 23 Jul 1979**.

4525   LAWRENCE, Andrew, jr, 31 Oct 1826–1907. From Old Deer, ABD. s/o Andrew L, qv, and Mary Murray, his first wife. To Ashburn Village, East Whitby Twp, Durham Co, ONT, <1854. Kept a harness shop along with bro James, qv. m Mary Keith, qv, in CAN, ch: 1. Beatrice or Betsy, b ca 1855; 2. Mary Ann, b ca 1858; 3. Margaret, b ca 1860; 4. John; 5. Andrew, twin with John.   **DC 23 Jul 1979**.

4526   LAWRENCE, James, 4 Feb 1832–2 May 1921. From Old Deer, ABD. s/o Andrew L, qv, and Mary Ann Sim, qv. To Ashburn Village, East Whitby Twp, Durham Co, ONT, <1854. Kept harness shop with bro Andrew, qv. m Jane Findlay, qv, ch: 1. Jane, dy; 2. Christine, res Toronto; 3. James, went to CA; 4. John, went to Detroit, MI.   **DC 23 Jul 1979**.

4527   LAWRENCE, John, 25 Aug 1834–27 Apr 1896. From Old Deer, ABD. s/o Andrew L, qv, and Mary Ann Sim, qv. To QUE on the *Beatrice*, Apr 1854; stld Ashburn, East Whitby Co, ONT. m Annie Calder, d 1914, ch: 1. Emily, unm; 2. John.   **DC 23 Jul 1979**.

LAWRIE. See also LAURIE.

4528   LAWRIE, Barbara. From Aberdeen. d/o David L, comb manufacturer. To ONT, prob <1850. m James Hogg.   **SH**.

4529   LAWRIE, John, b ca 1802. From LKS. To Scarborough, York Co, ONT, 1830. Weaver.   **DC 29 Mar 1981**.

4530   LAWRIE, Rev William. From ANS. Grad MA, Kings Coll, Aberdeen, 1825. Episcopal clergyman in CAN.   **KCG 281**.

4531   LAWRIN, John. To QUE on the *Brock*, ex Greenock, 9 Jul 1820; stld prob Lanark Co, ONT. **HCL 238**.

4532   LAWS, Valentine, b ca 1785. To Pictou, NS, 1815; res Pictou town, 1816. House carpenter, m with 2 ch.   **INS 39**.

4533   LAWSON, Angus, b ca 1825. From ANS. To CAN, 1854. m Mary Ann Herd, ch.   **SG xxviii/1 39**.

4534   LAWSON, Ann, 1804–31 Jul 1869. From PER. To Esquesing Twp, Halton Co, ONT, prob <1830. Bur Acton. Wife of Andrew Scott, qv.   **EPE 74**.

4535   LAWSON, David, d ca 1797. From Callendar, PER. To Richmond Bay, PEI, on the *Falmouth*, ex

Greenock, 8 Apr 1770; stld Stanhope, Queens Co. Miller, farmer and agent for Sir James Montgomery of Stanhope, Bt, proprietor of Lot 34. Wife Ellen with him, and ch: 1. William, qv; 2. James, qv; 3. John, qv; 4. Isabella, qv; 5. Elizabeth, qv. **DC 28 May 1980.**

4536 LAWSON, Elizabeth, 1756–1835. From Callendar, PER. d/o David L, qv. To PEI on the *Falmouth*, ex Greenock, 8 Apr 1770; stld Stanhope, Queens Co. m James Curtis, 1750–1819, agent for Sir James Montgomery of Stanhope, Bt, and Speaker of the House of Assembly. **DC 28 May 1980.**

4537 LAWSON, George, 12 Oct 1827–10 Nov 1895. From Newport, FIF. s/o Alexander L. and Margaret McEwen. Educ Univ of Edinburgh. Prof of Chemistry successively at Queens Univ, Kingston, ONT, and Dalhousie Univ, Halifax, NS. PhD, LLD, and author. m (i) Lucy, d 1871, d/o Charles Stapley, Tunbridge Wells, Kent, ENG, ch: (ii) 1876, Caroline Matilda, d/o William Jordan, Halifax, NS, and wid/o George A. Knox. **MDB 399.**

4538 LAWSON, Henry, ca 1789–20 Mar 1874. From PER. To Goshen, Upper Stewiacke, Colchester Co, NS. m Elizabeth, d/o Alexander Stewart, qv, and Elizabeth Taylor Fisher. Dau Esther. **NSN 9/5.**

4539 LAWSON, Isabella, ca 1755–17 Sep 1835. From Callendar, PER. d/o David L, qv. To Richmond Bay, PEI, on the *Falmouth*, ex Greenock, 8 Apr 1770; stld Stanhope, Queens Co. m ca 1777, Cornelius Higgins, 1735–1825, magistrate, Covehead, ch. **DC 28 May 1980.**

4540 LAWSON, James, ca 1760–10 Nov 1833. From Callendar, PER. s/o David L, qv. To Richmond Bay, PEI, on the *Falmouth*, ex Greenock, 8 Apr 1770; stld Covehead, Queens Co. m 20 Jul 1797, Elizabeth, 1771–1850, d/o John Miller, qv, and Catherine McIvor, qv, ch. **DC 28 May 1980.**

4541 LAWSON, John, b ca 1746. From Callendar, PER. s/o David L, qv. To Richmond Bay, PEI, on the *Falmouth*, ex Greenock, 8 Apr 1770; stld Stanhope, Queens Co. Farmer, and mem of first House of Assembly at Charlottetown. Son John, bap 3 Mar 1771 by Rev William Drummond, qv. **DC 28 May 1980.**

4542 LAWSON, Margaret G, 1802–90. From PER. To Halton Co, ONT, prob <1840; stld Esquesing Twp. Wife of David Somerville, qv. **EPE 76.**

4543 LAWSON, Martha, d 1849. To Hamilton, ONT, 1829. Wife of James Paterson, qv. **DC 23 Sep 1980.**

4544 LAWSON, William, 1744–1836. From Mill of Callendar, PER. s/o David L, qv. To Richmond Bay, PEI, on the *Falmouth*, ex Greenock, 8 Apr 1770; stld Stanhope, Queens Co. Farmer, and mem of first House of Assembly, Charlottetown, 1773. m (i) ca 1773, Mary Shaw, qv, ch; m (ii) 30 Nov 1792, Ann Graham, d 1824, from Halifax, further ch. **DC 28 May 1980.**

4545 LAYTON, David Stark, ca 1813–25 Oct 1866. From KRS. s/o Capt Thomas L, Lanarkshire Militia, and Sarah Spark. To ONT, and d Manitowaning, Manitoulin Is, Lake Huron. Surgeon. **Ts Kinross.**

LEACH. See also LEITCH.

4546 LEACH, Rev William Turnbull, 2 Mar 1805–18 Oct 1886. From Berwick-on-Tweed. Educ Univ of Edinburgh. To ONT as a missionary, and in 1835 adm min of St Andrews Ch, Toronto. Trans to York Mills, 1842, but joined Ch of England. Later prof at McGill Univ. m (i) d/o David Skirving, farmer, ELN, ch: 1. David, solicitor. m (ii) d/o Rev Robert Easton, Montreal; and (iii) Miss Gwilt, Montreal. **FES vii 639; CEG 222.**

4547 LEACHMAN, James. To Montreal, QUE, on the *Royal George*, ex Greenock, Jan 1827; stld Sarnia, Lambton Co, ONT. **DC 19 Nov 1978.**

4548 LEAPER, James, b ca 1770. To Pictou, NS, 1815; res Pictou town, 1816. Chainmaker, unm. **INS 39.**

4549 LEARMONTH, Agnes, 1799–1876. From Athelstaneford, ELN. d/o Alexander L, qv, and Margaret Pringle, qv. To Megantic Co, QUE, prob <1841. m — Harkness. **DC 15 Feb 1980.**

4550 LEARMONTH, Alexander, 1771–1851. From Athelstaneford, ELN. To Leeds Twp, Megantic Co, QUE, ca 1830. m Margaret Pringle, qv, ch: 1. William P, qv; 2. Agnes, qv; 3. Robert, qv; 4. Francis, ca 1802–ca 1874, d Fitzroy Harbour, Carleton Co, ONT; 5. George, qv; 6. Anne, qv; 7. James, qv. **DC 15 Feb 1980.**

4551 LEARMONTH, Anne, 1814–94. From Athelstaneford, ELN. d/o Alexander L, qv, and Margaret Pringle, qv. To Megantic Co, QUE, <1841; later to Arnprior, Renfrew Co, ONT. m George Young. **DC 15 Feb 1980.**

4552 LEARMONTH, George, 1810–82. From Athelstaneford, ELN. s/o Alexander L, qv, and Margaret Pringle, qv. To Megantic Co, QUE, prob <1841; stld later at Fitzroy Harbour, Carleton Co, ONT. m Anne Fraser, ch: 1. Elizabeth, 1857–1943; 2. Margaret P, 1867–1941; 3. Jessie Fraser, 1872–1950; 4. Mary Ann, 1869–1956; 5. Read, 1874–1916; 6. George, 1859–1907; 7. Alexander, 1861–1917; 8. Francis, 1862–1912; 9. John Fraser, 1864–1928. **DC 15 Feb 1980.**

4553 LEARMONTH, James. From Athelstaneford, ELN. s/o Alexander L, qv, and Margaret Pringle, qv. Prob to Megantic Co, QUE, <1840, but stld Fitzroy Harbour, Carleton Co, ONT. m Catherine, d/o Angus McGillvrey, qv, and Mary McDonald, ch. **DC 15 Feb 1980.**

4554 LEARMONTH, Robert, 1800–83. From Athelstaneford, ELN. s/o Alexander L, qv, and Margaret Pringle, qv. To Megantic Co, QUE, prob <1841, and d Quebec. m Christine Fair, qv, ch: 1. Alexander; 2. Gavin; 3. Janette; 4. Robert, who d at Buffalo, NY. **DC 15 Feb 1980.**

4555 LEARMONTH, William P, 22 Mar 1796–28 Mar 1883. From Athelstaneford, ELN. s/o Alexander L, qv, and Margaret Pringle, qv. To Leeds Twp, Megantic Co, QUE, ca 1830. m Agnes Dobie, qv, ch: 1. James, b 1843; 2. Margaret, b 1831; 3. Robert, b 1840; 4. James, b 1845; 5. George, b 1846. **DC 15 Feb 1980.**

4556 LEASK, Alexander, b 19 Jul 1827. From Ryland, Alvah par, BAN. s/o Peter L, qv, and Marjorie Ledingham, qv. To QUE, 1841, and stld Darlington Twp, Durham Co, ONT; later Brock Twp, Ontario Co. Farmer. **DC 9 Jun 1980.**

4557 LEASK, David, b 6 Oct 1833. From Ryland,

Alvah par, BAN. s/o Peter L, qv, and Marjorie Ledingham, qv. To Darlington Twp, Durham Co, ONT, 1841; stld later Uxbridge, Durham Co. Farmer. m Sarah J. Horn. **DC 9 Jun 1980**.

4558   LEASK, George, b 7 Jan 1822. From Ryland, Alvah par, BAN. s/o Peter L, qv, and Marjorie Ledingham, qv. To Darlington Twp, Durham Co, ONT, 1841. Farmer and miller. m Margaret Ledingham, qv. **DC 9 Jun 1980**.

4559   LEASK, Helen, b 30 Oct 1823. From Ryland, Alvah par, BAN. d/o Peter L, qv, and Marjorie Ledingham, qv. To Darlington Twp, Durham Co, ONT, ca 1841. m George Leask, farmer. **DC 9 Jun 1980**.

4560   LEASK, James, b 25 Oct 1825. From Ryland, Alvah par, BAN. s/o Peter L, qv, and Marjorie Ledingham, qv. To QUE, 1841; stld Darlington Twp, Durham Co, ONT. Farmer and sawyer. m Jane Ledingham, qv. **DC 9 Jun 1980**.

4561   LEASK, James. From SHI. To Windham Twp, Norfolk Co, ONT. Wife Jane Sinclair, qv, with him, and dau Ellen, 1837–1901. **DC 20 Jul 1979**.

4562   LEASK, John, b 4 Apr 1829. From Ryland, Alvah par, BAN. s/o Peter L, qv, and Marjorie Ledingham, qv. To Darlington Twp, Durham Co, ONT, 1841; stld later Greenbank, Reach Twp, Ontario Co. Farmer. m Marion O. Henry. **DC 9 Jun 1980**.

4563   LEASK, Margaret, b 8 May 1818. From Ryland, Alvah par, BAN, but poss b New Deer, ABD. d/o Peter L, qv, and Marjorie Ledingham, qv. To Whitby Twp, Ontario Co, ONT, ca 1841. m James Anderson, qv. **DC 9 Jun 1980**.

4564   LEASK, Peter, b 28 Jun 1784. From Ryland, Alvah par, BAN, but b New Deer par, ABD. To QUE, 1841; stld Darlington Twp, Durham Co, ONT. Farmer. m Marjorie Ledingham, qv, ch: 1. Margaret, qv; 2. William, qv; 3. George, qv; 4. Helen, qv; 5. James, qv; 6. Alexander, qv; 7. John, qv; 8. Rev Robert, qv; 9. David, qv; **DC 9 Jun 1980**.

4565   LEASK, Rev Robert, b 29 Jul 1831. From Ryland, Alvah par, BAN. s/o Peter L, qv, and Marjorie Ledingham, qv. To Darlington Twp, Durham Co, ONT, ca 1841, later to St Helens, Huron Co. **DC 9 Jun 1980**.

4566   LEASK, William, b 6 Apr 1820. From Ryland, Alvah par, BAN, but prob b Tookshill, New Deer, ABD. s/o Peter L, qv, and Marjorie Ledingham, qv. To Darlington Twp, Durham Co, ONT, ca 1841. Farmer. m Isabel Leask. **DC 9 Jun 1980**.

4567   LECK, Henry, b 1784. From Morebattle, ROX, but sometime in Aberdeen. To NS on the *Sir Edward Pillen*, arr 5 May 1817. m Mary Kirkwood, qv, ch: 1. William, b 1814; 2. John, b 1815; 3. Ellen; 4. Henry; 5. James; 6. Isabelle; 7. Robert; 8. Thomas; 9. Andrew. **DC 9 Sep 1981**.

4568   LECK, Robert, ca 1811–8 May 1876. From Hawick, ROX. To Toronto, ONT. m Mary Mitchelhill, 1814-55. **THS 1942/17**.

4569   LECKIE, David. To QUE on the *David of London*, ex Greenock, 19 May 1821; stld Ramsay Twp, Lanark Co, ONT. **HCL 85, 239**.

4570   LECKIE, John, 1778–1875. From Parkhead,

Glasgow. To QUE on the *Earl of Buckinghamshire*, ex Greenock, 29 Apr 1821; stld Lot 19, Con 8, Dalhousie Twp, Lanark Co, ONT. m Elizabeth McCracken, qv, ch: 1. Alice, b 1806; 2. Elizabeth, b 1808; 3. Ann, 1809-35; 4. Robert, 1811-91; 5. John, 1812-82; 6. William, b 1815; 7. Thomas, b 1816; 8. Margaret, b 1819; 9. Mary, b 1821; 10. Jane; 11. Rachel; 12. Sarah, d inf. **HCL 73; DC 5 Jan 1982**.

4571   LEDINGHAM, Jane. From BAN or ABD. To QUE, 1841; stld Darlington Twp, Durham Co, ONT. m James Leask, qv. **DC 9 Jun 1980**.

4572   LEDINGHAM, Margaret. Poss from Delgaty, ABD. To QUE, 1841; stld Darlington Twp, Durham Co, ONT. Wife of George Leask, qv. **DC 9 Jun 1980**.

4573   LEDINGHAM, Marjorie, b 23 May 1797. From Ryland, Alvah par, BAN, but poss b New Deer par, ABD. To QUE, 1841, and stld Darlington Twp, Durham Co, ONT. m ca 1817, Peter Leask, qv. **DC 9 Jun 1980**.

4574   LEE, James Paris, 9 Aug 1831–24 Feb 1904. b Hawick, ROX. s/o George L, qv, and Margaret Paris, qv. To Galt, Waterloo Co, ONT, 1836. Inventor of the Lee-Metford, Lee-Enfield, and other magazine rifles. Became pres of the Lee Arms Manufacturing Company at Bridgeport, CT. m Caroline Chrysler, of Chatham, who d 1888. Son George Miles, res Hartford, CT. **Hawick OPR 789/5; THS 23/1969; HGD 90, 265**.

4575   LEE, George. From Hawick, ROX. To Galt, Waterloo Co, ONT, 1836. Watchmaker, and second librarian of Galt Circulating Library. m Margaret Paris, qv, ch: 1. Mary, b 1827; 2. John, b 1829, d inf; 3. James Paris, qv; 4. John, b 1833; 5. Isabel, b 1833. **Hawick OPR 789/5; THS 23/1969; HGD 124**.

4576   LEES, John, d 1775. To QUE, ca 1763. Indian trader. Retr to SCT <1778. Son John, merchant in Quebec, and MLA. **MDB 403**.

4577   LEES, William. From ROX. To QUE on the *Rothiemuchus*, 1817; stld Bathurst Twp, Lanark Co, ONT. Farmer, Lot 25, Con 11. Son William, politician. **HCL 218**.

4578   LEISHMAN, Andrew. To Montreal, QUE, 1812. m Elizabeth Clapperton, qv. Dau Amelia. **DC 1 Apr 1974**.

4579   LEISHMAN, Rev William, d 18 Nov 1870. From Edinburgh, and educ there. To Montreal, QUE, 1846, and ind to St Gabriel Street FC. Resigned 1849, and went later to Victoria, AUS. m Miss Gibb, no ch. **SGC 519**.

LEITCH. See also LEACH.

4580   LEITCH, Alexander. From ARL. To Mosa Twp, Middlesex Co, ONT, 1830. **PMC 24**.

4581   LEITCH, Catherine, 1823-83. From ARL. To Mosa Twp, Middlesex Co, ONT, prob <1840. m Malcolm McKellar, qv. **DC 29 Oct 1979**.

4582   LEITCH, Donald, 1796–10 Aug 1840. From ARL. To Aldborough Twp, Elgin Co, ONT, prob 1818. **PDA 41**.

4583   LEITCH, Dugald. From Lochgilphead, ARL. To Caradoc Twp, Middlesex Co, ONT, 1840. Reeve of twp, later Warden of Middlesex Co. ch: 1. Malcolm; 2. John A; 3. Dugald; 4. Margaret; 5. Christina. **PCM 35**.

4584 LEITCH, Duncan, 1801-90. From ARL. To Aldborough Twp, Elgin Co, ONT, prob 1818. Farmer. Son Malcolm, 1835-99. **PDA 50**.

4585 LEITCH, Euphemia, 1824-94. From Craignish, ARL. d/o Lachlan L. and Elizabeth McLarty. To Mosa Twp, Middlesex Co, ONT, <1844. m Dugald McKellar, qv. **DC 29 Oct 1979**.

4586 LEITCH, Hugh. From ARL. To Metcalfe Twp, Middlesex Co, ONT, 1831. ch: 1. William; 2. Archibald. **PCM 26**.

4587 LEITCH, Hugh. From ARL. To Mosa Twp, Middlesex Co, ONT, 1841. ch: 1. Neil; 2. Isabella; 3. Sarah; 4. Donald. **PCM 24**.

4588 LEITCH, Hugh J, 1810-1900. From ARL. s/o John L, qv. To Aldborough Twp, Elgin Co, ONT, 1819; moved to Metcalfe Twp, 1819. ch: 1. John; 2. Hugh; 3. Alexander, teacher, Strathroy, Adelaide Twp; 4. Duncan, teacher; 5. Neil, d Mosa Twp; 6. Rev Malcolm, Stratford, Perth Co; 7. Catherine. **PCM 26**.

4589 LEITCH, James. To QUE on the *David of London*, ex Greenock, 19 May 1821; stld Ramsay Twp, Lanark Co, ONT. **HCL 70, 85**.

4590 LEITCH, John. From ARL. To Aldborough Twp, Elgin Co, ONT, 1819; moved to Mosa Twp, Middlesex Co, 1830. ch: 1. Neil; 2. Donald; 3. Hugh J, qv; 4. Alexander. **PMC 23**.

4591 LEITCH, John. From ARL. To Mosa Twp, Middlesex Co, ONT, 1844. **PMC 24**.

4592 LEITCH, Lachlan. From ARL. To Ekfrid Twp, Middlesex Co, ONT, prob <1850. **PCM 31**.

4593 LEITCH, Malcolm. From ARL. To Mosa Twp, Middlesex Co, ONT, 1849. m a d/o Archibald McNicholl. **PCM 24**.

4594 LEITCH, Neil. From ARL. To Ekfrid Twp, Middlesex Co, ONT, 1831. ch: 1. John; 2. Isabella. **PCM 30**.

4595 LEITCH, Peter, b ca 1750. From PER. Poss s/o Patrick or Peter L, weaver in Crieff, and Catherine Fenton. To Richmond Bay, PEI, on the *Falmouth*, ex Greenock, 8 Apr 1770; stld Lot 34; Stanhope, Queens Co. ch: 1. Peter; 2. John; 3. Neil. **DC 28 May 1980**.

4596 LEITCH, William. From Ardrossan, AYR. To Stormont Co, ONT, 1832. Contractor and militiaman. m Nicholes Bryden, Williamstown, Glengarry Co. Son James, 1850–1917, Judge of the Supreme Court of Ont. **DC 30 Aug 1977**.

4597 LEITCH, William, ca 1817–14 Feb 1876. From Guthrie, ANS. s/o Alexander L. and Elizabeth Petrie. Sometime merchant in Glasgow. To Montreal, QUE, and d there. m Ann Walker, qv. **Ts Guthrie**.

4598 LEITCH, Rev William, 1814–9 May 1864. From Rothesay, BUT. s/o John L, port custodian. Matric Univ of Glasgow, 1831; BA, 1837, MA, 1838. Ord min of Monimail, FIF, 1843. To Kingston, ONT, 1861, to become Principal and Prof of Divinity of Queens Coll. Astronomer, naturalist and mathematician. DD, Glasgow, 1860. m 1846, Euphemia, 1821-53, d/o George Paterson of Cunnoquhie, ch: 1. Moncrieff, b 1848; 2. John, b 1849; 3. William, b 1851; 4. George, b 1853. **RGG 329; GMA 12885; FES v 167, vii 639**.

4599 LEITH, George Gordon Browne, 1810-87. Educ Edinburgh Academy. s/o Maj Gen Sir George L, Bt. To Woodstock, Oxford Co, ONT. m 1843, Eleanor, d/o John Ferrier, WS, Edinburgh. **EAR 3**.

4600 LEITH, Rev Harry, ca 1796–28 Aug 1827. From ABD. s/o James L. of Balcairn, Meldrum, ABD. Grad MA, Kings Coll, Aberdeen, 1818. To Cornwall, Stormont Co, ONT, 1822, and was min and schoolmaster there until 1827. Retr to SCT and became min of Rothiemay, BAN. d unm. **KCG 276; FES vi 333, vii 639**.

4601 LEITH, James, 1777–1838. From ABD. s/o Alexander L. To Montreal, QUE, 1797. Wintering partner of XYCo, absorbed by NWCo. Chief Factor after merger with HBCo, and served at Folle Avoine, Michipocoten, Rainy Lake, Red River, and Monontague. **MDB 405**.

4602 LELLAND, Janet, b ca 1803. From KKD. To ONT, ca 1835; stld Cobourg Twp, Northumberland Co, later Dummer Twp, Peterborough Co. Wife of Robert Haighle, qv. **DC 29 Oct 1979**.

4603 LEMMON, Thomas. To QUE on the *Alexander*, 1816; stld Lot 3, Con 4, Drummond Twp, Lanark Co, ONT. **HCL 233**.

4604 LEMMOND, James, 1827–1909. From Ardlamond, Cairnie, ABD. To Hamilton, ONT, ca 1855. m Margaret Lovey, qv, ch. **DC 10 Nov 1981**.

4605 LESLEY, Isobel. From Banff. To QUE, ex Greenock, summer 1815; stld prob Lanark Co, ONT. Wife of George Gray, qv. **SEC 8**.

4606 LESLIE, Ann. From ABD. d/o George L, qv, and Ann Mitchell, qv. To Elora, Nichol Twp, Wellington Co, ONT, 1836. m James Davidson. **EHE 95**.

4607 LESLIE, Elizabeth. From Leslie, FIF. To Georgina Twp, York Co, ONT, ca 1825. Wife of Joseph Cockburn, qv. **DC 8 Nov 1981**.

4608 LESLIE, Rev George, ca 1795–ca 1875. From Aberdeen. To Dalhousie Twp, Lanark Co, ONT, <1830. Methodist preacher. m Mary, d/o Col Virtue, ch: 1. Jacob; 2. Mary; 3. Isaac, b 13 Jan 1831. **DC 3 Jul 1979**.

4609 LESLIE, George. From ABD. To Elora, Nichol Twp, Wellington Co, ONT, 1836. m Ann Mitchell, qv, ch: 1. Margaret, qv; 2. John; 3. Nancy; 4. Ann, qv; 5. Mary; 6. Jean, qv; 7. James, b Nichol Twp; 8. Beatrice; 9. George; 10. Rev Alexander; 11. Frank. **EHE 95**.

4610 LESLIE, James, ca 1748–15 Sep 1822. From Dunkeld, PER. To Shelburne Co, NS. **NSS No 2785**.

4611 LESLIE, James, 4 Sep 1786–6 Dec 1873. From Fordoun, KCD. s/o Capt James L. of Kair, 15th Regt. Educ Marischall Coll, Aberdeen, 1801-04, and went to Montreal, QUE. Merchant and a director of Bank of Montreal; MLA. m 1815, Julia, d/o dec Patrick Langan, Seignior of Bourchemin and Ramesay, ch: 1. Patrick; 2. Edward, d unm; 3. Mrs Nairn, Murray Bay; 4. Grace. **BNA 539; SGC 421; FAM ii 389; MDB 412; Ts Fordoun**.

4612 LESLIE, Jean. From ABD. d/o George L, qv, and Ann Mitchell, qv. To Elora, Nichol Twp, Wellington Co, ONT, 1836. m — Berwick. **EHE 95**.

4613 LESLIE, Margaret. From ABD. d/o George L, qv, and Ann Mitchell, qv. To Elora, Nichol Twp, Wellington Co, ONT, 1836. m Thomas Land. **EHE 95**.

4614 LESLIE, Robert. From Dornoch, SUT. To East Williams Twp, Middlesex Co, ONT, 1834. **PCM 43**.

4615 LESLIE, William, b 1823. Prob from Edinburgh. To PEI. **DC 21 Aug 1978**.

4616 LESSLIE, Edward, d 1828. From Dundee, ANS. To Dundas, Wentworth Co, ONT, 1822. Storekeeper. ch incl: 1. James, banker and proprietor of the *Toronto Examiner*; 2. John, emig 1820, storekeeper; 3. Joseph, editor; 4. William, d 1843; 5. Charles, went to Davenport, IA, 1839; 6. Mrs John Paterson; 7. Mrs Robert Holt; 8. Helen. **BNA 474, 1145-48**.

4617 LESSLIE, William. From ANS. bro/o Abram L, merchant in Dundee. To CAN, prob ONT, <1848. **SH**.

4618 LESTER, George. To Lanark Co, ONT, 1815, and stld Lot 11, Con 1, Bathurst Twp, 1816. **HCL 16**.

4619 LETHEIC, Adam, b ca 1802. Prob rel to Isabel L, qv. To St Gabriel de Valcartier, QUE, prob <1855. **Census 1861**.

4620 LETHEIC, Isabel, b ca 1826. Prob rel to Adam L, qv. To St Gabriel de Valcartier, QUE, prob <1855. **Census 1861**.

4621 LEVACK, Helen. From CAI. To Kingston, ONT, <1820. Wife of John Mowat, qv. **MDB 535**.

4622 LEVACK, Isabella, 24 Nov 1801–2 Mar 1867. From Dunnet, CAI. d/o George L. m at Edinburgh, 31 Mar 1826, Alexander McGowan, qv. To Montreal, QUE, 1836, with 2 ch, to join her husband. **LDW 21 Aug 1978**.

4623 LEWIS, John. To Colchester Co, NS, <1840. m Margaret Stevens. Son George, b 1862, manufacturer, Truro and Stewiacke. **HNS iii 388**.

4624 LIDDELL, Christina Blair, 20 Mar 1841–2 Dec 1911. From Glasgow. d/o Alexander L. To Wentworth Co, ONT, <1862, and d Toronto. m John Young, qv. **DC 6 Feb 1982**.

4625 LIDDELL, James, 1822–1900. From Haddington, ELN. s/o William L. and Mary Jamieson. To London on the steamer *Trident*, ex Granton, 11 Aug 1852; thence to Victoria, BC, on the *Norman Morrison*, ex East India Docks. m Helen Russell, qv, ch: 1. John, b 1852; 2. Mary, b 1854; 3. Ellen, b 1856; 4. Robert, 1857–1932. **DC 22 Apr 1978**.

4626 LIDDELL, Rev John, 1795–20 Jun 1844. From Dennyloanhead, STI. s/o John L. and Janet Martin. Matric Univ of Glasgow, 1809, and grad MA 1813. Secession min at Amherst, Cumberland Co, NS, 1817-20. Retr to SCT and was United Secession min at Johnshaven, KCD, 1825-38. d at Wardhead, Bonnybridge, STI, where he had some property. **UPC i 79; RGG 331; GMA 7805**.

4627 LIDDELL, Rev Thomas, 18 Oct 1800–11 Jun 1880. b St Ninians, STI. s/o John L. and Janet Martin. Matric Univ of Glasgow, 1817, and grad BA, Univ of Edinburgh, 1841. Min of Lady Glenorchys Chapel, Edinburgh, 1831-41. App first principal of Queens Coll, Kingston, ONT, 1841. Retr to SCT and became min of Lochmaben, DFS, 1850. m Susan Ann Jane, d/o Col Robert Stewart of Fincastle, PER, ch: 1. Susan, d 1884; 2. Louisa, d 1842. **GMA 9880; CEG 254; FES ii 215, vii 639; MDB 413**.

4628 LIGHTBODY, James. From LKS. To QUE on the *Prompt*, ex Greenock, 4 Jul 1820; stld Lanark Co, ONT. **HCL 238**.

4629 LILLIE, Rev Adam, 18 Jun 1803–10 Oct 1869. From Glasgow. s/o Adam L, craftsman. Matric Univ of Glasgow, 1821. To ONT, 1831, and was a Congregational min at Brantford, Dundas and Hamilton. **GMA 10828; MDB 414**.

4630 LILLIE, James, 2 Jan 1811–30 May 1880. From Ancrum, ROX. To QUE, 1830; stld nr Montreal. Farmer, in partnership with William Kerr. **SGC 625**.

4631 LILLIE, Robert. To Pictou, NS, on the *Lady Gray*, ex Cromarty, ROC, arr 16 Jul 1841. **DC 15 Jul 1979**.

4632 LILLY, John, 1739–5 Oct 1822. To Montreal, QUE, 1763. Merchant and JP. Dau Mrs Thomas Boston. **SGC 97**.

4633 LINDSAY, Charles, ca 1833–13 May 1857. From Balmaghie, KKD. s/o James L. in Lauriston. To St Catharines, Lincoln Co, ONT. **DGH 12 Jun 1857**.

4634 LINDSAY, George. To Aldborough Twp, Elgin Co, ONT, 1862. Son Dugald. **PDA 68**.

4635 LINDSAY, James. To QUE on the *Commerce*, ex Greenock, Jun 1820; stld Lanark Co, ONT. **HCL**.

4636 LINDSAY, Rev John, d 13 Jul 1857. To Kingston, ONT, and grad MA at Queens Coll, 1853. Adm min of Litchfield, 1854. **FES vii 639**.

4637 LINDSAY, John. Prob from ARL. To Ekfrid Twp, Middlesex Co, ONT, 1847. **PCM 31**.

4638 LINDSAY, Mary. To QUE on the *David of London*, ex Greenock, 19 Apr 1821; stld Ramsay Twp, Lanark Co, ONT. Wife of Walter Gardner, qv. **HCL 83**.

4639 LINDSAY, Peter. From Paisley, RFW. To ONT. Educ Queens Coll, Kingston, 1849-53, and grad BA. Min at Richmond, 1855-62; Cumberland, 1855-62; Arnprior, 1862; Caledon and Mono, 1871, and at Sherbrooke, QUE, 1872. **FES vii 639**.

4640 LINDSAY, Peter R, 1805–19 May 1885. s/o William L. To St John, NB, ca 1818; stld York Co. Went later to Fly Creek, Otsego Co, NY. m at Fredericton, 28 Oct 1828, Ann Griffith, 1812-94, and had, prob with other ch: 1. Eliza; 2. William F; 3. George Garling; 4. David G; 5. James; 6. Ellen; 7. Charles. **DC 13 Jan 1980**.

4641 LINDSAY, Rev Robert. App missionary by the Glasgow Colonial Society and stld Ayr, Waterloo Co, <1844, when he joined the FC. **FES vii 639**.

4642 LINDSAY, William. From Wishaw, LKS. To Ramsay Twp, Lanark Co, ONT, ca 1821. Wife with him, and ch, incl: 1. John, stonemason; 2. William, teacher. **HCL 85**.

4643 LINKLATER, George. From OKI. To Hudson Bay <1820, and was emp by the HBCo at Fort Albany. By wife Helen had ch: 1. Benjamen, b 1824; 2. Archibald, b 1826; 3. James, b 1832. **DC 16 May 1982**.

4644 LINTON, John James Edmonstone, ca 1804–23 Jan 1869. From Rothesay, BUT. To Stratford, Perth Co, ONT, 1833. Teacher, author and Clerk of the Peace. **MDB 415**.

4645 LINTON, Margaret. From Old Cumnock, AYR. To ONT, 1833. Wife of John Hunter, qv, m 11 Jul 1820. **Old Cumnock OPR 610/4; LDW 30 Aug 1976**.

4646 LINTON, Margaret. Poss from AYR. To Ottawa, ONT, <1841. Wife of Robert Cullen, qv. **LDW 20 May 1967**.

4647 LISTON, James, d 8 Jan 1867. From Lethendy, PER. s/o James L, farmer, and Isobel Soutar. To Montreal, QUE, and d there. **Ts Lethendy**.

4648 LITTLE, Helen. Poss from DFS. To QUE, summer 1815; stld prob Lanark Co, ONT. Wife of James Gibson, qv. **SEC 2**.

4649 LITTLE, James. From ROX. To QUE on the *Sarah Mary Jane*, 1831; stld Dumfries Twp, Waterloo Co, ONT. **HGD 60**.

4650 LITTLE, John, ca 1789–25 Aug 1845. From Knockwalloch, Kirkpatrick-Durham, DFS. To Galt, Waterloo Co, ONT. **DGH 13 Nov 1845**.

4651 LITTLE, Patrick. Poss from DFS. To QUE on the *Alexander*, 1816; stld Lot 12, Con 9, Bathurst Twp, Lanark Co, ONT. **HCL 233**.

4652 LITTLEJOHN, Janet. Prob from Bothwell par, LKS. To ONT, 1835. m (i) John McLellan, ch; m (ii) Peter Wardlaw, qv. **DC 13 Mar 1980**.

4653 LIVINGSTON, Alexander, ca 1787–20 Nov 1854. From ROC. To Pictou Co, NS, prob 1814; bur at Lovat. **DC 27 Oct 1979**.

4654 LIVINGSTON, Catherine, b ca 1784. Prob rel to Donald L, qv. To Charlottetown, PEI, on the *Rambler*, ex Tobermory, 20 Jun 1806. Margaret L, aged 1 ½ years, with her. **PLR**.

4655 LIVINGSTON, Donald, b ca 1751. To Charlottetown, PEI, on the *Rambler*, ex Tobermory, 20 Jun 1806. Wife Mary, aged 50, with him, and ch: 1. Duncan, aged 33; 2. John, aged 30; 3. Isabel, aged 22; 4. Flora, aged 17; 5. Alexander, aged 15. **PLR**.

4656 LIVINGSTON, Donald, b ca 1781. To Charlottetown, PEI, on the *Rambler*, ex Tobermory, 20 Jun 1806. Wife Flora, aged 24, with him, and inf s Malcolm. **PLR**.

4657 LIVINGSTON, Donald. From Dull par, PER. To Montreal, QUE, on the *Curlew*, ex Greenock, 21 Jul 1818; stld prob Beckwith Twp, Lanark Co, ONT. Wife Janet with him, and ch: 1. Ann, aged 13; 2. Margaret, aged 12; 3. Catherine, aged 7. **BCL**.

4658 LIVINGSTON, Flora, b ca 1803. From Is Mull, ARL. d/o John L, qv, and Catherine Campbell, qv. To Inverness Co, NS, with parents, and stld later Mull River. m — MacDonald. **MP ii 243**.

4659 LIVINGSTON, James, 1822–43. From Torthorwald, DFS. To PEI. **Ts Torthorwald**.

4660 LIVINGSTON, John. Prob from Is Mull, ARL. To Queens Co, PEI, prob <1806. Wife Isabella McGregor,

qv, with him. ch: 1. Ann, b 17 Jul 1806; 2. Dugald, b 30 Jul 1809; 3. Hector, b 30 Mar 1811; 4. Duncan, b 2 Apr 1813. **DC 11 Apr 1981**.

4661 LIVINGSTON, John, b ca 1786. To Charlottetown, PEI, on the *Humphreys*, ex Tobermory, 14 Jul 1806. **PLH**.

4662 LIVINGSTON, John, ca 1773–1840. From Is Mull, ARL. To Port Hood dist, Inverness Co, NS, 1803; stld Mull River, 1824. Weaver. m Catherine Campbell, qv, ch: 1. John, jr, qv; 2. Neil, qv; 3. Flora, qv; 4. Grace, b NS; 5. Ann; 6. Mary; 7. Allan. **CBC 1818; MP ii 240**.

4663 LIVINGSTON, John, jr, 1800–48. From Is Mull, ARL. To Inverness Co, NS, 1803; stld later Mull River. m Kate Livingston, 1808–1912, PEI, ch: 1. Duncan, b 1841; 2. Mary, b 1844; 3. John, 1847–1904; 4. Catherine, b 1847; 5. Jane, 1849-69; 6. Hugh, 1851–1943; 7. Flora, 1853–1922. **MP ii 241**.

4664 LIVINGSTON, Margaret, b ca 1774. Prob from Is Colonsay, ARL. To Charlottetown, PEI, on the *Spencer*, ex Oban, 22 Sep 1806. **PLSN**.

4665 LIVINGSTON, Margaret. From Is Rhum, ARL. To Kinloss Twp, Bruce Co, ONT, <1855. Wife of John McKinnon, qv. **DC 12 Apr 1979**.

4666 LIVINGSTON, Mary. From Lochaber, INV. To Salt Springs, Antigonish Co, NS, after 1781. m John Chisholm, jr, qv. **SG iii/4 97**.

4667 LIVINGSTON, Mary, b ca 1755. Prob from Is Colonsay, ARL. To Charlottetown, PEI, on the *Spencer*, ex Oban, 22 Sep 1806. **PLSN**.

4668 LIVINGSTON, Mary, 1800–42. From Ross, Is Mull, ARL. To Caledon Twp, Peel Co, ONT, <1840. **DC 21 Apr 1980**.

4669 LIVINGSTON, Nancy Ann, ca 1786–6 Jan 1867. From Knapdale, ARL. d/o Donald L. and Katherine McKillop. To QUE, 1837; later to Lobo Twp, Middlesex Co, ONT. Wife of John Graham, qv. **DC 25 Jan 1964 and 4 Feb 1982**.

4670 LIVINGSTON, Neil, d 1855. From Is Mull, ARL. s/o John L, qv, and Catherine Campbell, qv. To Inverness Co, NS, 1803; stld Mull River. m Ann, d/o Donald and Betsy Cameron, ch: 1. Catherine, b 1854; 2. Neil, b 1856; 3. Allan. **MP ii 243**.

4671 LIVINGSTON, Neil. From ARL. To Aldborough Twp, Elgin Co, ONT, 1812; moved to Mosa Twp, Middlesex Co, 1828. **PCM 23**.

4672 LIVINGSTONE, Angus. From Tobermory, Is Mull, ARL. To Wallace, Cumberland Co, NS, <1847. Wife Sarah with him. Son Joshua H, 1847–1932, merchant and MLA. **MLA 191**.

4673 LIVINGSTONE, Angus. From ARL. To Ekfrid Twp, Middlesex Co, ONT, 1849. **PCM 31**.

4674 LIVINGSTONE, Catherine, b ca 1789. From Caliach, Kilmore, Is Mull, ARL. To Hudson Bay and Red River <1815. Wife of Charles Campbell, qv. **RRS 24**.

4675 LIVINGSTONE, Catherine, ca 1786–16 Oct 1874. From ARL. To ONT, and d Lucknow, Kinloss Twp, Bruce Co. wid/o Duncan Graham, and mother of: 1. Mary; 2. Kate; 3. Alexander; 4. Donald; 5. Duncan; 6. Christie. **SG xxvi/3 92**.

4676   LIVINGSTONE, Donald. Prob from Is Mull, ARL. To Hudson Bay and Red River, <1813. Wife Ann with him, and s Donald.   **RRS 16**.

4677   LIVINGSTONE, Hugh, ca 1810-31. To Durham Co, ONT, and d Port Hope.   **DGC 15 Mar 1831**.

4678   LIVINGSTONE, James, 1810-94. From Is Mull, ARL. To Eldon Twp, Victoria Co, ONT, 1843, later to Arthur Twp, Wellington Co. m Mary McMillan, qv. Dau Anne.   **DC 1 Aug 1979**.

4679   LIVINGSTONE, John. From Fort William, INV. To Antigonish Co, NS; stld Cape George, 1812. Went later to Little Judique, Inverness Co. m Isabel MacDonald. Dau Anne.   **MP 503**.

4680   LIVINGSTONE, John. From Appin, ARL. To Ekfrid Twp, Middlesex Co, ONT, ca 1850; stld later Plympton Twp, Lambton Co. Tailor.   **PCM 31**.

4681   LIVINGSTONE, Malcolm. From Lochaber, INV. To Antigonish Co, NS, prob <1830. ch: 1. Angus, dy; 2. Malcolm.   **HCA 162**.

4682   LIVINGSTONE, Rev Martin Wilson, 30 Dec 1808–21 Mar 1887. From Kilsyth, STI. s/o Robert L, merchant. Matric Univ of Glasgow, 1826. Min of Mill Hill Relief and UP Ch, Musselburgh, 1837-53. To CAN, but had no stld charge until adm min of Presb Ch at Simcoe, ONT, 1858.   **UPC i 538; GMA 11920; FES vii 640**.

4683   LIVINGSTONE, Miles. Prob from Is Mull, ARL. To Hudson Bay, poss on the *Robert Taylor*, 1812. Went to Red River, but left and arr Holland River, 6 Sep 1815, with wife and 2 ch.   **LSS 187; LSC 324; RRS 16**.

4684   LIVINGSTONE, William. To ONT <1847; stld Delaware, Middlesex Co. Principal of Caradoc Academy.   **DC 21 Mar 1971**.

4685   LIZARS, Daniel, b 27 Feb 1797. From Edinburgh. s/o Daniel L, engraver, and Margaret Home, qv. To New York on the *Science*, 1833; stld Meadowlands, Colborne Twp, Huron Co, ONT. Publisher, farmer, and became Clerk of the Peace for Huron, 1842. m Robina Hutchison, qv, and had with other ch: 1. Daniel Home, b 1823, RFW, became county attorney for Perth, ONT; 2. Helen, b ca 1830; 3. George, b 27 Feb 1841.   **BNA 922; St Cuthberts OPR 685-2/35; DC 1 Jan 1968**.

LIZARS, Mrs Daniel. See HOME, Margaret.

4686   LIZARS, Henry. From Edinburgh. s/o Daniel L, engraver, and Margaret Home, qv. To Goderich Twp, Huron Co, ONT, arr 1833. Architect and surveyor. Became Registrar of Huron. Wife Jane with him.   **DC 1 Jan 1968**.

4687   LOCHHEAD, Rev Andrew, ca 1832–12 Jan 1864. From Paisley, RFW. Second s/o Robert L, craftsman. Matric Univ of Glasgow, 1846. Studied Theology at St Andrews, 1849-50. App by Colonial Committee, 1855, to be min at Georgetown, PEI, and arr 1856. Retr to SCT, 1860, and was chaplain at Paisley Prison. He later grad in medicine.   **GMA 15057; RRG 337; SAM 110; FES vii 620**.

4688   LOCHHEAD, Robert, 6 Feb 1820–11 Mar 1893. From Kilmarnock, AYR. To St-Thérèse-de-Blainville, Terrebonne Co, QUE, <1840. Farmer. m Janet Wylie, qv,

ch: 1. John, b 26 Feb 1855; 2. David, b 13 Dec 1856; 3. Agnes, b 16 Aug 1858; 4. Janet, b 28 Mar 1860; 5. Jane, b 26 Aug 1861; 6. Thomas, b 6 Aug 1863; 7. James, b 12 Dec 1865; 8. Helen, b 2 Feb 1868; 9. Eliza Ann, b 5 Jan 1870.   **DC 13 May 1980**.

4689   LOCHHEAD, William. From Glasgow. s/o William L, craftsman. Matric Univ of Glasgow, 1816, and studied theology. To CAN, later to Albany, NY.   **GMA 9592**.

4690   LOCHHEAD, William, b 1831. Poss from LKS. To ONT, ca 1852. By wife Helen had ch: 1. Euphemia, b 1853; 2. Robert, b 1856; 3. John, b 1860; 4. Alexander, b 1862; 5. William, 1864–1927, Professor of Biology at MacDonald Coll, Ste Anne de Bellevue, QUE; 6. George, b 1867.   **DC 17 Sep 1980**.

4691   LOCKERBIE, Jane. From Castle Douglas, KKD. d/o John L, qv, and Catherine Williamson, qv. To NS, 1835; stld Tatamagouche, Colchester Co. m Robert Purves.   **HT 71**.

4692   LOCKERBIE, John. From Castle Douglas, KKD. To NS, 1835; stld Tatamagouche, Colchester Co. m Catherine Williamson, qv, ch: 1. John; 2. Jane, qv; 3. Margaret; 4. Mary; 5. Martha Bell; 6. Cassie; 7. David; 8. Ninian.   **HT 71**.

4693   LOCKERBIE, Thomas, 4 Feb 1816–18 Apr 1884. To CAN, Apr 1839; stld Northumberland Co, NB. Bur Chatham. Wife Margaret, 1816-49. ch.   **DC 14 Jan 1980**.

4694   LOCKERBY, John, 7 Jan 1798–25 May 1900. From Annan, DFS. To Miramichi, Northumberland Co, NB, 1820; later to Charlottetown, PEI.   **CAE 70**.

4695   LOCKHART, Alexander MacDonald. From Edinburgh. s/o Norman L. of Tarbrax, WS, and Phyllis Barbara McMurdo. To ONT <1855.   **SH; HWS 223**.

4696   LOCKHART, John Hamilton, d 21 Sep 1842. From Castlehill, Lockerbie, DFS. s/o Robert L. To Woodstock, Oxford Co, ONT.   **DGH 27 Oct 1842**.

4697   LOCKIE, George. From Ashkirk, SEL. To CAN, Jun 1854; stld prob ONT. m Margaret Young, qv, ch: 1. John, b 10 Feb 1852; 2. Peter, b Whinfield, 13 Mar 1854.   **Ashkirk OPR 781/4**.

4698   LOGAN, Alexander. To Niagara, Lincoln Co, ONT, with wife Sabrina, prob <1860. Son Frank.   **DC 15 Sep 1960**.

4699   LOGAN, Dugal G, d 14 Nov 1820. To Halifax, NS, later to Cherry Garden Estate, Jamaica, and d there. **NSS No 2211**.

4700   LOGAN, Elizabeth Crawford. From LKS. To Sydney Mines, Cape Breton Co, NS, ca 1854. Wife of Andrew Anderson, qv, m 1829, poss at Glasgow.   **DC 25 Apr 1980**.

4701   LOGAN, George, b ca 1748. Prob from Spinningdale, SUT. To Charlottetown, PEI, on the *Elizabeth & Ann*, arr 8 Nov 1806. Wife Christian Gair, qv, with him, and ch: 1. Jean, aged 24; 2. James, aged 23; 3. George, aged 20; 4. Robert, aged 18; 5. Walter, aged 14; 6. Alexander, aged 12; 7. William, aged 10; 8. Peter, aged 8; 9. Dougald, aged 6.   **PLEA**.

4702   LOGAN, Hart. From STI. s/o James L, qv. To Montreal, QUE, ca 1784. Merchant, in partnership with

George Watt; Lt of Volunteers, War of 1812. Latterly in London, ENG. **SGC 131**.

4703   LOGAN, James, 1726–17 Jan 1806. From STI. To Montreal, QUE, 1784. Baker. ch: 1. William, qv; 2. Hart, qv. **SGC 117, 130**.

4704   LOGAN, John. From MLN. To QUE <1759, and fought under Gen Wolfe. Sometime in PA, but went as a Loyalist to St John, NB, 1783. By a second wife, ch: 1. James; 2. Alexander; 3. David; 4. Daniel; 5. Ann. **DC 23 Jul 1980**.

4705   LOGAN, Rev John Bulloch, ca 1824–15 Apr 1896. From DNB. s/o Robert L, tradesman. Matric Univ of Glasgow, 1839. Probationer of UP Ch. To Weston, York Co, ONT. Min there and later at Kentville, Kings Co, NS. **GMA 14097**.

4706   LOGAN, Thomas. Served in 82nd Regt and was gr land in Pictou Co, NS, 1784. **HPC App F**.

4707   LOGAN, William, ca 1759–14 Jun 1841. From STI. s/o James L, qv. To Montreal, QUE, 1784. Banker and property owner. Retr to SCT, 1815, and purchased estate of Clarkston, Polmont par, STI. m Janet E Edmond, qv, and had, poss with other ch: 1. James, who took charge of his father's interests in CAN; 2. Sir William Edmond, 1798–1875, geologist and cartographer, from whom Mount Logan in Yukon Territory–the highest point in CAN–is named; 3. Margaret, 1800-86; 4. Mary, 1806-32. **SGC 130; SAS 32; CBD 599; Ts Polmont**.

4708   LOGAN, Rev William, ca 1823–11 Apr 1896. From Longside, ABD. Schoolmaster at Cruden before emig to Toronto, ONT, 1845. Min at Cartwright and Manvers, Durham, and later at Huntsville and Fenelon Falls. Canon of St Albans, Toronto. **SNQ ii/2 10**.

4709   LOGIE, Rev John, ca 1823–19 Oct 1887. From Buckhaven, FIF. s/o William L, fisherman. Matric Univ of Glasgow, 1843. To London, Westminster Twp, Middlesex Co, ONT. Min of congregations at Warrensville, Brucefield, and Stanley. Went to NC, 1875, but retr to ONT and was ind to Tilbury, Kent Co. **UPC ii 202n; GMA 14538**.

4710   LOGIE, Margaret Lendrum, 7 May 1815–11 Mar 1904. From Lady, OKI. d/o Rev William L. and Elizabeth Scarth. To Fergus, Wellington Co, ONT, 1843. Wife of Rev George Smellie, qv. **FES vii 265**.

4711   LOGIE, Robert. From Bawds, Urquhart par, MOR. To PEI, <1780; later to Blackes Rock, Northumberland Co, NB. Farmer and fisherman. m Marjory Hay, qv, ch: 1. Alexander, b 1 Dec 1773; 2. Margaret, b 12 Oct 1775; 3. William, b 24 Jan 1778; 4. Patrick, b 19 Apr 1780. **LDW 24 Jun 1973; DC 27 Jun 1969**.

4712   LONG, Archibald. Served in 82nd Regt and was gr land in Pictou Co, NS, 1784. **HPC App F**.

4713   LONG, Phillip. To QUE <1792. Farmer. **DC 2 May 1980**.

4714   LORIMER, William, ca 1796–4 Aug 1868. From Annan, DFS. To St John, NB, <1830. **DC 11 May 1981**.

4715   LORRAINE, Francis, ca 1783–21 Jun 1815. From Kirkconnel, Kirkpatrick-Fleming, DFS. s/o Walter L. in Oakwoodhill, and Mary Currie. To Truro, Colchester Co, NS, 1805. m Elizabeth Smith, qv, ch. **Ts Kirkconnel**.

4716   LOTHIAN, Archibald, ca 1800–15 Oct 1865. From Glenlyon, PER. To ONT, 1817; stld Breadalbane, Lochiel Twp, Glengarry Co, 1824. m 4 Feb 1825, Catherine, d/o Rev Peter McDougall, Baptist clergyman. **DC 27 Oct 1979**.

4717   LOTHIAN, James. From PER. To ONT, 1817, and stld Lochiel Twp, Glengarry Co. m Janet Cameron, qv. **DC 27 Oct 1979**.

4718   LOTHIAN, Jane, 1802-80. From PER. To Osgoode Twp, Carleton Co, ONT, ca 1831. Wife of Robert McNab, qv. **DC 1 Aug 1979**.

4719   LOUGHTON, Charles, b ca 1801. To St Gabriel de Valcartier, QUE, prob <1855. **Census 1861**.

4720   LOUTTET, Magnus, b ca 1779. Prob from OKI. To Baddeck dist, Victoria Co, NS, 1817. Blacksmith, m and ch. **CBC 1818**.

4721   LOVE, Alexander. To Aldborough Twp, Elgin Co, ONT, 1821. Farmer. ch: 1. Alexander, d 1875; 2. Mrs Archibald McIntyre; 3. Mrs Duncan MacLean; 4. Mrs Duncan MacGregor; 5. Mrs Alexander Love; 6. Mrs Archibald Campbell; 7. Mrs John Pool; 8. Mrs John MacBride. **PDA 50**.

4722   LOVE, Alexander, b 1810. From Kilbride Bennan, Kilmory, Is Arran, BUT. To Dalhousie, NB, 1830. **MAC 18**.

4723   LOVE, Janet, d 1869. From Kilbarchan, RFW. To Pictou, NS, ca 1830. Prob sometime at St John, NB, but retr later to SCT. Wife of James Barr, qv. **FNQ iv 12-22**.

4724   LOVE, John, d 1896. From ARL. To West Williams Twp, Middlesex Co, ONT, 1846. Wife, who d 1891, with him, and s John. **PCM 46**.

4725   LOVE, Robert, 25 Apr 1779–22 Mar 1862. From Kilmarnock, AYR. s/o Robert L. and Elizabeth Lockhart. To QUE on the *Commerce*, ex Greenock, 11 May 1821; stld North Sherbrooke Twp, Lanark Co, ONT. Discharged soldier, 42nd Regt. m Deborah Donnahue, qv, ch: 1. James, b 11 Jan 1812; 2. Mary, b 1814; 3. Robert, b 9 Jun 1822; 4. William, b 1826; 5. John, b 30 Jul 1829; 6. Marion, b 20 Oct 1830. **HCL 74; SG xxiii/1 11; DC 26 Sep 1979**.

4726   LOVEY, Margaret, d 1912. From Ardlamond, Cairnie, ABD. To Hamilton, ONT, ca 1855. Wife of James Lemmond, qv. **DC 10 Nov 1981**.

4727   LOW, David, 1785–1868. From Cortachy, ANS. s/o Alexander L. and Isobel Stewart. To QUE on the *Brilliant*, ex Aberdeen, 16 Aug 1836; stld Argenteuil Co, nr Lachute. Farmer and piper. m Jean Duncan, qv, ch: 1. James, qv; 2. Margaret, 1824-82, emig 1841; 3. David, jr, 1827-63, emig 1841. **DC 15 Jan 1982**.

4728   LOW, James. From Aberargie, PER. To Montreal, QUE, on the *Royal George*, ex Greenock, Jan 1827; stld Sarnia, ONT. m Janet Baird, qv. **DC 19 Nov 1978**.

4729   LOW, James, 1820-96. From Cortachy, ANS. s/o David L, qv, and Jean Duncan, qv. To QUE on the *Brilliant*, ex Aberdeen, 16 Aug 1836; stld nr Lachute, Argenteuil Co. Farmer and militiaman. m Wilhelmina Elizabeth Schlaberg, qv. **DC 15 Jan 1982**.

4730   LOWDEN, William, d 20 Feb 1820. From DFS. To NS, ca 1787, and d at Pictou. **NSS No 1894**.

4731   LOWDETT, William. To Shelburne, Shelburne Co, NS, <25 Nov 1820, when m Elizabeth, d/o Capt McLean. **NSS No 2127**.

4732   LOWE, Silvania. From Is Arran, BUT. To Charlo, Restigouche Co, NB, prob <1840. **MAC 18**.

4733   LOWTHER, Thomas. To Pictou, NS, on the *Lulan*, ex Glasgow, 17 Aug 1848. **DC 12 Jul 1979**.

4734   LUCAS, John, ca 1818–1 Sep 1849. From DFS. s/o John L, hoop-maker, Wellgreen. To Welland Co, ONT, and d Port Colborne. **DGH 18 Oct 1849**.

4735   LUKE, Janet. From Fintry, STI. To QUE on the *Atlas*, ex Greenock, 11 Jul 1815; stld Bathurst Twp, Lanark Co, ONT. Wife of John Ritchie, qv. **SEC 2**.

4736   LUMSDEN, Magdalene, 26 May 1793–25 Oct 1864. From MacDuff, BAN. d/o John L. and Catharine Panton. To Halifax, NS, on the *Brilliant*, 1830. Went to Stanstead Twp, Richeleau Co, QUE, via Derby, VT. Wife of John Christie, qv. **DC 12 Jan 1980**.

4737   LUMSDEN, Mark, ca 1753–7 Apr 1820. To Halifax, NS, and d Haywood Mill. **NSS No 1921**.

4738   LUMSDEN, Margaret, 29 Mar 1785–1 Jul 1833. From Wester Kilbuckly, Banff par, BAN. d/o William L. and Katharine Panton. To QUE on the *Brilliant*, ex Aberdeen, 8 Aug 1832; stld Whitby Twp, Ontario Co, ONT. **DC 4 Feb 1982**.

4739   LUMSDEN, Thomas, b ca 1819. From Glasgow. To Montreal, QUE, <1850. Stonemason. m Elizabeth Wilson, ch. **DC 5 May 1981**.

4740   LUNAN, Henry, d 1870. From Blairgowrie, PER. To Montreal, QUE, 1854. Grocer, St Mary Street. m a d/o George Hutchison, Forres. **SGC 631**.

4741   LUNN, Thomas, ca 1799–5 Nov 1875. From Lilliesleaf, ROX. s/o James L. and Janet Reid. To ONT and d Owen Sound. **Ts Lilliesleaf**.

4742   LYALL, John. Prob from BEW. To ONT <1830. m Margaret Johnstone, qv. **DC 5 Aug 1970**.

4743   LYALL, Rev William, 11 Jun 1811–17 Jan 1890. Born Paisley, RFW. s/o William L, merchant. Matric Univ of Glasgow, 1825. FC min at Broxburn, 1844-48, and Uphall, 1845-48. To Toronto, ONT, 1848, and was a tutor at Knox Coll. Became Prof of Classics at FC Coll, Halifax, NS, 1850. Later Prof of Logic at Dalhousie Univ, Halifax. LLD, McGill Coll, 1864. **GMA 11571; AFC i 212; MDB 425**.

4744   LYALL, William. From BEW. To Kingston, ONT, <1829. m Jane Forgue, qv. Dau Sophia, 1829–1904. **DC 7 Jun 1980**.

4745   LYLE, Gavin. From Hamilton, LKS. To Clyde River, Shelburne Co, NS, <1770. m Isabella Curry, qv, and had, prob with other ch: 1. Gavin; 2. Alexander. **DC 18 Jul 1981**.

4746   LYMBURNER, Adam, 1746–1836. From Kilmarnock, AYR. s/o John L, merchant. Matric Univ of Glasgow, 1766. To QUE, ca 1775. Merchant and Loyalist agent. **BNA 398; GMA 2595**.

4747   LYMBURNER, John. From Kilmarnock, AYR. s/o John L, merchant. To Montreal, QUE, <1766. Merchant. Drowned, 1775. **DC 10 Jan 1980**.

4748   LYMBURNER, Matthew, 1725–17 Feb 1812. From Kilmarnock, AYR. To Penobscot, ME, ca 1767; stld later St Andrews, Charlotte Co, NB. Farmer and miller. m Margaret Glen, qv, ch: 1. Matthew, 1765–1832; 2. Margaret, b 1765; 3. John, b 1769; 4. Alexander, 1770–1812; 5. James, 1773–1812, res Caistor Twp, Lincoln Co, ONT; 6. Betsy; 7. Jenny; 8. Nancy; 9. William; 10. Robert, b 1793. **Ts Kilmarnock; DC 13 May 1980**.

4749   LYON, George. Prob from Inverary, ABD. To ONT <1837. **SH**.

4750   LYON, James. To Douglastown, Northumberland Co, NB, <1842. Son Alexander, farmer. **SH**.

4751   LYON, John. From PER. To Halton Co, ONT, prob <1840; stld Esquesing Twp. m Catherine McFarlane, qv. **EPE 75**.

4752   LYON, Margaret. Poss from Glasgow. To QUE, 1843; stld Huntingdon. Wife of Daniel MacFarlane, qv. **HCM 222**.

M

4753   McADAM, Archibald. From Arnisdale, INV. To NB <1800. **HCA 162**.

4754   McADAM, Henry, ca 1787–12 Jan 1828. To St John, NB, and d there. **NER viii 98**.

4755   McADAM, Hugh. From Arnisdale, INV. To Moidart, Antigonish Co, NS, ca 1790. m Mary MacDonald, ch: 1. Alexander; 2. John; 3. Allan; 4. Ronald; 5. Donald; 6. Sarah; 7. Ann; 8. Catherine; 9. Margaret, dy. **HCA 162**.

4756   McADAM, John. From Arnisdale, INV. To PEI <1800. **HCA 162**.

McALDER. See also McCALDER.

4757   McALDER, Margaret, b 12 Jun 1836. From Is Colonsay, ARL. d/o Archibald M. and Catherine Blue. To East Gwillimbury Twp, York Co, ONT, 1836, thence to Mariposa Twp, Victoria Co. Later in Elderslie Twp, Bruce Co. Wife of John Bell, qv. **DC 30 Jul 1979**.

4758   McALDRIDGE, Gilbert, b ca 1768. Prob from Is Colonsay, ARL. To Charlottetown, PEI, on the *Spencer*, ex Oban, 22 Sep 1806. ch with him: 1. John, aged 7; 2. Alexander, aged 5; 3. Peter, aged 3; 4. John, aged 1. **PLSN**.

4759   McALESTER, Ronald, 1800-95. From Is Arran, BUT. To Benjamen River, Restigouche Co, NB, 1833. **MAC 19**.

4760   MACALISTER, Alexander. Prob from RFW. To CAN <1854. **SH**.

4761   McALISTER, Archibald, b 1822. From Kilpatrick, Kilmory par, Is Arran, BUT. Prob bro/o Donald M, qv. To Restigouche Co, NB, ca 1843. **MAC 19**.

4762   McALISTER, Catherine, 1787–1868. From Is Arran, BUT. To Dalhousie, NB, prob <1833. Wife of William Murchy, qv. **MAC 25**.

4763   McALISTER, Donald, b 1822. From Kilpatrick, Kilmory par, Is Arran, BUT. Prob bro/o Archibald M, qv. To Restigouche Co, NB, ca 1843. **MAC 19**.

4764   McALISTER, Effy, b ca 1746. From Is Colonsay,

ARL. To Charlottetown, PEI, on the *Spencer*, ex Oban, arr Sep 1806. Wife of Angus Darroch, qv.   **PLSN**.

4765   McALISTER, Elizabeth, b 1828. From Kilpatrick, Kilmory par, Is Arran, BUT. Poss rel to Archibald M, qv, and Donald M, qv. To Blackland, Restigouche Co, NB, ca 1843.   **MAC 19**.

4766   MACALISTER, Henry Bowie. Prob from Paisley, RFW. bro/o John Bowie M, qv. To CAN <1855.   **SH**.

4767   MACALISTER, John Bowie. Prob from Paisley, RFW. bro/o Henry Bowie M, qv. To CAN <1855.   **SH**.

4768   McALISTER, Mary, 1798–1883. From Drimaginear, Kilmory par, Is Arran, BUT. To Escuminac, Bonaventure Co, QUE, <1846. Wife of Angus McKenzie, qv, whom she m 20 Jul 1821.   **MAC 21**.

4769   McALLISTER, Ann. From Skipness, ARL. To QUE, arr 3 Aug 1846; stld Erin Twp, Wellington Co, ONT. Wife of Hector McVannel, qv.   **DC 16 Mar 1978**.

4770   McALLISTER, Archibald. From Tarbert, ARL. To Lobo Twp, Middlesex Co, ONT, 1828. ch: 1. Flora; 2. Sarah; 3. Mary; 4. Kate; 5. Ellen; 6. Betsy.   **PCM 39**.

4771   McALLISTER, Catherine. From Is Islay, ARL. To Nottawa, Simcoe Co, ONT, prob <1853. Wife of John Currie, qv.   **DC 30 Aug 1977**.

4772   McALLISTER, Charles, 1794–1876. From Feorline, Kilmory par, Is Arran, BUT. To Benjamen River, Restigouche Co, NB, 1829. m 11 Mar 1824, Mary Ferguson, qv, ch: 1. Daniel, b 1826; 2. Isabella, b 1829.   **MAC 19**.

4773   McALLISTER, Donald, d 1890. From Is Arran, BUT. Poss rel to Charles M, qv. To Restigouche Co, NB, 1829. Postmaster at Newmills, ca 1866–ca 1876. Son Daniel, res Jacquet River.   **CUC 24**.

4774   McALLISTER, John, 1790–6 May 1862. From Dumfries. To Blissfield, Northumberland Co, NB, <1825. Physician. m Elizabeth Ogilvie, qv, ch: 1. James, b 1820; 2. William, 1825-56; 3. Elizabeth; 4. Jane; 5. John; 6. Margaret.   **LDW 6 May 1967**.

4775   McALLISTER, John, 1807-75. From Clauchog, Kilmory, Is Arran, BUT. To Heron Is, Chaleur Bay, NB, 1833.   **MAC 19**.

4776   McALLISTER, Rev William, b ca 1802. From Anderston, Glasgow. s/o William M, merchant. Matric Univ of Glasgow, 1818. To Dalhousie Twp, Lanark Co, ONT, 1830; stld Watsons Corners. Moved to Sarnia Twp, Lambton Co, 1842. Joined FC, 1844. Latterly at Woodlands, Metis, QUE.   **GMA 10156; HCL 196; FES vii 640**.

   McALLUM. See also McCALLUM.

4777   McALLUM, John. To QUE on the *Fancy*, 1816; stld Lot 14, Con 3, South Elmsley Twp, Leeds Co, ONT.   **HCL 234**.

4778   McALPIN, Catherine. From Letterfinlay, Loch Lochy, INV. To Montreal, QUE, ex Fort William, 3 Jul 1802; stld E ONT.   **MCM 1/4 23**.

4779   McALPIN, Catherine. From Aberchalder, INV. Poss wife of Alexander McPhee, qv. To Montreal, QUE, ex Fort William, 3 Jul 1802; stld E ONT.   **MCM 1/4 26**.

4780   McALPIN, Donald. From ARL. s/o Mrs Mary M, qv. To QUE on the *Tamerlane*, ex Greenock, 4 Jul 1831; stld Ekfrid Twp, Middlesex Co, ONT.   **PCM 31**.

4781   McALPIN, Duncan. From ARL. s/o Mrs Mary M, qv. To QUE on the *Tamerlane*, ex Greenock, 4 Jul 1831; stld Ekfrid Twp, Middlesex Co, ONT.   **PCM 31**.

4782   McALPIN, Elizabeth, 1805-68. From PER, prob Killin, and poss d/o Alpin M. and Jean Campbell. To Osgoode Twp, Carleton Co, ONT, 1833. m John Campbell, hostler, qv.   **DC 22 Nov 1978**.

4783   McALPIN, Hugh. Prob from ARL. To Ekfrid Twp, Middlesex Co, ONT, 1829. ch: 1. John; 2. Hugh; 3. Alexander; 4. Mrs Malcolm McAlpin; 5. Margaret.   **PCM 30**.

4784   McALPIN, James. From ARL. s/o Mrs Mary M, qv. To Ekfrid Twp, Middlesex Co, ONT, 1829.   **PCM 31**.

4785   McALPIN, John. From ARL. s/o Mrs Mary M, qv. To Ekfrid Twp, Middlesex Co, ONT, ca 1835.   **PCM 31**.

4786   McALPIN, Malcolm. From ARL. s/o Mrs Mary M, qv. To Ekfrid Twp, Middlesex Co, ONT, 1829.   **PCM 31**.

4787   McALPIN, Mary. From Greenfield, nr Loch Garry, INV. To Montreal, QUE, ex Fort William, 3 Jul 1802; stld E ONT.   **MCM 1/4 23**.

4788   McALPIN, Mary. From Letterfinlay, Loch Lochy, INV. To Montreal, QUE, ex Fort William, 3 Jul 1802; stld E ONT.   **MCM 1/4 23**.

4789   McALPIN, Mrs Mary, d 1837. From ARL. To QUE on the *Tamerlane*, ex Greenock, 4 Jul 1831; stld Ekfrid Twp, Middlesex Co, ONT. ch: 1. Malcolm, qv; 2. James, qv; 3. Peter, qv; 4. Duncan, qv; 5. Donald, qv; 6. John, qv.   **PCM 31**.

4790   McALPIN, Peter. From ARL. To QUE on the *Tamerlane*, ex Greenock, 4 Jul 1831; stld Ekfrid Twp, Middlesex Co.   **PCM 31**.

4791   McALPINE, Alexander. From Knapdale, ARL. bro/o James M, qv. To Eldon Twp, Victoria Co, ONT, ca 1830; stld Con 3.   **DC 21 Mar 1980**.

4792   McALPINE, Andrew. To Lanark Co, ONT, 1821; stld Lot 9, Con 2, North Sherbrooke Twp. Farmer and lay preacher.   **HCL 74, 201**.

4793   McALPINE, Archibald. From ARL. bro/o Robert M, qv. To Mosa Twp, Middlesex Co, ONT, 1831.   **PCM 24**.

4794   McALPINE, Donald. From ARL. To Aldborough Twp, Elgin Co, ONT, prob 1818. Farmer.   **PDA 93**.

4795   McALPINE, Donald. From ARL. bro/o John 'Ban' M, qv. To Metcalfe Twp, Middlesex Co, ONT, 1841. ch: 1. Capt Alexander; 2. Dr Dugald, res Vancouver, BC; 3. Donald, res London, Westminster Twp.   **PCM 26**.

4796   McALPINE, James, 1795–1851. From Knapdale, ARL. To Eldon Twp, Victoria Co, ONT, <1830; stld Lot 6, Con 2. Farmer. By wife Janet ch: 1. Duncan; 2. Colin; 3. Neil; 4. Gilbert; 5. Alexander; 6. Anne.   **EC 72**.

4797   McALPINE, John 'Ban'. From ARL. bro/o Donald M, qv. To Mosa Twp, Middlesex Co, ONT, 1841. Son Capt Alexander.   **PCM 24**.

4798   McALPINE, Malcolm. From ARL. To Aldborough Twp, Elgin Co, ONT, prob 1818. Farmer.   **PDA 93**.

4799   McALPINE, Mary, 1792–1865. From North Knapdale, ARL. d/o Alexander and Katherine M. To Talbot Settlement, ONT, 1819; stld Dunwich Twp, Elgin Co, 1820. Wife of Donald McGugan, qv, whom she m 29 Mar 1813.   **DC 8 Dec 1981**.

4800   McALPINE, Robert. From ARL. bro/o Archibald M, qv. To Mosa Twp, Middlesex Co, ONT, 1831. **PCM 23**.

4801   McALPINE, Sarah. Prob from ARL. To Metcalfe Twp, Middlesex Co, ONT, 1831. Wife of John Mitchell, qv.   **PCM 56**.

4802   MACARA, G, ca 1801–18 Nov 1828. To St John, NB, and d there. Was prob earlier in NS. **VSN No 3155**.

4803   MACARA, John, 1813-82. From Edinburgh. To Toronto, ONT, 1843, later to Goderich, Huron Co. Journalist and lawyer.   **MDB 427**.

4804   McARTHUR, Alexander. Poss from Is Skye, INV. To Charlottetown, PEI, prob 1803. Petitioner for Dr MacAulay, 1811.   **HP 74**.

4805   McARTHUR, Alexander. Poss from ARL. Prob bro/o John M, qv. To Pictou Co, NS, <1827; stld Wilkins Grant. m Catherine Campbell, ch: 1. Rachel, b 1827; 2. Janet, b 1830; 3. Mary, b 1836; 4. Alexander, b 1838.   **PAC 114**.

4806   McARTHUR, Alexander. From ARL. To Mosa Twp, Middlesex Co, ONT, 1832.   **PCM 24**.

4807   MACARTHUR, Allan. From Is Canna, INV. bro/o Duncan M, qv. To Cape Mabou, Inverness Co, NS, prob <1815. Son John.   **MP 385**.

4808   MACARTHUR, Angus, b 1805. From Carloway, Uig par, Is Lewis, ROC. To QUE, ex Stornoway, arr 4 Aug 1851; stld Huron Twp, Bruce Co, ONT, 1852. m Isabella McAulay (see ADDENDA), ch: 1. Kirsty; 2-3. Isabella and Mary, twins, b 1834; 4. John, b 1837; 5. Isabella, b 1840; 6. Effie, b 1841.   **WLC**.

4809   MACARTHUR, Anne. From Lochaber, INV. To Inverness Co, NS, 1816. Wife of Angus MacDonell, qv.   **MP 614**.

4810   McARTHUR, Archibald. From Kilmonivaig, par, INV. To Pictou, NS, on the *Sarah*, ex Fort William, Jun 1801. Farmer. Wife Christian with him, and an infant. **PLS**.

4811   McARTHUR, Archibald. From Lochaber, INV. To Antigonish Co, NS, ca 1818; stld Fraser Mountain. m Christine Campbell. Son Archibald.   **HCA 165**.

4812   McARTHUR, Archibald. Prob from ARL. To Eldon Twp, Victoria Co, ONT, 1833; stld Lot 19, Con 6. Farmer. Son Donald.   **EC 73**.

4813   McARTHUR, Charles. From Inverskilroy, ni, poss INV. Prob rel to Donald M, qv. To Montreal, QUE, ex Fort William, 3 Jul 1802; stld E ONT.   **MCM 1/4 24**.

4814   McARTHUR, Charles. From ARL. To Lobo Twp, Middlesex Co, ONT, 1840. ch: 1. John, reeve of Lobo; 2. Charles; 3. William; 4. Dugald; 5. Nancy; 6. Mary; 7. Rev Duncan; 8. Mrs Colin McArthur; 9. Mrs William Paul.   **PCM 39**.

4815   McARTHUR, Donald. From Inverskilroy, ni, poss INV. Prob rel to Charles M, qv. To Montreal, QUE, ex Fort William, 3 Jul 1802; stld E ONT.   **MCM 1/4 24**.

4816   McARTHUR, Donald. Prob from Lochaber, INV. To Antigonish Co, NS, prob <1830. ch: 1. John; 2. Angus; 3. James.   **HCA 166**.

4817   MACARTHUR, Donald, b 28 Apr 1814. From Kilmichael-Glassary, ARL. s/o Duncan M. and Emily MacArthur. To Southwold Twp, Elgin Co, ONT, summer 1843. m Ann MacCallum, qv.   **DC 5 Jan 1976**.

4818   McARTHUR, Donald, 1805-80. From Is Iona, ARL. To Caledon Twp, Peel Co, ONT, <1840. Wife Sarah McGillvery, qv, with him.   **DC 21 Apr 1980**.

4819   McARTHUR, Donald, 1818-90. From ARL. To East Nissouri Twp, Oxford Co, ONT, prob <1840; stld Lot 11, Con 12. m Janet McDonald, qv, ch: 1. Anne, 1844–1918; 2. Mary, b 1845; 3. Christine, 1848–1920; 4. Philip, 1850–1928; 5. Robert, 1856–1910; 6. James, 1861–1926; 7. John, unm.   **DC 25 Nov 1981**.

4820   McARTHUR, Donald. From Is Islay, ARL. To Galt, Waterloo Co, ONT, <1855; stld Dumfries Twp. m Jean Dickie, ch.   **DD 11**.

4821   MACARTHUR, Dugald. From ARL. To Aldborough Twp, Elgin Co, ONT, prob <1840. m Mary MacIntyre, qv, ch: 1. Duncan; 2. Belle; 3. John; 4. Dugald; 5. Kate; 6. Angus; 7. Amelia; 8. Daniel; 9. Archibald.   **PDA 64**.

4822   McARTHUR, Dugald A. From Camus, Inveraray, ARL. To Lobo Twp, Middlesex Co, ONT, 1820. ch: 1. Donald; 2. James; 3. John; 4. Archibald; 5. Colin; 6. Mary; 7. Janet.   **PCM 38**.

4823   McARTHUR, Duncan, b ca 1782. From Killin, PER. To QUE, ex Greenock, summer 1815, stld E ONT. Labourer. Wife Christian Campbell, qv, with him, and 2 ch.   **SEC 4**.

4824   MACARTHUR, Duncan. From Is Canna, INV. bro/o Allan M, qv. To Cape Mabou, Inverness Co, NS, prob <1815. ch: 1. Angus, 1808-78; 2. John; 3. Ronald.   **MP 380**.

4825   McARTHUR, Duncan. From ARL. bro/o Peter M, qv, and John M, qv. To Ekfrid Twp, Middlesex Co, ONT, 1824.   **PCM 31**.

4826   McARTHUR, Duncan, ca 1812–28 Apr 1837. From PER. To QUE and d Montreal.   **Ts Montreal**.

4827   McARTHUR, Effie. From Barvas, Is Lewis, ROC. To QUE, arr 4 Aug 1851; stld Huron Twp, Bruce Co, ONT, 1852. Wife of John McIver, qv.   **DC 25 Dec 1981**.

4828   McARTHUR, Hector, b 1822. From Is Rum, ARL. Poss rel to Peggy McLean, qv. To Gut of Canso, Cape Breton Is, NS, on the *St Lawrence*, ex Tobermory, 11 Jul 1828.   **SLL**.

4829   McARTHUR, Hugh, b ca 1800. Prob from ARL. bro/o Peter M, qv. To Eldon Twp, Victoria Co, ONT, 1842. m Jane McNab, qv, ch: 1. Rachel, qv; 2. Mary; 3. Margaret.   **EC 80**.

4830   MACARTHUR, Isabel. Prob from North Knapdale, ARL. To Aldborough Twp, Elgin Co, ONT, poss 1819. m 27 May 1811, Archibald MacIntyre, qv.   **DC 23 Nov 1981**.

4831   McARTHUR, James. From Comrie par, PER. To

Montreal, QUE, on the *Curlew*, ex Greenock, 21 Jul 1818; stld Con 7, Beckwith Twp, Lanark Co, ONT. Wife Ann with him, and ch: 1. Peter, aged 15; 2. Alexander, aged 11; 3. James, aged 3. **BCL; HCL 34**.

4832 McARTHUR, James. From ROC. To East Williams, Twp, Middlesex Co, ONT, 1832. **PCM 43**.

4833 McARTHUR, James. Prob from ARL. To Pictou, NS, <1835. Son James, b 1835. **HNS iii 308**.

4834 MACARTHUR, James. To QUE on the *Commerce*, ex Greenock, Jun 1820; stld Lanark Co, ONT. **HCL 238**.

4835 MACARTHUR, John, d 7 Jun 1811. From ARL. To Montreal, QUE, <1791. Grocer and spirit merchant. **SGC 125**.

4836 McARTHUR, John. From Inverskilroy, ni, prob INV. Prob s/o Charles M, qv. To Montreal, QUE, ex Fort William, 3 Jul 1802; stld E ONT. **MCM 1/4 24**.

4837 McARTHUR, John, b ca 1728. To Charlottetown, PEI, on the *Rambler*, ex Tobermory, arr 20 Jun 1806. Wife Mary, aged 60, with him. **PLR**.

4838 McARTHUR, John, b ca 1771. Prob s/o John M, qv, and wife Mary. To Charlottetown, PEI, on the *Rambler*, ex Tobermory, arr 20 Jun 1806. Wife Catherine, aged 30, with him, and ch: 1. John, aged 3; 2. Catherine, b 1805. **PLR**.

4839 McARTHUR, John. From ARL. bro/o Duncan M, qv, and Peter M, qv. To Ekfrid Twp, Middlesex Co, ONT, 1824. Went later to CA. **PCM 31**.

4840 McARTHUR, John. To Pictou Co, NS, <1830; stld Wilkins Grant. m Mary Kennedy, ch: 1. Elizabeth, b 1830; 2. Catherine, b 1832. **HNS iii 308**.

4841 McARTHUR, John 'Ruadh'. From Is Islay, ARL. To Eldon Twp, Victoria Co, ONT, <1840. **DC 21 Mar 1980**.

4842 McARTHUR, John. Prob from ARL. To North Dorchester Twp, Middlesex Co, ONT, 1850. **PCM 56**.

4843 McARTHUR, John. From Comrie, PER. To Montreal, QUE, on the *Curlew*, ex Greenock, 21 Jul 1818. Wife Catherine with him, and ch: 1. Duncan, aged 5; 2. Archibald, aged 2. They prob stld Beckwith Twp, Lanark Co, ONT. **BCL**.

4844 McARTHUR, John, b 1814. From Callanish, Is Lewis, ROC. To QUE, ex Stornoway, arr 4 Aug 1851; stld Huron Twp, Bruce Co, ONT, 1852. Farmer. m Christy McDonald, qv, ch: 1. Neil, b 1840; 2. Ann, b 1842; 3. John, b 1848; 4. Katherine, b 1851. **WLC**.

4845 McARTHUR, Lizzie. From Inverskilroy, ni, poss INV. Prob rel to Charles M, qv. To Montreal, QUE, ex Fort William, 3 Jul 1802; stld E ONT. **MCM 1/4 24**.

4846 McARTHUR, Marion, b ca 1781. Prob d/o John M, qv, and wife Mary. To Charlottetown, PEI, on the *Rambler*, ex Tobermory, arr 20 Jun 1806. **PLR**.

4847 McARTHUR, Mary, b ca 1786. Prob d/o John M, qv, and wife Mary. To Charlottetown, PEI, on the *Rambler*, ex Tobermory, arr 20 Jun 1806. **PLR**.

4848 MACARTHUR, Mary, 30 Nov 1782–15 Sep 1877. From Kilninian and Kilmore par, Is Mull, ARL. d/o Duncan M. and Flora Buchanan. To QUE, 1821; stld Markham Twp, York Co, ONT, later Caledon Twp, Peel

Co. d Saugeen Twp, Bruce Co. Pioneer woman settler, and wid/o Duncan Lamont, qv, who d at Long Sault. **DC 7 Jan 1982**.

4849 McARTHUR, Mary Ann, 1829-90. To Caledon Twp. Peel Co, ONT, <1840. Wife of Archibald Mackinnon, qv. **DC 21 Apr 1980**.

4850 McARTHUR, Nancy, 1810–1901. From Is Mull, ARL. To ONT <1820; stld prob Elgin Co. m Alexander Campbell. **SCN**.

4851 McARTHUR, Neil. From Is Lewis, INV. To QUE, ex Stornoway, arr 4 Aug 1851; stld Huron Twp, Bruce Co, ONT, 1852. Head of family. **DC 5 Apr 1967**.

4852 McARTHUR, Peggy, b 1816. From Is Rum, ARL. Poss rel to Peggy McLean, qv. To Gut of Canso, Cape Breton Is, NS, on the *St Lawrence*, ex Tobermory, 11 Jul 1828. **SLL**.

4853 McARTHUR, Peter. From ARL. bro/o Duncan M, qv, and of John M, qv. To Ekfrid Twp, Middlesex Co, ONT, 1824. m Catherine McLennan. Son Peter, 1866–1924, author and journalist. **PCM 31; MDB 428**.

4854 McARTHUR, Peter, 10 Nov 1809–26 Nov 1884. From Clonaig, Skipness, ARL. s/o Archibald M. and Kate Gilchrist. To ONT, prob <1850. m Catherine McLellan, qv, ch: 1. Jane; 2. Alexander; 3. Mary; 4. Catherine; 5. John; 6. Duncan; 7. Peter Gilchrist. **DC 21 Mar 1981**.

4855 McARTHUR, Peter, b 1798. Prob from ARL. bro/o Hugh M, qv. To Eldon Twp, Victoria Co, ONT, 1842. m Anne Muir, qv, ch: 1. John, b 1829; 2. Charles, b 1831; 3. Anne; 4. Mary, b prob Is Islay. **EC 80**.

4856 McARTHUR, Rachel, ca 1833–1933. From ARL. d/o Hugh M, qv, and Jane McNab, qv. To Eldon Twp, Victoria Co, ONT, prob 1842. m John MacMillan, qv. **EC 155**.

4857 McARTHUR, Sarah. From Inverskilroy, ni, prob INV. To Montreal, QUE, ex Fort William, 3 Jul 1802; stld E ONT. **MCM 1/4 24**.

4858 MACASKILL, Bannatyne. From Seilibost, Is Harris, INV. To Baddeck River, Victoria Co, NS, 1841. Farmer. m Elizabeth MacPhee, qv. Son Murdock D, b 1862, schoolteacher and merchant. **HNS iii 336**.

4859 McASKILL, Duncan, b ca 1789. From Is Harris, INV. To Hudson Bay, ca 1813, and prob to Red River. **RRS 13**.

4860 MACASKILL, Ellen. From Is Lewis, ROC. To Antigonish Co, NS, prob <1840. m Hugh MacDonald, qv. **HCA 233**.

4861 MACASKILL, John, 13 Dec 1811–9 Nov 1847. From Is Eigg, Small Isles, INV. s/o Dr Donald M. and Jane Campbell. To CAN, prob <1840. Physician. **CMM 2/16 26**.

4862 McASKILL, Malcolm. Prob from INV. To Montreal, QUE, arr Sep 1802. Petitioned for land on Ottawa River, ONT, 6 Aug 1804. **DC 15 Mar 1980**.

4863 McASKILL, Neil, ca 1803–6 Aug 1899. From Is Skye, INV. To Cape North, Victoria Co, NS. Wife Flora, 1816–1903. **DC 22 Jun 1979**.

4864 McASKILL, Norman. From Cuidinish, Is Harris, INV, but b Berneray. To Victoria Co, NS, 1831; stld St

Anns. Wife Christina Campbell, qv, with him, and family, incl Angus, 1825-63, the 'Cape Breton Giant.' **DC 19 Mar 1964**.

4865   MACASKILL, William. From Is Skye, INV. s/o Capt Kenneth M. of Rudha an Dunain. To CAN, prob <1830. **CMM 2/16 25**.

McAULAY. See also McAULEY and McCAULAY.

4866   MACAULAY, Rev Aneas, 1759–1827. From Applecross, ROC. s/o Rev Aneas M. and Mary MacLeod. To Orwell Bay, PEI, on the *Polly*, ex Portree, arr 7 Aug 1803; stld Belfast, Queens Co. Supervisor of Lord Selkirk's colonisation scheme; physician, grad MD, Glasgow, 1803; clergyman and schoolmaster. Settlers petitioned for him, 1811. m Mary MacDonald, qv, ch: 1. John; 2. William; 3. Ebenezer; 4. Charlotte; 5. Flora; 6. Alice. **RGG 348; HP 71; CMM 3/22 80**.

MACAULAY, Mrs Angus. See MACDONALD, Effie.

4867   MACAULAY, Archibald, b 1807. From Dunganichy, Is Benbecula, INV. s/o Angus M. and Effie MacDonald, qv. To Pictou, NS, on the *Lulan*, ex Glasgow, 17 Aug 1848. Wife Catherine Nicolson, qv, with him, and s Donald. **DC 12 Jul 1979**.

4868   McAULAY, Catherine. From Glenelg, INV. To QUE, ex Greenock, summer 1815; stld prob Lanark Co, ONT. Wife of John McCuaig, qv. **SEC 8**.

4869   MACAULAY, Catherine, 1821-51. From Crowlista, Is Lewis, ROC. To Montreal, QUE, ex Stornoway, 4 Aug 1851; stld Winslow Twp, Compton Co, QUE. Wife of Malcolm MacLeod, qv. **TFT 14; DC 5 Apr 1967**.

4870   McAULAY, Daniel, b ca 1784. To Baddeck dist, Victoria Co, NS, 1814. Prob farmer; m and ch. **CBC 1818**.

4871   McAULAY, Donald. From Frobost, Is South Uist, INV. To QUE on the *British Queen*, ex Arisaig, 16 Aug 1790; stld nr Montreal. Blacksmith. Wife and ch with him. **QCC 103**.

4872   McAULAY, Elizabeth. From Glasgow. sis/o Harry M, weaver. To Montreal, QUE, <1852. m William Ewing, qv. **SH**.

4873   MACAULAY, Rev Ewen, d 17 Apr 1907. From INV. To Kingston, ONT, <1860. Grad BA, Queens Coll, and ord min of Southwold, Elgin Co, 1866. Trans to Bolsover, 1871, and later held charges at London, Guelph, Puslinch, and East Gloucester, ONT, and Lingwick, QUE. **FES vii 640**.

4874   McAULAY, Flora. From Breanish, Uig, Is Lewis, ROC. To ONT, 1838. m Donald Mackay, qv. **Uig OPR 89/1**.

4875   McAULAY, Hugh. Prob from North Uist, INV. To Cape Breton Co, NS, 1844. m Flora McLeod, qv, ch: 1. Annie; 2. Norman, b 1817; 3. Murdoch; 4. John, b 1828. **NSN 7/1**.

4876   McAULAY, John. From Frobost, South Uist, INV. To QUE on the *British Queen*, ex Arisaig, 16 Aug 1790; stld nr Montreal. **QCC 103**.

4877   MACAULAY, Jessie. From Is Lewis, ROC. To Pictou Co, NS, <1790. Wife of Malcolm MacIver, qv. **NSN 38/26**.

4878   MACAULAY, Malcolm, b 1801. From Pennydonald, Uig, Is Lewis, ROC. s/o Angus M. and Kirsty McDonald. To QUE, arr Aug 1851; stld Weedon, Wolfe Co. m (i) Peggy McLean, ch: 1. John, b 1831; m (ii) Annie Buchanan, qv, further ch: 2. Donald; 3. Murdo, b 1836; 4. Margaret, b 1838; 5. Catherine, b 1844; 6. Roderick, b 1846; 7. Norman, b ca 1850. **MGC 2 Aug 1979; WLC; DC 25 Mar 1979**.

4879   McAULAY, Mary. From Glenshiel, ROC. To ONT, ca 1846. Wife of Christopher MacRae, qv. **Glenshiel OPR 67/2**.

4880   MACAULAY, Mary, b 1806. From Uachdar, Is Benbecula, INV. To Pictou, NS, on the *Lulan*, ex Glasgow, 17 Aug 1848. Wife of Neil MacCormick, qv. **DC 12 Jul 1979**.

4881   MACAULAY, Robertson, 20 Jan 1833–27 Sep 1915. From Fraserburgh, ABD. s/o Capt Kenneth M. and Margaret Noble. To Montreal, QUE, 1854. Manager, Sun Life Assurance Co. m Barbara Maria, d/o Thomas Bassett Reid. Son Thomas Bassett, 1860–1915, actuary. **MDB 429**.

4882   McAULEY, Murdock, ca 1789–17 Dec 1817. To St John, NB, and d, ch. **NER viii 98**.

4883   McBAIN, Alexander, ca 1765–29 May 1863. From INV. To Colchester Co, NS, prob <1830; bur East Colchester. Son Benjamen, ca 1820–19 Nov 1857. **DC 22 Jun 1980**.

4884   McBAIN, Donald, b ca 1823. Prob from INV. To Erin Twp, Wellington Co, ONT, <1847; moved to Arthur Twp. Went later to Oak Hill, Victoria Co. Schoolteacher, storekeeper, miller and farmer. m 4 Sep 1850, Catherine Turner, 1832–1915, ch: 1. Duncan, 1852–1931; 2. Jessie, 1855–1941; 3. Sarah, 1859–1951; 4. James Turner, 1861–1945; 5. Donald Turner, b 1863, d Everett, WA; 6. Kathie Edna, 1865–1940; 7. Mary Ellen, 1867–1942; 8. John Arthur, b 1869, d Julian, CA; 9. Christina Isabella, 1872–1955. **DC 27 Mar 1979**.

4885   McBAIN, Isabella, b ca 1807. From Rutherglen, LKS. d/o James M. m 1827, Andrew Hamilton, qv, and emig to McNab Twp, Renfrew Co, ONT. **LDW 2 Jul 1973**.

4886   McBAIN, John, 1817–1905. From Alvie, INV. s/o Lachlan M, tailor in Meadowside, and wife Margaret. To Teeswater, Culross Twp, Bruce Co, ONT. **Ts Alvie**.

4887   McBAIN, John, 1831–1904. From Rothiemurchus, INV. s/o Thomas M. and Janet MacIntyre. To Lucknow, Kinloss Twp, Bruce Co, ONT. Teacher. **Ts Rothiemurchus**.

4888   McBAIN, John. To Pictou Co, NS, <1815; stld East River St Marys. **CP 35**.

4889   McBAIN, Margery, ca 1799–5 Feb 1862. Prob from INV. To Elgin Co, ONT, <1832. m as his second wife, 1832, James Fraser, missionary, qv. **DC 11 Mar 1979**.

4890   McBAIN, William. To Montreal, QUE, 1809. **DC 22 Apr 1968**.

4891   McBANE, Duncan. From INV. To Lobo Twp, Middlesex Co, ONT, <1840. ch: 1. Alexander; 2. John; 3. Mrs Ross; 4. Mrs McLeish; 5. Mrs Scott; 6. Mrs Henderson. **PCM 40**.

4892 McBANE, Peter. From Loch Awe, ARL. To Lobo Twp, Middlesex Co, ONT, 1840. **PCM 40**.

4893 McBANE, William. Prob from ARL. To Lobo Twp, Middlesex Co, ONT, 1850. Weaver. **PCM 39**.

4894 McBEAN, Alexander. From Nairn. To Ekfrid Twp, Middlesex Co, ONT, 1835. **PCM 30**.

4895 McBEAN, Duncan, ca 1807–14 Mar 1880. From Moy, INV. To Colchester Co, NS, prob <1840. Bur East Earltown. m Helen Ross, 1809-45. **DC 22 Jun 1980**.

4896 McBEAN, Hugh, ca 1771–8 Feb 1859. Prob from Moy, INV. bro/o Margaret M, qv. To London Twp, Middlesex Co, ONT, ca 1828. **PCM 50**.

4897 McBEAN, Janet, ca 1775–10 Apr 1862. Prob from Moy, INV. sis/o Hugh M, qv, and Margaret M, qv. To London Twp, Middlesex Co, ONT, ca 1828. **PCM 50**.

4898 MACBEAN, Rev John, 1 Apr 1811–13 Aug 1897. From Nairn. s/o John M. Grad MA, Kings Coll, Aberdeen, 1832, and became a teacher. To Northumberland Co, NB, 1841. Min at Tabusintac and Burnt Ch until 1843, then trans to St Andrews, Chatham. Retr to SCT, 1847, and went later to AUS. **KCG 287; FES vii 593**.

4899 McBEAN, Margaret, ca 1773–22 Jul 1856. Prob from Moy, INV. sis/o Hugh M, qv, and Janet M, qv. To London Twp, Middlesex Co, ONT, ca 1828. m John Barclay, qv. **PCM 50**.

4900 McBEAN, Mary. From INV. To Inverness Twp, Megantic Co, QUE, 1833. m James McGillivray, qv. **AMC 48**.

4901 McBEAN, William, 27 Apr 1798–8 Sep 1883. From ABD. To Montreal, QUE, ca 1830. Miller and distiller. Session-clerk of St Gabriel Street Ch. ch. **SGC 560**.

4902 McBEAN, William. From Nairn. To Ekfrid Twp, Middlesex Co, ONT, 1835. Tailor. **PCM 30**.

McBEATH. See also McBETH.

4903 McBEATH, Alexander, b ca 1780. From Kildonan, SUT. To York Factory, Hudson Bay, arr 26 Aug 1815; thence to Red River. Pioneer settler. Wife Christian Gunn, qv, with him, and ch: 1. Margaret, aged 18; 2. Molly, aged 18; 3. George, aged 16; 4. Christian, aged 14; 5. Roderick, aged 12; 6. Robert, aged 10; 7. Adam, aged 6; 8. Morrison, aged 4. **LSC 326**.

4904 McBEATH, Andrew, b ca 1792. From Borrobol, Kildonan, SUT. s/o Mrs Barbara S, qv. To Fort Churchill, Hudson Bay, on the *Prince of Wales*, ex Stromness, 28 Jun 1813. Went to York Factory, Apr 1814, and then to Red River. Left settlement and arr Holland River, 6 Sep 1815, with wife Janet and 1 child. **LSS 185; RRS 26; LSC 322**.

4905 McBEATH, Mrs Barbara, b ca 1767. From Borrobol, Kildonan, SUT. wid/o John M. To Fort Churchill, Hudson Bay, on the *Prince of Wales*, ex Stomness, 28 Jun 1813. Trekked to Red River, spring 1814, with ch: 1. Janet or Hannah, aged 23; 2. Andrew, qv; 3. Charles, qv. Left settlement and arr Holland River, 6 Sep 1815. **LSS 185; RRS 26; LSC 322**.

4906 McBEATH, Charles, b ca 1797. From Borrobol, Kildonan, SUT. To Fort Churchill, Hudson Bay, on the *Prince of Wales*, ex Stromness, 28 Jun 1813. Went to Red River, spring 1814, but left settlement and arr Holland River, 6 Sep 1815. **LSS 185; RRS 26; LSC 322**.

4907 McBEATH, George, ca 1740–3 Dec 1812. To Montreal, QUE, ca 1758. Fur-trader, and became partner of NWCo. Sold out in 1787, and stld L'Assomption. MLC, 1793. m (i) Jane Graham, d 1787, ch; m (ii) 1801, Erie Smyth, Point-aux-Trembles, wid/o David McCrae. **SGC 96; MDB 429**.

4908 McBEATH, John. Prob from Kildonan, SUT. To Hudson Bay and Red River <1815. Pioneer settler. **LSC 327; RRS 192**.

4909 McBEATH, William, ca 1767–13 Aug 1840. From SUT. To Black River, Northumberland Co, NB, 1819. Wife Elizabeth, 1768–1837, with him. **DC 30 Jul 1980**.

4910 MACBETH, Rev James, b 1810. From Newton-on-Ayr, AYR. s/o James M, surgeon. Matric Univ of Glasgow, 1825. Min of Ladyloan, Arbroath, 1837-42; Lauriston QS, Kingston, Glasgow, 1842-43; and of Lauriston FC, 1843-50. Deposed in 1850 and went to CAN. m Mary Ann, d/o Capt McAllister. **GMA 11643; AFC i 215; FES iii 422**.

4911 McBETH, Neil. To Gairloch, Pictou Co, NS, prob <1830. m Catherine McKay, qv. **DC 10 Feb 1980**.

4912 McBRAYNE, Janet. From Campbeltown, ARL. To ONT, ca 1837. d/o John M. and Mary Campbell. To ONT 1837. m James McCorvie, qv. **DC 7 Jan 1983**.

4913 McBRIDE, Alexander, 20 Aug 1843–6 Apr 1924. From Shenochie, Kilmory par, Is Arran, BUT. s/o Donald M, qv, and Isabella McDonald, qv. To Nash Creek, Restigouche Co, NB, 1851, and d at Chilliwack, BC. **DC 23 May 1980**.

4914 McBRIDE, Anthony. To Lanark Co, ONT, 1821; stld Lot 13, Con 2, North Sherbrooke Twp. **HCL 74**.

4915 McBRIDE, Archibald, d 1890. From ARL. To Caledon Twp, Peel Co, ONT, <1840. **DC 21 Apr 1980**.

4916 McBRIDE, Christina, 11 Nov 1850–6 Jun 1914. From Kilmory par, Is Arran, BUT. d/o Donald M, qv, and Isabella McDonald, qv. To Nash Creek, Restigouche Co, NB, 1851. m John, s/o Hugh McKenzie, ch. **DC 23 May 1980**.

4917 McBRIDE, Donald, 1799–25 Nov 1879. From Shenachie, Kilmory par, Is Arran, BUT. s/o Thomas M. and Janet McMillan. To Nash Creek, Restigouche Co, NB, 1851. Wife Isabella McDonald, qv, with him. ch: 1. Thomas, qv; 2. John, qv; 3. Alexander, qv; 4. Janet, qv; 5. Donald or Daniel, qv; 6. Neil, 1850-76; 7. Christina, qv; 8. Margaret, 1853–1947; 9. Isabella, d inf; 10. Peter, 1863–1965. **DC 23 Mar 1980**.

4918 McBRIDE, Donald or Daniel, 7 Feb 1847–20 Dec 1931. From Kilmory par, Is Arran, BUT. s/o Donald M, qv, and Isabella McDonald, qv. To Nash Creek, Restigouche Co, NB, 1851; later to Spokane, WA. m Elizabeth Campbell Bell, ch: 1. Edwin Bell, b 1879; 2. Elizabeth Campbell, b 1885; 3. Clarence Smith, b 1885; 4. Kenneth Sidney, b 1892. **DC 23 May 1980**.

4919 McBRIDE, James, 1809-87. From ARL. To Caledon Twp, Peel Co, ONT, <1840. Wife Catherine Campbell, qv, with him. **DC 21 Apr 1980**.

4920   McBRIDE, Janet, 10 Nov 1845–3 Jun 1917. From Shenochie, Kilmory par, Is Arran, BUT. d/o Donald M, qv, and Isabella McDonald, qv. To Nash Creek, Restigouche Co, NB, 1851, and d Tabusintac, Northumberland Co. m Daniel McCormack, qv. **DC 23 May 1980**.

4921   McBRIDE, Janet, 1783–1872. From West Bennan, Kilmory par, Is Arran, BUT. To Restigouche Co, NB, <1835. Wife of Donald Murphy or Murchie, qv. **MAC 24**.

4922   McBRIDE, John, 23 Jan 1842–7 Aug 1873. From Shenochie, Kilmory par, Is Arran, BUT. s/o Donald M, qv, and Isabella McDonald, qv. To Nash Creek, Restigouche Co, NB, 1851, and d Antelope, Placer Co, CA. **DC 23 May 1980**.

4923   McBRIDE, Mary. From ARL. To Caledon Twp, Peel Co, ONT, prob <1835. Wife of James Brown, qv. **DC 21 Apr 1980**.

4924   McBRIDE, Mary, b ca 1776. From Kilbride par, Is Arran, BUT. To Charlo, Restigouche Co, NB, <1836. Wife of James Hamilton, qv. **MAC 14**.

4925   McBRIDE, Neil, d 1847. From ARL. To Caledon Twp, Peel Co, ONT, <1840. Wife Annie McKellar, qv, with him. **DC 21 Apr 1980**.

4926   McBRIDE, Samuel. To Westminster Twp, Middlesex Co, ONT, <1840; stld London. **PCM 55**.

4927   McBRIDE, Thomas, 7 Aug 1839–20 Oct 1892. From Shenochie, Kilmory par, Is Arran, BUT. s/o Donald M, qv, and Isabella McDonald, qv. To Nash Creek, Restigouche Co, NB, 1851. m Martha Emma Finley, ch: 1. Arthur Thomas, b 30 May 1881; 2. Agnes Finley, b 30 Oct 1882; 3. John Leslie, b 11 May 1886; 4. Bernice Ramsey, b 3 Apr 1890. **DC 23 May 1980**.

4928   McBURNIE, Robert, b ca 1754. From Fairgirth, Colvend par, KKD. Prob bro/o William M, qv. To Georgetown, PEI, on the *Lovely Nellie*, ex Annan, 1774. Joiner. **ELN**.

4929   McBURNIE, Robert. Prob from KKD. To Truro, Colchester Co, NS, <1820; later in Tatamagouche. Farmer and teacher. **HT 48**.

4930   McBURNIE, William, b ca 1748. From Fairgirth, Colvend par, KKD. Prob bro/o Robert M, qv. To Georgetown, PEI, on the *Lovely Nellie*, ex Annan, 1774. Joiner. **ELN**.

4931   McCABE, James. To Pictou Co, NS, and gr 300 acres on West River, 26 Aug 1783. **HPC App A**.

4932   McCABE, John. To Pictou Co, NS, <1776. **HPC App B**.

McCALDER. See also McALDER.

4933   McCALDER, Malcolm 'Og'. From Is Colonsay, ARL. s/o Malcolm 'Mor' M. To ONT <1855; stld Mariposa Twp, Victoria Co. Son Malcolm. **DC 23 Jul 1964**.

4934   McCALDER, Peter, 1790–1845. From Is Colonsay, ARL. To PEI, 1840. Fisherman. m Isabella Brown, qv, ch: 1. Mary, b ca 1825; 2. William, 1827-45; 3. Isabella. **DC 23 Jul 1964**.

4935   McCALL, Dugald. From Craignish, ARL. To Lobo Twp, Middlesex Co, ONT, 1824. ch: 1. Neil; 2. Duncan; 3. Malcolm; 4. Janet; 5. Nancy. **PCM 38**.

4936   McCALL, Duncan. From Craignish, ARL. To Lobo Twp, Middlesex Co, ONT, 1824. ch: 1. Donald; 2. Nancy; 3. Mrs John McLellan. **PCM 38**.

4937   McCALL, George, ca 1734–23 Feb 1812. From DFS. To St John, NB, <1800. Merchant. Wife Lydia, 1739–21 Nov 1829. **NER viii 98**.

4938   McCALL, Janet. From AYR. d/o James M, mason in Content, AYR. To Montreal, QUE, <1851. m — Goudie. **SH**.

4939   McCALLEY, Andrew, 10 Oct 1825–15 Sep 1891. Prob from FIF. s/o James M. and Ann McDonald. To PEI, 1850, but stld St John, NB, 1853. Went later to IL and IA, finally Springfield, OR. m Christina Miller, qv, ch: 1. Janette; 2. Christine, d inf; 3. Ann, b 1849; 4. Agnes, b 1852; 5. William Wallace, b 1853, NB; 6. Robert Morrison, b 1856; 7. Andrew, b 1857; 8. Theodore, b 1858, went to CA; 9. Walter Scott, b 1862; 10. Albert Edward, b 1864. **DC 2 Nov 1975**.

4940   McCALLOCH, William. To Pictou, NS, on the *Lulan*, ex Glasgow, 17 Aug 1848. **DC 12 Jul 1979**.

McCALLUM. See also McALLUM.

4941   McCALLUM, Alexander, d ca 1899. From Craignish, ARL. To Westminster Twp, Middlesex Co, ONT, 1836. ch incl: 1. Dr Hugh; 2. Prof A.B., physiologist, Univ of Toronto. **PCM 52**.

4942   McCALLUM, Angus. To QUE on the *Brock*, ex Greenock, 9 Jul 1820; stld prob Lanark Co, ONT. **HCL 238**.

4943   MACCALLUM, Ann, b ca 1815. From Kilmartin par, ARL. To Southwold Twp, Elgin Co, ONT, 1843. Wife of Donald MacArthur, qv, m 27 May 1843. **DC 5 Jan 1976**.

4944   McCALLUM, Ann, 1809-39. From ARL. To Caledon Twp, Peel Co, ONT, prob <1835. Wife of John Graham, qv. **DC 21 Apr 1980**.

4945   McCALLUM, Archibald 'Dalbuidhe'. From ARL. To Mosa Twp, Middlesex Co, ONT, 1831. **PCM 2**.

4946   McCALLUM, Archibald. From ARL. To Aldborough Twp, Elgin Co, ONT, 1819; moved to Mosa Twp, Middlesex Co, 1831. **PCM 23**.

4947   McCALLUM, Archibald, ca 1802–9 Jun 1880. From PER. To Halton Co, ONT, prob <1835; stld Esquesing Twp. Bur Boston cemetery. m Margaret McPherson, qv. **EPE 76**.

4948   McCALLUM, Catherine. Prob from Ross, Is Mull, ARL. To QUE, 1828; stld Lochaber, Ottawa Co. Wife of Neil Campbell, qv. **ELB 1**.

4949   MACCALLUM, Catherine, 1817–3 Sep 1883. From ARL. To Mosa Twp, Middlesex Co, ONT, <1843. m Duncan McKellar, qv. **DC 29 Oct 1979**.

4950   McCALLUM, Christina, 1812–1904. From Knapdale, ARL. To ONT, poss <1830; stld Dunwich Twp, Elgin Co. Wife of John Galbraith, qv. **GSO 33**.

4951   McCALLUM, Christina. Prob from Dull par, PER. To ONT, 1855. Wife of James Robertson, qv. **MDB 635**.

4952   MACCALLUM, Christine, b ca 1800. From Slackvullin, Kilmartin par, ARL. To Beverley Twp, Wentworth Co, ONT, 1847. Wife of Dougald MacPhail, qv.   **DC 11 Nov 1981**.

4953   McCALLUM, Donald, b 1773. Poss from ARL. To QUE on the *Oughton*, arr Jul 1804; stld Baldoon, Dover Twp, Kent Co, ONT. Wife Mary with him, and ch: 1. Hugh; 2. Jean, prob d 1805; 3. Flora, qv; 4. Isabella or Amelia; 5. Peggy; 6. Ann or Nancy.   **UCM 267, 302; DC 4 Oct 1979**.

4954   McCALLUM, Donald. From Skipness, ARL. To King Twp, York Co, ONT, 1831; moved to Dunwich Twp, Elgin Co, 1850. m Nancy McVannel, qv.   **DC 16 Mar 1978**.

4955   McCALLUM, Dugald, ca 1757–29 Jul 1829. From Southend, Kintyre, ARL. To Queens Co, PEI, <1815; stld Brackley Point. Farmer. m Margaret Shaw, qv, ch: 1. Janet, b 1786; 2. Dugald, b 1789; 3. Alexander, b 1791; 4. Neil, 1794–1850; 5. Donald, b 1799.   **DC 20 Dec 1981**.

4956   McCALLUM, Duncan, 2 Jan 1757–6 Jan 1844. From ARL. To PEI, 1771; stld Brackley Point, Queens Co. m 3 May 1784, Janet McGregor, qv, ch: 1. Neil, 1786–1879; 2. Margaret, b 1787; 3. Catherine, b 1789; 4. James, 1793–1871; 5. Elizabeth, b 1795; 6. Isabella, 1797–1878; 7. Mary, 1799–1853; 8. John, 1808-28.   **DC 27 Jul 1980**.

4957   McCALLUM, Duncan. From Comrie par, PER. To Montreal, QUE, on the *Curlew*, ex Greenock, 21 Jul 1818; stld prob Beckwith Twp, Lanark Co, ONT. Wife Christian with him, and s Robert, aged 10.   **BCL**.

4958   McCALLUM, Duncan. From Comrie par, PER. To Montreal, QUE, on the *Curlew*, ex Greenock, 21 Jul 1818; stld prob Beckwith Twp, Lanark Co, ONT. ch with him: 1. Angus, aged 10; 2. Duncan, aged 6.   **BCL**.

4959   McCALLUM, Duncan. Prob from Ross, Is Mull, ARL. To QUE, 1828; stld Lochaber, Ottawa Co.   **ELB 1**.

4960   McCALLUM, Duncan. From ARL. To Mosa Twp, Middlesex Co, ONT, prob <1832. Teacher. Drowned in Thames River.   **PMC 24**.

4961   McCALLUM, Duncan. From ARL. To Ekfrid Twp, Middlesex Co, ONT, 1832. ch: 1. Donald; 2. Archibald; 3. John; 4. Nebs.   **PCM 30**.

4962   McCALLUM, Duncan, 7 Jun 1800–1 Sep 1883. From Kenmore, PER. To Halton Co, ONT, prob <1850; stld Esquesing Twp. Bur Boston cemetery. m Susan Menzies, qv.   **EPE 75**.

4963   McCALLUM, Finlay, 1813–1 Dec 1881. From Kenmore, PER. To Halton Co, ONT, 1833; stld Esquesing Twp. Bur Boston cemetery.   **EPE 76**.

4964   McCALLUM, Flora, b 1790. Poss from ARL. d/o Donald M, qv, and wife Mary. To QUE on the *Oughton*, arr Jul 1804; stld Baldoon, Dover Twp, Kent Co, ONT. m Angus McDougall, qv.   **UCM 267; DC 4 Oct 1979**.

4965   MACCALLUM, George. From Jedburgh, ROX. To ONT. m Jane Sangster. Son George Alexander, physician.   **DC 29 Sep 1964**.

4966   McCALLUM, Hugh, b 1811. From ARL. To North Dorchester Twp, Middlesex Co, ONT, 1844. m Sarah

Tucker, ch: 1. Colin; 2. Mary; 3. George; 4. Angus; 5. Sarah.   **DC 30 Jul 1982**.

4967   McCALLUM, James, 1805–19 Oct 1863. From Kenmore, PER. To Halton Co, ONT, 1832; stld Esquesing Twp. d E. Oxford.   **EPE 76**.

4968   McCALLUM, James. From ARL. To North Dorchester Twp, Middlesex Co, ONT, 1844.   **PCM 57**.

4969   McCALLUM, Jane, ca 1791–2 Apr 1854. From ARL. To Pictou Co, NS. m William Dunbar Maxwell, qv.   **DC 10 Feb 1980**.

4970   McCALLUM, Janet, b ca 1791. Prob from Kilfinichen par, Is Mull, ARL. To QUE, 1829; stld Lochaber, Ottawa Co. Wife of Donald McLean, qv.   **ELB 1**.

4971   McCALLUM, Janet. From Is Tyree, ARL. To Cape Breton Is, NS, 1831. Wife of John Cameron, qv.   **DC 4 Mar 1981**.

4972   McCALLUM, John, 15 Mar 1764–ca 1835. From Kilmartin par, ARL. To Prince Co, PEI, poss 1770; moved to QUE, 1813, but retr 1831. Farmer and physician. m Catherine Shaw, qv, ch: 1. Neil, b 30 Nov 1787; 2. Christy, b 24 Jul 1789; 3. James, b 11 Oct 1791; 4. Daniel, b 23 Dec 1793; 5. John, d inf, 1797; 6. Ann, b 29 Oct 1798; 7. David, b 12 Apr 1800; 8. John J, b 18 Jun 1802; 9. Duncan, b 12 May 1805; 10. Alexander R, b 26 May 1808.   **DC 11 Apr 1981**.

4973   McCALLUM, John. From Carnbaan, Glenlyon, PER. To PEI, <1807.   **DC 21 Mar 1981**.

4974   McCALLUM, John, b ca 1771. To Pictou Co, NS, 1815; res Pictou Town, 1816. m, with 4 ch.   **INS 39**.

4975   McCALLUM, John, 1807-92. From ARL. To Mosa Twp, Middlesex Co, ONT, prob 1819. m 1 Apr 1834, Nancy McKellar, qv.   **DC 29 Oct 1979**.

4976   McCALLUM, Rev John, d 3 Oct 1849. Grad MA Kings Coll, Aberdeen, 1824, and became Ch of England clergyman. To Hudson Bay and served at Red River.   **KCG 280; DGH 11 Apr 1850**.

4977   McCALLUM, John, 1774–1863. From PER. To McNab Twp, Renfrew Co, ONT, poss <1825. m Janet Fisher, qv.   **DC 22 Aug 1978**.

4978   McCALLUM, John. Prob from Ross, Is Mull, ARL. To QUE, 1828; stld Lochaber, Ottawa Co.   **ELB 1**.

4979   McCALLUM, John. From ARL. s/o John M. To Ekfrid Twp, Middlesex Co, ONT, ca 1831. ch: 1. Donald; 2. Alexander; 3. Neil; 4. Mrs Dobie.   **PCM 30**.

4980   McCALLUM, John, 11 Apr 1806–15 Sep 1876. From Stranraer, WIG, but progenitors from ARL. To Montreal, QUE, on the *Oxford*, 1832. Pianoforte maker.   **SGC 558**.

4981   McCALLUM, John. From ARL. To Ekfrid Twp, Middlesex Co, ONT, 1832.   **PCM 30**.

4982   McCALLUM, John. Prob from ARL. To Eldon Twp, Victoria Co, ONT, <1840. Son Duncan, blacksmith.   **EC 81**.

4983   McCALLUM, Lachlan, b 15 Mar 1823. From ARL. To Haldimand Co, ONT, 1842. Contractor, shipbuilder and Conservative politician.   **BNA 1164**.

4984   McCALLUM, Malcolm. Prob from Ross, Is Mull, ARL. To QUE, 1828; stld Lochaber, Ottawa Co.   **ELB 1**.

4985   MACCALLUM, Mary, d ca 1860. From Tenga, nr Tobermory, Is Mull, ARL. To Mull River, Inverness Co, NS, 1820. Wife of Allan Campbell, qv.   **MP ii 119**.

4986   McCALLUM, Neil. From ARL. To PEI, 1771; stld Brackley Point, Queens Co. m Catherine McKay, qv. Son Duncan, qv.   **DC 27 Jul 1980**.

4987   McCALLUM, Neil, b ca 1775. From Is Mull, ARL. To Charlottetown, PEI, on the *Clarendon*, ex Oban, 6 Aug 1808. Wife Mary, aged 32, with him, and ch: 1. John, aged 12; 2. Finlay, aged 5; 3. Archibald, aged 5; 4. Mary, aged 3; 5. Donald, aged 1.   **CPL**.

4988   MacCALLUM, Neil. From Is Tyree, ARL. To Whycocomagh, Inverness Co, NS, prob 1820. m Elizabeth McDonald, qv.   **DC 23 Feb 1980**.

4989   McCALLUM, Neil. From Inverary, ARL. To Caradoc Twp, Middlesex Co, ONT, 1831. ch: 1. Neil; 2. Mrs James Crawford; 3. Christy.   **PCM 35**.

4990   McCALLUM, Neil. From ARL. To Metcalfe Twp, Middlesex Co, ONT, 1842. ch: 1. John; 2. Archibald; 3. Angus, res MI; 4. William, res MI.   **PCM 26**.

4991   McCALLUM, Neil. From Lochgilphead, ARL. To Lobo Twp, Middlesex Co, ONT, 1844. Sailor.   **PCM 39**.

4992   McCALLUM, Peter, b ca 1798. To Pictou Co, NS, 1815; res Lower Settlement, 1816. Clerk, unm.   **INS 38**.

4993   McCALLUM, Robert. From Bonhill, DNB. To ONT, ca 1855; later to IA. Wife Ann McKay, qv, with him, and ch.   **DC 23 Feb 1981**.

4994   McCANDLISH, Thomas. From Wigtown. To Perth Twp, Lanark Co, ONT, <1849. m Isabella Martin, qv.   **DGH 10 May 1859**.

McCARA. See also MACARA.

4995   McCARA, Anne. d/o Rev John McAra, Pathstruie, Forgandenny, PER. To Tatamagouche, Colchester Co, NS, <1840. m Rev Robert Blackwood, qv.   **HT 81**.

4996   McCARTER, Samuel, b ca 1758. To Richmond Co, NS, 1798.   **CBC 1818**.

4997   McCARTNEY, Agnes, b ca 1819. To St Gabriel de Valcartier, QUE, poss <1855.   **Census 1861**.

4998   McCARTNEY, James, b ca 1815. To St Gabriel de Valcartier, QUE, poss <1855.   **Census 1861**.

4999   McCARTNEY, Janet, b ca 1826. To St Gabriel de Valcartier, QUE, poss <1855.   **Census 1861**.

5000   McCARTNEY, Mary, b ca 1816. To St Gabriel de Valcartier, QUE, poss <1855.   **Census 1861**.

5001   McCAUGHTER, Janet, b ca 1739. From KKD. To Georgetown, Kings Co, PEI, on the *Lovely Nellie*, ex Carsethorn, May 1775. Went later to Pictou Co, NS. Wife of Anthony Culton, qv.   **ELN**.

5002   McCAUL, Archibald, 1800-80. Poss from Kilmartin par, ARL. s/o Malcolm M. and Christina Morrison. To West Zorra Twp, Oxford Co, ONT, <1820. m 1833, Ann McDonald, qv, ch: 1. Robert, b 1834; 2. Nancy; 3. Christine; 4. Archibald; 5. Malcolm. **DC 25 Nov 1981**.

McCAULAY. See also McAULAY, McAULEY.

5003   McCAULAY, Duncan, b 7 Dec 1792. From Cardross, DNB. s/o Aulay M, merchant, and Catherine Leitch. Matric Univ of Glasgow, 1808. App missionary by Glasgow Colonial Society, 1833, and went to QUE. Min at Leeds, 1833-34.   **GMA 7483; FES vii 640**.

McCLARTY. See also McLARTY.

5004   McCLARTY, William. To QUE, ca 1840; stld Richelieu Co. m Harriet Garfield. Son Lucius Lyman, b West Brome, 1869.   **MGC 2 Aug 1979**.

McCLEAN. See also McLEAN, McLAINE, and McLANE.

5005   McCLEAN, John. To Georgetown, Kings Co, PEI, on the *Lovely Nellie*, May 1775. Joined the ship at Kirkcudbright, with wife and son.   **ELN**.

5006   McCLEAN, Charles. To QUE on the *Brock*, ex Greenock, 9 Jul 1820; stld prob Lanark Co, ONT. **HCL 238**.

McCLELLAN. See also McLELLAN.

5007   McCLELLAN, Alexander. Prob from Gatehouse-of-Fleet, KKD. To Halifax, NS, <1815.   **SH**.

5008   McCLELLAN, Anthony, b 1720. From Colmonell, AYR. s/o Thomas M. of Craigneil, and Elizabeth Alexander. To Georgetown, Kings Co, PEI, on the *Lovely Nellie*, May 1775. Joined the ship at Kirkcudbright. 'A man of good character.' Wife and 5 ch with him, incl Anthony. They moved to West River, Pictou Co, NS. **HNS iii 126; HPC App D and E**.

5009   McCLELLAN, David, ca 1800-40. Prob from DFS. To St John, NB. Shipbuilder.   **DC 30 Jul 1981**.

5010   McCLESH, John. To QUE on the *Caledonian*, 1816; stld Lot 23, Con 9, Bathurst Twp, Lanark Co, ONT.   **HCL 234**.

5011   McCLIMENS, James. To Ekfrid Twp, Middlesex Co, ONT, <1828.   **PCM 29**.

5012   McCLUE, Charles, b ca 1836. From WIG. s/o Alexander and Jane M. To Reach Twp, Ontario Co, ONT, <5 Apr 1858, when he m Anna, aged 21, d/o Francis and Harriet Russell, of Whitchurch Twp, York Co.   **DC 24 Mar 1982**.

5013   McCLURE, Duncan, b ca 1783. From Glenelg, INV. To QUE, ex Greenock, summer 1815; stld prob Lanark Co, ONT. Farmer. Wife Janet Murchison, qv, with him, and 4 ch.   **SEC 7**.

5014   McCLURE, Mary. From Glenelg, INV. To QUE, ex Greenock, summer 1815; stld prob Lanark Co, ONT. Wife of John McIntosh, qv.   **SEC 7**.

5015   McCLUTCHEON, Kenneth. To Pictou, NS, <1776.   **HPC App B**.

5016   McCLYMONT, John, d 15 Sep 1858. From Glenluce, WIG. s/o Peter M, merchant. To St David, Charlotte Co, NB.   **DGH 17 Dec 1858**.

5017   McCOLL, Rev Alexander, ca 1804–16 Nov 1872. From Bridgetown, Glasgow. bro/o Rev John M, min of the Relief Ch, Patrick. To Lewiston, NY, 1847. Held charges at Seneca Falls and Niagara.   **UPC ii 306n**.

5018   McCOLL, Rev Alexander. From INV. s/o John M, farmer. Matric Univ of Glasgow, 1838. To QUE, 1842,

and became min at Aldborough, Elgin Co, ONT.
GMA 13900; FES vii 640.

5019 McCOLL, Ann, ca 1768–1840. From Is Mull,
ARL. To Charlottetown, PEI, on the *Phoenix*, ex
Tobermory, 1810; stld Queens Co. Wife of Archibald
McGregor, qv.   **DC 11 Apr 1981**.

5020 McCOLL, Donald. From Ardnamurchan, ARL. Rel
to Malcolm M, qv, and Samuel M, qv. To QUE, 1827;
moved to Westminster Twp, Middlesex Co, ONT, 1837.
PCM 52.

5021 McCOLL, Donald. From ARL. To Ekfrid Twp,
Middlesex Co, ONT, 1849. ch: 1. Donald Alexander;
2. Neil; 3. Mrs McKenzie.   **PCM 31**.

5022 McCOLL, Duncan. From ARL. s/o John M, qv.
To Ekfrid Twp, Middlesex Co, ONT, 1831. Catechist.
m 31 Mar 1836, Sarah McTaggart, qv, ch: 1. Hugh,
1837–1910, Postmaster of Strathroy, and historian of
Middlesex Co; 2. John D; 3. Mary; 4. Isabella; 5. Sarah;
6. Kate; 7. Christy.   **PCM 18, 30**.

5023 McCOLL, Duncan. From ARL. To Aldborough
Twp, Elgin Co, ONT, 1853. Son Dr Hugh.   **PDA 68**.

5024 McCOLL, Evan, 21 Sep 1808–25 Jul 1898. From
Kenmore par, PER. s/o — M. and — Cameron. To
Kingston, ONT, 1850. Customs official and Gaelic
poet.   **BNA 1143; MDB 432**.

5025 McCOLL, Hugh, d 1851. From ARL. To Ekfrid
Twp, Middlesex Co, ONT, ca 1849.   **PCM 31**.

5026 McCOLL, John. From Lismore, ARL. To Lobo
Twp, Middlesex Co, ONT. ch: 1. Duncan; 2. Thomas;
3. John; 4. Dugald; 5. Donald; 6. Archibald; 7. William;
8. Hugh; 9. Ellen; 10. Agnes; 11. Mary; 12. Christy;
13. Lizzie; 14. Barbara.   **PCM 38**.

5027 McCOLL, John. From ARL. To Ekfrid Twp,
Middlesex Co, ONT, 1831. ch: 1. Duncan, qv; 2. Hugh,
drowned in Niagara River; 3. Catherine; 4. Mary.
PCM 30.

5028 McCOLL, John. From Ardnamurchan, ARL. To
Westminster Twp, Middlesex Co, ONT, 1841. Son
Duncan, catechist, qv.   **PCM 52**.

5029 McCOLL, John B. From Appin, ARL. To ONT,
prob <1860. Son John H.   **DC 29 Sep 1964**.

5030 McCOLL, Louisa, b ca 1794. From RFW.
sis/o Mary M. To ONT, ca 1834; stld Huron Tract.
m Robert Graham Dunlop, qv.   **DC 10 Mar 1981**.

5031 McCOLL, Malcolm, d ca 1874. To
Ardnamurchan, ARL. Rel to Donald M, qv, and Samuel
M, qv. To QUE, 1827; moved to Westminster Twp,
Middlesex Co, ONT, 1837. ch: 1. Samuel, dentist,
Bellevue, MI; 2. Malcolm, physician, Detroit; 3. Duncan,
farmer.   **PCM 52**.

5032 McCOLL, Malcolm. From ARL. To Mosa Twp,
Middlesex Co, ONT, 1840. Son Neil, mill-owner and local
politician.   **PCM 24**.

5033 McCOLL, Margaret, 15 May 1805–28 Feb 1854.
From Balfron, STI. d/o William M, qv. To Montreal,
QUE, 1829; later to Peacham, VT. m Donald or Daniel
Sillars, qv.   **DC 15 Jul 1980**.

5034 McCOLL, Margaret, b 20 Sep 1817. From

Paisley, RFW. To ONT <1855. m Robert Collins, qv.
DC 7 Apr 1972.

5035 McCOLL, Samuel. From Ardnamurchan, ARL.
Rel to Donald M, qv, and Malcolm M, qv. To QUE, 1827;
moved to Westminster Twp, Middlesex Co, ONT, 1837.
Adopted s John S.   **PCM 52**.

5036 McCOLL, Samuel, b 1777. From Salachan, ARL.
s/o Samuel M. To ONT 1831. m Sarah Colquhoun, ch:
1. John S, b 22 Jul 1819; 2. Hugh, b ca 1821.
DC 20 Nov 1960.

5037 McCOLL, Samuel. From ARL. To Ekfrid Twp,
Middlesex Co, ONT, 1847. ch: 1. Daniel B, res Appin;
2. Catherine; 3. Duncan; 4. Mary; 5. John;
6. Samuel.   **PCM 31**.

5038 McCOLL, Thomas. From ARL. To QUE on the
Mars, ex Tobermory, 28 Jul 1818; stld Aldborough Twp,
Elgin Co. Schoolteacher, Brocks Creek.   **PDA 24, 60**.

5039 McCOLL, Thomas, b 1791. From Kilberry, ARL.
To Lobo Twp, Middlesex Co, ONT, <1830. Lay
preacher.   **PCM 15**.

5040 McCOLL, William, b ca 1763. From Drymen or
Balfron, STI. To Montreal, QUE, 1829; later to Peacham,
VT, and Peabody, MA. Dau Margaret.   **DC 15 Jul 1980**.

5041 McCOLLUM, Duncan. From ARL, poss Knapdale.
To QUE on the *Mars*, ex Tobermory, 28 Jul 1818; stld
Aldborough Twp, Elgin Co, ONT. ch: 1. Zachariah;
2. John; 3. Joseph; 4. Margaret; 5. Mrs Donald Currie;
6. Mrs Duncan Black; 7. Mrs Duncan Gillies; 8. Mrs
Archie MacIntyre; 9. Mrs J. Lumley.   **PDA 24, 30**.

5042 McCOLM, James, d 21 Jan 1857. From WIG,
prob Genoch, Old Luce par. s/o Charles M. To Pickering,
Durham Co, ONT, and d there.   **DGH 21 Oct 1864**.

5043 McCOLM, John, ca 1786–15 Sep 1866. From
Ayr. To Bay Chaleur, poss on the *Favourite*, ex Lamlash,
May 1833; stld New Richmond, Bonaventure Co, QUE.
Wright. m Margaret Sinclair, qv, ch: 1. John, b ca 1812;
2. Janet, b 10 Oct 1814; 3. Helen, b 7 Jun 1816;
4. William, b 29 Mar 1818; 5. Thomas, b 16 Jul 1822;
6. Mary, b 30 Aug 1823; 7. Margaret, b ca 1826;
8. Alexander, b 29 Jun 1828.   **DC 17 Dec 1981**.

McCONECHY. See also McCONNACHIE and
McCONNOCHIE.

5044 McCONECHY, Rev James, ca 1814–12 Apr 1878.
From BUT, prob Is Arran. s/o James M, farmer. Matric
Univ of Glasgow, 1836. To Henryville, Iberville Co, QUE,
<1854, when he moved to Leeds Twp, Megantic Co.
Presb min and schoolteacher.   **GMA 13531; AMC 123**.

5045 McCONECHY, Mary, ca 1808–26 Mar 1896. From
Killean and Kilchenzie par, Kintyre, ARL. To Elderslie
Twp, Bruce Co, ONT, <1855. Wife of Donald Blue, qv.
DC 6 Jan 1982.

5046 McCONNACHIE, Rev Donald, 1801–7 May 1864.
From Campbeltown, ARL. s/o Malcolm M, turner. Matric
Univ of Glasgow, 1820, and studied theology, 1824-26.
Min of Rogers Hill and Cape John, Pictou Co, NS,
<1844, when he retr to SCT. Became min of the 3rd
charge at Inverness, and later of Urquhart and
Glenmoriston. m 1833, Annie McLauchlan, d 1873, ch:
1. Flora Margaret, b 1834; 2. Rev Edward Murray, min of
Croick, b 1835; 3. Malcolm Samuel, b 1837; 4. Mary

Jane, b 1838; 5. Charlotte Lacon, b 1841; 6. Robert Williamson, b 1843; 7. Ewan, b 1844; 8. Susan Nicolson, b 1848; 9. Henrietta Grant, b 1849; 10. Carolina Grant, b 1851; 11. Joanna Charlotte Ogily Grant, b 1852; 12. Donalda, b 1859.   **GMA 10437; FES vii 615**.

5047   MACCONNACHIE, Flora. From ARL. To ONT, 1834. Wife of John Galbraith, jr, qv.   **DC 9 Mar 1980**.

5048   McCONNEL, George. To Pictou, NS, on the *Hector*, ex Glasgow, arr 17 Sep 1773; stld Ten Mile House, West River. ch.   **HPC App C**.

5049   McCONNELL, Allan. From ARL. To ONT, 1846; stld prob Huron Co. m Mary Graham, qv.
SG xxvi/3 92.

5050   McCONNELL, John. From WIG. To ONT ca 1829. Wife Henrietta, d 1833, with him.   **DGC 23 Oct 1833**.

McCONNOCHIE. See also McCONECHY and McCONNACHIE.

5051   McCONNOCHIE, John, b ca 1777. From Muirhouse, Kilbirnie, AYR. To QUE, summer 1815, ex Greenock; stld Point aux Trembles, Montreal Is. Farmer. m Janet Brodie, qv, ch: 1. John, b ca 1800; 2. Robert, b ca 1801; 3. William, b ca 1803; 4. Jean, b ca 1805; 5. James, b ca 1807; 6. Janet.   **SEC 3; DC 1 Apr 1979**.

5052   McCORD, Robert, ca 1801–15 Jan 1880. From AYR. To QUE <1840. Shipbuilder.   **DC 14 Jan 1980**.

McCORKINDALE. See also McCORQUODALE.

5053   McCORKINDALE, Angus, ca 1803–ca 1854. From Caolis Paible, North Uist, INV. To London Twp, Middlesex Co, ONT, 1852; moved to East Williams Twp, 1854. m Janet McEachen, qv, ch: 1. Lachland, b 1844; 2. Catherine, b 1846; 3. Alexander, b 1847; 4. Donald, b 1849; 5. Margaret.   **PCM 44; WLC**.

McCORMACK. See also McCORMICK and McCORMAIG.

5054   McCORMACK, Alexander, b 1811. From Uachdar, Is Benbecula, INV. s/o John M. and Kirsty McPherson. To East Williams Twp, Middlesex Co, ONT, 1848. m 1842, Annie McLeod, qv, ch: 1. Kirsty, b 1843; 2. Ewen, b 1844; 3. John, b 1847.   **PCM 44; WLC**.

5055   MACCORMACK, Allan. From Is South Uist, INV. s/o Neil M. To Grand River, PEI, ca 1809; later to Lake Ainslie, Inverness Co, NS. Farmer. m (i) Miss McIntyre, ch: 1. John; 2. Mary. m (ii) Margaret, d/o Farquhar McLellan, further ch: 3. Allan, schoolteacher; 4. Donald; 5. Angus, schoolteacher; 6. Ann; 7. Catherine; 8. Mary.   **MP ii 250**.

5056   MACCORMACK, Angus. From Frobost, Is South Uist, INV. Prob bro/o Donald M, qv. To PEI on the *Jane*, ex Loch nan Uamh, Arisaig, 12 Jul 1790; stld Kings Co.   **PLJ; MP ii 249**.

5057   McCORMACK, Daniel, 7 Feb 1832–29 Jun 1904. From Kilmory par, Is Arran, BUT. s/o John M, qv, and Catherine Kerr, qv. To Restigouche Co, NB. m Janet McBride, qv, ch: 1. John, b 1865; 2. Donald, b 1867; 3. Duncan, b 1869; 4. Isabella, b 1871; 5. Thomas, b 1873; 6. Duncan, b 1874; 7. Catherine, b 1877; 8. Margaret Emma, b 1884; 11. Percival W, b 1890.
DC 23 May 1980.

5058   McCORMACK, Donald. From Cleadale, Is Eigg, INV. To QUE on the *British Queen*, ex Arisaig, 16 Aug 1790; stld nr Montreal. Tenant.   **QCC 103**.

5059   McCORMACK, Donald. From Cleadale, Is Eigg, INV. To QUE on the *British Queen*, ex Arisaig, 16 Aug 1790; stld nr Montreal. Tenant. A child with him.
QCC 103.

5060   MACCORMACK, Donald. From Frobost, Is South Uist, INV. Prob bro/o Angus M, qv. To PEI on the *Jane*, ex Loch nan Uamh, Arisaig, 12 Jul 1790; stld Kings Co. Farmer.   **PLJ; MP ii 249**.

5061   McCORMACK, Donald, b ca 1788. Prob s/o Dougald M, qv. To Richmond Co, NS, 1814. Farmer, m and ch.   **CBC 1818**.

5062   McCORMACK, Donald. From INV. To Sydney, Cape Breton Co, NS, 1827. Son John, qv.   **HNS iii 321**.

5063   McCORMACK, Donald 'Beg', b 1806. From Uachdar, Is Benbecula, INV. s/o John M. and Kirsty McPherson. To East Williams Twp, Middlesex Co, ONT, 1848. m 1840, Mary McDonald, qv.   **PCM 44; WLC**.

5064   McCORMACK, Dougal, b ca 1768. To Port Hood dist, Inverness Co, NS, 1804. Farmer.   **CBC 1818**.

5065   McCORMACK, Dougald, b ca 1753. To Richmond Co, NS, 1813. Farmer, m and ch.   **CBC 1818**.

5066   McCORMACK, Dugald. From Gruilin, Is Eigg, INV. To PEI on the *Jane*, ex Loch nan Uamh, Arisaig, 12 Jul 1790. Pedlar.   **PLJ**.

5067   McCORMACK, Elizabeth, b ca 1782. From Fort William, INV. d/o John M, merchant, and — McLean. To Pictou, NS, <6 Dec 1804, when m Dr James Skinner, qv.   **RAM 21**.

5068   McCORMACK, Hugh, b ca 1790. Prob rel to Dougald M, qv. To Richmond Co, NS, 1813. Farmer. ch.   **CBC 1818**.

5069   McCORMACK, Janet. From WIG. To Shelburne Co, NS, ca 1773. m Gilbert McKenna, qv, in 1781.
DC 14 Nov 1981.

5070   McCORMACK, John, b 1818. From INV. s/o Donald M, qv. To Sydney, Cape Breton Co, NS, 1827. Miner. m Catherine McDonald, qv, ch: 1. Catherine; 2. Donald; 3. Flora; 4. Isabelle; 5. Charles; 6. Mary; 7. John; 8. Matilda; 9. Isabelle, jr; 10. Joseph; 11. Elizabeth; 12. Agnes; 13. Alexander, mayor of Sydney Mines, 1916.   **HNS iii 321**.

5071   McCORMACK, John, 1802–86. From Corrie, Is Arran, BUT. To Blackland, Restigouche Co, NB, 1832. m 22 Feb 1827, Catherine Kerr, qv, ch: 1. Duncan, 1827–90; 2. Margaret, 1829–1907; 3. Daniel, 1832–1904.
MAC 19.

5072   McCORMACK, Peter, b 1816. From Uachdar, Is Benbecula, INV. s/o John M. and Kirsty McPherson. To East Williams Twp, Middlesex Co, ONT, 1848. m 1844, Flora McMillan, qv, ch: 1. John, b 1845; 2. Alexander, b 1847. By Kirsty, his second wife, further ch: 3. Effie; 4. Flora; 5. Christy; 6. Katherine.   **PCM 44; WLC**.

5073   MACCORMACK, Sara. From Is Eigg, INV. To Little Mabou, Inverness Co, NS, <1818. Wife of John McQuarrie, qv.   **MP 796**.

5074   McCORMACK, William, b 1806. From Corrie, Is

Arran, BUT. To Blackland, Restigouche Co, NB, 1832.
MAC 20.

5075   McCORMAIG or McCORMICK, Duncan,
ca 1796–1879. From Is Danna, North Knapdale, ARL.
s/o Duncan M. and Isabella Lamond. To Southwold Twp,
Middlesex Co, ONT, 1833. Farmer. m Mary Kerr, qv, ch:
1. Janet, b 6 Mar 1833; 2. Isabella, 1834-71; 3. Duncan,
1838–1912; 4. Archibald, 1838–1929; 5. Mary,
1842–1918; 6. Colin, 1843–1929; 7. Catherine,
1844–1929; 8. Donald or Daniel, 1846-69; 9. Margaret,
1848-69.   **DC 18 Jul 1979**.

5076   McCORMICK, Angus, b ca 1784. To Western
Shore, Inverness Co, NS, ca 1811. Farmer. ch.
CBC 1818.

5077   McCORMICK, Donald. From Is South Uist, INV.
To West Williams Twp, Middlesex Co, ONT, 1849; stld
Con 14.   **PCM 48**.

5078   McCORMICK, Neil, b 1806. From Uachdar, Is
Benbecula, INV. To Pictou, NS, on the *Lulan*, ex
Glasgow, 17 Aug 1848. Wife Mary MacAulay, qv, with
him, and s Donald, b 1837.   **DC 12 Jul 1979**.

McCORQUODALE. See also McCORKINDALE.

5079   McCORQUODALE, Barbara. From Inverarary,
ARL. d/o Duncan M. in Kilmalieu, and Mary Campbell.
To NFD <1820. Wife of Archibald Campbell, qv.
SG xi/1 4.

5080   McCORQUODALE, Catherine. From North
Knapdale, ARL. sis/o Hugh M, qv. To QUE on the
Huntly, 1828; stld Eldon Twp, Victoria Co, ONT.
m Archibald Jackson, qv.   **EC 86; DC 21 Feb 1980**.

5081   McCORQUODALE, Christina, b 1830. From North
Knapdale, ARL. d/o Hugh M, qv, and Margaret McEwan,
qv. To Victoria Co, ONT, 1828. m Duncan Sinclair, qv.
DC 21 Feb 1980.

5082   McCORQUODALE, Donald. From ARL. To West
Zorra, Oxford Co, ONT, 1832; stld Lot 15, Con 1. Farmer.
Sons James and Alexander with him.   **DC 21 Mar 1981**.

5083   McCORQUODALE, Duncan, ca 1800–31 Jan
1863. From ARL. Said desc from the barons of
Phantilands. To Eldon Twp, Victoria Co, ONT, <1830;
stld Lot 2, Con 1. Farmer. m Sarah McCorquodale, qv,
ch.   **DC 21 Feb and 21 May 1980**.

5084   McCORQUODALE, Duncan. From North
Knapdale, ARL. bro/o Hugh M, qv. To QUE on the
Huntly, 1828; stld Eldon Twp, Victoria Co, ONT.
m Euphemia, d/o John Darroch alias Ray.   **EC 86;
DC 21 Mar 1980**.

5085   McCORQUODALE, Duncan, bap 18 Nov 1815.
From North Knapdale, ARL. s/o Hugh M, qv, and
Margaret McEwan, qv. To ONT 1828; stld Victoria Co.
Innkeeper. m Minnie Sinclair, qv.   **DC 21 Feb 1980**.

5086   McCORQUODALE, Hugh, ca 1792–Feb 1832.
From North Knapdale, ARL. To QUE on the *Huntly*,
1828; stld Victoria Co, ONT. Farmer, Lot 3, Con 2, Eldon
Twp. m Margaret McEwan, qv, ch: 1. Duncan, qv;
2. John, 1818-43; 3. Peter, 1820-99; 4. Janet, qv;
5. Donald, d 1850; 6. Christina, qv.   **EC 86; DC 21 Feb
1980**.

5087   McCORQUODALE, Hugh. From ARL. Prob rel to

Donald M, qv. To West Zorra, Oxford Co, ONT, 1832.
Farmer.   **DC 21 Mar 1981**.

5088   McCORQUODALE, Janet, 1822-95. From ARL.
d/o Hugh M, qv, and Margaret McEwan, qv. To ONT,
ca 1828; stld poss Victoria Co. m Archibald Smith, qv.
DC 21 Feb 1980.

5089   McCORQUODALE, Peter, 1807-50. From North
Knapdale, ARL. bro/o Hugh M, qv. To QUE on the
Huntly, 1828; stld Eldon Twp, Victoria Co, ONT, later
Oakville, Halton Co. Capt of a lake steamer. By wife
Sarah, from IRL, ch: 1. Robert, b 1832; 2. Duncan,
b 1834; 3. John, b 1836; 4. Peter, b 1838; 5. Hugh,
b 1840; 6. Elizabeth, b 1842; 7. Rebecca, b 1844;
8. Sarah, b 1846.   **EC 86; DC 21 Mar 1980**.

5090   McCORQUODALE, Sarah, ca 1800–20 Mar 1843.
From North Knapdale, ARL. sis/o Hugh M, qv. To ONT,
1832; stld Victoria Co. m Duncan McCorquodale, qv.
DC 21 Feb 1980.

5091   McCORVIE, James, b ca 1809. From
Campbeltown, ARL. bro/o Donald and Neil M. To ONT,
ca 1837. Farmer. m Janet McBrayne, qv, ch.   **DC 7 Jan
1983**.

5092   McCOSH, Alexander, 29 Aug 1806–10 Dec 1867.
From Ochiltree par, AYR. s/o William M. in Lawershill,
and Elizabeth Strathorn. To QUE on the *Glasgow*, ex
Glasgow, 23 Apr 1853; stld Toronto, ONT, later Huron
Twp, Bruce Co. Farmer and JP. m (i) ca 1830, Elizabeth
Gemmel, who d 1839, ch: 1. William, qv; 2. Robert, qv;
3. Thomas, qv; 4. John, qv; 5. Alexander Gemmel, qv.
m (ii) Mrs Margaret Brown.   **DC 20 May 1967**.

5093   McCOSH, Alexander Gemmel, 1839–1903. From
Ochiltree par, AYR. s/o Alexander M, qv, and Elizabeth
Gemmel. To QUE on the *Glasgow*, ex Glasgow, 23 Apr
1853; stld Toronto, ONT, later Bruce Co.   **DC 20 May
1967**.

5094   McCOSH, John, 1837-75. From Ochiltree par,
AYR. s/o Alexander M, qv, and Elizabeth Gemmel. To
QUE on the *Glasgow*, ex Glasgow, 23 Apr 1853; stld
Toronto, ONT, later Huron Twp, Bruce Co. m Maria
Jackson, ch: 1. Elizabeth; 2. Robert; 3. John.
DC 20 May 1967.

5095   McCOSH, Robert, b 1793. From AYR. To
Miramichi, Northumberland Co, NB, 1820. Shipbuilder
with Gilmour, Rankin & Co. Son Robert.   **DC 29 Apr
1968**.

5096   McCOSH, Robert, b 1833. From Ochiltree par,
AYR. s/o Alexander M, qv, and Elizabeth Gemmel. To
QUE on the *Glasgow*, ex Glasgow, 23 Apr 1853; stld
Toronto, ONT, later Huron Twp, Bruce Co. m Anne
Turnbull, ch: 1. Alexander Dawson, 1862–1943; 2. Mary,
1864–1946; 3. John William, 1866–1947; 4. Elizabeth
Ann, 1868–1946; 5. Janet Watson, 1870-90; 6. Agnes
Milne, 1872–1952; 7. Robert Thomas, 1874–1965.
DC 20 May 1967.

5097   McCOSH, Thomas, 1835–1914. From Ochiltree
par, AYR. s/o Alexander M, qv, and Elizabeth Gemmel.
To QUE on the *Glasgow*, ex Glasgow, 23 Apr 1853; stld
Toronto, later Bruce Co, ONT. m (i) Janet Watson
McColl, d 1884, ch: 1. Elizabeth Gemmel, 1860-65;
m (ii) Louise Tovell, d 1929, further ch: 2. Marion.
DC 20 May 1967.

5098 McCOSH, William, 1831–1914. From Ochiltree par, AYR. s/o Alexander M, qv, and Elizabeth Gemmel. To QUE on the *Glasgow*, ex Glasgow, 23 Apr 1853; stld Toronto, ONT. m Elizabeth, d/o Robert Cullen, qv, ch: 1. Alexander, b 2 Aug 1870; 2. Robert, b 8 Nov 1871; 3. William, b 3 Mar 1873; 4. Margaret, b 13 Mar 1875; 5. Bessie, b 27 Apr 1877; 6. Mary, b 22 May 1879; 7. Catherine, b 17 May 1883; 8. Thomas, b 29 Dec 1888. **DC 20 May 1967**.

5099 McCOWAN, Catherine, b 1795. From Kippen or Falkirk, STI. To Lanark Co, ONT, 1845. Wife of John Oswald, qv. **DC 29 Oct 1978**.

5100 McCOWAN, Christian. From Killin par, PER. To Montreal, QUE, on the *Curlew*, ex Greenock, 21 Jul 1818; stld Beckwith Twp, Lanark Co, ONT. Wife of Colin McLaurin, qv. **BCL; DC 10 Aug 1981**.

5101 McCOWAN, Duncan. From Comrie par, PER. Poss bro/o James M, qv. To Montreal, QUE, on the *Curlew*, ex Greenock, 21 Jul 1818; stld prob Beckwith Twp, Lanark Co, ONT. Wife Janet with him. **BCL**.

5102 McCOWAN, James. From Comrie par, PER. Poss bro/o Duncan M, qv. To Montreal, QUE, on the *Curlew*, ex Greenock, 21 Jul 1818; stld prob Beckwith Twp, Lanark Co, ONT. ch with him: 1. Peter, aged 6; 2. Duncan, aged 4. **BCL**.

5103 McCOWAN, James, 1773–1834. From Auchinbeg, Lesmahagow par, LKS. To Scarborough, York Co, ONT, 1833. Formerly coalmaster. **DC 29 Mar 1981**.

5104 MACCOY, Norman. From Glenelg, INV. To QUE, 1796; stld Lot 26, Con 7, Lochiel Twp, Glengarry Co, ONT. **MG 211**.

5105 McCRACKEN, Elizabeth, 1782–1875. From Glasgow. To QUE on the *Earl of Buckinghamshire*, ex Greenock, 29 Apr 1821; stld Dalhousie Twp, Lanark Co, ONT. Wife of John Leckie, qv. **DC 5 Jan 1982**.

5106 McCRACKEN, William. To Pictou Co, NS, <1776. **HPC App B**.

5107 McCRAW, Duncan. Prob from Knoydart, INV. To QUE on the *British Queen*, ex Arisaig, 16 Aug 1790; stld nr Montreal. Servant. **QCC 103**.

5108 McCREADY, William, d 1876. To Newcastle, Durham Co, ONT, 1836, when he stld Eldon Twp, Victoria Co. Ex-sergeant, 79th Regt; farmer, and postmaster at Portage. m Maria Parker, wid/o Capt William Dalgleish. She was poss his second wife. **EC 89**.

5109 McCREADY, Mary, b ca 1814. From Abbey par, RFW. Prob d/o James M. and Jean Pollock. To Lanark Co, ONT, ca 1841. Wife of Stevenson Blackburn, qv, m 3 Mar 1839. **Abbey OPR 559/8; DC 8 Sep 1980**.

5110 McCREAGH, Donald, d 1825. To Cape Breton Is, NS, and drowned in the Gut of Canso. **VSN No 1478**.

5111 McCREE, Andrew. From Edinburgh. To York Co, ONT, <1860. Engineer, Ontario, Simcoe & Huron Railroad. **DC 3 Dec 1981**.

5112 McCRIMMON, Alexander, b ca 1795. From Swordale, Glenelg, INV. s/o Donald M. and Anna McLeod. To ONT, 1816; stld Lot 34, Con 8, Lochiel Twp, Glengarry Co. m Jane Ross, ch. **GD50/225/1**.

5113 McCRIMMON, Angus, b ca 1792. From Swordale, Glenelg, INV. s/o Donald M. and Anna McLeod. To ONT, 1816; stld Lot 4, Con 9, Lochiel Twp, Glengarry Co. Farmer. m Arabella McDonald, ch. **GD50/225/1**.

5114 McCRIMMON, Catherine. From Glenelg, INV. To QUE, summer 1815; stld prob ONT. Wife of John McCrimmon, qv. **SEC 5**.

5115 McCRIMMON, Catherine. From Glenelg, INV. To QUE, ex Greenock, summer 1815; stld prob Lanark Co, ONT. Wife of Finlay McRae, qv. **SEC 8**.

5116 McCRIMMON, Christina, b ca 1798. From Swordale, Glenelg, INV. d/o Donald M. and Anna McLeod. To Lochiel Twp, Glengarry Co, ONT, poss 1816. m Angus McIntosh, veteran of the War of 1812, and moved to Kincardine Twp, Bruce Co. ch: 1. Donald; 2. Neil; 3. Donald; 4. Catherine; 5. Mary; 6. Margaret; 7. Sarah; 8. Christina. **GD50/225/1**.

5117 MACCRIMMON, Christy, 1763–5 Jul 1849. From Glenelg, INV. To Glengarry Co, ONT, 1796. Wife of Roderick D. MacLeod, qv. **MG 240**.

5118 MACCRIMMON, Donald Dubh, 1731–1822. From Is Skye, INV. To ONT <1820. Piper. **SN iii 71; IBD 318**.

5119 McCRIMMON, Donald Og, ca 1790–1890. From Innerghradan, Glenelg, INV. s/o Donald M. and Anna McLeod. To ONT, 1816; stld on half of Lot 34, Con 8, Lochiel Twp, Glengarry Co. Farmer. m Margaret McKay, Côte St George, ch. ***MacLeod Muniments*, Box 36/1; GD50/225/1**.

5120 McCRIMMON, Donald, b ca 1791. From Glenelg, INV. To QUE, ex Greenock, summer 1815; stld prob Lanark Co, ONT. Labourer. **SEC 7**.

5121 MACCRIMMON, Donald, ca 1787–13 Feb 1863. From Kilmuir, Duirinish par, Is Skye, INV. s/o Donald Ruadh M. To Victoria Co, ONT, <1851; stld Woodville. Farmer. m Catherine MacLeod, who d in Skye, having had, poss with other ch: 1. Elizabeth, qv; 2. Roderick, qv; 3. Margaret, b ca 1817; 4. Donald, jr, qv; 5. Hector, qv; 6. Sarah. **Duirinish OPR 110/2**.

5122 MACCRIMMON, Donald, jr, ca 1818–22 Jan 1902. From Kilmuir, Duirinish par, Is Skye, INV. s/o Donald M, qv, and Catherine McLeod. To Victoria Co, ONT, <1851; stld Woodville. m Rachel MacLeod, 1826–1907. **DC 5 Sep 1981**.

5123 McCRIMMON, Duncan, b ca 1794. From Swordale, Glenelg, INV. s/o Donald M. and Anna McLeod. To ONT, 1816; stld Lot 34, Con 8, Lochiel Twp, Glengarry Co. Farmer. m Isabella McLeod, ch. **GD 50/225/1**.

5124 McCRIMMON, Duncan, b ca 1783. To QUE, ex Greenock, summer 1815; stld prob Lanark Co, ONT. Labourer. **SEC 7**.

5125 MACCRIMMON, Elizabeth, b ca 1814. From Kilmuir, Duirinish par, Is Skye, INV. d/o Donald M, qv, and Catherine McLeod. To Victoria Co, ONT, <1851; stld Woodville. m Charles McDermott, ch. **DC 5 Sep 1981**.

5126 McCRIMMON, Farquhar, b ca 1787. From Glenelg, INV. To QUE, summer 1815; stld prob E ONT. Farmer. Wife Rachel McRae, qv, with him, and 1 child. **SEC 5**.

5127 MACCRIMMON, Hector, 2 May 1819–29 Nov

1876. From Kilmuir, Duirinish par, Is Skye, INV.
s/o Donald M, qv, and Catherine McLeod. To Victoria
Co, ONT, <1851; stld Woodville. m Christina Ferguson,
qv, ch.   **DC 5 Sep 1981**.

5128   McCRIMMON, John, b ca 1759. From Glenelg,
INV. To QUE, summer 1815; stld prob E ONT. Farmer and
weaver. m Catherine McCrimmon, qv, and emig with
4 ch.   **SEC 5**.

5129   MACCRIMMON, Roderick, ca 1815–16 Mar 1880.
From Kilmuir, Duirinish par, Is Skye, INV. s/o Donald M,
qv, and Catherine McLeod. To Victoria Co, ONT, <1851;
stld Woodville. m Sarah Murchison, qv. Son Malcolm,
1851–1928.   **DC 5 Sep 1981**.

McCUAIG. See also McLEOD.

5130   MACCUAIG, Catherine, ca 1809–24 Oct 1882.
From Glenelg, INV. d/o Patrick 'Post' M, qv. m, prob
1834, Rory MacLeod, qv.   **MG 304, 394**.

5131   McCUAIG, Duncan, b ca 1789. From Glenelg,
INV. To QUE, ex Greenock, summer 1815; stld prob
Lanark Co, ONT. Labourer. Wife Marion McRae, qv, with
him, and 2 ch. Other ch remained in SCT.   **SEC 8**.

5132   McCUAIG, Duncan, 1780–1837. From Is Islay,
ARL. To Eldon Twp, Victoria Co, ONT, <1830. m Janet
Campbell, qv, ch: 1. Donald, b 1807; 2. Colin, b 1808;
3. Hugh, b 1810; 4. Duncan, b 1813; 5. Elizabeth,
b 1813; 6. Ann, b 1814; 7. John, b 1819; 8. Peter,
1824-35; 9. Archibald, b 1829.   **EC 90**.

5133   McCUAIG, Ellen. From Is Islay, ARL. d/o Henry
M. and Janet Calder. To ONT, 1854, prob stld Oro Twp,
Simcoe Co. m Archibald Gilchrist, qv.   **DC 9 Oct 1979**.

5134   McCUAIG, Finlay. From Glenelg, INV. To QUE on
the *Nephton*, 1802; stld Chambly Mountain. Moved in
1812 to Williamstown.   **SAS 18**.

5135   McCUAIG, Henry. From Is Islay, ARL. To ONT,
<1855; prob stld Oro Twp, Simcoe Co. Wife Janet
Calder, qv, with him, and dau Ellen, qv.   **DC 9 Oct
1979**.

5136   McCUAIG, Janet, ca 1758–2 Nov 1846. From
Comrie par, PER. To QUE, and d Ormston, Ottawa East.
m Donald McEwan, qv.   **Ts Ormston**.

5137   McCUAIG, Jenny, bap 3 Nov 1787. From
Culedrain, Southend par, ARL. To ONT, 1845. wid/o John
McEachran, Pennyland Mill, m 24 Apr 1812, ch:
1. Janet, b 29 Jul 1813, emig <1845; 2. Neil, b 31 May
1815; 3. Thomas, b 6 Aug 1817, emig with mother.
Southend OPR, 532/1.

5138   McCUAIG, John, b ca 1790. From Glenelg, INV.
To QUE, summer 1815; stld prob Lanark Co, ONT.
Farmer. Wife Catherine McAulay, qv, with him, and
2 ch.   **SEC 8**.

5139   McCUAIG, Malcolm. From Glenmore, INV. To
Montreal, QUE, arr Sep 1802. Petitioned for land on the
Ottawa River, ONT, 6 Aug 1804.   **DC 15 Mar 1980**.

5140   McCUAIG, Malcolm, b ca 1765. From Glenelg,
INV. To QUE, ex Greenock, summer 1815; stld prob
Lanark Co, ONT. Farmer. Wife Catherine McLennan, qv,
with him, and 3 ch.   **SEC 8**.

5141   McCUAIG, Patrick 'Post'. From Glenelg, INV. To
Kenyon Twp, Glengarry Co, ONT, 1818. Dau Catherine,
qv.   **MG 304, 394**.

5142   McCUAIG, Sarah, 1788–1865. From Swordland,
Glenelg, INV. To Glengarry Co, ONT, <1810. Wife of
Norman McLeod, qv.   **MG 29**.

5143   McCUBBIN, James, b ca 1804. From Aberdeen.
To ONT <1831; stld Burford Twp, Brant Co. Farmer.
Wesleyan Methodist. By wife Maria ch: 1. Samuel,
b ca 1831; 2. Anna M, b ca 1836; 3. Mary C, b ca 1838;
4. William C, b ca 1840; 5. Maria, b ca 1844; 6. James,
b ca 1846; 7. Amelia, b ca 1847.   **DC 13 Apr 1847**.

5144   McCUISH, Archibald. From Is North Uist, INV. To
Loch Lomond, Richmond Co, NS, <1843. Wife Jane
McDonald, qv, with him. Son Alexander, b 1843,
merchant and MLA.   **MLA 198**.

5145   McCUISH, Donald, b 1796. From Knockintorran,
Is North Uist, INV. To East Williams Twp, Middlesex Co,
ONT, 1849. m Mary McDougall, ch: 1. Ann, b 1830;
2. Neil, b 1832; 3. Flora, b 1835; 4. Ann, b 1838.
PCM 44; WLC.

5146   McCULLOCH, Ann. From Kilbirnie, AYR. To QUE
on the *Atlas*, ex Greenock, 11 Jul 1815; stld Burgess
Twp, Lanark Co, ONT. Wife of Alexander McFarlane,
qv.   **SEC 1**.

5147   McCULLOCH, Edward. From ARL. To Middlesex
Co, ONT, 1830; stld Mosa Twp.   **PCM 24**.

5148   MACCULLOCH, Ferdinand. From Dornoch, SUT.
s/o William M, qv. To Montreal, QUE, 1823. Treas of St
Gabriel Street Ch, 1838-41, and became cashier, City of
Montreal Bank. m a d/o Dr William Robertson, qv.
SGC 498.

5149   McCULLOCH, James, b ca 1737. From Dumfries.
To Georgetown, Kings Co, PEI, on the *Lovely Nellie*, ex
Carsethorn, May 1775. Moved to Pictou Co, NS, and
was gr 240 acres on the east side of Middle River,
1783.   **ELN; HPC App A**.

5150   McCULLOCH, Hugh, b 19 Sep 1826. From AYR.
s/o Hugh M. and Jane Osborne. To Galt Twp, Waterloo
Co, ONT, arr 24 Aug 1850. m 1855, Janet, d/o Hugh
McCartney, ch: 1. Hugh; 2. Jessie; 3. Robert
Osborne.   **DC 29 Sep 1964**.

5151   McCULLOCH, James, 16 May 1834–11 Mar 1913.
From Port Patrick par, WIG. s/o David M. and Elizabeth
Anderson. To Blanshard Twp, Perth Co, ONT, 1855;
moved to Keppel Twp, Grey Co, 1864. m Margaret
McGill, qv.   **DC 11 Mar 1980**.

5152   McCULLOCH, Rev Thomas, ca 1776–9 Sep 1843.
From Neilston, RFW. s/o Michael M, craftsman. Matric
Univ of Glasgow, 1792, and became min of Secession
Ch at Stewarton, AYR. To Pictou Harbour, NS, arr Nov
1803. Min there and founder of Pictou Academy. Pres of
Dalhousie Coll, Halifax, 1838-43. DD, Glasgow, 1822.
m Isabella, d/o Rev David Walker, Pollokshaws. Son
William, 1811-95, min of Presb Ch at Truro, Colchester
Co, NS.   **GMA 5295; HNS iii 553; UPC ii 312;
PAC 236; MDB 435**.

5153   MACCULLOCH, William, d Nov 1856. From
Dornoch, SUT. To Montreal, QUE, 1823. Emp on the
Champlain Railway. Son Ferdinand, qv.   **SGC 501**.

5154   MACCULLOUGH, Mary, d 1906. To Pictou Co,
NS, <1850. m William Munro. Son Hector, went to NJ,
1882.   **NSN 27/196**.

5155   McCULLY, William. Prob from KKD. To French

River, Colchester Co, NS, 1830; later to New Annan. ch incl: 1. William, ships carpenter; 2. James, farmer; 3. Mary. **HT 43**.

5156   McCUNN, Robert, 1837–28 Feb 1895. From Greenock, RFW. s/o James M, merchant. Matric Univ of Glasgow, 1854; grad BA, 1856, and MA, 1857. To NS, 1863, and adm min of St Georges Ch, River John. Declined to join Union in 1875. **GMA 16387; RGG 359; FES vii 615**.

5157   McCURDIE, Ann. From Is Arran, BUT. sis/o Lachlan M, qv. To Inverness Twp, Megantic Co, QUE, <1850. m Peter Hamilton, qv. **AMC 42, 80; MAC 42**.

5158   McCURDIE, Lachlan. From Is Arran, BUT. bro/o Ann M, qv. To Inverness Twp, Megantic Co, QUE, 1851. m Janet Currie, qv, ch. **AMC 42; MAC 43**.

5159   McCURDY, Alexander, b 1811. From Is Arran, BUT. Prob bro/o Thomas M, qv. To Dalhousie, NB, prob <1840. **MAC 20**.

5160   McCURDY, John, b 1778. From Clauchog, Kilmory par, Is Arran, BUT. To Dalhousie, NB, prob 1832; stld Belledune, Gloucester Co. m Catherine MacDougald, qv, ch: 1. William, b 1805; 2. Margaret, b 1807; 3. James, b 1809. **MAC 20**.

5161   McCURDY, John, b 1796. From Levinhorroch, Kilmory par, Is Bute. To Dalhousie, NB, 1832; stld Point la Nim. m Catherine Cook, qv, ch: 1. John, b 1819; 2. Lauclan, 1821–1909; 3. Archibald, 1826–1923; 4. Donald, b 1829; 5. Margaret, 1831–1905. **MAC 20**.

5162   McCURDY, Rev John, 1815-99. From PER. To Chatham, Northumberland Co, NB. **DC 14 Jan 1980**.

5163   McCURDY, Thomas, b 1814. From Clauchog, Kilmory par, Is Arran, BUT. Prob bro/o Alexander M, qv. To Dalhousie, NB, prob <1840. **MAC 20**.

5164   McCUTCHEON, Peter, 1789–28 Sep 1860. From Creebridge, KKD. s/o John M, Newton-Stewart, and — McGill. To Montreal, QUE, 1809. Merchant, Peter McGill & Co. Assumed the surname of McGill at the request of his uncle John McGill, whose heir he was in 1835. m an adopted d/o John Shuter. **BNA 355; SGC 233, 382; MDB 452**.

5165   McCUSBIC, Finlay, b ca 1821. From Is Berneray, Harris, INV. To Richmond Co, NS, <1840. Wife Marion with him. ch: 1. Neil, b 1848; 2. Angus, b 1851; 3. Malcolm, b 1854; 4. Catherine, b 1858; 5. Marion, b 1860; 6. John, b 1861; 7. Flora, b 1863. **WLC**.

5166   McDERMID, Ann, b ca 1833. From Is Islay, ARL. To Minto Twp, Wellington Co, ONT, ca 1864. m William Ross, qv. **RFS 200**.

5167   McDERMID, Catherine. From Lesmahagow, LKS. To Scarborough, York Co, ONT, 1834. Wife of John Muir, qv, m 9 Sep 1829. **Lesmahagow OPR 649/4; MDB 536**.

5168   McDERMID, Donald 'Ossian', b 1778. From PER. To Glengarry Co, ONT, 1799. stld Williamstown. Schoolteacher, later merchant. Sometime postmaster at Coteau du Lac, Vaudreuil Co, QUE. m Isabella, d/o Hugh Macdonell, ch. **DC 21 Mar 1981**.

5169   McDERMID, Eliza. From PER. To Brant Co, ONT, via New York, ca 1851. wid/o John Marquis.

m (ii) Francis Fairchild. Son Duncan Marquis. **DC 23 Sep 1980**.

5170   McDERMID, Hugh. Prob from ARL. To QUE <1840; stld Ottawa Co, nr Buckingham. Flour miller. Son Duncan, schoolteacher. **ELB 3**.

5171   McDIARMAID, Cathrine. From PER, poss Killin. To McNab Twp, Renfrew Co, ONT, 1825. Wife of Peter McPherson, qv. **EMT 23**.

5172   McDIARMAID, Finlay. Poss from Edinburgh. Cous of Capt John M, Rifle Brigade. To Aldborough Twp, Elgin Co, ONT, <1847. **SH**.

5173   McDIARMED, Anne. To Wellington Co, ONT, <1854. m William Ross, qv. **DC 24 Jun 1979**.

5174   McDIARMED, Archibald. From Killin, PER. To Montreal, QUE, on the *Curlew*, ex Greenock, 21 Jul 1818; stld prob Beckwith Twp, Lanark Co, ONT. Wife Mary with him, and ch: 1. Donald, aged 4; 2. Catherine, aged 2. **BCL**.

5175   McDIARMED, Donald. From STI. To Osgoode Twp, Carleton Co, ONT, ca 1849. Dau Mary Ann, 1831-69. **DC 27 Oct 1979**.

5176   MACDIARMED, Donald, b 1840. From Killin, PER. To Lochiel Twp, Glengarry Co, ONT, with parents, 1845. Physician, teacher and Inspector of Schools. Son Dr William, MP for Glengarry, 1940-45. **SDG 330, 343**.

5177   McDIARMED, Duncan. From Comrie par, PER. To Montreal, QUE, on the *Curlew*, ex Greenock, 21 Jul 1818; stld Lot 22, Con 5, Beckwith Twp, Lanark Co, ONT. Farmer and leader of a group of emigrants. Wife Mary with him, and ch: 1. Catherine, aged 12; 2. John, aged 1. **BCL; HCL 33**.

5178   McDIARMED, Hugh. From Dull par, PER. To Montreal, QUE, on the *Curlew*, ex Greenock, 21 Jul 1818. Wife Janet with him, and ch: 1. Margaret, aged 8; 2. Janet. **BCL**.

5179   McDIARMED, Janet. From Breadalbane, PER. To Montreal, QUE, on the *Dorothy*, ex Greenock, 1815; stld Breadalbane, Lochiel Twp, Glengarry Co, ONT. **SDG 131**.

5180   McDIARMED, John. Prob from PER. To McNab Twp, Renfrew Co, ONT, ca 1834. Wife Mary Stewart, qv, with him. Son Peter d at sea. **DC 30 Nov 1979**.

5181   McDIARMED, Margaret. From Breadalbane, PER. To Montreal, QUE, on the *Dorothy*, ex Greenock, 1815; stld Breadalbane, Lochiel Twp, Glengarry Co, ONT. **SDG 131**.

5182   McDIARMID, Allan, b ca 1776. From Killin, PER. To QUE on the *Dorothy*, ex Greenock, 12 Jul 1815; stld Breadalbane, Lochiel Twp, Glengarry Co, ONT. Weaver, farmer, and elder of the Baptist Ch. m Janet McLaren, qv, ch. **SEC 4; SDG 131**.

5183   McDIARMID, Annabella. From Killin, PER. To QUE, summer 1815, ex Greenock, stld prob ONT. Wife of Duncan McLaren, qv. **SEC 6**.

5184   McDIARMID, Archibald, 1783–1 Dec 1859. From Killin par, PER. To ONT ca 1835; stld Reach Twp, Ontario Co. Farmer. m Jean Christie, qv, ch: 1. John, b ca 1825; 2. Donald, b ca 1827; 3. Jane, b ca 1829; 4. Colin, b ca 1829; 5. Janet, b ca 1831. **DC 31 Jan 1982**.

5185 McDIARMID, Colin. From Breadalbane, PER. To ONT, 1852, and stld prob Lambton Co. **DC 16 May 1979**.

5186 McDIARMID, Donald. Poss from PER. To Aldborough Twp, Elgin Co, ONT, prob 1818. Farmer, and in 1820, assessor. **PDA 93**.

5187 McDIARMID, Donald. From Snizort, Is Skye, INV. To Kinloss Twp, Bruce Co, ONT, 1852. **DC 6 Mar 1979**.

5188 McDIARMID, Donald. To Montreal, QUE, ex Glasgow, arr 2 Aug 1852. **DC 12 Apr 1979**.

5189 McDIARMID, Elizabeth. From Killin, PER. To QUE, ex Greenock, summer 1815; stld prob Lanark Co, ONT. Wife of Peter McIntosh, qv. **SEC 8**.

5190 McDIARMID, Elizabeth. From Dericambus, Glenlyon, PER. d/o Hugh M. To Esquesing Twp, Halton Co, ONT, ca 1844. **DC 21 Mar 1981**.

5191 MACDIARMID, Finlay. From PER. To Aldborough Twp, Elgin Co, ONT, ca 1814. Pioneer settler. **PDA 24, 93**.

5192 McDIARMID, John, ca 1790–1870. From Achleskine, Balquhidder par, PER. Prob s/o Archibald M. in Wester Ardchyle, Killin par, and Margaret McDiarmid. To Montreal, QUE, on the brig *Niagara*, ex Greenock, arr 28 May 1825; stld McNab Twp, Renfrew Co, ONT. m Margaret McDiarmid, qv, ch: 1. Margaret, b 1822; 2. Jean, b 1824; 3. Catherine, b 1826; 4. Archibald, b 1828; 5. Christian, b 1832; 6. Duncan, b 1834; 7. John, b 1836; 8. Angus, b 1838; 9. Jean, b 1841; 10. Isabella, b 1850. **Killin OPR 361/3; DC 26 Jun 1980**.

5193 McDIARMID, Margaret, 1802-51. From Killin par, PER. Prob d/o Duncan M. and Jean McEwen. To Montreal, QUE, on the *Niagara*, ex Greenock, arr 28 May 1825; stld McNab Twp, Renfrew Co, ONT. Wife of John McDiarmid, qv. **Killin OPR 361/3; DC 14 Mar 1980**.

5194 McDONALD, Alan. Prob from ARL. To Aldborough Twp, Elgin Co, ONT, poss 1818. Farmer. **PDA 93**.

5195 MACDONALD, Rev Alexander, 1753–15 Apr 1816. From Chlianaig, Glen Spean, INV. s/o Archibald M, desc from Keppoch family. Educ Scots Coll, Paris, and Valladolid, Spain, where ord to priesthood, 1781. To NS, 1783. Missionary at Merigomish, Margaree Harbour, and 1799–1801, at Judique. Par priest at Arisaig, Antigonish Co, 1802-16, and JP. **MP 21; HCA 198**.

5196 McDONALD, Alexander. To Pictou Co, NS, ca 1784. Discharged soldier, 82nd Regt. **HPC App F**.

5197 MACDONALD, Alexander. From Moidart, INV. s/o Alexander 'Baillie' M. To Antigonish Co, NS, ca 1784; stld nr Arisaig, and went later to Judique, Inverness Co. m Janet MacDonald, qv, ch: 1. Allan; 2. James; 3. Donald 'Dhu'; 4. Alexander; 5. John; 6. Donald Og; 7. Mary; 8. Anne; 9. Anne; 10. Margaret; 11. Susan; 12. Ellen. **DC 30 Mar 1981**.

5198 McDONALD, Alexander, ca 1762–11 Dec 1834. From Ardnamurchan, ARL. Served in British Army during American Revolutionary War, reaching the rank of Lt Col. Stld Bartibog River, Northumberland Co, NB, 1784. m Grace McLean, qv, and had with other ch: 1. Colin, dy; 2. John; 3. Dougal. **DC 2 Jun 1978**.

5199 MACDONALD, Alexander. From Glengarry, INV. To QUE on the *Alexander*, arr 5 Sep 1785; stld St Raphael West, Glengarry Co, ONT. Son John Sandfield, 1812-72, Prime Minister of Canada, 1862-64, and of ONT, 1867-71. **BNA 523; MDB 442**.

5200 MACDONALD, Alexander. From Is Skye, INV. To NS <1786. ch: 1. Donald, soldier, Revolutionary War; 2. Dr Alexander, Antigonish Co, qv. **HCA 249**.

5201 McDONALD, Alexander. From INV. To PEI on the *Jane*, ex Loch nan Uamh, Arisaig, 12 Jul 1790. Wife with him, and 4 ch. **PLJ**.

5202 McDONALD, Alexander. From Galmisdale, Is Eigg, INV. To PEI on the *Lucy*, ex Loch nan Uamh, Arisaig, 12 Jul 1790. Pedlar. Wife with him and 7 ch. **PLL**.

5203 McDONALD, Alexander. From Glenuig, Moidart, INV. To PEI on the *Lucy*, ex Loch nan Uamh, Arisaig, 12 Jul 1790. Tenant. Wife with him and 6 ch. **PLL**.

5204 McDONALD, Alexander, ca 1772–29 Nov 1848. From Arisaig, INV. To Miramichi, Northumberland Co, NB, 1790; stld Lower Bay du Vin. **DC 2 Jun 1978**.

5205 McDONALD, Alexander, b ca 1762. To Western Shore, Inverness Co, NS, 1799. Farmer, m and ch. **CBC 1818**.

5206 McDONALD, Alexander, b ca 1754. To Western Shore, Inverness Co, NS, 1800. Farmer, m and ch. **CBC 1818**.

5207 McDONALD, Alexander. From Appin, ARL. To Pictou, NS, on the *Sarah*, ex Fort William, Jun 1801. Labourer. **PLS**.

5208 McDONALD, Alexander. From Kilmorack, INV. To Pictou, NS, on the *Sarah*, ex Fort William, Jun 1801. Tenant. Wife Ann with him, and ch: 1. Alexander, aged 8; 2. John, aged 4. **PLS**.

5209 McDONALD, Alexander, b ca 1793. To Western Shore, Inverness Co, NS, 1802. Farmer, m and ch. **CBC 1818**.

5210 McDONALD, Alexander. From Moy, Glen Spean, INV. To Montreal, QUE, ex Fort William, 3 Jul 1802; stld E ONT. **MCM 1/4 26**.

5211 McDONALD, Alexander, ca 1775–31 Oct 1843. From Assynt, SUT. To Chatham, Northumberland Co, NB, 1803; stld Little Branch, Black River. **DC 2 Jun 1978**.

5212 McDONALD, Alexander, b ca 1786. To Port Hood dist, Inverness Co, NS, 1804. Farmer, m and ch. **CBC 1818**.

5213 McDONALD, Alexander, b 1769. To QUE on the *Oughton*, arr Jun 1804; stld Baldoon, Dover Twp, Kent Co, ONT. Farmer and piper. Wife Mary, aged 30, with him, and ch: 1. John, b 1791; 2. Unice, b 1793; 3-4. Angus and Ann, b 1799; 5. Catherine, b 1802. **UCM 267; DC 4 Oct 1979**.

5214 MACDONALD, Alexander. From Glen Nigg, Moidart, INV. bro/o Allan 'Mor' M, qv. To Antigonish Co, NS, ca 1804. Son Donald. **HCA 200**.

5215 McDONALD, Alexander. From Assynt or Edrachillis, SUT. To Boston, MA, arr 16 Aug 1803, but stld Scotch Ridge, Charlotte Co, NB, 1805. Formerly of the Reay Fencible Regt. **DC 29 Nov 1982**.

5216 MACDONALD, Alexander. From Brae-Lochaber, INV. s/o Donald 'Ban Onorach' M, qv, and Isabel Beaton, qv. To South West River, Inverness Co, NS, 1805. Farmer. m ca 1800, Catherine Campbell, qv, ch: 1. Donald; 2. Mary; 3. Isabel; 4. Mary, jr; 5. Jessie; 6. Angus; 7. Finlay. **MP 562**.

5217 MACDONALD, Alexander, b 1784. From Is Skye, INV. s/o Alexander M, qv. Studied medicine at Edinburgh and arr Antigonish Co, NS, 1805. Pioneer physician there. m 1812, Charlotte, d/o Daniel Harrington, ch: 1. Dr Archibald; 2. Donald, lawyer; 3. Alexander; 4. Anne. **HCA 30, 249**.

5218 McDONALD, Alexander, b ca 1778. To Port Hood dist, Inverness Co, NS, 1806. Farmer, m and ch. **CBC 1818**.

5219 McDONALD, Alexander, ca 1777–24 Dec 1812. From WIG. To St John, NB. Mariner. **NER viii 98**.

5220 McDONALD, Alexander, b ca 1787. From Is Mull, ARL. To Charlottetown, PEI, on the *Clarendon*, ex Oban, 6 Aug 1808. Labourer. **CPL**.

5221 McDONALD, Alexander, b ca 1780. To Inverness, Inverness Co, NS, 1809. Farmer, m and ch. **CBC 1818**.

5222 MACDONALD, Alexander. From Arisaig, INV. bro/o Lachlan M, qv, and Angus M, qv. To Arisaig, Antigonish Co, NS, <1810. ch: 1. Donald, mason; 2. Lachlan, mason. **HCA 208**.

5223 MACDONALD, Alexander. Prob from INV. s/o Donald M. To Antigonish Co, NS, prob <1810. m Miss MacIntyre, ch: 1. John; 2. Sarah; 3. Catherine; 4. Donald; 5. Allan; 6. Rory; 7. Lachlan; 8. Ann. **HCA 227**.

5224 McDONALD, Alexander, b ca 1772. To Western Shore, Inverness Co, NS, 1811. Farmer, m and ch. **CBC 1818**.

5225 McDONALD, Alexander, ca 1791–1853. From Glencoe, Lismore and Appin par, ARL. To Red River, MAN, 1813. An agent of Lord Selkirk, and afterwards emp with HBCo. **LDW 20 Nov 1979**.

5226 McDONALD, Alexander, b ca 1786. To Little Bras D'Or, Cape Breton Co, NS, <1815. Farmer, m and ch. **CBC 1818**.

5227 MACDONALD, Alexander. bro/o Deacon Thomas M, qv, Bigg Brook, west branch, East River. To Pictou Co, NS, <1815. Farmer. **PAC 12**.

5228 MACDONALD, Alexander. From INV. To South River, Antigonish Co, NS, <1815. Pioneer settler. m Catherine MacLennan, qv, ch: 1. Rev Kenneth, 1821–1910; 2. Flora; 3. Catherine; 4. Isabel; 5. John. By a second wife, ch: 6. Angus. **MP 47**.

5229 McDONALD, Alexander, b ca 1791. From Killin, PER. To QUE on the *Dorothy*, ex Greenock, 12 Jul 1815; stld South Elmsley Twp, Leeds Co, ONT. Mason. Wife Marjery Campbell, qv, with him. **SEC 4**.

5230 MACDONALD, Alexander. From Moidart, INV. s/o Hugh M. To Antigonish Co, NS, prob <1815; stld Browns Mountain. Dau Sarah. **HCA 172**.

5231 MACDONALD, Alexander 'Breac', ca 1777– ca 1872. From Fort William, INV. Said desc from the Keppoch family. To Pictou, NS, on the *Good Intent*,

1816; stld Arisaig, Antigonish Co. Farmer. m Katherine Kennedy, qv, ch: 1. Angus, b 1811; 2. Donald, b 1813; 3. John; 4. Ronald; 5. Alexander; 6. James; 7. Margaret. **HCA 190**.

5232 McDONALD, Alexander. To PEI <1816; stld Pinette, Queens Co. Farmer. **HP 49**.

5233 MACDONALD, Alexander 'Ruadh', b 1768. From Lochaber, INV. s/o Angus M, qv. To South West Mabou Ridge, Inverness Co, NS, 1816. Farmer. ch: 1. Angus, qv; 2. Allan, qv; 3. Donald; 4. Catherine; 5. Mary; 6. Flora; 7. Jessie; 8. Ann. His wife was Mary Campbell, qv. **CBC 1818; HCA 202; MP 512**.

5234 McDONALD, Alexander, b ca 1788. To Western Shore, Inverness Co, NS, 1816. Farmer, m and ch. **CBC 1818**.

5235 McDONALD, Alexander, b ca 1797. To Port Hood dist, Inverness Co, NS, 1816. Unm. **CBC 1818**.

5236 McDONALD, Alexander. From Breadalbane, PER. To QUE on the *Lady of the Lake*, Sep 1816; stld prob Beckwith Twp, Lanark Co, ONT. Farmer. **HCL 31, 237**.

5237 McDONALD, Alexander, b ca 1775. To Port Hood dist, Inverness Co, NS, 1817. Tailor, m and ch. **CBC 1818**.

5238 McDONALD, Alexander, b ca 1795. To Inverness Co, NS, 1817; prob stld Judique. Farmer, unm. **CBC 1818**.

5239 MACDONALD, Alexander. Prob from INV. s/o — M. and — MacLellan. To South River, Antigonish Co, NS, <1820. m Catherine MacLeod, and had, poss with other ch: 1. Rev Kenneth, b 1821; 2. John. **HCA 210**.

5240 MACDONALD, Alexander. Prob from INV. bro/o William M, qv. To Antigonish Co, NS, prob <1820; stld St Andrews. **HCA 223**.

5241 MACDONALD, Alexander 'Og'. Prob from Knoydart, INV. To Antigonish Co, NS, prob <1820. ch: 1. Rory; 2. Donald 'Mor'; 3. Charles; 4. John. **HCA 252**.

5242 MACDONALD, Alexander. From PER, poss Killin. To McNab Twp, Renfrew Co, ONT, 1825. Wife with him, and s John. **DC 3 Jan 1980**.

5243 MACDONALD, Alexander. From Glen Nigg, Moidart, INV. s/o Allan 'Mor' M. qv, and Ann Corbet, qv. To Antigonish Co, NS, 1829; stld Keppoch. Poet, known as 'Bard na Ceapach.' m Mary MacLean, ch: 1. Alexander; 2. John Duncan, dy; 3. Ann; 4. Allan; 5. Mary; 6. Catherine; 7. Margaret; 8. Marcella; 9. Roderick; 10. Allan. **HCA 200**.

5244 MACDONALD, Alexander. From Borrowdale, INV. To South River, Antigonish Co, NS, prob <1830. m a d/o Rory 'Ban' MacNeil, qv, ch: 1. Mrs Angus Macpherson; 2. Mrs John MacMillan. **HCA 216**.

5245 MACDONALD, Alexander 'Mor'. From INV. To Arisaig, Antigonish Co, NS, prob <1820; moved to Cloverville. m Catherine Kennedy, qv, ch: 1. Ronald; 2. Alexander; 3. James; 4. Donald; 5. Mrs W.M. Thompson; 6. Mrs Dougal Cameron. **HCA 222**.

5246 MACDONALD, Alexander. To East Bay, Cape Breton Co, NS, 1823. Dau Catherine. **HNS iii 204**.

5247 MACDONALD, Rev Alexander. From Is Skye,

INV. s/o John M, qv, and Janet MacLeod, qv. To Cape Breton Is, NS, 1827; later to Hampton, Kings Co. Baptist clergyman. m Jennie Crawford, no ch. **DC 23 Feb 1980**.

5248 McDONALD, Alexander. From Fort William, INV. To Antigonish Co, NS, <1830. Farmer. Dau Margaret. **HNS iii 310**.

5249 McDONALD, Alexander, 1771–1856. From INV. To Dundee, QUE, 1830; moved to Ekfrid Twp, Middlesex Co, ONT, 1835. m Ann Vass, qv, ch: 1. William, res Dundee, QUE; 2. Alexander, res Brooke; 3. John, went to IL; 4. James, stld London Twp, Middlesex Co; 5. David; 6. Mary; 7. Janetta. **PCM 30**.

5250 MACDONALD, Alexander 'Mor'. From INV, poss Is Skye. To Antigonish Co, NS, prob <1830. Son Donald. **HCA 213**.

5251 McDONALD, Alexander, ca 1792–8 Mar 1837. From Clyne par, SUT. To NS <1830; stld nr Earlton, Colchester Co. m (i) Christy Baillie, qv; (ii) Anne McDonald, 1799–1884. **DC 19 Mar 1980**.

5252 McDONALD, Alexander, ca 1795–18 Apr 1864. From ROC. To Upper Kemptown, Colchester Co, NS, <1830. Wife Isabella, ca 1795–1864. Son Hector, ca 1829-62. **DC 19 Mar 1981**.

5253 McDONALD, Alexander. Prob rel to Finlay M, qv. To London, Westminster Twp, Middlesex Co, ONT, 1831. **PCM 55**.

5254 MACDONALD, Alexander 'Mor'. From Lochaber, INV. s/o Donald 'Ruadh' M. To Mabou River, Inverness Co, NS, 1832. m Isabel MacDonald, who d on the voyage, ch: 1. Donald, qv; 2. Ronald, qv; 3. Angus, qv; 4. Allan, poet; 5. Alexander 'Ban', drowned; 6. John, dy. **HCA 194**.

5255 MACDONALD, Alexander, 1808-71. From Banff. s/o Lachlan M. and Elizabeth Imlach. To QUE, prob <1833. m Mary Stuart Douglas, qv. **DC 6 Jan 1977**.

5256 McDONALD, Alexander, d 1875. From Edinburgh. To ONT, 1834; stld London, Westminster Twp, Middlesex Co, 1850. **PCM 55**.

5257 McDONALD, Alexander, b 1786. To Dalhousie, NB, prob <1840. Wife Margaret with him. **MAC 20**.

5258 MACDONALD, Alexander. From Glen Roy, Kilmonivaig par, INV. To Antigonish Co, NS, prob <1840. m Mary Chisholm, ch: 1. Alexander; 2. John. **HCA 207**.

5259 McDONALD, Alexander. To Pictou, NS, on the *Lady Grey*, ex Cromarty, ROC, arr 16 Jul 1841. **DC 15 Jul 1979**.

5260 MACDONALD, Rev Alexander, 1801–21 May 1865. From Kilmonivaig par, INV. s/o Alexander M, said desc from the Keppoch family. Educ Valladolid, Spain, and ord to RC priesthood. Served at Moidart before going to Judique, Inverness Co, NS, 1842. Trans to Mabou, 1844. Gaelic writer, and became Vicar-General of Arichat. **HCA 196; MP 44**.

5261 McDONALD, Alexander, d 1846. To Bartibog River, Northumberland Co, NB. Farmer and fisherman. **DC 2 Jun 1978**.

5262 McDONALD, Alexander. To Pictou, NS, on the *London*, arr 11 Apr 1848. **DC 15 Jul 1979**.

5263 McDONALD, Alexander. From Is Lewis, INV. To QUE, ex Stornoway, arr 4 Aug 1851; stld Huron Twp, Bruce Co, ONT, 1852. Head of family. **DC 5 Apr 1967**.

5264 McDONALD, Alexander. From Is Benbecula, INV. To East Williams Twp, Middlesex Co, ONT, 1848. **PCM 44**.

5265 McDONALD, Alexander, b 1811. From Garrynamonie, Is South Uist, INV. To West Williams Twp, Middlesex Co, ONT, 1849; stld Con 14. Farmer. m Margaret McKinnon, ch: 1. Alexander; 2. Margaret; 3. Ann. **PCM 48; WLC**.

5266 MACDONALD, Alexander, b ca 1802. From Callanish, Uig, Is Lewis, ROC. To NS, 1851; stld Winslow Twp, later Whitton Twp, Compton Co. Farmer. m Mary McIver, qv, ch: 1. John, qv; 2. Annie, qv; 3. Kate, qv; 4. Mary, qv; 5. Maggie, qv; 6. Christy, qv; 7. Alexander, qv. **TFT 17**.

5267 MACDONALD, Alexander, jr, 1844–1909. From Callanish, Uig, Is Lewis, ROC. s/o Alexander M, qv, and Mary McIver, qv. To QUE, 1851; stld Winslow Twp, later Whitton Twp, Compton Co. Farmer. m 1867, Annie McRae, d 1890, ch: 1. Mary Elizabeth, 1868–1926; 2. Angus, 1870-92; 3. Alexander, 1873–1938; 4. Annie Bella, 1876–1904; 5. Katie, b 1879; 6. Christy Jane; 7. Bessie Ann, b 1886; 8. Maggie, d inf, 1888. **TFT 18**.

5268 MACDONALD, Alexander. From INV. s/o Duncan M, from Is Canna. To Foot Cape, Broad Cove Banks, Inverness Co, NS, prob <1840. m Miss MacDougall, ch: 1. Hugh; 2. John; 3. Allan; 4. Murdock; 5. Norman; 6. Neil; 7. Catherine; 8. Christine. **MP 476**.

5269 MACDONALD, Alexander 'Breac', 1827–10 Dec 1918. From Brae-Lochaber, INV. s/o Angus M, qv, and Catherine Cameron, qv. To Inverness Co, NS, 1831; stld North Lake Ainslie, later South East Mabou. m Margaret, d/o John 'Lord' MacDonald, qv, ch: 1. John; 2. Archibald; 3. Rev Angus, d 1897; 4. Allan; 5. Donald Cameron, b 1872; 6. Catherine; 7. Teresa; 8. Mary; 9. Jessie; 10. Maria. **MP 555**.

5270 MACDONALD, Alexander 'Mor'. From INV. s/o Roderick M, qv. To Port Hood, Inverness Co, NS, prob <1810. m Miss MacGillivray, ch: 1. Angus; 2. Margaret. **MP 438**.

5271 MACDONALD, Alexander 'Mor'. From INV. s/o Donald M, Lochaber. To Inverness Co, NS, 1832. m Isabel, d/o Malcolm Campbell, ch: 1. Donald, qv; 2. Angus, qv; 3. Allan, unm; 4. Alexander, b 1830; 5. Ronald, qv; 6. John, dy; 7. Flora, d in SCT. **MP 494**.

5272 McDONALD, Alexander 'Ruadh'. From Lochaber, INV. Desc from the *Sloihd an Taighe*, Bohuntin. To Mabou Ridge, Inverness Co, NS, 1816. m Mary Campbell, qv, ch: 1. Angus, qv; 2. Allan, qv; 3. Donald, qv; 4. Mary, qv; 5. Catherine, qv; 6. Flora, qv; 7. Anne, qv; 8. Jessie, qv. **MP 512**.

5273 McDONALD, Alexander B. From Is South Uist, INV. To East Williams Twp, Middlesex Co, ONT, ca 1849. **PCM 44**.

5274 McDONALD, Alexina. From South Uist, INV. d/o Allan M, qv, and Mary McLean, qv. To Mira Valley, Cape Breton Co, NS, 1823, but stld Whycocomagh,

Inverness Co. m John Dunlap, and d in ONT.
DC 23 Feb 1980.

5275   MACDONALD, Allan 'Ban'. From Glengarry, INV.
To PEI, 1776; stld later Indian Point, Judique, Inverness
Co, NS. Farmer and fisherman. m Catherine MacEachen,
qv, and had, poss with other ch: 1. James; 2. Teresa.
MP 21; NSN 32/363; DC 5 Feb 1961.

5276   McDONALD, Allan. From Ardnish, Arisaig, INV.
Prob rel to James M, qv. To PEI on the *Jane*, ex Loch
nan Uamh, Arisaig, 12 Jul 1790. Tenant. Family with
him. **PLJ.**

5277   McDONALD, Allan. From Cleadale, Is Eigg, INV.
To QUE on the *British Queen*, ex Arisaig, 16 Aug 1790;
stld nr Montreal. Tenant. Wife and ch with him.
QCC 103.

5278   McDONALD, Allan, b ca 1760. To Western
Shore, Inverness Co, NS, 1799. Farmer, m and ch.
CBC 1818.

5279   MACDONALD, Allan. From Knoydart, INV.
s/o Samuel M. and Johanna Hewitt. To Pictou, NS,
on the *Nora*, ex Fort William, 1801; stld Marydale,
Antigonish Co. **HCA 212.**

5280   McDONALD, Allan, b ca 1782. To Western
Shore, Inverness Co, NS, 1802. Farmer, m and ch.
CBC 1818.

5281   McDONALD, Allan, n 1786. s/o Angus M, qv,
and wife Nancy. To QUE on the *Oughton*, arr Jul 1804;
stld Baldoon, Dover Twp, Kent Co, ONT. Farmer.
m ca 1806, Belle McKay.   **UCM 267, 268; DC 4 Oct
1979.**

5282   MACDONALD, Allan 'Dhu'. From Lochaber, INV.
bro/o Donald 'Breac' M, qv. To Antigonish Co, NS, prob
<1810. m Mary MacDonald, and had, poss with other
ch: 1. John; 2. Donald; 3. Angus; 4. Alexander.
HCA 201.

5283   MACDONALD, Allan. Prob from INV. To
Antigonish Co, NS, poss <1815. Son John, qv.
HCA 219.

5284   McDONALD, Allan, b ca 1769. To Inverness,
Inverness Co, NS, 1816. Farmer, m and ch.   **CBC 1818.**

5285   McDONALD, Allan, b ca 1755. To St Andrews
dist, Cape Breton Co, NS, arr prob Apr 1817. Farmer,
m and ch.   **CBC 1818.**

5286   MACDONALD, Allan 'The Ridge', 1794–1868.
From Lochaber, INV. s/o Alexander 'Ruadh' M, qv, and
Mary Campbell, qv. To Inverness Co, NS, 1816. Farmer
and Gaelic poet. m Catherine Macpherson, ch:
1. Alexander; 2. Ronald; 3. Murdoch; 4. Donald;
5. John; 6. Alick; 7. Ann; 8. Janet.   **HCA 202.**

5287   MACDONALD, Allan, d 1834. From
Glenmoriston, INV. To ONT, 1816; stld Salmon River.
m Margaret Grant, qv, ch: 1. Mary; 2. Isabella;
3. Angus; 4. Margaret; 5. John 'Ban'.   **DC 4 Mar 1965.**

5288   MACDONALD, Allan, 1794–1868. From Lochaber,
INV. s/o Alexander 'Ruadh' M, qv, and Mary Campbell,
qv. To Mabou Ridge, Inverness Co, NS, 1816; moved in
1847 to Upper South River, Antigonish Co. m Catherine,
d/o Murdock MacPherson, qv, ch: 1. Alexander;
2. Ronald; 3. Murdoch; 4. Donald; 5. John;

6. Alexander; 7. Anne; 8. Jessie; 9. Angus.   **MP 526,
790.**

5289   MACDONALD, Allan. From Is South Uist, INV.
s/o John M. To Cape Breton Co, NS, 1823; moved to
Stewartdale, Whycocomagh, Inverness Co. Wife Mary
MacLean, qv, with him, and ch: 1. John, qv; 2. Norman,
qv; 3. James Edward, qv; 4. Susan, qv; 5. Mary, qv;
6. Alexina, qv; 7. Catherine, qv.   **NSN 27/194, 30/301;
DC 23 Feb 1980.**

5290   MACDONALD, Allan. From Is South Uist, INV.
s/o Donald M, qv. To St John, NB, 1826, but stld River
Denny, Cape Breton Is, NS. m Mary MacDonald, qv, ch:
1. William, b 1837, merchant, Glace Bay, and senator,
1872; 2. Malcolm.   **HNS iii 635.**

5291   MACDONALD, Allan. From Moidart, INV. To
Antigonish Co, NS, prob <1827; stld Fairmont. m Annie
MacDonald, qv, ch: 1. John; 2. Colin; 3. Roderick;
4. James; 5. Catherine; 6. Euphemia; 7. Margaret;
8. Mary.   **HCA 182, 259.**

5292   MACDONALD, Allan. From Is North Uist, INV. To
Cape Breton Is, NS, 1828; stld Catalone. Postmaster.
Dau Annie.   **HNS iii 195.**

5293   MACDONALD, Allan 'Mor'. From Glen Nigg,
Moidart, INV. bro/o Alexander M, qv. To Antigonish Co,
NS, 1829. m Ann Corbet, qv, ch: 1. Alexander, qv;
2. Roderick; 3. John; 4. Marcella; 5. Catherine;
6. Sarah.   **HCA 200.**

5294   MACDONALD, Allan. From INV. s/o Angus
Maclan Og Vic Ian, bro/o the laird of Morar. To South
River, Antigonish Co, NS, <1830. m Christina Cameron.
Son Hugh, 1827-99, PC under Sir John A.
Macdonald.   **HNS iii 634.**

5295   MACDONALD, Allan. Prob from INV.
bro/o Donald M, qv. To Lennox, Antigonish Co, NS,
prob <1830. m Ann MacDonald, ch: 1. John;
2. Alexander, dy; 3. Angus, qv; 4. Peggy; 5. Catherine;
6. Nancy; 7. Mary.   **HCA 250.**

5296   McDONALD, Allan, ca 1825–6 Jul 1915. From
INV, prob dist Ardnish, Arisaig. bro/o Donald M, qv, and
Angus M, qv. To PEI, ca 1837, but moved to East Bay,
Cape Breton Co, NS. Retr to SCT on the *Mary Ellen*,
1859, and led 60 families to Cape Breton Is and
Antigonish Co. Wife b 1828. ch: 1. Duncan A; 2. Mrs
Alexander McIntyre, East Bay; 3. Mrs John McCormack,
Bridgeport; 4. Mrs Margaret McDougall.   **NSN 37/134;
DC 8 Jul 1979.**

5297   MACDONALD, Allan. From INV. s/o Duncan M,
from Is Canna. To Foot Cape, Broad Cove Banks,
Inverness Co, NS, prob <1840. Farmer, and possessed
some medical skills. m Isabel, d/o Malcolm MacLean,
qv, ch: 1. Duncan; 2. Neil; 3. Malcolm; 4. Alexander;
5. Roderick; 6. James; 7. Elizabeth.   **MP 478, 739.**

5298   MACDONALD, Allan 'Mor'. From INV. To
Antigonish Co, NS, <1840; stld Beauly. m Miss
MacIntosh, ch: 1. Angus; 2. James; 3. Catherine;
4. Mary; 5. Margaret; 6. Mary.   **HCA 256.**

5299   McDONALD, Allan. To East Bay, Cape Breton Co,
NS, <1840. Son Allan.   **HNS iii 302.**

5300   MACDONALD, Allan, 1831–13 Sep 1899. From
Badenoch, INV. s/o Donald M, qv, and Jessie
MacDonald, qv. To Glenville, Inverness Co, NS, prob

<1840; stld later at Black River. Farmer. m 23 Jul 1865, Janet, d/o John MacDonald, ch: 1. Donald; 2. John; 3. Ronald; 4. Finlay; 5. Alexander; 6. Angus; 7. Kenneth Alexander; 8. Archibald Joseph. **MP 400**.

5301 McDONALD, Allan, d 1900. Prob from Duthill, INV. To London Twp, Middlesex Co, ONT, 1840; moved to West Williams Twp, 1850. **PCM 47**.

5302 MACDONALD, Allan. From Moidart, INV. bro/o Annie M, qv. To Monkshead, Antigonish Co, NS, 1842. ch. **HCA 182, 256**.

5303 MACDONALD, Allan. From Lochaber, INV. s/o Angus M, qv, and Mary Ann Rankin. To South West Mabou, Inverness Co, NS, 1854. m Margaret, d/o John MacPherson, ch: 1. Angus Anthony; 2. John Donald; 3. Mary; 4. Anne; 5. Christy Belle. **MP 586**.

5304 MACDONALD, Andrew, 1806-36. From Banff. s/o Lachlan M. and Elizabeth Imlach. To QUE prob <1833. **DC 6 Jan 1977**.

5305 MACDONALD, Andrew Robertson, b ca 1825. From Paisley, RFW. s/o Grant Steuart M. To Montreal, QUE. **Ts Paisley**.

5306 MACDONALD, Angus. From Moidart, INV. s/o Donald M. To Pictou, NS, ca 1784; stld Judique, Inverness Co. **DC 30 Mar 1981**.

5307 MACDONALD, Angus. From Lochaber, INV. To Pictou Co, NS, <1785. Soldier at Quebec, 1776; gr land at Merigomish and at Arisaig, Antigonish Co. Son Donald. **HNS iii 179**.

5308 McDONALD, Angus 'Ban'. From Munical, Loch Hourne, Knoydart, INV. To QUE on the *MacDonald*, arr 5 Sep 1785; stld nr Williamstown, Glengarry Co, ONT. By wife Elinor MacDonald, qv, ch: 1. James, qv; 2. John, qv; 3. Finan, qv. **GD 50/225/1**.

5309 MACDONALD, Angus. From Morar, INV. s/o — Gillis and — MacGillivray. To Merigomish, Pictou Co, NS, poss 1788, but moved to Antigonish Co. Pioneer settler at Arisaig, which he named, but retr to Pictou Co. Adopted surname McDonald at the instance of John McDonald of Glenaladale, qv, and m a sis/o Allan 'Dhu' M, qv. Son Donald, b Annapolis Co. **HCA 12, 142**.

5310 MACDONALD, Angus. From Moidart, INV. To Pictou Co, NS, <1790. Served in RN during American Revolutionary War, also French War, 1782. Became farmer. Son Donald, b Baileys Brook. **HNS iii 266**.

5311 MACDONALD, Angus. From Drumdarroch, Arisaig, INV. To PEI on the *Jane*, ex Loch nan Uamh, Arisaig, 12 Jul 1790. A large family with him. **PLJ**.

5312 McDONALD, Angus. From Is Eigg, INV. To PEI on the *Jane*, ex Loch nan Uamh, Arisaig, 12 Jul 1790. Wife with him and 2 ch. **PLJ**.

5313 MACDONALD, Angus, b ca 1769. From Is Skye, INV. s/o Ronald and Jenny M. To Musquodoboit, Halifax Co, NS, <17 Jan 1793, when m Martha, d/o James Fisher and Margaret McKeen. Dau Eleanor. **DC 30 Apr 1980**.

5314 McDONALD, Angus. From Knoydart, INV. To Pictou, NS, on the *Sarah*, ex Fort William, Jun 1801. Farmer. Wife Margaret with him, and ch: 1. Mary; 2. Allan; 3. Donald, aged 10; 4. Samuel, aged 6; 5. Peggy, aged 4; 7. Mary, aged 2. **PLS**.

5315 McDONALD, Angus. From Glengarry, INV. To Pictou, NS, on the *Sarah*, ex Fort William, Jun 1801. Labourer. Wife Janet with him, and ch: 1. Rachel; 2. Janet, aged 3. **PLS**.

5316 MACDONALD, Angus. From Knoydart, INV. s/o Samuel M. and Johanna Hewitt. To Pictou, NS, on the *Nora*, ex Fort William, 1801; stld Marydale, Antigonish Co. Pioneer settler. m Mary MacDonald, ch: 1. Donald; 2. Allan; 3. Archibald; 4. Mary; 5. Margaret; 6. Ann; 7. Marcella. **HCA 14, 212**.

5317 McDONALD, Angus, b ca 1748. To Western Shore, Inverness Co, NS, 1802. Farmer, m and ch. **CBC 1818**.

5318 McDONALD, Angus, d 1805. From ARL. To QUE on the *Oughton*, arr Jul 1804; stld Baldoon, Dover Twp, Kent Co, ONT. Farmer. Wife Nancy with him, and ch: 1. Allan, qv; 2. John; 3. Archibald, b 1791; 4. Donald, b 1789; 5. Hector, b 1800; 6. Neil, b 1802. **UCM 267, 302; DC 4 Oct 1979**.

5319 McDONALD, Angus 'Kirkland', b 1773. To QUE on the *Oughton*, arr Jul 1804; stld Baldoon, Dover Twp, Kent Co, ONT. Farmer. Wife Jean, 1764–1805, with him, and ch: 1. Reith, b 1796; 2. Andrew, b 1798; 3. Angus, b 1801; 4. Mary, b 1804. **UCM 268, 302; DC 4 Oct 1979**.

5320 McDONALD, Angus, ca 1755–4 Nov 1830. From Glen Roy, Kilmonivaig par, INV. To Miramichi, Northumberland Co, NB, 1805; stld Bay du Vin River. **DC 2 Jun 1978**.

5321 MACDONALD, Angus. From Glengarry, INV. s/o Allan M. To Arisaig, Antigonish Co, NS, <1805. ch: 1. Donald, qv; 2. Angus, res Lakevale; 3. Alexander, res Lakevale. **HCA 231**.

5322 McDONALD, Angus, b ca 1771. Poss from Is Mull, ARL. To Charlottetown, PEI, on the *Rambler*, ex Tobermory, 20 Jun 1806. Wife Mary, aged 30, with him, and ch: 1. Donald, aged 13; 2. John, aged 11; 3. Mary, aged 9; 4. Janet, aged 7; 5. Alexander, aged 6; 6. Katherine, aged 3; 7. Ann, b 1806. **PLR**.

5323 McDONALD, Angus, b ca 1746. To Charlottetown, PEI, on the *Humphreys*, ex Tobermory, arr 14 Jul 1806. Wife Ann, aged 50, with him, and ch: 1. Catherine, aged 24; 2. Christian, aged 22; 3. Donald, aged 20. **PLH**.

5324 MACDONALD, Angus. From Tulloch, Glenspean, INV. s/o Capt Angus M. To West Lake Ainslie, Inverness Co, NS, 1807. m Mary MacDonald, qv, ch: 1. Allan; 2. John; 3. Angus; 4. Neil; 5. Alexander; 6. Mary; 7. Margaret; 8. Ann. **HCA 199**.

5325 MACDONALD, Angus. From Arisaig, INV. bro/o Alexander M, qv, and Lachlan M, qv. To Arisaig, Antigonish Co, NS, <1820. Discharged soldier. m Ann, half-sister of Rev Allan MacLean, Judique, ch: 1. Alexander; 2. Donald; 3. Hugh; 4. Norman; 5. Lachlan; 6. Daniel; 7. Mary; 8. Margaret; 9. Ann. **HCA 209**.

5326 MACDONALD, Angus. From Morar, INV. s/o John 'Og' M. To South River, Antigonish Co, NS, prob <1810. ch: 1. Ronald; 2. Hugh; 3. Allan. **HCA 238**.

5327 MACDONALD, Angus. From Knoydart, INV. s/o Allan M. To Antigonish Co, NS, prob <1810. ch:

1. Alexander; 2. Angus; 3. John; 4. Donald; 5. Mary; 6. Ronald.   **HCA 180**.

5328   MACDONALD, Angus. From Lochaber, INV. s/o Angus M. To Caledonia, Antigonish Co, NS, prob <1810. ch: 1. Elizabeth; 2. Donald.   **MP 464**.

5329   MACDONALD, Angus 'Ruadh'. From Lochaber, INV. bro/o Allan 'Dhu' M, qv. To Antigonish Co, NS, prob <1810. m Kate, d/o Duncan Mackenzie.   **HCA 201**.

5330   McDONALD, Angus. Prob from Aberdeen. bro/o Hugh M, merchant. To NS <1812. Farmer.   **SH**.

5331   McDONALD, Angus. Prob from Is Mull, ARL. To Hudson Bay and Red River <1813. Pioneer settler. Wife and 2 ch with him.   **RRS 16**.

5332   McDONALD, Angus. Prob from Is Mull, ARL. To Hudson Bay and Red River <1813. Pioneer settler. Two sons with him.   **RRS 16**.

5333   McDONALD, Angus, b 1770. From Balinahard, Kilfinichen, ARL. To Hudson Bay and Red River, <1815. Wife Mary McLucas, qv, with him, and ch: 1. Donald, aged 18; 2. Jean, aged 16; 3. Archibald, aged 14; 4. Ann, aged 14; 5. Alexander, aged 8. Poss left settlement, summer 1815.   **RRS 24; LSS 187**.

5334   McDONALD, Angus, b ca 1781. From Knoydart, INV. To QUE, ex Greenock, summer 1815; stld prob Lanark Co, ONT. Farmer. Wife Jean McDougall, qv, with him, and 2 ch.   **SEC 7**.

5335   MACDONALD, Angus. From Arisaig, INV. s/o Donald M. To Cape George, Antigonish Co, NS, prob <1815; moved to Highfield, later to Double Hill, Arisaig.   **HCA 247**.

5336   MACDONALD, Angus. From Moidart, INV. s/o Lachlan M, qv. To Antigonish Co, NS, prob <1815. ch: 1. Hugh; 2. John; 3. Allan; 4. Donald; 5. Margaret.   **HCA 172**.

5337   McDONALD, Angus, ca 1764–31 Oct 1834. Poss from Is Iona, ARL. To Vaughan Twp, York Co, ONT, prob <1815. Wife Mary, ca 1766–1834.   **DC 24 Jan 1977**.

5338   MACDONALD, Angus, b ca 1792. From Lochaber, INV. s/o Alexander 'Ruadh' M, qv, and Mary Campbell, qv. To Mabou Ridge, Inverness Co, NS, 1816. m Mary, d/o Murdock MacPherson, qv, ch: 1. Angus; 2. Alexander; 3. Allan; 4. Archibald; 5. Hugh; 6. Alexander; 7. Catherine; 8. Jessie; 9. Mary; 10. Margaret; 11. Anne.   **HCA 202; MP 512, 790**.

5339   MACDONALD, Angus. From Moidart, INV. s/o Donald M, from Is Eigg, desc from the family of Clanranald. To Fox Brook, Pictou Co, NS, <1820. ch by first wife with him: 1. Isabel, qv; 2. Catherine, qv; m (ii) Isabel Campbell, qv, further ch: 3. Donald; 4. John; 5. William; 6. Colin; 7. Rory; 8. Christina; 9. Mary.   **HCA 185; MP 502**.

5340   MACDONALD, Angus 'Ban'. Prob from INV. To Antigonish Co, NS, prob <1820. ch: 1. Donald; 2. Angus; 3. Alexander, d at Miramichi; 4. Ann; 5. Jessie; 6. Catherine.   **HCA 243**.

5341   MACDONALD, Angus 'Ban'. From Arisaig, INV. bro/o Donald 'Mingary' M, qv. To Gut of Canso, NS, prob <1820; stld Lismore, Antigonish Co. Tailor. m Christina, d/o Hugh Cameron, shipowner, ch: 1. Hugh

C, shipbuilder; 2. Donald, 1819–1922; 3. Angus, building contractor, Halifax; 4. Roderick; 5. Mary; 6. Christina.   **HCA 235**.

5342   MACDONALD, Angus. From Lochaber, INV. s/o Alexander M. To Inverness Co, NS, ca 1822; stld Glencoe. Wife Margaret MacDonald, qv, with him, and ch: 1. Archibald, qv; 2. Alexander, dy; 3. Angus 'Og', qv; 4. Hugh, qv; 5. Catherine, qv; 6. Christina, qv; 7. Flora, unm; 8. Margaret, unm; 9. Mary, qv.   **MP 484**.

5343   MACDONALD, Angus, 30 May 1790–2 Jan 1843. From Lochaber, INV. s/o Capt Angus M. of Tulloch, Glen Spean, and Margaret MacDonald. Served as ensign in 6th West Indian Regt, and was gr land at West Lake Ainslie, Inverness Co, 1822. m Mary, d/o Allan MacDonald, 20 Feb 1820, ch: 1. Margaret; 2. Angus; 3. Anne; 4. Allan; 5. Mary; 6. John; 7. Angus; 8. Neil; 9. Alexander.   **MP 590**.

5344   MACDONALD, Angus, b ca 1821. From Is Coll, ARL. s/o Archibald M, qv. To Glencoe, Inverness Co, NS, ca 1824. m Margaret, d/o Alexander Beaton and Isabel MacDonald, ch: 1. John R; 2. Alexander; 3. Archie; 4. Archie A; 5. Angus; 6. John Alexander; 7. Daniel Francis; 8. Isabel.   **MP ii 371**.

5345   MACDONALD, Angus. Prob from INV. s/o Rory M. To Baileys Brook, Antigonish Co, NS, poss <1830. ch: 1. John; 2. Angus; 3. Ronald; 4. Donald; 5. Alexander; 6. Rory.   **HCA 254**.

5346   MACDONALD, Angus. From Borrodale, INV. To South River, Antigonish Co, NS, prob <1830. m Miss MacDonald, ch: 1. John; 2. Hugh; 3. Martin; 4. John Og.   **HCA 216**.

5347   MACDONALD, Angus. From Lochaber, INV. s/o Alexander 'Mor' M, qv, and Isabel MacDonald. To NS, prob 1832. m (i) Mary Campbell, ch: 1. Angus; 2. Alexis. m (ii) Isabel, d/o Alexander 'Dubh' MacDonald, further ch: 3. James, farmer, Strathlorne.   **HCA 194**.

5348   MACDONALD, Angus. From INV. To Antigonish Co, NS, <1840. m Janet MacNeill, ch: 1. Donald; 2. Malcolm, went to ONT; 3. James; 4. Michael, went to Newcastle, NB; 5. Mary; 6. Janet; 7. Annie; 8. Mary, dy; 9. Margaret; 10. Elizabeth.   **HCA 251**.

5349   MACDONALD, Angus, d 14 Apr 1880. From Brae-Lochaber, INV. s/o Alexander 'Dubh' M. and Ann MacDonald. To South East Mabou, Inverness Co, NS, 1831; prob later to Antigonish Co. m Catherine Cameron, qv, ch: 1. Alexander, qv; 2. Donald; 3. Archibald; 4. Allan; 5. Duncan; 6. Isabel; 7. Mary; 8. Jane; 9. Christina; 10. Anne.   **HCA 553; MP 553**.

5350   MACDONALD, Angus. From Moidart, INV. s/o Donald M, from Is Eigg, desc from the family of Clanranald. To Cape Mabou, Inverness Co, NS, poss <1830. m (i) Marjorie MacArthur, ch: 1. John; 2. Mary Anne. m (ii) Margaret MacLellan, Broad Cove, further ch: 3. James; 4. Angus; 5. Marcella.   **MP 473**.

5351   McDONALD, Angus. From Is Benbecula, INV. To East Williams Twp, Middlesex Co, ONT, 1848.   **PCM 44**.

5352   McDONALD, Angus 'Mor', b 1800. From Cheesebay, Is North Uist, INV. To West Williams Twp, Middlesex Co, ONT, 1850. Farmer and local councillor.

By wife Mary had ch: 1. Kirsty, b 1836; 2. Archibald, b 1839; 3. Margaret, b 1841; 4. Mary, b 1843; 5. Flora, b 1847. **PCM 48; WLC**.

5353 MACDONALD, Angus, b 1816. From Is Benbecula, INV. To West Williams Twp, Middlesex Co, ONT, ca 1850. m Ann McCormack, ch: 1. Ranald, b 1841; 2. John, b 1842; 3. John Og, b 1845; 4. Mary, b 1847; 5. Kirsty, b 1849. **WLC**.

5354 McDONALD, Angus, b 1811. From Stoneybridge, Is South Uist, INV. To Middlesex Co, ONT, ca 1856; stld Con 14, West Williams Twp. Farmer. m Ann Bowie, ch: 1. Allan, b 1844; 2. Marion, b 1846; 3. Archibald, b 1848; 4. Kirsty. **WLC**.

5355 McDONALD, Angus. From North Uist, INV. To Adelaide Twp, Middlesex Co, ONT, 1850. **PCM 28**.

5356 McDONALD, Angus (1). From Is Lewis, ROC. To QUE, ex Stornoway, arr 4 Aug 1851; stld Huron Twp, Bruce Co, ONT, 1852. Head of family. **DC 5 Apr 1967**.

5357 McDONALD, Angus (2). From Is Lewis, ROC. To QUE, ex Stornoway, arr 4 Aug 1851; stld Huron Twp, Bruce Co, ONT, 1852. Head of family. **DC 5 Apr 1967**.

5358 McDONALD, Angus (2). From Is Lewis, ROC. To QUE, ex Stornoway, arr 4 Aug 1851; stld Huron Twp, Bruce Co, ONT, 1852. Head of family. **DC 5 Apr 1967**.

5359 McDONALD, Angus (3). From Is Lewis, ROC. To QUE, ex Stornoway, arr 4 Aug 1851; stld Huron Twp, Bruce Co, ONT, 1852. Head of family. **DC 5 Apr 1967**.

5360 McDONALD, Angus (4). From Is Lewis, ROC. To QUE, ex Stornoway, arr 4 Aug 1851; stld Huron Twp, Bruce Co, ONT, 1852. Head of family. **DC 5 Apr 1967**.

5361 McDONALD, Angus (5). From Is Lewis, ROC. To QUE, ex Stornoway, arr 4 Aug 1851; stld Huron Twp, Bruce Co, ONT, 1852. Head of family. **DC 5 Apr 1967**.

5362 McDONALD, Angus. To Pictou, NS, on the *Lulan*, ex Glasgow, 17 Aug 1848. Wife Marion with him, and ch: 1. Ann; 2. Mary; 3. Neil; 4. Donald; 5. Christina. **DC 15 Jul 1979**.

5363 MACDONALD, Angus. From Lochaber, INV. s/o Donald M. of the *Sliochd an Taighe*, Bohuntin, and Mary MacDonald. To Inverness Co, NS, arr 31 Aug 1854; stld South West Mabou. m Mary Ann, d/o Donald Rankin, ch: 1. Donald, dy; 2. Donald Og, dy; 3. John, qv; 4. Allan, qv; 6. Anne, qv; 7. Margaret, qv; 8. Mary, dy; 9. Mary. **MP 585**.

5364 McDONALD, Angus. From INV. bro/o Allan M, qv, and Donald M, qv. To PEI <1855. **DC 3 Apr 1979**.

5365 McDONALD, Angus 'Cross'. From Glenturret, PER. Prob s/o Alexander 'Mor' M. To Mabou Bridge, Inverness Co, NS, 1835. Building contractor. m Anne MacDonald, qv, ch: 1. Alexander, dy; 2. Allan, dy; 3. Donald, d ca 1904; 4. Anne; 5. Mary; 6. Marcella; 7. Jessie. **MP 468**.

5366 McDONALD, Angus 'Mor'. From Lochaber, INV. s/o Alexander 'Mor' M, qv, and Isabel Campbell. To Mabou Bridge, Inverness Co, NS, 1832. Farmer. m (i) Mary, d/o Alexander Campbell, qv, and Lucy Kennedy, qv, ch: 1. Angus; 2. Alexina. m (ii) Isabel, d/o Angus MacDonald, further ch: 3. Alexander; 4. James. **MP 273, 498**.

5367 MACDONALD, Angus 'Og'. From Lochaber, INV. s/o Angus M, qv, and Margaret MacDonald, qv. To Inverness Co, NS, ca 1822. m Sara, d/o Alexander Beaton, Judique, ch: 1. Allan R; 2. Alexander; 3. Alexina; 4. Margaret; 5. Angus; 6. Anne. **MP 487**.

5368 McDONALD, Ann. From Is Shona, Moidart, INV. To PEI on the *Lucy*, ex Loch nan Uamh, Arisaig, 12 Jul 1790. Prob a widow with a family. **PLL**.

5369 McDONALD, Ann. From Kilmorack, INV. Poss wife of Roderick McDonell, qv. To Pictou, NS, on the *Sarah*, ex Fort William, Jun 1801. **PLS**.

5370 McDONALD, Ann. From Appin, ARL. Prob wife of rel of Alexander M, labourer, qv. To Pictou, NS, on the *Sarah*, ex Fort William, Jun 1801. Spinster. **PLS**.

5371 MACDONALD, Ann. From Is Mull, ARL. d/o Findlay M, qv, and Jessie Mackinnon, qv. To Charlottetown, PEI, on the *Dykes*, arr 9 Aug 1803. m Donald Og Murchison, qv. **HP 36**.

5372 McDONALD, Ann, b 1806. From Lairg par, SUT. d/o Finlay M, qv. To East Nissouri Twp, Oxford Co, ONT, ca 1830. m Archibald McCaul, qv. **DC 25 Nov 1981**.

5373 McDONALD, Ann, b 1777. From Is Skye, INV. To Glengarry Co, ONT, 1831. Wife of John McKenzie, qv. **DC 23 Nov 1981**.

5374 McDONALD, Ann, b 1811. From Dunganichy, Is Benbecula, INV. d/o Donald M. To Pictou, NS, on the *Lulan*, ex Glasgow, 17 Aug 1848. Wife of Malcolm McDonald, qv. **DC 12 Jul 1879**.

5375 McDONALD, Ann. From Nunton, Is Benbecula, INV. To East Williams Twp, Middlesex Co, ONT, ca 1852. Wife of James Buchanan, qv. **WLC**.

5376 McDONALD, Annabella. From Ardnafouran, Arisaig, INV. To PEI on the *Jane*, ex Loch nan Uamh, Arisaig, 12 Jul 1790. **PLJ**.

5377 MACDONALD, Anne. From Lochaber, INV. d/o Alexander 'Ruadh' M, qv, and Mary Campbell, qv. To Mabou Ridge, Inverness Co, NS, 1816. m Finlay Beaton, qv, Little Judique. **MP 544**.

5378 MACDONALD, Anne. From Lochaber, INV. d/o Angus M. To Arisaig, Antigonish Co, NS, 1816; moved to Black River, Inverness Co. wid/o Archibald MacDonald, saddler. ch: 1. Donald, qv; 2. Ronald, qv; 3. Alexander, saddler; 4. Jane, qv; 5. Margaret, qv; 6. Marcella, qv; 7. Mary, qv; 8. Anne, qv. **MP 467, 545**.

5379 MACDONALD, Anne. From Lochaber, INV. d/o Archibald M. and Anne MacDonald, qv. To Inverness Co, NS, prob 1816; stld Rear Little Judique. Wife of Alexander 'Mor' MacMillan, qv. **MP 554, 748**.

5380 McDONALD, Anne. From Lochaber, INV. sis/o John 'Mor' M, qv. To Inverness Co, NS, prob 1826. m Murdock MacPherson, qv. **MP 790**.

5381 MACDONALD, Anne. From Badenoch, INV. d/o Allan M. and Mary MacDonald, qv. To Inverness Co, NS, 1835; stld Mabou Bridge. Wife of Angus 'Cross' MacDonald, qv. **MP 412, 467**.

5382 MACDONALD, Anne. From Lochaber, INV. sis/o John M. To Inverness Co, NS. m Angus Campbell, qv. **MP 295, 437**.

5383 MACDONALD, Anne, d 1843. From Snizort par, Is Skye, INV. d/o Hugh M. To Inverness Co, NS, 1840. Wife of Lachlan Mackinnon, qv. **MP ii 526**.

5384 MACDONALD, Anne. From INV, prob Moidart. d/o Donald 'Mor' M, from Is Eigg, desc from the Clanranald family. To Cape Mabou, Inverness Co, NS, <1840. m John, s/o Allan MacArthur, qv. **MP 385, 475**.

5385 MACDONALD, Annie. From Moidart, INV. sis/o John M, qv. To Antigonish Co, NS, 1827; stld Monkshead. m Allan MacDonald, Fairmont, qv. **HCA 259**.

5386 MACDONALD, Annie. From Uig par, Is Lewis, ROC. d/o Alexander M, qv, and Mary MacIver, qv. To QUE, 1851; stld Winslow, Compton Co. m Murdo Smith, farmer, Spring Hill, ch. **TFT 17**.

5387 MACDONALD, Annie. From Eneclate, Uig par, Is Lewis, ROC. d/o Donald M, qv, and Christy MacArthur Campbell, qv. To Winslow Twp, Compton Co, QUE, 1851. m John C. Matheson, farmer, ch. **TFT 13**.

5388 McDONALD, Archibald, b ca 1788. To Western Shore, Inverness Co, NS, 1799. Farmer. **CBC 1818**.

5389 McDONALD, Archibald, b ca 1778. To Inverness Co, NS, 1808; stld Mabou. Farmer, m and ch. **CBC 1818**.

5390 McDONALD, Archibald, 1790–15 Jan 1853. From Appin, ARL. To Fort Churchill, Hudson Bay, on the *Prince of Wales*, ex Stromness, 28 Jun 1813. Second in command of a party of Lord Selkirks colonists, destined for Red River. Later he joined the HBCo and served in the Columbia dist. Retr to St Andrews, QUE. m d/o Chief Comcomby, of the Chinook tribe. Son Ranald. **MDB 436**.

5391 MACDONALD, Archibald, d 1851. From Badenoch, INV. s/o Donald M. To Mabou, Inverness Co, NS, <1815. Merchant. m Christina MacPherson, qv, ch: 1. Donald, 1847-88; 2. John C, 1850-79, store-keeper, Mull River. **MP ii 304**.

5392 McDONALD, Archibald. From Is Tyree, ARL. s/o Hugh M, qv, and Ann Campbell, qv. To Lake Ainslie, Inverness Co, NS, 1820. m Ann MacLean, no ch. **DC 23 Feb 1980**.

5393 MACDONALD, Archibald. From Is Barra, INV. s/o John 'Og' M. To Mabou, Inverness Co, NS, prob <1820. m (i) Jessie, d/o John MacQuarrie, ch: 1. John; 2. Margaret. m (ii) Miss MacDonald, further ch: 3. Donald; 4. Finlay; 5. Michael; 6. Catherine. **MP 420**.

5394 McDONALD, Archibald, ca 1776–6 Sep 1858. From Is Iona, ARL. s/o Donald M. To Mariposa Twp, Victoria Co, ONT, poss <1815; bur Maple, York Co. m Flora McNaughton, qv, and had, with other ch: 1. Flora; 2. Archibald; 3. Hugh. **DC 24 Jan 1977**.

5395 MACDONALD, Archibald. From Badenoch, INV. s/o Allan M. and Mary MacDonald. To Brook Village, Inverness Co, NS, <1820; stld later at Glencoe. m Mary, d/o Hector MacNeil, qv, ch: 1. Allan; 2. William; 3. Alexander; 4. Mary; 5. Anne; 6. Elizabeth; 7. Christina; 8. Janet; 9. Sarah; 10. Catherine; 11. Margaret; 12. Eunice. **MP 410**.

5396 MACDONALD, Archibald. From Lochaber, INV. s/o Angus M, qv, and Margaret MacDonald, qv. To Inverness Co, NS, ca 1822; stld Glencoe. m Mary, d/o John Campbell, ch: 1. Angus; 2. John; 3. Donald; 4. Dougald; 5. Angus Og; 6. Janet; 7. Archibald. **MP 484**.

5397 MACDONALD, Archibald. From Is Coll, ARL. To Glencoe, Inverness Co, NS, ca 1824. ch: 1. Angus, qv; 2. Janet, b 1823; 3. Mary; 4. Flora; 5. Archibald, d 1865; 6. Lauchlin; 7. John; 8. Roderick. **MP ii 371**.

5398 MACDONALD, Archibald. From PER. To McNab Twp, Renfrew Co, ONT, 1825. **DC 3 Jan 1980**.

5399 MACDONALD, Archibald. To Mira Valley, Cape Breton Co, NS, <1830. Son Ronald, qv. **HNS iii 200**.

5400 McDONALD, Archibald, 1812–12 Jul 1878. From Is Iona, ARL. To Vaughan Twp, York Co, ONT, prob <1830. **DC 24 Jan 1977**.

5401 McDONALD, Archibald. From North Uist, INV. To Ekfrid Twp, Middlesex Co, ONT, ca 1832. ch. **PCM 31**.

5402 McDONALD, Archibald, 9 Jan 1786–18 Jan 1854. From Morayshire. To Melbourne, Richmond Co, QUE, prob <1850. **MGC 16 Jul 1980**.

5403 MACDONALD, Archibald. From Moidart, INV. To Antigonish Co, NS, 1854. ch: 1. John; 2. Roderick; 3. Dougal; 4. Alexander; 5. Patrick; 6. Jane; 7. Ann. **HCA 200**.

MACDONALD, Mrs Archibald. See MACDONALD, Anne.

5404 McDONALD, Augustine. From INV. To PEI, 1803; stld Lot 8, Glenwood. Son Arthur, 1860–1940. **DC 23 Oct 1981**.

5405 McDONALD, Barbara, 1840–23 Dec 1913. From Is Skye, INV. Poss d/o Malcolm M, qv, and Flora Campbell, qv. To Victoria Co, NS, prob 1841. **DC 22 Jun 1979**.

5406 MACDONALD, Benjamen, 17 Mar 1828–6 Feb 1902. From Halkirk, CAI. s/o William M, qv, and Christina Mill, qv. To Markham Twp, York Co, ONT, ca 1840. Farmer, Con 4. m Hilda Lever, ch: 1. William, d 1922; 2. Henry, d 1911; 3. Janet; 4. Alice. **DC 5 Jul 1979**.

5407 MACDONALD, Catherine. To Pictou, NS, on the *Hector*, ex Lochbroom, arr 17 Sep 1773. Wife of Donald Grant, qv. **HCA 154**.

5408 McDONALD, Catherine. From Kilmorack, INV. To Pictou, NS, on the *Sarah*, ex Fort William, Jun 1801. Spinster. **PLS**.

5409 McDONALD, Catherine. From Kilmorack, INV. Poss wife or rel of Rory M, labourer, qv. To Pictou, NS, on the *Sarah*, ex Fort William, Jun 1801. Spinster. **PLS**.

5410 McDONALD, Catherine, b ca 1797. From Strathglass, INV. Prob rel to Alexander Chisholm, farmer, qv. To Pictou, NS, on the *Sarah*, ex Fort William, Jun 1801. **PLS**.

5411 McDONALD, Catherine, b ca 1782. From Is Mull, ARL. sis/o Donald M, qv. To Charlottetown, PEI, on the *Clarendon*, ex Oban, 6 Aug 1808. **CPL**.

5412 McDONALD, Catherine, b ca 1792. From Is Mull, ARL. To Hudson Bay, 1814; thence to Red River. Moved later to York Co, ONT. m John Puterbaugh, ch. **DC 12 Oct 1979**.

5413 McDONALD, Catherine, b ca 1756. To Pictou Co, NS, 1815; res Rogers Hill, 1816. Widow, with 1 child, and 'very poor.' **INS 38**.

5414 MACDONALD, Catherine. From Lochaber, INV. d/o Alexander 'Ruadh' M, qv, and Mary Campbell, qv. To Mabou Ridge, Inverness Co, NS, 1816. m Donald Beaton, qv. **MP 544**.

5415 MACDONALD, Catherine, ca 1750–9 Aug 1822. Prob from ARL. To Aldborough Twp, Elgin Co, ONT, poss 1818. **PDA 41**.

5416 MACDONALD, Catherine, ca 1797–19 Feb 1871. From INV. To Dundee Village, Charlottenburgh Twp, Glengarry Co, ONT, ca 1819; later to Ekfrid Twp, Middlesex Co. Wife of John McMaster, qv. **DC 14 Aug 1979**.

5417 MACDONALD, Catherine. From Is Eigg, INV. To Antigonish Co, NS, 1823. Wife of Lachlan MacIsaac, qv, m 1818. **HCA 299**.

5418 McDONALD, Catherine. To 'North America,' early Sep 1819. Wife of Donald Urquhart, qv. **Sandwich OPR 17/1**.

5419 MACDONALD, Catherine. From Lochaber, INV. Prob d/o Donald M. To Black River, Inverness Co, NS, 1821. Wife of Angus Campbell, qv. **MP 281**.

5420 MACDONALD, Catherine. From Lochaber, INV. d/o Angus M, qv, and Margaret MacDonald, qv. To Inverness Co, NS, ca 1822; stld Glencoe. m Donald, s/o Donald Beaton, Little Judique. **MP 95**.

5421 MACDONALD, Catherine. From Is South Uist, INV. d/o Allan M, qv, and Mary MacLean, qv. To Cape Breton Co, NS, 1823, but moved to Whycocomagh, Inverness Co. m John McKeigan. **DC 23 Feb 1980**.

5422 MACDONALD, Catherine. From Is Skye, INV. To Charlottetown, PEI, on the *Mary Kennedy*, arr 1 Jun 1829; stld Uigg, Queens Co. Wife of John Martin, qv. **SPI 149**.

5423 MACDONALD, Catherine. From Moidart, INV. d/o Angus M, qv, and first wife. To Inverness Co, NS, prob <1825; stld Port Hood. m (i) James, s/o Dennis Murphy, ch; (ii) Walter Whittie, further ch. **MP 503**.

5424 MACDONALD, Catherine. From Badenoch, INV. d/o Allan M. and Mary MacDonald. To Inverness Co, NS, <1830. m Ronald MacDonald, qv. **MP 412, 547**.

5425 McDONALD, Catherine. From Nunton, Is Benbecula, INV. To Sydney, Cape Breton Co, NS, <1830. m John McCormack, qv. **HNS iii 321**.

5426 McDONALD, Catherine, ca 1796–7 Sep 1847. From ROC. To Pictou Co, NS, prob <1830. m Duncan Murray, qv. **DC 20 Jan 1981**.

5427 MACDONALD, Catherine. From Knoydart, INV. d/o Samuel M. and Johanna Hewitt. To Antigonish Co, NS, poss <1830; stld St Andrews. **HCA 212**.

5428 MACDONALD, Catherine. From INV. d/o Alexander 'Dubh' M. To Mabou, Inverness Co, NS,

1831. Wife of Angus 'An Gobha Ban' Campbell, qv. **MP 291**.

5429 McDONALD, Catherine, b ca 1798. From Killin, PER. d/o John M. and Janet Menzies. To Osgoode Twp, Carleton Co, ONT, ca 1831. Wife of John McNab, qv. **DC 1 Aug 1979**.

5430 MACDONALD, Catherine. From INV, prob Arisaig. d/o Donald 'Mor' M. To Antigonish Co, NS, prob <1840. m Angus MacDonald. **HCA 201**.

5431 McDONALD, Catherine, b ca 1801. From Kallin, Is Grimsay, between Benbecula and North Uist. To Cape Breton Is, NS, ca 1842. Wife of Neil Johnson, qv. **LDW 9 Sep 1973; WLC**.

5432 McDONALD, Catherine, ca 1802–26 Apr 1877. From Denny, STI. To Melbourne, Richmond Co, QUE, 1846. m William Morrison, qv. **MGC 16 Jul 1980**.

5433 McDONALD, Catherine. To Pictou, NS, on the *London*, arr 14 Jul 1848. **DC 15 Jul 1979**.

5434 MACDONALD, Catherine, b 1807. From Is Coll, ARL. d/o Charles M. and Mary MacLean. To Pictou Co, NS, 1848. Wife of Hugh Mackinnon, qv, m 2 Jun 1829. **DC 16 Mar 1981**.

5435 MACDONALD, Catherine, b 1816. From Dunganichy, Is Benbecula, INV. d/o Angus M. and Marion MacKiggan. To Pictou, NS, on the *Lulan*, ex Glasgow, 17 Aug 1848. Wife of John MacIntyre, qv. **DC 12 Jul 1979**.

5436 McDONALD, Catherine, b ca 1803. From Breaclete, Bernera Is, Lewis, ROC. d/o Angus M. and Ann McLennan. To QUE, ex Stornoway, arr 4 Aug 1851; stld Huron Twp, Bruce Co, ONT. Wife of Donald McGregor, qv. **WLC**.

5437 McDONALD, Catherine, 1848–1926. From Laggan, INV. d/o Duncan M. and Katherine McDonald. To ONT, <1867; stld Caledon Twp, Peel Co. m Thomas R. Foster, 1845–1922, ch. **DC 17 Nov 1981**.

5438 McDONALD, Charles, b ca 1768. From PER. To Pictou, NS, on the *Commerce*, ex Port Glasgow, 10 Aug 1803. Farmer. Wife Agnes, aged 31, with him, and ch: 1. Eliza, aged 9; 2. Alexander, aged 2; 3. James, aged 9 mo. **PLC**.

5439 McDONALD, Charles. From Is Lewis, ROC. To QUE, ex Stornoway, arr 4 Aug 1851; stld Huron Twp, Bruce Co, ONT, 1852. Head of family. **DC 5 Apr 1967**.

5440 McDONALD, Christian. From Kilmorack, INV. Prob rel to Janet M, spinster, qv. To Pictou, NS, on the *Sarah*, ex Fort William, Jun 1801. Spinster. **PLS**.

5441 McDONALD, Christian, b ca 1770. To Charlottetown, PEI, on the *Spencer*, ex Oban, arr 22 Sep 1806. **PLSN**.

5442 McDONALD, Christiana, b 20 Jul 1818. To Sydney, Cape Breton Co, NS, <1840. m Charles Wittigan Ferdinand Augustus Dumaresque. Son James Charles Philip, b 1840. **HNS iii 453**.

5443 MACDONALD, Christie. From Lochaber, INV. d/o Angus M, qv, and Mary Ann Rankin. To South West Mabou, Inverness Co, NS, 1854. m Alexander, s/o Angus Beaton, Little Judique, ch. **MP 587**.

5444   MACDONALD, Christian. From Knoydart, INV. To QUE, ex Greenock, summer 1815; stld prob Lanark Co, ONT. Wife of Donald McDougall, qv. **SEC 7**.

5445   MACDONALD, Christina. From Lochaber, INV. d/o Angus M, qv, and Margaret MacDonald, qv. To Inverness Co, NS, ca 1822; stld Glencoe. m Duncan MacDonald, qv. **MP 409, 491**.

5446   MACDONALD, Christina, 1797–26 Jan 1873. From Kingussie, INV. sis/o John M, qv. To Southwest Mabou Ridge, Inverness Co, NS, 1831. Wife of John MacPherson, qv. **MP ii 375, 578**.

5447   MACDONALD, Christina, b 8 Apr 1833, Halkirk, CAI. d/o William M, qv, and Christina Mill, qv. To Markham Twp, York Co, ONT. ca 1840. m John Watson. Dau Christina Ogilvie, d unm. **DC 5 Jul 1979**.

5448   McDONALD, Christine. From PER. sis/o Donald M, qv. To QUE on the *Lady of the Lake*, Sep 1816; stld Drummond Twp, Lanark Co, ONT. Wife of Hugh Robertson, qv. **HCL 20**.

5449   McDONALD, Christine, 1830–1917. From Laggan, INV. d/o Duncan M. and Katharine McDonald. To ONT <1852, when m Malcolm McLachlan, qv. **DC 17 Nov 1981**.

5450   McDONALD, Christy, 1805-95. From Is Lewis, ROC. To Gulf Shore, Cumberland Co, NS, 1811. Wife of Donald McIvor, qv. **DC 29 Oct 1980**.

5451   MACDONALD, Christy. Prob from INV. sis/o Ronald 'Saor' M, qv. To Antigonish Co, NS, <1815. m Alexander Beaton, qv, Mabou. **MP 511**.

5452   McDONALD, Christy, ca 1770–27 Jun 1842. From SUT. To Pictou Co, NS. Wife of Robert Sutherland, qv. **DC 10 Feb 1980**.

5453   MACDONALD, Christy. From Lochaber, INV. sis/o Allan 'Dhu' M, qv. To Antigonish Co, NS, prob <1840. m Donald MacNaughton. **HCA 201**.

5454   McDONALD, Christy, b 1817. From Callanish, Is Lewis, ROC. To QUE, ex Stornoway, arr 4 Aug 1851; stld Huron Twp, Bruce Co, ONT. Wife of John McArthur, qv. **WLC**.

5455   MACDONALD, Christy. From Uig par, Is Lewis, ROC. d/o Alexander M, qv, and Mary McIver, qv. To Winslow Twp, Compton Co, QUE, 1851. m John MacLeod, farmer, Spring Hill, ch: 1. Alexander; 2. Daniel; 3. John; 4. Ellie. **TFT 17**.

5456   McDONALD, Colin, b ca 1790. To Western Shore, Inverness Co, NS, 1799. Farmer, m and ch. **CBC 1818**.

5457   MACDONALD, Colin. To Montreal, QUE, 1834. Formerly sergeant, 79th Regt, and became town major. **SGC 499**.

5458   McDONALD, Colin or Coll. Officer in 82nd Regt, and gr 500 acres at Merigomish, Pictou Co, NS, 1784. **HPC App F**.

5459   McDONALD, Colin. To Pictou, NS, on the *Lady Gray*, ex Cromarty, ROC, arr 16 Jul 1841. **DC 15 Jul 1979**.

5460   MACDONALD, Daniel. Prob from INV. bro/o John M, qv. To Antigonish Co, NS, prob <1840. m Janet, d/o Samuel MacDonald, miller, South River, ch: 1. Annie;

2. Catherine; 3. Allan; 4. Angus; 5. John; 6. Alexander; 7. Hugh; 8. Samuel; 9. Daniel; 10. Peter; 11. Sarah; 12. Mary. **HCA 232**.

5461   MACDONALD, Daniel, 18 Sep 1813–1 Mar 1883. From Halkirk, CAI. s/o William M, qv, and Christina Mill, qv. To Markham, York Co, ONT, 1836. Contractor. m Elizabeth MacDonald, qv, ch: 1. William, went to AUS; 2. Robert, res Toronto; 3. James, res Toronto; 4. Christina Elizabeth, d 1920; 5. Daniel. **DC 5 Jul 1979**.

5462   MACDONALD, Daniel, 1810–1903. From Dingwall, ROC. To Pugwash, Cumberland Co, NS, <1840. Physician. m Helen B. Lorraine, 1815-61. **DC 29 Oct 1980**.

5463   McDONALD, Donald. From INV. To Pictou, NS, on the *Hector*, ex Loch Broom, arr 17 Sep 1773; stld east side of Middle River, where gr 350 acres, 1783. ch incl: 1. Marion, qv; 2. Nancy, d 1774. **HPC App A and C**.

5464   MACDONALD, Donald 'Ban'. From Moidart, INV. s/o James 'Baillie' M. To Antigonish Co, NS, ca 1784; stld Arisaig, and went later to Judique, Inverness Co. ch incl: 1. James; 2. Allan; 3. Donald. **DC 30 Mar 1981**.

5465   MACDONALD, Donald. Prob from INV. s/o Donald M. To Pictou Co, NS, <1789. m Ann MacDougall, qv, ch: 1. Hugh; 2. John, 1789–1872; 3. Donald; 4. Angus, blacksmith; 5. Alexander; 6. Mary; 7. Sarah; 8. Ann; 9. Catherine. **HCA 230**.

5466   McDONALD, Donald, ca 1745–6 Apr 1850. Served in the 42nd Regt and was gr land at Nashwaak, York Co, NB, <1790. **DC 2 Jun 1978**.

5467   McDONALD, Donald. From Aberchalder, INV. To PEI on the *Jane*, ex Loch nan Uamh, Arisaig, 12 Jul 1790. Family with him. **PLJ**.

5468   McDONALD, Donald. From Is Eigg, INV. To PEI on the *Jane*, ex Loch nan Uamh, Arisaig, 12 Jul 1790. Wife and 4 ch with him. **PLJ**.

5469   McDONALD, Donald. From INV. To PEI on the *Jane*, ex Loch nan Uamh, Arisaig, 12 Jul 1790. Tenant. Wife with him. **PLJ**.

5470   McDONALD, Donald. From Drimlaogh, ni, INV. To PEI on the *Jane*, ex Loch nan Uamh, Arisaig, 12 Jul 1790. Tailor. Wife and a large family with him. **PLJ**.

5471   McDONALD, Donald. From Fiorlindach, ni, poss Moidart dist, INV. To PEI on the *Jane*, ex Loch nan Uamh, Arisaig, 12 Jul 1790. Tenant. **PLJ**.

5472   McDONALD, Donald. From Moidart, INV. To PEI on the *Lucy*, ex Loch nan Uamh, Arisaig, 12 Jul 1790. Family with him. **PLL**.

5473   McDONALD, Donald. From Arienskill, ni, INV. To PEI on the *Lucy*, ex Loch nan Uamh, Arisaig, 12 Jul 1790. Tenant. Family with him. **PLL**.

5474   McDONALD, Donald. From Is Shona, Moidart, INV. To PEI on the *Lucy*, ex Loch nan Uamh, Arisaig, 12 Jul 1790. Family with him. **PLL**.

5475   McDONALD, Donald. From Cleadale, Is Eigg, INV. To QUE on the *British Queen*, ex Arisaig, 16 Aug 1790; stld nr Montreal. Tenant. Wife and ch with him. **QCC 103**.

5476 McDONALD, Donald. From Lagganachdron, Glengarry, INV. To QUE on the *British Queen*, ex Arisaig, 16 Aug 1790; stld nr Montreal. Tenant. Wife and ch with him. **QCC 103**.

5477 McDONALD, Donald. From Cleadale, Is Eigg, INV. To QUE on the *British Queen*, ex Arisaig, 16 Aug 1790; stld nr Montreal. Tenant. **QCC 103**.

5478 MACDONALD, Donald 'Down'. From Glenelg, INV. To QUE, 1796; stld Lot 35, Con 6, Lochiel Twp, Glengarry Co, ONT. **MG 211**.

5479 McDONALD, Donald, b ca 1792. To Western Shore, Inverness Co, NS, 1799. Farmer. **CBC 1818**.

5480 McDONALD, Donald, ca 1760–ca 1840. From Moidart, INV. To Maryville, Antigonish Co, NS, <1800. Farmer. Son Allan. **HNS iii 675**.

5481 MACDONALD, Donald. From Knoydart, INV. s/o Samuel M. and Johanna Hewitt. To Pictou, NS, on the *Nora*, ex Fort William, 1801; stld Marydale, Antigonish Co. **HCA 212**.

5482 MACDONALD, Donald. From Kilmorack, INV. To Pictou, NS, on the *Dove*, ex Fort William, Jun 1801. Labourer. Prob stld in Antigonish Co. **PLD**.

5483 McDONALD, Donald. From Urquhart and Glenmoriston par, INV. To Pictou, NS, on the *Sarah*, ex Fort William, Jun 1801. Labourer. **PLS**.

5484 McDONALD, Donald. From Kilmorack, INV. To Pictou, NS, on the *Sarah*, ex Fort William, Jun 1801. Labourer. **PLS**.

5485 McDONALD, Donald. From Alness, ROC. To Pictou, NS, on the *Sarah*, ex Fort William, Jun 1801. Labourer. **PLS**.

5486 McDONALD, Donald. From Inchlaggan, Glengarry, INV. To Montreal, QUE, ex Fort William, 3 Jul 1802; stld E ONT. Wife and 2 ch with him. **MCM 1/4 26**.

5487 McDONALD, Donald, b ca 1801. To Western Shore, Inverness Co, NS, 1803, prob with relatives. Became farmer. **CBC 1818**.

5488 McDONALD, Donald, d 1813. To St Andrews, Charlotte Co, NB, <1803. Lawyer in Fredericton, and Crown land surveyor. Assisted members of the disbanded Reay Fencible Regt to settle at Scotch Ridge, Charlotte Co. **DC 29 Nov 1982**.

5489 McDONALD, Donald. From Assynt or Edrachillis, SUT. To Boston, MA, on the *Fortitude*, arr 16 Aug 1803, but stld at Scotch Ridge, Charlotte Co, NB, 1804. Family with him. Had served in the Reay Fencible Regt. **DC 29 Nov 1982**.

5490 McDONALD, Donald, b ca 1768. To Inverness Co, NS, 1804; stld nr Port Hood. Farmer, m and ch. **CBC 1818**.

5491 MACDONALD, Donald. From Is Eigg, INV. To Antigonish Co, NS, <1804. Discharged soldier, tailor and farmer. m (i) Isabella MacDonald, ch: 1. Duncan; 2. George; 3. John; 4. Mary; 5. Alexander; 6. Ann; 7. Kate, d on the voyage. m (ii) Annie MacDonald, no ch. **HCA 246**.

5492 McDONALD, Donald, 1759–1804. Prob from Laggan, INV. To QUE on the *Oughton*, arr Jul 1804; stld Baldoon, Dover Twp, Kent Co, ONT. Farmer. Wife Catherine, d 1767, with him, and ch: 1. Christy, b 1789; 2. Sarah, b 1791; 3. Angus, 1793–1856; 4. Mary, b 1795; 5. Catherine, 1797–1804; 6. Flora, b 1799; 7. Peggy, 1800-94. **UCM 267, 302; DC 4 Oct 1979**.

5493 McDONALD, Donald, 1759–1840. From Is Tyree, ARL. To QUE on the *Oughton*, arr Jul 1804; stld Baldoon, Dover Twp, Kent Co, ONT. Tailor. Wife Flora McDonald, qv, with him. ch: 1. John, qv; 2. Duncan, 1801-74; 3. Hugh, b 1803; 4. Mary; 5. Alexander; 6. Daniel; 7-8. Allan and Hector, twins; 9. Nancy, d 1875. **UCM 268, 302; DC 4 Oct 1979**.

5494 MACDONALD, Donald, b 1787. From Glengarry, INV. s/o Angus M, qv. To Arisaig, Antigonish Co, NS, <1805. m Catherine, d/o Angus 'Og' MacInnes, qv, ch: 1. Alexander; 2. Elizabeth. **HCA 231**.

5495 MACDONALD, Donald. From Brae-Lochaber, INV. s/o Donald 'Ban Onorach' M, qv, and Isabel Beaton, qv. To Mabou, Inverness Co, NS, 1805. m Sarah, d/o Alexander Beaton, ch: 1. Margaret; 2. Donald; 3. Angus; 4. John; 5. Alexander; 6. Archibald; 7. Sara; 8. Finlay; 9. Dougald; 10. Mary. **MP 568**.

5496 MACDONALD, Donald 'Ban Onorach'. From Bohuntin, INV. Desc from Donald M. of the *Sliochd an Taighe*. To Inverness Co, NS, 1805; stld South West River. Farmer. m Isabel Beaton, qv, ch: 1. Alexander, qv; 2. Donald, qv; 3. John, qv; 4. Finlay, qv; 5. Mary. **MP 562**.

5497 McDONALD, Donald, b ca 1782. To Charlottetown, PEI, on the *Humphreys*, ex Tobermory, arr 14 Jul 1806. **PLH**.

5498 McDONALD, Donald, 1770–1825. From Lochaber, INV. s/o Angus M. To Mabou Coal Mines, Inverness Co, NS, ca 1807. m Margaret J. MacDonald, qv, ch: 1. Angus, qv; 2. Ronald; 3. Flora; 4. Alexander; 5. Archibald; 6. Betty; 7. John; 8. Margaret; 9. Grace. **MP 457**.

5499 McDONALD, Donald, b ca 1776. From Is Mull, ARL. To Charlottetown, PEI, on the *Clarendon*, ex Oban, 6 Aug 1808. Wife Ann, aged 25, with him, and ch: 1. Catherine, aged 3; 2. Malcolm, aged 1. Mother Janet also with him, aged 57. Labourer. **CPL**.

5500 McDONALD, Donald, b ca 1781. From Foss, PER. To Charlottetown, PEI, on the *Clarendon*, ex Oban, 6 Aug 1808. Wife Margaret, aged 22, with him, and dau Elizabeth, aged 1. Labourer. **CPL**.

5501 MACDONALD, Donald. From Is Canna, INV. s/o Roderick M, qv. To Little Mabou, Inverness Co, NS, prob <1810. m Mary MacNeil, Judique, ch: 1. Donald; 2. Alexander; 3. Roderick; 4. Sara; 5. Christina; 6. Mary. **CBC 1818; MP 604**.

5502 MACDONALD, Donald 'Breac'. From Lochaber, INV. bro/o Allan 'Dhu' M, qv. To Antigonish Co, NS, prob <1810. m Miss MacDonald. **HCA 201**.

5503 MACDONALD, Donald. From Badenoch, INV. s/o Donald M. To Lower River Inhabitants, Richmond Co, NS, <1815. Farmer. m Catherine, d/o Alexander Beaton and Anne MacInnes, ch: 1. John; 2. Mary; 3. Donald; 4. Alexander. **MP ii 302, 304**.

5504 McDONALD, Donald, b ca 1770. From Glasgow. To QUE, ex Greenock, summer 1815; stld prob Lanark Co, ONT. Wife Mary McMillan, qv, with him, and s Donald, b 1798. **SEC 6**.

5505 McDONALD, Donald, b ca 1784. From Killin, PER. To QUE on the *Dorothy*, ex Greenock, 12 Jul 1815; stld North Elmsley Twp, Lanark Co, ONT. House carpenter, and became farmer. Wife Ann Campbell, qv, with him, and 2 ch. **SEC 4; HCL 232**.

5506 MACDONALD, Donald. From Moidart, INV. s/o Hugh M. To Antigonish Co, NS, prob <1815; stld Browns Mountain. **HCA 172**.

5507 MACDONALD, Donald. From Arisaig, INV. s/o Donald M. To Cape George, Antigonish Co, NS, prob <1815; moved to Highfield, later to Double Hill, Arisaig. **HCA 247**.

5508 MACDONALD, Donald 'Ban'. From INV. To Arisaig, Antigonish Co, NS, prob <1815. ch: 1. Michael; 2. John; 3. Duncan; 4. Archibald; 5. Catherine; 6. Janet; 7. Mary. **HCA 239**.

5509 MACDONALD, Donald, b 1796. From Lochaber, INV. s/o Alexander 'Ruadh' M, qv, and Mary Campbell, qv. To Mabou Ridge, Inverness Co, NS, 1816. m Sara, s/o Donald 'Ban' MacDonald, ch: 1-2. Alexander and Donald, twins; 3. Angus; 4. James; 5. Archibald; 6. John; 7. Allan; 8. Ranald; 9. Archibald; 10. Mary; 11. Catherine; 12. Anne; 13. Sara; 14. Janet. **MP 538**.

5510 McDONALD, Donald, b ca 1790. To Inverness Co, NS, 1816. Farmer. **CBC 1818**.

5511 McDONALD, Donald, ca 1793–16 Jun 1841. From Is Skye, INV. To Martintown, Glengarry Co, ONT, <1816. m Margaret Christie, qv. **SMB**.

5512 McDONALD, Donald. From PER. bro/o Christine M, qv. To Drummond Twp, Lanark Co, ONT, 1816. Farmer. m sis/o Hugh Robertson. Dau Isobel, qv. **HCL 20**.

5513 MACDONALD, Donald 'Diolladair'. From Lochaber, INV. s/o Archibald M. and Anne MacDonald, qv. To Arisaig, Antigonish Co, NS, 1816; moved to Inverness Co, 1818. m Sara, d/o Murdock MacPherson, qv, ch: 1. Archibald; 2. Murdock; 3. Alexander; 4. Angus; 5. John; 6. Elizabeth; 7. Anne; 8. Flora. **MP 545**.

5514 McDONALD, Donald, 1793–4 Jul 1893. From SUT. To Pictou Co, NS, prob <1820; stld nr Lansdowne. Veteran of Waterloo. m Catherine Ross, qv. **DC 10 Feb 1980**.

5515 McDONALD, Donald, b 1780. To St Andrews dist, Cape Breton Co, NS, 1818. Farmer, m and ch. **CBC 1818**.

5516 McDONALD, Donald, b 1786. To St Andrews dist, Cape Breton Co, NS, 1818. Farmer, m and ch. **CBC 1818**.

5517 McDONALD, Donald, ca 1785–27 Jan 1857. From CAI. To NS, 1818; stld nr Earlton, Colchester Co. m Esther Sinclair, qv, ch: 1. James, went to NY; 2. Donald, 1815-87; 3. Mary, d 1885; 4. Johanna. **DC 18 Mar 1981**.

5518 McDONALD, Donald. From Is Tyree, ARL. s/o John M. To Glengarry Co, ONT, <1820. **DC 23 Feb 1980**.

5519 MACDONALD, Donald 'Ban'. From Badenoch, INV. To Inverness Co, NS, <1820; stld Little Mabou. m Elizabeth MacDonald, qv, ch: 1. Archibald; 2. Alexander; 3. Allan; 4. Angus; 5. Donald; 6. Alexina; 7. Anne. **MP 412**.

5520 MACDONALD, Donald. From Is Barra, INV. s/o Iain 'Og' M. To Mabou Harbour, Inverness Co, NS, prob <1820. **MP 422**.

5521 MACDONALD, Donald 'Ban'. Prob from INV. To Antigonish Co, NS, poss <1820. Son Thomas. **HCA 227**.

5522 MACDONALD, Donald 'Mingary'. From Arisaig, INV, and Ardnamurchan, ARL. bro/o Angus 'Ban' M, qv. To Antigonish Co, NS, prob <1820. Formerly Keeper of Mingary Castle. m Marcella MacInnes. **HCA 235**.

5523 MACDONALD, Donald. From Moidart, INV. To Antigonish Co, NS, prob <1820. m Mary Gillis, ch: 1. Mary; 2. Alexander; 3. Mary. m (ii) Mary MacGillivray, further to: 4. John; 5. Christina; 6. Ann; 7. Sarah; 8. Catherine; 9. Isabella; 10. Mary. **HCA 173**.

5524 MACDONALD, Donald. From Lochaber, INV. s/o Alexander 'Mor' M, qv, and Isabel MacDonald. To NS, 1824. Sometime at Miramichi, Northumberland Co, NB. m Catherine MacDonald, Mabou, ch: 1. Alexander; 2. Angus; 3. John; 4. Major Daniel, surgeon; 5. Isabel; 6. Anne; 7. Flora; 8. Catherine; 9. Mary. **HCA 193**.

5525 McDONALD, Rev Donald, 1 Jan 1783–21 Feb 1867. From Drumcastle, Rannoch, PER. s/o Donald M. alias McKay, and Christian Stewart. Educ St Andrews Univ, 1807-08, and was a missionary in Glengarry, INV, before going to Bras d'Or Lake, Cape Breton Is, NS, in 1824. Went to PEI, 1827, and preached all over the province for 40 years. Estab 13 churches. **SAM 52; FES vii 620; MDB 437**.

5526 MACDONALD, Donald, ca 1783–1867. From Blair Atholl, PER. s/o William M, tenant in Ballintuim Foss, and Isabella Stewart. To PEI and stld New Perth. Farmer. **Ts Blair Atholl**.

5527 MACDONALD, Donald 'Mor', d 29 Mar 1877. From Lochaber, INV. s/o Alexander 'Mor' M, qv, and Isabel Campbell. To Miramichi, Northumberland Co, NB, 1824. Moved in 1832 to Mull River, Inverness Co, NS. Farmer. m Catherine, d/o John 'Mor' MacDonald, qv, Black River, ch: 1. Alexander; 2. Angus; 3. John; 4. Daniel; 5. Isabel; 6. Mary; 7. Margaret; 8. Flora; 9. Catherine; 10. Annie; 11. Mary, jr. **MP 494**.

5528 MACDONALD, Donald, b 1803. From North Uist, INV. To Whycocomagh, Inverness Co, NS, 1827. m Ann Morrison, qv, ch: 1. Peter, merchant; 2. James, merchant; 3. Ronald J. **DC 23 Feb 1980**.

5529 MACDONALD, Donald, b 1823. From Is Skye, INV. s/o John M, qv, and Janet MacLeod, qv. To Cape Breton Is, NS, 1827, and d Margaree, Inverness Co. m Catherine, d/o Daniel Carmichael, qv, ch. **DC 23 Feb 1980**.

5530 MACDONALD, Donald. From South Uist, INV. To St John, NB, 1826, but stld River Denny, Cape Breton Is, NS. Farmer. First wife d 1828. m (ii) Annie Battin,

Mabou. ch: 1. Eugene; 2. Allan, qv; 3. Peter; 4. Christy; 5. Sarah; 6. Lucy; 7. Euphemia. **HNS iii 634**.

5531 MACDONALD, Donald. From Is Skye, INV. To PEI on the *Mary Kennedy*, arr Jun 1829; stld Vernon River. Farmer and mem of the Baptist Ch. m Margaret Gordon, qv. Son Donald, 1843–1931. **HP 37**.

5532 McDONALD, Donald. From Knapdale, ARL. To Lobo Twp, Middlesex Co, ONT, 1830. ch: 1. Donald; 2. Archibald; 3. Angus; 4. Angus 'Og'; 5. Flora; 6. Isabella. **PCM 39**.

5533 MACDONALD, Donald. Prob from INV. bro/o Ronald M, qv, Hector M, qv, and John M, qv. To Mount Young, Mabou, Inverness Co, NS, <1830. m Miss MacDonald, West Lake Ainslie, s Donald or Daniel. **MP 504**.

5534 MACDONALD, Donald 'Straight'. From Moidart, INV. s/o Hugh M. To Antigonish Harbour, NS, <1830. m Sarah MacDonald, ch: 1. Rev Hugh, d 1865; 2. John; 3. Joseph. **HCA 259**.

5535 McDONALD, Donald, b 1799. Prob from INV. To Glengarry Co, ONT, <1830; later to Eldon Twp, Victoria Co. Shoemaker. m Mary 'Ban' McRae, ch: 1. Angus, b 1830; 2. Janet, b 1832; 3. Finlay, b 1834; 5. Mary Ann, b 1837; 5. Flora, b 1839; 6. John A, b 1843; 7. Colin, b 1845. **EC 91**.

5536 MACDONALD, Donald. Prob from INV. bro/o Allan M, qv. To Lennox, Antigonish Co, NS, prob <1830. ch: 1. John; 2. Allan; 3. Lachlan; 4. Ann; 5. Donald; 6. Ronald. **HCA 250**.

5537 MACDONALD, Donald. From Moidart, INV. s/o Hugh M. To Cape Breton Is, NS, prob <1830. m Sara MacAdam, ch: 1. Anne; 2. Christina; 3. Kate; 4. Joseph, res Williams Point; 5. John; 6. Angus; 7. Rev Hugh. **MP 448**.

5538 MACDONALD, Donald. From INV. s/o Allan M. To West South River, Antigonish Co, NS, prob <1830. m Margaret, d/o Donald 'Ban' Gillies, qv, and — MacGillivray, ch: 1. John, qv; 2. Donald; 3. Alexander; 4. Hugh; 5. Mary; 6. Margaret; 7. Catherine; 8. Liza; 9. Ann. **HCA 210**.

5539 MACDONALD, Donald. From Borrodale, INV. To South River, Antigonish Co, NS, prob <1830. m Elizabeth, d/o Allan MacDonald, ch: 1. Mary; 2. Margaret; 3. Angus; 4. Donald, teacher. **HCA 216**.

5540 MACDONALD, Donald. Prob from INV. s/o Rory M. To Gusset, Antigonish Co, NS, poss <1830. ch: 1. Michael; 2. Hugh; 3. John; 4. Duncan; 5. Rory; 6. Flora; 7. Sara; 8. Catherine; 9. Margaret; 10. Mary. **HCA 254**.

5541 McDONALD, Donald. From Is Skye, INV. s/o Malcolm M, qv. To Charlottetown, PEI, 1831. m Miss McMillan, ch: 1. Margaret, d inf; 2. Margaret; 3. Donald; 4. Malcolm; 5. Norman; 6. Janet; 7. Mary. **DC 11 Sep 1960**.

5542 McDONALD, Donald, b ca 1805. Poss from Ardnish, Arisaig, INV. bro/o Allan M, qv, and Angus M, qv. To PEI prob <1836, and moved later to East Bay, Cape Breton Co, NS. m Theresa, d/o Donald Gillis, and Mary MacDonald, ch: 1. Ronald, b 1836, sometime Collector of Customs at Sydney; 2. Ann, b 1839;

3. Catherine, b 1842; 4. Michael, b 1844; 5. Lachlan, b 1845; 6. Daniel, b 1852; 7. Agnes, b 1856; 8. Mary. **NSN 27/194; DC 3 Apr 1979**.

5543 McDONALD, Donald, 1810-74. From Inverness. To East Williams Twp, Middlesex Co, ONT, ca 1837. m Christine Cowie, qv, ch. **DC 10 Nov 1981**.

5544 McDONALD, Donald or Daniel, ca 1818–7 Jun 1882. From Edinburgh. To QUE on the *Malabar*, 15 May 1838. Soldier, 71st Regt. Served at St Jean, QUE, and at York, ONT, where he d. m Mary Shean, ch: 1. Caroline, b 1841; 2. Daniel, b Chambly, QUE, 1844; 3. Mary Ann, b 1849; 4. Susan, b 1851. **DC 9 Aug 1979**.

5545 McDONALD, Donald. Prob from Duthil, INV. To London Twp, Middlesex Co, ONT, 1840; moved to West Williams Twp, 1850, later to Port Huron, MI. **PCM 47**.

5546 MACDONALD, Donald. From Arisaig, INV. To Sydney, Cape Breton Co, NS, <1840. Dau Catherine. **HNS iii 637**.

5547 MACDONALD, Donald. From Arisaig, INV. s/o Alexander MacEachen M. and Catriona Gillies. To Port Hood, Inverness Co, NS, <1840. m (i) Miss Gillis, ch: 1. Alexander; 2. Mary. m (ii) Mary MacGillivray, further ch: 3. Hugh; 4. John; 5. Christina; 6. Sara; 7. Catherine; 8. Isabel; 9. Mary; 10. Anne. **MP 374**.

5548 MACDONALD, Donald, b ca 1850. From Badenoch, INV. s/o Allan M. and Mary MacDonald. To Glenville, Inverness Co, NS, <1840. m (i) Jessie MacDonald, qv, ch: 1. Allan, qv; 2. Sara, d unm; 3. Ranald, unm. m (ii) Miss Wilmot, no ch. m (iii) Mary, d/o Alexander McEachen, further ch: 4. John; 5. Alexander; 6. Alexander Og; 7. Mary. **MP 400, 440**.

5549 MACDONALD, Donald. From Glen Roy, Kilmonivaig par, INV. s/o Alexander M. To Antigonish Co, NS, prob <1840. m Mary MacDonald, ch: 1. Angus; 2. Donald; 3. John; 4. Andrew; 5. James; 6. Duncan; 7. Sarah; 8. Mary; 9. Kate; 10. Ann; 11. Janet. **HCA 207**.

5550 MACDONALD, Donald 'Og'. From Glen Roy, Kilmonivaig par, INV. To Antigonish Co, NS, prob <1840. m Catherine MacDonald, ch: 1. John; 2. Donald 'Ban'; 3. Mary. **HCA 207**.

5551 McDONALD, Donald. To London, Westminster Twp, Middlesex Co, ONT, <1840. **PCM 55**.

5552 MACDONALD, Donald, b ca 1788. From Halkirk, CAI. s/o Benjamen M. and Barbara Gunn. To Markham Twp, York Co, ONT, ca 1840. ch: 1. John; 2. Daniel, res Winnipeg; 3. Benjamen, res Chinguacousy Twp, York Co; 4. Elizabeth; 5. Williamina. **DC 5 Jul 1979**.

5553 MACDONALD, Donald. Poss from Is Benbecula, INV. To Pictou, NS, on the *Lulan*, ex Glasgow, 17 Aug 1848. **DC 12 Jul 1979**.

5554 McDONALD, Donald. From Is North Uist, INV. To West Williams Twp, Middlesex Co, ONT, ca 1848; stld Con 10. ch: 1. Murdock, farmer; 2. Rev Alexander, Chicago; 3. Maggie, teacher in Chicago. **PCM 48**.

5555 McDONALD, Donald. From Is South Uist, INV. To West Williams Twp, Middlesex Co, ONT, 1849; stld Con 12. **PCM 48**.

5556 McDONALD, Donald. From Is South Uist, INV. To West Williams Twp, Middlesex Co, ONT, 1849; stld Con 14. **PCM 48**.

5557 MACDONALD, Donald. From INV. To Whycocomagh, Inverness Co, NS, <1849. Wife Annie with him. Son James, 1849–1916, MLA. **MLA 205**.

5558 MACDONALD, Donald, b 1806. From Uachdar, Is Benbecula, INV. s/o Donald M, qv, and Mary MacLeod, qv. To Pictou, NS, on the *Lulan*, ex Glasgow, 17 Aug 1848. m Catherine MacMillan, qv, ch: 1. Mary, b 1832; 2. Donald, b 1834; 3. Angus, b 1837; 4. Margaret, b 1839; 5. Ann, b 1842; 6. Neil, b 1844; 7. Donald; 8. Christina. **DC 12 Jul 1979**.

5559 MACDONALD, Donald, b ca 1776. From Uachdar, Is Benbecula, INV. s/o Ranald M. To Pictou, NS, on the *Lulan*, ex Glasgow, 17 Aug 1848. Wife Mary MacLeod, qv, with him, and ch: 1. Donald, qv; 2. Peggy, b 1826. **DC 12 Jul 1979**.

5560 MACDONALD, Donald. From Is Skye, INV. To PEI <1850; stld Queens Co. m Margaret Alice Munro, qv, ch: 1. John, b 1858, Witten, SD; 2. Alexander, b 1863, ALB; 3. Peter Nicholson, b 1866, NE; 4. Katherine, b 1868, Seattle, WA; 5. Isabella Morrison, 1870–1915, res Creighton, NE; 6. George Robert Grey, b 1872, Billings, MT. **SPI 118**.

5561 MACDONALD, Donald, ca 1829–11 Jun 1892. From Is Skye, INV. s/o Angus and Ann M. To PEI <1850. m Catherine MacLeod, qv, and had, with other ch, s Murdock. **DC 9 Oct 1980**.

5562 MACDONALD, Donald, 1816–1901. From Eneclate, Uig, Is Lewis, INV. To Winslow Twp, Compton Co, QUE, 1851. m (i) Christy MacArthur Campbell, qv, ch: 1. Norman Donald, qv; 2. Christy, 1842-55; 3. John, qv; 4. Annie, qv; 5. Murdoch D, b 1855, stld Seattle, WA. **TFT 13**.

5563 McDONALD, Donald. From Barvas, Is Lewis, ROC. To QUE, ex Stornoway, arr 4 Aug 1851; stld 1852, Huron Twp, Bruce Co, ONT. Head of family. **DC 5 Apr 1967**.

5564 McDONALD, Donald, 1796–15 Mar 1861. From Barvas, Is Lewis, ROC. To QUE, ex Stornoway, arr 4 Aug 1851; stld Huron Twp, Bruce Co, ONT. Farmer, Con 6. Wife Mary, 1812-77, with him. ch: 1. Effie; 2. Amelia; 3. Mary; 4. Margaret; 5. Kate; 6. Annie; 7. Allan. **DC 5 Apr 1967 and 22 Jul 1982**.

5565 McDONALD, Donald, ca 1812–22 Oct 1881. From Barvas, Is Lewis, ROC. To QUE, ex Stornoway, arr 4 Aug 1851; stld Lot 26, Con 8, Huron Twp, Bruce Co, ONT. Farmer. m Katherine McDonald, qv, ch: 1. Annie; 2. Margaret; 3. John, dentist; 4. Effie; 5. Katherine; 6. Angus; 7. Murdoch; 8. Donald; 9. Mary. **DC 25 Dec 1981**.

5566 McDONALD, Donald 'Sly'. From Barvas, Is Lewis, ROC. To QUE, ex Stornoway, arr 4 Aug 1851; stld Huron Twp, Bruce Co, ONT, 1852. Head of family. **DC 5 Apr 1967**.

5567 McDONALD, Donald 'Yarrie', 1812-81. From Garry of Shader, Is Lewis, ROC. s/o John M. and Margaret McLean. To QUE, ex Stornoway, arr 4 Aug 1851; stld Huron Twp, Bruce Co, ONT, 1852. Farmer. m Catherine McDonald, ch: 1. Ann; 2. Margaret;

3. John; 4. Effie; 5. Catherine; 6. Angus; 7. Murdo; 8. Donald; 9. Mary. **WLC**.

5568 McDONALD, Donald, 1754–1858. From Glengarry, INV. To Pictou, NS, and stld Nine Mile River, Hants Co. Bur Old Catholic Cemetery there. **DC 20 Jan 1981**.

5569 MACDONALD, Rev Donald, 1830–28 Oct 1878. From North Uist, INV. s/o Donald M. Educ Univ of Edinburgh and at Queens Coll, Kingston, ONT. Min of Lochiel, Glengarry Co, ONT, 1856-59. Retr to SCT, 1859, but came again to CAN. m Harriet Ann Macpherson, d 1910, ch: 1. Lowther; 2. Donald; 3. William. **FES vii 176, 640**.

5570 McDONALD, Dougald, b ca 1758. From Moidart, INV. To Western Shore, Inverness Co, NS, 1802. Farmer and widower. **CBC 1818**.

5571 MACDONALD, Dougald. From Moidart, INV. bro/o Hector M, qv, and John M, qv. To Antigonish Co, NS, ca 1802. **HCA 173**.

5572 MACDONALD, Dougald 'Mor'. From Moidart, INV. s/o Hugh M. To Antigonish Co, NS, <1830. m Peggy MacDonald, ch: 1. Donald; 2. Alexander; 3. Rory; 4. Michael; 5. Ronald; 6. John; 7. Angus; 8. Catherine; 9. Margaret. **HCA 259; MP 448**.

5573 McDONALD, Dougall, b 1790. To St Andrews dist, Cape Breton Co, NS, 1818. Farmer, m and ch. **CBC 1818**.

5574 McDONALD, Duncan. Prob from INV. Served in the 84th Regt, and after discharge, 1784, was gr 100 acres on the west side of the east branch of East River, Pictou Co, NS. **HPC App G**.

5575 McDONALD, Duncan, b ca 1731. To Western Shore, Inverness Co, NS, 1799. Farmer, m <1818. **CBC 1818**.

5576 McDONALD, Duncan. From Urquhart, INV. To Pictou, NS, on the *Sarah*, ex Fort William, Jun 1801. Labourer. **PLS**.

5577 McDONALD, Duncan. From Kilmorack, INV. To Pictou, NS, on the *Sarah*, ex Fort William, Jun 1801. Farmer. Wife Janet with him. **PLS**.

5578 McDONALD, Duncan. From Urquhart, INV. To Pictou, NS, on the *Sarah*, ex Fort William, Jun 1801. Farmer. Wife Isobel with him, and ch: 1. Mary, aged 5; 2. John, aged 2. **PLS**.

5579 McDONALD, Duncan, b ca 1759. From Knoydart, INV. To QUE, ex Greenock, summer 1815; stld prob Lanark Co, ONT. Farmer. Wife Mary McLauchlan, qv, with him, and 5 ch. **SEC 7**.

5580 McDONALD, Duncan, ca 1806–28 Jul 1887. Poss from INV. Bur Old Elgin, Pictou Co, NS. m Jessie McKay. **DC 20 Nov 1976**.

5581 MACDONALD, Duncan. From Badenoch, INV. s/o Allan M. and Mary MacDonald. To Mabou, Inverness Co, NS, <1840. m Christina MacDonald, and had with other ch: 1. Allan; 2. Mary. **MP 409**.

5582 McDONALD, Duncan. To Pictou, NS, on the *Lady Gray*, ex Cromarty, ROC, arr 16 Jul 1841. **DC 15 Jul 1979**.

5583 McDONALD, Duncan, b ca 1807. From Alford,

ABD. s/o John M. To Saltfleet Twp, Wentworth Co, ONT, 1850. Gamekeeper. m Elizabeth Forbes, (see ADDENDA) ch: 1. Robert, b 1840; 2. John, 1842-49; 3. Elizabeth, 1844-45; 4. David, b 1846; 5. Arthur, b ca 1853. **DC 15 Feb 1983**.

5584 MACDONALD, Duncan, 1815-88. From Lairg, SUT. To North Shore, Cumberland Co, NS, prob <1850. Wife Jane, 1823-93.   **DC 29 Oct 1980**.

5585 MACDONALD, Effie, b ca 1740. From Glencoe, INV. To Pictou Co, NS, ca 1784; later to Inverness Co. Wife of John MacDonald, qv.   **DC 30 Mar 1981**.

5586 MACDONALD, Effie. From Glasphein, Staffin, Is Skye, INV. To Orwell Bay, PEI, on the *Polly*, ex Portree, arr 7 Aug 1803. Wife of Malcolm MacLeod, qv. **SPI 136**.

5587 MACDONALD, Effie, b ca 1785. From Dunganichy, Is Benbecula, INV. wid/o Angus MacAulay. To Pictou, NS, on the *Lulan*, ex Glasgow, 17 Aug 1848.   **DC 12 Jul 1979**.

5588 McDONALD, Elinor, called Nelly. From Stour, SUT. To QUE on the *MacDonald*, arr 5 Sep 1785; stld Williamstown, Glengarry Co, ONT. Wife of Angus 'Ban' McDonald, qv.   **DC 15 Feb 1968 and 27 Feb 1972**.

5589 McDONALD, Elizabeth. From Is Tyree, ARL. d/o John M. To Lake Ainslie, Inverness Co, NS, 1820. m Neil MacCallum, qv.   **DC 23 Feb 1980**.

5590 MACDONALD, Elizabeth, 1786–25 Nov 1840. From Brora, SUT. To Pictou Co, NS, prob 1831. Wife of Angus Murray, qv.   **DC 27 Oct 1979**.

5591 MACDONALD, Elizabeth, d 22 Oct 1900. From Edinburgh. To Markham, York Co, ONT, <1840. m Daniel MacDonald, qv.   **DC 5 Jul 1979**.

5592 MACDONALD, Elizabeth. From Badenoch, INV. To Inverness Co, NS, <1820; stld Little Mabou. Wife of Donald 'Ban' MacDonald.   **MP 412**.

5593 MACDONALD, Elizabeth. From Badenoch, INV. To Glencoe, Inverness Co, NS, 1820. Wife of John MacDonald, qv.   **MP ii 375**.

5594 McDONALD, Elizabeth, b ca 1800. From ABD. To Guelph Twp, Wellington Co, ONT, 1839. Wife of William Beattie, qv.   **SG xxiv/2 53**.

5595 McDONALD, Elizabeth, called Betsy. From Laggan, INV. d/o Duncan M. and Katharine McDonald. To ONT, prob <1858. m William Smith, teacher, Erin Twp, Wellington Co.   **DC 17 Nov 1981**.

5596 McDONALD, Ellen. From PER. To Halifax, NS, 1833; stld Lochaber, Antigonish Co. Wife of Donald Stewart, qv.   **HNS iii 681**.

5597 MACDONALD, Eoin. From Is Barra, INV. s/o Iain 'Og' M. To Mabou Harbour, Inverness Co, NS, prob <1820. m Euphemia, d/o John MacEachen, qv, and Sarah MacLellan, ch: 1. Ronald; 2. Donald; 3. Finlay; 4. John; 5. Neil; 6. Christy; 7. Mary; 8. Sara; 9. Anne; 10. Euphemia; 11. Margaret.   **MP 422**.

5598 McDONALD, Esther. From Dornoch, SUT. To Lanark Twp, Lanark Co, ONT, 1832. Wife of Alexander McKay, qv.   **DC 10 Jan 1980**.

5599 MACDONALD, Ewen. From Retland, South

Morar, INV. To PEI on the *Jane*, ex Loch nan Uamh, Arisaig, 12 Jul 1790. Family with him.   **PLJ**.

5600 McDONALD, Ewen. From Strathglass, INV. To Pictou, NS, on the *Sarah*, ex Fort William, Jun 1801. Labourer.   **PLS**.

5601 MACDONALD, Ewen, d ca 1806. From INV. To Gaspereaux Lake, Kings Co, NS, 1803. Family moved to Lochaber, Antigonish Co. m Mary Williams, qv, ch: 1. Kenneth; 2. John; 3. Alexander; 4. Donald, b 1804; 5. Katherine; 6. Ann; 7. Christine; 8. Mary.   **HCA 205**.

5602 MACDONALD, Ewen, 1813-95. Prob from INV. s/o John M. To Sydney Mines, Cape Breton Co, NS, 1828. Blacksmith. m Annie, d/o Allan MacDonald, Postmaster, Catalone, qv. Son Alexander, b 1861. **HNS iii 195**.

5603 McDONALD, Ewen, b 1838. From Is South Uist, INV. s/o John M, qv. To Richmond Co, NS, ca 1850. m Effie Morrison.   **DC 21 Mar 1981**.

5604 McDONALD, Farquhar. From ARL. To Ekfrid Twp, Middlesex Co, ONT, 1836.   **PCM 31**.

5605 McDONALD, Finan, 1782–3 Dec 1851. From Munical, Loch Hourne, Knoydart, INV, but poss b ABD. s/o Angus 'Ban' M, qv, and Elinor MacDonald. To QUE on the *MacDonald*, arr 5 Sep 1785; stld Glengarry Co, ONT. Joined NWCo at Lachine. Spent many years west of the Rocky Mountains and explored the basins of the Columbia, Kootenai and Snake rivers with David Thompson. Clerk with HBCo, 1821, and retr to Charlottenburg, Glengarry Co, ONT, 1827. m Margaret Ponderell, an Indian woman, ch.   **MDB 437; DC 15 Feb 1968 and 27 Feb 1972**.

5606 MACDONALD, Findlay, b ca 1750. From Is Mull, ARL. To Charlottetown, PEI, on the *Dykes*, arr 9 Aug 1803; stld Point Prim, Queens Co. m Jessie Mackinnon, qv, ch: 1. Hector, qv; 2. Ann, qv.   **HP 35**.

5607 McDONALD, Findlay. To Pictou Co, NS, <1830; stld East River. Dau Elizabeth.   **HNS iii 251**.

5608 McDONALD, Finlay. From Urquhart, INV. To Pictou, NS, on the *Sarah*, ex Fort William, Jun 1801. Farmer. Wife Ann with him, ch: 1. John, aged 13; 2. Ann, aged 10; 3. Donald, aged 6; 4. Christian, aged 4; 5. Duncan, aged 1 ½.   **PLS**.

5609 MACDONALD, Finlay, b ca 1773. From Brae-Lochaber, INV. s/o Donald 'Ban Onorach' M, qv, and Isabel Beaton, qv. To South West Mabou, Inverness Co, NS, ca 1805. Farmer. m Catherine Beaton, qv, ch: 1. Isabel; 2. Mary; 3. Sara; 4. Catherine; 5. Angus; 6. Flora; 7. Anne; 8. Donald; 9. Janet; 10. Sara, jr. **CBC 1818; MP 580**.

5610 MACDONALD, Finlay. From Is Barra, INV. s/o Iain 'Og' M. To Mabou, Inverness Co, NS, prob <1820. m Margaret MacDonald, qv, ch: 1. Neil; 2. Malcolm; 3. Janet; 4. Roderick; 5. Anne; 6. Mary.   **MP 426, 440**.

5611 McDONALD, Findlay, b 9 Nov 1772. From Lairg par, SUT. Poss s/o Angus M. To East Nissouri Twp, Oxford Co, ONT, ca 1830. Farmer, Lot 12, Con 4. ch: 1. Angus, remained in SCT; 2. Ann, qv; 3. James, qv; 4. William, qv; 5. Hugh, qv; 6. Janet, qv; 7. Robert, went to Cape Breton Is, NS.   **DC 25 Nov 1981**.

5612 McDONALD, Finlay. Prob rel to Alexander M, qv. To London Village, Westminster Twp, Middlesex Co, ONT, 1831. **PCM 55**.

5613 McDONALD, Flora, b 1778. From Is Tyree, ARL. To QUE on the *Oughton*, arr Jul 1804; stld Baldoon, Dover Twp, Kent Co, ONT. Wife of Donald McDonald, tailor, qv. **UCM 268, 302; DC 4 Oct 1979**.

5614 MACDONALD, Flora. From Lochaber, INV. d/o Alexander 'Ruadh' M, qv, and Mary Campbell, qv. To Mabou Ridge, Inverness Co, NS, 1816. m Donald, s/o Samuel Campbell, qv. **MP 544**.

5615 MACDONALD, Flora. From Knoydart, INV. To Antigonish Co, NS, poss <1830; stld Beaver Meadow. Wife of John MacLean, qv. **HCA 311**.

5616 McDONALD, Francis, 1714–25 Nov 1824. From CAI. To Fredericton, NB, ca 1784; stld Nashwaak. Prob discharged soldier. **VSN No 866**.

5617 McDONALD, George, ca 1766–1 Sep 1813. From Borrobol, Kildonan, SUT. To Fort Churchill, Hudson Bay, on the *Prince of Wales*, ex Stromness, 28 Jun 1813, and d there. Wife Janet McDonald, qv, with him. **LSS 186; RRS 27; LSC 323**.

5618 McDONALD, Grace, b ca 1775. From Aberfeldy, PER. To Osgoode Twp, Carleton Co, ONT, ca 1831. Wife of Alexander McNab, qv. **DC 1 Aug 1979**.

5619 McDONALD, Hector, 1791–1 Jun 1863. From Glen Urquhart, INV. To Pictou Co, NS, 1801; stld Hopewell. m Christy Thompson, qv, ch: 1. Alexander, 1825-77; 2. John, 1826–1910; 3. William, 1829–1907; 4. Margaret, 1832–1906; 5. Isabel, dy; 6. James, 1835-98; 7. Isabel, 1841–1918. **PAC 121**.

5620 MACDONALD, Hector. From Moidart, INV. bro/o Dougald M, qv. To Antigonish Co, NS, ca 1802. m Miss McAdam, ch: 1. John; 2. Alexander; 3. Joseph; 4. Hugh; 5. Kate. **HCA 173**.

5621 MACDONALD, Hector. From Is Mull, ARL. s/o Findlay M, qv, and Jessie Mackinnon, qv. To Charlottetown, PEI, on the *Dykes*, arr 9 Aug 1803; stld Point Prim, Queens Co. Petitioner for Dr Aneas MacAulay, 1811. m Catherine, d/o Murdoch MacLean, qv. Son Alexander Hector, master mariner. **HP 35, 73**.

5622 McDONALD, Hector. From Is Mull, ARL. To Hudson Bay <1813; thence to Red River. **RRS 16**.

5623 McDONALD, Hector. From Is Iona, ARL. Prob s/o Neil and Flora M. To Mariposa Twp, Victoria Co, ONT, poss <1818. ch: 1. Neil; 2. Gideon; 3. Hector; 4. Flora; 5. Katie; 6. Isabella; 7. Annie; 8. Janet. **DC 24 Jan 1977**.

5624 MACDONALD, Hector. Prob from INV. bro/o Ronald M, qv, Donald M, qv, and John M, qv. To Mount Young, Mabou, Inverness Co, NS, <1830. m Catherine Beaton, ch: 1. Alexander; 2. James; 3. Mary; 4. Christine; 5. Margaret; 6. Sara. **MP 504**.

5625 MACDONALD, Henry, 1789–17 Mar 1882. From Coupar-Angus, PER. Served at QUE in the 8th Regt during the War of 1812, and was gr land in Drummond Twp, Lanark Co, ONT 1821. Farmer and twp treasurer. m at Montreal, 1816, Ann Hyland, who d 1874. Son Henry. **DC 10 Nov 1981**.

5626 McDONALD, Hugh. Prob from INV. Served in the 84th Regt, and following discharge stld on east side of east branch of East River, where gr 100 acres. **HPC App G**.

5627 MACDONALD, Hugh 'Mor', 1778–27 Dec 1862. From Is South Uist, INV. To Inverness Co, NS, 1790, and d River Inhabitants. m (i) Jane, d/o Donald MacIntyre, ch: 1. Donald; 2. Alexander; 3. John; 4. Angus; 5. Archibald; 6. Donald 'Og'; 7. Mary; 8. Catherine; 9. Annie; 10. Margaret; 11. Jessie; 12. Jane. m (ii) Catherine MacInnes, with further ch: 13. Catherine; 14. Jane; 15. Margaret; 16. Christy. **WLC**.

5628 McDONALD, Hugh. To Glengarry Co, ONT, 1794; stld Lot 28, Con 15, Lancaster Twp. **MG 56**.

5629 McDONALD, Hugh. From Moidart, INV. To Pictou, NS, on the *Dove*, ex Fort William, Jun 1801. Tenant. Wife Ann with him, and 2 ch. **PLD**.

5630 McDONALD, Hugh, b ca 1766. To Western Shore, Inverness Co, NS, 1802. Farmer, m and ch. **CBC 1818**.

5631 MACDONALD, Hugh, ca 1771–16 Nov 1866. From PER. To Pictou, NS, and stld Lime Rock, West River. Bur Salt Springs. Wife Margaret, ca 1809–16 Apr 1897. **DC 27 Oct 1979**.

5632 MACDONALD, Hugh, ca 1789–1877. From Is Rum, INV. To NS, 1808; stld later at Guysborough Co. Postmaster, Registrar and MLA. m Elizabeth, d/o David Elliot and Sarah Archibald, of Truro, Colchester Co. **MLA 203**.

5633 McDONALD, Hugh, ca 1796–4 Apr 1881. From Lairg, SUT. To Pictou, NS, 1812. m Catherine Fraser, qv. **DC 10 Feb 1980**.

5634 McDONALD, Hugh. From Fort William, INV. To Fort Churchill, Hudson Bay, on the *Prince of Wales*, ex Stromness, Jun 1813, but d at sea, 3 Aug. **LSS 186; RRS 27; LSC 323**.

5635 McDONALD, Hugh. From Is Iona, ARL. Prob s/o Neil and Flora M. To York Co, ONT, poss <1815; stld Vaughan Twp, but went later to Brock Twp. Farmer. ch: 1. Flora; 2. Katie; 3. Christine; 4. Neil H; 5. Alexander. **DC 24 Jan 1977**.

5636 McDONALD, Hugh, b ca 1796. To St Andrews dist, Cape Breton Co, NS, prob arr Apr 1817. **CBC 1818**.

5637 McDONALD, Hugh. From Is Tyree, ARL. s/o John M. To Lake Ainslie, Inverness Co, NS, 1820. m Ann Campbell, qv, ch: 1. Ronald, qv; 2. John, qv; 3. Archibald, qv; 4. Malcolm; 5. Neil, 1823-95; 6. Mary; 7. Ann; 8. Elizabeth. **DC 23 Feb 1980**.

5638 MACDONALD, Hugh. From Arisaig, INV. bro/o Donald 'Mingary' M, qv. To NS, prob <1820; stld prob Antigonish Co. **HCA 235**.

5639 MACDONALD, Hugh, d 1841. From Glasgow, but b Rogart, SUT. To QUE on the *Earl of Buckinghamshire*, ex Greenock, arr 24 Jun 1820; stld nr Kingston, ONT. Merchant and farmer. m Ellen Shaw, qv, ch: 1. William, d inf; 2. Margaret, see ADDENDA; 3. John Alexander, qv; 4. James, d 22 May 1822; 5. Louisa, unm. **DC 5 Mar 1982**.

5640 MACDONALD, Hugh. From Lochaber, PER. s/o Angus M, qv, and Margaret MacDonald, qv. To Inverness Co, NS, ca 1822; stld Glencoe. m Flora, d/o Donald McEachen, ch: 1. Alexander; 2. Donald; 3. Angus; 4. Margaret; 5. Mary; 6. Christina. **MP 490**.

5641 McDONALD, Hugh, ca 1767–16 Feb 1865. From Glengarry, INV. To Nichol Twp, Wellington Co, ONT, ca 1830; stld later in Pilkington Twp. ch: 1. Alexander; 2. Allan; 3. Janet; 4. Margaret; 5. Jemima. **EHE 40**.

5642 McDONALD, Hugh, 1816-66. From Lairg par, SUT. s/o Finlay M, qv. To East Nissouri Twp, Oxford Co, ONT, ca 1830; stld Lot 11, Con 3. m Catherine McDonald, ch: 1. Phillip, 1844–1931; 2. Christine, 1845–1923; 3. Dougald, 1847–1908; 4. Elizabeth, 1849-91; 5. John, 1851–1912; 6. Annie, 1853–1934; 7. Donald, 1855–1935; 8. Robert, 1857–1923; 9. James, 1859-84; 10. William, 1862-64; 11. Alexander, 1865–1950. **DC 25 Nov 1981**.

5643 MACDONALD, Hugh. From Borrodale, INV. To South River, Antigonish Co, NS, prob <1830. m Ann, d/o Angus MacGillivray, ch: 1. Donald; 2. Mary. **HCA 216**.

5644 McDONALD, Hugh. From Petty, INV. To East Williams Twp, Middlesex Co, ONT, 1834. **PCM 43**.

5645 MACDONALD, Hugh, 1814-99. From SUT. To Cumberland Co, NS, prob <1840; stld nr Wallace. Wife Margaret, 1827–1904, with him. **DC 29 Oct 1980**.

5646 McDONALD, Hugh. To East Williams Twp, Middlesex Co, ONT, 1840. **PCM 44**.

5647 McDONALD, Hugh. From Assynt, SUT. To QUE on the *Panama*, ex Loch Laxford, 19 Jun 1847. Prob went to Owen Sound, ONT. *MacLeod Muniments*, **Box 36**.

5648 MACDONALD, Hugh 'Ban'. From Moidart, INV. s/o Hugh M. To Antigonish Co, NS, <1830. m Margaret, d/o John MacDonald, ch: 1. Alexander; 2. Angus; 3. Donald; 4. Duncan; 5. John; 6. Kate; 7. Ann; 8. Mary. **HCA 259; MP 447**.

5649 MACDONALD, Hugh. Prob from INV. bro/o Robert M, qv. To Morristown, Antigonish Co, NS, prob <1840. m Helen MacAskill, qv, ch: 1. Hugh; 2. Christina Ann; 3. Mrs M Patterson; 4. William. **HCA 233**.

5650 MACDONALD, Isabel. From Badenoch, INV. d/o Angus M. To Pictou, NS, on the *Dove*, ex Fort William, Jun 1801; stld Little Judique, Inverness Co. Wife of Angus Beaton, qv. **PLD; MP 95**.

5651 MACDONALD, Isabel. From Moidart, INV. d/o Angus M, qv, and first wife. To NS, prob <1820; stld Cape George, Antigonish Co, later Inverness Co. Wife of John Livingstone, qv. **MP 502**.

5652 McDONALD, Isabella. From Retland, South Morar, INV. To PEI on the *Jane*, ex Loch nan Uamh, 12 Jul 1790. **PLJ**.

5653 MACDONALD, Isabella, b 5 Apr 1786. From Lochaber, INV. d/o Capt Angus M. of Tulloch, Glen Spean, and Margaret MacDonald. To Mabou Coal Mines, Inverness Co, NS, prob <1815. m Andrew MacInnes. **MP 588**.

5654 McDONALD, Isabella. From Bedley Inn, Cadder par, LKS. To QUE, ex Greenock, summer 1815; stld Lochiel Twp, Glengarry Co, ONT. Wife of Thomas Duncan, qv. **SEC 1; DC 26 Jun 1981**.

5655 McDONALD, Isabella, d 16 May 1891. From West Bennan, Kilmory par, Is Arran, BUT. d/o Donald M. and Margaret Cook. To Nash Creek, Restigouche Co, NB, 1851, and d Archibald Settlement. Wife of Donald McBride, qv. **DC 23 May 1980**.

5656 McDONALD, Isobel, ca 1755–ca 1847. From Balquhidder, PER. Cous of Gerald M. To PEI ca 1803; stld Brudenell, Kings Co. Wife of James McLaren, qv. **BP 11, 42**.

5657 McDONALD, Isobel, b ca 1773. From Atholl, PER. To Charlottetown, PEI, on the *Clarendon*, ex Oban, 6 Aug 1808. Wife of James Donald, qv. **CPL**.

5658 McDONALD, Rev James. Prob from Is Skye, INV. To St John, PEI, on the *Alexander*, ex Arisaig and South Uist, 1 May 1772. Secular priest. **SG vii/4 15**.

5659 McDONALD, James. To Pictou, NS, and was gr 200 acres of West River, 26 Aug 1783. **HPC App A**.

5660 McDONALD, James. bro/o John M, qv. Served in the 84th Regt and after discharge, 1784, was gr land on the east side of the east branch of East River, Pictou Co, NS. Went later to Middlesex Co, ONT. ch. **HPC App G**.

5661 McDONALD, James. From Munical, Loch Hourne, Knoydart, INV. s/o Angus 'Ban' M, qv, and Elinor M, qv. To QUE on the *MacDonald*, arr 5 Sep 1785; stld nr Williamstown, Glengarry Co, ONT. Farmer. **DC 15 Feb 1968**.

5662 McDONALD, James. From Ardnish, Arisaig, INV. Prob rel to Allan M, qv. To PEI on the *Jane*, ex Loch nan Uamh, Arisaig, 12 Jul 1790. **PLJ**.

5663 McDONALD, James, b ca 1788. To Western Shore, Inverness Co, NS, 1800. Farmer. **CBC 1818**.

5664 MACDONALD, James. From Kilmorack, INV. To Pictou, NS, on the *Dove*, ex Fort William, Jun 1801. Labourer. **PLD**.

5665 McDONALD, James, b ca 1791. To Western Shore, Inverness Co, NS, 1801. Farmer, m and had ch. **CBC 1818**.

5666 McDONALD, James, b ca 1786. To Margaree, Inverness Co, NS, 1806. Farmer, unm. **CBC 1818**.

5667 MACDONALD, James, ca 1776–1842. Prob from INV. To Halifax, NS, 1810; stld Middle Musquodoboit. m Janet MacIntosh, qv, ch: 1. Margaret; 2. John. **NSN 6/1**.

5668 McDONALD, James. From Fort Augustus, INV. To Fort Churchill, Hudson Bay, on the *Prince of Wales*, ex Stromness, 28 Jun 1813. Went to York Factory, 14 Apr 1814, thence to Red River. Blacksmith. **LSS 186; RRS 27; LSC 323**.

5669 McDONALD, James, b ca 1778. From New Greyfriars par, Edinburgh. To QUE on the *Atlas*, ex Greenock, 11 Jun 1815; stld Lot 1, Con 10, North Burgess Twp, Lanark Co, ONT. Whitesmith, later farmer. Wife Margaret McDonald, qv, with him, and 4 ch. **SEC 1; HCL 15, 230, 232**.

5670 McDONALD, James. From INV. To Pictou, NS, <1820; later to Middlesex Co, ONT. Son Donald, 1787–1879, res London Twp. **PCM 49-50**.

5671 McDONALD, James. Prob from Kilmahog, Callander, PER. To Montreal, QUE, on the *Niagara*, ex Greenock, arr 28 May 1825; stld Flat River, McNab Twp, Renfrew Co. **EMT 18**.

5672 MACDONALD, James, ca 1793–12 Sep 1883. Prob from Is Skye, INV. To Queens Co, PEI, ca 1830. m d/o Norman MacLeod, qv, and Margaret MacPhee, qv, and had, prob with other ch: 1. Rev Donald, 1843–1929, Baptist min at Vancouver, BC; 2. Capt Malcolm, res Georgetown, Kings Co, PEI. **SPI 160**.

5673 McDONALD, James, 1809-85. From Lairg par, SUT. s/o Finlay M, qv. To East Nissouri Twp, Oxford Co, ONT, ca 1830. m Janet McKay, qv, ch: 1. Eliza, 1841–1919; 2. Alexander, 1843–1920; 3. Jessie, b 1843; 4. Ann, b 1844; 5. Philip, 1846–1939; 6. Hugh, 1849–1920; 7. Robert, 1851–1932. **DC 25 Nov 1981**.

5674 McDONALD, James. From ARL. To Middlesex Co, ONT, <20 Nov 1834, when m Janet Anderson, qv. stld in Mosa Twp. **PCM 18, 22**.

5675 MACDONALD, James, b 8 Sep 1817. From Halkirk, CAI. s/o William M, qv, and Christina Mill, qv. To Markham Twp, York Co, ONT, 1837. m Ann, b 1825, d/o William McMaster and Ann Robinson, ch: 1. William, b 1846; 2. Mary Anne, b 1851, d unm; 3. Christina Ogilvie, b 1853, d unm; 4. Johanna, b 1855; 5. Josephine Fenton, 1857-60; 6. Donald, b 1860; 7. Janet, b 1862, d unm; 8. Isabel Charleton, b 1864. **DC 5 Jul 1979**.

5676 McDONALD, James. Prob from Duthill, INV. To London Twp, Middlesex Co, ONT, 1840; moved to West Williams Twp, 1850. **PCM 47**.

5677 McDONALD, James. To Pictou, NS, on the *London*, arr 11 Apr 1848. Wife Janet with him. **DC 15 Jul 1979**.

5678 MACDONALD, James Edward. From Is South Uist, INV. s/o Allan M, qv, and Mary MacLean, qv. To Cape Breton Co, NS, 1823, but moved to Stewartdale, Whycocomagh, Inverness Co. m Mary Campbell, ch. **DC 23 Feb 1980**.

5679 McDONALD, Jane, b 1806. To NS, ex Glasgow, 1830; later to Louth, Lincoln Co, ONT. m William McKenzie, qv. **DC 5 Dec 1960**.

5680 MACDONALD, Jane. From Lochaber, INV. d/o Archibald M. and Anne MacDonald, qv. To Arisaig, Antigonish Co, NS, 1816; moved to Inverness Co, 1818. m Neil Mackinnon, Broad Cove Ponds, ch: 1. Charles; 2. Alexander, d unm; 3. Catherine. **MP 553**.

5681 McDONALD, Jane, 1807-77. From Reay, CAI. To Caledon Twp, Peel Co, ONT, <1840. **DC 21 Apr 1980**.

5682 McDONALD, Jane. From Is North Uist, INV. To Richmond Co, NS, <1843. Wife of Archibald McCuish, qv. **MLA 198**.

5683 McDONALD, Jane Jackson, ca 1840–22 Mar 1902. Prob from Glasgow. d/o John M. and Julia Ann Stewart. To Markham Twp, York Co, ONT, <1865; later to Parkhill, Middlesex Co. m Richard, s/o Richard and Jane Snowden, ch. **DC 18 May 1982**.

5684 MACDONALD, Janet. From Kinloch-Moidart, INV. To Antigonish Co, NS, ca 1784. Wife of Alexander MacDonald, qv. **DC 30 Mar 1981**.

5685 MACDONALD, Janet. From Frobost, South Uist, INV. To QUE on the *British Queen*, ex Arisaig, 16 Aug 1790. Poss widow with a child. **QCC 103**.

5686 McDONALD, Janet. From Kilmorack, INV. Prob rel to Christian M, qv. To Pictou, NS, on the *Sarah*, ex Fort William, Jun 1801. Spinster. **PLS**.

5687 McDONALD, Janet. From Urquhart, INV. Poss wife or rel of Duncan M, labourer, qv. To Pictou, NS, on the *Sarah*, ex Fort William, Jun 1801. Spinster. **PLS**.

5688 McDONALD, Janet. From Kilmorack, INV. To Pictou, NS, on the *Sarah*, ex Fort William, Jun 1801. Spinster. **PLS**.

5689 MACDONALD, Janet, b ca 1793. From Halkirk, CAI. d/o Benjamen M. and Barbara Gunn. To York Co, ONT, ca 1840; stld Toronto. m Hugh Sinclair, qv. **DC 5 Jul 1979**.

5690 McDONALD, Janet, b ca 1765. From Borrobol, Kildonan par, SUT. Wife of George M, qv. To Fort Churchill, Hudson Bay, on the *Prince of Wales*, ex Stromness, 28 Jun 1813. Went to York Factory, spring 1814, thence to Red River. **LSS 186; RRS 27; LSC 323**.

5691 McDONALD, Janet, 1818-76. From Gruids, Lairg, SUT. d/o Finlay M, qv. To East Nissouri Twp, Oxford Co, ONT, ca 1830. m 1843, Donald McArthur, qv. **DC 25 Nov 1981**.

5692 McDONALD, Janet, d 23 Sep 1896. Prob from PER. To Westchester, Cumberland Co, NS, 1832; stld Pugwash River. Wife of Donald Stewart, qv. **DC 1 Nov 1981**.

5693 MACDONALD, Jessie. From Lochaber, INV. d/o Alexander 'Ruadh' M, qv, and Mary Campbell, qv. To Mabou Ridge, Inverness Co, NS, 1816. m Donald Rankin, qv. **MP 544, 814**.

5694 MACDONALD, Jessie. From Glen Roy, Kilmonivaig par, INV. d/o Thomas M. To Glenville, Inverness Co, NS, prob <1840. Wife of Donald MacDonald, qv. **MP 400, 440**.

5695 MACDONALD, Jessie, b 1806. From Dunganichy, Is Benbecula, INV. To Pictou, NS, on the *Lulan*, ex Glasgow, 17 Aug 1848. Wife of Hugh MacLean, qv. **DC 12 Jul 1979**.

5696 McDONALD, Johanna. From Samalaman, Moidart, INV. To PEI on the *Lucy*, ex Loch nan Uamh, Arisaig, 12 Jul 1790. **PLL**.

5697 MACDONALD, Johanna, b 2 May 1826. From Halkirk, CAI. d/o William M, qv, and Christina Mill, qv. To Markham Twp, York Co, ONT, ca 1840. m William Ogilvie, and went to NY. Dau Johanna, d 1900. **DC 5 Jul 1979**.

5698 MACDONALD, John of Glenaladale, 1743–29 Dec 1811. From Moidart, INV. s/o Alexander M. of Glenaladale, and Margaret MacDonell. Educ Regensburg, and was sometime factor of the Clanranald estates. Promoted and organised a RC colony on PEI, at Tracadie Bay, and sent out emigrants from South Uist and Arisaig in 1772 on the ship *Alexander*. Sold his estate, 1773, and joined the emigrants. Capt 84th Regt. m (i) Isabella

Gordon, from Wardhouse, ABD, without surviving ch. m (ii) Margaret MacDonald, from Gernish, ch: 1. Flora Ann Marie; 2. Hon Donald, 1795–1854; 3. William, drowned off coast of IRL; 4. Rev John, 1808-74; 5. Lt Col Roderick C, British Army. **CD iii 265; MDC 2; DC 1 Oct 1960.**

5699 McDONALD, John. Served in the 84th Regt and after discharge, 1784, was gr 250 acres on the west side of the east branch of East River, Pictou Co, NS. **HPC App G.**

5700 McDONALD, John. bro/o James M, qv. Served in the 84th Regt, and following discharge, 1784, was gr 250 acres on the west side of the east branch of East River, Pictou Co, NS. **HPC App G.**

5701 MACDONALD, John, 1738–1811. From Moidart, INV. s/o Donald M. To Pictou Co, NS, ca 1784; stld Fishers Grant, and went later to Little Judique, Inverness Co. m (i) Effie MacDonald, qv, ch: 1. John; 2. Donald 'Ruadh'; 3. Mary; 4. Ronald; 5. Sara. m (ii) Annie Mackinnon. **DC 30 Mar 1981.**

5702 MACDONALD, John, ca 1746–7 Nov 1836. From INV. To Glengarry Co, ONT, 1784. **DGC 28 Dec 1836.**

5703 McDONALD, John 'le Borgue', 1770–8 Feb 1828. From Munical, Loch Hourne, Knoydart, INV. s/o Angus 'Ban' M, qv, and Elinor M, qv. To QUE on the *MacDonald*, arr 5 Sep 1785; stld Glengarry Co, ONT. Joined XYCo at Lachine as a clerk and became a wintering partner. Firm merged with NWCo, 1804, and at the merger with HBCo, 1821, became a chief factor. Bought land at Kempenfeldt Bay, Lake Simcoe, 1825. m Marie Poitras, ch. **MDB 439; DC 15 Feb 1818 and 27 Feb 1972.**

5704 MACDONALD, John. From Knoydart, INV. s/o Martin M, qv. To Halifax, NS, arr 1787; stld Knoydart, Antigonish Co. m Mary Robinson, ch: 1. Donald; 2. William; 3. Mary; 4. Sarah; 5. Martin; 6. Angus; 7. Ronald; 8. John. **HCA 178.**

5705 McDONALD, John. Poss from Aberdeen. To Kingston, ONT, <1789. Sometime Barrack-Master at Fort Michilimackinac, between Lakes Huron and Michigan. Dau Elizabeth, res Aberdeen. **Aberdeen OPR 168A/9.**

5706 MACDONALD, John. Prob from Arisaig, INV. s/o Angus M. To Arisaig, Antigonish Co, NS, 1790; moved to Lakeville, 1801. m Margaret MacDonald, qv, ch: 1. Ronald; 2. Colin; 3. Alexander 'Soloman'; 4. Isabella; 5. Catherine. **HCA 218.**

5707 McDONALD, John. From Fort William, INV. To PEI on the *Jane*, ex Loch nan Uamh, Arisaig, 12 Jul 1790. Wife and 3 ch with him. **PLJ.**

5708 McDONALD, John. From Scamadale, South Morar, INV. To PEI on the *Jane*, ex Loch nan Uamh, Arisaig, 12 Jul 1790. Family with him. **PLJ.**

5709 McDONALD, John. From Ardnafouran, Arisaig, INV. To PEI on the *Jane*, ex Loch nan Uamh, Arisaig, 12 Jul 1790. Wife with him, and 2 ch. **PLJ.**

5710 McDONALD, John. From Slochardnish, Arisaig, INV. To PEI on the *Jane*, ex Loch nan Uamh, Arisaig, 12 Jul 1790. Family with him. **PLJ.**

5711 McDONALD, John. From Slochardnish, Arisaig, INV. To PEI on the *Jane*, ex Loch nan Uamh, Arisaig, 12 Jul 1790. Wife with him. **PLJ.**

5712 McDONALD, John. From Glenuig, Moidart, INV. To PEI on the *Lucy*, ex Loch nan Uamh, Arisaig, 12 Jul 1790. Tenant. Wife with him, and 4 ch. **PLL.**

5713 McDONALD, John. From Borrodale, Moidart, INV. To PEI on the *Lucy*, ex Loch nan Uamh, Arisaig, 12 Jul 1790. Family with him. **PLL.**

5714 MACDONALD, John 'bras croche', ca 1772–1860. From Gart, Callander, PER. s/o Capt John M, 84th Regt. To Montreal, QUE, 1791. Joined NWCo and became a partner. Built Fort Augustus, nr Edmonton, 1798, and was present at the capture of Fort Astoria, 1813. Ret to Grays Creek, Glengarry Co, ONT, 1816. m (i) Indian woman; (ii) a niece of Hugh McGillis, Williamstown. ch: 1. Rolland, MLA, Cornwall, 1846; 2. De Bellefeuille; 3. Mrs James E. Campbell. **SGC 275; SDG 393; MDB 442.**

5715 McDONALD, John, b ca 1770. To Western Shore, Inverness Co, NS, 1799. Farmer, m and ch. **CBC 1818.**

5716 McDONALD, John, b ca 1783. To Western Shore, Inverness Co, NS, 1799. Farmer, m and ch. **CBC 1818.**

5717 MACDONALD, John. From Moidart, INV. s/o Rory M, of the Clanranald. To Pictou, NS, <1800; stld South Side Harbour, Antigonish Co. m Ann, d/o Dougald MacDonald, ch: 1. Rory 'Mor'; 2. Alexander; 3. Ann; 4. Janet; 5. Flora; 6. Mary; 7. Catherine; 8. Margaret. **HCA 245.**

5718 MACDONALD, John. From Arisaig, INV. To Malignant Cove, Antigonish Co, NS, prob <1800. m Margaret Mackinnon, qv, ch: 1. Donald; 2. Angus; 3. John; 4. Janet; 5. Catherine; 6. Mary. **HCA 244.**

5719 McDONALD, John. From Urquhart par, INV. To Pictou, NS, on the *Sarah*, ex Fort William, Jun 1801. Farmer. Wife Elizabeth with him, and ch: 1. Duncan, aged 6; 2. Janet, aged 3. **PLS.**

5720 McDONALD, John. From Glenmoriston, INV. To Pictou, NS, on the *Sarah*, ex Fort William, Jun 1801. Farmer. **PLS.**

5721 McDONALD, John. From Arisaig, INV. To Pictou, NS, on the *Dove*, ex Fort William, Jun 1801. Tenant. **PLD.**

5722 McDONALD, John, b 1758. To Western Shore, Inverness Co, NS, 1801. Farmer, m and ch. **CBC 1818.**

5723 McDONALD, John. From Moidart, INV. To Pictou, NS, on the *Dove*, ex Fort William, Jun 1801. Farmer. Wife Catherine with him, and ch: 1. Peggy, aged 14; 2. Catherine, aged 9; 3. James, aged 5; 4. Mary, aged 3. **PLD.**

5724 McDONALD, John. From Moidart, INV. To Pictou, NS, on the *Dove*, ex Fort William, Jun 1801. Labourer. Wife Marion with him, and ch: 1. Alexander, aged 8; 2. inf. **PLD.**

5725 McDONALD, John. From Moidart, INV. To Pictou, NS, on the *Dove*, ex Fort William, Jun 1801. Farmer. Wife Catherine with him, and inf dau. **PLD.**

5726 MACDONALD, John. From Kiltarlity, INV. To Pictou, NS, on the *Dove*, ex Fort William, Jun 1801. Labourer. **PLD.**

5727 McDONALD, John, b ca 1799. From Kilmorack, INV. Prob rel to Janet M, spinster, qv. To Pictou, NS, on the *Sarah*, ex Fort William, Jun 1801. **PLS.**

5728   MACDONALD, John. From Moidart, INV. bro/o Hector M, qv, and of Dougald M, qv. To Antigonish Co, NS, ca 1802.   **HCA 173**.

5729   McDONALD, John. From Inchlaggan, Glengarry, INV. To Montreal, QUE, ex Fort William, 3 Jul 1802; stld E ONT.   **MCM 1/4 23**.

5730   McDONALD, John. From Dores, INV. To Montreal, QUE, ex Fort William, 3 Jul 1802; stld E ONT.   **MCM 1/4 25**.

5731   McDONALD, John. Poss from Loch na Seilge, SUT. To Montreal, QUE, ex Fort William, 3 Jul 1802; stld E ONT. Wife with him, and family: 1. Alexander; 2. Donald; 3. Peggy.   **MCM 1/4 25**.

5732   McDONALD, John, b ca 1800. To Western Shore, Inverness Co, NS, ca 1802, prob with relatives. Farmer.   **CBC 1818**.

5733   McDONALD, John, b ca 1763. To Western Shore, Inverness Co, NS, 1803. Farmer, m and ch.   **CBC 1818**.

5734   McDONALD, John, b ca 1772. To Western Shore, Inverness Co, NS, 1803. Farmer, m and ch.   **CBC 1818**.

5735   MACDONALD, John. To PEI, poss 1803; stld Queens Co. Petitioner for Dr Aneas MacAulay, 1811. Son John.   **HP 73**.

5736   McDONALD, John, b ca 1773. To Inverness Co, NS, 1804; stld Judique. Tailor. ch.   **CBC 1818**.

5737   McDONALD, John, 1789–1861. From Is Tyree, ARL. s/o Donald M, qv, and Flora M, qv. To QUE on the *Oughton*, arr Jul 1804; stld Baldoon, Dover Twp, Kent Co, ONT. m Catherine McLean, qv. Dau Margaret, b 1827.   **UCM 268; DC 4 Oct 1979**.

5738   McDONALD, John, b ca 1788. To Western Shore, Inverness Co, NS, 1805. Farmer, m and ch.   **CBC 1818**.

5739   MACDONALD, John. From Brae-Lochaber, INV. s/o Donald 'Ban Onorach' M, qv, and Isabel Beaton, qv. To South West Mabou, Inverness Co, NS, 1805; stld later Rear Long Point. Farmer. m Mary, d/o Angus MacDonald, qv, and Isabel Campbell, qv, ch: 1. Isabel; 2. Mary; 3. Anne; 4. Sara; 5. Christina; 6. Catherine; 7. Flora.   **MP 577**.

5740   McDONALD, John, b ca 1781. To Inverness, Inverness Co, NS, 1806. Farmer, m and ch.   **CBC 1818**.

5741   McDONALD, John, b ca 1791. To Western Shore, Inverness Co, NS, ca 1806. Farmer.   **CBC 1818**.

5742   McDONALD, John, b ca 1793. To Inverness, Inverness Co, NS, 1806. Farmer, m and ch.   **CBC 1818**.

5743   McDONALD, John, ca 1771–11 Aug 1817. From Is Iona, ARL. Prob s/o Neil and Flora M. To York Co, ONT, <1812, when gr land in King and Vaughan Twps. Farmer, and had served in the Argyll Fencible Regt. m Sarah McInnes, qv, ch: 1. Dugald; 2. Archibald; 3. Neil; 4. John; 5. Daniel; 6. Anne; 7. Isabell; 8. Flora; 9. Mary; 10. Sarah.   **DC 24 Jan 1977**.

5744   MACDONALD, John. From South Uist, INV. s/o Alexander M. To PEI <1814, when he moved to West Lake Ainslie, Inverness Co, NS. Farmer. ch: 1. John; 2. Mary; 3. Sarah; 4. Anne; 5. Catherine; 6. Christie; 7. Mary, jr.   **MP 232, 596**:

5745   McDONALD, John, b ca 1785. From Fort Augustus, INV. To QUE, ex Greenock, summer 1815; stld prob Lanark Co, ONT. Labourer. Wife Elizabeth Fraser, qv, with him, and 2 ch.   **SEC 8**.

5746   McDONALD, John, b ca 1759. From Edinburgh. To QUE, ex Greenock, summer 1815; stld prob Lanark Co, ONT. Chelsea pensioner and labourer.   **SEC 5**.

5747   McDONALD, John, b ca 1767. From Callander, PER. To QUE on the *Dorothy*, ex Greenock, 12 Jul 1815; stld Lot 16, Con 4, South Elmsley Twp, Leeds Co, ONT. Labourer, later farmer. Wife Anne McPherson, qv, with him, and 6 ch.   **SEC 2; HCL 232**.

5748   McDONALD, John, b ca 1781. From Knoydart, INV. To QUE, ex Greenock, summer 1815; stld prob Lanark Co, ONT. Farmer. Wife Florence McKinnon, qv, with him, and 4 ch.   **SEC 7**.

5749   McDONALD, John, b ca 1787. From Killin, PER. To QUE, ex Greenock, summer 1815; stld ONT. Wife Christian Campbell, qv, with him, and 2 ch.   **SEC 4**.

5750   McDONALD, John, b 1794. From Edinburgh. To QUE, ex Greenock, summer 1815; stld ONT. Surgeon. Wife Margaret Motion, qv, with him.   **SEC 4**.

5751   McDONALD, John, b ca 1793. Prob from Kildonan, SUT. To York Factory, Hudson Bay, arr 26 Aug 1815, and went to Red River.   **LSC 327**.

5752   MACDONALD, John. From Moidart, INV. s/o Hugh M, qv. To Antigonish Co, NS, prob <1815; stld Lismore.   **HCA 172**.

5753   MACDONALD, John. Prob from INV. s/o Allan M, qv. To Antigonish Co, NS, poss <1815. ch: 1. Alexander; 2. Donald; 3. Alexander Og.   **HCA 220**.

5754   McDONALD, John, b ca 1790. To Western Shore, Inverness Co, NS, 1816. Farmer, m and ch.   **CBC 1818**.

5755   MACDONALD, John. From Is Tyree, ARL. s/o Hugh M, qv, and Ann Campbell, qv. To Lake Ainslie, Inverness Co, NS, 1820. m Margaret Mackinnon, qv. **DC 23 Feb 1980**.

5756   MACDONALD, John. From Kingussie, INV. bro/o Christina M, qv. To Glencoe, Inverness Co, NS, 1820. Farmer. m Elizabeth MacDonald, qv, ch: 1. John 'Seoc', qv; 2. Donald, d Judique.   **MP ii 375**.

5757   MACDONALD, John 'Seoc'. From Kingussie, INV. s/o John M, qv, and Elizabeth MacDonald, qv. To Glencoe, Inverness Co, NS, 1820. Farmer. m Jessie, d/o John Livingston, ch: 1. Donald; 2. James; 3. Colin; 4. John; 5. Eliza, b 1848; 6. Catherine; 7. Christy; 8. Nancy.   **MP ii 375**.

5758   MACDONALD, John. Prob from Lochaber, INV. s/o Archibald M. To Antigonish Co, NS, prob <1820. m Catherine Campbell, ch: 1. John; 2. Alexander; 3. Hugh; 4. Angus; 5. Catherine; 6. Janet.   **HCA 202**.

5759   MACDONALD, John 'Ban'. From INV. To Antigonish Co, NS, prob <1820; stld Georgeville. ch: 1. John; 2. Donald; 3. Allan.   **HCA 229**.

5760   McDONALD, John. From LKS. To QUE on the *David of London*, ex Greenock, 19 May 1821, and was in Lanark Co, ONT, for a short period. Retr to SCT. Author of *Narrative of a Voyage to Quebec*, which went through several editions and was reprinted at Ottawa, 1978.   **HCL 27, 70**.

5761 MACDONALD, John. From Is Mull, ARL. To QUE, arr 2 Aug 1821; stld Lanark Co, ONT. **SG xx/1 11**.

5762 McDONALD, John. From Oban par, ARL. To QUE on the *Duchess of Richmond*, 1821; stld Drummond Twp, Lanark Co, ONT, later Con 11, Ramsay Twp. Farmer. Wife Ishbel MacLaine, qv, with him, and ch: 1. Donald, d 1823; 2. Lachlan; 3. Neil; 4. Sarah; 5. Mary; 6. Flora; 7. Bell. **HCL 88**.

5763 MACDONALD, John, 1795–1864. From Is South Uist, INV. s/o Allan M, qv, and Mary MacLean, qv. To Cape Breton Co, NS, 1823, but moved to Stewartdale, Whycocomagh, Inverness Co. m Jane MacNiven, qv, ch. **DC 23 Feb 1980**.

5764 McDONALD, John, ca 1818-85. From DFS. To Miramichi, Northumberland Co, NB. Bur Moorfield, Miramichi. **DC 4 Dec 1978**.

5765 MACDONALD, John, b 1785. From Is Skye, INV. To Cape Breton Is, NS, 1827. m (i) Matilda Gordon, ch: 1. John, qv. m (ii) Janet MacLeod, qv, further ch: 2. Alexander, qv; 3. Lachlan, qv; 4. Flora, 1816–1905, unm; 5. Murdoch, qv; 6. Donald, qv. **DC 23 Feb 1980**.

5766 MACDONALD, John, jr. From Is Skye, INV. s/o John M, qv, and Matilda Gordon, his first wife. To Cape Breton Is, NS,1827. m Catherine MacIntosh, Pleasant Bay, Inverness Co, ch. **DC 23 Feb 1980**.

5767 MACDONALD, John. From Moidart, INV. bro/o Annie M, qv. To Monkshead, Antigonish Co, NS, 1827. m Annie MacDonald, qv, ch: 1. Daniel; 2. John; 3. Margaret; 4. Catherine; 5. Annie; 6. Mary. **HCA 182, 256**.

5768 MACDONALD, John. From Is North Uist, INV. To Cape Breton Co, NS, 1828; stld nr Louisbourg, later Sydney Mines. Son Ewen, b 1813, blacksmith. **HNS iii 195**.

5769 MACDONALD, John. Prob from INV. bro/o Donald M, qv, Hector M, qv, and Ronald M, qv. To Mount Young, Mabou, Inverness Co, NS, <1830. m Margaret, d/o Archibald Beaton, ch: 1. Angus; 2. Roderick; 3. Mary; 4. Alexander; 5. Margaret; 6. Flora; 7. Michael. **MP 506**.

5770 MACDONALD, John. From Moidart, INV. s/o Hugh M. To Inverness Co, NS, <1830. ch: 1. Donald; 2. John; 3. Mrs MacGillivray. **HCA 259**.

5771 McDONALD, John. From ARL. To Ekfrid Twp, Middlesex Co, ONT, 1830. **PCM 30**.

5772 MACDONALD, John. From Moidart, INV. s/o Hugh M. To Antigonish Co, NS, prob <1830; moved to Cape Mabou, Inverness Co. m Miss MacNeil, ch: 1. Lauchlan; 2. Angus; 3. Roderick; 4. Donald; 5. Mary. **MP 448**.

5773 McDONALD, John. From Perth. To Toronto, prob <1830. Formerly NCO, 93rd Regt. m Elizabeth Neilson, qv. Son John, 1824-90, Liberal politician. **MDB 439**.

5774 MACDONALD, John 'Ban'. From Moidart, INV. s/o Lachlan M. To Antigonish Co, NS, prob <1830. ch: 1. Donald; 2. Angus; 3. Dougal; 4. Mary; 5. Mrs John MacIsaac; 6. Mrs Donald 'Breac' MacDonald. **HCA 174**.

5775 MACDONALD, John, 1791–1858. From Milton, South Uist, INV. To Wallace, Cumberland Co, NS, prob

<1830. Wife Mary b East River, Pictou Co. Son Angus, 1835-58. **DC 29 Oct 1980**.

5776 MACDONALD, John. From INV. s/o Donald M, qv, and Margaret Gillis. To West South River, Antigonish Co, NS, prob <1830. m Ann Gillis, ch: 1. John; 2. Donald; 3. Andrew; 4. Hugh; 5. Allan; 6. Duncan; 7. Alexander; 8. Catherine; 9. Margaret; 10. Mary; 11. Ann. **HCA 210**.

5777 MACDONALD, John. From Brae-Lochaber, INV. To Hillsborough, Inverness Co, NS, 1831. Storekeeper. m Mary MacDonald, qv, ch: 1. Alexander, merchant; 2. John, merchant; 3. Allan, artist and photographer; 4. Angus, farmer; 5. Anne, unm; 6. Catherine; 7. Alexina. **MP 413**.

5778 MACDONALD, John. From INV. To ONT, 1831. m Mrs Alexander McBain. **DC 4 Mar 1965**.

5779 McDONALD, John. From INV. To Lobo Twp, Middlesex Co, ONT, ca 1832. ch: 1. Donald; 2. Alexander; 3. Hugh; 4. James; 5. Thomas; 6. Rev John; 7. Dr D.F.; 8. Mrs Noble; 9. Mrs John McNeil; 10. Mrs Struthers. **PCM 40**.

5780 MACDONALD, John. Prob from INV. bro/o Daniel M, qv. To Antigonish Co, NS, prob <1840. **HCA 232**.

5781 MACDONALD, John. From Badenoch, INV. s/o Allan M. and Mary MacDonald. To James River, Antigonish Co, NS, <1840. m Mary MacGregor, qv, ch: 1. Alexander; 2. Robert; 3. Duncan; 4. Allan; 5. William; 6. Mary; 7. Jessie; 8. Alexina; 9. Susan; 10-11 Mary Anne and Catherine, twins. **MP 393**.

5782 McDONALD, John, 1838–3 Apr 1923. From Uig, Snizort par, Is Skye, INV. Poss s/o Malcolm M, qv, and Flora Campbell, qv. To Victoria Co, NS, prob 1841. m Sarah McDonald, 1852–1937. **DC 22 Jun 1979**.

5783 MACDONALD, John 'Cannach'. From INV. s/o John M, from Is Canna, who d at sea on the voyage to NS, and Margaret MacArthur. To Glencoe, Inverness Co, NS, prob <1845. m (i) Mary MacDonald, qv, ch: 1. Margaret; 2. John; 3. Christina; 4. Archibald; 5. Alexander; 6. Mary Anne; 7. Jessie; 8. Mary; 9. Angus; 10. Mary, jr. m (ii) Sara, d/o Neil Stewart, further ch: 11. Mary Jane; 12. Margaret Anne; 13. Neil; 14. Alexander. **MP 442**.

5784 MACDONALD, John. From Is Mull, ARL. Prob s/o Neil and Catherine M. To Kingston, ONT; stld Sydenham Twp. **DC 27 Jan 1978**.

5785 McDONALD, John. To Pictou, NS, on the *London*, arr 14 Jul 1848. Wife Una with him, and ch: 1. Catherine; 2. June; 3. Murdoch. **DC 15 Jul 1979**.

5786 McDONALD, John. From South Uist, INV. To East Williams Twp, Middlesex Co, ONT, 1848. **PCM 44**.

5787 McDONALD, John 'Roy'. From Is North Uist, INV. To East Williams Twp, Middlesex Co, ONT, 1849. **PCM 44**.

5788 McDONALD, John, b 1835. From Is South Uist, INV. s/o Lachlan M, qv, and Catherine McMillan, qv. To West Williams Twp, Middlesex Co, ONT, ca 1849. Deputy reeve. m Mary McIntyre, qv, ch: 1. Lachlan; 2. Catherine; 3. Ann; 4. Effie; 5. Mary. **PCM 48**.

5789 McDONALD, John, b 1794. From Is South Uist,

INV. s/o Allan M. To Richmond Co, NS, ca 1850. Son Ewen, qv. **DC 21 Mar 1981**.

5790 McDONALD, John. From Is South Uist, INV. To QUE on the *Admiral*, ex Lochboisdale, Aug 1851; stld ONT. **DC 21 Mar 1981**.

5791 MACDONALD, John, b ca 1832. From Uig, Is Lewis, ROC. s/o Alexander M, qv, and Mary MacIver, qv. To QUE, 1851; stld Winslow Twp, Compton Co. m Margaret McIver, and had, prob with other ch: 1. Margaret; 2. Nancy; 3. Effie; 4. Donald; 5. Evander; 6. Mary. **TFT 17**.

5792 MACDONALD, John. Prob from ARL. To Aldborough Twp, Elgin Co, ONT, 1851. **PDA 68**.

5793 MACDONALD, John, b ca 1845. From Eneclate, Uig, Is Lewis, ROC. s/o Donald M, qv, and Christy MacArthur Campbell, qv. To Winslow Twp, Compton Co, QUE, 1851. Shoemaker. Moved to Flitchburg, MA. m Christy Nicholson, Lingwick, ch: 1. Christy; 2. Ann Jane; 3. Murdena; 4. Kenneth; 5. Donald Rory. **TFT 13**.

5794 McDONALD, John, ca 1819–ca 1870. From Is Skye, INV. To Kinloss Twp, Bruce Co, ONT, <1852. m Ann McKinnon, qv, ch: 1. Angus, b 1848; 2. Norman, b 1849; 3. Mary; 4. Sarah; 5. Peter, b 1855; 6. Christie, b 1856; 7. Betty, b 1857; 8. Catherine, b 1858; 9. Ann, b 1860; 10. Isobella, b 1865; 11. John. **DC 12 Apr 1979**.

5795 McDONALD, John (1). From Is Lewis, ROC. To QUE, ex Stornoway, arr 4 Aug 1851; stld Huron Twp, Bruce Co, ONT, 1852. Head of family. **DC 5 Apr 1967**.

5796 McDONALD, John (2). From Is Lewis, ROC. To QUE, ex Stornoway, arr 4 Aug 1851; stld Huron Twp, Bruce Co, ONT, 1852. Head of family. **DC 5 Apr 1967**.

5797 McDONALD, John (3). From Is Lewis, ROC. To QUE, ex Stornoway, arr 4 Aug 1851; stld Huron Twp, Bruce Co, ONT, 1852. Head of family. **DC 5 Apr 1967**.

5798 McDONALD, John (4). From Is Lewis, ROC. To QUE, ex Stornoway, arr 4 Aug 1851; stld Huron Twp, Bruce Co, ONT, 1852. Head of family. **DC 5 Apr 1967**.

5799 McDONALD, John (5). From Is Lewis, ROC. To QUE, ex Stornoway, arr 4 Aug 1851; stld Huron Twp, Bruce Co, ONT, 1852. Head of family. **DC 5 Apr 1967**.

5800 McDONALD, John (6). From Is Lewis, ROC. To QUE, ex Stornoway, arr 4 Aug 1851; stld Huron Twp, Bruce Co, ONT, 1852. Head of family. **DC 5 Apr 1967**.

5801 McDONALD, John (7). From Is Lewis, ROC. To QUE, ex Stornoway, arr 4 Aug 1851; stld Huron Twp, Bruce Co, ONT, 1852. Head of family. **DC 5 Apr 1967**.

5802 McDONALD, John 'Dorie'. From Is Lewis, ROC. To QUE, ex Stornoway, arr 4 Aug 1851; stld Huron Twp, Bruce Co, ONT, 1852. Head of family. **DC 5 Apr 1967**.

5803 McDONALD, John, b ca 1819. From Snizort par, Is Skye, INV. To ONT, 1852; stld Kinloss Twp, Bruce Co, ONT. Wife Ann McKinnon, qv, with him, and ch: 1. Angus, b ca 1847; 2. Norman, b ca 1849; 3. Mary, b ca 1850; 4. Sarah, b ca 1851. **DC 6 Mar 1979**.

5804 MACDONALD, John. From Lochaber, INV. s/o Angus M, qv, and Mary Ann Rankin. To South West Mabou, Inverness Co, NS, 1854. m Sara,

d/o Donald MacDonald, ch: 1. Angus; 2. Mary; 3. Sara. **MP 585**.

5805 MACDONALD, John, 1795–1853. From Lochaber, INV. s/o Donald M, of the *Sliochd an Taighe*, Bohuntin, and Mary MacDonald. To South West Mabou, Inverness Co, NS, arr 31 Aug 1854. Gaelic poet. m Mary Forbes, no ch. **MP 581**.

5806 MACDONALD, John 'Mor'. From INV. s/o Roderick M, qv. To Port Hood, Inverness Co, NS, prob <1810. Farmer. m Catherine MacNeil, Little Judique, ch: 1. Alexander; 2. Hugh; 3. John; 4. William; 5. Christina; 6. Mary; 7. Margaret; 8. Anne. **MP 438**.

5807 MACDONALD, John 'Mor'. From Is Canna, INV. s/o Roderick M, qv. To Little Mabou, Inverness Co, NS, <1810; stld later at Mabou Harbour. m Isabel MacInnes, ch: 1. Angus; 2. Roderick; 3. Robert; 4. Charles; 5. Donald; 6. Alexander; 7. Mary; 8. Jane; 9. Elizabeth; 10. Anne; 11. Catherine; 12. Mary, jr. **MP 606**.

5808 MACDONALD, John 'Lord'. From Kinlochlaggan, INV. s/o John M, of the *Sliochd an Taighe*, Bohuntin, and Margaret Beaton. To Sydney, Cape Breton Co, NS, 1818; stld Margaree, Inverness Co. Innkeeper in SCT; farmer and landowner in NS. m Mary MacIntosh, qv, ch: 1. John, d unm; 2. Donald; 3. Angus; 4. Margaret; 5. Mary; 6. Theresa; 7. Catherine; 8. Jessie. **MP 493**.

5809 MACDONALD, John 'Mor'. From Lochaber, INV. To Inverness Co, NS, 1826; stld Black River. m Margaret MacDonald, qv, ch: 1. Hugh; 2. Archibald; 3. Dougald; 4. Angus; 5. Elizabeth; 6. Catherine. **MP 431**.

5810 MACDONALD, John 'Mor'. To Pictou Co, NS, <1830; stld Big Brook. Farmer. m Margaret MacMillan, Irish Mountain, ch: 1. John, b 1827; 2. Mary, b 1830; 3. Alexander; 4. Hannah; 5. Donald, b 1837; 6. Jane, b 1842; 7. Sarah, b 1846. **PAC 115**.

5811 MACDONALD, Sir John Alexander, 10 Jan 1815–6 Jun 1891. From Glasgow. s/o Hugh M, qv, and Ellen Shaw, qv. To QUE on the *Earl of Buckinghamshire*, ex Greenock, arr 20 Jun 1820; stld nr Kingston, ONT. Became lawyer and Conservative politician. First Premier of CAN, 1867-73, and re-elected in 1878. Principal architect of the Constitution and the driving force behind Intercolonial and Pacific Railways. GCB, 1866; DCL (Oxon), and LL.D. m (i) Isabella Clerk, qv, ch: 1. John Alexander, d 21 Sep 1848; 2. Hugh John, b 13 Mar 1850, Prime Min of MAN, 1900, QC, KB, 1913. Sir John m (ii) 16 Feb 1867, Susan Agnes, 1836–1920, (cr Baroness Macdonald of Earnscliffe, 1891), d/o Hon T.J. Bernard, PC, Jamaica, further ch: 3. Mary Theodora Margaret, 1869–1933. **BNA 544-599; IBD 323; CBD 615; MOT 9/678; MDB 440**.

5812 MACDONALD, John L, 1806–31 Jul 1889. From Is Skye, INV. To Cape Breton Co, NS; stld Groves Point, Little Bras d'Or. Wright, farmer and shipowner. m Janet MacLeod, qv, ch. **DC 29 Dec 1981**.

5813 McDONALD, John McIsaac. From Fort Augustus, INV. s/o Ranald McIsaac M, qv, and Janet Cameron, qv. To QUE on the *Tamerlane*, ex Greenock, 4 Jul 1831; stld Greenfield, Glengarry Co, ONT. Wife Margaret Macdonell, qv, with him, and ch: 1. John; 2. Nancy. **DC 14 Jun 1968**.

5814 McDONALD, Kate. From Uig, Is Lewis, ROC.

d/o Alexander M, qv, and Mary McIver, qv, To QUE, 1851; stld Winslow Twp, Compton Co. m Murdo McLeay, and had with other ch: 1. Alexander; 2. Annie; 3. Keith; 4. Katie, res Barre, VT; 5. Alexander Og; 6. Rory; 7. Christie.   **TFT 17.**

5815   McDONALD, Katherine. From Glengarry, INV. Prob rel to Angus M, labourer, qv. To Pictou, NS, on the *Sarah*, ex Fort William, Jun 1801. Spinster.   **PLS.**

5816   McDONALD, Katherine, ca 1815–17 Sep 1898. From Barvas, Is Lewis, ROC. To QUE, ex Stornoway, arr 4 Aug 1851; stld Huron Twp, Bruce Co, ONT. Wife of Donald McDonald, qv.   **DC 25 Dec 1981.**

5817   McDONALD, Kenneth. To Tatamagouche, Colchester Co, NS, <1829. Teacher.   **HT 69.**

5818   McDONALD, Kenneth. From Is Lewis, ROC. To QUE, ex Stornoway, arr 4 Aug 1851; stld Huron Twp, Bruce Co, ONT, 1852. Head of family.   **DC 5 Apr 1967.**

5819   McDONALD, Lachlan. From Arisaig, INV. To PEI on the *Jane*, ex Loch nan Uamh, Arisaig, 12 Jul 1790. Wife with him.   **PLJ.**

5820   McDONALD, Lachlan. From INV. To PEI on the *Lucy*, ex Loch nan Uamh, Arisaig, 12 Jul 1790. Wife with him, and 4 ch.   **PLJ.**

5821   McDONALD, Lachlan, b ca 1801. To Inverness Co, NS, 1804. Farmer, and stld nr Port Hood.   **CBC 1818.**

5822   MACDONALD, Lachlan. From Arisaig, INV. bro/o Alexander M, qv, and Angus M, qv. To Arisaig, Antigonish Co, NS, <1810; moved to East Bay, Cape Breton Co. ch.   **HCA 208.**

5823   MACDONALD, Lachlan. Prob from INV. To Antigonish Co, NS, prob <1810. m Mary, d/o John Mackinnon, qv, and Eunice MacLeod, qv, ch: 1. John; 2. Joseph; 3. Donald; 4. Ronald; 5. Roderick; 6. Angus; 7. Alexander; 8. Colin; 9. Lachlan; 10. Mary; 11. Margaret; 12. Florence; 13. Annie; 14. Kate.   **HCA 171.**

5824   MACDONALD, Lachlan. From Moidart, INV. s/o Hugh M. To Antigonish Co, NS, prob <1815. ch: 1. Ronald, res Cape Breton Is; 3. Angus, qv.   **HCA 172.**

5825   MACDONALD, Lachlan. From Moidart, INV. To Antigonish Co, NS, prob <1820. m Mary Mackinnon, ch: 1. John; 2. Donald; 3. Angus; 4. Alexander; 5. Colin; 6. Joseph; 7. Lachlan; 8. Mary; 9. Flora; 10. Kate; 11. Ann.   **HCA 179.**

5826   MACDONALD, Lachlan, b 1815. From Is Skye, INV. s/o John M, qv, and Janet MacLeod, qv. To Cape Breton Is, NS, 1827. m Margaret Matheson, qv, ch.   **DC 23 Feb 1980.**

5827   MACDONALD, Lachlan. Prob from INV. s/o Donald M. To Antigonish Co, NS, <1830. m Miss Gillis. Son Donald, res Frasers Mills.   **HCA 211.**

5828   MACDONALD, Lachlan. Prob from INV. To Antigonish Co, NS, prob <1840. ch: 1. Hugh; 2. Kate; 3. Hugh; 4. Ronald; 5. Angus; 6. Alexander; 7. John; 8. Lachlan; 9. Mary.   **HCA 208.**

5829   McDONALD, Lachlan, ca 1800–ca 1879. From Bornish, Is South Uist, INV. To West Williams Twp,

Middlesex Co, ONT, ca 1849. m Catherine McMillan, qv, ch: 1. Ann, b 1830; 2. Mary, b 1832; 3. John, qv; 4. Margaret, b 1837; 5-6. Donald and Catherine, twins, b 1837; 7. Donald, b 1844; 8. Angus, b 1847.   **PCM 48; WLC.**

5830   MACDONALD, Lachlan. From Kilmuir, Is Skye, INV. To Margaree, Inverness Co, NS, <1850. Son John Archie, b 1851, lawyer and MLA.   **MLA 207.**

5831   McDONALD, Lauchlan. From Moidart, INV. To Pictou, NS, on the *Dove*, ex Fort William, Jun 1801. Tenant.   **PLD.**

5832   MACDONALD, Lewis. From INV. To Arisaig, Antigonish Co, NS, poss <1800. Pioneer settler. m Mary Grant, ch: 1. Donald; 2. John; 3. James; 4. Sandy; 5. Colin; 6. Ann; 7. Peggy; 8. Janet or Jessie; 9. Christina.   **HCA 241; MP 693.**

5833   MACDONALD, Lucy or Louisa. From Is Barra, INV. d/o Neil M. To Inverness Co, NS, 1831; stld West Lake Ainslie. Wife of Angus 'Og' MacInnis, qv.   **MP 660.**

5834   McDONALD, Ludovick. From Saunister, South Morar, INV. To PEI on the *Jane*, ex Loch nan Uamh, Arisaig, 12 Jul 1790. Wife with him, and 2 ch.   **PLJ.**

5835   MACDONALD, Maggie. From Uig, Is Lewis, ROC. d/o Alexander M, qv, and Mary MacIver, qv. To Winslow Twp, Compton Co, QUE, 1851. m John Murray, Granitville, VT, ch: 1. Mary; 2. Katie; 3. Maggie; 4. Alexander; 5. Rory; 6. Murdo; 7. Donald.   **TFT 17.**

5836   MACDONALD, Malcolm. Prob from Knoydart, INV. To Antigonish Co, NS, <1800; stld Knoydart.   **HCA 13.**

5837   MACDONALD, Malcolm. From Is Canna, INV. s/o Roderick M, qv. To Little Mabou, Inverness Co, NS, prob <1810. m Mary, d/o Hugh Gillis, qv, ch: 1. Hugh; 2. Roderick; 3. James; 4. Angus; 5. Mary; 6. Anne; 7. Catherine; 8. Elizabeth.   **MP 358; 610.**

5838   McDONALD, Malcolm. From Is Tyree, ARL. s/o John M. To Glengarry Co, ONT, <1820.   **DC 23 Feb 1980.**

5839   McDONALD, Malcolm. From Is Skye, INV. To PEI, 1831. ch: 1. Donald, qv; 2. John; 3. Alexander.   **DC 11 Sep 1960.**

5840   McDONALD, Malcolm, ca 1810–8 Feb 1890. From Uig, Snizort, Is Skye, INV. To Victoria Co, NS, 1841. m Flora Campbell, qv.   **DC 22 Jun 1979.**

5841   MACDONALD, Malcolm, b 1811. From Dunganichy, Is Benbecula, INV. s/o John and Mary M. To Pictou, NS, on the *Lulan*, ex Glasgow, 17 Aug 1848. m Ann MacDonald, qv, ch: 1. Ronald, b 1837; 2. Donald, b 1839; 3. Christina, b 1841; 4. Mary; 5. John.   **DC 12 Jul 1979; WLC.**

5842   McDONALD, Malcolm. From Is Lewis, INV. To QUE, ex Stornoway, arr 4 Aug 1851; stld Huron Twp, Bruce Co, ONT, 1852. Head of family.   **DC 5 Apr 1967.**

5843   McDONALD, Malcolm, 1808–24 Dec 1899. From Is Lewis, ROC. To QUE, ex Stornoway, arr 4 Aug 1851; stld Huron Twp, Bruce Co, ONT. Farmer, Lot 23, Con 8. Wife Annie with him. ch: 1. Jessie; 2. Margaret; 3. Mary; 4. Angus, 1847–1905; 5. John, 1851–1929; 6. Murdock, 1854–1931.   **DC 22 Jul 1982.**

5844 MACDONALD, Marcella. From Lochaber, INV. d/o Archibald M. and Anne MacDonald, qv. To Arisaig, Antigonish Co, NS, 1818. m Alexander McInnis, Upper West Lake, ch: 1. Duncan; 2. Alexander; 3. Hugh; 4. Marcella; 5. Catherine; 6. Anne. **MP 553**.

5845 McDONALD, Margaret. From INV. To Arisaig, Antigonish Co, NS, 1790. Wife of John MacDonald, qv. **HCA 218**.

5846 McDONALD, Margaret, b ca 1763. From PER. To Pictou, NS, on the *Commerce*, ex Port Glasgow, 10 Aug 1803. **PLC**.

5847 McDONALD, Margaret. From Anderston, Glasgow. To QUE, ex Greenock, summer 1815; stld prob Lanark Co, ONT. Wife of Donald MacPherson, qv. **SEC 8**.

5848 McDONALD, Margaret. From Edinburgh. To QUE on the *Atlas*, ex Greenock, 11 Jul 1815; stld North Burgess Twp, Lanark Co, ONT. Wife of James McDonald, qv. **SEC 1**.

5849 MACDONALD, Margaret. From Lochaber, INV. d/o Archibald M. and Anne MacDonald, qv. To Arisaig, Antigonish Co, NS, 1816; moved to Inverness Co, 1818. m John 'Mor' MacDonald, qv. **MP 431, 553**.

5850 MACDONALD, Margaret. From INV. d/o Roderick M, qv. To Port Hood, Inverness Co, NS, prob <1820. m Finlay MacDonald, qv. **MP 440**.

5851 MACDONALD, Margaret. From Lochaber, INV. To Inverness Co, NS, ca 1822; stld Glencoe. Wife of Angus MacDonald, qv. **MP 484**.

5852 MACDONALD, Margaret. From Geirinish, Is South Uist, INV. d/o Duncan M. and Mary MacIntyre. To Pictou, NS, on the *Lulan*, ex Glasgow, 17 Aug 1848. Wife of Allan Black, qv. **DC 12 Jul 1979**.

5853 MACDONALD, Margaret. From Is Lewis, ROC. To Scotch Hill, Brompton Twp, Richmond Co, QUE, ca 1850. m Kenneth Mackenzie, qv. **DC 14 Apr 1981**.

5854 MACDONALD, Margaret J, 14 Oct 1784–30 May 1870. From Lochaber, INV. d/o Capt Angus M. of Tulloch, Glen Spean, and Margaret MacDonald. To Mabou Coal Mines, Inverness Co, NS, ca 1807. Wife of Donald MacDonald, qv. **MP 457**.

5855 McDONALD, Margery. From Aberchalder, INV. To PEI on the *Jane*, ex Loch nan Uamh, Arisaig, 12 Jul 1790. **PLJ**.

5856 McDONALD, Marion, b 1753. From INV. d/o Donald M, qv. To Pictou, NS, on the *Hector*, ex Loch Broom, arr 17 Sep 1773. m Alexander Fraser, sr, Middle River. **HPC App C**.

5857 McDONALD, Marion. From Ross, Is Mull, ARL. sis/o Mary M, qv. To Lochaber, Ottawa Co, QUE, 1831. Wife of Duncan McEachern, qv. **ELB 3**.

5858 MACDONALD, Marion, b 1820. From Uskavagh, Is Benbecula, INV. d/o James M. and Kirsty Ferguson. To Pictou, NS, on the *Lulan*, ex Glasgow, 17 Aug 1848. Wife of Angus MacPhee, qv. **DC 12 Jul 1979**.

5859 MACDONALD, Martin. From Knoydart, INV. To Halifax, NS, 1787; stld Knoydart, Antigonish Co. ch: 1. John, qv; 2. Martin, jr, qv. **HCA 177**.

5860 MACDONALD, Martin, jr. From Knoydart, INV. s/o Martin M, qv. To Halifax, NS, 1787; stld Knoydart, Antigonish Co. ch: 1. Hugh; 2. Donald; 3. Ronald; 4. Angus; 5. Mary; 6. John; 7. Flora. **HCA 177**.

5861 McDONALD, Mary. From INV. To Pictou, NS, on the *Hector*, ex Loch Broom, arr 17 Sep 1773. Wife of Donald Cameron, qv. **HPC App C**.

5862 McDONALD, Mary. From Ardnafouran, Arisaig, INV. To PEI on the *Jane*, ex Loch nan Uamh, Arisaig, 12 Jul 1790. **PLJ**.

5863 McDONALD, Mary. From Arisaig, INV. Prob wife of John M, qv. To Pictou, NS, on the *Dove*, ex Fort William, Jun 1801. **PLD**.

5864 McDONALD, Mary. From Lochaber, INV. To Pictou, NS, on the *Dove*, ex Fort William, Jun 1801. Spinster. **PLJ**.

5865 MACDONALD, Mary, 1758–9 Apr 1857. From Sartill, Is Skye, INV. d/o Capt Soirle M. and first wife. To Orwell Bay, PEI, on the *Polly*, ex Portree, arr 7 Aug 1803; stld Queens Co. Wife of Rev Aneas MacAulay, qv. **HP 72; CMM 3/22 80**.

5866 McDONALD, Mary, b 1777. From Is Tyree, ARL. To QUE on the *Oughton*, arr Jul 1804; stld Baldoon, Dover Twp, Kent Co, ONT. Wife of Allan McLean, qv. **UCM 267, 302; DC 4 Oct 1979**.

5867 MACDONALD, Mary. From Glenspean, INV. d/o Allan M, desc from the Morar family. To West Lake Ainslie, Inverness Co, NS, 1807. Wife of Angus MacDonald, qv. **HCA 199**.

5868 MACDONALD, Mary. From INV. Said rel to the family of Glenaladale. To Mabou Coal Mines, Inverness Co, NS, ca 1809. Wife of Neil MacPhee, qv. **MP 773**.

5869 MACDONALD, Mary. From Tulloch, Glenspean, INV. d/o Capt Angus M. of Tulloch, and Margaret MacDonald. To Mabou, Inverness Co, NS, poss <1810. m John Beaton, qv. **HCA 199; MP 191, 595**.

5870 MACDONALD, Mary, ca 1762–1832. From Is Iona, ARL. d/o Donald M. To Vaughan Twp, York Co, ONT, poss <1815. m Neil McKay. **DC 24 Jan 1977**.

5871 MACDONALD, Mary. From Lochaber, INV. d/o Archibald M. and Anne MacDonald, qv. To Arisaig, Antigonish Co, NS, 1816. m there Hugh MacDonald, ch: 1. Alexander; 2. Donald; 3. Archibald; 4. Angus; 5. Stephen; 6. Margaret; 7. Mary; 8. Anne. **MP 553**.

5872 MACDONALD, Mary. From Lochaber, INV. d/o Alexander 'Ruadh' M, qv, and Mary Campbell, qv. To Mabou Ridge, Inverness Co, NS, 1816. m Malcolm, s/o Samuel Campbell, qv. **MP 544**.

5873 MACDONALD, Mary, 1786–1875. From Is Skye, INV. d/o — M. and — Douglas. To QUE on the *Young Norval*, ex Greenock, Apr 1820; stld Caledon Twp, Peel Co, ONT. **DC 19 Nov 1981**.

5874 MACDONALD, Mary. From INV. Desc from the Borrodale family. To Port Hood, Inverness Co, NS, prob <1820. m — MacLeod, Antigonish Co. Son Rev William. **MP 440**.

5875 MACDONALD, Mary. From INV. d/o Ronald M. To Mabou Ridge, Inverness Co, NS, ca 1822. Wife of Alexander 'Taillear' MacInnis, qv. **MP 654**.

5876 MACDONALD, Mary. From Lochaber, INV. d/o Angus M, qv, and Margaret MacDonald, qv. To Inverness Co, NS, ca 1822; stld Glencoe. m John 'Cannach' MacDonald, qv. **MP 442, 191**.

5877 MACDONALD, Mary. From Is South Uist, INV. d/o Allan M, qv, and Mary MacLean, qv. To Cape Breton Co, NS, 1823; moved to Whycocomagh, Inverness Co. m Murdock Mackinnon. **DC 23 Feb 1980**.

5878 McDONALD, Mary. From Is Skye, INV. d/o 'Tall' M. To Charlottetown, PEI, on the *Mary Kennedy*, ex Portree, arr Jun 1829. Wife of Donald Gordon, qv. **DC 21 Oct 1978**.

5879 MACDONALD, Mary. From Is Barra, INV. To River Denny, Cape Breton Is, NS, <1830. m Allan MacDonald, qv. **HNS iii 635**.

5880 MACDONALD, Mary. From Moidart, INV. d/o Hugh M. To Antigonish Co, NS, <1830. m Alexander Smith, Baileys Brook. **HCA 259**.

5881 MACDONALD, Mary. From Brae-Lochaber, INV. d/o Alexander 'Dubh' M. To Hillsborough, Inverness Co, NS, 1831. Wife of John MacDonald, qv. **MP 413**.

5882 McDONALD, Mary. From Ross, Is Mull, ARL. To QUE, 1831; stld Lochaber, Ottawa Co. m Robert McLachlan, qv. **ELB 3**.

5883 McDONALD, Mary, 1781–1865. From ARL. To Caledon Twp, Peel Co, ONT, <1840. Wife of Duncan McGillivray, qv. **DC 21 Apr 1980**.

5884 MACDONALD, Mary. From Glen Roy, Kilmonivaig par, INV. To Antigonish Co, NS, prob <1840. m Allan MacDonald. **HCA 209**.

5885 MACDONALD, Mary. From Lochaber, INV. sis/o Allan 'Dhu' M, qv. To Antigonish Co, NS, prob <1840. m Donald MacDonald, Glen Ray. **HCA 201**.

5886 MACDONALD, Mary, 1826-67. From Killearnan, ROC. d/o Murdoch M, qv, and Mary Cameron, qv. To Ashfield Twp, Huron Co, ONT, 1842. m Alexander McKenzie, qv. **DC 15 Jul 1979**.

5887 MACDONALD, Mary. From INV. d/o Duncan M, from Is Canna. To Broad Cove Banks, Inverness Co, NS, prob <1840. m John, s/o Duncan MacArthur, qv. **MP 381, 484**.

5888 McDONALD, Mary. From Uachdar, Is Benbecula, INV. To East Williams Twp, Middlesex Co, ONT, 1848. Wife of Donald 'Beg' McCormack, qv. **WLC**.

5889 MACDONALD, Mary. From Uig, Is Lewis, ROC. d/o Alexander M, qv, and Mary McIver, qv. To Winslow Twp, Compton Co, QUE, 1851. m Donald Smith, glover, VT, ch. **TFT 17**.

5890 McDONALD, Mary, b 1832. From Is Mull, ARL. d/o Malcolm M. and Flora Livingstone. To Minto Twp, Wellington Co, ONT, <1854. Wife of Peter McDougall, qv. **DC 30 Jul 1979**.

5891 McDONALD, Mary. From Laggan, INV. d/o Duncan M. and Katharine McDonald. To ONT, <1860; stld prob Peel Co, ONT. m David Kirkwood, ch. **DC 17 Nov 1981**.

5892 MACDONALD, Michael. From INV. To PEI <1774, and moved to Indian Point, Judique, Inverness

Co, NS. Pioneer settler, trader, ship-owner and poet. m sis/o Bishop Angus Bernard MacEachen, qv. Son Hugh. **MP 21; DC 5 Feb 1961**.

5893 McDONALD, Michael, 1816–1910. Poss from DFS. s/o John M. To Cape Breton Is, NS, stld Boisdale. m Catherine, d/o Alexander McDonald, qv, East Bay. Son Joseph, b 1863, lawyer. **HNS iii 205**.

5894 MACDONALD, Murdoch. From Is Skye, INV. s/o John M, qv, and Janet MacLeod, qv. To Cape Breton Is, NS, 1827, and d at Margaree, Inverness Co. m Mary Ingram, ch. **DC 23 Feb 1980**.

5895 MACDONALD, Murdoch, ca 1793–ca 1880. From Killearnan, ROC. To Ashfield Twp, Huron Co, ONT, 1845. m Mary Cameron, qv, ch: 1. Donald, b 1824, unm; 2. Mary, qv; 3. Ann, b 1 Aug 1833, unm; 4. Margaret, b ca 1836. **DC 15 Jul 1979**.

5896 McDONALD, Murdoch. To Pictou, NS, on the *London*, arr 14 Jul 1848. **DC 15 Jul 1979**.

5897 McDONALD, Murdock. To PEI, poss 1803; stld Queens Co. Petitioner for Dr MacAulay, 1811. **HP 74**.

5898 McDONALD, Murdock. From Is Lewis, INV. To QUE, ex Stornoway, arr 4 Aug 1851; stld Huron Twp, Bruce Co, ONT, 1852. Head of family. **DC 5 Apr 1967**.

McDONALD, Mrs. See CARMICHAEL, Mary.

5899 McDONALD, Nancy, ca 1780–8 Sep 1867. From INV. To Colchester Co, NS, 1801; later to Milltown, Pictou Co. Bur Old Elgin. Wife of Donald Gray, qv. **PAC 97; DC 20 Nov 1976**.

5900 MACDONALD, Neil. From Is Skye, INV. To Glengarry Co, ONT, <1812. Surveyor. **MG 394**.

5901 MACDONALD, Neil. From Is Barra, INV. s/o Iain 'Og' M. To Mabou, Inverness Co, NS, prob <1820. Wife Emily MacMillan, qv, with him. ch: 1. John; 2. Archibald; 3. Lucy; 4. Mary; 5. Catherine; 6. Jessie; 7. Jane. **MP 414**.

5902 MACDONALD, Neil, b 11 Sep 1793. From Kintyre, ARL. s/o John M. and Margaret MacAllister. To York Co, ONT, 1831, ex Campbeltown; stld Sutton. Farmer. m Betty McSporran, qv, ch: 1. Betty, b 1819; 2. Mary, b 1820; 3. Jean, b 1822; 4. Neil, b 1824; 5. Peggy, b 1826; 6. Katharine, b 1826; 7. John, b 1830; 8. Alexander, b 1833; 9. Annie, b 1838; 10. Susan, b 1841. **DC 3 Mar 1982**.

5903 MACDONALD, Neil. From INV. s/o Duncan M, from Is Canna. To Foot Cape, Broad Cove Banks, Inverness Co, NS, prob <1840. Mason. Son Duncan. **MP 476**.

5904 McDONALD, Neil, ca 1797–8 Mar 1893. From SUT. To NS, poss <1840; stld Central North River, Colchester Co. Wife Janet, 1817–23 Sep 1884. ch: 1. Robert, b 1845, d inf; 2. Roderick, 1848-60; 3. William, 1850-65; 4. Kenneth, 1851–1921; 5. Mary Margaret, 1859–1928. **DC 19 Mar 1981**.

5905 MACDONALD, Norman, 1799–1886. From South Uist, INV. s/o Allan M, qv, and Mary MacLean, qv. To Cape Breton Is, NS, 1823; moved to Stewartdale, Whycocomagh, Inverness Co. m Catherine Morrison, qv, ch: 1. Hugh; 2. Allan; 3. Alexia; 4. Margaret Ann; 5. Susan; 6. Catherine; 7. Mary; 8. Mary; 9. Annie; 10. John. **NSN 30/302; DC 23 Feb 1980**.

5906 MACDONALD, Norman. From Paible, Is North Uist, INV. To Cape Breton Co, NS, on the *Commerce*, ex Loch Maddy, 1 Aug 1828; Enon, Loch Lomond. m Miss McVicar. **DC 21 Mar 1981**.

5907 MACDONALD, Norman Donald, 1840–1925. From Eneclate, Uig, Is Lewis, ROC. s/o Donald M, qv, and Christy MacArthur Campbell, qv. To Winslow Twp, Compton Co, QUE, 1851. Farmer. m (i) 1867, Annie Smith, ch: 1. Donald, 1868-73; 2. Annie, b 1869; m (ii) 1872, Catherine MacLeod, qv, further ch: 3. Murdo Alexander; 4. Mary Bella; 5. Donald John, 1877-82; 6. Roderick M, 1879-82; 7. Christy Ann, b 1881; 8. Rev Malcolm Norman, family historian; 9. Arthur, d 1929; 10. John Angus, d 1900; 11. Catherine Ann. **TFT 15**.

5908 McDONALD, Patrick. From Urquhart, INV. To Pictou, NS, on the *Sarah*, ex Fort William, Jun 1801. Labourer. **PLS**.

5909 McDONALD, Paul. From Urquhart, INV. To Pictou, NS, on the *Sarah*, ex Fort William, Jun 1801. Farmer. Wife Ann with him, and ch: 1. John, aged 10; 2. Donald, aged 8; 3. Margaret, aged 6; 4. Alexander, aged 4. **PLS**.

5910 McDONALD, Paul. From SUT. To Colchester Co, NS, <1820; stld nr Earltown. Farmer. **HT 43**.

5911 McDONALD, Peter, d 1805. To QUE on the *Oughton*, arr Jul 1804; stld Baldoon, Dover Twp, Kent Co, ONT. Farmer. Wife Mary with him, and ch: 1. John, b 1791; 2. David, b 1793; 3. Peter, b 1798. **UCM 267, 302; DC 4 Oct 1979**.

5912 MACDONALD, Peter. From Is Islay, ARL. To ONT prob <1865; stld Lot 18, Con 8, Huron Twp, Bruce Co. Farmer. m Elizabeth Hamilton, qv, ch: 1. Daniel; 2. Robert; 3. Alexander; 4. Francis; 5. Mary Ann. **DC 25 Dec 1981**.

5913 McDONALD, Ranald. From Retland, South Morar, INV. To PEI on the *Jane*, ex Loch nan Uamh, Arisaig, 12 Jul 1790. Wife with him, and an inf. **PLJ**.

5914 McDONALD, Ranald, b ca 1782. To Port Hood dist, Inverness Co, NS, 1798. Farmer. m and ch. **CBC 1818**.

5915 McDONALD, Ranald, b ca 1795. To Inverness Co, NS, 1804; stld Port Hood. Trader, unm. **CBC 1818**.

5916 McDONALD, Ranald, b ca 1799. To Inverness Co, NS, 1816. Farmer, unm. **CBC 1818**.

5917 MACDONALD, Ranald, b 12 Jul 1788. From Lochaber, INV. s/o Capt Angus M. of Tulloch, and Margaret MacDonald. Served in 72nd Regt. Gr land at West Lake Ainslie, Inverness Co, NS, 1822. Sold out later and went to PEI. **MP 588**.

5918 McDONALD, Ranald. From Laggan, INV. s/o Donald M. To ONT <1840; stld prob Peel Co. m Lillie Lawson, ch: 1. Ann; 2. Donald; 3. Lillie; 4. Mary; 5. Margaret; 6. Graham; 7. Allan. **DC 17 Nov 1981**.

5919 McDONALD, Ranald McIsaac, b 1754. From Fort Augustus, INV. To Greenfield, Kenyon Twp, Glengarry Co, ONT, 1837. Farmer. m Janet Cameron, qv, ch: 1. Hugh; 2. Alexander; 3. Ranald J. McIsaac; 4. Jane; 5. Ellen; 6. John McIsaac, qv. **DC 14 Jun 1968**.

5920 McDONALD, Robert, ca 1786–23 Nov 1835. From SUT. To Pictou Co, NS, 1802. Bur Lansdowne. Schoolteacher. ch. **DC 10 Feb 1980**.

5921 McDONALD, Robert. Prob from Duthill, INV. To London Twp, Middlesex Co, ONT, 1840; moved to West Williams Twp, 1850. **PCM 47**.

5922 MACDONALD, Robert. From Dornoch, SUT. To Halifax, NS, poss <1840. Wife Catherine Gray, qv, with him. Son Charles John, 1841–1903, lawyer and MLA. **MLA 201**.

5923 MACDONALD, Robert. Poss from INV. bro/o Hugh M, qv. To Morristown, Antigonish Co, NS, prob <1840. **HCA 233**.

5924 MACDONALD, Robert, ca 1821–12 Dec 1848. From Crossmichael, KKD. To Richibucto, Kent Co, NB, and d at Galloway. **DGH 11 Jan 1849**.

5925 McDONALD, Roderick. To St John, PEI, on the *Alexander*, ex Arisaig and South Uist, May 1772. Physician. **SG vii/4 15**.

5926 McDONALD, Roderick. From Glenuig, Moidart, INV. To PEI on the *Jane*, ex Loch nan Uamh, Arisaig, 12 Jul 1790. Wife with him, and 4 ch. **PLJ**.

5927 McDONALD, Roderick. From Kyles, Morar, INV. To PEI on the *Lucy*, ex Loch nan Uamh, Arisaig, 12 Jul 1790. Wife with him. **PLL**.

5928 McDONALD, Roderick, b ca 1786. To Western Shore, Inverness Co, NS, 1802. Farmer, m and ch. **CBC 1818**.

5929 MACDONALD, Roderick. From INV. Desc from the family of Borrodale. To Port Hood, Inverness Co, NS, prob <1810. ch: 1. John 'Mor', qv; 2. Alexander 'Mor', qv; 3. Margaret, qv. **MP 438**.

5930 MACDONALD, Roderick. From Is Canna, INV. s/o Donald M. To Little Mabou, Inverness Co, NS, prob <1810. ch: 1. Donald, qv; 2. John, qv; 3. Malcolm, qv. **MP 604**.

5931 MACDONALD, Roderick, b ca 1810. From Scorraig, Little Loch Broom, ROC. s/o John M. and Mary Ross McIver. To Pictou, NS, 1830; later to Woodstock, Oxford Co, ONT. **DC 21 Mar 1981**.

5932 MACDONALD, Roderick, 1 Dec 1812–1 Feb 1894. From Harris, INV. To Pictou Co, NS, 1841; stld Gairloch Mountain. Farmer. m Rachel Nicholson, qv, ch. **DC 21 Mar 1981**.

5933 McDONALD, Roderick. From Is Benbecula, INV. To East Williams Twp, Middlesex Co, ONT, 1848. **PCM 44**.

5934 McDONALD, Roderick. From Barvas, Is Lewis, ROC. To QUE, ex Stornoway, arr 4 Aug 1851; stld Lot 27E, Con 8, Huron Twp, Bruce Co, ONT. Farmer. Wife Henrietta McLay, qv, with him. ch: 1. Isabelle; 2. Margaret; 3. John; 4. Colin; 5. Annie, dy; 6. Donald, 1885–1946; 7. Henrietta; 8. Roderick; 9. Annie; 10. Norman. **DC 25 Dec 1981**.

5935 MACDONALD, Ronald. From Moidart, INV. s/o James 'Baillie' M. To Antigonish Co, NS, ca 1784; stld nr Arisaig, but went later to Judique, Inverness Co. ch: 1. John, res Rear Judique Banks; 2. Ronald; 3. Donald; 4. James; 5. Alexander; 6. Mary. **DC 30 Mar 1981**.

5936 McDONALD, Ronald. To Glengarry Co, ONT, 1794; stld Lot 36, Con 15, Lancaster Twp. **MG 56**.

5937 McDONALD, Ronald. Poss from INV. To Delaware Twp, Middlesex Co, ONT, 1798. Pioneer settler, and formerly officer, British Army. **PCM 57**.

5938 McDONALD, Ronald, b ca 1766. To Western Shore, Inverness Co, NS, 1800. Farmer, m and ch. **CBC 1818**.

5939 MACDONALD, Ronald. From Arisaig, INV. To Pictou, NS, on the *Dove*, ex Fort William, Jun 1801. Farmer. Wife Katherine with him, and ch: 1. John, aged 6; 2. Janet, aged 3. **PLD**.

5940 MACDONALD, Ronald. Prob from INV. s/o Donald M. To Antigonish Co, NS, prob <1810. ch: 1. John; 2. Lachlan; 3. Donald; 4. Rory. **HCA 227**.

5941 MACDONALD, Ronald 'Saor'. Prob from INV. To Antigonish Co, NS, <1815; later to Margaree, Inverness Co. m Sara Beaton, qv, ch: 1. Angus; 2. Alexander; 3. Finlay; 4. James; 5. Donald; 6. Mary; 7. Flora; 8. Margaret; 9. Rachel; 10. Jessie. **MP 213, 508**.

5942 MACDONALD, Ronald 'Diolladair'. From Lochaber, INV. s/o Archibald M. and Anne MacDonald, qv. To Arisaig, Antigonish Co, NS, 1816; moved to Inverness Co, 1818. m Catherine MacDonald, qv, ch: 1. Archibald; 2. Allan; 3. Elizabeth; 4. Mary; 5. Margaret; 6. Alexander. **MP 547**.

5943 McDONALD, Ronald, b ca 1788. To St Andrews dist, Cape Breton Co, NS, prob arr Apr 1817. **CBC 1818**.

5944 McDONALD, Ronald. From Is Tyree, ARL. s/o Hugh M, qv, and Ann Campbell, qv. To Lake Ainslie, Inverness Co, NS, 1820. m (i) Sarah McDonald; (ii) Sarah Mackinnon. **DC 23 Feb 1980**.

5945 MACDONALD, Ronald, b ca 1826. Prob from INV. s/o Archibald M, qv. To Mira, Cape Breton Co, NS, <1830. Farmer. m Sarah MacPherson. Son Angus Ronald, b 1866, res Glace Bay. **HNS iii 200**.

5946 MACDONALD, Ronald. Prob from INV. bro/o Donald M, qv, Hector M, qv, and John M, qv. To Mount Young, Mabou, Inverness Co, NS, <1830. m Miss Mackay, Judique, ch: 1. John; 2. Peter; 3. Mary; 4. Anne; 5. Sheila; 6. Sara; 7. Catherine. **MP 504**.

5947 MACDONALD, Ronald 'Ban'. From Lochaber, INV. s/o Alexander 'Mor' M. and Isabel Campbell. To Mabou, Inverness Co, NS, ca 1832. m (i) Mary, d/o Donald Beaton, no ch; (ii) Elizabeth, d/o John Beaton, qv, Mull River, and Ellen Whitehead, ch: 1. Alexander; 2. Malcolm; 3. John; 4. James; 5. Daniel; 6. Angus; 7. Angus Og; 8. Isabel. **HCA 194; MP 500**.

5948 MACDONALD, Ronald. From Moidart, INV. bro/o Annie M, qv. To Monkshead, Antigonish Co, NS, 1842. ch: 1. Angus; 2. John; 3. Ronald; 4. Mary; 5. Flora; 6. Fanny. **HCA 183, 256**.

5949 McDONALD, Ronald. To Pictou, NS, on the *Lulan*, ex Glasgow, 17 Aug 1848. Family with him: 1. Donald; 2. Mary; 3. Peggy. **DC 15 Jul 1979**.

5950 McDONALD, Ronald. From Is South Uist, INV. To East Williams Twp, Middlesex Co, ONT, ca 1849. Tailor. **PCM 44**.

5951 MACDONALD, Ronald, ca 1815–10 Jun 1904. From Is Skye, INV. To Victoria Co, NS. m Marcella McPhee, qv, ch: 1. Donald R, 1853–1934; 2. Mary, 1855–1910; 3. Marcella, 1879–1924. **DC 22 Jun 1979**.

5952 MACDONALD, Ronald, 29 Mar 1824–20 Dec 1879. From Kilmuir, Is Skye, INV. To Victoria Co, NS. Wife Mary d 7 Jul 1918. ch incl: 1. Angus, 1857-85; 2. Katie, 1859-84; 3. Annabel, 1865-83; 4. Kenneth, 1874-83. **DC 22 Jun 1979**.

5953 MACDONALD, Rory. From Moidart, INV. s/o Donald M. To Pictou, NS, ca 1784; moved to Judique, Inverness Co, 1799. Farmer, m and ch. **CBC 1818; DC 30 Mar 1981**.

5954 McDONALD, Rory. From Kilmorack, INV. To Pictou, NS, on the *Sarah*, ex Fort William, Jun 1801. Labourer. **PLS**.

5955 McDONALD, Rory. From Urquhart, INV. To Pictou, NS, on the *Sarah*, ex Fort William, Jun 1801. Tenant. Wife Mary with him, and ch: 1. Catherine; 2. Janet. **PLS**.

5956 MACDONALD, Rory 'Beg'. From INV. To South River, Antigonish Co, NS, prob <1820. m Sarah, d/o Angus MacPherson, qv, ch: 1. Ronald; 2. Alexander; 3. John. **HCA 221, 345**.

5957 MACDONALD, Samuel C. To PEI on the *John Walker*, 1826; stld Dundas, Kings Co. **DC 1 Oct 1960**.

5958 MACDONALD, Sarah. From Is Mull, ARL. Prob d/o Neil and Catherine M. To Sydenham dist, Kingston, ONT, ca 1847. **DC 27 Jan 1978**.

5959 McDONALD, Suibhné, d ca 1863. To Dumfries Twp, Waterloo Co, ONT, <1836. Known as 'Sweden' M, roadmaker. m Alice Bell, qv, and had with other ch: 1. Robert S.; 2. William. **HGD 115; DC 26 Sep 1981**.

5960 MACDONALD, Susan. From Is South Uist, INV. d/o Allan M, qv, and Mary MacLean, qv. To Cape Breton Co, NS, 1823; moved to Whycocomagh, Inverness Co. m Malcolm MacLeod. **DC 23 Feb 1980**.

5961 McDONALD, Thomas, b ca 1778. To Port Hood dist, Inverness Co, NS, 1810. Farmer, m and ch. **CBC 1818**.

5962 McDONALD, Thomas 'Deacon', b ca 1794. bro/o Alexander M, qv, Big Brook. To Pictou Co, NS, <1815; stld Big Brook, west branch of East River. Farmer and sawyer. m Annie Fraser, ch: 1. John, b 1833; 2. Jane, b 1835; 3. William, b 1837; 4. Alexander, called 'Sandy Tom', b 1839. **PAC 12**.

5963 McDONALD, Thomas. From Kilmorack, INV. To Pictou, NS, on the *Sarah*, ex Fort William, Jun 1801. Labourer. Wife Janet with him. **PLS**.

5964 MACDONALD, Thomas, ca 1817–17 Jan 1859. To ONT. Secretary of the Trust & Loan Co. of Upper Canada. **DGH 28 Jan 1859**.

5965 McDONALD, Thomas, 1822–1922. To Pictou Co, NS; stld Middle River. Farmer. m Catherine McLeod, Wilkins Grant, ch: 1. Daniel, 1852-75; 2. William, 1854–1926; 3. Annie, d 1876; 4. Angus, 1857–1953; 5. Jessie; 6. John William, 1860–1933; 7. James Thomas, 1866-68. **PAC 116**.

5966 McDONALD, William. From Urquhart, INV. To

Pictou, NS, on the *Sarah*, ex Fort William, Jun 1801. Labourer. **PLS**.

5967   McDONALD, William. From Kiltarlity, INV. To Pictou, NS, on the *Sarah*, ex Fort William, Jun 1801. Wife Janet with him, and ch: 1. Mary, aged 13; 2. Ann, aged 10; 3. John, aged 8; 4. Catherine, aged 5; 5. Henry, aged 3; 6. inf.   **PLS**.

5968   McDONALD, William, 1750–23 Jul 1851. From Creich par, SUT. To NS, 1801. Bur Salt Springs, Pictou Co. m Catherine Campbell, qv.   **DC 22 Jun 1980**.

5969   MACDONALD, William, ca 1782–23 Mar 1867. From Rogart, SUT. To Pictou Co, NS, poss 1819. Bur at Lovat.   **DC 27 Oct 1979**.

5970   McDONALD, William, ca 1797–13 Nov 1879. From SUT. To Pictou Co, NS, <1830. Bur Lansdowne. m Isabella Ross, qv.   **DC 10 Feb 1980**.

5971   MACDONALD, William, 20 Oct 1786–18 Oct 1857. From Halkirk, CAI. s/o Benjamen M. and Barbara Gunn. To Markham Twp, York Co, ONT, and bur Necropolis, Toronto. m Christina Mill, qv, ch: 1. Daniel, qv; 2. Robert, 1815-66, went to Victoria, AUS; 3. James, qv; 4. Janet, 1819–1907, unm; 5. Margaret, 1821-76, unm; 6. Barbara, 1824–1917, unm; 7. Johanna, qv; 8. Benjamen, qv; 9. William, b 1830, went to AUS; 10. Christina, qv.   **DC 5 Jul 1979**.

5972   MACDONALD, William. To Pictou Co, NS, <1820. Farmer. Son William.   **HNS iii 421**.

5973   MACDONALD, William. Prob from INV. bro/o Alexander M, qv. To Antigonish Co, NS, prob <1820; stld St Andrews. ch: 1. John; 2. Rory; 3. Donald; 4. William; 5. Alexander or 'Sandy'; 6. Isobell; 7. Colin; 8. Catherine; 9. Margaret.   **HCA 223**.

5974   McDONALD, William. From PER. A minor, poss s/o Alexander M, qv. To McNab Twp, Renfrew Co, ONT, 1825.   **DC 3 Jan 1980**.

5975   McDONALD, William, b 1812. From Lairg par, SUT. s/o Finlay M, qv. To East Nissouri Twp, Oxford Co, ONT, ca 1830; stld later at Stratford, Perth Co. m Elizabeth McNaughton, b 1815, ch: 1. Philip, 1838–1907; 2. Isabella, b 1839; 3. Elizabeth, 1841-47; 4. John, 1843-57; 5. Ann, b 1846, prob dy; 6. Peter, 1849-57; 7. William, 1849-57; 8. Elizabeth, b 1857; 9. Robert W, 1859–1942.   **DC 25 Nov 1981**.

5976   McDONALD, William. Prob from Duthill, INV. To London Twp, Middlesex Co, ONT, 1840; moved to West Williams Twp, 1850.   **PCM 47**.

5977   McDONALD, William. To Pictou, NS, on the *Lady Gray*, ex Cromarty, ROC, arr 16 Jul 1841. **DC 15 Jul 1979**.

5978   MACDONALD, William. From SUT. To Megantic Co, QUE, 1842. m Margaret Johnstone, qv, ch: 1. John; 2. William; 3. Peter; 4. James; 5. Margaret; 6. Isabella.   **AMC 48**.

5979   McDONALD, William. From Is Lewis, ROC. To QUE, ex Stornoway, arr 4 Aug 1851; stld Huron Twp, Bruce Co, ONT, 1852. Head of family.   **DC 5 Apr 1967**.

5980   MACDONALD, William John, 29 Nov 1832– 25 Oct 1916. From Aird, Trotternish, Is Skye, INV. s/o Maj Alexander M. and Flora McRae. To Montreal, QUE, 1851. Entered service of HBCo and sent to Vancouver Is. MLA, 1859-66, and later Canadian senator. m, 1857, Catherine Valfour, d/o Capt Murray Reid, HBCo, ch: 1. Lt Col Reginald James; 2. William Balfour, RN; 3. Maj Alastair Douglas, RA; 4. Flora Alexandrina; 5. Edith Mary; 6. Lillias Christina, unm.   **BNA 736; MDB 442**.

5981   MACDONALD, Rev William Peter, 25 Mar 1771–2 Apr 1847. From Aberlour par, BAN. Educ Douai, France, and Vallidolid, Spain. Ord to priesthood in 1796, and served for a time in SCT. To ONT, 1827, and made Vicar-General by Bishop Alexander MacDonell, qv. He had charge of various parishes and founded the first RC newspaper in CAN.   **BNA 895; MDB 442**.

5982   MACDONELL, Rev Alexander 'Scotus', 1742–1803. From Knoydart, INV. To QUE on the *MacDonald*, ex Greenock, arr 5 Sep 1785; stld Glengarry Co, ONT. RC priest, and leader of over 500 emigrants from Knoydart and Glengarry. Founded St Raphaels par and was chaplain to the Glengarry Fencible Regiment. **SGD 50, 122; GD 50/225/1**.

5983   MACDONELL, Alexander, d 1819. From Greenfield, Lochgarry, INV. s/o Angus M. To 'Greenfield', Kenyon Twp, Glengarry Co, ONT, 1772. Emigrant leader; CO, 2nd Batt Glengarry Militia, War of 1812. m Janet, d/o Alexander MacDonell of Aberchalder and Mary MacDonald, ch: 1. Rev Hugh; 2. Angus, qv; 3. Duncan, qv; 4. Alexander, fur-trader; 5. John, qv; 6. Donald, qv; 7. Mrs Alexander McMillan.   **SDG 50; MDB 443**.

5984   McDONELL, Alexander, d 22 Jan 1850, 'at an advanced age', at Elora, Wellington Co, ONT. Formerly Capt, Glengarry Fencibles.   **DGH 6 Jun 1850**.

5985   McDONELL, Alexander. From Laggan, Loch Lochy, INV. To Montreal, QUE, ex Fort William, 3 Jul 1802; stld E ONT. Wife and 3 ch with him. **MCM 1/4 23**.

5986   McDONELL, Alexander. Prob from Boleskine, INV. To Montreal, QUE, ex Fort William, 3 Jul 1802; stld E ONT. Wife with him, and family: 1. Duncan; 2. Donald; 3. Catherine.   **MCM 1/4 23**.

5987   McDONELL, Alexander. From Invergarry, INV. To Montreal, QUE, ex Fort William, 3 Jul 1802; stld E ONT. Wife Mary McMillan, qv, with him, and 3 ch. **MCM 1/4 25**.

5988   McDONELL, Alexander, 1786–29 Nov 1861. From INV. Neph of Bishop Alexander M, qv, of Kingston. To ONT <1830; land and immigration agent for Northumberland and Durham counties.   **LDW 15 Jun 1969**.

5989   MACDONELL, Rev Alexander, called 'Maighster Alastair', 17 Jul 1762–14 Jun 1840. From Glen Urquhart, INV. Educ Valladolid Coll, Madrid, Spain, and ord to RC priesthood, 1787. Served at Badenoch, Lochaber and Glasgow, and as chaplain to the Glengarry Fencibles in IRL. When regt was disbanded he obtained land grants for the men in CAN. stld Glengarry Co, ONT, 1804, and was chaplain to the Glengarry Light Infantry during the War of 1812. Consecrated titular Bishop of Rosena, 1820, and Vicar Apostolic. First Bishop of Kingston, 1831. d at Dumfries on a visit to SCT. **BNA 888; SDG 127; MDB 443**.

5990 McDONELL, Alexander, b 1755. From Knoydart, INV. To QUE, ex Greenock, summer 1815; stld prob Lanark Co, ONT. Farmer. Wife Janet McDonell, qv, with him, and 7 ch incl Archibald, b ca 1791. **SEC 7**.

5991 MACDONELL, Alexander. From Lochaber, INV. s/o Alexander M, qv, Murlaggan. To Mabou Harbour, Inverness Co, NS, ca 1823. m Miss Morrison, ch: 1. Alexander; 2. Allan; 3. Angus; 4. Roderick; 5. John; 6. James; 7. Anne; 8. Flora. **MP 622**.

5992 MACDONELL, Alexander. From Lochaber, INV. s/o Angus M, of the Murlaggan family. To Mabou Harbour, Inverness Co, NS, ca 1823. ch: 1. Allan, retr to SCT; 2. Angus, qv; 3. Alexander, qv; 4. Anne, qv. **MP 622**.

5993 MACDONELL, Rev Alexander, 1782–1841. From Strathglass, INV. s/o Hugh M. and Mary Chisholm. To Arisaig, Antigonish Co, NS, 1811. Moved to Judique, Inverness Co, 1816. RC priest, ord Lismore, 1809. **MP 23**.

5994 MACDONELL, Alexander 'Og', 1794–24 Jan 1852. From Lochaber, INV. s/o Angus M, qv, and Ann MacArthur, qv. To Inverness Co, NS, 1816; stld South West Mabou. m Catherine, d/o Alexander Beaton, qv, Little Judique, ch: 1. Angus, b 1824; 2. Mary; 3. Sara; 4. John; 5. Archibald; 6. Anne; 7. Alexander; 8. Allan; 9. Donald; 10. Margaret. **MP 614**.

5995 McDONELL, Allan, 1722–26 Nov 1821. From Glengarry, INV. lo QUE, and d Three Rivers. **NSS No 2494**.

5996 MACDONELL, Allan, d 1843. Prob from INV. To Montreal, QUE, <1799. Fur-trader, XYCo. Joined NWCo as a clerk, 1804, and served at Swan River and Red River. Partner, 1816, and after the merger with HBCo, 1821, app a chief trader. App Councillor of Ruperts Land, 1839, and ret 1843. **MDB 444**.

5997 McDONELL, Allan. From Inchlaggan, Glengarry, INV. Prob s/o Donald M, qv. To Montreal, QUE, ex Fort William, 3 Jul 1802; stld E ONT. **MCM 1/4 23**.

5998 McDONELL, Allan. From Munerigg, Invergarry, INV. To Montreal, QUE, ex Fort William, 3 Jul 1802; stld E ONT. Wife with him, and ch: 1. Catherine; 2. Margaret; 3. Donald. **MCM 1/4 23**.

5999 McDONELL, Allan, b 1779. From Fort Augustus, INV. To QUE, ex Greenock, summer 1815; stld ONT. Wife Anne Kennedy, qv, with him, and 3 ch. **SEC 4**.

6000 McDONELL, Angus. From Glengarry, INV. s/o Alexander M, qv, Greenfield, and Janet Macdonell. To Glengarry Co, ONT, 1792. **SDG 50**.

6001 MACDONELL, Angus. From Glengarry, INV. To South River, Antigonish Co, NS, prob <1800. m Ann Bigelow, from Cornwallis, ch: 1. James; 2. Angus; 3. Charles; 4. William; 5. John; 6. Catherine; 7. Mary Ann; 8. Ellen. **HCA 264**.

6002 MACDONELL, Angus. From INV, poss Lochaber dist. To Montreal, QUE, arr Sep 1802. Petitioned for land on the Ottawa River, ONT, 6 Aug 1804. **DC 15 Mar 1980**.

6003 McDONELL, Angus. From Invervigar, Boleskine and Abertarff par, INV. To Montreal, QUE, ex Fort William, 3 Jul 1802; stld E ONT. Wife with him, and

family: 1. Duncan; 2. Katherine; 3. Margaret; 4. Alexander; 5. John. **MCM 1/4 25**.

6004 MACDONELL, Angus. From INV. To Glengarry Co, ONT, 1826. m at St Raphaels Ch, 29 Nov 1826, Amelia, d/o John Dewar and Margaret McPhee. **DC 10 Aug 1968**.

6005 MACDONELL, Angus. From Lochaber, INV. s/o Alexander M. To Inverness Co, NS, 1816; stld South West Mabou, 1819. Wife Ann MacArthur, qv, with him, and ch: 1. Alexander, qv; 2. Sara, qv; 3. Isabel, qv. **MP 614**.

6006 MACDONELL, Angus. From Lochaber, INV. s/o Alexander M, qv, Murlaggan family. To Mabou Harbour, Inverness Co, NS, ca 1823. m Miss Morrison, ch: 1. Alexander; 2. Mary; 3. Catherine. **MP 622**.

6007 MACDONELL, Angus 'Sandaig', d ca 1817. From Knoydart, INV. Cous of John 'Scotus' M. To Glengarry Co, ONT, 1786; stld Charlottenburg Twp. Officer, 71st Regt, and gr 500 acres. m Mme. Belletré, Montreal. Son John Belletré, res Montreal. **SDG 79**.

6008 MACDONELL, Anne. From Strathglass, INV. d/o Thomas 'Ban' M, qv. To Indian Point, Judique, Inverness Co, NS, prob <1810. m Patrick, s/o Neil MacDougall, Judique Interval. **MP 629**.

6009 MACDONELL, Anne. From Lochaber, INV. d/o Alexander M, qv, Murlaggan family. To Mabou Harbour, Inverness Co, NS, ca 1823. m Alexander MacNeil, qv. **MP 623**.

6010 McDONELL, Archibald. To Glengarry Co, ONT, 1794; stld Lot 25, Con 16, Lancaster Twp. **MG 57**.

6011 McDONELL, Archibald. From Paisley, RFW. To Montreal, QUE, ex Fort William, 3 Jul 1802; stld E ONT. Wife with him. **MCM 1/4 26**.

6012 McDONELL, Austin, 1795–16 Oct 1879. From Strathglass, INV. s/o John M. To St Agnes de Dundee, Huntingdon Co, QUE, ca 1818; moved to Chatham Twp, Kent Co, ONT, 1870. m Isabelle McRae, qv, ch: 1. Elizabeth, b 1835; 2. Augustine, b 1837; 3. Alexander, b 1839; 4. Flora, b 1841; 5. Mary, b 1846; 6. Isabella; 7. Annabelle. **DC 16 Jul 1979**.

6013 McDONELL, Catherine. From Moidart, INV. To Pictou, NS, on the *Dove*, ex Fort William, Jun 1801. Spinster. **PLD**.

6014 McDONELL, Catherine. Prob from Boleskine and Abertarff par, INV. To Montreal, QUE, ex Fort William, 3 Jul 1802; stld E ONT. **MCM 1/4 23**.

6015 McDONELL, Catherine. From Laddie, nr Loch Garry, INV. To Montreal, QUE, ex Fort William, 3 Jul 1802; stld E ONT. **MCM 1/4 26**.

6016 McDONELL, Catherine. From Knoydart, INV. To QUE, ex Greenock, summer 1815; stld prob Lanark Co, ONT. Wife of John McDonell, qv. **SEC 7**.

6017 MACDONELL, Catherine. From Lochaber, INV. d/o Thomas 'Ban' M, qv. To Indian Point, Judique, Inverness Co, NS <1810. m Alexander Chisholm. **MP 630**.

6018 MACDONELL, Christina. From INV. To Lochiel Twp, Glengarry Co, ONT, <1830. Wife of James McDonell, qv. **LDW 18 Jan 1964**.

6019   MACDONELL, Christopher. From Strathglass, INV. s/o Thomas 'Ban' M, qv. To Indian Point, Judique, Inverness Co, NS, prob <1810. Innkeeper. m Mary, d/o Hugh 'Mor' MacMaster and Margaret Graham, ch: 1. Hugh; 2. Alexander; 3. Donald; 4. Janet; 5. Jessie; 6. Anne; 7. Margaret; 8. Mary.   **MP 623**.

6020   MACDONELL, Daniel. From Kirkcaldy, FIF. To Halifax, NS, <1830. Son Rev George, qv.   **FES vii 641**.

6021   MACDONELL, Donald 'Ban', 1742–1839. From INV. To Montreal, QUE, 1783; stld Kingston, ONT. Discharged soldier. Son Col Ranald A.   **DC 21 Mar 1981**.

6022   MACDONELL, Donald. From Glengarry, INV. bro/o Mary M, qv. To Hants Co, NS, 1791; stld Ninemile River. m Mary Scott, ch: 1. Alexander, went to Ann Arbor, MI; 2. Donald, res Kansas City; 3. Allan, stld Antigonish Co, NS; 4. John; 5. Angus; 6. Duncan; 7. Archibald; 8. Margaret; 9. Mary; 10. Ann; 11. Catherine.   **HCA 263**.

6023   MACDONELL, Donald, 17 Jan 1778–13 Jun 1861. From Greenfield, Loch Garry, INV. s/o Alexander M, qv, and Janet MacDonell. To Clarlottenburg Twp, Glengarry Co, ONT, 1792. Capt Glengarry Militia, 1812-14. Became Registrar and Deputy Adjutant-General of Glengarry Co, also MLA. m Elizabeth, d/o Ranald MacDonell, Leek, ch: 1. Alexander G, barrister and reeve of Morrisburg; 2. John, barrister in Cornwall.   **SDG 167, 222**.

6024   McDONELL, Donald. To Glengarry Co, ONT, 1794; stld Lot 24, Con 16, Lancaster Twp.   **MG 57**.

6025   McDONELL, Donald. From Laddie, nr Loch Garry, INV. To Montreal, QUE, ex Fort William, 3 Jul 1802; stld E ONT.   **MCM 1/4 23**.

6026   McDONELL, Donald. From Inchlaggan, Glengarry, INV. To Montreal, QUE, ex Fort William, 3 Jul 1802; stld E ONT. Wife with him, and family: 1. Mary; 2. Janet; 3. Janet; 4. Catherine; 5. Peggy.   **MCM 1/4 23**.

6027   McDONELL, Donald. From Invervigar, Boleskine and Abertarff par, INV. To Montreal, QUE, ex Fort William, 3 Jul 1802; stld E ONT.   **MCM 1/4 24**.

6028   McDONELL, Donald. From Aberchalder, INV. To Montreal, QUE, ex Fort William, 3 Jul 1802; stld E ONT. Wife with him, and family: 1. Anne; 2. Duncan; 3. Ewen.   **MCM 1/4 25**.

6029   McDONELL, Donald. Prob from Glen Garry, INV. To Montreal, QUE, ex Fort William, 3 Jul 1802; stld E ONT. Wife with him.   **MCM 1/4 25**.

6030   McDONELL, Donald. From Thornhill, PER. To Montreal, QUE, ex Fort William, 3 Jul 1802; stld E ONT. Wife and 2 ch with him.   **MCM 1/4 26**.

6031   McDONELL, Donald. From Inchlaggan, Glengarry, INV. To Montreal, QUE, ex Fort William, 3 Jul 1802; stld E ONT. Wife and 2 ch with him.   **MCM 1/4 25**.

6032   McDONELL, Duncan. To Glengarry Co, ONT, 1794; stld Lot 15, Con 16, Lancaster Twp.   **MG 57**.

6033   MACDONELL, Duncan, d 1851. From Glengarry, INV. s/o Alexander M, qv, Greenfield, and Janet MacDonell. To Glengarry Co, ONT, 1792. Registrar of Deeds, Glengarry Co. m Harriet, d/o Col Archibald MacDonell. Son Archibald John, 1822-64, lawyer in Kingston.   **SDG 435**.

6034   McDONELL, Duncan. From Aviemore, INV. To Montreal, QUE, ex Fort William, 3 Jul 1802; stld E ONT.   **MCM 1/4 26**.

6035   McDONELL, Duncan. From Laddie, nr Loch Garry, INV. To Montreal, QUE, ex Fort William, 3 Jul 1802; stld E ONT.   **MCM 1/4 24**.

6036   McDONELL, Duncan, b ca 1777. From Fort Augustus, INV. To QUE, ex Greenock, summer 1815; stld prob Lanark Co, ONT. Labourer. Wife Isobel McPhee, qv, with him, and 3 ch.   **SEC 6**.

6037   McDONELL, Duncan, b ca 1783. From Knoydart, INV. To QUE, ex Greenock, summer 1815; stld prob Lanark Co, ONT. Farmer. Wife Janet with him, and 3 ch.   **SEC 8**.

6038   MACDONELL, Farquhar. From Dornie, ROC. s/o — M. and Margaret MacRae. To NS, ca 1820; stld St Anns, Victoria Co, later Long Point, Judique, Inverness Co. m Barbara MacRae, qv, ch: 1. Isabel; 2. Alexander; 3. Rev John Vincent, 1818-88; 4. Duncan, merchant; 5. Ellen; 6. Margaret; 7. Colin; 8. Catherine.   **DC 28 Aug 1981**.

6039   MACDONELL, Rev George, 1811–25 Apr 1871. From Kirkcaldy, FIF. s/o Daniel M, qv. Educ Univ of Edinburgh, 1830-38, and became min of St Lukes Ch, Bathurst, Northumberland Co, NB, 1840. Trans to Nelson and Watertown, ONT, 1852; and to Fergus, 1855. Latterly at Milton. ch: 1. Rev Daniel James, 1843-96, min at Peterborough; 2. Margaret.   **BNA 867; SGC 615; FES vii 641; MDB 446**.

6040   MACDONELL, Hugh. From Strathglass, INV. s/o Thomas 'Ban' M, qv. To Indian Point, Inverness Co, NS, poss <1810. m Margaret, d/o Donald MacIsaac, ch: 1. Donald; 2. John; 3. Colin; 4. Duncan; 5. Alexander; 6. Angus; 7. Thomas; 8. Donald Og; 9. Janet; 10. Mary; 11. Anne.   **MP 626**.

6041   MACDONELL, Isabel. From Lochaber, INV. d/o Thomas 'Ban' M, qv. To Indian Point, Judique, Inverness Co, NS, prob <1810. m John, s/o Donald, West Lake Ainslie, ch.   **MP 630**.

6042   MACDONELL, Isabel, ca 1804–10 Apr 1888. From Lochaber, INV. d/o Angus M, qv, and Ann MacArthur, qv. To South West Mabou, Inverness Co, NS, 1816. m Angus Boyle, qv.   **MP 224, 622**.

6043   McDONELL, James. To Glengarry Co, ONT, 1794; stld Lot 35, Con 16, Lancaster Twp.   **MG 57**.

6044   McDONELL, James. From Balnain, INV. To Montreal, QUE, ex Fort William, 3 Jul 1802; stld E ONT. Wife with him, and ch: 1. Katherine; 2. Allan.   **MCM 1/4 23**.

6045   MACDONELL, James. From INV. To Glengarry Co, ONT, <1830; stld Lot 15, Con 1, Lochiel Twp. m Christina MacDonell, qv. Son Rev Alexander, 1833–1905, Bishop of Alexandria.   **LDW 18 Jan 1964**.

6046   MACDONELL, James 'Stone'. From INV. To Kenyon Twp, Glengarry Co, ONT, <1830. m Eliza McPhee, qv, ch: 1. Col Angus; 2. Ranald; 3. Hector; 4. Mary; 5. Mrs Greeve; 6. Mrs Cameron.   **DC 10 Aug 1968**.

6047 MACDONELL, Janet. From Lochaber, INV. d/o Thomas 'Ban' M, qv. To Indian Point, Judique, Inverness Co, NS, poss <1810. m Alexander, s/o John 'Mor' Chisholm, River Denys. **MP 630**.

6048 McDONELL, Janet, b 1755. From Knoydart, INV. To QUE, ex Greenock, summer 1815; stld prob Lanark Co, ONT. Wife of Alexander McDonell, qv. **SEC 7**.

6049 McDONELL, John. From Invergosern, Knoydart, INV. To QUE on the *British Queen*, ex Arisaig, 16 Aug 1790; stld nr Montreal. Tenant. Wife and ch with him. **QCC 103**.

6050 MACDONELL, John, 19 Apr 1785–12 Oct 1812. From Greenfield, Loch Garry, INV. s/o Alexander M, qv, and Janet MacDonell. To Glengarry Co, ONT, 1792. Lawyer and MLA. Attorney-General, 1811-12, and was killed at Queenston Heights. **SDG 448; MDB 445**.

6051 McDONELL, John. From Glengarry, INV. To Montreal, QUE, ex Fort William, 3 Jul 1802; stld E ONT. **MCM 1/4 23**.

6052 McDONELL, John. From Laddie, nr Loch Garry, INV. To Montreal, QUE, ex Fort William, 3 Jul 1802; stld E ONT. **MCM 1/4 24**.

6053 McDONELL, John. From Divach, Urquhart and Glenmoriston par, INV. To Montreal, QUE, ex Fort William, 3 Jul 1802; stld E ONT. **MCM 1/4 24**.

6054 McDONELL, John. From Invervigar, Boleskine and Abertarff par, INV. To Montreal, QUE, ex Fort William, 3 Jul 1802; stld E ONT. Family with him: 1. Dugald; 2. Catherine; 3. Flora; 4. Peggy; 5. Donald. **MCM 1/4 24**.

6055 McDONELL, John. From Ardnable, ni, prob INV. To Montreal, QUE, ex Fort William, 3 Jul 1802; stld E ONT. Wife and child with him. **MCM 1/4 24**.

6056 McDONELL, John. From Errar, ni, prob INV. To Montreal, QUE, ex Fort William, 3 Jul 1802. Petitioned for land on Ottawa River, ONT, 6 Aug 1804. **DC 12 Mar 1980**.

6057 MACDONELL, John. From Bransauk, ni, poss ROC. To Montreal, QUE, arr Sep 1802. Petitioned for land on the Ottawa River, ONT, 6 Aug 1802. **DC 15 May 1980**.

6058 McDONELL, John, b 1755. From Knoydart, INV. To QUE, ex Greenock, summer 1815; stld prob Lanark Co, ONT. Farmer. Wife Catherine McDonell, qv, with him, and 4 ch. **SEC 7**.

6059 McDONELL, Kenneth. From INV. To Montreal, QUE, arr Sep 1802. Petitioned for land on Ottawa River, ONT, 6 Aug 1804. **DC 15 Mar 1980**.

6060 McDONELL, Lachlan. Prob from Glengarry, INV. To QUE, arr Sep 1802; stld prob E ONT. **DC 15 Mar 1980**.

6061 McDONELL, Margaret. From Aberchalder, INV. To Montreal, QUE, ex Fort William, 3 Jul 1802; stld E ONT. Poss widow with ch. **MCM 1/4 26**.

6062 McDONELL, John, b 1793. From Glengarry, INV. To Glengarry Co, ONT, <1830. m Margaret Elphinstone Harrower, ch. **DC 5 Apr 1982**.

6063 MACDONELL, Margaret. From Fort Augustus, INV. To QUE on the *Tamerlane*, ex Greenock, 4 Jul 1831; stld Greenfield, Kenyon Twp, Glengarry Co, ONT. Wife of John McIsaac McDonald, qv. **DC 14 Jun 1968**.

6064 MACDONELL, Mary. From Glengarry, INV. sis/o Donald M, qv. To Hants Co, NS, 1791; stld Ninemile River. m Archibald MacLellan. **HCA 263**.

6065 McDONELL, Mary. From Achluachrach, INV. To Montreal, QUE, ex Fort William, 3 Jul 1802; stld E ONT. Poss widow with several ch. **MCM 1/4 23**.

6066 McDONELL, Mary. From Kerrowdean, Glen Farrar, INV. To Montreal, QUE, ex Fort William, 3 Jul 1802; stld E ONT. **MCM 1/4 24**.

6067 McDONELL, Mary. From Lochaber, INV. d/o Thomas 'Ban' M, qv. To Indian Point, Judique, Inverness Co, NS, prob <1810. m Colin Chisholm. **MP 630**.

6068 MACDONELL, Ranald. From INV. To Glengarry Co, ONT, <1791; stld River Aux Raisins. Farmer. m Eliza, d/o Angus Macdonell, Leek, ch. **SDG 57, 413**.

6069 McDONELL, Ranald. From Auchterawe, nr Fort Augustus, INV. To Montreal, QUE, ex Fort William, 3 Jul 1802; stld E ONT. **MCM 1/4 24**.

6070 McDONELL, Roderick. From Kilmorack, INV. To Pictou, NS, on the *Sarah*, ex Fort William, Jun 1801. Labourer. **PLS**.

6071 MACDONELL, Roderick Dow. From INV, poss Lochaber dist. To Montreal, QUE, arr Sep 1802. Petitioned for land on the Ottawa River, ONT, 6 Aug 1804. **DC 15 Mar 1980**.

6072 McDONELL, Ronald. Prob from Lochaber, INV. To Montreal, QUE, arr Sep 1802. Petitioned for land on the Ottawa River, ONT, 6 Aug 1804. **DC 15 Mar 1980**.

6073 McDONELL, Ronald. To QUE on the *Fame*, 1815; stld Lot 7, Con 4, Drummond Twp, Lanark Co, ONT. **HCL 234**.

6074 McDONELL, Ronald, b 1785. From Knoydart, INV. To QUE, ex Greenock, summer 1815; stld prob Lanark Co, ONT. Wife Mary McDougall, qv, with him, and 2 ch. **SEC 7**.

6075 McDONELL, Ronald, b 1785. From Knoydart, INV. To QUE, ex Greenock, summer 1815; stld prob Lanark Co, ONT. Farmer. Wife Florence Gillies, qv, with him, and 6 ch. **SEC 7**.

6076 MACDONELL, Sara, ca 1798–28 May 1876. From Lochaber, INV. d/o Angus M, qv, and Ann MacArthur, qv. To South West Mabou, Inverness Co, NS, 1816. m (i) Angus McNeil; (ii) Alexander MacKillop, qv, Mabou Ridge. **MP 621, 715**.

6077 MACDONELL, Thomas 'Ban'. From Strathglass, INV. Cous of Rev Alexander M, qv. To Inverness Co, NS, prob <1810; stld Indian Point, Judique. ch: 1. Christopher, qv; 2. Hugh, qv; 3. Thomas, qv; 4. Anne, qv; 5. Mary, qv; 6. Catherine, qv; 7. Janet, qv; 8. Isabel, qv. **MP 623**.

6078 MACDONELL, Thomas, jr. From Strathglass, INV. s/o Thomas 'Ban' M, qv. To Indian Point, Judique, Inverness Co, NS, prob <1810. m Cecilia, d/o Alexander MacInnes, Judique, ch: 1. Angus; 2. Alexander; 3. Hugh. **MP 629**.

6079   McDOUALL, Alexander, d 6 Jul 1841. From Drummore, Kirkmaiden, WIG. To St Stephen, Charlotte Co, NB. **DGH 12 Aug 1841**.

McDOUGAL. See also McDOUGALD, McDOUGALL and McDUGALD.

6080   McDOUGAL, Alexander, d 16 Nov 1827. From Dumbarton. To Halifax, NS. Mate of the brig *Elizabeth*, and d at Kingston, Jamaica. **VSN No 2668**.

6081   McDOUGAL, Angus, b 1795. To Inverness Co, NS, 1800; stld nr Port Hood. Farmer. **CBC 1818**.

6082   McDOUGAL, Duncan. From Tarbet, ARL. To Caradoc Twp, Middlesex Co, ONT, 1842. ch incl: 1. Duncan; 2. Archie, res Sarnia. **PCM 35**.

6083   McDOUGAL, John, ca 1746–10 Aug 1826. Prob from ARL. To St David, Charlotte Co, NB, poss 1784. Discharged soldier (piper), 74th Regt. **VSN No 1825**.

6084   McDOUGAL, John. To St John, NB, <1825. Wife Jane, ca 1809–1831. **NER viii 98**.

6085   McDOUGAL, John. From Breadalbane, PER. To Montreal, QUE, on the *Dorothy*, ex Greenock, 12 Jul 1815; stld Breadalbane, Lochiel Twp, Glengarry Co, ONT. **SDG 131**.

6086   McDOUGAL, Neil, b ca 1761. To Port Hood dist, Inverness Co, NS, 1800. Farmer, m and ch. **CBC 1818**.

6087   McDOUGAL, Peter. From Breadalbane, PER. To QUE on the *Dorothy*, ex Greenock, 12 Jul 1815; stld Breadalbane, Lochiel Twp, Glengarry Co, ONT. Elder of Baptist Ch. **SDG 131**.

McDOUGALD. See also McDOUGAL, McDOUGALL and McDUGALD.

6088   McDOUGALD, Anne. From Knoydart, INV. To Pictou, NS, on the *Sarah*, ex Fort William, Jun 1801. Spinster. **PLS**.

6089   McDOUGALD, Archibald, b ca 1784. To Inverness, Inverness Co, NS, 1812. Farmer, m and ch. **CBC 1818**.

6090   McDOUGALD, Archibald, b ca 1788. To Western Shore, Inverness Co, NS, 1816. Farmer, m and ch. **CBC 1818**.

6091   McDOUGALD, Catherine. From Arisaig, INV. To Pictou, NS, on the *Dove*, ex Fort William, Jun 1801. **PLD**.

6092   McDOUGALD, Catherine. From Kilmory, Is Arran, BUT. To Dalhousie, NB, prob 1832; stld Belldune, Gloucester Co. Wife of John McCurdy, qv. **MAC 20**.

6093   McDOUGALD, Donald. From Fort Augustus, INV. To Montreal, QUE, ex Fort William, arr Sep 1802; stld E ONT. Wife with him, and ch: 1. Marjory; 2. Alexander; 3. John. **MCM 1/4 25**.

6094   McDOUGALD, Donald, b ca 1780. To Western Shore, Inverness Co, NS, 1816. Farmer. **CBC 1818**.

6095   McDOUGALD, Ereck. From Knoydart, INV. To Pictou, NS, on the *Sarah*, ex Fort William, Jun 1801. Spinster. **PLS**.

6096   McDOUGALD, Donald 'Ban', 1765–11 Feb 1844. From Is Eigg, INV. s/o Angus M. To Antigonish Co, NS, 1789, but went to Glengarry Co, ONT. Farmer.

m Catherine McKinnon, qv, ch: 1. Alexander, 1791–1866; 2. Malcolm, b 1800; 3. Angus, 1805-57; 4. Lachlan, 1806-81; 5. Dougald, 1808-91. **DC 29 Feb 1980**.

6097   McDOUGALD, Duncan, b ca 1768. To Inverness, Inverness Co, NS, 1813. Farmer, m and ch. **CBC 1818**.

6098   McDOUGALD, Hugh, b ca 1793. To Western Shore, Inverness Co, NS, 1816. Farmer, unm. **CBC 1818**.

6099   McDOUGALD, John, b ca 1786. To Western Shore, Inverness Co, NS, 1816. Farmer, m and ch. **CBC 1818**.

6100   McDOUGALD, Margaret, 1798–1884. From Morvern, ARL. d/o John M. and Catherine Mackinnon. To Charlottetown, PEI, on the *Catherine*, 1810. Schoolteacher, Charlottetown Royalty. m Malcolm McGregor, qv. **DC 1 Oct 1960**.

6101   McDOUGALD, Peter, b ca 1773. Prob from Is Colonsay, ARL. To Charlottetown, PEI, on the *Spencer*, arr 22 Sep 1806. **PLSN**.

McDOUGALL. See also McDOUGAL, McDOUGALD and McDUGALD.

6102   McDOUGALL, Agnes, b 1819. From Lochgoilhead, ARL. d/o John M, qv, and Agnes Campbell, qv. To North Sherbrooke, Lanark Co, ONT, 1828; later to Hibbert, Perth Co. m George Miller. **DC 21 Jan 1961**.

6103   McDOUGALL, Alexander. From STI. To Halifax, NS, 1795. Wife Catherine Buchanan, qv, with him. Son Alexander, 1804-55, lawyer and MLA. **MLA 210**.

6104   McDOUGALL, Alexander, d 1821. bro/o Lt Duncan M, 84th Regt. To Montreal, QUE, <1800. Served with NWCo and d at Lachine. **DC 21 Mar 1981**.

6105   McDOUGALL, Alexander. From Craignish, ARL. To Lobo Twp, Middlesex Co, ONT, 1824. m Margaret, d/o William Paul, qv, ch: 1. John; 2. Allan; 3. Mary. **PCM 39**.

6106   McDOUGALL, Alexander. From ARL. To Ekfrid Twp, Middlesex Co, ONT, 1831. ch: 1. Alexander; 2. Mrs Kennedy; 3. Mrs Angus Black; 4. Mrs de Cow. **PCM 30**.

6107   MACDOUGALL, Allan. From ARL. To Flat River, Queens Co, PEI, <1815. m Harriet Campbell, qv. **SPI 42; HP 85**.

6108   McDOUGALL, Allan, b 1783. Prob from Is Mull, ARL. To Baldoon, Dover Twp, Kent Co, ONT, 1804. Wife Nancy with him, ch: 1. John; 2. Mary; 3. Margaret. **UCM 267, 302; DC 4 Oct 1979**.

6109   McDOUGALL, Allan, b 23 Jul 1799, Is Jura, but emig from Is Islay, ARL. To ONT, and d Harrison, Wellington Co. m Janet Shaw, qv, ch: 1. John, b Tarbert, Jura, 18 Nov 1828; 2. Alexander, b Tarbert, Jura, 1830; 3. Margaret, b Tarbert, Jura, 13 May 1832; 4. Duncan, b Islay, 28 Jun 1844; 5. Flora Ann, b Islay, 12 Jun 1838; 6. Dugald, b Islay, 25 Nov 1840; 7. Mary, b Islay, 4 Aug 1843; 8. Duncan Og, b Islay 28 Jun 1844. **DC 19 Nov 1977**.

6110   McDOUGALL, Allan. From ARL. Prob bro/o Archibald M, qv, and Samuel M, qv. To Metcalfe Twp, Middlesex Co, ONT, 1848. **PCM 26**.

6111 McDOUGALL, Angus, b 1787. From ARL, prob Is Mull. To QUE on the *Oughton*, arr Jul 1804; stld Baldoon, Dover Twp, Kent Co, ONT. Farmer. m Flora McCallum, qv. **UCM 267; DC 4 Oct 1979**.

6112 McDOUGALL, Angus, 1816-96. From Snizort par, Is Skye, INV. Prob bro/o Murdoch M, qv, Catherine M, qv, and Peter M, qv. To Kinloss Twp, Bruce Co, ONT, 1852. Farmer. Wife Margaret with him, ch: 1. Flora, b 1850; 2. Margaret, b 1852; 3. Eric, b 1854; 4. Lachlan, b 1856; 5. Ann, b 1857; 6. Mary, b 1859; 7. Angus, b 1861; 8. Emily, b 1864; 9. John, b 1866. **DC 12 Apr 1979**.

6113 MACDOUGALL, Angus 'Ban'. From Moidart, INV. To Antigonish Co, NS, <1812, when he moved to West Lake Ainslie, Inverness Co. Dau Kate. **MP 596**.

6114 McDOUGALL, Ann. Poss from INV. To Pictou Co, NS, <1789. m Donald MacDonald, qv. **HCA 231**.

6115 MACDOUGALL, Ann. From Knoydart, INV. To QUE, ex Greenock, summer 1815; stld prob Lanark Co, ONT. Wife of Duncan McDougall, qv. **SEC 8**.

6116 McDOUGALL, Archibald. Rel to Duncan M, qv. To Lanark Co, ONT, 1821; stld Lot 11, Con 1, North Sherbrooke Twp. **HCL 74**.

6117 McDOUGALL, Archibald. From ARL. To Ekfrid Twp, Middlesex Co, ONT, 1831. ch: 1. Alexander P, twp clerk; 2. John; 3. Donald; 4. Nancy; 5. Mary. **PCM 30**.

6118 McDOUGALL, Archibald. From Is Islay, ARL. bro/o John M, qv. To Eldon Twp, Victoria Co, ONT, ca 1835; stld Lot 6, Con 2. ch: 1. Robert; 2. Flora; 3. Mary. **DC 21 Mar 1980**.

6119 McDOUGALL, Archibald. From ARL. Prob bro/o Allan M, qv, and Samuel M, qv. To Metcalfe Twp, Middlesex Co, ONT, 1848. **PCM 26**.

6120 McDOUGALL, Archibald, b 1799. Poss from Is Mull, ARL. To Vaughan Twp, York Co, ONT, poss <1835. By wife Catherine, ch: 1. Agnes, b 1835; 2. John, b 1836; 3. Christina, b 1837; 4. Mary, b 1840; 5. Charles, b 1842; 6. Catherine, b 1845; 7. Jane, b 1847; 8. Flora, b 1849; 9. Archibald, b 1850; 10. Donald, b 1854; 11. Sarah, b 1858. **DC 25 Feb 1976**.

6121 MACDOUGALL, Catherine. From Is Mull, ARL. To Upper West Lake Ainslie, Inverness Co, NS, <1820. Wife of Angus Walker, qv. **MP 865**.

6122 MACDOUGALL, Catharine. From Glasgow. To QUE, poss on the *Atlas*, ex Greenock, 11 Jul 1815; stld ONT. Wife of Alexander McNab, qv. **SEC 1**.

6123 McDOUGALL, Catherine, 1823-95. From Snizort par, Is Skye, INV. Prob sis/o Angus M, qv, Murdoch M, qv, and Peter M, qv. To Kinloss Twp, Bruce Co, ONT, 1852. m Norman Nicolson, qv, as his second wife. **DC 12 Apr 1979**.

6124 McDOUGALL, Clementina, 1811–31 Dec 1893. From PER. To Halton Co, ONT, prob <1840; stld Esquesing Twp, and bur Hillcrest, Norval. **EPE 77**.

6125 MACDOUGALL, Rev Daniel, 1831–22 Apr 1909. s/o Alexander M. and Margaret McDonald. Educ Univ of Edinburgh and was missionary at Buchlyvie, STI, 1858. To London, Middlesex Co, ONT, 1864, as missionary.

Retr to SCT, 1876, and became min at Berriedale, CAI. m Margaret Isabella, 1846–1918, d/o Andrew Milroy and Susannah Sawers Nixon. **FES vii 113, 641**.

6126 McDOUGALL, Donald. To Upper Nine Mile River, Hants Co, NS, 1784. Discharged soldier, 84th Regt. m Anne Reid. Son John, 1793–1873, farmer and MLA. **MLA 211**.

6127 MACDOUGALL, Donald. From Arisaig, INV. To Highfield, Arisaig, Antigonish Co, NS, <1810. ch: 1. Angus; 2. Donald; 3. James. **HCA 268**.

6128 McDOUGALL, Donald, b ca 1763. From Knoydart, INV. To QUE, ex Greenock, summer 1815; stld prob Lanark Co, ONT. Farmer. Wife Christian McDonald, qv, with him, ch: 1. James, qv; 2. Alexander, b ca 1794; 3. Archibald, b ca 1796. **SEC 7**.

6129 McDOUGALL, Donald. From ARL. To Lobo Twp, Middlesex Co, ONT, 1826. **PCM 39**.

6130 MACDOUGALL, Donald, b ca 1803. From Is Tyree, ARL. To ONT, ca 1847. Wife Sarah, b ca 1799, with him. **DC 8 Mar 1979**.

6131 McDOUGALL, Duncan, 1744-95. From ARL. To Montreal, QUE, ca 1768, later to Tryon Co, NY, and finally to St John, NB. m Nancy Weaver, 1755–1825. Son Nicolas Allen, b 1781. **DC 15 Apr 1961**.

6132 McDOUGALL, Duncan, b 1765. From Knoydart, INV. Rel to Archibald M, qv. To QUE, ex Greenock, summer 1815; stld Lot 11, Con 1, North Sherbrooke Twp, Lanark Co, ONT. Farmer. Wife Ann McDougall, qv, with him, and 4 ch, incl Donald, aged 21. **SEC 8; HCL 74**.

6133 McDOUGALL, Duncan. From ARL. To Lobo Twp, Middlesex Co, ONT, 1826. **PCM 39**.

6134 MACDOUGALL, Duncan. To Antigonish Co, NS, prob <1820. Son Angus. **HCA 265**.

6135 McDOUGALL, Duncan, b ca 1825. From Lochgoilhead, ARL. s/o John M, qv, and Agnes Campbell, qv. To Sherbrooke Twp, Lanark Co, ONT, 1828; moved to Hibbert, Perth Co, 1854. Farmer. **DC 21 Jan 1960**.

6136 MACDOUGALL, Duncan. From Is Mull, ARL. To Cape Breton Is, NS, <1830. m Mary Jane McLean, qv. Son Rev Donald, b 15 Aug 1837, min at Port Morien, 1866, later at West Bay. **HNS iii 614**.

6137 McDOUGALL, Duncan. From Kintyre, ARL. To Westminster Twp, Middlesex Co, ONT, 1832. **PCM 51**.

6138 McDOUGALL, Elizabeth, ca 1820–22 Nov 1850. From Foulden par, BEW. d/o John M, tenant in Foulden Mill. To QUE, and d Three Rivers. **Ts Foulden**.

6139 McDOUGALL, Ellen, b ca 1795. To Mosa Twp, Middlesex Co, ONT, <1840. Wife of Finlay Munro, qv. **DC 21 Nov 1968**.

6140 McDOUGALL, Flora, b ca 1824. Poss from Is Lewis, ROC. To Halifax, NS, <1855, when she m Edwin Broadbent, 76th Foot. **NS 35/24**.

6141 MACDOUGALL, George, d 1842. Prob from DFS. s/o Allan M. of Hayfield, Thornhill. To Peterborough, ONT. **DGH 7 Apr 1842**.

6142 McDOUGALL, Hugh, ca 1760–31 Oct 1827. From PER. To Black River, Northumberland Co, NB, 1817.

Wife Jane, 1781–1863, with him. Left ch. **DC 30 Jul 1980**.

6143   MACDOUGALL, Hugh. To Antigonish Co, NS, poss <1830. ch: 1. John; 2. Alexander; 3. Allan; 4. Angus; 5. Samuel; 6. Hugh. **HCA 269**.

6144   McDOUGALL, James, b ca 1790. From Knoydart, INV. s/o Donald M, qv, and Christian McDonald, qv. To QUE, ex Greenock, summer 1815; stld prob Lanark Co, ONT. Wife Mary with him. **SEC 7**.

6145   McDOUGALL, James W. From ARL. To Metcalfe Twp, Middlesex Co, ONT, 1850. **PCM 26**.

6146   McDOUGALL, Janet. From Port Ellen, Is Islay, ARL. To Brampton, Peel Co, ONT, 1841. Wife of Donald McLeod, qv, or McCuaig. **DC 29 Dec 1981**.

6147   McDOUGALL, Jean. From Knoydart, INV. To QUE, ex Greenock, summer 1815; stld prob Lanark Co, ONT. Wife of Angus McDonald, qv. **SEC 7**.

6148   MACDOUGALL, Jessie. From INV. To Pictou Co, NS, <1840; stld Blue Mountain. m John MacDougall, qv. **HNS iii 236**.

6149   McDOUGALL, John, 1754–1806. From ARL. To QUE on the *Oughton*, arr Jul 1804; stld Baldoon, Dover Twp, Kent Co, ONT. Wife Sarah McPherson, qv, with him, ch: 1. Allan, b 1783; 2. Ann, b 1785; 3. Mary, qv; 4. Angus, qv; 5. John, 1790–1855; 6. Hector, 1793–1859; 7. Lachlan, b 1796; 8. Archibald, b 1798; 9. Flora, b 1800; 10. James, b 1802; 11. Mary, b 1804. **UCM 267; DC 4 Oct 1979**.

6150   McDOUGALL, John. To QUE on the *Caledonian*, 1816; stld Lot 26, Con 9, Bathurst Twp, Lanark Co, ONT. **HCL 234**.

6151   MACDOUGALL, John. From ARL. To Aldborough Twp, Elgin Co, ONT, 1817. Farmer. **PDA 24**.

6152   McDOUGALL, John. From Craignish, ARL. To Lobo Twp, Middlesex Co, ONT, 1824. ch: 1. Alexander; 2. Allan; 3. Archibald; 4. John; 5. Duncan; 6. Mary; 7. Maisie; 8. Annabel; 9. Christy. **PCM 38**.

6153   McDOUGALL, John, 1792–1885. From Lochgoilhead, ARL. s/o Duncan M. and Agnes McNeish. To QUE, ex Greenock, 28 Jun 1828; stld North Sherbrooke Twp, Lanark Co, ONT, later Hibbert, Perth Co. Shoemaker, farmer. m 1818, Agnes Campbell, qv, ch: 1. Duncan, d inf; 2. Agnes, qv; 3. Archibald, dy; 4. Mary, d inf; 5. Duncan, qv; 6. Margaret, qv; 7. Mary, b CAN; 8. Helen; 9. John; 10. Lilly; 11. Isabella. **DC 21 Jan 1960**.

6154   McDOUGALL, John. From Is Islay, ARL. bro/o Archibald M, qv. To Eldon Twp, Victoria Co, ONT, ca 1835. Son Neil, sheriff of Victoria Co. **DC 21 Mar 1980**.

6155   McDOUGALL, John, 25 Jul 1805–21 Feb 1870. From Coldstream, BEW. s/o John M. and Janet Wilson. To QUE, ca 1834; stld Three Rivers. Industrialist. m Margaret Purvis, qv, ch: 1. John; 2. James; 3. Robert; 4. George; 5. David; 6. Alexander; 7. William, 1831-86, Judge of the Superior Court at Ottawa; 8. Thomas; 9. Ann; 10. Janet; 11. Margaret. **BNA 748; MDB 499**.

6156   McDOUGALL, John, b 1816. To ONT <1840; stld Lanark Co. m Mary Gibson, qv, ch: 1. James, b 1842;

2. John, b 1847; 3. Charles, b 1849; 4. Margaret, b 1850; 5. William, b 1851; 6. Thomas, b 1853; 7. Albert, b 1855; 8. Alexander, b 1857; 9. Hugh, b 1859; 10. Jane, b 1860. **DC 2 Nov 1979**.

6157   MACDOUGALL, John. From INV. To Pictou Co, NS, <1840; stld Blue Mountain. Farmer and storekeeper. m Jessie McDougall, qv. Son John. **HNS iii 192**.

6158   McDOUGALL, John D, 9 Sep 1835–1 Feb 1905. To Mosa Twp, Middlesex Co, ONT, ca 1853. m 1855, Christy Ann, d/o Finlay Munro, qv, ch: 1. Philip, 1857–1924; 2. Margaret Ann, 1859-91; 3. Catherine E, 1863–1936; 4. Lewis N, 1865–1935; 5. Loudice E, 1866-92; 6. William E, 1867–1933; 7. John, 1869–1931; 8. Almer Archibald, 1871–1937; 9. Mary C, 1873–1945; 10. Edward G, 1875–1944; 11. Chesley, 1877–1966; 12. Walter Earl, 1879-81; 13. Dolley Flora, b 1881. **DC 21 Nov 1968 and 8 Mar 1970**.

6159   McDOUGALL, John Lorne. To CAN <1830. Emp with HBCo, and stld later at Renfrew Village, Renfrew Co, ONT. m Catherine, d/o John Cameron. Son John Lorne, 1838–1909, Auditor General of CAN. **BNA 806; DC 12 Apr 1979**.

6160   McDOUGALL, John M. Poss from INV. To East River, Pictou Co, NS, <1797. Poss discharged soldier, and gr 250 acres. **HPC App H**.

6161   MACDOUGALL, Lachlan. To Antigonish Co, NS, poss <1830. ch: 1. Donald; 2. Angus; 3. John. **HCA 269**.

6162   McDOUGALL, Margaret, b ca 1826. From Lochgoilhead, ARL. d/o John M, qv, and Agnes Campbell, qv. To North Sherbrooke Twp, Lanark Co, ONT, 1828; later to Hibbert, Perth Co. m Henry Morril. **DC 21 Jan 1960**.

6163   McDOUGALL, Margaret, b 1830. From Is Colonsay, ARL. To Bruce Co, ONT, ca 1852. Wife of Donald Galbraith, qv. **DC 9 Mar 1980**.

6164   McDOUGALL, Mary, b 1786. From ARL. d/o John M, qv, and Sarah McPherson, qv. To Baldoon, Dover Twp, Kent Co, ONT, 1804. m ca 1806, Angus McDonell. **UCM 268; DC 4 Oct 1979**.

6165   McDOUGALL, Mary. From Knoydart, INV. To QUE, ex Greenock, summer 1815; stld prob Lanark Co, ONT. Wife of Ronald McDonell, qv. **SEC 7**.

6166   McDOUGALL, Murdoch, b ca 1822. From Snizort par, Is Skye, INV. Prob bro/o Angus M, qv, Catherine M, qv, and Peter M, qv. To Kinloss Twp, Bruce Co, ONT, 1852. Farmer. By wife Sarah, ch: 1. Lachlan, b 1855; 2. Roderick, b 1857. **DC 12 Apr 1979**.

6167   McDOUGALL, Neil, 1769–27 Feb 1843. b Is Muck, INV. s/o Patrick M, qv, and Ann McIsaac. To Pictou Co, NS, 1791; later to Judique, Inverness Co. m Flora McEachern, qv, ch: 1. Angus; 2. Donald; 3. Patrick; 4. Charles; 5. Ann; 6. Mary; 7. Jessie; 8. Catherine; 9. John; 10. Alexander; 11. Peggy; 12. Flora, 1817–1912. **DC 15 Mar 1982**.

6168   MACDOUGALL, Neil, 1790–1850. From ARL. To Aldborough Twp, Elgin Co, ONT, poss 1818. **PDA 42**.

6169   MACDOUGALL, Neil 'Ban'. From Moidart, INV. To Antigonish Co, NS, poss <1820. ch: 1. Donald 'Ban'; 2. John. **HCA 267**.

6170 McDOUGALL, Neil. From Is Islay, ARL. To Durham Co, ONT, ca 1853; stld Beaverton. Wife followed with ch: 1. Mary; 2. Annie; 3. Findlay. **DC 28 Feb 1979**.

6171 McDOUGALL, Rev Neil, 2 Apr 1829–30 Apr 1906. From Oban, ARL. s/o John M, teacher, and Christina McColloch. Matric Univ of Glasgow, 1854. To ONT, 1864. Missionary, Indian Lands, and adm min of Eldon Twp, Victoria Co. Retr to SCT and was min of Is Coll, ARL, 1877-95, later of Benbecula and of Gaelic Chapel, Rothesay, BUT. m (i) Miss Munro, ch: 1. Albert Lorne, b 1868; 2. Augustus Nigel, b 1870; 3. Alexander John Daniel, b 1872; 4. Somerled, b 1874. m (ii) 1884, Agnes MacRae, d/o John Brown, with further ch: 5. John Brown, b 1885; 6. Frederick George, b 1887; 7. Nigel William, b 1894. **GMA 16518; FES iv 44, vii 641**.

6172 McDOUGALL, Patrick, ca 1748–ca 1808. From Is Eigg, INV, but b South Uist. To Pictou Co, NS, 1791; later to Inverness Co. m Ann McIsaac, who d in SCT. Son Neil, qv. **DC 15 Mar 1982**.

6173 McDOUGALL, Peggy. From Cleadale, Is Eigg, INV. To QUE on the *British Queen*, ex Arisaig, 16 Aug 1790; stld nr Montreal. Poss widow, with a child. **QCC 103**.

6174 McDOUGALL, Peter. From Fernon, ni, but poss ARL. To QUE, ex Greenock, summer 1815; stld prob Lanark Co, ONT. Shoemaker Wife Catharine Campbell, qv, with him, and 3 ch. **SEC 3**.

6175 McDOUGALL, Peter, b 1825. From Is Mull, ARL. To Minto Twp, Wellington Co, ONT, <1854; moved to Keppel Twp, Grey Co, <1874. m Mary McDonald, qv, ch: 1. Duncan, b 1850; 2. Agnes, b 1852; 3. John, b 1855; 4. Jessie, b 1857; 5. Malcolm, b 1860; 6. Peter, b 1863; 7. Margaret, b 1865; 8. Jane, b 1867; 9. Hugh, b 1869; 10. Flora, b 1872. **DC 30 Jul 1979**.

6176 McDOUGALL, Peter, b ca 1825. From Snizort par, Is Skye, INV. Prob bro/o Angus M, qv, Catherine M, qv, and Murdoch M, qv. To Kinloss Twp, Bruce Co, ONT, 1852. m Mary McKinnon, qv, ch. **DC 6 Mar 1979**.

6177 MACDOUGALL, Rory. To Pictou Co, NS, prob <1830; stld Marydale, Antigonish Co. m (i) Jessie Smith, ch: 1. Archibald; 2. Mary; 3. Ann. m (ii) Lillian Chisholm, with further ch: 4. William; 5. Donald; 6. Flora; 7. John; 8. Catherine; 9. Lillian; 10. Jessie; 11. Hugh. **HCA 266**.

6178 McDOUGALL, Samuel. Prob from ARL. To Pictou Co, NS, on the *Hope*, ex Glasgow, 5 Apr 1848. Wife Ann with him, ch: 1. John; 2. Murdoch; 3. Agnes; 4. Euphemia. They went later to USA. **DC 12 Jul 1979**.

6179 McDOUGALL, Samuel. From ARL. Prob bro/o Allan M, qv, and Archibald M, qv. To Metcalfe Twp, Middlesex Co, ONT, 1848. **PCM 26**.

6180 McDOWALL, James, 1812-75. From Kirkconnel, DFS. Rel to Elizabeth Laidlaw, qv. To ONT, 1842; stld McKillop Twp, Huron Co. Weaver, later farmer. m Helen Esther Laidlaw, qv, ch: 1. Elizabeth, 1848-94; 2. James, 1850–1932; 3. John Laidlaw, 1851–1943; 4. William, b 1852, went to CO; 5. Thomas, 1853-55; 6. Thomas, 1857-92. **DC 26 May 1979**.

6181 McDOWALL, Susan, d 3 Apr 1835. From DFS. To Richibucto, Kent Co, NB. m Rev James Hannay, qv. **DGC 15 Jul 1835**.

6182 McDUFFIE, Duncan, b ca 1752. Prob from Is Colonsay, ARL. To Charlottetown, PEI, on the *Spencer*, ex Oban, arr 22 Sep 1806. ch: 1. Margaret, aged 20; 2. Nancy, aged 19; 3. Dugald, aged 17; 4. Janet, aged 14; 5. Catherine, aged 9; 6. Effie, aged 5; 7. Donald, aged 2 ½. **PLSN**.

6183 McDUFFIE, Flora, b ca 1765. Prob from Is Oronsay or Is Colonsay, ARL. To Charlottetown, PEI, on the *Spencer*, ex Oban, arr 22 Sep 1806. **PLSN**.

6184 McDUFFIE, Mary, b ca 1734. Prob from Is Oronsay or Is Colonsay, ARL. To Charlottetown, PEI, on the *Spencer*, ex Oban, arr 22 Sep 1806. **PLSN**.

McDUGALD. See also McDOUGAL, McDOUGALL and McDOUGALD.

6185 McDUGALD, Malcolm, d 1866. From Is Colonsay, ARL. To Arran Twp, Bruce Co, ONT, <1853. m Euphemia Currie, ch: 1. Donald, b 1833; 2. Hugh, b 1836; 3. Flora, b 1842; 4. Mary, b 1845; 5. Margaret; 6. Ann; 7. Malcolm. **DC 30 Jul 1979**.

6186 McEACHAN, Alexander. From Arienskill, ni, INV. To PEI on the *Lucy*, ex Loch nan Uamh, Arisaig, 12 Jul 1790. Tenant. Wife with him. **PLL**.

6187 McEACHAN, Angus. From Arienskill, ni, INV. To PEI on the *Lucy*, ex Loch nan Uamh, Arisaig, 12 Jul 1790. Smith. Family with him. **PLL**.

6188 McEACHAN, Angus, b 1791. To Western Shore, Inverness Co, NS, 1802. Farmer, m and had ch. **CBC 1818**.

6189 McEACHAN, Ann, b 1816. From Tomluachrach, Is Benbecula, INV. To Pictou, NS, on the *Lulan*, ex Glasgow, 17 Aug 1848. Wife of John Gillies, qv. **DC 12 Jul 1979**.

6190 McEACHAN, Eliza, b 1798. From Is South Uist, INV. To East Williams Twp, Middlesex Co, ONT, ca 1849. Wife of Archibald Currie, qv. **PCM 44; WLC**.

6191 McEACHAN, John. From Kinlochailort, Moidart, INV. To PEI on the *Lucy*, ex Loch nan Uamh, Arisaig, 12 Jul 1790. Family with him. **PLL**.

6192 McEACHAN, John. From Is Shona, INV. To PEI on the *Lucy*, ex Loch nan Uamh, Arisaig, 12 Jul 1790. **PLL**.

6193 McEACHAN, John. From Is Shona, INV. To PEI on the *Lucy*, ex Loch nan Uamh, Arisaig, 12 Jul 1790. Wife and 3 ch with him. **PLL**.

6194 McEACHAN, John, b ca 1800. Poss s/o Donald M. To Western Shore, Inverness Co, NS, 1802. Farmer. **CBC 1818**.

6195 McEACHAN, Lachland, b ca 1786. To Western Shore, Inverness Co, NS, 1802. Farmer, m and had ch. **CBC 1818**.

6196 MACEACHAN, Mary, b ca 1801. From Tomluachrach, Is Benbecula, INV. To Pictou on the *Lulan*, ex Glasgow, 17 Aug 1848. Wife of Duncan MacIntyre, qv. **DC 12 Jul 1979**.

6197 MACEACHEN, Alexander 'Gobha'. From Is South Uist, INV. bro/o John 'Gobha' M, qv, and Mary M, qv.

To Pictou Co, NS, 1791; stld Fishers Grant. Moved to Judique Banks, Inverness Co, and was later at Mabou Harbour. Farmer. m Mary, d/o Samuel Campbell, qv, and Jane MacGregor, qv, ch: 1. John; 2. Angus; 3. Allan; 4. Samuel; 5. Alexander; 6. Mary; 7. Catherine; 8. Anne. **MP 631**.

6198 McEACHEN, Angus, b ca 1758. To Western Shore, Inverness Co, NS, 1804. Farmer, m and had ch. **CBC 1818**.

6199 MACEACHEN, Rev Angus Bernard, 8 Feb 1759–22 Apr 1835. From Kinlochmoidart, ARL. s/o Hugh 'Ban' M, qv. Protégé of Bishop Hugh MacDonald, Highland dist, and educ Samalaman seminary and RC Coll, Valladolid, Madrid, Spain. Ord 1787, and after serving as a missionary in SCT, went to PEI in 1790. Consecrated Bishop of Rosen, with jurisdiction over Cape Breton Is, NB and PEI, at QUE, 17 Jun 1821. Bishop of Charlottetown, 1829. **HNS iii 465; MP 21**.

6200 MACEACHEN, Catherine. From Kinlochmoidart, ARL. d/o Hugh 'Ban' M, qv. To PEI, prob 1772; stld later Judique, Inverness Co, NS. m Allan 'Ban' MacDonald, qv. **MP 21; NSN 32/363**.

6201 McEACHEN, Donald. From Slochardnish, Arisaig, INV. To PEI on the *Jane*, ex Loch nan Uamh, 12 Jul 1790. Family with him. **PLJ**.

6202 McEACHEN, Donald, b ca 1758. To Western Shore, Inverness Co, NS, 1802. Farmer, m and had ch. **CBC 1818**.

6203 McEACHEN, Donald, b ca 1795. To Western Shore, Inverness Co, NS, 1802. Farmer. **CBC 1818**.

6204 McEACHEN, Donald, b ca 1791. To Western Shore, Inverness Co, NS, 1804. Farmer, m and had ch. **CBC 1818**.

6205 MACEACHEN, Ewen. From Kinlochmoidart, ARL. s/o Hugh 'Ban' M, qv. To PEI, 1772; later to Judique, Inverness Co, NS. Gr 600 acres at Indian Point, but later sold the land and went back to PEI. **HNS iii 465; MP 21; DC 5 Feb 1961**.

6206 McEACHEN, Hugh 'Ban'. From Kinlochmoidart, ARL. To Savage Harbour, PEI, prob on the *Alexander*, 1772. ch: 1. Hugh; 2. Margaret, qv; 3. Ewen, qv; 4. Mrs Michael McDonald, Judique; 5. Mary, qv; 6. Catherine, qv; 7. Rev Angus Bernard, qv. **HNS iii 465; MP 21; NSN 32/363; DC 5 Feb 1961**.

6207 MACEACHEN, Hugh. Prob from INV. To Mabou Harbour, Inverness Co, NS, poss <1810. m Miss Gillis, and had ch: 1. Andrew; 2. John; 3. Angus; 4. Ronald; 5. Alexander; 6. Donald. **MP 641**.

6208 McEACHEN, Janet. From Aird, Is Benbecula, INV. d/o Alexander M. and Rachel McLellan. To London Twp, Middlesex Co, ONT, 1852; later to East Williams Twp. Wife of Angus McCorkindale, qv. **WLC**.

6209 MACEACHEN, John 'Gobha', d ca 1800. From Is South Uist, INV. bro/o Alexander 'Gobha' M, qv, and Mary M, qv. To Pictou Co, NS, 1791; stld Fishers Grant, but moved later to Judique Banks, Inverness Co. m Sarah MacLellan, qv, ch: 1. John; 2. Mary. **MP 633; WLC**.

6210 McEACHEN, John, b 1754. To Western Shore,

Inverness Co, NS, 1802. Farmer, m and had ch. **CBC 1818**.

6211 MACEACHEN, John 'Ruadh'. From Arisaig, INV. To Port Hood, Inverness Co, NS, 1801. Wife Sara with him. ch: 1. John; 2. Angus; 3. Mary; 4. Margaret; 5. Catherine; 6. Anne. **MP 640**.

6212 McEACHEN, Katherine. From Airnapoul, ni, INV. To PEI on the *Jane*, ex Loch nan Uamh, Arisaig, 12 Jul 1790. **PLJ**.

6213 McEACHEN, Malcolm, b ca 1789. To Western Shore, Inverness Co, NS, 1804. Farmer, m and had ch. **CBC 1818**.

6214 McEACHEN, Margaret. From Kinlochmoidart, ARL. d/o Hugh 'Ban' M, qv. To Savage Harbour, PEI, prob on the *Alexander*, 1772. m Donald McIntyre. **DC 5 Feb 1961**.

6215 McEACHEN, Mary. From Kinlochmoidart, ARL. d/o Hugh 'Ban' M, qv. To PEI, prob on the *Alexander*, 1772. Went later to Judique, Inverness Co, NS. m Robert MacInnes, qv. **DC 5 Feb 1961**.

6216 MACEACHEN, Mary. From Is South Uist, INV. sis/o Alexander 'Gobha' M, qv, and John 'Gobha' M, qv. To Antigonish Co, 1791; later to PEI. m — Morrison. **MP 633**.

6217 McEACHERN, Alexander, b ca 1796. To Western Shore, Inverness Co, NS, 1802. Farmer. **CBC 1818**.

6218 McEACHERN, Alexander. From Is Mull, ARL. To Cape Breton Co, NS, <1850. Son John, b Boulardarie Is. **HNS iii 192**.

6219 McEACHERN, Allan, b ca 1781. To Western Shore, Inverness Co, NS, 1799. Farmer, m and had ch. **CBC 1818**.

6220 McEACHERN, Angus, b ca 1791. Poss s/o Duncan M, qv. To Western Shore, Inverness Co, NS, 1802. Farmer. **CBC 1818**.

6221 McEACHERN, Angus, b 1774. Prob from Is Colonsay, ARL. To Charlottetown, PEI on the *Spencer*, ex Oban, 22 Sep 1806. ch with him: 1. Neil, aged 7; 2. James, aged 1 ½. **PLSN**.

6222 MACEACHERN, Angus, b ca 1815. From Is Eigg, INV. s/o John M. and Mrs Mary M, qv. To Gut of Canso, Cape Breton, NS, on the *Catherine*, ex Tobermory, 13 Jul 1843; stld Upper Dalhousie, Inverness Co. **MP 635**.

6223 McEACHERN, Angus. From Is Jura, ARL. To Ekfrid Twp, Middlesex Co, ONT, ca 1852. **PCM 31**.

6224 McEACHERN, Ann, b 1756. To Charlottetown, PEI, on the *Humphreys*, ex Tobermory, 14 Jul 1806. Prob widow with s Charles with her. **PLH**.

6225 McEACHERN, Ann, b 1787. Poss from Is Colonsay, ARL, and prob rel to Archibald M, qv. To Charlottetown, PEI, on the *Spencer*, ex Oban, 22 Sep 1806. **PLSN**.

6226 McEACHERN, Archibald, b ca 1776. To Charlottetown, PEI, on the *Humphreys*, ex Tobermory, 14 Jul 1806. Wife Sarah, aged 30, with him, and ch: 1. Jane, aged 6; 2. Lachlan, aged 3; 3. Margaret, inf. **PLH**.

6227 McEACHERN, Archibald, b 1776. Poss from Is

Colonsay, ARL, and prob rel to Ann M, qv. To PEI on the *Spencer*, ex Oban, 22 Sep 1806. Son Malcolm, aged 3, with him. **PLSN**.

6228 MACEACHERN, Archibald. From Lochaber, INV. To Antigonish Co, NS, prob <1815; stld Lochaber Lake. m Mary Williams, ch: 1. Duncan; 2. Donald; 3. Allan, res Cape George; 4. John; 5. Neil; 6. Alexander; 7. Colin; 8. Mary; 9. Catherine; 10. Ann; 11. Flora. **HCA 270**.

6229 McEACHERN, Catherine, b 1779. Poss from Is Colonsay, ARL. To Charlottetown, PEI, on the *Spencer*, ex Oban, 22 Sep 1806. Poss rel to Angus M, qv. **PLSN**.

6230 MACEACHERN, Catherine. From Is Eigg, INV. d/o John M. and Mrs Mary M, qv. To Brantford, ONT, prob <1845. m Angus Campbell, and had ch. **MP 638**.

6231 MACEACHERN, Charles. To PEI, prob <1830; stld Queens Co. Schoolmaster at Newtown, 1834. **HP 28**.

6232 McEACHERN, Donald, b ca 1746. To Charlottetown, PEI, on the *Humpherys*, ex Tobermory, 14 Jul 1806. Wife Sarah, aged 52, with him, and ch: 1. Donald, aged 24; 2. Mary, aged 19; 3. Dugald, aged 18; 4. Janet, aged 12; 5. Hector, aged 9. **PLS**.

6233 McEACHERN, Donald. From Is Islay, ARL. s/o Malcolm M. To Megantic Co, QUE, 1833; later to St Croix. m Isabella Kerr, qv. **AMC 48**.

6234 MACEACHERN, Donald, 1821-87. From Is Islay, ARL. s/o Ronald M, qv, and his wife Rachel. To Eldon Twp, Victoria Co, ONT, 1845. Capt on Great Lakes. m Margaret McDougall, ch: 1. Mary Ellen, 1867 1916; 2. John D, 1863–1944; 3. Dan, 1868–1963; 4. Ronald, d 1944; 5. Archie, b 1865; 6. Neil, 1872–1953; 7. Robert. **EC 106**.

6235 McEACHERN, Donald. From Kintyre, ARL. To Ekfrid Twp, Middlesex Co, ONT, 1849. Son David, b 1817, emig 1850. **PCM 31**.

6236 MACEACHERN, Donald. Prob from Is Mull, ARL. To Eldon Twp, Victoria Co, ONT, <1850. m Isabel MacEachern. **EC 17**.

6237 McEACHERN, Donald. From ARL. To Ekfrid Twp, Middlesex Co, ONT, 1850. **PCM 31**.

6238 MACEACHERN, Dougald, b ca 1811. From Is Eigg, INV. s/o John M. and Mrs Mary M, qv. To Gut of Canso, Cape Breton, NS, on the *Catherine*, ex Tobermory, 13 Jul 1843; stld Upper Dalhousie, Inverness Co. m Catherine, d/o Lachlan MacEachern, ch: 1. Lachlan; 2. John; 3. Mary; 4. Margaret; 5. Anne; 6. Catherine. **MP 633**.

6239 MACEACHERN, Duncan, b 1748. To Western Shore, Inverness Co, NS, 1802. Farmer. Poss father of Hugh M, qv, Ronald M, qv, and Angus M, qv. **CBC 1818**.

6240 McEACHERN, Duncan. From Is Jura, ARL. To Ekfrid Twp, Middlesex Co, ONT, ca 1852. Blacksmith. **PCM 31**.

6241 MACEACHERN, Eachern. From Is Mull, ARL. bro/o Farquhar M, qv. To Eldon Twp, Victoria Co, ONT, <1830; stld Lot 5, Con 1, and Lot 10, Con 4. Farmer.

ch: 1. Hugh; 2. Dougal; 3. Malcolm; 5. John, female child. **EC 36; DC 21 Mar 1980**.

6242 McEACHERN, Flora, b ca 1775. From Moidart, INV. To Judique, Inverness Co, NS, <1800. m Neil McDougall, qv. **DC 15 Mar 1982**.

6243 McEACHERN, Farquhar. From Is Mull, ARL. bro/o Eachern M, qv. To Eldon Twp, Victoria Co, ONT, ca 1830. Son Alexander. **EC 112; DC 21 Mar 1980**.

6244 McEACHERN, Hector. Prob from Is Mull, ARL. To Hudson Bay and Red River <1813. Wife with him. **RRS 15**.

6245 MACEACHERN, Hector. From Is Islay, ARL. To Eldon Twp, Victoria Co, ONT, <1850. Farmer. m Martha Smith, qv, and had ch. **EC 118; DC 21 Feb 1980**.

6246 McEACHERN, Hugh, b ca 1785. To Western Shore, Inverness Co, NS, 1802. Farmer, m and had ch. **CBC 1818**.

6247 McEACHERN, Hugh, b ca 1791. Poss s/o Duncan M, qv. To Western Shore, Inverness Co, NS, 1802. Cooper. **CBC 1818**.

6248 MACEACHERN, Hugh, b ca 1812. From Is Eigg, INV. s/o John M. and Mrs Mary M, qv. To Gut of Canso, Cape Breton, NS, on the *Catherine*, ex Tobermory, 13 Jul 1843; stld Upper Dalhousie, Inverness Co. m Jessie MacEachen, and had ch. **MP 635**.

6249 McEACHERN, Hugh. Prob from ARL. To Minto Twp, Wellington Co, ONT, <1861. **RFS 148**.

6250 MACEACHERN, James, b ca 1825. From Is Eigg, INV. s/o John M. and Mrs Mary M, qv. To Gut of Canso, Cape Breton, NS, on the *Catherine*, ex Tobermory, 13 Jul 1843; stld Upper Dalhousie, Inverness Co. m Anne, d/o Archibald MacDonald, qv, and Mary MacNeil, ch: 1. Hugh; 2. Catherine; 3. Archibald; 4. Mary; 5. Janet; 6. Mary Anne; 7. John; 8. Jessie; 9. Allan; 10. Ranald; 11. Christina. **MP 411, 636**.

6251 MACEACHERN, John. From Dunmaglass, INV. s/o John 'Ruadh' M, qv, and Sarah MacGillivray, qv. To Antigonish Co, NS, 1792. m Isabella MacGillivray, ch: 1. Donald; 2. Mary; 3. Angus; 4. Isabella; 5. Hugh; 6. Kate; 7. Margaret; 8. Ann; 9. Sarah. **HCA 271**.

6252 MACEACHERN, John 'Ruadh'. From Dunmaglass, INV. To Antigonish Co, NS, 1792; stld at the Gusset. m Sarah MacGillivray, qv, ch: 1. John, qv; 2. Angus; 3. Donald. **HCA 271**.

6253 McEACHERN, John, b ca 1772. To Western Shore, Inverness Co, NS, 1800. Farmer, m and had ch. **CBC 1818**.

6254 McEACHERN, John, b 1771. To Charlottetown, PEI, on the *Rambler*, ex Tobermory, 20 Jun 1806. Wife Mary, aged 30, with him, and ch: 1. Hector, aged 3; 2. Allan, aged 2. **PLR**.

6255 McEACHERN, John, b ca 1784. Prob rel to Archibald M, qv. To Charlottetown, PEI, ex Tobermory, on the *Humphreys*, 14 Jul 1806. **PLH**.

6256 McEACHERN, John, b ca 1793. To Western Shore, Inverness Co, NS, 1817. Farmer. **CBC 1818**.

6257 MACEACHERN, John. Prob from Arisaig, INV. s/o Donald M. To Antigonish Co, NS, poss <1830. m Miss Macpherson, ch: 1. Mary; 2. Angus; 3. Ellen;

4. Isabel; 5. Sarah; 6. John; 7. Donald; 8. Lachlan; 9. Charles. **HCA 270**.

6258 McEACHERN, John. From Is Jura, ARL. To Kingston, ONT, 1832, and stld Ekfrid Twp, Middlesex Co. **PCM 31**.

6259 MACEACHERN, John, b ca 1817. From Is Eigg, INV. s/o John M. and Mrs Mary M, qv. To Gut of Canso, Cape Breton, NS, on the *Catherine*, ex Tobermory, 13 Jul 1843; stld Upper Dalhousie, Inverness Co. m Anne, d/o Donald, s/o Patrick MacEachen, ch: 1. John; 2. Mary; 3. Margaret; 4. Flora. **MP 635**.

6260 MACEACHERN, John, 1825–1903. From Is Islay, ARL. s/o Ronald M, qv, and wife Rachel. To Eldon Twp, Victoria Co, ONT, 1845. m Margaret Carmichael, ch: 1. Margaret; 2. Archibald; 3. Rachel; 4. Mary; 5. Ronald. **EC 106**.

6261 MACEACHERN, Lachlan, b ca 1825. Prob from Is Mull, ARL. To Eldon Twp, Victoria Co, ONT, <1850; stld Lot 23, Con 10. m Flora d/o John McInnes, qv, and Euphemia MacQuarrie, qv. **EC 116**.

6262 McEACHERN, Malcolm, b 1748. Prob from Is Colonsay, ARL. To Charlottetown, PEI, on the *Spencer*, ex Oban, 22 Sep 1806. Wife Flora Buchanan, qv, with him, and ch: 1. Mary, aged 28; 2. Donald, aged 22; 3. Angus, aged 12. **PLSN**.

6263 McEACHERN, Malcolm. From Kilcoman par, Is Islay, ARL. To Fort Churchill, Hudson Bay, on the *Prince of Wales*, ex Stromness, 28 Jun 1813. Went to York Factory, spring 1814, thence to Red River. Wife Mary with him. Left settlement, prob 1815. **LSS 186; RRS 27; LSC 323**.

6264 MACEACHERN, Malcolm. From Is Islay, ARL. To ONT, ca 1834; stld Lot 4, Con 20, Eldon Twp, Victoria Co. Farmer. m Elspie Smith, qv, ch: 1. Farquhar; 2. John; 3. Donald; 4. Angus; 5. Mary; 6. Catherine; 7. Margaret; 8. Sarah; 9. Flora; 10. Agnes; 11. Christina; 12. Elspie. **EC 102**.

6265 MACEACHERN, Malcolm, b ca 1800. From Is Islay, ARL. s/o Alan M. To York Co, ONT, <1830; stld Argyle, Eldon Twp, Victoria Co. **EC 112**.

6266 MACEACHERN, Margaret, called Peggy, b ca 1821. From Is Eigg, INV. d/o John M, and Mrs Margaret M, qv. To Gut of Canso, Cape Breton, NS, on the *Catherine*, ex Tobermory, 13 Jul 1843; stld Upper Dalhousie, Inverness Co. m Rory MacLean, Glencoe, ch: 1. John; 2. Norman; 3. Flora; 4. Mary. **MP 638**.

6267 MACEACHERN, Mary, 1833–1915. From Is Islay, ARL. d/o Ronald M, qv, and wife Rachel. To Eldon Twp, Victoria Co, ONT, 1845. m John Campbell, ch: 1. Rachel; 2. dau. **EC 106**.

6268 MACEACHERN, Mary. Prob from Is Mull, ARL. To Eldon Twp, Victoria Co, ONT, <1850. m — McFarlane. **EC 117**.

6269 MACEACHERN, Mrs Mary, b ca 1788. From Is Eigg, INV. wid/o John, s/o Hugh M. To Gut of Canso, Cape Breton, NS, on the *Catherine*, ex Tobermory, 13 Jul 1843; stld Upper Dalhousie, Inverness Co. ch with her: 1. Dougald, qv; 2. Hugh, qv; 3. Angus, qv; 4. John, qv; 5. Ronald, qv; 6. Roderick, qv; 7. James, qv; 8. Mary, qv; 9. Catherine, qv. **MP 633**.

6270 MACEACHERN, Mary, b ca 1828. From Is Eigg, INV. d/o John M. and Mrs Mary M, qv. To Gut of Canso, Cape Breton, NS, on the *Catherine*, ex Tobermory, 13 Jul 1843; stld Upper Dalhousie, Inverness Co. m John, s/o Lachlan McEachen, ch. **MP 637**.

6271 McEACHERN, Mrs. From Is Islay, ARL. To Megantic Co, QUE, 1833. wid/o Malcolm M. ch with her: 1. Archibald; 2. Peter; 3. Donald, qv; 4. Margaret; 5. Flora. **AMC 48**.

6272 MACEACHERN, Neil. From Is Islay, ARL. To ONT, 1834, stld Lot 3, Con 7, Eldon Twp, Victoria Co. Farmer. m Mary Smith, qv, ch: 1. John; 2. Angus; 3. Farquhar; 4. Donald; 5. Neil; 6. Mary; 7. Margaret; 8. Flora. **EC 100**.

6273 MACEACHERN, Neil, b 1829. Prob from Is Mull, ARL. To Eldon Twp, Victoria Co, ONT, <1850. m Kate McInnis. **EC 117**.

6274 MACEACHERN, Neil, 1836–1871. From Islay, ARL. s/o Ronald M, qv, and wife Rachel. To Eldon Twp, Victoria Co, ONT, 1845. m Ann McAlpine. **EC 106**.

6275 MACEACHERN, Peter, b 1841. From Is Islay, ARL. s/o Ronald M, qv, and wife Rachel. To Eldon Twp, Victoria Co, ONT, 1845. m Flora MacEachern, ch: 1. Archie; 2. Mary; 3. Rachel; 4. Ronald; 5. Peter, dy. **EC 106**.

6276 MACEACHERN, Roderick, b ca 1823. From Is Eigg, INV. s/o John M. and Mrs Mary M, qv. To Gut of Canso, Cape Breton, NS, on the *Catherine*, ex Tobermory, 13 Jul 1843; stld Upper Dalhousie, Inverness Co. m Mary, d/o Archibald MacDonald, qv, and Mary MacNeil, ch: 1. Mary; 2. Ann; 3. John; 4. Donald; 5. Archibald; 6. Donaly; 7. Ronald; 8. Hugh; 9. Hugh Og. **MP 635**.

6277 McEACHERN, Ronald, b ca 1788. Poss s/o Duncan M, qv. To Western Shore, Inverness Co, NS, 1802. Farmer, m and ch. **CBC 1818**.

6278 MACEACHERN, Ronald, 1794–1865. From Is Islay, ARL. To ONT, 1845; stld Woodville, Eldon Twp, Victoria Co. Moved to Con 3. Farmer. By wife Rachel, 1800-44, ch: 1. Donald, qv; 2. Archie, 1823–1910; 3. John, qv; 4. Margaret, 1827–1915; 5. Ronald, 1829-31; 6. Ronald, qv; 7. Mary, qv; 8. Neil, qv; 9. Peter, qv. **EC 106**.

6279 MACEACHERN, Ronald, b ca 1820. From Is Eigg, INV. s/o John M. and Mrs Mary M, qv. To Gut of Canso, Cape Breton, NS, on the *Catherine*, ex Tobermory, 13 Jul 1843; stld Upper Dalhousie, Inverness Co. m Mary, d/o Dougald Beaton, qv, ch. **MP, 94, 635**.

6280 MACEACHERN, Ronald, jr, 1832–1917. From Is Islay, ARL. s/o Ronald M, qv, and wife Rachel. To Eldon Twp, Victoria Co, ONT, ca 1845. m Margaret Bell, ch: 1. Mary; 2. Ronald; 3. Sarah; 4. Margaret; 5. Rachel. **EC 106**.

6281 McEACHERN, Sarah, 18 Mar 1808–9 Apr 1893. d/o Alexander M, 42nd Regt. To Charlottetown, PEI, ca 1839. m 8 Dec 1831, in Cromarty, John Foster, qv. **SCN**.

6282 MACEACHERN, Sarah, b 1813. From Is Islay, ARL. sis/o Hector M, qv. To Eldon Twp, Victoria Co, ONT, prob <1850; stld Lot 11, Con 4, later Lot 19,

Con 6. Farmer and weaver, and wid/o Duncan Morrison, by whom she had ch: 1. Jack, b 1835; 2. Malcolm, b 1839; 3. Donald, b 1841; 4. Katie; 5. Neil. **EC 118, 194**.

McEACHIN. See also McEACHAN and McEACHEN.

6283 McEACHIN, Alexander, 27 Jun 1833–14 Dec 1925. From Is Benbecula, INV. s/o Alexander M. and Sarah McLeod, qv. To Seaforth, Huron Co, ONT, ca 1837. m Margaret Campbell, 1833-95, ch: 1. Roderick, 1866–1933; 2. Annie, b 1868; 3. Sarah, b 1870; 4. John, b 1874; 5. Christena, 1880–1959; 6. Margaret, 1880–1901. **DC 12 Nov 1979**.

6284 McEACHIN, Christine, b ca 1826. From Is Benbecula, INV. d/o Alexander M. and Sarah McLeod, qv. To Seaforth, Huron Co, ONT, ca 1837. m Rory McLeod, ch: 1. Penny; 2. Margaret; 3. Rory; 4. Jack. **DC 12 Nov 1979**.

6285 McEACHIN, Donald. From Is South Uist, INV. To West Williams Twp, Middlesex Co, ONT, 1849. **PCM 47**.

6286 McEACHIN, Margaret, 25 Sep 1824–18 Nov 1910. From Is Benbecula, INV. d/o Alexander M. and Sarah McLeod, qv. To Seaforth, Huron Co, ONT, ca 1837. m Malcolm McNichol, qv. **DC 12 Nov 1979**.

6287 McEACHIN, Neil, b 1800. From Stoneybridge, Is South Uist, INV. To West Williams Twp, Middlesex Co, ONT, 1850. m Emily Ferguson, ch: 1. Neil, b 1829; 2. Catherine, b 1831; 3. Marion, b 1835; 4. Janet, b 1837; 5. John, b 1839; 6. Norman, b 1841; 7. Flora, b 1844; 8. John Og; 9. Jane. **PCM 47; WLC**.

6288 McEACHIN, Neil, b 1806. From Stoneybridge, Is South Uist, INV. To East Williams Twp, Middlesex Co, ONT, 1850; stld poss West Williams Twp. Farmer. m Christy McIntyre, b 1811, ch: 1. John, b 1830; 2. Roderick, b 1833; 3. Marion, b 1835; 4. Catherine, b 1839; 5. Neil, b 1841; 6. Mary, b 1844; 7. Donald. **PCM 44; WLC**.

McEACHIN, Mrs Alexander. See McLEOD, Sarah.

6289 McEACHIN, Sarah. From Is Benbecula, INV. d/o Alexander M. and Sarah McLeod, qv. To Seaforth, Huron Co, ONT, 1837. m David Dunbar, ch: 1. Sarah; 2. David. **DC 12 Nov 1979**.

6290 McEACHRAN, Alexander, b ca 1779. To Port Hood dist, Inverness Co, NS, 1804. Farmer. **CBC 1818**.

6291 McEACHRAN, Alexander, b 1773. To Inverness Co, NS, 1812; stld Mabou. Farmer, m and ch. **CBC 1818**.

6292 McEACHRAN, Angus. From Ardnamurchan, ARL. To PEI <1798. **DC 30 Sep 1960**.

6293 McEACHRAN, Archibald. From ARL. Prob rel to Donald M, qv. To Aldborough Twp, Elgin Co, ONT, 1850. ch incl: 1. Donald, physician, Seattle; 2. Archibald, physician, Minneapolis. **PDA 75**.

6294 McEACHRAN, Colin, b ca 1787. To Richmond Co, NS, 1814. Carpenter. ch. **CBC 1818**.

6295 McEACHRAN, Donald. From Ardnamurchan, ARL. To PEI <1798. **DC 30 Sep 1960**.

6296 McEACHRAN, Donald, b 1758. To St Andrews dist, Cape Breton Co, NS, <1817. Farmer, m and ch. **CBC 1818**.

6297 McEACHRAN, Donald. From ARL. Prob rel to Archibald M, qv. To Aldborough Twp, Elgin Co, ONT, 1850. ch incl: 1. Hugh, physician, Detroit; 2. John, physician, MI. **PDA 75**.

6298 McEACHRAN, Hugh, b ca 1777. To Port Hood dist, Inverness Co, NS, 1804. Tailor, m and ch. **CBC 1818**.

6299 McEACHRAN, John, b ca 1778. From Mull, ARL. To Charlottetown, PEI, on the *Clarendon*, ex Oban, 6 Aug 1808. Labourer. Wife Margaret, aged 35, with him, and ch: 1. Hugh, aged 10; 2. Alexander, aged 7; 3. Janet, aged 5. **CPL**.

6300 McEACHRAN, John. From Ardnamurchan, ARL. To PEI <1798. **DC 30 Sep 1960**.

McEACHRAN, Mrs. See McCUAIG, Jenny.

6301 McEACHRAN, Neil, b ca 1790. To Mabou, Inverness Co, NS, 1804. Farmer. **CBC 1818**.

6302 McEWAN, Alexander, b ca 1813. From Balquhidder par, PER. s/o Finlay M, qv, and Mary McLaren, qv. To Montreal, QUE, on the *Sophia*, ex Greenock, 26 Jul 1818; stld Beckwith Twp, Lanark Co, ONT. Went later to Ottawa. m Janet McNab, Osgoode Twp, 1839. Son Finlay, 1841-92, physician. **DC 30 Aug 1977**.

6303 McEWAN, Archibald. To QUE, 1821; stld North Sherbrooke Twp, Lanark Co, ONT. **HCL 74**.

6304 McEWAN, David, ca 1780–1833. From Ochtertyre, PER, but emig from PEE to ONT, 1832. m Helen Bruce, qv. **DC 23 Mar 1979**.

6305 McEWAN, Donald, 1750–29 Nov 1842. From Comrie par, PER. To QUE and stld Ormston, Ottawa East. m Janet McCuaig, qv. **Ts Ormston**.

6306 McEWAN, Finlay. From Lochearnhead, PER. s/o Finlay M. To Montreal, QUE, on the *Sophia*, ex Greenock, 26 Jul 1818; stld Lot 23, Con 7, Beckwith Twp, Lanark Co, ONT. m Mary McLaren, qv, ch: 1. John, b ca 1807; 2. Hugh, b ca 1809; 3. Alexander, qv; 4. James, b ca 1815; 5. Peter, b 1818. **SPL; HCL 33**.

6307 McEWAN, Janet. Poss from Lochearnhead, PER. To Montreal, QUE, on the *Niagara*, ex Greenock, arr 28 May 1825; stld McNab Twp, Renfrew Co, ONT. Wife of Archibald McNab, qv. **EMT 22**.

6308 McEWAN, Janet, 1778–1852. From Glen Quaich, Dull par, PER. To Osgoode Twp, Carleton Co, ONT, 1832. Wife of Thomas Dow, qv. **DC 1 Aug 1975**.

6309 McEWAN, Margaret. From Lochearnhead, PER. To Montreal, QUE, on the *Niagara*, ex Greenock, arr 28 May 1825; stld McNab Twp, Renfrew Co, ONT. Wife of Donald Fisher, qv. **MTE 18, 22**.

6310 McEWAN, Margaret, ca 1792–2 Jul 1871. From ARL. d/o Duncan M. and Kirsty Campbell. To ONT, 1828; stld Eldon Twp, Victoria Co. Wife of Hugh McCorquodale, qv. **DC 21 Feb 1980**.

6311 McEWAN or McKEOWN, Mary, 3 Aug 1778– 22 Feb 1821. From Falkirk, STI. d/o Alexander M. and Isabell Strathearn. To QUE on the *Rothiemurchus*, ex

Leith, 5 Apr 1817; stld York Co, ONT. Wife of Rev William Taylor, qv. **LDW 7 Dec 1974**.

6312 McEWAN, William. To QUE on the *George Canning*, ex Greenock, 14 Apr 1821; stld prob Lanark Co, ONT. **HCL 239**.

6313 McEWEN, Allan, b ca 1797. From Kilfinichen, Is Mull, ARL. To Hudson Bay and Red River <1815. **RRS 25**.

6314 McEWEN, Donald. Prob from PER. To Aldborough Twp, Elgin Co, ONT, ca 1814. Pioneer settler. **PDA 24**.

6315 McEWEN, Donald, b ca 1793. From Kilfinichen, Is Mull, ARL. To Hudson Bay and Red River <1815. Labourer. **RRS 25**.

6316 McEWEN, Dugald. From Breadalbane, PER. To East Williams Twp, Middlesex Co, ONT, 1832. **PCM 43**.

6317 McEWEN, Duncan, 1745–15 Mar 1831. From Muthil par, PER. To Richmond Bay, PEI, on the *Falmouth*, ex Greenock, 8 Apr 1770; stld Stanhope, but moved to St Peters, later to Campbellton. Farmer, landowner and mem of House of Assembly, 1784 and 1803. m (i) Jean McLaren, qv, ch: 1. Elizabeth, 1771–1825; 2. Duncan, 1773–1843; 3. John, 1775–1850; 4. Mary, 1777–1853; 5. James, 1779–1858; 6. David, 1781–1861; 7. Jane, b 1783; 8. William, b 1785; 9. Benjamen, 1789–1867; 10. Joseph, 1791–1843; 11. Margaret, b 1793. m (ii) Janet, d/o John McGregor, qv, further ch: 12. Edward, 1814–1909; 13. Theophilus; 14. Daniel. **DC 28 May 1980**.

6318 McEWEN, Effie, b ca 1803. From Kilfinichen, Is Mull, ARL. To Hudson Bay and Red River <1815. **RRS 25**.

6319 McEWEN, Hugh. Prob from PER. To McNab Twp, Renfrew Co, ONT, 1825. Wife with him. **EMT 18, 22**.

6320 McEWEN, Isabella, b ca 1802. From Kilfinichen, Is Mull, ARL. To Hudson Bay and Red River <1815. **RRS 25**.

6321 McEWEN, John. From Comrie par, PER. To Montreal, QUE, on the *Curlew*, ex Greenock, 21 Jul 1818; stld prob Beckwith Twp, Lanark Co, ONT. Dau Christian, aged 7, with him. **BCL**.

6322 McEWEN, John. From Little Dunkeld, PER. To Montreal, QUE, on the *Curlew*, ex Greenock, 21 Jul 1818; stld prob Beckwith Twp, Lanark Co, ONT. Wife Catherine with him, and ch: 1. Christian, aged 2; 2. Janet. **BCL**.

6323 McEWEN, Mary, b ca 1790. From Kilfinichen, Is Mull, ARL. To Hudson Bay and Red River <1815. **RRS 25**.

6324 McEWEN, Sarah, 1808–21 Feb 1895. Prob from Is Skye, Inverness Co. To Charlottetown, PEI, prob <1850; stld Hartsville. m John McLeod, qv. **DC 16 Aug 1980**.

6325 McEWEN, William, d 2 Aug 1770. From PER. To Richmond Bay, PEI, on the *Falmouth*; ex Greenock, 8 Apr 1770; stld Queens Co. Killed at Three Rivers by a rolling log. **DC 28 May 1980**.

6326 McEWEN, William. From Comrie, PER. To Montreal, QUE, on the *Curlew*, ex Greenock, 21 Jul

1818; stld prob Beckwith Twp, Lanark Co, ONT. Dau Helen, aged 8, with him. **BCL**.

McFADYEN. See also McPHADEN.

6327 McFADYEN, Alexander, b 1824. From Is Jura, ARL. To Hartley, Eldon Twp, Victoria Co, ONT, <1854. m Mary Shaw, ch: 1. Neil; 2. Kate. **EC 127**.

6328 McFADYEN, Angus, b ca 1827. From Is Jura, ARL. To Hartley, Eldon Twp, Victoria Co, ONT, <1854. m Sarah McMillan, 1849–1936, ch: 1. Duncan; 2. Jessie; 3. Minnie; 4. Kate; 5. Bessie; 6. Neil; 7. Mary; 8. Alexander; 9. Jack; 10. Samuel; 11. James; 12. Christena. **EC 127**.

6329 McFADYEN, Annie. From ARL. To Victoria Co, ONT, <1853. Wife of Alexander Ferguson, qv. **DC 5 Jun 1979**.

6330 McFADYEN, Duncan. Prob from ARL. bro/o Hugh M, qv. To Hartley, later Bolsover, Eldon Twp, Victoria Co, ONT, <1831. m Christina McLean, ch: 1. Gilbert; 2. Kate; 3. Donnie; 4. John; 5. Mary; 6. Hector; 7. Tena; 8. Margaret; 9. Minnie; 10. Duncan; 11. Andrew. **EC 129**.

6331 McFADYEN, Hugh, b ca 1817. Prob from ARL. bro/o Duncan M, qv. To Hartley, Eldon Twp, Victoria Co, ONT, <1841. ch incl: 1. Bella; 2. Bessie. **EC 129**.

6332 McFADYEN, John, b ca 1815. Prob from ARL. To Hartley, Eldon Twp, Victoria Co, ONT, <1841. By wife Flora had ch: 1. Mary, b 1841; 2. Katie, b 1843; 3. Ronald, b 1846; 4. Donald, b 1845; 5. Flora; 6. Margaret; 7. Ann, 1856–1937; 8. John, dy; 9. Allan. **EC 129**.

6333 McFADYEN, John. From Is Islay, ARL. To ONT <1850; stld Goose Lake, Eldon Twp, Victoria Co. m Mary Smith, ch: 1. Flora, b 1848; 2. Sarah, b 1849; 3. John Smith, steamship builder at Cameron Lake. **EC 123**.

6334 McFADYEN, Ronald. From Is Islay, ARL. To Hartley, Eldon Twp, Victoria Co, ONT, <1854. By wife Nancy had ch: 1. John; 2. Duncan; 3. Maggie. **EC 127**.

6335 McFADYEN, Samuel, b 1826. From Is Jura, ARL. To Hartley, Eldon Twp, Victoria Co, ONT, <1854, stld Lot 8, Con 10. m Peggy McMillan, ch: 1. Elizabeth; 2. Mary; 3. Kate. **EC 127**.

6336 McFARLAND, Agnes, 1798–1878. From ARL. To Caledon Twp, Peel Co, ONT, <1840. Wife of William Murdoch, qv. **DC 21 Apr 1980**.

6337 McFARLAND, John. To Montreal, QUE, on the *Royal George*, ex Greenock, Jan 1827; stld Sarnia, ONT. **DC 19 Nov 1978**.

6338 McFARLAND, John. Poss from LKS. To QUE, 1843; stld Aldborough Twp, Elgin Co, ONT. m a sis/o Duncan Somerville, qv. **DC 14 Aug 1979**.

6339 McFARLANE, Alexander, b ca 1779. From Kilbirnie, AYR. To QUE on the *Atlas*, ex Greenock, 11 Jul 1815; stld Lot 1, Con 1, North Burgess Twp, Lanark Co, ONT. Labourer, later farmer. Wife Ann McCulloch, qv, with him, and 7 ch. **SEC 1; HCL 15, 232**.

6340 McFARLANE, Alexander, 1803-69. From ARL. To Caledon Twp, Peel Co, ONT, <1840. Wife Jane Hunter, qv, with him. **DC 21 Apr 1980**.

6341 McFARLANE, Alexander, 3 Sep 1783–23 Mar 1869. From Thornhill, PER. s/o Donald M. and Mary McNee. To QUE, 1843; stld Huntingdon. **HCM 222**.

6342 McFARLANE, Andrew, b ca 1795. From Luss, DNB. To Hudson Bay, ca 1813, and prob to Red River. **RRS 13**.

6343 McFARLANE, Angus, b 1819. From Fivepenny, Borve, Is Lewis, ROC. s/o John M. and Ann McIver. To QUE, ex Stornoway, arr 4 Aug 1851; stld Con 10, Huron Twp, Bruce Co, ONT. Farmer. m Kirsty Murray. **WLC**.

6344 McFARLANE, Archibald. From Arisaig, INV. To Pictou, NS, on the *Dove*, ex Fort William, Jun 1801. Farmer. ch: 1. Dugald, labourer; 2. Peter, labourer; 3. John, labourer; 4. Peggy, aged 12; 5. Angus, aged 7. **PLD**.

6345 McFARLANE, Bell, b ca 1789. From Arisaig, INV. To Pictou, NS, on the *Dove*, ex Fort William, Jun 1801. **PLD**.

6346 McFARLANE, Catharine, 1788–11 Dec 1853. From PER, poss Port of Menteith. To Halton Co, ONT, prob <1840; stld Esquesing Twp, and bur Boston cemetery. Wife of John Lyon, qv. **EPE 75**.

6347 McFARLANE, Christina, b ca 1794. From Breadalbane, PER. sis/o Isabella M, qv, Margaret M, qv, and Donald M, qv. To Caledon Twp, Peel Co, ONT, 1833. Wife of John McGregor, qv. **DC 20 Jul 1979**.

6348 McFARLANE, Christina, d 1870. From Logierait, PER. To Eramosa Twp, Wellington Co, ONT, 1850. Wife of David Stewart, qv. **Lundie and Fowlis OPR 306/3; DC 24 Nov 1979**.

6349 MACFARLANE, Daniel, 1784–1849. From Glendochart, PER. To Wallace, Cumberland Co, NS, 1806. Magistrate. m Helen MacNab, qv. **DC 29 Oct 1980**.

6350 MACFARLANE, Daniel, 1821–29 Dec 1840. From Perth. s/o Alexander M, bailie and ironfounder, and Euphemia Watson. To Montreal, QUE, and d there. **Ts Greyfriars, Perth**.

6351 MACFARLANE, Daniel, 7 Sep 1775–16 Nov 1872. From Thornhill, PER. s/o Donald M. and Mary McNee. To QUE, 1843; stld Huntingdon. Merchant, later farmer. m Margaret Lyon, qv, ch: 1. Margaret, b 1822; 2. Daniel, jr, qv; 3. Jessie; 4. George Lyon, qv; 5. Elizabeth, b 1835; 6. John Alexander, b 1838. **HCM 222**.

6352 MACFARLANE, Daniel, jr, b 15 Jan 1824, Glasgow. s/o Daniel M, qv, and Margaret Lyon, qv. To QUE, 1843; stld Huntingdon. m 22 Dec 1850, Janet MacFarlane, ch: 1. Daniel, b 1851; 2. Parlan, b 1852; 3. George Lyon, b 1855; 4. Thomas, 1858-63; 5. Mary C, 1861-86; 6. Margaret Lyon, b 1863; 7. Janet, b 1865. **HCM 223**.

6353 McFARLANE, Donald, b 1756. From LKS. To Queens Co, PEI, 1784. Formerly sergeant, 84th Regt. Became mem of House of Assembly, 1790. m Marion Shaw, qv. **DC 11 Apr 1981**.

6354 McFARLANE, Donald, 13 Mar 1788–28 Dec 1866. From Arrocher, DNB. To ONT, <1834, when he stld Ekfrid Twp, Middlesex Co. Farmer. m Flora McNeil, qv, ch: 1. Donald, 1813-77; 2. John, 1814-76;

3. Margaret, 1816-93; 4. Malcolm, 1817-91; 5. Mary, b 17 Jan 1820; 6. Hector, b 24 Jan 1823. **PCM 30; DC 14 Aug and 29 Oct 1979**.

6355 McFARLANE, Donald. To Metcalfe Twp, Middlesex Co, ONT, 1831. **PCM 26**.

6356 McFARLANE, Donald. To Wallace, Cumberland Co, NS, <1850. Farmer and landowner. Son John, d 1896. **HNS iii 365**.

6357 McFARLANE, Donald. From Appin, ARL. To Ekfrid Twp, Middlesex Co, ONT, ca 1850; later to Plympton Twp, Lambton Co. **PCM 31**.

6358 McFARLANE, Donald or Daniel, b ca 1781. From Breadalbane, PER. bro/o Christine M, qv, Isabella M, qv, and Margaret M, qv. To Caledon Twp, Peel Co, ONT, ca 1836. **DC 20 Jul 1979**.

6359 MACFARLANE, Dougald. From Druimnaliaghart, ARL. To Pictou, NS, 1801; stld later Antigonish Harbour, afterwards at South River, Antigonish Co. m Margaret MacDonald, qv, ch: 1. Archibald; 2. Patrick; 3. John; 4. Angus; 5. Mary; 6. Catherine; 7. Isabel; 8. Margaret; 9. Janet. **HCA 275**.

6360 MACFARLANE, Duncan. Poss from ARL. To Aldborough Twp, Elgin Co, ONT, <1820. Farmer. **DPA 93**.

6361 McFARLANE, Duncan. From ARL. To East Williams Twp, Middlesex Co, ONT, 1831. **PCM 43**.

6362 MACFARLANE, Elizabeth, 1786–1852. From Kilmadock par, PER. To QUE, 1831; stld Lochaber, Ottawa Co. m 20 Jan 1809, James Lamb, qv. **Kilmadock OPR 362/4; DJL 1**.

6363 MACFARLANE, Elizabeth. From Cairneyhill, FIF. d/o John M. To Cobourg, Northumberland Co, ONT, <1840. m Robert Murray, qv. **DC 30 Aug 1977**.

6364 MACFARLANE, Euphemia, b 1806. From Is Mull, ARL. d/o Peter M, qv, and Sarah Buchanan, qv. To Port Hawkesbury, NS, 1819; stld Upper Southeast Mabou, Inverness Co. m Alexander MacInnes, qv. **MP ii 412, 438**.

6365 McFARLANE, Frank Walter. To NB <1833. m Eva Monture. Son John Walter, b 1833. **DC 20 Jan 1982**.

6366 McFARLANE, George. To St John, NB, <1830. Wife Margaret, ca 1803–24 Mar 1836. **NER viii 98**.

6367 MACFARLANE, George Lyon, b 11 Jun 1832, poss Glasgow. s/o Daniel M, qv, and Margaret Lyon, qv. To QUE, 1843; stld Huntingdon. m 1860, Christian Anderson. Son Daniel. **HCM 223**.

6368 McFARLANE, Henry, b ca 1825. To St John, NB, on the *Revenue*, Oct 1852. m Catherine Briggs. Son Charles Copperswaith, b NB. **DC 31 Aug 1979**.

6369 MACFARLANE, Henry Hepburn, ca 1813–1875. From Perth. s/o Alexander M, bailie and ironfounder, and Euphemia Watson. To Montreal, QUE, prob <1840. d at Alexandria. **Ts Greyfriars, Perth**.

6370 McFARLANE, Isabella, b ca 1791. From Breadalbane, PER. sis/o Christina M, qv, Donald M, qv, and Margaret M, qv. To Caledon Twp, Peel Co, ONT, ca 1836. **DC 20 Jul 1979**.

6371 **MACFARLANE, James**. From Perth. To Montreal, QUE, <1842. Master grocer. **SGC 487**.

6372 **McFARLANE, James**, b ca 1795. From PER. Poss s/o John M, qv, who went to Pictou on the *Commerce*, 1803. To Montague, Kings Co, PEI. m Isabel McLaren, qv, ch: 1. John; 2. Nancy; 3. James; 4-5. William and Benjamen, went to Victoria, AUS; 6. Jessie; 7. Alexander; 8. Jennie. **BP 42, 64**.

6373 **MACFARLANE, Janet**, 13 Sep 1793–25 Nov 1869. From Thornhill, PER. d/o Donald M. and Mary McNee. To QUE, 1821; stld Huntingdon. **HCM 223**.

6374 **McFARLANE, James**. Poss from Madderty, PER. To Montreal, QUE, on the *Niagara*, ex Greenock, arr 28 May 1825; stld McNab Twp, Renfrew Co. Wife Margaret Ker, qv, with him, and ch: 1. Duncan; 2. Alexander; 3. Walter. **EMT 18, 22**.

6375 **McFARLANE, James**. From Lochearnhead, PER. To Montreal, QUE, on the *Niagara*, ex Greenock, arr 28 May 1825; stld McNab Twp, Renfrew Co, ONT. Wife Anne Robertson, qv, with him, and ch: 1. Janet; 2. Ann; 3. Christian. **EMT 18, 22**.

6376 **McFARLANE, Jean**, 1773–1854. From Roseneath, DNB. To New York on the *Czar*, 1834; stld Ekfrid Twp, Middlesex Co, ONT. Wife of Robert Campbell, qv. **PCM 33**.

6377 **McFARLANE, John**, b ca 1762. From PER. To Pictou, NS, on the *Commerce*, ex Port Glasgow, 10 Aug 1803; poss went to PEI. Farmer. Wife Ann, aged 39, with him, and ch: 1. Eliza, aged 10; 2. James, aged 8; 3. John, aged 6; 4. Ann, aged 4; 5. Margaret, aged 2; 6. Janet, inf. **PLC**.

6378 **MACFARLANE, John**, 1793–1876. To North Shore, Cumberland Co, NS, <1830. Wife Amelia, 1806–94. **DC 29 Oct 1980**.

6379 **McFARLANE, John**. From Strathaven, LKS. To QUE <1842. m Elizabeth Cousins, from London, ENG, and had s William Henry, b L'Acadie, QUE, 21 Feb 1842. **MGC 2 Aug 1979**.

6380 **McFARLANE, Malcolm**. From Kilmartin, ARL. To Otonabee Twp, Peterborough Co, ONT, ca 1819. m Katherine Kerr, qv, ch: 1. Peter, 1798–1883; 2. Donald, b 1800; 3. John, b 1802-65; 4. Alexander, b 1803; 5. Duncan Alexander, 1806-52; 6. Mary, 1807-90. **DC 13 Sep 1982**.

6381 **McFARLANE, Margaret**, b ca 1801. From Breadalbane, PER. sis/o Christina M, qv, Donald M, qv, and Isabella M, qv. To Esquesing Twp, Halton Co, ONT, but stld Caledon Twp, Peel Co, ONT, 1833. **DC 20 Jul 1979**.

6382 **McFARLANE, Margaret**, ca 1788–24 Jan 1866. From STI. To Simcoe Co, ONT, 1831. Wife of Donald McLeod, qv, m 1810. **DC 8 Nov 1981**.

6383 **McFARLANE, Mary**, 1792–21 Aug 1876. From ARL. d/o Parlane M. To Halton Co, ONT, <1821, when m Walter Robertson, qv. Moved to Beverly Twp, Wentworth Co, 1837, and d there. **DC 29 Jun 1979**.

6384 **McFARLANE, Mary**. From ARL. To East Williams Twp, Middlesex Co, ONT, <1832, when m Malcolm Smith, qv. **PCM 45**.

6385 **McFARLANE, Mary**, b 1837. To ONT, ca 1855, later to Chicago, IL. m 1864, Joseph Bennet, ch. **DC 21 Mar 1981**.

6386 **McFARLANE, Mary Anne**, ca 1812–3 Nov 1886. From Perth. d/o Robert M, qv. To Montreal, QUE, prob <1833, when m Walter M. Peddie, qv. **SGC 495**.

6387 **McFARLANE, Matthew**. To Ramsay Twp, Lanark Co, ONT, 1821. Son Matthew. **HCL 85**.

6388 **McFARLANE, Mungo**, b ca 1785. From Strathbran, PER. To Charlottetown, PEI, on the *Clarendon*, ex Oban, 6 Aug 1808. Labourer. **CPL**.

6389 **McFARLANE, Murdock**. From Is Lewis, INV. To QUE, ex Stornoway, arr 4 Aug 1851; stld Huron Twp, Bruce Co, ONT, 1852. Head of family. **DC 5 Apr 1967**.

6390 **MACFARLANE, Nancy**, 1809-78. From Thornhill, PER. d/o Donald M. and Mary McNee. To QUE, prob 1843; stld Huntingdon. **HCM 228**.

6391 **MACFARLANE, Parlan**, 1782–1 Jun 1868. From Achnacroish, Kilninian and Kilmore par, Is Mull, ARL. s/o Peter M. and Mary MacGregor. To Port Hawkesbury, NS, 1819; stld Upper Southeast Mabou, Inverness Co. Farmer. m Ann Campbell, qv, ch: 1. Peter, qv; 2. Grace, 1823–1904; 3. Hugh, 1826–1908; 4. Mary, 1830-99. **MP 413**.

6392 **MACFARLANE, Parlane**, 25 Jun 1795–12 Jun 1860. From Thornhill, PER. s/o Donald M. and Mary McNee. To QUE, 1819; stld Huntingdon. ch: 1. Donald; 2. James; 3. Thomas; 4. Alexander, went to IN; 5. Parlane, went to Chicago, IL; 6. John; 7. Janet; 8. Mary. **HCM 224**.

6393 **MACFARLANE, Parlane**, ca 1800-74. From Pollokshaws, Glasgow. s/o Thomas M. To ONT <1829; later to St Paul, MN. Indian trader. ch: 1. Thomas; 2. John. **HCM 211**.

6394 **MACFARLANE, Peggy**. From Arisaig, INV. To Pictou, NS, on the *Dove*, ex Fort William, Jun 1801. **PLD**.

6395 **McFARLANE, Peter**, 1725–1811. To Montreal, QUE, <1769. Tailor. m (i) 1769, Mary Goodman; (ii) 1789, Mrs Mary Ann McNamara. **SGC 147**.

6396 **McFARLANE, Peter**, b ca 1783. From Caputh, PER. To Charlottetown, PEI, on the *Clarendon*, ex Oban, 6 Aug 1808. Wife Janet, aged 25, with him. Farmer. **CPL**.

6397 **MACFARLANE, Peter**, 1780–15 Jun 1867. From Achnacroish, Kilninian and Kilmore par, Is Mull, ARL. s/o Peter M. and Mary MacGregor. To Port Hawkesbury, NS, 1819; stld Upper Southeast Mabou, Inverness Co. Farmer of 600 acres. Mull River named after this family. m Sarah Buchanan, qv, ch: 1. Euphemia, qv; 2. Peter, jr, qv. **MP ii 412**.

6398 **MACFARLANE, Peter, jr**, b ca 1814. From Kilninian and Kilmore par, Is Mull, ARL. s/o Peter M, qv, and Sarah Buchanan, qv. To Port Hawkesbury, NS, 1819; stld Upper Southeast Mabou, Inverness Co. Farmer. m Isabella, d/o John Mackenzie and Katherine Calder, ch: 1. Duncan, b 1848; 2. John, b 1851; 3. Mary, b 1853; 4. Catherine, b 1858; 5. James, b 1860; 6. Sarah, b 1863; 7. Peter, b 1868; 8. Alexander, b 1871; 9. Daniel John, b 1872. **MP ii 412**.

6399 MACFARLANE, Peter, 25 Feb 1797–9 Oct 1870. From Thornhill, PER. s/o Donald M. and Mary McNee. To QUE, 1819; stld Huntingdon. ch: 1. James; 2. Peter. **HCM 224**.

6400 MACFARLANE, Peter, ca 1819–1879. From Perth. s/o Alexander M, bailie and ironfounder, and Euphemia Watson. To Montreal, QUE, prob <1840. **Ts Greyfriars, Perth**.

6401 MACFARLANE, Robert, ca 1767–23 Feb 1851. Poss from ABD. To Westmorland Co, NB, ca 1793; stld Dover. Farmer. m (i) Rachel Steeves, ch: 1. John, b 1796; 2. Jacob, b 1798; 3. Charles, b 1801. m (ii) Rose Anna, d/o Peter Lutz and Mary Ricker, further ch: 4. Rachel, b 1803; 5. Michael, 1806-80; 6. Peter, 1808-46; 7. William, b 1810; 8. Robert, b 1811. m (iii) 1812, Margaret Beatty, further ch: 9. Alexander, b 1813; 10. Jane, b 1814; 11. Margaret, b 1816; 12. James, b 1818; 13. Ralph, 1820–1904; 14. Joseph, 1822-62; 15. Nancy, b 1824; 16. Thomas Douglas, 1826-88. **DC 25 Oct 1980**.

6402 McFARLANE, Robert, b 1798. From RFW. To QUE, poss 1821; stld Lanark Co, ONT. m Catherine McLean, qv. **SG xx/1 11**.

6403 McFARLANE, Robert, ca 1786–1 May 1861. From Perth. To Montreal, QUE, <1844. Grain merchant. Dau Mary Anne, qv. **SGC 502**.

6404 McFARLANE, Rev Robert, b ca 1820. From Glasgow. s/o Robert M, merchant. Matric Univ of Glasgow, 1838, and ord 1847. To Montreal, QUE, 1850, and was min at Melbourne, Richmond Co. **GMA 13895; FES iii 282, vii 641**.

6405 McFARLANE, Sarah, ca 1788–16 Mar 1837. Prob from Buchlyvie, STI. To Galt, Waterloo Co, ONT. Wife of William McLauchlan, qv. **Ts Buchlyvie**.

6406 McFARLANE, Walter, ca 1815-94. To Eldon Twp, Victoria Co, ONT, 1835. Son Archibald, reeve of Eldon, 1895. **EC 133**.

6407 McFARLANE, Walter. From Stranraer, WIG. To Prescott, Grenville Co, ONT, <1841. Merchant. m 1841, Louisa, d/o Capt George Henderson, 4th Batt Militia. **DGH 14 Jan 1841**.

6408 MACFARLANE, Walter, 1831–22 May 1849. From Stranraer, WIG. s/o Alexander M, grocer. To Grey Co, ONT, and killed by lightning nr Owen Sound, along with Archibald Jamieson, qv. **DGH 5 Jul 1849**.

6409 MACFARLANE, William Stuart, ca 1815–1885. From Perth. s/o Alexander M, bailie and ironfounder, and Euphemia Watson. To Montreal, QUE, prob <1840. **Ts Greyfriars, Perth**.

McFEE. See also McFIE and McPHEE.

6410 McFEE, Allan, b 1798. To Little Bras D'Or dist, Cape Breton Co, NS, <1815. Servant. **CBC 1818**.

6411 McFEE, Angus, 1846–1922. From Is Colonsay, ARL. s/o John M, qv, and Hester Galbraith, qv. To Victoria Co, ONT, 1847. m Sarah Buchanan, ch: 1. Florence, 1885–1932; 2. Malcolm, 1889–1932; 3. John Wallace, 1892–1970, who carried on the representation of the McFees of Colonsay. **LDW 30 Jan 1974**.

6412 McFEE, Annie, 1803-77. From Dugary, Is Arran, BUT. To Inverness, Megantic Co, QUE, 1842. Wife of Finlay Kerr, qv, m 7 Jun 1825. **AMC 40; MAC 40**.

6413 McFEE, Archibald, b ca 1778. To Inverness Co, NS, 1817; stld nr Port Hood. Farmer, m and ch. **CBC 1818**.

6414 McFEE, James, ca 1785–1851. From BEW. To ONT, poss <1830; stld Peterborough Co. m Mary Forsyth, qv. Son James, b 1822. **DC 8 Nov 1981**.

6415 McFEE, John, 1814–1906. From Is Colonsay, ARL. s/o Malcolm M, chief of the family, and Ann Paterson. To Mariposa, Victoria Co, ONT, 1847; later to Paisley, Bruce Co. m 1845, Hester Galbraith, ch: 1. Angus, qv; 2. Malcolm, b Jura, d inf; 3. Annie, 1850–1920; 4. Katherine, 1853–1930; 5. John; 6. Neil, 1858–1932; 7. Alexander, d 1940. **LDW 30 Jan 1974**.

6416 McFEE, Margaret, ca 1784–6 Dec 1870. Poss from Is Colonsay, ARL. To West River, PEI, ca 1806. m Alexander McNeil, qv. **DC 27 Sep 1980**.

McFIE. See also McFEE and McPHEE.

6417 McFIE, Charles. From Glasgow. To Ekfrid Twp, Middlesex Co, ONT, 1844. Son James, farmer. **PCM 30**.

6418 McFIE, Donald, b 1819. From BUT. To Toronto, ONT, 1841; moved to London, Westminster Twp, Middlesex Co, 1850. Merchant. **PCM 55**.

6419 McFIE, Hugh. Prob from ARL. To London, Westminster Twp, Middlesex Co, ONT, <1850. **PCM 55**.

6420 McFIE, Robert. Prob from ARL. To London, Westminster Twp, Middlesex Co, ONT, <1850. **PCM 55**.

6421 McGEORGE, James. From Annan, DFS. To New Annan, Colchester Co, NS. Wife Janet, 1791–1869. **CAE 20**.

6422 McGEORGE, John, b ca 1751. From Lochend, Colvend par, KKD. To Georgetown, Kings Co, PEI, on the *Lovely Nellie*, ex Annan, 1774. **ELN**.

6423 McGEORGE, Rev Robert Jackson, ca 1808– 14 May 1884. From LKS. s/o Andrew M, solicitor in Glasgow. Matric Univ of Glasgow, 1821. Law clerk, poet, dramatist and a deacon of the Episcopal Ch. To Streetsville, ONT, 1841, and was curate of Trinity Ch until 1858, when he retr to SCT. stld Oban and became Dean of Argyll and the Isles. **BNA 886; GMA 10891; MDB 541**.

6424 McGIBBON, Alexander. Poss from Culdairbeg, Fortingall, PER. Cous of John M, qv. To QUE, prob 1818; stld Chatham Twp, Argenteuil Co. Farmer. m Nancy Campbell, qv, ch. **DC 30 Jun 1971**.

6425 McGIBBON, David, d 20 Aug 1826. Prob from South Queensferry, WLN. bro/o John M. To Montreal, QUE. Son David, in Muiravonside, STI, his heir. **SH**.

6426 McGIBBON, Dougald, 1795–1887. From ARL. To Caledon Twp, Peel Co, ONT, <1840. Wife Mary Stewart, qv, with him. **DC 21 Apr 1980**.

6427 McGIBBON, John, b 1781. From Rusgich, Glenlyon, PER. Cous of Alexander M, qv, and of Donald McGregor of Balhaldie. To QUE, ca 1818; stld Chatham

Twp, Argenteuil Co. Farmer. m Janet Wright, qv, ch:
1. Betty, b 1 Oct 1811; 2. Charlene, b 23 Aug 1813;
3. Finlay, b 15 Aug 1815; 4. Peter, b 14 Aug 1817, bap
Fortingall; 5. Alexander, b 5 Sep 1821; 6. James,
b 15 Feb 1823; 7. John, b 25 Feb 1825, d inf; 8. John,
1826-28.   **SH; DC 30 Jun 1971.**

6428   McGILL, Andrew, 1756–1 Aug 1805. From
Glasgow. s/o James M. and Margaret Gibson, and
bro/o James M, 1744–1813, founder of McGill Univ.
Matric Univ of Glasgow, 1765. Joined bros James and
John (from NC), in Montreal, QUE, and became
partner of firm of Todd & McGill. He m Anne,
d/o Dr George Wood, Cornwall. She m (ii) Rev John
Strachan, qv.   **GMA 2429; MDB 451.**

6429   McGILL, Anthony, 1799–1895. From Paisley,
RFW. s/o William M, weaver. Matric Univ of Glasgow,
1812, and grad MA, 1821. Studied theology, 1821-23. To
Woodside, Barton, ONT.   **GMA 8604.**

6430   McGILL, David. From ARL. Rel to Duncan M,
qv. To Westminster Twp, Middlesex Co, ONT, 1838.
PCM 52.

6431   McGILL, Duncan. From ARL. Rel to David M, qv.
To Westminster Twp, Middlesex Co, ONT, 1838.
PCM 52.

6432   McGILL, Francis. To Westminster Twp, Middlesex
Co, ONT, <1840.   **PCM 55.**

6433   McGILL, Margaret, 1772–1856. From Killean and
Kilchenzie par, ARL. To ONT, 1834. wid/o John Galbraith,
1780–1832, ch: 1. Archibald, 1802-36; 2. Daniel, qv;
3. David, 1809-76, physician; 4. Eliza, d SCT;
5. Alexander, qv; 6. Margaret, d SCT; 7. Jean, d 1847;
8. John, qv; 9. Roger.   **DC 9 Mar 1980.**

6434   McGILL, Margaret. From Inch par, WIG.
d/o James M. and Mary McQuaker. To Perth Co, ONT,
1855; stld later Grey Co. Wife of James McCulloch, qv,
m 31 May 1855.   **DC 11 Mar 1980.**

6435   McGILL, Peter. To QUE on the *David of London*,
ex Greenock, 19 May 1821; stld prob Lanark Co, ONT.
HCL 239.

McGILL, Peter. See McCUTCHEON, Peter.

6436   McGILL, Rev Robert, 21 May 1798–4 Feb 1856.
From Ayr. s/o William M, schoolmaster. Matric Univ of
Glasgow, 1819. To Lincoln Co, ONT, 1829, and became
Presb min at Niagara. Trans to St Pauls, Montreal, QUE,
1845. Author and editor.   **GMA 10416; FES vii 641;
MDB 453.**

6437   McGILL, William, b 1819. From Kirkmichael par,
DFS. s/o James M. To Charlottetown, PEI, 1835.
Merchant and politician.   **BNA 717.**

6438   McGILLAWEE, Alexander, b ca 1801. Prob from
PER. To ONT <1851. By wife Christian, b 1807, had dau
Margaret, b ca 1846.   **LDW 26 Jan 1973.**

6439   McGILLIS, Donald. Prob from INV. s/o John M.
To Glengarry Co, ONT, and gr land comprising Lot 31,
Con 13, 27 May 1797. Wife Mary with him. Son John,
d 1848.   **DC 1 Oct 1982.**

6440   McGILLIVRAY, Rev Alexander, 1801–16 Feb
1862. From Croy par, INV. s/o Alexander M. Matric Kings
Coll, Aberdeen, 1821, and was ord in 1832. To Pictou,

NS, same year, and was ind as min of Barneys River
and Merigomish. Trans to McLennans Mountain, 1837.
m 27 Jul 1837, Elizabeth, d/o Dr James Skinner, qv, and
Elizabeth McCormack, ch: 1. Elizabeth McCormack,
b 16 Jun 1838; 2. Mary Jane, b 14 Sep 1839;
3. Margaret, b 25 Jun 1840; 4. Donald, b 13 Apr 1842;
5. James Skinner, b 4 Nov 1843; 6. Margaret, b 2 Jun
1845; 7. John, b 2 Apr 1847; 8. Alexander, b 29 Dec
1848; 9. Anna Bella, b 29 Aug 1850; 10. Hugh William,
b 9 Nov 1852; 11. Carolina Amelia Skinner, b 29 Sep
1854; 12. James George, b 29 Nov 1856; 13. Caroline
Amelia, b 11 Feb 1862.   **AM 3, 14.**

6441   McGILLIVRAY, Alexander, ca 1788–26 Nov 1874.
From INV. To Pictou Co, NS. m Nancy McLeod, qv.
DC 27 Oct 1979.

6442   McGILLIVRAY, Rev Angus. To Pictou Co, NS,
1824; stld Springville.   **PAC 236.**

6443   McGILLIVRAY, Angus. Prob from INV. To Cribbins
Point, Antigonish Co, NS, <1830. Farmer. Son Rev
Alexander, min of Grand Narrows, Cape Breton.
HNS iii 436.

6444   McGILLIVRAY, Archibald. To Glengarry Co, ONT,
1794; stld Lot 7, Con 15, Lancaster Twp.   **MG 56.**

6445   MACGILLIVRAY, Archibald. From Glenelg, INV. To
QUE, 1796; stld Lots 27-28, Con 7, Lochiel Twp,
Glengarry Co, ONT.   **MG 211.**

6446   MACGILLIVRAY, Donald. Prob from Dunmaglass,
INV. s/o Hugh M. and Margaret MacEachern. To
Dunmaglass, Antigonish Co, NS, poss 1792. ch: 1. Capt
Alexander; 2. Angus 'Ruadh'; 3. Hugh; 4. Andrew.
HCA 276.

6447   McGILLIVRAY, Donald. Prob from INV. To
Glengarry Co, ONT, 1794; stld Lot 20, Con 15, Lancaster
Twp.   **MG 56.**

6448   McGILLIVRAY, Donald. To Glengarry Co, ONT,
1794; stld Lot 32, Con 15, Lancaster Twp.   **MG 56.**

6449   MACGILLIVRAY, Donald. From Glenelg, INV. Prob
rel to Archibald M, qv. To QUE, 1796; stld Lots 27-28,
Con 6, Lochiel Twp, Glengarry Co, ONT.   **MG 211.**

6450   MACGILLIVRAY, Donald 'Ban'. From Glenelg,
INV. To QUE, 1796; stld Lot 32, Con 6, Lochiel Twp,
Glengarry Co, ONT.   **MG 211.**

6451   McGILLIVRAY, Donald, b ca 1769. From
Barrowfield, Glasgow. To QUE, summer 1815; stld ONT.
Tailor. Wife Janet with him, and 3 ch.   **SEC 4.**

6452   MACGILLIVRAY, Dugald. To ONT ca 1830; stld
Eldon Twp, Victoria Co. Farmer. By wife Christina had ch:
1. John, qv; 2. Archibald, b 1830; 3. Hugh; 4. Malcolm,
b 1837; 5. Donald, b 1841.   **EC 134.**

6453   MACGILLIVRAY, Duncan, ca 1768–1808. From
Dunmaglass, Daviot and Dunlichity par, INV. s/o Donald
M, tacksman of Clovendale, and Ann McTavish. To
Montreal, 1792, and joined NWCo. Served at Upper Fort
des Prairies, and became a partner. Was also a partner
of McTavish, Frobisher & Co, agents for NWCo. d unm,
leaving a *Journal* covering 1794-95, which has been
published.   **SGC 104; MDB 154.**

6454   McGILLIVRAY, Duncan. Prob from INV. To
Glengarry Co, ONT. 1794; stld Lot 28, Con 16, Lancaster
Twp.   **MG 57.**

6455 McGILLIVRAY, Elizabeth. From INV. d/o Donald M, tacksman of Clovendale, Daviot and Dunlichity par, and Ann McTavish. To Montreal, QUE, <1798. m Hon James Reid, qv. **SGC 105, 242; LDW 15 Feb 1967**.

6456 MACGILLIVRAY, Flora, b ca 1765. From Morar, INV. To Merigomish, Pictou, NS, 1791; stld later Antigonish Co. Wife of John 'Ban' Gillis, qv. **HCA 143**.

6457 MACGILLIVRAY, Hugh. From INV. s/o William M. To Antigonish Co, NS, poss <1800. ch: 1. Archibald, merchant in Morristown; 2. Donald; 3. Angus. **HCA 279**.

6458 MACGILLIVRAY, Hugh. From Daviot and Dunlichity par, INV. bro/o John M, qv, and William M, qv. To Dunmaglass, Antigonish Co, NS, prob <1810. m Miss Cameron, ch: 1. John; 2. Hugh; 3. Angus; 4. Donald; 5. Alexander; 6. Margaret; 7. Catherine. **HCA 279**.

6459 MACGILLIVRAY, John. From Lochaber, INV. s/o Alexander M. and Katherine MacIntyre. To QUE, 1780, later to Albany, NY. m Janet McLeod, qv, ch: 1. Christine; 2. Katherine, d in SCT; 3. Alexander; 4. Daniel; 5. Ann; 6. John, blind from birth. **LDW 19 May 1972**.

6460 MACGILLIVRAY, John. From Daviot and Dunlichity par, INV. bro/o Hugh M, qv, and William M, qv. To Dunmaglass, Antigonish Co, NS, <1810. m (i) Miss MacDonald, from Knoydart; (ii) Miss MacDonald, from Strathglass. **HCA 279**.

6461 McGILLIVRAY, John, 1778–1855. From INV. s/o Farquhar M. of Dalcrombie. To Montreal, QUE, ca 1796, and joined NWCo. Became partner, 1801. Served at Athabaska River and Fort Dunvegan, Peace River. Became Commissioner for Crown Lands in Upper Canada. Retr to Williamstown, Glengarry Co, 1818. Heir to Dunmaglass, 1852. m Isabella, d/o Hon Neil McLean, qv, and had with other ch: 1. Neil John; 2. George H, 1837–1912. **SDG 401**.

6462 McGILLIVRAY, John, b ca 1786. From Glenelg, INV. To QUE, summer 1815; stld prob Lanark Co, ONT. Farmer. Wife Margaret Campbell, qv, with him. **SEC 8**.

6463 MACGILLIVRAY, John, b 1828. s/o Dugald M, qv. To Eldon Twp, Victoria Co, ONT, ca 1830. m Mary, d/o Alan MacEachern. Son Dougal. **EC 135**.

6464 MACGILLIVRAY, John Roy. From Glenelg, INV. To QUE, 1796; stld Lot 19, Con 6, Lochiel Twp, Glengarry Co, ONT. **MG 211**.

6465 MACGILLIVRAY, Malcolm. From Inverness. To Madoc, Hastings Co, ONT, ca 1860. Storekeeper. m (i) Mary Kelby, who d at sea, ch: 1. Mary, res Huron Twp, Bruce Co; 2. Neil; 3. Cornelius. m (ii) Margaret Sutherland, further ch. **DC 25 Dec 1981**.

6466 McGILLIVRAY, Margaret, ca 1819–9 Jul 1900. From Is Mull, ARL. To ONT <1852. m Andrew Currie, qv. **DC 6 May 1977**.

6467 McGILLIVRAY, Margerie, d 27 Mar 1820. From Dunmaglass, Daviot and Dunlichity par, INV. d/o Donald M, tacksman of Clovendale, and Ann McTavish. To Montreal, QUE, <1800. m Angus Shaw, qv. **MDB 685**.

6468 MACGILLIVRAY, Sarah. From Dunmaglass, Daviot and Dunlichity par, INV. d/o Hugh M. and Margaret MacEachern. To Antigonish Co, NS, 1792. Wife of John 'Ruadh' MacEachern, qv. **HCA 271**.

6469 McGILLIVRAY, Simon, 1783–1840. From Dunmaglass, Daviot and Dunlichity par, INV. s/o Donald M, tacksman of Clovendale, and Ann McTavish. To Montreal, QUE, ca 1808, and became a partner in NWCo and its subsidiary, McTavish, McGillivrays & Co. With Edward Ellice, qv, negotiated merger with HBCo, 1821. Went later to Mexico, and d London, ENG. m 1837, Miss Easthope, with ch, a dau Mary. **MDB 455; LDW 15 Feb 1967**.

6470 McGILLIVRAY, Rev Walter, 1807–30 Jun 1880. From Is Islay, ARL. s/o Malcolm M. Matric Univ of Glasgow, 1824. Min of St Marks, Glasgow, 1835-42; of Hope Street Free Gaelic Ch, 1843-46. To Glengarry Co, ONT, 1846, to become min of a Gaelic Ch there, but retr to SCT, 1848, and resumed his first charge. Later min of Gilcomston, Aberdeen. m 1846, Maria Hooker. **GMA 11445; FCS i 229; FES vii 642**.

6471 McGILLIVRAY, William, 1764–16 Oct 1825. From Dunmaglass, Daviot and Dunlichity par, INV. s/o Donald M, tacksman of Clovendale, and Ann McTavish. To Montreal, QUE, 1784, and became a clerk with the NWCo. Became partner and in 1799, Chief Superintendent. Reluctantly agreed to merger with HBCo, 1821. By Susan, a French-Cree woman, ch: 1-2. Simon and Joseph, b 1791; 3. Peter, dy; 4. Elizabeth. m Magdalen, d/o John McDonald of Gart and Julia McDonald, with surviving ch: 5. Ann Marie, b 1805; 6. Magdalene Julia, b 1808. **SGC 104; SDG 395, 401; MDB 155**.

6472 MACGILLIVRAY, William. From Daviot and Dunlichity par, INV. bro/o Hugh M, qv, and John M, qv. To Dunmaglass, Antigonish Co, NS, prob <1801. m Miss MacLellan. **HCA 279**.

6473 McGILLIVRAY, William. From Glasgow. To Lanark Co, ONT, 1815; stld North Burgess Twp, 1816. Wife with him and had 6 ch by 1818. **HCL 15, 231**.

6474 MACGILLIVRAY, William R, 15 Sep 1803–May 1890. From Kiltearn, ROC. s/o James M. and Ellen Rogers. To ONT, and d at Chatsworth, Grey Co. m Christian McKay, qv. **SG xxvi/3 90**.

6475 McGILLVERY, Duncan, 1774–1858. From ARL. To Caledon Twp, Peel Co, ONT, <1840. Wife Mary McDonald, qv, with him. **DC 21 Apr 1980**.

6476 McGILLVERY, Mary, 1807-71. From ARL. To Caledon Twp, Peel Co, ONT, <1840. **DC 21 Apr 1980**.

6477 McGILLVERY, Sarah, 1817–1901. From Is Iona, ARL. To Caledon Twp, Peel Co, ONT, <1840. Wife of Donald McArthur, qv. **DC 21 Apr 1980**.

6478 McGILVRAY, Marjery, b ca 1775. From Kilfinichen, Is Mull, ARL. To Hudson Bay and Red River, prob <1815. Wife of Neil McKinnon, qv. **RRS 25**.

6479 McGILVRAY, Alexander. s/o Angus M, qv, and Ann Matheson. To Inverness, Megantic Co, QUE, 1833. Shoemaker. m Catherine Brodie, qv. **AMC 48**.

6480 McGILVRAY, Angus. From South Morar, INV. To PEI on the *Jane*, ex Loch nan Uamh, Arisaig, 12 Jul 1790. Wife and ch with him. **PLJ**.

6481 McGILLVRAY, Angus, b ca 1798. From INV. s/o Malcolm M. and Christie McCoy. To ONT <1840;

stld poss Carleton Co. m Mary McDonald. Dau Catherine. **DC 15 Feb 1980**.

6482   McGILLVRAY, Angus. bro/o James M, qv. To Inverness, Megantic Co, QUE. m (i) Ann Matheson, ch: 1. Jessie; 2. Alexander, qv; 3. James, d in SCT; 4. Angus, qv; 5. Duncan; 6. Annie, qv. m (ii) Helen Morrison, qv, further ch: 7. John, dy; 8. Mary; 9. Isabella, qv; 10. Eliza, qv; 11. Agnes; 12. Jane, qv; 13. Peter, qv; 14. John, qv; 15. Margery; 16. Helen, qv. **AMC 48**.

6483   McGILLVRAY, Angus, jr. s/o Angus M, qv, and Ann Matheson. To Megantic Co, QUE, 1833. m Mary Kelso, qv. **AMC 11; MAC 30**.

6484   McGILLVRAY, Ann, b ca 1793. From Torosay, Is Mull, ARL. Prob rel to Archibald M, qv. To Hudson Bay and Red River <1815. **RRS 25**.

6485   McGILLVRAY, Annie. d/o Angus M, qv, and Ann Matheson. To Inverness, Megantic Co, QUE, 1833. m Angus McKillop, qv. **AMC 48; MAC 35**.

6486   McGILLVRAY, Archibald, b 1768. From Torosay, Is Mull, ARL. To Hudson Bay and Red River <1815. Labourer. Wife Mary McLean, qv, with him. **RRS 25**.

6487   McGILLVRAY, Catherine, b ca 1795. From Torosay, Is Mull, ARL. Poss rel to Archibald M, qv. To Hudson Bay and Red River <1815. **RRS 25**.

6488   McGILLVRAY, Donald. From Kyles, Morar, INV. To PEI on the *Lucy*, ex Loch nan Uamh, Arisaig, 12 Jul 1790. Carpenter. Wife with him. **PLL**.

6489   McGILLVRAY, Duncan. s/o James M, qv, and Mary McBean, qv. To Inverness, Megantic Co, QUE, 1833. m Margaret Kelso, qv. **AMC 48**.

6490   McGILLVRAY, Eliza. d/o Angus M, qv, and Helen Morrison, qv. To Inverness, Megantic Co, QUE, 1833. m Donald Bell. **AMC 48**.

6491   McGILLVRAY, Helen. d/o Angus M, qv, and Helen Morrison, qv. To Inverness, Megantic Co, QUE, 1833. m R. Drew. **AMC 48**.

6492   McGILLVRAY, Hugh. From Kylesmorar, Morar, INV. To PEI on the *Jane*, ex Loch nan Uamh, Arisaig, 12 Jul 1790. **PLJ**.

6493   McGILLVRAY, Hugh. Poss from Moidart, INV. Tenant. To PEI on the *Jane*, ex Loch nan Uamh, Arisaig, 12 Jul 1790. Wife and 3 ch with him. **PLJ**.

6494   McGILLVRAY, Hugh, b ca 1795. From Torosay, Is Mull, ARL. Prob rel to Archibald M, qv. To Hudson Bay and Red River <1815. Labourer. **RRS 25**.

6495   McGILLVRAY, Isabella. d/o Angus M, qv, and Helen Morrison, qv. To Inverness, Megantic Co, QUE, 1833. m Archibald Kelso, qv. **AMC 48; MAC 44**.

6496   McGILLVRAY, James. bro/o Angus M, qv. To Megantic Co, QUE; stld Inverness. Shoemaker. m Mary McBean, qv, ch: 1. Duncan, qv; 2. Mary, qv; 3. Jessie, qv; 4. Mysie, qv; 5. James, jr, qv. **AMC 48**.

6497   McGILLVRAY, James, jr. s/o James M, qv, and Mary McBean, qv. To Inverness, Megantic Co, QUE, 1833. m Elizabeth Kelso, qv. **AMC 48**.

6498   McGILLVRAY, Jane. d/o Angus M, qv, and Helen Morrison, qv. To Inverness, Megantic Co, QUE, 1833. m Alexander McKinnon, qv. **AMC 48; MAC 40**.

6499   McGILLVRAY, Janet, b ca 1787. To Charlottetown, PEI, on the *Rambler*, ex Tobermory, 20 Jun 1806; stld Queens Co. Wife of Neil Campbell, qv. **DC 11 Apr 1981**.

6500   McGILLVRAY, Jessie. d/o James M, qv, and Mary McBean, qv. To Inverness, Megantic Co, QUE, 1833. m Rev Simon Fraser. **AMC 48**.

6501   McGILLVRAY, John. From Moidart, INV. Tenant. To PEI on the *Jane*, ex Loch nan Uamh, Arisaig, 12 Jul 1790. Family with him. **PLJ**.

6502   McGILLVRAY, John. Poss from South Morar, INV. To PEI on the *Jane*, ex Loch nan Uamh, INV, 12 Jul 1790. Family with him, incl s John, jr, qv. **PLJ**.

6503   McGILLVRAY, John, jr. Poss from South Morar, INV. s/o John M, qv. To PEI on the *Jane*, ex Loch nan Uamh, Arisaig, INV, 12 Jul 1790. Wife and 2 ch with him. **PLJ**.

6504   McGILLVRAY, John, b ca 1790. From Torosay, Is Mull, ARL. Prob rel to Archibald M, qv. To Hudson Bay and Red River <1815. Pioneer settler. **RRS 25**.

6505   McGILLVRAY, John. s/o Angus M, qv, and Helen Morrison, qv. To Inverness, Megantic Co, QUE, 1833. m Mary A. McCullough. **AMC 48**.

6506   McGILLVRAY, Katherine. From INV. To PEI on the *Jane*, ex Loch nan Uamh, Arisaig, 12 Jul 1790. A child with her. **PLJ**.

6507   McGILLVRAY, Mary. From Kenlochnasale, ni, INV. To Montreal, QUE, ex Fort William, arr Sep 1802; stld E ONT. **MCM 1/4 25**.

6508   McGILLVRAY, Mary. d/o James M, qv, and Mary McBean, qv. To Inverness, Megantic Co, QUE, 1833. m James Johnston. **AMC 48**.

6509   McGILLVRAY, Mysie. d/o James M, qv, and Mary McBean, qv. To Inverness, Megantic Co, QUE, 1833. m James McEachern. **AMC 48**.

6510   McGILLVRAY, Peter. s/o Angus M, qv, and Helen Morrison, qv. To Inverness, Megantic Co, QUE, 1833. m Ann Bickford. **AMC 48**.

6511   McGILLVRAY, William. From INV. To PEI on the *Jane*, ex Loch nan Uamh, Arisaig, 12 Jul 1790. Family with him. **PLJ**.

6512   McGINNIS, Mary Margaret, ca 1792–27 Jul 1888. Prob from Glenelg, INV. To Glengarry Co, ONT, 1832. Wife of John McLeod, qv. **MG 291**.

6513   McGLASHAN, Charlotte. From Waterside, Fenwick par, AYR. To QUE on the *Atlas*, ex Greenock, 11 Jul 1815; stld North Burgess Twp, Lanark Co, ONT. Wife of John Ferrier, qv. **SEC 3**.

6514   McGLASHAN, James, ca 1817–4 Jun 1866. From Bonhill, DNB. s/o John M. and Mary Ferrie. To ONT and d there. **Ts Bonhill**.

6515   McGLASHAN, John, 1762–11 Apr 1845. From PER. To Niagara, Lincoln Co, ONT, 1795, and bur North Pelham. Carpenter, and owned land in 1810. m Mary Fletcher or McNab, 1779–1859, ch. **DC 26 May 1983**.

6516   McGLASHEN, John. To NB, 1810, and stld Cape Tormentine, Westmorland Co. Farmer. m Miss Seaman, from NS, ch.   **DC 17 Apr 1981**.

6517   McGOUN, Archibald, b 29 Oct 1817. From Douglas par, LKS. To QUE, 1831, and stld Montreal, 1833. Clerk and bookkeeper.   **SGC 513**.

6518   McGOWAN, Alexander, ca 1808–30 Apr 1868. From Edinburgh. To Montreal, QUE, 1836. Soldier and tailor. Moved to New York, 1848, and res Pearl Street, later Longacre, now Times Square. m Isabella Levack, qv, ch: 1. Alexander Bartholomew, qv; 2. Catherine Theresa Desirée, qv; 3. John Mowat, 1837–86; 4. Isabella Ida Vernon, 1843–1923, actress. **LDW 21 Aug 1978**.

6519   McGOWAN, Alexander Bartholomew, 16 Dec 1828–ca 1908. b Edinburgh. s/o Alexander M, qv, and Isabella Levack, qv. To Montreal, QUE, 1836; moved to New York City, 1848, and was naturalised 1853. Went to San Francisco, 1859. Soldier and lawyer. m (i) Frances Augusta, d/o Leonard A. Currier and Augusta Davenport, ch: 1. Charles Davenport, b 1860; 2. George Pierpont, b 1863. m (ii) Sarah —, ch: 3. Francis, dy. **LDW 21 Aug 1978**.

6520   McGOWAN, Catherine Theresa Desirée, 31 May 1831–13 Jan 1894. From Edinburgh. d/o Alexander M, qv, and Isabella Levack, qv. To Montreal, QUE, with mother, Aug 1836. m (i) John Campbell, qv; (ii) John Braneis.   **LDW 21 Aug 1978**.

6521   McGOWAN, James, b ca 1805. From WIG. To ONT, 1843. m Janet Martin, qv, and had with other ch: 1. Sarah, b 1833; 2. Jane.   **DC 4 Jun 1976**.

6522   McGOWAN, Robert. From Ballinton, Thornhill, PER. To Esquesing Twp, Halton Co. ONT, <1852. m Mary McGregor, qv, ch: 1. George, b 6 May 1827; 2. James, b 22 Jul 1829; 3. Walter, qv; 4. Gregor, b 25 Feb 1832, res Goderich; 5. Robert, b 30 Mar 1834; 6. Daniel, b 6 Dec 1836; 7. Sara, b 9 Mar 1836; 8. Janet, b 17 May 1842; 9. Alexander, b 10 Dec 1845.   **DC 15 Feb 1971**.

6523   McGOWAN, Thomas, b ca 1798. To ONT, poss <1830; stld Peterborough Co. m Margaret McNaughton, qv, ch: 1. Thomas, b ca 1828; 2. Ann, b ca 1835; 3. Jessie, 1843–1921; 4. John, b ca 1842; 5. William, b ca 1845.   **DC 8 Nov 1981**.

6524   McGOWAN, Walter, b 9 Feb 1830. From Ballinton, Thornhill, PER. s/o Robert M, qv, and Mary McGregor, qv. To Esquesing Twp, Halton Co, ONT, but stld Goderich Twp, Huron Co. m Rebecca, d/o William Cummings, qv, ch.   **DC 15 Feb 1971**.

6525   McGOWAN, Duncan. From Greenock, RFW. To ONT. m Margaret McIlwraith, qv.   **Ts Greenock**.

6526   McGRAW, Duncan. To Glengarry Co, ONT, 1794; stld Lot 22, Con 16, Lancaster Twp.   **MG 57**.

6527   McGRAW, Neil, 1756–May 1834. From ARL. To Black River, Northumberland Co, NB, ca 1784. Discharged soldier. m Mary Edwards, from ENG, ch. **DC 30 Jul 1980**.

6528   McGREGOR, Alexander. From Glen Lyon, PER. s/o — M. and Ellen Turnbull. To Glengarry Co, ONT, ca 1780. Discharged soldier, and gr land. m Ellen McGibbon. Son James.   **DC 8 Nov 1981**.

6529   McGREGOR, Alexander. From Urquhart, INV. To Pictou, NS, on the *Sarah*, ex Fort William, Jun 1801. Farmer. Wife Christian with him, and s William, aged 5.   **PLS**.

6530   MACGREGOR, Alexander. From Dunballoch, Beauly, INV. s/o Donald M. To Pictou, NS, 1801. Farmer. Son Rev Simon, 1831–1906, min at Appin, ARL, SCT. **GD50/184/113; FES iv 80**.

6531   McGREGOR, Alexander, b ca 1743. From PER. To Pictou, NS, on the *Commerce*, ex Port Glasgow, 10 Aug 1803. Farmer.   **PLC**.

6532   McGREGOR, Alexander. From Duneaves, PER. s/o Donald M, qv. To Queens Co, PEI, <1808. m Mary McGregor, who d prob 1829.   **DC 11 Apr 1981**.

6533   McGREGOR, Alexander, ca 1805–13 Jan 1871. From Appin, Aberfeldy, PER. s/o Archibald M, qv, and Christian Ann Anderson, qv. To Charlottetown, PEI, on the *Clarendon*, ex Oban, 6 Aug 1808; stld Hillsborough River, Queens Co. By wife Christiana, 1805-71, had with other ch: 1. Alexander, 1842–1927; 2. Jane, d 1937; 3. Christiana, d 1912; 4. Isabella, 1848-87.   **CPL; DC 11 Apr 1981**.

6534   McGREGOR, Alexander, 1785–20 Sep 1852. From Potterow, Edinburgh, but b PER. bro/o Sarah M, qv. Educ Edinburgh and went to Charlottetown, PEI, 1817. Surgeon and MLA. Moved to Sonora, CA, where he was murdered. m Catherine Stewart, qv, ch: 1. Peter; 2. John, unm; 3. Ann, schoolteacher, unm; 4. Isabella, unm; 5. Elizabeth, 1831–1921.   **DC 11 Apr 1981**.

6535   McGREGOR, Alexander. From Callander, PER. To Montreal, QUE, on the *Curlew*, ex Greenock, 21 Jul 1818; stld prob Beckwith Twp, Lanark Co, ONT. Wife Janet with him, and ch: 1. Peter, aged 4; 2. Alexander, aged 2; 3. Duncan, aged 9 mo.   **BCL**.

6536   McGREGOR, Alexander. From Balquhidder, PER. To Montreal, QUE, on the *Sophia*, ex Greenock, 26 Jul 1818; stld prob Beckwith Twp, Lanark Co, ONT. Wife Margaret with him, and dau Janet, aged 12.   **SPL**.

6537   McGREGOR, Alexander, b 1829. From Fortingall, PER. s/o John M, qv, and Christina McFarlane, qv. To Esquesing Twp, Halton Co, ONT, but stld Caledon Twp, Peel Co. m Bessie, d/o Robert Scott, London, ONT, ch: 1. Mary; 2. Godfrey; 3. Robert Lee.   **DC 20 Jul 1979**.

6538   MACGREGOR, Alexander. From Clashindrich, Glengairn, ABD. To Tilbury East, Kent Co, ONT, <1841. m 18 May 1834, Margaret Coutts, qv, ch: 1. James, b 18 May 1835; 2. Ann, b 1 Aug 1837; 3. John Alexander, b 1 Sep 1841; 4. William Charles, b 22 Oct 1843; 5. Allan Robert, b 7 Jan 1846; 6. Francis Colin, b 31 Mar 1849; 7. Mary Janet, b 10 Nov 1852. **SG ix/3 14**.

6539   McGREGOR, Rev Alexander, b 1834. From Glasgow. Educ Edinburgh and at Univ of Toronto. Ord as Congregational min, 1863, and adm to Brockville, Leeds Co, ONT. Trans to Yarmouth, NS, 1871. Associate editor of the *Christian Standard*, of St John, NB, and mem of senate of Halifax (Dalhousie) Univ.   **BNA 902**.

6540   McGREGOR, Andrew, 1802–11 Sep 1886. From Methven, PER. s/o Rev William M, qv, and wife Ann. To PEI, 1820; stld Lot 16. m Isabella, 1827-81, d/o Humphrey McLaurin and Isabella Fullerton. Son William, b ca 1850.   **DC 11 Apr 1981**.

6541   McGREGOR, Angus. From Appin, ARL. To Ekfrid Twp, Middlesex Co, ONT, ca 1850; later to Plympton Twp, Lambton Co.   **PCM 31**.

6542   McGREGOR, Archibald, ca 1780–23 Feb 1839. From Appin, Aberfeldy, PER. To Charlottetown, PEI, on the *Clarendon*, ex Oban, 6 Aug 1808; stld Hillsborough River, Queens Co. m Christian Ann Anderson, qv, ch: 1. Alexander, qv; 2. Catherine, 1809-87; 3. Margaret, b 1813; 4. Christian, alive 1839; 5. Jane, b 1818; 6. Grace; 7. Isobel, alive 1839; 8. Robert, alive 1873. **CPL; DC 11 Apr 1981**.

6543   McGREGOR, Archibald, ca 1765–1828. From Is Mull, ARL. To Charlottetown, PEI, on the *Phoenix*, ex Tobermory, 1810; stld Nine Mile Creek, Queens Co. Wife Ann McColl, qv, with him, and ch: 1. Isabella, qv; 2. Margaret, qv; 3. Mary, qv; 4. Elizabeth, qv; 5. Malcolm, qv.   **DC 11 Apr 1981**.

6544   McGREGOR, Archibald. From Balquhidder, PER. To Montreal, QUE, on the *Sophia*, ex Greenock, 26 Jul 1818; stld prob Beckwith Twp, Lanark Co, ONT. Wife Janet with him, and ch: 1. Duncan, aged 8; 2. Hugh, aged 6.   **SPL**.

6545   McGREGOR, Archibald, 1793–1891. From Moulin, PER. To Halifax, NS, ca 1851. m 7 Feb 1823, Anne Robertson, qv, ch: 1. Donald, b 4 Jul 1825; 2. Janet, b 29 May 1827; 3. Alexander, b 25 Sep 1828; 4. Elspeth, b 4 Sep 1830; 5. Anne, b 17 Nov 1835; 6. Archibald, b 28 Jul 1837; 7. Duncan, b 28 Sep 1840; 8. Christina.   **LDW 30 Dec 1970**.

6546   McGREGOR, Barbara, b ca 1791. From Strathconan, ROC. To Ashfield Twp, Huron Co, ONT, 1842. wid/o John McKenzie, Killearnan par. ch with her: 1. Colin, qv; 2. Roderick, d 1846; 3. Ann, qv; 4. Alexander, qv; 5. Christian, qv; 6. Isabella, qv. **DC 15 Jul 1979**.

6547   McGREGOR, Catharine. From Achallater, Braemar, ABD. d/o James M. To West Bay, Cape Breton Is, NS, 1846, after m to Rev Murdoch Stewart, qv. **FES vii 608**.

6548   McGREGOR, Catherine, 1787–1886. From Kenmore, PER. d/o John M. and Catherine McKercher. To Roxborough Twp, Stormont Co, ONT, 1828. Wife of Charles Robertson, qv, m 5 Jul 1807.   **DC 1 Aug 1975**.

6549   McGREGOR, Catherine. From Achton, Balquhidder, PER. d/o Gregor M. and Isabella Stewart. To Horton Twp, Renfrew Co, ONT, prob <1840. m John McGregor, shoemaker, ch: 1. Duncan; 2. Gregor; 3. John; 4. Catherine; 5. Margaret.   **GD 50/184/113**.

6550   McGREGOR, Charles. From Kilmaronock, DNB. Neph of John M, qv. To QUE <1829; stld Lachute, later Delhi, NY.   **DC 28 Jan 1961**.

6551   McGREGOR, Christine, b 1785. From Inver, Glen Lyon, PER. d/o Malcolm MacRobert M. To Osgoode Twp, Carleton Co, ONT, ca 1831. Wife of Patrick or Peter McNab, qv.   **DC 1 Aug 1979**.

6552   MACGREGOR, Daniel. From Glasgow. To Toronto, ONT, 1851. Bookbinder. Wife with him, and s Daniel.   **DC 29 Dec 1981**.

6553   McGREGOR, David, 1772–8 Mar 1868. From Rosskeen, ROC. s/o Alexander M, carpenter, and Janet Ross. To Queens Co, PEI, 1808. Schoolteacher, farmer and land surveyor. Retr to SCT, 1834, and d at Canisbay. m Janet Ross, qv, and had poss with other ch: 1. John, qv; 2. Annie, alive 1883, PEI; 3. Sybella, b 1807; 4. Rev Roderick, 1818-89, FC min at Canisbay.   **AFC i 230; DC 11 Apr 1981**.

6554   MACGREGOR, Donald, 1761–1825. s/o Hugh M. and Christian MacGregor. To Pictou, NS, <1800. m Isabella Fraser, qv, ch: 1. Andrew; 2. Alexander. **MacGregor Chart, SGSL**.

6555   McGREGOR, Donald, ca 1750–11 Oct 1816. From Duneaves, PER. To Queens Co, PEI, prob <1808, with ch: 1. Donald, jr, qv; 2. Alexander, qv; 3. Duncan, qv. **DC 11 Apr 1981**.

6556   McGREGOR, Donald, jr, ca 1779–10 Mar 1863. From Duneaves, PER. s/o Donald M, qv. To Queens Co, PEI, prob <1808. Farmer and deacon of the Baptist Ch. m Isabella Campbell, qv, ch: 1. Christiana, b ca 1811; 2. Catherine, b ca 1813; 3. Alexander, ca 1815-80; 4. John, 1819–1906; 5. Jane, 1820-86; 6. Jessie, res Boston; 7. Isabella, d 1905; 8. Elizabeth, alive 1880; 9. Ann, alive 1861.   **DC 11 Apr 1981**.

6557   McGREGOR, Donald, ca 1775–16 Jul 1836. From PER. To PEI, prob <1808; stld Queens Co. Shoemaker. m Susannah Kennedy, qv, ch: 1. Joseph, b ca 1810; 2. James, b ca 1815; 3. Catherine, b ca 1818; 4. Duncan, b ca 1820; 5. Jane, b ca 1822; 6. Daniel, 1826–1904; 7. Margaret, 1827-86; 8. Alexander; 9. John.   **DC 11 Apr 1981**.

6558   MACGREGOR, Donald, b 1802. From Aulich, Loch Rannoch, PER. To NS, Jul 1825; stld Antigonish Co. m 15 Nov 1830, Margaret MacIntosh, from Baileys Brook, ch: 1. Duncan, b 1831; 2. Alexander, b 1832; 3. Mary Ann, b 1834; 4. Rev Donald MacIntosh, 1837–1918; 5. James, b 1839; 6. Catherine, b 1841; 7. Janet, b 1843; 8. Margaret, b 1847; 9. Bella J, b 1850; 10. Alexander MacLeod, b 1852, d inf; 11. Alexander MacLeod, b 1854, d inf.   **HCA 282**.

6559   McGREGOR, Donald, 1806–3 Apr 1892. From Logierait, PER. s/o Donald 'Ruadh' M. and Margaret McGregor. To PEI, 1832, but moved later to South River Lake, Antigonish Co, NS. Baptist preacher. m Elizabeth, d/o John Stewart, ch.   **DC 21 Mar 1968**.

6560   McGREGOR, Donald, 1798–11 Jul 1869. From PER. To Esquesing Twp, Halton Co, ONT, prob <1830; bur Acton.   **EPE 74**.

6561   McGREGOR, Donald. From PER. Rel to John M, qv. To Westminster Twp, Middlesex Co, ONT, 1836. **PCM 51**.

6562   McGREGOR, Donald. From Torridon, ROC. To Charlottetown, PEI, 1842; stld Wood Islands, Queens Co. Farmer. ch at least two sons: 1. John, qv; 2. Roderick.   **DC 11 Apr 1981**.

6563   McGREGOR, Donald. From Strathspey. To West Williams Twp, Middlesex Co, ONT, 1846. Pioneer settler.   **PCM 46**.

6564   McGREGOR, Donald. From Is Lewis, ROC. To QUE, ex Stornoway, arr 4 Aug 1851; stld Huron Twp, Bruce Co, ONT, 1852. Head of family.   **DC 5 Apr 1967**.

6565   McGREGOR, Donald, b 1801. From Tolsta Chaolais, Is Lewis, ROC. s/o Murdo M. and Mary McDonald. To QUE, ex Stornoway, arr 4 Aug 1851; stld

Huron Twp, Bruce Co, ONT, 1852. Farmer. Wife Catherine McDonald, qv, with him, and ch: 1. Margaret, b 1826; 2. Murdo, b 1834; 3. John, b 1837; 4. Ann, b 1842; 5. Angus, b 1845. **WLC**.

6566 MACGREGOR, Duncan. From Rannoch, PER. To Merigomish, Pictou Co, NS, prob <1810; moved to Upper South River, Antigonish Co. ch: 1. Alexander; 2. Hugh; 3. Donald; 4. Duncan; 5. John, lawyer. **HCA 283**.

6567 McGREGOR, Duncan, b ca 1762. From PER. To Pictou, NS, on the *Commerce*, ex Port Glasgow, 10 Aug 1803. Farmer. Wife Margaret, aged 30, with him, and ch: 1. Charles, aged 6; 2. Hugh, aged 4; 3. Jessie, aged 1 ½. **PLC**.

6568 McGREGOR, Duncan, ca 1787–Feb 1860. From Duneaves, PER. s/o Donald M, qv. To Queens Co, PEI, <1808. m Elizabeth Stewart, ch: 1. John, 1812-96; 2. William, b 1814. **DC 11 Apr 1981**.

6569 McGREGOR, Duncan, b ca 1777. From Killin par, PER. To QUE, ex Greenock, summer 1815; stld ONT. Labourer, later farmer. Wife Christian McPherson, qv, with him, and 3 ch. **SEC 4**.

6570 McGREGOR, Duncan. From ARL. To Ekfrid Twp, Middlesex Co, ONT, 1831. **PCM 31**.

6571 McGREGOR, Elizabeth, called Betsy, b ca 1795. From Is Mull, ARL. d/o Archibald M, qv, and Ann McColl, qv. To Charlottetown, PEI, on the *Phoenix*, ex Tobermory, 1810. m Alexander Ross. Son William, b 1818. **DC 11 Apr 1981**.

6572 McGREGOR, George. To Restigouche Co, NB, ca 1784; stld Mission Point. Discharged soldier, 42nd Regt. **SR 15**.

6573 McGREGOR, Gregor. Poss from PER. To Aldborough Twp, Elgin Co, ca 1818. Son Gregor. **PDA 92**.

6574 McGREGOR, Gregor, b ca 1827. From Fortingall par, PER. s/o John M, qv, and Christian McFarlane, qv. To Esquesing Twp, Halton Co, ONT, but stld Caledon Twp, Peel Co, 1833. m Catherine McArthur, whose parents were from Is Islay, ARL. **DC 20 Jul 1979**.

6575 McGREGOR, Hugh, ca 1789–16 May 1847. To Kingston, ONT. Collector of Customs, Dickinsons Landing. **DGH 24 Jun 1847**.

6576 McGREGOR, Isabel, b 1759. From Dundurcas, MOR. d/o Peter M, qv, and Margaret Younie, qv. To Flat River, PEI, on the *John & Elizabeth*, arr 30 Jul 1775; stld Queens Co. m 1 Sep 1780, Gregory Kelly, mariner, Charlottetown, ch. **DC 27 Jul 1980**.

6577 McGREGOR, Isabella, b ca 1785. From Is Mull, ARL. d/o Archibald M, qv, and Ann McColl, qv. To Queens Co, PEI, <1806. Wife of John Livingston, qv. **DC 11 Apr 1981**.

6578 McGREGOR, James, 1765–2 Apr 1820. From Dundurcas, MOR. s/o Peter M, qv, and Margaret Younie, qv. To Flat River, PEI, on the *John & Elizabeth*, arr 30 Jul 1775; stld Queens Co, and d Brackley Point. Used surname Gregor. m 3 Apr 1798, Isabella Howat, qv, ch. **DC 27 Jul 1980**.

6579 McGREGOR, James. From Glen Lyon, PER.

s/o — M, and Ellen Turnbull. To NS ca 1780. **DC 8 Nov 1780**.

6580 McGREGOR, Rev James Drummond, 1759–3 Mar 1830. From Portmore, Lochearn, Comrie par, PER. s/o James Drummond M, farmer. Matric Univ of Glasgow, 1779. Ord by Secession Ch, 1786. To Halifax, NS, on the *Lily*, arr 11 Jul 1786, and went to Pictou Co. Pioneer Presb min there. DD, 1822. m (i) Ann Mackay, qv; (ii) Janet Auld, qv. ch: 1. James, b 1799; 2. Roderick; 3. Christian; 4. Jessie; 5. Sarah; 6. Robert, tanner in New Glasgow; 7. Mary; 8. Rev Peter, DD, min at Halifax; 9. Annabel. **BNA 276; GMA 3941; SG iii/4 96; MDB 456**.

6581 McGREGOR, Jane. From Methven, PER. d/o Rev William M, qv, and wife Ann. To Charlottetown, PEI, 1820. m Donald Campbell, 1808-82. **DC 11 Apr 1981**.

6582 McGREGOR, Janet, 1762–29 Feb 1844. From Dundurcas, MOR. d/o Peter M, qv, and Margaret Younie, qv. To Flat River, PEI, on the *John & Elizabeth*, arr 30 Jul 1775; stld Queens Co. m Duncan McCallum, qv. **DC 27 Jul 1980**.

6583 McGREGOR, Jean, b ca 1801. To St Gabriel de Valcartier, QUE, prob <1855. **Census 1861**.

6584 McGREGOR, John. To Granville, Annapolis, NS, <1780. Capt of Militia, 1812. m Mary McMillan, ch. **DC 23 May 1983**.

6585 McGREGOR, John, 1745–16 Feb 1832. From Killin par, PER. s/o Capt James 'Mor' M. (s/o the celebrated Rob Roy M.) and Annabella McNichol, Glenurchy. To Shelburne, NS, 1784; stld Stanhope, Queens Co, PEI. Discharged soldier, 42nd Regt. m (i) Annabella, d/o John Miller, qv, no ch. m (ii) 1790, Margaret McGregor, qv, ch: 1. Janet, 1792–1864; 2. Margaret, b 1794; 3. James, 1796–1874; 4. John, 1802-79. **DC 11 Apr 1981**.

6586 McGREGOR, John. To Restigouche Co, NB, ca 1784; stld Mission Point. Discharged soldier, 42nd Regt. **SR 15**.

6587 McGREGOR, John. From Lochbroom, ROC. To Pictou, NS, on the *Hector*, ex Loch Broom, arr 17 Sep 1773. **HPC App C**.

6588 McGREGOR, John, ca 1797–23 Apr 1857. From Drynie, ROC. s/o David M, qv, and Janet Ross, qv. To PEI, ca 1808; stld Queens Co. Merchant, estate factor, land surveyor and High Sheriff. Went to London, ENG, 1826, and became Secretary of the Board of Trade. Wrote a history of PEI. m 30 Jan 1833, Anne, d/o William P. Jillard. **MDB 457; DC 11 Apr 1981**.

6589 McGREGOR, John, b ca 1786. From Strathgarry, PER. To Charlottetown, PEI, on the *Clarendon*, ex Oban, 6 Aug 1808. Labourer. **CPL**.

6590 McGREGOR, John. From Comrie, PER. To Montreal, QUE, on the *Curlew*, ex Greenock, 21 Jul 1818; stld prob Beckwith Twp, Lanark Co, ONT. **BCL**.

6591 McGREGOR, John. From Balquhidder, PER. To Montreal, QUE, on the *Sophia*, ex Greenock, 26 Jul 1818; stld prob Beckwith Twp, Lanark Co, ONT. Wife Catherine with him, and s John, aged 11. **SPL**.

6592 McGREGOR, John, ca 1801–Sep 1880. From Methven, PER. s/o Rev William M, qv, and wife Ann. To

PEI, 1820; stld Lot 16. m 28 Jan 1835, Margaret Campbell, ch: 1. William, 1835–1901; 2. Charles Augustus.   **DC 11 Apr 1981.**

6593   McGREGOR, John, ca 1789–20 Dec 1869. From Fortingall par, PER. To Esquesing Twp, Halton Co, ONT, but stld Caledon Twp, Peel Co, 1833, on Lot 20, Con 5. m Christina McFarlane, qv, ch: 1. Gregor, qv; 2. Joseph, qv; 3. Alexander, qv; 4. John; 5. Jessie, b CAN, 21 Jun 1838.   **DC 20 Jul 1979.**

6594   McGREGOR, John. From PER. Rel to Donald M, qv. To Westminster Twp, Middlesex Co, ONT, 1836. **PCM 51.**

6595   McGREGOR, John. From Torridon, ROC. s/o Donald M, qv, Wood Is. To Charlottetown, PEI, 1842; stld Bangor, Lot 40. m (i) 30 Jun 1870, Mary Matheson, ch: 1. Murdock, accidentally killed, aged 31; 2. Catherine Isabella; 3. Mary, b 1875; 4. Christina. m (ii) Mary, d/o Allan Morrison, qv, and Effie McLean, further ch: 5. Effie, b 1880; 6. Eliza, a nurse; 7. Margaret, 1883–1934; 8. Ethel Blanche; 9. Daniel, dy; 10. Morrison, dy.   **DC 11 Apr 1981.**

6596   McGREGOR, John. From Is Lewis, INV. To QUE, ex Stornoway, arr 4 Aug 1851; stld Huron Twp, Bruce Co, ONT, 1852. Head of family.   **DC 5 Apr 1967.**

6597   MACGREGOR, Rev John Gibson, 1799–22 Dec 1881. From Alva, STI. Educ Edinburgh, and went to St Johns, NB, 1836. Moved in 1847 to Guelph, ONT, and adm min of Knox Ch. Headmaster of Elora Grammar School, 1852. m Jane Stirling, 1802-91, ch: 1. Helen; 2. Jane; 3. Malcolm O, barrister; 4. Alexander, res at Galt; 5. John, res Minneapolis, MN; 6. Robert, res MN.   **EHE 156.**

6598   McGREGOR, Joseph, 1828–21 Aug 1861. From Fortingall, PER. s/o John M, qv, and Christina McFarlane, qv. To Esquesing Twp, Halton Co, ONT, but stld Caledon Twp, Peel Co, 1833. m Susan McKee, from Erin Twp, Wellington Co, no ch.   **DC 20 Jul 1979.**

6599   McGREGOR, Malcolm, 1796–22 May 1878. From Tobermory, Is Mull, ARL. s/o Archibald M, qv, and Ann McColl, qv. To Charlottetown, PEI, on the *Phoenix*, ex Tobermory, 1810; stld Nine Mile Creek, Queens Co. m Margaret McDougald, qv. Son Archibald, 1827–1926.   **DC 11 Apr 1981.**

6600   MACGREGOR, Malcolm. Poss from PER. To Aldborough Twp, Elgin Co, ONT, prob 1818. Farmer. **PDA 93.**

6601   McGREGOR, Malcolm, 1806–17 Jun 1881. From PER. To Roxborough Twp, Stormont Co, ONT prob 1828. m Catherine Robertson, qv, ch.   **DC 1 Aug 1975.**

6602   McGREGOR, Margaret, 1760–1844. From Dundurcas, MOR. d/o Peter McGregor, qv, and Margaret Younie, qv. To Flat River, PEI, on the *John & Elizabeth*, arr 30 Jul 1775; stld Queens Co. m John McGregor, qv, Deputy Surveyor of PEI.   **DC 27 Jul 1980.**

6603   McGREGOR, Margaret, b ca 1787. From Is Mull, ARL. d/o Archibald M, qv, and Ann McColl, qv. To Charlottetown, PEI, on the *Phoenix*, ex Tobermory, 1810; stld Nine Mile Creek, Queens Co. m — De Frender. **DC 11 Apr 1981.**

6604   McGREGOR, Margaret, 1786–1872. From Killin, PER. d/o James M. and Catherine McNab. To Montreal,

QUE, <1816, when m Donald Fraser, qv.   **LDW 19 Aug 1970.**

6605   McGREGOR, Margaret. Prob from PER. To McNab Twp, Renfrew Co, ONT, 1825. Wife of James Robertson, qv.   **EMT 23.**

6606   McGREGOR, Margaret. To London, Westminster Twp, Middlesex Co, ONT, <6 Aug 1833, when m Hugh Fraser, qv.   **PCM 17.**

6607   McGREGOR, Mary, b ca 1791. From Is Mull, ARL. d/o Archibald M, qv, and Ann McColl, qv. To Charlottetown, PEI, on the *Phoenix*, ex Tobermory, 1810; stld Queens Co. m Peter McMahon.   **DC 11 Apr 1981.**

6608   McGREGOR, Mary. From Comrie par, PER. To Montreal, QUE, on the *Curlew*, ex Greenock, 21 Jul 1818; stld Beckwith Twp, Lanark Co, ONT. Wife of John Ferguson, qv.   **DC 29 Dec 1981.**

6609   McGREGOR, Mary, 1799–1899. From Applecross par, ROC. d/o Alexander M. and Ann McKenzie. To Boularderie, Victoria Co, NS, <1826, when m Gregor Kempt, qv. Went to Waipu, NZ, 1860.   **DC 21 Aug 1981.**

6610   MACGREGOR, Mary. From INV. d/o Rev Robert M. To James River, Antigonish Co, NS, <1840. Wife of John MacDonald, qv.   **MP 393.**

6611   McGREGOR, Mary. From Thornhill, PER. To Esquesing Twp, Halton Co, ONT, <1852. Wife of Robert McGregor, qv.   **DC 15 Feb 1971.**

6612   McGREGOR, Murdock. From Is Lewis, INV. To QUE, ex Stornoway, arr 4 Aug 1851; stld Huron Twp, Bruce Co, ONT, 1852. Head of family.   **DC 5 Apr 1967.**

6613   McGREGOR, Patrick or Peter, 1794–13 Jan 1846. Prob from PER. To London Village, Westminster Twp, Middlesex Co, ONT, 1826. Pioneer Scottish settler there; innkeeper and jailer. Bur Scottsville, where grave marker restored 1982.   **PCM 55.**

6614   McGREGOR, Patrick, ca 1816-82. From PER. To ONT, 1833, and became master of a grammar school at Kingston. Retr to SCT to study at Univ of Edinburgh, 1840-41. After a period in USA, he retr to CAN and practised law in Toronto.   **MDB 457.**

6615   McGREGOR, Patrick. Poss from ARL. To Mosa Twp, Middlesex Co, ONT, 1836. Schoolteacher. **PCM 24.**

6616   McGREGOR, Peter or Patrick, Oct 1721–29 Oct 1799. From Dundurcas, MOR. Prob s/o Peter M. To Flat River, PEI, on the *John & Elizabeth*, arr 30 Jul 1775; stld Queens Co. m Margaret Younie, qv, ch: 1. Isabel, qv; 2. Janet, qv; 3. James, qv; 4. Margaret, qv. **DC 27 Jul 1980.**

6617   McGREGOR, Peter. From Comrie par, PER. To Montreal, QUE, on the *Curlew*, ex Greenock, 21 Jul 1818; stld prob Beckwith Twp, Lanark Co, ONT. Wife Christian with him.   **BCL.**

6618   McGREGOR, Peter. From Balquhidder, PER. To Montreal, QUE, on the *Sophia*, ex Greenock, 26 Jul 1818; stld prob Beckwith Twp, Lanark Co, ONT. Wife Catherine with him, and ch: 1. Mary, aged 8; 2. Duncan, aged 6.   **SPL.**

6619   McGREGOR, Peter. From Balquhidder, PER. To Montreal, QUE, on the *Sophia*, ex Greenock, 26 Jul

1818; stld prob Beckwith Twp, Lanark Co, ONT. Wife Mary with him, and ch: 1. John, aged 6; 2. Mary, aged 3. **SPL**.

6620 McGREGOR, Peter, 1808-85. From Methven, PER. s/o Rev William M, qv, and wife Ann. To PEI, 1820, stld Lot 16. Farmer. m 12 Jul 1868, Harriet Green, 1819-85, Lot 17. **DC 11 Apr 1981**.

6621 McGREGOR, Peter. To Ramsay Twp, Lanark Co, ONT, 1821. **HCL 85**.

6622 McGREGOR, Richard, b 1802. From Assynt, SUT. To Cape Breton Co, NS. m Isabella McLeod, qv. **DC 14 Apr 1965**.

6623 McGREGOR, Robert. From Comrie par, PER. To Montreal, QUE, on the *Curlew*, ex Greenock, 21 Jul 1818; stld prob Beckwith Twp, Lanark Co, ONT. Wife Mary with him, and ch: 1. James, aged 12; 2. John, aged 10. **BCL**.

6624 McGREGOR, Sarah, ca 1797–21 May 1843. From PER. sis/o Alexander M, surgeon, qv. To Charlottetown, PEI, <15 Aug 1823, when m Alexander McRae, qv. **DC 11 Apr 1981**.

6625 McGREGOR, Thomas, b ca 1768. From Aberfeldy, PER. To Charlottetown, PEI, on the *Clarendon*, ex Oban, 6 Aug 1808. Son John, aged 12, with him. Labourer. **CPL**.

6626 McGREGOR, Rev William, 1775–10 Feb 1850. From Methven, PER. To PEI, 1820. Presb min, Richmond Bay. By wife Ann, who d 1845, ch: 1. John, qv; 2. Andrew, qv; 3. Jane, qv; 4. Peter, qv; 5. Mary, 1812-89, unm. **DC 11 Apr 1981**.

6627 McGREGOR, William, ca 1796–ca 1862. From INV. To Miramichi, Northumberland Co, NB, <1828, when he moved to Dalhousie, Restigouche Co, with wife Catherine. **DC 25 Feb 1982**.

6628 McGREGOR, William Malcolm. To ONT <1854. Son Robert Coll. **SH**.

6629 McGRIGOR, Donald. From Kiltarlity, INV. To Pictou, NS, on the *Sarah*, ex Fort William, Jun 1801. Farmer. Wife Isobel with him, and ch: 1. Mary, aged 11; 2. John, aged 9; 3. Jean, aged 8; 4. Alexander, aged 6; 5. Andrew, aged 4; 6. Kate, aged 2. **PLS**.

6630 McGUGAN, Archibald. From Caolasraide, South Knapdale, ARL. To Lobo Twp, Middlesex Co, ONT, 1828. ch: 1. John; 2. Archibald; 3. Duncan; 4. Flora; 5. Sarah; 6. Margaret; 7. Mary. **PCM 40**.

6631 McGUGAN, Archibald. From North Knapdale, ARL. To Lobo Twp, Middlesex Co, ONT, 1830. m Margaret, d/o Duncan 'Mor' Graham, qv, ch: 1. Donald; 2. Archibald; 3. Duncan; 4. Neil; 5. Nancy; 6. Maggie; 7. Flora. **PCM 39**.

6632 McGUGAN, Archibald. From ARL, prob South Knapdale. To Caradoc Twp, Middlesex Co, ONT, ca 1830. **PCM 34**.

6633 McGUGAN, Donald. From North Knapdale, ARL. To QUE on the *Mars*, ex Tobermory, 28 Jul 1818; stld Aldborough Twp, Elgin Co, ONT. Farmer. m Mary MacIntyre, qv, ch: 1. Angus; 2. Duncan; 3. Archie; 4. Daniel; 5. Effie; 6. Isabel. **PDA 28**.

6634 McGUGAN, Donald, 1791–1857. From

Coishindrochit, North Knapdale, ARL. s/o Neil M. and Elspeth Campbell. To Talbot Settlement, ONT, 1819; stld Dunwich Twp, Elgin Co. Farmer. m Mary McAlpine, qv, ch: 1. Neil, qv; 2. Catherine, b 1816; 3. Alexander, b 1818; 4. Katherine, b 1820; 5. Alexander, b 1822; 6. Elizabeth, b 1824; 7. John, b 1826; 8. Mary, b 1828; 9. Flora, b 1831; 10. Isabella, b 1834; 11. Donald, b 1835; 12. Sarah, b 1837. **DC 8 Dec 1981**.

6635 McGUGAN, Donald. From North Knapdale, ARL. To Caradoc Twp, Middlesex Co, ONT, 1829. Son Malcolm, politician. **PCM 34**.

6636 McGUGAN, Donald. From ARL. To Ekfrid Twp, Middlesex Co, ONT, 1849. ch: 1. John; 2. Malcolm; 3. Archie; 4. Donald; 5. Mrs John Kerr. **PCM 30**.

6637 McGUGAN, John. Prob from North Knapdale, ARL. To Caradoc Twp, Middlesex Co, ONT, 1830. m Sarah McTaggart, qv, ch: 1. Godfrey; 2. Annie. **PCM 34, 44**.

6638 McGUGAN, Neil. From North Knapdale, ARL. To Caradoc Twp, Middlesex Co, ONT, ca 1830. ch: 1. Angus; 2. Donald; 3. Duncan; 4. Malcolm; 5. John; 6. Isabella; 7. Nancy; 8. Nancy; 9. Margaret; 10. Sarah; 11. Kate; 12. Mary. **PCM 34**.

MACHATTIE. See also HATTIE.

6639 McHATTIE, Janet. From Forres, MOR. To Chatham, Deux-Montagnes, QUE, 1833. Wife of Alexander Alves, qv. **DC 17 Dec 1981**.

6640 McHATTIE, William. From Forres, MOR. Poss bro/o Janet M, qv. To York Co, ONT, 1832, with James Alves, qv. **DC 17 Dec 1981**.

6641 McHOLM, James. From Troqueer, KKD. To Cobourg, Northumberland Co, ONT, <1855. **DGC 4 Sep 1855**.

6642 McHOULL, Hugh. From Galston, AYR. s/o William M, merchant. To Oshawa, Durham Co, ONT, <1851. **SH**.

6643 McHUTCHISON, Hugh, b ca 1751. From AYR. To QUE on the *Friendship*, ex Port Glasgow, 30 Mar 1775. Ship carpenter, 'going out to build vessels.' **LSF**.

6644 McILRAITH, James. Prob from AYR. To QUE on the *Earl of Buckinghamshire*, ex Greenock, 29 Apr 1821; stld Lanark Co, ONT. **HCL 73**.

6645 McILWRAITH, Margaret, d 30 Jun 1871. From Greenock, RFW. d/o John M. and Susanna Boog. To Alma, Peel Twp, Wellington Co, ONT. Wife of Duncan McGown, qv. **Ts Greenock**.

6646 McILWRAITH, Thomas, 26 Dec 1824–31 Jan 1903. From Newton-upon-Ayr, AYR. s/o Thomas M, weaver, and Jean Adair. To Hamilton, ONT, 1853. Manager of gasworks, later carrier. Pioneer ornithologist and author of *Birds of Ontario*. m Mary Park, qv. Dau Jean, 1859–1938, authoress. **Newton OPR 612/3; MDB 458; DC 1 Jan 1968**.

6647 McINDOE, Mary, ca 1826–1909. Prob from Gourock, RFW. To Chatham, Northumberland Co, NB, ca 1850. Wife of Hugh Marquis, qv. **DC 2 Jun 1978**.

6648 McINNES, Alexander, b ca 1789. To Western Shore, Inverness Co, NS, 1802. Farmer, m and ch. **CBC 1818**.

6649 MACINNES, Alexander, b ca 1800. From Glendale, Durinish, Is Skye, INV. s/o Neil M. To Upper Southeast Mabou, Inverness Co, NS, ca 1822. Builder, and constructed bridges. m Euphemia Buchanan, qv, ch: 1. Mary, b 1834; 2. Neil; 3. Daniel; 4. John, mariner; 5. Peter, 1851–1915; 6. Angus, b 1852. **MP ii 438**.

6650 McINNES, Alexander. To QUE on the *Commerce*, ex Greenock, Jun 1820; stld prob Lanark Co, ONT. **HCL 239**.

6651 McINNES, Alexander. From Is Coll, ARL. To Portage Road, Eldon Twp, Victoria Co, ONT, ca 1853. m Mary McFadyen, ch: 1. Hector; 2. John; 3. Neil. **EC 140**.

6652 McINNES, Allan, b ca 1797. To Western Shore, Inverness Co, NS, 1816. Farmer, unm. **CBC 1818**.

6653 McINNES, Angus, b ca 1774. To Inverness Co, NS, 1802; stld prob Judique. Farmer, m and ch. **CBC 1818**.

6654 MACINNES, Angus, b ca 1780. To PEI, <1830, but moved to Mabou, Inverness Co, NS. Wife Jessie, b ca 1781, with him, and ch: 1. Angus, b 1808; 2. Ann, b 1816; 3. Donald, b 1821. **MP ii 438**.

6655 MACINNES, Archibald. Prob from INV. To Montreal, QUE, prob Sep 1802. Petitioned for land on the Ottawa River, ONT, 6 Aug 1804. **DC 15 Mar 1980**.

6656 MACINNES, Barbara. From Campbeltown, ARL. d/o John M. and — McTaggart. To Pictou Co, NS, ca 1845; stld Albion Mines, or Stellarton. **DC 21 Mar 1981**.

6657 MACINNES, Archibald, ca 1797–1872. From Ross of Mull, ARL. To Eldon Twp, Victoria Co, ONT, <1840. Farmer. m Catherine MacQuarrie, qv, ch: 1. Archie; 2. Lachie D; 3. John, b 1837; 4. Sarah, b 1839; 5. Catherine, b 1842. **EC 138**.

6658 McINNES, Catherine Ann. Prob from Is Mull, ARL. To Argyle, Eldon Twp, Victoria Co, ONT, ca 1852. Wife of James McQuarrie, qv. **EC 171**.

6659 McINNES, Colin, 1815–18 Jan 1898. From Campbeltown, ARL. s/o John M. and — McTaggart. To Pictou Co, NS, ca 1845; stld Albion Mines. Farmer at Brookville. m Sarah, 1825-90, d/o James 'Og' Fraser and Mary McIntosh, ch: 1. John Daniel; 2. Mary Catherine; 3. Sarah Ann. **DC 21 Mar 1981**.

6660 McINNES, Donald, b 1763. To Inverness Co, NS, 1800; stld Judique. Farmer, m and ch. **CBC 1818**.

6661 MACINNES, Donald. From Arisaig, INV. To Pictou, NS, on the *Dove*, ex Fort William, Jun 1801. Tenant. Wife Catherine with him, and ch: 1. Angus, labourer; 2. Jean, aged 7; 3. Duncan, aged 5. **PLD**.

6662 MACINNES, Donald. To Queens Co, PEI, poss 1803. Petitioner for Dr MacAulay, 1811. **HP 73**.

6663 McINNES, Donald, b 1774. To St Andrews dist, Cape Breton Co, NS, 1814. Farmer, m and ch. **CBC 1818**.

6664 McINNES, Donald, 26 May 1824–9 Dec 1900. From Oban, ARL. To Dundas, Wentworth Co, ONT; stld later in Hamilton. Merchant-banker and Canadian senator. m 1863, Mary Amelia, d/o Sir John B. Robinson, Bt. **MDB 458**.

6665 MACINNES, Donald. From Campbeltown, ARL. s/o John M. and — McTaggart. To Pictou Co, NS, ca 1845; stld nr Stellarton. **DC 21 Mar 1981**.

6666 MACINNES, Donald, b 1827. From Buaile Dubh, Is South Uist, INV. s/o Neil M. and wife Penny. To Pictou, NS, on the *Lulan*, ex Glasgow, 17 Aug 1848. **DC 12 Jul 1979**.

6667 McINNES, Donald, b ca 1825. From Is Skye, INV. s/o Malcolm and Ann M. To Baddeck, Victoria Co, NS, <1850. m Isobel Buchanan, ca 1825–ca 1902. Son Angus. **HNS iii 301**.

6668 McINNES, Duncan. To QUE on the *George Canning*, ex Greenock, 14 Apr 1821; stld Lanark Co, ONT. **HCL 191**.

6669 MACINNES, Finlay, b 1825. From Buaile Dubh, Is South Uist, INV. s/o Neil M. and wife Penny. To Pictou, NS, on the *Lulan*, ex Glasgow, 17 Aug 1848. **DC 12 Jul 1979**.

6670 MACINNES, Hector. Prob from Is Rum, ARL. s/o Donald M. To Cape Mabou, Inverness Co, NS, <1828. Farmer. m Miss Stevens, ch: 1. John; 2. John Lachie; 3. Alexander; 4. Donald. **MP ii 431**.

6671 MACINNES, Henrietta. From Creiff, PER. d/o Dr M, surgeon. To Montreal, QUE, >1 Mar 1816, when she m at Perth, William Peddie, merchant in Montreal. **Perth OPR 387/23**.

6672 McINNES, Hugh, b ca 1797. Poss s/o John M, b ca 1760, qv. To Western Shore, Inverness Co, NS, 1802. Farmer. **CBC 1818**.

6673 McINNES, Hugh, b ca 1800. Prob bro/o John M, qv. To Western Shore, Inverness Co, NS, 1817. Farmer, unm. **CBC 1818**.

6674 McINNES, James. From Callander, PER. To Montreal, QUE, on the *Curlew*, ex Greenock, 21 Jul 1818; stld prob Beckwith Twp, Lanark Co, ONT. Wife Marion with him, and inf dau Janet. **BCL**.

6675 McINNES, Janet, ca 1817–22 Mar 1893. From Ross of Mull, ARL. To Eldon Twp, Victoria Co, ONT, 1855. m Colin Stewart, qv. **EC 216**.

6676 McINNES, John. From Askernish, Is South Uist, INV. Prob rel to Peter M, qv. To PEI on the *Jane*, ex Loch nan Uamh, Arisaig, 12 Jul 1790. Wife and ch with him. **PLJ**.

6677 MACINNES, John. From Is Skye, INV. bro/o Murdock M, qv. To Inverness Co, NS, 1820; stld Malagawatch. **DC 21 Mar 1981**.

6678 MACINNES, John, b ca 1791. To Western Shore, Inverness Co, NS, 1800. Farmer, m and ch. **CBC 1818**.

6679 McINNES, John, b ca 1760. To Western Shore, Inverness Co, NS, 1802. Farmer, m and ch. **CBC 1818**.

6680 McINNES, John, b ca 1768. To Western Shore, Inverness Co, NS, 1817. Farmer, m and ch. **CBC 1818**.

6681 McINNES, John, b ca 1802. Prob bro/o Hugh M, qv. To Western Shore, Inverness Co, NS, 1817. Farmer. **CBC 1818**.

6682 McINNES, John. Prob from Is Rum, ARL. s/o Donald M. To Cape Mabou, Inverness Co, NS, <1828. Farmer. ch: 1. Angus; 2. Donald, shoemaker, d unm. **MP ii 435**.

6683 McINNES, John, 1810-89. From ARL. To Cumberland Co, NS, prob <1840; stld nr Wallace. Wife Mary, 1814–1903. **DC 29 Oct 1980**.

6684 MACINNES, John, ca 1798–1874. From Ross of Mull, ARL. To Eldon Twp, Victoria Co, ONT, <1840; purchased Lot 16, Con 8, in 1858. m Euphemia MacQuarrie, qv, ch: 1. Catherine, b 1827; 2. Allan, b 1831; 3. John, 1835–1913; 4. Flora, b 1841; 5. Lachlan, 1843–1921. **EC 138**.

6685 McINNES, John (1). To Pictou, NS, on the *London*, arr 14 Jul 1848. **DC 14 Jul 1848**.

6686 McINNES, John (2). To Pictou, NS, on the *London*, arr 14 Jul 1848. **DC 14 Jul 1848**.

6687 McINNES, John, b 1811. From Haclet, Is Benbecula, INV. s/o Finlay M. To East Williams Twp, Middlesex Co, ONT, poss 1849. m Catherine, d/o Malcolm Smith, ch: 1. Margaret, b 1845; 2. Malcolm, b 1847; 3. John, b 1849; 4. Malcolm, b 1851; 5. Sarah, b 1854; 6. Charles, b 1856; 7. Finlay, b 1857; 8. James, b 1859. **PCM 48; WLC**.

6688 McINNES, Lauchlan, b 1773. From Is Rum, ARL. To Gut of Canso, Cape Breton, NS, on the *St Lawrence*, ex Tobermory, 11 Jul 1828. Wife Mary, aged 48, with him, and ch: 1. Penny, aged 25; 2. Allan, aged 23; 3. Hector, aged 21; 4. Mary, aged 19; 5. Donald, aged 17; 6. Marion, aged 10; 7. Flory, aged 8; 8. Jessie, aged 6. **SLL**.

6689 MACINNES, Lachlan John, 1816-52. From Cliad, Is Coll, ARL. To QUE, ex Liverpool, 7 Jul 1847; stld Mara Twp, York Co, ONT, and d Uptergrove. Farmer. m Mary McLean, ch: 1. Margaret; 2. Alexander; 3. John; 4. Lachlan; 5. Christina. **DC 25 Apr 1983**.

6690 McINNES, Margaret, b ca 1770. From Cambus, Is Mull, ARL. Prob wid/o — McLean. To Hudson Bay, <1813. Pioneer settler. **RRS 25**.

6691 MACINNES, Margaret. From Campbeltown, ARL. d/o John M. and — McTaggart. To Pictou, NS, ca 1845; stld Albion Mines, now Stellarton. **DC 21 Mar 1981**.

6692 McINNES, Murdock. From Is Skye, INV. bro/o John M, qv. To Richmond Co, NS, 1820; stld West Bay. m Catherine MacLeod. Son Murdoch, 1842-93, master mariner. **DC 21 Mar 1981**.

6693 McINNES, Neil, b ca 1791. To Inverness Co, NS, 1803. Farmer, m and ch. **CBC 1818**.

6694 MACINNES, Mrs Penny, b ca 1788. From Buaile Dubh, Is South Uist, INV. wid/o Neil M. To Pictou, NS, on the *Lulan*, ex Glasgow, 17 Aug 1848. **DC 12 Jul 1979**.

6695 McINNES, Peter. From Askernish, Is South Uist, INV. Prob rel to John M, qv. To PEI on the *Jane*, ex Loch nan Uamh, Arisaig, 12 Jul 1790, poss calling at Loch Boisdale. **PLJ**.

6696 MACINNES, Robert. From Blair Atholl, PER. To PEI, poss on the *Alexander*, 1772; moved <1800 to Judique, Inverness Co, NS. Mason and pioneer settler. m Mary McEachen, qv, ch: 1. Alexander; 2. Donald; 3. Robert; 4. Margaret; 5. Mary; 6. Cecilia; 7. Isabel; 8. Elizabeth; 9. Jane; 10. Catherine; 11. Mary; 12. Ann. **DC 5 Feb 1961**.

6697 McINNES, Sarah, ca 1782–19 Aug 1845. From Is Iona, ARL. To York Co, ONT, <1812; stld Vaughan Twp. Wife of John McDonald, qv. **DC 24 Jan 1977**.

6698 McINNES, Rev Thomas G, ca 1791–26 Aug 1824. From Logie, STI. s/o Neil M, craftsman. Matric Univ of Glasgow, 1808. To Halifax, NS, 1815. Min of Relief Ch, 1815-20. Went to Philadelphia, 1820, to become min of 9th Presb Ch. **GMA 7534**.

6699 MACINNIS, Alexander 'Taillear'. From Glenfinnan, INV. s/o Alexander M. and Catherine Beaton. To Mabou Ridge, Inverness Co, NS, ca 1822. Wife Mary MacDonald, qv, with him, and ch: 1. John, qv; 2. Angus, qv; 3. Donald, qv; 4. Archibald; 5. Catherine, teacher, unm; 6. Sarah, qv. **MP 654**.

6700 McINNIS, Allan, b ca 1781. Prob s/o Angus M, qv. To Charlottetown, PEI, on the *Rambler*, ex Tobermory, arr 20 Jun 1806. **PLR**.

6701 MACINNIS, Angus. Prob from Morven, INV. To Pictou, NS, prob <1800; stld Pictou Is. m (i) Miss Gillis, ch: 1. John; 2. Angus; 3. Mary; 4. Ann; 5. Catherine. m (ii) Miss Smith, further ch: 6. Christy; 7. Donald; 8. John; 9. Alexander. **HCA 286**.

6702 McINNIS, Angus, b ca 1746. To Charlottetown, PEI, on the *Rambler*, ex Tobermory, arr 20 Jun 1806. Family prob with him. **PLR**.

6703 McINNIS, Angus, b ca 1793. Poss s/o Donald M, qv. To Charlottetown, PEI, on the *Rambler*, ex Tobermory, arr 20 Jun 1806. **PLR**.

6704 McINNIS, Angus, 1794–10 May 1872. From Glenfinnan, INV. s/o Alexander M, qv, and Mary McDonald, qv. To Mabou Ridge, Inverness Co, NS, ca 1822. Farmer and magistrate. m Catherine, d/o Alexander Beaton, qv, and Anne Beaton, ch: 1. Mary; 2. Mary, jr; 3. Alexander; 4. Sara; 5. John; 6. Donald; 7. Alexander T; 8. Anne; 9. Ronald. **MP 190, 655**.

6705 MACINNIS, Angus 'Ban'. From INV. s/o John 'Ban' M. To Cape George, Antigonish Co, NS, prob <1825. ch: 1. Donald, res South River; 2. Angus, res South River; 3. Hugh; 4. Harriet. **HCA 287**.

6706 MACINNIS, Angus 'Og'. From Is Barra, INV. To Inverness Co, NS, 1831; stld West Lake Ainslie. Printer, later farmer. m Lucy or Louisa MacDonald, qv, ch: 1. Charles, qv; 2. Neil, dy; 3. Angus, qv; 4. Christina, 1831–1906; 5. Margaret; 6. Emily; 7. Mary; 8. Flora. **MP 660**.

6707 MACINNIS, Angus, b ca 1829. From Rulios, Is Barra, INV. s/o Angus 'Og' M, qv, and Lucy MacDonald, qv. To Inverness Co, NS, 1831; stld West Lake Ainslie. m Margaret, d/o Angus MacDonald, ch: 1. Lucy; 2. Charles; 3. Angus; 4. Catherine; 5. Mary; 6. Flora; 7. Jessie Anne. **MP 285, 665**.

6708 McINNIS, Ann, b 1806. Poss d/o Donald M, qv. To Charlottetown, PEI, on the *Rambler*, ex Tobermory, arr 20 Jun 1806. **PLR**.

6709 MACINNIS, Anne. From Lochaber, INV. d/o Alexander M. To Pictou, NS, 1804; stld Mabou, Inverness Co. Wife of Alexander Beaton, qv. **MP 162**.

6710 MACINNIS, Charles, ca 1826-74. From Is Barra, INV. s/o Angus 'Og' M, qv, and Lucy MacDonald, qv. To

Inverness Co, NS, 1831; stld West Lake Ainslie. m Mary MacPherson, 1822–1920, from Cape Breton Co, ch: 1. Neil; 2. Angus; 3. Roderick; 4. Catherine; 5. Mary; 6. Matilda; 7. Joseph Charles; 8. Lucy.   **MP 661**.

6711   MACINNIS, Donald. To Antigonish Co, NS, prob <1790; stld OH. Discharged soldier. By first wife had ch: 1. Duncan 'Og'; 2. Angus; 3. Jane. m (ii) Sarah MacIsaac, further ch: 4. Hugh; 5. John; 6. Mary. By a third wife had ch: 7. Catherine; 8. Sarah; 9. Ann. **HCA 285**.

6712   McINNIS, Donald, b ca 1768. Prob s/o Angus M, qv. To Charlottetown, PEI, on the *Rambler*, ex Tobermory, arr 20 Jun 1806. Prob wife and ch with him.   **PLR**.

6713   MACINNIS, Donald. From Glenfinnan, INV. s/o Alexander M, qv. and Mary MacDonald, qv. To Mabou Ridge, Inverness Co, NS, ca 1822. m Margaret, d/o Alexander MacKillop, qv, and had, poss with other ch: 1. Alexander; 2. John; 3. Archibald; 4. Mary. **MP 658, 721**.

6714   MACINNIS, Donald. From INV. s/o John 'Ban' M. To Cape George, Antigonish Co, NS, prob <1825. ch: 1. John; 2. Ann.   **HCA 287**.

6715   McINNIS, Donald, b 1809. From Smerclett, Is South Uist, INV. To East Williams Twp, Middlesex Co, ONT, poss 1849, and d MI. m Margaret Morrison, ch: 1. Marion, b 1840; 2. Colin, b 1841; 3. Neil, b 1842; 4. Margaret; 5. Malcolm, b 1846; 6. John, b 1848; 7. Catherine, b 1850; 8. Effie, b 1852; 9. Margaret, b 1857; 10. Finlay, b 1859.   **PCM 44; WLC**.

6716   McINNIS, Finlay, b ca 1804. Poss s/o Donald M, qv. To Charlottetown, PEI, on the *Rambler*, ex Tobermory, arr 20 Jun 1806.   **PLJ**.

6717   McINNIS, Flora, b ca 1781. Poss d/o Angus M, qv. To Charlottetown, PEI, on the *Rambler*, ex Tobermory, arr 20 Jun 1806.   **PLJ**.

6718   McINNIS, Hector, b ca 1776. Prob s/o Angus M, qv. To Charlottetown, PEI, on the *Rambler*, ex Tobermory, arr 20 Jun 1806.   **PLR**.

6719   MACINNIS, Hugh. Prob from Morvern, INV. To Pictou, NS, poss <1800; stld Cape George, Antigonish Co.   **HCA 286**.

6720   McINNIS, Isabella, b ca 1790. Poss d/o Donald M, qv. To Charlottetown, PEI, on the *Rambler*, ex Tobermory, arr 20 Jun 1806.   **PLR**.

6721   McINNIS, John, b ca 1805. Poss s/o Donald M, qv. To Charlottetown, PEI, on the *Rambler*, ex Tobermory, arr 20 Jun 1806.   **PLR**.

6722   MACINNIS, John, b ca 1793. From Glenfinnan, INV. s/o Alexander M, qv, and Mary MacDonald, qv. To Mabou Ridge, Inverness Co, NS, ca 1822. m Mary, d/o Alexander 'Gobha' MacEachern, qv, and Mary Campbell, ch: 1. Mary; 2. Annie.   **MP 654**.

6723   MACINNIS, John. From INV. s/o John 'Ban' M. To Cape George, Antigonish Co, NS, prob <1825. Son Angus.   **HCA 287**.

6724   McINNIS, John, b ca 1777. To NS <1840; later to Cape Traverse, PEI.   **NSN 34/34**.

6725   MACINNIS, John. Prob from Morvern, INV. To NS, <1840; stld Antigonish Co. ch incl: 1. Donald James, res Gaspereaux Lake; 2. Angus; 3. Hugh; 4. John; 5. Catherine.   **HCA 284**.

6726   McINNIS, John. From INV. To Lake Ainslie, Inverness Co, NS, <1840. m Mary Hamilton, qv. Son Thomas Robert, 1840–1904, senator and physician. **DC 30 Aug 1977**.

6727   McINNIS, Lachlan. From Is South Uist, INV. To West Williams Twp, Middlesex Co, ONT, 1849; stld Con 14.   **PCM 48**.

6728   McINNIS, Margaret, b 1756. Poss wife of Angus M, qv. To Charlottetown, PEI, on the *Rambler*, ex Tobermory, arr 20 Jun 1806.   **PLR**.

6729   McINNIS, Margaret, b ca 1777. Poss wife of Donald M, qv. To Charlottetown, PEI, on the *Rambler*, ex Tobermory, arr 20 Jun 1806.   **PLR**.

6730   McINNIS, Margaret, b 1800. Poss d/o Donald M, qv. To Charlottetown, PEI, on the *Rambler*, ex Tobermory, arr 20 Jun 1806.   **PLR**.

6731   McINNIS, Mary, b 1778. Poss d/o Angus M, qv. To Charlottetown, PEI, on the *Rambler*, ex Tobermory, arr 20 Jun 1806.   **PLR**.

6732   McINNIS, Mary, b ca 1794. Poss d/o Donald M, qv. To Charlottetown, PEI, on the *Rambler*, ex Tobermory, arr 20 Jun 1806.   **PLR**.

6733   McINNIS, Sarah, b ca 1798. Poss d/o Donald M, qv. To Charlottetown, PEI, on the *Rambler*, ex Tobermory, arr 20 Jun 1806.   **PLR**.

6734   MACINNIS, Sarah. From Glenfinnan, INV. d/o Alexander M, qv, and Mary MacDonald, qv. To Mabou Ridge, Inverness Co, NS, ca 1822. m Alexander, s/o Alexander Beaton, qv, and Ann Beaton, ch. **MP 185, 659**.

6735   McINROY, Alexander, b 1781. Poss from Cargill, PER. To Huntingdon, Hastings Co, ONT, <1840. Wife Grace with him, and ch: 1. Donald, b ca 1820; 2. Isabelle, b ca 1823; 3. Alexander, b 1827; 4. John, b 1829; 5. Thomas, b 1832; 6. Charles, b 1834; 7. Andrew, 1837-38; 8. Duncan.   **DC 10 Nov 1981**.

6736   McINROY, Daniel or Donald, b ca 1820. Poss from PER. To Hastings Co, ONT, <1850. m Ellen Hill, qv, ch: 1. Barbara, b 1844; 2. Daniel, b 1846; 3. Ellen; 4. Thomas.   **DC 10 Nov 1981**.

McINTIRE. See also McINTYRE.

6737   McINTIRE, Angus, b ca 1770. To Inverness Co, NS, 1817; stld prob Mabou. Farmer, m and ch. **CBC 1818**.

6738   McINTOSH, Alexander. From INV. To Pictou Co, NS, prob 1784; gr 500 acres on East River. Prob discharged soldier, 84th Regt.   **HPC App H**.

6739   McINTOSH, Alexander. From Kilmorack, INV. Prob rel to Donald M, qv. To Pictou, NS, on the *Sarah*, ex Fort William, Jun 1801. Farmer.   **PLS**.

6740   McINTOSH, Alexander, b 1761. From PER. To Pictou, NS, on the *Commerce*, ex Port Glasgow, 10 Aug 1803. Farmer. Wife Agnes, aged 34, with him, and ch: 1. John, aged 13; 2. Margaret, aged 11; 3. James, aged 9; 4. William, aged 3.   **PLC**.

6741 MACINTOSH, Alexander. From Lochaber, INV.
bro/o John 'Og' M, qv, and Donald B. M, qv. To
South River, Antigonish Co, NS, prob <1820.
m a d/o Alexander Chisholm, soldier, ch: 1. Colin;
2. Christina; 3. Donald; 4. Peggy; 5. Katie; 6. Janet.
HCA 289.

6742 MACINTOSH, Alexander. Prob from INV.
bro/o Duncan M, qv. To South River, Antigonish Co,
NS, <1830. ch: 1. Duncan; 2. Hugh; 3. Kate;
4. Janet. **HCA 290**.

6743 McINTOSH, Alexander. Rel to Gilbert M, qv, and
John M, qv. To London, Westminster Twp, Middlesex
Co, ONT, prob <1840. Merchant. **PCM 55**.

6744 MAC(K)INTOSH, Alexander, 1823–1907. From
Auchindaar, Edinkillie par, MOR. To Perth Co, ONT, 1854.
Wife Isabella Whyte, qv, with him, and ch: 1. Margaret,
b 11 Jul 1851; 2. Janet, b 3 Jun 1854. **DC 17 Nov
1982**.

6745 MAC(K)INTOSH, Angus, ca 1756–25 Jan 1833.
From INV. s/o Duncan M. of Castle Leathers, and Agnes
Dallas. To Montreal, QUE, <1780, but was sometime in
Detroit before settling in Sandwich Twp, Essex Co, ONT,
as an agent for the NWCo. In 1827 he succ his brother
Alexander as 25th Chief of the Clan Mackintosh, and retr
to SCT to live at Moy Hall, Loch Moy, INV. w 1788,
Archange Marie, d 1827, d/o Jacques Baudry dit
Desbuttes dit St Martin, ch: 1. Donald, d unm;
2. Alexander, 26th Chief; 3. Aneas of Daviot;
4. James St Martin, who lived in CAN. **MDB 459;
LDW 12 Apr 1963**.

6746 McINTOSH, Rev Angus. App to mission of
Markham, York Co, ONT, 22 Apr 1833, by Glasgow
Colonial Society. Became min at Thorold, Welland dist,
1836. Joined FC, 1843. **FES vii 642**.

6747 McINTOSH, Angus. From Lower Bornish, Is
South Uist, INV. To West Williams Twp, Middlesex Co,
ONT, 1849. m Mary McPhee, ch. **DC 11 Apr 1983**.

6748 McINTOSH, Angus 'Mor'. From Is South Uist,
INV. To West Williams Twp, Middlesex Co, ONT, 1849.
PCM 48.

6749 McINTOSH, Ann. From Glenelg, INV. To Pictou,
NS, on the *Dove*, ex Fort William, Jun 1801. Prob wife
of John M, farmer, qv. **PLD**.

6750 McINTOSH, Mrs Ann. To Pictou, NS, on the
Ellen, ex Lochlaxford, 22 May 1848. ch with her:
1. Robina; 2. Donaldina; 3. Cina; 4. Roderick;
5. Hughina. **DC 15 Jul 1979**.

6751 McINTOSH, Catherine. From Kilmorack, INV.
Poss wife of Alexander M, farmer, qv. To Pictou, NS, on
the *Sarah*, ex Fort William, Jun 1801. **PLS**.

6752 McINTOSH, Catherine. From Glenelg, INV. To
QUE, summer 1815; stld prob E ONT. Wife of Alexander
McRae, qv. **SEC 5**.

6753 McINTOSH, Catherine. From Kerrowdoun,
Strathfarrar, INV. Prob rel to James M, qv. To Montreal,
ex Fort William, arr Sep 1802; stld E ONT.
MCM 1/4 24.

6754 McINTOSH, Charles. From Petty, INV. To
Cornwallis, NS, 1785; stld later east branch of East
River, Pictou Co. Farmer and landowner. m 2 Jun 1775,
Isabel Ross, qv, ch: 1. Donald, qv; 2. Hugh; 3. Duncan;
4. Isabell; 5. David; 6. Mary; 7. Margaret; 8. Elizabeth;
9. Sally. **SG iii/4 99; CP 54**.

6755 McINTOSH, Christina, ca 1797–ca 1880. From
Snizort par, Is Skye, INV. To Kinloss Twp, Bruce Co,
ONT, <1853. Wife of Peter McKinnon, qv. **DC 12 Apr
1979**.

6756 McINTOSH, David. From Edinburgh. To Leeds
Twp, Megantic Co, QUE, 1831. Farmer. m Christina
Anderson, qv, ch: 1. Andrew, stld Toronto; 2. Janet;
3. James; 4. Margaret. **AMC 144**.

6757 McINTOSH, Donald, b ca 1776. From Petty, INV.
s/o Charles M, qv, and Isabell Ross, qv. To Cornwallis,
NS, 1785; stld east branch of East River. Farmer. m Ann,
d/o Alexander Falconer, Pictou, ch: 1. Mary; 2. Margaret;
3. Isabell; 4. Charles; 5. Elizabeth; 6. Alexander;
7. Sally; 8. Jess; 9. Duncan; 10. Katie. **PAC 123;
CP 64**.

6758 McINTOSH, Donald. Prob from INV. To Halifax,
NS, <1784. Son William, b ca 1785. **NSN 12/3**.

6759 McINTOSH, Donald. From Urquhart and
Glenmoriston par, INV. To Pictou, NS, on the *Sarah*, ex
Fort William, Jun 1801. Wife Janet with him, and dau
Isobel, aged 3. **PLS**.

6760 McINTOSH, Donald. From Glenelg, INV. To
Pictou, NS, on the *Sarah*, ex Fort William, Jun 1801.
Farmer. Wife Mary with him, and ch: 1. Surmy, aged 12;
2. Anne, aged 8; 3. Donald, aged 5; 4. Mary,
aged 2 ½. **PLS**.

6761 McINTOSH, Donald. From Kilmorack, INV. To
Pictou, NS, on the *Sarah*, ex Fort William, Jun 1801.
Farmer. **PLS**.

6762 McINTOSH, Donald. From SUT. To Earltown,
Colchester Co, NS, <1817. Farmer. **HT 42**.

6763 McINTOSH, Donald, ca 1780–2 May 1842. From
Rannoch, PER. To Pictou Co, NS, prob <1830; bur Hill
Cemetery, West River Station. m Christie Fraser, qv.
DC 10 Feb 1980.

6764 McINTOSH, Donald. From MOR. To East
Williams Twp, Middlesex Co, ONT, 1832. **PCM 43**.

6765 MACINTOSH, Rev Donald, 1800–2 Jul 1859.
From Killearnan, ROC. s/o Alexander M, farmer, and
Isabel Noble. To Pictou, NS, 1833. Min at West River.
Retr to SCT, 1844, and adm min of Urray; trans to
Edderton, 1854. m 10 Apr 1839, Jane Lydiard, ch:
1. Lydiard, b 1840, dy; 2. Edward, b 6 May 1843;
3. Howard Lydiard, d 15 Jun 1845; 4. Flora Downie,
b 6 Oct 1846; 5. Mary Charlotte, b 19 Jul 1848;
6. Lydiard, b 20 May 1850; 7. Charles Downie,
b 25 Sep 1852. **FES vii 55**.

6766 MACINTOSH, Donald B. From Lochaber, INV.
bro/o John 'Og' M, qv, and Alexander M, qv. To
Antigonish Co, NS, prob <1820; stld Lismore. m Mary
Chisholm, ch: 1. Alexander; 2. Duncan; 3. Janet;
4. Ann; 5. Kate; 6. Flora; 7. Peggy; 8. Jane.
HCA 289.

6767 MACINTOSH, Duncan. Prob from INV.
bro/o Alexander M, qv. To South River, Antigonish Co,
NS, prob <1830. m Janet MacGregor, ch: 1. Peter;
2. John; 3. Alexander; 4. Donald; 5. Mary; 6. Ann;
7. Jane. **HCA 290**.

6768   McINTOSH, Finlay, ca 1780–1819. From INV. To Pictou, NS, ca 1790; later to ONT. Drowned near Port Dover, Norfolk Co. m ca 1800, Jerusha Robb, from Baltimore, ch: 1. Andrew, b 1801; 2. Alexander, 1803-78; 3. Daniel, 1809-65; 4. Samuel; 5. Benjamen, dy; 6. John Robb, 1807-73; 7. Agnes; 8. Annie Belle; 9. dau.   **DC 25 Jun and 22 Jul 1967**.

6769   McINTOSH, Finlay. From Glenelg, INV. To Pictou, NS, on the *Sarah*, ex Fort William, Jun 1801. Tenant. Wife Anne with him, and ch: 1. Anne, aged 4; 2. Donald, aged 2.   **PLS**.

6770   McINTOSH, Finlay. From Urquhart and Glenmoriston par, INV. To Pictou, NS, on the *Sarah*, ex Fort William, Jun 1801. Farmer. Wife Ann with him, and ch: 1. Elizabeth; 2. Isobel; 3. James, aged 14; 4. Christian, aged 8; 5. William, aged 8; 6. inf.   **PLS**.

6771   McINTOSH, Finlay. From INV. To Montreal, QUE, prob arr Sep 1802. Petitioned for land on the Ottawa River, ONT, 6 Aug 1804.   **DC 15 Mar 1980**.

6772   MACINTOSH, Flora. From Lochaber, INV. sis/o John 'Og' M, qv. To Antigonish Co, NS, prob <1820. m Christopher Chisholm.   **HCA 289**.

6773   MACINTOSH, George, ca 1750–12 Apr 1821. Poss from INV. To NS, and d at Spryfield, nr Halifax. **NSS No 2269**.

6774   McINTOSH, George. To Pictou, NS, on the *Ellen*, ex Lochlaxford, SUT, 22 May 1848. Wife Janet with him.   **DC 15 Jul 1979**.

6775   McINTOSH, Gilbert. Rel to Alexander M, qv, and John M, qv. To London, Westminster Twp, Middlesex Co, ONT, prob <1840. Merchant.   **PCM 55**.

6776   McINTOSH, Hugh, b 1746. To Pictou Co, NS, 1815; res Caribou, 1816. Labourer, m, with 1 child, and 'very poor.'   **INS 39**.

6777   McINTOSH, Hugh. To Pictou, NS, on the *Ellen*, ex Lochlaxford, SUT, 22 May 1848. Wife Barbara with him, and dau Elizabeth.   **DC 15 Jul 1979**.

6778   McINTOSH, James. From Kerrowdoun, Strathfarrar, INV. Prob rel to Catherine M, qv. To Montreal, QUE, ex Fort William, arr Sep 1802; stld E ONT.   **MCM 1/4 24**.

6779   MACINTOSH, James. Prob from INV. To Halifax, NS, 1810. Petitioned for land, 1811.   **NSN 6/4**.

6780   MAC(K)INTOSH, Rev James, d 9 Jun 1856. From ROC. Grad MA, Kings Coll, Aberdeen, 1818, and became asst min at Tain. App by Colonial Committee to be min of St James's Ch, Charlottetown, PEI, 1830. Res 1836, and was adm min of Burntisland, FIF, SCT. m 18 Mar 1835, Matilda Williams, d 1895, ch: 1. James Mackenzie, b 1836; 2. Henry Williams, b 1838; 3. John Scott, b 1839; 4. Eliza Male, b 1841.   **KCG 276; FES v 84, vii 621**.

6781   McINTOSH, Rev James, ca 1798–1875. From Coupar-Angus. Anti-burgher min at Shiels, ABD, 1828-50. To Amherst Is, Lennox and Addington Co, ONT, 1854.   **UPC i 28**.

6782   McINTOSH, Janet. From Kilmorack, INV. Poss d/o Alexander M, farmer, qv. To Pictou, NS, on the *Sarah*, ex Fort William, Jun 1801.   **PLS**.

6783   MACINTOSH, Janet. Prob from INV. To Halifax, NS, 1810; stld Middle Musquodoboit. Wife of James MacDonald, qv.   **NSN 6/1**.

6784   McINTOSH, John. From Glenelg, INV. To Pictou, NS, on the *Dove*, ex Fort William, Jun 1801. Farmer. **PLD**.

6785   McINTOSH, John. From Kilmorack, INV. To Pictou, NS, on the *Sarah*, ex Fort William, Jun 1801. Farmer. Wife Janet with him, and ch: 1. Flora, aged 5; 2. John, aged 3; 3. inf.   **PLS**.

6786   McINTOSH, John, b ca 1780. From Glenelg, INV. To QUE, ex Greenock, summer 1815; stld prob Lanark Co, ONT. Farmer. Wife Mary McClure, qv, with him, and 2 ch.   **SEC 7**.

6787   McINTOSH, John, 1792–22 Oct 1869. From Breadalbane, PER. To Breadalbane, Lochiel Twp, Glengarry Co, ONT, 1815. Pioneer settler.   **DC 27 Oct 1979**.

6788   MACINTOSH, John 'Og'. From Lochaber, INV. bro/o Alexander M, qv, and Donald B. M, qv. To South River, Antigonish Co, NS, prob <1820. m Margaret Chisholm, ch: 1. Alexander, physician; 2. Valentine; 3. John; 4. William; 5. Duncan; 6. Kate; 7. Margaret; 8. Mary; 9. Christina.   **HCA 289**.

6789   McINTOSH, John. From INV. To QUE, via NY, 1819; moved to Ekfrid Twp, Middlesex Co, ONT, 1821. m Bella, d/o Angus Campbell, qv. Dau Jane.   **PCM 29**.

6790   McINTOSH, John. From INV. To East Williams Twp, Middlesex Co, ONT, 1832.   **PCM 43**.

6791   McINTOSH, John. Poss from INV. To Pictou Co, NS, <1840; stld west branch of East River. m Catherine MacDonald, ch: 1. Angus, b 1839; 2. Margaret, b 1844; 3. Barbara; 4. Helen.   **PAC 124**.

6792   McINTOSH, John. Poss from ARL. To Mosa Twp, Middlesex Co, ONT, prob <1840. Merchant in Wardsville.   **PCM 24**.

6793   McINTOSH, John. Rel to Gilbert M, qv, and Alexander M, qv. To London, Westminster Twp, Middlesex Co, ONT, prob <1840. Merchant.   **PCM 55**.

6794   McINTOSH, John. From INV. Neph of James M, game-keeper, Culloden. To CAN <1843. Wright.   **SH**.

6795   McINTOSH, John. Prob from ARL. To Aldborough Twp, Elgin Co, ONT, 1850.   **PDA 68**.

6796   McINTOSH, Malcolm. Prob from INV. To Pictou Co, NS, <1828; stld nr West Branch Lake. By wife Isabel had ch: 1. James, b 1828; 2. Duncan, b 1829; 3. Anne or Nancy, b 1831; 4. Angus, b 1835; 5. Catherine, b 1840; 6. James Alexander, b 1842. **PAC 12**.

6797   McINTOSH, Malcolm. From Is South Uist, INV. To West Williams Twp, Middlesex Co, ONT, 1849; stld Con 4.   **PCM 48**.

6798   McINTOSH, Margaret, b ca 1787. From Kilmorack, INV. Poss d/o Alexander M, farmer, qv. To Pictou, NS, on the *Sarah*, ex Fort William, Jun 1801. **PLS**.

6799   McINTOSH, Margaret, 1818–1904. From SUT. To NS, 1854. Wife of Hugh Ross, qv.   **LDW 7 Feb 1973**.

6800 McINTOSH, Mary. From Glenelg, INV. To Pictou, NS, on the *Dove*, ex Fort William, Jun 1801. Spinster, and poss d/o John M, farmer, qv, and Ann McIntosh, qv. **PLD**.

6801 MACINTOSH, Mary. From Badenoch, INV. To Sydney, Cape Breton Co, NS, 1818; stld Margaree, Inverness Co. Wife of John 'Lord' MacDonald, qv. **MP 493**.

6802 McINTOSH, Mary. To Pictou, NS, on the *London*, arr 14 Jul 1848. **DC 15 Jul 1979**.

6803 McINTOSH, Peter, b 1768. From Killin, PER. To QUE, ex Greenock, summer 1815; stld prob Lanark Co, ONT. Shoemaker, later farmer. Wife Elizabeth McDiarmid, qv, with him, and 3 ch. **SEC 8**.

6804 MACINTOSH, Robert. From Urquhart and Glenmoriston par, INV. To Pictou, NS, on the *Sarah*, ex Fort William, Jun 1801. Farmer. Wife Janet with him, and dau Janet, aged 3. **PLS**.

6805 MACINTOSH, Robert, b 1850. From Insches, INV. To Pictou, NS, on the *Lord Brougham*, ex Cromarty, arr 10 Sep 1831. m Anne Robertson, qv, ch: 1. Mary; 2. Margaret; 3. Alexander; 4. John Arthur; 5. Charles. **DC 21 Mar 1981**.

6806 McINTOSH, William. From INV. To East Williams Twp, Middlesex Co, ONT, 1832. **PCM 43**.

6807 McINTOSH, William. From INV. To Lobo Twp, Middlesex Co, ONT, ca 1832. ch: 1. Alexander; 2. John; 3. Gilbert; 4. James; 5. William; 6. Mrs Cochrane; 7. Mrs Wilson. **PCM 40**.

6808 McINTOSH, William. To Pictou, NS, on the *Lady Gray*, ex Cromarty, ROC, 16 Jul 1841. **DC 15 Jul 1979**.

McINTYRE. See also McINTIRE.

6809 MACINTYRE, Rev Aeneas, 28 Sep 1815–24 Sep 1887. s/o Kenneth M. and Euphemia McPhee. To Charlottetown, PEI, 1840. Min of St James's Ch there until 1845, when retr to SCT to become min at Kinlochspelvie, ARL. m (ii) Hannah Binns, ch: 1. Norman, dy; 2. Mrs John C. Berrie, PEI; 3. Isabella Young; 4. Mary Jane Futton. **FES iv 115, vii 621**.

6810 McINTYRE, Alexander, b ca 1780. From Bowmore, Is Islay, ARL. To Parry Sound, ONT, <1840. Wife Catherine Turner, qv, with him, and 3 of their ch: 1. Jean, b 29 Dec 1810; 2. Catherine, b 27 Mar 1814; 3. Alexander, b 1821. ch Margaret, John, Agnes, Mary and Donald, remained in Islay. **DC 8 Jul 1966**.

6811 McINTYRE, Alexander. From ARL. To Aldborough Twp, Elgin Co, ONT, 1818; moved to Mosa Twp, 1827. m a sis/o Archibald Munro, qv. Their family went to USA. **PCM 23**.

6812 McINTYRE, Alexander. From ARL. To Mosa Twp, Middlesex Co, ONT, 1832. Son Duncan. **PCM 24**.

6813 McINTYRE, Alexander 'Mor'. To Aldborough Twp, Elgin Co, ONT, 1818; moved to Metcalfe Twp, 1827. Son Rev Dugald. **PCM 26**.

6814 McINTYRE, Alexander. From ARL. To Mosa Twp, Middlesex Co, ONT, <1840; stld Wardsville. Tailor. **PCM 24**.

MACINTYRE, Mrs Alexander. See CAMPBELL, Gormelia.

6815 McINTYRE, Andrew, b 1816. From ARL. bro/o Angus M, qv. To Eldon Twp, Victoria Co, ONT, <1840. m Catherine Fraser, b 1826, ch: 1. Duncan, b 1859; 2. Archie; 3. Angus; 4. Hugh; 5. Mary; 6. Jessie; 7. Annie; 8. Effie; 9. Jennie, b 1850; 10. Katie. **EC 142**.

6816 McINTYRE, Andrew, 1812–1900. From Sliddery, Kilmory par, Is Arran, BUT. Prob rel to Archibald M, qv. To Dalhousie, NB, 1835. **MAC 26**.

6817 McINTYRE, Angus. From South Uist, INV. To Kings Co, PEI, <1818. Farmer. m Sarah Mackinnon, qv. Son Rev Peter, b 29 Jun 1818, became RC Bishop of Charlottetown, 1860. **BNA 894**.

6818 McINTYRE, Angus, ca 1806–ca 1850. From ARL. bro/o Andrew M, qv. To Eldon Twp, Victoria Co, ONT, <1840. m Margaret Mitchell, qv, ch: 1. Mary; 2. Margaret; 3. Effie; 4. Sarah; 5. Isabelle; 6. William; 7. Daniel or Donald; 8. Elizabeth; 9. Annie. **EC 142**.

6819 MACINTYRE, Ann, b 1806. From Aird, Is Benbecula, INV. To Pictou, NS, on the *Lulan*, ex Glasgow, 17 Aug 1848. wid/o Allan Roy Morrison, by whom she had ch: 1. Ann, b 1829; 2. Mary, b 1831; 3. James, b 1833; 4. Allan, b 1837. **DC 12 Jul 1979**.

6820 MACINTYRE, Archibald, 1796–1824. From North Knapdale, ARL. s/o Duncan M, qv, and wife Katie. To Aldborough Twp, Elgin Co, ONT, 1818; moved to Dunwich Twp. Farmer. m Isabel MacArthur, qv. **PDA 27**.

6821 MACINTYRE, Archibald. From Is South Uist, INV. To Cape Breton Is, NS, 1820. Son James, res Glace Bay. **DC 9 Oct 1979**.

6822 McINTYRE, Archibald, 1815-67. From Sliddery, Kilmory par, Is Arran, BUT. Prob rel to Andrew M, qv. To Restigouche Co, NB, ca 1835. m Martha Hamilton. Son John, 1862–1938, engineer, Vancouver. **CUC 27; MAC 26**.

6823 McINTYRE, Archibald. From Kenmore, PER. To Glengarry Co, ONT, 1800. Dau Ann. **DC 10 Dec 1962**.

6824 McINTYRE, Archibald. From ARL. To Mosa Twp, Middlesex Co, ONT, 1831. Sailor. **PCM 24**.

McINTYRE, Mrs Archibald. See McINTYRE, Christian.

6825 McINTYRE, Archie, b 1811. From ARL. To Eldon Twp, Victoria Co, ONT, <1840. Wife Catherine, b 1820, with him. ch: 1. Malcolm, b 1837; 2. Mary, b 1839; 3. Donald, b 1842; 4. Gilbert, b 1844; 5. Duncan, b 1846; 6. Catherine, b 1847; 7. Angus, b 1849; 8. Peter, b 1850; 9. Andrew Archie. **EC 141**.

6826 MACINTYRE, Barbara, 1794–20 Aug 1852. From North Knapdale, ARL. d/o Duncan M, qv, and wife Katie. To Aldborough Twp, Elgin Co, ONT, 1818. m Donald MacIntyre, qv. **DC 23 Nov 1981**.

6827 McINTYRE, Betty. From PER, poss Killin par. Prob rel to John M, qv. To McNab Twp, Renfrew Co, ONT, 1825. **DC 3 Jan 1980**.

6828 McINTYRE, Catharine. From Callander, PER. Embarked at Greenock, summer 1815, for QUE, with husband, John Ferguson, qv, but d at sea or <Jul 1817.   **CEC 2; HCL 16, 230**.

6829   McINTYRE, Cathrine. From PER, poss Killin par. Prob rel to John M, qv. To McNab Twp, Renfrew Co, ONT, 1825.   **DC 3 Jan 1980**.

6830   McINTYRE, Christian. From Lochgilphead, ARL. To ONT, ca 1831. wid/o Archibald McIntyre, by whom she had ch: 1. Neil, b 1811; 2. Christian, b 1814; 3. Archibald, b 1817; 4. Donald, b 1819; 5. Margaret, b 1822; 6. John; 7. Mary; 8. Isobel.   **DC 22 Dec 1975**.

6831   McINTYRE, Daniel Eugene, 1812-96. From Oban, ARL. To Glengarry Co, ONT, 1836; stld Williamstown. Physician, and Sheriff of Stormont, Dundas and Glengarry. m 7 Apr 1837, Ann, d/o Alexander Fraser, qv, and Ann Macdonell. Son Alexander Fraser, 1847–1914.   **SDG 201, 249**.

6832   McINTYRE, Donald, d ca 1788. From Loch Sunart, ARL. To Cape Breton Is, NS, 1784. m Ann Cameron, qv. Dau Jane.   **WLC**.

6833   MACINTYRE, Donald, 30 Jul 1792–16 Mar 1886. From Keils, North Knapdale, ARL. To QUE on the *Mars*, ex Tobermory, 28 Jul 1818; stld Aldborough Twp, Elgin Co, ONT. Farmer. m Barbara MacIntyre, qv, ch: 1. Margaret, 1822-55; 2. Katherine, 1824-54; 3. John S, 1825-84; 4. Donald, 1827-61; 5. Duncan, 1830-63; 6. Barbara, 1831-57; 7. Mary, 1834–1904.   **DC 23 Nov 1981**.

6834   McINTYRE, Donald. From Arisaig, INV. To PEI on the *Jane*, ex Loch nan Uamh, Arisaig, 12 Jul 1790. Wife and child with him.   **PLJ**.

6835   McINTYRE, Donald. From Kyles, Morar, INV. To PEI on the *Lucy*, ex Loch nan Uamh, Arisaig, 12 Jul 1790. Wife and 7 ch with him.   **PLL**.

6836   McINTYRE, Donald. From Killin, PER. To Montreal, QUE, on the *Sophia*, ex Greenock, 26 Jul 1818; stld prob Beckwith Twp, Lanark Co, ONT. Wife Isabella with him, and ch: 1. Mary, aged 9; 2. Peter, aged 7.   **SPL**.

6837   McINTYRE, Donald. From ARL. To Aldborough Twp, Elgin Co, ONT, 1819; moved to Mosa Twp, 1828. ch: 1. Duncan C, res Glencoe; 2. Malcolm; 3. Dugald, stld East Williams Twp.   **PCM 23**.

6838   MACINTYRE, Donald. bro/o John M, qv. To Antigonish Co, NS, 1822. m Nancy Fraser. Son John.   **HCA 291**.

6839   McINTYRE, Donald. From PER, poss Killin par. To Montreal, QUE, on the *Niagara*, ex Greenock, arr 28 May 1825; stld Flat River, McNab Twp, Renfrew Co, ONT.   **EMT 18**.

6840   McINTYRE, Donald. From ARL. To Ekfrid Twp, Middlesex Co, ONT, 1830. Killed by a dry stump falling.   **PCM 30**.

6841   McINTYRE, Donald. From Is South Uist, INV. To East Williams Twp, Middlesex Co, ONT, ca 1849. **PCM 44**.

6842   MACINTYRE, Dougald. Prob from ARL. To Aldborough Twp, Elgin Co, ONT, <1820. Farmer. **PDA 93**.

6843   MACINTYRE, Duncan, b ca 1770. From North Knapdale, ARL. To QUE on the *Mars*, ex Tobermory, 28 Jul 1818; stld Aldborough Twp, Elgin Co, ONT. Farmer. Wife Katie with him, ch: 1. Barbara, qv; 2. Mary, qv; 3. Archibald, qv; 4. John, qv; 5. Malcolm, qv; 6. Katherine.   **PDA 24, 27; DC 23 Nov 1981**.

6844   McINTYRE, Duncan, b 1801. From ARL. To Eldon Twp, Victoria Co, ONT, <1840. Wife Mary, b 1817, with him. ch: 1. Donald, b 1835; 2. Alexander, b 1837; 3. Andrew, b 1839; 4. Duncan, b 1841; 5. Sarah, b 1843; 6. Mary, b 1845; 7. Laughlin, b 1847; 8. Catherine.   **EC 141**.

6845   McINTYRE, Duncan 'Og'. From Lismore, ARL. To Lobo Twp, Middlesex Co, ONT, 1820. ch: 1. Duncan; 2. John; 3. Donald; 4. Mary; 5. Lily; 6. Nancy. **PCM 38**.

6846   McINTYRE, Duncan 'Mor'. From Lismore, ARL. To Lobo Twp, Middlesex Co, ONT, 1820. ch: 1. Peter; 2. Archibald; 3. Donald; 4. Duncan; 5. Joseph; 6. Margaret.   **PCM 38**.

6847   MACINTYRE, Duncan, b ca 1800. From Tomluachrach, Is Benbecula, INV. To Pictou, NS, on the *Lulan*, 17 Aug 1848. m Mary MacEachan, qv, ch: 1. Mary, b 1829; 2. Catherine, b 1831; 3. Ann, b 1833; 4. Neil; 5. Matthew, b 1838, dy; 6. Effie, b 1841. **DC 12 Jul 1979**.

6848   McINTYRE, Duncan. Poss from ABD. To Montreal, QUE, 1849. Merchant and director, Canada Central Railroad.   **BNA 1076**.

6849   McINTYRE, Duncan. From Kintyre, ARL. To Aldborough Twp, Elgin Co, ONT, 1851.   **PDA 75**.

6850   MACINTYRE, Effie, b 1826. From Dunganichy, Is Benbecula, INV. d/o Donald M. To Pictou, NS, on the *Lulan*, ex Glasgow, 17 Aug 1848.   **DC 12 Jul 1979**.

6851   McINTYRE, Elizabeth, d 1857. From Comrie, PER. d/o Donald M, farmer, Wester Dundurn, and Margaret Ferguson. To CAN.   **Ts Comrie**.

6852   McINTYRE, Elizabeth, 1814-97. From Dunkeld, PER. To ONT, ca 1845. Wife of John B. Haliburton, qv.   **DC 2 Jun 1980**.

6853   McINTYRE, Finlay. From Is South Uist, INV. To East Williams Twp, Middlesex Co, ONT, prob 1849. **PCM 44**.

6854   McINTYRE, Mrs Flora, b 1746. To Charlottetown, PEI, on the *Humphreys*, ex Tobermory, arr 14 Jul 1806. ch: 1. Donald, aged 23; 2. Sarah, aged 20; 3. Mary, aged 18.   **PLH**.

6855   McINTYRE, Hugh. From ARL. To East Williams Twp, Middlesex Co, ONT, 1831.   **PCM 43**.

6856   McINTYRE, James. From PER, poss Killin par. Prob rel to John M, qv. To McNab Twp, Renfrew Co, ONT, 1825.   **DC 3 Jan 1980**.

6857   McINTYRE, James. From ARL. To Ekfrid Twp, Middlesex Co, ONT, <1828.   **PCM 29**.

6858   McINTYRE, James, ca 1827–5 Mar 1906. From Forres, MOR. To St Catharines, Lincoln Co, ONT, 1841; later to Ingersoll, Oxford Co. Undertaker and poet. **MDB 460**.

6859 McINTYRE, James. From ARL. To Metcalfe Twp, Middlesex Co, ONT, 1844. Drowned in Lake Huron. **PCM 24**.

6860 McINTYRE, James, b 1785. From Bornish, Is South Uist, INV. To West Williams Twp, Middlesex Co, ONT, 1849. m Catherine Boyd, qv, ch: 1. Effie; 2. Donald, b 1820; 3. Mary, b 1822; 4. Lachlan C, b 1824, bursar, Hamilton Asylum; 5. Ronald, b 1827, reeve; 6. Mary, b 1830; 7. Allan, res Chicago; 8. Mary, qv; 9. Alexander, b 1838. **PCM 48; WLC**.

6861 McINTYRE, Janet. From Craignavie, Killin par, PER. To QUE, ex Greenock, summer 1815; stld Bathurst Twp, Lanark Co, ONT. Wife of John McLaren, qv. **SEC 2**.

6862 McINTYRE, John. From Kyles, Morar, INV. To PEI on the *Lucy*, ex Loch nan Uamh, Arisaig, 12 Jul 1790. Tenant. Wife with him. **PLL**.

6863 McINTYRE, John, b ca 1772. To Western Shore, Inverness Co, NS, 1802. Farmer, m and had ch. **CBC 1818**.

6864 McINTYRE, John, b ca 1793. Prob from Paisley, RFW. To Fort Churchill, Hudson Bay, on the *Prince of Wales*, ex Stromness, 28 Jun 1813. Went to York Factory, 1814, and then to Red River. Joined HBCo. **LSS 186; RRS 27; LSC 323**.

6865 McINTYRE, John, b 1770. To Inverness, Inverness Co, NS, 1815. Farmer, m and had ch. **CBC 1818**.

6866 MACINTYRE, John, b 1800. From Knapdale, ARL. s/o Duncan M, qv, and wife Katie. To Aldborough Twp, Elgin Co, ONT, 1818; stld Southwold Twp. Miller. m Katie Blue, qv. **DC 23 Nov 1981**.

6867 MACINTYRE, John. bro/o Donald M, qv. To Antigonish Co, NS, 1822. m Eunice, d/o John MacPherson, qv, Clydesdale. Son Archibald. **HCA 291**.

6868 McINTYRE, John. From PER. To Brant Co, ONT, 1823. m Jeanette McNichol, qv, ch: 1. John, jr, qv; 2. Peter; 3. Nichol; 4. Robert; 5. Catherine; 6. Eleanor; 7. Elizabeth. **DC 23 Sep 1980**.

6869 McINTYRE, John, jr. From PER. s/o John M, qv, and Jeanette McNichol, qv. To Brant Co, ONT, 1823. m Lovice, d/o Eadie Burtch. **DC 23 Sep 1980**.

6870 McINTYRE, John. From PER, poss Killin par. To Montreal, QUE, on the *Niagara*, ex Greenock, arr 28 May 1825; stld Flat River, McNab Twp, Renfrew Co, ONT. **EMT 18**.

6871 McINTYRE, John. From ARL. To Ekfrid Twp, Middlesex Co, ONT, <1828. **PCM 29**.

6872 McINTYRE, John. From Petty, INV. To East Williams Twp, Middlesex Co, ONT, 1832. **PCM 43**.

6873 McINTYRE, John, ca 1806–2 Oct 1849. From Stranraer, WIG. To Hamilton, ONT, and d there. **DGH 13 Dec 1849**.

6874 McINTYRE, John. From Is Tyree, ARL. To Mariposa Twp, Victoria Co, ONT, 1847. m Margaret, d/o Archibald McInnes. Son Duncan John. **DC 29 Sep 1964**.

6875 McINTYRE, John, b 1821. From Dunganichy, Is

Benbecula, INV. s/o Donald M. To Pictou, NS, on the *Lulan*, ex Glasgow, 17 Aug 1848. Wife Catherine MacDonald, qv, with him, ch: 1. Marion, b 1843; 2. Effie, b 1845; 3. Donald, b 1847. **DC 12 Jul 1847**.

6876 McINTYRE, John. From INV. To Middlesex Co, ONT, 1849; stld McGillivray Twp. **PCM 56**.

6877 McINTYRE, John. From Is South Uist, INV. To East Williams Twp, Middlesex Co, ONT, 1849. **PCM 44**.

6878 McINTYRE, Joseph. From ARL. To Lobo Twp, Middlesex Co, ONT, 1838. **PCM 40**.

6879 MACINTYRE, Kirsty, b 1829. From Dunganichy, Is Benbecula, INV. d/o Donald M. To Pictou, NS, on the *Lulan*, ex Glasgow, 17 Aug 1848. **DC 12 Jul 1979**.

6880 MACINTYRE, Malcolm, b 1804. From North Knapdale, ARL. s/o Duncan M, qv, and wife Katie. To Aldborough Twp, Elgin Co, ONT, 1818. Farmer. m Mary Campbell, ch. **PDA 27**.

6881 McINTYRE, Malcolm, d 1832. From Callander, PER. To Montreal, QUE, ca 1822. Partner, Simpson & McIntyre, merchants. d in the cholera epidemic. **SGC 377**.

6882 McINTYRE, Malcolm. From ARL. To Ekfrid Twp, Middlesex Co, ONT, 1826. Tailor. ch: 1. Peter; 2. John; 3. James, went to IL; 4. Margaret. **PCM 29**.

6883 McINTYRE, Malcolm. From ARL. To Ekfrid Twp, Middlesex Co, ONT, <1828. **PCM 29**.

6884 McINTYRE, Malcolm. From ARL. To East Williams Twp, Middlesex Co, ONT, 1831. **PCM 43**.

6885 McINTYRE, Malcolm. To East Williams Twp, Middlesex Co, ONT, 1835. **PCM 44**.

6886 McINTYRE, Malcolm, called 'Callum Beag'. From ARL. To Metcalfe Twp, Middlesex Co, ONT, 1842. **PCM 26**.

6887 McINTYRE, Margaret. Poss from INV. To Glengarry Co, ONT, 1800; stld Martintown, Charlottenburgh Twp. m Malcolm McMartin, qv. **SDG 91**.

6888 MACINTYRE, Margaret, b 22 May 1800. From Appin, ARL. d/o Duncan M. To Wooler, Northumberland Co, ONT, 1821. Wife of John McPhail, qv. **DC 20 Nov 1960**.

6889 McINTYRE, Margaret, b 1785. From Bornish, Is South Uist, INV. To West Williams Twp, Middlesex Co, ONT, ca 1849. Wife of Alexander McMillan, qv. **WLC**.

6890 McINTYRE, Marion. From Dunganichy, Benbecula, INV. d/o Matthew M. To West Williams Twp, Middlesex Co, ONT, ca 1852. Wife of Malcolm Gillies, qv, whom she m 1836. **WLC**.

6891 MACINTYRE, Mary, 1795–19 Sep 1847. From North Knapdale, ARL. d/o Duncan M, qv, and wife Katie. To Aldborough Twp, Elgin Co, ONT, 1818. m Donald McGugan, qv, 26 Dec 1811. **DC 23 Nov 1981**.

6892 McINTYRE, Mary. From Is Islay, ARL. To ONT, 1833; stld Stayner, Simcoe Co. Wife of John McQueen, qv. **DC 31 May 1979**.

6893 MACINTYRE, Mary. From ARL. To Aldborough Twp, Elgin Co, ONT, prob <1840. m Dugald MacArthur, qv. **PDA 64**.

6894   MACINTYRE, Mary, b 1816. From Dunganichy, Is Benbecula, INV. d/o Donald M. To Pictou, NS, on the *Lulan*, ex Glasgow, 17 Aug 1848.   **DC 12 Jul 1979**.

6895   McINTYRE, Mary, b 1836. From Bornish, Is South Uist, INV. d/o James M, qv, and Catherine Bowie, qv. To West Williams Twp, Middlesex Co, ONT, ca 1849. Wife of John McDonald, qv.   **WLC**.

6896   McINTYRE, Neil. From ARL. To Martintown, Charlottenburgh Twp, Glengarry Co, ONT, 1817. ch: 1. James; 2. Malcolm; 3. Margaret; 4. Isabel; 5. John; 6. Donald; 7. Jane.   **DC 4 Mar 1965**.

6897   McINTYRE, Neil. From Is South Uist, INV. To West Williams Twp, Middlesex Co, ONT, 1849; stld Con 14.   **PCM 48**.

6898   McINTYRE, Neil. From Is South Uist, INV. To West Williams Twp, Middlesex Co, ONT, 1849; stld Centre Road.   **PCM 48**.

6899   McINTYRE, Peter. From Leny, PER. To Montreal, QUE, on the *Niagara*, ex Greenock, arr 28 May 1825; stld McNab Twp, Renfrew Co, ONT.   **HCL 102; EMT 18**.

6900   McINTYRE, Peter. From ARL. To Ekfrid Twp, Middlesex Co, ONT, <1828.   **PCM 29**.

6901   McINTYRE, Peter, b 1811. From Comrie par, PER. s/o Archibald M, weaver, and Helen McNab. To QUE, ex Greenock, Apr 1829; stld Keene, Peterborough Co, ONT. m Margaret Comrie, 1843.   **DC 5 Apr 1983**.

6902   McINTYRE, Peter. To St John, NB, <1830. Wife Martha.   **NER viii 98**.

6903   McINTYRE, Peter 'Mor'. From North Knapdale, ARL. To Caradoc Twp, Middlesex Co, ONT, 1830. ch: 1. Alexander; 2. John; 3. Peter; 4. Nancy; 5. Janet. **PCM 35**.

6904   McINTYRE, Peter. From Lismore, ARL. To QUE <1838, when he went to Lobo Twp, Middlesex Co, ONT. ch: 1. Duncan; 2. Donald; 3. Nichol; 4. Peter; 5. Mary; 6. Nancy; 7. Effie.   **PCM 40**.

6905   McINTYRE, Rev Peter, b 1810. From Kilchrenan, ARL. s/o Donald M, farmer. Grad MA, Univ of Glasgow, 1827, and studied theology. Adm min of St James's Ch, Charlotte Co, NB, 1833.   **RGG 379; GMA 11805; FES vii 610**.

6906   MACINTYRE, Peter. From ARL. To Aldborough Twp, Elgin Co, ONT, 1846. Miller. Son Alexander. **PDA 67**.

6907   McINTYRE, Peter. To Pictou, NS, on the *Lulan*, ex Glasgow, 17 Aug 1848. Family with him: 1. Gormal; 2. Donald; 3. Ann; 4. Angus; 5. John; 6. Peggy. **DC 15 Jul 1979**.

6908   McINTYRE, Robert, b 1769. To Western Shore, Inverness Co, NS, 1813. Farmer, m and had ch. **CBC 1818**.

6909   McINTYRE, Robert Lewis, b 12 Nov 1808. From Torlogrein, Croy and Dalcross par, INV. s/o Robert M. and Ann Falconer. To Stratford, Perth Co, ONT, ca 1854. Son Joseph.   **DC 26 Mar 1982**.

6910   McINTYRE, Soloman. From ARL. To Ekfrid Twp, Middlesex Co, ONT, 1834. ch: 1. John, reeve; 2. Archibald.   **PCM 30**.

6911   McINTYRE, William. To QUE on the *Commerce*, ex Greenock, Jun 1820; stld Lot 1, Con 11, Darling Twp, Lanark Co, ONT. Pioneer settler.   **HCL 76, 239**.

6912   McISAAC, Alexander, b 1794. To Inverness Co, NS, 1812. Weaver.   **CBC 1818**.

6913   MACISAAC, Allan. From Is Eigg, INV. s/o John M, qv. To Inverness Co, NS, ca 1820; stld Rear Judique. Farmer. ch: 1. John; 2. Hector; 3. James; 4. Donald; 5. Catherine; 6. Christine; 7. Malcolm; 8. Jane. **MP 671**.

6914   MACISAAC, Allan. From Is Canna, INV. s/o Neil M. To Inverness Co, NS, via PEI, ca 1820. m Mary MacDonald, ch: 1. John; 2. Alexander; 3. Donald; 4. Mary; 5. Catherine; 6. Isabel; 7. Margaret; 8. Anne.   **MP 697**.

6915   McISAAC, Angus, b ca 1770. To Inverness, Inverness Co, NS, 1805. Schoolmaster, m and had ch.   **CBC 1818**.

6916   McISAAC, Angus, b ca 1800. To Inverness, Inverness Co, NS, 1805, and became farmer. **CBC 1818**.

6917   McISAAC, Angus, b ca 1754. To Inverness, Inverness Co, NS, 1812. Farmer, m, ch.   **CBC 1818**.

6918   MACISAAC, Angus. From Is Canna, INV. s/o Neil M. To Inverness Co, NS, <1820. m Mrs MacPherson, ch: 1. Mary; 2. Archibald; 3. Donald; 4. Anne. **MP 692**.

6919   MACISAAC, Angus. From Is Eigg, INV. s/o Archibald M, qv. To Rear Judique, Inverness Co, NS, prob 1820. m (i) Miss MacInnes; (ii) Miss MacDonald, River Denys, ch: 1. Donald; 2. Archibald; 3. Margaret, called Peggy; 4. Mary 'Mhor'; 5. Mary 'Bheag'. **MP 683**.

6920   MACISAAC, Angus, b ca 1819. From Is Eigg, INV. s/o Lachlan M, qv, and Catherine MacDonald, qv. To Antigonish Co, NS, 1823. m Ann Mooney, and had with other ch: 1. Donald; 2. Annie; 3. Roderick; 4. George. **HCA 299**.

6921   MACISAAC, Angus. From Is Eigg, INV. s/o Duncan M. To Rear Judique, Inverness Co, NS, prob <1830. m Miss Campbell, Whycocomagh, ch: 1. Archie; 2. John; 3. Flora; 4. Catherine.   **MP 684**.

6922   McISAAC, Angus. From Is South Uist, INV. To West Williams Twp, Middlesex Co, ONT, 1849; stld Centre Road.   **PCM 48**.

6923   McISAAC, Ann. From Is Shona, Moidart, INV. To PEI on the *Lucy*, ex Loch nan Uamh, Arisaig, 12 Jul 1790.   **PLL**.

6924   McISAAC, Ann Campbell, b 30 Sep 1827. From Comrie, PER. d/o Rev Patrick M. and Amelia Wright. To CAN.   **FES iv 264**.

6925   MACISAAC, Annie. From Is Canna, INV. d/o Neil M. To Inverness Co, NS, ca 1820. m Roderick MacLean, Strathlorne.   **MP 710**.

6926   MACISAAC, Archibald. From Is Eigg, INV. s/o Duncan M. To Inverness Co, NS, 1820; stld Rear Judique. m Miss MacLellan, ch: 1. Duncan, qv; 2. Neil; 3. Angus, qv; 4. John, qv; 5. Mary, unm.   **MP 683**.

6927 MACISAAC, Archibald. From Is Eigg, INV.
s/o John M, qv. To Inverness Co, NS, prob 1820; stld
Rear Judique. Farmer. m Sara MacKay, ch: 1. Donald;
2. Neil; 3. Duncan; 4. Joseph; 5. John; 6. John J;
7. Catherine; 8. Mary; 9. Anne. **MP 676**.

6928 McISAAC, Donald, b ca 1768. To Inverness,
Inverness Co, NS, 1805. Farmer, m and had ch.
CBC 1818.

6929 McISAAC, Donald, b ca 1796. To Inverness,
Inverness Co, NS, 1805. Unm in 1818. **CBC 1818**.

6930 McISAAC, Donald, b ca 1799. To Inverness,
Inverness Co, NS, 1812. Farmer. **CBC 1818**.

6931 MACISAAC, Donald. To PEI <1817, later to East
Bay, Cape Breton Co, NS. Farmer. Son Roderick,
1817-80. **HNS iii 211**.

6932 McISAAC, Donald, b ca 1748. To Western Shore,
Inverness Co, NS, 1802. Farmer, m and had ch.
CBC 1818.

6933 MACISAAC, Donald. From Is Eigg, INV. To
Inverness Co, NS, prob 1820; stld Rear Judique.
m Catherine, d/o John 'Ban' Campbell, ch: 1. Duncan;
2. John; 3. Donald; 4. Hugh; 5. Catherine;
6. Christina. **MP 674**.

6934 MACISAAC, Duncan. From Is Eigg, INV.
s/o Archibald M, qv. To Rear Judique, Inverness Co, NS,
prob 1820. m Jessie, d/o Neil McDougall, ch:
1. Catherine; 2. Anne; 3. Janet; 4. Mary; 5. Mary, jr;
6. Flora; 7. Margaret; 8. Neil; 9. Archibald; 10. John.
MP 681.

6935 McISAAC, Hector, b ca 1795. Poss s/o Donald
M, qv. To Western Shore, Inverness Co, NS, 1802.
CBC 1818.

6936 MACISAAC, Hector. From Is Eigg, INV.
s/o Duncan M. To Inverness Co, NS, prob <1830, stld
Rear Judique. ch: 1. John; 2. Duncan; 3. Mrs Ronald
MacEachern; 4. Mrs Alexander McInnis; 5. Catherine;
6. Mrs Neil MacLeod; 7. Mrs Ronald MacDonald.
MP 684.

6937 MACISAAC, Hugh. From Is Eigg, INV. s/o Duncan
M, qv. To Inverness Co, NS, 1843; stld Upper South
West Mabou. ch: 1. Hugh; 2. Hector; 3. Donald;
4. John; 5. John, jr; 6. Angus; 7. Anne; 8. Sara.
MP 685.

6938 McISAAC, John, b ca 1777. To Western Shore,
Inverness Co, NS, 1799. Farmer, m and had ch.
CBC 1818.

6939 McISAAC, John, b ca 1782. To Inverness,
Inverness Co, NS, 1808. Farmer, m and had ch.
CBC 1818.

6940 MACISAAC, John. From Is Eigg, INV. s/o Duncan
M. To Inverness Co, NS, 1820; gr 800 acres at Rear
Judique. ch: 1. Allan, qv; 2. Donald, qv; 3. Alexander,
qv; 4. Catherine, d at an advanced age; 5. Mary;
6. Archibald, qv. **MP 671**.

6941 MACISAAC, John. From Is Eigg, INV.
s/o Archibald M, qv. To Inverness Co, NS, 1820; stld
Rear Judique. m Flora MacInnis, ch: 1. Angus;
2. Donald; 3. Janet; 4. Anne; 5. Alexander; 6. Mary
Anne; 7. Mary; 8. John; 9. Sara. **MP 863**.

6942 MACISAAC, John. Poss from Arisaig, INV. To
South River, Antigonish Co, NS, poss <1820. ch:
1. Ronald, stld Margaree, Inverness Co; 2. Hugh,
stld Margaree; 3. Archibald, stld Broad Cove Banks,
Inverness Co; 4. Duncan, South River; 5. Angus;
6. John; 7. Kate; 8. Mary. **HCA 291**.

6943 MACISAAC, John. From Is Eigg, INV. s/o Rory
M. To Antigonish Co, NS, ca 1827. **HCA 299**.

6944 McISAAC, Rev John, 1805–14 Jan 1847. From
ARL. s/o Robert M, merchant. Grad MA, Univ of
Glasgow, 1826. Missionary in RFW, and in 1835 adm
min of Lochiel Twp, Glengarry Co, ONT. Retr to SCT,
1845, and became min at Oban, ARL. Son Colin,
schoolmaster, Calicut, India. **RGG 379; GMA 11013;
FES iv 102, vii 642**.

6945 McISAAC, Kathrine. From Is Shona, Moidart,
INV. To PEI on the *Lucy*, ex Loch nan Uamh, Arisaig,
1790. With her were two other adults, and she may have
been a widow. **PLL**.

6946 MACISAAC, Lachlan. From Is Eigg, INV. s/o Rory
M. To Antigonish Co, NS, 1823. m Catherine
MacDonald, qv, ch: 1. Angus, qv; 2. Allan; 3. Isabella.
HCA 299.

6947 MACISAAC, Malcolm. From Is Eigg, INV.
s/o Rory M. To Antigonish Co, NS, <1830. **HCA 299**.

6948 McISAAC, Margaret, ca 1813–15 Dec 1895. Prob
from North Uist, INV. To Mira River, Cape Breton Co,
NS, ca 1828; stld Trout Brook. m ca 1834, Donald
McNeil, qv. **DC 7 Oct 1964**.

6949 McISAAC, Mary, b 1788. From Is Rum, ARL.
Prob d/o Rory M, qv. To Gut of Canso, Cape Breton,
NS, on the *Saint Lawrence*, ex Tobermory, 11 Jul
1828. **SLL**.

6950 MACISAAC, Maxwell, b ca 1799. To Western
Shore, Inverness Co, NS, 1801; stld prob Broad Cove.
Farmer. **CBC 1818**.

6951 MACISAAC, Murdock. Prob from ARL. To Broad
Cove, Inverness Co, NS, prob <1830. ch: 1. Angus;
2. Alexander; 3. Donald; 4. Isobel. **MP 710**.

6952 MACISAAC, Neil. From Is Eigg, INV. To NS prob
<1808; stld Antigonish Co. ch: 1. John, res Georgeville;
2. Donald, stld Cape Breton Is; 3. Allan; 4. Lachlan.
HCA 297.

6953 McISAAC, Norman, b ca 1766. To Western
Shore, Inverness Co, NS, 1800. Farmer, m and had
ch. **CBC 1818**.

6954 McISAAC, Norman. From Is South Uist, INV. To
West Williams Twp, Middlesex Co, ONT, 1849. Son
Finlay. **PCM 47**.

6955 McISAAC, Peggy. From Is Shona, Moidart, INV.
To PEI on the *Lucy*, ex Loch nan Uamh, Arisaig, 12 Jul
1790. **PLL**.

6956 McISAAC, Roderick, b ca 1794. To Western
Shore, Inverness Co, NS, 1817. Farmer, m and had
ch. **CBC 1818**.

6957 McISAAC, Ronald. From Rudha na Fochaig,
Moidart, INV. To Arisaig, Antigonish Co, NS, ca 1790.
HCA 297.

6958 McISAAC, Rory, b 1743. From Is Rum, ARL. To Gut of Canso, Cape Breton, NS, on the *Saint Lawrence*, ex Tobermory, 11 Jul 1828. **SLL**.

6959 McISAACK, John. From Arisaig, INV. To Pictou, NS, on the *Dove*, ex Fort William, Jun 1801. Labourer. Wife with him, and ch: 1. Angus; 2. Catherine; 3. Duncan; 4. Mary. **PLD**.

6960 McIVER, Angus. From Is Lewis, INV. To QUE, ex Stornoway, arr 4 Aug 1851. Stld Huron Twp, Bruce Co, ONT, 1852. Head of family. **DC 5 Apr 1967**.

6961 McIVER, Alexander. From Is Lewis, ROC. To QUE, ex Stornoway, on the *Lady Hood*, arr 29 Aug 1841; stld Lingwick, Compton Co. **MGC 15 Jul 1980**.

6962 McIVER, Allan, 1822–1906. From North Bragar, Is Lewis, ROC. s/o Donald M. and Kirsty McLeod or McPhail. To QUE, ex Stornoway, arr 4 Aug 1851; stld Huron Twp, Bruce Co, ONT, 1852. m Catherine McLeod, ch: 1. Malcolm; 2. John; 3. Mary; 4. Catherine; 5. Donald; 6. Norman; 7. Allan; 8. Kirsty. **WLC**.

6963 McIVER, Evander, ca 1787–1861. From Is Pabbay, off Lewis, ROC. To Melbourne, Richmond Co, QUE, poss 1841. Ret army sergeant. m Susannah Boyd, qv, and had, poss with other ch: 1. Thomas, 1822–41; 2. Evander, 1827–92; 3. Helen, b 1828; 4. Dorinda, b 1832. **MGC 15 Jul 1980**.

6964 McIVER, John, b 1808. To NS on the brig *Ann Shields*, 1811; stld Baddeck, later Barneys River, Pictou Co. m ca 1840, Christina Stewart, ch: 1. John; 2. Jessie; 3. Kenneth; 4. Alexander; 5. Angus. **NSN 26/163**.

6965 McIVER, John, ca 1815–7 Dec 1897. From Lower Barvas, Is Lewis, ROC. s/o John M. and Isabella Murray. To QUE, ex Stornoway, on the *Lady Hood*, arr 29 Aug 1841; stld Lingwick, Compton Co, later Melbourne, Richmond Co. m Margaret Gunn, see ADDENDA, ch: 1. Murdo, b 1849; 2. Kirsty, b 1851; 3. Isabella, b 1853; 4. John, b 1856; 5. Donald, b 1858; 6. Mary, b 1860; 7. Ann, b 1862; 8. Margaret, b 1864; 9. Flora, b 1869. **MGC 15 Jul 1980; WLC**.

6966 McIVER, John. From Barvas, Is Lewis, ROC. To QUE, arr 4 Aug 1851; stld Huron Twp, Bruce Co, ONT, 1852. Farmer, Lot 17, Con 8. m Effie McArthur, qv, ch: 1. Malcolm, remained in SCT; 2. Isabella; 3. Norman; 4. John. **DC 25 Dec 1981**.

6967 McIVER, Kenneth. From Is Lewis, ROC. To QUE on the *Lady Grey*, ex Stornoway, arr 29 Aug 1841; stld Lingwick, Compton Co. m Ann Nicholson. Son Kenneth Nicholson, b Gould, 1871. **MGC 2 Aug 1979**.

6968 McIVER, Lillias Anne, ca 1803–21 Oct 1905. From Stornoway, Is Lewis, ROC. To Melbourne, Richmond Co, QUE, prob 1841. **MGC 15 Jul 1980**.

6969 McIVER, Malcolm. From Is Lewis, ROC. To Pictou, NS, <1790. m Jessie MacAulay, qv, ch: 1. Murdoch; 2. John; 3. William; 4. William; 5. Norman; 6. Jessie; 7. Rachel; 8. Catherine; 9. Margaret; 10. Annie; 11. Mary. **NSN 38/26**.

6970 McIVER, Malcolm (1). From Is Lewis, ROC. To QUE, ex Stornoway, arr 4 Aug 1851; stld Huron Twp, Bruce Co, ONT, 1852. Head of family. **DC 5 Apr 1967**.

6971 McIVER, Malcolm (2). From Is Lewis, ROC. To

QUE, ex Stornoway, arr 4 Aug 1851; stld Huron Twp, Bruce Co, ONT. Head of family. **DC 5 Apr 1967**.

6972 McIVER, Malcolm 'Elder'. From Is Lewis, ROC. To QUE, ex Stornoway, arr 4 Aug 1851; stld Huron Twp, Bruce Co, ONT, 1852. Head of family. **DC 5 Apr 1967**.

6973 MACIVER, Mary. From Uig, Is Lewis, ROC. To QUE, 1851; stld Winslow Twp, later Whitton Twp, Compton Co. Wife of Alexander MacDonald, qv. **TFT 17**.

6974 McIVER, William, ca 1803–7 Oct 1876. From Is Lewis, ROC. To Melbourne, Richmond Co, QUE, poss 1841. **MGC 15 Jul 1980**.

6975 McIVOR, Angus. To NS on the brig *Ann*, 1811. Wife Christie McLeod, qv, with him. **NSN 30/310**.

6976 McIVOR, Donald, 1800–72. From Is Lewis, ROC. To Gulf Shore, Cumberland Co, NS, 1811. Wife Christy MacDonald, qv, with him. ch: 1. Daniel, 1843–72; 2. Kenneth, 1846–74. **DC 29 Oct 1980**.

6977 MACIVOR, John, 1794–1877. From Is Lewis, ROC. To Fox Harbour, Cumberland Co, NS, prob <1830. Wife Henrietta d 1876. **DC 29 Oct 1980**.

6978 McIVOR, Neil. To NS, poss on the brig *Ann*, 1811; stld Baddeck, Victoria Co. Son John. **NSN 30/310**.

6979 McIVOR, William. From ROC. To Lobo Twp, Middlesex Co, ONT, 1840. ch: 1. William; 2. Hugh; 3. Mrs Nichol McIntyre; 4. Mrs Jaynes; 5. Mrs Telfer; 6. Mrs McLeod; 7. Mrs Peter McIntyre. **PCM 40**.

6980 MACK, William, 20 Feb 1828–11 Dec 1897. From LKS. Gr-s of William M, writer in Airdrie, and rel to Aitchison Alexander M, WS. To Montreal, QUE, prob <1860; went later to Cornwall Twp, Stormont Co, ONT. Miller, reeve and MLA, 1879. ch incl: 1. Janet; 2. Margaret; 3. William. **BNA 800; SH; SDG 256**.

6981 McKAY, Adam, b ca 1800. From Kildonan, SUT. Poss rel to Christian Gunn, widow, qv. To York Factory, Hudson Bay, arr 26 Aug 1815; stld Red River. **LSC 323**.

6982 McKAY, Alexander. From Kilmorack, INV. s/o 'Squire' William M, qv, and Janet McKay, qv. To Pictou, NS, on the *Hector*, ex Loch Broom, arr 17 Sep 1773; stld Frasers Mountain. m Christian Cameron, qv, ch: 1. John; 2. William, 1799–1813. **HPC App C**.

6983 McKAY, Alexander, ca 1728–1821. From Beauly, INV. s/o Alasdair M. To Halifax, NS, on the brig *John*, arr 4 Jun 1784. Stld Fish Pools, East River, Pictou Co; moved to East River St Marys, 1815. Discharged soldier, Frasers Highlanders, and farmer. m Nellie Calder, qv, ch: 1. John, qv; 2. Alexander, qv; 3. Donald, qv; 4. Hugh, qv; 5. Catherine, qv; 6. Mary, qv. **HPC App 1; CP 35**.

6984 McKAY, Alexander, jr, 1769–1866. From Beauly, INV. s/o Alexander M, qv, and Nellie Calder, qv. To Halifax, NS, on the brig *John*, 1784; stld Fish Pools, Pictou Co, and moved in 1815 to East River St Marys. m Ann, d/o Hugh Fraser, ch: 1. Hugh; 2. Ann; 3. Roderick; 4. Alexander; 5. John; 6. Sophia; 7. Margaret; 8. Donald; 9. Helen; 10. James McGregor; 11. Catherine. **CP 47**.

6985 McKAY, Alexander, b ca 1798. From Kildonan, SUT. Poss rel to Christian Gunn, widow, qv. To York

Factory, Hudson Bay, arr 26 Aug 1815; thence to Red River. **LSC 323**.

6986 McKAY, Alexander. From Rogart, SUT. To Diamond, Pictou Co, NS, 1815. Wife Margaret with him, and dau Isabella, qv. **NSN 10/3**.

6987 McKAY, Alexander, b ca 1776. To Pictou Co, NS, 1815; res West River, 1816. Labourer, m with 5 ch, and 'very poor indeed.' **INS 38**.

6988 McKAY, Alexander, b ca 1786. To Pictou Co, NS, 1815; res Rogers Hill, 1816. Tailor. **INS 38**.

6989 McKAY, Alexander. From SUT. Stld nr Earltown, Colchester Co, NS, <1820. Farmer and tailor. **HT 43**.

6990 McKAY, Alexander, b ca 1795. From Loch Carron, ROC. To Baddeck, Victoria Co, NS, 1826. Carpenter, builder and farmer. m Mary Stewart, qv, ch: 1. Donald Alexander; 2. Mary; 3. Christine Isabella; 4. John Charles. **DC 10 Mar 1962**.

6991 McKAY, Alexander. To Halifax, NS, <17 May 1828, when he m Mary Ann, d/o John Potts, St Margarets Bay. **VSN 2891**.

6992 McKAY, Alexander. From Dornoch, SUT. To Lanark Twp, Lanark Co, ONT, 1832; stld Lot 21, Con 7. Soldier, Caithness Regt, later farmer. m Margaret Morrow, qv, ch: 1. Alexander, jr, qv; 2. Thomas, went to Buffalo; 3. Hugh, qv; 4. Marion, qv; 5. Jane. **DC 10 Jan 1980**.

6993 McKAY, Alexander, jr. From Dornoch, SUT. s/o Alexander M, qv, and Margaret Morrow, qv. To Lanark Twp, Lanark Co, ONT, 1832; stld Lot 24, Con 7. m Esther McDonald, qv, ch: 1. Catherine; 2. William; 3. Alexander; 4. Margaret; 5. Daniel, res Arnprior, Renfrew Co; 6. George, res Arnprior; 7. Elizabeth; 8. William Andrew; 9. Myra; 10. Anne Alice; 11. Esther S; 12. Mary; 13. Lexie; 14. Esther; 15. Thomas; 16. Nelson, res Almonte, Lanark Co. **DC 10 Jan 1980**.

6994 McKAY, Mrs Alice, b 1756. To Pictou, NS, 1815; res Harbourmouth, 1816. Widow, 'frequently sick,' with 5 ch, and 'a great object of charity.' **INS 39**.

6995 MACKAY, Allan. From Is Mull, ARL. To Antigonish Co, NS, 1840; stld Keppoch. m a d/o Angus MacInnis, ch: 1. Angus; 2. John; 3. James; 4. Ronald; 5. Charles. **HCA 301**.

6996 McKAY, Andrew. From Farr, SUT. bro/o Angus M, qv, Charles M, qv, and John M, qv. To York Co, ONT, 1836, later to Victoria Road, Eldon Twp, Victoria Co. m (i) Ann Ferguson, ch: 1. Mary; 2. Jessie; 3. Annie; 4. Christina. m (ii) Ann McCarroll, with further ch: 5. Margaret; 6. John; 7. Tena; 8. Hector; 9. Andrew; 10. Sarah; 11. Angus; 12. Lilly. **EC 274**.

6997 McKAY, Angus. From Shenieval, Glendessary, INV. To Montreal, QUE, ex Fort William, arr Sep 1802; stld E ONT. **MCM 1/4 26**.

6998 McKAY, Angus, b 1790. From Kildonan, SUT. To Fort Churchill, Hudson Bay, on the *Prince of Wales*, ex Stromness, 28 Jun 1813. Went to York Factory, 1814, and thence to Red River. Prob the man of this name who stld later in Dunwich Twp, Elgin Co, ONT. Wife Jean with him. Son John, res Aldborough Twp. **LSS 184; RRS 26; LSC 321; PDA 27, 64**.

6999 MACKAY, Angus. From Rogart, SUT. bro/o Alexander M, qv. To Pictou Co, NS, 1815; stld Lime Rock. **NSN 10/3**.

7000 McKAY, Angus. From ROC. s/o Donald M. To Victoria Co, NS, ca 1820; later to Waipu, North Is, NZ. **DC 15 Feb 1980**.

7001 McKAY, Angus. From Farr, SUT. bro/o John M, qv, Charles M, qv, and Andrew M, qv. To York Co, ONT, 1836; later to Mariposa Twp, Victoria Co. **EC 273**.

7002 McKAY, Angus, ca 1767–8 Jul 1840. From SUT. To Pictou, NS, 1803; stld West River. Bur Salt Springs. **DC 27 Oct 1979**.

7003 McKAY, Angus. To Pictou, NS, on the *Ellen*, ex Loch Laxford, SUT, 22 May 1848. Wife Elizabeth with him, ch: 1. Barbara; 2. William; 3. Georgina; 4. Margaret. **DC 15 Jul 1979**.

7004 McKAY, Angus (1). From Is Lewis, ROC. To QUE, ex Stornoway, arr 4 Aug 1851; stld Huron Twp, Bruce Co, ONT, 1852. Head of family. **DC 5 Apr 1967**.

7005 McKAY, Angus (2). From Is Lewis, ROC. To QUE, ex Stornoway, arr 4 Aug 1851; stld Huron Twp, Bruce Co, ONT, 1852. Head of family. **DC 5 Apr 1967**.

7006 McKAY, Angus 'Og'. From Is Lewis, INV. To QUE, ex Stornoway, arr 4 Aug 1851; stld Huron Twp, Bruce Co, ONT, 1852. Head of family. **DC 5 Apr 1967**.

7007 McKAY, Ann, d 6 Nov 1810. From Beauly, INV. d/o Roderick M, qv, and Christine Grant, qv. To Pictou, NS, on the *Hector*, ex Loch Broom, arr 17 Sep 1773. m Rev James Drummond McGregor, qv. **SG iii/4 96**.

7008 McKAY, Ann, b ca 1789. From Kilmorack, INV. To Pictou, NS, on the *Dove*, ex Fort William, Jun 1801. Spinster. **PLD**.

7009 McKAY, Ann, b ca 1793. From Cayn, Kildonan, SUT. To Fort Churchill, Hudson Bay, on the *Prince of Wales*, ex Stromness, 28 Jun 1813. To York Factory, following spring, with bro James, qv, and thence to Red River. **LSS 186; RRS 27; LSC 323**.

7010 McKAY, Ann, b ca 1796. To Pictou, NS, 1815; res Pictou Town, 1816. Unm servant, 'able to support herself.' **INS 39**.

7011 McKAY, Ann, b 1830. Rel to Elizabeth M, qv, and Margaret M, qv. To Pictou, NS, on the *Ellen*, ex Loch Laxford, SUT, 22 May 1848. **DC 15 Jul 1979**.

7012 McKAY, Ann. To ONT <1845; later to IA. Wife of Robert McCallum, qv. **DC 23 Feb 1981**.

7013 MACKAY, Mrs Ann. To NS <1819. wid/o Hector M, merchant in Dornoch, SUT. m (ii) 7 Mar 1819, R. Masters. **NSS No 1567**.

7014 McKAY, Barbara, 5 Mar 1852–3 Dec 1913. From Papa Westray, OKI. d/o John M. and Elizabeth Gunn. To Yarmouth Co, NS, spring 1852. Wife of George Foulis, qv. **DC 4 May 1979**.

7015 McKAY, Betsy. From Kildonan, SUT. Niece of Alexander Gunn, qv, from Ascaig. To Fort Churchill, Hudson Bay, on the *Prince of Wales*, ex Stromness, 28 Jun 1813. Went to York Factory, 1814, and to Red River. **LSS 185; RRS 27; LSC 322**.

7016 McKAY, Betsy, b 1771. To Charlottetown, PEI, on

the *Elizabeth & Ann*, ex Thurso, arr 8 Nov 1806. Wife of Kenneth McLeod, qv.   **PLEA**.

7017   McKAY, Caroline, ca 1803–9 Nov 1873. From Newtonhill, KCD. d/o Andrew M. To QUE, ca 1836, and stld St Francis. d at 'Newtonhill', Brompton, and was bur at Elmwood Cemetery, Sherbrooke. Wife of William Smith, qv.   **SAA 335; MGC 2 Aug 1979**.

7018   McKAY, Catherine. From ARL. To PEI, 1771; stld Brackley Point, Queens Co. Wife of Neil McCallum, qv.   **DC 27 Jul 1980**.

7019   McKAY, Catherine. From Beauly, INV. d/o Alexander M, qv, and Nellie Calder, qv. To Halifax, NS, on the brig *John*, arr 4 Jun 1784; stld Fish Pools, Pictou Co.   **CP 47**.

7020   McKAY, Mrs Catherine, b 1746. To Pictou, NS, 1815; res Harbourmouth 1816. Widow, 'very poor.'   **INS 39**.

7021   McKAY, Mrs Catherine, b 1764. To Pictou, NS, 1815; res Fishers Grant, 1816. Widow.   **INS 39**.

7022   MACKAY, Catherine, b ca 1751. To Pictou Co, NS, 1815; res Fishers Grant, 1816. Spinster, and 'poor.'   **INS 38**.

7023   McKAY, Catherine, b 1787. From Kildonan, SUT. Wife of John Bannerman, qv. To York Factory, Hudson Bay, arr 26 Aug 1815, then to Red River.   **LSC 326**.

7024   MACKAY, Catherine. Prob from LKS. d/o Daniel M. To Miramichi, Northumberland Co, NB, ex Greenock, 22 Sep 1816. Wife of Rev James Thomson, qv.   **DC 15 Sep 1982**.

7025   McKAY, Catherine, ca 1796–22 Aug 1863. From SUT. To Pictou Co, NS, prob <1830; bur Hill Cemetery, West River Station. m Neil McBeth, qv.   **DC 10 Feb 1980**.

7026   McKAY, Catherine, b 1768. From Is Rum, ARL. To Gut of Canso, Cape Breton, NS, on the *Saint Lawrence*, ex Tobermory, 11 Jul 1828.   **SLL**.

7027   McKAY, Catherine. To Pictou, NS, on the *Ellen*, ex Loch Laxford, SUT, 22 May 1848. Wife of Donald Morrison, qv.   **DC 15 May 1979**.

7028   McKAY, Charles, b 1804. From Is Rum, ARL. To Gut of Canso, Cape Breton, NS, on the *Saint Lawrence*, ex Tobermory, 11 Jul 1828.   **SLL**.

7029   McKAY, Charles. From Farr, SUT. bro/o Angus M, qv, John M, qv, and Andrew M, qv. To York Co, ONT, 1836; later to Mariposa Twp, Victoria Co.   **EC 274**.

7030   McKAY, Christena, 26 Mar 1811–24 Jan 1887. From ROC. To NS, 1839, and d Kingsley, MAN. m George Alexander Henderson, qv.   **DC 7 Nov 1980**.

7031   McKAY, Christian, b ca 1783. To Charlottetown, PEI, on the *Elizabeth & Ann*, arr 8 Nov 1806. Wife of William McKay, qv.   **PLEA**.

7032   McKAY, Christian, b 1792. To Pictou Co, NS, 1815; res Fishers Grant, 1816. Unm.   **INS 38**.

7033   McKAY, Christian, b ca 1796. From Kildonan, SUT. Poss rel to Christian Gunn, qv, widow. To York Factory, Hudson Bay, arr 26 Aug 1815, and went to Red River.   **LSC 323**.

7034   McKAY, Christian. From Crulivig, Is Lewis, ROC. d/o Donald and Ann M. To QUE, ex Stornoway, arr 4 Aug 1851; stld Huron Twp, Bruce Co, ONT. Wife of John McKay, qv.   **WLC**.

7035   McKAY, Christian, 2 Jun 1801–31 Oct 1871. From Clair, Kiltearn, ROC. d/o William M. and Jean Urquhart. To ONT and stld Grey Co. Wife of William R. MacGillivray, qv, whom she m at Kiltearn, 31 Mar 1826.   **SG xxvi/3 90**.

7036   McKAY, Colin, 1730–1804. From Beauly, INV, but b at Strathnaver, SUT. To Pictou, NS, on the *Hector*, ex Loch Broom, arr 17 Sep 1773. Served in the 78th Regt. at Louisburg and QUE, and became pioneer settler at East River of Pictou, where gr 400 acres, west side. Wife Helen Fraser, qv, with him, and s Colin.   **HPC App A and C; SG iii/4 96**.

7037   McKAY, Daniel. From Assynt or Eddrachillis, SUT. To Boston, MA, on the *Fortitude*, arr 16 Aug 1803; stld Scotch Ridge, Charlotte Co, NB, 1805. Formerly of the Reay Fencible Regt.   **DC 29 Nov 1982**.

7038   McKAY, David, d 7 Dec 1877. To Shelburne Co, NS, and stld nr Jordan River. m 11 Jan 1821, Janet, 1799–1883, sis/o John MacPherson, and had with other ch: 1. Mrs John Richardson; 2. Margaret; 3. David, b 1841; 4. Donald, res Roxbury, MA.   **HNS iii 501**.

7039   McKAY, David. Cabin passenger on the *Ellen*, ex Loch Laxford, SUT, 22 May 1848, bound for Pictou, NS.   **DC 15 Jul 1979**.

7040   McKAY, Dolina, 1803–8 Jul 1890. From Golspie, SUT. To Earltown, Colchester Co, NS, 1822. m 1823, John McKay, qv, miller.   **HNS iii 642**.

7041   McKAY, Donald, b ca 1730. From Beauly, INV. s/o Alasdair McAlasdair M. To Pictou, NS, on the *Hector*, ex Loch Broom, arr 17 Sep 1773; stld East River of Pictou. m Christy Fraser, qv, ch: 1. Donald, catechist; 2. Roderick; 3. Hugh, res Albion Mines or Stellarton; 4. Alexander, res Halifax; 5. Joseph, res Albion Mines; 6. William, res Millstream.   **HPC App C; CP 47; SG iii/4 96**.

7042   McKAY, Donald, 1755–1829. From Kilmorack, INV. s/o 'Squire' William M, qv, and Janet McKay, qv. To Pictou, NS, on the *Hector*, ex Loch Broom, arr 17 Sep 1773; stld Frasers Mountain. Farmer and Ch deacon. m Christina Fraser. Son William, surveyor, made a map of NS, which was published at London, ENG.   **HPC App C; SG iii/4 96**.

7043   McKAY, Donald. From Beauly, INV. s/o Alexander M, qv, and Nellie Calder, qv. To Halifax, NS, on the brig *John*, arr 4 Jun 1784; stld Fish Pools, later Fox Brook, Pictou Co. Son Roderick, 1818–1902.   **CP 47**.

7044   McKAY, Donald. Prob from INV. s/o Donald M. To Pictou Co, NS, <26 Aug 1783, when gr 80 acres on east side of East River.   **HPC App A**.

7045   McKAY, Donald. From Brora, SUT. bro/o John M. To CAN and joined HBCo, 1789. Retr later to SCT.   **DC 7 May 1976**.

7046   McKAY, Donald, b ca 1782. To Charlottetown, PEI, on the *Elizabeth & Ann*, ex Thurso, arr 8 Nov 1806. Wife Marion McKay, qv, with him, and s Hugh, aged 1.   **PLEA**.

7047 McKAY, Donald, b ca 1795. From Uig, Is Skye, INV. To York Factory, Hudson Bay, on the *Edward & Anne*, ex Stornoway, arr 24 Sep 1811, and went to Red River. Labourer, and pioneer settler. **LSS 184; RRS 13, 26; LSC 321**.

7048 McKAY, Donald, b ca 1754. To Pictou, NS, 1815; res Rogers Hill, 1816. Labourer, m with 1 child, and 'very poor.' **INS 38**.

7049 McKAY, Donald, b ca 1793. To Pictou Co, NS, 1815; res West River, 1816. **INS 38**.

7050 McKAY, Donald, b ca 1784. From Kildonan, SUT. To York Factory, Hudson Bay, arr 26 Aug 1815, and went to Red River. Wife Catherine Bruce, qv, with him, and s John, aged 1. **LSC 326**.

7051 McKAY, Donald, ca 1788–28 Jul 1861. From Lairg, SUT. To Pictou Co, NS, 1818, and bur at Lansdowne. **DC 10 Feb 1980**.

7052 McKAY, Donald, b 1774. From Is Rum, ARL. To Gut of Canso, Cape Breton, NS, on the *Saint Lawrence*, ex Tobermory, 11 Jul 1828. Wife Christine with him, aged 49, and ch: 1. Mary, aged 20; 2. Flora, aged 18; 3. John, aged 15; 4. Donald, aged 10; 5. Neil, aged 6. **SLL**.

7053 McKAY, Donald, b 1763. From Is Rum, ARL. To Gut of Canso, Cape Breton, NS, on the *Saint Lawrence*, ex Tobermory, 11 Jul 1828. **SLL**.

7054 McKAY, Donald, b 1800. From Is Rum, ARL. To Gut of Canso, Cape Breton Is, NS, on the *Saint Lawrence*, ex Tobermory, 11 Jul 1828. **SLL**.

7055 McKAY, Donald, ca 1784–13 Oct 1858. From SUT. To NS, poss <1830; stld Earltown, Colchester Co. Wife Marion, 1793–5 May 1870. **DC 19 Mar 1981**

7056 McKAY, Donald, 1770–19 May 1871. From SUT. Served in British Army, and was wounded at Battle of New Orleans, 1815. To NS, 1831, and stld Colchester Co. Bur East Colchester. Wife Barbara, 1792–12 Apr 1878, also from SUT. Son James, 1824-41. **DC 22 Jun 1980**.

7057 McKAY, Donald, 1810–1908. From Lairg, SUT. To Pictou Co, NS, 1831. m Elizabeth McLeod, qv, ch: 1. Neil, 1845-90; 2. George, 1847-87; 3. William, 1852–1921; 4. James C, 1855-98; 5. John, 1860–1948; 6. Lilly, b 1863; 7. Jane, b 1865; 8. Daniel, b 1870; 9. Kate. **PAC 108**.

7058 McKAY, Donald. From Kildonan, SUT. bro/o Edward M, qv, and Joseph M, qv. To Montreal, QUE, 1836. Merchant. **SGC 515**.

7059 MACKAY, Donald. From Mealista, Uig, Is Lewis, ROC. To ONT, 1838. m 26 Jun 1838, Flora McAulay, qv. **Uig OPR 89/1**.

7060 McKAY, Donald. To Pictou, NS, on the *Ellen*, ex Loch Laxford, SUT, 22 May 1848. Wife Jean with him, and ch: 1. Maria; 2. Elspet; 3. Georgina; 4. Diana. **DC 15 Jul 1979**.

7061 McKAY, Donald. To Earltown, Colchester Co, NS, <1850. Farmer. By wife Christina had s George. **HNS iii 176**.

7062 MACKAY, Donald, b 1831. To Dunakyn, Mabou, Inverness Co, NS, <1854. m Johanna MacKay, Big Baddeck, ch: 1. Christy Ann, b 1868; 2. Duncan, b 1871; 3. John Dan, b 1883. **MP ii 489**.

7063 McKAY, Duncan. From Killin, PER. To Montreal, QUE, on the *Curlew*, ex Greenock, 21 Jul 1818; stld prob Beckwith Twp, Lanark Co, ONT. Wife Janet with him, and dau Ann, aged 3. **BCL**.

7064 McKAY, Duncan, ca 1808–29 Oct 1834. From Wick, CAI. To St John, NB. Shipwright. **NER viii**.

7065 McKAY, Duncan, b 1808. From Is Rum, ARL. Poss rel to Neil M, qv. To Gut of Canso, Cape Breton, NS, on the *Saint Lawrence*, ex Tobermory, 11 Jul 1828. **SLL**.

7066 McKAY, Duncan 'Ban'. From ROC. To Victoria Co, NS, ca 1820, later to Waipu, North Is, NZ. **DC 15 Feb 1980**.

7067 McKAY, Edward, 1813–6 May 1883. From Kildonan, SUT. bro/o Donald M, qv, and Joseph M, qv. To Montreal, QUE, 1840. Merchant and philanthropist. **SGC 515**.

7068 McKAY, Elizabeth. From Kildonan, SUT. Niece of Alexander Gunn, qv, from Ascaig. To Fort Churchill, Hudson Bay, on the *Prince of Wales*, ex Stromness, 28 Jun 1813. To York Factory, 1814, thence to Red River. Left settlement and arr Holland River, ONT, 6 Sep 1815. **LSS 185; RRS 27; LSC 322**.

7069 McKAY, Elizabeth. Rel to Ann M, qv, and Margaret M, qv. To Pictou, NS, on the *Ellen*, ex Loch Laxford, SUT, 22 May 1848. **DC 15 Jul 1979**.

7070 McKAY, Evan. Poss from INV. To NS, ca 1803; stld Hants Co. **NSN 32/364**.

7071 McKAY, Fairly, b ca 1824. To Pictou, NS, on the *Ellen*, ex Loch Laxford, SUT, 22 May 1848. Wife Jean, b ca 1822, with him. **DC 15 Jul 1979**.

7072 MACKAY, Flora, b ca 1795. From Kilmorack, INV. To Pictou, NS, on the *Dove*, ex Fort William, Jun 1801. **PLD**.

7073 McKAY, George, ca 1794–9 Jul 1867. From SUT. To Pictou, NS, 1803; bur Mount Thom. **DC 10 Feb 1980**.

7074 McKAY, George, b ca 1765. From Kildonan, SUT. To York Factory, Hudson Bay, arr 26 Aug 1815, thence to Red River. Pioneer settler. Wife Isabella Matheson, qv, with him, ch: 1. Roderick; 2. Robert, aged 16; 3. Robert, aged 11. **LSC 326**.

7075 McKAY, George, 13 Feb 1809–19 Nov 1892. To South Nelson, Northumberland Co, NB, 1837. Farmer. m Margaret Robertson, qv, ch: 1. Isabella, d <1861; 2. William, qv; 3. Sarah, b 1837; 4. Margaret, b 1839; 5. Alexander, 1843–1920; 6. Mary Jane, b 1845; 7. Jessie, 1848–1926; 8. Eliza, 1850-85; 9. John Henry, 1854–1925. **SG xx/1 24**.

7076 McKAY, Hector, b ca 1753. To Margaree dist, Inverness Co, NS, 1810. Farmer, m and had ch. **CBC 1818**.

7077 McKAY, Hugh, b ca 1732. From Beauly, INV. s/o Alexander M, sr, qv, and Nellie Calder, qv. To Halifax, NS, on the brig *John*, arr 4 Jun 1784; stld Pictou Co, and gr 100 acres, east side of East River. Farmer. **HPC 286, App A and C; CP 47**.

7078 McKAY, Hugh, b 1782. From Gorbals, Glasgow. To QUE, poss on the *Atlas*, ex Greenock, 11 Jul 1815;

stld Lot 29, Con 10, North Elmsley Twp, Lanark Co,
ONT. Weaver. Wife Betty Ross, qv, with him, and
5 ch. **SEC 1; HCL 12, 17, 230**.

7079 McKAY, Hugh, b ca 1794. To Pictou, NS, 1815;
res Fishers Grant, 1816. Weaver, unm. **INS 38**.

7080 McKAY, Hugh. From Dornoch, SUT. s/o
Alexander M, qv, and Margaret Morrow, qv. To Lanark
Twp, Lanark Co, ONT, 1832, and went later to USA.
m Jane Dunlop. **DC 10 Jan 1980**.

7081 McKAY, Hugh, ca 1808–20 Jun 1867. From SUT.
To Pictou Co, NS, and stld New Lairg. **DC 10 Feb
1980**.

7082 McKAY, Hugh. To Pictou, NS, on the *Lady Gray*,
ex Cromarty, ROC, 16 Jul 1841. **DC 15 Jul 1979**.

7083 McKAY, Hugh. From Badnabay, Eddrachillis, SUT.
bro/o John M. To QUE on the *Panama*, ex Loch Laxford,
19 Jun 1847, and went to Zorra, Oxford Co, ONT.
MacLeod Muniments.

7084 McKAY, Hugh G, ca 1819–26 Jan 1907. From
ROC. To Pictou Co, NS, prob <1845; bur Mount
Thom. **DC 10 Feb 1980**.

7085 McKAY, Iain 'Ruadh'. From ROC. s/o Donald M.
To Victoria Co, NS, 1819; later to Waipu, North Is,
NZ. **DC 15 Feb 1980**.

7086 MACKAY, Isabella or Arabella, ca 1800–3 Jul
1837. From Rogart, SUT. d/o Alexander M, qv, and wife
Margaret. **NSN 10/3**.

7087 McKAY, James. From Kilmorack, INV.
s/o 'Squire' William M, qv, and Janet McKay, qv. To
Pictou, NS, on the *Hector*, ex Loch Broom, arr 17 Sep
1773; stld east side of East River, where gr 70 acres.
HPC App A and C.

7088 McKAY, James, d 20 Mar 1817. From CAI. To
Guysborough, NS, poss 1785. Discharged soldier, prob
of 42nd Regt, and became farmer. m Christian Stewart,
qv, ch: 1. Donald, b 15 Oct 1785; 2. Angus, b 22 Aug
1788; 3. Christian, b 17 Sep 1790; 4. Margaret,
b 22 Mar 1792; 5. Hannah, b 1794; 6. Helen, b 15 Sep
1797; 7. Christian, b 23 Dec 1799. **DC 29 Aug and
30 Oct 1980**.

7089 McKAY, James, b ca 1795. From Cayn, Kildonan
par, SUT. To Fort Churchill, Hudson Bay, on the *Prince of
Wales*, ex Stromness, 28 Jun 1813. Went to York
Factory, 1814, and on to Red River. Sist Ann, qv, with
him. **LSS 186; RRS 27; LSC 323**.

7090 McKAY, James, b 1795. To Pictou Co, NS, 1815;
res Lower Settlement, 1816. Tailor, unm. **INS 38**.

7091 McKAY, James, b ca 1798. To Pictou, NS, 1815;
res Fishers Grant, 1816. Labourer, unm. **INS 38**.

7092 McKAY, James. From Is Muck, INV. To Inverness
Co, NS, 1826; stld Lake Ainslie. Farmer. Son Hector,
went to NZ. **HNS iii 234**.

7093 McKAY, James, ca 1805–17 Apr 1878. From SUT.
To Pictou Co, NS, prob <1830. m Janet Graham, qv.
DC 10 Feb 1980.

7094 McKAY, Jean, b 1806. From Is Rum, ARL. To
Gut of Canso, Cape Breton, NS, on the *Saint Lawrence*,
ex Tobermory, 11 Jul 1828. **SLL**.

7095 MACKAY, Jean, d 11 Jun 1863. From Hurkedale,
Cummertrees par, DFS. d/o David M, farmer, and Mary
Dickson. To Galt, Dumfries Twp, Waterloo Co, ONT,
1844. Wife of William Tait, qv. **CAE 11; DC 21 Mar
1981**.

7096 McKAY, Jennie, 1808–1908. From CAI. To
Colchester Co, NS, prob <1840; bur East Earltown. Wife
of Hugh Gunn, qv. **DC 22 Jun 1980**.

7097 McKAY, Jessie, b 1795. From Is Rum, ARL.
d/o Neil M, qv, and wife Mary. To Gut of Canso, Cape
Breton, NS, on the *Saint Lawrence*, ex Tobermory, 11 Jul
1828. Inf child Ann with her. **SLL**.

7098 McKAY, Jessie. To Pictou Co, NS, ca 1773; stld
Dalhousie Mountain. Wife of William McKenzie, qv.
NSN 9/2.

7099 McKAY, John. From SUT. To Pictou, NS, on the
Hector, ex Loch Broom, arr 17 Sep 1773; stld
Shubenacadie, Colchester Co. **HPC App C**.

7100 McKAY, John. To Pictou Co, NS, <1 Apr 1793,
when gr 300 acres on west branch of East River.
HPC App H.

7101 McKAY, John, b 1767. From Beauly, INV.
s/o Alexander M, qv, and Nellie Calder, qv. To Halifax,
NS, on the brig *John*, arr 4 Jun 1784; stld New
Glasgow, Pictou Co. **CP 47**.

7102 McKAY, John, 1751–1839. From Reay, CAI. To
Montreal, QUE, ca 1784. Discharged soldier.
m Catherine, d/o John McDougall, arr 1779. Son
Angus, 1780–1853. **DC 29 Aug 1980**.

7103 McKAY, John. From Ardnafouran, Arisaig, INV. To
QUE on the *British Queen*, ex Arisaig, 16 Aug 1790; stld
nr Montreal. Tenant. **QCC 103**.

7104 McKAY, John. To Pictou Co, NS, <1 Apr 1793;
stld west branch of East River, and gr 300 acres.
HPC App H.

7105 McKAY, John, b ca 1759. To Charlottetown, PEI,
on the *Elizabeth & Anne*, ex Thurso, arr 8 Nov 1806.
Wife Jean Murray, qv, with him, and ch: 1. Murdoch,
aged 19; 2. Elizabeth, aged 16; 3. Christian, aged 14;
4. Hugh, aged 10; 5. Margaret, aged 8. **PLEA**.

7106 McKAY, John, b ca 1801. To Margaree dist,
Inverness Co, NS, 1810, and became farmer.
CBC 1818.

7107 McKAY, John. From Eddrachillis, Assynt, SUT. To
Hudson Bay, ca 1813, and prob to Red River. **RRS 13**.

7108 McKAY, John, b ca 1789. From Uig, Is Skye, INV.
To York Factory, Hudson Bay, on the *Edward & Anne*, ex
Stornoway, arr 24 Sep 1811. Boat-builder; pioneer settler,
Red River. **LSS 184; RRS 13, 26; LSC 321**.

7109 McKAY, John, b 1756. To Pictou, NS, 1815; res
Fishers Grant, 1816. Labourer and catechist. Had 8 ch
and was 'very poor.' **INS 38**.

7110 McKAY, John, b ca 1776. To Pictou, NS, 1815;
res Fishers Grant, 1816. Labourer, m with 7 ch, and
'very poor.' **INS 38**.

7111 McKAY, John, b ca 1781. To Pictou Co, NS, 1815;
res Lower Settlement, 1816. Labourer, m with 6 ch, and
'very poor.' **INS 38**.

7112 **McKAY, John**, b ca 1784. To Pictou Co, NS, 1815; res Fishers Grant, 1816. Labourer, m with 6 ch, and 'able to work.' **INS 38**.

7113 **McKAY, John**, b ca 1785. To Pictou Co, NS, 1815; res Middle River, 1816. Labourer, m with 1 ch, and 'very poor indeed.' **INS 38**.

7114 **McKAY, John**, b ca 1791. To Pictou Co, NS, 1815; res West River, 1816. Labourer, m, and 'poor.' **INS 38**.

7115 **McKAY, John**, b 1796. To Pictou Co, NS, 1815; res Fishers Grant, 1816. Labourer, unm. **INS 38**.

7116 **MACKAY, John**. From SUT. To Pictou Co, NS, 1815. Wife Margaret with him. Son Alexander, 1818-82, MLA. **MLA 217**.

7117 **MACKAY, John**. From Plockton, ROC. To Pictou Co, NS, 1817, with Rev Norman MacLeod, qv. **CMM 2/17 55**.

7118 **McKAY, John**. From SUT. To Colchester Co, NS, <1820; stld nr Earltown. Miller and farmer. m Dolina McKay, qv, and had with other ch: 1. William, physician; 2. Rev Neil. **HT 43; HNS iii 642**.

7119 **MACKAY, John**. From SUT. To Pictou Co, NS, 1822; stld Mount Dalhousie. m Barbara MacLean. Son Dr Alexander Howard, 1848–1929, Principal of Pictou Academy. **HNS iii 459**.

7120 **McKAY, John**, b 1809. From Is Rum, ARL. To Gut of Canso, Cape Breton, NS, on the *Saint Lawrence*, ex Tobermory, 11 Jul 1828. **SLL**.

7121 **MACKAY, John**, 1806–3 Jan 1873. From Dornoch par, SUT. bro/o Peter M. To Zorra Twp, Oxford Co, ONT, 1835. Weaver. m Marion MacKay, qv, ch: 1. Janet, 1836-56; 2. Jane, b 1838; 3. Catherine, b 1840; 4. Rev William, 1842–1905; 5. Rev James, 1845–1924; 8. Rev Donald G, 1851–1937; 9. George Duncan, 1853-81, student of divinity; 10. Marion, 1855-56. **DC 19 Nov 1981**.

7122 **McKAY, John**. From Farr, SUT. bro/o Angus M, qv, Charles M, qv, and Andrew M, qv. To York Co, ONT, 1836, later to Mariposa Twp, Victoria Co, and then to Woodville. Storekeeper, later farmer. ch. **EC 273**.

7123 **McKAY, John (1)**. To Pictou, NS, on the *Lady Gray*, ex Cromarty, ROC, arr 16 Jul 1841. **DC 15 Jul 1979**.

7124 **McKAY, John (2)**. To Pictou, NS, on the *Lady Gray*, ex Cromarty, ROC, arr 16 Jul 1841. **DC 15 Jul 1979**.

7125 **McKAY, John**. To Pictou, NS, on the *Ellen*, ex Loch Laxford, SUT, 22 May 1848. Wife Jess with him, and dau Georgina. **DC 15 Jul 1979**.

7126 **McKAY, John (1)**. From Is Lewis, ROC. To QUE, ex Stornoway, arr 4 Aug 1851; stld Huron Twp, Bruce Co, ONT, 1852. Head of family. **DC 5 Apr 1967**.

7127 **McKAY, John (2)**. From Is Lewis, ROC. To QUE, ex Stornoway, arr 4 Aug 1851; stld Huron Twp, Bruce Co, ONT, 1852. Head of family. **DC 5 Apr 1967**.

7128 **McKAY, John**, b 1788. From Is Lewis, ROC. s/o John M. and Christy McDonald. To QUE, ex Stornoway, arr 4 Aug 1851; stld Con 5, Huron Twp, Bruce Co, ONT. Farmer. m Christian McKay, qv, ch:

1. Catherine, b 1823; 2. John, b 1826; 3. Murdo, b 1827; 4. Donald, b 1829; 5. Norman, b 1830; 6. Margaret, b 1833; 7. Angus, b 1837. **WLC**.

McKAY, Mrs John. See CALDER, Ann.

7129 **MACKAY, John William**. From SUT. To Pictou, NS, on the *Hector*, ex Loch Broom, arr 17 Sep 1773. Piper. **HPC App C**.

7130 **McKAY, Joseph**, d 2 Jun 1881. From Kildonan, SUT. bro/o Edward M, qv, and Donald M, qv. To Montreal, QUE, 1832. Merchant and philanthropist. **SGC 514**.

7131 **McKAY, Kenneth**, b 1771. To Pictou Co, NS, 1815; res Fishers Grant, 1816. Shoemaker, m with 5 ch, and 'very poor.' **INS 38**.

7132 **McKAY, Lachlan**, b 1800. From Is Rum, ARL. To Gut of Canso, Cape Breton, NS, on the *St Lawrence*, ex Tobermory, 11 Jul 1828. **SLL**.

7133 **McKAY, Lily**. From North Knapdale, ARL. To Aldborough Twp, Elgin Co, ONT, 1819. Wife of Donald Paterson, qv. **DC 23 Nov 1981**.

7134 **McKAY, Malcolm**. From Is Lewis, ROC. To QUE, ex Stornoway, arr 4 Aug 1851; stld Huron Twp, Bruce Co, ONT, 1852. Head of family. **DC 5 Apr 1967**.

7135 **McKAY, Margaret**, ca 1731–18 Jan 1825. From Beauly, INV. d/o Alasdair McAlasdair M. To Halifax, NS, on the brig *John*, arr 4 Jun 1784; stld Churchville, East River, Pictou Co. Wife of John Robertson, qv. **CP 48; VSN No 965**.

7136 **McKAY, Margaret**, b ca 1786. To Pictou Co, NS, 1815; res Middle River, 1816. Unm servant. **INS 38**.

7137 **McKAY, Margaret**, b ca 1793. To Pictou Co, NS, 1815; res Pictou Town, 1816. Unm servant, 'able to support herself.' **INS 39**.

7138 **McKAY, Margaret**, b ca 1796. To Pictou Co, NS, 1815; res Fishers Grant, 1816. Unm. **INS 38**.

7139 **McKAY, Margaret**. Rel to Ann M, qv, and Elizabeth M, qv. To Pictou, NS, on the *Ellen*, ex Loch Laxford, SUT, 22 May 1848. **DC 15 Jul 1979**.

7140 **McKAY, Marion**, b 1776. To Charlottetown, PEI, on the *Elizabeth & Ann*, ex Thurso, arr 8 Nov 1806. Wife of Donald McKay, qv. **PLEA**.

7141 **McKAY, Marion**, b 1830. From Dornoch, SUT. d/o Alexander M, qv, and Margaret Morrow, qv. To Lanark Co, ONT, 1832. m John Munro, Darling Twp, ch: 1. Margaret, b ca 1859; 2. Alexander, b ca 1860; 3. John, b ca 1862; 4. Catherine, b ca 1864; 5. Hugh, b 1866; 6. Marion, b ca 1869. **DC 10 Jan 1980**.

7142 **MACKAY, Marion**, d 1901. From Dornoch par, SUT. To Zorra Twp, Oxford Co, ONT, 1835. Wife of John MacKay, qv, m 29 Apr 1835. **DC 19 Nov 1981**.

7143 **McKAY, Marjory**. To Pictou, NS, 1800; stld Big Brook, west branch of East River. m Charles McLean, qv. **PAC 125**.

7144 **McKAY, Mary**. From Beauly, INV. d/o Alexander M, qv, and Nellie Calder, qv. To Halifax, NS, on the brig *John*, arr 4 Jun 1784; stld Fish Pools, Pictou Co. m Andrew Fraser. **CP 47**.

7145   McKAY, Mary, b 1803. From Is Rum, ARL. Poss wife of Duncan M, qv. To Gut of Canso, Cape Breton, NS, on the *Saint Lawrence*, ex Tobermory, 11 Jul 1828. **SLL**.

7146   McKAY, Miss. From Beauly, INV. d/o Alasdair McAlasdair M. To NS, prob on the brig *John*, arr Halifax, 4 Jun 1784; stld Fish Pools, Pictou Co. m James Forbes, who went to Demerara. **CP 47**.

7147   McKAY, Murdoch, ca 1770–6 Sep 1850. From SUT. To Pictou Co, NS, 1819. Bur Lansdowne. **DC 10 Feb 1819**.

7148   McKAY, Murdock. From Is Lewis, ROC. To QUE, ex Stornoway, arr 4 Aug 1851; stld Huron Twp, Bruce Co, ONT, 1852. Head of family. **DC 5 Apr 1967**.

7149   McKAY, Neil, b 1768. From Is Rum, ARL. To Gut of Canso, Cape Breton, NS, on the *Saint Lawrence*, ex Tobermory, 11 Jul 1828. Wife Mary with him, aged 57, and family: 1. Mary, aged 35; 2. Jessie, aged 33, qv; 3. Peggy, aged 30; 4. Neil, aged 28; 5. John, aged 26; 6. Donald, aged 23; 7. Christina, aged 21. **SLL**.

7150   McKAY, Neil, b 1798. From Is Rum, ARL. To Gut of Canso, Cape Breton, NS, on the *Saint Lawrence*, ex Tobermory, 11 Jul 1828. **SLL**.

7151   MACKAY, Neil, 1800-82. From Rogart, SUT. To Earltown, Colchester Co, NS, ca 1819. m (i) Isabella or Arabella McKay, qv, ch: 1. John; 2. James; 3. Angus; 4. Alexander; 5. Margaret; 6. Janet. m (ii) Elizabeth MacDonald, b 1814. **NSN 10/3**.

7152   McKAY, Neil, b 1810. From Is Rum, ARL. Poss rel to Duncan M, qv. To Gut of Canso, Cape Breton, NS, on the *Saint Lawrence*, ex Tobermory, 11 Jul 1828. **SLL**.

7153   McKAY, Norman. To Glengarry Co, ONT, 1794; stld Lot 26, Con 16, Lancaster Twp. **MG 57**.

7154   McKAY, Norman, ca 1769–ca 1839. From Spinningdale, SUT. To Charlottetown, PEI, on the *Elizabeth & Anne*, ex Thurso, arr 8 Nov 1806; stld prob Pictou Co, NS. m Jean Logan, ch: 1. Jean, b ca 1802; 2. Ann, b ca 1803; 3. Isabell, b ca 1805. **PLEA**.

7155   McKAY, Norman. From Is Lewis, ROC. To QUE, ex Stornoway, arr Aug 1851; stld Huron Twp, Bruce Co, ONT, 1852. Head of family. **DC 5 Apr 1967**.

7156   McKAY, Peter, b 1783. From Is Rum, ARL. To Gut of Canso, Cape Breton, NS, on the *Saint Lawrence*, ex Tobermory, 11 Jul 1828. Wife Flora with him, and ch: 1. Lauchlin, aged 5; 2. Donald, aged 3; 4. John, inf. **SLL**.

7157   McKAY, Robert, b ca 1802. From Kildonan, SUT. Poss rel to Christian Gunn, widow, qv. To York Factory, Hudson Bay, arr 26 Aug 1815, and went to Red River. **LSC 323**.

7158   McKAY, Robert, b ca 1781. To Pictou, NS, 1815; res Lower Settlement, 1816. Labourer, m with 3 ch, and 'very poor.' **INS 38**.

7159   MACKAY, Robert, 1840–16 Dec 1916. From CAI. To Montreal, QUE, 1855. Dry goods merchant and Canadian senator. m 1871, Jean, d/o George Baptist, Three Rivers. ch incl: 1. Hugh, KC; 2. Edward; 3. Mrs Robert Loring. **MDB 462**.

7160   MACKAY, Robert Walter Stewart, ca 1809–9 Oct 1854. To Montreal, QUE, <1835. Founder of the *Montreal Directory* and other reference books. **MBD 462**.

7161   McKAY, Roderick, 1746–22 Nov 1829. From Beauly, INV. s/o Alasdair McAlasdair M. To Pictou, NS, on the *Hector*, ex Loch Broom, arr 17 Sep 1773. Blacksmith; pioneer settler, East River, gr 300 acres 1783, later 30 acres more. m Christina Grant, qv, ch: 1. Ann, qv; 2. dau; 3. James, d Albion Mines or Stellarton; 4. John, blacksmith; 5. Robert; 6. Roderick.   **HPC App E and C; HNS iii 656; SG iii/4 96; CP 47**.

7162   McKAY, Roderick. From ROC. s/o Donald M. To Victoria Co, NS, ca 1819. Went later to Waipu, North Is, NZ. **DC 15 Feb 1980**.

7163   McKAY, Roderick 'Og'. From ROC. s/o Donald M. To Victoria Co, NS, ca 1820, later to Waipu, North Is, NZ. **DC 15 Feb 1980**.

7164   McKAY, Roderick. To Pictou, NS, on the *Ellen*, ex Loch Laxford, SUT, 22 May 1848. Wife Barbara with him. **DC 15 Jul 1979**.

7165   McKAY, Roderick. From ROC. To East Williams Twp, Middlesex Co, ONT, <1850. **PCM 43**.

7166   McKAY, Sarah. From Kilmorack, INV. d/o 'Squire' William M, qv, and Janet M, qv. To Pictou, NS, on the *Hector*, ex Loch Broom, arr 17 Sep 1773. m William Fraser, surveyor. **HPC App C**.

7167   McKAY, Simon, ca 1786–10 Mar 1863. To Pictou, NS, <1820; stld Frasers Mountain. Farmer. m Janet Cameron, 1789–1866, and had, prob with other ch: 1. Margaret, 1820–1911; 2. Donald, 1824–1913; 3. James 'Miller,' 1826–1910; 4. William, 1836-60. **PAC 104; NSN 32/377**.

7168   McKAY, Thomas, b ca 1796. To Pictou, NS, 1815; res Harbourmouth, 1816. Labourer, unm. **INS 39**.

7169   McKAY, Thomas, 1 Sep 1792–9 Oct 1855. From Perth. To Montreal, QUE, 1817; later to Ottawa, ONT. Stonemason, and became building contractor on Lachine and Rideau canals. MLC, 1841, and trustee of Queens Coll, 1846. m 1813, Ann Crichton, qv, ch. **SGC 326; MDB 462**.

7170   MACKAY, Thomas, b 1794. From WLN. To Lanark Co, ONT, <1830; later to St Vincent Twp, Grey Co. **LDW 25 Sep 1973**.

7171   McKAY, Thomas. From Eddrachillis, SUT. To QUE on the *Panama*, ex Loch Laxford, 19 Jun 1847; stld Nissouri, Zorra Twp, Oxford Co, ONT. Wife appears to have been d/o Donald Morrison, Oldshoremore, Kinlochbervie, Eddrachillis. *MacLeod Muniments*, **Box 36**.

7172   McKAY, William. From SUT. To Pictou, NS, on the *Hector*, ex Loch Broom, arr 17 Sep 1773. Drowned in East River. Descendants took surname of McCabe, from an early settler for whom he worked. **HPC App C**.

7173   McKAY, 'Squire' William, 1731–2 Mar 1828. From Kilmorack, INV. To Pictou, NS, on the *Hector*, ex Loch Broom, arr 17 Sep 1773. Pioneer settler, East River, Pictou Co, where gr 550 acres, 26 Aug 1783. m Janet McKay, qv, ch: 1. Donald, qv; 2. Alexander, qv;

3. James, qv; 4. Sarah, qv; 5. John 'Collier,' b Pictou Co; 6. William, farmer, McLellans Brook; 7. Mrs John McKay. **HPC App A and C; SG iii/4 97; NSN 19/2.**

7174 McKAY, William, b ca 1748. To Charlottetown, PEI, on the *Elizabeth & Ann*, ex Thurso, arr 8 Nov 1806. Wife Jean Scobie, qv, with him, and ch: 1. Kenneth, aged 15; 2. George, aged 14; 3. Duncan, aged 13; 4. Jean, aged 12; 5. Hugh, aged 7; 6. John, aged 5; 7. William, aged 2. **PLEA.**

7175 McKAY, William, b ca 1766. To Charlottetown, PEI, on the *Elizabeth & Ann*, ex Thurso, arr 8 Nov 1806. Wife Christian McKay, qv, with him, and ch: 1. John, aged 16; 2. Neil, aged 13; 3. William, aged 12; 4. Janet, aged 6. **PLEA.**

7176 McKAY, William, b ca 1778. To Western Shore, Inverness Co, NS, 1816. Farmer, m and ch. **CBC 1818.**

7177 McKAY, William, b ca 1762. To Pictou, NS, 1815; res Rogers Hill, 1816. Labourer, m with 3 ch. **INS 38.**

7178 McKAY, William, b ca 1790. To Pictou Co, NS, 1815; res Pictou Town, 1816. Unm clerk, 'able to support himself.' **INS 39.**

7179 McKAY, William, b ca 1793. To Pictou Co, NS, 1815; res Rogers Hill, 1816. Labourer, m with 3 ch. **INS 38.**

7180 McKAY, William, b ca 1770. Prob from Kildonan, SUT, but embarked at Stromness, Orkney, taking out millstones. Arr York Factory, Hudson Bay, 26 Aug 1815, and went to Red River. Wife Barbara Sutherland, qv, with him, and ch: 1. Betty, aged 10; 2. Dorothy, aged 4; 3. Janet, aged 2. **LSC 327.**

7181 McKAY, William. From SUT. To NS, <1820; stld Earltown, Colchester Co. Farmer. **HT 43.**

7182 McKAY, William, ca 1802–27 Nov 1846. From SUT. To Pictou Co, NS, prob <1830; bur Mount Thom. Wife Elizabeth, 1806–29 Aug 1874. **DC 10 Feb 1980.**

7183 McKAY, William. From Dornoch, SUT. To East Williams Twp, Middlesex Co, ONT, 1834. **PCM 43.**

7184 McKAY, William, 1835–5 Jun 1920. s/o George M, qv, and Margaret Robertson, qv. To South Nelson, Northumberland Co, NB, 1837; stld later in Winnipeg, MAN, where he d. m Annie Tushing. **DC 25 Oct 1980.**

7185 McKAY, William. To Elzevir Twp, Hastings Co, ONT, ca 1846. Wife Margaret with him, and ch: 1. Margaret, b ca 1840; 2. Lucy, b ca 1843; 3. Garth, b ca 1845. **DC 10 Mar 1981.**

7186 McKAY, William. To Pictou, NS, on the *Ellen*, ex Loch Laxford, SUT, 22 May 1848. Wife Janet with him, and ch: 1. Catherine; 2. Neilina; 3. Roderick; 4. Murdo. **DC 15 Jul 1979.**

7187 McKAY, William, 1811–86. From Dornoch, SUT. To Wallace, Cumberland Co, NS, prob <1840. Wife Anne, 1818-54. Dau Jane, 1849-53. **DC 29 Oct 1980.**

7188 McKAY, William, ca 1823–19 Jun 1848. From Maxwelltown, KKD. s/o William M, draper. To Norfolk Co, ONT, and d Normandale. Farmer. **DGH 27 Jul 1848.**

7189 McKEACHY, Rev Thomas, d 14 Aug 1844. From Leswalt, WIG. To ONT, and d at res of William Hannah,

Yonge Street, Toronto. Missionary of the Reformed Presb Ch. **DGH 19 Sep 1844.**

7190 McKEAN, John, 1 Jan 1800–21 Mar 1868. From Newton Stewart, WIG. To Chatham, Northumberland Co, NB, <1820. Notary Public. **DC 14 Jan 1980.**

7191 McKEAND, James, ca 1814–3 Oct 1885. From Glasgow. s/o Anthony M, merchant-burgess, Trongate, and Annabella Ure. Matric Univ of Glasgow, 1829. To Hamilton, ONT. Merchant. **GMA 12534.**

7192 McKECHNIE, Archibald. To QUE on the *David of London*, ex Greenock, 19 May 1821; stld prob Lanark Co, ONT. **HCL 239.**

7193 McKECHNIE, Archibald. From Is Islay, ARL. s/o Neil M. and Martha Smith. To Chinguacousy Twp, Peel Co, ONT, 1833. Farmer. m Catherine Sinclair, qv, ch: 1. Mary; 2. Margaret; 3. Martha; 4. Janet; 5. Neil; 6. John; 7. Duncan; 8. Archibald. **DC 30 Dec 1981.**

7194 McKECHNIE, Catherine, 1826-88. From Is Islay, ARL. d/o Donald M, qv, and Margaret Sinclair, qv. Lived in Greenock before going to ONT, 1852. Wife of James Reid, qv. **DC 1 Dec 1980.**

7195 McKECHNIE, Donald, 1777–1857. From Is Islay, ARL. s/o Neil M. and Martha Smith. To ONT, 1847; stld Priceville, Artemesia Twp, Grey Co. Wife Margaret Sinclair, qv, with him, and ch: 1. Mary, qv; 2. John, qv; 3. Anne, remained in Islay; 4. Neil, qv; 5. Margaret, qv; 6. Martha, qv; 7. Catherine, qv; 8. Donald, jr, qv; 9. Dugald, dy. **DC 1 Dec 1980.**

7196 McKECHNIE, Donald, jr, 1835-72. From Is Islay, ARL. s/o Donald M, qv, and Margaret Sinclair, qv. To ONT, 1847; stld Artemesia Twp, Grey Co, later Priceville. m Mary McPhee, 1840–1906. **DC 1 Dec 1980.**

7197 McKECHNIE, Duncan. From Is Islay, ARL. s/o Neil M. and Martha Smith. To York Co, ONT, <1850; stld Cheltenham. Tailor. **DC 30 Dec 1981.**

7198 McKECHNIE, John, ca 1814-84. From Is Islay, ARL. s/o Donald M, qv, and Margaret Sinclair, qv. To Artemesia Twp, Grey Co. Bur Tryon. m Anne McPhee, 1817-99. **DC 1 Dec 1980.**

7199 McKECHNIE, Isobel. Prob from West Calder, MLN. To QUE on the *Atlas*, ex Greenock, 11 Jul 1815; stld Bathurst Twp, Lanark Co, ONT. Wife of Samuel Purdie, qv. **SEC 1.**

7200 McKECHNIE, Janet, b ca 1780. Prob from Glasgow. To QUE on the *Atlas*, ex Greenock, 11 Jul 1815; stld Bathurst Twp, Lanark Co, ONT. Wife of John Flood, qv. **SEC 1; HCL 16, 231.**

7201 McKECHNIE, Malcolm, 13 Jan 1815–30 Jun 1895. From Paisley, RFW. To Sherbrooke, QUE. m Jane Younie, qv. **MGC 2 Aug 1979.**

7202 McKECHNIE, Margaret, 1823–1916. From Is Islay, ARL. d/o Donald M, qv, and Margaret Sinclair, qv. To Wellington Co, ONT, <1850. Wife of Rev Hugh Reid, qv. **DC 1 Dec 1980.**

7203 McKECHNIE, Martha, 1824-97. From Is Islay, ARL. d/o Donald M, qv, and Margaret Sinclair, qv. To Artemesia Twp, Grey Co, ONT. m John Ferguson, and moved to Chicago, IL. **DC 1 Dec 1980.**

7204 McKECHNIE, Mary, 1819–1 Oct 1894. From Is

Iona or Is Mull, ARL. To QUE, 1830; stld New Glasgow, Terrebonne Co. Went to York Co, ONT, <1839. m Archibald Lamont, qv. **DC 7 Jan 1982**.

7205 McKECHNIE, Mary, 1812-89. From Is Islay, ARL. d/o Donald M, qv, and Margaret Sinclair, qv. To Artemesia Twp, Grey Co, ONT, 1847. m Neil Sinclair Clark, Boston Mills. **DC 1 Dec 1980**.

7206 McKECHNIE, Mary. From Greenock, RFW. d/o Dougald M, b Islay, ARL. To Wellington Co, ONT, <1860. m Hugh Smith, Acton. **DC 30 Dec 1981**.

7207 McKECHNIE, Neil, 1819-95. From Is Islay, ARL. s/o Donald M, qv, and Margaret Sinclair, qv. To Artemesia Twp, Grey Co, ONT, 1847; moved later to London, Middlesex Co. m 1843, Isabella Henderson. **DC 1 Dec 1980**.

7208 McKECHNIE, Peter. From RFW. bro/o Archibald M, Eaglesham. To Chambly, nr Montreal, QUE, <1826. Merchant. **SH**.

7209 McKEGAN, Angus, d ca 1852. Poss from Is North Uist, INV. To NS <1838; stld nr Ainslie, Inverness Co. Went later to ONT. By wife Sarah had, prob with other ch: 1. John; 2. Roderick; 3. Christina. **DC 2 Jan 1980**.

7210 McKEIGAN, Archibald, ca 1824–ca 1903. From Is Grimsay, off Is North Uist, INV. s/o — M. and wife Marion. To East Williams Twp, Middlesex Co, ONT, ca 1852. **PCM 44; WLC**.

7211 McKEIGAN, Callum. From Is Grimsay, off Is North Uist, INV. s/o — M. and wife Marion. To East Williams Twp, Middlesex Co, ONT, ca 1852. **WLC**.

7212 McKEIGAN, Finlay. From Is Benbecula, INV. To East Williams Twp, Middlesex Co, ONT, 1848. **PCM 44**.

7213 McKEITH, Duncan. From Lismore, ARL. To Lobo Twp, Middlesex Co, ONT, 1820. ch: 1. Duncan; 2. John, res MI; 3. Mary. **PCM 38**.

7214 McKEITH, Neil. From Lismore, ARL. To Lobo Twp, Middlesex Co, ONT, 1820. ch: 1. Duncan; 2. John; 3. Donald; 4. Peter; 5. Mary; 6. Isabella, went to MI. **PCM 38**.

7215 McKELLAIG, Donald. From INV, poss Moidart dist. To PEI on the *Lucy*, ex Loch nan Uamh, Arisaig, 12 Jul 1790. **PLL**.

7216 McKELLAIG, Mary. From Kyles, Morar, INV. To PEI on the *Lucy*, ex Loch nan Uamh, Arisaig, 12 Jul 1790. Family with her, and prob a widow. **PLL**.

7217 McKELLAR, Alexander. From ARL. To Ekfrid Twp, Middlesex Co, ONT, 1830. ch: 1. John; 2. Peggy; 3. Mrs William Graham. **PCM 30**.

7218 McKELLAR, Angus. From ARL. bro/o Douglas M, qv. To Ekfrid Twp, Middlesex Co, ONT, prob <1830. Physician. **PCM 23**.

7219 McKELLAR, Archibald. From ARL. To Aldborough Twp, Middlesex Co, ONT, 1818; moved to Mosa Twp, 1828. m Janet Black, qv, ch: 1. Donald, d MI, ca 1804; 2. Euphemia, nurse. **PCM 23**.

7220 McKELLAR, Archibald. From Fincharn, Lochgilphead, ARL. To Lobo Twp, Middlesex Co, ONT, 1820. ch: 1. Donald; 2. Archibald, a warden of Middlesex; 3. Kate; 4. Mary; 5. Margaret. **PCM 38**.

7221 McKELLAR, Archibald 'Arderie', 1776–1849. From Kilmichael-Glassary, ARL. To Mosa Twp, Middlesex Co, ONT, 1831, stld Lot 5, Con 9. Farmer. m Nancy McKellar, qv, ch: 1. Nancy, qv; 2. Christina, qv; 3. Duncan, qv; 4. Catherine, qv; 5. Dugald, qv; 6. Mary, qv; 7. Betsy, qv; 8. Malcolm, qv. **PCM 24; SG xxix/4 138**.

7222 McKELLAR, Archibald, 3 Feb 1816–12 Feb 1894. From Inverary, ARL. s/o Peter M. and Flora McNab. To Aldborough Twp, Elgin Co, ONT, 1817; later to Raleigh Twp, Kent Co. Farmer and politician. m (i) Lucy McNab, his second cousin; (ii) 1874, Catherine Mary Powell. **BNA 755; MDB 464**.

7223 McKELLAR, Betsy, b 1821. From Kilmichael-Glassary, ARL. d/o Archibald M, qv, and Nancy McKellar, qv. To Mosa Twp, Middlesex Co, ONT, 1831. m Malcolm McKellar, Lobo Twp. **DC 29 Oct 1979**.

7224 McKELLAR, Catherine, 1815–1902. From Kilmichael-Glassary, ARL. d/o Archibald M, qv, and Nancy M, qv. To Mosa Twp, Middlesex Co, ONT, 1831. m Hector McLarty. **DC 29 Oct 1979**.

7225 McKELLAR, Christina, b 1810. From Kilmichael-Glassary, ARL. d/o Archibald M, qv, and Nancy M, qv. To Mosa Twp, Middlesex Co, ONT, 1831. m Archibald McCallum. **DC 29 Oct 1979**.

7226 McKELLAR, Donald S, d 1870. Prob from ARL. To Mosa Twp, Middlesex Co, ONT, <1845. Physician and politician. Moved to Appin, and in 1862, to London, Westminster Twp. **PCM 24**.

7227 MACKELLAR, Dougald. From ARL. To Aldborough Twp, Elgin Co, ONT, prob 1818. Farmer. **PDA 93**.

7228 McKELLAR, Douglas. From ARL. bro/o Dr Angus M, qv. To Aldborough Twp, Elgin Co, ONT, 1818; moved later to Mosa Twp. **PCM 23**.

7229 McKELLAR, Dugald, 1817–4 Aug 1890. From Kilmichael-Glassary, ARL. s/o Archibald M, qv, and Nancy M, qv. To Mosa Twp, Middlesex Co, ONT, 1831. m Euphemia Leitch, qv. **DC 29 Oct 1979**.

7230 McKELLAR, Dugald. From ARL. To Metcalfe Twp, Middlesex Co, ONT, ca 1831. **PCM 24**.

7231 McKELLAR, Duncan. From ARL. To Kent Co, ONT, 1820. Farmer and miner. m Margaret Brodie, ch: 1. Peter; 2. Donald. **DC 29 Jun 1978**.

7232 McKELLAR, Duncan. From ARL. To Caradoc Twp, Middlesex Co, ONT, 1820. Son James, alive 1904. **PCM 34**.

7233 McKELLAR, Duncan. From ARL. To Lobo Twp, Middlesex Co, ONT, 1830. **PCM 39**.

7234 McKELLAR, Duncan, 1812–17 Feb 1888. From Kilmichael-Glassary, ARL. s/o Archibald M, qv, and Nancy M, qv. To Mosa Twp, Middlesex Co, ONT. m ca 1843, Catherine MacCallum, qv. **DC 29 Oct 1979**.

7235 McKELLAR, Duncan. From ARL. To Metcalfe Twp, Middlesex Co, ONT, 1831. **PCM 26**.

7236 McKELLAR, Rev Hugh, 11 Sep 1841–1 Apr 1932. From Appin, ARL. To Lambton Co, ONT, 1852; stld nr Sarnia. Presb min and biographer. Educ Sarnia and Knox Coll, Toronto; DD, 1874. Missionary at Prince Albert,

SAS, and at High Bluff, MAN, <1888. Min at Mount Forest, Wellington Co, ONT, and at Martintown, Glengarry Co. Trans 1903 to mission at Priddis and Red Deer Lake. Ret 1912, and went to live in Calgary. m 1874, Catherine McDiarmid, d 1906, Lambton Co, ONT, ch: 1. Hugh, d 1922; 2. Kate, teacher at Crescent Heights, Calgary.   **DC 16 Mar 1979.**

7237 McKELLAR, Jeanette. Poss from ARL. To Aldborough Twp, Elgin Co, ONT, 1849. Wife of James Jamieson, qv.   **PDA 64.**

7238 MACKELLAR, John. From ARL. To Aldborough Twp, Elgin Co, ONT, 1818. Farmer. Son John.   **PDA 93.**

7239 McKELLAR, John, b 6 Sep 1774. From Braevallich, Dalavich par, ARL. s/o Archibald M. and wife Margaret. To York Co, ONT, 1818; moved to Mosa Twp, Middlesex Co. Farmer. m Euphemia Black, qv, ch: 1. John, b 22 May 1798; 2. Archibald; 3. Dugald; 4. Neil, b 2 Jan 1805; 5. Capt Duncan, b 14 Jun 1807; 6. Mary, b 31 Oct 1808; 7. Peter, b ca 1810.   **PCM 23; DC 29 Oct 1979.**

7240 McKELLAR, John. From Fincharn, Lochgilphead, ARL. To Lobo Twp, Middlesex Co, ONT, 1820. ch: 1. Malcolm; 2. John; 3. Alexander; 4. Mary; 5. Christie.   **PCM 38.**

7241 McKELLAR, John. From ARL. To Ekfrid Twp, Middlesex Co, ONT, 1830; moved to Gore dist. **PCM 30.**

7242 McKELLAR, John. Poss from Killearn, STI. To Darlington Twp, Durham Co, ONT, 1841. Wife Agnes with him. ch: 1. Mary, b 10 Dec 1841; 2. Agnes, b 7 Nov 1843; 3. John, b 29 Dec 1845.   **DC 14 Nov 1974.**

7243 McKELLAR, Malcolm, called 'Callum Mor'. From Knapdale, ARL. To Caradoc Twp, Middlesex Co, ONT, 1830. Farmer. m Jane Morrison. Son Donald, res East Williams Twp, 1904.   **PCM 35.**

7244 McKELLAR, Malcolm, 1826-98. From Kilmichael-Glassary, ARL. s/o Archibald M, qv, and Nancy M, qv. To Mosa Twp, Middlesex Co, ONT, 1831. m Catherine Leitch, qv.   **DC 29 Oct 1979.**

7245 McKELLAR, Mary, b ca 1819. From Kilmichael-Glassary, ARL. d/o Archibald M, qv, and Nancy M, qv. To Mosa Twp, Middlesex Co, ONT, 1831. m Alexander McCallum.   **DC 29 Oct 1979.**

7246 McKELLAR, Nancy, 1784-1863. From Kilmichael-Glassary, ARL. To Mosa Twp, Middlesex Co, ONT, 1831. Wife of Archibald McKellar, qv.   **DC 29 Oct 1979.**

7247 McKELLAR, Nancy, 1809-16 Feb 1892. From Kilmichael-Glassary, ARL. d/o Archibald M, qv, and Nancy M, qv. To Mosa Twp, Middlesex Co, ONT, 1831. m John McCallum, qv.   **DC 29 Oct 1979.**

7248 MACKELLAR, Peter. From ARL. To Aldborough Twp, Elgin Co, ONT, 1817. Farmer and poet. ch incl: 1. Archibald, politician; 2. Peter, farmer.   **PDA 24, 27, 93.**

7249 McKELLAR, Peter. From Lochgilphead, ARL. To Lobo Twp, Middlesex Co, ONT, 1824. m Mary, d/o William Paul, qv.   **PCM 38.**

7250 McKELLAR, Rev W. To Middlesex Co, ONT, ca 1833. Presb clergyman.   **PCM 12.**

7251 McKELVIE, Alexander. From Auchincairn, Kilbride, Is Arran, BUT. To Inverness, Megantic Co, QUE, 1843. Blacksmith. ch: 1. Archibald; 2. Alexander; 3. Mary; 4. Elizabeth; 5. Donald, tailor; 6. Dugald. **AMC 48; MAC 43.**

7252 McKELVIE, Ann. From East Bennan, Is Arran, BUT. To QUE on the *Bowly*, 1846; stld Inverness, Megantic Co. m (i) 14 Apr 1829, James McKinnon, ch: 1. Mary, qv; 2. John, qv; 3. Donald, qv. m (ii) James Hunter, qv.   **AMC 49; MAC 43.**

7253 McKELVIE, Betsy, b 1819. From Knockan, Is Arran, BUT. d/o Duncan M, qv, and Mary Stewart, qv. To Inverness, Megantic Co, QUE, 1831. m John McGillvray.   **AMC 39; MAC 36.**

7254 McKELVIE, Duncan. From Knockan, Is Arran, BUT. To Inverness, Megantic Co, QUE, 1831. Sawyer. m Mary Stewart, qv, ch: 1. Mary, qv; 2. Jane, b 1817; 3. William, qv; 4. Betsy, qv; 5. Flora, qv; 6. John, qv; 7. Mysie, qv; 8. Robert, b 1828.   **AMC 39; MAC 36.**

7255 McKELVIE, Flora, b 1821. From Knochan, Is Arran, BUT. d/o Duncan M, qv, and Mary Stewart, qv. To Inverness, Megantic Co, QUE, 1831. m Donald Murchie, qv.   **AMC 39; MAC 36.**

7256 McKELVIE, Isabella, 1771-1820. From Kingscross or Brodick, Is Arran, BUT. To Charlo, Restigouche Co, NB, <1840. Wife of Peter Hamilton, qv.   **MAC 16.**

7257 McKELVIE, Isabella, ca 1815-29 Jan 1892. From Auchincairn, Kilbride par, Is Arran, BUT. Rel to Alexander McKelvie, qv. To Inverness, Megantic Co, QUE, 1843. m James Kelso, qv.   **AMC 44; MAC 43.**

7258 McKELVIE, John, b 1824. From Knockan, Is Arran, BUT. s/o Duncan M, qv, and Mary Stewart, qv. To Inverness, Megantic Co, QUE, 1831. m Mary Shaw. **AMC 39.**

7259 McKELVIE, Mary, b 1814. From Knockan, Is Arran, BUT. d/o Duncan M, qv, and Mary Stewart, qv. To Inverness, Megantic Co, QUE, 1831. m — Dunn. **AMC 39; MAC 36.**

7260 McKELVIE, Mary. From Is Arran, BUT. To QUE on the *Caledonia*, ex Greenock, 25 Apr 1829; stld Inverness, Megantic Co. Wife of Neil McKillop, sr, qv. **AMC 11.**

7261 McKELVIE, Mary. From Kilmory par, Is Arran, BUT. To Inverness, Megantic Co, QUE, 1831. m 1825, Archibald Cook, qv.   **AMC 39; MAC 37.**

7262 McKELVIE, Mary Margaret, 1808-95. From Auchenchairn, Kilbride, Is Arran, BUT. To Charlo, Restigouche Co, NB, <1832. Wife of William Hamilton, qv.   **MAC 16.**

7263 McKELVIE, Mysie, b 1826. From Is Arran, BUT. d/o Duncan M, qv, and Mary Stewart, qv. To Inverness, Megantic Co, QUE, 1831. m Donald McKillop, qv. **AMC 39; MAC 35.**

7264 McKELVIE, William, b 1819. From Knockan, Is Arran, BUT. s/o Duncan M, qv, and Mary Stewart, qv. To Inverness, Megantic Co, QUE, 1831. m Mary Stewart, qv.   **AMC 39; MAC 36.**

7265 McKENNA, Gilbert, 1751-1821. From WIG. To Shelburne Co, NS, ca 1783. Loyalist, sometime in NY, where m Janet McCormack, qv, ch: 1. Samuel, b 1783, sea-captain, West Indies; 2. Agnes, 1785–1878; 3. Mary, called Polly, 1787–1882; 4. Janet, 1789–1885; 5. James, b 1791; 6. Margaret, b 1793; 7. Rosanna, 1796–1891; 8. William, b 1798; 9. Gilbert, 1800-77; 10. Elizabeth, called Bessie, 1802-88; 11. Matthew Dripps, 1804-88, named after Rev Matthew Dripps, qv; 12. Archibald, 1807-26. **MLA 220; DC 14 Nov 1981**.

McKENZIE. See also McKINZIE.

7266 McKENZIE, Alexander. From Loch Broom, ROC. To Pictou, NS, on the *Hector*, ex Loch Broom, arr 17 Sep 1773. **HPC App C**.

7267 MACKENZIE, Sir Alexander, ca 1764–11 Mar 1820. From Stornoway, Is Lewis, ROC. s/o Kenneth M, who emig from NY, and Isabella McIver. To Montreal, QUE, via New York, and was educ there. Entered the service of Finlay, Gregory & Co, fur-traders, later Gregory, McLeod & Co, absorbed by NWCo, when he became a partner. Served at Fort Chipewyan, and made his historic journeys to the Arctic Sea and Pacific Coast from there. Severed connection with NWCo for some years, during which he wrote his *Voyages*. KB, 1802. Associated with the XYCo for a time, and at the merger with the NWCo again became a partner. MLA, rep Huntingdon, and retr to SCT, 1808. Purchased estate of Avoch, ROC. m (i) Indian woman, ch, among others Andrew, bapt Montreal, and served with NWCo. m (ii) 1812, Geddes, d/o George MacKenzie, ch: 1. Margaret, d 1888; 2. Alexander, d 1894; 3. George, d 1880. **IBD 305; CBD 616; SDG 402; MDB 464**.

7268 MACKENZIE, Alexander, ca 1768–17 Jan 1838. Prob from Stornoway, Is Lewis, ROC. Rel to–prob a cousin of–Sir Alexander M, qv. To Montreal, QUE, ca 1788, but was sometime in Detroit. Became a wintering partner of the XYCo, which was merged with the NWCo, 1804. Served at Athabaska, and was involved in the Red River troubles, 1815. Later an agent for McTavish, McGillivrays & Co. m Isabella Latour, ch: 1. John George, d 1838; 2. Ann or Nancy. **MDB 465**.

7269 McKENZIE, Alexander, ca 1795–11 Jan 1837. From Lochbroom par, ROC. Prob bro/o Murdoch M, 1798–1839, qv. To Pictou Co, NS, 1803; stld Watervale, West River. Bur Salt Springs. **DC 27 Oct 1979**.

7270 MACKENZIE, Alexander, ca 1748–28 Feb 1824. Prob from Is Skye, INV. To Belfast dist, Queens Co, PEI, ca 1803. **SPI 74**.

7271 MACKENZIE, Alexander, 1780–1868. From Contin par, ROC. s/o Roderick M. To Pictou Co, NS, 1808; stld Four Mile Brook, later River John. Lumberman and shipbuilder. m Elizabeth Archibald, and had, poss with other ch: 1. Charles, mariner; 2. Thomas, mariner; 3. George, mariner; 4. Amelia; 5. Annie; 6. Mary; 7. Archibald; 8. Maria. **DC 27 Feb 1979**.

7272 MACKENZIE, Alexander. To PEI, poss 1803; stld Queens Co. Petitioner for Dr MacAulay, 1811. **HP 73**.

7273 MACKENZIE, Alexander, 1797–1859. From Is Lewis, ROC. To North Shore, Cumberland Co, NS, poss 1811. **DC 29 Oct 1980**.

7274 MACKENZIE, Alexander, 1784–1851. From Is Lewis, ROC. To North Shore, Cumberland Co, NS, poss 1811. **DC 29 Oct 1980**.

7275 McKENZIE, Alexander, 1760–1844. From INV. To Pictou Co, NS, prob <1815; bur Churchville. m Ann Grant, 1758–1850, b Halifax, NS. **DC 20 Jan 1981**.

7276 McKENZIE, Alexander. To ONT, ca 1817; stld Lot 4, Con 8, Beckwith Twp, Lanark Co. **HCL 31**.

7277 McKENZIE, Alexander, 1769–1819. From ROC. To Pictou Co, NS, and bur Salt Springs. **DC 27 Oct 1979**.

7278 McKENZIE, Alexander, ca 1785–29 Mar 1845. From SUT. To Pictou Co, NS, and bur Salt Springs. m Catherine McPherson, qv. **DC 27 Oct 1979**.

7279 McKENZIE, Alexander, b 6 Jul 1816. From INV. s/o Duncan M, qv. To Antigonish Co, NS, prob <1825. Ploughman. m 18 Jun 1844, Hannah Chisholm, ch: 1. Mary; 2. Ellen; 3. Margaret, d 1922; 4. Isabel; 5. Kenneth; 6. Roderick; 7. William; 8. Mary Ellen; 9. Florence. **HCA 304**.

7280 McKENZIE, Alexander. Prob from ROC. To Pictou Co, NS, <1828; stld west branch of East River. m Mary Barclay. Son Duncan, b 1828. **PAC 111**.

7281 MACKENZIE, Alexander, ca 1785–10 Jan 1857. From Moy, INV. To London Twp, Middlesex Co, ONT, 1828. Wife Mary, 1792–1884, with him, and ch. **PCM 50**.

7282 MACKENZIE, Alexander, ca 1829–11 Feb 1921. From Is Skye, INV. s/o Donald M, qv, and Fanny Gollan, qv. To Belfast dist, Queens Co, PEI, ca 1830. Elder, St Johns Ch. m Mary McLeod, ch: 1. Kenneth; 2. Daniel; 3. John M; 4. Mrs Bertram. **DC 9 Oct 1980**.

7283 McKENZIE, Alexander, ca 1784–22 Nov 1841. From Ullapool, ROC. To QUE, prob <1830, and d at Melbourne, Richmond Co. Farmer. m Alexanderina McKenzie, qv. **MGC 15 Jul 1980**.

7284 MACKENZIE, Alexander. From Golspie, SUT. To Montreal, QUE, ca 1831; later to Waterloo Co, ONT, and stld Aberfoyle. Blacksmith. m Barbara Grant, qv, and had, prob with other ch: 1. George, b 29 Feb 1828; 2. Alexander, b 15 Aug 1829; 3. Mary. **DC 11 Mar 1982**.

7285 MACKENZIE, Alexander, 1788–1862. From Kilbride Bennan, Is Arran, BUT. To Restigouche Co, NB; stld Doyleville. m Janet Ferguson, qv. **MAC 20**.

7286 MACKENZIE, Alexander, ca 1812–25 Apr 1850. From Dingwall, ROC. To Montreal, QUE, <1835. Emp with HBCo, and was drowned at Godbout. m Marie Traversy. Son Alexander, b Three Rivers, 10 Nov 1843, educ Dingwall and joined HBCo, 1861. **DC 7 Sep 1979**.

7287 McKENZIE, Alexander, ca 1821–10 May 1896. From Killearnan, ROC. d/o John M. and Barbara McGregor, qv. To Ashfield Twp, Huron Co, ONT, 1842. m ca 1850, Mary Macdonald, 1826-67, ch: 1. Alexander, b 1851; 2. John, 1854-73; 3. Annie, 1855–1929; 4. Mary, 1857–1928; 5. Roderick, 1859–1931; 6. Barbara, 1862–1934; 7. Murdoch, 1864–1941. **DC 15 Jul and 4 Aug 1979**.

7288 MACKENZIE, Alexander, 22 Jan 1822–17 Apr 1892. From Logieraitt, PER. s/o Alexander M, wright, and Mary Fleming. To Kingston, ONT, 1842; later to Sarnia Twp, Lambton Co. Stonemason, journalist, politician. Prime Minister of CAN, 1873-78. m (i) Helen

Neil, qv, ch. m (ii) Jane Sym, qv. **Logieraitt**
OPR 376/4; BNA 577; CBD 616; MDB 465.

7289 McKENZIE, Alexander. From Glendhu,
Eddrachillis, SUT. To QUE on the *Panama*, ex Loch
Laxford, 19 Jun 1847. Went to Eldon Twp, Victoria Co,
ONT. *MacLeod Muniments*, **Box 36**.

7290 McKENZIE, Alexander. From Is Benbecula, INV.
To East Williams Twp, Middlesex Co, ONT, 1848.
PCM 44.

7291 McKENZIE, Alexander. From INV. To Middlesex
Co, ONT, 1849; stld McGillivray Twp. **PCM 56**.

7292 McKENZIE, Alexander. From Is Lewis, ROC. To
QUE, ex Stornoway, arr 4 Aug 1851; stld Huron Twp,
Bruce Co, ONT, 1852. Head of family. **DC 5 Apr 1967**.

7293 McKENZIE, Alexanderina, ca 1789–6 May 1878.
From Ullapool, ROC, but b poss Langwell, CAI. To QUE,
and d at Melbourne, Richmond Co. Wife of Alexander
McKenzie, qv. **MGC 15 Jul 1980**.

7294 McKENZIE, Alexandrina, ca 1803–16 Oct 1871.
From ROC. To Melbourne, Richmond Co, QUE, prob
<1850. **MGC 15 Jul 1980**.

7295 McKENZIE, Alexina, 11 Dec 1814–15 May 1851.
From Is Skye, INV. To Scotch Road, Sherbrooke Co,
QUE, ca 1838. m 24 Jan 1839, Allan McLeod, qv.
DC 7 Feb 1980.

7296 MACKENZIE, Allan, 1786–1850. From Lochs par,
Is Lewis, ROC. To North Shore, Cumberland Co, NS,
poss 1811. **DC 29 Oct 1980**.

7297 McKENZIE, Allan. To Pictou Co, NS, <1855.
m Nancy McKenzie. Son John W, 1855–1914. **PAC 111**.

7298 McKENZIE, Andrew, b ca 1781. To Pictou Co,
NS, 1815; res Caribou, 1816. Labourer, m with 4 ch, and
'sick and very poor.' **INS 39**.

7299 McKENZIE, Angus, b ca 1557. From SUT. To
Pictou, NS, on the *Hector*, ex Loch Broom, arr 17 Sep
1773; stld Windsor, Hants Co. Retr later to Pictou Co.
HPC App C.

7300 McKENZIE, Angus, b 1776. From Drimaginear,
Kilmory par, Is Arran, BUT. To Escuminac, Bonaventure
Co, QUE, <1846. m Mary McAlister, qv, ch: 1. George,
1822–1904; 2. Archibald, 1823-71; 3. John, 1825–1907;
4. Angus, 1829–1907. **MAC 21**.

7301 McKENZIE, Anne, b ca 1756. To Charlottetown,
PEI, on the *Elizabeth & Ann*, ex Thurso, arr 8 Nov 1806.
Wife of John McLeod, qv. **PLEA**.

7302 McKENZIE, Ann. From Edinburgh. To QUE, poss
on the *Atlas*, ex Greenock, 11 Jul 1815; stld prob Lanark
Co, ONT. Wife of William Anderson, qv. **SEC 1**.

7303 McKENZIE, Ann, ca 1820-85. From Killearnan,
ROC. d/o John M. and Barbara McGregor, qv. To
Ashfield Twp, Huron Co, ONT, 1842. m 9 Dec 1847,
Hector McGregor, 1821-93, ch: 1. Grace, b 1849;
2. Roderick, b 1850; 3. Christina, b 1853; 4. John,
b 1857; 5. Alexander, b 1862. **DC 15 Jul 1979**.

7304 MACKENZIE, Annabell, b 1784. From Contin par,
ROC. d/o Roderick M. To Pictou Co, NS, <1812; stld
Four Mile Brook. m — McDonald. **DC 27 Feb 1979**.

7305 McKENZIE, Annabell, ca 1807–25 Apr 1878.

From Assynt, SUT. sis/o Nancy M, qv, John M, qv, and
Kenneth M, qv. To Pictou Co, NS, <1830. Bur Old
Elgin. **PAC 111; DC 20 Nov 1976**.

7306 McKENZIE, Annabella, 1800–2 Oct 1888. Prob
from ROC. To Melbourne, Richmond Co, QUE, poss
<1840. **MGC 15 Jul 1980**.

7307 MACKENZIE, Anne. From Stornoway, Is Lewis,
ROC. sis/o Daniel M, qv. To Scotch Hill, Brompton Twp,
Richmond Co, QUE, ca 1850. **DC 14 Apr 1981**.

7308 McKENZIE, Archibald, 1817–1 Nov 1891. To
Pictou Co, NS; stld west branch of East River. Moved to
Centredale, 1849. Discharged soldier. Wife Catherine,
1820-95, with him. ch: 1. Mary, 1847–1903; 2. Daniel A,
1847–1903; 3. Alexander, 1852–1917. **PAC 112**.

7309 MACKENZIE, Barbara, 1795–1869. From Is
Lewis, ROC. To North Shore, Cumberland Co, NS, poss
1811. **DC 29 Oct 1980**.

7310 McKENZIE, Barbara, ca 1816–22 Feb 1887. From
SUT. To NS <1840; stld Miramichi, Northumberland Co,
NB. Wife of Alexander McLeod, qv. **DC 4 Oct 1978**.

7311 McKENZIE, Catherine. From Strathglass, INV.
Prob rel to William M, qv, labourer. To Pictou, NS, on
the *Sarah*, ex Fort William, Jun 1801. m Alexander
Urquhart, qv. **PLS; PAC 201, 231**.

7312 McKENZIE, Catherine, ca 1787–11 Jan 1837.
From Lochbroom par, ROC. To Pictou, NS, and bur Salt
Springs. **DC 27 Oct 1979**.

7313 McKENZIE, Ceaty. From Loch Inver, Assynt, SUT.
To QUE on the *Panama*, ex Loch Laxford, 19 Jun 1847.
Went to Woodstock, ONT. *MacLeod Muniments*, **Box
36**.

7314 McKENZIE, Charles, 1774–3 Mar 1855. From
Ferintosh, ROC. To Montreal, QUE, 1803. Clerk with
NWCo, and spent many years in dist between Rainy
Lake and Albany. Contd with HBCo, and retr 1854. Son
Hector. **MDB 466**.

7315 McKENZIE, Charles. From Is Lewis, ROC. To
Compton Co, QUE, 1851. m Isabella Stewart. Son
Murdock. **MGC 2 Aug 1979**.

7316 McKENZIE, Christian, b 16 Nov 1825, Contin par,
ROC. d/o John M. and Barbara McGregor, qv. To
Ashfield Twp, Huron Co, ONT, 1842. m ca 1849,
Alexander Young, b 1810, ch: 1. Jane, b 1850; 2. Julia,
b 1851; 3. Alexander, b 1852; 4. Roderick, b 1854;
5. John, b 1856; 6. William, b 1859; 7. Ann, b 1866;
8. Colin, b 1868. **DC 4 Aug 1979**.

7317 McKENZIE, Clementine. From Leith, MLN. To
QUE on the *Atlas*, ex Greenock, 11 Jul 1815; stld North
Burgess Twp, Lanark Co, ONT. Wife of David Oliphant,
qv. **SEC 2**.

7318 McKENZIE, Colin. From Lochbroom par, ROC. To
Pictou, NS, on the *Hector*, ex Loch Broom, arr 17 Sep
1773; stld East River, Pictou Co. Gr 300 acres on east
side of the river, 1783. Son Duncan, 1772–1871, last
survivor of the *Hector* passengers. **HPC App A and C**.

7319 MACKENZIE, Colin, 1778–1863. From Contin par,
ROC. s/o Roderick M. To Pictou Co, NS, 1808; stld
Rogers Hill. Farmer. **DC 27 Feb 1979**.

7320 McKENZIE, Colin. From Invergordon, ROC. To

East Williams Twp, Middlesex Co, ONT, 1832. Twp clerk for about 20 years.   **PCM 43**.

7321   McKENZIE, Colin, 1813-95. From Killearnan, ROC. s/o John M. and Barbara McGregor, qv. To Ashfield Twp, Huron Co, ONT, 1842. m ca 1847, Ann McLean, 1820-87, ch: 1. Isabella, 1848-90; 2. Roderick, b 1849; 3. Annie, 1850–1938; 4. John, 1852–1938; 5. Charles, 1855–1912; 6. Mary, 1858-72; 7. Donald, 1860–1937; 8. Murdoch, 1861–1928; 9. Alexander, 1865–1910.   **DC 4 Aug 1979**.

7322   MACKENZIE, Colquhoun, 1786–30 Aug 1828. From East Duthill, INV. s/o Alexander M, tenant, and Anne McQueen. To QUE and d there.   **Ts Duthill**.

7323   McKENZIE, Daniel, ca 1769–8 May 1832. To Montreal, QUE, ca 1790. Fur-trader, and became partner of NWCo. Involved in Red River troubles, 1815. Retr ca 1819, and res for some time at Augusta, GA.   **MDB 466**.

7324   MACKENZIE, Daniel. From Stornoway, Is Lewis, ROC. bro/o Murdoch M, qv. To Scotch Hill, Brompton Twp, Richmond Co, QUE, ca 1850. Farmer.   **DC 14 Apr 1981**.

7325   MACKENZIE, Rev David, b 1800, CAI. Educ Aberdeen, and was schoolmaster of Reay, CAI, 1821. Became min of Kinlochbervie, SUT. Deposed in 1833, and went to ONT. Min of St Thomas's Ch, Presb of York. m Ann Dodds.   **FES vii 108**.

7326   McKENZIE, David. To East Williams Twp, Middlesex Co, ONT, 1836.   **PCM 44**.

7327   McKENZIE, Donald. From SUT. To Pictou, NS, on the *Hector*, ex Loch Broom, arr 17 Aug 1773; stld Shubenacadie, Colchester Co.   **HPC App C**.

7328   MACKENZIE, Donald. From Strathglass, INV. To Malignant Cove, Antigonish Co, NS, 1799. m Mary MacDonell, ch: 1. Margaret; 2. Bella; 3. John; 4. John.   **HCA 301**.

7329   McKENZIE, Donald, 1783–20 Jan 1851. From Lochbroom, ROC. bro/o Henry M, qv, and Roderick M, qv. To Montreal, QUE, 1800. Clerk with NWCo, and joined John J. Astor's American Fur Co, 1810. Served at Fort Astoria until 1813, then re-joined NWCo. Governor of Assiniboia, 1825-33. Retr to Mayville, Chautauqua Co, NY.   **MDB 466; DC 15 Feb 1967**.

7330   McKENZIE, Donald. From Kilmorack, INV. To Pictou, NS, on the *Sarah*, ex Fort William, Jun 1801. Farmer.   **PLS**.

7331   McKENZIE, Donald. From Kilmorack, INV. To Pictou, NS, on the *Sarah*, ex Fort William, Jun 1801. Labourer. Wife Ann with him, and s John, aged 4.   **PLS**.

7332   MACKENZIE, Donald, 1775–1860. From Contin par, ROC. s/o Roderick M. To Pictou Co, NS, 1803; stld Four Mile Brook, later River John. m 19 Nov 1804, Barbara Mackenzie, ch. Both bur St Johns, Scotsburn.   **DC 27 Feb 1979**.

7333   McKENZIE, Donald (1). From Assynt or Eddrachillis, SUT. To Boston, MA, on the *Fortitude*, arr 16 Aug 1803; stld Scotch Ridge, Charlotte Co, NB, 1804. Formerly of the Reay Fencible Regt.   **DC 29 Nov 1982**.

7334   McKENZIE, Donald (2). From Assynt or Eddrachillis, SUT. To Boston, MA, on the *Fortitude*, arr

16 Aug 1803; stld Scotch Ridge, Charlotte Co, NB, 1804. Formerly of the Reay Fencible Regt.   **DC 29 Nov 1982**.

7335   McKENZIE, Donald, b 1792. To Pictou Co, NS, 1815; res Little Harbour, 1816. Labourer.   **INS 38**.

7336   MACKENZIE, Donald, b ca 1800. From Is Raasay, INV. To Belfast dist, Queens Co, PEI, ca 1830. m Fanny Gollan, qv, ch: 1. Alexander, qv; 2. Kenneth; 3. Janet; 4. Mrs J. McIntyre, Lorne Valley.   **DC 9 Oct 1980**.

7337   McKENZIE, Rev Donald, 2 Aug 1798–8 Apr 1884. From Dores par, INV. Ord at Dingwall, 1833, and went to Middlesex Co, ONT, as a missionary. Min of Knox Presb Ch, Zorra, Oxford Co, 1835-72. Built a stone house at Gleness farm, and d at Ingersoll.   **PCM 12, 13; FES vii 642**.

7338   MACKENZIE, Donald, 1808-70. From LKS. s/o James M, sometime moulder in Dublin, IRL. To Cape Breton Co, NS, <1840; stld Sydney Mines. Wife Margaret with him, and ch: 1. William; 2. Margaret.   **DC 20 May 1980**.

7339   McKENZIE, Donald. To Pictou, NS, on the *Lady Gray*, ex ROC, arr 16 Jul 1841.   **DC 15 Jul 1979**.

7340   McKENZIE, Donald, 1830-85. From Is Arran, BUT. s/o Peter M, qv, and Margaret Davidson, qv. To Inverness, Megantic Co, QUE, 1843. m Catherine, d/o Donald 'Valdie' McKillop, qv.   **AMC 40; MAC 40**.

7341   McKENZIE, Donald. To Pictou, NS, on the *Ellen*, ex Loch Laxford, 22 May 1848.   **DC 15 Jul 1979**.

7342   McKENZIE, Donald. To Pictou, NS, on the *Ellen*, ex Loch Laxford, SUT, 22 May 1848. Wife Mary with him, and ch: 1. Alexander; 2. Donald; 3. Murdoch; 4. Henry; 5. John; 6. Mary; 7. Flora.   **DC 15 Jul 1979**.

7343   McKENZIE, Donald. From ARL. Rel to William M, qv. To ONT, 1840; stld West Williams Twp, Middlesex Co, 1850.   **PCM 47**.

7344   MACKENZIE, Donald, b 13 Aug 1836. From Carnoch, Contin par, ROC. s/o Rev John M, par min, and Georgina Robertson Kennedy. To CAN, 1851; prob stld ONT. m 29 May 1864, Mary McAdam, ch: 1. John Joseph, b 25 Mar 1865; 2. James; 3. Winewood Ann.   **DRG 40; FES vii 29**.

7345   MACKENZIE, Daniel, d ca 1868. From INV, prob Is Skye. To Montague, Kings Co, PEI. m Ann, d/o — Campbell and Grace Stewart, ch: 1. Ann; 2. John; 3. Elizabeth; 4. Malcolm; 5. Peter; 6. Barbara; 7. Mary; 8. Jessie; 9. Jane; 10. Jane; 11. Catherine, 1861–1947; 12. Daniel; 13. Hannah.   **DC 25 Jan 1964**.

7346   McKENZIE, Dugald, 1798–1878. From Mid Sannox, Is Arran, BUT. To QUE on the *Caledonia*, ex Greenock, 25 Apr 1829; stld Inverness, Megantic Co. m Isabella McKillop, qv, ch: 1. John 'Dugald,' qv; 2. Neil, qv; 3. Dugald, first white child b in the Scotch settlement, 1829.   **AMC 12; MAC 33**.

7347   MACKENZIE, Duncan, ca 1786–2 Aug 1875. From Moy, INV. To Chatham, Northumberland Co, NB, 1817. Went to London Twp, Middlesex Co, ONT, via QUE, and stld Lot 23, Con 24. Farmer and twp clerk. Discharged soldier. m Margaret, d/o John Barclay, qv, and Margaret McBean, qv, and had with other ch: 1. Duncan; 2. Donald; 3. Anne, 1817-88.   **PCM 49**.

7348 MACKENZIE, Duncan. From INV. To NS, prob <1825; stld Pomquet River, Antigonish Co. ch: 1. Alexander, qv; 2. Archibald; 3. Duncan, went to St John, NB; 4. John; 5. John Og; 6. Margaret. **HCA 303**.

7349 MACKENZIE, Elizabeth. From Kilmorack, INV. To Pictou, NS, on the *Dove*, ex Fort William, Jun 1801. Spinster. **PLD**.

7350 McKENZIE, Ewen. From Knockintorran, North Uist, INV. To Sydney, Cape Breton Co, NS, on the *Tay*, ex Lochmaddy, 22 Aug 1841. m Catherine Ferguson, qv, ch: 1. Ann, b 1831; 2. Peggy, b 1833; 3. Mary, b 1836. **DC 19 Apr and 18 May 1968**.

7351 McKENZIE, Farquhar. From Strathglass, INV. To Pictou, NS, on the *Sarah*, ex Fort William, Jun 1801. Labourer. **PLS**.

7352 MACKENZIE, George. From Assynt or Eddrachillis, SUT. To Boston, MA, on the *Fortitude*, arr 16 Aug 1803; stld Scotch Ridge, Charlotte Co, NB, 1805. Formerly of the Reay Fencible Regt. **DC 29 Nov 1982**.

7353 McKENZIE, George, 1810–15 Feb 1894. From Garmouth, MOR. To ONT, 1829; stld Pilkington Twp, Wellington Co. Schoolteacher. m Ann, 1810-92, d/o Roderick McKay, ch: 1. Alexander, went to MI; 2. Margaret; 3. Louisa; 4. Isabella; 5. Roderick; 6. William; 7. George; 8. Elizabeth; 9. Catherine; 10. John, dy. **EHE 41**.

7354 MACKENZIE, George, 1800-75. From Is Lewis, ROC. To North Shore, Cumberland Co, NS, prob <1840. Wife Ellen, 1820-75, with him. **DC 29 Oct 1900**.

7355 McKENZIE, Grizel or Grace. From Tain, ROC. To Montreal, QUE, 1789. Wife of John Russel, qv. Retr to SCT after her husband was drowned in Lake Champlain, and m 15 Jul 1813, Rev Hugh McKay McKenzie, her cousin, min at Tongue, SUT. **SGC 79; FES vii 110**.

7356 MACKENZIE, Hector. To Flat River, Queens Co, PEI, poss 1803. Trader. **HP 55**.

7357 McKENZIE, Hector, b ca 1756. To Margaree dist, Inverness Co, NS, 1816. Farmer, m and ch. **CBC 1818**.

7358 MACKENZIE, Hector. From Lochbroom, ROC. To Big Bras d'Or, Cape Breton Is, NS, <1835. Son Donald, b ca 1836, blacksmith and JP. **HNS iii 442**.

7359 McKENZIE, Hector. To Pictou Co, NS, <1840; stld west branch of East River. m Janet McKay. Dau Ann, b 1840. **PAC 111**.

7360 McKENZIE, Henry, ca 1780–28 Jun 1832. From Lochbroom par, ROC. bro/o Donald M, qv, and Roderick M, qv. To Montreal, QUE, ca 1800, and joined NWCo. Factor of Terrebonne after d of Simon McTavish, and also acted for Sir Alexander Mackenzie, qv, and Joseph Frobisher, fur-trader. Director of Montreal Savings Bank, 1819-20, and JP. m 1815, Anne, d/o Rev William Bethune, Williamsburg, and had with other ch: 1. Simon McTavish; 2. Mrs Stow. **SGC 34, 366; MDB 467**.

7361 McKENZIE, Hugh. From ARL. To East Williams Twp, Middlesex Co, ONT, poss 1832. **PCM 43**.

7362 McKENZIE, Hugh. To Pictou, NS, on the *Ellen*, ex Loch Laxford, SUT, 23 May 1848. Wife Betty with him, and ch: 1. Hector; 2. Donald; 3. Angus; 4. Margaret. **DC 15 Jul 1979**.

7363 MACKENZIE, Rev Hugh Ross, 20 May 1798–31 Jan 1860. From Nigg, ROC. s/o John M, catechist, and Isabella Ross. Educ Univ of Edinburgh, and became min at Harthill, LKS, attached to Shotts. To Wallace, Cumberland Co, NS, 1832; trans to Lochaber, Antigonish Co, 1840. Retr to SCT, 1844. Min at Tongue, SUT, 1844-48, and trans to St Marys, Inverness. m 8 Apr 1833, Hectorina, d/o Dr James Skinner, qv, and Elizabeth McCormack, qv, ch: 1. Rev James, min at Little Dunkeld, PER; 2. Isabella, 1835-36; 3. John, 1837-73; 4. Isabella, 1839–1923, went to AUS; 5. Elizabeth, 1841–1919, went to AUS; 6. Margaret Ross, 1843-78; 7. Hugh Butler Gallie, b 1846, planter in Ceylon; 8. Sally Mitchell, 1848–1917, res Ceylon; 9. Hector, 1851–1901, went to AUS. **FES vi 466, vii 616**.

7364 McKENZIE, Isabella, ca 1820–30 Jul 1914. From Kintail, ROC. To Ontario Co, ONT, <1840. m Farquhar McRae, qv. **DC 20 Jul 1980**.

7365 McKENZIE, Isabella, b 1798. To Pictou, NS, 1815. Unm servant, 'able to support herself.' **INS 39**.

7366 MACKENZIE, Isabella, b ca 1800. From Is Lewis, ROC. To Gulf Shore, Cumberland Co, NS, prob <1825. m Alexander Ross, qv. **DC 29 Oct 1980**.

7367 MACKENZIE, Isabella, b ca 1827. From Contin par, ROC. d/o John M. and Barbara McGregor, qv. To Ashfield Twp, Huron Co, ONT, 1842. m Kenneth McKenzie, b 1820, ch: 1. Christie, b 1845; 2. Mary, b 1847; 3. Flora, b 1848; 4. John, b 1851; 5. Barbara, b 1852; 6. Rory, b 1853; 7. Margaret, b 1855; 8. John, b 1855; 9. Alick, b 1856; 10. Murdoch, b 1860; 11. Colin, b 1862; 12. Elizabeth, b 1864. **DC 15 Jul and 4 Aug 1979**.

7368 McKENZIE, Isabella, 27 Jul 1828–6 Oct 1898. From Appin, ARL. d/o John M. and Mary Livingstone. To Sarnia Twp, Lambton Co, ONT, <1854. m Archibald Gray, qv. **DC 30 Jul 1980**.

7369 McKENZIE, Isabella, b ca 1805. From Hamilton, LKS. To QUE on the *St George*, ex Glasgow, Apr 1863; stld ONT. wid/o James Wingfield, silk handloom weaver and sometime gardener, by whom she had ch: 1. James; 2. Mary, b ca 1826; 3. Ann, b ca 1827; 4. Janet, b ca 1828; 5. Marion, b ca 1832; 6. Elizabeth, b ca 1838. **DC 20 Sep 1982**.

7370 McKENZIE, James, d 1849. From Stornoway, Is Lewis, ROC. bro/o Roderick M, qv, and rel to Sir Alexander M, qv. To Montreal, QUE, 1794, and became clerk with the NWCo. Partner, 1802, and managed Kings Posts on the Lower St Lawrence. ch. **MDB 467; LDW 15 Feb 1967**.

7371 McKENZIE, James, b ca 1783. To Charlottetown, PEI, on the *Elizabeth & Ann*, ex Thurso, arr 8 Nov 1806. **PLEA**.

7372 MACKENZIE, James. From East Duthill, INV. s/o Alexander M, 1739–1825, and Anne McQueen, 1758–1845. To QUE <1830. **Ts Duthill**.

7373 McKENZIE, James. From Is Skye, INV. To PEI, ca 1829. **DC 18 Aug 1964**.

7374 MACKENZIE, James, b 3 Dec 1792. From Dumfries. To CAN, ca 1840. ch: 1. James, went to NZ; 2. Alexander, went to NZ. **SG xxiii/3 49**.

7375 MACKENZIE, James. From East Duthill, INV.

s/o Alexander M, 1739–1825, and Anne McQueen, 1758–1845. To QUE <1830. **Ts Duthill**.

7376   MACKENZIE, James Kay, ca 1836–27 Feb 1916. From Lochee, Dundee, ANS. s/o William M. and Elizabeth Kay. To CAN and d at North Portal, SAS. **Ts Balgay**.

7377   MACKENZIE, Janet. From Kilmorack, INV. To Pictou, NS, on the *Dove*, ex Fort William, Jun 1801. Spinster. **PLD**.

7378   MACKENZIE, Janet, ca 1807–18 May 1871. Poss from ROC. To Melbourne, Richmond Co, QUE, prob <1850. **MGC 15 Jul 1980**.

7379   MACKENZIE, Jessie. From Is Lewis, ROC. To Scotch Hill, Brompton Twp, Richmond Co, QUE, ca 1850. **DC 14 Apr 1981**.

7380   McKENZIE, John. To Pictou Co, NS, and was gr 500 acres on West River, 1784. Prob discharged soldier. **HPC App A**.

7381   MACKENZIE, John. From INV. Rel to–poss uncle of–Sir Alexander M, qv. To Charlottenburg Twp, Glengarry Co, ONT. Drowned in Salmon River, 1795. **SDG 402**.

7382   MACKENZIE, John. From Strathglass, INV. To Malignant Cove, Antigonish Co, NS, 1799; stld St Andrews. m Margaret Chisholm, ch: 1. Valentine; 2. Duncan; 3. John; 4. Christy. **HCA 303; NSN 32/372**.

7383   McKENZIE, John, b ca 1802. From Assynt, SUT. bro/o Kenneth M, qv, Annabell M, qv, and Nancy M, qv. To Pictou Co, NS, <1800; stld Big Brook, East River. **PAC 111, DC 20 Nov 1976**.

7384   McKENZIE, John. To Pictou Co, NS, <1801. Son Hugh, ca 1801–ca 1840, stld Blackland, Restigouche Co, NB.

7385   McKENZIE, John, ca 1752–6 Jan 1815. From Assynt, SUT. To Pictou Co, NS, 1803. Bur Old Elgin. **DC 20 Nov 1976**.

7386   McKENZIE, John. From Assynt or Eddrachillis, SUT. To Boston, MA, arr on the *Fortitude*, 16 Aug 1803; stld at Scotch Ridge, Charlotte Co, NB, 1804. Formerly of the Reay Fencible Regt. Wife with him. **DC 29 Nov 1982**.

7387   McKENZIE, John, b 1768. From ARL. To QUE on the *Oughton*, arr Jul 1804; stld Baldoon, Dover Twp, Kent Co, ONT. Farmer. Wife Ann, b 1768, with him, and ch: 1. Kenneth b 1794; 2. Donald, b 1796; 3. Flora, 1798–1805; 4. John. **UCM 268, 302; DC 4 Oct 1979**.

7388   McKENZIE, John, b 1785. To Charlottetown, PEI, on the *Elizabeth & Ann*, ex Thurso, arr 8 Nov 1806. **PLEA**.

7389   MACKENZIE, John, 1762–1849. From Is Lewis, ROC. To North Shore, Cumberland Co, NS, 1811. **DC 29 Oct 1900**.

7390   MACKENZIE, John, 1790–1863. From Is Lewis, ROC. To North Shore, Cumberland Co, NS, 1811. **DC 29 Oct 1900**.

7391   McKENZIE, John. From Lochbroom par, ROC. To Glengarry Co, ONT; stld nr Glen Sandfield. Farmer and landowner <1815. **LDW 15 Feb 1967**.

7392   McKENZIE, John, b ca 1787. To Pictou, NS, 1815; res Mount Thom, Pictou Co, 1816. Carpenter, unm. **INS 39**.

7393   McKENZIE, John, b 1791. To Pictou, NS, 1815; res Little Harbour, 1816. Labourer, m with 1 child. **INS 38**.

7394   McKENZIE, John, b ca 1791. To Pictou, NS, 1815; res Lower Settlement, Pictou Co, 1816. Labourer, m with 1 child. **INS 38**.

7395   McKENZIE, John, ca 1776–14 Dec 1846. From SUT, poss Assynt. To NS and stld Pictou Co. Bur Old Elgin. Wife Mary, 1769–1849. **DC 20 Nov 1976**.

7396   McKENZIE, Rev John, 5 May 1790–21 Apr 1855. From Fort Augustus, INV. Grad MA, Kings Coll, Aberdeen, 1813. After teaching for a time, he was ord for service in CAN and emig 1818. Adm min of St Andrews Ch, Williamstown, Glengarry, ONT, 1819. m Jessie Fraser. **KCG 274; SDG 120; FES vii 642**.

7397   McKENZIE, John, ca 1773–4 Dec 1856. From Urquhart, INV. To Hants Co, NS, prob <1820; stld Nine Mile River. Wife Sarah, 1788–1832, native of Pictou. **DC 20 Jan 1981**.

7398   McKENZIE, John, ca 1790–29 Nov 1873. From Tarbat, ROC. To Montreal, QUE, <1822. Merchant. ch: 1. Nancy; 2. Catherine Elizabeth. **SGC 382**.

7399   McKENZIE, John, 1787–1858. From North Sannox, Is Arran, BUT. To QUE on the *Albion*, ex Greenock, 5 Jun 1829; stld Inverness Twp, Megantic Co. m Margaret Robertson, qv, ch: 1. John, 1823–74; 2. Margery, 1825–70; 3. Mary, 1828–96; 4. Neil; 5. Margaret. **AMC 21; MAC 34**.

7400   McKENZIE, John, b ca 1828. Poss from Edinburgh. s/o William M, qv, and Jane McDonald, qv. To NS, ex Glasgow, 1830, but went to Louth, Lincoln Co, ONT. Ship carpenter and wheelwright. **DC 5 Dec 1960**.

7401   McKENZIE, John, b 1775. From Is Skye, INV. To Glengarry Co, ONT, 1831. Wife Ann McDonald, qv, with him. **DC 23 Nov 1981**.

7402   McKENZIE, John, 9 Oct 1810–5 Apr 1890. From Glasgow, but prob b Urray par, ROC. s/o Roderick M. and Janet McLennan. To QUE, 1832, later to Montreal. Moved to Glengarry Co, ONT, and latterly at Kirkfield. m (i) Mary McLauchlan, qv, ch: 1. Duncan, b 23 May 1833; 2. Catherine, b 1835; 3. Alexander, b 16 Sep 1837; 4. Roderick, b 1839; 5. John C, b 1841; 6. Janet, 1845–80; 7. Mary Ann, 1845–82; 8. Margaret, 1846–1928; 9. Sir William, 1849–1923, railway contractor; 10. Ewen, 1852–1927. m (ii) Margaret Anne Armstrong, d 1873, further ch: 11. Mary Jane Elizabeth; 12. Dr Robert, 1873–1945. **EC 148; DC 3 Dec 1979**.

7403   MACKENZIE, John, b ca 1813. From Is Eigg, INV. To Inverness Co, NS, <1840; stld Port Hood. m Theresa, d/o Allan 'Ban' MacDonald, qv, ch. **NSN 32/363**.

7404   McKENZIE, John. From Loch Inver, Assynt, SUT. To QUE on the *Panama*, ex Loch Laxford, 19 Jun 1847. Went to Woodstock, Oxford Co, ONT. Miller. *MacLeod Muniments*, **Box 36**.

McKENZIE, Mrs John. See CALDER, Ann.

7405 McKENZIE, John Dugald, 1826-74. From Mid Sannox, Is Arran, BUT. s/o Dugald M, qv, and Isabella McKillop, qv. To QUE on the *Caledonia*, ex Greenock, 25 Apr 1829; stld Inverness, Megantic Co. m Marion Brodie, qv. **AMC 12; MAC 33**.

7406 MACKENZIE, Kenneth, 1800-94. From Assynt, SUT. bro/o Annabell M, qv, John M, qv, and Nancy M, qv. To Pictou Co, NS, <1800. m Hughina Campbell, from Cape Breton, and stld Big Brook, west branch, East River of Pictou. **PAC 111; DC 20 Nov 1976**.

7407 McKENZIE, Kenneth. Prob from Is Skye, INV. To Queens Co, PEI, poss 1803. Petitioner for Dr MacAulay, 1811. Son Kenneth. **HP 74**.

7408 McKENZIE, Kenneth, d 1817. Rel to Roderick M, qv. To Montreal, QUE, <1805, and became partner of NWCo. Served at Fort William and was involved in the Red River troubles of 1815. Drowned in Lake Superior. **MDB 467**.

7409 McKENZIE, Kenneth. From ROC. To PEI on the *Northern Friends*, 1804; stld Queens Co. **DC 1 Oct 1960**.

7410 McKENZIE, Kenneth, b ca 1768. To Pictou Co, NS, 1815; res Caribou, 1816. Labourer, m with 6 ch, and 'poor.' **INS 39**.

7411 McKENZIE, Kenneth. From Loch Inver, Assynt, SUT. To QUE on the *Panama*, ex Loch Laxford, 19 Jun 1847. Went to Woodstock, Oxford Co, ONT. *MacLeod Muniments*, **Box 36**.

7412 MACKENZIE, Kenneth, ca 1838–11 Nov 1926. From Stornoway, Is Lewis, ROC. bro/o Daniel M. To Scotch Hill, Brompton Twp, Richmond Co, QUE, 1850. Farmer. m Margaret MacDonald, qv, ch: 1. John Alexander; 2. William Kenneth; 3. Mary Alice; 4. Roderick Duncan; 5. Christian Margaret. **DC 14 Apr 1981**.

7413 McKENZIE, Kenneth, 25 Oct 1811–10 Apr 1874. From Edinburgh. s/o Dr Kenneth M. of Morham, and Janet Blair. Educ Univ of Edinburgh, and went to Fort Victoria, BC, 1851, as emp of HBCo. Founded the farm of Craigflower. m Agnes Russel, qv, ch. **DC 22 Apr 1978 and 21 Mar 1981**.

7414 MACKENZIE, Rev Kenneth John, 1799–1838. From Stornoway, Is Lewis, ROC. Educ Kings Coll, Aberdeen, and grad MA, 1819. To Pictou, NS, 1823. Min of St Andrews Ch. **KCG 277; FES vii 616**.

7415 McKENZIE, Lachlan. To Inverness Twp, Megantic Co, QUE, <1829. Pioneer settler. **AMC 35**.

7416 MACKENZIE, Malcolm. From Portree, Is Skye, INV. To Cape Breton Is, NS, ca 1830; moved to Montague, Kings Co, PEI, <1840. m Christine MacPherson, qv, ch: 1. Emily; 2. Flora; 3. Roderick; 4. John; 5. Donald. **DC 18 Aug 1964 and 5 Mar 1979**.

7417 McKENZIE, Malcolm. To Pictou, NS, on the *London*, arr 14 Jul 1848. Wife Beth with him, and ch: 1. Marion; 2. Ewen. They may have gone to PEI. **DC 15 Jul 1979**.

7418 MACKENZIE, Rev Malcolm, 1835-96. From Brodick, Is Arran, BUT. s/o William M, fisherman. Matric Univ of Glasgow, 1850. To CAN, 1860, and was min of Lochiel, Glengarry Co, ONT, 1862. Later at Côte St George, QUE, and at Earltown, Colchester Co, NS. Sometime in Kenora, MAN, and latterly at Tyne Valley, PEI. **GMA 15863; FES vii 621**.

7419 McKENZIE, Margaret. Prob from Glasgow. To Drummond Twp, Lanark Co, ONT, 1831. Wife of John Headrick, qv. **DC 8 Aug 1979**.

7420 MACKENZIE, Margaret, b 8 Jun 1813. From Auchterblair, Duthill par, INV. d/o Peter M. in Lochanully, and Mary McDonald. To Grey Co, ONT, 1838. m 5 Jul 1838, Duncan Smith, qv. **Duthill OPR, 96b/1-2; DC 22 Jan 1980**.

7421 McKENZIE, Margaret, 1805–29 Sep 1894. From PER. To Halton Co, ONT, prob <1850; stld Esquesing Twp. m–as his second wife–James Duff, qv. **EPE 76**.

7422 McKENZIE, Mary. From Is Arran, BUT. To QUE on the *George Canning*, 1830. Wife of John McKillop, qv. **AMC 38; MAC 35**.

7423 McKENZIE, Mary, 1785–1870. From Lochranza, Is Arran, BUT. To Inverness, Megantic Co, QUE, 1831. Wife of William 'Voolies' McKenzie, qv. **AMC 39; MAC 37**.

7424 MACKENZIE, Mary. From Forres, MOR. To CAN, 1834. Wife of William Bain, qv, m 1807. **SG xx/1 26**.

7425 McKENZIE, Mary, ca 1807–28 May 1890. Prob from ROC. To QUE prob <1835; stld Racine. m John Rose, qv. **MGC 15 Jul 1980**.

7426 McKENZIE, Mary, 1821–1905. From Kilbride Bennan, Is Arran, BUT. To Restigouche Co, NB, prob <1840. **MAC 21**.

7427 McKENZIE, Mary. To Pictou, NS, on the *Ellen*, ex Loch Laxford, SUT, 22 May 1848. **DC Jul 1979**.

7428 McKENZIE, Mary, ca 1810–ca 1895. From ROC. To Melbourne, Richmond Co, QUE, prob <1850. m William McLeod, qv. **MGC 15 Jul 1980**.

7429 McKENZIE, Mary Elizabeth, b 1787. From Applecross, ROC. d/o Roderick M, qv. To Orwell Bay, PEI, on the *Polly*, ex Portree, arr 7 Aug 1803. Moved later to Wallace, Cumberland Co, NS. m Peter Ballem, Mount Albion. **NSN 25/124**.

7430 McKENZIE, Murdoch, 1757–6 Feb 1853. From Lochbroom par, ROC. To Pictou Co, NS, prob 1803. Wife Janet, ca 1770–27 Aug 1846. Dau Ellen, 1792–1879. All bur Salt Springs. **DC 27 Oct 1979**.

7431 McKENZIE, Murdoch, ca 1798–19 Dec 1839. From Lochbroom, ROC. Prob bro/o Alexander M, 1795–1837, qv. To Watervale, West River, Pictou Co, NS, 1803. Bur Salt Springs. **DC 27 Oct 1979**.

7432 McKENZIE, Murdoch. From Gairloch par, ROC. To NS, ca 1810. Wife Mary with him. **DC 11 Jan 1978**.

7433 McKENZIE, Murdoch, b ca 1793. Poss s/o Hector M, qv. To Margaree dist, Inverness Co, NS, 1816. Farmer, unm. **CBC 1818**.

7434 MACKENZIE, Murdoch. From Stornoway, Is Lewis, ROC. bro/o Daniel M, qv. To Scotch Hill, Brompton Twp, Richmond Co, QUE, ca 1850. Farmer. **DC 14 Apr 1981**.

7435 MACKENZIE, Nancy, ca 1790–24 Dec 1855. From Contin par, ROC. d/o Roderick M. To Pictou Co, NS, ca 1812. Wife of Alexander McLennan, qv. **DC 27 Feb 1979**.

7436 McKENZIE, Nancy, ca 1795–30 Apr 1855. From Assynt, SUT. sis/o Annabell M, qv, John M, qv, and Kenneth M, qv. To Pictou Co, NS, <1830. Bur Old Elgin. **PAC 111; DC 20 Nov 1976**.

7437 McKENZIE, Neil. From Assynt or Eddrachillis, SUT. To Boston, MA, on the *Fortitude*, arr 16 Aug 1803, but stld Scotch Ridge, Charlotte Co, NB, 1805. Formerly of the Reay Fencible Regt. **DC 29 Nov 1982**.

7438 McKENZIE, Neil, b 1781. To St Andrews dist, Cape Breton Co, NS, 1810. Farmer, m and ch. **CBC 1818**.

7439 McKENZIE, Neil, b 1827. From Mid Sannoch, Is Arran, BUT. s/o Dugald M, qv, and Isabella McKillop, qv. To QUE on the *Caledonia*, ex Greenock, 25 Apr 1829; stld Inverness Twp, Megantic Co. Son Dugald, physician, Holstein, Grey Co, ONT. **AMC 12; MAC 33**.

7440 McKENZIE, Paul. To Pictou Co, NS, <1828; stld west branch, East River. m Janet McDonald, ch: 1. Alexander, b 1828; 2. James, b 1829; 3. Mary Ann, b 1832; 4. Donald William, b 1834. **PAC 111**.

7441 McKENZIE, Peter, b ca 1799. From Is Arran, BUT. To NB, ca 1817; petitioned for 150 acres on the south side of Restigouche River, Restigouche Co, 9 Feb 1821. **DC 31 May 1980**.

7442 McKENZIE, Peter, 1784–1861. From Is Arran, BUT. To Inverness, Megantic Co, QUE, 1843. m Margaret Davidson, qv, ch: 1. Peter, jr, qv; 2. Robert, 1832–1910; 3. John, 1835–1901. **AMC 40; MAC 40**.

7443 McKENZIE, Peter, jr, 1824–1903. From Is Arran, BUT. s/o Peter M, qv, and Margaret Davidson, qv. To Inverness, Megantic Co, QUE, 1843. m Mary, d/o Donald 'Valdie' McKillop, qv. **AMC 40; MAC 40**.

7444 McKENZIE, Peter, 1 May 1820–31 Jan 1865. From Plockton, ROC. To Aldborough Twp, Elgin Co, ONT, 1851; moved 1852, to Huron Twp, Bruce Co. Mariner. m Annabel Gillies, qv, ch: 1. Donald; 2. Ann; 3. Christy, b 1851; 4. Katherine; 5. John. **DC 25 Dec 1981**.

7445 McKENZIE, Robert, ca 1760–8 Jul 1815. To St John, NB, and d there. **NER viii 98**.

7446 McKENZIE, Robert, b ca 1750. To Pictou Co, NS, 1815; res Fishers Grant, 1816. Labourer, m with 2 ch. **INS 38**.

7447 MACKENZIE, Robert, ca 1825–4 Apr 1879. To Ayr Village, Dumfries Twp, Waterloo Co, ONT, <1843. Sailor, later farmer. m 1843, Isabel, d/o John and Elizabeth Fraser, ch: 1. Catherine, 1844–1904; 2. Robert, 1847–1913; 3. Margaret, 1849-99; 4. Jane, 1851–1913; 5. Annie, b 1854; 6. Mary, 1857–1916. **DC 17 Jan 1967**.

7448 MACKENZIE, Robert. From Is Lewis, ROC. To Scotch Hill, Brompton Twp, Richmond Co, QUE, ca 1850. **DC 14 Apr 1981**.

7449 McKENZIE, Roderick, ca 1761–1844. From Lochbroom par, ROC. Cous of Sir Alexander M, qv. To Montreal, QUE, 1784. Associated with several fur companies and built Fort Chipewyan on Lake Athabasca, where he managed affairs for the NWCo. MLC, Lower Canada, 1817-38, and a historian of the fur trade. m 1803, Marie Louise Rachel, d/o Charles Jean Baptiste Chaboillez, and res afterwards at the Seignory of Terrebonne, which he purchased from Simon McTavish. ch incl: 1. Alexander, Lt Col, British Army; 2. Louisa. **SGC 104, 110; MDB 468**.

7450 McKENZIE, Roderick. To Glengarry Co, ONT, 1794; stld Lot 10, Con 16, Lancaster Twp. **MG 57**.

7451 McKENZIE, Roderick, ca 1778–21 Apr 1868. From Kilmorack, INV. To Pictou, NS, on the *Dove*, ex Fort William, Jun 1801. Labourer. Stld Mount Pleasant, West River. Bur at Lovat. Wife Ann, 1786–1867. **PLD; DC 10 Feb 1980**.

7452 McKENZIE, Roderick. From Applecross, ROC. To Orwell Bay, PEI, on the *Polly*, ex Portree, arr 7 Aug 1803. Moved to Wallace, Cumberland Co, NS, <1827. Dau Mary Elizabeth, qv. **NSN 25/124**.

7453 MACKENZIE, Roderick. Prob from ROC. To PEI, 1803; stld Queens Co. Leader of a group of emigrants. **HP 16**.

7454 MACKENZIE, Roderick, b ca 1776. From Contin par, ROC. s/o Roderick M. To Terrebonne, QUE, 1804. Emp with the firm of McKenzie, Oldham & Co. **DC 27 Feb 1979**.

7455 McKENZIE, Roderick, b ca 1778. To Baddeck dist, Victoria Co, NS, 1812. **CBC 1818**.

7456 McKENZIE, Roderick, 1772–2 Jan 1859. To CAN <1815, and joined HBCo as a clerk. Served at Fort Wedderburn and became a chief trader, 1821; later chief factor. d at the Red River settlement. **MDB 468**.

7457 McKENZIE, Roderick. From Strathan, Assynt, SUT. bro/o Allan M. To QUE on the *Panama*, ex Loch Laxford, 19 Jun 1847. Went to Zorra Twp, Oxford Co, ONT. *MacLeod Muniments*, **Box 36**.

7458 MACKENZIE, Roderick, 1800-58. From Assynt, SUT. To Melbourne, Richmond Co, QUE, 1806-55, with him. **MGC 15 Jul 1980**.

7459 McKENZIE, Sarah, b ca 1830. From Rentonhall, Morham, ELN. d/o Dr Kenneth M. To Victoria, BC, 1852. m Thomas Russell, qv. **DC 22 Apr 1978**.

7460 McKENZIE, Thomas. From Kirkhill, INV. To Halifax, NS, on the brig *John*, arr 4 Jun 1784; stld nr Fish Pools, East River, Pictou Co, and gr 100 acres, 1 Apr 1793. Farmer. m d/o Simon Fraser, qv, and Lydia Fraser, qv. Son Rev Alexander, min at McKillop, Huron Co, ONT. **HPC App H; NDF App p lii; CP 33**.

7461 McKENZIE, Thomas. From Dunkeld, PER. To QUE on the *Albion*, ex Greenock, 5 Jun 1829; stld Hamilton Range, Megantic Co, 1831. Stone-cutter. m Mary Burry, qv. **AMC 22**.

7462 MACKENZIE, William, b ca 1755. From Coigach, ROC. s/o Sir William M. of Ballone. To Pictou, NS, on the *Hector*, ex Loch Broom, arr 17 Sep 1773; stld later at Liverpool, Queens Co. Schoolmaster. m Kazia Peach. **HPC App C; SG iii/2 32**.

7463 McKENZIE, William. To Pictou Co, NS, ca 1774; stld Dalhousie Mountain. m Jessie McKay, qv, ch. **NSN 9/2**.

7464 McKENZIE, William. To Pictou Co, NS, <1793, and gr land on East River. Appears to have moved by 1797. **HPC App H**.

7465 McKENZIE, William, ca 1762–30 Aug 1826. From Dumfries. To NS and d there. **VSN No 1816**.

7466 McKENZIE, William. From Urquhart, INV. To Pictou, NS, on the *Sarah*, ex Fort William, Jun 1801. Farmer. Wife Flora with him, and ch: 1. Isobel, aged 5; 2. John, aged 2. **PLS**.

7467 McKENZIE, William. From Strathglass, INV. To Pictou, NS, on the *Sarah*, ex Fort William, Jun 1801. Labourer. **PLS**.

7468 McKENZIE, William, ca 1757–29 Apr 1822. From ROC. To Pictou Co, NS, 1803. Wife Nancy, 1755–9 Mar 1835. Both bur at Salt Springs. **DC 27 Oct 1979**.

7469 MACKENZIE, William, b ca 1756. To Pictou Co, NS, 1815; res Fishers Grant, 1816. Labourer, m and ch. **INS 38**.

7470 McKENZIE, William, b ca 1794. To Pictou Co, NS, 1815; res Little Harbour, 1816. Tailor, with a wife. **INS 38**.

7471 McKENZIE, William, b ca 1794. To Pictou Co, NS, 1815; res Lower Settlement, Pictou, 1816. Tailor, m and 'able to maintain himself.' **INS 38**.

7472 McKENZIE, William. To Glengarry Co, ONT, <1830. m Mary McPhail, ch. **MG 401**.

7473 McKENZIE, William, b ca 1804. Poss from Edinburgh. To NS, ex Glasgow, 1830, but went to Louth, Lincoln Co, ONT. m Jane McDonald, qv, ch: 1. John, qv; 2. Peter; 3. William; 4. Thomas; 5. David; 6. Andrew; 7. Alexander; 8. Mary, d aged 17; 9. Daniel. **DC 5 Dec 1960**.

7474 McKENZIE, William 'Voolies', 1786–1855. From Lochranza, Is Arran, BUT. To Inverness Twp, Megantic Co, QUE, 1831. m Mary McKenzie, qv, ch: 1. John, 1819-31; 2. Donald, 1822-90, unm; 3. Peter, 1824–1903, unm; 4. Margery, 1827–1914, unm. **AMC 39; MAC 37**.

7475 McKENZIE, William, 1816-94. From MOR. To Williamsburg, Stormont Co, ONT, 1834. Sawyer and reeve. **SDG 271**.

7476 McKENZIE, William. Poss from SUT. To Pictou Co, NS, <1835; stld Big Brook Lake. m Isabel McTavish, ch: 1. James, b ca 1835; 2. Anne, b ca 1836; 3. Duncan, b ca 1837; 4. Alexander, b ca 1839; 5. Duncan Finlay, b ca 1842. **PAC 114**.

7477 MACKENZIE, William, ca 1786–11 Dec 1895. From Gairloch, ROC. To Cape Breton Is, NS, <1840. **SNQ ix/1 141**.

7478 McKENZIE, William. Poss from SUT. To Pictou Co, NS, <1838; stld west branch of East River, but moved in 1849 to Glencoe, Middlesex Co, ONT. m Mary Chisholm, ch: 1. James, b 1838, res St Thomas; 2. Alexander; 3. Jessie; 4. Margaret; 5. Elizabeth; 6. Mary; 7. Daniel. **PAC 111, 113**.

7479 McKENZIE, William. From ARL. Rel to Donald M, qv. To ONT, 1840; stld West Williams Twp, Middlesex Co, 1850. **PCM 47**.

7480 MACKENZIE, William Lyon, 12 Mar 1795– 28 Aug 1861. From Springfield, Dundee, ANS. s/o Daniel M. and Elizabeth McKenzie. To Dundas, ONT, 1820; later to Queenston and Toronto. Storekeeper; editor-owner of the *Colonial Advocate*, founded 1824; MLA, 1828; Mayor of Toronto, 1835, but headed revolt against Assembly and fled to USA, 1837. Retr to CAN, 1849, and became MLA, rep Haldimand Co. m 1822, Isabel, d 1873, d/o Peter Baxter, Dundee. Dau Isabel Grace, mother of William Lyon Mackenzie King, 1874–1950, Prime Minister of Canada, 1921-26, 1926-30, 1935-48. **BNA 451; IBD 307; CBD 617; SDG 159, 334; MDB 469**.

7481 MACKENZIE, William Rattray. From ABD. To CAN <1846. **SH**.

7482 McKEOWN, Peter. Poss from Is Islay, ARL. To Eldon Twp, Victoria Co, ONT, ca 1853. m Sarah, d/o John Gillespie, qv, ch: 1. Hugh; 2. Sandy; 3. George; 4. Annie; 5. Mary; 6. John. **EC 149**.

7483 McKERCHAR, Alexander. From Breadalbane, PER. To Martintown, Charlottenburg Twp, Glengarry Co, ONT, <1816. **SMB**.

7484 McKERCHAR, Mrs Alexander. From Glenelg, INV. sis/o John Dewar, qv. To QUE on the *Liscard*, 1849; stld Glengarry Co, ONT. **MG 355**.

7485 McKERCHAR, Christine. Poss from Glenlyon, PER. To Dumfries Twp, Waterloo Co, ONT, <1845. m Andrew Thomson. **DC 15 May 1982**.

7486 McKERCHAR, William S, b 1810. From Fortingall, PER. s/o Duncan M. and Mary Stewart. To Huron Co, ONT; stld Wroxeter. **Ts Fortingall**.

7487 McKERCHER, Duncan. To QUE on the *Harmony*, 1817; stld Lot 15, Con 3, Beckwith Twp, Lanark Co, ONT. **HCL**.

7488 McKERECHER, John. To QUE on the *David of London*, ex Greenock, 19 May 1821; stld prob Lanark Co, ONT. **HCL 239**.

7489 MACKERRAS, Rev John Hugh, 1832–9 Jan 1880. From Nairn. s/o John M, schoolmaster. To Williamstown, Glengarry Co, ONT. Grad BA, 1850, and MA, 1852, Queens Coll, Kingston. Ord min of Bowmanville, 1853. Became Prof of Classical Literature at Queens Coll, 1866. **BNA 833; FES vii 643; MDB 470**.

7490 MACKERY, Archibald. From Kilmorack, INV. To Pictou, NS, on the *Dove*, ex Fort William, Jun 1801. Farmer. **PLD**.

7491 MACKERY, Barbara. From Kilmorack, INV. To Pictou, NS, on the *Dove*, ex Fort William, Jun 1801. Spinster. **PLD**.

7492 MACKERY, Isobel. From Kilmorack, INV. To Pictou, NS, on the *Dove*, ex Fort William, 1801. Spinster. **PLD**.

7493 MACKEY, Jane, 1744–1841. From DFS or KKD. To PEI on the *Lovely Nellie*, ex IOM, May 1775; moved in 1776 to Pictou Co, NS. Wife of Thomas Turnbull, qv. **DC 7 Mar 1982**.

7494 McKICHAN, Angus. From Is North Uist, INV. To West Williams Twp, Middlesex Co, ONT, ca 1848; stld Con 10. Clerk of twp, 1860. **PCM 48**.

7495 McKICHAN, Rev Dugald, ca 1801–5 Dec 1858. From Ardchattan, ARL. s/o Finlay M, merchant, and

Catherine Thomson. Matric Univ of Glasgow, 1815, and studied theology. To Arichat, NS, on the brig *Thetis*, ex Greenock, 28 Apr 1829. Adm Presb min of Barneys River, Pictou Co, 1829, and trans to River Inhabitants, Cape Breton, 1831. Retr to Barneys River, 1840. Went back to SCT, 1845, and was ind to Daviot and Dunlichity, INV. m Isabella McPhie, qv, ch: 1. Finlay Hugh, b 6 Sep 1832, who studied at St Andrews; 2. Catherine Isabella, b 30 Apr 1834; 3. Rev Alexander John, b 31 Dec 1835, min at Kinlochluichart, went to Barneys River, 1874; 4. Rev Peter Neil, b 7 Nov 1837, min at Lochgilphead, later at Inveraray; 5. James Archibald, b 23 Jul 1839; 6. Mary Dugalda, b 4 Apr 1841; 7. Isabella Christina, b 21 Mar 1843. **SAM 115; GMA 9345; FES iv 13, 19, vi 449, vii 45, 607, 616.**

7496 McKICHAN, Peter. From Oban, ARL. Neph of Rev Dugald M, qv. To Cape Breton Is, NS, <1850. ch. **DC 18 May 1982.**

7497 MACKID, Rev Thomas Alexander, ca 1804–22 May 1873. From Watten, CAI. Missionary in OKI, and educ Kings Coll, Aberdeen, where grad MA, 1842. To Colborne Twp, Huron Co, ONT, 1833. Min of St Andrews Ch, Ottawa, 1844; trans to Hamilton, 1845, and to Goderich, 1848. Ret 1866. m 1851, Julia, d 1877, d/o George Brown, shipowner, Huron Co, ch: 1. Aitcheson; 2. Jack; 3. Henry Goodsir; 4. Perceval. **KCG 295; FES vii 643; DC 5 Oct 1979.**

7498 MACKIE, David, b 1800. From Glasgow. To ONT, ca 1828. Widower. Son David, b 14 Apr 1826, with him. Retr to SCT for second wife Eliza, who went with him to CAN, 1831. **DC 31 Aug 1979.**

7499 MACKIE, Jane. From ABD. To Nichol Twp, Wellington Co, ONT, 1837. m 1855, Edmund Wollis, from LIN, ENG, ch: 1. Margaret; 2. Mary; 3. George; 4. Annie; 5. Edmund; 6. Elizabeth; 7. Sarah. **EHE 16.**

7500 MACKIE, Thomas, 1794–1 Mar 1871. Prob LKS. To Beckwith Twp, Lanark Co, ONT, 1821. m 1826, Jane Snedden, ch: 1. Mary, b 1827; 2. Thomas, b 1829; 3. James, b 1831. **DC 11 Mar 1979.**

7501 MACKIE, William. From ABD. To Nichol Twp, Wellington Co, ONT, 1835. **EHE 91.**

7502 McKIE, William, b 1744. From Cassiend, Kelton, KKD. To Georgetown, Kings Co, PEI, on the *Lovely Nellie*, ex Annan, 1774. Mason. Wife Isabell with him, ch: 1. John, aged 6; 2. Elizabeth, aged 4; 3. Mary, aged 1. **ELN.**

7503 McKILLICAN, John. From INV. To East Williams Twp, Middlesex Co, ONT, 1831. **PCM 43.**

7504 McKILLICAN, Rev William, 1802–24 Jun 1847. From BAN. Grad MA, Kings Coll, Aberdeen, 1822, and was schoolmaster at Walton. Ord min of West Gwillimbury, Simcoe Co, ONT, 1834. Trans to St Thomas, 1840. Retr to SCT, and adm min of Kildonan, SUT, 1845. m 21 May 1834, Margaret Anderson. Son William, 1839-54. **KCG 279; FES vii 91, 643.**

7505 McKILLICAN, Rev William, 1777–1849. From Breadalbane, PER. To Lochiel Twp, Glengarry Co, ONT. Min of Congregational Ch. **DGH 20 Dec 1849.**

7506 MACKILLOP, Alexander. From Lochaber, INV. To Inverness Co, NS, ca 1805; stld Mabou Ridge. m (i) Margaret MacPherson, qv, ch: 1. Duncan;

2. Hugh; 3. Ellen; 4. Margaret. m (ii) Mrs Sara MacDonell MacNeil, with further ch: 5. Alexander; 6. Donald; 7. Angus; 8. Sandy; 9. John; 10. Archibald; 11. Catherine. **MP 715.**

7507 McKILLOP, Alexander, b 1812. From Corrie, Is Arran, BUT. s/o John M. and Mary Crawford, qv. To QUE on the *Albion*, ex Greenock, 5 Jun 1829; stld Inverness, Megantic Co, QUE, and went later to Chatham, Kent Co, ONT. m Emma Gammage. **AMC 21; MAC 33.**

7508 McKILLOP, Alexander. From Urinbeg, Is Arran, BUT. s/o Mrs Catherine M, qv. To Inverness, Megantic Co, QUE, 1831. Baptist lay preacher. **AMC 38; MAC 35.**

7509 McKILLOP, Angus. From Is Arran, prob Glen Sannox, BUT. s/o Archibald M, qv, and Janet McMillan, qv. To QUE on the *Caledonia*, ex Greenock, 25 Apr 1829; stld Inverness, Megantic Co, but went later to Hamilton, ONT. m Catherine McKinnon, qv. **AMC 11, 40; MAC 29.**

7510 McKILLOP, Angus. From Urinbeg, Is Arran, BUT. s/o Mrs Catherine M, qv. To Inverness, Megantic Co, QUE, 1831. m Annie McGillvray, qv. **AMC 38; MAC 35.**

7511 McKILLOP, Ann, 1802–11 Jan 1898. From Is Arran, BUT. Prob sis/o Flora M, qv. To Megantic Co, QUE, <1840; later to ONT. Wife of Donald Blue, qv. **AMC 132.**

7512 McKILLOP, Ann, b ca 1824. From Laggan, Is Arran, BUT. d/o Neil M, qv, and Mary McKelvie, qv. To QUE on the *Caledonia*, ex Greenock, 25 Apr 1824; stld Inverness Twp, Megantic Co. m Donald Nichol, qv. **AMC 11; MAC 30.**

7513 McKILLOP, Anne. From Lochaber, INV. d/o Duncan M. and — Beaton. To South West Mabou, Inverness Co, NS, 1805. Wife of John 'Donn' Cameron, qv. **MP 249.**

7514 MACKILLOP, Anne. From Lochaber, INV. d/o Duncan M. To Inverness Co, NS, <1854. wid/o of Duncan Campbell. ch: 1. Angus, qv; 2. John, qv; 3. Donald, qv; 4. Duncan; 5. Mary, qv; 6. Allan. **MP 330.**

7515 McKILLOP, Archibald, 17 Aug 1782–18 Jun 1867. From Glen Sannox, Is Arran, BUT. To QUE on the *Caledonia*, ex Greenock, 25 Apr 1829; stld Inverness, Megantic Co. Emigrant leader, officer of militia and magistrate. m Flora McKillop, qv, ch: 1. Flora, dy; 2. Mary; 3. Catherine, 1817-43, teacher; 4. Margery, qv; 5. Malcolm, qv; 6. Jane, d 1820; 7. Jane; 8. Donald Alexander, d 1831; 9. Archibald. **AMC 11; MAC 29.**

7516 McKILLOP, Archibald. From Is Arran, prob Glen Sannox, BUT. To QUE on the *Caledonia*, ex Greenock, 25 Apr 1829; stld Inverness, Megantic Co. m Janet McMillan, qv, ch: 1. Donald 'Valdie', qv; 2. Mary, qv; 3. Malcolm, d ca 1835; 4. Angus, qv; 5. Archibald. **AMC 11; MAC 29.**

7517 McKILLOP, Archibald, 1821–15 Sep 1899. From Is Arran, prob Glen Sannox, BUT. s/o Donald M, qv, and Catherine Kelso, qv. To QUE on the *Caledonia*, ex Greenock, 25 Apr 1829; stld Inverness, Megantic Co. Farmer. m 1848, Margery McKelvie, ch: 1. Catherine; 2. Margaret; 3. Mary; 4. Elizabeth; 5. Donald; 6. Flora; 7. John; 8. Archibald. **AMC 10, 21; MAC 29.**

7518 McKILLOP, Archibald, 1824–1904. From Lochranza, Is Arran, BUT. s/o Archibald M, qv, and Flora

McKillop, qv. To QUE on the *Caledonia*, ex Greenock, 25 Apr 1829; stld Inverness, Megantic Co. Went later to Maxville, Dundas Co, ONT. Poet, linguist and inventor. Unm. **AMC 11, 145; MAC 30**.

7519 McKILLOP, Archibald. From Urinbeg, Kilmory par, Is Arran, BUT. s/o Mrs Catherine M, qv. To Inverness Twp, Megantic Co, QUE, 1831. Schoolteacher, Inverness, 1833-35. m Isabella Bannerman.   **AMC 38; MAC 35**.

7520 McKILLOP, Catherine, b ca 1804. From Corrie, Is Arran, BUT. d/o John M. and Mary Crawford, qv. To QUE on the *Albion*, ex Greenock, 5 Jun 1829; stld Inverness, Megantic Co. m Sinclair Goudie, qv. **AMC 21; MAC 33**.

7521 McKILLOP, Catherine, b 1814. From Laggan, Is Arran, BUT. d/o Neil M, qv, and Mary McKelvie, qv. To QUE on the *Caledonia*, ex Greenock, 25 Apr 1829; stld Inverness, Megantic Co. m Robert Stewart, Proton, Grey Co, ONT. **AMC 11; MAC 30**.

7522 McKILLOP, Mrs Catherine. From Urinbeg, Kilmory par, Is Arran, BUT. To Inverness, Megantic Co, QUE, 1831, with 4 sons: 1. Angus, qv; 2. Archibald, qv; 3. Alexander, qv; 4. Donald, qv. **AMC 38; MAC 35**.

7523 MACKILLOP, Donald. From ARL. To QUE, prob on the *Mars*, ex Tobermory, 28 Jul 1818; stld Aldborough Twp, Elgin Co, ONT. Farmer. Wife Catherine, 1760-1820, with him. **PDA 41, 44**.

7524 McKILLOP, Donald, 1775-1847. From Is Arran, prob Glen Sannox, Is Arran, BUT. To QUE on the *Caledonia*, ex Greenock, 25 Apr 1829; stld Inverness Twp, Megantic Co. m Catherine Kelso, qv, ch: 1. Mary, qv; 2. James, qv; 3. Margery, qv; 4. Catherine, b ca 1810; 5. Malcolm, qv; 6. Flora, b 1820; 7. Archibald, qv. **AMC 10; MAC 29**.

7525 McKILLOP, Donald, b ca 1800. From Corrie, Is Arran, BUT. s/o John M. and Mary Crawford, qv. To QUE on the *Albion*, ex Greenock, 5 Jun 1829; stld Inverness Twp, Megantic Co. m Ann Hamilton, ch: 1. John, teacher; 2. Mrs Treusdell; 3. Rev Peter, Baptist min; 4. Rev Donald, Baptist min, b 1846. **AMC 21, 57; MAC 33**.

7526 McKILLOP, Donald. From Urinbeg, Kilmory par, Is Arran, BUT. s/o Mrs Catherine M, qv. To Inverness, Megantic Co, QUE, 1831. m Mysie McKelvie, qv. **AMC 38; MAC 35**.

7527 McKILLOP, Donald 'Valdie', b 1808. From Is Arran, prob Glen Sannox, BUT. s/o Archibald M, qv, and Janet McMillan, qv. To QUE on the *Caledonia*, ex Greenock, 25 Apr 1829; stld Inverness, Megantic Co, and d SD. m (i) Flora McEachern; (ii) Ann McMillan, qv. ch: 1. Catherine; 2. Mary. **AMC 11; MAC 29**.

7528 McKILLOP, Donald, ca 1813-6 Jun 1895. From Is Arran, BUT. s/o Neil M, qv, and Mary McKelvie, qv. To QUE on the *Caledonia*, ex Greenock, 25 Apr 1829. Farmer. m Margery McKillop, qv, ch: 1. Neil; 2. Archibald; 3. Donald; 4. Catherine E; 5. Dugald McKenzie, historian of Megantic Co; 6. William Anderson; 7. John A; 8. Margery; 9. Malcolm A. **AMC 11, 73, 146; MAC 30**.

7529 McKILLOP, Duncan. From ARL. To QUE on the *Mars*, ex Tobermory, 28 Jul 1818; stld Aldborough Twp,

Elgin Co, ONT. Farmer and miller. ch: 1. John; 2. Archibald, lumberman; 3. Daniel, farmer. **PDA 24, 50, 93**.

7530 McKILLOP, Elizabeth, 1829-1915. From Is Arran, BUT. d/o John M, qv, and Mary McKenzie, qv. To QUE on the *George Canning*, 1830; stld Inverness Twp, Megantic Co. m William Mowat, qv. **AMC 38; MAC 35**.

7531 McKILLOP, Flora, ca 1791–16 Mar 1861. From Lochranza, Is Arran, BUT. To QUE on the *Caledonia*, ex Greenock, 25 Apr 1829; stld Inverness Twp, Megantic Co. Wife of Archibald McKillop, qv. **AMC 11; MAC 29**.

7532 McKILLOP, Isabella, 1805-87. From Glen Sannox, Is Arran, BUT. To QUE on the *Caledonia*, ex Greenock, 25 Apr 1829; stld Inverness Twp, Megantic Co. m 9 Mar 1825, Dugald McKenzie, qv. **AMC 12; MAC 33**.

7533 McKILLOP, James, b 5 Aug 1805. From Is Arran, prob Glen Sannox, BUT. s/o Donald M, qv, and Catherine Kelso, qv. To QUE on the *Caledonia*, ex Greenock, 25 Apr 1829; stld Inverness Twp, Megantic Co. m 4 Sep 1838, Catherine Kelso, qv, ch: 1. Mary E; 2. Donald; 3. Margaret; 4. James; 5. Robert; 6. Alexander; 7. Catherine; 8. Malcolm; 9. John. **AMC 10, 144; MAC 29**.

7534 McKILLOP, John, 1783–1859. From Corrie, Is Arran, BUT. To QUE on the *George Canning*, 1830; stld Inverness Twp, Megantic Co. m Mary McKenzie, qv, ch: 1. Mary, b 1824; 2. Kate, b 1825; 3. Alexander, b 1827, schoolteacher; 4. Elizabeth, qv; 5. John, b 1833. **AMC 38; MAC 35**.

7535 McKILLOP, John, 1802–28 Oct 1878. From Laggan, Is Arran, BUT. s/o Neil M, qv, and Mary McKelvie, qv. To QUE on the *Caledonia*, ex Greenock, 25 Apr 1829; stld Inverness Twp, Megantic Co. m Catherine McKinnon, qv, ch: 1. Mary; 2. Catherine; 3. Isabella; 4. Neil 'Yock.' **AMC 38; MAC 35**.

7536 MACKILLOP, John. From ARL. To Aldborough Twp, Elgin Co, ONT, 1846. Local politician. Son James B, attorney. **PDA 67**.

7537 McKILLOP, Malcolm, 1812–1905. From Corrie, Is Arran, BUT. s/o John M. and Mary Crawford, qv. To QUE on the *Albion*, ex Greenock, 5 Jun 1829; stld Inverness, Megantic Co, QUE. m Ellen Martin. **AMC 21; MAC 33**.

7538 McKILLOP, Malcolm, b ca 1813. From Is Arran, prob Glen Sannox, BUT. s/o Donald M, qv, and Catherine Kelso, qv. To QUE on the *Caledonia*, ex Greenock, 25 Apr 1829; stld Inverness Twp, Megantic Co. m Catherine Cook, qv. **AMC 10; MAC 29**.

7539 McKILLOP, Malcolm, ca 1823–28 Dec 1857. From Lochranza, Is Arran, BUT. s/o Archibald M, qv, and Flora McKillop, qv. To QUE on the *Caledonia*, ex Greenock, 25 Apr 1829; stld Inverness Twp, Megantic Co. Divinity student. m Ann Kelso, qv, ch: 1. Flora Ann, b 14 Mar 1850; 2. Catherine Elizabeth. **AMC 11; MAC 33**.

7540 McKILLOP, Margery, b ca 1808. From Is Arran, prob Glen Sannox, BUT. d/o Donald M, qv, and Catherine Kelso, qv. To QUE on the *Caledonia*, ex Greenock, 25 Apr 1829; stld Inverness Twp, Megantic Co. m Alexander Kerr, qv. **AMC 10; MAC 29**.

7541 McKILLOP, Margery, 26 Feb 1815–13 Feb 1900.

From Lochranza, Is Arran, BUT. d/o Archibald M, qv,
and Flora McKillop, qv. To QUE on the *Caledonia*, ex
Greenock, 25 Apr 1829; stld Inverness, Megantic Co. m
27 Mar 1839, Donald McKillop, qv.   **AMC 11, 146;
MAC 29**.

7542   McKILLOP, Mary, b ca 1808. From Corrie, Is
Arran, BUT. d/o John M. and Mary Crawford, qv. To
QUE on the *Albion*, ex Greenock, 5 Jun 1829; stld
Inverness Twp, Megantic Co. m Allan McLean.
AMC 21; MAC 33.

7543   McKILLOP, Mary, 1791–1860. From Mid Sannox,
Is Arran, BUT. To QUE on the *Caledonia*, ex Greenock,
25 Apr 1829; stld Inverness, Megantic Co. Wife of
William Kelso, qv.   **AMC 11; MAC 31**.

7544   McKILLOP, Mary, 1801-80. From Laggan, Is
Arran, BUT. d/o Neil M, qv, and Mary McKelvie, qv. To
QUE on the *Caledonia*, ex Greenock, 25 Apr 1829; stld
Inverness, Megantic Co. m Archibald McLean, qv.
AMC 11; MAC 30.

7545   McKILLOP, Mary, 1803-82. From Is Arran, prob
Glen Sannox, BUT. d/o Donald M, qv, and Catherine
Kelso, qv. To QUE on the *Caledonia*, ex Greenock,
25 Apr 1829; stld Inverness Twp, Megantic Co.
m 1830, John Cook.   **AMC 10; MAC 29**.

7546   McKILLOP, Mary, b ca 1806. From Is Arran,
prob Glen Sannox, BUT. d/o Archibald M, qv, and Janet
McMillan, qv. To QUE on the *Caledonia*, ex Greenock,
25 Apr 1829; stld Inverness Twp, Megantic Co.
m H. Thurber, and d MO.   **AMC 11; MAC 29**.

7547   McKILLOP, Mary. From Lochranza, Is Arran,
BUT. To Inverness Twp, Megantic Co, QUE, 1831. Wife of
Dugald Campbell, qv.   **AMC 40; MAC 35**.

7548   McKILLOP, Mary. Prob from Berneray, off Harris,
INV. To Mira River, Cape Breton Co, NS, ca 1828.
m ca 1809, Norman MacNeil, qv.   **DC 7 Oct 1964**.

7549   McKILLOP, Neil, 1767–1858. From Laggan, Is
Arran, BUT. To QUE on the *Caledonia*, ex Greenock,
25 Apr 1829; stld Inverness Twp, Megantic Co.
m Mary McKelvie, qv, ch: 1. Mary; 2. John, qv;
3. Neil, jr, qv; 4. Donald, qv; 5. Catherine, qv;
6. Isabella; 7. Ann, qv.   **AMC 11; MAC 30**.

7550   McKILLOP, Neil, jr, 1808–28 Jan 1873. From
Laggan, Is Arran, BUT. s/o Neil M, qv, and Mary
McKelvie, qv. To QUE on the *Caledonia*, ex Greenock,
5 Apr 1829; stld Inverness Twp, Megantic Co.
m Sarah McKinnon, qv, ch: 1. James, 1839-68;
2. Mary L, 1841-87; 3. Catherine, 1843-86;
4. Neil N; 5. Sarah; 6. John, 1848-76; 7. Alexander,
1850-61; 8. Donald W, 1854-80.   **AMC 11, 146; MAC 30**.

7551   McKILLOP, Peter, 1796–7 Feb 1864. From Corrie,
Is Arran, BUT. s/o John M. and Mary Crawford, qv. To
QUE on the *Albion*, ex Greenock, 5 Jun 1829; stld
Inverness, Megantic Co. m Margaret Currie, qv. Dau
Margery.   **AMC 21; MAC 33**.

7552   MACKINLAY, Donald. Prob from ARL, and poss
rel to Duncan M, qv, and Peter M, qv. To Aldborough
Twp, Elgin Co, ONT, <1820. Farmer.   **PDA 93**.

7553   MACKINLAY, Duncan. Prob from ARL, and poss
rel to Donald M, qv, and Peter M, qv. To Aldborough
Twp, Elgin Co, ONT, <1820. Farmer.   **PDA 93**.

7554   McKINLAY, Ellen, ca 1784–18 Aug 1869. From

Lochaber, INV. d/o James M, farmer, and Eleanor
Cameron. To Glengarry Co, ONT, 1829. m James
McMillan, qv, fur-trader.   **MCM 1/4 14**.

7555   McKINLAY, Ewen, ca 1796–16 Mar 1845. From
ARL. To Aldborough Twp, Elgin Co, ONT, poss 1818.
PDA 41.

7556   MACKINLAY, James. From ARL. To Aldborough
Twp, Elgin Co, ONT, <1820. Wife Mary with him. Son
John, dy.   **PDA 41, 93**.

7557   MACKINLAY, Peter. Prob from ARL, and poss rel
to Donald M, qv, and Duncan M, qv. To Aldborough
Twp, Elgin Co, ONT, <1820. Farmer.   **PDA 93**.

7558   MACKINLAY, William. From Tranent, ELN.
s/o Matthew M, collier. To ONT. Heir to his father,
1859.   **SH**.

7559   McKINNEE, Gilbert, ca 1752–6 Feb 1821. From
Galloway. To Carleton, Shelburne Co, NS. Prob
discharged soldier. Son William, lost with the ship
Countess of Dalhousie.   **NSS No 2221**.

7560   McKINNON, Alexander. Served in the 82nd Regt,
and was gr land in Pictou Co, NS, 1784.   **HPC App F**.

7561   McKINNON, Alexander. From Arisaig, INV. To PEI
on the *Jane*, ex Loch nan Uamh, Arisaig, 12 Jul 1790.
PLJ.

7562   McKINNON, Alexander. From INV. Prob rel to
Duncan M, qv. To Montreal, QUE, ex Fort William, arr
Sep 1802; stld E ONT.   **MCM 1/4 24**.

7563   MACKINNON, Alexander, ca 1819–5 Mar 1887.
From Is Skye, INV. s/o Malcolm M, qv, and —
Campbell. To Charlottetown, PEI, on the *Mary Kennedy*,
ex Portree, arr 1 Jun 1829; stld Uigg, Queens Co.
m Jessie MacDonald, ch: 1. Archibald; 2. Mary;
3. Angus; 4. Catherine; 5. Margaret; 6. Anne.
SPI 127.

7564   McKINNON, Alexander, b 1800. From Is Rum,
ARL. To Gut of Canso, Cape Breton, NS, on the *Saint
Lawrence*, ex Tobermory, 11 Jul 1828.   **SLL**.

7565   McKINNON, Alexander, called 'Sandy', 1804-86.
From Corriecrevie, Is Arran, BUT. s/o James M, qv, and
Catherine McKinnon, qv. To Inverness Twp, Megantic Co,
QUE, 1832. m (i) Bell Ross; (ii) Jane McGillvray, qv.
AMC 40; MAC 40.

7566   MACKINNON, Alexander, b ca 1773. From
Snizort par, Is Skye, INV. s/o Charles 'Og' M. and Mary
Gillis. To PEI <1840.   **MP ii 526**.

7567   MACKINNON, Alexander. From Is Mull, ARL.
bro/o Lachlan M, qv, and Allan M, qv, and Flora M, qv.
To Finch Twp, Stormont Co, ONT, ca 1843.   **DC 15 Aug
1979**.

7568   McKINNON, Allan, b ca 1784. From Mull, ARL.
bro/o Donald M, qv. To Charlottetown, PEI, on the
Clarendon, ex Oban, 6 Aug 1808.   **CPL**.

7569   MACKINNON, Allan 'Ban', 1786–1856. From Is
Muck, INV. s/o Neil M. To East Lake Ainslie, Inverness
Co, NS, 1820. Sea captain. m Mary MacLean, qv, ch:
1. Neil, 1817-22; 2. John, 1819-22; 3. Charles, b East
Lake, went to Bruce Co, ONT; 4. Christina; 5. Peggy;
6. Neil 'Og'; 7. Lachlan; 8. Mary; 9. Flora;
10. Breadalbane; 11. Anne.   **DC 23 Feb 1980**.

7570 McKINNON, Allan, b 1810. From Is Rum, ARL. Prob rel to Catherine M, qv. To Gut of Canso, Cape Breton, NS, on the *Saint Lawrence*, ex Tobermory, 11 Jul 1828. **SLL**.

7571 MACKINNON, Allan. From Is Mull, ARL. bro/o Alexander M, qv, Flora M, qv, and Lachlan M, qv. To Finch Twp, Stormont Co, ONT, 1843. **DC 15 Aug 1979**.

7572 McKINNON, Angus, b ca 1799. Prob bro/o Hector M, qv. To Inverness, Inverness Co, NS, 1806, and became farmer. **CBC 1818**.

7573 MACKINNON, Ann. From Is Eigg, INV. d/o Neil M, qv, and Mary Campbell. To NS <1797. m John, s/o Angus Macpherson. **HCA 318**.

7574 McKINNON, Ann, b 1816. From Is Rum, ARL. Prob rel of Catherine M, qv. To Gut of Canso, Cape Breton, NS, on the *Saint Lawrence*, ex Tobermory, 11 Jul 1828. **SLL**.

7575 McKINNON, Ann, ca 1822-94. From Snizort, Is Skye, INV. d/o Peter M, qv, and Christina McIntosh, qv. To Kinloss Twp, Bruce Co, ONT, 1852. m John McDonald, qv. **DC 6 Mar and 12 Apr 1979**.

7576 MACKINNON, Anne. From Snizort par, Is Skye, INV. d/o Lachlan M, qv, and Anne MacDonald, qv. To PEI <1840. m Angus MacPherson, qv. **MP ii 529**.

7577 MACKINNON, Archibald, b ca 1775. From Torinbeg, Kilfinichen, Is Mull, ARL. To Hudson Bay and Red River <1815. Wife Marion McLean, qv, with him, and ch: 1. John, aged 14; 2. Hector, aged 12; 3. Duncan, aged 10; 4. Effie, aged 6. **RRS 24**.

7578 McKINNON, Archibald, b ca 1795. From Is Mull, ARL. To Charlottetown, PEI, on the *Clarendon*, ex Oban, 6 Aug 1808. Labourer. Mother Margaret, aged 40, with him, and sist Mary, aged 10. **CPL**.

7579 MacKINNON, Archibald, 1784–1873. From Is Muck, INV. s/o Neil M, desc from the family of Strath, Is Skye. To East Lake Ainslie, Inverness Co, NS, 1820. Unm. **DC 23 Feb 1980**.

7580 MACKINNON, Archibald, b 1816. From Is Mull, ARL. s/o Neil M. and — McLean. To Charlottetown, PEI, on the *Amity*, ex Tobermory, 1833. Tailor. **DC 26 Dec 1964**.

7581 McKINNON, Archibald, b 1800. From Is Rum, ARL. To Gut of Canso, Cape Breton, NS, on the *Saint Lawrence*, ex Tobermory, 11 Jul 1828. Wife Mary, aged 26 with him, ch: 1. Ann, aged 5; 2. John, aged 3; 3. Flora, inf. **SLL**.

7582 MACKINNON, Archibald, 1816-98. From ARL. To Caledon Twp, Peel Co, ONT, <1840. Wife Mary McArthur, qv, with him. **DC 21 Apr 1980**.

7583 McKINNON, Catherine, b ca 1770. From Is Eigg, INV. d/o John M. and Catherine McDonald. To Antigonish Co, NS, 1789, but went to Glengarry Co, ONT. Wife of Donald 'Ban' McDougald, qv. **DC 29 Feb 1980**.

7584 McKINNON, Catherine, b ca 1788. From Is Mull, ARL. sis/o Donald M, qv, and Allan M, qv. To Charlottetown, PEI, on the *Clarendon*, ex Oban, 6 Aug 1808. **CPL**.

7585 McKINNON, Mrs Catherine, b 1778. From Is Rum, ARL. Perhaps d/o Marion McMillan, qv. To Gut of Canso, Cape Breton, NS, on the *Saint Lawrence*, ex Tobermory, 11 Jul 1828. Widow, with ch. **SLL**.

7586 McKINNON, Catherine, b 1800. From Is Rum, ARL. To Gut of Canso, Cape Breton, NS, on the *Saint Lawrence*, ex Tobermory, 11 Jul 1828. **SLL**.

7587 McKINNON, Catherine, b 1812. From Is Rum, ARL. To Gut of Canso, Cape Breton, NS, on the *Saint Lawrence*, ex Tobermory, 11 Jul 1828. **SLL**.

7588 McKINNON, Catherine, b 1813. From Is Rum, ARL. To Gut of Canso, Cape Breton, NS, on the *Saint Lawrence*, ex Tobermory, 11 Jul 1828. **SLL**.

7589 McKINNON, Catherine, b 1820. Prob from Is Arran, BUT. d/o John M, qv, and Annie Robertson, qv. To Inverness Twp, Megantic Co, QUE, 1831. m Angus McKillop, qv. **AMC 40**.

7590 McKINNON, Catherine. Prob from Is Arran, BUT. d/o James M, qv, and Catherine McKinnon, qv. To QUE on the *Caledonia*, ex Greenock, 25 Apr 1829; stld Leeds Twp, Megantic Co. m 10 Oct 1835, John McKillop, qv. **AMC 40; MAC 30**.

7591 MACKINNON, Catherine, 1814-92. Prob from ARL. To Caledon Twp, Peel Co, ONT, <1840. Wife of Archibald Campbell, qv. **DC 21 Apr 1980**.

7592 McKINNON, Charles, b 1788. To Western Shore, Inverness Co, NS, 1811. Farmer, m and had ch. **CBC 1818**.

7593 MACKINNON, Charles. To PEI <1815; stld Pinette, Queens Co. Labourer. **HP 49**.

7594 MACKINNON, Charles. To Pictou Co, NS, poss <1815; stld at Balleys Brook, later Lismore, Antigonish Co. ch: 1. Donald; 2. Alexander; 3. Malcolm; 4. John. **HCA 308**.

7595 MACKINNON, Charles, b ca 1778. From Snizort par, Is Skye, INV. s/o Charles 'Og' M, and Mary Gillis. To PEI <1840. **MP ii 526**.

7596 McKINNON, Charles, 1825–1901. From Is Skye, INV. s/o Peter M, qv, and Christine McIntosh, qv. To Kinloss Twp, Bruce Co, ONT, <1852. m Ann McQueen, qv, ch: 1. Alexander, b 1859; 2. Peter, b 1862; 3. Mary, b 1864; 4. Alexander, b 1866; 5. Catherine, b 1869; 6. John, b 1871; 7. Donald, b 1873; 8. Flora, b 1873; 9. James, b 1879; 10. Christena, b 1884. **DC 12 Apr 1979**.

7597 McKINNON, Christina. From Sliddery, Is Arran, BUT. To QUE on the *Caledonia*, ex Greenock, 25 Apr 1829; stld Inverness, Megantic Co, QUE. Wife of John McKinnon, sr, qv. **AMC 11; MAC 31**.

7598 MACKINNON, Christina. From Is Mull, ARL. To Pickering Twp, York Co, ONT, 1832. Wife of Colin Beaton, qv. **DC 30 Aug 1977**.

7599 MACKINNON, Christina, b ca 1810. From Is Mull, ARL, but emig from Kirkintilloch, DNB, to Finch Twp, Stormont Co, ONT. Wife of William Stark, qv. **SDG 460; DC 15 Aug 1979**.

7600 MACKINNON, Colin. From Ballachulish, ARL. To East Hawkesbury, Prescott Co, ONT, 1840. m his cous Margaret, d/o John Cameron, qv. **SMB**.

7601   MACKINNON, Donald. From Is Eigg, INV. To Pictou, NS, 1791; stld Baileys Brook. Son John. **HCA 304**.

7602   MACKINNON, Donald. From Is Skye, INV. To PEI, poss 1803; stld Queens Co. Petitioner for Dr Macaulay, 1811. **HP 73**.

7603   McKINNON, Donald, b 1780. To Charlottetown, PEI, on the *Humphreys*, ex Tobermory, arr 14 Jul 1806. Wife Marion, aged 25, with him, ch: 1. Marion, aged 4; 2. Catherine, aged 1. **PLH**.

7604   McKINNON, Donald, b 1774. From Is Mull, ARL. To Charlottetown, PEI, on the *Clarendon*, ex Oban, 6 Aug 1808. Labourer. Wife Mary, aged 22, with him, and dau Catherine, aged 2. **CPL**.

7605   MACKINNON, Donald. From Is Muck, INV. s/o Neil M, desc from the family of Strath, Is Skye. To Pictou Co, NS, ca 1817; later to East Lake Ainslie, Inverness Co. m Christy Mackinnon, ch: 1. Christy; 2. Julia; 3. Ann, d unm; 4. Arabella, d unm; 5. Neil; 6. John, went to PEI; 7. Farquhar. **DC 23 Feb 1980**.

7606   McKINNON, Donald, b 1781. From Is Rum, ARL. To Gut of Canso, Cape Breton, NS, on the *Saint Lawrence*, ex Tobermory, 11 Jul 1828. Wife Margaret, aged 46, with him, and ch: 1. Jessie, aged 21; 2. Lachlin, aged 20; 3. Donald, aged 16; 4. John, aged 13; 5. Catherine, aged 10; 6. Angus, aged 6; 7. Peter, aged 3. **SLL**.

7607   MACKINNON, Donald. From Is Mull, ARL. To Caledon Twp, Peel Co, ONT, 1818, res there 1851. Wife Christina McQuarrie, qv, with him. **DC 21 Apr 1980**.

7608   MACKINNON, Donald, 1801-74. From Sliddery, Is Arran, BUT. s/o John M, qv, and Christina M, qv. To QUE on the *Caledonia*, ex Greenock, 25 Apr 1829; stld Inverness Twp, Megantic Co. m Mary Sillars, qv, ch: 1. John; 2. Jessie; 3. Mary; 4. Christina; 5. Peter; 6. Donald; 7. Catherine; 8. James; 9. Annie; 10. Duncan. **AMC 11; MAC 32**.

7609   McKINNON, Donald, b 1807. From Corriecrevie, Is Arran, BUT. s/o James M, qv, and Catherine McKinnon, qv. To Inverness Twp, Megantic Co, QUE, 1832. m Kate Kerr, who d QUE, 1893. **AMC 40; MAC 40**.

7610   McKINNON, Donald, 1827–1901. From Is Skye, INV. s/o Peter M, qv, and Christena McIntosh, qv. To Kinloss Twp, Bruce Co, ONT, <1852. m Isobel Murcheson, qv, ch: 1. Colin, b 1857; 2. Christy, b 1859; 3. Peter, b 1861; 4. Donald, b 1863; 5. Mary, b 1865; 6. John, b 1867. **DC 12 Apr 1979**.

7611   McKINNON, Donald, b 1834. From East Bennan, Is Arran, BUT. s/o James M. and Ann McKelvie, qv. To QUE on the *Bowly*, 1846; stld Inverness Twp, Megantic Co. m Catherine Crawford. **AMC 49; MAC 43**.

7612   McKINNON, Donald, b ca 1836. From Is Rum, ARL. s/o John M, qv, and Margaret Livingston, qv. To Kinloss Twp, Bruce Co, ONT, <1855. m Effie McKinnon, qv, ch: 1. Mary, b 1865; 2. Peter, b 1866; 3. John, b 1868; 4. Alexander, b 1870; 5. Christena, b 1872; 6. Duncan, b 1874; 7. Kenneth, b 1876. The family moved to Mooreton, ND, USA, 1883. **DC 12 Apr 1979**.

7613   MACKINNON, Donald 'Sgoilear'. From Is Canna, INV. s/o John and Ann M. To Judique, Inverness Co,

NS, <1840. m (i) Christy Campbell, North Lake Ainslie, ch: 1. Rev John; 2. Bella; 3. Margaret; 4. Ann; 5. Mary; 6. Alexina; 7. Christina. m (ii) Mary MacLean, with further ch: 8. Hector, b 1860; 9. Charles, b 1864; 10. Kate, b 1866; 11. Sarah, b 1868; 12. Margaret, b 1869. **MP ii 519**.

7614   MACKINNON, Donald 'Og'. From Is Canna, INV. s/o John and Ann M. To Judique, Inverness Co, NS, <1840. m Margaret Campbell, Ashfield, ch: 1. Malcolm, b 22 Mar 1862; 2. Angus; 3. Christy Belle, b 1871; 4. Hugh, b 1873; 5. Annie; 6. John; 7. John Dan; 8. Flora Jane, b 1882. **MP ii 524**.

7615   McKINNON, Duncan, b ca 1777. From Is Mull, ARL. To Charlottetown, PEI, on the *Clarendon*, ex Oban, 6 Aug 1808. Labourer. Wife Julia, aged 28, with him, and sisters Mary, Margaret and Catherine. **CPL**.

7616   McKINNON, Duncan. From INV. Prob rel to Alexander M, qv. To Montreal, QUE, ex Fort William, arr Sep 1802; stld E ONT. **MCM 1/4 24**.

7617   McKINNON, Duncan. From INV. To Montreal, QUE, ex Fort William, arr Sep 1802; stld E ONT. Petitioned for land on the Ottawa River, 6 Aug 1804. Wife with him, and 6 ch. **MCM 1/4 24; DC 15 Mar 1980**.

7618   McKINNON, Duncan, b 1765. From Is Rum, ARL. To Gut of Canso, Cape Breton, NS, on the *Saint Lawrence*, ex Tobermory, 11 Jul 1828. Wife Mary, aged 58, with him, and family: 1. Alexander, aged 30; 2. Ann, aged 25; 3. Lachlan, aged 34; 4. Ann, aged 20; 5. Catherine, aged 15; 6. Donald. **SLL**.

7619   McKINNON, Duncan, 1790–1859. From Kildonan, Kilmory par, Is Arran, BUT. To Benjamen River, Restigouche Co, NB, 1829. m Catherine Murphie, qv, ch: 1. John, 1816-88; 2. Jean, 1817-81; 3. Ann, 1820-93. **MAC 21**.

7620   McKINNON, Duncan, 1835-81. From Is Skye, INV. s/o Peter M, qv, and Christena McIntosh, qv. To Kinloss Twp, Bruce Co, ONT, <1852. m Merry MacDonald, from PEI, ch: 1. Catherine, b 1866; 2. Mary, b 1867; 3. John, b 1871; 4. Peter, b 1872; 5. Christena, b 1873. **DC 12 Apr 1979**.

7621   McKINNON, Duncan, b 22 Mar 1840. From Corriecrevie, Kilmory par, Is Arran, BUT. s/o William M, qv, and Elizabeth Cook, qv. To Dundee, Restigouche Co, NB, 1852; went later to Lowell, MA, USA. m Mary Malcolm. **DC 1 Oct 1979**.

7622   McKINNON, Effie, 1837–1917. From Is Skye, INV. d/o Peter M, qv, and Christena McIntosh, qv. To Kinloss Twp, Bruce Co, ONT, <1852. m Donald McKinnon, qv. **DC 12 Apr 1979**.

7623   MACKINNON, Elizabeth, b 1845. From Sliddery, Kilmory par, Is Arran, BUT. d/o William M, qv, and Elizabeth Cook, qv. To NB, ca 1852; stld Dundee, Restigouche Co. m 15 Dec 1869, John Pettigrew. **DC 1 Oct 1979**.

7624   MACKINNON, Elizabeth. From Glasgow. To Morton, Leeds Co, ONT, <1855. m John Brown Somerville. Son Charles Ross, 1851–1931, financier. **DC 30 Aug 1977**.

7625   McKINNON, Euphemia, b ca 1768. From Is Mull, ARL. To Charlottetown, PEI, on the *Clarendon*, ex Oban, 6 Aug 1808. Spinster. **CPL**.

7626 MACKINNON, Euphemia, 1793–16 Feb 1864. From Kilfinichen par, Is Mull, ARL. To Mariposa Twp, Victoria Co, ONT, 1833. Wife of Angus McLean, qv. **DC 7 Dec 1968**.

7627 MACKINNON, Ewen, 1805-45. From Snizort par, Is Skye, INV. s/o Lachlan M, qv, and Anne MacDonald, qv. To Ainslie Glen, Inverness Co, NS, 1832. m Ann Beaton, ch: 1. Euphemia, 1829–1923; 2. Ann, 1832–1924; 3. Murdoch; 4. Lachlan, d 1915; 5. Flora; 6. Malcolm. **MP ii 526**.

7628 MACKINNON, Farquhar, 1784–1853. From ARL. To Caledon Twp, Peel Co, ONT, <1840. Wife Sarah, 1793–1835, with him. **DC 21 Apr 1980**.

7629 McKINNON, Finlay, b ca 1782. From Is Mull, ARL. To Charlottetown, PEI, on the *Clarendon*, ex Oban, 6 Aug 1808. Labourer. Wife Mary, aged 23, with him, ch: 1. Allan, aged 3; 2. Euphemia, aged 2. **CPL**.

7630 MACKINNON, Flora, b ca 1770. From Kilfinichen, Is Mull, ARL. Poss widow, and mother of Neil, John and Malcolm Campbell, qv. To Hudson Bay and Red River <1815. **RRS 24**.

7631 MACKINNON, Flora. From Is Mull, ARL. sis/o Alexander M, qv, Allan M, qv, and Lachlan M, qv. To Finch Twp, Stormont Co, ONT, ca 1843. m Donald McLean. **DC 15 Aug 1979**.

7632 McKINNON, Flora, b 1788. From Is Rum, ARL. To Gut of Canso, Cape Breton, NS, on the *Saint Lawrence*, ex Tobermory, 11 Jul 1828. **SLL**.

7633 McKINNON, Flora, b 1798. From Is Rum, ARL. To Gut of Canso, Cape Breton, NS, on the *Saint Lawrence*, ex Tobermory, 11 Jul 1828. **SLL**.

7634 McKINNON, Flora, b 1810. From Is Rum, ARL. To Gut of Canso, Cape Breton, NS, on the *Saint Lawrence*, ex Tobermory, 11 Jul 1828. **SLL**.

7635 McKINNON, Florence. From Knoydart, INV. To QUE, summer 1815; stld prob Lanark Co, ONT. Wife of John McDonald, qv. **SEC 7**.

7636 McKINNON, Hector, b ca 1803. Prob bro/o Angus M, qv. To Inverness, Inverness Co, NS, 1806, and became farmer. **CBC 1818**.

7637 McKINNON, Hector, b ca 1787. From Is Mull, ARL. To Charlottetown, PEI, on the *Clarendon*, ex Oban, 6 Aug 1808. Labourer. **CPL**.

7638 McKINNON, Hugh, b ca 1755. To Charlottetown, PEI, on the *Humphreys*, 14 Jul 1806. Wife Catherine, aged 45, with him, ch: 1. Mary, aged 20; 2. Neil, aged 19; 3. John, aged 14; 4. Malcolm, aged 12; 5. Catherine, aged 10; 6. Angus, aged 8; 7. Elizabeth, aged 6; 8. Roderick, aged 2. **PLH**.

7639 McKINNON, Hugh, b ca 1758. To Little Bras D'Or, Cape Breton Co, NS, <1815. Farmer. Son Alexander, b ca 1790. **CBC 1818**.

7640 MACKINNON, Hugh, 1790–1849. From Totamore, Is Coll, ARL. s/o Charles M. and Julia MacFadyen. To Pictou Co, NS, 1848. Sometime tenant in Totronald. m Catherine MacDonald, qv, ch: 1. Neil, b 1830, mate of the Allan Line ship *Moravia*; 2. Mary; 3. Ann; 4. Charles; 5. Julia; 6. Hector; 7. Catherine; 8. Flora, b NS. **DC 16 Mar 1981**.

7641 McKINNON, Isabel, b 28 Jan 1795. From Baladhuill, Is Tyree, ARL. d/o Hugh M. and Mary McLean. To QUE on the *Conrad*, ex Greenock, 18 Jun 1850; stld West Gwillimbury Twp, Simcoe Co, ONT. Wife of Alexander Kennedy, qv, whom she m 26 Dec 1815. **DC 30 Sep 1980**.

7642 McKINNON, Isobel, 1830–1925. From Is Skye, INV. d/o Peter M, qv, and Christena McIntosh, qv. To Kinloss Twp, Bruce Co, ONT, <1852. m (i) Charles Campbell; (ii) John McDougall, and had ch by both. The family moved to Mooreton, ND, USA, ca 1883. **DC 12 Apr 1979**.

7643 McKINNON, James, b ca 1784. From Kintyre, ARL. To Restigouche Co, NB, ca 1817. Petitioned for 150 acres–Lot 75–on the south side of the Restigouche River, 9 Feb 1821. **DC 31 May 1980**.

7644 McKINNON, James, 1800–21 Jul 1886. From Sliddery, Is Arran, BUT. s/o John M, qv, and Christina McKinnon, qv. To QUE on the *Caledonia*, ex Greenock, 25 Apr 1829; stld Inverness, Megantic Co. Schoolmaster, farmer and piper. m Janet Kelso, qv. Dau Christina. **AMC 11; MAC 31**.

7645 McKINNON, James. From Corriecrevie, Kilmory par, Is Arran, BUT. To Inverness Twp, Megantic Co, QUE, 1832. m Catherine McKinnon, qv, ch: 1. Alexander, qv; 2. Catherine, b 1802; 3. Donald, qv; 4. Sarah, b 1810; 5. William, b Sliddery, 1812. **AMC 40; MAC 40**.

7646 MACKINNON, James, 1824-87. From ARL. To Caledon Twp, Peel Co, ONT, <1840. **DC 21 Apr 1980**.

7647 MACKINNON, Jessie. From Is Mull, ARL. To Charlottetown, PEI, on the *Dykes*, arr 9 Aug 1803; stld Point Prim, Queens Co. Wife of Findlay MacDonald, qv. **HP 35**.

7648 McKINNON, Jessie, b 1802. From Is Rum, ARL. To Gut of Canso, Cape Breton, NS, on the *Saint Lawrence*, ex Tobermory, 11 Jul 1828. **SLL**.

7649 McKINNON, John. From Cleadale, Is Eigg, INV. To QUE on the *British Queen*, ex Arisaig, 16 Aug 1790; stld nr Montreal. Tenant farmer. **QCC 103**.

7650 MACKINNON, John. From Is Eigg, INV. To Pictou, NS, 1791; stld Parrsborough, Cumberland Co, later Williams Point, Antigonish Co. m Eunice MacLeod, qv, ch: 1. Neil; 2. Ewen; 3. Rev Colin Francis, 1810-79, Bishop of Arichat; 4. John; 5. Lachlan; 6. Eunice; 7. Catherine; 8. Mary; 9. Hugh. **HCA 57, 304**.

7651 MACKINNON, John, b 1794. To Inverness Co, NS, 1802; stld Western Shore. Farmer. **CBC 1818**.

7652 MACKINNON, John, b 1797. To Margaree dist, Inverness Co, NS, 1810. Farmer, m and had ch. **CBC 1818**.

7653 McKINNON, John, b 1776. To Inverness Co, NS, 1811. Farmer, m and had ch. **CBC 1818**.

7654 McKINNON, John, b 1804. From Is Rum, ARL. To Gut of Canso, Cape Breton, NS, on the *Saint Lawrence*, ex Tobermory, 11 Jul 1828. **SLL**.

7655 McKINNON, John, b 1780. From Is Rum, ARL. To Gut of Canso, Cape Breton, NS, on the *Saint Lawrence*, ex Tobermory, 11 Jul 1828. Wife Ann, aged 45, with him, ch: 1. Bell, aged 20; 2. Donald, aged 18;

3. Mary, aged 15; 4. Neil, aged 12; 5. John, aged 6;
6. Donald 'Og', aged 3. **SLL**.

7656 McKINNON, John. From Sliddery, Kilmory par, Is
Arran, BUT. To QUE on the *Caledonia*, ex Greenock,
25 Apr 1829; stld Inverness Twp, Megantic Co.
m Christina McKinnon, qv, ch: 1. Mary, b 1797;
2. James, qv; 3. Donald, qv; 4. John, jr, qv. **AMC 11;
MAC 31**.

7657 McKINNON, John, jr, 1 May 1803–31 Oct 1893.
From Sliddery, Kilmory par, Is Arran, BUT. s/o John M,
qv, and Christina McKinnon, qv. To QUE on the
Caledonia, ex Greenock, 25 Apr 1829; stld Inverness
Twp, Megantic Co. m Margaret Sillars, qv, ch: 1. Mary;
2. John; 3. Peter; 4. Janet; 5. Christina; 6. Margaret;
7. James; 8. Alexander; 9. Elizabeth; 10. Donald;
11. Catherine; 12. Flora. **AMC 11, 146; MAC 32**.

7658 McKINNON, John 'Somerset'. From Corriecrevie,
Kilmory par, Is Arran, BUT. To Inverness Twp, Megantic
Co, QUE, 1831. m Annie Robertson, qv, ch: 1. Donald,
b Sliddery, 1811; 2. Janet, b 1813, deaf-mute; 3. Mary,
b 1815, deaf-mute; 4. Neil, 1818-79; 5. Catherine,
b 1820; 6. John, jr, qv; 7. Elizabeth, b 1823. **AMC 40;
MAC 38**.

7659 McKINNON, John, jr, b ca 1821. From Sliddery,
Is Arran, BUT. s/o John 'Somerset' M, qv, and Annie
Robertson, qv. To Inverness Corners, Megantic Co,
QUE, 1831. Merchant. m Jane Campbell, qv. **AMC 40;
MAC 35**.

7660 MACKINNON, John, 1821-82. From ARL. To
Caledon Twp, Peel Co, ONT, <1840. **DC 21 Apr 1980**.

7661 MACKINNON, John, b 1821. From Is Canna, INV.
s/o John and Ann M. To Judique, Inverness Co, NS,
<1840. m Mary MacLeod, Orangedale, ch: 1. Ann,
b 1851; 2. Christy Ann, 1852-73; 3. Sarah, b 1855;
4. Flora, 1860-79; 5. Margaret, b 1859; 6. John J,
b 1860. **MP ii 520**.

7662 MACKINNON, John. From Annabast, Is Coll,
ARL. To QUE, ex Liverpool, 7 Jul 1847; stld Mara Twp,
Lake Simcoe, and d Uptergrove. Grasskeeper.
m Margaret Mackenzie, ch: 1. Margaret, b 1840;
2. Janet, b 1841; 3-4. Catherine and Flora, b 1842;
5. Lachlan John, 1846–1919. **DC 25 Apr 1983**.

7663 McKINNON, John, b 1803. From Sliddery,
Kilmory par, Is Arran, BUT. To Inverness Twp, Megantic
Co, QUE, prob <1840. **MAC 21**.

7664 McKINNON, John, 1832–1900. From East
Bennan, Is Arran, BUT. s/o James M. and Ann McKelvie,
qv. To QUE on the *Bowly*, 1846; stld Inverness Twp,
Megantic Co. m Isabella McKillop. **AMC 49; MAC 43**.

7665 McKINNON, John, 1829–1917. From Is Skye,
INV. s/o Peter M, qv, and Christena McIntosh, qv. To
Kinloss Twp, Bruce Co, ONT, <1852. m Margaret
Stewart, qv, ch: 1. Duncan, b 1852; 2. Donald, b 1855;
3. Peter, b 1857; 4. Sarah, b 1859; 5. Marion, b 1861;
6. Catherine, b 1862; 7. John, b 1863; 8. Alexander,
b 1865; 9. Mary, b 1867; 10. Christy, b 1870;
11. Margaret, b 1873; 12. Malcolm. **DC 12 Apr 1979**.

7666 McKINNON, John. From Is Rum, ARL. To
Kinloss Twp, Bruce Co, ONT, <1855. m Margaret
Livingston, qv, ch: 1. Donald, qv; 2. John, b ca 1837;
3. Dougald, b ca 1842; 4. Alexander, b ca 1844.
DC 12 Apr 1979.

7667 McKINNON, Jonathan, b 1798. From Is Rum,
ARL. To Gut of Canso, Cape Breton, NS, on the *Saint
Lawrence*, ex Tobermory, 11 Jul 1828. **SLL**.

7668 McKINNON, Lachlan. From Cleadale, Is Eigg,
INV. s/o Ewen M. To QUE on the *British Queen*, Arisaig,
16 Aug 1790; stld Lancaster Twp, Glengarry Co, ONT.
Received patent for Lot 22, Con 12, on 27 May 1797.
Wife Catherine with him, and ch: 1. Charles; 2. William;
3. Neil, d 1854; 4. John; 5. Flora, d 1861; 6. Donald;
7. Mary; 8. Sarah, b ca 1795; 9. Catherine, d 1856;
10. Janet, d 1862; 11. Christina, b ca 1779. **QCC 103;
DC 1 Oct 1982**.

7669 McKINNON, Lachland, b ca 1761. To
Charlottetown, PEI, on the *Humphreys*, ex Tobermory,
14 Jul 1806. Wife Catherine, aged 38, with him, ch:
1. Mary, aged 8; 2. Janet, aged 6; 3. John, aged 6;
4. Roderick, aged 2; 5. Duncan, inf. **PLH**.

7670 MACKINNON, Lachlan, b ca 1790. From Is Rum,
ARL. To NS, 1811; stld Port Hastings, Inverness Co.
Farmer. m Mary Mackinnon, ch: 1. Christy; 2. Mary;
3. Isobel; 4. Flora; 5. John. **CBC 1818; WLC**.

7671 MACKINNON, Lachlan, 1775–1855. From Snizort
par, Is Skye, INV. s/o Charles 'Og' M. and Mary Gillis.
To Inverness Co, NS, 1840. m Anne MacDonald, qv, ch:
1. Malcolm, qv; 2. Ewen, qv; 3. Anne, qv. **MP ii 526**.

7672 MACKINNON, Lachlan. From Is Mull, ARL.
bro/o Alexander M, qv, Allan M, qv, and Flora M, qv. To
Finch Twp, Stormont Co, ONT, ca 1843. **DC 15 Aug
1979**.

7673 MACMILLAN, Lauchlin. Poss from Is Muck,
ARL. To Cape Breton Is, NS, prob <1820. m Catherine
Campbell, qv. Dau Catherine. **NSN 32/379**.

7674 McKINNON, Lauchlin, b 1788. From Is Rum,
ARL. To Gut of Canso, Cape Breton, NS, on the *Saint
Lawrence*, ex Tobermory, 11 Jul 1828. Wife Marion, aged
35, with him, ch: 1. Lauchlin, aged 12; 2. Catherine,
aged 10; 3. Archie, aged 8; 4. Donald, aged 6; 5. Mary,
inf. **SLL**.

7675 McKINNON, Loddy, b 1811. From Is Rum, ARL.
To Gut of Canso, Cape Breton, NS, on the *Saint
Lawrence*, ex Tobermory, 11 Jul 1828. **SLL**.

7676 McKINNON, Malcolm, b 1788. From Is Mull,
ARL. To Charlottetown, PEI, on the *Clarendon*, ex Oban,
6 Aug 1808. Mother Margaret, aged 50, with him, and
brothers: 1. Lauchlan, aged 20; 2. Hector, aged 16;
3. John, aged 14. **CPL**.

7677 McKINNON, Malcolm, b 1791. From Is Mull,
ARL. bro/o Hector M, qv. To Charlottetown, PEI, on the
Clarendon, ex Oban, 6 Aug 1808. **CPL**.

7678 McKINNON, Malcolm, b 1783. From Is Rum,
ARL. To Gut of Canso, Cape Breton, NS, on the *Saint
Lawrence*, ex Tobermory, 11 Jul 1828. Wife Bell, aged
35, with him, ch: 1. Catherine, aged 18; 2. Christina,
aged 15; 3. John, aged 13; 4. Marion, aged 10;
5. Peggy, aged 6; 6. Flora, aged 4; 7. Bell, aged 2.
SLL.

7679 MACKINNON, Malcolm, b 1776. From Snizort
par, Is Skye, INV. s/o Charles 'Og' M. and Mary Gillis.
To PEI <1840. **MP ii 526**.

7680 MACKINNON, Malcolm. From Is Skye, INV. To
Charlottetown, PEI, on the *Mary Kennedy*, arr 1 Jun

1829; stld Uigg, Queens Co. m Miss Campbell, and had, poss with other ch: 1. Alexander, qv; 2. William, qv. **SPI 127**.

7681 MACKINNON, Malcolm, 1803-77. From Snizort par, Is Skye, INV. s/o Lachlan M, qv, and Anne MacDonald, qv. To Dunakym, Mabou, Inverness Co, NS, 1840. Wife Flora MacLeod, qv, with him, ch: 1. Ann, 1828-94; 2. Angus, 1830–1917. **MP ii 526**.

7682 MACKINNON, Margaret. From Portree, Is Skye, INV. d/o Neil M. To Lake Ainslie, Inverness Co, NS, 1820. m John MacDonald, qv. **DC 23 Feb 1980**.

7683 McKINNON, Margaret, 1792–1887. From Corriecrevie, Kilmory par, Is Arran, BUT. To Dickie, Restigouche Co, NB, 1829. Wife of John Cook, qv, whom she m 21 Dec 1814. **MAC 11**.

7684 MACKINNON, Margaret. From Is Eigg, INV. Prob sis/o John M, qv. To Antigonish Co, NS, poss 1791. m John MacDonald, qv. **HCA 244**.

7685 McKINNON, Margaret, b 1768. From Is Rum, ARL. To Gut of Canso, Cape Breton, NS, on the *Saint Lawrence*, ex Tobermory, 11 Jul 1828. **SLL**.

7686 McKINNON, Margaret, b 1769. From Is Rum, ARL. To Gut of Canso, Cape Breton, NS, on the *Saint Lawrence*, ex Tobermory, 11 Jul 1828. **SLL**.

7687 McKINNON, Margaret, b 1790. From Is Rum, ARL. To Gut of Canso, Cape Breton, NS, on the *Saint Lawrence*, ex Tobermory, 11 Jul 1828. **SLL**.

7688 McKINNON, Marion. From Arisaig, INV. To PEI on the *Jane*, ex Loch nan Uamh, Arisaig, 12 Jul 1790. **PLJ**.

7689 MACKINNON, Marion. Poss from INV. To Pictou Co, NS, 1801. Wife of William Fraser, qv. **PAC 61**.

7690 McKINNON, Marion, b 1800. From Is Rum, ARL. To Gut of Canso, Cape Breton, NS, on the *Saint Lawrence*, ex Tobermory, 11 Jul 1828. Inf dau Rachel with her. **SLL**.

7691 McKINNON, Marion, b 1800. From Is Rum, ARL. To Gut of Canso, Cape Breton, NS, on the *Saint Lawrence*, ex Tobermory, 11 Jul 1828. **SLL**.

7692 McKINNON, Marion, b 1812. From Is Rum, ARL. To Gut of Canso, Cape Breton, NS, on the *Saint Lawrence*, ex Tobermory, 11 Jul 1828. **SLL**.

7693 MACKINNON, Mary, 1789–24 Mar 1875. From Is Mull, ARL. To Charlottetown, PEI, <1810. m John Stewart, qv. **DC 16 Aug 1982**.

7694 McKINNON, Mary, b 1815. From Is Rum, ARL. Prob rel to Peggy M, qv. To Gut of Canso, Cape Breton, NS, on the *Saint Lawrence*, ex Tobermory, 11 Jul 1828. **SLL**.

7695 McKINNON, Mary, b 1802. From Is Rum, ARL. To Gut of Canso, Cape Breton, NS, on the *Saint Lawrence*, ex Tobermory, 11 Jul 1828. **SLL**.

7696 MACKINNON, Mary, 20 Aug 1812–14 Apr 1874. From Is Muck, INV. To Inverness Co, NS, 1831; stld Campbells Mountain. m Murdoch Campbell, qv. **DC 29 Apr 1960**.

7697 McKINNON, Mary, 1822–1920. From Is Skye, INV. d/o Peter M, qv, and Christena McIntosh, qv. To Kinloss Twp, Bruce Co, ONT, <1852. m Angus McLeod, qv. **DC 12 Apr 1979**.

7698 McKINNON, Mary, jr, 1832–1910. From Is Skye, INV. d/o Peter M, qv, and Christena McIntosh, qv. To Kinloss Twp, Bruce Co, ONT, <1852. m 12 Feb 1854, Peter McDougall, qv. **DC 12 Apr 1979**.

7699 MACKINNON, Mary S, 1785–1884. From ARL. To Caledon Twp, Peel Co, ONT, <1840. Bur St Andrews Cemetery. **DC 21 Apr 1980**.

7700 MACKINNON, Michael. From Is Barra, INV. To Cape Breton Is, NS, <1836. Farmer. Son John, b 1836, master mariner. **HNS iii 194**.

7701 McKINNON, Neil, b ca 1799. To St Andrews dist, Cape Breton Co, NS, ca 1805, and became a farmer. **CBC 1818**.

7702 McKINNON, Neil, b 1764. To Charlottetown, PEI, on the *Humphreys*, ex Tobermory, arr 14 Jul 1806. Wife Catherine, aged 40, with him, ch: 1. Donald, aged 26; 2. Marion, aged 25; 3. Ann, aged 18. **PLH**.

7703 McKINNON, Neil, b ca 1753. From Is Mull, ARL. To Charlottetown, PEI, on the *Clarendon*, ex Oban, 6 Aug 1808. Farmer. Wife Margaret McLean, qv, with him, ch: 1. John, aged 22; 2. Catherine, aged 20; 3. Margaret, aged 10. **CPL**.

7704 MACKINNON, Neil, b ca 1790. To Margaree dist, Inverness Co, NS, 1810. Farmer, m and had ch. **CBC 1818**.

7705 MACKINNON, Neil, b ca 1785. From Torinbeg, Kilfinichen, Is Mull, ARL. To Hudson Bay and Red River <1815. Pioneer settler. Wife Christina McLean, qv, with him. **RRS 25**.

7706 MACKINNON, Neil, b ca 1785. From Glenbaire, Kilfinichen, Is Mull, ARL. To Hudson Bay and Red River, <1815. Pioneer settler. Wife Marjery McGilvra, qv, with him. **RRS 25**.

7707 MACKINNON, Neil. Poss from Is Mull, ARL. To Cape Breton Is, NS, prob <1820. m Catherine, d/o Lauchlin MacMillan, qv, and Catherine Campbell, qv. Son Neil, tailor. **NSN 32/379**.

7708 MACKINNON, Neil. From Is Mull, ARL. To Esquesing, Halton Co, ONT, <1830. Farmer. m Christy, d/o Alexander McNaughton. **SG xi/4 15**.

7709 MACKINNON, Neil, 1826-54. From ARL. To Caledon Twp, Peel Co, ONT, <1840. **DC 21 Apr 1980**.

7710 McKINNON, Neil. From Is Benbecula, INV. To West Williams Twp, Middlesex Co, ONT, ca 1849. **PCM 48**.

7711 McKINNON, Neil. From Is Mull, ARL. To PEI on the *Amity*, 1853. **DC 1 Oct 1960**.

7712 MACKINNON, Neil 'Dubh', b 1816. From Is Canna, INV. s/o John and Anna M. To Judique, Inverness Co, NS, <1840. Farmer. m Annabelle Fraser, Cape Mabou, ch: 1. John, b 1856; 2. Donald; 3. Annie; 4. Marcella. **MP ii 519**.

7713 McKINNON, Peggy, b 1808. From Is Rum, ARL. To Gut of Canso, Cape Breton, NS, on the *Saint Lawrence*, ex Tobermory, 11 Jul 1828. **SLL**.

7714 McKINNON, Peter, 1787–1867. From Is Skye, INV. To Kinloss Twp, Bruce Co, ONT, <1853. Wife

Christena McIntosh, qv, with him, ch: 1. Ann, qv;
2. Mary, qv; 3. Charles, qv; 4. Donald, qv; 5. John, qv;
6. Isobel, qv; 7. Mary, jr, qv; 8. Sarah, qv; 9. Duncan,
qv; 10. Effie, qv; 11. Kinnon; 12. Angus.   **DC 12 Apr
1979**.

7715   MACKINNON, Col Ranald. From Is Skye, INV. To
Halifax, NS, 1766. m Letitia Piggot. Son John, b 1775,
MLA, Shelburne Co.   **MLA 225**.

7716   MACKINNON, Ranald, b ca 1786. To Margaree
dist, Inverness Co, NS, 1806. Farmer, m and had ch.
CBC 1818.

7717   McKINNON, Sarah, b ca 1804. From Is Mull,
ARL. Prob rel to Hector M, qv. To Charlottetown, PEI,
on the *Clarendon*, ex Oban, 6 Aug 1808.   **CPL**.

7718   MACKINNON, Sarah. From South Uist, INV. To
Kings Co, PEI, <1818. Wife of Angus McIntyre, qv.
BNA 894.

7719   McKINNON, Sarah, 1811–27 Jun 1880. Prob from
Is Arran, BUT. d/o James M, qv, and Catherine
McKinnon, qv. To QUE on the *Caledonia*, ex Greenock,
25 Apr 1829; stld Inverness, Megantic Co. m Neil
McKillop, jr, qv.   **AMC 40, 146; MAC 30**.

7720   McKINNON, Sarah, b 1833. From Is Skye, INV.
d/o Peter M, qv, and Christena McKinnon, qv. To Kinloss
Twp, Bruce Co, ONT, <1852. m, as his second wife,
James McQueen, qv.   **DC 12 Apr 1979**.

7721   MACKINNON, William. From Is Skye, INV.
s/o Malcolm M, qv, and — Campbell. To Charlottetown,
PEI, on the *Mary Kennedy*, ex Portree, arr 1 Jun 1829;
stld Uigg, Queens Co. m Katherine, sis/o Angus
Nicholson, ch: 1. Donald, 1863–1928, KC, MP, Lt Gov of
PEI; 2. Bella; 3. Margaret; 4. Charles, 1858–1911; 5. Dr
Artemus, stld Omaha, NE, USA; 6. Elizabeth,
1865–1907; 7. John; 8. Malcolm.   **SPI 128; HP 37**.

7722   MACKINNON, William, 1807–29 Jul 1896. From
Corriecrevie, Kilmory par, Is Arran, BUT. s/o Peter M.
and Betty Stewart. To NB, ca 1852; stld Dundee,
Restigouche Co. Farmer and tailor. m Elizabeth Cook, qv,
ch: 1. Duncan, qv; 2. Mary, 1842–1917; 3. Elizabeth, qv;
4. Peter, 1845-54; 5. John, 1850-54; 6. Catherine,
b 1853; 7. William, 1856–1955; 8. Peter, b 1859,
d at Vancouver, BC; 9. John, 1863–1943; 10. Ann,
b 1865.   **DC 1 Oct 1979**.

7723   MACKINVEN, Alexander. From Kintyre, ARL. To
QUE on the *Mars*, ex Tobermory, 28 Jul 1818; stld ONT,
poss Elgin Co. Descendants took the surname of
Love.   **SG xxv/1 30**.

McKINZIE. See also McKENZIE.

7724   McKINZIE, Alexander. From Urquhart and
Glenmoriston par, INV. To Montreal, QUE, ex Fort
William, arr Sep 1802; stld E ONT.   **MCM 1/4 24**.

7725   McKINSIE, John. To PEI, poss 1803; stld Queens
Co. Petitioner for Dr MacAulay, 1811.   **HP 74**.

7726   McKINSIE, Kenneth. To PEI, poss 1803; stld
Queens Co. Petitioner for Dr MacAulay, 1811.   **HP 73**.

7727   McKIRDY, John Lachlan. From Greenock, RFW.
s/o John M, writer, d 1821, and Janet McLachlan. To
QUE <1834.   **SH**.

7728   McKITTRICK, William. From DFS. Poss

s/o James M, mason. To Kings Co, NS, <1830.
Son James.   **HNS iii 68**.

7729   McKNIGHT, Rev Alexander, ca 1823–27 Apr
1894. From Dalmellington, AYR. s/o Samuel M, farmer.
Matric Univ of Glasgow, 1841, and studied theology at
New Coll, Edinburgh. To Halifax, NS, 1855. Teacher of
Hebrew, and in 1857 adm min of St James's Ch,
Dartmouth. Held posts in Halifax Free Coll, and after the
union of the Presb churches became Principal of the
Presb Coll of the Maritimes, at Halifax.   **BNA 839;
GMA 14336**.

7730   McKNIGHT, Susan. Prob from Montrose, ANS.
To ONT, 1854. Wife of William Strachan, qv, whom she
m 31 Dec 1845.   **DC 15 Apr 1961**.

McLACHLAN. See also McLACHLANE and
McLACHLIN.

7731   McLACHLAN, Alexander, 1818–30 Mar 1896.
From Johnstone, RFW. s/o Charles M, qv, and Jean
Sutherland, qv. To ONT, 1840; stld prob Peel Co. Farmer,
tailor and poet. m his cous Clamina McLachlan, qv, ch:
1. Jean; 2. Charles; 3. Malcolm; 4. Mary; 5. John,
1854-82; 6. Daniel, b ca 1858; 7. Ann, b 1861;
8. William; 9. Alexander; 10. Elizabeth; 11. Margaret,
b 1868.   **BNA 1154; MDB 471; DC 17 Nov 1981**.

7732   McLACHLAN, Archibald. From ARL. To Mosa
Twp, Middlesex Co, ONT, 1830. Son Capt Daniel.
PCM 24.

7733   McLACHLAN, Archibald. From ARL. To Mosa
Twp, Middlesex Co, ONT, 1834.   **PCM 30**.

7734   McLACHLAN, Archibald. From ARL. To
Westminster Twp, Middlesex Co, ONT, 1845.   **PCM 52**.

7735   McLACHLAN, Charles. From Johnstone, RFW,
but poss b Kilfinan, ARL. bro/o Daniel M, qv. To QUE on
the *Young Norval*, ex Greenock, Apr 1820; stld Caledon
Twp, Peel Co, but went later to NJ, USA, and d NY.
m Jean Sutherland, qv. Son Alexander, qv.   **DC 17 Nov
1981**.

7736   McLACHLAN, Charles, 1813-86. From
Johnstone, RFW. s/o Daniel M, qv, and Mary McDonald,
qv. To QUE on the *Young Norval*, ex Greenock, Apr
1820; stld Caledon Twp, Peel Co. ONT. m Miss Faed,
1820-62, ch: 1. Daniel; 2. Elizabeth, 1842-99; 3. Simon,
1850–1937; 4. Malcolm, 1856- 60; 5. James,
1860–1901; 6. Lachlan; 7. Jeanette; 8. Thomas,
1862–1932.   **DC 17 Nov 1981**.

7737   McLACHLAN, Clamina, b 1817. From Johnstone,
RFW. d/o Daniel M, qv, and Mary McDonald, qv. To QUE
on the *Young Norval*, ex Greenock, Apr 1820; stld
Caledon Twp, Peel Co, ONT. Teacher. m ca 1841, her
cous Alexander McLachlan, qv.   **DC 17 Nov 1981**.

7738   McLACHLAN, Donald. From Cowal dist, ARL. To
Lobo Twp, Middlesex Co, ONT, 1838. ch: 1. Duncan;
2. Hugh, stld Williams Twp; 3. John; 4. Janet;
5. Isabella; 6. Kate.   **PCM 39**.

7739   McLACHLAN, Daniel, ca 1785–1884. From
Johnstone, RFW. bro/o Charles M, qv. To QUE on the
Young Norval, ex Greenock, Apr 1820; stld Caledon Twp,
Peel Co, ONT. Farmer, and gr land. m Mary McDonald,
qv, ch: 1. John, qv; 2. Charles, qv; 3. Malcolm, qv;
4. Clamina, qv; 5. Daniel, 1819-96; 7. Mary; 8. Nancy;
9. Lachlan.   **DC 17 Nov 1981**.

7740 McLACHLAN, Dugald. From ARL. To Ekfrid Twp, Middlesex Co, ONT, 1830. ch: 1. Lachlan; 2. Duncan; 3. Mrs Duncan McKeith. **PCM 30**.

7741 McLACHLAN, Duncan. From ARL. To Lobo Twp, Middlesex Co, ONT, <1850; stld later West Williams Twp. ch: 1. Hector; 2. Donald; 3. Duncan; 4. Archibald; 5. John; 6. Hugh; 7. James; 8. Mary. **PCM 47**.

7742 McLACHLAN, Hugh. From ARL. To Mosa Twp, Middlesex Co, ONT, 1830. ch: 1. Donald; 2. Duncan; 3. Hugh; 4. Alexander; 5. Flora. **PCM 23**.

7743 McLACHLAN, Rev James, b ca 1803. From Glasgow. s/o David M, craftsman. Matric Univ of Glasgow, 1819, and ord by the Secession Ch as a missionary. To CAN, 1833. **GMA 10310**.

7744 McLACHLAN, John, d 11 Apr 1771. Prob from PER. To Richmond Bay, PEI, on the *Falmouth*, ex Greenock, 8 Apr 1770; stld Queens Co. Drowned along with Alexander, s/o John Jamieson, qv. **DC 28 May 1980**.

7745 McLACHLAN, John. Prob from Glasgow. To QUE on the *Brock*, ex Greenock, 9 Jul 1820; stld Lanark Co, ONT. Leader of a group of emigrants sponsored by the Trans-Atlantic Society. **HCL 62, 238**.

7746 McLACHLAN, John, 1809-82. From Johnstone, RFW. s/o Daniel M, qv, and Mary McDonald, qv. To QUE on the *Young Norval*, ex Greenock, Apr 1820; stld Caledon Twp, Peel Co, ONT. m Miss Hunter, ch: 1. Agnes, b 1842; 2. James, b 1844. **DC 17 Nov 1981**.

7747 McLACHLAN, John. From ARL. To Ekfrid Twp, Middlesex Co, ONT, 1831. ch: 1. Archibald; 2. John; 3. Angus; 4. Duncan; 5. Betsy. **PCM 30**.

7748 McLACHLAN, John. Prob from Kilfinichen par, Is Mull, ARL. To QUE, 1831; stld Breadalbane, later Lochaber, Ottawa Co. Son Robert, qv. **ELB 1**.

7749 McLACHLAN, John. From INV. To East Williams Twp, Middlesex Co, ONT, 1832. **PCM 43**.

7750 McLACHLAN, Lachlan. To QUE on the *Neptune*, arr May 1816; stld Lanark Co, ONT. **DC 31 Jan 1983**.

7751 McLACHLAN, Malcolm, 1815-84. From Johnstone, RFW. s/o Daniel M, qv, and Mary McDonald, qv. To QUE on the *Young Norval*, ex Greenock, Apr 1820; stld Caledon Twp, Peel Co, ONT. m (i) Jane Kirkwood, 1817-48, ch: 1. Margaret, 1838-87; 2. Daniel, 1840–1916; 3. William, 1842–1905; 4. Robert, 1844–1907; 5. Mary. m (ii) Christine McDonald, qv, with further ch: 6. Duncan, 1852–1932; 7. Catherine, 1855-56; 8. John, 1856–1928; 9. Alexander, 1858–1940; 10. Charles, 1861–1944; 11. Malcolm, 1865–1918; 12. James, 1868–1922; 13. Chalmers, 1870-86. **DC 17 Nov 1981**.

7752 McLACHLAN, Mary. Prob from Kilfinichen par, Is Mull, ARL. Rel to Robert M, qv. To QUE, ca 1831; stld Breadalbane, later Lochaber, Ottawa Co. m James McArthur, qv. **ELB 3**.

7753 McLACHLAN, Robert. Prob from Kilfinichen par, Is Mull, ARL. s/o John M, qv. To QUE, ca 1831; stld Breadalbane, later to Lochaber, Ottawa Co. Ship blacksmith. m Mary McDonald, qv, ch: 1. John; 2. Sarah, qv. **ELB 1**.

7754 McLACHLAN, Sarah. Prob from Kilfinichen par, Is Mull, ARL. d/o Robert M, qv, and Mary McDonald, qv. To QUE, ca 1831; stld Breadalbane, later Lochaber, Ottawa Co. m — McQueen. **ELB 1**.

7755 McLACHLANE, Angus. Poss from ARL. To Montreal, QUE, prob arr Sep 1802. Petitioned for land on the Ottawa River, 6 Aug 1804. **DC 15 Mar 1980**.

7756 McLACHLIN, Archibald, b 1827. Prob from ARL. To Aldborough Twp, Elgin Co, ONT, 1843. Schoolteacher, Brocks Creek, later editor and registrar. **PDA 18, 58**.

7757 McLAGAN, Elizabeth. From Dundee, ANS. To Huron Co, ONT, 1834. Wife of Colin Ross, qv. **MDB 647**.

MACLAINE. See also MACLEAN, McLEAN and McLANE.

7758 MACLAINE, Ishbel. From Oban par, ARL. To QUE on the *Duchess of Richmond*, 1821; stld Drummond Twp, later Ramsay Twp, Lanark Co, ONT. Wife of John McDonald, qv. **HCL 87**.

7759 McLANE, Angus, b 1751. To Charlottetown, PEI, on the *Humphreys*, ex Tobermory, arr 14 Jul 1806. Wife Ann, aged 50, with him, ch: 1. Christy, aged 18; 2. John, aged 16; 3. James, aged 14; 4. Mary, aged 12. **PLH**.

7760 McLATTERN, Finlay, b ca 1771. To Richmond Co, NS, 1811. Farmer, m and had ch. **CBC 1818**.

McLAREN. See also McLAUREN and McLAURIN.

7761 McLAREN, Alexander, b 1803. From PER, poss Dunkeld. bro/o Donald M, qv, and William M, qv. To Melrose, Tyendinaga Twp, Hastings Co, ONT, <1835. Son Alexander. **DC 30 Jan 1980**.

7762 McLAREN, Ann, d 1875. From Comrie par, PER. To Montreal, QUE, on the *Curlew*, ex Greenock, 21 Jul 1818; stld Beckwith Twp, Lanark Co, ONT. Wife of Duncan Ferguson, qv. **BCL; DC 29 Dec 1981**.

7763 McLAREN, Archibald, b ca 1784. From Killin, PER. To QUE, ex Greenock, summer 1815; stld prob Lanark Co, ONT. Mason. Wife Christian Brown, qv, with him, and 4 ch. **SEC 3**.

7764 McLAREN, Catherine. Prob from Strathyre, PER, and poss rel to James M, qv. To QUE on the *Niagara*, ex Greenock, 22 Apr 1825; stld McNab Twp, Renfrew Co, ONT. **DC 3 Jan 1980**.

7765 McLAREN, Catherine. To CAN <1854. m Robert Smith. **SH**.

7766 McLAREN, Christian. From Comrie par, PER. To Montreal, QUE, on the *Curlew*, ex Greenock, 21 Jul 1818; stld Beckwith Twp, Lanark Co, ONT. Wife of James Ferguson, qv. **BCL; DC 29 Dec 1981**.

7767 McLAREN, Christian. From PER, prob Lochearnhead. A minor, poss rel to Malcolm M, qv. To McNab Twp, Renfrew Co, ONT, prob 1825. **DC 3 Jan 1980**.

7768 McLAREN, Christian. Prob from PER, and poss rel to Robert M, qv. To McNab Twp, Renfrew Co, ONT, 1825. **DC 3 Jan 1980**.

7769 McLAREN, Christina, 1772–1804. From Balquhidder, PER. d/o James M, qv, and Isobel

McDonald, qv. To Pictou, NS, on the *Commerce*, ex Port Glasgow, 10 Aug 1803; stld Brudenell, Kings Co, PEI. Wife of Donald Gordon, qv. **PLC; BP 3, 8, 30**.

7770 McLAREN, David, 1789–1870. From Blackford, PER. s/o James M. and Mary Jean McCaunie. To ONT, 1821; stld Torbolton Twp, Carleton Co, and later Wakefield, Ottawa Co, QUE. Farmer, sawyer and merchant. m 1817, Elizabeth Barnet, ch: 1. James, qv; 2. John; 3. David; 4. Henry; 5. Rev William; 6. Rev Alexander. **DC 10 Mar 1980**.

7771 McLAREN, Donald, b ca 1780. From Balquhidder, PER. s/o James M, qv, and Isobel McDonald, qv. To Pictou, NS, on the *Commerce*, ex Port Glasgow, 10 Aug 1803; stld Brudenell, Kings Co, PEI. m Elizabeth Stewart, qv, ch: 1. James, qv; 2. Janet, b 1799; 3. John, qv; 4. Archibald; 5. Christina; 6. Betsy; 7. Robina. **PLC; BP 52**.

7772 McLAREN, Donald, b ca 1767. From Killin, PER. To QUE, ex Greenock, summer 1815; stld prob Lanark Co, ONT. Farmer. Wife Catherine McTavish, qv, with him, and 6 ch. **SEC 3**.

7773 McLAREN, Donald. From Balquhidder, PER. To Montreal, QUE, on the *Sophia*, ex Greenock, 26 Jul 1818; stld Beckwith Twp, Lanark Co, ONT. Wife Mary with him, ch: 1. John, aged 11; 2. Duncan, aged 8; 3. Peter, aged 5; 4. Mary, aged 3 ½; 5. Donald, aged 2; 6. Nicolas, b 1817. **SPL**.

7774 McLAREN, Donald. Prob from PER, and poss rel to Robert M, qv. To McNab Twp, Renfrew Co, ONT, 1825. **DC 3 Jan 1980**.

7775 McLAREN, Donald, b 1805. From PER, poss Dunkeld. bro/o Alexander M, qv, and William M, qv. To Melrose, Tyendinaga Twp, Hastings Co, ONT, <1835. **DC 30 Jan 1980**.

7776 McLAREN, Duncan. From PER. To Richmond Bay, PEI, on the *Falmouth*, ex Greenock, 8 Apr 1770; stld Queens Co. Wife with him, and several ch, incl Jean, qv. **DC 28 May 1980**.

7777 McLAREN, Duncan, b ca 1779. From Killin, PER. To QUE, summer 1815; ex Greenock, stld prob Lanark Co, ONT. Wife Annabella McDiarmid, qv, with him, and 5 ch. **SEC 6**.

7778 McLAREN, Duncan, 1773–1847. From Monzie par, PER. To Glengarry Co, ONT, and d there. Wife Margaret d at Gilmerton, Monzie, 1846. ch: 1. Alexander, d 25 Dec 1871; 2. Duncan, d 1874; 3. Helena, d Glengarry Co, 7 Mar 1868. **Ts Monzie**.

7779 McLAREN, Elizabeth. From Balquhidder, PER. d/o James M, qv, and Isobel McDonald, qv. To Brudenell, Kings Co, PEI, prob 1803. m James McFarlane, qv, and d WI, USA. **BP 42, 64**.

7780 McLAREN, Ellen. From Edinburgh. To PEI <1850. m Alexander Crawford, qv. **AMC 82**.

7781 McLAREN, Hector. Poss from ARL. To Mosa Twp, Middlesex Co, ONT, 1843. **PCM 24**.

7782 McLAREN, Helen. From PER, prob Lochearnhead. A minor, poss rel to Malcolm M, qv. To McNab Twp, Renfrew Co, ONT, 1825. **DC 3 Jan 1980**.

7783 McLAREN, Isabel, ca 1813–12 Oct 1902. From PER, poss Balquhidder. To PEI, prob <1828, with her uncle, Peter Robertson, qv. m Alexander Kennedy. **BP 25**.

7784 McLAREN, James, 1742–1818. From Balquhidder, PER. s/o Donald M, Invernenty, who fought in the '45 Rebellion, and Robina Stewart. To PEI, ca 1803; stld Brudenell, Kings Co. Farmer, and patriarch of the Brudenell McLarens. m Isobel McDonald, qv, ch: 1. James, qv; 2. William, qv; 3. Christina, qv; 4. Donald, qv; 5. Elizabeth, qv; 6. Janet, qv; 7. John, qv. **BP 11, 42**.

7785 McLAREN, James, jr, 1776–1863. From Balquhidder, PER. s/o James M, qv, and Isobel McDonald, qv. To Brudenell, Kings Co, PEI, ca 1803. m Elizabeth McFarlane, d 1846, ch: 1. Robina; 2. Nancy; 3. Lavinia; 4. Eliza; 5. Isabel; 6. Lydia; 7. Christina; 8. John. m (ii) Jane Cook. **BP 42, 59**.

7786 McLAREN, James, b 1797. From Balquhidder, PER. s/o Donald M, qv, and Elizabeth Stewart, qv. To Pictou, NS, on the *Commerce*, ex Port Glasgow, 10 Aug 1803; stld Brudenell, Kings Co, PEI, later Montague. m his cous Isobel Gordon, qv, who d in childbed. m (ii) Annie Stewart, 1808–72, ch: 1. Alexander; 2. Daniel; 3. Margaret; 4. Archibald; 5. Amelia; 6. Elizabeth; 7. William; 8. Anne; 9. John. **PLC; BP 53**.

7787 McLAREN, James, b ca 1782. From Callander, PER. To QUE on the *Dorothy*, ex Greenock, 12 Jul 1815; stld Lot 28, Con 10, North Elmsley Twp, Lanark Co, ONT. Weaver, labourer, farmer. Wife Euphemia Jamieson, qv, with him, and 5 ch. **SEC 1; HCL 17, 230, 232**.

7788 MACLAREN, James. Poss from PER. To Aldborough Twp, Elgin Co, ONT, prob 1818. **PDA 92**.

7789 McLAREN, James, 1818–92. From Glasgow. s/o David M, qv, and Elizabeth Barnet, qv. To Torbolton Twp, Carleton Co, ONT, 1821, later to Wakefield, Ottawa Co, QUE. Lumberman and banker. m Ann Sully, ch: 1. David, 1848–1916, banker; 2. John, 1853–1903, Pres of Bank of Ottawa; 3. Alexander; 4. James; 5. Albert; 6. Mrs W. Waring; 7. Mrs T. Raphael. **DC 30 Aug 1977**.

7790 McLAREN, James. From Strathyre, PER. Poss rel to Catherine M, qv. To Montreal on the *Niagara*, ex Greenock, arr 28 May 1825; stld McNab Twp, Renfrew Co, ONT. **EMT 22**.

7791 McLAREN, Jane. From Kirkintilloch, DNB. To Medonte Twp, Simcoe Co, ONT, <1836. Wife of Alexander Miller, qv. **DC 8 Nov 1981**.

7792 McLAREN, Janet, called Jessie, b ca 1766. From PER. d/o James M, qv, and Isobel McDonald, qv. To Pictou, NS, on the *Commerce*, ex Port Glasgow, 10 Aug 1803; stld Kings Co, PEI. m James Stewart, qv. **PLC; BP 42, 62**.

7793 McLAREN, Janet. From Killin, PER. To QUE, ex Greenock, summer 1815; stld ONT. Wife of Allan McDiarmid, qv. **SEC 4**.

7794 McLAREN, Janet. Prob from PER, and poss rel to Robert M, qv. To McNab Twp, Renfrew Co, ONT, 1825. **DC 3 Jan 1980**.

7795 McLAREN, Janet, 28 Oct 1810–10 Jan 1877. From Glasgow. To Ramsay Twp, Lanark Co, ONT, <1 Jan 1834, when she m Robert Yuill, qv. **DC 7 Dec 1981**.

7796 McLAREN, Jean, ca 1750–ca 1810. From PER. d/o Duncan M, qv. To Richmond Bay, PEI, on the *Falmouth*, ex Greenock, 8 Apr 1770; stld Queens Co. m Duncan McEwen, qv, ca 1770. **DC 28 May 1980**.

7797 McLAREN, Jean. From Killin, PER. To Reach Twp, Ontario Co, ONT, 1845. Wife of John Christie, qv. **DC 12 Jul 1979**.

7798 McLAREN, John, 1801-89. From Balquhidder, PER. s/o Donald M, qv, and Elizabeth Stewart, qv. To Pictou, NS, on the *Commerce*, ex Port Glasgow, 10 Aug 1803; stld Brudenell, Kings Co, PEI. m Catherine Ann Dewar, ca 1805-58, ch: 1. Daniel; 2. Sophia; 3. Anne; 4. Clementine; 5. Margaret; 6. Martha; 7. Elizabeth; 8. Lydia; 9. John; 10. Nathaniel. **PLC; BP 55**.

7799 McLAREN, John, 1786–1863. From Balquhidder, PER. s/o James M, qv, and Isobel McDonald, qv. To PEI, ca 1803; stld Brudenell, PEI. m Margaret Stewart, qv, ch: 1. James; 2. Charles; 3. Mysie; 4. Isabelle; 5. Elizabeth; 6. Christina. **BP 42, 62**.

7800 MACLAREN, John. From PER. To PEI, ca 1804; stld Hermitage Grove, Charlottetown Royalty. ch incl: 1. Christene, b 1805, res Vernon River; 2. Marjory, b 1821, res Vernon River. **HP 87**.

7801 McLAREN, John, b ca 1792. From Ledcharry, Crieff, PER. To QUE, ex Greenock, summer 1815; stld ONT, prob Lanark Co. Carpenter and farmer. Wife Susan McMartin, qv, with him, and 7 ch. **SEC 3**.

7802 McLAREN, John. To QUE on the *Caledonian*, 1816; stld Lot 14, Con 1, Bathurst Twp, Lanark Co, ONT. **HCL 234**.

7803 McLAREN, John. From Killin, PER. To Montreal, QUE, on the *Curlew*, ex Greenock, 21 Jul 1818; stld prob Beckwith Twp, Lanark Co, ONT. Wife Catherine with him, and ch: 1. Christian, aged 4; 2. Archibald, aged 2. **BCL**.

7804 McLAREN, John. From Comrie, PER. To Montreal, QUE, on the *Curlew*, ex Greenock, 21 Jul 1818; stld prob Beckwith Twp, Lanark Co, ONT. Wife Janet with him, and dau Catherine, aged 1. **BCL**.

7805 McLAREN, John. From Comrie, PER. To Montreal, QUE, on the *Curlew*, ex Greenock, 21 Jul 1818; stld prob Beckwith Twp, Lanark Co, ONT. Wife Janet with him, and ch: 1. Isabella, aged 6; 2. Malcolm, aged 3. **BCL**.

7806 McLAREN, Rev John, 1807–22 Mar 1855. From Balquhidder, PER. s/o Peter M. Matric Univ of Glasgow, 1834. Missionary in St Columbas par, Glasgow, and went to Martintown, Glengarry Co, ONT. **GMA 13294; FES vii 643**.

7807 McLAREN, John, ca 1830–25 Nov 1905. Poss from STI. s/o Peter M. and Agnes Stewart. To Dalhousie Lake, Lanark Co, ONT. m Mary, d/o John Brown, qv, and Isabella Whyte, qv, ch. **LDW 13 Feb 1978**.

7808 McLAREN, Malcolm. From Lochearnhead, PER. To Montreal, QUE, on the *Niagara*, ex Greenock, arr 28 May 1825; stld McNab Twp, Renfrew Co, ONT. m Janet Fisher, qv, ch: 1. Margaret; 2. Mary; 3. Janet; 4. Annie; 5. Peter. **EMT 18, 22**.

7809 McLAREN, Malcolm, 1812-98. From STI. To Galt, Waterloo Co, ONT, <1850. Went later to MAN. m Lily MacPhail, ch. **DC 11 Nov 1981**.

7810 MACLAREN, Margaret, b ca 1773. From Lochaber, INV. To PEI <1809, but moved to Mabou Coal Mines, Inverness Co, NS. Wife of Finlay 'Mor' Beaton, qv. **MP 190**.

7811 McLAREN, Mary. From Killin par, PER. To Martintown, Glengarry Co, ONT. Wife of Finlay Sinclair, qv. **SMB**.

7812 McLAREN, Mary. From Balquhidder, PER. To Montreal, QUE, on the *Sophia*, ex Greenock, 26 Jul 1818; stld Beckwith Twp, Lanark Co, ONT. Wife of Finlay McEwan, qv. **SPL; HCL 33**.

7813 McLAREN, Mary, 1790–1873. From PER. To Middlesex Co, ONT, 1818; stld London Twp. Wife of John Carmichael, qv. **PCM 50**.

7814 McLAREN, Mary. From PER. A minor, poss rel to James M, qv, from Strathyre. To Montreal, QUE, on the *Niagara*, ex Greenock, arr 28 May 1825; stld McNab Twp, Renfrew Co, ONT. **EMT 23**.

7815 McLAREN, Peter. To QUE on the *Brock*, ex Greenock, 9 Jul 1820; stld Beckwith Twp, Lanark Co, ONT. **HCL 238**.

7816 McLAREN, Peter. From PER. A minor, poss rel to James M, qv, from Strathyre. To McNab Twp, Renfrew Co, ONT, 1825. **DC 3 Jan 1980**.

7817 McLAREN, Robert. To QUE on the *George Canning*, ex Greenock, 14 Apr 1821; stld Ramsay Twp, Lanark Co, ONT. **HCL 86, 239**.

7818 McLAREN, Robert. Poss from Meiklewood, Gargunnock, STI. To Montreal, QUE, on the *Niagara*, ex Greenock, arr 28 May 1825; stld McNab Twp, Renfrew Co, ONT. **EMT 18**.

7819 McLAREN, Robert. From PER. A minor, poss rel to James M, qv, from Strathyre. To McNab Twp, Renfrew Co, ONT, 1825.

7820 McLAREN, Rev Robert G, ca 1830–6 Jun 1882. From CAI. Matric Univ of St Andrews, 1847. Ord 1857, and became min at Three Rivers, QUE, 1862. Widow d Chatham, Kent Co, ONT, 1895. **SAM 107; FES vii 643**.

7821 McLAREN, Thomas. To QUE on the *George Canning*, ex Greenock, 14 Apr 1821; stld Lot 20, Con 11, Ramsay Twp, Lanark Co, ONT. **HCL 88, 239**.

7822 McLAREN, Thomas, ca 1811–15 Feb 1864. From Perth. m in Bridgend. To Montreal, QUE, <1850. m Mary Taylor, qv, ch: 1. Thomas; 2. John, 1849-99; 3. Christy; 4. Benjamen; 5. William Barrett, b 1851, res New York, USA. **DC 24 Oct 1975**.

7823 McLAREN, Thomas J, 14 Aug 1830–18 Jul 1914. To Dundas, Wentworth Co, ONT, <1855. m Margaret Gray, qv. Son Alexander, 1855–1929, d Detroit, MI, USA. **DC 20 Feb 1981**.

7824 McLAREN, William, 1778–1850. From Balquhidder, PER. s/o James M, qv, and Isobel McDonald, qv. To Pictou, NS, on the *Commerce*, ex Port Glasgow, 10 Aug 1803; stld Brudenell, Kings Co, PEI. m Janet or Jessie Robertson, qv, ch: 1. Donald, b 1802; 2. Peter; 3. James; 4. John, b New Perth; 5. Lawrence; 6. Margaret; 7. Belle; 8. Jessie; 9. Nathaniel; 10. Daniel. **PLC; BP 43**.

7825 McLAREN, William, b 27 Jan 1827. From STI. To Montreal, QUE, with his parents, 1830. Baker. Dau Mrs James Fleck. **SGC 566**.

7826 McLAREN, William, b 1808. From PER, poss Dunkeld. bro/o Donald M, qv, and Alexander M, qv. To Melrose, Tyendinaga Twp, Hastings Co, ONT, <1835. **DC 30 Jan 1980**.

7827 McLARTY, Angus, 1 May 1821–5 Oct 1905. From ARL. s/o Archibald M, qv, and Isabel McTavish, qv. To QUE, prob on the *Deveron*, 1831; stld Howard Twp, Kent Co, ONT. Farmer and carpenter. m (i) 1854, Janet Campbell, ch: 1. Archibald, 1854–1934; 2. Isabella, 1856–1948; 3. John, 1858–1938; 4. Alexander, 1860–1943; 5. James, 1863–1941. **AMA 19**.

7828 McLARTY, Ann, 1827–11 Nov 1873. From Castleton, nr Lochgilphead, ARL. d/o Archibald M, qv, and Isabel McTavish, qv. To QUE, prob on the *Deveron*, 1831; stld Howard Twp, Kent Co, ONT. m Archibald McDiarmid, ca 1829–1909, farmer, ch: 1. John, 1853-72; 2. Isabel, 1854–1942; 3. Catherine Amantha, 1856–1913; 5. Archibald D, 1859–1910; 6. Eliza, 1861–1946; 7. Peter, 1863-93; 8. Malcolm, 1865-68; 9. Hugh, 1866–1903; 10. Anabel, 1868–1956. **AMA 24**.

7829 McLARTY, Archibald, 15 Mar 1795–23 May 1884. From Castleton, nr Lochgilphead, ARL. s/o Angus M. amd Anne Sinclair. To QUE, prob on the *Deveron*, 1831; stld Howard Twp, Kent Co, ONT. Cooper. m Isabel McTavish, qv, ch: 1. Angus, qv; 2. Jenat, qv; 3. Isabel, qv; 4. Ann, qv; 5. William, b 1831; 6. Margaret; 7. Mary; 8. Archibald. **AMA 11**.

7830 McLARTY, Catherine, 1799–2 Aug 1881. From ARL. To Aldborough Twp, Elgin Co, ONT, prob 1818. m Alexander Gray, qv. **PDA 24, 43**.

7831 McLARTY, Christina, b ca 1830. Prob from ARL, and poss rel to John McLarty, qv. To Ottawa Co, QUE, ca 1850; later to Minto Twp, Wellington Co, ONT. m James McMaster, qv. **DC 23 Apr 1967**.

7832 McLARTY, Dugald, d 1818. From ARL. To QUE on the *Mars*, ex Tobermory, 28 Jul 1818. Drowned when attempting to go ashore at New Glasgow, Elgin Co, ONT. **PDA 24**.

7833 McLARTY, Isabel, 20 Sep 1824–11 May 1917. From Castleton, nr Lochgilphead, ARL. d/o Archibald M, qv, and Isabel McTavish, qv. To QUE, prob on the *Deveron*, 1831; stld Howard Twp, Kent Co, ONT. m Peter Campbell, farmer, ch: 1. Archibald Peter, 1846–1930; 2. Isabelle Mary, 1848-88; 3. Margaret Anne, 1851–1909; 4. Mary, 1853–1944; 5. Sarah Catherine, 1855-56; 6. Malcolm Benjamen, 1857–1943; 7. Peter Neil, 1859–1941; 8. Edward, 1862–1954; 9. Florence Jennie, 1866–1910; 10. Rev George Alexander, 1869–1943. **AMA 22**.

7834 McLARTY, Jenat, 12 Oct 1822–1 Jan 1880. From Castleton, nr Lochgilphead, ARL. d/o Archibald M, qv, and Isabel McTavish, qv. To QUE, prob on the *Deveron*, 1831; stld Howard Twp, Kent Co, ONT. Hand-loom weaver. m ca 1845, Francis, s/o Michael Ogletree and Annabella Scott, ch: 1. Annabella, d inf; 2. Annabella, 1847-75; 3. Michael; 4. Hugh, dy; 5. Mary Ann; 6. Isabel Frances, 1857–1948; 7. Henry, 1860–1952; 8. Sarah, 1862-91, unm; 9. Evaline Frances, 1864-77; 10. Archibald, 1868–1928. **AMA 22**.

7835 McLARTY, John, b ca 1824. Prob from ARL. To Ottawa Co, QUE, ca 1850; prob later in Wellington Co, ONT. m Euphemia McMaster, qv, ch: 1. Flora; 2. Catherine; 3. Ann; 4. Archibald; 5. Malcolm; 6. Mary; 7. John; 8. Euphemia; 9. Amelia; 10. Elizabeth. **DC 23 Apr 1967**.

7836 McLARTY, Neil. From ARL. To Mosa Twp, Middlesex Co, ONT, 1831. **PCM 24**.

7837 MACLARTY, Neil. From ARL. To Aldborough Twp, Elgin Co, ONT, 1853. Son John, blacksmith and local politician. **PDA 68**.

7838 McLARTY, Peter. Prob from ARL. To Montreal, QUE, prob <1836; moved later to Lobo Twp, Middlesex Co, ONT. Discharged soldier. m Miss McNeil. **PCM 39**.

7839 McLAUCHLAN, Duncan. Prob from ARL. To North Dorchester Twp, Middlesex Co, ONT, 1839. **PCM 56**.

7840 McLAUCHLAN, John. To Westminster Twp, Middlesex Co, ONT, 1837. Shoemaker in London. **PCM 55**.

7841 McLAUCHLAN, John. Prob from Glasgow. bro/o Mary M, qv. To York Co, ONT, <1839; stld Kirkfield. **LDW 23 Aug 1979**.

7842 McLAUCHLAN, Lauchlin, b ca 1785. To PEI, ca 1817, afterwards to Miramichi, Northumberland Co, NB. Petitioned for 150 acres–Lot 65–on the south side of the Restigouche River, Restigouche Co, NB, 9 Feb 1821. **DC 31 May 1980**.

7843 McLAUCHLAN, Mary. From Knoydart, INV. To QUE, ex Greenock, summer 1815; stld prob Lanark Co, ONT. Wife of Duncan McDonald, qv. **SEC 7**.

7844 McLAUCHLAN, Mary, ca 1813–2 Jun 1852. Prob from Glasgow. To QUE, 1832; stld Montreal, later Glengarry Co, ONT. Went to Victoria Co, and stld Kirkfield. Wife of John McKenzie, qv, and sis/o John M. **LDW 23 Aug 1979**.

7845 McLAUCHLAN, William, ca 1793–11 Mar 1882. From Buchlyvie, STI. To Galt, Waterloo Co, ONT, <1837. m Sarah McFarlane, qv. Son James, d Cleveland, OH, 1870. **Ts Buchlyvie**.

7846 McLAUGHLIN, Donald, b ca 1785. To Charlottetown, PEI, on the *Rambler*, ex Tobermory, arr 20 Jun 1806. Wife Mary, aged 26, with him, and ch: 1. Isobel, aged 3; 2. Dugald, b 1805. **PLR**.

7847 MACLAUGHLIN, Elizabeth. From PER. d/o — M. and — Stewart. To NS, prob <1845; stld Lochaber, Antigonish Co. m George, s/o Alexander Manson, qv, ch. **HCA 350**.

7848 McLAUGHLIN, James, b 28 Sep 1834. From KKD. s/o William amd Nicolas M. To Hamilton, ONT, 1854. Baker and confectioner. m 1855, Hetty, d/o William Delaine, ch: 1. Mary Ann; 2. Lilley; 3. William; 4. Hetty Alice; 5. James Murray; 6. Joseph Kent; 7. John H; 8. George D. **DC 29 Sep 1964**.

7849 McLAUGHLIN, John, b ca 1756. To Charlottetown, PEI, on the *Rambler*, ex Tobermory, 20 Jun 1806. Wife Christian, aged 46, with him, and ch: 1. Duncan, aged 21; 2. Colin, aged 18; 3. Donald, aged 16; 4. Alexander, aged 14; 5. James, aged 5. **PLR**.

McLAUREN. See McLAREN and McLAURIN.

7850 McLAUREN, Christy, 1798–1878. From Craignavie, Killin par, PER. d/o John M, qv, and first wife. To QUE on the *Dorothy*, ex Greenock, 12 Jul 1815; stld Lochiel Twp, Glengarry Co, ONT. m John Mackinnon. **DC 9 Jan and 15 Jul 1981**.

7851 McLAUREN, Colin, b 1776. From Comrie par, PER. Prob s/o Peter M, Craignavie, Killin par, and Christian Campbell. To Montreal, QUE, on the *Curlew*, ex Greenock, 21 Jul 1818; stld Lot 21, Con 5, Beckwith Twp, Lanark Co, ONT. Shoemaker, later farmer. Wife Christian McCowan, qv, with him, and ch: 1. Elizabeth, b 1815; 2. John, b 1817. **BCL; HCL 33**.

7852 McLAUREN, Colin, 1814-98. From Craignavie, Killin par, PER. s/o John M, qv, and Janet McIntyre, qv. To QUE on the *Dorothy*, ex Greenock, 12 Jul 1815; stld Breadalbane, Lochiel Twp, Glengarry Co, ONT. m Sarah McIntosh, ch: 1. James; 2. Christy Ann; 3. John Lawrence; 4. Angus; 5. Peter; 6. Janet; 7. Margaret; 8. Colin Archie. **DC 15 Jul 1981**.

7853 McLAUREN, John, 3 Mar 1773–18 Sep 1869. From Craignavie, Killin, PER. s/o Peter M, and Christian Campbell. To QUE on the *Dorothy*, ex Greenock, 12 Jul 1815; stld Breadalbane, Lochiel Twp, Glengarry Co, ONT. Farmer and stonemason. m (i) —, ch: 1. Christy, qv. m (ii) Janet McIntyre, qv, further ch: 2. Rev John, qv; 3. Peter, qv; 4. Laurence, 1812–1900; 5. Colin, qv; 6. Janet, 1817-94; 7. Archibald, 1819-94. **SEC 2; DC 9 Jan and 15 Jul 1981**.

7854 McLAUREN, Rev John, 1805-55. From Craignavie, Killin, PER. s/o John M, qv, and Janet McIntyre, qv. To QUE on the *Dorothy*, ex Greenock, 12 Jul 1815; stld Breadalbane, Lochiel Twp, Glengarry Co, ONT. Became a clergyman. m Hannah, d/o Robert Leslie Drake, Montreal, ch: 1. John; 2. James; 3. Robert; 4. Peter; 5. Hannah; 6. Elizabeth; 7. Janet; 8. Annie; 9. William; 10. Louise. **DC 10 Aug 1981**.

7855 McLAUREN, Peter, 1810-43. From Craignavie, Killin, PER. s/o John M, qv, and Janet McIntyre, qv. To QUE on the *Dorothy*, ex Greenock, 12 Jul 1815; stld Breadalbane, Lochiel Twp, Glengarry Co, ONT. m Ann Buchanan, qv. Son John James, editor. **DC 15 Jul 1981**.

McLAURIN. See also McLAREN and McLAUREN.

7856 McLAURIN, Alexander, b 5 Jan 1789. From Killin par, PER. s/o Peter M. and Christian Campbell. To QUE on the *Dorothy*, ex Greenock, 12 Jul 1815; stld Lot 21, Con 5, Beckwith Twp, Lanark Co, ONT. Carpenter. Wife Margaret Dewar, qv. Son John, lumberman, East Templeton, QUE. **SEC 4; DC 15 Jul 1981**.

7857 McLAURIN, Annie. From PER. To Lochiel Twp, Glengarry Co, ONT, <1832. m John Stewart, qv. **SDG 272**.

7858 McLAURIN, Donald R, ca 1812–9 Apr 1868. From Breadalbane, PER. To Breadalbane, Lochiel Twp, Glengarry Co, ONT, ca 1815. **SDG 131**.

7859 McLAURIN, Mrs J. From Breadalbane, PER. Prob rel to Annie M, qv. To QUE on the *Dorothy*, ex Greenock, 12 Jul 1815; stld Breadalbane, Lochiel Twp, Glengarry Co, ONT. **SDG 131**.

7860 McLAURIN, Rev John, 1794–15 Jan 1847. From Breadalbane, PER. Ord Edinburgh and went to Glengarry

Co, ONT, where he commenced the building of Presb Ch at Kirk Hill, Lochiel Twp. Trans to L'Orignal and Hawkesbury, 1832. **SDG 121; FES vii 643; MG 428**.

7861 McLAURIN, Peter Roy, d 1898. From PER. To Glengarry Co, ONT, 1806. m Susan McLaurin. Son John. **DC 29 Sep 1964**.

7862 McLAWS, Eliza, d 1863. From Glasgow. To Brant Co, ONT, 1842; stld Oakland Twp. Wife of Robert Eadie, qv. **SG xxvi/4 142**.

7863 McLAWSON, James, b ca 1743. From PER. To Pictou, NS, on the *Commerce*, ex Port Glasgow, 10 Aug 1803. Farmer. Wife Isabella, aged 58, with him, and ch: 1. John, aged 21; 2. James, aged 18; 3. Eliza, aged 11. **PLC**.

7864 McLAY, Henrietta. From Barvas, Is Lewis, ROC. To QUE, ex Stornoway, arr 4 Aug 1851; stld Huron Twp, Bruce Co, ONT. Wife of Roderick McDonald, qv. **DC 25 Dec 1981**.

7865 McLAY, Janet, ca 1790–12 Jan 1853. From Calton, Glasgow. To ONT, 1812. Wife of William Paul, qv. **DC 29 Oct 1981**.

7866 McLAY, Margaret, ca 1796–19 May 1885. From INV. To Miramichi, Northumberland Co, NB, 1835, and d at Taymouth, York Co. Wife of Donald Hossack, qv. **DC 4 Dec 1978**.

7867 McLEA, Catherine, ca 1808–22 Mar 1866. From Greenock, RFW. d/o Kenneth M, shipmaster. To St Johns, NFD, and d there. **Ts Greenock**.

7868 McLEA, Kenneth, ca 1800–27 Jun 1862. From Greenock, RFW. Poss s/o Kenneth M, shipmaster. To St Johns, NFD. Merchant. m Elizabeth Brine, who d at Greenock, 17 Aug 1844. **Ts Greenock**.

McLEAN. See also McCLEAN, McLAINE and McLANE.

7869 McLEAN, —. From Kilfinichen, Is Mull, ARL. To Hudson Bay and Red River, <1813. Pioneer settler. Wife and two servants with him. **RRS 16, 25**.

7870 McLEAN, —. From Is Benbecula, INV. To East Williams Twp, Middlesex Co, ONT, 1848. Blacksmith. **PCM 44**.

7871 McLEAN, Adam, 6 Aug 1825–10 Jul 1909. From Kilmarnock, AYR. s/o John M, qv, and Jean Gilchrist, qv. To QUE on the *Renfrewshire*, 1842; stld Aldborough Twp, Elgin Co, ONT. Farmer. m 1855, Mary McKinlay. **DC 23 Nov 1981**.

7872 McLEAN, Alexander. From Lochbroom par, ROC. To Pictou, NS, on the *Hector*, ex Loch Broom, arr 17 Sep 1773; stld above Irishtown, East River, Pictou Co. Gr land 1783. Son Alexander. **HPC App A and C; PAC 154**.

7873 McLEAN, Alexander. To Pictou Co, NS, 1784; stld west branch of East River. Formerly ensign, 2nd Batt, 84th Regt. **NSN 27/195**.

7874 McLEAN, Alexander. From Urquhart and Glenmoriston par, INV. bro/o Hector M, qv. Gr 500 acres opposite Stellarton, on west branch of East River, 1 Apr 1793. ch. **HPC App H**.

7875 McLEAN, Alexander, b ca 1792. To Port Hood dist, Inverness Co, NS, 1799. Farmer, unm. **CBC 1818**.

7876   McLEAN, Alexander. From Urquhart and Glenmoriston par, INV. To Pictou, NS, on the *Sarah*, ex Fort William, Jun 1801. Tenant farmer. Wife Margaret with him, and ch: 1. Becky, aged 4; 2. Ann, aged 1 ½. **PLS**.

7877   McLEAN, Alexander. From Moidart, INV. To Pictou, NS, on the *Dove*, ex Fort William, Jun 1801. Farmer. Wife Marian with him, and 2 ch. **PLD**.

7878   MACLEAN, Alexander. From Kilmorack, INV. To Pictou, NS, on the *Dove*, ex Fort William, Jun 1801. Labourer. **PLD**.

7879   McLEAN, Alexander, ca 1792–1 Jun 1862. To Pictou Co, NS. Bur Old Elgin. **DC 20 Nov 1976**.

7880   McLEAN, Alexander, b ca 1780. From Kilfinichen, Is Mull, ARL. To Hudson Bay and Red River, <1813. Pioneer settler. **RSS 25**.

7881   McLEAN, Alexander. From Borve, Is Barra, INV. s/o Hector M. To Little Mabou, Inverness Co, NS, ca 1818. m Mary McNeil, qv, ch: 1. John, b 1814; 2. Roderick; 3. Peter, b 1818; 4. Angus; 5. Hector; 6. Elizabeth. **MP 727**.

7882   McLEAN, Alexander, b 1802. From Is Rum, ARL. To Gut of Canso, Cape Breton, NS, on the *Saint Lawrence*, ex Tobermory, 11 Jul 1828. **SLL**.

7883   MACLEAN, Alexander, ca 1798–10 Dec 1878. From Is Skye, INV. To Charlottetown, PEI, on the *Mary Kennedy*, ex Portree, arr 1 Jun 1829; stld Montague River, Kings Co. m Margaret MacDonald. Dau Catherine. **SPI 161**.

7884   McLEAN, Alexander. Prob from ARL. To Lobo Twp, Middlesex Co, ONT, 1838. ch: 1. Donald; 2. Hugh. **PCM 40**.

7885   McLEAN, Alexander. From INV. To Middlesex Co, ONT, 1849; stld McGillivray Twp. **PCM 56**.

7886   McLEAN, Rev Alexander, 1827–24 May 1864. From Is North Uist, INV. To Waterloo Co, ONT, and d at Morriston. Author. **MDB 473**.

7887   McLEAN, Allan, b 1772. From Is Tyree, ARL. To QUE on the *Oughton*, arr Jul 1804; stld Baldoon, Dover Twp, Kent Co, ONT. Wife Mary McDonald, qv, with him. ch: 1. Catherine, qv; 2. Hector, b 1796; 3. Mary, b 1801; 4. Euphemia, b 1803; 5. Henrietta; 6. Margaret. **UCM 267, 302; DC 4 Oct 1979**.

7888   McLEAN, Allan, b ca 1770. From Is Mull, ARL. Poss s/o Angus M, qv. To Charlottetown, PEI, on the *Clarendon*, ex Oban, 6 Aug 1808. Labourer. **CPL**.

7889   McLEAN, Allan, b ca 1794. To Inverness, Inverness Co, NS, 1812. Carpenter, unm. **CBC 1818**.

7890   McLEAN, Allan, b 1739. From Is Rum, ARL. To Gut of Canso, Cape Breton, NS, on the *Saint Lawrence*, ex Tobermory, 11 Jul 1828. **SLL**.

7891   McLEAN, Allan, b 1770. From Is Rum, ARL. To Gut of Canso, Cape Breton, NS, on the *Saint Lawrence*, ex Tobermory, 11 Jul 1828. **SLL**.

7892   MACLEAN, Allan, 1820-88. From Is Harris, INV. To Victoria Co, NS, 1828; stld Hunters Mountain, Baddeck. m Margaret Nicholson, qv. **DC 10 Mar 1980**.

7893   McLEAN, Allan, b ca 1805. To Megantic Co,

QUE, 1829. Farmer. Wife Margaret, b IRL. ch: 1. Allan, b 1855; 2. Susanna, b 1857; 3. Margaret, b 1859. **DC 11 Feb 1980**.

7894   McLEAN, Allan. From Caolasraide, South Knapdale, ARL. To Caradoc Twp, Middlesex Co, ONT, 1831. ch: 1. John; 2. Hector; 3. Allan; 4. Archie; 5. Charles; 6. Duncan, physician, Dockerville, MI, USA; 7. Isabella. **PCM 35**.

7895   MACLEAN, Allan. From Duart, Is Mull, ARL. To NS <1838; stld Stewartdale. Wife Margaret with him. ch: 1. Mary, b 1838; 2. John; 3. Jennie; 4. Donald. **NSN 30/301**.

7896   McLEAN, Allan. From Is Tyree, ARL. To Victoria Co, ONT, 1845. Wife and ch with him. **GD50/225/1**.

7897   McLEAN, Rev Allan, 6 May 1804–1 Oct 1877. From Arisaig, ARL. s/o Alexander M. and Catherine McVarish. Educ Lismore and at Valladolid, Spain. Ord to RC priesthood, 1836, and served in SCT at Is Barra, Is South Uist and Fort Augustus. To Judique, Inverness Co, NS, 1854. **MP 726**.

7898   McLEAN, Angus. From Laide, Gairloch, ROC. Rel to Archibald M, qv. To Montreal, QUE, ex Fort William, arr Sep 1802; stld prob E ONT. **MCM 1/4 24**.

7899   McLEAN, Angus. From Munerigg, Invergarry, INV. To Montreal, QUE, ex Fort William, arr Sep 1802; stld prob E ONT. **MCM 1/4 25**.

7900   McLEAN, Angus, b ca 1748. From Is Mull, ARL. To Charlottetown, PEI, on the *Clarendon*, ex Oban, 6 Aug 1808. Labourer. **CPL**.

7901   McLEAN, Angus, d 1879. From Killinaig, Kinfinichen, Is Mull, ARL. To Mariposa Twp, Victoria Co, ONT, 1833. Miller. Wife Euphemia Mackinnon, qv, with him, and s Lachlan, b 21 Jun 1831. **DC 7 Dec 1968**.

7902   McLEAN, Angus, ca 1777–ca 1857. From Kilfinichen, Is Mull, ARL. s/o Neil M. To QUE, ca 1811; moved ca 1820, to Blackland, Restigouche Co, NB. Farmer and fisherman, gr 200 acres, 1831. m Mary Sinclair, qv, ch: 1. Neil, b 1809; 2. John, qv; 3. Angus, b 1813, QUE; 4. Agnes, b 1815; 5. Daniel, b 1818; 6. Elizabeth, b ca 1823, d WI, USA. **RCP 5, 7**.

7903   MACLEAN, Angus. From Moidart, INV. s/o Angus M. To Antigonish Co, NS, prob <1840; stld OH. m (i) Johanna Hewitt, ch: 1. John; 2. Hugh; 3. Catherine; 4. Janet; 5. Marcella; 6. John; 7. James; 8. Donald; 9. William. m (ii) Mary Fraser, further ch: 10. Donald; 11. Alexander; 12. Kate; 13. Christy; 14. Mary. **HCA 310**.

7904   McLEAN, Angus. To Pictou, NS, on the *Lady Gray*, ex Cromarty, ROC, arr 16 Jul 1841. **DC 15 Jul 1979**.

7905   McLEAN, Angus. Prob from ARL. To Metcalfe Twp, Middlesex Co, ONT, 1854. Son Alexander, teacher, and studied law. **PCM 26**.

7906   McLEAN, Ann, b ca 1772. Poss rel to Archibald M, qv. To Charlottetown, PEI, on the *Rambler*, ex Tobermory, 20 Jun 1806. **PLR**.

7907   McLEAN, Ann, b ca 1776. Poss rel to Duncan M, qv. To Charlottetown, PEI, on the *Rambler*, ex Tobermory, 20 Jun 1806. **PLR**.

7908 McLEAN, Ann, b ca 1783. From Is Mull, ARL. d/o Angus M. To Charlottetown, PEI, on the *Clarendon*, ex Oban, 6 Aug 1808. **CPL**.

7909 McLEAN, Ann, b ca 1785. From Is Mull, ARL. sis/o Charles M, qv. To Charlottetown, PEI, on the *Clarendon*, ex Oban, 6 Aug 1808. Wife of Donald Campbell, qv. **DC 11 Apr 1981**.

7910 McLEAN, Ann, b ca 1791. From Kilfinichen par, Is Mull, ARL. sis/o Donald M, qv, seaman. To Hudson Bay and Red River <1815. **RRS 25**.

7911 McLEAN, Ann. From North Knapdale, ARL. To Aldborough Twp, Elgin Co, ONT, 1819. Wife of John Paterson, qv. **DC 23 Nov 1981**.

7912 McLEAN, Ann, b 1766. From Is Rum, ARL. Prob d/o Allan M, qv. To Gut of Canso, Cape Breton, NS, on the *Saint Lawrence*, ex Tobermory, 11 Jul 1828. **SLL**.

7913 McLEAN, Archibald. From Laide, Gairloch, ROC. Rel to Angus M, qv. To Montreal, QUE, ex Fort William, arr Sep 1802; stld prob E ONT. **MCM 1/4 24**.

7914 McLEAN, Archibald, b ca 1771. Prob rel to Duncan M, qv. To Charlottetown, PEI, on the *Rambler*, ex Tobermory, 20 Jun 1806. **PLR**.

7915 McLEAN, Archibald, b 1776. From Is Mull, ARL. bro/o Malcolm M, qv. To Leeds Twp, Megantic Co, QUE, 1809. Formerly of the Argyll Fencible Regt. Pioneer settler and served in War of 1812 as a scout. m 1830, Mary McKillop, qv, ch: 1. Archibald, physician and teacher at Lambton; 2. John; 3. Mary; 4. Neil. **AMC 35, 95**.

7916 McLEAN, Archibald, b ca 1790. From Kilbranian, Kilmore, Is Mull, ARL. To Hudson Bay, ca 1812, and thence to Red River. Wright and pioneer settler. **RRS 25**.

7917 MACLEAN, Archibald. Prob from ARL. To Aldborough Twp, Elgin Co, ONT, <1820. Farmer. **PDA 93**.

7918 McLEAN, Archibald. Poss from Is Skye, INV. To NS <1840; moved to Kincardine Twp, Bruce Co, ONT. Wife Mary, b ca 1812, with him. ch: 1. Murdock, 1838–1910; 2. Rachel, b 1842; 3. Angus, b 1844; 4. Christy, b 1849. **NSN 32/364**.

7919 McLEAN, Archibald. From Glasgow. s/o William M, 1798–1837, and Elizabeth Wilkinson, 1798–1841. To St John, NB, prob <1840. **Ts North St, Glasgow**.

7920 McLEAN, Archibald. From Is North Uist, INV. To East Williams Twp, Middlesex Co, ONT, 1848. **PCM 44**.

7921 McLEAN, Archibald John, b 1814. From Is Mull, ARL. To Pictou, NS, ca 1820. **DC 30 Jul 1979**.

7922 McLEAN, Catherine. From INV. To Montreal, QUE, ex Fort William, arr Sep 1802; prob stld E ONT. **MCM 1/4 25**.

7923 McLEAN, Catherine, b 1793. From Is Tyree, ARL. d/o Allan M, qv, and Mary MacDonald, qv. To QUE on the *Oughton*, arr Jul 1804; stld Baldoon, Dover Twp, Kent Co, ONT. m John McDonald, qv. **UCM 268; DC 4 Oct 1979**.

7924 McLEAN, Catherine. From Port Dundas, Glasgow. To QUE on the *Atlas*, ex Greenock, 11 Jul 1815;

stld North Burgess Twp, Lanark Co, ONT. Wife of John Brash, qv. **SEC 1**.

7925 McLEAN, Catherine. From Ardgour, ARL. To QUE, summer 1815, ex Greenock; stld prob E ONT. Wife of Donald McPhee, qv. **SEC 6**.

7926 McLEAN, Catherine, b 1801. From Rothesay, BUT. To QUE, poss 1821; stld Lanark Co, ONT. m Robert McFarlane, qv. **SG xx/1 11**.

7927 McLEAN, Catherine, b 1768. From Is Rum, ARL. To Gut of Canso, Cape Breton, NS, on the *Saint Lawrence*, ex Tobermory, 11 Jul 1828. **SLL**.

7928 McLEAN, Catherine, b 1795. From Is Rum, ARL. To Gut of Canso, Cape Breton, NS, on the *Saint Lawrence*, ex Tobermory, 11 Jul 1828. **SLL**.

7929 McLEAN, Catherine Isabella, d 8 Mar 1877. From Crosspool, Is Coll, ARL. d/o Allan M. To Halifax, NS, 1817. Wife of Rev Donald Allan Fraser, qv. **FES vii 659**.

7930 McLEAN, Cathrine, b ca 1771. To Charlottetown, PEI, on the *Spencer*, ex Oban, 22 Sep 1806. Poss wife of Dougald M, qv. **PLSN**.

7931 McLEAN, Charles. From Frobost, Is South Uist, INV. To PEI on the *Jane*, ex Loch nan Uamh, Arisaig, 12 Jul 1790, poss calling at Loch Boisdale. **PLJ**.

7932 McLEAN, Charles. From ARL. s/o John M, of the Drimnin family, and Margaret Campbell, of the family of Scamadale. To NS, prob <1800. ch. **NSN 19/2**.

7933 McLEAN, Charles, b ca 1786. From Fortingall, PER. To Charlottetown, PEI, on the *Clarendon*, ex Oban, 6 Aug 1808. Labourer. Wife Mary McVean, qv, with him, and inf dau Christian. **CPL**.

7934 McLEAN, Charles, b ca 1787. From Is Mull, ARL. bro/o Ann M, qv. To Charlottetown, PEI, on the *Clarendon*, ex Oban, 6 Aug 1808. Labourer. **CPL**.

7935 McLEAN, Charles. Prob from ARL. To Pictou Co, NS, 1800; stld Big Brook, west branch, East River. Farmer, gr 309 acres, 1809. m Marjory McKay, qv, ch: 1. Donald, b 1800; 2. Gregor, b 1805; 3. Kenneth, 1809-87; 4. Isabel; 5. Anne; 6. Janet; 7. Jane, 1820–1902. **PAC 125**.

7936 McLEAN, Charles, b ca 1792. To Inverness, Inverness Co, NS, 1812. Farmer, m and ch. **CBC 1818**.

7937 McLEAN, Charles, b 1798. From Is Rum, ARL. To Gut of Canso, Cape Breton, NS, on the *Saint Lawrence*, ex Tobermory, 11 Jul 1828. **SLL**.

7938 McLEAN, Charles. From Caolasraide, South Knapdale, ARL. To Caradoc Twp, Middlesex Co, ONT, 1831, and d at Enniskillen. ch: 1. Malcolm; 2. Allan; 3. Annie; 4. Sarah; 5. Mary; 6. Catherine; 7. Bella. **PCM 35**.

7939 McLEAN, Christian, b ca 1775. From Balimore, Lochgilphead, ARL. To QUE, ex Greenock, summer 1815; stld ONT. Wife of Peter Stewart, qv. **SEC 3**.

7940 McLEAN, Christina, b ca 1790. From Kilfinichen, Is Mull, ARL. To Hudson Bay and Red River <1815. Wife of Neil Mackinnon, qv. **RRS 25**.

7941 McLEAN, Christina. From Is Tyree, ARL. To QUE on the *Conrad*, ex Greenock, 18 Jun 1850; stld Carrick

Twp, later Bruce Twp, Bruce Co, ONT. Wife of Neil Kennedy, qv. **DC 30 Sep 1980**.

7942   McLEAN, Christy. From Invergarry, INV. To Montreal, QUE, ex Fort William, arr Sep 1802; stld prob E ONT. **MCM 1/4 25**.

7943   McLEAN, Christy, ca 1795–6 Jul 1850. From Is Lewis, ROC. To Pictou Co, NS. Bur Old Elgin. m John Fraser. **DC 20 Nov 1976**.

7944   McLEAN, David. To Pictou Co, NS, <1793, when gr 500 acres on East River. Farmer, surveyor and magistrate. m Isabelle Fraser, qv, Middle River. **HPC App H**.

7945   McLEAN, David. To Pictou on the *Hope*, ex Glasgow, 5 Apr 1848. Wife Martha with him, and s Robert. **DC 12 Jul 1979**.

7946   MACLEAN, Donald, d 1782. From ARL. s/o John M, of the family of Drimnin, and Margaret Campbell, of the family of Scamadale. To NS. Physician. ch. **NSN 19/2**.

7947   McLEAN, Donald. From INV, poss Kilmorack. s/o Roderick M, qv, and Mary Chisholm, qv. To Pictou Co, NS, 1784, and stld Hopewell. m Elizabeth McLean, ch: 1. Roderick; 2. Murdoch. **PAC 150**.

7948   MACLEAN, Donald, ca 1758–6 Aug 1825. From Is Mull, ARL. s/o Capt Hector M, Shuna, and Janet MacLean. To St Andrews, Charlotte Co, NB, 1784. Half-pay officer, 74th Regt. Gr 2,600 acres on the St Francis River, Drummond Co, QUE, 1813, and d at Durham. m at Fort George, nr Castine, ME, 1782, Susannah Haney, ch: 1. Catherine; 2. Susannah, b 1784; 3. Janet; 4. Hector; 5. Archibald, b ca 1794; 6. Eleanor, b 1795; 7. Elizabeth, b 1798; 8. Margaret, b ca 1801; 9. John, 1803-83, ferryman, McLeans Ferry, St Francis River. **SG xxiii/1 11; DC 5 Oct and 1 Nov 1980**.

7949   MACLEAN, Donald. From Is Barra, INV. s/o Hugh M. To Arisaig, Antigonish Co, NS, ca 1798. m Mary Morrison, qv, ch: 1. John; 2. Malcolm; 3. Donald; 4. Kenneth; 5. Hugh; 6. Angus; 7. Flora; 8. Mary. **HCA 312**.

7950   MACLEAN, Donald, b ca 1775. From Kilmorack, INV. s/o Roderick M. and Margaret Chisholm. To Pictou, NS, on the *Dove*, ex Fort William, Jun 1801; stld nr Hopewell. m Elizabeth MacLean, qv. Son Neil, res Port Hood. **PLD; SG xii/1 26; NSN 18/5**.

7951   McLEAN, Donald, b ca 1746. To Western Shore, Inverness Co, NS, 1804. Farmer, m and ch. **CBC 1818**.

7952   McLEAN, Donald, b ca 1780. From Fortingall, PER. To Charlottetown, PEI, on the *Clarendon*, ex Oban, 6 Aug 1808. Labourer. **CPL**.

7953   MACLEAN, Donald, b 1768. To St Andrews dist, Cape Breton Co, NS, 1811. Farmer, m and ch. **CBC 1818**.

7954   McLEAN, Donald, b ca 1796. To Inverness, Inverness Co, NS, 1812. Farmer. **CBC 1818**.

7955   McLEAN, Donald. Prob from ARL. To Megantic Co, QUE, 1812. **AMC 87**.

7956   McLEAN, Donald, 1806-76. To Pictou Co, NS, stld Elgin. m Jessie McKay, 1817-93, ch: 1. Hector, 1843–1924; 2. Norman. **PAC 152**.

7957   McLEAN, Donald, b ca 1793. From Kilfinichen, Is Mull, ARL. To Hudson Bay and Red River <1815. Seaman and pioneer settler. **RRS 25**.

7958   McLEAN, Donald, b ca 1785. From Kilfinichen, Is Mull, ARL. To Hudson Bay and Red River, <1815. Wright and pioneer settler. Wife Margaret Morrison, qv, with him. **RSS 24**.

7959   MACLEAN, Donald. Prob from ARL. To Aldborough Twp, Elgin Co, ONT, prob 1818. Farmer. **PDA 93**.

7960   McLEAN, Donald. To QUE on the *David of London*, ex Greenock, 19 May 1821; stld North Sherbrooke Twp, Lanark Co, ONT. **HCL 74, 239**.

7961   McLEAN, Donald, b 1780. From Is Rum, ARL. To Gut of Canso, Cape Breton, NS, on the *Saint Lawrence*, ex Tobermory, 11 Jul 1828. **SLL**.

7962   McLEAN, Donald, b 1786. From Kilfinichen, Is Mull, ARL. To QUE, 1829; stld Lochaber, Ottawa Co. Farmer. m at Bunessan, 1807, Janet McCallum, qv, ch: 1. Neil; 2. John; 3. Allan; 4. Hector; 5. Janet; 6. Marion; 7. Flora; 8. Alexander; 9. Mary; 10. Hugh, b CAN; 11. Donald. **ELB 1**.

7963   MACLEAN, Donald. Poss from INV. To Antigonish Co, NS, prob <1830. ch: 1. Mary; 2. Sarah; 3. Jane; 4. Christina; 5. Flora; 6. Catherine; 7. Ann; 8. John, stld Cape Breton Is; 9. Hugh 'Ban', stld Cape Breton Is. **HCA 312**.

7964   McLEAN, Donald. From ARL. To Aldborough Twp, Elgin Co, ONT, 1833; moved to Mosa Twp, 1836. ch: 1. Malcolm; 2. Catherine. **PCM 23**.

7965   MACLEAN, Donald. To Bras D'Or, Cape Breton Co, NS, <1841. By wife Mary had, poss with other ch: 1. Thomas S, b 1841; 2. Alexander W, b 1846; 3. Kate; 4. Donald; 5. Murdoch. **NSN 34, 35**.

7966   McLEAN, Donald. To Pictou, NS, on the *Lady Gray*, ex Cromarty, ROC, 16 Jul 1841. **DC 15 Jul 1979**.

7967   McLEAN, Donald. From ARL. To Ekfrid Twp, Middlesex Co, ONT, 1842. ch: 1. Samuel; 2. Mrs D. Campbell. **PCM 31**.

7968   McLEAN, Donald. From Is South Uist, INV. To West Williams Twp, Middlesex Co, ONT, 1849. **PCM 48**.

7969   McLEAN, Donald, ca 1817–17 Feb 1879. From ARL. To QUE, prob <1850. Bur Flodden Station. m Catherine Cameron, qv. **MGC 15 Jul 1980**.

7970   McLEAN, Dougald, b ca 1774. To Charlottetown, PEI, on the *Spencer*, ex Oban, 22 Sep 1806. Wife with him, and ch: 1. Allan, aged 6; 2. Alexander, aged 2; 3. Gilbert, aged 3 mo. **PLSN**.

7971   MACLEAN, Dougald. From ARL. Prob rel to Duncan M, qv. To Aldborough Twp, Elgin Co, ONT, 1850. Local politician. Son James. **PDA 68**.

7972   McLEAN, Duncan. From Caum, ni, INV. To Montreal, QUE, ex Fort William, arr Sep 1802; stld E ONT. Wife with him. **MCM 1/4 24**.

7973   McLEAN, Duncan. From Munerigg, Invergarry, INV. To Montreal, QUE, ex Fort William, arr Sep 1802; stld E ONT. Wife with him. **MCM 1/4 26**.

7974 McLEAN, Duncan. From Munerigg, Invergarry, INV. To Montreal, QUE, ex Fort William, arr Sep 1802. Petitioned for land on the Ottawa River, 6 Aug 1804. **MCM 1/4 25; DC 15 Mar 1980**.

7975 McLEAN, Duncan, b ca 1780. Prob rel to Archibald M, qv. To Charlottetown, PEI, on the *Rambler*, ex Tobermory, 20 Jun 1806. **PLR**.

7976 McLEAN, Duncan, ca 1809–23 Jan 1852. From ARL. To Aldborough Twp, Elgin Co, ONT, 1819; moved to Ekfrid Twp, 1824. ch: 1. Alexander; 2. John; 3. Archibald; 4. Neil; 5. Gilbert; 6. Effie; 7. Janet; 8. Bella; 9. Annie. **PCM 29**.

7977 McLEAN, Duncan. From Loch Awe, ARL. To ONT <1826, when stld in Lobo Twp, Middlesex Co. ch: 1. Archibald; 2. Duncan; 3. John; 4. Donald; 5. Christy; 6. Sarah; 7. Katie; 8. Mary. **PCM 39**.

7978 McLEAN, Duncan. From Caolasraide, South Knapdale, ARL. To Caradoc Twp, Middlesex Co, ONT, 1831. m Sarah Sinclair, qv, ch: 1. John L, res Strathroy, Adelaide Twp; 2. Charles A. **PCM 35**.

7979 MACLEAN, Duncan. From ARL. Prob rel to Dougald M, qv. To Aldborough Twp, Elgin Co, ONT, 1850. **PDA 68**.

7980 McLEAN, Duncan. To Montreal, QUE, <1853. Studied for the ministry at Knox Coll, Toronto, and retr to SCT. **SGC 561**.

7981 McLEAN, Edward. To Pictou Co, NS, <1783, when he was listed as 'capable to bear arms.' **HPC App E**.

7982 McLEAN, Effie, b 1768. From Is Rum, ARL. To Gut of Canso, Cape Breton, NS, on the *Saint Lawrence*, ex Tobermory, 11 Jul 1828. **SLL**.

7983 McLEAN, Mrs Eliza, ca 1775–28 Jan 1855. From Forres, MOR. To Hamilton, ONT. **Ts Mount Albion**.

7984 McLEAN, Elizabeth. From Kilmorack, INV. To Pictou Co, NS, ca 1801; stld nr Hopewell. Wife of Donald MacLean, qv. **NSN 18/5**.

7985 McLEAN, Ewen. From Aberchalder, INV. To Montreal, QUE, ex Fort William, arr Sep 1802; stld E ONT. Wife with him, and family: 1. Donald; 2. Catherine; 3. Mary; 4-8. names unknown. **MCM 1/4 26**.

7986 McLEAN, Flora, b 1766. From Is Rum, ARL. To Gut of Canso, Cape Breton, NS, on the *Saint Lawrence*, ex Tobermory, 11 Jul 1828. **SLL**.

7987 McLEAN, George. To St John, NB, <1820. m Jemima, 1800-21, d/o Joshua Hughson, qv. **NER viii 98**.

7988 McLEAN, George Norris, b 1806. Perhaps rel to Donald Livingston, qv. To Charlottetown, PEI, on the *Rambler*, ex Tobermory, 20 Jun 1806. **PLR**.

7989 McLEAN, Gillean. From ARL. To Lobo Twp, Middlesex Co, ONT, 1838. **PCM 40**.

7990 McLEAN, Grace, 1759–31 Dec 1835. From Is Eigg, ARL. To New England, prob <1784, but stld Bartibog River, Miramichi, Northumberland Co, NB. Wife of Lt Col Alexander McDonald, qv. **DC 2 Jun 1978**.

7991 McLEAN, Hector, 1772–1854. From INV, poss Kilmorack. s/o Roderick M, qv, and Mary Chisholm, qv.

To Pictou Co, NS, 1784, and stld Hopewell. m Ann, d/o Kenneth Fraser, ch: 1. Roderick; 2. Donald; 3. John; 4. Kenneth, 1816–1908; 5. Neil; 6. Rev Alexander, 1822–1916. **PAC 152; SG xxii/1 26**.

7992 McLEAN, Hector, b 1799. Prob bro/o John M, qv. To Western Shore, Inverness Co, NS, 1802. Farmer, unm. **CBC 1818**.

7993 MACLEAN, Hector. From Urquhart and Glenmoriston par, INV. bro/o Alexander M, qv. Gr 400 acres on west branch of East River, 1 Apr 1793. **HPC App H**.

7994 McLEAN, Hector, 2 Apr 1769–28 Apr 1810. From ARL. s/o Hugh M, 14th feudal baron of Kingairloch, and Beatrix McLachlan. Succeeded his bro Donald in 1799 as 16th baron of Kingairloch, but sold estate to James Forbes and stld Pictou, NS, 1812. Merchant, Deacons Wharf, in partnership with Simon Fraser. m 1 Jul 1801, Elizabeth, d/o Capt John Fraser, 82nd Regt, ch: 1. Harriet, b 1804; 2. Elizabeth, b 1805; 3. Murdoch Hector, 1807-65, High Sheriff of Guysborough Co, NS; 4. Simon Fraser, b 1809, master mariner. **DGC 28 Aug 1810**.

7995 McLEAN, Hector, b ca 1788. From Cambus, Kilfinichen, Is Mull, ARL. s/o — M. and Margaret McInnes, qv. To Hudson Bay and Red River, <1813. Pioneer settler. **RRS 25**.

7996 McLEAN, Hector, b 1796. From Is Rum, ARL. To Gut of Canso, Cape Breton, NS, on the *Saint Lawrence*, ex Tobermory, 11 Jul 1828. Wife Catherine, aged 29, with him, and inf dau Mary. **SLL**.

7997 McLEAN, Hector, b 1768. From Is Rum, ARL. To Gut of Canso, Cape Breton, NS, on the *Saint Lawrence*, ex Tobermory, 11 Jul 1828. **SLL**.

7998 McLEAN, Hector. From ARL. To London Twp, Middlesex Co, ONT, 1830. **PCM 50**.

7999 McLEAN, Hector. From ARL. To Mosa Twp, Middlesex Co, ONT, 1831. **PCM 24**.

8000 McLEAN, Hugh, b ca 1789. To Inverness, Inverness Co, NS, 1800. Farmer, m and ch. **CBC 1818**.

8001 McLEAN, Hugh, b ca 1757. To Inverness Co, NS, 1799; stld Port Hood dist. Farmer, m and ch. **CBC 1818**.

8002 McLEAN, Hugh, b ca 1779. To Inverness Co, NS, 1803; stld Port Hood dist. Farmer, m and ch. **CBC 1818**.

8003 McLEAN, Hugh, b ca 1796. From Kilfinichen, Is Mull, ARL. To Hudson Bay and Red River <1813. Pioneer settler. **RRS 25**.

8004 McLEAN, Hugh. To Lanark Co, ONT, 1821; stld Lot 5, Con 3, North Sherbrooke Twp. **HCL 74**.

8005 McLEAN, Hugh, b 1784. From Is Rum, ARL. To Gut of Canso, Cape Breton, NS, on the *Saint Lawrence*, ex Tobermory, 11 Jul 1828. Wife Marion with him, and ch: 1. Flora, aged 19; 2. John, aged 13; 3. Angus, aged 10; 4. Mary, aged 6; 5. Catherine, aged 4; 6. Hector, aged 3; 7. Allan, inf. **SLL**.

8006 McLEAN, Hugh, jr, b 1801. From Is Rum, ARL. Prob rel to Hugh M, qv, and wife Marion. To Gut of Canso, Cape Breton, NS, on the *Saint Lawrence*, ex Tobermory, 11 Jul 1828. **SLL**.

8007   McLEAN, Hugh, b 1799. From Is Rum, ARL. To Gut of Canso, Cape Breton, NS, on the *Saint Lawrence*, ex Tobermory, 11 Jul 1828. **SLL**.

8008   MACLEAN, Hugh 'Ban'. From Is Eigg, INV. To Judique, Inverness Co, NS, prob <1830. Son Alexander, bard. **MP 726**.

8009   McLEAN, Hugh. From Inverary, ARL. s/o Neil M, qv, and Mary McIntyre. To Caradoc Twp, Middlesex Co, ONT, 1831. ch: 1. Neil, farmer; 2. Maggie. **PCM 35**.

8010   McLEAN, Hugh, b 1802. From South Uist, INV. To Richmond Co, NS, <1839; stld L'Ardoise. Wife Sarah with him. They had, poss with other ch: 1. Neil, b 1829; 2. Donald, b 1839. **NSN 14/3**.

8011   McLEAN, Rev Hugh, 12 Jul 1830–12 Nov 1901. From Kilmorack, AYR. s/o John M, qv, and Jean Gilchrist, qv. To QUE on the *Renfrewshire*, 1842; stld Aldborough Twp, Elgin Co, ONT. Became a Methodist preacher, and d Toronto. m Margaret McNairn. **DC 23 Nov 1981**.

8012   MACLEAN, Hugh, b ca 1806. From Dunganichy, Is Benbecula, INV. s/o Donald M. and Catherine MacPherson. To Pictou, NS, on the *Lulan*, ex Greenock, 17 Aug 1848. Wife Jessie MacDonald, qv, with him, and some of the following ch: 1. Mary; 2. Charles; 3. Effie, b 1835; 4. Catherine, b 1838; 5. Donald, b 1841; 6. Mary, b 1845. **DC 12 Jul 1979; WLC**.

8013   MACLEAN, Hugh, b ca 1825. From Tain, ROC. s/o William M, labourer in Balnagall, and Grizel Ross. To NS, 1843; stld prob Pictou Co. **DC 14 Sep 1974**.

8014   McLEAN, Isabella, 1764–12 Aug 1791. d/o Daniel M, sometime Collector of Customs, Montego Bay, Jamaica, West Indies. To Miramichi, Northumberland Co, NB. m Patrick Taylor. **DC 4 Dec 1978**.

8015   McLEAN, James, b ca 1763. To Charlottetown, PEI, on the *Rambler*, ex Tobermory, 20 Jun 1806. Wife Peggy, aged 43, with him, and ch: 1. Donald, aged 20; 2. Christian, aged 18; 3. Hugh, aged 14; 4. Mary, aged 7; 5. Alexander, aged 6; 6. Angus, aged 4. **PLR**.

8016   McLEAN, James. From Killin, PER. To Montreal, QUE, on the *Curlew*, ex Greenock, 21 Jul 1818; stld prob Beckwith Twp, Lanark Co, ONT. Wife Janet with him, and inf dau Margaret. **BCL**.

8017   MACLEAN, James. From ARL. To Aldborough Twp, Elgin Co, ONT, 1850. **PDA 75**.

8018   McLEAN, Janet, ca 1755–12 Dec 1833. From ARL. To Pictou Co, NS. Bur Old Elgin. Wife of Allan McQuarry, qv. **DC 20 Nov 1976**.

8019   McLEAN, Janet. From Beauly, INV. To Pictou, NS, on the *Sarah*, ex Fort William, Jun 1801. Spinster. **PLS**.

8020   McLEAN, Janet, ca 1831–9 Nov 1877. To Wellington Co, ONT, ca 1854. m Francis Peffers, qv, and d in Minto Twp. **DC 30 Apr 1980**.

8021   McLEAN, Jean. From Munerigg, Invergarry, INV. To QUE, ex Fort William, arr Sep 1802; stld E ONT. **MCM 1/4 25**.

8022   MACLEAN, John. From Is Mull, ARL. To Shelburne Co, NS, <1776. m Margaret Allen, qv, ch. **DC 5 Mar 1979**.

8023   McLEAN, John. From DFS or KKD. To Pictou Co, NS, <12 Feb 1783, when listed as 'capable to bear arms.' Stld West River. Farmer and Ch elder. Son John. **HPC App D and E**.

8024   MACLEAN, John. From Is Mull, ARL. To Shelburne Co, NS, <1785. m Margaret Allen, ch: 1. Alexander; 2. Margaret; 3. Samuel; 4. Susanna. **DC 25 Jan 1964**.

8025   McLEAN, John. From Kildonan, Is Eigg, INV. To PEI on the *Lucy*, ex Loch nan Uamh, Arisaig, 12 Jul 1790. Tenant farmer. Wife with him, and 6 ch. **PLL**.

8026   McLEAN, John. From Kiltearn, ROC. To Pictou, NS, on the *Sarah*, ex Fort William, Jun 1801. Labourer. Wife Ann with him, and dau Isobel. **PLS**.

8027   MACLEAN, John, b ca 1791. From Kilmorack, INV. To Pictou, NS, on the *Dove*, ex Fort William, Jun 1801. **PLD**.

8028   McLEAN, John, 1784–1867. From ROC. To Pictou Co, NS, ca 1801. m Margaret McCabe, 1785–1831. **DC 21 Oct 1970**.

8029   McLEAN, John, b 1763. To Western Shore, Inverness Co, NS, 1802. Farmer, m and ch. **CBC 1818**.

8030   McLEAN, John, b ca 1801. Prob bro/o Hector M, qv. To Western Shore, Inverness Co, NS, 1802. Farmer. **CBC 1818**.

8031   McLEAN, John, b ca 1785. Poss s/o Donald M, qv. To Western Shore, Inverness Co, NS, 1804. Farmer, m and ch. **CBC 1818**.

8032   McLEAN, John. From Arisaig, INV. To Antigonish Co, NS, <1810, when m Jane Grant, Merigomish. **DC 21 Mar 1981**.

8033   McLEAN, John, 1811–ca 1883. From Kilfinichen, Is Mull, ARL. s/o Angus M, qv, and Mary Sinclair, qv. To QUE, ca 1810; moved ca 1820 to Blackland, Restigouche Co, NB, and later to Heron Is. Farmer and fisherman. m (i) Mary Miller, 1810–64, ch: 1. John, b ca 1839; 2. Angus, b ca 1840; 3. Catherine, b ca 1842; 4. Jane, b ca 1845; 5. William, b ca 1849. m (ii) Jessie Anderson, b ca 1840, further ch: 6. Elizabeth, b ca 1866; 7. David, b ca 1868; 8. Thomas, b 1869; 9. Arthur, b 1872; 10. Jessie Ann, b 1875; 11. Margaret Jane, b 1876; 12. Georgina, b 1878. **RCP 6**.

8034   McLEAN, John, b ca 1786. To Inverness, Inverness Co, NS, 1812. Farmer, m and ch. **CBC 1818**.

8035   McLEAN, John, b ca 1792. From Kilfinichen, Is Mull, ARL. To Hudson Bay and Red River <1813. Pioneer settler. **RSS 25**.

8036   McLEAN, John, ca 1786–1872. From Annan, DFS. To Miramichi, Northumberland Co, NB, ca 1816; stld Napan. Farmer. m Elizabeth Aitchison, qv. Son Thomas. **DC 2 Jun 1878**.

8037   McLEAN, John, ca 1799–13 Apr 1874. From INV. To Pictou Co, NS. Bur Old Elgin. **DC 20 Nov 1976**.

8038   McLEAN, John, ca 1801–20 Dec 1860. Poss from INV. To Pictou Co, NS. Bur Old Elgin. **DC 20 Nov 1976**.

8039   McLEAN, John, b ca 1787. From Kilbrianain, Kilmore, Is Mull, ARL. To Hudson Bay and Red River <1815. Wife and two ch with him. **RRS 24**.

8040 McLEAN, John, b ca 1795. To North End, Gut of Canso, Cape Breton, NS, 1816. Cooper, unm. **CBC 1818**.

8041 MACLEAN, John, 8 Jan 1787–26 Jan 1848. From Caolis, Is Tyree, ARL. To Pictou, NS, on the *Economy*, ex Tobermory, 1 Oct 1819. Shoemaker, poet and song-writer. m Isabella Black, qv, ch: 1. Christy; 2. Charles; 3. Archibald; 4. John; 5. John, b Ballard; 6. Allan; 7. Elizabeth. **DC 13 Apr 1966**.

8042 MACLEAN, John. Prob from ARL. Poss rel to Neil M, qv, and Duncan M, qv. To Aldborough Twp, Elgin Co, ONT, <1820. Farmer. **PDA 92**.

8043 McLEAN, John, 1799–8 Mar 1890. From Dervaig, Kilninian par, Is Mull, ARL. Neph of Col Neil M, Stormont Militia, qv. To Montreal, QUE, 1820, via NY and Hudson River. Emp with HBCo from 1821. Explored in NWT and Labrador, and discovered Hamilton or Churchill Falls, 1839. Ret in 1846, and stld Elora, Nichol Twp, Wellington Co, ONT. Left a journal. m (i) d/o Donald Ross, chief trader, ch: 1. John. m (ii) Eugenia, d/o Rev James Evans, Wesleyan missionary to the Cree Indians, further ch: 2. Archibald, journalist, d 1925; 3. Clara; 4. Margaret; 5. Eugenie. **MDB 474; EHE 152; DC 1 Jan 1968**.

8044 McLEAN, John. Prob from Edinburgh. s/o John M. and Margaret Reid. To Halifax, NS, <1822. **SH**.

8045 McLEAN, John, d 15 May 1840. From Dunscore, DFS. To North Elmsley Twp, Lanark Co, ONT. Surgeon, sometime in RN. **DGH 29 Oct 1840**.

8046 MACLEAN, John. Prob from ARL. s/o Angus M, qv. To Antigonish Co, NS, poss <1830. m (i) d/o Donald MacDonald, Williams Point, ch: 1. Daniel. m (ii) d/o Donald MacDonald, OH, further ch: 2. Mary; 3. Kate; 4. Maggie; 5. Sarah; 6. Jane; 7. Charles; 8. Angus. **HCA 310**.

8047 MACLEAN, John. From Knoydart, INV. To Antigonish Co, NS, poss <1830; stld Beaver Meadow. m Flora MacDonald, qv, ch: 1. Ann; 2. John; 3. Archibald; 4. Donald; 5. Jane; 6. Flora. **HCA 311**.

8048 McLEAN, John 'Roy'. From Ardgour, ARL. To Ekfrid Twp, Middlesex Co, ONT, 1835. **PCM 31**.

8049 McLEAN, John. From ARL. To Ekfrid Twp, Middlesex Co, ONT, 1835. Weaver. **PCM 31**.

8050 McLEAN, John, 2 Jan 1807–7 Apr 1882. From Kilmarnock, AYR. s/o Adam M, weaver, and Elizabeth Fraser. To QUE on the *Renfrewshire*, ex Glasgow, 1842; stld Aldborough Twp, Elgin Co, ONT. Weaver, later farmer. m Jean Gilchrist, qv, ch: 1. Adam, qv; 2. James, 1826–90, lumberman; 3. John, jr, qv; 4. Rev Hugh, qv; 5. William, qv; 6. Andrew, 1835–1928, blacksmith; 7. Robert, qv; 7-8. Jean and Mathew, twins, b 1839. **DC 1 Dec 1980**.

8051 McLEAN, John, jr, 8 Aug 1828–16 Sep 1908. From Kilmarnock, AYR. s/o John M, qv, and Jean Gilchrist, qv. To QUE on the *Renfrewshire*, 1842; stld Aldborough Twp, Elgin Co, ONT. Lawyer. Bur St Thomas. m Jane Ann Ward, 1828–1908. **DC 23 Nov 1981**.

8052 McLEAN, John, 5 Nov 1815–16 Jan 1889. From Torosay, Is Mull, ARL. s/o Roderick M. and Margaret McLean, qv. To ONT, 1848; stld Kincardine Twp, Bruce Co. m Christina McMaster, qv, ch. **Torosay OPR 551/1; DC 7 Nov 1980**.

8053 MACLEAN, John. From Arisaig, INV. To Antigonish Co, NS, poss <1850. m Jane Grant, from Merigomish, ch: 1. John; 2. Archibald; 3. John; 4. Ronald, lawyer; 5. John W; 6. Dougald; 7. Annie; 8. Mary; 9. Zita; 10. Margaret; 11. Sadie. **HCA 313**.

8054 McLEAN, John (1). From Is Lewis, ROC. To QUE, ex Stornoway, arr 4 Aug 1851; stld Huron Twp, Bruce Co, ONT, 1852. Head of family. **DC 5 Apr 1967**.

8055 McLEAN, John (2). From Is Lewis, ROC. To QUE, ex Stornoway, arr 4 Aug 1851; stld Huron Twp, Bruce Co, ONT, 1852. Head of family. **DC 5 Apr 1967**.

8056 MACLEAN, Rev John, 1828–7 Nov 1886. From Portsoy, BAN. s/o Charles M. Grad MA, Kings Coll, Aberdeen, 1851. To ONT, 1858, and app curate of St Pauls Ch, London, Middlesex Co. Rector of St Johns, Winnipeg, 1866, and Archdeacon of Assiniboia. Bishop of Saskatchewan, 1874. DCL, Trinity Coll, Toronto, and of Bishops Coll, Lennoxville; DD, Kenyon Coll, OH. **MOT 1875/684; BNA 1055; KCG 303**.

McLEAN, Mrs John. See McNAIR, Catherine.

8057 McLEAN, John B, ca 1804–19 Jan 1858. To QUE, prob <1850. Bur Flodden Station. m Margaret McNaughton, qv. **MGC 15 Jul 1980**.

8058 McLEAN, Rev John C, b 15 Aug 1800. From Is Tyree, ARL. s/o Allan M, tailor. Matric Univ of Glasgow, 1833. Entered United Secession Theological Hall, but went to Pictou, NS, before completing his studies. Became Presb min and moved to Newburyport, MA, 1852. Went later to NC, and d Wheeling, WV. **GMA 13195**.

8059 McLEAN, John Wesley, b 9 Nov 1818. To ONT <1828, prob with parents and other members of the family. **DC 10 Feb 1978**.

8060 MACLEAN, Katherine. From Kilmorack, INV. To Pictou, NS, on the *Dove*, ex Fort William, Jun 1801. Spinster. **PLD**.

8061 McLEAN, Katherine. Poss from Drumnadrochit, INV. To Montreal, QUE, ex Fort William, arr Sep 1802; stld E ONT. **MCM 1/4 26**.

8062 MACLEAN, Katherine. From Kilmorack, INV. Poss wife of Alexander M, labourer, qv. To Pictou, NS, on the *Dove*, ex Fort William, Jun 1801. **PLD**.

8063 McLEAN, Katrine, b 1806. Poss d/o Archibald M, qv. To Charlottetown, PEI, on the *Rambler*, ex Tobermory, 20 Jun 1806. **PLR**.

8064 McLEAN, Kenneth. From Is Mull, ARL. To Montreal, QUE, ex Fort William, arr Sep 1802; stld E ONT. **MCM 1/4 26**.

8065 MACLEAN, Lachlan. To PEI, poss 1803; stld Queens Co. Petitioner for Dr MacAulay, 1811. **HP 74**.

8066 McLEAN, Lachlan, b ca 1783. From Is Mull, ARL. To Charlottetown, PEI, on the *Clarendon*, ex Oban, 6 Aug 1808. Labourer. Wife Ann, aged 30, with him, and dau Janet, aged 2. **CPL**.

8067 MACLEAN, Lachlan. From Is Coll, ARL. To Antigonish Co, NS, <1820; stld Keppoch. ch: 1. Archibald; 2. John; 3. Norman; 4. Neil, res Guysborough Co; 5. Alexander; 6. Mary; 7. Christina; 8. Isabel. **HCA 309**.

8068   McLEAN, Lachlan. Prob from Glasgow. To Pictou Co, NS, 1821. m Elizabeth Campbell, qv.   **PAC 53**.

8069   McLEAN, Lachlan, b ca 1779. From Glenforsa, Kilninian and Kilmore par, Is Mull, ARL. Served in the Lochaber Regt, 1798–1801, and stld New Kilpatrick, DNB, as a weaver. To QUE on the *Earl of Buckinghamshire*, Apr 1821; stld Ramsay Twp, Lanark Co, ONT. Farmer and poet. m Christine Campbell, qv, ch: 1. Jean; 2. Alexander; 3. Robert; 4. Christy.   **DC 8 Aug 1978**.

8070   McLEAN, Lachlan. From Is Mull, ARL. To Finch Twp, Stormont Co, ONT. Farmer. Son George, 1863–1937, cheese-maker.   **SDG 488, 506**.

8071   McLEAN, Lachlan. From Lochbuie, Is Mull, ARL. To Port Elgin, Bruce Co, ONT, 1849. Storekeeper.   **DC 21 Mar 1981**.

8072   McLEAN, Lachlan, 25 Jun 1801–1 Mar 1894. From Caolis, Is Tyree, ARL. s/o Hector and Margaret M. To Kincardine Twp, Bruce Co, ONT, prob <1850. Wife Marion McLean, qv, with him, and ch: 1. Mary, b 8 Aug 1833; 2. Alexander; 3. John, b 28 Apr 1837; 4. Margaret, b 16 Jun 1839; 5. Lachlan, b 17 Nov 1841; 6. Archibald, b 4 Jul 1844; 7. Annabell, b 28 Aug 1846.   **DC 15 Nov 1980**.

8073   McLEAN, Lauchlan, b ca 1791. Poss rel to Archibald M, qv. To Charlottetown, PEI, on the *Rambler*, ex Tobermory, 20 Jun 1806.   **PLR**.

8074   McLEAN, Lauchlan, b ca 1749. From Is Mull, ARL. To Charlottetown, PEI, on the *Clarendon*, ex Oban, 6 Aug 1808. Wife Catherine, aged 56, with him, and family: 1. Flora, aged 30; 2. Hugh, aged 25; 3. Ann, aged 20; 4. Hector, aged 15; 5. John, aged 12; 6. Euphemia, aged 10.   **CPL**.

8075   MACLEAN, Lauchlan, b 23 Sep 1754. From Kilninian and Kilmore par, Is Mull, ARL. s/o Rev Alexander M. and Christian MacLean, of the family of Torloisk. To Halifax, NS, <1780. Civil servant.   **FES iv 115**.

8076   McLEAN, Lauchlan, b 1783. From Is Rum, ARL. To Gut of Canso, Cape Breton, NS, on the *Saint Lawrence*, ex Tobermory, 11 Jul 1828. Wife Mary, aged 48, with him.   **SLL**.

8077   McLEAN, Malcolm, b ca 1776. To Mabou, Inverness Co, NS, 1804. Farmer, m and ch.   **CBC 1818**.

8078   McLEAN, Malcolm. From Is Mull, ARL. bro/o Archibald M, qv. To Leeds Twp, Megantic Co, QUE, 1809. Pioneer settler. Killed by a falling tree.   **AMC 93**.

8079   MACLEAN, Malcolm. From Is Barra, INV. s/o Hector M. To Poplar Grove, Mabou Harbour, NS, ca 1818. ch: 1. Hector; 2. Angus; 3. Alexander; 4. John; 5. Julia; 6. Isabel; 7. Mary.   **MP 731**.

8080   McLEAN, Malcolm. From Is Lewis, INV. To QUE, ex Stornoway, arr 4 Aug 1851; stld Huron Twp, Bruce Co, ONT, 1852. Head of family.   **DC 5 Apr 1967**.

8081   MACLEAN, Margaret. From Kilmorack, INV. Poss rel to William M, qv. To Pictou, NS, on the *Dove*, ex Fort William, Jun 1801. Spinster.   **PLD**.

8082   McLEAN, Margaret, b ca 1800. To Port Hawkesbury, Inverness Co, NS, 1824. m William,

s/o William Philpotts and Elizabeth Shave, from Hampshire, ENG, ch: 1. William; 2. Angus; 3. James; 4. Jeremiah; 5. Catherine; 6. Elizabeth; 7. Susan; 8. Charlotte; 9. Martha.   **DC 10 Sep 1977**.

8083   McLEAN, Margaret, ca 1800–16 Jun 1874. From Is Lewis, ROC. To Richmond Co, NS, <1840. Wife of John Smith, qv.   **NSN 9/2**.

8084   McLEAN, Mrs Margaret, b ca 1791. From Torosay par, Is Mull, ARL. To ONT, 1848; stld Kincardine Twp, Bruce Co. wid/o Roderick M. ch with her: 1. Charles, b 1814; 2. John, qv.   **Torosay OPR 551/1; DC 7 Nov 1980**.

8085   McLEAN, Margaret, b ca 1815. From Uig par, Is Lewis, ROC. To Lingwick Twp, Compton Co, QUE, <1855. Wife of Peter Gillies, qv.   **WLC**.

8086   McLEAN, Marian, ca 1825–31 May 1912. Poss from ARL. To QUE, prob <1850. m John McLeod, qv.   **MGC 15 Jul 1980**.

8087   McLEAN, Marion, b ca 1787. Poss rel to Archibald M, qv. To Charlottetown, PEI, on the *Rambler*, ex Tobermory, 20 Jun 1806.   **PLR**.

8088   McLEAN, Mrs Marion, b ca 1746. To Pictou, NS, 1815. Widow, maintained by charity in 1816.   **INS 37**.

8089   McLEAN, Marion, b ca 1779. From Kilfinichen, Is Mull, ARL. To Hudson Bay and Red River <1815. Pioneer woman, and wife of Archibald Mackinnon, qv.   **RRS 24**.

8090   McLEAN, Marion, b 1804. From Is Rum, ARL. To Gut of Canso, Cape Breton, NS, on the *Saint Lawrence*, ex Tobermory, 11 Jul 1828.   **SLL**.

8091   McLEAN, Marion, b 1807. From Caolis, Is Tyree, ARL. d/o Archibald M. and Mary McConnel. To Kincardine Twp, Bruce Co, ONT, <1850. Wife of Lachlan McLean, qv, m 25 Apr 1832.   **DC 7 Nov 1980**.

8092   MACLEAN, Mary. From Kilmorack, INV. To Pictou, NS, on the *Dove*, ex Fort William, Jun 1801. Spinster.   **PLD**.

8093   McLEAN, Mary, ca 1783–6 Jul 1843. From Inverness. To Pictou Co, NS, 1801. m Donald Murray, qv.   **DC 10 Feb 1980**.

8094   McLEAN, Mary, b ca 1781. Poss rel to Archibald M, qv. To Charlottetown, PEI, on the *Rambler*, ex Tobermory, 20 Jun 1806.   **PLR**.

8095   McLEAN, Mary. Poss from Drumnadrochit, INV. To Montreal, QUE, ex Fort William, arr Sep 1802; stld E ONT.   **MCM 1/4 26**.

8096   McLEAN, Mary, b ca 1803. Poss d/o Archibald M, qv. To Charlottetown, PEI, on the *Rambler*, ex Tobermory, 20 Jun 1806.   **PLR**.

8097   McLEAN, Mary, b ca 1798. From Cambus, Kilfinichen, ARL. d/o — M. and Margaret McInnes, qv. To Hudson Bay and Red River, <1813.   **RRS 25**.

8098   McLEAN, Mary, b ca 1773. From Torosay par, Is Mull, ARL. To Hudson Bay and Red River <1815. Wife of Archibald McGillivray, qv.   **RRS 25**.

8099   MACLEAN, Mary, 1791–1884. From Is Coll, ARL. s/o Charles M, tenant there. To East Lake Ainslie, Inverness Co, NS, 1820. Wife of Allan Mackinnon, qv.   **DC 23 Feb 1980**.

8100 MACLEAN, Mary. From Is South Uist, INV. To Cape Breton Co, NS, 1823. Wife of Allan MacDonald, qv. **DC 23 Feb 1980**.

8101 McLEAN, Mary, b 1788. From Is Rum, ARL. Poss wife of Donald M, qv. To Gut of Canso, Cape Breton, NS, on the *Saint Lawrence*, ex Tobermory, 11 Jul 1828. **SLL**.

8102 McLEAN, Mary, b 1778. From Is Rum, ARL. To Gut of Canso, Cape Breton, NS, on the *Saint Lawrence*, ex Tobermory, 11 Jul 1828. **SLL**.

8103 McLEAN, Mary. To Dundas Co, ONT, <1853. m John Johnston, qv. **SDG 442**.

8104 McLEAN, Mary. Prob from ARL. To Cape Breton Co, NS, <1855. m Malcolm Ferguson, qv. **HNS iii 330**.

8105 McLEAN, Mary, b ca 1782. From Is Mull, ARL. d/o Angus M, qv. To Charlottetown, PEI, on the *Clarendon*, ex Oban, 6 Aug 1808. **CPL**.

8106 McLEAN, Mary. From Cummertrees, DFS. d/o William M, qv. To Watford, Lambton Co, ONT, ca 1845. m James Hamilton, qv. **DC 18 Jul 1979**.

8107 McLEAN, Mary Isabella, b 1812. From Is Coll, ARL. To NS <1845; stld Irish Cove, Cape Breton Co. m John Gillies, qv. **HNS iii 280**.

8108 McLEAN, Mary Jane. From Is Mull, ARL. To Cape Breton Is, NS, <1830. m Duncan MacDougall, qv. **HNS iii 613**.

8109 McLEAN, Mary Julia, d 24 May 1854. From Scallastle, Torosay par, Is Mull, ARL. d/o John and Margaret M. To Pictou Co, NS, 1838; later to Pittsburgh, PA, USA. m 1822, Rev John Campbell Sinclair, qv. **SCI 410**.

8110 MACLEAN, Matthew Witherspoon, b 11 Jun 1842. From Glasgow. s/o Malcolm M, beadle. Matric Univ of Glasgow, 1853. To Kingston, ONT, as a divinity student, and studied at Queens Coll, later Princeton. Adm min of St Andrews Presb Ch, Paisley, Bruce Co, ONT, 1866. Later min at Port Hope and Belleville. **BNA 1175; GMA 16352**.

8111 McLEAN, Mrs, d 24 Aug 1837. From Dunscore, DFS. To North Elmsley Twp, Lanark Co, ONT. Wife of William M, sometime farmer in Chapel. **DGC 8 Nov 1837**.

8112 McLEAN, Murdoch, b ca 1790. To Inverness, Inverness Co, NS, 1816. Farmer. **CBC 1818**.

8113 MACLEAN, Murdoch. To PEI <1818; stld Point Prim, Queens Co. m Mary Martin. Dau Catherine. **HP 35**.

8114 McLEAN, Murdoch, 1806-70. From INV. To Pictou Co, NS, 1827; stld west branch, East River. Farmer. m Jean McKay, qv, ch: 1. Betsy, b 1837; 2. Hugh, b 1839; 3. Neil, b 1840; 4. Christy Ann; 5. Roderick, b ca 1851; 6. Catherine, 1856–1901. **PAC 151**.

8115 McLEAN, Murdoch. From Is Lewis, ROC. To QUE, ex Stornoway, arr 4 Aug 1851; stld Huron Twp, Bruce Co, ONT, 1852. Head of family. **DC 5 Apr 1967**.

8116 McLEAN, Neil, 1757–1832. Born Mingarry, Is Mull, ARL. s/o John M. of Hyskier, and Elizabeth McLean. To Cornwall, Stormont Co, ONT, <1785.

Ensign, 84th Regt; Capt, Royal Canadian Volunteers, 1796–1802; Sheriff of East Cornwall and Col of Militia. m Isabella, d/o John Macdonell of Leek, ch: 1. John, Sheriff of Kingston; 2. Archibald, 1791–1865, Chief Justice of ONT; 3. Alexander, 1793–1875, MPP; 4. Isabella; 5. Mrs Hopper. **BNA 343; SDG 106, 109, 176**.

8117 McLEAN, Neil, b ca 1788. To Inverness, Inverness Co, NS, 1812. Carpenter, unm. **CBC 1818**.

8118 MACLEAN, Neil, 1784–19 Oct 1828. Prob from ARL. Poss rel to Duncan M, qv, and John M, qv. To Aldborough Twp, Elgin Co, ONT, <1820. Farmer. **PDA 92**.

8119 McLEAN, Neil, b 1788. From Is Rum, ARL. To Gut of Canso, Cape Breton, NS, on the *Saint Lawrence*, ex Tobermory, arr 11 Jul 1828. Wife Mary, aged 30, with him, and ch: 1. Margaret, aged 10; 2. John, aged 6; 3. Alexander, aged 5; 4. Ann, aged 3; 5. Donald, inf. **SLL**.

8120 McLEAN, Neil, b 1800. From Is Rum, ARL. To Gut of Canso, Cape Breton, NS, on the *Saint Lawrence*, ex Tobermory, 11 Jul 1828. **SLL**.

8121 McLEAN, Neil. From Inveraray, ARL. To Caradoc Twp, Middlesex Co, ONT, 1831; stld Lot 21, Con 9. Weaver and farmer. Wife Mary McIntyre, d Montreal, QUE. Son Hugh, qv. **PCM 35**.

8122 McLEAN, Norman. From Is Lewis, ROC. To QUE, ex Stornoway, arr 4 Aug 1851; stld Huron Twp, Bruce Co, ONT, 1852. Head of family. **DC 5 Apr 1967**.

8123 McLEAN, Rev Patrick 'Mor', 1800–20 Mar 1868. From Uig par, Is Lewis, ROC. Schoolmaster there. To Patricks Channel and Whycocomagh Bay, Cape Breton Is, NS, arr 26 Aug 1837. Retr to SCT because of ill-health, 1841, and in 1843, became FC min at Tobermory, Is Mull, ARL. m Flora Campbell. **AFC i 245; FES vii 607**.

8124 McLEAN, Peggy, b 1748. From Is Rum, ARL. To Gut of Canso, Cape Breton, NS, on the *Saint Lawrence*, ex Tobermory, 11 Jul 1828. **SLL**.

8125 McLEAN, Peggy, b 1788. From Is Rum, ARL. To Gut of Canso, Cape Breton, NS, on the *Saint Lawrence*, ex Tobermory, 11 Jul 1828. **SLL**.

8126 McLEAN, Peter. From ARL. To Ekfrid Twp, Middlesex Co, ONT, 1834. **PCM 30**.

8127 McLEAN, Ranald, b ca 1788. To Inverness, Inverness Co, NS, 1816. Farmer, m and ch. **CBC 1818**.

8128 McLEAN, Robert, 19 Feb 1837–8 Feb 1915. From Kilmarnock, AYR. s/o John M, qv, and Jean Gilchrist, qv. To QUE on the *Renfrewshire*, 1842; stld Aldborough Twp, Elgin Co, ONT. Bur Glencoe. m Margaret Davidson. **DC 23 Nov 1981**.

8129 McLEAN, Roderick. From INV. To Pictou Co, NS, 1784; stld Milltown, or Hopewell, Pictou Co. m Mary Chisholm, qv, ch: 1. Hector, qv; 2. Donald, qv; 3. Neil, went to AUS. **PAC 150**.

8130 McLEAN, Roderick, b ca 1750. To Inverness, Inverness Co, NS, 1812. Farmer, m and ch. **CBC 1818**.

8131 McLEAN, Roderick, b ca 1756. To Western Shore, Inverness Co, NS, 1802. Farmer, m and ch. **CBC 1818**.

McLEAN, Mrs Roderick. See McLEAN, Margaret.

8132   McLEAN, Sarah, b ca 1784. From Is Mull, ARL. To Charlottetown, PEI, on the *Clarendon*, ex Oban, 6 Aug 1808. Spinster.   **CPL**.

8133   McLEAN, Thomas, b ca 1792. From Dunscore, DFS. To QUE, on the *Atlas*, ex Greenock, 11 Jul 1815; stld Lot 23, Con 6, North Elmsley Twp, Lanark Co, ONT, along with Archibald Morrison, qv. Farmer.   **SEC 3; HCL 12, 230, 232**.

8134   McLEAN, Thomas, b ca 1810. From Annan, DFS. s/o John M, qv, and Elizabeth Aitchison, qv. To Miramichi, Northumberland Co, NB. Farmer at Napan. m at Chatham, 1843, Margaret Isabella McGraw, b IRL, 1826, ch: 1. John; 2. George, 1848–1931; 3. William, 1854–1936; 4. James.   **DC 2 Jun 1978**.

8135   MACLEAN, William. From Kilmorack, INV. To Pictou, NS, on the *Dove*, ex Fort William, Jun 1801. Farmer.   **PLD**.

8136   MACLEAN, William, b ca 1793. From Kilmorack, INV. To Pictou, NS, on the *Dove*, ex Fort William, Jun 1801.   **PLD**.

8137   McLEAN, William. From Beauly, INV. Prob rel to Janet M, qv. To Pictou, NS, on the *Sarah*, ex Fort William, Jun 1801. Labourer.   **PLS**.

8138   McLEAN, William, b ca 1779. To Margaree, Inverness Co, NS, 1810. Farmer, m and ch.   **CBC 1818**.

8139   McLEAN, William, b ca 1778. To Inverness, Inverness Co, NS, 1812. Farmer, m and ch.   **CBC 1818**.

8140   McLEAN, William. From Glasgow. s/o William M, 1798–1837, and Elizabeth Wilkinson, 1798–1841. To St John, NB, prob <1841.   **Ts North Street, Glasgow**.

8141   MACLEAN, William. From Kilmuir-Easter, ROC. To NS, 1842.   **DC 22 Aug 1980**.

8142   McLEAN, William, 10 Jun 1832–5 Jan 1929. From Kilmarnock, AYR. s/o John M, qv, and Jean Gilchrist, qv. To QUE on the *Renfrewshire*, 1842; stld Aldborough Twp, Elgin Co, ONT. Moved to Wardsville, 1846, and d London. Railwayman. m (i) 1855, Ann Maxwell; (ii) Jessie Muir, 1845–1902.   **DC 23 Nov 1981**.

8143   McLEAN, William. From Cummertrees, DFS. To Plympton Twp, Lambton Co, ONT, ca 1845. Wife Rachel with him, and dau Mary, qv.   **DC 18 Jul 1979**.

8144   McLEAN, William. From Is Lewis, ROC. To QUE, ex Stornoway, arr 4 Aug 1851; stld Huron Twp, Bruce Co, ONT, 1852. Head of family.   **DC 5 Apr 1967**.

8145   McLEAY, Allan, b 1822. From Upper Shader, Is Lewis, ROC. s/o John M. and Ann McDonald. To QUE, ex Stornoway, arr 4 Aug 1851; stld Huron Twp, Bruce Co, ONT, 1852. Farmer. m Ann McDonald, see ADDENDA, ch: 1. John, b 1849; 2. Ann, b 1851; 3. Kenneth, b 1855; 4. Donald; 5. Allan; 6. Margaret; 7. Murdo; 8. Malcolm; 9. Angus.   **WLC**.

8146   McLEAY, Kenneth, 1802–20 Aug 1862. From ROC. To Melbourne, Richmond Co, QUE, prob <1851.   **MGC 15 Jul 1980**.

8147   McLEAY, Lachlan, ca 1780–19 Jan 1874. From Garve, ROC. To Melbourne, Richmond Co, QUE, prob <1851. m Barbara Munroe, qv.   **MGC 15 Jul 1980**.

8148   McLEAY, Roderick, ca 1819–6 May 1855. From Gairloch, ROC. To QUE, prob <1850, and bur Flodden Station. m Janet McNaughton, qv. Son Donald, 1852-63.   **MGC 15 Jul 1980**.

8149   McLEISH, Alexander, 1788–1873. From Kilfinan par, ARL. s/o Alexander M, ferryman, and Catherine Whyte. To Caledon Twp, Peel Co, ONT, <1840. m Sarah Brown, qv, ch: 1. John, b 1819; 2. James, b 1822; 3. Alexander, b 1825; 4. Mary, b 1827; 5. Donald, b 1832; 6. Sarah, 1836-70; 7. Margaret, b 1838.   **DC 26 Sep 1981**.

8150   McLEISH, Alexander, 1817-93. Poss from ARL. To Bruce Co, ONT, <1851. Bur at Nairn. m Mary Galbraith, qv, ch: 1. Archibald, 1849–1931; 2. Lachlan, 1852–1903; 3. Elizabeth, 1853–1948; 4. Mary, 1857–1930; 5. Alexander, 1858-77; 6. Margaret, 1861–1949.   **GSO 31**.

McLEISH, Mrs Archibald. See WHYTE, Elizabeth.

8151   McLEISH, Donald. From ARL. bro/o John M, qv. To West Williams Twp, Middlesex Co, ONT, 1848. Son Angus, reeve.   **PCM 47**.

8152   McLEISH, John. From ARL. bro/o Donald M, qv. To West Williams Twp, Middlesex Co, ONT, 1848. Cattle-breeder. Son John.   **PCM 47**.

McLELLAN. See also McCLELLAN.

8153   McLELLAN, Alexander, b ca 1790. Prob rel to Neil M, qv. To Margaree dist, Inverness Co, NS, 1816. Farmer.   **CBC 1818**.

8154   McLELLAN, Angus. From Lagganachdron, Glengarry, INV. To QUE on the *British Queen*, ex Arisaig, 16 Aug 1790; stld nr Montreal. Tailor. Wife and ch with him.   **QCC 103**.

8155   MACLELLAN, Angus. From Morar, INV. s/o Archibald M. To South River, Antigonish Co, NS, 1804; moved later to Inverness Co.   **HCA 314**.

8156   McLELLAN, Angus. From Is South Uist, INV. To West Williams Twp, Middlesex Co, ONT, 1849. d aged 90.   **PCM 48**.

8157   McLELLAN, Angus. From Is South Uist, INV. To West Williams Twp, Middlesex Co, ONT, 1849; stld Con 12.   **PCM 48**.

8158   McLELLAN, Angus. From Is South Uist, INV. To West Williams Twp, Middlesex Co, ONT, 1849; stld Con 14.   **PCM 48**.

8159   McLELLAN, Archibald. From INV. To Pictou, NS, on the *Sarah*, ex Fort William, Jun 1801. Farmer. Wife Isobel with him, and ch: 1. Mary, aged 3; 2. Angus, aged 2.   **PLS**.

8160   MACLELLAN, Archibald. From Morar, INV. s/o Archibald M. To Antigonish Co, NS, prob stld South River, 1804. m Mary MacDonald, ch: 1. James; 2. Donald; 3. Angus; 4. Catherine; 5. Mary; 6. Margaret; 7. Nancy.   **HCA 314**.

8161   MACLELLAN, Archibald. From Is Eigg, INV. To Antigonish Co, NS, 1825; stld Eigg Mountain. m Miss MacIsaac, ch: 1. Ronald; 2. Angus; 3. Donald; 4. Bella; 5. Kate; 6. Mary.   **HCA 316**.

8162   MACLELLAN, Archibald. Prob from INV. To Cape

George, Antigonish Co, NS, 1828. m Margaret Mackinnon, qv, ch: 1. Malcolm, teacher, emig before parents; 2. John, emig to Sydney, Cape Breton Co, <1828; 3. John; 4. Thomas, who d in SCT; 5. Elizabeth Ann; 6. Jessie; 7. Jane. **HCA 317**.

8163   McLELLAN, Archibald. From Lochgilphead, ARL. To Lobo Twp, Middlesex Co, ONT, 1830. ch: 1. Duncan; 2. John Peter; 3. James. **PCM 39**.

8164   McLELLAN, Archibald. From ARL. To Mosa Twp, Middlesex Co, ONT, 1831. **PCM 24**.

8165   McLELLAN, Archibald, b ca 1815. From Is South Uist, INV. To West Williams Twp, Middlesex Co, ONT, 1849; stld Con 14. **PCM 48**.

8166   McLELLAN, Catherine. From Clonaig, Skipness, ARL. To ONT, prob <1850. Wife of Peter McArthur, qv. **DC 21 Mar 1981**.

8167   McLELLAN, Christian. From Glenelg, INV. To QUE, ex Greenock, summer 1815; stld prob Lanark Co, ONT. Wife of William Campbell, qv. **SEC 8**.

8168   McLELLAN, Donald. To Pictou Co, NS, <26 Aug 1783, when his heirs were gr 260 acres on the east side of East River. **HPC App A**.

8169   McLELLAN, Donald. From Glenelg, INV. To Montreal, QUE, ex Fort William, arr Sep 1802; stld E ONT. **MCM 1/4 26**.

8170   McLELLAN, Donald. Poss from PER. To ONT, 1817; stld Lot 3, Con 8, Beckwith Twp, Lanark Co. **HCL 31**.

8171   McLELLAN, Donald. From Arisaig, INV. To Pictou, NS, on the *Dove*, ex Fort William, Jun 1801. Tenant farmer. Wife Marin with him, and ch: 1. Margaret, aged 7; 2. Patrick, aged 3; 3. Alexander, aged 2. **PLD**.

8172   MACLELLAN, Donald, b 1826. From Balivanich, Is Benbecula, INV. s/o John M. and Anne McAulay. To Pictou, NS, on the *Lulan*, ex Glasgow, 17 Aug 1848. **DC 12 Jul 1979**.

8173   McLELLAN, Duncan, b ca 1765. From Glenelg, INV. To QUE, ex Greenock, summer 1815; stld prob Lanark Co, ONT. Farmer. Wife Ann Campbell, qv, with him, and 3 ch. **SEC 8**.

8174   McLELLAN, Duncan. Prob from Knapdale, ARL. To Aldborough Twp, Elgin Co, ONT, 1819; moved to Ekfrid Twp, 1829. **PCM 29**.

8175   McLELLAN, Duncan. From Knapdale, ARL. To Caradoc Twp, Middlesex Co, ONT, 1831. ch: 1. Archibald Y, res Strathroy, Adelaide Twp; 2. Mrs Alexander McIntyre. **PCM 35**.

8176   McLELLAN, Evan. To Pictou Co, NS, <1790; stld McLellans Brook. **HNS iii 669**.

8177   McLELLAN, Finlay. From Glenelg, INV. To Pictou, NS, on the *Dove*, ex Fort William, Jun 1801. Labourer. **PLD**.

8178   McLELLAN, Finlay. To Pictou, NS, on the *Lulan*, ex Glasgow, 17 Aug 1848. Wife Anne with him, and dau Penny. **DC 15 Jul 1979**.

8179   McLELLAN, Hugh, b 1816. From Torlum, Is

Benbecula, INV. s/o Roderick M, qv, and Flora MacMillan, qv. To Pictou, NS, on the *Lulan*, ex Glasgow, 17 Aug 1848. Wife Catherine MacLeod, qv, with him, and s Rory. **DC 12 Jul 1979**.

8180   McLELLAN, Isabella, 1752–1836. From Castle Swin, North Knapdale, ARL. wid/o Donald Campbell. To Lobo Twp, later to Caradoc Twp, Middlesex Co, ONT. Mother of 1. Nancy, b 1775; 2. Margaret, b 1777; 3. Mary, b 1779; 4. John, 1781-83; 5-6. Christy and Archibald, qv; 7. Malcolm, qv; 8. John, qv. **PCM 35; DC 20 Jul 1982**.

8181   McLELLAN, James. To Pictou Co, NS, <26 Aug 1783, when gr 100 acres on West River. **HPC App A**.

8182   McLELLAN, James. From INV. To Pictou Co, NS, <18 Dec 1797; stld nr Fish Pools, East River. **HPC App H**.

8183   McLELLAN, James. From ARL. To Ekfrid Twp, Middlesex Co, ONT, 1831. ch: 1. Isaac; 2. Nathaniel; 3. Dugald; 4. Mary; 5. Duncan; 6. Kate; 7. Nancy; 8. Flora. **PCM 30**.

8184   McLELLAN, John. From Lochbroom par, ROC. To Pictou, NS, on the *Hector*, ex Loch Broom, arr 17 Sep 1773; stld McLellans Brook. Farmer. **HPC App C**.

8185   McLELLAN, John. From INV. To Pictou Co, NS, <18 Dec 1797, and gr 100 acres on East River. Prob discharged soldier. **HPC App H**.

8186   McLELLAN, John. From Lochgilphead, ARL. To ONT, 1830; stld Lobo Twp, Middlesex Co. m Katherine McVicar, qv, ch: 1. Janet; 2. Archie; 3. Sarah; 4. Catherine; 5. Nevin; 6-7. Mary and John, twins. **PCM 38; DC 25 Jan 1964**.

8187   McLELLAN, John, b ca 1807. From LKS, poss Lesmahagow par. To Scarborough, York Co, ONT, 1835. Farmer. **DC 29 Mar 1981**.

8188   McLELLAN, John. To Pictou, NS, on the *Lady Gray*, ex Cromarty, ROC, arr 16 Jul 1841. **DC 15 Jul 1979**.

8189   MACLELLAN, Malcolm. Poss from Is Benbecula, INV. To Pictou, NS, on the *Lulan*, ex Glasgow, 17 Aug 1848. **DC 12 Jul 1979**.

8190   MACLELLAN, Marion, b 1821. From Balivanich, Is Benbecula, INV. d/o John M. and Ann MacAulay. To Pictou, NS, on the *Lulan*, ex Glasgow, 17 Aug 1848. Wife of James Wilson, qv. **DC 12 Jul 1979; WLC**.

8191   McLELLAN, Neil, b ca 1791. To Pictou Co, NS, 1815. Labourer, res Merigomish, 1816. Wife and child with him. **INS 37**.

8192   McLELLAN, Neil, b ca 1788. Prob rel to Alexander M, qv. To Margaree dist, Inverness Co, NS, 1816. Farmer, m and ch. **CBC 1818**.

8193   MACLELLAN, Penny, b 1831. From Balivanich, Is Benbecula, INV. d/o John M. and Ann MacAulay. To Pictou, NS, on the *Lulan*, ex Glasgow, 17 Aug 1848. **DC 12 Jul 1979**.

8194   MACLELLAN, Roderick, b 1786. From Torlum, Is Benbecula, INV. To Pictou, NS, on the *Lulan*, ex Glasgow, 17 Aug 1848. m Flora McMillan, qv, ch: 1. Hugh, qv; 2. Margaret, b 1821; 3. Mary, b 1826; 4. Donald, b 1828. **DC 12 Jul 1979**.

8195   MACLELLAN, Sarah. From Is South Uist, INV. To Pictou Co, NS, 1791; later to Judique Banks, Inverness Co. Wife of John 'Gobha' MacEachen, qv.   **MP 633**.

8196   McLELLAN, William. From Lochbroom par, ROC. Rel to John M, qv. To Pictou, NS, on the *Hector*, ex Loch Broom, arr 17 Sep 1773; stld West River, Pictou Co. ch.   **HPC App C**.

8197   McLELLAND, John. From Cambuslang, LKS. To QUE on the *Brock*, ex Greenock, 9 Jul 1820; stld Lanark Twp, Lanark Co, ONT. Wife and 4 ch with him.   **HCL**.

8198   MACLENNAN, Alexander. To Glengarry Co, ONT, 1794; stld Lot 14, Con 15, Lancaster Twp.   **MG 56**.

8199   McLENNAN, Alexander. From Inverness. To Montreal, QUE, prob arr Sep 1802. Petitioned for land on the Ottawa River, 6 Aug 1804.   **DC 15 Mar 1980**.

8200   McLENNAN, Alexander, ca 1773–5 Sep 1843. From Contin par, ROC. To Pictou Co, NS, ca 1812; stld Rogers Hill. Farmer. m Nancy Mackenzie, qv, ch: 1. Roderick, b 1808; 2. Isabella; 3. Margaret; 4. Nancy; 5. Charles; 6. Donald; 7. Annabella; 8. Colin; 9. William; 10. John.   **DC 27 Feb 1979**.

8201   MACLENNAN, Alexander Stewart, 1822-73. From Killilan, Kintail par, ROC. s/o Roderick M. and Charlotte Stewart. To ONT, ca 1855, stld prob Glengarry Co. **DC 24 Nov 1979**.

8202   MACLENNAN, Alexander Stewart. Poss from Kintail par, ROC. Gr-s of Roderick M. and Charlotte Stewart. To ONT, ca 1855.   **DC 24 Nov 1979**.

8203   McLENNAN, Catherine, ca 1794–17 Jun 1812. From ROC. To Pictou Co, NS, 1803. m Murdoch Munro, and d soon afterwards. Bur Salt Springs.   **DC 22 Jun 1980**.

8204   MACLENNAN, Catherine. From INV. To South River, Antigonish Co, NS, <1815. Wife of Alexander MacDonald, qv.   **MP 47**.

8205   McLENNAN, Catherine. From Glenelg, INV. To QUE, ex Greenock, summer 1815; stld prob Lanark Co, ONT. Wife of Malcolm McCuaig, qv.   **SEC 8**.

8206   McLENNAN, Donald. Prob from INV. To Montreal, QUE, prob arr Sep 1802. Petitioned for land on the Ottawa River, 6 Aug 1804.   **DC 15 Mar 1980**.

8207   McLENNAN, Donald. From Is Lewis, ROC. To QUE, ex Stornoway, arr 4 Aug 1851; stld Huron Twp, Bruce Co, ONT, 1852.   **DC 5 Apr 1967**.

8208   MACLENNAN, Donald, b 20 Jan 1822. From Kishorn, Applecross, ROC. s/o Neil M. and Isabella Mackenzie. To ONT prob <1857; stld Moore Twp, Lambton Co, where he bought a farm in 1860. m at Sarnia, 1862, Elizabeth Wilkin, ch.   **DC 18 Feb 1972**.

8209   MACLENNAN, Duncan. From ROC, prob Kintail par. To Cape Breton Is, NS, poss <1820; stld River Denys. m Kate Matheson, qv. Son Hugh.   **NSN 32/379**.

8210   McLENNAN, Duncan, b 1803. From Tolsta Chaolais, Is Lewis, ROC. s/o John M. and Catherine McNeil. To QUE, ex Stornoway, arr 4 Aug 1851; stld Huron Twp, Bruce Co, ONT, 1852. Farmer. m Anne McLeod, qv, ch: 1. Donald, b 1836; 2. John, b 1838; 3. Alexander, b 1840; 4. Neil, b 1842; 5. John Og, b 1845; 6. Mary, b 1850.   **WLC**.

8211   McLENNAN, Farquhar. From Kintail, ROC. To Glengarry Co, ONT, 1802. Son Roderick, res Charlottenburgh Twp.   **SDG 282**.

8212   MACLENNAN, Farquhar. Prob from ROC. To Montreal, QUE, arr Sep 1802. Petitioned for land on the Ottawa River, 6 Aug 1804.   **DC 15 Mar 1980**.

8213   McLENNAN, Farquhar, b 1796. Prob from Kintail, ROC. To Charlottenburgh Twp, Glengarry Co, ONT, <1850. Tanner. By wife Sophia had ch: 1. Alexander, b ca 1836; 2. Duncan, b ca 1841; 3. Isabella, b ca 1846.   **DC 2 Jan 1980**.

8214   MACLENNAN, Hector, b 1818. To Gulf Shore, Cumberland Co, NS, <1840. Wife Annie, 1825–1903, with him. ch incl: 1. Elizabeth, 1840-54; 2. John, 1855-71; 3. Hector, 1856-77, d in Rio de Janiero. **DC 29 Oct 1980**.

8215   McLENNAN, Hector. From Is South Uist, INV. To East Williams Twp, Middlesex Co, ONT, 1851. m Mary Currie, qv, and had, prob with other ch: 1. Effie, b 1846; 2. Donald, b 1850.   **WLC**.

8216   McLENNAN, Hugh, ca 1776–23 Dec 1820. From INV. To NS.   **NSS No 2156**.

8217   McLENNAN, Hugh, b ca 1788. Prob from Kintail par, ROC. To Charlottenburgh Twp, Glengarry Co, ONT, <1851. Farmer. Wife Mary, b ca 1798 with him, and several ch.   **DC 2 Jan 1980**.

8218   McLENNAN, Hugh, b ca 1793. Poss from Kintail par, ROC. To Charlottenburgh Twp, Glengarry Co, ONT, <1830. Farmer. By wife Christy had ch: 1. Andrew, b ca 1831; 2. Catherine, b ca 1833; 3. Donald, b ca 1834; 4. Hannah, b ca 1843; 5. Isabella, b ca 1845; 6. Margaret, b ca 1849.   **DC 2 Jan 1980**.

8219   McLENNAN, Jessie, 1842–1917. Prob from Is Lewis, ROC. To Victoria Co, NS. m Murdock Morrison, qv.   **DC 22 Jun 1979**.

8220   McLENNAN, John. From Aird, INV. To Pictou, NS, on the *Sarah*, ex Fort William, Jun 1801. Labourer. Wife Christian with him, and dau Kate, aged 3.   **PLS**.

8221   McLENNAN, John. Prob from Kintail par, ROC. To Williamstown, Lancaster Twp, Glengarry Co, ONT, 1802. Farmer, teacher and officer of militia, 1812 and 1837. ch incl: 1. John, politician; 2. Hugh, b 1825, merchant.   **SDG 260; DC 2 Jan 1980**.

8222   McLENNAN, John, b ca 1788. From ROC. To York Factory, Hudson Bay, on the *Edward & Anne*, ex Stornoway, Is Lewis, arr 24 Sep 1811. Pioneer settler, Red River, 1812.   **LSS 184; RRS 26; LSC 321**.

8223   McLENNAN, Rev John, ca 1797–11 Feb 1852. From ROC. Grad MA, Kings Coll, Aberdeen, 1818. To Belfast dist, Queens Co, PEI, 1823, and became min of St Johns Presb Ch. He also taught school. Preached at Georgetown, Wood Is, Murray Harbour and other places. Retr to SCT 1849, and became min of the Gaelic Chapel at Cromarty, ROC. d in ARL. Wife Catherine McNab, qv. Dau Mrs Daniel M. Gordon.   **KCG 276; FES vii 7; HP 28**.

8224   McLENNAN, John. s/o — M. and — Montgomery. To Eldon Twp, Victoria Co, ONT, prob <1854. m Mary Ann, d/o Donald Mitchell, ch: 1. John; 2. Annie; 3. Minnie; 4. Donald; 5. Liza; 6. Charles; 7. George; 8. Alvin.   **EC 151**.

8225 **McLENNAN, John Roy**. From Glenelg, INV. To QUE on the *Nepthon*, 1802; stld Chambly Mountain, but moved in 1812 to Williamstown. **SAS 18**.

8226 **McLENNAN, Kenneth**, 1760–1836. From Kintail par, ROC. To CAN, ca 1791; stld <1825 at Charlottenburgh Twp, Glengarry Co, ONT. Farmer, Lots 1-3, Con 3. m Sarah Dickson, 1770–1810, Lancaster Twp, ch: 1. Barbara; 2. Robert, 1797–1878; 3. Jane, b 1798; 4. John, b 1800; 5. Flora, b 1802; 6. Murdoch, b 1805; 7. William, b 1807. **DC 2 Jan 1980**.

8227 **McLENNAN, Margaret**. From Is South Uist, INV. To West Williams Twp, Middlesex Co, ONT, ca 1849. Wife of Alexander McMillan, jr, qv. **WLC**.

8228 **McLENNAN, Margaret**, ca 1784–19 Dec 1881. From ROC. To QUE <1850. Wife of Murdoch McLeod, qv. **MGC 15 Jul 1980**.

8229 **McLENNAN, Murdo**. From Aird, INV. To Pictou, NS, on the *Sarah*, ex Fort William, Jun 1801. Farmer. Wife Janet with him, and s Murdo, aged 3. **PLS**.

8230 **McLENNAN, Murdo**, b 1779. From Benigarry, Lower Shader, Barvas par, Is Lewis, ROC. To QUE, ex Stornoway, arr 4 Aug 1851; stld Lot 9, Con 8, Huron Twp, Bruce Co, ONT. Farmer. m Janet Martin, ch: 1. Margaret, b 1820; 2. Catherine; 3. Kirsty; 4. Roderick; 5. Ann; 6. Flora. **WLC**.

8231 **McLENNAN, Murdoch**. From Kintail par, ROC, or Glenelg, INV. To Glengarry Co, ONT, ca 1804. **SDG 50**.

8232 **MACLENNAN, Roderick**. From Glenelg, INV. To QUE, 1796; stld Lot 33, Con 6, Lochiel Twp, Glengarry Co, ONT. **MG 211**.

8233 **McLENNAN, Roderick**. Poss from Kintail, ROC. To Montreal, QUE, arr prob Sep 1802. Petitioned for land on the Ottawa River, 6 Aug 1804. **DC 15 Mar 1980**.

8234 **McLENNAN, Roderick**, b ca 1787. From Glenelg, INV. To QUE, ex Greenock, summer 1815; stld prob Lanark Co, ONT. Labourer. **SEC 8**.

8235 **MACLENNAN, Roderick**. From Is Lewis, INV. To QUE, ex Stornoway, arr 4 Aug 1851; stld Huron Twp, Bruce Co, ONT, 1852. Head of family. **DC 5 Apr 1967**.

8236 **McLEOD, —**. To Pictou, NS, on the *Ellen*, ex Loch Laxford, 22 May 1848. Wife Marion with him. **DC 15 Jul 1979**.

8237 **MACLEOD, Alasdair 'Og'**. From Glenelg, INV. bro/o Alexander M, qv. To Lochiel Twp, Glengarry Co, ONT, prob <1800. **MG 30**.

8238 **McLEOD, Alexander**. From SUT. To Pictou, NS, on the *Hector*, ex Loch Broom, arr 17 Sep 1773. Drowned in the Shubenacadie River, Colchester Co. Son Donald, passenger on the *Hector*, stld West River. **HPC App C**.

8239 **MACLEOD, Alexander**, ca 1768–4 Mar 1850. From Glenelg, INV. s/o Kenneth M, qv, from Myle. To PEI, arr 18 Oct 1793, but went to original destination of Glengarry Co, ONT, 1794. Emigrant leader, farmer and Capt of Militia. m (i) Miss MacDonell, who d at sea, 1793, ch: 1. John, qv; 2. Neil, qv; 3. Alexander, qv. m (ii) Margaret, d/o John Cameron, UEL, further ch: 4. Donald, b 1799; 5. Kenneth, 1802-57; 6. Alexander

Og, 1802-94; 7. Angus, 1804-69; 8. Roderick, 1806-84; 9. Norman Roy, 1810-87; 10. Mary, 1812-87; 11. Janet, b 1814; 12. John, 1818–1903; 13. Catherine, b 1821. **MG 28, 36, 63**.

8240 **MACLEOD, Alexander, jr**, 1793–1885. From Glenelg, INV. s/o Capt Alexander M, qv, and first wife. To PEI, arr 18 Oct 1793, but went to Lochiel Twp, Glengarry Co, ONT, 1794. Farmer, Lot 38, Con 8. m 27 Mar 1820, Catherine Fraser, from Prescott, ch: 1. Mary, b 1823; 2. William, b 1825; 3. Nancy, b 1827; 4. Alexander Norman, b 1830; 5. Kenneth, b 1839; 6. Lillie, b 1841. **MG 64, 72**.

8241 **MACLEOD, Alexander**. From Glenelg, INV. Eld bro/o Alasdair 'Og' M, qv. To Lochiel Twp, Glengarry Co, ONT, 1796. Farmer. **MG 29**.

8242 **McLEOD, Alexander**. Prob from Glasgow. To St John, NB, <1800. Wife Elizabeth with him, and dau Ann, 1797–1812. **NER viii 98**.

8243 **MACLEOD, Alexander**, b 1760. From Glenelg, INV. To QUE <1800; stld Argenteuil Co. Moved ca 1825 to Glengarry Co, ONT. ch: 1. Alexander, d unm; 2. William, 1791–1882, stld Kenyon Twp, Glengarry Co. **MG 252**.

8244 **MACLEOD, Alexander**. Prob from INV. To Montreal, QUE, prob Sep 1802. Petitioned for land on the Ottawa River, ONT, 6 Aug 1804. **DC 15 Mar 1980**.

8245 **MACLEOD, Alexander**. From Kendrum, Kilmaluag, Is Skye, INV. s/o Donald M, qv, and Catherine MacDonald. To Orwell Bay, PEI, on the *Polly*, ex Portree, arr 7 Aug 1803; stld Belfast. m a d/o Maj MacLeod, ch: 1. Flora; 2. Mary; 3. William. **CMM 3/22 97, 88; HP 73**.

8246 **MACLEOD, Alexander**. From INV. To Pictou Co, NS, 1814; stld East Forks, Middle River. By wife Annie had s William. **PAC 126**.

8247 **MACLEOD, Alexander**, b ca 1791. To Richmond Co, NS, 1817. **CBC 1818**.

8248 **MACLEOD, Alexander**, b ca 1750. Swordland, Glenelg, INV. s/o Olaus M. and Penelope MacLeod. To Glengarry Co, ONT, prob <1820, and was drowned there. m Janet MacRae, qv, ch: 1. Norman, qv; 2. Angus; 3. Donald; 4. Neil; 5. Penelope; 6. Mary. **MG 29, 269**.

8249 **MACLEOD, Alexander 'Tailor'**. b Is Skye, INV, and sometime on Is Raasay. To Queens Co, PEI, 1821; stld Orwell River. Son Murdo, qv. **SPI 162**.

8250 **MACLEOD, Alexander**. From Is Skye, INV. To PEI <1825; stld Orwell Cove, Queens Co. Schoolmaster. **HP 26**.

8251 **McLEOD, Alexander**, d 1841. From Angus. To Lincoln Co, ONT, ca 1825. Deputy Sheriff of Niagara dist, 1837. **MDB 476**.

8252 **MACLEOD, Alexander**. From Kiltarlity, INV. s/o William M. and Margaret McKay. To Pictou Co, NS, 1832; stld Middle River, later Big Brook, west branch, East River. Farmer. m Annie Fraser, qv, ch: 1. William, qv; 2. Catherine, qv; 3. Malcolm, qv; 4. Archibald, qv; 5. Alexander; 6. Simon; 7. Margaret; 8. Daniel; 9. Annie, unm; 10. Thomas; 11. Jessie Bell. **PAC 156**.

8253   McLEOD, Alexander, d ca 1892. From SUT. To NS <1840, when he stld Miramichi, Northumberland Co, NB. Farmer and shoemaker. m Barbara McKenzie, qv, ch: 1. Murdoch; 2. Jane; 3. John; 4. Fanny. **DC 4 Oct 1978**.

8254   McLEOD, Alexander. From INV. To Victoria Co, NS. Wife Christina, 1825–16 Oct 1891, with him. **DC 22 Jun 1979**.

8255   MACLEOD, Alexander M. From Glenelg, INV. To QUE, 1796; stld Lot 31, Lochiel Twp, Glengarry Co, ONT. **MG 211**.

8256   McLEOD, Alexander Roderick, d 11 Jun 1840. To Montreal, QUE, <1802. Served with the NWCo as a clerk in the Peace River dist, and after the merger with the HBCo, 1821, was a chief trader on the Pacific coast. **MDB 477**.

8257   MACLEOD, Alexander William, b 1760. From Glenelg, INV. To QUE, ca 1798; stld Lost River, Argenteuil Co. Moved ca 1823 to Glengarry Co, ONT. Farmer. ch: 1. Alexander, d unm; 2. William, qv. **MG 252**.

8258   McLEOD, Allan, ca 1803–19 Dec 1858. From Is Skye, INV. To Scotch Road, Sherbrooke Co, QUE, ca 1837. Farmer. m Alexina McKenzie, qv, ch. **DC 7 Feb 1980**.

8259   McLEOD, Allan. From Is Skye, INV. To NS <1850. m Sarah Marshall, Annapolis Co. Dau Minnie, b ca 1856. **NSN 22/12**.

8260   McLEOD, Andrew, b ca 1795. To Richmond Co, NS, 1817. **CBC 1818**.

8261   MACLEOD, Angus 'Mor', ca 1797–28 Jan 1885. From Glasphein, Staffin, Is Skye, INV. s/o Malcolm M, qv, and Effie MacDonald, qv. To Orwell Bay, PEI, on the *Polly*, ex Portree, arr 7 Aug 1803. Farmer, and petitioner for Dr MacAulay, 1811. m Margaret O'Docherty, qv, ch: 1. Katherine; 2. John, 1819–1908; 3. Mary; 4. Donald, 1826–1916; 5. Anne; 6. Christina, 1828–1924; 7. Mary, jr; 8. Malcolm; 9. Margaret; 10. Angus; 11. Effie; 12. Sarah. **SPI 136; HP 17, 73**.

8262   McLEOD, Angus. To Pictou, NS, on the *Lady Gray*, ex Cromarty, ROC, arr 16 Jul 1841. **DC 15 Jul 1979**.

8263   McLEOD, Angus, 1837–1906. From Is Islay, ARL. To Caledon Twp, Peel Co, ONT, prob <1850. m Sarah Walker, 1837–1927. **DC 21 Apr 1980**.

8264   McLEOD, Angus, ca 1820–15 Feb 1856. From Is Skye, INV. To Kinloss Twp, Bruce Co, ONT, <1852. m Mary McKinnon, qv, ch: 1. John, b 1857; 2. Alexander; 3. Peter, b 1863; 4. Christena, b 1865. **DC 12 Apr 1979**.

8265   MACLEOD, Ann. From INV. d/o Neil M, qv, and Mary Campbell. To Antigonish Co, NS, <1797. m John MacPherson, qv. **HCA 341**.

8266   McLEOD, Ann, b ca 1820. From Uisgarry, South Uist, INV. To Cape Breton Is, NS, ca 1842. m 1841, James Johnston, qv. **LDW 9 Sep 1973**.

8267   MACLEOD, Anna. From Is Skye, INV. To ONT, <1855. m Alexander MacQueen, qv. **DC 31 Aug 1979**.

8268   MACLEOD, Annabella, 1792–1852. From Cuidrach, Is Skye, INV. d/o Capt Murdo M, tacksman, and Marion MacDonald. To PEI on the *Ruther*, arr 8 Sep 1840. wid/o Dr James Munro, who d at Tobermory, Is Mull, 1840. ch: 1. Marion, qv; 2. George, b 1815, went to AUS, 1855; 3. Donald, qv; 4. Malcolm James, ca 1822–ca 1849, d New Orleans; 5. Jacobina Annabella, qv; 6. Margaret Alice, qv. **SPI 116; HP 89**.

8269   MACLEOD, Anne. From Glasphein, Staffin, Is Skye, INV. d/o Malcolm M, qv, and Effie MacDonald, qv. To Orwell Bay, PEI, on the *Polly*, ex Portree, arr 7 Aug 1803. m Alexander MacLeod. **SPI 136**.

8270   MACLEOD, Anne. From Oldshoremore, Kinlochbervie, SUT. d/o John M. To NS <1830. **DC 10 Feb 1962**.

8271   McLEOD, Anne. From Balivanich, Is Benbecula, INV. d/o Ewen M. To East Williams Twp, Middlesex Co, ONT, 1848. Wife of Alexander McCormack, qv. **WLC**.

8272   McLEOD, Anne, b 1809. From Is Vuia Mor, off Is Lewis, ROC. To QUE, ex Stornoway, arr 4 Aug 1851; stld Huron Twp, Bruce Co, ONT. Wife of Duncan McLennan, qv. **WLC**.

8273   MACLEOD, Archibald, b ca 1829. From Kiltarlity, INV. s/o Alexander M, qv, and Annie Fraser, qv. To Pictou Co, NS, 1832; stld Middle River. m 1870, Elizabeth Morrison, widow McCarthy, from Sheet Harbour, ch: 1. Bessie; 2. Rev Albert Morrison, d 1934; 3. James, farmer; 4. Susan; 5. Alexander Robert; 6. Grant, went to WY, USA. **PAC 160**.

8274   MACLEOD, Archibald Norman, b 17 Mar 1772. From Kilfinichen, Is Mull, ARL. s/o Rev Neil M. and Margaret MacLean. To Montreal, QUE, <1815, and joined NWCo. **FES iv 113**.

8275   MACLEOD, Asa. From Is Harris, INV. s/o James M, qv. To Mabou Ridge, Inverness Co, NS, <1820. m Jane, d/o John Campbell, and Janet Livingstone, ch: 1. Donald; 2. John; 3. James; 4. Catherine; 5. Ellen; 6. Margaret, dy. **MP 746**.

8276   MACLEOD, Barbara. From Oldshoremore, Kinlochbervie, SUT. d/o John M. To NS <1830. **DC 10 Feb 1962**.

8277   MACLEOD, Catherine. From Glasphein, Staffin, Is Skye, INV. s/o Malcolm M, qv, and Effie MacDonald, qv. To Orwell Bay, PEI, on the *Polly*, ex Portree, arr 7 Aug 1803; stld Pinette, Queens Co. m Angus O'Docherty, ch. **SPI 138; HP 74**.

8278   MACLEOD, Catherine, jr. From Glasphein, Staffin, Is Skye, INV. To Orwell Bay, PEI, on the *Polly*, ex Portree, arr 7 Aug 1803. m — McFadyen, West River. **SPI 138**.

8279   MACLEOD, Catherine. From Glenelg, INV. To QUE, ex Greenock, summer 1815; stld prob Lanark Co, ONT. Wife of John McRae, qv. **SEC 8**.

8280   MACLEOD, Catherine, b ca 1825. From Kiltarlity, INV. d/o Alexander M, qv, and Annie Fraser, qv. To Pictou Co, NS, 1832; stld Middle River, later Big Brook, west branch, East River. **PAC 156**.

8281   McLEOD or McCUAIG, Catherine. From Is Islay, ARL. d/o Donald M, qv, and Jane McDougall, qv. To QUE, ex Port Glasgow, 17 Jul 1842; stld Brampton, Peel Co, ONT, later Chinguacousy Twp. m Duncan Hunter, qv. **DC 29 Dec 1981**.

8282 MACLEOD, Catherine. From Torlum, Is Benbecula, INV. To Pictou, NS, on the *Lulan*, ex Glasgow, 17 Aug 1848. Wife of Hugh MacLellan, qv. **DC 12 Jul 1979**.

8283 MACLEOD, Catherine, ca 1834–3 Jan 1895. From Is Raasay, INV. d/o Alexander and Janet M. To PEI <1850. m Donald MacDonald, qv. **DC 9 Oct 1980**.

8284 MACLEOD, Catherine, 1850–1929. From Crowlista, Is Lewis, ROC. d/o Malcolm M, qv, and Catherine MacAulay, qv. To Winslow Twp, Compton Co, QUE, 1851. m Norman Donald MacLeod, qv. **TFT 15**.

8285 McLEOD, Christian, d 1773. From Assynt, SUT. To Pictou, NS, on the *Hector*, ex Loch Broom, 10 Jul 1773, and d soon after her arrival. Wife of Hugh McLeod, qv. **HPC App C**.

8286 McLEOD, Christie. To NS on the brig *Ann*, 1811. Wife of Angus McIvor, qv. **NSN 30/310**.

8287 McLEOD, Christina, b ca 1814. Poss d/o William M. To Chatham par, Miramichi, Northumberland Co, NB, <1840. m 9 Mar 1840, Alexander Fenton, qv. **LDW 18 Jun 1978**.

8288 MACLEOD, Christina, ca 1782–ca 1862. From Glasphein, Staffin, Is Skye, INV. d/o Malcolm M, qv, and Effie MacDonald, qv. To Orwell Bay, PEI, on the *Polly*, ex Portree, arr 7 Aug 1803; stld Pinette, Queens Co, later Orwell River. m Donald McQueen, qv. **SPI 136; HP 17**.

8289 MACLEOD, Christine. From Glenelg, INV. d/o Kenneth M, qv. To PEI, arr 18 Oct 1793, and moved in 1794 to Lochiel Twp, Glengarry Co, ONT. m 2 Jun 1795, John McGinnis, Charlottenburgh Twp. **MG 37**.

8290 MACLEOD, Christine, 1825–56. From STI. d/o Donald M, qv, and Margaret McFarlane, qv. To Simcoe Co, ONT, 1831. m 28 Jul 1848, Alexander McPherson, qv. **DC 8 Nov 1981**.

8291 MACLEOD, Donald, b 1794. From Glenelg, INV. s/o Roderick Roy M, qv, and Mary MacLeod, qv. To Lochiel Twp, Glengarry Co, ONT, 1796. Became farmer, Lot 24, Con 26. m Janet Urquhart, ch: 1. Catherine, b 1825; 2. Donald; 3. John; 4. Mary. **MG 30, 211**.

8292 MACLEOD, Donald. From Is Eigg, INV. s/o Neil M, qv, and Mary Campbell. To Parrsboro, Cumberland Co, NS, <1797. m Mary, d/o Donald MacLean and Euphemia MacLeod, ch: 1. James, 1820-56, lawyer; 2. Rev Alexander, bur Arisaig, Antigonish Co; 3. Rev William, Pubnico, Yarmouth Co; 4. John; 5. Duncan; 6. Mary. **HCA 320**.

8293 MACLEOD, Donald. From Kilmorack, INV. To Pictou, NS, on the *Dove*, ex Fort William, Jun 1801. Wife Ann with him, and ch: 1. Ann, aged 10; 2. Alexander, aged 8; 3. Andrew, aged 5; 4. David, aged 3. **PLD**.

8294 McLEOD, Donald, b ca 1758. To Port Hood dist, Inverness Co, NS, 1803. Farmer, m and ch. **CBC 1818**.

8295 MACLEOD, Donald. From Glasphein, Staffin, Is Skye, INV. s/o Malcolm M, qv, and Effie MacDonald, qv. To Orwell Bay, PEI, on the *Polly* ex Portree, arr 7 Aug 1803; stld Queens Co. m Miss MacLeod, ch. **SPI 138**.

8296 MACLEOD, Donald. From Kendrum, Kilmaluag, Is Skye, INV. To Orwell Bay, PEI, on the *Polly*, ex Portree, arr 7 Aug 1803; stld Queens Co. m Catherine MacDonald, d SCT, ch: 1. Malcolm, qv; 2. Murdoch, qv; 3. Roderick, qv; 4. Alexander, qv. **CMM 3/22 93; HP 73**.

8297 MACLEOD, Donald. Prob from Is Skye, INV. To Queens Co, PEI, poss 1803. Petitioner for Dr MacAulay, 1811. **HP 74**.

8298 McLEOD, Donald. From Assynt or Eddrachillis, SUT. To Boston, MA, arr on the *Fortitude*, 16 Aug 1803; stld Scotch Ridge, Charlotte Co, NB, 1805. Formerly of the Reay Fencible Regt. **DC 29 Nov 1982**.

8299 MACLEOD, Donald, 1751–1839. From Is Lewis, ROC. To Gulf Shore, Cumberland Co, NS, 1811. **DC 29 Oct 1980**.

8300 McLEOD, Donald, 1 Jan 1779–22 Jul 1879. From Fort Augustus, INV. Matric Kings Coll, Aberdeen, 1796, and trained for the ministry. Entered RN 1803, and went afterwards to ONT. Fought in War of 1812, and in Europe as a soldier, but retr to CAN, 1816. stld Augusta Twp, Grenville Co. Became a farmer and founded the *Grenville Gazette*. Also opened a classical school at Prescott, but was involved in the insurrection of 1837, and res latterly in Cleveland, OH, USA. **KCG 264; MDB 477; DC 10 Jan 1980**.

8301 McLEOD, Donald, ca 1789–11 Feb 1869. From Lairg, SUT. To Pictou Co, NS, 1819. Bur Lansdowne. Wife Christy Matheson, qv, with him. **DC 10 Feb 1980**.

8302 MACLEOD, Donald. From Is Harris, INV. s/o James M, qv. To Mabou Ridge, Inverness Co, NS, <1820. m Christina MacNeil, qv, ch: 1. James; 2. Roderick; 3. Neil; 4. Donald; 5. Thomas; 6. Sara; 7. Flora. **MP 740, 754**.

8303 MACLEOD, Donald, b 17 Jan 1806. Poss from Glenelg, INV. To Montreal, QUE, 1825; stld Glengarry Co, ONT. m 1837, Seraphina Curry, ch: 1. John, b 1837; 2. James Olaus, b 1839; 3. Mary; 4. Margaret. **MG 400**.

8304 MACLEOD, Donald, ca 1800–17 Jan 1889. From Harris, INV. s/o John M. and Christina Morrison. To St Anns, Victoria Co, NS, poss <1828. m Ann Morrison, qv, and then went to Waipu, NZ, ca 1860. Dau Sarah, d 1858. **DC 20 Mar 1981**.

8305 MACLEOD, Donald 'Ban Oig'. From Is Skye, INV. To Charlottetown, PEI, on the *Mary Kennedy*, arr 1 Jun 1829; stld Murray Harbour Road. m Mary Martin, qv, ch: 1. Donald, qv; 2. John; 3. Malcolm; 4. Roderick, qv; 5. Samuel; 6. Nancy; 7. Margaret; 8. Catherine. **SPI 141**.

8306 MACLEOD, Donald, 1818-96. From Stenscholl, Kilmuir par, Is Skye, INV. s/o Donald 'Ban Oig' M, qv, and Mary Martin, qv. To Charlottetown, PEI, on the *Mary Kennedy*, arr 1 Jun 1829; stld Murray Harbour Road, later moved to Middlesex Co, ONT, and taught school at Parkhill. m at Lingwick, Compton Co, QUE, Mary Noble, ch: 1. Emma, res Windsor; 2. Martha, res Calgary; 3. David Noble, res Edmonton; 4. Mary Priscilla, res Marshall, MN, USA; 5. Matilda, res Winnipeg; 6. Frederick, res Los Angeles, USA; 7. Edward Alexander, res Parkhill; 8. Katalena, res Minneapolis, MN. **SPI 141**.

8307 MACLEOD, Donald. From Oldshoremore, Kinlochbervie, SUT. s/o John M. To NS <1830. **DC 10 Feb 1962**.

8308   MACLEOD, Donald, 1788–18 Mar 1855. From Glenelg, INV. To Lochiel Twp, Glengarry Co, ONT, ca 1830; stld Lot 7, Con 4. m Sybella Forbes, qv, ch: 1. William, b 1834; 2. Alexander, 1836–1906; 3. Sarah, 1841-83. **MG 288**.

8309   McLEOD, Donald, ca 1784–14 Mar 1861. From Kilmuir, Is Skye, INV, and Buchanan, STI. To Simcoe Co, ONT, 1831. m Margaret McFarlane, qv, ch: 1. Norman, 1810-23; 2. Mary, qv; 3. Margaret, qv; 4. Isabella, qv; 5. William, 1819-38; 6. Marion, qv; 7. Christine, qv; 8. Duncan, 1827-31; 9. Jane, dy. **DC 8 Nov 1981**.

8310   McLEOD or McCUAIG, Donald. From Port Ellen, Is Islay, ARL. To Brampton, Peel Co, ONT, 1841. m Janet McDougall, qv, ch: 1. Catherine, qv; 2. Anne; 3. James; 4. Peter; 5. Alexander. **DC 29 Dec 1981**.

8311   McLEOD, Donald. To Pictou, NS, on the *Ellen*, ex Loch Laxford, SUT, 22 May 1848. Wife Betty with him, and ch: 1. Hugh; 2. Christy; 3. Ann; 4. Donald; 5. Johan. **DC 15 Jul 1979**.

8312   McLEOD, Donald. To Pictou, NS, on the *Ellen*, ex Loch Laxford, SUT, 22 May 1848. Wife Mary with him, and ch: 1. George; 2. Mary. **DC 15 Jul 1979**.

8313   McLEOD, Donald. To Pictou, NS, on the *Ellen*, ex Loch Laxford, 22 May 1848. Wife Margaret with him, and ch: 1. Colin; 2. Simon; 3. Thomas; 4. Janet. **DC 15 Jul 1979**.

8314   McLEOD, Donald. From Is Benbecula, INV. To East Williams Twp, Middlesex Co, ONT, 1848. **PCM 44**.

8315   MACLEOD, Donald. From Glenelg, INV. s/o Donald M. amd Mary MacCaskill. To QUE on the *Liscard*, 1849; stld Kenyon Twp, Glengarry Co, ONT. Farmer. m Catherine Bethune, qv, ch: 1. Donald, sailor; 2. Duncan, qv; 3. Duncan; 4. John; 5. Mary Ann, qv; 6. Katharine; 7. Margaret; 8. Mary; 9. Farquhar. **MG 317**.

8316   McLEOD, Donald 'Doun'. From Is North Uist, INV. To East Williams Twp, Middlesex Co, ONT, 1849. **PCM 44**.

8317   McLEOD, Rev Donald, 1800–19 May 1868. From Luss, DNB. s/o John M, farmer. Matric Univ of Glasgow, 1818. Min at Gourock, RFW, 1833-43, and of Gourock FC, 1843-49. To Cobourg, Northumberland Co, ONT, 1851. Min there until 1860. m Elizabeth Cochran, 1829. **GMA 10023; FES iii 196, vii 643**.

8318   MACLEOD, Donald, b 1806. From Ballaglom, Bernera, off Is Lewis, ROC. To QUE, prob on the *Mary Blanche*, ex Stornoway, arr 4 Aug 1851; stld Scotstown, Compton Co. m Rachel MacLeod, qv, ch: 1. Effie, b 1837; 2. Donald, b 1841; 3. Angus, b 1843; 4. John, b 1847; 5. Murdo, b 1849. **MGC 15 Jul 1980; WLC**.

8319   McLEOD, Donald (1). From Is Lewis, ROC. To QUE, ex Stornoway, arr 4 Aug 1851; stld Huron Twp, Bruce Co, ONT, 1852. Head of family. **DC 5 Apr 1967**.

8320   McLEOD, Donald (2). From Is Lewis, ROC. To QUE, ex Stornoway, arr 4 Aug 1851; stld Huron Twp, Bruce Co, ONT, 1852. Head of family. **DC 5 Apr 1967**.

8321   McLEOD, Donald. From Is Islay, ARL. To Sullivan Twp, Grey Co, ONT, 1851. m Elizabeth Gilchrist. Son Alexander Gilchrist, 1844–1919, master mariner. **DC 20 Jul 1982**.

8322   McLEOD, Donald, 1790–1852. From Tolsta Chaolais, Is Lewis, ROC. s/o Evander M. and Mary McGregor. To QUE, ex Stornoway, arr 4 Aug 1851; stld Huron Twp, Bruce Co, ONT. Farmer. m Effie McLeod, qv, ch: 1. Margaret, b 1817; 2. Malcolm, b 1821; 3. Kirsty, b 1822; 4. Donald, b 1825; 5. Catherine, b 1827; 6. Evander. **WLC**.

8323   McLEOD or McCUAIG, Donald, 1809-99. From Glenegedale, Kildalton par, Is Islay, ARL. s/o Donald McCuaig and Catherine Campbell. To Grey Co, ONT, poss 1854. Bur Greenwood cemetery, Owen Sound. m Elizabeth Gilchrist, qv, ch: 1. Peter, b ca 1841; 2. Isabella, b 1843; 3. Dugald, b 1846; 4. Mary, b 1848; 5. Grace, b 1850; 6. Ronald, b 1852; 7. Alexander, b 1854, navigator, Great Lakes. **LDW 4 Jun 1976**.

8324   MACLEOD, Donald William, b 1808. From Gesto, Is Skye, INV. s/o Neil M, tacksman, and Flora Mackinnon. To Ottawa, ONT, <1840; stld Hogs Back. m Isabella Murray. Son Neil Kenneth, farmer, Glengarry Co. **CMM 2/20 193**.

8325   McLEOD, Duncan, b ca 1783. To Western Shore, Inverness Co, NS, 1811. Farmer, m and ch. **CBC 1818**.

8326   MACLEOD, Duncan, b ca 1811. Prob from INV. To Gut of Canso, Cape Breton, NS, on the *Catherine*, ex Tobermory, 13 Jul 1843. Wife Ann, aged 26, with him, and inf s Duncan. **MP 639**.

8327   McLEOD, Duncan. From Is South Uist, INV. To West Williams Twp, Middlesex Co, ONT, 1849; stld Con 14. **PCM 48**.

8328   MACLEOD, Duncan. From Glenelg, INV. s/o Donald M, qv, and Catherine Beaton, qv. To QUE on the *Liscard*, 1849; stld Glengarry Co, ONT. m Jessie McIntosh, 1864, ch: 1. Donald Duncan; 2. Catherine; 3. Bella; 4. Isabella; 5. Farquhar; 6. Margaret; 7. Neil; 8. Mary; 9. Jessie. **MG 318, 319**.

8329   McLEOD, Duncan. From Is Lewis, ROC. To QUE, ex Stornoway, arr 4 Aug 1851; stld Huron Twp, Bruce Co, ONT, 1852. Head of family. **DC 5 Apr 1967**.

8330   MACLEOD, Duncan A, 1827–1906. From Is Skye, INV. s/o Angus M. and — MacIntosh. To Glengarry Co, ONT, poss 1849. m Catrien Fraser. Son Duncan J, 1864–1943. **MG 388**.

8331   McLEOD, Effie, b ca 1797. From Tolsta Chaolais, Is Lewis, ROC. To QUE, ex Stornoway, arr 4 Aug 1851; stld Huron Twp, Bruce Co, ONT, 1852. Wife of Donald McLeod, qv. **WLC**.

8332   McLEOD, Elizabeth. From SUT. To Pictou, NS, 1831. m Donald McKay. **PAC 108**.

8333   MACLEOD, Eunice. From Is Eigg, INV. d/o Neil M, qv, and Mary Campbell. To NS <1797. m John Mackinnon, qv. **HCA 304, 318**.

8334   McLEOD, Evander. From Is Lewis, ROC. To QUE, ex Stornoway, arr 4 Aug 1851; stld Huron Twp, Bruce Co, ONT, 1852. Head of family. **DC 5 Apr 1967**.

8335   McLEOD, Finlay, b ca 1771. To Richmond Co, NS, 1817. **CBC 1818**.

8336   MACLEOD, Flora. From Is Skye, INV. d/o Peter M, and Mary MacDiarmid. To Dunakym, Mabou, Inverness Co, NS, 1840. m 1827, Malcolm Mackinnon, qv. **MP ii 526**.

8337 McLEOD, Flora. Prob from Is Lewis, ROC. To Cape Breton Co, NS, 1844. Wife of Hugh McAulay, qv. **NSN 7/1**.

8338 McLEOD, George. From Assynt or Eddrachillis, SUT. To Boston, MA, on the *Fortitude*, arr 16 Aug 1803; stld Scotch Ridge, Charlotte Co, NB, 1805. Formerly of the Reay Fencible Regt. Son Rev Thomas, Miramichi, Northumberland Co. **DC 29 Nov 1982**.

8339 McLEOD, George, b 26 Dec 1882. From Clyne par, SUT. bro/o James M, qv. To Pictou Co, NS, 1814; stld Middle River. Farmer and magistrate, 1840. m Anne Sutherland, ch. **DC 27 Jan 1983**.

8340 McLEOD, George, ca 1788–1 Jan 1847. Prob from SUT. To Pictou Co, NS, and stld nr Lansdowne. Wife Elizabeth, 1802–16 Dec 1882, with him. **DC 10 Feb 1980**.

8341 McLEOD, George. To Pictou, NS, on the *Ellen*, ex Loch Laxford, SUT, 22 May 1848. Wife Nancy with him, and dau Margaret. **DC 15 Jul 1979**.

8342 MACLEOD, Harry. Prob from Is Skye, INV. To Queens Co, PEI, poss 1803. Petitioner for Dr MacAulay, 1811. **HP 74**.

8343 McLEOD, Hector, b ca 1795. From Kildonan, SUT. To Fort Churchill, Hudson Bay, on the *Prince of Wales*, ex Stromness, 28 Jun 1813. Went to York Factory, Apr 1814, thence to Red River. Left settlement and arr Holland River, ONT, 6 Sep 1815. **LSS 186; RRS 27; LSC 323**.

8344 McLEOD, Hector. Prob from Eddrachillis, SUT. To Oxford Co, ONT, <2 Nov 1847; stld Zorra Twp. *MacLeod Muniments*, **Box 36**.

8345 MACLEOD, Hector, b ca 1786. From Balivanich, Is Benbecula, INV. Prob rel to Archibald M, qv. To Pictou, NS, on the *Lulan*, ex Glasgow, arr 17 Aug 1848. Cooper. m Flora MacNeil, ch: 1. Marion, b 1816; 2. Christine, b 1821; 3. Jessie, b 1826; 4. John, b 1827; 5. Ewen, b 1829; 6. Mary. **DC 12 Jul 1979**.

8346 McLEOD, Henrietta, ca 1783–1860. From SUT. Poss sis/o John M, qv. To Earltown, Colchester Co, NS, prob <1824. **DC 19 Mar 1981**.

8347 McLEOD, Hugh. From Assynt, SUT. To Pictou, NS, on the *Hector*, ex Loch Broom, arr 17 Sep 1773; stld West River, Pictou Co. Farmer and teacher. m (i) Christian McLeod, qv, ch: 1. dau, stld Cornwallis; 2. Mrs Donald Ross; 3. Mrs Shiels. m (ii) Widow McLeod, further ch: 4. David. **HPC App C**.

8348 McLEOD, Hugh. From Assynt or Eddrachillis, SUT. To Boston, MA, on the *Fortitude*, arr 16 Aug 1803; stld Scotch Ridge, Charlotte Co, NB. Formerly of the Reay Fencible Regt. **DC 29 Nov 1982**.

8349 McLEOD, Hugh, b ca 1770. To Charlottetown, PEI, on the *Elizabeth & Anne*, ex Thurso, arr 8 Nov 1806. Wife Mary McPherson, qv, with him, and ch: 1. Isabel, aged 12; 2. Hugh, aged 10; 3. Christian, aged 8; 4. Margaret, aged 2; 5. Cathrine, aged 1. **PLEA**.

8350 McLEOD, Hugh. To Pictou, NS, on the *Ellen*, ex Loch Laxford, SUT, 22 May 1848. Wife Lucy with him, and ch: 1. Robina; 2. David; 3. Betty. **DC 15 Jul 1979**.

8351 MACLEOD, Rev Hugh, 23 Apr 1803–23 Jan 1894. b Tongue, SUT. Grad MA, Kings Coll, Aberdeen, 1826. Schoolmaster at Tongue; min in Edinburgh, then Logie-Easter. To CAN as missionary, 1845, and called to Mira Ferry or Albert Bridge, Cape Breton Co, NS, as FC min, to settle there, 1850. Moderator of the Presb Ch of Canada, 1877. DD. m 6 Apr 1841, Catherine Ross, qv, ch: 1. Hugh, b 1842; 2. Barbara, b 1844; 3. George, b 1846; 4. Anne, b 1849; 5. Barbara, b 1851; 6. William Mackenzie, b 1854; 7. Anne, b 1857; 8. Catherine, b 1860. **KCG 282; AFC i 250; FES vii 64, 607**.

8352 McLEOD, Isabella, 4 Aug 1816–4 Oct 1839. From STI. d/o Donald M, qv, and Margaret MacFarlane, qv. To Simcoe Co, ONT, 1831. m 4 Oct 1839, Archibald Leitch, qv. **DC 8 Nov 1981**.

8353 McLEOD, Isabella, b 1807. From Assynt, SUT. To Cape Breton Co, NS, prob <1850. **DC 14 Apr 1965**.

8354 McLEOD, James. From SUT. To Pictou, NS, on the *Hector*, ex Loch Broom, arr 17 Sep 1773; gr 150 acres on east side of Middle River, 1783. **HPC App A and C**.

8355 McLEOD, James, ca 1783–9 Feb 1844. From Clyne, SUT. bro/o George M, qv. To Pictou Co, NS, 1814; stld Fox Brook. Discharged soldier, later farmer. m Marion Sutherland, ch. **DC 27 Jan 1983**.

8356 MACLEOD, James. From Is Harris, INV. To Mabou Ridge, Inverness Co, NS, <1820. Pioneer settler. ch: 1. Donald, qv; 2. William, qv; 3. Asa, qv; 4. Sara, qv. **MP 740**.

8357 MACLEOD, Janet. To CAN, ca 1780; later to Albany, NY. Wife of John MacGillivray, qv. **LDW 19 May 1972**.

8358 MACLEOD, Janet. From Is Skye, INV. To Cape Breton Is, NS, 1827. Second wife of John MacDonald, qv. **DC 23 Feb 1980**.

8359 MACLEOD, Janet, 1814–19 Feb 1872. From Glasgow. To Cape Breton Co, NS, ca 1835. Wife of John L. MacDonald, qv. **DC 29 Dec 1981**.

8360 MACLEOD, Jessie. From Glenelg, INV. d/o Duncan M. and Mary MacCaskill. To Glengarry Co, ONT, 1832. m Donald Dewar, qv. **MG 317**.

8361 MACLEOD, John, called 'Iain Breac', b ca 1789. From Glenelg, INV. s/o Capt Alexander M, qv. To PEI, arr 18 Oct 1793, but went to Lochiel Twp, Glengarry Co, ONT, 1794. Farmer. m Margaret Morrison, ch: 1. Catherine; 2. William; 3. Allan; 4. Alexander; 5. Christy; 6. Norman; 7. Janet; 8. Mary. **MG 66**.

8362 McLEOD, John. To Glengarry Co, ONT, 1794; stld Lot 24, Con 15, Lancaster Twp. **MG 56**.

8363 MACLEOD, John. From Is Eigg, INV. s/o Neil M, qv, and Mary Campbell. To Parrsboro, Cumberland Co, NS, <1797. Moved to Arisaig, Antigonish Co, 1801. m Mary MacDonald, ch: 1. Rev William, b 1797; 2. Rev Neil; 3. Eunice; 4. Sarah; 5. John. **HCA 318**.

8364 McLEOD, John. From Is Skye, INV. To Orwell Bay, PEI, on the *Polly*, ex Portree, 7 Aug 1803; stld Belfast dist. Petitioner for Dr MacAulay, 1811. **HP 73**.

8365 McLEOD, John, b ca 1748. To Charlottetown, PEI, on the *Elizabeth & Ann*, ex Thurso, arr 8 Nov 1806.

Wife Ann McKenzie, qv, with him, and ch: 1. Donald, aged 25; 2. Barbara, aged 18; 3. Hugh, aged 15; 4. Urie, aged 14; 5. Williamina, aged 9; 6. Angus, aged 6. **PLEA**.

8366 McLEOD, John, b ca 1771. To Charlottetown, PEI, on the *Elizabeth & Ann*, ex Thurso, arr 8 Nov 1806. Wife Nancy Morrison, qv, with him, and ch: 1. Isobel, aged 12; 2. Hugh, aged 10; 3. Donald, aged 4; 4. Andrew, aged 2; 5. Nancy, aged 1. **PLEA**.

8367 McLEOD, John, 1788–24 Jul 1849. From Stornoway, Is Lewis, ROC. To CAN, 1811, and joined HBCo. In charge of Red River post and defended it against the Nor' Westers. Chief trader, 1821, and served in the Columbia dist. Ret 1848, and res Hochelaga. **MDB 478**.

8368 McLEOD, John, b ca 1773. From Glasgow. To QUE, ex Greenock, summer 1815; stld Lot 13, Con 10, Bathurst Twp, Lanark Co, ONT. Labourer, later farmer. Wife Jane Campbell, qv. **SEC 3; HCL 16**.

8369 MACLEOD, John, b 1807. From INV. To Glengarry Co, ONT, 1815; stld Glen Norman, Lancaster Twp. m Catherine MacRae, 1821–93, ch: 1. Donald, b 1845; 2. Harriet, b 1843; 3. Margaret, b 1847; 4. John; 5. Duncan, b 1852; 6-7. Sarah and Anne, b 1852; 8. Janet; 9. Mary; 10. Christine. **MG 261**.

8370 MACLEOD, John. From Is Lewis, ROC. To Glengarry Co, ONT, ca 1815. Son John. **MG 30**.

8371 MACLEOD, John. Poss from SUT. Said rel to Rev Norman M, qv. To NS, 1817; stld Gairloch, Pictou Co. Discharged soldier, veteran of Waterloo. m Sarah, d/o Angus MacLeod, ch: 1. Donald; 2. John; 3. Mary; 4. Catherine; 5. Jane; 6. Christy; 7. Sarah; 8. Flora; 9. Alexander Roderick. **DC 21 Mar 1981**.

8372 McLEOD, John, ca 1795–16 Aug 1869. From SUT. To Earltown, Colchester Co, NS, <1824. First wife Ann, 1794–1824; second wife Margaret, 1779–1849. **DC 19 Mar 1981**.

8373 MACLEOD, John. From Is Skye, INV. s/o Norman M, qv, and Margaret MacPhee, qv. To Charlottetown, PEI, on the *Mary Kennedy*, arr 1 Jun 1829; stld Queens Co. m Rachel, d/o Donald Gordon, no ch. **SPI 160**.

8374 MACLEOD, John, 1809–91. From Is Skye, INV. s/o Malcolm M, qv. To Glengarry Co, ONT, 1832; stld Kenyon Twp. m Catherine, d/o Angus Campbell, qv, and Margaret McGinnis, qv, ch: 1. Malcolm, b 1844; 2. Donald, b 1846; 3. John, b 1849; 4. Angus, b 1851; 5. Mary Ann, b 1858. **MG 292**.

8375 McLEOD, John, 1812–25 Jan 1893. From Is Rona, off Is Lewis, ROC. To Charlottetown, PEI, prob <1840; stld Hartsville, Queens Co. m Sarah Gillis, 1809–94. **DC 16 Aug 1982**.

8376 McLEOD, John. From Is Skye, INV. To Middlesex Co, ONT, 1841; stld West Williams Twp, Con 16, 1844. ch: 1. James; 2. Archibald; 3. Neil; 4. Mary; 5. Sara; 6. Annie; 7. Mrs Clark. **PCM 48**.

8377 McLEOD, John. From ARL. To ONT, prob 1846; stld poss Huron Co. m Kate Graham, qv. **SG xxvi/3 92**.

8378 McLEOD, John, 1821–8 Oct 1874. To QUE, prob <1850; and bur Flodden Station. m Marian McLean, qv. **MGC 15 Jul 1980**.

8379 McLEOD, John, 1800–22 Sep 1865. From Is Skye, INV. To Charlottetown, PEI, prob <1850; stld Hartsville, Queens Co. m Sarah McEwen. **DC 16 Aug 1982**.

8380 McLEOD, John. From Is Lewis, ROC. To QUE, ex Stornoway, arr 4 Aug 1851; stld Huron Twp, Bruce Co, ONT, 1852. Son John. **DC 5 Apr 1967**.

8381 McLEOD, John. From Carloway, Is Lewis, ROC. To QUE, ex Stornoway, arr 4 Aug 1851; stld Huron Twp, Bruce Co, ONT, 1852. Farmer. m Marion Morrison, ch: 1. Donald, b 1833; 2. Duncan, b 1838; 3. John, b 1841; 4. Malcolm, b 1842; 5. Angus; 6. Kenneth; 7. Mary Ann. **WLC**.

8382 McLEOD, John. To Pictou, NS, on the *Ellen*, ex Loch Laxford, SUT, 22 May 1848. Wife Ann with him, and ch: 1. Isabella; 2. Jean; 3. Barbara. **DC 15 Jul 1979**.

8383 McLEOD, John (1). From Is Lewis, ROC. To QUE, ex Stornoway, arr 4 Aug 1851; stld Huron Twp, Bruce Co, ONT, 1852. Head of family. **DC 5 Apr 1967**.

8384 McLEOD, John (2). From Is Lewis, ROC. To QUE, ex Stornoway, arr 4 Aug 1851; stld Huron Twp, Bruce Co, ONT, 1852. Head of family. **DC 5 Apr 1967**.

8385 McLEOD, John (3). From Is Lewis, ROC. To QUE, ex Stornoway, arr 4 Aug 1851; stld Huron Twp, Bruce Co, ONT, 1852. Head of family. **DC 5 Apr 1967**.

8386 McLEOD, John, 1791–27 Jul 1874. From Assynt, SUT. To Victoria Co, NS, and stld Cape North. **DC 22 Jun 1979**.

8387 McLEOD, John. Prob from Port Dundas, Glasgow. To Miramichi, Northumberland Co, NB, <1855; stld Tabusintac River. **DC 4 Oct 1978**.

8388 MACLEOD, John, 15 Jun 1824–5 Jun 1913. From Lochinver, SUT. To Victoria Co, NS. m Sarah MacIntosh, from Pleasant Bay. **DC 22 Jun 1979**.

8389 McLEOD, Rev John Neil Macaulay, 1826–30 Dec 1872. From Is Harris, INV. s/o Neil M. Matric Univ of Glasgow, 1846. Min of Cryston, Glasgow, 1853-63. Taught at a private school, and in 1866 was adm min of East Williams Twp, Middlesex Co, ONT. Trans to Glencoe, 1868. m 1853, Jessie, d/o Rev James Fleming, Troon, AYR. Son James Fleming. **GMA 15077; FES iii 384**.

8390 McLEOD, Joseph, ca 1787–9 Sep 1879. From SUT. To Pictou Co, NS. m Ellen Grant, qv. Both bur at Salt Springs. **DC 27 Oct 1979**.

8391 McLEOD, Kanaugh or Kavenaugh, b ca 1754. To Baddeck dist, Victoria Co, NS, 1812. Blacksmith. ch incl: 1. John, b ca 1792; 2. Kanaugh, b ca 1795. **CBC 1818**.

8392 MACLEOD, Kenneth. From Myle, Glenelg, INV. s/o Alexander M, of the Drynoch family, and Sybella MacLeod. To PEI, arr 18 Oct 1793; moved in spring of 1794 to Lochiel Twp, Glengarry Co, ONT. Farmer, Lot 18, Con 6. ch: 1. Capt Alexander, qv; 2. Norman 'Mor', qv; 3. Mary, qv; 4. Christine, qv. **MG 28, 35**.

8393 MACLEOD, Kenneth. Poss from Glenelg, INV. To Glengarry Co, ONT, 1794; stld Lot 19, Con 16, Lancaster Twp. **MG 57**.

8394 MACLEOD, Kenneth. From Kilmorack, INV. To

Pictou, NS, on the *Dove*, ex Fort William, Jun 1801. Labourer. **PLD**.

8395 McLEOD, Kenneth, b ca 1769. To Charlottetown, PEI, on the *Elizabeth & Ann*, ex Thurso, arr 8 Nov 1806. Wife Betsy McKay, qv, with him, and ch: 1. John, aged 12; 2. George, aged 5; 3. Kenneth, aged 3; 4. James, aged 1. **PLEA**.

8396 MACLEOD, Kenneth, b ca 1831. From Glenelg, INV. s/o Donald M, qv, and Catherine Bethune, qv. To QUE on the *Liscard*, 1849; stld Kenyon Twp, Glengarry Co, ONT. m 11 Aug 1863, Rebecca, d/o Norman MacLeod and Christie MacRae, ch: 1. Donald, 1864–1947; 2. Norman, 1866–1961; 3. Farquhar, d inf; 4. Duncan, 1870–1939; 5. Frederick, 1872–1956; 6. John Angus, 1864–1941; 7. Kenneth, 1877–1956; 8. Roderick, 1883–1940. **MG 318, 327**.

8397 MACLEOD, Malcolm. From Kendrum, Kilmaluag, Is Skye, INV. s/o Donald M, qv, and Catherine Macdonald. To Orwell Bay, PEI, prob on the *Polly*, ex Portree, arr 7 Aug 1803; stld Belfast dist. m Rachel MacQueen, ch: 1. Alexander; 2. William; 3. Neil; 4. Donald; 5. John; 6. Mary; 7. dau. **CMM 3/22 93**.

8398 MACLEOD, Malcolm. From Glasphein, Staffin, Is Skye, INV. To Orwell Bay, PEI, on the *Polly*, ex Portree, arr 7 Aug 1803; stld Pinette, Queens Co. wife Effie McDonald, qv, with him, and ch: 1. Christina, qv; 2. William, qv; 3. Anne, qv; 4. Malcolm, jr, qv; 5. Donald, qv; 6. Catherine, qv; 7. Mary, qv; 8. Catherine, qv; 9. Angus 'Mor', qv; 10. William 'Og', qv. **SPI 136; HP 17**.

8399 MACLEOD, Malcolm, jr. From Glasphein, Staffin, Is Skye, INV. s/o Malcolm M, qv, and Effie MacDonald, qv. To Orwell Bay, PEI, on the *Polly*, ex Portree, arr 7 Aug 1803; stld Queens Co. m Miss MacLean. **SPI 138**.

8400 McLEOD, Malcolm, b ca 1787. From Glenelg, INV. To QUE, ex Greenock, summer 1815; stld prob Lanark Co, ONT. Wife Ann Campbell, qv, with him, and 3 ch. **SEC 7**.

8401 MACLEOD, Malcolm, b ca 1790. From Cuidrach, Is Skye, INV. s/o Capt Murdoch M. and Marion MacDonald. To Cape Breton Is, NS, poss <1830. **SPI 135**.

8402 MACLEOD, Malcolm, b ca 1827. From Kiltarlity, INV. s/o Alexander M, qv, and Annie Fraser, qv. To Pictou Co, NS, 1832; stld west branch of East River. Went later to Truro, Colchester Co. Ship-painter. m Harriet Hill, ch: 1. Hedley Vickers; 2. Charles Simon; 3. Thomas; 4. Hattie; 5. Minnie; 6. Douglas; 7. Jessie; 8. Bert. **PAC 156**.

8403 MACLEOD, Malcolm. From Is Skye, INV. To Glengarry Co, ONT, 1832; stld Lot 23, Con 9, Kenyon Twp. Farmer and widower. ch: 1. John, qv; 2. Meriom, qv. **MG 29, 291**.

8404 McLEOD, Malcolm. From INV. To Middlesex Co, ONT, 1849; stld McGillivray Twp. **PCM 56**.

8405 MACLEOD, Malcolm. From Crowlista, Is Lewis, ROC. To Montreal, QUE, 1851; stld Middle dist, Winslow Twp, Compton Co. Stonemason. m Catherine MacAulay, qv, ch: 1. John, went to Klondyke, 1898; 2. Malcolm, jr, qv; 3. Catherine, qv; 4. Christena; 5. Margaret; 6. Annie; 7. Jessie; 8. Murdo. **TFT 14**.

8406 MACLEOD, Malcolm, jr, b ca 1848. From Crowlista, Is Lewis, ROC. s/o Malcolm M, qv, and Catherine MacAulay, qv. To Montreal, QUE, 1851; stld Winslow Twp, Compton Co. m Isabel MacDonald, ch: 1. John, res Littleton, NH, USA; 2. Murdo, res Corinth, VT, USA; 3. Mary; 4. Angus, res Barre, VT; 5. Lydia; 6. Katie; 7. David, res Corinth, VT; 8. Hector; 9. Albert. **TFT 14**.

8407 McLEOD, Malcolm (1). From Is Lewis, ROC. To QUE, ex Stornoway, arr 4 Aug 1851; stld Huron Twp, Bruce Co, ONT, 1852. Head of family. **DC 5 Apr 1967**.

8408 McLEOD, Malcolm (2). From Is Lewis, ROC. To QUE, ex Stornoway, arr 4 Aug 1851; stld Huron Twp, Bruce Co, ONT, 1852. Head of family. **DC 5 Apr 1967**.

8409 MACLEOD, Margaret, ca 1783–6 Jan 1876. From ROC. To NS, poss <1830; stld nr Earltown, Colchester Co. Wife of Hugh Munro, qv. **DC 19 Mar 1981**.

8410 MACLEOD, Margaret, 1825–31 Mar 1903. From Is Skye, INV. To Victoria Co, NS. Wife of William MacPherson, qv. **DC 22 Jun 1979**.

8411 MACLEOD, Margaret, b 1815. From Solitot, Kilmuir par, Is Skye, INV. d/o Angus 'Ruadh' M. and Anne Tolmie. To PEI, prob <1850. Wife of Allan Nicholson, qv. **SG xxvii/3 125**.

8412 McLEOD, Marian, 9 Jun 1823–14 Apr 1905. From STI. d/o Donald M, qv, and Margaret McFarlane, qv. To Simcoe Co, ONT, 1831. m 9 Dec 1845, Charles Harvie, qv. **DC 8 Nov 1981**.

8413 MACLEOD, Marion, ca 1768–1845. From Applecross, ROC. To Orwell Bay, PEI, on the *Polly*, ex Portree, arr 7 Aug 1803; stld Point Prim, later Newton River. Wife of Donald Martin, qv. **SPI 41; HP 78**.

8414 MACLEOD, Mary. From Glenelg, INV. d/o Kenneth M, qv. To PEI, arr 18 Oct 1793; moved in 1794 to Lochiel Twp, Glengarry Co, ONT. m Capt John Hay, UEL. Son Rev George A, 1807-76, RC priest. **MG 37**.

8415 MACLEOD, Mary. From Glenelg, INV. To Lochiel Twp, Glengarry Co, ONT, 1796. Wife of Roderick Roy MacLeod, qv. **MG 30**.

8416 MACLEOD, Mary. From Glasphein, Staffin, Is Skye, INV. d/o Malcolm M, qv, and Effie MacDonald, qv. To Queens Co, PEI, poss 1803. m Findlay O'Docherty, Seal River, ch. **SPI 138**.

8417 MACLEOD, Mary. From Is Skye, INV. To Orwell Cove, PEI, <1810. m John Nicholson, qv. **HP 16**.

8418 McLEOD, Mary, ca 1734–18 May 1801. From Glasgow. To St John, NB, and d there. **NER viii 99**.

8419 MACLEOD, Mary. From Stoer, Assynt, SUT. To Pictou, NS, prob summer 1818, to join her husband; stld Middle River, Pictou Co. Moved in 1821 to St Anns, Victoria Co, and later to Waipu, North Is, NZ. Wife of Rev Norman MacLeod, qv. **CMM 2/17 55; CP 98**.

8420 McLEOD, Mary, 13 Sep 1812–18 Sep 1866. From STI. d/o Donald M, qv, and Margaret McFarlane, qv. To Simcoe Co, ONT, 1831. m (i) James Horn; (ii) William Rutherford. **DC 8 Nov 1981**.

8421 MACLEOD, Mary, b 1775. From Uachdar, Is Benbecula, INV. To Pictou, NS, on the *Lulan*, ex

Glasgow, 17 Aug 1848. Wife of Donald MacDonald, qv.   **DC 12 Jul 1979**.

8422   MACLEOD, Mary Ann. From Glenelg, INV. d/o Donald M, qv, and Catherine Bethune, qv. To QUE on the *Liscard*, 1849; stld Glengarry Co, ONT. m John Dewar, qv.   **MG 355**.

8423   McLEOD, Matilda. From Is Skye, INV. d/o Norman 'Cypress' M. and second wife Jessie McDonald. To Cape Breton Is, NS. Wife of Archibald Campbell, qv.   **MacLeod Muniments**.

8424   MACLEOD, Meriom, ca 1817–25 Feb 1885. From Is Skye, INV. d/o Malcolm M, qv. To Glengarry Co, ONT, 1832; stld Kenyon Twp. m Donald Campbell, qv.   **MG 291**.

8425   MACLEOD, Murdo. To PEI, poss 1803; stld Queens Co. Petitioner for Dr MacAulay, 1811.   **HP 74**.

8426   MACLEOD, Murdo. From Is Raasay, INV. s/o Alexander 'Tailor' M, qv. To Queens Co, PEI, 1821. Farmer. m Miss Martin, ch.   **SPI 162**.

8427   MACLEOD, Murdo, b 1780. From Balivanich, Is Benbecula, INV. To Pictou, NS, on the *Lulan*, ex Glasgow, 17 Aug 1848. Wife Catherine, b 1785, with him, and ch: 1. Margaret, b 1821; 2. Mary, b 1826.   **DC 12 Jul 1979**.

8428   McLEOD, Murdoch, ca 1760–17 Aug 1813. From Portree, Is Skye, INV. To Kings Co, PEI. Farmer, and poss discharged army officer. m Jane Auld, qv, ch.   **DC 27 Jul 1980**.

8429   McLEOD, Murdoch. From Kendrum, Kilmaluag, Is Skye, INV. s/o Donald M, qv, and Catherine Macdonald. To Orwell Bay, PEI, prob on the *Polly*, ex Portree, arr 7 Aug 1803; stld Orwell Cove. m Flora, d/o Donald Nicholson, ch: 1. Donald; 2. Malcolm; 3. Roderick; 4. William; 5. Charles; 6. Donald 'Og'; 7. Margaret; 8. Catherine; 9. Mary; 10. Catherine, jr; 11. Christy.   **CMM 3/22 93, 96**.

8430   MACLEOD, Murdoch 'Tailor', ca 1784–23 May 1860. From Is Harris, INV. To Orwell Bay, PEI, 1816; stld Flat River, Queens Co. Farmer. m Mary MacLeod, rel to Neil M, of Orwell Bridge, ch: 1. Rachel; 2. Margaret; 3. Donald; 4. John; 5. William; 6. Bella, 1835–1927; 7. Neil, 1829–1910; 8. Catherine, d 1803; 9. Murdoch, 1832–1917; 10. Norman, d 1889; 11. Anne, b 1842; 12. Alexander, 1823-93, master mariner.   **SPI 139; HP 34**.

8431   McLEOD, Murdoch, d 10 Feb 1883. From Snizort par, Is Skye, INV. To Whycocomagh, Inverness Co, NS. m Mary Campbell, qv. Dau Jessie, 1838–1919.   **LDW 19 Nov 1977**.

8432   MACLEOD, Murdoch 'Mor', 1815–29 Jul 1889. From Is Skye, INV. s/o Norman M, qv, and Margaret MacPhee, qv. To Charlottetown, PEI, on the *Mary Kennedy*, arr 1 Jun 1829; stld Queens Co. Farmer. m 6 Oct 1837, Margaret Gunn, Miramichi, NB, and had, poss with other ch: 1. John Murdoch, b 1848; 2. William, res Bridgetown, Dundas.   **SPI 160**.

8433   McLEOD, Murdoch, ca 1786–13 Feb 1850. From ROC. To QUE, and bur Flodden Station. m Margaret McLennan, qv.   **MGC 15 Jul 1980**.

8434   MACLEOD, Murdoch. Poss from ARL. To Aldborough Twp, Elgin Co, ONT, 1855.   **PDA 68**.

8435   MACLEOD, Murdock. From INV. To Glengarry Co, ONT, <1820; stld Lochiel Twp. Farmer. m Annie MacMillan, ch: 1. Malcolm; 2. Murdock.   **MG 398**.

8436   McLEOD, Murdock (1). From Is Lewis, ROC. To QUE, ex Stornoway, arr 4 Aug 1851; stld Huron Twp, Bruce Co, ONT, 1852. Shepherd. Head of family.   **DC 5 Apr 1967**.

8437   McLEOD, Murdock (2). From Is Lewis, ROC. To QUE, ex Stornoway, arr 4 Aug 1851; stld Huron Twp, Bruce Co, ONT, 1852. Head of family.   **DC 5 Apr 1967**.

8438   McLEOD, Murdock (3). From Is Lewis, ROC. To QUE, ex Stornoway, arr 4 Aug 1851; stld Huron Twp, Bruce Co, ONT, 1852. Head of family.   **DC 5 Apr 1967**.

8439   McLEOD, Nancy, ca 1788–1874. From INV. To Pictou Co, NS, and bur with husband Alexander McGillivray, qv, at Salt Springs.   **DC 27 Oct 1979**.

8440   MACLEOD, Neil, ca 1791–1874. From Glenelg, INV. s/o Capt Alexander M, qv. To PEI, arr 18 Oct 1793, but went in 1794 to Lochiel Twp, Glengarry Co, ONT. Farmer. By his wife Harriet had ch: 1. Catherine; 2. William; 3. Mary; 4. Norman; 5. John; 6. Roderick; 7. Donald.   **MG 71**.

8441   MACLEOD, Neil. From Is Eigg, INV. To Parrsboro, Cumberland Co, NS, <1797. m Mary Campbell, from Is Skye, who may have d in SCT, ch: 1. John, qv; 2. Donald, qv; 3. Neil; 4. Hugh; 5. Eunice, qv; 6. Ann, qv.   **HCA 318**.

8442   McLEOD, Neil. To Pictou, NS, on the *London*, arr 14 Jul 1848.   **DC 15 Jul 1979**.

8443   McLEOD, Neil. To Pictou, NS, on the *Ellen*, ex Loch Laxford, SUT, 22 May 1848. Wife Bessy with him.   **DC 15 Jul 1979**.

8444   McLEOD, Ninian, d 27 Jan 1796. From Is Skye, INV. To Montreal, QUE, and d there.   **DC 15 May 1977**.

8445   McLEOD, Norman. To Glengarry Co, ONT, 1794; stld Lot 18, Con 16, Lancaster Twp.   **MG 57**.

8446   McLEOD, Norman. To Glengarry Co, ONT, 1794; stld Lot 32, Con 16, Lancaster Twp.   **MG 57**.

8447   McLEOD, Norman. To Glengarry Co, ONT, 1794; stld Lot 31, Con 15, Lancaster Twp.   **MG 57**.

8448   MACLEOD, Norman, 1786–22 Apr 1870. From Swordland, Glenelg, INV. s/o Alexander M, qv, and Janet MacRae, qv. To Kenyon Twp, Glengarry Co, ONT, 1817. Farmer. m Sarah MacCuaig, qv, ch: 1. Olaus, qv; 2. Norman; 3. Angus; 4. Donald; 5. Neil; 6. Harriet; 7. Ellen.   **MG 269, 285**.

8449   MACLEOD, Rev Norman, 1780–1866. From Clachtoll, Stoer, Assynt par, SUT. To Pictou, NS, on the *Francis Ann*, ex Loch Broom, Jul 1817; stld Middle River, Pictou Co. Moved, 1821, to St Anns, Victoria Co. Teacher and emigrant leader, ord to ministry at Genesee, Livingston Co, NY. In 1851 went with his followers to Waipu, North Is, NZ. m Mary MacLeod, qv, and had, poss with other ch: 1. John Luther; 2. Bunyan; 3. Donald; 4. Margaret.   **CMM 2/17 55; CP 98; GD50/225/1; FES vii 606**.

8450   MACLEOD, Norman, ca 1762–1837. From Is Skye, INV. s/o Neil M. and Sophia Nicholson. To Charlottetown, PEI, on the *Mary Kennedy*, ex Portree, arr 1 Jun 1829; stld Uigg, Queens Co. m Margaret

MacPhee, qv, ch: 1. Samuel, qv; 2. Roderick, qv; 3. John, qv; 4. Murdoch 'Mor', qv; 5. Mrs Angus MacDonald; 6. Mrs James MacDonald; 7. Mrs Cameron; 8. Neil, res Vernon River. **SPI 159**.

8451 McLEOD, Rev Norman. To Megantic Co, QUE, 1847. Ord Congregational min of Inverness, 23 Feb 1848. **AMC 112**.

8452 MACLEOD, Norman 'Miannaich'. From Glenelg, INV. To QUE, 1794; stld Lot 19, Con 7, Lochiel Twp, Glengarry Co, ONT. **MG 211**.

8453 MACLEOD, Norman 'Mor'. From Glenelg, INV. s/o Kenneth M, qv. To PEI, arr 18 Oct 1793; moved in 1794 to Lot 15, Con 15, Lancaster Twp, Glengarry Co, ONT. Son Donald stld Lochiel Twp. **MG 37, 54, 56**.

8454 McLEOD, Normand, d 1796. Prob from Durinish, Is Skye, INV. Fur-trader in Great Lakes area poss <1755, and prob res for a time at Detroit. Became a partner of Gregory, McLeod & Co, in Montreal, QUE, 1783; absorbed by NWCo in 1787, when he became a dormant partner. Sold his shares, 1790, and ret. m Cecile Roberts. **MDB 479**.

8455 McLEOD, Normanda or Norma. From Is Skye, INV. d/o Neil M. To Kenyon Twp, Glengarry Co, ONT. m Rev Adam Fraser MacQueen, qv. **DC 31 Aug 1979**.

8456 MACLEOD, Olaus, 1 Jan 1816–16 Feb 1896. From Glenelg, INV. s/o Norman M, qv, and Sarah MacCuaig, qv. To Kenyon Twp, Glengarry Co, ONT, 1817. m Christy MacIntosh, 1841, ch: 1. Catherine; 2. Alexander; 3. Donald; 4. Angus; 5. Duncan, res Ottawa; 6. Ann; 7. Janet; 8. John, artist, NY. **MG 284**.

8457 McLEOD, Philip. From SUT. To Pictou, NS, on the *Hector*, ex Loch Broom, arr 17 Sep 1773; stld Pictou Co. **HPC App C**.

8458 MACLEOD, Rachel, b 1811. From Bellaglom, Is Bernera, off Is Lewis, ROC. To QUE, 1851. Wife of Donald MacLeod, qv. **WLC**.

8459 MACLEOD, Roderick. From Kendrum, Kilmaluag, Is Skye, INV. s/o Donald M, qv, and Catherine Macdonald. To Orwell Bay, PEI, prob on the *Polly*, ex Portree, arr 7 Aug 1803; stld Belfast dist, Queens Co. m Miss Mackenzie, ch: 1. Jessie; 2. Christy; 3. Mary; 4. William. **CMM 3/22 96, 97**.

8460 MACLEOD, Roderick, ca 1803-88. From Is Skye, INV. s/o Norman M, qv, and Margaret MacPhee, qv. To Charlottetown, PEI, on the *Mary Kennedy*, ex Portree, arr 1 Jun 1829; stld Queens Co. By wife Catherine, d 1882, he had, poss with other ch: 1. Malcolm, KC; 2. John; 3. Ann; 4. Katherine, d 1929. **SPI 160**.

8461 MACLEOD, Roderick, 1822-96. From Stenscholl, Kilmuir par, Is Skye, INV. s/o Donald 'Ban Oig' M, qv, and Mary Martin, qv. To Charlottetown, PEI, on the *Mary Kennedy*, ex Portree, arr 1 Jun 1829; stld Murray Harbour Road. m Marjory Martin, a rel, ch: 1. Flora, b 1848; 2. Marjorie; 3. Charles; 4. Christy; 5. Donald, b 1859; 6. Malcolm; 7. Mary. **SPI 143**.

8462 McLEOD, Roderick. From Achmelvich, Assynt, SUT. s/o Roderick M. To QUE on the *Panama*, Jun 1847; stld Woodstock, Oxford Co, ONT. ***MacLeod Muniments*, Box 36**.

8463 McLEOD, Roderick. To Glengarry Co, ONT, 1794; stld Lot 30, Con 16, Lancaster Twp. **MG 57**.

8464 McLEOD, Roderick. To Glengarry Co, ONT, 1794; stld Lot 16, Con 16, Lancaster Twp. **MG 57**.

8465 McLEOD, Roderick, ca 1824–7 Mar 1912. From Is Harris, INV. To Victoria Co, NS. Wife Margaret, ca 1828–8 Apr 1902. **DC 22 Jun 1979**.

8466 MACLEOD, Roderick D, ca 1752–14 Dec 1848. From Glenelg, INV. To Glengarry Co, ONT, 1796; stld Lancaster Twp, but moved to Lot 37, Con 7, Lochiel Twp. Farmer. m Christy MacCrimmon, qv, ch: 1. John, stld QUE; 2. Neil, res Kingston; 3. Kenneth; 4. Donald; 5. Christy; 6. Sara; 7. Mary; 8. Finlay. **MG 29, 240**.

8467 MACLEOD, Roderick Roy. From Glenelg, INV. To Lochiel Twp, Glengarry Co, ONT, 1796; stld Lot 30, Con 7, later Lot 24, Con 6. Farmer. m Mary MacLeod, qv, and had, with other ch: 1. Donald, qv; 2. Harriet; 3. Malcolm; 4. Catherine; 5. John; 6. Kenneth; 7. Norman. **MG 30, 210**.

8468 MACLEOD, Rory, ca 1797–6 May 1868. From INV, poss Is Skye. To Lochiel Twp, Glengarry Co, ONT, <1812. Farmer. m Catherine MacCuaig, qv. Issue confused at source. **MG 304, 394**.

8469 MACLEOD, Rory. From Glenelg, INV. To QUE, ca 1833; stld Peveril. m Miss Bethune, ch: 1. Mary, unm; 2. Murdock, 1846–1916; 3. Donald; 4. Catherine; 5. Janet; 6. Janet; 7. Kate; 8. Annie; 9. Margaret. **MG 294**.

8470 MACLEOD, Samuel. From Glenelg, INV. s/o John M. To ONT, 1786; stld Lot 17, Con 2, Lancaster Twp, Glengarry Co. Farmer. Son Angus Roderick. **MG 203**.

8471 MACLEOD, Rev Samuel, ca 1796–23 Aug 1881. From Is Skye, INV. s/o Norman M, qv, and Margaret MacPhee, qv. To Charlottetown, PEI, on the *Mary Kennedy*, arr 1 Jun 1829; stld Pinette, Queens Co. Schoolteacher, and became Baptist clergyman. m Margaret Currie, qv, ch: 1. Norman, 1837–1928; 2. Malcolm, 1839–1903; 3. Dr James, d 1927; 4. Duncan, barrister; 5. Sarah; 6. Mary. **SPI 159**.

8472 MACLEOD, Sarah. From Is Benbecula, INV. wid/o Alexander McEachin, who d at sea. To Seaforth, Huron Co, ONT, ca 1837. ch with her: 1. Margaret, qv; 2. Christina, qv; 3. Sarah, qv; 4. Alexander, qv. **DC 12 Nov 1979**.

8473 McLEOD, Sarah, called Sally. From Is Harris, INV. To Mabou, Inverness Co, NS, <1820. m Joseph Basker, Mull River, ch. **MP 81, 747**.

8474 McLEOD, Simon. From ROC. To Adelaide Twp, Middlesex Co, ONT, ca 1850; stld Strathroy, later Nairn. Local councillor. **PCM 56**.

8475 McLEOD, William. To Pictou Co, NS, <12 Feb 1783, when listed as capable of bearing arms. Gr 270 acres on the east side of East River. **HPC App A and E**.

8476 MACLEOD, William, 1791–10 Sep 1882. From Glenelg, INV. s/o Alexander William M, qv. To QUE, ca 1798; later to Glengarry Co, ONT. Farmer, Lot 3, Con 9, Kenyon Twp. m Christina Grant, Williamstown, ch: 1. Donald; 2. Annie; 3. Alexander William; 4. James; 5. Isobel. **MG 253**.

8477 MACLEOD, William. From Glenelg, INV. To Kenyon Twp, Glengarry Co, ONT, <1810. **MG 30**.

8478 MACLEOD, William. From Is Harris, INV. s/o James M, qv. To Mabou Ridge, Inverness Co, NS, <1820. m Anne, d/o John Campbell and Janet Livingstone, ch: 1. David; 2. Alexander; 3. William; 4. James; 5. Malcolm; 6. Janet. **MP 746**.

8479 MACLEOD, William, 1783–1850. From Glasphein, Staffin, Is Skye, INV. s/o Malcolm M, qv, and Effie MacDonald, qv. To PEI, 1831; stld Uigg, Queens Co. m Catherine MacPherson, qv, ch: 1. Malcolm; 2. John; 3. Donald; 4. Angus; 5. Alexander; 6. Norman; 7. Effie; 8. Mary; 9. Katherine; 10. Jessie. **SPI 138**.

8480 MACLEOD, William 'Og', 1800-85. From Glasphein, Staffin, Is Skye, INV. s/o Malcolm M, qv, and Effie MacDonald, qv. To Orwell Bay, PEI, on the *Polly*, ex Portree, arr 7 Aug 1803; stld Queens Co. m Mary Lamont. Dau Eunice. **SPI 138**.

8481 MACLEOD, William, 17 Jul 1823–7 May 1902. From Kiltarlity, INV. s/o Alexander M, qv, and Annie Fraser, qv. To Pictou Co, NS, 1832; stld Middle River. Farmer. m 1847, Mary, d/o Donald McLean, Big Brook, and Marjory McKay. Dau Christy Ann. **PAC 126, 157**.

8482 McLEOD, William, ca 1769–9 Feb 1861. From SUT. To Tabusintac, Northumberland Co, NB, 1837. From Christina, 1771–1862, and ch: 1. Catherine, b ca 1801; 2. Flora, b ca 1818. **DC 4 Dec 1978**.

8483 McLEOD, William, 1813-99. From Branahuie, Is Lewis, ROC. s/o Donald M. and Mary McKenzie. To Lingwick Twp, Compton Co, QUE, ca 1842; later to Marston. Farmer and fisherman. m Rachel Finlayson, ch: 1. Donald, 1841-99; 2. Allan, b 1842; 3. Colin, b 1845; 4. Margaret, b 1847; 5. Mary Ann, b 1849; 6. John, b 1851; 7. George, b 1853; 8. Isabella, b 1855. **WLC**.

8484 McLEOD, William, d <1895. Prob from ROC. To Melbourne, Richmond Co, QUE, <1850. **MGC 15 Jul 1980**.

8485 McLEOD, William. From Is Lewis, INV. To QUE, ex Stornoway, arr 4 Aug 1851; stld Huron Twp, Bruce Co, ONT, 1852. Head of family. **DC 5 Apr 1967**.

8486 McLEVEN, Christina. From Kilmichael-Glassary, ARL. To Caledon Twp, Peel Co, ONT, <1840. m 24 May 1819, Donald Cameron, qv. **DC 21 Apr 1980**.

8487 McLORE, John. To Glengarry Co, ONT, 1794; stld Lot 29, Con 16, Lancaster Twp. **MG 57**.

8488 McLUCAS, Mary, b ca 1775. From Kilfinichen, Is Mull, ARL. To Hudson Bay and Red River, <1815. Wife of Angus McDonald, qv. **RRS 24; LSS 187**.

8489 McLUCKIE, Colin. To Pictou, NS, on the *Lulan*, ex Glasgow, 17 Aug 1848. **DC 12 Jul 1979**.

8490 McMARTIN, Alexander, 1788–1853. Prob from INV. s/o Malcolm M, qv, and Margaret McIntyre, qv. To Martintown, Glengarry Co, ONT, 1800. MP, 1812-24, 1828-34; postmaster, 1828; Sheriff of Stormont, Dundas and Glengarry, 1838-47. **SDG 91**.

8491 McMARTIN, Malcolm. Prob from INV. To Martintown, Glengarry Co, ONT, 1800. m Margaret McIntyre, qv. Son Alexander, qv. **SDG 91**.

8492 McMARTIN, Susan. From Ledcharry, Crieff, PER. To QUE, ex Greenock, summer 1815; stld ONT. Wife of John McLaren, qv. **SEC 3**.

8493 McMASTER, Alexander, ca 1804–4 Sep 1894. From INV. Rel to John M, qv. To QUE, 1817; stld Dundee Village, Charlottenburgh Twp, Glengarry Co, ONT, 1819. Moved to Ekfrid Twp, Middlesex Co. m at Williamstown, 1 Oct 1832, Margaret Stewart, ch: 1. Mary, b 1833; 2. Donald, 1837-75; 3. Catherine, 1839-1912; 4. Angus, b 1841; 5. John, 1843–1913; 6. Ann, b 1845; 7. Alexander, 1847–1923; 8. Margaret, 1849-88; 9. Jeanette, 1851–1919; 10. Jane, 1853-77; 11. James, 1858–1947. **PCM 30; DC 29 Oct 1979**.

8494 MACMASTER, Angus, b ca 1783. From Lochaber, INV. s/o Donald M, qv. To Inverness Co, NS, 1802; stld Queensville. m Miss MacEachen, and had with other ch: 1. James; 2. Isabel; 3. Catherine. **CBC 1818; WLC**.

8495 McMASTER, Rev Angus, 10 Sep 1801–6 Apr 1886. From Upper Feorline, Kilmory, Is Arran, BUT. s/o Alexander M, farmer, and Flora M. Tailor, but matric Univ of Glasgow, 1828, and ord in Ch of Scotland. To St Stephens Ch, Black River, and Kouchibouguac, Restigouche Co, NB, 1842. Joined FC and ind to New Mills, 1848, where he served for about 30 years. Ret to SCT, and d unm at Shiskin, Is Arran. **GMA 12225; FES vii 611; CUC 13; Ts Clachan**.

8496 MACMASTER, Angus. From Lochaber, INV. To Antigonish Co, NS, prob <1850. m Margaret Cameron, and had with other ch, s Rev John Francis, parish priest, Mabou, Inverness Co. **MP 50**.

8497 McMASTER, Archibald, 20 Dec 1785–12 Nov 1875. From Upper Feorline, Kilmory, Is Arran, BUT. To QUE, 1832; stld Hull Twp, Ottawa Co. Farmer. m Catherine Cook, qv, ch: 1. Euphemia, qv; 2. Flora, qv; 3. Charles; 4. James, qv; 5. Malcolm, qv; 6. Catherine; 7. Alexander; 8. Mary Cook; 9. John. **DC 23 Apr 1967**.

8498 McMASTER, Charles, 7 Mar 1827–13 Dec 1874. From Upper Feorline, Kilmory, Is Arran, BUT. s/o Archibald M, qv, and Catherine Cook, qv. To QUE, 1832; stld Hull Twp, Ottawa Co, later Minto Twp, Wellington Co, ONT. Farmer, unm. **DC 23 Apr 1967**.

8499 McMASTER, Christena, ca 1820–4 Dec 1894. From Is Mull, ARL. d/o John M. and Anna Weir. To ONT, 1848; stld Kincardine Twp, Bruce Co. Wife of John McLean, qv. **DC 7 Nov 1980**.

8500 MACMASTER, Donald, b ca 1764. From Lochaber, INV. Prob rel to John M, qv. To Inverness Co, NS, 1802; stld Queensville. ch: 1. Angus, qv; 2. John, qv; 3. Donald, jr, qv; 4. Hugh, qv. **CBC 1818; WLC**.

8501 MACMASTER, Donald, jr, b ca 1792. From Lochaber, INV. s/o Donald M, qv. To Inverness Co, NS, 1816; stld Western Shore. m Mary MacDonald, from Antigonish Co, ch: 1. Hugh; 2. Duncan; 3. Alexander; 4. Donald; 5. Samuel; 6. Anne; 7. Jessie. **CBC 1818; WLC**.

8502 McMASTER, Donald, b ca 1744. To Western Shore, Inverness Co, NS, 1808. Farmer, m and ch. **CBC 1818**.

8503 McMASTER, Donald, b ca 1789. Poss s/o Donald M, qv. To Western Shore, Inverness Co, NS, 1802. Farmer, m and ch. **CBC 1818**.

8504   McMASTER, Donald, 1811–21 Nov 1846. From INV. Rel to Alexander M, qv. To Dundee Village, Charlottenburgh Twp, Glengarry Co, ONT, 1819; moved to Ekfrid Twp, Middlesex Co, <1850. Farmer. m Mary Cameron, qv, ch: 1. Helen, 1842–1913; 2. Ann, 1844–1935; 3. Sir Donald, 1846–1922, QC, MLA. **BNA 804; DC 29 Oct 1979**.

8505   McMASTER, Duncan, b ca 1793. To Western Shore, Inverness Co, NS, 1802. Farmer.   **CBC 1818**.

8506   McMASTER, Euphemia, b 12 Feb 1824. From Upper Feorline, Kilmory, Is Arran, BUT. d/o Archibald M, qv, and Catherine Cook, qv. To QUE, 1832; stld Hull Twp, Ottawa Co, prob later Wellington Co, ONT. m John McLarty, qv.   **DC 23 Apr 1967**.

8507   McMASTER, Flora, b 3 Jul 1825. From Feorline, Kilmory, Is Arran, BUT. d/o Archibald M, qv, and Catherine Cook, qv. To QUE, 1832; stld Hull Twp, Ottawa Co; moved later to Wellington Co, ONT, and next to Drayton, ND, USA. m Peter Stewart, who emig to NY, 1833.   **DC 23 Apr 1967**.

8508   MACMASTER, Hugh, b ca 1788. From Lochaber, INV. s/o Donald M, qv. To Inverness Co, NS, 1816; stld Western Shore. m Isabel Cameron, qv, ch: 1. Donald, merchant, Princeville; 2. John; 3. Angus; 4. Duncan; 5. Catherine; 6. Mary; 7. Anne.   **CBC 1818; WLC**.

8509   McMASTER, James, 13 Jan 1829–13 Mar 1875. From Feorline, Kilmory, Is Arran, BUT. s/o Archibald M, qv, and Catherine Cook, qv. To QUE, 1832; stld Hull Twp, Ottawa Co, later Minto Twp, Wellington Co, ONT. Farmer. m Christine McLarty, qv, ch: 1. Archibald; 2. Ellen; 3. Mary; 4. Christina; 5. Catherine; 6. Flora; 7. Euphemia; 8. Janet; 9. Isabelle; 10. Dugald Donald. **DC 23 Apr 1967**.

8510   McMASTER, John, b ca 1776. Prob rel to Donald M, qv. To Western Shore, Inverness Co, NS, 1802. Farmer, m and ch.   **CBC 1818**.

8511   MACMASTER, John, b ca 1790. From Lochaber, INV. s/o Donald M, qv. To Inverness Co, NS, 1816; stld Western Shore. m Miss Macdonald, Creignish, and had, poss with other ch: 1. Hugh; 2. John; 3. Angus; 4. Alexander; 5. Donald.   **CBC 1818; WLC**.

8512   McMASTER, John, ca 1789–26 Sep 1847. From INV. To Dundee Village, Charlottenburgh Twp, Glengarry Co, ONT, ca 1819; moved to Ekfrid Twp, Middlesex Co, 1834. m Catherine MacDonald, qv, ch: 1. Alexander, 1817–1910; 2. Janet, b 1822; 3. Mary, 1826–1907; 4. Donald, b 1827; 5. Catherine, b 1828; 6. John, 1829–82; 7. Agnes, 1832–1901; 8. Janet, b 1834; 9. Christy, 1837–1912; 10. Margaret, b 1839; 11. Angus, 1839–1912.   **PCM 30; DC 14 Aug and 29 Oct 1979**.

8513   McMASTER, Rev John, 17 Feb 1787–9 Mar 1874. From Upper Feorline, Kilmory, Is Arran, BUT. To QUE <1840; stld Hull, Ottawa Twp. Anglican clergyman. m Mrs Isobella Moffat.   **DC 23 Apr 1967**.

8514   McMASTER, Malcolm, b ca 1831. From Feorline, Kilmory, Is Arran, BUT. s/o Archibald M, qv, and Catherine Cook, qv. To QUE, 1832; stld Hull Twp, Ottawa Co. Moved later to Lot 33, Con 2, Minto Twp, Wellington Co, ONT. Farmer. m Margaret Shaw, from IRL, ch: 1. Archibald; 2. Mary; 3. James; 4. John; 5. Thomas; 6. Catherine; 7. Flora; 8. Annie; 9. Angus. **DC 23 Apr 1967**.

8515   McMASTER, Mary. From Glenpean, INV. To QUE, ex Fort William, arr Sep 1802; stld E ONT. **MCM 1/4 25**.

8516   McMASTER, Mary. From Oban, ARL. To Montreal, QUE, ex Fort William, arr Sep 1802; stld E ONT.   **MCM 1/4 26**.

8517   McMEEKIN, John. From AYR. To PEI <1836; stld Cape Traverse, Prince Co. Wife Janet Milliken, qv, with him. ch: 1. Margaret; 2. Isabel; 3. John; 4. James; 5. Thomas; 6. Donald, b 14 Oct 1836.   **DC 30 Jun 1976**.

8518   McMICHAEL, Abraham, ca 1840–17 Nov 1881. From Kirkconnel, DFS. s/o Robert M, qv, and Grizel Nivison, qv. To ONT, 1842; stld McKillop Twp, Huron Co. Physician. m Mary Dow, Tuckersmith Twp.   **DC 26 May 1979**.

8519   McMICHAEL, Gilbert, ca 1817–30 Jun 1899. From Kirkconnel, DFS. Prob rel to Robert M, qv. To ONT, 1843; stld Hullett Twp, Huron Co. Farmer. m Jane McMillan, qv, ch: 1. Jane, 1841-71; 2. Elizabeth, 1843–1900; 3. Jane, 1844-80; 4. William, 1850–1924; 5. Margaret, b 1852; 6. Gilbert, b 1855; 7. Marion, b 1857; 8. Mary, b 1861.   **DC 26 May 1979**.

8520   McMICHAEL, James, 9 Mar 1823–13 Jan 1913. From Kirkconnel, DFS. s/o Robert M, qv, and Grizel Nivison, qv. To ONT, 1842; stld McKillop Twp, Huron Co. m Margaret Laidlaw, qv.   **DC 26 May 1979**.

8521   McMICHAEL, Janet, 1831-67. From Kirkconnel, DFS. d/o Robert M, qv, and Grizel Nivison, qv. To ONT, 1842; stld McKillop Twp, Huron Co. m John McMillan, qv.   **DC 26 May 1979**.

8522   McMICHAEL, Robert, 15 Nov 1793–3 Oct 1871. From Kirkconnel par, DFS. s/o Thomas M. and Margaret Hyslop. To ONT, 1842; stld McKillop Twp, Huron Co. Farmer. m Grizel Nivison, qv, ch: 1. Thomas, qv; 2. James, qv; 3. Alison, remained in SCT; 4. Janet, qv; 5. Robert, jr, qv; 6. William; 7. Alexander; 8. Abraham, qv.   **DC 26 May 1979**.

8523   McMICHAEL, Robert, jr, 1834–17 Feb 1895. From Kirkconnel, DFS. s/o Robert M, qv, and Grizel Nivison, qv. To ONT, 1842; stld McKillop Twp, Huron Co. m Jane Nivison.   **DC 26 May 1979**.

8524   McMICHAEL, Thomas, ca 1821–11 Apr 1875. From Kirkconnel, DFS. s/o Robert M, qv, and Grizel Nivison, qv. To ONT, 1840; stld Huron Co, ONT. Clerk in Sheriffs Office, Goderich, and farmer. m Elizabeth McMillan, qv, ch: 1. Elizabeth, b 1843; 2. Margaret, b 1844; 3. Robert, b 1848; 4. Grace, b 1850; 5. Jane, 1852–1929; 6. Mary, b 1855; 7. Marion, b 1857; 8. Thomas, 1859–1936; 9. Janet, 1861–1937; 10. James G, 1863–1936.   **DC 26 May 1979**.

8525   McMILLAN, Alexander. From INV. To PEI on the *Lucy*, ex Loch nan Uamh, Arisaig, 12 Jul 1790. Family with him.   **PLL**.

8526   McMILLAN, Alexander, ca 1760–ca 1840. From Glenpeanmore, nr Loch Arkaig, INV. s/o Ewen M, tacksman, and — Cameron. To QUE, ca 1790; stld Cornwall Twp, Glengarry Co, ONT. Farmer, and Col of Militia, War of 1812. m (i) —, ch: 1. Alexander Allan, shoemaker; (ii) Marcella, d/o Angus Macdonell, Greenfield, further ch: 2. Ann, b 1808; 3. Aneas, b 1813, Indian agent, St Regis.   **MCM 1/4 12**.

8527   **McMILLAN, Alexander**. From Callich, Loch Arkaig, INV. To QUE, ex Fort William, arr Sep 1802. Wife and child with him. Petitioned for 200 acres in Finch Twp, Stormont Co, ONT, 18 Feb 1804.   **MCM 1/4 25; 1/5 25**.

8528   **McMILLAN, Alexander**. From INV. To Montreal, QUE, ex Fort William, arr Sep 1802. Formerly soldier, Lochaber Regt. Petitioned for 200 acres in Finch Twp, Stormont Co, ONT, 18 Feb 1804.   **MCM 1/4 26**.

8529   **MACMILLAN, Alexander 'Mor'**. From Lochaber, INV. To Inverness Co, NS, <1820; stld Rear Little Judique. m Anne MacDonald, qv, ch: 1. Hugh, qv; 2. Duncan, qv; 3-4. Archibald and William, drowned at sea; 5. Catherine, qv; 6. Isabel, qv.   **MP 748**.

8530   **McMILLAN, Alexander**, b ca 1780. From Bornish, Is South Uist, INV. To West Williams Twp, Middlesex Co, ONT, ca 1849. m Margaret McIntyre, qv, ch: 1. Donald, b 1814; 2. Alexander, qv; 3. Neil, b 1822; 4. Mary, b 1820; 5. Flora, b 1824; 6. Michael, b 1827.   **PCM 47; WLC**.

8531   **McMILLAN, Alexander, jr**, b 1816. From Bornish, Is South Uist, INV. s/o Alexander M, qv, and Margaret McIntyre, qv. To West Williams Twp, Middlesex Co, ONT, ca 1849. m Margaret McLennan, qv, ch: 1. Catherine, b 1848; 2. Christy, b 1849.   **WLC**.

8532   **McMILLAN, Allan**, 1752–1823. From Glenpeanmore, nr Loch Arkaig, INV. s/o Ewen M, tacksman, and — Cameron. To Montreal, QUE, ex Fort William, arr Sep 1802; stld Lachine, but went afterwards to Finch Twp, Stormont Co, ONT. Farmer, and emigrant leader with cous Archibald M. of Murlaggan, qv. m Margaret Cameron, qv, ch: 1. Margaret, b 1775; 2. Ewen, b 1777; 3. John, b 1778; 4. Alexander, b 1780; 5. James, qv; 6. Donald, b 1784; 7. Archibald, b 1787; 8. Helen, b 1789; 9. Janet, b 1792.   **SDG 84; MCM 1/4 12, 26**.

8533   **MACMILLAN, Allan**. From Lochaber, INV. To Antigonish Co, NS, ca 1817; moved to Rear Little Judique, Inverness Co, 1820. Dancing master. m Catherine Rankine, qv, ch: 1. John; 2. Donald; 3. Anne; 4. Sara.   **MP 751; MCM 1/5 27**.

8534   **McMILLAN, Angus**. From Callich, Loch Arkaig, INV. To QUE, ex Fort William, arr Sep 1802. Petitioned for 200 acres in Finch Twp, Stormont Co, ONT, 18 Feb 1804. Wife emig with him, and 2 ch.   **MCM 1/4 25; 1/5 25**.

8535   **McMILLAN, Angus**. Prob from Callich, Loch Arkaig, INV. To Montreal, QUE, prob arr 1802. Petitioned for land on Ottawa River, ONT, 6 Aug 1804.   **DC 15 Mar 1980**.

8536   **MACMILLAN, Angus**. From Is Eigg, INV. s/o Donald M, qv. To Judique, Inverness Co, NS, prob <1820; moved to Guysborough Co, later to Antigonish Co. m Sarah, d/o John MacDonald, ch: 1. Hugh; 2. Alexander; 3. Margaret; 4. Sarah; 5. Jessie; 6. Ronald; 7. John; 8. Donald; 9. Allan; 10. William; 11. Mary; 12. Mary Ann.   **HCA 322**.

8537   **McMILLAN, Angus**. From Is Mull, ARL. To Port Hastings, Inverness Co, NS, on the *Commerce*, ex Tobermory, 1822.   **MCM 1/5 27**.

8538   **McMILLAN, Angus**, b 1790. From Is Rum, ARL.

To Gut of Canso, Cape Breton, NS, on the *Saint Lawrence*, ex Tobermory, 11 Jul 1828.   **SLL**.

8539   **McMILLAN, Angus**. From ARL. To West Williams Twp, Middlesex Co, ONT, 1849.   **PCM 47**.

8540   **McMILLAN, Angus**, b 1815. From Balivanich, Is Benbecula, INV. s/o John and Marion M. To QUE on the *Admiral*, ex Lochboisdale; stld Glenelg, Grey Co, ONT, 1849. m Flora McMillan, qv, ch: 1. John A, b ca 1843; 2. Donald or Daniel, b 1847; 3. Norman, b 1851; 4. Sarah, b 1852; 5. Michael, b 1854; 6. Alexander, b 1856; 7. Neil, b 1858.   **WLC; DC 23 Oct 1979**.

8541   **McMILLAN, Angus**. From Lochaber, INV. To ONT, <1850; stld Finch Twp, Stormont Co. Son Hugh, 1859–1917, reeve.   **SDG 483**.

8542   **McMILLAN, Ann**, b 1800. From Is Rum, ARL. Poss rel to Angus M, qv. To Gut of Canso, Cape Breton, NS, on the *Saint Lawrence*, ex Tobermory, 11 Jul 1828.   **SLL**.

8543   **McMILLAN, Ann**, b 1805. From Is Rum, ARL. Poss d/o John M, qv. To Gut of Canso, Cape Breton, NS, on the *Saint Lawrence*, ex Tobermory, 11 Jul 1828.   **SLL**.

8544   **McMILLAN, Ann**. From North Sannox, Is Arran, BUT. To Inverness, Megantic Co, QUE, 1831. Wife of John Kelso, qv.   **AMC 39; MAC 38**.

8545   **McMILLAN, Ann**, b 1802. From Is Arran, BUT. d/o Neil M, qv, and Catherine Kerr, qv. To QUE on the *Caledonia*, ex Greenock, 25 Apr 1829; stld Inverness Twp, Megantic Co. Wife of Donald 'Valdie' McKillop, qv.   **AMC 11; MAC 29**.

8546   **McMILLAN, Ann**, d 1846. From Kilmarnock, AYR. Prob d/o Mrs Margaret M, qv. To Pictou, NS. Drowned in wreck of the *Sutlej*, of Pictou, bound for Fall River.   **DGH 30 Jul 1846**.

8547   **MACMILLAN, Anne**. From Is Barra, INV. To South East Mabou, Inverness Co, NS, 1818. Wife of Hector 'Mor' MacNeil, qv.   **MP 770**.

8548   **McMILLAN, Annie**. From Paisley, RFW. Prob rel to Donald M, qv. To Montreal, QUE, arr Sep 1802; stld E ONT.   **MCM 1/4 26**.

8549   **McMILLAN, Archibald**, 1762–1832. From Murlaggan, Kilmallie par, INV. s/o Alexander M, tacksman, and Margaret Cameron. To Montreal, QUE, on the *Friends*, 3 Jun 1802. Gr 744 acres in Templeton Twp, 26 Mar 1807, and 420 acres in Grenville Twp, Argenteuil Co, 28 Jan 1808. Res also in Montreal. Emigrant leader, with cous Allan M, qv; merchant and postmaster. m Isabella Gray, qv, ch: 1. Alexander, b 1795; 2. Archibald, b 1796; 3. Mary, b 1797; 4. Margaret, b 1799; 5. Ewen, alive 1815; 6. John, b 1805; 7. William, b 1808; 8. Thomasina, b 1814; 9. Duncan, 1812–1901.   **MCN 1/4 18, 26**.

8550   **McMILLAN, Archibald**. From Corriebrough, Moy and Dalarossie par, INV. To QUE, ex Fort William, arr Sep 1802; stld E ONT.   **MCM 1/4 25**.

8551   **McMILLAN, Archibald**. From INV. To Montreal, QUE, ex Fort William, arr Sep 1802; stld E ONT.   **MCM 1/4 24**.

8552   **McMILLAN, Archibald**, 1800-33. From ARL. To Eldon Twp, Victoria Co, ONT, 1818. m Annie Campbell, qv. Dau Flora.   **EC 58**.

8553 McMILLAN, Archibald, ca 1816–ca 1900. From Bornish, Is South Uist, INV. s/o Lachlan M. and Julia McDonald. To West Williams Twp, Middlesex Co, ONT, ca 1849. Blacksmith. m Catherine Morrison, qv, ch: 1. Lachland, b 1841; 2. Kirsty, b 1842; 3. Cecily, b 1843; 4. Margaret, b 1845; 5. Kirsty, b 1846. **PCM 48; WLC**.

8554 MACMILLAN, Archibald, 1830-89. From Lagavulin, Is Islay, ARL. bro/o Neil M, qv. To Eldon Twp, Victoria Co, ONT, 1852. Mason. m Margaret Calder, qv, ch: 1. James; 2. Colin; 3. William; 4. Effie; 5. John, 1847-89. **EC 160**.

8555 McMILLAN, Archie, b 1801. From Is Rum, ARL. To Gut of Canso, Cape Breton, NS, on the *Saint Lawrence*, ex Tobermory, 11 Jul 1828. Wife Jessie, aged 28, with him, and ch: 1. Donald, aged 2; 2. Neil, inf. **SLL**.

8556 McMILLAN, Betty, b 1788. To Charlottetown, PEI, on the *Spencer*, ex Oban, arr 22 Sep 1806. **PLSN**.

8557 McMILLAN, Catherine. From INV. To Montreal, QUE, ex Fort William, arr Sep 1802; stld E ONT. **MCM 1/4 24**.

8558 McMILLAN, Catherine. sis/o Donald M, 'The Turner', qv. To Port Hastings, Inverness Co, NS, on the *Commerce*, ex Tobermory, 1822. **MCM 1/5 27**.

8559 MACMILLAN, Catherine. From Lochaber, INV. d/o Alexander 'Mor' M, qv, and Anne MacDonald, qv. To Rear Little Judique, Inverness Co, NS, <1820. m Angus MacFachen, ch. **MP 751**.

8560 McMILLAN, Catherine, b 1776. From Kilbride Bennan, Is Arran, BUT. To Restigouche Co, NB, <1834'. Wife of John Ferguson, qv. **MAC 13**.

8561 McMILLAN, Catherine, b 1802. From Is Rum, ARL. Poss d/o John M, qv. To Gut of Canso, Cape Breton, NS, on the *Saint Lawrence*, ex Tobermory, 11 Jul 1828. **SLL**.

8562 McMILLAN, Catherine, b 1810. From Shennochie, Kilmory par, Is Arran, BUT. d/o Donald M, qv, and Barbara Shaw, qv. To Restigouche Co, NB, 1830. m James Murdoch, qv. **MAC 22; DC 7 Feb 1981**.

8563 McMILLAN, Catherine, b 1804. From Auchenchairn, Kilbride par, Is Arran, BUT. To Archibald Settlement, Restigouche Co, NB, 1832. m 18 Jan 1831, Robert Cook, qv. **MAC 12**.

8564 MACMILLAN, Catherine. From Port Ellen, Is Islay, ARL. To Eldon Twp, Victoria Co, ONT, <1845. m Michael Moran, ch: 1. Ellen; 2. Roger; 3. Hannah; 4. Annie; 5. Duncan; 6. John. **EC 155**.

8565 MACMILLAN, Catherine, b 1811. From Aird, Is Benbecula, INV. To Pictou, NS, on the *Lulan*, ex Glasgow, 17 Aug 1848. Wife of Donald MacDonald, qv. **DC 12 Jul 1979**.

8566 McMILLAN, Catherine. From Is South Uist, INV. To West Williams Twp, Middlesex Co, ONT, ca 1849. Wife of Lachlan McDonald, qv. **WLC**.

8567 McMILLAN, Christie. From Glen Albyn, INV. d/o John M, qv. To Antigonish Co, NS, 1803, prob on the *Nora*; stld Glen Alpine. m John Cameron. **CP 30**.

8568 McMILLAN, Christina, b 1768. From Is Rum,

8569 MACMILLAN, Donald. Prob from Lochaber. To ONT, via NY, 1777. By wife Catherine had dau Susannah, gr 200 acres in Dundas Co, 1801, and a dau Catherine. **MCM 1/5 21**.

8570 McMILLAN, Donald. From INV. To Pictou Co, NS, 1801. Went later to Antigonish Co, and to Little Judique, Inverness Co. **MCM 1/5 27**.

8571 McMILLAN, Donald. From Loch Arkaig, INV. To Pictou, NS, on the *Dove*, ex Fort William, Jun 1801. Wife Marian with him, and ch: 1. Angus, labourer; 2. John. **PLD**.

8572 McMILLAN, Donald. From Callop, Glenfinnan, INV. To Montreal, QUE, ex Fort William, arr Sep 1802. Petitioned for 200 acres in Finch Twp, Stormont Co, ONT, 18 Feb 1804. Farmer. **MCM 1/4 26; 1/5 25**.

8573 McMILLAN, Donald. From Tomdoun, INV. To QUE, ex Fort William, arr Sep 1802; stld E ONT. Wife and 4 ch with him. **MCM 1/4 25**.

8574 McMILLAN, Donald. From Achintore, nr Fort William, INV. To QUE, ex Fort William, arr Sep 1802. Petitioned for 200 acres in Finch Twp, Stormont Co, ONT, 18 Feb 1804. Wife with him. **MCM 1/4 25**.

8575 McMILLAN, Donald. From Paisley, RFW. Prob rel to Annie M, qv. To Montreal, QUE, arr Sep 1802; stld E ONT. Wife and 2 ch with him. **MCM 1/4 26**.

8576 McMILLAN, Donald. From Aberchalder, INV. To Montreal, QUE, ex Fort William, arr Sep 1802; stld E ONT. wife with him, and ch: 1. John; 2. Margaret. **MCM 1/4 26**.

8577 McMILLAN, Donald. From Rellen, Loch Arkaig, INV. To Montreal, QUE, ex Fort William, arr Sep 1802; stld Finch Twp, Stormont Co, ONT. Farmer. **MCM 1/4 26**.

8578 McMILLAN, Donald, b ca 1800. To Western Shore, Inverness Co, NS, 1805. Farmer. **CBC 1818**.

8579 McMILLAN, Donald. Prob from Is Mull, ARL. To Hudson Bay and Red River, <1813. Sailor. **RRS 16**.

8580 MACMILLAN, Donald. From Is Eigg, INV. s/o John M. To Judique, Inverness Co, NS, prob <1820; moved later to Mulgrave, Guysborough Co, and afterwards to Maple Ridge. ch: 1. Angus, qv; 2. John 'Saor'; 3. John; 4. Hugh; 5. Flora; 6. Margaret; 7. Ann. **HCA 322**.

8581 McMILLAN, Donald. From Is Mull, ARL. To Port Hastings, Inverness Co, NS, on the *Commerce*, ex Tobermory, 1822. **MCM 1/5 27**.

8582 McMILLAN, Donald 'The Turner'. From Is Mull, ARL. bro/o Catherine M, qv. To Port Hastings, Inverness Co, NS, on the *Commerce*, ex Tobermory, 1822. **MCM 1/5 27**.

8583 McMILLAN, Donald, b 1771. From Is Rum, ARL. Prob rel to John M, qv. To Gut of Canso, Cape Breton, NS, on the *Saint Lawrence*, ex Tobermory, 11 Jul 1828. **SLL**.

8584 McMILLAN, Donald, b 1780. From Is Rum, ARL. To Gut of Canso, Cape Breton, NS, on the *Saint Lawrence*, ex Tobermory, 11 Jul 1828. **SLL**.

ARL. To Gut of Canso, Cape Breton, NS, on the *Saint Lawrence*, ex Tobermory, 11 Jul 1828. **SLL**.

8585 McMILLAN, Donald, 3 Aug 1779–13 Aug 1863. From Shannochie, Kilmory par, Is Arran, BUT. s/o John M. and Elspeth Cook. To Blackland, Restigouche Co, NB, 1830. Farmer. m Barbara Shaw, qv, ch: 1. Elizabeth, qv; 2. Isabella, qv; 3. Catherine, qv; 4. John, qv; 5. James, qv; 6. Mary, qv; 7. Donald, jr, qv. **MAC 22; SG xxvii/3 127**.

8586 McMILLAN, Donald, jr, 1822–1910. From Shannochie, Kilmory par, Is Arran, BUT. s/o Donald M, qv, and Barbara Shaw, qv. To Blackland, Restigouche Co, NB, 1830. Farmer. m Margaret McCormack, ch: 1. Barbara; 2. Donald; 3. Catherine; 4. John; 5. James. **MAC 22; DC 7 Feb 1981**.

8587 McMILLAN, Dougald. From Dalelea, Moidart, INV. To QUE on the *British Queen*, ex Arisaig, 16 Aug 1790; stld Montreal. Tenant farmer. Wife and ch with him. **QCC 103**.

8588 McMILLAN, Dugald. From Oban, ARL. To Montreal, QUE, ex Fort William, arr Sep 1802. Petitioned for 200 acres in Finch Twp, Stormont Co, ONT, 18 Feb 1804. Farmer. **MCM 1/4 26**.

8589 McMILLAN, Dugald. From Inchlaggan, INV. To Montreal, QUE, ex Fort William, arr Sep 1802; stld E ONT. Wife and child with him. **MCM 1/4 26**.

8590 McMILLAN, Duncan. From Arienskill, ni, INV. To PEI on the *Lucy*, ex Loch nan Uamh, Arisaig, 12 Jul 1790. Tenant farmer. Wife and inf with him. **PLL**.

8591 McMILLAN, Duncan 'Ban Og', 1766–1854. From INV. To Lochiel Twp, Glengarry Co, ONT, 1794. Son Donald. **DC 21 Mar 1981**.

8592 McMILLAN, Duncan. From Shenieval, Glendessary, INV. To Montreal, QUE, ex Fort William, arr Sep 1802; stld prob Finch Twp, Stormont Co, ONT. Wife with him, and ch: 1. Catherine; 2. Effie. **MCM 1/4 24; 1/5 25**.

8593 McMILLAN, Duncan, b ca 1785. From Glasgow. To QUE, ex Greenock, Jul 1815; stld ONT, poss Lanark Co. Farmer and weaver. **SEC 1**.

8594 McMILLAN, Duncan. From Glen Urquhart, INV. To Pictou, NS, prob 1820; stld Blue Mountain, Pictou Co. **MCM 1/5 27**.

8595 McMILLAN, Duncan. From Is Mull, ARL. To Port Hastings, Inverness Co, NS, on the *Commerce*, ex Tobermory, 1822. **MCM 1/5 27**.

8596 McMILLAN, Duncan. Poss from PER. To Lochiel Twp, Glengarry Co, ONT, <1835. m Mary 'Oig' Macdonell. Son Donald, b 1835, physician and senator. **SDG 455**.

8597 McMILLAN, Rev Duncan, d 25 Jan 1889. From Is Islay, ARL. To Caledon Twp, Peel Co, ONT, 1831. Moved to East Williams Twp, Middlesex Co, 1839. Presb min and schoolmaster. **PCM 12, 46; FES vii 644**.

8598 McMILLAN, Duncan. Prob from Is Muck, INV. To NS, ca 1820. m Julia Campbell, qv. **DC 1 Jul 1968**.

8599 MACMILLAN, Duncan. From Lochaber, INV. s/o Alexander 'Mor' M. and Anne MacDonald, qv. To Inverness Co, NS, <1820; stld Rear Little Judique. m Mary, d/o Alexander MacNeil, ch: 1. William; 2. Hugh; 3. Angus; 4. Alexander; 5. Archibald; 6. Neil; 7. Anne; 8. Alexina; 9. Annabella; 10. Sara. m (ii) Catherine, d/o Angus Beaton, no ch. **MP 749**.

8600 McMILLAN, Duncan. From South Sannox, Is Arran, BUT. s/o Neil M, qv, and Catherine Kerr, qv. To QUE on the *Caledonia*, ex Greenock, 25 Apr 1829; stld Inverness, Megantic Co. Prob the man who m Katherine Crawford, qv, no ch. **AMC 82; MAC 32**.

8601 MACMILLAN, Duncan 'Red'. From Port Ellen, Is Islay, ARL. bro/o John M, qv, and Neil M, qv. To Eldon Twp, Victoria Co, ONT, prob <1845. m Eliza Birmingham, ch: 1. John; 2. Archie; 3. Michael; 4. William; 5. Hannah; 6. Mary. **EC 155**.

8602 McMILLAN, Elizabeth, b 1797. From Kings Corse, Kilbride, Is Arran, BUT. To Dalhousie, NB, 1829; stld Nash Creek, Restigouche Co. Wife of James Black, qv. **MAC 9**.

8603 McMILLAN, Elizabeth, 10 Jan 1807–9 Mar 1891. From Kilmory par, Is Arran, BUT. d/o Donald M, qv, and Barbara Shaw, qv. To Blackland, Restigouche Co, NB, 1830. m Robert 'Valdie' McMillan, qv. **MAC 22; DC 7 Feb 1981**.

8604 McMILLAN, Elizabeth, b 28 Mar 1821. From Kirkconnel, DFS. d/o Robert M, qv, and Elizabeth Laidlaw, qv. To ONT, 1842; stld McKillop Twp, Huron Co. m Thomas McMichael, qv. **DC 26 May 1979**.

8605 McMILLAN, Elizabeth, d 1846. From Kilmarnock, AYR. Prob d/o Mrs Margaret M, qv. To Pictou, NS. Drowned in wreck of the *Sutlej*, of Pictou, bound for Fall River. **DGH 30 Jul 1846**.

8606 McMILLAN, Elizabeth, b 1797. From Kilmory par, Is Arran, BUT. To Dalhousie, NB, 1829; stld Nash Creek, Restigouche Co. Wife of James Black, qv. **MAC 9**.

8607 McMILLAN, Elizabeth, 1800-97. From Mid Kiscadale, Kilbride par, Is Arran, BUT. To Black Point, Restigouche Co, NB, 1829. Wife of Alexander Hamilton, qv. **MAC 16**.

8608 MACMILLAN, Emily. From ABD. To Mabou, Inverness Co, NS, poss <1820. Wife of Neil MacDonald, qv, from Is Barra. **MP 414**.

8609 McMILLAN, Ewen. Poss from Tomatin, INV. To QUE, ex Fort William, arr Sep 1802. Petitioned for land on the Ottawa River, ONT, 6 Aug 1804. Wife and 4 ch with him. **DC 6 Aug 1980**.

8610 McMILLAN, Ewen. From Craigellachie, BAN. To QUE, ex Fort William, arr Sep 1802; stld E ONT. Wife and child with him. **MCM 1/4 25**.

8611 McMILLAN, Ewen. From Quarter, ni, INV. To QUE, ex Fort William, arr Sep 1802; stld poss Lochaber Twp, Ottawa Co, QUE. **MCM 1/4 25**.

8612 McMILLAN, Ewen. From Cunich, Loch Arkaig, INV. To QUE, ex Fort William, arr Sep 1802. Wife and 3 ch with him. Petitioned for 200 acres in Finch Twp, Stormont Co, ONT, 18 Feb 1804. **MCM 1/4 25; 1/5 25**.

8613 McMILLAN, Ewen. From Lubriach, ni, INV. To QUE, ex Fort William, arr Sep 1802; stld poss Lochaber Twp, Ottawa Co. Wife with him, and ch: 1. Mary; 2. Peggy; 3. Donald; 4. Ewen. **MCM 1/4 25; 1/5 25**.

8614 McMILLAN, Ewen. From Ardgour, ARL. To QUE on the *British Queen*, ex Arisaig, 16 Aug 1790; stld nr Montreal. Tenant farmer. Wife and ch with him. **QCC 103**.

8615 McMILLAN, Ewen. From Is Mull, ARL. To Charlottetown, PEI, ca 1807. Mother with him. **DC 1 Oct 1962**.

8616 McMILLAN, Finlay. From Glen Urquhart, INV. To Pictou Co, NS, 1784; stld East River.   **MCM 1/5 27**.

8617 McMILLAN, Flora, b 1755. To Charlottetown, PEI, on the *Spencer*, ex Oban, arr 22 Sep 1806. Poss wife of Dougald McNeil, qv.   **PLSN**.

8618 McMILLAN, Flora, b 1816. From Balivanich, Is Benbecula, INV. d/o Donald and Kirsty M. To QUE, ex Lochboisdale, on the *Admiral*, 1851; stld Hamilton, ONT. m Angus McMillan, qv.   **DC 23 Oct 1979**.

8619 McMILLAN, Flora. From Balivanich, Is Benbecula, INV. To East Williams Twp, Middlesex Co, ONT, 1848. Wife of Peter McCormack, qv.   **WLC**.

8620 MACMILLAN, Flora, b 1786. From Torlum, Is Benbecula, INV. To Pictou, NS, on the *Lulan*, ex Glasgow, 17 Aug 1848. Wife of Roderick MacLellan, qv.   **DC 12 Jul 1979**.

8621 McMILLAN, Flora, b 1811. From Is Rum, ARL. Poss rel to Donald M, qv. To Gut of Canso, Cape Breton, NS, on the *Saint Lawrence*, ex Tobermory, 11 Jul 1828.   **SLL**.

8622 McMILLAN, Grace. Prob from ARL. d/o Donald M. To Aldborough Twp, Elgin Co, ONT, <1840. m Duncan Paterson, qv.   **PDA 64**.

8623 McMILLAN, Hugh. From Glen Albyn, INV s/o John M, qv. To Antigonish, NS, prob on the *Nora*, 1803; stld Glen Alpine. m Miss Cameron, Salt Springs. **CP 30**.

8624 MACMILLAN, Hugh. From Lochaber, INV. To Western Shore, Inverness Co, NS, <1818. Farmer, merchant and shipowner. m Christian Cummings, ch: 1. Donald; 2. John; 3. Angus; 4. Mary; 5. Alexander; 6. Jane.   **CBC 1818**.

8625 MACMILLAN, Hugh. From Lochaber, INV. s/o Alexander 'Mor' M, qv, and Anne MacDonald, qv. To Inverness Co, NS, <1820; stld Little Rear Judique. m Isabel, d/o Donald MacMillan, ch: 1. Archibald; 2. William; 3. Sara; 4. Marcella; 5. Jane.   **MP 748**.

8626 MACMILLAN, Hugh 'Ban'. Prob from Lochaber, INV. bro/o John M, qv. To Antigonish Co, NS, poss <1820; stld Livingston Cove. ch: 1. John; 2. Margaret; 3. Mary.   **HCA 323**.

8627 McMILLAN, Hugh, d 1846. From Kilmarnock, AYR. Rel to Mrs Margaret M, qv. To Pictou, NS. Drowned in the wreck of the *Sutlej*, of Pictou, bound for Fall River.   **DGH 30 Jul 1846**.

8628 MACMILLAN, Hugh. From Tarbolton, AYR. To Bruce Co, ONT, <1855. Farmer. By wife — Ross had s John.   **MCM 1/5 31**.

8629 McMILLAN, Isabel. From Loch Arkaig, INV. To Pictou, NS, on the *Dove*, ex Fort William, Jun 1801. Prob a widow, with ch: 1. Mary; 2. Martha; 3. Marian. **PLD**.

8630 McMILLAN, Isabel. From Lochaber, INV. d/o Alexander 'Mor' M, qv, and Anne MacDonald, qv. To Little Rear Judique, Inverness Co, NS, <1820. m Ronald, s/o Alexander Beaton, ch.   **MP 126, 751**.

8631 McMILLAN, Isabella. Prob from Loch Arkaig, INV. To QUE, prob 1802. Petitioned for land in Templeton Twp, Ottawa Co, QUE, 26 Mar 1807. Poss rel to Archibald M. of Murlaggan, qv.   **MCM 1/5 25**.

8632 McMILLAN, Isabella, 1809-88. From Shannochie, Kilmory par, Is Arran, BUT. d/o Donald M, qv, and Barbara Shaw, qv. To Blackland, Restigouche Co, NB, 1830. m Archibald McNair, qv.   **MAC 22; DC 7 Feb 1981**.

8633 McMILLAN, James. From Knoydart, INV. To Montreal, QUE, ex Fort William, arr Sep 1802. Petitioned for 200 acres in Finch Twp, Stormont Co, ONT, 18 Feb 1804.   **MCM 1/4 26; 1/5 25**.

8634 McMILLAN, James, 8 Aug 1782–26 Jan 1858. From Glenpeanmore, INV. s/o Allan M, qv, and Margaret Cameron, qv. To Montreal, QUE, ex Fort William, 3 Jun 1802. Joined NWCo as a clerk. Served at Fort des Prairies, and with David Thompson was one of the pioneers of the fur trade on the Columbia. After the merger with the HBCo, 1821, was in charge of an experimental farm on the Red River. m (i) an Indian woman, ch: 1. William. m (ii) 1829, Ellen McKinley, qv, further ch: 2. Mrs Dease; 3. Ewen Alexander; 4. James, res Esquemaux Bay; 5. Eleanor; 6. dau.   **MCM 1/4 14; MDB 481**.

8635 McMILLAN, James, 10 Jul 1817–3 Mar 1892. From Shannochie, Kilmory par, Is Arran, BUT. s/o Donald M, qv, and Barbara Shaw, qv. To Blackland, Restigouche Co, NB, 1830; went later to San Luis, Obispo Co, CA, USA. m Helen Cook, b 1847, ch: 1. Donald; 2. Helen; 3. Barbara; 4. Catherine; 5. John; 6. James; 7. Alexander; 8. Ebenezer; 9. Peter; 10. Arnold Cook.   **MAC 22; DC 7 Feb 1981**.

8636 McMILLAN, James, 1819–6 Apr 1904. From Auchincairn, Kilbride par, Is Arran, BUT. s/o John M. and Mary Nichol. To Restigouche Co, NB, prob <1840; stld Jacquet River. Farmer. m Mary Cook, qv, ch: 1. John, b 1849; 2. Robert, b 1850; 3. Finlay, b 1852; 4. Catherine, b 1853; 5. Mary, b 1855; 6. William, b 1856; 7. James, b 1858; 8. Donald, b 1860; 9. Isabella, b 1862; 10. Alexander, b 1863, d Portland, OR, USA.   **DMC 1 Oct 1979**.

8637 McMILLAN, James. To Whitby, York Co, ONT, <1840. m Eleanor Crawford, from IRL. Son Sir Daniel Hunter, 1846–1933, Lt Gov of MAN.   **DC 20 Jul 1982**.

8638 McMILLAN, Jane. From INV. To Montreal, QUE, ex Fort William, arr Sep 1802. Petitioned for 1,200 acres, 26 Mar 1807, and stld Lochaber Twp, Ottawa Co. Prob a widow.   **MCM 1/4 25**.

8639 McMILLAN, Jane, b ca 1817. From Kirkconnel, DFS. d/o Robert M, qv, and Elizabeth Laidlaw, qv. To ONT, ca 1843; stld McKillop Twp, Huron Co. m Gilbert McMichael, qv.   **DC 26 May 1979**.

8640 McMILLAN, Janet. From Is Arran, poss Glen Sannox, BUT. To QUE on the *Caledonia*, ex Greenock, 25 Apr 1829; stld Inverness, Megantic Co. Wife of Archibald McMillan, qv.   **AMC 11; MAC 29**.

8641 McMILLAN, Janet, d 1846. From Kilmarnock, AYR. Prob d/o Mrs Margaret M, qv. To Pictou, NS. Drowned in the wreck of the *Sutlej*, of Pictou, bound for Fall River.   **DGH 30 Jul 1846**.

8642 McMILLAN, Jean. From Loch Arkaig, INV. Prob d/o John M, farmer, qv. To Pictou, NS, on the *Dove*, ex Fort William, Jun 1801. Spinster. **PLD**.

8643 McMILLAN, John. Prob from Arisaig, INV. To PEI on the *Lucy*, ex Loch nan Uamh, Arisaig, 12 Jul 1790. Tenant farmer. Wife with him. **PLL**.

8644 McMILLAN, John. From Urquhart or Strathglass, INV. To Pictou, NS, on the *Sarah*, ex Fort William, Jun 1801; stld Irish Mountain, Springville. Blacksmith. m Catherine Campbell, qv, ch: 1. Elizabeth, d at sea; 2. William, d at sea; 3. William, b 1803; 4. Mary, b 1808; 5. Donald, went to ONT, later to CA, USA; 6. John, b 1812; 7. Alexander, d 1833; 8. Elizabeth, 1813-64, unm. **PLS; CP 86**.

8645 McMILLAN, John. From Urquhart, INV. To Pictou, NS, on the *Sarah*, ex Fort William, Jun 1801. Labourer. **PLS**.

8646 McMILLAN, John. From Loch Arkaig, INV. To Pictou, NS, on the *Dove*, ex Fort William, Jun 1801. Farmer. **PLD**.

8647 McMILLAN, John. From Loch Arkaig, INV. Prob s/o John M, farmer, qv. To Pictou, NS, on the *Dove*, ex Fort William, Jun 1801. Labourer. **PLD**.

8648 McMILLAN, John. From Loch Arkaig, INV. To Pictou, NS, on the *Dove*, ex Fort William, Jun 1801. Tenant farmer. ch with him: 1. Alexander, aged 12; 2. Donald. **PLD**.

8649 McMILLAN, John. From Corsuck, ni, INV. To QUE, ex Fort William, arr Sep 1802; stld poss Lochaber Twp, Ottawa Co, QUE. Wife with him, and s Ewen. **MCM 1/4 24**.

8650 McMILLAN, John. Prob from Is Muck, INV. To QUE, ex Fort William, arr Sep 1802; stld poss Lochaber Twp, Ottawa Co, QUE. Dau Catherine. **MCM 1/4 25**.

8651 McMILLAN, John. From Glengarry, INV. To QUE, ex Fort William, arr Sep 1802; stld poss Lochaber Twp, Ottawa Co, QUE. Wife with him, and family: 1. Duncan; 2. Dugald; 3. Alexander; 4. Bell. **MCM 1/4 25; 1/5 25**.

8652 McMILLAN, John. Poss from Ardersier, INV. To Pictou Co, NS, ca 1802; stld 'Kerrowgair'. **MCM 1/5 27**.

8653 McMILLAN, John. From Camusine, nr North Ballachulish, INV. To QUE, ex Fort William, arr Sep 1802; stld E ONT. He had 3 ch with him. **MCM 1/4 25**.

8654 McMILLAN, John. From Cunich, Loch Arkaig, INV. To QUE, ex Fort William, arr Sep 1802; stld poss Finch Twp, Stormont Co, ONT. Wife with him and ch: 1. Duncan; 2. Betty. **MCM 1/4 25; 1/5 25**.

8655 McMILLAN, John. From Shenieval, Glendessary, INV. To Montreal, QUE, ex Fort William, arr Sep 1802; stld poss Finch Twp, Stormont Co, ONT. Wife with him. **MCM 1/4 24; 1/5 25**.

8656 McMILLAN, John. From Glendessary, INV. To Montreal, QUE, ex Fort William, prob 1802. Petitioned for land on the Ottawa River, 6 Aug 1804. **DC 15 Mar 1980**.

8657 McMILLAN, John. From Glen Albyn, INV. s/o John M, qv. To Antigonish, NS, prob on the *Nora*, 1803; stld Glen Alpine. m Miss Kennedy. **CP 30**.

8658 McMILLAN, John. From Glen Albyn, INV. To Antigonish, NS, prob on the *Nora*, 1803; stld Glen Alpine. ch: 1. Malcolm, qv; 2. John, qv; 3. Duncan, qv; 4. Hugh, qv; 5. Peggy, qv; 6. Mary, qv; 7. Christy, qv; 8. Kate. **CP 30; SG iii/4 97**.

8659 McMILLAN, John, b ca 1751. To St Andrews dist, Cape Breton Co, NS, ca 1811. Farmer; m and ch incl Neil, b ca 1784. **CBC 1818**.

8660 MACMILLAN, John. From Lochaber, INV. To Mull River, Inverness Co, NS, <1820. Wife Margaret Rankin, qv, with him. ch: 1. John; 2. Duncan. **MP 831**.

8661 MACMILLAN, John. Prob from Lochaber, INV. bro/o Hugh 'Ban' M, qv. To Antigonish Co, NS, poss <1820. **HCA 324**.

8662 McMILLAN, John, b 1761. From Is Rum, ARL. Poss rel to Donald M, qv. To Gut of Canso, Cape Breton, NS, on the *Saint Lawrence*, ex Tobermory, 11 Jul 1828. **SLL**.

8663 McMILLAN, John, d 1840. From Inverness. To Pictou Co, NS, and bur Churchville. **DC 20 Jan 1981**.

8664 McMILLAN, Rev John, 1824–1900. From South Sannox, Is Arran, BUT. s/o Neil M, qv, and Catherine Kerr, qv. To QUE on the *Caledonia*, ex Greenock, 25 Apr 1829; stld Inverness, Megantic Co. Became Presb min at Mount Forest, Wellington Co, ONT. m Catherine Walker, ch: 1. Isabella, dy; 2. Malvina; 3. Rev John Walker, 1868–1932, Professor of Sociology, Victoria Coll, Toronto; 4. Rev Kerr Duncan, b 1871. **AMC 11; MAC 32**.

8665 McMILLAN, John, 23 Oct 1814–17 May 1895. From Shannochie, Kilmory par, Is Arran, BUT. s/o Donald M, qv, and Barbara Shaw, qv. To Blackland, Restigouche Co, NB, 1830; bur New Mills. Postmaster and JP. m Jean McNair, qv, ch: 1. Daniel; 2. Nathaniel; 3. Jean; 4. Barbara; 5. Margaret; 6. James, prob, dy; 7. James; 8. Ebenezer; 9. Mary; 10. John; 11. Isabella; 12. David. **MAC 22; DC 7 Feb 1981**.

8666 McMILLAN, John, called **'Iain mac Ruaridh'**. Poss from Is South Uist, INV. To Cape Breton, NS, <1840; stld prob River Denys, Inverness Co. **MCM 1/5 27**.

8667 McMILLAN, John. From Is South Uist, INV. To Orangedale, Inverness Co, NS, with his family, 1840. **MCM 1/5 27**.

8668 McMILLAN, John, 1824–1901. From Kirkconnel, DFS. s/o Walter M, qv, and Mary Laidlaw, qv. To McKillop Twp, Huron Co, ONT, 1843. Shoemaker and farmer; MP for Huron for 20 years. m (i) Janet McMichael, qv, ch: 1. Grizel, 1851-61; 2. Mary, 1853-73; 3. Agnes, 1855-75; 4. Walter, 1856-85; 5. Robert, 1856–1948; 6. John, 1860-77; 7. Thomas, 1862–1932, MP for Huron; 8. Grace, 1864–1925. m (ii) Ann Lang, qv. **DC 26 May 1979**.

8669 McMILLAN, John, b ca 1821. From Balivanich, Is Benbecula, INV. s/o Donald and Kirsty M. To QUE on the *Admiral*, ex Lochboisdale; stld Glenelg, Grey Co, ONT, 1849. m Mary Black, b 1833, ch: 1. Donald, b 1857; 2. Joseph, b 1859; 3. Kirsty, b 1869; 4. Donald, b 1864; 5. Angus, b 1864; 6. Mary. **DC 23 Oct 1979; WLC**.

8670 McMILLAN, John, b 1808. From Bornish, Is South Uist, INV. Poss eld s/o Alexander M, qv, and

Margaret McIntyre, qv. To West Williams Twp, Middlesex Co, ONT, ca 1849. m 1838, Flora Morrison, qv, ch: 1. Effie, b 1839; 2. Margaret, b 1841; 3. Mary, b 1843; 4. Catherine, b 1846; 5. Michael, b 1848. **WLC**.

8671 MACMILLAN, John, b 1831. From Port Ellon, Is Islay, ARL. bro/o Duncan M, qv, and Neil M, qv. To Eldon Twp, Victoria Co, ONT, prob <1845. m Rachel McArthur, qv, ch: 1. Duncan, b 1861; 2. Archie; 3. Hugh; 4. Jane; 5. Anne; 6. John. **EC 155**.

8672 MACMILLAN, John. Prob from INV. To Pictou, NS, prob <1854, and stld Upper South River, Antigonish Co. Farmer. m Ann MacGregor. Son Allan. **HCA 324**.

8673 McMILLAN, John B. From Is Benbecula, INV. To East Williams Twp, Middlesex Co, ONT, 1848. **PCM 44**.

8674 McMILLAN, John G. From Is Benbecula, INV. To East Williams Twp, Middlesex Co, ONT, 1848. **PCM 44**.

8675 McMILLAN, John Willie, b 1775. From Auchencairn, Kilbride par, Is Arran, BUT. To Dalhousie, NB, on the *Alice*, 1832; stld Jacquet River, Restigouche Co. m Mary McNicol, qv, ch: 1. Robert, 1809-93; 2. John, b 1811; 3. William, 1815-96; 4. Isabel, 1816–1905; 5. James, 1819–1904. **MAC 22**.

8676 McMILLAN, Julia. Prob from ARL. To Cape Breton Is, NS, <1850. Wife of Duncan Campbell, qv. **NSN 22/10**.

8677 McMILLAN, Kate. From Glen Albyn, INV. d/o John M, qv. To Antigonish, NS, prob on the *Norah*, 1803; stld Glen Alpine. m — Robertson, St Joseph. **CP 30**.

8678 McMILLAN, Katherine. From Shenieval, Glendessary, INV. To Montreal, QUE, ex Fort William, arr Sep 1802; stld poss Finch Twp, Stormont Co, ONT. **MCM 1/4 24**.

8679 McMILLAN, Lachlan. From Lochaber, INV. To Orwell Bay, PEI, on the *Polly*, ex Portree, arr 7 Aug 1803; stld Belfast dist, Queens Co; later Black Point, Covehead. Farmer. m Sarah McPherson, qv, ch: 1. Donald; 2. John; 3. Ewen; 4. Marion; 5. Catherine. **DC 28 May 1980**.

8680 McMILLAN, Lachlan. From Is Islay, ARL. To Oro Twp, Simcoe Co, ONT, prob <1853. m Mary Smith, qv. **DC 21 Mar 1980**.

8681 McMILLAN, Lauchlin, b 1751. Prob from Is Mull, ARL. To Charlottetown, PEI, on the *Rambler*, ex Tobermory, 20 Jun 1806. Wife Sarah, aged 50, with him, and ch: 1. Donald, aged 25; 2. Margaret, aged 20; 3. Hugh, aged 18; 4. Catherine, aged 12; 5. John, aged 7. **PLR**.

8682 MACMILLAN, Lauchlin. From Is Muck, INV. To Cape Breton Is, NS, prob <1820. Wife Catherine Campbell, qv, with him. Dau Catherine. **NSN 32/379**.

8683 McMILLAN, Malcolm, 1781–1840. From Glen Albyn, INV. s/o John M, qv. To Antigonish, NS, prob on the *Norah*, 1803; stld near Lochaber Lake, which he named. Farmer. m Margaret McMillan, South River, ch: 1. Angus; 2. Donald, 1808-81. **CP 30**.

8684 MACMILLAN, Malcolm, b 1758. From Is Colonsay, ARL. To Charlottetown, PEI, on the *Spencer*, ex Oban, 22 Sep 1806. Wife–poss Grizel McNeil,

qv–with him, and ch: 1. James, aged 19; 2. Alexander, aged 14; 3. Hector 'Colonsay', aged 13; 4. Malcolm, aged 10; 5. Flora, aged 8; 6. Duncan, aged 4; 7. Sophia, aged 3; 8. Catherine, aged 1. **PLSN; HP 41, 74**.

8685 MACMILLAN, Malcolm, b ca 1780. From Lochaber, INV. To Lochaber, Antigonish Co, NS, 1810. **HCA 240**.

8686 McMILLAN, Malcolm, 1810-97. From Is Arran, BUT. s/o Mrs Margaret M, qv. To QUE, on the *Caledonia*, ex Greenock, 25 Apr 1829; stld Inverness Twp, Megantic Co. m Elizabeth Bellingham. **AMC 11; MAC 32**.

8687 MACMILLAN, Malcolm. Prob from INV. To Antigonish Co, NS, prob <1830; stld Lochaber. ch incl: 1. Angus, who went to East River St Marys; 2. Donald; 3. John. **HCA 324**.

8688 McMILLAN, Malcolm. From ARL. To Ekfrid Twp, Middlesex Co, ONT, 1853. **PCM 31**.

8689 McMILLAN, Mairead. From Aberchalder, INV. To QUE, ex Fort William, arr Sep 1802; stld poss Finch Twp, Stormont Co, ONT. **MCM 1/4 25**.

8690 McMILLAN, Margaret. Prob from Is Muck, INV, and poss d/o John M. To QUE, ex Fort William, arr Sep 1802; stld E ONT. **MCM 1/4 25**.

8691 McMILLAN, Margaret, called Peggy, ca 1780–12 Feb 1853. From Is Colonsay, ARL. To Charlottetown, PEI, on the *Spencer*, ex Oban, 22 Sep 1806. Wife of Duncan Darroch, qv, m 6 Feb 1798. **PLSN; DC 18 Nov 1981**.

8692 MACMILLAN, Margaret. From Is Eigg, INV. To Ainslie Glen, Whycocomagh, Inverness Co, NS, ca 1820. Wife of Neil Stewart, qv. **MP 852**.

8693 McMILLAN, Mrs Margaret. From Is Arran, BUT. To QUE on the *Caledonia*, ex Greenock, 25 Apr 1829; stld Inverness Village, Megantic Co. ch with her: 1. Malcolm, qv; 2. James. **AMC 11; MAC 32**.

8694 McMILLAN, Margaret. Poss from Lochaber, INV. To Antigonish Co, NS, prob 1830. Wife of John 'Ruadh' Cameron, qv. **HCA 85**.

8695 McMILLAN, Margaret, 1794–1850. From Kintyre, ARL. To Eldon Twp, Victoria Co, ONT, <1840. Wife of William Mitchell, qv. **EC 180**.

8696 McMILLAN, Margaret, 1811-93. From Kilberry, South Knapdale, ARL. To ONT, 1847. Wife of John Galbraith, qv. **DC 9 Mar 1980**.

8697 McMILLAN, Margaret. From DFS. To CAN, poss NS, <1852. m John McConnell. **SH**.

8698 McMILLAN, Mrs Margaret, d 1846. From Kilmarnock, AYR. To Pictou, NS. Drowned–prob with some of her ch–in the wreck of the *Sutlej*, of Pictou, bound for Fall River. **DGH 30 Jul 1846**.

8699 McMILLAN, Marian, b 1748. From Is Rum, ARL. Poss rel to Catherine McKinnon, qv. To Gut of Canso, Cape Breton, NS, on the *Saint Lawrence*, ex Tobermory, 11 Jul 1828. **SLL**.

8700 McMILLAN, Marion, b 1776. From Is Rum, ARL. Poss wife of Donald M, qv. To Gut of Canso, Cape Breton, NS, on the *Saint Lawrence*, ex Tobermory, 11 Jul 1828. **SLL**.

8701 McMILLAN, Marion, b 1820. From Kirkconnel, DFS. d/o Robert M, qv, and Elizabeth Laidlaw, qv. To McKillop Twp, Huron Co, ONT, ca 1843. m Alexander Broadfoot, qv. **DC 26 May 1979**.

8702 McMILLAN, Marion, b 1788, Is Rum, ARL. Poss wife of Angus M, qv. To Gut of Canso, Cape Breton, NS, on the *Saint Lawrence*, ex Tobermory, 11 Jul 1828. **SLL**.

8703 McMILLAN, Marion, b 1811. From Is Rum, ARL. Poss rel to Angus M, qv. To Gut of Canso, Cape Breton, NS, on the *Saint Lawrence*, ex Tobermory, 11 Jul 1828. **SLL**.

8704 McMILLAN, Marion. From Balivanich, Is Benbecula, INV. To West Williams Twp, Middlesex Co, ONT, ca 1849. Wife of Ronald Monk, qv. **WLC**.

8705 McMILLAN, Mary. From ARL. To Malpeque, Prince Co, PEI, on the *Annabelle*, ex Campbeltown, arr Sep 1770. m Donald Ramsay, qv. **DC 24 Oct 1979**.

8706 McMILLAN, Mary. From INV. To Montreal, QUE, ex Fort William, arr Sep 1802; stld E ONT. **MCM 1/4 24**.

8707 McMILLAN, Mary. Prob from Is Muck, INV, and poss d/o John M. To QUE, ex Fort William, arr Sep 1802; stld E ONT. **MCM 1/4 25**.

8708 McMILLAN, Mary. From Munerigg, Invergarry, INV. To QUE, ex Fort William, arr Sep 1802; stld E ONT. Wife of Alexander McDonell, qv. **MCM 1/4 25**.

8709 McMILLAN, Mary. From Glen Albyn, INV. d/o John M, qv. To Antigonish, NS, prob on the *Nora*; stld Glen Alpine. m Archibald MacEachern. **CP 30**.

8710 McMILLAN, Mary. From Glasgow. To QUE, ex Greenock, summer 1815; stld prob Lanark Co, ONT. Wife of Donald McDonald, qv. **SEC 6**.

8711 McMILLAN, Mary, b 1804, Is Rum, ARL. Poss d/o John M, qv. To Gut of Canso, Cape Breton, NS, on the *Saint Lawrence*, ex Tobermory, 11 Jul 1828. **SLL**.

8712 McMILLAN, Mary, b 1785. From Glen, Kilbride par, Is Arran, BUT. To Nash Creek, Restigouche Co, NB, 1829. Wife of Archibald Kelso, qv. **MAC 18**.

8713 McMILLAN, Mary. From South Sannox, Is Arran, BUT. d/o Neil M, qv, and Catherine Kerr, qv. To QUE on the *Caledonian*, ex Greenock, 25 Apr 1829; stld Inverness Twp, Megantic Co. m James Fullerton, jr, qv. **AMC 11; MAC 32**.

8714 McMILLAN, Mary, 21 Mar 1819–10 Jan 1857. From Shannochie, Kilmory par, Is Arran, BUT. d/o Donald M, qv, and Barbara Shaw, qv. To Blackland, Restigouche Co, NB, 1830. m John Murchie, and had ch. **MAC 22; DC 7 Feb 1981**.

8715 McMILLAN, Mary, 1824–1910. From Is Mull, ARL. To Eldon Twp, Victoria Co, ONT, 1843. Wife of James Livingstone, qv. **DC 1 Aug 1979**.

8716 McMILLAN, Miles. From INV. To Montreal, QUE, ex Fort William, arr Sep 1802; stld E ONT. **MCM 1/4 24**.

8717 MACMILLAN, Miles. Prob from INV. To South River, Antigonish Co, NS, poss <1820. m Mary, d/o Rory MacPherson, qv, and — MacDonald, ch: 1. Duncan; 2. Donald; 3. Alexander; 4. Mary. **HCA 323, 339**.

8718 McMILLAN, Murdoch, b 1751. Prob from Is Colonsay, ARL. To Charlottetown, PEI, on the *Spencer*, ex Oban, 22 Sep 1806. **PLSN**.

8719 McMILLAN, Murdock, b ca 1817. From Balivanich, Is Benbecula, INV. s/o Donald 'Og' M. To QUE, ex Lochboisdale, on the *Admiral*; stld Glenelg, Grey Co, ONT, 1849. m (i) Effie —; (ii) 1842, Mary McPherson, ch: 1. Malcolm; 2. John; 3. Neil; 4. Donald; 5. Archibald; 6. Mary Flora; 7. Mary; 8. Ranald. **DC 23 Oct 1979**.

8720 McMILLAN, Myles. To Nashwaak River, York Co, NB, 1784. Discharged soldier, 42nd Regt. **DC 30 Mar 1981**.

8721 McMILLAN, Neil, b 1769. From Bornish, Is South Uist, INV. To Pictou, NS, 1799, then to PEI, but stld Judique, Inverness Co, NS. m and left ch. **MCM 1/5 27**.

8722 McMILLAN, Neil. From Is Mull, ARL. To Port Hastings, Inverness Co, NS, on the *Commerce*, ex Tobermory, 1822. **MCM 1/5 27**.

8723 McMILLAN, Neil, 1785–1861. From South Sannox, Is Arran, BUT. To QUE on the *Caledonian*, ex Greenock, 25 Apr 1829; stld Inverness Twp, Megantic Co, QUE. m Catherine Kerr, qv, ch: 1. Ann; 2. Duncan, qv; 3. Catherine; 4. Mary, qv; 5. Rev John, qv; 6. Margaret; 7. Janet; 8. Donald, JP. **AMC 11; MAC 32**.

8724 McMILLAN, Neil, b 1804, Is Rum, ARL. Poss rel to Angus M, qv. To Gut of Canso, Cape Breton, NS, on the *Saint Lawrence*, ex Tobermory, 11 Jul 1828. **SLL**.

8725 McMILLAN, Neil, b 1815, Is Rum, ARL. Poss rel to Donald M, qv. To Gut of Canso, Cape Breton, NS, on the *Saint Lawrence*, ex Tobermory, 11 Jul 1828. **SLL**.

8726 MACMILLAN, Neil. From Port Ellon, Is Islay, ARL. bro/o John M, qv, and Duncan M, qv. To Eldon Twp, Victoria Co, ONT, prob <1845. m Miss MacEachern, ch: 1. Sarah; 2. John. **EC 155**.

8727 McMILLAN, Neil. Prob from ARL. To Aldborough Twp, Elgin Co, ONT, prob <1845. ch: 1. Edward; 2. Donald; 3. John; 4. Malcolm; 5. Mrs Robert Graham; 6. Mrs Duncan Ferguson; 7. Mrs Dougald Campbell, res Huron Co. **PDA 64**.

8728 MACMILLAN, Neil. From Lagavulin, Is Islay, ARL. bro/o Archibald M, qv. To Eldon Twp, Victoria Co, ONT, 1852. m Nellie Black, ch: 1. Neil; 2. Colin; 3. John; 4. Margaret; 5. Mrs Gilchrist; 6. Mrs Archie Campbell. **EC 160**.

8729 McMILLAN, Norman. From Is Benbecula, INV. To East Williams Twp, Middlesex Co, ONT, 1848. **PCM 44**.

8730 McMILLAN, Peggy. From Shenieval, Glendessary, INV. To Montreal, QUE, ex Fort William, arr Sep 1802; stld prob Finch Twp, Stormont Co, ONT. A child with her. **MCM 1/4 24**.

8731 McMILLAN, Peggy. From Glen Albyn, INV. d/o John M, qv. To Antigonish, NS, prob on the *Nora*; stld Glen Alpine. m John 'Squire' Cameron, qv. **CP 30**.

8732 McMILLAN, Peter. From PER. To Montreal, QUE, on the *Niagara*, ex Greenock, arr 28 May 1825; stld McNab Twp, Renfrew Co, ONT. **HCL 103; EMT 18**.

8733 McMILLAN, Peter. From ARL. To Woodstock, Oxford Co, ONT, <1830. m Mary Keith, qv, and had dau Elizabeth. **DC 16 Jun 1980**.

8734 McMILLAN, Peter. From Is South Uist, INV. bro/o Rory M, qv. To Inverness Co, NS, prob <1840. **MCM 1/4 27**.

8735 McMILLAN, Robert 'Valdie', 1803–24 Dec 1885. From Mid Kiscadale, Kilbride par, Is Arran, BUT. s/o Archibald M. To Blackland, Restigouche Co, NB, 1830. Farmer. m Elizabeth McMillan, qv, ch: 1. John, 1830–1916; 2. Donald, 1832–1914; 3. Archie, 1834-83; 4. Betsy, 1836–1924; 5. Barbara, 1838–1929; 6. Robert, 1841–1922; 7. James, 1843–1928; 8. Kate, 1845–1922; 9. Mary, 1847-69; 10. Belle, 1851–1929. **MAC 22; DC 7 Feb 1981**.

8736 McMILLAN, Robert, ca 1782–Jun 1859. From Kirklandhill, Kirkconnel, DFS. bro/o Walter M, qv. To ONT, ca 1842; stld McKillop Twp, Huron Co. Weaver. m Elizabeth Laidlaw, qv, ch: 1. Jane, qv; 2. Marion, qv; 3. Elizabeth. **SG xxvii/2 80; DC 26 May 1979**.

8737 McMILLAN, Robert, 22 Apr 1821–23 Aug 1902. From Kirkconnel, DFS. s/o Walter M, qv, and Mary Laidlaw, qv. To ONT, 1843; stld McKillop Twp, Huron Co. Farmer and livestock importer. m Mary Dods, qv, ch: 1. Margaret, 1850–1915; 2. Walter, 1852–1903, went to KS, USA; 3. John, 1853–1930; 4. Mary, 1856–1933; 5. Robert, 1858-96; 6. Peter, 1860-96; 7. Agnes, 1864–1943. **DC 26 May 1979**.

8738 McMILLAN, Rory. From Is South Uist, INV. bro/o Peter M, qv. To Inverness Co, NS, prob <1840. Blacksmith. **MCM 1/5 27**.

8739 MACMILLAN, Thomas, 1771–1836. From Kilmory par, Is Arran, BUT. To Archibald Settlement, Restigouche Co, NB, <1834. m Margaret Duncan, qv, ch: 1. Mary, 1805-92; 2. Janet, b Shenoch, 1808; 3. Donald, b 1810; 4. Margaret, b 1812; 5. John, 1816–1900; 6. Christian, b 1819. **MAC 23**.

8740 McMILLAN, Walter, ca 1795–13 Jul 1869. From Kirklandhill, Kirkconnel, DFS. bro/o Robert M, qv. To ONT, ca 1844; stld McKillop Twp, Huron Co. m Mary Laidlaw, qv, ch: 1. Agnes, remained in SCT; 2. Robert, qv; 3. John, qv. **SG xxvii/2 80; DC 26 May 1979**.

8741 McMILLAN, Walter, b 1830. From ARL. To Chaleur Bay, QUE, 1844; moved to Puslinch Twp, Wellington Co, ONT. Farmer and mariner. m Elizabeth Stewart, qv, ch: 1. Mary; 2. John; 3. Dugald; 4. Jean; 5. Alexander, qv; 6. Sarah; 7. Dugald W. **DC 23 Apr 1967**.

8742 McMILLAN, William. To Pictou Co, NS, ca 1802; stld 'Kerrowgair'. **MCM 1/5 27**.

8743 McMILLAN, William. From Glen Urquhart, INV. To Pictou Co, NS, 1818. **MCM 1/5 27**.

8744 McMILLAN, William. From Glen Urquhart, INV. To Pictou Co, NS, prob 1820; stld Blue Mountain. **MCM 1/5 27**.

8745 McMILLAN, William, 1795–1879. From Stragail, Kilmory par, Is Arran, BUT. s/o Donald M. and Elspa Jamieson. To Restigouche Co, NB, 1826; stld Black Point. m Elizabeth Hamilton, qv, ch: 1. Donald, b ca 1830; 2. Elizabeth, b ca 1834; 3. Robert,

b ca 1836; 4. Mary, b ca 1838; 5. Thomas, b ca 1840; 6. Jane, b ca 1842; 7. William, b ca 1845. **MAC 23; DC 13 Oct 1980**.

8746 McMILLAN, William, ca 1803–4 Feb 1879. From INV. To London Twp, Middlesex Co, ONT, poss 1830. m Ann, d/o Duncan Mackenzie, qv, and Margaret Barclay, and had ch. **PCM 50**.

8747 McMILLAN, William, d 2 Mar 1871. To Dummer Twp, Peterborough Co, ONT, prob <1835. Wife Margaret with him, and ch: 1. William, b ca 1812; 2. Francis, b ca 1813; 3. John, b 1815; 4. Sarah, b ca 1818; 5. James, b ca 1821. **DC 19 Nov 1981**.

8748 McMILLAN, William, d 1846. From Kilmarnock, AYR. Prob s/o Mrs Margaret M, qv. To Pictou, NS. Drowned in the wreck of the *Sutlej*, of Pictou, bound for Fall River. **DGH 30 Jul 1846**.

8749 McMILLAN, Williamina, d 24 Dec 1839. From DFS. To Montreal, QUE. Wife of Rev Edward Black, qv, whom she m 11 Oct 1836. **DGC 19 Oct 1836**.

8750 McMORINE, Catherine, 1826–1908. From DFS. To Melbourne, Richmond Co, QUE, <1850. Wife of Simon Beattie, qv. **MGC 15 Jul 1980**.

8751 McMORINE, Jane, ca 1818–24 Apr 1902. From DFS. To QUE, and stld prob Sherbrooke Co. Wife of William Main, qv. **MGC 15 Jul 1980**.

8752 McMORINE, Rev John, 1799–22 May 1867. From Sanquhar, DFS. bro/o Robert M, qv. Educ Univ of Edinburgh. To QUE, 1837. Min at Melbourne, Richmond Co, 1839-44, when he became a teacher in the High School of QUE. Ind min of Ramsay, Lanark Co, ONT, 1846. DD, Queens Coll, 1865. **FES vii 644; MGC 2 Aug 1979**.

8753 McMORINE, John, 1822–1901. From Penpont or Sanquhar, DFS. To Melbourne, Richmond Co, QUE, 1842. Farmer and cabinet-maker. m Margaret Munro, qv, ch: 1. Catherine, 1854–1942; 2. Alexander, d inf; 3. George, 1861–1912; 4. John, 1862–1933, merchant; 5. Alexander, 1864–1906; 6. Annie, 1868–1942; 7. Finlay, 1869–1912. **MGC 2 Aug 1979 and 15 Jul 1980**.

8754 McMORINE, Robert, 1795–16 Mar 1865. From Sanquhar, DFS. bro/o Rev John M, qv. To Melbourne, Richmond Co, QUE, ca 1850. m Catherine Burnet, qv. Dau Jane. **MGC 15 Jul 1980**.

8755 McMURCHY, Archibald, 1832–27 Apr 1912. From Clachan, Kintyre, ARL. To ONT with parents, 1840. Educ Rockwood Academy and Univ of Toronto: BA 1861, MA 1868. Master of Toronto Grammar School, and served in Queens Own Rifles, 1866. m Marjory Jardine Ramsay, qv, and had, poss with other ch: 1. Dr Helen, 1862–1953, physician and author; 2. Marjory. **MDB 481, 803; SG xxx/1 19**.

8756 MACMURCHY, Rev John, 1800–22 Sep 1866. From Killean, ARL. Third s/o Thomas M, farmer. Educ Univs of Edinburgh and Glasgow. To ONT, 1840. Min of West Gwillimbury, 1842; trans to Eldon, Victoria Co, 1844, and d there. **FES vii 644; GMA 10085**.

8757 McMURCHY, John, b 1835. From Kintyre, ARL. To Aldborough Twp, Elgin Co, ONT, 1852; stld Lot 2, Con A. Farmer, m and left ch. **PDA 85**.

8758 McMURDO, Henry Douglas, d 1 Feb 1847. Poss from DFS or KKD. To Haldimand Co, ONT, and d Dunnville. **DGH 25 Mar 1847**.

8759 McMURDO, James, b ca 1813. To St Gabriel de Valcartier, QUE, prob <1855. **Census 1861**.

8760 McMURDO, Thomas, ca 1811–1 Apr 1880. From Closeburn, DFS. s/o Andrew M. and Ann Sharpe. To St John, NFD. **Ts Closeburn**.

8761 McMURPHY, Angus. From Tarbet, ARL. To Lobo Twp, Middlesex Co, ONT, 1846. ch: 1. John; 2. Archibald; 3. Angus; 4. Dugald; 5. Donald; 6. Allan; 7. Duncan; 8. Nancy; 9. Kate; 10. Jane; 11. Isabella. **PCM 39**.

8762 McMURPHY, Dugald. From Caolasraide, South Knapdale, ARL. To Lobo Twp, Middlesex Co, ONT, 1842. ch: 1. John; 2. Archibald; 3. Duncan; 4. Dugald; 5. Donald; 6. Alexander; 7. Christie; 8. Nancy; 9. Flora; 10. Bella; 11. Mary. **PCM 39**.

8763 McMURRICH, John, b 1804. From Port Glasgow, RFW. To Toronto, ONT, 1833. Merchant, rep firm of Bryce, McMurrich & Co, and founded branches at Toronto, Kingston and Hamilton. Alderman of Toronto and MLA, Saugeen. **BNA 733**.

8764 McNAB, Alexander. From PER. To Richmond Bay, PEI, on the *Falmouth*, ex Greenock, 8 Apr 1770; stld Queens Co. Wife with him. Prob parents of Donald and Hugh M, recorded 1798. **DC 28 May 1980**.

8765 McNAB, Alexander, b ca 1777. From Glasgow. To QUE, poss on the *Atlas*, ex Greenock, 11 Jul 1815; stld ONT. Farmer. Wife Catharine McDougall, qv, with him, and 2 ch. **SEC 1**.

8766 MACNAB, Alexander, 27 Sep 1762–11 May 1824. From Suie, Glendochart, PER. To Malagash, Cumberland Co, NS, <1818. Shipbuilder at Tatamagouche, Colchester Co. m Catherine Waugh, qv. **HT 35; DC 29 Oct 1980**.

8767 MACNAB, Alexander. Prob from PER. To Aldborough Twp, Elgin Co, ONT, <1820. Farmer. **PDA 42**.

8768 McNAB, Alexander. From Strathyre, PER. To Montreal, QUE, on the *Niagara*, ex Greenock, arr 28 May 1825; stld McNab Twp, Renfrew Co, ONT. Wife Catherine Dewar, qv, with him, and ch: 1. Catherine; 2. Margaret; 3. Duncan. **HCL 103; EMT 18**.

8769 McNAB, Alexander. Poss from Lochearnhead, PER. To Montreal, QUE, on the *Niagara*, ex Greenock, arr 28 May 1825; stld McNab Twp, Renfrew Co, ONT. An inf, poss s/o Archibald M, qv, and Janet McEwan, qv. **EMT 23**.

8770 McNAB, Alexander, b ca 1775. From Killin, PER. To Osgoode Twp, Carleton Co, ONT, ca 1831. Farmer. m 1795, Grace McDonald, qv, ch: 1. John, qv; 2. Colin, b 1798, retr to SCT; 3. Allan, b 1800; 4. Robert, qv; 5. James, b 1804; 6. Duncan, qv; 7. Alexander, b 1809; 8. Patrick or Peter, qv; 9. Janet, qv; 10. Grace, b 1817. **DC 1 Aug 1979**.

8771 MACNAB, Allan. From PER. s/o Robert M. of Dundurn, and Mary Stewart. Lt, 3rd Dragoons, and aide-de-camp to Gen Simcoe, Gov of Upper Canada. Res Newark or Niagara, Lincoln Co, ONT, <1796. m Anne, d/o Capt William Napier, Commissioner of the Port of

QUE. Son Allan Napier, 1798–1862, soldier and politician. **BNA 347, 532; IBD 314; SN iii 53; MDB 483**.

8772 MACNAB, Archibald, ca 1777–22 Apr 1860. From Easter Torry, PER. s/o Dr Robert M. of Bovain, Glendochart, bro/o 'The MacNab', and Anne Maule. Succ to the chiefship of the clan, and an encumbered estate, 1816. Fled to CAN, 1823, to avoid writ of caption, and obtained a grant of land on Madawaska River, ONT, where he attempted to establish a feudal lordship in the twp, which he named McNab, in Renfrew Co. App Col of 20th Batt, Carleton Light Infantry, 1837. Left the settlement in disgrace, ca 1851, and went to Hamilton, ONT, thence to his wife's property at Rendall, OKI, SCT. d at Lanion, Boulogne, France, in reduced circumstances. m Margaret Robertson; ch: a dau, Sophia Frances, chief of the clan, who d 1894. He had a natural s in CAN, by Catherine Fisher, named Allan Francis. **SN iii 53; IFB 108; MDB 483; HCL 102**.

8773 McNAB, Archibald. Poss from Lochearnhead, PER. To Montreal, QUE, on the *Niagara*, ex Greenock, arr 28 May 1825; stld McNab Twp, Renfrew Co, ONT. Wife Janet McEwan, qv, with him, ch: 1. Cathrine; 2. John; 3. James. **EMT 18**.

8774 McNAB, Archibald, 1812–18 Feb 1882. From PER. To Esquesing Twp, Halton Co, ONT, prob 1844; bur Acton. Wife Betty, 1784–1847. **EPE 74**.

8775 McNAB, Betty. From PER, poss Killin. Prob rel to John McNee, qv, alias McNab. To McNab Twp, Renfrew Co, ONT, 1825. **DC 3 Jan 1981**.

8776 McNAB, Catherine, ca 1804–24 Oct 1890. To PEI, 1823; stld Queens Co. Wife of John MacLennan, qv. **HP 44**.

8777 McNAB, Charles, b ca 1766. To St Andrews dist, Cape Breton Co, NS, 1810. Farmer, m and had ch. **CBC 1818**.

8778 McNAB, Dougald, b ca 1795. Poss s/o Charles M, qv. To St Andrews dist, Cape Breton Co, NS, 1810. Farmer. **CBC 1818**.

8779 MACNAB, Dugald. From Killin, PER. To QUE, 1823; stld Madawaska River, McNab Twp, Renfrew Co, ONT. Factor to Archibald MacNab of MacNab, qv, until 1835. **DC 3 Jan 1980**.

8780 McNAB, Duncan. From Killin par, PER. To Montreal, QUE, on the *Curlew*, ex Greenock, 21 Jul 1818; stld Beckwith Twp, Lanark Co, ONT, but moved to North Elmsley Twp, 1833. Weaver. Wife Catherine with him, ch: 1. Colin; 2. Thomas; 3. Janet. **BCL; HCL 34**.

8781 McNAB, Duncan. From PER. To McNab Twp, Renfrew Co, ONT, 1825. Farmer. **DC 3 Jan 1980**.

8782 McNAB, Duncan. From PER, prob Killin par. A minor, poss s/o Duncan M, qv. To McNab Twp, Renfrew Co, ONT, 1825. **DC 3 Jan 1825**.

8783 McNAB, Duncan, 1806-83. From Killin, PER. s/o Alexander M, qv, and Grace McDonald, qv. To Osgoode Twp, Carleton Co, ONT, ca 1831. m Janet Fisher, qv. **DC 1 Aug 1979**.

8784 McNAB, Grace Buchanan. To McNab Twp, Renfrew Co, ONT, 1825. A minor, poss rel to Alexander M, qv. **DC 3 Jan 1980**.

8785 McNAB, Helen, d <Jul 1817. From Callander, PER. To QUE, on the *Eliza*, ex Greenock, 3 Aug 1815, and d soon afterwards. Wife of Peter McPherson, qv. **SEC 1; HCL 230**.

8786 McNAB, Helen, 1795–1849. From Glendochart, PER. To Wallace, Cumberland Co, NS, prob <1820. m Daniel MacFarlane, qv.   **DC 29 Oct 1980**.

8787 McNAB, Hugh. From PER, poss Lochearnhead. An inf, poss s/o Archibald M, qv, and Janet McEwan, qv. To McNab Twp, Renfrew Co, ONT, 1825.   **DC 3 Jan 1980**.

McNAB, James. See McNEE, James.

8788 MACNAB, James, ca 1817–24 May 1894. From Callander, PER. s/o John M. and Christian Buchanan. To Arthur Twp, Wellington Co, ONT.   **Ts Buchanan**.

8789 McNAB, Jane. Poss from PER. To Caledon Twp, York Co, ONT, ca 1810. m James MacLaren. **DC 15 May 1982**.

8790 McNAB, Jane. From Killin, PER. d/o Colin, s/o Alexander M, qv. To Osgoode Twp, Carleton Co, ONT, 1840. Wife of John Stuart, qv.   **DC 1 Aug 1979**.

8791 McNAB, Janet, b 1814. From Killin, PER. d/o Alexander M, qv, and Grace McDonald, qv. To Osgoode Twp, Carleton Co, ONT, ca 1831. m Alexander McEwan, qv.   **DC 1 Aug 1979**.

8792 McNAB, Janet. Prob from ARL. To Eldon Twp, Victoria Co, ONT, 1842. Wife of Hugh McArthur, qv. **EC 80**.

8793 McNAB, John, b ca 1789. From Inverkeithing, FIF. To QUE, ex Greenock, summer 1815; stld ONT. Farmer. Wife Hannah Balmain, qv, with him, and 2 ch. **SEC 2**.

8794 McNAB, John. To CAN <1820. Surgeon, HBCo.   **SH**.

8795 McNAB, John, b 1796. From Killin, PER. s/o Alexander M, qv, and Grace McDonald, qv. To Osgoode Twp, Carleton Co, ONT, ca 1831. Farmer. m Catherine McDonald, qv.   **DC 1 Aug 1979**.

8796 McNAB, Patrick or Peter, b ca 1812. From Killin, PER. s/o Alexander M, qv, and Grace McDonald, qv. To Osgoode Twp, Carleton Co, ONT, ca 1831. m Christine McGregor, qv.   **DC 1 Aug 1979**.

8797 McNAB, Robert, b ca 1798. Poss s/o Charles M, qv. To St Andrews dist, Cape Breton Co, NS, 1810. Farmer.   **CBC 1818**.

8798 McNAB, Robert. From PER, prob Killin par. A minor, poss rel to Duncan M, qv. To McNab Twp, Renfrew Co, ONT, 1825.   **DC 3 Jan 1980**.

8799 McNAB, Robert, 1801-59. From Killin, PER. s/o Alexander M, qv, and Grace McDonald, qv. To Osgoode Twp, Carleton Co, ONT, ca 1831. m Jane Lothian, qv.   **DC 1 Aug 1979**.

8800 McNABB, Archibald. Poss from ARL. To Eldon Twp, Victoria Co, ONT, prob <1853. m Annie Livingstone, qv, ch: 1. Neil, 1846–1921; 2. Janet; 3. Maggie; 4. Malcolm, b 1848.   **EC 161**.

McNAIR. See also McNAYR.

8801 McNAIR, Alexander, b 5 May 1817. From

Kintyre, ARL. s/o Nathaniel M, qv, and Margaret Galbraith, qv. To Miramichi, Northumberland Co, NB, 1821; stld later Durham par, Restigouche Co. m Catherine Kelso, ch: 1. Mary; 2. Nathaniel; 3. Margaret; 4. Alexander; 5. Catherine; 6. Archibald; 7. Jane; 8. Elizabeth.   **DC 7 Feb 1981**.

8802 McNAIR, Archibald, b 13 Mar 1803. From Campbeltown, ARL. s/o Nathaniel M, qv, and Margaret Galbraith, qv. To Miramichi, Northumberland Co, NB, 1821; moved later to Heron Is, Restigouche Co. m Isabella McMillan, qv, ch: 1. Nathaniel; 2. Margaret; 3. Barbara; 4. Donald; 5. Mary; 6. John; 7. Jean; 8. James; 9. Barbara; 10. Archibald.   **CUC 16; DC 7 Feb 1981**.

8803 McNAIR, Catherine, b 12 Sep 1803, Paisley, RFW. d/o Duncan M. and Isabel McGregor, and estranged wife of John McLean, sawyer in Glasgow, whom she m 3 Oct 1836. To NY, 1855, and went to Mormon settlement at Cardston, ALB. ch with her: 1. Duncan, b 1837; 2. James W, b 1843; 3. Hugh, b 1847.   **DC 1 Nov 1973**.

8804 McNAIR, David, b 13 Jan 1805. From Kintyre, ARL. s/o Nathaniel M, qv, and Margaret Galbraith, qv. To Miramichi, Northumberland Co, NB, 1821; moved later to Durham par, Restigouche Co. Farmer. m Janet Ferguson, ch: 1. Jane; 2. Nathaniel; 3. John; 4. Ebenezer; 5. David; 6. James; 7. Alexander. **DC 7 Feb 1981**.

8805 McNAIR, James, b 18 Sep 1813. From Kintyre, ARL. s/o Nathaniel M, qv, and Margaret Galbraith, qv. To Miramichi, Northumberland Co, NB, 1821; stld later Durham par, Restigouche Co. m (i) 1837, Elizabeth Black; (ii) 1847, Lydia Bishop. ch: 1. Margaret; 2. Elizabeth; 3. Catherine; 4. Janet; 5. Mary; 6. James; 7. Nathaniel; 8. Robert.   **DC 7 Feb 1981**.

8806 McNAIR, Janet. From Culter, LKS. d/o James M. and Jane Kerr. To QUE on the *Norton*, ex Glasgow, 1 Jun 1851, and stld Whitby, Ontario Co, ONT. m 29 Jan 1857, John Shiels, qv.   **DC 29 Oct 1979**.

8807 McNAIR, Jean, b 5 May 1817. From Kintyre, ARL. d/o Nathaniel M, qv, and Margaret Galbraith, qv. To Miramichi, Northumberland Co, NB, 1821; stld later New Mills, Restigouche Co. m John McMillan, qv. **DC 7 Feb 1981**.

8808 McNAIR, John, b 15 Oct 1809. From Kintyre, ARL. s/o Nathaniel M, qv, and Margaret Galbraith, qv. To Miramichi, Northumberland Co, NB, 1821; moved later to Restigouche Co. m Elizabeth Kelso.   **DC 20 Apr 1981**.

8809 McNAIR, Margaret, b 1 Oct 1807. From Kintyre, ARL. d/o Nathaniel M, qv, and Margaret Galbraith, qv. To Miramichi, Northumberland Co, NB, 1821; later to Restigouche Co. m Nathaniel McNair, qv, her cous, and went to Omaha, NE.   **DC 7 Feb 1981**.

8810 McNAIR, Nathaniel, 6 Jan 1763–13 Sep 1857. From Campbeltown, Kintyre. s/o Archibald M. To Miramichi, Northumberland Co, NB, 1821; moved later to Restigouche Co, and stld New Mills. Farmer. m Margaret Galbraith, qv, ch: 1. Archibald, qv; 2. David, qv; 3. Margaret, qv; 4. John, qv; 5. Mary, b 1811; 6. James, qv; 7. Nathaniel, jr, qv; 8. Alexander, qv; 9. Jean, qv; 10. Janet, incapacitated.   **DC 7 Feb 1981**.

8811 McNAIR, Nathaniel, jr, 25 Jan 1815–9 Jun 1880. From Kintyre, ARL. s/o Nathaniel M, qv, and Margaret Galbraith, qv. To Miramichi, Northumberland Co, NB, 1821; moved later to Durham par, Restigouche Co. Farmer. m Martha Archibald, qv, ch: 1. Margaret, b 1847; 2. William, b 1848; 3. Nathaniel, b 1850; 4. Jane, b 1852; 5. Isabella, b 1854; 6. David, b 1856; 7. Robert, b 1858; 8. Elizabeth, b 1861; 9. Mary, b 1864; 10. James, b 1865. **DC 7 Feb 1981**.

8812 McNAIR, Nathaniel. Prob from Kintyre, ARL. s/o Archibald M. To Restigouche Co, NB, <1830. Went later to Omaha, NE, USA. m his cous, Margaret McNair, qv. **DC xxvii/3 127; DC 7 Feb 1981**.

8813 McNAUGHT, John, 1811-73. From Penpont, DFS. s/o David M. and Margaret Corrie. To ONT, ca 1842. m Sarah Kilpatrick, qv, ch: 1. Elizabeth, went to AUS; 2. Margaret; 3. David, b ca 1839; 4. Thomas, 1841–1921. **DC 23 Oct 1981**.

8814 McNAUGHT, John. From Uroch, Balmaghie par, KKD. To Dumfries Twp, Waterloo Co, ONT, <1847. m Euphemia Crosbie, qv. **DGH 20 May 1847**.

8815 McNAUGHTON, Alexander, ca 1770–ca 1851. From Kenmore, PER. To Williamstown, Glengarry Co, ONT, ca 1802. Shoemaker. m 1802, Catherine, d/o Peter Ferguson, UEL, ch: 1. Donald; 2. Christian, b 1805; 3. Peter; 4. John; 5. Ann; 6. William; 7. Margaret, b 1814; 8. Jane; 9. Donald 'Og'; 10. Alexander. **LDW 10 Nov 1974**.

8816 McNAUGHTON, Alexander. From Dull par, PER. To Montreal, QUE, on the *Curlew*, ex Greenock, 21 Jul 1818; stld prob Beckwith Twp, Lanark Co, ONT. Wife Elizabeth with him. **BCL**.

8817 McNAUGHTON, Rev Alexander, 1806-64. Prob from Perth. s/o Donald M, dyer, and Jane Menzies. Ord by Presb of Paisley, 1833, and sailed to QUE on the *Canada*, ex Greenock, 31 Aug 1833. Became min of Lancaster, Glengarry Co, ONT. Retr to SCT and was min of Is Colonsay, ARL, 1842-43, when trans to Kirkhill, INV. m 1839, Juliana Edmonston Campbell McTaggart, who d without ch, 1846. **FES vi 475**.

8818 McNAUGHTON, Alexander, b 7 Sep 1822. From PER. s/o Duncan M. To Middlesex Co, ONT, Jun 1833. m 1861, Christina Campbell, ch: 1. Duncan; 2. James. **DC 1 Aug 1979**.

8819 McNAUGHTON, Alexander, 14 Apr 1822–19 Jun 1921. From Killin par, PER. To Prescott and Russell Co, ONT, 1845; stld L'Orignal. Moved later to Finch Twp, Stormont Co. Farmer and schoolteacher. Inspector of Schools, Stormont, Dundas and Glengarry, 1871–1909. m (i) Jean McKay, ch. m (ii) Margaret Anderson, no ch. **SDG 343**.

8820 McNAUGHTON, Catherine. From Kilmonivaig, INV. d/o Duncan and Catherine M. in Letterfinlay. To Hemmingford, Huntingdon Co, QUE, Jun 1821. Wife of John McPhee, qv. **DC 1 Aug 1979**.

8821 McNAUGHTON, Daniel. To Montreal, QUE, <1846. Dau Elizabeth. **SH**.

8822 McNAUGHTON, Donald. Poss from PER. To Aldborough Twp, Elgin Co, ONT, <1820. Farmer. **PDA 93**.

8823 McNAUGHTON, Donald. From Cardross Moss, nr Port of Monteith, PER. To Montreal, QUE, on the *Niagara*, ex Greenock, arr 28 May 1825; stld Flat River, McNab Twp, Renfrew Co, ONT. Wife Cathrine with him, and ch: 1. Duncan; 2. John; 3. Robert; 4. Mary; 5. Alexander. **EMT 18, 22**.

8824 McNAUGHTON, Donald, b 1779. Prob from Glenlyon, PER. To Antigonish Co, NS, 1826. Farmer. Son Donald, b 1807. **DC 21 Mar 1981**.

8825 McNAUGHTON, Donald, ca 1803–15 Aug 1876. From PER. To Vaughan Twp, York Co, ONT, prob <1830. By wife Isabella, 1816-90, ch: 1. Archibald, 1838-95; 2. Flora, b 1840; 3. Peter, 1845-95; 4. James, 1849–1926. **DC 24 Jan 1977**.

8826 McNAUGHTON, Donald, b 1776. From Kilmonivaig, INV. s/o Duncan and Catherine M. in Letterfinlay. To Hemmingford, Huntingdon Co, QUE, 1831. m (i) ca 1815, Elizabeth Kennedy, d 1827, ch: 1. Margaret, b 1817; 2. Alexander, b 1820; 3. Catherine, b 1823; 4. Thomas, b 1825; 5. Elizabeth, b 1827. m (ii) 1828, Anna Cameron, qv, further ch: 6. Jessie, b 1829; 7. Christina, b 1831; 8. Hughena, b CAN, 1833; 9. Donald, b 1835; 10. Andria, b 1838. **DC 1 Aug 1979**.

8827 MACNAUGHTON, Donald. From PER. To Antigonish Co, NS, poss <1840; stld Loch Catherine. m Christy MacDonald, ch: 1. Donald; 2. John; 3. Peter; 4. Angus; 5. Allan; 6. James; 7. Janet; 8. Elizabeth; 9. Jane. **HCA 325**.

8828 McNAUGHTON, Duncan. Poss from Is Mull, ARL. To Hudson Bay and Red River, <1813. Pioneer settler. **RRS 16**.

8829 McNAUGHTON, Duncan. Prob from PER. Poss rel to John M, qv. To QUE on the *Fame*, 1815; stld Lot 24, Con 6, Drummond Twp, Lanark Co, ONT. **HCL 20, 233**.

8830 McNAUGHTON, Duncan. Prob from PER. To ONT, 1817; stld Lot 4, Con 8, Beckwith Twp, Lanark Co. **HCL**.

8831 McNAUGHTON, Duncan, ca 1810–1908. From PER. To Martintown, Glengarry Co, ONT, 1847. Son Finlay, warden, Finch Twp, 1884. **SDG 268**.

8832 McNAUGHTON, Finlay. Poss from PER. s/o — M. and — Gordon. To ONT <1820. ch: 1. Robert; 2. Matthew; 3. Christina. **DC 21 Mar 1981**.

8833 McNAUGHTON, Finlay, d 1851. From Kilmonivaig, INV. s/o Duncan and Catherine M. in Letterfinlay. To Hemmingford, Huntingdon Co, QUE, Jun 1821. m 1807, Andrea Black, qv, and had with other ch: 1. Duncan, b 1814; 2. John, b 1816; 3. Peter, b 1820; 4. Alexander, d 1905; 5-6. Donald and Catherine, twins, b 1826; 7. Adelia; 8. Jane. **DC 1 Aug 1979**.

8834 McNAUGHTON, Flora, ca 1785–7 Jul 1869. From Is Iona, ARL. To Mariposa Twp, Victoria Co, ONT, poss <1815. Wife of Archibald McDonald, qv. **DC 24 Jan 1977**.

8835 McNAUGHTON, Janet, 1821–10 Apr 1880. From PER. To QUE <1850. Bur Flodden Station. m Roderick MacLeay, qv. **MGC 15 Jul 1980**.

8836 McNAUGHTON, John. Prob from PER. Poss rel

to Duncan M, qv. To QUE on the *Fame*, 1815; stld Lot 24, Con 6, Drummond Twp, Lanark Co, ONT. **HCL 20, 233**.

8837 McNAUGHTON, John. From Breadalbane, PER. To East Williams Twp, Middlesex Co, ONT, 1832. **PCM 43**.

8838 MACNAUGHTON, Malcolm. Poss from PER. To Aldborough Twp, Elgin Co, ONT, prob 1818. Farmer. **PDA 93**.

8839 McNAUGHTON, Margaret, b 1798. To ONT, poss <1830; stld Peterborough Co. Wife of Thomas McGowan, qv. **DC 8 Nov 1981**.

8840 McNAUGHTON, Margaret, ca 1816–24 Feb 1884. Poss from PER. To QUE, prob <1850, and bur Flodden Station. m John B. McLean, qv. **MGC 15 Jul 1980**.

8841 McNAUGHTON, Peter. Poss from ARL. To St John, NB, ex Glasgow, 1816. Engineer and ships chandler. ch: 1. John; 2. James; 3. Duncan; 4. Alexander; 5. Peter, who joined the firm of McNaughton & Grey, chandlers. **DC 1 Aug 1979**.

8842 McNAUGHTON, Rev Peter, 1799–10 May 1878. From Comrie, PER. s/o John M, farmer. Matric Univ of Glasgow, 1813, and grad MA, 1821. To Vaughan, York Co, ONT, 1833, but retr to SCT and became min at Dores, INV. Again to Vaughan, 1847, and trans to Pickering, 1848. m 1835, Agnes Elizabeth Monteith, d 1889, ch: 1. Marie Ann Innes, b 1836; 2. Sarah Frances, b 1838; 3. Grace Elizabeth, b 1841; 4. John, 1843-44; 5. Peter, b 1854. **RGG 407; GMA 8892; FES vi 452, vii 644**.

8843 MACNAUGHTON, Peter, 8 Aug 1810–16 Feb 1881. From PER. To QUE, prob <1850; bur Flodden Station. m Julia Cameron, qv. **MGC 15 Jul 1980**.

8844 McNAUGHTON, William, b ca 1780. From Fortingall par, PER. To Charlottetown, PEI, on the *Clarendon*, ex Oban, 6 Aug 1808. Labourer. Wife Margaret, aged 17, with him. **CPL**.

McNAYR. See also McNAIR.

8845 McNAYR, Boyd, b 29 Oct 1778. Prob from Glasgow. To Halifax, NS, ca 1786, with his father, who was a soldier. Res later at Lawrencetown, Annapolis Co, and at Springfield. Blacksmith. ch: **DC 29 Dec 1980**.

8846 McNEE, Rev Daniel, d ca 1860. From PER. Adm min of Teviothead, ROX, 1847. To Hamilton, ONT, ca 1850, but retr later to SCT. **FES ii 141, vii 644**.

8847 McNEE, James, alias James McNab. From Killin, PER. To QUE, 1823; stld Madawaska River, McNab Twp, ONT. Personal piper to Archibald McNab, clan chief, qv. **DC 3 Jan 1980**.

8848 McNEE or McNAB, Janet. Poss from Killin, PER, and prob d/o John M, qv, alias McNab. To McNab Twp, Renfrew Co, ONT, 1825. **DC 3 Jan 1980**.

8849 McNEE, John. To QUE on the *Caledonian*, 1816; stld Lot 14, Con 1, Bathurst Twp, Lanark Co, ONT. **HCL 16, 233**.

8850 McNEE or McNAB, John. Poss from Killin, PER. To McNab Twp, Renfrew Co, ONT, 1825. **DC 3 Jan 1980**.

8851 McNEIL, Alexander, b ca 1800. To Inverness Co, NS, 1802; stld nr Port Hood. Farmer, unm. **CBC 1818**.

8852 MACNEIL, Alexander. From Is Barra, INV. To Pictou, NS, 1802; stld Mabou, Inverness Co, 1805. m (i) Ann, d/o Capt Alexander Macdonell, ch: 1. Neil; 2. Alexander; 3. Donald; 4. Anne; 5. Mary. m (ii) Sara, d/o Lauchlin MacNeil, further ch: 6. Lauchlin; 7. Michael; 8. Roderick; 9. Anne; 10. Katie. **CBC 1818; MP 766**.

8853 McNEIL, Alexander, ca 1779–8 Sep 1863. From Is Colonsay, ARL. s/o Dougald M, qv. To PEI on the *Spencer*, ex Oban, 22 Sep 1806. Discharged soldier, poss 3rd Argyll Fencible Regt. Stld Lot 65, West River, Queens Co. m Margaret McFee, qv, and had with other ch: 1. Catherine, 1813-93; 2. Margaret, 1819–1913; 3. Sarah; 4. Anne, 1823–1908; 5. Flora, ca 1827-68. **PLSN; SG xx/1 23; DC 25 Oct 1980**.

8854 McNEIL, Alexander, b ca 1778. Prob s/o John M, qv. To Judique, Inverness Co, NS, 1808. Farmer, m and ch. **CBC 1818**.

8855 MACNEIL, Alexander 'Sergeant'. From Is Barra, INV. To Mabou, Inverness Co, NS, 1808. ch: 1. Donald; 2. James; 3. John; 4. Catherine; 5. Margaret; 6. Sara. **MP 767**.

8856 McNEIL, Alexander, b ca 1806. From INV. To Lobo Twp, Middlesex Co, ONT, ca 1832. ch: 1. John; 2. Alexander; 3. James B, res Strathroy, Adelaide Twp; 4. Jessie; 5. Ann. **PCM 40**.

8857 McNEIL, Alexander. From ARL. Prob rel to John M, qv. To Ekfrid Twp, Middlesex Co, ONT, 1842. **PCM 31**.

8858 MACNEIL, Alexandrina. From Is Pabbay, off Harris, INV. d/o Roderick M, yr of St Kilda, and Christina MacLean. To Mira Valley, Cape Breton Co, NS, 1828. **DC 7 Oct 1964**.

8859 McNEIL, Allan, b 1826. From Ballymenach, Kilmory par, Is Arran, BUT. To Benjamen River, Restigouche Co, NB, <1840. **MAC 23**.

8860 McNEIL, Angus. From ARL. To Adelaide Twp, Middlesex Co, ONT, 1849. ch: 1. John; 2. Mary; 3. Janet. **PCM 28**.

8861 McNEIL, Archibald. From Knapdale, ARL. To Caradoc Twp, Middlesex Co, ONT, 1831. **PCM 35**.

8862 McNEIL, Archibald, b 1817. From Is Colonsay, ARL. To ONT, ca 1853; stld Bruce Co. Wife Janet, b 1827, with him. ch: 1. Hugh, b 1852; 2. Lachlan, b 1854; 3. John, b 1856; 4. Margaret, b 1858; 5. Donald, b 1860; 6. Isabella, b 1862; 7. Janet, b 1864; 8. Archibald, b 1866; 9. Flora, b 1868. **DC 30 Sep 1981**.

8863 McNEIL, Catherine, 1812-52. From Is Arran, BUT. To Benjamen River, Restigouche Co, NB, 1829. **MAC 23**.

8864 MACNEIL, Christina. From Is Barra, INV. d/o Neil M, qv. To Pictou Is, NS, 1802, but moved to Mabou, Inverness Co. m Donald MacLeod, qv. **MP 740, 754**.

8865 McNEIL, Daniel, b ca 1785. To Baddeck dist, Victoria Co, NS, 1817. Prob farmer; m and ch. **CBC 1818**.

8866 MACNEIL, Donald 'Og'. Prob from Is Barra, INV. To Cape George, Antigonish Co, NS, prob <1805. ch: 1. Ann; 2. Neil; 3. John; 4. Angus; 5. Hector; 6. Michael; 7. Catherine; 8. Donald. **HCA 333**.

8867 McNEIL, Donald, b ca 1772. Prob from Is Colonsay, ARL. To Charlottetown, PEI, on the *Spencer*, ex Oban, 22 Sep 1806. ch with him: 1. Malcolm, aged 5; 2. Donald, aged 2. **PLSN**.

8868 McNEIL, Donald, b ca 1799. To St Andrews dist, Cape Breton Co, NS, 1809. Became farmer. **CBC 1818**.

8869 McNEIL, Donald, b ca 1797. To Port Hood dist, Inverness Co, NS, 1810. Farmer, m and ch. **CBC 1818**.

8870 MACNEIL, Donald John. From Is Pabbay, off Harris, INV. s/o Roderick M, yr of St Kilda, and Christian MacLean. To Mira River, Cape Breton Co, NS, 1828. m Miss Campbell, ch. **DC 7 Oct 1964**.

8871 MACNEIL, Donald, called 'Domhnall a' Chaolais', 1793–1874. From Is Pabbay, off Harris, INV. s/o Roderick M, yr of St Kilda, and Christian MacLean. To Mira River, Cape Breton Co, NS, prob on the *Abercrombie*, 1828. Capt-Lt, Cape Regt; farmer and JP. m Margaret McIsaac, qv, ch: 1. Ewan; 2. Isabel; 3. Roderick, 1837–1912; 4. Margaret; 5. Catherine; 6. Donald William; 7. Alexander Farquharson; 8. Hector; 9. Merrin; 10. Mary, 1851–1946; 11. John James; 12. Kenneth Norman. **DC 7 Oct 1964**.

8872 MACNEIL, Donald. Poss from Is Barra, INV. bro/o Rory 'Ban' M, qv. To Antigonish Co, NS, poss <1830; stld Doctors Brook. **HCA 327**.

8873 McNEIL, Donald. To East Williams Twp, Middlesex Co, ONT, 1831. **PCM 44**.

8874 McNEIL, Donald. From ARL. To East Williams Twp, Middlesex Co, ONT, 1832. **PCM 43**.

8875 McNEIL, Donald. From Knapdale, ARL. To Lobo Twp, Middlesex Co, ONT, 1836. **PCM 39**.

8876 McNEIL, Donald. From ARL. To Mosa Twp, Middlesex Co, ONT, 1840. **PCM 24**.

8877 McNEIL, Donald. From North Knapdale, ARL. To Caradoc Twp, Middlesex Co, ONT, 1842. ch: 1. Donald; 2. Mary; 3. Margaret; 4. Malcolm; 5. John; 6. Nancy. **PCM 35**.

8878 McNEIL, Dougald, b 1746. Prob from Is Colonsay, ARL. To Charlottetown, PEI, on the *Spencer*, ex Oban, 22 Sep 1806. ch with him: 1. Alexander, qv; 2. Charles, aged 15; 3. Dougald, aged 12. **PLSN; DC 19 Sep 1977**.

8879 MACNEIL, Duncan. From ARL. To Aldborough Twp, Elgin Co, ONT, 1850. **PDA 68**.

8880 McNEIL, Duncan, b 1807. From Is Arran, BUT. To Benjamen River, Restigouche Co, NB, 1829. **MAC 23**.

8881 MACNEIL, Ewan A. From Is Pabbay, off Harris, INV. s/o Roderick M, yr of St Kilda, and Christian MacLean. To Mira River, Cape Breton Co, NS, 1828. Mariner, drowned in Bay Chaleur, unm. **DC 7 Oct 1964**.

8882 McNEIL, Flora, ca 1784–15 Aug 1853. From Arrocher, DNB. To ONT, poss 1819; stld Ekfrid Twp, Middlesex Co. Wife of Donald McFarlane, qv. **DC 14 Aug and 29 Oct 1979**.

8883 McNEIL, Grizel, b 1766. Prob from Is Colonsay, ARL, and poss wife of Malcolm McMillan, qv. To Charlottetown, PEI, on the *Spencer*, ex Oban, 22 Sep 1806. **PLSN**.

8884 McNEIL, Hector, b ca 1770. To St Andrews dist, Cape Breton Co, NS, 1802. Farmer, m and ch. **CBC 1818**.

8885 McNEIL, Hector, b 1779. Prob from Is Colonsay, ARL. To Charlottetown, PEI, on the *Spencer*, ex Oban, 22 Sep 1806. **PLSN**.

8886 McNEIL, Hector, b 1783. Poss s/o John B. M, qv. To St Andrews dist, Cape Breton Co, NS, 1812. Farmer; m and ch. **CBC 1818**.

8887 MACNEIL, Hector 'Mor'. From Is Barra, INV. To South East Mabou, Inverness Co, NS, 1818. m Anne MacMillan, qv, ch: 1. John; 2. Hugh; 3. William; 4. Anne; 5. Mary; 6. Catherine; 7. Sara. **MP 770**.

8888 MACNEIL, Hector 'Ban'. To Antigonish Co, NS, poss <1820; stld Doctors Brook. ch incl: 1. James; 2. John. **HCA 331**.

8889 MACNEIL, Hector, 1810–85. From Is Pabbay, off Harris, INV. s/o Norman M, qv, and Mary MacKillop, qv. To Mira River, Cape Breton Co, NS, prob on the *Abercrombie*, 1828. Farmer. m Maria Lamond, qv, ch: 1. Mary; 2. Margaret, 1844–85; 3. Marjory, 1846–1928; 4. Norman Hector, 1847–1919; 5. Neil, 1850–1902; 6. Marybelle, 1852–1937; 7. Effie, 1854–1929. **DC 7 Oct 1964**.

8890 McNEIL, Hugh, b 1787. From Is Mull, ARL. To Charlottetown, PEI, on the *Clarendon*, ex Oban, 6 Aug 1808. Labourer. **CPL**.

8891 McNEIL, Hugh, b ca 1790. Prob s/o John M, qv. To Judique, Inverness Co, NS, 1807. Farmer. **CBC 1818**.

8892 McNEIL, James, b 1796. Poss s/o John B. M, qv. To St Andrews dist, Cape Breton Co, NS, 1809. **CBC 1818**.

8893 McNEIL, James, b ca 1796. To Inverness Co, NS, 1817; stld Mabou. Fisherman. **CBC 1818**.

8894 McNEIL, Janet, b ca 1786. Prob from Is Colonsay, ARL. To Charlottetown, PEI, on the *Spencer*, ex Oban, 22 Sep 1806. **PLSN**.

8895 McNEIL, John. Officer of 82nd Regt, gr 300 acres in Pictou Co, NS, 1784. Son John seems also to have served in the 82nd, and also stld Pictou Co. **HPC App F**.

8896 McNEIL, John, ca 1748–24 Nov 1833. From Knockando, BAN. Served in 82nd Regt and was discharged at Halifax, NS, 1783. Gr land, and after a journey to SCT stld at Merigomish, Pictou Co. m Jean Grant, qv, ch: 1. James, 1781-90, b Buckie; 2. Peter, d 1801; 3. John, jr, qv. m (ii) Nancy McInnis, further ch: 4. Peter, 1825-88; 5. Margaret, unm; 6. Alexander, unm; 7. Robert, 1831-90, merchant; 8. Amelia, 1834-85. **Rathven OPR 164/1; DC 18 Jul 1981**.

8897 McNEIL, John, jr, ca 1784–25 Aug 1835. From Buckie, BAN. s/o John M, qv, and Jean Grant, qv. To Merigomish, Pictou Co, NS, prob 1788. Farmer. m Margaret Robertson, qv, ch: 1. James, 1815-49, stld NB; 2. Jean Grant, 1816–1907; 3. John, 1819-46, d Campbellton, Restigouche Co, NB; 4. Mary; 5. Christina. **DC 14 Nov 1981**.

8898 MACNEIL, John 'Breac'. From Knoydart, INV. To Antigonish Co, NS, 1788. m Margaret, d/o Donald MacDonald, ch: 1. Catherine, b Gulf Shore; 2. Stephen;

3. Angus; 4. Donald; 5. Hector; 6. John; 7. Alexander; 8. Michael; 9. Mary. **HCA 329**.

8899 McNEIL, John, b ca 1781. To Charlottetown, PEI, on the *Rambler*, ex Tobermory, 20 Jun 1806. **PLR**.

8900 McNEIL, John, b 1755. To Judique, Inverness Co, NS, 1808. Farmer. Son John. **CBC 1818**.

8901 McNEIL, John, b ca 1791. From Is Mull, ARL. To Charlottetown, PEI, on the *Clarendon*, ex Oban, 6 Aug 1808. Labourer. **CPL**.

8902 McNEIL, John, b ca 1793. To St Andrews dist, Cape Breton Co, NS, ca 1809. Farmer. **CBC 1818**.

8903 McNEIL, John, b ca 1795. To St Andrews dist, Cape Breton Co, NS, 1809. Farmer. **CBC 1818**.

8904 McNEIL, John, b 1786. To St Andrews dist, Cape Breton Co, NS, 1810. Farmer, m and ch. **CBC 1818**.

8905 McNEIL, John, b ca 1789. To Inverness Co, NS, 1817; stld nr Port Hood. Farmer. **CBC 1818**.

8906 McNEIL, John, b ca 1795. To Port Hood dist, Inverness Co, NS, 1817. Farmer, m and ch. **CBC 1818**.

8907 MACNEIL, John. bro/o Murdoch M, qv. To Antigonish Co, NS, prob <1820. ch incl: 1. John; 2. Charles; 3. Joseph; 4. Alexander. **HCA 332**.

8908 McNEIL, John, b 1822. From Is Arran, BUT. To Benjamen River, Restigouche Co, NB, 1829. **MAC 23**.

8909 MACNEIL, John. Prob from INV. To Antigonish Co, NS, poss <1840; stld St Peters. Farmer. ch: 1. Donald, went to MI, USA; 2. Peter; 3. Michael, dy; 4. Archibald, went to Glengarry Co, ONT; 5. Neil; 6. Mary; 7. Janet; 8. Mrs John Fraser; 9. Mary. **HCA 331**.

8910 McNEIL, John. From Knapdale, ARL. Prob rel to Alexander M, qv. To Ekfrid Twp, Middlesex Co, ONT, 1842. **PCM 31**.

8911 McNEIL, John B, b 1762. Prob rel to Hector M, qv. To St Andrews dist, Cape Breton Co, NS, 1809. Farmer. **CBC 1818**.

8912 MACNEIL, Malcolm 'Dubh'. To Halifax, NS, and stld Arisaig, Antigonish Co. Discharged soldier, res Georgeville, 1779. m Janet MacDonald, Widow MacLean, ch: 1. Rory; 2. John; 3. Lachlan; 4. Robert; 5. Sarah; 6. Jessie. **HCA 332, 334**.

8913 McNEIL, Malcolm, b ca 1755. Prob from Is Colonsay, ARL. To Charlottetown, PEI, on the *Spencer*, ex Oban, 22 Sep 1806. Son John, aged 14, with him. **PLSN**.

8914 McNEIL, Malcolm. From ARL. To Metcalfe Twp, Middlesex Co, ONT, 1840. Son Rev Dugald. **PCM 26**.

8915 McNEIL, Malcolm. From ARL. To Adelaide Twp, Middlesex Co, ONT, 1849; stld later at Brooke. **PCM 28**.

8916 McNEIL, Margaret, b ca 1785. To Charlottetown, PEI, on the *Spencer*, ex Oban, 22 Sep 1806. **PLSN**.

8917 McNEIL, Margaret, 1817-56. From Is Arran, BUT. To Benjamen River, Restigouche Co, NB, 1829. **MAC 23**.

8918 McNEIL, Mary, b ca 1766. Prob from Is Colonsay, ARL. To Charlottetown, PEI, on the *Spencer*,

ex Oban, 22 Sep 1806. Poss wife of Duncan McDuff(ie), qv. **PLSN**.

8919 MACNEIL, Mary. From Is Pabbay, off Harris, INV. d/o Roderick M, yr of St Kilda, and Christian MacLean. To Mira River, Cape Breton Co, NS, 1828. m Dr Jeans, of the Associated Mining Co, ch. **DC 7 Oct 1964**.

8920 McNEIL, Mary, 1849–1927. To Hamilton, ONT. m John Turner, qv. **Ts Mt Albion**.

8921 McNEIL, Murdoch, b 1783. To St Andrews dist, Cape Breton Co, NS, ca 1817. Farmer, m and ch. **CBC 1818**.

8922 MACNEIL, Murdoch. bro/o John M, qv. To Antigonish Co, NS, prob <1820; stld Clydesdale. Son Alexander. **HCA 332**.

8923 McNEIL, Nancy or Ann, b 1788. From North Knapdale, ARL. To Aldborough Twp, Elgin Co, ONT, 1819. Wife of Duncan Paterson, qv. **DC 23 Nov 1981**.

8924 MACNEIL, Neil, d 1812. From Is Barra, INV. To Pictou Co, NS, 1802; stld Mabou, Inverness Co, 1805. Farmer. ch: 1. Roderick, qv; 2. Alexander, qv; 3. Christina, qv. **MP 754**.

8925 McNEIL, Neil, b ca 1770. From Is Mull, ARL. To Charlottetown, PEI, on the *Clarendon*, ex Oban, 6 Aug 1808. Labourer. Wife Ann, aged 38, with him, and ch: 1. Torquil, aged 13; 2. Mary, aged 10; 3. John, aged 8; 4. Duncan, aged 6; 5. Catherine, aged 4. **CPL**.

8926 McNEIL, Neil, b 1801. Poss rel to Hector M, qv. To St Andrews dist, Cape Breton Co, NS, 1809. **CBC 1818**.

8927 McNEIL, Neil, b 1778. To St Andrews dist, Cape Breton Co, NS, ca 1810. Farmer. **CBC 1818**.

8928 McNEIL, Neil. From Is Barra, ARL. To Grand Narrows, Cape Breton Is, NS, <1840. Dau Ann. **HNS iii 319**.

8929 MACNEIL, Norman, called 'Tharmaid Hirt'. From Is Pabbay, off Harris, INV. s/o William M, tacksman of St Kilda. To Cape Breton Co, NS, 1828. Farmer, gr 250 acres. m Mary MacKillop, qv, ch: 1. Hector, qv; 2. Mary Louise, res Victoria Co, ONT. **DC 7 Oct 1964**.

8930 McNEIL, Peter. From ARL. To Mosa Twp, Middlesex Co, ONT, 1832. **PCM 24**.

8931 McNEIL, Peter. From Crinan, ARL. To Aldborough Twp, Elgin Co, ONT, prob <1860. **PDA 78**.

8932 MACNEIL, Roderick. From Is Barra, INV. s/o Neil M, qv. To Pictou Is, NS, 1802, but stld Mabou, Inverness Co, 1805. m Catherine, d/o John Campbell, Cape George, and Janet Livingstone, ch: 1. Neil; 2. Donald; 3. Malcolm; 4. John; 5. Lauchlin; 6. Alexander; 7. Janet; 8. Catherine; 9. Margaret; 10. Flora. **HNS iii 328; MP 754**.

8933 McNEIL, Rory, b ca 1793. To Inverness Co, NS, 1802; stld Mabou. Farmer. **CBC 1818**.

8934 MACNEIL, Rory 'Ban'. Poss from Is Barra, INV. bro/o Donald M, qv. To Antigonish Co, NS, poss <1830; stld nr Frasers Grant. ch: 1. Capt Donald; 2. John, blacksmith; 3. Angus; 4. Capt Alexander; 5. Mrs Colin Chisholm; 6. Mrs Alexander MacDonald; 7. Mrs John Chisholm. **HCA 216, 327**.

8935 McNEILL, Donald. Prob from ARL. Neph of James Stewart, Auchnaba. To Sunnidale, Simcoe Co, ONT, <1855. **SH**.

8936 McNEILL, William Dunn. From Edinburgh. s/o Alexander Kennedy M, solicitor. Educ Edinburgh High School. To Plantagenet, Prescott Co, ONT, ca 1856; later in Montreal, QUE. Treasury official. ch. **HSC 74**.

McNEISH. See also McNISH.

8937 McNEISH, Alexander, b 1820. From Lamlash, Is Arran, BUT. To Dalhousie, NB, 1839. **MAC 24**.

8938 McNEISH, Daniel, 1793–1858. From Kings Corse, Kilbride par, Is Arran, BUT. To Pointe-à-la-Garde, Bonaventure Co, QUE, 1831. m Margaret Hamilton, qv, ch: 1. Catherine, b 1824; 2. Thomas, 1827-99; 3. Elizabeth, b 1830. **MAC 24**.

8939 McNEISH, John, 20 Feb 1802–11 Sep 1890. From Kilmory par, Is Arran, BUT. s/o John M. and Agnes McDougall. To Point La Nim, Restigouche Co, NB, 1829. Farmer. m Mary Kerr, qv, ch: 1. John, jr, qv; 2. William, b 27 Apr 1829; 3. Mary, b 1 Aug 1832; 4. Thomas, b 28 May 1834; 5. Alexander, b 19 Apr 1836; 6. Ann, b 1 Jan 1840; 7. Daniel, b 23 Aug 1842; 8. Nancy, b 1 Jan 1846. **Kilmory OPR 554/2; DC 26 Nov 1967**.

8940 McNEISH, John, jr, 1827–1911. From Kilmory par, Is Arran, BUT. s/o John M, qv, and Mary Kerr, qv. To Point La Nim, Restigouche Co, NB, 1829. Farmer. m Ann McDonald, ch: 1. Alexander, 1855-82, unm; 2. Thomas, 1857-82, unm; 3. John, 1860-69; 4. Angus, 1864–1940; 5. Annie, 1868–1954. **DC 26 Nov 1967**.

8941 McNEVIN, —. To Sydney, Cape Breton Co, NS, <1810, and d at Barrie, Simcoe Co, ONT. Discharged soldier. Dau Isabella. **HNS iii 71**.

8942 McNICHOL, Jeanette. From PER. To Brant Co, ONT, 1823. Wife of John McIntyre, qv. **DC 23 Sep 1980**.

8943 McNICHOL, John. Prob from ARL. To Delaware Twp, Middlesex Co, ONT, ca 1852. **PCM 57**.

8944 McNICHOL, Malcolm, ca 1816–5 Feb 1901. Poss from ARL. To Ethel, Grey Twp, Huron Co, ONT, and stld Lot 26, Con 4. m Margaret McEachin, qv, ch: 1. Annie, b 1864; 2. Roderick; 3. Donald. **DC 12 Nov 1979**.

8945 McNICHOLL, Donald. From ARL. To Mosa Twp, Middlesex Co, ONT, 1830. **PCM 24**.

8946 McNICOL, Alexander, b 1823. To St Gabriel de Valcartier, QUE, prob <1855. **Census 1861**.

8947 McNICOL, Donald, b 1791. To St Gabriel de Valcartier, QUE, prob <1855. **Census 1861**.

8948 McNICOL, Donald, b 1787. From Knockankelly, Kilbride par, Is Arran, BUT. To Blackland, Restigouche Co, NB, 1829. m Helen Kennedy, qv, ch: 1. John, b 1818; 2. Mary; 3. James, b 1822; 4. Elizabeth, b 1824; 5. Helen, qv. **MAC 26**.

8949 McNICOL, Helen, 1828–1909. From Knockankelly, Kilbride par, Is Arran, BUT. d/o Donald M, qv, and Helen Kennedy, qv. To Blackland, Restigouche Co, NB, 1829. m William Archibald, qv. **MAC 26; DC 1 Oct 1979**.

8950 McNICOL, John, 1767–1849. From ARL. To QUE on the *Commerce*, ex Greenock, Jun 1820; stld Lot 11, Con 1, Dalhousie Twp, Lanark Co, ONT. Farmer. m Flora Munroe, qv, ch: 1. John; 2. Colin; 3. Duncan; 4. Donald; 5. Archibald; 6. Nicol; 7. Mary, qv; 8. Alexander. **HCL 67, 238; DC 2 Nov 1979**.

8951 McNICOL, John, 5 Aug 1807–20 Nov 1893. From Barachastian, Glenurchy, ARL. s/o Malcolm M. and Catherine McLennan. To Aldborough Twp, Elgin Co, ONT, <1847. Farmer. m (i) 1854, Margaret McIntyre, 1822-55, d/o Duncan M, qv, and Barbara M, qv, ch: 1. Malcolm McIntyre, 1855–1926. m (ii) 1860, Margaret McDiarmid, further ch: 1. John, 1860-61; 2. James, 1862–1931; 3. John, 1864–1928; 4. Peter Donald, b 1866. **DC 23 Nov 1981**.

8952 McNICOL, Mary, 1813-61. From ARL. d/o John M, qv, and Flora Munroe, qv. To Dalhousie Twp, Lanark Co, ONT, 1820. m John McDougall, ch: 1. Duncan, d 1917; 2. Ellen; 3. Elizabeth; 4. Janet; 5. Agnes, 1842-62. **DC 2 Nov 1979**.

8953 McNICOL, Mary, b 1775. From Auchenchairn, Kilbride, Is Arran, BUT. To Jacquet River, Restigouche Co, NB, 1832. Wife of John Willie MacMillan, qv. **MAC 22**.

8954 McNIDEN, James. From LKS. To QUE on the *Prompt*, ex Greenock, 4 Jul 1820; stld Lanark Co, ONT. **HCL 238**.

8955 McNIDER, Ann. From AYR. sis/o William M, tailor in Ayr. To QUE <1797. **DC 2 Aug 1982**.

8956 McNIDER, John. From AYR. bro/o Ann M, qv, and Matthew M, qv. To QUE <1797. **DC 2 Aug 1982**.

8957 McNIDER, Margaret. From Kilmarnock, AYR. d/o William M. and Ann Vallance. To QUE <1797. **DC 2 Aug 1982**.

8958 McNIDER, Matthew. From AYR. bro/o Ann M, qv, and John M, qv. To QUE <1797. Merchant. **DC 2 Aug 1982**.

McNIE. See also McNEE.

8959 McNIE, John. From Balquhidder, PER. To Montreal, QUE, on the *Sophia*, ex Greenock, 26 Jul 1818; stld prob Beckwith Twp, Lanark Co, ONT. Wife Janet with him, and ch: 1. Duncan, aged 10 ½; 2. Isabella, aged 9; 3. Mary, aged 7; 4. Catherine, aged 5; 5. Malcolm, aged 2. **SPL**.

8960 McNIE, John. From Comrie, PER. To Montreal, QUE, on the *Curlew*, ex Greenock, 21 Jul 1818; stld prob Beckwith Twp, Lanark Co, ONT. Wife Janet with him, and ch: 1. Donald, aged 4; 2. Janet, aged 1. **BCL**.

McNISH. See also McNEISH.

8961 MACNISH, Rev Neil, d 11 May 1905. From ARL. Educ Univ of Edinburgh, and grad BD, 1867. Studied also at Glasgow and Toronto. Adm min of Cornwall, ONT, 1868. LLD, Toronto, 1874. Gaelic scholar. **FES vii 644**.

8962 McNIVEN, Archibald, d ca 1830. From Comrie, PER. bro/o William M, qv. To Otonabee Twp, Peterborough Co, ONT, 1829. **DC 13 Sep 1982 and 3 Apr 1983**.

8963 McNIVEN, Colin, 1763–1823. From INV. To Cape Breton Is, NS, ca 1822, and d Bras d'Or Lake. m Flora

Campbell, qv, ch: 1. Colin, d 1823; 2. Julia, qv;
3. Katherine, qv; 4. Jessie, qv; 5. James, d 1835, unm;
6. Archibald, d 1861, Chicago, IL, USA; 7. Malcolm.
DC 23 Feb 1980.

8964 McNIVEN, Donald. From Grimsary, Is Coll, ARL.
To PEI ca 1820. m Catherine McLean, ch.
SG xxx/2 68.

8965 McNIVEN, Hope, 19 Mar 1803–26 Apr 1888.
s/o John M, flesher-burgess of Glasgow, and Susanna
Campbell. To Ingersoll Village, Oxford Co, ONT, <1850.
Poet. m (i) Agnes Woodrow, qv, ch: 1. John Hope;
2. James Woodrow; 3. Susan; 4. Arabella. m (ii)
Catherine Fraser, qv. **DC 22 Jun 1968 and 5 Sep 1979**.

8966 MACNIVEN, Isabella, b ca 1805. From Dunblane,
PER. To ONT, arr Jul 1849. m Jan 1827, John Stewart,
qv. **DC 31 Aug 1979**.

8967 MACNIVEN, Jane, 1808-95. From Is South Uist,
INV. To Cape Breton Co, NS, 1823. Wife of John
MacDonald, qv. **DC 23 Feb 1980**.

8968 McNIVEN, Jessie. From INV. d/o Colin M, qv,
and Flora Campbell, qv. To Cape Breton Is, NS; stld
McNiven Is, Whycocomagh, Inverness Co. m Angus
McDonald. **DC 23 Feb 1980**.

8969 McNIVEN, Julia, b 1805. From INV. d/o Colin M,
qv, and Flora Campbell, qv. To Inverness Co, NS, 1822;
stld 'McNiven Is', Whycocomagh. m Dr John Noble,
qv. **DC 23 Feb 1980**.

8970 McNIVEN, Katherine. From INV. d/o Colin M, qv,
and Flora Campbell, qv. To Inverness Co, NS, 1822; stld
'McNiven Is', Whycocomagh. m Alexander McDonald.
DC 23 Feb 1980.

8971 McNIVEN, Mary, b ca 1799. From Scour,
Kilninian and Kilmore par, Is Mull, ARL. To ONT <1848.
Wife of Neil Beaton, qv, m 18 Jun 1828. **DC 25 Feb
1976**.

8972 McNIVEN, William. From Comrie, PER.
bro/o Archibald M, qv. To Otonabee Twp,
Peterborough Co, ONT, 1829. Wife and ch with him.
DC 13 Sep 1982.

8973 McNORTON, Duncan. Prob from INV. Rel to
William M, qv. To London Twp, Middlesex Co, ONT,
1820. Pioneer settler. **PCM 50**.

8974 McNORTON, William. Prob from INV. Rel to
Duncan M, qv. To London Twp, Middlesex Co, ONT,
1820. Pioneer settler. **PCM 50**.

8975 McOWEN, Catherine. From PER. Prob rel to
Peter M, qv. To CAN, poss QUE, <1848. **SH**.

8976 McOWEN, Peter. From PER. Prob rel to
Catherine M, qv. To CAN <1855. m John Oswald. **SH**.

McPHADEN. See also McFADYEN.

8977 McPHADEN, Christian, b ca 1779. Prob from Is
Colonsay, ARL. To Charlottetown, PEI, on the *Spencer*,
ex Oban, arr 22 Sep 1806. **PLSN**.

8978 McPHADEN, Donald, b 1774. From Is Rum,
ARL. To Gut of Canso, Cape Breton, NS, on the *Saint
Lawrence*, ex Tobermory, 11 Jul 1828. Wife Flora, aged
50, with him, and ch: 1. Hector, aged 19; 2. Ann, aged
13; 3. Donald, aged 10; 4. John, aged 8; 5. Angus,
aged 6. **SLL**.

8979 McPHADEN, Mary, 1824–1909. From Is Islay,
ARL. To Oro Twp, Simcoe Co, ONT, <1842, when
m Peter Smith, qv. **DC 21 Mar 1980**.

8980 McPHAIL, Alexander. From ARL. To Ramsay
Twp, Lanark Co, ONT, ca 1822; stld Lot 20, Con 11.
HCL 88.

8981 MACPHAIL, Alexander, b 14 Mar 1831. From
Kilmartin, ARL. s/o Dougald M, qv, and Christine
MacCallum, qv. To Beverley Twp, Wentworth Co, ONT.
1847; later to Proton Twp, Grey Co. m (i) Miss Fettes;
(ii) Jean Jack, ch. **DC 11 Nov 1981**.

8982 McPHAIL, Alexander, 1831–1915. From ARL.
s/o William M, qv, and Catherine Johnston, qv. To
Nassagaweya Twp, Halton Co, ONT, <1849. Cartwright.
m (i) Caroline Hirst, 1835-68, no ch. m (ii) Elizabeth
Warren, 1848–1926, ch: 1. William Hirst, b 1879;
2. Alexander Lawton, 1881–1963; 3. Nancy Catherine,
1883–1939; 4. Francis Herbert, 1885–1938; 5. Mary
Maud, 1880-94. **DC 9 Nov 1981**.

8983 MACPHAIL, Ann, b 7 Mar 1823. From Kilmartin,
ARL. d/o Dougald M, qv, and Christine MacCallum, qv.
To Beverley Twp, Wentworth Co, ONT, 1847. m Duncan
Gillies, ch. **DC 11 Nov 1981**.

8984 McPHAIL, Annabella, b 1807. From Is Islay,
ARL. To Oro Twp, Simcoe Co, ONT, ca 1833. Wife of
Angus Galbraith, qv. **DC 9 Nov 1980**.

8985 McPHAIL, Archibald. From PER. To Carleton
Place, Lanark Co, ONT, 1828. Son John. **DC 4 Mar
1965**.

8986 McPHAIL, Archibald, 1812–1905. From ARL.
s/o William M, qv, and Catherine Johnston, qv. To
Nassagaweya Twp, Halton Co, ONT, <1849. Farmer.
m Margaret Campbell, qv, ch: 1. Katherine, b 1849;
2. Peter, b 1851; 3. William, 1853–1933; 4. John,
1855–1921; 5. Duncan, 1857-63; 6. Mary Hirst,
b 1863. **DC 9 Nov 1981**.

8987 McPHAIL, Catherine, ca 1811–19 Apr 1876. From
Kenmore, PER. To Esquesing Twp, Halton Co, ONT, prob
<1850. Wife of John McPherson, qv. **EPE 74**.

8988 McPHAIL, Colin, 1828–1906. From ARL.
s/o William M, qv, and Catherine Johnston, qv. To
Nassagaweya Twp, Halton Co, ONT, <1849. m Nancy
Mitchell, 1830–1911, ch: 1. William, 1855-85;
2. Alexander, 1857–1934; 3. Neil, b 1858;
4. Catherine, 1861–1932; 5. Nancy, 1861–1941;
6. Janet, 1863–1950; 7. Margaret, 1865–1917;
8. Charles John, 1868–1951; 9. Caroline, 1870–1947;
10. Peter Reid, 1872–1942; 11. Euphemia Jane,
1874–1969. **DC 9 Nov 1981**.

8989 MACPHAIL, Dougald, 1796–1887. From
Carnassarie, Kilmartin, ARL. To Beverley Twp,
Wentworth Co, ONT, 1847; Lot 30, Con 9. Farmer.
m Christine MacCallum, qv, ch: 1. Ann, qv; 2. Archie,
d inf; 3. Lily; 4. Sara, 1829–1918; 5. Alexander, qv;
6. John, qv; 7. Margaret, d inf; 8. Margaret; 9. Archie,
d inf; 10. Mary; 11. Archie, b 1843; 12. Carmel,
b 1846. **DC 11 Nov 1981**.

8990 MACPHAIL, Flora, b 1827. From ARL. To
Toronto, ONT, ca 1854. m at Glasgow, 16 May 1853,
David Wilkinson, qv. **DC 8 Mar 1974**.

8991 McPHAIL, John, 20 Nov 1799–29 Jan 1860.

From ARL, poss Appin. To Wooler, Northumberland Co,
ONT, 1821. m 23 Jan 1821, Margaret MacIntyre, qv.
DC 20 Nov 1960.

8992   McPHAIL, John, b 1816. From ARL. s/o William
M, qv, and Catherine Johnston, qv. To Nassagaweya
Twp, Halton Co, ONT, <1849; stld Erin Twp, Wellington
Co. Farmer. m Mary Campbell, qv, ch: 1. John, b 1843;
2. William, b 1847; 3. Alexander, b 1849; 4. Mary Ann,
b 1855; 5. Neil. **DC 9 Nov 1981**.

8993   MACPHAIL, William, 1800-52. From Inverurie,
ABD. To Pictou Co, NS, 1832; later to Belle Creek,
Queens Co, PEI. Schoolmaster. m Mary MacPherson,
qv. Son William, jr, qv. **HP 38**.

8994   MACPHAIL, William, jr, 1830–1905. From
Inverurie, ABD. s/o William M, qv, and Mary
MacPherson, qv. To Pictou Co, NS, 1832; later to Belle
Creek, Queens Co, PEI. Teacher at Uigg, 1862-67, and
farmer. m Catherine Moore, 1834–1920, d/o Findlay
Smith, ch: 1. John Andrew, b 1864; 2. Isabel, b 1866;
3. Janetta Clark, b 1868; 4. James Alexander, b 1869;
5. William Matheson, b 1872; 6. John Goodwill, b 1877;
7. Margaret; 8. Catherine. **HP 39**.

8995   McPHAIL, William, 1788–29 Aug 1875. From
ARL. To Nassagaweya Twp, Halton Co, ONT, <1849.
Farmer. m Catherine Johnston, qv, ch: 1. Archibald, qv;
2. John, qv; 3. Ann or Nancy; 4. Neil; 5. Colin, qv;
6. Alexander, qv. **DC 9 Nov 1981**.

8996   McPHAILL, Archibald. To London, Westminster
Twp, Middlesex Co, ONT, prob <1840. **PCM 55**.

8997   McPHAILL, Mary. Prob from Is Mull, ARL. To
Queens Co, PEI, 1808. Wife of Roderick Campbell, qv.
DC 11 Apr 1981.

8998   McPHARDON, Alexander, b ca 1778. To
Charlottetown, PEI, on the *Humphreys*, ex Tobermory,
14 Jul 1806. Wife Elizabeth, aged 24, with him, and s
Angus, aged 2. **PLH**.

8999   McPHEDERAN, John. To Montreal, QUE, on the
Royal George, ex Greenock, Jan 1827; stld Sarnia,
Lambton Co, ONT. Wife with him. **DC 19 Nov 1978**.

McPHEE. See also McFEE and McFIE.

9000   McPHEE, Alexander. From Aberchalder, INV. To
Montreal, QUE, ex Fort William, 3 Jul 1802; stld E ONT.
Wife was prob Catherine McAlpin, qv. Son Alexander.
MCM 1/4 26.

9001   McPHEE, Angus. From Crieff, PER. To QUE, ex
Fort William, arr Sep 1802; stld E ONT. Wife and 3 ch
with him. **MCM 1/4 25**.

9002   MACPHEE, Angus, b 1815. From Uskavagh, Is
Benbecula, INV. s/o John M. and Mary Morrison. To
Pictou, NS, on the *Lulan*, ex Glasgow, 17 Aug 1848.
Wife Marion MacDonald, qv, with him, and ch:
1. Ronald, b 1841; 2. Angus, b 1843; 3. Christina,
b 1846. **DC 12 Jul 1979**.

9003   McPHEE, Angus. From Is South Uist, INV. To
West Williams Twp, Middlesex Co, ONT, 1849.
PCM 48.

9004   McPHEE, Annie. From Aberchalder, INV. Prob
d/o Alexander M. To Montreal, QUE, ex Fort William,
arr Sep 1802; stld E ONT. **MCM 1/4 23**.

9005   MACPHEE, Archibald. From Is South Uist, INV.
bro/o Neil M, qv. To PEI, but moved ca 1809 to Mabou
Coal Mines, Inverness Co, NS. m Margaret Cameron,
qv, ch: 1. Angus; 2. Donald; 3. Angus 'Og';
4. Catherine; 5. Mary. **MP 778**.

9006   McPHEE, Archibald. Prob from Is Islay, ARL.
s/o Neil M. and Martha Mackenzie. To ONT, <1850;
moved to ALB, 1892, and res nr Edmonton. m Ann
Reid, qv. **DC 1 Dec 1980**.

9007   McPHEE, Archibald. From Is South Uist, INV. To
East Williams Twp, Middlesex Co, ONT, prob 1849.
PCM 44.

9008   McPHEE, Donald. From Aberchalder, INV. To
Montreal, QUE, ex Fort William, arr Sep 1802; stld E
ONT. Wife with him. **MCM 1/4 23**.

9009   MACPHEE, Donald. Poss from Is Skye, INV. To
Queens Co, PEI, <1811, when a petitioner for Dr
MacAulay. **HP 73**.

9010   McPHEE, Donald, b ca 1775. From Ardgour,
ARL. To QUE, summer 1815; ex Greenock; stld prob
Lanark Co, ONT. Wright and labourer. Wife Catherine
McLean, qv, with him, and 6 ch. **SEC 6**.

9011   McPHEE, Donald. From Is South Uist, INV. To
West Williams Twp, Middlesex Co, ONT, 1849.
PCM 47.

9012   MACPHEE, Dougal, ca 1749–1834. Born Loch
Arkaig, INV. To NB, 1803; moved to Upper South River,
Antigonish Co, NS, 1808. ch: 1. Donald, sergeant,
79th Regt, emig 1826; 2. Allan. **HCA 337**.

9013   McPHEE, Eliza. From INV. To Kenyon Twp,
Glengarry Co, ONT, <1830. Wife of James 'Stone'
Macdonell, qv. **DC 10 Aug 1968**.

9014   MACPHEE, Elizabeth. From Is Skye, INV. To
Baddeck River, Victoria Co, NS, ca 1841. m Bannatyne
MacAskill, qv. **HNS iii 336**.

9015   McPHEE, Hugh, b ca 1770. Prob from Is Mull,
ARL. To Charlottetown, PEI, on the *Rambler*, ex
Tobermory, 20 Jun 1806. **PLR**.

9016   MACPHEE, Hugh. From Lochaber, INV. To NB,
1808; moved to Avondale, Antigonish Co, NS. ch:
1. John; 2. Hugh; 3. Allan; 4. Alexander; 5. Margaret;
6. Christine; 7. Isabel; 8. Janet; 9. Mary. **HCA 337**.

9017   McPHEE, Hugh. From Is South Uist, INV. To
West Williams Twp, Middlesex Co, ONT, 1849.
PCM 48.

9018   McPHEE, Isobel. From Fort Augustus, INV. To
QUE, ex Greenock, summer 1815; stld prob Lanark Co,
ONT. Wife of Duncan McDonell, qv. **SEC 6**.

9019   MACPHEE, John 'Gibralter'. From Glenelg, INV.
To QUE, 1796; stld Lot 30, Con 6, Lochiel Twp,
Glengarry Co, ONT. **MG 211**.

9020   McPHEE, John, ca 1742–3 Jun 1821. To NS,
prob <1800. Cooper. **NSS No 2355**.

9021   McPHEE, John, b 1773. Prob from Is Mull, ARL.
To Charlottetown, PEI, on the *Rambler*, ex Tobermory,
arr 20 Jun 1806. **PLR**.

9022   McPHEE, John, 1770–9 Aug 1838. From
Lochaber, INV. To Hemmingford, Huntingdon Co, QUE,

Jun 1821. Farmer. m Catherine McNaughton, qv, ch:
1. Alexander, b 1801; 2. Donald; 3. Samantha;
4. Duncan, 1804-20; 5. Jane; 6. John; 7. Finlay, d inf;
8. Mary; 9. Hugh, went to AUS; 10. Finlay; 11. Coll;
12. Malcolm; 13-14. Charles and Peter, twins.
DC 1 Aug 1979.

9023 McPHEE, John. From Is South Uist, INV. To West
Williams Twp, Middlesex Co, ONT, 1849; stld Con 12.
PCM 47.

9024 McPHEE, John. From Is South Uist, INV. To West
Williams Twp, Middlesex Co, ONT, 1849; stld Con 14.
PCM 48.

9025 McPHEE, Marcella, ca 1824–11 Jul 1912. Prob
from Is Skye, INV. To Inverness Co, NS. Wife of Ronald
MacDonald, qv.   **DC 22 Jun 1979**.

9026 McPHEE, Margaret. From Aberchalder, INV. Poss
d/o Alexander M. To Montreal, QUE, ex Fort William, arr
Sep 1802; stld poss Finch Twp, Stormont Co, ONT.
MCM 1/4 23.

9027 McPHEE, Margaret, ca 1734–5 Jun 1837. From
North Uist, INV. To Orwell Bay, PEI, prob on the *Polly*,
arr 7 Aug 1803. Wife of Angus Beaton, qv.   **DC 9 Oct
1980**.

9028 MACPHEE, Margaret. From Is Skye, INV.
d/o Donald M. To Charlottetown, PEI, on the *Mary
Kennedy*, arr 1 Jun 1829; stld Uigg, Queens Co. Wife of
Norman MacLeod, qv.   **SPI 159**.

9029 McPHEE, Mary. From Aberchalder, INV. Poss
d/o Alexander M. To Montreal, QUE, ex Fort William,
arr Sep 1802; stld E ONT.   **MCM 1/4 23**.

9030 MACPHEE, Neil. From Is South Uist, INV.
bro/o Archibald M, qv. To PEI, but moved to Mabou
Coal Mines, Inverness Co, NS, ca 1809. m Mary
MacDonald, qv, ch: 1. Donald; 2. Angus; 3. John;
4. Angus 'Og'; 5. Mary; 6. Euphemia; 7. Matilda;
8. Mary; 9. Margaret.   **MP 773**.

9031 McPHEE, Sarah, b ca 1794. Prob rel to Hugh M,
qv. To Charlottetown, PEI, on the *Rambler*, ex
Tobermory, 20 Jun 1806.   **PLR**.

9032 McPHEE, William, b 1 Feb 1770. From Easter
Bunloit, Glen Urquhart, INV. To NS, <1780. Tailor.
m, prob at Newport, Hants Co, 3 Nov 1791, Margaret
Cochrane.   **NSN 19/2**.

9033 McPHERSON, Adam, b 18 Jun 1815. From
Portsoy, BAN. s/o William M. and Elspet Duff. To ONT,
1836.   **LDW 21 Sep 1971**.

9034 MACPHERSON, Alexander 'Mor'. b Is Eigg, INV.
s/o John M, sometime in Knoydart, and Mary
MacDonald. To Antigonish Co, NS, <1810. m Catherine
Gillis, qv, ch: 1. James, res Cape George; 2. Martin, res
Broad Cove; 3. John, res Broad Cove; 4. Alexander, res
Cape George; 5. Mary; 6. Ann.   **HCA 343**.

9035 McPHERSON, Alexander, b ca 1806. From
Miltown of Muinas, NAI. s/o James M, qv, and Ann
Rose, qv. To Restigouche Co, NB, 1819; stld Charlo.
Farmer and officer of militia. m 1834, Jane McIntosh,
ch: 1. Alexander; 2. James; 3. David; 4. Helen.
DC 7 Feb 1981.

9036 McPHERSON, Alexander, d 30 Aug 1862. From
Blairdrummond, STI. s/o John M, qv, and Christine

Fisher, qv. To Oro Twp, Simcoe Co, ONT, 1832.
m Christine McLeod, qv.   **DC 18 Nov 1981**.

9037 McPHERSON, Alexander, b 12 May 1807. From
Portsoy, BAN. s/o William M. and Elspet Duff. To
Stanstead, QUE, 1836, and stld Georgeville, 1843.
LDW 21 Sep 1971.

9038 McPHERSON, Alexander, b 20 Aug 1836. From
Is Skye, INV. To NS, 1841; stld Baddeck, Victoria Co.
Soldiered in American Civil War and discharged 1863;
miner, Glace Bay, later farmer, Baddeck. m Elizabeth,
d/o John McLean and Elizabeth Campbell, 1871, ch:
1. William; 2. Beatrice; 3. Charles; 4. Edward;
5. Everett; 6. Gordon; 7. Alexander; 8. Donald John;
9. Mary; 10. Elizabeth.   **HNS iii 517**.

9039 MACPHERSON, Alexander, 1816-72. From
Inverkip, RFW. s/o Robert M. in Bogside, and Eliza
Holm. To Toronto, ONT.   **Ts Inverkip**.

9040 McPHERSON, Allan. From Appin, ARL. To Ekfrid
Twp, Middlesex Co, ONT, ca 1850; later to Plympton
Twp, Lambton Co.   **PCM 31**.

9041 MACPHERSON, Andrew, d 16 Aug 1847. To CAN
<1807, and served with HBCo. d Montreal, QUE.
DGH 23 Sep 1947.

9042 McPHERSON, Andrew. From Badenoch, INV. To
Eldon Twp, Victoria Co, ONT, ca 1825. Pioneer settler.
DC 21 Mar 1980.

9043 McPHERSON, Angus. Prob from INV. To
Antigonish Co, NS, poss <1800; stld Moidart. Pioneer
settler.   **HCA 13**.

9044 MACPHERSON, Angus. Prob from INV. s/o John
M. To Antigonish Co, NS, ca 1801. m Isobella
MacFarlane, ch: 1. John; 2. Donald; 3. Flora,
4. Catherine.   **HCA 342**.

9045 McPHERSON, Angus, 1755–1804. Prob from
INV. To QUE on the *Oughton*, arr Jul 1804; stld Baldoon,
Dover Twp, Kent Co, ONT. Farmer. Wife Christy with
him, and ch: 1. Alexander, b 1785; 2. Donald, b 1787;
3. Mary, b 1795; 4. Dougald, b 1799.   **UCM 267, 302;
DC 4 Oct 1979**.

9046 MACPHERSON, Angus. Prob from INV.
bro/o Dougald M, qv. To Antigonish Co, NS, poss
<1820; stld OH. m Janet MacInnis, ch: 1. Sarah;
2. Annie; 3. Mary; 4. Catherine; 5. John; 6. Donald;
7. Alexander.   **HCA 345**.

9047 MACPHERSON, Angus. From Loch Enort,
Lochaber, INV. s/o Donald M. To Black River, Inverness
Co, NS, <1840.   **MP 790**.

9048 MACPHERSON, Angus. From Is Skye, INV. To
PEI prob <1840. m Anne Mackinnon, qv.   **MP ii 529**.

9049 MACPHERSON, Angus. Prob from INV.
bro/o Kate M, qv, John M, qv, and Lachlan M, qv. To
Antigonish Co, NS, poss <1840; stld South River.
m Catherine MacDonald. Son John.   **HCA 344**.

9050 McPHERSON, Ann. From Callander, PER. To QUE
on the *Dorothy*, ex Greenock, 12 Jul 1815; stld North
Elmsley Twp, Lanark Co, ONT. Wife of John McDonald,
qv.   **SEC 2**.

9051 McPHERSON, Ann. From Breadalbane, PER. To
CAN, prob ONT, 1831. Wife of Duncan McVean, qv, m at
Callander, 22 Apr 1831.   **DC 21 Jun 1981**.

9052   McPHERSON, Anne, ca 1812–15 Oct 1892. From Miltown of Muinas, NAI. d/o James M, qv, and Ann Rose, qv. To Restigouche Co, NB, 1819. m 1829, James Reid, qv.   **DC 7 Feb 1981**.

9053   McPHERSON, Archibald. From ARL. bro/o Malcolm M, qv. To London Twp, Middlesex Co, ONT, 1842. d unm.   **PCM 51**.

9054   McPHERSON, Catherine, ca 1792–29 Nov 1862. From SUT. To Pictou, NS, and bur at Salt Springs. Wife of Alexander McKenzie, qv.   **DC 27 Oct 1979**.

9055   McPHERSON, Catherine, b ca 1788. From Gailable, Kildonan, SUT. sis/o John M, qv. To Fort Churchill, Hudson Bay, on the *Prince of Wales*, ex Stromness, 28 Jun 1813. Went to York Factory, 1814, thence to Red River.   **LSS 186; RRS 27; LSC 323**.

9056   MACPHERSON, Catherine. From Is Skye, INV. To Uigg, Queens Co, PEI, 1831. m William MacLeod, qv.   **SPI 138**.

9057   McPHERSON, Charles, b 1786. To Madawaska Co, NB, arr Aug 1830. Farmer. Wife Sarah, b 1802, with him. They had, poss with other ch: 1. James, b ca 1826; 2. Christianna, b 1835; 3. William, b 1837.   **DC 18 Feb 1980**.

9058   MACPHERSON, Charlotte. From Glen Roy, INV. sis/o Murdock M, qv. To Mull River, Inverness Co, NS, 1823. m Angus, s/o Angus 'Cleireach' Beaton, qv.   **MP 790**.

9059   MACPHERSON, Christina, 1823-78. From Kingussie, INV. d/o John M, qv, and Christina MacDonald, qv. To Mabou Ridge, Inverness Co, NS, <1835. m (i) Archibald MacDonald; (ii) Allan Cameron, miller.   **MP ii, 302, 578**.

9060   MACPHERSON, Christine. From Is Skye, INV. To Cape Breton Is, NS, ca 1830; went later to Montague, Kings Co, PEI. Wife of Malcolm MacKenzie, qv.   **DC 5 Mar 1979**.

9061   McPHERSON, Colin. Poss from ARL. To Aldborough Twp, Elgin Co, ONT, 1855.   **PDA 68**.

9062   MACPHERSON, Daniel, 24 Apr 1795–5 Mar 1855. From Greenock, RFW. s/o Alexander M, mariner, and Agnes Campbell. To NFD, ca 1804. Family went to CA, 1849.   **DC 20 Jan 1966**.

9063   McPHERSON, David, b ca 1791. To Richmond Co, NS, 1811. Farmer, m and ch.   **CBC 1818**.

9064   MACPHERSON, Sir David Louis, 12 Sep 1818–16 Aug 1896. From Castle Leathers Farm, Inverness. s/o David M, tenant, and Naomi Grant. Educ Inverness Academy. To Montreal, QUE, 1835; later to Toronto, ONT. Politician, railway projector and industrialist. KCMG, 1884. m 18 Jun 1844, Sarah Badgeley, 1820-94, d/o William Mason, Montreal, and Elizabeth Badgeley, ch: 1. Elizabeth, b 31 May 1845; 2. William Mason, b 24 Sep 1848; 3. Helen, b 4 May 1845; 4. Isobel, b 17 Feb 1853; 5. Christina, b 14 Sep 1854.   **BNA 731; MDB 486; DC 15 Aug 1979**.

9065   McPHERSON, Donald. From Strathglass, INV. To Pictou, NS, on the *Sarah*, ex Fort William, Jun 1801. Wife Mary with him, and ch: 1. Ann; 2. Hugh.   **PLS**.

9066   MACPHERSON, Donald. From INV. s/o John M.

To Antigonish Co, NS, ca 1801; stld later Rear Judique, Inverness Co.   **HCA 342**.

9067   MACPHERSON, Donald. Poss from Is Skye, INV. To Belfast, Queens Co, PEI, <1811.   **HP 74**.

9068   McPHERSON, Donald, b ca 1784. From Anderston, Glasgow. To QUE, ex Greenock, summer 1815; stld prob Lanark Co, ONT. Labourer. Wife Margaret McDonald, qv, with him, and 2 ch.   **SEC 8**.

9069   MACPHERSON, Donald. Prob from INV. bro/o Angus M, qv, and Dougald M, qv. To Broad Cove, Inverness Co, NS, poss <1820.   **HCA 345**.

9070   MACPHERSON, Donald. From INV. bro/o John M, qv, and Marcella M, qv. To Antigonish Co, NS, poss <1820; stld Cloverville. m Mary Macdonald, ch: 1. Mary; 2. Ann; 3. Ellen.   **HCA 344**.

9071   MACPHERSON, Donald, b 1790. From Is Skye, INV. To Victoria Co, NS, 1829; stld later Margaree, Inverness Co. m Sarah Campbell, qv, ch: 1. Norman, qv; 2. John, qv; 3. Flora, qv; 4. Margaret, qv; 5. Elizabeth, d unm; 6. Isabel, d unm; 7. Rachel.   **DC 23 Feb 1980**.

9072   McPHERSON, Donald. Poss from ARL. To Aldborough Twp, Elgin Co, ONT, prob <1840. m Sarah, d/o Duncan Paterson, qv, and Grace McMillan, qv, ch: 1. Lily; 2. Donald; 3. Dugald; 4. Malcolm; 5. Hector; 6. Elizabeth.   **PDA 64**.

9073   McPHERSON, Donald, d 1843. From Is Skye, INV. To Baddeck, Victoria Co, NS, arr 18 Aug 1843. m Mary Findelson, qv, ch: 1. Margaret, qv; 2. Archibald; 3. Christie; 4. Alexander.   **HNS iii 517**.

9074   McPHERSON, Donald. From Is Benbecula, INV. To East Williams Twp, Middlesex Co, ONT, 1848.   **PCM 44**.

9075   McPHERSON, Donald. To Metcalfe Twp, Middlesex Co, ONT, ca 1850.   **PCM 26**.

9076   McPHERSON, Donald. Poss from INV. Prob rel to Duncan M, qv, and Hugh M, qv. To Delaware Twp, Middlesex Co, ONT, ca 1850.   **PCM 57**.

9077   MACPHERSON, Dougald, b ca 1725. From Moidart, INV. To NS on the *Aurora*, 1792; stld Moidart, Antigonish Co. m Miss MacDonald, ch: 1. Rory, qv; 2. John, qv; 3. Donald; 4. Mary.   **HCA 338**.

9078   MACPHERSON, Dougald. Prob from INV. s/o John M, qv. To Antigonish Co, NS, ca 1801, but stld Cape Breton Is.   **HCA 342**.

9079   MACPHERSON, Dougald. Prob from INV. bro/o Angus M, qv. To Antigonish Co, NS, poss <1820; stld OH. m Miss MacInnes, ch: 1. Mrs MacInnes; 2. Sarah; 3. Stephen; 4. John; 5. Donald; 6. Ann; 7. Mary; 8. Christy.   **HCA 345**.

9080   MACPHERSON, Duncan. Poss from INV. To QUE on the *Commerce*, ex Greenock, Jun 1820; stld prob Lanark Co, ONT.   **HCL 238**.

9081   MACPHERSON, Duncan. From Gairloch par, ROC. s/o John M. in Melvaig. To Cape Breton Is, NS, prob <1830.   **DC 28 Sep 1980**.

9082   McPHERSON, Duncan. From Carradale, Kintyre, ARL. To Westminster Twp, Middlesex Co, ONT, 1848. ch: 1. Archibald; 2. Hugh; 3. John; 4. Dugald.   **PCM 52**.

9083 McPHERSON, Duncan. Poss from INV. Prob rel to Donald M, qv, and Hugh M, qv. To Delaware Twp, Middlesex Co, ONT, ca 1850. **PCM 57**.

9084 MACPHERSON, Flora. From Is Skye, INV. d/o Donald M, qv, and Sarah Campbell, qv. To Victoria Co, NS, 1829; later to Margaree, Inverness Co. m Peter Ross. **DC 23 Feb 1980**.

9085 McPHERSON, Forbes Watson, b 8 Mar 1817. From Portsoy, BAN. s/o William M. and Elspet Duff. To ONT, 1836; later to VT, USA. **LDW 21 Sep 1971**.

9086 McPHERSON, Frances. From INV. To Kingston, ONT, <1826, when m John, s/o Robert Hamilton, qv, and Mary Herkimer, qv. **DC 2 Aug 1982**.

9087 McPHERSON, Gellen, b 1768. To Charlottetown, PEI, on the *Humphreys*, ex Tobermory, 14 Jul 1806. Wife Flora, aged 33, with him, and ch: 1. Archibald, aged 9; 2. Mary, aged 4; 3. Margaret, aged 2; 4. Jane, inf. **PLH**.

9088 McPHERSON, Helen, b 7 Aug 1822. From Ropshaw, ni. To QUE, ca 1830; stld Toronto, later London, ONT. m Alexander Campbell, qv. **DC 7 Apr 1980**.

9089 McPHERSON, Hugh, ca 1779–12 Oct 1843. From Golspie, SUT. To Pictou Co, NS, 1814. Bur at Lovat. Wife Ann Sutherland, qv. **DC 27 Oct 1979**.

9090 McPHERSON, Hugh. From Loch Awe, ARL. To Lobo Twp, Middlesex Co, ONT, 1832. ch: 1. Alexander; 2. Archibald; 3. John; 4. Margaret; 5. Kate; 6. Sarah; 7. Janet; 8. Nancy; 9. Mary. **PCM 39**.

9091 MACPHERSON, Hugh. Prob from INV. bro/o Angus M, qv. To Antigonish Co, NS, poss <1840; stld South River. m Miss MacMillan. **HCA 344**.

9092 MACPHERSON, Hugh. Poss from INV. Prob rel to Donald M, qv, and Duncan M, qv. To Delaware Twp, Middlesex Co, ONT, ca 1850. **PCM 57**.

9093 McPHERSON, James, 19 Nov 1780–26 Jul 1857. From Miltown of Muinas, NAI. s/o William M. and Julia Brodie. To Restigouche Co, NB, 1819. Farmer and officer of Militia. m Ann Rose, qv, ch: 1. Alexander, qv; 2. William, qv; 3. Anne, qv; 4. John, qv; 5. Margaret, qv; 6. Mary. **SG xxvii/3 126; DC 7 Feb 1981**.

9094 McPHERSON, James. From Badenoch, INV. To Eldon Twp, Victoria Co, ONT. ca 1825. Pioneer settler. **DC 21 Mar 1980**.

9095 McPHERSON, James. From Invergordon, ROC. To East Williams Twp, Middlesex Co, ONT, 1832. s/o Rev Lachan, min at Nairn. **PCM 43**.

9096 McPHERSON, James. To Pictou, NS, on the *Lady Gray*, ex Cromarty, ROC, arr 16 Jul 1841. **DC 15 Jul 1979**.

9097 McPHERSON, James, b Alvie par, INV, 1819. s/o Donald M, Chelsea pensioner, and Jean Cruikshank, qv. To Puslinch Twp, Wellington Co, ONT, ca 1843. **DC 7 Apr 1975**.

9098 McPHERSON, Jane, 1827–10 Jul 1858. Prob from Duthil, INV. To Sombra Twp, Lambton Co, ONT, ca 1851. Wife of Dr James Grant, qv. **DC 4 Oct 1979**.

9099 McPHERSON, Jane or Jean, b ca 1795. From Strathaven, LKS. To Southwold Twp, Elgin Co, ONT,

1835. m 12 Aug 1817, John Campbell, qv. **DC 17 Jun 1979**.

9100 McPHERSON, John. From Kyles Morar, INV. To PEI on the *Lucy*, ex Loch nan Uamh, Arisaig, 12 Jul 1790. Family with him. **PLL**.

9101 MACPHERSON, John. From Moidart, INV. s/o Dougald M, qv, and Miss MacDonald. To NS on the *Aurora*, 1792; stld Pictou Co, later Antigonish Co. Farmer. ch. **HCA 388**.

9102 MACPHERSON, John. From INV. To Antigonish Co, NS, poss <1800; stld Moidart. ch incl: 1. Angus; 2. Donald. **HCA 340**.

9103 MACPHERSON, John. From INV. s/o John M. To Antigonish Co, NS, ca 1801; stld Hallowell Grant. m Miss MacIsaac. Son Angus. **HCA 342**.

9104 MACPHERSON, John. Prob from Is Skye, INV. To Queens Co, PEI, poss 1803. Petitioner for Dr MacAulay, 1811. **HP 74**.

9105 MACPHERSON, John, 22 Feb 1790–29 Sep 1847. From Greenock, RFW. s/o Alexander M, mariner, and Agnes Campbell. To NFD, ca 1804. Son Capt John, d 1850. **DC 20 Jan 1966**.

9106 MACPHERSON, John. From INV. To Antigonish Co, NS, poss <1805. m Ann MacLeod, qv, ch: 1. John; 2. Angus; 3. Kenneth; 4. Allan; 5. Eunice. **HCA 341**.

9107 McPHERSON, John, b ca 1796. From Gailable, Kildonan, SUT. To Fort Churchill, Hudson Bay, on the *Prince of Wales*, ex Stromness, 28 Jun 1813. Sist Catherine M, qv, with him. Went to York Factory, 1814, thence to Red River. Left settlement and arr Holland River, ONT, 6 Sep 1815. **LSS 186; RRS 27; LSC 323**.

9108 McPHERSON, John, ca 1784–9 Sep 1824. From Edinburgh. To Cape North, Labrador, and d there. Merchant. **DGC 25 Jan 1825**.

9109 MACPHERSON, John. Prob from INV. To Antigonish Co, NS, prob <1815; stld Arisaig. Son Donald. **HCA 346**.

9110 McPHERSON, John, b ca 1815. From Miltown of Muinas, NAI. s/o James M, qv, and Ann Rose, qv. To Restigouche Co, NB, 1819. m Miss Hall, from Port Daniel, Bonaventure Co, QUE, and had, poss with other ch: 1. John, res Minneapolis, MN, USA; 2. Mary. **DC 7 Feb 1981**.

9111 MACPHERSON, John. From INV. bro/o Donald M, qv, and Marcella M, qv. To Antigonish Co, NS, poss <1820; stld Cloverville. m Margaret, d/o Allan MacDonald, ch: 1. Annie; 2. Mary; 3. Alexander. **HCA 344**.

9112 McPHERSON, John. To QUE on the *George Canning*, ex Greenock, 14 Apr 1821; stld Ramsay Twp, Lanark Co, ONT. **HCL 86, 239**.

9113 MACPHERSON, John. From Is Skye, INV. s/o Donald M, qv, and Sarah Campbell, qv. To Victoria Co, NS, 1829; later to Inverness Co, NS. m Elizabeth Mackenzie. **DC 23 Feb 1980**.

9114 McPHERSON, John, ca 1776–ca 1841. From Kenmore, PER. To Oro Twp, Simcoe Co, ONT, 1832. m Christine Fisher, qv, ch: 1. Duncan, d 1832; 2. John, qv; 3. Catherine, 1808-67; 4. Alexander, qv; 5. Peter,

1814-34; 6. William, d ca 1846; 7. Margaret; 8. Jane Moffatt. **DC 8 Nov 1981**.

9115 MACPHERSON, John, 1802-25 May 1880. s/o Donald M. From Loch Enort, INV. To Black River, Inverness Co, NS, <1840. m Margaret, d/o John Rankin, qv, ch: 1. Donald; 2. John; 3. Duncan; 4. Mary; 5. Catherine; 6. Janet. **MP 783, 830**.

9116 MACPHERSON, John. Prob from INV. bro/o Angus M, qv, Kate M, qv, and Lachlan M, qv. To Antigonish Co, NS, poss <1840; stld South River. m d/o Donald MacGillivray, ch: 1. Angus; 2. Donald; 3. Alexander; 4. John; 5. Kate; 6. Isabella. **HCA 344**.

9117 McPHERSON, John. From INV. To Middlesex Co, ONT, 1849; stld McGillivray Twp. **PCM 56**.

9118 McPHERSON, John. From Appin, ARL. To Ekfrid Twp, Middlesex Co, ONT, ca 1850; later to Plympton Twp, Lambton Co. **PCM 31**.

9119 McPHERSON, John, 1804-20 May 1883. From PER, prob Kenmore. To Esquesing Twp, Halton Co, ONT, prob <1850; bur Acton. m Catherine McPhail, qv. **EPE 74**.

9120 McPHERSON, Kate. From Arisaig, INV. To Pictou, NS, on the *Dove*, ex Fort William, Jun 1801. Spinster. **PLD**.

9121 MACPHERSON, Kate. Prob from INV. sis/o Angus M, qv, John M, qv, and Lachlan M, qv. To Antigonish Co, NS, poss <1840; stld South River. **HCA 344**.

9122 MACPHERSON, Lachlan. Prob from INV. bro/o Kate M, qv, Angus M, qv, and John M, qv. To Antigonish Co, NS, poss <1830; stld South River. Tailor. m Margaret, d/o Hugh Boyd, ch: 1. Donald; 2. Dr Hugh; 3. Margaret; 4. Mary; 5. Jessie; 6. Sarah; 7. Kate. **HCA 344**.

9123 McPHERSON, Rev Lachlan, ca 1814-Mar 1886. Poss from SUT. To Toronto, ONT, <1849. Missionary in Huron and Bruce counties, and ord min of Williams Twp, Middlesex Co. **PCM 14; DC 7 Apr 1980**.

9124 McPHERSON, Malcolm. Prob from Kenmore, PER. To Esquesing Twp, Halton Co, ONT, poss 1821. m Catherine Anderson, qv. **EPE 74**.

9125 McPHERSON, Malcolm. From ARL. bro/o Archibald M, qv. To London Twp, Middlesex Co, ONT, 1842; stld Lot 5, Con 2. Farmer. Wife with him, and s John, b 1830, mariner. **PCM 51**.

9126 MACPHERSON, Marcella. From INV. sis/o John M, qv, and Donald M, qv. To Antigonish Co, NS, poss <1820; stld Cloverdale. m Donald, s/o Donald MacDonald. **HCA 344**.

9127 McPHERSON, Margaret. To South River, Antigonish Co, NS, prob <1800. m John Boyd, qv. **HCA 79**.

9128 McPHERSON, Margaret, ca 1818-14 Jun 1868. From Miltown of Muinas, NAI. s/o James M, qv, and Ann Rose, qv. To Restigouche Co, NB, 1819. m John Cook, River Charlo, ch. **DC 7 Feb 1981**.

9129 McPHERSON, Margaret, 1823-9 Dec 1888. From PER. To Halton Co, ONT, prob <1835; stld Esquesing Twp. Wife of Archibald McCallum, qv. **EPE 76**.

9130 MACPHERSON, Margaret, 1824-29 Apr 1885. From Loch Enort, Lochaber, INV. d/o Donald M. To Black River, Restigouche Co, NB, <1840. **MP 783**.

9131 MACPHERSON, Margaret. From Is Skye, INV. d/o Donald M, qv, and Sarah Campbell, qv. To Victoria Co, NS, 1829, later to Inverness Co. m David, s/o Daniel or Donald Carmichael, qv, ch. **DC 23 Feb 1980**.

9132 McPHERSON, Margaret. From Is Skye, INV. d/o Donald M, qv, and Mary Findelson, qv. To Baddeck, Victoria Co, NS, 1841. m Dr Christie, and d Boston, MA, USA. **HNS iii 175**.

9133 MACPHERSON, Mary. Prob from INV. d/o John M. To Antigonish Co, NS, ca 1801. m Hugh MacDonald, Ballantynes Cove. **HCA 342**.

9134 McPHERSON, Mary, b ca 1774. To Charlottetown, PEI, on the *Elizabeth & Ann*, ex Thurso, arr 8 Nov 1806. Wife of Hugh McLeod, qv. **PLEA**.

9135 MACPHERSON, Mary, 1804-88. From Badenoch, INV. To Pictou Co, NS, 1832; stld later Belle Creek, Queens Co, PEI. Wife of William MacPhail, qv. **HP 38**.

9136 McPHERSON, Mary. From Is Skye, INV. To Margaree Forks, Inverness Co, NS, 1832. wid/o Donald Chisholm, by whom she had ch: 1. Malcolm, teacher, dy; 2. Alexander, qv; 3. Angus, qv; 4. James, farmer; 5. Archibald, tailor, went to Chicago, IL, USA; 6. Alexander 'Og', qv; 7. Colin, qv. **MP ii 186**.

9137 MACPHERSON, Moses. To Williamsburg Twp, Dundas Co, ONT, <1830. m 22 Jun 1819, Ann McMartin, ch: 1. Alexander, b 1820; 2. Hugh, b 1823. **DC 4 Mar 1965**.

9138 McPHERSON, Murdoch. From Noid, Badenoch, INV. To Montreal, QUE, ex Fort William, arr Sep 1802; stld poss Finch Twp, Stormont Co, ONT. **MCM 1/4 26**.

9139 MACPHERSON, Murdock, ca 1796-1863. From Gairloch, ROC. To Montreal, QUE, and joined NWCo, 1816. Served at Athabaska, and after merger with HBCo, 1821, in the Mackenzie River dist. Chief trader, 1834, and ret 1851. **MDB 486**.

9140 MACPHERSON, Murdock. From Glen Roy, INV. bro/o Charlotte M, qv. To Mull River, Inverness Co, NS, 1823; stld Glengarry, South West Mabou. m Anne MacDonald, qv, ch: 1. John; 2. Angus; 3. Catherine; 4. Mary; 5. Isabel; 6. Sara; 7. Margaret; 8. Anne; 9. Mary; 10. Janet. **MP 790**.

9141 McPHERSON, Neil. To Pictou, NS, on the *Lulan*, ex Glasgow, 17 Aug 1848. Wife Catherine with him, and ch: 1. Donald; 2. Samuel; 3. Marion; 4. Angus; 5. Fergus. **DC 15 Jul 1979**.

9142 MACPHERSON, Norman. From Is Skye, INV. s/o Donald M, qv, and Sarah Campbell, qv. To Victoria Co, NS, 1829, later to Inverness Co. m Sara Burton. **DC 23 Feb 1980**.

9143 MACPHERSON, Peter, 1787-1868. From Greenock, RFW. s/o Alexander M, mariner, and Agnes Campbell. To St Johns, NFD. Clerk, later merchant. m 17 Dec 1811, Lucinda Herbert Furneaux, ch: 1. Agnes Jane, b 1813; 2. Lucinda, b 1814; 3. Peter, b 1819, merchant; 4. Caroline, b 1822. **DC 20 Jan 1966**.

9144 McPHERSON, Peter, b ca 1773. From Callander, PER. To QUE, on the *Eliza*, ex Greenock, 3 Aug 1815; stld Lot 10, Con 10, North Elmsley Twp, Lanark Co, ONT. Labourer, later farmer. Wife Helen McNab, qv, with him, and 6 ch, incl William, who stld Lot 27, Con 10. **SEC 1; HCL 17, 230, 232.**

9145 McPHERSON, Peter. From PER. To McNab Twp, Renfrew Co, ONT, 1825. Wife Cathrine McDiarmid, qv, with him, and ch: 1. John; 2. Annabella; 3. Cathrine; 4. Peter; 5. Duncan; 6. Margaret; 7. Lorne; 8. Hugh. **EMT 18, 23.**

9146 MACPHERSON, Rory. From Moidart, INV. s/o Dougald M, qv, and Miss MacDonald. To NS on the *Aurora*, 1792; stld Antigonish Co. m Miss MacDonald, ch: 1. Hugh; 2. Donald; 3. John; 4. Mary; 5. Peggy. **HCA 338.**

9147 McPHERSON, Sarah. Poss from Is Skye, INV. To Orwell Bay, PEI, on the *Polly*, ex Portree, arr 7 Aug 1803; stld Belfast, Queens Co, later Covehead. Wife of Lachlan McMillan, qv. **DC 28 May 1980.**

9148 McPHERSON, Sarah, 1757–1833. From ARL. To Baldoon, Dover Twp, Kent Co, ONT, 1804. Wife of John McDougall, qv. **UCM 267; DC 4 Oct 1979.**

9149 MACPHERSON, Sophia, d 8 Oct 1800. From Kiltarlity, INV. To Pictou, NS, on the *Hector*, ex Loch Broom, arr 17 Sep 1773. Wife of Hugh Fraser, qv. **SG iii/4 96.**

9150 McPHERSON, Rev Thomas, b ca 1808. From ROC. Grad MA, Univ of Aberdeen, 1827. To Beechridge, ONT, 1836; trans to Lancaster, 1843. Declined to join Union, 1875. Min of Côte St George, 1877-86. **KCG 283; FES vii 645.**

9151 McPHERSON, William, ca 1808–8 Aug 1882. From Miltown of Muinas, NAI. s/o James M, qv, and Ann Rose, qv. To Restigouche Co, NB, 1819. Shipowner and lumberman. m (i) Agnes Miller; (ii) Mary Smith. ch: 1. William A, res Port Daniel, Bonaventure Co, QUE; 2. Isabella; 3. Cluny; 4. Agnes; 5. Mary; 6. Julia. **DC 7 Feb 1981.**

9152 MACPHERSON, William, 1818-72. From Is Skye, INV. To Victoria Co, NS, prob 1841. m Margaret MacLeod, qv. **DC 22 Jun 1979.**

McPHIE. See also McFEE and McPHEE.

9153 McPHIE, Isabella, ca 1808–24 Mar 1867. From ARL. d/o Hugh M, yeoman, and Mary M. To River Inhabitants, Cape Breton Is, NS, <1832. m Rev Dugald McKichan, qv. Retr to SCT, 1845, and d at Lochgilphead, ARL. **FES vi 449.**

9154 McPHIE, John. From Frobost, Is South Uist, INV. To PEI on the *Jane*, ex Loch nan Uamh, Arisaig, 12 Jul 1790, poss calling at Loch Boisdale. **PLJ.**

9155 McQUARRIE, Alexander. From Breadalbane, PER. To Halton Co, ONT, poss 1833; stld Esquesing Twp. Wife Isabella, ca 1808-35, d at Norval. **EPE 75.**

9156 McQUARRIE, Allan, b 1751. From Is Rum, ARL. s/o Lachlan M, qv. To Pictou, NS, 1791; stld Big Brook, west branch, East River. Farmer, gr 300 acres. By wife Janet had ch: 1. John; 2. Charles; 3. Donald; 4. Evan or Hugh, 1803-72; 5. Eunice; 6. Nancy. **PAC 11.**

9157 McQUARRIE, Allan, b ca 1792. Prob from ARL.

To Western Shore, Inverness Co, NS, 1816. Farmer. **CBC 1818.**

9158 McQUARRIE, Allan, b 1798. From Is Rum, ARL. Prob s/o John M, qv, and Marion M, qv. To Gut of Canso, Cape Breton, NS, on the *Saint Lawrence*, ex Tobermory, 11 Jul 1828. **SLL.**

9159 McQUARRIE, Angus. From Is Rum, ARL. s/o Malcolm M. To Pictou Co, NS, 1791; stld Iron Rock, East River. m Una, d/o Allan McDonald, Is Eigg, ch: 1. Allan; 2. Ronald; 3. Nancy; 4. Catherine; 5. Mary; 6. John. **PAC 184.**

9160 McQUARRIE, Bell, b 1808. From Is Rum, ARL. Prob d/o John M, qv, and Marion M, qv. To Gut of Canso, Cape Breton, NS, on the *Saint Lawrence*, ex Tobermory, 11 Jul 1828.

9161 MACQUARRIE, Catherine, b ca 1795. From Is Iona, ARL. To Eldon Twp, Victoria Co, ONT, <1840. Wife of Archibald MacInnes, qv. **EC 138.**

9162 McQUARRIE, Christina. From Is Mull, ARL. To Caledon Twp, Peel Co, ONT, 1818, and res there 1851. Wife of Donald Mackinnon, qv. **DC 21 Apr 1980.**

9163 MACQUARRIE, Donald, b ca 1790. From INV. s/o John M, qv, and Sara MacCormack, qv. To Little Mabou, Inverness Co, NS, <1818. m Jane, d/o John 'Mor' MacDonald, qv, ch: 1. John; 2. Neil; 3. Angus; 4. Dougald; 5. John 'Og'; 6. Mary; 7. Flora; 8. Sara; 9. Catherine; 10. Mary. **MP 610, 799.**

9164 McQUARRIE, Donald, b 1800. From Is Rum, ARL. Prob s/o John M, qv, and Marion M, qv. To Gut of Canso, Cape Breton, NS, on the *Saint Lawrence*, ex Tobermory, 11 Jul 1828. **SLL.**

9165 MACQUARRIE, Euphemia, ca 1810-51. From Is Iona, ARL. To Eldon Twp, Victoria Co, ONT, <1840. Wife of John MacInnes, qv. **EC 138.**

9166 MACQUARRIE, Flora. From INV. d/o John M, qv, and Sara MacCormack, qv. To Little Mabou, Inverness Co, NS, <1818. m Alexander, s/o Angus MacDonald, Port Hood, ch. **MP 802.**

9167 McQUARRIE, Hector, b ca 1785. From Is Mull, ARL. To Charlottetown, PEI, on the *Clarendon*, ex Oban, 6 Aug 1808. Labourer. **CPL.**

9168 McQUARRIE, Hector, b 1757. To Western Shore, Inverness Co, NS, <1818. Farmer, m and ch. **CBC 1818.**

9169 McQUARRIE, Hector. Prob from ARL. To Caledon Twp, Peel Co, ONT, ca 1820. Purchased land, 1839. **DC 21 Apr 1980.**

9170 McQUARRIE, James, 1814-86. From Is Iona, ARL. To Argyle, Eldon Twp, Victoria Co, ONT, ca 1852. Farmer. m Catherine Ann McInnes, qv, ch: 1. Archie, b 1834; 2. Lachlan, qv; 3. John, qv; 4. Donald; 5. Allan; 6. Angus; 7. Euphemia; 8. Hector. **EC 171.**

9171 MACQUARRIE, Jessie, b 1795. From INV. d/o John M, qv, and Sara MacCormack, qv. To Little Mabou, Inverness Co, NS, <1818. m Archibald MacDonald, qv, from Is Barra. **MP 420, 820.**

9172 MACQUARRIE, John. From INV. To Little Mabou, Inverness Co, NS, prob 1804. Pioneer settler. m Sara MacCormack, qv, ch: 1. Neil, qv; 2. Donald, qv; 3. Lachlan, qv; 4. Jessie, qv; 5. Flora, qv. **MP 796.**

9173   MACQUARRIE, John. From ARL. To NS on the *Highland Lad*, 1826; stld nr Port Hastings, Inverness Co. m Rachel Campbell, qv, ch: 1. Donald; 2. Malcolm; 3. Mary; 4. Christina; 5. John.   **DC 28 Jul 1981**.

9174   McQUARRIE, John. Prob from ARL. To Pictou Co, NS, <1827; stld Lansdowne. By wife Janet had ch: 1. Janet, b 1827; 2. Donald, b 1829; 3. Margaret, b 1834; 4. Polly, b 1836.   **PAC 180**.

9175   McQUARRIE, John. Prob from ARL. To Pictou Co, NS, poss <1820; stld Scotch Hill. m Mary McMillan. Son Malcolm.   **PAC 170**.

9176   McQUARRIE, John, b 1763, Is Rum, ARL. To Gut of Canso, Cape Breton, NS, on the *Saint Lawrence*, ex Tobermory, 11 Jul 1828. Prob hus/o Marion M, qv. **SLL**.

9177   McQUARRIE, John, 1836–1927. From Is Iona, ARL. s/o James M, qv, and Catherine Ann McInnes, qv. To Argyle, Eldon Twp, Victoria Co, ONT, ca 1852; moved later to Bowmanville, Durham Co. m Henrietta Lytle, ch: 1. Walter; 2. Angus; 3. John; 4. Joseph; 5. James; 6. George; 7. Thomas; 8. Sadie; 9. Jane; 10. Mary; 11. Euphemia; 12. Henrietta; 13. Elizabeth; 14. Azilla. **EC 171**.

9178   McQUARRIE, Lachlan. From Is Rum, ARL. To Pictou Co, NS, 1791; stld east branch of East River. Farmer. ch: 1. Allan, qv; 2. Neil, qv; 3. Mary; 4. Marion.   **PAC 180**.

9179   McQUARRIE, Lachlan, b ca 1795. From INV. s/o John M, qv, and Sara MacCormack, qv. To Little Mabou, Inverness Co, NS, prob 1804. Farmer. m Miss Mackinnon, ch: 1. Neil; 2. Malcolm; 3. John; 4. Dougald; 5. Sara; 6. Janet; 7. Margaret; 8. Angus. **CBC 1818; MP 802**.

9180   McQUARRIE, Lachlan, b ca 1887. From Is Mull, ARL. To Charlottetown, PEI, on the *Clarendon*, ex Oban, 6 Aug 1808. Labourer.   **CPL**.

9181   McQUARRIE, Lachlan, b ca 1758. Prob from ARL. To Western Shore, Inverness Co, NS, 1816. Farmer, m and ch.   **CBC 1818**.

9182   McQUARRIE, Lachlan, 1834–1922. From Is Iona, ARL. s/o James M, qv, and Catherine Ann McInnes, qv. To Argyle, Eldon Twp, Victoria Co, ONT, ca 1852. Farmer. m Isobel Campbell, 1849–1918, ch: 1. Catherine; 2. Duncan; 3. Christina; 4. James; 5. Isabel; 6. Donald or Daniel; 7. John Allan.   **EC 171**.

9183   McQUARRIE, Malcolm, b 1825. From Aird, Is Benbecula, INV. s/o Roderick M, qv, and wife Catherine. To East Williams Twp, Middlesex Co, ONT, ca 1850. Wife Mary with him.   **WLC**.

9184   McQUARRIE, Margaret, b 1804. From Is Rum, ARL. Prob d/o John M, and Marion M, qv. To Gut of Canso, Cape Breton, NS, on the *Saint Lawrence*, ex Tobermory, 11 Jul 1828.   **SLL**.

9185   McQUARRIE, Marion, b 1763, Is Rum, ARL. To Gut of Canso, Cape Breton, NS, on the *Saint Lawrence*, ex Tobermory, 11 Jul 1828. Prob wife of John M, qv. **SLL**.

9186   McQUARRIE, Neil. From Is Rum, ARL. s/o Lachlan M, qv. To Pictou Co, NS, 1791; stld Caledonia. m Flora McQuarrie, ch: 1. Lachlan;

2. Donald; 3. Christy; 4. Nancy; 5. Annabell. **PAC 184**.

9187   McQUARRIE, Neil. To Cornwall, ONT, via NY, <1815. m 1809, Nancy Laing, ch: 1. Donald, b 1809; 2. Thomas, b 1811; 3. John, b 1816; 4. Nichol Laing, b 1820; 5. Adam, b 1822, dy; 6. Duncan, b 1824; 7. Nancy, b 1826; 8. Neil, 1828-89; 9. George, b 1830; 10. David Gordon, b 1832.   **DC 18 May 1982**.

9188   McQUARRIE, Neil, b 1773, Is Rum, ARL. To Gut of Canso, Cape Breton, NS, on the *Saint Lawrence*, ex Tobermory, 11 Jul 1828. Wife Marion, aged 50, with him.   **SLL**.

9189   McQUARRIE, Neil, b ca 1783. Prob from ARL. To Western Shore, Inverness Co, NS, <1818. Farmer. **CBC 1818**.

9190   MACQUARRIE, Neil, b 1788. From INV. s/o John M, qv, and Sara MacCormack, qv. To Little Mabou, Inverness Co, NS, <1818. m Mary MacIsaac, ch: 1. Allan; 2. Jessie.   **MP 796**.

9191   McQUARRIE, Rachel, b 1802, Is Rum, ARL. Prob d/o John M, qv, and Marion M, qv. To Gut of Canso, Cape Breton, NS, on the *Saint Lawrence*, ex Tobermory, 11 Jul 1828.   **SLL**.

9192   McQUARRIE, Roderick, ca 1796–ca 1891. From Aird, Is Benbecula, INV. To East Williams Twp, Middlesex Co, ONT, ca 1850. Wife Catherine with him, and ch: 1. Malcolm, qv; 2. Flora, b 1827; 3. Donald, b 1830; 4. Neil, b 1832; 5. Angus, b 1835; 6. John, b 1838. **PCM 44; WLC**.

9193   McQUARRY, Allan, ca 1753–26 Feb 1840. From ARL. To Pictou Co, NS. Bur Old Elgin. m Janet McLean, qv.   **DC 20 Nov 1976**.

9194   McQUARRY, Hector. Poss from INV. To Queens Co, PEI, prob 1803. Petitioner for Dr MacAulay, 1811. **HP 74**.

9195   McQUARRY, Hector, b 1756. To North End, Gut of Canso, Inverness Co, NS, 1811. Farmer. ch: 1. Donald, b ca 1795; 2. Hector, b 1797.   **CBC 1818**.

9196   McQUARRY, Neil, b 1788. To Inverness Co, NS, 1804; stld nr Port Hood. Farmer, m and ch.   **CBC 1818**.

9197   McQUEARY, Alexander, b ca 1766. To Charlottetown, PEI, on the *Humphreys*, ex Tobermory, 14 Jul 1806. Wife Isabel, aged 33, with him, and ch: 1. Flora, aged 13; 2. Sarah, aged 11; 3. John, aged 8; 4. Sandy, aged 6; 5. Margaret, aged 4; 6. Una, inf. **PLH**.

9198   MACQUEEN, Rev Adam Fraser, 12 Dec 1824– 16 Feb 1898. From Snizort par, Is Skye, INV. s/o Murdo M. in Uig, and Mary Fraser. To QUE, 1849. Educ Knox Coll, Toronto and ord at Montreal, QUE, 1858. Min of Kenyon Twp, Glengarry Co, ONT, and trans to Ripley, Huron Twp, Bruce Co, ONT, 1874; and to Hampden, Compton Co, QUE, 1893. m 1859, Normanda MacLeod, qv. Son Rev Murdoch.   **SDG 347; CMM 2/16 7; DC 31 Aug 1979**.

9199   MACQUEEN, Alexander. From Snizort par, Is Skye, INV. s/o Murdo M. in Uig, and Mary Fraser. To ONT <1855, and prob stld Stormont Co. m Anna MacLeod, qv, ch: 1. Donald, b 1865; 2. Murdoch, b 1867; 3. Catharine, b 1869; 4. Mary, b 1871; 5. Bella, b 1873; 6. Adam, b 1875; 7. Alexander, b 1877; 8. Malcolm, b 1880; 9. John, b 1882. **DC 31 Aug 1979**.

9200 McQUEEN, Angus, 1790–14 Oct 1864. Prob from INV. s/o Alexander M, soldier, and Isabella McDonald. To NS <1815, when m Susan Robertson, 1792–1861, ch: 1. Mary; 2-3. Alexander and Daniel, twins; 4. Susan, b 1821; 5. Annabella; 6. Angus; 7. Duncan; 8. Thomas; 9. Janet; 10. Eliza; 11. John. **DC 14 Nov 1981**.

9201 McQUEEN, Ann, 1841–1921. From Is Skye, INV. d/o James M, qv, and Mary Stevens, qv. To Kinloss Twp, Bruce Co, ONT, <1841. m Charles McKinnon, qv, her step-uncle. **DC 12 Apr 1979**.

9202 MACQUEEN, Christina, b 1802. From Is Skye, INV. d/o Donald M, qv, and Christina MacLeod, qv. To Orwell Bay, PEI, on the *Polly*, ex Portree, arr 7 Aug 1803; stld Pinette, Queens Co. m John MacLeod, prob her cous, ch. **SPI 144**.

9203 MACQUEEN, David. From Is Skye, INV. To QUE, <1810. Officer, Canadian Fencibles. m d/o Hon Thomas Fraser. Son David S, b 1811, became county court judge of Oxford, ONT. **BNA 917**.

9204 MACQUEEN, Donald, ca 1780–ca 1813. From Is Skye, INV. To PEI on the *Polly*, ex Portree, arr Orwell Bay, 7 Aug 1803; stld Pinette, Queens Co. m Christina MacLeod, qv, ch: 1. Christina, qv; 2. Malcolm, 1804-86; 3. John, 1806-79; 4. Flora, b 1808; 5. Angus, 1809-76, farmer, Orwell River; 6. Catherine, ca 1812-71. **SPI 143; HP 33, 89**.

9205 McQUEEN, Donald. From INV. To East Williams Twp, Middlesex Co, ONT, 1832. **PCM 43**.

9206 McQUEEN, James, 1810-81. From Kilmuir, Is Skye, INV. s/o Alexander M. and Catherine Campbell. To Kinloss Twp, Bruce Co, ONT, <1847. m (i) Mary Stevens, qv, and had, prob with other ch: 1. Ann. m (ii) Sarah McKinnon, qv, with further ch: 2. Mary Ann, b 1864; 3. Christena. **DC 12 Apr 1879**.

9207 MACQUEEN, John. Prob from Is Skye, INV. To Queens Co, PEI, <1811, when petitioner for Dr MacAulay. **HP 74**.

9208 McQUEEN, John. From Is Islay, ARL. To ONT, 1833; stld Stayner, Simcoe Co. Wife Mary McIntyre, qv, with him, and ch: 1. Neil; 2. Flora; 3. Isabelle; 4. James; 5. James; 6. John; 7. Donald. **DC 31 May 1979**.

9209 MACQUEEN, Thomas, 9 Oct 1803–25 Jun 1861. From Kilbirnie, AYR. To Fitzroy Twp, Carleton Co, ONT, 1842; later to Goderich Twp, Huron Co. Stonemason, farmer, journalist and poet. **BNA 1129; MDB 486**.

9210 MACQUILLAN, Neil, b ca 1788. To Margaree dist, Inverness Co, NS, 1815. Farmer, m and ch. **CBC 1818**.

9211 McQUIN, Ronald, b 1790. To St Andrews dist, Cape Breton Co, NS, 1817. Farmer, m and ch. **CBC 1818**.

9212 McRAE, Alexander. From Glenshiel par, ROC. To Montreal, QUE, prob arr Sep 1802. Petitioned for land on the Ottawa River, 6 Aug 1804. **DC 15 Mar 1980**.

9213 McRAE, Alexander, 1789–1869. Poss from ROC. s/o Donald M. and Mary McLeod. To PEI, 1805; stld Pownal, Queens Co. m Sarah McGregor, qv, ch:

1. Daniel, b 26 Oct 1824; 2. Peter, b 2 Aug 1826; 3. Alexander, b 9 Mar 1828; 4. Mary, b 29 May 1829; 5. John, b 1 Mar 1831; 6. Margaret, b 10 Nov 1832; 7. James McGregor, b 3 May 1834; 8. Alexander Malcolm, b 21 Mar 1836; 9. Sarah, b 14 Feb 1838; 10. George, b 15 Jul 1840; 11. Christy Ann, b 18 Feb 1842. **DC 11 Apr 1981**.

9214 McRAE, Alexander. From Kintail, ROC. To QUE, 1821; stld Huntingdon Co, and moved later to Glen Nevis, Glengarry Co, ONT. Tanner. Son Alexander, res Lancaster Twp. **SDG 254**.

9215 McRAE, Alexander, 30 Nov 1792–3 May 1871. From Moulin, PER. s/o David M. and Janet Strong. To Westmorland Co, NB, 1814. Schoolteacher. m Nancy Terris. **DC 19 Feb 1979**.

9216 McRAE, Alexander, b ca 1747. From Glenelg, INV. To QUE, summer 1815; stld prob ONT. Farmer and labourer. Wife Catherine McIntosh, qv, with him, and ch: 1. Roderick, b ca 1790; 2. Archibald, b ca 1793. **SEC 5**.

9217 McRAE, Alexander, b ca 1769. From Glenelg, INV. To QUE, summer 1815; stld prob Lanark Co, ONT. Farmer. Wife Margaret McRae, qv, with him, and 8 ch, incl John, b ca 1794. **SEC 7**.

9218 MACRAE, Alexander, 1826–1907. To Pictou Co, NS, <1850, and stld Middle River. m Annie MacLean, ch: 1. Jane Ruth; 2. Alexander; 3. Catherine Ann. **PAC 231**.

9219 McRAE, Alexander. From Kintail, ROC. To Eldon Twp, Victoria Co, ONT, prob <1850. m Annie MacIsaac, ch: 1. John; 2. Hugh; 3. Donald; 4. Duncan; 5. Farquhar; 6. Flora; 7. Mary Anne; 8. Clementina. **EC 175**.

9220 McRAE, Alexander, ca 1822–24 Nov 1880. To ONT, ca 1853, poss first to Kingston, but stld Wolfe Is. Moved in 1857 to Lambton Co, and was latterly in Sarnia Twp. m 1857, Agnes Cameron, ch: 1. Jane, b 1858; 2. Isabella, b 1860; 3. Mary Elizabeth, b 1870. **DC 1 Feb 1980**.

9221 McRAE, Alexander or Alistair, ca 1778–30 Jan 1859. From ROC. s/o Alexander or Alistair M. To Lancaster Twp, Glengarry Co, ONT, <1833; stld Lot 28, Con 4. Wife Annabella with him, and ch: 1. Isabelle, qv; 2. James, b 1811; 3. Catherine, b 1816; 4. Patrick, b ca 1818; 5. Donald, b ca 1820. **DC 16 Jul 1979**.

9222 MACRAE, Angus, b 1816. From Back, Is Lewis, ROC. To Lingwick Twp, Compton Co, QUE, 1842. Farmer. m Bess Stewart, qv, ch: 1. John, qv; 2. George, qv; 3. Johnnie; 4. Maggie; 5. Katie; 6. Annie, 1848-90. **TFT 15**.

9223 McRAE, Betsey. From Strathglass, INV. To Pictou, NS, on the *Sarah*, ex Fort William, Jun 1801. Spinster. **PLS**.

9224 McRAE, Christopher, b ca 1765. From Glenshiel par, ROC. To QUE, ex Greenock, summer 1815; stld prob Lanark Co, ONT. Farmer. Wife Margaret McRae, qv, with him, and 4 ch. **SEC 8**.

9225 MACRAE, Christopher. From Glenshiel par, ROC. To ONT, 1846; stld poss Aldborough Twp, Elgin Co, ONT. Shepherd. Wife Mary McAulay, qv, with him, and ch: 1. Christy, b 1839; 2. John, b 1841; 3. Donald, b 1843; 4. John, b 1846. **Glenshiel OPR 67/2; PDA 75**.

9226   MACRAE, Donald. Prob from Is Skye, INV. To PEI <1811. m Mary, d/o Roderick Campbell and Anne Morrison, and stld Pinette, Queens Co.   **HP 33, 74**.

9227   McRAE, Donald. From Lochalsh, ROC. To Richmond Co, NS, <1846. Son Murdoch, 1846–1909, merchant and MLA.   **MLA 239**.

9228   McRAE, Donald. From ROC. Prob rel to Hugh M, qv. To Dundee, QUE, <1850; moved then to Ekfrid Twp, Middlesex Co, ONT.   **PCM 31**.

9229   McRAE, Donald. From Kintail, ROC. To Eldon Twp, Victoria Co, ONT, prob <1850.   **EC 175**.

9230   McRAE, Donald A, ca 1815–26 May 1904. From Edinburgh. To Glengarry Co, ONT, 1826; moved 1830 to Middlesex Co. Pioneer teacher in twps of Lobo and London. ch: 1. Catherine; 2. Jane; 3. Arthur; 4. John H, postmaster of Ilderton; 5. Effie; 6. Annie; 7. Eliza; 8. Jessie; 9. Mary.   **PCM 50**.

9231   McRAE, Duncan. From Glenshiel par, ROC. To Montreal, QUE, ex Fort William, arr Sep 1802; stld E ONT.   **MCM 1/4 26**.

9232   McRAE, Duncan. From Inverinate, ROC. To Montreal, QUE, prob arr 1802. Petitioned for land on the Ottawa River, 6 Aug 1804.   **DC 15 Mar 1980**.

9233   McRAE, Duncan, d 1879. From Kintail, ROC. To Bolsover, Eldon Twp, Victoria Co, <1850. Farmer, reeve of Eldon Twp and warden of Victoria Co. m Maria Dalgleish, ch: 1. Norman; 2. Walter; 3. William; 4. John; 5. Duncan; 6. Andrew; 7. Agnes; 8. Susan; 9. Maria; 10. Maggie; 11. Isabella.   **EC 174**.

9234   MACRAE, Evander. To Queens Co, PEI, poss 1803. Petitioner for Dr MacAulay, 1811.   **HP 73**.

9235   McRAE, Farquhar, 1757–25 Jun 1825. Poss from INV. To Lower Miramichi, Northumberland Co, NB, prob <1800. Discharged soldier, 78th Regt, and became farmer. m Emily Cameron, qv. Dau Margaret, 1820-61, res Bay du Vin.   **DC 14 Jan 1980**.

9236   McRAE, Farquhar, ca 1815–ca 1909. From Kintail par, ROC. s/o John Roy M, qv, and wife Isabella. To NS <1820; stld prob Antigonish Co. Went to Brechin, Ontario Co, ONT, <1840. m Isobella McKenzie, qv.   **DC 20 Jul 1980**.

9237   McRAE, Farquhar. From Kintail, ROC. To Eldon Twp, Victoria Co, ONT, <1850; stld Lot 27, Con 1.   **EC 174**.

9238   MACRAE, Finlay. To Queens Co, PEI, poss 1803. Petitioner for Dr MacAulay, 1811.   **HP 74**.

9239   McRAE, Finlay, b ca 1778. From Glenelg, INV. To QUE, ex Greenock, summer 1815; stld prob Lanark Co, ONT. Farmer. Wife Catharine McCrimmon, qv, with him, and 1 child.   **SEC 8**.

9240   MACRAE, George, b ca 1838. From Is Lewis, ROC. s/o Angus M, qv, and Bess Stewart, qv. To Lingwick Twp, Compton Co, QUE, 1842. m Annie MacLeay, and had with other ch: 1. Mabel; 2. Angus, res Seattle, WA, USA; 3. Caroline; 4. George.   **TFT 15**.

9241   McRAE, Gilchrist. From Lianish, Kintail, ROC. To Montreal, QUE, ex Fort William, arr Sep 1802; stld poss Finch Twp, Stormont Co, ONT.   **MCM 1/4 26**.

9242   McRAE, Hannah Margaret, ca 1813–ca 1899. From Is Skye, INV. To Ontario Co, ONT, <1840. m John McRae, qv.   **DC 20 Jul 1980**.

9243   McRAE, Hugh. From ROC. Prob rel to Donald M, qv. To Dundee, QUE, <1850, then to Ekfrid Twp, Middlesex Co, ONT.   **PCM 31**.

9244   MACRAE, Isabella, b 15 May 1786, ROC. d/o Rev John M, par min, and Madeline MacRae. To NS <1835. wid/o Capt John Campbell of Glentulm, Breadalbane Fencibles. Son Charles, b 1819, with her.   **FES vii 151; SG xviii/2 25**.

9245   McRAE, Isabelle, 1815-53. From ROC. d/o Alexander or Alistair M, qv, and wife Annabella. To Lancaster Twp, Glengarry Co, ONT, <1833. m Austin McDonell, qv.   **DC 16 Jul 1979**.

9246   McRAE, James, b 8 Sep 1787. From Moulin, PER. s/o David M. and Janet Strong. To Westmorland Co, NB, <1815. Shipbuilder at Hopewell.   **DC 19 Feb 1979**.

9247   McRAE, James 'Ban'. From ROC. To Ekfrid Twp, Middlesex Co, ONT, 1835.   **PCM 30**.

9248   MACRAE, Janet. From Glenelg, INV. d/o Farquhar M. in Fadoch, and Mary M. To Kenyon Twp, Glengarry Co, ONT, 1817. Wife of Norman MacLeod, qv.   **MG 269, 285**.

9249   MACRAE, John. To Queens Co, PEI, poss 1803. Petitioner for Dr MacAulay, 1811.   **HP 74**.

9250   McRAE, John, 29 Jun 1783–3 Jan 1838. From Moulin, PER. s/o David M. and Janet Strong. To Hillsborough, Westmorland Co, NB, 1815. Became shipbuilder at Hopewell. Unm.   **DC 19 Feb 1979**.

9251   McRAE, John, b ca 1777. From Glenelg, INV. To QUE, ex Greenock, summer 1815; stld prob Lanark Co, ONT. Farmer. Wife Catharine McLeod, qv, with him, and 5 ch.   **SEC 8**.

9252   McRAE, John, b ca 1780. From Glenelg, INV. To QUE, ex Greenock, summer 1815; stld prob Lanark Co, ONT. Wife Marion Campbell, qv, with him, and 4 ch.   **SEC 5**.

9253   McRAE, John, b ca 1785. From Glenelg, INV. s/o Roderick M, qv, and Marion Murchison, qv. To QUE, summer 1815; stld prob Lanark Co, ONT. Farmer. Wife Janet Cameron, qv, with him.   **SEC 5**.

9254   McRAE, John, ca 1802–1909. From Kintail par, ROC. s/o John Roy M, qv, and wife Isabella. To NS <1820; stld Brechin, Ontario Co, ONT, <1840. m Hannah Margaret McRae, qv, ch: 1. John, b ca 1840; 2. Margaret, b ca 1841; 3. Alexander, b ca 1843; 4. Farquhar, b 1849; 5. Duncan, b ca 1853; 6. James, b ca 1855.   **NSN 24/85; DC 20 Jul 1980**.

9255   MACRAE, John. From Strathglass, INV. To Antigonish Co, NS, poss <1820. m Miss Mackenzie, qv, ch: 1. Mary; 2. Catherine; 3. Mary; 4. John.   **HCA 349**.

9256   MACRAE, John. From Gairloch par, ROC. s/o John M. in Melvaig. To Cape Breton Is, NS, <1830.   **DC 28 Sep 1980**.

9257   McRAE, Rev John. From Kiltarlity, INV. To Pictou Co, NS, 1827. Min there until 1844, when retr to SCT. m on PEI, 10 Jul 1829, Julia C. MacDougall, ch.

1. William, 1830-31; 2. Isabella, b 1832; 3. Rev Donald, b 1833; 4. Archibald, b 1835; 5. Alexander, b 1837; 6. Elizabeth Ann, b 1843. **PAC 12, 214**.

9258 McRAE, John 'Garbh'. From ROC. To Ekfrid Twp, Middlesex Co, ONT, 1835. **PCM 30**.

9259 MACRAE, John, 1836–1916. From Is Lewis, ROC. s/o Angus M, qv, and Bess Stewart, qv. To Lingwick Twp, Compton Co, QUE, 1842; later to Winslow Twp. Farmer. m Catherine Morrison, and had, poss with other ch: 1. Effie, res VT, USA; 2. Bessie; 3. Katie, res Detroit, MI, USA; 4. Kenneth; 5. George, res St Johnsbury, VT, USA; 6. Maggie. **TFT 15**.

9260 McRAE, John Roy, b ca 1778. From Kintail par, ROC. s/o Duncan M. To NS <1820; stld prob Antigonish Co. Farmer and teacher. Wife Isabella, 1779–1864, with him, and she d at Brechin, Ontario Co, ONT. Known ch: 1. John, qv; 2. Farquhar, qv. **DC 20 Jul 1980**.

9261 McRAE, John Roy. From ROC. To Ekfrid Twp, Middlesex Co, ONT, 1835. **PCM 30**.

9262 McRAE, Kenneth, b ca 1781. From Glenelg, INV. To QUE, ex Greenock, summer 1815; stld prob Lanark Co, ONT. Farmer. Wife Marion Cameron, qv, with him, and 3 ch. **SEC 8**.

9263 McRAE, Kenneth. From Badenoch, INV. To Ekfrid Twp, Middlesex Co, ONT, 1835. **PCM 30**.

9264 McRAE, Malcolm, b ca 1780. From Glenelg, INV. To QUE, summer 1815; stld prob Lanark Co, ONT. Farmer and labourer. Wife Rebecca Morrison, qv, with him, and 4 ch. **SEC 5**.

9265 McRAE, Malcolm, b ca 1809. To Huron Twp, Bruce Co, ONT, <1851. Farmer. Wife Nancy with him. **DC 18 May 1982**.

9266 McRAE, Margaret. From Glenshiel par, ROC. To QUE, ex Greenock, summer 1815; stld prob Lanark Co, ONT. Wife of Christopher McRae, qv. **SEC 8**.

9267 McRAE, Margaret. From Miltown, Glenelg, INV. To QUE, summer 1815, ex Greenock; stld West Hawkesbury, Prescott Co, ONT. Wife of John Fraser, qv. **SEC 5; DC 21 Jan 1980**.

9268 McRAE, Margaret, ca 1790–1 Jan 1862. From Moulin, PER. d/o David M. and Janet Strong. To Westmorland Co, NB, 1829. Wife of Thomas Ross, qv. **DC 19 Feb 1979**.

9269 McRAE, Marion, b ca 1790. From Glenelg, INV. To QUE, ex Greenock, summer 1815; stld prob Lanark Co, ONT. Wife of Duncan McCuaig, qv. **SEC 8**.

9270 McRAE, Mary. From Kilmorack, INV. Prob wife or widow, with ch: 1. Mary; 2. Murdoch, aged 7; 3. Ann; 4. Duncan, aged 5; 5. Margaret, aged 4; 6. Farquhar, aged 1 ½. All to Pictou, NS, on the *Sarah*, ex Fort William, Jun 1801. **PLS**.

9271 MACRAE, Mary, 1813–1902. Prob from INV. d/o Kenneth M. To ONT, 1815. m John MacLeod, ch. **MG 411**.

9272 McRAE, Rachel. From Glenelg, INV. To QUE, summer 1815, ex Greenock; stld prob Lanark Co, ONT. Wife of Farquhar McCrimmon, qv. **SEC 5**.

9273 MACRAE, Roderick. To Queens Co, PEI, poss 1803. Petitioner for Dr MacAulay, 1811. **HP 73**.

9274 McRAE, Roderick, b ca 1755. From Glenelg, INV. To QUE, summer 1815, ex Greenock; stld prob Lanark Co, ONT. Wife Marion Murchison, qv, with him, and ch: 1. John, qv; 2. Donald, b ca 1787, house-carpenter; 3. Alexander, b ca 1789, farmer; 4. Malcolm, b ca 1794, labourer; 5. Ann, b ca 1792. **SEC 5**.

9275 McRAE, Roderick, b ca 1830. From Kintail, ROC. To Victoria Co, NS. Wife Ann, ca 1832–11 May 1886. **DC 22 Jun 1979**.

9276 McREA, Daniel, b ca 1760. To Baddeck, Victoria Co, NS, 1812; stld prob Middle River. ch: 1. John, b ca 1785; 2. Finley, b ca 1788; 3. Duncan, b ca 1792; 4. Daniel, b ca 1797; 5. Alexander, b ca 1801. **CBC 1818**.

9277 McRITCHIE, Charles, b 31 Jul 1783. From Peterhead, ABD. s/o Duncan M. and Ann Anderson. To Lanark Co, ONT, 1841; stld Merrickville. m Jane Henderson, qv, ch: 1. James, 1815-94; 2. Ann, remained in SCT; 3. Jane, 1818–1910; 4. Charles, 1820-88; 5. George, 1822–1900; 6. Isabella, 1824-95; 7. Alexander, 1825–1901; 8. William, 1827–1905; 9. Elizabeth Reed, 1829-73; 10. Maria, 1832-69. **DC 10 Oct 1982**.

9278 McRITCHIE, Kenneth. From Lochbroom, ROC. To Pictou, NS, on the *Hector*, ex Loch Broom, arr 17 Sep 1773. **HPC App C**.

9279 McROBBIE, Andrew, 1814-85. From PER. s/o — M. amd Margaret Douglas. To QUE, 1832. Emp on Lachine Canal, and went later to ONT. Worked as a foreman on the Dundas-Galt road, and afterwards farmed at Puslinch Twp, Wellington Co. m Margaret Grey, ch: 1. Margaret, d inf: 2. Mrs William Kerr; 3. Isabella; 4. Mrs James Stevenson; 5. John; 6-7. Catherine and Gilbert, twins; 8. Andrew; 9. James; 10. Mrs John Harbottle. **DC 31 Jul 1979**.

9280 McROBBIE, James. From PER. s/o — M. and Margaret Douglas, qv. To QUE, 1832; later to Puslinch Twp, Wellington Co, ONT. Farmer. m Christina, d/o John Clark, no ch. **DC 31 Jul 1979**.

9281 McROBBIE, John. From PER. s/o — M. and Margaret Douglas. To QUE, 1832; later to Puslinch Twp, Wellington Co, ONT. Farmer. m Margaret Morrison, Widow Cameron. **DC 31 Jul 1979**.

9282 McROBBIE, Ludovick, 1818-52. From PER. s/o — M. and Margaret Douglas, qv. To QUE, 1832; later to Puslinch Twp, Wellington Co, ONT. Farmer. m Janet McPherson. **DC 31 Jul 1979**.

McROBBIE, Mrs. See DOUGLAS, Margaret.

9283 McROBERT, Isabella, 1814-76. Prob from AYR. To Hamilton, ONT. Wife of Peter Reid, qv. **Ts Mt Albion**.

9284 McROBERT, Jane, d 17 Apr 1877. From Galloway. To QUE on the *Portia*, 1834; stld Wentworth Co, later in Huron Co, ONT. m 23 Jan 1829, John Murray, qv. **DC 12 Mar 1980**.

9285 McROBIE, Rev William, d 1820. From Muthill, PER. s/o John M, artisan. Matric Univ of Glasgow, 1844. Adm min of Gartmore, PER, 1856. To NB, 1857, and was min of Tabusintac and Burnt Ch. **GMA 1471; FES iv 346, vii 611**.

9286 **McRURY, John**, b ca 1811. From Knockline, Is North Uist, INV. s/o Angus M. To ONT <1850. m Sarah McAulay, ch: 1. Mary; 2. Archibald; 3. Marion. **LDW 12 Jan 1971**.

9287 **McSHANNON, Mary**, 1730–1824. From Lepenstrath, Southend, Kintyre, ARL. To Prince Co, PEI, ca 1772. Wife of Hugh Montgomery, qv. **DC 20 Dec 1981**.

9288 **McSPORRAN, Betty**. From Kintyre, ARL. To York Co, ONT, 1831; stld Sutton. Wife of Neil MacDonald, qv, whom she m 8 Mar 1817. **DC 3 Mar 1982**.

9289 **McSWAIN, Jane**, d 13 Mar 1925. From Is Skye, INV. To Charlottetown, PEI, prob on the brig *Ruther*, ex Portree, 14 Jul 1840; stld Queens Co. m John Munro, qv. **SPI 120**.

9290 **MACSWEYN, Donald**, 1764–1850. From Moy and Dalarossie par, INV. s/o Roderick Dhu Revan M. in Corrybrough. To QUE, 1804; stld Glengarry Co, ONT. Farmer. m Catherine McCaskill, from Rouen, France, ch: 1. Findlay, b 1802; 2. Donald, b 1804; 3. Anne; 4. Malcolm; 5. John; 6. Angus. **DC 18 Jul 1963**.

9291 **McTAGGART, Barbara**, 1803-92. From ARL. d/o Godfrey M, qv. To East Williams Twp, Middlesex Co, ONT, 1831. m A. McCallum, and had ch. **PCM 44**.

9292 **McTAGGART, Donald**. From ARL. To Ekfrid Twp, Middlesex Co, ONT, 1831. ch: 1. Lachlan; 2. Angus, b ca 1825; 3. Mary; 4. Nancy; 5. Mrs Archibald McDougall. **PCM 30**.

9293 **McTAGGART, Godfrey**, d 1837. From ARL. To East Williams Twp, Middlesex Co, ONT, 1831. ch: 1. Neil, d 1831; 2. Barbara, qv; 3. Sarah, qv; 4. Mary, qv. **PCM 44**.

9294 **McTAGGART, John**, d 8 Jan 1830. Poss from Tors, KKD, where he d. To ONT, <1826. Civil Engineer engaged in the construction of the Rideau Canal, and author of *Three Years in Canada* (1829). **HCL 28; DGC 12 Jan 1830**.

9295 **MACTAGGART, John**, b 1785. From Campbeltown, ARL. To Mariposa Twp, Victoria Co, ONT, 1835. Wife Elizabeth with him, and ch: 1. Lachlan, b 1823; 2. Alexander, b 1829. **DC 21 Nov 1981**.

9296 **McTAGGART, Lachlan**. From Knapdale, ARL. To Lobo Twp, Middlesex Co, ONT, 1829. m Ishbel, d/o Dugald Graham, qv, ch: 1. John; 2. Lachlan; 3. Dugald; 4. Mary; 5. Bella; 6. Ann; 7. Sarah; 8. Margaret. **PCM 38**.

9297 **McTAGGART, Mary**, 1811–1901. From ARL. d/o Godfrey M, qv. To Middlesex Co, ONT, 1831. m Donald McDonald, Lobo Twp, and had ch. **PCM 44**.

9298 **McTAGGART, Sarah**. From ARL. To Ekfrid Twp, Middlesex Co, ONT, 1829. m Duncan McColl, qv. **PCM 38**.

9299 **McTAGGART, Sarah**. From ARL. d/o Godfrey M, qv. To Middlesex Co, ONT, 1831. m John McGugan, qv. **PCM 44**.

9300 **McTAVISH, Alexander**, ca 1784–9 Dec 1832. From INV. To Montreal, QUE, <1813, when he went to Astoria as a clerk with the NWCo. After 1821 merger with HBCo, was stationed at the Pic, on Lake Superior. Chief trader, 1828, and d Lake Nipigon. **MDB 487**.

9301 **McTAVISH, Alexander**. From Dull par, PER. To Montreal, QUE, on the *Curlew*, ex Greenock, 21 Jul 1818; stld prob Beckwith Twp, Lanark Co, ONT. Wife Catherine with him, ch: 1. Duncan, aged 8; 2. Peter, aged 6. **BCL**.

9302 **McTAVISH, Alexander**, ca 1797–26 Sep 1847. From ARL. To Aldborough Twp, Elgin Co, prob <1830. **PDA 42**.

9303 **McTAVISH, Angus**. From INV. To Lobo Twp, Middlesex Co, ONT, ca 1832. ch: 1. Tavish; 2. William; 3. John; 4. Alexander; 5. Duncan; 6. Bella; 7. Katie. **PCM 40**.

9304 **McTAVISH, Catherine**. From Killin, PER. To QUE, ex Greenock, summer 1815; stld prob E ONT. Wife of Donald McLaren, qv. **SEC 3**.

9305 **MACTAVISH, Christene**. To Orwell Bay, PEI, on the *Polly*, ex Portree, Is Skye, 7 Aug 1803. Wife of Donald Fraser, qv. **HP 36**.

9306 **McTAVISH, Donald**, 1772–22 May 1814. From Stratherrick, INV. s/o Alexander M, and cous of the famous Simon M, fur-trader, who went first to Albany Co, NY. To QUE <1790, and became a clerk with the NWCo. Partner by 1799, and served at English River and Fort Dunvegan. He commanded the expedition to Fort Astoria, 1813, and brought the post under the care of the NWCo. Drowned in the Columbia River. **NSS 643; DGC 17 Oct 1815; MDB 487**.

9307 **McTAVISH, Dugald**, 10 Aug 1817–24 May 1871. From Kilchrist, Kintyre, ARL. s/o Dugald M, WS, Sheriff-Substitute at Campbeltown, and Letitia Lockhart. To Hudson Bay, 1833, and joined HBCo. Served on the Columbia and became a chief factor in 1851. Unm. **MDB 487; DC 28 Oct 1978**.

9308 **McTAVISH, Isabel**, ca 1796–29 Apr 1867. From Castleton, Lochgilphead, ARL. Poss d/o William M. To QUE, prob on the *Deveron*, 1831; stld Howard Twp, Kent Co, ONT. Wife of Archibald McLarty, qv, whom she m 21 Feb 1818. **AMC 12**.

9309 **McTAVISH, James Chisholm**, d 26 Dec 1827. From INV. To Montreal, QUE, and joined NWCo. Accompanied Donald M, qv, to Fort Astoria, 1813. Served at Fort William, 1816, and after 1821 merger with HBCo, was in charge of the Kings Posts on the Lower St Lawrence. **MDB 488**.

9310 **McTAVISH, Janet**. From ARL. To ONT, ca 1835. Wife of John McVicar, qv. **MDB 489**.

9311 **McTAVISH, John**, d 21 Jun 1852. From INV. s/o Alexander M. To QUE, ca 1808, and became a partner in the fur firm of McTavish, McGillivrays & Co. He went later to USA and in 1834 was app British Consul at Baltimore. In 1816 m Emily, d/o Richard Caton. **MDB 488**.

9312 **McTAVISH, John**. To Queens Co, PEI, <1815; stld Pinette. Day labourer. **HP 49**.

9313 **McTAVISH, John**. From Dull par, PER. To Montreal, QUE, on the *Curlew*, ex Greenock, 21 Jul 1818; stld prob Beckwith Twp, Lanark Co, ONT. Wife Catherine with him. **BCL**.

9314 **McTAVISH, John**. From Dull par, PER. To Montreal, QUE, on the *Curlew*, ex Greenock, 21 Jul 1818; stld prob Beckwith Twp, Lanark Co, ONT. **BCL**.

9315 McTAVISH, Rev John, 1814-97. From Is Islay, ARL. s/o Archibald M. Matric Univ of Glasgow, 1829, and became min at Ballachulish, 1844. Trans to Killean, 1851. Resigned and led some emigrants to ONT. Min at Woodville, Victoria Co, 1859, and was Moderator of the Canadian General Assembly. Retr to SCT in 1876 and became min of Inverness East FC. m 1851, Elizabeth Russell, and d at Dunardarigh.   **AFC i 259; GMA 12546; DC 21 Mar 1980**.

9316 McTAVISH, John. Poss from ARL. To Aldborough Twp, Elgin Co, ONT, 1818; moved to Mosa Twp, 1830. ch: 1. John; 2. Alexander; 3. Duncan; 4. Dugald, went to MI; 5. Christie. **PCM 23**.

9317 MACTAVISH, John George, ca 1782–20 Jul 1847. From Kintyre, ARL. s/o Lachlan M. of Dunardry. To Montreal, QUE, and in 1798 entered the service of the NWCo as a clerk. Sometime at Athabaska and on the Columbia, and became a partner, 1813. Involved in Red River troubles, 1815. App a chief factor after the merger with HBCo, and served at York Factory, Moose Factory, and at Two Mountains, nr Montreal.   **MDB 489; DC 28 Oct 1978**.

9318 MACTAVISH, Letitia, 1813-54. From Kilchrist, Kintyre, ARL. d/o Dugald M, WS, Sheriff-Substitute of Campbeltown, and Letitia Lockhart. To Hudson Bay, ex Gravesend, 7 Jun 1840, on the *Prince Albert*. Wife of James Hargrave, qv. In 1851 they went to Sault Ste Marie, Lake Superior, and she d there. Her *Letters* were printed by the Champlain Society.   **HWS 249; MDB 299; DC 28 Oct 1978**.

9319 McTAVISH, Mary, ca 1805–12 Apr 1846. From ARL. To Aldborough Twp, Elgin Co, ONT, poss <1830. m John Blue, qv.   **PDA 42**.

9320 MACTAVISH, William, ca 1811-70. From Kilchrist, Kintyre, ARL. s/o Dugald M, WS, Sheriff-Substitute of Campbeltown, and Letitia Lockhart. To Ruperts Land, 1833. Clerk with HBCo, and a chief factor, 1851. Became Gov of Assiniboia and Ruperts Land. Served heir to his father, 1858.   **SH; MDB 489; DC 20 Oct 1978**.

9321 McVANNEL, Hector. From Skipness, ARL. s/o Duncan M, d ca 1848, and Jean McArthur, qv. To QUE, arr 3 Aug 1846; stld Erin Twp, Wellington Co, ONT. m Ann McAllister, qv.   **DC 16 Mar 1978**.

McVANNEL, Mrs Duncan. See McARTHUR, Jean.

9322 McVANNEL, Nancy. From Skipness, ARL. d/o Duncan M, d ca 1848, and Jean McArthur, qv. To Kings Twp, York Co, ONT, 1831; later to Dunwich Twp, Elgin Co. Wife of Donald McCallum, qv.   **DC 16 Mar 1978**.

9323 McVANNEL, Jean. From Skipness, ARL. d/o Duncan M, d ca 1848, and Jean McArthur, qv. To ONT, ca 1846; stld poss Erin Twp, Wellington Co. Wife of Peter Hyndman, qv.   **DC 16 Mar 1978**.

9324 McVEAN, Duncan, b ca 1800. From Kenmore, PER. To CAN, prob ONT, 1831. m Ann McPherson, qv.   **DC 21 Jun 1981**.

9325 McVEAN, Jane, b ca 1788. From Fortingall, PER. To Charlottetown, PEI, on the *Clarendon*, ex Oban, 6 Aug 1808. sis/o Mary M, qv.   **CPL**.

9326 McVEAN, Malcolm, b ca 1777. From Callander,

PER. To QUE, Jul 1815, ex Greenock; stld poss Lanark Co, ONT. Wife Elizabeth Fletcher, qv, with him, and 6 ch.   **SEC 1**.

9327 McVEAN, Mary, b ca 1787. From Fortingall, PER. sis/o Jane M, qv, and wife of Charles McLean, qv. To Charlottetown, PEI, on the *Clarendon*, ex Oban, 6 Aug 1808.   **CPL**.

9328 McVEAN, Mrs Mary. From Killin, PER. To Montreal, QUE, on the *Curlew*, ex Greenock, 21 Jul 1818; stld prob Beckwith Twp, Lanark Co, ONT.   **BCL**.

9329 McVICAR, Alexander, 16 Feb 1770–8 Aug 1851. From Glasgow, but b prob AYR. To QUE on the *Earl of Buckinghamshire*, ex Greenock, 9 Apr 1821; stld Lanark Twp, Lanark Co, ONT. ch: 1. Archibald; 2. Sarah; 3. Elizabeth; 4. Jane or Jean; 5. Alexander; 6. John; 7. Archibald; 8. William; 9. Murray; 10. Margaret; 11. Sarah; 12. Alan.   **DC 18 May 1982**.

9330 McVICAR, Alexander. From PER, poss Killin par. Prob rel to James M, qv. To McNab Twp, Renfrew Co, ONT, 1825.   **DC 3 Jan 1980**.

9331 McVICAR, Archibald, ca 1792–1869. From ARL. To St George, Charlotte Co, NB, arr Jun 1820. Petitioned for land, 1 Sep 1821. Wife Ann, 1807-83, with him. ch: 1. Peter; 2. Ann; 3. Catharine; 4. Isabella; 5. Christina; 6. Janet; 7. Margaret; 8. Elizabeth.   **DC 4 Nov 1980**.

9332 McVICAR, Archibald, b ca 1795. From ARL. Rel to Archibald M, qv. To St George, Charlotte Co, NB, arr Jun 1820. Petitioned for land, 1 Sep 1821.   **DC 4 Nov 1980**.

9333 McVICAR, Archibald. From ARL. To Mosa Twp, Middlesex Co, ONT, prob <1840; stld Wardsville.   **PCM 24**.

9334 McVICAR, Archibald. From ARL. To Mosa Twp, Middlesex Co, ONT, 1842.   **PCM 24**.

9335 McVICAR, David. From ARL. To Ekfrid Twp, Middlesex Co, ONT, ca 1832.   **PCM 31**.

9336 McVICAR, Donald. From ARL. To Mosa Twp, Middlesex Co, ONT, ca 1848.   **PCM 24**.

9337 McVICAR, Donald. From ARL. To Caradoc Twp, Middlesex Co, ONT, 1850. ch: 1. Allan, farmer; 2. John, res Red Deer, ALB; 3. Rev Donald; 4. Rev Archibald.   **PCM 35**.

9338 McVICAR, Donald Harvey, 29 Nov 1831–15 Dec 1902. From ARL. s/o John M, qv, and Janet McTavish, qv. Educ Knox Coll, Univ of Toronto, and became head of the Presb Coll at Montreal. LLD, McGill, 1870, DD, Knox Coll, 1883. m 1860, Eleanor, d/o Robert Goulding, Toronto, and had ch.   **BNA 835; MDB 489**.

9339 McVICAR, Elizabeth. From PER, poss Killin par. Prob rel to Alexander M, qv, and James M, qv. To McNab Twp, Renfrew Co, ONT, 1825.   **DC 3 Jan 1980**.

9340 McVICAR, George, b ca 1794. From ARL. Rel to Archibald M, qv. To St George, Charlotte Co, NB, arr Jun 1820. Wife with him. Petitioned for land, 1 Sep 1821.   **DC 4 Nov 1980**.

9341 McVICAR, James. From PER, poss Killin par. Prob rel to Alexander M, qv, and Elizabeth M, qv.   **DC 3 Jan 1980**.

9342 McVICAR, John, 1760–22 Jul 1823. Poss from ARL. To Queens Co, NS, and d at Port Midway. **VSN No 252**.

9343 McVICAR, John. Prob from Is Mull, ARL. To Hudson Bay and Red River, <1813. Wright and pioneer settler. Wife with him. **RRS 16**.

9344 McVICAR, John, b ca 1800. From ARL. To St George, Charlotte Co, NB, arr Jun 1820. Petitioned for land, 30 Jul 1822. **DC 4 Nov 1980**.

9345 McVICAR, John. From ARL. To ONT, ca 1835, stld prob nr Toronto. Wife Janet McTavish, qv, with him, ch: 1. Malcolm, qv; 2. Donald Harvey, qv. **MDB 489**.

9346 McVICAR, Katherine. Prob from ARL. d/o Nevin M. and Janet Scott. To ONT, <1830; stld Middlesex Co. Wife of John McLellan, qv. **DC 25 Jan 1964**.

9347 McVICAR, Malcolm, 30 Sep 1829–18 May 1904. From ARL. s/o John M, qv, and Janet McTavish, qv. To ONT with parents. Educ Rochester, and grad BA, 1859. First chancellor of McMaster Univ. Inventor of the McVicar tellurian globe. PhD, NY, 1870; LLD, Rochester. **MDB 489**.

9348 McVICAR, Margaret, b ca 1747. From Lochend, Colvend, KKD. To Georgetown, Kings Co, PEI, on the *Lovely Nellie*, ex Annan, 1774. Wife of John Smith, qv. **ELN**.

9349 McVICAR, Neil. To Cape Breton Co, NS, <1820. Farmer. Son Donald drowned 1859. **HNS iii 299**.

9350 McVICAR, Peter. From Lochgilphead, ARL. To Lobo Twp, Middlesex Co, ONT, 1829. ch: 1. James; 2. John; 3. Peter; 4. Archibald; 5. Elizabeth; 6. Isabella; 7. Nancy. **PCM 38**.

9351 McVICAR, Peter. From Lochgilphead, ARL. To Lobo Twp, Middlesex Co, ONT, 1844. **PCM 39**.

9352 McVICHIE, Donald. From Ardradnaig, Kenmore par, PER. s/o Donald M, alias McDonald. To Glengarry Co, ONT, <1840; stld Bainsville. Son John D, d 1929. **IFB 372**.

9353 McVIE, William. Served in 82nd Regt, and was gr land in NS, 1784. **HPC App F**.

9354 McWATT, Daniel, b ca 1768. To Margaree, Inverness Co, NS, 1788. Farmer, m and had ch. **CBC 1818**.

9355 McWATTIE, Rev Alexander, b ca 1790. From Bonhill, DNB. s/o Duncan M, tradesman. Matric Univ of Glasgow, 1804, and ord to Original Secession Ch, Kennoway, FIF, 1811. Suspended, 1820, and after a period at Newcastle, went to CAN and d there. **GMA 6631**.

9356 McWHINNIE, John. To QUE on the *Alexander*, 1816; stld Lot 13, Con 9, Bathurst Twp, Lanark Co, ONT. **HCL 233**.

9357 McWILLIAM, Rev Alexander, 1827–8 Mar 1889. From Mortlach, BAN. s/o Alexander M, farmer. Matric Marischall Coll, Aberdeen, 1844. Schoolmaster successively at Ythan Wells and Culsamond, ABD. Ord 1863 and adm min of St Davids, Georgetown, PEI. Retr to SCT, 1871, and ind min of Ythan Wells. Demitted the charge, 1887. m 1864, Barbara Anderson, with ch dau Elizabeth. **FAM ii 526; FES vi 273, vii 622**.

9358 McWILLIAM, Charles. From KKD. To Orwell Bay, PEI, on the *Dykes*, arr 9 Aug 1803. Blacksmith employed by Lord Selkirk to assist his Belfast colonists. **HP 14**.

9359 McWILLIAM, Charles, ca 1799–10 Jan 1850. From Greenock, RFW, but b Kirkcolm, WIG. To Hamilton, ONT. **DGH 28 Feb 1850**.

9360 McWILLIAM, John, ca 1832–7 Dec 1858. From Stranraer, WIG. To Montreal, QUE, and d there. Printer. **DGH 7 Jan 1859**.

9361 McWILLIAM, Rev William, 20 Jul 1837–6 Jan 1907. From WIG. s/o Alexander M. Matric Univ of Glasgow, 1851, and studied at Knox Coll, Toronto, where he grad BA, 1862. Min at Roseneath and Bethesda, Northumberland Co; trans to Port Hope, 1887-93. **GMA 16055**.

9362 MABON, William, b ca 1783. From BEW. To PEI, prob ca 1840. m Elizabeth Cairns, qv. Son Ralph, b 1832, Galashiels, SEL. **SG xxvii/4 170; DC 17 Jan 1980**.

9363 MACHAN, James, 11 Jul 1788–4 Dec 1873. From Abbey par, RFW. s/o James M. and Martha Clark. To Dalhousie Twp, Lanark Co, ONT, 1821. m Margaret Forbes, qv, ch: 1. Janet, qv; 2. James; 3. John, qv; 4. William, 1822-29; 5. Martha, 1826–1901; 6. David, 1827–1904; 7. Margaret, b 12 Dec 1829; 8. Jane, 1832–1924; 9. Andrew, 1834-93. **DC 2 Nov 1979**.

9364 MACHAN, Janet, 10 Feb 1816–27 Jul 1902. From Abbey par, RFW. d/o James M, qv, and Margaret Forbes, qv. To Dalhousie Twp, Lanark Co, ONT, 1821. m 13 Mar 1837, James Horn. **DC 2 Nov 1979**.

9365 MACHAN, John, 13 Jan 1819–28 Feb 1859. From Abbey par, RFW. s/o James M, qv, and Margaret Forbes, qv. To Dalhousie Twp, Lanark Co, ONT, 1821. m Margaret Arnott, qv, ch: 1. James, 1849–1933; 2. John, 1850-53; 3. Margaret, b 1 Dec 1852; 4. George Arnott, 1854–1921; 5. David, 1856–1927; 6. Jane, 1859-94. **DC 2 Nov 1979**.

9366 MACHAN, Rev John, 16 Dec 1796–7 Feb 1863. b Tannadice, ANS. s/o John M, farmer. Matric Kings Coll, Aberdeen, and grad MA, 1814. Family tutor, and asst min at Logie, STI. To Kingston, ONT, 1827, and was min of St Andrews Ch. Principal of Queens Coll, 1846-53, and DD, Glasgow, 1847. Dau Agnes Maule, 1837–1927, writer of prose and verse. **KCG 274; FES vii 642; MDB 458; SNQ ii/2 171; Memorial plaque, Tannadice**.

9367 MACHRAY, Rev Robert, 1832–1904. From Dyce, ABD. s/o Robert M, advocate in Aberdeen, and Christian Allan. Grad MA, Kings Coll, Aberdeen, 1851, and BA, Sidney Coll, Cambridge. Consecrated Bishop of Ruperts Land, 1865. Primate of CAN, 1893. DD, LLD. d Winnipeg, MAN. **BNA 847, 1053; KCG 303; SAA 259**.

9368 MAGRAY, John. To Chebogue, Yarmouth Co, NS, <1774. m Margaret, d/o Capt John Allan. **NSN 14/3**.

9369 MAIN, Andrew. From Dunfermline, FIF. To Pictou, NS, on the *Hector*, ex Glasgow, arr 17 Sep 1773; stld Noel, Hants Co. Son Andrew, b ca 1772. **HPC App C**.

9370 MAIN, David. From Langholm, DFS. bro/o James M. in Lochmaben. To Rexton, Kent Co, NB, 1821. Son James, b 1821; stld Galloway, Kent Co. **SH; DC 17 Apr 1981**.

9371 MAIN, Janet, ca 1812–21 May 1884. From Canonbie, DFS. To Melbourne, Richmond Co, QUE, prob <1850. m Andrew Morrison. **MGC 15 Jul 1980**.

9372 MAIN, William, ca 1825–ca 1879. From Canonbie, DFS. Prob rel to Janet M, qv. To QUE, and stld Richmond Co. or Sherbrooke Co. Bur Lower Brampton. m Jane McMorine, qv. Dau Jane Dickson. **MGC 15 Jul 1980**.

9373 MAIN, William Dick, 19 Jan 1837–12 Jul 1903. From Maybole, AYR. s/o James M. and Helen Dick. To Amherst, Cumberland Co, NS. Dry goods merchant; Collector of Customs for Amherst, 1886–1903. m Margaret Baird Steel, qv, ch: 1. Clarence William, b 1858; 2. James Gordon, b 1859; 3. Ronald, b 1860; 4. Cuthbert, b 1861; 5. Helen Mary, b 1864; 6. Gertrude Isabel, b 1866; 7. Margaret Ethel, b 1868; 8. Charles Harold, b 1870; 9. Geoffrey Neilson, b ca 1872; 10. Gwendoline, b ca 1874. **DC 18 Nov 1978**.

9374 MAIR, James. Prob from LKS. s/o John M, qv. To Lanark Co, ONT, ca 1820. Lumberman and storekeeper, Lanark Village, later Perth. m Margaret Holmes, ch: 1. Holmes, lumberman; 2. James, lumberman; 3. Charles, 1838–1927, author and poet. **HCL 179, 222; MDB 491**.

9375 MAIR, Rev James, 1832–4 Feb 1875. From Savoch of Deer, ABD. s/o Rev James M, par schoolmaster, and Christian Johnston. Educ Marischall Coll, Aberdeen, and grad MA, 1846. Adm min of Barneys River, Pictou Co, NS, 1858; trans to Martintown, Glengarry Co, ONT, 1860. m Margaret Beveridge, ch: 1. Margaret, b 1864; 2. James, b 1866; 3. David Beveridge, b 1868; 4. Janetta Maria, b 1870; 5. Robert Beveridge, b 1872; 6. William, b 1875. **FAM ii 535; FES vii 645**.

9376 MAIR, John. Prob from LKS. To QUE on the *Commerce*, ex Greenock, Jun 1820; stld Lanark Village, Lanark Co, ONT. Shoemaker. Son James, qv. **HCL 179, 222, 239**.

9377 MAIR, John. From Ellon, ABD. s/o George M, shipowner. Alumnus, Marischall Coll, Aberdeen 1811-15. To CAN, prob ONT, <1855. Physician and author. **FAM ii 411; SH**.

9378 MAIR, Thomas, b ca 1798. From Milton of Birness, Ellon, ABD. s/o James M, from Mill of Tarty, Logie-Buchan. To Nichol Twp, Wellington Co, ONT, 1835. m and had ch: 1. James; 2. Thomas; 3. John, warden of Wellington Co; 4. Jane; 5. Isabella; 6. Elsie; 7. Eliza. **SH; SAA 265; EHE 91**.

9379 MAIR, Rev William, ca 1798–17 Oct 1860. From Glasgow. s/o William M, craftsman. Matric Univ of Glasgow, 1812. Mission and teaching work in Glasgow until 1833, when ord to Chatham and Grenville, QUE. **GMA 8527; FES vii 645**.

9380 MAITLAND, Agnes, b 4 Nov 1814. From Gimmershiels, Stenton par, ELN. d/o Dr Alexander M. and Jean Hamilton, his second wife. To CAN, prob <1850. **SA viii 94**.

9381 MAITLAND, David, b 9 Sep 1817. From Gimmershiels, Stenton par, ELN. s/o Dr Alexander M. and Jean Hamilton, his second wife. To CAN, prob <1850. **SA viii 94**.

9382 MAITLAND, James. From RFW. To Kilmarnock, Perth Co, ONT, ca 1830. Dau Rebecca Lauderdale, qv. **SG xvii/2 40**.

9383 MAITLAND, James, 20 Jul 1812–7 May 1875. s/o William M. To ONT, 1831. Ship carpenter. m at Darlington, Durham Co, Sarah Renwick, qv. **DC 7 Jan 1971**.

9384 MAITLAND, James. Prob from AYR. To Montague Twp, Lanark Co, ONT. Lock-keeper on Rideau River, <1840. **HCL 221**.

9385 MAITLAND, Rebecca Lauderdale, b 1829. From RFW. d/o James M, qv. To ONT <1856, when she m James Wylie, Almonte. **SG xvii/2 40**.

9386 MALCOLM, Elizabeth, d 1887. Poss from Edinburgh. To Lachute, QUE, 1833; later to Alexandria, Glengarry Co, ONT. Wife of Dr James Simpson, qv. **SDG 450**.

9387 MALCOLM, Elizabeth. d/o Robert M, poss res Aberdeen, and Elizabeth Henderson. To ONT, 1829. Wife of James Fife, qv. **DC 11 Dec 1967**.

9388 MALCOLM, Elspet, ca 1815–23 Sep 1839. From Dyke, MOR. To QUE, 1836; later to Lockland, OH, USA. Wife of James Taylor, qv, whom she m 7 May 1836. **DC 3 Aug 1983**.

9389 MALCOLM, Francis, 1791–1866. Prob from ABD. To ONT 1831; stld East Zorra Twp, Oxford Co, 1845. m Jessie Mitchell, qv, ch: 1. David, 1826-93; 2. Francis; 3. James; 4. John. **LDW 24 Sep 1974**.

9390 MALCOLM, James. From Dollar, CLK. To Pictou, NS, ca 1830; thence to St John, NB. m Margaret Barr, qv. Son Thomas, farmer, Rush City, MN, USA. **FNQ iv 12-22**.

9391 MALCOLM, Thomas. Prob from PER. To Brule, Tatamagouche, Colchester Co, NS, 1854. m Elizabeth Donaldson, qv. Son Robert D, farmer. **HT 83**.

9392 MALCOLM, William. From Kingskettle, FIF. To ONT, 1831; stld prob Oro Twp, Simcoe Co. m Margaret Lathange. **DC 9 Oct 1979**.

9393 MALLOCH, Donald. Poss from ARL. To St Andrews, Charlotte Co, NB, 1784. Discharged soldier, old 74th Regt. m 1792, Jane Greenlaw, ch: 1. Hannah; 2. John; 3. Peter; 4. Mary; 5. Daniel; 6. William; 7. Jane; 8. James. **SG xxx/2 65**.

9394 MALLOCH, Peter. From PER. To Dundas Co, ONT, 1843. Son Neil. **DC 4 Mar 1965**.

9395 MANN, Rev Alexander, ca 1800–15 Sep 1884. From Tarland, ABD. s/o James M, dyer, and Margaret Rennie. Grad MA, Kings Coll, Aberdeen, 1819, and emig to ONT. Min of Fitzroy, Pakenham, Torbolton, McNab and Horton. DD, Queens, 1876. **KCG 277; FES vii 645; Ts Tarland**.

9396 MANN, Anne. From Insch par, ABD. To QUE, ca 1836; stld Elora Twp, Wellington Co, ONT. Wife of James Milne, qv. **DC 27 Nov 1981**.

9397 MANN, Hugh. From INV. To Acton, Halton Co, ONT, 1834. Farmer. m Ellen Macdonell. Son Sir Donald, 1853–1934, railroad contractor. **DC 15 May 1982**.

9398 MANN, Jane Rainee. d/o — M. and Sarah Cowie. To QUE <1852. **SH**.

9399 MANSON, Alexander. From Wick, CAI. To Halifax, NS, prob <1815; moved to Stillwater, Guysborough Co. Farmer. m Jean Waters, ch: 1. John; 2. Ellen; 3. George, stld Lochaber, Antigonish Co, ca 1840; 4. Gilbert; 5. Allan. **HCA 350**.

9400 MANSON, Donald, b ca 1785. Prob bro/o Henry M, qv. To Charlottetown, PEI, on the *Elizabeth & Ann*, ex Thurso, 8 Nov 1806. **PLEA**.

9401 MANSON, Donald, 6 Apr 1796–7 Jan 1880. From Thurso, CAI. s/o Donald M. and Jean Gunn. To CAN and joined HBCo, 1817. Served in the English River, South Saskatchewan and Columbia dists, and established new trading posts. Chief trader, 1837, and in charge at Stuart Lake, 1844-57. Ret to a farm in OR, USA. m Félecité Lucier, and had ch. **MDB 495**.

9402 MANSON, Helen, 1809–3 Feb 1894. From Thurso, CAI. To Melbourne, Richmond Co, QUE, prob <1850. Wife of Henry Watters, qv. **MGC 15 Jul 1980**.

9403 MANSON, Henry, b ca 1788. Prob bro/o Donald M, qv. To Charlottetown, PEI, on the *Elizabeth & Ann*, ex Thurso, 8 Nov 1806. **PLEA**.

9404 MANSON, Jane, 1824–1911. From Lochmaben, DFS. d/o William M, qv. To Montreal, QUE, 1832. m Duncan Saunders, qv. **DC 31 Dec 1979**.

9405 MANSON, Mary. From AYR. To ONT, 1849, and d prob Amherstburg, Essex Co. Wife of James Gibb, qv. **DC 5 Jun 1981**.

9406 MANSON, William. To Montreal, QUE, <1800. Discharged soldier, and became farmer. Son Thomas. **SGC 140**.

9407 MANSON, William, d ca 1833. From Lochmaben, DFS. To Montreal, QUE, 1832. Wife d at sea. ch: 1. Jane, qv; 2. Esther. **DC 31 Dec 1979**.

9408 MANSON, William. Poss from Ringford, KKD. To Simcoe Co, ONT, <1850. Wife Jane McClucas, 1827-50, d at Rosemount. **DGH 2 May 1850**.

9409 MARJORIBANKS, Thomas, 1733–13 Jun 1793. To St John, NB, <1788. m Thomas Edward, 1738-93. **NER vii 96**.

9410 MARQUIS, Duncan, b 1842. From ARL. s/o John M, dec, and Eliza McDermid, qv. To Brant Co, ONT, via NY, ca 1851; stld Oakland Twp. Physician. m Eliza, d/o George Bryce, teacher, Mount Pleasant, ch. **DC 23 Sep 1980**.

9411 MARQUIS, Hugh, ca 1828–15 Nov 1899. Prob from Gourock, RFW. To Chatham, Northumberland Co, NB, ca 1850. Sailor. m 12 Mar 1849, Mary McIndoe, qv, ch: 1. Hugh; 2. John; 3. Margaret; 4. Mary; 5. Andrew; 6. Thomas; 7. George. **DC 2 Jun 1978**.

MARQUIS, Mrs John. See McDERMID, Eliza.

9412 MARSHALL, Rev Alexander Porter, 1824–1908. From ARL. s/o Alexander M, carrier. Matric Univ of Glasgow, 1838. Studied medicine, but went to CAN as a missionary, 1840. Retr to SCT and resumed medical studies. Res latterly at Campbeltown, ARL. **GMA 13959; FES vii 645**.

9413 MARSHALL, Janet. From Aberchalder, INV. Poss rel to Donald McPhee, qv. To Montreal, QUE, ex Fort William, arr Sep 1802; stld E ONT. **MCM 1/4 23**.

9414 MARSHALL, John, b 25 Oct 1813. From Tullibody, CLK. s/o John and Marion M. To Toronto, ONT, 1832. Coachman. Retr to SCT, 1840, to m Margaret Archibald, qv. They stld in Trafalgar Twp, Halton Co, ONT, where descendants still farm. ch: 1. Janet, b 18 Apr 1843; 2. John, b 30 Jun 1844; 3. Robert, b 22 Oct 1845; 4. Marion, b 22 Mar 1847; 5. Mary, 1848-54; 6. Ann Roselia, b 2 Apr 1850; 7. Margaret, b 24 Sep 1853; 8. Mary Jane, b 24 Mar 1855; 9. James, b 25 Sep 1856; 10. William, b 16 Apr 1861. **DC 31 Mar 1980**.

9415 MARSHALL, Robert, b ca 1742. From Troqueer, KKD. To Georgetown, Kings Co, PEI, on the *Lovely Nellie*, ex Carse Bay, May 1775; moved to Middle River, Pictou Co, NS, <1783. Weaver, later farmer, and gr 350 acres. Wife Elizabeth, aged 32, with him, and ch: 1. John, aged 8; 2. Andrew, aged 4; 3. James, inf; 4. David, b CAN. **ELN; HPC App A, D and E; NSN 9/6**.

9416 MARTIN, Abraham, ca 1588–8 Sep 1664. To QUE, 1614, and gr land in area later known as Plains of Abraham. River pilot. m 1613, poss in France, Marguerite Langlois, and had with other ch: 1. Ann; 2. Eustache, b 1621; 3. Marguerite, b 1624; 4. Hélène, b 1627; 5. Rev Charles-Amador. **SAS 16; MDB 499; ENA 1**.

9417 MARTIN, Alexander. From Is Skye, INV. To PEI, poss 1803; stld Queens Co. Petitioner for Dr MacAulay, 1811. **HP 74**.

9418 MARTIN, Catherine, b ca 1772. From Strath, Is Skye, INV. To Queens Co, PEI, 1821. Wife of Lachlan Ross, qv. **SPI 156**.

9419 MARTIN, Donald, 1783–1 Jul 1861. From Is Skye, INV. To Orwell Bay, PEI, on the *Polly*, ex Portree, arr 7 Aug 1803; stld Queens Co. Wife Ann, 1785–1850. **SPI 41**.

9420 MARTIN, Donald, 1759–1848. From Snizort par, Is Skye, INV. s/o Peter M. and Margaret McAulay. To Orwell Bay, PEI, on the *Polly*, ex Portree, arr 7 Aug 1811. m Marion MacLeod, qv, ch: 1. Mary; 2. Katherine; 3. Kenneth; 4. Margaret, 1806-92; 5. Peter, 1809-77; 6. John, 1811-62. **SPI 41; CMM 3/22; HP 74, 78**.

9421 MARTIN, Isabella, d 19 Mar 1849. From WIG. To Perth Twp, Lanark Co, ONT. Wife of Thomas McCandlish, qv. **DGH 10 May 1849**.

9422 MARTIN, James, 1814-85. From Penpont, DFS. s/o John M. and Janet Jackson. To Guelph Twp, Wellington Co, ONT, 1837. Cabinet-maker, later farmer. m Janet Roddick, qv, ch: 1. Thomas, 1840–1917; 2. James, 1842-91; 3. John, 1844–1922; 4. William, 1846–1932; 5. Robert, 1848–1918; 6. David, 1850–1926; 7. Janet, 1852–1929; 8. Hugh, 1854-73; 9. Mary, 1857–1941. **DC 31 Dec 1979**.

9423 MARTIN, Jane. From Stenscholl, Kilmuir par, Is Skye, INV. sis/o John M, qv. To Orwell Bay, PEI, on the *Polly*, ex Portree, arr 7 Aug 1803; stld Newtown River. Wife of John Nicholson, qv. **SPI 153; HP 16**.

9424 MARTIN, Janet, 1831-91. From Penpont, DFS. d/o Thomas M, qv, and Agnes Broadfoot, qv. To Guelph Twp, Wellington Co, ONT, 1837. m 1857, Thomas Laidlaw, qv. **DC 31 Dec 1979**.

9425 MARTIN, Janet, b 1803. From WIG. To ONT, 1843. Wife of James McGowan, qv. **DC 4 Jun 1976**.

9426 MARTIN, Rev John, 1790–1865. From Airdrie, LKS. s/o John M, merchant. Matric Univ of Glasgow, 1813. To Halifax, NS, 1821, to become min of St Andrews Ch. **GMA 8878; FES vii 617**.

9427 MARTIN, John, ca 1794–29 Jun 1877. From Westerkirk, DFS. To York Co, ONT, and d Scarborough. **CAE 39**.

9428 MARTIN, John. From Stenscholl, Kilmuir par, Is Skye, INV. bro/o Mary M, qv, and Jane M, qv. To Charlottetown, PEI, on the *Mary Kennedy*, arr 1 Jun 1829; stld Uigg, Queens Co. m Catherine MacDonald, qv, ch: 1. Samuel, qv; 2. Hugh, surgeon; 3. Catherine; 4. Malcolm; 5. Donald; 6. Charles; 7. John. **SPI 149**.

9429 MARTIN, John, 1810-83. From Penpont, DFS. s/o John M. and Janet Jackson. To Guelph Twp, Wellington Co, ONT, 1837. Miller. m 1840, Jean Munro, qv, ch: 1. Agnes, 1841–1927; 2. Elizabeth, 1843–1908; 3. John, 1846–1912; 4. David, 1847-86; 5. William Mutch, 1850–1933; 6. Thomas, 1850–1907; 7. Alexander Munro, 1852–1915; 8. Janet Jackson, 1855–1934; 9. Robert, 1858–1942; 10. Donald McLean, 1860–1931. **DC 31 Dec 1979**.

9430 MARTIN, John, 1833-91. From Penpont, DFS.. s/o Thomas M, qv, and Agnes Broadfoot, qv. To Guelph Twp, Wellington Co, ONT, 1831. Carriage trimmer, later miner. **DC 31 Dec 1979**.

9431 MARTIN, John Gillies, 1827–3 Aug 1854. Poss from Lesmahagow, LKS. To Brant Co, ONT, 1852, and d at Paris. m Margaret Buie, ch: 1. Catherine; 2. Helen, who emig later. **DC 9 Nov 1981**.

9432 MARTIN, Joseph. To Pictou, NS, on the *Hope*, ex Glasgow, 5 Apr 1848. Wife Jane with him, and s Joseph. May have gone to USA. **DC 12 Jul 1979**.

9433 MARTIN, Martin. From Is Skye, INV. To PEI, poss 1803; stld Queens Co. Petitioner for Dr MacAulay, 1811. **HP 74**.

9434 MARTIN, Mary. From Stenscholl, Kilmuir par, Is Skye, INV. bro/o John M, qv. To Charlottetown, PEI, on the *Mary Kennedy*, ex Portree, arr 1 Jun 1829; stld Murray Harbour Road. Wife of Donald 'Ban Oig' MacLeod, qv. **SPI 141**.

9435 MARTIN, Murdock. From Is Lewis, ROC. To QUE, ex Stornoway, arr 4 Aug 1851; stld Huron Twp, Bruce Co, ONT. Head of family. **DC 5 Apr 1967**.

9436 MARTIN, Robert, 1808-99. From Penpont, DFS. s/o John M. and Janet Jackson. To Guelph Twp, Wellington Co, ONT, 1837. Tailor. m Elizabeth Whigham Kennedy, qv, ch: 1. Robina Elizabeth, 1842–1916; 2. John Peter, 1844–1935; 3. Robert, 1845–1916; 4. Jeanette Jackson, 1847–1935; 5. David, 1850–1928; 6. Thomas William, 1852–1913; 7. George Ross, 1854–1909. **DC 31 Dec 1979**.

9437 MARTIN, Samuel. From Is Skye, INV. To Orwell Bay, PEI, on the *Polly*, ex Portree, arr 7 May 1803; stld

nr Belfast. Petitioner for Rev Dr MacAulay, 1811. **HP 74**.

9438 MARTIN, Samuel, b 1821. From Stenscholl, Kilmuir par, Is Skye, INV. s/o John M, qv, and Catherine MacDonald, qv. To Charlottetown, PEI, on the *Mary Kennedy*, ex Portree, arr 1 Jun 1829; stld Uigg, Queens Co. m Sarah, d/o James Campbell, Point Prim, ch: 1. Margaret, 1850-71; 2. Hugh, 1853–1923, went to WI, USA; 3. John Samuel, b 1855, politician; 4. Christy Ann, b 1857; 5. Catherine; 6. Rev James Campbell, b 1861; 7. Marjory; 8. Emily; 9. Sarah; 10. John Donald, 1868–1922; 11. Malcolm Campbell, b 1871; 12. Rev Samuel Angus, b 1873, stld MAN. **SPI 150; HP 38**.

9439 MARTIN, Thomas, 1805-36. From Penpont, DFS. s/o John M. and Janet Jackson. To Guelph Twp, Wellington Co, ONT, 1836. Tailor. m Agnes Broadfoot, qv, ch: 1. Janet, qv; 2. John, qv. **DC 31 Dec 1979**.

9440 MARTIN, Thomas. From Lochgelly, FIF. s/o James M, smith. To ONT, <1852; stld Dumfries Twp, Waterloo Co. **SH**.

9441 MARTIN, William, 1816-82. From Penpont, DFS. s/o John M. and Janet Jackson. To Guelph Twp, Wellington Co, ONT, 1836. **DC 31 Dec 1979**.

9442 MARTYN, Donald, 1814-93. From Benigary Farm, Lower Shader, Is Lewis, ROC. s/o Angus M. and Ann McIver. To QUE, ex Stornoway, arr 4 Aug 1851; stld Huron Twp, Bruce Co, ONT, 1852. Farmer. m (i) Margaret Morrison, d 1848, ch: 1. Malcolm, b 1840; 2. Christy, b 1841; 3. Murdo, b 1843; 4. Annie, b 1845; 5. Norman, b 1846. m (ii) Annie McKay, Widow McLean, further ch: 6. Murdo, b 1853; 7. Angus, b 1855; 8. Christina, b 1857; 9. Annie, b 1859; 10. John, b 1862. **WLC**.

9443 MARTYN, John. From Is Lewis, ROC. To QUE, ex Stornoway, arr 4 Aug 1851; stld Huron Twp, Bruce Co, ONT, 1852. Head of family. **DC 5 Apr 1967**.

9444 MARWICK, James. Prob from OKI. To Hudson Bay <1821. Emp by HBCo as labourer, smith, steersman and canoe builder. **DC 20 Mar 1983**.

9445 MARWICK, Jean, b ca 1775. From OKI. To Hudson Bay, prob 1791. m Oman Norquoy, qv. **DC 20 Mar 1983**.

9446 MARWICK, John, b 1 Dec 1842. From Rousay, OKI. To Nanaimo, Vancouver Is, BC, ca 1860. **DC 18 May 1982**.

9447 MASON, Robert. To Lanark Co, ONT, <1823; stld Lanark Twp. Schoolmaster. **HCL 177**.

MASSON, Mrs Alexander. See HARDY, Isobel.

9448 MASSON, Alexander Hardy, 14 Oct 1804–21 Apr 1885. From Newlands of Brodie, Dyke and Moy par, MOR. s/o Alexander M. and Isobel Hardy, qv. To Montreal, QUE, ca 1825; moved in 1832 to Huntingdon Twp, Hastings Co, ONT. Stonemason, later farmer. m Mary, d/o John and Mary Armstrong, ch: 1. Catherine, b 1832; 2. Mary, b 1835; 3. Elizabeth, b 1837; 4. Isabella, b 1839; 5. Jane, b 1841; 6. Hannah, b 1846; 7. Jemima, b 1848; 8. Matilda, b 1849; 9. Margaret, b 1852; 10. Caroline, b ca 1854. **DC 20 Jan 1980**.

9449 MASSON, Catherine. From Newlands of Brodie, Dyke and Moy par, MOR. d/o Alexander M. and Isobel

Hardy, qv. To Montreal, QUE, poss 1831; stld ONT. Wife of John Paul, qv. **DC 22 Sep 1979**.

9450 MASSON, Elizabeth, ca 1821–9 Apr 1894. To QUE, and stld Melbourne, Sherbrooke Co. Wife of Alexander Stewart, qv. **MGC 2 Aug 1979**.

9451 MASSON, Elizabeth. From Newlands of Brodie, Dyke and Moy par, MOR. d/o Alexander M. and Isobel Hardy, qv. Wife of or wid/o — Chalmers. To Montreal, QUE, poss 1831, prob later to ONT. **DC 22 Sep 1979**.

9452 MASSON, Isobella, 28 Dec 1796–27 Apr 1890. From Newlands of Brodie, Dyke and Moy par, MOR. d/o Alexander M. and Isobel Hardy, qv. To Montreal, QUE, poss 1831; stld Thurlow Twp, Hastings Co, ONT. Wife of 'Squire' William Campbell, qv. **DC 22 Sep 1979**.

9453 MASSON, Rev William, 1831–4 Apr 1909. From Rothes, MOR. s/o John M, builder, and Jane Suter. Educ Univ of St Andrews, and became a schoolmaster. To Hamilton, ONT, 1856, and adm min of St Johns Ch. Trans to Russeltown Flats, 1860, and to Galt, 1874. Retr to SCT, and was latterly min at Duffus, MOR. m 1854, Ann Cruden Anderson, qv, dau Edith Anne. **SAM 104; FES vi 387, vii 645**.

9454 MASTERTON, Janet. To CAN on the *Ellen McCarthy*, 1830; stld prob NB. Wife of John Burgess, qv. **DC 4 Oct 1979**.

9455 MATHER, Alexander, b 1806. bro/o James M. To NB, ca 1830; later to Morrow Co, OH, USA. Left ch. **DC 21 Sep 1981**.

9456 MATHER, David E, 1827–24 May 1905. From Dundee, ANS. To Waterloo Co, ONT. Bur Troy. **DC 12 May 1982**.

9457 MATHER, James Addison, ca 1838–15 Mar 1915. From Farnel, or perhaps Arbroath, ANS. s/o Alexander M. and Ann Mitchell. To QUE, ca 1855; stld Picton, Prince Edward Co, ONT. Moved to Sunnidale, Simcoe Co, 1860. Storekeeper. By first wife Isabelle, had no ch. m (ii) Christina Prentice, d 1872, ch: 1. Alexander Prentice, 1873–1930; 2. James, b 1875; 3. John William, 1877–1944; 4. Norman Lorne Campbell, b 1881. **DC 26 Oct 1979**.

9458 MATHER, Janet, b ca 1819. To St Gabriel de Valcartier, QUE, poss <1855. **Census 1861**.

9459 MATHER, John, 29 Oct 1827–10 Jun 1907. From Craig par, ANS. s/o James M. and Jean Low. To QUE, ca 1855; stld Gatineau Mills. Manager of Gilmour Lumber Co. m Jane Low, qv, ch: 1. Robert Addison, b 1851; 2. Annie Weir, 1853–70; 3. David Low, b 1855; 4. Jemima Jane, 1857–1933; 5. Allan Gilmour, 1862–1954. **DC 26 Oct 1979**.

9460 MATHER, John, 12 Aug 1835–1 Jan 1915. From Farnell, ANS. s/o Alexander M. and Ann Mitchell. To QUE, ca 1855; stld Angus, Simcoe Co, ONT. Storekeeper. m Margaret, d/o James Jack and Jean Hood, ch: 1. Jane Ann, 1863–1959; 2. Charles Douglas, b 1864; 3. Margaret, 1868–1933; 4. John Alexander, 1869–1960; 5. Isabella, 1871–91; 6. Agnes Elizabeth, 1872–1927; 7. Margaret Louisa, 1876–1975. **DC 26 Oct 1979**.

9461 MATHERS, John, b ca 1783. To St Gabriel de Valcartier, QUE, poss <1855. **Census 1861**.

9462 MATHERS, Margaret, b ca 1812. To St Gabriel de Valcartier, QUE, poss <1855. **Census 1861**.

MATHESON. See also MATHISON, MATHIESON and MATHEWSON.

9463 MATHESON, Alexander. From Kidonan par, SUT. To Fort Churchill, Hudson Bay, on the *Prince of Wales*, ex Stromness, 28 Jun 1813; thence to Red River. Pioneer settler. **LSS 186; RSS 27; LSC 323**.

9464 MATHESON, Alexander. From Lochalsh, ROC. To Eldon Twp, Victoria Co, ONT, prob <1840. m Miss McKenzie, ch: 1. Catherine; 2. Margaret; 3. Kenneth; 4. William; 5. Murdoch; 6. Donald, dy. **EC 71**.

9465 MATHESON or MATHEWSON, Alexander, b ca 1780. From Kildonan, SUT. To York Factory, Hudson Bay, arr 26 Aug 1815, and went to Red River. Overseer of passengers and pioneer settler. Wife Ann, aged 34, with him, and ch: 1. Hugh, aged 10; 2. Angus, aged 6; 3. Catherine, aged 2; 4. John, aged 1. **LSC 236**.

9466 MATHESON, Angus, b ca 1785. From Kildonan, SUT. To York Factory, Hudson Bay, arr 26 Aug 1815, thence to Red River. Pioneer settler. **LSC 325**.

9467 MATHESON, Angus, b ca 1815. Poss from Is Lewis, ROC. To St Anns, Victoria Co, NS, <1840. Moved in 1857 to Omaha or Leigh, North Is, NZ. Shipbuilder. Son Duncan, sea captain. **DC 15 Feb 1980**.

9468 MATHESON, Ann. From Gairloch par, ROC. To NS, ca 1839. m John McKenzie. **DC 11 Jan 1978**.

9469 MATHESON, Ann. From Is Skye, INV. To CAN, 1841; stld prob PEI. Wife of Donald Bruce, qv. **DC 1 Aug 1979**.

9470 MATHESON, Anne, ca 1790–1 Jan 1865. Prob from Rogart par, SUT. To NS, and stld Earltown, Colchester Co, <1841. **DC 19 Mar 1981**.

9471 MATHESON, Charles. From Lochbroom par, ROC. To Pictou, NS, on the *Hector*, ex Loch Broom, arr 17 Sep 1773; stld prob Pictou Co. **HPC App C**.

9472 MATHESON, Christian, b 1795. From Kildonan, SUT. Prob rel to Angus M, qv. To York Factory, Hudson Bay, arr 26 Aug 1815; thence to Red River. **LSC 325**.

9473 MATHESON, Christian, ca 1779–18 Apr 1844. From Shinness, Lairg par, SUT. To Pictou Co, NS, 1819. **DC 10 Feb 1980**.

9474 MATHESON, Christina, ca 1795–25 Dec 1882. From Rogart par, SUT. To Pictou, NS, 1822; stld Truro, Colchester Co. Wife of John William Murray, qv. **DC 15 May 1982**.

9475 MATHESON, Christy, ca 1787–11 Nov 1854. From SUT. To Pictou Co, NS, poss 1819; stld nr Lansdowne. Wife of Donald McLeod, qv. **DC 10 Feb 1980**.

9476 MATHESON, David, 1800–5 Jul 1848. From ROC. To Melbourne, Richmond Co, QUE. Discharged soldier, 79th Regt. **MGC 15 Jul 1980**.

9477 MATHESON, Donald. From Plockton, ROC. To St Peters, Richmond Co, NS, <1800. Son John. **HNS iii 71**.

9478 MATHESON, Donald. From Is North Uist, INV. To East Williams Twp, Middlesex Co, ONT, 1849. **PCM 44**.

9479 MATHESON, Donald. From Is Lewis, ROC. To QUE, ex Stornoway, arr 4 Aug 1851; stld Huron Twp, Bruce Co, ONT, 1852. Head of family. **DC 5 Apr 1967**.

9480 MATHESON, Dougald. From Lochalsh, ROC. To Inverness Co, NS, prob <1830; stld nr River Denys. Farmer. m Katherine McIntosh, Malagawatch. Dau Catherine, 1832-77. **MP ii 117**.

9481 MATHESON, Duncan, ca 1797–30 Apr 1879. From SUT. To Pictou Co, NS, 1819; stld Wilkins Grant or Lansdowne. m Jane Matheson, qv, ch: 1. Catherine, b 1826; 2. Anne, b 1828; 3. William, 1830-90; 4. Neil, b 1831; 5. Duncan, b 1844. **PAC 121; DC 10 Feb 1980**.

9482 MATHESON, Duncan. From Plockton, ROC. To St Esprit, Richmond Co, NS, 1820. m Jessie McLennan. Son Alexander, b 1846, postmaster, Sydney. **HNS iii 238**.

9483 MATHESON, Harriet, 1815–25 Jan 1906. Prob from Is Skye, INV. d/o Capt John M. To Charlottetown, PEI, 1828. m Malcolm Gillis, qv. **DC 16 Aug 1982**.

9484 MATHESON, Isabel, b ca 1803. From Lauderdale, BEW. To Dummer Twp, Peterborough Co, ONT, 1832. Wife of George Inglis, qv, whom she m 28 May 1831. **DC 14 Jul 1980**.

9485 MATHESON, Mrs Isabella. Prob from Lairg, SUT. To New Lairg, Pictou Co, NS, 1802. Widow with ch: 1. John; 2. Donald; 3. Finlay; 4. dau. **DC 30 Sep 1977**.

9486 MATHESON, Isabella, b ca 1765. From Kildonan, SUT. Wife of George McKay, qv. To York Factory, Hudson Bay, arr 26 Aug 1815, thence to Red River. **LSC 323**.

9487 MATHESON, Jane, ca 1798–20 Jan 1874. From SUT. To Pictou, NS, 1818. m Duncan Matheson, qv. **DC 2 Feb 1980**.

9488 MATHESON, John, b ca 1770. From SUT. s/o William M, qv. To Pictou, NS, on the *Hector*, ex Loch Broom, arr 17 Sep 1773; stld Londonderry, Colchester Co, later Rogers Hill, Pictou Co. **HPC App C; CP 35**.

9489 MATHESON, John. From Assynt or Eddrachillis, SUT. To Boston, MS, on the *Fortitude*, arr 16 Aug 1803; stld Scotch Ridge, Charlotte Co, NB, 1804. Formerly of the Reay Fencible Regt. Son Robert. **DC 29 Nov 1982**.

9490 MATHESON, John. From Kildonan, SUT. To Fort Churchill, Hudson Bay, on the *Prince of Wales*, ex Stromness, 28 Jun 1813. Went to York Factory, Apr 1814; thence to Red River. Pioneer settler. **LSS 186; RRS 27; LSC 323**.

9491 MATHESON, John, b ca 1792. From Auldbreakachy, Kildonan, SUT. To Fort Churchill, Hudson Bay, on the *Prince of Wales*, ex Stromness, 28 Jun 1813. Went to York Factory, Apr 1814, and on to Red River. Prob left settlement, 1815. **LSS 186; RRS 27; LSC 323**.

9492 MATHESON, John, b ca 1793. From Kildonan, SUT. To York Factory, Hudson Bay, arr 26 Aug 1815; and on to Red River. **LSC 327**.

9493 MATHESON, John, b 1790. From SUT. To Montreal, QUE, ca 1820; later to Tiverton, Bruce Co,

ONT. Carpenter. By wife Barbara had s Hugh. **DC 20 May 1962**.

9494 MATHESON, John. From ROC. To Shelburne, Shelburne Co, NS, <16 Jul 1827, when he m Mary Barber, from IRL. **VSN No 2343**.

9495 MATHESON, John. Poss from ARL. To Metcalfe Twp, Middlesex Co, ONT, 1831. **PCM 26**.

9496 MATHESON, John. To Pictou, NS, on the *Ellen*, ex Lochlaxford, SUT, 22 May 1848. Wife Johan with him, ch: 1. William; 2. John; 3. John; 4. Patrick; 5. Kenneth; 6. Elspet; 7. Robert. **DC 15 Jul 1979**.

9497 MATHESON, John Donald, 1802-65. From Is Skye, INV. To Charlottetown, PEI, prob on the *Mary Kennedy*, arr 1 Jun 1829; stld Uigg, Queens Co. m Isabella, d/o Donald Nicholson, qv, and Isabella Nicholson, qv. Son Roderick. **SPI 155; DC 31 Jul 1961**.

9498 MATHESON, Kate. From ROC. To Cape Breton, NS, poss <1820. Wife of Duncan MacLennan, qv. **NSN 32/379**.

9499 MATHESON, Margaret. From Lochalsh, ROC. To Victoria Co, NS, prob <1840; stld Middle River. m Lachlan MacDonald, qv. **DC 23 Feb 1980**.

9500 MATHESON, Neil, ca 1790–10 May 1866. From Lairg, SUT. To Pictou Co, NS, and bur Lansdowne. Wife Catherine, ca 1797–27 Aug 1866. **DC 10 Feb 1980**.

9501 MATHESON, Roderick. To ONT <1810. Served in Glengarry Light Infantry during War of 1812, and stld later in Perth, Lanark Co. Banker and politician. m 1823, Mary Robertson, Brockville. **BNA 731; HCL 56**.

9502 MATHESON, Sarah, 1828–22 Nov 1902. Prob from Is Lewis, ROC. To Victoria Co, NS. Wife of Alexander Morrison, qv. **DC 22 Jun 1979**.

9503 MATHESON, Widow, b ca 1755. From Kildonan, SUT. To York Factory, Hudson Bay, arr 26 Aug 1815; thence to Red River. ch with her: 1. Helen, aged 21; 2. John, aged 18, schoolteacher. **LSC 325**.

9504 MATHESON, William. From SUT. To Pictou, NS, on the *Hector*, ex Loch Broom, arr 17 Sep 1773; stld Londonderry, Colchester Co; later Pictou Co. ch: 1. John, qv; 2. William. **HPC App C**.

9505 MATHESON, William. From SUT. To Pictou Co, NS; stld nr Lansdowne. Wife Christy, ca 1765–16 Dec 1843. **DC 10 Feb 1980**.

9506 MATHEWS, Thomas, b ca 1768. To Little Bras D'Or, Cape Breton Co, NS, <1810. Farmer, m and had ch. **CBC 1818**.

MATHEWSON. See also MATHESON, MATHIESON and MATHISON.

9507 MATHEWSON, John, b ca 1795. To Pictou Co, NS, 1815; res Lower Settlement, 1816. Unm labourer. **INS 38**.

9508 MATHIE, David. From Forfar, ANS. To NB <1826. m Margaret Easton, qv. **Ts Forfar**.

MATHIESON. See also MATHISON, MATHESON and MATHEWSON.

9509 MATHIESON, Rev Alexander, 1 Oct 1795–14 Feb 1870. From Renton, DNB. s/o George M, copperplate printer, and Janet Ewing. Matric Univ of Glasgow, 1810, and grad MA, 1815. To Montreal, QUE, 1826. Min of St Andrews Ch. DD, Glasgow, 1837. **BNA 851; GMA 8038; RGG 426; FES vii 645; MDB 503.**

9510   MATHIESON, John. From SUT. To ONT, 1835; stld West Zorra, Oxford Co, ONT. Farmer. m 1839, Jean Middleton. Son John Hugh. **DC 29 Sep 1964.**

9511   MATHISON, Mary. Poss from Edinburgh. To CAN <1851. m — Johnston. **SH.**

9512   MATTHEW, George, ca 1749–27 Apr 1832. From Dundee, ANS. To St John, NB, <1800. Harbour-master. m Jane, 1761–1841, d/o Miles and Elizabeth Hamlin. Son David, 1778–1825, d Carthagena, Columbia. **NER viii 97.**

9513   MAUGHAN, Philip, 9 Nov 1831–29 Oct 1897. From Edinburgh. s/o Capt Philip M, HEIC Marine Service. Educ Edinburgh Academy, 1841-45. To CAN, ca 1855. Later in London, ENG. Insurance secretary. **EAR 118.**

9514   MAXTON, Alexander, ca 1812-39. From Alloa, CLK. s/o Rev John M, min of Alloa and Tullibody, and Elizabeth Bald. To Montreal, QUE. **FES iv 293; Ts Alloa.**

9515   MAXWELL, Alexander, d 1 Aug 1834. From Carruchan, Troqueer, KKD. s/o Lt Col M. To Galt, Wellington Co, ONT. **DGC 10 Sep 1834.**

9516   MAXWELL, Christina, ca 1797–8 Aug 1836. From Langholm, DFS. d/o Dr Charles M. and Jean Jardine. To CAN. **Ts Langholm.**

9517   MAXWELL, Duncan, 20 Jul 1810–20 Apr 1869. From Lochbroom, ROC. To NS, 1838, and bur Ebenezer Cemetery, Salt Springs, Pictou Co. **DC 10 Feb 1980.**

9518   MAXWELL, George, ca 1807–14 Jan 1902. Poss from Tayport, FIF. s/o Alexander M. and Elizabeth Dutch, sis/o Alexander and George D, qv. To NB, prob 1826; stld nr Dalhousie, Restigouche Co, 1829. m Margaret Miller, ch: 1. Mary Isabella, 1857–1921; 2. William, 1859–1942, postmaster, New Mills. **CUC 6; LDW 6 May 1967.**

9519   MAXWELL, Helen. From STI. To QUE on the *David of London*, ex Greenock, 19 May 1821; stld Lanark Co, ONT. Wife of Thomas Dods, qv, whom she m 13 Feb 1803. **DC 1 Nov 1979.**

9520   MAXWELL, Hugh. To Pictou, NS, on the *Lulan*, ex Glasgow, 17 Aug 1848. **DC 12 Jul 1979.**

9521   MAXWELL, Isabella. Poss from Edinburgh. To Halifax, NS, 1749. Wife of William Allan, qv. **MLA 10.**

9522   MAXWELL, Jean. From Rutherglen, LKS. To QUE on the *Prompt*, ex Greenock, 4 Jul 1820; stld Lanark Co, ONT. Wife of James Park, qv. **DC 12 Mar 1980.**

9523   MAXWELL, John, 1817–1904. Poss from DFS. To Napanee Twp, Addington Co, ONT, 1842. Physician. **DC 13 Jan 1982.**

9524   MAXWELL, Patrick, ca 1771–10 Jul 1790. From DFS. s/o Sir William M. of Sprinkell, 3rd Bt, and Margaret Stewart. Drowned at Shelburne, NS. Ensign, Warwickshire Regt. **DGH 13 Sep 1849.**

9525   MAXWELL, William Dunbar, ca 1789–6 Oct 1852. From DFS. To Pictou Co, NS, and bur Ebenezer

Cemetery, Salt Springs. Wife Jane McCallum, qv. **DC 10 Feb 1980.**

9526   MEEK, James, b 2 Feb 1820. From Longridge, WLN. Prob s/o George M. and Isabella Wallace. To Scott Twp, York Co, ONT, 1847. Farmer. m Frances Somerville, qv, ch: 1. John, b 15 Sep 1846; 2. Catherine Wilson, b 16 Jun 1848; 3. Janet, b 2 May 1851; 4. Mary Jane, b 25 Aug 1852; 5. James Cleland, b 4 Aug 1854; 6. William, b 11 Sep 1862; 7. Agnes, b 29 Dec 1856; 8. Robert Wilson, b 3 Oct 1858; 9. George, b 30 Jul 1860; 10. William, b 4 Sep 1862; 11. George, b 28 Jul 1864; 12. Frances, b 7 Dec 1867. **DC 15 Jul 1979.**

9527   MEIKLE, Alison, 15 Jul 1800–26 Mar 1880. Prob from LKS. To Dummer Twp, Peterborough Co, ONT, <1830. Wife of Menan Forsyth, qv. **DC 8 Nov 1981.**

9528   MEIKLE, Mary. Prob from AYR. Gr-dau of James McClure, Galston, who d 1837. To CAN <1855. m Robert McHoull. **SH.**

9529   MEIKLEJOHN, James. From Edinburgh. To PEI <1850; later to North Is, NZ. Shipbuilder. **DC 18 May 1982.**

9530   MELDRUM, John. From ABD. To Waterloo Co, ONT. Farmer. m Elsie Smith. Son William Hewitt. **DC 29 Sep 1964.**

9531   MELDRUM, Rev William, d 22 Nov 1889. From ABD. To Puslinch Twp, Wellington Co, ONT, 1840. Min there. Joined FC, 1844, and was afterwards at Vaughan and Harrington. **FES vii 646.**

9532   MELLANSON, Charles. Prob from ABD. bro/o Peter M, qv. To Port Royal, NS, ca 1657. Wrote several letters in 1696 to the Governor of Massachusetts Bay Colony, in one of which he refers to French privateers wintering at Port Royal, and pretending 'to take possession of this Country against our wills.' **DC 8 Mar and 14 May 1958.**

9533   MELLANSON, Peter. Prob from ABD. bro/o Charles M, qv. To Port Royal, NS, ca 1657. **DC 8 Mar and 14 May 1958.**

9534   MELROSE, Alexander. From Chirnside, BEW. bro/o William M, qv. To QUE, prob 1830. Worked as a mason on the Erie Canal, and stld ca 1835 in Megantic Co. m Williamina Forbes, qv, ch: 1. Janet; 2. John; 3. Mary, b QUE; 4. Agnes; 5. Margaret; 6. Williamina. **DC 11 Feb 1980.**

9535   MELROSE, William. From Chirnside, BEW. bro/o Alexander M, qv. To Inverness Twp, Megantic Co, QUE, 1831. Tailor. **DC 11 Feb 1980.**

9536   MELVILL, Alexander, d 31 Oct 1823. To Halifax, NS, and drowned in St Margarets Bay. **VSN 366.**

9537   MELVILLE, Catherine, d 10 Sep 1891. Poss from Glenelg, INV. d/o William M. and Katherine MacLeod. To QUE on the *Liscard*, 1849, and stld Glengarry Co, ONT. m Duncan, s/o Norman MacLeod and Christie MacRae, and had ch. **MG 30, 349.**

9538   MELVILLE, Peter. From Breadalbane, PER. To East Williams Twp, Middlesex Co, ONT, 1832. **PCM 43.**

9539   MELVIN, Ann. From ABD. To Burford Twp, Brant Co, ONT, 1843. Wife of Stephen Wilson, qv. **DC 23 Sep 1980.**

9540 MELVIN, Robert. From ABD. To QUE on the *Fania*, ex Glasgow, 30 Jun 1834; stld Bon Accord, Nichol Twp, Wellington Co, ONT. **EHE 64**.

9541 MENNIE, John. From Insch, ABD. To Elora, Nichol Twp, Wellington Co, ONT, 1836. m Elizabeth Sorrie, qv, ch: 1. John, dry goods merchant, Fergus; 2. Alexander, Assessor, Fergus; 3. George, res Bessemer, MI; 4. Peter; 5. James; 6. William; 7. Catharine; 8. Mary Ann; 9. Maria. **EHE 95**.

9542 MENNIE, Margaret, d 19 Feb 1865. From Rayne, ABD. To Nichol Twp, Wellington Co, ONT, ca 1836; stld later Pilkington Twp. m 31 Dec 1833, James Cruickshank, qv. **EHE 40**.

9543 MENZIE, William. From PER. To Pictou Co, NS, 1849; stld Fox Harbour, Cumberland Co; later Tatamagouche, Colchester Co. m Agnes Donaldson, qv. **HT 83**.

9544 MENZIES, Archibald. From Blair Drummond, PER. To ONT, prob <1852; stld Goderich, Huron Co. Farmer. **DC 15 Feb 1971**.

9545 MENZIES, Elizabeth, 4 Sep 1813–26 Feb 1886. Poss from PER. To Hamilton, ONT. Wife of John Colville, qv. **Ts Mt Albion**.

9546 MENZIES, George, d 4 Mar 1847. To Oxford Co, ONT. Journalist, and in 1840 founded the *Herald*, in Woodstock. **MDB 507**.

9547 MENZIES, John. Prob from PER. To Aldborough Twp, Elgin Co, ONT, ca 1814. Pioneer settler. **PDA 24**.

9548 MENZIES, John, 22 Nov 1779–2 Dec 1859. From PER. To Halton Co, ONT, poss <1830; stld Esquesing Twp. Bur Hillcrest, Norval. **EPE 77**.

9549 MENZIES, Mary. Prob from BAN. To Pictou, NS, 1817. Wife of John Geddes, qv. **DC 21 Mar 1981**.

9550 MENZIES, Susan, 30 Nov 1801–11 Oct 1876. From Fortingall, PER. To Halton Co, ONT, <1850; stld Esquesing Twp. m Duncan Menzies. **EPE 75**.

9551 MENZIES, Thomas. From Comrie, PER. s/o James M, d 1849, shoemaker, and Isabella MacIntyre, d 1841. To Peterborough Co, ONT, <1855. **Ts Comrie**.

9552 MENZIES, William. To East Williams Twp, Middlesex Co, ONT, 1844. **PCM 44**.

9553 MENZIES, William Cunningham, 14 Jun 1833–10 Apr 1876. From Maybole, AYR. s/o Rev William M, par min, and Margaret Pagan. Matric Univ of Glasgow, 1848. Emp with Bank of British North America, later with Bank of Nova Scotia, Halifax, NS. d at Hyères, France. **GMA 15487; FES iii 54**.

9554 MERCER, Isabella. From Tillicoultry, CLK. To CAN, prob ONT, 1852. Wife of Robert Philip, qv. **Tillicoultry OPR 486/3**.

9555 MERCER, William, 1808–27. s/o John and Ann M. To St John, NB, and d there. **NER viii 97**.

9556 MERRIMAN, George, b ca 1791, Harray, OKI. To Hudson Bay, ca 1813, and prob to Red River. **RRS 13**.

9557 MERTON, Agnes, b ca 1798. From Eccles, BEW. d/o — M. and Elizabeth Aitchison. To ONT <1832. **Ts Eccles**.

9558 MERTON, Elizabeth, b ca 1795. From Eccles, BEW. d/o — M. and Elizabeth Aitchison. To ONT <1832. **Ts Eccles**.

9559 MICHIE, Ann. From ABD. To Nichol Twp, Wellington Co, ONT, ca 1842. m John Thacker. **EHE 23**.

9560 MICHIE, Charles. From ABD. To Elora, Nichol Twp, Wellington Co, ONT, 1836. **EHE 92**.

9561 MICHIE, James, 29 Feb 1828–13 Jan 1883. From Corgarff, Strathdon, ABD. To ONT and d Toronto. **SG xxx/1 22**.

9562 MICHIE, John, 1789–1861. From BAN. To NS, 1818; stld Cumberland Co. **DC 29 Oct 1980**.

9563 MICHIE, William, ca 1792–19 Apr 1885. Prob from Northhouse, Hawick, ROX. To Esquesing Twp, Halton Co, ONT, and d there. **THS 1938/57**.

9564 MIDDLEMISS, Rev James, 23 Feb 1823–11 Mar 1907. From Duns, BEW. Educ Univ of Edinburgh. To Hamilton, ONT, but stld Elora, Nichol Twp, Wellington Co. Min there. m 23 Aug 1855, Mary, 1802–91, d/o Capt Duncan Menzies, RN, of Dura Den, Cupar, FIF. **MDB 512; EHE 156**.

9565 MIDDLETON, Catherine Robeson, 18 Sep 1816–5 Mar 1878. From ABD. d/o Rev James M, qv, and Catherine Robeson, qv. To Nichol Twp, Wellington Co, ONT, 1838. m 1 Nov 1838, John Alexander Davidson, qv. **EHE 89; DC 7 Jun 1980**.

9566 MIDDLETON, Christina, 2 Apr 1829–14 Apr 1853. From Aberdeen. d/o Rev James M, qv, and Catherine Robeson, qv. To Nichol Twp, Wellington Co, ONT, 1838. m 14 Apr 1853, Charles Keeling, 1819–95, from Derby, ENG. **EHE 95; DC 7 Jun 1980**.

9567 MIDDLETON, Gavin, 22 Dec 1831–6 Feb 1910. From Aberdeen. s/o Rev James M, qv, and Catherine Robeson, qv. To Nichol Twp, Wellington Co, ONT, prob 1838, and d Carnduff, SAS. m Jean Graham. **EHE 95; DC 7 Jun 1980**.

9568 MIDDLETON, James, ca 1816–7 Jun 1844. From Arbroath, ANS. s/o Charles M. and Elizabeth Williamson. To St John, NB, and d there. **Ts Arbroath Abbey**.

9569 MIDDLETON, Rev James, 28 Mar 1788–28 Nov 1873. From Aberdeen. To Nichol Twp, Wellington Co, ONT, 1838; stld Lot 16, Con 12. Min of religion. m Catherine Robeson, qv, ch: 1. William Gavin, qv; 2. Catherine Robeson, qv; 3. Capt Lewis, qv; 4. James, 1820-25; 5. John, 1822-41; 6. Mary Ann, qv; 7. James, qv; 8. Christina, qv; 9. Gavin, qv; 10. Jane Smith, qv. **EHE 95; DC 7 Jun 1980**.

9570 MIDDLETON, James, 25 Dec 1826–10 Jan 1905. From Aberdeen. s/o Rev James M, qv, and Catherine Robeson, qv. To Nichol Twp, Wellington Co, ONT, 1838. m Margaret Elmslie, qv. **EHE 95; DC 7 Jun 1980**.

9571 MIDDLETON, James Taylor, b 28 Nov 1840. From Alloa, CLK. s/o Arthur M. and Jeanette Stuart Taylor. To St Catharines, Lincoln Co, ONT, arr 3 Jul 1851. Wholesaler, and became Sheriff. m 1865, Catherine, d/o William O. Eastman and Catherine Keefer. **DC 29 Sep 1964**.

9572 MIDDLETON, Jane Smith, 9 Nov 1834–25 Aug

1862. From Aberdeen. d/o Rev James M, qv, and Catherine Robeson, qv. To Nichol Twp, Wellington Co, ONT, 1838. m 27 May 1856, William H. Fraser. **EHE 95; DC 7 Jun 1980**.

9573 MIDDLETON, Jessie. From PER. d/o William M. To Halifax, NS, 1849. Wife of Rev Robert Sedgwick, qv. **HNS iii 164**.

9574 MIDDLETON, Lewis, 12 Jul 1818–1 Jan 1888. From Aberdeen. d/o Rev James M, qv, and Catherine Robeson, qv. To Nichol Twp, Wellington Co, ONT. m Sophia, d/o William Lyall, qv, and Jane Forgue, qv. **EHE 95; DC 7 Jun 1980**.

9575 MIDDLETON, Mary Ann, 1 Nov 1824–28 May 1907. From Aberdeen. d/o Rev James M, qv, and Catherine Robeson, qv. To Nichol Twp, Wellington Co, ONT, 1838. m William Robert, 1820–1900, s/o Joseph Field and Esther Pallet. **EHE 95; DC 7 Jun 1980**.

9576 MIDDLETON, William Gavin, 7 Apr 1815–26 Oct 1881. From Aberdeen. s/o Rev James M, qv, and Catherine Robeson, qv. To Nichol Twp, Wellington Co, ONT, 1838, and d Amherst Is. m Henrietta, d/o Charles Allan, qv, and Grace Irons, qv. **EHE 95**.

9577 MILL, Christina, ca 1790–ca 1870. From Halkirk, CAI. d/o William M. and Margaret Polson. To Markham Twp, York Co, ONT, ca 1840. m 1 Jan 1813, William MacDonald, qv. **DC 5 Jul 1979**.

9578 MILL, John, ca 1800–5 Mar 1858. From Lochmaben, DFS. To Richibucto, Kent Co, NB, 1824. Merchant. **CAE 18**.

9579 MILLAR, Alexander, 1823–1901. From Kilmory par, Is Arran, BUT. s/o Thomas M, qv. To Restigouche Co, NB, <1853, when m Anne Hamilton. **DC 10 Jul 1980**.

9580 MILLAR, Andrew. From Edinburgh. To Pictou, NS, prob <1820. Son John, b 1824, stld Tatamagouche, Colchester Co. **HT 73**.

9581 MILLAR, Janet. From Comrie, PER. To Otonabee Twp, Peterborough Co, ONT, 1829. Wife of Duncan Comrie, qv. **DC 13 Sep 1982**.

9582 MILLAR, Margaret, 1827–1908. From SEL. To Waterloo Co, ONT, <1 Feb 1850, when she m Thomas Baird, qv. **DC 2 Dec 1979**.

9583 MILLAR, Thomas, 1786–1879. From Kilmory par, Is Arran, BUT. s/o Alexander M. and Margaret Neish. To Restigouche Co, NB, <1855. Bur New Mills. Wife Catharine, 1793–1886, with him, and ch: 1. Margaret, b ca 1821; 2. Alexander, qv; 3. Ann, b ca 1824; 4. Janet, b ca 1826; 5. Kathy, b ca 1828; 6. James, b ca 1830; 7. John, b ca 1832. **DC 10 Jul 1980**.

9584 MILLAR, William Gillies. From DFS. To St John, NB. m there, 1 Aug 1857, Agnes, d/o Robert Beattie. **DGC 28 Aug 1857**.

9585 MILLER, Agnes, 26 Feb 1826–15 Dec 1901. From Kirkintilloch, DNB. d/o Robert M, qv, and Janet Rowat, qv. To Perth Twp, Lanark Co, ONT, 1827; stld later Medonte Twp, Simcoe Co. m David Brotherston. **DC 8 Nov 1981**.

9586 MILLER, Agnes, ca 1790–20 Jun 1863. From STI. To South Orillia Twp, Simcoe Co, ONT, 1832. Wife of John Harvie, qv. **DC 8 Nov 1981**.

9587 MILLER, Alexander, ca 1802–7 Jul 1823. bro/o John M. To NB, and d Nepisiguit, Chaleur Bay. **VSN No 226**.

9588 MILLER, Alexander. From Arnprior, STI. To Montreal, QUE, on the *Niagara*, ex Greenock, arr 28 May 1825; stld Flat River, McNab Twp, Renfrew Co, ONT. Schoolteacher, farmer and emigrant leader. Wife Agnes Moir, qv, with him, and ch: 1. Janet; 2. Peter. **HCL 103; EMT 18**.

9589 MILLER, Alexander, 23 May 1772–11 Aug 1845. From Kirkintilloch, DNB. s/o Alexander M. and Margaret Frew. To Perth Twp, Lanark Co, ONT, 1827; went to Medonte Twp, Simcoe Co, 1835. Weaver. m (i) Susanna Burnie, ch: 1. Robert, qv. m (ii) Jane McLaren, qv, with further ch: 2. Alexander, jr, qv; 3. James, qv; 4. William; 5. Mary; 6. John, 1835–89; 7. Margaret; 8. Thomas, b 1837; 9. Robert McLaren, 1840–1922. **DC 8 Nov 1981**.

9590 MILLER, Alexander, jr, b 1819. From Kirkintilloch, DNB. s/o Alexander M, qv, and Jane McLaren, qv. To Lanark Co, ONT, 1827; moved to Medonte Twp, Simcoe Co, 1835. m 1840, Rebecca French. **DC 8 Nov 1981**.

9591 MILLER, Andrew. From Aberdeen. To ONT, 1843. m Catherine McKillop, ch: 1. James; 2. Colin. **DC 21 Mar 1981**.

9592 MILLER, Andrew F, ca 1818–19 Apr 1862. From Riggfoot, Cummertrees, DFS. s/o William M. To St Catharines, Lincoln Co, ONT, and d there. **Ts Cummertrees**.

9593 MILLER, Catherine, ca 1758–Apr 1828. From Crieff, PER. d/o John M, qv, and wife Catherine. To Richmond Bay, PEI, on the *Falmouth*, ex Greenock, 8 Apr 1770; stld Stanhope, Queens Co. m ca 1779, William Douglas, qv. **DC 28 May 1980**.

9594 MILLER, Cecilia. From Dysart, FIF. To Guelph Twp, Wellington Co, ONT, 1834. Later in Pilkington Twp. Wife of James Ross, qv. **EHE 40**.

9595 MILLER, Christina, 1 Apr 1829–18 Sep 1865. Poss from Edinburgh. d/o Alexander M. and Christina Stuart. To PEI, 1850; but stld St John, NB, 1853. Went later to USA, and d Salem, OR. Wife of Andrew McCalley, qv, whom she m at Edinburgh, 1 May 1845. **DC 2 Nov 1975**.

9596 MILLER, Elizabeth, ca 1794–26 Apr 1838. From Wintersheugh, Cummertrees, DFS. d/o John M. and Euphemia Story, qv. To ONT, and d Markham, York Co. **Ts Cummertrees**.

MILLER, Mrs John. See STORY, Euphemia.

9597 MILLER, George. To QUE on the *Fame*, 1815; stld Lot 22, Con 1, Drummond Twp, Lanark Co, ONT. **HCL 233**.

9598 MILLER, George, 7 Feb 1790–10 Jun 1848. From Kippen, STI. To Halton Co, ONT, prob <1830; stld Esquesing Twp, and bur Boston cemetery. **EPE 75**.

9599 MILLER, George. From Riggfoot, Cummertrees, DFS. Prob rel to William M, qv. To ONT, ca 1831; stld Markham Twp, York Co. Farmer and stockman. Dau Mary. **CAE 5, 7**.

9600 MILLER, Isabella, ca 1764–ca 1820. From Crieff,

PER. d/o John M, qv, and wife Catherine. To Richmond Bay, PEI, on the *Falmouth*, ex Greenock, 8 Apr 1770; stld Stanhope, Queens Co. m 15 Jan 1785, Duncan Shaw, qv.   **DC 28 May 1980**.

9601   MILLER, Isabella. From Murrayshall, PER. d/o George M. To ONT <1851.   **SH**.

9602   MILLER, James, b ca 1767. From West Kilbride, AYR. To QUE, ex Greenock, summer 1815; stld North Burgess Twp, Lanark Co, ONT. Mariner, later farmer. Wife Mary Friend, qv, with him, and 3 ch.   **SEC 3; HCL 230**.

9603   MILLER, James, 1821-92. From Kirkintilloch, DNB. s/o Alexander M, qv, and Jane McLaren, qv. To Perth Twp, Lanark Co, ONT, 1827. Moved in 1835 to Medonte Twp, Simcoe Co. m Isabella Johnston. **DC 8 Nov 1981**.

9604   MILLER, Janet. From AYR. To Galt, ONT, 1833; stld Dumfries Twp. m John Dickie, jr, qv.   **DD 14**.

9605   MILLER, Jean. From PER. To PEI, 1808; stld Marshfield. Wife of James Robertson, qv.   **HP 102**.

9606   MILLER, Jean. Prob from Edinburgh. d/o Joseph M. To CAN <1833. m — Stark.   **SH**.

9607   MILLER, Jean, 10 Mar 1794–14 Feb 1863. From Glasgow. To QUE, ex Greenock, 24 Jun 1847; stld Ancaster Twp, Wentworth Co, ONT. Wife of James Young, qv.   **DC 6 Feb 1982**.

9608   MILLER, John, ca 1730–ca 1810. From Muthil par, PER. To Richmond Bay, PEI, on the *Falmouth*, ex Greenock, 8 Apr 1770; stld Covehead, Queens Co. Wife Catherine with him. ch: 1. Catherine, qv; 2. Isabella, qv; 3. Mary, qv; 4. Annabella; 5. Elizabeth; 6. Helen; · 7. Margaret; 8. Janet; 9. John, 1782–1856. **DC 28 May 1980**.

9609   MILLER, John, b ca 1794. From Reston or Coldingham, BEW. To QUE on the *Atlas*, ex Greenock, 11 Jul 1815; stld Lot 4, Con 10, North Burgess Twp, Lanark Co, ONT. Farmworker.   **SEC 1; HCL 16, 231**.

9610   MILLER, John, b ca 1795. From Sorn, AYR. To QUE <1816. m Isabella Torrance, qv, ch.   **DC 30 Jul 1980**.

9611   MILLER, John, ca 1823–10 Sep 1891. From PER. To Halton Co, ONT, poss <1850; stld Esquesing Twp, and bur Greenwood cemetery, Georgetown.   **EPE 76**.

9612   MILLER, John. From Cummertrees, par, DFS. To Toronto, ONT, <8 Mar 1848, when m Margaret Whiteside, from Pickering, where he may have stld. **DGH 13 Apr 1848**.

9613   MILLER, Margaret, 1793–1866. From ROX. To ONT <1804; stld prob Huron Co. Wife of Peter Dods, qv.   **DC 26 May 1979**.

9614   MILLER, Margaret, 1798–1874. From Annan, DFS. To New Annan, Colchester Co, NS, 1832. Wife of William Aitchison, qv.   **SG xxvii/2 76**.

9615   MILLER, Margaret, ca 1808–27 May 1869. From PER. To Halton Co, ONT, <1840; stld Esquesing Twp. m George Barnes.   **EPE 76**.

9616   MILLER, Margaret Cook, ca 1825–22 Mar 1910. From Gorbals, Glasgow. d/o Walter and Margaret M. To Hibbert Twp, Perth Co, ONT, 1850. Wife of John Whyte, qv.   **DC 26 May 1979 and 10 Jul 1980**.

9617   MILLER, Marian. From Mangrel, Is Arran, BUT. To Inverness, Megantic Co, QUE, 1831. m 1819, Duncan Sillers, qv   **MAC 41**.

9618   MILLER, Mary, ca 1767–22 Feb 1852. From Crieff, PER. d/o John M, qv, and wife Catherine. To Richmond Bay, PEI, on the *Falmouth*, ex Greenock, arr 8 Apr 1770; stld Stanhope, Queens Co. m 13 Feb 1790, William Simpson, qv.   **DC 28 May 1980**.

9619   MILLER, Mary, 1824–9 Oct 1904. From Kirkintilloch, DNB. d/o Robert M, qv, and Jane Rowat, qv. To Perth, Lanark Co, ONT, 1827; moved to Medonte Twp, Simcoe Co, 1835. m William Thompson. **DC 8 Nov 1981**.

9620   MILLER, Mary Ann. From Murrayshall, PER. d/o George M. To ONT <1851. m — Hunt.   **SH**.

9621   MILLER, Rev Matthew, 1806–15 Feb 1834. From Glasgow. s/o James M, merchant. Matric Univ of Glasgow, 1820, and grad MA, 1824. App by Glasgow Colonial Society, and ord min of Cobourg and Colborne, ONT, 19 Jun 1833. Drowned through ice breaking on the Bay of Quinte.   **GMA 10549; FES vii 646**.

9622   MILLER, Mrs. Cabin passenger on the *London*, arr Pictou, NS, 11 Apr 1848.   **DC 15 Jul 1979**.

9623   MILLER, Peter, ca 1796–1 Aug 1832. From Cullen, BAN. To Montreal, QUE, and d there. **Ts Cullen**.

9624   MILLER, Peter, ca 1803–14 Apr 1876. From Blackford, PER. To Halton Co, ONT, prob <1850; stld Esquesing Twp, and bur at Limehouse.   **EPE 76**.

9625   MILLER, Robert. Served in the 82nd Regt and was gr land in Pictou Co, NS.   **HPC App F**.

9626   MILLER, Robert, 1802–3 Sep 1882. Prob from DNB. s/o Alexander M, qv, and first wife Susanna Burnie. To Perth, Lanark Co, ONT, 1827; moved to Medonte Twp, Simcoe Co, 1835, and stld Lot 11W, Con 6. Farmer. m Jane Rowat, qv, ch: 1. Mary, qv; 2. Agnes, qv; 3. Jessie; 4. Christine, 1830–1909; 5. Robert, 1832-77; 6. Margaret, 1834–1918; 7. Alexander, b 1836; 8. Susanna, 1840–1930; 9. Jane; 10. David, 1842–1918.   **DC 8 Nov 1981**.

9627   MILLER, Robert. From Stewarton, AYR. To QUE, 1832, and stld Galt, Waterloo Co, ONT. Surgeon; MD, New York, 1850, and MRCP, London, 1860.   **HGD 95**.

9628   MILLER, Walter. Prob from Stevenston, AYR. bro/o Bryce M. To QUE, arr May 1841; stld Megantic Co. Stock-breeder.   **DC 20 Apr 1981**.

9629   MILLER, William. From Glasgow. To QUE on the *Prompt*, ex Greenock, 4 Jul 1820; stld Lot 14, Con 2, Dalhousie Twp, Lanark Co, ONT.   **HCL 68**.

9630   MILLER, Rev William, 1786–1861. From AYR. To Pictou Co, NS, ca 1821. Ord at West River, and became Presb min at Hillsborough, Mabou, Inverness Co. Resigned 1851. m Maria, b 1804, d/o Peter and Charlotte Sarah Renouf, ch: 1. John, b 1826; 2. William, b 1828; 3. Alexander, 1832–1901; 4. Elizabeth, b 1835, d unm; 5. Grace, b 1836; 6. James, b 1839; 7. Rachel, b 1847; 8. Mary Jane, b 1848; 9. Peter, b 1850.   **MP ii 591, 652; DC 11 Apr 1981**.

9631 MILLER, William, ca 1793–22 Jun 1879. From Riggfoot, Cummertrees, DFS. To ONT, prob 1831; stld York Co, and d Pickering. m Helen Parish, qv. **CAE 47**.

9632 MILLER, Rev William. Prob from Duns, BEW. Relief Ch min elected to Kilmarnonock, DNB, 1844, but refused the call and came to CAN. **UPV i 219**.

9633 MILLER, William. From Murrayshall, PER. s/o George M. To ONT <1851. **SH**.

9634 MILLIGAN, Rev Archibald H, d 7 Feb 1855. From Thornhill, DFS. Educ Univ of Edinburgh. Min of East Chapel, Airdrie, LKS, 1846-51; Pultneytown, CAI, 1852-53. To Montreal, QUE, 1853, and was min at Russeltown Flats. **FES iii 221, vii 646; DGC 13 Mar 1855**.

9635 MILLIGAN, Elizabeth, ca 1747–26 Feb 1820. From KKD. To NS. **NSS No 1881**.

9636 MILLIGAN, John, ca 1774–1 May 1821. From DFS. To St John, NB. Architect and Civil Engineer. Son John. **NER viii 97; DGC 4 Sep 1821**.

9637 MILLIGAN, Peter. From Nether Locharwoods, Ruthwell, DFS. To Clarke, Durham Co, ONT, <1843. Dau Ann. **DGC 18 Jan 1844**.

9638 MILLIGAN, Robert, 1784–3 Feb 1871. From DFS. To PEI 1819. **CAE 25**.

9639 MILLIKEN, Janet. From AYR. To Cape Traverse, Prince Co, PEI, <1836. Wife of John McMeekin, qv. **DC 30 Jun 1976**.

9640 MILLOY, Duncan, ca 1825–20 Oct 1871. From Oban, ARL. To ONT, 1843; stld Brant Co, but went later to Niagara, Lincoln Co. Capt and owner of a lake steamer. **DC 18 May 1982**.

9641 MILNE, Alexander, 5 Aug 1777–18 Oct 1844. From Crimond par, ABD. To Uxbridge Twp, York Co, ONT, ca 1840. m Isabella Park, qv, ch: 1. Margaret, qv; 2. William, 1814-45, d IL, USA; 3. James, qv; 4. Alexander, 1818-44; 5. Robert, 1820-91, d Garafraxa Twp, Wellington Co; 6. Isabella, 1825-87, d Buffalo, NY; 7. Harriet, 1835-82. **DC 12 Sep 1979**.

9642 MILNE, Andrew, 1 Apr 1790–3 Mar 1873. From Rothiemay, BAN. s/o William and Ann Milne. To Pictou, NS, ex Leith, 11 May 1811; stld Frasers Mountain. m Ann Small, 1823, ch: 1. John, d inf; 2. John, 1825-59; 3. William, 1827-59, schoolteacher; 4. Ann, 1829-71; 5. Anthony, 1832–1928; 6. Marian, 1834-79; 7. Andrew, 1837-40; 8. James, 1839-76; 9. George, 1842-1935; 10. Mary Jane, 1845-1931. **DC 20 Nov 1981**.

9643 MILNE, Ann. From Auchinblae, Fordoun, KCD. d/o David M, qv, and Ann Scott, qv. To Nichol Twp, Wellington Co, ONT, <1844. m David Black. **EHE 43**.

9644 MILNE, David, d 29 Oct 1822. To Hants Co, NS, and d at Shubenacadie. **VSN No 9**.

9645 MILNE, David, 1792–28 Jun 1887. From Auchinblae, Fordoun, KCD. To Nichol Twp, Wellington Co, ONT, <1844. m Ann Scott, qv, ch: 1. William, qv; 2. James, qv; 3. Mary, qv; 4. Ann, qv; 5. Margaret, qv; 6. Elspet, qv; 7. Jean, qv; 8. David, jr, qv; 9. Isabella, qv; 10. Jessie, qv; 11. George, qv; 12. Helen, qv. **EHE 43**.

9646 MILNE, David, jr. From Auchinblae, Fordoun,

KCD. s/o David M, qv, and Ann Scott, qv. To Nichol Twp, Wellington Co, ONT, <1844. m Jane Richardson. **EHE 43**.

9647 MILNE, Elspet, 1828-97. From Auchinblae, Fordoun, KCD. d/o David M, qv, and Ann Scott, qv. To Nichol Twp, Wellington Co, ONT, <1844. m Arthur Ross, qv. **EHE 42**.

9648 MILNE, Fairly, 20 Sep 1812–7 Dec 1865. From ABD. To QUE, 1836; stld Elora, Wellington Co, ONT. Farmer. m Isabella Booth Scott, qv, ch: 1. John, b 1837; 2. William, b 1838; 3. David, 1839–1910; 4. Alexander, 1841–1911; 5. Fairly, 1842-58; 6. Margaret, 1844-84; 7. Robert, b 1846; 8. James Scott, b 1848; 9. Isabella, 1850–1919; 10. Mary, b 1852; 11. Ellan, 1854-91; 12. Jane, 1859-97; 13. Elizabeth, 1859-87, twin. **DC 27 Nov 1981**.

9649 MILNE, George. From Auchinblae, Fordoun, KCD. s/o David M, qv, and Ann Scott, qv. To Nichol Twp, Wellington Co, ONT, <1844. m Helen Hay. **EHE 43**.

9650 MILNE, Helen. From Edinburgh. sis/o Charles M, baker. To CAN, prob ONT, <1851. m Robert Fairbairn, qv. **SH**.

9651 MILNE, Isabella. From Auchinblae, Fordoun, KCD. d/o David M, qv, and Ann Scott, qv. To Nichol Twp, Wellington Co, ONT, <1844. m Robert Fasken, qv. **EHE 43**.

9652 MILNE, Rev James. From Aberdeen. s/o George M. Matric Marischall Coll, 1775. Episcopal min at Banff, 1797, later at Marnoch. To NS, ca 1816. **FAM ii 349; SNQ ii/2 138**.

9653 MILNE, James. From Insch par, ABD. To QUE, ca 1836; stld Elora, Nichol Twp, Wellington Co, ONT. m Anne Mann, qv, ch: 1. James, b 1831; 2. Betty, b 1832; 3. Scott Alexander, b 1833; 4. Ann, b 1835; 5. Margaret, b 1836; 6. George, b 1839; 7. Robert, b 1841. **DC 27 Nov 1981**.

9654 MILNE, James. From Auchinblae, Fordoun, KCD. s/o David M, qv, and Ann Scott, qv. To Elora, Nichol Twp, Wellington Co, ONT, <1844. m Mary Barclay. **EHE 43**.

9655 MILNE, James, 17 Jan 1816–3 May 1898. From Crimond par, ABD. s/o Alexander M, qv, and Isabella Park, qv. To Uxbridge Twp, York Co, ONT, ca 1840. Blacksmith and farmer. m Ann Cowie, qv, ch: 1. Margaret, 1843-78; 2. Isabella Ann, 1845-46; 3. Eliza Ann, 1847–1927; 4. Harriet, 1849–1923, d Winnipeg; 5. Mary Jean, 1855–1936, d Agincourt; 6. Isabella Park, 1857–1938, d Toronto; 7. William Milne, 1860–1912, d Toronto; 8. John, 1866–1945, d Vancouver, BC; 9. Annie, b 1867; 10. Louisa, b 1870, d inf. **DC 12 Sep 1979**.

9656 MILNE, James, 1821-98. From Kincardine O'Neil, ABD. s/o James M. and Margaret Forbes. To Nissouri Twp, Middlesex Co, ONT, <1855. Farmer. m Margaret Adam, qv. **DC 1 Aug 1979**.

9657 MILNE, Jean. From Auchinblae, Fordoun, KCD. d/o David M, qv, and Ann Scott, qv. To Nichol Twp, Wellington Co, ONT, <1844. m Hugh Kilpatrick. **EHE 43**.

9658 MILNE, Jessie. From Auchinblae, Fordoun, KCD.

d/o David M, qv, and Ann Scott, qv. To Nichol Twp, Wellington Co, ONT, <1844. m Alexander Dalgarno. **EHE 43**.

9659 MILNE, John, b 1838. s/o Thomas M. and Jane McKay. To Waterloo Co, ONT, <1842. m 1860, Barbara Ann, d/o David Wismer, ch: 1. Arthur; 2. John; 3. Ariadne.   **DC 29 Sep 1964**.

9660 MILNE, John. From ABD. To QUE, ca 1846; stld Elora, Nichol Twp, Wellington Co, ONT. m Margaret Anderson. Dau Christian.   **DC 27 Nov 1981**.

9661 MILNE, Margaret. From Aberdeen. m in NS, Capt Edward Smith, qv.   **NSS No 345**.

9662 MILNE, Margaret, 6 Feb 1812–Aug 1892. From Crimond par, ABD. d/o Alexander M, qv, and Isabella Park, qv. To Uxbridge, York Co, ONT, ca 1840. m James Walker, and d at Fergus.   **DC 12 Sep 1979**.

9663 MILNE, Margaret. From Auchinblae, Fordoun, KCD. d/o David M, qv, and Ann Scott, qv. To Nichol Twp, Wellington Co, ONT, <1844. m Andrew Smith, and retr to SCT.   **EHE 43**.

9664 MILNE, Mary. From Auchinblae, Fordoun, KCD. d/o David M, qv, and Ann Scott, qv. To Nichol Twp, Wellington Co, ONT, <1844. m James Ross, Guelph. **EHE 43**.

9665 MILNE, Robert. From Aberdeen. To Halifax, NS, <24 Jan 1828, when m Jane Hutton, Edwards Valley. **VSN No 2681**.

9666 MILNE, Thomas, 1825–1908. From Laurencekirk, KCD. To Wellington Co, ONT, and stld Fergus. m Mary Croll, 1825-74.   **DC 21 Mar 1981**.

9667 MILNE, William, ca 1753 - 1825. From Falkirk, STI. s/o Alexander M, solicitor. To Ancaster Twp, Wentworth Co, ONT, <1825. Ret naval officer. By first wife ch: 1. William, 1783–1851, RN. m (ii) 1797, Johanna Gallwey, further ch: 2. Anna Maria; 3. James Pickmore, b 1806; 4. Alexander Stover, b 1809; 5. Sarah Rosine, b 1814.   **DC 21 Feb 1980**.

9668 MILNE, William. From Auchinblae, Fordoun, KCD. s/o David M, qv, and Ann Scott, qv. To Nichol Twp, Wellington Co, ONT, <1844. m Helen Milne. **EHE 43**.

9669 MITCHELL, Andrew. To Montreal, QUE, <1854. Discharged NCO, 26th Regt.   **SGC 564**.

9670 MITCHELL, Ann. From ABD. To Elora, Nichol Twp, Wellington Co, ONT, 1836. Wife of George Leslie, qv.   **EHE 95**.

9671 MITCHELL, Ann. From Inverurie, ABD. To Kingston, ONT, <1843; stld later Northumberland Co. m James Stewart.   **SG xxiii/3 53**.

9672 MITCHELL, Archibald, 1834–1904. From Kintyre, ARL. s/o William M, qv, and Margaret McMillan, qv. To Eldon Twp, Victoria Co, ONT, <1840. m Betsy Mitchell, 1841-93, ch: 1. Janet, 1862–1944; 2. William, 1863–1943; 3. Donald, 1869–1955; 4. Maggie, 1872–1945; 5. Hughena, 1876–1947.   **EC 180**.

9673 MITCHELL, Charles, 1821-67. From Kintyre, ARL. s/o William M, qv, and Margaret McMillan, qv. To Eldon Twp, Victoria Co, ONT, <1840. m Margaret Sherry, ch: 1. Brigit; 2. William J, 1859–1936; 3. Eliza, 1866-83; 4. Margaret.   **EC 180**.

9674 MITCHELL, David, 1750–1830. Educ Edinburgh and grad MD, 1773. To CAN as Surgeon-General to the Indian Dept, and served at Mackinaw, Drummond Is, and other stations along what is now the US border. Moved to Penetanguishene, Simcoe Co, ONT, 1828. m at Montreal, 20 Jul 1776, Elizabeth Bertrand, and by her who d 1827 at Drummond Is, had ch: 1. Andrew; 2. Dr George, b 1794; 3. Louisa; 4. Elizabeth; 5. Jessie; 6. William.   **DC 17 Mar 1980**.

9675 MITCHELL, David. Prob from Livingston, WLN. s/o Andrew M. and Elizabeth Anderson. To CAN <1802.   **SH**.

9676 MITCHELL, Donald, 1823-86. From Kintyre, ARL. s/o William M, qv, and Margaret McMillan, qv. To Eldon Twp, Victoria Co, ONT, <1840. Postmaster at Argyle. By wife Ann had ch: 1. Mary Ann; 2. Maggie; 3. Christine; 4. Charles; 5. William; 6. James.   **EC 180**.

9677 MITCHELL, Eliza, ca 1827–30 Aug 1863. From Alloa, CLK. d/o William M. To Montreal, QUE. m Robert Schaw Miller.   **Ts Alloa**.

9678 MITCHELL, Elizabeth. sis/o Sarah M, wife of George Selkirk, wright in Jedburgh, ROX. To QUE <1826. m Daniel Fraser, qv.   **SH**.

9679 MITCHELL, Isobell. Poss from Killean par, ARL. To ONT, 1834. Wife of Alexander Galbraith, qv. **DC 9 Mar 1980**.

9680 MITCHELL, James. Educ Univ of Edinburgh and emig to ONT <1812. Family tutor, militiaman, farmer and magistrate, Brant Co. Son James, physician. **DC 23 Sep 1980**.

9681 MITCHELL, James. From Inverurie, ABD. To Kingston, ONT, <1843; stld later Northumberland Co. **SG xxiii/3 53**.

9682 MITCHELL, James, b ca 1816. Prob from Lundie and Fowlis par, ANS. To Eramosa Twp, Wellington Co, ONT, <1851. Clothier. By wife Grace had ch: 1. John; 2. William; 3. Peter; 4. Janet; 5. Isabella; 6. Christian; 7. Grace; 8. Ann; 9. David.   **DC 24 Nov 1979**.

9683 MITCHELL, Jean, 1831–1912. From Cullen par, BAN. d/o Alexander M. and Janet Wilson. To Hamilton, ONT, 1854; stld Sullivan Twp, Grey Co. m James Fraser, qv.   **DC 17 Aug 1982**.

9684 MITCHELL, Jessie. Prob from ABD. To ONT, 1831; stld East Zorra Twp, Oxford Co, 1845. Wife of Francis Malcolm, qv.   **LDW 24 Sep 1974**.

9685 MITCHELL, John. Prob from ARL. To Metcalfe Twp, Middlesex Co, ONT, 1831. m Sarah McAlpine, qv, ch: 1. Peter; 2. William; 3. Duncan; 4. Donald; 5. Margaret, remained in SCT; 6. Catherine; 7. Betsy; 8. Ann.   **PCM 56**.

9686 MITCHELL, Margaret, ca 1743–7 Jun 1812. From Glenmoriston, INV. To Nine Mile River, Hants Co, NS, poss <1800. Wife of Alexander Grant, qv.   **DC 20 Jan 1981**.

9687 MITCHELL, Margaret. From Forgue, ABD. To Nichol Twp, Wellington Co, ONT, 1839; later to Pilkington Twp. Wife of William Fasken, qv.   **EHE 42**.

9688 MITCHELL, Margaret, ca 1818–6 Oct 1891. From PER. d/o William M, qv. To Oro Twp, Simcoe Co, ONT, prob <1835. m Isaac Fell, 1811-79, ch: 1. Sarah,

1836-96; 2. Ann, 1841-95; 3. William, 1843–1928.
DC 29 Dec 1981.

9689   MITCHELL, Margaret, ca 1818-90. From Kintyre, ARL. d/o William M, qv, and Margaret McMillan, qv. To Eldon Twp, Victoria Co, ONT, <1840. m Angus McIntyre, qv.   **EC 142, 180.**

9690   MITCHELL, May. From Inverurie, ABD. To Kingston, ONT, <1843; stld Northumberland Co. m Arthur Knox.   **SG xxiii/3 53.**

9691   MITCHELL, Peter. Prob from ARL. To QUE on the *Retrench*, 1835; stld Metcalfe Twp, Middlesex Co, ONT. ch: 1. John; 2. Isabella; 3. Catherine; 4. Duncan; 5. Euphemia; 6. Donald.   **PCM 56.**

9692   MITCHELL, Peter James, 9 Nov 1832–5 Aug 1882. From Nethergate, Dundee, ANS. s/o Peter M. and Mary Chisholm. To QUE on the *Inkerman*, ex Greenock, 3 Jul 1857; stld Montreal and d at Galt, ONT. Printer. m at St Pauls Ch, Montreal, 30 Jan 1863, Helen Honeyman Boyle, ch: 1. Mary Margaret, 1864–1928; 2. Peter Chisholm, 1865–1937; 3. William, 1865–1933; 4. Helen Honeyman, 1868–1916; 5. James Benjamin, 1870–1944; 6. Benjamin Black, b 1876.   **DC 27 Aug 1982.**

9693   MITCHELL, Thomas, d 10 Aug 1848. From St Andrews, FIF. s/o Robert M. and Ann Carmichael, 1775–1847. To Montreal, QUE, and d there.
Ts St Andrews; SH.

9694   MITCHELL, William, ca 1782–ca 1862. From PER. To Oro Twp, Simcoe Co, ONT, prob <1835. Dau Margaret, qv.   **DC 29 Dec 1981.**

9695   MITCHELL, William. To Sherbrooke Co, QUE, 1835. m Annie Wood. Son Robert, b Lennoxville, 1845.   **MGC 2 Aug 1979.**

9696   MITCHELL, William, 1786–1850. From Kintyre, ARL. To Eldon Twp, Victoria Co, ONT, <1840; stld Con 4. Farmer. m Margaret McMillan, qv, ch: 1. Mary, qv; 2. Charles, qv; 3. Donald, qv; 4. Ann, b 1827; 5. William, 1828-99; 6. Elizabeth, b 1833; 7. Archibald, qv.   **EC 180.**

9697   MITCHISON, Andrew. From Lauder, BEW. s/o Andrew M, innkeeper. To CAN <1853.   **SH.**

9698   MOAR, George. Prob from PER. To Brudenell, Kings Co, PEI, poss 1803. ch: 1. John; 2. James.
BP 14.

9699   MOFFAT, George. Prob from ABD. To Montreal, QUE, <1830. Merchant. Son George, educ Marischall Coll, Aberdeen, 1836-40.   **FAM ii 499.**

9700   MOFFAT, Jane, 1787–25 Jun 1840. From DFS. To Charlottetown, PEI, 1820; stld Brookfield. Wife of Alexander Johnstone, qv.   **DC 16 Aug 1982.**

9701   MOFFAT, John, b 30 Jan 1794. From Kilmarnock, AYR. s/o John M, merchant, and Elizabeth McNeil, Saltcoats. To ONT <1840. Merchant. m Jane, d/o Alexander McVicar, qv, and Jean Donald, qv, ch: 1. Jane, b 23 Jun 1822; 2. Margaret, b 11 Jan 1824; 3. Ann, b 8 Jun 1825; 4. John, b 30 Nov 1827; 5. Alexander McVicar, b 1 Mar 1830.   **SH; DC 24 Jun 1980.**

9702   MOFFAT, John. From Angus. bro/o George M,

tailor, Almericloss, Arbroath. To Garafraxa Twp, Wellington Co, ONT, <1841.   **SH.**

9703   MOFFAT, John Alston, b 1825. From LKS. To Hamilton, ONT, 1836; stld later London, Middlesex Co. Merchant tailor and entomologist.   **DC 1 Jan 1968.**

9704   MOFFAT, Thomas. From DFS. To ONT, ca 1842; stld prob Dundas Co.   **DC 4 Mar 1965.**

9705   MOIR, Agnes. From PER, poss Killin. To QUE on the *Niagara*, ex Greenock, 22 Apr 1825; stld McNab Twp, Renfrew Co, ONT. Wife of Alexander Miller, qv.
DC 3 Jan 1980.

9706   MOIR, Alexander Leith. From ABD. To Elora, Nichol Twp, Wellington Co, ONT, 1836.   **EHE 94.**

9707   MOIR, Annie. From Aberdeen. sis/o James Moir, qv. To Elora, Nichol Twp, Wellington Co, ONT, 1835. m George Pirie, Dundas.   **EHE 89.**

9708   MOIR, Archibald. To Montreal, QUE, <1854. Grocer, later customs officer.   **SGC 564.**

9709   MOIR, George, 22 Aug 1784–6 May 1855. From Thornhill, STI. s/o George M. and Janet Adam. To Huron Co, ONT, ca 1844; stld Con 2, Usborne Twp. Farmer. m Jane Stirling, qv, ch: 1. George; 2. Margaret; 3. John; 4. Alexander; 5. Robert; 6. James; 7. Jean; 8. Janet; 9. Peter; 10. Andrew; 11. Thomas; 12. William.
DC 18 May 1982.

9710   MOIR, Jacqueline. From Aberdeen. sis/o James M, qv. To Elora, Nichol Twp, Wellington Co, ONT, 1835. m (i) — Jamieson, who d in Aberdeen; (ii) James Leslie, postmaster at Dundas.   **EHE 89.**

9711   MOIR, John. To QUE <1842. Son David Walter, b Graniteville, QUE.   **MGC 2 Aug 1979.**

9712   MOIR, James, 28 Oct 1815–1 Apr 1906. From Aberdeen. To Elora, Nichol Twp, Wellington Co, ONT, 1835. App watchmaker in Aberdeen, but became farmer. m Margaret Pellet, Dundas, ch: 1. Mrs Troxel; 2. William, res Winnipeg; 3. Alexander; 4. Mrs Mann; 5. Mrs Qua; 6. Jacqueline; 7. James; 8. John; 9. Leslie; 10. Mrs G. Tower Fergusson.   **EHE 89.**

9713   MOIR, Margaret. From Aberdeen. sis/o James M, qv. To Elora, Nichol Twp, Wellington Co, ONT, 1835. m John Gartshore, sawyer, Bon Accord.   **EHE 89.**

9714   MONCRIEFF, Rev William Glen, ca 1835–19 Jul 1891. From Glasgow. s/o Rev John M, Professor of Hebrew, Andersonian Coll. Seccesion min at Musselburgh, 1839-52. To London, Middlesex Co, ONT, where he appears to have been engaged in secular work.   **UPC i 534.**

9715   MONDAY, Robert. To QUE on the *Commerce*, ex Greenock, Jun 1820; stld prob Lanark Co, ONT.
HCL 238.

9716   MONK, Ronald, 1806-96. From Balivanich, Is Benbecula, INV. s/o Neil M. in Aird. To West Williams Twp, Middlesex Co, ONT, ca 1849. m Marion McMillan, qv, ch: 1. Neil, b 1832; 2. Roderick, b 1834; 3. Catherine, b 1837; 4. Effie, b 1840; 5. Neil, b 1842; 6. Donald, b 1844; 7. Malcolm, b 1848; 8. Effie, b 1853; 9. Peggy, b 1859.   **PCM 48; WLC.**

MONRO. See also MUNRO, MUNROE and MONROE.

9717   MONRO, Alexander, 1813-96. From BAN. To NB, ca 1832. Surveyor and author. d at Baie Verte. **MDB 520**.

9718   MONRO, Rev Donald, d 1867. From ARL. To Finch Twp, Stormont Co, ONT, <1850. Presb missionary, and became min of St Lukes Ch. ch: 1. John C, qv; 2. Margery. **SDG 455**.

9719   MONRO, James, ca 1771–Sep 1843. From Cromarty, ROC. s/o Rev James M, min there, and Mary Stark. To Pictou, NS, <1820. Cabinet-maker. m Helen Gordon, qv, and had, poss with other ch: 1. George, solicitor in Edinburgh; 2. James, d 1841; 3. Mrs Grant. **NDF 202**.

9720   MONRO, John C, b 1827. From ARL. s/o Rev Donald M, qv. To Finch Twp, Stormont Co, ONT, ca 1849. Educ Queens Univ and became physician. **SDG 455**.

9721   MONROE, Margaret, ca 1778–8 May 1860. From ROC. To Pictou Co, NS, prob <1830; stld Mount Thom. m John Fraser, qv. **DC 19 Mar 1981**.

9722   MONTEITH, Margaret. From ARL. d/o Thomas M. To QUE on the *David of London*, ex Greenock, 19 May 1821; stld Lanark Twp, Lanark Co, ONT. Wife of James Bowes, qv, m 29 Apr 1791. **HCL 72**.

9723   MONTEITH, Rev Robert, ca 1815–23 Jan 1893. From Dunblane, PER. s/o George M, craftsman. Matric Univ of Glasgow, 1831. Antiburgher min at Greenlaw, BEW, 1841-54. To Prince Albert, SAS, and was min there. Res latterly at Toronto. **UPC i 417; GMA 12875**.

9724   MONTGOMERIE, Robert, b ca 1794. From Kilmaurs, AYR. To Hudson Bay, ca 1812, and prob to Red River. **RRS 13**.

9725   MONTGOMERY, Christina, b ca 1770. From LKS. To QUE on the *Commerce*, ex Greenock, 11 May 1821; stld Ramsay Twp, Lanark Co, ONT. Wife of James Sneddon, qv. **DC 11 Mar 1979**.

9726   MONTGOMERY, Donald, ca 1760–27 Feb 1845. From Southend, Kintyre, ARL. s/o Hugh M, qv, and Mary McShannon, qv. To Prince Co, PEI, prob 1772. m ca 1788, Nancy Penman, 1768-1837. **DC 28 Apr 1980**.

9727   MONTGOMERY, Helen, 1768–20 Jun 1853. d/o Hugh M, qv, and Mary McShannon, qv. To Prince Co, PEI, prob 1772. m 26 Feb 1788, Archibald Ramsay, qv. **DC 28 May 1980**.

9728   MONTGOMERY, Henry. Prob rel to James M, qv. To QUE on the *Alexander*, 1816; stld Lot 23, Con 8, Bathurst Twp, Lanark Co, ONT. **HCL 233**.

9729   MONTGOMERY, Hugh, ca 1725–ca 1805. From Southend, Kintyre, ARL. To Prince Co, PEI, ca 1772. m Mary McShannon, qv, ch: 1. Donald, qv; 2. John, qv; 3. Margaret, qv; 4. Helen, qv; 5. Hugh, jr, qv. **DC 28 May 1980**.

9730   MONTGOMERY, Hugh, jr, ca 1770–ca 1830. s/o Hugh M, qv, and Mary McShannon, qv. To Prince Co, PEI, ca 1772. m ca 1795, Christie Penman, d 1811, from New England. **DC 28 Apr 1980**.

9731   MONTGOMERY, Hugh. Rel to John M, qv. To Dalhousie, Restigouche Co, NB, <1826. Shipbuilder and timber exporter. **SR 19**.

9732   MONTGOMERY, James. Prob rel to Henry M, qv. To QUE on the *Alexander*, 1816; stld Lot 23, Con 8, Bathurst Twp, Lanark Co, ONT. **HCL 233**.

9733   MONTGOMERY, James, b ca 1811. To St Gabriel de Valcartier, QUE, prob <1855. **Census 1861**.

9734   MONTGOMERY, John, b ca 1763. s/o Hugh M, qv, and Mary McShannon, qv. To Prince Co, PEI, prob 1772. m, ca 1788, Ann Hooper, b 1765. **DC 28 May 1980**.

9735   MONTGOMERY, John. Rel to Hugh M, qv. To Dalhousie, Restigouche Co, NB, <1826. Shipbuilder and timber exporter. **SR 19**.

9736   MONTGOMERY, Margaret, b ca 1765. From Southend, Kintyre, ARL. d/o Hugh M, qv, and Mary McShannon, qv. To Prince Co, PEI, ca 1772. m (i) Capt Norman McLeod; (ii) Thomas Archibald, Rose Hill. **DC 28 May 1980**.

9737   MONTGOMERY, Mary, b 1824. Poss from Paisley, RFW. To Toronto, ONT, ca 1844; later to Peoria Co, IL. Wife of John Alexander, qv. **DC 10 Sep 1974**.

9738   MONTGOMERY, William, ca 1797–17 Jul 1817. From Hutton par, DFS. s/o John M. and Margaret Davidson. To Miramichi, Northumberland Co, NB, and d there. **Ts Hutton**.

9739   MOODIE, Alexander. From Dumfermline, FIF. Neph of Thomas M, qv. To Perth, Drummond Twp, Lanark Co, ONT, <1850. **DC 25 Jul 1972**.

9740   MOODIE, James. From Dunfermline, FIF. Neph of Thomas M, qv. To Perth, Drummond Twp, Lanark Co, ONT, <1850. **DC 25 Jul 1972**.

9741   MOODIE, John Wedderburn Dunbar, 7 Oct 1797–22 Oct 1869. From Melsetter, Hoy, OKI. s/o Maj James M. To Montreal, QUE, on the brig *Anne*, ex Leith 1 July 1832; stld nr Cobourg, Northumberland Co. Moved to Douro Twp, Peterborough Co, and in 1840 to Belleville, Hastings Co. Lt, 21st Fusiliers; Sheriff of Hastings Co, 1839-63; author. m 1831, Susanna, 1803-85, authoress, d/o Thomas Strickland of Reydon Hall, Suffolk, ENG, ch: 1. Catherine, b 1832; 2. Agnes, b 1833; 3. Dunbar, b 1834; 4. Donald, b 1836; 5. John, b 1838; 6. George Arthur, b 1840; 7. Robert Baldwin. **BNA 1185-89**.

9742   MOODIE, Robert, ca 1791–2 May 1868. From SHI. To Miramichi, Northumberland Co, NB, and d Point Aux Carr. **DC 4 Oct 1978**.

9743   MOODIE, Robert, d 4 Dec 1837. From Dunfermline, FIF. To York Co, ONT, prob <1820. Discharged soldier, 28th Foot and 104th Regt. m at Fredericton, NB, 1811, Frances, d/o Hon George Sproule, Surveyor-General of NB. **MDB 524**.

9744   MOODIE, Robert. From Dunfermline, FIF. Neph of Thomas M, qv. To Perth, Drummond Twp, Lanark Co, ONT, <1850. **DC 25 Jul 1972**.

9745   MOODIE, Thomas, ca 1784–19 Sep 1880. From FIF. To North Burgess Twp, Lanark Co, ONT, ca 1822. m Christian Drysdale, qv, ch: 1. Andrew Toshack, b 11 Apr 1811; 2. Thomas, b 31 Oct 1813; 3. John, b 19 Dec 1818; 4. Helen Fergus, b 25 May 1821. **DC 18 Mar 1968 and 24 Sep 1969**.

9746   MOODIE, Thomas. From Dunfermline, FIF. Neph

of Thomas M, qv. To Drummond Twp, Lanark Co, ONT, <1850.   **DC 25 Jul 1850**.

9747   MOODIE, William. From Dunfermline, FIF. To Perth, Drummond Twp, Lanark Co, ONT, <1850. **DC 25 Jul 1972**.

9748   MOODY, Rev Duncan, ca 1798–5 Jan 1855. From Kilmallie, INV. s/o William M, craftsman. Matric Univ of Glasgow, 1814. To Dundee, Charlottenburgh Twp, Glengarry Co, ONT, <1835, as missionary. Became min of Dundee. m 1837, Ann, d/o Nicholas Farlinger, ch: 1. Duncan MacGregor; 2. Sarah.   **GMA 9091; FES vii 646; DC 4 Mar 1965**.

9749   MOON, Christian, b ca 1786. From Blair, PER. To PEI on the *Clarendon*, ex Oban, 6 Aug 1808. Spinster. **CPL**.

9750   MOON, George, b ca 1781. From Strathgarry, PER. To Charlottetown, PEI, on the *Clarendon*, ex Oban, 6 Aug 1808. Labourer.   **CPL**.

9751   MOORE, Francis, ca 1841–1 May 1928. From Newmilns, AYR. s/o William M, surgeon, and Margaret Gilmour Findlay. To Kent Co, ONT, 1854; stld Morpeth, but went later to CO, USA. Brig Gen, US Army. m Agnes Dougall, ch: 1. Francis, dy; 2. Jessie, b 1884. **DC 15 Apr 1960**.

9752   MOORE, William. To East Williams Twp, Middlesex Co, ONT, 1831.   **PCM 43**.

9753   MOORE, William J, 2 Sep 1777–17 Mar 1841. From Glasgow. To Huntingdon Co, QUE, <1837; stld Elgin. Farmer. m Mary Elizabeth Boyd, qv, ch. **DC 21 Nov 1981**.

9754   MORE, Robert. From Glasgow. To Hamilton, ONT, <1850. Dry goods merchant. m Jeanette Brown. Son Andrew.   **DC 29 Sep 1964**.

9755   MORINE, Mrs Janet Corrie, d 22 Feb 1842. From DFS. wid/o Thomas M, turnkey, Dumfries jail, who was killed by a prisoner. To Montreal, QUE, and d there.   **DGH 14 Apr 1842**.

MORISON. See also MORRISON.

9756   MORISON, Alexander, b ca 1803. Prob from INV. To Gut of Canso, Cape Breton, NS, on the *Catherine*, ex Tobermory, 13 Jul 1843. Wife Flora, b ca 1811, with him, and ch: 1. Mary, b ca 1844; 2. Peggy, b ca 1846; 3. Donald, b ca 1848; 4. Effie, b ca 1841; 5. John, b ca 1842.   **MP 639**.

9757   MORISON, Anne. To Pictou, NS, on the *Lulan*, ex Glasgow, 17 Aug 1848. Family with her: 1. Anna; 2. Mary; 3. James; 4. Allan.   **DC 15 Jul 1979**.

9758   MORISON, George, 1825–1901. From Auchaber, Forgue par, ABD. s/o John Young M, qv, and Jean M, qv. To QUE, 1834; stld Bristol. Blacksmith and storekeeper; postmaster and magistrate at Glengyle. m Jean Smith, qv, and had with other ch: 1. John Young, 1856–1922; 2. David, 1867–1936; 3. Andrew, 1869–1940, physician; 4. George.   **Fergus OPR 194/3; DC 15 Mar 1971**.

9759   MORISON, Hector. To PEI, poss 1803; stld nr Belfast, Queens Co. Petitioner for Dr MacAulay, 1811. **HP 74**.

9760   MORISON, Jean, b ca 1798. From Forgue par,

ABD. To QUE, 1834; stld Bristol. Wife of John Young M, qv.   **DC 15 Mar 1971**.

9761   MORISON, John, b ca 1769. To Richmond Co, NS, 1802. Farmer, m and ch.   **CBC 1818**.

9762   MORISON, John. From Alloa, CLK. s/o John M, d 1846, and Isabella Gilmour. To Toronto, ONT, <1853.   **Ts Alloa**.

9763   MORISON, John Young, 6 May 1794–21 Dec 1870. From Auchaber, Forgue, ABD. s/o Alexander M, blacksmith. To QUE, 1834; stld Bristol. Blacksmith with a lumber firm. m Jean Morison, qv, ch: 1. Alexander, b 1821; 2. James, 1822-70; 3. John, 1834-91; 5. Margaret, b 1827; 6. Katherine, 1831–1913.   **Fergus OPR 194/3; DC 15 Mar 1971**.

9764   MORISON, Mary. To Pictou, NS, on the *Lulan*, ex Glasgow, 17 Aug 1848.   **DC 15 Jul 1979**.

9765   MORISON, Peter, b ca 1781. From Finlarig, PER. To QUE, ex Greenock, summer 1815; stld prob Lanark Co, ONT. Mason and farmer. Wife Mary Campbell, qv, with him, and 4 ch.   **SEC 8**.

9766   MORISON, Peter, b ca 1790. To Little Bras D'Or dist, Cape Breton Co, NS, 1817. Farmer, m and ch. **CBC 1818**.

9767   MORISON, William. From ABD. Said desc from the Morisons of Bognie. To QUE <1780. Lawyer. Moved to the Bahamas where he became Chief Justice and was knighted. m a French lady.   **SNQ xi/1 133**.

9768   MORNER, Thomas. To QUE on the *Fame*, 1815; stld Lot 7, Con 4, Drummond Twp, Lanark Co, ONT. **HCL 234**.

9769   MORRICE, David. From PER. To Montreal, QUE, <1860. Textile manufacturer. Son James Wilson, 1841–1914, impressionist painter.   **DC 15 May 1982**.

9770   MORRIS, Alexander. From Paisley, RFW. To Montreal, QUE, ca 1801. Merchant there, later farmer nr Brockville, ONT. ch incl: 1. Alexander, merchant; 2. William, qv; 3. James, qv.   **MDB 529; HCL 151**.

9771   MORRIS, James, 1798–29 Sep 1865. From Paisley, RFW. s/o Alexander M, qv. To Montreal, QUE, ca 1801, later to Perth, Lanark Co, ONT. Merchant and politician; Postmaster-General, 1853-54, Receiver-General, 1862-63. m 1827, Emily Rosamund, d/o Henry Murney, Kingston.   **MDB 529; HCL 151**.

9772   MORRIS, William, 31 Oct 1786–29 Jun 1858. From Paisley, RFW. s/o Alexander M, qv. To Montreal, QUE, ca 1801; later to Perth, Lanark Co, ONT. Merchant and MLA; Receiver-General, 1844-46. m Elizabeth, d/o John Cochran, qv. Son Alexander, 1826-89, Lt Gov of MAN and NWT, 1872-77.   **BNA 365, 535, 738; MDB 530; HCL 46, 52, 56, 151**.

MORRISON. See also MORISON.

9773   MORRISON, Alexander. From Is South Uist, INV. To West Williams Twp, Middlesex Co, ONT, 1849; stld Centre Road.   **PCM 48**.

9774   MORRISON, Alexander, ca 1830–1916. From Harris, INV. Poss s/o Peter M, qv, and wife Annie. To Inverness Co, NS, and d Wreck Cove. m Sarah Matheson, qv.   **DC 22 Jun 1979**.

9775   MORRISON, Alexander, 1 Nov 1838–18 Jun

1877. To Sherbrooke, QUE. m Elizabeth Youngston, qv. Dau Sophia Jean, 1867–1946. **MGC 2 Aug 1979**.

9776 MORRISON, Allan. From Is Skye, INV. To PEI <1850; stld Queens Co. m Effie McLean. Dau Mary. **DC 11 Apr 1981**.

MORRISON, Mrs Allan Roy. See MACINTYRE, Ann.

9777 MORRISON, Andrew, ca 1804–23 Dec 1882. From Denny, STI. To Melbourne, Richmond Co, QUE, prob <1850. m Janet Main, qv. **MGC 15 Jul 1980**.

9778 MORRISON, Angus, 20 Jan 1822–10 Jun 1882. b Edinburgh. s/o Hugh M, from SUT, qv. To QUE, 1834; stld ONT, 1842. Barrister; QC, 1873; MLA, rep North Simcoe, 1854-63, and Niagara, 1864-74. **BNA 748; MDB 530**.

9779 MORRISON, Angus. From Is South Uist, INV. To West Williams Twp, Middlesex Co, ONT, 1849; stld Con 14. **PCM 48**.

9780 MORRISON, Angus, 1830–25 May 1913. From Kyles of Scalpay, Harris, INV. Prob s/o Peter M, qv, and wife Annie. To Victoria Co, NS. Wife Christy, 1835–1912. **DC 22 Jun 1979**.

9781 MORRISON, Ann, b 1808. From Is North Uist, INV. To Whycocomagh, Inverness Co, NS, 1827. Wife of Donald McDonald, qv. **DC 23 Feb 1980**.

9782 MORRISON, Ann, ca 1810–29 Apr 1900. Poss from Is Lewis, ROC, or Is Harris, INV. d/o William and Ann M. To St Annes, Victoria Co, NS, poss <1828. m Donald MacLeod, qv, and went later to Waipu, NZ. **DC 20 Mar 1981**.

9783 MORRISON, Archibald, b ca 1777. From Glasgow. To QUE on the *Atlas*, ex Greenock, 11 Jul 1815; stld with Thomas McLean, qv, on Lot 23, Con 6, North Elmsley Twp, Lanark Co, ONT. Ship carpenter, and became farmer. **SEC 1; HCL 12, 230, 232**.

9784 MORRISON, Catherine. From Glenelg, INV. To QUE, ex Greenock, summer 1815; stld prob Lanark Co, ONT. Wife of Donald Campbell, qv. **SEC 7**.

9785 MORRISON, Catherine, 1808-84. From Is South Uist, INV. To Cape Breton Is, NS, 1823. Wife of Norman MacDonald, qv. **DC 23 Feb 1980**.

9786 MORRISON, Catherine, ca 1819–1916. From Lanark. To Aldborough Twp, Elgin Co, ONT, 1843. Wife of Duncan Somerville, qv. **DC 14 Aug 1979**.

9787 MORRISON, Catherine. From Bornish, Is South Uist, INV. To West Williams Twp, Middlesex Co, ONT, <1849. Wife of Angus Ross, qv. **PCM 48; WLC**.

9788 MORRISON, Catherine. From Bornish, Is South Uist, INV. To West Williams Twp, Middlesex Co, ONT, ca 1849. Wife of Archibald McMillan, qv. **WLC**.

9789 MORRISON, Charles, b 1755. To QUE on the *Oughton*, arr Jul 1804; stld Baldoon, Dover Twp, Kent Co, ONT. Wife Peggy, b 1770, with him, ch: 1. Flora, b 1790; 2. James, b 1791; 3. Christian, b 1801; 4. Isabell; 5. Maryanne; 6. Catherine; 7. John. **UCM 268, 302; DC 4 Oct 1979**.

9790 MORRISON, Daniel, b ca 1761. To Port Hood dist, Inverness Co, NS, 1804. Farmer. ch incl: 1. Allan, b ca 1795; 2. Patrick, b ca 1797. **CBC 1818**.

9791 MORRISON, Rev David, 4 Oct 1841–3 May 1894. From Denny, STI. s/o William M, qv, and Catherine McDonald, qv. To Melbourne, Richmond Co, QUE, 1846. Educ McGill Univ, Montreal, and grad BA, 1870, also studied Morrin Coll, QUE. Adm min of Ormstown, 4 Mar 1874. DD, Queens Univ, 1903. d at Beauharnois. **Denny OPR 476/3; FES vii 646**.

9792 MORRISON, Donald. To Pictou, NS, on the *Ellen*, ex Loch Laxford, SUT, 22 May 1848. Wife Catherine McKay, qv, with him. **DC 15 Jul 1979**.

9793 MORRISON, Donald. From Is South Uist, INV. To West Williams Twp, Middlesex Co, ONT, 1849. Son Angus 'Mor'. **PCM 48**.

9794 MORRISON, Rev Duncan, ca 1816–3 May 1894. Educ Queens Coll, Kingston, ONT, and grad BA. Ord min of Beckwith, Lanark Co, 1851, and trans to Brockville, 1856. DD, Montreal, 1890. **FES vii 646**.

9795 MORRISON, Ellen Jane, b ca 1838. From Glasgow. d/o Rev Samuel M. and wife Margaret. To Hamilton Twp, Northumberland Co, ONT. m 13 Feb 1860, William Scott King, qv. **DC 18 Jan 1980**.

9796 MORRISON, Fingal. To Pictou, NS, on the *Ellen*, ex Loch Laxford, SUT. **DC 15 Jul 1979**.

9797 MORRISON, George. From Banff. To Pictou, NS, on the *Hector*, ex Glasgow, arr 17 Sep 1773; stld Barneys River, Pictou Co. Dau Mrs David Ballantyne, res Cape George. **HPC App C**.

9798 MORRISON, Helen. From INV. To Inverness Twp, Megantic Co, QUE, 1833. Wife of Angus McGillivray, qv, m <1825. **AMC 48**.

9799 MORRISON, Hugh. From Stonebridge, Is South Uist, INV. To PEI on the *Jane*, ex Loch nan Uamh, Arisaig, 12 Jul 1790, poss calling at Loch Boisdale. **PLJ**.

9800 MORRISON, Hugh. From Assynt or Eddrachillis, SUT. To Boston, MA, on the *Fortitude*, arr 16 Aug 1803; stld 1805 at Scotch Ridge, Charlotte Co, NB. Formerly of the Reay Fencibles Regt. **DC 29 Nov 1982**.

9801 MORRISON, Hugh. To Toronto, ONT, 1832. Formerly officer, 42nd Regt. ch: 1. Joseph Curran, 1816-85, Solicitor-General, 1860-62; 2. Angus, qv. **DC 20 Apr 1970**.

9802 MORRISON, Hugh. From Is South Uist, INV. To East Williams Twp, Middlesex Co, ONT, 1849. **PCM 44**.

9803 MORRISON, James. From Drumnaguie, SUT. To ONT, and stld Zorra, Oxford Co, <2 Nov 1847. May have sld on the *Panama*, ex Loch Laxford, 19 Jun 1847. *MacLeod Muniments, Box 36*.

9804 MORRISON, Rev James, 1789–16 Aug 1849. b Glasgow. s/o James M, craftsman. Matric Univ of Glasgow, 1810. Ord by Presb of Glasgow, and adm min of Dartmouth, Halifax Harbour, NS, 1829. Trans to Lawrencetown, 1833. Went to Bermuda, 1843, and joined FC. **GMA 8158; FES vii 617, 661**.

9805 MORRISON, Jane, ca 1802–8 Jul 1882. From Denny, STI. To Melbourne, Richmond Co, QUE, prob <1850. m John Watson. **MGC 15 Jul 1980**.

9806 MORRISON, Jessie. From ROC. To Cape Breton Is, NS, 1835. Wife of Rev James Fraser, qv. **MLA 129**.

9807 MORRISON, John. To Pictou, NS, on the *Hope*, ex Glasgow, 5 Apr 1848. Wife Jane with him, and ch: 1. Elizabeth; 2. Robert; 3. John; 4. Jane. They went to USA. **DC 12 Jul 1979.**

9808 MORRISON, John. From Lochdar, Is South Uist, INV. s/o Donald M. To Pictou, NS, on the *Lulan*, ex Glasgow, 17 Aug 1848. Wife Isabella Gillies, qv, with him, and ch: 1. Ann, b 1845; 2. Angus. **DC 12 Jul 1979.**

9809 MORRISON, John. From Is South Uist, INV. To West Williams Twp, Middlesex Co, ONT, 1849. **PCM 48.**

9810 MORRISON, John, 1832–30 Jun 1910. From INV. s/o Kenneth M. and Annie Kennedy. To ONT, ca 1850; stld Ingersoll, Oxford Co. Magistrate. m Mary Jane, d/o — Irwin and Elizabeth Dundas, ch. **DC 22 Apr 1981.**

9811 MORRISON, John. From North Galson, Is Lewis, ROC. To QUE, 1855. m Effie Campbell, qv. **DC 22 Jun 1979.**

9812 MORRISON, John, b 1837. From Harris, INV. s/o John M 'Gobha na Hearadh', hymn-writer, and his third wife Mary McAulay. To Kincardine, Huron Twp, Bruce Co, ONT, <1857. **WLC.**

9813 MORRISON, Margaret, b ca 1793. From Kilninian, Is Mull, ARL. To Hudson Bay and Red River <1815. Wife of Donald McLean, qv. **RRS 24.**

9814 MORRISON, Mary. From Is Barra, INV. To Arisaig, Antigonish Co, NS, ca 1798. Wife of Donald MacLean, qv. **HCA 312.**

9815 MORRISON, Mary. Poss from Edinburgh. To Boulardarie, Victoria Co, NS, 1821; later to Waipu, NZ. m Duncan Kemp, qv. **DC 25 Sep 1981.**

9816 MORRISON, Mary, 1764–1804. To Baldoon, Dover Twp, Kent Co, ONT, 1804. Wife of Donald McCallum, qv. **UCM 267; DC 4 Oct 1979.**

MORRISON, Mrs Duncan. See MACEACHERN, Sarah.

9817 MORRISON, Murdo. To Pictou, NS, on the *Ellen*, ex Loch Laxford, SUT, 22 May 1848. Wife Elizabeth with him, and ch: 1. Ann; 2. Alexander; 3. John; 4. Donald. **DC 15 Jul 1979.**

9818 MORRISON, Murdo, 1817-95. From Valtos, Uig par, Is Lewis, ROC. s/o Norman M. To Gould, Whitton Twp, Compton Co, QUE, ca 1843; moved to Lake Megantic. Farmer. m Sibella Mackenzie, see ADDENDA, ch: 1. Kirsty, b 1845; 2. Norman, b 1847; 3. Malcolm, b 1849, went to ND, USA; 4. Kate, b 1851; 5. Murdo, b 1853; 6. John, b 1855; 7. Donald, 1857-94, the 'Megantic outlaw'. **WLC.**

9819 MORRISON, Murdoch. Poss from Is Lewis, ROC. To Glen Morris, Brant Co, ONT, <1800. **DC 23 Sep 1980.**

9820 MORRISON, Murdock, 1824–1907. Prob from Is Lewis, ROC. To Victoria Co, NS. m Jessie McLennan, qv, and had, poss with other ch: 1. Murdock, 1871-92; 2. Donald, 1886-92, d Cape North. **DC 22 Jun 1979.**

9821 MORRISON, Nancy, b ca 1776. To Charlottetown, PEI, on the *Elizabeth & Ann*, ex Thurso, arr 8 Nov 1806. Wife of John McLeod, qv. **PLEA.**

9822 MORRISON, Neil, d 1826. From Assynt or Eddrachillis, SUT. To Boston, MA, on the *Fortitude*, arr 16 Aug 1803; stld Scotch Ridge, Charlotte Co, NB, 1804. Formerly of the Reay Fencible Regt; group leader and lay preacher. Son Donald. **DC 29 Nov 1982.**

9823 MORRISON, Neil, b 1828. From Is Harris, INV. To Englishtown, Victoria Co, NS, ca 1853. By wife Margaret had ch: 1. Murdock Daniel, b 1868, physician; 2. Katie; 3. John Charles, b 1875, physician. **HNS iii 187.**

9824 MORRISON, Norman. From Glenelg, INV. To Montreal, QUE, ex Fort William, arr Sep 1802. Petitioned for land on the Ottawa River, 6 Aug 1804. **MCM 1/4 26.**

9825 MORRISON, Peter, 1796–30 Sep 1868. From Harris, INV. To Victoria Co, NS, prob <1840; stld nr Wreck Cove. Wife Annie, 1796–1894, with him, and s John, 1838–1917. **WLC; DC 22 Jun 1979.**

9826 MORRISON, Peter. To Pictou, NS, on the *Ellen*, ex Loch Laxford, SUT, 22 May 1848. **DC 15 Jul 1979.**

9827 MORRISON, Rebecca. From Glenelg, INV. To QUE, summer 1815; stld prob ONT. Wife of Malcolm McRae, qv. **SEC 5.**

9828 MORRISON, Robert. To PEI on the *Valiant*, ex Hull, arr 22 Mar 1817; stld Sussex, Kings Co, NB. **DC 1 Oct 1960.**

9829 MORRISON, Robert. Poss from Lanark. bro/o Catherine M, qv. To QUE, 1834; stld Aldborough Twp, Elgin Co, ONT. **DC 14 Aug 1979.**

9830 MORRISON, Robert, 1788–1874. From Tarbert, ARL. To Aldborough Twp, Elgin Co, ONT, 1843. Carpenter and violinist. m Jean Crawford, qv. Son Robert, b 1828. **DC 14 Feb 1980.**

9831 MORRISON, Roderick. From Assynt or Eddrachillis, SUT. To Boston, MA, on the *Fortitude*, arr 16 Aug 1803; stld Scotch Ridge, Charlotte Co, NB, 1805. Formerly of the Reay Fencible Regt. **DC 29 Nov 1982.**

9832 MORRISON, Rory, b ca 1787. To Port Hood, Inverness Co, NS, 1802. Farmer, m and ch. **CBC 1818.**

9833 MORRISON, Rev Thomas. Educ Univ of Edinburgh. App by Colonial Committee, and adm to Melbourne Presb Ch, Middlesex Co, ONT, 1853. Retr to SCT, 1855. **FES vii 646.**

9834 MORRISON, William. To QUE on the *Commerce*, ex Greenock, Jun 1820; stld prob Lanark Co, ONT. **HCL 238.**

9835 MORRISON, William, ca 1833–9 Nov 1906. From Denny, STI. To Melbourne, Richmond Co, QUE, <1850. m Agnes Beattie. **MGC 15 Jul 1980.**

9836 MORRISON, William. From Denny, STI. To Melbourne, Richmond Co, QUE, poss 1846. m Catherine McDonald. Son Rev David, qv. **FES vii 646; MGC 15 Jul 1980.**

9837 MORRISON, Williamina. From Is Handa, Eddrachillis, SUT. To QUE, on the *Panama*, ex Loch Laxford, 19 Jun 1847; stld Nissouri, Oxford Co, ONT. *MacLeod Muniments,* Box 36.

9838 MORROW, Catherine. From Dornoch, SUT. sis/o Margaret M, qv. To Lanark Co, ONT, ca 1830; stld

prob Ramsay Twp. Wife of Donald Munro, qv.
DC 10 Jan 1980.

9839 MORTIMER, Christina. Prob from Kincardine
O'Neil, ABD. To QUE, 1854, with 4 ch, to join her
husband, David Duncan, qv.   **DC 29 Jun 1977**.

9840 MORTIMER, Edward, 1767–10 Oct 1819. From
Keith, BAN. s/o Alexander M, burgess of Forres, and
Mary Smith. To Halifax, NS, 1788; stld later Pictou.
Merchant, shipowner and MLA. m Sarah, d/o John
Patterson, qv.   **BNA 280; SAS 20; MLA 256; Ts Keith**.

9841 MORTIMER, Jane, d 12 Jan 1895. From
Aberdeen. wid/o John Clark, broker. To Toronto, ONT,
1858. Wife of Rev Alexander Topp, qv.   **FES vi 391**.

9842 MORTIMER, William. From Aberdeen. s/o John
M, baker. Grad MA, Marischall Coll, Aberdeen, 1816. To
Pictou, NS. Merchant.   **FAM ii 414**.

9843 MORTON, James, b 11 Aug 1813, Dalsangan
Farm, Mauchline, AYR. s/o Robert M. and Helen
McClelland. To QUE on the *Gondola*, ex Liverpool,
20 Apr 1841; stld prob Waterloo Co, ONT. Farmer.
m Jane Morton, of Ayr Twp, poss a relative.
LDW 23 Sep 1976.

9844 MORTON, James. To St John, NB, prob <1840.
m at Paisley, 27 Aug 1842, Janet Risk.   **Paisley Low
OPR 573-3/5**.

9845 MORTON, John. Served as an NCO in the 82nd
Regt and was gr land in Pictou Co, NS, 1784.
HPC App F.

9846 MORTON, John, b 14 Nov 1811, Dalsangan Farm,
Mauchline, AYR. s/o Robert M. and Helen McClelland.
Farmer. To Huron Co, ONT, 1832; stld later Williams Twp,
Middlesex Co.   **LDW 23 Sep 1976**.

MORTON, Mrs John. See RUSSELL, Catherine.

9847 MORTON, Robert, 1795–1873. From Coupar-
Angus, PER. s/o John M. and Catherine Russell, qv. To
Montreal, QUE, <1850. m Helen Young, ch.   **DC 11 Jul
1966**.

9848 MORTON, Robert, b 27 Sep 1801, Dalsangan
Farm, Mauchline, AYR. s/o Robert M. and Helen
McClelland. To Huron Co, ONT, prob 1832; stld
MacGillivray Twp.   **LDW 23 Sep 1976**.

9849 MORTON, Samuel. From Stranraer, WIG.
s/o Charles M. and Rosanna Ballantine. To Halifax, NS,
<1834. m Maryanne, d/o John Spence and Mary Cuddy.
Son Samuel Horatio, b ca 1840.   **DC 21 Mar 1981**.

9850 MOSES, David. To Pictou, NS, on the *Lulan*, ex
Glasgow, 17 Aug 1848.   **DC 12 Jul 1979**.

9851 MOTION, Margaret. From Edinburgh. To QUE, ex
Greenock, summer 1815; stld prob Lanark Co, ONT. Wife
of John McDonald, surgeon, qv.   **SEC 4**.

9852 MOUBRAY, Robert, ca 1806–4 Mar 1844. To
Aldborough Twp, Elgin Co, ONT, prob <1830.
Schoolteacher. Son William.   **PDA 41**.

9853 MOULTON, John. To QUE on the *Brock*, ex
Greenock, 9 Jul 1820; stld prob Lanark Co, ONT.
HCL 238.

9854 MOUNCEY, Janette, ca 1803–30 Oct 1862. From
DFS. To York Co, ONT, and d at Sutton. m Edward
Latimer.   **CAE 8**.

9855 MOUNCEY, Lancelot, b ca 1813. Poss from DFS.
To Roseneath, Alnwick Twp, Northumberland Co, ONT,
ca 1845. m Elizabeth, b ca 1822, d/o William Harris,
from ENG, ch.   **SG xxvi/4 142**.

MOUNT STEPHEN, Lord. See STEPHEN, George.

9856 MOWAT, Alexander Henderson. From Lerwick,
SHI. s/o James M, merchant. To ONT <1855.   **SH**.

9857 MOWAT, John, b ca 1730. To NS, 1785; stld
Margaree dist, Inverness Co. Farmer, and widowed by
1818.   **CBC 1818**.

9858 MOWAT, John. From Canisbay, CAI. To Kingston,
ONT, 1816. Discharged soldier. m Helen Levack, qv, and
had, prob with other ch: 1. Sir Oliver, 1820–1903,
Premier of ONT, 1872-96; 2. Rev John, 1825–1900,
Professor of Biblical Criticism at Queens Coll,
Kingston.   **BNA 580; FES vii 646; MDB 535**.

9859 MOWAT, Lawrence. Prob from Is Arran, BUT.
Half-bro of William M, qv. To Megantic Co, QUE,
1841.   **AMC 48**.

9860 MOWAT, Thomas. Prob from Is Arran, BUT.
Half-bro of William M, qv. To Megantic Co, QUE, 1841.
Tailor.   **AMC 48**.

9861 MOWAT, William. Prob from Is Arran, BUT.
Half-bro of Lawrence M, qv, and Thomas M, qv. To
Megantic Co, QUE, 1841. m Elizabeth McKillop, qv.
AMC 38; MAC 35.

9862 MOYES, John, d 19 Apr 1841. From DFS. To St
John, NB, and d there.   **DGH 1 Jul 1841**.

9863 MOYSE, Robert, b ca 1821. Poss from
Burntisland, FIF. To Dartmouth, Halifax Co, NS, prob
<1860. m Isabella Taylor. Dau Euphemia, b 1853.
LDW 29 Sep 1981.

9864 MUDIE, Margaret. Prob from Dunning, PER.
d/o — M. and Christian Robertson. To NS; stld
Douglas, Hants Co.   **SH**.

9865 MUGGAH, John. From BAN. To Sydney, Cape
Breton Co, NS. Construction engineer, Sydney Barracks.
m Miss Meloney. Son William, master mariner.
HNS iii 297.

9866 MUIR, Agnes, 1812–4 May 1864. From
Kilmarnock, AYR. To Elgin Co, ONT, 1842; later to Mosa
Twp, Middlesex Co. Wife of David Webster, qv.
DC 8 Nov 1981.

9867 MUIR, Alexander, 3 Apr 1830–26 Jun 1906.
From Lesmahagow, LKS. s/o John M, qv, and Catherine
McDonald, qv. To Scarborough, ONT, and educ Queens
Univ, Kingston, where he grad BA in 1851.
Schoolteacher in Toronto, and in 1867 composed the
words and music of *The Maple Leaf Forever*.
Lesmahagow OPR 649/4; MDB 536; ENA 22.

9868 MUIR, Andrew, b 1763. From RFW. s/o John
and Agnes M. To Niagara, Lincoln Co, ONT, 1797.
Mariner. m Anna, d/o Adam Green, and moved to
Grimsby.   **DC 23 Sep 1980**.

9869 MUIR, Allan. To Brant Co, ONT, 1835. Farmer.
Son John.   **DC 29 Sep 1964**.

9870 MUIR, Anne. Prob from ARL. To Eldon Twp,
Victoria Co, ONT, 1842. Wife of Peter McArthur, qv.
EC 80.

9871 MUIR, Christina, 22 Mar 1824–25 Oct 1910. From Lady par, Sanday, OKI. d/o Edward M. and Sibella Fotheringham. To Blanshard Twp, Perth Co, ONT, ca 1855, and d Goderich, Huron Co. m James Cutt, qv. **DC 20 Jul 1979**.

9872 MUIR, Duncan, d 1868. Poss from Kintyre, ARL. To Caledon Twp, Peel Co, ONT, <1840. **DC 21 Apr 1980**.

9873 MUIR, George, b 1781. From West Calder, MLN. s/o James M. and Elizabeth Graham. To Grimsby, Lincoln Co, ONT, <1850. **DC 12 May 1972**.

9874 MUIR, James. From LKS. Prob rel to William M, qv. To QUE on the *Prompt*, ex Greenock, 4 Jul 1820; stld Dalhousie Twp, Lanark Co, ONT. **HCL 238**.

9875 MUIR, James, b 1826. From West Calder, MLN. s/o James M. and Agnes Stewart. To ONT, 1852; stld Port Elgin, Bruce Co. Carpenter. m Jane Fleming. **DC 12 May 1972**.

MUIR, Mrs James. See STEUART, Agnes.

9876 MUIR, Rev James Creighton, d 1881. Educ Univ of Edinburgh. Ord min of Georgetown, Halton Co, ONT, 1836. Moderator of the Synod, 1849; DD, Queens Univ, 1858. **FES vii 647**.

9877 MUIR, John, 1802-65. From Lesmahagow, LKS. To Scarborough, York Co, ONT, 1833. Schoolteacher. Wife Catherine McDermid, qv, with him, and ch: 1. Alexander, qv; 2. John, b 4 Jan 1832. **Lesmahagow OPR 649/4; MDB 536**.

MUIR, Mrs John. See REID, Margaret.

9878 MUIR, John. From West Calder, MLN. s/o James M. and Agnes Stewart. To ONT, 1853; stld nr Port Elgin, Bruce Co. Farmer. m Jane McTavish. **DC 12 May 1972**.

9879 MUIR, Margaret, ca 1800–9 Mar 1875. From Dunfermline, FIF. To Simcoe Co, ONT, <1832; bur Craighurst. Wife of Donald Jamieson, qv, m at Colinton, nr Edinburgh, 17 Mar 1828. **DC 10 Dec 1981**.

9880 MUIR, Mary, 1815-93. From ARL. To Caledon Twp, Peel Co, ONT, <1840. m Peter Ferguson, qv. **DC 21 Apr 1980**.

9881 MUIR, Robert. From RFW. s/o John M. and Diana Winnet. To ONT, 1821; stld later in Brant Co. Farmer. Son Robert, b ca 1813, res Burford. **DC 23 Sep 1980**.

9882 MUIR, William. From LKS. Prob rel to James M, qv. To QUE on the *Prompt*, ex Greenock, 4 Jul 1820; stld Dalhousie Twp, Lanark Co, ONT. **HCL 238**.

9883 MUIR, William, b 1787. From West Calder, MLN. s/o James M. and Elizabeth Graham. To Norwich Twp, Oxford Co, ONT, <1850. **DC 12 May 1972**.

9884 MUIR, William Ker, 1829-92. From Kilmarnock, AYR. To ONT <1855. Emp with Great Western Railway. Moved to Detroit, MI. **SNQ vi/1 50**.

9885 MUIRHEAD, Ann. From New Abbey, KKD. d/o James M. To St Andrews, Charlotte Co, NB, <1837, when m Berwick Douglas. **DGC 3 May 1837**.

9886 MUNDLE, David, 1805–4 May 1871. From Annan, DFS. To Kent Co, NB, prob <1830. Ships carpenter. m Mary Room, qv, ch: 1. John, qv; 2. Mary; 3. Agnes, unm; 4. David; 5. Alexander; 6. Margaret. **DC 5 Aug 1980**.

9887 MUNDLE, John, 28 Aug 1827–12 May 1898. From Annan, DFS. s/o David M, qv, and Mary Room, qv. To Kent Co, NB, ca 1829. m Mary Hannay, qv, ch. **DC 5 Aug 1980**.

9888 MUNDLE, Margaret, b 18 Jun 1788. From Ruthwell, DFS. d/o Edward M. and Jean Beattie. To Smiths Falls, North Elmsley Twp, Lanark Co, ONT, 1817. Wife of Gabriel Chalmers, qv. **DC 14 Jan 1980**.

9889 MUNN, Alexander, 26 Sep 1766–19 May 1812. From Irvine, AYR. s/o John M, carpenter, and Katherine Edwards. To QUE <1794. Shipbuilder. m Agnes Galloway, 6 Dec 1797, ch: 1. Catherine, b 1801; 2. Helenore, b 1800; 3. Agnes, b 1801; 4. John, b 1802; 5. Alexander, b 1804; 6. Agnes, b 1805; 7. Alexander, b 1806; 8. Elizabeth, b 1807; 9. Maria, b 1808; 10. James, b 1810; 11. John, b 1811, dy. **LDW 29 Sep 1979**.

9890 MUNN, Angus. Poss from Is Colonsay, ARL. To PEI, prob 1806; stld nr Belfast, Queens Co. Petitioner for Dr MacAulay, 1811. **HP 74**.

9891 MUNN, Archibald, ca 1811–ca 1903. From ARL. To Ekfrid Twp, Middlesex Co, ONT, 1831. ch: 1. Duncan; 2. John; 3. Catherine; 4. Mary; 5. Effie. **PCM 30**.

9892 MUNN, Catherine, b 1806. Poss from Is Colonsay, ARL, and prob rel to Duncan M, qv. To Charlottetown, PEI, on the *Spencer*, ex Oban, 22 Sep 1806. **PLSN**.

9893 MUNN, David, 9 Aug 1783–13 Mar 1829. b Irvine, AYR. s/o John M, carpenter, and Katherine Edwards. To QUE <1803. Shipbuilder. m Jane Bryan, 1784–1820. Son John, b 1813. **LDW 29 Sep 1979**.

9894 MUNN, Duncan, b ca 1746. Prob from Is Colonsay, ARL. To Charlottetown, PEI, on the *Spencer*, ex Oban, 22 Sep 1806. Wife Flora Brown, qv, with him, and ch: 1. Angus, aged 31; 2. Neil, aged 28; 3. Malcolm, aged 23; 4. James, aged 20; 5. Ann, aged 17; 6. Effie, aged 15. **PLSN**.

9895 MUNN, James, 1783–5 Jun 1867. From Is Colonsay, ARL. bro/o Malcolm M, qv. To PEI, 1806; stld Belle Creek. Farmer. ch. **HP 15, 74**.

9896 MUNN, John, 1769–1815. b Irvine, AYR. s/o John M, carpenter, and Katharine Edwards. To QUE <1798; stld St Roch. Shipbuilder. m Frances Farrie. Son James, dy, 1806. **LDW 29 Sep 1979**.

9897 MUNN, John, 2 Nov 1788–20 Mar 1859. From Irvine, AYR. Natural s/o John M, sailor, and Mary Gemmill. To QUE <1803. Shipbuilder, and d unm. Benefactor of Queens Univ, Kingston. **DC 16 Mar 1970**.

9898 MUNN, John, b 1760. From Is Colonsay, ARL. To Charlottetown, PEI, on the *Clarendon*, ex Oban, 6 Aug 1808. Labourer. Wife Catherine, aged 42, with him, and ch: 1. Donald, aged 16; 2. Duncan, aged 14; 3. Sarah, aged 12; 4. Catherine, aged 7; 5. Barbara, aged 5; 6. John, aged 4. **CPL; HP 74**.

9899 MUNN, Malcolm. From Is Colonsay, ARL. bro/o James M, qv. To PEI, prob 1806; stld Wood Is, Queens Co. **HP 15, 74**.

9900 MUNN, Mary. From Kilmarnock, AYR. To QUE, ex Greenock, summer 1815; stld prob Lanark Co, ONT. Wife of John Oliver, qv. **SEC 4**.

MUNRO. See also MONRO, MUNROE.

9901 MUNRO, Alexander, ca 1754–27 Mar 1828. To St John, NB. Wife Margaret, 1763–2 Oct 1826. **NER viii 98**.

9902 MUNRO, Alexander. Poss from ROC. To ONT, 1811. Fought in War of 1812, and stld afterwards at Portage Road, Eldon Twp, Victoria Co. Farmer and Ch precentor. m 1810, Margaret Gunn, qv, ch: 1. Donald, b 1811; 2. Sarah; 3. George; 4. Jeanette; 5. Isabel. **EC 200**.

9903 MUNRO, Alexander, b ca 1786. To Pictou, NS, 1815; res Caribou, 1816. Labourer, with 1 ch. 'Industrious, but now very poor.' **INS 39**.

9904 MUNRO, Alexander, b ca 1794. To Pictou Co, NS, 1815; res Lower Settlement, 1816. Unm carpenter. **INS 38**.

9905 MUNRO, Alexander. From Inverary, ARL. To Matilda Twp, Dundas Co, ONT. ch: 1. William; 2. John; 3, Jennie; 4. Catherine Rose; 5. Isabella; 6. Mary Ann. **DC 4 Mar 1965**.

9906 MUNRO, Alexander, d 1869. From Glasgow. To Lanark Co, ONT, prob <1830. Physician. m Elizabeth Bain, qv, ch: 1. James, b 1834; 2. William, 1836–1916; 3. Janet, d inf, 1839; 4. John, 1839–1918; 5. Dr David, 1842–1903; 6. Alexander, 1844–1911; 7. Margaret, 1848-51; 8. Mary Cullen, 1850–1930; 9. George, 1853-54. **DC 2 Nov 1979**.

9907 MUNRO, Alexander, ca 1797–9 May 1874. From Ullapool, ROC. To Melbourne, Richmond Co, QUE, prob <1840. Wife Hannah, 1814–10 Nov 1859. **MGC 15 Jul 1980**.

9908 MUNRO, Alexander 'Mor', 1774–11 Nov 1856. From Strath, Is Skye, INV. s/o George M, miller, and Jessie Nicholson. To PEI, 1842; stld Valleyfield, Queens Co. Moved later to Lorne Valley. m Euphemia Campbell, qv, ch: 1. Janet, remained in Skye; 2. Thomas Boston, qv; 3. George, qv; 4. Flora, qv; 5. Catherine, qv; 6. John, qv; 7. Ann, qv; 8. Mary, qv; 9. Donald, qv; 10. Christy, qv. **SPI 118; HP 90**.

9909 MUNRO, Allan, b ca 1785. To Baddeck, Victoria Co, NS, 1814. Prob farmer, m and ch. **CBC 1818**.

9910 MUNRO, Ann, 1834–1926. From Is Skye, INV. d/o Alexander 'Mor' M, qv, and Euphemia Campbell, qv. To PEI, prob 1842; stld Queens Co. m John McSwain, Lorne Valley, ch. **SPI 121**.

9911 MUNRO, Annabella, ca 1799 -1 May 1829. From Gairloch, ROC. To Pictou Co, NS. Wife of Alexander Fraser, qv. **DC 27 Oct 1979**.

9912 MUNRO, Archibald. From ARL. To QUE on the Mars, ex Tobermory, 28 Jul 1818; stld Aldborough Twp, Elgin Co, ONT. Farmer. ch incl: 1. George; 2. Duncan, teacher. **PDA, 24, 36, 72, 93**.

9913 MUNRO, Archibald 'Mor'. Poss from ARL. To Aldborough Twp, Elgin Co, ONT, 1818; moved to Mosa Twp, 1827. Son John Malcolm. **PCM 23**.

9914 MUNRO, Archibald. Poss from ARL. bro/o Sheriff M, Elgin Co, ONT. To Mosa Twp, Middlesex Co, ca 1850. **PCM 24**.

9915 MUNRO, Betsy. Poss from Is Skye, INV. To Aldborough Twp, Elgin Co, ONT, 1836. Wife of Dougald Smith, qv, m 1832. **PDA 63**.

9916 MUNRO, Catherine, d 26 Jul 1854. From Is Skye, INV. d/o Alexander 'Mor' M, qv, and Euphemia Campbell, qv. To Charlottetown, PEI, prob on the Ruther, ex Portree, 14 Jul 1840. m John Shaw, Lorne Valley, ch. **SPI 120**.

9917 MUNRO, Christy, ca 1793–18 Nov 1883. From ROC. To Pictou Co, NS. Wife of Alexander Graham, qv. **DC 27 Oct 1979**.

9918 MUNRO, Christy. From Is Skye, INV. d/o Alexander 'Mor' M, qv, and Euphemia Campbell, qv. To Queens Co, PEI, prob 1842. m Neil MacLeod. **SPI 121**.

9919 MUNRO, Donald. From INV. To Pictou, NS, on the Hector, ex Loch Broom, arr 17 Sep 1773; stld Halifax, later West Branch, East River, Pictou Co. Son Henry. **HPC App C**.

9920 MUNRO, Donald. From Dornoch, SUT. To Lanark Co, ONT, 1830; stld prob Ramsay Twp. m Catherine Morrow, qv. **DC 10 Jan 1980**.

9921 MUNRO, Donald, ca 1782–13 Apr 1863. From ROC. To Pictou, NS, 1831; bur Salt Springs. **DC 27 Oct 1979**.

9922 MUNRO, Donald, 1799–22 Jan 1881. From SUT. To Lanark Co, ONT, prob <1840; stld nr Middleville. **DC 5 Dec 1981**.

9923 MUNRO, Donald, 1819-84. From Uig, Trotternich, Is Skye, INV. s/o Dr James M, d Iobermory, 1840, and Annabella MacLeod, qv. To Charlottetown, PEI, on the Ruther, arr 8 Sep 1840. Physician, legislator and officer of militia. m Jessie Robertson, 1833–1910, Montague Bridge, ch: 1. Margaret; 2. Alice. **HP 26**.

9924 MUNRO, Donald. From Is Skye, INV. s/o Alexander 'Mor' M, qv, and Euphemia Campbell, qv. To Queens Co, PEI, prob 1842. m Catherine Cameron, Whim Road Cross, ch. **SPI 121**.

9925 MUNRO, Rev Donald, 1789–15 Feb 1867. From Kilmichael-Glassary, ARL. s/o Malcolm M, farmer. Educ Univ of Glasgow and Edinburgh. Missionary in ARL, and adm min of Finch Twp, Stormont Co, ONT, 19 Dec 1850. m Mary Campbell. Son Robert. **GMA 7240; FES vii 647**.

9926 MUNRO, Dugald. Poss from ARL. To Mosa Twp, Middlesex Co, ONT, 1831. **PCM 24**.

9927 MUNRO, Finlay, b ca 1785. To Mosa Twp, Middlesex Co, ONT, <1840. m Ellen McDougall, qv. Dau Christy Ann. **DC 21 Nov 1968**.

9928 MUNRO, Flora. From Is Skye, INV. d/o Alexander 'Mor' M, qv, and Euphemia Campbell, qv. To Charlottetown, PEI, on the Ruther, ex Portree, 14 Jul 1840; stld Queens Co. m Neil Shaw, Cardigan, ch. **SPI 120**.

9929 MUNRO, George, b ca 1780. To Pictou, NS, 1815; res Caribou, 1816. Weaver, m with 3 ch, and 'very poor.' **INS 39**.

9930 MUNRO, George, 1804-92. Prob from ARL. To Aldborough Twp, Elgin Co, ONT, <1830. m Mary, poss d/o John Menzies, qv. ch: 1. Mary, 1834-97; 2. Donald, 1841–1906. **PDA 42**.

9931 MUNRO, George, b 1821. From Is Skye, INV. s/o Alexander 'Mor' M, qv, and Euphemia Campbell, qv. To PEI, prob on the *Ruther*, ex Portree, 14 Jul 1840; stld Queens Co. m (i) Louise Swan; (ii) Hattie Wadman, ch by both. **SPI 120**.

9932 MUNRO, Hector, b 21 Jan 1807. From ROX. To Montreal, QUE, 1832. Stonemason and contractor. **SGC 564**.

9933 MUNRO, Henry, d 6 Jan 1781. From ROC. bro/o Sir George M. To Annapolis Co, NS, 1765. Lt, Montgomerys Highlanders and gr 2,000 acres. MLA, rep Granville Twp. m Sarah, d/o Thomas Hooper. **MLA 260**.

9934 MUNRO, Henry, 1754–14 Jun 1799. To Halifax, NS, <1785, later to west branch, East River, Pictou Co. Farmer, and gr 300 acres. m Nancy Fraser, qv, ch: 1. Thomas; 2. Donald; 3. Catherine; 4. Betsy; 5. Jennie; 6. Isabel; 7. Nancy. **PAC 179**.

9935 MUNRO, Hugh, ca 1788–15 Nov 1859. From ROC. To NS poss <1830; stld nr Earltown, Colchester Co. m Margaret MacLeod, qv. ch incl: 1. Jane, 1823–1911; 2. Margaret, ca 1827-98. **DC 19 Mar 1981**.

9936 MUNRO, Hugh, b 1814. From Tain, ROC. To Cape Breton Is, NS, 1837; moved to Halifax, 1839. Teacher, and MLA, rep Victoria Co, 1851-61. Went later to Livingstone, MT, and was in grain business there. **MLA 261**.

9937 MUNRO, Isabella. From Aberdeen. To Charlottetown, PEI, <1841. m Donald Stewart, ch. **LC 21 Oct 1976**.

9938 MUNRO, Jacobina Annabella, 1831–1911. From Uig, Trotternish, Is Skye, INV. d/o Dr James M, d Tobermory, 1840, and Annabella MacLeod, qv. To PEI, 1841; stld Queens Co. m Charles Crawford, Cardigan, a distant relative, ch. **SPI 117**.

9939 MUNRO, James, b 1 Jul 1772. s/o Rev James M, Cromarty, and second wife Mary Stark. To Pictou, NS. Cabinet-maker. **FES vii 5**.

9940 MUNRO, James. To Pictou Co, NS, 1815; res Pictou Town, 1816. Joiner, m with 1 ch. **INS 39**.

9941 MUNRO, Jean, 1820-81. From Dufftown, BAN. d/o John M, qv, and Elizabeth Dunbar, qv. To Nichol Twp, Wellington Co, ONT, 1832. m John Martin, qv. **DC 31 Dec 1979**.

9942 MUNRO, John. From Lochbroom par, ROC. To Pictou, NS, on the *Hector*, ex Loch Broom, arr 17 Sep 1773. Family with him. **HPC App C**.

9943 MUNRO, John, 1799–1879. From Assynt, SUT. To Pictou, NS, 1817, with Rev Norman MacLeod, qv. Teacher, merchant, shipbuilder and MLA. Went to Waipu, NZ, on his own ship, the *Gertrude*, 1856. **MLA 261**.

9944 MUNRO, John, ca 1806–31 Oct 1884. From INV. To Colchester Co, NS, and bur East Earltown. m Nancy McBain, 1815-89. **DC 22 Jun 1980**.

9945 MUNRO, John. Prob from ARL. To Aldborough Twp, Elgin Co, ONT, <1820. Farmer. **PDA 93**.

9946 MUNRO, John. From Melfort, ARL. To Westminster Twp, Middlesex Co, ONT, 1831. ch: 1. Malcolm; 2. Archibald; 3. John, jr, qv. **PCM 51**.

9947 MUNRO, John, jr, b ca 1824. From Melfort, ARL. s/o John M, qv. To Westminster Twp, Middlesex Co, ONT, 1831. ch: 1. Dr George; 2. John, architect; 3. Kenneth; 4. Edward. **PCM 51**.

9948 MUNRO, John. Poss from ARL. To Mosa Twp, Middlesex Co, ONT, 1832. **PCM 24**.

9949 MUNRO, John, 1784–1866. From Dufftown, BAN. To Nichol Twp, Wellington Co, ONT, 1832. Carpenter, later farmer. m Elizabeth Dunbar, qv, ch: 1. Jean, qv; 2. Alexander, b 1813; 3. Margaret; 4. David, carpenter; 5. Anne. **DC 31 Dec 1979**.

9950 MUNRO, John, 1831–1917. From Is Skye, INV. s/o Alexander 'Mor' M, qv, and Euphemia Campbell, qv. To Charlottetown, PEI, prob on the *Ruther*, ex Portree, 14 Jul 1840; stld Queens Co. d Lorne Valley. Farmer and schoolmaster. m Jane McSwain, qv, ch: 1. Catherine, b 1861; 2. Euphemia Catherine, b 1864; 3. James Allan, b 1868; 4. Annabella, 1870-98; 5. Donald, b 1872; 6. Mary, 1876–1927; 7. Jacobina, b 1878. **SPI 120**.

9951 MUNRO, John Campbell. From Golspie, SUT. To Stormont Co, ONT, 1830. Merchant. m Lucretia Valentine Crysler. Son John Malcolm. **DC 29 Sep 1964**.

9952 MUNRO, Margaret, ca 1778–12 Jun 1862. From Clyne, SUT. To Pictou Co, NS, and bur Salt Springs. Wife of Alexander Sutherland, qv. **DC 27 Oct 1979**.

9953 MUNRO, Margaret, b 1829. From Loch Broom, ROC. To Melbourne, Richmond Co, QUE, <1852, when m John McMorine, qv. **MGC 2 Aug 1979**.

9954 MUNRO, Margaret Alice, 1836–1912. From Uig, Trotternish, Is Skye, INV. d/o Dr James M, d Tobermory, 1840, and Annabella MacLeod, qv. To Queens Co, PEI, 1841. m Donald MacDonald. **SPI 118**.

9955 MUNRO, Marion, 1812-97. From Kilmuir, Is Skye, INV. d/o Dr James M, d Tobermory, 1840, and Annabella MacLeod, qv. To PEI, prob on the *Ruther*, 1840; stld Queens Co. m Peter, s/o Donald Nicholson, qv, and Isabella Nicholson, qv, ch. **SPI 116; HP 26**.

9956 MUNRO, Mary. From INV. d/o George Ross M. To Pictou Co, NS, <1835. m James Grant, qv. **FES vii 636**.

9957 MUNRO, Mary, b 1834. From Is Skye, INV. Twin d/o Alexander 'Mor' M, qv, and Euphemia Campbell, qv. To PEI, prob 1842; stld Queens Co. m Capt Allan McSwain, Lorne Valley. **SPI 121**.

9958 MUNRO, Mary Ann, b ca 1817. From Jemimaville, nr Resolis, ROC. To ONT, 1834; stld Carleton Co. Wife of William Ross, qv. **LDW 2 Apr 1978**.

9959 MUNRO, Neil 'Ban'. Poss from ARL. Prob bro/o Archibald 'Mor' M, qv. To Aldborough Twp, Elgin Co, ONT, 1818; moved to Mosa Twp, 1827. Son Archibald. **PCM 23**.

9960 MUNRO, Neil. Poss from ARL. To Mosa Twp,

Middlesex Co, ONT, 1831. ch: 1. Neil, reeve of Mosa; 2. Rev Donald, Presb min. **PCM 24**.

9961 MUNRO, Peter. To QUE on the *Commerce*, ex Greenock, Jun 1820; stld prob Lanark Co, ONT. **HCL 239**.

9962 MUNRO, Robert, ca 1771–5 Jul 1841. From Rogart par, SUT. To NS, and stld nr Earltown, Colchester Co. m Ann Matheson, qv. **DC 19 Mar 1981**.

9963 MUNRO, Thomas Boston, 17 Oct 1817–31 Jun 1888. From Triaslan, Is Skye, INV. s/o Alexander 'Mor' M, qv, and Euphemia Campbell, qv. To Charlottetown, PEI, on the *Ruther*, ex Portree, 14 Jul 1840; stld Queens Co. Schoolmaster. m Sarah Shaw, 1827–97, Flat River, ch: 1. Janet, 1852–1913; 2. Alexander, b 1854; 3. Allan, b 1857; 4. George, 1862–1914; 5. Donald, 1864–99; 6. Catherine Elizabeth, 1867–1923. **SPI 118; HP 90**.

9964 MUNROE, Barbara, ca 1803–26 Jan 1890. From Garve, ROC. To Melbourne, Richmond Co, QUE. Wife of Lachlan McLeay, qv. **MGC 15 Jul 1980**.

9965 MUNROE, Donald. From Balquhidder par, PER. To Montreal, QUE, on the *Sophia*, ex Greenock, 26 Jul 1818; stld prob Beckwith Twp, Lanark Co, ONT. Wife Mary with him, and ch: 1. Thomas, aged 10; 2. John, aged 7; 3. Catherine, aged 4. **SPL**.

9966 MUNROE, Flora, 1783–1866. From ARL. Said to have been a cous of James M, fifth president of the USA. To Lanark Twp, Lanark Co, ONT, 1820. Wife of John McNichol, qv. **HCL 67; DC 2 Nov 1979**.

9967 MUNROE, Hugh, 15 Jul 1833–11 Mar 1919. From Lochbroom, ROC. To Melbourne, Richmond Co, QUE, m Janet Allan, qv, ch: 1. Alexander, 1863–1941; 2. George D, d inf, 1866; 3. William F, 1875–1943; 4. Frederick A, 1875–1939; 5. Elisha J, 1879–1956. **MGC 15 Jul 1980**.

9968 MUNROE, Murdock, 1844-83. Prob from ROC. To Melbourne, Richmond Co, QUE. By wife Nancy had s Daniel T, 1877–1900. **MGC 15 Jul 1980**.

9969 MURCHESON, Isobel, 1828-75. From Is Skye, INV. Poss d/o Colin M. To Kinloss Twp, Bruce Co, ONT, <1852. m Donald McKinnon, qv. **DC 12 Apr 1979**.

9970 MURCHIE, Donald. From Ballymichael, Is Arran, BUT. To Inverness, Megantic Co, QUE, 1831. m Flora McKelvie, qv. **AMC 42; MAC 41**.

9971 MURCHIE or MURPHY, Donald, 1773–1837. From Cloined, Kilmory par, Is Arran, BUT. s/o Donald M. and Jean McCurdy. To Durham Co, NB, 1833. m Janet McBride, qv, ch: 1. Mary, 1812-76; 2. Catherine, b 1814; 3. John, 1816-94; 4. Archibald; 5. Donald; 6. Alexander; 7. Margaret. **LDW 6 May 1967**.

9972 MURCHIE or MURPHY, Peter, b 1792. From Cloined, Kilmory par, Is Arran, BUT. s/o Donald M. and Jean McCurdy. To Restigouche Co, NB, 1831; stld Blackland. m 19 Jun 1824, Mary Cook, qv, ch: 1. Donald; 2. Archibald, b 1826; 3. John, b 1828; 4. James, b 1831; 5. Mary, 1834–1925; 6. Margaret, b 1836; 7. Alexander, b 1839; 8. Peter, b 1842. **MAC 25; LDW 6 Nov 1967**.

9973 MURCHIE, William. From Ballymichael, Is Arran, BUT. To Inverness Twp, Megantic Co, QUE, 1831. m Elizabeth Sillers, qv. **AMC 42; MAC 41**.

9974 MURCHISON, Donald. Prob rel to the Murchisons of Achtertyre, Lochalsh, ROC. To Orwell Bay, PEI, on the *Polly*, ex Portree, arr 7 Aug 1803; stld Point Prim, Queens Co. m (ii) Ann MacGillivray, 1751–1838. Dau Mary. **HP 28**.

9975 MURCHISON, Donald 'Og'. To Charlottetown, PEI, 1803; stld Point Prim, Queens Co. m Ann MacDonald, qv. Son William, banker, Charlottetown. **HP 36, 73**.

9976 MURCHISON, Janet. From Glenelg, INV. To QUE, ex Greenock, summer 1815; stld prob Lanark Co, ONT. Wife of Duncan McClure, qv. **SEC 7**.

9977 MURCHISON, John. Prob from INV. To PEI, prob 1803; stld Queens Co. Petitioner for Dr MacAulay, 1811. **HP 73**.

9978 MURCHISON, Marion. From Glenelg, INV. To QUE, summer 1815; stld prob Lanark Co, ONT. Wife of Roderick McRae, qv. **SEC 5**.

9979 MURCHISON, Murdock. To Glengarry Co, ONT, 1794; stld Lot 34, Con 15, Lancaster Twp. **MG 56**.

9980 MURCHISON, Peter. To Queens Co, PEI, poss 1803. Petitioner for Dr MacAulay, 1811. **HP 74**.

9981 MURCHISON, Sarah. From Is Skye, INV. To Victoria Co, ONT, <1851; stld Woodville. Wife of Roderick MacCrimmon, qv. **DC 5 Sep 1981**.

MURCHY. See also MURCHIE.

9982 MURCHY, Archibald, 1755–1836. From Is Arran, BUT. To Dalhousie, NB, prob <1833. **MAC 25**.

9983 MURCHY, Archibald, b 1806. From Is Arran, BUT. Prob s/o Archibald M, qv. To Dalhousie, NB, <1836. **MAC 25**.

9984 MURCHY, Charles, 1804-36. From Is Arran, BUT. Prob s/o Archibald M, qv. To Dalhousie, NB, <1836. **MAC 25**.

9985 MURCHY, Elizabeth, 1805-82. From Is Arran, BUT. Prob d/o Archibald M, qv. To Dalhousie, NB, <1836. **MAC 25**.

9986 MURCHY, Isabella. From Is Arran, BUT. To NB, poss <1840; stld prob Restigouche Co. **MAC 25**.

9987 MURCHY, John, 1807-92. From Lag of Torrilin, Kilmory par, Is Arran, BUT. To Benjamen River, Restigouche Co, NB, 1829. **MAC 24**.

9988 MURCHY, William, 1781–1866. From Corriecrevie, Is Arran, BUT. To Dalhousie, NB, prob <1833. m (i) 30 Jan 1812, Janet Hamilton, ch: 1. John, 1812-96; 2. Mary, b 1815; 3. Janet, b 1818; 4. Donald, b 1825. m (ii) 1823, Catherine McAlister, qv, further ch: 5. Alexander, 1824-69; 6. Catherine, b 1825. **MAC 25**.

9989 MURDOCH, James, b 1805. From Is Arran, BUT. To River Charlo, Restigouche Co, NB, 1827. Farmer. m Catherine McMillan, qv, ch: 1. Duncan; 2. Barbara; 3. Donald; 4. Mary; 5. James; 6. Catherine. **MAC 22; DC 7 Feb 1981**.

9990 MURDOCH, William. To Pictou, NS, <1822. m Mary Tanner. Son William, ca 1822-90, d Providence, RI. **NSN 5/3**.

9991 MURDOCH, William, 1806-86. From ARL. To Caledon Twp, Peel Co, ONT, <1840. Wife Agnes McFarland, qv, with him. **DC 21 Apr 1980**.

9992 MURDOCH, William. Poss from Hawick, ROX. To Halifax, NS, <1851. **SH**.

9993 MURDOCH, William, 1823–4 May 1887. From Paisley, RFW. To NB, 1854. On staff of marine station, Partridge Is. Journalist and poet. **MDB 538**.

9994 MURDOCK, David. Poss from KKD. To Wauchs River, Colchester Co, NS, 1840. Game-keeper, and became farmer. m Sara Wilson, qv. **HT 81**.

9995 MURDOCK, Isabella, ca 1791–19 Jul 1865. From Kilmarnock, AYR. To Cleveland Twp, Richmond Co, QUE, 1820; later to Sherbrooke, and bur Maple Grove. Wife of John Smellie, qv. **MGC 2 Aug 1979; DC 11 Jan 1980**.

9996 MURDOCK, Rev James. To Halifax, NS, <1790. Presb min. Believed drowned in Musquodoboit River. Dau Susan. **HNS iii 61**.

9997 MURPHIE, Catherine, 1796–1870. From Kildonan, Kilmory par, Is Arran, BUT. To Benjamen River, Restigouche Co, NB, 1829. Wife of Duncan McKinnon, qv. **MAC 21**.

MURPHY. See also MURCHIE.

9998 MURPHY or MURCHIE, Margaret, b 1802. From Drimaginear, Is Arran, BUT. To Dalhousie, NB, <1840. m 19 Aug 1823, Archibald Cook, qv. **MAC 9**.

9999 MURPHY, Margaret. Prob from Campbeltown, ARL. To Malpeque, Prince Co, PEI, on the *Annabella*, ex Campbeltown, 27 Jul 1770. m Malcolm Ramsay, qv. **DC 18 May 1981**.

10000 MURPHY, Mary, b ca 1800. From Corrie, Is Arran, BUT. To QUE on the *Albion*, ex Greenock, 5 Jun 1829; stld Inverness, Megantic Co. Wife of James Fullerton, sr, qv. **AMC 21; MAC 34**.

10001 MURRAY, —. From Dornoch, SUT. To Halifax, NS, 1816. Merchant. m Jane Hardy, qv. Son William H, 1822-67, father of George Henry M, Premier of NS, 1896. **HNS iii 638**.

10002 MURRAY, Adam, b 1 Aug 1808. From Castleton, ROX. s/o Charles M. and Elizabeth Armstrong. To York Co, NB, poss 1819; moved to Westminster Twp, Middlesex Co, ONT. Farmer and schoolteacher. m Jane, d/o William Beattie, qv, and Janet Hogg, qv. **DC 16 Jul 1979**.

10003 MURRAY, Agnes, b ca 1812. From Castleton, ROX. d/o Charles M. and Elizabeth Armstrong. To York Co, NB, poss 1820. m Thomas Armstrong, qv. **DC 16 Jul 1979**.

10004 MURRAY, Alexander, b ca 1763. From Kildonan, SUT. To York Factory, Hudson Bay, arr 26 Aug 1815, and went to Red River. Wife Elizabeth, aged 54, with him, and ch: 1. Catherine, aged 27; 2. Christian, aged 25; 3. Isabella, aged 18; 4. James, aged 16; 5. Donald, aged 13. **LSC 326**.

10005 MURRAY, Alexander, b ca 1793. From Suisguill, Kildonan par, SUT. bro/o John M, qv. To Fort Churchill, Hudson Bay, on the *Prince of Wales*, ex Stromness, 28 Jun 1813. Went to York Factory, Apr 1814, thence to Red River. Left settlement and arr Holland River, ONT, 6 Sep 1815. **LSS 186; RRS 27; LSC 323**.

10006 MURRAY, Alexander, b ca 1809. To Cumberland Co, NS, <1838. m Jane Ross, b ca 1820, ch: 1. James,

b 1839; 2. Hugh, b 1841; 3. Catherine, b 1845; 4. William, b 1848; 5. Isabella, b 1853; 6. Mary, b 1855. **NSN 11/2**.

10007 MURRAY, Alexander, ca 1809–8 Jul 1871. From Dornoch, SUT. To ONT, ca 1830, and d at Beeton, Tecumseth Twp, Simcoe Co. House carpenter. m Ellen Bannerman, qv, ch: 1. Robert, ca 1829–1915; 2. William, d New York City; 3. James, 1834-79; 4. Catherine, 1837-65; 5. Elizabeth, b ca 1840; 6. John, ca 1845-66. **DC 28 Nov 1980**.

10008 MURRAY, Alexander, b 14 Dec 1813. From Clyne par, SUT. s/o Angus M, qv, and Elizabeth MacDonald, qv. To Pictou, NS, 1831; stld Mount Thom. Farmer. m 3 Dec 1868, Isabella, d/o Kenneth and Nancy Munro, ch: 1. Elizabeth; 2. Ann; 3. Alexander; 4. Hugh Ross; 5. Kenneth; 6. Angus. **DC 31 Dec 1979**.

10009 MURRAY, Alexander, ca 1810–22 Sep 1883. From Glasgow. s/o Thomas M, Muirkirk, AYR, and Janet Ferguson. To Wentworth Co, ONT, ca 1841; stld Dundas. Res later in Toronto. **NDF 209**.

10010 MURRAY, Alexander. From Dalbeattie, KKD. To CAN, ca 1842. m Janet Brown, qv. **DC 22 Nov 1981**.

10011 MURRAY, Alexander Hunter, 1818-74. From Kilmun, ARL. s/o Comm M, RN. To Hudson Bay, 1846, and joined HBCo. Served in Mackenzie River dist and conducted explorations on the Peel, Porcupine and Pelly rivers. Established Fort Yukon, and became a chief trader. Ret 1867. m Anne, d/o Colin Campbell, chief trader, Athabasca, and had with other ch: 1. Alexander C, who served with HBCo; 2. Mrs W.J. McLean. **DC 18 May 1982**.

10012 MURRAY, Angus, b ca 1744. To Pictou Co, NS, 1815, res Rogers Hill, 1816. Labourer; 'very poor'. **INS 38**.

10013 MURRAY, Angus, ca 1777–16 Dec 1844. From Golspie, SUT. To Pictou, NS, 1831; stld Mount Thom. Blacksmith. But at Lovat. m Elizabeth MacDonald, qv, ch: 1. Janet, qv; 2. Alexander, qv; 3. Betsy Anderson, qv; 4. Isabel, qv; 5. Margaret, qv; 6. John, qv; 7. Ann, qv; 8. Georgina Anderson, qv; 9. Jane, b 17 Mar 1830. **Clyne OPR 45/1-2; DC 27 Oct and 31 Dec 1979**.

10014 MURRAY, Angus, 1819-94. From Glen Tolsta, Is Lewis, ROC. s/o Angus M. and Ann McDonald. To QUE, ex Stornoway, arr 4 Aug 1851; stld Lot 13, Con 8, Huron Twp, Bruce Co, ONT. Farmer. m Margaret McIver, see ADDENDA; ch: 1. Isabella, b 1841; 2. Kirsty, b 1844, d inf; 3. Norman, b 1848; 4. Kirsty, b 1851; 5. Ann, b 1853; 6. Catherine, b 1855; 7. Effie, b 1857; 8. Angus, b 1859. **WLC**.

10015 MURRAY, Ann, b 12 May 1825. From Clyne, SUT. d/o Angus M, qv, and Elizabeth MacDonald, qv. To Pictou, NS, 1831; stld Mount Thom. m Tom Johnston, ch: 1. John; 2. Elizabeth. **DC 31 Dec 1979**.

10016 MURRAY, Archibald. From Glen Quaich, PER. s/o John M, Kinloch. To ONT <1847. **SH**.

10017 MURRAY, Betsy Anderson, 5 Aug 1815–24 May 1879. From Clyne par, SUT. s/o Angus M, qv, and Elizabeth MacDonald, qv. To Pictou, NS, 1831; stld Mount Thom. m 10 Apr 1840, Alexander McPherson, ch. **DC 31 Dec 1979**.

10018 MURRAY, Donald, ca 1768–15 Feb 1848. From Lairg, SUT. To Pictou Co, NS, 1802; stld New Lairg. m Mary McLean, qv. **DC 10 Feb 1980**.

10019 MURRAY, Donald, b ca 1776. To Pictou Co, NS, 1815; res Rogers Hill, 1816. Labourer, m with 5 ch, and 'very poor'. **INS 39**.

10020 MURRAY, Donald, b ca 1791. To Pictou Co, NS, 1815; res West River, 1816. Labourer, m with 2 ch, and 'very poor indeed'. **INS 38**.

10021 MURRAY, Donald. To NS, <1830; stld Loganville. ch: 1. William H; 2. Donald George; 3. John; 4. Robert. **HNS iii 79**.

10022 MURRAY, Donald. From Dornoch, SUT. To Halifax, NS, <1820. Gr-uncle of George Henry M, Premier of NS, 1896. **HNS iii 638**.

10023 MURRAY, Donald, b 1805. From Glasgow. s/o — M. and — Gunn. To Montreal, QUE, <1837. Forwarding agent, Montreal and Kingston. m at Montreal, 25 Aug 1837, Matilda Sophia Ray, ch: 1. Catherine Sophia, 1838-39; 2. Donald, b 1840, went to USA; 3. Alexander William, 1842-43; 4. Ericson, 1843-82, d Fort Garry, MAN; 5. Amy Frances, 1845-75, unm; 6. Albert, 1849–1928. **DC 27 Jul 1982**.

10024 MURRAY, Donald. Prob from ARL. To Ekfrid Twp, Middlesex Co, ONT, prob <1850. **PCM 31**.

10025 MURRAY, Donald. From South Dell, Ness, Is Lewis, ROC. To QUE, 1855. m Mary Campbell, qv. **DC 22 Jun 1975**.

10026 MURRAY, Duncan, ca 1796–6 Jul 1852. From ROC. To Pictou Co, NS, prob <1830; bur Churchville. m Catherine McDonald, ca 1796–7 Sep 1847, and had, prob with other ch: 1. Jessy, 1852-57; 2. Mary, d 1857. **DC 22 Jun 1980**.

10027 MURRAY, Elizabeth, b 1793. From Dumfries. To Pictou Co, NS, 1823. Wife of Samuel Brown, qv, m 19 Dec 1813. **HNS iii 695**.

10028 MURRAY, Elizabeth, 1813–1901. From Castleton, ROX. d/o John M. and Margaret Murray. To Dumfries Twp, Waterloo Co, ONT, 1840. Wife of William Pattison Telford, qv. **DC 10 Jul 1979**.

10029 MURRAY, Elizabeth, ca 1806–15 Feb 1884. From DFS. To Melbourne, Richmond Co, QUE, prob <1850. Wife of Charles Beattie, qv. **MGC 15 Jul 1980**.

10030 MURRAY, Sir George, 6 Feb 1772–28 Jul 1846. From Crieff, PER. s/o Sir William M. of Ochtertyre, and Lady Augusta Mackenzie. Held various staff appointments in British Army, and in 1815, with the rank of Lt Gen, became Lt Gov of Upper Canada. KCB, 1813; GCB, 1815; LLD, Oxford, 1820. m Lady Louisa Erskine, ch: Louisa. **BNA ii 357; SP iii 81; MDB 540**.

10031 MURRAY, Rev George, ca 1805–26 Apr 1869. From Glasgow. s/o Dr George M. Matric Univ of Glasgow, 1821. Attended theological course in United Secession Hall, and became missionary at Blenheim Twp, Oxford Co, ONT. **GMA 10727**.

10032 MURRAY, Georgina Anderson, b 25 Jun 1827. From Clyne, SUT. d/o Angus M, qv, and Elizabeth MacDonald, qv. To Pictou, NS, 1831; stld Mount Thom. m Roderick Mackenzie, no ch. **DC 31 Dec 1979**.

10033 MURRAY, Grizel. sis/o Richard M. To Montreal, QUE, <1838. m — Sutherland. **SH**.

10034 MURRAY, Hugh. To Pictou, NS, on the *Lady Gray*, ex Cromarty, ROC, arr 16 Jul 1841. **DC 15 Jul 1979**.

10035 MURRAY, Hugh, b 26 Jun 1843. From Paisley, RFW. s/o Daniel M. and Bethia Fleming. To Dewart, Kent Co, ONT. m Elizabeth Ann, d/o Alfred Crisp, ch: 1. Elizabeth; 2. Bethia; 3. Jessie; 4. Mary; 5. Hugh. **DC 29 Sep 1964**.

10036 MURRAY, Isabel, 1817–1901. From Clyne par, SUT. d/o Angus M, qv, and Elizabeth MacDonald, qv. To Pictou, NS, 1831; stld Mount Thom. m Malcolm Sillers, ch: 1. Angus; 2. Margaret; 3. Elizabeth; 4. Annie; 5. Jessie. **DC 31 Dec 1979**.

10037 MURRAY, Sir James, 1719–18 Jun 1794. From SEL. s/o Alexander, 4th Lord Elibank, and Elizabeth Stirling. Served with distinction as an officer in the 15th and 60th Regts, and prom to Maj Gen, 1762. Administrator of QUE, 1763-66, and in charge of all the troops in CAN. Later app Gov of Minorca, and d London, ENG. m (i) Cordelia Collier, d 1779; (ii) 1780, Ann, d/o Abraham Whitham. Son James Patrick, MP for Yarmouth. **BNA i 296; SAS 16; SP iii 515; MDB 541**.

10038 MURRAY, James. From SUT. To Pictou, NS, on the *Hector*, ex Loch Broom, arr 17 Sep 1773; stld Londonderry, Colchester Co. ch. **HPC App C**.

10039 MURRAY, James. Prob from Kildonan, SUT. To Hudson Bay and Red River <1815. Pioneer settler. Son James, b 1839, MPP, rep Assiniboia. **BNA 1098; LSS 192; LSC 327**.

10040 MURRAY, James, ca 1805–21 Jan 1844. From Castleton, DFS. s/o James M. and Elizabeth Main. To Galt, Waterloo Co, ONT, and d there. Mason. **Ts Castleton**.

10041 MURRAY, James. Prob from ARL. To Ekfrid Twp, Middlesex Co, ONT, 1831. ch: 1. John; 2. Margaret; 3. Mary. **PCM 30**.

10042 MURRAY, James A, ca 1811–6 Nov 1834. From Edinburgh. s/o Professor Alexander M, Orientalist. Drowned at Cape Gaskie, Gulf of St Lawrence. Surgeon on the HEIC ship *Elizabeth*. **DGH 24 Jun 1835**.

10043 MURRAY, Jane, 22 Dec 1809–2 Mar 1897. Prob from Hawick par, ROX. To Toronto, ONT, <1833, when m William Edward Campbell, qv. d at Brampton, Peel Co. **DC 7 Jul 1981**.

10044 MURRAY, Janet, 12 Oct 1811–1 May 1901. From Clyne par, SUT. d/o Angus M, qv, and Elizabeth MacDonald, qv. To Pictou, NS, 1831; stld Mount Thom. m James Dawson. Son Charles. **DC 31 Dec 1979**.

10045 MURRAY, Jean, b 1758. To Charlottetown, PEI, on the *Elizabeth & Ann*, ex Thurso, arr 8 Nov 1806. Wife of John McKay, qv. **PLEA**.

10046 MURRAY, Joan, 22 Feb 1809–2 Jan 1897. From Westerkirk par, DFS. To Vaughan Twp, York Co, ONT, 1841. Wife of William Ritchie, qv. **DC 21 Mar 1980**.

10047 MURRAY, John, b ca 1793. From Suisgill, Kildonan par, SUT. bro/o Alexander M, qv. To Fort

Churchill, Hudson Bay, on the *Prince of Wales*, ex Stromness, 28 Jun 1813. Went to York Factory, Apr 1814, thence to Red River. Left settlement and arr Holland River, ONT, 6 Sep 1815. **LSS 186; RRS 27; LSC 323.**

10048 MURRAY, John, 9 Sep 1822–25 Jan 1894. From Clyne par, SUT. s/o Angus M, qv, and Elizabeth MacDonald, qv. To Pictou, NS, 1831; stld Mount Thom. Farmer. m 18 Jul 1876, Jessie, d/o Alexander Murray and Jane Ross, ch: 1. Angus; 2. Allan; 3. Alexander H; 4. James W; 5. Jean; 6. Robert F; 7. Annie Belle; 8. John Martin. **DC 31 Dec 1979.**

10049 MURRAY, John. From DFS. To Miramichi, Northumberland Co, NB, poss <1830; stld later Westmorland Co. ch: 1. William; 2. James; 3. David; 4. John; 5. Mary; 6. Jane; 7. Eliza; 8. Isabella; 9. Agnes; 10. Maria; 11. Janet. **DC 17 Apr 1981.**

10050 MURRAY, John, 26 Jan 1799–24 May 1874. From Galloway. s/o Phillip M. and Agnes McKnight. To QUE on the *Portia*, arr Jul 1834; stld Flamborough Twp, Wentworth Co, ONT, later Tuckersmith Twp, Huron Co. Farmer. m Jane McRobert, qv, ch: 1. William, b 22 Nov 1829; 2. Agnes, b 10 Oct 1832. **DC 12 Mar 1890.**

10051 MURRAY, John, 1801–4 May 1884. From CAI. To NS, poss <1840; stld Central North River, Colchester Co. Wife Ellen, 1805–1905. Son John, 1837–1917. **DC 19 Mar 1971.**

10052 MURRAY, John. To Pictou, NS, on the *Lady Gray*, ex Cromarty, ROC, arr 16 Jul 1841. **DC 15 Jul 1979.**

10053 MURRAY, John, d 20 Apr 1848. From Urrall, Kirkcowan par, WIG. s/o William M, farmer. To Lincoln Co, ONT, and d Port Robinson. **DGH 1 Jun 1848.**

10054 MURRAY, John. From Is Lewis, ROC. To QUE, ex Stornoway, arr 4 Aug 1851; stld Huron Twp, Bruce Co, ONT, 1852. Head of family. **WLC.**

10055 MURRAY, Rev John Clark, 19 Mar 1836–20 Nov 1917. From Paisley, RFW. s/o David M. and Elizabeth Clark. Educ Univs of Heidelberg, Gottingen, Edinburgh and Glasgow. Professor of Moral Philosophy at Queens Univ, Kingston, ONT, 1862-92, later at McGill Univ, Montreal. LLD, Glasgow; author. m Margaret Polson, qv, ch. **GMA 15859; FES vii 647.**

10056 MURRAY, John William, 1784–1842. From Rogart par, SUT. s/o John M. and Annie Sutherland. To Pictou, NS, and stld Truro, Colchester Co. Farmer. m Christina Matheson, qv, ch: 1. Nancy, 1822-93; 2. Christina, 1827–1917; 3. William, 1829-86; 4. John, 1829-88; 5. Alexander, 1831–1916; 6. Robert, 1832–1910; 7. Katherine. **DC 15 May 1982.**

10057 MURRAY, Malcolm. From ARL. To Ekfrid Twp, Middlesex Co, ONT. ch: 1. Angus; 2. Dugald; 3. John. **PCM 30.**

10058 MURRAY, Margaret, 23 Jan 1820–20 Mar 1906. From Clyne par, SUT. d/o Angus M, qv, and Elizabeth MacDonald. To Pictou, NS, 1831; stld Mount Thom. m James Frazer, ch. **DC 31 Dec 1979.**

10059 MURRAY, Margaret, d 12 Jul 1854. From Edinburgh. To Oshawa, Durham Co, ONT, <1854. Wife of James Borrowman, qv. **DC 6 Sep 1979.**

10060 MURRAY, Mrs Mary, b 1758. To Charlottetown, PEI, on the *Rambler*, ex Tobermory, 20 Jun 1806. ch with her: 1. Archibald, aged 21; 2. Margaret, aged 13; 3. Janet, aged 5. **PLR.**

10061 MURRAY, Mary, ca 1791–5 Dec 1869. To Kent Co, NB, <1830. m William Hannay, qv. **DC 5 Aug 1980.**

10062 MURRAY, Mary, 25 Dec 1804–23 Aug 1853. From Muirkirk, AYR. d/o Thomas M. and Janet Ferguson. To Stratford, Perth Co, ONT, 1841. m 9 Mar 1827, David Ballantyne, qv. **NFD 12.**

10063 MURRAY, Peter. From SUT. To Earltown, Colchester Co, NS, <1820. Farmer. **HT 43.**

10064 MURRAY, Peter, d 1850. From Kirkinner par, WIG. bro/o Rev Robert M, qv. To Ashfield, Huron Co, ONT, and d there. **DGH 1 Aug 1850.**

10065 MURRAY, Robert, 1783–4 Dec 1862. From SUT. To NS poss <1820; stld Colchester Co. Farmer and tailor. Wife Mary, 1800-52. ch: 1. William, dy; 2. Elizabeth; 3. John, 1833-74. **HT 43; DC 19 Mar 1980.**

10066 MURRAY, Robert. To ONT, 1834; stld Cobourg, Northumberland Co. Accountant. m Elizabeth McFarlane, qv. Son Sir John, 1841–1914, marine naturalist, res Edinburgh. **DC 30 Aug 1977.**

10067 MURRAY, Rev Robert, d 13 Mar 1853. From Kirkinner par, WIG. bro/o Peter M, qv. To Halton Co, ONT, <1842. Superintendent of Schools, and became Professor of Mathematics and Moral Philosophy at Kings Coll, Toronto. d at Port Albert, Ashfield Twp, Huron Co. **MDB 542.**

10068 MURRAY, Thomas, b 3 Oct 1830. From BEW. s/o — M. and wife Grace. To Northumberland Co, ONT, 1854. m at Coldstream, 23 Nov 1854, Janet Watt, qv. **DC 20 Nov 1960.**

10069 MURRAY, Walter. From SUT. To Pictou, NS, on the *Hector*, ex Loch Broom, arr 17 Sep 1773; stld East River, Pictou Co, later Merigomish. Discharged soldier. Wife Christy with him and dau Elizabeth. **HPC App C.**

10070 MURRAY, Walter 'Morton'. To Pictou Co, NS, <26 Aug 1784, when gr 280 acres on east side of Middle River. **HPC App A.**

10071 MURRAY, William. From Buckhaven, FIF. s/o William M. To QUE <1805. ch: 1. Amelia; 2. Elizabeth. **SH.**

10072 MURRAY, William, 1769–24 May 1873. From SUT. To Pictou Co, NS, ca 1823, and d west branch, River John. m Mrs Jane Morrison, 7 Sep 1824. **VSN No 701; CAE 30.**

10073 MURRAY, William, ca 1750–14 Apr 1833. From KKD. To Montreal, QUE. Ret to estate of Glencaird, KKD, and d at Bath. **DGC 23 Apr 1833.**

10074 MURRAY, William, b ca 1791. To Pictou Co, NS, 1815; res Merigomish, 1816. Farmer. **INS 37.**

10075 MURRAY, William, ca 1790–24 Nov 1835. From Rogart par, SUT. To NS <1830; stld nr Earltown, Colchester Co. m Christy Sutherland, qv, ch. **DC 19 Mar 1980.**

10076 MURRAY, William, 31 Nov 1798–12 May 1814. From Edinburgh. To Montreal, QUE, 1832. Bookkeeper with firm of Gillespie, Moffatt & Co, and res Westmount. **SGC 477**.

10077 MURRAY, William, d ca 1842. From Kirkcowan, WIG. s/o William M, farmer in Urrall. To Queenston, Lincoln Co, ONT. **DGH 28 Dec 1843**.

10078 MURRAY, Rev William, d 14 Feb 1904. To Moncton, Westmorland Co, NB, 1855, as missionary. Min of Dalhousie, Restigouche Co, 1859-65, when he became asst at Fredericton. Adm min of St Andrews Ch, Campbelltown, Restigouche Co, 1869. Retr to SCT >1875. **FES vii 611**.

10079 MURRAY, William Allan, 5 Aug 1814–7 Sep 1891. From Ravelston, Edinburgh. To ONT, 1854. Merchant. m 8 Dec 1844, Jane Ann, d/o William Macnamara, ch: 1. Mary Jane; 2. Charles Stuart; 3. William Thomas; 4. James Peter; 5. John Alexander; 6. Elizabeth Honora; 7. Margaret Helena. **DC 29 Sep 1964**.

10080 MUSTARD, George, b 1771. From Peddieston, Cromarty par, ROC. s/o Alexander M. To ONT, poss 1830. Farmer. **DC 27 Dec 1979**.

10081 MUSTARD, Hugh, 1778–1854. From Peddieston, Cromarty par, ROC. s/o Alexander M. To Scott Twp, Durham Co, ONT, poss 1830. Farmer. m Isabella Hood, qv, and had with other ch: 1. James; 2. Hugh. **DC 27 Dec 1979**.

10082 MUSTARD, James, b 1768. From Peddieston, Cromarty par, ROC. To York Co, ONT, via USA, 1795. Farmer. m Elizabeth, d/o Peter Gordon, Ancaster Twp, Wentworth Co. Dau Nancy. **DC 27 Dec 1979**.

10083 MUSTARD, James. From Cromarty par, ROC. To Kings Co, PEI, <1840. m Jessie, 1819-98, d/o Donald Gordon, qv, and second wife, Jessie McLaren, and had with other ch: 1. John; 2. James; 3. Isabel; 4. Jessie; 5. Alexander; 6. Barbara. **BP 40**.

10084 MUTCH, Alexander, 1754–1828. From ABD. To PEI, 1783. Army officer during Revolutionary War, later farmer. m (i) Elizabeth Crowell, Widow Brown, ch: 1. Margaret; 2. James, 1793–1865; 3. Robert, 1796–1869; 4. Rev Alexander, 1799–1875; 5. Jane, 1800-49; 6. Maria, 1802-43. m (ii) 1805, Catherine Nicholson, further ch: 7. John, 1806-79; 8. Capt Samuel, 1807-82; 9. William, d inf; 10. William, 1811-84; 11. Mary, 1812-91; 12. George, 1816-43; 13. Joseph, 1817-47; 14. Rebecca, 1819-93; 15. David, 1821-90. **GMF 14**.

10085 MUTCH, Alexander. From Ellon, ABD. s/o James and Ann M. To ONT, 1853. **SNQ iii/3 69**.

N

10086 NAIRN, Archibald. From RFW. bro/o John N, qv. To Lanark Co, ONT, ca 1820; stld Ramsay Twp. m Beatrice Anderson, qv, ch: 1. James, qv; 2. William, b 1806; 3. Elizabeth, qv; 4. John, qv; 5. Archibald, jr, qv; 6. Mary, qv. **DC 21 Mar 1980**.

10087 NAIRN, Archibald, jr, 1816–18 Mar 1888. From LKS. s/o Archibald N, qv, and Beatrice Anderson, qv. To Lanark Co, ONT, 1820. m Grace Galbraith, 1815-90. **DC 21 Mar 1980**.

10088 NAIRN, Christian, d <1821. sis/o Capt Thomas N, 49th Regt. To Murray Bay, QUE, <1815. **SH**.

10089 NAIRN, Elizabeth, b 2 Aug 1808. From LKS. d/o Archibald N, qv. To Lanark Co, ONT, ca 1820. m William Penman, qv. **DC 21 Mar 1980**.

10090 NAIRN, James, 1805–8 Jul 1878. From LKS. s/o Archibald N, qv, and Beatrice Anderson, qv. To Lanark Co, ONT, 1820. m Margaret Nairn. **DC 21 Mar 1980**.

10091 NAIRN, John, 1 Mar 1731–14 Jul 1802. Served in the Scots Brigade in Holland, and obtained a commission in the 78th Regt. Fought at Louisbourg and Quebec, and in 1761 purchased the seignory of Murray Bay, QUE. m 1766, Christianna Emery. **MDB 544**.

10092 NAIRN, John, d 1830. From RFW. bro/o Archibald N, qv. To Lanark Co, ONT, ca 1820; stld Lot 1W, Con 11, Ramsay Twp. Farmer. m Janet, called Jessie, d/o James Dewart and Janet Penman, qv, and had, poss with other ch: 1. Mary; 2. Margaret. **DC 21 Mar 1980**.

10093 NAIRN, Magdalene. sis/o Capt Thomas N, 49th Regt. To Murray Bay, QUE, <1815. m Peter McNicol. **SH**.

10094 NAIRN, Mary. sis/o Capt Thomas N, 49th Regt. To Murray Bay, QUE, <1820. m Austin Blackburn. **SH**.

10095 NAIRN, Mary, b 1815. From LKS. d/o Archibald N, qv, and Beatrice Anderson, qv. To Lanark Co, ONT, ca 1820. m James Penman, qv. **DC 21 Mar 1980**.

10096 NAIRN, Thomas McIntyre, b 1836. From Balloch, DNB. To St John, NB, 1850, and worked as a publishers asst. Went later to Boston, MA, afterwards to Aylmer, Elgin Co, ONT. Merchant, grain-dealer and notary. **BNA 797**.

10097 NAVIN, Margaret, 1805-90. From LKS. To Cumberland Co, NS, prob <1840; stld nr Wallace. m John Stevenson, qv. **DC 29 Oct 1980**.

10098 NEIL, Helen, d 1852. From Irvine, AYR. d/o William N. To Kingston, ONT, <1850. m Alexander MacKenzie, qv. **MDB 465**.

10099 NEILL, Rev Robert, 1804–23 Jan 1890. From Dunipace, STI. s/o Andrew N. Matric Univ of Glasgow, 1818. To QUE, 1837. Asst min, St Andrews, Montreal, Valcartier, and Kingston. Ord min of Seymour, 1840. DD, Queens Univ, 1872. **GMA 10104; FES vii 647**.

10100 NEILSON, Alexander, ca 1760–1850. From LKS. poss Strathavon or Lesmahagow. To Scarborough, York Co, ONT, ca 1833. **DC 29 Mar 1981**.

10101 NEILSON, Andrew. Prob rel to James N, qv. To Pictou, NS, on the *Lulan*, ex Glasgow, 17 Aug 1848. **DC 12 Jul 1979**.

10102 NEILSON, Elizabeth. Poss from PER. To Toronto, prob <1830. Wife of John McDonald, qv. **MDB 439**.

10103 NEILSON, James. Prob rel to Andrew N, qv. To Pictou, NS, on the *Lulan*, ex Glasgow, 17 Aug 1848. **DC 12 Jul 1979**.

10104 NEILSON, John, 17 Jul 1776–1 Feb 1848. From Balmaghie, WIG. s/o William N. and Isobel Brown. To QUE <1793, to join his uncle William Brown, qv, owner of the Quebec *Gazette*. Became co-proprietor. MLA, 1818-34, and MLC, 1844. **BNA 489; MDB 546**.

10105   NEILSON, John. From Paisley, RFW. To Lanark Co, ONT, 1820; stld Lot 6, Con 12, Ramsay Twp. Wife Agnes and ch with him. **HCL 80**.

10106   NEILSON, John, b 29 Oct 1773. From Bogside, Carluke, LKS. s/o William N, farmer in Law, and Elizabeth Chalmer. To Otonabee Twp, Peterborough Co, ONT, ca 1819. Farmer, Cons 4 and 5. m Jul 1799, Janet Weir, qv, ch: 1. William, 1797–1870; 2. Andrew, 1799–1840; 3. William, yr, 1801-78; 4. John, 1803-36; 5. Archibald, 1805-84; 6. David, 1807-82; 7. Robert, 1809-83; 8. Hugh, 1811-64. **DC 8 Aug 1979**.

10107   NEILSON, Johnathan, 1800–23 Sep 1825. From Annan, DFS. s/o Walter N, shipbuilder, and Isobella Stothart. To Richibucto, Northumberland Co, NB. Ships carpenter. **Ts Annan**.

10108   NEILSON, Samuel, ca 1771–12 Jul 1793. From Balmaghie, WIG. s/o William N. and Isabel Brown. To QUE, ca 1784, to learn the printing trade with his uncle William Brown. Became proprietor of the Quebec *Gazette*. **BNA 489; MDB 546**.

10109   NEILSON, William, ca 1797–ca 1842. From Lochmaben, DFS. To Rainham, Haldimand Co, ONT. Farmer. **DGH 7 Apr 1842**.

10110   NEISH, Janet, b ca 1723. From New Abbey, KKD. To Georgetown, Kings Co, PEI, on the *Lovely Nellie*, ex Carsethorn Bay, May 1775. Wife of James Douglas, qv. **ELN**.

NELSON. See also NEILSON.

10111   NELSON, John, ca 1810–27 Nov 1846. From Annan, DFS. s/o Johnathan N. and Annie Wise. To Whitechurch, Huron Co, ONT. Land surveyor. **Ts Annan**.

NESBIT. See also NISBET.

10112   NESBIT, James. To North Sherbrooke Twp, Lanark Co, ONT, 1821; stld Lot 10, Con 1. **HCL 74**.

10113   NESBITT, John W. Poss from LKS. To Holbrook, Norwich Co, ONT, 1837. m Mary Wallace, from IRL. Son Hon Wallace, 1858–1930, b nr Woodstock, Justice of the Supreme Court of Canada. **DC 30 Aug 1977**.

10114   NESS, Angus. To Queens Co, PEI, <1811, when a petitioner for Dr Aneas MacAulay. **HP 74**.

10115   NESS, Margaret. To Inverness Co, NS, <1823. m (i) Alexander Boyd; (ii) John Boyd. **MP ii 246**.

10116   NEWALL, Homer. From Dalbeattie, DFS. s/o — N. and wife Hannah. To CAN, ca 1840. Discharged soldier, 93rd Regt. **SG xxiii/3 49**.

10117   NEWALL, John, d 10 Oct 1829. From Airdrie, Kirkbean, KKD. s/o Robert N. To Cornwall, ONT. **DGC 8 Dec 1829**.

10118   NEWALL, Robert, b ca 1785. From Hawick, ROX. To QUE, Jul 1815, ex Greenock; stld prob Lanark Co, ONT. Farmer. Wife Sarah Blair, qv, with him, and 2 ch. **SEC 1**.

10119   NEWALL, Robert, d 18 Nov 1835. From Airdrie, Kirkbean, KKD. s/o Robert N. To Cornwall, Stormont Co, ONT, and d at Williamstown, Glengarry Co. **DGC 20 Jan 1836**.

10120   NEWBIGGING, Barbara, 1786–1867. From LKS. To Lanark Co, ONT, 1820. Wife of James Brooke, qv. **DC 27 Jan 1977**.

10121   NEWTON, Agnes, b 1789. From Pollokshaws, RFW. To QUE on the *Earl of Buckinghamshire*, 1821. Wife of James Nisbet, qv. **Nisbet Chart, SGS**.

10122   NICHOL, Donald. From West Bennan, Kilmory par, Is Arran, BUT. To Inverness, Megantic Co, QUE, 1831. Wife Janet Currie, d at sea, and he afterwards m Ann McKillop, qv. Son John, b 1829. **AMC 39; MAC 37**.

10123   NICHOL, Janet. From ROX. To Chatham Twp, Argenteuil Co, QUE, 1818. Wife of George Brown, Northumberland, ENG, miller and militiaman, who founded Brownsburg. Dau Jane Frances, b at sea, 1818. **DC 30 Jun 1971**.

10124   NICHOL, John, b 1818. From Knockonkelly, Kilbride par, Is Arran, BUT. To Blackland, Restigouche Co, NB, <1841, later to Marinette, WI. m Elizabeth, d/o Angus McLean, qv, and Mary Sinclair, qv, ch: 1. Donald, b ca 1849; 2. Mary, b ca 1850; 3. James, b ca 1852; 4. John, b ca 1856; 5. Ellen, b ca 1859; 6. Elizabeth, b ca 1861; 7. Angus, b ca 1867. **RCP 8**.

10125   NICHOL, Margaret, b ca 1792. From Hawick, ROX. To Galt, Waterloo Co, ONT, 1829. Wife of James Cowan, qv. **DC 9 May 1979**.

10126   NICHOL, Robert, ca 1774–6 May 1824. To Norfolk Co, ONT, <1795, as agent for Col Thomas Talbot. Nichol Twp, Wellington Co, named in his honour. Moved to Lundys Lane, Lincoln Co. Served in militia during War of 1812. Attorney-at-Law, and became Judge of Surrogate Court of Niagara dist. Accidentally killed. m Maria Julian, d/o Dr Wright and Theresa Grant, ch. **MDB 549; EHE 51, 173**.

10127   NICHOLSON, Allan. From Kilmuir par, Is Skye, INV. To PEI, prob <1850. m Margaret MacLeod, qv. **SG xxvii/3 125**.

10128   NICHOLSON, Angus, ca 1790–13 Jan 1874. From Is Barra, INV. To Mabou, Inverness Co, NS, prob <1820. m Mary, d/o Neil MacDonald, qv, and Emily MacMillan, ch: 1. Hector; 2. Neil; 3. John; 4. Neil, jr; 5. Christina; 6. Emily; 7. George; 8. Michael; 9. Roderick; 10. Janet. **MP 418, 804**.

10129   NICHOLSON, Catherine. From Lochaber, INV. To Glencoe, Inverness Co, NS, prob <1820. Wife of Angus Campbell, qv. **MP 285**.

10130   NICHOLSON, Christy, ca 1836–1917. Prob from ARL. To ONT <1855; stld poss Victoria Co. m John Smith, qv. **DC 21 Feb 1980**.

10131   NICHOLSON, Donald, ca 1780–26 Sep 1820. From Stenscholl, Kilmuir par, Is Skye, INV. s/o John N, qv, and Jane Martin, qv. To Orwell Bay, PEI, on the *Polly*, ex Portree, arr 7 Aug 1803; stld Orwell River. Emigrant agent, 1803 and 1806, miller and magistrate. m Isabella Nicholson, qv, ch: 1. Hannah; 2. Flora, 1808-95; 3. Peter, 1809-84; 4. Mary, dy; 5. Margaret; 6. Isabella; 7. Jane, 1814-99; 8. John, dy; 9. Christina, 1815-93. **SPI 1815-93; HP 16, 74**.

10132   NICHOLSON, Donald. To Pictou, NS, on the *London*, arr 11 Apr 1848. **DC 15 Jul 1979**.

10133   NICHOLSON, Duncan, b 1808. From Lochalsh,

ROC. To Richmond Co, NS, 1828; stld St Georges Channel. m Catherine Stewart, qv, and went later to Catalone, Cape Breton Co. ch: 1. John, b 1834; 2. Christian, b 1835; 3. Catherine, b 1837; 4. Lachlan, b 1839; 5. Elizabeth, b 1841; 6. Donald, b 1842; 7. Donald, b 1844; 8. Alexander, b 1845; 9. Mary, b 1851; 10. Duncan, b 1844. **NSN 27/196**.

10134   NICHOLSON, Isabella, ca 1789–3 May 1854. From Kilmuir par, Is Skye, INV. To PEI, poss 1805; stld Orwell River. m Donald Nicholson, qv. **SPI 153; HP 16**.

10135   NICHOLSON, John. From Stenscholl, Kilmuir par, Is Skye, INV. s/o Malcolm N, tacksman. To Orwell Bay, PEI, on the *Polly*, ex Portree, arr 7 Aug 1803; stld Newton River, and gr 500 acres. m Jane Martin, qv, ch: 1. Hannah; 2. Rachel; 3. Donald, qv; 4. John, jr, qv. **SPI 153; HP 16**.

10136   NICHOLSON, John, jr, ca 1792–10 Nov 1866. From Stenscholl, Is Skye, INV. s/o John N, qv, and Jane Martin, qv. To Orwell Bay, PEI, on the *Polly*, ex Portree, arr 7 Aug 1803; stld Orwell Cove. m Mary MacLeod, qv. Son Donald. **SPI 155; HP 16, 74**.

10137   NICHOLSON, John, 1815–1905. Prob from Is Skye, INV. bro/o Angus N. To Pictou Co, NS, 1841; stld Gairloch Mountain. m Catherine MacRitchie, b Little Narrows, Cape Breton, 1828. **DC 21 Mar 1981**.

10138   NICHOLSON, Malcolm. From Uig, Is Skye, INV. To Richmond Co, QUE, <1840. m Marion Stalker, qv. **DC 7 Mar 1980**.

10139   NICHOLSON, Margaret, 1824-83. From Is Harris, INV. To Baddeck, Victoria Co, NS, 1828. Wife of Allan MacLean. **DC 10 Mar 1980**.

10140   NICHOLSON, Mary. From Dornoch, SUT. d/o Thomas N, weaver. To CAN <1855. m William Jardine. **SH**.

10141   NICHOLSON, Neil. From Is Skye, INV. To Orwell Bay, PEI, on the *Polly*, ex Portree, arr 7 May 1803. m Mary Stewart, qv, ch. **LDW 11 Oct 1974**.

10142   NICHOLSON, Rachel, 1818–1901. From Harris, INV. To Pictou, NS, 1841; stld Gairloch Mountain. Wife of Roderick MacDonald, qv. **DC 21 Mar 1981**.

10143   NICHOLSON, Samuel, 9 Jun 1814–9 Jun 1891. From Tailanotighean, Uig, Kilmuir par, Is Skye. s/o Armiger N. and Margaret Mackenzie. To Mount Hope, PEI, 1840. Farmer. m Mary MacDougal. Son Armiger, 1841–1926, d Murrayville, BC. **DC 22 Mar 1982**.

10144   NICHOLSON, Soirle. From Is Skye, INV. To Orwell Bay, PEI, on the *Polly*, ex Portree, arr 7 May 1803. Petitioner for Dr McAulay, 1811. Son James. **HP 74; LDW 4 Nov 1974**.

10145   NICHOLSON, Rev Thomas, 1823–1908. From FIF. To NB, and ord at Fredericton, 1858. Missionary. Chaleur Bay area, and called to Charlo and Jacquet River, 1862. Inspector of Schools, Restigouche Co, <1879, and owned property at River Charlo. m Janet Kerr, from Napan, Miramichi. **CUC 20**.

10146   NICKLESON, Donald, b ca 1782. To North End, Gut of Canso, Inverness Co, NS, 1815. Fisherman, unm. **CBC 1818**.

10147   NICOL, Francis, 1782–1868. From

Newcastleton, ROX. To ONT, 1833. m Janet, ch: 1. John, b ca 1823; 2. Thomas, b ca 1826; 3. Francis, b ca 1828; 4. Mary, b ca 1830; 5. Adam, b ONT; 6. William, b ONT. **DC 6 Sep 1967**.

10148   NICOL, Rev Francis, 1823–30 Oct 1873. From AYR. s/o Adam N, merchant. Matric Univ of Glasgow, 1838, and attended course at Relief Ch Theological Hall. App by Colonial Committee as third min for Halifax, NS, 1837. Trans to St Johns, NFD, 1851, and to London, Middlesex Co, ONT, 1859. **GMA 13913; FES vii 647**.

10149   NICOL, Helen, 15 Jul 1796–17 Nov 1875. From Selkirk, SEL. d/o William N. and Katherine Bruce. To North Dumfries Twp, Waterloo Co, ONT, poss 1857. Wife of or wid/o James Brown, carter. Dau Margaret, qv. **DC 7 Dec 1981**.

10150   NICOL, James Stewart. To Perth, Drummond Twp, Lanark Co, ONT, 1827. Physician, educ Edinburgh. **HCL 142**.

10151   NICOL, Janet. Prob from Stobo, PEE. To QUE, ex Greenock, summer 1815; stld prob Lanark Co, ONT. Wife of William Johnston, qv. **SEC 6**.

10152   NICOL, Jessie, ca 1815–3 Aug 1849. From Thornoelaw, Lilliesleaf, ROX. d/o Robert N, farmer, and Mary Smith. To Tunisbank, ONT, and d there. **Ts Lilliesleaf**.

10153   NICOL, William, b ca 1776. To Pictou Co, NS, 1816; res Rogers Hill, 1816. Labourer, 'poor', and m with 4 ch. **INS 39**.

10154   NICOLL, Duncan, ca 1752–5 Apr 1821. To Shelburne Co, NS, and was latterly in Grafton Street, Halifax. **NSS No 2259**.

10155   NICOLL, James, b ca 1797. From Is Arran, BUT. To Restigouche Co, NB, ca 1817; petitioned for 150 acres–on Lot 70–on the south side of the Restigouche River, 9 Feb 1821. ch: 1. Dorothy Ann, 1826–1912; 2. Eliza. **DC 31 May 1980**.

10156   NICOLSON, Ann. From Portree, Is Skye, INV. d/o Malcolm N. and Flora McQueen. To PEI, Jul 1841. m James Kennedy, qv. **DC 13 Nov 1968**.

10157   NICOLSON, Catherine, b ca 1827. From Dunganichy, Is Benbecula, INV. d/o Donald and Ann N. To Pictou, NS, on the *Lulan*, ex Glasgow, 17 Aug 1848. Wife of Archibald MacAulay, qv. **DC 12 Jul 1979**.

10158   NICOLSON, Donald. From Is Skye, INV. To Orwell Bay, PEI, 1803; stld Queens Co. Schoolmaster, gr 100 acres of land. Petitioner for Dr MacAulay, 1811. **HP 27, 74**.

10159   NICOLSON, Flora. From Is Skye, INV. sis/o James N, MLA, qv. To Queens Co, PEI, <1846; stld Eldon. m — McSwain. Son Dr Angus, 1846-93. **HP 34**.

10160   NICOLSON, James. From Is Skye, INV. bro/o Flora N, qv. To Queens Co, PEI, <1846; stld Eldon. MLA. m Mary Jane Munro, from NFD. Son John Alexander, 1860–1940, Registrar of McGill Univ, 1902-30. **HP 34**.

10161   NICOLSON, Murdoch, 1785–1850. Prob from Uig, Is Lewis, ROC. To NS <1820; stld Wallace, Cumberland Co. **DC 29 Oct 1980**.

10162 NICOLSON, Norman, b ca 1820. Prob from Snizort par, Is Skye, INV. To Kinloss Twp, Bruce Co, ONT, 1852. m (i) Ann Cameron, qv, ch: 1. Margaret, b ONT, 1852; 2. Malcolm, b 1854; 3. John, b 1855; 4. Alexander, b 1856; 5. Mary A, b 1858. m (ii) ca 1862, Catherine McDougall, qv. **DC 12 Apr 1979**.

10163 NICOLSON, Roderick. From Is Lewis, ROC. To Gulf Shore, Cumberland Co, NS, <1830. Wife Margaret, 1801-32, also from Lewis. **DC 29 Oct 1980**.

10164 NIMMO, Mary. From LKS. To QUE <1830. Wife of Andrew Russell, qv. **SG xxvii/2 80**.

NISBET. See also NESBIT.

10165 NISBET, Ann, 1797–1866. From Rutherglen, LKS. d/o David N. and second wife Helen Main. To Plympton Twp, Lambton Co, ONT, and res with bro James N, qv. **Nisbet Chart, SGS**.

10166 NISBET, David, 1814-95. From Pollokshaws, RFW. s/o James N, qv, and Agnes Newton, qv. To QUE on the *Earl of Buckinghamshire*, 1821; stld Plympton Twp, Lambton Co, ONT. m Agnes Donald, 1822–1905, ch: 1. James, 1849–1920; 2. Marian, 1851–1927; 3. John, 1853–1900; 4. William, 1855–1928; 5. Thomas, 1857–1927; 6. Agnes, 1860–1940; 7. Jeanette, 1862–1915; 8. Jean, 1864–1931. **Nisbet Chart, SGS**.

10167 NISBET, James. To St John, NB, 1798. m Mary Roulston, ch. **DC 21 Mar 1981**.

10168 NISBET, James, 1789–1846. From Rutherglen, LKS. s/o David N. and second wife, Helen Main. To QUE on the *Earl of Buckinghamshire*, ex Greenock, 29 Apr 1821. Merchant. m 19 Jun 1813, Agnes Newton, qv, ch: 1. David, qv; 2. James, b 1816; 3. William, b 1818; 4. Jennie, b 1820. **Nisbet Chart, SGS**.

10169 NISBET, Rev James, 8 Sep 1823–30 Sep 1874. From Hutchisontown, Glasgow. s/o Thomas N, qv, and Jean Crawford, qv. Matric Univ of Glasgow, 1842. To Oakville, Halton Co, ONT, 1844. Studied at Knox Coll, Toronto, and ord 1850. Missionary among the Indians, and founded Prince Albert, SAS. m Mary, d/o Robert McBeth, Kildonan, ch: 1. Mary, 1866–1942; 2. Isabella, 1868–1907; 3. Thomas, 1870–1928; 4. Robert, 1872–1931. **BNA 1052; GMA 14507; MDB 551; Nisbet Chart, SGS**.

10170 NISBET, Janet, 1807-84. From Glasgow. d/o Thomas N, qv, and Jean Crawford, qv. To Oakville, Halton Co, ONT, 1844. m Robert Patterson. **Nisbet Chart, SGS**.

10171 NISBET, Thomas, 1783–1871. From Rutherglen, LKS. s/o David N. and Jean Parkhill. To Oakville, Halton Co, ONT, 1844. Smith, later shipbuilder. m Jean Crawford, qv, ch: 1. Jean, 1805-87; 2. Janet, qv; 3. Mary, 1810-41; 4. David, 1812-27; 5. Sarah, 1814-97, res Sarnia; 6. Thomas, jr, qv; 7. Henry, b 1818; 8. Isabella, 1820-89; 9. Ebenezer, 1822-40; 10. Rev James, qv. **Nisbet Chart, SGS**.

10172 NISBET, Thomas, jr, 1816-73. From Glasgow. s/o Thomas N, qv, and Jean Crawford, qv. To Oakville, Halton Co, ONT, 1844. m Hannah Eastwood. **Nisbet Chart, SGS**.

10173 NIVEN, Archibald. To Pictou, NS, on the *Hope*, ex Glasgow, 5 Apr 1848. **DC 12 Jul 1979**.

10174 NIVEN, Elizabeth, b 1835. From Lochgilphead, ARL. To Mariposa Twp, Victoria Co, ONT, ca 1857. Wife of John Jackson, qv. **EC 256**.

10175 NIVEN, Hugh. Poss from ARL. To Hamilton, ONT, 1845. Teacher. m Jessie Kennedy, ch. **DC 21 Mar 1981**.

10176 NIVEN, Rev Hugh. Educ Univ of Edinburgh, and became min of Gartmore quoad sacra par, PER, 1850. To ONT, and was adm min of Saltfleet and Binbrook, Wentworth Co, 1857. Demitted charge, 1867. **FES iv 346, vii 648**.

10177 NIVISON, Grizel, 17 Jun 1799–9 Apr 1868. From Durrisdeer par, DFS. To ONT, 1842; stld McKillop Twp, Huron Co. Wife of Robert McMichael, qv. **DC 26 May 1979**.

10178 NOBLE, Colin, b 20 Jul 1828. From INV. s/o Alexander N. To Compton Co, QUE, 1838; stld Winslow Twp. Storekeeper, later farmer and merchant. m 1854, Maria Gaymer Hunt, from ENG, ch: 1. Lucy Matilda, b 1855; 2. Jane Elizabeth, b 1856; 3. Frederick Alexander, b 1864; 6. Edward Colin, b 1867; 8. Clara Malvina, b 1868; 8. Alberta, b 1874. **WLC; MGC 2 Aug 1979**.

10179 NOBLE, Flora, b 1824. From INV. d/o John N, qv, and Julia MacNiven, qv. To Inverness Co, NS, prob <1830. m Archibald MacIntyre. **DC 23 Feb 1980**.

10180 NOBLE, James, b ca 1810. Prob from ROC, and poss rel to Margaret N, qv. To Scott Twp, York Co, ONT, <1851. **RFS 116**.

10181 NOBLE, John, 1783–1854. From INV. To Whycocomagh, Inverness Co, NS, prob <1830; moved later to Little Judique, and aferwards to Malta, ONT. m Julia MacNiven, qv, ch: 1. Flora, b 1824, qv; 2. Colin, b 1826; 3. Janet, b 1828; 4. Mary, b 1830; 5. Colina, b 1833; 6. John, b 1835; 7. James, b 1838; 8. Catherine, d 1841; 9. James T, b 1843. **DC 23 Feb 1980**.

10182 NOBLE, Margaret, 1784–1866. From Killearnan par, ROC. s/o Alexander N. and Margaret McRae. To Minto Twp, Wellington Co, ONT, 1860. Wife of Alexander Ross, qv. **RFS 54, 146**.

10183 NORQUOY, Oman, 1773–1820. From South Ronaldsay, OKI. To Hudson Bay on the *Seahorse*, Jul 1791. Served with HBCo at Red River, MAN. m Jean Marwick, qv, ch. **DC 20 Mar 1983**.

10184 NORVAL, Janet. From FIF. To QUE, <1850; stld Clarendon Twp, Pontiac Co. Wife of Alexander Kilgour, qv. **DC 21 Mar 1981**.

10185 NORVAL, John. Prob from Glasgow. To CAN <1841. **SH**.

10186 NOURSE, William, ca 1795–1855. From Edinburgh. s/o John N, confectioner, and Elizabeth Burn. To CAN, 1817, and joined HBCo. Served in southern dept, Ruperts Land. In charge of outpost at Crows Nest Lake, 1820-21, later clerk at La Cloche, in Lake Huron dist. App a chief trader, 1838. m Ann, d/o Jacob Corrigal, qv, ch: 1. Joseph; 2. John; 3. Jacob; 4. Charles; 5. William; 6. Eliza; 7. Mary; 8. Catherine. **LDW 19 Jan 1979**.

O

10187 ODOCHARDY, Angus. From Is Skye, INV, but of Irish ancestry. bro/o Donald O, qv, and Finlay O, qv. To Queens Co, PEI, ca 1803. m Catherine MacLeod, qv. Son Malcolm, res Cardigan, Kings Co. **HP 74**.

10188 ODOCHARDY, Donald. From Is Skye, INV. bro/o Finlay O, qv, and Angus O, qv. To Queens Co, PEI, ca 1803. **HP 74**.

10189 ODOCHARDY, Finlay. From Is Skye, INV. bro/o Angus O, qv, and Donald O, qv. To Queens Co, PEI, ca 1803. **HP 74**.

10190 O'DOCHERTY, Margaret, 1799–11 Dec 1863. From Staffin, Is Skye, INV. To Orwell Bay, PEI, on the *Polly*, ex Portree, arr 7 Aug 1803. Wife of Angus 'Mor' MacLeod, qv. **SPI 136**.

10191 OGILVIE, Archibald, d 1839. From STI. To QUE, 1800; stld Chateauguay, later Côte St Michael, Montreal. Farmer, and served in the Lachine Cavalry. m Agnes Watson. Son Alexander, flour miller. **BNA 803; OSG 803**.

10192 OGILVIE, David, ca 1796–9 Jan 1828. To St John, NB, and d there. May have been previously in NS. **VSN No 2671**.

10193 OGILVIE, Elizabeth, ca 1790–1876. From Old Meldrum, ABD. To Blissfield, Northumberland Co, NB, <1825. m Dr John McAllister, qv. **LDW 6 May 1967**.

10194 OGILVY, Charles, ca 1813–27 Jan 1838. From Montrose, ANS. s/o David O. of Parkconnon, and Ann Mitchell. To ONT and d there. **Ts Montrose**.

10195 OGILVY, John, ca 1769–28 Sep 1819. Poss from ANS. To Montreal, QUE, 1790. Fur-trader, associated with firms of Parker, Gerrard & Ogilvy, and Forsyth, Richardson & Co, which merged to form the old XYCo. Signed an agreement in 1804 to merge with the NWCo, and acquired an indirect interest. In 1817 he was app a commissioner to determine the boundaries of British North America under the Treaty of Ghent. **MDB 561**.

10196 OGILVY, Mary, 1817–16 May 1904. From Castleton, ROX. To Westminster Twp, Middlesex Co, ONT, ca 1833, and d McKillop Twp, Huron Co. m John Bell Grieve, ch. **SG xxix/4 135**.

10197 O'HENLEY, Angus, d 1793. From Upper Bornish, South Uist, INV. To West Williams Twp, Middlesex Co, ONT, ca 1850. Farmer. Wife Kirsty McDonald, see ADDENDA, with him, and ch: 1. Donald, b 1815; 2. Marion, b 1818; 3. Catherine, b 1820; 4. Donald, b 1826; 5. Mary. **WLC**.

10198 O'HENLEY, John. From Upper Bornish, South Uist, INV. To East Williams Twp, Middlesex Co, ONT, ca 1850. m Catherine Morrison, see ADDENDA, ch: 1. Angus, b 1834; 2. Mary, b 1835; 3. Mary, b 1838; 4. Donald, b 1840; 5. Michael, b 1843; 6. Angus Og, b 1844; 7. Michael, b 1847; 8. John, b 1849; 9. Janet. **PCM 44; WLC**.

10199 OLD, John B, ca 1811–28 May 1893. Poss from Dundee, ANS. s/o John O. To Middlesex Co, ONT, <1835; stld London. Went later to Sault Ste Marie, and d there. **SG xxvii/2 81**.

10200 OLD, William, b ca 1782. From Canongate,

Edinburgh. To QUE on the *Atlas*, ex Greenock, 11 Jul 1815; stld Lot 21, Con 1, Bathurst Twp, Lanark Co, ONT. Shopkeeper, labourer, later farmer. Wife Agnes Brackenridge, qv, with him, and 5 ch. **SEC 1; HCL 12, 231, 232**.

10201 OLIPHANT, David, b ca 1782. From Leith, MLN. To QUE on the *Atlas*, ex Greenock, 11 Jul 1815; stld Lot 1, Con 9, North Burgess Twp, Lanark Co, ONT. Printer. Wife Clementine McKenzie, qv, with him, and 3 ch. **SEC 2; HCL 232**.

10202 OLIPHANT, John. s/o William O, farmworker. To Kingston, ONT, <1828. **SH**.

10203 OLIVER, Andrew. From DFS. To Brampton, Peel Co, ONT, 1842. m Barbara Hyslop, ch: 1. Robert; 2. Frank. **DC 15 May 1982**.

10204 OLIVER, James, b ca 1752. From AYR. To QUE on the *Friendship*, ex Port Glasgow, 30 Mar 1775. Ship carpenter, 'going out to build vessels.' **LSF; OM 3/8**.

10205 OLIVER, Jean, b 30 Oct 1816. From Castleton, ROX. d/o John O, qv, and Janet Armstrong, qv. To Scotch Lake, York Co, NB, 1819. m James Blair, qv. **DC 16 Jul 1979**.

10206 OLIVER, John, b ca 1775. From Kilmarnock, AYR. To QUE, ex Greenock, summer 1815; stld ONT, prob Lanark Co. Farmer. Wife Mary Munn, qv, with him, and 5 ch. **SEC 4**.

10207 OLIVER, John, 9 Jun 1795–15 Aug 1841. From Castleton par, ROX. s/o James O. and Jean Armstrong. To Scotch Lake, York Co, NB, and gr 182 acres in Queensbury par. Moved to Pond Mills, Westminster Twp, Middlesex Co, ONT, 1836. m (i) Janet Armstrong, qv, ch: 1. Jean, qv; 2. John, b 18 Aug 1818; 3. James, b 1821, York Co, NB; 4. Adam, sawyer, went to Ingersoll, ONT; 5. Walter, b 1826; 6. Peter, b 1829. m (ii) Isabella Beattie, qv, further ch: 7-8. Janet and Margaret, b 7 Aug 1838. **DC 16 Jul 1979**.

10208 OLIVER, Robert, 1766–1863. From ROX. To Howick, Montreal, 1840; later to Galt Twp, Waterloo Co, ONT. Shepherd in various places in SCT. m Isabella Telfer, qv, ch: 1. Mary, b Ellesden, NBL, 3 May 1810; 2. Walter, b 15 Jun 1811; 3. James, b 15 Jan 1813, stld Brantford Twp, Brant Co, ONT; 4. William, b 28 Jun 1814; 5. Isabella, b Farr, SUT, 31 Jan 1816; 6. Jane, b Rogart, SUT; 7. Ellen, b Cromarty, 18 Jun 1819; 8. George, twin with Ellen, stld Shakespeare Twp; 9. Johanna, b Kildonan, SUT, 10 Jun 1821; 10. Robert, b 5 Jan 1823, grain merchant, Montreal; 11. Jessie, b 16 Jan 1825; 12. Andrew, b 29 Sep 1826; 13. Adam, b 3 May 1828; 14. Thomas, b 17 May 1830; 15. Mary Ann, b Farr, SUT, 22 May 1832; 16. Elizabeth, b 13 Mar 1834, dy. **OM 5/17**.

10209 OLIVER, Robert, 1786–1871. From Eddenside, nr Lilliesleaf, ROX. s/o John O. and Margaret Douglas. To Pictou, NS, ex Greenock, arr 28 Oct 1814; stld Middle River. Farmer. m Elizabeth Hardy, qv, ch: 1. John, b 18 Jul 1813; 2. James Douglas; 3. Helen; 4. Isobel; 5. William, 1826-61, d CA. **OM 4/3**.

10210 OLIVER, Robert Wallace, 15 Nov 1822–8 Feb 1881. From Dalkeith, MLN. To Trafalgar Twp, Halton Co, ONT, 1838; moved later to Lambton Co. Farmer. m 17 May 1850, Rebecca, 1823-98, d/o Isaac Weylie and Nancy Bell, ch: 1. Jane, 1851–1920; 2. John Wallace,

1852–1939; 3. Agnes, b 1854; 4. Margaret, 1856–1932; 5. Frances Mary, 1858–1929; 6. Isaac Weylie, 1860–1959; 7. Robert Wallace, b 1863; 8. Alexander, b 1866. **DC 22 Jan 1983**.

10211 OLIVER, Thomas. To Oxford Co, ONT, <1860. School teacher and became reeve of Woodstock and warden of the county. **BNA 749**.

10212 OLIVER, Violet. From Liddesdale, ROX. To Scotch Lake, York Co, NB, poss 1819; later to Westminster Twp, Middlesex Co, ONT. Wife of Thomas Blair, qv. **DC 16 Jul 1979**.

10213 OLIVER, William. Prob from ROX. To Leeds Twp, Megantic Co, QUE, 1831. m Margaret Allan, qv, ch: 1. James; 2. Robert; 3. Elizabeth; 4. Janet; 5. Samuel; 6. Annie; 7. Andrew. **AMC 147; OM 3/8**.

10214 OLIVER, William. To Montreal, QUE; stld Farnham Centre, Missisquoi Co. Son William, res Mansonville, 1873. **MGC 2 Aug 1979**.

10215 OLIVER, William. Prob from ROX. s/o Thomas O. To Blanshard Twp, Perth Co, ONT, ca 1853. Farmer. **DC 29 Sep 1964; OM 3/8**.

10216 OLIVER, William. From Langholm, DFS. To ONT, poss >1855; stld Bobcaygeon, Victoria Co. m Mary Forsyth Gibson, ch: 1. George, b 1840; 2. Alexander, b 1842; 3. James; 4. William, b 1851; 5. John, b 1853; 6. Adam, b 1855. **DC 16 May 1982**.

10217 ORD, Jane. From INV. To Martintown, Glengarry Co, ONT, ca 1832. Wife of Dr James Grant, qv. **MDB 277**.

10218 ORMISTON, Frank. To Dartmouth, Halifax Co, NS, <1800. Discharged soldier, gr land; engaged also in road building. Son Andrew. **HNS iii 651**.

10219 ORMISTON, Rev William, 23 Apr 1821–9 Mar 1899. From Symington, LKS. s/o Thomas O, farmer, and Margaret Smith. To Darlington Twp, Durham Co, ONT, ca 1834. Educ Victoria Univ, Cobourg, and became Professor of Moral Philosophy there. Went later to USA as a pastor of the Dutch Reformed Ch, and d Gladstone, CA. **Symington OPR 657/2; MDB 565**.

10220 ORR, James Ramsay, ca 1807–16 Mar 1852. From Stirling. To Montreal, QUE. Merchant. m Martha Thomson, ch: 1. Margaret; 2. James, 1841-50; 3. Jane, d 1906; 4. Thomas William, 1847–1922; 5. Mary, d 1916. **Ts Stirling**.

10221 ORR, John, ca 1807–20 Apr 1850. From Edinburgh. s/o Thomas O. and Catherine Denholme. To Montreal, QUE, and d there. **Ts New Calton**.

10222 ORR, Thomas. Poss from RFW. To QUE on the *Brock*, ex Greenock, 9 Jul 1820; stld prob Lanark Co, ONT. **HCL 238**.

10223 ORROCK, John Muir, 15 Jul 1830–21 Dec 1909. From Muiryhall, Kirkliston par, WLN. s/o Robert O, qv, and Janet Fairie, qv. To Montreal, QUE, 1832; stld Durham. Went later to Orrock Twp, Shelburne Co, MN, and d Brookline, MA. m (i) Josephine Johnson, 1829-82; (ii) Elizabeth —, d 1913. **LDW 23 Dec 1978**.

10224 ORROCK, Robert, 5 Jul 1802–4 Jan 1885. From Muiryhall, Kirkliston, WLN. s/o Robert O. and Janet Lawrie. To Montreal, QUE, 1832; stld Durham. Went

later to Orrock Twp, Shelburne Co, MN. Farmer. m Janet Fairie, qv, ch: 1. 1. John Muir, qv; 2. Margaret, b 29 Nov 1832, QUE; 3. Robert, b 25 Jun 1834, dy; 4. Janet, b 19 Dec 1836, Montreal; 5. Elizabeth, b 20 May 1839, Durham, QUE; 6. Harriet Gertrude, b 4 Jan 1842, Durham, QUE; 7. Robert James, b 28 May 1842; 8. George Swinton, b 9 Sep 1847; 9. William Henry, b 23 Apr 1851. **Kirkliston OPR 667/2; LDW 23 Dec 1978**.

10225 OSBORNE, James. Prob from Newmilns, AYR. s/o Robert O. in Waterhaughs. To ONT <1855. **SH**.

10226 OSBORNE, Rev John, ca 1788–6 Jul 1850. To Hamilton, ONT. m Miss Murray, from Dalbeattie, KKD. **DGH 1 Aug 1850**.

10227 OSWALD, George. Served in the 82nd Regt and was gr land in Pictou Co, NS, 1784. **HPC App F**.

10228 OSWALD, John, b 1794. From Kippen, STI. To Hamilton, ONT, summer 1845. Wife Catherine McCowan, qv, with him, and ch: 1. Findlay, b 29 Jun 1829; 2. Jean; 3. Lillias. **DC 29 Oct 1978**.

10229 OUTRAM, Joseph, 20 May 1833–14 Aug 1886. From Glasgow. s/o Joseph O, merchant-burgess. Matric Univ of Glasgow, 1847. To Halifax, NS. Merchant; later Government official. **GMA 15385**.

P

10230 PAISLEY, Ellen, 17 Aug 1841–17 Feb 1922. From Hawick, ROX. To Sherbrooke, QUE. m John Baird, qv. **MGC 2 Aug 1979**.

10231 PAISLEY, James, 1 Dec 1795–27 Aug 1847. From DFS. To QUE, ca 1832; stld Buckingham, and d there. m Helen Denham, qv, ch: 1. Margaret, qv; 2. John, qv; 3. Elizabeth, d 1837; 4. James, qv; 5. Mary, qv; 6. Jane, b QUE; 7. Hugh, b 1837; 8. George; 9. Elizabeth, b 1840. **DC 11 Jul 1979**.

10232 PAISLEY, James, jr, b ca 1827. From DFS. s/o James P, qv, and Helen Denham, qv. To QUE, ca 1832; stld Buckingham. Went later to Ancaster Twp, Wentworth Co, ONT. m Agnes Proudfoot. **DC 11 Jul 1979**.

10233 PAISLEY, John, b ca 1821. From DFS. s/o James P, qv, and Helen Denham, qv. To QUE, ca 1832; stld Buckingham. m in ONT, Mary Cameron. **DC 11 Jul 1979**.

10234 PAISLEY, Margaret, 13 Jun 1819–2 Feb 1889. From DFS. d/o James P, qv, and Helen Denham, qv. To QUE, ca 1832; stld Buckingham, and d Barton Twp, Wentworth Co, ONT. **DC 11 Jul 1979**.

10235 PAISLEY, Mary, b 2 Feb 1830. From DFS. d/o James P, qv, and Helen Denham, qv. To QUE, ca 1832; stld Buckingham, but went later to Ancaster Twp, Wentworth Co, ONT. m 10 Nov 1853, David Smith. **DC 11 Jul 1979**.

10236 PARIS, Margaret. From Hawick, ROX. To Galt, Waterloo Co, ONT, 1836. Wife of George Lee, qv. **Hawick OPR 789/5**.

10237 PARISH, Helen, ca 1795–20 May 1979. Prob from Annandale, DFS. To ONT, prob 1831. Wife of William Miller, qv. **CAE 47**.

10238 PARK, Andrew. From LKS. Prob rel to James P,

qv. To QUE on the *Prompt*, ex Greenock, 4 Jul 1820; stld Dalhousie Twp, Lanark Co, ONT. **HCL 68**.

10239 PARK, Ann, b 17 Feb 1805. From Rutherglen, LKS. d/o James P, qv, and Jean Maxwell, qv. To QUE on the *Prompt*, ex Greenock, 4 Jul 1820; stld Dalhousie Twp, Lanark Co, ONT. m 1828, Robert Wallace, qv. **DC 12 Mar 1980**.

10240 PARK, Isabella, 29 Oct 1787–14 May 1863. From Crimond par, ABD. To Uxbridge Twp, York Co, ONT, ca 1840. Wife of Alexander Milne, qv. **DC 12 Sep 1979**.

10241 PARK, James. From Rutherglen, LKS. Prob rel to Andrew P, qv. To QUE on the *Prompt*, ex Greenock, 4 Jul 1820; stld Dalhousie Twp, Lanark Co, ONT. m Jean Maxwell, qv, ch: 1. Ann, qv; 2. Andrew; 3. Alexander. **HCL 68, 228; DC 12 Mar 1980**.

10242 PARK, John, ca 1800–5 Jul 1842. From Eskdalemuir, DFS. Gr-s of William P. in Netheralbie, and Barbara Rogerson. To Galt, Waterloo Co, ONT, and d there. **Ts Eskdalemuir**.

10243 PARK, Margaret. From Eskdalemuir, DFS. d/o William P. and Janet Laidlaw, qv. To Scarborough, York Co, ONT. m Alexander Glendenning. **Ts Eskdalemuir**.

10244 PARK, Marion, b 17 Jul 1794. From Cambuslang, LKS. d/o James P. and Marion Allan. To Dalhousie Twp, Lanark Co, ONT, 1828. Wife of William Umpherston, qv. **DC 17 Jul 1979**.

10245 PARK, Martha, 31 Dec 1799–21 Jan 1880. From Cambuslang, LKS. d/o James P. and Marion Allan. To Dalhousie Twp, Lanark Co, ONT, <1826. m William Hood, qv. **DC 21 Mar 1980**.

10246 PARK, Mary. Prob from LKS. d/o Hugh P. To Hamilton, ONT, <1853, when m Thomas McIlwraith, qv. **MDB 458**.

10247 PARK, Rev William. From Eskdalemuir, DFS. s/o William P. in Halmains, and Janet Laidlaw, qv. To Durham, Grey Co, ONT, <1855. **Ts Eskdalemuir**.

10248 PARKER, David, 4 Jul 1828–30 Jul 1859. From Edinburgh. s/o John P, solicitor, 7 Mary Place. Educ Edinburgh Academy, 1839-44, and emig to CAN. m Isabella, d/o Robert Paul, banker, and d Madeira. **EAR 105**.

10249 PARKER, George, 10 Aug 1806–3 Sep 1860. From Kilmarnock, AYR. s/o Charles Stewart of Fairlie, and Margaret Rainy. To Hamilton, ONT, <1854; later to New York, and d there. m Ann Traill, qv, ch: 1. George, 1837-57; 2. Emily Traill, 1839-57; 3. Ada, 1839-63; 4. Charles Edward, 1842-64; 5. Evelyn Margaret, 1844-56, bur Hamilton; 6. Ida Roslie, 1854-55. **DRG 23**.

10250 PARKER, John William Hogg. From Calton, Glasgow. To Hibbert Twp, Perth Co, ONT, <1854. m Jean Lawrie. **Ayr PRS 376 21**.

10251 PARKER, William. From Kilmarnock, AYR. s/o Hugh P, merchant. To Montreal, QUE, <1787. Merchant. **SH**.

10252 PARLANE, Alexander, d 12 May 1847. From Helensburgh, DNB. bro/o Robert P. To Montreal, QUE, <1845. Merchant. **SH**.

PATERSON. See also PATTERSON.

10253 PATERSON, Agnes, 18 Mar 1832–Jan 1910. From Cockburnspath, BEW. d/o John P, qv, and Agnes Johnstone, qv. To Wellington Co, ONT, 1851. m — Main. **DC 29 Dec 1970**.

10254 PATERSON, Allan. Poss from LKS. bro/o Charles P, qv, fur-trader. To Montreal, QUE, <1784. m Cornelia, d/o Capt John Munro. **MDB 582**.

10255 PATERSON, Anne, 30 Jun 1845–23 May 1918. From Cockburnspath, BEW. s/o John P, qv, and Agnes Johnstone, qv. To Wellington Co, ONT, 1851. m 22 Feb 1863, at Wallace, Perth Co, James Reuben, s/o Eli and Lucinda Phillips, Napanee, Lennox Co. **DC 29 Dec 1970**.

10256 PATERSON, Archibald, 22 Dec 1816–8 Jul 1897. From North Ardbeig, North Knapdale, ARL. s/o Duncan P, qv, and Ann McNeil, qv. To Aldborough Twp, Elgin Co, ONT, 1819. Farmer. m Christian Sinclair. **DC 23 Nov 1981**.

10257 PATERSON, Archibald. Poss from LKS. To QUE on the *David of London*, ex Greenock, 19 May 1821; stld prob Lanark Co, ONT. **HCL 239**.

10258 PATERSON, Charles, d 10 Sep 1788. Poss from LKS. bro/o Allan P, qv. To Montreal, QUE, <1770. Pioneer fur-trader on the Saskatchewan and in Assiniboia. Formed a partnership with John McGill which held shares in the NWCo, 1779, but withdrew, 1783. Drowned in Lake Michigan. **MDB 582**.

10259 PATERSON, Charles, ca 1779–1848. From Kirkstyle, Ruthwell, DFS. To St John, NB. m Jane Glover, ca 1773–1826, and had, poss with other ch: 1. Anthony, 1802-22; 2. James, d 1857 in Cuba; 3. Jane Henderson, 1804-57. **Ts Ruthwell; DGH 23 Mar 1848**.

10260 PATERSON, Donald, 1788–15 Oct 1826. Poss from ARL. To Aldborough Twp, Elgin Co, ONT, prob 1818. Son Hector, qv. **PDA 41, 66**.

10261 PATERSON, Donald, 1776–24 Nov 1866. From Ardbeig, North Knapdale, ARL. s/o John P, qv, and Ann McLean, qv. To Aldborough Twp, Elgin Co, ONT, 1819. Farmer. m Lily McKay, qv. **DC 23 Nov 1981**.

10262 PATERSON, Duncan, b 1 Jun 1786. From North Ardbeig, North Knapdale, ARL. To Aldborough Twp, Elgin Co, ONT, 1819. Farmer. m Ann or Nancy McNeil, qv, ch: 1. John, qv; 2. Isabella, qv; 3. Archibald, qv; 4. Nancy, qv; 5. Margaret, 1823–1910; 6. Donald, 1824-68; 7. Mary, 1826–1915. **DC 23 Nov 1981**.

10263 PATERSON, Duncan. From ARL. To Aldborough Twp, Elgin Co, ONT, <1840. m Grace McMillan, qv, ch: 1. Margaret; 2. Lily; 3. Mary; 4. Agnes; 5. Sarah; 6. Jennie; 7. Daniel; 8. Archibald. **PDA 64**.

10264 PATERSON, Elizabeth, ca 1779–2 Dec 1866. From West Linton, PEE. d/o John P. and Jean Tweedie. To ONT, but stld later Long Grove, IA, and d there. **Ts West Linton**.

10265 PATERSON, Elizabeth, 28 Nov 1833–1868. From Cockburnspath, BEW. d/o John P, qv, and Agnes Johnstone, qv. To Wellington Co, ONT, 1851. m — Hutchinson, and d Buffalo, NY. **DC 29 Dec 1970**.

10266 PATERSON, George, b 1780. To Pictou, NS, 1815. House carpenter, m and ch. **INS 39**.

10267 PATERSON, George, 26 Sep 1836–5 Jan 1918. From Cockburnspath, BEW. s/o John P, qv, and Agnes Johnstone, qv. To Wellington Co, ONT, 1851. m Jane Dobbie, ch: 1. John; 2. William George; 3. Mark; 4. Isabella McDonald. **DC 29 Dec 1970**.

10268 PATERSON, Hector. Poss from ARL. To Aldborough Twp, Elgin Co, ONT, prob 1818. m 1852, Sarah MacPherson, ch: 1. Duncan; 2. John; 3. Mary Ann; 4. Alexander; 5. Daniel. **PDA 66**.

10269 PATERSON, Hugh, 1777–12 Nov 1834. Poss from ARL. To Aldborough Twp, Elgin Co, ONT, prob <1820. **PDA 41**.

10270 PATERSON, Isabella, 23 Apr 1815–20 Apr 1905. From North Ardbeig, North Knapdale, ARL. d/o Duncan P, qv, and Ann McNeil, qv. To Aldborough Twp, Elgin Co, ONT, 1819. m Dugald McLarty. **DC 23 Nov 1981**.

10271 PATERSON, James, d 1849. From Midmar, ABD. s/o Rev James P, Burgher min. To Hamilton, ONT, 1829, and d there of cholera. m Martha Lawson, qv. Son William, 1839–1914, manufacturer, Mayor of Brantford, 1872. **UPC i 31; MDB 582; DC 23 Sep 1980**.

10272 PATERSON, James, 1813-88. To ONT <1850, when he purchased land at Lot 27-28, Con 9, Euphrasia Twp, Grey Co. Weaver and farmer. Wife Ann, 1818–1904, with him. Son James, 1852–1932. **DC 15 Nov 1979**.

10273 PATERSON, James, 1814-95. From Kirriemuir, ANS. s/o James and Margaret P. To York Co, ONT, 1842, and stld Euphrasia Twp, Grey Co, ONT, 1853. Weaver, later storekeeper and postmaster at Blantyre. m Ann Warden, qv, ch: 1. James, 1836-40; 2. Robert Warden, 1838–1917; 3. William Stephen, 1841–1907; 4. Eliza Ann, b 1843; 5. John Warden, 1845–1909; 6. George, d inf 1847; 7. Alexander Johnston Warden, b 1849; 8. Flora, d inf 1851; 9. James Craig, 1852–1912; 10. Albert Craig, 1854–1934; 11. James Mason, 1858-62; 12. Noble Livingston, b 1861. **DC 15 Nov 1979**.

10274 PATERSON, John, d 1825. From North Knapdale, ARL. Perhaps rel to Duncan P, qv. To Aldborough Twp, Elgin Co, ONT, 1819. Farmer. m Ann McLean, qv, ch: 1. Donald, qv; 2. Duncan, b 1786; 3. Anne, b 1780; 4. Catherine. **DC 23 Nov 1981**.

10275 PATERSON, John, 12 Nov 1813–27 Aug 1897. From North Ardbeig, Knapdale, ARL. s/o Duncan P, qv, and Ann McNeil, qv. To Aldborough Twp, Elgin Co, ONT, 1819. Farmer. m Nancy McKellar, 6 Apr 1847. **DC 23 Nov 1981**.

10276 PATERSON, John, 21 Dec 1807–15 Dec 1864. From Cockburnspath, BEW. s/o George P, hedger, and Agnes White. To Wellington Co, ONT, 1851. m 5 Feb 1830, Agnes Johnstone, qv, ch: 1. Margaret, qv; 2. Agnes, qv; 3. Elizabeth, qv; 4. George, qv; 5. Mary, qv; 6. Mark James, qv; 7. Anne, qv; 8. John, jr, qv. **DC 29 Dec 1970**.

10277 PATERSON, John, jr, 18 Mar 1848–10 May 1914. From Cockburnspath, BEW. s/o John P, qv, and Agnes Johnstone, qv. To Wellington Co, ONT, 1851. Machinist. m Christina Armstrong, ch: 1. John A, d NY, 1964; 2. Agnes. **DC 29 Dec 1970**.

10278 PATERSON, Margaret, 14 Aug 1830–1 Jan 1913. From Cockburnspath, BEW. d/o John P, qv, and Agnes Johnstone, qv. To Wellington Co, ONT, 1851. m — Reid. **DC 29 Dec 1970**.

10279 PATERSON, Mark James, b 20 Sep 1842. From Cockburnspath, BEW. s/o John P, qv, and Agnes Johnstone, qv. To Wellington Co, ONT, 1851. Miller. m Mary Ann Korman, ch: 1. John Martin; 2. Mary Ann; 3. Catherine Margaret Elizabeth; 4. Agnes Johnstone. **DC 29 Dec 1970**.

10280 PATERSON, Mary, ca 1801–11 Nov 1852. From Kirkmichael par, DFS. To Kent Co, ONT, and d there. Wife of James Potter, who d at Templand, Lochmaben, DFS, 1880. Dau Elizabeth, ca 1823-52, d QUE. **DC 29 Dec 1970**.

10281 PATERSON, Mary, 21 Mar 1840–1901. From Cockburnspath, BEW. d/o John P, qv, and Agnes Johnstone, qv. To Wellington Co, ONT, 1851, and d Avon, Livingston Co, NY. **DC 29 Dec 1970**.

10282 PATERSON, Mary. From Galson, Barvas par, Is Lewis, ROC. d/o John P, Carloway. To Whitton Twp, Compton Co, QUE, 1863. Wife of John Graham, qv. **WLC**.

10283 PATERSON, Nancy, 21 Nov 1818–15 Apr 1900. From North Ardbeig, North Knapdale, ARL. d/o Duncan P, qv, and Ann McNeil, qv. To Aldborough Twp, Elgin Co, ONT, 1819. m Neil McLarty. **DC 23 Nov 1981**.

10284 PATERSON, Rev Nathaniel, ca 1830–2 Aug 1896. From Glasgow. s/o Rev Nathaniel P, min of St Andrews Ch, and Margaret Laidlaw. Matric Univ of Glasgow, 1847, and became FC min at Merrickville, Leeds and Grenville Co, ONT. d at Hamilton. **GMA 15240; FES iii 434**.

10285 PATERSON, Peter, 1806–12 Apr 1883. From Blantyre, LKS. s/o Peter P. and Jean Fraser. To Toronto, ONT, 1819. Dry goods merchant. m 1835, Hannah Wilson, from Kingston, ch: 1. John Henry; 2. James Frederick; 3. Rev Thomas Wilson, 1847–1934; 4. Elizabeth; 5. Emily Jane; 6. Mary Louise. **DC 15 May 1982**.

10286 PATERSON, Robert B. From Kinneswood, Portmoak, KRS. s/o Robert P, 1811-97, and Margaret Low, 1812-51. To CAN, poss St John, NB. **Ts Portmoak**.

10287 PATERSON, William, ca 1788–18 Nov 1823. From Hayberries, Ruthwell, DFS. s/o John P. To St John, NB, and d there. **Ts Ruthwell**.

10288 PATERSON, William, ca 1778–21 Jul 1834. From West Linton, PEE. s/o John P. and Jean Tweedie. To Montreal, QUE, and d there. **Ts West Linton**.

10289 PATERSON, William, d 2 Aug 1860. From Preston, Kirkbean, KKD. To ONT, and drowned on River St Clair. Chief engineer on a steamboat. m d/o Joseph Nicholson, baker in Dumfries. **CAE 5**.

10290 PATON, Alexander, 22 Dec 1848–18 Dec 1933. From Galston, AYR. s/o David P, qv, and Christina Woodburn. To Amherstburg, Essex Co, ONT, 1852; later to Almont, Lapeer Co, MI. m 1870, Harriet Martha Wilson; m (ii) 1896, Gertrude Beryl Pierce. **DC 30 Sep 1960**.

10291 PATON, Rev Andrew, b 17 Jun 1839, Ballingry, FIF. s/o James P, Balbedie, and Ann Deas. Educ Univ of Edinburgh, and became asst min at Haddington. To Montreal, QUE, 1865, and ord to St Andrews Ch. Retr to SCT and adm min of Penpont par, DFS, 1870. **FES ii 324, vii 648**.

10292 PATON, Annie, b 22 Nov 1839. From Kilmarnock, AYR. d/o John P, qv, and Margaret Wilson, qv. To Amherstburg, Essex Co, ONT, 1843; later to Cheyboygan, MI. m at Armada, MI, 22 Nov 1867, Harry A. Blake. **DC 30 Sep 1960**.

10293 PATON, Annie Allan, 29 Dec 1846–7 Dec 1938. From Galston, AYR. d/o David P, qv, and Christina Woodburn. To Amherstburg, Essex Co, ONT, 1852; thence to Lapeer Co, MI. **DC 30 Sep 1960**.

10294 PATON, Christina, 20 Jun 1836–23 Oct 1868. From Galston, AYR. d/o David P, qv, and Christina Woodburn. To Amherstburg, Essex Co, ONT, 1852; thence to Almont, Lapeer Co, MI. m 1853, William Millikin. **DC 30 Sep 1960**.

10295 PATON, David, b 18 Nov 1812. From Burnhead, Galston, AYR. s/o John P. and Ann Allan, qv. To Amherstburg, Essex Co, ONT, 1852; thence to Almont, Lapeer Co, MI. Flesher, later farmer. m (i) 1833, Christina Woodburn, 1812-49, ch: 1. John, b 1835, dy; 2. Christina, qv; 3. David, jr, qv; 4. John H, qv; 5. William Woodburn, qv; 6. Annie Allan, qv; 7. Alexander, qv. m (ii) 1849, his widow's sist, Elizabeth Woodburn, qv, further ch: 8. Andrew, 1851–1924; 9. Elizabeth, 1853–1916; 10. Janet, 1854–1943; 11. Jean, 1855–1943; 12. Margaret Ann, 1857–1933; 13. Agnes, 1858-66; 14. Rev Robert, 1860–1959; 15. Mary Gertrude, 1861–1947; 16. James Woodburn, 1863–1943; 17. Allan Hamilton, 1864–1938; 18. Grace, 1866–1928; 19. Thomas Woodburn, 1869–1939. **DC 30 Sep 1960**.

10296 PATON, David, jr, 3 Jan 1839–8 Oct 1932. From Galston, AYR. s/o David P, qv, and Christina Woodburn. To Amherstburg, Essex Co, ONT, 1852; thence to Almont, Lapeer Co, MI. m 13 Jun 1866, Agnes McKail. **DC 30 Sep 1960**.

10297 PATON, Elizabeth, 28 Mar 1804–1 Mar 1875. From Burnhead, Galston, AYR. d/o John P. and Ann Allan, qv. To Amherstburg, Essex Co, ONT, 1852; later to Almont, Lapeer Co, MI. m John F. Hamilton, qv, no ch. **DC 30 Sep 1960**.

10298 PATON, Jean, 8 Aug 1841–25 Mar 1925. From Kilmarnock, AYR. d/o John P, qv, and Margaret Wilson, qv. To Amherstburg, Essex Co, ONT, 1843; later to Memphis, MI. m 8 Aug 1865, Henry Pawson Leighton. **DC 30 Sep 1960**.

10299 PATON, John, 21 Apr 1809–2 Aug 1887. From Burnhead, Galston, AYR. s/o John P. and Ann Allan, qv. To Amherstburg, Essex Co, ONT, 1843; moved in 1846 to Armada, MI. m Margaret Wilson, qv, ch: 1. Margaret, qv; 2. John, d inf; 3. Annie, qv; 4. Jean, qv; 5. James, 1844-57; 6. Alexander W, b 1846; 7. John Allan, 1849–1914; 8. Jessie, 1852–1938; 9. William, 1854-96. **DC 30 Sep 1960**.

10300 PATON, John, 26 May 1831–30 Mar 1901. From Ancrum, ROX. s/o Rev John P, par min, and Mary Paton, his cous. Educ Univ of Edinburgh, and went to Kingston, ONT. Banker, and hon secretary of Queens

Coll. Also officer of Militia. Later in NY. m d/o Hon John Hamilton, Kingston. **EAR 118; FES ii 101**.

PATON, Mrs John. See ALLAN, Ann.

10301 PATON, Rev John H, 7 Apr 1843–6 Sep 1922. From Galston, AYR. s/o David P, qv, and Christina Woodburn. To Amherstburg, Essex Co, ONT, 1852; thence to Almont, Lapeer Co, MI. m Sarah E. Wilson. **DC 30 Sep 1960**.

10302 PATON, Margaret, 8 Feb 1836–18 Jul 1933. From Kilmarnock, AYR. d/o John P, qv, and Margaret Wilson, qv. To Amherstburg, Essex Co, ONT, 1843. m 8 Feb 1859, Richard Golden. **DC 30 Sep 1960**.

10303 PATON, Thomas, b 1806. From Lasswade, MLN. s/o Rev John P, par min, and Margaret Main. To CAN, later to NZ. Banker. Heir to his bro Peter, 1857. **FES i 330**.

10304 PATON, William Woodburn, 21 Jan 1845–29 Nov 1935. From Galston, AYR. s/o David P, qv, and Christina Woodburn. To Amherstburg, Essex Co, ONT, 1852; thence to Almont, Lapeer Co, MI. m 25 Nov 1874, Jean Hunter Millikin, b 1851. **DC 30 Sep 1960**.

10305 PATRICK, Rev William, ca 1771–25 Nov 1844. b Kilsyth, STI. s/o John P, farmer. Matric Univ of Glasgow, 1792. Antiburgher min at Lockerbie, DFS, 1802-15. To NS, 1815, and was min at Merigomish, Pictou Co. m d/o Rev John Young, Antiburgher min at Hawick, ROX. **UPC i 43, ii 456; GMA 5305**.

10306 PATTEN, Henry William, ca 1835–19 May 1855. From Devonshaw, Fossoway, KRS. s/o Capt William P. To ONT, and d Benares. **Ts Fossoway**.

10307 PATTEN, Thomas. Rel to John P. in Jamaica, West Indies. To NFD, <1838. **SH**.

PATTERSON. See also PATERSON.

10308 PATTERSON, Andrew, d ca 1860. Prob from LKS. To Montreal, QUE, <1800. Mem of mercantile firm of Gillespie, Moffat & Co. Moved to QUE, 1815. **SGC 249**.

10309 PATTERSON, Archibald, 1800-21. From Paisley, RFW. To Pictou, NS, and d there. **Ts Paisley**.

10310 PATTERSON, Archibald, d 1 Mar 1850. Prob from DFS. s/o John P. To Toronto, ONT. **DGH 11 Apr 1850**.

10311 PATTERSON, David. Poss from ARL. Prob rel to John P, qv. To Aldborough Twp, Elgin Co, ONT, 1845. **PDA 67**.

10312 PATTERSON, Dolly, b ca 1736. To Charlottetown, PEI, on the *Spencer*, ex Oban, arr 22 Sep 1806. **PLSN**.

10313 PATTERSON, Dugald. Prob from ARL. To Ekfrid Twp, Middlesex Co, ONT, 1834. ch: 1. Alexander; 2. Malcolm; 3. Archibald. **PCM 30**.

10314 PATTERSON, Duncan. From ARL. Prob bro/o John P, qv. To West Williams Twp, Middlesex Co, ONT, 1848. **PCM 47**.

10315 PATTERSON, Edward, d 27 Jan 1850. From Glensome, New Abbey, KKD. To Cobourg, Northumberland Co, ONT, and d at Hamilton. Schoolmaster. **DGH 11 Apr 1850**.

10316 PATTERSON, Eliza. From Ballater, ABD. To Sarnia, Lambton Co, ONT, 1855. Wife of Francis O. Laird, qv. **DC 30 Aug 1977**.

10317 PATTERSON, James. To QUE, ca 1820; stld Lot 22, Con 6, Ramsay Twp, Lanark Co, ONT. **HCL 72**.

10318 PATTERSON, James. To QUE on the *George Canning*, ex Greenock, 14 Apr 1821; stld Ramsay Twp, Lanark Co, ONT. Tailor. **HCL 86, 239**.

10319 PATTERSON, James. To Kent Co, NB, <1835; stld Kouchibouguac. m Janet Potter, qv, ch: 1. James; 2. John, 1837–1911; 3. Archibald; 4. David, d inf; 5. Elizabeth; 6. Mary; 7. Jessie; 8. Margaret. **DC 15 Nov 1980**.

10320 PATTERSON, John. From Linwood, RFW. To Pictou, NS, on the *Hector*, ex Greenock, arr 17 Sep 1773. Carpenter, merchant and magistrate. m Ann, d/o Matthew Harris, ch: 1. James; 2. David; 3. John; 4. Abraham, father of Dr George P, historian of Pictou Co. **HPC App C; HT 77**.

10321 PATTERSON, John. Poss from ARL. Prob rel to David P, qv. To Aldborough Twp, Elgin Co, ONT, 1845. **PDA 67**.

10322 PATTERSON, John. From ARL. Prob bro/o Duncan P, qv. To West Williams Twp, Middlesex Co, ONT, 1848. Son Duncan, physician. **PCM 47**.

10323 PATTERSON, Peter. From ARL. bro/o Roger P, qv, and Sarah P, qv. To Ekfrid Twp, Middlesex Co, ONT, 1842. Widowed mother with him. **PCM 31**.

10324 PATTERSON, Rebecca. From Kiltarlity, INV. To Pictou, NS, on the *Hector*, ex Loch Broom, arr 17 Sep 1773. Wife of Hugh Fraser, qv. **HPC App C**.

10325 PATTERSON, Robert. To Pictou Co, NS, <16 Aug 1783, when gr 480 acres on West River. **HPC App A**.

10326 PATTERSON, Robert, d 10 Mar 1863. From Caerlaverock, DFS. To West McGillivray Twp, Middlesex Co, ONT. Farmworker. **CAE 10**.

10327 PATTERSON, Robert, ca 1824–ca 1905. From ROX, prob Hassendean, Minto par. To ONT <1855, when stld on Lot 8, Con 7, Bentinck Twp, Grey Co. Farmer and stone-mason. m (ii) Christina Gillis, sis/o his first wife, ch. **DC 9 Nov 1981**.

10328 PATTERSON, Robert, 10 Mar 1848–21 Jul 1921. From Kelso, ROX. To Stratford, Perth Co, ca 1866. Engineer, Grand Trunk Railway. m Mary Young, 1853–1925, ch: 1. Harry Murray, 1880–1942; 2. Alice, res Los Angeles, CA; 3. Helen, res Toronto. **DC 25 Nov 1981**.

10329 PATTERSON, Roger. From ARL. bro/o Peter P, qv, and Sarah P, qv. To Ekfrid Twp, Middlesex Co, ONT, 1842. m Isabella, d/o Neil Leitch, qv. **PCM 31**.

10330 PATTERSON, Sarah. From ARL. sis/o Peter P, qv, and Roger P, qv. To Ekfrid Twp, Middlesex Co, ONT, 1842. **PCM 31**.

10331 PATTERSON, William. To Dundas Co, ONT, 1820. m Margaret, d/o Walter Barrigar. **DC 4 Mar 1865**.

PATTON. See also PATON.

10332 PATTON, Andrew. From St Andrews, FIF. Prob the man of this name who matric at Univ of St Andrews, 1786. To Prescott Twp, Grenville Co, ONT, <1824. Ret Major, 45th Regt. Son James, 1824-88, journalist and politician. **BNA 598; SAM 35; MDB 585**.

10333 PATTON, George, ca 1770–1854. From LKS, poss Lesmahagow. To Scarborough, York Co, ONT, 1833. **DC 29 Mar 1981**.

10334 PATTON, Lydia. To QUE, and stld Rouville Co. m Robert Gillespie, qv, and d soon after emigrating. **MGC 2 Aug 1979**.

10335 PATULLO, Alexander, ca 1775–8 Dec 1828. From Kirriemuir, ANS. To Peel Co, ONT, 1820; stld Caledon Twp. Soldier, 42nd Regt, later farmer. m (i) Sadie Hewie, ch: 1. Alexander, b 13 May 1799; 2. Mary, b 25 Feb 1801; 3. James, b 23 Jun 1807; 4. Halket, b 31 Jul 1809; 5. Jean, b 9 Feb 1812; 6. Margaret, b 23 Dec 1813; 7. Thomas, b 8 Apr 1817, Inveresk, Musselburgh, MLN. **DC 20 Jul 1979**.

10336 PATULLO, Robert. Prob from ANS. To St John, NB. Poss mariner. Wife Susannah, ca 1748–2 Feb 1801. **NER viii 99**.

10337 PAUL, Andrew. From LKS. To Ramsay Twp, Lanark Co, ONT, ca 1821. Farmer and lime merchant. m 2 Feb 1827, Euphemia Yuill, qv, ch. **HCL 87**.

10338 PAUL, Duncan. To Metcalfe Twp, Middlesex Co, ONT, 1832. **PCM 26**.

10339 PAUL, James. Poss from ARL. To Aldborough Twp, Elgin Co, ONT, prob 1818. Farmer. **PDA 93**.

10340 PAUL, James. To QUE on the *George Canning*, ex Greenock, 14 Apr 1821; stld Dalhousie Twp, Lanark Co, ONT. Pioneer settler. **HCL 227**.

10341 PAUL, Rev James T. To Kingston, ONT, and attended Queens Coll, 1843-44. Ord min of St Louis de Gonzaque, 1850, but demitted his charge, 1865. Adm min of Dummer, Peterborough Co, 1872; trans to Bolsover, Victoria Co, ONT, 1875. **FES vii 648**.

10342 PAUL, John, ca 1750–29 Apr 1833. From Lanark. To St John, NB, <1800. In the service of the Ordnance Department. **NER viii 99**.

10343 PAUL, John. From ABD. s/o John P, farmer, Dyce. Matric Marischall Coll, Aberdeen, 1816. To York Co, ONT. Engaged in rebellion, 1836-37, and was afterwards Clerk of Court at Weston. **FAM ii 428**.

10344 PAUL, John. From MOR, poss par of Dyke. To Montreal, QUE, prob 1831; stld ONT. Wife Catherine Masson, qv, with him. **DC 22 Sep 1979**.

10345 PAUL, William, 20 Mar 1789–29 Jul 1849. From Paisley, RFW. s/o William P. and Tamar Whittaker. To ONT, ca 1812; stld Newburgh, Lennox and Addington Co. Soldier and farmer. m Janet McLay, qv, ch. **DC 29 Oct 1981**.

10346 PAUL, William. From Loch Awe, ARL. To Lobo Twp, Middlesex Co, ONT, 1830. ch: 1. Malcolm; 2. William; 3. Archy; 4. Dugald; 5. Mary; 6. Janet; 7. Margaret. **PCM 39**.

10347 PEACOCK, James. Served as an NCO in 82nd Regt, and was gr 200 acres in Pictou Co, NS, 1784. Res nr Chance Harbour. **HPC App F**.

10348   PEARSON, Charles. Prob from Glasgow. bro/o William P, writer. To Montreal, QUE, <1819.   **SH**.

10349   PEARSON, James, ca 1764–23 May 1845. From Dormont Mill, Dalton, DFS. To ONT; stld poss Perth Co. m Elizabeth Calvert, qv. Dau Henrietta, d Mossburn, Lochmaben, DFS, 1846, aged 37.   **Ts Dalton**.

10350   PEARSON, John, 9 Jan 1833–12 Apr 1888. From PER. To ONT, <1855.   **DC 8 Nov 1981**.

10351   PEDDIE, James, ca 1806–25 Feb 1843. From PER. To Halton Co, ONT, prob <1840; stld Esquesing Twp. Bur Boston Cemetery.   **EPE 75**.

10352   PEDDIE, Stuart. From Perth. bro/o Walter Miller P, qv. To Montreal, QUE, <1797. Dry goods merchant, with bro William P, qv.   **SGC 494**.

10353   PEDDIE, Walter Miller, 12 Feb 1797–19 Aug 1876. From Perth. bro/o Stuart P, qv, and William P, qv. To Montreal, QUE, 1814. Dry goods merchant. m Mary Ann McFarlane, qv, and ret to Sault-aux-Recollets.   **SGC 494**.

10354   PEDDIE, William, ca 1789–27 Jul 1834. From Perth. bro/o Stuart P, qv, and Walter Miller P, qv. To Montreal, QUE, <1800. Dry goods merchant with bro Stuart P. Said to have d unm.   **SGC 494**.

10355   PEDEN, Hugh. To QUE on the *Caledonian*, 1816; stld Lot 26, Con 2, Bathurst Twp, Lanark Co, ONT. **HCL 234**.

10356   PEDEN, Rev Robert, 1816–10 Jan 1883. From Kilmarnock, AYR. s/o John P, craftsman. Matric Univ of Glasgow, 1833, and studied at United Secession Hall. To Amherstburg, Essex Co, ONT, 1844, and joined FC the same year.   **GMA 13138; FES vii 648**.

10357   PEFFERS, Francis, 1832–1914. To Wellington Co, ONT. m Janet McLean, qv, and d Pickford, MI, ch: 1. John, b ca 1856; 2. Margaret, b 1858; 3. James, b 1859; 4. Janet, b 1862; 5. Agnes, b 1863; 6. William, b 1865; 7. Mary Jane, b ca 1869.   **DC 30 Apr 1980**.

10358   PEFFERS, Walter, b ca 1813. To Eldon Twp, Victoria Co, ONT, 1833, afterwards to Scarborough Twp, York Co, and later in Mornington Twp, Perth Co. Farmer and magistrate. m Maria Arkins. Son Neil.   **DC 13 Apr 1971 and 6 Jan 1972**.

10359   PENMAN, Ann, b 1808. From LKS. d/o Robert Penman, qv, and Grizel Cuthbertson, qv. To QUE on the *Prompt*, ex Greenock, 4 Jul 1820; stld Lanark Twp, Lanark Co, ONT. m William Watson, b 1802. **DC 21 Mar 1980**.

10360   PENMAN, James, 1815–3 Apr 1891. From LKS. s/o Robert P, qv, and Grizel Cuthbertson, qv. To QUE on the *Prompt*, ex Greenock, 4 Jul 1820; stld Lanark Twp, Lanark Co, ONT. m Mary Nairn, qv.   **DC 21 Mar 1980**.

10361   PENMAN, Janet, 1796–1887. From LKS. d/o Robert P, qv, and Grizel Cuthbertson, qv. To Lanark Co, ONT, prob 1820; stld Lanark Twp. m (i) William Galbraith, ch; (ii) James Dewart, ch; and (iii) Thomas Taylor.   **DC 21 Mar 1980**.

10362   PENMAN, John. From LKS. s/o Robert P, qv, and Grizel Cuthbertson, qv. To QUE on the *Prompt*, ex Greenock, 4 Jul 1820; stld Lanark Twp, Lanark Co, ONT. Went to Niagara <1839.   **DC 22 Oct 1980**.

10363   PENMAN, Margaret, 6 Jun 1806–6 Jul 1877. From LKS. d/o Robert P, qv, and Grizel Cuthbertson, qv. To QUE on the *Prompt*, ex Greenock, 4 Jul 1820; stld Lanark Twp, Lanark Co, ONT. m James Scoular, b 1802.   **DC 21 Mar 1980**.

10364   PENMAN, Robert. From LKS. To QUE on the *Prompt*, ex Greenock, 4 Jul 1820; stld Lot 21E, Con 9, Lanark Twp, Lanark Co, ONT. Farmer. m Grizel Cuthbertson, qv, ch: 1. Janet, qv; 2. Robert, jr, qv; 3. William, qv; 4. Margaret, qv; 5. Ann, qv; 6. James, qv; 7. John, qv.   **HCL 238; DC 22 Oct 1980**.

10365   PENMAN, Robert, jr, 1799–1863. From LKS. s/o Robert P, qv, and Grizel Cuthbertson, qv. To QUE on the *Prompt*, ex Greenock, 4 Jul 1820; Lot 20E, Con 9, Lanark Twp, Lanark Co, ONT. m Sarah (called Sally) Jane Menarey, b 1809, Co Tyrone, IRL. **DC 21 Mar 1980**.

10366   PENMAN, William, 1802–26 Jul 1885. From LKS. s/o Robert P, qv, and Grizel Cuthbertson, qv. To QUE on the *Prompt*, ex Greenock, 4 Jul 1820; stld Lanark Twp, later Dalhousie Twp, Lanark Co, ONT. m (i) Elizabeth Nairn, qv; (ii) Ellen Ogilvie.   **DC 22 Oct 1980**.

10367   PENMAN, William, b ca 1811. From LKS. Poss rel to Robert P, qv. To Lanark Twp, Lanark Co, ONT, <21 Jul 1834, when m Jane Somerville.   **DC 22 Oct 1980**.

10368   PENNEY, Robert, ca 1790–24 Apr 1828. From STI. To NS, and d there.   **VSN No 2854**.

10369   PENNEY, Rev Robert, 1 Oct 1808–10 Jan 1883. From Glasgow. s/o William P, merchant-burgess. Educ Univ of Glasgow, matric 1822. App a catechist by the Glasgow Colonial Committee for service in CAN, 1846. Retr to SCT and built a mission Ch at Irvine, AYR, mainly for seamen.   **GMA 11153; FES vii 648**.

10370   PETRIE, Alexander Oliphant. From Dundee, ANS. To Belleville, Hastings Co, ONT, <1836.   **SH**.

10371   PETRIE, Margaret. From Rothes, MOR. To QUE, ex Greenock, summer 1815; stld Bathurst Twp, Lanark Co, ONT. Wife of John Simpson, qv.   **SEC 2; HCL 230**.

10372   PETTIGREW, James, ca 1775–29 Mar 1826. To NS, and d there leaving a widow and 10 ch. **VSN No 1636**.

10373   PETTIGREW, Rev John, b 8 Apr 1802. From Cathkin Mill, Carmunnoch, LKS. s/o John P. and Agnes Cumming. To ONT, 1850; stld Blandford Twp, Oxford Co. m Margaret Scoullar, qv, ch: 1. John, b 17 Mar 1833; 2. Margaret, b 5 May 1835; 3. James, b 15 Dec 1836; 4. Joseph, b 7 Aug 1840; 5. Agnes, 1842-43; 6. Agnes, b 8 Apr 1844; 7. Robert, b 19 Jul 1847.   **DC 27 Aug 1981**.

10374   PETTIGREW, William, 1798–1853. From Is Arran, BUT. To Dalhousie, NB, 1829; stld Heron Is, Restigouche Co.   **MAC 26**.

10375   PHEMISTER, William, b 21 Dec 1851. From Aberdeen. s/o William P. and Jane Buchan. To ONT, 1854. Postmaster. m Sarah, d/o Henry Zimmerman, ch: 1. William Henry; 2. George Stanley.   **DC 29 Sep 1964**.

10376   PHILIP, James, 1812–23 Aug 1889. From Old Meldrum, ABD. s/o James P. of Kingindee. To CAN,

1839, and worked as a bookkeeper for contractors for the Welland Canal. Stld later at Elora, Nichol Twp, Wellington Co, ONT, and purchased a store there. m Mary Brown, qv, ch.   **EHE 135**.

10377   PHILIP, Robert. From Tillicoultry, CLK. To CAN, prob ONT, 1852. m Isabella Mercer, qv, ch: 1. Catherine, b 6 Feb 1837; 2. Elizabeth Goodfellow, b 30 Dec 1838; 3. Margaret, b 6 Aug 1840; 4. John, b 25 Aug 1842; 5. Helen, b 2 Aug 1844; 6. Isabella, b 17 Jan 1847; 7. Robert, b 23 May 1849; 8. Janet, b 6 Nov 1851. **Tillicoultry OPR 486/3**.

10378   PHILIP, Robert, b ca 1815. From Old Meldrum, ABD. s/o James Philip of Kingindee. To Elora, Nichol Twp, Wellington Co, ONT, <1854. Storekeeper. m d/o George Emslie, qv, and Agnes Gibbon, qv. **EHE 135**.

10379   PHILLIPS, Edward, b 5 Oct 1790. From Bo'ness, WLN. He served in RN for 8 years, and afterwards emig to NB.   **DC 16 Apr 1983**.

10380   PHILLIPS, Susan, d 5 Apr 1839. From Ruthwell, DFS. d/o John P. in Aiket. To Galt, Waterloo Co, ONT. m — Young, merchant.   **DGH 31 May 1839**.

10381   PHINNEY, Susan. To Montreal, QUE, on the *Royal George*, ex Greenock, Jan 1827; stld Sarnia, Lambton Co, ONT. Second wife of Henry Jones, qv. **DC 19 Nov 1978**.

10382   PICKEN, Andrew Belfrage, 5 Nov 1802–1 Jul 1849. From Edinburgh. s/o Ebenezer P, teacher and poet. To Montreal, QUE, 1830. Art teacher and author. **IBD 409; SGC 563**.

10383   PICKEN, Catherine. From Edinburgh. d/o Ebenezer P, teacher and poet. To Montreal, QUE, prob <1840, and established a high-class boarding school.   **SGC 563**.

10384   PICKEN, Henry Belfrage, 1809-87. s/o Ebenezer P, teacher and poet. To Montreal, QUE, 1832. Emp for 35 years with the Bank of Montreal. ch incl: 1. Henry Belfrage, treas of Knox Ch; 2. John Belfrage, elder of Knox Ch.   **SGC 562**.

10385   PICKEN, Janet, 1840–1920. From Kilmarnock, AYR. sis/o Sarah P, qv. To Mosa Twp, Middlesex Co, ONT, and bur Oakland Cemetery, nr Glencoe.   **DC 8 Nov 1981**.

10386   PICKEN, Joanna Belfrage, 8 May 1798–24 Mar 1859. From Edinburgh. d/o Ebenezer P, teacher and poet. To Montreal, QUE, 1842. Associated with sist Catherine in running a boarding school; musician and poetess.   **IBD 409; SGC 563**.

10387   PICKEN, John. Prob rel to Margaret P, qv. To Pictou, NS, on the *Hope*, ex Glasgow, 5 Apr 1848, but went to USA.   **DC 12 Jul 1979**.

10388   PICKEN, Margaret. Prob rel to John P, qv. To Pictou, NS, on the *Hope*, ex Glasgow, 5 Apr 1848. **DC 12 Jul 1979**.

10389   PICKEN, Sarah, 1821–1905. From Kilmarnock, AYR. sis/o Janet P, qv. To Mosa Twp, Middlesex Co, ONT, ca 1865. m William Webster, qv.   **DC 8 Nov 1981**.

10390   PINSSALL, John. Prob from PER. To McNab Twp, Renfrew Co, ONT, 1825. Family with him: 1. James; 2. David; 3. Thomas.   **DC 3 Jan 1980**.

10391   PIRIE, George. From Aberdeen. To Bon Accord, Nichol Twp, Wellington Co, ONT, ca 1838; stld later in Guelph. Newspaper editor and lyrical poet. m d/o William Robeson, shipmaster, Aberdeen, and Mary Gavin, ch: 1. George, res Dundas; 2. William, res Elora; 3. Catherine; 4. Mary; 5. Gavin; 6. Thomas.   **SAS 40; EHE 95**.

10392   PIRIE, John, b 1805. From ABD. To ONT, ca 1825. m Janet Anderson.   **DC 19 Feb 1959**.

10393   PIRIE, John, 20 Feb 1821–23 Nov 1874. From Old Deer, ABD. To ONT, 1854; bur Campbellford, Northumberland Co. m Janet Hacket, qv, and had ch in CAN: 1. John; 2. Jessie; 3. Isabella Wilson; 4. Margaret; 5. Christine.   **DC 22 Aug 1974**.

10394   PIRIE, Mary Dunbar, b ca 1832. From ABD. To QUE, 1850; later to Peel Twp, Wellington Co, ONT. m Neil, s/o Walter Peffers, qv.   **DC 5 Jun 1978**.

10395   PIRIE, Robert, 13 Oct 1812–1 Mar 1876. From Old Deer, ABD. To ONT, 1857, and stld Campbellford, Northumberland Co. m Margaret Fyfe, qv, ch: 1. Jane or Jean, b Skene, 1846, dy; 2. Alexander Fyfe, b Newhills par, 1848; 3. Isabella, b 1850; 4. Elspet, b 1852; 5. Robert, b 1854; 6. Jean, b 1856; 7. Charles Wilson, b 1860, d inf.   **DC 22 Aug 1974 and 18 Apr 1983**.

10396   PITBLUDIE, James. Rel to John P, qv. To Pictou, NS, on the *London*, arr 11 Apr 1848. Wife Catherine with him, and ch: 1. Ann K; 2. Alexander. **DC 15 Jul 1979**.

10397   PITBLUDIE, John. Rel to James P, qv. To Pictou, NS, on the *London*, arr 11 Apr 1848. Wife Anne with him, and ch: 1. Charles B; 2. P. McD; 3. Anne; 4. Catherine; 5. John; 6. Janet.   **DC 15 Jul 1979**.

10398   PITT, Mary Ann, 1819–13 Apr 1885. From Kilmarnock, AYR. To Sherbrooke Co, QUE, 1843. Wife of William Giffen, qv.   **DC 31 Dec 1981**.

10399   PLAYFAIR, Ann, 4 Jun 1822–27 Jan 1881. To Darlington Twp, Durham Co, ONT, <1840. m 1847, Samuel McElwain, from CAV, IRL, ch: 1. Samuel Michael, b 1849; 2. John William, b ca 1852; 3. Margaret Jane, b 1855; 4. Robert, b 1856; 5. George, b 1856, twin; 6. Charles James, b 1858; 7. Martha Ann, b 1860; 8. Eliza Jane, b 1863.   **DC 17 May 1969**.

10400   POLLOCK, Alexander, b 1807. Poss from Fraserburgh, ABD. s/o John P, surveyor. To NB, ca 1816.   **DC 3 Apr 1981**.

10401   POLLOCK, James. Poss from RFW, and prob rel to Thomas P, qv. To QUE on the *David of London*, ex Greenock, 19 May 1821; stld Ramsay Twp, Lanark Co, ONT.   **HCL 239**.

10402   POLLOCK, John. To Pictou, NS, on the *Lulan*, ex Glasgow, 17 Aug 1848.   **DC 12 Jul 1979**.

10403   POLLOCK, Robert, 24 May 1852–17 Aug 1929. From Kilmarnock, AYR. s/o John P. and Anne Kennedy. To Galt, Waterloo Co, ONT, prob <1867. Moved to BC, 1889, later to Los Angeles, CA. m Agnes Gilchrist, ch.   **DC 8 Aug 1983**.

10404   POLLOCK, Thomas. Poss from RFW, and prob rel to James P, qv. To QUE on the *David of London*, ex Greenock, 19 May 1821; stld Ramsay Twp, Lanark Co, ONT.   **HCL 239**.

10405 POLLOCK, William, 1820-92. To Ottawa, ONT, <1846. Farmer. m (i) Margery Smith Bayne, qv, ch; (ii) 1859, Mary Robertson, Widow Browne, his first wife's cous, further ch. He was sometime at Syracuse, NY, but returned to ONT and stld Nepean Twp, Carleton Co. **DC 15 Aug 1967**.

10406 POLLOK, Rev Allan, 19 Oct 1829–7 Jul 1918. From Glasgow, but b Buckhaven, FIF. s/o Rev Robert P. and Janet Carlaw. Matric Univ of Glasgow, 1843. To New Glasgow, Pictou Co, NS, 1852. Min of St Andrews Ch there, later Principal of Pine Hill Coll, Halifax. DD, Queens Univ, 1900; LLD, Dalhousie, 1902. m Catherine, d/o Hon James Fraser, ch: 1. Robert, dy; 2. Elizabeth. **GMA 14640; FES iii 420, vii 617; MDB 598**.

10407 POLSON, Alexander, b ca 1785. From Cayn, Kildonan par, SUT. To York Factory, Hudson Bay, arr 26 Aug 1815; thence to Red River. Pioneer settler. Wife Catherine with him, and ch: 1. Hugh, aged 10; 2. Ann, aged 7; 3. John, aged 5; 4. Donald, aged 1. **LSC 326**.

10408 POLSON, Margaret. From Paisley, RFW. d/o William P. To Kingston, ONT. m 1865, Rev John Clark Murray, qv, and founded the Daughters of the Empire. **FES vii 647**.

10409 POLSON, Mary, b 1767. From Kildonan par, SUT. To York Factory, Hudson Bay, arr 25 Aug 1815; thence to Red River. Wife of James Sutherland, qv. **LSC 325**.

10410 PONTON, Mungo, d 16 Mar 1849. From Edinburgh, but sometime in Inverness. To Belleville, Hastings Co, ONT. Physician. **DGH 31 May 1849**.

10411 POOL, John. From Annan, DFS. To Ekfrid Twp, Middlesex Co, ONT, 1841. Wife Janet, 1789–1875. Son Irving, res Strathroy, Adelaide Twp. **CAE 35**.

10412 POOL, William, ca 1769–5 Nov 1813. From Annan, DFS. s/o William P, North Street. To Markham, York Co, ONT, and d there. **Ts Annan**.

10413 PORTER, John. To Lanark Co, ONT, 1821; stld Lot 8, Con 1, North Sherbrooke Twp. **HCL 74**.

10414 PORTER, John, ca 1792–1843. From ABD. To Chatham, Northumberland Co, NB. Wife Catherine, ca 1800–11 Jan 1868. They had, prob with other ch: 1. George, 1827-59; 2. Mary, 1840-77. **DC 4 Dec 1978**.

10415 PORTEOUS, Alexander, b ca 1836. From PEE. s/o William and Margaret P. To East Whitby Twp, Durham Co, ONT. m Margaret Burns, 8 Nov 1861. **DC 18 Jan 1980**.

10416 PORTEOUS, James, ca 1820–1 May 1848. From Hoddam, DFS. s/o William P. in Kirtlebridge. To ONT, ca 1840. Drowned in the Madawaska River, Nipissing Co. **Ts Hoddam**.

10417 PORTEOUS, John. Poss from Aberdeen. To Chatham, Northumberland Co, NB, <1827. m Helenor Perley, who d 1 Aug 1828. **DC 4 Oct 1978**.

10418 PORTEOUS, John. From Kilmarnock, AYR. To Tatamagouche, Colchester Co, NS, prob <1835. m Miss Wilson. Dau Elizabeth. **NSN 5/3**.

10419 PORTEOUS, Rev John, b 1816. From Maybole, AYR. s/o Thomas P, craftsman. Matric Univ of Glasgow, 1831, and studied theology at the United Secession Hall.

To St Catharines, Lincoln Co, ONT, and was min there. **GMA 12769; SH**.

10420 PORTEOUS, Mary, ca 1801–4 Oct 1881. From Kilmarnock, AYR. To Hamilton, ONT. m Henry Cowan. **Ts Mt Albion**.

10421 PORTEOUS, Thomas, b ca 1770. From LKS. To Montreal, QUE, ca 1785. m Olive Everett, ch. **DC 6 Jan 1981**.

10422 PORTEOUS, William, ca 1800-38. Poss from Aberdeen. To Chatham, Northumberland Co, NB. Carpenter. m Elspeth Brayden, d 1839. Son William, d 1838. **DC 4 Oct 1978**.

PORTEOUS, Mrs William. See JOHNSTONE, Jean.

10423 POTTER, Agnes. From Kirkmichael, DFS. Niece of Janet P, qv. To Kent Co, 1831. m (i) Joseph Jardine, ch; (ii) William McNaught, further ch. **DC 15 Nov 1980**.

POTTER, Mrs James. See PATERSON, Mary.

10424 POTTER, Janet, 1802–1909. From Kirkmichael par, DFS. d/o James P, weaver. To CAN on the *Isabella*, 1833; stld Kouchibouguac, Kent Co, NB. m James Patterson, qv. **DC 15 Nov 1980**.

10425 POTTER, William, ca 1818–23 May 1855. From Torthorwald, DFS. s/o James P, farmer in East Roucan, and Agnes Kirkpatrick. To Montreal, QUE, and d there. **Ts Torthorwald**.

10426 POTTS, Mary. From Jedburgh, ROX. To QUE <1766; stld Woodfield. Wife of Thomas Ainslie, qv. **Jedburgh OPR 792/4**.

10427 POWRIE, James. From PER. To ONT, ca 1850. m Jessie Maitland. **DC 12 Apr 1970**.

10428 PRENTICE, George. To Pictou, NS, on the *Lulan*, ex Glasgow, 17 Aug 1848. Wife Jane with him. **DC 12 Jul 1979**.

10429 PRENTICE, James. Prob from RFW. s/o James P. To ONT <1855. **SH**.

10430 PRIMROSE, Alexander. From Rothiemay, BAN. bro/o James P, merchant. To Halifax, NS, <1829. Barrister. **HNS iii 259**.

10431 PRIMROSE, James, b 24 Jun 1802. Prob b Grange, BAN. s/o Rev John P, Antiburgher min, and Helen Grant. To Halifax, NS, 1822; stld later in Pictou. m (i) 1829, Annie, d/o John Gordon, ch: 1. Clarence, b 1830; 2. Howard, b 1832; 3. Gordon, dy. m (ii) 1834, Eliza Brown. **SA ix 188; HNS iii 259**.

10432 PRIMROSE, John Wilson, 1801-68. From East Calder, MLN. s/o Rev John P, Burgher min, and Janet Wilson. To Halifax, NS, 1830; stld poss Cornwallis. Physician. m Ann Chipman, ch: 1. John, b 1836; 2. Samuel, b 1838; 3. Thomas H, b 1840; 4. William, b 1843; 5. James, b 1846; 6. Edward, b 1850; 7. Frederick, b 1855; 8. Elizabeth. **UPC i 611; HNS iii 259**.

10433 PRINGLE, Alexander, ca 1777–17 Sep 1850. From ROX. To Kingston, ONT. **DGH 17 Oct 1850**.

10434 PRINGLE, James. Prob from ELN. To CAN <1843. **SH**.

10435 PRINGLE, John, 1798–1868. From Eildon, Melrose par, ROX. To Waterloo Co, ONT, ca 1854; stld Ayr. Wife Jane, b 1820, with him, and ch: 1. Robert; 2. Helen; 3. Agnes; 4. William, qv; 5. Margaret; 6. John, b ca 1838. **DC 8 Nov 1981**.

10436 PRINGLE, Margaret. From Athelstaneford, ELN. To Megantic Co, QUE, ca 1830. Wife of Alexander Learmonth, qv. **DC 15 Feb 1980**.

PRINGLE, Mrs Thomas. See BROWN, Margaret, in the ADDENDA.

10437 PRINGLE, William, ca 1835–1914. From Eildon, Melrose par, ROX. s/o John P, qv, and wife Jane. To Waterloo Co, ONT, ca 1854; stld Ayr. m Margaret Young, 1843–1923, ch: 1. John, 1866–1949; 2. Adam, 1870–1936; 3. Margaret, 1873–1928; 4. Helen, 1876–1968; 5. Isabella, 1873–1928; 6. Grace, d 1965. **DC 8 Nov 1981**.

10438 PROUDFOOT, James, ca 1797–5 Oct 1866. From DFS. To Pictou Co, NS, 1830, and bur Salt Springs. Wife Mary Reid, qv, with him. Son Thomas, ca 1835–9 May 1877. **DC 22 Jun 1980**.

10439 PROUDFOOT, Rev John James Aitchison, 1821–1903. From Pitrodie, PER. s/o Rev William P, qv, and Isobel Aitchison, qv. To Middlesex Co, ONT, 1832. Min at Avonbank, later London, and lecturer at Knox Coll, Toronto. m 1854, Alathea Mary Coleman, St Marys, ch. **HGD 214; MDB 609**.

10440 PROUDFOOT, Robert. From PER. s/o Rev William P, qv, and Isobel Aitchison, qv. To ONT, 1832, and stld Colborne Twp, Huron Co. m Margaret Darlington. Son William, 1859–1922, Canadian senator. **MDB 609**.

10441 PROUDFOOT, Rev William, 1787–16 Jan 1851. From Manor, PEE. Burgher min at Pitrodie, PER, 1813-32. To ONT, 1832; stld London, Middlesex Co. App Professor of Theology at Knox Coll, Toronto. m Isobel Aitchison, qv, ch: 1. Rev John James Aitchison, qv; 2. William, jr, qv; 3. Robert, qv. **BNA 827; UPC ii 579; HGD 214; MDB 609**.

10442 PROUDFOOT, William, jr, 9 Nov 1823–4 Aug 1903. s/o Rev William P, qv, and Isobel Aitchison, qv. To ONT, 1832. Lawyer, and became Professor of Roman Law, Jurisprudence and English Law at Univ of Toronto. m (i) 1853, d/o John Thomson, Toronto; (ii) Emily, d/o Adam Cook, Hamilton, ONT. **BNA 912; MDB 609**.

10443 PROWD, Elizabeth. From Glasgow. To Kincardine, Bruce Co, ONT, 1849. Wife of James Reid, qv. **DC 17 Nov 1981**.

10444 PURCELL, Archibald. To Aldborough Twp, Elgin Co, ONT, 1848. Farmer, Lot 5, Con 3. **PDA 67**.

10445 PURCELL, Dugald. Prob from ARL. To Aldborough Twp, Elgin Co, ONT, ca 1836. m Mrs Jean Anderson. Son William, res Rodney. **PDA 65**.

10446 PURDIE, Jane. From West Calder, MLN. Prob sis/o Samuel P, qv. To QUE on the *Atlas*, ex Greenock, 11 Jul 1815; stld Bathurst Twp, Lanark Co, ONT. Wife of James Bryce, qv. **SEC 1; HCL 16, 232**.

10447 PURDIE, Samuel, b ca 1770. From West Calder, MLN. Prob bro/o Jane P, qv. To QUE on the *Atlas*, ex Greenock, 11 Jul 1815; stld Lot 12, Con 1, Bathurst Twp,

Lanark Co, ONT. Wright. Wife Isobel McKechnie, qv. **SEC 1; HCL 16, 232**.

10448 PURDIE, William. From Bridgeton, Glasgow. To QUE on the *Commerce*, ex Greenock, 11 May 1821, and d at Prescott, ONT, on the way to Lanark Co. Agent for the Trongate Emigration Society. Wife d on voyage, leaving 2 ch. **DC 20 Jul 1982**.

10449 PURDIE, William, 1808-97. From LKS, poss Lesmahagow. To Scarborough, York Co, ONT, 1832. Farmer. **DC 29 Mar 1981**.

10450 PURDOM, Alexander. From Hawick, ROX. s/o Richard P, joiner, and Isabella Elliot. To Middlesex Co, ONT, 1849. m Margaret Hunter, qv, ch: 1. Richard; 2. John, contractor; 3. Thomas, 1853–1923, QC; 4. Alexander, solicitor. **THS 1848/23; 1935/75; DC 29 Sep 1964**.

10451 PURDON, Robert, b 1786. From Trongate, Glasgow. To QUE, ex Greenock, on the *George Canning*, 14 Apr 1821; stld poss Lanark Co, ONT. Wife Jane Hunter, qv, with him. **DC 26 Nov 1980**.

10452 PURSE, John, b 12 Dec 1732. From Elgin. s/o Alexander P, tailor, and Isabel Blenshel. To QUE <1769. Merchant. **SG xiii/3 33**.

10453 PURVES, John, 1770–1847. From Swinton, BEW. To Halifax, NS, prob <1815; stld later Pictou Co. **DC 28 Jan 1981**.

10454 PURVIS, George, ca 1839–27 Oct 1876. From Arbroath, ANS. s/o John P. and Elizabeth Findlay. To ONT. **Ts Arbroath Abbey**.

10455 PURVIS, John, ca 1823–28 Mar 1864. From Arbroath, ANS. s/o John P. and Elizabeth Findlay. To ONT. **Ts Arbroath Abbey**.

10456 PYPER, George A. From Edinburgh. Rel to William P, 1797–1861, Professor of Humanity, St Andrews. To Montreal, QUE, <1844, later to Toronto, ONT. **SGC 526**.

Q

10457 QUARRIE, Agnes, 10 Jul 1795–13 Nov 1879. From ROX. To Halton Co, ONT, ca 1818; stld Esquesing Twp. Wife of Andrew Laidlaw, qv, m 24 May 1816. **LDW 15 Mar 1968**.

R

10458 RAE, Cecilia, d <1860. From Swinton, BEW. wid/o John Strauchon, 1761–1840, parochial schoolmaster. To ONT, and d Sydenham, Grey Co. **Ts Swinton**.

10459 RAE, David, b 1821. From DFS. To Glengarry Co, ONT, <1837. Served in the Patriots War, 1837/38. **DC 4 Mar 1965**.

10460 RAE, Helen, ca 1790–22 Oct 1863. Prob from Blackwoodhouse, Middlebie par, DFS. To Ekfrid Twp, Middlesex Co, ONT. m John Beckton. **CAE 10**.

10461 RAE, James. To QUE on the *David of London*, ex Greenock, 19 May 1821; stld prob Lanark Co, ONT. **HCL 239**.

10462 RAE, James, ca 1811–25 Jan 1904. From Ecclefechan, DFS. To QUE, 1852; stld Hamilton, ONT.

Farmer and magistrate. m Isabella Lockerby, who d ca 1852; and re-m. ch incl: 1. John; 2. Andrew; 3. James; 4. George; 5. Robert; 6. Matthew; 7. William.   **CAE 75**.

10463   RAE, John, 1 Jun 1796–14 Jul 1872. From Footdee, Aberdeen. s/o John R. and Margaret Cuthbert. Grad MA, Marischall Coll, Aberdeen, 1815, and studied medicine at Edinburgh, 1815-17. To Montreal, QUE, 1822; later to Boston, MA. Author and scientist. **FAM ii 407; SNQ i/2 174; MDB 616**.

10464   RAE, John, 30 Sep 1813–22 Jul 1893. From Stromness, OKI. s/o John R, HBCo agent. Grad as a surgeon at Edinburgh, 1833, and joined HBCo. Took part in first land expedition in search of Sir John Franklin, 1847, and in 1851 commanded a search party which examined Wolaston Land. Various explorations and telegraphic surveys. FRS, 1880; Hon LLD, Edinburgh. m 1860, Catharine Jane Alicia, d/o Maj George Ash Thompson, no ch.   **IBD 420; CBD 774; MDB 616**.

10465   RAE, Robert, 1803-32. From LKS, poss Lesmahagow. To Scarborough, York Co, ONT, 1832. **DC 29 Mar 1981**.

10466   RAE, William Glen, ca 1809–Oct 1845. From Wyre, OKI. s/o John R. To Montreal, QUE. Emp with HBCo, and d CA.   **DGH 6 Nov 1845**.

10467   RAEBURN, Catherine. Prob from Aberdeen. d/o — R. and — Marnoch. To Montreal, QUE. m James Morice.   **SH**.

10468   RALPH, Jane, b ca 1795. From Yarrow, SEL. To Montreal, QUE, arr 22 Aug 1831; stld Port Dover, Norfolk Co, ONT. Wife of Robert Turnbull, qv. **DC 29 Jun 1979**.

10469   RALSTON, Jane, 1826–1919. From Campbeltown, ARL. To Niagara Twp, Lincoln Co, ONT, ca 1842.   **DC 17 May 1972**.

10470   RALSTON, Nathaniel, d 3 Mar 1858. From Sorbie, WIG. To Montreal, QUE, ca 1846. Emp with Muir & Sons, merchants.   **DGH 5 Mar 1858**.

10471   RAMSAY, Archibald, 1756–1839. From Ugadale, Campbeltown, ARL. s/o John R, qv, and Margaret Taylor, qv. To Malpeque, Prince Co, PEI, on the Annabella, ex Campbeltown, 27 Jul 1770; stld Beech Point. m 26 Feb 1788, Helen Montgomery, qv, ch: 1. Mary, b 1788; 2. John, b 1790, Mem of the House of Assembly; 3. Margaret, 1792–1861; 4. Hugh, 1795–1881; 5. Donald, 1798–1879, MLC; 6. Archibald, 1800-73; 7. Helen, 1804-70; 8. Norman McLeod, 1808-60.   **DC 18 May 1981**.

10472   RAMSAY, Donald, b May 1748. From Ugadale, Campbeltown, ARL. s/o John R, qv, and Margaret Taylor, qv. To Malpeque, Prince Co, PEI, on the Annabella, ex Campbeltown, 27 Jul 1770; stld Low Point. Farmer. m Mary McMillan, qv, ch: 1. John; 2. Neil; 3. Donald; 4. Malcolm; 5. Michael; 6. Archibald; 7. Angus; 8. Mary; 9. Eleanor.   **DC 18 May 1981**.

10473   RAMSAY, Edward. Prob from Campbeltown, ARL. Neph of John R, qv. To Malpeque, Prince Co, PEI, on the Annabella, ex Campbeltown, 27 Jul 1770; stld Malpeque. m Flora McKay, 13 Feb 1790, ch: 1. Margaret, b 1791; 2. Barbara; 3. Neil, b 1794; 4. Malcolm, b 1796; 5. Archibald, b 1798; 6. John, b 1800; 7. Jane, b 1802; 8. Nancy, b 1804; 9. Flora, b 1806; 10. Elizabeth,

b 1809; 11. Mary, b 1811; 12. Donald, b 1814; 13. Rachael, b 1817.   **DC 18 May 1981**.

10474   RAMSAY, George, 23 Oct 1770–21 Mar 1838. From Dalhousie Castle, Cockpen, MLN. s/o George, 8th Earl of Dalhousie, and Elizabeth Glen. Succ as 9th Earl, 1807. Lt Gov of NS, 1816; Gov Gen of CAN, 1819-28. m 1805, Christian, d/o Charles Broun of Colstoun, ch: 1. George, Lord Ramsay; 2. Charles, 1807-17; 3. James Andrew, 10th Earl.   **BNA 493; SP iii 105; Dalhousie Papers, SRO**.

10475   RAMSAY, George, 1816–26 Mar 1891. To Sombra Twp, Lambton Co, ONT, <1836. m 26 Jan 1841, Jane Ann Mary, d/o Peter Grant, qv, and Elizabeth Jane Grant, qv, ch.   **DC 4 Oct 1979**.

10476   RAMSAY, Hew. From Edinburgh. To Montreal, QUE, <6 Sep 1842, when m Agnes, d/o Robert Armour.   **DGH 6 Oct 1842**.

10477   RAMSAY, John. From Ugadale, Campbeltown, ARL. To Malpeque, Prince Co, PEI, on the Annabella, ex Campbeltown, 27 Jul 1770; stld Malpeque. Farmer. m Margaret Taylor, qv, ch: 1. Donald, qv; 2. Neil, qv; 3. Malcolm, qv; 4. Archibald, qv; 5. John, jr, qv; 6. Janet, b 1760; 7. Angus, b 1764, went to USA; 8. Janet, b 1766; 9-10. Mary and Catherine, twins, b 1768.   **SG vii/4 15; DC 20 Dec 1981**.

10478   RAMSAY, John, jr, b ca 1758. s/o John R, qv, and Margaret Taylor, qv. To Malpeque, Prince Co, PEI, on the Annabella, ex Campbeltown, 27 Jul 1770; stld Cape Malpeque. m Catherine McKay, ch: 1. Mary; 2. Nellie; 3. Christy; 4. Donald; 5. John, drowned in early manhood; 6. Alexander; 7. Jennie; 8. Sarah. **DC 18 May 1981**.

10479   RAMSAY, Malcolm, b ca 1753, nr Campbeltown, ARL. s/o John R, qv, and Malcolm Taylor, qv. To Malpeque, Prince Co, PEI, on the Annabella, ex Campbeltown, 27 Jul 1770. Magistrate. m Margaret Murphy, qv, ch: 1. Jennie; 2. Nellie; 3. John; 4. Donald; 5. Mary; 6. Margaret; 7. Archibald; 8. Charles; 9. James.   **DC 18 May 1981**.

10480   RAMSAY, Malcolm. Prob from Campbeltown, ARL. Neph of John R, qv. To Malpeque, Prince Co, PEI, on the Annabella, ex Campbeltown, 27 Jul 1770; stld Indian River. m Miss McNeil, ch: 1. Betsy, b 1788; 2. Malcolm, b 1789; 3. Nellie, b 1790; 4. Penny, b 1793; 5. James, b 1795; 6. Nancy, b 1797, dy; 7. Flora, b 1799; 8. Charles, b 1802; 9. Barbara, b 1804; 10. Jennie, b 1806; 11. Edward, b 1808.   **DC 18 May 1981**.

10481   RAMSAY, Marjory Jardine, 1832-89. From Linlithgow, WLN. d/o James R. and Helen Christie. To Toronto, ONT, <1859, when m Archibald McMurchy, qv.   **SG xxx/1 19**.

10482   RAMSAY, Neil, b May 1751. From Campbeltown, ARL. s/o John R, qv, and Margaret Taylor, qv. To Malpeque, Prince Co, PEI, on the Annabella, ex Campbeltown, 27 Jul 1770; stld Malpeque Bay. m Mary Cole, ch: 1. John; 2. George; 3. Dougald; 4. Edward; 5. Neil; 6. Donald; 7. Benjamen; 8. Jennie; 9. Mary.   **DC 18 May 1981**.

10483   RAMSAY, Robert. Prob from Edinburgh. bro/o David R, merchant in Leith. To Montreal, QUE, <1850.   **SH**.

10484 RAMSAY, Thomas Kennedy, 2 Sep 1826–22 Dec 1886. From Ayr. To QUE <1855. Founded the *Lower Canada Jurist* in 1857, and became an asst judge of the superior Court of Quebec. **BNA 925; MDB 618.**

10485 RAMSAY, William, 1775–1835. To Annapolis Royal, Annapolis Co, NS, 1818. Army sergeant, discharged. **DC 29 Jan 1980.**

10486 RAMSEY, George, b 23 Nov 1816. To ONT ca 1836; stld poss Kent Co. m Isabella Hermiston, qv. **DC 15 Apr 1980.**

10487 RANKIN, Alexander. From Carnach, Glencoe, ARL. To Montreal, QUE, ex Fort William, arr Sep 1802; stld E ONT. Wife and 2 ch with him. **MCM 1/4 25.**

10488 RANKIN, Alexander, b 7 Feb 1820. From INV. To PEI <1840; later to Pictou Is, NS. **NSN 10/3.**

10489 RANKIN, Angus. From Lochaber, INV. s/o John R. To Mabou, Inverness Co, NS, <1820. m Catherine Rankin, ch: 1. Alexander; 2. Finlay; 3. Donald; 4. Duncan; 5. John; 6. Jessie; 7. Anne; 8. John. **MP 831.**

10490 RANKIN, C.D. b ca 1777. To Charlottetown, PEI, on the *Humphreys*, ex Tobermory, 14 Jul 1806. Wife Flora, aged 24, with him, and inf s George. **PLH.**

10491 RANKIN, Duncan, b 1812. From Lochaber, INV. s/o John R. To Inverness Co, NS, 1843. m Isobel, d/o Finlay MacDonald, qv, ch: 1. Donald; 2. Finlay; 3. John; 4. Anne; 5. Angus; 6. Alexander; 7. Allan; 8. Catherine; 9. Margaret; 10. Mary. **MP 580, 810.**

10492 RANKIN, Hugh. From ARL. To Ekfrid Twp, Middlesex Co, ONT, 1835. **PCM 31.**

10493 RANKIN, John, b 1775. From Lochaber, INV. s/o John R. To Inverness Co, NS, 1801. m Catherine Beaton, qv, ch: 1. Donald; 2. John; 3. Duncan; 4. Hugh; 5. Margaret, 1800–89; 6. Mary. **MP 600, 814.**

10494 RANKIN, Margaret, 1782–18 Apr 1866. From Lochaber, INV. d/o John R. To Mabou, Inverness Co, NS, <1820. m James Fanning, farmer, no ch. **MP 843.**

10495 RANKIN, Margaret. From Lochaber, INV. sis/o Catherine R, wife of Angus R, qv. To Inverness Co, NS, <1820. m John MacMillan, qv. **MP 831.**

10496 RANKIN, William, ca 1783–30 Dec 1827. From STI. To Pictou Co, NS, and d there. **VSN No 2648.**

10497 RANNIE, Rev John, 1828–1910. From Walls, OKI. s/o John R, schoolmaster. Grad MA, Kings Coll, Aberdeen, 1846, and became schoolmaster at Coull, ABD. Ord for service in CAN and adm min of Chatham, Kent Co, ONT, 1859. Trans to All Saints Ch, British Guiana, 1876. Classical scholar. Son Dr Arthur, d Demerara. **KCG 297; FES vii 648, 673.**

10498 RATTRAY, Charles, d 1872. From PER. To Cornwall Twp, Stormont Co, ONT. Physician, educ Edinburgh. m Miss Chesley, ch. **SDG 449.**

10499 RAY, Jessie, b ca 1801. Prob rel to Margaret R, qv. To St Gabriel de Valcartier, QUE, poss <1855. **Census 1861.**

10500 RAY, Margaret, b ca 1807. Prob rel to Jessie R, qv. To St Gabriel de Valcartier, QUE, poss <1855. **Census 1861.**

10501 REACH, Annie. From Rothes, ABD. To Halifax, NS; stld Musquodoboit Harbour, 1819. m John Anderson, qv. **HNS iii 521.**

10502 REDPATH, John, b 1796. From Earlston, BEW. To Montreal, QUE, 1816. Stonemason, and associated with Thomas McKay, qv, in building contracts, incl Rideau Canal, 1826-32. Sugar refiner, and Director of the Bank of Montreal, 1833-69. m 19 Dec 1818, Janet Macphie, and had, poss with other ch: 1. Betsy, b 1819; 2. Peter, 1821-94, merchant and philanthropist; 3. Mary; 4. Jane; 5. Helen; 6. Elizabeth. **SGC 388.**

REED. See also REID.

10503 REED, James. To QUE on the *Commerce*, Jun 1820; stld prob Lanark Co, ONT. **HCL 238.**

10504 REED, Jane. From Old Deer, ABD. To ONT, prob <1854. Wife of Alexander Clubb, qv. **DC 20 Sep 1979.**

10505 REED, William, b 18 Aug 1826. From Kilmarnock, AYR. s/o Dr James R, physician. To Montreal, QUE, arr Aug 1846. Customs broker; mem of Board of Trustees, St Gabriel Street Ch. **SGC 794.**

10506 REEKIE, George, 1795–1877. From Dundee, ANS. To Collingwood, Grey Co, ONT, ca 1848; later to Parry Sound. Capt of a lake steamer. m (i) Magdalene Cooper, qv, ch: 1. John, qv; 2. George, 1821-90. m (ii) Nancy McGuire Eaton, further ch: 3. Charles; 4. Albert; 5. Nancy; 6. dau. **DC 24 May 1979.**

10507 REEKIE, John, 1820-99. From Dundee, ANS. s/o George R, qv, and Magdalene Cooper, qv. To Collingwood Twp, Grey Co, ONT, ca 1848; stld Lot 26N, Con 7, and d at Heathcote. Farmer and weaver. m Agnes Kennedy, qv, ch: 1. George, 1846–1935; 2. Jessie, 1848-91; 3. Agnes; 4. Flora; 5. James; 6. William; 7. Mary; 8. Elizabeth; 9. John; 10. David; 11. Alexander, farmer. **DC 24 May 1979.**

10508 REEKIE, Rev Thomas Miller, ca 1820–ca 1904. From Glasgow. s/o Andrew R, merchant-burgess. Matric Univ of Glasgow, 1838. To CAN <1850. Congregational min. **GMA 13878.**

REID. See also REED.

10509 REID, Mrs Agnes. From BAN. Aunt of Andrew and Alexander MacDonald, qv. To QUE, prob <1833. **DC 6 Jan 1977.**

10510 REID, Agnes, b 21 Nov 1835, Johnstone, RFW. d/o Matthew R, qv, and Margaret Blackburn, qv. To Lanark Co, ONT, ca 1841. m 11 Sep 1868, William Miller. **DC 5 Feb 1981.**

10511 REID, Agnes, b ca 1811. From Dysart par, FIF. To Ashfield Twp, Huron Co, ONT, ca 1848. Wife of James Bogie, qv, m 3 Nov 1832. **Dysart OPR 426/6; DC 15 Jul 1979.**

10512 REID, Ann, b 1822. From Kildalton, Is Islay, ARL. d/o Robert R, qv, and Catherine Sinclair, qv. To ONT <1850. m Archibald McPhee, qv. **DC 1 Dec 1980.**

10513 REID, Elizabeth. Prob from DFS. d/o Robert R, qv, and wife Elizabeth. To Restigouche Co, NB, 1818. m 30 Aug 1829, David, s/o Robert Henderson. **DC 7 Feb 1981.**

10514 REID, Elizabeth Erskine, 22 Sep 1839–6 Feb 1905. From Elderslie, RFW. d/o Matthew R, qv, and

Margaret Blackburn, qv. To Lanark Co, ONT, ca 1841. m James Walker. **DC 5 Feb 1981**.

10515 REID, Francis, ca 1792–30 Mar 1888. From AYR. To ONT, prob <1850; stld poss Grey Co. m Ann Scott, qv. **DC 8 Mar 1977**.

10516 REID, George, 11 Feb 1755–Feb 1780. From New Machar, ABD. s/o Rev Thomas R, par min, and Elizabeth Reid, his cous. To NFD, and d there. **FES vi 67**.

10517 REID, George, b 31 Aug 1812. From Minto par, ROX. s/o James R, qv, and Margaret Scott. To ONT, ca 1843; stld prob Grey Co. Labourer. m Janet Grierson, qv, ch: 1. Helen, b 1839; 2. Margaret, b 1842, Jedburgh par. **DC 8 Mar 1977**.

10518 REID, Helen, 21 Apr 1811–16 Oct 1884. From Edinburgh. d/o John R. To Brantford, Brant Co, ONT, and d there. m William Keir, lawyer. **Ts Greyfriars**.

10519 REID, Rev Hugh, 1818-95. From Kildalton par, Is Islay, ARL. s/o Robert R, qv, and Catherine Sinclair, qv. To Wellington Co, ONT, <1850. Bur Erin Twp. m his cous, Margaret McKechnie, qv. **DC 1 Dec 1980**.

10520 REID, James, 1769–19 Jan 1848. From New Deer, ABD. s/o William R, feuar, and Jean Hatt. To Montreal, QUE, 1788. Studied law and was called to the Bar, 1794. App Judge of Court of Kings Bench at Montreal, and became Chief Justice, 1825. m Elizabeth McGillivray, qv. **SGC 105, 242; MDB 623**.

10521 REID, James, b 1788. To Pictou Co, NS, 1815; res Mount Thom, 1816. Labourer, 'poor but industrious,' m with 4 ch. **INS 39**.

10522 REID, James, 16 Mar 1805–8 Jun 1879. From DFS. s/o Robert R, qv, and wife Elizabeth. To Restigouche Co, NB, 1818, and bur New Mills. Farmer and blacksmith. m Anne McPherson, qv, ch:
1. Elizabeth, 1833-49; 2. Robert; 3. Margaret;
4. James McPherson; 5. John; 6. Alexander; 7. Mary;
8. Barbara; 9. Jane. **DC 7 Feb 1981**.

10523 REID, James. To Montreal, QUE, on the *Royal George*, ex Greenock, Jan 1827; stld Sarnia, ONT. Wife and 3 ch with him. **DC 19 Nov 1978**.

10524 REID, James, ca 1804–7 Aug 1883. From Inveravon, BAN. To Sombra Twp, Lambton Co, ONT, 1836, via NY and the Erie Canal. Farmer and lumberman. m Jane Grant, qv, ch: 1. John, b 20 Oct 1829; 2. George, 1831–1917; 3. William, b 1832, dy; 4. James, b 10 Feb 1835; 5. Margaret, b 14 May 1838; 6-7. Charles and Elspet, twins, b 12 May 1840; 8. Alexander, b 7 Jun 1842; 9. Elizabeth, b 31 Jul 1844. **DC 4 Oct 1979**.

10525 REID, James, 1781–1853. From Minto par, ROX. To ONT, ca 1843; stld prob Grey Co. Ploughman. m Margaret Scott, 1778–1836, ch: 1. James, b 1809; 2. George, qv; 3. Robert, b 1814; 4. John, b 1817; 5. William, b 1819; 6. Francis, b 1822; 7. Helen, b 1825; 8. David, b 1828; 9. Peter Purves, b 1830. **DC 8 Mar 1977**.

10526 REID, James. To Pictou, NS, on the *London*, arr 11 Apr 1848. **DC 15 Jul 1979**.

10527 REID, James. From Glasgow. To Kincardine, Bruce Co, ONT, 1849. m Elizabeth Prowd, qv, ch:

1. John, b 1843; 2. William; 3. Elizabeth. **DC 17 Nov 1981**.

10528 REID, James, 1823-81. From Kildalton, Is Islay, ARL. s/o Robert R, qv, and Catherine Sinclair, qv. To ONT, 1849; stld Cheltenham, later Erin Twp, Wellington Co. m his cous, Catherine McKechnie, qv, and had ch. **DC 1 Dec 1980**.

10529 REID, John, b ca 1778. From PER. To Pictou, NS, on the *Commerce*, ex Port Glasgow, 10 Aug 1803. Farmer. Wife Eliza, aged 23, with him, ch: 1. Alexander, aged 3 ¼; 2. Ann, aged 1 ¼. **PLC**.

10530 REID, John. Prob rel to William R, qv. To QUE on the *William & Ann*, 1815; stld Lot 8, Con 11, Drummond Twp, Lanark Co, ONT. **HCL 234**.

10531 REID, John, 1778–1851. From Kirriemuir, ANS. To Ormestown, Dorchester Co, QUE, 1847. Farmer. m Mary Guthrie, qv. Dau Mary, qv. **DC 21 Jul 1969**.

10532 REID, Margaret. Prob from DFS. d/o Robert R, qv, and wife Elizabeth. To Restigouche Co, NB, 1818. m 30 Aug 1829, Daniel Malcolm. **DC 7 Feb 1981**.

10533 REID, Margaret, ca 1797–1869. From Lesmahagow, LKS. To Scarborough, York Co, ONT, 1833. wid/o John Muir, mason. **DC 29 Mar 1981**.

10534 REID, Margaret, 22 Aug 1841–26 Mar 1911. From Elderslie, RFW. d/o Matthew R, qv, and Margaret Blackburn, qv. To Lanark Co, ONT, ca 1841. m Danny Munro. **DC 5 Feb 1981**.

10535 REID, Mary. Prob from DFS. d/o Robert R, qv, and wife Elizabeth. To Restigouche Co, NB, 1818. m James McDonald, <1851. **DC 7 Feb 1981**.

10536 REID, Mary, ca 1801–18 Aug 1881. From DFS. To NS, 1830; stld Salt Springs, Pictou Co. Wife of James Proudfoot, qv. **DC 10 Dec 1980**.

10537 REID, Mary. From Kirriemuir, ANS. d/o John R, qv, and Mary Guthrie, qv. To QUE, 1841. Wife of Charles Steele, qv. **DC 21 Jul 1969**.

10538 REID, Matthew, 1815-93. From Inchinnan, RFW. s/o William R. and Elizabeth Erskine. To Lanark Co, ONT, ca 1841; stld nr Middleville. m (i) Margaret Blackburn, qv, ch: 1. Agnes, qv; 2. William, qv; 3. Elizabeth Erskine, qv; 4. Margaret, qv; 5. Mary, b Bathurst, 1843; 6. Robert, b 1845, Lanark Co; 7. Isabella, 1848–1931; 8. Jane, qv; 9. Bertha, b 1852; 10. Matthew, 1855–1927. m (ii) Mary, d/o Matthew Baird, qv, and Ann Robertson. **Abbey OPR 599/7; DC 5 Feb 1981**.

10539 REID, Peter, b 1776. From Old Patrick, DNB. To QUE, prob 1830; stld Lanark Co, ONT. Dau Agnes, b ca 1824. **SG xx/1 11**.

10540 REID, Peter, ca 1806–23 Feb 1887. Prob from AYR. To Hamilton, ONT. m Isabella McRobert, qv. Dau Isabella, 1845-88. **Ts Mt Albion**.

10541 REID, Robert, b ca 1774. Prob from DFS. To Restigouche Co, NB, 1818; stld Lots 49-50. Wife Elizabeth with him, ch: 1. Robert, jr, qv; 2. James, qv; 3. Elizabeth, qv; 4. Margaret, qv; 5. Mary, qv. **SG xxvii/2 126; DC 7 Feb 1981**.

10542 REID, Robert, jr. Prob from DFS. s/o Robert R, qv, and wife Elizabeth. To Restigouche Co, NB, 1818. m 18 Mar 1833, Mary Alexander, and res nr Maple Green. **DC 7 Feb 1981**.

10543 REID, Robert, 1810-80. From LKS, poss Lesmahagow or Strathaven. To Scarborough, York Co, ONT, ca 1833. **DC 29 Mar 1981**.

10544 REID, Robert. From Lower Kildean, Kildalton, Is Islay, ARL. To Erin Twp, Wellington Co, ONT, 1844. m 26 Mar 1817, Catherine Sinclair, qv, ch: 1. Rev Hugh, qv; 2. Peter, b 1819; 3. Ann, qv; 4. James, qv; 5. Donald, b 1824. **DC 1 Dec 1980**.

10545 REID, Susan, ca 1818–1905. From Sanquhar, DFS. To Melbourne, Richmond Co, QUE, prob <1850. Wife of John Scot, qv. **MGC 15 Jul 1980**.

10546 REID, William. Prob rel to John R, qv. To QUE on the *William & Ann*, 1815; stld Lot 8, Con 11, Drummond Twp, Lanark Co, ONT. **HCL 234**.

10547 REID, William, ca 1813–20 Apr 1884. Prob from DFS. To Egremont, Grey Co, ONT, <1835. m Helen Gillespie, qv, ch: 1. Helen, b 1835; 2. Mary, b 1838; 3. Jane Patterson, b 1839; 4. William, b 1841; 5. Hugh, b 1843; 6. Margaret, b 1844; 7. Jane, b 1845; 8. Hugh, b 1847; 9. John, b 1849; 10. Janet, b 1851; 11. Thomas James, b 1853; 12. Henry, b 1855; 13. Godfrey MacDonald, b 1858. **DC 20 Feb 1978**.

10548 REID, Rev William, 10 Dec 1816–21 Jan 1896. From Kildrummy, ABD. Grad MA, Kings Coll, Aberdeen, 1833. Adm min of Grafton and Colborne, Northumberland Co, ONT, 1840. Joined FC, 1843. Min of Picton, Prince Edward Co. Moderator of Presb Ch, 1879; DD, Queens Univ, 1876. **KCG 288; FES vii 648; MDB 624**.

10549 REID, William, 20 Sep 1837–7 Mar 1905. From Elderslie, RFW. s/o Matthew R, qv, and Margaret Blackburn, qv. To Lanark Co, ONT, ca 1841. m Jessie Browning. **DC 5 Feb 1981**.

10550 RENNIE, Alexander. From ABD. To Bon Accord, Nichol Twp, Wellington Co, ONT, 1836. m Margaret Webster, ch: 1. Margaret; 2. John; 3. Christina; 4. Jean. **EHE 93**.

10551 RENNIE, Hercules. From Montrose, ANS. To Halifax, NS. Army officer. m Margaretta Ness, ch: 1. Hercules; 2. Thomas, b Halifax, 28 Feb 1815; 3. Robert, b Mouse Is, 17 Apr 1817. **Montrose OPR 312/5**.

10552 RENNY, Agnes. From Falkirk, STI. d/o George R. To Sydney, Cape Breton Co, NS, 1815. Wife of John 'Agricola' Young, qv. **MLA 375; MDB 819**.

10553 RENTON, John, 1816-98. From Lauder, BEW. To Guelph Twp, Wellington Co, ONT, 1831, and d Egremont Twp. Farmer and blacksmith. m Isabella Elliott, qv, and had ch. **DC 11 Nov 1981**.

10554 RENTON, Thomas. From DFS. To Pictou Co, NS, <1825. Wool-carder, later lumberman. m Jane Fullarton, qv, ch: 1. James, went to AUS; 2. Dougal, b 1829; 3. Fergus A, b 1833; 4. John, 1842-93. **HNS iii 247; DC 24 Mar 1979**.

10555 RENWICK, Sarah, d 1892. From DFS. d/o Walter and Mary R. To Darlington, Durham Co, ONT, 1835. m James Maitland, qv, in 1841. **DC 7 Jan 1971**.

10556 RETTIE, John, ca 1793–16 May 1875. From BAN. To Pictou, NS, and d Salt Springs. m Christina Callie, qv. **DC 27 Oct 1979**.

10557 RICHARDS, Joseph, b 20 Mar 1743. s/o James R. and Rachel Taylor, Innerpeffray, PER. To PEI, Apr 1770. **Muthill OPR 386A/1**.

10558 RICHARDSON, Andrew. From Haddington, ELN. To Halifax, NS, ca 1790. Wife Catherine with him, and s Andrew, b Portsmouth, ENG, 15 Mar 1787. **DC 10 Nov 1982**.

10559 RICHARDSON, Charles, ca 1806–15 Jul 1855. From Lammonbie, Applegirth par, DFS. To Chatham, Northumberland Co, NB, and d there. **DGC 7 Aug 1855**.

10560 RICHARDSON, Cochrane Ray, b 7 Mar 1812. From ELN. d/o John R, gardener, Newbyth House, and Margaret Schulier. m at Edinburgh, 1833, James Dunlop, qv, and emig to Perth, Lanark Co, ONT, the same year. **DC 15 Aug 1967**.

10561 RICHARDSON, Isabella, 1815–5 Sep 1854. From Hawick, ROX. d/o John R, spinner, and Esther Robson. To Galt Twp, Waterloo Co, ONT, and d at Doon. **THS 1936/34**.

10562 RICHARDSON, James, 29 Mar 1810–18 Nov 1883. From PER. To QUE, prob <1854; stld Beauharnois Co. Farmer and geologist. Worked in the north-west with the Geological Survey of Canada. Richardson Inlet, Queen Charlotte Islands, named after him. **MDB 627**.

10563 RICHARDSON, John, ca 1755–18 May 1831. From Portsoy, BAN. s/o John R. and — Phyn. To Montreal, QUE, 1787, having been sometime in NY State. Became partner in firm of Forsyth, Richardson & Co, merchants who supplied the XYCo traders. MLA and a founder mem of the Bank of Montreal. ch: 1. Eweretta, d 1808; 2. Mrs Ogden. **SGC 86**.

10564 RICHARDSON, Sir John, 5 Nov 1787–5 Jun 1865. From DFS. s/o Gabriel R, a friend of the poet Burns, and Anne Mundle. Grad MD, Univ of Edinburgh, 1816, and qualified MRCS. Served as a naval surgeon before joining Sir John Franklin on his journeys in North America, 1819-27, and assisted in the exploration of the Arctic shores. Author, and knighted 1846. m (i) 1818, d/o William Stiven, Leith; (ii) 1833, d/o John Booth, Stickney; (iii) 1847, d/o Archibald Fletcher, Edinburgh. **IBD 423; CBD 789; MDB 627**.

10565 RICHARDSON, Margaret, ca 1796–26 May 1877. From Lochmaben, DFS. To ONT, 1833, and d Roseville, Dumfries Twp, Waterloo Co. m Alexander Thomson. **CAE 39**.

10566 RICHARDSON, Thomas, b ca 1833. From Parton, KKD. s/o William R, qv. To Nichol Twp, Wellington Co, ONT, 1852. Son William, b Peel Twp. **DC 19 Sep 1979**.

10567 RICHARDSON, William. From Parton, KKD. To Nichol Twp, Wellington Co, ONT, 1852. Wife Margaret with him. Son Thomas, qv. **DC 19 Sep 1979**.

10568 RICHARDSON, William, ca 1775–3 Mar 1840. From Roberton par, ROX. To Oxford Co, ONT, ca 1833, and d there. Widower of Margaret Laing, d 1831. Son Robert, b 28 Aug 1804, stld Oxford Co. **Ts Borthwick Wa's; Roberton OPR 777/1**.

10569 RICHMOND, James. Prob from Mauchline, AYR. bro/o George R. in Carleith. To NB <1758. Mason. **SH**.

10570 RICHMOND, George, d 1821. From LKS. To QUE, summer 1820; stld Dalhousie Twp, Lanark Co. Schoolteacher. Killed by a falling tree. **HCL 68**.

10571 RICHMOND, Henry, d 16 Sep 1833. From Sorn, AYR. s/o Henry R, farmer in Montgarswood, and Agnes Murray. To CAN, poss ONT, <1855. **DC 21 Mar 1981**.

10572 RICHMOND, James, b 1832. From Sorn, AYR. s/o Henry R, farmer in Montgarswood, and Agnes Murray. To CAN, prob <1855. **DC 21 Mar 1981**.

10573 RICHMOND, Janet, b 23 Nov 1817. From Sorn, AYR. d/o Henry R, farmer in Montgarswood, and first wife. To CAN <1855. **DC 21 Mar 1981**.

10574 RICHMOND, John, b 25 Jul 1837. From Sorn, AYR. s/o Henry R, farmer in Montgarswood, and Agnes Murray. To CAN, prob <1855. **DC 21 Mar 1981**.

10575 RICHMOND, Mary, b 13 Jan 1819. From Sorn, AYR. d/o Henry R, farmer in Montgarswood, and first wife. To CAN, prob <1855. **DC 21 Mar 1981**.

10576 RIDDELL, Andrew, d 1885. From Lilliesleaf, ROX. To St Catharines, Lincoln Co, ONT, 1850. Woollen manufacturer. m Catherine Cameron. Son Andrew. **DC 29 Sep 1964**.

10577 RIDDELL, Mary, b 1827. From Jedburgh, ROX. d/o — R. and — Scott. To CAN, prob ONT, <1850. m then, William Latham Blacker-Hamlin, from Drogheda, IRL, and had ch. **DC 6 Apr 1967**.

10578 RIDDELL, Walter, 1813–1904. From Eskdalemuir, DFS. To Northumberland Co, ONT, 1833. Farmer. m Mary Renwick. Son William. **DC 29 Sep 1964**.

10579 RIDDELL, William. From Hawick, ROX. s/o Walter R, tailor, who d 1849. To CAN. **SH**.

10580 RIDDELL, William. From Galashiels, SEL. s/o Robert R, grocer. To ONT <1855. **SH**.

10581 RIDDICK, Mrs Mary, ca 1766–ca 1857. From Bellridding, Ruthwell, DFS. To Stormont Co, ONT; stld Greenfield. wid/o James R. **DGH 20 Nov 1857**.

10582 RICHARD, Joseph. From DFS or KKD. To Pictou Co, NS, and stld west side of West River. Prob the man of this name listed as capable to bear arms, 1783. **HPC App C, D and E**.

10583 RINTOUL, Rev David. Missionary at Eday and Pharay, OKI, 1834. Min at St Catharines, Lincoln Co, ONT, 1841-45. **FES vii 648**.

10584 RINTOUL, Rev William, 30 Oct 1797–13 Sep 1851. From Kincardine-on-Forth, PER. s/o Robert R, merchant. Matric Univ of Glasgow, 1813. Min at Maryport, Cumberland, 1821. To Toronto, ONT, 1830, to become min of St Andrews Ch. Trans to Streetsville, 1834, and joined FC, 1844. Professor of Biblical Criticism, Knox Coll, Toronto, 1848-49. Adm min of St Gabriel Street Ch, Montreal, QUE, 1850. Son David. **GMA 8743; SGC 531; FES vii 649; SG xxx/1 20; MDB 631**.

10585 RITCHIE, Adam. From Johnstone, RFW. s/o John R. To Greenock Twp, Bruce Co, ONT, <1838. Farmer. By wife Elizabeth, ch: 1. John B; 2. Sterling; 3. William. **SH; DC 4 Oct 1980**.

10586 RITCHIE, Arthur. Rel to Robert R, qv. To Miramichi, Northumberland Co, NB, <1830; moved to Dalhousie, Restigouche Co, 1832. Lumber agent. **SR 20**.

10587 RITCHIE, Daniel. To Lanark Co, ONT, 1821; stld Lot 12, Con 1, North Sherbrooke Twp. **HCL 74**.

10588 RITCHIE, Elizabeth. Gr-dau of John R, qv, and Elizabeth Sterling. To Horton, Kings Co, NS, <1840. m 1841, John Christopher Taylor, of West Brook, Cumberland Co. **NSN 15/6**.

10589 RITCHIE, Jean, 1834–1909. From Glasgow. To Pugwash, Cumberland Co, NS, prob <1854. m Daniel C. Fraser. **DC 29 Oct 1980**.

10590 RITCHIE, John, b ca 1768. From Fintry, STI. To QUE on the *Atlas*, ex Greenock, 11 Jul 1815; stld Lot 10, Con 1, Bathurst Twp, Lanark Co, ONT. Blacksmith and farmer. Wife Janet Luke, qv, with him, and 9 ch, incl John. **SEC 2; HCL 16, 232**.

10591 RITCHIE, John. Poss from Johnstone, RFW. To Horton, Kings Co, NS, <1840. m Elizabeth Sterling or Stirling. **NSN 15/6**.

10592 RITCHIE, John. From Ecclefechan, DFS. To Toronto, ONT, autumn 1849; stld later Elmvale, Simcoe Co. **CAE 69**.

10593 RITCHIE, Mary, b 1807. From Sliddery, Kilmory par, Is Arran, BUT. To Charlo, Restigouche Co, NB, <1844. Wife of John Henderson, qv. **MAC 17**.

10594 RITCHIE, Robert. Rel to Arthur R, qv. To Miramichi, Northumberland Co, NB, <1830; moved to Dalhousie, Restigouche Co, 1832. Lumber agent. **SR 20**.

10595 RITCHIE, Thomas. From Brechin, ANS. s/o David R. Alumnus, Univ of Aberdeen, 1785. To NS. Magistrate. **FAM ii 63**.

10596 RITCHIE, William, d Jan 1865. From Wisebyhill, Kirkpatrick-Fleming, DFS. To Vaughan Twp, York Co, ONT, 1841. Moved ca 1851, to Flos Twp, Simcoe Co, where he purchased 200 acres. Became Postmaster at Elmvale. m Joan Murray, qv. **DC 21 Mar 1980**.

10597 ROACH, Rev Walter, 1808–27 Aug 1849. From Edinburgh. s/o Walter R. Educ Univ of Edinburgh. Ord at QUE as min of Beauharnois, St Louis and Chateauguay. Clerk to Presb of QUE, 1838-41, and to the Presb of Montreal, 1842-48. Moderator, Ch of Scotland Synod, 1847. **FES vii 649**.

10598 ROBB, Andrew, ca 1833–1907. From Abedeen. To ONT, and d Hamilton. m 1860, Catherine, d/o James Jackson, qv, and Jane Rutherford, qv, ch: 1. Jenny; 2. William; 3. John Archibald; 4. James A; 5. Minnie Anne; 6. Edwin G; 7. Andrew; 8. Belle; 9. Lillian; 10. Emma. **DC 23 Mar 1979**.

10599 ROBB, Rev Ralph, ca 1800-50. From Alloa, CLK. s/o William R, farmer, Logie. Matric Univ of Glasgow, 1815. Min of Strathkinnes Secession Ch, FIF, 1827-39, and of the Par Ch there, 1839-43, when he joined FC. To Halifax, NS, later to Hamilton, ONT, where min of Free Colonial Ch. **GMA 9438; FES v 244; UPC i 206**.

ROBERTON. See also ROBERTSON, ROBINSON and ROBSON.

10600 ROBERTON, James, 23 Jun 1810–25 Nov 1888. From LKS. s/o John R. of Lauchop, and Catherine Hozier. Matric Univ of Glasgow, 1823. To Thurlow Twp, Hastings Co, ONT, <1846. Farmer and officer of militia. Succ to estate of Lauchop, 1850, and retr to SCT. m 2 May 1846, Anastatia, 1825–1906; d/o Robert Hopkins and Ann Person, ch: 1. Catherine, 1846–1927; 2. Victoria, 1847–1927; 3. John of Lauchop, 1850–1906; 4. Mary Elizabeth, b 1848; 5. Robert Hopkins, b 1854; 6. Grace; 7. Isaiah, 1864-89, who purchased Lauchop. **GMA 11348; LDW 4 Oct 1971**.

ROBERTSON. See also ROBERTON, ROBINSON and ROBSON.

10601 ROBERTSON, Alexander, d 1822. From Crieff, PER. s/o Duncan R. of Struan, and Mey Nairn. Served as Col of the 82nd Regt, and was gr Is Merigomish, Pictou Co, NS. Seems not to have stld, but caused a large house to be built, called Struan. d unm, leaving his Canadian property to his neph, Lawrence Oliphant of Gask. **HPC App F; Burkes Landed Gentry, 1846, 1124**.

10602 ROBERTSON, Alexander, b 1771. From Fortingall, PER. s/o James R, qv, and wife Cathrine. To Charlottetown, PEI, on the Clarendon, ex Oban, 7 Aug 1808. Labourer. Wife Cathrine, aged 31, with him. **CPL**.

10603 ROBERTSON, Alexander, 1800-75. From Blair Atholl, PER. s/o James R, qv, and Jean Miller, qv. To PEI, 1808; stld Marshfield. m his cous Margaret, d/o John Fergusson, qv, and Margaret Robertson, qv. Son Alexander, 1842–1910. **HP 103**.

10604 ROBERTSON, Alexander. To Lochiel Twp, Glengarry Co, ONT. Farmer. m Mary Adams, from IRL. Son David, 1861–1933, station agent and reeve. **SDG 491**.

10605 ROBERTSON, Alexander, ca 1766–1 Feb 1840. From PER. To Halton Co, ONT, prob <1820; stld Esquesing Twp. Bur Boston cemetery. By wife Cecilia, ca 1772–1847, ch: 1. Robert, 1803-26; 2. Duncan, 1806-55. **EPE 74**.

10606 ROBERTSON, Alexander, 1786–16 Jan 1853. From Rannoch, PER. To Esquesing Twp, Halton Co, ONT, prob <1840. Son Dr David, b 1841, MPP, rep Halton. **BNA 800; EPE 74**.

10607 ROBERTSON, Anne. From Lochearnhead, PER. To Montreal, QUE, on the Niagara, ex Greenock, arr 28 May 1825; stld McNab Twp, Renfrew Co, ONT. Wife of James Robertson, qv. **EMT 18**.

10608 ROBERTSON, Anne, 1802–12 Apr 1894. From Insches, INV. To Pictou, NS, on the Lord Brougham, ex Cromarty, arr 10 Sep 1831. Wife of Robert MacIntosh, qv. **DC 21 Mar 1981**.

10609 ROBERTSON, Anne, b ca 1793. From Moulin, PER. To Halifax, NS, ca 1851; later to Seaforth, Huron Co, ONT. Wife of Archibald McGregor, qv. **LDW 30 Dec 1970**.

10610 ROBERTSON, Annie. From Sliddery, Is Arran, BUT. To Inverness Twp, Megantic Co, QUE, 1831; later to Somerset Twp. Wife of John McKinnon, qv, whom she m 27 Mar 1810.

10611 ROBERTSON, Arthur. From Insches, INV. s/o William R. and — Cockeral. To Halifax, NS, poss

1796. Collector of Customs. **Burkes Landed Gentry, 1846, 1126**.

10612 ROBERTSON, Arthur John. From Insches, INV. s/o Masterton R. and Mary Sherar. To ONT, where he held extensive lands by grant from 18 Indian chiefs, 15 Mar 1796. m (i) 1824, Marianne, only child of Richard Pattison, Petite Côte, and Julia Chabert, and by her who d 1836, ch: 1. Arthur Masterton, b 1826; 2. Thomas Gilzean, b 1827; 3. Julia Isabella; 4. Ellen Rose. m (ii) 1840, Charlotte Maria Bearda, d/o T.B. Batard, Sydenham, Kent, and by her who d 1842, ch: 5. Charlotte Caroline Bearda. **Burkes Landed Gentry, 1846, 1124**.

10613 ROBERTSON, Catherine, 1812-73. From Scone, PER. d/o Charles R, qv, and Catherine McGregor, qv. To Roxborough Twp, Stormont Co, ONT, 1828. m Malcolm McGregor, qv. **DC 1 Aug 1975**.

10614 ROBERTSON, Charles. From Lude, PER. Served as an NCO in 82nd Regt, and was gr 200 acres in Pictou Co, NS, ca 1784. Left ch. **HPC App F**.

10615 ROBERTSON, Charles, 1777–1857. From Lawers, PER, but res sometime at Scone. To QUE, 1828; stld Roxborough Twp, Stormont Co, ONT. Shoemaker. m Catherine McGregor, qv, ch: 1. Catherine, qv; 2. Isabel, qv; 3. Charles, jr, qv; 4. Ellen, qv; 5. Hugh, qv; 6. Janet, qv; 7. Alexander; 8. John; 9. Christy; 10. Duncan. **SMB; DC 1 Aug 1975**.

10616 ROBERTSON, Charles, jr, 1816–17 Aug 1885. From Scone, PER. s/o Charles R, qv, and Catherine McGregor, qv. To Roxborough Twp, Stormont Co, ONT, 1828. m Catherine Sinclair, 1826-93, and had ch. **DC 1 Aug 1975**.

10617 ROBERTSON, Colin, ca 1779–1842. To Montreal, QUE, 1804. Clerk with NWCo, but dismissed and joined HBCo. With William Auld, he re-organised the settlement at Red River for Lord Selkirk, qv, 1816. Chief factor, 1821, and served at Fort Churchill, Island Lake, Swan River, and in NB. Ret to Montreal, 1840. Son Colin, jr, d 1844. **MDB 634**.

10618 ROBERTSON, Daniel. To Pictou, NS, on the London, arr 11 Apr 1848. Wife Grace with him, and s James. **DC 15 Jul 1979**.

10619 ROBERTSON, David, 20 Oct 1838–6 May 1903. From Liff and Benvie par, ANS. s/o John R, grocer, and Elizabeth Wilson. To Montreal, QUE. **Ts Liff**.

10620 ROBERTSON, Donald. From Rannoch, PER. To Pictou, NS, on the Sarah, ex Fort William, Jun 1801. Farmer. Wife Janet with him, and ch: 1. Peggy, aged 6; 2. Janet, aged 4; 3. John, aged 2. **PLS**.

10621 ROBERTSON, Donald. From Dull par, PER. To Montreal, QUE, on the Curlew, ex Greenock, 21 Jul 1818; stld prob Beckwith Twp, Lanark Co, ONT. Wife Janet with him. **BCL**.

10622 ROBERTSON, Donald. From Dull par, PER. To Montreal, QUE, on the Curlew, ex Greenock, 21 Jul 1818; stld prob Beckwith Twp, Lanark Co, ONT. Wife Catherine with him. **BCL**.

10623 ROBERTSON, Duncan, b ca 1761. From PER. To Pictou, NS, on the Commerce, ex Port Glasgow, 10 Aug 1803. Farmer. Wife Isabella, aged 31, with him, and ch: 1. Alexander, aged 6; 2. Eliza, aged 4; 3. Margaret, aged 1; 4. Isabella. **PLC**.

10624 ROBERTSON, Duncan, b ca 1787. From Strathbran, PER. To Charlottetown, PEI, on the *Clarendon*, ex Oban, 6 Aug 1808. Labourer. **CPL**.

10625 ROBERTSON, Duncan. From Dull par, PER. To Montreal, QUE, on the *Curlew*, ex Greenock, 21 Jul 1818; stld prob Beckwith Twp, Lanark Co, ONT. Wife Margaret with him, and ch: 1. Janet, aged 5; 2. Mary, aged 3. **BCL**.

10626 ROBERTSON, Edward. To Pictou, NS, on the *Hope*, ex Glasgow, 5 Apr 1848. Wife Margaret with him, and ch: 1. Mary; 2. Peter; 3. Barbara; 4. George. **DC 12 Jul 1979**.

10627 ROBERTSON, Elizabeth, 1792–10 Jul 1881. From PER. sis/o John R, qv. To Ottawa, ONT, 1826. Wife of George Thomas Bayne, qv. **DC 3 May 1967**.

10628 ROBERTSON, Ellen, 1820–1 Dec 1902. From Scone, PER. d/o Charles R, qv, and Catherine McGregor, qv. To Roxborough Twp, Stormont Co, ONT, 1828. m Donald Sinclair, and had ch. **SMB; DC 1 Aug 1975**.

10629 ROBERTSON, Farquhar, d 1875. Prob from PER. To West Hawkesbury Twp, Prescott & Russell Co, ONT, <1830. Farmer and Liberal politician. Son William, d 1894. **DC 19 Feb 1980**.

10630 ROBERTSON, George, ca 1794–28 Sep 1859. From Dumfries. To Hamilton, ONT. Provision dealer. **DGH 18 Nov 1859**.

10631 ROBERTSON, George. To Pictou, NS, on the *Hope*, ex Glasgow, 5 Apr 1848. Wife Anne with him, and ch: 1. Margaret; 2. Anne; 3. Sarah; 4. Charles. **DC 12 Jul 1979**.

10632 ROBERTSON, George. To Pictou, NS, on the *Hope*, ex Glasgow, 5 Apr 1848. Wife Mary with him, and ch: 1. Anne; 2. Mary. They stld in USA. **DC 12 Jul 1979**.

10633 ROBERTSON, Henry, 1819–89. Prob from PER. To Pictou, NS; stld Middle River. m Catherine MacNaughton, 1827–1908, ch: 1. Ellen; 2. John; 3. Marjory; 4. Alexander; 5. Mary Ann; 6. William; 7. Dan Philip, d NY; 8. Elizabeth; 9. Christy Margaret; 10. Catherine Ruth; 11. James Roderick. **PAC 187**.

10634 ROBERTSON, Hugh. From PER. To QUE on the *Lady of the Lake*, Sep 1816; stld Drummond Twp, Lanark Co, ONT. Estate factor, bookkeeper and farmer. m Christine McDonald, qv. **HCL 20**.

10635 ROBERTSON, Hugh, 1826–1902. From Scone, PER. s/o Charles R, qv, and Catherine McGregor, qv. To Roxborough Twp, Stormont Co, ONT, 18.8. m Isobel Campbell, and had ch. **DC 1 Aug 1975**.

10636 ROBERTSON, Hugh, ca 1822–24 Jul 1906. From LKS. s/o Hugh R. of Gartloch, Garnkirk, merchant-burgess of Glasgow. Matric Univ of Glasgow, 1835. To Owen Sound, ONT, and d Brookholm. **GMA 13498**.

10637 ROBERTSON, Isobel, 1815–14 Jun 1890. From Scone, PER. d/o Charles R, qv, and Catherine McGregor, qv. To Roxborough Twp, Stormont Co, ONT, 1828. m James McNaughton, and had ch. **SMB; DC 1 Aug 1975**.

10638 ROBERTSON, James. Served in the 82nd Regt and was gr land in Pictou Co, NS, 1784. **HPC App F**.

10639 ROBERTSON, James. From Rannoch, PER. To Pictou, NS, on the *Sarah*, ex Fort William, Jun 1801. Labourer. **PLS**.

10640 ROBERTSON, James. From Rannoch, PER. To Pictou, NS, on the *Sarah*, ex Fort William, Jun 1801. Farmer. Wife Christian with him, and ch: 1. Elizabeth, aged 6; 2. Janet, aged 3; 3. Duncan, aged 2. **PLS**.

10641 ROBERTSON, James, b ca 1730. From Fortingall, PER. To Charlottetown, PEI, on the *Clarendon*, ex Oban, 7 Aug 1808. Labourer. Wife Cathrine, aged 71, with him, and sons: 1. Alexander, qv; 2. James, b 1776, stld Queens Co. **CPL**.

10642 ROBERTSON, James, b ca 1784. From Strathbran, PER. To Charlottetown, PEI, on the *Clarendon*, ex Oban, 6 Aug 1808. Labourer. **CPL**.

10643 ROBERTSON, James, ca 1770–1842. From Blair Atholl, PER. s/o James R. To PEI, 1808; stld Marshfield. m Jean Miller, qv, and had, prob with other ch: 1. Alexander, qv; 2. Margaret, 1802-75. **HP 103**.

10644 ROBERTSON, James, b ca 1793. From Sandwick, OKI. To Hudson Bay, ca 1813, and poss to Red River. **RRS 13**.

10645 ROBERTSON, James, b ca 1790. From Kilmaurs, AYR. To Hudson Bay, ca 1813, and prob to Red River. **RRS 13**.

10646 ROBERTSON, James, ca 1784–22 Feb 1867. From BAN. To Pictou Co, NS, and stld Eight Mile Brook. m Abigail Stewart, qv, and had, prob with other ch: 1. James, 1833-36; 2. James H, d inf, 1847. All bur Salt Springs. **DC 27 Oct 1979**.

10647 ROBERTSON, James. From Edinburgh. To McNab Twp, Renfrew Co, ONT, 1825. Wife Margaret McGregor, qv, with him, and family: 1. John; 2. Peter; 3. Elizabeth; 4. Christian; 5. Donald; 6. Duncan, inf. **HCL 103; EMT 18, 23**.

10648 ROBERTSON, Rev James, ca 1800–19 Jan 1878. From Perth. Grad MA, Kings Coll, Aberdeen, 1826, and became a priest of the Ch of England. To NS, as missionary, 1829, and became rector of Wilmot, Annapolis Co. LLD, Kings Coll, 1856. **KCG 117, 282; MDB 635**.

10649 ROBERTSON, Rev James. From Stuartfield, ABD. To Sherbrooke, QUE, 1832. Congregational min at Stuartfield, 1802-32, afterwards at Sherbrooke until ca 1857. Son Joseph Gibb, b 1820, Conservative politician. **BNA 762**.

10650 ROBERTSON, James. To Pictou, NS, on the *Hope*, ex Glasgow, 5 Apr 1848. Wife Jane with him, and ch: 1. George; 2. Jane; 3. James; 4. Anne; 5. Charles; 6. John. They went to USA. **DC 12 Jul 1979**.

10651 ROBERTSON, James. From Dull par, PER. To ONT, 1855. Wife Christina McCallum, qv, with him, and s Rev James, qv. **MDB 635**.

10652 ROBERTSON, Rev James, 24 Apr 1839–4 Jan 1902. From Dull par, PER. s/o James R, qv, and Christina McCallum, qv. To ONT, 1855. Educ Univs of Toronto and Princeton, and became min at Norwich, Oxford Co, ONT, 1869. Trans to Knox Coll, Winnipeg, 1874, and later app superintendent of missions in Western CAN. DD. m 1869, Mary Anne Cowing, and had ch. **MDB 635**.

10653   ROBERTSON, James. b Old Kilpatrick, DNB. To Montreal, QUE, ca 1855. Lead pipe manufacturer. m 1864, Amelia, d/o David Morris, Seignior of St Thérèse de Blainville.   **SGC 573**.

10654   ROBERTSON, Jane, ca 1765–ca 1808. From PER. d/o William R, qv. To Malpeque, PEI, on the *Falmouth*, ex Greenock, 8 Apr 1770. m ca 1785, Elisha Coffin, jr, 1763–1851.   **DC 28 May 1980**.

10655   ROBERTSON, Jane, 15 Oct 1826–3 Jun 1907. From Largie, Insch par, ABD. d/o John R. and Janet Harvey, qv. To Wellington Co, ONT. m as his second wife, Sem Wissler, 1819–65, wealthy founder of Salem Village, ch: 1. John; 2. Ezra.   **EHE 124**.

10656   ROBERTSON, Janet or Jessie, 1783–1851. From PER, poss Balquhidder par. sis/o Peter R, qv. To Pictou, NS, on the *Commerce*, ex Port Glasgow, 10 Aug 1803; stld Brudenell, Kings Co, PEI. Wife of William McLaren, qv.   **PLC; BP 43**.

10657   ROBERTSON, Janet. From Blair Atholl, PER. To Pictou Co, NS, ca 1812, soon after her m to James Haggart, qv.   **DC 27 May 1981**.

10658   ROBERTSON, Janet. From PER. sis/o Hugh R, qv. To QUE on the *Lady of the Lake*, Sep 1816; stld Drummond Twp, Lanark Co, ONT. Wife of Donald Campbell, qv.   **HCL 20**.

10659   ROBERTSON, Janet, ca 1780–1865. From Redhall, Lochmaben, DFS. To London, Middlesex Co, ONT, and d there. Wife of George Gowanlock, qv.   **DGB 9 Sep 1865**.

10660   ROBERTSON, Janet, 1828–25 Dec 1874. From Scone, PER. d/o Charles R, qv, and Catherine McGregor, qv. To Roxborough Twp, Stormont Co, ONT, 1828. m James Dow, qv.   **DC 1 Aug 1975**.

10661   ROBERTSON, Janet. Prob from PER. sis/o Farquhar R, qv. To West Hawkesbury Twp, Prescott & Russell Co, ONT, <1830. m Alexander Roderick Fraser, qv.   **DC 19 Feb 1980**.

10662   ROBERTSON, John. From Farley, Kilmorack, INV, but seems to have had some connection with Ballinloan Dunkeld, PER. To Halifax, NS, on the *John*, arr 4 Jun 1784; stld nr Churchville, west branch of East River, where gr 450 acres. m Margaret McKay, qv, ch: 1. William, gr 200 acres; 2. James; 3. Catherine; 4. Nancy; 5. Margaret; 6. Mary.   **HPC App H and I; CP 48; VSN No 965**.

10663   ROBERTSON, John. From Rannoch, PER. To Pictou, NS, on the *Sarah*, ex Fort William, Jun 1801. Tenant. Wife Janet with him, and ch: 1. Alexander; 2. Elizabeth; 3. Donald, aged 13; 4. Janet, aged 11; 5. Duncan, aged 5.   **PLS**.

10664   ROBERTSON, John. From Dull, PER. To Montreal, QUE, on the *Curlew*, ex Greenock, 21 Jul 1818; stld prob Beckwith Twp, Lanark Co, ONT. Wife Catherine with him.   **BCL**.

10665   ROBERTSON, John. From Killin, PER. To Montreal, QUE, on the *Curlew*, ex Greenock, 21 Jul 1818; stld prob Beckwith Twp, Lanark Co, ONT. Wife Janet with him, and ch: 1. John, aged 16; 2. Daniel, aged 14.   **BCL**.

10666   ROBERTSON, John, b 1802. From Blair Atholl,

PER. Poss rel to John Stewart, qv, or his wife. To Montreal, QUE, on the *Curlew*, ex Greenock, 21 Jul 1818.   **BCL**.

10667   ROBERTSON, John. From Breadalbane, PER. To QUE, 1818; stld Beckwith Twp, Lanark Co, ONT. Farmer and leader of a group of emigrants.   **HCL 32**.

10668   ROBERTSON, John. To QUE on the *Commerce*, ex Greenock, Jun 1820; stld Lot 18, Con 2, Lanark Twp, Lanark Co, ONT.   **HCL 65, 239**.

10669   ROBERTSON, John. To QUE on the *David of London*, ex Greenock, 19 May 1821; stld Lot 5, Con 8, Lavant Twp, Lanark Co, ONT. Robertson Lake named after him.   **HCL 76, 239**.

10670   ROBERTSON, John. From Barracks Street, Glasgow. To QUE, 1821; stld Lanark Co, ONT. m Jane Kyle, qv.   **SG xx/1 11**.

10671   ROBERTSON, John, b 1810. From Glasgow. To QUE, prob 1821; stld Lanark Co, ONT. m Janet Dow, qv.   **SG xx/1 11**.

10672   ROBERTSON, John, 1791–1880. From PER. bro/o Elizabeth R, qv. To Ottawa, ONT, arr May 1827. Weaver, mechanical engineer and farmer. By wife Jean had dau Emilia.   **DC 3 May 1967**.

10673   ROBERTSON, John, 1799–3 Aug 1876. From Dowally, PER. s/o John R. and wife Margaret. To St John, NB, <1830. Shipping clerk, and acquired business interests. Mayor of St John, 1836, and Canadian senator, 1867. m Sophia Dobie, and ret to ENG.   **Ts Dowally; DC 21 Mar 1981**.

10674   ROBERTSON, John, 1785–27 Nov 1861. From PER. To Halton Co, ONT, poss <1830; stld Esquesing Twp, and bur Hillcrest, Norval.   **EPE 77**.

10675   ROBERTSON, John. From NAI. To Toronto, ONT, 1833. m Margaret Sinclair, qv. Son John Ross, 1841–1918, journalist and legislator.   **MDB 636; DC 30 Aug 1977**.

10676   ROBERTSON, John, 1807-72. From RFW. To Pictou Co, NS, ca 1840. Left ch.   **NSN 5/1**.

10677   ROBERTSON, John, 1805–1902. From Is Arran, BUT. To Restigouche Co, NB, prob <1841, and d New Mills.   **MAC 26**.

10678   ROBERTSON, John. To Pictou Co, NS, on the *Hope*, ex Glasgow, 5 Apr 1848. Wife Maria with him, and s James.   **DC 12 Jul 1979**.

10679   ROBERTSON, John, b 1833. From Eassie and Nevay par, ANS. To Seneca Twp, Haldimand Co, ONT. m, ca 1860, Annie Brown.   **DC 14 Nov 1978**.

10680   ROBERTSON, John, b ca 1803. To St Gabriel de Valcartier, QUE, prob <1855.   **Census 1861**.

ROBERTSON, Mrs John. See MACKAY, Margaret.

10681   ROBERTSON, John Palmerston, 23 May 1841–11 Apr 1919. From Fortingall, PER. To CAN, 1845, with parents. Schoolteacher, and became provincial librarian of MAN.   **MDB 636**.

10682   ROBERTSON, John S, b 11 Aug 1811. From Govan, Glasgow. To ONT, ca 1846. m Margaret Barr, qv.   **DC 23 Feb 1981**.

10683 ROBERTSON, Joseph. To Pictou, NS, on the *Hope*, ex Glasgow, 5 Apr 1848. Wife Rosanna with him, and ch: 1. Joseph; 2. George; 3. William; 4. Mary; 5. James; 6. Jane; 7. Isabella. **DC 12 Jul 1979**.

10684 ROBERTSON, Kenneth. Prob from PER. To Galt, Waterloo Co, ONT, prob <1827. Factor for Hon William Dickson, qv. **HGD 53**.

10685 ROBERTSON, Malcolm, ca 1796–ca 1818. From Ballachulish, ARL. s/o Donald R, 76th Highlanders, and Mary McCall. To CAN. **Ts Isla Munda**.

10686 ROBERTSON, Malcolm. Prob from ARL. To Aldborough Twp, Elgin Co, ONT, poss 1818; stld Lot 7, Con 12. Farmer and schoolteacher. **PDA 18, 93**.

10687 ROBERTSON, Margaret. From PER. d/o William R, qv. To Malpeque, PEI, on the *Falmouth*, ex Greenock, 8 Apr 1770. m 26 Jan 1790, John McEachern. **DC 28 May 1980**.

10688 ROBERTSON, Margaret. From PER. d/o James R. To PEI, 1808. Wife of John Fergusson, qv. **HP 103**.

10689 ROBERTSON, Margaret, 1797–1875. Poss from PER. d/o Alexander R. and Margaret McDonald. To Merigomish, Pictou Co, NS, <1815. m John McNeil, jr, qv. **DC 14 Nov 1981**.

10690 ROBERTSON, Margaret. From Is Arran, BUT. To QUE on the *Albion*, ex Greenock, 5 Jun 1829. Wife of John McKenzie, qv. **AMC 21**.

10691 ROBERTSON, Margaret, 3 Aug 1809–18 Oct 1887. To NB, 1837. Wife of George McKay, qv. **DC 27 Sep 1980**.

10692 ROBERTSON, Margaret. From Blair Atholl, PER. To Halifax, NS, 1833; stld Lochaber, Antigonish Co. m John Stewart, qv. **HNS iii 681**.

10693 ROBERTSON, Margaret Murray, 1823-97. From Old Deer, ABD. To QUE, 1832. Teacher and novelist. **SNQ xii/1 22**.

10694 ROBERTSON, Marjory, 1820–19 Dec 1866. From Longforgan, PER. d/o Andrew R, baker and brewer. To QUE, and d Melbourne. m C.R. Christie. **Ts Longforgan**.

10695 ROBERTSON, Mrs. Cabin passenger on the *London*; returning to Pictou, NS, and arr 11 Apr 1848. **DC 15 Jul 1979**.

10696 ROBERTSON, Peter. From Dull par, PER. To Montreal, QUE, on the *Curlew*, ex Greenock, 21 Jul 1818; stld prob Beckwith Twp, Lanark Co, ONT. **BCL**.

10697 ROBERTSON, Peter. From PER, prob Balquhidder par. bro/o Janet or Jessie R, qv. To PEI prob <1828; stld New Perth, Kings Co. **BP 43**.

10698 ROBERTSON, Peter. Prob from OKI. To CAN <1808, and served with HBCo. **SH**.

10699 ROBERTSON, Pettigrew. To Pictou, NS, on the *Hope*, ex Glasgow, 5 Apr 1848. Wife Martha with him, and ch: 1. John; 2. Elizabeth; 3. Jane. They went to USA. **DC 12 Jul 1979**.

10700 ROBERTSON, Robert, d 1859. From Kilmaurs, AYR. To Belleville, Hastings Co, ONT. m Bessie Ross. Son David. **DC 29 Sep 1964**.

10701 ROBERTSON, Sarah. From Aberdeen. To

Montreal, QUE, <1834, when she m James Moir Ferris, qv. **MDB 465**.

10702 ROBERTSON, Walter, 7 May 1791–Jan 1864. From RFW. To Niagara-on-the-Lake, ONT, 1820; later to Halton Co. Farmer and manager, 1821-27, of the estate of Chief Joseph Brant. m Mary McFarlane, qv, and had ch. **DC 29 Jun 1979**.

10703 ROBERTSON, Walter. To Pictou, NS, on the *Hope*, ex Glasgow, 5 Apr 1848. Wife Isabella with him, and ch: 1. Isabella; 2. Elizabeth; 3. William. They went to USA. **DC 12 Jul 1979**.

10704 ROBERTSON, William, ca 1738–23 Dec 1805. From PER. To Malpeque, PEI, on the *Falmouth*, ex Greenock, 8 Apr 1770; stld Stanhope, later St Peters. Wife with him, and ch incl: 1. Margaret, qv; 2. Jane, qv. **DC 28 May 1980**.

10705 ROBERTSON, William, 1746–1812. From Struan, PER. To NS, ca 1783. Loyalist; merchant and MLA, rep Annapolis Twp, 1808-11. By wife Mary Adelia had s John, 1784–1872, merchant and MLA, 1820-26. **MLA 297, 298**.

10706 ROBERTSON, William. To Pictou Co, NS, <1 Apr 1793; stld East River. **HPC App H**.

10707 ROBERTSON, William, 15 Mar 1774–18 Jul 1844. From Kindrochit, nr Struan, PER. Surgeon, 49th Regt, and stationed at Halifax, NS, 1805. Went to Montreal. Founder mem of the old medical school which was incorporated in McGill Coll. m 21 Jan 1806, Elizabeth Amelia, d/o William Campbell, qv, and Hannah Hadley, and had with other ch: 1. Duncan, res Lachine; 2. Mrs Ferdinand McCulloch; 3. Mrs John Pangman; 4. Mrs A.C. Cooper; 5. Mrs William McDonald; 6. Hannah Carolina (Lady Cunningham of Milncraig, AYR). **SGC 369**.

10708 ROBERTSON, William. Poss from Glasgow. To QUE, prob 1821; stld Lanark Co, ONT. m Mary Dow, qv. **SG xx/1 11**.

10709 ROBERTSON, William. To Lanark Co, ONT, <1832. Farmer. **SH**.

10710 ROBERTSON, Rev William, d 22 Sep 1832. From Haddington, ELN. Antiburgher min at Cupar, FIF, 1829-32. To Montreal, QUE, but d of cholera soon after arrival, leaving a widow who retr to SCT and had a posthumous child. **UPC i 186**.

10711 ROBERTSON, William. From Is Arran, BUT. To Restigouche Co, NB, prob <1841. **MAC 26**.

10712 ROBERTSON, William. To Pictou, NS, on the *Hope*, ex Glasgow, 5 Apr 1848. **DC 12 Jul 1979**.

10713 ROBERTSON, William Forbes, ca 1828–8 Jul 1849. From Rosehall, SUT. s/o William R. To Montreal, QUE, and d there. **DGH 16 Aug 1849**.

10714 ROBESON, Catherine, 16 Oct 1793–6 Feb 1841. From Aberdeen. d/o William R, shipmaster, and Mary Gavin. To Nichol Twp, Wellington Co, ONT, 1838. Wife of Rev James Middleton, qv. **DC 7 Jun 1980**.

ROBINSON. See also ROBERTSON, ROBERTON and ROBSON.

10715 ROBINSON, Colin. Poss bro/o William R, qv. To Pictou Co, NS, <1 Apr 1793, when gr land on East

River. He seems to have moved <18 Dec 1797. **HPC App H**.

10716 ROBINSON, Francis. Prob from Paisley, RFW. To ONT, 1837; stld poss Elgin Co. Wife Margaret with him. **SG xxvii/2 78**.

10717 ROBINSON, James, b ca 1785. To St Gabriel de Valcartier, QUE, prob <1855. Teacher. **Census 1861**.

10718 ROBINSON, William. Poss bro/o Colin R, qv. To Pictou Co, NS, <1 Apr 1793, when gr land on East River. He seems to have moved <18 Dec 1797. **HPC App H**.

ROBSON. See also ROBESON, ROBERTSON, ROBERTON and ROBINSON.

10719 ROBSON, Rev James, d 8 Dec 1838. Prob from Kelso, ROX. To NS <1836. Clergyman. **SH**.

10720 ROBSON, John. Served as an NCO in 82nd Regt, and was gr 200 acres in Pictou Co, NS, 1784. Had some surgical skills. Left ch. **HPC App F**.

10721 ROBSON, Thomas, b 1814. From Minto par, ROX. s/o James R. To Burford Twp, Brant Co, ONT, 1834. m 1847, Margaret, d/o Alexander Johnston, qv, and had ch. **DC 23 Dec 1980**.

10722 ROBSON, Thomas Oliver, b 11 Aug 1844. From Jedburgh, ROX. s/o Thomas R. and Frances Oliver. To Blanshard Twp, Perth Co, ONT, 1853. Cattle dealer. **DC 29 Sep 1964**.

10723 RODDICK, Janet, 1816-79. From Annan par, DFS. To Guelph Twp, Wellington Co, ONT, 1837. m at Fort Jackson, 1840, James Martin, qv. **DC 31 Dec 1979**.

10724 RODDICK, John, d 17 Jan 1855. From Meikle Kirkland, Urr, KKD. To Cobourg, Northumberland Co, ONT, <1846. m Isabella Davidson, qv. **DGC 20 Feb 1855**.

10725 RODDICK, John, 1792–1876. From DFS. To ONT, ca 1842; stld Brockville, Leeds Co, and moved in 1853 to Brantford Twp, Brant Co. Wife was d/o Robert Courtland. Son William, qv. **DC 23 Sep 1980**.

10726 RODDICK, John Irvine. To Harbour Grace, NFD, <1846. Schoolmaster. m Emma Jane Martin. Son Sir Thomas, 1846–1923, surgeon and legislator, Montreal, QUE. **MDB 642**.

10727 RODDICK, William, b 1840. From DFS. To ONT, 1842. s/o John R, qv. To Brantford Twp, Brant Co, ONT, 1853. m 1873, Mary, d/o John Aulsebrook, ch: 1. William, b 1878; 2. James, b 1882. **DC 23 Sep 1980**.

RODGER. See also ROGER and ROGERS.

10728 RODGER, Agnes Berry. From FIF. Gr-dau of Andrew R, weaver in St Monance. To Chatham, Northumberland Co, NB. m John Johnston, farmer. **SH**.

10729 RODGER, David. From Edinburgh. To Montreal, QUE, 1848. Teacher in the High School for 27 years. Left ch. **SGC 569**.

10730 RODGER, John. Poss from Greenock, RFW. To NB <1839. Merchant. **SH**.

RODGERSON. See also ROGERSON.

10731 RODGERSON, James. From Annandale, DFS. To PEI, 1832; stld prob Breadalbane, Queens Co. m Janet Milligan, qv. Dau Mary, qv. **CAE 46; DC 25 Nov 1981**.

10732 RODGERSON, Mary, 1797–1882. From Annandale, DFS. d/o James R, qv, and Janet Milligan, qv. To PEI, prob <1836. Wife of John Biggar, qv. **DC 25 Nov 1981**.

10733 RODGIE, Margaret, b 1 May 1782. From Edinburgh. d/o Thomas R, weaver in Perth, and Margaret Wright. To Montreal, QUE, on the *Jean*, ex Glasgow, Apr 1822; stld English River. Wife of John Stewart, qv, whom she m 5 Jul 1809. **DC 3 Jun 1980**.

ROGER. See also ROGERS and RODGER.

10734 ROGER, Charles, ca 1819–ca 1880. From Dundee, ANS. s/o Charles R, librarian, and Ann Cruickshank. Matric Univ of St Andrews, 1832. Studied theology and medicine, but joined Royal Artillery and went to CAN. Discharged at own request, 1842, and became librarian and journalist. m at QUE, 29 Feb 1840, Dorothy MacRobie, and had ch. **SAM 85; MDB 642**.

10735 ROGER, Rev John Morrice, 14 Sep 1807–9 Jan 1878. From Kincardine O'Neil, ABD. s/o Rev John R, par min, and Jane Morrice. Grad MA, Kings Coll, Aberdeen, 1827, and went on to study medicine and divinity. Ord min of Peterborough, ONT, 1833, and joined FC, 1844. m 1835, his cous, Eliza Morrice, and by her who d 1864, left ch. **KCG 283; SNQ ii/2 186; FES vi 102, vii 649**.

10736 ROGERS, Archibald, 1800-35. Prob Falkirk, STI. To Scarborough, York Co, ONT, <1835. Wife Isabella Wilson, qv, with him, and s Thomas, qv. **SCN**.

10737 ROGERS, Charles, 1816-91. From Glasgow. s/o David R. and Margaret Jackson. To Toronto, ONT, 1851. Cabinet-maker. m Janet Ferguson, qv. Son Charles, 1845–1915. **DC 29 Dec 1981**.

10738 ROGERS, James. From LKS. Prob rel to Robert R, qv. To QUE on the *Prompt*, ex Greenock, 4 Jul 1820; stld Lanark Co, ONT. **HCL 238**.

10739 ROGERS, John. To Pictou Co, NS, <8 Nov 1775. ch: 1. James; 2. John; 3. David. **HPC App B**.

10740 ROGERS, Robert. From LKS. Prob rel to James R, qv. To QUE on the *Prompt*, ex Greenock, 4 Jul 1820; stld Lanark Co, ONT. **HCL 238**.

10741 ROGERS, Thomas, 15 Aug 1827–16 Sep 1896. From Falkirk, STI. s/o Archibald R, qv, and Isabella Wilson, qv. To Scarborough, York Co, ONT, <1835; later to Salt Lake City, UT. m 27 Mar 1851, Aurelia Spencer, and had ch.

ROGERSON. See also RODGERSON.

10742 ROGERSON, Janet, b ca 1750. From Dryfesdale, DFS. To Georgetown, Kings Co, PEI, on the *Lovely Nellie*, ex Carsethorn, May 1775. **ELN**.

10743 ROGERSON, John Nichols, ca 1832–22 Apr 1861. From Johnstone par, DFS. s/o Alexander J, merchant in St Petersburgh, Russia. To QUE, and d Lake Beaufort. **Ts Johnstone**.

10744 ROGERSON, Mrs Mary, ca 1814–5 Apr 1858. From DFS. To Carleton, Kent Co, NB. Wife of Thomas R. **DGH 21 May 1858**.

10745 ROGERSON, Peter, 13 Nov 1789–27 Sep 1858. From Johnstone par, DFS. s/o James R, tenant in Upper Fenton, and Margaret Halliday. To St Johns, NFD, 1814. Merchant. Son Peter. **Johnstone OPR 832/1; Ts Johnstone; DGH 22 Oct 1858**.

10746 ROGERSON, Samuel, d 27 Nov 1854. From Dumfries. To Montreal, QUE, and d there. Saddler. **DGC 2 Jan 1855**.

10747 ROLLO, James. From Glasgow. To Newmarket, York Co, ONT, <7 Jan 1858, when he m Mary Ford, b USA. **DC 24 Mar 1982**.

10748 ROLLO, Major, ca 1803–14 Feb 1844. From AYR. s/o Roger R. To Ottawa, ONT, and d there. **DGH 21 Mar 1844**.

10749 ROOM, Mary, ca 1805–14 Jan 1861. Prob from Annan, DFS. To Kent Co, NB, ca 1829. Wife of David Mundle, qv. **DC 5 Aug 1980**.

10750 ROMANES, Rev George, 1806-71. From Edinburgh, and grad MA there, 1826. To ONT to become min of Smiths Falls, Lanark Co, 1834. Trans to St Francis, 1839, but was again at Smiths Falls and Elmsley <1846, when app Professor of Classical Literature at Queens Coll, Kingston. Retr to Britain, 1850, and stld London. LLD, Queens Coll, 1866. m Isabella Gair Smith, qv, ch: 1. James, 1836–1902; 2. Robert, dy; 3. Georgina, 1842-78; 4. Prof George John, d 1894; 5. Charlotte, d unm 1911. **CEG 221; FES vii 6, 649; MGC 2 Aug 1979**.

ROME, Mrs Andrew. See BELL, Mary.

10751 ROME, John, ca 1788–9 Jul 1857. From Longlands, Dornock, DFS. s/o David R, cabinet-maker, and Elizabeth Irving. To Truro, Colchester Co, NS. **Ts Dornock**.

10752 RONALDSON, William, ca 1805–7 Sep 1834. From Leith, MLN. s/o Archibald R. To QUE, and d there. **Ts South Leith**.

10753 ROSE, Alexander, 1819-97. Prob from ROC. s/o — R. and Isabella Robertson. To QUE, prob <1835; stld Racine. m Euphemia Allan, 1830-85. Dau Margaret, 1867-85. **MGC 15 Jul 1980**.

10754 ROSE, Rev Alexander, 1823–14 May 1871. From Dunoon, ARL. s/o Robert R, shopkeeper. Matric Univ of Glasgow, 1838. App by Colonial Committee for missionary service in CAN. Retr to SCT, 1866, and res latterly at Irvine, AYR. **GMA 13974; FES vii 649**.

10755 ROSE, Amelia. From INV. To Pictou Co, NS, 1785; stld Big Brook, west branch of East River. Wife of William Dunbar, qv. **SH**.

10756 ROSE, Anne, 1778–1851. From Brodie, MOR, but poss b ROC. To Blackland, Restigouche Co, NB, 1819. Wife of James MacPherson, qv. **DC 7 Feb 1981**.

10757 ROSE, Anne, ca 1803–30 May 1877. From ROC. To Melbourne, Richmond Co, QUE. m Finlay Munroe. **MGC 15 Jul 1980**.

10758 ROSE, George MacLean, 14 Mar 1829–10 Feb 1898. From Wick, CAI. To Montreal, QUE, 1851. Printer, journalist and publisher. m 1856, Margaret, d/o William Manson, and had ch. **BNA 1138; MDB 646**.

10759 ROSE, Hugh. Prob from INV. To London, Westminster Twp, Middlesex Co, ONT, 1844. **PCM 55**.

10760 ROSE, James H, d 28 Mar 1840. From ROC. s/o William R. in Rhynie, Fearn par. To Markham, York Co, ONT, and d Rose Hill. **DGH 11 Jun 1840**.

10761 ROSE, John, 1809–5 Jul 1880. From ROC. To QUE, prob <1835; stld Racine. m Mary McKenzie, qv. Dau Mary, 1851-82. **MGC 15 Jul 1980**.

10762 ROSE, Sir John, 2 Aug 1820–24 Aug 1888. From Turriff, ABD. s/o William R, qv, and Elizabeth Fyfe, qv. To Huntingdon Village, QUE, 1836. Schoolteacher, lawyer, banker and politician. KCMG, 1872; GCMG, 1878; PC, 1886. Went to London, ENG, 1869, and stld there. m (i) 1843, Charlotte, d/o Robert Emmet Temple, of Rutland, VT, with ch. m (ii) 1887, Julia, d/o Keith Stewart Mackenzie of Seaforth, wid/o Arthur, 9th Marquess of Tweeddale. **BNA 597; SNQ xii/1 22; IBD 445; MDB 646**.

10763 ROSE, Murdoch, 1813-35. Prob from ROC. s/o — R. and Isabella Robertson. To QUE <1835, and d at Racine. **MGC 15 Jul 1980**.

10764 ROSE, Walter, ca 1795–12 Apr 1843. From MOR. s/o James R. in Muirtown of Drainie, and Mary Grant. To ONT, and stld poss York Co. Landowner. Bur at Toronto. **Ts Kinnedar**.

10765 ROSE, William. From Turriff, ABD. To Huntingdon Village, QUE, 1836. Wife Elizabeth Fyfe, qv, with him, and s John, qv. **DC 11 Nov 1979**.

10766 ROSE, William, ca 1807–18 Aug 1841. From MOR. s/o James R. in Muirtown of Drainie, and Mary Grant. To ONT. Bur at Toronto. **Ts Kinnedar**.

10767 ROSE, William. From ABD. s/o James R. and Jane Davie. To ONT, 1854; later to Manton, MI. **DC 21 Mar 1981**.

10768 ROSIE, Murdoch, b ca 1793. From Burray, OKI. To Hudson Bay, ca 1813; and prob to Red River. **RRS 13**.

10769 ROSS, Alexander. From Lochbroom, ROC. To Pictou, NS, on the *Hector*, ex Loch Broom, arr 17 Sep 1773; stld east side of Middle River, and gr 300 acres, 26 Aug 1783. Son Alexander, jr, qv. **HPC App A and C**.

10770 ROSS, Alexander, jr. From Lochbroom, ROC. To Pictou, NS, on the *Hector*, ex Loch Broom, arr 17 Sep 1773; stld east side of Middle River. Farmer. m Katherine Fraser, ch: 1. Donald, Olivers Farm, emig to OH; 2. Alexander, Middle River Point; 3. Mary; 4. Mrs Blair, East River. **HPC App A and C**.

10771 ROSS, Alexander. From Kincardine, INV. To Pictou, NS, on the *Dove*, ex Fort William, Jun 1801. Labourer. **PLD**.

10772 ROSS, Alexander, 9 May 1783–23 Oct 1856. From NAI. To Glengarry Co, ONT, ca 1805. Schoolteacher, but joined Pacific Fur Co, 1810. After the capture of Fort Astoria, he became a clerk with the NWC, and remained on the Pacific coast after the merger with the HBCo, 1821. Ret 1825, and was thereafter Sheriff of Assiniboia. Author. m d/o an Okanagan chief, and had ch. **MDB 647**.

10773 ROSS, Alexander, b 1756. To Pictou Co, NS, 1815; res West River, 1816. Millwright, m with 5 ch, and 'poor'. **INS 38**.

10774 ROSS, Alexander, b ca 1781. Prob from SUT. To

Pictou, NS, 1815. Blacksmith, m with 5 ch. Poor, but 'very industrious'. **INS 39**.

10775   ROSS, Alexander, b ca 1800. From Tain, ROC. To NS, and stld Big Brook, west branch of East River. Farmer. m (i) Isabella McKay, ch: 1. Margaret, b ca 1833; 2. Isabella; 3. Daniel, 1839–1912; 4. Jessie. m (ii) Betsy Gunn, and had further ch: 5. John, b 1846; 6. Catherine. **PAC 196**.

10776   ROSS, Alexander, 1793–1872. From Is Lewis, ROC. s/o David R. and Mary Smith. To Gulf Shore, Cumberland Co, NS, prob <1825. m Isabella Mackenzie, qv, and had, prob with other ch: 1. David, 1824–1901; 2. Roderick, 1826–91. **DC 29 Oct 1980**.

10777   ROSS, Alexander, ca 1784–24 Aug 1866. From INV. To Middlesex Co, ONT, prob <1830. Wife Isabella, 1790–1879. **PCM 50**.

10778   ROSS, Rev Alexander, 1794–14 Mar 1857. From ROC. Educ at Aberdeen. Became first Presb min of Aldborough, Elgin Co, ONT, 1830. Trans to Woolwich, 1843, and to Innisfil and Gwillimbury, 1846. Ret about 1855, and d at Bradford. **FES vii 650; PDA 55**.

10779   ROSS, Alexander. From ROC. bro/o John R, qv, George R, qv, Hugh R, qv, Thomas R, qv, and William R, qv. To Barrochois, Colchester Co, NS, 1833. ch: 1. William; 2. Jefferson. **HT 70**.

10780   ROSS, Alexander, 1781–1863. From Killearnan, ROC. s/o David R. and Isabella Dingwall. To ONT, 1860; stld Minto Twp, Wellington Co. Farmer. m Margaret Noble, qv, ch: 1. Alexander, jr, qv; 2. David, d inf; 3. Margaret, d ca 1840; 4. Donald, qv; 5. Isabella, qv; 6. Elizabeth, qv; 7. Roderick, qv; 8. William, qv; 9. Catherine, qv; 10. Agnes, d in SCT. **RFS 44, 106, 146**.

10781   ROSS, Alexander, jr, 11 Jan 1814–8 Oct 1886. From Knockbain par, ROC, but b Killearnan par. s/o Alexander R, qv, and Margaret Noble, qv. To QUE, prob on the *Brilliant*, ex Cromarty, arr 23 May 1842; stld Scott Twp, York Co, ONT. Farmer Lot 13, Con 6. m Janet Fraser, qv, ch: 1. Donald, d at sea; 2. Agnes, d Whitby, ONT, 1842; 3. Alexander Fraser, b 1842, farmer, Minto Twp, Wellington Co; 4. James, b ca 1845, farmer and stonemason; 5. William, b ca 1846; 6. John, b ca 1848; 7. Margaret Isabel, b ca 1850; 8. Rev John Alexander, b 1854; 9. Rev Hugh; 10. Mary Ann; 11. Donald; 12-13. Colin and Allan, b 1862. **RFS 77, 82, 122**.

10782   ROSS, Alexander R, 1771–1840. From Tarbet, ROC. To Wallace, Cumberland Co, NS, 1833. Wife Elizabeth, 1780–1849, with him. Dau Jane, 1866-73. **DC 29 Oct 1980**.

10783   ROSS, Alexandrina. From Dornoch, SUT. To Lanark Co, ONT, 1831. Wife of William Sutherland, qv. **DC 11 Nov 1981**.

10784   ROSS, Angus. From Bornish, Is South Uist, INV. To West Williams Twp, Middlesex Co, ONT, <1849. Wife Catherine Morrison, qv, with him. ch: 1. Ewen, b 1834; 2. Marion, b 1835; 3. Isabella, b 1838; 4. John, b 1840; 5. Ann, b 1842; 6. Donald, b 1844; 7. Finlay, b 1846; 8. Ann, b 1849. **PCM 48; WLC**.

10785   ROSS, Arthur. Prob rel to Donald R, qv. To Metcalfe and Adelaide Twps, Middlesex Co, ONT, 1832.

Discharged soldier, 78th Regt. ch: 1. Andrew, Reeve of London East; 2. Donald, res East Williams Twp; 3. Isabella. **BNA 1091; PCM 26**.

10786   ROSS, Arthur, 1821–1900. From Arnage, Ellon, ABD. To Nichol Twp, Wellington Co, ONT, 1838. Farmer and merchant. m Elspet Milne, qv, ch: 1. Ann; 2. William; 3. Rev John, Port Dalhousie; 4. David, went to Portland, OR; 5. Robert, went to SAS; 6. Elizabeth; 7. Jane; 8. Alexander, res Port Arthur; 9. Arthur, res Miniota, MAN; 10. Margaret; 11. Elsie; 12. James, res Toronto. **EHE 43**.

10787   ROSS, Betty. From Gorbals, Glasgow. To QUE, prob on the *Atlas*, ex Greenock, 11 Jul 1815; stld North Elmsley Twp, Lanark Co, ONT. Wife of Hugh McKay, qv. **SEC 1**.

10788   ROSS, Catherine, ca 1808–22 Apr 1863. From SUT. To Pictou, NS. Bur Lansdowne. Wife of Donald McDonald, centenarian, qv. **DC 10 Feb 1980**.

10789   ROSS, Catherine, b 3 Nov 1821. From Fearn, ROC. d/o Rev Hugh R, par min, and Ann Ross. To Mira Ferry, now Albert Bridge, Cape Breton Co, NS, 1850. Wife of Rev Hugh MacLeod, qv. **FES vii 57, 64**.

10790   ROSS, Catherine, b 1 Jun 1831. From Kilmuir, Knockbain par, ROC. d/o Alexander R, qv, and Margaret Noble, qv. To Scott Twp, York Co, ONT, 1860. m 20 Mar 1862, Malcolm Ferguson, jr, qv. **RFS 147**.

10791   ROSS, Charles, ca 1794–27 Jun 1844. From Kincraig, Roskeen par, ROC. To Montreal, QUE, and joined NWCo. Served at Norway House as a clerk, and after the merger with HBCo, 1821, stationed at Rainy Lake, New Caledonia and Fort Victoria. Chief trader, 1843. m Isabella Melville, 1822, and had ch. **MDB 648**.

10792   ROSS, Colin. From Dundee, ANS. To Goderich Twp, Huron Co, ONT, 1834. Wife Elizabeth McLagan, qv, with him. Son Alexander McLagan, 1829–1900, banker and politician. **BNA 798; MDB 647**.

10793   ROSS, David. From Tain, ROC. s/o John R, 78th Regt. To Montreal, <1800. Attorney. m 1803, Jane, d/o Arthur Davidson, qv, and Jane Fraser. Son Arthur. **SGC 148**.

10794   ROSS, David. From Is Skye, INV. To Queens Co, PEI, 1821. m Ann Martin, Belle River. Son Donald C, lawyer in Toronto. **HP 38**.

10795   ROSS, Donald. To Queens Co, PEI, <1811, when a petitioner for Dr MacAulay. Farmer nr Pinette. **HP 49**.

10796   ROSS, Donald, b ca 1796. From Rogart, SUT. s/o Donald R. To Pictou, NS, 1815; stld Earltown, Colchester Co. Farmer. m Catherine McBain, ch: 1. Mary, b 1823; 2. Isabella; 3. Alexander; 4. Donald; 5. Donald; 6. Christian; 7. George; 8. James; 9. Angus. **SG xxvi/4 143**.

10797   ROSS, Donald. From Eddrachillis, SUT. To Pictou Co, NS, <1815; stld Irish Mountain. **DC 30 Mar 1981**.

10798   ROSS, Donald, b 1756. To Pictou, NS, 1815; res there 1816, when described as a labourer, m with 1 child. **INS 39**.

10799   ROSS, Donald, b 1794. To Pictou Co, NS, 1815;

res Fishers Grant, 1816. Unm labourer, 'sick from fall,' and the 'only support of his family.' **INS 38**.

10800 ROSS, Donald, ca 1797–19 Nov 1852. From Stornoway, Is Lewis, ROC. To Norway House, MAN, 1816, and became confidential secretary to Sir George Simpson, qv, HBCo. He was in charge of Norway House dept, 1830-51, having become a chief trader in 1829, and a chief factor in 1839. Dau Jessy. **DC 8 Oct 1980**.

10801 ROSS, Donald, 27 Jul 1804–9 Dec 1856. From Strath par, Is Skye, INV. s/o Lachlan R, qv, and Catherine Martin, qv. To Queens Co, PEI, 1821. m Flora, 1808-95, d/o Donald Nicholson, qv, and Isabella Nicholson, qv, ch: 1. Donald, 1824-92; 2. Walter; 3. Katherine; 4. Isabel; 5. Alexander; 6. John, 1835–1908; 7. David, 1837–1913. **SPI 157**.

10802 ROSS, Donald. Prob rel to Arthur R, qv. To Metcalfe Twp, Middlesex Co, ONT, 1832. Fought at Waterloo, 1815. ch: 1. Arthur, politician; 2. William H, barrister; 3. James, teacher; 4. Donald, farmer. **PCM 26**.

10803 ROSS, Donald. To Pictou, NS, on the *Lady Gray*, ex Cromarty, ROC. arr 16 Jul 1841. **DC 15 Jul 1979**.

10804 ROSS, Donald, 17 Mar 1820–26 Aug 1914. From Knockbain, ROC, but b Killearnan par. s/o Alexander R, qv, and Margaret Noble, qv. To QUE on the *Brilliant*, ex Cromarty, arr 23 May 1842; stld Scott Twp, York Co, ONT. Farmer. m 30 May 1854, Mary Ann, 1831–1905, d/o Henry Madill, from MOG, IRL, and Elizabeth Quin, ch: 1. Alexander, b 1855; 2. Henry, b 1856; 3. John, b 1858, went to Brandon, MAN; 4. Donald, b 1860; 5. Benjamen, b 1863; 6. Elizabeth, b 1863; 7. Francis Roderick, b 1870; 8. William, b 1873; 9. Margaret, b 1876. **RFS 116, 132; DC 24 Jun 1979**.

10805 ROSS, Donald. To Pictou, NS, on the *London*, arr 14 Jul 1848. **DC 15 Jul 1979**.

10806 ROSS, Donald, b 1825. To Cumberland Co, NS. m Margaret Fraser, Port Philip, and went to Thorburn, Pictou Co. ch: 1. Matilda; 2. James; 3. Alexander; 4. Ann; 5. Margaret; 6. Charles; 7. William; 8. Janet. **NSN 26/165**.

10807 ROSS, Duncan. From Alyth, PER. To West River, Pictou Co, NS, <1802. Farmer and lay preacher. Founded an Agricultural society. Son Rev James, 1811-86, Principal of Dalhousie Coll, Halifax. **BNA 837; HNS iii 90; PAC 236**.

10808 ROSS, Elizabeth, 1823-67. From Kilmuir, Knockbain par, ROC, but b Killearnan par. d/o Alexander R, qv, and Margaret Noble, qv. To Oct 1854; stld Scott Twp, York Co, and moved to Minto Twp, Wellington Co. Wife of Donald Fraser, qv. **RFS 164**.

10809 ROSS, Finlay, b 1766. To Pictou, NS, 1815; res there in 1816, when recorded as a shoemaker, m with 7 ch, and 'an industrious man.' **INS 39**.

10810 ROSS, Georgina, 21 Mar 1815–4 May 1901. From Loch Broom, ROC. d/o Rev Thomas R, par min, and Jane Mackenzie. To St John, NB, poss 1850; later to Galt, Waterloo Co, ONT, and afterwards to NY. m Rev John Thomson, qv. **FES vi 363, vii 159, 612**.

10811 ROSS, George, ca 1793–25 Jul 1838. From Rogart, SUT. s/o Donald R. To Pictou Co, NS, 1813; stld

West River, later in Earltown, Colchester Co. Schoolmaster, innkeeper and farmer. m Margaret, 1796–1868, d/o John McLellan, and Margaret McMillan, ch: 1. Isabelle, 1815-30; 2. Donald, 1816-86; 3. Margaret, 1819-54; 4. William, 1821-88, went to PEI; 5. John, 1823-56, went to PEI; 6. James, 1827–1902; 7. Nancy, 1828–1914; 8. Ada Christian, 1830–1921; 9. George, d inf. **SG xxvi/4 143**.

10812 ROSS, George. To Hudson Bay and Red River <1815. Pioneer settler. **LSS 192; LSC 327**.

10813 ROSS, George. From ROC. bro/o Alexander R, qv, Hugh R, qv, John R, qv, Thomas R, qv, and William R, qv. To Waldegrave, Colchester Co, NS, 1841. Farmer. **HT 70**.

10814 ROSS, George, ca 1741–5 May 1816. From Aberdeen. To Shelburne, Shelburne Co, NS. Merchant. **NSS 796**.

10815 ROSS, George. From SUT. To Colchester Co, NS, <1820; stld nr Earltown. Farmer. **HT 43**.

10816 ROSS, Rev Hugh, 1796–1858. From ABD. To Ross Point, Colchester Co, NS, <1823. Educ Pictou Academy, and licensed to preach by the Anti-Burgher Presb, 1824. After missionary work in Cape Breton Is, adm min of Tatamagouche and New Annan, 1827. Joined Ch of Scotland and became min at Georgetown, PEI. Embraced FC, 1844. m Flora McKay, 1794–1874, ch: 1. Mary Ann; 2. Margaret; 3. Caroline; 4. Isabella; 5. Jessie; 6. Flora; 7. Elizabeth; 8. James; 9. John; 10. Peter; 11. Alexander. **HT 67; FES vii 622**.

10817 ROSS, Hugh. From Strathdearn, INV. To East Williams Twp, Middlesex Co, ONT, 1832. **PCM 43**.

10818 ROSS, Hugh (1). To Pictou, NS, on the *Lady Gray*, ex Cromarty, ROC, arr 16 Jul 1841. **DC 15 Jul 1979**.

10819 ROSS, Hugh (2). To Pictou, NS, on the *Lady Gray*, ex Cromarty, ROC, arr 16 Jul 1841. **DC 15 Jul 1979**.

10820 ROSS, Hugh. From ROC. bro/o Alexander R, qv, George R, qv, John R, qv, Thomas R, qv, and William R, qv. To Waldegrave, Colchester Co, NS, 1841. Farmer. **HT 70**.

10821 ROSS, Hugh, 1797–1889. From SUT. To NS, 1854. Shepherd. m (i) Mary McLean; (ii) Margaret McIntosh, qv. **LDW 7 Feb 1973**.

10822 ROSS, Isabell. From Flemington, nr Fort George, INV. d/o John R. To Cornwallis, Annapolis Co, NS; later to east branch, East River, Pictou Co. Wife of Charles McIntosh, qv. **SG iii/4 99; CP 54**.

10823 ROSS, Isabella, ca 1804–6 May 1845. From Abernethy, INV. To Pictou Co, NS, prob <1830. m William McDonald, qv. **DC 10 Feb 1980**.

10824 ROSS, Isabella. To Middlesex Co, ONT, <30 Sep 1834; stld Williams Twp. m Donald Fraser, qv. **PCM 17**.

10825 ROSS, Isabella, ca 1821–19 Oct 1898. From Knockbain par, ROC, but b Killearnan par. d/o Alexander R, qv, and Margaret Noble, qv. To QUE on the *John McKenzie*, ex Glasgow, 25 Jun 1857; stld Scott Twp, York Co, ONT, later Minto Twp, Wellington Co. Wife of William Young, qv. **RFS 200**.

10826   ROSS, James, b 1765. To Pictou Co, NS, 1815; res Fishers Grant, 1816. Labourer, m with 9 ch. **INS 38**.

10827   ROSS, James, b 5 Oct 1793. From Dalkeith, MLN. s/o William R, labourer, and Agnes Wilkieson. To QUE, ca 1817. m at Montreal, 1823, Mary, d/o Joseph Hargrieve and Jane Melrose. **Dalkeith OPR 683/4; LDW 14 Apr 1973**.

10828   ROSS, James. From BAN. s/o — R. and — Stewart. To Antigonish Co, NS, prob <1830. m Mary, d/o Peter Grant, Merigomish, ch: 1. Catherine; 2. John, dy; 3. Colin; 4. Patrick; 5. Donald; 6. James; 7. Betsy. **HCA 356**.

10829   ROSS, James. From Edderton, ROC. To East Williams Twp, Middlesex Co, ONT, 1834. m Ellen Mackinnon. Son George William, 1841–1914, Prime Minister of ONT, 1899–1905. **BNA 753; PCM 44**.

10830   ROSS, James, ca 1794–21 Dec 1869. From Dysart, FIF. To Guelph, Wellington Co, ONT, 1834; later to Pilkington Twp, and ret to Elora, Nichol Twp. m Cecilia Miller, qv, ch: 1. James, jr, qv; 2. George, d 1879; 3. John, res Pasadena, CA. **EHE 40**.

10831   ROSS, James, jr. From Dysart, FIF. s/o James R, qv, and Cecilia Miller, qv. To Guelph Twp, Wellington Co, ONT, 1834; later to Pilkington Twp. Farmer. m Jean Bissett, ch: 1. Cecilia; 2. James; 3. Jane; 4. John; 5. George Miller; 6. Margaret. **EHE 40**.

10832   ROSS, James, 1819-95. From Ellon, ABD. s/o John Leith R. of Arnage and Elizabeth Young. Grad MA, Marischall Coll, Aberdeen, 1841. To Wellington Co, ONT. Warden of Wellington; MLA, North Wellington, 1859-61, and elected to the Commons, 1868. m 1846, Mary Milne, ch. **BNA 754; FAM 479; HWS 305**.

10833   ROSS, James. To Pictou, NS, on the *Lady Gray*, ex Cromarty, ROC, arr 16 Jul 1841. **DC 15 Jul 1979**.

10834   ROSS, James. From ARL. To North Dorchester Twp, Middlesex Co, ONT, 1844. **PCM 57**.

10835   ROSS, James, 1812-86. From Tain, ROC. Prob s/o Alexander R, tenant. To Zorra Twp, Oxford Co, ONT, <1850. Purchased with bro John, qv, 200 acres, Lot 9, Con 16. Son Alexander. **DC 26 Feb 1977**.

10836   ROSS, Jane, 22 Jul 1826–27 Feb 1916. From ROC. To Pictou Co, NS, prob <1845; bur Mount Thom. m Alexander Ross, 1826–27 Feb 1887. **DC 10 Feb 1980**.

10837   ROSS, Janet. From Drynie, ROC. To Queens Co, PEI, ca 1808. Retr to SCT <1818, and again in 1834. Wife of David McGregor, qv. **DC 11 Apr 1981**.

10838   ROSS, Janet, 1780–28 Sep 1876. From PER. To Lanark Co, ONT, poss 1821. m at Glasgow, 7 Jun 1805, William Bain, qv. **DC 2 Nov 1979**.

10839   ROSS, Jessie. From Tain, ROC. Prob d/o Alexander R, tenant. To Zorra Twp, Oxford Co, ONT, <1851. m Andrew Emmerson, a widower. **DC 26 Feb 1977**.

10840   ROSS, John. From Dingwall, ROC. To Pictou, NS, on the *Hector*, ex Loch Broom, arr 17 Sep 1773, but seems not to have stld. Merchant in Dingwall, appointed by the Board of Trustees of the Forfeited Estates to manage a linen factory at Lochbroom; emigration agent for John Pagan, 1773. **LDW 19 Nov 1979**.

10841   ROSS, John. To York Co, ONT, ca 1796, and gr 200 acres of land for military services. Served 26 years in British Army, 19 as a Sgt in the 26th Regt (Cameronians). ch: 1. Mary, b Dublin, IRL, 1784; 2. James, b 1786; 3. William, b QUE, 1787; 4. Katherine, b 1788; 5. John, b Niagara, 1789; 6. Susanna, b Jole-aux-noire, 1793; 7. William, b Lachine, 1795, d inf; 8. Robert, b Newark, 1797; 9. George, b York, 1799; 10. Thomas, b York, 1803. **DC 4 Jul 1979**.

10842   ROSS, John. From Tain, ROC. s/o John R, 78th Highlanders. To Montreal, QUE, <1800. Prothonotary of the Court of Kings Bench. Son Hon David, politician. **SGC 148**.

10843   ROSS, John. To Queens Co, PEI, poss 1803. Petitioner for Dr A. MacAulay, 1811. **HP 74**.

10844   ROSS, John, b 1746. To Pictou Co, NS, 1815; res Rogers Hill, 1816. Farmer, m with 3 ch. **INS 39**.

10845   ROSS, John, 1761–1856. From ROC. To Pictou, NS, 1813; stld west branch, East River. m Mary Smith, qv, ch: 1. Christy, 1813-30; 2. Peter, qv. **PAC 199; DC 20 Nov 1976**.

10846   ROSS, Sir John, 24 Jun 1777–30 Aug 1856. b Inch, WIG. s/o Rev Andrew R. of Barsarroch, and Elizabeth Corsane. Served in RN, and in 1818 commanded expedition to Baffin's Bay. Made other journeys in quest for North-West Passage and in search of Sir John Franklin; KB, 1834. m (i) 1816, Miss Adair, Edinburgh, who d 1822, ch; (ii) 1834, Miss Jones, London. **SN iii 371; IBD 446; CBD 803; FES ii 337**.

10847   ROSS, John. From ROC. To Pugwash, Cumberland Co, NS, 1832. Wife Margaret, 1802-98. **DC 29 Oct 1980**.

10848   ROSS, John, ca 1790–24 Nov 1874. From SUT. To Pictou Co, NS, and bur Salt Springs. m Mary Ross, qv. **DC 27 Oct 1979**.

10849   ROSS, John. From ROC. bro/o Alexander R, qv, George R, qv, Hugh R, qv, Thomas R, qv, and William R, qv. To Tatamagouche, Colchester Co, NS, 1832. Farmer, wright and shipbuilder. **HT 70**.

10850   ROSS, Rev John, 1807-71. From ROC. s/o Simon R, shoemaker, poss in Cromarty par. Educ at Marischall Coll, Aberdeen. To Shelburne and Yarmouth, NS, 1836, and adm min. Trans to Greenock Presb Ch, St Andrews, Charlotte Co, NB, 1845. **FAM ii 445; FES vii 611; DC 14 Jan 1980**.

10851   ROSS, John. To Pictou, NS, on the *Lady Gray*, ex Cromarty, ROC, arr 16 Jul 1841. **DC 15 Jul 1979**.

10852   ROSS, John, 1811-91. From Tain, ROC. Prob s/o Alexander R, tenant. To Zorra Twp, Oxford Co, ONT, <1850. Purchased with bro James R, qv, 200 acres, Lot 9, Con 16. Son Alexander. **DC 26 Feb 1977**.

10853   ROSS, Joseph. From Aberdeen. bro/o Thomas R, qv. To Montreal, QUE, prob 1818. Grocer, St Joseph St. **SGC 376, 433**.

10854   ROSS, Kenneth. To Pictou Co, NS, <1850; stld Millbrook. Dau Catherine. **HNS iii 388**.

10855 ROSS, Lachlan, ca 1770–15 Jul 1848. From Strath par, Is Skye, INV. To PEI, 1821; stld Queens Co. m Catherine Martin, qv, ch: 1. Donald, qv; 2. David; 3. Isabell; 4. Alexander; 5. Walter; 6. Katherine; 7. Donald Og, 1824-75. **SPI 156**.

10856 ROSS, Malcolm, 11 Jan 1815–22 Aug 1895. From ROC. To Sherbrooke, QUE. m Janet Beattie, qv, ch: 1. Katherine, ca 1852–1936; 2. Robert, ca 1858–2 Jul 1885, killed in a railway accident in MO. **MGC 2 Aug 1979**.

10857 ROSS, Margaret. To London, Westminster Twp, Middlesex Co, ONT, <6 Aug 1833, when m Neil Ross, qv. **PCM 17**.

10858 ROSS, Marion, ca 1815-34. From SUT. To Pictou, NS, 1819. Wife of William MacDonald, West River. Bur at Lovat. **DC 27 Oct 1979**.

10859 ROSS, Mary, ca 1790–18 Dec 1858. From Creich, SUT. To Pictou Co, NS, and bur Salt Springs. Wife of John Ross, qv. **DC 27 Oct 1979**.

10860 ROSS, Murdock. To Cape Breton, NS, <1820; stld Bras d'Or. Moved later to Margaree, Inverness Co. m a French woman, ch: 1. Donald; 2. Hugh, miner; 3. Rev Malcolm, Baptist min, PEI; 4. John; 5. James; 6. William. **HNS iii 630**.

10861 ROSS, Neil. To Middlesex Co, ONT, <6 Aug 1833, when m Margaret Ross, qv. **PCM 17**.

10862 ROSS, Peter, 1798–11 May 1879. From Strathspey. s/o John R, qv, and Mary Smith, qv. To Pictou, NS, 1813; stld West Branch, East River. Land surveyor and Ch elder for 52 years. Bur at Old Elgin. m Catherine McLean, 1796–1876. Son Andrew. **PAC 199; DC 20 Nov 1976**.

10863 ROSS, Robert, b ca 1804. To St Gabriel de Valcartier, prob <1855. **Census 1861**.

10864 ROSS, Roderick, b ca 1814. From ROC. To QUE <1855; stld Bristol, Ottawa Co. m Mary Ross. **DC 2 Apr 1978**.

10865 ROSS, Roderick. From Fortrose, MOR. s/o Donald R, dyker, Hill of Fortrose. To CAN <1855. **SH**.

10866 ROSS, Roderick, 15 Jul 1825–13 Feb 1919. From Knockbain par, but b Killearnan par, ROC. s/o Alexander R, qv, and Margaret Noble, qv. To QUE on the *John McKenzie*, ex Glasgow, arr 25 Jun 1857; stld Scott Twp, York Co, ONT. Moved to Minto Twp, Wellington Co, 1858. Farmer. m Christian Junor, qv, ch: 1. Margaret Ann, b 1857; 2. Alexander, b 1860; 3. Ellen, b ca 1863; 4. John, b ca 1855. **RFS 158**.

10867 ROSS, Thomas, b 21 Mar 1793. From Dalkeith, MLN. s/o William R. and Agnes Wilkieson. To CAN <1818. **Dalkeith OPR 683/4; LDW 14 Apr 1973**.

10868 ROSS, Thomas. From ROC. bro/o Alexander R, qv, George R, qv, Hugh R, qv, John R, qv, and William R, qv. To Waldegrave, Colchester Co, NS, 1841. Farmer. **HT 70**.

10869 ROSS, Thomas, ca 1780–15 Dec 1864. From Aberdeen. bro/o Joseph R, qv. To Montreal, QUE, prob 1818. Cooper. ch: 1. Thomas B; 2. Joseph M; 3. Mrs Whitehead. **SGC 433; DC 4 Jan 1965**.

10870 ROSS, Thomas, 1790–1871. From ROC. To Westmorland Co, NB, 1829; stld Hopewell. m Margaret McRae, qv. **DC 19 Feb 1979**.

10871 ROSS, Thomas. From Tain, ROC. Prob s/o Alexander R, tenant. To Zorra Twp, Oxford Co, ONT, prob <1855, but went to Bruce Peninsula. **DC 26 Feb 1977**.

10872 ROSS, Rev Walter R. Matric Kings Coll, Aberdeen, 1848. Adm min of Pickering, York Co, ONT, 1861. **FES vii 650**.

10873 ROSS, William, ca 1734–7 Nov 1808. From ROC. s/o Alexander R. and Helen Bain. To CAN as an NCO in the 78th Regt, and fought at Quebec. Stld QUE, 1763. m in St Thomas de Montmagny, 9 Jan 1764, Marie-Josephe Proulx, ch: 1. Guillaume, b 1764; 2. Jean-Baptiste, b 1766; 3. Alexander, b 1768; 4. Hector, b 1770; 5. Laughlin, b 1775; 6. Joseph, b ca 1778. **DC 7 May 1975 and 6 Apr 1981**.

10874 ROSS, William, b 1786. To Pictou, NS, 1815; res Fishers Grant, 1816. Labourer, m with 3 ch. Poor, but 'able to work.' **INS 38**.

10875 ROSS, William, d 27 Apr 1824. To Truro, Colchester Co, NS, and d there. **VSN No 568**.

10876 ROSS, William, 1799–17 Mar 1875. From Stornoway, Is Lewis, ROC. To Victoria Co, NS. **DC 22 Jun 1979**.

10877 ROSS, William, ca 1780–12 Jan 1855. From ROC. Served as an ensign in the 11th Regt and entered the service of the HBCo. Emp at Oxford House, Nelson House and Fort Churchill. Retr to Ottawa. **MDB 651**.

10878 ROSS, William. From ROC. bro/o Alexander R, qv, Hugh R, qv, John R, qv, George R, qv, and Thomas R, qv. To Waldegrave, Colchester Co, NS, 1841. Farmer. **HT 70**.

10879 ROSS, William, 9 Aug 1828–ca 1909. From Redcastle, Killearnan par, ROC. s/o Alexander Ross and Margaret Noble, qv. To QUE, 1851; stld Minto Twp, Wellington Co, ONT. Farmer. m Anne McDiarmed, qv, ch: 1. Anna, b 1855; 2. Alexander, b 1867; 3. Margaret, b 1869; 4. Flora. **DC 24 Jun 1979**.

10880 ROSS, William, d 1855. From ROC. To Montreal, QUE, but retr to SCT, and res nr Kirriemuir, ANS. **SH**.

10881 ROSS, William, b ca 1804. From Jemimaville, nr Resolis, ROC. To Carleton Co, ONT, 1834. m Mary Ann Munro, qv, in 1831. **LDW 2 Apr 1978**.

10882 ROSS, William. From ROC. To East Williams Twp, Middlesex Co, ONT, 1836. ch: 1. George M; 2. David; 3. Ellen; 4. Margaret; 5. Jessie. **PCM 43, 44**.

10883 ROSS, William. To Pictou, NS, on the *Lady Gray*, ex Cromarty, ROC, arr 16 Jul 1841. **DC 15 Jul 1979**.

10884 ROSS, William, b 14 Mar 1815. From Tain, ROC. To CAN <1850. m 2 Feb 1838, Christine Urquhart, qv, ch: 1. Harry, b 1839; 2. Jane, b 1840; 3-4. John and William, b 1842; 5-6. Jessie and Isabella; 7. Alexander, b 1849; 8. Walter, b 1851; 9. Isabella, b 1856. **DC 27 Sep 1974**.

10885 ROSS, William Aird, 24 Oct 1816–31 Dec 1904. From Roskeen, ROC. s/o Donald R, farmer, Strathrusdale, and Janet Aird. Educ Tain Academy and Queens Univ, ONT. Headmaster of Williamstown Grammar School, Glengarry Co, <1850, afterwards of Ottawa Grammar School. Practised law after 1855 in Ottawa, in partnership with Hon Richard W. Scott, QC. App Judge of Carleton Co, 1874. m Janet Durie, who d 1893. **Roskeen OPR 81/1; DC 2 Apr and 9 Oct 1978**.

10886 ROTHNEY, William. From ABD. To Leeds Twp, Megantic Co, QUE, 1819. Farmer. m Elizabeth Smith, qv. Son George. **DC 11 Feb 1980**.

10887 ROWAL, Christian. From Waterside, Fenwick par, AYR. To QUE, prob on the *Atlas*, ex Greenock, 11 Jul 1815; stld North Burgess Twp, Lanark Co, ONT. Wife of Abraham Ferrier, qv. **SEC 3**.

10888 ROWAN, William, ca 1803–21 Jan 1874. From Strathaven, LKS. To Montreal, QUE, <1848. Discharged soldier, 79th Regt, and became town sergeant. **SGC 529**.

10889 ROWAT, John, b 10 Feb 1792. From Kilsyth, STI. To ONT <1820; again with his family, 1826. Farmer. m (i) Agnes Scott, d 1820; (ii) Margaret Drysdale, in CAN. **DC 21 Mar 1981**.

10890 ROXBURGH, Euphemia. From KKD. To ONT <1854. **SH**.

10891 ROY, Rev David, b ca 1795. From Muthill par, PER. s/o John R, craftsman. Matric Univ of Glasgow, 1811. Probationer of the Secession Ch. To NS and became min of New Glasgow, Pictou Co. **GMA 8513**.

10892 ROY, Henry, b 25 Apr 1813. From Edinburgh. s/o William R. of Nenthorn, 22 Drummond Place. Educ Edinburgh Academy, 1824-30, and afterwards went to CAN. **EAR 19**.

10893 ROY, Rev James, ca 1799–15 May 1852. From Denny, STI. s/o Alexander R, farmer. Matric Univ of Glasgow, 1808. Ord Secession min in 1827, and went to ONT, where he was min at Dumfries and Beverly. **GMA 7506**.

10894 ROY, John. From Glasgow. To Pictou Co, NS, prob <1853; stld Albion Mines or Stellarton. Miner. m Fannie Brown. Son James, Town Clerk of New Glasgow, 1898. **HNS iii 422**.

10895 RUSSEL, John, d ca 1801. From Tain, ROC. bro/o William R, qv, and Robert R, qv. To Montreal, QUE, <1790. Merchant. Accidentally drowned. m Grizel McKenzie, qv, ch. **SGC 79**.

10896 RUSSEL, Robert. From Tain, ROC. bro/o William R, qv, and John R, qv. To Montreal, QUE, <1791. Lawyer. **SGC 89**.

10897 RUSSEL, William. From Tain, ROC. bro/o John R, qv, and Robert R, qv. To Montreal, QUE, <1891. **SGC 80**.

10898 RUSSELL, Agnes, b 1823. From Haddington, ELN. d/o Robert R. To London on the steamboat *Trident*, ex Granton, 11 Aug 1852; thence to Victoria, BC, on the *Norman Morrison*, ex India Docks, 20 Aug 1852. m Kenneth McKenzie, qv. **DC 22 Apr 1978**.

10899 RUSSELL, Alexander, 1777–1852. To Miramichi, Northumberland Co, NB, 1787. Wife Catherine, 1787–1827. **DC 4 Dec 1978**.

10900 RUSSELL, Alexander. Poss from BEW. To Pictou Co, NS, <1843; stld Middle River. Farmer. m (i) Margaret Kerr, ch: 1. Mary; 2. Elizabeth; 3. James; 4. Robert. m (ii) Margaret McKenzie, ch: 5. Jessie. m (iii) Mrs Brown, further ch: 6. Calder; 7. Annie. **PAC 203**.

10901 RUSSELL, Andrew. Poss from LKS. To QUE <1830. m Mary Nimmo, qv. **SG xxvii/2 80**.

10902 RUSSELL, Anna, 26 Aug 1791–Mar 1872. From Elgin, MOR. To ONT <1855; stld Sarnia, Lambton Co. **DC 21 Mar 1981**.

10903 RUSSELL, Annabella, b 8 Dec 1811. From Gairloch, ROC. d/o Rev James R, par min, and Isabella Munro. To Perth, Lanark Co, ONT. m Col Roderick Matheson. **FES vii 148**.

10904 RUSSELL, Alexander Jamieson, 1807-87. From Glasgow. To Megantic Co, QUE, 1822. Engineer and surveyor. **MDB 657**.

10905 RUSSELL, Catherine. From Coupar-Angus, PER. To Montreal, QUE, <1850. wid/o John Morton, 1766–1840, by whom she had ch: 1. Ann, b 1794; 2. Robert; 3. Mrs Peacock; 4. Alexander; 5. Andrew. **DC 11 Jul 1966**.

10906 RUSSELL, Elizabeth. From Is Arran, BUT. To Megantic Co, QUE, and stld Halifax Twp <1850. Wife of John Kean. **AMC 49**.

10907 RUSSELL, Helen or Ellen, 1827-93. From Haddington, ELN. d/o Robert R, stabler, and Agnes Cameron. To London on the steamer *Trident*, ex Granton, 11 Aug 1852; thence to Victoria, BC, on the *Norman Morrison*, ex East India Docks, 20 Aug 1852. Wife of James Liddell, qv, m Dec 1850. **DC 22 Apr 1979**.

10908 RUSSELL, Isobel. From Haddington, ELN. d/o Robert R, stabler, and Agnes Cameron. To London on the steamer *Trident*, ex Granton, 11 Aug 1852; thence to Victoria, BC, on the *Norman Morrison*, ex East India Docks, 20 Aug 1852. **DC 4 Oct 1981**.

10909 RUSSELL, Jane. From BAN. To Halifax, NS, <1808. Wife of William Annand, qv. **MLA 14**.

10910 RUSSELL, John, 1822-64. Prob from BEW. To Pictou Co, NS, <1843; stld Middle River. m Margaret Dryden, 1818-90. **PAC 203**.

10911 RUSSELL, John. To Montreal, QUE, <1853. Merchant. Son Hector. **SH**.

10912 RUSSELL, Robert. From BEW. To Pictou, NS, <1843; stld Middle River. Farmer, gr 300 acres. m (i) Miss McLeod, ch: 1. Robert, b 1843, dy. m (ii) Margaret McLellan, West River, further ch: 2. Walter Robert, b 1857; 3. Thomas, d 1869. **PAC 202**.

10913 RUSSELL, Robert. From Chirnside, BEW. To Pictou Co, NS, <1840; stld Middle River, later New Glasgow. Farmer and sawyer. ch: 1. Elizabeth; 2. William; 3. Mary; 4. Annie; 5. Alison. **PAC 204**.

10914 RUSSELL, Rev Thomas. From Slamannan, STI. s/o William R, farmer. Matric Univ of Glasgow, 1772. To Halifax, NS, 1783. Min of Protestant Dissenting Ch there until 1787, when lost on a voyage to SCT. **GMA 3264; FES vii 618**.

10915 RUSSELL, Thomas, b 29 Feb 1836. From Haddington, ELN. s/o Robert R, stabler, and Agnes Cameron. To London on the steamer *Trident*, ex Granton, 11 Aug 1852; thence to Victoria, BC, on the *Norman Morrison*, ex East India Docks, 20 Aug 1852. m Sarah McKenzie, qv. **DC 22 Apr 1978**.

10916 RUTHERFORD, Elizabeth, 21 Jul 1808–25 Jun 1894. From Kelso, ROX. d/o Walter R. and Margaret Redpath. To York Co, ONT, 1831; stld Scarborough Twp. Wife of William Hood, qv, m 1826. **DC 27 Aug 1975**.

10917 RUTHERFORD, Jane. From Blairgowrie, PER. To ONT, 1843. Wife of James Jackson, qv. **DC 23 Mar 1979**.

10918 RUTHERFORD, Lumsden, d 1876. To Ottawa, ONT, 1836 and 1850. m Catherine Stevenson. Son George. **DC 29 Sep 1964**.

10919 RUTHERFORD, Mary, 25 Dec 1801–14 Sep 1885. From Jedburgh, ROX, but b Northumberland, ENG. To South Elmsley Twp, Leeds Co, ONT, 1831. Wife of Archibald Brown, qv. **DC 9 Nov 1981**.

10920 RUTHERFORD, Peter, d 1848. From Dunfermline, FIF. To Toronto, ONT, 1832. Builder. Son John. **DC 29 Sep 1964**.

10921 RUTHERFORD, William, b ca 1790. From Liff and Benvie par, ANS. To QUE, ex Greenock, summer 1815; stld North Burgess Twp, Lanark Co, ONT. Wright. **SEC 4; HCL 15, 230**.

10922 RUTHERFORD, William. Poss from LKS. To QUE on the *Commerce*, ex Greenock, 11 May 1821; stld North Sherbrooke Twp, Lanark Co, ONT. Wife d on voyage, ch: 1. Thomas; 2. Mary; 3. William, d 1821. **DC 28 Dec 1978**.

10923 RUTHVEN, Colin. Poss from PER. Prob rel to Hugh R, qv, and James R, qv. To Aldborough Twp, Elgin Co, ONT, 1818. Farmer. **PDA 92**.

10924 RUTHVEN, Hugh. Poss from PER, and prob rel to James R, qv, and Colin R, qv. To Aldborough Twp, Elgin Co, ONT, 1818. Farmer. **PDA 92**.

10925 RUTHVEN, James. Poss from PER, and prob rel to Colin R, qv, and Hugh R, qv. To QUE on the *Mars*, ex Tobermory, 28 Jul 1818. Drowned when attempting to go ashore at New Glasgow, Elgin Co. **PDA 24**.

10926 RUTHVEN, Robert, 1777–1852. From Glasgow. To Essa Twp, Simcoe Co, ONT, ca 1825. Farmer. m Margaret Thompson, qv, ch: 1. John, b 1799, remained in SCT; 2. Alexander; 3. Robert, 1803–79; 4. George, b 1804; 5. William, 1815–73. **DC 24 May 1979**.

10927 RUXTON, Margaret. From Foveran, ABD. To Nichol Twp, Wellington Co, ONT, 1836. Wife of James Findlay, qv. **EHE 92**.

S

10928 SAMSON, Peter. To Pictou, NS, on the *Lulan*, ex Glasgow, 17 Aug 1848. Wife Janet with him, and ch: 1. Peter; 2. Margaret; 3. Agnes; 4. Jane; 5. Robert. **DC 12 Jul 1979**.

10929 SANDERS, James, d 4 May 1855. From Wamphray par, DFS. s/o William S, surgeon, and Mary Jardine. To Ellesmere, Scarborough Twp, York Co, ONT. **Ts Wamphrey**.

10930 SANDILANDS, George, 1811-64. From Kirkcaldy, FIF. To Huntingdon Co, QUE, 1827; stld Athelstan, and d Hinchinbrooke. Farmer. **DC 19 Nov 1982**.

10931 SANDILANDS, Robert, ca 1822–1840. From DFS. s/o William S, mason. To QUE and d there. **DGH 3 Dec 1840**.

10932 SANDISON, James, 1811–29 Dec 1875. From CAI. To Raleigh Twp, Kent Co, ONT, ca 1825. Brewer. m (i) 28 Jul 1836, Christian Duncan, 1818-37, ch: 1. James, b Cornwall, ONT, 12 Jul 1837. m (ii) 21 Aug 1838, Frances, d/o Samuel Cherry and Abigail Delano, further ch: 2. Christie Ann, b 27 May 1839; 3. William Wilbur, b 26 Oct 1840; 4. Samuel, b 21 Dec 1842; 5. Edwin Wallace, b 2 Nov 1845; 6. Thomas Stuart, b 7 May 1848; 7. Francis Adelaide, b 25 Dec 1851. **DC 27 Jan 1969**.

10933 SANDY, William, 4 Sep 1812–17 Jul 1893. From Alyth, PER. s/o Gilbert S. and Jane Drummond. To Garafraxa Twp, Wellington Co, ONT, <1844. Stonemason and farmer. m 1838, Maria, d/o John Wardell and Sarah Dutton, ch: 1. James, b 20 May 1839; 2. Sarah, b 13 Aug 1841; 3. Maria, b 24 Oct 1843; 4. John, b 25 May 1846; 5. Jane, b 7 May 1849; 6. Isabella, b 29 Jun 1851; 7. Margaret, b 9 Jun 1854; 8. William, b 6 Jun 1860. **DC 13 Nov 1979**.

10934 SANGSTER, John. From Aberdeen. To Hants Co, NS, <1795; stld Falmouth. m Susan, d/o Rev James Murdock, qv. Son James Murdock, 1796–1866, farmer and MLA. **HNS iii 60; MLA 309**.

10935 SANGSTER, Jean, 1808-67. From ABD. To Wellington Co, ONT, 1835. Wife of Alexander Burnett, qv. **DC 11 Nov 1981**.

10936 SAUNDERS, Mrs Catherine, ca 1797–2 Mar 1866. From CLK. wid/o Thomas S, d 1845. To CAN, and d there. **Ts Clackmannan**.

10937 SAUNDERS, Donald, b ca 1820, poss Is Arran, BUT. To Garafraxa Twp, Wellington Co, ONT, <1854. Farmer. By first wife had ch: 1. Mary, b 11 May 1843; 2. Henrietta. m (ii) Margaret, d/o Malcolm Smith and Mary McIntyre, with further ch: 3. Margaret, b 1854; 4. Christena, b 1856; 5. Sarah, b 1859; 6. Robert, b 1867; 7. Mary Emily, b 1870. **DC 13 Nov 1979**.

10938 SAUNDERS, Duncan, 1824-72. From Blairgowrie, PER. s/o John S, qv, and Margaret Seaton, qv. To Montreal, QUE, 1843. Plasterer, later farmer. m Jane Manson, qv, ch: 1. Jane, 1848-49; 2. John, 1849-50; 3. Elizabeth, 1852–1927; 4. William, 1855–1927; 5. Mary, 1857–1944; 6. Isabella, 1860-61; 7. Duncan Douvin, 1861–1940; 8. John, 1864–1944. **DC 31 Dec 1979**.

10939 SAUNDERS, Elizabeth, 1830–1907. From Blairgowrie, PER. d/o John S, qv, and Margaret Seaton, qv. To Hamilton, ONT, 1852. m James Duncan Seaton, qv. **DC 31 Dec 1979**.

10940 SAUNDERS, Isabella, 1820-92. From Blairgowrie, PER. d/o John S, qv, and Margaret Seaton, qv. To Hamilton, ONT, 1852. Handloom weaver. m Peter Reid, b ca 1818, ch: 1. John, b ca 1852; 2. David, b ca 1854; 3. Margaret, b ca 1856; 4. Janet, b ca 1859; 5. Peter, b ca 1861. **DC 31 Dec 1979**.

10941   SAUNDERS, James, 1824-92. From Blairgowrie, PER. s/o John S, qv, and Margaret Seaton, qv. To Hamilton, ONT, 1852. Tinsmith and ironmonger. m Catherine Kennedy, qv, ch: 1. Margaret, b ca 1843; 2. Arthur, b ca 1847; 3. James Harrison, qv; 4. Thomas, b ca 1852; 5. Alexander, 1854–1928; 6. Catherine Jean, 1858–1935.   **DC 31 Dec 1979**.

10942   SAUNDERS, James Harrison, 1849–1937. From Blairgowrie, PER. s/o James S, qv, and Catherine Kennedy, qv. To Hamilton, ONT, 1852. Farmer. m 25 Feb 1875, Margaret Isabel Saunders, ch: 1. Catherine Ann, 1875–1952; 2. Jennie Mabel, b 1878; 3. Margaret Alice, 1882–1959; 4. Thomas William, 1884–1968; 5. Bertha, b 1887; 6. Maude Lilliam, b 1888.   **DC 31 Dec 1979**.

10943   SAUNDERS, Janet or Jessie, 1839–1910. From Blairgowrie, PER. d/o John S, qv, and Margaret Seaton, qv. To Hamilton, ONT, 1852. m James Bartlet Wales, qv.   **DC 31 Dec 1979**.

10944   SAUNDERS, John, 1793–1872. From Blairgowrie, PER. To Hamilton, ONT, 1852. Weaver, later farmer. m Margaret Seaton, qv, ch: 1. Isabella, qv; 2. James, qv; 3. Duncan, qv; 4. Margaret, b 1826; 5. William, b 1828; 6. Elizabeth, qv; 7. Thomas, d inf, 1832; 8. Mary Coleville, qv; 9. John, qv; 10. Janet or Jessie, qv.   **DC 31 Dec 1979**.

10945   SAUNDERS, John, jr, 1836–1900. From Blairgowrie, PER. s/o John S, qv, and Margaret Seaton, qv. To Hamilton, ONT, 1852. Tinsmith, later farmer. m Mary Rebecca, 1845–1921, d/o William Fleming, and Eliza Ellis, ch: 1. William Fleming, 1871–1918; 2. Margaret Elizabeth, 1873–1947; 3. John Elmer, 1876–1939; 4. Mary Adella, 1878–1904; 5. Duncan Stewart, 1881–1947; 6. Charles Reid, 1883–1960; 7. Dora Alice, 1886–1969; 8. Anna Bella, 1889–1953. **DC 31 Dec 1979**.

10946   SAUNDERS, Mary Coleville, 1834–1915. From Blairgowrie, PER. d/o John S, qv, and Margaret Seaton, qv. To Hamilton, ONT, 1852. m James Dalrymple, qv. **DC 31 Dec 1979**.

10947   SAWERS, George, b ca 1792. To Western Shore, Inverness Co, NS, 1812. Farmer, m and ch. **CBC 1818**.

10948   SCHLABERG, Wilhelmina Elizabeth, 1824-83. b Leith, MLN. d/o Charles Frederick S, merchant, from Hildesheim, GER, and Rebecca Wilson. To QUE, 1828; stld poss Argenteuil Co. m James Low, qv. **SG xxx/2 69; DC 15 Jan 1982**.

SCLATER. See also SLATER.

10949   SCLATER, Alexander, 13 Mar 1819–4 May 1876. From Saltcoats, AYR. To QUE, and stld Montreal, 1858. Sea Capt, and became port warden. m d/o Dr Grant, Martintown.   **SGC 636**.

10950   SCOBIE, Hugh, 29 Apr 1811–4 Dec 1853. From Fort George, INV. Educ Tain Academy and emig to Toronto, ONT, 1832. Journalist, and founded the *British Colonist*.   **MDB 673**.

10951   SCOBIE, Jean, b ca 1756. To Charlottetown, PEI, on the *Elizabeth & Ann*, ex Thurso, arr 8 Nov 1806. Wife of William McKay, qv.   **PLEA**.

10952   SCOT, Alexander. From Urquhart and Glenmoriston par, INV. To Montreal, QUE, ex Fort William, arr Sep 1802; stld poss Finch Twp, Stormont Co, ONT.   **MCM 1/4 24**.

10953   SCOT, Donald. From Aberchalder, INV. To Montreal, QUE, ex Fort William, arr Sep 1802; stld E ONT. Wife with him, and ch: 1. Alexander; 2. Duncan; 3. Janet; 4. Mary.   **MCM 1/4 23**.

10954   SCOT, John, b ca 1772. To Pictou Co, NS, 1815; res Mount Thom, 1816. Labourer, m but family in SCT.   **INS 39**.

10955   SCOT, William, d <1905. Poss from Sanquhar, DFS. To Melbourne, Richmond Co, QUE, prob <1850. m Susan Reid, qv.   **MGC 15 Jul 1980**.

10956   SCOTT, Adam, b 26 Nov 1793. From Hawick, ROX. To Botsford, Westmorland Co, NB, 1834. m Janet Armstrong, qv, ch: 1. James Amos; 2. Ellen; 3. Robert; 4. Agnes; 5. Barbara; 6. Adam.   **DC 11 Dec 1979**.

10957   SCOTT, Adam, ca 1823–22 Oct 1881. From Canonbie, DFS. To St Johns, NFD, 1851.   **DGC 17 Jan 1882**.

10958   SCOTT, Alexander McDonald, 1809–4 Aug 1909. From Fraserburgh, ABD. s/o Alexander S, blacksmith, and Elizabeth Robb. To NS, ca 1830. Lumber merchant. Retr to SCT <26 Jul 1859, when m Grace, 1834–1906, d/o Alexander Cassie and Mary Philip. They went to Middlesex Co, ONT, ca 1870, ch: 1. Christie; 2. Ann, d 1943; 3. Alexander M, 1862–1933; 4. James Cassie, b ca 1863; 5. Mary P, d unm 1890; 6. Jessie; 7. Catherine, d 1919; 8. William Ironside, d unm 1900.   **DC 21 Jul 1979**.

10959   SCOTT, Andrew, 1803–26 Feb 1880. From PER. To Esquesing Twp, Halton Co, ONT, prob <1830; bur Acton. m Ann Lawson, qv.   **EPE 74**.

10960   SCOTT, Andrew. From ROX. bro/o Dr John S, qv. To Galt, Waterloo Co, ONT, poss 1831.   **HGD 105**.

10961   SCOTT, Andrew, 8 Nov 1800–10 Oct 1870. b Burnmouth, Castleton, ROX. s/o William S, schoolmaster, and Isabella Veitch. To Brockville, Leeds and Grenville Co, ONT, 1841. Schoolteacher. Retr to SCT, 1844, and became Prof of Hebrew in the Univ of Aberdeen.   **KCG 74; FES vii 369**.

10962   SCOTT, Archibald. From Aberchalder, nr Daviot, INV. To PEI on the *Jane*, ex Loch nan Uamh, Arisaig, 12 Jul 1790.   **PLJ**.

10963   SCOTT, Ann, ca 1798–1865. From Auchinblae, Fordoun, KCD. To Nichol Twp, Wellington Co, ONT, <1844. Wife of David Milne, qv.   **EHE 42**.

10964   SCOTT, Ann, b ca 1803. From Paisley, RFW. To ONT, prob <1850. m Francis Reid, qv.   **DC 8 Mar 1977**.

10965   SCOTT, Charles, 1824-96. From Hawick, ROX. s/o Charles S, weaver. To Winnipeg, MAN, 1854. m Ann Knox, qv. Dau Margaret, qv.   **THS 1936/96**.

10966   SCOTT, Christopher. From RFW. bro/o James and William S, shipbuilders in Greenock. To St John, NB, 1797; stld St Andrews, Charlotte Co, 1805. Master mariner, engineer and timber merchant. Built Greenock Presb Ch, St Andrews.   **FES vii 610**.

10967   SCOTT, Helen. Prob from Innerleithen, PEE. To QUE, ex Greenock, summer 1815; stld ONT. Wife of Robert Hood, qv.   **SEC 2**.

10968 SCOTT, Helen, ca 1790–16 Mar 1872. From Hawick, ROX. To ONT, and stld prob Galt, Waterloo Co. **THS 1936/27**.

10969 SCOTT, Helen, 14 May 1818–19 Jun 1888. From Hawick, ROX. To King Twp, York Co, ONT, ca 1846. Wife of William Anderson, qv. **DC 2 Aug 1979**.

10970 SCOTT, Isabella Booth, 20 Oct 1812–6 May 1896. From ABD. To QUE, 1836; stld Elora Twp, Wellington Co, ONT. Wife of Fairly Milne, qv. **DC 27 Nov 1981**.

10971 SCOTT, James. Poss from LKS. To Aldborough Twp, Elgin Co, ONT, <1843. ch. **PDA 67**.

10972 SCOTT, John. Served as an NCO in the 82nd Regt and was gr 200 acres in Pictou Co, NS, 1784. Sold land later to John Fraser, qv, late of same regt. **HPC App F**.

10973 SCOTT, John. From Dull par, PER. To Montreal, QUE, on the *Curlew*, ex Greenock, 21 Jul 1818; stld prob Beckwith Twp, Lanark Co, ONT. Wife Margaret with him. **BCL**.

10974 SCOTT, John, d 19 May 1827. From ABD. To NS and d there. **VSN No 2264**.

10975 SCOTT, John, d 10 Jan 1827. Sometime in New Galloway, KKD, and at Whinny Hill, New Abbey, DFS. To Charlottetown, PEI. Farmer. **DGC 28 Jul 1827**.

10976 SCOTT, John. To Galt, Waterloo Co, ONT, 1817, but moved to Chinguacousy Twp, Peel Co. Son Alexander Forsyth, b Brampton, 1828, became judge of the county court of Peel. **BNA 919**.

10977 SCOTT, John. From ROX. bro/o Andrew S, qv. To Galt, Waterloo Co, ONT, summer 1834. Physician, Berlin Village. **HGD 97**.

10978 SCOTT, Rev John, b ca 1817. From Kirkintilloch, DNB. s/o Robert S, craftsman. Matric Univ of Glasgow, 1832. Licentiate of the Secession Ch, and ord for CAN, 1845. **GMA 13001**.

10979 SCOTT, Rev Joseph, ca 1800–22 May 1857. From Hawick, ROX, but poss some connection with Selkirk. Burgher min at Lochgelly, FIF, 1824-33. To Blandford Twp, Oxford Co, ONT, ca 1853. Presb min there. **UPC i 219; DGH 26 Jun 1857**.

10980 SCOTT, Margaret. From Hawick, ROX. d/o Charles S, qv, and Annie Knox, qv. To Winnipeg, MAN, 1854. m Robert Grant, estate agent, Vancouver, BC. **THS 1936/96**.

10981 SCOTT, Margaret, ca 1828–7 Dec 1897. From East Boonraw, Hawick, ROX. d/o Robert S, farmer, and Agnes S. To Galt, Waterloo Co, ONT later to Owen Sound. **THS 1937/74**.

10982 SCOTT, Montague. From Edinburgh. To Megantic Co, QUE, <1850. Physician and teacher. **AMC 128**.

10983 SCOTT, Robert. From Dull par, PER. To Montreal, QUE, on the *Curlew*, ex Greenock, 21 Jul 1818; stld prob Beckwith Twp, Lanark Co, ONT. Wife Nelly with him. **BCL**.

10984 SCOTT, Robert. From Dull par, PER. To Montreal, QUE, on the *Curlew*, ex Greenock, 21 Jul 1818; stld prob Beckwith Twp, Lanark Co, ONT. Wife Margaret with him, and s Alexander, aged 16. **BCL**.

10985 SCOTT, Robert, 1784–1866. From Tranent, ELN. To Wallace, Cumberland Co, NS, prob <1830. Wife Jane, 1793–1867, b London, ENG. **DC 20 Jan 1981**.

10986 SCOTT, Robert, ca 1833-98. From East Boonraw, Hawick, ROX. s/o Robert S, farmer, and second wife Janet Douglas. To Toronto, ONT. m Martha Craig, d 1897, ch. **THS 1937/74**.

10987 SCOTT, Thomas, ca 1774–14 Feb 1823. From Edinburgh. s/o Walter S, WS, and Ann Rutherford. To QUE, and d there. Extractor, HM Register House, Edinburgh, later Paymaster, 70th Regt. m 1799, Elizabeth, d/o David McCulloch of Ardwall, KKD, ch: 1. Walter, 1807-76; 2. Jessie, 1801-70; 3. Ann Rutherford, b 1803; 4. Eliza Charlotte, b 1811. **HWS 314; DGC 1 Apr 1823**.

10988 SCOTT, Thomas, 1746–1824. From Kingoldrum, ANS. s/o Rev Alexander S, par min, and Euphemia Henderson. To ONT. Studied divinity, afterwards law, and became Chief Justice of Upper Canada. **FES v 271; MDB 675; Ts Meigle**.

10989 SCOTT, Thomas, b ca 1788. From Tundergarth, DFS. To QUE, ex Greenock, summer 1815; stld Lot 12, Con 1, Bathurst Twp, Lanark Co, ONT. Tailor, labourer, farmer. Wife Janet Gardiner, qv, with him, and 2 ch. **SEC 6; HCL 16**.

10990 SCOTT, Thomas. From Lesmahagow, LKS. To QUE on the *Prompt*, ex Greenock, 4 Jul 1820; stld Con 4, Dalhousie Twp, Lanark Co, ONT. Farmer, and leader of a group of 170 persons sponsored by the Lesmahagow Society. Wife and 7 ch with him. **HCL 62, 68, 238; DC 13 Feb 1978**.

10991 SCOTT, William, b ca 1783. From Strathbran, PER. To Charlottetown, PEI, on the *Clarendon*, ex Oban, 6 Aug 1808. Labourer. **CPL**.

10992 SCOTT, William, ca 1784–13 Jan 1820. From ROX. s/o William S, sometime in Wooler, NBL, ENG. To QUE. Poss lawyer. **NSS No 1861**.

10993 SCOTT, William. To Dumfries Twp, Waterloo Co, ONT, 1824. Farmer. m Janet Burnet, qv, ch. **DC 17 Mar 1980**.

10994 SCOTT, William, ca 1811-61. From LKS, poss Lesmahagow. To Scarborough, York Co, ONT, 1834. **DC 29 Mar 1981**.

10995 SCOTT, William. From Burnfoot, Hawick, ROX. s/o Robert S, East Boonraw, and first wife, Agnes Scott. To Toronto, ONT, 1848. Drover and farmer. Moved to Columbus, OH, and m Martha Rice, ch. **THS 1937/74**.

10996 SCOTT, William. From Boonraw, Hawick, ROX. s/o John S, farmer, and Euphemia Elliot, d 1850. To Toronto, ONT. Physician. **THS 1937/75**.

10997 SCOTT, William, b 1846. From Ashkirk, SEL. s/o William S. and Helen Inglis. To Durham Co, ONT, 1853. Teacher. m 1870, Mary, d/o John Hughes, ch: 1. Wallace, physician; 2. John William. **DC 29 Sep 1964**.

10998 SCOTT, William W. To Brockville, Leeds and Grenville Co, ONT, 1815; later to Lanark Co. **HCL 12**.

10999   SCOTT, William Henry, b ca 1799. s/o William S. and Catherine Ferguson. To Montreal, QUE. Merchant and politician. Son James.   **DC 14 Nov 1973**.

11000   SCOULAR, Mary, b 19 May 1823. From Wishaw, LKS. d/o Thomas S, weaver, Dykend, Avondale par, LKS, and Isobell Torrance. To ONT <1854. m 1842, Burns Steel, qv.   **DC 5 Sep 1979**.

11001   SCOULAR, Robert. To QUE on the *Prompt*, ex Greenock, 4 Jul 1820; stld prob Lanark Co, ONT. **HCL 238**.

11002   SCOULAR, Thomas, b 5 Oct 1820. From Wishaw, LKS. s/o Thomas S, weaver, Dykend, Avondale par, LKS, and Isobell Torrance. To ONT, prob ca 1853. **DC 5 Sep 1979**.

11003   SCOULLAR, Margaret, 1802-82. From Carmunnock, LKS. To ONT, 1850; stld Blandford Twp, Oxford Co. Wife of Rev John Pettigrew, qv.   **DC 27 Aug 1981**.

11004   SEATH, John, 6 Jan 1844–17 Mar 1919. From Auchtermuchty, FIF. s/o John S. and Isobel Herkless. Matric Univ of Glasgow, 1858, and grad BA, Queens Univ, Belfast, 1861. To Brampton, Peel Co, ONT, 1862; later at Oshawa, Dundas and St Catharines. Teacher, Inspector of Schools, and author. m 1873, Caroline Louisa Mackenzie, Dundas. Son John.   **GMA 16931**.

11005   SEATON, Donald. Poss from PER. To Westminster Twp, Middlesex Co, ONT, prob <1840. **PCM 55**.

11006   SEATON, James Duncan, 1822–1903. From Tynich Ballinluig, Dunkeld, PER. s/o Robert S. and Margaret Douglas. To Hamilton, ONT, 1854. Shoemaker, later farmer. m Elizabeth Saunders, qv, ch: 1. Stewart Manson, 1859–1938; 2. George; 3. Mary Jane; 4. Mina Isabel; 5. Elizabeth.   **DC 31 Dec 1979**.

11007   SEATON, John. From INV. To QUE, 1815; moved to Ekfrid Twp, Middlesex Co, ONT, 1837. ch: 1. Donald; 2. Alexander; 3. John; 4. Susan; 5. Margaret. **PCM 30**.

11008   SEATON, Margaret, 1797–1881. From Tynich, Ballinluig, Dunkeld, PER. d/o Duncan S. and Margaret Cameron. To Hamilton, ONT, 1852. Wife of John Saunders, qv.   **DC 31 Dec 1979**.

11009   SEDGWICK, Rev Robert, 1804–2 Apr 1885. From Paisley, RFW. s/o Thomas S, craftsman. Educ East Greenock, and matric Univ of Glasgow, 1828. Secession min at Belmont St, Aberdeen, 1836-49. Ind min of Musquodoboit, Halifax Co, NS, 4 Sep 1849, and remained there until 1882. DD, Queens Univ, 1877. m Jessie Middleton, qv, ch: 1. Thomas, qv; 2. Agnes, res Dundee, SCT; 3. John, merchant in Leith, SCT; 4. Jane; 5. George, dy; 6. Jessie; 7. Robert, lawyer in Ottawa; 8. William; 9. Henry; 10. Ann; 11. James, b 1860, grad Univ of Dalhousie.   **GMA 12308; UPC i 7; HNS iii 165**.

11010   SEDGWICK, Rev Thomas, b ca 1838, prob Aberdeen. s/o Rev Robert S, qv, and Jessie Middleton, qv. To Tatamagouche, Colchester Co, NS, 1849. Became min there. DD, Presb Coll, Halifax, 1893. m Christina P, d/o Roderick MacGregor, ch: 1. William Middleton, res New Glasgow; 2. Sarah. **HNS iii 164**.

SELKIRK, Lord. See DOUGLAS, Thomas.

11011   SELLAR, Alexander. From LKS. To Toronto, ONT, <1853. Estate factor and farmer. m Isabella Grant, qv. Son Robert, qv.   **LDW 16 Apr 1970**.

11012   SELLAR, Robert, 1 Aug 1841–30 Nov 1919. From Glasgow. s/o Alexander S, qv, and Isabella Grant, qv. To Toronto, ONT, as a child. Journalist, and founded the *Canadian Gleaner* at Huntingdon, QUE, 1836. m 1886, Mary, d/o Rev James Watson, ch: 1. Leslie; 2. R. Watson; 3. Adam L; 4. Gordon; 5. Elsie Margaret.   **MDB 680**.

11013   SEMPLE, James. Poss from PER. To Pictou Co, NS, 1849; stld Tatamagouche, Colchester Co. Farmer. m Cecilia Donaldson, qv.   **HT 83**.

11014   SHACKLETON, Anna, b Jul 1826. To CAN <1850. Wife of Alexander Forsyth, qv.   **SG xxvii/2 84**.

11015   SHAND, Janet, ca 1790–7 Nov 1856. From Slains par, ABD. To QUE on the *Amity*, ex Aberdeen, spring 1835, and went to Seymour, Northumberland Co, ONT. Moved to Upper Pilkington Twp, Wellington Co. Wife of Peter Hay, qv.   **EHE 96**.

11016   SHANKS, Rev David, ca 1801–12 Nov 1871. From Hartloup, New Monkland par, LKS. s/o William S, craftsman. Matric Univ of Glasgow, 1820, and became a probationer of the Secession Ch. Missionary to Montreal, QUE, 1832; min of St Eustache Secession Ch, 1833-47, and joined Ch of Scotland, 1841. Trans to St Gabriel de Valcartier, QUE, 1847.   **GMA 10466; FES vii 650; Census 1861, Valcartier**.

11017   SHANNON, Henry, b ca 1755. From Drum, New Abbey, KKD. To Georgetown, Kings Co, PEI, on the *Lovely Nellie*, ex Annan, 1774.   **ELN**.

11018   SHARP, James, 1765–1840. From Balmonth, Anstruther, FIF. bro/o Andrew S, farmer. To Glen Morris, South Dumfries Twp, Brant Co, ONT, 1818. Farmer and cabinet-maker. m Betty Brown, qv, ch: 1. James, d inf; 2. John, stld Chatham Twp, Kent Co; 3. Horace, res Whitemans Creek; 4. Andrew, storekeeper at Mount Pleasant; 5. James, farmer.   **DC 31 Jan 1982**.

11019   SHARP, John, b 31 Jul 1791. From Errol par, PER. To ONT, spring 1832. Wife Margaret Kinmond, qv, with him, and ch: 1. Charles, b 29 Nov 1814; 2. Betty, b 11 Nov 1816; 3. Elizabeth, b 1 Nov 1818; 4. William, b 16 Dec 1820; 5. Maidy, b 14 Dec 1822; 6. Isabella, b 25 May 1827; 7. Peter, b 26 Jul 1829.   **DC 31 Aug 1979**.

11020   SHARPE, James, ca 1825–14 Jan 1884. Poss from PER. To QUE, 1847. Stonemason. m Isabella Alexander, b ca 1829.   **DC 28 Nov 1981**.

11021   SHAW, Alexander. From Is Skye, INV. s/o Duncan S, Sheriff of Skye, and — McLeod. To CAN <1850. *Crathienaird chart*.

11022   SHAW, Andrew, 27 Jul 1775–11 May 1862. From Glasgow. s/o William S, merchant. To Montreal, QUE, 1810. Originator of the Montreal Telegraph Co, and its first president. m 14 Mar 1821, Hanna Ferguson. Dau Anne.   **SGC 491**.

11023   SHAW, Angus, d 25 Jul 1832. From INV. To Montreal, QUE, <1787, and joined NWCo. Partner. Became mem of firm of McTavish, McGillivrays & Co, 1808. Involved in Red River troubles, 1815. After merger of NWCo and HBCo in 1821, his firm were agents for the

latter, but failed in 1825. m Margerie McGillivray, qv.
MDB 685.

11024 SHAW, Annabella, ca 1758–ca 1789. From
Southend, Kintyre, ARL. d/o Neil S, qv. To PEI, 1772;
stld Queens Co. Poss first wife of John McGregor, qv.
DC 28 May 1980.

11025 SHAW, Barbara, 22 Jul 1805–11 Oct 1866. From
Kilmory par, Is Arran, BUT. d/o James S. To Blackland,
Restigouche Co, NB, 1830. Wife of Donald McMillan, qv,
m 22 Jul 1805.   **MAC 22; DC 7 Feb 1981**.

11026 SHAW, Catherine, 16 May 1766–23 Sep 1827.
From Southend, Kintyre, ARL. d/o Neil S, qv. To Queens
Co, PEI, 1772. m 17 Jan 1787, at Covehead, John
McCallum, qv.   **DC 11 Apr 1981**.

11027 SHAW, Donald. From INV. To Pictou, NS,
<1797; stld East River, where gr 300 acres. Prob
discharged soldier, 84th Regt. ch.   **HPC App H**.

11028 SHAW, Donald. From Is Colonsay, ARL. To
Pictou Co, NS, <1789; stld Elgin. Army tailor,
afterwards farmer. m d/o Donald Roy Cameron, ch:
1. Margaret; 2. Betsy; 3. Catherine; 4. Christy; 5. Mary;
6. Hugh; 7. Donald; 8. John.   **PAC 201**.

11029 SHAW, Donald, b ca 1776. Prob from Colonsay,
ARL. To Charlottetown, PEI, on the *Spencer*, ex Oban,
arr 22 Sep 1806.   **PLSN**.

11030 SHAW, Donald. From Is Colonsay, ARL. To
Pictou, NS, 1815; stld River John. Moved in 1819 to
Brudenell, Kings Co, PEI. m Christian Amos or McVane,
ch: 1. John; 2. Robert; 3. Stephen; 4. Donald;
5. Margaret; 6. Archibald.   **DC 25 Oct 1980**.

11031 SHAW, Donald, ca 1783–9 Feb 1867. Prob from
INV. To Pictou Co, NS; bur Old Elgin. m Catherine
Chisholm, qv, ch.   **DC 20 Nov 1976**.

11032 SHAW, Donald. From Corrigills, Kilbride par, Is
Arran, BUT. To Inverness Twp, Megantic Co, QUE, 1839.
m 25 Jan 1825, Flora Henry, qv, ch: 1. John; 2. Mary;
3. Donald; 4. Elizabeth; 5. William.   **AMC 48; MAC 42**.

11033 SHAW, Donald, b 1816. From Is Skye, INV. To
ONT, 1844; stld Southwold Twp, later Aldborough Twp,
Elgin Co. Farmer. m 1854, Betsy Smith, midwife, ch:
1. Rev Neil; 2. Dugald, farmer; 3. John, barrister;
4. Mrs Marcus; 5. Mrs Cunningham; 6. Mrs Bisnett;
7. Mrs Lindsay.   **PDA 63**.

11034 SHAW, Duncan, ca 1760–ca 1811. From
Southend, Kintyre, ARL. s/o Neil S, qv. To PEI, 1772;
stld Stanhope, Queens Co. Farmer. m Isabella Miller, qv,
and moved to Brackley Point, ca 1809. ch: 1. John;
2. Catherine; 3. Neil; 4. James; 5. Mary; 6. Malcolm;
7. Duncan.   **DC 11 Apr 1981**.

11035 SHAW, Ellen, b ca 1778. From Glasgow, but
b Dalnavert, Alvie par, INV. d/o James S. To QUE on the
Earl of Buckinghamshire, ex Greenock, arr 24 Jun 1820;
stld nr Kingston, ONT. Wife of Hugh MacDonald, qv.
DC 5 Mar 1982.

11036 SHAW, Janet. From Is Jura, but emig from Is
Islay, ARL, to ONT, <1855. m 20 Jun 1826, Allan
McDougall, qv.   **DC 19 Nov 1977**.

11037 SHAW, John. From Houston, RFW. s/o Robert
S, 1799–1866, and Ann McEwing, 1801–82. To Forest,
Lambton Co, ONT. Merchant.   **Ts Houston**.

11038 SHAW, John, d 26 Oct 1843. From Colmonell
par, AYR. To St Catharines, Lincoln Co, ONT. Joiner.
DGH 28 Dec 1843.

11039 SHAW, Malcolm, ca 1755–21 May 1833. From
Southend, Kintyre, ARL. s/o Neil S, qv. To PEI, 1772;
stld Parsons Creek, Queens Co. m Margaret Murphy, ch:
1. Neil; 2. Jenny; 3. Marian.   **DC 11 Apr 1981**.

11040 SHAW, Margaret, ca 1758–29 Sep 1840. From
Southend, Kintyre, ARL. To Queens Co, PEI, <1815;
stld Brackley Point. Wife of Dugald McCallum, qv, m at
Southend, Mar 1786.   **DC 20 Dec 1981**.

11041 SHAW, Margaret. From PER. sis/o William S. To
QUE, ca 1833.   **DC 8 May 1979**.

11042 SHAW, Marion, ca 1768–4 Feb 1846. From
Southend, Kintyre, ARL. d/o Neil S, qv. To PEI, 1772;
stld Queens Co. m 17 Jan 1787, Sgt Donald McFarlane,
qv.   **DC 11 Apr 1981**.

11043 SHAW, Mary, ca 1753–ca 1790. From Southend,
Kintyre, ARL. d/o Neil S, qv. To PEI, 1772. m William
Lawson, qv, Stanhope, Queens Co.   **DC 28 May 1980**.

11044 SHAW, Neil, d 15 Dec 1799. From Southend,
Kintyre, ARL. To PEI, 1772; stld Stanhope, Queens Co.
Farmer. m prob 3 times, ch: 1. Mary, qv; 2. Malcolm,
qv; 3. Annabella, qv; 4. Duncan, qv; 5. Catherine, qv;
6. Marion, qv.   **DC 28 May 1980 and 11 Apr 1981**.

11045 SHAW, Rebecca, 1802–67. From Hamilton, LKS.
To ONT, ca 1842; stld Lambton Co. Wife of Alexander
Chalmers, qv.   **DC 12 Jul 1979**.

11046 SHAW, Thomas, ca 1790–13 Feb 1827. From
Dumbarton. To NS, and d there.   **VSN No 2077**.

11047 SHAW, William. From Doune, PER. To QUE,
1832; stld Drummond Twp, Lanark Co, ONT. m Agnes
Dunn, qv, ch: 1. Alexander, called Sandy; 2. Jane;
3. Margaret, d 1882; 4. James, 1840–1922; 5. Janet;
6. Sarah; 7. John, 1842–1926.   **DC 6 Jun and 3 Aug
1979**.

SHEARER. See also SHERAR.

11048 SHEARER, Alexander, 1814–1901. From Little
Hareshaw, Shotts par, LKS. s/o Archibald S. and Anne
Wilson. To Northumberland Co, ONT, ca 1828. m Lydia
Sweet, 1830–1906.   **DC 17 Jan 1981**.

11049 SHEARER, Andrew, 1802–88. From Little
Hareshaw, Shotts par, LKS. s/o Archibald S. and Anne
Wilson. To Asphodel Twp, Peterborough Co, ONT, ca
1828. Farmer. m Ellen Waddell, ch.   **DC 17 Jan 1981**.

11050 SHEARER, Archibald, 1797–1867. From Little
Hareshaw, Shotts par, LKS. s/o Archibald S. and Anne
Wilson. To Otonabee Twp, Peterborough Co, ONT, ca
1828. Farmer. m Agnes Blackstock, ch: 1. Archibald,
1829–93; 2. Janet, 1834–1906; 3. Andrew, 1836–1920;
4. Ann, 1843-61.   **DC 25 Mar 1981**.

11051 SHEARER, Gavin, 1811-96. From Little
Hareshaw, Shotts par, LKS. s/o Archibald S. and Anne
Wilson. To Peterborough Co, ONT, ca 1828; stld Con 2,
Otonabee Twp. Farmer. m Janet Gilchrist, 1811-71.
DC 17 Jan 1981.

11052 SHEARER, Helen or Nellie. From Little
Hareshaw, Shotts par, LKS. d/o Archibald S. and Anne
Wilson. To Peterborough Co, ONT, ca 1828. Wife of
Thomas Davidson, qv.   **DC 17 Jan 1981**.

11053   SHEARER, James, 1810-92. From Little Hareshaw, Shotts par, LKS. s/o Archibald S. and Anne Wilson. To ONT, ca 1828; stld prob Peterborough Co, but went to KS. m Mary Marshall, 1815-97.   **DC 17 Jan 1981**.

11054   SHEARER, Janet, d 1847. From Little Hareshaw, Shotts par, LKS. d/o Archibald S. and Anne Wilson. To Asphodel Twp, Peterborough Co, ONT, ca 1828. m John Yetts, 1803-91.   **DC 17 Jan 1981**.

11055   SHEARER, John, 1805-84. From Little Hareshaw, Shotts par, LKS. s/o Archibald S. and Anne Wilson. To Peterborough Co, ONT, ca 1828; stld Con 7, Otonabee Twp. Farmer. m Sarah Bradley, 1810-66, ch.   **DC 17 Jan 1981**.

11056   SHEARER, John Sharp, b ca 1830. From Banff. To CAN. Naturalist.   **SNQ vii/1 101**.

11057   SHEARER, Margaret. To New Annan, Colchester Co, NS. Wife of George Drysdale, qv.   **MLA 109**.

11058   SHEARER, Matthew, 1817-99. From Little Hareshaw, Shotts par, LKS. s/o Archibald S. and Anne Wilson. To ONT ca 1828; stld Northumberland Co. Farmer. m Charlotte Brown, 1833-98.   **DC 17 Jan 1981**.

11059   SHEDDEN, John, 1825-16 May 1873. From Kilbirnie, AYR. To Montreal, QUE, ca 1855, via PA. Railway contractor and freight agent, in partnership with William Hendrie. Unm, and was succ by neph, Hugh Paton.   **DC 15 May 1982**.

11060   SHEDDON, Robert. Prob from Glasgow. To Montreal, QUE, <1853. Merchant.   **SH**.

11061   SHEED, Rev George, 1790-1832. From Aberdeen. s/o William S, shoemaker. Grad MA, Marischall Coll, Aberdeen, 1807. Ord by Presb of Aberdeen, and adm min of Ancaster and Flamboro, Wentworth Co, ONT, 1827.   **FAM ii 392; FES vii 650**.

11062   SHEPHERD, John, 1815-1908. From Aberdeen. To QUE on the *Hercules*, 1834; stld Brantford Twp, Brant Co, ONT. Tanner, later farmer. m 1840, Sarah Edmonds, d 1890, ch.   **DC 23 Sep 1980**.

SHERAR. See also SHEARER.

11063   SHERAR, Elspeth. From Rothes, MOR. To Halifax, NS, <26 Apr 1825, when m James Finlay, qv.   **VSN No 1126**.

SHERIFFS. See also SHIRREFF and SHEREFFS.

11064   SHERIFFS, John. From ABD. bro/o James S, keeper of the Court House. To NS <1840; stld Whiteburn.   **SH**.

11065   SHIELDS, Peter. From LKS. To QUE on the *Prompt*, ex Greenock, 4 Jul 1820; stld Dalhousie Twp, Lanark Co, ONT.   **HCL 68**.

11066   SHIELL, John, b ca 1813. From Dalkeith, MLN, but prob b Cavers, ROX. To QUE on the *Niagara*, ex Greenock, 3 Sep 1852; stld Oxford Co, ONT. Wife Mary Telfer, qv, with him, and 3 ch.   **DC 27 Aug 1981**.

11067   SHIELS, George, 20 Oct 1828-19 Jan 1906. From Culter, LKS. s/o Thomas S. and Barbara Cranston. To QUE on the *Norton*, ex Glasgow, 1 Jun 1851, and went to Whitby, Durham Co, ONT. Moved, ca 1853, to Grey Twp, Huron Co. m 4 Sep 1857, Susanna, d/o Benjamen and Mary Wortley, from ENG, ch:

1. Barbara, b 24 Mar 1859; 2. Jane, b 10 Aug 1860; 3. Thomas E, b 24 May 1862; 4. Susanna, b 22 Jun 1864; 5. Robert, b 1 Apr 1867; 6. Mary, b 22 May 1869; 7. George, b 18 Oct 1871; 8. Jemima, b 11 Apr 1874; 9. Ellen, b 12 Jul 1877; 10. William John, b 10 Apr 1880; 11. David, b 19 Nov 1883.   **DC 29 Oct 1979**.

11068   SHIELS, John, 8 Jul 1826-5 Feb 1908. From Culter, LKS. s/o Thomas S. and Barbara Cranston. To QUE on the *Norton*, ex Glasgow, 1 Jun 1851; stld Whitby, Durham Co, ONT. Moved, ca 1853, to Grey Twp, Huron Co. Farmer. m Janet McNair, qv, ch: 1. Thomas, b ca 1858; 2. Jane, b ca 1859; 3. Barbara Anne, b ca 1860; 4. James, b ca 1862; 5. Janet, b ca 1866; 6. John, b ca 1868; 7. Jack, b ca 1869; 8. Robert Douglas, b 1871; 9. William, b ca 1875.   **DC 29 Oct 1979**.

11069   SHIELS, Moses, b ca 1779. From Old Kilpatrick, DNB. To QUE, poss on the *Atlas*, ex Greenock, 11 Jul 1815; stld prob Lanark Co, ONT. Farmer and teacher.   **SEC 1**.

11070   SHIER, John, 16 Aug 1808-14 May 1882. From Peterculter, ABD. To Whitby Twp, Durham Co, ONT. Civil engineer. m Clara Slade, 1818-81, from Bristol, ENG, ch: 1. William, 1841-49; 2. Clara, 1843-1922; 3. Edward, b 1845, clerk; 4. James, b 1847, printer.   **DC 6 Sep 1979**.

SHIRREFF. See also SHERIFFS.

11071   SHIRREFF, Charles, 26 May 1768-May 1849. From Leith, MLN. s/o — S. and Barbara Menzies. To Fitzroy Twp, Carleton Co, ONT. Property owner. ch incl: 1. Alexander; 2. Robert, powder manufacturer.   **SH; DC 27 Oct 1980**.

11072   SHIRREFF, John. Rel to Charles S, qv. To ONT, prob Fitzroy Twp, Carleton Co, <1849.   **SH**.

11073   SHIRREFFS, John, ca 1803-28 Jun 1882. To Sherbrooke, QUE. m Henrietta McGillivray, ca 1797-15 Oct 1884. Son John, 1836-90.   **MGC 2 Aug 1979**.

11074   SHORTT, John, ca 1803-18 Jul 1853. To Pictou Co, NS, 1817; bur Salt Springs. m Catherine Chisholm, qv.   **DC 27 Oct 1979**.

11075   SIBBALD, Charles, b 1819. From Pinnacle, Ancrum par, ROX. s/o Lt Col William S. and Susan Mein. To 'Eildon Hall,' Sutton West, Simcoe Co, ONT. Officer of Militia, 1837.   **ABC 447**.

11076   SIBBALD, Thomas, b ca 1811. From Pinnacle, Ancrum par, ROX. s/o Lt Col William S. and Susan Mein. To Sutton West, Simcoe Co, ONT, prob <1837; stld 'Eildon Hall.' Commander, RN, ret. m Mary, d/o Rev Waddon Martyn, of Lifton, DBY, ch: 1. William M; 2. Thomas Mein, surgeon, RN.   **ABC 446**.

11077   SIDEY, David. From PER. To Northumberland Co, ONT, <1830; stld Cold Springs.   **DC 20 Dec 1975**.

11078   SIDEY, George. Prob from PER. To ONT <1830; stld St. Catharines, Lincoln Co.   **DC 20 Dec 1975**.

11079   SIDEY, John. From Dundee, ANS. To Binbrook Twp, Wentworth Co, ONT, 1822. Farmer. Dau Isabella.   **DC 29 Sep 1964**.

11080   SIDEY, Peter. Prob from PER. To Northumberland Co, ONT, <1840; stld Cold Springs.   **DC 20 Dec 1975**.

11081 SIEVEWRIGHT, Rev James, b 1832. From Aberdeen. s/o William S, merchant. Educ Marischall Coll, Aberdeen, 1848-52, and grad BA, Queens Coll, Kingston, ONT, 1856. Ord min of Melbourne, Middlesex Co, 1857; trans to Ormstown, 1862; to Chelsea and Ironside, 1865; and to Goderich, 1869. Missionary at Prince Albert, MAN, 1880-83. Ind to Scots Ch, Quebec. m 1859, Frances Ann Petrie. **FAM ii 544; FES vii 650**.

11082 SILLARS, Angus, 1763–1836. From Is Arran, BUT. To Restigouche Co, NB, prob 1829. m Mary Graham, qv, ch: 1. James, b 1804; 2. Margaret, b 1810. Family bur at Atholville. **MAC 27**.

11083 SILLARS, Daniel or Donald, 26 Jul 1809–14 Mar 1862. From Is Arran, BUT. s/o Malcolm S. and Margaret Craig. To Inverness Co, QUE, ca 1831; later to VT. m 28 Apr 1835, Margaret McColl, qv, ch: 1. Margaret, b 1836; 2. Malcolm, b 1837; 3. dau; 4. William, b 1841; 5. Elizabeth Jane, b 1845; 6. Archibald Walter, b 1846. **DC 15 Jul 1980**.

11084 SILLARS, Robert. To Pictou, NS, on the *Lulan*, ex Glasgow, 17 Aug 1848. **DC 15 Jul 1979**.

11085 SILLERS, Donald, 1800–19 Mar 1894. From Is Arran, BUT. bro/o Peter S, qv. To QUE on the *Newfoundland*, 12 Jun 1829; stld Inverness Twp, Megantic Co. Tailor. m Catherine Ferguson, 1842-93. **AMC 12; MAC 35**.

11086 SILLERS, Duncan. From Mangrel, Is Arran, BUT. To Inverness Twp, Megantic Co, QUE, 1831. m Marian Miller, qv, ch: 1. John; 2. Mary, d 1911. **MAC 41**.

11087 SILLERS, Duncan. From Is Arran, BUT. s/o Peter S, qv, and Janet Kelso, qv. To QUE on the *Newfoundland*, ex Greenock, 12 Jun 1829; stld Inverness Twp, Megantic Co. m Jane Sillars. **AMC 22; MAC 34**.

11088 SILLERS, Elizabeth, 1819–1913. From Is Arran, BUT. d/o Peter S, qv, and Janet Kelso, qv. To QUE on the *Newfoundland*, ex Greenock, 12 Jun 1829; stld Inverness Twp, Megantic Co. m William Murchie, qv. **AMC 22; MAC 34**.

11089 SILLERS, John. From Is Arran, BUT. s/o Peter S, qv, and Janet Kelso, qv. To QUE on the *Newfoundland*, ex Greenock, 12 Jun 1829; stld Inverness Twp, Megantic Co, QUE, later Atchison Co, MO. m (i) Janet McKillop; (ii) Catherine McKillop. **AMC 22; MAC 35**.

11090 SILLERS, John. From Is Arran, BUT. bro/o Peter S, sr, qv. To Inverness Twp, Megantic Co, QUE, <1831. **AMC 22**.

11091 SILLERS, Margaret, 1818–1910. From Is Arran, BUT. d/o Peter S, qv, and Janet Kelso, qv. To QUE on the *Newfoundland*, ex Greenock, 12 Jun 1829; stld Megantic Co. m 15 Feb 1838, John McKinnon, jr, qv. **AMC 11; MAC 34**.

11092 SILLERS, Mary, b ca 1816. From Is Arran, BUT. d/o Peter S, qv, and Janet Kelso, qv. To QUE on the *Newfoundland*, ex Greenock, 12 Jun 1829; stld Inverness Twp, Megantic Co. m 20 Mar 1839, Donald McKinnon, qv. **AMC 11; MAC 34**.

11093 SILLERS, Peter. From Is Arran, BUT. bro/o Donald S, qv. To QUE on the *Newfoundland*, ex Greenock, 12 Jun 1829; stld Inverness Twp, Megantic Co. Shoemaker. m Janet Kelso, qv, ch: 1. Margaret, qv; 2. Elizabeth, qv; 3. Mary, qv; 4. Catherine; 5. Duncan, qv; 6. John, qv; 7. Peter, jr, qv; 8. Janet, went to Boston, MA. **AMC 22; MAC 34**.

11094 SILLERS, Peter, jr, b 1809. From Is Arran, BUT. s/o Peter S, qv, and Janet Kelso, qv. To QUE on the *Newfoundland*, ex Greenock, 12 Jun 1829; stld Inverness Twp, Megantic Co. m Annie Stewart. **AMC 22; MAC 35**.

11095 SIM, Francis, b ca 1828. Prob from ABD. Rel–poss neph–to Francis Malcolm, qv. To East Zorra Twp, Oxford Co, ONT, 1840. **LDW 24 Sep 1974**.

11096 SIM, Mary Ann, ca 1803–8 May 1884. From Longside, ABD. To QUE on the *Beatrice*, 8 Apr 1854; stld Ashburn Village, East Whitby Twp, Durham Co, ONT. Bur Oshawa Union Cemetery. Wife of Andrew Lawrence, qv. **DC 23 Jul 1979**.

11097 SIM, Robert. From Loch Broom, ROC. To Pictou, NS, on the *Hector*, ex Loch Broom, arr 17 Sep 1773. Moved later to NB. **HPC App C**.

11098 SIMPSON, Aemilius. From Dingwall, ROC. To Hudson Bay, 1826. s/o Alexander S. Served with HBCo. **DC 17 May 1982**.

11099 SIMPSON, Alexander, b ca 1761. Poss from MOR. To QUE, ex Greenock, 11 Jul 1815, on the *Atlas*; stld Lot 29, Con 10, North Elmsley Twp, Lanark Co, ONT. Labourer, later farmer. **SEC 4; HCL 12, 17, 232**.

11100 SIMPSON, Alexander. From Dingwall, ROC. s/o Alexander S. To Hudson Bay, and joined HBCo. **DC 17 May 1982**.

11101 SIMPSON, Andrew, d 1871. From CAI. To Montreal, QUE, 1834. Brewer, firm of Simpson & Dawson. m Mrs Graham. **SGC 488**.

11102 SIMPSON, David. Served as an NCO in the 82nd Regt and was gr 200 acres at Merigomish, Pictou Co, NS, 1784. Became a schoolmaster. ch. **HPC App F**.

11103 SIMPSON, Sir George, 1792–7 Sep 1860. From Lochbroom par, ROC. s/o George S. To CAN, 1820, and emp by HBCo at Athabasca. Afterwards chosen to command northern dept of Ruperts Land. Later in charge of other areas and ultimately of all territories of HBCo. Organised explorations and knighted in 1841; FRGS; author. m 1827, his cous, Frances Ramsay, d/o Geddes Mackenzie Simpson, Stamford Hill, Middlesex, ENG, ch. **BNA 999; SN iii 454; IBD 472; MDB 693**.

11104 SIMPSON, Hannah. From Kilbride, LKS. To PEI, 1809; stld Charlottetown. m ca 1800, Robert Jones, qv. **HP 78**.

11105 SIMPSON, James, 13 Mar 1770–18 Dec 1850. From Dundurcas, MOR. s/o William S, qv, and Janet Winchester, qv. To Flat River, PEI, on the *John & Elizabeth*, arr 30 Jul 1775; stld later Cavendish, Queens Co. m 1798, Agnes or Nancy, d/o James Woodside and Ann Love, see ADDENDA. **DC 20 Dec 1981**.

11106 SIMPSON, James. To Tatamagouche, Colchester Co, NS, <1828. Farmer. **HT 68**.

11107 SIMPSON, James, d 1884. From MOR. To Lachute, QUE, 1833; later to Alexandria, Glengarry Co, ONT. Physician, grad Edinburgh. m Elizabeth Malcolm, qv. Son John, merchant, Alexandria. **SDG 450**.

11108 SIMPSON, James F. To Pictou, NS, on the *Lady Gray*, ex Cromarty, ROC, arr 16 Jul 1841. **DC 15 Jul 1979**.

11109 SIMPSON, John, d 1747. From Marnoch, BAN. s/o James S. in Foggieloan, or Aberchirder, and Isobel Mackie. To QUE <1793. Merchant. **Ts Marnoch**.

11110 SIMPSON, John, b 1754. To Pictou Co, NS, 1815, res Mount Thom, 1816. Farmer, m with 7 ch, 3 'able to support themselves.' **INS 39**.

11111 SIMPSON, John, b ca 1770. From Rothes, MOR. To QUE, ex Greenock, summer 1815; stld Lot 26, Con 1, Bathurst Twp, Lanark Co, ONT. Shoemaker, later farmer. Wife Margaret Petrie, qv, with him, and 5 ch, incl John, 1812-85, Canadian senator, 1867. **SEC 2; BNA 735; HCL 16; MDB 693**.

11112 SIMPSON, John, ca 1769–16 Jan 1820. From Eastwood, RFW. s/o Rev James S. To NS and d there. **NSS No 1830**.

11113 SIMPSON, Mary, b ca 1830. To St Gabriel de Valcartier, QUE, <1856. **Census 1861**.

11114 SIMPSON, Peter, 1797–10 Jun 1868. From Aberdeen. bro/o — S, printer, Fredericton, NB. To NB prob <1830; stld poss Northumberland Co. **DC 14 Jan 1980**.

11115 SIMPSON, Thomas. To Malpeque, Prince Co, PEI, ca 1793; moved to Cape Tormentine, Westmorland Co, NB. m Margaret McLean, ch. **DC 17 Apr 1981**.

11116 SIMPSON, Thomas, 2 Jul 1808–14 Jun 1840. From Dingwall, ROC. s/o Alexander S. Grad MA, Kings Coll, Aberdeen, 1829, and entered service of HBCo. For a time he was secretary to his kinsman, Sir George S, qv. Later in Red River dist and was involved in Arctic explorations. Killed in IA. **BNA 999; KCG 284; MDB 694**.

11117 SIMPSON, Thomas, 1790–1861. To Gulf Shore, Cumberland Co, NS, 1832. Wife Barbara, 1787–1862, with him. **DC 29 Oct 1980**.

11118 SIMPSON, William. From Rothes, MOR. To Flat River, PEI, on the *John & Elizabeth*, arr 30 Jul 1775; stld prob Kings Co. m Janet Winchester, qv, and had, prob with other ch: 1. William, jr, qv; 2. James, qv. **DC 28 May 1980**.

11119 SIMPSON, William, jr, 15 Jun 1762–22 Feb 1840. From Rothes, MOR. To Flat River, PEI, on the *John & Elizabeth*, arr 30 Jul 1775; stld prob Kings Co. m Mary Miller, qv, ch. **DC 28 May 1980**.

11120 SIMPSON, Rev William, b 1806. From STI. Educ Univ of St Andrews, and Original Secession Theological Hall. Joined Ch of Scotland, 1839, and ind min of Lachine, QUE, 1844. Declined to join Union of 1875. **SAM 76; FES vii 650**.

11121 SIMS, James. From ABD, poss Insh par. To Galt, Waterloo Co, ONT, 1838; stld Hawkesville. m Janet Harvey, qv, wid/o of John Robertson. **EHE 124**.

11122 SIMSON or SIMPSON, Ann, b 28 Jul 1763. From Eastwood, RFW. d/o Rev James S. To NS, ca 1790. m William Lyon, merchant in Halifax. **FES iii 136**.

11123 SIMSON, Agnes, ca 1743–27 Jun 1827. From Midlem, Bowden par, ROX. To Bradford Village, Simcoe Co, ONT. Wife or wid/o of William Goodfellow, m 1770. **MGC 2 Aug 1979**.

11124 SIMSON, Robert. From Leith, MLN. s/o Walter S, customs officer. Educ Edinburgh High School. To Montreal, QUE, 1849. Farmer. Moved to NJ <1862. **HSC 91**.

11125 SIMSON, Walter. From Kirkcaldy, FIF. s/o William S. and Helen Reddie. To ONT <1847. **SH**.

11126 SINCLAIR, Rev Alexander, 14 Mar 1834–22 Feb 1885. b Is Mull, ARL. s/o Rev John Campbell S, qv, and Mary Julia McLean, qv. To Pictou, NS, with parents, 1838; later to USA, and d Salisbury, MD. Presb min. m (i) Nellie Plummer, who d without ch; (ii) Mary Laura, d/o Adam Brevard Davidson, ch: 1. Rev Brevard Davidson, b 1859; 2. Mary Duart, b 1861; 3. John Campbell, dy; 4. Alexander McLean, dy; 5. Alexander Peter, b 1867; 6. Laura Virginia, b 1870; 7. Richard Springs, dy; 8. Annie Harley, b 1875. **SCI 410**.

11127 SINCLAIR, Alexander, 1818–17 Dec 1897. To ONT, 1831; stld prob Kent Co. Farmer and author. **MDB 694**.

11128 SINCLAIR, Alexander. s/o Finlay S. and Mary McLaren. To CAN, 1850. **DC 4 Mar 1965**.

11129 SINCLAIR, Archibald. From Lawers, PER. s/o Peter S, qv, and Ann McIntyre, qv. To Bruce Co, ONT, 1800. Farmer, timber and flour merchant, and reeve. m Mary, d/o Peter Grant. Son Alexander Grant, b 30 Jul 1842, Charlottenburgh, Glengarry Co, physician. **DC 10 Dec 1962**.

11130 SINCLAIR, Archibald. From ARL. To Aldborough Twp, Elgin Co, ONT, 1816; stld Mosa Twp, 1827. **PCM 23**.

11131 SINCLAIR, Archibald, b 22 Jul 1787. From Is Islay, ARL. s/o Duncan S. and Margaret Mary Dougall. To ONT, ca 1830, stld Victoria Co. m Peggy Kirkland, qv, ch. **DC 21 Feb 1980**.

11132 SINCLAIR, Archibald. From Mullindry, Is Islay, ARL. s/o Archibald S. To Victoria Co, ONT, prob 1847; stld Cannington. **DC 30 Dec 1981**.

11133 SINCLAIR, Rev Archibald, 30 Jan 1803–20 Jan 1867. b Edinburgh. s/o Malcolm S, cabinet-maker. Tutor to the Scotts of Scalloway, SHI, and became min of Walls and Sandness, 1833. Demitted charge, 1840, and joined FC, 1843. Min of St Andrews Ch, NFD, 1847. Retr to SCT, 1848, and d Edinburgh. m 21 May 1833, Jessie, d/o Arthur Gifford of Busta. **AFC i 317; FES vii 318**.

11134 SINCLAIR, Catherine. From Mullindry, Is Islay, ARL. d/o Duncan S. To Chinguacousy Twp, Peel Co, ONT, 1833. Wife of Archibald McKechnie, qv. **DC 1 Dec 1980**.

11135 SINCLAIR, Catherine. From Is Islay, ARL. d/o Donald S. and Anne Clark. To Erin Twp, Wellington Co, ONT, 1844. Wife of Robert Reid, qv. **DC 1 Dec 1980**.

11136 SINCLAIR, Christina, 1803–9 Aug 1888. From Lochgilphead, ARL. To QUE, prob on the *Deveron*, 1831; stld Lobo Twp, Middlesex Co, ONT. Wife of Rev Dugald Sinclair, qv. **DC 18 May 1982**.

11137 SINCLAIR, Donald. Prob from ARL. To

Aldborough Twp, Elgin Co, ONT, <1820. Farmer. **PDA 93**.

11138 SINCLAIR, Donald, 1785–3 Mar 1868. From Knapdale, ARL. bro/o Rev Dugald S, qv. To Mosa Twp, Middlesex Co, ONT, 1830. **PCM 23**.

11139 SINCLAIR, Rev Donald, ca 1800–19 Apr 1871. s/o Duncan S, farmer, and Margaret Sinclair. Ord min of Côte St George, QUE, 1 Jun 1843. Retr to SCT, and was min of Duror, ARL, 1847-71. m Catherine Jane Sinclair. Son John A. **FES iv 84, vii 650**.

11140 SINCLAIR, Donald. From Mullindry, Is Islay, ARL. s/o Neil S. To ONT, ca 1847; stld Walkerton, Bruce Co. **DC 30 Dec 1981**.

11141 SINCLAIR, Donald, d 1812. Prob from PER. s/o Finlay S. To ONT, 1850. m Ellen Robertson. **DC 4 Mar 1966**.

11142 SINCLAIR, Donald M, b 1829. Poss from Is Islay, ARL. To Minto Twp, Wellington Co, ONT, <1861. Farmer. Wife Margaret with him. ch: 1. Margaret, b ca 1855; 2. Euphemia, 1857–1918; 3. Sarah, b ca 1858; 4. Elizabeth. **RFS 145**.

11143 SINCLAIR, Rev Dugald, 25 May 1777–18 Oct 1870. From Lochgilphead or Ardrishaig, ARL. bro/o Donald S, qv. To QUE, prob on the *Deveron*, 1831; stld Lobo Twp, Middlesex Co, ONT, and was active in Kent Co. Baptist preacher and leader of a group of emigrants. m Christina Sinclair, qv, ch: 1. Dugald, 1826-92; 2. Maria Donalda, 1828-80; 3. John, 1829-59; 4. Malcolm, 1831-45; 5. Rev Colin, b 1834; 6. Mary Ann, b 1836; 7. Rev Archibald, b 1838; 8. Duncan, b 1840. **PCM 17; AMA 13; DC 18 May 1982**.

11144 SINCLAIR, Duncan. Prob from ARL. To ONT <1840. Capt of a lake steamer. m Christina, d/o Hugh McCorquodale, qv. Son Hugh, lawyer. **DC 21 Mar 1980**.

11145 SINCLAIR, Duncan. From Mullindry, Is Islay, ARL. s/o Archibald S. To Toronto, ONT, prob <1850. **DC 30 Dec 1981**.

11146 SINCLAIR, Duncan, d 1810. Prob from PER. s/o Finlay S. To ONT, poss Glengarry Co, <1850. **DC 30 Dec 1981**.

11147 SINCLAIR, Effie. From Mullindry, Is Islay, ARL. d/o Archibald S. To York Co, ONT, <1850. m — Campbell, res Toronto. **DC 30 Dec 1981**.

11148 SINCLAIR, Elizabeth, ca 1834–10 Oct 1909. From Glenelg, INV. d/o Alexander S, stonemason. To Puslinch Twp, Wellington Co, ONT, <1855. m James Stewart, ch: 1. Catherine; 2. John K; 3. Jane; 4. Mary; 5. Alexander; 6. Elizabeth; 7. James; 8. Archibald; 9. Peter. **DC 23 Apr 1967**.

11149 SINCLAIR, Esther, ca 1790–29 Jan 1829. From CAI. To NS, 1818; stld nr Earltown, Colchester Co. Wife of Donald McDonald, qv. **DC 18 Mar 1981**.

11150 SINCLAIR, Finlay. From Killin or Lawers, PER. To Martintown, Glengarry Co, ONT, 1816. Wife Mary McLaren, qv, with him, and ch: 1. John; 2. Donald; 3. Peter, qv; 4. Archibald; 5. Mrs Robertson; 6. Mrs Campbell; 7. Mrs Finlayson; 8. Mrs McKerchar. **DC 10 Dec 1962; SMB; SH**.

11151 SINCLAIR, Hugh. From Halkirk, CAI. To York Co,

ONT, prob <1840. m Janet MacDonald, qv. ch incl: 1. William; 2. Donald; 3. Minnie. **DC 5 Jul 1979**.

11152 SINCLAIR, James, b ca 1783. From CAI. To Charlottetown, PEI, on the *Elizabeth & Ann*, ex Thurso, arr 8 Nov 1806. **PLEA**.

11153 SINCLAIR, Jane. From SHI. To Windham Twp, Norfolk Co, ONT. Wife of James Leask, qv. **DC 20 Jul 1979**.

11154 SINCLAIR, John. From Clacha Dubha, ni, ARL. To Lobo Twp, Middlesex Co, ONT, 1820. ch: 1. Alexander; 2. Neil; 3. Eliza; 4. Nancy; 5. Sarah; 6. Kate; 7. Mary; 8. Margaret. **PCM 38**.

11155 SINCLAIR, John. Prob from ARL. To Aldborough Twp, Elgin Co, ONT, <1820. Farmer. **PDA 93**.

11156 SINCLAIR, John. From Coire Buidhe, ni, ARL. To Lobo Twp, Middlesex Co, ONT, 1820. ch: 1. Archibald; 2. Lachlan; 3. Sarah. **PCM 38**.

11157 SINCLAIR, John, 20 May 1797–27 Jun 1875. From Glenaladale, Moidart, INV. s/o John and Janet S. To Pictou, NS, on the *Industry*, ex Cromarty, 6 Jul 1831. Farmer at Goshen. m (i) Mary, d/o John Inglis and Maria Lambert, ch: 1. Janet; 2. John; 3. George. m (ii) Christy, d/o John MacLean, qv, and Isabella Black, qv. **DC 13 Apr 1966**.

11158 SINCLAIR, John, 1780–17 Jun 1869. From Breadalbane, PER. To ONT, 1831; stld Breadalbane, Lochiel Twp, Glengarry Co. **DC 27 Oct 1979**.

11159 SINCLAIR, John. To Middlesex Co, ONT, <17 Mar 1834, when m Eliza Donaldson, qv. **PCM 17**.

11160 SINCLAIR, John. From Mullindry, Is Islay, ARL. s/o Archibald S. To Eldon Twp, Victoria Co, ONT, prob 1847. Farmer. **DC 30 Dec 1981**.

11161 SINCLAIR, John. From Culloden, INV. Rel to Donald McPherson, farmer, Balchree of Petty. To NS <1850. **SH**.

11162 SINCLAIR, John. Poss from Is Islay, ARL. To Minto Twp, Wellington Co, ONT, <1855, when he transferred Lot 1, Con 5, to Benjamin Madill. **RFS 138**.

11163 SINCLAIR, Rev John Campbell, 15 Aug 1797–23 Apr 1878. From Is Tyree, ARL. s/o Peter S, farmer, and Margaret Campbell. Matric Univ of Glasgow, 1822. To Pictou, NS, 1838. Min there, later in Newburyport, MA, and in NC. d at Wheeling, WV. m Mary Julia McLean, qv, ch: 1. Rev Alexander, qv. 2. Mrs D.A. Cunningham, Wheeling. **GMA 10923; SAS 33; SCI 410**.

11164 SINCLAIR, Lachlan. From ARL. To Caradoc Twp, Middlesex Co, ONT, 1825. ch: 1. Peter; 2. Duncan. **PCM 34**.

11165 SINCLAIR, Margaret, ca 1786–18 Jan 1867. From Ayr. To Chaleur Bay, poss on the *Favourite*, ex Lamlash, May 1833; stld New Richmond, Bonaventure Co, QUE. Wife of John McColm, qv. **DC 17 Dec 1981**.

11166 SINCLAIR, Margaret. From Stornoway, Is Lewis, ROC. d/o Hector S. To Toronto, ONT, 1840. m John Robertson, qv. **DC 30 Aug 1977**.

11167 SINCLAIR, Margaret, 1779–1875. From Is Islay, ARL. d/o Donald S. and Ann Clark. To ONT, 1847; stld Priceville, Artemesia Twp, Grey Co. Wife of Donald McKechnie, qv. **DC 1 Dec 1980**.

11168 SINCLAIR, Margaret. From Glenelg, INV. d/o Alexander S, stonemason. To Puslinch Twp, Wellington Co, ONT, <1855. m John Stewart, ch: 1. Duncan; 2. Jean; 3. Catherine; 4. John A; 5. Alexander. **DC 23 Apr 1967**.

11169 SINCLAIR, Mary, b 8 May 1788. From Glasgow. d/o John S. and Susanna Fleckfield. To QUE, ca 1811; moved ca 1820 to Restigouche Co, NB. Wife of Angus McLean, qv. **RCP 6**.

11170 SINCLAIR, Mary. Poss from Killin, PER. To Montreal, QUE, on the *Niagara*, ex Greenock, arr 28 May 1825; stld McNab Twp, Renfrew Co, ONT. Wife of James Carmichael, qv. **EMT 18, 22**.

11171 SINCLAIR, Mary. From Angus. To Toronto Twp, Peel Co, ONT, 1827. Wife of William Gibson, qv. **DC 30 Aug 1977**.

11172 SINCLAIR, Neil. From Mullindry, Is Islay, ARL. bro/o Alexander S. To Fenelon Falls, Victoria Co, ONT, 1847. **DC 30 Dec 1981**.

11173 SINCLAIR, Neil. From Mullindry, Is Islay, ARL. s/o Archibald S. To Eldon Twp, Victoria Co, ONT, prob 1847. Farmer. **DC 30 Dec 1981**.

11174 SINCLAIR, Peter. From Glenduarel, Kilmodan par, ARL. s/o Peter S, 1808-71. To Queens Co, PEI, <1860. Farmer and Liberal politician. **BNA 717; Ts Glenduarel**.

11175 SINCLAIR, Peter. From Killin, PER. s/o Finlay S, qv, and Mary McLaren, qv. To Charlottetown, Glengarry Co, ONT. m Ann, d/o Archibald McIntyre, qv. Son Archibald. **DC 10 Dec 1962; SMB**.

11176 SINCLAIR, Peter. From ARL. To London Twp, Middlesex Co, ONT, 1828. Son Peter, farmer. **PCM 50**.

11177 SINCLAIR, Peter. From ARL. To Mosa Twp, Middlesex Co, ONT, 1831. Weaver. **PCM 24**.

11178 SINCLAIR, Sarah. From South Knapdale, ARL. To Caradoc Twp, Middlesex Co, ONT, 1831. Wife of Duncan McLean, qv. **PCM 35**.

11179 SINCLAIR, Thomas. From Assynt or Eddrachillis, SUT. To Boston, MA, on the *Fortitude*, arr 16 Aug 1803; stld South Ridge, Charlotte Co, NB, 1804. Formerly of the Reay Fencible Regt. ch incl: 1. William; 2. Alexander. **DC 29 Nov 1982**.

11180 SINCLAIR, William. From OKI. bro/o Thomas S. To CAN <1825. Emp with HBCo. **SH**.

11181 SINCLAIR, William, b 21 Apr 1780. From Balmaclellan par, KKD. s/o William S. and Agnes McDoual. To Burlington, Nelson Twp, Halton Co, ONT, 1817. Wife Jane Gordon, qv, with him, and ch: 1. Agnes, b 1802; 2. Janet, b 1808; 3. Mary, b 1809; 4. Samuel, b 1812; 5. Margaret, b 1813; 6. Elizabeth, b 1816. **DC 18 Feb 1980**.

11182 SINCLARE, Ann, b 1792. From Kilbride Bannan, Is Arran, BUT. To Dalhousie, NB, 1827. Wife of Daniel Kerr, qv. **MAC 18**.

11183 SINCLARE, Robert, b ca 1792. From OKI. To Inverness Co, NS, 1814; stld Mabou. Farmer, m and ch. **CBC 1818**.

11184 SIVEWRIGHT, John, ca 1779–4 Sep 1856. From Cairnie, ABD. To Montreal, QUE, <1800. Fur-trader,

XYCo and NWCo, and involved in Red River troubles, 1815. Chief trader after merger with HBCo, 1821, and became council mem. Retr to SCT, 1849, and d at Edinburgh. **MDB 695; Ts Warriston**.

11185 SIVEWRIGHT, John. From Inverkeithing, FIF. s/o James S, shoemaker. To McLellans Brook, Pictou Co, NS, <1852. **SH**.

11186 SKAE, Edward, ca 1804–5 Jun 1848. From Leith, MLN. To Oshawa, Durham Co, ONT. Wife Mary, 1807-82. **DC 6 Sep 1979**.

11187 SKAKEL, Alexander, ca 1775–13 Aug 1846. From Fochabers, MOR. Educ Kings Coll, Aberdeen, and grad MA, 1793. To QUE, 1798, but stld Montreal, where he founded a grammar school, which was the forerunner of Montreal High School. Secretary of Montreal General Hospital. m (i) Isobel Skakel, his cous; (ii) Christian Dalrymple, qv. **KCG 118, 252, 263; SGC 235, 502; MDB 695; DC 9 Jan and 2 Aug 1979**.

11188 SKAKEL, George. Prob from Aberdeen. bro/o William S, qv. To Montreal, QUE, <1800. Cooper. **SGC 250**.

11189 SKAKEL, William. From Fochabers, MOR. bro/o Alexander S, qv. To QUE, prob 1798; stld Montreal. **SGC 502; DC 9 Jan 1977**.

11190 SKAKEL, William, d 31 Dec 1807. Prob from Aberdeen. bro/o George S, qv. To Montreal, QUE <1800. Tailor. **SGC 250**.

11191 SKEOCH, James. From Kilwinning, AYR. bro/o John S, qv. To ONT, ca 1842; stld Wellington Co. m Margaret Davidson, ch. **DC 14 Feb 1982**.

11192 SKEOCH, John, ca 1807–6 Apr 1886. From Kilwinning, AYR. bro/o James S, qv. To ONT, ca 1842; stld Nichol Twp, Wellington Co, ONT. m Agnes Watt, qv, ch. **DC 8 Nov 1981**.

11193 SKIEFF, Mary, b 10 Oct 1821. From Ballater, ABD. To QUE on the *Berbice*, 1848; stld Elora, Nichol Twp, Wellington Co, ONT, 1849. Wife of Andrew Gordon, qv. **EHE 131**.

11194 SKINNER, Hugh B, b 9 Apr 1784. From Ardnamurchan, ARL. s/o Donald S. and Mary McLean. To Port Hastings, Inverness Co, NS, on the *Aurora*, 1802. Collector of light dues. m Catherine Beaton, poss from North Uist, INV, ch: 1. John; 2. Donald; 3. Archibald; 4. Hugh; 5. James; 6. Kenneth; 7. Hector; 8. Janet; 9. Elizabeth; 10. Mary; 11. Jessie. **CBC 1818; FES iv 107**.

11195 SKINNER, James, b 17 Oct 1781. From Ardnamurchan, ARL. s/o Rev Donald S. and Mary McLean. To Port Hastings, Inverness Co, NS, on the *Aurora*, 1802; stld Pictou. m his cous, Elizabeth McCormack, qv, ch: 1. James, b 1805; 2. Donald, b 1808; 3. Hectorina, b 1810; 4. Margaret, b 1812; 5. John, b 1814; 6. Elizabeth, b 1815; 7. Colin; 8. Hugh, b 1818; 9. John, b 1820; 10. Michael Wallace, b 1823, res Charlottetown, PEI. **FES iv 107; RAM 21**.

11196 SKINNER, James Acheson, b 1826. From Tain, ROC. To Hamilton, ONT, <1855. Farmer and officer of militia. **BNA 812**.

11197 SLACKS, William, ca 1818–3 Mar 1849. From Langholm, DFS. s/o Thomas S, mason. To ONT, poss Northumberland Co. **Ts Wauchope**.

SLATER. See also SCLATER.

11198 SLATER, William, 1800-85. From Jedburgh par, ROX. To Montreal, QUE, 1828; stld Almonte, Ramsay Twp, Lanark Co, ONT, 1829. Farmworker with the Gemmill family. m 1837, Isobel, d 1851, sis/o John Gilmour, and had, poss with other ch: 1. Allan, 1840–1934, who went to Waskada, MAN, 1882; 2. Margaret; 3. Mary; 4. William J, 1849–1926. **DC 26 Feb 1982**.

11199 SLATER, William, ca 1805–6 Jun 1876. From ROX. To ONT, <1839. Wife Mary with him. **DC 14 Jan 1980**.

11200 SLESSOR, James. From Aberdeen. To CAN <1865. Son Robert Ewen. **DC 8 Sep 1975**.

11201 SMAILL, Alexander, ca 1807–5 Apr 1864. From Lilliesleaf, ROX. To QUE, and stld prob Huntingdon Co. **DC 19 Nov 1982**.

11202 SMAILL, James William, b 1824. To ONT, and d Goderich, Huron Co. Son James Wellington. **DC 29 Oct 1983**.

11203 SMALL, Janet, d 29 Jul 1865. From Dirnanean, Kirkmichael par, PER. d/o Andrew S. and Ann Spalding. To St John, NB, 1833. Wife of James Inches, qv, m 11 Oct 1814. **DC 2 Mar 1980**.

11204 SMALL, John, ca 1732–18 Oct 1819. From East Kilbride, LKS. Served in 77th Regt from its recruitment in 1757, until disbanded, 1763, having fought at Quebec, 1759. Stld nr Fredericton, NB. **NSS No 1753**.

11205 SMALL, John, 1726–3 Oct 1794. From Strathardle, PER. Served with the Scots Brigade in Holland, ca 1747, and obtained a commission in the 42nd Regt. After action at Ticonderoga and Montreal, he was associated with Lt Col Allan MacLean, qv, in raising the Royal Highland Emigrant Regiment, afterwards the 84th, and commanded the 2nd Batt, which he raised in NS. Held rank of Lt Col and attained that of Maj Gen. **MDB 696**.

11206 SMALL, Patrick, d ca 1810. From PER. s/o John S. To Montreal, QUE, 1779, and joined NWCo. Served at Churchill River and Isle à la Crosse. Later merchant in London, ENG, and inherited property belonging to his uncle, Lt Col John S, qv. By a Cree woman had ch: 1. Patrick; 2. Nancy; 3. Charlotte. **MDB 697**.

11207 SMART, Alexander, 9 Oct 1805–1 Feb 1868. From Brechin, ANS. s/o Thomas S, qv, and first wife. To QUE, 1824, and stld Portage du Fort, or Shawville. m June Long, from Almonte, Lanark Co, ONT, 1 Mar 1831, ch: 1. Jane; 2. Thomas; 3. Janet; 4. Arthur; 5. Mary; 6. John; 7. Alexander; 8. William; 9. Lois, 1846-69; 10. Amelia; 11. Robert; 12. Bemsley. **DC 20 Jun and 20 Jul 1979**.

11208 SMART, Thomas, 22 Mar 1780–12 Jan 1838. From Brechin, ANS. To Ramsay Twp, Lanark Co, ONT, and stld Lot 12, Con 9, in 1821. Discharged soldier. By a first wife had ch: 1. Alexander, qv; 2. John, remained in SCT; 3. William, remained in SCT; 4-5. daughters. m (i) Mrs Lois Murdoch, d/o Bemslee Buell and Lois Sherwood, further ch: 6. Bemslee Buell, 1830–1904; 7. Thomas, 1831-43; 8. Lois Anne, 1834-83; 9. John James, d inf, 1837. **DC 20 Jun 1979**.

11209 SMART, Rev William, 14 Sep 1788–9 Sep 1876. From Haddington, ELN. s/o Alexander S. Educ Gosport, Hampshire, and ord at Scots Ch, London. To Brockville, Leeds Co, ONT, 1811, and was min there, joining Ch of Scotland, 1840. m (i) 1816, Philena, d 1855, wid/o Israel Jones, Brockville; (ii) 1862, Mrs Bush, Gananoque. Son William, judge, Hastings Co. **FES vii 651; MDB 697; HCL 189**.

11210 SMELLIE, Rev George, 14 Jun 1811–22 Nov 1896. From Deerness, OKI. s/o Rev James S. and Margaret Spence. Asst min of Lady par, OKI. Joined FC, 1843, and became min of Melville Ch, Fergus, Wellington Co, ONT. DD, Queens Univ, 1885. m 19 Jun 1843, Margaret Lendrum Logie, qv, ch: 1. Dr James, Fort William; 2. Elizabeth Logie, Toronto. **SGC 642; FES vii, 265, 651; MDB 697**.

11211 SMELLIE, John, ca 1791–19 Jul 1865. From Kilmarnock, AYR. To Cleveland Twp, Richmond Co, QUE, 1820; later to Melbourne Twp, Sherbrooke Co. Weaver, farmer. m Isabella Murdock, qv, ch: 1. John; 2. James Murdock, qv; 3. Nelson; 4. Isabella; 5. Eleanora; 6. Janet; 7. Suzanna; 8. Jessie. **MGC 2 Aug 1979; DC 11 Jan 1980**.

11212 SMELLIE, John Murdock, 1817–1911. From Kilmarnock, AYR. s/o John S, qv, and Isabella Murdock, qv. To Cleveland Twp, Richmond Co, QUE, 1820. m 1847, Violet Wilson, ch: 1. Jessie; 2. Jack; 3. Bell; 4. Andrew; 5. Violet; 6. Agnes; 7. James Albert, 1864–1957; 8. George; 9. Maggie. **DC 11 Jan 1980**.

11213 SMELLIE, James, 23 Nov 1807–4 Dec 1885. From Edinburgh. To QUE, with parents, 1821, and went later to NY. Engraver. **MDB 697**.

11214 SMITH, Agnes. From Kilmarnock, AYR. d/o William S, merchant. To Montreal, QUE, <May 1798. m William Parker. **Ayr Sasines, 42, 25**.

11215 SMITH, Alexander. From Is South Uist, INV. To West Williams Twp, Middlesex Co, ONT, 1849; stld Con 14. **PCM 48**.

11216 SMITH, Andrew, 1839–1914. From Brechin, ANS. s/o David S, qv, and Cecilia Kydd, qv. To QUE, 1850; stld Bristol. m 1870, Catherine Telfer, 1843–1918, ch: 1. David Kydd, 1871–1923; 2. John W, 1873–1954; 3. William Gordon, 1875–1961; 4. Sidney S, 1881–1968. **DC 15 Mar 1971**.

11217 SMITH, Angus, b ca 1758. To Margaree dist, Inverness Co, NS, 1807. Farmer, m and ch. **CBC 1818**.

11218 SMITH, Angus. From Moidart, INV. s/o Donald S, qv. To Moidart, Antigonish Co, NS, <1784. ch incl: 1. Ronald; 2. John. **HCA 362**.

11219 SMITH, Angus. From Is Lewis, INV. To QUE, ex Stornoway, arr 4 Aug 1851; stld Huron Twp, Bruce Co, ONT, 1852. Head of family. **DC 5 Apr 1967**.

11220 SMITH, Ann. From Killarrow par, Is Islay, ARL. d/o John S, qv, and Ann MacLachlan. To Eldon Twp, Victoria Co, ONT, <1840. Wife of John Spence, qv. **EC 214**.

11221 SMITH, Ann, ca 1813–9 Sep 1904. From Is Islay, ARL. d/o Gilbert S, qv, and Martha Smith, qv. To ONT, ca 1830; stld Victoria Co. m Duncan Smith, qv. **DC 21 Feb 1980**.

11222　SMITH, Ann, b 1811. Prob from Glasgow. To Cape Breton Co, NS, <1834; stld Bras d'Or Lake. Wife of John Christie, qv, m 7 Oct 1833. **HNS iii 418**.

11223　SMITH, Archibald, ca 1810–ca 1886. From Is Islay, ARL. s/o Gilbert S, qv, and Martha Smith, qv. To ONT, ca 1810; stld prob Victoria Co. Farmer. m Janet McCorquodale, qv, ch. **DC 21 Feb 1980**.

11224　SMITH, Catherine, b 1813. Prob from Kilmeny, Is Islay, ARL. To Eldon Twp, Victoria Co, ONT, ca 1835. Wife of Donald Campbell, qv. **EC 46**.

11225　SMITH, Cecilia, 1822–4 Jan 1882. From Cambusnethan par, LKS. To ONT and d Elderslie, Bruce Co. Wife of William Bell, qv. **Ts Carbarns**.

11226　SMITH, Charles. From Is Lewis, ROC. To QUE, 1841; stld prob Wolfe Co. m Catherine Buchanan, qv. Son Charles, b Red Mountain, 1878. **WLC; MGC 2 Aug 1979**.

11227　SMITH, Charles Farquharson, ca 1827–13 Aug 1883. From Lumphanan, ABD. s/o Alexander S, advocate in Aberdeen, proprietor of Glemillan, and Elizabeth Lamond. Educ Marischall Coll, Aberdeen, 1841-45, and grad MA. To QUE. Banker, British Bank of North America. **FAM ii 514; SAA 330**.

11228　SMITH, Christiana Charlotte. From Aberdeen. d/o John S. To NS <1825, when m James Ross. **VSN No 1180**.

11229　SMITH, Mrs Christina. From Is Lewis, ROC. To QUE, ex Stornoway, arr 4 Aug 1851; stld Huron Twp, Bruce Co, ONT, 1852. Widow and head of family. **DC 5 Apr 1967**.

11230　SMITH, Rev David, ca 1732–25 Mar 1795. From Auchtermuchty, FIF. Burgher min at St Andrews, 1763-69. To Londonderry, Colchester Co, NS, 1770. m Agnes Spear, qv. Son James, qv. **UPC i 172; MLA 322**.

11231　SMITH, David, 1801-83. From Brechin, ANS. s/o David S, Aberlemno, and Mary Gouck. To QUE, 1850; stld Bristol. Shoemaker. m Cecilia Kydd, ch: 1. Jean Whyte, qv; 2. Margaret, qv; 3. John, qv; 4. Andrew, qv. **DC 15 Mar 1971**.

11232　SMITH, Donald. From Moidart, INV. To Moidart, Antigonish Co, NS, 1784. Farmer. ch: 1. John, qv; 2. Angus, qv. **HCA 361**.

11233　SMITH, Donald. From Rannoch, PER. To Pictou, NS, on the *Sarah*, ex Fort William, Jun 1801. Tenant. Wife with him. **PLS**.

11234　SMITH, Donald. From INV. To Antigonish Co, NS, poss <1830; stld Georgeville. m Christina, d/o Angus MacDonald, ch: 1. Angus; 2. Margaret; 3. Mary; 4. John; 5. Catherine; 6. Elizabeth; 7. Ann. **HCA 363**.

11235　SMITH, Donald. From Is Lewis, ROC. To QUE, ex Stornoway, arr 4 Aug 1851; stld Huron Twp, Bruce Co, ONT, 1852. Head of family. **DC 5 Apr 1967**.

11236　SMITH, Donald Alexander, 6 Aug 1820–21 Jan 1914. From Archieston, MOR. s/o Alexander S. and Barbara Stewart. To Lachine, Montreal, QUE, 1838. Clerk, later chief factor, HBCo, and Governor, 1889–1914. Mem of Federal Parliament, 1871-79, and Vice Pres of Bank of Montreal. Cr Baron as Lord Strathcona and Mount Royal, 1897. GCMG, GCVO, LLD, FRS. m Isabella Sophia, d/o Richard Hardisty, chief factor, HBCo, with ch: dau Margaret Charlotte, b 17 Jan 1854, Baroness, who left ch. **BNA 1077; MDB 722; DC 15 Mar 1971**.

11237　SMITH, Dougald, d 1881. Poss from Is Skye, INV. To Aldborough Twp, Elgin Co, ONT, 1836. Farmer. m (i) Betsy Munro; (ii) Marge Cameron; ch by both. **PDA 63**.

11238　SMITH, Dugald, ca 1780–3 Dec 1837. From Ardrishaig, ARL. To Caradoc Twp, Middlesex Co, ONT, 1833. m Christina Campbell, qv, ch: 1. Donald, 1816-40; 2. Christina. **PCM 35**.

11239　SMITH, Duncan. From Knapdale, ARL. To Lobo Twp, Middlesex Co, ONT, 1828. ch: 1. John; 2. Malcolm; 3. Archibald; 4. Mattie; 5. Kate. **PCM 38**.

11240　SMITH, Duncan. From Culmakyle, Abernethy par, INV. To Grey Co, ONT, autumn 1838. Servant. m Margaret Mackenzie, qv, ch: 1. John, d 1917; 2. Lewis, farmer, d 10 May 1904; 3. Mary; 4. Annie; 5. Duncan, went to MAN; 6. Maggie. **Duthil OPR 96b/1-2; DC 22 Jan 1980**.

11241　SMITH, Duncan, ca 1801–1 May 1885. From Is Islay, ARL. To ONT <1830; stld prob Eldon Twp, Victoria Co. Farmer. m Ann Smith, qv. **DC 21 Feb 1980**.

11242　SMITH, Edward. From Aberdeen. Master of the schooner *Pictou*. m in NS, 29 Oct 1814, Margaret Milne, qv. **NSS No 345**.

11243　SMITH, Elizabeth, ca 1777–14 Apr 1869. From Half Morton par, DFS. To Truro, Colchester Co, NS, 1805; later to Onslow. Wife of Francis Lorraine, qv. **CAE 20**.

11244　SMITH, Elspet. From Knockando par, MOR. d/o John S. To Montreal, QUE, 1848, to join her husband William Stephen, qv, having with her 4 ch. **DC 15 Mar 1971**.

11245　SMITH, Elspie, b 13 Jan 1822. From Is Islay, ARL. d/o Gilbert S, qv, and Martha S, qv. To ONT, ca 1830; stld Victoria Co. m Malcolm MacEachern, qv. **DC 21 Feb 1980**.

11246　SMITH, Farquhar, b ca 1767. From Barrowfield, Glasgow. To QUE, ex Greenock, summer 1815; stld poss Lanark Co, ONT. Farmer. Wife Margaret Baillie, qv, with him, and 2 ch. **SEC 4**.

11247　SMITH, Francis, 1806-63. To Pictou Co, NS, <1840; stld west branch of East River. m 13 Dec 1841, Isabella McKay, ch: 1. John, 1844-90; 2. David, 1848-95; 3. Joanna, 1861–1913. **PAC 124**.

11248　SMITH, George, d 14 Nov 1850. From Banff. To Halifax, NS, <1815. Lumberman, merchant and MLA. **MLA 320**.

11249　SMITH, Gilbert, ca 1766–18 Mar 1846. From Is Islay, ARL. To ONT, ca 1830; stld poss Victoria Co. Farmer. m (i) Sarah Lamont; (ii) Martha Smith, qv. ch: 1. John, qv; 2. Mary, qv; 3. Archibald, qv; 4. Ann, b 1813; 5. Neil, qv; 6. James, b 1817; 7. Martha, qv; 8. Elspie, qv; 9. Margaret, qv. **DC 21 Feb 1980**.

11250　SMITH, Gilbert, 1771–1834. From Is Islay, ARL. To Oro Twp, Simcoe Co, ONT, 1834, and d soon after arrival. Wife Janet, 1782–1877, with him, and family:

1. Peter, qv; 2. William, qv; 3. Mary, qv. **DC 21 Mar 1980**.

11251   SMITH, Helen, 14 Dec 1804–28 Oct 1852. From Cromarty, ROC. d/o Rev Robert S, par min, and Isabella Gair Ross. To QUE on the *Canada*, ex Greenock, 31 Aug 1833; stld Beckwith Twp, Lanark Co, ONT. m 1852, Dr John James Aitchison, Elmsley Twp. **FES vii 6; MGC 2 Aug 1979**.

11252   SMITH, Helen McKean, d 15 Oct 1857. From Gatehouse-of-Fleet, KKD. To Laprairie, QUE. Wife of Lt L Fleming S. **DGH 27 Nov 1857**.

11253   SMITH, Isabella Gair, 10 Jan 1811–2 Jan 1883. From Cromarty, ROC. d/o Rev Robert S, par min, and Isabella Gair Rose. To QUE on the *Canada*, ex Greenock, 31 Aug 1833; stld Beckwith Twp, Lanark Co, ONT. m 1835, Rev George Romanes, qv. **FES vii 6, 649; MGC 2 Aug 1979**.

11254   SMITH, James, ca 1780–18 Apr 1820. From DFS. To Onslow, Colchester Co, NS. **NSN 30/307**.

11255   SMITH, James, b ca 1757. s/o Rev David S, qv, and Agnes Spear. To NS, 1770; stld Colchester Co, at Londonderry, later Stewiacke. Farmer and MLA. m Elizabeth, d/o William and Dorothy Putnam. **MLA 322**.

11256   SMITH, James, d 28 Jul 1815. From Ayr. To Montreal, QUE, <1804. General merchant. m Susanna McClemont. Son James, 1806–68, lawyer, was in SCT, 1815–23, but retr to Montreal. **SGC 238**.

11257   SMITH, James, b ca 1791. Poss s/o Angus S, qv. To Margaree dist, Inverness Co, NS, 1807. Farmer, m and ch. **CBC 1818**.

11258   SMITH, James. Poss from Is Mull, ARL. To Hudson Bay and Red River, <1813. Wife and 3 ch with him. **RRS 16**.

11259   SMITH, Rev James, ca 1800–16 May 1871. From Methven, PER. s/o John S, craftsman. Matric Univ of Glasgow, 1814. Prob of Secession Ch, and became min of Stewiacke, Colchester Co, NS, 1829. App Professor of Theology of the Lower Provinces of British North America. **GMA 9125**.

11260   SMITH, James. To Lanark Co, ONT, 1821; stld Lot 13, Con 3, North Sherbrooke Twp. Farmer. **HCL 74**.

11261   SMITH, James. From ABD. To Westmorland Co, NB, poss <1840. Farmer. m Isabella Bruce. **DC 17 Apr 1981**.

11262   SMITH, James. From Shotts, LKS. To ONT, ca 1830; stld prob Uxbridge, Ontario Co. m Christian Somerville, qv, ch: 1. James; 2. Maureen. **DC 27 Dec 1979 and 30 Sep 1983**.

11263   SMITH, Rev James, d 28 Jan 1853. Educ Univ of Edinburgh. To ONT and ord at Guelph, Wellington Co, 9 Feb 1832. Joined FC, 1844. d at Puslinch. **FES vii 651**.

11264   SMITH, James, ca 1801–3 Jan 1867. From Lunan, ANS. s/o Alexander S, feuar in Macduff. To NB <1852, later to Toronto. Tutor, sometime of Knox Coll. m Jane Tocher, qv. Son Alexander, 1823–55, d Toronto. **SH; Ts Lunan**.

11265   SMITH, James. From Orchardton, KKD. Son and heir of Andrew S. To CAN <1855. Saddler. **SH**.

11266   SMITH, James, s 22 Sep 1858. From Long Beoch, Irongray, DFS. To Cobourg, Northumberland Co, ONT. **DGH 26 Nov 1858**.

11267   SMITH, James Lamond, d 13 Jan 1883. From Lumphanan, ABD. s/o Alexander S, advocate in Aberdeen, and Elizabeth Lamond. To Toronto, ONT, <1855. **SAA 330**.

11268   SMITH, Mrs Jane, ca 1784–1 Nov 1857. From Lockerbie Hill, Lockerbie, DFS. Wife of William S. To Warwick Twp, Lambton Co, ONT, and d there. **DGH 4 Dec 1857**.

11269   SMITH, Janet, ca 1794–ca 1866. From SEL. To Westminster Twp, Middlesex Co, ONT, 1833. Wife of James Crinklaw, qv, m 1814. **DC 11 Nov 1981**.

11270   SMITH, Jean Whyte, 1833–1908. From Brechin, ANS. d/o David S, qv, and Cecilia Kydd, qv. To QUE, 1850, stld Bristol. m 1852, George Morison, qv. **DC 15 Mar 1971**.

11271   SMITH, Jessie, ca 1802–8 Feb 1869. From Dunscore, DFS. To Kent Co, NB, prob <1840, and d Kouchibouguac. m D. Clark. **DC 14 Jan 1980**.

11272   SMITH, Jessie, 6 Dec 1818–23 Oct 1902. From Ayr. To QUE and stld Melbourne, Sherbrooke Co. Wife of John Ewing, qv. **MGC 2 Aug 1979**.

11273   SMITH, John, b ca 1730. From Preston Merse, Kirkbean, KKD. To Georgetown, PEI, on the *Lovely Nellie*, ex Annan, 1774. Mason. Wife Janet Sturgeon, qv, with him and ch: 1. Mary, aged 16; 2. Jane, aged 9; 3. Janet, aged 6; 4. Agnes, aged 5; 5. Isabella, aged 3; 6. Nellie, aged 1. **ELN**.

11274   SMITH, John, bapt 8 Apr 1750. From Lochend, Colvend par, KKD, but b Lockerbie, DFS. s/o David S. in Netherplace. To Georgetown, Kings Co, PEI, on the *Lovely Nellie*, ex Annan, 1774. Moved later to Middle River, Pictou Co, NS, where he had a grant of land. Afterwards at Tatamagouche, Colchester Co. Blacksmith, farmer and landowner. Wife Margaret McVicar, qv, with him, and ch: 1. William, aged 6; 2. Mary, aged 5. **ELN; Lockerbie OPR 820/1; HPC 287; HT 69**.

11275   SMITH, John. From Moidart, INV. s/o Donald S, qv. To Moidart, Antigonish Co, NS, <1784. m Margaret Gillis, qv, ch: 1. Alexander; 2. Allan; 3. Angus; 4. John; 5. Catherine. **HCA 361**.

11276   SMITH, John, d 1872. From Athelstaneford, ELN. To Montreal, QUE, <1811. Merchant, in partnership with Charles Bowman. **SGC 381**.

11277   SMITH, John. From Kildalton, Is Islay, ARL. To Fort Churchill, Hudson Bay, on the *Prince of Wales*, 1813. Went to Red River, 1814. Wife Mary with him, and ch: 1. Neil, qv; 2. John; 3. Mary; 4. Jean. **LSS 184; RRS 27; LSC 323**.

11278   SMITH, John. To Lanark Co, ONT, 1821; stld Lot 6, Con 2, North Sherbrooke Twp. **HCL 74**.

11279   SMITH, Rev John. To Kingston, ONT; later to Brockville. m (i) Mary Bland, qv; (ii) Eliza Blaind, qv. **DGC 7 May 1834 and 30 Sep 1835**.

11280   SMITH, John, 1788–31 Jul 1872. From ARL. To Euphemia Twp, Kent Co, ONT, 1830; stld Lot 25, Con 10. Farmer. Wife Lucy with him, and s Angus. **DC 24 Mar 1982**.

11281 SMITH, John, ca 1807–8 Jan 1869. From Is Islay, ARL. s/o Gilbert S, qv, and Martha S, qv. To ONT, ca 1830; stld poss Victoria Co. m Christy Nicholson, qv, ch. **DC 21 Dec 1982**.

11282 SMITH, Rev John, 19 Jan 1801–18 Apr 1851. b Cromarty, ROC. s/o Rev Robert S, par min, and Isabella Gair Rose. Educ Aberdeen, and ord Fortrose, May 1833. To QUE on the *Canada*, ex Greenock, 31 Aug 1833; stld Beckwith Twp, Lanark Co, ONT. Min of St Andrews Presb Ch, 7th line. m 1838, Jane, 1816–99, d/o Thomas Morson, lawyer, ch: 1. Robert, b 1839, lawyer; 2. Isabella Rose, 1840–1913; 3. Mary Matilda Ottley Fellowes, 1842–1922; 4. Margaret Crawford, 1844–1920; 5. Jane Morson, 1847–1915; 6. Rev John Rose, 1847–1947, Britannia Bay. **FES vii 651; HCL 203**.

11283 SMITH, John. From DFS. To PEI <1840; stld Summerside, Prince Co. Moved later to Truro, Colchester Co, NS. Millwright and farmer. Son Daniel C. **HNS iii 369**.

11284 SMITH, John, ca 1765–23 Jan 1844. From Ayr. To QUE, and stld Melbourne, Sherbrooke Co. m Marion Wilson, qv. Both bur Maple Grove. **MGC 2 Aug 1979**.

11285 SMITH, John, ca 1796–4 Feb 1872. From Is Lewis, ROC. To Black River, Richmond Co, NS, <1840. m Margaret McLean, qv. Son Richard, 1838–1912. **NSN 9/2**.

11286 SMITH, John, 1784–1847. From Killarrow par, Is Islay, ARL. To Eldon Twp, Victoria Co, ONT, <1843. m Ann McLachlan. ch: 1. Ann, qv; 2. John, jr, qv. **EC 210**.

11287 SMITH, John, jr, 1813–1903. From Is Islay, ARL. s/o John S, qv, and Ann McLachlan. To Eldon Twp, Victoria Co, ONT, <1843. m Mary McCarroll, 1827–99, ch: 1. John, 1852–1917; 2. Hugh, 1853–54; 3. Dougald, 1855–1924; 4. Hugh, 1857–1928; 5. Isabella, 1859–1924; 6. Minnie, 1862–1942; 7. Caleb, 1864–1955; 8. Silas, 1866–87; 9. Gilbert, b 1871. **EC 210**.

11288 SMITH, John. From Brechin, ANS. s/o David S, qv, and Cecilia Kydd, qv. To QUE, 1850; stld Bristol. m Jean Reid, ch: 1. David; 2. Alexander. **DC 15 Mar 1971**.

11289 SMITH, John. From Knapdale, ARL. To Adelaide Twp, Middlesex Co, ONT, ca 1850. ch: 1. John; 2. Malcolm. **PCM 28**.

11290 SMITH, John, ca 1807–24 Nov 1879. From Duns, BEW. s/o John S, surgeon, and Elizabeth Martin. To ONT, and d Torbolton Twp, Carleton Co. **Ts Duns**.

11291 SMITH, John H. From Alloa, CLK. To QUE, and stld Richmond. m Malvina C. Denison, b Cleveland, QUE. Son John Denison, b 1875. **MGC 2 Aug 1979**.

11292 SMITH, Rev John Malcolm, ca 1823–8 Aug 1856. Min of Garelochhead, DNB. To Galt, ONT, Nov 1848. Min there, and in 1850 app Prof of Classical Literature and Moral Philosophy at Queens Coll, Kingston. Dau Mary Jane Ewing, 1853–1913. **FES vii 651; Ts Grange, Edinburgh**.

11293 SMITH, Laughlin, 1723–1823. To Halifax, NS, poss 1784. Discharged soldier; veteran of QUE. **VSN No 310**.

11294 SMITH, Malcolm. From Knapdale, ARL. To Lobo Twp, Middlesex Co, ONT, 1828. Sailor. m 1832, Mary McFarlane, qv, ch: 1. John; 2. Duncan; 3. Malcolm; 4. Donald; 5. Archibald; 6. Peter; 7. Flora; 8. Christy. **PCM 39, 45**.

11295 SMITH, Malcolm. From Is Lewis, ROC. To QUE, ex Stornoway, arr 4 Aug 1851; stld Huron Twp, Bruce Co, ONT. Head of family. **DC 5 Apr 1967**.

11296 SMITH, Malcolm, b 1816. From Ungshader, Is Lewis, ROC. s/o Kenneth S. and Marion McDonald. To QUE, ex Stornoway, arr 4 Aug 1851; stld Huron Twp, Bruce Co, ONT, 1852. Wife Ann with him, and ch: 1. Marion, b 1839; 2. Christy, b 1840; 3. Ann, b 1842; 4. Malcolm, b 1846; 5. Kenneth. **WLC**.

11297 SMITH, Margaret, b ca 1824. From Is Islay, ARL. d/o Gilbert S, qv, and Martha S, qv. To ONT, ca 1830; stld prob Victoria Co. m — Eastwood. **DC 21 Feb 1980**.

11298 SMITH, Margaret. From Brechin, ANS. d/o David S, qv, and Cecilia Kydd, qv. To QUE, 1850; stld Bristol. m George Graham. **DC 15 Mar 1971**.

11299 SMITH, Margaret Dunlop. From AYR. d/o James S, Monkwood Grove. To Galt, Waterloo Co, ONT, 1844; stld Ayr Village. Wife of John Goldie, qv, m 1815. **MDB 269**.

11300 SMITH, Martha, ca 1775–15 Jul 1873. From Is Islay, ARL. To ONT, ca 1830; stld poss Victoria Co. Wife of Gilbert S, qv. **DC 21 Feb 1980**.

11301 SMITH, Martha, bapt 23 Nov 1820. From Is Islay, ARL. d/o Gilbert S, qv, and Martha S, qv. To ONT, ca 1830; stld poss Victoria Co. m Hector MacEachern, qv. **EC 118; DC 21 Feb 1980**.

11302 SMITH, Mary, ca 1765–ca 1841. From Strathspey. To Pictou Co, NS, 1813; stld west branch of East River. m John Ross, 1761–1856, qv. **PAC 199**.

11303 SMITH, Mary, 28 May 1786–6 Apr 1881. From Tayvallich, North Knapdale, ARL. d/o John S. and Kirsty McMillan. To Caradoc Twp, Middlesex Co, ONT, 1819. Wife of Malcolm Campbell, qv. **DC 20 May 1980**.

11304 SMITH, Mary, b ca 1809. From Is Islay, ARL. d/o Gilbert S, qv, and Martha S, qv. To ONT, ca 1830; stld poss Victoria Co. m Neil MacEachern, qv. **DC 21 Feb 1980**.

11305 SMITH, Mary. From Is Islay, ARL. d/o Gilbert S, qv, and wife Janet. To Oro Twp, Simcoe Co, ONT, 1834. m Lachlan McMillan. **DC 21 Mar 1980**.

11306 SMITH, Murdoch. To Cape Breton Co, NS, <1820; stld St Anns, Victoria Co. Wife Ann with him. **NSN 7/5**.

11307 SMITH, Neil. From Kildalton, Is Islay, ARL. To Fort Churchill, Hudson Bay, on the *Prince of Wales*, ex Stromness, 28 Jun 1813. Went to York Factory, spring 1814, thence to Red River. Entered service of HBCo, Jul 1814. **LSS 186; RRS 27; LSC 323**.

11308 SMITH, Neil, b 1814. From Is Islay, ARL. s/o Gilbert S, qv, and Martha Smith, qv. To ONT, ca 1830; stld prob Victoria Co. m Christie Carmichael. **DC 21 Feb 1980**.

11309 SMITH, Norman. From Is Lewis, ROC. To QUE,

ex Stornoway, arr 4 Aug 1851; stld Huron Twp, Bruce Co, 1852. Head of family. **DC 5 Apr 1967**.

11310 SMITH, Peter, d 19 Mar 1816. From Galloway. To Halifax, NS, ca 1786. Merchant. **NSS No 784**.

11311 SMITH, Peter, 1816-90. From Is Islay, ARL. s/o Gilbert S, qv, and wife Janet. To Oro Twp, Simcoe Co, ONT, 1834. m Mary McPhaden, qv, ch: 1. Gilbert, b 1843; 2. Mary, 1844-1931; 3. Janet, 1846-1909; 4. Donald, b 1847; 5. Margaret, b 1849; 6. John, 1852-1932; 7. Betsy, dy; 8. Peter, b 1856; 9. Catherine, 1858-1941; 10. Archibald, 1860-1933; 11. Christina Ann, b 1862; 12. Sarah, b 1865; 13. Hugh, 1870-1909; 14. William, b 1867. **DC 21 Mar 1980**.

11312 SMITH, Peter, 1799-1885. From Lochgilphead, ARL. To Westminster Twp, Middlesex Co, ONT, 1836. **PCM 52**.

11313 SMITH, Rachel, 1770-5 Dec 1845. From Aberdeen. sis/o William and Alexander S, merchants in Liverpool. To Halifax, NS, <1820. Retr later to Aberdeen. m James Thom, qv. **NDF 227**.

11314 SMITH, Robert. Served as an NCO in the 82nd Regt, and was gr 200 acres at Merigomish, Pictou Co, 1784. ch. **HPC App F**.

11315 SMITH, Robert. To QUE on the *David of London*, ex Greenock, 19 May 1821; stld Lot 10, Con 3, North Sherbrooke Twp, Lanark Co, ONT. Son Robert. **HCL 74, 239**.

11316 SMITH, Robert, 1768-24 Apr 1841. From Glasgow. s/o William S. To Montreal, QUE, 1832. Merchant. Son William Primrose, qv. **SGC 566**.

11317 SMITH, Robert, 14 Aug 1804-16 May 1842. From RFW. s/o James S, merchant in Greenock, and Ann Farm. To QUE <1840. Merchant. **Ts Johnstone**.

11318 SMITH, Rev Robert Primrose, b 1835. From Aberdeen. s/o David S, shipmaster. Matric Marischall Coll, Aberdeen, 1853. To QUE, later to NZ. **FAM ii 563; FES vii 651**.

11319 SMITH, Robert Robertson, 21 Sep 1810-22 Jul 1899. From Peterhead, ABD. s/o John S. and Christian Pratt. To QUE on the *Champlain of Quebec*, Sep 1831. Went to Leeds Co, ONT, but stld Bromley and Wilberforce Twps, Renfrew Co. m Elizabeth Callachan, qv, ch: 1. John, b 16 Aug 1832; 2. Richard, b 20 Sep 1834; 3. Christian, b 29 Feb 1836; 4. Catharine, b 28 Jul 1838; 5. Elizabeth, b 29 Feb 1840; 6. Jean, b 19 Mar 1841; 7. Mary, b 22 Mar 1842; 8. Robert John, b 21 Jan 1844; 9. James, b 28 Oct 1845; 10. Alexander, b 16 Jun 1847; 11. Jane, b 14 Mar 1849; 12. William, b 26 Apr 1851; 13. George, b 10 Mar 1853; 14. Thomas, b 18 Feb 1854; 15. Harriet Ann, b 26 Apr 1856; 16. Grace Ellen, b 26 Jun 1858. **DC 15 Sep 1979**.

11320 SMITH, Ronald. From INV. To Antigonish Co, NS, poss <1830. Violinist. ch: 1. Donald; 2. Archibald; 3. Angus, dy; 4. Ann; 5. Mary. **HCA 363**.

11321 SMITH, Thomas, b ca 1793. From Barrowfield, Glasgow. To QUE, ex Greenock, summer 1815; stld prob Lanark Co, ONT. Unm labourer. **SEC 4**.

11322 SMITH, William. Prob from ABD. To Chaleur Bay, NB, ca 1773; stld Mission Point, Restigouche River. Agent for John Schoolbread, merchant. **SR 13**.

11323 SMITH, William, b ca 1750. From Corsock, Colvend par, KKD. To Georgetown, Kings Co, PEI, on the *Lovely Nellie*, ex Annan, 1774; later to Pictou Co, NS, where listed, 1783, as capable of bearing arms. Son Anthony, res West River. **ELN; HPC App D and E**.

11324 SMITH, William, ca 1797-26 Jan 1867. From Aberdeen. s/o George S, glazier. Grad MA at Marischall Coll, Aberdeen, 1813. Appr to Alexander Smith, Advocate, and adm Advocate, 1817. Burgess of Aberdeen, 1826, and Notary Public. To QUE, ca 1836, and stld St Francis. Legal adviser and JP. Bur Elmwood, Sherbrooke. m Caroline McKay, qv, ch: 1. Caroline Isabella, ca 1825-1902; 2. George, ca 1825-59; 3. Jane Farquhar, ca 1826-1904; 4. William, ca 1828-71; 5. Katherine Ann, ca 1831-87. **SAA 335; FAM ii 406**.

11325 SMITH, William, d 7 Jan 1819. From BAN. To NS and d there. **NSS No 1519**.

11326 SMITH, William, 1818-80. From Is Islay, ARL. s/o Gilbert S, qv, and wife Janet. To Oro Twp, Simcoe Co, ONT, 1834. m Barbara Currie, qv, ch: 1. Kate, 1859-1929; 2. Gilbert, 1857-1923; 3. Janet; 4. Mary; 5. John; 6. William; 7. Rose; 8. Lillian; 9. Annie. **DC 21 Mar 1980**.

11327 SMITH, William, ca 1814-26 Dec 1854. From MOR. To Durham Co, ONT, and stld Oshawa. m Elizabeth Laing, qv. **DC 6 Sep 1979**.

11328 SMITH, William. To Ramsay Twp, Lanark Co, ONT, <1855, and stld Almonte. m Jean Neilson. Son Robert, 1859-1942, Justice of High Court of ONT, 1922-27, and of Supreme Court of CAN, 1927-33. **SDG 304**.

11329 SMITH, William. From Is Lewis, INV. To QUE, ex Stornoway, arr 4 Aug 1851; stld Huron Twp, Bruce Co, 1852. Head of family. **DC 5 Apr 1967**.

11330 SMITH, William, b ca 1831. From Lumphanan, ABD. s/o Alexander S. of Glenmillan, advocate, and Elizabeth Lamond. Alumnus, Marischall Coll, 1848-52, and went to Montreal, QUE. Agent of the Standard Assurance Co, and banker, Canadian Bank of Commerce. m 7 Oct 1863, Ann Sophia, d/o Dr W.H. Smith, Philadelphia. **FAM ii 543; SAA 330**.

11331 SMITH, William A. From BAN. To QUE, ca 1830; stld Stanstead. Farmer at Cassville. m Jane Boynton. Son Henry Havelock, b 1858. **MGC 2 Aug 1979**.

11332 SMITH, William Primrose, d 13 Dec 1877. b Stirling. s/o Robert S, qv. To Montreal, QUE, 1832. Physician. **SGC 566**.

11333 SMITH, William S. From Torthorwald, DFS. To QUE <1845. Schoolmaster. Lost his villa in great fire in the city, Jun 1845. **DGH 3 Jul 1845**.

11334 SMYTHE, Mary. From Huntleywood, Gordon, BEW. To New Glasgow, Terrebonne Co, QUE, 1833. Wife of George Edward Guthrie, qv. **DC 22 Jul 1979**.

11335 SNEDDEN, Alexander, ca 1795-12 Aug 1867. From Cambuslang, LKS. s/o James S, qv, and Christina Montgomery, qv. To Beckwith Twp, Lanark Co, ONT, 1819. m Mary Whyte, qv, and had, prob with other ch: 1. Mary, b 1827; 2. William, b 1829; 3. James, b 21 Apr 1831; 4. Alexander, jr. **HCL 39, 84; DC 11 Mar 1979**.

11336 SNEDDEN, David, ca 1797-ca 1834. From

Cambuslang, LKS. s/o James S, qv, and Christina Montgomery, qv. To Beckwith Twp, Lanark Co, ONT, 1819; stld Lot 26, Con 11. Farmer. m 30 Dec 1820, Nancy Whyte, qv, ch: 1. James, b 1821; 2. Mary, b 1823; 3. John; 4. William. **HCL 84; DC 11 Mar 1979**.

11337 SNEDDEN, James, b ca 1761. From Cambuslang, LKS. To QUE on the *Commerce*, ex Greenock, 11 May 1821; stld Ramsay Twp, Lanark Co, ONT, on Lot 25, Con 9. Soldiered with the 82nd Regt in North America during the Revolutionary War. m Christina Montgomery, qv, and had with other ch: 1. Alexander, qv; 2. David, qv. **DC 11 Mar 1979**.

11338 SNEDDEN, James. From Cambuslang, LKS. Rel to Alexander S, qv, and David S, qv. To Ramsay Twp, Lanark Co, ONT, ca 1820. Son James, farmer and lumberman. **HCL 84**.

11339 SNODGRASS, Andrew. From Gorbals, Glasgow. To Digby Co, NS, <1826. **SH**.

11340 SNODGRASS, Rev William, 4 Sep 1827–22 Jul 1906. From Paisley, RFW. s/o John S, Cardonald Mills, and Agnes Miller. Matric Univ of Glasgow, 1844. Min of St James's Ch, Charlottetown, PEI, 1852-56; trans to St Pauls, Montreal, QUE. Prof of Divinity at Queens Univ, 1864-77, when he retr to SCT to become min of Canonbie, DFS. m 1852, Jessie Calder, qv, ch: 1. Rev John Allan, b 1853, min of Demorestville, Prince Edward Co, ONT, 1888; 2. Janet Elizabeth, b 1855; 3. Agnes Miller, b 1856; 4. Robert Pollock, b 1858; 5. William George, b 1860; 6. Elizabeth Allan, b 1863; 7. Margaret, d inf 1865; 8. Mary, d inf 1867. **GMA 14825; FES ii 230, vii 651; MDB 705**.

11341 SOMERS, James. From DFS. bro/o Robert S, qv. To PEI, ca 1825. **DC 26 Feb 1981**.

11342 SOMERS, Robert. From DFS. bro/o James S, qv. To PEI, ca 1825; moved to NB. **DC 26 Feb 1981**.

11343 SOMERVILLE, Alexander, 15 Mar 1811–17 Jun 1885. From Oldhamstocks, ELN. s/o James S. and Mary Orkney. To Toronto, ONT, ca 1860. Discharged soldier, Scots Greys, and became editor of the *Canadian Illustrated News*, at Hamilton. **BNA 1135; MDB 706**.

11344 SOMERVILLE, Rev Alexander Carnegie, 1798–1872. From Brechin, ANS. s/o Rev James S, Episcopal clergyman, and Margaret Campbell. Grad MA, Kings Coll, Aberdeen, 1826. To NB, and was Episcopal incumbent at Bathurst, Gloucester Co, 1827-42. Retr to SCT and d Fettercairn, KCD. **KCG 282; SNQ ii/2 126**.

11345 SOMERVILLE, Andrew. From Kenmore, PER. s/o Robert S. and Isobell Scotland. To NB, 1816. Wife Janet Buchanan, qv, with him. **LDW 16 Dec 1980**.

11346 SOMERVILLE, Andrew, ca 1823-97. To Dundee, Charlottenburgh Twp, Glengarry Co, ONT, prob <1850. **DC 4 Mar 1965**.

11347 SOMERVILLE, Ann, 1825-93. From PER. d/o David S, qv, and Margaret G. Lawson, qv. To Halton Co, ONT, prob <1840; stld Esquesing Twp. m William Ross. **EPE 76**.

11348 SOMERVILLE, Christian, b 2 Feb 1795. From LKS. To ONT, ca 1830. Wife of James Smith, qv. **DC 27 Sep 1979**.

11349 SOMERVILLE, Colin Campbell, 22 Apr 1826–28 Jun 1903. From Edinburgh. s/o Alexander S, wine-merchant, 9 Malta Terrace. Educ Edinburgh Academy, 1835-40. To CAN, 1846, and moved in 1852 to Savannah, MO. Banker. m 1854, Mary Woodcock, Savannah. **EAR 90**.

11350 SOMERVILLE, David, 1788–1838. From PER. To Halton Co, ONT, prob <1840; stld Esquesing Twp. m Margaret G. Lawson, qv. Dau Ann, qv. **EPE 76**.

11351 SOMERVILLE, Duncan, ca 1812–12 Feb 1912. From Lanark, but family had some connection with Edinburgh. To QUE, ca 1843; stld Aldborough Twp, Elgin Co, ONT. Farmer. m Catherine Morrison, qv, and had, poss with other ch: 1. dau, d 1841; 2. Robert, 1843–1910, bur Rodney; 3. Duncan; 4. Thomas; 5. John. **PDA 66; DC 29 Oct 1979**.

11352 SOMERVILLE, Francis, 1825-98. From Whitburn par, WLN. To Scott Twp, York Co, ONT, 1847. Wife of James Meek, qv. **DC 15 Jul 1979**.

11353 SOMERVILLE, Rev James. From Brechin, ANS. s/o Rev James C, Episcopal min, and Margaret Campbell. Grad MA, Kings Coll, Aberdeen, 1795. To NB, 1811. Episcopal clergyman at Fredericton, and sometime Pres and Prof of Divinity at the Coll of NB. LLD, Kings Coll, Aberdeen, 1829. **KCG 117, 264; SNQ ii/2 125**.

11354 SOMERVILLE, Rev James, 1 Apr 1775–2 Jun 1837. From Tollcross, Glasgow. s/o William S, merchant. Matric Univ of Glasgow, 1789, and licensed to preach by the Relief Presb of Glasgow. To Montreal, QUE. Schoolmaster, but became min of St Gabriel St Ch, 1803. Retr 1822. m (i) 8 Jul 1805, Marianne Veitch, qv, ch: 1. Marianne, 1806-33, who gave a silver communion service to St Gabriel St Ch. m (ii) 4 Apr 1808, Charlotte Blaney, d 1819, further ch: 2. Alexander William, 1814-32, student of medicine. **SGC 154, 166, 585; GMA 4964; FES vii 652**.

11355 SOMERVILLE, James, ca 1809–5 Feb 1904. From LKS. To ONT, poss 1830. m Ann Smith. **DC 27 Dec 1979**.

11356 SOMERVILLE, John. To Restigouche River, NB, ca 1780, and acquired land on the south bank. **SR 15**.

11357 SOMERVILLE, John. Prob from ELN. bro/o Robert S, qv. To Dundee, Charlottenburgh Twp, Glengarry Co, ONT, <1800. **DC 4 Mar 1965**.

11358 SOMERVILLE, Peter, 1807-47. From Dunfermline, FIF. s/o James S, cooper in Clackmannan, and Christian Smith. To Wentworth Co, ONT, 1833; stld Dundas. m Agnes Bennett, qv, ch: 1. Isabel, 1829–1905; 2. Christina, 1832–1910; 3. James, 1834–1916; 4. Agnes, 1839–1930. **DC 4 Oct 1980**.

11359 SOMERVILLE, Robert. Prob from ELN. bro/o John S, qv. To Dundee, Charlottenburgh Twp, Glengarry Co, ONT, <1800. **DC 4 Mar 1965**.

11360 SOMERVILLE, Robert, 24 Jan 1800–29 Oct 1881. From Dunfermline, FIF. s/o James S, cooper in Clackmannan, and Christian Smith. To Wentworth Co, ONT, ca 1841; and bur Dundas. m Christian Bennett, qv, ch: 1. James, b 30 Jan 1826; 2. Christian, b 21 Jul 1828; 3. Thomas Bennett, b 29 Oct 1834. **DC 4 Oct 1980**.

11361   SOMERVILLE, Sarah, ca 1791–ca 1863. From LKS. To QUE on the *George Canning*, ex Greenock, 14 Apr 1821; stld Lanark Co. Wife of James Headrick, qv. **DC 27 Oct 1980**.

11362   SORRIE, Elizabeth. From Insch par, ABD. To Elora, Nichol Twp, Wellington Co, ONT, 1836. Wife of John Mennie, qv. **EHE 95**.

11363   SOUTAR, Rev James, d 6 Apr 1846. From ABD. Grad MA, Kings Coll, Aberdeen, 1830. Ord to St James's Ch, Newcastle, Northumberland Co, NB, 11 Jun 1830. Retr to SCT and adm min of Borthwick par, MLN, 1844. m 1831, Helen Ogilvie, d/o James Dyce, ch: 1. William Henry McGregor, b 1832; 2. Helen Ogilvie, b 1834; 3. Margaret Dyce, b 1839; 4. Ann Elizabeth, b 1841. **KCG 286; FES i 303, vii 611**.

11364   SPALDING, Alexander, b ca 1799. From Liff and Benvie par, ANS. bro/o William S, qv. To QUE, ex Greenock, summer 1815; stld prob Bathurst Twp, Lanark Co, ONT. **SEC 4**.

11365   SPALDING, William, b ca 1789. From Liff and Benvie par, ANS. bro/o Alexander S, qv. To QUE, ex Greenock, summer 1815; stld Lot 25, Con 1, Bathurst Twp, Lanark Co, ONT. Mason, later farmer. Wife and child still in SCT, Jul 1817. **SEC 4; HCL 16, 230**.

11366   SPARK, Rev Alexander, 7 Jan 1762–7 Jul 1819. From Marykirk, KCD. s/o Alexander S. Grad MA, Kings Coll, Aberdeen, 1776. To QUE, and was a teacher there until 1784, when he retr to SCT. Ord by Presb of Ellon, 1784, and went again to QUE to become min of St Andrews Ch. **SGC 172; KCG 252; FES vii 652; MDB 707**.

11367   SPEAR, Agnes. From Auchtermuchty, FIF. To Londonderry, Colchester Co, NS, 1770. Wife of Rev David Smith, qv. **MLA 322**.

11368   SPEDON, Andrew Learmont, 21 Aug 1831–26 Sep 1884. From Edinburgh. To QUE, with parents, <1855, and stld Chateauguay. Author and journalist. **MDB 707**.

11369   SPEEDY, Ellen, b 1835. From STI. To York Co, ONT, 1850. m Job Lambourn, b 1820, Reading, ENG, ch. **DC 17 Nov 1981**.

11370   SPIERS, Patrick, b 1787. From Bridge of Weir, RFW. s/o Peter S, 1769–1821. To Brampton, ONT, ca 1833, with family. **LDW 30 Jun 1971**.

11371   SPENCE, Rev Alexander, ca 1802–4 Sep 1878. b Huntly, ABD. Poss s/o Alexander S. Educ Aberdeen and Edinburgh. Presb min of St Vincent, West Indies, 1841-48. To Ottawa, ONT, and adm min of St Andrews Ch, 1848. DD, Queens Coll, 1864. Demitted his charge, 1867, and retr to Elgin, SCT. **FES vii 652**.

11372   SPENCE, Charles, b 1821. From Edinburgh. s/o Charles S, solicitor, 10 Saxe-Coburg Place. Educ Edinburgh Academy, 1832-36, and went to Goderich Twp, Huron Co, ONT. m Ellen Sawtell. **EAR 67**.

11373   SPENCE, James, b 21 Dec 1756. From Orwell, KRS. s/o Rev John S, par min, and Jean Clow. To QUE. Merchant. **FES v 72**.

11374   SPENCE, James. To CAN <1831, when neph William Shaw in Leith served heir to him. Wheelwright. **SH**.

11375   SPENCE, John. From Kilmany, Is Islay, ARL. To Eldon Twp, Victoria Co, ONT, <1840. Farmer. m Ann Smith, qv, and had, poss with other ch: 1. John; 2. Alexander; 3. Donald; 4. Hugh. **EC 214**.

11376   SPENCE, Peter, b ca 1793. From Sandwick, OKI. To Hudson Bay, ca 1813, and prob to Red River. **RRS 13**.

11377   SPIERS, Agnes, b ca 1822. To Plympton Twp, Lambton Co, ONT, <1848. Wife of William Bain, qv. **DC 7 Nov 1979**.

11378   SPIERS, John. Poss from STI. Gr-s/o James Wilson in Denny, who d 1815. To Waterloo Co, ONT, <1851. Smith. **SH**.

11379   SPREULL, Samuel, ca 1800–17 Dec 1879. From Glasgow. s/o James S, City Chamberlain. Matric Univ of Glasgow, 1815. To ONT <1850; stld Toronto. **GMA 9532**.

11380   SPROAT, George, ca 1794–ca 1870. From KKD. To ONT, ca 1842; stld prob Tuckersmith Twp, Huron Co. Farmer and stockbreeder. m Agnes Hastie, qv, ch: 1. John, qv; 2. William, qv; 3. George, jr, qv; 4. James, res Kippen, Tuckersmith Twp; 5. Agnes; 6. Agnes; 7. David; 8. Alexander; 9. Marion. **DC 29 Oct 1979**.

11381   SPROAT, George, jr, 1826–17 Aug 1879. From KKD. s/o George S, qv, and Agnes Hastie, qv. To Huron Co, ONT, ca 1842; stld Seaforth, Tuckersmith Twp. m Mary Black, 1829-97, ch: 1. Sarah, b 1851; 2. Isabella, b 1854; 3. Adam Black, b 1856; 4. Agnes Hastie, b 1858; 5. George A, b 1861; 6. James, b 1863; 7. John, b 1865; 8. David Douglas, b 1867; 9. Mary Black, b 1869; 10. Thomas, b 1876; 11. Myrtle. **DC 29 Oct 1979**.

11382   SPROAT, John, 1821-82. From KKD. s/o George S, qv, and Agnes Hastie, qv. To Huron Co, ONT, ca 1842; stld Tuckersmith Twp. m Jane Ross, ch: 1. John, b 1851; 2. James, b 1853; 3. Thomas, b 1855; 4. Jane, b 1858; 5. Mary, b 1860. **DC 29 Oct 1979**.

11383   SPROAT, William, 1824-92. From KKD. s/o George S, qv, and Agnes Hastie, qv. To Huron Co, ONT, ca 1842; stld Tuckersmith Twp. m Margaret Gerrund, b 1829, ch: 1. Annie, b 1851; 2. William, b 1853; 3. George, b 1856; 4. Agnes, b 1860; 5. John, b 1863; 6. Jessie, b 1867; 7. Alexander. **DC 29 Oct 1979**.

11384   SPROTT, Rev John, 3 Feb 1780–15 Sep 1869. From Stoneykirk, WIG. s/o James S, Caldon Park. Educ Univ of Edinburgh. To Halifax, NS, 1822, and became min at Musquodoboit, 1826. m 11 Apr 1821, Lemoira, d/o Archibald Smith, Kennetcook, Hants Co. Son Rev George Washington, 1829–1909, Halifax. **SH; NSS No 2639; VSN No 452; MDB 452**.

11385   SPROTT, Gilbert Malcolm, 1834–1913. From DFS. s/o Alexander S. and Hectorina Shaw. To Vancouver Is, BC, 1860. Government agent and author. **DC 17 May 1982**.

11386   SQUAIR, Francis. From Newmill, Auldearn, NAI. bro/o Robert S, qv. To Bowmanville, Durham Co, ONT, 1843. m Ann Margach. Son John, 1850–1928, linguist. **DC 30 Aug 1977**.

11387   SQUAIR, Robert. From Newmill, Auldearn, NAI. bro/o Francis S, qv. To Bowmanville, Durham Co, ONT, <1843. **DC 30 Aug 1977**.

11388   STALKER, Donald, ca 1813–11 Nov 1891. From Campbeltown, ARL. Prob rel to Gilbert S, qv. To Melbourne, Richmond Co, QUE, 1830. m Jane Beattie, qv. Son Donald S, 1862–1946.   **MGC 15 Jul 1980**.

11389   STALKER, Duncan. From Kintyre, ARL. Prob rel to Gilbert S, qv. To Aldborough Twp, Elgin Co, ONT, 1851.   **PDA 75**.

11390   STALKER, Flora. From Campbeltown, ARL. d/o Gilbert S, qv, and Marion Blue, qv. To Richmond Co, QUE, 1830. m Neil Bruce.   **DC 7 Mar 1980**.

11391   STALKER, Gilbert, d 1837. From Campbeltown, ARL. To QUE, 1830; stld Richmond Co. Wife Marion Blue, qv, with him, and ch: 1. John, d 1815; 2. Neil, d 1833; 3. Dugald; 4. Duncan, d 1867; 5. Marion, qv; 6. Nancy, qv; 7. Flora, qv.   **DC 7 Mar 1980**.

11392   STALKER, Gilbert. From Kintyre, ARL. Prob rel to Duncan S, qv. To Aldborough Twp, Elgin Co, ONT, 1851.   **PDA 75**.

11393   STALKER, Rev Hugh McLellan, 5 Aug 1807–17 Sep 1861. From Perth. To Inverness, Megantic Co, QUE, arr 23 Oct 1855. Congregational min. m Annie Tyler, qv, and had with other ch: 1. Margaret; 2. Annie; 3. Elizabeth; 4. Jane.   **AMC 117**.

11394   STALKER, James. From ARL. To Aldborough Twp, Elgin Co, ONT, 1850.   **PDA 75**.

11395   STALKER, John, ca 1787–3 Sep 1877. From PER. To Esquesing Twp, Halton Co, ONT, prob <1850; bur Acton.   **EPE 74**.

11396   STALKER, Marion. From Campbeltown, ARL. d/o Gilbert S, qv, and Marion Blue, qv. To Richmond Co, QUE, 1830. m Archibald Stewart.   **DC 7 Mar 1980**.

11397   STALKER, Nancy. From Campbeltown, ARL. d/o Gilbert S, qv, and Marion Blue, qv. To Richmond Co, QUE, 1830. m Malcolm Nicholson, qv.   **DC 7 Mar 1980**.

11398   STARK, Alexander, 1841–1905. From Kirkintilloch, DNB. s/o William S, qv, and Christina Mackinnon, qv. To Finch Twp, Stormont Co, ONT. Educ Queens Coll. Physician. m Martha Robertson, ch: 1. William Duncan James, 1878–1964; 2. Alexander, 1879–1963; 3. Robertson, 1880–1962; 4. Allan, 1885–1957; 5. James, 1886–1961.   **DC 15 and 31 Aug 1979**.

11399   STARK, Helen, 1778–1856. To QUE on the *David of London*, ex Greenock, 19 May 1821; stld Lanark Twp, Lanark Co, ONT. Bur at Middleville. Wife of James Gillies, qv.   **HCL 70; DC 2 Nov 1979**.

11400   STARK, John, b ca 1790. From Westruther, BEW. s/o William S. and Margaret Hervey, d 1806. To CAN <1830. m Margaret Cockburn.   **Ts Westruther**.

11401   STARK, Rev Mark Young, 9 Jan 1799–24 Jan 1866. b Cleish Castle, KRS. s/o Robert S, merchant in Dunfermline, FIF. Matric Univ of Glasgow, 1815, and grad MA, 1821. To Dundas, Wentworth Co, ONT, 1833. Joined FC, 1843, as min of Dundas and Ancaster.   **RGG 574; GMA 9424; FES vii 652; MDB 711**.

11402   STARK, William, b ca 1801. From Kirkintilloch, DNB. To Finch Twp, Stormont Co, ONT, 1849. Farmer. m Christina Mackinnon, qv, ch: 1. William, b ca 1839; 2. Alexander, qv; 3. Flora, b ca 1842; 4. James, b ca 1845; 5. Mary, b ca 1847; 6. Thomas Duncan, b CAN, hotelier.   **DC 15 and 31 Aug 1979; SDG 460**.

11403   STEEL, Burns, b 4 May 1821. From Wishaw, LKS, but prob b RFW. To ONT <1854. m Mary Scoular, qv, and had, prob with other ch: 1. Matthew, b 22 Jun 1843; 2. Robert, qv.   **DC 5 Sep 1979**.

11404   STEEL, James, d 1910. From PEE. To Haldimand Co, ONT, ca 1856; moved to Huron Twp, Bruce Co. Blacksmith. m Isabel Young, qv, ch: 1. James; 2. Isabel; 3. Walter; 4. Elsie.   **DC 25 Dec 1981**.

11405   STEEL, John, b ca 1782. To Richmond Co, NS, 1813. Farmer, m and ch.   **CBC 1818**.

11406   STEEL, Margaret Baird, 7 May 1832–17 Jun 1920. From Barony par, Glasgow. d/o John S. and Mary Neilson. To Amherst, Cumberland Co, NS. m 2 Dec 1857, William Dick Main, qv.   **DC 18 Nov 1978**.

11407   STEEL, Robert. From Wishaw, LKS. s/o Burns S, qv, and Mary Scoular, qv. To ONT <1854. m Emma Coleman. Dau Kate, b 1897.   **DC 5 Sep 1979**.

11408   STEELE, Charles, 22 Apr 1815–1895. From The Roods, Kirriemuir, ANS. s/o Thomas S. and Betty Mair. To QUE, 1841; stld River aux Outardes, Labrador. Farmer. m Mary Reid, qv, ch: 1. David, qv; 2. Alexander, b 1843; 3. Thomas Lindsay, b 1845; 4. John, b 1848; 5. Charles, b 1852; 6. Mary, 1854–1920; 7. George, 1860–1941.   **Kirriemuir OPR 299/2; DC 5 Aug 1969**.

11409   STEELE, David, 28 May 1840–1922. b Tannadice, ANS. s/o Charles S, qv, and Mary Reid, qv. To QUE, 1841. Became a farmer at Mount Pleasant, QUE. m at Ormstoun, Chateauguay Co, Catherine McNeil. Son Charles Alexander, b 1865, Three Rivers.   **DC 5 Aug 1969**.

11410   STEELE, Donald. From Is South Uist, INV. To West Williams Twp, Middlesex Co, ONT, 1849; stld Con 12.   **PCM 48**.

11411   STEELE, Donald. From Is South Uist, INV. To West Williams Twp, Middlesex Co, ONT, 1849; stld Con 14.   **PCM 48**.

11412   STEELE, John, 1786–1829. From DFS. To Cumberland Co, NS. Bur Methodist cemetery, Wallace.   **DC 29 Aug 1980**.

11413   STEELE, John. Poss from AYR. To Lanark Co, ONT, 1821; stld Lot 22, Con 7, Ramsay Twp. Farmer. m Mary Johnstone.   **HCL 82**.

11414   STEELE, Peter. From Is South Uist, INV. To West Williams Twp, Middlesex Co, ONT, 1849.   **PCM 48**.

11415   STEIN, Thomas. To Montreal, QUE, on the *Royal George*, ex Greenock, Jan 1827; stld Sarnia, Lambton Co, ONT. wife and 3 ch with him.   **DC 19 Nov 1978**.

STEPHEN. See also STEVENS.

11416   STEPHEN, Alexander, 1814–12 Mar 1884. From Rothes, MOR. s/o John S, baker, and Ann Booth. To Halifax, NS, ca 1829; later to Musquodoboit, Halifax Co. Retr to Halifax, 1845, where in partnership with John Esson, qv, in grocery trade. Established a furniture factory, 1862. By first wife Jean Eliza, ch: 1. John, b 1841. m (ii) Mary Ann Guild, d 1897, further ch: 2. Alexander, b 1845; 3. Annie; 4. Matthew; 5. Jessie; 6. James H; 7. William F; 8. Eliza; 9. Fannie Maud.   **DC 31 Aug 1979**.

11417 STEPHEN, Christina, 20 Apr 1841–29 May 1887. From Rayne, Garioch par, ABD. d/o Alexander S. and Christine Inglis. To Toronto, ONT, <1860. m John Vert, qv. **DC 1 Jan 1982**.

11418 STEPHEN, George, 5 Jun 1829–29 Nov 1921. From Dufftown, BAN. s/o William S, qv, and Elspet Smith, qv. Appr silk mercer, Aberdeen, 1814, and became cloth merchant. To Montreal, QUE, ex London, on the *John Bull*, 16 Mar 1850. Became banker and railroad director, later financier associated in particular with the Canadian Pacific Railroad. Baronet, 1886, as Lord Mount Stephen. Legacies to Dufftown, for a cottage hospital, and to Univ of Aberdeen. m (i) 1853, Annie Charlotte, d/o Benjamen Kane, Portsmouth, ENG, no ch. m (ii) 1897, Gian, d/o Capt George Tufnell, RN, no ch. Adopted dau Alice Brooke. **BNA 1074; SNQ vii/1 101; MDB 713; DC 15 Mar 1971**.

11419 STEPHEN, James, 1817-83. From Rothes, MOR. s/o John S, baker, and Ann Booth. To Middle Musquodoboit, Halifax Co, NS, ca 1844. Farmer. m Mary Jean Rhynd, Horton, Kings Co. Dau Emma, b ca 1853. **DC 31 Aug 1979**.

11420 STEPHEN, William, b 25 Mar 1801, Torvanich, Ineravon, BAN. s/o William S, builder, and Elizabeth Cameron. To Montreal, QUE, on the *Saint Lawrence*, ex Aberdeen, 1847. Carpenter. m Elspet Smith, qv, ch: 1. George, qv; 2. Elizabeth, who sailed with her father; 3. Eleanora; 4. Elsie; 5. James; 6. William; 7. Francis. **DC 15 Mar 1971**.

11421 STEPHEN, William, b 19 Jan 1812. From Croft Glass, Ineravon par, BAN. s/o George S. and Barbara Innes. To Montreal, QUE, <1847. Dry goods merchant. **Ineravon OPR 157/1; DC 15 Mar 1971**.

11422 STEPHENS, James. To Halifax, NS, <1785, when he requested help in returning to SCT, where he had a wife and 3 ch. Offered 200 acres on Windsor Road, 1787. **DC 31 Aug 1979**.

11423 STEPHENSON, Jean, b ca 1709. From Lochend, Colvend, KKD. To Georgetown, Kings Co, PEI, on the *Lovely Nellie*, ex Annan, 1774. **ELN**.

11424 STEPHENSON, Robert, 1841–1920. To Normanby Twp, Grey Co, ONT, ca 1854. m Isabella Jeffrey, qv, ch: 1. Mary Ann, b 1864; 2. William, b 1866; 3. George, b 1868; 4. Robert, b 1870; 5. Peter, b 1871; 6. Jessie Isabelle, 1873–1942; 7. James Henry, 1875–1949; 8. Thomas, b 1877; 9. Margaret, b 1880; 10. Charles; 11. Elizabeth; 12. Christina; 13. Ethel. **DC 3 Jul 1981**.

STEUART. See also STEWART and STUART.

11425 STEUART, Agnes. From Blackbrae, West Calder, MLN. wid/o James Muir. To Port Elgin, Bruce Co, ONT, ca 1854. **DC 12 May 1972**.

11426 STEUART, Donald, b ca 1790. From Athol, PER. To Charlottetown, PEI, on the *Clarendon*, ex Oban, 6 Aug 1808. Labourer. **CPL**.

11427 STEUART, James Hope, b ca 1783. From Edinburgh. To Charlottetown, PEI, on the *Clarendon*, ex Oban, 6 Aug 1808. Supercargo. **CPL**.

STEVENS. See also STEPHEN.

11428 STEVENS, James, 1764–1832. From Glasgow. To Newport, Hants Co, NS, 1781, and acquired land at Rawdon Twp. m (i) Sarah Mercer, 1768–1811, ch: 1. Samuel, b 1792; 2. Joseph; 3. William. m (ii) Esther, d/o Levi Loomer and Lois Chase, Cornwallis. **DC 31 Aug 1979**.

11429 STEVENS, Rev James, 1801-64. From Galston, AYR. s/o James S, craftsman. Matric Univ of Glasgow, 1813. To Cambelltown, Restigouche Co, NB. First Presb missionary in northern NB, and min of Prince William Street Ch, Campbelltown, from 1831. **GMA 8986; FES vii 611; SR 23**.

11430 STEVENS, James Gray, 25 Jan 1822–16 Oct 1906. From Edinburgh. To St Stephen, Charlotte Co, NB. Lawyer, judge, 1867, and politician. **BNA 930; MDB 714**.

11431 STEVENS, Mary, d 1849. From Is Skye, INV. To Kinloss Twp, Bruce Co, ONT. Wife of James McQueen, qv. **DC 12 Apr 1979**.

11432 STEVENS, Moses. To Tracadie, Antigonish Co, NS, <1812. Gr land, 1819, when he had a wife and 6 ch. **DC 31 Aug 1979**.

11433 STEVENS, William, ca 1816-75. Prob from Brechin, ANS. To Halifax, NS, <1843. Wheelwright and landowner. m 7 Mar 1845, Jane Catharine Roxby, 1819-90, Horton, Kings Co, ch: 1. William, b 1847; 2. Jane Henrietta; 3. Mary Ann. **DC 31 Aug 1979**.

11434 STEVENSON, Alexander Allan, b 1829. From Riccarton, AYR. To Montreal, QUE, 1846. Learned the printing trade and became co-owner of the *Sun* newspaper. Commanded the Montreal Field Battery of Artillery. **BNA 1173; SNQ vi/1 50**.

11435 STEVENSON, Allan. Prob from ARL. To Fkfrid Twp, Middlesex Co, ONT, 1831. ch: 1. James; 2. Robert; 3. Archy; 4. Kate; 5. Flora. **PCM 30**.

11436 STEVENSON, Barbara. Prob from Duns, BEW. d/o — S. and Catherine Kirkwood. To CAN <1855. m John Henderson, cabinet-maker. **SH**.

11437 STEVENSON, Francis. To Pictou, NS, on the *Hope*, ex Glasgow, 5 Apr 1848. **DC 12 Jul 1979**.

11438 STEVENSON, Helen. Rel to Francis S, qv. To Pictou, NS, on the *Hope*, ex Glasgow, 5 Apr 1848. **DC 12 Jul 1979**.

11439 STEVENSON, Isobel. From Redford Green, MLN. To QUE, ex Greenock, summer 1815; stld prob Lanark Co, ONT. Wife of John Broad, qv. **SEC 2**.

11440 STEVENSON, James, ca 1777–ca 1826. From ABD. To Annapolis Co, NS, and d there. **VSN No 1646**.

11441 STEVENSON, James, b ca 1750. From Beith, AYR. To QUE, ex Greenock, summer 1815; stld prob Lanark Co, ONT. Farmer and widower. **SEC 9**.

11442 STEVENSON, James, b 1810. From Campbeltown, ARL. To Montreal, QUE, 1840. Bookkeeper. Son James. **SGC 574**.

11443 STEVENSON, James. Rel to Francis S, qv. To Pictou, NS, on the *Hope*, ex Glasgow, 5 Apr 1848, but went to USA. **DC 12 Jul 1979**.

11444 STEVENSON, James. To Pictou, NS, on the *Hope*, ex Glasgow, 5 Apr 1848. Wife Helen with him. **DC 12 Jul 1979**.

11445 STEVENSON, Jane, 6 Apr 1813–12 Sep 1843. From Wilton, ROX. d/o Rev David ?. par min, and Christian Taylor. To Montreal, QUE, <1840, when m James Farish, merchant. She was sometime in Seneca, Haldimand Twp, Northumberland Co, ONT. **DGH 26 Oct 1843; FES ii 144**.

11446 STEVENSON, Janet. From Beith, AYR. Prob d/o James S, qv. To QUE, summer 1815; stld prob Lanark Co, ONT. Wife of David Wilson, qv. **SEC 9**.

11447 STEVENSON, Janet. Rel to Francis S, qv. To Pictou, NS, on the *Hope*, ex Glasgow, 5 Apr 1848. **DC 12 Jul 1979**.

11448 STEVENSON, John, 1799–1890. Prob from Aberdour, FIF. To Cumberland Co, NS, poss <1840; stld nr Wallace. m Margaret Navin, qv. **DC 29 Oct 1980**.

11449 STEVENSON, John. Poss from RFW. s/o William S. To ONT <1838. Retr to SCT, 1840. **SH**.

11450 STEVENSON, Rev Robert, b 1828. From Kilwinning, AYR. s/o John S, farmer. Matric Univ of Glasgow, 1844, and trained at Original Secession Hall. Joined Ch of Scotland, 1849. To East Williams Twp, Middlesex Co, ONT, 1855. **GMA 14753; FES vii 652**.

11451 STEVENSON, Samuel. To QUE on the *David of London*, ex Greenock, 19 May 1821; stld prob Lanark Co, ONT. **HCL 239**.

11452 STEVENSON, William, b 26 May 1821. From Kilmarnock, AYR. To Paris Twp, Brant Co, ONT, 1843. Cooper. m Janet Fulton, qv, ch: 1. Thomas, b 5 Nov 1843; 2. Sarah, b 27 Jul 1845; 3. John, b 11 Jun 1847; 4. Elizabeth, b 30 Aug 1849; 5. Margaret, b 30 Sep 1851; 6. James Wallace, b 15 Nov 1853; 9. Ann, b 7 May 1861; 10. William, b 13 Apr 1863; 11. Robert Fulton, b 28 Jul 1867. **DC 31 Jul 1979**.

11453 STEVENSON, William. To Pictou, NS, on the *London*, arr 14 Jul 1848. **DC 15 Jul 1979**.

STEWARD. See also STEUART, STEWART, and STUART.

11454 STEWARD, Isabel. To NB. m John Sinclair, b NS. Son John R, b 1859. **DC 10 Jun 1980**.

11455 STEWART, Abigail, ca 1799–2 Dec 1887. Prob from BAN. To Pictou Co, NS. Wife of James Robertson, qv, Eight Mile Brook. **DC 27 Oct 1979**.

11456 STEWART, Alexander. Served in 82nd Regt and was gr land in Pictou Co, NS, 1784. **HPC App F**.

11457 STEWART, Alexander, d 23 Mar 1853. From Glasgow. To Colchester Co, NS, and stld Upper Stewiacke. Moved later to Upper Musquodoboit, Halifax Co. Served in 82nd Regt, 1778-83. m Elizabeth Taylor, d/o John Fisher. Dau Elizabeth, 1798–1869. **NSN 9/5**.

11458 STEWART, Alexander. From Atholl, PER. To Pictou, NS, on the *Dove*, ex Fort William, Jun 1801. Tenant. **PLD**.

11459 STEWART, Alexander. From Fort Augustus, INV. To Montreal, QUE, ex Fort William, arr Sep 1802; stld E ONT. A child with him. **MCM 1/4 23**.

11460 STEWART, Alexander, b ca 1783. From PER. To Pictou, NS, on the *Commerce*, ex Port Glasgow, 10 Aug 1803. **PLC**.

11461 STEWART, Alexander, 1793–1892. From Blair Atholl, PER. To Montreal, QUE, on the *Curlew*, ex Greenock, 21 Jul 1818; stld Blacks Corners, Beckwith Twp, Lanark Co, ONT. Pioneer settler. Wife Margaret with him. **BCL; HCL 35**.

11462 STEWART, Alexander. From ARL. To QUE on the *Gestian*, ex Oban, 1820; stld prob Lobo Twp, Middlesex Co, ONT. Wife Margaret Graham, qv, with him. **PCM 41**.

11463 STEWART, Rev Alexander, d 19 Jun 1840. Poss from INV. To ONT as a missionary, <1827. Became Baptist min at Toronto. **MDB 715**.

11464 STEWART, Alexander. From Knapdale, ARL. To Lobo Twp, Middlesex Co, ONT, 1828. ch: 1. Dr Peter, d in Detroit, MI; 2. Donald; 3. Alexander; 4. Archibald; 5. Duncan; 6. Jane; 7. Margaret; 8. Mary; 9. Jessie. **PCM 39**.

11465 STEWART, Alexander, b 1802. From Minginish, Is Skye, INV. s/o Archibald Charles S. and John Morrison. To Glengarry Co, ONT, 1832. Schoolteacher. m 1833, Mary Stewart, qv, ch: 1. John; 2. Charles; 3. Alexander; 4. Mary; 5. Janet; 6. Janet, jr; 7. Adam; 8. Ann; 9. Maggie; 10. Harriet; 11. Donald. **DC 18 Jul 1963**.

11466 STEWART, Alexander, 2 Jan 1810–16 Dec 1850. From Balhastle, Blair Atholl, PER. s/o John S. and Grizel Stewart, qv. To Westchester, Cumberland Co, NS, 1832. m 24 Dec 1837, Jane Renwick. **DC 1 Nov 1981**.

11467 STEWART, Rev Alexander, ca 1804–15 Apr 1896. From Huntly, ABD. s/o John S, physician. Grad MA, Kings Coll, Aberdeen, 1829. To NS, <1840. Became rector of St James's Ch, Orillia, Simcoe Co, ONT, 1842. **KCG 285; SNQ ii/2 10**.

11468 STEWART, Alexander, 1789–1879. From Ross, Is Mull, ARL. To Caledon Twp, Peel Co, ONT, <1840. Wife Catherine Ferguson, qv, with him. **DC 21 Apr 1980**.

11469 STEWART, Alexander, b 1798. From STI, but was sometime in Glasgow. To Guelph, Wellington Co, ONT, ca 1842. m Rachel Kennedy, qv, ch: 1. Susanna, b 1820; 2. John, b 1821; 3. William, b 1825; 4. Jane Nicol, b 1827; 5. Alexander, b 1829; 6. David, b 1831; 7. Henry, b 1833; 8. Mary, b 1835; 9. Janet, b 1837. **LDW 4 Jun 1973**.

11470 STEWART, Alexander, ca 1781–6 Oct 1860. Poss from Comrie, PER. To QUE, and stld Melbourne, Sherbrooke Co. m Elizabeth Masson, qv. Both bur Maple Grove. **MGC 2 Aug 1979**.

11471 STEWART, Alexander, ca 1796–ca 1866. From Blair Atholl, PER. To Grey Twp, Huron Co, ONT, 1852. m Margaret Fleming, qv, ch: 1. Elizabeth, 1830–1907; 2. Margaret; 3. John Archibald, 1836-97; 4. Alexander, 1838–1915; 5. Ann; 6. Christine; 7. Isabella. **DC 15 May 1969**.

11472 STEWART, Alexander D, b 1827. From Blair Atholl, PER. s/o Donald S, qv, and Ellen McDonald, qv. To Halifax, NS, 1833; stld Lochaber, Antigonish Co. m 17 Mar 1857, Christina, d/o John Stewart, qv, and Margaret Robertson, qv. Son James H, b 1863, merchant. **HNS iii 681**.

11473 STEWART, Andrew, ca 1789–24 May 1822. From Glasgow. To CAN, 1811, and entered service of HBCo. Worked at Moose Factory, Missakama Lake, Kenogamissee and Michipicoten. Chief trader, 1821. **MDB 715**.

11474 STEWART, Andrew, b 8 Aug 1811, Methven, PER. s/o John S, qv, Castlehill, Edinburgh, and Margaret Rodgie, qv. To Montreal, QUE, on the *Jean*, ex Glasgow, 1822; stld Howick, English River. m 18 Feb 1842, Elizabeth, d/o John Gordon, qv, and Sarah Henderson, qv, ch. **DC 3 Jun 1981**.

11475 STEWART, Andrew Buchanan, b 11 Sep 1816. From Glasgow. To Montreal, QUE, 1833. Sometime in Guelph, Wellington Co, but retr to Montreal. Merchant, later accountant, and was session-clerk of St Gabriel St Ch, 1867-74. **SGC 629**.

11476 STEWART, Angus, b 1780. From PER. To QUE, 1828; but moved in 1835 to Mosa Twp, Middlesex Co, ONT. Farmer, Lot 3, Longmans Road. Son Duncan, b ca 1820. **PCM 24**.

11477 STEWART, Angus. From PER. To East Williams Twp, Middlesex Co, ONT, 1832. **PCM 43**.

11478 STEWART, Ann. From PER, poss Killin. Prob d/o Archibald S, qv. To McNab Twp, Renfrew Co, ONT, 1825. **DC 3 Jan 1980**.

11479 STEWART, Annabella. Prob from PER. sis/o Col Robert S, qv. To Malpeque, Prince Co, PEI, on the *Annabella*, ex Campbeltown, ARL, 27 Jul 1770. Wife of Robert Stewart, qv. **DC 18 May 1981**.

11480 STEWART, Archibald. From PER, poss Killin. To McNab Twp, Renfrew Co, ONT, 1825. **DC 3 Jan.1960**.

11481 STEWART, Bess. From Is Lewis, ROC. To Lingwick Twp, Compton Co, QUE, 1842. Wife of Angus MacRae, qv. **TFT 15**.

11482 STEWART, Catherine, 1808-76. From Is North Uist, INV. To Richmond Co, NS, 1828. Wife of Duncan Nicholson, qv. **NSN 27/196**.

11483 STEWART, Catherine, ca 1787–Sep 1862. From Aberfeldy, PER. sis/o Charles S. To Charlottetown, PEI, and remained there. m Alexander McGregor, qv. **DC 11 Apr 1981**.

11484 STEWART, Charles, b ca 1802. From PER, poss Balquhidder. s/o James S, qv, and Janet McLaren, qv. To Pictou, NS, on the *Commerce*, ex Port Glasgow, 10 Aug 1803; stld Brudenell, Kings Co, PEI, later Roseneath. m Esther Gay, ch: 1. Mary; 2. Jessie; 3. Henry; 4. Lemuel; 5. Katharine; 6. Dr James. **PLC; BP 62**.

11485 STEWART, Charles, b 1760. From Aberfeldy, PER. To Kings Co, PEI, 1804. m 7 Oct 1780, Ann Nicolson, prob d <1804, ch: 1. Isabel, 1781–1865; 2. John, b 1782; 3. Donald, 1784–1875; 4. Catherine, 1787–1862; 5. Charles, ca 1790–1877; 6. Jennie, 1796–1864; 7. Malcolm, 1800-49. **SG xxiii 4/91**.

11486 STEWART, Charles, b ca 1794. From Aberfeldy, PER. To Charlottetown, PEI, on the *Clarendon*, ex Oban, 6 Aug 1808. Labourer. **CPL**.

11487 STEWART, Rev Charles James, 15 Apr 1775–13 Jul 1837. From WIG. s/o John, 7th Earl of Galloway, and his second Countess, Ann Dashwood. Educ Oxford,

and grad MA, 1799. Became rector of Orton, HUN. To QUE <1819 as missionary successively in the eastern townships, and in the diocese of Quebec. Succ Bishop Jacob Mountain 1826. Author; DD, Oxford, 1817. **BNA 498; SP iv 168; MDB 715**.

11488 STEWART, Christian or Christina, ca 1762–27 Dec 1837. Prob from PER. To Guysborough Co, NS, ca 1785. m James McKay, qv. **DC 30 Oct 1980**.

11489 STEWART, Christian, b ca 1771. From Glengoe, PER. sis/o Neil S, qv. To Charlottetown, PEI, on the *Clarendon*, ex Oban, 6 Aug 1808. **CPL**.

11490 STEWART, Christian, b ca 1753. From Comrie par, PER. To Montreal, QUE, on the *Curlew*, ex Greenock, 21 Jul 1818; stld Beckwith Twp, Lanark Co, ONT. Wife of Donald Ferguson, qv. **DC 29 Dec 1981**.

11491 STEWART, Christina, b 1768. From Blair Atholl, PER. d/o Donald and Janet S. To PEI, ca 1806. m Alexander Scott. **DC 1 Nov 1981**.

11492 STEWART, Christy, b 18 Jul 1832. From Blair Atholl, PER. d/o James S, qv, and Janet Stewart, qv. To Lochaber, Antigonish Co, NS, 1833. m 24 Mar 1854, Robert Stewart. **DC 1 Nov 1981**.

11493 STEWART, Clementina. From ABD. To Bon Accord, Nichol Twp, Wellington Co, ONT, 1836. Wife of William Gerrie, qv. **EHE 93**.

11494 STEWART, Colin. From Maryburgh, Dingwall, ROC. bro/o George S. To Eldon Twp, Victoria Co, ONT, 1855. m Janet McInnes, qv. Dau Flora. **EC 216**.

11495 STEWART, Daniel, 1803-83. From Dunblane, PER. To Hamilton, ONT, but retr later to SCT. **Ts Dunblane**.

11496 STEWART, David. From DFS or KKD. To Pictou, NS, <12 Feb 1783, when listed as capable of bearing arms. Gr 300 acres, east side of West River. **HPC App A, D and E**.

11497 STEWART, David. From Muthill par, PER. To Montreal, QUE, on the *Curlew*, ex Greenock, 21 Jul 1818; stld prob Beckwith Twp, Lanark Co, ONT. Wife Catherine with him, and ch: 1. James, aged 8; 2. William, aged 2. **BCL**.

11498 STEWART, David. From PER, poss Killin. Prob s/o Archibald S, qv. To McNab Twp, Renfrew Co, ONT, 1825. **DC 3 Jan 1980**.

11499 STEWART, David. Prob from PER. bro/o John S, qv, Scotsburn, Pictou Co, NS. To Antigonish Co, NS, <1838. **HNS iii 179**.

11500 STEWART, David, 29 Dec 1813–29 Jul 1904. From Nether Smiston, Lundie and Fowlis par, ANS. To Eramosa Twp, Wellington Co, ONT, 1850. Tailor. m (i) 1834, Elspeth, d/o David Mitchell and Janet James, ch: 1. Margaret, b 1 Apr 1835; 2. Jane, b 29 Dec 1836; 3. Elizabeth, b 14 Dec 1838; 4. Isabella, b 7 Feb 1841; 5. Hannah, b 15 Dec 1842; 6. James, b 6 Oct 1846. m (ii) 1847, Christina McFarlane, qv, further ch: 7. Margaret, b 21 Oct 1848; 8. Christina, b 13 Jan 1850. m (iii) Effie McMillan McIntosh, further ch: 9. Mary; 10. George; 11. Alexander. **Lundie & Fowlis OPR 306/3; SG xxiii/3 50; DC 24 Nov 1979**.

11501 STEWART, Donald, b ca 1792. From PER, poss Balquhidder. s/o James S, qv, and Janet McLaren, qv. To

Pictou, NS, on the *Commerce*, ex Port Glasgow, 10 Aug 1803; stld Brudenell, Kings Co, PEI. m Christian Stewart. **PLC; BP 62**.

11502   STEWART, Donald, b 28 Aug 1784. From Aberfeldy, PER. s/o Charles S, qv, and Ann Nicolson. To PEI, 1804. m 1813, Ellen Stewart. **SG xxiii/4 91**.

11503   STEWART, Donald, b ca 1784. From Blair Atholl, PER. To Charlottetown, PEI, on the *Clarendon*, ex Oban, 6 Aug 1808. Labourer. **CPL**.

11504   STEWART, Donald, b ca 1762. From Glengoe, PER. To Charlottetown, PEI, on the *Clarendon*, ex Oban, 6 Aug 1808. Labourer. **CPL**.

11505   STEWART, Donald, d 20 Aug 1813. From Ballachulish, ARL. To Fort Churchill, Hudson Bay, on the *Prince of Wales*, ex Stromness, 28 Jun 1813, and d there. Wife Catherine with him, and ch: 1. Margaret, aged 8; 2. Mary, aged 5; 3. Ann, aged 2. They went to York Factory, spring 1814, thence to Red River. **LSS 184; RRS 26; LSC 321**.

11506   STEWART, Donald. From PER, poss Killin. Prob s/o Archibald S, qv. To McNab Twp, Renfrew Co, ONT, 1825. **DC 3 Jan 1980**.

11507   STEWART, Donald, 24 Jun 1800–11 Dec 1889. From Balhastle, Blair Atholl, PER. s/o John S. and Grizel Stewart, qv. To NS, 1832; stld Westchester, Cumberland Co, later Pugwash. m 26 Dec 1827, Janet McDonald, qv. Son John, 1834-97. **HNS iii 681; DC 1 Nov 1981**.

11508   STEWART, Donald Robert. From Blair Atholl, PER. s/o Robert S. To Lochaber, Antigonish Co, NS, poss 1832. **DC 1 Nov 1981**.

11509   STEWART, Dougald, 1797–25 Jan 1852. From Callander, PER. To Montreal, QUE, 1816. Dry goods merchant. **SGC 378**.

11510   STEWART, Dugald. From Kintyre, ARL. To Aldborough Twp, Elgin Co, ONT, 1851. **PDA 75**.

11511   STEWART, Duncan. Poss from PER. To Aldborough Twp, Elgin Co, ONT, <1820; prob moved to Mosa Twp. **PDA 92**.

11512   STEWART, Duncan. From PER. To East Williams Twp, Middlesex Co, ONT, 1832. **PCM 43**.

11513   STEWART, Duncan, ca 1804–17 Apr 1887. From PER. To Halton Co, ONT, prob <1850; stld Esquesing Twp. Bur Boston cemetery. **EPE 76**.

11514   STEWART, Elizabeth, 1781–1843. From Balquhidder, PER. To Pictou, NS, on the *Commerce*, ex Port Glasgow, 10 Aug 1803; stld Brudenell, Kings Co, PEI. Wife of Donald McLaren, qv. **PLC; BP 32**.

11515   STEWART, Elizabeth. From ARL. To Puslinch Twp, Wellington Co, ONT, 1844. d/o John and Jane S. m Walter McMillan, qv. **DC 23 Apr 1967**.

11516   STEWART, Ellen, 1807-55. To Carleton Place, Lanark Co, ONT. Wife of John Galbraith, qv. **DC 9 Mar 1980**.

11517   STEWART, Flora. From PER, poss Killin. Prob rel to Archibald S, qv. To McNab Twp, Renfrew Co, ONT, 1825. **DC 3 Jan 1980**.

11518   STEWART, George. To Colchester Co, NS, <1829; stld on Wauchs River. Farmer. **HT 69**.

11519   STEWART, George, 1802-79. From PER, poss Logierait. To Ancaster Twp, Wentworth Co, ONT, prob <1860. Wife Margaret, 1815-95. **DC 11 Dec 1981**.

11520   STEWART, Grace. Prob from ARL. To Charlottetown, PEI, <1810. Wife of Donald Campbell, qv. **DC 11 Apr 1981**.

11521   STEWART, Grace Anne. From Findynate, PER. To Montreal, QUE, <1850. m Duncan, s/o Dr William Robertson, qv, and Elizabeth Amelia Campbell, and stld Lachine. ch. **SGC 370**.

11522   STEWART, Grizel, 1778–29 Jun 1861. From Balnald, Blair Atholl, PER. To Westchester, Cumberland Co, NS, 1832. wid/o John Stewart, by whom she had ch: 1. Janet, qv; 2. Donald, qv; 3. Margaret, qv; 4. Christina, 1804-75, unm; 5. Helen, d inf, 1806; 6. William, qv; 7. Alexander, qv; 8. Grizel, qv; 9. Isabel, qv. **DC 1 Nov 1981**.

11523   STEWART, Grizel, 29 May 1812–12 Jul 1868. From Balhastle, Blair Atholl, PER. d/o John S. and Grizel S, qv. To Westchester, Cumberland Co, NS, 1832. m 17 Apr 1863, Isaiah Singer. **DC 1 Nov 1981**.

11524   STEWART, Mrs Isabel, 1771–1849. From Corriecrevie, Is Arran, BUT. To QUE on the *Caledonia*, ex Greenock, 25 Apr 1829; stld Inverness Twp, Megantic Co. wid/o William S, m 8 Dec 1801, ch: 1. James, b 1802; 2. Robert, b 1806; 3. Donald, 1808-86, sawyer; 4. Alexander, 1809-90; 5. Mary, 1811-57; 6. Catherine, 1812-78; 7. Isabella, b 1814. **AMC 40; MAC 33**.

11525   STEWART, Isabel, 3 Apr 1815–16 Aug 1880. From Balhastle, Blair Atholl, PER. d/o John S. and Grizel S, qv. To Cumberland Co, NS, 1832; stld Pugwash River. m Hugh McPherson. **DC 1 Nov 1981**.

11526   STEWART, James, b ca 1766. From PER, poss Balquhidder. To Pictou, NS, on the *Commerce*, ex Port Glasgow, 10 Aug 1803; stld Kings Co, PEI. m Janet or Jessie McLaren, qv, ch: 1. Donald, qv; 2. Isabella, b 1795; 3. Janet, b 1797; 4. Charles, qv; 5. John; 6. James; 7. Catherine; 8. Christina. **PLC; BP 42, 62**.

11527   STEWART, James. To Ramsay Twp, Lanark Co, ONT, 1821. **HCL 86**.

11528   STEWART, James, 1787–6 Jun 1874. From North Kiscadale, Is Arran, BUT. To Inverness Twp, Megantic Co, QUE, 1831. Tailor. m Mary Cook, qv, ch: 1. Mary, qv; 2. John, 1827-47; 3. Donald; 4. Catherine; 5. Ann; 6. Robert, merchant; 7. Duncan, 1836-97. **AMC 39; MAC 38**.

11529   STEWART, James, d 16 Nov 1857. From Blair Atholl, PER. To Lochaber, Antigonish Co, NS, 1833. m Janet Stewart, qv, ch: 1. Jane, qv; 2. Margaret, qv; 3. Janet, qv; 4. Christy, qv; 5. Isabel, b 30 Aug 1834; 6. John A, b 22 May 1836; 7. James D, b 12 Jun 1838; 8. Helen, b 24 Feb 1840. **DC 1 Nov 1981**.

11530   STEWART, James, 1820-99. From Thornhill, PER. s/o Walter S. and Agnes Buchanan. To Montreal, QUE, on the *Cluthe*, ex Glasgow, 1851; stld Huron Co, and d Kippen. m Margaret Wingate Doig, qv, ch: 1. Walter; 2. Henry; 3. James; 4. Jean; 5. Agnes; 6. John; 7. Peter; 8. Helen. **DC 10 Nov 1966**.

11531   STEWART, James Affleck, d 15 May 1867. From Forgan, FIF. s/o Henry S. and Jane Fraser. To Brantford,

Brant Co, ONT. Sometime Capt, 11th Hussars.   **Ts Ferry Port-on-Craig**.

11532   STEWART, James David. Prob from Edinburgh. s/o James S. To Charlottetown, PEI, <1820. m 1822, Christian McLure, ch: 1. Margaret, schoolteacher; 2. John; 3. Hannah; 4. Alexander; 5. David James. **DC 10 Aug 1965**.

11533   STEWART, Jane, b 20 Jun 1827. From Balhastle, Blair Atholl, PER. d/o James S, qv, and Janet Stewart, qv. To Lochaber, Antigonish Co, NS, 1833. m 1848, William H. Brown.   **DC 1 Nov 1981**.

11534   STEWART, Janet, b ca 1760. From Knockhooley, Kirkbean, KKD. Prob sis/o Robert S, qv. To Georgetown, Kings Co, PEI, on the *Lovely Nellie*, ex Annan, 1774. **ELN**.

11535   STEWART, Mrs Janet. From Killin, PER. To Montreal, QUE, on the *Curlew*, ex Greenock, 21 Jul 1818; stld prob Beckwith Twp, Lanark Co, ONT.   **BCL**.

11536   STEWART, Janet, 28 Nov 1798–17 Jun 1875. From Balhastle, Blair Atholl, PER. d/o John S. and Grizel S, qv. To Lochaber, Antigonish Co, NS, 1833. m James Stewart, qv, 28 May 1826.   **DC 1 Nov 1981**.

11537   STEWART, Janet, b 18 Jul 1832. From Blair Atholl, PER. d/o James S, qv, and Janet S, qv. To Lochaber, Antigonish Co, NS, 1833. m 1857, John McLaughlin, d 1907.   **DC 1 Nov 1891**.

11538   STEWART, Janet, 1820-86. From PER, prob Logierait. To Ancaster Twp, Wentworth Co, ONT, <1853. m Robert, 1819-91, s/o Donald Forbes, qv, ch. **DC 11 Dec 1981**.

11539   STEWART, John. Poss from Boleskine, INV. To Montreal, QUE, ex Fort William, arr Sep 1802; stld E ONT. Wife with him, and dau Catherine.   **MCM 1/4 24**.

11540   STEWART, John, 1779–30 Jan 1852. From Blair Atholl, PER. To Charlottetown, PEI, <1810; stld North River. Farmer and carpenter. m Mary Mackinnon, qv, ch: 1. Neil, b 1810; 2. John, b 1813; 3. Jessie, b 1815; 4. Isabella, b 1817; 5. Catherine, b 1819; 6. Charles, alive 1852; 7. William, alive 1852; 8. Eleanor, b 1829. **DC 16 Aug 1982**.

11541   STEWART, John, 1774–1 May 1854. From Perth. Desc from the Stewarts of Crossmount, Kinloch Rannoch. To Halton Co, ONT, 1817; stld Esquesing Twp. m Margaret Lamond, qv.   **HPE 75**.

11542   STEWART, John. From Blair Atholl, PER. To Montreal, QUE, on the *Curlew*, ex Greenock, 21 Jul 1818; stld prob Beckwith Twp, Lanark Co, ONT. Wife Ellen with him, and inf dau Isabella.   **BCL**.

11543   STEWART, John. From Dull par, PER. To Montreal, QUE, on the *Curlew*, ex Greenock, 21 Jul 1818; stld prob Beckwith Twp, Lanark Co, ONT. Wife Elizabeth with him.   **BCL**.

11544   STEWART, John, d Nov 1788. From Castlehill, Edinburgh. s/o John and Helen S, Methven, PER. To Montreal, QUE, on the brig *Jean*, ex Glasgow, Apr 1822; stld Williamstown or Howick, English River. Bookseller, farmer. m Margaret Rodgie, qv, ch: 1. Andrew, qv; 2. Thomas, b Edinburgh, 13 Dec 1813; 3. John, b 28 Mar 1816; 4. Alexander Bishop, b 7 Jul 1818; 5. Margaret Wright, 1820-21; 6. Margaret, b 24 Jun

1823; 7. William, b 30 Aug 1825; 8. Ellen, b 23 Oct 1827.   **DC 3 Jun 1981**.

11545   STEWART, John. To Montreal, QUE, on the *Royal George*, ex Greenock, Jan 1827; stld Sarnia, Lambton Co, ONT.   **DC 19 Nov 1978**.

11546   STEWART or STUART, John, 1779–14 Jan 1847. From Abernethy, INV. s/o Donald S, tacksman of Leanichle, and Janet Grant. To Montreal, QUE, ca 1799. Emp with NWCo and became a partner, 1813. Served on Peace River, and accompanied Simon Fraser on his epic journey down the Fraser River, 1806. After the merger with the HBCo, 1821, was chief factor in charge of Caledonia. Ret to SCT, 1839, and d Springfield, nr Forres, MOR. Interred at Abernethy, where he had erected a family memorial in 1830. Lake Stuart, BC, named after him.   **Ts Abernethy; MDB 724**.

11547   STEWART, John. From PER. To Lochiel Twp, Glengarry Co, ONT, <1832. m Annie McLaurin, qv. Son Peter A, 1832–1908.   **SDG 272**.

11548   STEWART, John. From PER. To East Williams Twp, Middlesex Co, ONT, 1832. Son John.   **PCM 43**.

11549   STEWART, John. From Blair Atholl, PER. To Halifax, NS, 1833; stld Lochaber, Antigonish Co. m Margaret Robertson, qv. Dau Christina. **HNS iii 681**.

11550   STEWART, Rev John, 1800–4 May 1880. From Little Dunkeld, PER. Studied medicine at Edinburgh, later theology, and was licensed to preach in 1832. Teacher in Edinburgh, 1832-34. To Plaster Cove, NS, and was ord at Pictou. Adm min of West Bay, 1835; trans to New Glasgow, 1838. Joined FC, 1844. m 1836, Alicia Murray Drysdale, qv.   **FES vii 608, 618**.

11551   STEWART, John. Prob from PER. bro/o David S, qv, Antigonish Co. To Scotsburn, Pictou Co, NS, <1838. Farmer. m Dorothy McLeod. Son Donald, schoolmaster.   **HNS iii 383**.

11552   STEWART, John, 1787–1859. Poss from Ross, Is Mull, ARL. To Caledon Twp, Peel Co, ONT, <1840. **DC 21 Apr 1980**.

11553   STEWART, John. From Minginish, Is Skye, INV. s/o Archibald Charles S. and Mary Morrison. To ONT <1840; stld prob Glengarry Co.   **DC 18 Jul 1963**.

11554   STEWART, John, ca 1789–7 Feb 1866. From PEE. To QUE and stld Melbourne, Sherbrooke Co. Bur Maple Grove.   **MGC 2 Aug 1979**.

11555   STEWART, John, b ca 1800. From Dumblane, PER. To ONT, 1849. Wife Isabella MacNiven, qv, with him, and ch: 1. Jean, b 12 May 1827; 2. Isabella, b 15 Mar 1831; 3. Elizabeth, b 7 Feb 1837; 4. Janet, b Jul 1839; 5. John, b 14 Oct 1843; 6. Peter, b 28 Sep 1846.   **DC 31 Aug 1979**.

11556   STEWART, John. To Sight Point, Inverness Co, NS, <1855; later to Stearns Co, MN. m Sara MacDonald, ch: 1. John; 2. Alexander; 3. Donald; 4. Allan; 5. Dougald; 6. Catherine; 7. Mary; 8. Flora. **MP 850**.

11557   STEWART, John, 1827–1906. From PER, poss Logierait. To Ancaster Twp, Wentworth Co, ONT, prob <1860. m Jessie Harvey, 1837–1906, and had ch incl: 1. Jessie, 1860–1905; 2. Alison, 1872–1919. **DC 11 Dec 1981**.

11558 STEWART, Margaret. From Blair Atholl, PER. To Pictou, NS, on the *Dove*, ex Fort William, Jun 1801. Prob wife of Alexander S, qv, tenant. **PLD**.

11559 STEWART, Margaret. From PER, poss Balquhidder. sis/o Peter S. To Kings Co, PEI, poss <1810. m John McLaren, qv. **BP 42, 61**.

11560 STEWART, Margaret, 26 Sep 1802–3 Jun 1896. From Balhastle, Blair Atholl, PER. d/o John S. and Grizel S, qv. To Cumberland Co, NS, ca 1832. m 8 Feb 1838, John Ross. **DC 1 Nov 1981**.

11561 STEWART, Margaret, b 20 Dec 1830. From Blair Atholl, PER. d/o James S, qv, and Janet S, qv. To Lochaber, Antigonish Co, NS, 1833. m William K. Inglis, d 1891. **DC 1 Nov 1981**.

11562 STEWART, Margaret, 1829–1904. Prob from Is Skye, INV. To Kinloss Twp, Bruce Co, ONT, <1852. m John McKinnon, qv. **DC 12 Apr 1979**.

11563 STEWART, Marion, b 1808. From Is Rum, ARL. Prob wife of Neil S, qv. To Gut of Canso, Cape Breton, NS, on the *Saint Lawrence*, ex Tobermory, 11 Jul 1828. **SLL**.

11564 STEWART, Mary. From Is Skye, INV. To Orwell Bay, PEI, on the *Polly*, ex Portree, arr 7 May 1803. Wife of Neil Nicholson, qv. **LDW 11 Oct 1974**.

11565 STEWART, Mary. From PER, poss Killin. Prob d/o Archibald S, qv. To McNab Twp, Renfrew Co, ONT, 1825. **DC 3 Jan 1980**.

11566 STEWART, Mary, b ca 1805. From Portree, Is Skye, INV. d/o Murdock S. and Mary McDonald. To Glengarry Co, ONT, <1832. m Alexander S, schoolteacher, qv. **DC 18 Jul 1963**.

11567 STEWART, Mary, 1812-72. From Is Arran, BUT. To Dalhousie, NB, prob 1833; stld Escuminac, Bonaventure Co, QUE. m 24 Jan 1832, James Crawford, qv. **MAC 13**.

11568 STEWART, Mary, b ca 1826. From Kiscadale, Is Arran, BUT. d/o James S, qv, and Mary Cook, qv. To Inverness, Megantic Co, QUE, 1831. m William McKelvie, qv. **AMC 39; MAC 38**.

11569 STEWART, Mary, 1795–1903. From Lochcarron, ROC. To Baddeck, Victoria Co, NS, 1826. Wife of Alexander McKay, qv. **DC 10 Mar 1962**.

11570 STEWART, Mary. From Knockan, Is Arran, BUT. To Inverness, Megantic Co, QUE, 1831. Wife of Duncan McKelvie, qv. **AMC 39; MAC 36**.

11571 STEWART, Mary. Prob from PER. To ONT, ca 1834; stld McNab Twp, Renfrew Co, ONT. Wife of John McDiarmed, qv. **DC 30 Nov 1979**.

11572 STEWART, Mary, 1803-63. From ARL. To Caledon Twp, Peel Co, ONT, <1840. Wife of Dougeld McGibbon, qv. **DC 21 Apr 1980**.

11573 STEWART, Rev Murdoch, 18 May 1810–30 Jul 1884. From Contin, ROC. s/o John S. and Catherine S. Grad MA, Kings Coll, Aberdeen, 1834, and became a schoolteacher. To West Bay, St Georges Channel, Cape Breton, NS, and was FC min there, 1843-68; when trans to Whycocomagh, Inverness Co. Ret 1882. m Catherine McGregor, qv, ch: 1. Dr John, 1848–1933, Lecturer in Surgery at Halifax; 2. Margaret Mary, 1850–1937; 3. Donald Alexander, 1851-97, CE; 4. James McGregor,

1853-97, lawyer; 5. Rev Thomas, 1855–1923; 6. Katherine Isabel, 1857–1938; 7. Anne Amelia, b 1859, res Halifax; 8. Elizabeth Helen, b 1860; 9. Maria Louisa Jessie, b 1862; 10. Alexander Forrester, 1864–1937, CE. **KCG 289; FES vii 608, viii 735**.

11574 STEWART, Neil, b 1773. From Glengoe, PER. To Charlottetown, PEI, on the *Clarendon*, ex Oban, 6 Aug 1808. Labourer. Wife Mary, aged 27, with him, and ch: 1. Christian, aged 5; 2. Margaret, aged 3; 3. Mary, aged 1 ½. **CPL**.

11575 STEWART, Neil. From Is Eigg, INV. To Ainslie Glen, Whycocomagh, Inverness Co, NS, ca 1820. m Margaret McMillan, qv, ch: 1. John; 2. Alexander; 3. Donald; 4. Donald Og; 5. Sara; 6. Anne; 7. Mary; 8. Flora; 9. Margaret. **MP 852**.

11576 STEWART, Neil, b 1802. From Is Rum, ARL. To Gut of Canso, Cape Breton, NS, on the *Saint Lawrence*, ex Tobermory, 11 Jul 1828. **SLL**.

11577 STEWART, Peter. From ARL. To Prince Co, PEI, 1775. Magistrate. Son John, landowner and historian. **SG xxx/2 68**.

11578 STEWART, Peter, b 1757. From Blair Atholl, PER. To Charlottetown, PEI, on the *Clarendon*, ex Oban, 6 Aug 1808. Labourer. Wife Ann, aged 51, with him, and ch: 1. Ann, aged 16; 2. John, aged 13; 3. Neil, aged 10. **CPL**.

11579 STEWART, Peter, b ca 1775. From Balimore, Lochgilphead, ARL. To QUE, ex Greenock, on the *Dorothy*, 12 Jul 1815; stld Breadalbane, Lochiel Twp, Glengarry Co, ONT. Farmer. Wife Christian McLean, qv, with him, and 5 ch. **SDG 131; SEC 3**.

11580 STEWART, Peter. Prob from PER. bro/o John S, qv, Scotsburn, Pictou Co, and of David S, qv, Antigonish Co, NS. To PEI <1838. **HNS iii 383**.

11581 STEWART, Peter. From Strichen, ABD. s/o Peter S, innkeeper. To ONT, 1839. Contractor. **SH**.

11582 STEWART, Peter, 1807-94. From Is Arran, BUT. To Restigouche Co, NB, 1841; stld Black Point. m Christian Ferguson, qv. Son John, b 1839. **MAC 26**.

11583 STEWART, Col Robert. From PER or ARL. bro/o Annabella S, qv. Gr Lot 18, Malpeque, Prince Co, PEI, 1767, and divided the title among members of his family. **DC 18 May 1981**.

11584 STEWART, Robert. Prob from PER. To Malpeque, Prince Co, PEI, on the *Annabella*, ex Campbeltown, 27 Jul 1770. m Annabella Stewart, qv. **DC 18 May 1981**.

11585 STEWART, Robert, b ca 1758. From Knockhooley, Southwick, Kirkbean, KKD. Prob bro/o Janet S, qv. To Georgetown, Kings Co, PEI, on the *Lovely Nellie*, ex Annan, 1774. Labourer. **ELN**.

11586 STEWART, Robert 'Smashem'. Served as an NCO in 82nd Regt and gr 200 acres at Merigomish, Pictou Co, NS, 1784. Factor to Col Alexander Robertson, qv. **HPC App F**.

11587 STEWART, Robert. Poss from PER. To Usborne Twp, Huron Co, ONT, 1835. Pioneer settler. m Jane Ross. Son Duncan, b 1867, farmed in MAN. **DC 27 Dec 1968**.

11588 STEWART, Robert. From Is Arran, BUT. Stld Inverness, Megantic Co, QUE, <1840. Carpenter. **AMC 48**.

11589 STEWART, Robert. Prob from Blair Atholl, PER. s/o Robert S. To Lochaber, Antigonish Co, NS, poss 1832. **DC 1 Nov 1981**.

11590 STEWART, Robert, ca 1820–ca 1898. From Logierait, PER. To Ancaster Twp, Wentworth Co, ONT, prob <1860. By wife Jane, 1833-86, ch: 1. James, 1862–1910; 2. Christina, 1863-80. **DC 11 Dec 1981**.

11591 STEWART, Robert Bruce, b ca 1770. From Callander, PER. s/o Robert S, Ardcheanochrochan, Kilmahog. To Queens Co, PEI, 1846, and stld on lands previously gr to the family, which he named Strathgartney. **SG xvii/3 89; DC 18 Jan 1980**.

11592 STEWART, Susan, d 25 Jul 1839. From KKD. d/o Hon Montgomery Granville S. of Castramont, and Catherine Honeyman. To QUE. m Rev Edmund Willoughby Sewell. **DGH 30 Aug 1839**.

11593 STEWART, William, ca 1753–3 Dec 1797. From Glasgow. To Montreal, QUE, <1791. Merchant. m Isabella Cowan, who m (ii) William Hunter, qv. ch incl: 1. Isabella, d 1821; 2. Jane, b 1797, d unm. **SGC 71**.

11594 STEWART, William, d 1860. From Ayr. To Pictou, NS, prob 1830; stld Merigomish, later Little Harbour. Miller. m Agnes Brown, qv, ch: 1. William, res Galt, ONT; 2. Thomas, miller, Galt, ONT; 3. Adam; 4. Andrew, miller. **HNS iii 391**.

11595 STEWART, William, 4 May 1808–14 Dec 1889. From Balhastle, Blair Atholl, PER. s/o John S, and Grizel S, qv. To NS, 1832; stld Westchester, Cumberland Co. m 1 Nov 1836, Sarah E. Peppard, who d 1859, ch. **DC 1 Nov 1859**.

11596 STEWART, Rev William. To Galt, Waterloo Co, ONT, 1832. First min of St Andrews Ch there. Went to Demerara, 1835. **HGD 75; FES vii 652**.

11597 STEWART, William. To QUE, and stld Melbourne, Sherbrooke Co. m Janet Wilson, qv. Both bur Maple Grove. **MGC 2 Aug 1979**.

11598 STEWART, Rev William, d 20 Jun 1892. From Glasgow. s/o John S, merchant. Matric Univ of Glasgow, 1830. Missionary to Presb of St John, NB, 1848-49, and became min of St Andrews Ch, Chatham. After 1860 in Halton Co, ONT, and d at Toronto. **GMA 12693; FES vii 611, 652**.

11599 STEWART, Rev William, 1835–1912. From Ecclefechan, DFS. To ONT, ca 1855. Baptist clergyman and Principal of Toronto Bible Training School. **MDB 717**.

11600 STEWART, Rev William, 1831–26 May 1920. From Foss, PER. Educ Univs of St Andrews and Edinburgh. Asst min at Blair Atholl, 1859-63, when he went to NS. Min of McLennans Mountain. Declined to join union of 1875. **SAM 114; FES vii 618**.

11601 STILL, John, b ca 1788. From ABD. To ONT, 1834, and stld Mona Centre, Dufferin Co. Wife Margaret d 1836. ch: 1. Jacob, dy; 2. John; 3. James; 4. George; 5. Alexander; 6. Robert; 7. David; 8. William; 9. Peter. **DC 19 Jul 1978**.

11602 STIRLING, Fergus, ca 1786–6 Aug 1853. From Glasgow. To Hamilton, ONT, and d there. **Ts Mt Albion**.

11603 STIRLING, Jane. From Thornhill, STI. d/o Peter S. To Huron Co, ONT, ca 1844. Wife of George Moir, qv. **DC 18 May 1982**.

11604 STIRLING, Jane, b 12 Apr 1802. From Tillicoultry, CLK. d/o Rev Dr Alexander S, par min, and Euphemia Auld. To St John, NB, 1836; later to Guelph, Wellington Co, ONT. Wife of Rev John Gibson MacGregor, qv, m 3 Dec 1830. **SH; FES iv 362**.

11605 STIRLING, John. To Glengarry Co, ONT, <1812. Soldier during War of 1812. Son John, b ca 1807. **DC 21 Mar 1981**.

11606 STIRTON, Grace, ca 1787–29 Dec 1878. From Gartmore, PER. To ONT and d there. m Peter Slater. **Ts Gartmore**.

11607 STITT, Catherine, 1786–16 Oct 1878. From New Cumnock, AYR. wid/o John Farquhar, 1772–1841. To Richmond Co, QUE, 1847; stld Windsor Mills, and d there. **DC 11 Nov 1981**.

STIVEN. See also STEVEN.

11608 STIVEN, Andrew, d 19 Mar 1883. From Arbroath, ANS. Prob s/o William S, shipmaster, and Margaret Air. To Goderich, Huron Co, ONT. m Elizabeth Gibson, 1815-76. Son William, d 1846. **Ts Arbroath**.

11609 STOBIE, George, d 15 Oct 1855. From Balneathill, Portmoak, KRS. s/o Thomas S. and Margaret Condie. To Etobicoke, York Co, ONT, and d there. **Ts Portmoak**.

11610 STOBO, Elizabeth, b 26 Jun 1790. From Strathaven, LKS. To Scarborough, York Co, ONT, 1830. Wife of Robert Hamilton, qv. **DC 31 Jan 1982**.

11611 STOBO, Robert, ca 1764–1834. From LKS, poss Strathaven or Lesmahagow. To Scarborough, York Co, ONT, 1824. Farmer. **DC 29 Mar 1981**.

11612 STOCKS, James. From Perth. s/o — S. and Ann Hutton. To Elora, Wellington Co, ONT, <1853. **SH**.

11613 STOCKS, James, 1825–1907. From ABD. To ONT ca 1854; stld prob Durham Co. m Elizabeth Keith, qv. **DC 23 Jul 1979**.

STODDART. See also STOTHART.

11614 STODDART, Margaret. From Ashkirk, SEL. To ONT, 1830. Wife of James Hutson, qv. **Ashkirk OPR 781/4**.

11615 STOKES, Arthur. From Paisley, RFW. To ONT, 1821, under the sponsorship of the Lesmahagow Society, and stld Lanark Co. Gamekeeper. ch incl: 1. Arthur; 2. David; 3. Mary. **LDW 13 Feb 1978**.

11616 STORIE, James. Prob from DFS. Rel to Robert S, qv. To Montreal, QUE, on the *Niagara*, ex Greenock, arr 28 May 1825; stld McNab Twp, Renfrew Co, ONT. **EMT 18**.

11617 STORIE, Robert. Prob from DNB. Rel to James S, qv. To Montreal, QUE, on the *Niagara*, ex Greenock, arr 28 May 1825; stld McNab Twp, Renfrew Co, ONT. **EMT 23**.

11618 STORIE, William. To Pictou, NS, on the *Hope*, ex Glasgow, 5 Apr 1848. **DC 12 Jul 1979**.

11619 STORY, Andrew, 1801-58. From Annan, DFS. To York Co, ONT, 1831; stld Pickering. Farmer. ch. **CAE 2**.

11620 STORY, Euphemia, ca 1760–4 Feb 1847. From Wintersheugh, Cummertrees, DFS. wid/o John Miller. To York Co, ONT, poss 1831, and d at Pickering. Dau Elizabeth, qv. **Ts Cummertrees**.

STOTHART. See also STODDART.

11621 STOTHART, John, d Oct 1825. Poss from DFS. To Miramichi, Northumberland Co, NB, 1815; stld Douglastown. Storekeeper and property owner. Perished with his wife in Great Miramichi Fire. **DC 4 Dec 1978**.

11622 STOTT, Rev David, 1826–8 Dec 1898. Prob from FIF. s/o John S, leather merchant, and Christina Fife. Educ Univ of St Andrews, 1846-47. To Woodstock, Carleton Co, NB, 1856. Min there until 1858, when he went as a missionary to Brantford, Brant Co, ONT. Retr to SCT, 1866, and became min of Deerness, OKI. m (i) 1857, Elizabeth Jane Dibble, NB, who d 1886, ch: 1. Ellen, b 1859; 2. John, b 1862; 3. Henry, d 1866. m (ii) 1889, Christina, d/o George Gordon, merchant in Fearn. **SAM 106; FES vii 214, 611, 653**.

11623 STOUT, William. From INV. To QUE, 1831; stld Ottawa Co, nr Lochaber. **ELB 3**.

11624 STRACHAN, Agnes Simpson, 22 Nov 1846– 5 Dec 1936. From Montrose, ANS. d/o William S, qv, and Susan McKnight, qv. To ONT, 1854; stld prob Haldimand Co. m 30 Nov 1872, at Newport, MN, Harvey Benjamen Scofield, ch. **DC 15 Apr 1961**.

11625 STRACHAN, James, b 22 Jan 1739. From Kinkell, ABD. s/o Rev James S. and Barbara S. To Halifax, NS. Merchant. **FES vi 165**.

11626 STRACHAN, Rev John, 12 Apr 1778–1 Nov 1867. b Aberdeen. s/o John S. and Elizabeth Findlayson. Grad MA, Kings Coll, Aberdeen, 1797, and became schoolmaster of Kettle par, FIF. Studied theology and emig to Kingston, ONT, 1779, to become tutor to the family of Richard Cartwright. Candidate for the min of St Gabriel Street Presb Ch, Montreal, but was ord in the Anglican Ch by Bishop Jehoshaphat Mountain. Became rector of Cornwall, where he opened a school for boys. Trans to Toronto, 1813, and made archdeacon, 1827. Consecrated Bishop of Toronto, with Upper Canada his diocese, 1839. Mem of the 'Family Compact', author and DD, Kings Coll, Aberdeen, 1811. m 1807, Ann, wid/o Andrew McGill, qv, and d/o Dr George Wood, ch: 1. Elizabeth; 2. James. **SGC 183-200; KCG 106, 265; SDG 104, 445; MDB 720**.

11627 STRACHAN, Mary, 3 Feb 1822–27 Apr 1905. From BAN. d/o James S. and Jane Watt. To Campbellford, Hastings Co, ONT, 1842. m 22 Dec 1841, John, qv. **DC 17 Dec 1970**.

11628 STRACHAN, Mary, b 15 Apr 1847. From Montrose, ANS. d/o William S, qv, and Susan McKnight, qv. To ONT, 1854; stld prob Haldimand Co. m 25 Feb 1866, David Peter Hess, Caledonia. **DC 15 Apr 1961**.

11629 STRACHAN, Thomas. Prob from ARL. To Ekfrid Twp, Middlesex Co, ONT, 1855. Weaver. **PCM 31**.

11630 STRACHAN, William, 1820-59. From Brechin, ANS. To ONT, 1854; stld prob Haldimand Co. m Susan McKnight, qv, ch: 1. Agnes Simpson, qv; 2. Mary, qv;

3. Charles, dy; 4. Alexander, dy; 5. William, d Newport, MN; 6-7. Isabella and John, twins. **DC 15 Apr 1961**.

11631 STRAHAN, Mary, 1801-34. From Is Arran, BUT. To Nash Creek, Restigouche Co, NB, 1831. Wife of Robert Harvie, qv. **MAC 17**.

11632 STRAITH, Rev John, 1826–10 Jan 1885. From ABD. To ONT, and after studying at Knox Coll, Toronto, became min of a Presb Ch, 1857. d at Shelburne, Dufferin Co. **MDB 720**.

11633 STRANG or STRANGE, James, b 27 Jun 1776, Brankamhall, East Kilbride, LKS. s/o Maxwell S. and Catherine Warnock. To QUE, ex Greenock, prob May 1823. Went to NY. **LDW 27 Sep 1975**.

11634 STRANG or STRANGE, John, b 2 Sep 1788. From East Kilbride, LKS. s/o Maxwell S. and Catherine Warnock. To Kingston, ONT, prob <1810. Lt, Lanarkshire Militia, and Major, 1st Regt Frontenac Militia, 1812. m 2 Feb 1818, May, d/o William McGill, Albany, NY, ch: 1. Maxwell, b 1820; 2. Orlando Sampson, physician. **East Kilbride OPR 643/2; LDW 27 Sep 1975**.

11635 STRANG, John, 1819–1904. From Thornhill, PER. s/o Peter S. and Margaret Sands. To Hamilton, ONT; later to Exeter, Huron Co. Stonemason and farmer. m 1852, Janet Dougall, qv, ch: 1. Margaret; 2. Elizabeth; 3. Peter; 4. Janet; 5. Henry; 6. John; 7. James. **DC 19 Sep 1960**.

11636 STRANG or STRANGE, Mary, b 12 Jan 1782, Brankamhall, East Kilbride, LKS. d/o Maxwell S. of Whitefield, Cambuslang, and Catherine Warnock. To QUE, ex Greenock, prob May 1823; stld later at Jackson, Washington Co, NY. Wife of Robert Alexander, qv. **East Kilbride OPR 643/2; LDW 27 Sep 1975**.

11637 STRANG or STRANGE, Maxwell, b 6 Jul 1786, Hutt, East Kilbride, LKS. s/o Maxwell S. and Catherine Warnock. To QUE, ex Greenock, prob May 1823. Went to Albany, NY, and m d/o William McGill, ch. **LDW 27 Sep 1975**.

STRATHCONA AND MOUNT ROYAL, Lord. See SMITH, Donald Alexander.

11638 STRATHEARN, Elizabeth, 8 Dec 1811–23 Jun 1867. From AYR. d/o John S. To ONT, 1834, and d Whitby Twp, Durham Co. m 13 Feb 1836, William Dow, jr, qv. **DC 4 Feb 1982**.

11639 STRONACH, George, ca 1766–1849. Poss from Barony par, Glasgow. To Annapolis Co, NS, <1790. Farmer and magistrate. m (i) Mary, sis/o Benjamen Fales, ch: 1. Rev Ebenezer, 1792–1858; 2. Sarah, 1795–1865; 3. Elizabeth; 4. William; 5. Nelson; 6. Reis, 1808-68; 7. Rev Abraham; 8. Margaret; 9. Rachel. m (ii) Elizabeth Merrit, Widow O'Connor, 1800-68. **LDW 9 Oct 1980; DC 31 Mar 1983**.

11640 STRUTHERS, Alexander. From Ayr. To Dumfries Twp, Waterloo Co, ONT, <1848. **DGH 27 Apr 1848**.

11641 STRUTHERS, Andrew. From Glasgow. s/o Alexander S, cottonwaste dealer. To ONT <1848. **SH**.

11642 STRUTHERS, Rev George, 1783–19 Mar 1857. From Sorn, AYR. s/o John S, farmer. Matric Univ of Glasgow, 1807. Adm min of Horton and Cornwallis, NS, 1827. Trans to St Marks, British Guiana, 1832, but demitted and retr to NS. Again at Cornwallis, and was Moderator of the Synod in 1838. Son John, 1841-82. **GMA 7261; FES vii 618.**

11643 STRUTHERS, James. Prob from LKS. Served in 82nd Regt and was gr land in Pictou Co, NS, 1784. **HPC App F.**

11644 STRUTHERS, Jean, 1819–2 Jan 1894. From RFW. d/o — S. and — Miller. To ONT, 1843, and d King Twp, York Co. Wife of John Gillies, qv. **DC 17 Nov 1979.**

11645 STRUTHERS, Matthew, d 27 Oct 1845. From Glasgow. To Montreal, QUE, 1815. Bequeathed £200 to the City of Montreal, 'to assist in building a house of industry.' **DGH 4 Dec 1845.**

STUART. See also STEUART and STEWART.

11646 STUART, Alexander. From Kiltearn, ROC. To Pictou, NS, on the *Sarah*, ex Fort William, Jun 1801. Tenant. Wife Mary with him, and ch: 1. Murdo, aged 9; 2. Donald, aged 4; 3. Ann, aged 2; 4. inf. **PLS.**

11647 STUART, Rev Alexander. From Inveravon, BAN. Grad MA, Kings Coll, Aberdeen, 1843, and became Congregational min at Halifax, NS. **KCG 296.**

11648 STUART, David, ca 1765–18 Oct 1853. From Callendar, PER. s/o Alexander S. To Montreal, QUE, <1800. Fur-trader, and in 1810 became a partner of John J. Astors Pacific Fur Co. d at Detroit. **MDB 723.**

11649 STUART, Isabella, ca 1755–6 May 1828. From PER. To NS, and d there. **VSN No 2876.**

11650 STUART, Isaiah. From Greenock, RFW. s/o Robert S. and Ann Campbell. To NS, prob <1840. **DC 18 May 1982.**

11651 STUART, James. From Is Arran, BUT. To Megantic Co, QUE, 1851. m Christina Cook, qv. **AMC 49.**

11652 STUART, John, 1752–1835. From PER. To Guysborough Co, NS, 1783. Lt, 71st Regt, later lawyer and MLA. **MLA 334.**

11653 STUART, John. From Weem, Kenmore, PER. s/o Alexander S, 1780–1858, and Jessie McNaughton, 1795–1848. To Osgoode Twp, Carleton Co, ONT, 1840. Shoemaker. m Jane McNab, qv. **DC 1 Aug 1979.**

11654 STUART, John Campbell, b 1809. From Greenock, RFW. s/o Robert S. and Ann Campbell. To NS prob <1840; later to NSW, AUS. Shipbuilder. **DC 18 May 1982.**

11655 STUART, Margaret. From Is South Uist, INV. To Whycocomagh, Inverness Co, NS, <1834. m Angus Beaton, qv. **MP 218.**

11656 STUART, Nancy, ca 1792–14 Dec 1861. Prob from INV. To Pictou, NS. Wife of Hugh Fraser, qv. **DC 27 Oct 1979.**

11657 STUART, Robert, 19 Feb 1785–29 Oct 1848. From Callandar, PER. s/o John S. and Mary Buchanan, and neph of David S, qv. To Montreal, QUE, 1807. Fur-trader. Joined John J. Astors Pacific Fur Co, 1810, and was afterwards agent of its successor, the American Fur Co, at Michilimackinac. Ret to Detroit. m 1813, Elizabeth Emma Sullivan, of Brooklyn, NY. Son Gen David, 1816-68. **DC 21 Mar 1981.**

11658 STURGEON, Janet, b ca 1740. From Preston Merse, Kirkbean, KKD. To Georgetown, Kings Co, PEI, on the *Lovely Nellie*, ex Annan, 1774. Wife of John Smith, qv. **ELN.**

11659 SUTHERLAND, Adam, b ca 1798. From Borrobol, Kildonan par, SUT. bro/o George S, qv. To Fort Churchill, Hudson Bay, on the *Prince of Wales*, ex Stromness, 28 Jun 1813. Went to York Factory, spring 1814, thence to Red River. **LSS 186; RRS 27; LSC 323.**

11660 SUTHERLAND, Alexander, b ca 1790. From Balnavaillich, Kildonan par, SUT. To Fort Churchill, Hudson Bay, on the *Prince of Wales*, ex Stromness, 28 Jun 1813. Went to York Factory, 1814, thence to Red River. **LSS 186; RRS 186; LSC 323.**

11661 SUTHERLAND, Alexander, b ca 1790. From Kildonan par, SUT. To York Factory, Hudson Bay, arr 26 Aug 1815, thence to Red River. Overseer of a group of settlers. **LSC 327.**

11662 SUTHERLAND, Alexander, 28 Feb 1802–23 Mar 1882. From Kildonan, SUT. s/o John S, qv, and Katherine Grant, qv. To Fort Churchill, Hudson Bay, on the *Prince of Wales*, ex Stromness, 28 Jun 1813. Went to Red River, and later to Bradford, Simcoe Co, ONT. m 27 Feb 1827, Ann, 1807-87, d/o Joseph Johnston and Catherine Gower, ch: 1. Jane, b Holland Landing, 1 Dec 1827; 2. Joseph, 1829-33; 3. John, 1832-33; 4. Mary, 1832-35; 5. Catherine, 1836–1905; 6. Margaret Ann, d inf, 1840. **LSS 184; RRS 26; LSC 321; DC 11 Sep 1977.**

11663 SUTHERLAND, Alexander, b ca 1776. To Pictou, NS, 1815; res Lower Settlement, 1816. Labourer. m with 3 ch, and 'very poor.' **INS 38.**

11664 SUTHERLAND, Alexander, b ca 1771. To Pictou, NS, 1815, res Scots Hill, 1816. Labourer, m with 4 ch, and 'very poor.' **INS 38.**

11665 SUTHERLAND, Alexander, ca 1782–23 Aug 1870. From SUT. To Pictou Co, NS, and bur Salt Springs. m Margaret Munro, qv. **DC 27 Oct 1979.**

11666 SUTHERLAND, Alexander, 1800-63. From CAI. To NS, 1817; stld Lower Caledonia, Guysborough Co. m Eleanor MacDonald, 1820. **NSN 30/308.**

11667 SUTHERLAND, Alexander, d 3 Feb 1881. From Rogart par, SUT. To NS, poss <1840; stld nr Earltown, Colchester Co. **DC 19 Mar 1981.**

11668 SUTHERLAND, Alexander, ca 1788–1870. From CAI or SUT. To Wentworth Co, ONT, ca 1841; stld ca 1844, Sydenham Twp, Grey Co. Farmer. m Christina Gunn, qv, ch: 1. Christian, 1825–1910; 2. Donald, 1829-56; 3. Ann, 1832–1914; 4. Janet, 1834–1908; 5. Ellen, 1836–1914; 6. Wilhelmina, 1838–1927; 7. Catherine, 1841–1900; 8. John, 1842–1904. **DC 11 Mar 1980.**

11669 SUTHERLAND, Alexander, ca 1826-96. From Dornoch, SUT. s/o William S, qv, and Alexandrina Ross, qv. To Lanark Co, ONT, 1831, and d at Hybla. m Eliza Smith, ch. **DC 11 Nov 1981.**

11670 SUTHERLAND, Alexander. From Dornoch, SUT. To East Williams Twp, Middlesex Co, ONT, 1833. **PCM 43.**

11671 SUTHERLAND, Alexander. To Pictou, NS, on the *Lady Grey*, ex Cromarty, ROC, arr 16 Jul 1841. **DC 15 Jul 1979.**

11672   SUTHERLAND, Andrew. From Fraserburgh, ABD. s/o 'Fiddler' F. To St Marys Twp, Perth Co, ONT. Dau Janet.   **DC 1 Apr 1966**.

11673   SUTHERLAND, Angus. From SUT. To Earltown, Colchester Co, NS, 1813. Farmer.   **HT 42**.

11674   SUTHERLAND, Angus. From SUT. To Ramsay Twp, Lanark Co, ONT, ca 1831. Farmer. m Margaret Fraser, qv, ch: 1. John, qv; 2. Alexander, b 28 Jul 1833; 3. Angus, b 21 Jul 1835; 4. Margaret, b 30 Apr 1837; 5. Helen or Ellen, b 20 May 1839.   **DC 11 Mar 1980**.

11675   SUTHERLAND, Angus, b ca 1794. From Auchraich, Creich, SUT. s/o Mrs Elizabeth S, qv. To Fort Churchill, Hudson Bay, on the *Prince of Wales*, ex Stromness, 28 Jun 1813. Went to York Factory, spring 1814, thence to Red River. Left settlement and arr Holland River, ONT, 6 Sep 1815.   **LSS 185; RRS 26; LSC 322**.

11676   SUTHERLAND, Angus. From Dornoch, SUT. bro/o John S, qv. To ONT, ca 1831; stld Almonte, Lanark Co.   **DC 11 Nov 1981**.

11677   SUTHERLAND, Ann, ca 1783–8 Sep 1857. From Golspie, SUT. To Pictou Co, NS, 1814. Wife of Hugh McPherson, qv.   **DC 27 Nov 1979**.

11678   SUTHERLAND, Mrs Ann, b ca 1768. To Pictou, NS, on the *Ellen*, ex Loch Laxford, SUT, 22 May 1848. Widow.   **DC 15 Jul 1979**.

11679   SUTHERLAND, Barbara, b ca 1780. Prob from Kildonan par, SUT. Wife of William McKay, qv. To York Factory, Hudson Bay, arr 26 Aug 1815, thence to Red River.   **LSC 327**.

11680   SUTHERLAND, Barbara, b ca 1794. From Kennageall, SUT. d/o James S, catechist. To Fort Churchill, Hudson Bay, on the *Prince of Wales*, ex Stromness, 28 Jun 1813. Went to York Factory, Apr 1814, thence to Red River. May have moved with her bro Hannan, qv, to West Gwillimbury, ONT.   **LSS 186; RRS 27; LSC 323**.

11681   SUTHERLAND, Catherine, ca 1789–30 Dec 1837. From Clyne, SUT. To NS, prob <1830; stld nr Earltown, Colchester Co. m John Graham.   **DC 19 Mar 1981**.

11682   SUTHERLAND, Christian, b ca 1790. From Borrobol, Kildonan par, SUT. sis/o William S, qv. To Fort Churchill, Hudson Bay, on the *Prince of Wales*, ex Stromness, 28 Jun 1813, and may have d soon after arrival.   **LSS 185; RRS 27; LSC 323**.

11683   SUTHERLAND, Christian. From SUT. To NS <30 Oct 1824, when m James Thompson, qv.   **VSN No 778**.

11684   SUTHERLAND, Christian, ca 1764–16 Apr 1849. From SUT. To NS <1830; stld nr Earltown, Colchester Co. Wife of William Baillie, qv.   **DC 19 Mar 1981**.

11685   SUTHERLAND, Christie, ca 1794–18 Dec 1857. From SUT. To Pictou Co, NS, and stld nr Lansdowne. Wife of John Fraser, qv.   **DC 10 Feb 1980**.

11686   SUTHERLAND, Christy, b ca 1780. To Pictou, NS, 1815; res there 1816. Unm servant and 'able to support herself.'   **INS 39**.

11687   SUTHERLAND, Christy or Christine, ca 1808–

30 Jul 1854. Prob from Rogart par, SUT. To NS, poss <1840; stld nr Earltown, Colchester Co. Wife of William Murray, qv.   **DC 19 Mar 1981**.

11688   SUTHERLAND, Daniel, 1756–19 Aug 1832. Poss from SUT. To Montreal, QUE, <1770, and became a partner of NWCo. App Postmaster at Montreal, 1812, and in 1817 became Deputy Postmaster-General of British North America. m 1771, Margaret Robertson.   **MDB 727**.

11689   SUTHERLAND, David. From SUT. Prob bro/o James S, qv. To Glengarry Co, ONT, 1824, with parents. Moved to Ekfrid Twp, Middlesex Co, 1834.   **PCM 31**.

11690   SUTHERLAND, David, 12 Feb 1828–28 Jun 1912. From Dornoch, SUT. s/o William S, qv, and Alexandrina Ross, qv. To Lanark Co, ONT, 1831, and d Wilberforce Twp, Renfrew Co. m Elizabeth King, ch.   **DC 11 Nov 1981**.

11691   SUTHERLAND, Donald, ca 1782–18 May 1848. From Lairg, SUT. To Pictou Co, NS, 1802; stld New Lairg. m Isabella Gordon, qv.   **DC 10 Feb 1980**.

11692   SUTHERLAND, Donald, b 15 Feb 1796. From Kildonan, SUT. s/o John S, qv, and Katherine Grant, qv. To Fort Churchill, Hudson Bay, on the *Prince of Wales*, ex Stromness, 28 Jun 1813. Went to Red River, later to Bradford, Simcoe Co, ONT, and afterwards to Galena, IL.   **LSS 184; RRS 26; LSC 321; DC 11 Sep 1977**.

11693   SUTHERLAND, Donald, b ca 1794. To Western Shore, Inverness Co, NS, 1816. Farmer.   **CBC 1818**.

11694   SUTHERLAND, Donald, d 28 Mar 1847. From Golspie, SUT. To Drummondville, Drummond Twp, QUE, ca 1817, to join his s Donald. d at Durham.   **DC 5 Oct 1980**.

11695   SUTHERLAND, Donald, 1790–1877. From Rangag, Latheron, CAI. To Guysborough Co, NS, Jun 1817; stld St Marys River. m 11 Jan 1820, Eleanor, 1797–1877, d/o Angus McDonald, qv, and Martha Fisher, ch: 1. John Angus, b 1820; 2. Donald M, b 1822; 3. Alexander, b 1825; 4. Martha, b 1827; 5. Margaret, b 1829; 6. James D, b 1831; 7. Janet, b 1832; 8. William, b 1834; 9. Christy E, b 1837; 10. Elizabeth, b 1841.   **DC 31 Mar 1980**.

11696   SUTHERLAND, Donald, ca 1767–30 Nov 1874. From Lairg, SUT. To Pictou Co, NS, 1818, and bur Lansdowne.   **DC 10 Feb 1980**.

11697   SUTHERLAND, Donald. From Creich, SUT. To Pictou, NS, ex Cromarty, 4 Jul 1818; stld New Lairg. m (i) Jane Ross, ch: 1. Christy; 2. James, b 1800. m (ii) Jessie McKay, further ch: 3. William, b 1803; 4. Jane; 5. Donald; 6. John Hugh; 7. Roderick, b 18 Aug 1815.   **DC 24 Nov 1983**.

11698   SUTHERLAND, Donald. From SUT. Prob bro/o James S, qv. To Glengarry Co, ONT, with parents, 1824; moved to Ekfrid Twp, Middlesex Co, 1834.   **PCM 31**.

11699   SUTHERLAND, Donald, d 1831. From Golspie, SUT. To Eldon Twp, Victoria Co, ONT, ca 1830. Discharged soldier, 72nd Regt. Wife Ann with him, and later m — Fraser and went to Buffalo, NY. Son John, Postmaster at Argyle, ca 1860.   **EC 218**.

11700 SUTHERLAND, Donald. To Pictou, NS, on the *Lady Gray*, ex Cromarty, ROC, arr 16 Jul 1841. **DC 15 Jul 1979**.

11701 SUTHERLAND, Eleanor, b ca 1795. To Pictou, NS, 1815; res there 1816. Unm servant, 'able to support herself.' **INS 39**.

11702 SUTHERLAND, Mrs Elizabeth. From Auchraich, Kildonan par, SUT. To Fort Churchill, Hudson Bay, on the *Prince of Wales*, ex Stromness, 28 Jun 1813. Widow. Son Angus, qv, with her, and dau Betsy, who d Fort Churchill, 26 Oct 1813. Went to York Factory, Apr 1814, thence to Red River. Left settlement and arr Holland River, ONT, 6 Sep 1815. **LSS 185; RRS 26; LSC 322**.

11703 SUTHERLAND, Ellen, ca 1791–Sep 1849. Poss from SUT. To Pictou, NS, prob <1830. m John Graham, qv. **DC 10 Feb 1980**.

11704 SUTHERLAND, George, 23 Nov 1783–11 Sep 1863. From Golspie, SUT. s/o Donald S, qv. To QUE, and stld Drummondville, Drummond Twp, 1815. Discharged soldier, 49th Regt, and formerly of the Ross-shire Militia. Farmer, gr land on the St Francis River. m 24 Dec 1822, Sarah Drye, wid/o Archibald Hamilton, soldier, ch: 1. Elizabeth, b 29 Sep 1823; 2. John, b 15 Feb 1826; 3. Christiana, b 21 Apr 1828; 4. Donald, b 8 Feb 1830; 5. Sarah Elspeth, b 12 Sep 1834; 6. George Joseph, b 17 Jan 1837; 7. James McKeown, b 12 Sep 1838. **DC 1 Nov 1980**.

11705 SUTHERLAND, George, ca 1793–16 Dec 1868. From SUT. To Pokemouche, Gloucester Co, NB. **DC 4 Oct 1978**.

11706 SUTHERLAND, George, b 4 Jan 1794. From Kildonan, SUT. s/o John S, qv, and Katherine Grant, qv. To Fort Churchill, Hudson Bay, on the *Prince of Wales*, ex Stromness, 28 Jun 1813. Went to York Factory, Apr 1814, thence to Red River. Moved later to Bradford, Simcoe Co, ONT. m Henrietta Gunn. **LSS 184; RRS 26; LSC 321; DC 11 Sep 1977**.

11707 SUTHERLAND, George, b ca 1796. From Borrobol, Kildonan par, SUT. bro/o Adam S, qv. To Fort Churchill, Hudson Bay, on the *Prince of Wales*, ex Stromness, 28 Jun 1813. Went to York Factory, Apr 1814, thence to Red River. Left settlement and arr Holland River, ONT, 6 Sep 1815. **LSS 186; RRS 27; LSC 323**.

11708 SUTHERLAND, Hannan, b ca 1795. From Kennageall, SUT. s/o James S, catechist. To Fort Churchill, Hudson Bay, on the *Prince of Wales*, ex Stromness, 28 Jun 1813. Went to York Factory, Apr 1814, thence to Red River. Moved to West Gwillimbury, Simcoe Co, ONT. **LSS 186; RRS 27; LSC 323**.

11709 SUTHERLAND, Hector, d 24 Mar 1840. Prob from PER. To Montreal, QUE, and d there. Sometime Sgt-Maj, 7th Hussars. **Ts Greyfriars, Perth**.

11710 SUTHERLAND, Hugh, ca 1828–14 Feb 1865. From Rogart par, SUT. To NS, poss <1840; stld nr Earltown, Colchester Co. **DC 19 Mar 1981**.

11711 SUTHERLAND, Isabella, ca 1786–29 Sep 1850. From SUT. To Pictou, NS, and stld New Lairg. m D. Matheson. **DC 10 Feb 1980**.

11712 SUTHERLAND, James, 1778–1 Oct 1844. From South Ronaldsay, OKI. s/o George S, tenant in Knockhall. To Hudson Bay, 1797 and entered service of HBCo. Served at York Factory, Cumberland House, Red River and Swan River. Mem of Council of Assiniboia, and was app a chief factor, 1821. Ret 1827, and d Red River Settlement where he had a farm. m formally, 1832, Jane Flett, of Orkney ancestry, but had ch before then: 1. William; 2. James; 3. John; 4. Roderick; 5. George; 6. Jane or Jessie; 7. Nancy; 8. Elizabeth; 9. Letitia. **MDB 727; DC 21 Mar 1971**.

11713 SUTHERLAND, James, b ca 1755. To Charlottetown, PEI, on the *Elizabeth & Ann*, ex Thurso, arr 8 Nov 1806. ch: 1. Ann, aged 19; 2. Mary, aged 15; 3. Janet, aged 12; 4. Isobel, aged 3; 5. Ann, aged 1. **PLEA**.

11714 SUTHERLAND, James, b ca 1768, Kildonan par, SUT. To York Factory, Hudson Bay, arr 26 Aug 1815, thence to Red River. Pioneer settler and ch elder, authorised to baptize and marry. Wife Mary Polson, qv, with him, and ch: 1. Janet, aged 16; 2. Catherine, aged 14; 3. James, aged 12; 4. Isabella, aged 13. **LSC 325; LSS 193**.

11715 SUTHERLAND, James G, b 1822. From SUT. To Glengarry Co, ONT, with parents, 1824; moved to Ekfrid Twp, Middlesex Co, ONT, poss 1834. Woollen manufacturer and farmer. Son William H, res Toronto. **PCM 31**.

11716 SUTHERLAND, Jean, 1793–1860. Prob from Johnstone, RFW. To ONT, 1858; stld Caledon Twp, Peel Co, ONT. wid/o Alexander McLachlan, qv. **DC 17 Nov 1981**.

11717 SUTHERLAND, John. From SUT. To Pictou, NS, on the *Hector*, ex Loch Broom, arr 17 Sep 1773; stld Windsor, Hants Co, later Sutherland River, Pictou Co, which received its named from him. **HPC App C**.

11718 SUTHERLAND, John. From SUT. To Pictou, NS, on the *Hector*, ex Loch Broom, arr 17 Sep 1773. Prob the person gr 180 acres on east side of West River, 1783, later another 70 acres. **HPC App A and C**.

11719 SUTHERLAND, John, ca 1763–2 Sep 1813. From Kildonan, SUT. To Fort Churchill, Hudson Bay, on the *Prince of Wales*, ex Stromness, 28 Jun 1813. Wife Katherine Grant, qv, with him. ch: 1. John, b 17 Feb 1792; 2. George, qv; 3. Donald, qv; 4. Janet, b 7 Feb 1798; 5. William, b 6 Aug 1800; 6. Alexander, qv. **LSS 184; RRS 26; LSC 321; DC 11 Sep 1977**.

11720 SUTHERLAND, John, b ca 1771. To Pictou Co, NS, 1815; res Caribou, 1816. Labourer, m with 4 ch. **INS 39**.

11721 SUTHERLAND, John, b ca 1794. To Pictou, NS, 1815; res there 1816, and m. Tailor. **INS 39**.

11722 SUTHERLAND, John, b ca 1784. To St Andrews dist, Cape Breton Co, NS, arr prob Apr 1817. Farmer, m and ch. **CBC 1818**.

11723 SUTHERLAND, John. To Colchester Co, NS, <1820; stld Earltown, later Rogers Hill, Pictou Co. Farmer. Son Rev Alexander. **HT 43**.

11724 SUTHERLAND, John. To Delaware Twp, Middlesex Co, ONT, prob 1820. Pioneer settler. **PCM 57**.

11725   SUTHERLAND, John. From SUT. Prob bro/o James G. S, qv. To Glengarry Co, ONT, 1824, with parents; moved to Ekfrid Twp, Middlesex Co, ONT, 1834.   **PCM 31**.

11726   SUTHERLAND, John, ca 1789–6 Apr 1852. From Rogart par, SUT. To NS, poss <1830; stld nr Earltown, Colchester Co. Wife Jane, 1779–1875. ch incl: 1. Catherine, ca 1818–1901; 2. Donald, 1821-28. **DC 19 Mar 1981**.

11727   SUTHERLAND, John. From Dornoch, SUT. To Pictou Co, NS, <1830; stld Six Mile Brook. Farmer, and built the first stone house in eastern NS. Son Hector. **HNS iii 660**.

11728   SUTHERLAND, John, 14 Feb 1822–12 Mar 1910. From SUT. s/o Angus S, qv, and Margaret Fraser, qv. To Ramsay Twp, Lanark Co, ONT, ca 1831. Farmer. m Jessie, d/o Alexander Nicholson, ch: 1. Alexander; 2. John; 3. Jessie; 4. Angus.   **DC 11 Mar 1980**.

11729   SUTHERLAND, John. From Dornoch, SUT. bro/o Angus S, qv. To NS, ca 1831.   **DC 11 Nov 1981**.

11730   SUTHERLAND, John, ca 1790–1 Sep 1838. From SUT. To NS, 1833; stld nr Lansdowne, Pictou Co. **DC 10 Feb 1980**.

11731   SUTHERLAND, John. To Pictou, NS, on the *Lady Gray*, ex Cromarty, ROC, 16 Jul 1841.   **DC 15 Jul 1979**.

11732   SUTHERLAND, Joseph, ca 1748–15 Oct 1835. From Dornoch, SUT. bro/o Walter S, qv. To QUE, 1764; later to ONT. Maj, Glengarry Militia, and enlisted in 26th Regt. d at Lancaster Twp.   **DGC 6 Jan 1836**.

11733   SUTHERLAND, Katie, b ca 1793. From Balnavailich, Kildonan par, SUT. sis/o Alexander S, qv, and William S, qv. To Fort Churchill, Hudson Bay, on the *Prince of Wales*, ex Stromness, 28 Jun 1814, thence to Red River.   **LSS 186; RRS 27; LSC 322**.

11734   SUTHERLAND, Margaret. From Thurso, CAI. To Shelburne Co, NS, 1785. Wife of Robert Inness, qv. **LC 22 Dec 1962**.

11735   SUTHERLAND, Margaret, b ca 1776. To Charlottetown, PEI, on the *Elizabeth & Ann*, ex Thurso, arr 8 Nov 1806.   **PLEA**.

11736   SUTHERLAND, Margaret, b ca 1797. To Pictou, NS, 1815; res there 1816. Unm servant, 'able to support herself.' **INS 39**.

11737   SUTHERLAND, Maria, ca 1816–9 Mar 1897. From Clyne, SUT. To NS, poss <1840. m John Ferguson, qv.   **DC 19 Mar 1981**.

11738   SUTHERLAND, Mary. To Fredericton, York Co, NB, <1795. Heir to her aunt, Marjory Stuart, in Canongate, Edinburgh. m Rev F. Lauder.   **SH**.

11739   SUTHERLAND, Robert, ca 1797–1854. From Borrobol, Kildonan par, SUT. bro/o William S, qv. To Fort Churchill, Hudson Bay, on the *Prince of Wales*, ex Stromness, 28 Jun 1813. Went to York Factory, Apr 1814, thence to Red River. Left settlement and arr Holland River, ONT, 6 Sep 1815. Stld at West Gwillimbury, Simcoe Co. m Isabella Bannerman, qv, ch: 1. William, b 15 Apr 1816; 2. Barbara, b 1818; 3. Christine, b 1822.   **LSS 184; RRS 26; LSC 321; DC 1 Jan 1979**.

11740   SUTHERLAND, Robert. From SUT. Prob bro/o James S, qv. To Glengarry Co, ONT, with parents, 1824; moved to Ekfrid Twp, Middlesex Co, 1834. **PCM 31**.

11741   SUTHERLAND, Robert, ca 1765–26 Apr 1843. From SUT. To Pictou Co, NS, and bur Lansdowne. m Christy McDonald, qv.   **DC 10 Feb 1980**.

11742   SUTHERLAND, Robert, b ca 1770. To Pictou, NS, 1815; res Caribou, 1816. Labourer, m with 6 ch, and 'very poor.' **INS 39**.

11743   SUTHERLAND, Robert. To Pictou Co, NS, <1844; stld Middle River. By wife Lexy had s Donald. **PAC 207**.

11744   SUTHERLAND, Robert Dundas, 1815-68. To ONT, and stld Ernestown, Lennox Co, ca 1835. Physician. m Anne Crowe, 1818-87.   **DC 6 Jan 1977**.

11745   SUTHERLAND, Sarah, b 1839. From Is Skye, INV. d/o John S. To NS ca 1853.   **DC 19 Feb 1970**.

11746   SUTHERLAND, Spencer, ca 1788–4 Mar 1874. From SUT. To Shubenacadie, Hants Co, NS. Railway contractor.   *The Highlander*, **28 Mar 1874**.

11747   SUTHERLAND, Walter, d <1835. From Dornoch, SUT. bro/o Joseph S, qv. To QUE, 1764, later to ONT. Maj, Glengarry Militia, and enlisted in 26th Regt.   **DGC 6 Jan 1836**.

11748   SUTHERLAND, Wilhelmina. From Kintradwell or Loth, SUT. m 1817, Gordon Bannerman, qv, and stld Pictou Co, NS, 1822.   **DC 3 Sep 1979**.

11749   SUTHERLAND, William, b 1756. To Pictou Co, NS, 1815; res Scots Hill, 1816. Farmer, m with 2 ch, and 'very poor.' **INS 39**.

11750   SUTHERLAND, William, b ca 1760. To Pictou Co, NS, 1815; res West branch, East River, 1816. Labourer, m with 3 ch, and 'very poor.' **INS 38**.

11751   SUTHERLAND, William, b ca 1761. From Kildonan, SUT. To York Factory, Hudson Bay, arr 26 Aug 1815; thence to Red River. Wife Isobel, aged 50, with him, and ch: 1. Jeremiah; 2. Ebenezer, aged 11; 3. Donald, aged 7; 4. Helen, aged 12.   **LSC 325**.

11752   SUTHERLAND, William, b ca 1791. From Borrobol, Kildonan, SUT. To Fort Churchill, Hudson Bay, on the *Prince of Wales*, ex Stromness, 28 Jun 1813. Wife Margaret with him. Went to Red River, 1814, but left settlement and arr Holland River, ONT, 6 Sep 1815, with his young wife and a child.   **LSS 185; RRS 26; LSC 322**.

11753   SUTHERLAND, William, b ca 1795. From Balnavailich, Kildonan par, SUT. bro/o Alexander S, qv. To Fort Churchill, Hudson Bay, on the *Prince of Wales*, ex Stromness, 28 Jun 1814. d on his way to York Factory.   **LSS 186; RRS 27; LSC 322**.

11754   SUTHERLAND, William. From SUT. Prob bro/o James G.S, qv. To Glengarry Co, ONT, with parents, 1824; moved to Ekfrid Twp, Middlesex Co, 1834.   **PCM 31**.

11755   SUTHERLAND, William, 1804-81. From Dornoch, SUT. To Lanark Co, ONT, 1831; stld later Wilberforce Twp, Renfrew Co. Farmer. m Alexandrina Ross, qv, ch: 1. Alexander, qv; 2. David, qv; 3. James,

1832–1906; 4. Angus, 1835–1917; 5. John, b 1835; 6. Donald, 1838–1916; 7. Margaret, b 1841. **DC 11 Nov 1981**.

11756   SUTHERLAND, Rev William, d 1848. To Earltown, Colchester Co, NS, and West Branch, River John, Pictou Co, 1836. After 1843, min at Earltown only. **FES vii 618**.

11757   SUTHERLAND, William. To Westminster Twp, Middlesex Co, ONT, prob <1840. Founder of the *Free Press*. **PCM 55**.

11758   SUTHERLAND, William G, ca 1812–30 May 1895. Prob from Wick, CAI. To Pictou, NS, and d at Watervale, West River. Physician. Wife Eliza Ann, ca 1826–6 Apr 1857. Both bur Salt Springs. **DC 27 Oct 1979**.

11759   SWAN, Archibald, 12 Mar 1829–12 Aug 1885. From Dollar, CLK. To Montreal, QUE, <1849. Dry goods merchant, in partnership sometime with James Brown, qv. **SGC 567**.

11760   SWAN, James, ca 1805–10 Apr 1842. From Stevenston, AYR. To Halifax, NS, and d there leaving a wife and an aged mother. Superintendent, Government Buildings. **DGH 9 Jun 1842**.

11761   SWAN, Mary, ca 1760–10 Mar 1836. From Mouswald, DFS. wid/o James Farish in Oldmill. To Westminster Twp, Middlesex Co, ONT, and d there. **Ts Mouswald**.

11762   SWANSON, George, ca 1823–28 May 1897. From ABD. To Sherbrooke, QUE. m Mary Smith, ca 1830–11 Dec 1914. **MGC 2 Aug 1979**.

11763   SWANSTON, Margaret. From Bowden, ROX. d/o John S, mason. To Montreal, QUE, <1833. m — Bain. **SH**.

11764   SWANSTON, Walter, b 1819. From Galashiels, SEL. To Eramosa Twp, Wellington Co, ONT, prob <1850. m Elizabeth Fielding, ch. **DC 4 Oct 1980**.

11765   SWEET, Sarah A, b ca 1838. To St John, NB, <1861, when m John R. Douglass, by whom she had ch. **DC 25 Jan 1983**.

11766   SWINTON, John, 12 Dec 1829–15 Dec 1901. From Saltoun, ELN. s/o William S. and Jane Currie. To Montreal, QUE, 1843; later to NY. War correspondent, managing editor, *New York Sun*, and publisher. m 1877, Mrs Orsena Smith, d/o Prof Orson Squire Fowler. **AMC 99**.

11767   SWINTON, William, 23 Apr 1833–24 Oct 1892. From Saltoun, ELN. s/o William S. and Jane Currie. To Montreal, QUE, <1850; later to NY and CA. War correspondent, *New York Times*; author and linguist. m 4 May 1853, Catherine, d/o James Linton and Margaret Loudon, ch. **AMC 99**.

11768   SYM, Jane. From Perth. d/o Robert S. To Kingston, ONT, and m as his second wife, Alexander McKenzie, qv. **MDB 465**.

11769   SYM, Robert. To Lanark Co, ONT, 1821; stld Lot 9, Con 2, North Sherbrooke Twp. Went later to NY. **HCL 74; DC 27 Oct 1979**.

SYME, Mrs William J. See BABINGTON, Lilias.

11770   SYMINGTON, James, ca 1800–25 Jul 1877. From Lanark. s/o John S. and Martha Paterson. To Montreal, QUE. m Mary Thomson, d 1841. Son John, railwayman, Edinburgh. **Ts Lanark**.

T

11771   TAIT, David, d 25 Mar 1877. From Haddington, ELN. To Montreal, QUE, 1831. Clerk with a firm of notaries, later emp in Stamp Office. **SGC 631**.

11772   TAIT, Rev James, 6 Apr 1829–22 Dec 1899. To ONT, with parents, <1845. Educ Edinburgh and at Knox Coll, Toronto. Became Presb min at Fitzroy Harbour, Carleton Co. Author. **MDB 734**.

11773   TAIT, Janet. From Meggatknowes, PEE. To QUE, 1831; stld Guelph Twp, Wellington Co, ONT. Wife of William Elliot, qv. **DC 11 Nov 1981**.

11774   TAIT, William, d 14 Jun 1832. From Newton Stewart, WIG. To QUE and d there of cholera. **DGC 17 Jul 1832**.

11775   TAIT, William. From DFS. To Galt, Dumfries Twp, Waterloo Co, ONT, 1844. Farmer. m Jean Mackay, qv. **CAE 11**.

11776   TAIT, William L, ca 1808–16 Apr 1897. From Kirkpatrick-Fleming, DFS. To ONT, 1848, and d Coldwater, Simcoe Co. Son Andrew. **CAE 67**.

11777   TATLOCK, William. Prob from Glasgow. To QUE on the *Prompt*, ex Greenock, 4 Jul 1820; stld Lanark Co, ONT, poss in South Sherbrooke Twp. **HCL 238**.

11778   TAWSE, Alexander McLaughlan, ca 1833–22 Mar 1873. From Dundee, ANS. s/o George T, Stobswell, and wife Catherine. To Toronto, ONT, and d there. **Ts Dundee**.

11779   TAWSE, Rev John, 1801–8 Apr 1877. From Towie, ABD. s/o James T, farmer. Grad MA, Marischall Coll, Aberdeen, 1821. To York Co, ONT, 1837. Min at King for 40 years. **FAM ii 431; SNQ ii/2 186; FES vii 653**.

11780   TAYLOR, Alexander. Prob from Grange, BAN. To Halifax, NS, 1818. m Margaret Johnstone. **DC 22 Jul 1965**.

11781   TAYLOR, Alexander. To Pictou, NS, on the *Lady Gray*, ex Cromarty, ROC, arr 15 Jul 1979. **DC 15 Jul 1979**.

11782   TAYLOR, Alexander. From Kilcalmonell, Kintyre, ARL. To Elderslie Twp, Bruce Co, ONT, <1855. Farmer. m Margaret Walker, qv. Son Neil, b 1832. **DC 6 Jan 1982**.

11783   TAYLOR, Ebenezer. From PER. Prob bro/o William T, qv. To Richmond Bay, PEI, on the *Falmouth*, ex Greenock, 8 Apr 1770; stld Stanhope, Queens Co. **DC 28 May 1980**.

11784   TAYLOR, Elizabeth. From Wick, CAI. To Guelph Twp, Wellington Co, ONT, 1836. Wife of John Bruce, qv. **DC 11 Nov 1981**.

11785   TAYLOR, George. Prob from Grange, BAN. To Halifax, NS, on the *Pillan*, ex Greenock, 1810. **DC 22 Jul 1965**.

11786   TAYLOR, James, b ca 1749. From Southwick, Kirkbean, KKD. To Georgetown, Kings Co, PEI, on the *Lovely Nellie*, ex Annan, 1774. Wright. **ELN**.

11787   TAYLOR, James, b ca 1769. From Carnwath, LKS. To QUE on the *Atlas*, ex Greenock, 11 Jul 1815; stld North Elmsley Twp, Lanark Co, ONT, 1816. Dyer and clothier, later farmer, Lot 28, Con 10. Wife Margaret Cowie, qv, with him and 5 ch.   **SEC 2; HCL 12, 17, 230, 232**.

11788   TAYLOR, Rev James, 20 Dec 1805–28 Jun 1865. From Tibbermore, PER. s/o Rev Dr Thomas T. and Mary Alison. To Lachine, QUE, 1836. Min there until 1842. m 14 Jul 1835, Eleanor Kay Hick, ch: 1. Mary Alison, b 1836; 2. Eleanor Janet, b 1837; 3. James Keith, 1840-98; 4. Horatio Carwell, 1841-61; 5. Edward Willgress, 1843-59.   **FES i 270, iv 255**.

11789   TAYLOR, James, 6 Nov 1814–16 Jul 1901. From Forres, MOR. To QUE, 1836; moved in 1838 to Locland, OH, and later to Rock Is Co, IL. Master tailor. m (i) Elspet Malcolm, qv, ch: 1. John, d 1844; 2. Ann. m (ii) 22 Apr 1840, Rachel A. Vancamp, from NJ, further ch: 3. Catherine; 4. William R, 1841-61; 5. Louisa; 6. James P, b 1843; 7. Nettie; 8. Samuel Cleland, 1849–1939; 9. Flora; 10. John C, b 1852; 11. Martha, 1860-63.   **DC 7 Jun and 3 Aug 1983**.

11790   TAYLOR, Jessie, b ca 1828. To St Gabriel de Valcartier, QUE, prob <1855.   **Census 1861**.

11791   TAYLOR, John. From PER, poss Killin. To McNab Twp, Renfrew Co, ONT, 1825.   **DC 3 Jan 1980**.

11792   TAYLOR, John, 1816–14 Jun 1881. From Montrose, ANS. To Halifax, NS. Shipmaster and MLA, 1873-74.   **MLA 336**.

11793   TAYLOR, Rev John. From Stow, MLN. Burgher Ch min at Auchtermuchty, FIF, 1827-52, when app Prof of Theology at Toronto, ONT. DD. Retr to SCT and became min at Busby, AYR, 1863. m (i) Marion Antill Wardlaw, qv. Son Sir Thomas Wardlaw, qv. m (ii) a d/o Rev John Richardson, Freuchie Burgher Ch, PER. **UPC i 164, 202, ii 146**.

11794   TAYLOR, Rev Lachlan, 1816-61. From Killean and Kilchenzie par, ARL. s/o — T, schoolmaster, and — McLean. To QUE <1840; stld St Andrews, Argenteuil Co. Schoolmaster, but became Methodist clergyman, successively at Ottawa, Kingston, Hamilton, Toronto and Montreal.   **BNA 899; SGC 329**.

11795   TAYLOR, Margaret, b ca 1730. From Campbeltown, ARL. To Malpeque, Prince Co, PEI, on the *Annabella*, ex Campbeltown, 27 Jul 1770; stld Malpeque. Wife of John Ramsay, qv.   **DC 20 Dec 1981**.

11796   TAYLOR, Margaret, b 1828. From Galston, AYR. To Port Morien, Cape Breton Co, NS, 1855. m John Johnstone, qv.   **NSN 7/3**.

11797   TAYLOR, Maria. From Edinburgh. d/o John T. To ONT <1848, when m Rev Hugh John Borthwick, qv. **FES vii 656**.

11798   TAYLOR, Mary. To Montreal, QUE, <1850. Wife of Thomas McLaren, qv.   **DC 24 Oct 1975**.

11799   TAYLOR, Samuel. Prob from Papa Westray, OKI. Rel to William T, qv. To Hudson Bay <1850. **LDW 18 Mar 1968**.

11800   TAYLOR, Sir Thomas Wardlaw, 25 Mar 1833–1 Mar 1917. b Auchtermuchty, FIF. s/o Rev John T, qv, and Marion Antill Wardlaw, qv. Grad BA, Univ of Edinburgh, 1852, and went to ONT with parents, 1853. Lawyer; QC, 1876, and became Chief Justice of MAN. KB, 1897. m (i) 1858, Jessie, d/o Dr John Cameron, Wilmington, SC, ch: 1. Marion Antill, d 1865; 2. Isabella, d 1901; 3. Capt John, RNWMP, d 1910. m (ii) 1864, Margaret, d/o Hugh Vallance, Hamilton, ONT, further ch: 4. Rev Thomas Wardlaw, Goderich; 5. Anne; 6. George Vallance, killed in action, 1916; 7. Janet Catherine; 8. Alexander; 9. Margaret; 10. William Calven.   **CEG 234; UPC i 164, ii 147; MDB 740**.

11801   TAYLOR, William. From PER. Prob bro/o Ebenezer T, qv. To Richmond Bay, PEI, on the *Falmouth*, ex Greenock, 8 Apr 1770; stld Stanhope, Queens Co.   **DC 28 May 1980**.

11802   TAYLOR, Rev William, ca 1768–1837. From Falkirk, STI. s/o John T, farmer, and Elizabeth Gardner. Matric Univ of Glasgow, 1790, and became Secession min at Stonehouse, LKS, 1798. To QUE on the *Rothiemurchus*, ex Leith, 5 Apr 1817; stld Osnaburgh and Gwillimbury, York Co, ONT. Went to NY, later to Madrid Ch, Waddington. m (i) Mary McEwan, qv, ch: 1. Eliza, b ca 1795; 2. William; 3. Ann; 4. David; 5. Mary, b 1805; 6. James, b 1809; 7. Margaret, b 1811. m (ii) Mary Armstrong, 1782–1869.   **GMA 5030; UPC i 233; FES vii 653**.

11803   TAYLOR, Rev William, ca 1804–4 Sep 1876. From Slammanan, STI. s/o Alexander T, farmer. Matric Univ of Glasgow, 1817. Min of Secession Ch, PEE, 1831-33. To Montreal, QUE, arr 3 Jun 1833, and was min of Erskine Ch there until his d at Portland, ME. Moderator of the United Synod of Canada, 1861, and author.   **SGC 523; GMA 9851; MDB 740**.

11804   TAYLOR, William, 25 Jan 1786–Aug 1870. From KCD. To Windsor Forks, Hants Co, NS, <1850. By wife Catherine, 1805-74, had s John.   **HNS iii 66; DC 4 Dec 1978**.

11805   TAYLOR, William. Prob from Papa Westray, OKI. Rel to Samuel T, qv. To Fort Albany, Hudson Bay, <1826. Emp by HBCo, prob from 1829.   **LDW 18 Mar 1968**.

11806   TELFER, Isabella, 1791–1877. From ROX. To Howick, Chateauguay Co, QUE, 1840; later to Galt Twp, Waterloo Co, ONT. Wife of Robert Oliver, qv.   **OM 5/17**.

11807   TELFER, James, 14 May 1810–24 Sep 1883. From Armadale, SUT. s/o William T, qv, and Mary Davidson. To ONT <1840; stld Collingwood Twp, Grey Co, and became a merchant. m 24 Dec 1840, Alice Keeler, 1818-89, from Heydon, Norfolk, ENG, ch: 1. William, b 21 Sep 1841; 2. John, b 10 Jan 1844; 3. James Hall, b 19 Jun 1846; 4. Sophia Alice, b 7 Jun 1848; 5. John Alfred, b 20 Oct 1849; 6. Emily, b 2 May 1852; 7. Louise Esther, b 12 Apr 1854; 8. Charles Andres, b 29 Jan 1856; 9. Frederick Jarrett, b 29 Apr 1858; 10. George Gilbert, b 24 Jan 1865. **DC 2 Dec 1979**.

11808   TELFER, Mary, b 1818. From Dalkeith, MLN, but b poss NBL. To QUE on the *Niagara*, ex Greenock, 3 Sep 1852; stld Oxford Co, ONT. Wife of John Shiell, qv.   **DC 27 Aug 1981**.

11809   TELFER, William, ca 1780–10 Oct 1851. From Armadale, SUT, but b prob ROX. To Halton Co, ONT,

prob <1840, and d Trafalgar Twp. Farmer. m Mary
Davidson, ch: 1. John, b Tongue par, 1806; 2. George,
1808-92; 3. James, qv; 4. William, b 1812; 5. Janet,
b 1814; 6. Andrew, 1817-85; 7. Gilbert, b 1819;
8. Hall, 1822-1902; 9. Elizabeth, 1825-99.   **DC 13 Sep
1983**.

11810   TELFORD, James Pattison, 1839-1933. From
Newcastleton, ROX. s/o William Pattison T, qv, and
Elizabeth Murray, qv. To Dumfries Twp, Waterloo Co,
ONT, 1840; later to Annan, Sydenham Twp, Grey Co.
m Catherine McDonald, 1851-1933, ch: 1. Elizabeth,
1869-1930; 2. Jean, 1870-1851; 3. Catherine,
1871-1962; 4. William Murray, 1873-1955; 5. Maxwell,
1875-1929; 6. Margaret, 1877-78; 7. John McDonald,
1879-1960, KC; 8. Richard Rennelson, 1885-1954;
9. James Edward, 1889-1951.   **DC 3 Aug 1979**.

11811   TELFORD, Margaret, 1835-1917. From
Newcastleton, ROX. d/o William Pattison T, qv, and
Elizabeth Murray, qv. To Dumfries Twp, Waterloo Co,
ONT, 1840; later to Annan, Sydenham Twp, Grey Co.
m William Ross, res Leith, Sydenham Twp, ch: 1. David;
2. John; 3. William, 1865-1950; 4. Margaret; 5. Allan
Harkness, 1874-1938; 6. Elizabeth, 1869-1960;
7. Jessie, 1871-1961.   **DC 3 Aug 1979**.

11812   TELFORD, William, 6 Jan 1828-13 Apr 1895.
From Leitholm, BEW. To Peterborough Co, ONT, and
d Smith Twp. Farmer and poet.   **MDB 741**.

11813   TELFORD, William Pattison, 1797-1879. From
Newcastleton, ROX. s/o William T. and Isabel Pattison.
To Dumfries Twp, Waterloo Co, ONT, 1840; later to
Annan, North Sydenham Twp, Grey Co. Schoolmaster,
cabinet-maker, draughtsman and musician. m Elizabeth
Murray, qv, ch: 1. Margaret, qv; 2. William Pattison, jr,
qv; 3. James Pattison, qv; 4. Isabella, 1843-1932;
5. Elizabeth, 1845-1935; 6. Mary, b 1848; 7. John
Pattison, 1855-1920.   **DC 10 Jul 1979**.

11814   TELFORD, William Pattison, jr, 1836-1922.
From Newcastleton, ROX. s/o William Pattison T, qv, and
Elizabeth Murray. To Dumfries Twp, Waterloo Co, ONT,
1840; later to Annan, Sydenham Twp, Grey Co.
m Margaret, d/o John Couper, ch: 1. William Pattison,
1867-1955, politician; 2. John Couper, 1870-1931;
3. Robert, 1875-1937; 4. Euphemia, 1883-1975.
DC 29 Sep 1964 and 3 Aug 1979.

11815   TENNANT, James, b 1796. From DFS.
bro/o William T, qv, and Thomas T, qv. To Brockville,
Leeds Co, ONT, 1817.   **DC 30 Jan 1980**.

11816   TENNANT, Lillias. To East Whitby Twp, Durham
Co, ONT. m ca 1840, Robert Dempster, qv.   **DC 18 Jan
1980**.

11817   TENNANT, Thomas, b 20 Jun 1797. From DFS.
bro/o James T, qv, and of William T, qv. To Brockville,
Leeds Co, ONT, 1833. Wife with him–d poss Montreal,
1833–and ch: 1. David, b 1826; 2. Susanna, b 1829;
3. William, b 1831; 4. Isabella, b 17 Sep 1833.
m (ii) Grace Wood, qv.   **DC 30 Jan 1980**.

11818   TENNANT, William, b 1794. From DFS.
bro/o James T, qv, and Thomas T, qv. To NB, 1814; later
to Montreal, QUE, and stld Brockville, Leeds Co, ONT.
Prob ex-soldier.   **DC 30 Jan 1980**.

11819   THAIN, Thomas, d 6 Jan 1832. Poss from ABD.
s/o — T. and — Richardson. To CAN <1804. Clerk with

XYCo, and later served with NWCo. Became partner of
McTavish, McGillivrays, & Co, 1813, and Montreal agent
for HBCo. Retr to SCT in poor health and d Aberdeen.
MDB 743.

11820   THOM, Adam, ca 1803-21 Feb 1890. From
Brechin, ANS. Grad MA, Kings Coll, Aberdeen, 1823. To
Montreal, QUE, on the *Rosalind*, ex London, 1832.
Studied law and engaged in journalism. App Recorder of
Ruperts Land, 1838, and became a Councillor of
Assiniboia. LLD, Kings Coll, 1840. Retr to Britain, 1854,
and d at London, ch.   **KCG 117, 280; SA vii 139;
MDB 744**.

11821   THOM, Alexander. From Old Machar, ABD.
s/o Alexander T, farmer. To Perth, Lanark Co, ONT,
<1821. Surgeon.   **SH**.

11822   THOM, James, 1763-1834. From Belhelvie,
ABD. s/o John T, farmer. To Halifax, NS, <1800.
Merchant. Retr later to Aberdeen, and res Albyn Place.
m Rachel Smith, qv, and had, poss with other ch:
1. Rachel; 2. Barbara, 1812-63; 3. Sophia; 4. Mrs
Hurchison, Peterhead.   **NDF 238**.

11823   THOM, William. From Glasgoforest, Kinellar par,
ABD. s/o William T, sometime farmer in Auchmacoy,
Logie- Buchan. To QUE, ex Aberdeen, arr 14 Jul 1843;
stld St Charles, Kane Co, IL. Farmer. Wife Isobel with
him.   **DC 25 Mar 1980**.

11824   THOMAS, Francis Tracey, d 6 Jun 1843. From
Edinburgh. To Montreal, QUE, <1830. Sometime Capt
and Brigade Maj, Scots Greys and 100th Regt. In public
service in CAN, ch.   **DGH 10 Aug 1843**.

THOMPSON. See also THOMSON.

11825   THOMPSON, Alexander. To ONT <1818.
m Janet Carmichael, qv, ch: 1. John, b 1818; 2. Donald,
b 1820; 3. Helen, b 1824; 4. Archibald, 1826-98;
5. Alexander, b 1828; 6. Janet, b 1829; 7. James,
b 1831; 8. Duncan, b 1833.   **DC 2 Sep 1981**.

11826   THOMPSON, Alexander. From INV. Prob rel to
John T, qv. To East Williams Twp, Middlesex Co, ONT,
1832.   **PCM 43**.

11827   THOMPSON, Andrew, ca 1795-24 May 1873.
From KKD. To Pictou Co, NS, and bur Salt Springs.
Wife Elizabeth, ca 1796-13 May 1870, native of CAI.
DC 27 Oct 1979.

11828   THOMPSON, Andrew. From ROC. To East
Williams Twp, Middlesex Co, ONT, <1842, when elected
twp clerk.   **PCM 43, 46**.

11829   THOMPSON, Andrew. From Glasgow. To
Farnham, Missisquoi Co, QUE, prob <1850. Son
Alexander, res Brome, 1881.   **MGC 2 Aug 1979**.

11830   THOMPSON, Archibald. From ARL. To Delaware
Twp, Middlesex Co, ONT, ca 1852.   **PCM 57**.

11831   THOMPSON, Charles, ca 1807-13 Jul 1832.
s/o William T, res Woodhouse, poss Colvend, DFS. To
Port Stanley, Elgin Co, ONT.   **DGC 21 Aug 1832**.

11832   THOMPSON, Christy, 1799-1874. Prob from
INV. To Pictou Co, NS, 1801; stld Hopewell. m Hector
McDonald, qv.   **PAC 121**.

11833   THOMPSON, David, 1796-1868. To Niagara,
Lincoln Co, ONT, after service with the Royal Scots.
Schoolteacher and historian.   **MDB 746**.

11834   THOMPSON, David, 1781–1841. From Dumfries. Rel to James T, qv. To Wallace, Cumberland Co, NS, prob <1830.   **DC 29 Oct 1980**.

11835   THOMPSON, Donald, 15 Sep 1763–3 Nov 1825. To NS, prob 1784. Discharged soldier, 2nd Batt, 84th Regt. Dau Rebecca, b 13 Jun 1795.   **NSN 23/49**.

11836   THOMPSON, Dougald, 1805-75. From ARL. To Pictou Co, NS, <1840; stld Middle River. m and ch: 1. Robert; 2. Donald, 1848-99.   **PAC 208**.

11837   THOMPSON, James. From SUT. To NS <30 Oct 1824, when m Christian Sutherland, qv.   **VSN No 778**.

11838   THOMPSON, James, 1816-56. From Dumfries. Poss s/o David T, qv. To Wallace, Cumberland Co, NS, prob <1830.   **DC 29 Oct 1980**.

11839   THOMPSON, John, b ca 1762. To Pictou, NS, 1815; res there 1816. Mason, m with 4 ch.   **INS 39**.

11840   THOMPSON, John, ca 1777–1840. From Dumfries. To St John, NB, and d there. Merchant. **DGH 27 Mar 1840**.

11841   THOMPSON, John, 1800-82. From LKS. To Dalhousie Twp, Lanark Co, ONT, <1825; later to Perth Co. Stonemason. ch: 1. Thomas George; 2. John; 3. Robert; 4. Elizabeth; 5. Martha; 6. Agnes; 7. Hannah; 8. Adelaide.   **DC 13 Jan 1978**.

11842   THOMPSON, John. From Inverness. Prob rel to Alexander T, qv. To East Williams Twp, Middlesex Co, ONT, 1832.   **PCM 43**.

11843   THOMPSON, John, d 1858. To Dundas Co, ONT, 1835. Hardware merchant. m Margaret Ewing. Son Alexander.   **DC 29 Sep 1964**.

11844   THOMPSON, Margaret, 1770–1863. Prob from Glasgow. To West Essa Twp, Simcoe Co, ONT, ca 1825. Wife of Robert Ruthven, qv.   **DC 24 May 1979**.

11845   THOMPSON, Margaret, ca 1813–28 Oct 1897. To Pictou Co, NS, 1841; stld East Forks, Middle River. m William Campbell, qv.   **PAC 36**.

11846   THOMPSON, Robert, ca 1828–9 Oct 1861. From Chirnside, BEW. s/o John T. and Catherine Lunham. To CAN.   **Ts Chirnside**.

11847   THOMPSON, Thomas, ca 1801-89. From LKS. To Dalhousie Twp, Lanark Co, ONT, <1825; later to Perth Co. Stonemason. ch: 1. Mary, 1833–1913; 2. Thomas, 1835–1908; 3. John, 1838–1935; 4. Jane, 1842–1909; 5. Robert, 1844–1930; 6. Martha, 1845–1932; 7. George, 1848–1927; 8. James, d 1873; 9. Margaret, 1858–1913.   **DC 13 Jan 1978**.

11848   THOMPSON, William, ca 1830–12 Dec 1887. Prob from Cummertrees, DFS. To Middlesex Co, ONT; stld Whyton Village. m Elizabeth Patton, qv, ch: 1. Lydia, 1855–1910; 2. John, 1858-74; 3. Robert, 1859–1953; 4. James, 1860–1941; 5. Mary; 6. William, 1866–1941; 7. David, 1872–1943; 8. Charles; 9. Ann; 10. Daniel; 11. Elizabeth, 1881–1947; 12. Jenny, d 1960.   **DC 7 Nov 1981**.

THOMSON. See also THOMPSON.

11849   THOMSON, Andrew, b 25 May 1751, Netherknock, Westerkirk par, DFS. s/o Andrew T, tenant farmer, and Janet Scott. To Scarborough Twp, York Co, ONT, ca 1802. Farmer. m (i) Betty Borthwick, and by her who d 1786 had ch: 1. John, b 1782; 2. Janet, b 1784; 3. Christopher, b 1786. m (ii) 21 Sep 1792, Jean Henderson, qv, further ch: 4. Margaret, b 1792; 5. William, b 1803; 6. Hannah; 7. Mary; 8. Andrew; 9. James; 10. Ellen; 11. Elizabeth.   **Westerkirk OPR 854/1; LDW 22 Jan 1976**.

11850   THOMSON, Ann. From Kilmorack, INV. To Pictou, NS, on the *Dove*, ex Fort William, Jun 1801. Spinster.   **PLD**.

11851   THOMSON, Archibald, b 7 May 1749, Netherknock, Westerkirk par, DFS. s/o Andrew T, tenant farmer, and Janet Scott. To Scarborough Twp, ONT, ca 1802. Stonemason. m Elizabeth McKay, from QUE, ch: 1. Edward; 2. Elizabeth; 3. Janet; 4. Ellen; 5. Mary; 6. Andrew; 7. Agnes; 8. Hugh; 9. Alexander; 10. John; 11. George, b 1801, ancestor of Lord Thomson of Fleet, newspaper magnate (for descendants see *Burkes Peerage & Baronetage*, 1970).   **Westerkirk OPR 854/1; LDW 22 Jan 1976**.

11852   THOMSON, Archibald, 1784–1819. From Bonese, Westerkirk, DFS. s/o William T, tenant farmer, and first wife Margaret Anderson. To Scarborough Twp, York Co, ONT, 1802, bur retr later to SCT.   **LDW 22 Jan 1976**.

11853   THOMSON, Archibald, ca 1784–1875. From Dunadd, North Knapdale, ARL. To QUE, 1819, stld West Lorne, Elgin Co, ONT. Wife Margaret Gillies, qv, with him, and s Donald, b 1814.   **DC 11 Nov 1981**.

11854   THOMSON, Archibald. From Houston, RFW. s/o Archibald T, 1774–1868, and wife Mary. To ONT, ca 1830.   **Ts Houston**.

11855   THOMSON, Christopher, b 31 Aug 1796, Bonese, Westerkirk, DFS. s/o William T, tenant farmer, and second wife Ann Little. To Scarborough Twp, York Co, ONT, ca 1819. Journalist. m his cous, Mary, d/o Andrew T, qv, and Betty Borthwick, qv. **Westerkirk OPR 854/1**.

11856   THOMSON, David, b 18 Jul 1799, Bonese, Westerkirk par, DFS. s/o William T, tenant farmer, and second wife Ann Little. To Scarborough Twp, York Co, ONT, ca 1832. m Jean Edgar, qv, ch: 1. William, b 1826; 2. Archibald, b 1828; 3. George, b 1832; 4. Robert, b 1830; 5. James, b 1835; 6. Janet, b 1837; 7. Ann, b 1841; 8. James, b 1843; 9. Margaret Anne, b 1845. **Westerkirk OPR 854/1; LDW 22 Jan 1976**.

11857   THOMSON, David, 1763–1834. From Netherknock, Westerkirk par, DFS. s/o Andrew T, tenant farmer, and Janet Scott. To Scarborough Twp, York Co, ONT, via Niagara-on-the-Lake, 1795. Stonemason. m Mary Glendinning, qv, ch: 1. James, b 1789; 2. Andrew, b 1790; 3. Isobel, b 1793; 4. Richard, b 1794; 5. Archibald, 1796–1877; 6. David, b 1798; 7. Janet, b 1800; 8. John; 9. Mary; 10. Helen; 11. William.   **Westerkirk OPR 854/1; LDW 22 Jan 1976**.

11858   THOMSON, George, ca 1787–1841. From DFS. To Portland par, St John, NB. Shipbuilder.   **DGH 12 Aug 1841**.

11859   THOMSON, Rev George, ca 1802–31 Dec 1870. From Aberdeen. s/o George T. Grad MA, Kings Coll, Aberdeen, 1822. To Renfrew Co, ONT, 1851. Adm min of McNab and Horton. m Sarah McKay, 1805-72, ch: 1. Sarah, b 1834; 2. George, b 1839; 3. Alexander,

b 1840; 4. William, 1841-68; 5. Susan, b 1843;
6. Margaret, 1845–1918; 7. Harriet; 8. John. **KCG 279;
FES vii 654; DC 18 May 1982**.

11860 THOMSON, George, b ca 1807. From Blantyre,
LKS. To Waterloo Co, ONT, and stld Ayr. m Agnes
Johnston, d 1889, ch: 1. George, b 9 Jan 1837;
2. Robert, b 26 Aug 1843; 3. John, b 26 Aug 1847.
DC 27 Jan 1969.

11861 THOMSON, Hector. From Kilmorack, INV. To
Pictou, NS, on the *Sarah*, ex Fort William, Jun 1801.
Tenant. Wife Janet with him, and s Simon, aged 3.
PLS.

11862 THOMSON, Hugh Christopher, ca 1791–23 Apr
1834. To ONT, ca 1815; stld Kingston. Printer, journalist
and founder of the *Upper Canada Herald*, 1819. MLA,
rep Frontenac, 1824-34. **DC 17 May 1982**.

11863 THOMSON, James, 1772–20 Nov 1854. From
Dunfermline, FIF. To Windsor, Hants Co, NS. Son
James, ca 1798–1863. **DC 4 Dec 1978**.

11864 THOMSON, James, ca 1828–26 Sep 1856. From
Methil, FIF. s/o Andrew T. and Ann White. To QUE.
Drowned in the St Lawrence River. **Ts Methilhill**.

11865 THOMSON, Rev James, 1779–11 Oct 1830.
From Wamphray par, DFS. To Miramichi,
Northumberland Co, NB, ex Greenock, 22 Sep 1816. Min
of Auchtergaven Antiburgher Ch, PER, 1806-15; adm to
Miramichi, Aug 1817. m 1 Jul 1807, Catherine Mackay,
qv, ch incl: 1. John, 1808-84, physician; 2. Daniel
Mackay, 1810-64; 3. Catherine, 1810-64, unm;
4. Alexandrina, alive 1851; 5. Joseph, b 1823;
6. Samuel, 1815–1904, KC. **UPC ii 646; DC 15 Sep
1982**.

11866 THOMSON, James, ca 1802-36. From
Lesmahagow, LKS. To QUE and d there.
Ts Lesmahagow.

11867 THOMSON, Janet, 5 Jan 1792–16 Jul 1864.
From Innerleithen, PEE. d/o John T. and Janet Pow. To
QUE <1821; stld St Gabriel de Valcartier. m Robert
Goodfellow, qv. **MGC 2 Aug 1979**.

11868 THOMSON, Rev John, 7 Jan 1819–1 Mar 1893.
From St Andrews, FIF. s/o John T, builder, and Margaret
Nicoll. Educ Univ of St Andrews, 1841-42, and became
min of St Davids Ch, St John, NB, 1848. Trans to Fourth
Presb Ch, New York, 1853; to Knox Ch, Galt, ONT, 1861.
Went again to New York, 1864, and retr to SCT, 1878.
Min at Inverallan, MOR. m Georgina Ross, qv, ch:
1. John Ross, physician, Plockton; 2. Thomas Ross;
3. Jean Mackenzie; 4. Bradbury; 5. Alexander Stewart
Duff, b 1854, Sheriff-Substitute of LKS. **SAM 98;
FES vi 363, vii 612; FAS 207**.

11869 THOMSON, John. From Leith, MLN. s/o John T,
merchant, and Margaret Robertson. To Montreal, QUE,
<1834. **SH**.

11870 THOMSON, John, d 27 Sep 1847. From Urr,
KKD. s/o William T. in Bushiebiel. To Toronto, ONT, and
res King Street. Merchant. **DGH 11 Oct 1847**.

11871 THOMSON, John, 13 Nov 1818–2 May 1900.
From PER. To Montreal, QUE, ca 1855; stld North
Easthope, Perth Co, ONT. Farmer, Lot 44, Con 3.
m Elspeth Easson, qv, ch: 1. Grace, d 1953; 2. Elizabeth,
d 1848; 3. Margaret, 1865–1943; 4. John R, 1868–

1939; 5. Andrew, 1870–1901; 6. James Burns, 1872–
1948; 7. Martha or Matilda, d 1938; 8. Jennie, d 1948.
DC 15 Jul 1978 and 24 May 1979.

11872 THOMSON, John James Johnston, ca 1833–
4 Aug 1877. From Kirkpatrick-Fleming, DFS. To
Chatham, Kent Co, ONT. Major, Canadian Militia.
Ts Kirkpatrick-Fleming.

11873 THOMSON, Margaret, 16 Dec 1799–25 Feb
1887. From Carnock, FIF. d/o James T. and Agnes
Steedman. To QUE on the *Commerce*, Jun 1820; stld
Lanark Co, ONT. m Robert Drysdale. **DC 7 Apr 1962**.

11874 THOMSON, Margaret, called Peggy. Prob from
Cambusnethan, LKS. To ONT, 1826, with her husband,
James Brownlee, qv, but retr to SCT after his death.
LDW 13 Feb 1978.

11875 THOMSON, Marion, b ca 1803. From Glasgow.
To CAN, 1824. Wife of Thomas William Downs, qv.
SG xxvii/4 170.

11876 THOMSON, Mary, d 27 Jan 1826. From Dalton
par, DFS. d/o John T. in Hargrovehill. To Richibucto,
Kent Co, NB. m George Platt, merchant. **DGC 2 May
1826**.

11877 THOMSON, Mary. From AYR. To Carbonear,
NFD. m <1870, William Duff, qv. **HNS iii 644**.

11878 THOMSON, Mary. From Ayr. To ONT, 1854, and
d prob Amherstburg Twp, Essex Co. Wife of William
Gibb, qv, m 29 Nov 1833. **DC 5 Jun 1981**.

11879 THOMSON, Robert, ca 1762–12 Oct 1858. From
KKD. To Pictou Co, NS, and bur Salt Springs. Dau
Marion, d 1869. **DC 27 Oct 1979**.

11880 THOMSON, Simon, b 10 Mar 1795, Bonese,
Westerkirk par, DFS. s/o William T, tenant farmer, and
second wife Ann Little. To Orillia Twp, York Co, ONT, ca
1820. m Janet Thomson, poss his cous. **Westerkirk
OPR 854/1**.

11881 THOMSON, Walter, b 1834. From Kelso, ROX.
s/o Andrew T. and Agnes Vass. To ONT, 1843.
Millwright, Howland Mills. m 1869, Christina Hossie,
d/o James Elder, ch: 1. Walter Warren; 2. Howard W;
3. Frederick L; 4. Mabel V; 5. J. Hossie; 6. Violet F;
7. Christina H; 8. Charles Gordon; 9. A. Lorraine.
DC 29 Sep 1964.

11882 THOMSON, William, ca 1832–12 Aug 1909.
From Tannadice, ANS. s/o David T. in East Howmuir, and
Martha Sime. To Vancouver Is, BC, and d there.
Ts Tannadice.

11883 THOMSON, William, d 27 May 1842. From
Ashkirk, SEL. s/o Andrew T. and Janet Paterson. To
Montreal, QUE, and d there. **Ts Ashkirk**.

11884 THOMSON, William, ca 1835–11 Nov 1855.
Poss from DFS. s/o Robert T. To Elgin Co, ONT, and
d Port Stanley. **DGC 1 Jan 1856**.

11885 THORBURN, Jessie, ca 1811-88. From Bowden,
ROX. d/o Robert T. in Midlem, and Margaret Ridford. To
CAN, prob ONT. **Ts Bowden**.

11886 THORBURN, John, 1777–5 Mar 1866. From
Roadhead, Quothquhan, LKS. s/o David T. and Agnes
Steuart. To Montreal, QUE, poss 1843, and d there. Bur
Mount Royal. Farmer. Wife Mary Wilson, 1794–1840,
bur Carnwath, LKS. **Ts Carnwath**.

11887 THORBURN, Mungo, ca 1809–18 Mar 1888. From Bowden, ROX. s/o Robert T. in Midlem, and Margaret Ridford. To CAN, prob ONT. **Ts Bowden**.

11888 THORBURN, Sir Robert, 28 Mar 1836–12 Apr 1906. From PEE. To NFD, 1852. Merchant and MLA. Prime Minister of NFW, 1885-89; KCMG 1894. m Susanna Janetta, d/o Andrew Milroy, Hamilton, ONT, ch. **MDB 748**.

11889 THORBURN, William, b ca 1770. To Montreal, QUE, <1789, and became a partner of the NWCo. Served for a time on the Saskatchewan River. Sold his shares, 1805. **SGC 81; MDB 748**.

11890 THORNTON, Janet, b ca 1812. sis/o Rev Robert Hill T, qv. To Oshawa, East Whitby Twp, Durham Co, ONT. Wife of Alexander Burnet, qv. **DC 18 Jan 1980**.

11891 THORNTON, Rev Robert Hill, 1806-75. From West Calder, MLN. bro/o Janet T, qv. To CAN, ex Greenock, 8 May 1833; stld Oshawa, East Whitby Twp, Durham, Co, ONT. UP min and Inspector of Schools. DD and LLD, Princeton. By wife Margaret had ch: 1. John, b ca 1836; 2. Agnes; 3. Jessie; 4. Robert; 5. Eliza; 6. Margaret; 7. Edward; 8. George. **DC 18 Jan 1980**.

11892 TILLOCH, Elizabeth. From Glasgow. d/o Alexander T, 1759–1825, printer, and Margaret Simson. To ONT, 1826. Wife of John Galt, qv. **DC 1 Jan 1968**.

11893 TOCHER, Jane. From Macduff, BAN. d/o Alexander T, 1755–1844, schoolmaster, and Ann Hislop, 1767–1850. To CAN <1852. Wife of John Smith, qv. **Ts Lunan**.

11894 TOD, John, 1791–1882. From Strathleven, DNB. To CAN and joined HBCo. Served in Thompson River dist of BC, and ret in 1849. Mem of the first council of Vancouver Is, and d at Victoria. **MDB 750**.

11895 TODD, Barbara. From Errol, PER. m there, 1823, Robert Dawson of Pictou, NS. **Errol OPR 351/7**.

11896 TODD, Charles, 1796–12 Mar 1851. From Glasgow. s/o John T, qv. To Dalhousie Twp, Lanark Co, ONT, ca 1821. m Isabella Malcolm, 1806-95. **DC 21 Mar 1980**.

11897 TODD, Davidson, d 20 Apr 1847. From Glasgow. s/o John T, qv. To Dalhousie Twp, Lanark Co, ONT, prob 1821. m (i) 12 Aug 1814, Margaret Hood, qv. **DC 21 Mar 1980**.

11898 TODD, Ebenezer, 1814–5 Dec 1884. From Glasgow. s/o John T, qv. To Dalhousie Twp, Lanark Co, ONT, ca 1821. m Ann Tivy, 1823-88. **DC 21 Mar 1980**.

11899 TODD, George, b ca 1817. To St Gabriel de Valcartier, QUE, prob <1855. **Census 1861**.

11900 TODD, Hugh, 1811–4 Aug 1863. From Glasgow. s/o John T, qv. To Dalhousie Twp, Lanark Co, ONT, ca 1821. m Margaret Allan, 1811-80. **DC 21 Mar 1980**.

11901 TODD, James, ca 1800-85. From BEW. To Hastings Co, ONT, 1831. Lumberman. m Christina Clerke, ch: 1. Isabel, b ca 1827; 2. Walter, b ca 1829, farmer; 3. Joseph, res Kamloops, BC. **DC 14 Jan 1971**.

11902 TODD, John, d 1851. From Glasgow. To QUE on the *Prompt*, ex Greenock, 4 Jul 1820; stld Dalhousie Twp, Lanark Co, ONT. Weaver and farmer. m (i) Marion Gordon, and (ii) Elizabeth Hood, qv. Known ch:

1. William, b 1795; 2. Charles, qv; 3. Hugh, b 1802; 4. Thomas, b 1805; 5. John, went to MA; 6. Ebenezer; 7. Susanna; 8. Elizabeth; 9. Davidson, qv; 10. Ebenezer, qv; 11. Hugh, qv; 12. Samuel; 13. Joseph. **HCL 68; DC 21 Mar 1980**.

11903 TODD, Thomas, ca 1834–27 Mar 1866. From Dunfermline, FIF. s/o William T. and Janet Christie. To ONT. **Ts Dunfermline**.

11904 TODD, Walter Clark, 1829–1902. From BEW. s/o James T. To ONT, 1830. **DC 1 Aug 1979**.

11905 TOLMIE, Anne. Poss from ARL. To ONT, 1846. Wife of Alexander Graham, qv. **SG xxvi/3 92**.

11906 TOLMIE, William Fraser, 3 Feb 1812–8 Dec 1886. From INV. s/o Alexander T, merchant, and Marjory Fraser. Studied medicine, and emig to CAN on the *Ganymede*, Sep 1832. Surgeon with HBCo, on Pacific coast, and became mem of the board of management at Victoria. MLA and farmer. m 1850, Jane, 1827-80, d/o John Work, chief factor, HBCo, and Josette Lagacee, ch: 1. William Fraser, b 1853; 2. John Work, 1854–1936; 3. Alexander John, 1857–1916; 4. Roderick Finlayson, 1858–1934; 5. Jane Work, 1862–1935; 6. Mary Fraser; 7. Annie Fraser, 1863-65; 8. Margaret Cecilia, 1865-66; 9. Simon Fraser, 1867–1937, Prime Minister of BC, 1928-33; 10. Josette, 1869–1944. **BNA 1121; MDB 751; DC 24 Nov 1964**.

11907 TOMISON, William, ca 1739–ca 1811. From South Ronaldsay, OKI. To CAN, 1760, as a labourer, and served with the HBCo at York Fort, Severn and Cumberland House. Chief factor and resisted the advance of the Nor' Westers. Assisted natives during a smallpox epidemic, 1781-82. Retr to Orkneys, 1811, and founded Tomisons School. **MDB 751**.

11908 TOPP, Rev Alexander, 1 Apr 1814–5 Oct 1879. From Sheriffhall, Elgin. s/o Alexander T, farmer. Grad MA, Kings Coll, Aberdeen, 1831. Family tutor, and adm min of Elgin FC, 1843. To Toronto, ONT, 1858, to become min of Knox Ch. m 1850, Jane Mortimer, qv, ch: 1. Agnes, b 1850; 2. Alexander, b 1852; 3. Margaret, b 1854; 4. William, b 1855. **BNA 861; KCG 286; AFC i 345; FES vi 381, vii 654**.

TORRANCE, Mrs Andrew. See GIBB, Marion.

11909 TORRANCE, Benjamen, 5 May 1797–18 Jun 1857. From Catrine, AYR. s/o Andrew T. and Marion Gibb, qv. To QUE, 1817. Merchant here and at Toronto, where he d. m 23 Apr 1825, at Burlington, VT, Mary Mead, ch: 1. John Andrew, 1826-29; 2. Mary Mead, 1829–1904; 3. Eliza, b 1830. **DC 15 Jul 1980**.

11910 TORRANCE, Isabella, b 6 Apr 1794. From Catrine, AYR. d/o Andrew T. and Marion Gibb, qv. To QUE <1816. m John Miller, qv. **DC 15 Jul 1980**.

11911 TORRANCE, James, ca 1789–10 Sep 1817. From Catrine, AYR, but prob b Larkhall, LKS. s/o Andrew T. and Marion Gibb, qv. To Kingston, ONT, via NY, 1805. Merchant. m Elizabeth Kissock, qv. Son David, 1805-76, banker, sometime in business with his uncle John T, qv. **MDB 752; MGC 15 Jul 1980**.

11912 TORRANCE, John, 8 Jun 1786–20 Jan 1870. From Catrine, AYR, but b poss Larkhall, LKS. s/o Andrew T, merchant, and Marion Gibb, qv. To QUE on the *Dunlop*, arr 26 Jun 1807. Shipowner and merchant. m 28 May 1811, Elizabeth, d/o Duncan Fisher, qv, and Catherine Embury, ch incl: 1. Frederick William, QC, b 1823; 2. Elizabeth; 3. Amy; 4. Mrs David Torrance. **BNA 926; SGC 314; DC 15 Jul 1980**.

11913 TORRANCE, Thomas, 1776–1823. From Larkhall, LKS. s/o Andrew T. and Marion Gibb, qv. To Montreal, QUE, via NY, 1804. Merchant. Wife emig 1805. ch incl: 1. Marion; 2. Mrs John Stephenson. **SGC 313; DC 13 Jul 1980**.

11914 TORRANCE, William, b ca 1791. From Larkhall, LKS. s/o Andrew T. and Marion Gibb, qv. To QUE, ca 1814. Merchant. m 6 May 1815, Isabella Gibb, ch. **DC 15 Jul 1980**.

11915 TOSHACH, James, 1827-87. From Dron, PER. s/o James T, miller, and Isabella Stewart. To CAN. **Ts Dron**.

11916 TOSHACH, John. Prob from Glasgow. To Lanark Co, ONT, 1821; stld Ramsay Twp. Wife with him, and ch, incl: 1. Margaret; 2. Andrew; 3. Helen; 4. Aneas. **RPE 105; HCL 83**.

11917 TOUGH, Jasper. From ABD. To Montreal, QUE, <1803. Merchant, firm of Gillespie, Moffatt & Co. **SGC 239**.

11918 TOWART, Jane. From Glasgow. d/o William T, innkeeper. To NB <1820. m J. Paterson, teacher. **SH**.

11919 TOWER, Jessy. From Aberdeen. d/o George T, merchant. To ONT, 1833. m Adam Fergusson, qv. **FAS 69**.

11920 TRAILL, Ann, 3 Aug 1812–10 Jan 1873. Prob from Edinburgh. d/o Dr Thomas Stewart T, prof of Medicine, and Christian Robertson. To Hamilton, ONT, <1854. Went later to NY, and retr to SCT. Wife of George Parker, qv, m 24 May 1836. **DRG 23**.

11921 TRAILL, Thomas, Jun 1793–21 Jun 1859. From OKI. s/o Rev Walter T. of Westhove, min of Burness, and Margaret McBeath. To QUE on the *Laurel*, ex Greenock, 7 Jul 1832; stld Peterborough Co, ONT. m (i) 1814, Ann Traill Fotheringham, ch: 1. Walter, b 1815; 2. John Heddle, 1819-47. m (ii) Catherine Parr, 1802-99, authoress, d/o Thomas Strickland, Reydon, Suffolk, further ch: 3. James George, 1833-67; 4. Catherine Agnes Strickland, b 1836; 5. Thomas Henry Strickland, 1837-70; 6. Ann Traill Fotheringham, b 1838; 7. Mary Elizabeth, b 1841; 8. William Edward, emp with HBCo; 9. Walter John, b 1848. **TOO 39; FES vii 264; MDB 754**.

11922 TRAQUAIR, Marion. To Huron Co, ONT, 1853. Widow of John Drover, qv. **DC 6 Dec 1967**.

11923 TROOP, John, b ca 1752. From Cassiend, Kelton, KKD. Prob bro/o William T, qv. To Georgetown, Kings Co, PEI, on the *Lovely Nellie*, ex Annan, 1774. Labourer. **ELN**.

11924 TROOP, William, b ca 1750. From Cassiend, Kelton, KKD. Prob bro/o John T, qv. To Georgetown, Kings Co, PEI, on the *Lovely Nellie*, ex Annan, 1774. Mason. **ELN**.

11925 TROTTER, Rev Thomas, ca 1781–20 Apr 1855. From Lauder, BEW. Educ Univ of Edinburgh, and became Burgher min at Johnshaven, KCD. To Antigonish, NS, 1818, and adm as colleague and successor to Rev James Munroe. Opened a grammar school, 1879, and

was also a miller and farmer. **UPC i 78; HCA 27; MDB 755**.

11926 TUDHOPE, Catherine, 1816-85. From Lesmahagow, LKS. d/o James T, qv, and Christian Brockett, qv. To Oro Twp, Simcoe Co, ONT, 1831. m George Ingram, qv. **DC 5 Aug 1979**.

11927 TUDHOPE, Elizabeth. From Lesmahagow, LKS. d/o James T, qv, and Christian Brockett, qv. To Oro Twp, Simcoe Co, ONT, 1831. m James Ingram, qv. **DC 5 Aug 1979**.

11928 TUDHOPE, James, d 1833. From Lesmahagow, LKS. To Oro Twp, Simcoe Co, ONT, 1831. Farmer. m Christian Brockett, qv, 11 Sep 1811, ch: 1. George; 2. Jean; 3. Catherine, qv; 4. Margaret; 5. Elizabeth, qv; 6. James; 7. Janet; 8. John; 9. William. **DC 18 Aug 1979**.

11929 TUDHOPE, Walter. Prob from Lesmahagow, LKS. To Simcoe Co, ONT, <1840. m a cous, d/o James Tudhope, qv, and Christian Brockett, qv. **DC 5 Aug 1979**.

11930 TULLIS, Janet, 22 Dec 1779–12 Nov 1866. From Cupar, FIF. d/o James T. and Janet Wilson. To Pickering Twp, York Co, ONT, 1816. Wife of Rev George Barclay, qv. **BOP 2, 5, 6**.

11931 TULLOCH, John. To Pictou, NS, poss 1773. Son Peter, 1778–1860, res Belnan, Hants Co. **NSN 22/12, 24/93**.

11932 TULLOCH, Patrick. From Callander, PER. To Pictou, NS, on the *Dove*, ex Fort William, Jun 1801. Tenant. **PLD**.

11933 TURNBULL, Alexander. From LKS. To Dalhousie Twp, Lanark Co, ONT, 1829. Farmer. Wife Elizabeth with him, and ch: 1. David, qv; 2. Alexander; 3. Janet, qv; 4. Ann; 5. Isobella; 6. Elizabeth. **DC 21 Jan 1960**.

11934 TURNBULL, Christina, 1840–1922. From Glasgow. Prob rel to Robert T, qv, and William T, qv. To QUE on the *Bowling*, 1842; stld East Williams Twp, Middlesex Co, ONT. m John Bryce Cowie, qv. **DC 10 Nov 1981**.

11935 TURNBULL, David, 4 Jun 1815–8 Nov 1896. From LKS. s/o Alexander T, qv, and wife Elizabeth. To Dalhousie Twp, Lanark Co, ONT, 1829; later to Huron Co, and stld Lot 18, Con 10, Usborne Twp. Farmer. m 2 Apr 1841, Isabella Aitken, qv, ch: 1. Margaret; 2. Jane; 3. Annie; 4. Elizabeth; 5. Alexander; 6. Mary; 7. John; 8. Janet; 9. Alexander; 10. Isabella; 11. Agnes; 12. William. **DC 21 Jan 1960**.

11936 TURNBULL, Euphemia. From SEL. To NS <17 Jun 1818, when m Francis Dobson, qv. **NSS No 1376**.

11937 TURNBULL, Helen. From Melrose, ROX. To Port Hood, Inverness Co, NS, <1840. Wife of George C. Laurence, qv. **MLA 184**.

11938 TURNBULL, Jane. From Swinton, BEW. To Fredericton, NB, 1834; stld Stanley, York Co. Wife of John Kerr, qv. **DC 19 Jun 1980**.

11939 TURNBULL, Janet, b ca 1818. From LKS, poss Govan. d/o Alexander T, qv, and wife Elizabeth. To Lanark Twp, Lanark Co, ONT, 1832. m Robert Munn. **DC 21 Jan 1960**.

11940   TURNBULL, John, ca 1768–1791. From Bunkle, BEW. s/o John T, tenant in Wedderburn West Mains, and Alison Hunter. To NS, and d there. **Ts Bunkle**.

11941   TURNBULL, John. To QUE on the *Brock*, ex Greenock, 9 Jul 1820; stld prob Lanark Co, ONT. **HCL 238**.

11942   TURNBULL, Rev John, ca 1815–2 Jun 1881. From DNB. s/o John T, craftsman. Matric Univ of Glasgow, 1830. Secession min at Perth, 1838-39, when he joined Ch of Scotland. Presb min at St John, NB, 1841-74, when he retr to SCT. **GMA 12669**.

11943   TURNBULL, Robert, 16 Jun 1794–22 Aug 1831. From Catslacknowe, Yarrow, SEL. s/o Walter T. and Agnes Wright. To Montreal, QUE, and was accidentally drowned there. m Jane Ralph, qv, who went on to Port Dover, Norfolk Co, ONT, with her ch: 1. Walter, b 16 Jul 1819; 2. Janet, b 10 Sep 1820; 3. James, b 16 Jul 1822; 4. Nancy, b 20 May 1824; 5. Margaret, b 25 Apr 1826; 6. Robert, b 5 Mar 1828; 7. Alexander, b 27 Jan 1830; 8. Elsie, b ca 1831. **DC 29 Jun 1979**.

11944   TURNBULL, Robert, 1816–1902. From Glasgow. Prob rel to William T, qv, and Christina T, qv. To QUE on the *Bowling*, 1842; stld East Williams Twp, Middlesex Co, ONT. m Janet Cowie, qv, and emig with ch: 1. William, 1839–1919; 2. Robert, 1841–1918. **DC 10 Nov 1981**.

11945   TURNBULL, Thomas. From DFS or KKD. To PEI on the *Lovely Nellie*, ex IOM, May 1775; moved to Pictou Co, NS, 1776, and stld McLellans Brook. Farmer, and in 1783 listed as capable of bearing arms. m Jane Mackey, qv, ch: 1. James; 2. Donald; 3. Margaret; 4. Thomas; 5. Benjamen. **ELN; HPC App A, D and E**.

11946   TURNBULL, Thomas, d 1881. From Bowden, ROX. s/o Adam T. and Betty Scott in Hassendean. To Wellington Co, ONT; stld Bosworth. **Ts Bowden**.

11947   TURNBULL, William, 1813-74. From Springbank, Glasgow. Prob rel to Robert T, qv, and Christina T, qv. To QUE on the *Bowling*, 1842; stld East Williams Twp, Middlesex Co, ONT. m Elizabeth Cowan, qv, ch. **DC 10 Oct 1981**.

11948   TURNBULL, William, d 1857. From Hawick, ROX. To Wentworth Co, ONT; stld Waterdown. Manufacturer. **DGH 29 May 1857**.

11949   TURNER, Alexander, b 8 Jun 1831. From Glasgow. s/o John T. To ONT, 1855. Wholesale grocer. m 1865, Margaret J. Strang, ch: 1. Katherine; 2. Agnes; 3. Mary; 4. Lucie; 5. John A; 6. Campbell S. **DC 29 Sep 1964**.

11950   TURNER, Archibald, ca 1777–1 Dec 1817. From Greenock, RFW. To Aylesford, Kings Co, NS. **NSS 1261**.

11951   TURNER, Catherine. From Bowmore, Is Islay, ARL. To Georgian Bay, ONT, <1840. Wife of Alexander McIntyre, qv. **DC 8 Jul 1966**.

11952   TURNER, Daniel, d 30 Aug 1825. To Halifax, NS, and d NY. **VSN No 1386**.

11953   TURNER, Dougald, 1815-99. Poss from Glasgow. To Hamilton, ONT. m Sarah Kenney, 1817-98. Dau Sarah Jane, 1857-73. **Ts Mt Albion**.

11954   TURNER, Duncan, ca 1793–19 Jun 1864. Poss from Glasgow. To Hamilton, ONT. Wife Ann, 1797–1867. **Ts Mt Albion**.

11955   TURNER, Gavin, 1805–11 Dec 1879. From Glasgow. To QUE, 1832; stld Medonte Twp, Simcoe Co, ONT, and had grants of land west of the Penetanguishene Road between 1842 and 1860. Farmer and local politician. m Elizabeth Johnston, qv, ch: 1. Gavin, b 1825; 2. Elizabeth, b 1829; 3. James, b 1831; 4. Gavin, 1835–1907; 5. John, 1837–1918; 6. Margaret, 1839–1909; 7. Thomas, b 1842. **DC 8 Nov 1981**.

11956   TURNER, James, 1801–10 Nov 1849. Poss from Oxton, BEW. To Montreal, QUE, 1833. Veterinary surgeon, in partnership with George Bertram, qv. Dau Mrs Cruikshank. **SGC 485**.

11957   TURNER, James, ca 1821–4 Feb 1855. Prob from Glasgow. To Hamilton, ONT. Stone-cutter. Wife Elizabeth, ca 1830-73. **Ts Mt Albion**.

11958   TURNER, James. From Glasgow. s/o John T. To ONT, 1849. Wholesale grocer. **DC 29 Sep 1964**.

11959   TURNER, John, 20 Feb 1834–26 May 1896. Poss from Glasgow. To Hamilton, ONT. m Mary McNeil, qv. Dau Elizabeth A, d 30 Jul 1928. **Ts Mt Albion**.

11960   TURNER, John, ca 1776–1828. From DFS. s/o James T. To Pictou Co, NS, 1815; stld Barneys River. m Nicolas Couliard, ch: 1. John, 1816-84; 2. William, b 1818; 3. James, b 1820; 4. Ann, b 1822, poss dy; 5. Robert, b 1824; 6. Nicolas, poss dy. **DC 12 Mar 1979**.

11961   TURNER, John. From Glasgow. s/o John T. To ONT, 1844. Wholesale grocer. **DC 29 Sep 1964**.

11962   TURNER, John Visey. Prob from Aberdeen. s/o Major Alexander T, HEICS. To Seymour, Northumberland Co, ONT. **SH**.

11963   TURNER, Marion, ca 1802–ca 1860. From Glasgow. To QUE on the *George Canning*, ex Greenock, 21 Apr 1821; stld Ramsay Twp, Lanark Co, ONT. Wife of James Yuill, jr, qv. **DC 7 Dec 1981**.

11964   TURNER, Peter. Prob from Glasgow. To QUE <1825; stld prob Huntingdon Twp. **SH**.

11965   TURNER, Robert, 1784–1852. From ROX. s/o Thomas T, farm grieve, and Janet Murray. To York Co, ONT, <1850. ch. **DC 21 Mar 1981**.

11966   TURNER, Thomas Andrew, ca 1775–21 Jul 1834. From ABD. To Montreal, QUE, prob <1810. Merchant, and a founder of the Bank of Montreal, 1817, of which he was Vice-Pres, 1817-18. Pres of the Bank of Canada, 1820, absorbed by Bank of Montreal in 1831. May have rep USA interests. Proprietor of the *Montreal Gazette* for some years. **MDB 760**.

11967   TURRIFF, John. Prob rel to William T, qv. To QUE on the *Commerce*, ex Greenock, Jun 1820; stld prob Lanark Co, ONT. **HCL 238**.

11968   TURRIFF, William. Prob rel to John T, qv. To QUE on the *Commerce*, ex Greenock, Jun 1820; stld prob Lanark Co, ONT. **HCL 238**.

11969   TWADDELL, James. Prob from LKS. Rel to Robert T, qv. To Lanark Co, ONT, 1821; stld Lot 12, Con 2, North Sherbrooke Twp, and estab 1836. **HCL 74**.

11970 TWADDELL, Robert. Prob from LKS. Rel to James T, qv. To Lanark Co, ONT, 1821; stld Lot 12, Con 2, North Sherbrooke Twp, and estab 1836. **HCL 74**.

11971 TWEEDIE, George, ca 1793–17 Apr 1869. From DFS. To Fenelon Falls, Victoria Co, ONT. **CAE 20**.

11972 TYLER, Alexander. To Westminster Twp, Middlesex Co, ONT, prob <1840; stld London. **PCM 55**.

11973 TYLER, Annie, ca 1810–16 Nov 1898. Prob from Perth. To Inverness Twp, Megantic Co, QUE, 1855, and d Sedelia, CO. Wife of Rev Hugh McLellan Stalker, qv, m 1 Jan 1833. **AMC 117**.

11974 TYRE, James, 1807–8 May 1876. From Largs, AYR. To Niagara, Lincoln Co, ONT, 1825, but moved to Montreal, QUE. Merchant and in 1837 treas of St Gabriel Street Ch. m Miss Clarke. **SGC 503**.

11975 TYTLER, Joseph. From Kincardine O'Neil, ABD. bro/o William T, qv. To Bon Accord, Nichol Twp, Wellington Co, ONT, 1836. Storekeeper, and postmaster of Elora. **EHE 93**.

11976 TYTLER, William. From Kincardine O'Neil, ABD. bro/o Joseph T, qv. To Bon Accord, Nichol Twp, Wellington Co, ONT, 1835. m Jane Inglis Forbes, qv, ch: 1. William, res Guelph; 2. Alexander, res Rochester, NY; 3. Barbara, schoolteacher. **EHE 93**.

11977 TYTLER, William. From Ferryhill, Aberdeen. s/o John T. To CAN, prob ONT, <1846. **SH**.

U

11978 UMIACHE, John, ca 1732–6 Jul 1821. To NS, and d St Margarets Bay, Halifax Co. **NSS No 2355**.

11979 UMPHERSTON, James, ca 1764–ca 1839. From Glasgow. Prob s/o James U. and Katherine Graham. To Dalhousie Twp, Lanark Co, ONT, ca 1830. Discharged soldier, 2nd Batt, RA, later farmer. Gr land in Lot 25, Con 6. ch: 1. William, qv; 2. Mary, qv. **DC 17 Jul 1979**.

11980 UMPHERSTON, James, 2 Mar 1824–22 Jan 1894. From Cambuslang, LKS. s/o William U, qv, and Marion Park, qv. To Dalhousie Twp, Lanark Co, ONT, 1828. m (i) 31 Aug 1845, Agnes Waddell, ch; (ii) Maria Conroy, further ch. **DC 17 Jul 1979**.

11981 UMPHERSTON, Mary, b ca 1805. From LKS. d/o James U, qv. To Dalhousie Twp, Lanark Co, ONT, ca 1830. m Peter McAnally. **DC 17 Jul 1979**.

11982 UMPHERSTON, William, b ca 1801. From LKS. s/o James U, qv. To Dalhousie Twp, Lanark Co, ONT, 1828; stld Lot 25, Con 8. Discharged soldier, later farmer. m Marion Park, qv. Son James, qv. **DC 17 Jul 1979**.

11983 URE, George P, d 1860. To CAN and became a journalist on the staff of the *North American*. Later with the *Toronto Globe*, and wrote a *Handbook of Toronto*. In 1859 he founded at Montreal, QUE, *The Family Herald*, a weekly. **MDB 764**.

11984 URE, Rev Robert, b 1823. From LKS. To Hamilton, ONT, 1842. Studied at Knox Coll, Toronto, and became min at Streetsville. Trans to Goderich, 1862. DD, Queens Coll, Kingston. **BNA 865**.

11985 URE, Rev Thomas, b ca 1830. From STI. s/o Thomas U, merchant. Matric Univ of Glasgow, 1847, and studied at the Theological Hall of the UP Ch, 1850. To CAN <1855. Clergyman and linguist. **GMA 15297**.

11986 URQUHART, Alexander. From Cawdor, NAI. To Pictou, NS, on the *Dove*, ex Fort William, Jun 1801; stld Centredale. Tenant. m Catherine McKenzie, qv, ch: 1. John, 1814-87; 2. Kenneth, b 1816; 3. William, b 1818; 4. Isabella, 1821-79; 5. Alexander, 1823-46; 6. James, 1826-45; 7. Donald, b 1829. **PLD; PAC 201, 231**.

11987 URQUHART, Alexander, ca 1789–9 Mar 1830. From Ferintosh, ROC. To Nine Mile River, Hants Co, NS, prob <1820. **DC 20 Jan 1981**.

11988 URQUHART, Alexander, b 14 Apr 1816. From Cawdor, NAI. To QUE, 1840; moved to Montreal, 1844. Wholesale grocer. **SGC 483**.

11989 URQUHART, Andrew McNair, 6 Jun 1835–29 Dec 1879. From Hamilton, LKS. s/o John U. of Fairhill, and Jane McNair. Matric Univ of Glasgow, 1850. To ONT, but retr later to SCT. Commission merchant. m 1857, Abigail Young, who survived him. **GMA 15770**.

11990 URQUHART, Christine, b 12 Apr 1812. To CAN <1851. Wife of William Ross, qv. **DC 27 Sep 1974**.

11991 URQUHART, David. From SUT. To Pictou, NS, on the *Hector*, ex Loch Broom, arr 17 Sep 1773; stld Londonderry, Colchester Co. Dau Mrs Davidson, res Pictou. **HPC App C**.

11992 URQUHART, David. From ROC. To QUE on the *Cleopatra*, 14 Jun 1831; stld ONT. Wife Jane Fraser, qv, with him, and s Donald, b 1830. **DC 27 Dec 1979**.

11993 URQUHART, Donald, b ca 1789. To Pictou, NS, 1815. Wife with him. Res Harbourmouth, 1816. Labourer. **INS 39**.

11994 URQUHART, Donald. To 'North America,' early Sep 1819. Wife Catherine McDonald, qv, with him, and s Donald, b OKI, 29 Aug 1819. **Sandwick OPR 17/1**.

11995 URQUHART, George. From ROC. To QUE on the *Cleopatra*, 14 Jun 1831; stld ONT. **DC 27 Dec 1979**.

11996 URQUHART, Rev Hugh, ca 1793–5 Feb 1871. From ROC. Grad MA, Kings Coll, Aberdeen, 1815. To Montreal, QUE, 1822. Teacher, Montreal Academy, and became min of St Johns, Cornwall, Stormont Co, ONT, 1827. App Prof of Ch History at Queens Coll, Kingston, 1846. DD, Kings Coll, 1856. **SGC 287, 310; KCG 108, 274; SNQ ii/2 186; FES vii 654**.

11997 URQUHART, Robert. To QUE on the *Brock*, ex Greenock, 9 Jul 1820; stld Lot 11, Con 1, Dalhousie Twp, Lanark Co, ONT. Farmer. **HCL 67, 238**.

11998 URQUHART, Thomas, 22 May 1816–21 Nov 1881. From Cullicudden, ROC. s/o Thomas U. and Janet Murray. To Mornington Twp, Perth Co, ONT. m Martha Jack, qv, ch: 1. Martha; 2. Jessie; 3. Janet; 4. Alexander; 5. Helen Bertha; 6. Mary; 7. William Thomas. **DC 16 Jul 1974**.

V

11999 VAIR, William, b 29 May 1829. From Melrose, ROX. s/o James V. and Louisa Ireland. To ONT, poss 1855. Dau Catherine Telfer, b Kelso, 1854. **Kelso OPR 793/7**.

12000 VALENTINE, Andrew, b ca 1762. From AYR. To QUE on the *Friendship*, ex Port Glasgow, 30 Mar 1775. Ship carpenter, 'going to build vessels.' **LSF**.

12001 VASS, Ann, 1777–1857. From INV. To Dundee, Huntingdon Twp, QUE, 1830; moved to Ekfrid Twp, Middlesex Co, ONT, 1835. Wife of Alexander McDonald, qv. **PCM 30**.

12002 VAUGHAN, Mary Ann. From Parkhead, Glasgow. To QUE, 1820; and stld Lanark Co, ONT. Wife of David Caldwell, qv. **DC 17 Nov 1973**.

12003 VEITCH, James, d 1832. From Inveresk, MLN. s/o David V, farmer. To CAN, and d Moose Factory, James Bay. **Ts Inveresk**.

12004 VEITCH, John. From ROX. To CAN on the *Sarah Mary Jane*, 1831; stld Dumfries Twp, Waterloo Co, ONT. Plasterer. **HGD 60**.

12005 VEITCH, Marianne, d 16 Aug 1806. From Edinburgh. To QUE <1805. m Rev James Somerville, qv. **SGC 162**.

12006 VEITCH, Rev Samuel, 9 Nov 1668–30 Apr 1732. From Edinburgh. s/o Rev William V, min successively at Morebattle, Peebles and Manor, and Marion Fairley. Sometime officer in 26th Regt, and involved in Darien Scheme, 1698. Went to QUE on a diplomatic mission in 1705, and in 1710 was Adj Gen of an expedition sent to conquer Acadia. Governor of NS, 1710-17. m Margaret, d/o Robert Livingston, NY. **FES ii 265; MDB 770**.

12007 VEITCH, William. From ROX. Prob rel to John V, qv. To CAN on the *Sarah Mary Jane*, 1831; stld Dumfries Twp, Waterloo Co, ONT. **HGD 60**.

12008 VERT, John, 18 Jul 1810–9 Aug 1887. From South Leith, MLN. s/o John V. and Helen Ritchie. To York Co, ONT, <1839; stld Pickering, later Mimico. Teacher. m 29 May 1839, at Toronto, Caroline Scott, 1820-50, ch: 1. Helen, b 1841, teacher, Dundalk; 2. John Ritchie, 1843–1900, teacher; 3. Sarah Elizabeth, dy; 4. Aquilla, dy. m (ii) 1860, Christine Stephen, qv, further ch: 5. Emma; 6. Calvin, 1863–1921; 7. Dorinda, 1865–1947; 8. Luther, b 1867; 9. Caroline, 1869–1948, midwife; 10. Christina, 1872–1922; 11. John Alexander, 1876–1945; 12. Jerome, b 1878. **DC 1 Jan 1982**.

12009 VIRTUE, William, ca 1833–21 Jun 1863. From Lanark. To Montreal, QUE, and d there. **Ts Lanark**.

W

12010 WADDELL, George, ca 1782–30 Aug 1872. From LKS. To QUE on the *Brock*, ex Greenock, 9 Jul 1820; stld Lanark Co, ONT. m Margaret Anderson, qv, ch: 1. Elisabeth, b 1803; 2. Helen, b 1806; 3. Jean, d inf 1806; 4. William, b 1808; 5. Matilda Mary, b 1810, dy; 6. Matilda, b 1812; 7. John, b 1814; 8. Margaret, b 1816; 9. George, b 1819. **HCL 238; DC 27 Jan 1977**.

12011 WADDELL, James. To Pakenham Twp, Lanark

Co, ONT, prob 1820. ch: 1. Margaret; 2. Elizabeth. **HCL 224**.

12012 WADDELL, James. From Leadloch, Auchtermuir, LKS. s/o James W. To CAN <1854. Merchant. **SH**.

12013 WADDELL, James. Cabin passenger on the *Lulan*, ex Glasgow, 17 Aug 1848, bound for Pictou, NS. **DC 12 Jul 1979**.

12014 WADDELL, Rev John, ca 1770–13 Nov 1842. From Shotts, LKS. Matric Univ of Glasgow, 1788, and grad MA, 1793. To Truro, Colchester Co, NS, 1798. Secession min. **GMA 4858; RGG 623**.

12015 WADDELL, Thomas. From Shotts par, LKS. To Clarke Twp, Durham Co, ONT, 1835. m Mary Gardner, qv, ch: 1. Catherine, b 28 Feb 1832; 2. Jane Jack, b 28 May 1834; 3. John Gardner, b 30 Jul 1836. **Shotts OPR 655/4**.

12016 WALDIE, James, b ca 1814. From SEL. To ONT, 1831. Farmer. Wife Isabella, b 1817, Northumberland. **DC 12 Oct 1979**.

12017 WALDIE, William. From Yarrow par, SEL. To ONT, summer 1831. Wife Isabel Crozier, qv, with him. **DC 12 Oct 1979**.

12018 WALES, James Bartlet, 1832-93. From Banff. To Arthur Twp, Wellington Co, ONT, 1855. Brewery worker, seaman and farmer. m Jane or Jessie Saunders, qv, ch: 1. Margaret, 1864-77; 2. William Bartlet, b 1866, d inf; 3. Robert Powrie, 1867–1914; 4. Mary Elizabeth Bartlet, 1869–1938; 5. Arthur, 1875–1959; 6. James, 1878–1944; 7. Jessie, 1881–1967. **DC 31 Dec 1979**.

12019 WALKER, Angus. From Is Mull, ARL. Prob bro/o John W, qv. To Upper West Lake Ainslie, Inverness Co, NS, <1820. m Catherine MacDougall, qv, ch: 1. Effie; 2. Catherine; 3. Anne; 4. Flora; 5. Margaret; 6. Mary; 7. John. **MP 865**.

12020 WALKER, Angus. From Is South Uist, INV. To West Williams Twp, Middlesex Co, ONT, 1849; stld Con 14. **PCM 48**.

12021 WALKER, Ann, ca 1829–18 Mar 1899. From Arbroath, ANS. d/o James W, merchant and shipowner, and Jessie Spink. To Montreal, QUE, and d Hamilton, ONT. m William Leitch, qv. **Ts Arbroath Abbey**.

12022 WALKER, Rev Archibald, ca 1827–1 Mar 1881. From Cardross, DNB. s/o William A, tradesman. Matric Univ of Glasgow, 1843. To Belleville, Hastings Co, ONT. Min of St Andrews Ch there, from 1854. Retr later to SCT, and res at Row, DNB. **GMA 14582; FES iv 297, vii 654**.

12023 WALKER, David. From Mearns Village, RFW. s/o James W. and Margaret Murray. To Toronto, ONT, <1850. **Ts Mearns**.

12024 WALKER, Duncan. Prob bro/o James W, qv. To Metcalfe Twp, Middlesex Co, ONT, 1831. **PCM 26**.

12025 WALKER, George, d 1777. To Chaleur Bay, NB, <1767. Master mariner and pioneer trader in Restigouche Co. Sometime in partnership with Hugh Baillie, qv, and for a period overseer with John Schoolbred. **SR 13**.

12026 WALKER, Rev George, ca 1805–1 Feb 1884. From Greenock, RFW. s/o Andrew W, publican. Matric Univ of Glasgow, 1821. Secession min at Muirkirk, AYR,

1840-42; Johnshaven, KCD, 1842-48. App min of New Glasgow, Pictou Co, NS, by the Mission Board, 1842. **GMA 10732; UPC i 80, ii 346**.

12027 WALKER, George. To Pictou, NS, as cabin passenger on the *Hope*, ex Glasgow, 5 Apr 1848. Wife with him, and ch: 1. Janet; 2. Anne; 3. Andrew; 4. Robert; 5. George; 6. Mary Jane. **DC 12 Jul 1979**.

12028 WALKER, Hugh. From Is South Uist, INV. To East Williams Twp, Middlesex Co, ONT, ca 1849. **PCM 44**.

12029 WALKER, Isabella, 1800–26 Jun 1881. From Mid Sannox, Is Arran, BUT. d/o Neil W, qv. To QUE on the *Caledonia*, ex Greenock, 25 Apr 1829; stld Inverness Twp, Megantic Co. Wife of Angus Brodie, qv, m 1822. **AMC 12; MAC 32**.

12030 WALKER, James, b ca 1775. To Little Bras D'Or dist, Cape Breton Co, NS, <1818. Farmer, m and ch. **CBC 1818**.

12031 WALKER, James. Prob bro/o Neil W, qv. To Metcalfe Twp, Middlesex Co, ONT, 1831. ch: 1. Archibald; 2. John; 3. Duncan; 4. Colin; 5. Dugald; 6. Duncan; 7. Euphemia. **PCM 26**.

12032 WALKER, James. From Johnstone, RFW. s/o James W. To CAN <1855. Cotton-spinner. **SH**.

12033 WALKER, John. From Askernish, Is South Uist, INV. To PEI on the *Jane*, ex Loch nan Uamh, Arisaig, 12 Jul 1790, poss calling at Loch Boisdale. **PLJ**.

12034 WALKER, John, b ca 1792. From Bonhill par, DNB. To Hudson Bay, ca 1813, and prob to Red River. **RRS 13**.

12035 WALKER, John. From South Uist, INV. To Hay River, Inverness Co, NS, <1815. m Miss MacDonald, ch: 1. Donald; 2. Flora; 3. Effie; 4. Alexander; 5. Roderick; 6. Angus; 7. Margaret; 8. Sara. **MP 855**.

12036 WALKER, John, b 1800. To Megantic Co, QUE, ca 1831. Farmer. Wife Mary, b 1800, with him, and s William, b 1823. **DC 11 Feb 1980**.

12037 WALKER, John, ca 1803–3 Aug 1855. From Glengap, Balmaghie par, KKD. To Huron Co, ONT, prob <1840. Farmer. **DGC 25 Sep 1855**.

12038 WALKER, John, b 1832. From ARL. To Middlesex Co, ONT, ca 1846. Land agent at Bothwell, Chatham Co, afterwards manufacturer at London, Westminster Twp. **BNA 1172**.

12039 WALKER, John. From Aberdeen. s/o John W, flaxdresser. To PEI <1852. **SH**.

12040 WALKER, John Dickson, ca 1834–3 Aug 1854. From Dollar, CLK. s/o James W. and Jane Smith. To QUE, and d there. **Ts Dollar**.

12041 WALKER, Margaret, d 13 Mar 1859. From Lockerbie, DFS. To South Dumfries, Brant Co, ONT. wid/o William Dobie, draper. **DGC 12 Apr 1859**.

12042 WALKER, Margaret, ca 1835–15 Jul 1873. From Arbroath, ANS. d/o James W, merchant and shipowner, and Jessie Spink. To Hamilton, ONT. m William Hendrie. **Ts Arbroath**.

12043 WALKER, Margaret, b 1800. From Kilcalmonell,

Kintyre, ARL. To Elderslie Twp, Bruce Co, ONT, <1855. Wife of Alexander Taylor, qv. **DC 6 Jan 1982**.

12044 WALKER, Neil, 1749–1830. Prob from Is Arran, BUT. To QUE on the *Caledonia*, ex Greenock, 25 Apr 1829; stld Inverness, Megantic Co. Dau Isabella, qv. **AMC 12; MAC 33**.

12045 WALKER, Peter. From South Uist, INV. To West Williams Twp, Middlesex Co, ONT, 1849; stld Con 14, so prob rel to Angus W, qv. **PCM 48**.

12046 WALKER, Sarah, 1837–1927. From Is Islay, ARL. To Caledon Twp, Peel Co, ONT, prob <1850. m Angus McLeod, qv. **DC 21 Apr 1980**.

12047 WALKER, William, 1793–18 May 1863. To Montreal, QUE, ca 1815. Fur-trader, and part owner of the *Royal William*, the first steamship to cross the Atlantic. MLA, 1842, and Chancellor of Bishops Coll, Lennoxville. **DC 18 May 1982**.

12048 WALKER, William. From Glasgow. s/o Matthew W, carter, Cowcaddens. To QUE <1826. Son Matthew, carter, Montreal. **SH**.

12049 WALKER, Rev William Montgomery, ca 1803–24 Apr 1880. From Irvine, AYR. s/o Dr Thomas W. and Mary Fleeming. Matric Univ of Glasgow, 1818. To Huntingdon, QUE, 1834, and was min there. Retr to SCT, 1844, and was min at Ochiltree, AYR. m Jane Walker, 1835, ch: 1. Mary Fleeming; 2. Margaret Laird, b 1839; 3. Thomas, b 1841; 4. Jane, b 1844; 5. William Hugh, b 1847; 6. Josiah, b 1851; 7. Frances, b 1854; 8. Patrick, b 1858. **GMA 10164; SH; FES iii 62, vii 654**.

12050 WALLACE, Rev Alexander, d 4 Jul 1870. From Glasgow. To Kingston, ONT, and grad BA, Kings Coll, 1843. Ord min of Huntingdon, QUE. **FES vii 654**.

12051 WALLACE, Alexander, d ca 1862. From Murraygate, Dundee. To Montreal, QUE, <1844. Wood plane-maker. Wife Isabella, and s Alexander with him. **DC 6 Jan 1982**.

12052 WALLACE, Catherine. To Pictou, NS, on the *London*, arr 14 Jul 1848. **DC 15 Jul 1979**.

12053 WALLACE, Rev Finlay. To Inverness Twp, Megantic Co, QUE, 1851. Congregational min, 1851-52. **AMC 118**.

12054 WALLACE, James, 3 Mar 1814–10 Jul 1882. From KCD. To Whitby, Durham Co, ONT, <1846. Merchant, and Mayor of Whitby, 1856. m Elspeth Dow, qv, ch: 1. Mary; 2. Margaret; 3. William, 1846–1937; 4. James; 5. Annie F, 1853–1905. **DC 4 Feb 1982**.

12055 WALLACE, Janet. From DFS. To ONT, 1817. Wife of William Cowan, qv. **DC 4 Dec 1970**.

12056 WALLACE, Robert, 7 Jun 1798–17 Mar 1864. From Mearns, RFW. s/o Hugh W. and Janet Hamilton. To QUE on the *Prompt*, ex Greenock, 4 Jul 1820; stld Dalhousie Twp, Lanark Co, ONT. Farmer. Moved, ca 1832, to Innisfil, Simcoe Co. m Ann Park, qv, ch: 1. Hugh, 1829–1914; 2. Jean, 1831-39; 3. Janet, 1832–1915; 4. James, 1834–1913; 5. Robert, 1836–1915; 6. Andrew, 1839–1929; 7. Margaret, d inf 1841; 8. William, 1842-66; 9. George, 1844–1912; 10. John, 1847-72. **DC 12 Mar 1980**.

12057 WALLACE, William, b ca 1790. From Riccarton, AYR. To York Factory, Hudson Bay, on the *Edward &*

Anne, ex Stornoway, Lewis, arr 24 Sep 1811. Pioneer settler, Red River. **LSS 184; RRS 26; LSC 321**.

12058　WALLACE, William, b ca 1776. From Cowlin, ni but possibly in RFW. To QUE, on the *Atlas*, ex Greenock, 11 Jul 1815; stld Lot 10, Con 7, North Burgess Twp, Lanark Co, ONT. Farmer. Wife Martha Blackwood, qv, with him, and 1 child. **SEC 3; HCL 232**.

12059　WALLACE, William. From Is Arran, BUT. To Inverness, Megantic Co, QUE, <1840. Blacksmith. **AMC 48**.

12060　WALLACE, William Young. To Seaforth, Huron Co, ONT, 1854. Publisher, with Alexander Young, of *The British Canadian* newspaper. **DC 2 Jan 1962**.

12061　WALLS, Lawrence. To CAN <1852. Son Lawrence. **SH**.

12062　WARD, Rev Robert G, 1803-70. From OKI. To Kingston, ONT, <1841, but res in QUE while studying. Went afterwards to Lower Ireland Twp, Megantic Co, QUE. Schoolteacher and Ch of Eng clergyman. m Mary Ann Turriff, Little Metis. Son Lt Col W.J, b Kingston. **AMC 122; MGC 2 Aug 1979**.

12063　WARD, Ann, 1816-97. From Kinnettles, ANS. Prob d/o Robert W. To York Co, ONT, 1842; stld later Euphrasia Twp, Grey Co. Wife of James Paterson, qv. **DC 15 Nov 1979**.

12064　WARDLAW, Marion Antill. From Dalkeith, MLN. d/o John W, banker. To ONT, 1853; stld Toronto. Wife of Dr John Taylor, qv. Retr to SCT, 1863. **UPC i 164, 201**.

12065　WARDLAW, Peter. From LKS. To ONT, 1835. m Janet Littlejohn, qv, and had with other ch: 1. Margaret; 2. James Lamont; 3. Peter; 4. Ellen; 5. Gavin; 6. Alexander. **DC 13 Mar 1980**.

12066　WARDLAW, Walter, b ca 1847. To St Gabriel de Valcartier, QUE, prob <1855. Poss s/o William W, qv. **Census 1861**.

12067　WARDLAW, William, b ca 1812. To St Gabriel de Valcartier, QUE, prob <1855. **Census 1861**.

12068　WARDROPE, James, b ca 1749. From Lochmaben par, DFS. To Georgetown, Kings Co, PEI, on the *Lovely Nellie*, ex Annan, 1774. Mason. **ELN**.

12069　WARDROPE, Rev Thomas, ca 1819–17 Jun 1914. From Ladykirk, BEW. To ONT, 1834. Educ Queens Coll, Kingston, and Univ of Edinburgh. Schoolteacher, but ord and became min of Knox Ch, Ottawa. Trans to Chalmers Ch, Guelph. Moderator of the Presb Ch in CAN, 1892. **MDB 784**.

12070　WARNOCK, John. To Lanark Co, ONT, 1821; stld North Sherbrooke Twp, Lot 7, Con 1. **HCL 74**.

12071　WATSON, Agnes, b ca 1832. From Kettins, ANS. d/o Alexander W, qv, and Mary Anderson, qv. To Ancaster Twp, Wentworth Co, ONT, 1844; later to Pilkington Twp, Wellington Co. m Francis Frank, journalist. **EHE 41**.

12072　WATSON, Alexander, 1803-81. From Kettins, ANS. To Ancaster Twp, Wentworth Co, ONT, 1844; later to Pilkington Twp, Wellington Co. m Mary Anderson, qv, ch: 1. George, qv; 2. Mary, qv; 3. Janet; 4. Agnes, qv; 5. Alexander, jr, qv; 6. John, qv; 7. James, qv; 8. Marjery, qv; 9. Ann, qv. **EHE 41**.

12073　WATSON, Alexander, jr, b ca 1834. From Kettins, ANS. s/o Alexander W, qv, and Mary Anderson, qv. To Ancaster Twp, Wentworth Co, ONT, 1844; later to Pilkington Twp, Wellington Co. m (i) Johanna Marigold, and went to Elora, Nichol Twp; (ii) Ann Weadick. **EHE 41**.

12074　WATSON, Angus. To East Williams Twp, Middlesex Co, ONT, 1843. **PCM 44**.

12075　WATSON, Ann. From Kettins, ANS. d/o Alexander W, qv, and Mary Anderson, qv. To Ancaster Twp, Wentworth Co, ONT, 1844; later to Pilkington Twp, Wellington Co. m William Wilson, res Elora, Nichol Twp. **EHE 41**.

12076　WATSON, Archibald, 1 Sep 1817–2 Dec 1873. From Glasgow. s/o Archibald W. and Margaret Ure. To Waterloo Co, ONT, ca 1842; stld Ayr. m Janet Gibb, qv, ch: 1. Archibald, b 16 Jan 1838, dy; 2. William, 1839-47; 3. James, 1841–1915. **DC 31 Jul 1979**.

12077　WATSON, Dickson, ca 1791–29 Jul 1849. From Urr par, KKD. s/o Charles W. in Auchengibbert. To NS, and d Pugwash, Cumberland Co. **DGH 13 Sep 1849**.

12078　WATSON, George, d 1846. From Hawick, ROX. s/o William W, hozier, Wiltonbank, and wife Margaret. To Hamilton, ONT. **THS 1938/29**.

12079　WATSON, George, 1826-95. From Kettins, ANS. s/o Alexander W, qv, and Margaret Anderson, qv. To Ancaster Twp, Wentworth Co, ONT, 1844; later to Pilkington Twp, Wellington Co. m Maria Carder, and afterwards stld Elora, Nichol Twp. **EHE 41**.

12080　WATSON, James. To Pictou Co, NS, <8 Nov 1775. **HPC App B**.

12081　WATSON, James. From LKS. To QUE on the *Prompt*, ex Greenock, 4 Jul 1820; stld Dalhousie Twp, Lanark Co, ONT. Watsons Corners named after him. **HCL 68, 238**.

12082　WATSON, Rev James, ca 1804–12 Dec 1881. From Glasgow. s/o John W, stone-cutter. Matric Univ of Glasgow, 1817. Relief Ch min at Waterbeck, DFS, 1830-39. To Economy, Colchester Co, NS, ca 1843; trans to West River, Pictou Co, 1852; and in 1859 to New Annan, Colchester Co. **GMA 9935; UPC i 56**.

12083　WATSON, James. From Kettins, ANS. s/o Alexander W, qv, and Mary Anderson, qv. To Ancaster Twp, Wentworth Co, ONT, 1844; later to Pilkington Twp, Wellington Co. m Pauline Hayes, and went to MAN. **EHE 41**.

12084　WATSON, James, d Apr 1845. Poss from DFS. s/o James W, lawyer. To Toronto, ONT. **DGH 29 May 1845**.

12085　WATSON, Jean, 3 May 1771–8 Aug 1852. Prob from Musselburgh, MLN. d/o James W. and Jean Dickson. m (i) — Thompson, ch: 1. Thomas, b 8 Nov 1799; 2. William, b 28 Jan 1801. m (ii) Alexander Patullo, qv, and emig to Peel Co, ONT, 1820. **DC 20 Jul 1979**.

12086　WATSON, Joanna, 1815–4 Aug 1854. From Edinburgh. d/o Robert W. m at London, ENG, 7 Jun 1841, James Bain, qv, and went to Toronto, ONT. **DC 27 Mar 1979**.

12087   WATSON, Rev John, d 6 May 1820. s/o Rev William W, Burgher min at East Campbell St, Glasgow. Matric Univ of Glasgow, 1803, and studied theology. To Montreal, QUE, and d Point St Charles.   **UPC i 221, ii 39, 191; GMA 3317, 6578**.

12088   WATSON, John, ca 1793–1 Jul 1820. From Aberdeen. To Halifax, NS, and d at Truro, Colchester Co. Millwright.   **NSS No 2059**.

12089   WATSON, John, b 1820. From Glasgow. s/o Archibald W. and Margaret Ure. To Waterloo Co, ONT, 1848. Founded Ayr Agricultural Works. m (i) Marie Urie, ch; (ii) Elizabeth Ann Dolman, ch; (iii) Harriet McKellar, no ch. ch: 1. Alfred E; 2-3. Elizabeth Dolman and Mary Urie, twins.   **DC 31 Jul 1979**.

12090   WATSON, John. From Kettins, ANS. s/o Alexander W, qv, and Mary Anderson, qv. To Ancaster Twp, Wentworth Co, ONT, 1844; later to Pilkington Twp, Wellington Co. m (i) Mary Hayes; (ii) Anna Blyth.   **EHE 41**.

12091   WATSON, Marion. From Lesmahagow, LKS. To ONT, 1833. Wife of Robert Lang, qv.   **DC 6 May 1978**.

12092   WATSON, Marjery. From Kettins, ANS. d/o Alexander W, qv, and Mary Anderson, qv. To Ancaster Twp, Wentworth Co, ONT, 1844; later to Pilkington Twp, Wellington Co. m James Buchan, res Elora, Nichol Twp.   **EHE 41**.

12093   WATSON, Mary. From Kettins, ANS. d/o Alexander W, qv, and Mary Anderson, qv. To Ancaster Twp, Wentworth Co, ONT, 1844, later to Pilkington Twp, Wellington Co. m William Veitch.   **EHE 41**.

12094   WATSON, Rev Peter, d 1899. From INV. To Kingston, ONT, and grad BA, Queens Coll, 1854. Ord min of Williamstown, Glengarry Co, 1856. Declined to enter Union of 1875.   **FES vii 654**.

12095   WATSON, Robert. To Pictou Co, NS, <8 Nov 1775. Son Robert.   **HPC App B**.

12096   WATSON, Thomas. From Irvine, AYR. To QUE, 1844; stld Laprairie, later Napierville. Moved to Ottawa, ONT, 1881. Dau Mrs George Jeffrey, Petite Côte.   **SGC 636**.

12097   WATT, Agnes, ca 1808–28 Mar 1885. From Kilwinning, AYR. Prob rel to John Watt, qv. To Nichol Twp, Wellington Co, ONT, ca 1842. Wife of John Skeoch, qv.   **DC 8 Nov 1981**.

12098   WATT, Alexander. From LKS. To QUE, summer 1820, and stld Dalhousie Twp, Lanark Co, ONT. Farmer.   **HCL 69**.

12099   WATT, Alexander, b ca 1810. From Auchreddie, New Deer, ABD. bro/o Christian W, qv. To QUE on the *Fania*, ex Glasgow, 30 Jun 1834; stld Bon Accord, Nichol Twp, Wellington Co, ONT. Cattle-breeder. m Barbara Argo, qv, ch: 1. Margaret; 2. Barbara; 3. James, d 1873; 4. Isabella; 5. Elspeth; 6. William Barrie, d 1903; 7. Annie.   **EHE 88**.

12100   WATT, Ann, b 1791. From Old Deer, ABD. To QUE, ex Greenock, summer 1815; stld Beech Ridge, Chateauguay Co. Wife of Alexander Laing, qv.   **SEC 4; DC 27 May 1980**.

12101   WATT, Christian, 1811-89. From Auchreddie, New Deer, ABD. sis/o Alexander W, qv. To QUE on the *Fania*, ex Glasgow, 30 Jun 1834; stld Bon Accord, Nichol Twp, Wellington Co. ONT. Wife of John Keith, qv.   **EHE 85**.

12102   WATT, Elspet, ca 1801–18 Feb 1894. From Auchreddie, New Deer, ABD. sis/o Alexander W, qv, and Christian W, qv. To Bon Accord, Nichol Twp, Wellington Co, ONT, prob 1834. m 1835, George Barron, qv.   **EHE 92**.

12103   WATT, George, b ca 1781. From St Andrews par, Glasgow. To QUE, ex Greenock, summer 1821; stld prob Lanark Co, ONT. Weaver and farmer. Wife Catherine Gilmour, qv, with him, and ch: 1. George, aged 14; 2. John, aged 12; 3. Janet, aged 10; 4. James, aged 7; 5. Catharine, aged 3; 6. Michael, aged 1 ½.   **RPE 62**.

12104   WATT, Helen. From Lochearnhead, PER. To Montreal, QUE, on the *Niagara*, ex Greenock, arr 28 May 1825; stld McNab Twp, Renfrew Co, ONT. Wife of Duncan Campbell, qv.   **EMT 18, 22**.

12105   WATT, James, b ca 1830. From Glasgow. s/o John and Ann W. To Ingersoll Twp, Oxford Co, ONT. m Isabella King, qv.   **DC 18 Jan 1980**.

12106   WATT, Janet, 2 Sep 1830–17 Mar 1894. From Blackadder, BEW. d/o Alexander W. and Janet Alexander. To Northumberland Co, ONT, 1854. m 23 Nov 1854, Thomas Murray, qv.   **DC 20 Nov 1960**.

12107   WATT, John, ca 1809–4 Jan 1879. From Kilwinning, AYR. Prob rel to Agnes W, qv. To Galt Twp, Waterloo Co, ONT, ca 1834; moved to Fergus Village, Wellington Co, 1836. Schoolteacher.   **DC 8 Nov 1981**.

12108   WATT, John, b 10 Sep 1827. From BEW. To Hamilton, ONT, ca 1854. Wife Margaret.   **DC 20 Nov 1960**.

12109   WATT, Mary, b ca 1809. To St Gabriel de Valcartier, QUE, prob <1855.   **Census 1861**.

12110   WATT, Robert, ca 1817–7 Mar 1858. From Glasgow. s/o James W, architect. Matric Univ of Glasgow, 1832. To Paris, Brant Co, ONT.   **GMA 13004**.

12111   WATT, Robert, 31 Dec 1820–7 Sep 1897. Prob from AYR. To Hamilton, ONT. Farmer at Saltfleet. By first wife Janet had ch: 1. William, 1845–1908. m (ii) Isabella Innes, qv, further ch: 2. Alexander, 1854-61; 3. Janet, 1856-68.   **Ts Mt Albion**.

12112   WATTERS, Henry, 1806–31 Oct 1882. From Thurso, CAI. To Melbourne, Richmond Co, QUE, prob <1850. m Helen Manson, qv.   **MGC 15 Jul 1980**.

12113   WATTS, Hugh, 1746–1815. To Port Hood, Inverness Co, NS, ca 1784. Discharged officer, RN; gr land and was an officer of Militia. m Sarah or Sally Heather, ch: 1. Isabella; 2. Ada; 3. Sally, d unm; 4. William, b 1776.   **DC 23 Feb 1980**.

12114   WAUGH, Alexander, 1766–1804. From Brownmoor, Annan, DFS. s/o Wellwood W, qv, and Helen Henderson, qv. To Georgetown, Kings Co, PEI, on the *Lovely Nellie*, ex Annan, 1774; moved to Pictou Co, NS, later to Colchester Co, and stld Tatamagouche. Farmer and magistrate. m Hannah Wilson, 1781–1865, who m (ii) William Wilson. ch: 1. William; 2. Wellwood; 3. Eleanor.   **HT 35**.

12115   WAUGH, Catherine, 5 Apr 1771–10 Jun 1853. From Brownmoor, Annan, DFS. d/o Wellwood W, qv, and Helen Henderson, qv. To Georgetown, Kings Co, PEI, on the *Lovely Nellie*, ex Annan, 1774; moved to Pictou Co, later to Colchester Co, NS. m Alexander MacNab, qv. **HT 35; DC 29 Oct 1980**.

12116   WAUGH, Thomas, b 1763. From Brownmoor, Annan, DFS. s/o Wellwood W, qv, and Helen Henderson, qv. To Georgetown, Kings Co, PEI, on the *Lovely Nellie*, ex Annan, 1774; moved to Pictou Co, later to Colchester Co, NS, and stld Tatamagouche. m Mary, d/o Capt Brown, US Navy, ch: 1. Wellwood; 2. Donald; 3. Murray; 4. George. **ELN; HT 34**.

12117   WAUGH, Wellwood, 1741–1824. From Brownmoor, Annan, DFS. s/o Alexander W, dec, and Catherine Colvin, qv. To Georgetown, Kings Co, PEI, on the *Lovely Nellie*, ex Annan, 1774; moved to Pictou Co, later to Colchester Co, NS. Joiner, estate factor, farmer and magistrate. m Helen Henderson, qv, ch: 1. Thomas, qv; 2. Alexander, qv; 3. William, qv; 4. Wellwood, jr; 5. Catherine, qv; 6. Mary. **ELN; HPC App D, 288; HT 32**.

12118   WAUGH, William, 1768–1857. From Brownmoor, Annan, DFS. s/o Wellwood W, qv, and Helen Henderson, qv. To Georgetown, Kings Co, PEI, on the *Lovely Nellie*, ex Annan, 1774; moved to Pictou Co, later to Colchester Co, NS. Farmer and officer of Militia. m Elizabeth Rood, and had with other ch: 1. Samuel, 1794–1894; 2. William; 3. Wellwood; 4. John; 5. Soloman; 6. Alexander. **ELN; HT 35, 52**.

12119   WEAL, Andrew, 1776–2 Jul 1846. From Langholm, DFS, where he was bailie to the Duke of Buccleuch. To ONT. **DGH 15 Oct 1846**.

12120   WEATHERHEAD, James, ca 1803–5 Feb 1867. From Duns, BEW. To Nine Mile River, Hants Co, NS, prob <1850. Wife Isabella, d 26 Jun 1872. **DC 20 Jan 1981**.

12121   WEBSTER, Alexander. From ABD. To Nichol Twp, Wellington Co, ONT, 1835, but retr later to SCT. **EHE 91**.

12122   WEBSTER, Charles, ca 1817–9 Sep 1863. Poss from Blairgowrie, PER. To Vaughan Twp, York Co, ONT, ca 1846. m Jane Gilray, qv, ch: 1. John, qv; 2. James, qv; 3. Arthur, 1846-47; 4. Margaret, 1848-49; 5. Christina, b 1850; 6. Catherine, 1853–1940; 7. Jemima, d inf 1855; 8. Philmore, b 1858; 9. Margaret Ann, 1860–1931. **DC 11 Jan 1980**.

12123   WEBSTER, David, 1808–28 Jul 1897. From Kilmarnock, AYR. To Elgin Co, ONT, 1842; stld Fingal Twp. Moved later to Mosa Twp, Middlesex Co. Farmer. Retr to Newbury, 1864. m (i) Agnes Muir, qv, ch: 1. William, qv; 2. David, went to Salina, CA; 3. Jean; 4. Janette, res Lexington, MI; 5. Agnes, 1842–1918; 6. Robert, 1843–1919; 7. Elizabeth, res Detroit, MI; 8. James, 1847–1931; 9. Isabelle, 1850–1910; 10. John, farmer nr Brandon, MAN; 11. Minnie, res nr Brandon, MAN. David m (ii) Sarah Picken, 1821–1905. **DC 8 Nov 1981**.

12124   WEBSTER, James, ca 1809-69. From Liff, ANS. s/o James W. of Balruddery, and Agnes Hunter. To ONT, and d prob Wellington Co. **Ts Liff**.

12125   WEBSTER, James, 4 Dec 1845–22 May 1913. From PER. s/o Charles W, qv, and Jane Gilray, qv. To Vaughan Twp, York Co, ONT, ca 1846. m Anne Turkington. **DC 11 Jan 1980**.

12126   WEBSTER, John, 20 Jan 1809–18 Feb 1895. From ABD. To Hamilton, ONT. **Ts Mt Albion**.

12127   WEBSTER, John, 1 Feb 1843–20 Dec 1895. From PER. s/o Charles W, qv, and Jane Gilray, qv. To Vaughan Twp, York Co, ONT, ca 1846. m his wife Ida at Toronto. **DC 11 Jan 1980**.

12128   WEBSTER, Margaret. From ABD. Prob sis/o Alexander W, qv. To Bon Accord, Nichol Twp, Wellington Co, ONT, 1836. Wife of Alexander Rennie, qv. **EHE 93**.

12129   WEBSTER, Thomas, ca 1813–2 Oct 1857. From Liff, ANS. s/o James W. of Balruddery, and Agnes Hunter. To Arthur Twp, Wellington Co, ONT. **Ts Liff**.

12130   WEBSTER, William, 1834–1910. From Kilmarnock, AYR. s/o David W, qv, and Agnes Muir, qv. To Elgin Co, ONT, 1842; stld later Mosa Twp, Middlesex Co. Farmer. m Janet Ferguson, 1843–1908. **DC 8 Nov 1981**.

12131   WEDDERBURN, Alexander, ca 1796–19 Jun 1843. From Aberdeen. To St John, prob <1820. Emigration officer and author. Son William, b 1834, lawyer and journalist. **BNA 699; MDB 787**.

12132   WEDDERBURN, William. From ABD. To Nichol Twp, Wellington Co, ONT, 1835. m Miss Webster. **EHE 91**.

12133   WEIR, Adam, 1788–27 Jun 1873. From ROX. To Glenelg Twp, Grey Co, ONT, ca 1850. Farmer, Lot 51-52, Con 3. m Jane Hyndmarsh, qv, ch: 1. Mary, b 1831; 2. Margaret, b 1833; 3. John, b 1835; 4. Adam, b 1840. **DC 28 Dec 1981**.

12134   WEIR, Agnes. To Pictou, NS, on the *Hope*, ex Glasgow, 5 Apr 1848, with ch: 1. Mary; 2. Agnes. **DC 12 Jul 1979**.

12135   WEIR, Andrew. Poss from Edinburgh. To Ottawa, ONT, <1850. m Rebecca Bisland. Son John, 1850–1936. **DC 1 Oct 1983**.

12136   WEIR, Rev George, d 1891. From Aberlour, BAN. Grad MA, Kings Coll, Aberdeen, 1848. To Frontenac Co, ONT, 1853, and became Prof of Classics at Queens Univ, Kingston. LLD, Aberdeen, 1881. **KCG 300; SNQ ii/2 186**.

12137   WEIR, James, 1817-97. From LKS, poss Lesmahagow. To Scarborough, York Co, ONT, 1833. Farmer and landowner. **DC 29 Mar 1981**.

12138   WEIR, Janet, b ca 1774. From Lanark par, LKS. Prob d/o Archibald W. and Janet Aitken. To Otonabee Twp, Peterborough Co, ONT, ca 1819. Wife of John Neilson, qv. **DC 8 Aug 1979**.

12139   WEIR, John, ca 1808–6 Dec 1834. From Troon, AYR. s/o William W. To Montreal, QUE; later to Hamilton, ONT. **DGC 11 Feb 1835**.

12140   WEIR, John Blackwood. From Grahamston, Falkirk, STI. s/o John W. in Larbert par, and Helen Blackwood. To CAN <1853. **SH; Ts Larbert**.

12141 WEIR, William, 28 Oct 1823–25 Mar 1905. From Brechin, ANS. To Montreal, QUE, 1842. Exchange broker there; afterwards publisher at Toronto, ONT, of the *Canadian Merchants Magazine*. **MDB 789**.

12142 WELLS, Elspeth, ca 1832–12 Jun 1858. From Dalry, KKD. To Dundas, Wentworth Co, ONT. m James Cowan. **DGH 9 Jul 1858**.

12143 WELLS, Rev John, b ca 1832. From DFS. s/o Robert W, husbandman. Matric Univ of Glasgow, 1852, and grad MA, 1856. Asst min at Campbeltown, ARL, <1861, when adm min of New Richmond, Restigouche Co, NB. **GMA 16211; RGG 638; FES vii 612**.

12144 WELSH, George, 19 Jul 1811–6 Mar 1856. From Pollokshaws, RFW. s/o William W, weaver, and Elizabeth Sanderson. To Huron Twp, Bruce Co, ONT, <1854. **Ts Pollokshaws; DC 28 Jan 1981**.

12145 WELSH, John, ca 1800–14 Apr 1864. From Pollokshaws, RFW. s/o William W, weaver, and Elizabeth Sanderson. To Huron Twp, Bruce Co, ONT, <1854. **Ts Pollokshaws; DC 28 Jan 1981**.

12146 WELSH, Matthew, ca 1816–10 Sep 1888. From Pollokshaws, RFW. s/o William W, weaver, and Elizabeth Sanderson. To Huron Twp, Bruce Co, ONT, <1854. m Catherine Wright. Son Thomas. **Ts Pollokshaws; DC 28 Jan 1981**.

12147 WEMYSS, Kate. From Kirkcaldy, FIF. d/o John W, solicitor, and wife Esther. To CAN, prob >1860, when m her cous, Robert W, qv. **Ts Kirkcaldy; DC 21 Mar 1981**.

12148 WEMYSS, Robert, b 16 Aug 1824. Prob from Kirkcaldy, FIF. s/o John W. and Margaret Morison. To CAN, poss <1850. Shipowner. m Kate W, qv. **DC 21 Mar 1981**.

12149 WESLEY, Andrew. To Pictou, NS, on the *Hector*, ex Glasgow, arr 17 Sep 1773. **HPC App C**.

12150 WEST, John. From Riccarton Farm, Linlithgow, WLN. To Montreal, QUE, ca 1850. Moved later to OR, where he built a sawmill on the Columbia River, which he named West Port. **DC 21 Mar 1981**.

12151 WEST, Thomas, b 1817. To ONT. m Margaret McGhaughy, ch: 1. John; 2. Thomas; 3. Charles; 4. Margaret; 5. James; 6. George; 7. Isabella; 8. Samuel. **DC 16 Jul 1974**.

12152 WEST, William. Served in 82nd Regt, and was gr land in Pictou Co, NS, 1784. **HPC App F**.

12153 WHALE, Agnes. From Dundee, ANS. To QUE, ex Greenock, summer 1815; stld Bathurst Twp, Lanark Co, ONT. Wife of Thomas Barrie. **SEC 2**.

12154 WHALEN, David, b ca 1821. To St Gabriel de Valcartier, QUE, prob <1855. Poss rel to Ellen Whalen, qv. **Census 1861**.

12155 WHALEN, Ellen, b ca 1795. To St Gabriel de Valcartier, QUE, prob <1855. Poss wife of Andrew Kerr, qv. **Census 1861**.

12156 WHAN, Thomas. From Stranraer, WIG. s/o James W, weaver. To CAN <1850. **SH**.

WHITE. See also WHYTE.

12157 WHITE, Alison. Prob from Gordon, BEW. To Medonte Twp, Simcoe Co, ONT, 1833. Wife of George Ingram, qv. **DC 5 Aug 1979**.

12158 WHITE, Christian. From Blackburn, WLN. To QUE, ex Greenock, summer 1815; stld Bathurst Twp, Lanark Co, ONT. Wife of Alexander Kidd, qv. **SEC 8**.

12159 WHITE, Donald, b ca 1773. To St Andrew dist, Cape Breton Co, NS, arr prob Apr 1817. Weaver. **CBC 1818**.

12160 WHITE, George, 1720–1807. From Jedburgh, ROX. To Kennetcook, Hants Co, NS, <1790. Served in 84th Regt. **NSN 6/6**.

12161 WHITE, Joanna Olive. From Kilmarnock, AYR. d/o Alexander W. To Vancouver, BC, 1851. Wife of Robert Dunsmuir, qv, m 1847. **MDB 208**.

12162 WHITE, John. From ARL. To West Williams Twp, Middlesex Co, ONT, ca 1850. ch: 1. Hugh; 2. John; 3. Mrs Donald McLachlan. **PCM 47**.

12163 WHITE, Robert, b 6 Mar 1806. From Linlithgow, WLN. s/o Robert W, baker, and Christian Sim. To CAN, prob ONT, ca 1840. **SG xvi/2 39; DC 2 Jun 1968**.

12164 WHITEFORD, William. From Lesmahagow, LKS. To Montreal, QUE, <1852. **SH**.

12165 WHITEHEAD, Jane. From Mellerstain, BEW. To QUE, ex Greenock, summer 1815; stld poss Lanark Co, ONT. Wife of John Cockburn, qv. **SEC 2**.

12166 WHITEHEAD, William, 1767–1842. From Bannockburn, STI. To NB, 1820; stld later PEI. m Mary Hosea, qv, ch: 1. Mary, 1792–1886; 2. Jane, b 1793; 3. John, 1794–1862; 4. Ann, 1795–1875; 5. Margaret, 1797–1886; 6. William, 1800-80; 7. Andrew, 1804-85; 8. James, 1809-99; 9. Christina, 1812-90. **DC 25 Nov 1981**.

12167 WHITELAW, Andrew. From Merton, BEW. Poss bro/o William W. To Guelph Twp, Wellington Co, ONT, 1833. m Isabella Gladstone, qv, ch: 1. William, b 1814; 2. Mrs George Aitchison; 3. George, b 1819; 4. Andrew; 5. Robert; 6. Ellen. **SG xxiv/2 53**.

12168 WHITELAW, John, 22 Feb 1774–25 Jan 1853. From Bothwell, LKS. s/o James W, tenant in Ridgehead, and Elison Jenkins. Studied medicine at Edinburgh, and came to QUE, where he practised <1807, when he moved to ONT. Headmaster successively of the grammar schools of Kingston, Frontenac Co, and Niagara, Lincoln Co. **Bothwell OPR 625/1; MDB 795**.

12169 WHITELAW, Thomas. To QUE on the *Brock*, ex Greenock, 9 Jul 1820; stld prob Lanark Co, ONT. **HCL 238**.

12170 WHITLAW, John, d 22 Sep 1867. From Gifford, ELN. To Montreal, QUE, 1816. Carpenter, and an alderman of the city, 1852-53. **SGC 637**.

12171 WHITTON, John. Rel to William W, qv. To Lanark Co, ONT, 1821; stld Darling Twp, Lot 1, Con 10. **HCL 76**.

12172 WHITTON, Robert. To QUE on the *David of London*, ex Greenock, 19 May 1821; stld poss Darling Twp, Lanark Co, ONT. **HCL 239**.

12173 WHITTON, William. Rel to John W, qv. To Lanark Co, ONT, 1821; stld Lot 1, Con 10, Darling Twp. **HCL 76**.

WHYTE. See also WHITE.

12174 WHYTE, Elizabeth, b ca 1783. From Kilfinan par, ARL. To ONT, 1842; stld prob Caledon Twp, Peel Co. wid/o Archibald McLeish, by whom she had ch: 1. Jean, b 1815; 2. Alexander, 1817-93; 3. John, 1820–1907; 4. Donald, b 1822; 5. Peter, b 1823; 6. Betsy, b 1816; 7. Catherine, b 1828; 8. Archibald, b 1831; 9. Cathcart, b 1833; 10. Hector. Most of them emig with her. **DC 26 Sep 1981**.

12175 WHYTE, Isabella, b 12 Mar 1799–28 Feb 1869. From South Knapdale, ARL. d/o Neil W. To Dalhousie Lake, Lanark Co, ONT, ca 1835. Wife of John Brown, qv. **DC 13 Feb 1978**.

12176 WHYTE, Isabella, b ca 1831. From Pitsligo, ABD. d/o William W. and Margaret Blackie. To Perth Co, ONT, 1854. Wife of Alexander Mackintosh, qv. **DC 17 Nov 1982**.

12177 WHYTE, Jean. To Lanark Co, ONT, 1822; stld Middleville, Lanark Twp. Wife of James Campbell, qv. **HCL 65**.

12178 WHYTE, John, b 4 Jan 1838. From Dunfermline, FIF. s/o John W. and Elizabeth Simpson. To CAN, ca 1854. Sometime at Cariboo, Pictou Co, NS, but stld Leeds Twp, Megantic Co, QUE. General merchant; MLA, 1884. m 22 Jun 1859, Harriet, d/o Duncan Donaldson, Leeds, ch: 1. Mary Ann, b 1860; 2. John D, b 1862; 3. Andrew, b 1865; 4. Peter D, b 1862; 5. George, b 1871; 6. Effie, b 1880. **MGC 2 Aug 1979**.

12179 WHYTE, John, ca 1821–13 Oct 1907. From Ardlui, DNB. To Hibbert Twp, Perth Co, ONT, 1850; stld Lot 17, Con 12. Farmer and stone-cutter. m Margaret Cook Miller, qv, ch: 1. John, jr, qv; 2. Margaret Cook, 1848–1926; 3. Walter, b 1850; 4. David, b 1853; 5. Janet, b 1855; 6. Helen, 1860-97; 7. Elizabeth, b 1864; 8. Robert, b 1867. **DC 25 Nov 1981**.

12180 WHYTE, John, jr, b 1846. From Ardlui, DNB. s/o John W, qv. and Margaret Cook Miller, qv. To Perth Co, ONT, 1850. m (i) 1879, Lucinda Amelia Rogers, who d 1886; (ii) 1888, Sarah Jane Howe, who d 1950, ch. **DC 10 Jul 1980**.

12181 WHYTE, Rev John, ca 1821–9 Dec 1893. From Girvan, AYR. s/o David W. Matric Univ of Glasgow, 1842. To Brockville, Leeds Co, ONT, 1851. Min there until 1856, afterwards at Arthur, Wellington Co. Retr to SCT, 1872, and adm min of South Queensferry. m (i) 1845, Joanna Finlay, who d 1866, ch: 1. Mary Ruth; 2. John McClymont; 3. Col Albert; 4. Joanna, 1857-62. m (ii) 1878, Robina, d/o John Cameron, farmer, Ardchapple, wid/o Capt Harkness, sometime of Greenock. **GMA 14510; FES i 227, vii 654**.

12182 WHYTE, Joseph, ca 1780–8 Jul 1851. From Banff. Surgeon in RN, afterwards medical practitioner in Banff. To Huntingdon, QUE, 1835. **DC 24 Jul 1978**.

12183 WHYTE, Mary, b ca 1800. Prob from Cambuslang, LKS. To Beckwith Twp, Lanark Co, ONT, ca 1819. m Alexander Snedden, qv. **DC 11 Mar 1979**.

12184 WHYTE, Nancy or Agnes, b ca 1805. Prob from Cambuslang, LKS. To Beckwith Twp, Lanark Co, ONT, ca 1819. m David Snedden, qv. **DC 11 Mar 1979**.

12185 WHYTE, Patrick. From Dundee, ANS. bro/o Alexander W, manufacturer. To CAN <1850. Banker. **SH**.

12186 WHYTE, Robert. From Stirling. To New Westminster, BC, ca 1863. m Jean Connal. Son Lt Col John C, b 1861, warden of BC Penitentiary. **DC 19 Jul 1983**.

12187 WHYTE, Sir William, 15 Sep 1843–14 Apr 1914. From Dunfermline, FIF. s/o William W. and Christina Methven. To ONT, 1863; stld Toronto. Superintendent of ONT division of Canadian Pacific Railway, and became a Vice-pres of the company. KB, 1911. m 1872, Jane, d/o Adam Scott, ch. **DC 11 May 1980**.

12188 WILKIE, Ann, b ca 1738. From Sanquhar, DFS. To Georgetown, Kings Co, PEI, on the *Lovely Nellie*, ex Carsethorn, May 1775. Wife of Joseph Clark, qv. **ELN**.

12189 WILKIE, Rev Daniel, 1777–10 May 1851. From Bothwell, LKS. s/o James W, farmer. Matric Univ of Glasgow, 1794, and grad MA, 1803. Licentiate of Ch of Scotland, and became a teacher in QUE, 1804. Conducted the *Star* newspaper, and became rector of the High School of Quebec, 1843. LLD, Glasgow, 1837. Son Daniel. **BNA 904; RGG 645; GMA 5516; FES vii 654; MDB 798**.

12190 WILKINSON, David. Prob from Glasgow. To Toronto, ONT, ca 1854. Wife Flora McPhail, qv, with him. Son Neil, b 1854. **DC 8 Mar 1974**.

12191 WILLIAMS, Martha. Prob from FIF. To Charlottetown, PEI, ca 1848. Wife of Rev James Mac(k)intosh, qv, m 18 Mar 1835. **FES v 84**.

12192 WILLIAMS, Mary. From INV. To Gaspereaux Lake, Kings Co, NS, 1803. Moved later to Antigonish Co. Wife of Ewen MacDonald, qv. **HCA 205**.

12193 WILLIAMS, Samuel May, 1774–1 Aug 1827. To Charlottetown, PEI, on the *Humphreys*, ex Tobermory, 14 Jul 1806. Farmer and merchant. m Maria, b 1777, prob sis/o John Allen, qv, ch: 1. Samuel May; 2. Joshua; 3. John May; 4. Henry; 5. Thomas R; 6. Matilda; 7. Alicia. **PLH; DC 3 Sep 1982**.

12194 WILLIAMSON, Catherine. From KKD. sis/o David W, qv. To Tatamagouche, Colchester Co, NS, 1835. Wife of John Lockerbie, qv. **HT 71**.

12195 WILLIAMSON, Catherine, 1820–13 Jul 1886. Prob from Sanquhar, DFS. To Melbourne, Richmond Co, QUE, prob <1840. m Thomas Kerr. **MGC 15 Jul 1980**.

12196 WILLIAMSON, David. From KKD. bro/o Catherine W, qv. To Tatamagouche, Colchester Co, NS, ca 1840. Farmer. m Mary Carruthers. Son Alexander, d Buenos Aires, South America. **HT 71**.

12197 WILLIAMSON, George, 1833–1911. From Sanquhar, DFS. To Montreal, QUE, 1848; stld Melbourne, Richmond Co. Afterwards he purchased Clark Mills, Salmon River. d Kingsbury Village. Sometime Mayor of Melbourne and Gore, and bur St Andrews Cemetery, Melbourne. **MGC 2 Aug 1979 and 15 Jul 1980**.

12198 WILLIAMSON, James, b ca 1800. From Sanquhar, DFS. bro/o Robert W, qv. To Eldon Twp, Victoria Co, ONT, 1831; stld Lot 21, Con 3. m Jessie Galloway, qv, ch: 1. Robert; 2. George; 3. William; 4. Janet; 5. Bella; 6. Catherine. **EC 223**.

12199 WILLIAMSON, James. Prob from ABD. Gr-s/o James W. in St Fergus. To CAN <1838. Mason. **SH**.

12200 WILLIAMSON, Rev James, 19 Oct 1806–26 Sep 1895. From Edinburgh. s/o James W. Grad MA, Univ of Edinburgh, 1827. Sometime tutor to French Royal Family at Holyroodhouse. To Kilsyth, Derby Twp, Grey Co, ONT, <1840. Became Prof of Mathematics and Natural Philosophy at Queens Coll, Kingston, 1842, and was ord 1845. Later Prof of Astronomy. LLD, Glasgow, 1855. m Margaret Macdonald, see ADDENDA. **CEG 222; FES vii 655; MDB 801**.

12201 WILLIAMSON, Margaret, ca 1801–1 Feb 1867. From Sanquhar, DFS. d/o William W, wool-merchant, and Marjorie Cringan. To ONT, 1831; stld prob Hullett, Huron Co. m William Sloan. **DGC 12 Mar 1837**.

12202 WILLIAMSON, Marion, d 1836. From Gorbals, Glasgow. To Brockville, Leeds Co, ONT, 1835. Wife of Rev Thomas Woodrow, qv. **Gorbals OPR 644-2/5**.

12203 WILLIAMSON, Rev Robert, 1798–1870. From ROC. s/o John W, farmer, and Catherine Ross. Grad MA, Kings Coll, Aberdeen, 1818. Ord min of Croick, ROC, 1828. Trans to St Andrews Ch, Pictou, NS, 1840. Retr to SCT, 1843, and adm min of Knockbain, ROC. m 26 May 1834, Charlotte Priscilla Lacon, who d without ch, 1876. **KCG 276; FES vii 16, 52**.

12204 WILLIAMSON, Robert, b 16 Feb 1796. From Sanquhar, DFS. bro/o James W, qv. To Eldon Twp, Victoria Co, ONT, 1831; stld Lot 21, Con 3. m Isabella Cringen, qv, ch: 1. Ann, b 1821; 2. William, b 1823; 3. Marion, b 1825; 4. James. **EC 223**.

12205 WILLIAMSON, Robert. From Sanquhar, DFS. To Melbourne, Richmond Co, QUE, prob <1840. Wife Marion, 1794–1888. **MGC 15 Jul 1980**.

12206 WILLIS, Rev Michael, 1799–19 Aug 1879. From Greenock, RFW. s/o Rev William W, Burgher min at Burntshields, Paisley, and — Jamieson. Matric Univ of Glasgow, 1813. Min at Renfield St, Glasgow, 1821-47. DD, Glasgow, 1839. To ONT, 1847, to become Prof of Divinity and Principal of Knox Coll. He retr to SCT, 1871, and res Aberlour, BAN. m Agnes McHaffie. **BNA 823; RGG 647; GMA 8886; UPC ii 169, 513, 669; FES iii 431, vii 655**.

12207 WILSON, Sir Adam, 22 Sep 1814–28 Dec 1891. From Edinburgh. s/o Andrew W, flesher-burgess, and Jane Chalmers. To Halton Co, ONT, 1830. Jurist; Solicitor-General, 1862-64; Mayor of Toronto, 1859; KB, 1887. m d/o Thomas Dalton, Toronto. **BNA 596; Edinburgh OPR 658-1/42; MDB 805**.

12208 WILSON, Agnes, d 15 Oct 1841. From DFS. To Bedeque, Prince Co, PEI. Wife of Thomas Cairns, qv. **DGH 25 Nov 1841**.

12209 WILSON, Agnes, d 1863. From Hamilton, LKS. To Dalhousie Twp, Lanark Co, ONT, prob 1820. wid/o John Donald. Son John, qv. **DC 11 Nov 1981**.

12210 WILSON, Agnes, 23 Mar 1819–11 Apr 1898. From New Cumnock, AYR. To Richmond Co, QUE, 1847; stld Windsor Mills. Wife of Gilbert Farquhar, qv. **DC 11 Nov 1981**.

12211 WILSON, Agnes Rankin, ca 1829–3 Jun 1913. Prob from Edinburgh. To Algoma Co, ONT, but d Edinburgh. Wife of George Hart Downie, qv. **Ts Grange, Edinburgh**.

12212 WILSON, Andrew, 1822–24 Oct 1879. From MLN. To Montreal, QUE, 1834. Emp in a newspaper office and became a shareholder of the Montreal *Herald*. m 1852, Esther Matthews. **SGC 490**.

12213 WILSON, Andrew, ca 1784–26 Feb 1866. From DFS. To Melbourne, Sherbrooke Co, QUE. Wife Janet Hogg, qv, with him. Both bur Maple Grove. **MGC 2 Aug 1979**.

12214 WILSON, Archibald. Served in 82nd Regt and was gr land in Pictou Co, NS, 1784. **HPC App F**.

12215 WILSON, Bethia, ca 1805-59. From AYR. To Guelph Twp, Wellington Co, ONT, 1828. Wife of George Burt, qv. **DC 11 Dec 1981**.

12216 WILSON, Colin, b ca 1811. Poss from LKS. To Darling Twp, Lanark Co, ONT, ca 1843. Shoemaker. m Mary Colquhoun, qv, ch: 1. John, b ca 1842; 2. Mary, b ca 1844; 3. James, b ca 1846; 4. Daniel, b ca 1849; 5. Hugh. **DC 5 Feb 1981**.

12217 WILSON, Sir Daniel, 5 Jan 1816–6 Aug 1892. From Edinburgh. s/o Archibald W, vintner, and Janet Aitken. Educ Univ of Edinburgh, and became secretary and a Fellow of the Society of Antiquaries of SCT. App Prof of History and English Literature in University Coll, Toronto, 1853. Pres of Coll, 1880, and on re-organisation, 1887, Pres of Univ of Toronto. Pres of Royal Society of Canada, 1885; KB, 1888, and LLD. An eminent archaeological writer and educational reformer. m 1840, Margaret, d/o Hugh Mackay, ch. **MOT, 1887/1053; IBD 551; CBD 976; MDB 806**.

12218 WILSON, David, b ca 1780. From Beith, AYR. To QUE, summer 1815; stld prob Lanark Co, ONT. Farmer. Wife Janet Stevenson, qv, with him, and 6 ch. **SEC 9**.

12219 WILSON, Ebenezer. From Paisley, RFW. To QUE on the *Buchan*, 1821; stld nr Dalhousie Lake, Lanark Co. Farmer, miller, innkeeper and magistrate. Son John, qv. **HCL 75**.

12220 WILSON, Elizabeth, 1801-87. From DFS. To York Co, ONT, <1843; stld Markham. Wife of John Calvert, qv. **DC 17 Apr 1978**.

12221 WILSON, Francis. Prob from Edinburgh. To Halifax, NS, <1817; stld later Tatamagouche, Colchester Co. Farmer and innkeeper. ch: 1. James, res Pugwash, Cumberland Co; 2. John, stld Waughs River; 3. William, stld Waughs River; 4. Alexander. **HT 48**.

12222 WILSON, Gage. Prob from LKS. To NB <1845. m William Scott. **SH**.

12223 WILSON, Hugh McKenzie, b 1840. From ABD. s/o Stephen W, qv, and Ann Melvin, qv. To ONT, 1843; stld Burford Twp, Brant Co. Educ Hamilton, and became a lawyer. m Mary Selina Nelles. **DC 23 Sep 1980**.

12224 WILSON, Isaac. To Lanark Co, ONT, 1815; stld Lot 15, Con 1, Bathurst Twp. **HCL 16**.

12225 WILSON, Isabella, 1801-85. From Pollokshaws, RFW. To QUE on the *Anchor*, summer 1847; stld Woodbridge, York Co, ONT. Wife of Robert Graham, qv. **DC 22 Nov 1981**.

12226 WILSON, Isabella, 14 Dec 1802–18 Aug 1872. From Falkirk, STI. d/o John W. and Marion Miller. To Scarborough, York Co, ONT, <1835; later to Salt Lake

City, UT. Wife of Archibald Rogers, qv, m 25 Mar 1825. **SCN**.

12227   WILSON, Isobella. From Edinburgh. To QUE, ex Greenock, summer 1815; stld prob Lanark Co, ONT. Wife of Thomas Jeffreys, qv. **SEC 6**.

12228   WILSON, James. To QUE on the *David of London*, ex Greenock, 19 May 1821; stld Perth, Drummond Twp, Lanark Co, ONT. Physician and mineralogist. **HCL 58, 239**.

12229   WILSON, James, b 1811. From Balivanich, Is Benbecula, INV. Prob s/o Ranald 'Ruadh' W. and Flora MacDonald. To Pictou, NS, on the *Lulan*, ex Glasgow, 17 Aug 1848. m Marion MacLellan, qv, ch: 1. Mary, b 1839; 2. Catherine, b 1842; 3. John, b 1844; 4. Ranald, b 1847, prob dy. **DC 12 Jul 1979**.

12230   WILSON, Rev James, d 30 Aug 1905. From Tyrie, ABD. Grad MA, Kings Coll, Aberdeen, 1849. To Musquodoboit, Halifax Co, NS, ca 1856, as missionary. Retr to SCT and adm to Maxwelltown Chapel, DFS, 1859. To Lanark, Lanark Co, ONT, 1862, and adm to St Andrews Ch. **KCG 302; FES vii 655**.

12231   WILSON, Jane, 1816–1904. From Douglas, LKS. To PEI, 1844. Wife of William Brown, qv. **DC 2 Dec 1981**.

12232   WILSON, Janet. Prob from DFS. To Markham, York Co, ONT, <1843. Wife of John Calvert, qv. **LDW 17 Apr 1978**.

12233   WILSON, Janet, b ca 1795. To St Gabriel de Valcartier, QUE, prob <1855. **Census 1861**.

12234   WILSON, Janet, 1820–79. From ROX. To QUE, and stld Melbourne, Sherbrooke Co. Wife of William Stewart, qv. **MGC 2 Aug 1979**.

12235   WILSON, Jean, 25 Oct 1805–10 Apr 1884. From Galston, AYR. d/o Hugh W. and Helen Hood. To ONT, ca 1855, and d Toronto. wid/o James Ewing, d 1854, East Burnside. ch with her: 1. Robert D, 1828-93, sawyer, d Buffalo, NY; 2. Hugh Wilson, b 15 Feb 1830, miller; 3. Helen, qv; 4. Margaret Ann, qv; 5. William Brydone, b 1842; 6. Isabella, qv; 7. Jane Hood, qv. **Ts Galston; DC 12 Aug 1980**.

12236   WILSON, John, 18 Apr 1738–22 Aug 1766. From Coldstream, BEW. s/o Rev William W, par min, and Agnes Chatto. To CAN, prob NB, <1765. m Ann, d/o William Oake. **FES ii 41**.

12237   WILSON, John, b ca 1753. From Boreland, Colvend, KKD. Prob bro/o William W, qv. To Georgetown, Kings Co, PEI, on the *Lovely Nellie*, ex Annan, 1774. Labourer. **ELN**.

12238   WILSON, John, 1809–3 Jun 1869. From Paisley, RFW. s/o Ebenezer W, qv. To QUE on the *Buchan*, 1821; stld Lanark Co, later Middlesex Co, ONT. Lawyer, and became a Judge of the Court of Common Pleas for Upper Canada. m Elizabeth Hughes. **HCL 75, 137; MDB 806**.

12239   WILSON, John, 1833-99. From Hawick, ROX. s/o Walter W, baker in Howgate, and Isabel Richardson. To CAN, and d Nanaimo, BC. **THS 1935/59**.

12240   WILSON, John. From BEW. To ONT <1851; stld poss Oshawa, Durham Co. **SH**.

12241   WILSON, Malcolm. From Is South Uist, INV. To Middlesex Co, ONT, ca 1849; stld prob East Williams Twp. m Catherine Currie, qv. **WLC**.

12242   WILSON, Margaret, 28 Aug 1811–17 May 1894. From Kilmarnock, AYR. d/o James W. and Margaret McSkimming. To Amherstburg, Essex Co, ONT, 1843; later to Armada, MI. Wife of John Paton, qv, m 8 Apr 1834. **DC 30 Sep 1960**.

12243   WILSON, Margaret, d 1871. From BEW. To Guelph, Wellington Co, ONT, <1855. m John Carter, qv. **DC 18 Apr 1962**.

12244   WILSON, Maria. From Campbellfield, Glasgow. d/o William Wilson, merchant. To Ramsay Twp, Lanark Co, ONT, after m at Glasgow, 17 Aug 1837, to Rev John Fairbairn, qv. **Glasgow OPR 644/42**.

12245   WILSON, Marion, ca 1787–4 Dec 1861. Prob from Ayr. To QUE, and stld Melbourne, Sherbrooke Co. Wife of John Smith, qv. **MGC 2 Aug 1979**.

12246   WILSON, Mary, b ca 1725. From Corsock, Colvend, KKD. To Georgetown, Kings Co, PEI, on the *Lovely Nellie*, ex Annan, 1774. **ELN**.

12247   WILSON, Mary, 1821–1903. From DFS. To Nichol Twp, Wellington Co, ONT, <1850, when m Thomas Dow, qv. **DC 4 Oct 1979**.

12248   WILSON, Rev Matthew, 1 Jan 1806–13 Dec 1884. From Cadder par, LKS. Seventh s/o Alexander W, farmer. Matric Univ of Glasgow, 1826. Studied theology and became missionary in Glasgow. Ord by Presb of Glasgow and app by Colonial Committee to serve at Sydney Mines, Cape Breton Co, NS, 1842. Resigned 1883. **GMA 11832; FES vii 608**.

12249   WILSON, Robert. To Pictou, NS, on the *Hope*, ex Glasgow, 5 Apr 1848. **DC 12 Jul 1979**.

12250   WILSON, Rev Robert, 13 May 1805–5 May 1894. From Glasgow. s/o Thomas W, architect. Glasgow High School Dux, 1816-19, and matric Univ of Glasgow, 1819. Grad MA, 1826. To St John, NB, and min of St Andrews Ch there, 1832-42. Retr to SCT, and was FC min at Ronaldsay, OKI, 1846-94. m Margaret Elizabeth, d/o John Wilmot, NB. **RGG 653; GMA 10418; AFC i 359**.

12251   WILSON, Rev Robert, 18 Feb 1833–24 Jun 1912. From Fort George, INV. To PEI <1855. Educ Prince of Wales Coll, Charlottetown. Ord to min of Methodist Ch and served various pastorates in the Maritimes. Author: pseud 'Mark Mapleton.' **MDB 807**.

12252   WILSON, Robert. From Bridge of Don, Aberdeen. To ONT, 1854; stld poss Wentworth Co. Farmer. m Jean Anderson, qv. **DC 23 Nov 1981**.

12253   WILSON, Sara. Poss from KKD. To Waughs River, Colchester Co, NS, 1841. Wife of David Murdock, qv. **HT 81**.

12254   WILSON, Stephen. From BAN. To Burford Twp, Brant Co, ONT, 1843. Wife Ann Melvin, qv, with him, and s Hugh McKenzie, qv. **DC 23 Sep 1980**.

12255   WILSON, Thomas, ca 1828–25 Jun 1886. From Ruthwell, DFS. s/o Matthew W, farmer in Cockpool. To ONT. **Ts Ruthwell**.

12256 WILSON, Rev Thomas Clark, 22 Dec 1806–3 Aug 1877. From Lesmahagow, LKS. s/o Rev John W, par min, and Agnes Clark. To Perth, Drummond Twp, Lanark Co, ONT, after educ at Univ of Glasgow. Min of St Andrews congregation ca 1830-45. Retr to SCT and became min of New Ardrossan, AYR. Trans to Dunkeld, 1846. m (i) 1832, Anne Macdonald, d 1852, ch: 1. John Norman, b 1833, went to NZ; 2. Mary, b 1835; 3. David Clark, 1837-53; 4. Henry, 1843-88; 5. Colin, 1847-80. m (ii) 1855, Agnes, d 1889, d/o John Johnston and Agnes Urquhart, further ch: 6. Thomas Clark, 1856–1911; 7. Agnes Clark, 1858-71; 8. Mary, b 1860; 9. Jessie Elizabeth, b 1861; 10. Georgina Murray, b 1864; 11. Jane Macfarlane, b 1866; 12. Dr John Johnston, Anstruther, b 1867; 13. Archibald, b 1870; 14. Hugh, 1877–1906. **GMA 10570; FES iii 317, iv 156, vii 655; HCL 202**.

12257 WILSON, William, b ca 1751. From Boreland, Colvend, KKD. Prob bro/o John W, qv. To Georgetown, Kings Co, PEI, on the *Lovely Nellie*, ex Annan, 1774. Labourer. **ELN**.

12258 WILSON, William, 1800-70. From LKS. To Nelson Twp, Halton Co, ONT, ca 1826. m Janet Carr, qv, ch: 1. Andrew, b 1823; 2. Samuel, b 1825; 3. George, b 1827; 4. Janet; 5. Agnes, 1832–1902; 6. Mary Ann; 7. Isabel, b 1838. **DC 21 Mar 1981**.

12259 WILSON, William, ca 1782–10 Sep 1857. From Glenaggan, Parton, KKD. To ONT; poss Wellington Co. m Sarah Shaw, 1787–1857. **DGH 16 Oct 1857**.

12260 WILSON, Rev William Macknight, 1831–6 Jan 1914. From Ayr. s/o Henry W, shoemaker, and Elizabeth Macknight. Educ Glasgow, and became min of St Andrews Ch, Campbelltown, Restigouche Co, NB. Trans to Chatham, Northumberland Co, 1868. Retr to SCT and was min of North Ch, Aberdeen, 1879–1904. m 1860, Mary Ann Russell Robertson, who d 2 Feb 1923. **FES vi 16, vii 612**.

12261 WINCHESTER, Janet. From Rothes, MOR. To Flat River, PEI, on the *John & Elizabeth*, arr 30 Jul 1775; stld prob Kings Co. Wife of William Simpson, qv. **DC 28 May 1980**.

12262 WINGFIELD, George Gordon, b 30 May 1859, Burnbank, Hamilton, LKS. To QUE on the *St George*, ex Glasgow, Apr 1863, with his grandmother, Isabella Wingfield or McKenzie, qv. Stld ONT. **DC 20 Sep 1982**.

WINGFIELD, Mrs James. See McKENZIE, Isabella.

12263 WINTON, Alexander. Poss from AYR. To River Louison, Restigouche Co, NB, Jun 1831. **CUC 21**.

12264 WISHART, Alexander. Rel to Christopher W, qv. To Miramichi, Northumberland Co, NB, 1775. **DC 4 Dec 1978**.

12265 WISHART, Alexander, ca 1792–10 Dec 1823. From Edinburgh. s/o Capt Alexander W. and Mary McGregor. To York Co, ONT. **Ts Preston St, Edinburgh**.

12266 WISHART, Christopher. To Miramichi, Northumberland Co, NB, 1775. Rel to Alexander W. m (i) Janet Bell, qv; (ii) Helen Milne, 1808–19 Sep 1843. **DC 4 Dec 1978**.

12267 WISHART, Philadelphia Anne, 13 Feb 1814–29 Oct 1890. From Edinburgh. d/o Patrick W. of Foxhall, WS, and Margaret Robertson. To Montreal, QUE. m Dr W. Mackinder. **HWS 369; Ts Greyfriars, Edinburgh**.

12268 WISHART, Rev William Thomas, 9 Jun 1809–21 Jan 1853. From Edinburgh. s/o Patrick W, of Foxhall, WS, and Margaret Robertson. To Shelburne, Shelburne Co, NS, <1842, when he became min of St Stephens Ch, St John, NB. Author of theological works. **HWS 369; FES vii 612; MDB 612; Ts Greyfriars, Edinburgh**.

12269 WOOD, Alexander. From Stonehaven, KCD. To Toronto, ONT, 1836. Merchant, and Vice-President of St Andrews Society of Toronto. Retr to SCT, and had property in ABD. **DC 20 Apr 1970**.

12270 WOOD, Andrew, ca 1809–21 Feb 1881. From PER. To Windsor, Hants Co, NS. Bur Maplewood. m Fanny Barnes, d 1887, from BRK, ENG. **DC 4 Dec 1978**.

12271 WOOD, Ann, b ca 1826. To St Gabriel de Valcartier, QUE, prob <1855. **Census 1861**.

12272 WOOD, Francis, ca 1793–26 Nov 1854. From Jardineton, KKD. To Mill Creek, Galt, Wellington Co, ONT. Farmer. **DGC 2 Jan 1855**.

12273 WOOD, George. From FIF. Gr-s/o Andrew W, weaver in Drumeldrie Muir, nr Largo. To St John, NB, <1849. Ships carpenter. **SH**.

12274 WOOD, Grace. Prob from DFS. To Brockville, Leeds Co, ONT, 1833. m Thomas Tennant, qv. **DC 30 Jan 1980**.

12275 WOOD, Isabel, b 20 Dec 1793, Saltcoats, AYR. d/o Robert W, mariner, and Isabel Robinson. To Restigouche Co, NB, Jun 1831. Wife of William Archibald. **Ardrossan OPR 576/1; DC 1 Oct 1979**.

12276 WOOD, Robert. To QUE on the *Baltic Merchant*, ex Greenock, 12 Jul 1815; stld Lot 7, Con 3, Drummond Twp, Lanark Co, ONT. **HCL 232**.

12277 WOOD, William Wadell, b 1812. From Earlston, BEW. s/o Robert W, farm steward, Legerwood par, and Janet Deans. To Hamilton, ONT, 1852; stld Onondaga Twp, Brant Co. Sawyer. m Mary Gill, qv, ch: 1. William; 2. Janet; 3. Elizabeth Vallance; 4. George. **DC 23 Sep 1980**.

12278 WOODBURN, Elizabeth, 3 Jul 1825–18 May 1895. From Galston, AYR. d/o William W. and Christian Ferguson. To Amherstburg, Essex Co, ONT, 1852. Moved to Lapeer Co, MI. Wife of David Paton, qv. **DC 30 Sep 1960**.

12279 WOODROW, Agnes. Prob from RFW. To Ingersoll, Oxford Co, ONT, <1850. Wife of Hope McNiven, qv. **DC 5 Sep 1969**.

12280 WOODROW, Rev Thomas, 15 Mar 1793–27 Apr 1877. From Paisley, RFW. s/o John W, craftsman, and Janet Morton. Matric Univ of Glasgow, 1815, and grad MA, 1819. Min at Carlisle, 1820-35. To Brockville, Leeds Co, ONT, 1835; moved in 1836 to Chillicothe, OH. m (i) Marion Williamson, qv, ch: 1. Robert, b 1820; 2. John, b 1822; 3. Thomas; 4. William, 5. Janet or Jeannie, b 1826, mother of Pres Woodrow Wilson, 1856–1934; 6. James, 1828–1907, res Columbus, SC; 7. George; 8. Marion. m (ii) 1843, Harriet L. Renick. **GMA 9445; RGG 658; LDW 12 Apr 1973**.

12281   WRIGHT, Agnes, 1820-95. From SEL. To ONT <1839 and stld <1850 at Hullett Twp, Huron Co. Wife of George Cunningham, qv. **DC 20 Jun 1979**.

12282   WRIGHT, Alexander, b ca 1812. To St Gabriel de Valcartier, QUE, prob <1855. **Census 1861**.

12283   WRIGHT, Daniel, ca 1788–31 Aug 1851. From PER. To Halton Co, ONT, prob <1840; stld Esquesing Twp, and bur Limehouse. **EPE 76**.

12284   WRIGHT, Isobel. To QUE on the *Eliza*, ex Greenock, 3 Aug 1815; stld Bathurst Twp, Lanark Co, ONT. Wife of John Christie, qv. **SEC 1**.

12285   WRIGHT, James, b 1796. From Is Arran, BUT. To Campbellton, Restigouche Co, NB, 1829. **MAC 27**.

12286   WRIGHT, James. From Stranraer, WIG. s/o Archibald W. To Richibucto, Kent Co, NB. Dau Mrs McBeath, d there, 24 Sep 1864. **DGH 21 Oct 1864**.

12287   WRIGHT, Janet. From PER. To QUE, prob 1818; stld Chatham Twp, Argenteuil Co. Wife of John Gibbon, qv. **DC 30 Jun 1971**.

12288   WRIGHT, Janet Grey, 1832–1906. From Glasgow. To Toronto, ONT, ca 1855. Wife of William Galbraith, qv. **GSO 19**.

12289   WYLD, James Charles, 11 Jul 1813–11 Jul 1892. From Leith, MLN. s/o James W. of Gilston, merchant-burgess of Edinburgh. Educ Edinburgh Academy, Edinburgh Univ. and the Military Academy. To ONT, 1834; stld Toronto. m 1844, Dorothea, d/o Henry Moston. **EAR 5**.

12290   WYLIE, Rev Alexander L, 1818–30 Jan 1892. From Montrose, ANS. s/o John W, farmer. Matric Univ of Glasgow, 1844. To Londonderry, Colchester Co, NS, 1852, and was UP Ch min at Great Village for nearly 40 years. **UPC ii 156n; GMA 14718**.

12291   WYLIE, Ann, ca 1819–6 Jan 1892. From PER. To QUE, and d Russelltown Flats, Beauharnois. Wife of Josiah Black, qv. **Ts Russelltown Flats**.

12292   WYLIE, David. To Lanark Co, ONT, 1821; stld Lot 11, Con 3, North Sherbrooke Twp, and estab 1836. **HCL 74**.

12293   WYLIE, David, 23 May 1811–21 Dec 1891. From Paisley, RFW. s/o William W. in Johnstone, and Mary Orr. To Montreal, QUE, 1845; moved to Leeds Co, ONT, and became editor and proprietor of the *Brockville Recorder*. Chairman of school board at Brockville for many years. Author and poet. **BNA 1141; SGC 527; MDB 816**.

12294   WYLIE, Janet, 1833–26 Jan 1870. From Kilmarnock, AYR. To St Thérèse-de-Blainville, Terrebonne Co, QUE, <1855. m Robert Lochhead, qv. **DC 13 May 1980**.

12295   WYLIE, John, 1791–1877. From Gretna par, DFS. s/o Thomas and Jane W. To Durham Co, ONT, ca 1851. Cotton weaver. m Margaret Philips, 1790–1850, ch: 1. Thomas, 1817–1902; 2. Jane, 1820-95; 3. Mary, 1825-51, bur Dornock, DFS; 4. Elizabeth, 1826-55; 5. Janet, 1827-85; 6. James, 1832–1911. **DC 29 Dec 1982**.

12296   WYLIE, Margaret. From DFS. To ONT <1855. Wife of John Irving, qv. **SDG 243**.

12297   WYLIE, William, 9 Sep 1824–7 Aug 1853. From Carluke, LKS. s/o Rev John W, par min, and Caroline Ann Dick. To QUE, and drowned in the St Lawrence River. **FES iii 286**.

12298   WYLLIE, James, 1818–23 May 1893. From AYR. To NS on the *Isobel*, of Glasgow, 1838. Moved to Germantown, PA, 1839, and <1863 to Sierra Co, CA. Miner. m 30 Jun 1845, Margaret Galloway or McGregor, ch: 1. Janetta Russel, b 4 May 1846; 2. William James, b 12 Apr 1848; 3. John Edward, b 10 Jan 1852; 4. Michael Galloway, b 2 Oct 1853; 5. Abraham Lincoln, b 1 Sep 1863; 6. Helen Thompson, b 21 Sep 1865; 7. Anne Elizabeth, b 5 Feb 1869. **DC 13 Apr 1978**.

Y

12299   YEOMAN, Jennet. Prob from ABD. To QUE, but stld Sydney, Cape Breton Co, NS, <1853. Wife of John Forbes, qv. **HNS iii 243**.

12300   YORSTON, William. From Kirkwall, OKI. To Miramichi, NB, 1843. Engaged in shipbuilding. m Isabelle Henderson, qv. Son Frederick P, d Douglastown, 27 Mar 1870. **MGC 2 Aug 1979**.

12301   YOUNIE, Margaret, b 1737. From Dundurcas, MOR. To Flat River, PEI, on the *John & Elizabeth*, arr 30 Jul 1775; stld Queens Co. Wife of Peter McGregor, qv. **DC 27 Jul 1980**.

12302   YOUNG, Alexander, 23 Nov 1783–31 May 1856. From Abernethy, PER. s/o Andrew Y, farmer, and Jean Reid. To CAN <1825; later to SC. Jeweller. m Miss Gardiner, from Auchtermuchty, ch. **DC 21 Mar 1981**.

12303   YOUNG, Alexander, 1819-61. From Edinburgh. To Seaforth, Huron Co, ONT, but d Simcoe, Norfolk Co. Co-partner in stone-cutting business. m ca 1843, Margaret Sinclair Hill, qv, ch: 1. Alexander, jr, qv; 2. Margaret, d unm; 3. Robert, jeweller, d unm; 4. William, dy. **DC 2 Jan 1962**.

12304   YOUNG, Alexander, jr, 1844–1930. From Edinburgh. s/o Alexander Y, qv, and Margaret Sinclair Hill, qv. To Seaforth Twp, Huron Co, ONT, 1854. Writer and editor. m 1868, Hannah McMichael, d/o David Smith, and Jane More Backus, ch: 1. Anne Hill; 2. David Alexander; 3. Charles Robery; 4. Jean Gillon. **DC 2 Jan 1962**.

12305   YOUNG, Andrew. To QUE, prob 1854; stld Stanstead. Associated with Col. Kilburn in utilizing water power on Tomofobia River, at Rock Is. Son Robert. **MGC 2 Aug 1979**.

12306   YOUNG, Andrew Houston, ca 1800–8 Aug 1859. From Irvine, AYR. s/o William Y, solicitor, and Marion Paterson. To QUE <1845. Merchant. m Janet Greenshields, qv, ch: 1. William, b 1846, d inf; 2. William Andrew, 1850-57; 3. Eliza, 1845-68; 4. Marion, 1850–1926, d Prestwick, AYR; 5. Mary Isabella Grace, 1856–1917, d Kilmarnock, AYR. **Ts Irving**.

12307   YOUNG, Charles, b 1812. From Falkirk, STI. s/o John 'Agricola' Y, qv, and Agnes Renny, qv. To Pictou, NS, prob 1815. Educ Dalhousie Coll, Halifax, and became lawyer. Moved to Charlottetown, PEI. QC, LLD. **BNA 713**.

12308   YOUNG, David. To QUE on the *David of London*,

ex Greenock, 19 May 1821; stld prob Lanark Co, ONT.
HCL 239.

12309 YOUNG, George, ca 1800–19 Sep 1869. From
ROX. To North Monaghan Twp, Peterborough Co, ONT,
<1851. m Mary Brunton, qv, ch: 1. William, qv;
2. John, 1825–1913; 3. George, b 1830; 4. Janet,
b 1833; 5. Margaret, b 1836; 6. Elizabeth, b 1838;
7. Andrew, 1840–1900; 8. Mary, b 1843; 9. Isabel,
b 1845. **DC 25 Mar 1981**.

12310 YOUNG, George Renny, 4 Jul 1802–30 Jun
1853. From Falkirk, STI. s/o John 'Agricola' Y, qv, and
Agnes Renny, qv. To Pictou, NS, 1815. Lawyer, MLA,
and founder of the *Nova Scotian*, which he edited
1824-28. **MLA 374; MDB 819**.

12311 YOUNG, Helen, 1850–5 Apr 1941. From Galston,
AYR. d/o Robert Y, qv, and Grizel Gillies, qv. To Keppel
Twp, Grey Co, ONT, poss 1854. m 17 May 1876, Andrew
Brown, 1852–1926. **DC 11 Dec 1979**.

12312 YOUNG, Helen, b 12 Jan 1843. From Knockbain
par, ROC. d/o William Y, qv, and Isabella Ross, qv. To
QUE on the *John McKenzie*, ex Glasgow, 25 Jun 1857;
stld Scott Twp, York Co; later Minto Twp, Wellington Co,
ONT. m 1865, David Halliday, who d 1866. She lived 'to
an advanced age' at Sarnia. **RFS 207**.

12313 YOUNG, Isabel. From ROX. To Haldimand Co,
ONT, ca 1856; moved to Huron Twp, Bruce Co, 1867.
Wife of James Steel, qv. **DC 25 Dec 1981**.

12314 YOUNG, James, 1 Mar 1793–10 Jun 1841. From
Dundee, ANS. Slater, and served in 3rd Regt of Foot
Guards, 1812-31, reaching the rank of Sgt-Maj. Trans to
the West Suffolk Militia, 1831, and was commissioned.
Gr land in ONT, and arr Toronto, 7 Aug 1837. m at
London, ENG, 1819, and by his wife Elizabeth Jemima,
ch: 1. James, 1820–1906; 2. Sophia, b 1822, d inf;
3. Elizabeth Jemima, b 1824, d inf; 4. John William,
1826-91; 5. Alfred Joseph Brittnor, b 1830, d inf;
6. Helen Jane, 1825–1914; 7. Elizabeth Euston, 1837–
1917; 8. Hugh Thomas, 1840-63. **DC 9 Nov 1981**.

12315 YOUNG, James. From ABD. To Nichol Twp,
Wellington Co, ONT, 1836, with ch: 1. Jean; 2. Ann;
3. Kirstie; 4. George. **EHE 94**.

12316 YOUNG, James, 10 Apr 1791–6 May 1868. From
Glasgow. s/o William Y, from AYR, and Margaret Paton.
To QUE, ex Greenock, 24 Jun 1847; stld Ancaster Twp,
Wentworth Co, ONT. m Jean Miller, qv, ch: 1. William
Paton; 2. Agnes Miller; 3. Margaret Wallace; 4. Hugh;
5. John, qv; 6. Robert; 7. Jean Miller; 8. Agnes Miller;
9. Elizabeth. **DC 6 Feb 1982**.

12317 YOUNG, Janet, b 16 Jun 1791. From
Kittochside, East Kilbride par, LKS. d/o William and
Margaret Y. To Ramsay Twp, Lanark Co, ONT, prob
summer 1832. m Angus Sutherland. **DC 17 Oct 1979**.

12318 YOUNG, Joan, 21 Dec 1839–24 May 1907. From
Galston, AYR. d/o Robert Y, qv, and Grizel Gillies, qv. To
Keppel Twp, Grey Co, ONT, poss 1854. m James
Burrows, 1839–1916, in 1859, at Eversley, King Twp, and
d at Russell, MAN. **DC 11 Dec 1979**.

12319 YOUNG, John 'Agricola', 1773–6 Oct 1837.
From Falkirk, STI. s/o William Y, merchant. Matric Univ
of Glasgow, 1790, and took theological course. To
Sydney, Cape Breton Co, NS, 1815; later to Halifax.

Secretary of NS Board of Agriculture, farmer, journalist
and MLA. m Agnes Renny, qv, and had, prob with other
ch: 1. Sir William, qv; 2. George Renny, qv; 3. Charles,
qv. **BNA 282, 504, 664, 712; GMA 5059; MLA 375;
MDB 819**.

12320 YOUNG, John. To QUE on the *David of London*,
ex Greenock, 19 May 1821; stld Lanark Co, ONT.
Schoolmaster, Ramsay Twp. **HCL 180, 239**.

12321 YOUNG, John, 1811–21 Feb 1859. From
Melrose, ROX. To Dumfries Twp, Waterloo Co, ONT,
1834. Innkeeper, road contractor, and town councillor of
Galt, 1857. m Janet Bell, qv. Son James, 1835–1913,
editor of the *Dumfries Reformer*. **BNA 750; HGD 115,
162; DC 26 Sep 1981**.

12322 YOUNG, John, 10 May 1827–20 Dec 1904. From
Glasgow. s/o James Y, qv, and Jean Miller, qv. To QUE,
ex Greenock, 24 Jun 1847; stld Ancaster Twp,
Wentworth Co. m Christina Blair Liddell, qv, ch:
1. James Miller, 1863–1920; 2. Margaret Denniston;
3. Alexander Liddell; 4. Marion Agnes; 5. William
Edgar; 7-8. Elizabeth and Christina May; 9. Elizabeth
Liddell; 10-11. Mabel Hamilton and John Liddell;
12. Lily Irene. **DC 6 Feb 1982**.

12323 YOUNG, John. From Neilston, RFW. s/o Robert
Y, farmer in Parkhouse. To ONT <1855. **SH**.

12324 YOUNG, Margaret, b ca 1747. From Colvend
par, KKD. d/o John Y. To Georgetown, Kings Co, PEI, on
the *Lovely Nellie*, ex Annan, 1774. Wife of John
Crockett, qv. **ELN; PAC 44**.

12325 YOUNG, Margaret, b 1842. From Galston, AYR.
d/o Robert Y, qv, and Grizel Gillies, qv. To Keppel Twp,
Grey Co, ONT, poss 1854. m William Cuddy.
DC 11 Dec 1979.

12326 YOUNG, Margaret, b 4 Sep 1845. From
Knockbain par, ROC. d/o William Y, qv, and Isabella
Ross, qv. To Minto Twp, Wellington Co, ONT, 1860.
m John Hewer, from PEI. **RFS 200**.

12327 YOUNG, Mary, b 18 Jun 1809. Poss from
Grahamston, Falkirk, STI. d/o William and Margaret Y.
To Ramsay Twp, Lanark Co, ONT, summer 1832.
m Walter Wood. **DC 17 Oct 1979**.

12328 YOUNG, Peter, 9 Oct 1804–8 Feb 1886. From
Grahamston, Falkirk, STI. s/o William and Margaret Y.
To Ramsay Twp, Lanark Co, ONT, summer 1832. Farmer.
m Jean Erskine, qv, ch: 1. William Peter, qv; 2. Agnes,
b 1831; 3. Alexander E, b 1834; 4. Margaret, b 1837;
5. Maxanne; 6. Peter C, b 1839; 7. John; 8. Stephen;
9. Jean, b 1846; 10. Robert, b 1849; 11. Andrew;
12. Janet. **DC 17 Oct 1979**.

12329 YOUNG, Robert, ca 1813–9 May 1873. From
Galston, AYR. To Keppel Twp, Grey Co, ONT, poss 1854.
m Feb 1839, Grizel or Grace Gillies, qv, ch: 1. Joan, qv;
2. Margaret, qv; 3. William, qv; 4. Isobel; 5. Helen, qv;
6. Grace; 7. Robert. **DC 17 Nov and 11 Dec 1979**.

12330 YOUNG, Robert. To Lanark Co, ONT, 1821; stld
Lot 4, Con 2, North Sherbrooke Twp. **HCL 74**.

12331 YOUNG, Sir William, 29 Jul 1799–8 May 1887.
From Falkirk, STI. s/o John 'Agricola' Y, qv, and Agnes
Renny, qv. Matric Univ of Glasgow, 1813, and emig to
Sydney, Cape Breton Co, NS, 1815. Later in Halifax.
Barrister; QC, 1843, and MLA; Chief Justice of NS,

1860-81; KB, 1869, and LLD, Dalhousie, 1881. m 10 Aug 1830, Anne, d/o Hon Michael Tobin, Halifax. **BNA 664; GMA 8762; MLA 376; MDB 819**.

12332   YOUNG, William, 1817-83. From LKS, poss Lesmahagow. To Scarborough Twp, York Co, ONT, 1842. **DC 29 Mar 1981**.

12333   YOUNG, William, 1826-8 Nov 1886. From ROX. s/o George Y, qv, and Mary Brunton, qv. To North Monaghan Twp, Peterborough Co, ONT, <1851. m Janet, d/o Archibald Haggart, qv, ch: 1. John; 2. William, 1871-1945; 3. Archibald, 1867-1941; 4. Andrew, 1870-1929; 5. Isabelle, 1857-1931; 6. George;`7. Mary, d 1928; 8. Margaret; 9. Elizabeth. **DC 25 Mar 1981**.

12334   YOUNG, William, 1844-27 Sep 1908. From Galston, AYR. s/o Robert Y, qv, and Grizel Gillies, qv. To Keppel Twp, Grey Co, ONT, poss 1854; stld later at Wiarton. Owner of sawmills. m (i) Sarah Carley; (ii) Vina —. No ch. **DC 11 Dec 1979**.

12335   YOUNG, William, 1806-79. From Drumspittal, Knockbain par, ROC. To QUE on the *John McKenzie*, ex Glasgow, 25 Jun 1857; stld Scott Twp, York Co, ONT, later Minto Twp, Wellington Co. Farmer. m Isabella Ross, qv, ch: 1. Helen, qv; 2. Margaret, qv; 3. Roderick, b 1848; 4. Isabella, b 1850; 5. Elizabeth, b 1853; 6. Colin, b 1857; 7. child, d 1860. **RFS 200**.

12336   YOUNG, Rev William C, b ca 1829. From Annan, DFS. s/o James Y, tradesman. Matric Univ of Glasgow, 1844. Licentiate of UP Ch, 1853. To ONT, and was a min in the Presbytery of Durham. **GMA 14832**.

12337   YOUNG, William Peter, 25 Sep 1830-24 Nov 1905. From Glasgow. s/o Peter Y, qv, and Jean Erskine, qv. To Ramsay Twp, Lanark Co, ONT, summer 1832. Farmer. m (i) Margaret, d/o Angus Sutherland and Margaret Fraser; (ii) Agnes Nicholson; and (iii) Mary, d/o Edward Clint and Mary Chalmers. ch: 1. Margaret, b 1862; 2. Peter E, b 1865; 3. Janet; 4. Mary Erskine, b 1877. **DC 17 Oct 1979**.

12338   YOUNGSTON, Elizabeth, 1836-1913. To Sherbrooke, QUE. m Alexander Morrison, qv. **MGC 2 Aug 1979**.

12339   YOUNIE, Jane, 25 Jan 1828-12 Feb 1913. From Knockando, MOR. To Sherbrooke, QUE. m Malcolm McKechnie, qv. **MGC 2 Aug 1979**.

12340   YUILE, Jessie. To Hants Co, NS, <1855. m Capt David Morris, ch. **HNS iii 122**.

12341   YUILL, Alexander. From Glasgow. s/o James Y, qv, and Barbara Colton, qv. To QUE on the *George Canning*, ex Greenock, 14 Apr 1821; stld Ramsay Twp,

Lanark Co, ONT. Weaver and farmer. m Ellen Aitkenhead, ch. **DC 7 Dec 1981**.

12342   YUILL, David, 24 Sep 1818-8 Jul 1902. From Glasgow. s/o James Y, qv, and Barbara Colton, qv. To QUE on the *George Canning*, ex Greenock, 14 Apr 1821; stld Ramsay Twp, Lanark Co, ONT. m Agnes Aitkenhead, 1818-1908, ch. **DC 7 Dec 1981**.

12343   YUILL, Euphemia, 1805-14 May 1897. From Glasgow. d/o James Y, qv, and Barbara Colton, qv. To QUE on the *George Canning*, ex Greenock, 14 Apr 1821; stld Ramsay Twp, Lanark Co, ONT. m Andrew Paul, qv. **HCL 87**.

12344   YUILL, James, 1774-26 Nov 1858. From Glasgow. To QUE on the *George Canning*, ex Greenock, 14 Apr 1821; stld Ramsay Twp, Lanark Co, ONT. Weaver. m Barbara Colton, qv, ch: 1. James, jr, qv; 2. Euphemia, qv; 3. Alexander, qv; 4. Robert, qv; 5. Jessie, qv; 6. Joseph, qv; 7. John, unm; 8. David, qv; 9. William, qv. **HCL 87; DC 7 Dec 1981**.

12345   YUILL, James, jr, 1803-84. From Glasgow. s/o James Y, qv, and Barbara Colton, qv. To QUE on the *George Canning*, ex Greenock, 14 Apr 1821; stld Ramsay Twp, Lanark Co, ONT. Weaver and farmer. m Marion Turner, qv, ch. **DC 7 Dec 1981**.

12346   YUILL, Jessie. From Glasgow. d/o James Y, and Barbara Colton, qv. To QUE on the *George Canning*, ex Greenock, 14 Apr 1821; stld Ramsay Twp, Lanark Co, ONT. m — Witherspoon, New York City. **DC 7 Dec 1981**.

12347   YUILL, Joseph, d ca 1855. From Glasgow. s/o James Y, qv, and Barbara Colton, qv. To QUE on the *George Canning*, ex Greenock, 14 Apr 1821; stld Ramsay Twp, Lanark Co, ONT. m Mary Paris, ch. **DC 7 Dec 1981**.

12348   YUILL, Robert, 28 May 1808-26 Jan 1896. From Glasgow. s/o James Y, qv, and Barbara Colton, qv. To QUE on the *George Canning*, ex Greenock, 14 Apr 1821; stld Ramsay Twp, Lanark Co, ONT, later Brantford Twp, Brant Co. Master tailor. m Janet McLaren, qv, ch. **DC 7 Dec 1981**.

12349   YUILL, William, 1819-28 Dec 1893. From Glasgow. s/o James Y, qv, and Barbara Colton, qv. To QUE on the *George Canning*, ex Greenock, 14 Apr 1821; stld Ramsay Twp, Lanark Co, ONT. m Isabella Browning, 1822-1906, ch. **DC 7 Dec 1981**.

12350   YULE, William. To QUE on the *Commerce*, ex Greenock, Jun 1820; stld poss Lanark Co, ONT. **HCL 238**.

ADDENDA

12351 ANDERSON, Margaret, 1792–1888. From PEE. d/o Peter A. and Isobel Henderson. To Hay Twp, Huron Co, ONT, 1834. Wife of James Murray, qv. **DC 18 May 1982.**

12352 BEATON, John, 1810-94. From Tobson, Is Bernera, Lewis, ROC. s/o Angus B. and Kirsty McNeil. To Whitton Twp, Compton Co, QUE, poss 1863. Farmer. m Ann McAulay, qv, ch: 1. Donald, b 1832; 2. Norman, b 1836; 3. Angus, b 1839; 4. Kirsty, b 1840; 5. Ann, b 1843; 6. Murdo, b 1847; 7. Kate, b 1850; 8. Neil, b 1854; 9. Zachary, b 1858. **WLC.**

12353 BROWN, Margaret, b 1 Mar 1780. From Papple, Whittinghame par, ELN. d/o William B, farmer, and Janet Lee. To ONT, ca 1835, poss Kingston, but may have retr later to SCT. wid/o Thomas Pringle, 1789–1834, poet and miscellaneous writer, who d in South Africa. **LDW 30 Apr 1982.**

12354 BUCHANAN, Jean, b ca 1790. From Johnstone, RFW. d/o John B. and Jean Hutchins. To Grey Co, ONT, 1842. m 1811, David Wilson, qv. **DC 1 May 1982.**

12355 BUCHANAN, Kenneth, 1805-87. From Carnish, Is Lewis, ROC. s/o Norman B. and Kirsty McDonald. To Wolfe Co, QUE, 1851. m Peggy Nicholson, qv, ch: 1. Murdo, b 1837; 2. Marion, b 1839; 3. Catherine, 1841–1912; 4. Mary Ann, b 1844; 5. Norman, b 1848; 6. John, b 1851. **WLC.**

12356 CADDEL, Donald, 1811–25 Feb 1855. From Glasgow. bro/o Peter C, qv. To Oneida Twp, Haldimand Co, ONT, 1855. m Janet McDonald, qv, ch: 1. Peter, b 10 Mar 1851; 2. John, b 22 Jun 1852; 3. Donald, b 16 Mar 1854. **DC 22 Mar 1982.**

12357 CADDEL, Peter. From Glasgow. bro/o Donald C, qv. To Oneida Twp, Haldimand Co, ONT, <1855. **DC 22 Mar 1982.**

12358 CAIRNS, Robert, 4 Aug 1765–28 Aug 1836. From PEE. s/o Robert C, miller, and Ann Hope. To QUE, ca 1789. Tailor, emp with Archibald Ferguson, qv, and succ him in business. ch. **DC 18 Apr 1982.**

12359 CAMERON, Angus. From INV. To Three Rivers, QUE, <1805. Discharged soldier. m Euphemia McGregor. Son Malcolm, 1808-76, merchant and politician. **BNA 530.**

12360 CAMERON, Daniel, b 1786. From Glasgow. To CAN, 1831. Wife Barbara with him, and ch: 1. Jean; 2. Barbara; 3. John; 4. Daniel; 5. Helen; 6. Duncan. **DC 28 May 1982.**

12361 CAMERON, Duncan, b 12 Jul 1803. From Crieff, PER. To Montreal, QUE, 1824. **DC 28 May 1982.**

12362 CAMPBELL, John, b ca 1796. From Is Bute, BUT. To Restigouche Co, NB, ca 1818. Petitioned 9 Feb 1821 for 150 acres in Lot 73, south side of the Restigouche River. **DC 31 May 1980.**

12363 CAMPBELL, Robert, ca 1811–15 Sep 1848. From Dalry, KKD. To Kent Co, ONT, apparently with mother, who d at Harwich, also in Sep 1848. **DGH 2 Nov 1848.**

12364 CARSEWELL, David Allan, 1788–11 May 1860. From Glasgow. To Pakenham Twp, Lanark Co, ONT. <1827; later to Horton Twp, Renfrew Co. Farmer.

m Janet Mitchell, 30 Nov 1829, ch: 1. Margaret; 2. Allan; 3. David; 4. James; 5. Ann. **DC 18 May 1982.**

12365 COCHRANE, Margaret, b 16 May 1786. From Dunbar, ELN. d/o John C. and Margaret Henderson. To Toronto, ONT, ca 1836. Wife of John Riddel, qv. **DC 15 May 1982.**

12366 COULTARD, Robert. Prob from LKS. To QUE on the *Aide*, 1815; stld Lot 10, Con 11, Drummond Twp, Lanark Co, ONT. **HCL 234.**

12367 CRAIGIE, John. From Edinburgh. s/o John and Ann C, of the Kilgraston family. To QUE <1812. Commissary General of Lower Canada. m Susan Coffin, wid/o James Grant. Son John Moreton of Jedbank, d 1871, Sheriff-Substitute of SEL. **ABC 92; FAS 44.**

12368 CROSS, Robert, d ca 1827. From Old Monkland par, LKS. To Montreal, QUE, 1826. Farmer. Son Alexander, b 1821, lawyer, and became judge, 1877. **BNA 923; SGC 584; DC 4 May 1982.**

12369 DEWAR, William. From PER. To Richmond Bay, PEI, on the *Falmouth*, ex Greenock, 8 Apr 1770; stld Queens Co. Wife and ch with him. **DC 20 Dec 1981.**

12370 DICKIE, John. From Peterhead, ABD. To Montreal, QUE, 1844; later to Kingston, ONT. Shipbuilder. ch: 1. James, lumberman in IA; 2. John, b 1843, lumberman in IA; 3. Mary; 4. Catherine; 5. Mrs Chestnut. **DC 21 Jun 1983.**

12371 DOBIE, Richard. Poss from Gilmerton, MLN. To Montreal, QUE, <1764. He was active as a fur-trader in the Timiskaming dist in association with William Grant, qv, of Three Rivers. **LDW 15 Sep 1972.**

12372 DONALD, Lewis, 8 Feb 1836–11 Oct 1915. From ABD. To ONT <1866; later to Oil City, PA. m 25 Dec 1869, Sarah Bowlin, ch: 1. Andrew; 2. Lewis. **LDW 15 Dec 1970.**

12373 DOUGALL, John, 14 Jan 1783–20 Jan 1867. From Parkhead, Mid Calder, MLN. To St Andrews, Argenteuil Co, QUE, 1832. Farmer. m Marion Hastie, qv, ch: 1. Thomas, b 1811; 2. Margaret, b 1813; 3. John, b 1814; 4. James, b 1816; 5. George, b 1818; 6. Margaret, b 1819; 7. Jean, b 1822; 8. Peter, b 1824; 9. Marion, b 1826; 10. Marion, b 1829; 11. Helen, b 1832. **DC 18 May 1982.**

12374 FORBES, Elizabeth, b 1815. From Towie, ABD. d/o Arthur F. To Saltfleet Twp, Wentworth Co, ONT, 1850. Wife of Duncan McDonald, qv, m 28 Jun 1840. **DC 5 Feb 1983.**

12375 GEDDES, James, b ca 1829. From Rathlin, ABD. s/o James G. and Margaret Hepburn. To Pickering, Durham Co, ONT, <16 Dec 1858, when m Eliza Phillip, qv. **DC 24 Mar 1982.**

12376 GERRARD, Adam, 1772–25 Nov 1832. From ABD. To Chaleur Bay, NB, ca 1795; stld Restigouche Co. Bur Atholville. **DC 8 Aug 1982.**

12377 GILLIES, Duncan. From ARL. To Dundee, Huntingdon Co, QUE, 1818. Son Rev Archibald, b 1812, Baptist min at Eaton, Compton Co. **WLC.**

12378   GORDON, Elizabeth. Poss from ABD. d/o John G. and Mary Milne. To Reach Twp, Durham Co, ONT, <29 Oct 1861, when m William Lough, qv. **DC 24 Mar 1982**.

12379   GORRIE, Daniel, ca 1805–2 Jul 1872. From Glasgow, but family previously in PER. To Montreal, QUE, 1820. Brewer, and an alderman of Montreal, 1859-64. **SGC 500**.

12380   GRAHAM, Alexander Aitken, 13 Mar 1810– 4 Mar 1879. From Edinburgh. s/o John G, silversmith-burgess, and Isabella Aitken. To ONT, ca 1827; stld Ottawa. m Harriet Frost, b Devonshire, ENG, ca 1816, ch: 1. Martha, b 1843; 2. Isabella, b 1846; 3. Alexander, b ca 1849; 4. Elizabeth, b 1852.   **DC 5 Apr 1982**.

12381   GRAHAM, Kenneth. Prob from Is Raasay, off Is Skye, INV. To Charlottetown, PEI, on the *James Gibbs*, ex Uig Bay, 26 May 1858. Wife Rachel McLeod, qv, with him, and ch: 1. Alexander; 2. Murdo; 3. Annie; 4. Donald; 5. Mary.   **DC 6 Mar 1982**.

12382   GRANT, Andrew. From Clachaig, Abernethy, INV. s/o Duncan G, 1771–1831, tenant in Ballintuime, and Margaret Fraser, 1777–1851. To Hamilton, ONT, 1851. **Ts Abernethy**.

12383   GUNN, Margaret, b 1823. From South Dell, Is Lewis, ROC. d/o John G. and Margaret McLean. To Compton Co, QUE, 1841. m John McIver, qv.   **WLC**.

12384   HASTIE, Marion, 27 Jul 1790–Jul 1879. From Heads, Whitburn par, WLN. d/o John H, tenant farmer, and Margaret Brown. To St Andrews, Argenteuil Co, QUE, 1832. Wife of John Dougall, qv.   **SG xxvi/1 24 and xxvi/3 92; DC 18 May 1982**.

12385   HECTOR, Dr James, 16 Mar 1834–5 Nov 1907. From Edinburgh. s/o Alexander H, solicitor, and Margaret Macrostie. Grad MD, Univ of Edinburgh. App surgeon and geologist in the Palliser Expedition to the Canadian Rockies, and served 1857-60. Named Kicking Horse Pass. Went later to Wellington, NZ, and became a director of the New Zealand Institute. CMG, 1875, KCMG, 1887. m 1868, Maria Munro.   **DC 18 May 1982**.

12386   HILL, Margaret, 1814-88. From Greenlaw, BEW. d/o Thomas H. and Margaret Sparks. To Oxford Co, ONT, 1843. Wife of George Wilson, qv.   **DC 18 May 1982**.

12387   HOPE, Brig Gen Henry, ca 1747–13 Apr 1789. From Cramond par, Edinburgh. s/o Hon Charles H. of Craigiehall, and Lady Ann Vane. Commissary General of the troops in CAN, 1786. Lt Gov of QUE, 1786-89. m Sarah, d/o Rev John Jones, Prebendary of Mullaghbrack, no ch.   **SP iv 496**.

12388   IRVING, George. From Annan, DFS. To Montreal, QUE, 1838. Paymaster, Grand Trunk Railroad.   **SGC 573**.

12389   JOHNSTON, Angus, d 8 May 1860. From Kintyre, ARL. To Yarmouth Twp, Elgin Co, ONT, <1836. Farmer. Wife Ann, 1794–1859, with him. ch: 1. Donald; 2. James; 3. Mary, b 1822; 4. Catherine; 5. Ann; 6. Isabella; 7. Janet.   **DC 6 Jun 1982**.

12390   KENNEDY, Rev Andrew, 1789–19 May 1882. b Leadhills, LKS. Adm min of Keith Burgher Ch, BAN. To QUE, 1841, and became min at Lachute. Moved to Philadelphia, PA, and later to London, ONT. m Mary

Mutter, qv, ch: 1. Jessie Pew, 1826-35; 2. John, 1828-74; 3. Margery Mutter, 1829–1923; 4. Catherine Ainslie, b 1831; 5. William Erskine, b 1834, d inf; 6. Jessie Allan, b 1835; 7. Eliza Helen, b 1837; 8. Mary Ann, 1839–1913; 9. Margaret Georgina, 1843-45. **UPC i 122**.

12391   LOUGH, William, b ca 1839. s/o William L. and Jane Mason. To Reach Twp, Durham Co, ONT, <29 Oct 1861, when m Elizabeth Gordon, qv.   **DC 24 Mar 1982**.

12392   LOVE, Ann, ca 1745–ca 1825. From Campbeltown, ARL. To PEI, prob 1772; stld Prince Co. Wife of James Woodside, qv, m 4 Apr 1765. **DC 20 Dec 1981**.

12393   McARTHUR, Mary. From Carnish, Uig par, Is Lewis, ROC. d/o John M. and Kirsty McLeod. To Scotstown, Compton Co, QUE, 1851. Third wife of Neil Buchanan, qv.   **WLC**.

12394   McAULAY, Ann, 1814–1902. From Bosta, Is Bernera, off Lewis, ROC. d/o Zachary M. and Margaret Mackenzie. To Whitton Twp, Compton Co, QUE, poss 1863. Wife of John Beaton, qv.   **WLC**.

12395   McAULAY, Isabella, b ca 1808. From Carloway, Uig par, Is Lewis, ROC. To QUE, ex Stornoway, arr 4 Aug 1851; stld Huron Twp, Bruce Co, ONT, 1852. Wife of Angus McArthur, qv.   **WLC**.

12396   McAULAY, Malcolm, 1797–1852. From Swainibost, Is Lewis, ROC. To Lingwick Twp, Compton Co, QUE, poss 1841. Farmer. m Kirsty McRitchie, qv, ch: 1. Margaret, b 1825; 2. Ann, b 1828; 3. Donald 'Gad,' b 1829; 4. Angus, b 1833; 5. Kenneth, b 1835; 6. John 'Gael,' b 1837; 7. Jane, b 1839; 8. Donald Og, b 1841; 9. Lt Col Malcolm, b 1845, lumberman and officer of militia.   **WLC**.

12397   McCALLUM, D. Prob from PER. To Richmond Bay, PEI, on the *Falmouth*, ex Greenock, 8 Apr 1770; stld Stanhope, Queens Co. Weaver.   **DC 28 May 1980**.

12398   McCODRUM, Donald, ca 1790–27 Mar 1852. From Hougharry, Is North Uist, INV. s/o Hugh M. To Mira Valley, Cape Breton Co, NS, 1831; stld Mineral Rock. m Catherine McLean, qv, ch: 1. Hugh, b 1820; 2. Flora, b 1822; 3. Neil, b 1824; 4. Murdo, b 1828; 5. John; 6. Archibald; 7. Sarah.   **WLC**.

12399   McCRACKAN, John, b ca 1751. From Thorneyhill, Colvend, KKD. To Georgetown, Kings Co, PEI, on the *Lovely Nellie*, ex Annan, 1774. Farmer. **ELN**.

12400   McCUSBIC, Margaret, b 1801. From Is Berneray, Harris, INV. d/o John M. To Fergusons Lake, Richmond Co, NS, ca 1841. Wife of Kenneth Morrison, qv.   **WLC**.

12401   McDERMID, Donald. From Is Grimsay, North Uist, INV. To Whitton, Compton Co, QUE, 1863. m Marion Smith, qv, ch: 1. Charles, b 1835; 2. Margaret, b 1836; 3. Neil, b 1838; 4. John, b 1843; 5. Archie, b 1847.   **WLC**.

12402   McDIARMID, Peter. Prob from PER. To ONT <1848; stld Kemptville, Leeds and Grenville Co, later Adelaide Twp, Middlesex Co; finally Brooke Twp, Lambton Co. m Elizabeth Fraser, qv, ch: 1. Andrew; 2. Peter; 3. Mary, b 1850; 4. Margaret; 5. Elizabeth. **DC 18 May 1982**.

12403   McDONALD, Ann, b ca 1822. From Garry of Shader, Is Lewis, ROC. d/o John M. and Margaret McLean. To QUE, ex Stornoway, arr 4 Aug 1851; stld Huron Twp, Bruce Co, ONT, 1852. Wife of Allan McLeay, qv. **WLC**.

12404   McDONALD, Catherine, b ca 1810. From Is Tyree, ARL. d/o Archibald and Catherine M. To Brock Twp, Durham Co, ONT, <5 May 1858, when m Lachlan McLean, qv. **DC 24 Mar 1982**.

12405   McDONALD, Janet, 1828–8 Nov 1903. From Glasgow. To Oneida Twp, Haldimand Co, ONT, 1855. Wife of Donald Caddel, qv, m 1 Jun 1850.   **DC 22 Mar 1982**.

12406   McDONALD, John, called 'Iain Laghach', 1789–1889. From Gisla, Is Lewis, ROC. s/o Norman and Effie M. To Winslow Twp, Compton Co, QUE, poss 1841. m Annie Mackenzie, qv, ch: 1. Donald, b 1815; 2. John, b 1818; 3. Angus, b 1820; 4. William, b 1825; 5. Catherine, b 1827; 6. Norman, b 1831; 7. Allan, b 1831.   **WLC**.

12407   MACDONALD, John Duff, 18 Nov 1819–26 Dec 1850. From Cromarty par, ROC. s/o John Duff M. and Catherine Smith. To Perth, Drummond Twp, Lanark Co, ONT, <1850. Surgeon, sometime of 23rd Fusiliers. m Sarah Ann Malloch, ch.   **DC 18 May 1982**.

12408   McDONALD, Kate. From Upper Shader, Is Lewis, ROC. To QUE, ex Stornoway, arr 4 Aug 1851; stld Huron Twp, Bruce Co, ONT, 1852. Wife of Allan McLeay, qv. **WLC**.

12409   McDONALD, Kirsty. From Upper Bornish, Is Lewis, ROC. To West Williams Twp, Middlesex Co, ONT, ca 1850. Wife of Angus O'Henley, qv. **WLC**.

12410   MACDONALD, Margaret, b Glasgow. d/o Hugh M, qv, and Ellen Shaw, qv. To QUE on the *Earl of Buckinghamshire*, ex Greenock, arr 24 Jun 1820; stld nr Kingston, ONT. m Rev Prof James Williamson, qv. **DC 5 Mar 1982**.

12411   McDONALD, Murdo, 1797–1862. From Callanish, Is Lewis, ROC. s/o John and Ann M. To Hampden Twp, Compton Co, QUE, 1851. m Isabella McLeod, qv, ch: 1. John 'Boston,' 1828-93; 2. Mary, b 1831; 3. Jane, b 1834; 4. Angus, b 1838; 5. Alexander, b 1842; 6. Ann, b 1844; 7. Kirsty, b 1847. **WLC**.

12412   McGILLIVRAY, Mary. From Dunmaglas, Daviot and Dunlichity par, INV. d/o Donald M, tacksman of Clovendale, and Ann McTavish. To Montreal, QUE, <1810. After the d of Magdalen, wife of her bro William M, qv, she became châtelaine of his home at St Antoines, Montreal, and reared his ch.   **LDW 15 Feb 1967**.

12413   McGILLIVRAY, Peter, d 31 May 1884. From Is Mull, ARL. s/o John and Mary M. To Saugeen Twp, York Co, ONT, <1840. Moved later to Vaughan Twp. Farmer. Wife Mary, d 1861, with him.   **DC 11 Jan 1980**.

12414   McINNES, John. To Grand Narrows, Cape Breton Co, NS, <1850. Son Alexander.   **HNS iii 191**.

12415   McINTYRE, Mary, b ca 1800. From Stoneybridge, Is South Uist, INV. To East Williams Twp, Middlesex Co, ONT, ca 1850. Wife of John O'Henley, qv. **WLC**.

12416   McINTYRE, Peter, d 1854. From Comrie, PER. s/o Donald M, farmer, and Margaret Ferguson, tenants in Dundurn. To CAN, prob ONT.   **Ts Comrie**.

12417   McIVER, Anna, b 1822. From Gress, Is Lewis, ROC. d/o Donald and Catherine M. To Lingwick Twp, Compton Co, QUE, ca 1841. Wife of Malcolm Mackay, qv. **WLC**.

12418   McIVER, Anna, b 1825. From Stornoway par, Is Lewis, ROC. To Compton Co, QUE, <1851. Wife of Donald Stewart, qv. **WLC**.

12419   McIVER, John, d ca 1890. From North Tolsta, Is Lewis, ROC. s/o Donald and Catherine M. To Lingwick, Compton Co, QUE, ca 1842; later to Marston. ch: 1. John; 2. Alexander.   **DC 12 Dec 1975**.

12420   McIVER, Margaret, 1821–1903. From Glen Tolsta, Is Lewis, ROC. d/o Donald M, Barvas par. To QUE, ex Stornoway, arr 4 Aug 1851; stld Huron Twp, Bruce Co, ONT, 1852. Wife of Angus Murray, qv. **WLC**.

12421   McIVER, Murdo. From North Tolsta, Is Lewis, ROC. s/o Donald and Catherine M. To Lingwick Twp, Compton Co, QUE, ca 1842; later to Marston. **DC 12 Feb 1975**.

12422   McIVER, Roderick, b 1806. From North Tolsta, Is Lewis, ROC. s/o Donald and Catherine M. To Lingwick Twp, Compton Co, QUE, ca 1842; later to Marston. Farmer. m Isabella McLeod, qv, ch. **WLC**.

12423   McKAY, Alexander, d 1811. To Montreal, QUE, <1797, and sometime at Sault Ste Marie, Algoma Dist, ONT. Fur-trader with Pacific Fur Co, 1810. m Margaret Wadin, who m (ii) Dr John McLoughlin, HBCo. Son Thomas, 1797–1850, fur-trader and frontier scout in ID and OR.   **DC 29 Dec 1966**.

12424   McKAY, Ann. From Valtos, Uig par, Is Lewis, ROC. d/o John M. and Ann Smith. To Winslow Twp, Compton Co, QUE, ca 1855. Wife of John Smith, qv. **WLC**.

12425   MACKAY, Malcolm, b 1813. From Is Lewis, ROC. To Lingwick Twp, Compton Co, QUE, ca 1841; stld later at Victoria Bay, Lake Megantic. Farmer. m Anna McIver, qv, ch: 1. Rachel, prob dy; 2. John, b 1847; 3. Donald, b 1849; 4. Catherine, b 1851; 5. Mary, b 1853; 6. Bella, b 1859; 7. Effie, b 1860; 8. Murdo J, b 1862; 9. Roderick, b 1865; 10. Rachel, b 1867. **WLC**.

12426   McKAY, Murdo, b 1818. From Is Lewis, ROC. s/o Norman M. and Kirsty Buchanan. To Lingwick Twp, Compton Co, QUE, ca 1838. Son Angus, 1863–1923, pseud 'Oscar Dhu,' poet of the Eastern Twps of QUE. **WLC**.

12427   MACKAY, Robert, d ca 1835. From DFS. bro/o Anthony M. To York Co, NB, 1815.   **DC 23 Jun 1982**.

12428   McKELLAR, Alexander, b ca 1765. From Fincharn, Loch Awe, ARL. To Lobo Twp, Middlesex Co, ONT, <1830. m Mary Muir, qv, ch: 1. John, 1789–1869; 2. Duncan, 1795–1882; 3. Archibald, 1799–1852. **DC 18 May 1982**.

12429   MACKENZIE, Annie, 1789–1878. From Gisla, Is Lewis, ROC. To Winslow Twp, Compton Co, QUE, poss 1841. Wife of John McDonald, qv. **WLC**.

12430 MACKENZIE, Hope Fleming. From Logieraitt, PER. s/o Alexander M, wright, and Mary Fleming. To Kingston, ONT, 1843. Politician, rep Lambton and North Oxford. **BNA 577.**

12431 MACKENZIE, Lachlan, 1816-92. From Is Coll, ARL. s/o Murdock M, qv, and Jessie Mackinnon, qv. To York Co, ONT, <1820; stld Mara Twp. m Sarah McLean, 1824-1901. **DC 4 Mar 1982.**

12432 MACKENZIE, Murdock, 1785-1872. From Is Coll, ARL. To York Co, ONT, <1820; stld Mara Twp. Farmer. m Jessie Mackinnon, qv, ch: 1. Lachlan, qv; 2. John; 3. Mary; 4. Margaret; 5. Sibbie; 6. James; 7. Bella. **DC 4 Mar 1982.**

12433 MACKENZIE, Sibella, 1818-1906. From Barvas, Is Lewis, ROC. d/o Malcolm M, weaver. To Whitton Twp, Compton Co, QUE, ca 1843. Wife of Murdo Morrison, qv. **WLC.**

12434 McKERRACHER, William. Poss from PER. To Port Stanley, Elgin Co, ONT, via New York and Buffalo, NY, 1833. m Agnes McFarlane. Son Daniel. **DC 5 Dec 1983.**

12435 McKINNON, Jessie, 1789-1872. From Is Coll, ARL. To York Co, ONT, <1820; stld Mara Twp. Wife of Murdock Mackenzie, qv. **DC 4 Mar 1982.**

12436 McLAREN, Donald, b ca 1830. From Callander, PER. s/o Donald and Jane M. To Mariposa Twp, Victoria Co, <3 Oct 1858, when m Janet Gillies, qv. **DC 24 Mar 1982.**

12437 McLEAN, Archibald, 1820-24 Apr 1897. From ARL, prob Campbeltown. To Lambton Co, ONT, ca 1862; stld Bonsaquet Twp, later Plympton Twp. Farmer. m Barbara Beith, ch: 1. Barbara; 2. Mary; 3. Charles; 4. Donald; 5. Dougal; 6. Alexander; 7. Robert; 8. Archibald; 9. Elizabeth. **DC 18 May 1982.**

12438 McLEAN, Catherine, 1786-1894. From Hougharry, Is North Uist, INV. To Mira Valley, Cape Breton Co, NS, 1831. Wife of Donald McCodrum, qv. **WLC.**

12439 MACLEAN, Hector, 1750-1828. From Glen Urquhart, INV. To Pictou Co, NS, 1784. Discharged soldier. m Isabell McIntosh, ch: 1. Alexander; 2. Finlay; 3. Mary; 4. John; 5. Donald; 6. Hector; 7. Jerusha; 8. Andrew; 9. Hugh. **NSN 26/163.**

12440 McLEAN, Lachlan, b ca 1812. From Is Tyree, ARL. s/o Alexander and Catherine M. To Brock Twp, Durham Co, ONT, <5 May 1858, when m Catherine McDonald, qv. **DC 24 Mar 1982.**

12441 McLEAN, Peggy. From Is Pabay, off Lewis, ROC. s/o Malcolm M. and Peggy McIver. To Huron Twp, Bruce Co, ONT, <1864. Wife of Murdo Matheson, qv. **WLC.**

12442 McLELLAN, Mary, b ca 1803. From Geshader, Is Lewis, ROC. To Huron Twp, Bruce Co, ONT, <1865. Wife of Neil Matheson, qv. **WLC.**

12443 McLENNAN, Robert Stewart, b ca 1816. From Killilan, Kintail par, ROC. s/o Roderick M. and Charlotte Stewart. To Charlottenburgh Twp, Glengarry Co, ONT, <1855. Teacher. By wife Elspeth, b ca 1830, ch: 1. Roderick, b ca 1850; 2. Kenneth, b ca 1851; 3. John, b ca 1854; 4. Colin, b ca 1856; 5. Charlotte, b ca 1858; 6. Flora; 7. Isabella. **DC 24 Jan 1979 and 2 Jan 1980.**

12444 McLEOD, Alexander, b 1800. From Back, Stornoway, Is Lewis, ROC. s/o Murdo M. To Winslow Twp, Compton Co, QUE, <1851. Schoolteacher. m Isabella Stewart, qv, ch: 1. Marion, b 1833; 2. Rev Finlay, went to MAN; 3. Ann, b 1835; 4. Murdo, b 1837; 5. Donald, b 1840; 6. Kirsty, b 1843; 7. Duncan L, b 1846, storekeeper; 8. John, b 1848. **WLC.**

12445 McLEOD, Isabella. From Branahuie, Is Lewis, ROC. d/o Donald M. and Mary Mackenzie. To Lingwick Twp, Compton Co, QUE, ca 1842. Wife of Roderick McIver, qv. **WLC.**

12446 McLEOD, Isabella, 1806-93. From Carloway, Uig par, Is Lewis, ROC. d/o Angus M. To Hampden Twp, Compton Co, QUE, 1851. Wife of Murdo McDonald, qv. **WLC.**

12447 McLEOD, Isabella, b 1819. From Enaclete, Uig par, Is Lewis, ROC. d/o Donald and Mary M. To Winslow Twp, Compton Co, QUE, 1851. Wife of Donald Campbell, qv. **WLC.**

12448 McLEOD, Rachel. Prob from Is Raasay, off Is Skye, INV. To Charlottetown, PEI, on the *James Gibbs*, ex Uig Bay, 26 May 1858. Wife of Kenneth Graham, qv. **DC 6 Mar 1982.**

12449 MACPHERSON, Samuel, 1814-39. From Kingussie, INV. s/o James M, farmer in Culfern, and Elspeth M. To Yaira, ONT. **Ts Kingussie; CSL 182.**

12450 McRITCHIE, Kirsty, b 1805. From Swainbost, Is Lewis, ROC. To Lingwick Twp, Compton Co, QUE, poss 1841. Wife of Malcolm McAulay, qv. **WLC.**

12451 McRITCHIE, Margaret, b 1837. From Barvas, Is Lewis, ROC. d/o John M. and Catherine McLeod. To Lingwick Twp, Compton Co, QUE, 1858; stld Red Mountain. Wife of Donald Morrison, qv. **WLC.**

12452 MARTIN, James. From Glasgow. To QUE on the *Prompt*, ex Greenock, 4 Jul 1820; stld Dalhousie Twp, Lanark Co, ONT. Farmer. **HCL 68.**

12453 MATHESON, Murdo, b 1801. From Reef, Is Lewis, ROC. s/o Murdo M. and Rachel McLeod. To Huron Twp, Bruce Co, ONT, <1864. Farmer. Con 8. m Peggy McLean, qv, ch: 1. Donald, b 1832; 2. Peggy, b 1834; 3. Flora, b 1837; 4. Annabella, b 1838; 5. Murdo, b 1840; 6. Malcolm, b 1842; 7. Ann, b 1844; 8. John, b 1847; 9. Murdo. **WLC.**

12454 MATHESON, Neil, b 1795. From Geshader, Is Lewis, ROC. s/o Norman M. and Catherine McLeod. To Huron Twp, Bruce Co, ONT, <1865. Farmer. m Mary McLellan, qv, ch: 1. Eory or Dorothy, b 1821; 2. Donald, b 1825; 3. Catherine, b 1827; 4. John, remained in Lewis; 5. Kirsty, b 1832; 6. Duncan, b 1835; 7. Mary, b 1836; 8. Margaret, b 1838; 9. Donald, b 1840; 10. Norman, b 1842; 11. Ann, b 1844. **WLC.**

12455 MONTGOMERY, Daniel. From ARL. To Prince Co, PEI, <1795. Son Donald, b 1800, Speaker in the Legislature. **BNA 720.**

12456 MORRISON, Angus, 1820-91. From Licisto, Harrish, INV. s/o Neil and Catherine M. To Bruce Co, ONT, 1863. m Lexy Ross, qv, ch: 1. Neil, b 1855; 2. Mary, b 1857; 3. Margaret, b 1859; 4. Mary, b 1860; 5. Kirsty, b 1862. **WLC.**

12457 MORRISON, Donald, b 14 Jun 1835. From Tolsta, Is Lewis, ROC. s/o Norman M. and Mary McIver.

To Lingwick Twp, Compton Co, QUE, 1858; stld Red Mountain. Farmer. m Margaret Ritchie, qv, ch: 1. Mary Ann, b 1872; 2. Margaret E, 1874-92; 3. John, b 1876; 4. Norman, b 1878; 5. Catherine, b 1880; 6. Murdo, b 1882; 7. Donald, b 1884. **WLC**.

12458 MORRISON, Kenneth, b 1794. From Is Berneray, Harris, INV. s/o John M. To Fergusons Lake, Richmond Co, NS, ca 1841. m Margaret McCusbic, qv, ch: 1. John, b 1823; 2. Flora, b 1826; 3. Roderick, b 1829; 4. Roderick 'Og,' b 1831; 5. Donald, b 1835; 6. John, b 1838; 7. Murdo, b 1840, author of Gaelic poems and songs. **WLC**.

12459 MUIR, Mary, 1762–9 Apr 1846. From Fincharn, Loch Awe, ARL. To Lobo Twp, Middlesex Co, ONT, <1830. Wife of Alexander McKellar, qv. **DC 18 May 1982**.

12460 MURRAY, James, 1791–2 Jun 1874. From Tweedsmuir, PEE. To ONT, 1834; stld Hay Twp, Huron Co. Farmer. m Margaret Anderson, qv, ch: 1. Peter, 1817–1910; 2. James, 1817–1908; 3. Agnes, 1819-63; 4. Robert, 1822-76; 5. John; 6. Isabella, 1830-80; 7. Janet, 1832-68; 8. Thomas, b 1835. **DC 18 May 1982**.

12461 MURRAY, Norman, b 1829. From Is Lewis, ROC. To Lingwick Twp, Compton Co, QUE, ca 1842. Farmer. m Jane Eliza Hanwright, from PEI, ch: 1. Esther Marion, b 1855; 2. Ann, b 1858; 3. Alice, b 1860; 4. Malvina, b 1862; 5. Robert, b 1864; 6. Frederick William, b 1866; 7. Daniel Cyrus, b 1868; 8. David L. **WLC**.

12462 MUTTER, Mary. From Coates, Edinburgh. d/o William M. m 28 Jun 1824, Rev Andrew Kennedy, qv, and emig to Lachute, QUE. **UPC I 122**.

12463 NICHOLSON, Peggy, 1809-81. From Vuia Mor Is, Lewis, ROC. d/o Norman N, and Marian McDonald. To Wolfe Co, QUE, 1851. Wife of Kenneth Buchanan, qv. **WLC**.

12464 O'HENLEY, John, b 1796. From Stoneybridge, Is South Uist, INV. To East Williams Twp, Middlesex Co, ONT, ca 1850. m Mary McIntyre, qv, ch: 1. Kirsty, b 1824; 2-3. Neil and Flora, twins, b 1827; 4. Marion, b 1828; 5. Michael, b 1829; 6. Janet, b 1832; 7. John, b 1834. **WLC**.

12465 PHILLIP, Eliza. From Monquhitter, ABD. d/o Thomas P. and Jane Patterson. To Whitby, Durham Co, ONT, <16 Dec 1858, when m James Geddes, qv. **DC 24 Mar 1982**.

12466 RAMSAY, James, ca 1811-33. From DFS. s/o James R, solicitor. To NFD and drowned off coast. **DGC 18 Dec 1833**.

12467 RANKIN, Janet, b ca 1839. From Glasgow. d/o Robert R. and Mary Donaldson. To Whitby, ONT, <2 Dec 1858, when m William, b ca 1836, Co Antrim, IRL, s/o Patrick H. and Margaret Logan, Cartwright Twp, Durham Co. **DC 24 Mar 1982**.

12468 REID, James, b ca 1835. s/o Alexander R. and Elizabeth Chalmers. To McKillop Twp, Huron Co, ONT, <11 Jan 1861, when m Ann Rennie, qv. **DC 24 Mar 1982**.

12469 RENNIE, Ann, b ca 1836. d/o Charles R. and Mary Kirton. To Brock Twp, Durham Co, ONT, <11 Jan 1861, when m James Reid, qv. **DC 24 Mar 1982**.

12470 RENNIE, Charles, b ca 1833. s/o Charles R. and Mary Kirton. To Reach Twp, Durham Co, ONT, <8 Feb 1861, when m Christina Wallace, qv. **DC 24 Mar 1982**.

12471 RIDDEL, Archibald Alexander, 10 Dec 1819–15 Dec 1883. From Peterhead, ABD. To Toronto, ONT, ca 1836. Printer, physician and alderman. m 12 Dec 1842, Ann Devlin, from IRL, ch: 1. Charles James, b 1843; 2. Mary Ann, b 1848; 3. Margaret Emily, b 1850; 4. Sarah Jane, b 1853; 5. Isabel, b 1856. **DC 15 May 1982**.

12472 RIDDEL, John, b ca 1785. From Peterhead, ABD. To Toronto, ONT, ca 1836. Wife Margaret Cochrane, qv, with him, and s Archibald Alexander, qv. **DC 15 May 1982**.

12473 ROBERTSON, Thomas. From Paisley, RFW. To QUE on the *Carleton*, ex Glasgow, arr 5 Jun 1842; stld prob Drummond Twp, Lanark Co, ONT. **DC 19 Apr 1982**.

12474 ROBINS, William, ca 1738–23 Dec 1805. From Crieff, PER. Poss s/o James R, weaver. To Richmond Bay, PEI, on the *Falmouth*, ex Greenock, 8 Apr 1770; stld Stanhope. Moved to St Peters, 1787. Wife with him, and ch, incl: 1. Jane, ca 1767–ca 1808; 2. Margaret, b ca 1769. **DC 28 May 1980**.

12475 ROGERSON, Samuel, 5 Feb 1802–19 Aug 1864. From Gillesbie, Hutton and Corrie par, DFS. s/o Samuel R. and Janet Mounsey. To St Johns, NFD, arr 4 Sep 1820, ex Greenock. Appr to Hunter & Co, merchants. Retr later to SCT, and d Leithen Hall, Wamphray, DFS. **SRO GD1/620/66**.

12476 ROSS, Sir James Clark, 15 Apr 1800–3 Apr 1862. From Kirkholm, WIG. s/o George R. of Balsarroch. Served in RN, and went to the Arctic with William Edward Parry, 1824-25. With uncle Sir John R, qv, on expedition, 1829-33, and discovered the magnetic pole. Knighted, 1843. **SN iii 373; IBD 447; CBD 803**.

12477 ROSS, Lexy. From Finsbay, Harris, INV. d/o William R. and Christy McLean. To Bruce Co, ONT, 1863. Wife of Angus Morrison, qv. **WLC**.

12478 ROSS, William, b 1831. From Melbost Borve, Is Lewis, ROC. s/o Donald R. and Margaret Nicholson. To Whitton Twp, Compton Co, QUE, 1863. Farmer. Wife Margaret with him. ch: 1. Donald, b 1853; 2. Margaret, b 1855; 3. Kirsty, b 1861; 4. Mary, b 1865; 5. Ann, b 1867; 6. Murdo, b 1869; 7. Malcolm. **WLC**.

12479 SANDERSON, George, 25 Apr 1808–28 Apr 1903. From Earlston, BEW. s/o John S. and Margaret Pringle. To Kemptville, Leeds and Grenville Co, ONT, 1831. Carpenter. m 15 Apr 1831, Mary Clark, ch: 1. John, b 1832; 2. Elisabeth, 1834-40; 3. Margaret, 1836-40; 4. William, 1838-71; 5. Margaret, 1840-70; 6. Elisabeth, 1843-90; 7. Mary, b 1845; 8. Jane, 1847–1931; 9. Isabella, 1850–1919; 10. George, b 1852. **DC 18 May 1982**.

12480 SINCLAIR, Donald. From Is Islay, ARL. To Elderslie Twp, Bruce Co, ONT, prob 1851; stld Paisley. Merchant and MLA. **BNA 799**.

12481 SINCLAIR, Janet, 1819-63. From Auchareuch, Kilmory par, Is Arran, BUT. To Restigouche Co, NB, ca 1855; stld Dundee. Wife of William Wright, 1825-93, from IRL, by whom she had ch. **DC 21 Mar 1982**.

12482 SMITH, Agnes or Ann, 1810-81. Prob from Is Islay, ARL. To ONT, 1847; stld Wellington Co. Wife of Daniel Spence, qv. **DC 18 May 1982**.

12483 SMITH, James Sinclair, 1816-97. From Bridge of Forss, Thurso par, CAI. s/o Alexander S, farmer in Lieurary, and Charlotte Cormack. To McGillivray Twp, Huron Co, ONT, <1846, and stld Maple Grove. Farmer. m Agnes Wilson, qv, ch: 1. Jane, 1847–1934; 2. Charlotte, 1850–1913; 3. Janet, 1852–1934; 4. Alexander, 1854–1913; 5. Agnes, 1858–1935. **DC 1 May 1982**.

12484 SMITH, John, b 1816. From Valtos, Uig par, Is Lewis, ROC. s/o Donald S. and Kirsty Morrison. To Winslow Twp, Compton Co, QUE, ca 1855. m Ann McKay, qv, ch: 1. Donald, 1842–1913; 2. Kirsty, b 1845; 3. Norman, b 1848; 4. Roderick, b 1851; 5. John, b 1853; 6. Malcolm, b 1856; 7. Angus, b 1859. **WLC**.

12485 SMITH, Marion. From Tarbet, DNB. To Whitton Twp, Compton Co, QUE, 1863. Wife of Donald McDermid, qv. **WLC**.

12486 SPENCE, Daniel, 1802-75. From Is Islay, ARL. s/o David S. To ONT, 1847; stld Arthur Twp, Wellington Co. Farmer. m Agnes or Ann Smith, qv, ch: 1. David, b 1832; 2. Gilbert, b 1834; 3. Peter, b 1836; 4. Daniel, b 1838; 5. Charles, b 1840; 6. Alexander, b 1842; 7. Janet, b 1844; 8. Margaret, b 1847. **DC 18 May 1982**.

12487 STEWART, Donald, b 1812. From Stornoway par, Is Lewis, ROC. To Compton Co, QUE, <1851. m Anna McIver, qv, ch: 1. John, b 1845; 2. Anna, b 1847; 3. Malcolm, b 1849; 4. Mary, b 1851; 5. Alexander, b 1854; 6. Isabella, b 1857; 7. George, b 1859; 8. Angus, b 1862; 9. Donald, b 1864; 10. Alexander, b 1866; 11. Catherine, b 1868; 12. Johanna, b 1870. **WLC**.

12488 STEWART, Isabella. From Back, Stornoway, Is Lewis, ROC. d/o Duncan S. To Winslow Twp, Compton Co, QUE, <1851. Wife of Alexander McLeod, qv. **WLC**.

12489 STRANG, Struthers, 9 Feb 1806–18 Apr 1856. From Glasgow. s/o Robert S. and Mary Smith. To Montreal, QUE, ca 1830. m 22 Nov 1831, Janet, 1809-52, d/o Adam Ferrie, qv, and Rachel Campbell, qv, ch: 1. Rachel Campbell, 1832-81; 2. Robert, 1833–1900; 3. Adam Ferrie, 1835-60; 4. Mary Smith, 1837-61; 5. Janet Ferrie, 1838–1926; 6. Struthers, d inf, 1840; 7. Margaret Jane, b 1844; 8. Struthers, 1847-48; 9. Andrew, 1849–1913, res Winnipeg; 10. Colin Ferrie, 1850–1900, res Edmonton; 11. John, 1851-62. **DC 5 Apr 1982**.

12490 WALLACE, Christina, b 1837. d/o George W. and Christina Alexander. To Reach Twp, Durham Co, ONT, <8 Feb 1861, when m Charles Rennie, qv. **DC 24 Mar 1982**.

12491 WATERS, John, 1829–1922. From Thurso, CAI. s/o David W. and Margaret Rosie. To Pictou, NS, 1850; stld later at New Glasgow. Sea captain. m 19 Sep 1851, Maria Anna, d/o Adam Merkel and Elizabeth Dorman, ch: 1. Elizabeth; 2. David; 3. Margaret; 4. Adam; 5. James; 6. George; 7. William. **DC 31 May 1982**.

12492 WHYTE, Andrew G, 5 Nov 1826–4 Nov 1908. From Glasgow. s/o William W. and Margaret Galetti. To ONT <1853. m Annie, d/o John Harvie and Mary Mason, ch: 1. Mary, 1854–1922; 2. Margaret, 1856–1925; 3. William, b 1857; 4. Elizabeth, b 1859; 5. John, b 1861; 6. Andrew, b 1863; 7. Jessie, b 1864; 8. James Galetti, b 1867; 9. Isabella, 1869–1906; 10. Mathew Mason, b 1871; 11. Jennie, b 1873; 12. Robert Young, 1875–1966; 13. Annie, b 1878. **DC 18 May 1982**.

12493 WILSON, Agnes, 1821–1914. From Elderslie, RFW. d/o David W, qv, and Jean Buchanan, qv. To Grey Co, ONT, 1842. m at Toronto, 18 Jun 1846, James Sinclair Smith, qv. **DC 1 May 1982**.

12494 WILSON, David, 1790–1854. From Elderslie, RFW> s/o John W. Rutherglen, LKS, and Jane Alcorn. To Grey Co, ONT, 1842. m Jean Buchanan, qv, ch: 1. Jean; 2. Janet; 3. David; 4. Agnes, qv; 5. John. **DC 1 May 1982**.

12495 WILSON, George, 1810-89. From Greenlaw par, BEW. s/o Thomas W, and Isabel Huddlestone. To Blenheim Twp, Oxford Co, ONT, 1843. Farmer. m Margaret Hill, qv, ch: 1. Margaret, b 1835; 2. Isabella, b 1837; 3. Thomas, b 1839; 4. James, b 1840; 5. Mary, b 1843; 6. George, 1845-46, b CAN; 7. George, 1846-48; 8. George, b 1849; 9. Helen, b 1851; 10. Elizabeth, 1854-56; 11. Robert, b 1856; 12. W. Jeffery, b 1860. **DC 18 May 1982**.

12496 WILSON, Robert, b ca 1839. From Strathaven, LKS. s/o John W. and Jane Hamilton. To Whitby, Ontario Co, ONT, <17 Dec 1858, when m Janet, d/o William Miller and Elizabeth Robinson. **DC 24 Mar 1982**.

12497 WOODSIDE, James, 1736–1824. From Ardrossan, AYR. To PEI, prob 1772; stld Prince Co. Served in RN, 1756-63. Farmer, and mem of House of Assembly, 1784. m Ann Love, qv, ch: 1. John, b ca 1766; 2. Rebecca, 1768–1823; 3. Robert, b 1770; 4. James, b ca 1772; 5. Andrew, b ca 1775; 6. Agnes, or Nancy, b ca 1778; 7. Margaret, b ca 1780; 8. Archibald, 1782–1860; 9. William, b ca 1874. **DC 20 Dec 1980**.

12498 WYLIE, Robert, d 1831. From Annan, DFS. Drowned at Smiths Falls, on the Rideau Canal, Lanark Co, ONT. Master of the ship *Jane*, of Annan. *Carlisle Journal*, 5 Nov 1831.

12499 WYLIE, William, ca 1788–12 Jun 1838. From Dornock, DFS. To QUE. m Margaret Irving, ca 1775–1855, left ch in SCT. **Ts Dornock**.

12500 YOUNG, John, 4 Mar 1811–12 Apr 1878. From Ayr. To Montreal, QUE, 1826. Clerk in the office of John Torrance, qv, and became partner of David Torrance, at Quebec. MLA, 1851-57; MPP, 1872-74; Chairman of Board of Trade and later of Harbour Commissioners at Montreal. **BNA 600; SNQ vi/1 49**.

12501 YOUNG, Henry. To Montreal, QUE, on the *Royal George*, ex Greenock, Jan 1827; stld Sarnia, ONT. Wife with him, and 2 sons. **DC 19 Nov 1978**.

BIBLIOGRAPHY AND GUIDE TO THE REFERENCES

ABC   *The Annals of a Border Club*, by George Tancred. Edinburgh, Glasgow and Jedburgh, 1903.

AFC   *Annals of the Free Church of Scotland*, 1843–1900, edited by Rev. William Ewing. 2 vols. Edinburgh, 1914.

AM   *Rev Alexander McGillivray*, D.D., by Hon John Doull. Halifax, 1838.

AMA   *Archibald McLarty of Argyll*, by Minnie E. Burley. Kingston, 1963.

AMC   *Annals of Megantic County, Quebec*, by Dugald McKenzie McKillop. Lynn, Massachusetts, 1902. New edition, Inverness, Que, 1962.

AJM   *Autograph of James R. McDonald*. Grayston, California. 1898. Not published. Typescript copy from the original in the Library of the California Historical Society, San Francisco.

BCL   *Passenger List of the brig Curlew, Greenock to Quebec*, 1818. Copy in the Public Archives of Canada, Ottawa, ref. CO 384, vol. 3.

BNA   *The Scot in British North America*, by W.J. Rattray. 4 vols. Toronto, 1880-83.

BOP   *The Barclays of Pickering*, by Robert M. Fuller and Kathleen Bowley. Typewriter script. Windsor, 1976.

BP   *Brudenell Pioneers*. Anniversary celebration booklet about early settlers in P.E.I. 1953.

CAE   *Calendar of Annandale Emigration*, by R.A. Shannon. Mimeographed. Annan, 1971.

CAG   *Abridged Compendium of American Genealogy*, by Frederick Adams Virkus. 7 vols. American Institute of Genealogy, 1925-42.

CBC   *Cape Breton Census*, 1818. Printed with *Holland's Description of Cape Breton*, edited by D.C. Harvey. Halifax, 1935.

CBD   *Chamber's Biographical Dictionary*, edited by David Patrick and Francis Hindes Groome. London and Edinburgh, 1897.

CD   *The Clan Donald*, by Angus J. MacDonald and Archibald A. MacDonald. 3 vols. Inverness, 1896–1904.

CEG   *Catalogue of the Graduates in Arts, Divinity and Law, of the University of Edinburgh*, 1587–1858, edited by David Laing. Edinburgh, 1858.

CMM   *Clan MacLeod Magazine*. Clan MacLeod Society, Edinburgh.

CP   *Certain Pioneers of the Family of Angus Williams of Goldenville, N.S., and Elizabeth (MacLeod) Williams of Westville and New Glasgow*. Manuscript presented to the Scottish Genealogy Society, 1956, by the author, Mrs M.E. Williams, Vancouver, B.C.

CPL   *Clarendon Passenger List*, 1808. Oban to Charlottetown, P.E.I. Colonial Office Papers, Public Record Office, London, ref. CO 226, vol. 23. Copy in the Public Archives of Canada, and published in *The Island Magazine*, 1977.

CSL   *Church and Social Life in the Highlands in the Olden Times*, by Alexander Macpherson. Edinburgh, 1893.

CUC   *A History of the Charlo, New Mills, and Jacquet River Congregations of the United Church of Canada*, edited by Fleming Holm. Mimeographed. Dalhousie, 1861.

DC   *Dictionary Correspondence*. Letters to the author regarding emigrants to Canada, contained in 9 lever-arch files.

DD   *The Dickies of Dumfries*, by Catherine Stewart. Ottawa (ca. 1972). Typewriter script. Copy presented by the author as a contribution to this work.

DGB   *Dumfries & Galloway Courier*.

DGC   *The Dumfries & Galloway Courier*.

DGH   *Dumfries and Galloway Herald & Advertiser* (merged in 1844 with the *Galloway Register* to become the *Dumfries & Galloway Herald & Register*).

DJL	*The Lambs of Quebec and Ontario, being Descendants of James Lamb of Scotland*, by Rev. J. William Lamb. Mimeographed for private circulation. Belleville, 1970.
DMC	*Correspondence with Donald W. MacLean*, Fredericton, N.B., filed 1st October, 1979.
DRG	*The Douglas and Robertson Genealogies* (attributed to Gustav Aird). Dingwall, 1895.
EAR	*Edinburgh Academy Register*, 1824–1914. Edinburgh, 1914.
EC	*Eldon Connections*, by Rae Fleming. Woodville, 1975.
EHE	*Early History of Elora and Vicinity*, by John Robert Connon. 2nd edition. Waterloo, 1975.
ELB	*Early Lochaber Bay*, by Dorothy Lamb. Buckingham, 1937. Mimeographed. Appended to DJL.
ELN	*List of Emigrants on the Lovely Nellie*. Solway Firth to St John's Island, 1774-75 (two voyages). Original in the Public Record Office, London, ref. T47/12, and copy in the Public Archives of Canada, ref. MG15.
EMT	*The Original Emigrants to McNab Township, Upper Canada*, 1825, by Dr Garnet McDiarmid. Typescript copy presented to the compiler of this work by the author, 1980. Printed in *Families* (1980) and in *The Scottish Genealogist* (1981).
ENA	*Emigration to North America*, by Donald Whyte. Salt Lake City (World Conference lecture), 1969.
EPE	*Emigration from the Perth Estate to Ontario*, by Donna L. Baker. Unpublished thesis. Waterloo, 1979.
ERT	*Index to Edinburgh Register of Testaments*, 1701–1800, edited by Francis J. Grant. Edinburgh: Scottish Record Society, 1922.
FAM	*Fasti Academiae Mariscallanae Aberdonensis*, edited by Peter J. Anderson. 3 vols. Aberdeen: New Spalding Club, 1889-98.
FAS	*The Faculty of Advocates in Scotland*, 1532–1943, edited by Francis J. Grant. Edinburgh: Scottish Record Society, 1944.
FES	*Fasti Ecclesiae Scoticanae*, by Rev. Hew Scott. Revised edition. 8 vols. Edinburgh, 1915-50.
FNQ	*Falkirk Antiquarian Notes and Queries*, by James Love, reprinted from *The Falkirk Herald*. 4 vols. Falkirk, 1928.
GMA	*Matriculation Albums of the University of Glasgow*, 1728–1858, edited by W. Innes Addison. Glasgow, 1913.
GMF	*Genealogy of the Mutch Family*, James Robert Mutch. Charlottetown, 1929.
GNL	*Glasgow & West of Scotland Family History Society Newsletter*.
GSO	*Galbraith Settlers in 19th Century Ontario*, by Edwin A.S. Galbraith. Weston, 1978. Typescript copy in the Library of the Scottish Genealogy Society, Edinburgh.
HCA	*A History of the County of Antigonish*, Nova Scotia, by Rev. D.J. Rankin. Toronto, 1929.
HCM	*History of the Clan McFarlane*, by C.M. Little. New York, 1893.
HFM	*Hattie Family Memoirs*, by Robert Connell Hattie and Joseph Howe Kirk. Halifax, 1936.
HGD	*Reminiscences of the Early History of Galt and the Settlement of Dumfries, in the Province of Ontario*, by James Young. Toronto, 1880.
HNS	*History of Nova Scotia*, by David Allison. 3 vols. Halifax, 1916.
HP	*Hebridean Pioneers*, by Malcolm A. MacQueen. Winnipeg, 1957.
HPC	*History of Pictou County*, by Rev. George Patterson. Montreal, 1877.
HSC	*History of Dr Boyds's Fourth High School Class*, by James Colston. Edinburgh, 1873.
HT	*A History of Tatamagouche, Nova Scotia*, by Frank H. Patterson. Halifax, 1917.
HWS	*History of the Writers to H.M. Signet*. 2nd edition. Edinburgh, 1936.

IBD   *Biographical Dictionary of Eminent Scotsmen*, by Joseph Irving. Paisley, 1881.

IFB   *In Famed Breadalbane*, by Rev. William Gillies. Perth, 1938.

INS   *Immigration to and Emigration from Nova Scotia*, 1815–1838.

ISL   *Passenger List of the ship Isle of Skye*, 1806. Tobermory to Charlottetown, P.E.I. Copy in the Public Archives of N.S., ref MG18, vol. 16, No. 67, and another in the Public Archives of P.E.I., ref 2702. Published in *The Island Magazine*.

KCG   *Officers and Graduates of University and King's College*, Aberdeen, by Peter J. Anderson. Aberdeen: New Spalding Club, 1893.

LC   *Library Correspondence*, Scottish Genealogy Society.

LDW   *Letters to Donald Whyte.* Personal correspondence of the author. Not indexed.

LFA   *Letters from America*, 1822-45. Copy of a manuscript in the possession of M.C. Wilson, 11 Richard Street, Titahi Bay, Wellington, New Zealand.

LSC   *The Romantic Settlement of Lord Selkirk's Colonists: the Pioneers of Manitoba*, by Dr George Bryce. New York. Toronto, ca. 1909.

LSF   *List of Passengers on the Friendship*, 1775. Port Glasgow to Quebec. Copy in the Public Archives of Canada, ref MG15, T.47, pp. 33-39. Original in Public Record Office, London.

LSS   *The Hudson Bay Company's Tenures and the Occupation of Assiniboia by Lord Selkirk's Settlers, with a List of Grantees*, by Archer Martin. London, 1898.

MAC   *Memorial of the Arran Clearances*, compiled by George H. Cook. Saint John, N.B., 1977.

MCM   *Clan MacMillan Magazine*, edited by Rev. Somerled McMillan, Paisley.

MDB   *The MacMillan Dictionary of Canadian Biography*, edited by W. Stewart Wallace. 3rd edition. Toronto, 1963. A 4th edition of this excellent reference work, revised and enlarged by W.A. McKay, was published in 1978. Our page references are for the 3rd edition.

MDC   *MacDonald College of McGill University*, by J.F. Snell. Montreal, 1963.

MG   *The MacLeods of Glengarry, 1793–1971: The Genealogy of a Clan*, by the Historical Committee of the Clan MacLeod Society of Glengarry. Dunvegan, Ont., 1971.

MGC   *Correspondence with Marjory Goodfellow*, Sherbrooke, Que., filed 2 Aug 1979.

MLA   *A Directory of the Members of the Legislative Assembly of Nova Scotia*, 1758–1858, edited by Bruce Fergusson. Halifax, 1958.

MOT   *Men of the Time: A Dictionary of Contempories*. Various editions, London, 1867, etc.

MP   *Mabou Pioneers*, by Rev. A.D. MacDonald. Privately printed. Mabou, N.S., 1957. A supplementary volume, issued in 1977 by the Mabou Pioneer Committee (with additional material by James O. St. Clair), is referred to by volume and page.

MSK   *Memorials of Sanquhar Kirkyard*, by Tom Wilson, Dumfries, 1912.

MSM   *Memorials of St Michael's Churchyard, Dumfries*, by William McDowall. Edinburgh, 1876.

NDF   *Family Record of the Name of Dingwall Fordyce in Aberdeenshire*, by Alexander Dingwall Fordyce, Fergus, 1885.

NER   *New England Historical and Genealogical Register*. From 1847. Complete set in National Library of Scotland.

NSN   *Genealogical Newsletter of the Genealogical Committee of the Nova Scotia Historical Society*, 1972-82. This is now the *Nova Scotia Genealogist*, issued by the Genealogical Association of Nova Scotia, formed in 1982, of which the author is a member.

NSS   *Certain Extracts from Nova Scotia Vital Statistics from Newspapers*, 1813-22, compiled by Terrence Punch. Halifax, 1980.

OEC   *The Memorial Catalogue of the Old Glasgow Exhibition*, 1894. Glasgow, 1894. An index volume published 1903.

OM   *The Oliver Magazine*, edited by Col. Winston Oliver. Blain, Blainslie, Galashiels.

OSG   *Note on the origin of the surname of Gemmill or Gemmell*, by J.A. Gemill. Privately printed. Montreal, 1898.

PCM   *Some Sketches of the Early Highland Pioneers of the County of Middlesex*, by Hugh McColl. Toronto, 1904.

PDA   *The Pioneer Days in Aldborough*, edited by J.H. MacIntyre. Aldborough, ca. 1934. Reprinted by West Elgin Historical and Genealogical Society, 1981.

PLC   *Passenger List of the Commerce*, 1803. Port Glasgow to Pictou, N.S. Original among the *Melville Papers: Scotland*, 1784–1807, MS. 1053, National Library of Scotland, Edinburgh. Published by the author in *Family History*, vol. 9 (1975).

PLD   *Passenger List of the ship Dove*, 1801. Fort William to Pictou, N.S. Original in the Public Record Office, London, ref. HO, vol. 18. Copy in the Public Archives of Canada, ref. CMG II, Supp. I, vol. 10. Another in the Scottish Record Office, Edinburgh, ref. RH2/4/87.

PLEA   *Passenger List of the Elizabeth & Ann*, 1806. Thurso to Charlottetown, P.E.I. Copy in the Public Archives of N.S., ref MG 100-16, 66. Another list, probably the original, in the Public Archives of P.E.I., Charlottetown, ref. 2702.

PLH   *Passenger List of the brig Humphreys*, 1806. Tobermory to Charlottetown. Copy in the Public Archives of N.S., ref. MG 100-16, 64, and another, probably the original, in the Public Archives of P.E.I., ref. 2702.

PLJ   *Passenger List of the ship Jane*, 1790. Arisaig to P.E.I. Original in the Scottish Catholic Archives, Edinburgh. List from the papers of Colin S. MacDonald, in the Public Archives of N.S., published in *The Island Magazine*.

PLL   *Passenger List of the ship Lucy*, 1790. Arisaig to P.E.I. Original in the Scottish Catholic Archives, Edinburgh. List from the papers of Colin S. MacDonald, in the Public Archives of N.S., published in *The Island Magazine*.

PLR   *Passenger List of the ship Rambler*, 1806. Tobermory to Charlottetown. Copy in the Provincial Archives of N.S., ref. MG 100-16, 63, and in the library of the author.

PLS   *Passenger List of the ship Sarah*, 1801. Fort William to Pictou, 1806. Original in the Public Record Office, London. Copy in the Public Archives of N.S., ref. CMG II, Supp. 1, vol. 10. Another list in the Scottish Record Office, ref. RH2/4/87, 66-71.

PLSN   *Passenger List of the ship Spencer*, 1806. Oban to Charlottetown. Copy in the Public Archives of N.S., ref MG 100, vol. 16, No. 65. Also in the Public Archives of P.E.I.

PRS   *Particular Register of Sasines*, various districts. Scottish Record Office, Edinburgh.

QCC   *Quebec Colonial Correspondence*. Public Archives of Canada, ref. MG-11, 2/48.

RCP   *Angus MacLean and his wife Mary Sinclair: Restigouche County Pioneers*, by Donald W. MacLean. Mimeographed for private circulation. Fredericton, N.B., 1978.

RFS   *Our Ross Family Story*, by J. Douglas Ross. Willowdale, 1978.

RGG   *A Roll of the Graduates of the University of Glasgow*, 1727–1897, by W. Innes Addison. Glasgow, 1898.

RPE   *A Narrative of the Rise and Progress of Emigration from the Counties of Lanark and Renfrew to the New Settlements in Upper Canada*, by Robert Lamont. Glasgow, 1921.

RRS   *Red River Settlement: Papers in the Canadian Archives Relating to the Pioneers*, by Chester Martin. Ottawa, 1910.

SA   *The Scottish Antiquary*, or *Northern Notes and Queries*. 17 vols. Edinburgh.

SAA   *The Society of Advocates in Aberdeen*, by John A. Henderson. Aberdeen: New Spalding Club, 1912.

SAM   *The Matriculation Roll of the University of St Andrews*, 1747–1897, edited by James Maitland Anderson. Edinburgh, 1905.

SAS   *Scotland and the Scots*, by Peter Ross. New York, 1889.

SCI   *The St. Clairs of the Isles*, by R.W. Sinclair. Auckland, N.Z., 1898.

SCN   *Notes on Scottish Emigrants*, contributed by Sidney Cramer, and filed in *Dictionary Correspondence*, July, 1960.

SDG   *Stormont, Dundas and Glengarry*, by John Graham Harkness, Oshawa, 1946.

SEC   *Scottish Emigrants to Canada: General List of Settlers*, 1815. Transcribed by Estelle Leeson from Audit Office Records, Public Record Office, London, ref. AO-3/144. Typescript, 1971, contributed by Francis Leeson.

SH   *Services of Heirs: Decennial Indexes*, vols. 1-4, 1700–1859. Edinburgh, 1863-91.

SLL   *Passenger List of the ship St. Lawrence*, 1828. Is. Rum to Cape Breton. Copy in the author's library. Printed in *The History of Inverness County, Cape Breton*, by John L. MacDougall.

SMB   *Sinclair Manuscript: Stories from the Memory of Charles R. Sinclair*, Glengarry, Ont. Preserved by Clark Barret, 2336 N. 81st Street, Scottsville, Arizona, U.S.A.

SN   *The Scottish Nation*, edited by William Anderson. 3 vols. Edinburgh, 1878-80.

SNQ   *Scottish Notes & Queries*. Series 1-3. 1888–1935.

SP   *The Scots Peerage*, edited by Sir James Balfour Paul. 9 vols. Edinburgh, 1904-14.

SPI   *Skye Pioneers and the Island*, by Malcolm A. MacQueen. Winnipeg, 1929.

SPL   *Copy of the Passenger List of the Sophia*, 1818. Greenock to Montreal. Microfilm in the Public Archives of Canada, ref. CO 384, vol. 3.

SR   *The Story of the Restigouche*, by George B. MacBeath, Saint John, N.B., 1954.

TFC   *The Family of Clouston*, by J. Storer Clouston. Privately circulated. Kirkwall, 1948.

TFT   *The Family Tree, and Some Reminiscences of Early Days in Winslow and Whitton*, Que., by Rev. M.N. MacDonald. Avonmore, 1945, reprinted Sherbrooke, 1973.

THS   *Transactions of the Hawick Archaelogical Society*.

TOO   *Genealogical Account of the Trails of Orkney*, by William Traill of Woodwick, M.D. Kirkwall, 1883.

UCM   *Upper Canada Memoranda*, in the *Selkirk Papers*. Public Archives of Canada, MG 19. E.1., vol. 52.

UPC   *History of the Congregation of the United Presbyterian Church from 1733 to 1900*, by Rev. Robert Small. 2 vols. Edinburgh, 1904.

VSN   *Certain Extracts from Nova Scotia Vital Statistics from 1823-28*, compiled by Jean M. Holder. Halifax, 1980.

WLC   *William Lawson Collection*. MS. material, historical and genealogical, relating to the Long Island, collected by William McF. Lawson, B.L., F.R.I.C.S., Project Manager, Outer Isles Integrated Development Programme, 82 Keith Street, Stornoway, Is Lewis.